COMICS VALUES ANNUAL

2004 EDITION
THE COMIC BOOK PRICE GUIDE

by Alex G. Malloy

edited by Stuart W. Wells III

Intro: Robert J. Sodaro

©2004 by Alex G. Malloy & Stuart W. Wells III
Published by
Antique Trader Books, a division of

krause publications
An F+W Publications Company

700 East State Street • Iola, WI 54990-0001
715-445-2214 • 888-457-2873
www.krause.com

Our toll-free number to place an order or
obtain a free catalog is (800) 258-0929.

All rights reserved. No portion of this publication may be
reproduced or transmitted in any form or by any means,
electronic or mechanical, including photocopy, recording,
or any information storage and retrieval system, without
permission in writing from the publisher, except by a
reviewer who may quote brief passages in a critical article
or review to be printed in a magazine or newspaper, or
electronically transmitted on radio or television.

Library of Congress Catalog Number:
1062-4503

ISBN:
0-87349-802-X

Designed by Stuart W. Wells III
Edited by Alex G. Malloy

Printed in the U.S.A.

CONTENTS

Preface, *by Alex G. Malloy and Robert J. Sodaro* 5
CVA Grading Guide. 8
Artist and General Terms: Name–Abbreviation. 12
Artist and General Terms: Abbreviation–Name. 16
Bibliography 20
DC Comics Listings & Values 21
Amalgam Comics Listings & Values. 186
Marvel Comics Listings & Values. 187
Golden Age Comics Listings & Values 358
Dark Horse Comics Listings & Values 489
Image Comics Listings & Values 523
Other Publishers Listings & Values (Color). 560
Other Publishers Listings & Values (Black & White) 694
Classics Illustrated Comics Listings & Values. 791
Underground Comix Listings & Values. 804
Index. 811
CVA Grading/Price Guide 840

741.5
M

11/6/04

DEMCO

Making the Grade:
Comics has Another Banner Year

By Alex G. Malloy, with Bob Sodaro

As we reported last year, more and more collectors are turning to acquiring "certified" grading of their comics. Needless to say, the surge of actual graded comics in auctions has continued to cause the significant rise of classical Silver Age prices. This, plus the renewed interest in Silver Age comics themselves, has helped to breathe new life into the classic tales, and has convinced publishers to collect (or in some instances, re-collect), these heady tales into new bound volumes. As we rush pell-mell towards the end of 2003 and this editorial is being penned, *Comic Shop News* has released a special issue on the gaggle of bound volumes of collected works that are now or soon will become available.

Still, many titles have—over the course of numerous auctions—achieved new records to prove the true values of these wondrous titles. This is nowhere more notable than with Silver Age Marvel comics, where the values continue to rise at each succeeding auction. Then, as these cyclic fires tend to fan themselves, the more interest they generate in the field, the more that executives in Hollywoodland fall over themselves to extend the franchise, and invite new properties to make the jump from four-color pulp to the giant Silver Screen. Already we're seeing posters, one-sheets, and trailers for Marvel's The Punisher, Spider-Man 2 (hey, Features Editor—and resident Spidey-head Bob Sodaro tells me that the new wall banner for Spidey 2 is simply awesome!), and Dark Horse's Hellboy (which looks like it could either go either way).

Still, even if isn't the blockbuster of Spidey or X2 and simply does decent business like Daredevil and The League of Extraordinary Gentlemen; we certainly hope that it steers clear of the unfortunate pitfalls that befell Hulk (more later). These movies are still fanning the fire. X-Men 2 was very, very hot (Okay, anyone who really thinks that Jean Grey died go back and re-read the entire Phoenix saga—you can't be born again unless you kick the bucket at least once, eh?). High auction records and extensive offerings of fine quality early X-Men comics have followed in the wake of these two great films.

Spider-Man is white hot (the film set the movie industry on its collective ear, and forever altered the way movies are released, and how the world looks at comics). Prices are up—up across the board. Daredevil is very also hot (the film hit mixed reviews, but comicbook fans generally agree that it was a fair treatment of the characters, and that the film accurately reflected the dual natures of Daredevil—a little bit Spider-Man, and a little bit Batman).

Other silver age characters that are up—but not as high as the first three—

include The Avengers, Capt America, Conan the Barbarian, Early Thor, Fantastic Four—all hot but, unfortunately, not many high grade, early comics are currently being offered at auctions. Perhaps a round of films featuring these characters will help revive interest in not only their current stories, but in the classic Silver Age market on their titles. (As an unavoidable aside, Mike Richards, head man over at Dark Horse, must be the angriest man in California these days, ever since Arnold Schwarzenegger won the Gubernatorial race. Richards landed the rights to a new Conan movie entitled *King Conan: Crown of Iron,* due to appear in 2005, which was supposed to star the newly-elected Governor. It is now up in the air, as he takes over his new office and duties.) (Ed. Note: Dark Horse headquarters are in Milwaukie, Oregon.)

Interestingly enough, early Incredible Hulk is very hot in spite of the tepid reception of the Ang Lee film (those of us who attended opening night felt that the film failed on two levels, as during the first half of the film we waited for Bruce to get mad and start smashing stuff, and then when he did Hulk out, his CGI self was simply not realistic enough—still we did enjoy it much better than apparently the rest of the non-comicbook-buying public did, Ah well.)

Star Wars—as always—is eternally very hot due to the popularity and crossover collectible interest with Science Fiction and Movie collectors (and those very neat Legos certainly don't hurt).

Another sure-fire marker that the Silver Age is returning to pre-eminence is the appearance of pricey coffee table art books featuring historical perspectives on that era. So, while it isn't often that we recommend books by other authors (especially ones from other publishers) it is in the spirit of "Damn, we wish we wrote that book", we'd like to draw attention to the outstanding work of one of our esteemed colleagues, Arlen Schumer, who, at the end of 2003, released his weighty The Silver Age of Comic Book Art (Collector Press). This book is without a doubt the finest treatment of this era that we have ever seen.

In closing, we truly believe that the industry has turned a very powerful corner, and what with solid (and rising) sales of both Silver Age and current books, combined with the recent (and up-coming) crop of comicbook-related films that are being so well received, we feel that we are on the verge of a new era of comics, and—as always—we look longingly towards the future.

The fearless creators of this book have also written others. Among them are:
American Games by Alex G. Malloy (Krause, May 2000, ISBN 0-930615-60-9);
Kiddy Meal Collectibles by Robert J. Sodaro (Krause, ISBN 0-930625-16-1);
A Universe of Star Wars Collectibles, Identification and Price Guide, 2nd Edition,
by Stuart W. Wells III (Krause, July 2002, ISBN 0-87349-415-6),
all available from Krause (see the copyright page for Web site and catalog information).

CVA GRADING GUIDE

In David Brin's science fiction–fantasy novel, *The Practice Effect*, things improve with use. You start with a crudely made tool and keep using it until it becomes a fine instrument. If our world worked that way, you could read your golden age comics as often as you liked and they would just get better looking each time. Unfortunately, our world does not work that way, and reading your comics (along with just about everything else) causes comics to deteriorate.

Even if you could protect your comics from external light, heat, cold, moisture, pressure and everything else, you couldn't protect them from their own paper. Most comic books were printed on pulp paper, which has a high acid content. This means that the paper slowly turns brittle with age, no matter what you do to it, short of special museum-style preservation.

Very old, well-preserved comics are coveted collector's items. In most cases, people did not save their comic books for future generations. They read them and discarded them. Comic books were considered harmless ephemera for children. When these children outgrew their comics, their parents often threw them away. If everybody kept all of their comics, comics would not be valuable because everybody would have them scattered about the house!

The value of any comic depends on scarcity, popularity and condition. Scarcity increases with age and popularity depends on the whim of the public — only condition automatically decreases with age. Newer comics are generally available in near-mint condition, so newer comics in lesser condition have little collector potential. However, older comics are scarce, so they are still collectible in less than near-mint condition, but the value is obviously less. This is a basic tenet of all collectibles. A car is more valuable with its original paint. A baseball card is more valuable if it has not been marred by bicycle spokes. Coke bottles, stamps, coins, and toys in good condition are all more valuable than their abused counterparts. Comic books are no exception.

New comic book collectors should learn how to assess the prospective value of a comic in order to protect themselves from being fleeced by unscrupulous dealers or hucksters. Yet, a majority of dealers, especially store owners, can be considered reliable judges of comic grade. Because comic retail may be their primary source of income, certain dealers are particularly adept at noticing comic book imperfections, especially in issues they intend to purchase. As such, hobbyists and collectors must understand that dealers need to make a minimum profit on their investments. Buying collectible comics entails certain risks. Therefore, dealers must scrutinize a comic to determine if the particular book will stand a chance of resale. Well-preserved comics are invariably more desirable to dealers because they are more desirable to collectors.

There are eight standard comic grades: mint, near mint, very fine, fine, very good, good, fair, and poor. Clearly, these eight grades could be split into even finer categories when haggling over an exceptionally rare or coveted Golden Age comic. In most cases, however, comic books can be evaluated using these eight standard grades. The values listed in *Comics Values Annual* are all for comics in "Near Mint" condition. The grading/price chart given at the back of this book should be used to adjust this price for comics in different grades.

Mint

Finding new comics in true mint condition can be difficult. Finding old comics in mint condition is almost impossible. Mint condition comics usually fetch prices higher than price guide listings. Mint comics can sell for 120% or more of *Comics Values Annual* listed prices. The reason for this is the strict criteria reserved for mint comics.

Mint comics are perfect comics and allow no room for imperfections. Pages and covers must be free of discoloration, wear, and wrinkles. A mint comic is one that looks like it just rolled off the press. Staples and spine must meet perfectly without cover "rollover." The cover must be crisp, bright, and trimmed perfectly. The staples must not be rusted and the cover should not have any visible creases.

The interior pages of a mint comic are equally crisp and new. A mint comic must not show any signs of age or decay. Because of the paper stock used on many older comics, acid and oxygen cause interior pages to yellow and flake. It is much harder to find pre-1970 mint comics because of inferior storage techniques and materials. In the early days of collecting, few people anticipated that the very boxes and bags in which they stored their comics were contributing to decay. Acid from bags, backing boards, and boxes ate away at many comics.

Near Mint

A near mint comic and a mint comic are close siblings, with their differences slight, even to an experienced eye. Most of the new comics on the shelf of the local comic shop are in near mint condition. These are comics that have been handled gingerly to preserve the original luster of the book.

Near mint comics are bright, clean copies with no major or minor defects. Slight stress lines near the staples and perhaps a very minor printing defect are permissible. Corners must still be sharp and devoid of creases. Interior pages of newsprint stock should show almost no discernible yellowing. Near mint comics usually trade for 100% of the suggested *Comics Values Annual* listed prices.

Very Fine

A very fine comic is one that is routinely found on the shelves and back issue bins of most good direct market comic shops. This grade comic has few defects, none of them major. Stress around the staples of a very fine comic are visible but not yet radical enough to create wrinkles. Both the cover and interior pages should still be crisp and sharp, devoid of flaking and creases. Interior pages may be slightly yellowed from age.

Most high-quality older comics graded as very fine can obtain 80-90% of *Comics Values Annual* listed prices. Newer comics graded as very fine get about 70-85% because many near mint copies probably exist. Despite that, very fine comics are desirable for most collectors.

Fine

Fine comics are often issues that may have been stored carefully under a bed or on a shelf by a meticulous collector. This grade of comic is also very desirable because it shows little wear and retains much of its original sharpness. The cover may be slightly off center from rollover. The cover retains less of its original gloss and may even possess a chip or wrinkle. The comers should be sharp but may also have a slight crease. Yellowing begins to creep into the interior pages of a comic graded as fine.

Fine comics are respectable additions to collections and sell for about 40-60% of the listed prices.

Very Good

A very good comic may have been an issue passed around or read frequently. This grade is the common condition of older books. Its cover will probably have lost some luster and may have two or three creases around the staples or edges. The corners of the book may begin to show the beginnings of minor rounding and chipping, but it is by no means a damaged or defaced comic. Comics in very good condition sell for about 30-40% of *Comics Values Annual* listed prices.

Good

A good comic is one that has been well-read and is beginning to show its age. Although both front and back covers are still attached, a good grade comic may have a number of serious wrinkles and chips. The corners and edges of this grade comic may show clear signs of rounding and flaking. There should be no major tears in a good comic nor should any pages be clipped out or missing. Interior pages may be fairly yellowed and brittle. Good comics sell for about 15-25% of the *Comics Values Annual* listed prices.

Fair

A fair comic is one that has definitely seen better days and has considerably limited resale value for most collectors. This comic may be soiled and damaged on the cover and interior. Fair comics should be completely intact and may only be useful as a comic to lend to friends. Fair comics sell for about 10-20% of the *Comics Values Annual* listed prices.

Poor

Comics in poor condition are generally unsuitable for collecting or reading because they range from damaged to unrecognizable. Poor comics may have been water damaged, attacked by a small child, or worse, perhaps, gnawed on by the family pet! Interior and exterior pages may be cut apart or missing entirely. A poor comic sells for about 5-15% of the *Comics Values Annual* listed price.

Sniffing Out Grades

Despite everything that is mentioned about comic grading, the process remains relative to the situation. A comic that seems to be in very good condition may actually be a restored copy. A restored copy is generally considered to be inbetween the grade it was previous to restoration and the grade it has become. Many collectors avoid restored comics entirely.

Each collector builds his collection around what he believes is important. Some want every issue of a particular series or company. Others want every issue of a favorite artist or writer. Because of this, many collectors will purchase lower-grade comics to fill out a series or to try out a new series. Mint and near mint comics are usually much more desirable to hard-core collectors. Hobbyists and readers may find the effort and cost of collecting only high-grade comics financially prohibitive.

Getting artists or writers to autograph comics has also become a source of major dispute. Some collectors enjoy signed comics and others consider those very comics defaced! The current trends indicate that most collectors do enjoy signed comics. A signature does not usually change the grade of the comic.

As mentioned, comic grading is a subjective process that must be agreed upon by the buyer and seller. Buyers will often be quick to note minor defects in order to negotiate a better price. Sellers are sometimes selectively blind to their comic's defects. *Comics Values Annual:2004* provides this grading guide as a protection for both parties.

NAME–ABBREVIATION

Comics Values Annual

Name	Abbr
Abel, Jack	**JA**
Abell, Dusty	DAb
Abnett, Dan	DAn
Abrams, Paul	PIA
Adams, Art	AAd
Adams, Neal	NA
Addeo, Stephen	StA
Adkins, Dan	DA
Adlard, Charlie	CAd
Albano, John	JAo
Albrecht, Jeff	JAl
Alcala, Alfredo	AA
Alcazar, Vincent	VAz
Alexander, Chris	CAx
Alibaster, Jo	JoA
Allred, Michael	MiA
Alstaetter, Karl	KlA
Althorp, Brian	BAp
Amaro, Gary	GyA
Amendola, Sal	Sal
Ammerman, David	DvA
Anderson, Bill	BAn
Anderson, Brent	BA
Anderson, Murphy	MA
Andriola, Alfred	AlA
Andru, Ross	RA
Aparo, Jim	JAp
Aragones, Sergio	SA
Arcudi, John	JAr
Artis, Tom	TAr
Ashe, Edd	EA
Asamiya	KiA
Augustyn, Brian	BAu
Austin, Terry	TA
Avison, Al	AAv
Ayers, Dick	DAy
Bachalo, Chris	**CBa**
Badger, Mark	MBg
Bagley, Mark	MBa
Baikie, Jim	JBa
Bailey, Bernard	BBa
Bair, Michael	MlB
Baker, Kyle	KB
Baker, Matt	MB
Balent, Jim	JBa
Banks, Darryl	DBk
Barks, Carl	CB
Baron, Mike	MBn
Barr, Mike	MiB
Barras, John	DBs
Barreiro, Mike	MkB
Barreto, Ed	EB
Barry, Dan	DBa
Batista, Chris	CsB
Battlefield, D.	DB
Beatty, John	JhB
Beatty, Terry	TBe
Beauvais, Denis	DB
Beeston, John	JBe
Belardinelli, M.	MBe
Bell, Bob Boze	BBB
Bell, George	GBl
Bell, Julie	JuB
Benefiel, Scott	ScB
Benes, Ed	EBe
Benitez, Joe	JBz
Benjamin, Ryan	RBn
Bennett, Joe	JoB
Bennett, Richard	RiB
Benson, Scott	StB
Berger, Charles	ChB
Bernado, Ramon	RBe
Bernstein, Robert	RbB
Bierbaum, Mary	MBm
Bierbaum, Tom	TBm
Biggs, Geoffrey	GB
Binder, Jack	JaB
Bingham, Jerry	JBi
Birch, JJ	JJB
Biro, Charles	CBi
Bisley, Simon	SBs
Bissette, Stephen	SBi
Blaisdell, Tex.	TeB
Blasco, Jesus	JBl
Blevins, Bret	BBl
Blum, Alex	AB
Bode, Vaughn.	VB
Bogdanove, Jon	JBg
Bolland, Brian	BB
Bolle, Frank	FBe
Boller, David	DdB
Bolton, John	JBo
Bond, Philip	PBd
Booth, Brett	BBh
Boring, Wayne.	WB
Bossart, William	WmB
Boxell, Tim	TB
Bradstreet, Tim	TBd
Braithwaite, Doug	DBw
Brasfield, Craig	CrB
Braun, Russell	RsB
Breeding, Brett	BBr
Brereton, Daniel	DlB
Brewster, Ann	ABr
Breyfogle, Norm	NBy
Bridwell, E. Nelson	ENB
Briefer, Dick	DBr
Bright, Mark	MBr
Brigman, June	JBr
Broderick, Pat	PB
Brodsky, Allyn	AyB
Broom, John	JBm
Broome, Matt	MtB
Brothers, Hernandez	HB
Brown, Bob	BbB
Browne, Dick	DkB
Brunner, Frank	FB
Bryant, Rick	RkB
Buckingham, Mark	MBu
Buckler, Rich	RB
Budget, Greg	GBu
Bugro, Carl.	CBu
Bulanadi, Danny	DBl
Burchett, Rick	RBr
Burgard, Tim	TmB
Burke, Fred	FBk
Burns, John	JBn
Burns, Robert	RBu
Burroughs, W.	WBu
Buscema, John	JB
Buscema, Sal	SB
Busiek, Kurt	KBk
Butler, Jeff	JBt
Butler, Steve	SBt
Buzz	Buzz
Byrd, Mitch.	MBy
Byrne, John	JBy
Calafiore, Jim.	**JCf**
Caldes, Charles	CCa
Callahan, Jim.	JiC
Calnan, John	JCa
Cameron, Don	DCn
Cameron, Lou	LC
Campbell, Eddie	ECa
Campbell, J. Scott	JSC
Campbell, Stan	StC
Campenella, Robert	RbC
Campos, Marc	MCa
Capullo, Greg	GCa
Cardy, Nick	NC
Carey, Mike	MCy
Cariello, Sergio	SCi
Carlin, Mike	MCr
Carpenter, Brent D.	BDC
Carralero, Ricky	RCl
Carrasco, Dario	DoC
Carter, Joe.	JCt
Case, Richard	RCa
Casey, Joe	JoC
Castellaneta, Dan	DaC
Castellini, Claudio	CCt
Castrillo, Anthony	ACa
Chadwick, Paul	PC
Chan, Ernie	ECh
Chang, Bernard	BCh
Charest, Travis	TC
Chase, Bobbie	BCe
Chaykin, Howard	HC
Check, Sid	SC
Chen, Mike	MCh
Chen, Sean	SCh
Chestney, Lillian	LCh
Chiarello, Mark	MCo
Chichester, D.G.	DGC
Chiodo, Joe	JCh
Choi, Brandon	BCi
Chriscross	Ccs
Christopher, Tom	TmC
Chua, Ernie	Chu
Chun, Anthony	ACh
Churchhill, Ian	IaC
Cirocco, Frank	FC
Citron, Sam	SmC
Claremont, Chris	CCl
Clark, Mike	MCl
Clark, Scott	ScC
Cockrum, Dave	DC
Cohn, Gary	GCh
Coker, Tomm	TCk
Colan, Gene	GC
Colby, Simon	SCy
Cole, Jack	JCo
Cole, Leonard B.	LbC
Colletta, Vince	ViC
Collins, Max Allan	MCn
Collins, Mike	MC
Collins, Nancy	NyC
Colon, Ernie	EC
Conner, Amanda	ACo
Conway, Gerry	GyC
Cooper, Dave	DvC
Cooper, John	JCp
Corben, Richard	RCo
Costanza, Peter	PrC
Cowan, Denys	DCw
Cox, Jeromy	JCx
Craig, Johnny	JCr
Crandall, Reed	RC
Crespo, Steve	SCr
Crilley, Mark	MCi
Crumb, Robert	RCr
Cruz, E. R.	ERC
Cruz, Jerry	JCz
Cruz, Roger	RCz
Culdera, Chuck	CCu
Cullins, Paris	PCu
Currie, Andrew	ACe
Damaggio, Rodolfo	**RDm**
Daniel, Tony	TnD
Danner, Paul	PuD
Darrow, Geof	GfD
David, Peter	PDd
Davis, Alan	AD
Davis, Dan	DDv
Davis, Guy	GyD
Davis, Jack	JDa
Davis, Malcolm	MDa
Davison, Al	ADv
Day, Dan	Day
Day, Gene	GD
DeFalco, Tom	TDF
Deitch, Kim	KDe
Delano, Jamie	JaD
DeLaRosa, Sam	SDR
Delgado, Richard	RdD
Dell, John	JhD
DeMatteis, J. M.	JMD
DeMulder, Kim	KDM
Deodato, Jr., Mike	MD2
Derenick, Tom	TDr
DeZago, Todd	TDz
DeZuniga, M.	MDb
DeZuniga, Tony	TD
Diaz, Paco	PaD
Dillin, Dick	DD
Dillon, Glyn	GlD
Dillon, Steve	SDi
Dini, Paul	PDi
Ditko, Steve	SD
Dixon, Chuck	CDi
Dixon, John	JDx
Dobbyn, Nigel	ND
Dodson, Terry	TyD
Doherty, Peter	PD
Dominguez, Luis	LDz
Doran, Colleen	CDo
Dorey, Mike	MDo
Dorkin, Evan	EDo
Dorman, Dave	DvD
Doucet, Julie	JDo
Drake, Stan	SDr
Dresser, Larry	LDr
Dringenberg, Mike	MDr
Drucker, Mort	MD
DuBerkr, Randy	RDB
Duffy, Jo	JDy
Dumm, Gary	GDu
Dunn, Ben	BDn
Duranona, Leo	LDu
Duursema, Jan	JD
Dwyer, Kieron	KD
Eastman, Kevin	**KEa**
Eaton, Scott	SEa
Edginton, Ian	IEd
Edlund, Ben	BEd
Egeland, Marty	MEg
Eisner, Will	WE
Elder, Bill	BE
Eldred, Tim	TEl
Elias, Lee	LE
Elliot, D.	DE
Ellis, Warren	WEl
Ellison, Harlan	HaE
Emberlin, Randy	RyE

Comics Values Annual — NAME–ABBREVIATION

Name	Abbr.	Name	Abbr.	Name	Abbr.	Name	Abbr.
Englehart, Steve	SEt	Goodman, Till	TGo	Hobbs, Bill	BIH	Kolins, Scott	ScK
Ennis, Garth	GEn	Goodwin, Archie	AGw	Hoberg, Rick	RHo	Krause, Peter	PKr
Epting, Steve	SEp	Gordon, Al	AG	Hoffer, Mike	MkH	Krenkel, Roy	RKu
Erskine, Gary	GEr	Gottfredson, Floyd	FG	Hogarth, Burne	BHg	Krigstein, Bernie	BK
Erwin, Steve	StE	Gould, Chester	ChG	Holcomb, Art	AHo	Kristiansen, Teddy H.	TKr
Esposito, Mike	ME	Grant, Alan	AlG	Holdredge, John	JHo	Kruse, Brandon	BKr
Estes, John	JEs	Grant, Steve	StG	Hoover, Dave	DHv	Kubert, Adam	AKu
Estrada, Ric	RE	Grau, Peter	PGr	Hopgood, Kevin	KHd	Kubert, Andy	NKu
Evans, George	GE	Gray, Mick	MGy	Horie, Richard	RHe	Kubert, Joe	JKu
Everett, Bill	BEv	Green, Dan	DGr	Hotz, Kyle	KHt	Kupperberg, Paul	PuK
Ewins, Brett	BEw	Green, Randy	RGr	Howarth, Matt	MHo	Kurtzman, Harvey	HK
Ezquerra, Carlos	CE	Greene, Sid	SGe	Howell, Rich	RHo	Kwitney, Alisa	AaK
Fabry, Glenn	**GF**	Grell, Mike	MGr	Hudnall, James	JHl	**LaBan, Terry**	**TLa**
Fago, Al	AFa	Griffith, Bill	BG	Hughes, Adam	AH	Lago, Ray	RyL
Farmer, Mark	MFm	Griffiths, Martin	MGs	Hund, Dave	DeH	Laird, Peter	PLa
Fegredo, Duncan	DFg	Grindberg, Tom	TGb	Hunt, Chad	CH	Lanning, Andy	ALa
Feldstein, Al	AF	Gross, Daerick	DkG	**Immonen, Stuart**	**SI**	Lansdale, Joe	JLd
Ferry, Pascual	PFe	Gross, Peter	PrG	Infantino, Carmine	CI	Lapham, Dave	DL
Fine, Lou	LF	Grossman, R.	RGs	Ingles, Graham	Grl	Lark, Michael	MLr
Fingeroth, Danny	DFr	Gruenwald, Mark	MGu	Iorio, Medio	MI	Larkin, Bob	BLr
Finnocchiaro, Sal	SF	Grummett, Tom	TG	Isherwood, Geoff	GI	LaRocque, Greg	GrL
Fleisher, Michael	MFl	Guardineer, Frank	FG	Ivie, Larry	LI	Larroca, Salvador	SvL
Fleming, Robert	RFl	Guay, Rebecca	RGu	Ivy, Chris	CIv	Larsen, Erik	EL
Flemming, Homer	HFl	Guice, Jackson	JG	**Jackson, Julius**	**JJn**	Lash, Batton	BLs
Foreman, Dick	DiF	Guichet, Yvel	YG	Jaffee, Al	AJ	Lashley, Ken	KeL
Forte, John	JF	Guinan, Paul	PGn	Janke, Dennis	DJa	Lavery, Jim	JLv
Forton, Gerald	GFo	Gulacy, Paul	PG	Janson, Klaus	KJ	Lawlis, Dan	DLw
Fosco, Frank	FFo	Gustovich, Mike	MG	Javinen, Kirk	KJa	Lawrence, Terral	TLw
Foster, Alan Dean	ADF	**Ha, Gene**	**GeH**	Jenkins, Paul	PJe	Lawson, Jim	JmL
Fox, Gardner	GaF	Haley, Matt	MHy	Jenney, Robert	RJ	Layton, Bob	BL
Fox, Gill	GFx	Hall, Bob	BH	Jensen, Dennis	DJ	Leach, Garry	GL
Fox, Matt	MF	Halsted, Ted	TeH	Jimenez, Leonardo	LJi	Leach, Rick	RkL
Fraga, Dan	DaF	Hama, Larry	LHa	Jimminiz, Phil	PJ	Lee, Elaine	ELe
Franchesco	Fso	Hamilton, Tim	TH	Johnson, Dave	DvJ	Lee, Jae	JaL
Frank, Gary	GFr	Hamner, Cully	CHm	Johnson, Jeff	JJ	Lee, Jim	JLe
Frazetta, Frank	FF	Hampton, Bo	BHa	Johnson, Paul	PuJ	Lee, Patrick	PtL
Freeman, John	JFr	Hampton, Scott	SHp	Johnson, Todd	TJn	Lee, Scott	ScL
Freeman, Simon	SFr	Hanna, Scott	SHa	Jones, Casey	CJ	Lee, Stan	StL
Frenz, Ron	RF	Hannigan, Ed.	EH	Jones, Gerard	GJ	Leeke, Mike	MLe
Friedman, Michael Jan	MFr	Hanson, Neil	NHa	Jones, J.B.	JJo	Leialoha, Steve	SL
Friedrich, Mike	MkF	Harras, Bob	BHs	Jones, Jeff	JeJ	Leon, John Paul	JPL
Frolechlich, A.	AgF	Harris, N. Steven	NSH	Jones, Kelley	KJo	Leonardi, Rick	RL
Fry III, James	JFy	Harris, Tim	THa	Jones, Malcolm	MJ	Levins, Rik	RLe
Fujitani(Fuje), Bob	BF	Harris, Tony	TyH	Jones, R.A.	RAJ	Lieber, Larry	LLi
Furman, Simon	SFu	Harrison, Lou	LuH	Jones, Robert	RJn	Liefeld, Rob	RLd
Gaiman, Neil	**NGa**	Harrison, Simon	SHn	Jurgens, Dan	DJu	Lightle, Steve	SLi
Galan, Manny	MaG	Hart, Ernest	EhH	Jusko, Joe	JJu	Lim, Ron	RLm
Gallant, Shannon	ShG	Hartsoe, Everette	EHr	**Kaluta, Mike**	**MK**	Linsner, Joseph M.	JLi
Gammill, Kerry	KGa	Hathaway, Kurt	KtH	Kamen, Jack	JKa	Livingstone, R.	RLv
Garcia, Dave	DaG	Hawkins, Matt	MHw	Kaminski, Len	LKa	Lloyd, David	DvL
Garner, Alex	AGo	Hayes, Drew	DHa	Kane & Romita	K&R	Lobdell, Scott	SLo
Garney, Ron	RG	Haynes, Hugh	HH	Kane, Bob	Bka	Locke, Vince	VcL
Garzon, Carlos	CG	Hazlewood, Douglas	DHz	Kane, Gil	GK	Loeb, Jeph	JLb
Gascoine, Phil	PGa	Heath, Russ	RH	Kanigher, Bob	BbK	Lopez, Jose	JL
Gaudino, Stefano	SGa	Hebbard, Robert	RtH	Kaniuga, Trent	TKn	Lopresti, Aaron	AaL
Gaughan, Jack	JGa	Heck, Don	DH	Karounos, Paris T.	PaK	Louapre, Dave	DLp
Gecko, Gabe	GG	Heisler, Mike	MHs	Katz, Jack	JKz	Lowe, John	Low
Geggan	Ggn	Hempel, Mark	MaH	Kavanagh, Terry	TKa	Lubbers, Bob	BLb
Gerard, Ruben	RGd	Henry, Flint	FH	Kelly, Walt	WK	Lustbader, Eric Van.	ELu
Gerber, Steve	SvG	Herman, Jack	JH	Kennedy, Cam	CK	Luzniak, Greg	GLz
Giacoia, Frank	FrG	Hernandez, Gilbert	GHe	Keown, Dale	DK	Lyle, Tom	TL
Giarrano, Vince	VGi	Hernandez, Jaime	JHr	Kerschl, Karl	KlK	**Macchio, Ralph**	**RMc**
Gibbons, Dave	DGb	Herrera, Ben	BHr	Kesel, Barbara	BKs	Mack, David	DMk
Gibson, Ian	IG	Hester, Phil	PhH	Kesel, Karl	KK	Mackie, Howard	HMe
Giella, Joe	JoG	Hewlett, Jamie	JHw	Kieth, Sam	SK	Madan, Dev	DeM
Giffen, Keith	KG	Hibbard, E.E.	EHi	King, Hannibal	HbK	Madureira, Joe	JMd
Gilbert, Michael T.	MGi	Hicklenton, John	JHk	Kinsler, Everett R.	EK	Maggin, Elliot S.	ESM
Giordano, Dick	DG	Higgins, Graham	GHi	Kirby, Jack	JK	Maguire, Kevin	KM
Glanzman, Sam	SG	Higgins, John	JHi	Kisniro, Yukito	YuK	Magyar, Rick	RM
Golden, Michael	MGo	Higgins, Michael	MHi	Kitson, Barry	BKi	Mahlstedt, Larry	LMa
Gonzalez, Jorge	JGz	Hitch, Bryan	BHi	Kobasic, Kevin	KoK	Mahnke, Doug	DoM

NAME–ABBREVIATION   Comics Values Annual

Name	Abbr	Name	Abbr	Name	Abbr	Name	Abbr
Mandrake, Tom	TMd	Montano, Steve	SeM	Pascoe, James	JmP	Rodier, Denis	DRo
Maneely, Joe	JMn	Mooney, Jim	JM	Pasko, Martin	MPk	Rogers, Marshall	MR
Manley, Mike	MM	Moore, Alan	AMo	Patterson, Bruce	BrP	Romita, John	JR
Mann, Roland	RMn	Moore, Jeff	JMr	Pearson, Jason	JPn	Romita, John Jr.	JR2
Mann, Roland	Man	Moore, Jerome	JeM	Pelletier, Paul	PaP	Rosenberger, J.	JRo
Manning, Russ	RsM	Moore, John Francis	JFM	Pence, Eric	ErP	Ross, Alex	AxR
Marais, Raymond	RdM	Moore, Terry	TMr	Pennington, Mark	MPn	Ross, David	DR
Mariotte, Jeff	JMi	Morales, Rags	RgM	Pensa, Shea Anton	SAP	Ross, John	JRs
Maroto, Esteban	EM	Moretti, Mark	MMo	Perez, George	GP	Ross, Luke	LRs
Marrinan, Chris	ChM	Morgan, Tom	TMo	Perham, James	JPh	Roth, Werner	WR
Marrs, Lee	LMr	Morisi, Pete	PMo	Perlin, Don	DP	Royle, Jim	JRl
Martin, Gary	GyM	Morosco, Vincent	VMo	Perryman, Edmund	EP	Royle, John	JRe
Martin, Joe	JMt	Morrison, Grant	GMo	Peterson, Brandon	BPe	Rozum, John	JRz
Martinbrough, Shawn	SMa	Morrow, Gray	GM	Peterson, Jonathan	JPe	Rubi, Melvin	MvR
Martinez, Henry	HMz	Mortimer, Win	WMo	Petrucha, Stefan	SPr	Rubinstein, Joe	JRu
Martinez, Roy Allan	RMr	Motter, Dean	DMt	Peyer, Tom	TPe	Rude, Steve	SR
Marz, Ron	RMz	Moy, Jeffrey	JMy	Phillips, Joe	JoP	Ruffner, Sean	SRf
Marzan, Jose	JMz	Murray, Brian	BrM	Phillips, Scott	SPl	Russell, P. Craig	CR
Mason, Tom	TMs	Musial, Joe	JoM	Phillips, Sean	SeP	Russell, Vince	VRu
Massengill, Nathan	NMa	Muth, Jon J.	JMu	Pini, Richard	RPi	Ryan, Matt	MRy
Matsuda, Jeff	JMs	Mychaels, Marat	MMy	Pini, Wendy	WP	Ryan, Paul	PR
Mattsson, Steve	SMt	**Naifeh, Ted**	**TNa**	Platt, Stephen	SPa	Ryder, Tom	TmR
Maus, Bill	BMs	Napolitano, Nick	NNa	Pleece, Warren	WaP	Sakakibara, Mizuki	MiS
Mayer, Sheldon	ShM	Napton, Bob	BNa	Ploog, Mike	MP	Sakai, Stan	SS
Mayerik, Val	VMk	Nauck, Todd	TNu	Plunkett, Kilian	KPl	Sale, Tim	TSe
Mazzucchelli, David	DM	Neary, Paul	PNe	Pollack, Rachel	RaP	Salmons, Tony	TSa
McCarthy, Brendon	BMy	Nebres, Rudy	RN	Pollard, Keith	KP	Saltares, Javier	JS
McCloud, Scott	SMI	Nelson	Nel	Pollina, Adam	AdP	Sanders, Jim III	JS3
McCorkindale, B	BMC	Netzer, Mike	MN	Pope, Paul	PPo	Sasso, Mark	MSo
McCraw, Tom	TMw	Newton, Don	DN	Porch, David	DPo	Saviuk, Alex	AS
McCrea, John	JMC	Nguyen, Hoang	HNg	Portacio, Whilce	WPo	Schaffenberger, Kurt	KS
McDaniel, Scott	SMc	Nichols, Art	ANi	Porter, Howard	HPo	Schane, Tristan	TnS
McDaniel, Walter	WMc	Nicieza, Fabian	FaN	Post, Howard	HwP	Schiller, Fred	FdS
McDonnell, Luke	LMc	Nino, Alex	AN	Potts, Carl	CP	Schmitz, Mark	MaS
McDuffie, Dwayne	DMD	Nocenti, Ann	ANo	Powell, Bob	BP	Schultz, Mark	MSh
McFarlane, Todd	TM	Nocon, Cedric	CNn	Power, Dermot	DPw	Scoffield, Sean	SSc
McGregor, Don	DMG	Nodell, Martin	MnN	Pratt, George	GgP	Scott, Jeffery	JSc
McKean, Dave	DMc	Nolan, Graham	GN	Priest, Christopher	CPr	Scott, Trevor	TvS
McKeever, Ted	TMK	Nord, Cary	CNr	Prosser, Jerry	JeP	Seagle, Steven T.	SSe
McKenna, Mike	MkK	Norem, Earl	EN	Pugh, Steve	StP	Sears, Bart	BS
McKie, Angus	AMK	Nostrand, Howard	HN	Pulido, Brian	BnP	Sekowsky, Mike	MSy
McKone, Mike	MMK	Novick, Irv	IN	**Queen, Randy**	**RQu**	Semeiks, Val	VS
McLaughlin, Frank	FMc	Nowlan, Kevin	KN	Quesada, Joe	JQ	Senior, Geoff	GSr
McLaughlin, Sean	SML	Nutman, Philip	PNu	Quinn, David	DQ	Serpe, Jerry	JyS
McLeod, Bob	BMc	**O'Barr, James**	**JOb**	Quinones, Peter	PQ	Severin, John	JSe
McMahon, M.	MMc	O'Neil, Denny	DON	**Raab, Ben**	**BRa**	Shamray, Gerry	GSh
McManus, Shawn	SwM	O'Neill, Kevin	KON	Raboy, Mac	MRa	Shanower, Eric	EiS
McWilliams, Al	AMc	Olbrich, Dave	DO	Ramos, Humberto	HuR	Sharp, Liam	LSh
Medina, Angel	AMe	Olivetti, Ariel	AOl	Ramos, Rodney	RyR	Shaw, Sean	SSh
Medley, Linda	LiM	Olliffe, Patrick	PO	Randall, Ron	RoR	Sherman, Jim	JSh
Mercadoocasio, H.	HMo	One, Dark	DOe	Raney, Tom	TR	Shoemaker, Terry	TSr
Meskin, Mort	MMe	Ordway, Jerry	JOy	Rankin, Rich	RRa	Shooter, Jim	JiS
Messner-Loebs, Bill	BML	Orlando, Joe	JO	Rapmund, Norm	NRd	Shum, Howard	HSm
Michelinie, David	DvM	Ortiz, Jose	JOt	Raymond, Alex	AR	Shuster, Joe	JoS
Miehm, Grant	GtM	Oskner, Bob	BO	Redondo, Nestor	NR	Sibal, Jonathan	JSb
Mighten, Duke	DMn	Ostrander, John	JOs	Reed, David	DvR	Siegel & Shuster	S&S
Mignola, Michael	MMi	Owen, James	JOn	Reeves-Stevens, Judith	JRv	Sienkiewicz, Bill	BSz
Miki, Danny	DaM	Ozkan, Tayyar	TOz	Reinhold, Bill	BR	Silvestri, Eric	EcS
Milgrom, Al	AM	**Pace, Richard**	**RPc**	Richards, Ted	TR	Silvestri, Mark	MS
Millar, Mark	MMr	Pacella, Mark	MPa	Richardson, Mike	MRi	Sim, Dave	DS
Miller, Frank	FM	Pacheco, Carlos	CPa	Ricketts, Mark	MRc	Simon & Kirby	S&K
Miller, Mike S.	MsM	Palais, Rudy	RP	Rico, Don	DRi	Simon, Joe	JSm
Miller, Steve	SM	Palmer, Tom	TP	Ridgeway, John	JRy	Simonson, Louise	LSi
Milligan, Peter	PrM	Palmiotti, Jimmy	JP	Rieber, John Ney	JNR	Simonson, Walt	WS
Mills, Pat	PMs	Pamai, Gene	GPi	Riley, John	JnR	Simpson, Don	DSs
Minor, Jason	JnM	Panalign, Noly	NPl	Riply	Rip	Simpson, Howard	HSn
Mitchel, Barry	BM	Paniccia, Mark	MPc	Robbins, Frank	FR	Simpson, Will	WSm
Moder, Lee	LMd	Panosian, Dan	DPs	Robbins, Trina	TrR	Sinnott, Joe	JSt
Moebius	Moe	Parkhouse, Annie	APh	Robertson, Darrick	DaR	Skroce, Steve	SSr
Moeller, Chris	CsM	Parkhouse, Steve	SvP	Robinson, James	JeR	Smith, Andy	ASm
Moench, Doug	DgM	Parobeck, Mike	MeP			Smith, Barry W.	BWS

NAME–ABBREVIATION

Name	Abbr.	Name	Abbr.	Name	Abbr.	Name	Abbr.
Smith, Beau	BSt	Sweetman, Dan	DSw	Vance, Steve	SVa	Williams, David	DdW
Smith, Cam	CaS	**Taggart, Tom**	**TTg**	VanHook, Kevin	KVH	Williams, J.H.	JWi
Smith, Jeff	JSi	Takenaga, Francis	FTa	Vargas, Vagner	VV	Williams, Keith	KWi
Smith, John	JnS	Takezaki, Tony	ToT	Veitch, Rick	RV	Williams, Kent	KW
Smith, Kevin	KSm	Talbot, Bryan	BT	Velez, Ivan, Jr.	IV	Williams, Scott	SW
Smith, Malcolm	MSt	Tallarico, Tony	TyT	Velluto, Sal	SaV	Williamson, Al	AW
Smith, Paul	PS	Tan, Billy	BTn	Vess, Charles	CV	Williamson, Skip	SWi
Smith, Robin	RSm	Tanaka, Masashi	MTk	Vey, Al	AV	Willingham, Bill	BWg
Smith, Ron	RS	Tanghal, Romeo	RT	Vigil, Tim	TV	Willis, Damon	DaW
Snejbjerg, Peter	PSj	Tappin, Steve	SeT	Vokes, Neil	NV	Wilshire, Mary	MW
Sniegoski, Tom	TSg	Taylor, David	DTy	Von Eeden, Trevor	TVE	Wilson, Colin	CWi
Spark	Spk	Taylor, R.G.	RGT	Vosburg, Mike	MV	Wilson, Gahan	GW
Sparling, Jack	JkS	Templeton, Ty	TTn	**Wagner, Matt**	**MWg**	Wilson, Keith S.	KSW
Spiegelman, Art	ASp	Teney, Tom	TmT	Wagner, Ron	RoW	Woch, Stan	SnW
Spiegle, Dan	DSp	Tenney, Mark	MaT	Waid, Mark	MWa	Woggin, Bill	BWo
Spinks, Frank	FrS	Texeira, Mark	MT	Walker, Kevin	KeW	Wojtkiewicz, Chuck	Woj
Springer, Frank	FS	Thibert, Art	ATi	Waltrip, Jason	JWp	Wolf, Chance	CWf
Sprouse, Chris	CSp	Thomas, Dann	DTs	Waltrip, John	JWt	Wolfe, Joseph	JWf
St.Pierre, Joe	JPi	Thomas, Roy	RTs	Ward, Bill	BWa	Wolfman, Marv	MWn
Starlin, Jim	JSn	Thomason, Derek	DeT	Warner, Chris	CW	Wolverton, Basil	BW
Starr, Leonard	LSt	Thompson, Jill	JIT	Warren, Adam	AWa	Wood, Bob	BoW
Staton, Joe	JSon	Thorne, Frank	FT	Washington 3, Robert	3RW	Wood, Teri Sue	TWo
Steacy, Ken	KSy	Tinker, Ron	RnT	Watkiss, John	JWk	Wood, Wally	WW
Steffan, Dan	DnS	Torres, Angelo	AT	Weeks, Lee	LW	Woodring, Jim	JWo
Stelfreeze, Brian	BSf	Toth, Alex	ATh	Wein, Len	LWn	Wormer, Kirk Van	KWo
Stephenson, Eric	ErS	Totleben, John	JTo	Weinstein, Howard	HWe	Wright, Greg	GWt
Steranko, Jim	JSo	Trimpe, Herb	HT	Welch, Larry	LyW	Wrightson, Berni	BWr
Stern, Roger	RSt	Truman, Timothy	TT	Wendel, Andrew	AdW	Wyman, M.C.	MCW
Stern, Steve	SSt	Truog, Chas	ChT	Wenzel, David	DWe	**Yaep, Chap**	**CYp**
Stevens, Dave	DSt	Tucci, Bill	BiT	Weringo, Mike	MeW	Yeates, Tom	TY
Stiles, Steve	SvS	Turner, Dwayne	DT	West, Kevin	KWe	Yeowell, Steve	SY
Story, Karl	KlS	Tuska, George	GT	Weston, Chris	CWn	**Zabel, Joe**	**JZe**
Stout, William	WiS	**Ulm, Chris**	**CU**	Wheatley, Mark	MkW	Zachary, Dean	DZ
Stradley, Randy	RSd	**Vachss, Andrew**	**AVs**	Whitney, Ogden	OW	Zaffino, Jorge	JZ
Strazewski, Len	LeS	Vado, Dan	DVa	Wiacek, Bob	BWi	Zeck, Mike	MZ
Stroman, Larry	LSn	Valentino, Jim	JV	Wiesenfeld, Aron	AWs	Zick, Bruce	BZ
Sullivan, Lee	LS	Vallejo, Boris	BV	Wildey, Doug	DW	Zulli, Michael	MZi
Sutton, Tom	TS	Van Fleet, John	JVF	Wildman, Andrew	Wld	Zyskowski, Joseph	JZy
Swan, Curt	CS	Vancata, Brad	BVa	Williams, Anthony	AWi	Zyskowski, Steven	SZ

GENERAL ABBREVIATIONS FOR COMICS LISTINGS

Adaptation	Adapt.	Giant Size	G-Size	Prestige Format	PF
Appearance of	A:	Golden Age	G.A.	Preview	Prev.
Anniversary	Anniv.	Graphic Album	GAm	Reprinted issue	rep.
Annual	Ann.#	Graphic Novel	GN or GNv	Retold	rtd.
Art & Cover	(a&c)	Hardcover	HC	Return/Revival of	R:
Art & Plot	(a&pl)	Identity Revealed	IR:	Scripted/Written by	(s)
Art & Script	(a&s)	Inks by	(i)	Scripts & inks	(s&i)
Artist	(a)	Introduction of	I:	Silver Age	S.A.
Back-Up Story	BU:	Joins of	J:	Softcover	SC
Beginning of	B:	King Size	K-Size	Special	Spec.
Birth of	b:	Leaving of	L:	Team-up	T.U.
Cameo Appearance	C:	New Costume	N:	Trade Paperback	TPB
Cover	(c)	No Issue Number	N#	Versus	V: or vs.
Cover and Script	(c&s)	Origin of	O:	Wedding of	W:
Crossover with	x-over	Painted Cover	P(c)	With	w/
Death/Destruction of	D:	Part	pt. or Pt.	Without	w/o
Edition	Ed.	Pencils by	(p)		
Ending of	E:	Photographic cover	Ph(c)		
Features	F:	Plotted by	(pl)		

CVA Page 15

ABBREVIATION–NAME   Comics Values Annual

3RW. Robert Washington 3	BDn. . . . . Ben Dunn	CE. . . . . Carlos Ezquerra	DHz . . Douglas Hazlewood
AA. . . . . Alfredo Alcala	BE . . . . Bill Elder	CG . . . . . . Carlos Garzon	DiF . . . . Dick Foreman
AAd . . . . Art Adams	BEd . . . . Ben Edlund	CH. . . . . Chad Hunt	DJ . . . . Dennis Jensen
AaK . . . . . . Alisa Kwitney	BEv . . . . Bill Everett	ChB. . . . . . . Charles Berger	DJa . . . . Dennis Janke
AaL . . . . . . Aaron Lopresti	BEw . . . . Brett Ewins	ChG . . . . . Chester Gould	DJu. . . . . Dan Jurgens
AAv . . . . Al Avison	BF . . . . Bob Fujitani(Fuje)	ChM. . . . . Chris Marrinan	DK . . . . Dale Keown
AB. . . . . Alex Blum	BG . . . . Bill Griffith	CHm . . . . . Cully Hamner	DkB. . . . . . . Dick Browne
ABr . . . . Ann Brewster	BH. . . . . Bob Hall	ChT . . . . Chas Truog	DkG . . . . . . Daerick Gross
ACa . . . . Anthony Castrillo	BHa. . . . . . . Bo Hampton	Chu. . . . . Ernie Chua	DL. . . . . . Dave Lapham
ACe . . . . . Andrew Currie	BHg . . . . . . Burne Hogarth	CI . . . . . Carmine Infantino	DlB . . . . Daniel Brereton
ACh . . . . . . Anthony Chun	BHi . . . . Bryan Hitch	Clv . . . . Chris Ivy	DLp. . . . . . . Dave Louapre
ACo . . . . . Amanda Conner	BHr . . . . Ben Herrera	CJ. . . . . Casey Jones	DLw. . . . . Dan Lawlis
AD . . . . Alan Davis	BHs. . . . . . . Bob Harras	CK . . . . . Cam Kennedy	DM . . . David Mazzucchelli
ADF. . . . Alan Dean Foster	BiT . . . . Bill Tucci	CNn . . . . . . Cedric Nocon	DMc . . . . . Dave McKean
AdP . . . . Adam Pollina	BK . . . . . . Bernie Krigstein	CNr. . . . . Cary Nord	DMD . . . Dwayne McDuffie
ADv . . . . Al Davison	Bka . . . . Bob Kane	CP. . . . . Carl Potts	DMG . . . Don McGregor
AdW. . . . . Andrew Wendel	BKi. . . . . Barry Kitson	CPa . . . . . Carlos Pacheco	DMk . . . . David Mack
AF . . . . Al Feldstein	BKr . . . . . . Brandon Kruse	CPr . . . . . Christopher Priest	DMn . . . . . . Duke Mighten
AFa . . . . Al Fago	BKs . . . . . . Babara Kesel	CR . . . . . P. Craig Russell	DMt . . . . Dean Motter
AG . . . . Al Gordon	BL. . . . . Bob Layton	CrB . . . . . . Craig Brasfield	DN. . . . . Don Newton
AgF . . . . . . A. Frolechlich	BLb. . . . . . . Bob Lubbers	CS . . . . Curt Swan	DnS . . . . Dan Steffan
AGo . . . . Alex Garner	BlH . . . . Bill Hobbs	CsB . . . . . . Chris Batista	DO . . . . Dave Olbrich
AGw . . . . . Archie Goodwin	BLr . . . . Bob Larkin	CsM . . . . . . Chris Moeller	DoC. . . . . . Dario Carrasco
AH . . . . . . Adam Hughes	BLs . . . . Batton Lash	CSp . . . . . . Chris Sprouse	DOe. . . . . Dark One
AHo . . . . Art Holcomb	BM . . . . Barry Mitchel	CU. . . . . Chris Ulm	DoM . . . . . . Doug Mahnke
AIA. . . . . . Alfred Andriola	BMc . . . . Bob McLeod	CV . . . . . . Charles Vess	DON . . . . . O'Neil, Denny
AJ. . . . . Al Jaffee	BMC . . . B. McCorkindale	CW. . . . . . Chris Warner	DP . . . . Don Perlin
AKu . . . . . Adam Kubert	BML . . Bill Messner-Loebs	CWf . . . . . . Chance Wolf	DPo . . . . Porch, David
ALa . . . . . . Andy Lanning	BMs . . . . Bill Maus	CWi . . . . . . Colin Wilson	DPs. . . . . . . Dan Panosian
AlG . . . . Alan Grant	BMy . . . Brendon McCarthy	CWn . . . . . . Chris Weston	DPw. . . . . . Power, Dermot
AM . . . . Al Milgrom	BNa . . . . Bob Napton	CYp . . . . Chap Yaep	DQ. . . . . David Quinn
AMc . . . . . Al McWilliams	BnP . . . . Brian Pulido	**DA. . . . . Dan Adkins**	DR . . . . Ross, David
AMe. . . . . . . Angel Medina	BO . . . . Bob Oskner	DAb. . . . . . . Dusty Abell	Rd. . . . . . Richard Delgado
AMK . . . . . . Angus McKie	BoW . . . . Bob Wood	DaC . . . Dan Castellaneta	DRi. . . . . Don Rico
AMo . . . . Alan Moore	BP . . . . Bob Powell	DaF . . . . Dan Fraga	DRo . . . . . Denis Rodier
AN . . . . Alex Nino	BPe . . . Brandon Peterson	DaG . . . . . Dave Garcia	DS . . . . Dave Sim
ANi . . . . Art Nichols	BR. . . . . . . Bill Reinhold	DaM . . . . . Danny Miki	DSp . . . . Dan Spiegle
ANo . . . . Ann Nocenti	BRa . . . . Ben Raab	DAn . . . . . Dan Abnett	DSs . . . . Don Simpson
AOl. . . . . Ariel Olivetti	BrM. . . . . . . Brian Murray	DaR . . . Darrick Robertson	DSt . . . . Dave Stevens
APh . . . Annie Parkhouse	BrP . . . . . Bruce Patterson	DaW. . . . . . . Damon Willis	DSw . . . . Dan Sweetman
AR . . . . Alex Raymond	BS . . . . Bart Sears	Day . . . . Dan Day	DT . . . . Dwayne Turner
AS . . . . Alex Saviuk	BSf. . . . . . Brian Stelfreeze	DAy . . . . Dick Ayers	DTs . . . . . . Dann Thomas
ASm . . . . Andy Smith	BSt . . . . Beau Smith	DB . . . . D. Battlefield	DTy . . . . David Taylor
ASp. . . . . . Art Spiegelman	BSz. . . . . . Bill Sienkiewicz	DB . . . . . Denis Beauvais	DvA. . . . David Ammerman
AT . . . . Angelo Torres	BT . . . . Bryan Talbot	DBa . . . . Dan Barry	DVa . . . . Dan Vado
ATh. . . . . Alex Toth	BTn . . . . Billy Tan	DBk . . . . . . Darryl Banks	DvC . . . . . . Dave Cooper
ATi . . . . Art Thibert	Buzz . . . . Buzz	DBl . . . . . . Danny Bulanadi	DvD. . . . . . . Dave Dorman
AV. . . . . Al Vey	BV . . . . Boris Vallejo	DBr. . . . . . . Dick Briefer	DvJ. . . . . . . Dave Johnson
AVs . . . . . Andrew Vachss	BVa . . . . . . Brad Vancata	DBs . . . . John Barras	DvL. . . . . David Lloyd
AW. . . . . . Al Williamson	BW . . . . . . Basil Wolverton	DBw . . . Doug Braithwaite	DvM. . . . . David Michelinie
AWa . . . . . Adam Warren	BWa . . . . Bill Ward	DC. . . . . . Dave Cockrum	DvR . . . . David Reed
AWi . . . Anthony Williams	BWg. . . . . Bill Willingham	DCn . . . . . . Don Cameron	DW . . . . Doug Wildey
AWs . . . . Aron Wiesenfeld	BWi . . . . . . Bob Wiacek	DCw . . . . . . Denys Cowan	DWe . . . . . David Wenzel
AxR. . . . . Alex Ross	BWo . . . . Bill Woggin	DD. . . . . Dick Dillin	DZ . . . . Dean Zachary
AyB . . . . Allyn Brodsky	BWr . . . . . . Berni Wrightson	DdB . . . . David Boller	**EA . . . . Edd Ashe**
BA . . . . . Brent Anderson	BWS . Barry Windsor-Smith	DDv . . . . Dan Davis	EB . . . . Ed Barreto
BAn . . . . . . Bill Anderson	BZ . . . . Bruce Zick	DdW . . . . . . David Williams	EBe . . . . Ed Benes
BAp . . . . . . Brian Althorp	**CAd . . . . . Charlie Adlard**	DE . . . . D. Elliot	EC . . . . Ernie Colon
BAu . . . . . . Brian Augustyn	CaS . . . . Cam Smith	DeH. . . . . . . Dave Hund	ECa . . . . . Eddie Campbell
BB . . . . Brian Bolland	CAx . . . . Chris Alexander	DeM . . . . . . Dev Madan	ECh. . . . . Ernie Chan
BBa . . . . . . Bernard Bailey	CB . . . . Carl Barks	DeT . . . . Derek Thomason	EcS . . . . Eric Silvestri
BbB . . . . Bob Brown	CBa. . . . . . Chris Bachalo	DFg. . . . . Duncan Fegredo	EDo . . . . Evan Dorkin
BBB . . . . . . Bob Boze Bell	CBi . . . . Charles Biro	DFr. . . . . Danny Fingeroth	EH . . . . Ed Hannigan
BBh. . . . . Brett Booth	CBu . . . . Carl Bugro	DG . . . . . . Dick Giordano	EhH. . . . . Ernest Hart
BbK . . . . . . Bob Kaniger	CCa . . . . . Charles Caldes	DGb . . . . . Dave Gibbons	EHi . . . . . . E.E. Hibbard
BBl . . . . Bret Blevins	CCl . . . . . Chris Claremont	DGC . . . . D.G. Chichester	EHr . . . . . Everette Hartsoe
BBr. . . . . . . Brett Breeding	Ccs. . . . . Chriscross	DgM . . . . . Doug Moench	EiS . . . . . . Eric Shanower
BCe . . . . . . Bobbie Chase	CCt . . . . Claudio Castellini	DGr . . . . Dan Green	EK . . . . . Everett R. Kinsler
BCh . . . . . . Bernard Chang	CCu . . . . . . Chuck Culdera	DH. . . . . Don Heck	EL . . . . Erik Larsen
BCi . . . . Brandon Choi	CDi . . . . Chuck Dixon	DHa . . . . Drew Hayes	ELe . . . . Elaine Lee
BDC . . . Brent D Carpenter	CDo . . . . . . Colleen Doran	DHv . . . . . . Dave Hoover	ELu . . . Eric Van Lustbader

CVA Page 16

Comics Values Annual — ABBREVIATION–NAME

Abbr	Name
EM	Esteban Maroto
EN	Earl Norem
ENB	E. Nelson Bridwell
EP	Edmund Perryman
ERC	E.R. Cruz
ErP	Eric Pence
ErS	Eric Stephenson
ESM	Elliot S. Maggin
FaN	**Fabian Nicieza**
FB	Frank Brunner
FBe	Frank Bolle
FBk	Fred Burke
FC	Frank Cirocco
FdS	Fred Schiller
FF	Frank Frazetta
FFo	Frank Fosco
FG	Frank Guardineer
FG	Floyd Gottfredson
FH	Flint Henry
FM	Frank Miller
FMc	Frank McLaughlin
FR	Frank Robbins
FrG	Frank Giacoia
FrS	Frank Spinks
FS	Frank Springer
Fso	Franchesco
FT	Frank Thorne
FTa	Francis Takenaga
GaF	**Gardner Fox**
GB	Geoffrey Biggs
GBl	George Bell
GBu	Greg Budget
GC	Gene Colan
GCa	Greg Capullo
GCh	Gary Cohn
GD	Gene Day
GDu	Gary Dumm
GE	George Evans
GeH	Gene Ha
GEn	Garth Ennis
GEr	Gary Erskine
GF	Glenn Fabry
GfD	Geof Darrow
GFo	Gerald Forton
GFr	Gary Frank
GFx	Gill Fox
GG	Gabe Gecko
Ggn	Geggan
GgP	George Pratt
GHe	Gilbert Hernandez
GHi	Graham Higgins
GI	Geoff Isherwood
GJ	Gerard Jones
GK	Gil Kane
GL	Garry Leach
GlD	Glyn Dillon
GLz	Greg Luzniak
GM	Gray Morrow
GMo	Grant Morrison
GN	Graham Nolan
GP	George Perez
GPi	Gene Pamai
GrI	Graham Ingles
GrL	Greg LaRocque
GSh	Gerry Shamray
GSr	Geoff Senior
GT	George Tuska
GtM	Grant Miehm
GW	Gahan Wilson
GWt	Greg Wright
GyA	Gary Amaro
GyC	Gerry Conway
GyD	Guy Davis
GyM	Gary Martin
HaE	**Harlan Ellison**
HB	Hernandez Brothers
HbK	Hannibal King
HC	Howard Chaykin
HFl	Homer Flemming
HH	Hugh Haynes
HK	Harvey Kurtzman
HMe	Howard Mackie
HMo	H. Mercadoocasio
HMz	Henry Martinez
HN	Howard Nostrand
HNg	Hoang Nguyen
HPo	Howard Porter
HSm	Howard Shum
HSn	Howard Simpson
HT	Herb Trimpe
HuR	Humberto Ramos
HWe	Howard Weinstein
HwP	Howard Post
IaC	**Ian Churchhill**
IEd	Ian Edginton
IG	Ian Gibson
IN	Irv Novick
IV	Ivan Velez, Jr.
JA	**Jack Abel**
JaB	Jack Binder
JaD	Jamie Delano
JaL	Jae Lee
JAl	Jeff Albrecht
JAo	John Albano
JAp	Jim Aparo
JAr	John Arcudi
JB	John Buscema
JBa	Jim Baikie
JBa	Jim Balent
JBe	John Beeston
JBg	Jon Bogdanove
JBi	Jerry Bingham
JBl	Jesus Blasco
JBm	John Broom
JBn	John Burns
JBo	John Bolton
JBr	June Brigman
JBt	Jeff Butler
JBy	John Byrne
JBz	Joe Benitez
JCa	John Calnan
JCf	Jim Calafiore
JCh	Joe Chiodo
JCo	Jack Cole
JCp	John Cooper
JCr	Johnny Craig
JCt	Joe Carter
JCx	Jeromy Cox
JCz	Jerry Cruz
JD	Jan Duursema
JDa	Jack Davis
JDo	Julie Doucet
JDx	John Dixon
JDy	Jo Duffy
JeJ	Jeff Jones
JeM	Jerome Moore
JeP	Jerry Prosser
JeR	James Robinson
JEs	John Estes
JF	John Forte
JFM	John Francis Moore
JFr	John Freeman
JFy	James Fry III
JG	Jackson Guice
JGa	Jack Gaughan
JGz	Jorge Gonzalez
JH	Jack Herman
JhB	John Beatty
JhD	John Dell
JHi	John Higgins
JHk	John Hicklenton
JHl	James Hudnall
JHo	John Holdredge
JHr	Jaime Hernandez
JHw	Jamie Hewlett
JiC	Jim Callahan
JiS	Jim Shooter
JJ	Jeff Johnson
JJB	JJ Birch
JJn	Julius Jackson
JJo	J.B. Jones
JJu	Joe Jusko
JK	Jack Kirby
JKa	Jack Kamen
JkS	Jack Sparling
JKu	Joe Kubert
JKz	Jack Katz
JL	Jose Lopez
JLb	Jeph Loeb
JLd	Joe Lansdale
JLe	Jim Lee
JLi	Joseph M. Linsner
JIT	Jill Thompson
JLv	Jim Lavery
JM	Jim Mooney
JMC	John McCrea
JMd	Joe Madureira
JMD	J.M. DeMatteis
JMi	Jeff Mariotte
JmL	Jim Lawson
JMn	Joe Maneely
JmP	James Pascoe
JMr	Jeff Moore
JMs	Jeff Matsuda
JMt	Joe Martin
JMu	Jon J. Muth
JMy	Jeffrey Moy
JMz	Jose Marzan
JnM	Jason Minor
JnR	John Riley
JNR	John Ney Rieber
JnS	John Smith
JO	Joe Orlando
JoA	Jo Alibaster
JoB	Joe Bennett
JoC	Joe Casey
JOb	James O'Barr
JoG	Joe Giella
JoM	Joe Musial
JOn	James Owen
JoP	Joe Phillips
JoS	Joe Shuster
JOs	John Ostrander
JOt	Jose Ortiz
JOy	Jerry Ordway
JP	Jimmy Palmiotti
JPe	Jonathan Peterson
JPh	James Perham
JPi	Joe St.Pierre
JPL	John Paul Leon
JPn	Jason Pearson
JQ	Joe Quesada
JR	John Romita
JR2	John Romita, Jr.
JRe	John Royle
JRl	Jim Royle
JRo	J. Rosenberger
JRs	John Ross
JRu	Joe Rubinstein
JRv	Judith Reeves-Stevens
JRy	John Ridgeway
JRz	John Rozum
JS	Javier Saltares
JS3	Jim Sanders III
JSb	Jonathan Sibal
JSc	Jeffery Scott
JSC	J. Scott Campbell
JSe	John Severin
JSh	Jim Sherman
JSi	Jeff Smith
JSm	Joe Simon
JSn	Jim Starlin
JSo	Jim Steranko
JSon	Joe Staton
JSt	Joe Sinnott
JTo	John Totleben
JuB	Julie Bell
JV	Jim Valentino
JVF	John Van Fleet
JWf	Joseph Wolfe
JWi	J.H. Williams
JWk	John Watkiss
JWo	Jim Woodring
JWp	Jason Waltrip
JWt	John Waltrip
JyS	Jerry Serpe
JZ	Jorge Zaffino
JZe	Joe Zabel
JZy	Joseph Zyskowski
K&R	**Kane & Romita**
KB	Kyle Baker
KBk	Kurt Busiek
KD	Kieron Dwyer
KDe	Kim Deitch
KDM	Kim DeMulder
KEa	Kevin Eastman
KeL	Ken Lashley
KeW	Kevin Walker
KG	Keith Giffen
KGa	Kerry Gammill
KHd	Kevin Hopgood
KHt	Kyle Hotz
KiA	Kia Asamiya
KJ	Klaus Janson
KJa	Kirk Javinen
KJo	Kelley Jones
KK	Karl Kesel
KlA	Karl Alstaetter
KlK	Karl Kerschl
KlS	Karl Story
KM	Kevin Maguire
KN	Kevin Nowlan
KoK	Kevin Kobasic
KON	Kevin O'Neill
KP	Keith Pollard
KPl	Kilian Plunkett
KS	Kurt Schaffenberger
KSm	Kevin Smith
KSW	Keith S. Wilson
KSy	Ken Steacy
KtH	Kurt Hathaway
KVH	Kevin VanHook
KW	Kent Williams
KWe	Kevin West

CVA Page 17

ABBREVIATION–NAME — Comics Values Annual

Abbr	Name	Abbr	Name	Abbr	Name	Abbr	Name
KWi	Keith Williams	MG	Mike Gustovich	NKu	Andy Kubert	RG	Ron Garney
KWo	Kirk Van Wormer	MGi	Michael T. Gilbert	NMa	Nathan Massengill	RGd	Ruben Gerard
LbC	**Leonard B. Cole**	MGo	Michael Golden	NNa	Nick Napolitano	RgM	Rags Morales
LC	Lou Cameron	MGr	Mike Grell	NPl	Noly Panalign	RGr	Randy Green
LCh	Lillian Chestney	MGs	Martin Griffiths	NR	Nestor Redondo	RGs	R. Grossman
LDr	Larry Dresser	MGu	Mark Gruenwald	NRd	Norm Rapmund	RGT	R.G. Taylor
LDu	Leo Duranona	MGy	Mick Gray	NSH	N. Steven Harris	RGu	Rebecca Guay
LDz	Luis Dominguez	MHi	Michael Higgins	NV	Neil Vokes	RH	Russ Heath
LE	Lee Elias	MHo	Matt Howarth	NyC	Nancy Collins	RHe	Richard Horie
LeS	Len Strazewski	MHs	Mike Heisler	**OW**	**Ogden Whitney**	RHo	Rick Hoberg
LF	Lou Fine	MHw	Matt Hawkins	**PaD**	**Paco Diaz**	RHo	Rich Howell
LHa	Larry Hama	MHy	Matt Haley	PaK	Paris T. Karounos	RiB	Richard Bennett
LI	Larry Ivie	MI	Medio Iorio	PaP	Paul Pelletier	Rip	Riply
LiM	Linda Medley	MiA	Michael Allred	PB	Pat Broderick	RJ	Robert Jenney
LJi	Leonardo Jimenez	MiB	Mike Barr	PBd	Philip Bond	RJn	Robert Jones
LKa	Len Kaminski	MiS	Mizuki Sakakibara	PC	Paul Chadwick	RkB	Rick Bryant
LLi	Larry Lieber	MJ	Malcolm Jones	PCu	Paris Cullins	RkL	Rick Leach
LMa	Larry Mahlstedt	MK	Mike Kaluta	PD	Peter Doherty	RKu	Roy Krenkel
LMc	Luke McDonnell	MkB	Mike Barreiro	PDd	Peter David	RL	Rick Leonardi
LMd	Lee Moder	MkF	Mike Friedlich	PDi	Paul Dini	RLd	Rob Liefeld
LMr	Lee Marrs	MkH	Mike Hoffer	PFe	Pascual Ferry	RLe	Rik Levins
Low	John Lowe	MkK	Mike McKenna	PG	Paul Gulacy	RLm	Ron Lim
LRs	Luke Ross	MkW	Mark Wheatley	PGa	Phil Gascoine	RLv	R. Livingstone
LS	Lee Sullivan	MlB	Michael Bair	PGn	Paul Guinan	RM	Rick Magyar
LSh	Liam Sharp	MLe	Mike Leeke	PGr	Peter Grau	RMc	Ralph Macchio
LSi	Louise Simonson	MLr	Michael Lark	PhH	Phil Hester	RMn	Roland Mann
LSn	Larry Stroman	MM	Mike Manley	PJ	Phil Jimminiz	RMr	Roy Allan Martinez
LSt	Leonard Starr	MMc	M. McMahon	PJe	Paul Jenkins	RMz	Ron Marz
LuH	Lou Harrison	MMe	Mort Meskin	PKr	Peter Krause	RN	Rudy Nebres
LW	Lee Weeks	MMi	Michael Mignola	PIA	Paul Abrams	RnT	Ron Tinker
LWn	Len Wein	MMK	Mike McKone	PLa	Peter Laird	RoR	Ron Randall
LyW	Larry Welch	MMo	Mark Moretti	PMo	Pete Morisi	RoW	on Wagner
MA	**Murphy Anderson**	MMr	Mark Millar	PMs	Pat Mills	RP	Rudy Palais
MaG	Manny Galan	MMy	Marat Mychaels	PNe	Paul Neary	RPc	Richard Pace
MaH	Mark Hempel	MN	Mike Netzer	PNu	Philip Nutman	RPi	Richard Pini
Man	Roland Mann	MnN	Martin Nodell	PO	Patrick Olliffe	RQu	Randy Queen
MaS	Mark Schmitz	Moe	Moebius	PPo	Paul Pope	RRa	Rich Rankin
MaT	Mark Tenney	MP	Mike Ploog	PQ	Peter Quinones	RS	Ron Smith
MB	Matt Baker	MPa	Mark Pacella	PR	Paul Ryan	RsB	Russell Braun
MBa	Mark Bagley	MPc	Mark Paniccia	PrC	Peter Costanza	RSd	Randy Stradley
MBe	M. Belardinelli	MPk	Martin Pasko	PrG	Peter Gross	RsM	Russ Manning
MBg	Mark Badger	MPn	Mark Pennington	PrM	Peter Milligan	RSm	Robin Smith
MBm	Mary Bierbaum	MR	Marshall Rogers	PS	Paul Smith	RSt	Roger Stern
MBn	Mike Baron	MRa	Mac Raboy	PSj	Peter Snejbjerg	RT	Romeo Tanghal
MBr	Mark Bright	MRc	Mark Ricketts	PtL	Patrick Lee	RtH	Robert Hebbard
MBu	Mark Buckingham	MRi	Mike Richardson	PuD	Paul Danner	RTs	Roy Thomas
MBy	Mitch Byrd	MRy	Matt Ryan	PuJ	Paul Johnson	RV	Rick Veitch
MC	Mike Collins	MS	Mark Silvestri	PuK	Paul Kupperberg	RyE	Randy Emberlin
MCa	Marc Campos	MSh	Mark Schultz	**RA**	**Ross Andru**	RyL	Ray Lago
MCh	Mike Chen	MsM	Mike S. Miller	RAJ	R.A. Jones	RyR	Rodney Ramos
MCi	Mark Crilley	MSo	Mark Sasso	RaP	Rachel Pollack	**S&K**	**Simon & Kirby**
MCl	Mike Clark	MSt	Malcolm Smith	RB	Rich Buckler	S&S	Siegel & Shuster
MCn	Max Allan Collins	MSy	Mike Sekowsky	RbB	Robert Bernstein	SA	Sergio Aragones
MCo	Mark Chiarello	MT	Mark Texeira	RbC	Robert Campenella	Sal	Sal Amendola
MCr	Mike Carlin	MtB	Matt Broome	RBe	Ramon Bernado	SAP	Shea Anton Pensa
MCW	M.C. Wyman	MTk	Masashi Tanaka	RBn	Ryan Benjamin	SaV	Sal Velluto
MCy	Mike Carey	MV	Mike Vosburg	RBr	Rick Burchett	SB	Sal Buscema
MD	Mort Drucker	MvR	Melvin Rubi	RBu	Robert Burns	SBi	Stephen Bissette
MD2	Mike Deodato, Jr.	MW	Mary Wilshire	RC	Reed Crandall	SBs	Simon Bisley
MDa	Malcolm Davis	MWa	Mark Waid	RCa	Richard Case	SBt	Steve Butler
MDb	M. DeZuniga	MWg	Matt Wagner	RCl	Ricky Carralero	SC	Sid Check
MDo	Mike Dorey	MWn	Marv Wolfman	RCo	Richard Corben	ScB	Scott Benefiel
MDr	Mike Dringenberg	MZ	Mike Zeck	RCr	Robert Crumb	ScC	Scott Clark
ME	Mike Esposito	MZi	Michael Zulli	RCz	Roger Cruz	SCh	Sean Chen
MEg	Marty Egeland	**NA**	**Neal Adams**	RDB	Randy DuBerkr	SCi	Sergio Cariello
MeP	Mike Parobeck	NBy	Norm Breyfogle	RdM	Raymond Marais	ScK	Scott Kolins
MeW	Mike Weringo	NC	Nick Cardy	RDm	Rodolfo Damaggio	ScL	Scott Lee
MF	Matt Fox	ND	Nigel Dobbyn	RdD	Richard Delgado	SCr	Steve Crespo
MFl	Michael Fleisher	Nel	Nelson	RE	Ric Estrada	SCy	Simon Colby
MFm	Mark Farmer	NGa	Neil Gaiman	RF	Ron Frenz	SD	Steve Ditko
MFr	Michael Jan Friedman	NHa	Neil Hanson	RFl	Robert Fleming	SDi	Steve Dillon

ABBREVIATION–NAME

Abbr	Name	Abbr	Name	Abbr	Name	Abbr	Name
SDr	Stan Drake	SSc	Sean Scoffield	TGo	Till Goodman	TTn	Ty Templeton
SDR	Sam DeLaRosa	SSe	Steven T. Seagle	TH	Tim Hamilton	TV	Tim Vigil
SEa	Scott Eaton	SSh	Sean Shaw	THa	Tim Harris	TVE	Trevor Von Eeden
SeM	Steve Montano	SSr	Steve Skroce	TJn	Todd Johnson	TvS	Trevor Scott
SeP	Sean Phillips	SSt	Steve Stern	TKa	Terry Kavanagh	TWo	Teri Sue Wood
SEp	Steve Epting	StA	Stephen Addeo	TKn	Trent Kaniuga	TY	Tom Yeates
SeT	Steve Tappin	StB	Scott Benson	TKr	Teddy H. Kristiansen	TyD	Terry Dodson
SEt	Steve Englehart	StC	Stan Campbell	TL	Tom Lyle	TyH	Tony Harris
SF	Sal Finnocchiaro	StE	Steve Erwin	TLa	Terry LaBan	TyT	Tony Tallarico
SFr	Simon Freeman	StG	Steve Grant	TLw	Terral Lawrence	**VAz**	**Vincent Alcazar**
SFu	Simon Furman	StL	Stan Lee	TM	Todd McFarlane	VB	Vaughn Bode
SG	Sam Glanzman	StP	Steve Pugh	TmB	Tim Burgard	VcL	Vince Locke
SGa	Stefano Gaudino	SVa	Steve Vance	TmC	Tom Christopher	VGi	Vince Giarrano
SGe	Sid Greene	SvG	Steve Gerber	TMd	Tom Mandrake	ViC	Vince Colletta
SHa	Scott Hanna	SvL	Salvador Larroca	TMK	Ted McKeever	VMk	Val Mayerik
ShG	Shannon Gallant	SvP	Steve Parkhouse	TMo	Tom Morgan	VMo	Vincent Morosco
ShM	Sheldon Mayer	SvS	Steve Stiles	TmR	Tom Ryder	VRu	Vince Russell
SHn	Simon Harrison	SW	Scott Williams	TMr	Terry Moore	VS	Val Semeiks
SHp	Scott Hampton	SWi	Skip Williamson	TMs	Tom Mason	VV	Vagner Vargas
SI	Stuart Immonen	SwM	Shawn McManus	TmT	Tom Teney	**WaP**	**Warren Pleece**
SK	Sam Kieth	SY	Steve Yeowell	TMw	Tom McCraw	WB	Wayne Boring
SL	Steve Leialoha	SZ	Steven Zyskowski	TNa	Ted Naifeh	WBu	W. Burroughs
SLi	Steve Lightle	**TA**	**Terry Austin**	TnD	Tony Daniel	WE	Will Eisner
SLo	Scott Lobdell	TAr	Tom Artis	TnS	Tristan Schane	WEl	Warren Ellis
SM	Steve Miller	TB	Tim Boxell	TNu	Todd Nauck	WiS	William Stout
SMa	Shawn Martinbrough	TBd	Tim Bradstreet	ToT	Tony Takezaki	WK	Walt Kelly
SmC	Sam Citron	TBe	Terry Beatty	TOz	Tayyar Ozkan	Wld	Andrew Wildman
SMc	Scott McDaniel	TBm	Tom Bierbaum	TP	Tom Palmer	WmB	William Bossart
SMl	Scott McCloud	TC	Travis Charest	TPe	Tom Peyer	WMc	Walter McDaniel
SML	Sean McLaughlin	TCk	Tomm Coker	TR	Tom Raney	WMo	Win Mortimer
SMt	Steve Mattsson	TD	Tony DeZuniga	TR	Ted Richards	Woj	Chuck Wojtkiewicz
SnW	Stan Woch	TDF	Tom DeFalco	TrR	Trina Robbins	WP	Wendy Pini
SPa	Stephen Platt	TDr	Tom Derenick	TS	Tom Sutton	WPo	Whilce Portacio
Spk	Spark	TDz	Todd DeZago	TSa	Tony Salmons	WR	Werner Roth
SPl	Scott Phillips	TeB	Tex Blaisdell	TSe	Tim Sale	WS	Walt Simonson
SPr	Stefan Petrucha	TeH	Ted Halsted	TSg	Tom Sniegoski	WSm	Will Simpson
SR	Steve Rude	TEl	Tim Eldred	TSr	Terry Shoemaker	WW	Wally Wood
SRf	Sean Ruffner	TG	Tom Grummett	TT	Timothy Truman	**YG**	**Yvel Guichet**
SS	Stan Sakai	TGb	Tom Grindberg	TTg	Tom Taggart	YuK	Yukito Kisniro

GENERAL ABBREVIATIONS FOR COMICS LISTINGS

A:	Appearance of	GAm	Graphic Album	pt. or Pt.	Part
(a)	Artist	GN or GNv	Graphic Novel	rep.	Reprinted issue
Adapt.	Adaptation	G-Size	Giant Size	R:	Return/Revival of
Anniv.	Anniversary	HC	Hardcover	rtd	Retold
Ann.#	Annual	I:	Introduction of	(s)	Scripted/Written by
(a&c)	Art & Cover	(i)	Inks by	S.A.	Silver Age
(a&pl)	Art & Plot	IR:	Identity Revealed	SC	Softcover
(a&s)	Art & Script	J:	Joins of	(s&i)	Scripts & inks
B:	Beginning of	K-Size	King Size	Spec.	Special
b:	Birth of	L:	Leaving of	TPB	Trade Paperback
BU:	Back-Up Story	N:	New Costume	T.U.	Team-up
C:	Cameo Appearance	N#	No Issue Number	V: or vs.	Versus
(c)	Cover	O:	Origin of	W:	Wedding of
(c&s)	Cover and Script	P(c)	Painted Cover	w/	With
D:	Death/Destruction of	(p)	Pencils by	w/o	Without
Ed.	Edition	PF	Prestige Format	x-over	Crossover with
E:	Ending of	Ph(c)	Photographic cover		
F:	Features	(pl)	Plotted by		
G.A.	Golden Age	Prev.	Preview		

BIBLIOGRAPHY

Daniels, Les. *Comix: A History of Comic Books in America.* New York, NY: Bonanza Books, 1971.

Gerber, Ernst. *The Photo Journal Guide to Comic Books.* Minden, NV: Gerber Publishing, 1989. Vols. 1 & 2.

Gerber, Ernst. *The Photo Journal Guide to Marvel Comics.* Minden, NV: Gerber Publishing, 1991. Vols. 3 & 4.

Goulart, Ron. *The Adventurous Decade.* New Rochelle, NY: Arlington House, 1975.

Goulart, Ron. *Comic Book Culture, An Illustrated History.* Portland, OR: Collectors Press, 2000

Goulart, Ron. *The Encyclopedia of American Comics.* New York, NY. Facts on File Publications, 1990.

Goulart, Ron. *Over 50 Years of American Comic Books.* Lincolnwood, IL: Mallard Press, 1991.

Hegenburger, John. *Collectors Guide to Comic Books.* Radnor, PA: Wallace Homestead Book Company, 1990.

Kennedy, Jay. *The Official Underground and Newave Price Guide.* Cambridge, MA: Boatner Norton Press, 1982.

Malan, Dan. *The Complete Guide to Classics Collectibles.* St. Louis, MO: Malan Classical Enterprises, 1991.

Miller, John Jackson et al. *The Standard Catalog of Comic Books.* Iola, WI: Krause Publications, 2002.

O'Neil, Dennis. *Secret Origins of DC Super Heroes.* New York, NY: Warner Books, 1976.

Overstreet, Robert. *The Overstreet Comic Book Price Guide (28th Edition).* New York, NY. Avon Books, 1998

Rovin, Jeff. *The Encyclopedia of Super Heroes.* New York, NY: Facts on File Publications, 1985.

Rovin, Jeff. *The Encyclopedia of Super Villians.* New York, NY: Facts on File Publications, 1987.

Thompson, Don & Maggie. *The Golden Age of Comics, Summer 1982.* Tainpa, FL: New Media Publishing, 1982.

DC COMICS

A. BIZARRO
1999
1 (of 4) SvG,MBr,F:Al Bizarro 2.50
2 SvG,MBr,A:Superman. 2.50
3 SvG,MBr, ... 2.50
4 SvG,MBr, Viva Bizarro 2.50

ABSOLUTE VERTIGO
1995
Ashcan: Invisibles, other samples . . 6.00

ACCELERATE
DC/Vertigo, June, 2000
1 (of 4) Great Escape 3.00
2 Great Escape,pt.2. . . . . 3.00
3 Great Escape,pt.3. . . . . 3.00
4 Great Escape,pt.4,concl. 3.00

Action Comics #15 © DC Comics, Inc.

ACTION
June, 1938
1 JoS,I&O:Superman;Rescues Evelyn Curry from electric chair . 400,000.00
2 JoS,V:Emil Norvell 50,000.00
3 JoS,V:Thorton Blakely 30,000.00
4 JoS,V:Coach Randall 18,000.00
5 JoS,Emergency of Vallegho Dam 18,000.00
6 JoS,I:Jimmy Olsen, V:Nick Williams 18,000.00
7 JoS,V:Derek Niles 32,000.00
8 JoS,V:Gimpy 12,000.00
9 JoS,A:Det.Captain Reilly . . 12,000.00
10 JoS,Superman fights for prison reform 25,000.00
11 JoS,Disguised as Homer Ramsey 6,000.00
12 JoS,Crusade against reckless drivers 7,000.00
13 JoS,I:Ultra Humanite 11,000.00
14 JoS,BKa,V:Ultra Humanite, B:Clip Carson 6,000.00
15 JoS,BKa,Superman in Kidtown 9,000.00
16 JoS,BKa,Crusade against Gambling. 4,500.00
17 JoS,BKa,V:Ultra Humanite . 7,000.00
18 JoS,BKa,V:Mr.Hamilton O:Three Aces 4,500.00
19 JoS,BKa,V:Ultra Humanite B:Superman (c) 7,500.00
20 JoS,BKa,V:Ultra Humanite . 6,500.00
21 JoS,BKa,V:Ultra Humanite . 4,000.00
22 JoS,BKa,War between Toran and Galonia. 4,000.00
23 JoS,BKa,SMo,I:Lex Luthor. 11,000.00
24 JoS,BKa,BBa,SMo,FG,Meets Peter Carnahan 4,000.00
25 JoS,BKa,BBa,SMo,V:Medini 4,000.00
26 JoS,BKa,V:Clarence Cobalt. 4,000.00
27 JoS,BKa,V:Mr & Mrs.Tweed 3,000.00
28 JoS,BKa,JBu,V:Strongarm Bandit 3,000.00
29 JoS,BKa,V:Martin 3,500.00
30 JoS,BKa,V:Zolar 3,000.00
31 JoS,BKa,JBu,V:Baron Munsdorf 2,000.00
32 JoS,BKa,JBu,I:Krypto Ray Gun V:Mr.Preston 2,000.00
33 JoS,BKa,JBu,V:Brett Hall, O:Mr. America 2,000.00
34 JoS,BKa,V:Jim Laurg 2,000.00
35 JoS,BKa,V:Brock Walter . . . 2,000.00
36 JoS,BKa,V:StuartPemberton 2,000.00
37 JoS,BKa,V:Commissioner Kennedy, O:Congo Bill. . . . 2,100.00
38 JoS,BKa,V:Harold Morton . . 2,000.00
39 JoS,BKa,Meets Britt Bryson 2,000.00
40 JoS,BKa,Meets Nancy Thorgenson 2,000.00
41 JoS,BKa,V:Ralph Cowan, E:Clip Carson 1,600.00
42 V:Lex Luthor,I&O:Vigilante. . 2,300.00
43 V:Dutch O'Leary,Nazi(c) . . . 1,600.00
44 V:Prof. Steffens,Nazi(c) 1,600.00
45 V:Count Von Henzel, I:Stuff,Nazi(c) 1,600.00
46 V:The Domino 1,600.00
47 V:Lex Luthor—1st app. w/super powers,I:Powerstone 2,500.00
48 V:The Top 1,600.00
49 I:Puzzler 1,650.00
50 Meets Stan Doborak 1,600.00
51 I:Prankster 1,700.00
52 V:Emperor of America 2,100.00
53 JBu,V:Night-Owl 1,600.00
54 JBu,Meets Stanley Finchcomb. 1,400.00
55 JBu,V:Cartoonist Al Hatt . . . 1,400.00
56 V:Emil Loring 1,400.00
57 V:Prankster. 1,400.00
58 JBu,V:Adonis 1,400.00
59 I:Susie Thompkins,Lois Lane's niece 1,350.00
60 JBu,Lois Lane-Superwoman 1,500.00
61 JBu,Meets Craig Shaw 1,300.00
62 JBu,V:Admiral Von Storff . . . 1,300.00
63 JBu,V:Professor Praline . . . 1,300.00
64 I:Toyman. 1,600.00
65 JBu,V:Truman Treadwell . . . 1,200.00
66 JBu,V:Mr.Annister 1,200.00
67 JBu,Superman School for Officer's Training 1,200.00
68 A:Susie Thompkins 1,200.00
69 V:Prankster. 1,200.00
70 JBu,V:Thinker 1,200.00
71 Superman Valentine's Day Special 1,000.00
72 V:Mr. Sniggle 1,000.00
73 V:Lucius Spruce 1,000.00
74 Meets Adelbert Dribble 1,000.00
75 V:Johnny Aesop 1,000.00
76 A Voyage with Destiny 1,000.00
77 V:Prankster. 1,000.00
78 The Chef of Bohemia 1,000.00
79 JBu,A:J. Wilbur Wolfingham 1,000.00
80 A:Mr. Mxyzptlk (2nd App.) . . 1,400.00
81 Meets John Nicholas. 1,000.00
82 JBu,V:Water Sprite. 900.00
83 I:Hocus and Pocus. 900.00
84 JBu,V:Dapper Gang 900.00
85 JBu,V:Toyman 900.00
86 JBu,V:Wizard of Wokit 900.00
87 V:Truck Hijackers. 900.00
88 A:Hocus and Pocus 900.00
89 V:Slippery Andy 900.00
90 JBu,V:Horace Rikker and the Amphi-Bandits 900.00
91 JBu,V:Davey Jones 875.00
92 JBu,V:Nowmie Norman 875.00
93 Superman Christmas story . . . 875.00
94 JBu,V:Bullwer `Bull' Rylie 875.00
95 V:Prankster 875.00
96 V:Mr. Twister 875.00
97 A:Hocus and Pocus 875.00
98 V:Mr. Mxyzptlk, A:Susie Thompkins 875.00
99 V:Keith Langwell 875.00
100 I:InspectorErskineHawkins 1,300.00
101 V:Specs Dour,A-Bomb(c). . 1,900.00
102 V:Mr. Mxyzptlk 800.00
103 V:Emperor Quexo 800.00
104 V:Prankster 800.00
105 Superman Christmas story . . 800.00
106 Clark Kent becomes Baron Edgestream 800.00
107 JBu,A:J.Wilbur Wolfingham . 800.00
108 JBu,V:Vince Vincent. 800.00
109 V:Prankster 800.00
110 A:Susie Thompkins. 800.00
111 Cameras in the Clouds 800.00
112 V:Mr. Mxyzptlk 800.00
113 Just an Ordinary Guy 800.00
114 V:Mike Chesney 800.00
115 Meets Arthur Parrish 800.00
116 A:J. Wilbur Wolfingham . . . 800.00
117 Superman Christmas story . 800.00
118 The Execution of Clark Kent. 800.00
119 Meets Jim Banning 800.00
120 V:Mike Foss 800.00
121 V:William Sharp 800.00
122 V:Charley Carson 800.00
123 V:Skid Russell 800.00
124 Superman becomes radioactive 750.00

Action Comics #31 © DC Comics, Inc.

All comics prices listed are for *Near Mint* condition.

CVA Page 21

Action Comics

Action Comics #76 © DC Comics, Inc.

125 V:Lex Luthor	750.00
126 V:Chameleon	750.00
127 JKu,Superman on Truth or Consequences	800.00
128 V:`Aces' Deucey	750.00
129 Meets Gob-Gob	750.00
130 V:Captain Kidder	750.00
131 V:Lex Luthor	750.00
132 Superman meets George Washington	750.00
133 V:Emma Blotz	750.00
134 V:Paul Strong	750.00
135 V:John Morton	750.00
136 Superman Show-Off!	750.00
137 Meets Percival Winter	750.00
138 Meets Herbert Hinkle	750.00
139 Clark Kent...Daredevil!	750.00
140 Superman becomes Hermit	750.00
141 V:Lex Luthor	750.00
142 V:Dan the Dip	750.00
143 Dates Nikki Larve	750.00
144 O:Clark Kent reporting for Daily Planet	750.00
145 Meets Merton Gloop	700.00
146 V:Luthor	700.00
147 V:`Cheeks' Ross	700.00
148 Superman, Indian Chief	700.00
149 The Courtship on Krypton!	700.00
150 V:Morko	700.00
151 V:Mr.Mxyzptlk,Lex Luthor and Prankster	700.00
152 I:Metropolis Shutterbug Society	700.00
153 V:Kingpin	700.00
154 V:Harry Reed	700.00
155 V:Andrew Arvin	700.00
156 Lois Lane becomes Superwoman,V:Lex Luthor	700.00
157 V:Joe Striker	700.00
158 V:Kane Korrell O:Superman (retold)	1,600.00
159 Meets Oswald Whimple	700.00
160 I:Minerva Kent	700.00
161 Meets Antara	700.00
162 V:`IT!'	650.00
163 Meets Susan Semple	650.00
164 Meets Stefan Andriessen	650.00
165 V:Crime Czar	650.00
166 V:Lex Luthor	650.00
167 V:Prof. Nero	650.00
168 O:Olaf	650.00
169 Caveman Clark Kent!	650.00
170 V:Mad Artist of Metropolis	650.00
171 The Secrets of Superman	650.00
172 Lois Lane..Witch!	650.00
173 V:Dragon Lang	650.00
174 V:Miracle Twine Gang	650.00
175 V:John Vinden	650.00
176 V:Billion Dollar Marvin Gang	650.00
177 V:General	650.00
178 V:Prof. Sands	650.00
179 Superman in Mapleville	650.00
180 V:Syndicate of Five	650.00
181 V:Diamond Dave Delaney	600.00
182 The Return from Planet Krypton	600.00
183 V:Lex Luthor	600.00
184 Meets Donald Whitmore	600.00
185 V:Issah Pendleton	600.00
186 The Haunted Superman	600.00
187 V:Silver	600.00
188 V:Cushions Raymond gang	600.00
189 Meets Mr.&Mrs. John Vandeveir	600.00
190 V:Mr. Mxyzptlk	600.00
191 V:Vic Vordan	600.00
192 Meets Vic Vordan	600.00
193 V:Beetles Brogan	600.00
194 V:Maln	600.00
195 V:Tiger Woman	600.00
196 Superman becomes Mental Man	600.00
197 V:Stanley Stark	600.00
198 The Six Lives of Lois Lane	600.00
199 V:Lex Luthor	600.00
200 V:Morwatha	600.00
201 V:Benny the Brute	600.00
202 Lois Lane's X-Ray Vision	500.00
203 Meets Pietro Paresca	500.00
204 Meets Sam Spulby	500.00
205 Sergeant Superman	500.00
206 Imaginary story featuring Lois Lane	500.00
207 Four Superman Medals!	500.00
208 V:Mr. Mxyzptlk	500.00
209 V:`Doc' Winters	500.00
210 V:Lex Luthor,I:Superman Land	500.00
211 Superman Spectaculars	500.00
212 V:Thorne Varden	500.00
213 V:Paul Paxton	500.00
214 Superman,Sup.Destroyer!	500.00
215 I:Superman of 2956	500.00
216 A:Jor-El	500.00
217 Meets Mr&Mrs.Roger Bliss	500.00
218 I:Super-Ape from Krypton	500.00
219 V:Art Shaler	500.00
220 The Interplanetary Olympics	500.00
221 V:Jay Vorrell	400.00
222 The Duplicate Superman	400.00
223 A:Jor-El	400.00
224 I:Superman Island	400.00
225 The Death of Superman	400.00
226 V:Lex Luthor	400.00
227 The Man with the Triple X-Ray Eyes	400.00
228 A:Superman Museum	400.00
229 V:Dr. John Haley	400.00
230 V:Bart Wellins	400.00
231 Sir Jimmy Olsen, Knight of Metropolis	400.00
232 Meets Johnny Kirk	400.00
233 V:Torm	400.00
234 Meets Golto	400.00
235 B:Congo Bill, B:Tommy Tomorrow	400.00
236 A:Lex Luthor	400.00
237 V:Nebula Gang	400.00
238 I:King Krypton,the Gorilla	400.00
239 `Superman's New Face'	400.00
240 V:Superman Sphinx	400.00
241 WB,A:Batman,Fortress of Solitude (Fort Superman)	350.00
242 I&O:Brainiac	2,500.00
243 Lady and the Lion	350.00
244 CS,A:Vul-Kor,Lya-La	350.00

Action Comics #102 © DC Comics, Inc.

245 WB,V:Kak-Kul	350.00
246 WB,A:Krypton Island	350.00
247 WB,Superman Lost Parents	350.00
248 B&I:Congorilla	350.00
249 AP,A:Lex Luthor	350.00
250 WB,`The Eye of Metropolis'	350.00
251 AP,E:Tommy Tomorrow	350.00
252 I&O:Supergirl	2,500.00
253 B:Supergirl	650.00
254 I:Adult Bizarro	500.00
255 I:Bizarro Lois	400.00
256 `Superman of the Future'	250.00
257 WB,JM,V:Lex Luthor	250.00
258 A:Cosmic Man	250.00
259 A:Lex Luthor,Superboy	250.00
260 A:Mighty Maid	250.00
261 I:Streaky,E:Congorilla	250.00
262 A:Bizarro	250.00
263 O:Bizarro World	300.00
264 V:Bizarro	250.00
265 A:Hyper-Man	250.00
266 A:Streaky,Krypto	250.00
267 JM,3rd A:Legion,I:Invisible Kid	650.00
268 WB,A:Hercules	225.00
269 A:Jerro	225.00
270 CS,JM,A:Batman	250.00
271 A:Lex Luthor	225.00
272 A:Aquaman	225.00
273 A:Mr.Mxyzptlk	225.00
274 A:Superwoman	225.00
275 WB,JM,V:Brainiac	225.00
276 JM,6th A:Legion,I:Brainiac 5, Triplicate Girl,Bouncing Boy	350.00
277 CS,JM,V:Lex Luthor	175.00
278 CS,Perry White Becomes Master Man	175.00
279 JM,V:Hercules,Samson	175.00
280 CS,JM,V:Braniac, A:Congorilla	175.00
281 JM,A:Krypto	175.00
282 JM,V:Mxyzptlk	175.00
283 CS,JM,A:Legion of Super Outlaws	200.00
284 A:Krypto,Jerro	175.00
285 JM,Supergirl Existence Revealed, C:Legion (12th app.)	200.00
286 CS,JM,V:Lex Luthor	150.00
287 JM,A:Legion	150.00
288 JM,A:Mon-El	150.00
289 JM,A:Adult Legion	150.00
290 JM,C:Phantom Girl	150.00
291 JM,V:Mxyzptlk	150.00
292 JM,I:Superhorse	150.00
293 JM,O:Comet-Superhorse	150.00
294 JM,V:Lex Luthor	150.00

Action Comics

#	Description	Price
295	CS,JM,O:Lex Luthor	150.00
296	V:Super Ants	150.00
297	CS,JM,A:Mon-El	150.00
298	CS,JM,V:Lex Luthor	150.00
299	O:Superman Robots	150.00
300	JM,A:Mxyzptlk	150.00
301	CS(c),JM,O:Superhorse	100.00
302	CS(c),JM,O:Superhorse	100.00
303	CS(c),Red Kryptonite story	100.00
304	CS,JM,I&O:Black Flame	125.00
305	CS(c),O:Supergirl	100.00
306	JM,C:Mon-El,Brainiac 5	100.00
307	CS,JM,A:Saturn Girl	100.00
308	CS(c),V:Hercules	100.00
309	CS,A:Batman,JFK,Legion	125.00
310	CS,JM,I:Jewel Kryptonite	90.00
311	CS,JM,O:Superhorse	90.00
312	CS,JM,V:Metallo-Superman	90.00
313	CS,A:Supergirl,Lex Luthor,Batman	90.00
314	JM,A:Justice League	90.00
315	JM,V:Zigi,Zag	90.00
316	JM,A:Zigi,Zag,Zyra	90.00
317	JM,V:Lex Luthor	90.00
318	CS,JM,A:Brainiac	90.00
319	CS,JM,A:Legion,V:L.Luthor	90.00
320	CS,JM,V:Atlas,Hercules	90.00
321	CS,JM,A:Superhorse	90.00
322	JM,'Coward of Steel'	90.00
323	JM,A:Superhorse	90.00
324	JM,A:Abdul	90.00
325	CS,JM,SkyscraperSuperman	90.00
326	CS,JM,V:Legion of Super Creatures	90.00
327	CS,JM,C:Brainiac	90.00
328	JM,Hands of Doom	90.00
329	JM,V:Drang	90.00
330	CS,JM,Krypto	90.00
331	CS,V:Dr.Supernatural	90.00
332	CS,A:Brainiac	90.00
333	CS(c),A:Lex Luthor	90.00
334	JM(c),A:Lex Luthor,80pgs.	150.00
335	CS,V:Lex Luthor	85.00
336	CS,O:Akvar	85.00
337	CS,V:Tiger Gang	85.00
338	CS,JM,V:Muto	85.00
339	CS,V:Muto,Brainiac	85.00
340	JM,I:Parasite	85.00
341	CS,V:Vakox,A:Batman	50.00
342	WB,JM,V:Brainiac	50.00
343	WB,V:Eterno	50.00
344	WB,JM,A:Batman	50.00
345	CS(c),A:Allen Funt	50.00
346	WB,JM	50.00
347	CS(c),A:Supergirl, 80pgs.	100.00
348	WB,JM,V:Acid Master	50.00
349	WB,JM,V:Dr.Kryptonite	50.00
350	A:JLA	50.00
351	WB,I:Zha-Vam	50.00
352	WB,V:Zha-Vam	50.00
353	WB,JM,V:Zha-Vam	50.00
354	JM,A:Captain Incredible	50.00
355	WB,JM,V:Lex Luthor	50.00
356	WB,JM,V:Jr. Annihilitor	50.00
357	WB,JM,V:Annihilitor	50.00
358	NA(c),CS,JM,A:Superboy	50.00
359	NA(c),CS,KS,C:Batman	50.00
360	CS(c),A:Supergirl, 80pgs.	100.00
361	NA(c),A:Parasite	45.00
362	RA,KS,V:Lex Luthor	45.00
363	RA,KS,V:Lex Luthor	45.00
364	RA,KS,V:Lex Luthor	45.00
365	A:Legion & J.L.A.	45.00
366	RA,KS,A:J.L.A.	45.00
367	NA(c),CS,KS,A:Supergirl	45.00
368	CS,KS,V:Mxyzptlk	45.00
369	CS,KS,Superman's Greatest Blunder	45.00
370	NA(c),CS,KS	45.00
371	NA(c),CS,KS	45.00
372	NA(c),CS,KS	45.00
373	A:Supergirl,(giant size)	90.00
374	NA(c),CS,KS,V:Super Thief	40.00
375	CS,KS,The Big Forget	40.00
376	CS,KS,E:Supergirl	40.00
377	CS,KS,B:Legion	40.00
378	CS,KS,V:Marauder	40.00
379	CS,JA,MA,V:Eliminator	40.00
380	KS,Confessions of Superman	40.00
381	CS,Dictators of Earth	40.00
382	CS,Clark Kent-Magician	35.00
383	CS,The Killer Costume	35.00
384	CS,The Forbidden Costume	35.00
385	CS,The Mortal Superman	35.00
386	CS,Home For Old Supermen	35.00
387	CS,A:Legion,Even Supermen Die	35.00
388	CS,A:Legion,Puzzle of The Wild Word	35.00
389	A:Legion,The Kid Who Struck Out Superman	35.00
390	CS,`Self-Destruct Superman'	35.00
391	CS,Punishment of Superman's Son	35.00
392	CS,E:Legion	35.00
393	CS,MA,RA,A:Super Houdini	35.00
394	CS,MA	35.00
395	CS,MA,A:Althera	35.00
396	CS,MA	35.00
397	CS,MA,Imaginary Story	35.00
398	NA(c),CS,MA,I:Morgan Edge	35.00
399	NA(c),CS,MA,A:Superbaby	35.00
400	NA(c),CS,MA,Kandor Story	45.00
401	CS,MA,V:Indians	35.00
402	NA(c),CS,MA,V:Indians	40.00
403	CS,MA,Vigilante rep.	40.00
404	CS,MA,Aquaman rep	40.00
405	CS,MA,Vigilante rep.	40.00
406	CS,MA,Atom & Flash rep.	40.00
407	CS,MA,V:Lex Luthor	40.00
408	CS,MA,Atom rep.	40.00
409	CS,MA,T.Tommorrow rep.	40.00
410	CS,MA,T.Tommorrow rep.	40.00
411	CS,MA,O:Eclipso rep.	40.00
412	CS,MA,Eclipso rep.	40.00
413	CS,MA,V:Brainiac	40.00
414	CS,MA,B:Metamorpho	20.00
415	CS,MA,V:Metroplis Monster	20.00
416	CS,MA	20.00
417	CS,MA,V:Luthor	20.00
418	CS,MA,V:Luthor,E:Metamorpho	20.00
419	CS,MA,CI,DG,I:HumanTarget.	22.00
420	CS,MA,DG,V:Towbee	18.00
421	CS,MA,B:Green Arrow	20.00
422	CS,DG,O:Human Target	18.00
423	CS,MA,DG,A:Lex Luthor	18.00
424	CS,MA,Green Arrow	20.00
425	CS,DD,NA,DG,B:Atom	35.00
426	CS,MA,Green Arrow	15.00
427	CS,MA,DD,DG,Atom	15.00
428	CS,MA,DG,Luthor	15.00
429	CS,BO,DG,C:JLA	15.00
430	CS,MA,DD,DG,Atom	15.00
431	CS,MA,Green Arrow	15.00
432	CS,MA,DG,Toyman	18.00
433	CS,BO,DD,DG,A:Atom	15.00
434	CS,DD,Green Arrow	15.00
435	FM(c),CS,DD,DG,Atom	15.00
436	CS,DD,Green Arrow	15.00
437	CS,DG,Green Arrow,100-pg	45.00
438	CS,BO,DD,Atom	15.00
439	CS,BO,DD,Atom	15.00
440	1st MGr Green Arrow	22.00
441	CS,BO,MGr,A:Green Arrow,Flash,R:Krypto	15.00
442	CS,MS,MGr,Atom	15.00
443	CS,A:JLA(100 pg.giant)	45.00
444	MGr,Green Arrow	15.00
445	MGr,Green Arrow	15.00
446	MGr,Green Arrow	15.00
447	CS,BO,RB,KJ,Atom	15.00
448	CS,BO,DD,JL,Atom	15.00
449	CS,BO	20.00
450	MGr,Green Arrow	10.00
451	MGr,Green Arrow	8.00
452	CS,MGr,Green Arrow	8.00
453	CS,Atom	8.00
454	CS,E:Atom	8.00
455	CS,Green Arrow	8.00
456	CS,MGr,Green Arrow	8.00
457	CS,MGr,Green Arrow	8.00
458	CS,MGr,I:Black Rock	8.00
459	CS,BO,Blackrock	8.00
460	CS,I:Karb-Brak	8.00
461	CS,V:Karb-Brak	8.00
462	CS,V:Karb-Brak	8.00
463	CS,V:Karb-Brak	8.00
464	CS,KS,V:Pile-Driver	8.00
465	CS,FMc,Luthor	8.00
466	NA(c),CS,V:Luthor	8.00
467	CS,V:Mzyzptlk	8.00
468	NA(c),CS,FMc,V:Terra-Man	8.00
469	CS,TerraMan	8.00
470	CS,Flash Green Lantern	8.00
471	CS,V:Phantom Zone Female	8.00
472	CS,V:Faora Hu-Ul	8.00
473	NA(c),CS,Phantom Zone Villians	8.00
474	KS,V:Doctor Light	8.00
475	CS,V:Karb-Brak,A:Vartox	8.00
476	KS,V:Vartox	8.00
477	CS,DD,Land Lords of Earth	8.00
478	CS,Earth's Last	8.00
479	CS	8.00
480	CS,A:JLA,V:Amazo	8.00
481	CS,A:JLA,V:Amazo	8.00
482	CS,Amazo	8.00
483	CS,Amazo,JLA	8.00
484	CS,W:Earth 2 Superman & Lois Lane	15.00
485	NA(c),CS,rep.Superman#233.	10.00
486	GT,KS,V:Lex Luthor	8.00
487	CS,AS,O:Atom	8.00
488	CS,AS,A:Air Wave	8.00
489	CS,AS,A:JLA,Atom	8.00
490	CS,Brainiac	8.00
491	CS,A:Hawkman	8.00
492	CS,`Superman's After Life'	8.00
493	CS,A:UFO	8.00
494	CS	8.00
495	CS	8.00
496	CS,A:Kandor	8.00
497	CS	8.00
498	CS,Vartox	8.00
499	CS,Vartox	8.00

Action Comics #247 © DC Comics Inc.

All comics prices listed are for *Near Mint* condition.

Action Comics

Action Comics #483 © DC Comics, Inc.

500 CS,Superman's Life Story
    A:Legion. 14.00
501 KS. 4.00
502 CS,A:Supergirl,Gal.Golem 4.00
503 CS,`A Save in Time'. 4.00
504 CS,`The Power and Choice'. . . 4.00
505 CS. 4.00
506 CS. 4.00
507 CS,A:Jonathan Kent 4.00
508 CS,A:Jonathan Kent 4.00
509 CS,JSn,DG 4.00
510 CS,Luthor 4.00
511 CS,AS,V:Terraman,
    A:Air Wave. 4.00
512 CS,RT,V:Luthor,A:Air Wave . . . 4.00
513 CS,RT,V:Krell,A:Air Wave. 4.00
514 CS,RT,V:Brainiac,A:Atom 4.00
515 CS,AS,A:Atom 4.00
516 CS,AS,V:Luthor,A:Atom 4.00
517 CS,DH,A:Aquaman 4.00
518 CS,DH,A:Aquaman 4.00
519 CS,DH,A:Aquaman 4.00
520 CS,DH,A:Aquaman 4.00
521 CS,AS,I:Vixen,A:Atom 4.00
522 CS,AS,A:Atom 4.00
523 CS,AS,A:Atom 4.00
524 CS,AS,A:Atom 4.00
525 JSon,FMc,AS,I:Neutron
    A:Air Wave. 4.00
526 JSon,AS,V:Neutron 4.00
527 CS,AS,I:Satanis,A:Aquaman . . . 4.50
528 CS,AS,V:Brainiac,A:Aq'man . . . 4.00
529 GP(c),CS,DA,AS,A:Aquaman,
    V:Brainiac. 4.00
530 CS,DA,Brainiac. 4.00
531 JSon,FMc,AS,A:Atom 4.00
532 CS,C:New Teen Titans. 4.00
533 CS,V:The. 4.00
534 CS,AS,V:Satanis,A:Air Wave . 4.00
535 GK(c),JSon,AS,
    A:Omega Men 4.00
536 JSon,AS,FMc,A:Omega Men . . 4.00
537 IN,CS,AS,V:Satanis
    A:Aquaman 4.00
538 IN,AS,FMc,V:Satanis,
    A:Aquaman 4.00
539 KG(c),GK,AS,DA,A:Flash,
    Atom,Aquaman 4.00
540 GK,AS,V:Satanis 4.00
541 GK,V:Satanis 4.00
542 AS,V:Vandal Savage 4.00
543 CS,V:Vandal Savage 4.00
544 CS,MA,GK,GP,45th Anniv.
    D:Ardora,Lexor. 6.00
545 GK,Brainiac. 4.00

DC

546 GK,A:JLA,New Teen Titans . . . 4.00
547 GK(c),CS. 4.00
548 GK(c),AS,Phantom Zone 4.00
549 GK(c),AS 4.00
550 AS(c),GT 4.00
551 GK,Starfire becomes
    Red Star 4.00
552 GK,Forgotten Heroes
    (inc.Animal Man) 9.00
553 GK,Forgotten Heroes (inc.
    Animal Man). 9.00
554 GK(a&c) 4.00
555 CS,A:Parasite (X-over
    Supergirl #20) 4.00
556 CS,KS,C:Batman. 4.00
557 CS,Terra-man 4.00
558 KS 4.00
559 KS,AS 4.00
560 AS,KG,BO,A:Ambush Bug 4.00
561 KS,WB,Toyman 4.00
562 KS,Queen Bee. 4.00
563 AS,KG,BO,A:Ambush Bug 4.00
564 AS,V:Master Jailer 4.00
565 KG,KS,BO,A:Ambush Bug 4.00
566 BO(i),MR. 4.00
567 KS,AS,PB 4.00
568 CS,AW,AN. 4.00
569 IN,The Force of Revenge. 4.00
570 KS, Jimmy Olsen's Alter-Ego . . 4.00
571 BB(c),AS,A:Thresh 222 . . . . . . 4.00
572 WB,BO 4.00
573 KS,BO,AS 4.00
574 KS. 4.00
575 KS,V:Intellax 4.00
576 KS,Earth's Sister Planet. 4.00
577 KG,BO,V:Caitiff 4.00
578 KS,Parasite 4.00
579 KG,BO,Asterix Parody 4.00
580 GK(c),KS,Superman's Failure . 4.00
581 DCw(c),KS,Superman
    Requires Legal aid 4.00
582 AS,KS,Superman's Parents
    Alive. 4.00
583 CS,KS,AMo(s),Last Pre
    Crisis Superman. 12.00
584 JBy,DG,A:NewTeenTitans,
    I:Modern Age Superman. 6.00
585 JBy,DG,Phantom Stranger 4.50
586 JBy,DG,Legends,V:New
    Gods,Darkseid 4.50
587 JBy,DG,Demon 4.50
588 JBy,DG,Hawkman 4.50
589 JBy,DG,Gr.Lant.Corp. 4.50
590 JBy,DG,Metal Men. 4.50
591 JBy,V:Superboy,A:Legion 4.50
592 JBy,Big Barda 4.50
593 JBy,Mr. Miracle 4.50
594 JBy,A:Booster Gold 4.50
595 JBy,A:M.Manhunter,
    I:Silver Banshee. 4.50
596 JBy,A:Spectre,Millenium. 4.50
597 JBy,L.Starr(i),Lois V:Lana. 4.50
598 JBy,TyT,I:Checkmate 6.00
599 RA,JBy(i),A:MetalMen,
    BonusBook. 4.50
600 JBy,GP,KS,JOy,DG,CS,MA,
    MMi,A:Wonder Woman;
    Man-Bat,V:Darkseid 7.00
Becomes:

ACTION WEEKLY
1988–89
601 GK,DSp,CS,DJu,TD,
    B:Superman,Gr.Lantern,
    Blackhawk,Deadman,Secret
    Six,Wilddog 3.50
602 GP(c),GK,DSp,CS,DJu,TD. . . 3.50
603 GK,CS,DsP,DJu,TD. 3.50
604 GK,DSp,CS,DJu,TD. 3.50
605 NKu/AKu(c),GK,DSp,CS,
    DJu,TD 3.50

Comics Values Annual

Action Comics #507 © DC Comics, Inc.

606 DSp,CS,DJu,TD. 3.50
607 SLi(c),TD,DSp,CS,DJu. 3.50
608 DSp,CS,DJu,TD,E:Blackhawk . 3.50
609 BB(c),DSp,DJu,TD,CS,
    E:Wild Dog,B:Black Canary . . . 3.50
610 KB,DJu,CS,DSp,TD,CS
    A:Phantom Stranger. 3.50
611 AN(c),DJu,DSp,CS,BKi,TD,
    BKi,B:Catwoman 3.75
612 PG(c),DSp,CS,BKi,TD,
    E:Secret Six,Deadman 3.50
613 MK(c),BKi,CS,MA,TGr,
    Nightwing,B:Phantom Stranger . 3.50
614 TG,CS,Phantom Stranger
    E:Catwoman 3.50
615 MMi(c),CS,MA,BKi,TGr,
    Blackhawk,B:Wild Dog 3.50
616 ATh(c),CS,MA,E:Bl.Canary. . . . 3.50
617 CS,MA,JO,A:Ph.Stranger. 3.50
618 JBg(c),CS,MA,JKo,TD,
    B:Deadman,E:Nightwing. 3.50
619 CS,MA,FS,FMc,KJo,TD,FMc,
    B:Sinister Six. 3.50
620 CS,MA,FS,FMc,KJo,TD 3.50
621 JO(c),CS,MA,FS,FMc,KJo,
    TD,MBr,E:Deadman 3.50
622 RF(c),MBr,TL,CS,MA,FS,
    FMc,A:Starman,E:Wild
    Dog,Blackhawk 3.50
623 MBr,TD,CS,MA,FS,FMc,JL,
    JKo,A:Ph.Stranger,
    B:Deadman,Shazam 3.50
624 AD(c),MBr,FS,FMc,CS,MA,
    TD,B:Black Canary. 3.50
625 MBr,FS,FMc,CS,MA,
    TD,FMc 3.50
626 MBr,FS,FMc,CS,MA,JKo,TD,
    E:Shazam,Deadman 3.50
627 GK(c),MBr,RT,FS,FMc,CS,
    MA,TMd,B:Nightwing,Speedy . . 3.50
628 TY(c),MBr,RT,TMd,CS,MA,
    FS,FMc,B:Blackhawk 3.50
629 CS,MA,MBr,RT,FS,FMc,TMd . . 3.50
630 CS,MA,MBr,RT,FS,FMc,TMd,
    E:Secret Six 3.50
631 JS(c),CS,MA,MBr,RT,TMd,
    B:Phantom Stranger. 3.50
632 TGr(c),CS,MA,MBr,RT,TMd . . 3.50
633 CS,MA,MBr,RT,TMd. 3.50
634 CS,MA,MBr,RT,TMd,E:Ph.Strangr,
    Nightwing/Speedy,Bl.hawk . . . 3.50
635 CS,MA,MBr,RT,EB,E:Black
    Canary,Green Lantern 3.50
636 DG(c),CS,MA,NKu,MPa,FMc,
    B:Demon,Wild Dog,Ph.Lady,

DC — Action Comics

Speedy,A:Phantom Stranger . . . 3.50
637 CS,MA,KS,FMc,MPa,
    B:Hero Hotline 3.50
638 JK(c),CS,MA,KS,FMc,MPa 3.50
639 CS,MA,KS,FMc,MPa 3.50
640 CS,KS,MA,FS,FMc,MPa,
    E:Speedy,Hero Hotline 3.50
641 CS,MA,JL,DG,MPa,E:Demon,
    Phant.Lady,Superman,Wild Dog,
    A:Ph.Stranger,Hum.Target 3.50
642 GK,SD,ATi,CS,JAp,JM,CI,KN,
    Green Lantern,Superman 3.50
Becomes:

ACTION COMICS
1989–2002

643 B:RSt(s),GP,BBr,V:Intergang . . 4.50
644 GP,BBr,V:Matrix 3.50
645 GP,BBr,I:Maxima 3.50
646 KG,V:Alien Creature,
    A:Brainiac 4.00
647 GP,KGa,BBr,V:Brainiac 3.50
648 GP,KGa,BBr,V:Brainiac 3.50
649 GP,KGa,BBr,V:Brainiac 3.50
650 JOy,BBr,CS,BMc,GP,KGa,
    ATi,DJu,JLA,C:Lobo 5.50
651 GP,KGa,BBr,Day of Krypton
    Man #3,V:Maxima 3.50
652 GP,KGa,BBr,Day of Krypton
    Man #6,V:Eradicator 5.00
653 BMc,BBr,D:Amanda 3.50
654 BMc,BBr,A:Batman Pt.3 . . . . . 3.50
655 BMc,BBr,V:Morrisson,Ma
    Kent's Photo Album 3.50
656 BMc,BBr,Soul Search #1,
    V:Blaze 3.50
657 KGa,BBr,V:Toyman 3.50
658 CS,Sinbad Contract #3 . . . . . 3.50
659 BMc,BBr,K.Krimson
    Kryptonite #3 . . . . 5.00
660 BMc,BBr,D:Lex Luthor 4.50
661 BMc,BBr,A:Plastic Man 3.50
662 JOy,JM,TG,BMc,V:Silver
    Banshee,Clark tells
    Lois his identity 5.50
662a 2nd printing 5.00
663 BMc,Time & Time Again,pt.2,
    A:JSA,Legion 3.50
664 BMc,Time & Time Again,pt.5 . . 3.50
665 TG,V:Baron Sunday 3.50
666 EH,Red Glass Trilogy,pt.3 . . . . 3.50
667 JOy,JM,TG,ATi,DJu,Revenge
    of the Krypton Man,pt.4 . . . . 3.75
668 BMc,Luthor confirmed dead . . . 3.50
669 BMc,V:Intergang,A:Thorn 3.50
670 BMc,A:Waverider,JLA,JLE 3.50
671 KD,Blackout,pt.2 . . . . 3.50
672 BMc,Superman Meets Lex
    Luthor II 3.50
673 BMc,V:Hellgramite 3.50
674 BMc,Panic in the Sky (Prologue)
    R:Supergirl(Matrix) 7.00
675 BMc,Panic in the Sky #4,
    V:Brainiac 3.50
676 B:KK(s),JG,A:Supergirl,Lex
    Luthor II 3.50
677 JG,Supergirl V:Superman 3.50
678 JG,O:Lex Luthor II 3.50
679 JG,I:Shellshock 3.50
680 JG,Blaze/Satanus War,pt.2 . . . 3.50
681 JG,V:Hellgramite 3.50
682 DAb,TA,V:Hi-Tech 3.50
683 JG,I:Jackal,C:Doomsday 3.50
683a 2nd printing 3.00
684 JG,Doomsday Pt.4 . . . . 4.50
684a 2nd printing 3.00
685 JG,Funeral for a Friend#2 . . . 3.50
686 JG,Funeral for a Friend#6 . . . 3.50
687 JG,Reign of Superman #1,Direct
    Sales,Die-Cut(s),Mini-Poster,
    F:Last Son of Krypton 3.00

687a newsstand Ed. 3.00
688 JG,V:Guy Gardner 3.00
689 JG,V:Man of Steel,A:Superboy,
    Supergirl,R:Real Superman . . . 3.50
690 JG,Cyborg Vs. Superboy 3.00
691 JG,A:All Supermen,V:Cyborg
    Superman,Mongul 3.00
692 JG,A:Superboy,Man of Steel . . 3.00
693 JG,A:Last Son of Krypton 3.00
694 JG,Spilled Blood#2,V:Hi-Tech . . 3.00
695 JG,Foil(c),I:Cauldron,A:Lobo . . 3.50
695a Newsstand Ed. 3.00
696 JG,V:Alien,C:Doomsday 3.00
697 JG,Bizarro's World #3,
    V:Bizarro 3.00
698 JG,A:Lex Luthor 3.00
699 JG,A:Project Cadmus 3.00
700 JG,Fall of Metropolis#1 . . . . . . 4.00
700a Platinum Edition 13.00
701 JG,Fall of Metropolis#5,
    V:Luthor 3.00
702 JG,DvM,B:DyM(s),R:Bloodsport 3.00
703 JG,DvM,Zero Hour 3.00
704 JG,DvM,Eradicator 3.00
705 JG,DvM,Supes real? 3.00
706 JG,DvM,A:Supergirl 3.00
707 JG,DvM,V:Shado Dragon 3.00
708 JG,DvM,R:Deathtrap 3.00
709 JG,DvM,A:Guy Gardner,
    Warrior 3.00
710 JG,DvM,Death of Clark Kent,pt.3
    [new Miraweb format begins] . . 3.00
711 JG,DvM,Death of Clark
    Kent,pt.7 . . . . 3.00
712 Rescue Jimmy Olsen 3.00
713 Scarlet Salvation 3.00
714 R:The Joker 3.00
715 DvM,DaR,V:Parasite 3.00
716 DvM,DaR,Trial of Superman . . 3.00
717 DvM,DaR,Trial of Superman . . 3.00
718 DvM,DRo,mystery of Demolitia 3.00
719 DvM,DRo 3.00
720 DvM,DRo,Lois ends
    engagement 3.50
721 DvM,DRo,lottery fever 3.00
722 DvM,DaR,Tornados in
    Smallville 3.00
723 V:Brainiac 3.00
724 V:S.T.A.R.labs monster 3.00
725 Tolos 3.00
726 DvM(s),TMo,DRo,Krisis of the
    Krimson Kryptonite follow-up . . 3.00
727 DvM(s),TMo,DRo,brutal weather
    in Metropolis, Final Night tie-in . 3.00
728 DvM(s),TG,DRo, Some

Action Comics #706 © DC Comics Inc.

    Honeymoon! 3.00
729 DvM(s),TG,DRo, in Fortress of
    Solitude 3.00
730 DvM(s),TG,Ro, ... 3.00
731 DvM(s),TG,DRo, R:Cauldron . . 3.00
732 DvM(s),TG,DRo, Atomic Skull
    rampages through Metropolis . . 3.00
733 DvM(s),TG,DRo, V:Matallo,
    A:Ray 3.00
734 DvM(s),TG,DRo, Superman &
    Atom in Kandor 3.00
735 DvM(s),TG,DRo, V:Savior 3.00
736 DvM(s),TG,DRo 3.00
737 MWa(s),TG,DRo, Luthor gets
    day in court 3.00
738 SI,JMz,Lois sent to Australia . . 3.00
739 SI,JMz,Superman imprisoned . 3.00
740 SI,JMz,Lucy Lane disappears . 3.00
741 SI,JMz,V:C.O.M.P.U.T.O. 3.00
742 SI,JMz 3.00
743 SI,JMz,F:Slam Bradley 3.00
744 SI,JMz,Millennium Giants
    x-over 3.00
745 SI,JMz,The Prankster 2.50
746 SI,JMz,The Prankster,pt.2 . . . . 2.50
747 SI,JMz,The Prankster,pt.3 . . . . 2.50
748 SI,JMz,Dominus Theory 2.50
749 RMz(s),TGb,TP,City of the
    Future, pt.1 x-over 2.50
750 SI,JMz,I:Crazytop, 48-page . . . 3.50
751 SI,JMz,A:Geo-Force 2.50
752 SI,JMz,Supermen of
    America x-over 2.50
753 SI,JMz,A:JLA 2.50
754 SI,JMz,R:Dominus,
    A:Wonder Woman 2.50
755 SI&MMr(s),King of the
    World aftermath 2.50
756 VGi,old villain is back. 2.50
757 TPe(s),TGb,Hawkworld,pt.3 . . . 2.50
758 SI,JMz,V:Boss Moxie 2.50
759 RF,SB,Strange Visitor,pt.3 . . . . 2.50
760 JRu,F:Encantadora 2.50
761 JRu 2.50
762 JRu,V:Demon Etrigan 2.50
763 JRu,V:Brainiac 13 . . . . 2.50
764 JRu,marital troubles 2.50
765 JRu,V:Joker & Harley Quinn . . 2.50
766 F:Batman 2.50
767 CriticalCondition,pt.4,x-over . . . 2.50
768 F:Marvel Family 3.00
769 Superman:Arkham,concl 3.00
770 Superman:Emperor,48-pg 4.50
771 CDi(s),F:Nightwing 2.50
772 V:Ra's al Ghul,pt.1 . . . . 2.50
773 V:Ra's al Ghul,pt.2 . . . . 2.50
774 A:Martian Manhunter 2.50
775 48-page 6.00
776 Return to Krypton,pt.4 . . . . . . 2.50
777 Kancer 2.50
778 MWm,Infestation x-over,pt.4 . . . 2.50
779 V:Killer,pt.1 . . . . 2.50
780 V:Killer,pt.2 . . . . 2.50
781 Our Worlds at War,All-OutWar . 2.50
782 Our Worlds at War,Casualties . 2.50
783 V:Ocean Master,Scorch 2.50
784 Joker:Last Laugh tie-in 2.50
785 R:Bizarro 2.50
786 PFe,kidnapped by aliens 2.50
787 PFe,Byakko, Gunshin, Sakki . . 2.50
788 PFe,Jikei Ketsuki,pt.1 . . . . 2.50
789 Evil from the Gorge 2.50
790 Krypto vs. Kancer 2.50
791 Smallville, flash-back tale 2.50
792 Superman, detective 2.50
793 PFe,Return to KryptonII,concl . . 2.50
794 F:Quintescence 2.50
795 Ending Battle,pt.4 . . . . 2.50
796 Ending Battle,pt.8 . . . . 2.50
797 New General Zod 2.50
798 Lost Hearts, pt.4 x-over 2.50

All comics prices listed are for *Near Mint* condition.

Action–Adventure DC Comics Values Annual

799 TR,SHa,F:Girl 13 . . . . 2.50
800 64-page, life re-examined 4.50
801 metahumans 2.50
802 PFe,CaS,The Harvest,pt.1 . . . . 2.50
803 PFe,CaS,The Harvest,pt.2 . . . . 2.50
804 PFe,CaS,The Harvest,pt.3 . . . . 2.50
805 PFe,CaS,The Harvest,pt.4 . . . . 2.50
806 PFe,CaS,The Harvest,pt.5 . . . . 2.50
807 PFe,CaS,Supergirls 2.50
808 PFe,CaS,Supergirls 2.50
809 PFe,CaS,murder suspect. 2.50
Ann.#1 AAd,DG,A:Batman 8.00
Ann.#2 MMi,CS,GP,JOy,DJu,BBr,
  V:Mongul 4.00
Ann.#3 TG,Armageddon X-over . . . 3.50
Ann.#4 Eclipso,A:Captain
  Marvel 3.50
Ann.#5 MZ(c),Bloodlines, I:Loose
  Cannon 3.50
Ann.#6 Elseworlds,JBy(a&S) 3.50
Ann.#7 Year One Annual 4.50
Ann.#8 DvM,Legends of the Dead
  Earth 3.50
Ann.#9 DvM,VGi,BBr,Pulp Heroes . 4.50
Gold.Ann.rep.#1 . . . . 2.50
#0 Peer Pressure,pt.4 (1994) 2.50
Spec.#1,000,000 MSh(s),RLm,JMz. 2.50

ADAM STRANGE
1990
1 NKu,A.Strange on Rann 5.00
2 NKu,Wanted:Adam Strange 4.00
3 NKu,final issue 4.00
TPB Man of Two Worlds (2003) . . 19.95

Advanced Dungeons & Dragons #1
© DC Comics, Inc.

ADVANCED
DUNGEONS & DRAGONS
1988–91
1 JD,I:Onyx,Priam,Timoth,
  Cybriana,Vajra,Luna 5.00
2 JD,V:Imgig Zu,I:Conner 4.00
3 JD,V:Imgig Zu. 4.00
4 JD,V:Imgig Zu,I:Kyriani 3.00
5 JD,Spirit of Myrrth I. 3.00
6 JD,Spirit of Myrrth II 3.00
7 JD,Spirit of Myrrth III. 2.50
8 JD,Spirit of Myrrth IV 2.50
9 JD,Catspawn Quartet I 2.50
10 JD,Catspawn Quartet II 2.50
11 JD,Catspawn Quartet III. 2.50
12 JD,Catspawn Quartet IV 2.50
13 JD,Spell Games I. 2.50

14 JD,Spell Games II 2.50
15 JD,Spell Games III. 2.50
16 JD,Spell Games IV 2.50
17 JD,RM,Kyriani's Story I 2.50
18 JD,RM,Kyriani's Story II. 2.50
19 JD,RM,Luna I 2.50
20 JD,RM,Luna II 2.50
21 JD,RM,Luna III 2.50
22 JD,RM,Luna IV 2.50
23 TMd,RM,Siege Dragons I. 2.50
24 Scavengers 2.50
25 JD,RM,Centaur Village 2.25
26 JD,Timoth the Centaur. 2.25
27 JD,Kyriani,Dragons Eye #1 . . . 2.25
28 JD,Dragons Eye #2 . . . . 2.25
29 JD,RM,Dragons Eye #3 . . . . . . 2.25
30 JD,RM,Carril's Killer
  Revealed 2.25
31 TMd,Onyx'Father,pt.1 . . . . 2.25
32 TMd,Onyx'Father,pt.2 . . . . 2.25
33 JD,Waterdeep,pt.1. . . . . 2.25
34 JD,Waterdeep,pt.2. . . . . 2.25
35 JD,RM,Waterdeep,pt.3. . . . . . . 2.25
36 JD,RM,final issue. 2.25
Ann.#1 JD,RM,Tmd 4.00

ADVENTURE COMICS
Nov., 1938–83
[Prev: New Comics]
32 CF(c) 4,000.00
33 . . . . 2,000.00
34 FG(c) 2,000.00
35 FG(c) 2,000.00
36 Giant Snake(c) 2,000.00
37 Rampaging Elephant(c). . . . 2,000.00
38 Tiger(c). 2,000.00
39 Male Bondage(c). 2,100.00
40 CF(c),1st app. Sandman . . 60,000.00
41 Killer Shark(c) 7,500.00
42 CF,Sandman(c) 10,000.00
43 CF(c) 4,000.00
44 CF,Sandman(c) 10,000.00
45 FG(c) 4,000.00
46 CF,Sandman(c). 6,500.00
47 Sandman (c). 6,500.00
48 1st app.& B:Hourman 35,000.00
49 . . . . 3,000.00
50 Hourman(c). 3,000.00
51 BBa(c),Sandman(c). 4,500.00
52 BBa(c),Hourman(c) 2,800.00
53 BBa(c),1st app. Minuteman . 2,800.00
54 BBa(c),Hourman(c) 2,800.00
55 BBa(c),same. 2,800.00
56 BBa(c),same. 2,800.00
57 BBa(c),same. 2,800.00
58 BBa(c),same. 2,800.00
59 BBa(c),same. 2,800.00
60 Sandman(c) 4,500.00
61 CF(c),JBu,Starman(c) 17,000.00
62 JBu(c),JBu,Starman(c) 2,400.00
63 JBu(c),JBu,same. 2,400.00
64 JBu(c),JBu,same. 2,400.00
65 JBu(c),JBu,same. 2,400.00
66 JBu(c),JBu,O:Shining Knight,
  Starman(c) 2,900.00
67 JBu(c),JBu,O:Mist 2,400.00
68 JBu(c),JBu,same. 2,400.00
69 JBu(c),JBu, 1st app. Sandy,
  Starman(c) 2,700.00
70 JBu(c),JBu,Starman(c) 2,400.00
71 JBu(c),JBu,same. 2,200.00
72 JBu(c),S&K,JBu,Sandman. 18,000.00
73 S&K(c),S&K,I:Manhunter. . 19,000.00
74 S&K(c),S&K,You can't Escape
  your Fate-The Sandman . . 2,200.00
75 S&K(c),S&K,Sandman and
  Sandy Battle Thor 2,200.00
76 S&K(c),Sandman(c),S&K . 2,200.00
77 S&K,(c),S&K,same 2,200.00
78 S&K(c),S&K,same. 2,200.00

Adventure Comics #41
© DC Comics, Inc.

79 S&K(c),S&K,Manhunter. . . . 2,400.00
80 S&K(c),Sandman(c),S&K . . 2,200.00
81 S&K(c),MMe,S&K,same . . . 1,500.00
82 S&K(c),S&K,Sandman
  X-Mas story. 1,500.00
83 S&K(c),S&K,Sandman
  Boxing(c),E:Hourman. 1,500.00
84 S&K(c),S&K 1,500.00
85 S&K(c),S&K,Sandman in
  `The Amazing Dreams of
  Gentleman Jack' 1,500.00
86 S&K(c),Sandman(c) 1,500.00
87 S&K(c),same. 1,500.00
88 S&K(c),same. 1,500.00
89 S&K(c),same. 1,500.00
90 S&K(c),same. 1,500.00
91 S&K(c),JK 1,400.00
92 S&K(c) 1,300.00
93 S&K(c),Sandman in `Sleep
  for Sale'. 1,300.00
94 S&K(c),Sandman(c) 1,300.00
95 S&K(c),same. 1,300.00
96 S&K(c),same. 1,300.00
97 S&K(c),same. 1,300.00
98 JK(c),Sandman in `Hero
  of Dreams'. 1,300.00
99 JK(c) 1,300.00
100 . . . . 1,700.00
101 S&K(c) 1,300.00
102 S&K(c) 1,300.00
103 B:Superboy stories,(c),BU:
  Johnny Quick,Aquaman,Shining
  Knight,Green Arrow 4,000.00
104 S&S,ToyTown USA 1,400.00
105 S&S,Palace of Fantasy . . . 1,000.00
106 S&S,Weather Hurricane . . 1,000.00
107 S&S,The Sky is the Limit. . 1,000.00
108 S&S,Proof of the Proverbs 1,000.00
109 S&S,You Can't Lose 1,000.00
110 S&S,The Farmer Takes
  it Easy. 1,000.00
111 S&S,The Whiz Quiz Club. . 1,000.00
112 S&S,Super Safety First . . . 1,000.00
113 S&S,The 33rd Christmas . . . 900.00
114 S&S,Superboy Spells
  Danger 900.00
115 S&S,The Adventure of
  Jaguar Boy. 900.00
116 S&S,JBu,Superboy Toy
  Tester. 900.00
117 S&S,JBu,Miracle Plane 900.00
118 S&S,JBu,The Quiz Biz
  Broadcast. 900.00
119 WMo,JBu,Superboy
  Meets Girls 900.00
120 S&S,JBu,A:Perry White;

CVA Page 26 All comics prices listed are for *Near Mint* condition.

Comics Values Annual — DC Adventure Comics

- I:Ringmaster 950.00
- 121 S&S,Great Hobby Contest . . 800.00
- 122 S&S,Superboy-Super-Magician 800.00
- 123 S&S,Lesson For a Bully 800.00
- 124 S&S,Barbed Wire Boys Town 800.00
- 125 S&S,The Weight Before Christmas 800.00
- 126 S&S,Superboy:Crime Fighting Poet 800.00
- 127 MMe,O:Shining Knight; Super Bellboy 800.00
- 128 WMo,How Clark Kent Met Lois Lane' 800.00
- 129 WMo,Pupils of the Past 800.00
- 130 WMo,Superboy Super Salesman 800.00
- 131 WMo,The Million Dollar Athlete 700.00
- 132 WMo,Superboy Super Cowboy 700.00
- 133 WMo,Superboy's Report Card 700.00
- 134 WMo,Silver Gloves Sellout . . 700.00
- 135 WMo,The Most Amazing of All Boys 700.00
- 136 WMo,My Pal Superboy 700.00
- 137 WMo,Treasure of Tondimo . . 700.00
- 138 WMo,Around the World in Eighty Minutes 700.00
- 139 WMo,Telegraph Boy 700.00
- 140 Journey to the Moon 700.00
- 141 WMo,When Superboy Lost His Powers 700.00
- 142 WMo,The Man Who Walked With Trouble 700.00
- 143 WMo,The Superboy Savings Bank,A:Wooden Head Jones 700.00
- 144 WMo,The Way to Stop Superboy 700.00
- 145 WMo,Holiday Hijackers 700.00
- 146 The Substitute Superboy . . . 700.00
- 147 Clark Kent,Orphan 700.00
- 148 Superboy Meets Mummies . . 700.00
- 149 Fake Superboys 700.00
- 150 FF,Superboy's Initiation 800.00
- 151 FF,No Hunting(c) 800.00
- 152 Superboy Hunts For a Job . . 600.00
- 153 FF,Clark Kent,Boy Hobo 800.00
- 154 The Carnival Boat Crimes . . 600.00
- 155 FF,Superboy-Hollywood Actor 800.00
- 156 The Flying Peril 600.00
- 157 FF,The Worst Boy in Smallville 600.00
- 158 The Impossible Task 600.00
- 159 FF,Superboy Millionaire? . . . 850.00
- 160 Superboy's Phoney Father . . 600.00
- 161 FF 600.00
- 162 Super-Coach of Smallville High 600.00
- 163 FF,Superboy's Phoney Father 800.00
- 164 Discovers the Secret of a Lost Indian Tribe 600.00
- 165 Superboy's School for Stunt Men 600.00
- 166 Town That Stole Superboy . . 600.00
- 167 Lana Lang, Super-Girl 600.00
- 168 The Boy Who Out Smarted Superboy 600.00
- 169 Clark Kent's Private Butler . . 600.00
- 170 Lana Lang's Big Crush 500.00
- 171 Superboy's Toughest Tasks . 500.00
- 172 Laws that Backfired 500.00
- 173 Superboy's School of Hard Knocks 500.00
- 174 The New Lana Lang 500.00
- 175 Duel of the Superboys 500.00
- 176 Superboy's New Parents . . . 500.00
- 177 Hot-Rod Chariot Race 500.00
- 178 Boy in the Lead Mask 500.00
- 179 World's Whackiest Inventors 500.00
- 180 Grand Prize o/t Underworld . 500.00
- 181 Mask for a Hero 500.00
- 182 Super Hick from Smallville . . 475.00
- 183 Superboy and Cleopatra . . . 475.00
- 184 Shutterbugs of Smallville . . . 475.00
- 185 The Mythical Monster 475.00
- 186 . . . . 475.00
- 187 25th Century Superboy 475.00
- 188 Bull Fighter from Smallville . . 475.00
- 189 Girl of Steel(Lana Lang) 475.00
- 190 The Two Clark Kents 475.00
- 191 . . . . 475.00
- 192 The Coronation of Queen Lana Lang 475.00
- 193 Superboy's Lost Costume . . 475.00
- 194 Super-Charged Superboy . . . 475.00
- 195 Lana Lang's Romance on Mars 475.00
- 196 Superboy vs. King Gorilla . . . 475.00
- 197 V:Juvenile Gangs 475.00
- 198 Super-Carnival from Space . 475.00
- 199 Superboy meets Superlad . . 475.00
- 200 Superboy and the Apes 700.00
- 201 Safari in Smallville 450.00
- 202 Superboy City, U.S.A 450.00
- 203 Uncle Superboy 475.00
- 204 Super-Brat of Smallville 450.00
- 205 The Journey of the Second Superboy 450.00
- 206 The Impossible Creatures . . 450.00
- 207 Smallville's Worst Athlete . . . 450.00
- 208 Rip Van Winkle of Smallville? 450.00
- 209 Superboy Week 450.00
- 210 I:Krypto,The Superdog from Krypton 4,800.00
- 211 Superboy's Most Amazing Dream 400.00
- 212 Superboy's Robot Twin 400.00
- 213 Junior Jury of Smallville 400.00
- 214 A:Krypto 700.00
- 215 Super-Hobby of Superboy . . 400.00
- 216 The Wizard City 400.00
- 217 Superboy's Farewell to Smallville 400.00
- 218 Two World's of Superboy . . . 400.00
- 219 Rip Van Winkle of Smallville 400.00
- 220 The Greatest Show on Earth A:Krypto 400.00
- 221 The Babe of Steel 350.00
- 222 Superboy's Repeat Performance 350.00
- 223 Hercules Junior 350.00
- 224 Pa Kent Superman 350.00
- 225 Bird with Super-Powers 350.00
- 226 Superboy's Super Rival 350.00
- 227 Good Samaritan of Smallville 350.00
- 228 Clark Kent's Body Guard . . . 350.00
- 229 . . . . 350.00
- 230 Secret of the Flying Horse . . 325.00
- 231 Super-Feats of Super-Baby . 325.00
- 232 The House where Superboy was Born 325.00
- 233 Joe Smith, Man of Steel 325.00
- 234 1,001 Rides of Superboy . . . 325.00
- 235 Confessions of Superboy . . . 325.00
- 236 Clark Kent's Super-Dad 325.00
- 237 Robot War of Smallville 325.00
- 238 The Secret Past of Superboy's Father 325.00
- 239 The Super-Tricks of the Dog of Steel 325.00
- 240 Super Teacher From Krypton 325.00
- 241 Super-Outlaw of Smallville . . 325.00
- 242 The Kid From Krypton 325.00
- 243 Super Toys From Krypton . . . 325.00
- 244 Poorest Family in Smallville . 325.00
- 245 The Mystery of Monster X . . 325.00
- 246 Girl Who Trapped Superboy . 325.00
- 247 I&O:Legion 7,000.00
- 248 Green Arrow 275.00
- 249 CS,Green Arrow 275.00
- 250 JK,Green Arrow 275.00
- 251 JK,Green Arrow 275.00
- 252 JK,Green Arrow 275.00
- 253 JK,1st Superboy & Robin T.U 400.00
- 254 JK,Green Arrow 275.00
- 255 JK,Green Arrow 275.00
- 256 JK,O:Green Arrow 850.00
- 257 CS,LE,A:Hercules,Samson . . 250.00
- 258 LE,Aquaman,Superboy 250.00
- 259 I:Crimson Archer 250.00
- 260 1st S.A. O:Aquaman 1,000.00
- 261 GA,A:Lois Lane 200.00
- 262 O:Speedy 200.00
- 263 GA,Aquaman,Superboy 200.00
- 264 GA,A:Robin Hood 200.00
- 265 GA,Aquaman,Superboy 200.00
- 266 GA,I:Aquagirl 200.00
- 267 N:Legion(2nd app.) 1,200.00
- 268 I:Aquaboy 200.00
- 269 I:Aqualad,E:Green Arrow . . . 350.00
- 270 2nd A:Aqualad,B:Congorilla . 200.00
- 271 O:Lex Luthor rtd 350.00
- 272 I:Human Flying Fish 200.00
- 273 Aquaman,Superboy 200.00
- 274 Aquaman,Superboy 200.00
- 275 O:Superman/Batman T.U. rtd 300.00
- 276 Superboy,3rd A:Metallo 200.00
- 277 Aquaman,Superboy 200.00
- 278 Aquaman,Superboy 200.00
- 279 CS,Aquaman,Superboy 200.00
- 280 CS,A:Lori Lemaris 200.00
- 281 Aquaman,Superboy E:Congorilla 200.00
- 282 5th A:Legion,I:Starboy 275.00
- 283 I:Phantom Zone 250.00
- 284 CS,JM,Aquaman,Superboy . 150.00
- 285 WB,B:Bizarro World 250.00
- 286 I:Bizarro Mxyzptlk 250.00
- 287 I:Dev-Em,Bizarro Perry White, Jimmy Olsen 150.00
- 288 A:Dev-Em 150.00
- 289 Superboy 150.00
- 290 8th A:Legion,O&J:Sunboy, I:Brainiac 5 . . . . 275.00
- 291 A:Lex Luthor 150.00
- 292 Superboy,I:Bizarro Lucy Lane, Lana Lang 150.00
- 293 CS,O&I:Marv-El,I:Bizarro Luthor 250.00

Adventure Comics #165
© *DC Comics Inc.*

All comics prices listed are for *Near Mint* condition.

Adventure Comics — DC — Comics Values Annual

Adventure Comics #326
© DC Comics, Inc.

294 I:Bizarro M.Monroe,JFK 200.00
295 I:Bizarro Titano. 150.00
296 A:Ben Franklin,George
    Washington 150.00
297 Lana Lang Superboy Sister . 150.00
298 The Fat Superboy 150.00
299 I:Gold Kryptonite 150.00
300 B:Legion,J:Mon-El,
    E:Bizarro World 650.00
301 CS,O:Bouncing Boy 225.00
302 CS,Legion 150.00
303 I:Matter Eater Lad 150.00
304 D:Lightning Lad 150.00
305 A:Chameleon Boy 150.00
306 I:Legion of Sub.Heroes 150.00
307 I:Element Lad 150.00
308 I:Light Lass 150.00
309 I:Legion of Super Monsters . 150.00
310 A:Mxyzptlk 150.00
311 CS,V:Legion of Substitue
    Heroes 125.00
312 R:Lightning Lad 150.00
313 CS,J:Supergirl 125.00
314 A:Hitler. 125.00
315 A:Legion of Substitute
    Heroes. 125.00
316 O:Legion 100.00
317 I&J:Dreamgirl 100.00
318 Legion 100.00
319 Legion 100.00
320 A:Dev-Em 100.00
321 I:Time Trapper 125.00
322 JF,A:Legion of Super Pets . . . 90.00
323 JF,BU:Kypto. 90.00
324 JF,I:Legion of
    Super Outlaws 90.00
325 JF,V:Lex Luthor 90.00
326 BU:Superboy. 90.00
327 I&J:Timber Wolf 90.00
328 Legion 90.00
329 I:Legion of Super Bizarros . . . 90.00
330 Legion 90.00
331 Legion 75.00
332 Legion 75.00
333 Legion 75.00
334 Legion 75.00
335 Legion 75.00
336 Legion 75.00
337 Legion 75.00
338 Legion 75.00
339 Legion 75.00
340 I:Computo 75.00
341 CS,D:Triplicate Girl (becomes
    Duo Damsel) 65.00
342 CS,Star Boy expelled. 60.00

343 CS,V:Lords of Luck 60.00
344 CS,Super Stalag,pt.1. . . . . . 60.00
345 CS,Super Stalag,pt.2 . . . . . . 60.00
346 CS,I&J:Karate Kid,Princess
    Projectra,I:Nemesis Kid 75.00
347 CS,Legion 60.00
348 I:Dr.Regulus. 75.00
349 CS,I:Rond Vidar. 60.00
350 CS,I:White Witch 75.00
351 CS,R:Star Boy 60.00
352 CS,I:Fatal Fire 60.00
353 CS,D:Ferro Lad 75.00
354 CS,Adult Legion. 60.00
355 CS,J:Insect Queen. 50.00
356 CS,Five Legion Orphans 50.00
357 CS,I:Controller 50.00
358 I:Hunter 50.00
359 CS,Outlawed Legion,pt.1 . . . 50.00
360 CS,Outlawed Legion,pt.2 . . . 50.00
361 I:Dominators (30th century) . . 50.00
362 I:Dr.Mantis Morto 50.00
363 V:Dr.Mantis Morlo 50.00
364 A:Legion of Super Pets 50.00
365 CS,I:Shadow Lass,
    V:Fatal Five 50.00
366 CS,J:Shadow Lass. 50.00
367 N:Legion H.Q.,I:Dark Circle . . 50.00
368 CS. 50.00
369 CS,JAb,I:Mordru 50.00
370 CS,JAb,V:Mordru. 50.00
371 CS,JAb,I:Chemical King 55.00
372 CS,JAb,J:Timber Wolf,
    Chemical King 55.00
373 I:Tornado Twins 45.00
374 WM,I:Black Mace. 45.00
375 I:Wanderers 45.00
376 Execution of Cham.Boy 45.00
377 Heroes for Hire 45.00
378 Twelve Hours to Live 45.00
379 Burial In Space 45.00
380 The Amazing Space Odyssey
    of the Legion,E:Legion 45.00
381 The Supergirl Gang
    C:Batgirl,B:Supergirl 125.00
382 NA(c),The Superteams Split
    Up,A:Superman 40.00
383 NA(c),Please Stop my Funeral,
    A:Superman,Comet,Streaky . . 40.00
384 KS,The Heroine Haters,
    A:Superman. 40.00
385 Supergirl's Big Sister 40.00
386 The Beast That Loved
    Supergirl 40.00
387 Wolfgirl of Stanhope;
    A:Superman;V:Lex Luthor. . . . 40.00
388 Kindergarten Criminal;
    V:Luthor,Brainiac 40.00
389 A:Supergirl's Parents,
    V:Brainiac. 40.00
390 Linda Danvers Superstar
    (80 page giant). 75.00
391 The Super Cheat;A:Comet. . . 40.00
392 Supergirls Lost Costume 40.00
393 KS,Unwanted Supergirl 40.00
394 KS,Heartbreak Prison 40.00
395 Heroine in Haunted House . . . 40.00
396 Mystery o/t Super Orphan . . . 40.00
397 Now Comes Zod,N:Supergirl,
    V:Luthor 40.00
398 Maid of Doom,A:Superman,
    Streaky,Krypto,Comet. 40.00
399 CI,Johnny Dee,Hero Bum . . . 50.00
400 MSy,35th Anniv.,Return of the
    Black Flame 30.00
401 MSy,JAb,The Frightened
    Supergirl,V:Lex Luthor 30.00
402 MSy,JAb,TD,I:Starfire,
    Dr.Kangle 40.00
403 68 page giant. 75.00
404 MSy,JAb,V:Starfire 25.00
405 V:Starfire,Dr.Kangle 25.00

406 MSy,JAb,Suspicion 25.00
407 MSy,JAb,Suspicion Confirmed
    N:Supergirl. 25.00
408 The Face at the Window 25.00
409 MSy,DG,Legion rep. 40.00
410 N:Supergirl 40.00
411 CI,N:Supergirl 40.00
412 rep.Strange Adventures #180
    (I:Animal Man). 45.00
413 GM,JKu,rep.Hawkman 40.00
414 Animal Man rep. 40.00
415 BO,GM,CI,Animal Man rep. . . 40.00
416 CI,All women issue,giantsize . 40.00
417 GM,inc.rep.Adventure #161,
    Frazetta art. 35.00
418 ATh,Black Canary 35.00
419 ATh,Black Canary 40.00
420 Animal Man rep. 35.00
421 MSy,Supergirl 20.00
422 MSy,Supergirl 20.00
423 MSy,Supergirl 20.00
424 MSy,E:Supergirl,A:JLA 20.00
425 AN,ATh,I:Captain Fear 35.00
426 MSy,DG,JAp,Vigilante 20.00
427 TD 20.00
428 TD,I:Black Orchid. 75.00
429 TD,AN,Black Orchid 35.00
430 A:Black Orchid. 35.00
431 JAp,ATh,B:Spectre. 75.00
432 JAp,AN,A:Spectre,Capt.Fear . 35.00
433 JAp,AN 35.00
434 JAp 35.00
435 MGr(1st work),JAp,Aquaman . 35.00
436 JAp, MGr,Aquaman. 35.00
437 JAp,MGr,Aquaman. 35.00
438 JAp,HC,DD,7 Soldiers 35.00
439 JAp 35.00
440 JAp,O:New Spectre 55.00
441 JAp,B:Aquaman 15.00
442 JAp,A:Aquaman. 15.00
443 JAp 18.00
444 JAp 15.00
445 JAp,RE,JSon,Creeper 15.00
446 JAp,RE,JSon,Creeper 15.00
447 JAp,RE,JSon,Creeper 18.00
448 JAp,Aquaman 15.00
449 JAp,MN,TA,Jonn J'onz 15.00
450 JAp,MN,TA,Supergirl 15.00
451 JAp,MN,TA,Hawkman 15.00
452 JAp,Aquaman 15.00
453 MA,CP,JRu,B:Superboy
    & Aqualad 15.00
454 CP,DG,A:Kryptonite Kid 15.00
455 CP,DG,A:Kryptonite Kid
    E:Aqualad 15.00
456 JSon,JA 15.00
457 JSon,JA,JO,B:Eclipso 15.00
458 JAp,JAp,JO,BL,E:Superboy
    & Eclipso 15.00
459 IN,FMc,JAp,JSon,DN,JA,A:Wond.
    Woman,New Gods,Green Lantern,
    Flash,Deadman,(giant size) . . 25.00
460 IN,FMc,JAp,DN,DA,JSon,JA,
    D:Darkseid 25.00
461 IN,FMc,JAp,JSon,DN,JA,
    B:JSA & Aquaman 25.00
462 IN,FMc,DH,JL,DG,JA,
    D:Earth 2,Batman 25.00
463 DH,JL,JSon,FMc 20.00
464 DH,JAp,JSon,DN,DA,
    Deadman 20.00
465 DN,JSon,DG,JL 20.00
466 MN,JL,JSon,DN,DA 20.00
467 JSon,SD,RT,I:Starman
    B:Plastic Man 25.00
468 SD,JSon 8.00
469 SD,JSon,O:Starman 8.00
470 SD,JSon,O:Starman 8.00
471 SD,JSon,I:Brickface. 8.00
472 SD,RT,JSon 8.00
473 SD,RT,JSon 8.00

CVA Page 28   All comics prices listed are for *Near Mint* condition.

DC — Adventure–Adventures

Adventure Comics #448
© DC Comics, Inc.

Adventures of Dean Martin and Jerry Lewis © DC Comics Inc.

issue 4.00
6 F:Ocean Master, Power Girl 4.00
7 SVa(s),F:Shazam Family 4.00
8 SVa(s),F:Blue Beetle &
 Booster Gold 4.00
9 SVa(s),F:Flash,V:Grodd,Cipher .. 4.00
10 SVa(s),Legion month 4.00
11 SVa(s),F:Green Lantern &
 Wonder Woman 4.00
12 SVa(s) 4.50
13 SVa(s),A:Martian Manhunter ... 4.00
14 SVa(s),Flash races Superboy... 4.00
15 SVa(s),Shazam,Aquaman 4.00
16 SVa(s),F:Green Lantern 4.00
17 SVa(s),F:Batman, Creeper 4.00
18 SVa(s),F:JLA 4.50
19 F:Catwoman, Wonder Woman .. 4.00
Ann.#1 magic amulets,5 stories ... 5.00

ADVENTURES IN THE RIFLE BRIGADE
DC/Vertigo, Aug., 2000
1 (of 3) GEn, ... 2.50
2 F:Gerta Gash 2.50
3 GEn,Up Yours Fritz, concl. 2.50

ADVENTURES IN THE RIFLE BRIGADE: OPERATION BOLLOCK
DC/Vertigo, Aug., 2001
1 GEn,find Hitler's testicle! 2.50
2 GEn, still looking 2.50
3 GEn,concl. 2.50

ADVENTURES OF ALAN LADD
1949–51
1 Ph(c) 1,200.00
2 Ph(c) 600.00
3 Ph(c) 450.00
4 Ph(c) 450.00
5 Ph(c),inc.Destination Danger.. 400.00
6 Ph(c) 400.00
7 .... 400.00
8 Grand Duchess takes over ... 400.00
9 Deadlien in Rapula 400.00

ADVENTURES OF BOB HOPE
1951–68
1 Ph(c) 2,200.00
2 Ph(c) 1,000.00
3 Ph(c) 600.00
4 Ph(c) 600.00
5 thru 10 .... @450.00
11 thru 20 .... @300.00
21 thru 40 .... @200.00
41 thru 60 .... @150.00
61 thru 90 .... @75.00
91 thru 93 .... @50.00
94 C:Aquaman 60.00
95 thru 105 .... @50.00
106 thru 109 NA .... @85.00

474 SD,RT,JSon. 8.00
475 BB(c),SD,RT,JSon,DG,
 B:Aquaman 8.00
476 SD,RT,JSon,DG. 8.00
477 SD,RT,JSon,DG. 8.00
478 SD,RT,JSon,DG. 8.00
479 CI,DG,JSon,Dial H For Hero,
 E:Starman and Aquaman 8.00
480 CI,DJ,B:Dial H for Hero 8.00
481 CI,DJ. 8.00
482 CI,DJ,DH. 8.00
483 CI,DJ,DH. 8.00
484 GP(c),CI,DJ,DH 8.00
485 GP(c),CI,DJ 8.00
486 GP(c),DH,RT,TVE 8.00
487 CI,DJ,DH. 8.00
488 CI,DJ,TVE 8.00
489 CI,FMc,TVE 8.00
490 GP(c),CI,E:Dial H for Hero.... 8.00
491 KG(c),DigestSize,DN,
 Shazam,rep.other material ... 20.00
492 KG(c),DN,E:Shazam 20.00
493 KG(c),GT,B:Challengers of
 the Unknown,reprints 20.00
494 KG(c),GT,Challengers,
 reprints. 20.00
495 ATh,reprints,Challengers 20.00
496 GK(c),ATh,reprints,
 Challengers 20.00
497 ATh,DA,reps.,E:Challengers.. 20.00
498 GK(c),reprints,Rep.Legion ... 20.00
499 GK(c),reprints,Rep. 20.00
500 KG(c),Legion reprints,Rep ... 20.00
501 reprints,Rep. 20.00
502 reprints,Rep. 20.00
503 reprints,final issue 20.00
Giant #1, 80 page, 7 tales (1998) . 15.00

ADVENTURE COMICS
1999
1 JeR,PSj,F:Starman & The Atom . 2.00

ADVENTURES IN THE DC UNIVERSE
1997–98
1 F:New JLA 6.00
2 F:The Flash,Catwoman. 4.00
3 Wonder Woman vs. Cheetah;
 Poison Ivy vs. Batman 4.00
4 F:Green Lantern vs. Glorious
 Godfrey; Mister Miracle 4.00
5 F:Martian Manhunter, all alien

ADVENTURES OF DEAN MARTIN AND JERRY LEWIS
1952–57
1 .... 1,200.00
2 .... 600.00
3 thru 10 .... @300.00
11 thru 20 .... @200.00
21 thru 40 .... @125.00

Becomes:

ADVENTURES OF JERRY LEWIS
1957–71
41 thru 55 .... @125.00
56 thru 69 .... @100.00
70 thru 87 .... @75.00
88 A:Bob Hope 75.00
89 thru 91 .... @50.00
92 C:Superman 70.00
93 thru 96 .... @60.00
97 A:Batman & Joker 125.00
98 thru 100 .... @55.00
101 and 102 .... @75.00
103 and 104 NA .... @75.00
105 A:Superman. 70.00
106 thru 111 .... @45.00
112 A:Flash 55.00
113 thru 116 .... @40.00
117 A:Wonder Woman 75.00
118 thru 124 .... @35.00

ADVENTURES OF FORD FAIRLANE
1990
1 DH,DG 2.00
2 thru 4 DH .... @2.00

ADVENTURES OF THE OUTSIDERS
(see BATMAN & THE OUTSIDERS)

ADVENTURES OF OZZIE AND HARRIET
1949–50
1 Ph(c) 1,200.00
2 .... 600.00
3 thru 5 .... @500.00

ADVENTURES OF REX, THE WONDERDOG
1952–59
1 ATh 1,500.00
2 ATh. 750.00
3 ATh. 600.00
4 .... 450.00
5 .... 450.00

All comics prices listed are for *Near Mint* condition.

Adventures–All-American — DC — Comics Values Annual

6 thru 11 . . . . @350.00	41 . . . . 1,500.00	85 . . . . 1,000.00
12 thru 20 . . . . @200.00	42 . . . . 1,500.00	86 V:Crime of the Month Club . 1,000.00
21 thru 46 . . . . @150.00	43 . . . . 1,500.00	87 `The Strange Case of
	44 `I Accuse the Green Lantern!1,500.00	Professor Nobody' 1,000.00
ADVENTURES	45 . . . . 1,500.00	88 `Canvas of Crime' 1,000.00
OF SUPERBOY	46 . . . . 1,500.00	89 O:Harlequin 1,500.00
See: SUPERBOY	47 Hop Harrigan meets the	90 O:Icicle 1,500.00
	Enemy,(c) 1,500.00	91 `Wedding of the Harlequin' . 1,500.00
ADVENTURES	48 . . . . 1,500.00	92 `The Icicle goes South' 1,500.00
OF SUPERMAN	49 . . . . 1,500.00	93 `Double Crossing Decoy' . . . 1,500.00
See: SUPERMAN	50 E:Sargon 1,500.00	94 A:Harlequin 1,500.00
	51 `Murder Under the Stars' . . . 1,200.00	95 `The Unmasking of the
AGENT LIBERTY	52 . . . . 1,200.00	Harlequin' 1,500.00
SPECIAL	53 Green Lantern delivers	96 ATh(c),`Solve the Mystery
1992	the Mail 1,200.00	of the Emerald Necklaces!' 1,500.00
1 DAb,O:Agent Liberty 2.00	54 . . . . 1,200.00	97 ATh(c),`The Country Fair
	55 `The Riddle of the	Crimes' 1,500.00
	Runaway Trolley' 1,200.00	98 ATh,ATh(c),`End of Sports!' . 1,500.00
	56 V:Elegant Esmond 1,200.00	99 ATh,ATh(c),E:Hop Harrigan . 1,500.00
	57 V:The Melancholy Men 1,200.00	100 ATh,I:Johnny Thunder 2,500.00
ALIEN NATION	58 . . . . 1,200.00	101 ATh,ATh(c),E:Mutt & Jeff . . 1,800.00
1988	59 `The Story of the Man Who	102 ATh,ATh(c),E:GrnLantern . 5,000.00
1 JBi,movie adaption 2.50	Couldn't Tell The Truth' . . . 1,200.00	Becomes:
	60 . . . . 1,200.00	**ALL-AMERICAN**
ALL-AMERICAN COMICS	61 O:Soloman Grundy,`Fighters	**WESTERN**
1939–48	Never Quit' 7,000.00	1948–52
1 B:Hop Harrigan,Scribbly,Mutt&Jeff,	62 `Da Distrik Attorney' 1,100.00	103 A:Johnny Thunder,`The City
Red,White&Blue,Bobby Thatcher,	63 . . . . 1,100.00	Without Guns,`All Johnny
Skippy,Daiseybelle,Mystery Men	64 `A Bag of Assorted Nuts!' . . 1,100.00	Thunder stories 700.00
of Mars,Toonerville 7,500.00	65 `The Man Who Lost	104 ATh(c),`Unseen Allies' 450.00
2 B:Ripley's Believe It or Not . . 2,500.00	Wednesday' 1,100.00	105 ATh(c),`Hidden Guns' 400.00
3 Hop Harrigan (c) 1,700.00	66 `The Soles of Manhattan!' . . 1,100.00	106 ATh(c),`Snow Mountain
4 Flag(c) 1,700.00	67 V:King Shark 1,100.00	Ambush' 350.00
5 B:The American Way 1,700.00	68 Meets Napoleon&Joe	107 ATh(c),`Cheyenne Justice' . . 400.00
6 ShM(c),Fredric Marchin in	Safeen 1,100.00	108 ATh(c),`Vengeance of
`The American Way' 1,500.00	69 `Backwards Man!' 1,100.00	the Silver Bullet' 350.00
7 E:Bobby Thatcher,C.H.	70 JKu,I:Maximillian O'Leary,	109 ATh(c),`Secret of
Claudy's `A Thousand Years	V:Colley, the Leprechaun . . 1,100.00	Crazy River' 350.00
in a Minute' 1,500.00	71 E:Red,White&Blue,`The	110 ATh(c),`Ambush at
8 B:Ultra Man 2,700.00	Human Bomb' 1,000.00	Scarecrow Hills' 350.00
9 . . . . 1,500.00	72 B:Black Pirate 1,000.00	111 ATh(c),`Gun-Shy Sheriff' . . . 350.00
10 ShM(c),E:The American Way,	73 B:Winkey,Blinky&Noddy,	112 ATh(c),`Double Danger' . . . 350.00
Santa-X-Mas(c) 1,400.00	`Mountain Music Mayhem' . 1,000.00	113 ATh(c),`Johnny Thunder
11 Ultra Man(c) 1,500.00	74 . . . . 1,000.00	Indian Chief' 375.00
12 E:Toonerville Folks 1,200.00	75 . . . . 1,000.00	114 ATh(c),`The End of
13 `The Infra Red Des'Royers' . 1,200.00	76 `Spring Time for Doiby' 1,000.00	Johnny Thunder' 350.00
14 . . . . 1,200.00	77 Hop Harrigan(c) 1,000.00	115 ATh(c),`Cheyenne Mystery' . . 350.00
15 E:Tippie and Reg'lar Fellars 1,500.00	78 . . . . 1,000.00	116 ATh(c),`Buffalo Raiders
16 O&1st App:Green Lantern,	79 Mutt & Jeff 1,000.00	of the Mesa' 350.00
B:Lantern(c) 140,000.00	80 . . . . 1,000.00	117 ATh(c),V:Black Lightnin 250.00
17 SMo(c) 21,000.00	81 . . . . 1,000.00	118 ATh(c),`Challenge of
18 SMo(c) 14,000.00	82 . . . . 1,000.00	the Aztecs' 250.00
19 SMo(c),O&I: Atom, E:Ultra	83 Mutt & Jeff 1,000.00	119 GK(c),`The Vanishing
Man 22,000.00	84 `The Adventure of the Man	Gold Mine' 250.00
20 I:Atom's costume,Hunkle	with Two Faces' 1,000.00	120 GK(c),`Ambush at
becomes Red Tornado 6,500.00		Painted Mountain' 250.00
21 E:Wiley of West Point		121 ATh(c),`The Unmasking of
& Skippy 3,500.00		Johnny Thunder' 250.00
22 . . . . 3,000.00		122 ATh(c),`The Real
23 E:Daieybelle 3,500.00		Johnny Thunder' 250.00
24 E:Ripley's Believe It or Not . 4,000.00		123 GK(c),`Johnny Thunder's
25 O&I:Dr. Mid-Nite 14,000.00		Strange Rival' 250.00
26 O&I:Sargon the Sorcerer . . . 5,000.00		124 ATh(c),`The Iron Horse's
27 I:Doiby Dickles 5,000.00		Last Run' 250.00
28 . . . . 2,200.00		125 ATh(c),`Johnny Thunder's
29 ShM(c) 2,200.00		Last Roundup' 250.00
30 ShM(c) 2,200.00		126 ATh(c),`Phantoms of the
31 Adventures of the underfed		Desert' 250.00
orphans 2,200.00		Becomes:
32 . . . . 1,800.00		**ALL-AMERICAN**
33 . . . . 1,800.00		**MEN OF WAR**
34 . . . . 1,800.00		1952–66
35 Doiby discovers Lantern's ID 1,800.00		127 (0) 1,500.00
36 . . . . 1,800.00		128 (1) 900.00
37 . . . . 1,800.00		2 JGr(c),Killer Bait 750.00
38 . . . . 1,800.00		3 Pied Piper of Pyong-Yang . . . 700.00
39 . . . . 1,800.00	*All-American Comics #8*	4 JGr(c),The Hills of Hate 700.00
40 . . . . 1,800.00	© DC Comics, Inc.	5 One Second to Zero 700.00
		6 IN(c),Jungle Killers 600.00

Comics Values Annual — DC — All-American–All-Flash

All-American Western #115
© *DC Comics, Inc.*

7 IN(c),Beach to Hold 600.00
8 IN(c),Sgt. Storm Cloud 600.00
9 . . . . 600.00
10 . . . . 600.00
11 JGr(c),Dragon's Teeth 600.00
12 . . . . 500.00
13 JGr(c),Lost Patrol. 500.00
14 IN(c),Pigeon Boss 500.00
15 JGr(c),Flying Roadblock. 500.00
16 JGr(c),The Flying Jeep. 500.00
17 JGr(c),Booby Trap Ridge 500.00
18 JKu(c),The Ballad of
    Battling Bells 500.00
19 JGr(c),IN,Torpedo Track. 350.00
20 JGr(c),JKu,Lifenet to
    Beach Road. 350.00
21 JGr(c),IN,RH,The
    Coldest War 350.00
22 JGr(c),IN,JKu,Snipers Nest . . 350.00
23 JGr(c),The Silent War 350.00
24 JGr(c),The Thin Line 350.00
25 JGr(c),IN,For Rent-One
    Foxhole 350.00
26. . . . . 350.00
27 JGr(c),RH,Fighting Pigeon . . . 350.00
28 JGr(c),RA,JKu,Medal
    for A Dog 350.00
29 IN(c),JKu,Battle Bridges. 350.00
30 JGr(c),Frogman Hunt 350.00
31 JGr(c),Battle Seat 275.00
32 JGr(c),RH,Battle Station. 275.00
33 JGr(c),IN,Sky Ambush 275.00
34 JGr(c),JKu,No Man's Alley . . . 250.00
35 JGr(c),IN, Battle Call 250.00
36 JGr(c),JKu,Battle Window . . . 250.00
37 JGr(c),JKu,The Big Stretch . . 250.00
38 JGr(c),RH,JKu,The
    Floating Sentinel. 250.00
39 JGr(c),JKu,The Four Faces
    of Sgt. Fay 250.00
40 JGr(c),IN,Walking Helmet. . . . 250.00
41 JKu(c),RH,JKu,The 50-50 War 225.00
42 JGr(c),JKu,Battle Arm 225.00
43 JGr(c),JKu,Command Post. . . 225.00
44 JKu(c),The Flying Frogman . . 225.00
45 JGr(c),RH,Combat Waterboy . 225.00
46 JGr(c),IN,RH,Tank Busters. . . 225.00
47 JGr(c),JKu,MD,Battle Freight. 225.00
48 JGr(c),JKu,MD,Roadblock . . . 225.00
49 JGr(c),Walking Target. 225.00
50 IN,RH,Bodyguard For A Sub . 225.00
51 JGr(c),RH,Bomber's Moon . . . 175.00
52 JKu(c),RH,MD,Back
    Seat Driver. 175.00
53 JKu(c),JKu,Night Attack 175.00
54 JKu(c),IN,Diary of a
    Fighter Pilot 175.00
55 JKu(c),RH,Split-Second Target 175.00
56 JKu,IN,RH,Frogman Jinx 175.00
57 Pick-Up for Easy Co. 175.00
58 JKu(c),RH,MD,A Piece of Sky 175.00
59 JGr(c),JKu,The Hand of War . 175.00
60 JGr(c),The Time Table 175.00
61 JGr(c),IN,MD,Blind Target . . . 175.00
62 JGr(c),RH,RA,No(c) 175.00
63 JGr(c),JKu,Frogman Carrier . . 175.00
64 JKu(c),JKu,RH,The Other
    Man's War 175.00
65 JGr(c),JKu,MD,Same
    Old Sarge. 175.00
66 JGr(c),The Walking Fort 175.00
67 JGr(c),RH,A:Gunner&Sarge,
    The Cover Man 500.00
68 JKu(c),Gunner&Sarge,
    The Man & The Gun. 200.00
69 JKu(c),A:Tank Killer,
    Bazooka Hill 200.00
70 JKu(c),IN,Pigeon
    Without Wings 175.00
71 JGr(c),A:Tank Killer,Target
    For An Ammo Boy 125.00
72 JGr(c),A:Tank Killer,T.N.T.
    Broom 125.00
73 JGr(c),JKu,No Detour. 125.00
74 The Minute Commandos 125.00
75 JKu(c),Sink That Flattop. 125.00
76 JGr(c),A:Tank Killer,
    Just One More Tank 125.00
77 JKu(c),IN,MD,Big Fish-
    little Fish. 125.00
78 JGr(c),Tin Hat for an
    Iron Man. 125.00
79 JKu(c),RA,Showdown Soldier. 125.00
80 JGr(c),RA,The Medal Men . . . 125.00
81 JGr(c),IN,Ghost Ship of
    Two Wars 100.00
82 IN(c),B:Johnny Cloud,
    The Flying Chief 200.00
83 IN(c),Fighting Blind 125.00
84 IN(c),Death Dive 100.00
85 RH(c),Battle Eagle. 100.00
86 JGr(c),Top-Gun Ace 100.00
87 JGr(c),Broken Ace 100.00
88 JGr(c),The Ace of Vengeance 100.00
89 JGr(c),The Star Jockey 100.00
90 JGr(c),Wingmate of Doom 75.00
91 RH(c),Two Missions To Doom . 75.00
92 JGr(c),The Battle Hawk 75.00
93 RH(c),The Silent Rider. 75.00
94 RH(c),Be Brave-Be Silent 75.00
95 RH(c),Second Sight
    For a Pilot 75.00
96 RH(c),The Last Flight
    of Lt. Moon. 75.00
97 IN(c),A 'Target' Called
    Johnny 75.00
98 The Time-Bomb Ace 75.00
99 IN(c),The Empty Cockpit 75.00
100 RH(c),Battle o/t Sky Chiefs. . . 75.00
101 RH(c),Death Ship of
    Three Wars 55.00
102 JKu(c),Blind Eagle-Hungry
    Hawk 55.00
103 IN(c),Battle Ship-
    Battle Heart 55.00
104 JKu(c),The Last Target. 55.00
105 IN(c),Killer Horse-Ship 55.00
106 IN(c),Death Song For
    A Battle Hawk. 55.00
107 IN(c),Flame in the Sky 55.00
108 IN(c),Death-Dive of the Aces . 55.00
109 IN(c),The Killer Slot 55.00
110 RH(c),The Co-Pilot was
    Death. 55.00
111 RH(c),E:Johnny Cloud, Tag–
    You're Dead 55.00
112 RH(c),B:Balloon Buster,Lt.
    Steve Savage-Balloon Buster . 55.00
113 JKu(c),The Ace of
    Sudden Death 55.00
114 JKu(c),The Ace Who
    Died Twice 55.00
115 IN(c),A:Johnny Cloud,
    Deliver One Enemy Ace-
    Handle With Care. 55.00
116 JKu(c),A:Baloon Buster,
    Circle of Death 55.00
117 Sept.–Oct., 1966 . . . . 55.00

ALL-AMERICAN COMICS
1999
1 RMz(s),F:Green Lantern &
   Johnny Thunder 2.00

ALL-FLASH
1941–47
1 EHi,O:Flash,I:The Monocle 22,000.00
2 EHi,The Adventure of Roy
   Revenge 4,500.00
3 EHi,The Adventure of
   Misplaced Faces 2,400.00
4 EHi,Tale of the Time
   Capsule. 2,400.00
5 EHi,The Case of the Patsy
   Colt! Last Quarterly 1,700.00
6 EHi,The Ray that Changed
   Men's Souls. 1,400.00
7 EHi,Adventures of a Writers
   Fantasy, House of Horrors . 1,400.00
8 EHi,Formula to Fairyland!. . . 1,400.00
9 EHi,Adventure of the Stolen
   Telescope 1,400.00
10 EHi,Case of the Curious Cat 1,400.00
11 EHi,Troubles come
    in Doubles 1,200.00
12 EHi,Tumble INN to Trouble,
    Becomes Quarterly on orders
    from War Production Board
    O:The Thinker 1,200.00
13 EHi,I:The King. 1,200.00
14 EHi,I:Winky, Blinky & Noddy
    Green Lantern (c) 1,400.00
15 EHi,Secrets of a Stranger . . 1,200.00
16 EHi,A:The Sinister. 1,200.00
17 Tales of the Three Wishes. . 1,200.00
18 A:Winkly,Blinky&Noddy
    B:Mutt & Jeff reprints 1,200.00
19 No Rest at the Rest Home . 1,200.00
20 A:Winky, Blinky & Noddy . . . 1,200.00

All-Flash #7
© *DC Comics Inc.*

All-Flash–All-Star — DC — Comics Values Annual

21 I:Turtle 900.00	becomes chairman 44,000.00	82 thru 98 . . . . @125.00
22 The Money Doubler,E:Mutt & Jeff reprints 900.00	9 JSA in Latin America 4,500.00	99 FF 150.00
23 The Bad Men of Bar Nothing . 900.00	10 C:Flash & Green Lantern, JSA Time Travel story 4,500.00	100 . . . . 125.00
24 I:Worry Wart,3 Court Clowns Get Caught 900.00	11 Wonder Women joins; I:Justice Battalion 6,000.00	101 thru 104 . . . . @100.00
25 I:Slapsy Simmons, Flash Jitterbugs 900.00	12 V:Black Dragon society 3,500.00	105 O:JSA, March, 1987 . . . . 100.00
26 I:The Chef,The Boss,Shrimp Coogan,A:Winky, Blinky & Noddy 900.00	13 V:Hitler 3,500.00	106 and 107 . . . . @100.00
27 A:The Thinker,Gangplank Gus story 900.00	14 JSA in occupied Europe . . . 3,500.00	108 O:Johnny Thunder 225.00
28 A:Shrimp Coogan,Winky, Blinky & Noddy 900.00	15 I:Brain Wave,A:JSA's Girl Friends 3,500.00	109 thru 116 . . . . @100.00
29 The Thousand-Year Old Terror, A:Winky,Blinky & Noddy 900.00	16 Propaganda/relevance issue 2,400.00	117 CI,O:Super-Chief 125.00
30 The Vanishing Snowman 900.00	17 V:Brain Wave 2,400.00	118 . . . . 100.00
31 A:Black Hat,Planet of Sport . . 900.00	18 I:King Bee 2,500.00	119 . . . . 100.00
32 I:Fiddler,A:Thinker 1,200.00	19 Hunt for Hawkman 2,400.00	

ALL FUNNY COMICS
1943–48

1 Genius Jones 600.00	20 I:Monster 2,400.00	
2 same 250.00	21 Time travel story 2,000.00	### ALL-STAR COMICS
3 same 175.00	22 Sandman and Dr. Fate leave, I:Conscience, Good Fairy. . 2,000.00	#### 1976–78
4 same 175.00	23 I:Psycho-Pirate 2,000.00	58 RE,WW,R:JSA,I:Power Girl . . . 65.00
5 thru 10 . . . . @175.00	24 Propaganda/relevance issue, A:Conscience&Wildcat,Mr.Terrific; L:Starman & Spectre; Flash & Green Lantern return . . 2,000.00	59 RE,WW,Brain Wave 50.00
11 Genius Jones 175.00		60 KG,WW,I:Vulcan 50.00
12 same 175.00		61 KG,WW,V:Vulcan 50.00
13 same 100.00		62 KG,WW,A:E-2 Superman 50.00
14 . . . . 100.00	25 JSA whodunit issue 1,800.00	63 KG,WW,A:E-2 Superman, Solomon Grundy 50.00
15 . . . . 100.00	26 V:Metal Men from Jupiter . . 1,800.00	64 WW,Shining Knight 50.00
16 A:DC Superheroes 350.00	27 Handicap issue,A:Wildcat . . 1,800.00	65 KG,WW,E-2 Superman, Vandal Savage 50.00
17 thru 23 . . . . @100.00	28 Ancient curse comes to life . 1,600.00	66 JSon,BL,Injustice Society 50.00
	29 I:Landor from 25th century . 1,600.00	67 JSon,BL 50.00
	30 V:Brain Wave 1,600.00	68 JSon,BL 50.00
### ALL-STAR COMICS	31 V:Zor 1,600.00	69 JSon,BL,A:E-2 Superman, Starman,Dr.Mid-Nite 60.00
#### Summer, 1940–51	32 V:Psycho-Pirate 1,600.00	70 JSon,BL,Huntress 50.00
1 B:Flash,Hawkman,Hourman, Sandman,Spectre,Red White & Blue 19,000.00	33 V:Soloman Grundy,A:Doiby Dickles, Last appearance Thunderbolt 4,500.00	71 JSon,BL 50.00
	34 I:Wizard 1,500.00	72 JSon,A:Golden.Age Huntress . . 50.00
2 B:Green Lantern and Johnny Thunder 7,500.00	35 I:Per Degaton 1,500.00	73 JSon 50.00
3 First meeting of Justice Society with Flash as Chairman . . 55,000.00	36 A:Superman and Batman . 4,000.00	74 JSon 50.00
4 First mission of JSA 8,000.00	37 I:Injustice Society of the World 2,000.00	### ALL STAR COMICS
5 V:Mr. X,I:Hawkgirl 6,500.00	38 V:Villians of History, A:Black Canary 2,200.00	#### 1999
6 Flash leaves 4,000.00	39 JSA in magic world, Johnny Thunder leaves . . . 1,500.00	1 JeR(s),F:Justice Society of America, V:Stalker's Seven . . 3.00
7 Green Lantern becomes Chairman, L:Hourman, C:Superman, Batman & Flash 4,500.00	40 A:Black Canary,Junior Justice Society of America 1,500.00	2 JeR(s) conclusion 3.00
	41 Black Canary joins,A:Harlequin, V:Injustice Society of the World 1,500.00	Giant #1 80-page 5.00
8 I:Wonder Women;Starman and Dr. Mid-Nite join,Hawkman	42 I:Alchemist 1,400.00	### ALL STAR SQUADRON
	43 V:Interdimensional gold men 1,400.00	#### 1981–87
	44 I:Evil Star 1,400.00	1 RB,JOy,JSa,I:Degaton 8.00
	45 Crooks develop stellar JSA powers 1,400.00	2 RB,JOy,Robotman 5.00
	46 Comedy issue 1,400.00	3 RB,JOy,Robotman 5.00
	47 V:Billy the Kid 1,400.00	4 RB,JOy,Robotman 5.00
	48 Time Travel story 1,400.00	5 RB/JOy,I:Firebrand(Dannette) . . 5.00
	49 V:Comet-being invaders . . 1,400.00	6 JOy,Hawkgirl 5.00
	50 V:Flash's College classmate 1,500.00	7 JOy,Hawkgirl 5.00
	51 V:Diamond men from center of the Earth 1,400.00	8 DH/JOy,A:Steel 5.00
	52 JSA disappears from Earth for years 1,400.00	9 DH/JOy,A:Steel 5.00
	53 Time Travel issue 1,400.00	10 JOy,V:Binary Brotherhood 5.00
	54 Circus issue 1,400.00	11 JOy,V:Binary Brotherhood 5.00
	55 JSA fly to Jupiter 1,400.00	12 JOy,R:Dr.Hastor O:Hawkman . . 5.00
	56 V:Chameleons from 31st Century 1,400.00	13 JOy,photo(c) 5.00
	57 I:Key 2,100.00	14 JOy,JLA crossover 5.00
	Becomes:	15 JOy,JLA crossover 5.00
		16 I&D:Nuclear 5.00
	### ALL STAR WESTERN	17 Trial of Robotman 5.00
	#### April-May, 1951	18 V:Thor 5.00
	58 Trigger Twins 600.00	19 V:Brainwave 5.00
	59 . . . . 300.00	20 JOy,V:Brainwave 5.00
	60 . . . . 300.00	21 JOy,I:Cyclotron (1st JOy Superman) 7.00
	61 thru 64 ATh 250.00	22 JOy,V:Deathbolt,Cyclotron 5.00
	65 . . . . 250.00	23 JOy,I:Amazing-Man 5.00
	66 . . . . 275.00	24 JOy,I:Brainwave,Jr 7.00
	67 GK,B:Johnny Thunder 300.00	25 JOy,I:Infinity Inc 5.00
All-Star Comics #1 © DC Comics, Inc.	68 thru 81 . . . . @125.00	26 JOy,Infinity Inc 7.00
		27 Spectre 5.00
		28 JOy,Spectre 5.00
		29 JOy,retold story 5.00
		30 V:Black Dragons 5.00
		31 All-Star gathering 5.00
		32 O:Freedom Fighters 5.00
		33 Freedom Fighters,I:Tsunami . . . 5.00

DC All-Star–Animal

All Star Squadron #58
© DC Comics Inc.

34 Freedom Fighters	5.00
35 RB,Shazam family	5.00
36 Shazam family	5.00
37 A:Shazam Family	5.00
38 V:The Real American	5.00
39 V:The Real American	5.00
40 D:The Real American	5.00
41 O:Starman	5.00
42 V:Tsunami,Kung	5.00
43 V:Tsunami,Kung	5.00
44 I:Night & Fog	5.00
45 I:Zyklon	5.00
46 V:Baron Blitzkrieg	5.00
47 TM,O:Dr.Fate	10.00
48 A:Blackhawk	5.00
49 A:Dr.Occult	5.00
50 Crisis	7.00
51 AA,Crisis	5.00
52 Crisis	5.00
53 Crisis,A:The Dummy	5.00
54 Crisis,V:The Dummy	5.00
55 Crisis,V:Anti-Monitor	5.00
56 Crisis	5.00
57 A:Dr.Occult	5.00
58 I:Mekanique	5.00
59 A:Mekanique,Spectre	5.00
60 Crisis 1942, conclusion	5.00
61 O:Liberty Belle	5.00
62 O:The Shining Knight	5.00
63 O:Robotman	5.00
64 WB/TD,V:Funny Face	5.00
65 DH/TD,O:Johnny Quick	5.00
66 TD,O:Tarantula	5.00
67 TD,Last Issue,O:JSA	5.00
Ann.#1 JOy,O:G.A.,Atom	5.00
Ann.#2 JOy,Infinity Inc.	5.00
Ann.#3 WB,JOy,KG,GP,DN	5.00

ALL STAR WESTERN
See: WEIRD WESTERN TALES

ALPHA CENTURION
1996
Spec.#1 .... 3.00

AMBER: THE GUNS OF AVALON
Aug., 1996
1 (of 3) adapt. of Roger Zelazny classic 7.00

2 and 3 conclusion .... @7.00

AMBUSH BUG
1985
1 KG,I:Cheeks	3.00
2 KG thru 4	@3.00
Spec.#1 Stocking Stuffer, KG,R:Cheeks (1986)	3.00
Spec.#1 Nothing Special KG,A:Sandman,Death (1992)	3.50

AMERICA vs. JUSTICE SOCIETY
Jan.–April, 1985
1 AA,R,Thomas Script	7.00
2 AA	5.00
3 AA	5.00
4 AA	5.00

AMERICAN CENTURY
DC/Vertigo, March, 2001
1 HC,vet hijacks plane	5.00
2 HC,Hell hotter for Harry	3.00
3 HC,Guatemalan Revolution	3.00
4 HC,Bananarama	3.00
5 HC,The Protector,pt.1	3.00
6 HC,The Protector,pt.2	3.00
7 HC,The Protector,pt.3	3.00
8 HC,The Protector,pt.4	3.00
9 HC,Route 66	3.00
10 HC,White Lightning,pt.1	3.00
11 HC,White Lightning,pt.2	3.00
12 HC,White Lightning,pt.3	3.00
13 HC,White Lightning,pt.4	3.00
14 HC,An American in Paris,pt.1	3.00
15 HC,An American in Paris,pt.2	3.00
16 HC,An American in Paris,pt.3	3.00
17 HC,Coming Home,pt.1	3.00
18 HC,Coming Home,pt.2	3.00
19 HC,Coming Home,pt.3	3.00
20 HC,Coming Home,Pt.4	3.00
21 HC,Coming Home,pt.5	3.00
22 HC,Tramps,pt.1	3.00
23 HC,Tramps,pt.2	3.00
24 HC,one-shot	3.00
25 HC,Bite the Big Apple,pt.1	3.00
26 HC,Bite the Big Apple,pt.2	3.00
27 HC,Bite the Big Apple,pt.3	3.00
TPB Scars and Stripes, HC	8.95
TPB Hollywood Babylon	12.95

AMERICAN FREAK: A TALE OF THE UN-MEN
DC/Vertigo, 1994
1 B:DLp,(s),VcL,R:Un-Men	2.25
2 VcL,A:Crassus	2.25
3 VcL,A:Scylla	2.25
4 VcL,A:Scylla	2.25
5 VcL,Final Issue	2.25

AMETHYST
[Limited Series], 1983–84
[PRINCESS OF GEMWORLD]
1 Origin	2.50
2 thru 7 EC	@2.50
8 EC,O:Gemworld	2.50
9 thru 12 EC	@2.50
Spec.#1 KG	2.50

[Regular Series], 1985–86
1 thru 12 EC	@2.50
13 EC,Crisis,A:Dr.Fate	2.50
14 EC	2.50
15 EC,Castle Amethyst Destroyed	2.50
16 EC	2.50
Spec.#1 EM	2.50

[Mini-Series], 1987–88
1 EM	2.00
2 EM	2.50
3 EM	2.00
4 EM,O:Mordru	2.00

ANARKY
March, 1997
1 AlG(s),NBy,JRu,Anarky vs. Etrigan	4.00
2 AlG(s),NBy,JRu,V:Darkseid	2.50
3 AlG(s),NBy,JRu,A:Batman	2.50
4 AlG(s),NBy,JRu,A:Batman,concl.	2.50

ANARKY
1999
1 AlG(s),NBy,JRu,F:JLA	2.50
2 AlG(s),NBy,JRu,F:GreenLantern	2.50
3 AlG(s),NBy,JRu,F:GreenLantern	2.50
4 AlG(s),NBy,JRu,V:Ra's al Ghul	2.50
5 AlG(s),NBy,JRu,V:Ra's al Ghul,pt.2	2.50
6 AlG(s),NBy,JRu,F:Ra's al Ghul,pt.3	2.50
7 AlG,NBy,JRu,Day of Judgment	2.50
8 AlG(s),NBy,JRu, final issue	2.50

ANGEL & THE APE
1991
1 Apes of Wrath,pt.1	3.00
2 Wrath pt.2,A:G.Gardner	3.00
3 Wrath,pt.3,A:InferiorFive	3.00
4 Wrath,pt.4,A:InferiorFive	3.00

ANGEL AND THE APE
DC/Vertigo, Aug., 2001
1 (of 4) HC,F:Angel O'Day	3.00
2 thru 4 HC	@3.00

ANIMA
DC/Vertigo, 1994–95
1 R:Anima	2.50
2 V:Scarecrow	2.50
3 V:Scarecrow	2.50
4 A:Nameless one	2.50
5 CI,V:Arkana	2.50
6 CI,V:Arkana	2.50
7 Zero Hour	2.50
8 Nameless One	2.50
9 Superboy & Nameless One	2.50
10 A:Superboy	2.50
11 V:Nameless One	2.50
12 A:Hawkman,V:Shrike	2.50
13 A:Hawkman,Shrike	2.50
14 Return to Gotham City	2.50
15 V:Psychic Vampire, final issue	3.00

ANIMAL ANTICS
1946–49
1	450.00
2	250.00
3 thru 10	@150.00
11 thru 23	@100.00

ANIMAL-MAN
1988–95
1 BB(c),B:GMo(s),ChT,DHz, B:Animal Rights,I:Dr.Myers	12.00
2 BB(c),ChT,DHz,A:Superman	6.00
3 BB(c),ChT,DHz,A:B'wana Beast	3.00
4 BB(c),ChT,DHz,V:B'wana Beast, E:Animal Rights	3.00
5 BB(c),ChT,DHz, I&D:Crafty Coyote	3.50
6 BB(c),ChT,DHz,A:Hawkman	3.00

Animal–Aquaman · DC · Comics Values Annual

Animal Man #63 © DC Comics, Inc.

7 BB(c),ChT,DHz,D:Red Mask 3.00
8 BB(c),ChT,DHz,V:Mirror Master . 3.00
9 BB(c),DHz,TG,A:Martian
   Manhunter 3.00
10 BB(c),ChT,DHz,A:Vixen,
   B:O:Animal Man 3.00
11 BB(c),ChT,DHz,I:Hamed Ali,
   Tabu,A:Vixen 3.00
12 BB(c),D:Hamed Ali,A:Vixen,
   B'wanaBeast 3.00
13 BB(c),I:Dominic Mndawe,R:B'wana
   Beast,Apartheid 3.00
14 BB(c),TG,SeM,A:Future Animal
   Man,I:Lennox 3.00
15 BB(c),ChT,DHz,A:Dolphin 3.00
16 BB(c),ChT,DHz,A:JLA. 3.00
17 BB(c),ChT,DHz,A:Mirr.Master. . . 3.00
18 BB(c),ChT,DHz,A:Lennox 3.00
19 BB(c),ChT,DHz,D:Ellen,
   Cliff,Maxine 3.00
20 BB(c),ChT,DHz,I:Bug-Man 3.00
21 BB(c),ChT,DHz,N&V:Bug-Man . . 3.00
22 BB(c),PCu,SeM,A:Rip Hunter. . . 3.00
23 BB(c),A:Phantom Stranger. 3.00
24 BB(c),V:Psycho Pirate 3.00
25 BB(c),ChT,MFm,I:Comic
   Book Limbo 3.00
26 BB(c),E:GMo(s),ChT,MFm,
   A:Grant Morrison 3.00
27 BB(c),B:PMi(s),ChT,MFm 3.00
28 BB(c),ChT,MFm,I:Nowhere Man,
   I&D:Front Page 3.00
29 ChT,SDi,V:National Man 3.00
30 BB(c),ChT,MFm,V:Angel Mob . . 3.00
31 BB(c),ChT,MFm 3.00
32 BB(c),E:PMi(s),ChT,MFm 3.00
33 BB(c),B:TV(s),SDi,A:Travis
   Cody 3.00
34 BB(c),SDi,Requiem 3.00
35 BB(c),SDi,V:Radioactive Dogs . . 3.00
36 BB(c),SDi,A:Mr.Rainbow 3.00
37 BB(c),SDi,Animal/Lizard Man. . . 3.00
38 BB(c),SDi,A:Mr.Rainbow 3.00
39 BB(c),TMd,SDi,Wolfpack in
   San Diego 3.00
40 BB(c),SDi,War of the Gods
   x-over. 3.00
41 BB(c),SDi,V:Star Labs
   Renegades,I:Winky 3.00
42 BB(c),SDi,V:Star Labs
   Renegades. 3.00
43 BB(c),SDi,I:Tristess,A:Vixen. . . . 3.00
44 BB(c),SDi,A:Vixen 3.00
45 BB(c),StP,SDi,I:L.Decker 3.00
46 BB(c),SDi,I:Frank Baker. 3.00
47 BB(c),SDi,I:Shining Man,
   (B'wana Beast). 3.00
48 BB(c),SDi,V:Antagon 3.00
49 BB(c),SDi,V:Antagon 3.00
50 BB(c),E:TV(s),SDi,I:Metaman. . . 5.00
51 BB(c),B:JaD(s),StP,B:Flesh
   and Blood. 3.00
52 BB(c),StP,Homecoming 3.00
53 BB(c),StP,Flesh and Blood. 3.00
54 BB(c),StP,Flesh and Blood. 3.00
55 BB(c),StP,Flesh and Blood. 3.00
56 BB(c),StP,E:Flesh and Blood,
   Double-sized 6.00

DC/Vertigo, 1993
57 BB(c),StP,B:Recreation,
   Ellen in NY. 3.00
58 BB(c),StP,Wild Side 3.00
59 BB(c),RsB,GHi(i),Wild Town. . . . 3.00
60 RsB,GHi(i),Wild life 3.00
61 BB(c),StP,Tooth and Claw#1 . . . 3.00
62 BB(c),StP,Tooth and Claw#2 . . . 3.00
63 BB(c),V:Leviathan 3.00
64 DIB(c),WSm,DnS(i),
   Breath of God. 3.00
65 RDB(c),WSm,
   Perfumed Garden. 3.00
66 A:Kindred Spirit 3.00
67 StP,Mysterious Ways #1 . . . . . . 3.00
68 StP,Mysterious Ways #2 . . . . . . 3.00
69 Animal Man's Family 3.00
70 GgP(c),StP 3.00
71 GgP(c),StP,Maxine Alive? 3.00
72 StP 3.00
73 StP,Power Life Church 3.00
74 StP,Power Life Church 3.00
75 StP,Power Life Church 3.00
76 StP,Pilgrimage problems 3.00
77 Cliff shot 3.00
78 StP,Animal Man poisoned 3.00
79 New Direction 3.00
80 New Direction 3.00
81 Wild Type,pt.1 . . . . 3.00
82 Wild Type,pt.2 . . . . 3.00
83 Wild Type,pt.3 . . . . 3.00
84 F:Maxine,SupernaturalDreams. . 3.00
85 Animal Mundi,pt.1 . . . . 3.00
86 Animal Mundi,pt.2 . . . . 3.00
87 Animal Mundi,pt.3 . . . . 3.00
88 Morphogenetic Fields. 3.00
89 final issue 3.00
Ann.#1 BB(c),JaD,TS(i),RIB(i),
   Children Crusade,F:Maxine . . . 4.25
TPB Rep.#1 thru #10 . . . . 19.95
TPB Animal Man, 2nd pr. 19.95
TPB Origin of the Species. 19.95
TPB Deus Ex Machina (2003) . . . 19.95

ANIMANIACS
Warner Bros./DC May, 1995
1 F:Yakko,Wakko,Dot 8.00
2 thru 20 . . . . @4.00
21 thru 59. . . . . @3.00
Christmas Spec. 4.00

ANTHRO
1968–69
1 HwP. 75.00
2 HwP 45.00
3 thru 5 HwP . . . . @50.00
6 HwP,WW(c&a) 50.00

AQUAMAN
[1st Regular Series], 1962–78
1 NC,I:Quisp. 1,300.00
2 NC,V:Captain Sykes. 500.00
3 NC,Aquaman from Atlantis . . . 250.00
4 NC,A:Quisp 200.00
5 NC,The Haunted Sea 200.00

Aquaman 1st Series #60
© DC Comics, Inc.

6 NC,A:Quisp 175.00
7 NC,Sea Beasts of Atlantis 175.00
8 NC,Plot to Steal the Seas 175.00
9 NC,V:King Neptune. 175.00
10 NC,A:Quisp 175.00
11 I: Mera. 150.00
12 NC,The Cosmic Gladiators. . . 150.00
13 NC,Invasion of the Giant
   Reptiles 150.00
14 NC,AquamanSecretPowers . . 150.00
15 NC,Menace of the Man-Fish . 150.00
16 NC,Duel of the Sea Queens. . 150.00
17 NC,Man Who Vanquished
   Aquaman 150.00
18 W:Aquaman & Mera. 150.00
19 NC,Atlanteans for Sale. 150.00
20 NC,Sea King's DoubleDoom . 150.00
21 NC,I:Fisherman 80.00
22 NC,The Trap of the Sinister
   Sea Nymphs 80.00
23 NC,I:Aquababy. 80.00
24 NC,O:Black Manta. 80.00
25 NC,Revolt of Aquaboy 80.00
26 NC,I:O.G.R.E. 80.00
27 NC,Battle of the Rival
   Aquamen'. 80.00
28 NC,Hail Aquababy,King of
   Atlantis 80.00
29 I:Ocean Master 75.00
30 NC,C:JLA 75.00
31 NC,V:O.G.R.E. 75.00
32 NC,V:Tryton. 75.00
33 NC,I:Aquagirl 100.00
34 NC,I:Aquabeast 60.00
35 I:Black Manta. 60.00
36 NC,What Seeks the
   Awesome Threesome? 60.00
37 I:Scavenger. 60.00
38 NC,I:Liquidator. 60.00
39 NC,How to Kill a Sea King . . . 60.00
40 JAp,Sorcerers from the Sea. . 60.00
41 JAp,Quest for Mera,pt.1. . . . . 50.00
42 JAp,Quest for Mera,pt.2. . . . . 50.00
43 JAp,Quest for Mera,pt.3. . . . . 50.00
44 JAp,Quest for Mera,pt.4. . . . . 50.00
45 JAp,Quest for Mera,pt.5. . . . . 50.00
46 JAp,Quest for Mera concl. . . . 50.00
47 JAp,Revolution in Atlantis #1
   rep.Adventure #268 . . . . 50.00
48 JAp,Revolution in Atlantis #2
   rep.Adventure #260 . . . . 65.00
49 JAp,As the Seas Die 50.00
50 JAp,NA,A:Deadman. 90.00

51 JAp,NA,A:Deadman......... 90.00
52 JAp,NA,A:Deadman......... 90.00
53 JAp,Is California Sinking?.... 20.00
54 JAp,Crime Wave........... 20.00
55 JAp,Return of the Alien..... 20.00
56 JAp,I&O:Crusader (1970)..... 20.00
57 JAp,V:Black Manta (1977).... 20.00
58 JAp,O:Aquaman rtd......... 25.00
59 JAp,V:Scavenger........... 20.00
60 DN,V:Scavenger........... 20.00
61 DN,BMc,A:Batman......... 20.00
62 DN,A:Ocean Master......... 15.00
63 DN,V:Ocean Master,
  final issue................ 15.00

[2nd Regular Series], 1991–92
1 Poseidonis Under Attack,
  C:J'onn J'onzz,Blue Beetle.... 3.00
2 V:Oumland................ 2.50
3 I:Iqula.................... 2.50
4 V:Iqula,A:Queequeg......... 2.50
5 A:Aqualad,Titans,M.Manhunter,
  R:Manta................. 2.50
6 V: Manta................. 2.50
7 R:Mera................... 2.50
8 A:Batman,V:NKV Demon..... 2.50
9 Eco-Wars#1,A:Sea Devils..... 2.50
10 Eco-Wars#2,A:Sea Devils.... 2.50
11 V:Gigantic Dinosaur......... 2.50
12 A:Iaula.................. 2.50
13 V:The Scavenger........... 2.50
14 V:The Scavenger........... 2.50

[3rd Regular Series], 1994–97
0 B:PDd(s),Paternal secret..... 7.00
1 PDd(s),R:Aqualad,I:Charybdis.. 6.00
2 V:Charybdis............... 7.00
3 B:PDd(s),Superboy......... 4.00
4 B:PDd(s),Lobo............. 4.00
5 New Costume.............. 4.00
6 V:The Deep Six............ 4.00
7 Kako's Metamorphosis...... 4.00
8 V:Corona and Naiad........ 4.00
9 JPi(c&a),V:Deadline,A:Koryak.. 3.00
10 A:Green Lantern,Koryak..... 3.00
11 R:Mera.................. 3.00
12 F:Mera.................. 3.00
13 V:Thanatos............... 3.00
14 PDd,V:Major Disaster,Underworld
  Unleashed tie-in........... 3.00
15 PDd,V:Tiamat............ 3.00
16 PDd,A:Justice League....... 3.00
17 PDd,V:underwater gargoyles.. 3.00
18 .... 3.00
19 PDd,V:Ocean Master........ 3.00
20 PDd,V:Ocean Master........ 3.00
21 PDd,JCf,A:Dolphin,
  V:ThiernaNaOge........... 3.00
22 PDd(s).................. 3.00
23 PDd(s),I:Deep Blue (Neptune
  Perkins)................. 3.00
24 PDd(s),A:Neptune Perkins.... 3.00
25 PDd(s),MEg,HSm,Atlantis united,
  Aquaman king?............ 3.00
26 PDd(s),MEg,HSm,Oceans
  threatened, Final Night tie-in... 3.00
27 PDd(s),MEg,HSm,V:Demon
  Gate, dolphin killer........ 3.00
28 PDd(s),JCf,JP,A:J'onn J'onzz... 3.00
29 PDd(s),MEg,HSm,........... 3.00
30 PDd(s),MEg,HSm,The Pit..... 3.00
31 PDd(s),V:The Shark, mind-
  controlled aquatic army..... 3.00
32 PDd(s),A:Swamp Thing...... 3.00
33 PDd(s),Aquaman's dark powers
  affect him physically....... 3.00
34 PDd(s),V:Triton........... 3.00
35 PDd(s),JCf,I:Gamesman,
  A:Animal Man............ 3.00
36 PDd(s),JCf,R:Poseidonis,
  Tempest,Vulko............ 3.00
37 PDd,JCf,Genesis,V:Darkseid... 3.00

38 PDd,JCf,capitalism........ 3.00
39 PDd,JCf,Perkins Family Reunion 3.00
40 PDd,JCf,Dr. Polaris......... 3.00
41 PDd,JCf,BSf,F:Power Girl.... 2.50
42 PDd,JCf................. 2.50
43 PDd,JCf,Millennium Giants,
  pt.2 x-over, A:Superman Red.. 2.50
44 PDd,JCf,F:Golden Age Flash,
  Sentinel................. 2.50
45 PDd,JCf,V:Triton.......... 2.50
46 PDd,JCf,news of Mera...... 2.50
47 DAn,Shadows on Water,pt.1.. 2.50
48 DAn,Shadows on Water,pt.2.. 2.50
49 DAn,ALa,JCf,V:Tempest..... 2.50
50 EL,NRd,New Costume...... 2.50
51 EL,NRd,V:King Noble....... 2.50
52 EL,V:Fire Trolls........... 2.50
53 EL,A:Superman........... 2.50

Aquaman 3rd Series #38
© DC Comics Inc.

54 EL,A:Landlovers........... 2.50
55 EL,wooing Mera............ 2.50
56 EL,V:Piranha Man,pt.1...... 2.50
57 EL,V:Piranha Man,pt.2...... 2.50
58 EL,V:DemonGate & BlackManta 2.50
59 EL,drugs in Atlantis........ 2.50
60 NRd,W:Tempest & Dolphin... 2.50
61 NRd,Day of Judgment x-over.. 2.50
62 EL(s),NRd................ 2.50
63 NRd.................... 2.50
64 DJu,SEp,NRd............ 2.50
65 DJu,SEp,NRd............ 2.50
66 DJu,PR,NRd,F:JLA........ 2.50
67 DJu,SEp,NRd............ 2.50
68 DJu,SEp,NRd,V:Cerdia..... 2.50
69 DJu,SEp,NRd,.............. 2.50
70 DJu,new alliance.......... 3.00
71 DJu,SEp,NRd,A:Warlord.... 3.00
72 DJu,SEp,NRd,V:Ch'Rinn.... 3.00
73 DJu,SEp,NRd,V:Valgos..... 3.00
74 DJu,SEp,NRd,death of friend.. 3.00
75 DJu,SEp,NRd,final issue..... 3.00
Ann.#1 Year One Annual, V:Triton,
  A:Superman,Mera......... 4.00
Ann.#2 Legends o/t Dead Earth.. 3.50
Ann.#3 Pulp Heroes (Hard Boiled). 5.00
Ann.#4 PDa, Ghosts.......... 3.50
Ann.#5 JOs(s),MBr,DG, JLApe
  Gorilla Warfare........... 3.50
Spec.#1,000,000 DAn&ALa(s),TGb,
  BAn, King of Waterworld.... 3.00
Secret Files #1 EL........... 5.00
TPB Time and Tide.......... 10.00

AQUAMAN
[1st Limited Series], 1986
1 V:Ocean Master............ 6.00
2 V:Ocean Master............ 4.00
3 V:Ocean Master............ 4.00
4 V:Ocean Master............ 4.00
[2nd Limited Series], 1989
1 CS,Atlantis Under Siege...... 3.50
2 CS,V:Invaders............. 3.00
3 CS,Mera turned Psychotic.... 3.00
4 CS,Poseidonis Under Siege... 3.00
5 CS,Last Stand,final issue..... 3.00
Spec#1 MPa,Legend o/Aquaman.. 3.00

AQUAMAN
Dec. 2002
1 Obsidian Age aftermath...... 3.00
2 F:Martian Hunter.......... 3.00
3 New look and costume...... 3.00
4 F:Tempest............... 3.00
5 V:The Thirst.............. 3.00
6 V:The Thirst.............. 3.00
7 undead pirates............ 3.00
8 V:Black Mantra............ 3.00
9 V:Black Mantra............ 3.00
10 V:The Thirst............. 3.00
11 V:The Thirst............. 3.00
12 V:The Thirst............. 3.00
TPB Aquaman: The Water Bearer. 12.95
Spec. Secret Files 2003....... 4.95

AQUAMAN: TIME & TIDE
1993–94
1 PDd(s),O:Aquaman......... 3.00
2 and 3 PDd(s),O:Aquaman
  contd................... @3.00
4 PDd(s),O:Aquaman,final issue.. 3.00
TPB rep.#1–4............... 10.00

ARAK
1981–85
1 EC,O:Ara................ 3.00
2 EC.................... 2.50
3 EC,I:Valda............... 2.50
4 thru 10 EC............... @2.50
11 EC,AA................. 2.50
12 EC,AA,I:Satyricus........ 2.50
13 thru 19 AA............. @2.50
20 AA,O:Angelica........... 2.50
21 thru 23 AA.............. 2.50
24 Double size.............. 2.50
25 thru 30............... @2.50
31 D Arak,becomes shaman.... 2.50
32 thru 48............... @2.50
49 CI/TD.................. 2.50
50 TD.................... 2.50
Ann.#1................... 2.50

ARCANA: THE BOOKS OF MAGIC
DC/Vertigo, 1994
Ann.#1 JBo(c),JNR(s),PrG,Children's
  Crusade,R:Tim Hunter,
  A:Free Country............ 4.00

ARGUS
[Mini-Series], 1995
1 R:Argus,I:Raver............ 2.00
2 Blinded by metahuman hitmen.. 2.00
3 Spy Satellite.............. 2.00
4 The Watcher.............. 2.00
5 Data Highways............ 2.00
6 Restored Sight............ 2.00

Arion–Azrael / DC / Comics Values Annual

Argus #1 © DC Comics, Inc.

ARION, LORD OF ATLANTIS
1982–85
1 JDu,Star Spawn Sun Death 3.00
2 JDu,I:Mara 2.50
3 JDu 2.50
4 JDu,O:Arion 2.50
5 & 6 JDu .... @2.50
7 thru 12 .... @2.50
13 thru 35 .... @2.50
Spec. 2.50

ARION THE IMMORTAL
1992
1 RWi,R:Arion 3.00
2 RWi,V:Garffon 2.25
3 RWi,V:Garn Daanuth 2.25
4 RWi,V:Garn Daanuth 2.25
5 RWi,Darkworlet. 2.25
6 RWi,MG,A:Power Girl 2.25

ARKHAM ASYLUM: LIVING HELL
May 2003
1 (of 6) F:Warren White 3.00
2 Food Fight 3.00
3 Humphry Dumpler 3.00
4 F:Killer Croc 3.00
5 F:Jason Blood 3.00
6 Concl.. .... 3.00

ARMAGEDDON 2001
May, 1991
1 DJu,DG,I&O:Waverider. 4.00
1a 2nd printing 2.50
1b 3rd printing (silver) 2.50
2 DJu,ATi,Monarch revealed as Hawk,
 D:Dove,L:Capt Atom(JLE) 3.00
Spec.#1 MR 3.00

ARMAGEDDON 2001 ARMAGEDDON: THE ALIEN AGENDA
1991–92
1 DJu,JOy,A:Monarch,Capt.Atom. 2.50
2 V:Ancient Romans 2.50
3 JRu(i),The Old West. 2.50
4 DG,GP,V:Nazi's,last issue... 2.50

ARMAGEDDON: INFERNO
1992
1 TMd,LMc,A:Creeper,Batman,
  Firestorm 2.50
2 AAd,LMc,WS,I:Abraxis,A:Lobo .. 2.50
3 AAd,WS,LMc,TMd,MN,R:Justice
  Society. 2.50
4 AAd,WS,LMc,TMd,MN,DG,
  V:Abraxis,A:Justice Society . 2.50

ARSENAL
Aug., 1998
1 (of 4) F:Black Canary 2.50
2 F:Green Arrow 2.50
3 F:Vandal Savage 2.50
4 conclusion 2.50

ARTEMIS: REQUIEM
1996
1 BML(s) (of 6) 3.00
2 thru 6 BML(s),EBe, ... @3.00

ATARI FORCE
1984–85
1 JL,I:TempestDart 5.00
2 JL. 3.00
3 JL. 3.00
4 RA/JL/JO 3.00
5 RA/JL/JO 3.00
6 thru 12 JL .... @3.00
13 KG 3.00
14 thru 21 EB .... @3.00

ATLANTIS CHRONICLES
1990
1 EM,Atlantis 50,000 years ago ... 3.50
2 EM,Atlantis Sunk 3.25
3 EM,Twin Cities of Poseidonis
  & Tritonis 3.25
4 EM,King Orin's Daughter
  Cora Assumes Throne 3.25
5 EM,Orin vs. Shalako. 3.25
6 EM,Contact with Surface
  Dwellers. 3.25
7 EM,Queen Atlanna gives Birth to
  son(Aquaman)48 pg.final issue. 3.25

ATOM, THE
1962–68
1 MA,GK,I:Plant Master 1,300.00
2 MA,GK,V:Plant Master 500.00
3 MA,GK,I:Chronos 300.00
4 MA,GK,Snapper Carr 250.00
5 MA,GK 250.00
6 MA,GK 250.00
7 MA,GK,1st Atom & Hawkman
  team-up 400.00
8 MA,GK,A:JLA,V:Doctor Light. . 200.00
9 MA,GK 200.00
10 MA,GK. 200.00
11 MA,GK. 125.00
12 MA,GK. 125.00
13 MA,GK. 125.00
14 MA,GK. 125.00
15 MA,GK. 125.00
16 MA,GK. 100.00
17 MA,GK. 100.00
18 MA,GK. 100.00
19 MA,GK,A:Zatanna 100.00
20 MA,GK. 100.00
21 MA,GK 75.00
22 MA,GK 75.00
23 MA,GK 75.00
24 MA,GK,V:Jason Woodrue 75.00
25 MA,GK 75.00
26 GK. 60.00
27 GK. 60.00
28 GK. 60.00
29 GK,A:E-2 Atom,Thinker. 250.00
30 GK. 75.00
31 GK,A:Hawkman 60.00
32 GK. 60.00
33 GK. 60.00
34 GK,V:Big Head 60.00
35 GK. 60.00
36 GK,A:Golden Age Atom 100.00
37 GK,I:Major Mynah 60.00
38 Sinister stopover Earth. 60.00
Becomes:

ATOM & HAWKMAN
1968–69
39 MA, V:Tekla 75.00
40 DD,JKu,MA 65.00
41 DD,JKu,MA 65.00
42 MA,V:Brama 65.00
43 MA,I:Gentleman Ghost. 65.00
44 DD. 65.00
45 DD. 65.00

ATOM SPECIAL
1 SDi,V:Chronos (1993). 3.00
2 Zero Hour Atom (1994). 3.00

AVATAR
1991
1 A:Midnight & Allies 7.00
2 Search for Tablets 6.00
3 V:Cyric, Myrkul, final issue 6.00

AVENGERS/JLA
DC/Marvel 2003
2 (of 4) KBk,GP(c), 48-pg. 5.95

AZRAEL
1994
1 I:New Azrael,Brian Bryan 5.00
2 A:Batman,New Azreal. 3.50
3 V:Order of St. Dumas 3.50
4 The System 3.00
5 BKi(c&a),R:Ra's al Ghul,Talia
  [new Miraweb format begins] . 3.00
6 BKi(c&a),Ra's al Ghul,Talia . 3.00
7 Sister Lily's Transformation. . 3.00
8 System Secret 2.50
9 Jean Paul Vanishes 2.50
10 DON,BKi,JmP,F:Neron,
  Underworld Unleashed tie-in... 2.50
11 DON,BKi,JmP,A:Batman 2.50
12 DON,BKi,JmP,Azrael looks
  for Shondra 2.50
13 DON,BKi,JmP,Demon Time,pt.1 . 2.50
14 DON,BKi,JmP,Demon Time,pt.2 . 2.50
15 DON,BKi,Contagion,pt.5 ..... 3.00
16 DON,BKi,Contagion,pt.10 .... 2.50
17 DON,BKi,JmP,A:Dr.Orchid 2.50
18 DON,BKi,JmP,A:Dr.Orchid 2.50
19 DON(s) 2.50
20 DON(s) 2.50
21 DON(s) 2.50
22 DON(s),BKi,JmP,Angel in
  Hiding, pt.2 (of 3) 2.50
23 DON(s),BKi,JmP,Angel in
  Hiding, pt.3 .... 2.50
24 DON(s),BKi,JmP,The Order's
  return 2.50
25 DON(s),BKi,JmP,V:Brother
  Rollo 2.50
26 .... 2.50
27 DON(s),BKi,JmP,Angel Insane,
  pt.1 .... 2.50
28 DON(s),BKi,JmP,Joker, Riddler

DC — Azrael–Batgirl

Azrael #47 © DC Comics Inc.

& Two-Face escape from Arkham Asylum	2.50
29 DON(s),DBw,JmP, F:Ra's Al Ghul, pt.1	2.50
30 DON(s),DBw,JmP, F:Ra's Al Ghul, pt.2	2.50
31 DON(s),JmP Angel and the Monster Maker, pt.1 (of 3)	2.50
32 DON(s),JmP Angel and the Monster Maker, pt.2	2.50
33 DON(s),JmP Angel and the Monster Maker, pt.3 concl.	2.50
34 DON(s),JmP,Genesis, a parademon	2.50
35 DON(s),JmP,F:Hitman	2.50
36 DON,JmP,Return of Bane,pt.1	2.50
37 DON,JmP,Return of Bane,pt.2	2.50
38 DON(s),JmP,Return of Bane,pt.3	2.50
39 DON,JmP	2.50
40 DON,JmP,Cataclysm,pt.4,x-over	4.50
41 DON,JmP,A:Devil Latour	2.50
42 DON,JmP,Madame Kalypso	2.50
43 DON,JmP,Lilhy,Brian Bryan	2.50
44 DON,JmP,Luc & Lilhy disappear	2.50
45 DON,JmP,V:Deathstroke, A:Calibax	2.50
46 DON(s),JmP,V:Calibax	2.50
47 Road to No Man's Land, flip-book Batman:Shadow of the Bat	5.00
48 DON(s),JmP,No Man's Land	2.50
49 DON(s),JmP,New Costume	2.50
50 DON(s),JmP,New Costume	2.50
51 DON(s),JmP,V:Demonic Trio	2.50
52 DON(s),JmP,No Man's Land	2.50
53 DON(s),JmP,V:Joker	2.50
54 DON(s),JmP,V:Death Dancer	2.50
55 DON(s),JmP,V:Death Dancer	2.50
56 DON(s),JmP,A:Batgirl	2.50
57 DON(s),JmP,No Man's Land	2.50
58 DON(s),JmP,Day of Judgment x-over	2.50
59 DON(s),JmP,F:Catwoman	2.50
60 DON(s)	2.50
61 DON(s),F:Batgirl,V:Joker	2.50
62 DON(s)	2.50
63 DON(s),F:Huntress	2.50
64 DON(s),F:Huntress	2.50
65 DON(s),Nicholas Scratch	2.50
66 DON(s),F:Lilhi	2.50
67 DON(s),JmP,to Africa	2.50
68 DON(s),JmP,	2.50
69 DON(s),JmP,stranded	2.50
70 DON(s),SCi,JmP,Prophet,pt.1	2.50
71 DON(s),SCi,JmP,Prophet,pt.2	2.50
72 DON(s),SCi,JmP,Prophet,pt.3	2.50
73 DON(s),SCi,JmP,Batman,pt.1	2.50
74 DON(s),SCi,JmP,Batman,pt.2	2.50
75 DON(s),SCi,JmP,N:Azrael, F:Batman	4.50
76 DON(s),SCi,JmP,A:Batman	2.50
77 DON(s),SCi,V:Mr. Prymm	2.50
78 DON(s),SCi,Captain Death	2.50
79 DON(s),SCi,F:Jean Paul	2.50
80 DON(s),SCi,JmP,F:Jean Paul	2.50
81 DON(s),SCi,JmP,imprisoned	2.50
82 DON(s),SCi,JmP,escape	2.50
83 DON(s),SCi,JmP,Jokerized	2.50
84 DON(s),SCi,JmP,madman	2.50
85 DON(s),SCi,JmP,new villain	2.50
86 DON(s),SCi,JmP,Spartan	2.50
87 DON(s),SCi,new foe	2.50
88 DON(s),JmP,SCi,F:Nightwing	2.50
89 DON(s),F:Nightwing	2.50
90 DON(s),F:Nightwing	2.50
91 Bruce Wayne:Fugitive,pt.15	2.50
92 DON(s),SCi,F:Batman	2.50
93 DON(s),SCi,war on crime	2.95
94 DON(s),SCi,Demon Biis	2.95
95 DON(s),SCi,Biis,Two-face	2.95
96 DON(s),SCi,A:Batman, V:Two-Face	2.95
97 DON(s),MZ,JOy,New costume	2.95
98 DON(s),MZ,JOy,on the brink	2.95
99 DON(s),MZ,JOy,	2.95
100 DON(s),MZ,JOy,final issue	2.95
Ann.#1 Year One Annual	3.00
Ann.#2 Legends o/t Dead Earth	4.00
Ann.#3 Pulp Heroes (Hard Boiled)	5.00
Spec.#1,000,000 DON(s),VGi,JmP F:Green Arrow,Robin,Hawkman	3.00
GN Azrael/Ash	5.00

AZRAEL/ASH
March, 1997

1 one-shot DON(s),JQ,V:Surtr, A:Batman, x-over ... 5.00

AZRAEL PLUS
Oct., 1996

1 one-shot, DON(s),VGi,F:Vic Sage, The Question ... 3.00

AZTEK: THE ULTIMATE MAN
1996–97

1 GMo&MMr(s),NSH,I:Aztek & Synth ... 6.00
2 GMo&MMr(s),NSH,A:Green Lantern ... 4.00
3 GMo&MMr(s),NSH,V:Doll-Face ... 4.00
4 GMo&MMr(s),NSH,I:Lizard King, Vanity ... 4.00
5 GMo&MMr(s),NSH,O:Aztek, V:Lizard King ... 4.00
6 GMo&MMr(s),NSH,V:Vanity, A: Joker ... 4.00
7 GMo&MMr(s),NSH,A:Batman ... 4.00
8 GMo&MMr(s),NSH,return to Brotherhood of Zuetzacoatl,A:Raptor ... 4.00
9 GMo&MMr(s),NSH,V:Parasite, A:Superman ... 4.00
10 GMo&MMr(s),NSH,A:Justice League, final issue ... 12.00

BABYLON 5
1995

1 From TV series ... 14.00
2 From TV series ... 8.00
3 Mysterious Assassin ... 8.00
4 V:Mysterious Assassin ... 8.00
5 Shadows of the Present,pt.1 ... 8.00
6 Shadows of the Present,pt.2 ... 8.00
7 Shadows of the Present,pt.3 ... 7.00
8 Laser-Mirror Starweb,pt.1 ... 7.00
9 Laser-Mirror Starweb,pt.2 ... 7.00
10 Laser-Mirror-Starweb,pt.3 ... 7.00
11 final issue ... 7.00
TPB The Price of Peace ... 10.00

Babylon 5: In Valen's Name #1 © DC Comics, Inc.

BABYLON 5: IN VALEN'S NAME
Jan., 1998

1 (of 3) PDd, from TV series ... 4.00
2 PDd ... 4.00
3 PDd ... 4.00

BAD GIRLS
Aug. 2003

1 (of 6) F:Lauren ... 2.50
2 thru 4 ... @2.50

BALL AND CHAIN
Homage/DC Sept., 1999

1 (of 4) SLo ... 2.50
2 thru 4 SLo ... @2.50

BATGIRL
1988

Spec.#1 V: Cormorant,I:Slash ... 10.00

BATGIRL
Feb., 2000

1 No Man's Land follow-up ... 10.00
1a 2nd printing ... 2.50
2 saves dying man ... 7.00
3 A:Batman ... 4.00
4 A:Batman ... 4.00
5 V:Ezra ... 4.00
6 A:Batman ... 4.00
7 A:Batman, ... 4.00
8 V:Lady Shiva ... 4.00
9 Batgirl questions her motives ... 3.50
10 Too slow to stop a killer ... 3.50
11 This Issue: Batman Dies! ... 3.50
12 Officer Down tie-in ... 3.50
13 Government trained killers ... 3.50
14 A:Batman ... 3.50
15 RbC,ghastly murders ... 3.50
16 RbC,young boy's father ... 3.50

Batgirl–Batman — DC Comics Values Annual

17 RbC,A:Oracle,Cassandra		3.50
18 RbC,A:Robin,V:Deadeye		3.50
19 RbC,Nobody dies tonight		3.50
20 CDi,F:The Spoiler		3.50
21 CDi,Joker:Last Laugh		3.50
22 RbC,F:Cain		3.50
23 RbC,F:Lady Shiva		3.50
24 RbC,BruceWayne:Murderer,pt.2		3.50
25 RbC,V:Lady Shiva,40-pg.		4.00
26 VGi,Spoiler		3.00
27 RbC,Bruce Wayne:Fugitive,pt.4		3.00
28 RbC,I:Sensor		3.00
29 RbC,Bruce Wayne:Fugitive,pt.13		3.00
30 CDi,KJ,Roman military cult		3.00
31 CDi,F:Robin, Spoiler		3.00
32 CDi,all-star issue		3.00
33 RbC,A:Batman,metahunt		3.00
34 RbC,A:Batman,detective skills		3.00
35 RbC,V:Alpha,A:Batman		3.00
36 RbC,V:Alpha		3.00
37 RbC,save the child		3.00
38 RbC,F:Spoiler		3.00
39 V:Black Wind		3.00
40 V:Black Wind		3.00
41 First date,A:Superboy		3.00
42 I:New Dr. Death		3.00
43 V:Dr. Death		3.00
44 V:Dr. Death		3.00
45 RL,drug Soul		3.00
46 RL,F:Oracle		3.00
Ann.#1 Planet DC,A:Batman		3.50
Spec. Secret Files #1, 48-pg.		5.00
TPB A Knight Alone, 160-page		12.95
TPB Silent Running, 144-page		12.95
TPB Death Wish		14.95

BATGIRL ADVENTURES
Dec., 1997
1-shot RBr,V:Poison Ivy,A:Harley Quinn............ 4.00

BATGIRL: YEAR ONE
Dec. 2002

1 CDi(s),F:Barbara Gordon		3.00
2 CDi(s),meets JSA		3.00
3 CDi(s),Dynamic Duo		3.00
4 CDi(s),Dynamic Duo		3.00
5 CDi(s),Killer Moth		3.00
6 CDi(s),F:Black Canary		3.00
7 CDi(s),A:Robin		3.00
8 CDi(s),V:Blockbuster		3.00
9 CDi(s),Origin concl.		3.00
TPB O:Barbara Gordon		17.95

BATMAN
Spring, 1940

1 I:Joker,Cat(Catwoman), V:Hugo Strange		120,000.00
2 V:Joker/Catwoman team		20,000.00
3 V:Catwoman		12,000.00
4 V:Joker		10,000.00
5 V:Joker		7,000.00
6 V:`Clock Maker'		6,500.00
7 V:Joker		6,000.00
8 V:Joker		5,000.00
9 V:Joker		5,000.00
10 V:Catwoman		5,000.00
11 V:Joker,Penguin		9,500.00
12 V:Joker		4,000.00
13 V:Joker		4,200.00
14 V:Penguin;Propaganda sty		4,000.00
15 V:Catwoman		4,000.00
16 I:Alfred,V:Joker		7,000.00
17 V:Penguin		3,000.00
18 V:Tweedledum & Tweedledee		3,500.00
19 V:Joker		3,000.00
20 V:Joker		3,000.00

Batman #40 © DC Comics, Inc.

21 V:Penguin		2,000.00
22 V:Catwoman,Cavalier		2,000.00
23 V:Joker		2,800.00
24 I:Carter Nichols, V:Tweedledum & Tweedledee		2,000.00
25 V:Joker/Penguin team		2,800.00
26 V:Cavalier		2,000.00
27 V:Penguin		4,000.00
28 V:Joker		1,600.00
29 V:Scuttler		1,600.00
30 V:Penguin,I:Ally Babble		1,600.00
31 I:Punch and Judy		1,400.00
32 O:Robin,V:Joker		1,400.00
33 V:Penguin,Jackall		1,500.00
34 A:Ally Babble		1,400.00
35 V:Catwoman		1,400.00
36 V:Penguin,A:King Arthur		1,400.00
37 V:Joker		2,000.00
38 V:Penguin		1,700.00
39 V:Catwoman,Xmas Story		1,400.00
40 V:Joker		1,900.00
41 V:Penguin		1,000.00
42 V:Catwoman		1,000.00
43 V:Penguin		1,000.00
44 V:Joker,A:Carter Nichols,Meets ancester Silas Wayne		1,900.00
45 V:Catwoman		1,000.00
46 V:Joker,A:Carter Nichols, Leonardo Da Vinci		1,000.00
47 O:Batman,V:Catwoman		4,200.00
48 V:Penguin, Bat-Cave story		1,400.00
49 I:Mad Hatter & Vicki Vale		2,200.00
50 V:Two-Face,A:Vicki Vale		1,200.00
51 V:Penguin		1,000.00
52 V:Joker		1,300.00
53 V:Joker		1,300.00
54 V:`The Treasure Hunter'		1,000.00
55 V:Joker		1,300.00
56 V:Penguin		1,000.00
57 V:Joker		1,000.00
58 V:Penguin		1,000.00
59 I:Deadshot		1,000.00
60 V:`Shark' Marlin		1,000.00
61 V:Penguin		1,100.00
62 O:Catwoman,I:Knight & Squire		1,500.00
63 V:Joker		1,000.00
64 V:Killer Moth		800.00
65 I:Wingman,V:Catwoman		850.00
66 V:Joker		850.00
67 V:Joker		850.00
68 V:Two-Face,Alfred story		800.00
69 I:King of the Cats, A:Catwoman		850.00
70 V:Penguin		800.00
71 V:Mr. Cipher		800.00
72 `The Jungle Batman'		800.00
73 V:Joker,A:Vicki Vale		1,000.00
74 V:Joker		800.00
75 I:The Gorilla Boss		800.00
76 V:Penguin		800.00
77 `The Crime Predictor'		800.00
78 `The Manhunter from Mars'		1,000.00
79 A:Vicki Vale		800.00
80 V:Joker		800.00
81 V:Two-Face		800.00
82 `The Flying Batman'		750.00
83 V:`Fish' Frye		750.00
84 V:Catwoman		850.00
85 V:Joker		750.00
86 V:Joker		750.00
87 V:Joker		750.00
88 V:Mr. Mystery		750.00
89 I:Aunt Agatha		750.00
90 I:Batboy		750.00
91 V:Blinky Grosset		750.00
92 I:Ace, the Bat-Hound		750.00
93 `The Caveman Batman'		700.00
94 Alfred has Amnesia		600.00
95 `The Bat-Train'		600.00
96 `Batman's College Days'		600.00
97 V:Joker		600.00
98 A:Carter Nichols,Jules Verne		600.00
99 V:Penguin,A:Carter Nichols, Bat Masterson		600.00
100 `Great Batman Contest'		3,000.00
101 `The Great Bat-Cape Hunt'		600.00
102 V:Mayne Mallok		550.00
103 A:Ace, the Bat-Hound		550.00
104 V:Devoe		550.00
105 A:Batwoman		750.00
106 V:Keene Harper gang		600.00
107 V:Daredevils		600.00
108 Bat-cave story		600.00
109 1,000 Inventions of Batman		600.00
110 V:Joker		550.00
111		450.00
112 I:Signalman		450.00
113 I:Fatman		450.00
114		450.00
115		450.00
116		450.00
117		450.00
118		450.00
119		450.00
120		450.00
121 I:Mr.Zero (Mr.Freeze)		600.00
122		300.00
123 A:Joker		325.00
124 `Mystery Seed from Space'		300.00
125		300.00
126		300.00
127 A:Superman & Joker		325.00
128		300.00
129 O:Robin (Retold)		350.00
130		300.00
131 I:2nd Batman		250.00
132 `Lair of the Sea-Fox'		250.00
133		250.00
134		250.00
135		250.00
136 A:Joker,Bat-Mite		275.00
137 V:Mr.Marvel,The Brand		250.00
138 A:Bat-Mite		250.00
139 I:Old Batgirl		250.00
140 A:Joker		250.00
141 V:Clockmaster		225.00
142 Batman robot story		225.00
143 A:Bathound		225.00
144 A:Joker,Bat-Mite,Bat-Girl		225.00
145 V:Mr.50,Joker		250.00
146 A:Bat-Mite,Joker		250.00
147 Batman becomes Bat-Baby		200.00
148 A:Joker		250.00
149 V:Maestro		200.00
150 V:Biff Warner,Jack Pine		200.00

All comics prices listed are for Near Mint condition.

Comics Values Annual — DC — Batman

Batman #160 © DC Comics, Inc.

#	Description	Price
151	V:Harris Boys	150.00
152	A:Joker	165.00
153	Other Dimension story	150.00
154	V:Dr. Dorn	150.00
155	1st S.A. Penguin	500.00
156	V:Gorilla Gang	165.00
157	V:Mirror Man	165.00
158	A:Bathound,Bat-Mite	165.00
159	A:Joker,Clayface	175.00
160	V:Bart Cullen	165.00
161	A:Bat-Mite	165.00
162	F:Robin	165.00
163	A:Joker	165.00
164	CI,A:Mystery Analysts,new Batmobile	150.00
165	V:The Mutated Man	150.00
166	Escape story	150.00
167	V:Karabi & Hydra, the Crime Cartel	150.00
168	V:Mr. Mammoth	150.00
169	A:Penguin	175.00
170	V:Getaway Genius	150.00
171	CI,1st S.A. Riddler	650.00
172	V:Flower Gang	100.00
173	V:Elwood Pearson	100.00
174	V:Big Game Hunter	100.00
175	V:Eddie Repp	100.00
176	Giant rep.A:Joker,Catwom	125.00
177	BK,A:Elongated Man,Atom	100.00
178	CI	100.00
179	CI,2nd Riddler(Silver)	250.00
180	BK,A:Death-Man	100.00
181	CI,I:Poison Ivy	250.00
182	A:Joker,(giant size rep)	150.00
183	CI,A:Poison Ivy	150.00
184	CI,Mystery of the Missing Manhunters	100.00
185	Giant rep	125.00
186	A:Joker	100.00
187	Giant rep.A:Joker	125.00
188	CI,A:Eraser	65.00
189	CI,A:Scarecrow	125.00
190	CI,A:Penguin	75.00
191	CI,The Day Batman Soldout	65.00
192	CI,The Crystal ball that betrayed Batman	65.00
193	Giant rep	90.00
194	MSy,BK,A:Blockbuster,Mystery Analysts of Gotham City	65.00
195	CI	65.00
196	BK,Psychic Super-Sleuth	65.00
197	MSy,A:Bat Girl,Catwoman	100.00
198	A:Joker,Penguin,Catwoman, O:Batman rtd,(G-Size rep)	100.00
199	CI,`Peril o/t Poison Rings'	65.00
200	NA(c),O:rtd,A:Joker,Pengiun, Scarecrow	200.00
201	A:Batman Villains	65.00
202	BU:Robin	50.00
203	NA(c),(giant size)	70.00
204	FR(s),IN,JG	50.00
205	FR(s),IN,JG	50.00
206	FR(s),IN,JG	50.00
207	FR(s),IN,JG	50.00
208	GK,new O:Batman, A:Catwoman	75.00
209	FR(s),IN,JG	75.00
210	A:Catwoman	75.00
211	FR(s),IN,JG	50.00
212	FR(s),IN,JG	50.00
213	RA,30th Anniv.Batman,new O:Robin,rep.O:Alfred,Joker	125.00
214	IN,A:Batgirl	50.00
215	IN,DG	50.00
216	IN,DG,I:DaphnePennyworth	50.00
217	NA(c)	50.00
218	NA(c),giant	75.00
219	NA,IN,DG,Batman Xmas	75.00
220	NA(c),IN	40.00
221	IN,DG	40.00
222	IN,Rock'n Roll story	65.00
223	NA(c),giant	65.00
224	NA(c)	40.00
225	NA(c),IN,DG	40.00
226	IN,DG I:10-Eyed Man	40.00
227	IN,DG,A:Daphne Pennyworth	40.00
228	giant Deadly Traps rep	75.00
229	IN	40.00
230	NA(c),Robin	40.00
231	F:Ten-Eyed Man	40.00
232	DON(s),NA,DG, I:Ras al Ghul	150.00
233	giant Bruce Wayne iss	75.00
234	NA,DG,IN,1stS.A.Two-Face	200.00
235	CI,V:Spook	40.00
236	NA	50.00
237	NA,I:The Reaper	90.00
238	NA,JC,JKu,giant	75.00
239	NA,RB	40.00
240	NA(c),RB,giant,R-Ghul	40.00
241	IN,DG,RB,A:Kid Flash	40.00
242	RB,MK	40.00
243	NA,DG,Ras al Ghul	75.00
244	NA,Ras al Ghul	75.00
245	NA,IN,DG,FMc,Ras al Ghul	75.00
246		35.00
247	Deadly New Year	35.00
248		35.00
249	`Citidel of Crime'	35.00
250	IN,DG	35.00
251	NA,V:Joker	100.00
252		35.00
253	AN,DG,A:Shadow	35.00
254	NA,GK,B:100 page issues	65.00
255	GK,CI,NA,DG,I:CrazyQuilt	65.00
256	Catwoman	60.00
257	IN,DG,V:Penguin	60.00
258	IN,DG	60.00
259	GK,IN,DG,A:Shadow	60.00
260	IN,DG,Joker	75.00
261	CI,GK,E:100 page issues	75.00
262	A:Scarecrow	40.00
263	DG(i),A:Riddler	20.00
264	DON(s),DG,A:Devil Dayre	20.00
265	RB,BWr	25.00
266	DG,Catwoman(old Costume)	22.00
267	DG	20.00
268	DON(s),IN,TeB,V:Sheikh	20.00
269	A:Riddler	20.00
270	B:DvR(s)	20.00
271	IN,FMc	20.00
272	JL	20.00
273	V:Underworld Olympics/76	20.00
274		20.00
275		20.00
276		20.00
277		20.00
278		20.00
279	A:Riddler	22.00
280		20.00
281		20.00
282		20.00
283	V:Camouflage	20.00
284	JA,R:Dr.Tzin Tzin	20.00
285		20.00
286	V:Joker	30.00
287	BWi,MGr,Penguin	25.00
288	BWi,MGr,Penguin	25.00
289	MGr, V:Skull	20.00
290	MGr,V:Skull Dagger	20.00
291	B:Underworld Olympics #1, A:Catwoman	30.00
292	A:Riddler	20.00
293	A:Superman & Luthor	20.00
294	E:DvR(s),E:Underworld Olympics:A:Joker	30.00
295	GyC(s),MGo,JyS,V:Hamton	20.00
296	B:DvR(s),V:Scarecrow	20.00
297	RB,Mad Hatter	20.00
298	JCA,DG,V:Baxter Bains	20.00
299	DG	20.00
300	WS,DG,A:Batman E-2, Robin E-2	35.00
301	JCa,TeB	15.00
302	JCa,DG,V:Human Dynamo	15.00
303	JCa,DG	15.00
304	E:DvR(s),V:Spook	15.00
305	GyC,JCa,DeH,V:Thanatos	16.00
306	JCa,DeH,DN,V:Black Spider	20.00
307	B:LWn(s),JCa,DG, I:Limehouse Jack	20.00
308	JCa,DG,V:Mr.Freeze	16.00
309	E:LWn(s),JCa,FMc, V:Blockbuster	16.00
310	IN,DG,A:Gentleman Ghost	16.00
311	SEt,FMc,IN,Batgirl, V:Dr.Phosphorus	16.00
312	WS,DG,Calenderman	16.00
313	IN,FMc,VTwo-Face	16.00
314	IN,FMc,V:Two-Face	16.00
315	IN,FMc,V:Kiteman	16.00
316	IN,FMc,F:Robin, V:Crazy Quilt	16.00
317	IN,FMc,V:Riddler	17.00
318	IN,I:Fire Bug	16.00
319	JKu(c),IN,DG,A:Gentleman Ghost,E:Catwoman	16.00
320	BWr(c)	17.00
321	DG,WS,A:Joker,Catwoman	17.00
322	V:Cap.Boomerang,Catwoman	16.00

Batmm#296 © DC Comics Inc.

All comics prices listed are for *Near Mint* condition.

Batman — DC Comics Values Annual

Batman #476 © DC Comics, Inc.

Batman #497 © DC Comics, Inc.

#	Description	Price
323	IN,A:Catwoman	16.00
324	IN,A:Catwoman	16.00
325		16.00
326	A:Catwoman	16.00
327	IN,A:Proffessor.Milo	16.00
328	A:Two-Face	16.00
329	IN,A:Two-Face	16.00
330		16.00
331	DN,FMc,V:Electrocutioner	16.00
332	IN,DN,Ras al Ghul.1st solo Catwoman story	17.00
333	IN,DN,A:Catwoman, Ras al Ghul	15.00
334	FMc,Ras al Ghul,Catwoman	15.00
335	IN,FMc,Catwoman,Ras al Ghul	15.00
336	JL,FMc,Loser Villains	15.00
337	DN,V:Snow Man	15.00
338	DN,Deathsport	15.00
339	A:Poison Ivy	15.00
340	GC,A:Mole	15.00
341	A:Man Bat	15.00
342	V:Man Bat	15.00
343	GC,KJ,I:The Dagger	15.00
344	GC,KJ,Poison Ivy	15.00
345	I:New Dr.Death,A:Catwoman	15.00
346	DN,V:Two Face	15.00
347	A:Alfred	15.00
348	GC,KJ,Man-Bat,A:Catwoman	15.00
349	GC,AA,A:Catwoman	15.00
350	GC,TD,A:Catwoman	15.00
351	GC,TD,A:Catwoman	15.00
352	Col Blimp	15.00
353	JL,DN,DA,A:Joker	20.00
354	DN,AA,V:HugoStrange,A:Catwoman	15.00
355	DN,AA,A:Catwoman	15.00
356	DG,DN,Hugo Strange	15.00
357	DN,AA,I:Jason Todd	16.00
358	A:King Croc	15.00
359	DG,O:King Croc,Joker	17.00
360	I:Savage Skull	15.00
361	DN,Man-Bat,I:Harvey Bullock	15.00
362	V:Riddler	15.00
363	V:Nocturna	15.00
364	DN,AA,J.Todd 1st full solo story (cont'd Detective #531)	15.00
365	DN,AA,C:Joker	15.00
366	DN,AA,Joker,J.Todd in Robin Costume	17.00
367	DN,AA,PoisonIvy	14.00
368	DN,AA,I:2nd Robin (Jason Todd)	15.00
369	DN,AA,I:Dr.Fang,V:Deadshot	12.00
370	DN,AA	12.00
371	DN,AA,V:Catman	10.00
372	DN,AA,A:Dr.Fang	7.00
373	DN,AA,V:Scarecrow	7.00
374	GC,AA,V:Penguin	8.00
375	GC,AA,V:Dr.Freeze	7.00
376	DN,Halloween issue	7.00
377	DN,AA,V:Nocturna	7.00
378	V:Mad Hatter	7.00
379	V:Mad Hatter	7.00
380	AA,V:Nocturna	7.00
381	V:Batman	7.00
382	A:Catwoman	8.00
383	GC	7.00
384	V:Calender Man	7.00
385	V:Calender Man	7.00
386	I:Black Mask	7.00
387	V:Black Mask	7.00
388	V:Capt.Boomerang & Mirror Master	7.00
389	V:Nocturna,Catwoman	7.00
390	V:Nocturna,Catwoman	7.00
391	V:Nocturna,Catwoman	7.00
392	A:Catwoman	7.00
393	PG,V:Cossack	6.00
394	PG,V:Cossack	6.00
395	V:Film Freak	6.00
396	V:Film Freak	6.00
397	V:Two-Face,Catwoman	7.00
398	V:Two-Face,Catwoman	7.00
399	HaE(s),Two-Face	6.00
400	BSz,AAd,GP,BB,A:Joker	25.00
401	JBy(c),TVE,Legends, A:Magpie	6.00
402	JSn,Fake Batman	6.00
403	DCw,Batcave discovered	6.00
404	DM,FM(s),B:Year 1,I:Modern Age Catwoman	20.00
405	FM,DM,Year 1	14.00
406	FM,DM,Year 1	14.00
407	FM,DM,E:Year 1	14.00
408	CW,V:Joker, new O:Jason Todd	10.00
408a	2nd printing	3.00
409	DG,RA,V:Crime School	10.00
409a	2nd printing	3.00
410	DC,Jason Todd	10.00
411	DC,DH,V:Two Face	6.00
412	DC,DH,I:Mime	6.00
413	DC,DH	6.00
414	JAp,Slasher	6.00
415	JAp,Millenium Week #2	6.00
416	JAp,1st Batman/Nightwing T.U.	6.00
417	JAp,B:10 Nights,I:KGBeast	12.00
418	JAp,V:KGBeast	12.00
419	JAp,V:KGBeast	12.00
420	JAp,E:10 Nights,D:KGBeast	12.00
421	DG	7.00
422	MBr,V:Dumpster Slayer	6.00
423	TM(c),DC,Who is Batman	7.00
424	MBr,Robin	6.00
425	MBr,Gordon Kidnapped	6.00
426	JAp,B:Death in the Family, V:Joker	20.00
427	JAp,V:Joker	18.00
428	JAp,D:2nd Robin	18.00
429	JAp,A:Superman, E:Death in the Family	15.00
430	JAp,JSn,V:Madman	5.00
431	JAp,Murder Investigation	4.00
432	JAp	4.00
433	JBy,JAp,Many Deaths of the Batman #1	5.00
434	JBy,JAp,Many Deaths #2	4.50
435	JBy,Many Deaths #3	4.50
436	PB,B:Year#3,A:Nightwing,I:Tim Drake as child	5.00
436a	2ndPrint(green DC logo)	3.00
437	PB,year#3	4.00
438	PB,year#3	3.50
439	PB,year#3	3.50
440	JAp,Lonely Place of Dying #1, A:Tim Drake (face not shown)	4.00
441	JAp,Lonely Place Dying	4.00
442	JAp,I:3rd Robin(Tim Drake)	5.00
443	JAp,I:Crimesmith	3.00
444	JAp,V:Crimesmith	3.00
445	JAp,I:K.G.Beast Demon	3.00
446	JAp,V:K.G.Beast Demon	3.00
447	JAp,D:K.G.Beast Demon	3.00
448	JAp,A:Penguin#1	3.50
449	MBr,A:Penguin#3	3.50
450	JAp,I:Joker II	3.00
451	JAp,V:Joker II	3.00
452	KD,Dark Knight Dark City#1	3.00
453	KD,Dark Knight Dark City#2	3.00
454	KD,Dark Knight Dark City#3	3.00
455	Identity Crisis#1, A:Scarecrow	3.00
456	IdentityCrisis#2	4.00
457	V:Scarecrow,A:Robin, New Costume	6.00
457a	2nd printing	3.00
458	R:Sarah Essen	3.00
459	A:Sarah Essen	3.00
460	Sisters in Arms,pt.1 A:Catwoman	3.50
461	Sisters in Arms,pt.2 Catwoman V:Sarah.Essen	3.50
462	Batman in San Francisco	3.00
463	Death Valley	3.00
464	V:Two-Hearts	3.00
465	Batman/Robin T.U.	3.50
466	Robin Trapped	3.00
467	Shadowbox #1(sequel to Robin Mini-Series)	3.50
468	Shadowbox #2	3.00
469	Shadowbox #3	3.00
470	War of the Gods x-over	3.00
471	V:Killer Croc	3.00
472	The Idiot Root,pt.1	3.00
473	The Idiot Root,pt.3	3.00
474	Destroyer,pt.1 (LOTDK#27)	3.50
475	R:Scarface,A:VickiVale	3.00
476	A:Scarface	3.00
477	Ph(c),Gotham Tale,pt.1	3.00
478	Ph(c),Gotham Tale,pt.2	3.00
479	TMd,I:Pagan	3.00
480	JAp,To the father I never knew	3.00
481	JAp,V:Maxie Zeus	3.00
482	JAp,V:Maxie Zeus	3.00
483	JAp,I:Crash & Burn	3.00
484	JAp,R:Black Mask	3.00
485	TGr,V:Black Mask	3.00
486	JAp,I:Metalhead	3.00

All comics prices listed are for *Near Mint* condition.

Comics Values Annual — DC — Batman

#	Description	Price
487	JAp,V:Headhunter	3.00
488	JAp,N:Azrael	10.00
489	JAp,Bane vs Killer Croc, I:Azrael as Batman	6.00
489a	2nd Printing	3.00
490	JAp,Bane vs.Riddler	7.00
490a	2nd Printing	2.50
490b	3rd Printing	2.00
491	JAp,V:Joker,A:Bane	4.50
491a	2nd Printing	2.00
492	B:DgM(s),NB,Knightfall#1, V:Mad Hatter,A:Bane	5.00
492a	Platinum Ed.	10.00
492b	2nd Printing	2.00
493	NB,Knightfall,#3,Mr.Zsasz	4.00
494	JAp,TMd,Knightfall #5,A:Bane, V:Cornelius,Stirk,Joker	3.50
495	NB,Knightfall#7,V:Poison Ivy,A:Bane	3.50
496	JAp,JRu,Knightfall#9,V:Joker, Scarecrow,A:Bane	3.50
497	JAp,DG,Knightfall#11,V:Bane, Batman gets back broken	5.50
497a	2nd Printing	2.50
498	JAp,JRu,Knightfall#15,A:Bane, Catwoman,Azrael Becomes Batman	3.00
499	JAp,SHa,Knightfall#17, A:Bane,Catwoman	3.00
500	JQ(c),JAp,MM,Die Cut(c), Direct Market,Knightfall#19, V:Bane,N:Batman	6.00
500a	KJo(c),Newstand Ed.	3.50
501	MM,I:Mekros	3.00
502	MM,V:Mekros	3.00
503	MM,V:Catwoman	3.00
504	MM,V:Catwoman	3.00
505	MM,V:Canibal	3.00
506	KJo(c),MM,A:Ballistic	3.00
507	KJo(c),MM,A:Ballistic	3.00
508	KJo(c),MM,V:Abattior	3.00
509	KJo(c),MM,KnightsEnd#1, A:Shiva	3.50
510	KJo(c),MM,Knights End #7, V:Azrael	3.00
511	Zero Hour, A:Batgirl	3.00
512	Killer Croc sewer battles	3.00
513	Two-Face and convicts	3.00
514	Identity Crisis	3.00
515	KJo,Return of Bruce Wayne, Troika,pt.1	3.00
515	Collector's Edition	3.50
516	V:The Sleeper	3.00
517	V:The Sleeper	3.00
518	V:The Black Spider	3.00
519	KJo,V:The Black Spider [new Miraweb format begins]	3.00
520	EB,A:James Gordon	3.00
521	R:Killer Croc	3.00
522	R:Scarecrow	3.00
523	V:Scarecrow	3.00
524	DgM,KJo,V:Scarecrow	3.00
525	DgM,KJo,Underworld Unleashed tie-in	3.00
526	DgM,A:Alfred,Nightwing,Robin	3.00
527	DgM,V:Two-Face,I:Schism	3.00
528		3.00
529	DgM,KJo,Contagion,pt.6	3.50
530	DgM,KJo,The Aztec Connection,pt.1	3.50
530a	collector's edition	3.50
531	DgM,KJo,The Aztec Connection,pt.2	3.00
531a	collectors edition	3.50
532	DgM(s),KJo,The Aztec Connection,pt.3, A:Deadman	3.00
532a	card stock cover	3.50
533	DgM(s),KJo,Legacy prelude	3.00
534	DgM(s),KJo,Legacy, pt.5	3.00
535	DgM(s),KJo,JhB,I:The Ogre, double sides	4.00
535a	Collector's edition, gatefold cover	5.00
536	DgM(s),KJo,JhB,V:Man-Bat, Final Night tie-in	3.00
537	DgM(s),KJo,JhB,A:Man-Bat,pt.2	3.00
538	DgM(s),KJo,JhB,A:Man-Bat,pt.3	3.00
539		3.00
540	DgM(s),KJo,JhB,Spectre,pt.1	3.00
541	DgM(s),KJo,JhB,Spectre,pt.2	3.00
542	DgM(s),KJo,JhB,V:Faceless, pt. 1	3.00
543	DgM(s),KJo,JhB,pt. 2	3.00
544	DgM(s),KJo,JhB, F:Joker,pt.1	3.00
545	DgM(s),KJo, F:Joker, Demon, pt.2	3.00
546	DgM(s),KJo,JhB,F:Joker, Demon, pt.3 concl.	3.00
547	DgM,KJo,JhB,Genesis tie-in	3.00
548	DgM,KJo,JhB,V:Penguin, pt.1	3.00
549	DgM,KJo,JhB,V:Penguin, pt.2	3.00
550	DgM,KJo,JhB,I:Chase	3.50
550a	deluxe, with file card inserts	3.50
551	DgM,KJo,JhB,F:Ragman	2.50
552	DgM,	2.50
553	DgM,KJo,SB, Cataclysm x-over, pt.3	4.50
554	DgM,KJo,SB,Cataclysm,	3.00
555	DGm,JhB,SB,BSf,Aftershock	2.50
556	DGm,NBy,BSf,Aftershock	2.50
557	DGm,VGi,SB,BSf,F:Ballistic	2.50
558	DGm,JAp,SB,doubts	2.50
559	DgM(s),BH,SB,Aftershock	2.50
560	CDi,SB,A:Nightwing & Robin	2.50
561	CDi(s),JAp, No Man's Land	2.50
562	CDi(s),JAp, No Man's Land	2.50
563	No Law and A New Order, pt.3	6.00
564	F:Batgirl, Mosaic,pt.1	2.50
565	F:Batgirl, Mosaic,pt.3	2.50
566	JBg,A:Superman	2.50
567	SCi,F:Batgirl, pt.1,x-over	2.50
568	DJu,BSz,Fruit of the Earth, pt.2	2.50
569	F:Batgirl.	2.50
570	MD2,No Man's Land, The Code, pt.1	2.50
571	CDi,MtB,Goin'Downtown,pt.1	2.50
572	Jurisprudence,pt.1	2.50
573		2.50
574	Endgame, pt.2 x-over	2.50
575	LHa,SMc,KIS	2.50
576	LHa,SMc,KIS,kidnapping	2.50
577	LHa,SMc,KIS,rodents	2.50
578	LHa,SMc,MPn,serial killer	2.50
579	LHa,SMc,KIS,V:Orca,pt.1	2.50
580	LHa,SMc,KIS,V:Orca,pt.2	2.50
581	LHa,SMc,KIS,V:Orca,pt.3	2.50
582	SMc,KIS,Fearless,pt.1	2.50
583	SMc,KIs,Fearless,pt.2	2.50
584	SMc,KIS,A:Penguin	2.50
585	SMc,KIS,V:Penguin	2.50
586	SMc,KIS,V:Penguin, This issue: Batman Dies!	2.50
587	RBr,RyR,Officer Down,pt.1	2.50
588	SMc,KIS,Close Before Striking	2.50
589	SMc,KIS,Close Before Striking	2.50
590	SMc,KIS,Close Before Striking	2.50
591	SMc,KIS,Shot thru the Heart	2.50
592	SMc,KIS,Shot thru the Heart	2.50
593	SMc,KIS,Worlds at War tie-in	2.50
594	SMc,KIS,Worlds at War tie-in	2.50
595	SMc,F:Lew Moxon	2.50
596	SMc,Joker:Last Laugh	2.50
597	SMc,V:Zeiss	2.50
598	SMc,Christmas in Gotham	2.50
599	Bruce Wayne:Murderer,pt.7	2.50
600	Bruce Wayne:Fugitive,pt.1	6.00
600a	2nd printing	4.00
601	Bruce Wayne:Fugitive,pt.3	2.50
602	SMc,V:Nicodemus	2.50
603	Bruce Wayne:Fugitive,pt.11	2.50
604	SMc,Crime Alley	2.50
605	Bruce Wayne:Fugitive,concl.	3.50
606	SMc,F:Deadshot	2.50
607	SMc,F:Deadshot,pt.2	2.50
608	JLb,JLe,SW,Hush,pt.1	3.50
609	JLb,JLe,SW,Hush,pt.2	2.50
610	JLb,JLe,SW,Hush,pt.3	2.50
611	JLb,JLe,SW,Hush,pt.4	2.50
612	JLb,JLe,SW,Hush,pt.5	4.00
612a	2nd printing, B&W(c)	15.00
613	JLb,JLe,SW,Hush,pt.6	4.00
614	JLb,JLe,SW,Hush,pt.7	4.00
615	JLb,JLe,SW,Hush,pt.8	4.00
616	JLb,JLe,SW,Hush,pt.9	4.00
617	JLb,JLe,SW,Hush,pt.10	2.50
618	JLb,JLe,SW,Hush,pt.11	2.50
619	JLb,JLe,SW,Hush,pt.12	2.50
620	Broken City, pt.1	2.50
621	Broken City, pt.2	2.50
Ann.#1	CS,O:BatCave	1,000.00
Ann.#2		450.00
Ann.#3	A:Joker	450.00
Ann.#4		200.00
Ann.#5		200.00
Ann.#6		150.00
Ann.#7		150.00
Ann.#8	TVE,A:Ras al Ghul	10.00
Ann.#9	JOy,AN,PS	9.00
Ann.#10	DCw,DG,V:HugoStrange	9.00
Ann.#11	JBy(c),AMo(s),V:Penguin	10.00
Ann.#12	RA,V:Killer	7.00
Ann.#13	A:Two-Face	8.00
Ann.#14	O:Two-Face	6.00
Ann.#15	Armageddon,pt.3	8.00
Ann.#15a	2nd printing(silver)	4.00
Ann.#16	SK(c),Eclipso,V:Joker	4.00
Ann.#17	EB,Bloodline#8, I:Decimator	4.00
Ann.#18	Elseworld Story	5.00
Ann.#19	Year One, O:Scarecrow	6.00
Ann.#20	Legends o/t Dead Earth	5.00
Ann.#21	Pulp Heroes (Weird Mystery) DgM(s)	6.00
Ann.#22	BWr(c) Ghosts	5.00
Ann.#23	CDi(s),GN,MPn, JLApe Gorilla Warfare	5.00
Ann.#24	Planet DC	5.00

Specials & 1-shots

Giant Ann.#1 Facsimile edition		6.00
Spec.#0 (1994)		4.00
Spec.#1 MGo,I:Wrath		5.00
Spec.#1,000,000 DgM(s),SB, F:Toy Wonder		3.00

Batman #558 © DC Comics Inc.

All comics prices listed are for Near Mint condition.

Batman — DC Comics Values Annual

Batman/Harley Quinn Graphic Novel © DC Comics, Inc.

Spec.#1 Our Worlds at War (2001) . 4.00
Giant #1, 7 tales, 80-page (1998) . . 6.00
Giant #2, 80-page (1999) 6.00
Giant #3 CDi(s) 80-page (2000) . . . 7.00
Batman: Arkham Asylum — Tales
   of Madness, AIG, Cataclysm
   tie-in (1998) 4.00
Batman: Batgirl, JBa,RBr,
   Girlfrenzy (1998) 3.00
Batman: Blackgate, CDi(s), JSon,
   in Blackgate prison (1996) 4.50
Batman: Blackgate — Isle of Men,
   DgM, JAp,BSf,BSz,
   Cataclysm (1998) 3.00
Batman Dark Knight Gallery (1995). 3.50
Batman: Day of Judgment 4.00
Batman: Death of Innocents, DON(s),
   JSt, BSz, (1996) 4.00
Batman Gallery,collection of past
   (c),posters,pin-ups,JQ(c) (1992) 4.00
Batman: Gotham By Gaslight,MMi,
   V:Jack the Ripper 6.00
Gotham City Secret Files #1 . . . . . . 5.00
Batman: The Hill (2000) 3.00
Batman: Joker's Apprentice 4.00
Batman: The Killing Joke,BB,AMo(s),
   O:Joker,Batgirl paralyzed
   (1988) 15.00
   2nd thru 6th Printings . . . . . . @5.00
Batman: Mitefall, V:Bane
   Mite (1995). 5.00
Batman: Penguin Triumphant
   (1992) 5.00
Batman: Plus (1997). 3.00
Batman Record Comic (1996) 2.00
Batman/Riddler: The Riddle
   Factory (1995) 5.00
Secret Files #1 SMc(c) inc.
   O:Batman (1997) 6.00
Batman: Seduction of the Gun,
   V:Illegal Gun Control (1992) . . 3.00
Spec. The 10-Cent Adventure 0.10
3-D Batman:Scarecrow. 4.00
Batman/Two-Face: Crime and
   Punishment (1995) 5.00
   2nd printing (1998) 5.00
Two-Face Strikes Twice #1 . . . . . . 5.25
Two-Face Strikes Twice #2 . . . . . . 5.25
Batman: Vengeance of Bane,
   GN,I:Bane (1992) 30.00
   2nd Printing 5.00
Batman: Vengeance of Bane II
   (1995) 4.00

Batman Villains Secret Files,
   AIG,CDi,RMz,BB,F:Greatest Foes
   (1998) 5.00
Elseworld 1-shots
Batman of Arkham (2000). 6.00
Batman: The Blue, The Grey, and
   The Bat, JL (1992) 6.00
Batman: Brotherhood of the Bat
   (1995) 6.00
Batman: Castle of the Bat. 6.00
Batman: Dark Allegiances (1996) . . 6.00
Batman: Holy Terror (1991). 6.50
Batman: I, Joker, BH, in
   2083 (1998) 5.00
Batman: In Darkest Knight
   MiB(s),JBi (1994). 5.50
Batman Knightgallery (1995). 3.50
Batman: Masque, MGr, in turn of
   the century Gotham 7.00
Batman: Master of the Future,EB,
   Sequel to Goth.by Gaslight
   (1991) 6.00
Batman: Scar of the Bat (1996). . . . 5.00
Batman: Two Faces (1998). 5.00
Batman: Master of the Future(1998) 6.00
Graphic Novels
The Abduction 6.00
Batman A Lonely Place of Dying
   (1990) rep. Batman #440–442
   & New Titans #60–61 . . . . 4.00
Batman: Blind Justice, rep. Detective
   Comics #598–#600 (1992) . . . 7.50
Batman: Bloodstorm 13.00
Batman: Bullock's Law 5.00
The Book of Shadows 6.00
Child of Dreams, manga 19.95
Crimson Mist, Elseworlds (2001). . 14.95
Batman: Dark Joker, KJo 12.00
Many Deaths of the Batman;
   rep. #433-#435 (1992) 4.00
Batman: Dreamland (2000) 6.00
Batman: Ego (2000) 7.00
Batman: Full Circle AD,
   A:Reaper (1992). 7.00
Batman/Joker: Switch 6.95
Golden Steets of Gotham 6.95
Gotham Noir, 64-page (2001) 7.00
Batman: Harley Quinn (1998) 6.00
Batman: Mr. Freeze 5.00
Batman/Nightwing: Bloodborne
   48-pg. (2002) 5.95
No Man's Land, 48-page No Law
   and a New Order, pt.1 . . . . 3.00
No Man's Land, lenticular (c) 4.00
No Man's Land Gallery 4.00
Nosferatu 6.00
Batman: Poison Ivy. 5.00
Reign of Terror 5.00
Batman: Scar of the Bat 5.00
Scarface—A Psychodrama (2001) . 5.95
The Scottish Connection. 6.00
Batman: Ten Knights of the Beast,
   rep. #417–#420 (1994) 5.95
Batman: Two Faces 5.00
Batman: The Ultimate Evil:
   1 Novel adaptation (of 2) 5.95
   2 Novel adaptation, finale 5.95
Trade Paperbacks
Batman: Absolution 17.95
The Batman Adventures 8.00
Batman: Anarky 13.00
Batman: Arkham Asylum,DMc . . . 15.00
The Arrow, The Ring & The Bat . . 19.95
Birth of the Demon, O:Ras al
   Ghul (1993) 13.00
Batman: Black and White 19.95
Black and White, Vol.2 . . . . 19.95
Batman: Bloodstorm,KJo,V:Joker,
   Vampires 12.95
Bride of the Demon, TGr, V:Ra's
   al Ghul 13.00

Bruce Wayne-Fugitive, Vol. 1 . . . . 12.95
Bruce Wayne-Fugitive, Vol. 2 . . . . 12.95
Bruce Wayne-Fugitive, Vol. 3 . . . . 12.95
Bruce Wayne-Murderer? 12.95
Batman: Cataclysm. 18.00
Batman: The Chalice (2000) 14.95
Batman: Contagion. 13.00
Contagion. 19.95
Batman: The Cult 19.95
The Dark Knight Adventures 8.00
Batman: Dark Knight Dynasty, three
   elseworlds stories (1999) 14.95
Batman: Dark Victory (2002) 19.95
Batman: A Death in the Family,
   rep. Batman #426-429 (1988)
   TPB 8.00
   2nd printing 5.00
   3rd printing 4.00
Batman/Deathblow: After the Fire . 12.95
Batman: Evolution (2001) 12.95
Batman: Faces (1995) 10.00
Batman: Fortunate Son (1999) . . . 14.95
Batman: Gothic, rept. Legends of
   the Dark Knight #6–#10 (1992) 13.00
Greatest Batman Stories. 16.00
Greatest Batman Stories, Vol. 2 . . 17.95
Harvest Breed 17.95
Batman/Huntress: Cry For Blood. . 12.95
Batman in the Fifties. 19.95
Batman in the Sixties 19.95
Batman in the Seventies. 19.95
Greatest Joker Stories 15.00
Batman: Knight's End, rep. Batman
   #509–#510, Shadow of the Bat
   #29–#30, Detective #676–#677,
   Legends #62–#63, Catwoman
   #12, Robin #8–#9 . . . . 14.95
Knightfall rep. #1–#11 . . . . 12.95
Knightfall rep. #12-#19 . . . . 12.95
Batman: The Last Angel, F:Catwoman
   V:Aztec bat-god (1994). 12.95
Batman: The Last Arkham 12.95
Legacy, seq.to Contagion 18.00
Batman: Night Cries,SHa 13.00
Batman: Nine Lives 17.95
Batman: Officer Down (2001) 12.95
Batman: Prodigal, rep, ... 15.00
Batman: Son of the Demon,JBi . . 17.00
   2nd thru 4th printings . . . . . . @8.95
Batman: Strange Apparitions
   (1999) 12.95
Batman/Superman: World'sFinest . 19.95
Batman: Tales of the Demon (1991)
   TPB 20.00
   TPB (1999) 17.95
Batman: Terror 12.95
Batman: Thrillkiller 13.00
Batman: Year One Rep. Batman
   #404-#407 (1998). 14.00
   Later Printings 10.00
Batman: Four of a Kind, from
   Year One annuals (1998) 15.00
Year Two (1990) rep. Detective
   Comics #575–#578 . . . . 10.00
Year Two: Fear the Reaper(2002). 17.95
Movies
TPB The Movies, (all 4) (1997) . . . 20.00
Batman, JOy, Movie adaptation . . . 3.00
   Perfect Bound 6.00
Batman Returns, SE,JL Movie
   Adaption. 6.00
   Newsstand Format 4.00
Batman: Mask of the Phantasm,
   animated movie adapt. 5.25
   Newstand Ed. 3.25
Batman Forever, Movie Adaptation . 5.95
   Newsstand version 3.95
Batman and Robin, DON(s), Movie
   Adaptation (1997) 3.95
   Collector's edition, ... 5.95
GN Batman: Bane, BSz(c) movie

CVA Page 42   All comics prices listed are for *Near Mint* condition.

DC

Batman–Batman And

tie-in (1997) 4.95
GN Batman: Batgirl, BSz(c) movie
tie-in (1997) 4.95
GN Batman: Mr. Freeze, BSz(c)
movie tie-in (1997) 4.95
GN Batman: Poison Ivy, BSz(c)
movie tie-in (1997) 4.95

X-overs
Batman & Superman Adventures:
World's Finest (1997) adaptation
of animated adventures, 64pg . 7.00
Batman/Captain America (DC/Marvel
1996) Elseworlds 6.00
Batman/Deadman, Death and
Glory, JeR(s),JEs (1996). 12.95
Batman/Demon (1996) 5.95
Batman/Demon: A Tragedy (2000) . 5.95
Batman/Dracula: Red Rain KJo,MJ,
Batman becomes Vampire,
SC (1992) 12.00
TPB Elseworlds (1999). 12.95
Batman/Green Arrow: The Poison
Tomorrow,MN,JRu,V:Poison
Ivy (1992). 6.25
GN rep. (2000). 5.95
Batman/Houdini: The Devil's
Workshop (1993) 6.50
Batman: Huntress/Spoiler—Blunt
Trauma, CDi,Cataclysm (1988). 3.00
Batman/Judge Dredd: Judgement on
Gotham, SBs,V:Scarecrow, Judge
Death (1991) 9.00
Batman/Judge Dredd: Vendetta in
Gotham, AIG(s),V:Ventriliquist
(1993) 5.25
Batman/Judge Dredd: The Ultimate
Riddle (1995). 5.00
Batman/Lobo, Elseworlds (2000) . . 5.95
Batman/Phantom Stranger, AIG(s),
Lemurian artifact (1997) 5.00
Batman/Punisher: Lake of Fire,
DON(s),BKi,A:Punisher,V:Jigsaw
(DC/Marvel 1994). 5.25
Batman/Spawn: War Devil, DgM,CDi,
AIG(s), KJ,V:Croatoan (1994) . . 6.00
Batman/Spawn: War Devil (1999). . 4.95
Batman/Spider-Man JMD,GN,KK,
V:Kingpin&Ra's al Ghul(1997). . 5.00
Batman vs. The Incredible Hulk
(DC/Marvel 1995). 4.00

BATMAN ADVENTURES
1992–95
(Based on TV cartoon series)
1 MeP,V:Penguin. 5.00
2 MeP,V:Catwoman 4.00
3 MeP,V:Joker. 3.00
4 MeP,V:Scarecrow 3.00
5 MeP,V:Scarecrow 3.00
6 MeP,A:Robin 3.00
7 MeP,V:Killer Croc,w/card. 6.00
8 MeP,Larceny my Sweet 3.00
9 MeP,V:Two Face. 3.00
10 MeP,V:Riddler 3.00
11 MeP,V:Man-Bat 3.00
12 MeP,F:Batgirl 3.00
13 MeP,V:Talia 3.00
14 MeP,F:Robin 3.00
15 MeP,F:Commissioner Gordon . . 3.00
16 MeP,V:Joker 3.00
17 MeP,V:Talia 3.00
18 MeP,R:Batgirl 3.00
19 MeP,V:Scarecrow 3.00
20 MeP,V:Mastermind,Mr.Nice,
Perfssor 3.00
21 MeP,V:Man-Bat,Tygrus. 3.00
22 MeP,V:Two-Face 3.00
23 MEP,V:Poison Ivy 3.00
24 MeP,I:Kyodi Ken 3.00
25 MeP,dbl.size,Superman 3.50

Batman Adventures #3
© *DC Comics Inc.*

26 MeP,A:Robin,Batgirl. 3.00
27 MeP,I:Doppleganger 3.00
28 Joker 3.00
29 A:Talia 3.00
30 O:Mastermind, Mr. Nice 3.00
31 I:Anarchy 3.00
32 Criminals dressed as
Napoleonic Soldiers 3.00
33 Bruce and date mugged. 2.50
34 V:Dr. Hugo Strange 2.50
35 A:Catwoman 2.50
36 V:Joker, Final issue 2.50
Ann.#1 Roxy Rocket. 3.00
Ann.#2 JBa,BBl,DG,TG,SHa,BKi,MM,
GN,JRu,V:Demon,Ra's al
Ghul,Etrigan. 3.50
Holiday Special. 2.95
Spec. Mad Love 3.95
TPB Collected Adventures #1 . . . . 6.00
TPB Collected Adventures #2 . . . . 6.00

BATMAN ADVENTURES:
THE LOST YEARS
Nov., 1997
1 (of 5) BHa,TBe,Batgirl. 2.50
2 BHa,TBe,Dick Grayson quits . . . 2.50
3 . . . . 2.50
4 BHa,TBe, Batman & Robin 2.50
5 BHa,TBe,Tim Drake new Robin . 2.50

BATMAN ADVENTURES:
THE LOST YEARS
1999
1 (of 6) TBe. 2.50
2 thru 6 . . . . @2.50
TPB series rep. 5.95

BATMAN ADVENTURES
May 2003
1 TTn 2.25
1a newsstand edition. 2.25
2 TTn,F:Riddler. 2.25
3 F:Joker & Harley. 2.25
4 TTn,RBr,V:Ra's Al Ghul 2.25
5 TTn,V:Deadshot 2.25
6 TTn,TBe,V:Black Mask 2.25
7 RBr, TBe,V:Phantasm 2.25
8 RBr, TBe,V:Black Mask 2.25
TPB Dangerous Dames & Demons 14.95

BATMAN/ALIENS II
DC/Dark Horse Dec. 2002
GN #1 (of 3) IEd(s). 5.95
GN #2 IEd(s) 5.95
GN #3 IED(s). 5.95
TPB Batman/Aliens II 14.95

BATMAN AND
THE OUTSIDERS
Aug., 1983
1 B:MiB(s),JAp,O:Outsiders,
O:Geo Force 4.50
2 JAp,V:Baron Bedlam 3.00
3 JAp,V:Agent Orange. 2.50
4 JAp,V:Fearsome Five 2.50
5 JAp,A:New Teen Titans. 3.00
6 JAp,V:Cryonic Man 2.50
7 JAp,V:Cryonic Man 2.50
8 JAp,A:Phantom Stranger 2.50
9 JAp,I:Master of Disaster 2.50
10 JAp,A:Master of Disaster 2.50
11 JAp,V:Takeo. 2.50
12 JAp,DG,O:Katana 2.50
13 JAp,Day,O:Batman 2.50
14 BWg,Olympics,V:Maxi Zeus. . . . 2.50
15 TVE,Olympics,V:Maxi Zeus . . . 2.50
16 JAp,L:Halo. 2.50
17 JAp,V:Ahk-Ton. 2.50
18 JAp,V:Ahk-Ton. 2.50
19 JAp,A:Superman 2.50
20 JAp,V:Syonide,R:Halo 2.50
21 TVE,JeM,Solo Stories 2.50
22 AD,O:Halo,I:Aurakles 2.50
23 AD,O:Halo,V:Aurakles 2.50
24 AD,C:Kobra 2.50
25 AD,V:Kobra 2.50
26 AD. 2.50
27 AD,V:Kobra 2.50
28 AD,I:Lia Briggs(Looker) 2.50
29 AD,V:Metamorpho 2.50
30 AD,C:Looker 2.50
31 AD,I&J:Looker 2.50
32 AD,L:Batman. 2.50
Ann.#1 JA N:Geo-Force,
I:Force of July 2.50
Ann.#2 V:Tremayne,W:Metamorpho
& Sapphire Stagg 2.50
Becomes:

ADVENTURES OF
THE OUTSIDERS
May, 1986
33 AD,V:Baron Bedlam. 2.25
34 AD,Masters of Disaster 2.25
35 AD,V:Adolph Hitler. 2.25
36 AD,A:Masters of Disaster. 2.25
37 . . . . 2.25
38 . . . . 2.25
39 thru 47 JAp,reprints
Outsiders #1-#9 . . . . @2.25

BATMAN AND ROBIN
ADVENTURES, THE
Nov., 1995
1 TTn 3.00
2 TTn,V:Two-Face 3.00
3 TTn,V:The Riddler 3.00
4 TTn,V:The Penguin. 3.00
5 TTn 3.00
6 TTn,Robin Fired?. 2.50
7 TTn,V:Scarface. 2.50
8 TTn(s) 2.50
9 TTn(s),F:Batgirl & Talia 2.50
10 TTn(s),F:Ra's Al Ghul 2.50
11 TTn(s),Alfred & Robin look
for monster in Batcave 2.50
12 TTn(s),BKr,RBr, sequel to

All comics prices listed are for Near Mint condition.

Batman: And–Dark — DC Comics Values Annual

Batman & Robin Adventures #24
© DC Comics Inc.

iBaneî TV episode 2.50
13 TTn(s),BKr,RBr,V:Scarecrow . . . 2.50
14 TTn(s),BKr,RBr,young criminal
 turns to Batman for help 2.50
15 TTn(s) 2.50
16 TTn(s),V:Catman,A:Catwoman . . 2.50
17 PDi&TTn(s),JSon,RBr,Mad
 Hatter dies in Arkham 2.50
18 TTn(s),BKr,TBe,A:Joker,
 Harley Quinn 2.50
19 TTn(s),BKr,TBe,The Huntress . . 2.50
20 TTn(s),BKr,TBe, office pool 2.50
21 TTn(s),JSon,Riddler kidnaps
 Commissioner Gordon 2.50
22 TTn(s),BKr,TBe,V:Two-Face. . . . 2.50
23 TTn(s),TBe,V:Killer Croc 2.50
24 TTn(c),F:Poison Ivy 2.50
25 TTn,TBe,final issue, 48pg 3.50
Ann.#1 PDi(s),TTn, sequel to
 Batman: Mask of the Phantasm 3.00
Ann.#2 JSon,TBe,V:Hypnotist. . . . 4.00
Sub-Zero one-shot, F:Mr. Freeze,
 Nora, 64pg. 3.95

BATMAN & SUPERMAN: WORLD'S FINEST
1999
1 (of 10) KK(s),DTy,RbC,48-page . 6.00
2 KK(s),DTy,RbC 3.50
3 KK(s),DTy,RbC,Arkham Asylum . . 3.00
4 KK(s),DTy,RbC,Metropolis 3.00
5 KK(s),DTy,RbC,Batgirl 3.00
6 KK(s),DTy,RbC,trade identities . . 3.00
7 KK(s),PD,RbC 3.00
8 KK(s),PD,RbC 3.00
9 KK(s),RbC,split issue 3.00
10 concl. 3.00
GN 6.95

BATMAN: THE ANKH
Nov., 2001
1 (of 2) CDi,JVF,ancient Egypt. . . . 5.95
2 CDi,JVF,V:Khatera, concl. 5.95

BATMAN: BANE OF THE DEMON
Feb., 1998
1 (of 4) CDi,GN,TP, Bane &
 Ra's al Ghul 2.50
2 CDi,GN,TP,Talia 2.50

3 CDi,GN,TP,the Lazarus Pit 2.50
4 CDi,GN,TP,Bane imprisoned. . . . 2.50

BATMAN BEYOND
Mini-series 1999
1 (of 6) RBr,TBe,Rebirth 2.50
2 RBr,TBe,Rebirth,pt.2. . . . . 2.50
3 RBr,TBe,V:Blight. 2.50
4 JSon,TBe,F:Demon Etrigan 2.50
5 JSon,TBe,V:Mummy 2.50
6 JSon,TBe,V:Inque. 2.50
TPB rep. mini-series 10.00

BATMAN BEYOND
1999
1 Batman: Classic vs. Future 3.00
2 V:Inque. 2.50
3 . . . . 2.50
4 V:Royal Flush Gang 2.50
5 V:Shriek 2.50
6 V:Stalker 2.50
7 V:Jokerz 2.50
8 V:Vendetta 2.50
9 V:Curare. 2.50
10 V:Golem 2.50
11 nanotechnology 2.50
12 F:Terminal 2.50
13 Commissioner Barbara Gordon . 2.50
14 F:Etrigan the Demon 2.50
15 BSf(s),F:Erica Electra 2.50
16 BSf(c),V:Kobra. 2.50
17 BSf(c),F:Dana 2.50
18 BSf(c),V:Stalker,Blight 2.50
19 BSf(c),V:Ma Mayhem,Carl,Slim . 2.50
20 BSf(c),V:Jokerz 2.50
21 I:Justice League Unlimited 2.50
22 In Blackest Day, concl. 2.50
23 New Royal Flush Gang 2.50
24 final issue 2.50
Spec. Return of the Joker. 3.00

BATMAN BLACK & WHITE
1996
1 JLe(c) numerous artists 5.00
2 thru 4 . . . . @4.00

BATMAN: BOOK OF THE DEAD
1999
1 (of 2) DgM(s),BKi,Elseworlds . . . 5.00
2 DgM(s),BKi,Conclusion. 5.00

BATMAN CHRONICLES
1995
1 CDi,LW,BSz, multiple stories. . . . 5.00
2 V:Feedback 4.00
3 All villains issue 4.00
4 F:Hitman 15.00
5 Oracle, Year One story 3.50
6 Ra's Al Ghul 3.50
7 JOy,LW, woman on death row. . . 3.50
8 Talia goes to Gotham to
 eliminate Batman 3.50
9 CDi(s),F:Batgirl, Mr. Freeze,
 Poison Ivy 3.50
10 BSn, anthology 3.50
11 CDi,JFM, Elseworlds stories. . . . 3.00
12 Cataclysm x-over. 3.00
13 F:GCPD 3.00
14 SB(c),F:Alfred,Huntress 3.00
15 Road to No Man's Land 3.00
16 F:Batgirl,No Man's Land tie-in . . 3.00
17 V:Penguin,No Man's Land 3.00
18 No Man's Land 3.00
19 . . . . 3.00
20 SBe(s)&IEd(s),48-pg. 3.00

Batman Chronicles #17
© DC Comics, Inc.

21 DG,JRu,3 Elseworlds tales 3.00
22 F:Lady Shiva,48-pg. 3.00
23 BSf(c) final issue 3.00
Gallery #1, Pin-ups. 3.50
GN The Gauntlet 5.00

BATMAN: CITY OF LIGHT
Oct. 2003
1 (of 8) Gotham transformed 2.95
2 new Gotham City 2.95

BATMAN: THE CULT
1988
1 JSn,BWr,V:Deacon Blackfire . . . 8.00
2 JSn,BWr,V:Deacon Blackfire. . . . 6.00
3 JSn,BWr,V:Deacon Blackfire. . . . 6.00
4 JSn,BWr,V:Deacon Blackfire. . . . 5.00
TPB Rep.#1-#4. . . . . 14.95

BATMAN: DARK KNIGHT OF THE ROUND TABLE
1998
1 (of 2) BL,DG,Elseworlds,48pg. . . 5.00
2 BL,DG, conclusion 5.00

BATMAN: THE DARK KNIGHT RETURNS
1986
1 FM,KJ,V:Two-Face 30.00
1a 2nd printing 5.00
1b 3rd printing 3.00
2 FM,KJ,V:Sons of the Batman . . 10.00
2a 2nd printing 3.00
3 FM,KJ,D:Joker 7.00
3a 2nd printing 3.00
4 FM,KJ,Batman vs.Superman,
 A:Green Arrow,D:Alfred 7.00
Paperback book 20.00
Warner paperback 17.00
 2nd-8th printing 13.00
TPB 10th Anniv. Spec, 224 pg. . . . 15.00

BATMAN: THE DARK KNIGHT STRIKES AGAIN
Dec., 2001
1 (of 3) FM,80-pg. 8.00

2 FM, 80-pg. 8.00
3 FM, 80-pg. concl. 8.00

BATMAN: DARK VICTORY
Oct., 1999
1 (of 13) JLb,TSe,48-pg. 6.00
2 JLb,TSe 5.00
3 JLb,TSe,V:Scarecrow 3.00
4 JLb,TSe,V:Two-Face 3.00
5 JLb,TSe,F:Catwoman 3.00
6 JLb,TSe,F:Penguin. 3.00
7 JLb,TSe,V:Calendar Man 3.00
8 JLb,TSe,V:Hang Man 3.00
9 JLb,TSe,F:Bruce & Dick 3.00
10 JLb,TSe,V:Two-Face 3.00
11 JLb,F:Scarecrow 3.00
11 JLb,TSe,V:Poison Ivy 3.00
12 JLb,TSe,Revenge 3.00
13 JLb,TSe, conclusion 5.00

BATMAN: DEATH AND THE MAIDENS
Aug. 2003
1 (of 9) KJ,V:Ra's al Ghul 2.95
2 KJ,F:Nyssa. 2.95
3 KJ,Ra's al Ghul, Nyssa. 2.95
4 KJ,Ra's al Ghul 2.95

BATMAN/DEATHBLOW: AFTER THE FIRE
DC/Wildstorm March, 2002
1 (of 3)TBd,x-over,48-pg. 6.00
2 TBd, 48-pg. 6.00
3 TBd, 48-pg., concl. 6.00

BATMAN: THE DOOM THAT CAME TO GOTHAM
Sept., 2000
1 (of 3) Elseworlds. 5.00
2 MMi,DJa, return from the Arctic. . 5.00
3 Elseworlds, concl 5.00

BATMAN FAMILY
Sept.–Oct., 1975
1 MGr,NA(rep.) Batgirl &
  Robin begins,giant 30.00
2 V:Clue Master. 15.00
3 Batgirl & Robin reveal ID 15.00
4 I:Fatman. 15.00
5 I:Bat Hound 15.00
6 Joker Daughter. 22.00
7 CS,A:Sportsmaster,
  G.A.Huntress 13.00
8 First solo Robin story,
  C:Joker's Daughter. 13.00
9 Joker's Daughter 22.00
10 R:B'woman,1st solo Batgirl sty. 25.00
11 MR,Man-Bat begins 22.00
12 MR 22.00
13 MR,DN,BWi 22.00
14 HC/JRu,Man-Bat 20.00
15 MGo,Man-Bat 20.00
16 MGo,Man-Bat 20.00
17 JA,DH,MG,Batman, B:Huntress
  A:Demon,MK(c),A:Catwoman . 22.00
18 MGo,JSon,BL,Huntress,BM . . 22.00
19 MGo,JSon,BL,Huntress,BM . . 22.00
20 MGo,JSon,DH,A:Ragman,
  Elongat'dMan, Oct.–Nov.,1978 22.00

BATMAN: FAMILY
Oct., 2002
1 (of 8) JFM,SFa,RHo,The Tracker 3.50
2 JFM,SFa,RHo,Athena. 2.25
3 JFM,SFa,RHo,Bugg & Dr.Excess 2.25

Batman GCPD #2
© DC Comics, Inc.

4 JFM,SFa,RHo,Suicide King 2.25
5 JFM,SFa,RHo,Freeway 2.25
6 JFM,RHo,The Technician 2.25
7 JFM,Mr. Fun. 2.25
8 JFM,RHo,Blackout, 48-pg. 3.50

BATMAN: GCPD
Mini-Series Aug., 1996
1 CDi(s),JAp,BSz 2.50
2 CDi(s),JAp,BSz 2.50
3 CDi(s), JAp, BSz,F:Montoya,
  Kitch & Bullock. 2.50
4 CDi(s), JAp, BSz, finale 2.50

BATMAN: GORDON'S LAW
October, 1996
1 CDi(s),KJ,Gordon looks for
  bad cops 2.50
2 CDi(s),KJ,Gordon combats
  corruption. 2.50
3 CDi(s),KJ,. 2.50
4 (of 4) CDi(s),KJ, concl. 2.50

BATMAN: GORDON OF GOTHAM
April, 1998
1 (of 4) DON,DG,KJ,F:Jim Gordon. 2.50
2 DON,DG,KJ,Cuchulain 2.50
3 DON,DG,KJ,break-in 2.50
4 DON,DG,KJ,past revealed 2.50

BATMAN: GOTHAM ADVENTURES
April, 1998
1 TTn,RBr,TBe,F:Joker 3.50
2 TTn,RBr,TBe,F:Two-Face 2.50
3 TTn,RBr,TBe,V:Scarecrow 2.50
4 TTn,RBr,TBe,A:Catwoman 2.50
5 RBr,TBe,TTn,A:Mr.Freeze. 2.50
6 TTn,RBr,TBe,O:Deadman. 2.50
7 TTn,RBe,TBe,V:Danger Dixon . . 2.50
8 TTn,RBe,TBe,Batgirl. 2.50
9 TTn,RBe,TBe,V:League
  of Assassins. 2.50
10 TTn,RBe,TBe,F:Nightwing
  & Robin, A:Harley Quinn 2.50
11 TTn,RBe,TBe,V:Riddler 2.50

Batman: Gordon of Gotham #4
© DC Comics Inc.

12 TTn,RBe,TBe,V:Two-Face 2.50
13 RBe,TBe,V:Mastermind 2.50
14 TTn(s),TBe,V:Harley Quinn . . . 2.50
15 V:Bane 2.50
16 TBe,Alfred Kidnapped 2.50
17 TBe 2.50
18 TBe,R:Man-Bat 2.50
19 TBe,Eden's Own,Poison Ivy . . . 2.50
20 TBe, ... 2.50
21 TBe, ... 2.50
22 TBe,F:Comm.Gordon & Batgirl. . 2.50
23 TBe,V:Ra's al Ghul 2.50
24 TBe,F:Killer Croc 2.50
25 TBe,A:Flash. 2.50
26 TBe,F:Kristov. 2.50
27 TBe, ... 2.50
28 TBe,V:Riddler 2.50
29 CDi(s),TBe,Batman poisoned. . . 2.50
30 TBe,F:Clayface 2.50
31 TTn,TBe,Blackout in Gotham. . . 2.50
32 TBe,V:Scarecrow. 2.50
33 A:Phantom Stranger 2.50
34 V:Maxie Zeus 2.50
35 TBe,On the jury. 2.50
36 TBe,A:Superman. 2.50
37 TBe,V:Joker, Penguin 2.50
38 TBe,F:Robin, Batgirl 2.50
39 TBe,V:Clayface 2.50
40 TBe,V:Mr. Freeze. 2.50
41 TBe,The Man called Joe 2.50
42 Tuesday Night 2.50
43 TBe,F:Harley Quinn 2.50
44 TBe,F:Two-Face 2.50
45 TBe,Running the Asylum 2.50
46 TBe,Saving Face. 2.50
47 TBe,Gotham's Underworld 2.50
48 TBe,RBr,F:Dick Grayson 2.50
49 TBe,Facade. 2.50
50 TBe,Catwoman returns 2.50
51 TA,Mr. Freeze 2.50
52 TBe,Bane 2.50
53 TBe,Poison Ivy superplant 2.50
54 TBe,crime spree 2.50
55 TBe,RBr,mobsters 2.50
56 TBe,V:Riddler? 2.50
57 TBe,V:Riddler 2.50
58 TTn,V:Ventriloquist. 2.50
59 TBe,financial scandal. 2.50
60 TBe,final issue. 2.50
TPB Batman: Gotham Adventures . 9.95

BATMAN: GOTHAM KNIGHTS
Feb., 2000
1 WEl,JLe 5.00
2 JBy,BB(c),F:Batgirl 3.00
3 PPo,PR,BB(c),Samsara,pt.1 . . . . 3.00
4 PR,BB(c),Samsara,pt.2 . . . . 3.00
5 BB(c)V:The Key 3.00
6 WS,PR,JPL,F:Oracle 3.00
7 SD,PR, ... 3.00
8 Transference,pt.1 . . . . 3.00
9 Transference,pt.2 . . . . 3.00
10 Transference,pt.3, ... 3.00
11 BB(c),Transference,pt.4,48-pg. . . 3.50
12 This issue: Batman dies! 3.00
13 Officer Down,x-over,concl. 3.00
14 V:Double Dare 3.00
15 TPe,GC,V:Poison Ivy 3.00
16 Matatoa,pt.1 . . . . 3.00
17 Matatoa,pt.2 . . . . 3.00
18 Cavernous,F:Aquaman 3.00
19 CDi,MSh,DG,F:Titus 3.00
20 A:Superman 3.00
21 TA,Retribution, pt.2 . . . . 3.00
22 TA,Chemical attack 3.00
23 BB(c),F:Scarecrow 3.00
24 TDz,KIs,F:Bruce Wayne 3.00
25 Bruce Wayne:Murderer,pt.4 . . . . 3.50
26 Bruce Wayne:Murderer,pt.10 . . . 3.50
27 DCw,A:Man of Steel 3.00
28 Bruce Wayne:Fugitive,pt.7 . . . . . 3.00
29 Mortician,pt.2 . . . . 3.00
30 Bruce Wayne:Fugitive,pt.14 . . . . 3.00
31 Bruce Wayne:Fugitive,pt.17 . . . . 3.00
32 MK,lives Batman impacts 3.00
33 SBe(s),BSz,F:Bane 3.00
34 SBe(s),Tabula Rasa,pt.1 . . . . . . 3.00
35 SBe(s),Tabula Rasa,pt.2 . . . . . . 3.00
36 SBe(s),F:Robin,Nightwing 3.00
37 SBe(s),F:Spoiler 3.00
38 SBe(s),V:Checkmate 3.00
39 SBe(s),V:Checkmate 3.00
40 SBe(s),Knight Moves 3.00
41 SBe(s),V:Elongated Man 3.00
42 SBe(s),Alfred's illness 3.00
43 SBe(s),F:Batgirl,Robin 3.00
44 SBe(s),death of Jason Todd 3.00
45 SBe(s),Knights Passed 3.00
46 SBe(s),F:Nightwing,Robin 3.00
47 WPo,F:Bane,Nightwing 3.00

(BATMAN:) GOTHAM NIGHTS
[Mini-Series], 1992
1 Gotham City 2.50
2 Lives of Gotham Citizens 2.50
3 Lives of Gotham Citizens 2.50
4 Lives of Gotham Citizens 2.50

BATMAN: GOTHAM NIGHTS II
1995
1 Sequel to Gotham Nights 2.50
2 F:Carmine Sansone 2.50
3 Fire 2.50
4 JQ(c) Decisions 2.50

BATMAN/GRENDEL
[First Series]
DC/Comico, 1993
1 MWg,Devil's Riddle 5.25
2 MWg,Devil's Masque 5.25

[Second Series]
DC/Dark Horse, 1996
1 MWg,Devil's Bones 5.00
2 MWg,Devil's Dance 5.00

Batman/Grendel #2
© DC Comics, Inc.

BATMAN: HAUNTED GOTHAM
Dec., 1999
1 (of 4) DgM,KJo,JhB,Elseworlds. . 5.00
2 DgM,KJo,JhB 5.00
3 DgM,KJo,JhB,V:Ophidus 5.00
4 DgM,KJo,JhB,concl. 5.00

BATMAN/HELLBOY/ STARMAN
DC/Dark Horse 1998
1 JeR(s),MMi, x-over 2.50
2 JeR(s),MMi, conclusion. 2.50

BATMAN: HOLLYWOOD KNIGHT
Feb., 2001
1 (of 3) DG,Elseworlds 2.50
2 DG,F:Byron Wyatt 2.50
3 DG, concl. 2.50

BATMAN/HUNTRESS: CRY FOR BLOOD
April, 2000
1 (of 6) RBr,O:Huntress 2.50
2 RBr,A:Question. 2.50
3 RBr,A:Richard Dragon 2.50
4 RBr, ... 2.50
5 RBr, ... 2.50
6 RBr,Claudio's killer,concl. 2.50

BATMAN: IT'S JOKER TIME
May, 2000
1 (of 3) BH 4.95
2 BH 4.95
3 BH, concl. 4.95

BATMAN: JAZZ
Mini-Series 1995
1 I:Blue Byrd 2.50
2 V:Brotherhood of Bop 2.50
3 F:Blue Byrd 2.50

BATMAN/JUDGE DREDD: DIE LAUGHING
1998
1 (of 2) AIG(s),GF 48-pg. 5.00
2 AIG(s),GF conclusion 5.00

BATMAN: LEAGUE OF BATMEN
April, 2001
1 MBr,RT,48-page, Elseworlds 5.95
2 MBr,RT,48-page, concl. 5.95

BATMAN: LEGENDS OF THE DARK KNIGHT
1989
1 EH,Shaman of Gotham,pt.1, Yellow(c) 5.00
1a Blue,Orange or Pink(c) 4.00
2 EH,Shaman of Gotham,pt.2 . . . . 3.00
3 EH,Shaman of Gotham,pt.3 . . . . 3.00
4 EH,Shaman of Gotham,pt.4 . . . . 3.00
5 EH,Shaman of Gotham,pt.5 . . . . 3.00
6 KJ,Gothic,pt.1 . . . . 3.00
7 KJ,Gothic,pt.2 . . . . 3.00
8 KJ,Gothic,pt.3 . . . . 3.00
9 KJ,Gothic,pt.4 . . . . 3.00
10 KJ,Gothic,pt.5 . . . . 3.00
11 PG,TA,Prey,pt.1 . . . . 6.00
12 PG,TA,Prey,pt.2 . . . . 5.00
13 PG,TA,Prey,pt.3 . . . . 5.00
14 PG,TA,Prey,pt.4 . . . . 5.00
15 PG,TA,Prey,pt.5 . . . . 4.00
16 TVE,Venom,pt.1 . . . . 5.00
17 TVE,JL,Venom,pt.2 . . . . 5.00
18 TVE,JL,Venom,pt.3 . . . . 5.00
19 TVE,JL,Venom,pt.4 . . . . 5.00
20 TVE,JL,Venom,pt.5 . . . . 5.00
21 BS,Faith,pt.1 . . . . 3.00
22 BS,Faith,pt.2 . . . . 3.00
23 BS,Faith,pt.3 . . . . 3.00
24 GK,Flyer,pt.1 . . . . 3.00
25 GK,Flyer,pt.2 . . . . 3.00
26 GK,Flyer,pt.3 . . . . 3.00
27 Destroyer,pt.2 (Batman#474) . . . 3.50
28 MWg,Faces,pt.1,V:Two-Face . . . 4.00
29 MWg,Faces,pt.2,V:Two-Face . . . 4.00
30 MWg,Faces,pt.3,V:Two-Face . . . 4.00
31 BA,Family 3.00
32 Blades,pt.1 . . . . 3.00
33 Blades,pt.2 . . . . 3.00
34 Blades,pt.3 . . . . 3.00
35 BHa,Destiny Pt.1 . . . . 3.00
36 BHa,Destiny Pt.2 . . . . 3.00
37 I:Mercy,V:The Cossack 3.00
38 KON,R:Bat-Mite 3.00
39 BT,Mask#1 . . . . 3.00
40 BT,Mask#2 . . . . 3.00
41 Sunset 3.00
42 CR,Hothouse #1 . . . . 3.00
43 CR,Hothouse #2,V:Poison Ivy . . 3.00
44 SMc,Turf #1 . . . . 3.00
45 Turf#2 . . . . 3.00
46 RH,A:Catwoman,V:Catman 3.00
47 RH,A:Catwoman,V:Catman 3.00
48 RH,A:Catwoman,V:Catman 3.00
49 RH,A:Catwoman,V:Catman 3.00
50 BBl,JLe,KN,KM,WS,MZ,BB, V:Joker 6.00
51 JKu,A:Ragman 3.00
52 Tao #1,V:Dragon 3.00
53 Tao #2,V:Dragon 3.00
54 MMi 3.00
55 B:Watchtower 3.00
56 CDi(s),V:Battle Guards 3.00
57 CDi(s),E:Watchtower 3.00
58 Storm 3.00
59 DON(s),RoW,B:Qarry 3.00

DC — Batman: Legends–Outlaws

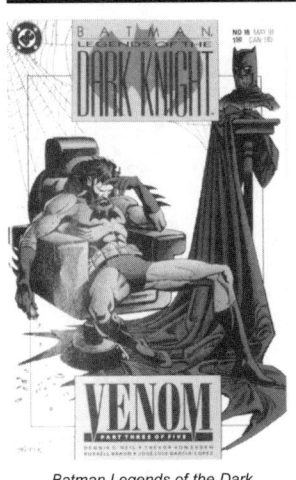

Batman Legends of the Dark Knight #18 © DC Comics, Inc.

60 RoW,V:Asp	3.00
61 RoW,V:Asp	3.00
62 RoW,KnightsEnd#4,A:Shiva, Nightwing	4.50
63 Knights End #10,V:Azrael	3.00
64 CBa	3.00
65 Joker	3.00
66 Joker	3.00
67 Going Sane,pt.3	3.00
68 Going Sane,pt.4	3.00
69 Criminals,pt.1	3.00
70 Criminals,pt.2	3.00
71 Werewolf,pt.1	3.00
72 JWk(c&a),Werewolf,pt.2 [new Miraweb format begins]	3.00
73 JWk(c&a),Werewolf,pt.3	3.00
74 Engis,pt.1	3.00
75 Engins,pt.2	3.00
76 The Sleeping,pt.1	3.00
77 The Sleeping,pt.2	3.00
78 The Sleeping,pt.3	3.00
79 Favorite Things	3.00
80 Idols,pt.1	3.00
81 Idols,pt.2	3.00
82 Idols, climax	3.00
83 new villain	3.00
84 WEI(s)	3.00
85 JeR(s)	3.00
86 DgM,JWi,MGy,Conspiracy,pt.1	3.00
87 DgM,JWi,MGy,Conspiracy,pt.2	3.00
88 DgM,JWi,MGy,Conspiracy,pt.3	3.00
89 AIG(s),Clay,pt. 1	3.00
90 AIG(s),Clay,pt. 2	3.00
91 Freakout, pt.1	3.00
92 GEn(s),WSm,Freakout, pt.2	3.00
93 GEn(s),WSm,Freakout, pt.3	3.00
94 MGi(s),Saul Fisher's story	3.00
95 DAn&ALa(s),AWi,ALa,Dirty Tricks, pt.1	3.00
96 DAn&ALa(s),AWi,ALa,Dirty Tricks, pt.2	3.00
97 DAn&ALa(s),AWi,ALa,,Dirty Tricks, concl.	3.00
98 PJe(s),SeP,Steps, pt.1	3.00
99 PJe(s),SeP,Steps, pt.2	3.00
100 DON,JRo,F:Robin, 64pg	6.00
101 CE,KN(c)100 years in future	3.00
102 JRo,PuJ,Spook, pt.1	3.00
103 JRo,PuJ,Spook, pt.2	3.00
104 JRo,PuJ,Spook, pt.3	3.00
105 TVE,JRu,Duty, pt.1	3.00
106 TVE,JRu,Duty, pt.2	3.00
107 LMr,Stalking, pt.1	3.00
108 LMr,Stalking, pt.2	3.00
109 SEt,DAb,Primal Riddle,pt.1	3.00
110 SEt,DAb,Primal Riddle,pt.2	3.00
111 SEt,DAb,Primal Riddle,pt.3	3.00
112 DVa,FC,V:Lord Demise,pt.1	3.00
113 DVa,FC,V:Lord Demise,pt.2	3.00
114 JeR(s),DIB,TBd	3.00
115 LMc,DIB(c)	3.00
116 IEd,Bread and Circuses,pt.1	5.00
117 IEd,Bread and Circuses,pt.2	3.00
118 JPn,Alfred in No Man's Land	2.50
119 MD2,Claim Jumping,pt.1	2.50
120 MD2,Assembly	4.00
121 RBr,V:Mr.Freeze	2.50
122 LHa(s),PG, Low Road to Golden Mountain,pt.1	2.50
123 PR,ALa,Underground Railroad,pt.1	2.50
124 CDi(s),MkK,No Man's Land	2.50
125 No Man's Land	2.50
126 Endgame, pt.1 x-over	2.50
127 MRy,F:Green Arrow,pt.1	2.50
128 MRy,F:Green Arrow,pt.2	2.50
129 MRy,F:Green Arrow,pt.3	2.50
130 MRy,F:Green Arrow,pt.4	2.50
131 MRy,F:Green Arrow,pt.5	2.50
132 AGw,JeR,MR,BWi,Siege,pt.1	2.50
133 AGw,JeR,MR,BWi,Siege,pt.2	2.50
134 AGw,JeR,MR,BWi,Siege,pt.3	2.50
135 AGw,JeR,MR,BWi,Siege,pt.4	2.50
136 AGw,JeR,MR,BWi,Siege,pt.5	2.50
137 DgM,PG,JP,Terror,pt.1	2.50
138 DgM,PG,JP,Terror,pt.2	2.50
139 DgM,PG,JP,Terror,pt.3	2.50
140 DgM,PG,JP,Terror,pt.4	2.50
141 DgM,PG,JP,Terror,pt.5	2.50
142 CDi,JAp,Demon Laughs,pt.1	2.50
143 CDi,JAp,Demon Laughs,pt.2	2.50
144 CDi,JAp,Demon Laughs,pt.3	2.50
145 CDi,JaP,Demon Laughs,pt.4	2.50
146 DgM,BKi,Bad,pt.1	2.50
147 DgM,BKi,Bad,pt.2	2.50
148 DgM,BKi,Bad,pt.3	2.50
149 JMD,TVE, Grimm, pt.1	2.50
150 JMD,TVE, Grimm, pt.2	2.50
151 JMD,TVE, Grimm, pt.3	2.50
152 JMD,TVE, Grimm, pt.4	2.50
153 JMD, TVE, Grimm, pt.5	2.50
154 MBn,BR,Colossus,pt.1	2.50
155 MBn,BR,Colossus,pt.2	2.50
156 DGr,Blink,pt.1	2.50
157 DGr,Blink,pt.2	2.50
158 DGr,Blink,pt.3	2.50
159 JOs,DGr,Loyalties,pt.1	2.50
160 JOs,DGr,Loyalties,pt.2	2.50
161 JOs,DGr,Loyalties,pt.3	2.50
162 JAr(s),Auterism,pt.1	2.50
163 JAr(s),Auterism,pt.2	2.50
164 DMD,DGr,Don't Blink,pt.1	2.50
165 DMD,DGr,Don't Blink,pt.2	2.50
166 DMD,DGr,Don't Blink,pt.3	2.50
167 DMD,DGr,Don't Blink,pt.4	2.50
168 Urban Legend	2.50
169 TyH,Irresistible,pt.1	2.50
170 TyH,Irresistible,pt.2	2.50
171 TyH,Irresistible,pt.3	2.50
172 V:Rough Justice	2.50
173 V:Rough Justice	2.50
Ann.#1 JAp,KG,DSp,TL,JRu, MGo,JQ,`Duel',C:Joker	5.50
Ann.#2 MN,LMc,W:Gordn&Essen	5.00
Ann.#3 MM,I:Cardinal Sin	5.00
Ann.#4 JSon(c),Elseworlds Story	5.00
Ann.#5 CDi(s)Year One Annuals, O:Man-Bat	5.00
Ann.#6 Legends o/t Dead Earth	4.00
Ann.#7 Pulp Heroes (War)	5.00
Halloween Spec.I	8.00
Halloween Spec.II	5.00
Ghosts, Halloween Special	5.00
TPB Shaman rep.#1-#5 (1993)	12.95
TPB Batman: Gothic, rep. #6-#10 (1992)	12.95
TPB Prey, rep.Legends of the Dark Knight #11–#15 (1992)	12.95
TPB Batman: Venom, TVE, rep. #16–#20 (1993)	9.95
TPB Collected Legends of the Dark Knight,BB(c),rep.#32-#34,#38, #42–#43 (1994)	12.95
TPB Other Realms	13.00

BATMAN: THE LONG HALLOWEEN
Oct., 1996

1 (of 13) JLb,TSe,Who is Holiday? F: usual suspects	11.00
2 JLb(s),TSe,V:Holiday,A:Solomon Grundy	8.00
3 JLb,TSe,	9.00
4 JLb(s),TSe,New Year's Eve	9.00
5 JLb(s),TSe,F:Poison Ivy, Search for Holiday	6.00
6 JLb(s),TSe,F:Poison Ivy, Catwoman	6.00
7 JLb(s),TSe,V:The Riddler	5.00
8 JLb(s),TSe,V:Scarecrow	5.00
9 JLb(s),TSe,A:Holiday,Scarecrow	5.00
10 JLb(s),TSe,V:Scarecrow,Mad Hatter	5.00
11 JLb(s),TSe,V:Holiday	5.00
12 JLb(s),TSe,Harvey Dent	5.00
13 JLb(s),TSe,concl.,48pg	7.00
TPB Haunted Knight, rep. Fears, Madness & Ghosts	12.95
TPB The Long Halloween	19.95

BATMAN: MAN-BAT
1995

1 R:Man-Bat, painted series	5.00
2 F:Marilyn Muno.	5.00
3 JBo,Elseworlds story, concl.	5.00
TPB rep. mini-series	14.95

BATMAN: NEVERMORE
April 2003

1 (of 5) Elseworlds,BWr(c)	2.50
2 GyD,BWr(c),Raven Murders	2.50
3 GyD,BWr(c),Raven Murders	2.50
4 GyD,BWr(c),Raven Murders	2.50
5 GyD,BWr(c),concl.	2.50

BATMAN: NO MAN'S LAND
Sept., 1999

0 F:Huntress	4.95
Secret Files #1	4.95
TPB Vol. 1, x-over rep.	12.95
TPB Vol. 2, x-over rep.	12.95
TPB Vol. 3, x-over rep.	12.95
TPB Vol. 4, x-over rep.(2001)	12.95
TPB Vol. 5, x-over rep.(2001)	12.95

BATMAN: ORPHEUS RISING
Aug., 2001

1 (of 5) DT,DaM	2.50
2 DT,DaM,caught in cross-fire	2.50
3 DT,DaM,who's behind it	2.50
4 DT,DaM,The Deacons	2.50
5 DT,DaM,concl.	2.50

BATMAN: OUTLAWS
July, 2000

1 (of 3) DgM,PG	4.95

All comics prices listed are for Near Mint condition.

Batman: Outlaws–Vs. — DC Comics Values Annual

2 DgM,PG,V:Bloodhawks....... 4.95
3 DgM,PG,concl............. 4.95

BATMAN: RUN, RIDDLER RUN
1992
1 MBg,Batman V:Riddler........ 5.50
2 MBg,Batman V:Riddler........ 5.25
3 MBg,V:Perfect Securities...... 5.25

BATMAN: SHADOW OF THE BAT
1992–97
1 NB,Last Arkham Pt.1......... 5.00
1a Collector set,w/posters,pop-up . 6.00
2 NB,Last Arkham Pt.2......... 4.00
3 NB,Last Arkham Pt.3......... 4.00
4 NB,Last Arkham Pt.4......... 4.00
5 NB,A:Black Spider........... 3.00
6 NB,I:Chancer............... 3.00
7 Misfits Pt.1................ 3.00
8 Misfits Pt.2................ 3.00
9 Misfits Pt.3................ 3.00
10 MC,V:Mad Thane of Gotham... 3.00
11 V:Kadaver................. 2.50
12 V:Kadaver,A:Human Flea..... 2.50
13 NB,`The Nobody'........... 2.50
14 NB,Gotham Freaks#1........ 2.50
15 NB,Gotham Freaks#2........ 2.50
16 BBI,MM,A:Anarchy,Scarecrow . 2.50
17 BBI,V:Scarecrow........... 2.50
18 BBI,A:Anarchy,Scarecrow..... 2.50
19 BBI,Knightquest:The Crusade,pt.2, V:Gotham criminals....... 2.50
20 VGi,Knightquest:The Crusade, V:Tally Man............. 2.50
21 BBI,Knightquest:The Search, V:Mr.Asp............... 2.50
22 BBI,Knightquest:The Search, In London.............. 2.50
23 BBI,Knightquest:The Search .. 2.50
24 BBI,Knightquest:The Crusade . 2.50
25 BSf(c),BBI,Knightquest: Crusade, A:Joe Public,V:Corrosive Man . 2.50
26 BSf(c),BBI,Knightquest: Crusade, V:Clayface.............. 2.50
27 BSf(c),BBI,Knightquest: Crusade, I:Clayface Baby.......... 2.50
28 BSf(c),BBI................ 2.50
29 BSf(c),BBI,KnightsEnd#2,

Batman: Shadow of the Bat #51
© DC Comics, Inc.

A:Nightwing.............. 4.00
30 BSf(c),BBI,KnightsEnd#8, V:Azrael................ 2.50
31 Zero Hour, V:Butler......... 2.50
32 Ventriloquist,Two-Face....... 2.50
33 Two-Face................ 2.50
34 V:Tally Man............... 2.50
35 BKi,Return of Bruce Wayne, Troika,pt.2.............. 2.50
35a Collectors Edition........... 3.50
36 Black Canary.............. 2.50
37 Joker Hunt................ 2.50
38 V:The Joker............... 2.50
39 BSf(c),R:Solomon Grundy [new Miraweb format begins] . . 2.50
40 BSf(c), F:Anarky............ 2.50
41 Explosive Dirigible.......... 2.50
42 .... 2.50
43 Secret of the Universe,pt1.... 2.50
44 AIG,BSz(c) Secret of the Universe,pt.3............ 2.50
45 AIG,BSz(c) 100 year old corpse . 2.50
46 AIG,BSz(c) V:Cornelius Stirk ... 2.50
47 AIG,BSz(c) V:Cornelius Stirk .. 2.50
48 AIG...................... 2.50
49 AIG,Contagion,pt.7......... 2.50
50 AIG,Nightmare on Gotham,pt.1 . 2.50
51 AIG,DTy, Nightmare on Gotham,pt.2 (of 3)........ 2.50
52 AIG(s),Nightmare on Gotham, pt.3................... 2.50
53 AIG(s),Legacy, prelude....... 2.50
54 AIG(s),Legacy, pt. 4, x-over ... 2.50
55 AIG(s),RBr,KJ,Bruce Wayne a murderer? A:Nightwing...... 2.50
56 AIG(s),DTy,SnW,Leaves of Grass,pt.1,V:Poison Ivy..... 2.50
57 AIG(s),DTy,SnW,Grass,pt.2 .... 2.50
58 AIG(s),DTy,SnW,Grass,pt.3 .... 2.50
59 AIG(s),DTy,SnW,Killer, Killer, pt.1................ 2.50
60 AIG(s),DTy,SnW,Killer, pt.2..... 2.50
61 AIG(s),JAp,SnW,night of second chances........... 2.50
62 AIG(s),DTy,SnW,Two-Face,pt.1 . 2.50
63 AIG(s),DTy,SnW,Two-Face,pt.2 . 2.50
64 AIG(s),DTy,SnW,A:Jason Blood . 2.50
65 AIG(s),NBy,JRu, A:Oracle, pt.1.. 2.50
66 AIG(s),NBy,JRu, V:Thinker, Cheat, pt.2............... 2.50
67 AIG(s),NBy,SnW,CsM,V:Thinker, Cheat, pt.3, concl........... 2.50
68 AIG(s),JAp,SnW,annual killer ... 2.50
69 AIG(s),MBu,WF,CsM, The Spirit of 2000, pt. 1...... 2.50
70 AIG(s),MBu,WF,CsM, pt.2 ..... 2.50
71 AIG(s),MBu,WF,CsM,detective .. 2.50
72 AIG(s),MBu,WF............ 2.50
73 AIG(s),MBu,WF,Cataclysm x-over,pt.1.............. 3.50
74 AIG(s),MBu,WF,Cataclysm cont........................ 2.50
75 AIG(s),MBu,WF,Aftershock..... 3.50
76 AIG(s),MBu,WF,Aftershock..... 2.50
77 AIG(s),MBu,WF,quake-torn. ... 2.50
78 AIG(s),MBu,Aftershock....... 2.50
79 AIG(s),MBu,V:Mad Hatter, Narcosis................ 2.50
80 Road to No Man's Land, flip-book Azrael:Agent of the Bat #47 ... 5.00
81 AIG(s),MBu,No Man's Land ... 2.50
82 AIG(s),MBu,No Man's Land 2.50
83 No Law and a New Order, pt.2.. 14.00
84 IEd,Bread and Circuses, pt.2... 5.00
85 IEd(s),Bread & Circuses,concl... 5.00
86 GyD,No Man's Land......... 3.00
87 MD2, Claim Jumping, pt.2..... 3.00
88 DJu,BSz,Fruit of the Earth,pt.1.............. 3.00
89 IEd(s),SB,No Man's Land...... 3.00
90 LHa(s),PG,No Man's Land..... 3.00
91 PR,ALa,Underground Railroad,pt.2............. 3.00
92 No Man's Land,A:Superman ... 3.00
93 No Man's Land 3.00
94 final issue 3.00
Ann.#1 TVE,DG,Bloodlines#3, I:Joe Public.............. 4.00
Ann.#2 Elseworlds story....... 4.00
Ann.#3 Year One Annual....... 4.00
Ann.#4 Legends of the Dead Earth................... 3.00
Ann.#5 AIG(s), Pulp Heroes..... 4.00
Spec.#1,000,000 AIG(s),MBu, Origin of 853rd-century Dark Knight.... 2.00

BATMAN/SUPERMAN/ WONDER WOMAN: TRINITY
June 2003
1 (of 3) MWg, first meeting...... 6.95
2 MWg,V:Bizarro.............. 6.95
3 MWg,concl................ 6.95

BATMAN: SWORD OF AZRAEL
1992–93
1 JQ,KN,I:Azrael............. 12.00
2 JQ,KN,A:Azrael............. 9.00
3 JQ,KN,V:Biis,A:Azrael........ 8.00
4 JQ,KN,V:Biis,A:Azrael........ 8.00
TPB rep.#1–#4.............. 11.00
TPB Platinum................ 25.00

BATMAN: TENSES
Aug. 2003
1 (of 2) JoC(s)............... 6.95
2 JoC(s), concl................ 6.95

BATMAN: TOYMAN
1998
1 (of 4) LHa(s),AWi,KJ.......... 2.50
2 LHa(s),AWi,KJ.............. 2.50
3 LHa(s),AWi,KJ.............. 2.50
4 LHa(s),AWi,KJ conclusion...... 2.50

BATMAN: TURNING POINTS
Nov., 2000
1 (of 5) F:Gordon & Batman..... 2.50
2 TTn(c),Robin arrives.......... 2.50
3 DG,JKu(c),Batgirl dead........ 2.50
4 CDi,BA,HC(c),Azrael......... 2.50
5 No Man's Land.............. 2.50

BATMAN vs. PREDATOR
DC/Dark Horse 1991–92
1 NKu,AKu,inc.8 trading cards bound in (Prestige).......... 5.00
1a Newsstand................ 4.00
2 NKu,AKu,Inc. pinups (prestige).. 4.00
2a Newsstand................ 3.00
3 NKu,AKu,conclusion,inc. 8 trading cards (Prestige)..... 4.00
3a Newsstand................ 3.00
TPB,rep.#1–#3............... 5.95

BATMAN vs. PREDATOR II BLOODMATCH
1994–95
1 R:Predators................ 3.00
2 A:Huntress................. 3.00
3 Assassins.................. 3.00

DC — Batman–Birds

4 V:Head Hunters 3.00
TPB Rep.#1-#4. . . . . 6.95

BATMAN/PREDATOR III: BLOOD TIES
DC/Dark Horse 1997
1 (of 4) CDi,RDm,RbC, vs. pair of Predators 2.50
2 CDi,RDm,RbC, pt.2 . . . . 2.50
3 CDi,RDm,RbC, pt.3 . . . . 2.50
4 CDi,RDm,RbC, concl. 2.50
TPB rep. 8.00

BATMAN/WILDCAT
Feb., 1997
1 (of 3) CDi&BSt(s),SCi,ATi, Batman and Robin discover Secret Ring of combat 2.50
2 CDi&BSt(s),SCi,V:KGBeast, Willis Danko 2.50
3 CDi&BSt(s),SCi, Batman vs. Wildcat, concl. 2.50

BEAST BOY
Nov., 1999
1 (of 4)BRa,Clv 3.00
2 BRa,Clv,A:Nightwing 3.00
3 BRa,Clv,V:Nightwing. 3.00
4 BRa,Clv,F:Flamebird 3.00

BATTLEAXES
DC/Vertigo, March, 2000
1 (of 4) female sword & sorcery . . . 2.50
2 . . . . 2.50
3 . . . . 2.50
4 conclusion 2.50

BATTLE CLASSICS
Sept.–Oct., 1978
1 JKu, reprints. 7.00

BEAUTIFUL STORIES FOR UGLY CHILDREN
Piranha Press 1989–91
1 thru 11 . . . . @3.00
12 thru 14. . . . . @3.00
15 Blood Day 3.50
16 thru 20. . . . . @3.00

21 thru 30 . . . . @4.00

BEOWOLF
April-May, 1975
1 . . . . 25.00
2 thru 3 . . . . @10.00
4 Dracula. 15.00
5 . . . . 10.00
6 Flying Saucer,Feb.–Mar.1976 . . 12.00

BEST OF THE BRAVE & THE BOLD
1988
1 JL(c),NA,rep.B&B #85. . . . . . . 5.00
2 JL(c),NA,rep.B&B #81 . . . . 5.00
3 JL(c),NA,rep.B&B #82 . . . . 5.00
4 JL(c),NA,rep.B&B #80 . . . . 5.00
5 JL(c),NA,rep.B&B #93 . . . . 5.00
6 JL(c),NA,rep.B&B #83 . . . . 5.00

BEWARE THE CREEPER
1968–69
1 . . . . 150.00
2 thru 6 . . . . 75.00

BEWARE THE CREEPER
DC/Vertigo April 2003
1 (of 5) 2.95
2 thru 5 . . . . @2.95

BIG ALL-AMERICAN COMIC BOOK
Dec., 1944
1 JKu 20,000.00

BIG BOOK OF FUN COMICS
Spring, 1936
1 . . . . 20,000.00

THE BIG BOOK OF ...:
DC/Paradox Press B&W 1994–2001
TPB Conspiracies (1995) 12.95
TPB Death (1994). 12.95
TPB Hoaxes (1996) 14.95
TPB Little Criminals (1996). 14.95
TPB Losers 14.95
TPB Martyrs (1997) 15.00
TPB Scandal (1997) 15.00
TPB Thugs (1996) 14.95
TPB Unexplained DgM(s) (1997) . 14.95
TPB Urban Legends (1994) 12.95
TPB Weirdos (1995) 15.00
TPB Weird Wild West (1998) . . . 15.00
TPB Big Book of the '70s (2000). . 14.95
TPB Wild Women,192-page(2001) 14.95

BIG DADDY DANGER
Aug., 2002
1 (of 9) AdP,masked wrestler . . . 2.95
2 AdP,Danny Danger 2.95
3 AdP,Diablo X 2.95
4 AdP,Diablo X 2.95
5 AdP,home dimension 2.95
6 AdP,V:Danny Danger 2.95
7 AdP,Diablo X 2.95
8 AdP,Daddy's soul 2.95
9 AdP,concl. 2.95

BIGG TIME
DC/Vertigo, Aug., 2002
TPB TTn, 128-pg. (b&w) 14.95

BIRDS OF PREY: MANHUNT
1996
1 CDi(s),MHy,F:Black Canary, Oracle 10.00
2 CDi(s),MHy,V,Archer Braun, A:Catwoman 7.00
3 CDi(s),MHy,V:Catwoman, Huntress 7.00
4 CDi(s),MHy,V:Lady Shiva 7.00
1-shot Birds of Prey: Batgirl CDi, Batgirl & Black Canary (1997). . 3.00
1-shot Birds of Prey: Revolution CDi(s),BMc. 3.00
1-shot Birds of Prey: The Ravens, CDi, Girlfrenzy (1998). 3.00
1-shot Birds of Prey: Wolves CDi,DG (1997) 3.00

Birdes of Prey #55 © DC Comics Inc.

BIRDS OF PREY
1998
1 CDi(s),Black Canary & Oracle. . 7.00
2 CDi(s),V:Jackie Pajamas 5.00
3 CDi(s),V:Hellbound 5.00
4 CDi(s),V:Ravens. 5.00
5 CDi(s),V:Ravens,pt.2 . . . . 3.00
6 CDi(s),V:Ravens,pt.3 . . . . 3.00
7 CDi(s),PKr, ... 3.00
8 CDi(s),F:Nightwing 30.00
9 CDi(s),V:Iron Brigade 3.00
10 CDi(s),DG,V:Dr.Pop 3.00
11 CDi(s),DG 3.00
12 CDi(s),DG,F:Catwoman 3.00
13 CDi(s),DG 3.00
14 CDi(s),DG,V:Lashina 3.00
15 CDi(s),JG 3.00
16 CDi(s),JG,V:maniac 2.50
17 CDi(s),JG,V:Joker 2.50
18 CDi(s),JG,Transbelvia 2.50
19 CDi(s),JG,A:Nightwing,Robin . 2.50
20 CDi(s),Hunt for Oracle,pt.2. . . 2.50
21 CDi(s),Hunt for Oracle,concl. . 2.50
22 CDi(s),Gorilla City 2.50
23 CDi(s),Gorilla City 2.50
24 CDi,search for heart donor. . . 3.00
25 CDi,Deathstroke,Blue Beetle . . 2.50
26 CDi,This issue Batman dies! . . 2.50
27 Officer Down x-over,pt.3 . . . . 2.50

Beowulf #2 © DC Comics Inc.

All comics prices listed are for *Near Mint* condition.

Birds–Blackhawk

28 CDi,History Lession,pt.1 . . . . 2.50
29 CDi,History Lession,pt.2 . . . . 2.50
30 CDi,History Lession,pt.3 . . . . 2.50
31 CDi,star-crossed love 2.50
32 CDi,love, and marriage? 2.50
33 CDi,Black Canary,Ra's Al Ghul . . 2.50
34 CDi,A:Power Girl,Blue Beetle . . . 2.50
35 CDi,rescue Black Canary 2.50
36 CDi,Joker: Last Laugh 2.50
37 CDi,Last Laugh aftermath 2.50
38 CDi,F:Dinah 2.50
39 CDi,BruceWayne:Murderer,pt.5 . 5.00
40 CDi,BruceWayne:Murderer,pt.12 6.00
41 CDi,BruceWayne:Fugitive,pt.2 . . 6.00
42 CDi,GF,F:Power Girl 2.50
43 CDi,BruceWayne:Fugitive,pt.10 . 2.50
44 CDi,Deathstroke 2.50
45 CDi,Deathstroke, dinosaurs 2.50
46 CDi,Deathstroke 2.50
47 TMr(s),JP,Heartache,pt.1 . . . . . . 2.50
48 TMr(s),JP,Heartache,pt.2 . . . . . . 2.50
49 TMr(s),JP,Heartache,pt.3 . . . . . . 2.50
50 GHe,CJ 2.50
51 GHe,CJ 2.50
52 GHe,CJ 2.50
53 GHe,CJ 2.50
54 GHe,CJ 2.50
55 GHe,CJ 2.50
56 EBe,V:Savant 2.50
57 EBe,V:Savant 2.50
58 EBe,V:Savant 2.50
59 EBe,V:Savant 2.50
60 EBe,R:Huntress 2.50
61 EBe,consequences 2.50
TPB Birds of Prey 18.00
New edition (2002) 17.95
TPB Old Friends, New Enemies . . 17.95
Spec. Secret Files 2003 . . . . 4.95

BIRDS OF PREY: CATWOMAN/BATGIRL
Feb. 2003
1 JFM,JP,DaR 5.95
2 . . . . 5.95
GN Catwoman/Oracle 5.95

BIZARRO COMICS
March 2003
TPB 19.95

BLACK CANARY
[Limited Series], 1991–92
1 TVE/DG,New Wings,pt.1 . . . . . . 2.50
2 TVE/DG,New Wings,pt.2 . . . . . . 2.50
3 TVE/DG,New Wings,pt.3 . . . . . . 2.50
4 TVE/DG,New Wings,pt.4,Conc . . 2.50
[Regular Series], 1993
1 TVE,Hero Worship,pt.1 . . . . 3.00
2 TVE,Hero Worship,pt.2 . . . . 3.00
3 TVE,Hero Worship,pt.3 . . . . 3.00
4 TVE,V:Whorrsman 3.00
5 . . . . 3.00
6 Blynde Woman's Bluff 3.00
7 TVE,V:Maniacal Killer 3.00
8 . . . . 3.00
9 A:Huntress 3.00
10 TVE,A:Nightwing,Huntress 3.00
11 TVE,A:Nightwing 3.00
12 final issue 3.00

BLACK CANARY/ORACLE: BIRDS OF PREY
1996
1-shot DDi, double size 10.00

BLACK CONDOR
1992–93
1 I&O:Black Condor 3.00
2 V:Sky Pirate 3.00
3 V:Sky Pirate 3.00
4 V:The Shark 3.00
35 V:Mind Force 3.00
6 V:Mind Force 3.00
7 Forest Fire 3.00
8 MG,In Jail 3.00
9 A:The Ray 3.00
10 . . . . 3.00
11 O:Black Condor 3.00

BLACKHAWK
Prev: Golden Age
1957–1984
108 DD,CCu,DD&CCu(c),The
Threat from the Abyss
A:Blaisie 650.00
109 DD,CCu,DD&CCu(c),The
Avalance Kid 225.00
110 DD,CCu,DD&CCu(c),Mystery
of Tigress Island 225.00
111 DD,CCu,DD&CCu(c),Menace
of the Machines 225.00
112 DD,CCu,DD(c),The Doomed
Dog Fight 225.00
113 DD,CCu,CCu(c),Volunteers
of Doom 225.00
114 DD,CCu,DD&CCu(c),Gladiators
of Blackhawk Island 225.00
115 DD,CCu,DD&CCu(c),The
Tyrant's Return 225.00
116 DD,CCu,DD&CCu(c),Prisoners
of the Black Island 225.00
117 DD,CCu,DD&CCu(c),Menace
of the Dragon Boat 225.00
118 DD,CCu,DD&SMo(c),FF,The
Bandit With 1,000 Nets 250.00
119 DD,CCu,DD&SMo(c),
V:Chief Blackhawk 200.00
120 DD,CCu,DD&SMo(c),The
Challenge of the Wizard 200.00
121 DD,CCu,DD&CCu(c),Secret
Weapon of the Archer 200.00
122 DD,CCu,DD&CCu(c),The
Movie That Backfired 200.00
123 DD,CCu,DD&CCu(c),The
Underseas Gold Fort 200.00
124 DD,CCu,DD&CCu(c),Thieves
With A Thousand Faces 200.00
125 DD,CCu,DD&CCu(c),Secrets
o/t Blackhawk Time Capsule . 200.00
126 DD,CCu,DD&CCu(c),Secret
of the Glass Fort 200.00
127 DD,CCu,DD&CCu(c),Blackie-
The Winged Sky Fighter 200.00
128 DD,CCu,DD&CCu(c),The
Vengeful Bowman 200.00
129 DD,CCu,DD&CCu(c),The
Cavemen From 3,000 B.C. . . 200.00
130 DD,CCu,DD&SMo(c),The
Mystery Missle From Space . 200.00
131 DD,CCu,DD&CCu(c),The
Return of the Rocketeers . . . 150.00
132 DD,CCu,DD&CCu(c),Raid
of the Rocketeers 150.00
133 DD,CCu,DD&CCu(c),Human
Dynamo 150.00
134 DD,CC,DD&CC(c),The
Sinister Snowman 150.00
135 DD,CCu,DD&CCu(c),The
Underworld Supermarket . . . 150.00
136 DD,CCu,DD&CCu(c),The
Menace of the Smoke-Master 150.00
137 DD,CCu,DD&CCu(c),The
Weapons That Backfired 150.00
138 DD,CCu,DD&SMo(c),The
Menace of the Blob 150.00
139 DD,CCu,DD&CCu(c),The
Secret Blackhawk 150.00
140 DD,CCu,DD&CCu(c),The
Space Age Marauders 150.00
141 DD,CCu,DD&CCu(c),Crimes
of the Captive Masterminds . 100.00
142 DD,CCu,DD&CCu(c),Alien
Blackhawk Chief 100.00
143 DD,SMo,DD&CCu(c),Lady
Blackhawk's Rival 100.00
144 DD,CCu,DD&CCu(c),The
Underworld Sportsmen 100.00
145 DD,CCu,DD&CCu(c),The
Deadly Lensman 100.00
146 DD,CCu,DD&CCu(c),
Blackhawk's Fantastic Fables 100.00
147 DD,SMo,DD&CCu(c),The
Blackhawk Movie Queen . . . 100.00
148 DD,CCu,DD&CCu(c),Four
Dooms For The Blackhawks . 100.00
149 DD,CCu,DD&CCu(c),Masks
of Doom 100.00
150 DD,CCu,DD&SMo(c), Black-
hawk Mascot from Space . . . 100.00
151 DD,CCu,Lost City 125.00
152 DD,CCu,DD&SMo(c),Noah's
Ark From Space 100.00
153 DD,CCu,DD&SMo(c),
Boomerang Master 100.00
154 DD,CCu,DD&SMo(c),The
Beast Time Forgot 100.00
155 DD,CCu,DD&CCu(c),Killer
Shark's Land Armada 100.00
156 DD,CCu,DD&SMo(c),Peril of
the Plutonian Raider 100.00
157 DD,CCu,DD&SMo(c),Secret
of the Blackhawk Sphinx 100.00
158 DD,CCu,DD&SMo(c),Bandit
Birds From Space 100.00
159 DD,CCu,DD&SMo(c),Master
of the Puppet Men 100.00
160 DD,CCu,DD&CCu(c),The
Phantom Spy 100.00
161 DD,SMo,DD&SMo(c),Lady
Blackhawk's Crime Chief . . . 100.00
162 DD,CCu,DD&CCu(c),The
Invisible Blackhawk 100.00
163 DD,CCu,DD&SMo(c),
Fisherman of Crime 100.00
164 DD,O:Blackhawk retold 125.00
165 DD,V:League of Anti
Blackhawks 75.00

Blackhawk #247
© DC Comics, Inc.

DC

Blackhawk–Black Lightning

166 DD,A:Lady Blackhawk 75.00
167 DD,The Blackhawk Bandits . . 75.00
168 DD,Blackhawk Time
   Travelers 60.00
169 DD,Sinister Hunts of Mr.
   Safari. 60.00
170 DD,A:Lady Blackhawk,V:Killer
   Shark 60.00
171 DD,Secret of Alien Island 60.00
172 DD,Challenge of the
   GasMaster 60.00
173 DD,The Super Jungle Man. . . 60.00
174 DD,Andre's Impossible
   World 60.00
175 DD,The Creature with
   Blackhawk's Brain 60.00
176 DD,Stone Age Blackhawks. . . 55.00
177 DD,Town that time Forgot . . . 55.00
178 DD,Return of the Scorpions . . 55.00
179 DD,Invisible Dr.Dunbar. 55.00
180 DD,Son of Blackhawk 55.00
181 DD,I:Tom Thumb Blackhawk . 60.00
182 DD,A:Lady Blackhawk 60.00
183 DD,V:Killer Shark. 60.00
184 DD,Island of Super
   Monkeys 60.00
185 DD,Last 7 days of the
   Blackhawks 60.00
186 DD,A:Lady Blackhawk 60.00
187 DD,V:Porcupine 60.00
188 DD,A:Lady Blackhawk 60.00
189 DD:O:rtd 60.00
190 DD,FantasticHumanStarfish . . 60.00
191 DD,A:Lady Blackhawk 60.00
192 DD,V:King Condor 35.00
193 DD,The Jailer's Revenge 35.00
194 DD,The Outlaw Blackhawk. . . 35.00
195 DD,A:Tom Thumb Blackhawk. 35.00
196 DD,Blackhawk WWII Combat
   Diary story 35.00
197 DD:new look 35.00
198 DD:O:rtd 40.00
199 DD,Attack with the Mummy
   Insects 40.00
200 DD,A:Lady Blackhawk,
   I:Queen Killer Shark 40.00
201 DD,Blackhawk Detached Diary
   Story,F:Hendrickson 40.00
202 DD,Combat Diary,F:Andre . . . 40.00
203 DD:O:Chop-Chop. 40.00
204 DD,A:Queen Killer Shark 40.00
205 DD,Combat Diary story 40.00
206 DD,Combat Diary,F:Olaf 40.00
207 DD,Blackhawk Devil Dolls . . . 40.00
208 DD,Detached service diary
   F:Chuck 40.00
209 DD,V:King Condor 40.00
210 DD,Danger..Blackhawk Bait
   rep.Blackhawk #139. . . . . . . 30.00
211 DD,GC,Detached service
   diary. 30.00
212 DD,Combat Diary,
   F:Chop-Chop 30.00
213 DD,Blackhawk goes
   Hollywood 30.00
214 DD,Team of Traitors. 30.00
215 DD,Detached service diary
   F:Olaf 30.00
216 DD,A:Queen Killer Shark 30.00
217 DD,Detached service diary
   F:Stanislaus 30.00
218 DD,7 against Planet Peril 30.00
219 DD,El Blackhawk Peligroso . . 30.00
220 DD,The Revolt of the
   Assembled Man 30.00
221 DD,Detach service diary
   F:Hendrickson 30.00
222 DD,The Man from E=MC2 . . 30.00
223 DD,V:Mr.Quick CHange 30.00
224 DD,Combat Diary,
   F:Stanislaus 30.00

Blackhawk 3rd Series #12
© DC Comics, Inc.

225 DD,A:Queen Killer Shark 30.00
226 DD,Secret Monster of
   Blackhawk Island 30.00
227 DD,Detached Service diary
   F:Chop-Chop 30.00
228 DD (1st art on JLA characters)
   Blackhawks become super-heroes,
   Junk-Heap heroes #1(C:JLA). . 35.00
229 DD,Junk-Heap Heroes #2
   (C:JLA). 30.00
230 DD,Junk-Heap Heroes concl.
   (C:JLA). 30.00
231 DD,A:Lady Blackhawk 30.00
232 DD,A:Lady Blackhawk 30.00
233 DD,Too Late,The Leaper 30.00
234 DD,The Terrible Twins 30.00
235 DD,A Coffin for
   a Blackhawk. 30.00
236 DD,Melt,Mutant, Melt 30.00
237 DD,Magnificent 7 Assassins . . 30.00
238 DD,Walking Booby-Traps 30.00
239 DD,The Killer That Time
   Forgot 30.00
240 DD,He Who Must Die. 30.00
241 DD,A Blackhawk a Day 30.00
242 Blackhawks back in blue &
   black costumes 30.00
243 Mission Incredible (1968) 30.00
244 GE,new costumes,Blackhawks
   become mercenaries (1976) . . 10.00
245 GE,Death's Double Deal 10.00
246 RE,GE,Death's Deadly Dawn . 10.00
247 RE,AM,Operation:Over Kill. . . 10.00
248 JSh,Vengeance is Mine!..
   Sayeth the Cyborg 10.00
249 RE,GE,V:Sky-Skull. 10.00
250 RE,GE,FS,D:Chuck(1977) . . . 10.00
251 DSp,Back to WWII(1982). . . . 10.00
252 thru 258 DSp . . . . @10.00
259 . . . . 10.00
260 HC,ATh 10.00
261 thru 271 DSp . . . . @10.00
272. . . . . 10.00
273 DSp. 10.00
274 DSp. 10.00

[2nd Series], 1988

1 HC Mini-series,Blackhawk accused
   of communism 5.00
2 HC,visits Soviet Union 4.00
3 HC,Atom Bomb threat to N.Y. . . . 4.00

[3rd Series], 1989

1 All in color for a Crime,pt.1
   I:The Real Lady Blackhawk . . . 4.00

2 All in color for a Crime,pt.2 . . . . 2.50
3 Agent Rescue Attempt in Rome . 2.50
4 Blackhawk's girlfriend murdered . 2.50
5 I:Circus Organization 2.50
6 Blackhawks on false mission . . . 2.50
7 V:Circus,A:Suicide Squad, rep.
   1st Blackhawk story 3.00
8 Project: Assimilation 2.50
9 V:Grundfest 2.50
10 Blackhawks Attacked 2.50
11 Master plan revealed 2.50
12 Raid on BlackhawkAirwaysHQ. . 2.50
13 Team Member Accused of 2.50
14 Blackhawk test pilots 2.50
15 Plans for independence 2.50
16 Independence, final issue 2.50
Ann.#1 Hawks in Albania 2.95
Spec.#1 Assassination of JFK
   to Saigon,1975. . . . . 3.50

BLACK HOOD
Impact, 1991–92

1 O:Black Hood. 4.00
2 Nick Cray becomes Black Hood . 3.00
3 New Year's Eve,A:Creeptures. . . 3.00
4 Nate Cray become Black Hood,
   Dr.M.Harvey becomes Ozone. . 3.00
5 E:Nate Cray as Black Hood
   V:Ozone. 3.00
6 New Black Hood. 3.00
7 History of Seaside City 3.00
8 V:Hit Coffee 3.00
9 V:Hit Coffee 3.00

Black Hood Ann. #1
© DC Comics Inc.

10 Slime of Your Life #1 . . . . 3.00
11 Slime of Your Life #2 . . . . 3.00
12 Final Issue. 3.00
Ann#1 Earthquest,w/trading card . . 3.00

BLACK LAMB, THE
DC/Helix, Sept., 1996

1 TT,Vampire saga. 2.50
2 TT,war between werewolf clans . 2.50
3 TT,O:Black Lamb,V:Lykaon. . . . 2.50
4 TT thru 6. . . . . @2.50

BLACK LIGHTNING
1977–78

1 TVE/FS,I&O:Black Lightning . . . 12.00
2 TVE/FS,A:Talia. 6.00

Black–Blue / DC / Comics Values Annual

3 TVE,I:Tobias Whale 6.00
4 TVE,A:Jimmy Olsen 7.00
5 TVE,A:Superman 7.00
6 TVE,I:Syonide 5.00
7 TVE,V:Syonide 5.00
8 TVE,V:Tobias Whale 5.00
9 TVE,V:Annihilist 5.00
10 TVE,V:Trickster 5.00
11 TVE,BU:The Ray 7.00

[2nd Series], 1995–96
1 He's Back..................... 3.00
2 V:Painkiller 3.00
3 V:Painkiller 3.00
4 V:Painkiller,Royal Family...... 3.00
5 Flashbacks of Past............ 3.00
6 V:Gangbuster 3.00
7 V:Gangbuster 3.00
8 V:Tobias Whale 3.00
9 I&V:Demolition 3.00
10 Jefferson Pierce becomes Black Lightning full time 3.00
11 Hunt for Sick Nick 3.00
12 V:Sick Nick's death squad 3.00
13 final issue 3.00

BLACK MASK
1993–94
1 I:Black Mask.................. 5.00
2 V:Underworld 5.00
3 V:Valentine................... 5.00

BLACK ORCHID
1993–95
1 DMc,O:Black Orchid, A:Batman,Luthor,Poison Ivy ... 6.00
2 DMc,O:cont,Arkham Asylum.... 7.00
3 DMc,A:SwampThing,conc...... 6.00
TPB rep. #1 thru #3 .... 20.00

DC/Vertigo
1 DMc(c),B:DiF(s),JIT,SnW,I:Sherilyn Somers,I:Logos,F:Walt Brody .. 2.50
1a Platinum Ed................. 12.00
2 JIT,SnW,Uprooting,V:Logos..... 2.50
3 JIT,SnW,Tainted Zone, V:Fungus 2.50
4 JIT,SnW,I:Nick & Orthia........ 2.50
5 DMc(c),JIT,SnW, A:Swamp Thing 2.50
6 JIT,BMc(i),God in the Cage..... 2.50
7 JIT,RGu,SnW, Upon the Threshold 2.50
8 DMc(c),RGu,A:Silent People.... 2.50
9 DMc(c),RGu 2.50
10 DMc(c),RGu 2.50
11 DMc(c),RGu,In Tennessee..... 2.50
12 DMc(c),RGu 2.50
13 DMc(c),RGu,F:Walt Brody 2.50
14 DMc(c),RGu,Black Annis 2.50
15 DMc(c),RGu,Kobolds.......... 2.50
16 DMc(c),RGu,Suzy,Junkin 2.50
17 Twisted Season,pt.1 .... 2.50
18 Twisted Season,pt.2 .... 2.50
19 Twisted Season,pt.3 .... 2.50
20 Twisted Season,pt.4 .... 2.50
21 Twisted Season,pt.5 .... 2.50
22 Twisted Season,pt.6, final iss. .. 2.50
Ann.#1 DMc(c),DiF(s),GyA,JnM,F:Suzy, Childrens Crusade,BU:retells Adventure Comics#430 ...... 4.00

BLASTERS SPECIAL
1989
1 A:Snapper Carr, Spider Guild ... 2.00

BLOOD: A TALE
DC/Vertigo, Sept., 1996
[Mini-series, re-release of Marvel Epic]
1 JMD(s),KW, quest for truth begins 3.00
2 JMD(s),KW, Blood falls in love .. 3.00
3 JMD(s),KW, companion dies.... 3.00
4 JMD(s),KW, finale.............. 3.00

BLOOD & SHADOWS
DC/Vertigo, 1996
1 .... 6.00
2 Journal of Justice Jones 6.00
3 Chet Daley flung into 21st century 6.00
4 V:God of the Razor, finale..... 6.00

BLOOD AND WATER
DC/Vertigo March 2003
1 (of 5) F:Adam Heller.......... 2.95
2 vampire 2.95
3 sex for Adam 2.95
4 past, present, future 2.95
5 concl......................... 2.95

BLOODBATH
1993
1 A:Superman 4.00
2 A:New Heroes, Hitman 8.00

BLOODPACK
[Mini-Series], 1995
1 I:Blood Pack, V:Demolition 2.25
2 A:Superboy................... 2.25
3 Loira's Corpse 2.25
4 Real Heroes Final Issue 2.25

BLOOD SYNDICATE
DC/Milestone, 1993–96
1 I:Blood Syndicate,Rob Chaplick, Dir.Mark.Ed.,w/B puzzle piece, Skybox card,Poster 3.50
1a Newstand Ed................ 2.50
2 I:Boogieman,Tech-9 Vs. Holocaust 2.50
3 V:S.Y.S.T.E.M.,I:Mom,D:Tech-9 .. 2.50
4 V:S.Y.S.T.E.M. 2.50
5 I:John Wing,Kwai,Demon Fox... 2.50
6 V:John Wing.................. 2.50
7 I:Edmund,Cornelia 2.50
8 V:Demon Fox 2.50
9 O:Blood Syndicate,I:Templo 2.50
10 WS(c),Ccs,Shadow War,I:Iota, Sideshow,Rainsaw,Slag,Ash, Bad Betty,Oro................ 2.75
11 IV(s),Ccs,A:Aquamaria........ 2.50
12 IV(s),Ccs,V:Dinosaur 2.50
13 IV(s),Ccs,B:Roach War 2.50
14 IV(s),Ccs,V:Roaches 2.50
15 IV(s),Ccs,E:Roach War 2.50
16 IV(s),Ccs,Worlds Collide#6, A:Superman................. 2.50
17 Ccs,Worlds Collide#13,V:Rift ... 2.50
18 Ccs,V:S.Y.S.T.E.M. 2.50
19 .... 2.50
20 .... 2.50
21 .... 2.50
22 .... 2.50
23 F:Boogieman 2.50
24 L:Third Rail,Brickhouse 2.50
25 R:Tech-9 .... 3.50
26 Return of the Dead 2.50
27 R:Masquerade............... 2.50
28 Tech-9 takes control.......... 2.75

29 Reader's Choice 2.50
30 Long Hot Summer 2.50
31 V:New Threat................ 2.50
32 MC(c),V:Soulbreaker 2.50
33 Kwai returns to paris Island ... 2.50
34 Visit to Kwen Lun 2.50
35 final issue 3.50

BLOODY MARY
DC/Helix, Aug., 1996
1 (of 4) GEn(s),CE, near-future war...................... 3.00
2 thru 4 GEn(s),CE, near-future war, concl. .... @3.00

Bloody Mary: Lady Liberty #1
© DC Comics, Inc.

BLOODY MARY: LADY LIBERTY
DC/Helix, July, 1996
1 (of 4) GEn(s),CE, ... 4.00
2 GEn(s),CE,V:Achilles Seagal ... 4.00
3 GEn(s),CE,V:Vatman 4.00
4 GEn(s),CE,V:Vatman, concl..... 4.00

BLUE BEETLE
1986–88
1 O:Blue Beetle................. 4.00
2 V:Fire Fist.................... 2.25
3 V:Madmen 2.25
4 V:Doctor Alchemy 2.25
5 A:Question 2.25
6 V:Question 2.25
7 A:Question 2.25
8 A:Chronos 2.25
9 A:Chronos 2.25
10 Legends, V:Chronos 2.25
11 A:New Teen Titans 2.25
12 A:New Teen Titans 2.25
13 A:New Teen Titans 2.25
14 Pago Island,I:Catalyst 2.25
15 RA:V:Carapax 2.25
16 RA,Chicago Murders 2.25
17 R:Dan Garrett/Blue Beetle.... 2.25
18 D:Dan Garrett 2.25
19 RA,R:Dr. Cyber 2.25
20 RA,Millennium,A:JLI. 3.00
21 RA,A:Mr.Miracle, Millennium tie in 2.25
22 RA,Prehistoric Chicago 2.25
23 DH,V:The Madmen 2.25
24 DH,final issue 2.25

CVA Page 52 — All comics prices listed are for *Near Mint* condition.

DC

Blue–Booster

BLUE DEVIL
1984–86
- 1 O:Blue Devil 4.00
- 2 . . . . 2.50
- 3 A:Superman 2.50
- 4 A:JLA 2.50
- 5 . . . . 2.50
- 6 EC,I:Bolt 2.50
- 7 KG 2.50
- 8 GV 2.50
- 9 thru 16 . . . . @2.50
- 17 Crisis 3.00
- 18 Crisis 3.00
- 19 . . . . 2.50
- 20 RM,Halloween 2.50
- 21 RM,I:Roadmaster 2.50
- 22 RM,A:Jorj & Lehni 2.50
- 23 A:Jorj & Lehni 2.50
- 24 V:Blue Devil Toys 2.50
- 25 Mary Frances Cassidy 2.50
- 26 Special Baseball issue 2.50
- 27 Godfrey Goose 2.50
- 28 real live fan guest star 2.50
- 29 . . . . 2.50
- 30 Double sized 2.50
- 31 BSz,V:Seraph 2.50
- Ann.#1 . . . . 2.50

BOB, THE GALACTIC BUM
[Mini-Series], 1995
- 1 A:Lobo 2.50
- 2 Planet Gnulp,A:Lobo 2.50
- 3 V:Khunds 2.50
- 4 Rando's Coronation 2.50

BODY DOUBLES
Aug., 1999
- 1 (of 4) DAn,ALa,JoP 2.50
- 2 DAn,ALa,JoP 2.50
- 3 DAn,ALa,JoP 2.50

BOGIE MAN, THE
DC/Paradox/Pocket 1998
- TPB 6"x8" AlG,b&w 14.00

BOMBA, THE JUNGLE BOY
1967–68
- 1 CI,MA,I:Bomba 50.00
- 2 thru 7 . . . . @35.00

BOOK OF FATE, THE
1997–98
- 1 KG(s),RoW,BR, ... 3.00
- 2 KG(s),RoW,BR,The Chaos-Order War, pt.1 (of 4) 3.00
- 3 KG(s),RoW,BR,The Chaos-Order War, pt.2 . . . . 3.00
- 4 KG(s),RoW,BR,The Chaos-Order War, pt.3, A:Two-Face . . 3.00
- 5 KG(s),RoW,BR,The Chaos-Order War, pt.4 . . . . 3.00
- 6 KG(s),RoW,BR,Convergence, pt.1 x-over 3.00
- 7 KG(s),RoW,BR, Signs, pt.1 . . . . 3.00
- 8 KG(s),RoW,BR, Signs, pt.2 . . . . 3.00
- 9 KG,AlG,BR,Signs, pt.3 . . . . 3.00
- 10 KG,AlG,BR,Signs,pt.4 . . . . 3.00
- 11 KG,AlG, in a Swiss Jail 3.00
- 12 AlG,KG,F:Lobo, final issue 3.00

BOOKS OF FAERIE, THE
DC/Vertigo, Jan., 1997
- 1 PrG,F:Titania and Auberon 3.00
- 2 PrG, ... 3.00
- 3 (of 3) PrG 3.00
- TPB 15.00

BOOKS OF FAERIE, THE: AUBERON'S TALE
DC/Vertigo, June, 1998
- 1 (of 3) PrG,VcL,F:Early life of King Auberon 3.00
- 2 PrG,VcL, early life 3.00
- 3 PrG,VcL, early life, concl 3.00
- TPB Books of Faerie 15.00

BOOKS OF FAERIE, THE: MOLLY'S STORY
DC/Vertigo, 1999
- 1 (of 4) JNR(s) 3.00
- 2 CV(c) 3.00
- 3 CV(c) 3.00
- 4 CV(c) conclusion 3.00

BOOKS OF MAGIC
[Limited Series], 1990–91
- 1 B:NGa(s),JBo,F:Phantom Stranger, A:J.Constantine,Tim Hunter, Doctor Occult,Mister E 11.00
- 2 SHp,F:J.Constantine,A:Spectre, Dr.Fate,Demon,Zatanna 11.00
- 3 CV,F:Doctor Occult, A:Sandman 8.00
- 4 E:NGa(s),PuJ,F:Mr.E,A:Death . . . 9.00
- TPB rep.#1-#4 . . . . 20.00

[Regular Series] DC/Vertigo, 1994–97
- 1 MkB,B:Bindings,R:Tim Hunter . . 13.00
- 1a Platinum Edition 25.00
- 2 CV(c),MkB,V:Manticore 6.00
- 3 CV(c),MkB,E:Bindings 6.00
- 4 CV(c),MkB,A:Death 7.00
- 5 CV(c),I:Khara 4.00
- 6 Sacrifices,pt.I 4.00
- 7 Sacrifices,pt.II 4.00
- 8 Tim vs. evil Tim 4.00
- 9 Artificial Heart,pt.1 . . . . 4.00
- 10 Artificial Heart,pt.2 . . . . 4.00
- 11 Artificial Heart,pt.3 . . . . 4.00
- 12 Small Glass Worlds,pt.1 . . . . . . 4.00
- 13 Small Glass Worlds,pt.2 . . . . . . 4.00
- 14 CV(c),A:The Wobbly 4.00
- 15 Hell and Back,pt.1 . . . . 4.00
- 16 Hall and Back,pt.2 . . . . 3.50
- 17 Playgrounds,pt.1 . . . . 3.50
- 18 JNR,PrG,Playgrounds,cont. . . . 3.50
- 19 JNR,PrG,Playgrounds,concl. . . 3.50
- 20 Barabatos gives the orders . . . 3.50
- 21 JNR,PrG,Molly seeks Mayra . . . 3.50
- 22 . . . . 3.50
- 23 JNR,V:Margraves Strafenkinder . 3.50
- 24 JNR,PrG,F:Molly vs. Amadan . . 3.50
- 25 JNR,PrG,Death and the Endless 3.50
- 26 JNR,PrG,Rites of Passage, pt.1 . 3.00
- 27 JNR,PrG,Rites of Passage, pt.2 . 3.00
- 28 JNR,PrG,Rites of Passage, pt.3, Cupid & Psyche 3.00
- 29 JNR,PrG,Rite of Passage 3.00
- 30 JNR,PrG,Rite of Passage 3.00
- 31 JNR,PrG,Rite of Passage 3.00
- 32 JNR(s),PSj,Rites of Passage . . 3.00
- 33 JNR(s),PSj,Rites of Passage . . 3.00
- 34 JNR(s),PSj,Rites of Passage . . 3.00
- 35 JNR(s),PrG,Rites of Passage . . 3.00
- 36 JNR,Rites of Passage, cont . . . 3.00
- 37 JNR,Rites of Passage, cont . . . 3.00
- 38 JNR,Rites of Passage, concl . . . 3.00
- 39 PrG, at Sphinx casino 3.00
- 40 JNR(s),F:Tim & Molly 3.00
- 41 JNR(s),V:Gargoyles 3.00
- 42 JNR(s),JIT,magical havok 3.00
- 43 JNR(s),PrG,F:The Wobbly 3.00
- 44 JNR(s),goodbye to Zatanna . . . 3.00
- 45 JNR(s) Slave of Heavens, pt.1 . 3.00
- 46 JNR(s) Slave of Heavens, pt.2 . 3.00
- 47 JNR(s) Slave of Heavens, pt.3 . 3.00
- 48 JNR(s) Slave of Heavens, pt.4 . 3.00
- 49 JNR(s) Slave of Heavens, pt.5 . 3.00
- 50 JNR(s) Slave of Heavens, pt.6 . 3.00
- 51 PrG,MK,an Opener 2.50
- 52 PrG,MK,Homecoming 2.50
- 54 PrG,MK,V:Thomas 2.50
- 55 PrG,MK,Coming of the Other . . 2.50
- 56 PrG,MK,Last Molly Story 2.50
- 57 PrG,MK,after car crash 2.50
- 58 PrG,MK,The Other 2.50
- 59 PrG,MK,The Other 2.50
- 60 PrG,MK,The Other 2.50
- 61 PrG,MK(c),The Other, concl. . . 2.50
- 62 PrG,MK(c),crossroads 2.50
- 63 GyA,MK(c), ... 2.50
- 64 PrG,MK(c),Wild Hunt 2.50
- 65 PrG,MK,new life cont. 2.50
- 66 PrG,A Day,A Night & A Dream,pt.1 . . . . 2.50
- 67 PrG,A Day, A Night & A Dream,concl. 2.50
- 68 PrG 2.50
- 69 PrG 2.50
- 70 PrG 2.50
- 71 PrG,MK(c) 2.50
- 72 PrG,MK(c),F:Timothy Hunter . . . 2.50
- 73 PrG,MK(c),V:Other self 2.50
- 74 PrG,MK(c),V:Other self 2.50
- 75 PrG,MK(c), final issue 2.50
- Ann.#2 JNR(s) Minotaur 4.00
- Ann.#3 PrG 4.00
- TPB Rep. #5-#13 & Rave #1 . . 12.95
- TPB Reckonings, rep. #14–#20 . 12.95
- TPB Reckonings, new printing . . 14.95
- TPB Bindings, GyA,PrG,WK . . . 13.00
- TPB Transformations PrG,MK. . . 13.00
- TPB The Books of Magic 20.00
- TPB Girl in the Box 15.00
- TPB The Burning Girl 17.95
- TPB Death After Death 19.95

BOOSTER GOLD
1986–88
- 1 DJ,V:Blackguard 3.00
- 2 DJ,V:Minddancer 2.50
- 3 DJ,V:Minddancer 2.50
- 4 DJ,V:Minddancer 2.50

Books of Magic #54
© DC Comics Inc.

All comics prices listed are for *Near Mint* condition.

Booster–Brave — DC — Comics Values Annual

5 DJ,V:Fascinator 2.50
6 DJ,A:Superman 2.50
7 DJ,A:Superman 2.50
8 DJ,A:Braniac 5,Cham.Boy,
   Ultra Boy,pt.1 . . . . 2.50
9 DJ,A:Braniac 5,Cham.Boy,
   Ultra Boy,pt.2 . . . . 2.50
10 DJ,V:1000 . . . . 2.50
11 DJ,V:Shockwave 2.50
12 DJ,Booster Weakening 2.50
13 DJ,I:Rip Hunter(modern) 2.50
14 DJ,Rip Hunter 2.50
15 DJ,Rip Hunter 2.50
16 DJ,Boosters new company 2.50
17 DJ,A:Cheshire & Hawk 2.50
18 DJ,V:Broderick. 2.50
19 DJ,V:Rainbow Raider. 2.50
20 DJ,V:Rainbow Raider. 2.50
21 DJ,Goldstar captured by aliens . 2.50
22 DJ,A:J.L.I.,D:Goldstar 2.50
23 DJ,A:Superman & Luthor 2.50
24 DJ,Millenium 2.50
25 DJ,last issue 2.50

BOY COMMANDOS
Winter, 1942–43
1 S&K,O:Liberty Belle;Sandman
   & Newsboy Legion 7,500.00
2 S&K,Hitler(c) 2,500.00
3 S&K,WWII(c) 1,500.00
4 WWII(c) 1,000.00
5 WWII(c) 1,000.00
6 S&K,WWII(c) 750.00
7 S&K,WWII(c) 650.00
8 S&K,WWII(c) 650.00
9 WWII(c) 650.00
10 S&K,WWII(c) 650.00
11 WWII(c) 650.00
12 WWII(c) 450.00
13 WWII(c) 450.00
14 . . . . 350.00
15 1st Crazy Quilt 450.00
16 . . . . 350.00
17 Science Fiction(c) 350.00
18 . . . . 350.00
19 . . . . 375.00
20 Science Fiction (c) 375.00
21 . . . . 250.00
22 . . . . 250.00
23 S&K,S&K,(c) 350.00
24 . . . . 325.00
25 superhero(c) 275.00
26 Science Fiction(c) 300.00
27 . . . . 250.00
28 . . . . 250.00
29 S&K story 275.00
30 Baseball Story 275.00
31 . . . . 250.00
32 A:Dale Evans(c) 260.00
33 . . . . 250.00
34 I:Wolf. 250.00
35 . . . . 250.00
36 Sci-Fi(c),Nov.–Dec., 1949 . . . 450.00

BRAINBANX
DC/Helix, Jan., 1997
1 ELe(s),Down Upon the
   Darkness 2.50
2 ELe(s),Anna flees to the Sheol . . 2.50
3 Ele(s),Anna stranded 2.50
4 ELe(s),Anna & Logan 2.50
5 ELe(s),To Enter the Kingdom . . . 2.50
6 (of 6) 2.50

BRAVE AND THE BOLD
Aug.–Sept., 1955
1 JKu,RH,IN,I:VikingPrince,Golden
   Gladiator,Silent Knight 4,500.00

The Brave and the Bold #34
© *DC Comics, Inc.*

2 F:Viking Prince 1,800.00
3 F:Viking Prince 1,000.00
4 F:Viking Prince 1,000.00
5 B:Robin Hood 1,100.00
6 JKu,F:Robin Hood,E:Golden
   Gladiator 750.00
7 JKu,F:Robin Hood 750.00
8 JKu,F:Robin Hood 750.00
9 JKu,F:Robin Hood 750.00
10 JKu,F:Robin Hood 750.00
11 JKu,F:Viking Prince 550.00
12 JKu,F:Viking Prince 550.00
13 JKu,F:Viking Prince 550.00
14 JKu,F:Viking Prince 500.00
15 JKu,F:Viking Prince 500.00
16 JKu,F:Viking Prince 500.00
17 JKu,F:Viking Prince 500.00
18 JKu,F:Viking Prince 500.00
19 JKu,F:Viking Prince 500.00
20 JKu,F:Viking Prince 500.00
21 JKu,F:Viking Prince 500.00
22 JKu,F:Viking Prince 500.00
23 JKu,O:Viking Prince 750.00
24 JKu,E:Viking Prince,Silent
   Knight. 500.00
25 RA,I&B:Suicide Squad 650.00
26 F:Suicide Squad 450.00
27 Creature of Ghost Lake 450.00
28 I:Justice League of
   America,O:Snapper Carr . . 7,700.00
29 F:Justice League. 3,300.00
30 F:Justice League. 2,500.00
31 F:Cave Carson 600.00
32 F:Cave Carson 350.00
33 F:Cave Carson 350.00
34 JKu,I&O:S.A. Hawkman . . . 3,500.00
35 JKu:F:Hawkman 750.00
36 JKu:F:Hawkman 750.00
37 F:Suicide Squad 400.00
38 F:Suicide Squad 300.00
39 F:Suicide Squad 300.00
40 JKu,F:Cave Carson 250.00
41 F:Cave Carson 250.00
42 JKu,F:Hawkman 450.00
43 JKu,O:Hawkman 550.00
44 JKu,F:Hawkman 400.00
45 CI,F:Strange Sports 125.00
46 CI,F:Strange Sports 125.00
47 CI,F:Strange Sports 125.00
48 CI,F:Strange Sports 125.00
49 CI,F:Strange Sports 125.00
50 F:GreenArrow & JonnJ'onzz . . 275.00
51 F:Aquaman & Hawkman 275.00
52 JKu,F:Sgt.Rock 275.00

53 ATh,F:Atom & Flash 125.00
54 I&O:Teen Titans 450.00
55 F:Metal Man & Atom 100.00
56 F:Flash & J'onn J'onzz. 100.00
57 I&O:Metamorpho 275.00
58 F:Metamorpho 135.00
59 F:Batman & Green Lantern . . 150.00
60 A:Teen Titans,I:Wonder Girl . . 150.00
61 MA,O:Starman,BlackCanary . . 200.00
62 MA,O:Starman,BlackCanary . . 200.00
63 F:Supergirl&WonderWoman . . 100.00
64 F:Batman,V:Eclipso 125.00
65 DG,FMc,F:Flash & Doom
   Patrol 75.00
66 F:Metamorpho & Metal Men . . 75.00
67 CI,F:Batman & Flash 90.00
68 F:Batman,Metamorpho,Joker,
   Riddler,Penguin 125.00
69 F:Batman & Green Lantern . . . 75.00
70 F:Batman & Hawkman 75.00
71 F:Batman & Green Arrow 75.00
72 CI,F:Spectre & Flash 85.00
73 F:Aquaman & Atom 75.00
74 B:Batman T.U.,A:Metal Men . . 75.00
75 F:Spectre 75.00
76 F:Plastic Man 75.00
77 F:Atom 75.00
78 F:Wonder Woman 75.00
79 NA,F:Deadman 125.00
80 NA,DG,F:Creeper 100.00
81 NA,F:Flash 100.00
82 NA,F:Aquaman,O:Ocean
   Master 100.00
83 NA,F:Teen Titans 100.00
84 NA,F:Sgt.Rock 100.00
85 NA,F:Green Arrow 100.00
86 NA,F:Deadman 100.00
87 F:Wonder Woman 50.00
88 F:Wildcat 50.00
89 RA,F:Phantom Stranger 50.00
90 F:Adam Strange 50.00
91 F:Black Canary 50.00
92 F:Bat Squad 50.00
93 NA,House of Mystery 75.00
94 NC,F:Teen Titans 65.00
95 F:Plastic Man 65.00
96 F:Sgt.Rock. 50.00
97 NC(i),F:Wildcat 50.00
98 JAp,F:Phantom Stranger 50.00
99 NC,F:Flash 50.00
100 NA,F:Green Arrow 75.00
101 JA,F:Metamorpho 40.00
102 NA,JA,F:Teen Titans 40.00
103 FMc,F:Metal Men 25.00

The Brave and the Bold #106
© *DC Comics, Inc.*

CVA Page 54   All comics prices listed are for *Near Mint* condition.

Comics Values Annual — DC — Brave–Camelot

The Brave and the Bold #183
© DC Comics Inc.

104 JAp,F:Deadman. 25.00
105 JAp,F:Wonder Woman. 25.00
106 JAp,F:Green Arrow 25.00
107 JAp,F:Black Canary 25.00
108 JAp,F:Sgt.Rock 25.00
109 JAp,F:Demon. 25.00
110 JAp,F:Wildcat. 25.00
111 JAp,F:Joker 30.00
112 JAp,F:Mr.Miracle. 50.00
113 JAp,F:Metal Men 50.00
114 JAp,F:Aquaman 50.00
115 JAp,O:Viking Prince 50.00
116 JAp,F:Spectre 50.00
117 JAp,F:Sgt.Rock 50.00
118 JAp,F:Wildcat,V:Joker 50.00
119 JAp,F:Man-Bat 20.00
120 JAp,F:Kamandi 20.00
121 JAp,F:Metal Men 20.00
122 JAp,F:Swamp Thing. 20.00
123 JAp,F:Plastic Man 20.00
124 JAp,F:Sgt.Rock 20.00
125 JAp,F:Flash 20.00
126 JAp,F:Aquaman 20.00
127 JAp,F:Wildcat 20.00
128 JAp,F:Mr.Miracle 20.00
129 F:Green Arrow,V:Joker. 22.00
130 F:Green Arrow,V:Joker. 22.00
131 JAp,F:WonderWoman,
    A:Catwoman. 20.00
132 JAp,F:King Fu Foom 18.00
133 JAp,F:Deadman. 18.00
134 JAp,F:Green Lantern 18.00
135 JAp,F:Metal Men 18.00
136 JAp,F:Metal Men,Green Arr. . . 18.00
137 F:Demon 18.00
138 JAp,F:Mr.Miracle 18.00
139 JAp,F:Hawkman 18.00
140 JAp,F:Wonder Woman. 18.00
141 JAp,F:Bl.Canary,A:Joker 25.00
142 JAp,F:Aquaman 10.00
143 O:Human Target 10.00
144 JAp,F:Green Arrow 10.00
145 JAp,F:Phantom Stranger 10.00
146 JAp,F:E-2 Batman 10.00
147 JAp,A:Supergirl 10.00
148 JSon,JAp,F:Plastic Man 10.00
149 JAp,F:Teen Titans 12.00
150 JAp,F:Superman 10.00
151 JAp,F:Flash 12.00
152 JAp,F:Atom 10.00
153 DN,F:Red Tornado 10.00
154 JAp,F:Metamorpho 10.00
155 JAp,F:Green Lantern 10.00
156 DN,F:Dr.Fate 10.00
157 JAp,F:Kamandi 10.00
158 JAp,F:Wonder Woman. 10.00
159 JAp,A:Ras al Ghul 10.00
160 JAp,F:Supergirl 10.00
161 JAp,F:Adam Strange 10.00
162 JAp,F:Sgt.Rock 10.00
163 DG,F:Black Lightning 10.00
164 JL,F:Hawkman 10.00
165 DN,F:Man-bat 10.00
166 DG,TA,DSp,F:Black Canary
    A:Penguin,I:Nemesis 10.00
167 DC,DA,F:Blackhawk. 10.00
168 JAp,DSp,F:Green Arrow. 7.00
169 JAp,DSp,F:Zatanna 7.00
170 JA,F:Nemesis 7.00
171 JL,DSp,V:Scalphunter 7.00
172 CI,F:Firestorm 7.00
173 JAp,F:Guardians 7.00
174 JAp,F:Green Lantern 7.00
175 JAp,A:Lois Lane 7.00
176 JAp,F:Swamp Thing. 7.00
177 JAp,F:Elongated Man 7.00
178 JAp,F:Creeper 7.00
179 EC,F:Legion o/Superheroes . . . 7.00
180 JAp,F:Spectre,Nemesis 7.00
181 JAp,F:Hawk & Dove. 7.00
182 JAp,F:E-2 Robin 7.00
183 CI,V:Riddler 8.00
184 JAp,A:Catwoman. 8.00
185 F:Green Arrow 7.00
186 JAp,F:Hawkman 7.00
187 JAp,F:Metal Men 7.00
188 JAp,F:Rose & Thorn 7.00
189 JAp,A:Thorn 7.00
190 JAp,F:Adam Strange 7.00
191 JAp,V:Joker,Penguin 10.00
192 JAp,F:Superboy. 7.00
193 JAp,D:Nemesis 7.00
194 CI,F:Flash 7.00
195 JA,I:Vampire 7.00
196 JAp,F:Ragman 7.00
197 JSon,W:Earth II Batman &
    Catwoman 7.00
198 F:Karate Kid 7.00
199 RA,F:Spectre 7.00
200 DGb,JAp,A:Earth-2 Batman,I:
    Outsiders (GeoForce,Katana,Halo),
    E:Batman T.U.,final issue 15.00
Ann. #1-1969 80-page giant (2001) . 5.95
    [Limited Series]
1 SAP,Green Arrow/Butcher T.U. . . 2.50
2 SAP,A:Black Canary,Question. . . 2.50
3 SAP,Green Arrow/Butcher. 2.50
4 SAP,GA on Trial;A:Black
    Canary. 2.50
5 SAP,V:Native Canadians,I.R.A. . . 2.50

BRAVE OLD WORLD
DC/Vertigo, Dec., 1999
1 (of 4) BML,GyD,PhH,Y2K story . . 2.50
2 BML,GyD,PhH 2.50
3 BML,GyD,PhH 2.50
4 BML,GyD,PhH 2.50

BREATHTAKER
1990
1 I:Breathtaker(Chase Darrow) . . . 6.00
2 Chase Darrow captured 6.00
3 O:Breathtaker. 6.00
4 V:The Man, final issue 5.00
TPB Breathtaker. 15.00

BROOKLYN DREAMS
DC/Paradox April 2003
TPB 12.95

BROTHER POWER, THE GEEK
Sept.–Oct., 1968
1 . . . . 75.00
2 Nov.–Dec., 1968. . . . . 50.00

BUGS BUNNY
1990
1 Search for Fudd Statues. 3.50
2 V:WitchHazel 3.50
3 Bugs&Co.in outer space, final. . . 3.50
TPB Bugs Bunny & Friends: A Comic
    Celebration (2000) 14.95

Butcher #1 © DC Comics Inc.

BUTCHER, THE
[Limited Series], 1990
1 MB,I:John Butcher 3.50
2 MB,in San Francisco 3.00
3 MB,V:Corporation 3.00
4 MB,A:Green Arrow 2.50
5 MB,A:Corvus,final issue 2.25

BUZZY
1944–58
1 . . . . 350.00
2 . . . . 175.00
3 thru 5 . . . . @125.00
6 thru 10 . . . . @75.00
11 thru 15 . . . . @65.00
16 thru 25 . . . . @65.00
26 thru 35 . . . . @50.00
36 thru 45 . . . . @40.00
46 thru 77 . . . . @40.00

CAMELOT 3000
Dec., 1982
1 BB,O:Arthur,Merlin 3.50
2 BB,A:Morgan LeFay 3.00
3 BB,J:New Knights. 3.00
4 BB,V:McAllister. 3.00
5 BB,O:Morgan Le Fay 3.00
6 BB,TA,W:Arthur 3.00
7 BB,TA,R:Isolde. 3.00
8 BB,TA,D:Sir Kay 3.00
9 BB,TA,L:Sir Percival 3.00
10 BB,TA,V:Morgan Le Fay 3.00
11 BB,TA,V:Morgan Le Fay. 3.00
12 BB,TA,D:Arthur 3.00

All comics prices listed are for Near Mint condition.

Caper–Catwoman — DC — Comics Values Annual

CAPER
Oct. 2003
1 (of 12) organized crime. 2.95
2 . . . . 2.95

CAPTAIN ACTION
[Based on toy] Oct.–Nov., 1968
1 WW,I:Captain Action,Action Boy,A:Superman. 175.00
2 GK,WW, V:Krellik. 125.00
3 GK,I:Dr.Evil. 125.00
4 GK,A:Dr.Evil. 125.00
5 GK,WW,A:Matthew Blackwell . . 75.00

CAPTAIN ATOM
March, 1987
1 PB,O:Captain Atom 4.50
2 PB,C:Batman 2.50
3 PB,O:Captain Atom 2.50
4 PB,A:Firestorm 2.50
5 PB,A:Firestorm 2.50
6 PB,Dr.Spectro 2.50
7 R:Plastique 2.50
8 PB,Capt.Atom/Plastique 2.50
9 V:Bolt 2.50
10 PB,A:JLI 2.50
11 PB,A:Firestorm 2.50
12 PB,I: Major Force 2.50
13 PB,Christmas issue 2.50
14 PB,A:Nightshade 2.50
15 PB,Dr.Spectro, Major Force. . . . 2.50
16 PB,A:JLI,V:Red Tornado 2.50
17 V:Red Tornado;A:Swamp Thing,JLI 2.50
18 PB,A:Major Force 2.50
19 PB,Drug War 2.50
20 FMc,BlueBeetle 2.50
21 PB,A:Plastique,Nightshade . . . 2.50
22 PB,A:MaxLord,Nightshade, Plastique 2.50
23 PB,V:The Ghost 2.50
24 PB,Invasion X-over 2.50
25 PB,Invvasion X-over 2.50
26 A:JLA,Top Secret,pt.1 . . . . 2.50
27 A:JLA,Top Secret,pt.2 . . . . 2.50
28 V:Ghost, Top Secret,pt.3 . . . . . 2.50
29 RT,Captain Atom cleared (new direction) 2.50
30 Janus Directive #11,V:Black Manta. 2.50
31 RT,Capt. Atom's Powers,
A:Rocket Red. 2.50
32 Loses Powers 2.50
33 A:Batman. 3.00
34 C:JLE 2.50
35 RT,Secret o/t Silver Shield, A:Major Force 2.50
36 RT,Las Vegas Battle,A:Major Force 2.50
37 I:New Atomic Skull. 2.50
38 RT,A:Red Tornado, Black Racer 2.50
39 RT,A:Red Tornado 2.50
40 RT,V:Kobra 2.50
41 RT,A:Black Racer, Red Tornado 2.50
42 RT,A:Phantom Stranger,Red Tornado,Black Racer, Death from Sandman 2.50
43 RT,V:Nekron 2.50
44 RT,V:Plastique 2.50
45 RT,A:The Ghost,I:Ironfire 2.50
46 RT,V:Superman 2.50
47 RT,A:SupermanV:Ghost 2.50
48 RT,R:Red Tornado 2.50
49 RT,Plastique on trial 2.50
50 RT,V:The Ghost,DoubleSize. . . 3.00
51 RT. 2.50
52 RT,Terror on RTE.91' 2.50
53 RT,A:Aquaman 2.50
54 RT,A:Rasputin,Shadowstorm . . 2.50
55 RT,Inside Quantum Field 2.50
56 RT,Quantum Field cont. 2.50
57 RT,V:ShadowStorm, Quantum.Field 2.50
Ann.#1 I:Maj.Force 2.50
Ann.#2 A:RocketRed,Maj.Force . . . 2.50

CAPTAIN CARROT
March, 1982
1 RA,A:Superman,Starro 2.50
2 AA 2.50
3 thru 19 . . . . @2.50
20 A:Changeling,Nov., 1983 . . . . . 2.50

CAPTAIN STORM
May-June, 1964
1 IN(c),Killer Hunt 75.00
2 IN(c),First Shot-Last Shot 50.00
3 JKu,Death of a PT Boat 50.00
4 IN(c),First Command-Last Command 50.00
5 IN(c), Killer Torpedo 50.00
6 JKu,IN(c),Medals for an Ocean . 50.00
7 IN(c),A Bullet For The General . 50.00
8 IN(c), Death of A Sub. 50.00
9 IN(c),Sink That Flattop 50.00
10 IN(c),Only The Last Man Lives . 50.00
11 IN(c),Ride a Hot Torpedo 50.00
12 JKu(c),T.N.T. Tea Party Abroad PT 47 . . . . 50.00
13 JKu,Yankee Banzai 50.00
14 RH(c),Sink Capt. Storm 50.00
15 IN(c),My Enemy-My Friend . . . 50.00
16 IN(c),Battle of the Stinging Mosquito 50.00
17 IN(c),First Shot for a Dead Man 50.00
18 March-April, 1967 . . . . 50.00

CARTOON CARTOONS
Jan., 2001
1 thru 24 from TV Shows . . . . . . @2.50

CARTOON NETWORK PRESENTS
Warner Bros./DC June, 1997
1: From TV Shows. 4.50
2: thru 24 . . . . @2.50

CARTOON NETWORK STARRING
Warner Bros./DC, 1999
1 From TV Shows 4.00
2 thru 18 . . . . @2.50

CATWOMAN
[Limited Series], 1989
1 O:Catwoman. 11.00
2 Catwoman'sSister kidnapped . . . 8.00
3 Battle 7.00
4 Final,V:Batman 7.00

[Regular Series], 1993
0 JBa,O:Catwoman 3.50
1 B:JDy(s),JBa,DG,A:Bane 5.00
2 JBa,DG,A:Bane 3.50
3 JBa,DG,at Santa Prisca 3.50
4 JBa,DG,Bane's Secret 3.00
5 JBa,V:Ninjas 3.00
6 JBa,A:Batman 3.00
7 JBa,A:Batman 3.00
8 JBa,V:Zephyr 3.00
9 JBa,V:Zephyr 3.00
10 JBa,V:Arms Dealer 3.00
11 JBa 3.00
12 JBa,Knights End #6,A:Batman . . 5.00
13 JBa,Knights End,Aftermath#2 . . 3.00
14 JBa,Zero Hour 3.00
15 JBa,new path. 3.00
16 JBa,Island forterss 3.00
17 . . . . 3.00
18 . . . . 3.00
19 Amazonia 3.00
20 Hollywood 3.00
21 JBa(c&a)V:Movie Monster [new Miraweb format begins] . . 2.50
22 JBa(c&a) Family Ties,pt.1 . . . . 2.50
23 Family Ties,pt.2 . . . . 2.50
24 . . . . 2.50
25 A:Robin,Psyba-Rats. 3.00
26 AIG,JBa,The Secret of the Universe,pt.2 (of 3). 2.50
27 CDi,Underworld Unleashed tie-in 2.50
28 CDi,Catwoman enlists help 2.50
29 CDi,A:Penguin 2.50
30 . . . . 2.50
31 . . . . 3.00
32 CDi,JBa,Contagion,pt.9 . . . . . . 3.00
33 CDi,JBa,Hellhound,pt.1 . . . . . . 2.50
34 CDi,JBa,Hellhound,pt.2 (of 3). . . 2.50
35 CDi,JBa 2.75
36 CDi,JBa, Legacy, pt.2 x-over . . 2.50
37 CDi,JBa, Panara, the Leopard Woman 2.50
38 DgM(s),JBa,MPn,Catwoman, Year One, pt.1 (of 3). 2.50
39 DgM(s),JBa,MPn,Catwoman, Year One, pt. 2 . . . . 2.50
40 DgM(s),JBa,MPn,Catwoman, Year One, pt. 3 . . . . 2.50
41 DgM(s),JBa,I:MorelandMcShane 2.50
42 DgM(s),JBa,RedFangClaw,pt.1 . 2.50
43 DgM(s),JBa,RedFangClaw,pt.2 . 2.50
44 DgM(s),JBa,Red FangClaw,pt.3 . 2.50
45 DgM(s),JBa,Nine Deaths of the Cat. 2.50
46 DgM(s),JBa,F:Two Face,pt.1 . . . 2.50
47 DgM(s),JBa,F:Two Face,pt.2 . . . 2.50
48 DgM(s),JBa,V:Morella,pt.1 . . . . 2.50
49 DgM(s),JBa,V:Morella,pt. 2 . . . 2.50
50 DgM(s),JBa,V:Cybercat 3.00
50a metallic cover, collectors ed. . . . 3.00
51 DgM(s),JBa,F:Huntress,pt.1 . . . 2.50
52 DgM(s),JBa,F:Huntress,pt.2 . . . 2.50
53 DgM(s),JBa,F:identity learned . . 2.50
54 JBa,improving security. 2.50

Captain Atom #43
© DC Comics, Inc.

Comics Values Annual — DC — Catwoman–Challengers

Catwoman #2 © DC Comics Inc.

CATWOMAN
Nov., 2001
1 MiA,R:Selina Kyle.............7.00
2 MiA,serial murders............4.00
3 MiA,Selina undercover........3.00
4 MiA,V:Serial killer..............3.00
5 Selina & Holly..................2.50
6 F:Holly.............................2.50
7 Holly in danger.................2.50
8 RBr,East End's Crooked Cops..2.50
9 RBr,Disguises..................2.50
10 RBr,Death's Row killer......2.50
11 F:Slam Bradley................2.50
12 F:Slam Bradley, Bruce Wayne..2.50
13 F:Slam Bradley, Holly........2.50
14 Holly.............................2.50
15 V:Black Mask..................2.50
16 V:Black Mask..................2.50
17 No Easy Way Down,pt.1....2.50
18 No Easy Way Down,pt.2....2.50
19 No Easy Way Down,pt.3....2.50
20 A: Wildcat......................2.50
21 V:Captain Cold................2.50
22 V:Captain Cold................2.50
23 Opal City........................2.50
24 Wild Ride, concl..............2.50
25 JP,PG,back to Gotham......2.50
TPB The Dark End of the Street..12.95
TPB Crooked Little Town.....14.95
TPB Selina's Big Score........17.95
Spec. Secret Files #1..........4.95

CATWOMAN: GUARDIAN OF GOTHAM
1999
1 (of 2) Elseworlds,V:Bat-Man....6.00
2 DgM,JBa.........................6.00

CATWOMAN/WILDCAT
June, 1998
1 (of 4) CDi,TP,SCi,BSf,
   V:Claw Hammer...............3.00
2 CDi,BSt,TP,SCi,BSf............3.00
3 CDi,BSt,TP,SCi,BSf............3.00
4 CDi,BSt,TP,SCi,BSf............3.00

CENTURIONS
June, 1987
1 DH,V:Doc Terror................2.50
2 DH,O:Centurions...............2.50
3 DH,V:Doc Terror................2.50
4 DH,Sept., 1987..................2.50

CHAIN GANG WAR
1993–94
1 I:Chain Gang....................3.00
2 V:8-Ball..........................2.50
3 C:Deathstroke..................2.50
4 C:Deathstroke..................2.50
5 Embossed(c),A:Deathstroke..3.00
6 A:Deathstroke,Batman.......2.50
7 V:Crooked Man.................2.50
8 B:Crooked Man.................2.50
9 V:Crooked Man.................2.50
10 A:Deathstroke,C:Batman...2.50
11 A:Batman......................2.50
12 E:Crooked Man,D:Chain Gang,
   Final Issue...................2.50

CHALLENGERS OF THE UNKNOWN
1958–78
1 JK&JK(c),The Man Who
   Tampered With Infinity...3,500.00
2 JK&JK(c),The Monster

55 JBa,..................................2.50
56 JBa,Cataclysm x-over,pt.6....2.50
57 JBa,Cataclysm,V:Poison Ivy..2.50
58 JBa,F:Scarecrow, pt.1..........2.50
59 JBa,F:Scarecrow, pt.2..........2.50
60 JBa,F:Scarecrow, pt.3..........2.50
61 JBa,Bank robbery...............2.50
62 JBa,A:Nemesis..................2.50
63 JBa,A:Batman & Joker, pt.1..2.50
64 JBa,A:Batman & Joker, pt.2..2.50
65 JBa,A:Batman & Joker, pt.3..2.50
66 JBa,I'll Take Manhattan,pt.1..2.50
67 JBa,I'll Take Manhattan,pt.2..2.50
68 JBa,I'll Take Manhattan,pt.3..2.50
69 JBa,I'll Take Manhattan,pt.4..2.50
70 JBa,I'll Take Manhattan,pt.5..2.50
71 JBa,I'll Take Manhattan,pt.6..2.50
72 JOs(s),JBa,A:Batman..........2.50
73 JOs(s),JBa,No Man's Land....2.50
74 JOs(s),JBa,No Man's Land....2.50
75 JOs(s),JBa,No Man's Land....2.50
76 JOs(s),JBa,No Man's Land....2.50
77 JOs(s),JBa,No Man's Land....2.50
78 ....2.50
79 A:Batman........................2.50
80 going to jail.....................2.50
81 solitary confinement..........2.50
82 payback time...................2.50
83 A:Batman,CommissionerGordon..2.25
84 F:Harley Quinn.................2.25
85 anger & revenge...............2.25
86 V:Banner........................2.25
87 NSH, from Catwoman's past..2.25
88 V:Banner........................2.25
89 This issue: Batman dies!......2.25
90 Officer Down x-over,pt.4......2.25
91 Second Catwoman.............2.25
92 JFM(s), V:Scarecrow,pt.1.....2.25
93 JFM(s), V:Scarecrow,pt.2.....2.25
94 JFM(s), final issue.............2.25
Ann.#1 Elseworlds Story,A:Ra's Al
   Ghul.............................3.50
Ann.#2 JBa(c&a) Year One Annuals,
   Young Selina Kyle............4.50
Ann.#3 Legends of the Dead Earth..3.50
Ann.#4 Pulp Heroes (Macabre)..4.50
Spec. Catwoman Defiant,TGr,DG,
   V:Mr.Handsome..............6.00
Spec. Catwoman Plus, LKa,AWi,
   ALa, F:Screamqueen (1997)..3.00
Spec.#1,000,000 JBa, on prison
   planet of Pluto................2.00
TPB The Catfile, rep.#15–#19....10.00

   Maker..........................1,200.00
3 JK&JK(c),The Secret of the
   Sorcerer's Mirror..........1,000.00
4 JK,WW,JK(c),The Wizard of
   Time............................750.00
5 JK,WW&JK(c),The Riddle of
   the Star-Stone..............750.00
6 JK,WW,JK(c),Captives of
   the Space Circus..........750.00
7 JK,WW,JK(c),The Isle of
   No Return...................750.00
8 JK,WW,JK&WW(c),The
   Prisoners of the Robot Planet..750.00
9 The Plot To Destroy Earth....400.00
10 The Four Faces of Doom....400.00
11 The Creatures From The
   Forbidden World...........275.00
12 The Three Clues To Sorcery..275.00
13 The Prisoner of the
   Tiny Space Ball.............275.00
14 O: Multi Man.................275.00
15 Lady Giant and the Beast..275.00
16 Prisoners of the Mirage World..200.00
17 The Secret of the
   Space Capsules............200.00
18 Menace of Mystery Island..200.00
19 The Alien Who Stole a Planet..200.00
20 Multi-Man Strikes Back....200.00
21 Weird World That Didn't Exist..200.00
22 The Thing In
   Challenger Mountain......200.00
23 The Island In The Sky.......100.00
24 The Challengers Die At Dawn..100.00
25 Captives of the Alien Hunter..100.00
26 Death Crowns the
   Challenge King..............100.00
27 Master of the Volcano Men..100.00
28 The Riddle of the
   Faceless Man................100.00
29 Four Roads to Doomsday..100.00
30 Multi-Man...Villain Turned
   Hero.............................100.00
31 O:Challengers................125.00
32 One Challenger Must Die....50.00
33 Challengers Meet Their Master..50.00
34 Beachhead, USA.............50.00
35 War Against The Moon Beast..50.00
36 Giant In Challenger Mountain..50.00
37 Triple Terror of Mr. Dimension..50.00
38 Menace the Challengers Made..50.00
39 Phantom of the Fair..........50.00
40 Super-Powers of the
   Challengers...................50.00
41 The Challenger Who Quit....40.00

Challengers of the Unknown #52 © DC Comics Inc.

All comics prices listed are for *Near Mint* condition.

Challengers–Cinder / DC / Comics Values Annual

DC COMICS

42 The League of
  Challenger-Haters 40.00
43 New look begins 40.00
44 The Curse of the Evil Eye 40.00
45 Queen of the
  Challenger-Haters 40.00
46 Strange Schemes of the
  Gargoyle 40.00
47 The Sinister Sponge 40.00
48 A:Doom Patrol 40.00
49 Tyrant Who Owned the World . 40.00
50 Final Hours for the
  Challengers 40.00
51 A:Sea Devil 40.00
52 Two Are Dead - Two To Go ... 40.00
53 Who is the Traitor Among Us? . 40.00
54 War of the Sub-Humans...... 40.00
55 D:Red Ryan................ 40.00
56 License To Kill 40.00
57 Kook And The Kilowatt Killer .. 40.00
58 Live Till Tomorrow 40.00
59 Seekeenakee - The Petrified
  Giant 40.00
60 R:Red Ryan................ 40.00
61 Robot Hounds of Chang 40.00
62 Legion of the Weird 40.00
63 None Shall Escape the
  Walking Evil 40.00
64 JKu(c),Invitation to a Hanging . 40.00
65 The Devil's Circus 25.00
66 JKu(c),Rendezvous With
  Revenge 25.00
67 NA(c),The Dream Killers 25.00
68 NA(c),One of Us is a Madman . 25.00
69 JKu(c),I:Corinna............ 25.00
70 NA(c),Scream of Yesterdays .. 25.00
71 NC(c),When Evil Calls....... 25.00
72 NA(c),A Plague of Darkness... 25.00
73 NC(c),Curse of the Killer
  Time Forgot 25.00
74 GT&NA(c),A:Deadman....... 40.00
75 JK(c),Ultivac Is Loose 15.00
76 JKu(c),The Traitorous
  Challenger 15.00
77 JK(c),Menace of the
  Ancient Vials 15.00
78 JK(c),The Island of No Return . 15.00
79 JK(c),The Monster Maker.... 15.00
80 NC(c),The Day The Earth
  Blew Up 15.00
81 MN&NA(c),Multi-Man's
  Master Plan 12.00
82 MN&NA(c),Swamp Thing..... 12.00
83 Seven Doorways to Destiny ... 12.00
84 To Save A Monster......... 12.00
85 The Creature From The End
  Of Time 12.00
86 The War At Time's End 12.00
87 final issue, July, 1978........ 12.00

CHALLENGERS OF THE UNKNOWN
[Mini-Series], 1991

1 BB(c) In The Spotlight 2.50
2 .... 2.50
3 Challengers `Split Up'........ 2.50
4 `Separate Ways'............. 2.50
5 Moffet...................... 2.50
6 GK(c),Challengers reunited.... 2.50
7 AAd(c),June pregnant........ 2.50
8 final issue.................. 2.50

CHALLENGERS OF THE UNKNOWN
1997

1 StG(s),JPL................. 3.00
2 StG(s),LKa,JPL,SMa,Zombies . 2.50
3 StG(s),JPL,death of Challenger . 2.50

4 StG&LKa(s),JPL,SMa,
  O:Challengers 2.50
5 StG&LKa(s)JPL,SMa, V:The
  Fearslayer 2.50
6 StG(s),JPL,SMa,Convergence
  pt. 3 x-over............... 2.50
7 StG(s),JPL,PastPerfect,pt.1 ... 2.50
8 StG(s),JPL,PastPerfect,pt.2 ... 2.50
9 StG(s),JPL,PastPerfect,pt.3 ... 2.50
10 StG(s),JIT,F:Brenda Ruskin 2.50
11 StG(s),JPL,in Gothan, pt.1 .... 2.50
12 StG(s),JPL,in Gothan, pt.2 .... 2.50
13 StG(s),F:Marlon Corbett....... 2.50
14 .... 2.50
15 StG(s),JPL,Millennium Giants
  pt. 3, x-over 2.75
16 StG(s),JPL,MZ, original Chalis .. 2.75
17 StG(s),JPL,disappearances ... 2.75
18 StG(s),DRo,MZ, final issue 2.75

CHASE
Dec., 1997

1 JWi,MGy,from Batman #550 .... 2.50
2 JWi,MGy................... 2.50
3 JWi,MGy,Rocket Reds 2.50
4 JWi,MGy,F:Teen Titans....... 2.50
5 JWi,MGy,flashback story...... 2.50
6 JWi,MGy,Chase's past 2.50
7 JWi,Shadowing the Bat,pt.1 ... 2.50
8 JWi,Shadowing the Bat,pt.2 ... 2.50
9 JWi,MBr,MGy,A:Green Lantern .. 2.50
Spec.#1,000,000 Final Issue...... 2.50

Checkmate #3 © DC Comics, Inc.

CHECKMATE
April, 1988

1 From Vigilante & Action Comics . 3.00
2 Chicago Bombings cont........ 2.50
3 V:Terrorist Right 2.50
4 V:Crime Lords Abroad,B.U.Story
  `Training of a Knight' begins ... 2.50
5 Renegade nation of Quarac 2.50
6 Secret Arms Deal 2.50
7 Checkmate Invades Quarac 2.50
8 Consequences-Quarac Invasion . 2.50
9 Checkmate's security in doubt ... 2.50
10 V:Counterfeiting Ring......... 2.50
11 Invasion X-over 2.50
12 Invasion Aftermath extra 2.50
13 CommanderH.Stein's vacation .. 2.50
14 R:Blackthorn................ 2.50
15 Janus Directive #1........... 2.50
16 Janus Directive #3........... 2.50
17 Janus Directive #6........... 2.50

18 Janus Directive #9........... 2.50
19 Reorganization of Group 2.50
20 `Shadow of Bishop'
  A:Peacemaker,pt.1 .... 2.50
21 Peacemaker behind Iron
  Curtain,pt.2 .... 2.50
22 Mystery of Bishop Cont.,pt.3 ... 2.50
23 European Scientists
  Suicides,pt.4 .... 2.50
24 Bishop Mystery cont.,pt.5...... 2.50
25 Bishop's Identity Revealed..... 2.50
26 Mazarin kidnaps H.Stein's kids . 2.50
27 Stein rescue attempt,I:Cypher .. 2.50
28 A:Cypher, Bishop-Robots...... 2.50
29 A:Cypher,Blackthorn 2.50
30 Irish Knight W.O'Donnell/British
  Knight L.Hawkins team-up 2.50
31 V:Cypher International 2.50
32 V:Cypher International 2.50
33 final issue (32 pages)......... 2.50

CHIAROSCURO: THE PRIVATE LIVES OF LEONARDO DaVINCI
DC/Vertigo, 1995–96

1 Biographical, Adult 2.50
2 Two of Da Vinci Sisters........ 2.50
3 .... 2.50
4 F:Salari 3.00
5 Crazy Leonardo 3.00
6 Salai schemes,O:Mona Lisa ... 3.00
7 V:Borgia & Machiavelli 3.00
8 daVinci returns to Florence..... 3.00
9 .... 3.00
10 finale...................... 3.00

CHILDREN'S CRUSADE
DC/Vertigo, 1993–94

1 NGa(s),CBa,MkB(i),F:Rowland,
  Payne (From Sandman)...... 4.75
2 NGa(s),AaK(s),JaD(s),PSj,A:Tim
  Hunter,Suzy,Maxine,final issue . 4.50

CHRISTMAS WITH THE SUPER-HEROES
1988–89

1 JBy(c)..................... 5.00
2 PC,GM,JBy,NKu,DG A:Batman
  Superman,Deadman,(last
  Supergirl appearance) 4.00

CHRONOS
Jan., 1998

1 JFM,PGn,SL,Time Travel 2.50
2 JFM,PGn,SL................. 2.50
3 JFM,PGn,SL, in 1873......... 2.50
4 JFM,PGn,SL,in Chronopolis 2.50
5 JFM,PGn,DHz,SL,WalkerGabriel 2.50
6 JFM,PGn,Tattooed man 2.50
7 JFM,PGn,DRo,SL,Star City..... 2.50
8 JFM,PGn,DRo,SL,
  V:Metrognomes 2.50
9 JFM(s),PGn,SL, The Man
  Who Chose Not to Exist...... 2.50
10 JFM(s),PGn,SL,Forever Engin .. 2.50
11 JFM(s),PGn,SL final issue 2.50
Spec.#1,000,000 JFM(s) Steals
  time gauntlets.............. 2.50

CINDER & ASHE
March, 1988

1 JL,I:Cinder & Ashe 2.50
2 JL,Viet Nam Flashbacks........ 2.50
3 JL,Truth About Lacey revealed .. 2.50
4 JL,final issue, June, 1988 ...... 2.50

CVA Page 58 All comics prices listed are for *Near Mint* condition.

CINNAMON: EL CICLO
Aug. 2003
1 (of 5) RbC, New West. 2.50
2 thru 4 RbC,HC(c) . . . . @2.50

CLASH
1991
1 AKu,I:Joe McLash(b/w) 5.00
2 AKu,Panja-Rise to Power 5.00
3 AKu,V:Archons,conclusion 5.00

CLAW THE UNCONQUERED
May-June, 1975
1 . . . . 15.00
2 . . . . 8.00
3 Nudity panel 10.00
4 . . . . 8.00
5 . . . . 8.00
6 . . . . 8.00
7 . . . . 8.00
8 KG 8.00
9 KG/BL,Origin 8.00
10 KG 8.00
11 KG 8.00
12 KG/BL,Aug.–Sept., 1978. . . . 8.00

COMET, THE
Impact, 1991–92
1 TL,I&O:Comet I:Applejack, Victoria Johnson, Ben Lee 3.00
2 TL,A:Applejack,Lance Perry . . . 2.50
3 TL,V:Anti-nuclear terrorists . . . 2.50
4 TL,I&V:Black Hood,I:Inferno . . . 2.50
5 V:Cyborg Soldier 2.50
6 TL,I:The Hangman 2.50
7 `Press Problems' 2.50
8 TL,Comet ID discovered 2.50
9 TL,`Bad Judgment' 2.50
10 Fly/Comet T.U.,V:Dolphus . . . 2.50
11 V:Inferno 2.50
12 V:Inferno 2.50
13 O:Comet's Powers. 2.50
14 O:Comet's Powers Pt.2 . . . . . 2.50
15 Rob finds his mother 2.50
16 V:Aliens 2.50
17 "Shocking Truth" 2.50
18 Last Issue 2.50
Ann.#1 Earthquest,w/trading card . . 2.50

CODENAME: KNOCKOUT
DC/Vertigo, April, 2001
0 sexy spy thriller satire 3.00
1 MFm,JCh,Devil You Say,pt.1. . . . 3.00
1a variant JCh(c) (1:2). 3.00
2 MFm,JCh,Devil You Say,pt.2. . . . 2.50
3 MFm,Little Orphan Angela 2.50
4 MFm,St. Grace Under Fire 2.50
5 MFm,Arms & Legs for Hostages . 2.50
6 MFm,Arms & Legs for Hostages . 2.50
7 MFm,Go-Go-A-Go-Go 2.50
8 MFm,A is for Anarchy 2.50
9 JP,ACo,Enigma Variations 2.50
10 Undressed to Kill,pt.1. . . . . 2.50
11 Undressed to Kill,pt.2. . . . . 2.50
12 Undressed to Kill,pt.3. . . . . 2.50
13 Fleshback 1932:Roma. 2.50
14a JP,JLe(c) 2.50
14b variant JSC(c) 2.50
15 EBe,F:Whole cast 2.50
16 EBe,Amok in America,pt.1 . . . 2.75
17 EBe,Amok in America,pt.2 . . . 2.75
18 EBe,Amok in America,pt.3 . . . 2.75
19 Fleshback '69 . . . . 2.75
20 Rebel Yell 2.75
21 Secrets & Thighs,pt.1 . . . . 2.75

Comic Cavalcade #6
© DC Comics Inc.

22 Secrets & Thighs,pt.2 . . . . 2.75
23 final issue 2.75

COMIC CAVALCADE
1942–43
1 Green Lantern, Flash, Wildcat, Wonder Woman, Black Pirate. 14,000.00
2 ShM,B:Mutt & Jeff 3,000.00
3 ShM,B:HotHarrigan,Sorcerer 2,100.00
4 Gay Ghost, A:Scribby, A:Red Tornado. 2,000.00
5 Green Lantern, Flash Wonder Woman. 1,900.00
6 Flash, Wonder Woman Green Lantern 1,500.00
7 A:Red Tornado, E:Scribby . . 1,500.00
8 Flash, Wonder Woman Green Lantern 1,500.00
9 Flash, Wonder Woman Green Lantern 1,500.00
10 Flash, Wonder Woman Green Lantern 1,500.00
11 Flash, Wonder Woman Green Lantern 1,200.00
12 E:Red, White & Blue 1,200.00
13 A:Solomon Grundy 2,000.00
14 Flash, Wonder Woman, Green Lantern 1,200.00
15 B:Johnny Peril 1,300.00
16 Flash, Wonder Woman, Green Lantern 1,200.00
17 Flash, Wonder Woman, Green Lantern 1,200.00
18 Flash, Wonder Woman, Green Lantern 1,200.00
19 Flash, Wonder Woman, Green Lantern 1,200.00
20 Flash, Wonder Woman, Green Lantern 1,200.00
21 Flash, Wonder Woman, Green Lantern 1,200.00
22 A:Atom 1,200.00
23 A:Atom 1,200.00
24 A:Solomon Grundy 1,500.00
25 A:Black Canary 1,000.00
26 ATh, E:Mutt & Jeff 1,000.00
27 ATh,ATh(c) 1,000.00
28 ATh E:Flash, Wonder Woman Green Lantern 1,000.00
29 E:Johnny Peril. 1,200.00
30 RG,B:Fox & Crow 500.00
31 thru 39 RG . . . . @300.00
40 RG,ShM 200.00
41 thru 49 RG,ShM . . . . @175.00
50 thru 62 RG,ShM . . . . @225.00
63 RG,ShM, July, 1954 . . . . 400.00

CONGO BILL
Aug.–Sept., 1954
1 . . . . 2,000.00
2 . . . . 1,500.00
3 thru 6 . . . . @1,500.00
7 Aug.–Sept.,1955 . . . . 1,500.00

CONGO BILL
DC/Vertigo, 1999
1 (of 4) RCo(c) 3.00
2 RCo(c) 3.00
3 RCo(c) 3.00
4 . . . . 3.00

CONGORILLA
1992–93
1 R:Congo Bill 2.50
2 BB(c),V:Congo Bill 2.50
3 BB(c),V:Congo Bill 2.50
4 BB(c),V:Congo Bill 2.50

CONJURORS
1999
1 (of 3) CDi(s),EB, Elseworlds . . . 3.00
2 CDi(s),EB, ... 3.00
3 CDi(s),EB, concl. 3.00

Conqueror of the Barren Earth #4
© DC Comics Inc.

CONQUEROR OF THE BARREN EARTH
1985
1 thru 4 . . . . @3.00

COOL WORLD
1992
1 Prequel to Movie 2.25
2 Movie Adapt. 2.25
3 Movie Adapt. 2.25
4 . . . . 2.25

COPS
1988–89
1 PB,O:Cops,double-size. 3.50

Cops–Dale

2 PB,V:Big Boss 2.50
3 PB,RT,V:Dr.Bad Vibes 2.50
4 BS,A:Sheriff Sundown 2.50
5 PB,Blitz the Robo-Dog 2.50
6 PB,A:Ms.Demeaner 2.50
7 PB,A:Tramplor 2.50
8 PB,V:BigBoss & Ally 2.50
9 PB,Cops Trapped 2.50
10 PB,Dr.Bad Vibes becomes
 Dr.Goodvibes 2.50
11 PB,V:Big Boss 2.50
12 PB,V:Dr.Badvibe's T.H.U.G.S. . . 2.50
13 Berserko/Ms.Demeanor
 marriage proposal 2.50
14 A:Buttons McBoom-Boom 2.50
15 Cops vs. Crooks, final issue. . . . 2.50

COSMIC BOY
Dec., 1986

1 KG,EC,Legends tie-in 2.50
2 KG,EC,'Is History Destiny' 2.50
3 KG,EC,'Past,Present,Future' . . . 2.50
4 KG,EC,Legends 2.50

COSMIC ODYSSEY
1988

1 MMi,A:Superman,Batman,John
 Stewart,Starfire,J'onn J'onzz,
 NewGods,Demon,JSn story . . . 5.00
2 MMi,'Disaster'(low dist) 5.00
3 MMi,Return to New Genesis 5.00
4 MMi,A:Dr.Fate, final 5.00
TPB Cosmic Odyssey (2003) 19.95

COWBOY WALLY SHOW, THE
DC/Vertigo June 2003

TPB KB 14.95

Creature Commandos #1
© DC Comics, Inc.

CREATURE COMMANDOS
March, 2000

1 (of 8) TT,SEa 2.50
2 TT,SEa,V:Saturna 2.50
3 TT,SEa, ... 2.50
4 TT,SEa, ... 2.50
5 TT,SEa,F:Claw 2.50
6 TT,SEa,V:Saturna 2.50
7 TT,SEa,V:Claw 2.50
8 TT,SEa,War Movie, concl. 2.50

DC

CREEPER, THE
Oct., 1997

1 LKa,SMa,SB,R:Creeper 3.00
2 LKa,SMa,SB,A:Dr. Skolos. 3.00
3 LKa,SMa,SB,V:Proteus. 3.00
4 LKa,SMa,SB. 3.00
5 LKa,SMa,SB, new job. 3.00
6 LKa,SMa,SB, strange meals 3.00
7 LKa,SMa,SB,F:Joker, pt.1 . . . . . . 3.00
8 LKa,SMa,SB,F:Joker, pt.2 . . . . . . 3.00
9 DAn,ALa,All-star issue 3.00
10 LKa,SB,Jack Ryder 3.00
11 LKa,SB,SMa,Creeper splits
 again 3.00
Spec.#1,000,000 LKa,SB,final issue 3.00

CRIMSON AVENGER
1988

1 Mini-series 2.50
2 V:Black Cross. 2.50
3 'V:Killers of the Dark Cross' 2.50
4 'V:Dark Cross,final issue 2.50

CRISIS ON INFINITE EARTHS
April, 1985

1 B:MWn(s),GP,DG,I:Pariah,I&O:Alex
 Luthor,D:Crime Syndicate 18.00
2 GP,DG,V:Psycho Pirate,
 A:Joker,Batman 12.00
3 GP,DG,D:Losers 12.00
4 GP,D:Monitor,I:2nd Dr.Light 10.00
5 GP,JOy,I:Anti-Monitor 10.00
6 GP,JOy,I:2nd Wildcat,A:Fawcett,
 Quality & Charlton heroes 10.00
7 GP,JOy,DG,D:Supergirl 25.00
8 GP,JOy,D:1st Flash 22.00
9 GP,JOy,D:Aquagirl 10.00
10 GP,JOy,D:Psimon,A:Spectre . . 10.00
11 GP,JOy,D:Angle Man 12.00
12 E:MWn(s),GP,JOy,D:Huntress,Kole,
 Kid Flash becomes 2nd Flash,
 D:Earth 2 . . . . 15.00
TPB MWn,GP,DG,JOy,(2001) . . . 29.95

CRISIS ON MULTIPLE EARTHS
July, 2002

TPB Justice League rep. 14.95
TPB Vol. 2 . . . . 14.95

CRUCIBLE
Impact, 1993

1 JQ,F:The Comet 2.50
2 JQ,A:Black Hood,Comet 2.50
3 JQ,Comet Vs.Black Hood 2.50
4 JQ,V:Tomorrow Men 2.50
5 JQ,Black Hod vs Shield 2.50
6 JQ,V:The Crucible 2.50

CRUEL AND UNUSUAL
DC/Vertigo, 1999

1 (of 4) JaD&TPe(s),JMC,satire . . . 3.00
2 thru 4 JaD&TPe(s),JMC . . . . . @3.00

CRUSADERS
Impact, May, 1992

1 DJu(c),I:Crusaders,inc Trading
 cards 2.50
2 V:Kalathar 2.50
3 V:Kalathar 2.50
4 Crusaders form as group 2.50
5 V:Cyber-Punks 2.50
6 V:Cyborg Villains 2.50

Comics Values Annual

Crusaders #7
© DC Comics, Inc.

7 Woj,Low,F:Fireball 2.50
8 Last Issue. 2.50

CRUSADES, THE
DC/Vertigo, March, 2001

1 KJo,F:Venus. 5.00
2 KJo,V:Dark Ages Knight 3.50
3 KJo,MBu,in San Francisco 3.50
4 KJo,MBu,Anton Marx 3.00
5 KJo,Marx eats crow 3.00
6 KJo,second Crusade 3.00
7 KJo,V:The Knight 3.00
8 KJo,Knight's lair 3.00
9 KJo,Godfrey 3.00
10 KJo,sex, sin, subjugation 3.00
11 KJo,origin of the Knight? 3.00
12 KJo,Knight's hidden enclave . . 3.00
13 KJo,Third Crusade begins 3.00
14 KJo,Ash Wednesday Killer 3.00
15 KJo,Ash Wednesday Killer 3.00
16 KJo,Ash Wednesday Killings . . 3.00
17 KJo,Venus Kostopikas 3.00
18 KJo,Shockjock Anton 3.00
19 KJo,back to Medieval times . . . 3.00
20 KJo,final issue 3.00
Spec. Urban Decree, KJo,48-page . 3.95

CYBERELLA
DC/Helix, Sept., 1996

1 HC(s),DCn, ... 2.25
2 HC(s),DCn,Secret history
 revealed 2.25
3 HC(s),DCn,Sunny goes on
 rampage. 2.25
4 HC(s),DCn,Attack on MacroCorp 2.25
5 HC(s),DCn,V:Army of
 Necronauts. 2.25
6 HC(s),DCn, ... 2.25
7 HC(s),DCn,Trip to Hell 2.25
8 HC(s),DCn,V:BTIII, concl. 2.50
9 DCn, The Informers 2.25
10 HC(s),DCn,Wuvzums,
 Digitina,pt.1 . . . . 2.25
11 HC(s),DCn,Wuvzums,pt.2 . . . . 2.25
12 HC(s),final issue 2.50

DALE EVANS COMICS
1948–52

1 Ph(c),ATh,B:Sierra Smith . . . 1,200.00
2 Ph(c),ATh 600.00
3 ATh 350.00

All comics prices listed are for *Near Mint* condition.

Comics Values Annual — DC — Dale–DC Comics

4 thru 11 .... @325.00
12 thru 24 .... @150.00

DAMAGE
1994–96
1 I:Damage,V:Metallo 4.00
2 V:Symbolix 3.00
3 V:Troll 3.00
4 V:Troll 3.00
5 A:New Titans,V:Baron 3.00
6 Zero Hour,A:New Titans 3.00
7 Trial 3.00
8 Fragments,pt.1 .... 3.00
9 Fragments,pt.2 .... 3.00
10 Fragments,pt.3 .... 3.00
11 Fragments,pt.4 .... 3.00
12 Fragments,pt.5 .... 3.00
13 Picking Up The Pieces,pt.1 . 3.00
14 Picking Up The Pieces,pt.2
   A:The Ray 3.00
15 Picking Up the Pieces,pt.3 . 3.00
16 .... 3.00
17 V:Bounty 3.00
18 Underworld Unleashed tie-in. 3.00
19 Underworld Unleashed tie-in. 3.00
20 final issue 3.00

DANGER TRAIL
July-Aug., 1950
1 CI,Ath,I:King For A Day 1,500.00
2 ATh 1,200.00
3 ATh 1,400.00
4 ATh 900.00
5 March-April, 1951 .... 900.00

DANGER TRAIL
[Mini-Series], 1993
1 thru 4 CI,FMc,F:King Faraday
   V:Cobra 2.25

DARK MANSION OF FORBIDDEN LOVE, THE
Sept.–Oct., 1971
1 .... 250.00
2 and 4 March-April, 1972 ... @100.00

DARKSEID VS. GALACTUS THE HUNGER
1995
1-shot Orion vs. Silver Surfer .. 5.00
GN JBy,in Apokolips 6.00

DARKSTARS
1992–96
0 History 2.00
1 TC(c),LSn,I:Darkstars 3.50
2 TC(c),LSn,F:Ferin Colos 2.50
3 LSn,J:Mo,Flint,V:Evil Star .. 2.50
4 TC,V:Evilstar 3.00
5 TC,A:Hawkman,Hawkwoman 3.00
6 TC,A:Hawkman 2.50
7 TC,V:K'llash 2.50
8 F:Ferris Colos 2.50
9 Colos vs K'lassh 2.50
10 V:Con Artists 2.50
11 TC,Trinity#4,A:Green Lantern,
   L.E.G.I.O.N. 2.50
12 TC(c),Trinity#7,A:Green Lantern,
   L.E.G.I.O.N. 2.50
13 TC(c),V:Alien Underworld ... 2.50
14 I:Annihilator 2.50
15 V:Annihilator 2.50
16 V:Annihilator 2.50
17 Murders 2.50
18 B:Eve of Destruction 2.50

Darkstars #19 © DC Comics Inc.

19 A:Flash 2.50
20 E:Eve of Destruction 2.50
21 A:John Stewart,Donna Troy .. 2.50
22 A:Controllers 2.50
23 Donna Troy is new Darkstar . 2.50
24 Zero Hour,V:HalJordan,Entropy. 2.50
25 Stewart 2.50
26 Alien criminals 2.50
27 and 28 .... @2.50
29 V:Alien Syndicate 2.50
30 A:Green Lantern 2.50
31 V:Darkseid 2.50
32 Crimelord/Syndicate War,pt.3,
   A:New Titans,Supergirl,
   Deathstroke 2.50
33 V:Jeddigan 2.50
34 .... 2.50
35 A:Flash 2.50
36 MkF,MC,A:Flash 2.50
37 MkF,MC,Colos vs. Warrior ... 2.50
38 final issue 2.50

DAY OF JUDGMENT
Sept., 1999
1 (of 5) Spectre x-over 4.00
2 F:Wonder Woman,Supergirl 3.00
3 F:Superman & Green Lantern .. 3.00
4 F:Superman's team 3.00
5 conclusion 3.00
Spec. Secret Files #1 .... 5.00

DC CHALLENGE
Nov., 1985
1 GC,Batman 3.00
2 Superman 2.50
3 CI,Adam Strange 2.50
4 GK/KJ,Aquaman 2.50
5 DGb,Dr.Fate,Capt.Marvel 2.50
6 Dr. 13 .... 2.50
7 Gorilla Grodd 2.50
8 DG,Outsiders, New Gods 2.50
9 New Teen Titans,JLA 2.50
10 CS,New Teen Titans,JLA 2.50
11 KG,Outsiders 2.50
12 DCw,TMd,DSp,New Teen Titans,
   Oct., 1986 .... 2.50

DC COMICS PRESENTS
July-Aug., 1978
[all have Superman]
1 JL,DA,F:Flash 20.00
2 JL,DA,F:Flash 15.00
3 JL,F:Adam Strange 15.00
4 JL,F:Metal Men,A:Mr.IQ 15.00
5 MA,F:Aquaman 7.00
6 CS,F:Green Lantern 7.00
7 DD,F:Red Tornado 7.00
8 MA,F:Swamp Thing 7.00
9 JSon,JA,RH,F:Wonder Woman ... 7.00
10 JSon,JA,F:Sgt.Rock 7.00
11 JSon,F:Hawkman 5.00
12 RB,DG,F:Mr.Miracle 5.00
13 DD,DG,F:Legion 6.00
14 DD,DG,F:Superboy 5.00
15 JSon,F:Atom,C:Batman 5.00
16 JSon,F:Black Lightning 5.00
17 JL,F:Firestorm 5.00
18 DD,F:Zatanna 5.00
19 JSon,F:Batgirl 5.00
20 JL,F:Green Arrow 4.00
21 JSon,JSa,F:Elongated Man 4.00
22 DD,FMc,F:Captain Comet 4.00
23 JSon,F:Dr.Fate 4.00
24 JL,F:Deadman 4.00
25 DD,FMc,F:Phantom Stranger ... 4.00
26 GP,DG,JSn,I:New Teen Titans,
   Cyborg,Raven,Starfire
   A:Green Lantern 25.00
27 JSn,RT,I:Mongul 6.00
28 JSn,RT,GK,F:Mongul 5.00
29 JSn,RT,AS,F:Spectre 5.00
30 CS,AS,F:Black Canary 4.00
31 JL,DG,AS,F:Robin 4.00
32 KS,AS,F:Wonder Woman 4.00
33 RB,DG,AS,F:Captain Marvel ... 4.00
34 RB,DG,F:Marvel Family 4.00
35 CS,GK,F:Man-bat 4.00
36 JSn,F:Starman 5.00
37 JSn,AS,F:Hawkgirl 4.00
38 GP(c),DH,AS,DG,D:Crimson
   Avenger,F:Flash 4.00
39 JSon,AS,F:PlasticMan,Toyman . 4.00
40 IN,FMc,AS,F:Metamorpho 4.00
41 JL,FMc,GC,RT,I:New Wonder
   Woman,A:Joker 8.00
42 IN,FMc,F:Unknown Soldier 4.00
43 BB(c),CS,F:Legion 4.00
44 IN,FMc,F:Dial H for Hero 5.00
45 RB,F:Firestorm 4.00
46 AS,I:Global Guardians 4.00
47 CS,I:Masters of Universe ... 10.00
48 GK(c),AA,IN,FMc,F:Aquaman ... 4.00
49 RB,F:Shazam!,V:Black Adam ... 4.00
50 KS,CS,F:Clark Kent 4.00
51 AS,FMc,CS,F:Atom,Masters
   of the Universe 7.00
52 KG,F:Doom Patrol,
   I:Ambush Bug 4.00
53 CS,TD,RA,DG,I:Atari Force ... 4.00
54 DN,DA,F:Gr.Arrow,Bl.Canary .. 4.00
55 AS,F:Air Wave,A:Superboy 4.00
56 GK(c),F:Power Girl 4.00
57 AS,FMc,F:Atomic Knights 4.00
58 GK(c),AS,F:Robin,Elongated
   Man 4.00
59 KG,KS,F:Ambush Bug 4.00
60 GK(c),IN,TD,F:Guardians 4.00
61 GP,F:Omac 4.00
62 GK(c),IN,F:Freedom Fighters. 4.00
63 AS,EC,F:Amethyst 4.00
64 GK(c),AS,FMc,F:Kamandi 4.00
65 GM,F:Madame Xanadu 4.00
66 JKu,F:Demon 4.00
67 CS,MA,F:Santa Claus 4.00
68 GK(c),CS,MA,F:Vixen 4.00
69 IN,DJ,F:Blackhawk 4.00
70 AS,TD,F:Metal Men 4.00
71 CS,F:Bizarro 4.00
72 AS,DG,F:Phant.Stranger,Joker. 5.00
73 CI,F:Flash 4.00
74 AS,RT,F:Hawkman 4.00
75 TMd,F:Arion 4.00

All comics prices listed are for Near Mint condition.

CVA Page 61

DC Comics–DC Special

DC Comics Presents #20
© DC Comics, Inc.

76 EB,F:Wonder Woman 4.00
77 CS,F:Forgotten Heroes 5.00
78 CS,F:Forgotten Villains 5.00
79 CS,AW,F:Legion 4.00
80 CS,F:Clark Kent 4.00
81 KG,BO,F:Ambush Bug 4.00
82 KJ,F:Adam Strange 4.00
83 IN,F:Batman/Outsiders 4.00
84 JK,ATh,MA,F:Challengers 7.00
85 RV,AW,AMo(s),
   F:Swamp Thing 7.00
86 Crisis,F:Supergirl 4.00
87 CS,AW,Crisis,I:Earth Prime
   Superboy 4.00
88 KG,Crisis,F:Creeper 4.00
89 MMi(c),AS,F:Omega Men 4.00
90 DCw,F:Firestorm,Capt.Atom. . . 4.00
91 CS,F:Captain Comet 4.00
92 CS,F:Vigilante 4.00
93 JSn(c),AS,KS,F:Elastic Four . . 4.00
94 GP(c),TMd,DH,Crisis,F:Lady
   Quark,Pariah,Harbinger 4.00
95 MA(i),F:Hawkman 4.00
96 JSon,KS,F:Blue Devil 4.00
97 RV,F:Phantom Zone Villians,
   final issue,double-sized 4.00
Ann.#1,RB,F:Earth 2 Superman . . . 4.00
Ann.#2 GK(c),KP,I:Superwoman . . 4.00
Ann.#3 GK,F:Captain Marvel 4.00
Ann.#4 EB,JOy,F:Superwoman. . . 4.00

DC/MARVEL:
ALL ACCESS
October 1996
sequel to DC Versus Marvel
1 (of 4) RMz(s),JG,JRu, crossover
   crisis again, 48pg 4.00
2 RMz(s),JG,JRu,F:Jubilee,Robin,
   Daredevil,Two-Face 3.00
3 RMz(s),JG,JRu,F:Doctor
   Strange, X-Men 3.00
4 RMz(s),JG,JRu,48pg 3.50

DC/MARVEL
CROSSOVER CLASSICS
TPB rep. all x-overs 17.95
TPB Vol. 2 (1998). 14.95
TPB Vol. 4 . . . . 14.95

DC FIRST
May, 2002
Superman/Lobo, 48-pg. 3.50
The Flash/Superman, 48-pg. 3.50
Batgirl/The Joker, 48-pg. 3.50
Green Lantern/Green Lantern 3.50

DC GRAPHIC NOVEL
Nov., 1983
1 JL,Star Raiders 15.00
2 Warlords 15.00
3 EC,Medusa Chain 15.00
4 JK,Hunger Dogs 50.00
5 Me and Joe Priest 15.00
6 Space Clusters 15.00

DC MILLENNIUM
EDITIONS
Dec., 1999–2000
Action Comics #1 . . . . 3.95
Action Comics #252 . . . . 2.50
Adventure Comics #247 . . . . 2.50
Adventure Comics #761 . . . . 3.95
All-Star Comics #3 . . . . 3.95
All-Star Comics #3, chromium . . . 5.00
All Star Comics #8 . . . . 3.95
All-Star Western #10 . . . . 2.95
Batman #1 . . . . 3.95
Batman #1 chromium 5.00
Batman: Dark Knight Returns #1. . 5.95
The Brave and the Bold #28 . . . . 2.50
The Brave and the Bold #85 . . . . 2.50
Crisis on Infinte Earths #1 . . . . . . 2.50
Detective Comics #27 . . . . 3.95
Detective Comics #38 . . . . 3.95
Detective Comics #327 . . . . 2.50
Detective Comics #359 . . . . 2.50
Detective Comics #395 . . . . 2.50
Flash Comics #1 . . . . 3.95
Flash #123 . . . . 2.50
Gen 13 #1 . . . . 2.50
Green Lantern/Green Arrow #76 . . 2.50
Hellblazer #1 . . . . 2.95
House of Mystery #1 . . . . 2.50
House of Secrets #92 . . . . 2.50
JLA #1 . . . . 2.50
Justice League #1 . . . . 2.50
Justice League #1, chromium . . . 5.00
Kingdom Come #1 . . . . 5.95
The Man of Steel #1 . . . . 2.50
Military Comics #1 . . . . 3.95
More Fun Comics #101 . . . . 2.95
Mysterious Suspense #1 . . . . 2.50
New Gods #1 . . . . 2.50
New Teen Titans #1 . . . . 2.50
Our Army at War #81 . . . . 2.50
Plop! #1 . . . . 2.50
Police Comics #1 . . . . 3.95
Preacher #1 . . . . 2.95
Saga of the Swamp Thing #21 . . . 2.50
Sandman #1. . . . . 2.95
Sensation Comics #1 . . . . 3.95
The Shadow #1 . . . . 2.50
Showcase #22 . . . . 2.50
Showcase #4 . . . . 2.50
Spirit #1 . . . . 3.95
Superboy #1 . . . . 2.95
Superman #1 . . . . 3.95
Superman #1 Chromium edition . . . 5.00
Superman #76 . . . . 2.95
Superman #75 Death of Superman. 2.50
Superman's Pal Jimmy Olsen #1 . . 2.50
Watchmen #1 . . . . 2.50
Whiz Comics #2 . . . . 3.95
WildC.A.T.S #1 . . . . 2.50
Wonder Woman 1st.Series #1 . . . 3.95
Wonder Woman #1 . . . . 2.50
World's Finest Comics #71 . . . . . . 2.50

Young Romance #1, JK, JSm 2.95

DC ONE MILLION
1998
1 GMo(s),VS,in 853rd-century 3.00
2 GMo(s),VS,V:Hourman Virus . . . 2.50
3 GMo(s),VS,V:Solaris 2.50
4 GMo(s),VS,finale 2.50
TPB series rep 14.95

DC REPLICA EDITIONS
1999–2000
DC 100-Page Super-Spectacular:
   Love Stories 7.00
Justice Society of America
   100-page Super Spectacular #1 7.00
Teen Titans Annual #1 (1967) 5.00
Sgt. Rock's Prize Battle Tales
   80-pg. Giant 6.00

DC SCIENCE FICTION
GRAPHIC NOVEL
1985–87
1 KG,Hell on Earth 15.00
2 Nightwings 15.00
3 Frost and Fire 15.00
4 Merchants of Venus 15.00
5 Metalzoic 15.00
6 MR,Demon-Glass Hand 15.00
7 Sandkings 15.00

DC SPECIAL
Oct.–Dec., 1968
[All reprint]
1 CI,F:Flash,Batman,Adam Strange,
   (#1 thru #21 reps) 100.00
2 F:Teen Titans 125.00
3 GA,F:Black Canary 100.00
4 Mystery 50.00
5 JKu,F:Viking Prince/Sgt.Rock . . 50.00
6 Wild Frontier 50.00
7 F:Strange Sports 50.00
8 Wanted 50.00
9 . . . . 50.00
10 LAW 50.00
11 NA,BWr,F:Monsters 50.00
12 JKu,F:Viking Prince 50.00
13 F:Strange Sports 50.00
14 Wanted,F:Penguin/Joker 60.00
15 GA,F:Plastic Man 60.00
16 F:Super Heroes & Gorillas . . . 25.00
17 F:Green Lantern 25.00
18 Earth Shaking Stories 25.00
19 F:War Against Gianta 25.00
20 Green Lantern 25.00
21 F:War Against Monsters 25.00
22 Three Musketeers 25.00
23 Three Musketeers 25.00
24 Three Musketeers 25.00
25 Three Musketeers 25.00
26 F:Enemy Ace(rep) 25.00
27 RB,JR,F:Captain Comet 25.00
28 DN,DA,Earth disasters 25.00
29 JSon,BL,O:JSA 25.00

DC SPECIAL SERIES
Sept., 1977
1 MN,DD,IN,FMc,JSon,JA,BMc,
   JRu,F:Batman,Flash,Green
   Lantern,Atom,Aquaman 25.00
2 BWr(c),BWr,F:Swamp
   Thing rep 12.00
3 JKu(c),F:Sgt.Rock 15.00
4 AN,RT,Unexpected Annual 15.00
5 CS,F:Superman 20.00
6 BMc(i),Secret Society Vs.JLA . . 15.00

Comics Values Annual — DC — DC Special–Death

7 AN,F:Ghosts. 15.00
8 RE,DG,F:Brave&Bold,Deadman 15.00
9 SD,RH,DAy,F:Wonder Woman . 22.00
10 JSon,MN,DN,TA,Secret Origins,
    O:Dr.Fate 15.00
11 JL,KS,MA,IN,WW,AS,F:Flash . . 15.00
12 MK(c),RT,RH,TS,Secrets of
    Haunted House 17.00
13 JKu(c),RT,SBi,RE,F:Sgt.Rock. . 17.00
14 BWr(c),F:Swamp Thing rep. . . . 15.00
15 MN,JRu,MR,DG,MGo,
    F:Batman 20.00
16 RH,D:Jonah Hex 60.00
17 F:Swamp Thing rep. 12.00
18 JK(c),digest,F:Sgt.Rock rep. . . . 15.00
19 digest,Secret Origins
    O:Wonder Woman 15.00
20 BWr(c),F:Swamp Thing rep. . . . 12.00
21 FM,JL,DG,RT,DA,F:Batman,
    Legion 25.00
22 JKu(c),F:G.I.Combat 15.00
23 digest size,F:Flash 15.00
24 F:Worlds Finest 15.00
25 F:Superman II,Photo Album . . . 15.00
26 RA,F:Superman's Fortress. 18.00
27 JL,DG,F:Batman vs.Hulk 30.00

DC SUPER-STARS
1976–78

1 F:Teen Titans rep. 25.00
2 F:DC Super-Stars of Space . . . 12.00
3 CS,F:Superman,Legion. 12.00
4 DC,MA,F:Super-Stars of Space 12.00
5 CI,F:Flash rep. 12.00
6 MA,F:Super-Stars of Space . . . 12.00
7 F:Aquaman rep. 12.00
8 CI,MA,F:Adam Strange. 14.00
9 F:Superman rep. 12.00
10 DD,FMc,F:Superhero Baseball
    Special,A:Joker 14.00
11 GM,Super-Stars of Magic. 12.00
12 CS,MA,F:Superboy 12.00
13 SA. 22.00
14 RB,BL,JA,JRu,Secret Origins. . 12.00
15 JKu(c),RB,RT(i),War Heroes . . 12.00
16 DN,BL,I:Star Hunters 12.00
17 JSon,MGr,BL,I&O:Huntress,O:Gr.
    Arrow,D:EarthII Catwoman . . . 35.00
18 RT,DG,BL,F:Deadman,Phantom
    Stranger. 20.00

DC Super-Stars #12
© DC Comics, Inc.

DC TWO THOUSAND
July, 2000

1 (of 2) TPe,VS 6.95
2 TPe,VS,JLA & Golden age JSA . 6.95

DC UNIVERSE
1997–2003

Heroes, Secret Files #1 . . . . 5.00
Villains, Secret Files #1 . . . . 5.00
TPB Christmas, Tyt(c) (2000) 19.95
GN Holiday Bash #1 (1997) 4.00
GN Holiday Bash #2 (1998) 4.00
GN Holiday Bash #3 (1999) 5.00
TPB The DC Universe Stories
    of Alan Moore (2003) 19.95

DC UNIVERSE: TRINITY
1993

1 TC,GeH,BKi,F:Darkstars,Green
    Lantern,L.E.G.I.O.N.,V:Triarch . 4.00
2 BKi,SHa,F:Darkstars,Green Lantern,
    L.E.G.I.O.N.,V:Triarch 4.00

DC VS. MARVEL
1996

1 RMz 5.50
1 2nd printing 4.00
2 & 3 see Marvel
4 PDa 5.00

DEAD CORPS(E)
DC/Helix, July, 1998

1 StP, C.J.Rataan 2.50
2 StP, CJ becomes an expired. . . . 2.50
3 StP,Death is not the end 2.50
4 StP, conclusion 2.50

DEADENDERS
DC/Vertigo, Jan., 2000

1 WaP,Stealing the Sun,pt.1 . . . . . 2.50
2 WaP,Stealing the Sun,pt.2 . . . . . 2.50
3 WaP,Stealing the Sun,pt.3 . . . . . 2.50
4 WaP,Stealing the Sun,pt.4 . . . . . 2.50
5 WaP,Now and Then,pt.1 . . . . . . 2.50
6 WaP,Now and Then,pt.2 . . . . . . 2.50
7 WaP,Now and Then,pt.3 . . . . . . 2.50
8 WaP,scooter races 2.50
9 More Fun in New World,pt.1 . . . . 2.50
10 More Fun in New World,pt.2 . . . 2.50
11 Sector 9 . . . . 2.50
12 V:Science Corp.. . . . . 2.50
13 Scooter race 2.50
14 Behind the Wheel, pt.1 . . . . 2.50
15 Behind the Wheel, pt.2 . . . . 2.50
16 Behind the Wheel, pt.3 . . . . 2.50
TPB Stealing the Sun 10.00

DEADMAN
May, 1985

1 CI,NA,rep 4.00
2 NA,rep.. . . . . 3.00
3 NA,rep.. . . . . 3.00
4 NA,rep.. . . . . 3.00
5 NA,rep.. . . . . 3.00
6 NA,rep.. . . . . 3.00
7 NA,rep.Nov., 1985. . . . . 3.00

[Mini-Series], 1986

1 JL,A:Batman. 3.00
2 JL,V:Sensei,A:Batman 3.00
3 JL,D:Sensei 3.00
4 JL,V:Jonah, final issue 3.00

Deadman #3
© DC Comics Inc.

DEADMAN
Dec., 2001

1 SVa(s) F:Boston Brand 2.50
2 SVa(s),Sirna 2.50
3 SVa(s),F:Duroc, drugs 2.50
4 SVa(s),nuclear submarine. 2.50
5 SVa(s),Death & the Maiden,pt.1 . 2.50
6 SVa(s),Death & the Maiden,pt.2 . 2.50
7 SVa(s),children of Nanda Parbat. 2.50
8 SVa(s),Nanda Parbat,Onyx 2.50
9 SVa(s),final issue 2.50

DEADMAN: DEAD AGAIN
Aug., 2001

1 SVa,RBr,A:Flash 2.50
2 SVa,RBr,JAp,A:Robin 2.50
3 SVa,RBr,A:Superman,Doomsday 2.50
4 SVa,RBr,MBr,A:Green Lantern . . 2.50
5 SVa,RBr,concl., ... 2.50

DEADMAN: EXORCISM
[Limited-Series], 1992

1 KJo,A:Phantom Stranger 5.25
2 KJo,A:Phantom Stranger 5.25

DEADMAN: LOST SOULS
TPB MBn, KJo, rep. Exorcism
    and Love After Death 19.95

DEADMAN: LOVE AFTER DEATH
1989–90

1 KJo,Circus of Monsters. 4.25
2 KJo,Circus of Monsters. 4.25

DEADSHOT
1988–89

1 LMc,From Suicide Squad 2.50
2 LMc,Search for Son 2.50
3 LMc,V:Pantha 2.50
4 LMc,final issue 2.50

DEATH GALLERY
DC/Vertigo

1 DMc(c),NGa Death Sketch
    Various Pinups 3.50

All comics prices listed are for *Near Mint* condition.

Death–Demon — DC — Comics Values Annual

DEATH: THE HIGH COST OF LIVING
DC/Vertigo, 1993

1 B:NGa(s),CBa,MBu(i),Death becomes Human,A:Hettie 6.00
1a Platinum Ed. 18.00
2 CBa,MBu(i),V:Eremite,A:Hettie .. 4.00
3 E:NGa(s),CBa,MBu(i),V:Eremite, A:Hettie 3.50
3a Error Copy 7.00
TPB w/Tori Amos Intro 13.00

DEATH: THE TIME OF YOUR LIFE
DC/Vertigo, 1995

1 NGa,MBu,four-issue miniseries.. 3.00
2 NGa,MBu,F:Foxglove 3.00
3 NGa,MBu,conclusion 3.00
TPB NGa(s),rep. 13.00

Deathstroke: The Terminator #31
© DC Comics Inc.

DEATHSTROKE: THE TERMINATOR
1991–94

1 MZ(c),(from New Teen Titans) SE,I:2nd Ravager 4.00
1a Second Printing,Gold 3.00
2 MZ(c),SE,Quraci Agents 3.50
3 SE,V:Ravager. 3.00
4 SE,D:2ndRavager(Jackel). 3.00
5 Winter Green Rescue Attempt .. 3.00
6 MZ(c),SE,B:City of Assassins, A:Batman. 3.00
7 MZ(c),SE,A:Batman 2.50
8 MZ(c),SE,A:Batman 2.50
9 MZ(c),SE,E:City of Assassins, A:Batman,I:2nd Vigilante 2.50
10 MZ(c),ANi,GP,A:2nd Vigilante .. 2.50
11 MZ(c),ANi,GP,A:2nd Vigilante... 2.50
12 MGo,Short Stories re:Slade 2.50
13 SE,V:Gr.Lant.,Flash,Aquaman .. 2.50
14 ANi,Total Chaos#1,A:New Titans, Team Titans,V:Nightwing 2.50
15 ANi,Total Chaos#4,A:New Titans, Team Titans,I:Sweet Lili 2.50
16 ANi,Total Chaos#7 .... 2.50
17 SE,Titans Sell-Out #2 A:Brotherhood of Evil 2.50
18 SE,V:Cheshire,R:Speedy 2.50
19 SE,V:Broth.of Evil,A:Speedy ... 2.50
20 SE,MZ(c),V:Checkmate 2.50
21 SE,MZ(c),A:Checkmate 2.50

22 MZ(c),Quality of Mercy#1. ..... 2.50
23 MZ(c),Quality of Mercy#2. ..... 2.50
24 MZ(c),V:The Black Dome. 2.50
25 MZ(c),V:The Black Dome. 2.50
26 MZ(c),SE,in Kenya. 2.50
27 MZ(c),SE,B:World Tour, in Germany 2.50
28 MZ(c),SE,in France 2.50
29 KM(c),SE,in Hong Kong. 2.50
30 SE,A:Vigilante 2.50
31 SE,in Milwaukie 2.50
32 SE,in Africa 2.50
33 SE,I:Fleur de Lis 2.50
34 SE,E:World Tour 2.50
35 V:Mercenaries 2.50
36 V:British General 2.50
37 V:Assassin. 2.50
38 A:Vigilante 2.50
39 A:Vigilante 2.50
40 Wedding in Red. 2.50
Ann.#1 Eclipso,A:Vigilante 4.00
Ann.#2 SE,I:Gunfire 4.00
Ann.#3 Elseworlds Story. 4.25
TPB Full Circle rep#1–#4, New Titans#70 .... 12.95

Becomes:

DEATHSTROKE: THE HUNTED
1994–95

0 Slade 2.50
41 Bronze Tiger 2.50
42 Wounded. 2.50
43 .... 2.50
44 .... 2.50
45 A:New Titans 2.50

Becomes:

DEATHSTROKE
1995–96

46 Checkmate,Wintergreen 2.50
47 I:New Vigilante 2.50
48 Crimelord/Syndicate War,pt.1 .. 2.50
49 Crimelord/Syndicate War,pt.4 A:Supergirl, New Titans, Hawkman Blood Pack 2.50
50 A:Titans,Outsiders,Steel. 3.50
51 No Fate or Future,pt.1 .... 2.50
52 No Fate or Future,pt.2 .... 2.50
53 The Borgia Plague,pt.1 ...... 2.50
54 The Borgia Plague,pt.2 ...... 2.50
55 MWn,Rebirth? 2.50
56 MWn,Night of the Karrion,pt.2 .. 2.50
57 .... 2.50
58 MWn,V:The Joker 2.50
59 MWn,F:Hellriders 2.50
60 MWn,final issue 2.50

DEATHWISH
1994–95

1 New mini-series 2.50
2 F:Rahme 2.50
3 .... 2.50
4 V:Boots 2.50

DEMOLITION MAN
1993–94

1 thru 4 Movie Adapt 2.50

DEMON
[1st Regular Series], 1972–74

1 JK,I:Demon 60.00
2 JK 30.00
3 JK 25.00
4 JK 25.00
5 JK 25.00
6 JK 20.00
7 JK 20.00

8 JK 20.00
9 JK 20.00
10 JK 20.00
11 JK 20.00
12 JK 20.00
13 JK 20.00
14 JK 20.00
15 JK 20.00
16 JK 20.00

[Limited Series], 1987

1 MWg,B:Jason Blood's Case 3.00
2 MWg,Fight to Save Gotham ... 3.00
3 MWg,Fight to Save Gotham ... 3.00
4 MWg,final issue 3.00

[2nd Regular Series], 1990–95

0 Relationships 2.50
1 VS,A:Etrigan (32 pages) 4.00
2 VS,V:TheCrone 3.00
3 VS,A:Batman 3.00
4 VS,A:Batman 3.00
5 VS,ThePit. 3.00
6 VS,In Hell. 3.00
7 VS,Etrigan-King of Hell. 3.00
8 VS,Klarion the Witch Boy 3.00
9 VS,Jason Leaves Gotham 3.00
10 VS,A:PhantomStranger 3.00
11 VS,A:Klarion,C:Lobo 3.00
12 VS,Etrigan Vs. Lobo 3.00
13 VS,Etrigan Vs. Lobo 3.00
14 VS,V:Odd Squad,A:Lobo 3.00
15 VS,Etrigan Vs.Lobo 3.00
16 VS,Etrigan & Jason Blood switch bodies 3.00
17 VS, War of the Gods x-over ... 3.00
18 VS,V:Wotan,A:Scape Goat. ... 3.00
19 VS,O:Demon,Demon/Lobo pin-up. 3.50
20 VS,V:Golden Knight. 2.50
21 VS,Etrigan/Jason, A:Lobo,Glenda 2.50
22 MWg,V:Mojo & Hayden 2.50
23 VS,A:Robin 2.50
24 VS,A:Robin 2.50
25 VS,V:Gideon Ryme 2.50
26 VS,B:America Rules 2.50
27 VS,A:Superman. 2.50
28 VS,A:Superman. 2.50
29 VS,E:America Rules 2.50
30 R:Asteroth 2.50
31 VS(c),A:Lobo. 2.50
32 VS(c),A:Lobo,W.Woman 2.50
33 VS(c),A:Lobo,V:Asteroth 2.50
34 A:Lobo. 2.50
35 A:Lobo,V:Belial 2.50
36 A:Lobo,V:Belial 2.50
37 A:Lobo,Morax 2.50
38 A:Lobo,Morax 2.50
39 A:Lobo. 2.50
40 New Direction,B:GEn(s). 3.50
41 V:Mad Bishop 3.00
42 V:Demons 3.00
43 A:Hitman 10.00
44 V:Gotho-Demon,A:Hitman ... 15.00
45 V:Gotho-Demon,A:Hitman ... 15.00
46 R:Haunted Tank. 5.00
47 V:Zombie Nazis 5.00
48 A:Haunted Tank,V:Zombie Nazis 5.00
49 b:Demon's Son,A:Joe Gun. ... 2.50
50 GEn(s). 3.00
51 GEn(s),Son & Lovers. 2.50
52 Etrigan & son–Hitman 4.00
53 Glenda & child–Hitman 4.00
54 Suffer the Children. 4.00
55 Rebellion 2.50
56 F:Etrigan 2.50
57 Last Stand. 2.50
58 Last issue 2.50
Ann.#1 Eclipso,V:Klarion. 3.25
Ann.#2 I:Hitman 15.00

CVA Page 64 — All comics prices listed are for *Near Mint* condition.

DEMON, THE: DRIVEN OUT
Sept. 2003
1 (of 6) ATi,F:Etrigan 2.50
2 ATi 2.50
3 ATi 2.50

DESPERADOES: EPIDEMIC
Homage/DC Sept., 1999
GN Epidemic, 48-pg (1999) 6.00

DESPERADOES: QUIET OF THE GRAVE
Homage/DC May, 2001
1 (of 5) JMi,JSe 3.00
2 JMi,JSe 3.00
3 JMi,JSe 3.00
4 JMi,JSe 3.00
5 JMi,JSe, concl. 3.00
TPB JMi,JSe series rep. 15.00

DESTINY: A CHRONICLE OF DEATHS FORETOLD
DC/Vertigo, Sept., 1997
1 (of 3) F:Destiny of the Endless .. 6.00
2 Destiny of the Endless, pt.2 .... 6.00
3 Destiny of the Endless, pt.3 .... 6.00
TPB series rep. 14.95

DETECTIVE COMICS
March, 1937
1 I:Slam Bradley 75,000.00
2 JoS 20,000.00
3 JoS 15,000.00
4 JoS 8,000.00
5 JoS 7,500.00
6 JoS 6,000.00
7 JoS 6,000.00
8 JoS,Mr. Chang(c). 8,500.00
9 JoS 6,000.00
10 .... 6,000.00
11 .... 4,500.00
12 .... 4,500.00
13 .... 4,500.00
14 .... 4,500.00
15 .... 4,500.00
16 .... 4,500.00
17 I:Fu Manchu 4,500.00
18 Fu Manchu(c) 7,000.00
19 .... 4,000.00
20 I:Crimson Avenger 6,500.00
21 .... 3,500.00
22 .... 4,500.00
23 .... 3,500.00
24 .... 3,500.00
25 .... 3,500.00
26 .... 3,500.00
27 BK,I:Batman 350,000.00
28 BK,V:Frenchy Blake 27,000.00
29 BK,I:Doctor Death 44,000.00
30 BK,V:Dr. Death 10,000.00
31 BK,I:Monk 44,000.00
32 BK,V:Monk 8,500.00
33 O:Batman,V:Scarlet Horde 55,000.00
34 V:Due D'Orterre 6,500.00
35 V:Sheldon Lenox. 15,000.00
36 I:Hugo Strange 9,500.00
37 V:Count Grutt, last Batman solo 9,000.00
38 I:Robin, the Boy Wonder .. 50,000.00
39 V:Green Dragon 8,000.00
40 I:Clayface (Basil Karlo) 9,000.00
41 V:Graves. 4,500.00
42 V:Pierre Antal 3,000.00
43 V:Harliss Greer 3,000.00
44 Robin Dream Story 3,000.00
45 V:Joker 4,500.00
46 V:Hugo Strange 2,700.00
47 Meets Harvey Midas 2,700.00
48 Meets Henry Lewis 2,700.00
49 V:Clayface 2,700.00
50 V:Three Devils 2,700.00
51 V:Mindy Gang 2,000.00
52 V:Loo Chung. 2,000.00
53 V:Toothy Hare gang 2,000.00
54 V:Hook Morgan 2,000.00
55 V:Dr. Death 2,000.00
56 V:Mad Mack 2,000.00
57 Meet Richard Sneed 2,000.00
58 I:Penguin 5,500.00
59 V:Penguin 2,100.00
60 V:Joker,I:Air Wave. 2,100.00
61 The Three Racketeers ... 1,800.00
62 V:Joker 3,000.00
63 I:Mr. Baffle 1,800.00
64 I:Boy Commandos,V:Joker . 5,000.00
65 Meet Tom Bolton 3,800.00
66 I:Two-Face 4,800.00
67 V:Penguin 3,000.00
68 V:Two-Face 2,100.00
69 V:Joker 2,100.00
70 Meet the Amazing Carlo .. 1,500.00
71 V:Joker 1,800.00
72 V:Larry the Judge 1,400.00
73 V:Scarecrow 1,700.00
74 I:Tweedledum & Tweedledee 1,400.00
75 V:Robber Baron 1,400.00
76 V:Joker 2,100.00
77 V:Dr. Matthew Thorne ... 1,400.00
78 V:Baron Von Luger 1,400.00
79 `Destiny's' Auction. 1,400.00
80 V:Two-Face. 1,600.00
81 I:Cavalier 1,200.00
82 V:Blackee Blondeen 1,200.00
83 V:Dr. Goodwin. 1,300.00
84 V:Ivan Krafft 1,200.00
85 V:Joker 1,500.00
86 V:Gentleman Jim Jewell .. 1,200.00
87 V:Penguin 1,300.00
88 V:Big Hearted John 1,200.00
89 V:Cavalier 1,200.00
90 V:Capt. Ben 1,200.00
91 V:Joker 1,500.00
92 V:Braing Bulow 1,000.00
93 V:`Tiger' Ragland 1,000.00
94 V:Lefty Goran 1,000.00
95 V:The Blaze 1,000.00
96 F:Alfred. 1,000.00
97 V:Nick Petri 1,000.00
98 Meets Casper Thurbridge .. 1,000.00
99 V:Penguin 1,500.00
100 V:Digger 1,600.00
101 V:Joe Bart. 1,000.00
102 V:Joker 1,500.00
103 Meet Dean Gray 1,000.00
104 V:Fat Frank gang 1,000.00
105 V:Simon Gurlan. 1,000.00
106 V:Todd Torrey 1,000.00
107 V:Bugs Scarpis 1,000.00
108 Meet Ed Gregory. 1,000.00
109 V:Joker 1,000.00
110 V:Prof. Moriarty 1,000.00
111 `Coaltown, USA' 1,000.00
112 `Case Without A Crime' ... 1,000.00
113 V:Blackhand 1,000.00
114 V:Joker 1,000.00
115 V:Basil Grimes 1,000.00
116 A:Carter Nichols, Robin Hood 1,000.00
117 `Steeplejack's Slowdown' . 1,000.00
118 V:Joker 1,300.00
119 V:Wiley Derek 1,000.00
120 V:Penguin 2,100.00
121 F:Commissioner Gordon .. 1,000.00
122 V:Catwoman 1,700.00
123 V:Shiner. 900.00
124 V:Joker 1,200.00
125 V:Thinker. 900.00
126 V:Penguin 900.00
127 V:Dr. Agar 900.00
128 V:Joker 1,200.00
129 V:Diamond Dan mob 900.00
130. .... 900.00
131 V:`Trigger Joe' 750.00
132 V:Human Key. 750.00
133 Meets Arthur Loom. 750.00
134 V:Penguin 750.00
135 A:Baron Frankenstein, Carter Nichols 750.00
136 A:Carter Nichols. 750.00
137 V:Joker 1,100.00
138 V:Joker,O:Robotman 1,500.00
139 V:Nick Bailey 750.00
140 I:Riddler 6,000.00
141 V:`Blackie' Nason. 750.00
142 V:Riddler. 1,500.00
143 V:Pied Piper. 750.00
144 A:Kay Kyser (radio personality). 750.00
145 V:Yellow Mask mob 750.00
146 V:J.J. Jason. 750.00
147 V:Tiger Shark. 750.00
148 V:Prof. Zero. 750.00
149 V:Joker 1,000.00

Detective Comics — DC — Comics Values Annual

Detective Comics #143
© DC Comics, Inc.

Detective Comics #279
© DC Comics, Inc.

#	Entry	Price
150	V:Dr. Paul Visio	750.00
151	I&O:Pow Wow Smith	900.00
152	V:Goblin	750.00
153	V:Slits Danton	900.00
154	V:Hatch Marlin	750.00
155	A:Vicki Vale	750.00
156	'The Batmobile of 1950'	750.00
157	V:Bart Gillis	750.00
158	V:Dr. Doom	750.00
159	V:T. Worthington Chubb	750.00
160	V:Globe-Trotter	750.00
161	V:Bill Waters	750.00
162	Batman on railroad	750.00
163	V:Slippery Jim Elgin	750.00
164	Bat-signal story	750.00
165	'The Strange Costumes of Batman'	750.00
166	Meets John Gillen	750.00
167	A:Carter Nichols, Cleopatra	750.00
168	O:Joker	4,500.00
169	V:`Squint' Tolmar	750.00
170	Batman teams with Navy and Coast Guard	750.00
171	V:Penguin	1,100.00
172	V:Paul Gregorian	700.00
173	V:Killer Moth	700.00
174	V:Dagger	700.00
175	V:Kangaroo Kiley	700.00
176	V:Mr. Velvet	700.00
177	Bat-Cave story	650.00
178	V:Baron Swane	650.00
179	`Mayor Bruce Wayne'	650.00
180	V:Joker	650.00
181	V:Human Magnet	650.00
182	V:Maestro Dorn	650.00
183	V:John Cook	650.00
184	I:Firefly(Garfield Lynns)	650.00
185	`Secret's of Batman's Utility Belt'	650.00
186	'The Flying Bat-Cave'	650.00
187	V:Two-Face	650.00
188	V:William Milden	650.00
189	V:Styx	650.00
190	Meets Dr. Sampson, O:Batman	1,000.00
191	V:Executioner	650.00
192	V: Nails Riley	650.00
193	V:Joker	650.00
194	V:Sammy Sabre	650.00
195	Meets Hugo Marmon	650.00
196	V:Frank Lumardi	650.00
197	V:Wrecker	650.00
198	Batman in Scotland	650.00
199	V:Jack Baker	650.00
200	V:Brand Keldon	900.00
201	Meet Human Target	650.00
202	V:Jolly Roger	650.00
203	V:Catwoman	650.00
204	V:Odo Neral	650.00
205	O:Bat-Cave	900.00
206	V:Trapper	650.00
207	Meets Merko the Great	650.00
208	V:Groff	650.00
209	V:Inventor	650.00
210	V:`Brain' Hobson	650.00
211	V:Catwoman	650.00
212	Meets Jonathan Bard	650.00
213	O:Mirror-Man	750.00
214	'The Batman Encyclopedia'	650.00
215	I:Ranger, Legionary, Gaucho & Musketeer,A:Knight & Squire (See: World's Finest 89)	550.00
216	A:Brane Taylor	550.00
217	Meets Barney Barrows	550.00
218	V:Dr. Richard Marston	550.00
219	V:Marty Mantee	550.00
220	A:Roger Bacon, historical scientist/philosopher	550.00
221	V:Paul King	550.00
222	V:`Big Jim' Jarrell	550.00
223	V:`Blast' Varner	550.00
224		550.00
225	I&O:Martian Manhunter (J'onn J'onzz)	7,400.00
226	O:Robin's costume, A:J'onn J'onzz	1,700.00
227	A:Roy Raymond,J'onnJ'onzz	700.00
228	A:Roy Raymond,J'onnJ'onzz	700.00
229	A:Roy Raymond,J'onnJ'onzz	700.00
230	A:Martian Manhunter, I:Mad Hatter	750.00
231	A:Batman,Jr.,Roy Raymond J'onn J'onzz	500.00
232	A:J'onn J'onzz	500.00
233	I&O:Batwoman	1,500.00
234	V:Jay Caird	500.00
235	O:Batman's Costume	850.00
236	V:Wallace Walby	650.00
237	F:Robin	500.00
238	V:Checkmate(villain)	500.00
239	Batman robot story	500.00
240	V:Burt Weaver	500.00
241	The Rainbow Batman	500.00
242	Batcave story	350.00
243	V:Jay Vanney	350.00
244	O:Batarang	350.00
245	F:Comm.Gordon	350.00
246		350.00
247	I:Professor Milo	350.00
248		350.00
249	V:Collector	350.00
250	V:John Stannor	350.00
251	V:Brand Ballard	350.00
252	Batman in a movie	350.00
253	I:Terrible Trio	350.00
254	A:Bathound	350.00
255	V:Fingers Nolan	350.00
256	Batman outer-space story	350.00
257	Batman sci-fi story	350.00
258	Batman robot story	350.00
259	I:Calendar Man	350.00
260	Batman outer space story	350.00
261	I:Dr. Double X	300.00
262	V:Jackal-Head	300.00
263	V:The Professor	300.00
264		300.00
265	O:Batman retold	400.00
266	V:Astro	300.00
267	I&O:Bat-Mite	425.00
268	V:iBig Joeî Foster	300.00
269	V:Director	300.00
270	Batman sci-fi story	300.00
271	V:Crimson Knight,O:Martian Manhunter(retold)	300.00
272	V:Crystal Creature	300.00
273	A:Dragon Society	250.00
274	V:Nails Lewin	250.00
275	A:Zebra-Man	250.00
276	A:Batmite	250.00
277	Batman Monster story	250.00
278	A:Professor Simms	250.00
279	Batman robot story	250.00
280	A:Atomic Man	250.00
281	Batman robot story	200.00
282	Batman sci-fi story	200.00
283	V:Phantom of Gotham City	200.00
284	V:Hal Durgan	200.00
285	V:Harbin	200.00
286	A:Batwoman	200.00
287	A:Bathound	200.00
288	V:Multicreature	200.00
289	A:Bat-Mite	200.00
290	Batman's robot story	200.00
291	Batman sci-fi story	200.00
292	Last Roy Raymond	200.00
293	A:Aquaman,J'onn J'onzz	200.00
294	V:Elemental Men, A:Aquaman	200.00
295	A:Aquaman	200.00
296	A:Aquaman	200.00
297	A:Aquaman	200.00
298	I:Clayface(Matt Hagen)	350.00
299	Batman sci-fi stories	150.00
300	I:Mr.Polka-dot,E:Aquaman	175.00
301	A:J'onn J'onzz	150.00
302	A:J'onn J'onzz	125.00
303	A:J'onn J'onzz	125.00
304	A:Clayface,J'onnJ'onz	125.00
305	Batman sci-fi story	125.00
306	A:J'onn J'onzz	125.00
307	A:J'onn J'onzz	125.00
308	A:J'onn J'onzz	125.00
309	A:J'onn J'onzz	125.00
310	A:Bat-Mite,J'onn J'onzz	125.00
311	I:Cat-Man,Zook	135.00
312	A:Clayface,J'onn J'onzz	100.00
313	A:J'onn J'onzz	100.00
314	A:J'onn J'onzz	100.00
315	I:Jungle Man	100.00
316	A:Dr.Double X,J'onn J'onzz	100.00
317	A:J'onn J'onzz	100.00
318	A:Cat-Man,J'onn J'onzz	100.00
319	A:J'onn J'onzz	100.00
320	A:Vicki Vale	100.00
321	I:Terrible Trio	125.00
322	A:J'onn J'onzz	110.00
323	I:Zodiac Master, A:J'onn J'onzz	110.00
324	A:Mad Hatter,J'onn J'onzz	110.00
325	A:Cat-Man,J'onn J'onzz	100.00
326	Batman sci-fi story	110.00

All comics prices listed are for *Near Mint* condition.

Detective Comics

#	Description	Price
327	CI,25th ann,symbol change	150.00
328	D:Alfred,I:WayneFoundation	150.00
329	A:Elongated Man	110.00
330	"Fallen Idol of Gotham"	110.00
331	A:Elongated Man	110.00
332	A:Joker	75.00
333	A:Gorla	75.00
334		75.00
335		75.00
336		75.00
337	"Deep Freeze Menace"	75.00
338		75.00
339		75.00
340		75.00
341	A:Joker	75.00
342		75.00
343	BK,CI,Elongated Man	75.00
344		75.00
345	CI,I:Blockbuster	75.00
346		75.00
347	CI,Elongated Man	75.00
348	Elongated Man	75.00
349	BK(c),CI,Blockbuster	75.00
350	Elongated Man	75.00
351	CI,A:Elongated Man, I:Cluemaster	75.00
352	BK,Elongated Man	75.00
353		75.00
354	BK,Elongated Man,I:Dr. Tzin-Tzin	75.00
355	CI,Elongated Man	75.00
356	BK,Outsider,Alfred	75.00
357		75.00
358	BK,Elongated Man	75.00
359	I:new Batgirl	150.00
360		75.00
361	CI	75.00
362	CI,Elongated Man	75.00
363	CI,Elongated Man	75.00
364	BK,Elongated Man	75.00
365	A:Joker	75.00
366	Elongated Man	75.00
367	Elongated Man	75.00
368	BK,Elongated Man	75.00
369	CA,Elongated Man, Catwoman	90.00
370	BK,Elongated Man	75.00
371	BK,Elongated Man	90.00
372	BK,Elongated Man	60.00
373	BK,Elongated Man	60.00
374	BK,Elongated Man	60.00
375	CI,Elongated Man	60.00
376		60.00
377	MA,Elongated Man, V:Riddler	60.00
378	Elongated Man	60.00
379	CI,Elongated Man	60.00
380	Elongated Man	60.00
381	GaF,Marital Bliss Miss	60.00
382	FR(s),BbB,JoG,GaF(s),SGe	60.00
383	FR(s),BbB,JoG,GaF(s),SGe	60.00
384	FR(s),BbB,JoG,SGe, BU:Batgirl	60.00
385	E:FR(s),BbB,JoG,NA(c),GK,MA, MkF,BU:Batgirl	60.00
386	BbK,MkF,BbB,JoG, BU:Batgirl	60.00
387	RA,rep.Detective #27	75.00
388	JBr(s),BbB,JoG, GK,MA,FR(s)	70.00
389	FR(s),BbB,JoG,GK,MA	60.00
390	FR(s),BbB,JoG,GK,MA, A:Masquerader	60.00
391	FR(s),NA(c),BbB, JoG,GK,MA	50.00
392	FR(s),BbB,JoG,I:Jason Bard	50.00
393	FR(s),BbB,JoG,GK,MA	50.00
394	FR(s),BbB,JoG,GK,MA	50.00
395	FR(s),NA,DG,GK,MA	55.00
396	FR(s),BbB,JoG,GK,MA	50.00
397	DON(s),NA,DG,GK,MA	55.00
398	FR(s),BbB,JoG,GK,ViC	50.00
399	NA(c),DON(s),BbB,JoG, GK,ViC,Robin	55.00
400	FR(s),NA,DG,GK,I:Man-Bat	100.00
401	NA(c),FR(s),JoG, BbB,JoG,GK,ViC	50.00
402	FR(s),NA,DG,V:Man-Bat	55.00
403	FR(s),BbB,JoG,NA(c),GK,ViC, BU:Robin	55.00
404	NA,GC,GK,A:Enemy Ace	60.00
405	IN,GK,I:League of Assassins	55.00
406	DON(s),BbB,FrG	55.00
407	FR(s),NA,DG,V:Man-bat	60.00
408	MWn(s),LWn(s),NA,DG, V:DrTzin Tzin	60.00
409	B:FR(s),BbB,FrG,DH,DG	45.00
410	DON(s),FR(s),NA,DG,DH	45.00
411	NA(c),DON(s),BbB,DG,DH	35.00
412	NA(c),BbB,DG,DH	35.00
413	NA(c),BbB,DG,DH	35.00
414	DON(s),IN,DG,DH	40.00
415	BbB,DG,DH	40.00
416	DH	40.00
417	BbB,DG,DH,BU:Batgirl	40.00
418	DON(s),DH,IN,DG,A:Creeper	40.00
419	DON(s),DH	40.00
420	DH	40.00
421	DON(s),BbB,DG,DH,A:Batgirl	35.00
422	BbB,DG,DH,Batgirl	35.00
423	BbB,DG,DH	35.00
424	BbB,DG,DH,Batgirl	35.00
425	BWr(c),DON(s),IN,DG,DH	35.00
426	LWn(s),DG,A:Elongated Man	25.00
427	IN,DG,DH,BU:Batgirl	25.00
428	BbB,DG,ENB(s),DD,JoG, BU:Hawkman	25.00
429	DG,JoG,V:Man-Bat	25.00
430	BbB,NC,ENS(s),DG, A:Elongated Man	25.00
431	DON(s),IN,MA	25.00
432	MA,A:Atom	25.00
433	DD,DG,MA	25.00
434	IN,DG,ENB(s),RB,DG	25.00
435	E:FR(s),DG,IN	25.00
436	MA,(i),DG,A:Elongated Man	25.00
437	JA,WS,I:Manhunter	45.00
438	JA,WS,Manhunter	70.00
439	DG,WS,O:Manhunter,Kid Eternity rep.	70.00
440	JAp,WS	70.00
441	HC,WS	70.00
442	ATh,WS	70.00
443	WS,D:Manhunter	70.00
444	JAp,B:Bat-Murderer, A:Ra's Al Ghul	70.00
445	JAp,MGr,A:Talia	70.00
446	JAp,last giant	22.00
447	DG(i),A:Creeper	22.00
448	DG(i),E:Bat-Murderer, A:Creeper,Ra's Al Ghul	22.00
449	'Midnight Rustler in Gotham'	22.00
450	WS	25.00
451		22.00
452		22.00
453		22.00
454		22.00
455	MGr,A:Hawkman,V:Vampire	22.00
456	V:Ulysses Vulcan	22.00
457	O:Batman rtd	25.00
458	A:Man Bat	22.00
459	A:Man Bat	22.00
460		22.00
461	V:Capt.Stingaree	18.00
462	V:Capt.Stingaree,A:Flash	18.00
463	MGr,Atom,I:Calc.,BI.Spider	18.00
464	MGr,TA,BlackCanary	18.00
465	TA,Elongated Man	18.00
466	MR,TA,V:Signalman	24.00
467	MR,TA	24.00
468	MR,TA,A:JLA	24.00
469	WS,I:Dr.Phosphorus	18.00
470	WS,AM,V:Dr.Phosphorus	18.00
471	MR,TA,A:Hugo Strange	24.00
472	MR,TA,A:Hugo Strange	24.00
473	MR,TA,R:Deadshot	24.00
474	MR,TA,A:Penguin, N:Deadshot	25.00
475	MR,TA,A:Joker	70.00
476	MR,TA,A:Joker	70.00
477	MR,DG,rep.NA	25.00
478	MR,DG,I:3rd Clayface	24.00
479	MR,DG,A:3rd Clayface	24.00
480	DN,MA	18.00
481	JSt,CR,DN,DA,MR, A:ManBat	24.00
482	HC,MGo,DG,A:Demon	20.00
483	DN,DA,SD,A:Demon, 40 Anniv.	22.00
484	DN,DA,Demon,O:1st Robin	18.00
485	DN,DA,D:Batwoman,A:Demon A:Ras al Ghul	18.00
486	DN,DA,DG,I:Odd Man, V:Scarecrow	18.00
487	DN,DA,A:Ras Al Ghul	18.00
488	DN,V:Spook,Catwoman	18.00
489	IN,DH,DN,DA,Ras Al Ghul	18.00
490	DN,DA,PB,FMc,A:Black Lightning;A:Ras Al Ghul	18.00
491	DN,DA,PB,FMc,A:Black Lightning;V:Maxie Zeus	18.00
492	DN,DA,A:Penguin	18.00
493	DN,DA,A:Riddler	18.00
494	DN,DA,V:Crime Doctor	18.00
495	DN,DA,V:Crime Doctor	18.00
496	DN,DA,A:Clayface I	10.00
497	DN,DA	10.00
498	DN,DA,V:Blockbuster	10.00
499	DN,DA,V:Blockbuster	10.00
500	DG,CI,WS,TY,JKu,Deadman, Hawkman,Robin	20.00
501	DN,DA	10.00
502	DN,DA	10.00
503	DN,DA,Batgirl,Robin, V:Scarecrow	10.00
504	DN,DA,Joker	12.00
505	DN,DA	10.00
506	DN,DA	10.00
507	DN,DA	10.00
508	DN,DA,V:Catwoman	11.00
509	DN,DA,V:Catman,Catwoman	11.00
510	DN,DA,V:Madhatter	10.00
511	DN,DA,I:Mirage	10.00
512	GC,45th Anniv.	10.00
513	V:Two-Face	11.00

Detective Comics #417
© DC Comics Inc.

All comics prices listed are for *Near Mint* condition.

Detective Comics

#	Description	Price
514		10.00
515		10.00
516		10.00
517		10.00
518	V:Deadshot	10.00
519		10.00
520	A:Hugo Strange,Catwoman	11.00
521	IN,TVE,A:Catwoman,B: BU:Green Arrow	12.00
522	D:Snowman	10.00
523	V:Solomon Grundy	10.00
524	2nd A:J.Todd	11.00
525	J.Todd	10.00
526	DN,AA,A:Joker,Catwoman 500th A:Batman	20.00
527	V:Man Bat	6.00
528	Green Arrow,Ozone	6.00
529	I:Night Slayer,Nocturna	6.00
530	V:Nocturna	6.00
531	GC,AA,Chimera,J.Todd (see Batman #364)	6.00
532	GC,V:Joker	8.00
533		6.00
534	GC,A:Gr.Arrow,V:PoisonIvy	6.00
535	GC,A:Gr.Arrow,V:Crazy Quitt 2nd A:New Robin	7.00
536	GC,A:Gr.Arrow,V:Deadshot	6.00
537	GC,A:Gr.Arrow	6.00
538	GC,A:Gr.Arrow,V:Catman	6.00
539	GC,A:Gr.Arrow	6.00
540	GC,A:Gr.Arrow,V:Scarecrow	6.00
541	GC,A:Gr.Arrow,V:Penguin	7.00
542	GC,A:Gr.Arrow	6.00
543	GC,A:Gr.Arrow,V:Nightslayer	6.00
544	GC,A:Gr.Arrow,V:Nightslayer Nocturna	6.00
545		6.00
546		6.00
547		6.00
548	PB	6.00
549	PB,KJ,AMo(s),Gr.Arrow	7.00
550	KJ,AMo(s),Gr.Arrow	7.00
551	PB,V:Calendar Man	6.00
552	V:Black Mask	6.00
553	V:Black Mask	6.00
554	KJ,N:Black Canary	6.00
555	GC,DD,GreenArrow	6.00
556	GC,Gr.Arrow,V:Nightslayer	6.00
557	V:Nightslayer	6.00
558	GC,Green Arrow	6.00
559	GC,Green Arrow	6.00
560	GC,A:Green Arrow	6.00
561		6.00
562	GC,V:Film Freak	6.00
563	V:Two Face	6.00
564	V:Two Face	6.00
565	GC,A:Catwoman	7.00
566	GC,Joker	8.00
567	GC,HarlanEllison	6.00
568	KJ,Legends tie-in,A:Penguin	7.00
569	AD,V:Joker	7.00
570	AD,EvilCatwoman,A:Joker	7.00
571	AD,V:Scarecrow	6.00
572	AD,CI,A:Elongated Man,Sherlock Holmes,SlamBradley,50thAnn.	6.00
573	AD,V:Mad Hatter	6.00
574	AD,End old J.Todd/Robin sty	6.00
575	AD,Year 2,pt.1,I:Reaper	18.00
576	TM,AA,Year 2,pt.2, R:Joe Chill	17.00
577	TM,AA,Year 2,pt.3,V:Reaper	17.00
578	TM,AA,Year 2,pt.4, D:Joe Chill	17.00
579	I:NewCrimeDoctor	4.00
580	V:Two Face	4.00
581	V:Two Face	4.00
582	Millennium X-over	4.00
583	I:Ventriloquist	4.00
584	V:Ventriloquist	4.00
585	I:Rat Catcher	4.00
586	V:Rat Catcher	4.00
587	NB,V:Corrosive Man	4.00
588	NB,V:Corrosive Man	4.00
589	Bonus Book #5	5.00
590	NB,V:Hassan	4.00
591	NB,V:Rollo	4.00
592	V:Psychic Vampire	4.00
593	NB,V:Stirh	4.00
594	NB,A:Mr.Potato	4.00
595	IN,bonus book #11	4.00

Detective Comics #658
© DC Comics, Inc.

#	Description	Price
596	V:Sladek	4.00
597	V:Sladek	4.00
598	DCw,BSz,Blind Justice #1	5.00
599	DCw,BSz,Blind Justice #2	5.00
600	DCw,BSz,Blind Justice #3, 50th Anniv.(double size)	5.00
601	NB,I:Tulpa	3.00
602	NB,A:Jason Blood	3.00
603	NB,A:Demon	3.00
604	NB,MudPack #1,V:Clayface, poster insert	3.00
605	NB,MudPack #2,V:Clayface	3.00
606	NB,MudPack #3,V:Clayface	3.00
607	NB,MudPack #4,V:Clayface, poster insert	3.00
608	NB,I:Anarky	3.00
609	NB,V:Anarky	3.00
610	NB,V:Penguin	3.00
611	NB,V:Catwoman,Catman	4.00
612	NB,A:Vicki Vale	3.00
613	Search for Poisoner	3.00
614	V:Street Demons	3.00
615	NB,Return Penguin #2 (see Batman #448-#449)	3.50
616	NB	3.00
617	A:Joker	3.00
618	NB,DG,A:Tim Drake	3.00
619	NB,V:Moneyspider	3.00
620	NB,V:Obeah,Man	3.00
621	NB,SM,Obeah,Man	3.00
622	Demon Within,pt.1	3.00
623	Demon Within,pt.2	3.00
624	Demon Within,pt.3	3.00
625	JAp,I:Abattior	3.00
626	JAp,A:Electrocutioner	3.00
627	600th issue w/Batman,rep. Detective #27	5.00
628	JAp,A:Abattior	3.00
629	JAp,`The Hungry Grass'	3.00
630	JAp,I:Stiletto	3.00
631	JAp,V:Neo-Nazi Gangs	3.00
632	JAp,V:Creature	3.00
633	TMd,Fake Batman?	3.00
634	`The Third Man'	3.00
635	Video Game,pt.1	3.00
636	Video Game,pt.2	3.00
637	Video Game,pt.3	3.00
638	JAp,Walking Time Bomb	3.00
639	JAp,The Idiot Root,pt.2	3.00
640	JAp,The Idiot Root,pt.4	3.00
641	JAp,Destroyer,pt.3 (see LOTDK#27)	3.00
642	JAp,Faces,pt.2	3.00
643	JAp,`Librarian of Souls'	3.00
644	TL,Electric City,pt.1 A:Electrocutioner	3.00
645	TL,Electric City,pt.2	3.00
646	TL,Electric City,pt.3	3.00
647	TL,V:Cluemaster	3.00
648	MWg(c),TL,V:Cluemaster	4.00
649	MWg(c),TL,V:Cluemaster	3.00
650	TL,A:Harold,Ace	3.00
651	TL,`A Bullet for Bullock'	3.00
652	GN,R:Huntress	3.00
653	GN,A:Huntress	3.00
654	MN,The General,pt.1	3.00
655	MN,The General,pt.2	3.00
656	MN,The General,pt.3,C:Bane	4.00
657	MN,A:Azrael,I:Cypher	5.00
658	MN,A:Azrael	3.50
659	MN,Knightfall#2, V:Ventriloquist,A:Bane	3.50
660	Knightfall#4,Bane Vs. Killer Croc	3.00
661	GN,Knightfall#6,V:Firefly, Joker,A:Bane	3.00
662	GN,Knightfall#8,V:Firefly, Joker,A:Huntress,Bane	3.00
663	GN,Knightfall#10,V:Trogg, Zombie,Bird,A:Bane	3.00
664	GN,Knightfall#12,A:Azrael	3.00
665	GN,Knightfall#16,A:Azrael	3.00
666	GN,SHa,A:Azrael,Trogg, Zombie,Bird	3.00
667	GN,SHa,Knightquest:Crusade, V:Trigger Twins	3.00
668	GN,SHa,Knightquest:Crusade, Robin locked out of Batcave	3.00
669	GN,SHa,Knightquest:Crusade, V:Trigger Twins	3.00
670	GN,SHa,Knightquest:Crusade, F:Rene Montoya	3.00
671	GN,SHa,V:Joker	3.00
672	KJ(c),GN,SHa,Knightquest: Crusade,V:Joker	3.00
673	KJ(c),GN,SHa,Knightquest: Crusade,V:Joker	3.00
674	KJ(c),GN,SHa,Knightquest: Crusade	3.00
675	Foil(c),KJ(c),GN,SHa,Knightquest: Crusade,V:Gunhawk,foil(c)	4.00
675a	Newsstand ed.	3.00
675b	Platinum edition	5.00
676	KJ(c),GN,SHa,Knights End #3, A:Nightwing	4.00
677	KJ(c),GN,SHa,Knights End #9 V:Azrael	3.00
678	GN,SHa,Zero Hour	3.00
679	Ratcatcher	3.00
680	Batman,Two-Face	3.00
681	CDi,GN,KJ,Jean-Paul Valley	3.00
682	CDi,GN,SHa,Return of Bruce Wayne,Troika,pt.3	3.00
682a	Collector's Edition	3.50
683	R:Penguin,I:Actuary	3.00
684	Daylight Heist	3.00
685	Chinatown War	3.00
686	V:King Snake,Lynx	3.00
687	CDi,SHa,V:River Pirate	2.50
688	V:Captian Fear	2.50
689	F:Black Mask,Firefly	2.50
690	F:Black Mask,Firefly	2.50
691	V:Spellbinder	2.50
692	CDi,SHa,Underworld	

Comics Values Annual — DC — Detective–Doctor

Unleashed tie-in 2.50	754 Officer Down x-over,pt.6 . . . . . . 2.50	
693 CDi,SHa,V:Poison Ivy	755 SMa,DPs,V:Two-Face 2.50	
& Agent Orange 2.50	756 Lord of the Ring x-over pt.2 . . . 2.50	
694 CDi,find plant-killer 2.50	757 RBr,RyR,DPs,Air Time 2.50	
695 CDi 3.00	758 SMa,Crooked Cops in Gotham . . 2.50	
696 CDi,GN,SHa,Contagion,pt.8 . . . 3.00	759 SMa,BU:Catwoman,pt.1 . . . . . . 2.50	
697 CDi,GN,SHa,pt.1 (of 3)	760 SMa,V:Mad Hatter,BU:pt.2 . . . . 2.50	
V:Lock-up 2.50	761 SMa,BU:Catwoman,pt.3 . . . . . . 2.50	
698 CDi(s),A:Two-Face 2.50	762 RBr,BU:Catwoman,concl 2.50	
699 CDi(s), ... 2.50	763 SMa,F:Sasha,V:Cucilla 2.50	
700 double size, Legacy, pt.1	764 SMa,F:Vesper 2.50	
x-over, R:Bane 3.50	765 RBr,James Gordon 2.50	
700a cardstock cover 6.00	766 Bruce Wayne:Murderer,pt.1 . . . 2.50	
701 Legacy, pt. 6 x-over, V:Bane . . 2.50	767 Bruce Wayne:Murderer,pt.8 . . . 5.00	
702 CDi(s),GN,SHa,Legacy	768 MGy,shipment of heroin 2.50	
aftermath 2.50	769 Bruce Wayne:Fugitive,pt.5 . . . . 2.50	
703 CDi(s),GN,SHa, riots in Gotham	770 Bruce Wayne:Fugitive,pt.8 . . . . 2.50	
City, Final Night tie-in 2.50	771 BruceWayne:Fugitive,pt.12 . . . . 2.50	
704 CDi(s),GN,TP,V:Al Gabone . . . 2.50	772 BruceWayne:Fugitive,pt.16 . . . . 2.75	
705 CDi(s),GN,Riddler & Cluemaster	773 F:Sasha Bordeaux in prison . . . 2.75	
clash 2.50	774 BSz(c),Checkmate 2.75	
706 CDi(s),GN, ... 2.50	775 BSz(c),V:Checkmate 48-pg 3.50	
707 CDi(s),GN,Riddler/Cluemaster	776 BWi,A cop's vendetta 2.75	
concl 2.50	777 Dead Reckoning,pt.1 . . . . 2.75	
708 CDi(s),GN,BSz,F:Deathstroke,	778 Dead Reckoning,pt.2 . . . . 2.75	
R:Gunhawk, pt.1 (of 3) 2.50	779 Dead Reckoning,pt.3 . . . . 2.75	
709 CDi(s),GN,BSz,F:Deathstroke,	780 Dead Reckoning,pt.4 . . . . 2.75	
Gunhawk,pt.2 . . . . 2.50	781 Dead Reckoning,pt.5 . . . . 2.75	*Doc Savage #3*
710 CDi(s),GN,BSz,F:Deathstroke,	782 Dead Reckoning,pt.6 . . . . 2.75	© DC Comics, Inc.
Gunhawk,pt.3 . . . . 2.50	783 SMa,KJ,More Perfect 2.75	
711 CDi(s),GN,CaS,Bruce Wayne	784 Made of Wood,pt.1 . . . . 2.75	**DOC SAVAGE**
fights crime 2.50	785 Made of Wood,pt.2 . . . . 2.75	**1987–88**
712 CDi(s),GN,I:Gearhead 2.50	786 Made of Wood,pt.3 . . . . 2.75	1 AKu/NKu,D:Orig. Doc Savage . . . 3.00
713 CDi(s),GN,V:Gearhead,pt.2 . . . 2.50	787 RBr,Low,Mad Hatter,Man-Bat . . 2.75	2 AKu/NKu,V:Nazi's 3.00
714 CDi(s),GN,F:MartianManhunter 2.50	788 Randori Stone, pt.1 . . . . 2.75	3 AKu/NKu,V:Nazi's 3.00
715 CDi(s),GN,F:MartianManhunter	Ann.#1 KJ,TD,A:Question,Talia,	4 AKu/NKu,V:Heinz 3.00
pt.2 . . . . 2.50	V:Penguin 6.00	**[2nd Series], 1988–90**
716 CDi,JAp,SNw,BSf, ... 2.50	Ann.#2 VS,A:Harvey Harris 6.00	1 `Five in the Sky'(painted cov.) . . . 3.00
717 CDi,GN,BSf,V:Gearhead,pt.1 . . 2.50	Ann.#3 DJu,DG,Batman in Japan . . 2.50	2 Chip Lost in Himalayas 3.00
718 CDi,GN,BSf,V:Gearhead,pt.2 . . 2.50	Ann.#4 Armageddon,pt.10 . . . . 3.00	3 Doc declares war on USSR 3.00
719 . . . . 3.00	Ann.#5 SK(c),TMd,Eclipso,V:The	4 Doc Savage/Russian team-up . . . 3.00
720 CDi,GN,KJ,Cataclysm	Ventriloquist,Joker 3.00	5 V:The Erisians 3.00
x-over,pt.5 . . . . 4.00	Ann.#6 JBa,I:Geist 2.75	6 U.S.,USSR,China Alliance
721 CDi,GN,KJ,Cataclysm 3.00	Ann.#7 CDi,Elseworlds Story 3.25	vs. Erisians 3.00
722 CDi,JAp,BSf,Aftershock 3.00	Ann.#8 CDi,KD(c) Year One Annual	7 Mind Molder,pt.1, I:Pat Savage . . 3.00
723 CDi,BSz,Brotherhood of	O:The Riddler 3.95	8 . . . . 3.00
the Fist x-over, pt.2 . . . . 3.00	Ann.#9 Legends o/t Dead Earth . . . 2.95	9 In Hidalgo 3.00
724 CDi,JAp,BSf,F:Nightwing 3.00	Ann.#10 Pulp Heroes (War) CDi(s),	10 V:Forces of the Golden God . . . 3.00
725 CDi,TP,BSf,Aftershock 3.00	SB,KJ 3.95	11 Sunlight Rising,pt.1 . . . . 3.00
726 CDi(s),BSf,V:Joker 3.00	Spec.#1,000,000 CDi(s) 2.00	12 Sunlight Rising,pt.2 . . . . 3.00
727 . . . . 3.00	TPB Manhunter AGw,WS 10.00	13 Sunlight Rising,pt.3 . . . . 3.00
728 CDi(s),BSf,SB,No Man's Land . 3.00		14 Sunlight Rising,pt.4 . . . . 3.00
729 CDi(s),SB,No Man's Land 3.00	**DETENTION COMICS**	15 SeaBaron #1 . . . . 3.00
730 No Law and a New Order,	**Aug., 1996**	16 EB,Shadow & Doc Savage 3.50
concl 4.00	one-shot DON(s) 64pg, 3 stories . . . 3.50	17 EB,Shadow & Doc Savage 4.00
731 F:Batgirl, Mosaic, pt.2 . . . . 3.00		18 EB,Shadow/Doc Savage conc . . 4.00
732 F:Batgirl, Mosaic, pt.4 . . . . 3.00	**DEXTER'S LABORATORY**	19 All new 1930's story 2.50
733 SB,Alfreds advice 3.00	**Warner Bros./DC, 1999**	20 V:Airlord & his Black Zepplin . . . 2.50
734 F:Batgirl,pt.2 x-over 3.00	1 Kirbytron 6000 . . . . 5.00	21 Airlord (30's story conc.) 2.50
735 DJu,BSz,Fruit of	2 Let's Save the World, You Jerk . . 4.00	22 Doc Savages Past,pt.1 . . . . 2.50
the Earth,pt.3 . . . . 3.00	3 thru 10 . . . . @3.00	23 Doc Savages Past,pt.2 . . . . 2.50
736 LHa(s),MD2,V:Bane 3.00	11 thru 24 . . . . @2.50	24 Doc Savages Past,pt.3 (final). . . 2.50
737 TMo, No Man's Land,	25 Action Hank, spec. price 1.00	Ann.#1 1956 Olympic Games 4.50
The Code, concl 3.00	26 thru 34 . . . . @2.25	
738 CDi,MtB,Goin'Downtown,pt.2 . . 3.00		**DOCTOR FATE**
739 Jurisprudence,concl 3.00	**DHAMPIRE: STILLBORN**	**July, 1987**
740 . . . . 3.00	**DC/Vertigo, Sept., 1996**	1 KG,V:Lords of Chaos 3.00
741 Endgame, pt.3,40-pg.x-over . . . 3.00	GN Nancy A. Collins adaptation . . . 6.00	2 KG,New Dr. Fate 3.00
742 SMa, 40-pg. 2.50		3 KG,A:JLI 3.00
743 SMa,40-pg,new logo 2.50	**DISAVOWED**	4 KG,V:Lords of Chaos Champion . 3.00
744 SMa,40-pg 2.50	**Homage/DC Jan., 2000**	**[2nd Series], 1988–92**
745 SMa,V:Whisperer 2.50	1 BCi 2.50	1 New Dr.Fate,V:Demons 4.00
746 SMa,B.U.:The Jacobian 2.50	2 BCi(s) 2.50	2 A:Andrew Bennett(I,Vampire) . . . 3.00
747 JJ,F:Renee Montoya 2.50	3 BCi(s) 2.50	3 A:Andrew Bennett(I,Vampire) . . . 3.00
748 JJ,Urban Renewal,pt.1 . . . . 2.50	4 BCi(s),F:Iven 2.50	4 V:I, Vampire 3.00
749 JJ,PhH,Urban Renewal,pt.2 . . . 2.50	5 BCi(s) 2.50	5 Dr.Fate & I,Vampire in Europe . . 3.00
750 V:Ra's Al Ghul,64-pg 6.00	6 BCi(s) 2.50	6 A:Petey 3.00
751 SMa,JJ,DPS,F:Poison Ivy 2.50		7 Petey returns home dimension . . 3.00
752 SMa,JJ,DPs,F:Poison Ivy 2.50		8 Linda become Dr.Fate again 3.00
753 SMa,JJ,DPs,This issue:		9 Eric's Mother's Ghost,
Batman dies! 2.50		A:Deadman 3.00

All comics prices listed are for *Near Mint* condition.

CVA Page 69

DC COMICS

Doctor Fate #23 © DC Comics, Inc.

10 Death of Innocence,pt.1	3.00
11 Return of Darkseid, Death of Innocence,pt.2	3.00
12 Two Dr.Fates Vs.Darkseid, Death of Innocence,pt.3	3.00
13 Linda in the Astral Realm, Death of Innocence,pt.4	3.00
14 Kent & Petey vs. Wotan	3.00
15 V:Wotan,A:JLI	3.50
16 Flashback-novice Dr.Fate	2.50
17 Eric's Journey thru afterlife	2.50
18 Search for Eric	2.50
19 A:Dr.Benjamine Stoner, Lords of Chaos, Phantom Stranger, Search for Eric continued	2.50
20 V:Lords of Chaos,Dr.Stoner, A:Phantom Stranger	2.50
21 V:Chaos,A:PhantomStranger	2.50
22 A:Chaos and Order	2.50
23 Spirits of Kent & Inza Nelson	2.50
24 L:Dr.Fate Characters	2.50
25 I:New Dr. Fate	2.50
26 Dr.Fate vs. Orig.Dr.Fate	2.50
27 New York Crime	2.50
28 `Diabolism'	2.50
29 Kent Nelson	2.50
30 `Resurrection'	2.50
31 `Resurrection' contd.	2.50
32 War of the Gods x-over	2.50
33 War of the Gods x-over	2.50
34 A:T'Gilian	2.50
35 Kent Nelson in N.Y.	2.50
36 Search For Inza,A:Shat-Ru	2.50
37 Fate Helmet Powers revealed	2.50
38 `The Spirit Motor,'Flashback	2.50
39 U.S.Senate Hearing	2.50
40 A:Wonder Woman	2.50
41 O:Chaos and Order,last issue	2.50
Ann.#1 TS,R:Eric's dead mother	3.00

DR. FATE
Aug. 2003

1 (of 5) Hector Hall	2.50
2 Salem mystics	2.50
3 Nabu disappeared	2.50
4 The Curse	2.50

DOCTOR MID-NITE
1999

1 (of 3) MWg,F:Dr. Piter Cross.	6.00
2 MWg	6.00
3 MWg, conclusion	6.00
TPB	19.95

DOME, THE: GROUND ZERO
DC/Helix, July, 1998

1-shot DGb,AMK	8.00

DOOM FORCE
1992

Spec.#1 MMi(c),RCa,WS,PCu,KSy, I:Doom Force	3.00

DOOM PATROL
[1st series]
See: MY GREATEST ADVENTURE

DOOM PATROL
[2nd Regular Series], 1987

1 SLi,R:Doom Patrol,plus Who's Who background of team, I:Kalki	5.00
2 SLi,V:Kalki	3.50
3 SLi,I:Lodestone	3.50
4 SLi,I:Karma	3.50
5 SLi,R:Chief	3.50
6 B:PuK(s),EL,GyM(i), I:Scott Fischer	4.50
7 EL,GyM(i),V:Shrapnel	3.50
8 EL,GyM(i),V:Shrapnel	3.50
9 E:PuK(s),EL,GyM(i),V:Garguax, & Bonus Book	3.50
10 EL,A:Superman	3.50
11 EL,R:Garguax	3.00
12 EL,A:Garguax	3.00
13 EL,A:Power Girl	3.00
14 EL,A:Power Girl	3.00
15 EL,Animal-Veg-.Mineral Man	3.00
16 V:GenImmotus,Animal-Veg.-Mineral Man	3.00
17 D:Celsius,R:Aquaman & Sea Devils, Invasion tie-in	4.00
18 Invasion	3.00
19 B:GMo(s),New Direction, I:Crazy Jane	8.00
20 I:Rebis(new Negative-Being), A:CrazyJane,Scissormen	4.00
21 V:Scissormen	3.50
22 City of Bone,V:Scissormen	3.50
23 A:RedJack,Lodestone kidnap	3.50
24 V:Red Jack	3.50
25 Secrets of New Doom Patrol	3.50
26 I:Brotherhood of Dada	3.00
27 V:Brotherhood of Dada	3.00
28 Trapped in nightmare,V:Dada	3.00
29 Trapped in painting, A:Superman	3.00
30 SBs(c),V:Brotherhood of Dada	3.00
31 SBs(c),A:The Pale Police	3.00
32 SBs(c),V:Cult of Unwritten Book	3.00
33 SBs(c),V:Cult,A:Anti-God the DeCreator	3.00
34 SBs(c),Robotman vs. his brain, R:The Brain & Mr.Mallah	3.00
35 SBs(c),A:Men from N.O.W.H.E.R.E.	3.00
36 SBs(c),V:Men from N.O.W.H.E.R.E.	3.25
37 SBs(c),Rhea Jones Story	2.50
38 SBs(c),V:Aliens	2.50
39 SBs(c),V:Aliens	2.50
40 SBs(c),Aliens	2.50
41 SBS(c),Aliens	2.50
42 O:Flex Mentallo	2.50
43 SBs(c),V:N.O.W.H.E.R.E.	2.50
44 SBs(c),V:N.O.W.H.E.R.E.	2.50
45	2.50
46 SBs(c),RCa,MkK,A:Crazy Jane, Dr.Silence	2.50

Doom Patrol #9 © DC Comics, Inc.

47 Scarlet Harlot (Crazy Jane)	2.50
48 V:Mr.Evans	2.50
49 TTg(c),RCa,MGb,I:Mr.Nobody	2.50
50 SBs(c),V:Brotherhood of Dada & bonus artists portfolio	3.00
51 SBs(c),Mr.Nobody Runs for President	2.50
52 SBs(c),Mr.Nobody saga conc.	2.50
53 SBs(c),Parody Issue,A:Phantom Stranger,Hellblazer,Mr.E	2.50
54 Rebis'Transformation	2.50
55 SBs(c),V:Crazy Jane, Candle Maker	2.50
56 SBs(c),RCa,V:Candle Maker	2.50
57 SBs(c),RCa,V:Candle Maker, O:Team,Double-sized	3.00
58 SBs(c),V:Candle Maker	2.50
59 TTg(c),RCa,SnW(i),A:Candlemaker D:Larry Trainor	2.50
60 JHw(c),RCa,SnW(i), V:Candlemaker,A:Magnus	2.50
61 TTg(c),RCa,SnW(i),A:Magnus D:Candlemaker	2.50
62 DFg(c),RCa,SnW(i), V:Nanomachines	2.50
63 E:GMo(s),RCa,R:Crazy Jane, V:Keysmiths,BU:Sliding from the Wreckage	2.50

DC/Vertigo, 1993

64 BB(c),B:RaP(s),RCa,SnW(i), B:Sliding from the Wreckage, R:Niles Caulder	3.00
65 TTg(c),RCa,SnW(i),Nannos	3.00
66 RCa,E:Sliding from the Wreckage	3.00
67 TTg(c),LiM,GHi(i),New HQ,I:Charlie, George, Marion,V:Wild Girl	3.00
68 TTg(c),LiM,GHi(i),I:Indentity Addict	3.00
69 TTg(c),LiM,GHi(i),V:Identity Addict	3.00
70 TTg(c),SEa,TS(i),I:Coagula, V:Codpiece	3.00
71 TTg(c),LiM,TS(i),Fox & Crow	3.00
72 TTg(c),LiM,TS(i),Fox vs Crow	3.00
73 LiM,GPi(i),Head's Nightmare	3.00
74 LiM,TS(i),Bootleg Steele	3.00
75 BB(c),TMK,Teiresias Wars#1, Double size	3.00
76 Teiresias Wars#2	3.00
77 BB(c),TMK,N:Cliff	3.00
78 BB(c),V:Tower of Babel	3.00
79 BB(c),E:Teiresias Wars	3.00
80 V:Yapping Dogs	3.00

DC

Doom–Eclipso

#	Title	Price
81	B:Masquerade	3.00
82	E:Masquerade	3.00
83	False Memory	3.00
84	The Healers	3.00
85	Charlie the Doll	3.00
86	Imagine Ari's Friends	3.00
87	KB(c),Imagine Ari's Friends,pt.4,final issue	3.00
Ann.#1	A:Lex Luthor	3.00
Ann.#2	RaP(s),MkW,Children's Crusade,F:Dorothy,A:Maxine	4.25
	Doom Patrol/Suicide Squad #1 EL, D:Mr.104,Thinker,Psi,Weasel	2.50
	TPB Crawling From the Wreckage, SBs(c),rep.#19-#25	19.95

DOOM PATROL
Oct., 2001

#	Title	Price
1	JAr,R:Doom Patrol	3.00
2	JAr,F:Robotman, Thayer	2.50
3	JAr,V:Gomz	2.50
4	JAr,new Doom Patrol?	2.50
5	JAr,Doom Force	2.50
6	JAr,Robotman gone	2.50
7	JAr,search for Robotman	2.50
8	JAr,new Robotman	2.50
9	JAr,Cliff Steele, Robotman	2.50
10	JAr,Black Vulture,Amazo	2.50
11	JAr,in Hell	2.50
12	JAr,V:Demon Raum	2.50
13	JAr(s),Monsters,pt.1	2.50
14	JAr(s),Monsters,pt.2	2.50
15	JAr(s),F:Robotman	2.50
16	JAr(s),V:Purple Purposeless	2.50
17	JAr(s),R:Tycho	2.50
18	JAr(s),ancient China	2.50
19	JAr(s),R:Tycho	2.50
20	television studios	2.50
21	O:Tycho	2.50
22	final issue	2.50

DOOMSDAY
1995

#	Title	Price
Ann.#1	Year One annuals	4.00

DOORWAY TO NIGHTMARE
1978

#	Title	Price
1	I:Madame Xanadu	15.00
2		10.00
3		10.00
4	JCr	10.00
5		10.00

DOUBLE ACTION COMICS
Jan., 1940

#	Title	Price
2	Pre-Hero DC	17,000.00

DRAGONLANCE
1988–91

#	Title	Price
1	Krynn's Companion's advent.	4.00
2	Vandar&Riva vs.Riba's brother	3.50
3	V:Takhesis,Queen of Darkness	3.50
4	V:Lord Soth & Kitiara	3.50
5	V:Queen of Darkness	3.50
6	Gnatch vs. Kalthanan	3.50
7	Raistlin's Evil contd.	3.50
8	Raistlin's Evil concl.	3.00
9	Journey to land o/t Minotaurs A:Tanis, Kitiara	3.00
10	Blood Sea,`Arena of Istar'	3.00
11	Cataclysm of Krynn Revealed `Arena of Istar' contd.	3.00
12	Horak vs.Koraf, Arena contd.	3.00
13	Test of High Sorcery #1	3.00

Dragonlance #28 © DC Comics Inc.

#	Title	Price
14	Test of High Sorcery #2	3.00
15	Test of High Sorcery #3	3.00
16	Test of High Sorcery #4	3.00
17	Winter'sKnight:DragonkillPt.1	3.00
18	Winter'sKnight:DragonkillPt.1	3.00
19	Winter'sKnight:DragonkillPt.1	3.00
20	Winter'sKnight:DragonkillPt.1	3.00
21	Move to New World	3.00
22	Taladas,pt.1,A:Myrella	3.00
23	Taladas,pt.2,Riva vs. Dragon	3.00
24	Taladas,pt.3,V:Minotaur Lord	3.00
25	Taladas,pt.4,V:Axantheas	3.00
26	Rune Discovery,V:Agents of Eristem	3.00
27	V:Agents of Eristem	3.00
28	Riva continued	3.00
29	Riva continued	3.00
30	Dwarf War,pt.1	3.00
31	Dwarf War,pt.2	3.00
32	Dwarf War,pt.3	3.00
33	Dwarf War,pt.4	3.00
34	conc., last issue	3.00
Ann.#1	Myrella of the Robed Wizards	2.95

DREAMING, THE
DC/Vertigo, June, 1996

#	Title	Price
1	TLa(s),PSj,GoldieFactor,pt.1	4.50
2	TLa(s),PSj,GoldieFactor,pt.2	4.00
3	TLa(s),PSj,GoldieFactor,pt.3	4.00
4	SvP,The Lost Boy,pt.1	3.50
5	SvP,The Lost Boy,pt.2	2.50
6	SvP,The Lost Boy,pt.3	2.50
7	SvP,The Lost Boy,pt.4	2.50
8	AaK(s),MZi,visitor from past	2.50
9	BT(s),PD,TOz,Weird Romance, pt.1	2.50
10	BT(s),PD,TOz,Romance,pt.2	2.50
11	BT(s),PD,TOz,Romance,pt.3	2.50
12	BT(s),PD,TOz,Romance,pt.4	2.50
13	TLa, JIT,Coyote's Kiss,pt.1	2.50
14	TLa, JIT,Coyote's Kiss,pt.2	2.50
15		2.50
16	GyA,F:Nuala	2.50
17	PD,DMc,Souvenirs, pt.1	2.50
18	PD,DMc,Souvenirs, pt.2	2.50
19	PD,DMc,Souvenirs, pt.3	2.50
20	ADv, The Dark Rose, pt.1	2.50
21	ADv, The Dark Rose, pt.2	2.50
22	The Unkindness of One, pt.1	2.50
23	The Unkindness of One, pt.2	2.50
24	The Unkindness of One, pt.3	2.50
25	My Life as a Man	2.50
26	Restitution	2.50
27	Caretaker Cain	2.50
28	Victims of famous fires	2.50
29	PSj,DMc,Abel'sHouse ofSecrets	2.50
30	DMc(c),Lucien's mysteries	2.50
31	House of Secrets, 48-pg.	4.00
32	DG,SvP	2.50
33	The Little Mermaid	2.50
34	MaH, Cave of Nightmares	2.50
35	DMc(c),Kaleidoscope	2.50
36	DMc(c),The Gyres, pt.1	2.50
37	DMc(c),The Gyres, pt.2	2.50
38	DMc(c),The Gyres, pt.3	2.50
39	DMc(c),Lost Language of Flowers	2.50
40	DMc(c),Foxes & Hounds,pt.1	2.50
41	DMc(c),Foxes & Hounds,pt.2	2.50
42	DMc(c),Foxes & Hounds,pt.3	2.50
43	DMc(c),Foxes & Hounds,pt.4	2.50
44	Trinket,pt.1	2.50
45	Trinket,pt.2	2.50
46	Trinket,pt.3	2.50
47	CV,RoR	2.50
48		2.50
49	DMc(c),The Dawn Stone	2.50
50	DMc(c),rebuilding	2.50
51	DMc(c),in Manhattan	2.50
52	Exiles,pt.1	2.50
53	Exiles,pt.2	2.50
54	Exiles,pt.3	2.50
55	F:Danny Nod	2.50
56	1stAdventure of CatterinaPoe	2.50
57	Rise,pt.1	2.50
58	Rise,pt.2	2.50
59	Rise,pt.3	2.50
60	Rise,pt.4	2.50
	TPB Beyond the Shores of Night	20.00
	TPB Through the Gates of Horn & Ivory	20.00
	GN Trial and Error	6.00

DROPSIE AVENUE: THE NEIGHBORHOOD
Jan., 2001

#	Title	Price
	TPB 176-page	14.95

DYNAMIC CLASSICS
Sept-Oct., 1978

#	Title	Price
1	NA,WS,rep.Detective 395&438	15.00

ECLIPSO
1992–94

#	Title	Price
1	BS,MPn,V:South American Drug Dealers	2.50
2	BS,MPn,A:Bruce Gordon	2.25
3	BS,MPn,R:Amanda Waller	2.25
4	BS,A:Creeper,Cave Carson	2.25
5	A:Creeper,Cave Carson	2.25
6	LMc,V:Bruce Gordon	2.25
7	London,1891	2.25
8	A:Sherlock Holmes	2.25
9	I:Johnny Peril	2.25
10	CDo,V:Darkseid	2.25
11	A:Creeper,Peacemaker,Steel	2.25
12	V:Shadow Fighters	2.25
13	D:Manhunter,Commander Steel, Major Victory,Peacemaker, Wildcat,Dr.Midnight,Creeper	2.25
14	A:JLA	2.25
15	A:Amanda Waller	2.25
16	V:US Army	2.25
17	A:Amanda Waller,Martian Manhunter,Wonder Woman,Flash, Bloodwynd,Booster Gold	2.25
18	A:Spectre,JLA,final issue	2.25
Ann.#1	I:Prism	2.50

All comics prices listed are for Near Mint condition.

Eclipso–Essential — DC — Comics Values Annual

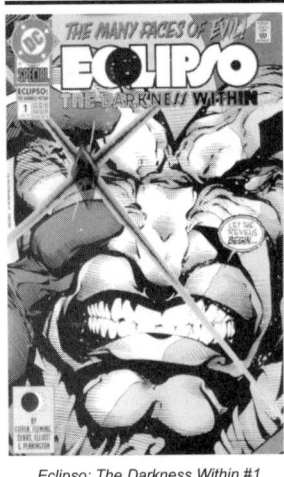

Eclipso: The Darkness Within #1
© DC Comics, Inc.

ECLIPSO: THE DARKNESS WITHIN
1992
1 BS,Direct w/purple diamond,
 A:Superman,Creeper 4.00
1a BS,Newstand w/out diamond . . 3.00
2 BS,MPn,DC heroes V:Eclipso,
 D:Starman 3.00

EGYPT
1995–96
1 College Experiments. 3.50
2 College Experiments. 3.00
3 New York Haunt 3.00
4 V:Seth,Isis 3.00
5 V: The Priests. 3.00
6 . . . . 3.00
7 finale 3.00

80 PAGE GIANTS
Aug., 1964
1 Superman. 650.00
2 Jimmy Olsen. 400.00
3 Lois Lane 300.00
4 Golden Age-Flash. 300.00
5 Batman. 300.00
6 Superman. 250.00
7 JKu&JKu(c),Sgt. Rock's Prize
 Battle Tales. 250.00
8 Secret Origins,O:JLA,Aquaman,
 Robin,Atom, Superman . . . 550.00
9 Flash 225.00
10 Superboy. 225.00
11 Superman,A:Lex Luthor 225.00
12 Batman 225.00
13 Jimmy Olsen 225.00
14 Lois Lane. 225.00
15 Superman & Batman 225.00
16 thru 89 in regular series runs

EL DIABLO
1989–91
1 I:El Diablo, double-size 3.00
2 V:Crime Lord Benny Contreras . . 2.50
3 'Day of the Dead' Celebration . . . 2.50
4 thru 7 Storm #1–#4 . . . . @2.50
8 V:Car-Theft Ring. 2.50
9 V:Crime Lord of Dos Rios 2.50
10 The Franchise #1. . . . . 2.50
11 The Franchise #2. . . . . 2.50

12 A:Greg Sanders (golden age). . . 2.50
13 thru 15 The River #1–#3. . . . . @2.50
16 Final Issue. 2.50

EL DIABLO
DC/Vertigo, Jan., 2001
1 (of 4) Weird Western Tales 2.50
2 thru 4 . . . . @2.50

ELECTRIC WARRIOR
1986–87
1 SF series,I:Electric Warriors 2.50
2 'Bloodstalker Mode' 2.25
3 Rogue Warrior vs. Z-Primes . . . 2.25
4 Primmies vs. Electric Warriors . . 2.25
5 Lek 0-03 Rebels. 2.25
6 Lek 0-03 vs. Masters 2.25
7 Lek'sFate,Derek Two-Shadows. . 2.25
8 Derek Two-Shadows Betrayed . . 2.25
9 Fate of Derek Two-Shadows. . . 2.25
10 Two-Shadows as one 2.25
11 Rebellion. 2.25
12 Rebellion continued 2.25
13 V:Prime One 2.25
14 Mutants Join Rebellion. 2.25
15 Invaders Arrival 2.25
16 Unified Warriors vs. Invaders . . . 2.25
17 V:Terrans, O:Electric Warriors . . 2.25
18 Origin continued, final issue 2.25

ELFQUEST: 25th ANNIVERSARY EDITION
DC 2003
Spec. WP,RPi, rep. Elfquest #1. . . . 2.95

ELFQUEST: WOLFRIDER
Sept. 2003
TPB Vol. 1 . . . . 9.95
TPB Vol. 2 . . . . 9.95

ELONGATED MAN
1992
1 A:Copperhead 2.25
2 Modora,A:Flash,I:Sonar 2.25
3 A:Flash,V:Wurst Gang 2.25

ELSEWORLD'S FINEST
DC/Elseworlds 1998
1 (of 2) JFM,KD,F:Bruce Wayne
 and Clark Kent, ... 5.00
2 JFM,KD,concl. 5.00
GN Supergirl & Batgirl 6.00

ELVIRA
1986–87
1 DSp,BB(c) 5.00
2 thru 10 . . . . @4.00
11 DSt(c)Find Cain 5.00

EMPIRE
June 2003
0 JmP,from Gorilla Comics. 4.95
1 (of 6) JmP,V:Golgoth. 2.50
2 thru 5 BKi,JmP . . . . @2.50

ENEMY ACE: WAR IN HEAVEN
March, 2001
1 (of 2) GEn, 48-page 5.95
2 GEn,48-page 5.95
TPB Enemy Ace:War in Heaven . . 14.95

ENIGMA
DC/Vertigo, 1993
1 B:PrM(s),DFg,I:Enigma,Michael
 Smith,V:The Head 3.00
2 DFg,I:The Truth 3.00
3 DFg,V:The Truth,I:Envelope Girl,
 Titus Bird 3.00
4 DFg,D:The Truth,I:Interior
 League. 3.00
5 DFg,I:Enigma's Mother 3.00
6 DFg,V:Envelope Girl 3.00
7 DFg,V:Enigma's Mother,D:Envelope
 Girl,O:Enigma. 3.00
8 E:PrM(s),DFg,final issue 3.00
TPB Rep. #1–#8 . . . . 19.95

ERADICATOR
1996
1 IV,Low, ... 2.50
2 IV,Low, ... 2.50
3 IV,Low,Reign of the Superman
 concl.,A:Superboy 2.50

ESSENTIAL VERTIGO: SWAMP THING
DC/Vertigo, Sept., 1996
B&W reprints
1 AMo(s), rep. Saga of
 the Swamp Thing #21. . . . . . . 3.00
2 thru 11 AMo(s), rep. Saga of
 the Swamp Thing #22–#31. . @3.00
12 AMo(s) rep. Saga Ann. #2 . . . . 3.00
13 AMo(s) rep. Saga #32–#42. . @3.00
24 AMo,Windfall, final issue 3.00

ESSENTIAL VERTIGO: THE SANDMAN
DC/Vertigo, 1996
3 NGa(s),SK,MDr,rep. 3.00
4 NGa(s),SK,MDr,rep. F:Etrigan . . 3.00
5 NGa(s),SK,MJ,F:Morpheus,
 John Dee 3.00
6 NGa(s),SK,MJ,V:Dr. Destiny 3.00
7 . . . . 3.00
8 NGa(s),MDr,MJ,The Sound
 of Her Wings 3.00
9 NGa(s),MDr,MJ,The Doll's
 House, F:Nada. 3.00
10 NGa(s),MDr,MJ, Doll's House . . . 3.00
11 NGa(s),MDr,RT 3.00
12 NGa(s),CBa,MJ,Doll'sHouse . . 3.00
13 NGa,rep.Doll's House,pt.4 . . . . 3.00
14 NGa,rep.Doll's House,pt.5 . . . . 3.50
15 NGa,rep.Doll's House,pt.6 . . . . 3.00
16 NGa,rep.Lost Hearts 3.00
17 NGa,rep.Dream Country 3.00
18 NGa,Dream of Thousand Cats. . 3.00
19 NGa,rep.Sandman #19 . . . . . . 3.00
20 NGa,rep.Sandman #20 . . . . . . 3.00
21 NGa,rep.Sandman #21 . . . . . . 3.00
22 NGa,rep.Season of Mists pt.1 . . 3.00
23 NGa,rep.Season of Mists pt.2 . . 3.00
24 NGa,rep.Season of Mists pt.3 . . 3.00
25 NGa,rep.Season of Mists pt.4 . . 3.00
26 NGa,rep.Season of Mists pt.5 . . 3.00
27 NGa,rep.Season of Mists,pt.6 . . 3.00
28 NGa,rep.Season of Mists,epilog. 3.00
29 NGa,rep.Thermidor 3.00
30 NGa,rep.August. 3.00
31 NGa,rep.Three Septembers
 and a January 3.00
32 NGa,rep. Sandman Special #1
 final issue. 4.50

CVA Page 72 — All comics prices listed are for *Near Mint* condition.

Comics Values Annual — DC — Extreme–Final

EXTREME JUSTICE
1995–96
- 0 New Group ... 3.50
- 1 V:Captain Atom ... 3.00
- 2 V:War Cyborgs ... 3.00
- 3 V:Synge ... 3.00
- 4 R:Firestorm the Nuclear Man ... 3.00
- 5 Firestorm & Elementals ... 3.00
- 6 Monarch,Captain Atom, Booster Gold, Maxima ... 3.00
- 7 F:Monarch,Captain Atom ... 3.00
- 8 ... 3.00
- 9 F:Firestorm ... 3.00
- 10 Underworld Unleashed tie-in ... 3.00
- 11 Underworld Unleashed tie-in ... 3.00
- 12 Monarch's scheme revealed ... 3.00
- 13 Monarch vs. Captain Atom ... 3.00
- 14 ... 3.00
- 15 TMo,V:The Slavemaster from the Stars ... 3.00
- 16 TMo,V:Legion of Doom ... 3.00
- 17 TMo,V:Legion of Doom ... 3.00

EXTREMIST
DC/Vertigo, 1993
- 1 B:PrM(s),TMK,I:The Order, Extremist(Judy Tanner) ... 2.50
- 1a Platinum Ed. ... 5.00
- 2 TMK,D:Extremist(Jack Tanner) ... 2.25
- 3 TMK,V:Patrick ... 2.25
- 4 E:PrM(s),TMK,D:Tony Murphy ... 2.25

FABLES
DC/Vertigo, May, 2002
- 1 SL, Legends in Exile,pt.1 ... 9.00
- 2 SL, Legends in Exile,pt.2 ... 6.00
- 3 SL, Legends in Exile,pt.3 ... 4.00
- 4 BWg,Legends in Exile,pt.4 ... 4.00
- 5 SL, Legends in Exile,pt.5 ... 4.00
- 6 MBu,SL,Animal Farm,pt.1 ... 3.00
- 7 MBu,SL,Animal Farm,pt.2 ... 3.00
- 8 MBu,SL,Animal Farm,pt.3 ... 3.00
- 9 MBu,SL,Animal Farm,pt.4 ... 3.00
- 10 MBu,SL,Animal Farm,pt.5 ... 2.50
- 11 Jack of the Tales ... 2.50
- 12 Fables caper,pt.1 ... 2.50
- 13 Fables caper,pt.2 ... 2.50
- 14 Storybook Love,pt.1 ... 2.50
- 15 Storybook Love,pt.2 ... 2.50
- 16 Storybook Love,pt.3 ... 2.50
- 17 Storybook Love,pt.4 ... 2.50
- 18 The Barley Corn Brides ... 2.50
- 19 MBu,SL ... 2.50
- TPB Fables: Legends in Exile ... 14.95
- TPB Fables: Animal Farm ... 12.95
- Spec. The Last Castle ... 5.95

FACE, THE
- GN DFg,PrM ... 5.50

FAITH
DC/Vertigo, Sept., 1999
- 1 (of 5) TMK ... 2.50
- 2 TMK ... 2.50
- 3 TMK ... 2.50
- 4 TMK ... 2.50
- 5 TMK ... 2.50

FALLEN ANGEL
July 2003
- 1 PDd(s),Bete Noire ... 2.50
- 2 PDd(s),Asia Minor ... 2.50
- 3 PDd(s),Little Better,pt.1 ... 2.50
- 4 PDd(s),Little Better,pt.2 ... 2.50
- 5 PDd(s),Little Better,pt.3 ... 2.50

FAMILY MAN
Paradox 1995
- 1 I:Family Man ... 5.50
- 2 V:Brother Charles ... 5.50
- 3 Escape ... 5.50

Fanboy #2 © DC Comics, Inc.

FANBOY
1999
- 1 (of 6) SA, various artists ... 2.50
- 2 ... 2.50
- 3 A:JLA ... 2.50
- 4 SA, A:Sgt. Rock ... 2.50
- 5 SA, A:Batman ... 2.50
- 6 SA, A:Wonder Woman, concl. ... 2.50
- TPB F:Finster, 144-page(2001) ... 12.95

FAREWELL MOONSHADOW
DC/Vertigo, 1997
- GN JMD(s),JMu, prose & pictures ... 8.50

FATE
1994–96
- 1 Dr. Fate ... 2.50
- 2 Nabu,Astral plane ... 2.25
- 3 Bloodstain ... 2.25
- 4 Decisions ... 2.25
- 5 Judged by Enclave ... 2.25
- 6 V:Grimoire ... 2.25
- 7 V:Dark Agent ... 2.25
- 8 V:Dark Agent ... 2.25
- 9 Tries to change his destiny ... 2.25
- 10 A:Zatanna ... 2.25
- 11 ... 2.25
- 12 A:Sentinel ... 2.25
- 13 V:Blaze ... 2.25
- 14 LKa,ALa,AWi,Underworld Unleashed tie-in ... 2.25
- 15 LKa,ALa,AWi,V:Charnelle ... 2.25
- 16 LKa,ALa,AWi,canibal drug-cult. ... 2.25
- 17 LKa,ALa,AWi ... 2.25
- 18 LKa,ALa,AWi,V:Charnelle ... 2.25
- 19 LKa,ALa,AWi,V:men in black ... 2.25

FAULT LINES
DC/Vertigo, March, 1997
Mini-series
- 1 LMr(s),F:Tracey Farrand ... 2.50
- 2 LMr(s) ... 2.50
- 3 LMr(s) ... 2.50
- 4 LMr(s) ... 2.50
- 5 (of 6) LMr(s) ... 2.50
- 6 LMrs(s) concl. ... 2.50

FIGHT FOR TOMORROW
DC/Vertigo, Sept., 2002
- 1 (of 6) DCw,JLe(c) kung-fu ... 2.50
- 2 DCw,KW, more kung-fu ... 2.50
- 3 thru 6 DCw ... @2.50

Fighting American #6 © DC Comics, Inc.

FIGHTING AMERICAN
1994
- 1 GrL,R:Fighting American ... 2.50
- 2 GrL,Media Circus ... 2.50
- 3 GrL,I&V:Gross Nation Product, Def Iffit ... 2.50
- 4 GrL,V:Gross Nation Product, Def Iffit ... 2.50
- 5 GrL,PhorOptor ... 2.50
- 6 Final Issue ... 2.50

FILTH, THE
DC/Vertigo, June, 2002
- 1 (of 13) GMo ... 3.00
- 2 GMo, Perfect Victim ... 3.00
- 3 GMo, unexpected guest ... 3.00
- 4 GMo, Otto Von Vermun ... 3.00
- 5 GMo, Pornomancer ... 3.00
- 6 GMo,World of Anders Klimaaks ... 3.00
- 7 GMo,Libertania ... 3.00
- 8 GMo,Libertania ... 3.00
- 9 GMo,Answers ... 3.00
- 10 GMo,Mother Dirt ... 3.00
- 11 GMo,Greg Feely ... 3.00
- 12 GMo,Mother Dirt ... 3.00
- 13 GMo,concl. ... 3.00

FINAL NIGHT, THE
Sept., 1996
[Cross-Over Series]
- 1 KK(s),SI,JMz, Alien crash lands on Earth ... 4.00
- 2 KK(s),SI,JMz, Earth's sun extinguished ... 2.50
- 3 KK(s),SI,JMz, Attempts to stave off inevitable ... 2.50
- 4 KK(s),SI,JMz, Can they save the world, and at what price? ... 2.50
- TPB rep. ... 13.00

All comics prices listed are for Near Mint condition.

FINALS
DC/Vertigo, 1999
1 (of 4) College satire 3.00
2 JIT,pt.2 .... 3.00
3 JIT,pt.3 .... 3.00
4 JIT,conclusion 3.00

FIREBRAND
1995
1 SaV,Alex Sanchez becomes Firebrand 2.25
2 SaV 2.25
3 SaV,Generation Prime case climax 2.25
4 SaV,Young gang member 2.25
5 SaV,V;serial killer(s) 2.25
6 BAu,SaV 2.25
7 .... 2.25
8 .... 2.25
9 final issue 2.25

FIRESTORM
March, 1978
1 AM,JRu,I&O:Firestorm 12.00
2 AM,BMc,A:Superman 7.00
3 AM,I:Killer Froat 7.00
4 AM,BMc,I:Hyena 7.00
5 AM,BMc,Hyena 7.00

FIRESTORM, THE NUCLEAR MAN
See: **FURY OF FIRESTORM**

FIRST ISSUE SPECIAL
April, 1975
1 JK,Atlas 12.00
2 Green Team 10.00
3 Metamorpho 10.00
4 Lady Cop 7.00
5 JK,Manhunter 17.00
6 JK,Dingbats 12.00
7 SD,Creeper 12.00
8 MGr,Warlord 25.00
9 WS,Dr.Fate 10.00
10 Outsiders(not Batman team) ... 8.00
11 NR,AM Code:Assassin 8.00
12 new Starman 8.00
13 return of New Gods 25.00

First Issue Special #4
© *DC Comics, Inc.*

FLASH COMICS
Jan., 1940
1 SMo,SMo(c),O:Flash,Hawkman,The Whip & Johnny Thunder,B:Cliff Cornwall,Minute Movies .. 95,000.00
2 B:Rod Rain 10,000.00
3 SMo,SMo(c),B:The King 7,500.00
4 SMo,SMo(c),F:The Whip ... 5,500.00
5 SMo,SMo(c),F:The King 4,500.00
6 F:Flash 6,500.00
7 Hawkman(c) 6,000.00
8 Male bondage(c) 3,800.00
9 Hawkman(c) 4,000.00
10 SMo,SMo(c),Flash(c) 4,000.00
11 SMo,SMo(c) 2,500.00
12 SMo,SMo(c),B:Les Watts .. 2,500.00
13 SMo,SMo(c) 2,500.00
14 SMo,SMo(c) 3,000.00
15 SMo,SMo(c) 2,500.00
16 SMo,SMo(c) 2,500.00
17 SMo,SMo(c),E:CliffCornwall 2,500.00
18 SMo,SMo(c) 2,500.00
19 SMo,SMo(c) 2,500.00
20 SMo,SMo(c) 2,500.00
21 SMo(c) 2,400.00
22 SMo,SMo(c) 2,200.00
23 SMo,SMo(c) 2,200.00
24 SMo,SMo(c),Flash V:Spider-Men of Mars,A:Hawkgirl ... 2,600.00
25 SMo,SMo(c) 1,500.00
26 SMo,SMo(c) 1,500.00
27 SMo,SMo(c) 1,500.00
28 SMo,SMo(c),Flash goes to Hollywood 1,500.00
29 SMo,SMo(c) 1,700.00
30 SMo,SMo(c),Flash in`Adventure of the Curiosity Ray!' 1,500.00
31 SMo,SMo(c),Hawkman(c) .. 1,500.00
32 SMo,SM(c),Flash in`Adventure of the Fictious Villians' 1,500.00
33 SMo,SMo(c) 1,500.00
34 SMo,SMo(c),Flash in `The Robbers of the Round Table' 1,500.00
35 SMo,SMo(c) 1,500.00
36 SMo,SMo(c),F:Flash, The Mystery of the Doll Who Walks Like a Man' 1,500.00
37 SMo,SMo(c) 1,500.00
38 SMo,SMo(c) 1,500.00
39 SMo,SMo(c) 1,500.00
40 SMo,SMo(c),F:Flash, Man Who Could Read Man's Souls!.. 1,500.00
41 SMo,SMo(c) 1,200.00
42 SMo,SMo(c),Flash V:The Gangsters Baby! 1,200.00
43 SMo,SMo(c) 1,200.00
44 SMo,SMo(c),Flash V:The Liars Club 1,200.00
45 SMo,SMo(c),F:Hawkman,Big Butch Makes Hall of Fame . 1,200.00
46 SMo,SMo(c) 1,200.00
47 SMo,SMo(c),Hawkman in Crime Canned for the Duration... 1,200.00
48 SMo,SMo(c) 1,200.00
49 SMo,SMo(c) 1,200.00
50 SMo,SMo(c),Hawkman, Tale of the 1,000 Dollar Bill 1,200.00
51 SMo,SMo(c) 1,100.00
52 SMo,SMo(c),Flash, Machine that Thinks Like a Man 1,100.00
53 SMo,SMo(c),Hawkman, Simple Simon Met the Hawkman .. 1,100.00
54 SMo,SMo(c),Flash, Mysterious Bottle from the Sea 1,100.00
55 SMo,SMo(c),Hawkman, Riddle of the Stolen Statuette! 1,100.00
56 SMo,SMo(c) 1,100.00
57 SMo,SMo(c),Hawkman, Adventure of the Gangster & the Ghost 1,100.00
58 SMo,SMo(c),`Merman meets the Flash' 1,100.00
59 SMo,SMo(c),Hawkman V:Pied Piper 1,100.00
60 SMo,SMo(c),Flash V:The Wind Master 1,100.00
61 SMo,SMo(c),Hawkman V:The Beanstalk 1,100.00
62 JKu,Flash in `High Jinks on the Rinks' 1,400.00
63 JKu(c),Hawkman in `The Tale of the Mystic Urn' 1,000.00
64 .... 1,000.00
65 JKu(c),Hawkman in `Return of the Simple Simon' 1,000.00
66 .... 1,000.00
67 JKu(c) 1,000.00
68 Flash in `The Radio that Ran Wild' 1,000.00
69 .... 1,000.00
70 JKu(c) 1,000.00
71 JKu(c),Hawkman in `Battle of the Birdmen' 1,000.00
72 JKu 1,000.00
73 JKu(c) 1,000.00
74 JKu(c) 1,000.00
75 JKu(c),Hawkman in `Magic at the Mardi Gras' 1,000.00
76 A:Worry Wart 1,000.00
77 Hawkman in `The Case of the Curious Casket' 1,000.00
78 .... 1,000.00
79 Hawkman in `The Battle of the Birds' 1,000.00
80 Flash in `The Story of the Boy Genius' 1,000.00
81 JKu(c),Hawkman's Voyage to Venus 1,000.00
82 A:Walter Jordan 1,000.00
83 JKu,JKu(c),Hawkman in `Destined for Disaster' ... 1,000.00
84 Flash V:`The Changeling' .. 1,000.00
85 JKu,JKu(c),Hawkman in Hollywood 1,000.00
86 JKu,1st Black Canary,Flash V:Stone Age Menace 3,500.00
87 Hawkman meets the Foil... 1,500.00
88 JKu,Flash in `The Case of the Vanished Year!' 1,500.00
89 I:The Thorn 1,500.00
90 Flash in `Nine Empty Uniforms' 1,500.00
91 Hawkman V:The Phantom Menace 1,700.00
92 1st full-length Black Canary story 4,500.00

Flash Comics #1
© *DC Comics, Inc.*

DC — Flash

93 Flash V:Violin of Villainy . . . 1,700.00
94 JKu(c) 1,700.00
95 . . . . 1,700.00
96 . . . . 1,700.00
97 Flash in 'The Dream
 that Didn't Vanish' 1,700.00
98 JKu(c),Hawkman in
 `Crime Costume!' 1,700.00
99 Flash in 'The Star Prize
 of the Year' 1,700.00
100 Hawkman in 'The Human
 -Fly Bandits!' 3,800.00
101 . . . . 3,000.00
102 Hawkman in 'The Flying
 Darkness' 3,000.00
103 . . . . 3,800.00
104 JKu,Hawkman in `Flaming
 Darkness' Feb., 1949 . . . . . 9,000.00

FLASH
Feb.–March, 1959

105 CI,O:Flash,I:Mirror
 Master 8,000.00
106 CI,I&O:Gorilla Grodd,
 O:Pied Piper 2,500.00
107 CI,A:Grodd 1,300.00
108 CI,A:Grodd 1,100.00
109 CI,A:Mirror Master 800.00
110 CI,MA,I:Kid Flash,
 Weather Wizard 2,000.00
111 CI,A:Kid Flash,The Invasion
 Of the Cloud Creatures 600.00
112 CI,I&O:Elongated Man,
 A:Kid Flash 700.00
113 CI,I&O:Trickster 600.00
114 CI,A:Captain Cold 450.00
115 CI,A:Grodd 350.00
116 CI,A:Kid Flash,The Man
 Who Stole Central City 350.00
117 CI,MA,I:Capt.Boomerang . . . 425.00
118 CI,MA 350.00
119 CI,W:Elongated Man 350.00
120 CI,A:Kid Flash,Land of
 Golden Giants 350.00
121 CI,A:Trickster 250.00
122 CI,I&O:The Top 250.00
123 I:Earth 2,R:G.A.Flash 1,900.00
124 CI,A:Capt.Boomerang 225.00
125 CI,A:Kid Flash,The
 Conquerors of Time 200.00
126 CI,A:Mirror Master 200.00
127 CI,A:Grodd 200.00
128 CI,O:Abra Kadabra 200.00
129 CI,A:Capt.Cold,Trickster,A:Gold.
 Age Flash,C:JLA (flashback). 425.00
130 CI,A:Mirror Master,
 Weather Wizard 200.00
131 CI,A:Green Lantern 175.00
132 CI,A:Daphne Dean 175.00
133 CI,A:Abra Kadabra 175.00
134 CI,A:Captain Cold 175.00
135 CI,N:Kid Flash 175.00
136 CI,A:Mirror Master 175.00
137 CI,Vandal Savage,R:JSA,
 A:G.A.Flash 650.00
138 CI,A:Pied Piper 200.00
139 CI,I&O:Prof.Zoom(Reverse
 Flash) 200.00
140 CI,O:Heat Wave 200.00
141 CI,A:Top 150.00
142 CI,A:Trickster 150.00
143 CI,A:Green Lantern 150.00
144 CI,A:Man Missile,Kid Flash . . 150.00
145 CI,A:Weather Wizard 150.00
146 CI,A:Mirror Master 150.00
147 CI,A:Mr.Element,A:Reverse
 Flash 150.00
148 CI,A:Capt.Boomerang 150.00
149 CI,A:Abra Kadabra 150.00
150 CI,A:Captain Cold 150.00

Flash #185 © DC Comics Inc.

151 CI,A:Earth II Flash,
 The Shade 175.00
152 CI,V:Trickster 125.00
153 CI,A:Mr.Element,Rev.Flash . . 125.00
154 CI,The Day Flash Ran Away
 with Himself 125.00
155 CI,A:MirrorMaster,Capt.Cold,Top
 Capt. Boomerang,Grodd 125.00
156 CI,A:Kid Flash,The Super Hero
 who Betrayed the World 125.00
157 CI,A:Doralla Kon,The Top . . . 125.00
158 CI,V:The Breakaway Bandit
 A:The Justice League 125.00
159 CI,A:Kid Flash 125.00
160 CI,giant 175.00
161 CI,A:Mirror Master 100.00
162 CI,Who Haunts the Corridor
 of Chills 100.00
163 CI,A:Abra kadabra 100.00
164 CI,V:Pied Piper,A:Kid Flash . 100.00
165 CI,W:Flash,Iris West 110.00
166 CI,A:Captain Cold 100.00
167 CI,O:Flash,I:Mopee 100.00
168 CI,A:Green Lantern 100.00
169 CI,O:Flash rtd,giant 150.00
170 CI,A:Abra Kadabra,
 G.A.Flash 100.00
171 CI,A:Dexter Myles,Justice
 League,Atom;V:Dr Light 100.00
172 CI,A:Grodd 100.00
173 CI,A:Kid Flash,EarthII Flash
 V:Golden Man 100.00
174 CI,A:Mirror Master,Top
 Captain Cold 100.00
175 2nd Superman/Flash race,
 C:Justice League o/America . 250.00
176 giant-size 100.00
177 RA,V:The Trickster 100.00
178 CI,(giant size) 125.00
179 RA,Fact or Fiction 100.00
180 RA,V:Baron Katana 100.00
181 RA,V;Baron Katana 75.00
182 A:Abra Kadabra 75.00
183 RA,V:The Frog 75.00
184 RA,V:Dr Yom 75.00
185 RA,Threat of the High Rise
 Buildings 75.00
186 RA,A:Sargon 75.00
187 CI,AbraKadabra,giant 100.00
188 A:Mirror Master 75.00
189 JKu(c),RA,A:Kid Flash 75.00
190 JKu(c),RA,A:Dexter Myles . . . 75.00
191 JKu(c),RA,A:Green Lantern . . 75.00
192 RA;V:Captain Vulcan 75.00

193 A:Captain Cold 75.00
194 . . . . 75.00
195 GK,MA 75.00
196 CI,giant 100.00
197 GK 75.00
198 GK 75.00
199 GK 75.00
200 IN,MA 75.00
201 IN,MA,A:G.A. Flash 45.00
202 IN,MA,A:Kid Flash 45.00
203 IN 45.00
204 . . . . 45.00
205 giant 75.00
206 A:Mirror Master 45.00
207 . . . . 45.00
208 . . . . 45.00
209 A:Capt.Boomerang,Grodd
 Trickster 45.00
210 CI 45.00
211 O:Flash 45.00
212 A:Abra Kadabra 45.00
213 CI 45.00
214 CI,rep.Showcase #37
 (O:Metal Men),giant size 50.00
215 IN,FMc,rep.Showcase #14 . . 50.00
216 A:Mr.Element 35.00
217 NA,A:Gr.Lant,Gr.Arrow 45.00
218 NA,A:Gr.Lant,Gr.Arrow 45.00
219 NA,L:Greeen Arrow 45.00
220 IN,DG,A:KidFlash,Gr.Lantern . 40.00
221 IN 25.00
222 IN 25.00
223 DG,Green Lantern 25.00
224 IN,DG,A:Green Lantern 25.00
225 IN,DG,A:Gr.Lant,Rev.Flash . . 20.00
226 NA,A:Capt. Cold 25.00
227 IN,FMc,DG,Capt.Boomerang,
 Green Lantern 20.00
228 IN 20.00
229 IN,FMc,A:Green Arrow,
 V:Rag Doll (giant size) 45.00
230 A:VandalSavage,Dr.Alchemy . 20.00
231 FMc 20.00
232 giant 50.00
233 giant 50.00
234 V:Reverse Flash 16.00
235 . . . . 15.00
236 MGr 15.00
237 IN,FMc,MGr,A:Prof Zoom,
 Green Lantern 16.00
238 MGr 15.00
239 . . . . 15.00
240 MGr 15.00
241 A:Mirror Master 15.00
242 MGr,D:Top 15.00
243 IN,FMc,MGr,TA,O:Top,
 A:Green Lantern 15.00
244 IN,FMc,A:Rogue's Gallery . . . 15.00
245 IN,FMc,DD,TA,I:PlantMaster . 15.00
246 IN,FMc,DD,TA,I:PlantMaster . 15.00
247 . . . . 15.00
248 FMc,IN,I:Master 15.00
249 FMc,IN,V:Master 15.00
250 FMc,IN,I:Golden Glider 15.00
251 FMc,IN,V:Golden Glider 12.00
252 FMc,IN,I:Molder 12.00
253 FMc,IN,V:Molder 12.00
254 FMc 12.00
255 FMc,A:MirrorMaster 12.00
256 FMc,V:Top 12.00
257 FMc,A:Green Glider 12.00
258 FMc,A:Black Hand 12.00
259 FMc,IN 12.00
260 FMc,IN 12.00
261 FMc,IN,V:Golden Glider 12.00
262 FMc,IN,V:Golden Glider 12.00
263 FMc,IN,V:Golden Glider 12.00
264 FMc,IN,V:Golden Glider 12.00
265 FMc,IN 12.00
266 FMc,IN,V:Heat Wave 12.00
267 FMc,IN,V:Heat Wave 12.00

All comics prices listed are for Near Mint condition.

Flash — DC

Flash #344 © DC Comics, Inc.

268 FMc,IN,A:E2 Flash 12.00
269 FMc,IN,A:Kid Flash 12.00
270 FMc,IN,V:Clown 12.00
271 RB,V:Clown 12.00
272 RB,V:Clown 12.00
273 RB 12.00
274 RB 12.00
275 AS,D:Iris West,PCP story ... 14.00
276 AS,A:JLA 12.00
277 AS,FMc,A:JLA,
 V:MirrorMaster 12.00
278 A:Captain.Boomerang
 & Heatwave 12.00
279 A:Captain.Boomerang
 & Heatwave 12.00
280 DH 12.00
281 DH,V:Reverse Flash 14.00
282 DH,V:Reverse Flash 14.00
283 DH,V:Reverse Flash 14.00
284 DH,Flash's life story
 I:Limbo Lord 12.00
285 DH,V:Trickster 12.00
286 DH,I:Rainbow Raider 12.00
287 DH,V:Dr.Alchemy 12.00
288 DH,V:Dr.Alchemy 12.00
289 DH,GP,1st GP DC art; V:Dr.
 Alchemy;B:B.U.Firestrom ... 15.00
290 GP 6.00
291 GP,DH,V:Sabretooth 6.00
292 GP,DH,V:Mirror Master. 6.00
293 GP,DH,V:Pied Piper 6.00
294 GP,DH,V:Grodd 6.00
295 CI,JSn,V:Grodd 6.00
296 JSn,A:Elongated Man 6.00
297 CI,A:Captain Cold 6.00
298 CI,V:Shade,Rainbowraider ... 6.00
299 CI,V:Shade,Rainbowraider ... 6.00
300 A:New Teen Titans 10.00
301 CI,A:Firestorm 6.00
302 CI,V:Golden Glider 6.00
303 CI,V:Golden Glider 6.00
304 CI,PB,I:Col.Computron;E.B.U.
 Firestorm 6.00
305 KG,CI,A:G.A.Flash,B:Dr.Fate . 6.00
306 CI,KG,V:Mirror Master 6.00
307 CI,KG,V:Pied Piper 6.00
308 CI,KG 6.00
309 CI,KG 7.00
310 CI,KG,V:Capt.Boomerang ... 6.00
311 CI,KG,V:Capt.Boomerang ... 6.00
312 CI,A:Heatwave 6.00
313 KG,A:Psylon,E:Dr.Fate 6.00
314 CI,I:Eradicator 6.00
315 CI,V:Gold Face 6.00
316 CI,V:Gold Face 6.00

317 CI,V:Gold Face 6.00
318 CI,DGb,V:Eradicator;B:
 B.U.Creeper 6.00
319 CI,DGb,V:Eradicator 6.00
320 CI,V:Eradicator 6.00
321 CI,D:Eradicator 5.00
322 CI,V:Reverse Flash 5.00
323 CI,V:Reverse Flash;E:
 B.U.Creeper 5.00
324 CI,D:Reverse Flash 5.50
325 CI,A:Rogues Gallery 5.00
326 CI,A:Weather Wizard 5.00
327 CI,A:JLA,G.Grodd 5.00
328 CI 5.00
329 CI,A:J.L.A.,G.Grodd 5.00
330 CI,FMc,V:G.Grodd 5.00
331 CI,FMc,V:G.Grodd 5.00
332 CI,FMc,V:Rainbow Raider ... 5.00
333 CI,FMc,V:Pied Piper 5.00
334 CI,FMc,V:Pied Piper 5.00
335 CI,FMc,V:Pied Piper 5.00
336 CI,FMc,V:Pied Piper 5.00
337 CI,FMc,V:Pied Piper 5.00
338 CI,FMc,I:Big Sir 5.00
339 CI,FMc,A:Big Sir 5.00
340 CI,FMc,Trial,A:Big Sir. 5.00
341 CI,FMc,Trial,A:Big Sir. 5.00
342 CI,FMc,Trial,V:RogueGallery .. 5.00
343 CI,FMc,Trial,A:GoldFace 5.00
344 CI,O:Kid Flash,Trial 5.00
345 CI,A:Kid Flash,Trial 5.00
346 CI,FMc,Trial,V:AbraKadabra .. 5.00
347 CI,FMc,Trial,V:AbraKadabra .. 5.00
348 CI,FMc,Trial,V:AbraKadabra .. 5.00
349 CI,FMc,Trial,V:AbraKadabra .. 5.00
350 CI,FMc,Trial,V:AbraKadabra .. 7.00
Ann.#1 O:ElongatedMan,
 G.Grodd 500.00

FLASH
[2nd Series] Oct., 1985

1 JG,Legends,C:Vandal Savage . 12.00
2 JG,V:Vandal Savage 5.00
3 JG,I:Kilgore 4.00
4 JG,A:Cyborg 4.00
5 JG,V:Speed Demon 4.00
6 JG,V:Speed Demon 4.00
7 JG,V:Red Trinity 4.00
8 JG,V:BlueTrinity,Millennium 4.00
9 JG,I:Chunk,Millennium 4.00
10 V:Chunk,Chunks World 3.00
11 Return to Earth 3.00
12 Velocity 9 .... 3.00
13 Vandal Savage,V:Velocity 9
 Adicts 3.00
14 V:Vandal Savage 3.00
15 A:Velocity 9 Junkies 3.00
16 C:V.Savage,SpeedMcGeePt.1 .. 3.00
17 GLa,Speed McGee,pt.2 .... 3.00
18 GLa,SpeedMcGeePt.3,
 V:V.Savage 3.00
19 JM:+bonus book,R:Rogue
 Gallery,O:Blue/Red Trinity 3.00
20 A:Durlan 3.00
21 A:Manhunter,Invasion x-over .. 3.00
22 A:Manhunter,Invasion x-over .. 3.00
23 V:Abrakadabra 3.00
24 GLa,FlashRegainsSpeed,
 A:L.Lane 3.00
25 GLa,Search for Flash 3.00
26 GLa,I:Porcupine Man 3.00
27 GLa,Porcupine Man as Flash ... 3.00
28 GLa,A:Golden Glider,
 Capt.Cold 3.00
29 A:New Phantom Lady 3.00
30 GLa,Turtle Saga,pt.1 .... 3.00
31 GLa,Turtle Saga,pt.2 .... 3.00
32 GLa,Turtle Saga,pt.3,
 R:G.A.Turtle 3.00
33 GLa,Turtle Saga,pt.4 .... 3.00

Flash 2nd Series #6 © DC Comics, Inc.

34 GLa,Turtle Saga,pt.5 .... 3.00
35 GLa,Turtle Saga,pt.6,
 D:G.A.Turtle 3.00
36 GLa,V:Cult 3.00
37 GLa,V:Cult 3.00
38 GLa,V:Cult 3.00
39 GLa,V:Cult 3.00
40 GLa,A:Dr.Alchemy 3.00
41 GLa,A:Dr.Alchemy 3.00
42 GLa,MechanicalTroubles 3.00
43 GLa,V:Kilgore 3.00
44 GLa,V:Velocity 3.00
45 V:Gorilla Grod 3.00
46 V:Gorilla Grod 3.00
47 V:Gorilla Grod 3.00
48 .... 3.00
49 A:Vandal Savage 3.00
50 N:Flash (double sz)V:Savage ... 5.00
51 I:Proletariat 3.00
52 I.R.S. Mission 3.00
53 A:Superman,Race to Save
 Jimmy Olsen 3.00
54 Terrorist Airline Attack 3.00
55 War of the Gods x-over 3.00
56 The Way of a Will,pt.1 .... 3.00
57 The Way of a Will,pt.2 .... 3.00
58 Meta Gene-activated Homeless . 3.00
59 The Last Resort 3.00
60 Love Song of the Chunk 3.00
61 Wally's Mother's Wedding Day . . 3.00
62 GLa,Year 1,pt.1 .... 4.00
63 GLa,Year 1,pt.2 .... 4.00
64 GLa,Year 1,pt.3 .... 4.00
65 GLa,Year 1,pt.4 .... 4.00
66 A:Aq'man,V:Marine Marauder .. 4.00
67 GLa,V:Abra Kadabra 4.00
68 GLa,V:Abra Kadabra 4.00
69 GLa,Gorilla Warfare#2 .... 4.00
70 Gorilla Warfare#4 .... 4.00
71 GLa,V:Dr.Alchemy 4.00
72 GLa,V:Dr.Alchemy,C:Barry
 Allen 4.00
73 GLa,Xmas Issue,R:Barry Allen .. 5.00
74 GLa,A:Barry Allen? 4.50
75 GLa,A:Reverse Flash,V:Mob
 Violence 4.50
76 GLa,A:Reverse Flash 4.00
77 GLa,G.A.Flash vs
 Reverse Flash 4.00
78 GLa,V:Reverse Flash 4.00
79 GLa,V:Reverse Flash,48 pgs. ... 5.00
80 AD(c),V:Frances Kane 5.00
80a Newstand Ed 3.00
81 AD(c) 4.00

Comics Values Annual — DC — Flash–Flash Plus

DC COMICS

82 AD(c),A:Nightwing 4.00
83 AD(c),A:Nightwing,Starfire 4.00
84 AD(c),I:Razer. 4.00
85 AD(c),V:Razer. 4.00
86 AD(c),A:Argus 4.00
86 V:Santa Claus 4.00
87 Christmas issue 4.00
88 . . . . 4.00
89 On Trial 4.00
90 On Trial#2 . . . . 4.00
91 Out of Time 5.00
92 I:3rd Flash 12.00
93 A:Impulse 5.00
94 Zero Hour 5.00
95 Terminal Velocity,pt.1 . . . . 4.00
96 Terminal Velocity,pt.2 . . . . 2.50
97 Terminal Velocity,pt.3 . . . . 4.00
98 Terminal Velocity,pt.4 . . . . 4.00
99 Terminal Velocity,pt.5 . . . . 4.00
100 I:New Flash 5.00
100a Collector's Edition 3.00
101 Velocity Aftermath 4.00
102 V:Mongul. 3.00
103 Supernatural threat from
    Linda's Past Secret 3.00
104 Exorcise Demons. 3.00
105 . . . . 3.00
106 R:Magenta. 3.00
107 MWa,Underworld Unleashed
    tie-in. 3.00
108 MWa,Dead Heat,pt.1 . . . . 3.00
109 MWa,Dead Heat,pt.2 . . . . 3.00
110 MWa,Dead Heat,pt.4 . . . . 3.00
111 MWa,Dead Heat,pt.6 . . . . 3.00
112 MWa,New Flash in town. 3.00
113 MWa,F:Linda 3.00
114 MWa,V:Chillblaine 3.00
115 thru 117 . . . . @3.00
118 MWa&BAu(s),Flash returns
    from the future 3.00
119 MWa&BAu(s),PR,Final Night
    tie-in. 3.00
120 MWa&BAu(s),PR,Presidential
    Race,pt.1 . . . . 3.00
121 MWa&BAu(s),PR,Presidential
    Race,pt.2 . . . . 3.00
122 MWa&BAu(s),PR, ... 3.00
123 MWa&BAu(s),PR,Flash moves
    to Santa Marta 3.00
124 MWa&BAu(s),PR,Wally doesn't
    know reality from illusion 3.00
125 MWa&BAu(s),PR,California,
    V:Major Disaster 3.00
126 MWa&BAu(s),PR,V:Major
    Disaster 3.00
127 MWa&Bau(s),PR,Hell to Pay,
    pt.1 . . . . 3.00
128 MWa&BAu(s),PR,Hell to Pay
    pt.2, A:JLA 3.00
129 MWa&BAu(s),PR,HellPay,pt.3 . 3.00
130 GMo&MMr(s),PR,new menace. 3.00
131 GMo&MMr(s),PR,V:The Suit . . 3.50
132 GMo&MMr(s),PR,V:The Suit . . 3.50
133 GMo&MMr(s),PR,V:Mirror
    Master 3.00
134 GMo&MMr(s),PR,V:Weather
    Wizard & Captain Cold 3.00
135 GMo&MMr(s), ... 3.00
136 GMo&MMr(s),PR,Human
    Race,pt.1 . . . . 3.00
137 GMo&MMr(s),PR,Human
    Race,pt.2 . . . . 3.00
138 GMo&MMr(s),PR,Human
    Race,pt.3 . . . . 3.00
139 MMr(s),ClV,Black Flash,pt.1 . . 3.00
140 MMr(s),ClV,Black Flash,pt.2 . . 3.00
141 MMr(s),ClV,Black Flash,pt.3 . . 3.00
142 MWa&BAu(s),ClV,SLi,wedding of
    Wally West & Linda Park 3.00
143 MWa&BAu(s),ClV,V:CobaltBlue 3.00
144 MWa&BAu(s),ClV,O:CobaltBlue 3.00

Flash 2nd Series #80
© DC Comics Inc.

145 MWa&BAu(s),PaP,VRu,
    Chain Lightning, pt.1 . . . . 3.00
146 MWa&BAu(s),PaP,VRu,
    Chain Lightning, pt.2 . . . . 3.00
147 MWa&BAu(s),PaP,VRu,
    Chain Lightning, pt.3 . . . . 3.00
148 MWa&BAu(s),PaP,VRu,
    Chain Lightning, pt.4 . . . . 3.00
149 MWa&BAu(s),PaP,VRu,
    Chain Lightning, pt.5 . . . . 3.00
150 MWa&BAu(s),PaP,VRu, Chain
    Lightning, pt.6, 48-page 4.00
151 MWa&BAu(s),PaP,A:Robin
    & Aqualad, flashback issue. . . . 2.50
152 MWa&BAu(s),PaP,VRu,
    new costume 2.50
153 MWa&BAu(s),PaP,JMz,
    V:Folded Man. 2.50
154 MWa&BAu(s),PaP,JMz, ... 2.50
155 MWa&BAu(s),PaP,JMz,
    V:Replicant. 2.50
156 MWa&BAu(s),PaP,JMz. 2.50
157 MWa&BAu(s),PaP,JMz,fate of
    Linda Park 2.50
158 MWa&BAu(s),PaP,DHz 2.50
159 MWa&BAu(s),PaP,Dark Flash . 2.50
160 BAu(s),Honeymoon on the Run 2.50
161 PaP,DHz,F:Original JSA. 2.50
162 PaP,DHz,R:Felix Faust. 2.50
163 RLm,DHz,A:JLA. 2.50
164 DHz,BBo(c),Wonderland,pt.1 . . 3.00
165 DHz,Wonderland,pt.2. . . . . 2.50
166 DHz,Wonderland,pt.3. . . . . 2.50
167 DHz,Wonderland,pt.4. . . . . 2.50
168 DHz,Wonderland,pt.5. . . . . 2.50
169 DHz,Wonderland,pt.6. . . . . 2.50
170 DHz,Blood Will Run,pt.1. . . . . . 2.50
171 DHz,Blood Will Run,pt.2. . . . . . 2.50
172 DHz,Blood Will Run,pt.3. . . . . . 2.50
173 DHz,Blood Will Run,pt.4. . . . . . 2.50
174 DHz,Moving Right Along 2.50
175 DHz,Deadly storm 2.50
176 DHz,The Rainmaker 2.50
177 DHz,interdimensional menace . 2.50
178 DHz,Caged,V:Gorilla Grodd . . . 2.50
179 DHz,Joker:Last Laugh 2.50
180 DHz,V:Peekaboo 2.50
181 DHz,BB(c),V:Fallout 2.50
182 DPs,Absolute Zero. 2.50
183 DHz,BB(c),new Trickster 2.50
184 DHz,BB(c),Crossfire,pt.1 . . . . . 2.50
185 DHz,BB(c),Crossfire,pt.2 . . . . . 2.50
186 DHz,BB(c),Crossfire,pt.3 . . . . . 2.50
187 DHz,BB(c),Crossfire,pt.4 . . . . . 2.50
188 DHz,BB(c),Crossfire,pt.5 . . . . . 3.00
189 RBr,DPs,F:Cyborg, ... 2.25
190 Rogues spotlight,Pied Piper . . . 2.25
191 ScK,DHz,F:Hawkman 2.25
192 ScK,DHz,Run Riot,pt.1. . . . . . . 2.25
193 ScK,DHz,Run Riot,pt.2. . . . . . . 2.25
194 ScK,DHz,Run Riot,pt.3. . . . . . . 2.25
195 ScK,DHz,The Top 2.25
196 V:Peek-a-Boo 2.25
197 ScK,Blitz,pt.1 . . . . 10.00
198 ScK,Blitz,pt.2 . . . . 5.00
199 ScK,Blitz,pt.3 . . . . 3.00
200 ScK,DHz,Blitz,concl.48-pg... . . 3.50
201 Ignition,pt.1 . . . . 2.25
202 Ignition,pt.2 . . . . 2.25
203 Ignition,pt.3 . . . . 2.25
204 Ignition,pt.4 . . . . 2.25
Ann.#1 JG,The Deathtouch. 4.00
Ann.#2 A:Wally's Father 3.00
Ann.#3 Roots 3.00
Ann.#4 Armageddon,pt7 . . . . 3.00
Ann.#5 TC(1st Full Work),Eclipso,
    V:Rogue's Gallery. 8.00
Ann.#6 Bloodlines#4,I:Argus. 3.00
Ann.#7 Elseworlds story 3.50
Ann.#8 Year One story 4.00
Ann.#9 Legends o/t Dead Earth . . . 3.50
Ann.#10 Pulp Heroes (Romance) . . 4.50
Ann.#11 BAu,BWr, Ghosts 3.50
Ann.#12 DBw,AAd(c),JLApe: Gorilla
    Warfare 3.50
Ann.#13 Planet DC. 4.00
Ann.#1 (1963) replica ed.(2001) . . . 7.50
Spec #1,IN,DG,CI,50th Anniv.,
    Three Flash's 5.00
Spec.#1,000,000 MWa(s),JMz,
    A:Capt.Marvel of 853rd-cent. . . 2.50
Spec.#1 Our Worlds at War,48-pg. . 3.50
T.V. Spec.#1,JS,w/episode guide . . 4.25
TPB Terminal Velocity. 12.95
TPB The Life Story of the Flash . . 13.00
TPB The Return of Barry Allen . . . 13.00
TPB Born to Run 13.00
TPB Dead Heat 14.95
TPB Race Against Time, 168-page 14.95
TPB Blood will Run (2002) 17.95
TPB Return of Barry Allen. 12.95
TPB Rogues. 14.95
TPB Terminal Velocity. 14.95
GN Iron Heights, 48-page. 5.95
GN Time Flies, 48-pg. (2002) 5.95
Secret Files #1 MWa,BAu,PRy,
    O:Flash family 5.00
Secret Files #2 (1999) 4.95
Secret Files #3, 48-page (2001) . . . 4.95
Giant #1 MWa,80-page (1998) 5.00
Giant #2 80-page 5.00

FLASH & GREEN LANTERN: THE BRAVE & THE BOLD

1999

1 (of 6) MWa&TPe(s),BKi 2.50
2 MWa&TPe(s),BKi 2.50
3 MWa&TPe(s),BKi 2.50
4 MWa&TPe(s),BKi 2.50
5 MWa&TPe(s),BKi 2.50
6 MWa&TPe(s),BKi,concl. 2.50
TPB Flash & Green Lantern,
    Brave and the Bold, 144-page 12.95

THE FLASH PLUS

Nov., 1996

1 MWa(s),F:Wally West, Dick
    Grayson 3.50

All comics prices listed are for Near Mint condition.

Flash Gordon #1 © DC Comics, Inc.

FLASH GORDON
1988
1 DJu,I:New Flash Gordon 3.00
2 DJu,A:Lion-Men,Shark-Men 3.00
3 DJu,V:Shark-Men 3.00
4 DJu,Dale Kidnapped by Voltan . . 3.00
5 DJu,Alliance Against Ming 3.00
6 DJu,Arctic City 3.00
7 DJu,Alliance vs. Ming 3.00
8 DJu,Alliance vs. Ming 3.00
9 DJu,V:Ming, final issue 3.00

FLASHPOINT
Oct., 1999
1 (of 3) NBy,Elseworlds 3.00
2 NBy,Flash in wheelchair 3.00
3 NBy 3.00

FLINCH
DC/Vertigo, 1999
1 JLe,RCo,horror anthology 2.50
2 BSz,RCo(c),3 horror tales 2.50
3 KJo,3 horror tales 2.50
4 TTn,PGu,3 horror tales 2.50
5 JLd(s),RBr,3 horror tales 2.50
6 WML(s) 2.50
7 WML(s) 2.50
8 . . . . 2.50
9 3 Tales of horror 2.50
10 . . . . 2.50
11 JLd(s) 2.50
12 . . . . 2.50
13 Hubris & dark whimsy 2.50
14 . . . . 2.50
15 3 grim tales 2.50
16 RCo(c) final issue 2.50

FLINTSTONES AND THE JETSONS, THE
Warner Bros./DC, 1997
1 Ancestors & Descendents meet . 3.00
2 thru 21 . . . . @3.00

FLY, THE
Impact, 1991–92
1 I&O:Fly I:Arachnus,Chromium . . . 3.00
2 V:Chromium 2.50
3 O:Arachnus, I:Lt.Walker Odell . . . 2.50
4 A:Black Hood, V:Arachnus 2.50
5 V:Arachnus 2.50

6 I:Blackjack 2.50
7 Oceanworld,V:Dolphus 2.50
8 A:Comet,Dolphus 2.50
9 F:Fireball, with trading card 2.50
10 V:General Mechanix 2.50
11 Suicide Issue 2.50
12 V:Agent from WEB. 2.50
13 I:Tremor. 2.50
14 and 15 V:Domino . . . . @2.50
16 V:Arachnus 2.50
17 Final Issue 2.50
Ann.#1 Earthquest,pt.4,w/card 3.00

FORBIDDEN TALES OF DARK MANSION
May-June, 1972
5 DH 65.00
6 JK 30.00
7 MK(c&a 25.00
8 MK(c&a) 25.00
9 NA(a),MK,AA 30.00
10 thru 15 Feb.–March, 1974 . . . 25.00

FOREVER MAELSTROM
Nov., 2002
1 (of 6) HC,EB,time-jumping 3.00
2 HC,EB,time past 3.00
3 HC,EB,V:Praetor 3.00
4 HC,EB,V:Ragnarok 3.00
5 HC,EB,robots 3.00
6 HC,EB,concl 3.00

FOREVER PEOPLE, THE
1971–72
1 JK,I:Forever People,A:Superman,
 A:Darkseid 100.00
2 JK,A:Darkseid 50.00
3 JK,A:Darkseid 50.00
4 JK,A:Darkseid 50.00
5 JK 40.00
6 thru 11 JK . . . . @25.00

FOREVER PEOPLE
1988
1 Return of Forever People 3.00
2 Return of Earth of Yesterday 3.00
3 A:Mark Moonrider 3.00
4 The Dark controls M.Moonrider . 3.00
5 R:MotherBox,Infinity Man 3.00
6 Donny's Fate, final issue 3.00

FORGOTTEN REALMS
1989–91
1 A:RealmsMaster,PriamAgrivar . . . 4.00
2 Mystic Hand of Vaprak,
 A:Ogre Mage 3.00
3 Mystic Hand of Vaprak contd . . . 2.75
4 Ogre Mage vs.Omen the Wizard . 2.75
5 Dragon Reach #1 . . . . 2.75
6 Dragon Reach #2 . . . . 2.50
7 Dragon Reach #3 . . . . 2.50
8 Dragon Reach #4 . . . . 2.50
9 V:Giant Squid 2.50
10 'Head Cheese' 2.50
11 Triangles #1. . . . . 2.50
12 Triangles #2. . . . . 2.50
13 Triangles #3. . . . . 2.50
14 A:Lich Viranton the Mage 2.25
15 Avatar Comics tie-in 2.25
16 Mad Gods and Paladins,pt.1 . . . 2.25
17 Mad Gods and Paladins,pt.2 . . . 2.25
18 Mad Gods and Paladins,pt.3 . . . 2.25
19 Mad Gods and Paladins,pt.4 . . . 2.25
20 Realms Master Crew captured . . 2.25
21 Catewere Tribe 2.25
22 V:The Akri 2.25

23 A:Sandusk the Leprechaun 2.25
24 'Everybody wants to rule
 the realms' 2.25
25 The Wake, final issue 2.25
Ann.#1 V:Advanced D&D crew 3.50

FORMERLY KNOWN AS THE JUSTICE LEAGUE
July 2003
1 (of 6) F:Maxwell Lord 2.50
2 JRu,KM 2.50
3 JRu,KM,V:Roulette 2.50
4 JRu,KM,F:Mary Marvel 2.50
5 JRu,R:G'nort 2.50

FOUR HORSEMEN
DC/Vertigo, Dec., 1999
1 (of 4) F:Famine 2.50
2 F:War 2.50
3 F:Pestilence 2.50
4 F:Death, concl 2.50

FOUR STAR BATTLE TALES
1973
1 MD 35.00
2 RH 20.00
3 MD 20.00
4 MD,JKo 20.00
5 MD,RH,BK 20.00

FOUR STAR SPECTACULAR
March-April, 1976
1 . . . . 20.00
2 thru 6 . . . . @10.00

FOURTH WORLD GALLERY
1-shot pin-up collection (1996) 3.50

FOUR WOMEN
Homage/DC Oct., 2001
1 (of 5) SK. 3.00
2 SK 3.00
3 SK 3.00
4 SK 3.00
5 SK 3.00
TPB SK rep. #1–#5 . . . . 17.95

FOX AND THE CROW
Dec.–Jan., 1951
1 . . . . 1,300.00
2 . . . . 600.00
3 . . . . 400.00
4 . . . . 400.00
5 . . . . 400.00
6 thru 10 . . . . @300.00
11 thru 20 . . . . @225.00
21 thru 40 . . . . @150.00
41 thru 60 . . . . @100.00
61 thru 80 . . . . @75.00
81 thru 94 . . . . @50.00
95 . . . . 65.00
96 thru 99 . . . . @35.00
100 . . . . 40.00
101 thru 108 . . . . @35.00
Becomes:

STANLEY & HIS MONSTER
109 thru 112 Oct.Nov.,1968 . . . @50.00

FREEDOM FIGHTERS
March-April, 1976
1 Freedom Fighters go to Earth 1 20.00
2 . . . . 10.00
3 . . . . 10.00
4 . . . . 10.00
5 A:Wonder Woman. 12.00
6 . . . . 10.00
7 . . . . 10.00
8 . . . . 10.00
9 . . . . 10.00
10 O:Doll Man 10.00
11 O:Ray 10.00
12 O:Firebrand 12.00
13 O:Black Condor 12.00
14 A:Batgirl. 12.00
15 O:Phantom Lady 12.00

From Beyond The Unknown #19
© DC Comics Inc.

FROM BEYOND THE UNKNOWN
Oct.–Nov., 1969
1 JKu,CI 65.00
2 MA(c),CI,ATh 30.00
3 NA(c),CI 25.00
4 MA(c),CI. 25.00
5 MA(c),CI. 25.00
6 NA(c),I:Glen Merrit 27.00
7 CI,JKu(c) 35.00
8 NA(c),CI 35.00
9 NA(c),CI 35.00
10 MA(c),CI 35.00
11 MA(c),CI 35.00
12 JKu(c),CI 35.00
13 JKu(c),CI,WW 35.00
14 JKu(c),CI 35.00
15 MA(c),CI 35.00
16 MA(c),CI 35.00
17 MA(c),CI 35.00
18 MK(c),CI 20.00
19 MK(c),CI 20.00
20 . . . . 20.00
21 . . . . 20.00
22 MA(c) 22.00
23 CI,Space Museum 20.00
24 CI 20.00

FUNNY STOCKING STUFFER
March, 1985
1 . . . . 2.00

FUNNY STUFF
Summer, 1944
1 B:3 Mouseketeer Terrific
  Whatzit 1,000.00
2 . . . . 450.00
3 . . . . 300.00
4 . . . . 200.00
5 . . . . 200.00
6 thru 10 . . . . @175.00
11 thru 20 . . . . @150.00
21 . . . . 125.00
22 C:Superman 350.00
23 thru 30 . . . . @125.00
31 thru 78 . . . . @100.00
79 July-Aug., 1954 . . . . 100.00

FURY OF FIRESTORM
June, 1982
1 PB,I:Black Bison. 7.00
2 PB,V:Black Bison 3.00
3 PB,V:Pied Piper, Killer Frost 2.50
4 PB,A:JLA,Killer Frost 2.50
5 PB,V:Pied Piper 2.50
6 V:Pied Piper 2.50
7 I:Plastique 2.50
8 V:Typhoon 2.50
9 V:Typhoon 2.50
10 V:Hyena 2.50
11 V:Hyena. 2.50
12 PB,V:Hyena. 2.50
13 . . . . 2.50
14 PB,I:Enforcer,A:Multiplex 2.50
15 V:Multiplex. 2.50
16 V:Multiplex. 2.50
17 I:2000 Committee,Firehawk 2.50
18 I:Tokamak,A:Multiplex 2.50
19 GC,V:Goldenrod 2.50
20 A:Killer Frost 2.50
21 D:Killer Frost 3.00
22 O:Firestorm 3.00
23 I:Bug & Byte 2.50
24 I:Blue Devil,Bug & Byte 2.75
25 I:Silver Deer 2.50
26 V:Black Bison 2.50
27 V:Black Bison 2.50
28 I:Slipknot 2.50
29 I:2000 C'tee,I:Breathtaker 2.50
30 V:2000 Committee 2.50
31 V:2000 Committee. 2.50
32 Phantom Stranger 2.50
33 A:Plastique 2.50
34 I:Killer Frost 2 . . . . 2.50
35 V:K.Frost/Plastique,I:Weasel . . 2.50
36 V:Killer Frost & Plastique 2.50
37 . . . . 2.50
38 V:Weasel. 2.50
39 V:Weasel. 2.50
40 . . . . 2.50
41 Crisis. 2.50
42 Crisis,A:Firehawk. 2.50
43 V:Typhoon 2.50
44 V:Typhoon 2.50
45 V:Multiplex. 2.50
46 A:Blue Devil 2.50
47 A:Blue Devil. 2.50
48 I:Moonbow. 2.50
49 V:Moonbow. 2.50
50 W:Ed Raymond 2.50
51 A:King Crusher 2.50
52 A:King Crusher 2.50
53 V:Steel Shadow 2.50
54 I:Lava 2.50
55 Legends,V:World's
  Luckiest Man 2.50
56 Legends,A:Hawk 2.50
57 . . . . 2.50
58 I:Parasite II 2.50
59 . . . . 2.50
60 Secret behind Hugo's accident. . 2.50
61 V:Typhoon 2.50

61a Superman Logo 40.00
62 A:Russian `Firestorm'. 2.50
63 A:Capt.Atom 2.50
64 A:Suicide Squad 2.50
Ann.#1 EC,A:Firehawk,
  V:Tokamak 2.50
Ann.#2 . . . . 2.50
Ann.#3 . . . . 2.50
Ann.#4 KG,CS,GC,DG 2.50
Becomes:

FIRESTORM, THE NUCLEAR MAN
Nov., 1987
65 A:New Firestorm 2.00
66 A:Green Lantern 2.00
67 Millenium, Week 1 . . . . 2.00
68 Millenium. 2.00
69 V:Zuggernaut,Stalnivolk USA. . . 2.00
70 V:Flying Dutchman 2.00
71 Trapped in the Timestream 2.00
72 V:Zuggernaut. 2.00
73 V:Stalnivolk & Zuggernaut 2.00
74 Quest for Martin Stein 2.00
75 Return of Martin Stein 2.00
76 Firestorm & Firehawk
  vs Brimstone 2.00
77 Firestorm & Firehawk in Africa . . 2.00
78 `Exile From Eden',pt.1 . . . . 2.00
79 `Exile From Eden',pt.2 . . . . 2.00
80 A:Power Girl,Starman,Invasion
  x-over. 2.00
81 A:Soyuz,Invasion aftermath 2.00
82 Invasion Aftermath. 2.00
83 V:Svarozhich 2.00
84 . . . . 2.00
85 Soul of Fire,N:Firestorm. 2.00
86 TMd,Janus Directive #7 . . . . . . 2.00
87 TMd. 2.00
88 TMd,E:Air Wave B:Maser. 2.00
89 TMd,V:Firehawk,Vandermeer
  Steel 2.00
90 TMd,Elemental War #1 . . . . . . 2.00
91 TMd,Elemental War #2 . . . . . . 2.00
92 TMd,Elemental War #3 . . . . . . 2.00
93 TMd,Elemental War concl. 2.00
94 TMd,A:Killer Frost 2.00
95 TMd,V:Captains of Industry . . . 2.00
96 TMd,A:Shango,African God &
  Obatala,Lord o/t White Cloth. . 2.00
97 TMd,A:Obatala,V:Shango. 2.00
98 TMd,A:Masar. 2.00
99 TMd,A:Brimstone,PlasmaGiant . 2.00

Firestorm The Nuclear Man #67
© DC Comics, Inc.

GHOSTDANCING
DC/Vertigo, 1995
[Mini-Series]
1 I:Snake,Ghost Dancing 2.50
2 Secrets 2.50
3 I:Father Craft 2.50
4 Coyote prisoner 2.50
5 F:Snot Boy 2.50

Ghosts #9 © DC Comics, Inc.

GHOSTS
Sept.–Oct., 1971
1 JAp,NC(c),Death's Bride-
    groom! 165.00
2 WW,NC(c),Mission
    Supernatural 75.00
3 TD,NC(c),Death is my Mother . . 50.00
4 GT,NC(c),The Crimson Claw . . . 50.00
5 NC(c),Death, The Pale
    Horseman 50.00
6 NC(c),A Specter Poured
    The Potion 30.00
7 MK(c),Death's Finger Points . . . 30.00
8 NC(c),The Cadaver In
    The Clock 30.00
9 AA,NC(c),The Last Ride
    Of Rosie The Wrecker 30.00
10 NC(c),A Specter Stalks Saigon. 30.00
11 NC(c),The Devils Lake 20.00
12 NC(c),The Macabre Mummy
    Of Takhem-Ahtem 20.00
13 NC(c),Hell Is One Mile High . . . 20.00
14 NC(c),The Bride Wore
    A Shroud 20.00
15 AA,NC(c),The Ghost That
    Wouldn't Die 20.00
16 NC(c),Death's Grinning Face . . 20.00
17 NC(c),Death Held the
    Lantern High 20.00
18 AA,NC(c),Graveyard of
    Vengeance 20.00
19 AA,NC(c),The Dead Live On . . 20.00
20 NC(c),The Haunting Hussar
    Of West Point 20.00
21 NC(c),The Ghost In The
    Devil's Chair 15.00
22 NC(c),The Haunted Horns
    Of Death 15.00
23 NC(c),Dead Is My Darling! 15.00
24 AA,NC(c),You Too, Will Die . . . 15.00
25 AA,NC(c),Three Skulls On
    The Zambezi 15.00
26 DP,NC(c),The Freaky Phantom
    Of Watkins Glen 15.00
27 NC(c),Conversation With
    A Corpse 15.00
28 DP,NC(c),Flight Of The
    Lost Phantom 15.00
29 NC(c),The Haunted Lady
    Of Death 15.00
30 NC(c),The Fangs of
    the Phantom 15.00
31 NC(c),Blood On The Moon 15.00
32 NC(c),Phantom Laughed Last . 15.00
33 NC(c),The Hangman of
    Haunted Island 15.00
34 NC(c),Wrath of the Ghost Apes 15.00
35 NC(c),Feud with a Phantom . . . 15.00
36 NC(c),The Boy Who Returned
    From The Gave 15.00
37 LD(c),Fear On Ice 15.00
38 LD(c),Specter In The Surf 15.00
39 LD(c),The Haunting Hitchhiker 15.00
40 LD(c),The Nightmare That
    Haunted The World 25.00
41 LD(c),Ship of Specters 20.00
42 LD(c),The Spectral Sentries . . . 20.00
43 LD(c),3 Corpses On A Rope . . . 20.00
44 LD(c),The Case of the
    Murdering Specters 20.00
45 LD(c),Bray of the
    Phantom Beast 20.00
46 LD(c),The World's Most
    Famous Phantom 20.00
47 LD(c),Wrath of the
    Restless Specters 20.00
48 DP,LD(c),The Phantom Head . . 20.00
49 The Ghost in the Cellar 20.00
50 Home Is Where The Grave Is . 20.00
51 The Ghost Who Would Not Die 20.00
52 LD(c),Thunderhead Phantom . . 20.00
53 LD(c),Whose Spirit Invades Me 20.00
54 LD(c),The Deadly Dreams
    Of Ernie Caruso 20.00
55 LD(c),The House That Was
    Built For Haunting 20.00
56 LD(c),The Triumph Of The
    Teen-Age Phantom 20.00
57 LD(c),The Flaming Phantoms
    of Oradour 20.00
58 LD(c),The Corpse in the Closet 20.00
59 LD(c),That Demon Within Me . . 20.00
60 LD(c),The Spectral Smile
    of Death 10.00
61 LD(c),When Will I Die Again . . . 10.00
62 LD(c),The Phantom Hoaxer! . . 10.00
63 LD(c),The Burning Bride 10.00
64 LD(c),Dead Men Do Tell Tales . 10.00
65 LD(c),The Imprisoned Phantom 10.00
66 LD(c),Conversation With A
    Corpse 10.00
67 LD(c),The Spectral Sword 10.00
68 LD(c),The Phantom of the
    Class of '76 . . . . 8.00
69 LD(c),The Haunted Gondola . . . 8.00
70 LD(c),Haunted Honeymoon . . . 8.00
71 LD(c),The Ghost Nobody Knew . 8.00
72 LD(c),The Ghost of
    Washington Monument 8.00
73 LD(c),The Specter Of The
    Haunted Highway 8.00
74 LD(c),The Gem That Haunted
    the World! 8.00
75 LD(c),The Legend Of The
    Lottie Lowry 8.00
76 LD(c),Two Ghosts of
    Death Row 8.00
77 LD(c),Ghost, Where Do
    You Hide? 8.00
78 LD(c),The World's Most
    Famous Phantom 8.00
79 LD(c),Lure of the Specter 8.00
80 JO(c),The Winged Specter 8.00

---

100 TMd,AM,V:Brimstone (Firestorm
    back-up story) final issue 3.00
Ann.#5 JLI,Suicide Squad
    I:New Firestorm 2.50

GAMMARAUDERS
1989
1 I:Animal-Warrior Bioborgs 2.25
2 V:The Slugnoids 2.25
3 V:Slugnoids,I:Squawk the
    Penguinoid 2.25
4 V:Slugnoids 2.25
5 V:Bioborg/Podnoid 2.25
6 Slash vs.Sassin,A:RadicalDebs . 2.25
7 Jok findsSword that was broken . 2.25
8 Jok's search for KirkwardDerby . . 2.25
9 Jok the Congressman 2.25
10 The Big Nada, final issue 2.25

GANG BUSTERS
1947–58
1 . . . . 1,000.00
2 . . . . 450.00
3 . . . . 325.00
4 . . . . 325.00
5 . . . . 325.00
6 . . . . 325.00
7 . . . . 325.00
8 . . . . 325.00
9 Ph(c) 250.00
10 Ph(c) 250.00
11 Ph(c) 200.00
12 Ph(c) 200.00
13 Ph(c) 200.00
14 Ph(c),FF 400.00
15 . . . . 150.00
16 . . . . 150.00
17 . . . . 400.00
18 . . . . 150.00
19 . . . . 150.00
20 . . . . 150.00
21 thru 25 . . . . @125.00
26 JK 125.00
27 thru 40 . . . . @125.00
41 thru 44 . . . . @100.00
45 Comics Code 100.00
46 thru 50 . . . . @100.00
51 MD 100.00
52 thru 67 . . . . @100.00

GANGLAND
April, 1998
1 (of 4) crime anthology 3.00
2 Platinum Nights 3.00
3 Gang Buff 3.00
4 conclusion 3.00
TPB series rep 12.95

GEMINI BLOOD
DC/Helix, 1996–97
1 Species: Paratwa, pt.1 . . . . 2.25
2 Species: Paratwa, pt.2 . . . . 2.25
3 Species: Paratwa, pt.3 . . . . 2.50
4 Species: Paratwa, pt.4 . . . . 2.25
5 WSi(c),Species: Paratwa,pt.5 . . 2.25
6 Species: Paratwa, pt.6 . . . . 2.50
7 BSz, Gillian's secret revealed . . . 2.50
8 Loothka BI-Modal,pt.1 . . . . 2.50
9 Loothka BI-Modal,pt.2 . . . . 2.50

GENESIS
Aug., 1997
1 (of 4) JBy,RoW,JRu,AD,MFm,
    Marvel x-over 3.00
2 JBy,RoW,JRu,AD,MFm,x-over . . 3.00
3 JBy,RoW,JRu,AD,MFm,x-over . . 3.00
4 JBy,RoW,JRu,AD,MFm,concl . . . 3.00

Comics Values Annual — DC — Ghosts–G.I. Combat

81 LD(c),Unburied Phantom 8.00	62 RH,JKu,Drop An Inch. 175.00	For A Tiger 100.00
82 LD(c),The Ghost Who Wouldn't Die. 8.00	63 MD,JKu(c),Last Stand 175.00	104 JA,JKu,RH(c),Blind Man's Radar. 100.00
83 LD(c),Escape From the Haunt of the Amazon Specter. 8.00	64 MD,RH,JKu,JKu(c),The Silent Jet 175.00	105 JA,JKu(c),Time Bomb Tank . 100.00
84 LD(c),Torment of the Phantom Face 8.00	65 JKu,Battle Parade 175.00	106 JA,JKu(c),Two-Sided War . . 100.00
85 LD(c),The Fiery Phantom of Faracutin 8.00	66 MD,The Eagle of Easy Company 200.00	107 JKu(c),The Ghost Pipers . . . 100.00
86 LD(c),The Ghostly Garden. 8.00	67 JKu(c),I:Tank Killer. 200.00	108 JKu(c),The Wounded Won't Wait,I:Sgt.Rock. 100.00
87 LD(c),The Phantom Freak 8.00	68 JKu,RH,The Rock 750.00	109 JKu(c),Battle of the Tank Graveyard 100.00
88 LD(c),Harem In Hell. 8.00	69 JKu,RH,The Steel Ribbon . . . 175.00	110 IN,JKu(c),Choose Your War . 100.00
89 JKu(c),Came The Specter Shrouded In Seaweed 8.00	70 JKu,Bull's-Eye Bridge. 175.00	111 JA,JKu(c),Death Trap. 100.00
90 The Ghost Galleon 8.00	71 MD,JKu(c),Last Stand 150.00	112 JA,JKu(c),Ghost Ace 90.00
91 LD(c),The Haunted Wheelchair . 8.00	72 MD,JKu(c),Ground Fire 150.00	113 JKu,RH(c),Tank Fight In Death Town 90.00
92 DH(c),Double Vision 8.00	73 RH,JKu(c),Window War 150.00	114 JA,RH(c),O:Haunted Tank . . 150.00
93 MK(c),The Flaming Phantoms of Nightmare Alley 8.00	74 RH,A Flag For Joey 150.00	115 JA,RH(c),MedalsForMayhem . 90.00
94 LD(c),Great Caesar's Ghost. . . . 8.00	75 RH,Dogtag Hill. 200.00	116 IN,JA,JKu(c),Battle Cry For A Dead Man. 90.00
95 All The Stage Is A Haunt 8.00	76 MD,RH,JKu,Bazooka For A Mouse. 200.00	117 JA,RH,JKu(c),Tank In The Ice Box 90.00
96 DH(c),Dread of the Deadly Domestic 8.00	77 RH,JKu,H-Hour For A Gunner 200.00	118 IN,JA,RH(c),My Buddy- My Enemy 90.00
97 JAp(c),A Very Special Spirit A:Spectre 15.00	78 MD,RH,JKu(c),Who Cares About The Infantry 200.00	119 RH,RH(c),Target For A Firing Squad 90.00
98 JAp(c),The Death of a Ghost A:Spectre 15.00	79 RH,JKu,Big Gun-Little Gun . . 200.00	120 IN,JA,RH(c),Pull a Tiger'sTail . 90.00
99 EC(c),Till Death Do Us Join A:Spectre 15.00	80 JKu,RH(c),Flying Horsemen. . 200.00	121 RH(c),Battle of Two Wars. . . . 50.00
100 EC&DG(c),The Phantom's Final Debt 10.00	81 Jump For Glory 175.00	122 JA,JKu(c),Who Dies Next?. . . 50.00
101 MK(c),The Haunted Hospital . . 5.00	82 IN,Get Off My Back 175.00	123 IN,RH(c),The Target of Terro . 50.00
102 RB&DG(c),The Fine Art Of Haunting 5.00	83 Too Tired To Fight 175.00	124 IN,RH(c),Scratch That Tank . . 50.00
103 RB&DG(c),Visions and Vengeance 5.00	84 JKu(c),Dog Company Is Holding 160.00	125 RH(c),Stay Alive-Until Dark . . 50.00
104 LD(c),The First Ghost 5.00	85 IN,JKu(c),The T.N.T. Trio 160.00	126 JA,RH(c),Tank Umbrella. 50.00
105 JKu(c) 5.00	86 JKu,RH(c),Not Return 160.00	127 JA,JKu(c),Mission-Sudden Death. 50.00
106 JKu(c) 5.00	87 RH(c),I:Haunted Tank. 750.00	128 RH(c),The Ghost of the Haunted Tank 50.00
107 JKu(c) 5.00	88 RH,JKu(c),Haunted Tank Vs. Ghost Tank. 300.00	129 JA,RH(c),Hold That Town For A Dead Man 50.00
108 JKu(c) 5.00	89 JA,RH,IN,Tank With Wings. . . 175.00	130 RH(c),Battle of the Generals . 50.00
109 EC(c). 5.00	90 JA,IN,RH,Tank Raiders 175.00	131 JKu&RH(c),Devil For Dinner. . 50.00
110 EC&DG(c) 5.00	91 IN,RH,Tank and the Turtle . . . 175.00	132 JA,RH(c),The Executioner. . . 50.00
111 JKu(c) 5.00	92 JA,IN,The Tank of Doom 175.00	133 JKu(c),Operation:Death Trap . 50.00
112 May, 1982 . . . . 5.00	93 RH(c),JA,No-Return Mission . 175.00	134 MD,JKu(c),Desert Holocaust . 50.00
	94 IN,RH(c),Haunted Tank Vs. The Killer Tank 175.00	135 GE,JKu(c),Death is the Joker. 50.00
GIANTKILLER **1999**	95 JA,RH(c),The Ghost of the Haunted Tank 175.00	136 JKu(c),Kill Now-Pay Later . . . 50.00
1 (of 6) 2.50	96 JA,RH(c),The Lonesome Tank 175.00	137 JKu(c),We Can't See 50.00
2 DIB. 2.50	97 IN,RH(c),The Decoy Tank . . . 175.00	138 JKu(c),I:The Losers 100.00
3 DIB. 2.50	98 JA,RH(c),Trap of Dragon's Teeth 175.00	139 JKu(c),Corner of Hell. 45.00
4 DIB,O:Jill 2.50	99 JA,JKu,RH(c),Battle of the Thirsty Tanks 175.00	140 RH,MD,JKu(c),The LastTank . 45.00
5 DIB,V:Nox. 2.50	100 JA,JKu,Return of the Ghost Tank. 175.00	141 MD,JKu(c),Let Me Live.. Let Me Die 30.00
6 . . . . 2.50	101 JA,The Haunted Tank Vs. Attila's Battle Tiger 100.00	142 RH,JKu(c),Checkpoint-Death . 30.00
	102 JKu(c),Haunted Tank Battle Window 100.00	143 RH,JKu(c),The Iron Horseman 30.00
G.I. COMBAT **Jan., 1957** **Prev: Golden Age**	103 JKu,JA,RH(c),Rabbit Punch	144 RH,MD,JKu(c),Every Man A Fort 30.00
44 RH,JKu,The Eagle and the Wolves. 750.00		145 MD,JKu(c),Sand,Sun and Death 30.00
45 RH,JKu,Fireworks Hill 375.00		146 JKu(c),Move the World. 30.00
46 JKu,The Long Walk To Wansan. 300.00		147 JKu(c),Rebel Tank 30.00
47 RH, The Walking Weapon . . . 300.00		148 IN,JKu(c),The Gold-Plated General 30.00
48 No Fence For A Jet 300.00		149 JKu(c),Leave The Fighting To Us 25.00
49 Frying Pan Seat. 300.00		150 JKu(c),The Death of the Haunted Tank. 25.00
50 Foxhole Pilot 300.00		151 JKu(c),A Strong Right Arm . . . 25.00
51 RH,The Walking Grenade . . . 300.00		152 JKu(c),Decoy Tank. 25.00
52 Jku,JKu(c),Call For A Tank . . . 225.00		153 JKu(c),The Armored Ark. 25.00
53 JKu,The Paper Trap. 225.00		154 JKu(c),Battle Prize. 25.00
54 RH,JKu,Sky Tank. 225.00		155 JKu(c),The Long Journey. . . . 15.00
55 Call For A Gunner 225.00		156 JKu(c),Beyond Hell 15.00
56 JKu,JKu(c),The D.I.-And the Sand Fleas. 250.00		157 JKu(c),The Fountain 15.00
57 RH,Live Wire For Easy 250.00		158 What Price War 15.00
58 JKu(c),Flying Saddle 250.00		159 JKu(c),Mission Dead End. . . . 15.00
59 JKu,Hot Corner 225.00		160 JKu(c),Battle Ghost 15.00
60 RH,Bazooka Crossroads 225.00		161 JKu(c),The Day of the Goth . . 15.00
61 JKu(c),The Big Run 175.00		162 JKu(c),The Final Victor. 15.00
		163 A Crew Divided 15.00
		164 Siren Song. 15.00
	G. I. Combat #164 © DC Comics Inc.	165 JKu(c),Truce,Pathfinder 15.00
		166 Enemy From Yesterday 15.00

All comics prices listed are for *Near Mint* condition.

G. I. Combat #288 © DC Comics, Inc.

167 JKu(c),The Finish Line 15.00
168 NA(c),The Breaking Point. ... 25.00
169 WS(c),The Death of the
    Haunted Tank............ 15.00
170 Chain of Vengeance........ 15.00
171 JKu(c),The Man Who
    Killed Jeb Stuart........... 12.00
172 RH(c),At The Mercy of
    My Foes................ 12.00
173 JKu(c),The Final Crash 12.00
174 JKu(c),Vow To A Dead Foe .. 12.00
175 JKu(c),The Captive Tank 12.00
176 JKu(c),A Star Can Cry 12.00
177 JKu(c),The Tank That
    Missed D-Day............ 12.00
178 JKu(c),A Tank Is Born 12.00
179 JKu(c),One Last Charge 12.00
180 JKu(c),The Saints Go
    Riding On............... 12.00
181 JKu(c),The Kidnapped Tank .. 12.00
182 JKu(c),Combat Clock........ 12.00
183 JKu(c),6 Stallions To
    Hell- And Back 12.00
184 JKu(c),Battlefield Bundle 12.00
185 JKu(c),No Taps For A Tank. .. 12.00
186 JKu(c),Souvenir
    From A Headhunter 12.00
187 JKu(c),The General
    Died Twice 12.00
188 The Devil's Pipers 12.00
189 The Gunner is a Gorilla 12.00
190 The Tiger and The Terrier.... 12.00
191 Decoy For Death 12.00
192 The General Has Two Faces . 12.00
193 JKu(c),The War That
    Had To Wait 12.00
194 GE(c),Blitzkrieg Brain........ 12.00
195 JKu(c),The War That
    Time Forgot 12.00
196 JKu(c),Dead Men Patrol..... 12.00
197 JKu(c),Battle Ark 12.00
198 JKu(c),The Devil
    Rides A Panzer........... 12.00
199 JKu(c),A Medal From A Ghost 12.00
200 JKu(c),The Tank That Died... 15.00
201 NA&RH(c),The Rocking
    Chair Soldiers............ 20.00
202 NA&RH(c),Walking Wounded
    Don't Cry 20.00
203 JKu(c),To Trap A Tiger 15.00
204 JKu(c),A Winter In Hell...... 15.00
205 JKu(c),A Gift From
    The Emperor 15.00
206 JKu(c),A Tomb For A Tank ... 15.00
207 JKu(c),Foxhole for a Sherman 15.00
208 JKu(c),Sink That Tank 15.00
209 JKu(c),Ring Of Blood 15.00
210 JKu(c),Tankers Also Bleed ... 15.00
211 JKu(c),A Nice Day For Killing . 12.00
212 JKu(c),Clay Pigeon Crew.... 12.00
213 JKu(c),Back Door To War.... 12.00
214 JKu(c),The Tanker Who
    Couldn't Die 12.00
215 JKu(c),Last Stand For Losers. 12.00
216 JKu(c),Ghost Squadron 12.00
217 JKu(c), The Pigeon Spies 12.00
218 JKu(c), 48 Hours to Die 12.00
219 thru 230 .... @12.00
231 thru 288 .... @10.00

GIFTS OF THE NIGHT
DC/Vertigo, 1999
1 (of 4) PC,JBo 3.00
2 PC,JBo................... 3.00
3 PC,JBo................... 3.00
4 PC,JBo, conclusion 3.00

GILGAMESH II
1989
1 JSn,O:Gilgamesh 5.00
2 JSn,V:Nightshadow 4.50
3 JSn,V:Robotic Ninja 4.50
4 JSn,final issue 4.00

GIRL WHO WOULD BE DEATH, THE
DC/Vertigo, 1998
1 (of 4) F:Plath 2.50
2 .... 2.50
3 .... 2.50
4 .... 2.50

GODDESS
DC/Vertigo, 1995–96
[Mini-Series]
1 I:Rosie Nolan 4.00
2 Rosie arrested 4.00
3 I:Jenny 4.00
4 CIA Chase 4.00
5 V:Agent Hooks 4.00
6 V:Harry Hooks 4.00
7 Mudhawks Past 4.00
8 finale 4.00
TPB Goddess, GEn, 256-page ... 19.95

GOLDEN AGE
Elseworld 1993–94
1 PS,F:JSA,All-Star Squadron 8.00
2 PS,I:Dynaman 7.00
3 PS,IR:Mr. Terrific is
    Ultra-Humanite........... 7.00
4 PS,D:Dynaman,Mr. Terrific 6.00
1 Secret Files,48-page(2000)..... 4.95

GON
DC/Paradox 1996
Book 1 .... 7.00
Book 2 Gon Again!............ 7.00
Book 3 Here Today,Gon Tomorrow . 7.00
Book 4 Going, Going, Gon 7.00
TPB Gon Swimmin' 7.00
TPB Gon Color Spectacular 6.00
TPB Gon Wild rep. books 3 & 4 .. 10.00
TPB 224-page (2001)........... 9.95

GOTHAM CENTRAL
Dec. 2002
1 MLr,F:Gotham Detectives 2.50
2 MLr,cop murdered 2.50
3 MLr,V:Firebug................ 2.50
4 MLr,V:Firebug................ 2.50
5 MLr,two cases 2.50
6 MLr,Half a Life,pt.1 .... 2.50
7 MLr,Half a Life,pt.2 .... 2.50
8 MLr,Half a Life,pt.3 .... 2.50
9 MLr,Half a Life,pt.4 .... 2.50
10 MLr,Half a Life,pt.5 .... 2.50
11 F:Stacy 2.50
12 A sniper strikes 2.50
13 shadow of the Joker 2.50

GOTHAM GIRLS
Aug., 2002
1 (of 5) F:Catwoman 2.25
2 Catwoman,Batgirl,P.Ivy,H.Quinn . 2.25
3 Poison Ivy, Harley Quinn 2.25
4 Batgirl..................... 2.25
5 Renee Montoya, concl........ 2.25

GREATEST STORIES EVER TOLD
TPB Superman (1989) 15.95
TPB Batman (1989) 16.00
TPB Vol.#2 Catwoman & Penguin. 16.95
TPB Joker (1989) BBo(c) 15.00
TPB Flash (1991) 15.00
TPB Golden Age (1990) 15.00
TPB Fifties 15.00
TPB Team-Up (1990) 15.00

GREEN ARROW
[Limited Series], 1983
1 TVE,DG,O:Green Arrow 5.00
2 TVE,DG,A:Vertigo............. 4.00
3 TVE,DG,A:Vertigo............. 4.00
4 TVE,DG,A:Black Canary........ 4.00
[Regular Series], 1988–97
1 EH,DG,V:Muncie 5.00
2 EH,DG,V:Muncie 4.00
3 EH,DG,FMc,V:Fyres........... 4.00
4 EH,DG,FMc,V:Fryes........... 4.00
5 EH,DG,FMc,Gauntlet 4.00
6 EH,DG,FMc,Gauntlet 4.00
7 EB,DG,A:Black Canary......... 4.00
8 DG,Alaska 3.50
9 EH,DG,FMc,R:Shado 3.50
10 EH,DG,FMc,A:Shado......... 3.50
11 EH,DG,FMc,A:Shado......... 3.50
12 EH,DG,FMc,A:Shado......... 3.00
13 DJu,DG,FMc,Moving Target.... 3.00
14 EH,DG,FMc................. 3.00
15 EH,DG,FMc,Seattle And Die ... 3.00
16 EH,DG,FMc,Seattle And Die ... 3.00
17 DJu,DG,FMc,The Horse Man... 2.50
18 DJu,DG,FMc,The Horse Man... 2.50
19 EH,DG,FMc,A:Hal Jordan 2.50
20 EH,DG,FMc,A:Hal Jordan 2.50
21 DJu,DG,B:Blood of Dragon,
    A:Shado................. 4.00
22 DJu,DG,A:Shado............ 2.50
23 DJu,DG,A:Shado............ 2.50
24 DJu,DG,E:Blood of Dragon ... 2.50
25 TVE,Witch Hunt #1 .... 2.50
26 Witch Hunt #2 .... 2.50
27 DJu,DG,FMc,R:Warlord 2.50
28 DJu,DG,FMc,A:Warlord 2.50
29 DJu,DG,FMc,Coyote Tears ... 2.50
30 DJu,DG,FMc,Coyote Tears ... 2.50
31 FMc,V:Drug Dealers 2.50
32 FMc,V:Drug Dealers 2.50
33 DJu,FMc,Psychology Issue ... 2.50
34 DJu,DG,A:Fryes,Arrested..... 2.50
35 B:Black Arrow Saga,A:Shade.. 2.50
36 Black Arrow Saga,A:Shade ... 2.50
37 Black Arrow Saga,A:Shade ... 2.50
38 E:Black Arrow Saga,A:Shade... 2.50
39 DCw,Leaves Seattle 2.50

DC — Green Arrow–Green Arrow

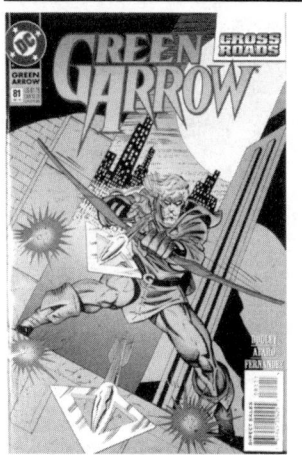

Green Arrow #81
© DC Comics, Inc.

Green Arrow #110
© DC Comics Inc.

40 MGr,Spirit Quest,A:
  Indian Shaman 2.50
41 DCw,I.R.A 2.50
42 DCw,I.R.A 2.50
43 DCw,I.R.A 2.50
44 DCw,Rock'n'Runes,pt.1 . . . . . . 2.50
45 Rock'n'Runes,pt.2 . . . . 2.50
46 DCw,Africa 2.50
47 DCw,V:Trappers 2.50
48 DCw,V:Trappers 2.50
49 V:Trappers 2.50
50 MGr(c),50th Anniv.,R:Seattle . . . 3.00
51 Tanetti's Murder,pt.1 . . . . 2.50
52 Tanetti's Murder,pt.2 . . . . 2.50
53 The List,pt.1,A:Fyres 2.50
54 The List,pt.2,A:Fyres 2.50
55 Longbow Hunters tie-in 2.50
56 A:Lt. Cameron 2.50
57 And Not A Drop to Drink,pt.1 . . 2.50
58 And Not A Drop to Drink,pt.2 . . 2.50
59 Predator,pt.1 . . . . 2.50
60 Predator,pt.2 . . . . 2.50
61 FS,F:Draft Dodgers 2.50
62 FS 2.50
63 FS,B:Hunt for Red Dragon 2.50
64 FS,Hunt for Red Dragon 2.50
65 MGr(c),Hunt for Red Dragon . . 2.50
66 MGr(c),E:Hunt for Red Dragon. . 2.50
67 MGr(c),FS,V:Rockband Killer . . . 2.50
68 MGr(c),FS,BumRap 2.50
69 MGr(c),Reunion Tour #1 . . . . . 2.50
70 Reunion Tour #2 . . . . 2.50
71 Wild in the Streets #1 . . . . 2.50
72 MGr(c),Wild in the Streets#2 . . 2.50
73 MGr(c),F:Vietnam Vet 2.50
74 SAP,MGr(c),V:Sniper 2.50
75 MGr(c),A:Speedy Shado,
  Black Canary 3.00
76 MGr(c),R:Eddie Fyers 2.50
77 MGr(c),A:Eddie Fyers 2.50
78 MGr(c),V:CIA 2.50
79 MGr(c),V:CIA 2.50
80 MGr(c),E:MGr(s),V:CIA 2.50
81 B:CDi(s),JAp,V:Shrapnel,
  Nuklon 2.50
82 JAp,I:Rival 2.50
83 JAp,V:Yakuza 2.50
84 E:CDi(s),JAp,In Las Vegas. . . . 2.50
85 AlG(s),JAp,A:Deathstroke 2.50
86 DgM(s),JAp,A:Catwoman. 2.50
87 JAp,V:Factory Owner. 2.50
88 JAp,A:M.Manhunter,Bl.Beetle. . 2.50
89 JAp,A:Anarky 2.50
90 Zero Hour 2.50
91 Hitman. 2.50
92 Partner attacked 2.50
93 Secrets of Red File 2.50
94 I:Camo Rouge 2.50
95 V:Camo Rouge 2.50
96 I:Slyfox,A:Hal Jordan 2.50
97 Where Angels Fear to
  Tread,pt.2. . . . . 2.50
98 Where Angels Fear to
  Tread,pt.3, A:Arsenal 2.50
99 Where Angels Fear to Tread . . . 2.50
100 . . . . 12.00
101 A:Superman,Black Canary . . . 35.00
102 CDi,RbC,Underworld
  Unleashed tie-in 3.00
103 CDi,RbC,Underworld
  Unleashed tie-in 3.00
104 CDi,RbC,A:Green Lantern . . . 3.00
105 CDi,RbC,A:Robin 3.00
106 . . . . 2.50
107 CDi,RbC,protects child-king . . . 2.50
108 CDi,A:Thorn 2.50
109 CDi,JAp,BSz,in Metropolis. . . . 2.50
110 CDi(s),RbC,I:Hatchet, Green
  Lantern x-over 3.50
111 CDi(s),RbC,I:Hatchet, Green
  Lantern x-over 3.50
112 CDi(s),RbC, ... 2.50
113 CDi(s),RbC,In the Mongolian
  wastes 2.50
114 CDi(s) RbC,airplane downed,
  Final Night tie-in 2.50
115 CDi(s),RbC,IronDeath,pt.1 . . . 2.50
116 CDi(s),RbC,IronDeath,pt.2 . . . 2.50
117 CDi(s),RbC,IronDeath,pt.3 . . . 2.50
118 CDi(s),DBw,RbC,Endangered
  Species, pt.1 . . . . 2.50
119 CDi(s),DBw,RbC,Endangered
  Species, pt.2 . . . . 2.50
120 CDi(s),RbC,at grandfather's
  ranch 2.50
121 CDi(s),RbC,V:The Silver
  Monkey 2.50
122 CDi(s),RbC, at Idaho ranch . . . 2.50
123 CDi(s),JAp,KJ,The
  Stormbringers, concl. 2.50
124 CDi(s),RbC,V:Milo Armitage. . . 2.50
125 CDi(s),DBw,Green Lantern
  x-over,pt.1, 48pg 3.50
126 CDi(s),DBw,x-over, pt.3 . . . . . 3.00
127 CDi(s),DBw,to San Francisco . . 3.00
128 CDi(s),DWb,Russian Mob 3.00
129 CDi,DBw,Jansen prisoner,pt.2 . . 3.00
130 CDi,DBw, ... 3.00
131 CDi,DBw,F:Crackshot 3.00
132 CDi,DBw,Eddie Fyers returns. . . 3.00
133 CDi,DBw,Eddie Fyers pt.2 . . . . 3.00
134 CDi,DBw,Brotherhood of
  the Fist x-over,pt.1 . . . . 3.00
135 CDi,DBw,Brotherhood of the
  Fist x-over, concl. 3.00
136 CDi,DBw,Green Pastures,pt.1 . . 2.50
137 CDi(s),A:Superman 2.50
Ann.#1 A:Question,FablesII 4.00
Ann.#2 EH,DG,FMc,A:Question . . . 3.50
Ann.#3 A:Question 3.50
Ann.#4 'The Black Alchemist' . . . 3.50
Ann.#5 TVE,FS,Eclipso,Batman . . 3.50
Ann.#6 JBa(c), I:Hook 3.50
Ann.#7 CDi, Year One 4.25
Spec. #0 Return 2.50
Spec.#1,000,000 CDi(s), A:Superman
  final issue. 2.50

GREEN ARROW
Feb., 2001

1 PhH,Quiver,pt.1 . . . . 17.00
1a 2nd printing 3.00
2 PhH,Quiver,pt.2 . . . . 8.00
3 PhH,Quiver,pt.3 . . . . 5.00
4 PhH,Quiver,pt.4,A:JLA 5.00
5 PhH,Quiver,pt.5,A:Batman 5.00
6 PhH,Quiver,pt.6,F:Arsenal 3.00
7 PhH,Quiver,pt.7 . . . . 3.00
8 PhH,Quiver,pt.8 . . . . 3.00
9 PhH,Quiver,pt.9 . . . . 3.00
10 PhH,Quiver,concl. 3.00
11 KSm(s),PhH,rediscovery 3.00
12 KSm(s),PhH,Ollie, Connor 3.00
13 KSm(s),PhH,Oliver & Connor. . . 3.00
14 KSm(s),PhH,Onomatopoeia. . . . 3.00
15 KSm(s),PhH,last Smith issue . . . 3.00
16 PhH,Archers Quest,pt.1 . . . . . 2.50
17 PhH,Archers Quest,pt.2. . . . . . 2.50
18 PhH,Archers Quest,pt.3 . . . . . 2.50
19 PhH,Archers Quest,pt.4,F:JLA . . 2.50
20 PhH,Archers Quest,pt.5 . . . . . 2.50
21 PhH,Archers Quest,pt.6 . . . . . 2.50
22 PhH,V:Count Vertigo 2.50
23 CAd,Urban Knights,pt.1 x-over. . 2.50
24 CAd,Urban Knights,pt.3 x-over. . 2.50
25 CAd,Urban Knights,pt.5 x-over. . 2.50
26 PhH,Straight Shooter,pt.1 . . . . 2.50
27 PhH,Straight Shooter,pt.2 . . . . 2.50
28 PhH,Straight Shooter,pt.3 . . . . 2.50
29 PhH,Straight Shooter,pt.4 . . . . 2.50
30 PhH,Straight Shooter,pt.5 . . . . 2.50
31 PhH,Straight Shooter,pt.6 . . . . 2.50
32 F:Arsenal,Green Arrow II 2.50
Spec. Secret Files #1,64-pg. 4.95
GN Green Arrow by Jack Kirby 5.95
TPB Traitor, 144-page. 12.95
TPB Quiver 17.95

GREEN ARROW LONGBOW HUNTERS
Aug., 1987

1 MGr,N:GreenArrow,I:Shado 7.00
1a 2nd printing 3.00
2 MGr,'Shadow' Revealed 5.00
2a 2nd printing 3.00
3 MGr,Tracking Snow 5.00
TPB, rep. #1-#3 . . . . 12.95
TPB Longbow Hunters, new pr. . . 14.95

GREEN ARROW: THE WONDER YEARS
1993

1 MGr,GM,B:New O:Green Arrow . 2.50
2 MGr,GM,I:Brianna Stone. 2.50

All comics prices listed are for *Near Mint* condition. CVA Page 83

Green–Green Lantern / DC / Comics Values Annual

3 MGr,GM,A:Brianna Stone 2.50
4 MGr,GM,Conclusion 2.50

GREEN CANDLES
1995
1 Paradox Mystery,F:John Halting 6.00
2 F:John Halting 6.00
3 finale 6.00
TPB B&W rep. #1–#3 .... 10.00

Green Lantern #25 © DC Comics, Inc.

GREEN LANTERN
Autumn, 1941
1 O:Green Lantern, V:Master of
   Light, Arson in the Slums . 50,000.00
2 V:Baldy,Tycoon's Legacy ... 9,000.00
3 War cover 7,000.00
4 Doiby and Green Lantern
   join the Army 5,500.00
5 V:Nazis and Black
   Prophet,A:General Prophet 3,500.00
6 V:Nordo & Hordes of War Hungry
   Henchmen,Exhile of Exiles,
   A:Shiloh................ 2,800.00
7 The Wizard of Odds....... 2,900.00
8 The Lady and Her Jewels,
   A:Hop Harrigan 2,800.00
9 V:The Whistler, The School
   for Vandals 2,300.00
10 V:Vandal Savage,The Man Who
   Wanted the World,O:Vandal
   Savage 2,300.00
11 The Distardly Designs of
   Doiby Dickles' Pals 1,700.00
12 O:The Gambler........... 1,700.00
13 A:Angela Van Enters 1,700.00
14 Case of the Crooked Cook . 1,700.00
15 V:Albert Zero, One...Two...
   Three...Stop Thinking..... 1,700.00
16 V:The Lizard 1,700.00
17 V:Kid Triangle, Reward for
   Green Lantern 1,700.00
18 V:The Dandy,The Connoisseur
   of Crime, X-mas(c) 1,900.00
19 V:Harpies, Sing a Song of
   Disaster A:Fate 1,700.00
20 A:Gambler.............. 1,700.00
21 V:The Woodman,The Good
   Humor Man 1,500.00
22 A:Dapper Dan Crocker 1,500.00
23 Doiby Dickles Movie
   Ajax Pictures 1,500.00
24 A:Mike Mattson,OnceA Cop. 1,500.00
25 The Diamond Magnet 1,500.00
26 The Scourge of the Sea ... 1,500.00

27 V:Sky Pirate 1,500.00
28 The Tricks of the
   Sports Master 1,500.00
29 Meets the Challange of
   the Harlequin 1,500.00
30 I:Streak the Wonder Dog... 1,500.00
31 The Terror of the Talismans . 1,200.00
32 The Case of the
   Astonishing Juggler 1,200.00
33 Crime goes West 1,200.00
34 Streak meets the Princess . 1,200.00
35 V:The Three-in-One Criminal 1,200.00
36 The Mystery of the
   Missing Messanger 1,500.00
37 A:Sargon. 1,500.00
38 DoublePlay,May-June,1949. 1,500.00

GREEN LANTERN
1960–72, 1976–86
1 GK,O:Green Lantern 4,500.00
2 GK,I:Qward,Pieface 1,100.00
3 GK,V:Qward 600.00
4 GK,Secret of GL Mask 450.00
5 GK,I:Hector Hammond 450.00
6 GK,I:Tomar-Re 450.00
7 GK,I&O:Sinestro.......... 400.00
8 GK,1st Story in 5700 A.D.... 400.00
9 GK,A:Sinestro............ 400.00
10 GK,O:Green Lantern's Oath.. 400.00
11 GK,V:Sinestro........... 250.00
12 GK,Sinestro,I:Dr.Polaris..... 250.00
13 GK,A:Flash,Sinestro....... 300.00
14 GK,I&O:Sonar,1st Jordan
   Brothers story........... 200.00
15 GK,Zero Hour story 200.00
16 GK,MA,I:Star Saphire,
   O:Abin Sur 200.00
17 GK,V:Sinestro........... 200.00
18 GK. 200.00
19 GK,A:Sonar 200.00
20 GK,A:Flash 200.00
21 GK,O:Dr.Polaris 175.00
22 GK,A:Hector Hammond,Jordan
   Brothers story........... 175.00
23 GK,I:Tattooed Man 175.00
24 GK,O:Shark 175.00
25 GK,V:Sonar,HectorHammond. 175.00
26 GK,A:Star Sapphire 175.00
27 GK. 175.00
28 GK,I:Goldface 175.00
29 GK,I:Black Hand 185.00
30 GK,I:Katma Tui 175.00
31 GK,Jordan brothers story.... 150.00
32 GK. 150.00
33 GK,V:Dr. Light 150.00
34 GK,V:Hector Hammond 150.00
35 GK,I:Aerialist 150.00
36 GK. 150.00
37 GK,I:Evil Star. 150.00
38 GK,A:Tomar-Re 150.00
39 GK,V:Black Hand........ 150.00
40 GK,O:Guardians,A:Golden
   Age Green Lantern........ 700.00
41 GK,A:Star Sapphire 125.00
42 GK,A:Zatanna 125.00
43 GK,A:Major Disaster 125.00
44 GK,A:Evil Star 125.00
45 GK,I:Prince Peril,A:Golden
   Age Green Lantern....... 175.00
46 GK,V:Dr.Polaris 125.00
47 GK,5700 A.D. V:Dr.Polaris ... 125.00
48 GK,I:Goldface 125.00
49 GK,I:Dazzler 125.00
50 GK,V:Thraxon the Powerful . . 125.00
51 GK,Green Lantern's Evil
   Alter-ego 100.00
52 GK,A:Golden Age Green
   Lantern Sinestro. 125.00
53 GK,CI,Jordon brothers story.. 100.00
54 GK,Menace in the Iron Lung . 100.00

Green Lantern #12 © DC Comics, Inc.

55 GK,Cosmic Enemy #1 ...... 100.00
56 GK. 100.00
57 GK,V:Major Disaster 100.00
58 GK,Perils of the Powerless
   Green Lantern 100.00
59 GK,I:Guy Gardner(imaginary
   story) 300.00
60 GK,I:Lamplighter 75.00
61 GK,A:Gold.Age Gr.Lantern.... 75.00
62 Steel Small,Rob Big......... 75.00
63 NA(c),This is the Way the
   World Ends 75.00
64 MSy,We Vow Death to Green
   Lantern................ 75.00
65 MSy,Dry up and Die....... 75.00
66 MSy,5700 AD story 75.00
67 DD,The First Green Lantern... 75.00
68 GK,I Wonder Where The
   Yellow Went? 75.00
69 GK,WW,If Earth Fails the
   Test.. It Means War 75.00
70 GK,A Funny Thing Happened
   on the way to Earth 75.00
71 GK,DD,MA,Jordan brothers ... 55.00
72 GK,Phantom o/t SpaceOpera.. 55.00
73 GK,MA,A:Star Sapphire,
   Sinestro............... 55.00
74 GK,MA,A:Star Sapphire,
   Sinestro............... 55.00
75 GK,Qward 55.00
76 NA,Gr.Lantern & Gr.Arrow
   team-up begins.......... 300.00
77 NA,Journey to Desolation.... 100.00
78 NA,A:Black Canary,A Kind of
   Loving..A Way to Death 90.00
79 NA,DA,A:Black Canary,Ulysses
   Star is Still Alive 75.00
80 NA,DG,Even an Immortal
   can die................. 75.00
81 NA,DG,A:Black Canary,Death
   be my Destiny 75.00
82 NA,DG,A:Black Canary,
   V:Sinestro,(BWr 1 page).... 75.00
83 NA,DG,A:BlackCanary,Gr.Lantern
   reveals I.D. to Carol Ferris ... 75.00
84 NA,BWr,V:Black Hand 75.00
85 NA,Speedy on Drugs,pt.1,
   rep.Green Lantern #1...... 100.00
86 NA,DG,Speedy on Drugs,pt.2,
   ATh(rep)Golden Age G.L.... 100.00
87 NA,DG,I:John Stewart,
   2nd Guy Gardner app....... 75.00
88 all reprints................. 40.00
89 NA,And Through Him Save
   the World 65.00
90 MGr,New Gr.Lantern rings 25.00

CVA Page 84 — All comics prices listed are for *Near Mint* condition.

Comics Values Annual — DC — Green Lantern

91 MGr,V:Sinestro 15.00
92 MGr,V:Sinestro 15.00
93 MGr,TA,War Against the
    World Builders 15.00
94 MGr,TA,DG,Green Arrow
    Assassin,pt.1 .... 15.00
95 MGr,Gr.Arrow Assassin,pt.2 ... 15.00
96 MGr,A:Katma Tui 15.00
97 MGr,V:Mocker 15.00
98 MGr,V:Mocker 15.00
99 MGr,V:Mocker 15.00
100 MGr,AS,I:Air Wave 25.00
101 MGr,A:Green Arrow 15.00
102 AS,A:Green Arrow 10.00
103 AS,Earth-Asylum for an Alien . 10.00
104 AS,A:Air Wave 10.00
105 AS,Thunder Doom 10.00
106 MGr,Panic..In High Places
    & Low. 10.00
107 AS,Green Lantern Corp.story . 10.00
108 MGr,BU:G.A.Green Lantern,
    V:Replikon 15.00
109 MGr,Replicon#2,GA.GL.#2 ... 10.00
110 MGr,GA.GL.#3 .... 10.00
111 AS,O:Green Lantern,
    A:G.A.Green Lantern 15.00
112 AS,O&A:G.A. Green Lantern . 20.00
113 AS,Christmas story 10.00
114 AS,I:Crumbler 10.00
115 AS,V:Crumbler 10.00
116 Guy Gardner as Gr.Lantern .. 50.00
117 JSon,I:KariLimbo,V:Prof.Ojo .. 12.00
118 AS,V:Prof.Ojo 12.00
119 AS,G.L.& G.A.solo storys ... 12.00
120 DH,A:Kari,V:El Espectro 6.00
121 DH,V:El Espectro 6.00
122 DH,A:Guy Gardner,Superman 10.00
123 JSon,DG,E:Green Lantern/Green
    Arrow T.U.,A:G.Gardner,
    V:Sinestro 12.00
124 JSon,V:Sinestro 6.00
125 JSon,FMc,V:Sinestro 6.00
126 JSon,FMc,V:Shark 6.00
127 JSon,FMc,V:Goldface 6.00
128 JSon,V:Goldface 6.00
129 JSon,V:Star Sapphire 6.00
130 JSon,FMc,A:Sonar,B:Tales of the
    Green Lantern Corps 6.00
131 JSon,AS,V:Evil Star 6.00
132 JSon,AS,E:Tales of GL Corps
    B:B.U.Adam Strange 6.00
133 JSon,V:Dr.Polaris 5.00
134 JSon,V:Dr.Polaris 5.00
135 JSon,V:Dr.Polaris 5.00
136 JSon,A:Space Ranger,
    Adam Strange 5.00
137 JSon,CI,MA,I:Citadel,A:Space
    Ranger,A.Strange 5.00
138 JSon,A&O:Eclipso 6.00
139 JSon,V:Eclipso 5.00
140 JSon,I:Congressman Block
    Adam Strange 5.00
141 JSon,I:OmegaMen 7.00
142 JSon,A:OmegaMen 6.00
143 JSon,A:OmegaMen 6.00
144 JSon,D:Tattooed Man,Adam
    Strange 5.00
145 JSon,V:Goldface 5.00
146 JSon,CI,V:Goldface
    E:B.U.Adam Strange 5.00
147 JSon,CI,V:Goldface 5.00
148 JSon,DN,DA,V:Quardians 5.00
149 JSon,A:GL.Corps 5.00
150 JSon,anniversary 6.00
151 JSon,GL.Exiled in space 5.00
152 JSon,CI,GL Exile #2 .... 5.00
153 JSon,CI,Gr.Lantern Exile #3 ... 5.00
154 JSon,Gr.Lantern Exile #4 ..... 5.00
155 JSon,Gr.Lantern Exile #5 ..... 5.00
156 GK,Gr.Lantern Exile #6 ...... 5.00
157 KP,IN,Gr.Lantern Exile #7 .... 5.00
158 KP,IN,Gr.Lantern Exile #8 .... 5.00
159 KP,Gr.Lantern Exile #9 .... 5.00
160 KP,Gr.Lantern Exile #10 ...... 5.00
161 KP,A:Omega Men,Exile #11 ... 5.00
162 KP,Gr.Lantern Exile #12 ...... 5.00
163 KP,Gr.Lantern Exile #13 ...... 5.00
164 KP,A:Myrwhidden,Exile #14 ... 5.00
165 KP,A:John Stewart & Gr.Arrow
    Green Lantern Exile #15 ..... 5.00
166 GT,FMc,DGi,Exile #16 .... 5.00
167 GT,FMc,G.L.Exile #17 .... 5.00
168 GT,FMc,G.L. Exile #18 .... 5.00
169 Green Lantern Exile #19 ..... 5.00
170 GT,MSy,GreenLanternCorps .. 5.00
171 ATh,TA,DGb,Green Lantern
    Exile #20 .... 5.00
172 DGb,E:Gr.Lant.Exile 5.00
173 DGb,I:Javelin,A:Congressman
    Bloch 5.00
174 DGb,V:Javelin 4.50
175 DGb,A:Flash 4.50
176 DGb,V:The Shark 4.50
177 DGb,rep. Gr.Lant #128 ...... 4.50
178 DGb,A:Monitor,V:Demolition
    Team 4.50
179 DGb,I:Predator 4.50
180 DGb,A:JLA 4.50
181 DGi,Hal Jordan quits as Green
    Lantern 5.00
182 DGi,John Stewart takes over
    V:Major Disaster 8.00
183 DGi,V:Major Disaster 3.50
184 DGb,Rep. Gr.Lant. #59 ...... 4.00
185 DGi,DH,V:Eclipso 4.00
186 DGi,V:Eclipso 4.00
187 BWi,John Stewart meets
    Katma Tui 3.50
188 JSon,C:GrArrow,V:Sonar,John
    Stewart reveals I.D. to world ... 4.00
189 JSon,V:Sonar 3.50
190 JSon,A:Green Arrow/Black
    Canary,Guy Gardner 3.50
191 JSon,IR:Predator is Star
    Sapphire 3.50
192 JSon,O:Star Sapphire 3.50
193 JSon,V:Replikon,
    A:G.Gardner 3.50
194 JSon,Crisis,R:G.Gardner 5.00
195 JSon,Guy Gardner as Green
    Lantern,develops attitude 12.00
196 JSon,V:Shark,Hal Jordan
    regains ring 3.50
197 JSon,V:Shark, Sonar,
    Goldface 3.50
198 JSon,D:Tomar-Re,Hal returns as
    Green Lantern,(double size) ... 3.50
199 JSon,V:Star Sapphire 3.50
200 JSon,final Gr.Lantern issue ... 5.00
Becomes:

GREEN LANTERN CORPS
1986–88
201 JSon,I:NewGr.LantCorps,V:Star
    Sapphire, Sonar, Dr.Polaris ... 3.50
202 JSon,set up headquarters 3.50
203 JSon,tribute to Disney 3.50
204 JSon,Arisia reaches puberty .. 3.50
205 JSon,V:Black Hand 3.50
206 JSon,V:Black Hand 3.00
207 JSon, Legends crossover. 3.00
208 JSon,I:Rocket Red Brigade,
    Green Lanterns in Russia#1 ... 3.00
209 JSon,In Russia #2 .... 3.00
210 JSon,In Russia #3 .... 3.00
211 JSon,John Stewart proposes
    to Katma Tui 3.00
212 JSon,W:J.Stewart&KatmaTui .. 3.00
213 JSon,For Want of a Male 3.00
214 IG,5700 A.D. Story 3.00
215 IG,Salaak and Chip quit 3.00

Green Lantern Corps #220
© DC Comics Inc.

216 IG,V:Carl 3.00
217 JSon,V:Sinestro 3.00
218 BWg,V:Sinestro 3.00
219 BWg,V:Sinestro 3.00
220 JSon,Millennium,pt.3 .... 3.00
221 JSon,Millennium 3.00
222 JSon,V:Sinestro 3.00
223 GK,V:Sinestro 3.00
224 GK,V:Sinestro 3.00
Ann.#1 GK 3.00
Ann.#2 JSa,BWg,S:AnM 3.50
Ann.#3 JBy,JL,JR 3.00
Spec.#1 A:Superman 3.00
Spec.#2 MBr,RT,V:Seeker 3.00
TPB rep.#84-#87,#89,Flash
    #217-#219 .... 12.95
TPB rep. reprints of #1-#7 ...... 8.95

GREEN LANTERN
[2nd Regular Series], 1990
1 PB,A:Hal Jordan,John Stuart,
    Guy Gardner 5.00
2 PB,A:Tattooed Man 4.50
3 PB,Jordan vs.Gardner 4.50
4 PB,Vanishing Cities 4.00
5 PB Return to OA 4.00
6 PB 3GL'sCaptive 4.00
7 PB R:Guardians 4.00
8 PB R:Guardians 4.00
9 JSon,G.Gardner,pt.1 .... 4.00
10 JSon,G.Gardner,pt.2 .... 4.00
11 JSon,G.Gardner,pt.3 .... 4.00
12 JSon,G.Gardner,pt.4 .... 4.00
13 Jordan,Gardner,Stuart(giant) .. 4.00
14 PB,Mosaic,pt.1 .... 4.00
15 RT,Mosaic,pt.2 .... 4.00
16 MBr,RT,Mosaic,pt.3 .... 4.00
17 MBr,RT,Mosaic,pt.4 .... 4.00
18 JSon,JRu,G.Gardner,
    A:Goldface 4.00
19 MBr,PB,JSon,A:All Four G.L.'s,
    O:Alan Scott,A:Doiby Dickles
    (D.Size-50th Ann.Iss.) 5.00
20 PB,RT,Hal Jordan G.L. Corp
    story begins, A:Flicker 3.00
21 PB,RT,G.L. Corp.,pt.2,
    V:Flicker 3.00
22 PB,RT,G.L. Corp.,pt.3,
    R:Star Sapphire 3.00
23 PB,RT,V:Star Sapphire,
    A:John Stuart 3.00
24 PB,RT,V:Star Sapphire 3.00

Green Lantern

Green Lantern 2nd Series #39
© DC Comics, Inc.

25 MBr,JSon,RT,Hal Vs.Guy,
   A:JLA 3.00
26 MBr,V:Evil Star,Starlings 3.00
27 MBr,V:Evil Star,Starlings 3.00
28 MBr,V:Evil Star,Starlings 3.00
29 MBr,RT,R:Olivia Reynolds 3.00
30 MBr,RT,Gorilla Warfare#1 . . . . . 3.00
31 MBr,RT,Gorilla Warfare#3 . . . . . 3.00
32 RT(i),A:Floro,Arisia 3.00
33 MBr,RT,Third Law#1,
   A;New Guardians 3.00
34 MBr,RT,Third Law#2,I:Entropy . . 3.00
35 MBr,RT,Third Law#3,V;Entropy . 3.00
36 V:Dr.Light 3.00
37 MBg,RT,A:Guy Gardner 3.00
38 MBr,RT,A:Adam Strange 3.00
39 MBr,RT,A:Adam Strange 3.00
40 RT(i),A:Darkstar,
   V:Reverse Flash 3.00
41 MBr,RT,V:Predator,
   C:Deathstroke 3.00
42 MBr,RT,V:Predator,
   Deathstroke 3.00
43 RT(i),A:Itty 3.00
44 RT(i),Trinity#2,A:L.E.G.I.O.N . . . 3.00
45 GeH,Trinity#5,A:L.E.G.I.O.N.,
   Darkstars 3.00
46 MBr,A:All Supermen,
   V:Mongul 8.00
47 A:Green Arrow 6.00
48 KM(c),B:Emerald Twilight,I:Kyle
   Rayner (Last Green Lantern) . . 7.00
49 KM(c),GJ(s),A:Sinestro 6.00
50 KM(c),GJ(s),D:Sinestro,Kiliwog,
   Guardians,I:Last Green
   Lantern (in Costume) 8.00
51 V:Ohm,A:Mongul 5.00
52 V:Mongul 4.00
53 A:Superman,V:Mongul 4.00
54 D:Alex, V:Major Force 4.00
55 Zero Hour,A:Alan Scott,
   V:Major Force 4.00
56 Green Lantern and ring 3.50
57 Psimon 3.50
58 Donna Troy,Felix Faust 3.50
59 V:Dr. Polaris 3.50
60 Capital Punishment,pt.3 . . . . 3.50
61 V:Kalibak,A:Darkstar 3.50
62 V:Duality,R:Ganthet 3.50
63 Parallax View: The Resurrection
   of Hal Jordan,pt.1 . . . . 3.00
64 Parallax View,pt.2,A:Superman,
   Flash,V:Parallax 3.00

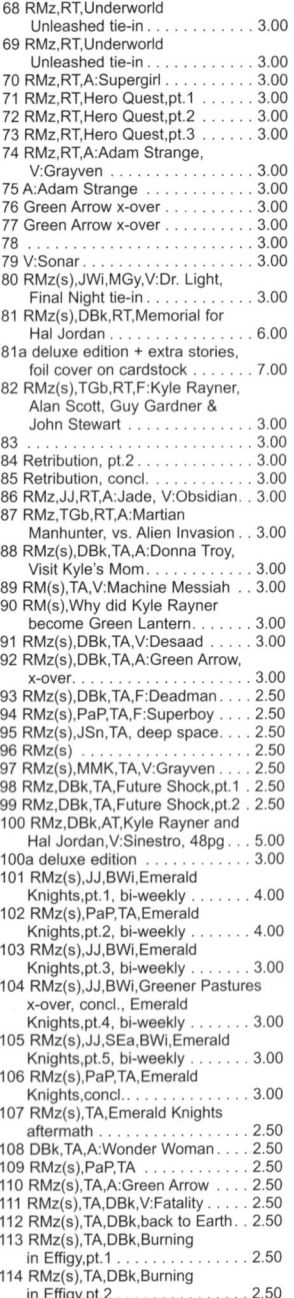

65 Siege of ZiCharan,pt.2 . . . . 3.00
66 V:Sonar 3.00
67 A:Flash,V:Sonar 3.00
68 RMz,RT,Underworld
   Unleashed tie-in 3.00
69 RMz,RT,Underworld
   Unleashed tie-in 3.00
70 RMz,RT,A:Supergirl 3.00
71 RMz,RT,Hero Quest,pt.1 . . . . . . 3.00
72 RMz,RT,Hero Quest,pt.2 . . . . . . 3.00
73 RMz,RT,Hero Quest,pt.3 . . . . . . 3.00
74 RMz,RT,A:Adam Strange,
   V:Grayven 3.00
75 A:Adam Strange 3.00
76 Green Arrow x-over 3.00
77 Green Arrow x-over 3.00
78 . . . . 3.00
79 V:Sonar 3.00
80 RMz(s),JWi,MGy,V:Dr. Light,
   Final Night tie-in 3.00
81 RMz(s),DBk,RT,Memorial for
   Hal Jordan 6.00
81a deluxe edition + extra stories,
   foil cover on cardstock 7.00
82 RMz(s),TGb,RT,F:Kyle Rayner,
   Alan Scott, Guy Gardner &
   John Stewart 3.00
83 . . . . 3.00
84 Retribution, pt.2 . . . . 3.00
85 Retribution, concl. 3.00
86 RMz,JJ,RT,A:Jade, V:Obsidian . . 3.00
87 RMz,TGb,RT,A:Martian
   Manhunter, vs. Alien Invasion . . 3.00
88 RMz(s),DBk,TA,A:Donna Troy,
   Visit Kyle's Mom 3.00
89 RM(s),TA,V:Machine Messiah . . 3.00
90 RM(s),Why did Kyle Rayner
   become Green Lantern 3.00
91 RMz(s),DBk,TA,V:Desaad 3.00
92 RMz(s),DBk,TA,A:Green Arrow,
   x-over 3.00
93 RMz(s),DBk,TA,F:Deadman . . . 2.50
94 RMz(s),PaP,TA,F:Superboy 2.50
95 RMz(s),JSn,TA, deep space . . . 2.50
96 RMz(s) 2.50
97 RMz(s),MMK,TA,V:Grayven 2.50
98 RMz,DBk,TA,Future Shock,pt.1 . 2.50
99 RMz,DBk,TA,Future Shock,pt.2 . 2.50
100 RMz,DBk,AT,Kyle Rayner and
   Hal Jordan,V:Sinestro, 48pg . . 5.00
100a deluxe edition 3.00
101 RMz(s),JJ,BWi,Emerald
   Knights,pt.1, bi-weekly 4.00
102 RMz(s),PaP,TA,Emerald
   Knights,pt.2, bi-weekly 4.00
103 RMz(s),JJ,BWi,Emerald
   Knights,pt.3, bi-weekly 3.00
104 RMz(s),JJ,BWi,Greener Pastures
   x-over, concl., Emerald
   Knights,pt.4, bi-weekly 3.00
105 RMz(s),JJ,SEa,BWi,Emerald
   Knights,pt.5, bi-weekly 3.00
106 RMz(s),PaP,TA,Emerald
   Knights,concl. 3.00
107 RMz(s),TA,Emerald Knights
   aftermath 2.50
108 DBk,TA,A:Wonder Woman 2.50
109 RMz(s),PaP,TA 2.50
110 RMz(s),TA,A:Green Arrow 2.50
111 RMz(s),TA,DBk,V:Fatality 2.50
112 RMz(s),TA,DBk,back to Earth . . 2.50
113 RMz(s),TA,DBk,Burning
   in Effigy,pt.1 . . . . 2.50
114 RMz(s),TA,DBk,Burning
   in Effigy,pt.2 . . . . 2.50
115 DJu(s),A:Plastic Man &
   Booster Gold, pt.1 . . . . 2.50
116 DJu(s),A:Plastic Man &
   Booster Gold, pt.1 . . . . 2.50
117 RMz(s),DBk,TA,R:Donna Troy . 2.50
118 RMz(s),DBk,TA,Day of

Green Lantern 2nd Series, Annual #2
© DC Comics, Inc.

   Judgment x-over 2.50
119 RMz,DBk,CaS,Day of
   Judgment aftermath 2.50
120 RMz,DBk,CaS 2.50
121 RMz,DBk,CaS 2.50
122 RMz,DBk,CaS 2.50
123 RMz,DBk,V:Controllers 2.50
124 RMz,DBk,V:Controllers 2.50
125 RMz,Unmooning secrets 2.50
126 Goes undercover 2.50
127 F:Effigy & Killer Frost 2.50
128 F:Arsenal 2.50
129 DBk,ASm,V:Manhunters 2.50
130 DBk,ASm,V:Manhunters 2.50
131 DBk,ASm,V:Manhunters 2.50
132 DBk,While Rome Burned,pt.1. . 2.50
133 DBk,MBr,Rome Burned,pt.2 . . . 2.50
134 DBk,While Rome Burned,pt.3. . 2.50
135 DBk,While Rome Burned,pt.4. . 2.50
136 DBk,While Rome Burned,pt.5. . 2.50
137 DBk,Friends & Lovers 2.50
138 DBk,Away From Home,pt.1 . . . 2.50
139 DBk,Away From Home,pt.2 . . . 2.50
140 DBk,A:Alan Scott 2.50
141 DBk,A:Jade,V:arsonist 2.50
142 V:Inferno 2.50
143 JLe,Joker:Last Laugh,tie-in . . . 2.50
144 Battle to control his powers . . . 2.50
145 V:Nero 2.50
146 incredible metamorphosis 2.50
147 F:John Stewart 2.50
148 A:Superman,R:Jade 2.50
149 F:JLA 2.50
150 End of Ion,48-pg. 5.00
151 JLe(c) Hand of God,aftermath . 2.50
152 RbC,uncontrollable madness . . 2.50
153 JLe(c),high school reunion 2.50
154 JLe&SW(c),attacked 2.50
155 JLe&SW(c),A:Flash,JLA 2.50
156 John Stewart back,A:Sentinel. . 2.50
157 Girl Talk 2.50
158 industrialist nomads 2.50
159 Boar Beasts 2.50
160 Child Guardians 2.50
161 V:Amazon 2.50
162 CAd,Urban Knights,pt.2 x-over. 2.50
163 CAd,Urban Knights,pt.4 x-over. 2.50
164 CAd,Urban Knights,pt.6 x-over. 2.50
165 RBr,A Tiny Spark 2.50
166 RBr,The Blind,pt.1 . . . . 2.50
167 RBr,The Blind,pt.2 . . . . 2.50
168 RBr 2.50
169 RBr,Kilowog's soul 2.50

170 RBr 2.50
171 Wanted, pt.1 . . . . 2.50
Ann.#1 Eclipso,V:Star Sapphire . . . 4.00
Ann.#1 80pg, rep. 5.00
Ann.#2 Bloodlines#7,I:Nightblade . . 4.00
Ann.#3 Elseworlds Story. 3.50
Ann.#4 Year One story 4.00
Ann.#5 Legends o/t Dead Earth . . . 3.50
Ann.#6 RMz(s),JJ,Low,Pulp
 Heroes, 64pg. 4.50
Ann.#7 SV,RLm,Clv,BWr,Ghosts. . . 3.50
Ann.#8 MCa,AAd(c),JLApe:Gorilla
 Warfare 3.50
Ann.#9 Planet DC. 4.00
Spec.#1,000,000 RMz(s),BHi,PNe . 2.50
Spec. 3-D #1 V:Dr. Light. 4.00
Spec.#1 Our Worlds at War(2001) . 2.95
Secret Files #1 . . . . 5.00
Secret Files Spec.#2 . . . . 5.00
Secret Files #3, 48-pg. 4.95
Green Lantern Plus, 1-shot RMz(s),
 F:The Ray,V:Dr. Polaris 3.00
Green Lantern/Silver Surfer, 1-shot
 DC/Marvel RMz,TA A:Thanos
 vs. Parallax 5.00
Green Lantern Gallery, 1 one-shot
 life in pictures 3.50
Green Lantern: Ganthet's Tale,
 1-shot, JBy,O:Guardians. 7.00
Giant #1 80-page 5.50
Giant #2 80-page 5.50
Giant #3 80-page 5.95
GN Ganthet's Tale, JBy 6.00
GN Green Lantern/Superman:
 Legends of the Green Flame . . 5.95
GN 1001 Emerald Nights(2001) . . . 6.95
GN Brightest Day/Blackest Night . . 5.95
TPB A New Dawn. 10.00
TPB Emerald Twilight 6.25
TPB Emerald Knights 13.00
TPB A New Dawn 10.00
TPB Baptism of Fire 13.00
TPB Fear Itself 14.95
TPB Emerald Allies, rep. 13.00
TPB New Journey, Old Path 12.95
TPB Circle of Fire 17.95
TPB Emerald Dawn (rep. 2003) . . 14.95
TPB The Power of Ion (2003) . . . 14.95
TPB Emerald Dawn II (2003) 12.95
TPB Brother's Keeper. 12.95
TPB The Road Back. 14.95
TPB Emerald Twilight/New Dawn . 19.95

GREEN LANTERN & SENTINEL: HEART OF DARKNESS
Feb., 1998
1 (of 3) RMz(s),PaP,DDv 3.00
2 RMz(s),PaP,DDv. 3.00
3 RMz(s),PaP,DDv. 3.00

GREEN LANTERN: CIRCLE OF FIRE
Aug., 2000
1 (of 2) NBy,64-pg. x-over 5.00
2 48-pg.x-over concl. 5.00
Spec.Gr.Lant.: Adam Strange #1. . . 2.50
Spec.Gr.Lant.: The Atom #1 . . . . . 2.50
Spec.Gr.Lant.: Firestorm #1 . . . . . 2.50
Spec.Gr.Lant.: Green Lantern #1 . 2.50
Spec.Gr.Lant.: Power Girl #1 . . . . 2.50

GREEN LANTERN CORPS QUARTERLY
1992–94
1 DAb,JSon,FH,PG,MBr,F:Alan

 Scott G'nort 3.00
2 DAb,JSon,PG,AG,Alan Scott . . . 2.75
3 DAb,RT,F:Alan Scott,G'Nort 2.75
4 TA,AG(i),F:H.Jordan,G'Nort 2.75
5 F:Alan Scott,I:Adam 2.75
6 JBa,TC,F:Alan Scott 3.25
7 Halloween Issue 3.25
8 GeH,SHa,final issue 3.25

GREEN LANTERN: DRAGON LORD
April, 2001
1 (of 3) PG, 48-page 5.00
2 PG, 48-page 5.00
3 PG, 48-page. 5.00

GREEN LANTERN: EMERALD DAWN
[1st Limited Series], 1989–90
1 MBr,RT,I:Mod.Age.Gr.Lantern . . . 5.00
2 MBr,RT,I:Legion (not group) 4.00
3 MBr,RT,V:Legion 3.00
4 MBr,RT,A:Green Lantern Corps . 3.00
5 MBr,RT,V:Legion. 3.00
6 MBr,RT,V:Legion. 3.00
TPB rep#1-#6. . . . . 5.50

*Green Lantern Emerald Dawn II #6
© DC Comics Inc.*

[2nd Limited Series], 1991
1 MBr,A:Sinestro,Guy Gardner. . . . 2.00
2 MBr,RT,V:Alien Aliance 2.00
3 MBr,RT,Sinestro's Home Planet . 2.00
4 MBr,RT,Korugar Revolt 2.00
5 MBr,RT,A:G.Gardner. 2.00
6 MBr,RT,Trial of Sinestro 2.00

GREEN LANTERN: EVIL'S MIGHT
Aug., 2002
1 (of 3) HC, Elseworlds, 48-pg. . . . 5.95
2 HC,F:Kyle Rayner. 5.95
3 HC,concl. 5.95

GREEN LANTERN/ GREEN ARROW
1983–84
1 NA rep. 5.00
2 NA,DG rep. 4.00
3 NA,DG rep. 4.00

4 NA,DG rep. 4.00
5 NA,DG rep. 4.00
6 NA,DG rep. 4.00
7 NA,DG rep. 4.00
TPB Roadback 9.00
TPB Traveling Heroes, Vol.1 . . . . 12.95
TPB Traveling Heroes, Vol.2 . . . . 12.95

GREEN LANTERN: MOSAIC
1992–93
1 F:John Stewart. 2.25
2 D:Ch'p 2.25
3 V:Sinestro. 2.25
4 F:The Children on Oa 2.25
5 V:Hal Jordan 2.25
6 A:Kilowog 2.25
7 V:Alien Faction 2.25
8 V:Ethereal Creatures 2.25
9 Christmas issue 2.25
10 V:Guardians 2.25
11 R:Ch'p 2.25
12 V:KKK 2.25
13 V:KKK,Racism. 2.25
14 A:Salaak,Ch'p 2.25
15 A:Katma Tui,Ch'p. 2.25
16 LMc,A:JLA,Green Lantern . . . 2.25
17 A:JLA 2.25
18 final issue 2.25

GREEN LANTERN: THE NEW CORPS
1999
1 (of 2) CDi(s),SEa 5.00
2 CDi(s),SEa, concl. 5.00

GREGORY
DC/Piranha
1 MaH, b&w 8.00
2 MaH 5.00
3 MaH Bookshelf Ed. 5.00
3a Platinum Ed. 8.00
4 MaH, b&w 5.00

GRIFFIN
1991–92
1 I:Matt Williams as Griffin 5.50
2 V:Carson 5.25
3 A:Mary Wayne 5.25
4 A:Mary Wayne 5.25
5 Face to Face with Himself 5.25
6 Final Issue 5.25

GRIP: THE STRANGE WORLD OF MEN
DC/Vertigo, Nov., 2001
1 (of 5) GHe 2.50
2 GHe 2.50
3 GHe 2.50
4 GHe 2.50
5 GHe, concl 2.50

GROSS POINT
July, 1997
1 MWa&BAu(s) parody 2.50
2 Independence Day picnic 2.50
3 Ed Gein High School 2.50
4 paranoid driving instructor. 2.50
5 Halloween 2.50
6 Trip to Chicago 2.50
7 Stuck in Gross Point. 2.50
8 Dru Hardly & Nancy Boys 2.50
9 . . . . 2.50
10 Businessman of the Year 2.50

DC

Gross Point #2
© DC Comics, Inc.

11 Mystery Meat 2.50
12 Cold Hands, Still Heart 2.50
13 Terminal illness 2.50
14 The Aisle of Doctor Morose 2.50

GUARDIANS OF METROPOLIS
Nov., 1994

1 Kirby characters 2.25
2 Donovan's creations 2.25
3 . . . . 2.25
4 Female Furies 2.25

GUNFIRE
1994–95

1 B:LWn(s),StE,I:Ricochet 2.25
2 StE,V:Ricochet 2.25
3 StE,I:Purge 2.25
4 StE,V:Maraud 3 . . . . 2.25
5 StE,I:Exomorphic Man 2.25
6 New costume 2.25
7 Ragnarok 2.25
8 V:Tattoo 2.25
9 V:Ragnarock 2.25
10 V:Yakuza 2.25
11 V:Yakuza 2.25
12 I:New Weapon 2.25
13 A:JLA,V:Ragnarok, final issue . . 2.25

GUNS OF THE DRAGON
Aug., 1998

1 (of 4) TT, set in 1920s 2.50
2 TT 2.50
3 TT 2.50
4 TT conclusion 2.50

GUY GARDNER
1992–94

1 JSon,A:JLA,JLE 2.50
2 JSon,A:Kilowog 2.50
3 JSon,V:Big,Ugly Alien 2.50
4 JSon,G.Gardner vs Ice 2.50
5 JSon,A:Hal Jordan,V:Goldface . . 2.50
6 JSon,A:Hal Jordan,V:Goldface . . 2.50
7 JSon,V:Goldface 2.50
8 JSon,V:Lobo 2.50
9 JSon,V:Boodikka 2.50
10 JSon,V:Boodikka 2.50
11 JSon,B:Year One 2.50
12 JSon,V:Batman,Flash,Green Lantern 2.50
13 JSon,Year One#3 . . . . 2.50
14 JSon,E:Year One 2.50
15 V:Bad Guy Gardner 2.50
16 B:CDi(s),MaT,V:Guy's Brother . . 2.50
Becomes:

GUY GARDNER: WARRIOR
1994–96

17 V:Militia 2.50
18 B:Emerald Fallout,N:Guy Gardner,
  V:Militia 4.00
19 A:G.A.Green Lantern,V:Militia . . 4.00
20 A:JLA,Darkstars 2.50
21 E:Emerald Fallout,V:H.Jordan . . 2.50
22 I:Dementor 2.50
23 A:Buck Wargo 2.50
24 Zero Hour 2.50
25 A:Buck Wargo 3.00
26 Zero Hour 2.50
27 Capital Punishment 2.50
28 Capital Punishment,pt.2 . . . . 2.50
29 I:Warriors Bar 2.50
29a Collector's Edition 3.25
30 V:Superman,Supergirl 2.50
31 A:Sentinel,Supergirl,
  V:Dementor 2.50
32 Way of the Warrior,pt.1,A:JLA . . 2.50
33 Way of the Warrior,pt.4 . . . . 2.50
34 . . . . 2.50
35 Return of an Old Foe 2.50
36 Underworld Unleashed tie-in . . . 2.50
37 Underworld Unleashed tie-in . . . 2.50
38 A new woman 2.50
39 Guest stars galore 2.50
40 . . . . 2.50
41 V:Dungeon 2.50
42 Martika revealed as Seductress . 2.50
43 V:5 Foes 2.50
Ann.#1 Year One Annual, Leechun
  vs. Vuldarians 4.00
Ann.#2 Dead Earth 3.50

GUY GARDNER: REBORN
1992

1 JSon,JRu,V:Goldface,C:Lobo . . . 6.00
2 JSon,JRu,A:Lobo,V:Weapons
  of Qward 5.50
3 JSon,JRu,A:Lobo,N:G.Gardner
  V:Qwardians 5.50

HACKER FILES
1992–93

1 TS,Soft Wars#1,I:Jack Marshall . 2.25
2 TS,Soft Wars#2 . . . . 2.25
3 TS,Soft Wars#3 . . . . 2.25
4 TS,Soft Wars#4 . . . . 2.25
5 TS,A:Oracle(Batgirl) 2.25
6 TS,A:Oracle,Green Lantern 2.25
7 TS,V:Digitronix 2.25
8 TS,V:Digitronix 2.25
9 TS,V:Digitronix 2.25
10 V:Digitronix 2.25
11 TS,A:JLE 2.25
12 TS,V:Digitronix,final issue 2.25

HAMMER LOCKE
1992–93

1 I:Hammerlocke 3.00
2 V:Tharn the Iron Spider 2.25
3 V:Tharn the Iron Spider 2.25
4 O:Hammerlocke 2.25
5 V:Sahara Skyhawk 2.25
6 V:Tharn the Iron Spider 2.25
7 V:Tharn 2.25
8 CSp,V:Iron Spider 2.25

HARDCORE STATION
May, 1998

1 (of 6) JSn,JRu,F:Maximillian 2.50
2 JSn,JRu,V:Synnar 2.50
3 JSn,JRu,F:Kyle Rayner 2.50
4 JSn,JRu,V:Synnar 2.50
5 JSn,JRu,F:JLA 2.50
6 JSn,JRu,conclusion 2.50

HARDWARE
DC/Milestone, 1993–96

1 DCw,I:Hardware,Edwin Alva,Reprise,
  Dir.Mark.Ed.,w/A puzzle piece,
  Skybox Card,Poster 4.00
1a NewsstandEd. 2.50
1b Platinum Ed 6.00
2 DCw,V:Repirise,I:Barraki Young . 2.50
3 DCw,O:EDwin Alva,
  I:S.Y.S.T.E.M. 2.50
4 DCw,V:S.Y.S.T.E.M. 2.50
5 DCw,I:Deathwish 2.50
6 DCw,V:Deathwish 2.50
7 DCw,O:Deathwish 2.50
8 DCw(c),O:Hardware 2.50
9 DCw(c),I:Technique 2.50
10 DCw(c),I:Harm,Transit 2.50
11 WS(c),DCw,Shadow War,
  I:Iron Butterfly,Dharma 2.50
12 RB,V:Harm 2.50
13 DCw,A:Reprise 2.50
14 DCw 2.50
15 DCw(c),HuR,V:Alva 2.50
16 Die-Cut(c),JBy(c),DCw,
  N:Hardware 4.25
16a Newsstand ED 2.50
17 Worlds Collide,pt.2,A:Steel 2.50
18 Worlds Collide,pt.9,V:Rift 2.50
19 I:Evan,Tetras 2.50
20 . . . . 2.50
21 Arcana,Helga 2.50
22 Curt & Assistant 2.50
23 . . . . 2.50
24 . . . . 2.50
25 V:Death Row, Sanction 3.00
26 Hunt For Deathwish,pt.1 . . . . . . 2.50
27 Hunt For Deathwish,pt.2 . . . . . . 2.50
28 Hunt For Deathwish,pt.3 . . . . . . 2.50
29 Long Hot Summer, A:The Blood
  Syndicate, spec.low price 2.50
30 Long Hot Summer 2.50
31 . . . . 2.50
32 Control of Alva 2.50

Hardware #1
© DC Comics, Inc.

DC

Hardware–Hawkman

33 HC(c), Cyborg 2.50
34 V:Huaca Aires 2.50
35 A:Sanction 2.50
36 A:Sanction 2.50
37 . . . . 2.50
38 V:Malleus, without armor 2.50
39 F:Sabrina Alva 2.50
40 V:Top Dog 2.50
41 . . . . 2.50
42 . . . . 2.50
43 . . . . 2.50
44 A:Heroes 2.50
45 DGC(s),Hardware & Hard
   Company go back to basics . . . 2.50
46 DGC(s),Discovery of Edwin
   Alva's artificial intelligence 2.50
47 DGC(s),The truth behind a
   brutal murder 2.50
48 . . . . 2.50
49 DGC(s),Moe(c),V:Tyrant. 2.50
50 DGC(s), 48pg. anniversary issue 3.95
51 DMc(s) final issue 2.50

HARLEY QUINN
October, 2000

1 KK,TyD,A:Batman,48 pg. 3.00
2 KK,TyD,A:Two-Face,Poison Ivy. . 2.50
3 KK,TyD,A:Catwoman 2.50
4 KK,TyD,I:Quinntettes 2.50
5 KK,TyD,F:Quinntettes 2.50
6 KK,TyD,A:Oracle 2.50
7 KK,TyD,F:Big Barda 2.50
8 KK,TyD,Harley's Past 2.50
9 KK,TyD,V:Quinntettes 2.50
10 KK,TyD,F:Barbara Gordon . . . 2.50
11 KK,TyD,F:Nightwing 2.50
12 KK,TyD,40-page 3.50
13 KK,Joker:Last Laugh 2.50
14 KK,TyD,to Metropolis 2.50
15 KK,TyD,Lovers advice 2.50
16 KK,TyD,City of Tomorrow 2.50
17 KK,TyD,F:Bizarro 2.50
18 KK,TyD,F:Bizarro 2.50
19 KK,TyD,A:Superman 2.50
20 KK,Harley pays price for evil . . . 2.50
21 KK,ultimate prison 2.50
22 KK,TyD,Highwater 2.50
23 KK,TyD,World Without Harley . . 2.50
24 KK,DDv,back from Hell 2.50
25 KK,DDv,F:Batman,A:Joker 2.50
26 wanted for murder 2.50
27 Harley a psychiatrist 2.50
28 new patient 2.50
29 a stalker 2.50
30 Who framed Harley? 2.50
31 Harley and Doc 2.50
32 A:Joker 2.50
33 Behind Blue Eyes,pt.1 . . . . . . 2.50
34 Behind Blue Eyes,pt.2 . . . . . . 2.50
35 Behind Blue Eyes,pt.3 . . . . . . 2.50
36 Behind Blue Eyes,pt.4 . . . . . . 2.50
37 Behind Blue Eyes,pt.5 . . . . . . 2.50
38 CAd,final issue 2.50
Spec.#1 Our Worlds at War,48-pg. . 3.25
GN Harley & Ivy, Love on the Lam . 6.50

HAVEN:
THE BROKEN CITY
Dec., 2001

1 (of 9) AOI,F:JLA 2.50
2 AOI,A:JLA. 2.50
3 AOI,A:Superman,I:HankVelveeda . 2.50
4 AOI,F:Nia 2.50
5 AOI,Eater of Filth 2.50
6 AOI,search for crash survivors . . 2.50
7 AOI,V:Ivas the ultra-powerful. . . . 2.50
8 AOI,Anathema 2.50
9 AOI,Valadin. 2.50

HAWK & DOVE
[1st Regular Series], 1968–69

1 SD 125.00
2 SD 75.00
3 GK 75.00
4 GK 75.00
5 GK,C:Teen Titans 75.00
6 GK 75.00

[Limited Series], 1988–89

1 RLd,I:New Dove 4.00
2 RLd,V:Kestrel 3.50
3 RLd,V:Kestrel 3.50
4 RLd,V:Kestrel 3.50
5 RLd,V:Kestrel,O:New Dove 3.50
TPB rep. #1-#5 . . . . 10.50

[2nd Regular Series], 1989–91

1 A:Superman,Green Lantern
  Hawkman 2.50
2 V:Aztec Goddess 2.50
3 V:Aztec Goddess 2.50
4 I:The Untouchables 2.50
5 I:Sudden Death, A:1st Dove's
  Ghost. 2.50
6 A:Barter,Secrets o/Hawk&Dove. . 2.50
7 A:Barter,V:Count St.Germain . . . 2.50
8 V:Count St.Germain 2.50
9 A:Copperhead 2.50
10 V:Gauntlet & Andromeda 2.50
11 A:New Titans,V:M.A.C.,
   Andromeda Gauntlet 2.50
12 A:New Titans,V:Scarab 2.50
13 1960's,I:Shellshock 2.50
14 Prelue to O:Hawk & Dove,
   V:Kestrel 2.50
15 O:Hawk & Dove begins 2.50
16 HawkV:Dove,V:Lord of Chaos . . 2.50
17 V:Lords-Order & Chaos 2.50
18 The Creeper #1 . . . . 2.50
19 The Creeper #2 . . . . 2.50
20 KM,DG,Christmas Story 2.50
21 Dove 2.50
22 V:Sudden Death 2.50
23 A:Velv.Tiger,SuddenDeath 2.50
24 A:Velv.Tiger,SuddenDeath 2.50
25 Recap 1st 2 yrs.(48 pg) 2.50
26 Dove's past 2.50
27 The Hunt for Hawk. 2.50
28 War of the Gods,A:Wildebeest
   A:Uncle Sam,final issue,
   double size. 3.00
Ann.#1 In Hell. 3.00
Ann.#2 CS,KGa,ArmageddonPt.5 . 3.00
TPB RLd 9.50

HAWK & DOVE
Sept., 1997

1 (of 5) MBn,DZ,DG,Sasha Martens
  & Wiley Wolverman 2.50
2 MBn,DZ,DG,Vixen & Vigilante. . . 2.50
3 MBn,DZ,DG,grave desecrations . 2.50
4 MBn,DZ,DG,V:Suicide Squad . . . 2.50

HAWKMAN
[1st Regular Series], 1964–68

1 MA,V:Chac 900.00
2 MA,V:Tralls 300.00
3 MA,V:Sky Raiders 175.00
4 MA,I&O:Zatanna 200.00
5 MA 175.00
6 MA 175.00
7 MA,V:I.Q. 175.00
8 MA 175.00
9 MA,V:Matter Master 175.00
10 MA,V:Caw 175.00
11 MA. 125.00
12 MA 125.00
13 MA 125.00
14 GaF,MA,V:Caw 125.00
15 GaF,MA,V:Makkar 125.00
16 GaF,MA,V:Ruthvol 125.00
17 GaF,MA,V:Raven 125.00
18 GaF,MA,A:Adam Strange . . . 100.00
19 GaF,MA,A:Adam Strange . . . 100.00
20 GaF,MA,V:Lionmane 70.00
21 GaF,MA,V:Lionmane 70.00
22 V:Falcon 70.00
23 V:Dr.Malevolo 70.00
24 Robot Raiders from
   Planet Midnight 70.00
25 DD,V:Medusa,G.A.Hawkman . . 70.00
26 RdM,CCu,DD. 70.00
27 DD,JKu(c),V:Yeti 70.00

[2nd Regular Series], 1986–87

1 DH,A:Shadow Thief 3.00
2 DH,V:Shadow Thief 2.50
3 DH,V:Shadow Thief 2.50
4 DH A:Zatanna 2.50
5 DH,V:Lionmane 2.50
6 DH,V:Gentleman Ghost,
  Lionmane 2.50
7 DH,Honor Wings 2.50
8 DH,Shadow War contd. 2.50
9 DH,Shadow War contd. 2.50
10 JBy(c),D:Hyatis Corp 2.50
11 End of Shadow War 2.50
12 Hawks on Thanagar. 2.50
13 DH,Murder Case 2.50
14 DH,Mystery o/Haunted Masks . . 2.50
15 DH,Murderer Revealed 2.50
16 DH,Hawkwoman lost 2.50
17 EH,DH,final issue 2.50
TPB rep.Brave & Bold apps. 19.95

[3rd Regular Series], 1993–96

1 B:JOs(s),JD,R:Hawkman,
  V:Deadline 5.00
2 JD,A:Gr.Lantern,V:Meta-Tech . . . 3.00
3 JD,I:Airstryke 2.75
4 JD,RM 2.50
5 JD(c),V:Count Viper 2.50
6 JD(c),A:Eradicator 2.50
7 JD(c),PuK(s),LMc,B:King of the
  Netherworld 2.50
8 LMc,E:King of the Netherworld . . 2.50
9 BML(s) 2.50
10 I:Badblood 2.50
11 V:Badblood 2.50
12 V:Hawkgod 2.75
13 V:Hawkgod 2.75
14 New abilities,pt.1 . . . . 2.50
15 New abilities,pt.2 . . . . 2.50
16 Eyes of the Hawk,pt.3 . . . . 2.50
17 Eyes of the Hawk,pt.4 . . . . 2.50

Hawkman #1 © DC Comics Inc.

All comics prices listed are for Near Mint condition.

Hawkman–Hellblazer

18 Seagle,Ellis, Pepoy 2.50
19 F:Hawkman 2.50
21 RLm,V:Shadow Thief,
  Gentleman Ghost 2.75
22 Way of the Warrior,pt.3
  A:Warrior,JLA 2.75
23 Way of the Warrior,pt.6 . . . . . . 2.75
24 . . . . 2.75
25 V:Lionmane,painted(c) 2.75
26 WML,Underworld
  Unleashed tie-in 2.75
27 WML,Underworld
  Unleashed tie-in 2.75
28 WML,V:Doctor Polaris 2.75
29 HC(c),V:Vandal Savage 2.75
30 . . . . 2.75
31 serial killer has Tangarian
  technology 2.75
32 MC,Search for serial killer 2.75
Ann.#1 JD,I:Mongrel. 3.75
Ann.#2 Year One Annual 3.95

[4th Regular Series], 2002
1 RgM,MiB,Hawkman & Hawkgirl . 2.50
2 RgM,MiB,F:Hawkgirl 2.50
3 RgM,MiB,inter-dimensional portal 2.50
4 RgM,MiB,trapped in Battlelands . 2.50
5 RgM,MiB,Slings and Arrows,pt.1 . 2.50
6 RgM,MiB,Slings and Arrows,pt.2 . 2.50
7 RgM,TT,Lives past 2.50
8 RgM,MiB,F:Atom 2.50
9 RgM,F:Dr.Fate 2.50
10 RgM,find Speed Saunders 2.50
11 RgM,V:Hath-Set. 2.50
12 RgM,V:Darkraven 2.50
13 Hawk vs. Hawk 2.50
14 Hawkgirl's parents' murderer . . 2.50
15 Shayera Thai 2.50
16 RgM,The Thanagarian,pt.1 . . . . 2.50
17 RgM,The Thanagarian,pt.2 . . . . 2.50
18 RgM,The Thanagarian,pt.3 . . . . 2.50
19 F:Black Adam 2.50
20 RgM,MIB,V:Headhunter,pt.1. . . 2.50
21 RgM,MIB,V:Headhunter,pt.2. . . 2.50
Spec. Secret Files #1, 48-pg. 4.95
TPB Endless Flight 12.95

HAWKWORLD
1989
1 TT,Hawkman, Origin retold 5.00
2 TT,Katar tried for treason 4.00
3 TT,Hawkgirl's debut 4.00

[1st Regular Series], 1990–93
1 GN,Byth on Earth,R:Kanjar Ro . . 3.00
2 GN,Katar & Shayera in Chicago . 2.50
3 GN,V:Chicago Crime 2.50
4 GN,Byth's Control Tightens. 2.50
5 GN,Return of Shadow Thief 2.50
6 GN,Stolen Thanagarian Ship . . . 2.50
7 GN,V:Byth 2.50
8 GN,Hawkman vs. Hawkwoman. . 2.50
9 GN,Hawkwoman in Prison 2.50
10 Shayera returns to Thanagar . . 2.50
11 GN,Blackhawk,Express 2.50
12 GN,Princess Treska 2.50
13 TMd,A:Firehawk,V:Marauder . . 2.50
14 GN,Shayera's Father 2.50
15 GN,War of the Gods X-over . . . 2.50
16 GN War of the Gods X-over . . . 2.50
17 GN,Train Terrorists. 2.50
18 GN,V:Atilla. 2.50
19 GN,V:Atilla. 2.50
20 V:Smir'Beau 2.50
21 GN,Thanagar Pt.1,
  A:J.S.A. Hawkman 2.50
22 GN,Thanagar Pt.2 . . . . 2.50
23 GN,Thanagar Pt.3 . . . . 2.50
24 GN,Thanagar Pt.4 . . . . 2.50
25 GN,Thanagar Pt.5 . . . . 2.50
26 GN,V:Attilla battle armor 2.50
27 JD,B:Flight's End 2.50

Hawkworld #30 © DC Comics, Inc.

28 JD,Flight's End #2 . . . . 2.50
29 TT(c),JDu,Flight's End #3 . . . . . 2.50
30 TT,Flight's End #4 . . . . 2.50
31 TT,Flight's End #5 . . . . 2.50
32 TT,V:Count Viper,final issue 3.00
Ann.#1 A:Flash 4.50
Ann.#2 Armageddon,pt.6 . . . . 4.00
Ann.#2a reprint (Silver) 3.50
Ann.#3 Eclipso tie-in 3.25

HAYWIRE
1988–89
1 . . . . 2.25
2 . . . . 2.25
3 thru 13 . . . . 2.25

HEARTLAND
DC/Vertigo, Jan., 1997
1 GEn(s),SDi,Kit faces childhood
  memories 4.95

HEART OF THE BEAST
DC/Vertigo
GN SeP 19.95

HEART THROBS
DC/Vertigo, 1998
1 (of 4) anthology 3.00
2 modern romance 3.00
3 . . . . 3.00
4 . . . . 3.00

HEAVY LIQUID
DC/Vertigo, 1999
1 PPo,pt 1 of 5 . . . . 6.00
2 PPo,pt.2 . . . . 6.00
3 PPo,pt.3 . . . . 6.00
4 PPo,pt.4 . . . . 6.00
5 PPo,pt.5 . . . . 6.00
TPB PPo, 240-page 29.95

HECKLER, THE
1992–93
1 KG,MJ,I:The Heckler 2.25
2 KG,MJ,V:The Generic Man 2.25
3 KG,MJ,V:Cosmic Clown 2.25
4 KG,V:Bushwacker 2.25
5 KG,Theater Date 2.25
6 KG,I:Lex Concord 2.25

7 KG,V:Cuttin'Edge 2.25

HELLBLAZER
Jan., 1988
1 B:JaD(s),JRy,F:John
  Constantine 15.00
2 JRy,I:Papa Midnight 8.00
3 JRy,I:Blathoxi 7.00
4 JRy,I:Resurrection Crusade,
  Gemma 7.00
5 JRy,F:Pyramid of Fear 7.00
6 JRy,V:Resurrection Crusade,
  I:Nergal 6.00
7 JRy,V:Resurrection Crusade,
  I:Richie Simpson 6.00
8 JRy,AA,Constantine receives
  demon blood,V:Nergal 6.00
9 JRy,A:Swamp Thing 6.00
10 JRy,V:Nergal 6.00
11 MBu,Newcastle Incident,pt.1 . . . 5.00
12 JRy,D:Nergal 5.00
13 JRy,John has a Nightmare 5.00
14 JRy,B:The Fear Machine,
  I:Mercury,Marj,Eddie 5.00
15 JRy,Shepard's Warning 5.00
16 JRy,Rough Justice 5.00
17 MkH,I:Mr. Wester 5.00
18 JRy,R:Zed 5.00
19 JRy,I:Simon Hughes 7.00
20 JRy,F:Mr.Webster 6.00
21 JRy,I:Jallakuntilliokan 6.00
22 JRy,E:The Fear Machine 6.00
23 I&D:Jerry O'Flynn 5.00
24 E:JaD(s),I:Sammy Morris 5.00
25 GMo(s),DvL,Early Warning 5.00
26 GMo(s) 5.00
27 NGa(s),DMc,Hold Me 15.00
28 B:JaD(s),RnT,KeW,F:S.Morris . 5.00
29 RnT,KeW,V:Sammy Morris 5.00
30 RnT,KeW,D:Sammy Morris 5.00
31 E:JaD(s),SeP,Constantine's
  Father's Funeral 5.00
32 DiF(s),StP,I&D:Drummond 4.50
33 B:JaD(s),MPn,F:Pat McDonell . . 4.50
34 SeP,R:Mercury,Marj 4.50
35 SeP,Constantine's Past 4.50
36 Future Death,(preview of
  World Without End) 4.50
37 Journey to England's Secret
  Mystics 4.50
38 Constantine's Journey contd. . . 4.50
39 Journey to Discovery 4.50
40 DMc,I:2nd Kid Eternity 5.00
41 B:GEn(s),WSm,MPn,Dangerous
  Habits 6.00
42 Dangerous Habits 4.50
43 I:Chantinelle 4.50
44 Dangerous Habits 4.50
45 Dangerous Habits 4.50
46 Dangerous Habits epilogue,
  I:Kit(John's girlfriend) 4.50
47 SnW(i),Pub Where I Was Born. . 4.00
48 Love Kills 4.00
49 X-mas issue,Lord o/t Dance . . . 4.00
50 WSm,Remarkable Lives,A:Lord
  of Vampires (48pgs) 6.00
51 JnS,SeP,Laundromat-
  Possession 5.00
52 GF(c),WSm, Royal Blood 5.00
53 GF(c),WSm, Royal Blood 5.00
54 GF(c),WSm, Royal Blood 5.00
55 GF(c),WSm, Royal Blood 5.00
56 GF(c),B:GEn(s),DvL,
  V:Danny Drake 5.00
57 GF(c),SDi,Mortal Clay#1,
  V:Dr. Amis 5.00
58 GF(c),SDi,Mortal Clay#2,
  V:Dr. Amis 5.00
59 GF(c),WSm,MkB(i),KDM,B:Guys
  & Dolls 5.00

Comics Values Annual — DC — Hellblazer–Heroes

Hellblazer #4 © DC Comics, Inc.

60 GF(c),WSm,MkB(i),F:Tali,
   Chantinelle 5.00
61 GF(c),WSm,MkB(i),E:Guys &
   Dolls, V:First of the Fallen. 5.00
62 GF(c),SDi,End of the Line,I:Gemma,
   AIDS storyline insert w/Death . . 5.00

DC/Vertigo, 1993
63 GF(c),SDi,C:Swamp Thing,Zatanna
   Phantom Stranger 5.00
64 GF(c),SDi,B:Fear & Loathing,
   A:Gabriel (Racism) 4.00
65 GF(c),SDi,D:Dez 4.00
66 GF(c),SDi,E:Fear and Loathing . 4.00
67 GF(c),SDi,Kit leaves John 4.00
68 GF(c),SDi,F:Lord of Vampires,
   Darius,Mary 4.00
69 GF(c),SDi,D:Lord of Vampires . . 4.00
70 GF(c),SDi,Kit in Ireland 4.00
71 GF(c),SDi,A:WWII Fighter Pilot . 4.00
72 GF(c),SDi,B:Damnation's
   Flame,A:Papa Midnight 4.00
73 GF(c),SDi,Nightmare NY,
   A:JFK. 4.00
74 GF(c),SDi,I:Cedella,A:JFK 4.00
75 GF(c),SDi,E:Damnation'sFlame . 4.00
76 GF(c),SDi,R:Brendan. 4.00
77 Returns to England 4.00
78 GF(c),SDi,B:Rake at the
   Gates of Hell 4.00
79 GF(c),SDi,In Hell 4.00
80 GF(c),SDi,In London 4.00
81 GF(c),SDi 4.00
82 Kit 4.00
83 Rake,Gates of Hell 4.00
84 John's past 4.00
85 Warped Notions,pt.1 . . . . 4.00
86 Warped Notions,pt.2 . . . . 4.00
87 Warped Notions,pt.3 . . . . 4.00
88 Warped Notions,pt.4 . . . . 4.00
89 Dreamtime 4.00
90 Dreamtime,pt.2 . . . . 4.00
91 Visits Battlefield 4.00
92 Critical Mass,pt.1 . . . . 4.00
93 Critical Mass,pt.2 . . . . 4.00
94 Critical Mass,pt.3 . . . . 4.00
95 SeP,Critical Mass,pt.4 . . . . 4.00
96 SeP,Critical Mass,pt.5 . . . . 4.00
97 SeP,Critical Mass epilogue. 4.00
98 SeP, helps neighbor. 4.00
99 SeP. 4.00
100 SeP, In a coma 5.00
101 SeP,deal with a demon 3.50
102 SeP,DifficultBeginnings,pt.1 . . 3.50
103 SeP,DifficultBeginnings,pt.2 . . 3.50
104 SeP,DifficultBeginnings,pt.3 . . . 3.50
105 . . . . 3.50
106 PJe(s),SEp,In the Line of
   Fire, pt.1 (of 2) 3.50
107 PJe(s),SEp,Line of Fire,pt.2 . . 3.50
108 PJe(s),SeP,a Bacchic
   celebration 3.50
109 PJe(s),SeP,cattle mutilations
   in Northern England 3.50
110 PJe(s),SeP,Last Man
   Standing,pt.1 . . . . 3.50
111 PJe(s),SeP,Last Man,pt.2 . . . . 3.50
112 PJe(s),SeP,Last Man,pt.3 . . . . 3.50
113 PJe(s),SeP,Last Man,pt.4 . . . . 3.50
114 PJe(s),SeP,Last Man,pt.5 . . . . 3.50
115 PJe(s),SeP(s),Dani's ex-
   boyfriend 3.50
116 SeP,Widdershins,pt.1 (of 2) . . 3.50
117 SeP,Widdershins,pt.2 . . . . 3.50
118 PJe(s),SeP,John's a Godfather. 4.00
119 PJe(s),SeP,disasters 3.50
120 PJe(s),SeP,10th anniv. 48pg . . 3.00
121 PJe(s),SeP, Up the Down
   Staircase pt.1 . . . . 3.00
122 PJe(s),SeP, Up the Down
   Staircase pt.2 . . . . 3.00
123 PJe(s),SeP, Up the Down
   Staircase pt.3 . . . . 3.00
124 PJe(s),SeP, Up the Down
   Staircase pt.4 . . . . 3.00
125 PJe(s),SeP, How to Play
   with Fire, pt.1 . . . . 3.00
126 PJe(s),SeP,Play/Fire,pt.2 . . . . 3.00
127 PJe(s),SeP,Play/Fire,pt.3 . . . . 3.00
128 PJe(s),SeP,Play/Fire,pt.4 . . . . 3.00
129 . . . . 3.00
130 GEn,JHi,GF,Son of Man,pt.2 . . 3.00
131 GEn,JHi,GF,Son of Man,pt.3 . . 2.75
132 GEn,JHi,GF,Son of Man,pt.4 . . 2.75
133 GEn,JHi,GF,Son of Man,pt.5 . . 2.75
134 WEl(s),JHi,Haunted,pt.1. . . . . . 2.75
135 WEl(s),JHi,Haunted,pt.2. . . . . . 2.75
136 WEl(s),JHi,Haunted,pt.3. . . . . . 2.75
137 WEl(s),JHi,Haunted,pt.4. . . . . . 2.75
138 WEl(s),JHi,Haunted,pt.5. . . . . . 2.75
139 WEl(s),JHi,Haunted,pt.6. . . . . . 2.75
140 WEl(s),Locked 2.75
141 WEl(s),ALa 2.75
142 WEl,TBd,Setting Sun 2.75
143 WEl,TBd,Telling Tales 2.75
144 GEr,ALa,Ashes & Honey,pt.1 . 2.75
145 GEr,ALa,Ashes & Honey,pt.2 . 2.75
146 RC,Hard Time 2.75
147 RC,Hard Time,pt.2. . . . . 2.75
148 RC,Hard Time,pt.3. . . . . 2.75
149 RC,Hard Time,pt.4. . . . . 2.75
150 RC,Hard Time,concl. 2.75
151 Good Intentions,pt.1. . . . . 2.75
152 Good Intentions,pt.2. . . . . 2.75
153 Good Intentions,pt.3. . . . . 2.75
154 Good Intentions,pt.4. . . . . 2.75
155 Good Intentions,pt.5. . . . . 2.75
156 Good Intentions,pt.6. . . . . 2.75
157 SDi,"...and buried?" 2.75
158 Freezes Over,pt.1 . . . . 2.75
159 Freezes Over,pt.2 . . . . 2.75
160 Freezes Over,pt.3 . . . . 2.75
161 Freezes Over,pt.4 . . . . 2.75
162 Lapdogs and Englishmen. 2.75
163 Lapdogs and Englishmen. 2.75
164 Highwater, pt.1. . . . . 2.75
165 Highwater, pt.2. . . . . 2.75
166 Highwater, pt.3. . . . . 2.75
167 Highwater, pt.4. . . . . 2.75
168 A Fresh Coat of Red Paint 2.75
169 Constantine in LA 2.75
170 Ashes and Dust,pt.1. . . . . 2.75
171 Ashes and Dust,pt.2. . . . . 2.75
172 Ashes and Dust,pt.3. . . . . 2.75
173 Ashes and Dust,pt.4. . . . . 2.75
174 Ashes and Dust,pt.5. . . . . 2.75
175 SDi,JP,High on Life,pt.1 . . . . . . 2.75
176 SDi,JP,High on Life, pt.2 . . . . . 2.75
177 Red Sepulchre,pt.1 . . . . 2.75
178 Red Sepulchre,pt.2 . . . . 2.75
179 Red Sepulchre,pt.3 . . . . 2.75
180 Red Sepulchre,pt.4 . . . . 2.75
181 Red Sepulchre,concl. 2.75
182 MCy(s),Black Flowers,pt.1 . . . . 2.75
183 MCy(s),Black Flowers,pt.2 . . . . 2.75
184 MCy(s),Wild Card 2.75
185 MCy(s),Ordeal 2.75
186 MCy(s),The Pit. 2.75
187 MCy(s),Bred in Bone,pt.1 . . . . 2.75
188 MCy(s),Bred in Bone,pt.2 . . . . 2.75
189 MCy(s),Staring at Wall,pt.1 . . . 2.75
190 MCy(s),Staring at Wall,pt.2 . . . 2.75
Ann.#1 JaD(s),BT,Raven Scar 7.00
Spec.#1 GF(s),GEn(s),SDi,John
   Constantine's teenage years . . 4.50
Secret Files #1 . . . . 4.95
TPB Original Sins,rep.#1–#9. . . . . 19.95
TPB Dangerous Habits,
   rep.#41–#46 . . . . 14.95
TPB Fear and Loathing. 14.95
TPB Damnation's Flame 17.00
TPB Hard Time, 128-page 9.95
TPB Good Intentions (2002) 12.95
TPB Haunted (2003). 12.95
TPB Hellblazer: Freezes Over. . . . 14.95
TPB Rake at the Gates of Hell . . . 19.95

HELLBLAZER/ THE BOOKS OF MAGIC
Oct., 1997
1 (of 2) PJe,JNR 2.50
2 PJe,JNR. 2.50

HELLBLAZER SPECIAL: BAD BLOOD
DC/Vertigo, July, 2000
1 (of 4) JaD,PBd 3.50
2 thru 4 JaD,PBd, ... @3.50

HELLBLAZER SPECIAL: LADY CONSTANTINE
DC/Vertigo Dec. 2002
1 (of 4) F:Johanna Constantine . . . 2.95
2 thru 4 . . . . @2.95

HERCULES UNBOUND
Oct.–Nov., 1975
1 WW 20.00
2 thru 8 . . . . @12.00
9 thru 12 WS,Aug.–Sept.,1977. . . 10.00

H-E-R-O
Feb. 2003
1 Jerry Feldon 10.00
2 life-saving mission 5.00
3 F:Molly 5.00
4 Powers and Abilities 5.00
5 F:Matt Allen 3.00
6 F:Andrea Allen 3.00
7 Chaos, Inc. 3.00
8 Chaos. Inc.,pt.2 . . . . 3.00
9 World Made of Glass,pt.1 . . . . . . 3.00
10 World Made of Glass,pt.2 . . . . 2.50
Spec. Double Feature,rep.#1&#2 . 4.95
TPB Powers and Abilities 9.95

HEROES
DC/Milestone, 1996
1 Six heroes join 3.50
2 thru 6 . . . . @2.50

All comics prices listed are for Near Mint condition.

HEROES AGAINST HUNGER
1986
1 NA,DG,JBy,CS,AA,BWr,BS,
  Superman,Batman 3.50

HERO HOTLINE
1989
1 thru 6, Mini-series . . . . @2.00

HEX
Sept., 1985
1 MT,I:Hex. 7.00
2 MT 5.00
3 MT,V:Conglomerate 5.00
4 MT,V:Conglomerate 5.00
5 MT,A:Chainsaw Killer 5.00
6 MT,V:Conglomerate 5.00
7 MT,Tries to Return to own era. . . 5.00
8 MT,The Future 6.00
9 MT,Future Killer Cyborgs 5.00
10 MT,V:Death Cult 5.00
11 MT,V:The Batman 6.00
12 MT,A:Batman,V:Terminators. . . . 6.00
13 MT,I:New Supergroup 5.00
14 MT,A:The Dogs of War. 5.00
15 KG,V:Chainsaw Killer. 5.00
16 KG,V:Dogs of War 5.00
17 KG,Hex/Dogs of War T.U.
  V:XXGG 5.00
18 KGr,Confronting the Past, ... 5.00

HISTORY OF DC UNIVERSE
Sept., 1986
1 GP, From start to WWII. 5.00
2 GP, From WWII to present 5.00
TPB MWn(s),GP,KK,AxR(c) (2002) . 9.95

A HISTORY OF VIOLENCE
DC/Paradox Press March, 1997
GN B&W 9.95

HITCHHIKER'S GUIDE TO THE GALAXY
1993
1 Based on Douglas Adams book . 7.00
2 Based on the book 6.50
3 Based on the book 6.50
GN from Douglas Adams book . . . 14.95

HITMAN
1996–2001
1 GEn, F:Tommy Monaghan 9.00
2 GEn, Attempt to kill Joker 7.00
3 GEn(s),JMC, Mawzin & The
  Arkanonne 4.50
4 GEn(s),JMC, ... 3.00
5 GEn(s),JMC, ... 3.00
6 GEn(s),JMC,A:Johnny Navarone,
  Natt the Hatt. 3.00
7 GEn(s),JMC, Pat's dead, Hitman
  wants revenge 3.00
8 GEn(s),JMC,barricaded in
  Noonan's Bar, Final Night tie-in. 3.00
9 GEn(s),JMC,A:Six-Pack 3.00
10 GEn(s),JMC,A:Green Lantern . 3.00
11 . . . . 2.50
12 GEn(s),JMC,Local Heroes,
  A:Green Lantern. 2.50
13 . . . . 2.50
14 GEn(s),JMC, Zombie Night at
  the Aquarium, concl. 2.50
15 GEn(s),JMC, Ace of

Killers, pt.1, V:Mawzir 2.50
16 GEn(s),JMC,Ace of Killers,pt.2 . . 2.50
17 GEn(s),JMC,Ace of Killers,pt.3,
  A:Catwoman, Demon Etrigan . 2.50
18 GEn(s),JMC,Ace of Killers,pt.4,
  A:Demon Etrigan, Baytor 2.50
19 GEn(s),JMC,Ace/Killers,pt.5, . . . 2.50
20 GEn(s),JMC,Ace/Killers,concl. . . 2.50
21 GEn(s),JMC,Romeo & Juliet . . . 2.50
22 GEn(s),JMC,holiday special 2.50
23 GEn(s),JMc,Who Dares
  Wins,pt.1 . . . . 2.50
24 GEn(s),JMc,Dares/Wins,pt.2 . . . 2.50
25 GEn(s),JMc,Dares/Wins,pt.3 . . . 2.50
26 GEn(s),JMC,Dares/Wins,pt.4 . . . 2.50
27 GEn(s),JMc,Dares/Wins,pt.5 . . . 2.50
28 GEn(s),JMC,aftermath 2.50
29 GEn(s),JMC,Tommy's
  Heroes, pt.1 . . . . 2.50
30 GEn(s),JMC,Heroes, pt.2 . . . . . . 2.50
31 GEn(s),JMC,Heroes, pt.3 . . . . . . 2.50
32 GEn(s),JMC,Heroes, pt.4 . . . . . . 2.50
33 GEn(s),JMC,Heroes, pt.5 . . . . . . 2.50
34 GEn(s),A:Superman. 2.50
35 GEn(s),Frances Monaghan 2.50
36 GEn(s), ... 2.50
37 GEn(s). 2.50
38 GEn(s),Dead Man's Land, concl. 2.50
39 GEn(s),JMC,A:RingoChen,pt.1. . 2.50
40 GEn(s),JMC,A:RingoChen,pt.2. . 2.50
41 GEn(s),JMC,A:RingoChen,pt.3. . 2.50
42 GEn(s),JMC,A:RingoChen,pt.4. . 2.50
43 GEn(s),JMC, ... 2.50
44 GEn(s),JMC, ... 2.50
45 GEn(s),JMC. 2.50
46 GEn(s),JMC. 2.50
47 GEn(s),JMC,Old Dog 2.50
48 GEn(s),JMC,Old Dog,pt.2 . . . . . 2.50
49 GEn(s),JMC,Old Dog,pt.3 . . . . . 2.50
50 GEn(s),JMC,Hitman's future . . . 2.50
51 GEn(s),JMC,Superguy,pt.1 . . . . 2.50
52 GEn(s),JMc,Superguy,pt.2 . . . . 2.50
53 GEn(s),JMc,ClosingTime,pt.1. . . 2.50
54 GEn(s),JMc,ClosingTime,pt.2. . . 2.50
55 GEn(s),JMc,ClosingTime,pt.3. . . 2.50
56 GEn,JMC,GL,O:Tommy
  Monaghan 2.50
57 GEn,JMC,GL,O:Natt 2.50
58 GEn,JMC,GL,Closing time 2.50
59 GEn,JMC,GL,Closing time 2.50
60 GEn,JMC,GL,Closing time,final . 2.50
Ann.#1 Pulp Heroes (Western) 3.95
Spec.#1,000,000 GEn(s),JMC 2.50
Spec. Hitman/Lobo: That
  Stupid Bastich! 3.95
TPB rep. Demon Annual #2, Batman
  Chronicles #4, Hitman #1–#3 . 10.00
TPB Hitman,rep.#1–#3,+other 9.95
TPB Ten Thousand Bullets,
  rep. #4–#8 . . . . 10.00
TPB Hitman: Ten Thousand Bullets 10.00
TPB Hitman: Local Heroes 18.00
TPB Hitman GEn(s),JMC 9.95
TPB Ace of Killers. 17.95
TPB Who Dares Wins, GEn,JMC . 12.95

HOPALONG CASSIDY
Feb., 1954
86 GC,Ph(c):William Boyd & Topper,
  'The Secret of the Tattooed
  Burro' 400.00
87 GC,Ph(c),'The Tenderfoot
  Outlaw' 225.00
88 Ph(c),GC,'15 Robbers of Rimfire
  Ridge' 150.00
89 GC,Ph(c),'One-Day
  Boom Town' 150.00
90 GC,Ph(c),'Cowboy Clown
  Robberies' 125.00
91 GC,Ph(c),'The Riddle of

the Roaring R Ranch' 150.00
92 GC,Ph(c),'The Sky-Riding
  Outlaws' 150.00
93 GC,Ph(c),'The Silver Badge
  of Courage' 150.00
94 GC,Ph(c),'Mystery of the
  Masquerading Lion' 150.00
95 GC,Ph(c),'Showdown at the
  Post-Hole Bank' 150.00
96 GC,Ph(c),'Knights of
  the Range' 150.00
97 GC,Ph(c),'The Mystery of
  the Three-Eyed Cowboy' . . . 150.00
98 GC,Ph(c),'Hopalong's
  Unlucky Day' 150.00
99 GC,Ph(c),'Partners in Peril' . . . 150.00
100 GC,Ph(c),'The Secrets
  of a Sheriff' 160.00
101 GC,Ph(c),'Way Out West
  Where The East Begins' 100.00
102 GC,Ph(c),'Secret of the
  Buffalo Hat' 100.00
103 GC,Ph(c),'The Train-Rustlers
  of Avalance Valley' 100.00
104 GC,Ph(c),'Secret of the
  Surrendering Outlaws' 100.00
105 GC,Ph(c),'Three Signs
  to Danger' 100.00
106 GC,Ph(c),'The Secret of
  the Stolen Signature' 100.00
107 GC,Ph(c),'The Mystery Trail
  to Stagecoach Town' 100.00
108 GC,Ph(c),'The Mystery
  Stage From Burro Bend' 100.00
109 GC,'The Big Gun on Saddletop
  Mountain' 100.00
110 GC,'The Dangerous Stunts
  of Hopalong Cassidy' 75.00
111 GC,'Sheriff Cassidy's
  Mystery Clue' 75.00
112 GC,'Treasure Trail to
  Thunderbolt Ridge 75.00
113 GC,'The Shadow of the
  Toy Soldier' 75.00
114 GC,'Ambush at
  Natural Bridge' 75.00
115 GC,'The Empty-Handed
  Robberies' 75.00
116 GC,'Mystery of the
  Vanishing Cabin' 75.00
117 GC,'School for Sheriffs' 75.00
118 GC,'The Hero of
  Comanche Ridge' 75.00
119 GC,'The Dream Sheriff of
  Twin Rivers' 75.00

Hopalong Cassidy #108
© DC Comics, Inc.

Comics Values Annual — DC — Hopalong–House

120 GC,`Salute to a Star-Wearer'. 75.00
121 GC,`The Secret of the
 Golden Caravan' 75.00
122 GC,`The Rocking
 Horse Bandits' 75.00
123 GK,`Mystery of the
 One-Dollar Bank Robbery' ... 75.00
124 GK,`Mystery of the
 Double-X Brand'............ 75.00
125 GK,`Hopalong Cassidy's
 Secret Brother'............ 75.00
126 GK,`Trail of the
 Telltale Clues'.............. 75.00
127 GK,`Hopalong Cassidy's
 Golden Riddle' 75.00
128 GK,`The House That
 Hated Outlaws'............ 75.00
129 GK,`Hopalong Cassidy's
 Indian Sign' 75.00
130 GK,`The Return of the
 Canine Sheriff' 75.00
131 GK&GK(c),`The Amazing
 Sheriff of Double Creek' 75.00
132 GK,`Track of the
 Invisible Indians'........... 75.00
133 GK,`The Golden Trail
 to Danger' 75.00
134 GK,`Case of the
 Three Crack-Shots'.......... 75.00
135 GK,May-June, 1959........ 75.00

HORRORIST
DC/Vertigo, 1995
1 I:Horrorist................... 6.50
2 conclusion 6.50

HOT WHEELS
March-April, 1970
1 ATh....................... 125.00
2 thru 5 ATh................ @75.00
6 NA(c) 80.00

HOURMAN
1999
1 TPe,RgM,A:JLA 2.50
2 TPe(s),RgM,F:Tomorrow Woman 2.50
3 TPe(s),RgM,Timepoint,pt.1 ..... 2.50
4 TPe(s),RgM,Timepoint,pt.2 ..... 2.50
5 TPe(s),RgM,Rex Tyler's life 2.50
6 TPe,RgM,JLAndroids,pt.1 ...... 2.50
7 TPe,RgM,JLAndroids,pt.2 ...... 2.50
8 TPe,RgM,Day of Judgment
 x-over..................... 2.50
9 TPe,RgM,F:Rick Tyler.......... 2.50
10 TPe,RgM................... 2.50
11 TPe,RgM,One Million,pt.1 ..... 2.50
12 TPe,RgM,One Million,pt.2 ..... 2.50
13 TPe,RgM,One Million,pt.3 ..... 2.50
14 TPe,RgM,V:Undersoul........ 2.50
15 TPe,RgM,human secrets 2.50
16 TPe,RgM,F:Snapper 2.50
17 TPe,100 Years of Solitude 2.50
18 TPe,RgM,High Society,pt.1 .... 2.50
19 TPe,RgM,High Society,pt.2 .... 2.50
20 TPe,RgM,F:Snapper 2.50
21 TPe,RgM,reduced to nothing ... 2.50
22 TPe,TyH 2.50
23 TPe,RgM,Unbelievable
 Truth,pt.1 .... 2.50
24 TPE,RgM,Unbel.Truth,pt.2 .... 2.50
25 TPE,RgM,final issue 2.50

HOUSE OF MYSTERY
Dec.–Jan., 1952
1 I Fell In Love With
 a Monster 2,700.00
2 The Mark of X 1,100.00

House of Mystery #1
© DC Comics, Inc.

3 The Dummy of Death 800.00
4 The Man With the Evil Eye ... 600.00
5 The Man With the Strangler
 Hands!.................. 600.00
6 The Monster in Clay!........ 500.00
7 Nine Lives of Alger Denham!.. 500.00
8 Tattoos of Doom 500.00
9 Secret of the Little Black Bag . 500.00
10 The Wishes of Doom 500.00
11 Deadly Game of G-H-O-S-T . 400.00
12 The Devil's Chessboard..... 400.00
13 The Theater Of A
 Thousand Thrills! 400.00
14 The Deadly Dolls 400.00
15 The Man Who Could Change
 the World 400.00
16 Dead Men Tell No Tales! 300.00
17 Man With the X-Ray Eyes ... 275.00
18 Dance of Doom 275.00
19 The Strange Faces of Death . 275.00
20 The Beast Of Bristol........ 275.00
21 Man Who Could See Death .. 275.00
22 The Phantom's Return...... 275.00
23 Stamps of Doom 275.00
24 Kill The Black Cat 275.00
25 The Man With Three Eyes!.. 275.00
26 The Man with Magic Ears... 250.00
27 Fate Held Four Aces!....... 250.00
28 The Wings Of Mr. Milo! 250.00
29 .... 250.00
30 .... 250.00
31 The Incredible Illusions!..... 250.00
32 Pied Piper of the Sea........ 250.00
33 Mr. Misfortune!............ 250.00
34 The Hundred Year Duel 250.00
35 .... 250.00
36 The Treasure of Montezuma!. 200.00
37 MD,The Statue That
 Came to Life.............. 200.00
38 The Voyage Of No Return ... 200.00
39 .... 200.00
40 The Coins That Came To Life. 200.00
41 The Impossible Tricks!...... 200.00
42 The Stranger From Out There 200.00
43 .... 200.00
44 The Secret Of Hill 14 .... 200.00
45 .... 200.00
46 The Bird of Fate........... 200.00
47 The Robot Named Think 200.00
48 The Man Marooned On Earth. 200.00
49 The Mysterious Mr. Omen ... 200.00
50 .... 225.00
51 Man Who Stole Teardrops ... 150.00
52 The Man With The Golden
 Shoes.................. 150.00
53 The Man Who Hated Mirrors . 150.00
54 The Woman Who Lived Twice 150.00
55 I Turned Back Time 150.00
56 The Thing In The Black Box.. 150.00
57 The Untamed............. 150.00
58 .... 150.00
59 The Tomb Of Ramfis 150.00
60 The Prisoner On Canvas 150.00
61 JK,Superstition Day 150.00
62 The Haunting Scarecrow ... 135.00
63 JK,The Lady & The Creature . 150.00
64 The Golden Doom 135.00
65 JK,The Magic Lantern 150.00
66 JK,Sinister Shadow 150.00
67 The Wizard of Water 135.00
68 The Book That Bewitched ... 135.00
69 The Miniature Disasters..... 135.00
70 JK,The Man With Nine Lives . 140.00
71 Menace of the Mole Man 140.00
72 JK,Dark Journey 140.00
73 Museum That Came to Life . 135.00
74 Museum That Came To Life . 135.00
75 Assignment Unknown! 135.00
76 JK,Prisoners Of The Tiny
 Universe................. 135.00
77 The Eyes That Went Berserk . 125.00
78 JK(c),The 13th Hour........ 135.00
79 JK(c),The Fantastic Sky
 Puzzle 135.00
80 Man With Countless Faces!.. 125.00
81 The Man Who Made Utopia .. 125.00
82 The Riddle of the Earth's
 Second Moon............. 125.00
83 The Mystery of the
 Martian Eye 125.00
84 JK,BK,100-Century Doom ... 175.00
85 JK(c),Earth's Strangest
 Salesman................ 125.00
86 The Baffling Bargains....... 100.00
87 The Human Diamond....... 100.00
88 Return of the Animal Man.... 125.00
89 The Cosmic Plant!.......... 125.00
90 The Invasion Of the Energy
 Creatures................ 125.00
91 DD&SMo(c),The Riddle of the
 Alien Satellite............. 125.00
92 DD(c),Menace of the
 Golden Globule 125.00
93 NC(c),I Fought The
 Molten Monster........... 125.00
94 DD&SMo(c),The Creature
 In Echo Lake 125.00

House of Mystery #178
© DC Comics Inc.

All comics prices listed are for *Near Mint* condition.

House Of Mystery — DC — Comics Values Annual

House of Mystery #269
© DC Comics, Inc.

House of Mystery #321
© DC Comics, Inc.

#	Description	Price
95	The Wizard's Gift	125.00
96	The Amazing 70-Ton Man	125.00
97	The Alien Who Change History	125.00
98	DD&SMo(c),The Midnight Creature	125.00
99	The Secret of the Leopard God	125.00
100	The Beast Beneath Earth	150.00
101	The Magnificent Monster	125.00
102	Cellmate to a Monster	125.00
103	Hail the Conquering Aliens	125.00
104	I was the Seeing-Eye Man	125.00
105	Case of the Creature X-14	125.00
106	Invaders from the Doomed Dimension	125.00
107	Captives o/t Alien Fisherman	125.00
108	RMo,Four Faces of Frank Forbes	125.00
109	ATh,JKu,Secret of the Hybrid Creatures	125.00
110	Beast Who Stalked Through Time	125.00
111	Operation Beast Slayer	125.00
112	Menace of Craven's Creatures	125.00
113	RMo,Prisoners of Beast Asteroid	125.00
114	The Movies from Nowhere	125.00
115	Prisoner o/t Golden Mask	125.00
116	RMo,Return of the Barsfo Beast	125.00
117	Menace of the Fire Furies	110.00
118	RMo,Secret o/SuperGorillas	110.00
119	Deadly Gift from the Stars	110.00
120	ATh,Catman of KarynPeale	110.00
121	RMo,Beam that Transformed Men	110.00
122	Menace fo the Alien Hero	110.00
123	RMo,Lure o/t Decoy Creature	110.00
124	Secret of Mr. Doom	110.00
125	Fantastic Camera Creature	110.00
126	The Human Totem Poles	110.00
127	RMo,Cosmic Game o/Doom	110.00
128	NC,The Sorcerer's Snares	110.00
129	Man in the Nuclear Trap	110.00
130	The Alien Creature Hunt	110.00
131	Vengeance o/t GeyserGod	75.00
132	MMe,Beware My Invisible Master	75.00
133	MMe,Captive Queen of Beast Island	75.00
134	MMe,Secret Prisoner of Darkmore Dungeon	75.00
135	MMe,Alien Body Thief	75.00
136	MMe,Secret o/t StolenFace	75.00
137	MMe,Tunnel to Disaster	75.00
138	MMe,Creature Must Die	75.00
139	MMe,Creatures of Vengeful Eye	75.00
140	I&Only app.:Astro.	75.00
141	MMe,The Alien Gladiator	75.00
142	MMe,The Wax Demons	75.00
143	J'onn J'onzz begins	300.00
144	J'onn J'onzz on Weird World of Gilgana	150.00
145	J'onn J'onzz app	100.00
146	BP,J'onn J'onzz	100.00
147	J'onn J'onzz	100.00
148	J'onn J'onzz	100.00
149	ATh,J'onn J'onzz	100.00
150	MMe,J'onn J'onzz	100.00
151	J'onn J'onzz	100.00
152	MMe,J'onn J'onzz	100.00
153	J'onn J'onzz	100.00
154	J'onn J'onzz	100.00
155	J'onn J'onzz	100.00
156	JM,I:Dial H for Hero (Giantboy Cometeer,Mole)J.J'onzz sty	125.00
157	JM,Dial H for Hero (Human Bullet,Super Charge,Radar Sonar Man) J.J'onzz sty	100.00
158	JM,Dial H for Hero (Quake MasterSquid)J'onn J'onzz sty	90.00
159	JM,Dial H for Hero (Human Starfish,Hypno Man,Mighty Moppet) J'onn J'onzz sty	90.00
160	JM,Dial H for Hero (King Kandy A:Plastic Man,I:Marco Xavier (J'onn J'onzz new secret I.D.)	150.00
161	JM,Dial H for Hero (Magneto, Hornet Man,Shadow Man)	75.00
162	JM,Dial H for Hero (Mr.Echo, Future Man) J'onnJ'onzz sty	75.00
163	JM,Dial H for Hero(Castor&Pollux, King Coil) J'onnJ'onzz sty	75.00
164	JM,Dial H for Hero (Super Nova Zip Tide) J'onnJ'onzz sty	75.00
165	JM,Dial H for Hero (Whoozis, Whatsis,Howzis) J'onn J'onzz story	75.00
166	JM,Dial H for Hero (Yankee Doodle Kid,Chief Mighty Arrow) J'onn J'onzz sty	75.00
167	JM,Dial H for Hero (Balloon Boy, Muscle Man,Radar Sonar Man) J'onn J'onzz sty	75.00
168	JM,Dial H for Hero (Thunderbolt, Mole,Cometeer,Hoopster) J'onn J'onzz sty	75.00
169	JM,I:Gem Girl in Dial H for Hero,J'onn J'onzz sty	75.00
170	JM,Dial H for Hero (Baron BuzzSaw,Don Juan,Sphinx Man) J'onn J'onzz sty	75.00
171	JM,Dial H for Hero (King Viking Whirl-I-Gig)J'onn J'onzz sty	65.00
172	JM,Dial H for Hero	65.00
173	E:Dial H for Hero,F:J'onn J'onzz	65.00
174	New direction,SA pg.13	50.00
175	I:Cain	40.00
176	SA,Cain's Game Room	40.00
177	Curse of the Car	40.00
178	NA,The Game	75.00
179	BWr,NA,JO,Widow'sWalk	100.00
180	GK,WW,BWr,SA,Room 13	60.00
181	BWr,The Siren of Satan	60.00
182	ATh,The Devil's Doorway	35.00
183	BWr,WW(i),DeadCanKill	60.00
184	ATh,GK,WW,Eye o/Basilisk	50.00
185	AW,The Beautiful Beast	50.00
186	BWr,NA,Nightmare	50.00
187	ATh,Mask of the Red Fox	25.00
188	TD,BWr,NA(c),House of Madness	50.00
189	WW(i),NA(c),Eyes of the Cat	35.00
190	ATh,Fright	35.00
191	BWr,TD,NA(c),Christmas Story	50.00
192	JAp,GM,DH,NA(c),Garnener of Eden	35.00
193	BWr(c)	35.00
194	ATh,NR,RH(rep),JK(rep) Born Loser	40.00
195	NR,BWr,ThingsOld..Things Forgotten	65.00
196	GM,GK,ATh(rep)A Girl & Her Dog	35.00
197	DD,NR,NA(c),House of Horrors	30.00
198	MSy,NC,Day of the Demon	35.00
199	WW,RB,NA(c),Sno'Fun	40.00
200	MK,TD,The Beast's Revenge	50.00
201	JAp,The Demon Within	35.00
202	MSy,GC(rep),SA,The Poster Plague,John Prentice?	35.00
203	NR,Tower of Prey	35.00
204	BWr,AN,All in the Family	40.00
205	The Coffin Creature	17.00
206	MSy,TP,The Burning	17.00
207	JSn,The Spell	20.00
208	Creator of Evil	17.00
209	AA,JAp,Tomorrow I Hang	20.00
210	The Immortal	17.00
211	NR,Deliver Us From Evil	20.00
212	MA,AN,Ever After	17.00
213	AN,Back from the Realm of the Damned	20.00
214	NR,The Shaggy Dog	20.00
215	The Man Who Wanted Power over Women	17.00
216	TD,Look into My Eyes & Kill	17.00
217	NR,AA,Swamp God	25.00
218	FT,An Ice Place to Visit	17.00
219	AA,NR,BWr(c),Pledge to Satan	30.00
220	AA,AN,They Hunt Butterflies Don't They?	17.00
221	FT,BWr,MK,He Who Laughs Last	30.00
222	AA,Night of the Teddy Bear	15.00
223	Demon From the Deep	15.00
224	FR,AA,SheerFear,B:100pg	50.00
225	AA,FT,AN,See No Evil	50.00
226	AA,FR,NR,SA,Monster in House	

All comics prices listed are for *Near Mint* condition.

DC — House Of

Tour of House of Mystery 50.00	292 TS,MS,TD,RE,DSp,Wendigo . 10.00	13 The Face in the Mist 175.00
227 NR,AA,The Carriage Man .. 50.00	293 GT,TS,A:I..Vampire #3 ...... 10.00	14 MMe,The Man who Stole Air . 175.00
228 FR,NA(i),The Rebel 50.00	294 CI,TY,GT,TD,The Darkness .. 10.00	15 The Creature in the Camera.. 175.00
229 NR,Nightmare Castle,	295 TS,TVE,JCr,I..Vampire #4 ... 10.00	16 NC,We matched wits with a
last 100 page 50.00	296 CI,BH,Night Women......... 10.00	Gorilla genius 150.00
230 Experiment In Fear 10.00	297 TS,DCw,TD,I..Vampire #5 ... 10.00	17 DW,Lady in the Moon....... 150.00
231 Cold,Cold Heart........... 10.00	298 TS,`Stalker on a Starless	18 MMe,The Fantastic
232 Last Tango in Hell 10.00	Night' 10.00	Typewriter 150.00
233 FR,Cake!................. 10.00	299 TS,DSp,I..Vampire #6 ...... 10.00	19 MMe,NC,Lair of the
234 AM,Lafferty's Luck 10.00	300 GK,DA,JSon,JCr,DSp,Anniv. . 15.00	Dragonfly 150.00
235 NR,Wings of Black Death.... 10.00	301 JDu,TVE,KG,TY `...Virginia' . 12.00	20 Incredible Fireball Creatures . 150.00
236 SD,NA(i),BWr(c),Death	302 TS,NR,DSp,I..Vampire #7... 12.00	21 Girl from 50,000 Fathoms ... 150.00
Played a Sideshow......... 20.00	303 TS,DSp,I..Vampire #8 ...... 12.00	22 MMe,Thing from Beyond 150.00
237 FT,Night of the Chameleon... 10.00	304 EC,RE,I..Vampire #9 .... 12.00	23 MMe,I&O:Mark Merlin 165.00
238......................... 10.00	305 TVE,EC,I..Vampire #10 .... 12.00	24 NC,Mark Merlin story....... 150.00
239 Day of the Witch 10.00	306 TS,TD,I..Vampire #11,	25 MMe,Mark Merlin story...... 135.00
240 The Murderer............. 10.00	A:Jack the Ripper.......... 12.00	26 NC,MMe, Mark Merlin story . 135.00
241 FR,NR,DeathPulls theStrings . 10.00	307 TS,I..Vampire #12 .... 12.00	27 MMe,Mark Merlin........... 135.00
242 FR,The Balloon Vendor 10.00	308 TS,MT,NR,I..Vampire #13... 12.00	28 MMe,Mark Merlin........... 135.00
243 Brother Bear 10.00	309 TS,I..Vampire #14 .... 12.00	29 NC,MMe,Mark Merlin 135.00
244 FT,Kronos..Zagros-Eborak... 10.00	310 TS(i),I..Vampire #15 .... 12.00	30 JKu,MMe,Mark Merlin 135.00
245 AN,Check the J.C.Demon	311 I..Vampire #16 .... 12.00	31 DD,MMe,RH,Mark Merlin ... 125.00
Catalogue Under...Death 10.00	312 TS(i),I..Vampire #17 .... 12.00	32 MMe,Mark Merlin........... 125.00
246 DeathVault of Eskimo Kings.. 10.00	313 TS(i),CI,I..Vampire #18...... 12.00	33 MMe,Mark Merlin........... 125.00
247 SD,Death Rides the Waves ... 10.00	314 TS,I..Vampire #19 .... 12.00	34 MMe,Mark Merlin........... 125.00
248 NightJamieGaveUp theGhost. 10.00	315 TS(i),TY,I..Vampire #20 .... 12.00	35 MMe,Mark Merlin........... 125.00
249 Hit Parade of Death 10.00	316 TS(i),GT,TVE,I..Vampire #21 . 12.00	36 MMe,Mark Merlin........... 125.00
250 AN,Voyage to Hell 10.00	317 TS(i),I..Vampire #22 .... 12.00	37 MMe,Mark Merlin........... 125.00
251 WW,AA,NA(c),The Collector,	318 TS(i),I..Vampire #23 .... 12.00	38 MMe,Mark Merlin........... 125.00
68-pages 20.00	319 TS,JOy,I..Vampire conc..... 15.00	39 JKu,MMe,Mark Merlin 125.00
252 DP,RT,AA,FR,AN,NA(c),	320 GM,Project: Inferior 15.00	40 NC,MMe,Mark Merlin....... 125.00
ManKillers 20.00	321 final issue 15.00	41 MMe,Mark Merlin........... 125.00
253 TD,AN,GK,KJ,NA(c),Beware	Welcome Back to the House of Mystery	42 MMe,Mark Merlin........... 125.00
the Demon Child 20.00	GN BWr(c) horror stories rep.. 15.00	43 RMo,MMe,CI,Mark Merlin ... 125.00
254 SD,AN,MR,NA(c),The		44 MMe,Mark Merlin........... 125.00
Devil's Place............... 20.00		45 MMe,Mark Merlin........... 125.00
255 RE,GM,BWr(c),Sometimes	**HOUSE OF SECRETS**	46 MMe,Mark Merlin........... 125.00
Leopards 20.00	**Nov.–Dec., 1956**	47 MMe,Mark Merlin........... 125.00
256 DAy,AN,BWr(c),Museum of	1 MD,JM,The Hand of Doom.. 2,000.00	48 ATh,MMe,Mark Merlin 125.00
Murders 20.00	2 JPr,RMo,NC,Mask of Fear ... 650.00	49 MMe,Mark Merlin........... 125.00
257 RE,MGo,TD(i),MBr,Xmas iss.. 18.00	3 JM,JK,MMe,The Three	50 MMe,Mark Merlin........... 125.00
258 SD,RB,BMc,DG(i),The Demon	Prophecies 550.00	51 MMe,Mark Merlin........... 125.00
and His Boy 18.00	4 JM,JK,MMe,Master of	52 MMe,Mark Merlin........... 125.00
259 RE,RT,MGo,DN,BL,Hair Today,	Unknown 400.00	53 CI,Mark Merlin............. 125.00
Gone Tomorrow, last giant ... 18.00	5 MMe,The Man Who	54 RMo,MMe,Mark Merlin...... 125.00
260 Go to Hades 10.00	Hated Fear............... 275.00	55 MMe,Mark Merlin........... 125.00
261 The Husker 10.00	6 NC,MMe,Experiment 1000 ... 275.00	56 MMe,Mark Merlin........... 125.00
262 FreedFrom Infernos of Hell .. 10.00	7 RMo,Island o/t Enchantress .. 275.00	57 MMe,Mark Merlin........... 125.00
263 JCr,Is There Vengeance	8 JK,RMo,The Electrified Man.. 325.00	58 MMe,O:Mark Merlin 125.00
After Death?............... 10.00	9 JM,JSt,The Jigsaw Creatures . 225.00	59 MMe,Mark Merlin........... 125.00
264 Halloween Issue 10.00	10 JSt,NC,I was a Prisoner	60 MMe,Mark Merlin........... 125.00
265 The Perfect Host 10.00	of the Sea 225.00	61 I:Eclipso,A:Mark Merlin 225.00
266 The Demon Blade 10.00	11 KJ(c),NC,The Man who	62 MMe,Eclipso,Mark Merlin.... 125.00
267 A Strange Way to Die....... 10.00	couldn't stop growing 225.00	63 GC,ATh,Eclipso,Mark Merlin . 100.00
269 Blood on the Grooves 10.00	12 JK,The Hole in the Sky 250.00	64 MMe,ATh,M Merlin,Eclipso... 100.00
270 JSh,JRu,JBi,Black Moss 10.00		65 MMe,ATh,M Merlin,Eclipso... 100.00
271 TS,HellHound of		66 MMe,ATh,M Merlin,Eclipso... 125.00
Brackenmoor 10.00		67 MMe,ATh,M Merlin,Eclipso... 100.00
272 DN,DA,theSorcerer's Castle.. 10.00		68 MMe,Mark Merlin,Eclipso.... 100.00
273 The Rites of Inheritance 10.00		69 MMe,Mark Merlin,Eclipso.... 100.00
274 MR,JBi,Hell Park 10.00		70 MMe,Mark Merlin,Eclipso.... 100.00
275 JCr,`Final Installment'....... 10.00		71 MMe,Mark Merlin,Eclipso.... 100.00
276 SD,MN,`Epode' 10.00		72 MMe,Mark Merlin,Eclipso. ... 100.00
277 HC,AMi,`LimitedEngagement' 10.00		73 MMe,D:Mark Merlin,I:Prince
278 `TV or Not TV' 10.00		Ra-Man; Eclipso.......... 100.00
279 AS,Trial by Fury 10.00		74 MMe,Prince Ra-Man,Eclipso . 100.00
280 VMK,DAy,Hungry Jaws		75 MMe,Prince Ra-Man,Eclipso . 100.00
of Death 10.00		76 MMe,Prince Ra-Man,Eclipso . 100.00
281 Now Dying in this Corner.... 10.00		77 MMe,Prince Ra-Man,Eclipso . 100.00
282 JSw,DG,Superman/Radio		78 MMe,Prince Ra-Man,Eclipso . 100.00
Shack ins 10.00		79 MMe,Prince Ra-Man,Eclipso . 100.00
283 RT,AN`Kill Me Gently' 10.00		80 MMe,Prince Ra-Man,Eclipso . 100.00
284 KG,King and the Dragon 10.00		81 I:Abel, new mystery format
285 Cold Storage 10.00		Don't Move It 75.00
286 Long Arm of the Law 10.00		82 DD,NA,One & only, fully guaran–
287 NR,AS,BL,Legend o/t Lost... 10.00		teed super-permanent 100%.. 50.00
288 DSp,Piper at Gates of Hell... 10.00		83 ATh,The Stuff that Dreams
289 Brother Bobby's Home for		are Made of 50.00
Wayward Girls & Boys 10.00		84 DD,If I had but world enough
290 TS,I:I..Vampire............. 20.00	*House of Secrets #7*	and time................. 50.00
291 TS,DAy,I..Vampire #2....... 10.00	© DC Comics Inc.	85 DH,GK,NA,Second Chance ... 60.00

All comics prices listed are for *Near Mint* condition.

86 GT,GM,Strain. 35.00
87 DD,DG,RA,MK,BWr,The Coming
  of Ghaglan 50.00
88 DD,The Morning Ghost 35.00
89 GM,DH,Where Dead MenWalk. 35.00
90 GT,RB,NA,GM,The Symbionts . 50.00
91 WW,MA,The Eagle's Talon. . . . 50.00
92 BWr,TD(i),I:Swamp Thing
  (Alex Olson). 750.00
93 JAp,TD,ATh(rep.)Lonely in
  Death. 35.00
94 TD,ATh(rep.)Hyde.and
  go Seek 35.00
95 DH,NR,The Bride of Death. . . . 35.00
96 DD,JAb,WW,BWr,the Monster . 40.00
97 JAp,Divide and Murder 35.00
98 MK,ATh(rep),Born Losers. 35.00
99 NR,TD(i),BWr,,Beyond His
  Imagination 35.00
100 TP,TD,AA,BWr,Rest in Peace. 50.00
101 AN,MK,Small Invasion 20.00
102 NR,MK,A Lonely Monstrosity . 20.00
103 AN,BWr,Village on Edge
  of Forever 18.00
104 NR,AA,GT,Ghosts Don't
  Bother Me...But... . . . . 18.00
105 JAp,AA,MK,An Axe to Grind. . 18.00
106 AN,AA,BWr,This Will Kill You . 25.00
107 AA,BWr(c),The Night of
  the Nebbish 25.00
108 A New Kid on the Block 18.00
109 AA,AN...And in Death, there
  is no Escape 18.00
110 Safes Have Secrets, Too 18.00
111 TD,Hair-I-Kari. 18.00
112 Case of the Demon Spawn . . 18.00
113 MSy,NC,NR,Spawns
  of Satan 18.00
114 FBe,Night Game 18.00
115 AA,AN,Nobody Hurts My
  Brother. 18.00
116 NR,Like Father,Like Son 18.00
117 AA,AN,Revenge for the Deadly
  Dummy 18.00
118 GE,Very Last Picture Show . . 18.00
119 A Carnival of Dwarves 18.00
120 TD,AA,The Lion's Share. 18.00
121 Ms.Vampire Killer. 18.00
122 AA,Requiem for Igor. 15.00
123 ATh,A Connecticut Ice Cream
  Man in King Arthur's Court . . 15.00
124 Last of the Frankensteins. . . . 15.00
125 AA,FR,Instant Re-Kill 15.00
126 AN,On Borrowed Time 15.00
127 MSy,A Test of Innocence 15.00
128 AN,Freak Out! 15.00
129 Almost Human 15.00
130 All Dolled Up!. 15.00
131 AN,Point of No Return 15.00
132 Killer Instinct 15.00
133 Portraits of Death. 15.00
134 NR,Inheritance of Blood. 15.00
135 BWr,The Vegitable Garden. . . 15.00
136 BWr,NR,Last Voyage of
  Lady Luck 15.00
137 BWr,The Harder They Fall . . . 15.00
138 Where Dreams are Born 20.00
139 SD,NR,A Real Crazy Kid 20.00
140 NR,O:Patchwork Man 25.00
141 You Can't Beat the Devil 10.00
142 Playmate 10.00
143 The Evil Side 10.00
144 The Vampire of Broadway . . . 10.00
145 Operation was Successful,But 10.00
146 GM,Snake's Alive. 10.00
147 AN,GM,See-Through Thief. . . 10.00
148 GM,SD,Sorcerer's Apprentice 10.00
149 MK,The Evil One 10.00
150 JSN(c),A:Phantom Stranger
  and Dr.13. . . . . 10.00
151 MGo,MK,Nightmare 10.00
152 Sister Witch. 10.00
153 VM,AN,Don't Look Now 10.00
154 TS,MK,JL,Last issue 10.00

HOUSE OF SECRETS
DC/Vertigo, Aug., 1996
1 SSe(s),TKr, judgments on your
  darkest secrets. 4.00
2 SSe(s),TKr, F:Rain 3.00
3 SSe(s),TKr,Seattle's citizens
  secrets. 3.00
4 SSe(s),TKr,Eric's secrets
  exposed 3.00
5 . . . . 3.00
6 SSe(s),DFg,Other rooms:
  Meeting 3.00
7 SSe(s),TKr,Blueprint:
  Elevation A. 3.00
8 SSe(s),TKr,Road to You,pt.1 . . . 3.00
9 SSe(s),TKr,Road to You,pt.2 . . . 3.00
10 SSe(s),TKr,Road to You,pt.3 . . . 3.00
11 The Book of Law, pt.1 (of 5) . . . 3.00
12 The Book of Law, pt.2 . . . . 3.00
13 SSe,The Book of Law, pt.3 . . . 3.00
14 SSe,The Book of Law, pt.4 . . . 3.00
15 SSe,The Book of Law, pt.5 . . . 3.00
16 SSe,Book of Law, epilogue . . . 3.00
17 SSe,The Road to You, pt.1 . . . 3.00
18 SSe,The Road to You, pt.2 . . . 3.00
19 SSe,The Road to You, pt.3 . . . 3.00
20 SSe,Other Rooms story. 3.00
21 SSe,Basement, pt.1. . . . . 3.00
22 SSe,Basement, pt.2. . . . . 3.00
23 SSe,Basement, pt.3. . . . . 3.00
24 SSe,TKr,Attic. 3.00
25 SSe,TKr, final issue 3.00
TPB Foundation, rep.#1–#5 . . . . . 14.95

HOUSE OF SECRETS: FACADE
DC/Vertigo, March, 2001
1 (of 2) TKr, 48-page 5.95
2 TKr,48-page 5.95

HOUSE ON THE BORDERLANDS, THE
DC/Vertigo May 2003
TPB from W.H.Hodgson book 19.95

HUMAN DEFENSE CORPS
May 2003
1 (of 6) TTn. 2.50
2 TTn,Parasitic aliens 2.50
3 TTn,What dreams may come . . 2.50
4 TTn,Seance 2.50
5 TTn,War is Hell. 2.50
6 TTn,concl. 2.50

HUMAN TARGET SPECIAL
1991
1 DG(i),Prequel to T.V. Series 2.25

HUMAN TARGET
DC/Vertigo, 1999
1 (of 4) PrM(s). 3.00
2 PrM(s) 3.00
3 PrM(s) 3.00
4 PrM(s), concl. 3.00
TPB 12.95

HUMAN TARGET
DC/Vertigo Aug. 2003
1 PrM(s),40-pg. 3.00
2 PrM(s),Unshredded Man,pt.1 . . . 3.00
3 PrM(s),Unshredded Man,pt.2 . . . 3.00
4 PrM(s),Ball Game, pt.1 . . . . 3.00
TPB Human Target: Final Cut 19.95

HUNTER: THE AGE OF MAGIC
DC/Vertigo, July, 2001
1 R:The Hunter 3.50
2 F:Kalesh. 3.00
3 The Worlds of The White School. 3.00
4 The Sardonyx Warriors 3.00
5 The Red Man's Devastation . . . 3.00
6 Whose funeral is it 3.00
7 Welcome Home Timothy Hunter . 3.00
8 The Evil Gene,pt.1 . . . . 3.00
9 The Evil Gene,pt.2 . . . . 3.00
10 The Evil Gene,pt.3. . . . . 3.00
11 The Evil Gene,pt.4 . . . . 3.00
12 F:Tim. 3.00
13 A Declaration of War 3.00
14 War begins 3.00
15 Tim vs. Arawn Kruder. 3.00
16 Tim vs. Arawn Kruder. 3.00
17 Ash Walker 3.00
18 Mr. Lily 3.00
19 Sefer Raziel. 3.00
20 Janosh-el. 3.00
21 art and magic 3.00
22 art and magic 3.00
23 Art of Magic 3.00
24 Stone of Albion 3.00
25 final issue 3.00

HUNTER'S HEART
1995
1 Cops vs. Serial Killer 4.95
2 . . . . 4.95
3 F:Lieutenant Slidell 4.95

HUNTRESS, THE
1989–90
1 JSon/DG 2.50
2 JSon,Search for Family's
  Murderer 2.50
3 JSon,A:La Bruja 2.50
4 JSon,Little Italy/Chinatown
  Gangs 2.50

DC

Huntress–Impulse

5 JSon,V:Doctor Mandragora	2.50	
6 JSon,Huntress'secrets revealed	2.50	
7 JSon,V:Serial Killer	2.50	
8 JSon,V:Serial Killer	2.50	
9 JSon,V:Serial Killer	2.50	
10 JSon,Nuclear Terrorists in NY	2.50	
11 JSon,V:Wyvern,Nuclear Terrorists contd.	2.50	
12 JSon,V:Nuclear Terrorists cont	2.50	
13 JSon,Violence in NY	2.50	
14 JSon,Violence contd.,New Mob boss	2.50	
15 JSon,I:Waterfront Warrior	2.50	
16 JSon,Secret of Waterfront Warrior revealed	2.50	
17 JSon,Batman+Huntress#1	2.50	
18 JSon,Batman+Huntress#2	2.50	
19 JSon,Batman+Huntress#3,final issue	2.50	

HUNTRESS
[Limited Series], 1994

1 CDi(s),MN,V:Redzone	2.25
2 MN,V:Redzone	2.25
3 MN,V:Redzone	2.25
4 MN,V:Spano,Redzone	2.25

iCANDY
Sept. 2003

1 DAn&ALa(s)	2.50
2 DAn&ALa(s)	2.50
3 DAn&ALa(s)	2.50

ICON
DC/Milestone, 1993–96

1 Direct Market Ed.,MBr,MG,I:Icon, Rocket,S.H.R.E.D.,w/poster, card,C puzzle piece	3.50
1a Newsstand Ed.	2.00
2 MBr,MG,I:Payback	2.50
3 MBr,MG,V:Payback	2.50
4 MBr,MG,Teen Pregnancy Issue.	2.50
5 MBr,MG,V:Blood Syndicate	2.50
6 MBr,MG,V:Blood Syndicate	2.50
7 MBr,MG	2.50
8 MBr,MG,O:Icon	2.50
9 WS(c),MBr,MG,Shadow War, I:Donner,Blitzen	2.50
10 MBr,MG,V:Holocaust	2.50
11 MBr,Hero Worship	2.50
12 Sanctimony	2.50
13 MBr,Rocket & Static T.U.	2.50

Icon #7 © DC Comics, Inc.

14 JBy(c)	2.50
15 Worlds Collide,pt.4,A:Superboy	2.50
16 Worlds Collide,pt.11, V:Superman,Rift	2.50
17 Mothership Connection	2.50
18 Mothership Connection,pt.2	2.50
19 Mothership Connection,pt.3	2.50
20 Rocket	2.50
21	2.50
22	2.50
23 New Rocket	2.50
24 F:Buck Wild	2.50
25 V:Oblivion	3.00
26 V:Oblivion	2.50
27 Move to Paris Island projects	2.50
28 Long Hot Summer	2.50
29 Long Hot Summer	2.50
30 Icon Leaves Earth	2.50
31 HC(c) Readers Choice comic.	2.50
32 Rocket, Galactic Corporate	2.50
33 V:Rocket	2.50
34 V:Cooperative	2.50
35	2.50
36 Rocket returns to Earth	2.50
37 MBr,RT,F:Rocket	2.50
38 DMD(s),RT	2.50
39 DMD(s),RT,V:Holocaust & Blood Syndicate	2.50
40 DMD(s),RT, V:Holocaust	2.50
41 DMD(s),RT, V:Blood Syndicate.	2.50
42 DMD(s),RT	2.50
43 DMD(s),RT,Blood Reign, concl.	2.50
44 DMD(s),RT,V:Smurphs	2.50
45 DMD(s),RT, final issue	2.50
TPB A Hero's Welcome	12.95

I DIE AT MIDNIGHT
DC/Vertigo, Dec., 1999

GN 64-pg.	6.95

IMMORTAL DR. FATE
1995

1 WS,KG,rep.	2.25
2 and 3 KG,rep.	@2.25

IMPACT WINTER SPECIAL
Impact, 1991

1 CI/MR/TL,A:All Impact Heros, President Kidnapped	2.50

IMPULSE
1995–2002

1 Young Flash Adventures	6.00
2 V:Terrorists	3.50
3 In School	3.00
4 V:White Lightning	3.00
5 V:White Lightning	3.00
6	3.00
7 V:Gridlock	3.00
8 MWa,Underworld Unleashed tie-in	3.00
9 MWa,F:XS,	3.00
10 MWa,Dead Heat,pt.3	3.00
11 MWa,Dead Heat,pt.5	3.00
12	3.00
13 MWa,new daredevil in town	2.50
14 AWi,A:White Lightning	2.50
15	2.50
16	2.50
17	2.50
18 MPk(s),AWi,Virtual reality nightmare	2.50
19 MWa(s),HuR, Bart's dreams	2.50
20 MWa(s),HuR, baseball	2.50
21 MWa(s),F:Legion of Super-Heroes	2.50

Impulse #15 © DC Comics Inc.

22 MWa(s)	2.50
23 MWa(s),HuR,Mercury at a crossroads	2.50
24 MWa(s),HuR,Impulse's mother comes from the future	2.50
25 MWa(s),HuR,Impulse & his mom in 30th century	2.50
26 MWa(s),Bart Allen back in the 20th century	2.50
27 MWa(s)	2.50
28	2.50
29 BML,Bart searches for Max Mercury	2.50
30 BML, pt.2, Genesis tie-in	2.50
31 BML, pt.3,V:Dr. Morlo.	2.50
32 BML,Max is home	2.50
33 BML,White Lightning	2.50
34 BML,Devonian Age, pt.1	2.50
35 BML	2.50
36 BML,Court Dates	2.50
37 BML,Dr. Morlo	2.50
38 BML,freak snow storm	2.50
39 BML,V:Trickster	2.50
40 BML,WF, kid picnic	2.50
41 Return of Arrowette	2.50
42 BML(s),virtual monsters	2.50
43 BML(s),F:Jamal	2.50
44 BML(s),V:Evil Eye	2.50
45 BML(s),Christmas	2.50
46 BML(s),Chain Lightning x-over	2.50
47 BML(s),A:Superman	2.50
48 BML(s),A:Riddler	2.50
49 BML(s),C:Flash	2.50
50 TDz(s),A:Batman, Joker	2.50
51 TDz(s),V:Frog Prince	2.50
52 TDz(s),WS,F:Kalibak,pt.1	2.50
53 TDz(s),WS,F:Kalibak,pt.2	2.50
54 TDz(s),Day of Judgment x-over	2.50
55 V:Sir Real	2.50
56	2.50
57 TDz(s),F:Plastic Man	2.50
58 TDz(s),F:Max Mercury	2.50
59 TDz(s),F:Arrowette	2.50
60 DMD(s),V:Alabama	2.50
61 F:Max Mercury,S.T.R.I.P.E.	2.50
62 TDz(s),Mercury Falling,pt.1	2.50
63 TDz(s),Mercury Falling,pt.2	2.50
64 TDz(s),Mercury Falling,pt.3	2.50
65 TDz(s),Mercury Falling,pt.4	2.50
66 TDz(s),Mercury Falling,pt.5	2.50
67 TDz,RyR,Mercury Falling epilogue	2.50
68 TDz,F:Green Lantern,pt.1	2.50
69 TDz,F:Green Lantern,pt.2	2.50

All comics prices listed are for Near Mint condition.

Impulse–Invisibles / DC / Comics Values Annual

```
70 TDz, . . . . . . . . . . . . . . . . . . . . . 2.50
71 TDz,V:Lucius Keller . . . . . . . . . . 2.50
72 TDz,Carol kidnapped . . . . . . . . . 2.50
73 TDz,The Dark Tomorrow . . . . . . 2.50
74 TDz,The Dark Tomorrow,pt.2 . . . 2.50
75 TDz,The Dark Tomorrow,pt.2 . . . 2.50
76 TDz,V:White Lightning . . . . . . . . 2.50
77 TDz,Our Worlds at War tie-in . . . 2.50
78 ImpulseNoMore,F:YoungJustice. 2.50
79 TDz,Joker:Last Laugh . . . . . . . . 2.50
80 TDz,V:White Lightning . . . . . . . . 2.50
81 TDz,V:Captain Saturn . . . . . . . . 2.50
82 TDz,Double Visions . . . . . . . . . . 2.50
83 TDz,fearsome monsters. . . . . . . 2.50
84 TDz,F:Jay Garrick . . . . . . . . . . . 2.50
85 World WithoutYoungJustice,pt.2. 2.50
86 TDz,Bedlam's Abilities . . . . . . . . 2.50
87 TDz,The power of Impulse . . . . . 2.50
88 TDz,TA,rescue Carol . . . . . . . . . 2.50
89 TDz,TA,final issue . . . . . . . . . . . 2.50
Ann.#2 Pulp Heroes (Western) . . . . 3.95
Spec.#1,000,000 BML(s) . . . . . . . . 2.25
GN Bart Saves the Universe. . . . . . 6.00
TPB Reckless Youth MWa(s) rep.
   Flash #92–#94 . . . . . . . . . . . . 14.95
Spec. Impulse/Atom Double-Shot
   DJu, x-over concl. (1997) . . . . . 3.00
Spec. Impulse Plus 48pg.
   with Grossout (1997) . . . . . . . . 2.95
```

INDUSTRIAL GOTHIC
DC/Vertigo, 1995

```
1 Jail Break Plans . . . . . . . . . . . . . 2.50
2 thru 5 Jail Break Plans . . . . . . @2.50
```

INFERIOR FIVE
March-April, 1967

```
1 MSy . . . . . . . . . . . . . . . . . . . . . 75.00
2 MSy,A:Plastic Man . . . . . . . . . . 40.00
3 . . . . . . . . . . . . . . . . . . . . . . . . 25.00
4 . . . . . . . . . . . . . . . . . . . . . . . . 25.00
5 . . . . . . . . . . . . . . . . . . . . . . . . 25.00
6 . . . . . . . . . . . . . . . . . . . . . . . . 25.00
7 . . . . . . . . . . . . . . . . . . . . . . . . 25.00
8 . . . . . . . . . . . . . . . . . . . . . . . . 25.00
9 . . . . . . . . . . . . . . . . . . . . . . . . 25.00
10 A:Superman. . . . . . . . . . . . . . . 30.00
11 JO(c&a) . . . . . . . . . . . . . . . . . 25.00
12 JO(c&a). . . . . . . . . . . . . . . . . . 25.00
```

INFERNO
Aug., 1997

```
1 (of 4) SI, from Legion . . . . . . . . . 4.00
2 SI,mall grrrls . . . . . . . . . . . . . . . . 3.00
3 SI,Legion Month tie-in. . . . . . . . . 3.00
4 SI, concl. . . . . . . . . . . . . . . . . . . 3.00
```

INFINITY, INC.
March, 1984

```
1 JOy,O:Infinity Inc. . . . . . . . . . . . . 4.00
2 JOy,End of Origin . . . . . . . . . . . . 3.50
3 JOy,O:Jade . . . . . . . . . . . . . . . . 3.00
4 JOy,V:JSA . . . . . . . . . . . . . . . . . 3.00
5 JOy,V:JSA . . . . . . . . . . . . . . . . . 3.00
6 JOy,V:JSA . . . . . . . . . . . . . . . . . 3.00
7 JOy,V:JSA . . . . . . . . . . . . . . . . . 3.00
8 JOy,V:Ultra Humanite . . . . . . . . . 3.00
9 JOy,V:Ultra Humanite . . . . . . . . . 3.00
10 JOy,V:Ultra Humanite. . . . . . . . . 3.00
11 DN,GT,O:Infinity Inc. . . . . . . . . . 3.00
12 Infinity Unmasks,I:Yolanda
   Montez (New Wildcat) . . . . . . . 3.00
13 DN,V:Rose & Thorn . . . . . . . . . . 3.00
14 1st TM DC art,V:Chroma . . . . . 10.00
15 TM,V:Chroma . . . . . . . . . . . . . . 4.00
16 TM,I:Helix (Mr. Bones) . . . . . . . . 3.50
17 TM,V:Helix. . . . . . . . . . . . . . . . . 4.00
```

Infinity Inc. #7 © DC Comics, Inc.

```
18 TM,Crisis. . . . . . . . . . . . . . . . . . 4.00
19 TM,JSA,JLA x-over,
   I:Mekanique . . . . . . . . . . . . . . 4.00
20 TM,Crisis. . . . . . . . . . . . . . . . . . 4.00
21 TM,Crisis,I:HourmanII,
   Dr.Midnight. . . . . . . . . . . . . . . 4.00
22 TM,Crisis. . . . . . . . . . . . . . . . . . 4.00
23 TM,Crisis. . . . . . . . . . . . . . . . . . 4.00
24 TM,Crisis. . . . . . . . . . . . . . . . . . 4.00
25 TM,Crisis,JSA . . . . . . . . . . . . . . 4.00
26 TM,V:Carcharo . . . . . . . . . . . . . 4.00
27 TM,V:Carcharo . . . . . . . . . . . . . 4.00
28 TM,V:Carcharo . . . . . . . . . . . . . 4.00
29 TM,V:Helix. . . . . . . . . . . . . . . . . 4.00
30 TM,Mourning of JSA . . . . . . . . . 4.00
31 TM,V:Psycho Pirate . . . . . . . . . . 4.00
32 TM,V:Psycho Pirate . . . . . . . . . . 4.00
33 TM,O:Obsidian . . . . . . . . . . . . . 4.00
34 TM,A: Global Guardians . . . . . . 4.00
35 TM,V:Infinitors . . . . . . . . . . . . . . 4.00
36 TM,V:Injustice Unl. . . . . . . . . . . . 4.00
37 TM,TD,O:Northwind . . . . . . . . . . 4.00
38 Helix on Trial . . . . . . . . . . . . . . . 3.00
39 O:Solomon Grundy . . . . . . . . . . 3.00
40 V:Thunderbolt . . . . . . . . . . . . . . 3.00
41 Jonni Thunder . . . . . . . . . . . . . . 3.00
42 TD,V:Hastor,L:Fury . . . . . . . . . . 3.00
43 TD,V:Hastor,Silver Scarab . . . . . 3.00
44 TD,D:Silver Scarab . . . . . . . . . . 3.00
45 MGu,A:New Teen Titans,
   V:Ultra-Humanite . . . . . . . . . . 3.00
46 TD,Millennium,V:Floronic Man . . 3.00
47 TD,Millennium,V:Harlequin. . . . . 3.00
48 TD,O:Nuklon . . . . . . . . . . . . . . . 3.00
49 Silver Scarab becomes
   Sandman . . . . . . . . . . . . . . . . 3.00
50 TD,V:The Wizard,O:Sandman . . 3.50
51 W:Fury & Sandman,D:Skyman. . 3.00
52 V:Helix. . . . . . . . . . . . . . . . . . . . 3.00
53 V:Justice Unlimited,last issue . . . 3.00
Ann.#1 TM,V:Thorn . . . . . . . . . . . . 4.00
Ann.#2 V:Degaton,x-over Young
   All-Stars Annual #1. . . . . . . . . 3.00
Spec.#1 TD,A:Outsiders,V:Psycho
   Pirate. . . . . . . . . . . . . . . . . . . 3.00
```

IN THE SHADOW OF EDGAR ALLAN POE
DC/Vertigo July 2003

```
TPB . . . . . . . . . . . . . . . . . . . . . . 17.95
```

INVASION!
1988–89

```
1 TM,I:Vril Dox,Dominators
   (20th century). . . . . . . . . . . . . 4.00
2 TM,KG,DG,I:L.E.G.I.O.N. . . . . . . 3.00
3 BS,DG,I:Blasters . . . . . . . . . . . . 3.00
Daily Planet-Invasion! 16p . . . . . . . 2.00
```

INVISIBLES
DC/Vertigo, 1994–96

```
1 GMo(s). . . . . . . . . . . . . . . . . . . . 7.00
2 GMo(s),Down & Out,pt.1. . . . . . . 4.00
3 GMo(s),Down & Out,pt.2. . . . . . . 4.00
4 GMo(s),Down & Out,pt.3. . . . . . . 4.00
5 Arcadia,pt.1 . . . . . . . . . . . . . . . . 4.00
6 Arcadia,pt.2 . . . . . . . . . . . . . . . . 4.00
7 Arcadia,pt.3 . . . . . . . . . . . . . . . . 4.00
8 Arcadia,pt.4 . . . . . . . . . . . . . . . . 4.00
9 SeP(c),L:Dane . . . . . . . . . . . . . . 3.00
10 SeP(c),CWn,Jim Crow v. 3
   Zombies. . . . . . . . . . . . . . . . . 3.00
11 V:New Breed of Hunter . . . . . . . 3.00
12 . . . . . . . . . . . . . . . . . . . . . . . . . 3.00
13 GMO,Sheman,pt.1. . . . . . . . . . . 3.00
14 GMo,SeP,Sheman,pt.2. . . . . . . . 3.00
15 GMo,Sheman,pt.3. . . . . . . . . . . 3.00
16 GMo,An offer from Sir Miles. . . . 3.00
17 GMo,Entropy in the U.K.,pt.1 . . . 3.00
18 GMo,Entropy in the U.K.,pt.2 . . . 3.00
19 GMo,Entropy in the U.K.,pt.3 . . . 3.00
20 GMo,F:RaggedRobin,Dane,Boy. 4.00
21 GMo,PuJ,F:Dane. . . . . . . . . . . . 4.00
22 GMo(s),MBu,MPn . . . . . . . . . . . 4.00
23 GMo(s),MBu,MPn . . . . . . . . . . . 4.00
24 GMo(s),MBu,MPn . . . . . . . . . . . 4.00
25 GMo(s),MBu,MPn,final issue
   Aug., 1996 . . . . . . . . . . . . . . . 5.00
```

[Volume 2] DC/Vertigo, 1996

```
1 GMo(s),PJ,Black Science,pt.1. . . 4.00
2 GMo(s),PJ,Black Science,pt.2. . . 3.00
3 GMo(s),PJ,Black Science,pt.3. . . 3.00
4 GMo(s),PJ,Black Science,pt.4. . . 3.00
5 GMo(s),PJ,In SanFrancisco,pt.1 . 3.00
6 GMo(s),PJ,In SanFrancisco,pt.2 . 3.00
7 GMo(s),PJ,BB(c),Time Machine
   Go, concl. . . . . . . . . . . . . . . . . 3.00
8 GMo(s),PJ,BB(c),Sensitive
   Criminals,pt.1. . . . . . . . . . . . . 3.00
9 GMo(s),PJ,BB(c),Criminals,pt.2 . 3.00
10 GMo(s),PJ,Criminals,pt.3, . . . . . 3.00
11 GMo(s),PJ,BB(c),Hand of Glory
   pt.1 . . . . . . . . . . . . . . . . . . . . . 3.00
12 GMo(s),PJ,BB(c),Glory,pt.2 . . . . 3.00
13 GMo(s),PJ,BB(c),Glory,concl. . . . 3.00
14 GMo(s),BB(c),Archons aftermath 3.00
15 GMo(s),BB(c), The Philadelphia
   Experiment, pt.1. . . . . . . . . . . 3.00
16 GMo(s),BB(c),Experiment,pt.2 . . 3.00
17 GMo,CWn,BB,Black Science II
   pt.1 . . . . . . . . . . . . . . . . . . . . . 3.00
18 GMo,CWn,BB,Science,pt.2 . . . . 3.00
19 GMo,CWn,BB,Science,pt.3 . . . . 3.00
20 GMo,CWn,BB(c),Science,pt.4 . . 2.50
21 GMo,CWn,BB(c),King Mob . . . . 2.50
22 GMo,CWn,BB(c) The Tower . . . . 2.50
TPB Counting to None . . . . . . . . . 20.00
TPB Say You Want a Revolution. . 20.00
TPB Bloody Hell in America . . . . . 13.00
TPB Kissing Mister . . . . . . . . . . . . 19.95
TPB Apocalipstick, 208-page . . . . 19.95
TPB Entropy in the U.K. . . . . . . . . 19.95
```

[Volume 3] DC/Vertigo, 1999

```
12 GMo,Satanstorm,pt.1. . . . . . . . . 3.00
11 GMo,Satanstorm,pt.2. . . . . . . . . 3.00
10 GMo,Satanstorm,pt.3. . . . . . . . . 3.00
9 GMo,Satanstorm,pt.4. . . . . . . . . 3.00
8 GMo,Karmageddon,pt.1 . . . . . . . 3.00
7 GMo,Karmageddon,pt.2 . . . . . . . 3.00
6 GMo,Karmageddon,pt.3 . . . . . . . 3.00
```

DC

Invisibles–JLA

5 GMo... 2.95
4 GMo,Invisible Kingdom,pt.1 ... 2.95
3 GMo,Invisible Kingdom,pt.2 ... 2.95
2 GMo,Invisible Kingdom,pt.3 ... 2.95
1 GMo,conclusion ... 2.95
GN The Mystery Play ... 9.95
TPB The Invisible Kingdom ... 19.95
TPB Kissing Mister Quimper ... 19.95

I, PAPARAZZI
DC/Vertigo, Sept., 2001
TPB ... 19.95

IRONWOLF
1986
1 HC,rep. ... 2.25

IRONWOLF: FIRES OF THE REVOLUTION
1992
Hardcov.GN MMi,CR,R:Ironwolf ... 29.95
TPB Fires of the Revolution ... 15.00

ISIS
Oct.–Nov., 1976
1 RE/WW ... 20.00
2 MN ... 10.00
3 ... 10.00
4 ... 10.00
5 ... 10.00
6 ... 10.00
7 O:Isis ... 12.00
8 Dec.–Jan., 1977–78 ... 10.00

IT'S GAMETIME
Sept.–Oct., 1955
1 ... 800.00
2 Dodo and the Frog ... 600.00
3 ... 600.00
4 March-April, 1956 ... 600.00

JACKIE GLEASON AND THE HONEYMOONERS
June-July, 1956
1 Based on TV show ... 1,100.00
2 ... 600.00
3 ... 450.00
4 ... 450.00
5 ... 450.00
6 ... 450.00
7 ... 450.00
8 ... 450.00
9 ... 450.00
10 ... 450.00
11 ... 450.00
12 April-May, 1958 ... 750.00

JACK KIRBY'S FOURTH WORLD
Jan., 1997
1 JBy,Worlds of New Genesis & Apokolips become one ... 2.25
2 JBy,F:Big Barda vs. Thor ... 2.25
3 JBy,at Wall of the Source ... 2.25
4 JBy,Can Highfather save his son 2.25
5 JBy,conflict between the gods ... 2.25
6 JBy,Cause of Orion's transformation ... 2.25
7 JBy,Orion taught lesson ... 2.25
8 JBy,WS,Genesis tie-in ... 2.25
9 JBy,WS(c),Genesis aftermath ... 2.25
10 JBy,WS, ... 2.25
11 JBy,WS,F:Orion ... 2.25

12 JBy,WS,F:Mister Miracle ... 2.25
13 JBy,WS ... 2.25
14 JBy,WS,Promethean Giant ... 2.25
15 JBy,WS,Armaghetto ... 2.25
16 JBy,WS,Kalibak vs. Darkseid ... 2.25
17 JBy,WS,Darkseid ... 2.25
18 JBy,WS,Darkseid freed ... 2.25
19 JBy,WS,two stories ... 2.25
20 JBy,WS,A:Superman,final issue .. 2.25
TPB JK ... 12.95

JAGUAR
Impact, 1991
1 I&O:Jaguar I: Timon De Guzman, Maxx 13,Prof.Ruiz, Luiza Timmerman ... 2.25
2 Development of Powers ... 2.25
3 A:Maxx-13 ... 2.25
4 A:Black Hood ... 2.25
5 V:Void,The Living Black Hole ... 2.25
6 `The Doomster,'A:Maxx-13 ... 2.25
7 Jaguar Secret Discovered, V:Void ... 2.25
8 V:Aryan League ... 2.25
9 I:Moonlighter(w/trading cards) ... 2.25
10 V:Invisible Terror ... 2.25
11 Defending Comedienne ... 2.25
12 V:The Bodyguard ... 2.25
13 V:Purge ... 2.25
14 'Frightmare in Rio',last iss ... 2.25
Ann.#1 Earthquest,w/trading card .. 2.50

JEMM, SON OF SATURN
Sept., 1984
1 GC/KJ mini-series ... 2.50
2 GC ... 2.50
3 GC,Origin ... 2.50
4 A:Superman ... 2.50
5 Kin ... 2.50
6 thru 12 GC, Aug., 1985 ... @2.50

JIMMY OLSEN: ADVENTURES
July 2003
TPB JK ... 19.95

Jack Kirby's Fourth World #9
© DC Comics, Inc.

Jemm, Son of Saturn #9
© DC Comics Inc.

JIMMY WAKELY
Sept.–Oct., 1949
1 Ph(c),ATh,The Cowboy Swordsman ... 1,400.00
2 Ph(c),ATh,The Prize Pony ... 550.00
3 Ph(c),ATh,The Return of Tulsa Tom ... 550.00
4 Ph(c),ATh,FF,HK,Where There's Smoke There's Gunfire ... 575.00
5 ATh,The Return of the Conquistadores ... 450.00
6 ATh,Two Lives of Jimmy Wakely ... 450.00
7 The Secret of Hairpin Canyon . 450.00
8 ATh,The Lost City of Blue Valley ... 450.00
9 ATh,The Return of the Western Firebrands ... 350.00
10 ATh,Secret of Lantikin'sLight . 350.00
11 ATh,Trail o/a Thousand Hoofs 350.00
12 ATh,JKU,The King of Sierra Valley ... 350.00
13 ATh,The Raiders of Treasure Mountain ... 350.00
14 ATh(c),JKu,The Badmen of Roaring Flame Valley ... 350.00
15 GK(c),Tommyguns on the Range ... 350.00
16 GK(c),The Bad Luck Boots ... 300.00
17 GK(c),Terror atThunderBasin . 300.00
18 July-Aug., 1952 ... 350.00

JLA
Nov., 1996
1 GMo(s),HPo,JhD,V:Hyperclan .. 16.00
2 ... 12.00
3 GMo(s),HPo,JhD,War of the Worlds ... 10.00
4 GMo(s),HPo,JhD,battle of the super-heroes, conc ... 10.00
5 GMo(s),HPo,JhD Woman of Tomorrow ... 7.00
6 GMo(s),HPo,JhD,Fire in theSky . 6.00
7 GMo(s),HPo,JhD,Heaven on Earth ... 6.00
8 GMo(s),HPo,JhD,Imaginary Stories, F:Green Arrow ... 6.00
9 GMo(s),V:The Key ... 6.00
10 GMo(s),HPo,JhD,R:Injustice Gang, pt.1 (of 6) ... 6.00
11 GMo(s),HPo,JhD,Rock of Ages, pt.2 ... 6.00

All comics prices listed are for Near Mint condition.

JLA–JLA:Scary — DC — Comics Values Annual

#	Description	Price
12	GMo(s),HPo,JhD,Rock of Ages, pt.3, A:Hourman	6.00
13	GMo(s),HPo,JhD,Rock of Ages, pt.4	6.00
14	GMo(s),HPo,JhD,Rock of Ages, pt.5	6.00
15	GMo(s),HPo,JhD,Rock of Ages pt.6, concl, 48 pg	6.00
16	GMo(s),HPo,JhD, new member	6.00
17	GMo(s),HPo,JhD,V:Prometheus	6.00
18	MWa,Engine of Chance, pt.1	6.00
19	MWa,Engine of Chance, pt.2	6.00
20	MWa,F:Adam Strange,pt.1	6.00
21	MWa,F:Adam Strange,pt.2	6.00
22	GMo(s),The Star Conqueror	2.50
23	GMo,V:Star Conqueror, A:Sandman	2.50
24	GMo,HPo,Ultra-Marines,pt.1	2.50
25	GMo,HPo,Ultra-Marines,pt.2	2.50
26	GMo,HPo,Ultra-Marines,pt.3	2.50
27	GMo,HPo,CrisisTimesFive,pt.1	2.50
28	GMo,HPo,CrisisTimesFive,pt.2	2.50
29	GMo,HPo,CrisisTimesFive,pt.3	2.50
30	GMo,HPo,CrisisTimesFive,pt.4	2.50
31	GMo,HPo,CrisisTimes Five,concl.	2.50
32	MWa(s),No Man's Land	2.50
33	MWa(s),No Man's Land	2.50
34	GMo,Super-villains riot.	2.50
35	JMD(s),F:New Spectre	2.50
36	GMo,HPo,World War 3,pt.1	2.50
37	GMo,HPo,World War 3,pt.2	2.50
38	GMo,HPo,World War 3,pt.3	2.50
39	GMo,HPo,World War 3,pt.4	2.50
40	GMo,HPo,World War 3,pt.5	2.50
41	GMo,HPo,World War 3, concl.48-pg.	3.00
42	Miniscule civilization	2.25
43	MWa(s),HPo,V:Ra's al Ghul	2.25
44	HPo,Tower of Babel,pt.2	2.25
45	HPo,Tower of Babel,pt.3	2.25
46	HPo,Tower of Babel,concl.	2.25
47	MWa,BHi,PNe,Queen ofFables	2.25
48	MWa,BHi,PNe,Queen ofFables	2.25
49	MWa,BHi,PNe,Queen ofFables	2.25
50	MWa,BHi,PNe,48-page	4.00
51	MWa,MsM,Man and Superman	2.25
52	MWa,BHi,PNe	2.25
53	MWa,BHi,PNe	2.25
54	MWa,BHi,PNe,Man & Superman	2.25
55	MWa,Terror Incongita,pt.1	2.25
56	MWa,Terror Incongita,pt.2	2.25
57	MWa,Terror Incongita,pt.3	2.25
58	MWa,Terror Incongita,pt.4	2.25
59	CDi,DBk,Joker:Last Laugh	2.25
60	MWa,F:Santa Claus	2.25
61	DoM,TG,+16-pg.PowerCompany	2.25
62	DoM,Golden Perfect,pt.1	2.25
63	DoM,Golden Perfect,pt.2	2.25
64	DoM,Golden Perfect,pt.3	2.25
65	DoM,Batman & Plastic Man	2.25
66	DoM,warrior priests	2.25
67	DoM,human sacrifice	2.25
68	DoM,Obsidian Age prologue	2.25
69	Hunt for Aquaman,pt.1	2.25
70	DoM,Hunt for Aquaman,pt.2	2.25
71	DoM,Hunt for Aquaman,pt.3	2.25
72	DoM,Hunt for Aquaman,pt.4	2.25
73	DoM,Hunt for Aquaman,pt.5	2.25
74	DoM,Hunt for Aquaman,pt.6	2.25
75	DoM,Hunt for Aquaman,64-pg.	4.50
76	DoM,after Obsidian Age	2.25
77	RV(s),memories stolen	2.25
78	DoM,	2.25
79	DoM,F:Faith	2.25
80	White Rage,pt.1	2.25
81	White Rage,pt.2	2.25
82	White Rage,pt.3	2.25
83	Qurac	2.25
84	Trial by Fire,pt.1	2.25
85	Trial by Fire,pt.2	2.25
86	Trial by Fire,pt.3	2.25
87	Trial by Fire,pt.4	2.25
88	Trial by Fire,pt.5	2.25
89	Trial by Fire,pt.6	2.25
90	F:Batman,Wonder Woman	2.25
Ann.#1	Pulp Heroes (Hard Boiled)	4.50
Ann.#2	TTn,BWr,Ghosts	3.50
Ann.#3	JLApe Gorilla Warfare	3.50
Ann.#4	Planet DC	4.00
Spec.#1,000,000	GMo(s),HPo, V:Justice Legion A	2.50
SuperSpec.#1	Justice League of America	6.00
Spec.#1	Our Worlds at War,48-pg.	2.95
Giant #1, 7 new stories, 80-pg.		5.00
Giant #2, 80-page.		4.95
Giant #3, 80-page, oversize		5.95
SC Secret Origins, oversize		7.95
JLA: Tomorrow Woman, 1-shot TPe,Girlfrenzy (1998)		2.00
GN New World Order GMo(s),HPo, JhD, rep. #1–#4		5.95
GN American Dreams rep.#5–#9		8.00
GN Secret Files		4.00
GN Secret Files deluxe		5.00
GN Secret Files #2		4.00
GN Secret Files #3 How Talia stole Batman's Secret Files		4.95
GN Foreign Bodies		6.00
GN JLA/WildC.A.T.S, GMo(s), VS,x-over		6.00
GN JLA/Haven: Arrival (2001)		5.95
GN JLA: Earth 2,96-page, F:Crime Syndicate (2000)		14.95
GN Gods and Monsters		6.95
GN Seven Caskets,DIB, 48-page		5.95
GN JLA: Superpower		5.95
GN JLA Primeval		5.95
GN Shogun of Steel,Elseworlds		6.95
GN JLA/Haven:Anathema (2002)		5.95
GN The Island of Dr. Moreau,GP Elseworlds (2002)		6.95
GN JLA: Liberty and Justice		9.95
JLA/Witchblade, x-over		6.00
TPB Heaven's Ladder		9.95
TPB JLA:Rock of Ages		10.00
TPB Strength in Numbers		13.00
TPB Justice League of America: The Nail, Elseworlds		13.00
TPB Secret Origins Featuring JLA		15.00
TPB JLA:World War III,208-page		12.95
TPB JLA vs. Predator x-over		5.95
TPB Tower of Babel, 160-page		12.95
TPB Divided We Fall (2002)		17.95
TPB A League of One, CsM (2002)		14.95
TPB Terra Incognita (2002)		12.95
JLA Showcase 80-pg Giant #1		4.95
TPB The Golden Perfect		12.95
TPB Riddle of the Beast		14.95
TPB The Obsidian Age, Vol.1		12.95
TPB The Obsidian Age, Vol.2		12.95
Spec. JLA: Workweek		6.95

JLA Ann. #3 © DC Comics, Inc.

JLA: ACT OF GOD
Nov., 2000
1 (of 3) Elseworlds,48-page 4.95
2 powers gone,48-page 4.95
3 concl.,48-page 4.95

JLA: AGE OF WONDER
April 2003
1 (of 2) Elseworlds 5.95
2 concl. 5.95

JLA: BLACK BAPTISM
March, 2001
1 (of 4) F:Faust 2.50
2 F:Faust 2.50
3 V:Daiblos 2.50
4 concl. 2.50

JLA: CREATED EQUAL
Feb., 2000
1 FaN,KM,JRu,Elseworlds 5.95
2 FaN,KM,JRu. 5.95

JLA: DESTINY
June, 2002
1 (of 4) TMd,48-pg. 5.95
2 JAr(s),TMd, Elseworlds. 5.95
3 JAr(s),TMd,Luthor,Mongul. 5.95
4 JAr(s),TMc,concl. 5.95

JLA: GATEKEEPER
Oct., 2001
1 (of 3) TT, 48-page. 4.95
2 TT, 48-page 4.95
3 TT,48-page, concl. 4.95

JLA: INCARNATIONS
May, 2001
1 (of 7) JOs,VS,V:Wotan 3.50
2 JOs,VS,Batman joins 3.50
3 JOs,VS,V:Lex Luthor, Kobra . . . 3.50
4 JOs,VS,F:Aquaman 3.50
5 JOs,VS,F:Aquaman 3.50
6 JOs,VS,two tales 3.50
7 JOs,VS,concl. 3.50

JLA/JSA
Nov., 2002
1 Secret files, Team-up, prelude,64-pg. 4.95
TPB Virtue and Vice 17.95

JLA: PARADISE LOST
Nov., 1997
1 (of 3) MMr,AOI,F:Zauriel 2.25
2 MMr,AOI,F:Zauriel,Martian Manhunter 2.25

JLA: SCARY MONSTERS
Mar. 2003
1 (of 6) CCI,V:Ancient spirits 2.50
2 CCI 2.50
3 CCI,ancient evil 2.50

Comics Values Annual — DC — JLA–Jonah Hex

4 CCI,Kishana secret 2.50
5 CCI,Kishana's origin 2.50
6 CCI,concl. 2.50

JLA/THE SPECTRE: SOUL WAR
Jan. 2003
1 (of 2) DBk,PNe 5.95
2 DBk,PNe 5.95

JLA/TITANS
1998
1 (of 3) JLA vs. Teen Titans 3.00
2 .... 3.00
3 conclusion, New Titans 3.00
TPB The Technis Imperative 12.95

JLA: WORLD WITHOUT GROWN-UPS
June, 1998
1 (of 2) I:Young Justice 48pg 5.00
2 Young Justice, concl. 5.00
TPB World Without Grown-Ups... 10.00

JLA: YEAR ONE
Nov., 1997
1 (of 12) MWa,BAu,BKi,48pg. 6.00
2 MWa,BAu,BKi,V:Vandal Savage . 4.00
3 MWa,BAu,BKi. 4.00
4 MWa,BAu,BKi,V:Locus 4.00
5 MWa,BAu,BKi,F:Doom Patrol ... 4.00
6 MWa,BAu,BKi,V:Doom Patrol ... 4.00
7 MWa,BAu,BKi,V:Weapon Master 4.00
8 MWa,BAu,BKi,MIB,V:Locus..... 4.00
9 MWa,BAu,BKi,MIB,V:Locus..... 3.00
10 MWa,BAu,BKi,MIB,V:Locus 3.00
11 MWa,BAu,BKi,MIB 3.00
12 MWa,BAu,BKi,MIB, concl. 3.50
TPB Year One 20.00

JLA-Z
Sept. 2003
1 (of 3) handbook 2.50
2 .... 2.50
3 conclusion 2.50

JOHNNY THUNDER
Feb.–March, 1973
1 ATh 25.00
2 GK,MD 15.00
3 ATh,GK,MD,July-Aug., 1973 ... 15.00

JOKER, THE
1975–76
1 IN,DG,A:TwoFace 50.00
2 IN,JL WillieTheWeeper 25.00
3 JL,A:Creeper 25.00
4 JL,A:GreenArrow 20.00
5 .... 20.00
6 V:Sherlock Holmes 20.00
7 IN,A:Luthor 20.00
8 .... 20.00
9 A:Catwoman 25.00
The Devil's Advocate HC GN 24.95
GN 12.95

JOKER, THE: LAST LAUGH
Oct., 2001
1 (of 6) CDi,Oracle vs. villains 3.00
2 CDi,Batman,Riot in the Slab 3.00
3 CDi,F:JLA vs. Joker army 3.00
4 CDi,F:Mr. Mind, Lex Luthor 3.00
5 CDi,Harley Quinn is last hope ... 3.00
6 CDi,Joker's final stand 3.00
Secret Files #1 64-page 6.00

JONAH HEX
1977–85
1 'Vengeance For A Fallen Gladiator' 125.00
2 'The Lair of the Parrot' 60.00
3 'The Fugitive' 50.00
4 'The Day of Chameleon' 50.00
5 'Welcome to Paradise' 50.00
6 'The Lawman'. 35.00
7 'Son of the Apache' 50.00
8 O:Jonah Hex 50.00
9 BWr(c) 40.00
10 GM(c),'Violence at Vera Cruz' . 40.00
11 'The Holdout' 25.00
12 JS(c) 25.00
13 'The Railroad Blaster' 25.00
14 'The Sin Killer'. 25.00
15 'Saw Dust and Slow Death' .. 25.00
16 'The Wyandott Verdict!' 20.00
17 .... 20.00
18 .... 20.00
19 'The Duke of Zarkania!' 20.00
20 'Phantom Stage to William Bend' 20.00
21 'The Buryin'!' 20.00
22 'Requiem For A Pack Rat' ... 20.00
23 'The Massacre of the Celestials!' 20.00
24 'Minister of the Lord' 20.00
25 'The Widow Maker' 20.00
26 'Death Race to Cholera Bend!' 15.00
27 'The Wooden Six Gun!' 15.00
28 'Night of the Savage' 15.00
29 'The Innocent' 15.00
30 O:Jonah Hex 15.00
31 A:Arbee Stoneham 15.00
32 A:Arbee Stoneham 15.00
33 'The Crusader' 15.00
34 'Christmas in an Outlaw Town'. 15.00
35 'The Fort Charlotte Brigade'.. 15.00
36 'Return to Fort Charlotte' 15.00
37 DAy,A:Stonewall Jackson 15.00
38 .... 15.00
39 'The Vow of a Samurai!'. 15.00
40 DAy 15.00
41 DAy,'Two for the Hangman!' . 15.00
42 'Wanted for Murder'. 15.00
43 JKu(c) 15.00
44 JKu(c),DAy 15.00
45 DAy,Jonah gets married 15.00
46 JKu(c),DAy 15.00
47 DAy,'Doom Rides the Sundown Town' 15.00
48 DAy,A:El Diablo 15.00
49 DAy 15.00
50 DAy,'The Hunter' 15.00
51 DAy,'The Comforter' 6.00
52 DAy,'Rescue!' 6.00
53 DAy 6.00
54 .... 6.00
55 'Trail of Blood' 6.00
56 DAy,'The Asylum' 6.00
57 B:El Diablo backup story 6.00
58 DAy,'The Treasure of Catfish Pond' 6.00
59 DAy,'Night of the White Lotus'.. 6.00
60 DAy,'Domain of the Warlord' ... 6.00
61 DAy,'In the Lair of the Manchus!'. 6.00
62 DAy,'The Belly of the Malay Tiger!'. 6.00
63 DAy 6.00
64 DAy,'The Pearl!' 6.00
65 DAy,'The Vendetta!' 6.00
66 DAy 'Requiem for a Coward' .. 6.00
67 DAy,'Deadman's Hand!' 6.00
68 DAy,'Gunfight at Gravesboro!' . 6.00
69 DAy,'The Gauntlet!' 6.00
70 DAy 6.00
71 DAy,'The Masquerades'. 6.00
72 DAy,'Tarantula' 6.00
73 DAy,Jonah in a wheel chair ... 6.00
74 DAy,A:Railroad Bill. 6.00
75 DAy,JAp,A:Railroad Bill 6.00
76 DAy,Jonah goes to Jail 5.00
77 DAy,'Over the Wall' 5.00
78 DAy,Me Ling returns 5.00
79 DAy,'Duel in the Sand'. 5.00
80 A:Turnbull 5.00
81 thru 89 DAy .... @7.00
90 thru 91 .... @7.00
92 .... 20.00

JONAH HEX AND OTHER WESTERN TALES
Sept.–Oct., 1979
1 .... 15.00
2 NA,ATh,SA,GK 18.00
3 Jan.–Feb., 1980 .... 15.00

Joker #1 © DC Comics Inc.

Jonah Hex, Riders of the Worm and Such #4 © DC Comics, Inc.

All comics prices listed are for *Near Mint* condition.

JONAH HEX: RIDERS OF THE WORM AND SUCH
[Mini-Series] DC/Vertigo, 1995
1 R:Ronah Hex 4.00
2 At Wildes West Ranch 4.00
3 History Lesson 4.00
4 I:Autumn Brothers. 4.00
5 V:Big worm, final issue 4.00

JONAH HEX: SHADOWS WEST
DC/Vertigo, 1998
1 (of 3) JLd(s),TTn. 4.00
2 JLd(s),TTn 4.00
3 JLd(s),TTn concl. 4.00

JONAH HEX: TWO-GUN MOJO
DC/Vertigo, 1993
1 B:JLd(s),TT,SG(i),R:Jonah Hex, I:Slow Go Smith 7.00
1a Platinum Ed. 17.00
2 TT,SG(i),D:Slow Go Smith,I:Doc Williams,Wild Bill Hickok. 4.00
3 TT,SG(i),Jonah captured 4.00
4 TT,SG(i),O:Doc Williams 4.00
5 TT,SG(i),V::Doc Williams. 4.00

JONNI THUNDER
Feb., 1985
1 DG,origin issue. 2.25
2 DG 2.25
3 DG 2.25

JONNY DOUBLE
DC/Vertigo, July, 1998
1 . . . . 3.00
2 MCo(c) detective 3.00
3 . . . . 3.00
4 . . . . 3.00
TPB series rep. 12.95

JSA
1999
1 JeR,V:Dark Lord 10.00
2 JeR,AD&Mfm(c),A:Hawkgirl 6.00
3 JeR,AD&MFm(c),V:Dark Lord . . . 5.00
4 JeR,AD&MFm(c),V:Mordru 5.00
5 JeR,AD&MFm(c), ... 5.00
6 . . . . 4.00
7 Darkness Falls, pt.1 . . . . 4.00
8 Darkness Falls, pt.2 . . . . 4.00
9 Darkness Falls, pt.3 . . . . 4.00
10 V:Injustice Society 4.00
11 V:Kobra 4.00
12 V:Kobra,Whitehorse project 4.00
13 Hunt for Extant,pt.1 . . . . 4.00
14 Hunt for Extant,pt.2 . . . . 4.00
15 Hunt for Extant,concl. 4.00
16 Injustice be Done, pt.1. . . . . 4.00
17 Injustice be Done, pt.2. . . . . 4.00
18 Injustice be Done, pt.3. . . . . 4.00
19 Injustice be Done, pt.4. . . . . 4.00
20 Injustice be Done, pt.5. . . . . 4.00
21 Hawkman prologue 4.00
22 Hawkman prologue 4.00
23 Return of Hawkman,pt.1 . . . . . . 4.00
24 Return of Hawkman,pt.2 . . . . . . 4.00
25 Return of Hawkman,pt.3,48-pg. . 4.50
26 Return of Hawkman,pt.4 . . . . . . 3.00
27 F:Captain Marvel,V:Black Adam . 3.00
28 V:Roulette 3.00
29 PSj,Joker:Last Laugh,tie-in 3.00
30 V:Roulette 3.00
31 RgM(c),MakingWaves,A:Batman 3.00
32 RgM(c),Stealing Thunder,prev. . . 3.00
33 RgM(c),Stealing Thunder,pt.1. . . 3.00
34 RgM(c),Stealing Thunder,pt.2. . . 3.00
35 RgM(c),Stealing Thunder,pt.3. . . 3.00
36 RgM(c),Stealing Thunder,pt.4. . . 3.00
37 RgM(c),Thunder,pt.5,40-pg. 3.00
38 RgM(c),F:Rick Tyler 3.00
39 RgM(c),F:Power Girl 3.00
40 RgM(c),Shadower's grandson . . 3.00
41 RgM(c),V:Black Barax 3.00
42 V:Black Barax 3.00
43 F:JSA B.C. 3.00
44 F:Vandal Savage 3.00
45 F:Doctor Fate 3.00
46 Princes of Darkness,pt.1 . . . . . . 3.00
47 Princes of Darkness,pt.2 . . . . . . 3.00
48 Princes of Darkness,pt.3 . . . . . . 3.00
49 Princes of Darkness,pt.4 . . . . . . 3.00
50 Princes of Darkness,concl. 4.50
51 Dr. Fate 3.00
52 F:Black Adam 3.00
53 V:Crimson Avenger 3.00
54 F:Superman,Batman 3.00
Ann.#1 Planet DC. 4.00
Spec.#1 Our Worlds at War,48-pg. . 3.50
Secret Files #1. . . . . 5.00
Secret Files #2, 64-page. 4.95
TPB Darkness Falls, 232-page . . . 19.95
TPB Justice be Done 14.95
TPB The Return of Hawkman . . . 19.95
TPB Fair Play. 14.95
TPB Stealing Thunder 14.95

JSA: ALL-STARS
May 2003
1 (of 8) SaV,past and present 2.50
2 JLb,TSe,F:Hawkgirl 2.50
3 Salem Mass. 2.50
4 F:Stargirl 2.50
5 F:Hourman 2.50
6 F:Dr. Mid-Nite. 2.50
7 40 pg.,BU: Mr. Terrific. 3.50

JSA: THE LIBERTY FILES
Dec., 1999
1 (of 2) Elseworlds. 7.00
2 TyH, concl. 7.00

JSA: THE UNHOLY THREE
Feb. 2003
1 (of 2) Elseworlds. 6.95
2 concl. 6.95

JUDGE DREDD
1994–96
1 R:Judge Dredd. 3.00
2 Silicon Dreams 2.50
3 Terrorists 2.75
4 Mega-City One crisis 2.50
5 Solitary Dredd 2.50
6 V:Richard Magg 2.50
7 . . . . 2.50
8 V:Ministry of Fear 2.50
9 V:Mister Synn. 2.50
10 D:Judge Dredd 2.50
11 Mega-City One Chaos 2.50
12 V:Wally Squad. 2.50
13 Block Wars,pt.1 . . . . 2.50
14 Block Wars,pt.2 . . . . 2.50
15 Block Wars,pt.3 . . . . 2.50
16 R:Judge with a Grudge 2.50
17 F:Judge Cadet Lewis, Nova Scotia 2.50
18 final issue 2.50
Movie Adaptation 5.95

JUDGE DREDD: LEGENDS OF THE LAW
1994–95
1 Organ Donor,pt.1 . . . . 3.00
2 Organ Donor,pt.2 . . . . 2.50
3 Organ Donor,pt.3 . . . . 2.50
4 Organ Donor,pt.4 . . . . 2.50
5 Trial By Gunfire,pt.1 . . . . 2.50
6 Trial By Gunfire,pt.2 . . . . 2.50
7 JHi(c),Trial By Gunfire,pt.3 . . . . 2.50
8 JBy(s),Fall From Grace,pt.1 . . . . 2.50
9 Fall From Grace,pt.2. . . . . 2.50
10 Fall From Grace,pt.3. . . . . 2.50
11 Dredd of Night,pt.1. . . . . 2.50
12 Dredd of Night,pt.2 . . . . 2.50
13 Dredd of Night,pt.3,final issue . . 2.50

JUNK CULTURE
DC/Vertigo, May, 1997
1 (of 2) TMK 2.50
2 (of 2) TMK, Deuces Wild. 2.50

JUST IMAGINE...
July 2001
TPB DC Universe, by StL,Vol.2. . 19.95

Justice #1 © DC Comics, Inc.

JUSTICE, INC.
May-June, 1975
1 AMc,JKu(c),O:Avenger 20.00
2 JK 15.00
3 JK 15.00
4 JK,JKu(c),Nov.–Dec., 1975. . . . . 15.00
[Mini-Series], 1989
1 PerfectBound `Trust & Betrayal' . 4.00
2 PerfectBound 4.00

JUSTICE LEAGUE ADVENTURES
Nov., 2001
1 TTn,based on Cartoon show. . . . 2.50
2 magical cult 2.25
3 travelers from Daxam 2.25
4 World War of the Sexes 2.25
5 Starro Wars 2.25
6 Super-Heroes for sale. 2.25
7 JSon,RBr,Fastest Fax Alive. 2.25
8 Moon used as monster incubator 2.25
9 Stepping Out 2.25

Comics Values Annual — DC — Justice League

10 Superman v. Martian Manhunter		2.25
11 back from the future,F:Atom		2.25
12 F:Mr. Freeze		2.25
13 I:All-Star		2.25
14 F:Aquaman		2.25
15 V:Kanjar-Ro		2.25
16 Hide and Seek		2.25
17 renegade Amazon		2.25
18 F:The Atom		2.25
19 F:Green Lantern		2.25
20 Psycho-Pirates		2.25
21 JOs,Dominators		2.25
22 Shayol		2.25
23 V:Kobra		2.25
24 boy or super-villain		2.25
25 F:Adam Strange		2.25
TPB Justice League Adventures		9.95

JUSTICE LEAGUE AMERICA
(see JUSTICE LEAGUE INTERNATIONAL)

JUSTICE LEAGUE EUROPE
1989–93

1 BS,A:Wonder Woman		4.00
2 BS,Search for Nazi-Killer		3.00
3 BS,A:Jack O'Lantern, Queen Bee		2.50
4 BS,V:Queen Bee		2.50
5 JRu,BS,Metamorpho's Baby, A:Sapphire Starr		2.50
6 BS,V:Injustice League		2.50
7 BS,Teasdale Imperative#2, A:JLA		2.50
8 BS,Teasdale Imperative#4, A:JLA		2.50
9 BS,ANi,A:Superman		2.50
10 BS,V:Crimson Fox		2.50
11 BS,C:DocMagnus&Metal Men		2.50
12 BS,A:Metal Men		2.50
13 BS,V:One-Eyed Cat, contd from JLA #37		2.50
14 I:VCR		2.50
15 BS,B:Extremists Vector saga, V:One-Eyed Cat,A:BlueJay		2.50
16 BS,A:Rocket Reds, Blue Jay		2.50
17 BS,JLI in Another Dimension		2.50
18 BS,Extremists Homeworld		2.50
19 BS,E:Extremist Vector Saga.		2.50

Justice League Europe #11
© DC Comics, Inc.

20 MR,I:Beefeater,V:Kilowog		2.50
21 MR,JRu,New JLE embassy in London,CS,A:Kilowog		2.50
22 MR,JLE's Cat stolen		2.50
23 BS,O:Crimson Fox		2.50
24 BS,Worms in London		2.50
25 BS,V:Worms		2.50
26 BS,V:Starro		2.50
27 BS,JLE V:JLE,A:JLA,V:Starro		2.50
28 BS, JLE V:JLE,A:J'onn J'onzz, V:Starro		2.50
29 BS,Breakdowns #2,V:Global Guardians		2.50
30 Breakdowns#4,V:J.O'Lantern		2.50
31 Breakdowns #6,War of the Gods tie-in		2.50
32 Breakdowns #8,A:Chief(Doom Patrol)		2.50
33 Breakdowns #10,Lobo vs. Despero		2.50
34 Breakdowns #12,Lobo vs.Despero		2.50
35 Breakdowns #14,V:Extremists, D:Silver Sorceress		2.50
36 Breakdowns #16,All Quit		2.50
37 B:New JLE,I:Deconstructo		2.50
38 V:Deconstructo,A:Batman		2.50
39 V:Deconstructo,A:Batman		2.50
40 J:Hal Jordan,A:Metamorpho		2.50
41 A:Metamorpho,Wond.Woman		2.50
42 A:Wonder Woman,V:Echidna		2.50
43 V:Amos Fortune		2.50
44 V:Amos Fortune		2.50
45 Red Winter#1,V:Rocket Reds		2.50
46 Red Winter#2		2.50
47 Red Winter#3,V:Sonar		2.50
48 Red Winter#4,V:Sonar		2.50
49 Red Winter #5,V:Sonar		2.50
50 Red Winter#6,Double-sized, V:Sonar,J:Metamorpho		3.50
Ann.#1 A:Global Guardians		2.50
Ann.#2 MR,CS,ArmageddonPt.7		3.00
Ann.#3 RT(i),Eclipso tie-in		2.75
Justice League Spectacular JLE(c) New Direction		2.50

Becomes:

JUSTICE LEAGUE INTERNATIONAL
[2nd Series]

JUSTICE LEAGUE [INTERNATIONAL]
[1st Series], 1987

1 KM,TA,New Team,I:Max. Lord		8.00
2 KM,AG,A:BlueJay & Silver Sorceress		6.00
3 KM,AG,J:Booster Gold, V:Rocket Lords		5.00
3a Superman Logo		60.00
4 KM,AG,V:Royal Flush		3.00
5 KM,AG,A:The Creeper		3.00
6 KM,AG,A:The Creeper		3.00

Becomes:

JUSTICE LEAGUE INTERNATIONAL
1988–89

7 KM,AG,L:Dr.Fate,Capt.Marvel, J:Rocket Red,Capt.Atom (Double size)		3.00
8 KM,AG,KG,Move to Paris Embassy, I:C.Cobert,B.U.Glob.Guardians		2.50
9 KM,AG,KG,Millennium,Rocket Red-Traitor		2.50
10 KG,KM,AG,A:G.L.Corps, Superman,I:G'Nort		2.50
11 KM,AG,V:Construct,C:Metron		2.50
12 KG,KM,AG,O:Max Lord		2.50
13 KG,AG,A:Suicide Squad		2.50

Justice League International #19
© DC Comics Inc.

14 SL,AG,J:Fire&Ice,L:Ron, I:Manga Kahn		2.50
15 SL,AG,V:Magna Kahn		2.00
16 KM,AG,I:Queen Bee		2.00
17 KM,AG,V:Queen Bee		2.00
18 KM,AG,MPn,A:Lobo,Guy Gardner (bonus book)		3.00
19 KM,JRu,A:Lobo vs.Guy Gardner, J:Hawkman & Hawkwoman		3.00
20 KM,JRu(i),A:Lobo,G.Gardner		2.50
21 KM,JRu(i),A:Lobo vs.Guy Gardner		2.50
22 KM,JRu,Imskian Soldiers		2.50
23 KM,JRu,I:Injustice League		2.50
24 KM,JRu,DoubleSize + Bonus Bk#13,I:JusticeLeagueEurope		4.00
25 KM(c),JRu(i),V:Vampire story		2.50
Ann.#1 BWg,DG,CR		2.50
Ann.#2 BWg,JRu,A:Joker		3.00
Ann.#3 KM(c),JRu,JLI Embassies		2.50
Spec.#1 Mr.Miracle		2.00
Spec.#2,The Huntress		2.95
TPB new beginning,rep.#1-#7		12.95
TPB The Secret Gospel of Maxwell Lord Rep. #8-#12, Ann.#1		12.95

Becomes:

JUSTICE LEAGUE AMERICA
1989–96

26 KM(c),JRu(i),Possessed Blue Beetle		3.00
27 KM(c),JRu,DG(i),'Exorcist', (c)tribute		2.50
28 KM(c),JRu(i), A:Black Hand		2.50
29 KM(c),JRu(i),V:Mega-Death		2.50
30 KM(c),BWg,JRu,J:Huntress, D:Mega-Death		2.50
31 ANi,AH,JRu,Teasdale Imperative #1,N:Fire,Ice,A:JLE		3.00
32 ANi,AH,Teasdale Imperative #3, A:JLE		3.00
33 ANi,AH,GuyGardner vs.Kilowog		2.50
34 ANi,AH,`Club JLI',`A:Aquaman		2.50
35 ANi,JRu,AH,A:Aquaman		2.50
36 Gnort vs. Scarlet Skier		2.50
37 ANi,AH,L:Booster Gold		2.50
38 JRu,AH,R:Desparo,D:Steel		2.50
39 JRu,AH,V:Desparo,D:Mr.Miracle, Robot		2.50
40 AH,Mr.Miracle Funeral		2.50
41 MMc,MaxForce		2.50
42 MMc,J:L-Ron		2.50

All comics prices listed are for *Near Mint* condition. — CVA Page 103

Justice League — DC — Comics Values Annual

43 AH,KG,The Man Who Knew Too Much #1 . . . . 2.50
44 AH,Man Knew Too Much #2 . . . 2.50
45 AH,MJ,JRu,Guy & Ice's 2nd date 2.50
46 Glory Bound #1,I:Gen.Glory. . . 2.50
47 Glory Bound #2,J:Gen.Glory . . . 2.50
48 Glory Bound #3,V:DosUberbot. . 2.50
49 Glory Bound #4 . . . . 2.50
50 Glory Bound #5 (double size). . . 3.00
51 JRu,AH,V:BlackHand, R:Booster Gold. 2.50
52 TVE,Blue Beetle Vs. Guy Gardner A:Batman 2.50
53 Breakdowns #1, A:JLE. 2.50
54 Breakdowns #3, A:JLE. 2.50
55 Breakdowns #5,V:Global Guardians 2.50
56 Breakdowns #7, U.N. revokes JLA charter. 2.50
57 Breakdowns #9,A:Lobo, V:Despero 2.50
58 BS,Breakdowns #11,Lobo Vs.Despero 2.50
59 BS,Breakdowns #13, V:Extremists 2.50
60 KM,TA,Breakdowns #15, End of J.L.A. 2.50
61 DJu,I:Weapons Master,B:New JLA Line-up,I:Bloodwynd 3.00
62 DJu,V:Weapons Master 2.50
63 DJu,V:Starbreaker 2.50
64 DJu,V:Starbreaker 2.50
65 DJu,V:Starbreaker 2.50
66 DJu,Superman V:Guy Gardner . 2.50
67 DJu,Bloodwynd mystery. 2.50
68 DJu,V:Alien Land Baron. 2.50
69 DJu, Doomsday Pt.1-A 10.00
69a 2nd printing 6.00
70 DJu,Funeral for a Friend#1 . . . 6.00
70a 2nd printing 2.50
71 DJu,J:Agent Liberty,Black Condor, The Ray,Wonder Woman 5.00
71a Newsstand ed. 2.50
71b 2nd Printing 2.50
72 DJu,A:Green Arrow,Black Canary,Atom,B:Destiny's Hand . 4.00
73 DJu,Destiny's Hand #2 . . . . 3.00
74 DJu,Destiny's Hand #3 . . . . 2.50
75 DJu,E:Destiny's Hand #4,Martian Manhunter as Bloodwynd 2.50
76 DJu,Blood Secrets#1, V:Weaponmaster 2.50
77 DJu,Blood Secrets#2, V:Weaponmaster 2.50
78 MC,V:The Extremists. 2.50
79 MC,V:The Extremists. 2.50
80 KWe,N:Booster Gold 2.50
81 KWe,A:Captain Atom 2.50
82 KWe,A:Captain Atom 2.50
83 KWe,V:Guy Gardner 2.50
84 KWe,A:Ice 2.50
85 KWe,V:Frost Giants 2.50
86 B:Cults of the Machine. 2.50
87 N:Booster Gold 2.50
88 E:Cults of the Machine. 2.50
89 Judgement Day#1, V:Overmaster. 2.50
90 Judgement Day#4 . . . . 2.50
91 Aftershocks #3 . . . . 2.50
92 Zero Hour,I:Triumph. 2.50
93 Power Girl and child 2.50
94 Scarabus 2.50
95 . . . . 2.50
96 Funeral 2.50
97 I:Judgment 2.50
98 J:Blue Devil, Ice Maiden 2.50
99 V:New Metahumes 2.50
100 GJ,Woj,V:Lord Havok,dbl.size . 4.50
100a Collector's Edition 4.50
101 GJ,Woj,Way of the Warrior,pt.2 . . . . 2.50
102 Way of the Warrior,pt.5 . . . . . . 2.50
103 . . . . 2.50
104 F:Metamorpho 2.50
105 GJ,Woj,Underworld Unleashed tie-in 2.50
106 GJ,Woj,Underworld Unleashed tie-in 2.50
107 GJ,Woj,secret of Power Girl's son 2.50
108 GJ,Woj,The Arcana revealed . . 2.50
109. . . . . 2.50
110 GJ,Woj,V:El Diablo. 2.50
111 GJ,Woj,The Purge,pt.1 (of 3) . . 2.50
112 GJ,Woj,The Purge,pt.2 (of 3) . . 2.50
113 GJ,Woj,The Purge,pt.3 (of 3) . . 2.50
Ann.#4 KM(c),I:JL Antartica 3.50
Ann.#5 MR,KM,DJu,Armageddon . 3.50
Ann.#5a 2nd Printing,silver. 2.50
Ann.#6 DC,Eclipso 3.00
Ann.#7 I:Terrorsmith 3.00
Ann.#8 Elseworlds Story. 3.50
Ann.#9 Year One Annual 4.00
Ann.#10 CPr(s),SCi,NNa,Legends of the Dead Earth. 3.50
Justice League Spectacular DJu, JLA(c) New Direction 2.50
Archives Vol. 4 . . . . 50.00

JUSTICE LEAGUE OF AMERICA: THE NAIL
June, 1998
Elseworlds
1 World without a Superman 5.00
2 AID,MFm,Robin & Batgirl dead . . 5.00
3 AID,MFm,concl. 5.00

JUSTICE LEAGUE INTERNATIONAL
[2nd Regular Series], 1993–94
Prev: Justice League Europe
51 Aztec Cult 2.25
52 V:Aztec Cult. 2.25
53 R:Fox's Husband. 2.25
54 RoR,I:Creator 2.25
55 RoR,A:Creator. 2.25
56 RoR,V:Terrorists 2.25
57 RoR,V:Terrorists 2.25
58 RoR,V:Aliens 2.25
59 RoR,A:Guy Gardner 2.25
60 GJ(s),RoR 2.25
61 GJ(s),V:Godfrey. 2.25
62 GJ(s),N:Metamorpho,V:Godfrey . 2.25
63 GJ(s),In Africa 2.25
64 GJ(s),V:Cadre 2.25
65 JudgmentDay#3,V:Overmaster . 2.25
66 JudgmentDay#6,V:Overmaster . 2.25
67 Aftershock #3. . . . . 2.25
68 Zero Hour, Final Issue 2.25
Ann.#4 Bloodlines#9,I:Lionheart . . 2.75
Ann.#5 . . . . 3.25
Ann.#6 Elseworlds Story. 2.95

JUSTICE LEAGUE [INTERNATIONAL] QUARTERLY
1990–94
1 I:Conglomerate. 4.00
2 MJ(i),R:Mr.Nebula. 3.50
3 V:Extremists,C:Original JLA 3.50
4 KM(c),MR,CR,A:Injustice League. 3.00
5 KM(c),Superhero Attacks 3.00
6 EB,Elongated Man,B.U.Global Guardians,Powergirl,B.Beetle . . 3.00
7 EB,DH,MR.Global Guardians . . . 3.00
8 . . . . 3.00
9 DC,F:Power Girl,Booster Gold . . 3.50
10 F:Flash,Fire & Ice 3.50
11 F:JL Women 3.50
12 F:Conglomerate. 3.50
13 V:Ultraa. 7.00
14 MMi(c),PuK(s),F:Captain Atom,Blue Beetle,Nightshade,Thunderbolt. 3.75
15 F:Praxis. 3.50
16 F:Gen Glory. 3.50
17 Final Issue. 3.50

JUSTICE LEAGUE: A MIDSUMMER'S NIGHTMARE
1996
1 (of 3) MWa(s),FaN,JJ,DaR, ... 5.00
2 MWa(s),FaN,JJ,DaR,Batman & Superman attempt to free other heroes. 4.00
3 MWa&FaN(s), Know-Man's plot revealed, finale. 4.00
TPB Rep. 3 issues 8.95

JUSTICE LEAGUE OF AMERICA
Oct.–Nov., 1960
1 MSy,I&O:Despero 5,500.00
2 MSy,A:Merlin 1,100.00
3 MSy,I&O:Kanjar Ro. 950.00
4 MSy,J:Green Arrow. 600.00
5 MSy,I&O:Dr.Destiny 450.00
6 MSy,Prof. Fortune. 400.00
7 MSy,Cosmic Fun-House 400.00
8 MSy,For Sale-Justice League . 400.00
9 MSy,O:JLA 600.00
10 MSy,I:Felix Faust 400.00
11 MSy,A:Felix Faust 275.00
12 MSy,I&O:Dr Light. 275.00
13 MSy,A:Speedy 275.00
14 MSy,J:Atom 275.00
15 MSy,V:Untouchable Aliens . . 275.00
16 MSy,I:Maestro 250.00
17 MSy,A:Tornado Tyrant 250.00
18 MSy,V:Terrane, Ocana 250.00
19 MSy,A:Dr.Destiny 250.00
20 MSy,V:Metal Being. 250.00
21 MSy,R:JSA,1st S.A Hourman, Dr.Fate. 500.00
22 MSy,R:JSA 450.00

Justice League America #77
© DC Comics, Inc.

23 MSy,I:Queen Bee 200.00
24 MSy,A:Adam Strange 200.00
25 MSy,I:Draad,the Conqueror . . 200.00
26 MSy,A:Despero 200.00
27 MSy,V:I,A:Amazo 200.00
28 MSy,I:Headmaster Mind,
  A:Robin 200.00
29 MSy,I:Crime Syndicate,A:JSA,
  1st S.A. Starman 250.00
30 MSy,V:Crime Syndicate,
  A:JSA. 200.00
31 MSy,J:Hawkman 150.00
32 MSy,I&O:Brain Storm 125.00
33 MSy,I:Endless One 100.00
34 MSy,A:Dr.Destiny,Joker 125.00
35 MSy,A:Three Demons 100.00
36 MSy,A:Brain Storm,
  Handicap story 100.00
37 MSy,A:JSA,x-over,
  1st S.A.Mr.Terrific 150.00
38 MSy,A:JSA,Mr.Terrific 150.00
39 Giant 150.00
40 MSy,A:Shark,Penguin 100.00
41 MSy,I:Key 100.00
42 MSy,A:Metamorpho 90.00
43 MSy,I:Royal Flush Gang 90.00
44 MSy,A:Unimaginable 90.00
45 MSy,I:Shaggy Man 90.00
46 MSy,A:JSA,Blockbuster,Solomon
  Grundy,1st S.A.Sandman . . 150.00
47 MSy,A:JSA,Blockbuster,
  Solomon Grundy 100.00
48 Giant 110.00
49 MSy,A:Felix Faust 75.00
50 MSy,A:Robin 75.00
51 MSy,A:Zatanna,Elong.Man. . . . 75.00
52 MSy,A:Robin,Lord of Time . . . 75.00
53 MSy,A:Hawkgirl 75.00
54 MSy,A:Royal Flush Gang 75.00
55 MSy,A:JSA,E-2 Robin 100.00
56 MSy,A:JSA,E-2 Robin 75.00
57 MSy,Brotherhood 75.00
58 Reprint(giant size). 85.00
59 MSy,V:Impossibles. 50.00
60 MSy,Queen Bee,Batgirl. 60.00
61 MSy,A:Lex Luthor,Penguin . . . 60.00
62 MSy,V:Bulleters 60.00
63 MSy,A:Key. 60.00
64 DD,I:Red Tornado,A:JSA 75.00
65 DD,A:JSA 75.00
66 DD,A:Demmy Gog 60.00
67 MSy,Giant reprints 75.00
68 DD,V:Choas Maker 60.00
69 DD,L:Wonder Woman 60.00
70 DD,A:Creeper 60.00
71 DD,L:J'onn J'onzz 60.00
72 DD,A:Hawkgirl 60.00
73 DD,A:JSA 60.00
74 DD,D:Larry Lance,A:JSA 60.00
75 DD,J:Black Canary 60.00
76 Giant,MA,two page pin-up 60.00
77 DD,A:Joker,L:Snapper Carr . . . 40.00
78 DD,R:Vigilante 40.00
79 DD,A:Vigilante 40.00
80 DD,A:Tomar-Re,Guardians. . . . 40.00
81 DD,V:Jest-Master. 40.00
82 DD,A:JSA 35.00
83 DD,A:JSA,Spectre 45.00
84 DD,Devil in Paradise 35.00
85 Giant reprint. 50.00
86 DD,V:Zapper 35.00
87 DD,A:Zatanna,I:Silver
  Sorceress,Blue Jay. 40.00
88 DD,A:Mera. 40.00
89 DD,A:Harlequin Ellis,
  (i.e. Harlan Ellison) 40.00
90 CI(c),MA(ci),DD,V:Pale People. 40.00
91 DD,A:JSA,V:Solomon Grundy . 40.00
92 DD,A:JSA,V:Solomon Grundy . 40.00
93 DD:A:JSA, (giant size) 40.00
94 DD,NA,O:Sandman,rep. . . . .

Justice League of America #35
© DC Comics Inc.

Adventure #40 . . . . 125.00
95 DD,rep.More Fun Comics #67,
  All American Comics #25 . . . 50.00
96 DD,I:Starbreaker 40.00
97 DD,MS,O:JLA 35.00
98 DD,A:Sargon,Gold.Age reps . . 40.00
99 DD,G.A. reps. 40.00
100 DD,A:JSA,Metamorpho,
  R:7 Soldiers of Victory 50.00
101 DD,A:JSA,7 Soldiers 35.00
102 DD,DG,A:JSA,7 Soldiers
  D:Red Tornado. 35.00
103 DD,DG,Halloween issue,
  A:Phantom Stranger 25.00
104 DD,DG,A:Shaggy Man,
  Hector Hammond. 25.00
105 DD,DG,J:ElongatedMan. 25.00
106 DD,DG,J:RedTornado. 25.00
107 DD,DG,I:Freedom Fighters,
  A:JSA. 30.00
108 DD,DG,A:JSA,
  Freedom Fighters 30.00
109 DD,DG,L:Hawkman 30.00
110 DD,DG,A:John Stewart,
  Phantom Stranger 50.00
111 DD,DG,I:Injustice Gang 50.00
112 DD,DG,A:Amazo 50.00
113 DD,DG,A:JSA 50.00
114 DD,DG,A:SnapperCarr. 50.00
115 DD,FMc,A:J'onn J'onzz 50.00
116 DD,FMc,I:Golden Eagle 50.00
117 DD,FMc,R:Hawkman 15.00
118 DD,FMc 15.00
119 DD,FMc,A:Hawkgirl 15.00
120 DD,FMc,A:Adam Strange. . . 15.00
121 DD,FMc,W:Adam Strange . . 15.00
122 DD,FMc,JLA casebook story
  V:Dr.Light 15.00
123 DD,FMc,A:JSA. 17.00
124 DD,FMc,A: JSA 17.00
125 DD,FMc,A:Two-Face 15.00
126 DD,FMc,A:Two-Face 15.00
127 DD,FMc,V:Anarchist. 15.00
128 DD,FMc,J:W.Woman 15.00
129 DD,FMC,D:RedTornado 15.00
130 DD,FMc,O:JLASatellite 15.00
131 DD,FMc,V:Queen Bee,Sonar . 15.00
132 DD,FMc,A:Supergirl 15.00
133 DD,FMc,A:Supergirl 15.00
134 DD,FMc,A:Supergirl 15.00
135 DD,FMc,A:Squad.of Justice . . 15.00
136 DD,FMc,A:E-2Joker. 17.00
137 DD,FMc,Superman vs.
  Capt. Marvel. 25.00

138 NA(c),DD,FMc,A:Adam
  Strange 15.00
139 NA(c),DD,FMc,A:AdamStrange,
  Phantom Stranger,doub.size. . 16.00
140 DD,FMc,Manhunters 16.00
141 DD,FMc,Manhunters 16.00
142 DD,FMc,F:Aquaman,Atom,
  Elongated Man 16.00
143 DD,FMc,V:Injustice Gang . . . 16.00
144 DD,FMc,O:JLA. 16.00
145 DD,FMc,A:Phant.Stranger . . . 16.00
146 J:Red Tornado,Hawkgirl 16.00
147 DD,FMc,A:Legion. 16.00
148 DD,FMc,A:Legion. 16.00
149 DD,FMc,A:Dr.Light. 16.00
150 DD,FMc,A:Dr.Light 16.00
151 DD,FMc,A:Amos Fortune . . . 15.00
152 DD,FMc. 15.00
153 GT,FMc,I:Ultraa 15.00
154 MK(c),DD,FMc. 15.00
155 DD,FMc. 15.00
156 DD,FMc. 15.00
157 DD,FMc,W:Atom 15.00
158 DD,FMc,A:Ultraa 15.00
159 DD,FMc,A:JSA,Jonah Hex,
  Enemy Ace. 10.00
160 DD,FMc,A:JSA,Jonah Hex,
  Enemy Ace. 10.00
161 DD,FMc,J:Zatanna. 10.00
162 DD,FMc. 10.00
163 DD,FMc,V:Mad Maestro 10.00
164 DD,FMc,V:Mad Maestro 10.00
165 DD,FMc. 10.00
166 DD,FMc,V:Secret Society. . . . 10.00
167 DD,FMc,V:Secret Society. . . . 10.00
168 DD,FMc,V:Secret Society. . . . 10.00
169 DD,FMc,A:Ultraa 10.00
170 DD,FMc,A:Ultraa 10.00
171 DD,FMc,A:JSA,D:Mr.Terrific . 10.00
172 DD,FMc,A:JSA,D:Mr.Terrific . 10.00
173 DD,FMc,A:Black Lightning . . 10.00
174 DD,FMc,A:Black Lightning . . 10.00
175 DD,FMc,V:Dr.Destiny. 10.00
176 DD,FMc,V:Dr.Destiny 7.00
177 DD,FMc,V:Desparo 7.00
178 JSn(c),DD,FMc,V:Desparo . . . 7.00
179 JSn(c),DD,FMc,J:Firestorm . . 7.00
180 JSn(c),DD,FMc,J:Satin Satan . 7.00
181 DD,FMc,L:Gr.Arrow,V:Star . . . 8.00
182 DD,FMc,A:Green Arrow,
  V:Felix Faust 8.00
183 JSn(c),DD,FMc,A:JSA,
  NewGods. 8.00
184 GP,FMc,A:JSA,NewGods. . . . 8.00
185 JSn(c),GP,FMc,A:JSA,
  New Gods 5.00
186 FMc,GP,V:Shaggy Man 5.00
187 DH,FMc,N:Zatanna 5.00
188 DH,FMc,V:Proteus 5.00
189 BB(c),RB,FMc,V:Starro 5.00
190 BB(c),RB,LMa,V:Starro 5.00
191 RB,V:Amazo 5.00
192 GP,O:Red Tornado 5.00
193 GP,RB,JOy,I:AllStarSquad . . . 5.00
194 GP,V:Amos Fortune 4.00
195 GP,A:JSA,V:Secret Society . . 4.00
196 GP,RT,A:JSA,V:Secret Soc. . . 4.00
197 GP,RT,KP,A:JSA,V:Secret
  Society. 4.00
198 DH,BBr,A:J.Hex,BatLash 4.00
199 GP(c),DH,BBr,A:Jonah Hex,
  BatLash 4.00
200 GP,DG,BB (1st Batman),PB,TA,
  BBr,GK,CI,JAp,JKu,Anniv.,A:Adam
  Strange,Phantom Stranger,
  J:Green Arrow 6.00
201 GP(c),DH,A:Ultraa 3.00
202 GP(c),DH,BBr,JLA in Space . . 3.00
203 GP(c),DH,RT,V:Royal
  Flush Gang 3.00
204 GP(c),DH,RT,V:R.FlushGang . . 3.00

Justice League–Kamandi — DC — Comics Values Annual

Justice League of America #242
© DC Comics, Inc.

205 GP(c),DH,RT,V:R.FlushGang . . 3.00
206 DH,RT,A:Demons 3 . . . . 3.00
207 GP(c),DH,RT,A:All Star
   Squadron,JSA 4.00
208 GP(c),DH,RT,A:All Star
   Squadron,JSA 4.00
209 GP(c),DH,RT,A:All Star
   Squadron,JSA 3.00
210 RB,RT,JLA casebook #1 . . . . . 3.00
211 RB,RT,JLA casebook #2. . . . . . 3.00
212 GP(c),RB,PCu,RT,c.book #3 . . 3.00
213 GP(c),DH,RT 3.00
214 GP(c),DH,RT,I:Siren Sist.h'd . . 3.00
215 GP(c),DH,RT 3.00
216 DH. 3.00
217 GP(c),RT(i) 3.00
218 RT(i),A:Prof.Ivo 3.00
219 GP(c),RT(i),A:JSA 4.00
220 GP(c),RT,O:Bl.Canary,A:JSA . 4.00
221 Beasts #1 . . . . 3.00
222 RT(i),Beasts #2 . . . . 3.00
223 RT(i),Beasts #3 . . . . 3.00
224 DG(i),V:Paragon 3.00
225 V:Hellrazor. 3.00
226 FMc(i),V:Hellrazor 3.00
227 V:Hellrazor,I:Lord Claw 3.00
228 GT,AN,R:J'onn J'onzz,War of
   the Worlds,pt.1. . . . . 3.00
229 War of the Worlds,pt.2 . . . . 3.00
230 War of the Worlds conc. 3.00
231 RB(i),A:JSA,Supergirl. 3.00
232 A:JSA Supergirl 3.00
233 New JLA takes over book,
   B:Rebirth,F:Vibe. 3.00
234 F:Vixen 3.00
235 F:Steel. 3.00
236 E:Rebirth,F:Gypsy. 3.00
237 A:Superman,Flash,WWoman . 3.00
238 A:Superman,Flash,WWoman . 3.00
239 V:Ox 3.00
240 MSy,TMd. 3.00
241 GT,V:Amazo 3.00
242 GT,V:Amazo,Mask(Toy tie-in)
   insert 3.00
243 GT,L:Aquaman,V:Amazo 3.00
244 JSon,Crisis,A:InfinityInc,JSA . . 4.00
245 LMc,Crisis,N:Steel 4.00
246 LMc,JLA leaves Detroit 3.00
247 LMc,JLA returns to old HQ. . . . 3.00
248 LMc,F:J'onn J'onzz 3.00
249 LMc,Lead-in to Anniv. 3.00
250 LMc,Anniv.,A:Superman,
   Green Lantern,Green Arrow,
   Black Canary,R:Batman 3.00
251 LMc,V:Despero 3.00
252 LMc,V:Despero,N:Elongated
   Man 3.00
253 LMc,V:Despero 3.00
254 LMc,V:Despero 3.00
255 LMc,O:Gypsy. 3.00
256 LMc,Gypsy 3.00
257 LMc,A:Adam,L:Zatanna 3.00
258 LMc,Legends x-over,D:Vibe . . . 3.00
259 LMc,Legends x-over 3.00
260 LMc,Legends x-over,D:Steel . . 6.00
261 LMc,Legends,final issue. 8.00
Ann.#1 DG(i),A:Sandman 3.50
Ann.#2 I:NewJLA 3.00
Ann.#3 MG(i),Crisis 3.00

JUSTICE LEAGUES
Jan., 2001
Pt.1 Justice Leagues #1,GP(c) . . . 2.50
Pt.2 Just.League of Amazons #1. . . 2.50
Pt.3 Just.League of Atlantis #1 . . . 2.50
Pt.4 Just.League of Arkham #1. . . . 2.50
Pt.5 Just.League of Aliens #1 . . . . 2.50
Pt.6 Just.League of America #1 . . . 2.50

Justice League Task Force #16
© DC Comics, Inc.

JUSTICE LEAGUE TASK FORCE
1993–96
1 F:Mart.Manhunter,Nightwing,
   Aquaman,Flash,Gr.Lantern. . . . 2.25
2 V:Count Glass,Blitz. 2.25
3 V:Blitz,Count Glass. 2.25
4 DG,F:Gypsy,A:Lady Shiva 2.25
5 JAI,Knightquest:Crusade,F:Bronze
   Tiger,Green Arrow,Gypsy 2.25
6 JAI,Knightquest:Search,F:Bronze
   Tiger,Green Arrow,Gypsy 2.25
7 PDd(s),F:Maxima,Wonder Woman,
   Dolphin,Gypsy,Vixen,V:Luta . . 2.25
8 PDd(s),SaV,V:Amazons 2.25
9 GrL,V:Wildman 2.25
10 Purification Plague#1 . . . . 2.25
11 Purification Plague#2 . . . . 2.25
12 Purification Plague#3 . . . . 2.25
13 Jugdement Day#2,
   V:Overmaster. 2.25
14 Jugdement Day#5,
   V:Overmaster. 2.25
15 Aftershocks #2. . . . . 2.25
16 Zero Hour,A:Triumph 2.25
17 Savage 2.25
18 Savage 2.25
19 Martian Manhunter. 2.25
20 Savage Legacy,pt.4 . . . . 2.25
21 F:Martian Manhunter. 2.25
22 F:Triumph 2.25
23 V:Vampire 2.25
24 F:Von Mauler, Gypsy 2.25
25 A:Impulse & Damage, V:Mystek. 2.25
26 Cut Day. 2.25
27 F:L-Ron. 2.25
28 Triumph vs. Manhunter 2.25
29 A:Glenn Gammeron. 2.25
30 Underworld Unleashed tie-in . . 2.25
31 Despero on trial. 2.25
32 Despero vs. terrorists. 2.25
33 . . . . 2.25
34 On Earth, or Skartaris? 2.25
35 A:Warlord Travis Morgan 2.25

JUSTICE RIDERS
1999
1-shot, Elseworlds 7.00

JUSTICE SOCIETY OF AMERICA
[Limited Series]
April–Nov., 1991
1 B:Veng.From Stars,A:Flash. 3.00
2 A:BlackCanary,V:Solomon Grundy,
   C:G.A.Green Lantern. 2.50
3 A:G.A.Green Lantern,Black Canary,
   V:Sol.Grundy 2.50
4 A:G.A.Hawkman,C:G.A.Flash . . 2.50
5 A:G.A.Hawkman,Flash 2.50
6 FMc(i),A:Bl.Canary,G.A.Gr.Lantern,
   V:Sol.Grundy,V.Savage. 2.50
7 JSA united,V:Vandal Savage. . . . 2.50
8 E:Veng.FromStar,V:V.Savage,
   Solomon Grundy 2.50
Spec.#1 DR,MG,End of JSA. 2.50

[Regular Series], 1992–93
1 V:The New Order 2.50
2 V:Ultra Gen 2.50
3 R:Ultra-Humanite 2.50
4 V:Ultra-Humanite 2.50
5 V:Ultra-Humanite 2.50
6 F:Johnny Thunderbolt. 2.50
7 ..Or give me Liberty 2.50
8 Pyramid Scheme 2.50
9 V:Kulak. 2.50
10 V:Kulak,final issue 2.50
TPB Justice Society
   Returns (2003) 19.95

JUST IMAGINE...
July, 2001
GN Aquaman, by StL & SMc 5.95
GN Batman, by StL & JKu 5.95
GN Catwoman, by StL & CBa. . . . 5.95
GN Crisis, by StL 5.95
GN The Flash, by StL & KM 5.95
GN Green Lantern, by StL & DGb. . 5.95
GN The JLA, by StL & JOy 5.95
GN Robin, by StL & JBy. 5.95
GN Sandman, by StL & WS 5.95
GN Shazam!, by StL & GFr. 5.95
GN Superman, by StL & JB 5.95
GN Wonder Woman, by StL & JLe . 5.95
GN Just Imagine Secret Files 4.95
TPB The DC Universe, by StL . . . 19.95

KAMANDI, THE LAST BOY ON EARTH
Oct.–Nov., 1972
1 JK,O:Kamandi 75.00
2 JK 40.00

CVA Page 106 — All comics prices listed are for *Near Mint* condition.

DC — Kamandi–Lab Rats

Kamandi, The Last Boy on Earth #22
© DC Comics, Inc.

3 JK 40.00
4 JK,I:Prince Tuftan 30.00
5 JK 30.00
6 JK 20.00
7 JK 20.00
8 JK 20.00
9 JK 20.00
10 JK 20.00
11 JK 15.00
12 JK 15.00
13 thru 24 JK .... @15.00
25 thru 28 JK .... @12.00
29 A:Superman 20.00
30 JK 12.00
31 .... 12.00
32 Double size 15.00
33 thru 57 .... @12.00
58 A:Karate Kid 12.00
59 JSn,A:Omac, Sept.–Oct,1978 . 15.00

KAMANDI: AT EARTH'S END
[Mini-Series], 1993
1 R:Kamandi 2.50
2 V:Kingpin,Big Q 2.50
3 A:Sleeper Zom,Saphira 2.50
4 A:Superman 2.50
5 A:Superman,V:Ben Boxer 2.50
6 final issue 2.50

KARATE KID
March-April, 1976
1 I:Iris Jacobs,A:Legion 15.00
2 A:Major Disaster 8.00
3 thru 10 .... @8.00
11 A:Superboy/Legion 8.00
12 A:Superboy/Legion 8.00
13 A:Superboy/Legion 8.00
14 A:Robin 8.00
15 July-Aug., 1978 .... 8.00

KENTS, THE
1997
1 (of 12) JOs(s),TT,MiB 3.00
2 JOs(s),TT,MiB, tragedy strikes . 3.00
3 JOs,TT,MiB,Jed & Nate Kent .. 3.00
4 JOs,TT,MiB,Bleeding Kansas, concl. 3.00
5 JOs,TT,Brother vs.Brother pt.1 . 3.00
6 JOs,TT,Brother vs.Brother pt.2 . 3.00
7 JOs,TT,MiB,Quantrill, Wild

Bill Hickcock 3.00
8 JOs, ... 3.00
9 JOs,TMd,To the Stars by Hard Ways,pt.1 .... 3.00
10 JOs,TMd,To the Stars,pt.2 .. 3.00
11 JOs,TMd,To the Stars,pt.3 .. 3.00
12 JOs,TMd,To the Stars,pt.4 .. 3.00
TPB The Kents, rep. 19.95

KID ETERNITY
1991
1 GMo(s),DFg,O:Kid Eternity ... 5.50
2 GMo(s),DFg,A:Mr.Keeper 5.50
3 GMo(s),DFg,True Origin revealed, final issue. 5.50

KID ETERNITY
DC/Vertigo, 1993–94
1 B:ANo(s),SeP,R:Kid Eternity, A:Mdm.Blavatsky,Hemlock 2.75
2 SeP,A:Sigmund Freud,Carl Jung, A:Malocchio 2.50
3 SeP,A:Malocchio,I:Dr.Pathos .. 2.25
4 SeP,A:Neal Cassady 2.25
5 SeP,In Cyberspace 2.25
6 SeP,A:Dr.Pathos,Marilyn Monroe 2.25
7 SeP,I:Infinity 2.25
8 SeP,In Insane Asylum 2.25
9 SeP,Asylum,A:Dr.Pathos 2.25
10 SeP,Small Wages 2.25
11 ANi(s),I:Slap 2.25
12 SeP,A:Slap 2.25
13 SeP,Date in Hell,pt.1 ..... 2.25
14 SeP,Date in Hell,pt.2 ..... 2.25
15 SeP,Date in Hell,pt.3 ..... 2.25
16 SeP,The Zone , ... 2.25

KILL YOUR BOYFRIEND
DC/Vertigo, 1995, 1999
GNv PBd(c) (1995) 4.95
1-shot GMo (1999) 6.00

KINGDOM, THE
1998
1 (of 2) MWa,AOl 5.00
2 MWa,MZ,JhB,V:Gog 4.00
Spec.#1 Kid Flash 2.25
Spec.#1 Offspring 2.25
Spec.#1 Nightstar 2.25
Spec.#1 Planet Krypton 2.25
Spec.#1 Son of the Bat 2.25
DirectCurrents Spec .... free
TPB 14.95

KINGDOM COME
Elseworlds 1996
1 MWa,AxR 8.00
2 MWa,AxR,R:JLA 7.00
3 MWa,AxR,A:Capt. Marvel 7.00
4 MWa,AxR, final issue 7.00
TPB MWa,AxR, rep. 15.00

KISSYFUR
1989
1 .... 2.25

KOBALT
DC/Milestone, 1994–95
1 JBy(c),I:Kobalt,Richard Page . 3.00
2 .... 2.50
3 I:Slick,Volt,Red Light 2.50
4 I:Slick,Volt,Red Light 2.50
5 Richard Page 2.50
6 Volt 2.50

Kobalt #10 © DC Comics Inc.

7 Static 2.50
8 A:Hardward 2.50
9 .... 2.50
10 A:Harvest 2.50
11 V:St.Cloud 2.50
12 V:Rabid 2.50
13 V:Harvester 2.50
14 Long Hot Summer, V:Harvester . 3.00
15 Long Hot Summer 3.00

KOBRA
1976–77
1 JK,I:Kobra & Jason Burr 15.00
2 I:Solaris 8.00
3 KG/DG,TA,V:Solaris 8.00
4 V:Servitor 8.00
5 RB/FMc,A:Jonny Double 8.00
6 MN/JRu,A:Jonny Double 8.00
7 MN/JRu,A:Jonny Double last iss. 8.00

KONG THE UNTAMED
June-July, 1975
1 AA,BWr(c) 15.00
2 AA,BWr(c) 12.00
3 AA 10.00
4 .... 10.00
5 Feb.–March, 1976 .... 10.00

KORAK, SON OF TARZAN
1975
(Prev. published by Gold Key)
46 JKu(c),B:Carson of Venus .. 25.00
47 JKu(c) 10.00
48 JKu(c) 10.00
49 JKu(c),Origin of Korak ... 15.00
50 thru 59 JKu(c),1975 ...... 10.00
Becomes:

TARZAN FAMILY

KRYPTON CHRONICLES
1981
1 CS,A:Superman 5.00
2 CS,A:Black Flame 4.00
3 CS,O:Name of Kal-El 4.00

LAB RATS
April, 2002
1 by the one and only JBy 7.00
1a 2nd printing 4.50
2 JBy, amusement park 6.00

All comics prices listed are for *Near Mint* condition.

Lab Rats–Legends / DC / Comics Values Annual

2a 2nd printing 4.50
3 JBy, ... 2.50
4 JBy,time travel,pt.1 .... 2.50
5 JBy,time travel,pt.2 .... 2.50
6 JBy,time travel,pt.3,A:Superman . 2.50
7 JBy,interplanetary adventure.... 2.50
8 JBy, final issue 2.50

LAST DAYS OF THE JUSTICE SOCIETY
1986
1 .... 5.00

LAST ONE
DC/Vertigo, 1993
1 B:JMD(s),DSw,I:Myrwann,Patrick
   Maguire's Story 3.25
2 DSw,Pat's Addiction to Drugs ... 3.00
3 DSw,Pat goes into Coma 3.00
4 DSw,In Victorian age 3.00
5 DSw,Myrwann Memories 3.00
6 E:JMD(s),DSw,final Issue 3.00

L.A.W.
1999
1 (of 6) BL,DG,Living Assault
   Weapons 2.50
2 BL,DG 2.50
3 BL,DG 2.50
4 BL,DG,rescue JLA 2.50
5 BL,DG 2.50
6 BL,DG,conclusion 2.50

LAZARUS FIVE
May, 2000
1 (of 5) THy,F:Inquisitors 2.50
2 THy,F:Hank the Swede......... 2.50
3 THy,The Decayed Ones,Digit ... 2.50
4 THy,The Decayed Ones 2.50
5 THy,conclusion 2.50

LEADING COMICS
Winter, 1941–42
1 O:Seven Soldiers of Victory,
   B:Crimson Avenger,Green Arrow
   & Speedy,Shining Knight,
   A:The Dummy 6,500.00
2 MMe,V:Black Star 2,100.00
3 V:Dr. Doome 1,600.00
4 'Seven Steps to Conquest',

Leading #4 © DC Comics, Inc.

V:The Sixth Sense....... 1,200.00
5 'The Miracles that Money
   Couldn't Buy'.............. 1,200.00
6 'The Treasure that Time
   Forgot'..................... 1,000.00
7 The Wizard of Wisstark 1,000.00
8 Seven Soldiers Go back
   through the Centuries ... 1,000.00
9 V:Mr. X,Chameleon of Crime 1,000.00
10 King of the Hundred Isles . 1,000.00
11 'The Hard Luck Hat!' 700.00
12 'The Million Dollar
   Challenge!'.............. 700.00
13 'The Trophies of Crime' 700.00
14 'Bandits from the Book' 700.00
15 (fa) 250.00
16 thru 22 (fa) .... @100.00
23 (fa),I:Peter Porkchops 250.00
24 thru 30 (fa) .... @100.00
31 (fa) 75.00
32 (fa) 75.00
33 (fa) 75.00
34 thru 40 (fa) .... @75.00
41 (fa),Feb.–March, 1950 .... 75.00

LEAGUE OF JUSTICE
1996
1 (of 2) Elseworlds............ 5.95
2 (of 2) Elseworlds............ 5.95

LEAVE IT TO BINKY
Feb.–March, 1948
1 Teen-age stories 300.00
2 .... 150.00
3 .... 75.00
4 .... 75.00
5 thru 14 .... @50.00
15 SM,Scribbly 55.00
16 thru 60 .... @40.00
61 thru 71 .... @35.00

LEGEND OF THE HAWKMAN
July, 2000
1 BRa,Hawkman & Hawkgirl 4.95
2 BRa,V:Thanagarian zealots 4.95
3 BRa,concl. 4.95

LEGEND OF THE SHIELD
DC/Impact, 1991–92
1 I:Shield,V:Mann-X,I:Big Daddy,
   Lt.Devon Hall,Arvell Hauser,Mary
   Masterson-Higgins 2.50
2 Shield in Middle East 2.50
3 Shield Goes A.W.O.L.......... 2.50
4 Hunt for Shield 2.50
5 A:Shield's Partner Dusty....... 2.50
6 O:Shield, V:The Jewels........ 2.50
7 Shield/Fly team-up 2.50
8 V:Weapon 2.50
9 Father Vs. Son 2.50
10 Arvell Hauser................ 2.50
11 inc,Trading cards 2.50
12 .... 2.50
13 Shield court martialed 2.50
14 Mike Barnes becomes Shield... 2.50
15 Shield becomes a Crusader.... 2.50
16 V:Soviets,final issue.......... 2.50
Ann.#1 Earthquest,w/trading card . 2.25

LEGEND OF WONDER WOMAN
1986
1 Return of Atomia............ 4.00

2 A:Queens Solalia & Leila 3.50
3 Escape from Atomia 3.50
4 conclusion 3.50

LEGENDS
1986–87
1 JBy,V:Darkseid 5.00
2 JBy,A:Superman.............. 4.00
3 JBy,I:Suicide Squad 4.00
4 JBy,V:Darkseid 4.00
5 JBy,A:Dr. Fate 4.00
6 JBy,I:Justice League........... 5.00
TPB rep.#1-#6 JBy(c)........... 9.95

LEGENDS OF DANIEL BOONE, THE
Oct., 1955–Jan., 1957
1 .... 750.00
2 .... 500.00
3 thru 8 .... 450.00

LEGENDS OF THE DARK KNIGHT
(see BATMAN)

LEGENDS OF THE DC UNIVERSE
Dec., 1997
1 JeR,VS,PNe,A:Superman, pt.1 . . 3.50
2 JeR,VS,PNe,A:Superman, pt.2 . . 4.00
3 JeR,VS,PNe,A:Superman, pt.3 . . 2.50
4 BML,MD2,VRu,Moments, pt.1. . . 2.50
5 BML,MD2,VRu,Moments, pt.2. . . 2.50
6 DTy,KN,Robin meets Superman . 2.50
7 DON,DG,Peacemakers, pt.1 .... 2.50
8 DON,DG,Peacemakers, pt.2 .... 2.50
9 DON,DG,Peacemakers, pt.3 .... 2.50
10 TyD,KN,F:Batman & Batgirl,pt.1 . 2.50
11 KN,TyD,F:Batman & Batgirl,pt.2 . 2.50
12 CPr(s),Critical Mass,pt.1 ...... 2.50
13 CPr(s),Critical Mass,pt.2 ...... 2.50
14 JK,BR,SR,64-page 5.00
15 RCa,Dark Matters, pt.1 .... 2.50
16 RCa,Dark Matters, pt.2 .... 2.50
17 RCa,Dark Matters, pt.3 .... 2.50
18 MWn(s),JG,F:New Teen Titans. . 2.50
19 RT,F:Impulse 2.50
20 StG(s),MZ,KJ,Trail of the
   Traitor, pt.1................ 2.50
21 StG(s),MZ,KJ,Trail of the
   Traitor, pt.2................ 2.50
22 Transilvane,pt.1 .... 2.50
23 Transilvane,pt.2 .... 2.50
24 StP,The Jump,pt.1 .... 2.50
25 StP,The Jump,pt.2 .... 2.50
26 TVE,JRu,Aquaman&Joker,pt.1. . 2.50
27 TVE,JRu,Aquaman&Joker,pt.2. . 2.50
28 GK,KJ,pt.1.................. 2.50
29 GK,KJ,pt.2,F:Traitor.......... 2.50
30 CPr(s),Wonder Woman,pt.1 .... 2.50
31 CPr(s),Wonder Woman,pt.2 .... 2.50
32 CPr(s),Wonder Woman,pt.3 .... 2.50
33 JMD,MZi,VcL,F:Spectre,pt.1 ... 2.50
34 JMD,MZi,VcL,F:Spectre,pt.2 ... 2.50
35 JMD,MZi,VcL,F:Spectre,pt.3 ... 2.50
36 JMD,MZi,VcL,F:Spectre,pt.4 ... 2.50
37 ScK,KJ,Traitor Trilogy,pt.1 .... 2.50
38 ScK,KJ,V:Traitor,pt.2 .... 2.50
39 RGr,Sole Survivor of Earth..... 2.50
40 RGr,Lessons in Time,pt.1...... 2.50
41 RGr,Lessons in Time,pt.2...... 2.50
Giant #1 JKu(c), 80 pg........... 5.00
Spec 3-D Gallery #1 .... 3.00
GN Crisis on Infinite Earths....... 5.00

CVA Page 108   All comics prices listed are for *Near Mint* condition.

LEGENDS OF THE LEGION
Dec., 1997
1 (of 4) BKi,TPe,TNu,O:Ultra Boy . 2.75
2 .... 2.50
3 BKi,TPe,O:Umbra............ 2.50
4 BKi,TPe,O:Star Boy 2.50

LEGENDS OF THE WORLD FINEST
1994
1 WS(s),DIB,V:Silver Banshee,
    Blaze,Tullus,Foil(c).......... 6.00
2 WS(s),DIB,V:Silver Banshee,
    Blaze,Tullus,Foil(c).......... 6.00
3 WS(s),DIB,V:Silver Banshee,
    Blaze,Tullus,Foil(c).......... 6.00
TPB 14.95

L.E.G.I.O.N. '89 #6 © DC Comics, Inc.

L.E.G.I.O.N. '89-94
1989–94
1 BKi,V:Computer Tyrants 6.00
2 BKi,V:Computer Tyrants 3.50
3 BKi,V:Computer Tyrants,
    A:Lobo......................... 3.50
4 BKi,V: Lobo 3.50
5 BKi,J:Lobo(in the rest of the
    series),V:Konis-Biz........... 3.50
6 BKi,V:Konis-Biz 3.50
7 BKi,Stealth vs. Dox............. 3.50
8 BKi,R:Dox 3.50
9 BKi,J:Phase (Phantom Girl)..... 3.00
10 BKi,Stealth vs Lobo 3.00
11 BKi,V:Mr.Stoorr 3.00
12 BKi,V:Emerald Eye 3.00
13 BKi,V:Emerald Eye 3.00
14 BKi,V:Pirates 3.00
15 BKi,V:Emerald Eye 3.00
16 BKi,J:LarGand 3.00
17 BKi,V:Dragon-Ro.............. 3.00
18 BKi,V:Dragon-Ro.............. 3.00
19 V:Lydea,L:Stealth.............. 3.00
20 Aftermath...................... 3.00
21 D:Lyrissa Mallor,V:Mr.Starr ... 3.00
22 V:Mr.Starr 3.00
23 O:R.J.Brande(double sized)... 3.50
24 BKi,V:Khunds 3.00
25 BKi,V:Khunds 3.00
26 BKi,V:Khunds 3.00
27 BKi,J:Lydea Mallor............ 3.00
28 KG,Birth of Stealth's Babies... 3.00
29 BKi,J:Capt.Comet,Marij'n Bek . . 3.00
30 BKi,R:Stealth.................. 3.00
31 Lobo vs.Capt.Marvel 4.00
32 V:Space Biker Gang 3.00
33 A:Ice-Man 3.00
34 MPn,V:Ice Man 3.00
35 Legion Disbanded 3.00
36 Dox proposes to Ignea........ 3.00
37 V:Intergalactic Ninjas 3.00
38 BKi,Lobo V:Ice Man........... 3.00
39 BKi,D:G'odd,V:G'oddSquad ... 3.00
40 BKi,V:Kyaltic Space Station ... 3.00
41 BKi,A:Stealth'sBaby........... 3.00
42 BKi,V:Yeltsin-Beta 3.00
43 BKi,V:Yeltsin-Beta 3.00
44 V:Yeltsin-Beta,C:Gr.Lantern ... 3.00
45 .... 3.00
46 BKi,A:Hal Jordan.............. 3.00
47 BKi,Lobo vs Hal Jordan 3.00
48 BKi,R:Ig'nea................... 3.00
49 BKi,V:Ig'nea................... 3.00
50 BKi,V:Ig'nea,A:Legion'67 ..... 4.00
51 F:Lobo, Telepath............... 3.00
52 BKi,V:Cyborg Skull of Darius ... 3.00
53 BKi,V:Shadow Creature 3.00
54 BKi,V:Shadow Creature 3.00
55 BKi,V:Shadow Beast 3.00
56 BKi,A:Masked Avenger 3.00
57 BKi,Trinity,V:Green Lantern ... 3.00
58 BKi,Trinity#6,A:Green Lantern,
    Darkstar....................... 3.00
59 F:Phase....................... 3.00
60 V:Phantom Riders 3.00
61 Little Party 3.00
62 A:R.E.C.R.U.I.T.S. 3.00
63 A:Superman................... 3.00
64 BKi(c),V:Mr.B................. 3.00
65 BKi(c),V:Brain Bandit.......... 3.00
66 Stealth and Dox name child ... 3.00
67 F:Telepath 3.00
68 .... 3.00
69 .... 3.00
70 Zero Hour, last issue 3.50
Ann.#1 A:Superman,V:Brainiac.... 5.50
Ann.#2 Armageddon 2001 .... 3.50
Ann.#3 Eclipso tie-in. 3.25
Ann.#4 SHa(i),I:Pax 3.75
Ann.#5 Elseworlds story 3.50

LEGION, THE
Oct., 2001
1 DAn,ALa, New era dawns...... 4.00
2 DAn,ALa,F:Oversight Watch 2.50
3 DAn,ALa,new headquarters 2.50
4 DAn,ALa,Footstep Drive Tech. ... 2.50
5 DAn,ALa,Return to Lost Galaxy . 2.50
6 DAn,ALa,Moon & Inhabitants ... 2.50
7 DAn,ALa,V:Ra's Al Ghul 2.50
8 DAn,ALa,V:Ra's Al Ghul 2.50
9 DAn,ALa,Apparition,Ultra-Boy... 2.50
10 DAn,ALa,Robotica to Earth ... 2.50
11 DAn,ALa,F:Robotica 2.50
12 DAn,ALa,F:JLA 2.50
13 DAn,ALa,V:Robotica 2.50
14 DAn,ALa,V:Robotica 2.50
15 DAn,ALa,F:Timber Wolf 2.50
16 DAn,ALa,F:Lone Wolf 2.50
17 DAn,ALa,The Fittest,pt.1 ..... 2.50
18 DAn,ALa,The Fittest,pt.2 ..... 2.50
19 DAn,MFm,Dream Crime,pt.1 ... 2.50
20 DAn,MFm,Dream Crime,pt.2 ... 2.50
21 DAn,MFm,Dream Crime,pt.3 ... 2.50
22 DAn,MFm,Dream Crime,pt.4 ... 2.50
23 DAn,MFm,Dream Crime,pt.5 ... 2.50
24 DAn,ALa,F:Umbra 2.50
25 Foundations,pt.1,48-pg....... 3.95
26 DAn,ALa,Foundations,pt.2 .... 2.50
27 DAn,ALa,Foundations,pt.3 .... 2.50
GN Legion Secret Files 3003 ..... 4.95

LEGION LOST
March, 2000
1 (of 12) DAn,ALa 5.50
2 DAn,ALa,V:Progeny 2.50
3 DAn,ALa,V:Progeny 2.50
4 DAn,ALa,........................ 2.50
5 DAn,ALa,Brainiac 5.1.......... 2.50
6 DAn,ALa,F:Umbra 2.50
7 DAn,ALa,F:Ultra Boy 2.50
8 DAn,ALa,........................ 2.50
9 DAn,ALa........................ 2.50
10 DAn,ALa 2.50
11 DAn,ALA 2.50
12 DAn,ALA conclusion 2.50

LEGIONNAIRES
1992
1 CSp,V:Mano and the Hand,Bagged
    w/SkyBox promo card........ 4.00
1a w/out card 3.00
2 CSp,V:Mano..................... 3.00
3 CSp,I:2nd Emerald Empress.... 3.00
4 CSp,R:Fatal Five 3.00
5 CSp,V:Fatal Five 3.00
6 CSp,V:Fatal Five 2.50
7 AH,V:Devil Fish 2.50
8 CDo,F:Brainiac 5 .... 2.50
9 CSp,A:Kid Quantum 2.50
10 CSp,A:Kono,I:2nd Kid Pyscho . 2.50
11 CSp,J:2nd Kid Pyscho 2.50
12 CSp,A:2nd Kid Pyscho........ 2.50
13 FFo,V:Grimbor 2.50
14 V:Grimbor 2.50
15 V:Grimbor 2.50
16 In Time 2.50
17 End of An Era #1 .... 2.50
18 Zero Hour, LSH 2.50
19 Problems...................... 2.50
20 Moon Battle................... 2.50
21 and 22 .... @2.50
23 Saturday Night................ 2.50
24 F:Triad........................ 2.50
25 F:Chameleon.................. 2.50
26 F:Apparition, Ultra Boy....... 2.50
27 V:The Daxamites 2.50
28 V:Daxamites 2.50
29 .... 2.50
30 Silbing Rivalry,pt.2 .... 2.50
31 Future Tense,pt.3............. 2.50
32 Two Timer, pt.2 .... 2.50
33 deadly new villain 2.50
34 Shrinking Violet killed?....... 2.50

Legionnairs #21 © DC Comics Inc.

Legionnaires–Legion Of DC Comics Values Annual

Legionnaires #66 © DC Comics, Inc.

35 . . . . 2.50
36 RSt,V:Fatal Five 2.50
37 RSt,A:Kinetix,The Empress 2.50
38 . . . . 2.50
39 . . . . 2.50
40 . . . . 2.50
41 RSt&TMw(s),JMy,Legion of
  Super-Heroes #84 aftermath . . 2.50
42 RSt&TMw(s),JMy,Mysa vs.
  Kinetix 2.50
43 RSt&TMw(s),JMy,Legionnaire
  try-outs 2.50
44 TPe&TMw(s),JMy,revenge by
  rejected applicants 2.50
45 . . . . 2.50
46 RSt&TMw(s),JMy,M'Onel's life
  hangs by a thread 2.50
47 TPe&TMw(s),JMy,Brainiac 5 has
  plan to return Legionnaires to
  the future 2.50
48 RSt&TMw(s),JMy,Dawn of the
  Dark Lord,pt.1 . . . . 2.50
49 RSt&TMw(s),JMy,Dawn of the
  Dark Lord,pt.2 . . . . 2.50
50 RSt&TMw(s),JMy,The Bride of
  Mordru, 48pg, with poster 5.00
51 Picking Up the Pieces 2.50
52 RSt&TMw(s),JMy,LeVlathan 2.50
53 RSt&TMw(s),JMy,F:Monstress . . 2.50
54 TPe&TMw(s),JMy,F:G.A. Legion   2.50
55 RSt&TMw(s),JMy,V:Composite
  Man 2.50
56 RSt&TMw(s),JMy,F:M'Onel 2.50
57 RSt&TMw(s),JMy,V:Khunds . . . 2.50
58 . . . . 2.50
59 RSt&TMw(s),JMy,date night 2.50
60 RSt&TMw(s),JMy,2 join, 2 leave. 2.50
61 RSt&TMw(s),JMy,Adventures
  in Action x-over 2.50
62 RSt&TMw(s),JMy,Dark
  Circle Rising x-over, pt.1 . . . . 2.50
63 RSt&TMw(s),JMy,Dark Circle
  Rising, x-over, pt.3 . . . . 2.50
64 RSt&TMw(s),JMy, Dark Circle
  Rising, x-over pt.5 . . . . 2.50
65 RSt&TMw(s),JMy,aftermath 2.50
66 F:Invisible Kid 2.50
67 RSt&TMw(s),JMy,Star Boy. 2.50
68 RSt&TMw(s),JMy,Cosmic Boy . 2.50
69 RSt&TMw(s),JMy,Lori Morning . . 2.50
70 RSt&TMw(s),JMy,Alux Cuspin . 2.50
71 RSt&TMw(s),JMy,Dragonmage . 2.50
72 RSt&TMw(s),JMy,V:Mordru 2.50
73 RSt&TMw(s),JMy,V:Mordru 2.50
74 RSt&TMw(s),JMy,V:Elements
  of Disaster 2.50
75 TPe(s),JMy, ... 2.50
76 RSt&TMw(s),JMy. 2.50
77 RSt,TMw(s),JMy 2.50
78 DAn&ALa(s),rescue mission . . . 2.50
79 ALa,Legion of the Damned,pt.2 . 2.50
80 ALa,Legion of the Damned,pt.4 . 2.50
81 DAn&ALa(s),final issue 2.50
Ann.#1 Elseworlds Story 3.50
Ann.#2 Year One Story 3.50
Ann.#3 RSt&TMw(s) Legends of the
  Dead Earth 4.00
Spec.#1,000,000 TPe(s),SeP, Justice
  Legion L 2.50

LEGIONNAIRES THREE
1986
1 EC,Saturn Girl,Cosmic Boy 4.00
2 EC,V:Time Trapper,pt.1 . . . . 3.00
3 EC,V:Time Trapper,pt.2 . . . . 3.00
4 EC,V:Time Trapper,pt.3 . . . . 3.00

LEGION OF SUBSTITUTE HEROES
1985
Spec.#1 KG 3.00

LEGION OF SUPER-HEROES
[Reprint Series], 1973
1 rep. Tommy Tomorrow 25.00
2 rep. Tommy Tomorrow 15.00
3 rep. Tommy Tomorrow 15.00
4 rep. Tommy Tomorrow 15.00

[1st Regular Series], 1980–84
Prev: SUPERBOY (& LEGION)
259 JSon,L:Superboy 15.00
260 RE,I:Circus of Death 8.00
261 RE,V:Circus of Death 8.00
262 JSh,V:Engineer 8.00
263 V:Dagon the Avenger 8.00
264 V:Dagon the Avenger 8.00
265 JSn,DG,Superman/Radio Shack
  insert 8.00
266 R:Bouncing Boy,Duo Damsel . 8.00
267 SD,V:Kantuu 8.00
268 SD,BWi,V:Dr.Mayavale 8.00
269 V:Fatal Five 8.00
270 V:Fatal Five 8.00
271 V:Tharok (Dark Man) 6.00
272 CI,SD,O:J:Blok, I:New
  Dial `H' for Hero 6.00
273 V:Stargrave 6.00
274 SD,V:Captain Frake 6.00
275 V:Captain Frake 6.00
276 SD,V:Mordru 6.00
277 A:Reflecto(Superboy) 6.00
278 A:Reflecto(Superboy) 6.00
279 A:Reflecto(Superboy) 6.00
280 R:Superboy 6.00
281 SD,V:Time Trapper 6.00
282 V:Time Trapper 6.00
283 O:Wildfire 6.00
284 PB,V:Organleggor 6.00
285 PB,KG(1st Legion)V:Khunds . . 8.00
286 PB,KG,V:Khunds 8.00
287 KG,V:Kharlak 8.00
288 KG,V:Kharlak 8.00
289 KG,Stranded 8.00
290 KG,B:Great Darkness Saga,
  J:Invisible Kid II 8.00
291 KG,V:Darkseid's Minions 6.00
292 KG,V:Darkseid's Minions 6.00
293 KG,Daxam destroyed 6.00
294 KG,E:Great Darkness Saga,
  V:Darkseid,A:Auron,Superboy . 8.00
295 KG,A:Green Lantern Corps . . . 3.50

Legion of Super-Heroes #270 © DC Comics, Inc.

296 KG,D:Cosmic Boys family 3.50
297 KG,O:Legion,A:Cosmic Boy . . . 3.50
298 KG,EC,I:Amethyst 3.50
299 KG,R:Invisible Kid I 3.50
300 KG,CS,JSon,DC,KS,DG 6.00
301 KG,R:Chameleon Boy 3.50
302 KG,A:Chameleon Boy 3.50
303 KG,V:Fatal Five 3.50
304 KG,V:Fatal Five 3.50
305 KG,V:Micro Lad 3.50
306 KG,CS,RT,O:Star Boy 3.50
307 KG,GT,Omen 3.50
308 KG,V:Omen 3.50
309 KG,V:Omen 3.50
310 KG,V:Omen 3.50
311 KG,GC,New Headquarters 3.50
312 KG,V:Khunds 3.50
313 KG,V:Khunds 3.50
Ann.#1 IT,KG,I:Invisible Kid 4.00
Ann.#2 DGb,W:Karate Kid and
  Princess Projectra 3.00
Ann.#3 CS,RT,A:Darkseid 3.00
Ann.#4 reprint. 3.00
Ann.#5 reprint. 3.00
Becomes:

TALES OF LEGION OF SUPER HEROES

LEGION OF SUPER-HEROES
[3rd Regular Series], 1984–89
1 KG,V:Legion of Super-Villians . . . 5.00
2 KG,V:Legion of Super-Villians . . . 4.00
3 KG,V:Legion of Super-Villians . . . 4.00
4 KG,D:Karate Kid 4.00
5 KG,D:Nemesis Kid 4.00
6 JO,F:Lightning Lass 3.00
7 SLi,A:Controller 3.00
8 SLi,V:Controller 3.00
9 Sli,V:Sklarians 3.00
10 V:Khunds 3.00
11 EC,KG,L:Orig 3 members 3.00
12 SLi,EC,A:Superboy 3.00
13 SLi,V:Lythyls,F:TimberWolf 3.00
14 SLi,J:Sensor Girl (Princess
  Projectra),Quislet,Tellus,Polar
  Boy,Magnetic Kid 3.00
15 GLa,V:Dr. Regulus 3.00
16 SLi,Crisis tie-in,F:Braniac5 . . . . . 3.00
17 GLa,O:Legion 3.00
18 GLa,Crisis tie-in,V:InfiniteMan . . 3.00
19 GLa,V:Controller 3.00

CVA Page 110 All comics prices listed are for *Near Mint* condition.

DC — Legion Of Super-Heroes

Legion of Super-Heroes 3rd Series #11
© DC Comics Inc.

Ann #5 I:2nd Legion Sub.Heroes . . 3.00

[4th Regular Series], 1989–97
1 KG,R:Cosmic Boy, Chameleon . . 5.00
2 KG,R:Ultra Boy,I:Kono 3.50
3 KG,D:Block,V:Roxxas 3.50
4 KG,V:Time Trapper 3.50
5 KG,V:Mordru,A:Glorith 3.50
6 KG,I:Laurel Gand 3.50
7 KG,V:Mordru 3.00
8 KG,O:Legion 3.00
9 KG,O:Laurel Gand 3.00
10 KG,V:Roxxas 3.00
11 KG,V:Roxxas 3.00
12 KG,I:Kent Shakespeare 3.00
13 KG,V:Dominators,posters. 3.00
14 KG,J:Tenzil Kem 3.00
15 KG,Khund Invasion 3.00
16 KG,V:Khunds. 3.00
17 KG,V:Khunds. 3.00
18 KG,V:Khunds. 3.00
19 KG,cont.from Adv.of Superman
  #478,A:Original Dr. Fate 3.00
20 KG,V:Dominators 3.00
21 KG,B:Quiet Darkness,
  A:Lobo,Darkseid. 3.50
22 KG,A:Lobo,Darkseid 3.00
23 KG,A:Lobo,Darkseid 3.00
24 KG,E:Quiet Darkness,A:Lobo,
  Darkseid,C:Legionairres 3.00
25 DAb,I:Legionairres 3.50
26 JPn,B:Terra Mosaic,V:B.I.O.N . . 2.50
27 JPn,V:B.I.O.N. 2.50
28 JPn,O:Sun Boy 2.50
29 JPn,I:Monica Sade. 2.50
30 JPn,V:Dominators 2.50
31 CS,AG,F:Shvaughn as man 2.50
32 JPn,D:Karate Kid,Prin.Projectra,
  Chameleon Boy(Legionaires) . . 2.50
33 R:Kid Quantum 2.50
34 R:Sun Boy. 2.50
35 JPN,V:Dominators 2.50
36 JPn,E:Terra Mosaic 2.50
37 JBr,R:Star Boy,Dream Girl 2.50
38 JPn,Earth is destroyed. 5.00
39 SI,A:Legionaires 2.50
40 SI,Legion meets Legionnaires . . 2.50
41 SI,F:The Legionnaires 2.50
42 SI,V:Glorith 2.50
43 SI,B:Mordru Arises. 2.50
44 SI,R:Karate Kid 2.50
45 SI,R:Roxxas 2.50
46 SI, ... 2.50
47 SI, ... 2.50
48 SI,E:Mordru Arises. 2.50
49 F:Matter Eater Lad. 2.50
50 W:Tenzil & Saturn Queen,
  R:Wildfire,V:B.I.O.N 4.00
51 R:Kent,Celeste,Ivy,V:Grimbor. . . 2.50
52 F:Timber Wolf 2.50
53 SI,V:Glorith 2.50
54 SI,Foil,Die-Cut(c),
  N:L.E.G.I.O.N. 5.00
55 SI,On Mordru. 2.50
56 SI,R:Espionage Squad. 2.50
57 SI,R:Khund Legionnaires 2.50
58 SI,D:Laurel Gand. 2.50
59 SI,R:Valor,Dawnstar. 2.50
60 SI,End of an Era#3 . . . . 2.50
61 SI,End of an Era#6 . . . . 2.50
62 I:New Team 2.50
63 Alien Attack 2.50
64 . . . . 2.50
65 . . . . 2.50
66 I:New Team Members 2.50
67 F:Leviathan 2.50
68 F:Leviathan 2.50
69 V:Durlan 2.50
70 A:Andromeda, Briainiac 5 . . . . . 2.50
71 Planet Trom 2.50
72 . . . . 2.50
73 Sibling Rivalry,pt.1 . . . . 2.50

20 GLa,V:Tyr 3.00
21 GLa,V:Emerald Empress 4.00
22 GLa,V:Restorer,A:Universo 4.00
23 SLi,GLa,A:Superboy,
  Jonah Hex 4.00
24 GLa,NBi,A:Fatal Five 4.00
25 GLa,V:FatalFive. 4.00
26 GLa,V:FatalFive,O:SensorGirl . . 3.00
27 GLa,GC,A:Mordru 3.00
28 GLa,L:StarBoy. 3.00
29 GLa,V:Starfinger 3.00
30 GLa,A:Universo 3.00
31 GLa,V:Ferro Lad,Karate Kid. . . . 3.00
32 GLa,V:Universo,I:Atmos. 3.00
33 GLa,V:Universo 3.00
34 GLa,V:Universo 3.00
35 GLa,V:Universo,R:Saturn Girl . . 3.00
36 GLa,R:Cosmic Boy 3.00
37 GLa,V:Universo,I:Superboy
  (Earth Prime) 12.00
38 GLa,V:TimeTrapper,
  D:Superboy 14.00
39 CS,RT,O:Colossal Boy. 3.00
40 GLa,I:New Starfinger 3.00
41 GLa,V:Starfinger 3.00
42 GLa,Millennium,V:Laurel Kent . . 3.00
43 GLa,Millennium,V:Laurel Kent . . 3.00
44 GLa,O:Quislet 3.00
45 GLa,CS,MGr,DC,30th Ann. 4.00
46 GLa,Conspiracy 3.00
47 GLa,PB,V:Starfinger 3.00
48 GLa,Conspiracy,A:Starfinger . . . 3.00
49 PB, Conspiracy,A:Starfinger 3.00
50 KG,V:Time Trapper,A:Infinite
  Man,E:Conspiracy 4.00
51 KG,V:Gorak,L:Brainiac5. . . . . . . 3.00
52 KG,V:Gil'Dishpan 3.00
53 KG,V:Gil'Dishpan. 3.00
54 KG,V:Gorak. 3.00
55 KG,EC,JL,EL,N:Legion 3.00
56 EB,V:Inquisitor. 3.00
57 KG,V:Emerald Empress 3.00
58 KG,V:Emerald Empress 3.00
59 KG,MBr,F:Invisible Kid 3.00
60 KG,B:Magic Wars 3.00
61 KG,Magic Wars 3.00
62 KG,D:Magnetic Lad 3.00
63 KG,E:Magic Wars #4,final iss. . . 3.50
Ann.#1 KG,Murder Mystery. 3.00
Ann.#2 KG,CS,O:Validus,
  A:Darkseid. 3.50
Ann.#3 GLa,I:2nd Karate Kid 3.00
Ann.#4 BKi,V:Starfinger 3.00

74 Future Tense,pt2 . . . . 2.50
75 Two Timer,pt.1 (of 2) 2.50
76 F:Valor & Triad. 2.50
77 F:Brainiac 5 . . . . 2.50
78 . . . . 2.50
79 Fatal Five attacks 2.50
80 V:Fatal Five 2.50
81 R:Dirk Morgna 2.50
82 . . . . 2.50
83 . . . . 2.50
84 . . . . 2.50
85 TPe&TMw(s),LMd,A:Superman,
  back in 20th century. 2.50
86 TPe&TMw(s),LMd,Final Night
  tie-in. 2.50
87 TPe&TMw(s),LMd,F:Deadman . . 2.50
88 TPe&TMw(s),LMd,A:Impulse . . . 2.50
89 TPe&TMw(s),LMd, ... 2.50
90 TPe&TMw(s),LMd,V:Dr. Psycho . 2.50
91 TPe&TMw(s),LMd,Legion back
  together, but trapped in
  timestream. 2.50
92 TPe&TMs(s),LMd,Displaced
  in Time. 2.50
93 TPe&TMw(s),MC, All-tragedy
  issue 2.50
94 TPe&TMw(s),LMd,22 short
  pages about the Legion of
  Super-Heroes. 2.50
95 MFm,F:Brainiac 5 . . . . 2.50
96 MFm,wedding 2.50
97 TPe,LMd,Genesis tie-in 2.50
98 TPe&TMC,LMd,C.O.M.P.U.T.O.
  the Conqueror, pt.1. . . . . 2.50
99 TPe&TMw,LMd,Computo, pt.2 . . 2.50
100 TPe&TMw,LMd,Computo, pt.3 . 7.50
101 TPe&TMs(s),AD&MFm(c),
  F:Sparks 2.50
102 . . . . 2.50
103 TPe&TMw,AD&MFm(c),Star
  Boy 2.50
104 TPe&TMw,AD&MFm(c),
  changes 2.50
105 TPe&TMw,AD&MFm(c),
  Adventures in Action x-over . . . 2.50
106 TPe&TMw,AD&MFm(c),Dark
  Circle Rising, x-over pt.2 . . . . . 2.50
107 TPe&TMw,AD&MFm(c),Dark
  Circle Rising, x-over pt.4 . . . . . 2.50
108 TPe&TMw,AD&MFm(c),Dark
  Circle Rising, x-over pt.6 . . . . . 2.50
109 DDv,AD,MFm,F:Violet 2.50
110 TPe,V:Thunder. 2.50
111 TPe&TMw(s),V:Daxamite 2.50
112 TPe&TMw(s),In Space 2.50
113 TPe&TMw(s),Kinetix. 2.50
114 TPe&TMw(s),Bizarro
  Legion,pt.1 . . . . 2.50
115 TPe&TMw(s),Bizarro
  Legion, pt.2 . . . . 2.50
116 TPe&TMw(s),V:Pernisius,pt.1 . . 2.50
117 TPe&TMw(s),V:Pernisius,pt.2 . . 2.50
118 TPe&TMw(s),V:Pernisius,pt.3 . . 2.50
119 TPe&TMw(s),A:Valor & Phase . 2.50
120 TPe,TMw,V:Fatal Four,pt.1 . . . . 2.50
121 TPe,TMw,V:Fatal Five,pt.2 . . . . 2.50
122 DAn,ALa,Legion of
  the Damned,pt.1. . . . . 2.50
123 DAn,ALa,Legion of
  the Damned,pt.3. . . . . 2.50
124 DAn,ALa,Legion of the Damned,
  aftermath 2.50
125 DAn,ALa,final issue 2.50
Ann.#1 O:Ultra Boy,V:Glorith. 3.50
Ann.#2 O:Valor. 3.50
Ann.#3 N:Timberwolf 4.00
Ann.#4 I:Jamm 3.50
Ann.#5 SI(c),CDo,MFm,TMc,
  Elseworlds Story 3.75
Ann.#6 Year One Annual + pin-ups . 3.95
Ann.#7 TPe(s),MC,MFm,Legends

All comics prices listed are for Near Mint condition.

CVA Page 111

Legion Of–Lobo · DC · Comics Values Annual

of the Dead Earth 3.50
Spec.#1,000,000 TPe(s),KG,AG . . . 2.50
TPB Great Darkness Saga 17.95
TPB GreatDarknessSaga,
  no poster 14.95
TPB Legion Archives, rep.#1-#3 . . 39.95
TPB Legion Archives, rep.#4 . . . . . 49.95
TPB The Beginnings of Tomorrow. 17.95
GN Secret Files, inc.O:Legion 5.00
GN Secret Files #2 . . . . 4.95

LEGION: SCIENCE POLICE
June, 1998

1 (of 4) DvM,PR,JRu,set in
  30th century 2.50
2 DvM,PR,JRu,Jarik Shadder . . . 2.50
3 DvM,PR,JRu, ... 2.50
4 DvM,PR,JRu 2.25

LEGION WORLDS
April, 2001

1 (of 6) DAn,ALa 3.95
2 DAn,ALa 3.95
3 DAn,ALa, On Braal 3.95
4 DAn,ALa, heading for Xanthu . . . 3.95
5 DAn,ALa, SDi, on Steele 3.95
6 DAn,ALa, concl. 3.95

Life, The Universe and Everything #2
© DC Comics, Inc.

LIFE, THE UNIVERSE AND EVERYTHING
1996

1 thru 3 Doug Adams adapt. . . . . . @6.95

LIMITED COLLECTORS EDITION
Summer, 1973

21 Shazam 40.00
22 Tarzan 30.00
23 House of Mystery 45.00
24 Rudolph, the Red-nosed
  Reindeer 100.00
25 NA,NA(c),Batman 50.00
27 Shazam 30.00
29 Tarzan 30.00
31 NA,O:Superman 30.00
32 Ghosts 50.00
33 Rudolph 100.00
34 X-Mas with Superheroes 30.00

35 Shazam 25.00
36 The Bible 25.00
37 Batman 30.00
38 Superman 25.00
39 Secret Origins 25.00
40 Dick Tracy 25.00
41 ATh,Super Friends 25.00
42 Rudolph 60.00
43 X-mas with Super-Heroes 25.00
44 NA,Batman 25.00
45 Secret Origins-Super Villians . . 25.00
46 ATh,JLA 25.00
47 Superman 25.00
48 Superman-Flash Race 25.00
49 Superboy & Legion of
  Super-Heroes 25.00
50 Rudolph 60.00
51 NA,NA(c),Batman 30.00
52 NA,NA(c),The Best of DC 30.00
57 Welcome Back Kotter 30.00
59 NA,BWr,Batman,1978 . . . . . . 30.00

LITTLE ENDLESS STORYBOOK
DC/Vertigo, June, 2001

GN JIT 5.95

LITTLE SHOP OF HORRORS
Feb., 1987

1 GC 2.50

LOBO
[1st Limited Series], 1990–91

1 SBs,Last Czarnian #1 . . . . 4.00
1a 2nd Printing 2.00
2 SBs,Last Czarnian #2 . . . . 3.00
3 SBs,Last Czarnian #3 . . . . 3.00
4 SBs,Last Czarnian #4 . . . . 3.00
Ann.#1 Bloodlines#1,I:Layla 3.75
Lobo Paramilitary X-Mas SBs 5.50
Lobo:Blazing Chain of Love,DCw . 2.00
TPB Last Czarnian,rep.#1-#4 . . . . 9.95
TPB Lobo's Greatest Hits 12.95

[Regular Series], 1993–97

1 VS,Foil(c),V:Dead Boys 3.25
2 VS 3.00
3 VS 2.75
4 VS,Quigly Affair 2.75
5 V:Bludhound 2.50

Lobo #4 © DC Comics, Inc.

6 I:Bim Simms 2.50
7 A:Losers 2.50
8 A:Losers 2.50
9 V:Lobo 2.50
10 Preacher 2.50
11 Goldstar vs. Rev.Bo 2.50
12 . . . . 2.50
13 . . . . 2.50
14 Lobo, P.I. 2.50
15 Lobo, P.I.,pt.2 . . . . 2.50
16 Lobo, P.I.,pt.3 . . . . 2.50
17 Lobo, P.I.,pt.4 . . . . 2.50
18 Lobo, P.I.,pt.5 . . . . 2.50
19 . . . . 2.50
20 Toilot Fight 2.50
21 AIG,KON,R:Space Cabby 2.50
22 AIG,UnderworldUnleashed tie-in. 2.50
23 AIG,Stargaze Rally,pt.1 . . . . . 2.50
24 AIG,Stargaze Rally,pt.2 . . . . . 2.50
25 AIG 2.50
26 AIG,V:Erik the Khund 2.50
27 AIG,V:Billy Krono 2.50
28 AIG,A:Great Big Fat Bastiches . . 2.50
29 . . . . 2.50
30 . . . . 2.50
31 . . . . 2.50
32 AIG(s),Lobo attends a seance,
  frags himself 2.50
33 AIG(s),Lobo returns from spirit
  world 2.50
34 AIG(s),vs. Japan, whaling, ... 2.50
35 AIG(s), Deathtrek 2.50
36 . . . . 2.50
37 AIG(s),BKi,Lobo's Guide to Girls 2.50
38 AIG(s),Bomandi The Last Boy
  on Earth 2.50
39 AIG(s),Belly of Behemoth,pt.1 . . 2.50
40 AIG(s),Belly of Behemoth,pt.2 . . 2.50
41 AIG(s),roommates 2.50
42 AIG(s),A:Perfidia 2.50
43 AIG(s),A:Jonas 2.50
44 AIG(s),Genesis tie-in 2.50
45 AIG(s),battle royale 2.50
46 AIG(s),Jackie Chin 2.50
47 AIG(s),V:Kiljoy Riggs 2.50
48 AIG(s),F:the penguins 2.50
49 AIG(s) 2.50
50 AIG(s),war on DC universe 2.50
51 AIG(s),Slater and Candy 2.50
52 AIG(s),Goldstar funeral 2.50
53 AIG(s),disrupted ceremony . . . 2.50
54 AIG(s),Good Vibes machine 2.50
55 AIG(s),Sheepworld 2.50
56 AIG(s),MPn,GLz,the wedding . . 2.50
57 AIG(s),MPn, GLz, Intergalactic
  Police convention 2.50
58 KG&AIG(s) 2.50
59 AIG(s),V:Bad Wee Bastards 2.50
60 AIG(s),All-New, Nonviolent
  Adventures of Superbo, pt.1 . . . 2.50
61 AIG(s),Superbo, pt.2 . . . . 2.50
62 AiG(s),Superbo, pt.3 . . . . 2.50
63 AIG(s),Soul Brothers,pt.1 . . . . . 2.50
64 AIG(s),Soul Brothers,pt.2
  final issue 2.50
Ann.#1 Bloodlines 4.00
Ann.#2 Elseworlds Story 3.50
Ann.#3 AIG Year One 4.95
Spec.#1,000,000 AIG(s),GLz 2.50
Spec. Lobo's Big Babe Spring Break,
  Miss Voluptuous Contest 2.50
Spec. Blazing Chains of Love 2.00
Spec. Bounty Hunting for Fun
  and Profit, F:Fanboy 4.95
Spec. Lobo: Chained AIG(s),
  Lobo in prison 2.50
Spec. Lobo/Demon: Hellowe'en,
  AIG(s),VGi 2.25
Spec. Lobo In the Chair, AIG(s). . . . 2.25
Spec. Lobo:I Quit,AIG,
  nicotine withdrawal 2.25

CVA Page 112 — All comics prices listed are for *Near Mint* condition.

Spec. Lobo/Judge Dredd: Psycho
 Bikers vs. Mutants From Hell . . 4.95
Spec. Lobo: Portrait of a Victim
 VS,I:John Doe 2.25
GN Fragtastic Voyage AGr,
 miniaturized 6.00
TPB Lobo's Back's Back. 10.00
TPB Lobo's Greatest Hits 13.00
Convention Special, comic con. . . . 2.00

LOBO: A CONTRACT ON GAWD
1994
1 AlG(s),KD 2.50
2 AlG(s),KD,A:Dave. 2.50
3 AlG(s),KD 2.50
4 AlG(s),KD,Final Issue 2.50

LOBO'S BACK
1992
1 SBs,w/3(c) inside,V:Loo 2.50
1a 2nd printing 2.00
2 SBs,Lobo becomes a woman . . . 2.50
3 SBs,V:Heaven 2.50
4 SBs,V:Heaven 2.50
TPB GF(c),rep.#1-#4 . . . . 9.95

LOBO: DEATH & TAXES
[Mini-Series], Aug., 1996
1 (of 4) KG&AlG(s) 2.25
2 KG&AlG(s),Interstellar Revenue
 learns Lobo doesn't pay taxes . 2.25
3 KG&AlG(s),Lobo walks into
 IRS trap 2.25
4 KG&AlG(s),Lobo destroys IRS . . 2.25

LOBO: INFANTICIDE
1992–93
1 KG,V:Su,Lobo Bastards 2.50
2 Lobo at Boot Camp 2.50
3 KG,Lobo Vs.his offspring 2.50
4 KG,V:Lobo Bastards. 2.50

LOBO/MASK
1 AlG&JAr(s),DoM,Kwi, humorous
 x-over. 5.95
2 AlG&JAr(s),DoM,Kwi, concl. 5.95

LOBO: UNAMERICAN GLADIATORS
1993
1 CK,V:Satan's Brothers 2.50
2 CK,V:Jonny Caesar 2.50
3 CK,MMi(c),V:Satan Brothers. . . . 2.50
4 CK,MMi(c),V:Jonny Caeser. 2.50

LOBO UNBOUND
June 2003
1 (of 6) mass-murder. 2.95
2 . . . . 2.95
3 Bling-Bling 2.95
4 Ambush Bug. 2.95
5 Dhabba Dhu 2.95

LOBOCOP
1 StG(s) 2.25

LOIS AND CLARK: THE NEW ADVENTURES OF SUPERMAN
TPB 9.95
TPB stories that became episodes 10.00

LOIS LANE
Aug., 1986
1 and 2 GM . . . . @3.00

LONG HOT SUMMER, THE
Milestone, 1995
[Mini-Series]
1 Blood Syndicate v. G.R.I.N.D. . . . 3.00
2 A:Icon,Xombi,Hardware 2.50

LOONEY TUNES MAG.
1 thru 6 . . . . @2.00

Looney Tunes #17 © DC Comics Inc.

LOONEY TUNES
1994
1 thru 6 Warner Bros. cartoons. . . @3.00
7 thru 11 Warner Bros. . . . . @3.00
12 thru 25 . . . . @2.50
26 thru 108 . . . . @2.25
Spec. Back in Action: Movie 3.95

LOOSE CANNON
[Mini-Series], 1995
1 AdP,V:Bounty Hunters. 2.50
2 V:Bounty Hunters & The
 Eradicator 2.25
3 A:Eradicator 2.25

LORDS OF THE ULTRAREALM
1986
1 PB 3.50
2 PB 2.25
3 thru 6 PB . . . . @2.25
Spec.#1 PB,DG,Oneshot 2.25

LOSERS
DC/Vertigo June 2003
1 crime espionage 3.00
2 thru 6 Goliath,pt.1–pt.5 . . . . . . @3.00

LOSERS SPECIAL
1985
1 Crisis,D:Losers 4.00

LUCIFER
DC/Vertigo, Apr., 2000
1 Lucifer struggles to regain power . 6.00
2 Living Tarot Deck 4.00
3 V:Jill Presto 4.00
4 WaP,F:Elaine Belloc 3.00
5 PrG,House of Windowless
 Rooms,pt.1. . . . . 3.00
6 PrG,Windowless Rooms,pt.2 . . . 3.00
7 PrG,Windowless Rooms,pt.3 . . . 3.00
8 PrG,Windowless Rooms,pt.4 . . . 3.00
9 Immortality 3.00
10 Children & Monsters,pt.1 . . . . . 3.00
11 Children & Monsters,pt.2 . . . . . 2.50
12 Children & Monsters,pt.3 . . . . . 2.50
13 Children & Monsters,pt.4 . . . . . 2.50
14 Triptych 2.50
15 Triptych,Two Edge Sword 2.50
16 Triptych,Ancestral Deed. 2.50
17 Dalliance with the Dead,pt.1 . . 2.50
18 Dalliance with the Dead,pt.2 . . 2.50
19 Dalliance with the Dead,pt.3 . . 2.50
20 The Thunder Sermon. 2.50
21 Paradiso,pt.1 . . . . 2.50
22 Paradiso,pt.2 . . . . 2.50
23 Paradiso,pt.3 . . . . 2.50
24 The Writing on the Wall 2.50
25 Purgatorio,pt.1 . . . . 2.50
26 Purgatorio,pt.2 . . . . 2.50
27 Purgatorio,pt.3 . . . . 2.50
28 F:Gaudium 2.50
29 MCy,Inferno,pt.1 . . . . 2.50
30 MCy,Inferno,pt.2 . . . . 2.50
31 MCy,Inferno,pt.3 . . . . 2.50
32 MCy,Inferno,pt.4 . . . . 2.50
33 MCy,robbery 2.50
34 MCy,Come to Judgment,pt.1 . . . 2.50
35 MCy,Come to Judgment,pt.2 . . . 2.50
36 MCy,Naglfar,pt.1 . . . . 2.50
37 MCy,Naglfar,pt.2 . . . . 2.50
38 MCy,Naglfar,pt.3 . . . . 2.50
39 MCy,Naglfar,pt.4 . . . . 2.50
40 MCy,Naglfar,pt.5 . . . . 2.50
41 MCy,Sisters of Mercy 2.50
42 MCy,Brothers in Arms,pt.1 . . . . 2.50
43 MCy,Brothers in Arms,pt.2 . . . . 2.50
44 MCy,Brothers in Arms,pt.3 . . . . 2.50
TPB Devil in the Gateway 14.95
TPB Children and Monsters 17.95
TPB A Dalliance with the Damned. 14.95
TPB The Divine Comedy 17.95
GN Nirvana, 48-pg.. . . . . 5.95

MADAME XANADU
1981
1 MR/BB 5.00

MAJOR BUMMER
June, 1997
1 JAr(s),DoM,I:Major Bummer 2.50
2 JAr(s),DoM,Major Bummer gets
 new costume 2.50
3 JAr(s),DoM,bad guys arrive 2.50
4 JAr(s),DoM,alien germs 2.50
5 JAr(s),DoM,dinosaurs, Nazis. . . . 2.50
6 JAr(s),DoM,Mutant bully 2.50
7 JAr(s),DoM 2.50
8 . . . . 2.50
9 JAr(s),DoM,epic fight 2.50
10 JAr(s),DoM,Nunzio dead? 2.50
11 JAr(s),DoM,everyone dies? . . . 2.50
12 JAr(s),DoM,Lou Martin dead . . . 2.50
13 JAr(s),DoM,Lauren 2.50
14 JAr(s),DoM,tells the future off. . . 2.50
15 JAr(s),DoM, final issue 2.50

MAN-BAT
1975–76
1 SD,AM,A:Batman 30.00
2 V:The Ten-Eyed Man 25.00
Reprint NA(c) 15.00

MAN-BAT
1996
1 CDi,terrorizes city 2.25
2 . . . . 2.25
3 CDi,V:Steeljacket, finale 2.25

MAN-BAT vs. BATMAN
1 NA,DG,reprint 4.00

A MAN CALLED AX
Aug., 1997
1 MWn(s),SwM, part rep. 2.50
2 MWn(s),SwM, ... 2.50
3 MWn(s),SwM, vs. DC universe . 2.50
4 MWn(s),SwM,killer cyborg 2.50
5 MWn(s),SwM,R-Mor 2.50
6 MWn(s),SwM, ... 2.50
7 MWn(s),SwM,battle in Bedlam . 2.50
8 MWn(s),SwM,final issue 2.50

MANHUNTER
1988–90
1 from Millennium-Suicide Squad. 2.50
2 in Tokyo,A:Dumas 2.25
3 The Yakuza,V:Dumas 2.25
4 Secrets Revealed-Manhunter,
  Dumas & Olivia 2.25
5 A:Silvia Kandery 2.25
6 A:Argent,contd.Suicide Squad
  Annual #1 . . . . 2.25
7 Vlatavia, V:Count Vertigo 2.25
8 FS,A:Flash,Invasion x-over 2.25
9 FS,Invasion Aftermath extra
  (contd from Flash #22) 2.25
10 Salvage,pt.1 . . . . 2.25
11 Salvage,pt.2. . . . . 2.25
12 . . . . 2.25
13 V:Catman 2.25
14 Janus Directive #5 . . . . 2.25
15 I:Mirage 2.25
16 V:Outlaw 2.25
17 In Gotham,A:Batman 2.25
18 Saints & Sinners,pt.1,R:Dumas 2.25

Manhunter #13 © DC Comics, Inc.

19 Saints & Sinners,pt.2,V:Dumas . 2.25
20 Saints & Sinners,pt.3,V:Dumas . 2.25
21 Saints & Sinners,pt.4,
  A:Manhunter Grandmaster . . . 2.25
22 Saints & Sinners,pt.5,
  A:Manhunter Grandmaster . . . 2.25
23 Saints & Sinners,pt.6,V:Dumas . 2.25
24 DG,Showdown, final issue 2.25

[2nd Series], 1994–95
0 . . . . 2.50
1 . . . . 2.50
2 N:Wild Huntsman 2.50
3 V:Malig. 2.50
4 Necrodyne 2.50
5 V:Skin Walker. 2.50
6 V:Barbarian,Incarnate 2.50
7 V:Incarnate,A:White Lotus
  & Capt. Atom 2.25
8 V:Butcher Boys. 2.25
9 V:Butcher Boys. 2.25
10 V:Necrodyne 2.25
11 Return of Old Enemy 2.25
12 Underworld Unleashed, finale . 2.25

Man of Steel #1 © DC Comics, Inc.

MAN OF STEEL
1986
1 JBy,DG,I:Modern Superman 5.00
1a 2nd edition 3.00
2 JBy,DG,R:Lois Lane 3.50
3 JBy,DG,A:Batman. 3.00
4 JBy,DG,V:Lex Luthor 3.00
5 JBy,DG,I:Modern Bizarro 3.00
6 JBy,DG,A:Lana Lang 3.00
TPB rep. Man of Steel #1–#6 . . . . 20.00
TPBa 2nd printing. 7.95

MANY LOVES OF DOBIE GILLIS
May-June, 1960
1 . . . . 300.00
2 . . . . 150.00
3 . . . . 100.00
4 . . . . 100.00
5 thru 9 . . . . @75.00
10 thru 25 . . . . @75.00
26 Oct., 1964 . . . . 75.00

MARTIAN MANHUNTER
1988
1 A:JLI. 3.00
2 A:JLI,V:Death God 2.50

3 V:Death God,A:Dr.Erdel 2.50
4 A:JLI,final issue 2.50

[Mini-Series]
1 EB,American Secrets #1. . . . . . 5.25
2 EB,American Secrets #2. . . . . . 5.25
3 EB,American Secrets #3. . . . . . 5.25

MARTIAN MANHUNTER
Aug., 1998
0 JOs,TMd,A:Batman,Superman . 3.00
1 JOs,TMd,V:Headman 2.50
2 JOs,TMd,V:Antares 2.50
3 JOs,TMd,V:Bette Noir 2.50
4 JOs,TMd,J'emm, Son of Saturn 2.50
5 JAr,JD,A:Chase 2.50
6 JOs,TMd,A:JLA,pt.1 . . . . 2.50
7 JOs(s),TMd,A:JLA,pt.2 . . . . 2.50
8 JOs(s),TMd,A:JLA,pt.3 . . . . 2.50
9 JOs(s),TMd,A:JLA,pt.4 . . . . 2.50
10 JOs(s),A:Fire 2.50
11 JOs,PNe,BHi, ... 2.50
12 JOs,TMd,Day of Judgment
  x-over. 2.50
13 JOs,TMd,Rings of Saturn,pt.1 . 2.50
14 JOs,TMd,Rings of Saturn,pt.2 . 2.50
15 JOs,TMd,Rings of Saturn,pt.3 . 2.50
16 JOs,TMd,Rings of Saturn,pt.4 . 2.50
17 JOs,TMd,Rings of Saturn,pt.5 . 2.50
18 JOs,TMd,V:Kanto 2.50
19 JOs,TMd,defeated, captured . . 2.50
20 JOs,TMd,year one on earth . . . 2.50
21 JOs,TT,A:Abin Sur 2.50
22 JOs,TMd,A:Batman 2.50
23 JOs,TMd,F:Spectre 2.50
24 JOs,TMd,F:Just.Leag.Int. 2.50
25 JOs,TMd,F:Gypsy 2.50
26 JOs,TMd,Renegades of Mars . 2.50
27 JOs,TMd,Renegades of Mars . 2.50
28 JOs,TMd,at Stonehenge 2.50
29 JOs,TMd,telepath 2.50
30 JOs,TMd,Altered Egos,pt.1 . . . 2.50
31 JOs,TMd,Altered Egos,pt.2 . . . 2.50
32 TMd,V:Bloodworms of Mars . . 2.50
33 TMd,J'onn J'onzz hidden life . . 2.50
34 JOs,V:Darkseid 2.50
35 JOs,V:Malefic 2.50
36 JOs,final issue 2.50
Ann.#1 TT,AOI,BWr,Ghosts x-over . 3.00
Ann.#2 AAd(c),JLApe:Gorilla
  Warfare 2.95
Spec.#1,000,000 JOs,TMd 2.00

MASK
Dec., 1985
1 HC(c),TV tie-in,I:Mask Team 2.50
2 HC(c),In Egypt,V:Venom 2.50
3 HC(c),`Anarchy in the U.K.'. . . . 2.50
4 HC(c),V:Venom, final issue,
  March, 1986 . . . . 2.50

[2nd Series], Feb.–Oct., 1987
1 CS/KS,reg.series 2.50
2 CS/KS,V:Venom 2.50
3 CS/KS,V:Venom 2.50
4 CS/KS,V:Venom 2.50
5 CS/KS,Mask operatives hostage. 2.50
6 CS/KS,I:Jacana 2.50
7 CS/KS,Mask gone bad? 2.50
8 CS/KS,Matt Trakker,V:Venom . . 2.50
9 CS/KS,V:Venom, last issue 2.50

MASTERS OF THE UNIVERSE
May, 1986
1 GT,AA,O:He-Man 6.00
2 GT,AA,V:Skeletor 5.00
3 GT,V:Skeletor 5.00

MASTERWORKS SERIES OF GREAT COMIC BOOK ARTISTS
May, 1983
1 .... 5.00
2 .... 4.00
3 Dec., 1983 .... 4.00

'MAZING MAN
Jan., 1986
1 I:Maze 3.00
2 .... 2.50
3 .... 2.50
4 .... 2.50
5 .... 2.50
6 Shea Stadium 2.50
7 Shea Stadium 2.50
8 Cat-Sitting 2.50
9 Bank Hold-up 2.50
10 .... 2.50
11 Jones Beach 2.50
12 FM(c),last issue, Dec., 1986 . 3.00
Spec.#1 .... 2.25
Spec.#2 .... 2.25
Spec.#3 KB/TM 2.25

MEK
DC/Vertigo, Nov., 2002
1 (of 3) WEI, ... 2.95

MEN OF WAR
Aug., 1977
1 I:Gravedigger,Code Name: Gravedigger,I:Enemy Ace 20.00
2 JKu(c),The Five-Walled War ... 10.00
3 JKu(c),The Suicide Strategem . 10.00
4 JKu(c),Trail by Fire 10.00
5 JKu(c),Valley of the Shadow .. 10.00
6 JKu(c),A Choice of Deaths ... 10.00
7 JKu(c),Milkrun 10.00
8 JKu(c),Death-Stroke 10.00
9 JKu(c),Gravedigger-R.I.P. 10.00
10 JKu(c),Crossroads 10.00
11 JKu(c),Berkstaten 10.00
12 JKu(c),Where Is Gravedigger?.. 7.00
13 JKu(c),Project Gravedigger - Plus One 7.00
14 JKu(c),The Swirling Sands of Death 7.00
15 JKu(c),The Man With the Opened Eye 7.00
16 JKu(c),Hide and Seek The Spy . 7.00
17 JKu(c),The River of Death ... 7.00
18 JKu(c),The Amiens Assault ... 7.00
19 JKu(c),An Angel Named Marie .. 7.00
20 JKu(c),Cry:Jerico 7.00
21 JKu(c),Home-Is Where The Hell Is 7.00
22 JKu(c),Blackout On The Boardwalk 7.00
23 JKu(c),Mission: Six Feet Under . 7.00
24 JKu&DG(c),The Presidential Peril 7.00
25 GE(c),Save the President 7.00
26 March, 1980 .... 7.00

MENZ INSANA
DC/Vertigo, 1998
GN JBo 7.95

MERCY
DC/Vertigo, 1993
Graphic Novel I:Mercy 8.00

Metal Men #15 © DC Comics Inc.

METAL MEN
1965–78
[1st Regular Series]
1 RA,I:Missile Men 900.00
2 RA,Robot of Terror 300.00
3 RA,Moon's Invisible Army 200.00
4 RA,Bracelet of Doomed Hero . 200.00
5 RA,Menace of the Mammoth Robots 200.00
6 RA,I:Gas Gang 150.00
7 RA,V:Solar Brain 125.00
8 RA,Playground of Terror 125.00
9 RA,A:Billy 125.00
10 RA,A:Gas Gang 125.00
11 RA,The Floating Furies 125.00
12 RA,A:Missle Men 100.00
13 RA,I:Nameless 100.00
14 RA,A:Chemo 100.00
15 RA,V:B.O.L.T.S. 100.00
16 RA,Robots for Sale 100.00
17 JKu(c),RA,V:Bl.Widow Robot . 100.00
18 JKu(c),RA 100.00
19 RA,V:Man-Horse of Hades ... 100.00
20 RA,V:Dr.Yes 100.00
21 RA,C:Batman & Robin,Flash Wonder Woman 75.00
22 RA,A:Chemo 75.00
23 RA,A:Sizzler 75.00
24 RA,V:Balloonman 75.00
25 RA,V:Chemo 75.00
26 RA,V:Metal Mods 75.00
27 RA,O:Metal Men,rtd 100.00
28 RA 75.00
29 RA,V:Robot Eater 75.00
30 RA,GK,in the Forbidden Zone . 75.00
31 RA,GK 50.00
32 RA,Robot Amazon Blues 45.00
33 MS,The Hunted Metal Men 45.00
34 MS 45.00
35 MS 45.00
36 MS,The Cruel Clowns 45.00
37 MS,To walk among Men 45.00
38 MS 45.00
39 MS,Beauty of the Beast 45.00
40 MS 45.00
41 MS 45.00
42 RA,reprint 20.00
43 RA,reprint 20.00
44 RA,reprint,V:Missile Men ... 20.00
45 WS 20.00
46 WS,V:Chemo 20.00
47 WS,V:Plutonium Man 20.00
48 WS,A:Eclipso 22.00
49 WS,A:Eclipso 22.00
50 WS,JSa 15.00
51 JSn,V:Vox 15.00
52 JSn,V:Brain Children 15.00
53 JA(c),V:Brain Children 15.00
54 JSn,A:Green Lantern 15.00
55 JSn,A:Green Lantern 15.00
56 JSn,V:Inheritor 15.00

[Limited Series], 1993–94
1 DJu,BBr,Foil(c) 5.00
2 DJu,BBr,O:Metal Men 3.00
3 DJu,BBr,V:Missile Men 3.00
4 DJu,BBr,final issue 3.00

METAMORPHO
July-Aug., 1965
[Regular Series]
1 A:Kurt Vornok 175.00
2 Terror from the Telstar 100.00
3 Who stole the USA 100.00
4 V:Cha-Cha Chaves 75.00
5 V:Bulark 75.00
6 .... 75.00
7 thru 9 .... @50.00
10 I:Element Girl 70.00
11 thru 17 March-April, 1968 .. @45.00

[Mini-Series], 1993
1 GN,V:The Orb of Ra 2.50
2 GN,A:Metamorpho's Son 2.50
3 GN,V:Elemental Man 2.50
4 GN,final Issue 2.50

METROPOLIS S.C.U.
Nov., 1994
1 Special Police unit 2.25
2 Eco-terror in Metropolis 2.25
3 Superman 2.25
4 final issue 2.25

MICHAEL MOORCOCK'S MULTIVERSE
DC/Helix, Sept., 1997
1 WS,three stories, inc. Eternal Champion adapt. 2.50
2 WS,Eternal Champion 2.50
3 WS,Moonbeams & Roses 2.50
4 WS,Moonbeams & Roses 2.50
5 .... 2.50
6 Duke Elric 2.50
7 Metatemporal Detective 2.50
8 Castle Silverskin 2.50
9 Duke Elric 2.50
10 Eternal Champion 2.50
11 WS, Silverskin 2.50
12 WS, concl. 2.50
TPB rep. #1–#12 .... 19.95

MIDNIGHT, MASS
DC/Vertigo, April, 2002
1 JRz,F:Adam & Julia 2.50
2 JRz,a lone farmhouse 2.50
3 JRz,JP 2.50
4 JRz,JP,The Four Sisters,pt.1 . 2.50
5 JRz,JP,The Four Sisters,pt.2 . 2.50
6 JRz,JP,The Four Sisters,pt.3 . 2.50
7 JRz,JP,3 uninvited visitors .. 2.50
8 JRz,Secrets 2.50

MILLENNIUM
Jan., 1988
1 JSa,SEt, The Plan 3.00
2 JSa,SEt, The Chosen 2.50
3 JSa,SEt, Reagen/Manhunters .. 2.50
4 JSa,SEt, Mark Shaw/Batman ... 2.50
5 JSa,SEt, The Chosen 2.50
6 JSa,SEt, Superman 2.50

Millennium–Mr. District

DC

Comics Values Annual

7 JSa,SEt, Boster Gold 2.50
8 JSa,SEt,I:New Guardians 2.50

MILLENNIUM FEVER
1995–96
1 Young Love 2.50
2 Nightmares Worsen 2.50
3 Worst Nightmare 2.50
4 . . . . 2.50

MINX, THE
DC/Vertigo, Aug., 1998
1 PrM,SeP,The Chosen, pt.1 . . . . 3.00
2 PrM,SeP,The Chosen, pt.2 . . . . 2.50
3 PrM,SeP,The Chosen, pt.3 . . . . 2.50
4 PrM,SeP,Monkey Quartet,pt.1 . . 2.50
5 PrM,SeP,Monkey Quartet,pt.2 . . 2.50
6 PrM,SeP,Monkey Quartet,pt.3 . . 2.50
7 PrM,SeP,Monkey Quartet,pt.4 . . 2.50
8 PrM,SeP,final issue 2.50

MISTER E
1991
1 (From Books of Magic) 2.50
2 A:The Shadower 2.50
3 A:The Shadower 2.50
4 A:Tim Hunter, Dr. Fate, Phantom Stranger, final issue 2.50

MISTER MIRACLE
1971–78
1 JK,I:Mr.Miracle 90.00
2 JK,I:Granny Goodness 50.00
3 JK,`Paraniod Pill' 50.00
4 JK,I:Barda 55.00
5 JK,I:Vermin Vundabar 55.00
6 JK,I:Female Furies 55.00
7 JK,V:Kanto 55.00
8 JK,V:Lump 55.00
9 JK,O:Mr.Miracle,C:Darkseid . . . 25.00
10 JK,A:Female Furies 25.00
11 JK,V:Doctor Bedlum 25.00
12 JK,`Mystivac' 25.00
13 JK,`The Dictator's Dungeon' . . 25.00
14 JK,I:Madame Evil Eye 25.00
15 JK,O:Shilo Norman 25.00
16 JK,F:Shilo Norman 25.00
17 JK,`Murder Lodge' 25.00
18 JK,W:Mr.Miracle & Barda 25.00
19 MR,NA,DG,TA,JRu,AM 25.00
20 MR 10.00

21 MR 10.00
22 MR 10.00
23 MG 10.00
24 MG,RH 10.00
25 MG,RH 10.00
Spec.#1 SR 3.50

[2nd Series], 1989–91
1 IG,O:Mister Miracle 3.00
2 IG 2.50
3 IG,A:Highfather,Forever People . 2.50
4 IG,A:The Dark,Forever People . 2.50
5 IG,V:TheDark,A:Forever People 2.50
6 A:G.L. Gnort 2.50
7 A:Blue Beetle, Booster Gold . . . 2.50
8 RM,A:Blue Beetle,Booster Gold 2.50
9 I:Maxi-Man 2.50
10 V:Maxi-Man 2.50
11 . . . . 2.50
12 . . . . 2.50
13 Manga Khan Saga begins,
   A:L-Ron,A:Lobo 3.00
14 A:Lobo 2.50
15 Manga Khan cont. 2.50
16 MangaKhan cont.,JLA#39tie-in . 2.50
17 On Apokolips,A:Darkseid 2.50
18 On Apokolips 2.50
19 Return to Earth, contd
   from JLA#42 . . . . 2.50
20 IG,Oberon 2.50
21 Return of Shilo 2.50
22 New Mr.Miracle revealed 2.50
23 Secrets of the 2 Mr. Miracles
   revealed, A:Mother Box 2.50
24 . . . . 2.50
25 . . . . 2.50
26 Monster Party,pt.1 . . . . 2.50
27 Monster Party,pt.2,
   A:Justice League 2.50
28 final issue 2.50

[3rd Series], 1996
1 JK, new mythology 2.25
2 V:Justice League 2.25
2 How can Scott Free save
   Big Barda 2.25
3 accepts his powers 2.25
4 corruption throughout
   the cosmos 2.25
5 thru 7 SCr . . . . @2.25
TPB Jack Kirby's Mister Miracle . . 13.00

MR. DISTRICT ATTORNEY
Jan.–Feb., 1948
1 The Innocent Forger 1,200.00
2 The Richest Man In Prison . . 500.00
3 The Honest Convicts 350.00
4 The Merchant of Death 350.00
5 The Booby-Trap Killer 350.00
6 The D.A. Meets Scotland Yard 300.00
7 The People vs. Killer Kane . . 300.00
8 The Rise and Fall of 'Lucky'
   Lynn 300.00
9 The Case of the Living
   Counterfeit 300.00
10 The D.A. Takes a Vacation . . . 225.00
11 The Game That Has
   No Winners 225.00
12 Fake Accident Racket 225.00
13 The Execution of Caesar
   Larsen 225.00
14 The Innocent Man In
   Murderers' Row 225.00
15 Prison Train 225.00
16 The Wire Tap Crimes 225.00
17 The Bachelor of Crime 225.00
18 The Case of the Twelve
   O'Clock Killer 225.00
19 The Four King's Of Crime . . . 225.00
20 You Catch a Killer 225.00

21 I Was A Killer's Bodyguard . . . 150.00
22 The Marksman of Crime 150.00
23 Diary of a Criminal 150.00
24 The Killer In The Iron Mask . . 150.00
25 I Hired My Killer 150.00
26 The Case of the Wanted
   Criminals 150.00
27 The Case of the Secret Six . . 150.00
28 Beware the Bogus Beggars . . 150.00
29 The Crimes of Mr. Jumbo 150.00
30 Man of a Thousand Faces . . . 150.00
31 The Hot Money Gang 150.00
32 The Case o/t Bad Luck Clues . 150.00
33 A Crime Is Born 150.00
34 The Amazing Crimes of Mr. X . 150.00
35 This Crime For Hire 150.00
36 The Chameleon of Crime 150.00
37 Miss Miller's Big Case 150.00
38 The Puzzle Shop For Crime . . 150.00
39 Man Who Killed Daredevils . . 150.00
40 The Human Vultures 150.00
41 The Great Token Take 150.00
42 Super-Market Sleuth 150.00
43 Hotel Detective 150.00
44 S.S. Justice,B:Comics Code . . 125.00
45 Miss Miller, Widow 125.00
46 Mr. District Attorney,
   Public Defender 125.00
47 The Missing Persons Racket . 125.00
48 Manhunt With the Mounties . . 125.00
49 The TV Dragnet 125.00
50 The Case of Frank Bragan,
   Little Shot 125.00
51 The Big Heist 125.00
52 Crooked Wheels of Fortune . . 125.00
53 The Courtroom Patrol 125.00
54 The Underworld Spy Squad . . 125.00
55 The Flying Saucer Mystery . . . 125.00
56 The Underworld Oracle 125.00
57 The Underworld Employment
   Agency 125.00
58 The Great Bomb Scare 125.00
59 Great Underworld Spy Plot . . . 125.00
60 The D.A.'s TV Rival 125.00
61 SMo(c),Architect of Crime . . . 125.00
62 A-Bombs For Sale 125.00
63 The Flying Prison 125.00
64 SMo(c),The Underworld
   Treasure Hunt 125.00
65 SMo(c),World Wide Dragnet . . 125.00
66 SMo(c),The Secret of the
   D.A.'s Diary 125.00
67 Jan.–Feb., 1959 . . . . 125.00

Mister Miracle #18 © DC Comics, Inc.

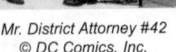

Mr. District Attorney #42 © DC Comics, Inc.

CVA Page 116 — All comics prices listed are for *Near Mint* condition.

MOBFIRE
1994–95
1 WaP,Gangsters in London 2.50
2 WaP, ... 2.50
3 WaP,The Bocor. 2.50
4 WaP,V:Bocor 2.50
5 WaP,Voice in My Head 2.50
6 WaP,Genetic Babies, final issue . 2.50

MODESTY BLAISE
1 DG,V:Gabriel 4.95
2 DG,V:Gabriel 4.95
GN Spy Thriller. 19.95

MOONSHADOW
DC/Vertigo, 1994–95
1 JMD(s),JMu,rep. 2.50
2 thru 4 JMD .... @2.50
5 fully painted 2.50
6 .... 2.50
7 F:Shady Lady. 2.50
8 Rep. Search for Ira. 2.50
9 JMD,JMu,A:Tittletat Twins. 2.50
10 JMD,JMu,Interplanetary
   Prostitutes 2.50
11 JMu,Ira's life story 2.50
12 Rep. w/6pg new material 3.50

MORE FUN COMICS
See: NEW FUN COMICS

MOVIE COMICS
April, 1939
1 `Gunga Din'. 4,500.00
2 `Stagecoach'. 3,000.00
3 `East Side of Heaven' 2,000.00
4 Captain Fury,B:Oregon Trail . 1,600.00
5 `Man in the Iron Mask'. 1,900.00
6 Phantom Creeps, Sept.,1939 2,500.00

MS. TREE QUARTERLY
1990
1 MGr,A:Batman 5.00
2 A:Butcher 4.00
3 A:Butcher 4.00
4 `Paper Midnight' 4.50
5 Murder/Rape Investigation ... 4.50
6 Gothic House 4.50
7 The Family Way 4.50
8 CI,FMc,Ms Tree Pregnant(c),
  B.U. King Faraday 4.50
9 Child Kidnapped. 4.50
10 V:International Mob 4.00

MUCHA LUCHA
April 2003
1 (of 3) 2.25
2 It's All Buena 2.25
3 Flea loses match 2.25

MUKTUK WOLFSBREATH:
HARD-BOILED SHAMAN
DC/Vertigo, June, 1998
1 (of 3) TLa,SvP,Lady Shaman ... 2.50
2 .... 2.50
3 TLa,SvP, concl. 2.50

MUTT AND JEFF
1939
1 .... 1,500.00
2 .... 750.00
3 Bucking Broncos. 550.00
4 and 5 .... @500.00

6 thru 10 .... @250.00
11 thru 20 .... @175.00
21 thru 30 .... @125.00
31 thru 50 .... @100.00
51 thru 70 .... @75.00
71 thru 80 .... @65.00
81 thru 99 .... @50.00
100 .... 65.00
101 thru 103 .... @50.00
104 thru 148 .... @45.00

MY GREATEST ADVENTURE
Jan.–Feb., 1955
1 LSt,I Was King Of
  Danger Island 2,000.00
2 My Million Dollar Dive. 800.00
3 I Found Captain
  Kidd's Treasure 600.00
4 I Had A Date With Doom. 600.00
5 I Escaped From Castle Morte . 475.00
6 I Had To Spend A Million. 475.00
7 I Was A Prisoner On Island X . 450.00
8 The Day They Stole My Face . 450.00
9 I Walked Through The Doors
  of Destiny. 450.00
10 We Found A World Of
   Tiny Cavemen 450.00
11 LSt(c),My Friend, Madcap
   Manning. 350.00
12 MMe(c),I Hunted Big Game
   in Outer Space 350.00
13 LSt(c),I Hunted Goliath
   The Robot 350.00
14 LSt,I Had the Midas
   Touch of Gold. 350.00
15 JK, I Hunted the Worlds
   Wildest Animals 350.00
16 JK,I Died a Thousand Times . 350.00
17 JK,I Doomed the World 350.00
18 JK(c),We Discovered The
   Edge of the World. 400.00
19 I Caught Earth's
   Strangest Criminal 350.00
20 JK,I Was Big-Game
   on Neptune 350.00
21 JK,We Were Doomed By
   The Metal-Eating Monster. .. 350.00
22 I Was Trapped In The
   Magic Mountains 325.00
23 I Was A Captive In
   Space Prison 325.00
24 NC(c),I Was The Robinson
   Crusoe of Space. 325.00
25 I Led Earth's Strangest
   Safari! 325.00
26 NC(c),We Battled The
   Sand Creature 325.00
27 I Was the Earth's First Exile . 325.00
28 I Stalked the Camouflage
   Creatures. 300.00
29 I Tracked the
   Forbidden Powers 200.00
30 We Cruised Into the
   Supernatural! 200.00
31 I Was A Modern Hercules. ... 175.00
32 We Were Trapped In A Freak
   Valley! 175.00
33 I Was Pursued by
   the Elements 175.00
34 DD,We Unleashed The Cloud
   Creatures. 175.00
35 I Solved the Mystery of
   Volcano Valley 175.00
36 I Was Bewitched
   By Lady Doom 175.00
37 DD&SMo(c),I Hunted the
   Legendary Creatures!..... 175.00
38 DD&SMo(c),I Was the Slave
   of the Dream-Master. 175.00

39 DD&SMo(c),We were Trapped
   in the Valley of no Return ... 175.00
40 We Battled the Storm
   Creature. 175.00
41 DD&SMo(c),I Was Tried
   by a Robot Court 150.00
42 DD&SMo(c),My Brother
   Was a Robot 150.00
43 DD&SMo(c),I Fought the
   Sonar Creatures 150.00
44 DD&SMo(c),We Fought the
   Beasts of Petrified Island . 150.00
45 DD&SMo(c),We Battled the
   Black Narwhal 150.00
46 DD&SMo(c),We Were Prisoners
   of the Sundial of Doom 150.00
47 We Became Partners of the
   Beast Brigade. 150.00
48 DD&SMo(c),I Was Marooned
   On Earth 150.00
49 DD&SMo(c),I Was An Ally
   Of A Criminal Creature 150.00
50 DD&SMo(c),I Fought the
   Idol King. 150.00
51 DD&SMo(c),We Unleashed
   the Demon of the Dungeon. . 135.00
52 DD&SMo(c),I Was A
   Stand-In For an Alien 135.00
53 DD&SMo(c),I, Creature Slayer 135.00
54 I Was Cursed With
   an Alien Pal 135.00
55 DD&SMo(c),I Beacame The
   Wonder-Man of Space 135.00
56 DD&SMo(c),My Brother-The
   Alien. 135.00
57 DD&SMo(c),Don't Touch Me
   Or You'll Die. 135.00
58 DD&SMo(c),ATh,I was Trapped
   in the Land of L'Oz. 150.00
59 DD&SMo(c),Listen Earth-I
   Am Still Alive 150.00
60 DD&SMo(c),ATh,I Lived in
   Two Worlds 150.00
61 DD&SMo(c),ATh,I Battled For
   the Doom-Stone 150.00
62 DD&SMo(c),I Fought For
   An Alien Enemy 100.00
63 DD&SMo(c),We Braved the
   Trail of the Ancient Warrior . 100.00
64 DD&SMo(c),They Crowned My
   Fiance Their King! 100.00
65 DD&SMo(c),I Lost the Life
   or Death Secret 100.00
66 DD&SMo(c),I Dueled with

My Greatest Adventure #35
© DC Comics Inc.

My Greatest–Mystery — DC — Comics Values Annual

My Greatest Adventure #40
© DC Comics, Inc.

the Super Spirits 100.00
67 I Protected the Idols
   of Idoro! 100.00
68 DD&SMo(c),My Deadly Island
   of Space 100.00
69 DD&SMo(c),I Was A Courier
   From the Past 100.00
70 DD&SMo(c),We Tracked the
   Fabled Fish-Man! 100.00
71 We Dared to open the Door
   of Danger Dungeon 100.00
72 The Haunted Beach 100.00
73 I Defeiller Mountain 100.00
74 GC(c),We Were Challenged
   By The River Spirit 100.00
75 GC(c),Castaway Cave-Men
   of 1950 . . . . 100.00
76 MMe(c),We Battled the
   Micro-Monster 100.00
77 ATh,We Found the Super-
   Tribes of Tomorrow 125.00
78 Destination-'Dead Man's Alley' 100.00
79 Countdown in Dinosaur Valley 100.00
80 BP,I:Doom Patrol 750.00
81 BP,ATh,I:Dr. Janus 250.00
82 BP,F:Doom Patrol 225.00
83 BP,F:Doom Patrol 225.00
84 BP,V:General Immortus 225.00
85 BP,ATh,F:Doom Patrol 225.00
Becomes:

DOOM PATROL
March, 1964

86 BP,I:Brogherhood of Evil 150.00
87 BP,O:Negative Man 125.00
88 BP,O:Chief 125.00
89 BP,I:Animal-Veg.-MineralMan . 125.00
90 BP,A:Brotherhood of Evil . . . 125.00
91 BP,I:Manto, Gargvax 125.00
92 BP,I:Dr.Tyme, A:Mento 125.00
93 BP,A:Brotherhood of Evil . . . 125.00
94 BP,I:Dr.Radich, The Claw . . . 125.00
95 BP,A:Animal-Vegetable
   -Mineral Man 125.00
96 BP,A:General Immortus,
   Brotherhood of Evil 125.00
97 BP,A:General Immortus,
   Brotherhood of Evil 125.00
98 BP,I:Mr.103 . . . . 125.00
99 I:Beast Boy 120.00
100 BP,O:Beast Boy,Robotman . 130.00
101 BP,A:Beast Boy 75.00
102 BP,A:Beast Boy,Challengers
   of the Unknown 60.00
103 BP,A:Beast Boy 60.00
104 BP,W:Elasti-Girl,Mento,
   C:JLA,Teen Titans 60.00
105 BP,A:Beast Boy 60.00
106 BP,O:Negative Man 60.00
107 BP,A:Beast Boy, I:Dr.Death . . 60.00
108 BP,A:Brotherhood of Evil . . . 60.00
109 BP,I:Mandred 60.00
110 BP,A:Garguax,Mandred,
   Brotherhood of Evil 50.00
111 BP,I:Zarox-13,A:Brotherhood
   of Evil 50.00
112 BP,O:Beast Boy,Madame
   Rouge 50.00
113 BP,A:Beast Boy,Mento 50.00
114 BP,A:Beast Boy 50.00
115 BP,A:Beast Boy 50.00
116 BP,A:Madame Rouge 50.00
117 BP,I:Black Vulture 50.00
118 BP,A:Beast Boy 50.00
119 BP,A:Madam Rouge 50.00
120 I:Wrecker 50.00
121 JO,D:Doom Patrol 150.00
122 rep.Doom Patrol #89 . . . . . 15.00
123 rep.Doom Patrol #95 . . . . . 15.00
124 rep.Doom Patrol #90 . . . . . 15.00

[2nd Series]
See: DOOM PATROL

MY NAME IS CHAOS
1992

1 JRy,Song Laid Waste to Earth . . 4.95
2 JRy,Colonization of Mars 4.95
3 JRy,Search for Eternal Beings . . 4.95
4 JRy,final issue 4.95

MY NAME IS HOLOCAUST
DC/Milestone, 1995
[Mini-Series]

1 F:Holocaust (Blood Syndicate) . . 2.50
2 V:Cantano 2.50
3 A:Blood Syndicate 2.50

MYSTERY IN SPACE
April-May, 1951

1 Cl&FrG(c),FF,B:Knights of the
   Galaxy,Nine Worlds to
   Conquer 4,500.00
2 Cl(c),MA,A:Knights of the
   Galaxy, Jesse James-
   Highwayman of Space 1,700.00
3 Cl(c),A:Knights of the
   Galaxy, Duel of the Planets 1,300.00
4 Cl(c),S&K,MA,A:Knights of the
   Galaxy, Master of Doom . . 1,100.00
5 Cl(c),A:Knights of the Galaxy,
   Outcast of the Lost World . 1,100.00
6 Cl(c),A:Knights of the Galaxy,
   The Day the World Melted . . 800.00
7 GK(c),ATh,A:Knights of the Galaxy,
   Challenge o/t Robot Knight . . 800.00
8 MA,It's a Women's World 800.00
9 MA(c),The Seven Wonders
   of Space 800.00
10 MA(c),The Last Time I
   Saw Earth 800.00
11 GK(c),Unknown Spaceman . . 600.00
12 MA,The Sword in the Sky . . . 600.00
13 MA(c),MD,Signboard
   in Space 600.00
14 MA,GK(c),Hollywood
   in Space 600.00
15 MA(c),Doom from Station X . 600.00
16 MA(c),Honeymoon in Space . 600.00
17 MA(c),The Last Mile of Space 600.00
18 MA(c),GK,Chain Gang
   of Space 600.00
19 MA(c),The Great

Mystery in Space #18
© DC Comics, Inc.

Space-Train Robbery 600.00
20 MA(c),The Man in the
   Martian Mask 500.00
21 MA(c),Interplanetary
   Merry-Go-Round 500.00
22 MA(c),The Square Earth . . . 500.00
23 MA(c),Monkey-Rocket
   to Mars 500.00
24 MA(c),A:Space Cabby,
   Hitchhiker of Space 500.00
25 MA(c),Station Mars on the Air 425.00
26 GK(c),Earth is the Target 425.00
27 The Human Fishbowl 425.00
28 The Radio Planet 425.00
29 GK(c),Space-Enemy
   Number One 425.00
30 GK(c),The Impossible
   World Named Earth 425.00
31 GK(c),The Day the Earth
   Split in Two 400.00
32 GK(c),Riddle of the
   Vanishing Earthmen 400.00
33 The Wooden World War 400.00
34 GK(c),The Man Who
   Moved the World 400.00
35 The Counterfeit Earth 400.00
36 GK(c),Secret of the
   Moon Sphinx 400.00
37 GK(c),Secret of the
   Masked Martians 400.00
38 GK(c),The Canals of Earth . . . 400.00
39 GK(c),Sorcerers of Space . . . 400.00
40 GK(c),Riddle of the
   Runaway Earth 400.00
41 GK(c),The Miser of Space . . . 300.00
42 GK(c),The Secret of the
   Skyscraper Spaceship 300.00
43 GK(c),Invaders From the
   Space Satellites 300.00
44 GK(c),Amazing Space Flight
   of North America 300.00
45 GK(c),MA,Flying Saucers
   Over Mars 300.00
46 GK(c),MA,Mystery of the
   Moon Sniper 300.00
47 GK(c),MA,Interplanetary Tug
   of War 300.00
48 GK(c),MA,Secret of the
   Scarecrow World 300.00
49 GK(c),The Sky-High Man 300.00
50 GK(c),The Runaway
   Space-Train 300.00
51 GK(c),MA,Battle of the
   Moon Monsters 300.00

DC — Mystery–New Fun

52 GK(c),MSy,Mirror Menace
    of Mars 300.00
53 GK(c),B:Adam Strange stories,
    Menace o/t Robot Raiders . 2,500.00
54 GK(c),Invaders of the
    Underground World 700.00
55 GK(c),The Beast From
    the Runaway World 550.00
56 GK(c),The Menace of
    the Super-Atom 300.00
57 GK(c),Mystery of the
    Giant Footsteps 300.00
58 GK(c),Chariot in in the Sky. . . 300.00
59 GK(c),The Duel of the
    Two Adam Stranges 300.00
60 GK(c),The Attack of the
    Tentacle World 300.00
61 CI&MA(c),Threat of the
    Tornado Tyrant 250.00
62 CI&MA(c),The Beast with
    the Sizzling Blue Eyes 250.00
63 The Weapon that
    Swallowed Men 250.00
64 The Radioactive Menace 250.00
65 Mechanical Masters of Rann . 250.00
66 Space-Island of Peril 250.00
67 Challenge of the
    Giant Fireflies. 250.00
68 CI&MA(c),Fadeaway Doom . 250.00
69 CI&MA(c),Menace of the
    Aqua-Ray Weapon 250.00
70 CI&MA(c),Vengeance of
    the Dust Devil. 250.00
71 CI&MA(c),The Challenge of
    the Crystal Conquerors. . . . 250.00
72 The Multiple Menace Weapon 200.00
73 CI&MA(c),The Invisible
    Invaders of Rann 200.00
74 CI&MA(c),The Spaceman
    Who Fought Himself. 200.00
75 CI&MA(c),The Planet That
    Came to a Standstill 350.00
76 CI&MA(c),Challenge of
    the Rival Starman 200.00
77 CI&MA(c),Ray-Gun in the Sky 200.00
78 CI&MA(c),Shadow People
    of the Eclipse 200.00
79 CI&MA(c),The Metal
    Conqueror of Rann. 200.00
80 CI&MA(c),The Deadly
    Shadows of Adam Strange . 200.00
81 CI&MA(c),The Cloud-Creature
    That Menaced Two Worlds . . 150.00
82 CI&MA(c),World War on
    Earth and Rann 150.00
83 CI&MA(c),The Emotion-Master
    of Space. 150.00
84 CI&MA(c),The Powerless
    Weapons of Adam Strange . . 150.00
85 CI&MA(c),Riddle of the
    Runaway Rockets. 150.00
86 CI&MA(c),Attack of the
    Underworld Giants 150.00
87 MA(c),The Super-Brain of
    Adam Strange,B:Hawkman. . 275.00
88 CI&MA(c),The Robot Wraith
    of Rann 250.00
89 MA(c),Siren o/t Space Ark . . . 225.00
90 CI&MA(c),Planets and
    Peril, E:Hawkman. 225.00
91 CI&MA(c),Puzzle of
    the Perilous Prisons 75.00
92 DD&SMo(c),The Alien Invasion
    From Earth,B:Space Ranger. . 75.00
93 DD&SMo(c),The Convict
    Twins of Space. 75.00
94 DD&SMo(c),The Adam
    Strange Story 75.00
95 The Hydra-Head From
    Outer Space. 75.00
96 The Coins That Doomed
    Two Planets 75.00
97 The Day Adam Strange
    Vanished 75.00
98 The Wizard of the Cosmos. . . . 75.00
99 DD&SMo(c),The World-
    Destroyer From Space 75.00
100 DD&SMo(c),GK,The Death
    of Alanna 75.00
101 GK(c),The Valley of
    1,000 Dooms 75.00
102 GK,The Robot World of Rann 75.00
103 The Billion-Dollar Time-
    Capsule(Space Ranger),I:Ultra
    the Multi-Agent 75.00
104 thru 109 . . . . @50.00
110 Series ends, Sept., 1966 . . . 50.00
[Series Revived], Sept., 1980
111 JAp,SD,MR,DSp. 10.00
112 JAp,TS,JKu(c) 10.00
113 JKu(c),MGo 10.00
114 JKu(c),JCr,SD,DSp 10.00
115 JKu(c),SD,GT,BB 10.00
116 JSn(c),JCr,SD 10.00
117 DN,GT,March, 1981 . . . . . 10.00

MYTHOS: THE FINAL TOUR
DC/Vertigo, Oct., 1996
1 JNR(s),GyA,PrG,F:Rock Star
    Adam Case 5.95
2 JNR(s),PSj,F:Rock Star Adam
    Case 5.95
3 JNR(s), finale 5.95

NAME OF THE GAME, THE
Dec. 2002
TPB WE. 19.95

NAMES OF MAGIC, THE
DC/Vertigo, Dec., 2000
1 (of 5) JBo(c),F:Tim Hunter 10.00
2 JBo(c) 10.00
3 JBo(c) 10.00
4 JBo(c) 10.00
5 JBo(c) concl. 10.00
TPB rep. 14.95

NATHANIEL DUSK
Feb., 1984
1 GC(p). 2.25
2 GC(p) 2.25
3 GC(p) 2.25
4 GC(p), May, 1984 . . . . 2.25

NATHANIEL DUSK II
Oct., 1985
1 thru 4 GC,Jan., 1986. . . . . . . @2.25

NATIONAL COMICS
1999
1 MWa(s),AAl,F:Flash &
    Mr. Terrific 2.25

NAZZ, THE
1990–91
1 Michael'sBook 5.50
2 Johnny'sBook 5.00
3 Search for Michael Nazareth. . . 5.00
4 V:Retaliators,final issue 5.00

NEVADA
DC/Vertigo, March, 1998
1 (of 6) SvG,SL,show girl. 2.50

2 SvG,SL,dismembered corpse . . . 2.50
3 SvG,SL,stabbed an inhuman . . . 2.50
4 SvG,SL,another dimension 2.50
5 SvG,SL 2.50
6 SvG,SL,Big Bang, concl. 2.50
TPB Nevada, rep. 15.00

NEW ADVENTURES OF SUPERBOY
See: SUPERBOY

NEW BOOK OF COMICS
1937
1 Dr.Occult 20,000.00
2 Dr.Occult 10,000.00

NEW COMICS
1935
1 . . . . 25,000.00
2 . . . . 10,000.00
3 thru 6 . . . . @7,500.00
7 thru 11 . . . . @6,000.00
Becomes:

NEW ADVENTURE COMICS
Jan., 1937
12 S&S 6,000.00
13 thru 20 . . . . @5,000.00
21 . . . . 4,000.00
22 thru 31 . . . . @3,000.00
Becomes:
ADVENTURE COMICS

NEW FUN COMICS
Feb., 1935
1 B:Oswald the Rabbit,
    Jack Woods. 60,000.00
2 . . . . 30,000.00
3 . . . . 15,000.00
4 . . . . 15,000.00
5 . . . . 15,000.00
6 S&S,B:Dr.Occult,
    Henri Duval 30,000.00
Becomes:
MORE FUN COMICS
Jan., 1936
7 S&S,WK 8,000.00
8 S&S,WK 7,500.00
9 S&S,E:Henri Duval 9,000.00

Nazz Book #2 © DC Comics Inc.

All comics prices listed are for *Near Mint* condition.

New Fun–New Gods — DC — Comics Values Annual

More Fun #40 © DC Comics, Inc.

10 S&S 5,000.00
11 S&S,B:Calling all Girls 4,800.00
12 S&S 4,000.00
13 S&S 3,800.00
14 S&S,Color,Dr.Occult 16,000.00
15 S&S 8,000.00
16 S&S,Christmas(c) 8,000.00
17 S&S 7,500.00
18 S&S 3,000.00
19 S&S 3,000.00
20 HcK,S&S 3,000.00
21 S&S 3,500.00
22 S&S 3,500.00
23 S&S 3,500.00
24 S&S 3,500.00
25 S&S 2,700.00
26 S&S 2,500.00
27 S&S 2,500.00
28 S&S 2,400.00
29 S&S 2,400.00
30 S&S 2,400.00
31 S&S 2,500.00
32 S&S,E:Dr. Occult 2,400.00
33 . . . . 2,400.00
34 . . . . 2,400.00
35 . . . . 2,400.00
36 B:Masked Ranger 2,400.00
37 thru 40 . . . . @3,000.00
41 E:Masked Ranger 2,000.00
42 thru 50 . . . . @2,000.00
51 I:The Spectre 7,000.00
52 O:The Spectre,pt.1,
   E:Wing Brady 80,000.00
53 O:The Spectre,pt.2,
   B:Capt.Desmo 42,000.00
54 E:King Carter,Spectre(c) . . 17,000.00
55 I:Dr.Fate,E:Bulldog Martin,
   Spectre(c) 20,000.00
56 B:Congo Bill,Dr.Fate(c) 9,000.00
57 Spectre(c) 7,000.00
58 Spectre(c) 7,000.00
59 A:Spectre 7,000.00
60 Spectre(c) 7,000.00
61 Spectre(c) 7,000.00
62 Spectre(c) 4,000.00
63 Spectre(c),E:St.Bob Neal . . 4,000.00
64 Spectre(c),B:Lance Larkin . . 4,000.00
65 Spectre(c) 4,000.00
66 Spectre(c) 4,000.00
67 Spectre(c),O:Dr. Fate,
   E:Congo Bill,Biff Bronson . . 9,000.00
68 Dr.Fate(c),B:Clip Carson . . . 2,800.00
69 Dr.Fate(c) 2,800.00
70 Dr.Fate(c),E:Lance Larkin . . 2,800.00
71 Dr.Fate(c),I:Johnny Quick . . 7,000.00
72 Dr.Fate has Smaller Helmet,
   E:Sgt. Carey,Sgt.O'Malley . 2,700.00
73 Dr.Fate(c),I:Aquaman,Green
   Arrow,Speedy 18,000.00
74 Dr.Fate(c),A:Aquaman 3,500.00
75 Dr.Fate(c) 2,900.00
76 Dr.Fate(c),MMe,E:Clip Carson,
   B:Johnny Quick 2,900.00
77 MMe,Green Arrow(c) 2,900.00
78 MMe,Green Arrow(c) 2,900.00
79 MMe,Green Arrow(c) 2,900.00
80 MMe,Green Arrow(c) 2,900.00
81 MMe,Green Arrow(c) 1,600.00
82 MMe,Green Arrow(c) 1,600.00
83 MMe,Green Arrow(c) 1,600.00
84 MMe,Green Arrow(c) 1,600.00
85 MMe,Green Arrow(c) 1,600.00
86 MMe 1,600.00
87 MMe,E:Radio Squad 1,600.00
88 MMe,Green Arrow(c) 1,600.00
89 MMe,O:Gr.Arrow&Speedy . 1,700.00
90 MMe,Green Arrow(c) 1,600.00
91 MMe,Green Arrow(c) 1,000.00
92 MMe,Green Arrow(c) 1,000.00
93 MMe,B:Dover & Clover 1,000.00
94 MMe,Green Arrow(c) 1,000.00
95 MMe,Green Arrow(c) 1,000.00
96 MMe,Green Arrow(c) 1,000.00
97 MMe,JKu,E:Johnny Quick . . 1,000.00
98 E:Dr. Fate 1,300.00
99 Green Arrow(c) 1,000.00
100 Anniversary Issue 1,500.00
101 O&I:Superboy,
    E:The Spectre 12,000.00
102 A:Superboy 1,500.00
103 A:Superboy 1,200.00
104 Superboy(c) 1,100.00
105 Superboy(c) 1,100.00
106 . . . . 1,100.00
107 E:Superboy 1,100.00
108 A:Genius Jones,'Genius
    Meets Genius' 250.00
109 A:Genius Jones, The
    Disappearing Deposits 250.00
110 A:Genius Jones, Birds,
    Brains and Burglary 250.00
111 A:Genius Jones, Jeepers
    Creepers 250.00
112 A:Genius Jones, The
    Tell-Tale Tornado 250.00
113 A:Genius Jones, Clocks
    and Shocks 250.00
114 A:Genius Jones, The
    Milky Way 250.00
115 A:Genius Jones,Foolish
    Questions 250.00
116 A:Genius Jones,Palette
    For Plunder 250.00
117 A:Genius Jones,Battle of
    the Pretzel Benders 250.00
118 A:Genius Jones,The
    Sinister Siren 250.00
119 A:Genius Jones,A
    Perpetual Jackpot 250.00
120 A:Genius Jones,The Man
    in the Moon 250.00
121 A:Genius Jones,The
    Mayor Goes Haywire 225.00
122 A:Genius Jones,When Thug-
    Hood Was In Floor 225.00
123 A:Genius Jones,Hi Diddle Diddle,
    the Cat and the Fiddle 225.00
124 A:Genius Jones,
    The Zany Zoo 225.00
125 Genius Jones,
    Impossible But True 1,000.00
126 A:Genius Jones,The Case
    of the Gravy Spots 225.00
127 Nov.–Dec., 1947 . . . . 400.00

NEW GODS, THE
Feb.–March, 1971

1 JK,I:Orion 125.00
2 JK 60.00
3 JK 50.00
4 JK,O:Manhunter, rep. 40.00
5 JK,I:Fastbak & Black Racer . . . 40.00
6 JK 40.00
7 JK,O:Orion 40.00
8 JK 40.00
9 JK,I:Forager 40.00
10 JK 40.00
11 JK 40.00
12 DN,DA,R:New Gods 10.00
13 DN,DA 10.00
14 DN,DA 10.00
15 RB,BMc 10.00
16 DN,DA 10.00
17 DN,DA 10.00
18 DN,DA 10.00
19 DN,DA 10.00

NEW GODS
(Reprints) 1984

1 JK reprint 3.00
2 thru 5 JK reprint . . . . @2.50
6 JK rep.+NewMaterial 2.50

NEW GODS
[2nd Series], 1989

1 From Cosmic Odyssey 3.00
2 A:Orion of New Genesis 2.50
3 A:Orion 2.50
4 Renegade Apokolyptian Insect
  Colony 2.50
5 Orion vs. Forager 2.50
6 A:Eve Donner, Darkseid 2.50
7 Bloodline #1 . . . . 2.50
8 Bloodline #2 . . . . 2.50
9 Bloodline #3 . . . . 2.50
10 Bloodline #4 . . . . 2.50
11 Bloodline #5 . . . . 2.50
12 Bloodlines #6 . . . . 2.50
13 Back on Earth 2.50
14 I:Reflektor 2.50
15 V:Serial Killer 2.50
16 A:Fastbak & Metron 2.50
17 A:Darkseid, Metron 2.50
18 A:YugaKhan,Darkseid,
   Moniters 2.50
19 V:Yuga Khan 2.50
20 Darkseid Dethroned,
   V:Yuga Khan 2.50
21 A:Orion 2.50
22 A:Metron 2.50
23 A:Forever People 2.50
24 A:Forever People 2.50
25 The Pact #1,R:Infinity Man 2.50
26 The Pact #2 . . . . 2.50
27 Assault on Apokolips,Pact#3 . . 2.50
28 Pact #4, final issue 2.50

[3rd Series], 1995–97

1 F:Orion vs. Darkseid 2.50
2 RaP,UnderworldUnleashed tie-in. 2.50
3 RaP,Darkseid destroyed 2.50
4 RaP,F:Lightray 2.50
5 RaP,F:Orion 2.50
6 . . . . 2.50
7 RaP,R:Darkseid 2.50
8 RaP,DZ,F:Highfather, Darkseid . . 2.50
9 thru 11 . . . . @2.50
12 JBy,BWi,F:Metron 2.50
13 JBy,BWi,Orion reappears
   on Earth 2.50
14 JBy,BWi,A:Forever People,
   Lightray 2.50
TPB rep. #1–#11,b&w 12.00
Secret Files #1 KK,JBy 5.00

Comics Values Annual — DC — New Guardians–New Titans

New Guardians #8 © DC Comics Inc.

NEW GUARDIANS
1988–89
1 JSon,from Millennium series.... 3.00
2 JSon,Colombian Drug Cartel ... 2.25
3 JSon,in South Africa,
  V:Janwillem's Army.......... 2.25
4 JSon,V:Neo-Nazi Skinheads
  in California 2.25
5 JSon,Tegra Kidnapped 2.25
6 JSon, In China, Invasion x-over . 2.25
7 JSon, Guardians Return Home .. 2.25
8 JSon, V:Janwillem 2.25
9 JSon, A:Tome Kalmaku,
  V:Janwillem 2.25
10 JSon, A:Tome Kalmaku 2.25
11 PB,Janwillem's secret 2.25
12 PB,New Guardians Future
  revealed, final issue 2.25

NEW TEEN TITANS
Nov., 1980
1 GP,RT,V:Gordanians (see DC
  Comics Presents #26 .... 15.00
2 GP,RT,I:Deathstroke the
  Terminator, I&D:Ravager..... 10.00
3 GP,I:Fearsome Five 6.00
4 GP,RT,A:JLA,O:Starfire........ 6.00
5 CS,RT,O:Raven,I:Trigon 6.00
6 GP,V:Trigon,O:Raven 6.00
7 GP,RT,O:Cyborg............. 6.00
8 GP,RT,A Day in the Life 6.00
9 GP,RT,A:Terminator,
  V:Puppeteer................ 6.00
10 GP,RT,A:Terminator 6.00
11 GP,RT,V:Hyperion 3.00
12 GP,RT,V:Titans of Myth 3.00
13 GP,RT,R:Robotman 3.00
14 GP,RT,I:New Brotherhood of
  Evil,V:Zahl and Rouge 3.00
15 GP,RT,D:Madame Rouge 3.00
16 GP,RT,I:Captain Carrot........ 3.00
17 GP,RT,I:Frances Kane 3.00
18 GP,RT,A:Orig.Starfire 3.00
19 GP,RT,A:Hawkman 3.00
20 GP,RT,V:Disruptor 3.00
21 GP,RT,GC,I:Brother Blood,
  Night Force 3.00
22 GP,RT,V:Brother Blood........ 3.00
23 GP,RT,I:Blackfire 3.00
24 GP,RT,A:Omega Men,I:X-hal ... 3.00
25 GP,RT,A:Omega Men.......... 3.00
26 GP,RT,I:Terra,Runaway #1 .... 3.00
27 GP,RT,A:Speedy,Runaway #2 . 3.00
28 GP,RT,V:Terra 4.00
29 GP,RT,V:Broth.of Evil......... 3.00
30 GP,RT,V:Broth.of Evil,J:Terra ... 3.00
31 GP,RT,V:Broth.of Evil 3.00
32 GP,RT,I:Thunder & Lightning ... 3.00
33 GP,I:Trident 3.00
34 GP,V:The Terminator 3.00
35 KP,RT,V:Mark Wright 3.00
36 KP,RT,A:Thunder & Lightning... 3.00
37 GP,RT,A:Batman/Outsiders(x-over
  BATO#5),V:Fearsome Five.... 3.00
38 GP,O:Wonder Girl 3.00
39 GP,Grayson quits as Robin ... 5.00
40 GP,A:Brother Blood 3.00
Ann.#1 GP,RT,Blackfire.......... 3.50
Ann.#2 GP,I:Vigilante 3.00
Ann.#3 GP,DG,D:Terra,A:Deathstroke
  V:The H.I.V.E............... 3.50
Ann.#4 rep.Direct Ann.#1 .... 2.50
TPB Judas Contract rep.#39-#44,
  Ann.#3,new GP(c).......... 14.95
TPB The Terror of Trigon 17.95

[Special Issues]
Keebler:GP,DG,Drugs........... 2.50
Beverage:Drugs,RA 2.50
IBM:Drugs 3.00
Becomes:

TALES OF THE TEEN TITANS
1984–88
41 GP,A:Brother Blood 3.00
42 GP,DG,V:Deathstroke 5.00
43 GP,DG,V:Deathstroke 5.00
44 GP,DG,I:Nightwing,O:Deathstroke
  Joe Wilson becomes Jericho .. 8.00
45 GP,A:Aqualad,V:The H.I.V.E. ... 3.00
46 GP,A:Aqualad,V:The H.I.V.E. ... 3.00
47 GP,A:Aqualad,V:The H.I.V.E. ... 3.00
48 SR,V:The Recombatants 3.00
49 GP,CI,V:Dr.Light,A:Flash 3.00
50 GP/DG W:Wonder Girl &
  Terry Long,C:Batman,
  Wonder Woman 4.00
51 RB,A:Cheshire.............. 2.50
52 RB,A:Cheshire.............. 2.50
53 RB,I:Ariel,A:Terminator. 2.50
54 RB,A:Terminator 2.50
55 A:Terminator 2.50
56 A:Fearsome Five 2.50
57 A:Fearsome Five 2.50
58 E:MWn(s),A:Fearsome Five.... 2.50
59 rep. DC presennts #26........ 2.50
60 thru 91 rep................. @2.50

NEW TEEN TITANS
[Direct sales series]
Aug., 1984
1 B:MWn(s),GP,L:Raven 6.00
2 GP,D:Azareth,A:Trigon 4.00
3 GP,V:Raven................. 4.00
4 GP,V:Trigon,Raven 4.00
5 GP,D:Trigon,Raven disappears .. 4.00
6 GP,A:Superman,Batman....... 3.00
7 JL,V:Titans of Myth 3.00
8 JL,V:Titans of Myth 3.00
9 JL,V:Titans of Myth,I:Kole 3.00
10 JL,O:Kole 3.00
11 JL,O:Kole 2.50
12 JL,Ghost story 2.50
13 EB,Crisis 2.50
14 EB,Crisis 2.50
15 EB,A:Raven................ 2.50
16 EB,A:OmegaMen............ 2.50
17 EB,V:Blackfire 2.50
18 E:MWn(s),EB,V:Blackfire 2.50
19 EB,V:Mento 2.50
20 GP(c),EB,V:Cheshire,J.Todd ... 2.50
21 GP(c),EB,V:Cheshire,J.Todd ... 2.50
22 GP(c),EB,V:Blackfire,Mento,

New Teen Titans #28 © DC Comics, Inc.

Brother Blood 2.50
23 GP(c),V:Blackfire 2.50
24 CB,V:Hybrid................ 2.50
25 EB,RT,V:Hybrid,Mento,A:Flash.. 2.50
26 KGa,V:Mento 2.50
27 KGa,Church of Br.Blood....... 2.50
28 EB,RT,V:BrotherBlood,A:Flash ... 2.50
29 EB,RT,V:Brother Blood,
  A:Flash,Robin............... 2.50
30 EB,Batman,Superman 2.50
31 EB,RT,V:Brother Blood,A:Flash
  Batman,Robin,Gr.Lantern Corps
  Superman 2.50
32 EB,RT,Murder Weekend 2.50
33 EB,V:Terrorists.............. 2.50
34 EB,RT,V:Mento,Hybird 2.50
35 PB,RT,V:Arthur & Eve 2.50
36 EB,RT,I:Wildebeest 2.50
37 EB,RT,V:Wildebeest.......... 2.50
38 EB,RT,A:Infinity 2.50
39 EB,RT,F:Raven 2.50
40 EB,RT,V:Gentleman Ghost..... 2.50
41 EB,V:Wildebeest,A:Puppeteer,
  Trident,Wildebeest 2.50
42 EB,RT,V:Puppeteer,Gizmo,
  Trident,Wildebeest 2.50
43 CS,RT,V:Phobia............. 2.50
44 RT,V:Godiva 2.50
45 EB,RT,A:Dial H for Hero....... 2.50
46 EB,RT,A:Dial H for Hero....... 2.50
47 O:Titans,C:Wildebeest........ 2.50
48 EB,RT,A:Red Star 2.50
49 EB,RT,A:Red Star 2.50
Ann.#1 A:Superman,V:Brainiac.... 2.50
Ann.#2 JBy,JL,O:Brother Blood.... 3.00
Ann.#3 I:Danny Chase 2.50
Ann.#4 V:Godiva 2.50
Becomes:

NEW TITANS
1988–96
50 B:MWn(s),GP,BMc,B:Who is
  Wonder Girl? 7.00
51 GP,BMc.................... 3.00
52 GP,BMc.................... 3.00
53 GP,RT 3.00
54 GP,RT,E:Who is Wonder Girl? .. 3.00
55 GP,RT,I:Troia 3.00
56 MBr,RT,Tale of Middle Titans ... 3.00
57 GP,BMc,V:Wildebeast 3.00
58 GP,TG,BMc,V:Wildebeast 3.00
59 GP,TG,BMc,V:Wildebeast 3.00
60 GP,TG,BMc,3rd A:Tim Drake

All comics prices listed are for Near Mint condition.

New Titans–Nightwing / DC / Comics Values Annual

(Face Revealed),Batman 5.00
61 GP,TG,BMc,A:Tim Drake,
    Batman 5.00
62 TG,AV,A:Deathstroke 3.00
63 TG,AV,A:Deathstroke 3.00
64 TG,AV,A:Deathstroke 3.00
65 TG,AV,A:Deathstroke,Tim Drake,
    Batman 3.00
66 TG,AV,V:Eric Forrester 2.50
67 TG,AV,V:Eric Forrester 2.50
68 SE,V:Royal Flush Gang 2.50
69 SE,V:Royal Flush Gang 2.50
70 SE,A:Deathstroke 3.00
71 TG,AV,B:Deathstroke,
    B:Titans Hunt 5.00
72 TG,AV,D:Golden Eagle 4.00
73 TG,AV,I:Phantasm 4.00
74 TG,AV,I:Pantha 3.00
75 TG,AV,IR:Jericho/Wildebeest .. 3.00
76 TG,AV,V:Wildebeests 2.50
77 TG,AV,A:Red Star,N:Cyborg... 2.50
78 TG,AV,V:Cyborg 2.50
79 TG,AV,I:Team Titans 3.00
80 KGa,PC,A:Team Titans 2.50
81 CS,AV,War of the Gods 2.50
82 TG,AV,V:Wildebeests 2.50
83 TG,AV,D:Jericho 3.00
84 TG,AV,E:Titans Hunt 2.50
85 TG,AV,I:Baby Wildebeest 2.50
86 CS,AV,E:Deathstroke 2.50
87 TG,AV,A:Team Titans 2.50
88 TG,AV,CS,V:Team Titans 2.50
89 JBr,I:Lord Chaos 2.50
90 TG,AV,Total Chaos#2,A:Team
    Titans,D'stroke,V:Lord Chaos .. 2.50
91 TG,AV,Total Chaos#5,A:Team
    Titans,D'stroke,V:Lord Chaos .. 2.50
92 E:MWn(s),TG,AV,Total Chaos#8,
    A:Team Titans,V:Lord Chaos .. 2.50
93 TG,AV,Titans Sell-Out#3 ...... 2.50
94 PJ,F:Red Star & Cyborg 2.50
95 PJ,Red Star gains new powers . 2.50
96 PJ,I:Solar Flare,
    V:Konstantine 2.50
97 TG,AV,B:The Darkening,R:Speedy
    V:Brotherhood of Evil 2.50
98 TG,AV,V:Brotherhood of Evil ... 2.50
99 TG,AV,I:Arsenal (Speedy) 2.50
100 TG,AV,W:Nightwing&Starfire,
    V:Deathwing,Raven,A:Flash,Team
    Titans,Hologram(c) 4.00
101 AV(i),L:Nightwing 2.50
102 AV(i),A:Prester John 2.50
103 AV(i),V:Bro. of Evil 2.50
104 Terminus #1 .... 2.50
105 Terminus #2 .... 2.50
106 Terminus #3 .... 2.50
107 Terminus #4 .... 2.50
108 A:Supergirl,Flash 2.50
109 F:Starfire 2.50
110 A:Flash,Serg.Steele 2.50
111 A:Checkmate 2.50
112 A:Checkmate 2.50
113 F:Nightwing 2.75
114 L:Starfire, Nightwing,Panthra,
    Wildebeest 2.50
115 A:Trigon 2.50
116 Changling 2.50
117 V:Psimon 2.50
118 V:Raven + Brotherhood 2.50
119 Suffer the Children,pt.1 ...... 2.50
120 Forever Evil,pt.2 .... 2.50
121 Forever Evil,pt.3 .... 2.50
122 Crimelord/Syndicate War,pt.2
    J:Supergirl 2.50
123 MWn(s),RRa,O:Minion 2.50
124 The Siege of Zi Charan 2.50
125 The Siege of Zi Charan 3.00
126 Meltdown,pt.1 .... 2.50
127 MWn,Meltdown, cont. 2.50
128 MWn,Meltdown, cont. 2.50

New Titans #86 © DC Comics, Inc.

129 MWn,Meltdown, cont. 2.50
130 MWn,Meltdown,final issue ... 2.50
Ann.#5 V:Children of the Sun 3.00
Ann.#6 CS,F:Starfire 3.00
Ann.#7 Armageddon 2001,I:Future
    Teen Titans 4.00
Ann.#8 PJ,Eclipso,V:Deathstroke . 3.75
Ann.#9 Bloodlines#5,I:Anima 3.75
Ann.#10 Elseworlds story 3.75
Ann.#11 Year One Annual 3.95
#0 Spec. Zero Hour,new team 2.50

NEW T.H.U.N.D.E.R. AGENTS, THE
July 2003
1 JP 3.00

NEW YEAR'S EVIL:
Dec., 1997
Body Doubles #1 DAn,ALa,JoP,
    JPn(c) 2.00
Dark Nemesis #1 DJu,Ccs,JPn(c). . 2.00
Darkseid #1 JBy,SB,JPn(c) 2.00
Gog #1 MWa,JOy,DJa,JPn(c) 2.00
Mr. Mxyzptlk #1 AlG,TMo,JPn(c) . 2.00
Prometheus #1 GMo,JPn(c) 2.00
Scarecrow #1 PrM,DFg,JPn(c) 2.00
The Rogues #1 BAu,RoW,JPn(c) . 2.00

NEW YORK WORLD'S FAIR
1 1939 .... 30,000.00
2 1940 .... 17,000.00

NIGHTFALL: THE BLACK CHRONICLES
Homage/DC Oct., 1999
1 monsters living among us 2.95
2 .... 2.95
3 .... 2.95

NIGHT FORCE
Aug., 1982
1 GC,1:Night Force 5.00
2 thru 13 GC .... @3.00
14 GC,Sept.,1983 .... 3.00

NIGHT FORCE
Oct., 1996
1 MWn(s),BA,Baron Winters leads. 2.50
2 MWn(s) 2.25
3 MWn(s) 2.25
4 MWn(s),EB,HellSeemsHeaven .. 2.25
5 MWn(s),Low,SMa,Dreamers of
    Dreams,pt.1 .... 2.25
6 MWn(s),Low,SMa,Dreamers,pt.2. 2.25
7 MWn(s),Low,SMa,Dreamers,pt.3. 2.25
8 MWn(s),Convergence, x-over .. 2.25
9 MWn(s),Low,Sma,The Eleventh
    Manî pt.1 (of 3) 2.25
10 MWn(s),Eleventh Man, pt.2 ... 2.50
11 MWn(s),Eleventh Man, pt.3 ... 2.50
12 MWn(s),Lady of the Leopard
    final issue,Sept., 1997 .... 2.50

NIGHTWING
1995
1 R:Nightwing 5.00
2 N:Nightwing 4.00
3 visit to Kravia 4.00
4 conclusion 4.00

NIGHTWING
Aug., 1996
1 CDi(s),SMc,KIS,Nightwing goes
    to Bluhaven 15.00
2 CDi(s),SMc,KIS,V:smugglers.... 7.00
3 CDi(s),SMc,KIS,run-down bank
    iheld upî 7.00
4 CDi(s),SMc,KIS,V:Lady Vick ... 4.00
5 CDi(s),SMc,KIS, ... 4.00
6 CDi(s),SMc,KIS,A:Tim Drake ... 4.00
7 CDi(s),SMc,KIS,Rough Justice .. 4.00
8 CDi(s),SMc,KIS,V: the kingpin
    of Bluhaven 4.00
9 CDi(s),SMc,KIS,kidnapping, pt.1 . 4.00
10 CDi(s),SMc,KIS,nightmare
    or dream? 4.00
11 CDi(s),SMc,V:Soames,
    Blockbuster 4.00
12 CDi(s),SMc,Mutt 3.00
13 CDi(s),SMc,KIS,A:Batman 3.00
14 CDi(s),SMc,KIS,A:Batman,pt.2.. 3.00
15 CDi(s),SMc,KIS,A:Batman,pt.3.. 3.00
16 CDi(s),SMc,KIS,Nightwingmobile 3.00
17 CDi(s),SMc,KIS,V:Man-Bat..... 3.00
18 CDi(s),SMc,KIS 3.00
19 CDi(s),SMc,KIS,Cataclysm
    x-over, pt.2 .... 4.00
20 CDi(s),SMc,KIS,Cataclysm..... 3.00
21 CDi(s),SMc,KIS,post Cataclysm 2.50
22 CDi(s),SMc,KIS,V:Lady Vic 2.50
23 Brotherhood of
    the Fist x-over, pt.4 .... 2.50
24 CDi(s),SMc,KIS,cop story 2.50
25 CDi(s),SMc,KIS,A:Robin 2.50
26 CDi(s),SMc,KIS,A;Huntress ... 2.50
27 CDi(s),SMc,KIS,V:Torque 2.50
28 CDi(s),SMc,KIS,V:Torque 2.50
29 CDi(s),SMc,KIS,A:Huntress ... 2.50
30 CDi(s),SMc,KIS,A:Superman .. 2.50
31 CDi(s),SMc,KIS,A:Nite-Wing .. 3.00
32 CDi(s),SMc,KIS,V:DoubleDare . 2.50
33 CDi(s),SMc,KIS,
    V:Electrocutioner 2.50
34 CDi(s),SMc,KIS,x-over 2.50
35 CDi(s),SMc,KIS,No
    Man's Land,pt.1 .... 2.50
36 CDi(s),SMc,No
    Man's Land,pt.2 .... 2.50
37 CDi(s),SMc,No Man's
    Land, concl. 2.50
38 CDi(s),SMc,KIS,F:Oracle 2.50
39 CDi(s),SMc,KIS 2.50
40 CDi(s),SMc,KIS,R:Tarantula ... 2.50
41 CDi(s),Police Academy grad ... 2.50

42 CDi(s),V:Nite-wing 2.50	**NUTSY SQUIRREL**	28 V:Psions 2.50
43 CDi(s),V:Torque 2.50	**Sept.–Oct., 1954**	29 V:Psions 2.50
44 CDi(s),F:Nite-wing 2.50	61 SM 100.00	30 R:Primus,I:Artin 2.50
45 CDi(s),Hunt for Oracle,pt.1 . . . . 2.50	62 thru 71 . . . . @50.00	31 Crisis tie-in 2.50
46 CDi(s),Hunt for Oracle,pt.3 . . . . 2.50	72 Nov., 1957 . . . . 50.00	32 Felicity. 2.50
47 CDi(s),showdown. 2.50		33 Regufe World 2.50
48 CDi(s),JMz,F:Slyph 2.50	**OMAC**	34 A:New Teen Titans. 2.50
49 CDi(s),JMz,F:Torque 2.50	**Sept.–Oct., 1974**	35 A:New Teen Titans. 2.50
50 CDi,JMz,at crossroads,48-pg. . . 4.00	1 JK,I&O:Omac 35.00	36 Last Days of Broot. 2.50
51 CDi,KD,O:Nite-wing 2.50	2 JK,I:Mr.Big 20.00	37 V:Spiderguild,A:Lobo 5.00
52 CDi,This issue: Batman dies! . . 2.50	3 JK,100,000 foes 20.00	38 A:Tweener Network 2.50
53 Officer Down x-over,pt.5 . . . . . . 2.50	4 JK,V:Kafka 20.00	Ann.#1 KG,R:Harpis 2.50
54 CDi,life-threatening accident . . 2.50	5 JK,New Bodies for Old 20.00	Ann.#2 KG,O:Primus 2.50
55 CDi,A:Blockbuster,Shrike 2.50	6 JK,The Body Bank 20.00	
56 CDi,V:Blockbuster,Shrike 2.50	7 JK,The Ocean Stealers. 20.00	**100 BULLETS**
57 CDi,RL,MFm,V:Shrike 2.50	8 JK,Last issue 20.00	**DC/Vertigo, 1999**
58 CDi,V:Shrike 2.50	**[2nd Series], 1991**	1 F:Dizzy Cordova & AgentGraves. 4.50
59 CDi,RL,Where's Freddy Minh. . . 2.50	1 JBy,B&W prestige. 5.00	2 . . . . 3.00
60 CDi,Low,V:Transbelvan mob . . . 2.50	2 JBy,The Great Depression era . . 4.50	3 F:Mr.Shepard 3.00
61 CDi,V:Bank Robbers 2.50	3 JBy,`To Kill Adolf Hitler'. 4.50	4 Shot, Water Back,pt.1. . . . . 3.00
62 CDi,Joker:Last Laugh 2.50	4 JBy,D:Mr.Big. 4.50	5 Shot, Water Back,pt.2. . . . . 3.00
63 CDi,Last Laugh, aftermath 2.50		6 Short Con, Long Odds,pt.1 . . . . 2.50
64 CDi,On a Christmas Evening . . 2.50	**OMEGA MEN**	7 Short Con, Long Odds,pt.2 . . . . 2.50
65 CDi,BruceWayne:Murderer,pt.3 . 2.50	**Dec., 1982**	8 F:Agent Graves 2.50
66 CDi,BruceWayne:Murderer,pt.9 . 2.50	1 KG,V:Citadel. 3.50	9 Right Ear,Left in the Cold,pt.1 . . 2.50
67 CDi,V:Amygdala 2.50	2 KG,O:Broot. 2.50	10 Right Ear,Left in the Cold,pt.2 . 2.50
68 CDi,BruceWayne:Fugitive,pt.6 . . 2.50	3 KG,I:Lobo. 8.00	11 F:Lilly Roach 2.50
69 CDi,BruceWayne:Fugitive,pt.9 . . 2.50	4 KG,D:Demonia,I:Felicity 2.50	12 Parlez Kung Vous,pt.1 . . . . 2.50
70 CDi,in Arizona 2.50	5 KG,V:Lobo 3.00	13 Parlez Kung Vous,pt.2. . . . . . . 2.50
71 RL,Something About Mary,pt.1 . 2.50	6 KG,V:Citadel,D:Gepsen 2.50	14 Parlez Kung Vous,concl. 2.50
72 RL,Something About Mary,pt.2 . 2.50	7 O:Citadel,L:Auron. 2.50	15 Hang Up on Hang Low,pt.1 . . . 2.50
73 RL,Something About Mary,pt.3 . 2.50	8 R:Nimbus,I:H.Hokum 2.50	16 Hang Up on Hang Low,pt.2 . . . 2.50
74 RL,Something About Mary,pt.4 . 2.50	9 V:HarryHokum,A:Lobo 2.50	17 Hang Up on Hang Low,pt.3 . . . 2.50
75 RL,MGo,40-pg. 3.50	10 A:Lobo (First Full Story). 6.00	18 Hang Up on Hang Low,pt.4 . . . 2.50
76 MGo(c) 2.50	11 V:Blackfire 2.50	19 Hang Up on Hang Low,pt.5 . . . 2.50
77 cops go bad. 2.50	12 R:Broots Wife 2.50	20 Hot House 2.50
78 V:new Tarantula. 2.50	13 A:Broots Wife. 2.50	21 Sell Fish & Out to Sea,pt.1 . . . 2.50
79 Source of madness 2.50	14 Karna 2.50	22 Sell Fish & Out to Sea,pt.2. . . . 2.50
80 Venn Diagram,pt.1 . . . . 2.50	15 Primus Goes Mad 2.50	23 Red Prince Blues,pt.1 . . . . 2.50
81 Venn Diagram,pt.2 . . . . 2.50	16 Spotlight Issue. 2.50	24 Red Prince Blues,pt.2 . . . . 2.50
82 Venn Diagram,pt.3 . . . . 2.50	17 V:Psions 2.50	25 Red Prince Blues,pt.3 . . . . 2.50
83 Murder of Chief Redhorn 2.50	18 V:Psions 2.50	26 Mr. Branch & the Family Tree. . 2.50
84 RL,Chief Redhorn case 2.50	19 V:Psions,C:Lobo 2.50	27 Idol Chatter 2.50
85 Tarantula or Nite-Wing 2.50	20 V:Psions,A:Lobo 2.50	28 Contrabandolero,pt.1 . . . . 2.50
86 Cyber-punks 2.50	21 Spotlight Issue. 2.50	29 Contrabandolero,pt.2 . . . . 2.50
87 V:Blockbuster 2.50	22 Nimbus 2.50	30 Contrabandolero,pt.3 . . . . 2.50
Ann.#1 Pulp Heroes (Romance) . . 4.50	23 Nimbus 2.50	31 Counterfeit Detective,pt.1. . . . . 2.50
Spec.#1,000,000 CDi(s),SMc,KIS . 2.50	24 Okaara 2.50	32 Counterfeit Detective,pt.2. . . . . 2.50
Secret Files #1 64-page 5.50	25 Kalista 2.50	33 Counterfeit Detective,pt.3. . . . . 2.50
Spec.#1 Our Worlds at War,48-pg. . 3.50	26 V:Spiderguild 2.50	34 Counterfeit Detective,pt.4. . . . . 2.50
Giant #1 80-pg.CDi,I:Hella 5.95	27 V:Psions 2.50	35 Counterfeit Detective,pt.5. . . . . 2.50
GN The Target,CDi,SMc,48-page . 5.95		36 Counterfeit Detective,pt.6. . . . . 2.50
TPB A Knight in Bludhaven,CDi, SMc,KIS, rep. #1–#8. . . . . 15.00		37 On Accidental Purpose 2.50
TPB Ties That Bind, DON,AIG, DG,KIS,rep. 13.00		38 Cole Burns Slow Hand. 2.50
TPB Rough Justice. 18.00		39 Ambition's Audition. 2.50
TPB Love and Bullets,rep. 17.95		40 Night of the Payday 2.50
TPB A Darker Shade of Justice. . . 19.95		41 A Crash 2.50
TPB Love and Bullets 17.95		42 V:Wylie Times 2.50
TPB The Hunt for Oracle 14.95		43 Chill in the Oven,pt.1 . . . . 2.50
		44 Chill in the Oven,pt.2 . . . . 2.50
NIGHTWING:		45 Chill in the Oven,pt.3 . . . . 2.50
ALFRED'S RETURN		46 Chill in the Oven,pt.4 . . . . 2.50
1995		47 In Stinked,pt.1 . . . . 2.50
1-shot DG. 5.00		TPB First Shot,Last Call 9.95
		TPB Split Second Chance 14.95
NIGHTWING		TPB Hang Up on the Hang Low . . 9.95
AND HUNTRESS		TPB A Foregone Tomorrow. 17.95
March, 1998		TPB The Counterfifth Detective. . . 12.95
1 (of 4) BSz,conflict 2.50		TPB Six Feet Under The Gun . . . 12.95
2 BSz,good cop, bad cop. 2.50		
3 BSz,Malfatti 2.50		**100%**
4 BSz,concl. 2.50		**DC/Vertigo, June, 2002**
		1 (of 5) PPo, 48-pg. b&w 6.00
		2 PPo, Sci-fi, 48-pg. b&w. 6.00
		3 PPo, 48-pg. b&w 6.00
		4 PPo, 48-pg. b&w 6.00
		5 PPo, 48-pg. b&w 6.00

Omega Men #4 © DC Comics Inc.

100%–Our Army — DC — Comics Values Annual

100% TRUE?
DC/Paradox Press, (B&W) 1996
1 rep. from Paradox Press books .. 5.00

ORION
April, 2000
1 WS,Darkseid 2.50
2 WS,V:Darkseid 2.50
3 WS,FM,V:Suicide Jockeys 2.50
4 WS,DGb,V:Darkseid 2.50
5 WS,V:Darkseid 2.50
6 WS,EL,AG,F:Mortalla 2.50
7 WS,HC,V:Kalibak 2.50
8 WS,RLe,JLb,V:Kalibak 2.50
9 WS,V:Desaad 2.50
10 WS,AAd,V:Desaad 2.50
11 WS,New Genesis,Anti-Life ... 2.50
12 WS,JLe,return to Apokolips ... 2.50
13 WS,TA,JBy,F:Captain Marvel ... 2.50
14 WS,TA,JBy,F:Captain Marvel .. 2.50
15 WS,JPL,48-page 4.50
16 WS,Abysmal Plane,V:Clockwerx 2.50
17 WS,Abysmal Plane,V:Clockwerx 2.50
18 WS,AM,F:Rakar............. 2.50
19 WS,ECa,Joker-crazed Deep Six 2.50
20 WS,fall from Grace 2.50
21 WS,V:Arnicus Wolfram........ 2.50
22 WS,young teen 2.50
23 WS,BWi,young teen.......... 2.50
24 WS,BWi,Tactical nuke 2.50
25 WS,BWi,48-pg.final issue..... 4.25
TPB The Gates of Apokolips..... 12.95

*Our Army at War #10 ©
DC Comics, Inc.*

OUR ARMY AT WAR
Aug., 1952
1 CI(c),Dig Your FoxholeDeep. 2,400.00
2 CI(c),Champ 1,000.00
3 GK(c),No Exit 750.00
4 IN(c),Last Man 600.00
5 IN(c),T.N.T. Bouquet 575.00
6 IN(c),Battle Flag 575.00
7 IN(c),Dive Bomber 575.00
8 IN(c),One Man Army 575.00
9 GC(c),Undersea Raider 575.00
10 IN(c),Soldiers on the
  High Wire 575.00
11 IN(c),Scratch One Meatball .. 575.00
12 IN(c),The Big Drop.......... 450.00
13 BK(c),Ghost Ace 450.00
14 BK(c),Drummer of Waterloo .. 600.00
15 IN(c),Thunder in the Skies ... 450.00
16 IN(c),A Million To One Shot .. 450.00
17 IN(c),The White Death 450.00
18 IN(c),Frontier Fighter 450.00
19 IN(c),The Big Ditch 450.00
20 IN(c),Abandon Ship 450.00
21 IN(c),Dairy of a Flattop...... 300.00
22 JGr(c),Ranger Raid 300.00
23 IN(c),Jungle Navy 300.00
24 IN(c),Suprise Landing 300.00
25 JGr(c),Take 'Er Down....... 300.00
26 JGr(c),Sky Duel 300.00
27 IN(c),MD,Diary of a Frogman. 300.00
28 JGr(c),Detour-War 300.00
29 IN(c),Grounded Fighter 300.00
30 JGr(c),Torpedo Raft 300.00
31 IN(c),Howitzer Hill 300.00
32 JGr(c),Battle Mirror 300.00
33 JGr(c),Fighting Gunner 300.00
34 JGr(c),Point-Blank War 300.00
35 JGr(c),Frontline Tackle 300.00
36 JGr(c),Foxhole Mascot...... 300.00
37 JGr(c),Walking Battle Pin 300.00
38 JGr(c),Floating Pillbox 300.00
39 JGr(c),Trench Trap......... 300.00
40 RH(c),Tank Hunter 300.00
41 JGr(c),Jungle Target 300.00
42 IN(c),Shadow Targets....... 200.00
43 JGr(c),A Bridge For Billy..... 200.00
44 JGr(c),Thunder In The Desert 200.00
45 JGr(c),Diary of a Fighter Pilot. 200.00
46 JGr(c),Prize Package....... 200.00
47 JGr(c),Flying Jeep 200.00
48 JGr(c),Front Seat.......... 200.00
49 JKu(c),Landing Postponed... 200.00
50 JGr(c),RH,Mop-Up Squad ... 200.00
51 JGr(c),Battle Tag 200.00
52 JGr(c),Pony Express Pilot ... 200.00
53 JGr(c),One Ringside-For War. 200.00
54 JKu(c),No-Man Secret 200.00
55 JGr(c),No Rest For A Raider . 200.00
56 JKu(c),You're Next......... 200.00
57 JGr(c),Ten-Minute Break 200.00
58 JKu(c),The Fighting SnowBird 200.00
59 JGr(c),The Mustang Had
  My Number 200.00
60 JGr(c),Ranger Raid 200.00
61 JGr(c),A Pigeon For Easy Co. 175.00
62 JKu(c),Trigger Man 175.00
63 JGr(c),The Big Toss 175.00
64 JKu(c),Tank Rider 175.00
65 JGr(c),Scramble-War Upstairs 175.00
66 RH(c),Gunner Wanted 175.00
67 JKu(c),MD,Boiling Point 175.00
68 JKu(c),MD,End of the Line ... 175.00
69 JGr(c),Combat Cage 175.00
70 JGr(c),Torpedo Tank 175.00
71 JGr(c),Flying Mosquitoes 175.00
72 JGr(c),No. 1 Pigeon........ 175.00
73 JKu(c),Shooting Gallery 175.00
74 JGr(c),Ace Without Guns 175.00
75 JGr(c),Blind Night Fighter.... 175.00
76 JKu(c),Clipped Hellcat 175.00
77 JGr(c),Jets Don't Dream 175.00
78 IN(c),Battle Nurse 175.00
79 JGr(c),MD,What's the Price
  of a B-17? 175.00
80 JKu(c),The Sparrow And
  The...Hawk 175.00
81 JGr(c),Sgt. Rock in The
  Rock of Easy Co.......... 3,500.00
82 JKu(c),MD,Gun Jockey...... 800.00
83 JGr(c),MD,B:Sgt.Rock Stories,
  The Rock and the Wall ... 2,700.00
84 JKu(c),Laughter On
  Snakehead Hill........... 400.00
85 RH(c),Ice Cream Soldier 500.00
86 RH(c),Tank 711 .... 350.00
87 RH(c),Calling Easy Co. 350.00
88 JKu(c),The Hard Way....... 350.00
89 RH(c),No Shoot From Easy .. 350.00
90 JKu(c),3 Stripes Hill 350.00
91 JGr(c),No Answer fromSarge 1,000.00
92 JGr(c),Luck of Easy 225.00
93 JGr(c),Deliver One Airfield ... 225.00
94 JKu(c),Target-Easy Company. 225.00
95 JKu(c),Battle of the Stripes... 225.00
96 JGr(c),MD,Last Stand
  For Easy 225.00
97 JKu(c),What Makes A
  Sergeant Run?........... 225.00
98 JKu(c),Soldiers Never Die ... 225.00
99 JKu(c),Easy's Hardest Battle . 225.00
100 JKu(c),No Exit For Easy.... 225.00
101 JKu(c),End Of Easy 200.00
102 JKu(c),The Big Star 200.00
103 RH(c),Easy's Had It 200.00
104 JKu(c),A New Kind Of War . 200.00
105 JKu(c),T.N.T. Birthday 200.00
106 JKu(c),Meet Lt. Rock 200.00
107 JKu(c),Doom Over Easy.... 200.00
108 JGr(c),Unknown Sergeant . 200.00
109 JKu(c),Roll Call For Heroes . 200.00
110 JKu(c),That's An Order..... 200.00
111 JKu(c),What's The Price
  Of A Dog Tag 200.00
112 JKu(c),Battle Shadow...... 200.00
113 JKu(c),Eyes Of A
  Blind Gunner 200.00
114 JKu(c),Killer Sergeant 200.00
115 JKu(c),Rock's Battle Family . 200.00
116 JKu(c),S.O.S. Sgt. Rock.... 200.00
117 JKu(c),Snafu Squad....... 200.00
118 RH(c),The Tank Vs. The
  Tin Soldier 200.00
119 JKu(c),A Bazooka For
  Babyface 200.00
120 JGr(c),Battle Tags
  For Easy Co. 125.00
121 JKu(c),New Boy In Easy ... 100.00
122 JKu(c),Battle of the
  Pajama Commandoes 100.00
123 JGr(c),Battle Brass Ring.... 100.00
124 JKu(c),Target-Sgt. Rock 100.00
125 JKu(c),Hold-At All Costs.... 100.00
126 RH(c),The End Of
  Easy Company.......... 100.00
127 JKu(c),4 Faces of Sgt. Rock. 100.00
128 JKu(c),O:Sgt. Rock 350.00
129 JKu(c),Heroes NeedCowards 100.00
130 JKu(c),No Hill For Easy 100.00
131 JKu(c),One Pair of
  Dogtags For Sale 100.00
132 JKu(c),Young Soldiers
  Never Die 100.00
133 JKu(c),Yesterday's Hero.... 100.00
134 JKu(c),The T.N.T. Book 100.00

*Our Army at War #16
© DC Comics, Inc.*

Our Army At War

135 JKu(c),Battlefield Double . . . 100.00
136 JKu(c),Make Me A Hero 100.00
137 JKu(c),Too Many Sergeants . 100.00
138 JKu(c),Easy's Lost Sparrow . 100.00
139 JKu(c),A Firing Squad
    For Easy 100.00
140 JKu(c),Brass Sergeant 100.00
141 JKu(c),Dead Man's Trigger. . 100.00
142 JKu(c),Easy's New Topkick . 100.00
143 JKu(c),Easy's T.N.T. Crop. . . 100.00
144 JKu(c),The Sparrow And
    The Tiger 100.00
145 JKu(c),A Feather For
    Little Sure Shot. 100.00
146 JKu(c),The Fighting Guns
    For Easy 100.00
147 JKu(c),Book One:Generals
    Don't Die 100.00
148 JKu(c),Book Two:Generals
    Don't Die:Generals Are
    Sergeants With Stars 100.00
149 JKu(c),Surrender Ticket 100.00
150 JKu(c),Flytrap Hill. 100.00
151 JKu(c),War Party,
    I:Enemy Ace. 600.00
152 Jku(c),Last Man-Last Shot . . 125.00
153 JKu(c),Easy's Last Stand . . . 250.00
154 JKu(c),Boobytrap Mascot . . . 100.00
155 JKu(c),No Stripes For Me. . . 200.00
156 JKu(c),The Human Tank Trap 100.00
157 JKu(c),Nothin's Ever
    Lost In War. 100.00
158 JKu(c),Iron Major-Rock
    Sergeant 100.00
159 JKu(c),The Blind Gun. 100.00
160 JKu(c),What's The Color
    Of Your Blood. 100.00
161 JKu(c),Dead End
    For A Dogface 100.00
162 JKu(c),The Price and
    The Sergeant 100.00
163 JKu(c),MD,RE,Kill Me-Kill Me 100.00
164 JKu(c),CE,No Exit For Easy,
    reprint from #100 . . . . 200.00
165 GE,JKu(c),The Return of the
    Iron Major. 100.00
166 GE,JKu(c),Half A Sergeant. . 100.00
167 GE,JKu(c),Kill One-
    Save One. 100.00
168 GE,JKu(c),I Knew The
    Unknown Soldier 200.00
169 GE,JKu(c),Nazi On My Back . 90.00
170 GE,JKu(c),Buzzard Bait Hill . . 90.00
171 GE,JKu(c),The Sergeant
    Must Die. 75.00
172 GE,JKu(c),A Slug for a
    Sergeant 75.00
173 GE,JKu(c),Easy's Hardest
    Battle, reprint from #99. . . . . . 75.00
174 GE,JKu(c),One Kill Too
    Many 75.00
175 JKu(c),T.N.T. Letter 75.00
176 MD,JKu(c),Give Me Your
    Stripes 75.00
177 RH,JKu(c),Target-Easy Company,
    reprint from #94, giant-size . . 125.00
178 RH,JKu(c),Only One Medal
    For Easy 75.00
179 RH,JKu(c),A Penny Jackie
    Johnson 75.00
180 RH,JKu(c),You Can't
    Kill A General 75.00
181 RH,Monday's Coward-
    Tuesday's Hero 75.00
182 NA,RH,The Desert Rats
    of Easy. 90.00
183 RH,NA,JKu(c),Sergeants
    Don't Stay Dead 90.00
184 RH,JKu(c),Candidate For A
    Firing Squad. 75.00
185 JKu(c),Battle Flag For
    A G.I. 75.00
186 RH,NA,JKu(c),3 Stripes Hill
    reprint from #90, Origin. 75.00
187 RH,JKu(c),Shadow of a
    Sergeant 65.00
188 RH,JKu(c),Death Comes for
    Easy. 65.00
189 RH,JKu(c),The Mission Was
    Murder. 65.00
190 RH,JKu(c),What Make's A
    Sergeant Run?, reprint
    from #97, giant-size 100.00
191 RH,JKu(c),Death Flies High,
    A:Johnny Cloud 100.00
192 RH,JKu(c),A Firing Squad
    For A Sergeant 100.00
193 RH,JKu(c),Blood in theDesert 100.00
194 RH,JKu(c),Time For
    Vengeance 100.00
195 RH,JKu(c),Dead Town 100.00
196 RH,JKu(c),Stop The War-
    I Want To Get Off 100.00
197 RH,JKu(c),Last Exit For Easy 100.00
198 RH,JKu(c),Plugged Nickel . . 100.00
199 RH,JKu(c),Nazi Ghost Wolf . 100.00
200 RH,GE,JKu(c),The
    Troubadour. 75.00
201 RH,JKu(c),The Graffiti Writer . 50.00
202 RH,JKu(c),The Sarge Is Dead 50.00
203 RH,MD,JKu(c),Easy's Had It,
    reprint from # 103, giant-size . 90.00
204 RH,JKu(c) 50.00
205 RH,JKu(c) 45.00
206 RH,JKu(c),There's A War On . 45.00
207 RH,JKu(c),A Sparrow's
    Prayer 45.00
208 RH,JKu(c),A Piece of Rag...
    And A Hank of Hair. 45.00
209 RH,JKu(c),I'm Still Alive 45.00
210 RH,JKu(c),I'm Kilroy. 45.00
211 RH,JKu(c),The Treasure of
    St. Daniel 45.00
212 RH,MD,JKu(c),The Quiet War 45.00
213 RH,JKu(c),A Letter For
    Bulldozer 45.00
214 RH,JKu(c),Where Are You? . . 45.00
215 RH,JKu(c),Pied Piper of Peril . 45.00
216 RH,JKu(c),Doom Over Easy,
    reprint from # 107, Giant-size . 75.00
217 RH,JKu(c),Surprise Party 35.00
218 RH,JKu(c),Medic! 35.00
219 RH,JKu(c),Yesterday's Hero . . 35.00
220 RH,JKu(c),Stone-Age War . . 35.00
221 RH,JKu(c),Hang-Up 35.00
222 RH,JKu(c),Dig In, Easy 35.00
223 RH,JKu(c),On Time 35.00
224 RH,JKu(c),One For The
    Money 35.00
225 RH,JKu(c),Face Front 35.00
226 RH,JKu(c),Death Stop 35.00
227 RH,JKu(c),Traitor's Blood. . . . 35.00
228 RH,JKu(c),It's A Dirty War . . . 35.00
229 RH,JKu(c),The Battle of the
    Sergeants, reprint #128,
    Giant-size. 50.00
230 RH,JKu(c),Home Is The
    Hunter 25.00
231 RH,JKu(c),My Brother's
    Keeper. 25.00
232 RH,JKu(c),3 Men In A Tub . . . 25.00
233 RH,JKu(c),Head Count 25.00
234 RH,JKu(c),Summer In Salerno 25.00
235 RH,ATh,JKu(c),Pressure
    Point, giant-size 35.00
236 RH,JKu(c),Face The Devil,
    giant-size 35.00
237 RH,JKu(c),Nobody Cares,
    giant-size 35.00
238 RH,JKu(c),I Kid You Not,
    giant-size 35.00
239 RH,JKu(c),The Soldier,
    giant-size 35.00
240 RH,JKu(c),NA, giant-size 50.00
241 RH,ATh,JKu(c),War Story,
    giant-size 35.00
242 RH,JKu(c),Infantry 35.00
243 RH,MD,JKu(c),24 Hour Pass . 30.00
244 RH,MD,JKu(c),Easy's First
    Tiger 30.00
245 RH,JKu(c),The Prisoner 30.00
246 RH,JKu(c),Naked Combat . . 30.00
247 RH,JKu(c),The Vision. 20.00
248 RH,JKu(c),The Firing Squad . 20.00
249 RH,JKu(c),The Luck of
    Easy,WW 22.00
250 RH,JKu(c),90 Day Wonder. . . 20.00
251 RH,JKu(c),The Iron Major . . . 20.00
252 RH,JKu(c),The Iron Hand. . . 20.00
253 RH,JKu(c),Rock and Iron . . . 20.00
254 RH,ATh,JKu(c),The Town . . . 20.00
255 RH,JKu(c),What's It Like . . . 20.00
256 RH,JKu(c),School For
    Sergeants. 20.00
257 RH,JKu(c),The Castaway . . . 20.00
258 RH,JKu(c),The Survivors 20.00
259 RH,JKu(c),Lost Paradise 20.00
260 RH,JKu(c),Hell's Island 20.00
261 RH,JKu(c),The Medal That
    Nobody Wanted 20.00
262 RH,JKu(c),The Return 20.00
263 RH,JKu(c),The Cage 20.00
264 RH,JKu(c),The Hunt. 20.00
265 RH,JKu(c),The Brother. 20.00
266 RH,GE,JKu(c),The Evacuees. 20.00
267 RH,JKu(c),A Bakers Dozen . . 20.00
268 RH,JKu(c),The Elite 20.00
269 RH,MD,GE,JKu(c), giant-size. 50.00
270 RH,JKu(c),Spawn of the
    Devil. 20.00
271 RH,JKu(c),Brittle Harvest 18.00
272 RH,JKu(c),The Bloody Flag . . 17.00
273 RH,JKu(c),The Arena 17.00
274 RH,GE,JKu(c),Home Is The
    Hero. 17.00
275 RH,MD,JKu(c),Graveyard
    Battleship, giant-size. 50.00
276 RH,GE,JKu(c),A Bullet For
    Rock 16.00
277 RH,JKu(c),Gashouse Gang . 16.00
278 RH,GE,JKu(c),Rearguard
    Action. 16.00
279 JKu(c),Mined City 16.00
280 RH,GE,MD,JKu(c),Mercy
    Mission. 30.00
281 RH,JKu(c),Dead Man's Eyes . 14.00
282 JKu(c),Pieces of Time 14.00

Our Army at War #219
© DC Comics Inc.

Our Army–Our Fighting

Our Army at War #282
© DC Comics, Inc.

283 JKu(c),Dropouts 14.00
284 JKu(c),Linkup 14.00
285 JKu(c),Bring Him Back 14.00
286 JKu(c),Firebird 12.00
287 MGr,JKu(c),The Fifth
    Dimension 12.00
288 JKu(c),Defend-Or Destroy . . . 12.00
289 JKu(c),The Line 12.00
290 JKu(c),Super-Soldiers 12.00
291 JKu(c),Death Squad. 12.00
292 JKu(c),A Lesson In Blood 12.00
293 JKu(c),It Figures 12.00
294 JKu(c),Coffin For Easy 12.00
295 JKu(c),The Devil in Paradise . 12.00
296 JKu(c),Combat Soldier 12.00
297 JKu(c),Percentages 12.00
298 JKu(c),Return to Chartres . . . 12.00
299 JKu(c),Three Soldiers 12.00
300 JKu(c),300th Hill 16.00
301 JKu(c),The Farm 12.00
Becomes:

SGT. ROCK
1977–88

302 JKu(c),Anzio-The Bloodbath,
    part I 40.00
303 JKu(c),Anzio, part II 20.00
304 JKu(c),Anzio, part III 20.00
305 JKu(c),Dead Man's Trigger,
    reprint from #141 . . . . 20.00
306 JKu(c),The Last Soldier 20.00
307 JKu(c),I'm Easy 20.00
308 JKu(c),One Short Step 20.00
309 JKu(c),Battle Clowns 20.00
310 JKu(c),Hitler's Wolf Children. . 20.00
311 JKu(c),The Sergeant and
    the Lady 15.00
312 JKu(c),No Name Hill 15.00
313 JKu(c),A Jeep For Joey 15.00
314 JKu(c),Gimme Sky 15.00
315 JKu(c),Combat Antenna 15.00
316 JKu(c),Another Hill... . . . . 15.00
317 JKu(c),Hell's Oven 15.00
318 JKu(c),Stone-Age War 15.00
319 JKu(c),To Kill a Sergeant 15.00
320 JKu(c),Never Salute a
    Sergeant 15.00
321 JKu(c),It's Murder Out Here . . 10.00
322 JKu(c),The Killer 10.00
323 JKu(c),Monday's Hero 10.00
324 JKu(c),Ghost of a Tank 10.00
325 JKu(c),Future Kill, part I 10.00
326 JKu(c),Future Kill, part II 10.00
327 JKu(c),Death Express 10.00
328 JKu(c),Waiting For Rock 10.00
329 JKu(c),Dead Heat 10.00
330 JKu(c),G.I. Trophy 10.00
331 JKu(c),The Sons of War 10.00
332 JKu(c),Pyramid of Death 10.00
333 JKu(c),Ask The Dead 10.00
334 JKu(c),What's Holding Up
    The War 10.00
335 JKu(c),Killer Compass 10.00
336 JKu(c),The Red Maple Leaf . . 10.00
337 JKu(c),A Bridge Called Charlie 10.00
338 JKu(c),No Escape From
    the Front 10.00
339 JKu(c),I Was Here Before . . . 10.00
340 JKu(c),How To Win A War . . . 10.00
341 JKu(c),High-Flyer 10.00
342 JKu(c), 6 sides of Sgt. Rock . . 10.00
343 thru 350 . . . . @10.00
351 thru 422 . . . . @7.00

OUR FIGHTING FORCES
Oct.–Nov., 1954

1 IN,JGr(c),Human Booby Trap 1,500.00
2 RH,IN,IN(c),Mile-Long Step. . . 600.00
3 RA,JKu(c),Winter Ambush 500.00
4 RA,JGr(c),The Hot Seat 400.00
5 IN,RA,JGr(c),The Iron Punch . 400.00
6 IN,RA,JGr(c),The Sitting Tank . 350.00
7 RA,JKu,JGr(c),Battle Fist 350.00
8 IN,RA,JGr(c),No War
    For A Gunner 350.00
9 JKu,RH,JGr(c),Crash-
    Landing At Dawn 350.00
10 WW,RA,JGr(c),Grenade
    Pitcher 350.00
11 JKu,JGr(c),Diary of a Sub . . . 250.00
12 IN,JKu,JGr(c),Jump Seat 250.00
13 RA,JGr(c),Beach Party 250.00
14 JA,RA,IN,JGr(c),Unseen War . 250.00
15 RH,JKu,JGr(c),Target For
    A Lame Duck 250.00
16 RH,JKu,JGr(c),Night Fighter 250.00
17 RA,JGr(c),Anchored Frogman 250.00
18 RH,JKu,JGr(c),Cockpit Seat . . 250.00
19 JA,JKu(c),StraightenThatLine 250.00
20 RA,MD,JGr(c),The
    Floating Pilot 300.00
21 RA,JGr(c),The Bouncing
    Baby of Company B 175.00
22 JKu,RA,JGr(c),3 Doorways
    To War 175.00
23 RA,IN,JA,JGr(c),Tin Fish Pilot 175.00
24 RA,RH,JGr(c),Frogman Duel . 175.00
25 RA,JGr(c),Dead End 175.00
26 IN,RH,JKu(c),Tag Day 175.00
27 MD,RA,JKu(c),TNT Escort . . . 175.00
28 RH,MD,JKu(c),AllQuiet atC.P. 175.00
29 JKu,JKu(c),Listen To A Jet . . . 175.00
30 IN,RA,JKu(c),Fort
    For A Gunner 175.00
31 MD,RA,JKu(c),Silent Sub 175.00
32 RH,MD,RH(c),PaperWorkWar 175.00
33 RH,JKu,JKu(c),Frogman
    In A Net 175.00
34 JA,JGr,JKu(c),Calling U-217 . . 175.00
35 JA,JGr,JKu(c),Mask of
    a Frogman 175.00
36 MD,JA,JKu(c),Steel Soldier . . 175.00
37 JA,JGr,JGr(c),Frogman
    In A Bottle 175.00
38 RH,RA,JA,JKu(c),Sub Sinker . 175.00
39 JA,RH,RH(c),Last Torpedo . . . 175.00
40 JGr,JA,JKu,JKu(c),The
    Silent Ones 175.00
41 RH,RA,JA,JKu(c),Battle
    Mustang 225.00
42 RH,MD,JGr(c),Sorry-
    Wrong Hill 150.00
43 MD,JA,JGr(c),Inside Battle . . 150.00
44 MD,RH,RA,JGr(c),Big Job
    For Baker 150.00

Our Fighting Forces #12
© DC Comics, Inc.

45 RH,RA,JGr(c),B:Gunner and
    Sarge, Mop-Up Squad 550.00
46 RH,RA,JGr(c),Gunner'sSquad 225.00
47 RH,JKu(c),TNT Birthday. 150.00
48 JA,RH,JGr(c),A Statue
    For Sarge. 150.00
49 MD,RH,JGr(c),Blind Gunner . . 175.00
50 JA,RH,JGr(c),I:Pooch,My
    Pal, The Pooch 150.00
51 RA,JA,RH(c),Underwater
    Gunner 125.00
52 MD,JKu,JKu(c),The Gunner
    and the Nurse 100.00
53 JA,RA,JGr(c),An Egg
    For Sarge 100.00
54 . . . . 100.00
55 MD,RH,JGr(c),The Last Patrol 100.00
56 RH,RA,JGr(c),Bridge of
    Bullets 100.00
57 JA,IN,JGr(c),A Tank For Sarge 100.00
58 JA,JGr(c),Return of the Pooch 100.00
59 RH,JA,JGr(c),Pooch-Patrol
    Leader 100.00
60 RH,JA,JGr(c),Tank Target . . . 100.00
61 JA,JGr(c),Pass to Peril 100.00
62 JA,JGr(c),The Flying Pooch . . 100.00
63 JA,RH,JGr(c),Pooch-Tank
    Hunter 100.00
64 JK,RH,JGr(c),A Lifeline
    For Sarge 100.00
65 IN,JA,JGr(c),Dogtag Patrol . . . 100.00
66 JKu,JA,JGr(c),Trail of the
    Ghost Bomber 100.00
67 IN,JA,JGr(c),Purple Heart
    For Pooch 100.00
68 JA,JGr(c),Col. Hakawa's
    Birthday Party 100.00
69 JA,JKu,JGr(c),
    Destination Doom 100.00
70 JA,JKu(c),The Last Holdout . . 100.00
71 JA,JGr(c),End of the Marines . . 75.00
72 JA,JGr(c),Four-Footed Spy . . . 75.00
73 IN,JGr(c),The Hero Maker 75.00
74 IN,JGr(c),Three On A T.N.T.
    Bull's-Eye 75.00
75 JKu(c),Purple Heart Patrol 75.00
76 JKu(c),The T.N.T. Seat 75.00
77 JKu(c),No Foxhole-No Home . . 75.00
78 JGr(c),The Last Medal 75.00
79 JA,JGr(c),Backs to the Sea . . . 75.00
80 JA,JGr(c),Don't Come Back . . . 75.00
81 JA,JGr(c),Battle of
    the Mud Marines 75.00
82 JA,JGr(c),Battle of the
    Empty Helmets 75.00

83 RA,JKu(c),Any Marine
   Can Do It................. 75.00
84 JA,JKu(c),The Gun of Shame . 75.00
85 Ja,JKu(c),The TNT Pin-Points . 75.00
86 JKu(c),3 Faces of Combat.... 75.00
87 JKu(c),Battle of the
   Boobytraps................ 75.00
88 GC,JKu(c),Devil Dog Patrol... 75.00
89 JKu(c),TNT Toothache........ 75.00
90 JKu(c),Stop the War.......... 75.00
91 JKu(c),The Human Shooting
   Gallery................... 50.00
92 JA,JKu(c),The Bomb That
   Stopped The War.......... 50.00
93 IN,JKu(c),The Human Sharks. . 50.00
94 RH(c),E:Gunner,Sarge & Pooch,
   The Human Blockbusters.... 50.00
95 GC,RH(c),B:The Fighting Devil
   Dog, Lt. Rock, The
   Fighting Devil Dog......... 50.00
96 JA,RH(c),Battle of Fire........ 50.00
97 IN(c),Invitation To A
   Firing Squad.............. 50.00
98 IN(c),E:The Fighting Devil
   Dog, Death Wore A Grin... 50.00
99 JA,JKu(c),B:Capt. Hunter,
   No Mercy in Vietnam....... 50.00
100 GC,IN(c),Death Also
    Stalks the Hunter.......... 50.00
101 JA,RH(c),Killer of Vietnam.... 35.00
102 RH,JKu(c),Cold Steel
    For A Hot War............ 35.00
103 JKu(c),The Tunnels of Death . 35.00
104 JKu(c),Night Raid In Vietnam. 35.00
105 JKu(c),Blood Loyalty......... 35.00
106 IN(c),Trail By Fury........... 35.00
107 IN(c),Raid Of The Hellcats... 35.00
108 IN(c),Kill The Wolf Pack...... 35.00
109 IN(c),Burn, Raiders, Burn.... 35.00
110 IN(c),Mountains Full of Death. 35.00
111 IN(c),Train of Terror......... 35.00
112 IN(c),What's In It For
    The Hellcats?............. 35.00
113 IN(c),Operation-Survival...... 35.00
114 JKu(c),No Loot For The
    Hellcats.................. 35.00
115 JKu(c),Death In The Desert. . 35.00
116 JKu(c),Peril From the Casbah 35.00
117 JKu(c),Colder Than Death ... 35.00
118 JKu(c),Hell Underwater...... 35.00
119 JKu(c),Bedlam In Berlin..... 35.00
120 JKu(c),Devil In The Dark..... 35.00
121 JKu(c),Take My Place........ 35.00
122 JKu(c),24 Hours To Die...... 35.00
123 JKu(c),B:Born Losers,No
    Medals No Graves......... 75.00
124 JKu(c),Losers Take All....... 25.00
125 Daughters of Death......... 25.00
126 JKu(c),Lost Town........... 25.00
127 JKu(c),Angels Over Hell's
    Corner................... 25.00
128 JKu(c),7 11 War............ 25.00
129 JKu(c),Ride The Nightmare.. 25.00
130 JKu(c),Nameless Target..... 25.00
131 JKu(c),Half A Man........... 25.00
132 JKu(c),Pooch, The Winner. .. 25.00
133 JKu(c),Heads or Tails,
    giant-size................. 35.00
134 JKu(c),The Real Losers,
    giant-size................. 35.00
135 JKu(c),Death Picks A Loser,
    giant-size................. 35.00
136 JKu(c),Decoy For Death,
    giant-size................. 35.00
137 JKu(c),God Of The Losers,
    giant-size................. 35.00
138 JKu(c),The Targets.......... 18.00
139 JKu(c),The Pirate........... 18.00
140 JKu(c),Lost...One Loser..... 18.00
141 JKu(c),Bad Penny, The..... 18.00
142 JKu(c),1/2 A Man........... 18.00

Our Fighting Forces #159
© DC Comics Inc.

143 JKu(c),Diamonds Are
    For Never................. 18.00
144 JKu(c),The Lost Mission..... 18.00
145 JKu(c),A Flag For Losers.... 18.00
146 JKu(c),The Forever Walk.... 18.00
147 NA(c),The Glory Road...... 22.00
148 JKu(c),The Last Charge..... 18.00
149 FT(c),A Bullet For A Traitor.. 18.00
150 JKu(c),Mark Our Graves.... 18.00
151 JKu(c),Kill Me With Wagner.. 20.00
152 JKu(c),A Small Place In Hell . 20.00
153 JK(c),Big Max.............. 20.00
154 JK(c),Bushido,Live By The
    Code, Die By The Code..... 20.00
155 JK(c),The Partisans......... 20.00
156 JK(c),Good-Bye Broadway... 20.00
157 JK(c),Panama Fattie........ 20.00
158 JK(c),Bombing Out On
    The Panama Canal........ 20.00
159 JK(c),Mile-A-Minute Jones... 20.00
160 JKu(c),Ivan................. 20.00
161 JKu(c),The Major's Dream... 20.00
162 Gung-Ho.................. 20.00
163 JKu(c),The Unmarked Graves 12.00
164 JKu(c),A Town Full Of Losers. 12.00
165 LD(c),The Rowboat Fleet.... 12.00
166 LD(c),Sword of Flame...... 12.00
167 LD(c),A Front Seat In Hell... 12.00
168 LD(c),A Cold Day To Die.... 12.00
169 JKu(c),Welcome Home-And
    Die...................... 12.00
170 JKu(c),A Bullet For
    The General.............. 12.00
171 JKu(c),A Long Day...
    A Long War.............. 12.00
172 JKu(c),The Two-Headed Spy. 12.00
173 JKu(c),An Appointment
    With A Direct Hit.......... 12.00
174 JKu(c),Winner Takes-Death.. 12.00
175 JKu(c),Death Warrant....... 12.00
176 JKu(c),The Loser Is A
    Teen-Ager................ 12.00
177 JKu(c),This Loser Must Die.. 12.00
178 JKu(c),Last Drop For Losers. 12.00
179 JKu(c),The Last Loser...... 12.00
180 JKu(c),Hot Seat In A
    Cold War................. 12.00
181 JKu(c),Sept.–Oct., 1978..... 18.00

OUTCASTS
Oct., 1987
1 .... 2.25
2 thru 11 .... @2.25

OUTLAW NATION
DC/Vertigo, Aug., 2000
1 JaD(s),F:pulp-fiction writer..... 2.50
2 JaD(s),Southern bayou........ 2.50
3 JaD,F:Devil Kid............... 2.50
4 JaD,F:Kid Gloves............. 2.50
5 JaD,F:Kid Gloves............. 2.50
6 JaD,........................ 2.50
7 JaD,........................ 2.50
8 JaD,Women,tequila & guns..... 2.50
9 JaD,Hell Holes............... 2.50
10 JaD,V:Gloves................ 2.50
11 JaD,Hate, Murder and Revenge. 2.50
12 JaD,Temptation.............. 2.50
13 JaD,Desperado.............. 2.50
14 JaD,The Devil Kid............ 2.50
15 JaD,The Devil Kid............ 2.50
16 JaD,Under siege............. 2.50
17 JaD,Quicksand.............. 2.50
18 JaD,Old Asa................ 2.50
19 JaD,final issue.............. 2.50

OUTLAWS
1991
1 LMc,I:Hood.................. 2.25
2 LMc,O:Hood................. 2.25
3 LMc,V:Evil King.............. 2.25
4 LMc,V:Lord Conductor........ 2.25
5 LMc,Archery contest.......... 2.25
6 LMc,Raid on King's Castle..... 2.25
7 LMc,Refuge, V:Lord Conductor. . 2.25

OUTSIDERS, THE
Nov., 1985
[1st Regular Series]
1 JAp,I:Looker................. 3.00
2 JAp,V:Nuclear Family......... 2.50
3 JAp,V:Force of July........... 2.50
4 JAp,V:Force of July........... 2.50
5 JAp,Christmas Issue.......... 2.50
6 JAp,V:Duke of Oil............ 2.50
7 JAp,V:Duke of Oil............ 2.50
8 JAp,Japan................... 2.50
9 JAp/SD/JOp,Bik Lightning..... 2.50
10 JAp,I:Peoples Heroes......... 2.50
11 JAp,Imprisoned in death camp.. 2.50
12 JAp,Imprisoned in death camp.. 2.50
13 JAp,Desert island............ 2.50
14 JAp,Looker/murder story...... 2.50
15 DJu,V:Bio-hazard............ 2.50
16 Halo vs.Firefly............... 2.50
17 JAp,J:Batman............... 2.50
18 JAp,BB,V:Eclipso............ 2.50
19 JAp,V:Windfall............... 2.50
20 JAp,Masters of Disaster...... 2.50
21 JAp,V:Kobra,I:Clayface IV.... 2.50
22 JAp,V:Strike Force Kobra...... 2.50
23 Return of People's Heroes..... 2.50
24 TVE,JAp,V:Skull,A:Duke of Oil. . 2.50
25 JAp,V:Skull.................. 2.50
26 JAp,in Markovia.............. 2.50
27 EL,Millennium............... 2.50
28 EL,Millennium,final issue...... 2.50
Ann.#1,KN,V:Skull,A:Batman..... 2.50
Spec.#1,A:Infinity,Inc........... 2.50

[2nd Regular Series], 1993–95
1 Alpha,TC(c),B:MiB(s),PaP,
   I:Technocrat,Faust,Wylde..... 3.00
1a Omega,TC(c),PaP,V:Vampires. 3.00
2 PaP,V:Sanction.............. 2.25
3 PaP,V:Eradicator............. 2.25
4 PaP,A:Eradicator............. 2.25
5 PaP,V:Atomic Knight,A:Jihad... 2.25
6 PaP,V:Jihad................. 2.25
7 PaP,C:Batman............... 2.25
8 PaP,V:Batman,I:Halo......... 2.25
9 PaP,V:Batman............... 2.25
10 PaP,B:Final Blood, R:Looker... 2.50

Outsiders–Plastic

11 PaP,Zero Hour,E:Final Blood ... 2.25
12 PaP.......................... 2.25
13 New base 2.25
14 Martial Arts Spectacular...... 2.25
15 V:New Year's Evil 2.25
16 R:Windfall 2.25
17 A:Green Lantern 2.25
18 Sins of the Father 2.25
19 Sins of the Father, pt.2....... 2.25
20 DvA,V:Metamorpho 2.25
21 A:Apokolips 2.25
22 Alien Assassin 2.25
23 V:Defilers..................... 2.25
24 finale......................... 2.25

OUTSIDERS
June 2003

1 TR,SHa 2.50
2 TR,SHa,F:Jade................. 2.50
3 TR,SHa,Gorilla Grodd.......... 2.50
4 Ccs,V:Brother Blood 2.50
5 CCs,V:Brother Blood 2.50
6 CCs,V:Brother Blood 2.50

PARALLAX: EMERALD NIGHT
Nov., 1996

1 RMz(s),MMK,MkK, pivotal tie-in
 to Final Night 4.50

PEACEMAKER
Jan., 1988

1 A:Dr.Tzin-Tzin................. 2.50
2 thru 4 .... @2.50

PENGUIN TRIUMPHANT

1 JSon,A:Batman,Wall Street..... 6.00

PETER CANNON: THUNDERBOLT
1992–93

1 thru 6 MC .... @2.25
7 MC,'Battleground'............. 2.25
8 MC,Cairo Kidnapped 2.25
9 MC........................... 2.25
10 MC,A:JLA 2.25
11 MC,V:Havoc,A:Checkmate..... 2.25
12 MC,final Issue 2.25

PETER PANDA
Aug.–Sept., 1953

1 .... 500.00
2 .... 250.00
3 thru 9 .... @200.00
10 Aug.–Sept., 1958............ 200.00

PETER PORKCHOPS
Nov.–Dec., 1949

1 .... 350.00
2 .... 175.00
3 thru 10 .... @125.00
11 thru 30 .... @100.00
31 thru 61 .... @75.00
62 Oct.–Dec., 1960............. 75.00

PHANTOM, THE
Oct., 1987

1 JO,A:Modern Phantom,13th
 Phantom 3.00
2 JO,Murder Trial in Manhattan ... 3.00
3 JO,A:Chessman 3.00
4 JO,V:Chessman,final issue..... 3.00

DC

PHANTOM, THE
1989–90

1 LMc,V:Gun Runners 3.00
2 LMc,V:Gun Runners 2.50
3 LMc,V:Drug Smugglers........ 2.50
4 LMc,In America,A:Diana Palner . 2.50
5 LMc,Racial Riots 2.50
6 LMc,in Africa,Toxic Waste
 Problem 2.50
7 LMc,`Gold Rush'.............. 2.50
8 LMc,`Train Surfing' 2.50
9 LMc,`The Slave Trade' 2.50
10 LMc,Famine in Khagana 2.50
11 LMc,Phantom/Diana Wedding
 proposal................... 2.50
12 LMc,Phantom framed for
 murder..................... 2.50
13 W:Phantom & Diana Palner
 C:Mandrake last issue 2.50

PHANTOM STRANGER
Aug.–Sept., 1952

1 .... 2,500.00
2 .... 1,500.00
3 .... 1,200.00
4 .... 1,200.00
5 .... 1,200.00
6, June-July, 1953........... 1,200.00

PHANTOM STRANGER
May-June, 1969

1 CI rep.&new material 150.00
2 CI rep.&new material 60.00
3 CI rep.&new material 60.00
4 NA,I:Tala,1st All-new issue 75.00
5 MSy,MA,A:Dr.13 .... 50.00
6 MSy,A:Dr.13 .... 50.00
7 JAp,V:Tala 50.00
8 JAp,A:Dr.13 .... 50.00
9 JAp,A:Dr.13 .... 50.00
10 JAp,I:Tannarak.............. 50.00
11 JAp,V:Tannarak 30.00
12 JAp,TD,Dr.13 solo story 30.00
13 JAp,TD,Dr.13 solo 30.00
14 JAp,TD,Dr.13 solo 30.00
15 JAp,ATh(rep),TD,Iron Messiah,
 giant-size 35.00
16 JAp,TD,MMes(rep)Dr.13 solo
 giant-size 35.00
17 JAp,I:Cassandra Craft,
 giant-size 35.00
18 TD,Dr.13 solo, giant-size 35.00

Phantom Stranger #36
© DC Comics, Inc.

Comics Values Annual

19 JAp,TD,Dr.13 solo, giant-size.. 35.00
20 JAp,`And A Child
 Shall Lead Them' 25.00
21 JAp,TD,Dr.13 solo 15.00
22 JAp,TD,I:Dark Circle 15.00
23 JAp,MK,I:Spawn-Frankenstein. 15.00
24 JAp,MA,Spawn Frankenstein.. 30.00
25 JAp,MA,Spawn Frankenstein.. 30.00
26 JAp,A:Frankenstein 35.00
27 V:Dr. Zorn 30.00
28 BU:Spawn of Frankenstein... 30.00
29 V:Dr.Zorn,BU:Frankenstein ... 30.00
30 E:Spawn of Frankenstein..... 30.00
31 B:BU:Black Orchid 35.00
32 NR,BU:Black Orchid 20.00
33 MGr,A:Deadman 20.00
34 BU:Black Orchid 20.00
35 BU:Black Orchid 20.00
36 BU:Black Orchid 20.00
37 Crimson Gold,BU:BlackOrchid. 20.00
38 Images of the Dead 20.00
39 A:Deadman 20.00
40 A:Deadman 20.00
41 A:Deadman 20.00

PHANTOM STRANGER
Oct., 1987–Jan., 1988

1 MMi,CR,V:Eclipso............. 3.00
2 and 4 MMi,CR,V:Eclipso ..... @3.00

PHANTOM ZONE, THE
Jan., 1982

1 GD/TD,A:Jax-Ur.............. 2.50
2 GC/TD,A:JLA 2.50
3 GC/TD,A:Mon-El.............. 2.50
4 GC/TD 2.50

PICTURE STORIES FROM THE BIBLE
Autumn, 1942–43

1 thru 4 Old Testament...... @250.00
1 thru 3 New Testament....... 225.00

PINKY AND THE BRAIN
Warner Bros./DC, 1996

1 from animated TV series....... 3.00
2 thru 27 .... @3.00

PLASTIC MAN
[1st Series]
Nov.–Dec., 1966

1 GK,I:Dr.Drome (1966 series
 begins)................... 125.00
2 V:The Spider 50.00
3 V:Whed 50.00
4 V:Dr.Dome 50.00
5 1,001 Plassassins............. 50.00
6 V:Dr.Dome 40.00
7 O:Plastic Man Jr.,A:Original
 Plastic Man,Woozy Winks.... 40.00
8 V:The Weasel................. 40.00
9 V:Joe the Killer Pro........... 40.00
10 V:Doll Maker(series ends) 40.00
11 (1976 series begins) 10.00
12 I:Carrot-Man 10.00
13 A:Robby Reed 10.00
14 V:Meat By-Product & Sludge .. 10.00
15 I:Snuffer,V:Carrot-Man 10.00
16 V:Kolonel Kool 10.00
17 O:Plastic Man 10.00
18 V:Professor Klean 10.00
19 I&Only App.Marty Meeker 10.00
20 V:Snooping Sneetches
 Oct.–Nov., 1977 .... 10.00

PLASTIC MAN
1988–89
1 Mini-series,Origin retold 2.25
2 V:The Ooze Brothers 2.25
3 In Los Angeles 2.25
4 End-series,A:Superman 2.25

PLASTIC MAN
1999
Spec.#1 TTn(s),ALo,RBr,48-page . . 4.00

PLOP!
Sept.–Oct., 1973
1 SA-AA,GE,ShM 40.00
2 AA,SA 20.00
3 AA,SA 20.00
4 BW,SA 25.00
5 MA,MSy,SA,BWr. 22.00
6 MSy,SA 18.00
7 SA 18.00
8 SA 18.00
9 SA 18.00
10 SA 18.00
11 ATh,SA 18.00
12 SA 18.00
13 WW(c),SA 20.00
14 WW,SA 20.00
15 WW(c),SA 20.00
16 SD,WW,SA 20.00
17 SA 20.00
18 SD,WW,SA 20.00
19 WW,SA 20.00
20 SA,WW 20.00
21 JO,WW 25.00
22 JO,WW,BW 25.00
23 BW,WW 25.00
24 SA,WW,Nov.–Dec., 1976 . . . . . 25.00

POWER COMPANY, THE
Jan., 2002
1 KBk,TG,V:Doctor Cyber 2.50
2 KBk,TG,V:Dragoneer 2.50
3 KBk,TG,V:Dragoneer, Godstone . 2.50
4 KBk,TG,offices under attack 2.50
5 KBk,TG,F:Manhunter 2.50
6 KBk,TG,F:Green Arrow 2.50
7 KBk,F:Striker Z 2.75
8 KBk,TG,Power Loss,pt.1 . . . . 2.75
9 KBk,TG,Power Loss,pt.2 . . . . 2.75
10 KBk,TG,anger aside 2.75
11 KBk,new member 2.75
12 KBk,F:Witchfire 2.75
13 KBk,TG,V:Dr. Polaris 2.75
14 KBk,TG,V:Dr.Polaris,Cadre 2.75
15 KBk,TG,V:Dark Knight 2.75
16 KBk,TG,Witchfire 2.75
17 KBk,TG,barbaric world 2.75
18 KBk,TG,final issue 2.75
Spec. Josiah Power,A:Superman . . 2.50
Spec. Striker Z,A:Superboy 2.50
Spec. Witchfire,A:Wonder Woman . 2.50
Spec. Skyrocket,A:Hal Jordan 2.50
Spec. Bork, A:Batman & Flash 2.50
Spec. Sapphire,A:JLA 2.50
Spec. Manhunter,A:Nightwing 2.50

POWER GIRL
[Mini-Series], 1988
1 . . . . 3.00
2 A:The Weaver, mongo Krebs . . . 3.00
3 V:The Weaver 3.00
4 V:Weaver, final issue 3.00

POWER OF SHAZAM!
1995–97
1 R:Captain Marvel 4.00

Power of Shazam #6
© DC Comics Inc.

2 V:Arson Fiend 3.00
3 V:Ibac 3.00
4 JOy,R:Mary Marvel,Tawky,
  Tawny 3.00
5 JOy(c&a),F:Mary Marvel,
  V:Black Adam 3.00
6 R:Captain Marvel 3.00
7 V:Captain Nazi 3.00
8 R:Captain Marvel,Jr. 3.00
9 JOy,MM,V:Black Adam 3.00
10 JOy,MM,V:Seven Deadly
  Enemies of Man 3.00
11 JOy,MM,R:Ibis as Capt.Marvel . . 3.00
12 JOy,MM,How Billy Batson's
  father met Shazam 3.00
13 JOy,MM 3.00
14 JOy,GK,MM,F:CaptainMarvelJr . 3.00
15 JOy,MM,V:Mr. Mind 3.00
16 thru 18 . . . . @3.00
19 JOy(s),GK,MM,Captain Marvel
  Jr. V:Captain Nazi 3.00
20 JOy(s),PKr,MM,A:Superman . . 3.00
21 JOy(s),PKr,MM,V:Liquidator . . . 2.50
22 JOy(s),PKr,MM,A:Batman 2.50
23 JOy(s),PKr,MM, ... 2.50
24 JOy(s),PKr,MM,V:Baron Blitz-
  krieg, prelude to new family . . 2.50
25 JOy(s),PKr,MM,The Marvel
  Family '97 . . . . 2.50
26 JOy(s),PKr,MM,new Capt.
  Marvel framed for murder 2.50
27 JOy(s),PKr,MM,D:Captain
  Marvel 2.50
28 JOy(s),DG, V:Patty Patty
  Bang Bang 2.50
29 JOy(c),DG,F:Hoppy 2.50
30 JOy(c),PKr,DG,V:Mr. Finish . . . 2.50
31 JOy,PKr,DG,Genesis x-over . . . 2.50
32 JOy,PKr,DG,Genesis aftermath . 2.50
33 JOy,PKr,DG,Madam M, Sin . . . 2.50
34 JOy,PKr,DG,F:Gangbuster 2.50
35 JOy,PKr,DG,Lightning &
  Stars, pt.2 x-over 2.50
36 JOy 2.50
37 JOy,MM,DG,F:Capt.Marvel Jr. . 2.50
38 JOy,PKr,DG,Monster Society
  of Evil, pt.1 . . . . 2.50
39 JOy,PKr,DG,Monster, pt.2 . . . . 2.50
40 JOy,PKr,DG,Monster, pt.3 . . . . 2.50
41 JOy,PKr,DG,Monster, pt.4 . . . . 2.50
42 JOy,DG,new logo & design . . . 2.50
43 JOy,DG,I:Bulletgirl 2.50
44 JOy,DG,V:Chain Lightning 2.50

45 JOy,DG,A:JLA 2.50
46 JOy,DG,A:Superman 2.50
47 JOy,V:Black Adam, final issue . . 2.50
Ann.#1 JOy(s),MM,Legends of
  the Dead Earth 2.95
Spec.#1,000,000 JOy,DG 2.50
GN Power of Shazam 7.50
GNv JOy(a&s),O:Captain Marvel . . 9.95
TPB JOy, reoffer 7.50

POWER OF THE ATOM
1988–89
1 1st Issue, Origin retold 2.25
2 Return of Powers 2.25
3 I:Strobe 2.25
4 A:Hawkman+bonus book #8 . . . 2.25
5 DT,A:Elongated Man 2.25
6 JBy,V:Chronos 2.25
7 GN,Invasion,V:Khunds,Chronos . 2.25
8 GN,Invasion,V:Chronos 2.25
9 GN,A:Justice League 2.25
10 GN,I:Humbug 2.25
11 GN,V:Paul Hoben 2.25
12 GN,V:Edg the Destroyer 2.25
13 GN,Blood Stream Journey 2.25
14 GN,V:Humbug 2.25
15 GN,V:Humbug 2.25
16 GN,V:The CIA 2.25
17 GN,V:The Sting 2.25
18 GN,V:The CIA, last issue 2.25

POWERPUFF GIRLS
Warner Bros./DC March, 2000
1 . . . . 3.50
2 DaF, ... 2.25
3 Mysterious meteor 2.25
4 Video game 2.00
5 thru 44 . . . . @2.25
Double Whammy, rep. #1 & #2 . . . 3.95
Spec.Powerpuff Girls movie comic . 2.95
TPB Titans of Townsville 6.95
TPB Go, Girls, Go 6.95

PREACHER
DC/Vertigo, 1995
1 I:Jesse Custer, Genesis 22.00
2 Saint of Killers 18.00
3 GF(c),I:Angels 15.00
4 GF(c),V:Saint of Killers 10.00
5 Naked City,pt.1 . . . . 10.00
6 Naked City,pt.2 . . . . 10.00
7 Naked City,pt.3 . . . . 8.00
8 GEn,SDi,All in the Family,pt.1 . . 5.00
9 GEn,SDi,All in the Family,pt.2 . . 5.00
10 GEn,SDi,All in the Family,pt.3 . 5.00
11 GEn,SDi,All in the Family,pt.4 . 5.00
12 GEn,SDi,All in the Family,pt.5 . 6.00
13 GEn,SDi,Hunters,pt.1 . . . . 5.00
14 GEn,SDi,Hunters,pt.2 (of 4) . . . 4.00
15 and 16 . . . . @4.00
17 Star captures Cassidy 3.00
18 GEn(s),SDi,secret of Jesse
  Custer's cigarette lighter 3.00
19 GEn(s),SDi,Crusaders, pt.1 . . . 3.00
20 GEn(s),SDi,Crusaders, pt.2 . . . 3.00
21 GEn(s),SDi,Crusaders, pt.3 . . . 3.00
22 GEn(s),SDi,Crusaders, pt.4 . . . 3.00
23 GEn(s),SDi,Crusaders, pt.5 . . . 3.00
24 GEn(s),SDi,Crusaders, concl. . . 3.00
25 GEn(s),SDi,Cry Blood, Cry
  Erin 3.00
26 GEn(s),SDi,To the Streets of
  Manhattan I Wandered Away . . 2.50
27 GEn(s),SDi, Jessie & Tulip in
  New York, pt.1 . . . . 2.50
28 GEn(s),SDi, Jessie & Tulip in
  New York, pt.2 . . . . 2.50
29 GEn(s),SDi, south to New

Preacher–Ragman — DC — Comics Values Annual

Orleans 2.50
30 GEn,SDi,in New Orleans 2.50
31 GEn,SDi,in New Orleans 2.50
32 GEn,SDi,in New Orleans 2.50
33 GEn,SDi,in New Orleans,concl. .. 2.50
34 GEn,SDi,War in the Sun,pt.1 ... 2.50
35 GEn,SDi,War in the Sun,pt.2 ... 2.50
36 GEn,SDi,War in the Sun,pt.3 ... 2.50
37 GEn,SDi,War in the Sun,pt.4 ... 2.50
38 GEn,SDi,GF,Utah radioactive. .. 2.50
39 GEn,SDi,GF,out of the desert. .. 2.50
40 GEn,SDi,GF,Arsefaced World .. 2.50
41 .... 2.50
42 GEn(s),SDi,GF,V:Meatman 2.50
43 GEn(s),SDi,GF,V:Meat Man ... 2.50
44 GEn(s),SDi,GF,Gunther Hahn .. 2.50
45 GEn(s),SDi,GF,V:Meat Man ... 2.50
46 GEn(s),SDi,GF,Miss Oatlash .. 2.50
47 GEn(s),SDi,GF,Salvation 2.50
48 GEn(s),SDi,GF,Salvation 2.50
49 GEn(s),SDi,GF,First Contact .. 2.50
50 GEn(s),SDi,GF,48-page
    I:100 Bullets 4.00
51 GEn(s),SDi,GF,Tulip's past,pt.1 . 4.00
52 GEn(s),SDi,GF,Tulip's past,pt.2 . 2.50
53 GEn(s),SDi,GF,road trip story. .. 2.50
54 GEn(s),SDi,GF,Jesse & Tulip .. 2.50
55 GEn(s),SKi,GF. 2.50
56 GEn(s),GF. 2.50
57 GEn(s), ... 2.50
58 GEn(s),SDi, ... 2.50
59 GEn(s),SDi,Alamo,pt.1. ...... 2.50
60 GEn(s),SDi,Alamo,pt.2. ...... 2.50
61 GEn(s),SDi,Alamo,pt.3. ...... 2.50
62 GEn(s),SDi,Alamo,pt.4. ...... 2.50
63 GEn(s),SDi,Alamo,pt.5. ...... 2.50
64 GEn(s),SDi,Alamo,pt.6. ...... 2.50
65 GEn(s),SDi,Alamo,pt.7. ...... 5.00
66 GEn(s),SDi,Alamo,pt.8,
    final issue............... 5.00
TPB Gone to Texas, rep.#1–#7 ... 15.00
TPB Proud Americans GEn(s). ... 15.00
TPB Until the End of the World ... 15.00
TPB Ancient History 15.00
TPB War in the Sun 15.00
TPB All Hell's A-Coming 17.95
TPB Alamo, GEn,SDi 17.95
TPB Dead or Alive 19.95
GN Preacher Spec. Cassidy: Blood
    and Whisky, GEn(s) (1997). .. 6.00
GN Tall in the Saddle 5.95
Spec. The Good Old Boys, parody . 5.50
Spec. The Story of You-Know-Who
    GEn(s),RCa,O:Arseface (1996) 5.00
Spec. One Man's War. 4.95

PREACHER SPECIAL: SAINT OF KILLERS
DC/Vertigo, 1996
1 GEn(s),StP. 5.00
2 GEn(s),StP 4.50
3 GEn(s),StP 3.50
4 GEn(s),StP 3.00

PREZ
Aug.–Sept., 1973
1 I:Prez (from Sandman #54).... 30.00
2 thru 4 F:Prez 20.00

PRIDE & JOY
DC/Vertigo, May, 1997
[Mini-series]
1 (of 4) GEn(s),JHi, ... 2.50
2 GEn(s),JHi. 2.50
3 GEn(s),JHi 2.50
4 GEn(s),JHi,concl. 2.50

Primal Force #3 © DC Comics, Inc.

PRIMAL FORCE
1994–95
O New Team 2.25
1 Claw. 2.25
2 Cataclysm 2.25
3 .... 2.25
4 Claw. 2.25
5 V:Demons 2.25
6 V:The Four Beasts 2.25
7 Trip to the Past........... 2.25
8 N.Choles(p),I:New Team..... 2.25
9 Maltis worsens, Tornado speaks . 2.25
10 V:August 2.25
11 .... 2.25
12 Black Condor vs. August ... 2.25
13 Underworld Unleashed tie-in . 2.25
14 final issue 2.25

PRINCE
DC/Piranha Press 1991
1 DCw,KW,based on rock star ... 10.00
1a Second printing 2.50
1b 3rd printing 2.00

PRISONER, THE
1988–89
1 Based on TV series 4.00
2 'By Hook or by Crook' 4.00
3 'Confrontation' 4.00
4 'Departure' final issue...... 4.00

PROPOSITION PLAYER
DC/Vertigo, Oct., 2000
1 (of 6) PGn,BWg,............ 2.50
2 PGn,BWg, ... 2.50
3 PGn,BWg, ... 2.50
4 PGn,BWg, ... 2.50
5 PGn,BWg, ... 2.50
6 PGn,BWg, poker game ends ... 2.50
TPB 14.95

PSYBA-RATS, THE
[Mini-Series], 1995
1 CDi,A:Robin 2.50
2 CDi,A:Robin 2.00
3 CDi,F:Razorsharp,final issue. .. 2.00

PSYCHO, THE
1991
1 I:Psycho................. 12.00
2 Sonya Rescue 10.00
3 'Psycho against the World'.... 7.00

PULP FANTASTIC
DC/Vertigo, Dec., 1999
1 (of 3) HC,RBr,detective....... 2.50
2 HC,RBr 2.50
3 HC,RBr,conclusion 2.50

QUEST FOR CAMELOT
June, 1998
1-shot movie adaptation 5.00

QUESTION, THE
Feb., 1987
1 DCw,R:Question,I:Myra,A:Shiva . 3.00
2 DCw,A:Batman,Shiva 2.50
3 DCw,I:Mayor Firman......... 2.50
4 DCw,V:Hatch 2.50
5 DCw,Hub City fall Apart 2.50
6 DCw,Abuse story 2.50
7 DCw,V:Mr.Volk 2.50
8 DCw,I:Mikado.............. 2.50
9 DCw,O:Rodor. 2.50
10 DCw,O:Rodor cont. 2.50
11 DCw,Transformation. 2.50
12 DCw,Poisoned Ground 2.50
13 DCw,V:The Spartans 2.50
14 DCw,V:The Spartans 2.50
15 DCw,The Klan in Hub City ... 2.50
16 DCw,'Butch Cassidy &
    Sundance Kid' 2.50
17 DCw,A:Green Arrow......... 2.50
18 DCw,A:Green Arrow. 2.50
19 DCw,V:Terrorists 2.50
20 DCw,Travelling Circus 2.50
21 DCw,V:Junior Musto 2.50
22 DCw,Election Night 2.50
23 DCw,Election Night contd. ... 2.50
24 DCw,Election Night contd. ... 2.50
25 DCw,Myra Critically Ill 2.50
26 A:Riddler................. 2.50
27 DCw 2.50
28 DCw,A:Lady Shiva. 2.50
29 DCw,V:Lady Shiva. 2.50
30 DCw,A:Lady Shiva. 2.50
31 DCw,Hub City Chaos contd ... 2.50
32 DCw,Identity Crisis. 2.50
33 DCw,Identity Crisis contd.... 2.50
34 DCw,Identity Crisis contd.... 2.50
35 DCw,Fate of Hub City 2.50
36 DCw,final issue (contd.G.A.Ann#3
    Question Quarterly #1)...... 2.50
Ann.#1 DCw,A:Batman,G.A. 3.00
Ann.#2 A:Green Arrow 4.00

QUESTION QUARTERLY
1 DCw. 4.50
2 DCw. 4.00
3 DCw(c) Film 3.00
4 DCw,MM,'Waiting for Phil' 3.00
5 DCw,MMi,MM,last issue 3.00

RAGMAN
[1st Limited Series], 1976–77
1 I&O:Ragman............... 20.00
2 I:Opal 12.00
3 V:Mr. Big 10.00
4 JKu(1st interior on character) .. 10.00
5 JKu,O:Ragman,final issue..... 10.00
[2nd Limited Series], 1991–92
1 PB,O:Ragman 3.00
2 PB,O:Ragman Powers 3.00

| 3 PB,Original Ragman......... 3.00
| 4 PB,Gang War............... 3.00
| 5 PB,V:Golem................ 3.00
| 6 PB,V:Golem,A:Batman....... 3.00
| 7 PB,V:Golem,A:Batman....... 3.00
| 8 PB,V:Golem,A:Batman....... 3.00

RAGMAN: CRY OF THE DEAD
1993–94
1 JKu(c),R:Ragman............ 3.00
2 JKu(c),A:Marinette.......... 2.50
3 JKu(c),V:Marinette.......... 2.50
4 JKu(c),Exorcism............. 2.50
5 JKu(c),V:Marinette.......... 2.50
6 JKu(c),final issue........... 2.50

THE RAY
[Limited Series], 1992
1 JQ,ANi,I&O:Ray(Ray Torril)..... 4.00
2 JQ,ANi,I:G.A. Ray........... 3.00
3 JQ,ANi,A:G.A. Ray........... 3.00
4 JQ,ANi,V:Dr.Polaris.......... 4.00
5 JQ,ANi,V:Dr.Polaris.......... 3.00
6 JQ,ANi,C:Lobo,final issue..... 3.00
TPB In A Blaze of Power....... 9.95

[Regular Series], 1994–96
1 JQ(c),RPr,V:Brinestone,
  A:Superboy............... 3.00
1a Newsstand Ed............. 2.25
2 RPr,V:Brinestone,A:Superboy... 2.25
3 RPr,I:Death Masque......... 2.25
4 JQ(c),RPr,I:Death Masque,
  Dr. Polarus............... 2.25
5 JQ(c),RPr,V:G.A.Ray......... 2.25
6 JQ(c),RPr,V:Black Canary..... 2.25
7 JQ(c),RPr,V:Canary/Ray...... 2.25
8 V:Lobo,Black Canary......... 2.25
9 Ray Undoes the past......... 2.25
10 F:Happy Terril.............. 2.25
11 30 years in future........... 2.25
12 V:Mystech................. 2.25
13 V:Death Masque............ 2.25
14 The Ray needs help, V:Death
  Masque.................. 2.25
15 F:Vandal Savage............ 2.25
16 D:Happy Terrill............. 2.25
17 I:Josh Terrill,V:Atomic Skull.... 2.25
18 Underworld Unleashed...... 2.25
19 Underworld Unleashed tie-in... 2.25
20 F:Black Condor............. 2.25
21 Black Condor captured...... 2.25

The Ray #1 © DC Comics, Inc.

| 22.................... 2.25
| 23 V:Death Masque........... 2.25
| 24...................... 2.25
| 25 double size.............. 3.50
| 26...................... 2.25
| 27...................... 2.25
| 28 CPr,final issue........... 2.25
| Ann.#1 Year One Annual...... 3.95

REAL FACT COMICS
March–April, 1946
1 S&K,Harry Houdini story..... 700.00
2 S&K, Rin-Tin-Tin story...... 450.00
3 H.G. Wells story........... 400.00
4 Jimmy Stewart story,B:Just
  Imagine................ 450.00
5 Batman & Robin(c)....... 2,200.00
6 O:Tommy Tomorrow...... 1,400.00
7 `The Flying White House'.... 200.00
8 VF,A:Tommy Tomorrow..... 750.00
9 S&K,Glen Miller story...... 300.00
10 `The Vigilante' by MMe.... 300.00
11 EK,`How the G-Men Capture
  Public Enemies!'......... 175.00
12 `How G-Men are Trained'... 175.00
13 Dale Evans story.......... 600.00
14 Will Rogers story,`Diary of
  Death'................. 150.00
15 A:The Master Magician-
  Thurston,A-Bomb........ 200.00
16 A:Four Reno Brothers,
  T.Tommorrow........... 600.00
17 `I Guard an Armored Car'... 150.00
18 `The Mystery Man of
  Tombstone'............. 150.00
19 `The Weapon that Won the
  West'................. 150.00
20 JKu,Daniel Boone......... 200.00
21 JKu,Kit Carson,July-Aug.,1949 150.00

REAL SCREEN COMICS
Spring, 1945
1 B:Fox & the Crow,Flippity
  & Flop............... 1,200.00
2 (fa).................... 550.00
3 (fa).................... 350.00
4 thru 7 (fa)............. @225.00
8 thru 11 (fa)............ @175.00
12 thru 20 (fa)........... @150.00
21 thru 30 (fa)........... @125.00
31 thru 40 (fa)........... @100.00
41 thru 128 (fa)........... @75.00
Becomes:

TV SCREEN CARTOONS
129 thru 137.............. @75.00
138 Jan.–Feb., 1961......... 75.00

REALWORLDS
March, 2000
GN Batman, 48-pg............ 6.00
GN Wonder Woman, 48-pg...... 6.00
GN JLA, 48-pg............... 6.00
GN Superman................ 6.00

R.E.B.E.L.S '94–'96
0 New team................. 2.50
1 L.E.G.I.O.N.,Green Lantern.... 2.50
2 Dissent................... 2.50
3....................... 2.50
4 Ship goes Insane............ 2.50
5 F:Dox.................... 2.25
6 Dox Defeated.............. 2.25
7 John Sin.................. 2.25
8 V:Galactic Bank............ 2.25
9 F:Dox,Ignea,Garv,Strata..... 2.25
10 V:World Bank.............. 2.25
11...................... 2.25

Rebels '94 #0 © DC Comics Inc.

12 F:Iceman Assassin.......... 2.25
13 Underworld Unleashed tie-in... 2.25
14 F:Lyrl Dox................ 2.25
15 V:Lyrl Dox................ 2.25
16 V:Lyrl Dox's satellite........ 2.25

RED TORNADO
1985
1 CI/FMc................... 3.00
2 CI/FMc,A:Superman......... 3.00
3 CI/FMc................... 3.00
4 CI/FMc................... 3.00

REIGN OF THE ZODIAC
Aug. 2003
1 BWi,CDo................. 2.75
2 BWi,CDo, Eidolon.......... 2.75
3 BWi,CDo................. 2.75
4 BWi,CDo................. 2.75

RELATIVE HEROES
Feb., 2000
1 (of 6) Olympian super-teens.... 2.50
2 Things to Do in Olympus
  When Your're Dead........ 2.50
3 F:Impulse................. 2.50
4 F:Blindside................ 2.50
5 O:Omni................... 2.50
6 Concl.................... 2.50

REMARKABLE WORLDS OF PHINEAS B. FUDDLE
DC/Paradox, 1999
1 (of 4) F:Angus & McKee....... 6.00
2........................ 6.00
3 ancient India.............. 6.00
4 concl.................... 6.00
TPB 192-page.............. 19.95

RESTAURANT AT THE END OF THE UNIVERSE
1994
1 Adapt. 2nd book in Hitchhikers'
  Guide to the Galaxy,
  I:The Restaurant........... 7.00
2 V:The Meal................ 7.00
3 Final issue................ 7.00

All comics prices listed are for Near Mint condition.

RESURRECTION MAN
March, 1997
1 DAn(s),JG,lenticular death's head cover............... 6.00
2 DAn(s),JG,V:Amazo........ 5.00
3 DAn(s),JG,Scorpion Memories pt.1 (of 3)................ 4.00
4 DAn(s),JG,Scorpion,pt.2...... 4.00
5 DAn(s),JG,Scorpion,pt.3...... 4.00
6 DAn&ALa(s),JoP,Genesis tie-in.. 3.00
7 DAn&ALa(s),TGb,BG,A:Batman. 3.00
8 DAn&ALa(s),BG,Big Howler... 3.00
9 DAn&ALa(s),F:Hitman, pt.1.... 3.00
10 DAn&ALa(s),F:Hitman, pt.2 ... 3.00
11 DAn&ALa(s), Origin of the Species, pt.1.............. 2.50
12 DAn&ALa(s), Origin of the Species, pt.2.............. 2.50
13 DAn&ALa(s),Candy Man..... 2.50
14 DAn&ALa(s),really dead?..... 2.50
15 DAn&ALa(s),JG,V:Rider...... 2.50
16 DAn&ALa(s),BG,Avenging Angels x-over pt.1.......... 2.50
17 DAn&ALa(s),BG,Avenging Angels x-over pt.3.......... 2.50
18 DAn&ALa(s),A:Phantom Stranger, Deadman................. 2.50
19 DAn&ALa(s),Cape Fear, pt.1 .. 2.50
20 DAn&ALa(s),Cape Fear, pt.2 .. 2.50
21 DAn&ALa(s),Cape Fear, pt.3 .. 2.50
22 DAn&ALa(s)............... 2.50
23 DAn&ALa(s),Resurrection Woman.................. 2.50
24 DAn&ALa(s)............... 2.50
25 DAn&ALa(s)Millennium Meteor,pt.1................ 2.50
26 DAn&ALa(s)Millennium Meteor, pt.2,A:Superman, Titans....... 3.50
27 DAn&ALa(s)Millennium Meteor, pt.3,final issue............ 2.50
Spec.#1,000,000 DAn&ALa(s) .. 2.50

RICHARD DRAGON, KUNG FU FIGHTER
April-May, 1975
1 O:Richard Dragon.......... 20.00
2 JSn/AM................. 15.00
3 JK..................... 12.00
4 RE/WW................. 10.00
5 RE/WW................. 10.00
6 RE/WW................. 10.00
7 RE/WW................. 10.00
8 RE/WW................. 10.00
9 RE..................... 8.00
10 RE.................... 8.00
11 RE.................... 8.00
12 RE.................... 8.00
13 thru 17 RE........... @8.00
18 Nov.–Dec., 1977......... 8.00

RIMA, THE JUNGLE GIRL
April-May, 1974
1 NR,I:Rima,O:Pt. 1.......... 20.00
2 NR,O:Pt.2................ 10.00
3 NR,O:Pt.3................ 10.00
4 NR,O:Pt.4................ 10.00
5 NR..................... 10.00
6 NR..................... 10.00
7 April-May, 1975........... 10.00

RING, THE [OF THE NIEBLUNG]
1989
1 GK,Opera Adaption......... 12.00
2 GK,Sigfried's Father's Sword .. 7.00
3 GK,to save Brunhilde........ 6.00
4 GK, final issue............. 6.00
TPB rep.#1 thru #4.......... 19.95

RIP HUNTER, TIME MASTER
March-April, 1961
1 .... 750.00
2 .... 350.00
3 thru 5 ....@250.00
6 and 7 Ath.............@150.00
8 thru 15...............@125.00
16 thru 20..............@125.00
21 thru 28..............@100.00
29 Nov.–Dec., 1965........ 100.00

ROAD TO PERDITION
DC/Paradox/Pocket, 1998
TPB 6"x8" 304pg., b&w....... 25.00
TPB b&w,new edition (2002)... 15.00
TPB Vol. 2 Sanctuary......... 7.95

ROBIN
[1st Limited Series], 1991
1 TL,BB(c),Trial,pt.1(&Poster) ... 5.00
1a 2nd printing.............. 2.50
1b 3rd printing.............. 2.25
2 TL,BB(c) Trial,pt.2.......... 2.50
2a 2nd printing.............. 2.25
3 TL,BB(c) Trial,pt.3.......... 2.50
4 TL,Trial,pt.4............... 2.50
5 TL,Final issue,A:Batman...... 2.50
TPB BB(c),rep.#1–#5,Batman #455–#457................ 7.95

[2nd Limited Series], 1991 [ROBIN II: THE JOKER'S WILD]
1 Direct,Hologram(c)Joker face .. 3.00
1a (c)Joker straightjacket....... 2.25
1b (c)Joker standing.......... 2.25
1c (c)Batman............... 2.25
1d Newsstand(no hologram) ... 2.25
1e collectors set,extra holo..... 10.00
2 Direct,Hologram(c) Robin/Joker Knife................... 2.25
2a (c)Joker/Robin-Dartboard..... 2.25
2b (c)Robin/Joker-Hammer..... 2.25
2c Newsstand(no hologram).... 2.25
2d collectors set,extra holo..... 9.00
3 Direct,Holo(c)Robin standing .. 2.25
3a (c)Robin swinging.......... 2.25
3b Newsstand(no hologram).... 2.25
3c collectors set,extra holo..... 7.00
4 Direct, Hologram............ 2.25
4a Newsstand (no hologram).... 2.25
4b collectors set,extra holo..... 2.25
Collectors set (#1 thru #4)...... 30.00

[3rd Limited Series], 1992–93 [ROBIN III: CRY OF THE HUNTRESS]
1 TL,A:Huntress,Collector's Ed. movable(c),poster.......... 3.00
1a MZ(c),Newsstand Ed........ 2.25
2 TL,V:KGBeast,A:Huntress..... 2.75
2a MZ(c),Newsstand Ed 2.25
3 TL,V:KGBeast,A:Huntress..... 2.75
3a MZ(c),newsstand Ed........ 2.25
4 TL,V:KGBeast,A:Huntress..... 2.75
4a MZ(c),newsstand Ed........ 2.25
5 TL,V:KGBeast,A:Huntress..... 2.75
5a MZ(c),newsstand Ed........ 2.25
6 TL,V:KGBeast,King Snake, A:Huntress................ 2.75
6a MZ(c),Newsstand Ed........ 2.25

[Regular Series], 1993–2002
1 B:CDi(s),TG,SHa,V:Speedboyz... 4.00
1a Newstand Ed............. 2.25
2 TG,V:Speedboyz........... 2.50
3 TG,V:Cluemaster, Electrocutioner............. 2.50
4 TG,V:Cluemaster,Czonk, Electrocutioner............. 2.50
5 TG,V:Cluemaster,Czonk, Electrocutioner............. 2.50
6 TG,A:Huntress............. 2.50
7 TG,R:Robin's Father......... 2.50
8 TG,KnightsEnd#5,A:Shiva..... 3.00
9 TG,Knights End:Aftermath 2.50
10 TG,Zero Hour,V:Weasel...... 2.50
11 New Batman............. 2.50
12 Robin vs. thugs............ 2.50
13 V:Steeljacket............. 2.50
14 CDi(s),TG,Return of Bruce Wayne,Troika,pt.4.......... 3.00
14a Collector's edition......... 3.00
15 Cluemaster Mystery......... 2.50
16 F:Spoiler................ 2.50
17 I:Silver Monkey,V:King Snake,Lynx [New Miraweb format begins].. 2.50
18 Gotham City sabotaged...... 2.50
19 V:The General............ 2.50
20 F:Robin................. 2.50
21 Ninja Camp,pt.1........... 2.50
22 CDi,TG,Ninja Camp,pt.2..... 2.50
23 CDi,Underworld Unleashed tie-in 2.50
24 CDi,V:Charaxes........... 2.50
25 CDi,F:Green Arrow......... 2.50
26 .... 2.50
27 .... 2.50
28 CDi,Contagion: conclusion.... 2.50
29 CDi,FFo,SnW,A:Maxie Zeus .. 2.50
30 CDi,FFo,SnW,A:Maxie Zeus .. 2.50
31 CDi(s),A:Wildcat........... 2.50
32 CDi(s),Legacy, pt. 3 x-over.... 2.50
33 CDi(s),Legacy, pt. 7 x-over.... 2.50
34 CDi(s),JhD,action at a Shakespear play........... 2.50
35 CDi(s),Robin & Spoiler, Final Night tie-in............... 2.50
36 CDi(s),V:Toyman, The General. . 2.50
37 CDi(s),V:The General, Toyman.. 2.50
38 CDi(s)................. 2.50
39 CDi(s), pt.2.............. 2.50
40 CDi(s),................ 2.50
41 CDi(s),F:Tim and Ariana..... 2.50
42 CDi(s),F:Crocky the Crocodile .. 2.50
43 CDi(s),A:Spoiler........... 2.50
44 CDi(s) Pt.2 (of 2)........... 2.50
45 CDi(s) Tim Drake grounded.... 2.50
46 CDi(s) Genesis tie-in........ 2.50
47 CDi,V:General, pt.1......... 2.50

Robin #12 © DC Comics, Inc.

48 CDi,V:General, pt.2 . . . . 2.50	Earth 2.95	1951 thru 1954. . . . . @125.00
49 CDi,to Paris 2.50	Ann.#5 Legends o/t Dead Earth . . . 2.95	1955 thru 1962 Winter . . . . . . @100.00
50 CDi(s),F:Lady Shiva & King	Ann.#6 Pulp Heroes (Western),	
Snake, 48pg. 3.50	CDi(s) 3.95	### RUSSIAN ROULETTE
51 CDi(s) 2.50	Spec.#1,000,000 CDi(s),SnW 2.00	**DC/Vertigo, 1999**
52 CDi(s) Cataclysm x-over,pt.7 . . . 2.50	Spec. Robin/Argent Double Shot	1 (of 3) 3.00
53 CDi(s),SnW,Cataclysm concl.. . . 2.50	DJu,CDi,V:Spoiler x-over (1997)2.00	
54 CDi(s),SnW,Aftershock 2.50	TPB A Hero Reborn,JAp,TL 4.95	### SAGA OF
55 CDi(s),SnW, Brotherhood of	TPB Tragedy and Triumph,	### RAS AL GHUL
the Fist x-over, pt.3. . . . . 2.50	TL,NBy. 9.95	**1988**
56 CDi(s),SnW,tearful turning point . 2.50	TPB Robin: Flying Solo. 12.95	1 NA,DG,reprints. 6.00
57 CDi(s),SnW,A:Spoiler. 2.50	80-page Giant #1 CDi. 5.95	2 rep. 5.00
58 CDi(s),SnW,A:Spoiler. 2.50		3 rep.Batman #242&#243 . . . . . . 5.00
59 CDi(s),SnW,V:Steeljacket. 2.50	### ROBIN PLUS	4 rep.Batman #244&#245,
60 CDi(s),SnW,Alvin Draper 2.50	**1996**	Detective #410 . . . . 5.00
61 CDi(s),SnW,V:Phil Delinger 2.50	1 MWa&BAu(s), F:Bart Allen, skiing	TPB reps. 17.95
62 CDi(s),SnW,A:Flash, pt.1. . . . . . 2.50	rips, V:Mystral 2.95	
63 CDi(s),SnW,A:Flash, pt.2 . . . . . . 2.50	2 LKa,CDi,AWi,ALa,F:Fang 3.00	
64 CDi(s),SnW,A:Flash, pt.3 . . . . . . 2.50		
65 CDi(s),SnW,A:Spoiler. 2.50	### ROBIN 3000	
66 CDi(s),SnW,V:demons 2.50	**1992**	
67 CDi(s),SnW,No Man's Land 2.50	1 CR,Elseworlds,V:Skulpt 5.25	
68 CDi(s),No Man's Land 2.50	2 CR,Elseworlds,V:Skulpt 5.25	
69 CDi(s),No Man's Land 2.50		
70 CDi(s),No Man's Land 2.50	### ROBIN: YEAR ONE	
71 CDi(s),V:Killer Croc 2.50	**October, 2000**	
72 CDi(s). 2.50	1 CDi,SBe,F:Dick Grayson 5.00	
73 CDi(s),F:Batgirl 2.50	2 CDi,SBe,F:Dick Grayson 5.00	
74 CDi(s),F:Batman & Nightwing . . 2.50	3 CDi,SBe,RbC,F:Dick Grayson. . . 5.00	
75 CDi(s),48-pg. 3.50	4 CDi,SBe,concl. 5.00	
76 CDi(s),R:Man-Bat 2.50	TPB series rep. 14.95	
77 CDi(s),I:Jaeger. 2.50		
78 CDi(s),V:Arrakhat. 2.50	### ROBIN HOOD TALES	
79 CDi(s),F:Green Arrow 2.50	**1957–58**	
80 CDi(s),A:Star. 2.50	7 . . . . 450.00	
81 CDi(s),MPn,. 2.50	8 thru 14 . . . . @400.00	
82 CDi(s),Spoiler,Star 2.50		
83 CDi,Vacation time 2.50	### ROBOTECH	
84 CDi,A:Lagoon Boy 2.50	### DEFENDERS	
85 CDi,This issue: Batman dies!. . . 2.50	**1985**	*Saga of Swamp Thing #39*
86 Officer Down x-over,pt.2 . . . . . . 2.50	1 MA,mini-series 3.50	*© DC Comics Inc.*
87 CDi,A:Spoiler. 2.50	2 MA. 3.00	
88 CDi,Road trip. 2.50		
89 CDi,to Himalayas. 2.50	### ROGAN GOSH	### SAGA OF THE
90 CDi,V:mini-yeti 2.50	**DC/Vertigo, 1994**	### SWAMP THING
91 CDi,F:Danny Temple 2.50	1 PF PrM(s) (From Revolver). 7.25	**1982–85**
92 CDi,SBe,A:Batman,Spoiler. 2.50		1 JmP(s),TY,DSp,O:Swamp Thing,
93 CDi,F:Spoiler. 2.50	### RONIN	BU:PhantomStranger 7.00
94 CDi,F:Spoiler,Wesley 2.50	**July, 1983**	2 Ph(c),TY,DSp,I:Grasp 4.00
95 CDi,Joker:Last Laugh tie-in 2.50	1 FM,1:Billy 6.00	3 TY,DSp,V:Vampires 4.00
96 CDi,Last Laugh aftermath 2.50	2 FM,I:Casey. 5.00	4 TY,TD,V:Demon 4.00
97 CDi,F:Normandy 2.50	3 FM,V:Agat 5.00	5 TY 4.00
98 Bruce Wayne:Murderer,pt.8 . . . . 2.50	4 FM,V:Agat 5.00	6 TY,I:General Sunderland. 4.00
99 Bruce Wayne:Murderer,pt.11 . . . 2.50	5 FM,V:Agat 6.00	7 TY 4.00
100 CDi,Spoiler,48-pg. 4.00	6 FM,D:Billy. 8.00	8 TY 4.00
101 WorldWithoutYoungJustice,pt.3 2.25	Paperback, FM inc. Gatefold. 12.00	9 TY 4.00
102 Spoiler. 2.25		10 TY 4.00
103 Nocturna's secret. 2.25	### ROOTS OF THE	11 TY,I:Golem. 4.00
104 Astrology Lady 2.25	### SWAMP THING	12 LWn(s),TY 4.00
105 riddle of Natalia 2.25	**July, 1986**	13 TY,D:Grasp 4.00
106 A:Batman. 2.25	1 BWr,rep.SwampThing#1&#2 . . . 3.50	14 A:Phantom Stranger 4.00
107 F:Charaxis 2.25	2 BWr,rep.SwampThing#3&#4 . . . 3.50	15 . . . . 4.00
108 F:Charaxis 2.25	3 BWr,rep.SwampThing#5&#6 . . . 3.50	16 SBi,JTo 5.00
109 V:Charaxis. 2.25	4 BWr,rep.SwampThing#7&#8 . . . 3.50	17 I:Matthew Cable. 5.00
110 F:Nightwing 2.25	5 BWr,rep.SwampThing#9&#10,	18 JmP(s),LWn(s),SBi,JTo,BWr,
111 F:Spoiler 2.25	H.O.S. #92, final issue 3.50	R:Arcane. 5.00
112 to Pennsylvania 2.25		19 JmP(s),SBi,JTo,V:Arcane 5.00
113 V:The Riddler. 2.25	### RUDOLPH THE RED–	20 B:AMo(s),Day,JTo(i),D:Arcane
114 The Wrong Town 2.25	### NOSED REINDEER	(Original incarnation) 20.00
115 The Wrong Town 2.25	**Dec., 1950**	21 SBi,JTo,O:Swamp Thing,I:Floronic
116 Identity compromised 2.25	1950 . . . . 250.00	Man,D:General Sunderland . . 17.00
117 Identity compromised 2.25		22 SBi,JTo,O:Floronic Man 11.00
118 Traitor's identity 2.25		23 SBi,JTo,V:Floronic Man 11.00
119 Traitor's identity 2.25		24 SBi,JTo,V:Floronic Man,A:JLA,
120 Hell in a handbasket 2.25		In Arkham. 11.00
Ann.#1 TL,Eclipso tie-in,V:Anarky . . 3.00		
Ann.#2 KD,JL,Bloodlines#10,		
I:Razorsharp 2.75		
Ann.#3 Elseworlds Story. 3.25		
Ann.#4 Year One Annual 2.95		
Ann.#5 CDi,Legends of the Dead		

Saga–Sandman DC Comics Values Annual

25 SBi,A:Jason Blood,I:Kamara . . 10.00
26 SBi,A:Demon,
 D:Matthew Cable 10.00
27 SBi,D:Kamara,A:Demon 7.00
28 SwM,Burial of Alec Holland . . . 7.00
29 SBi,JTo,R:Arcane. 7.00
30 SBi,AA,D:Abby,C:Joker,
 V:Arcane 9.00
31 RV,JTo,D:Arcane 6.00
32 SwM,Tribute to WK Pogo strip . . 6.00
33 rep.H.O.S.#92,A:Cain & Abel . . . 6.00
34 SBi,JTo,Swamp Thing & Abby
 Fall in Love 8.00
35 SBi,JTo,Nukeface,pt.1 . . . . . . 5.00
36 SBi,JTo,Nukeface,pt.2 . . . . . . 6.00
37 RV,JTo,I:John Constantine,
 American Gothic,pt.1 . . . . . . 17.00
38 SnW,JTo,V:Water-Vampires
 (Pt.1) A:J.Constantine. 9.00
39 SBi,JTo,V:Water-Vampires
 (Pt.2) A:J.Constantine. 9.00
40 SBi,JTo,C:J.Constantine,
 The Curse 9.00
41 SBi,AA,Voodoo Zombies #1. . . 4.00
42 SBi,JTo,RoR,
 Voodoo Zombies #2 . . . . 4.00
43 SnW,RoR,Windfall,
 I:Chester Williams 4.00
44 SBi,JTo,RoR,V:Serial Killer,
 C:Batman,Constantine,Mento . . 5.00
45 SnW,AA,Ghost Dance 4.00
Ann.#1 MT,TD,Movie Adaption . . . 2.00
Ann.#2 AMo(s),E:Arcane,A:Deadman,
 Phantom Stranger,Spectre,
 Demon,Resurrection of Abby . . 7.00
TPB rep.#21-#27 . . . . 12.95
TPB rep.#28-#34,Ann.#2 . . . . . . 14.95
TPB Love and Death 19.95
Becomes:

SWAMP THING

SAMURAI JACK
Warner Bros./DC July, 2002
Spec. #1 64-pg. 3.95

SANDMAN
[1st Regular Series], 1974–75
1 JK,I&O:Sandman,I:General
 Electric. 60.00
2 V:Dr.Spider. 25.00
3 Brain that Blanked
 out the Bronx 25.00
4 JK,Panic in the Dream Stream . 25.00
5 JK,Invasion of the Frog Men . . . 25.00
6 JK,WW,V:Dr.Spider. 32.00
[2nd Regular Series], 1989–93
1 B:NGa(s),SK,I:2nd Sandman . . 35.00
2 SK,A:Cain,Abel. 15.00
3 SK,A:John Constantine 12.00
4 SK,A:Demon. 12.00
5 SK,A:Mr.Miracle,J'onn J'onzz . . 12.00
6 V:Doctor Destiny. 10.00
7 V:Doctor Destiny. 10.00
8 Sound of her wings,F:Death . . 25.00
8a Guest Ed.Pin-Up Cover 50.00
9 Tales in the Sand,Doll's House
 prologue. 10.00
10 B:Doll's House,A:Desire
 & Despair,I:Brut & Glob 10.00
11 MovingIn,A:2ndS-man 10.00
12 Play House,D;2ndS'man 10.00
13 Men of Good Fortune,A:Death,
 Lady Constantine 10.00
14 Collectors,D:Corinthian 10.00
15 Into' Night,DreamVortex 10.00
16 E:Doll's House,Lost Hearts . . . 10.00
17 Calliope 10.00
18 Dream of a 1000 Cats 10.00
18a error pg.1. . . . . 20.00

Sandman #1 © DC Comics Inc.

19 Midsummer Nights Dream 6.00
19a error copy 15.00
20 Strange Death Element Girl,
 A:Death 7.00
21 Family Reunion,B:Season
 of Mists 8.00
22 Season of Mists,I:Daniel Hall . . 13.00
23 Season of Mists. 7.00
24 Season of Mists. 7.00
25 Season of Mists. 7.00
26 Season of Mists. 6.00
27 E:Season of Mists 6.00
28 Ownership of Hell 6.00
29 A:Lady J.Constantine. 5.00
30 Ancient Rome;A:Death,Desire . . 5.00
31 Ancient Rome,pt.2 . . . . 5.00
32 B:The Game of You 5.00
33 The Game of You 5.00
34 The Game of You 4.00
35 The Game of You 4.00
36 The Game of You,48pgs 5.00
37 The Game of You,Epilogue 4.00
38 Convergence. 4.00
39 Convergence,A:Marco Polo . . . 4.00
40 Convergence,A:Cain,Abel,Eve,
 Matthew the Raven 4.00
41 JIT,VcL,(i),B:Brief Lives,
 F:Endless. 4.00
42 JIT,VcL,(i),F:Delirium,Dream. . . 4.00
43 JIT,VcL,(i),A:Death,Etain 4.00
44 JIT,VcL,(i),R:Corinthian,
 Destruction 4.00
45 JIT,VcL,(i),F:Tiffany,
 Ishtar(Belli). 4.00
46 JIT,VcL,(i),F:Morpheus/Bast,
 A:Aids insert story,F:Death . . . 4.00
DC/Vertigo, 1994–96
47 JIT,VcL,(i),A:Endless 4.00
48 JIT,VcL,(i),L:Destruction 4.00
49 JIT,VcL,(i),E:Brief Lives,
 F:Orpheus 4.00
50 DMc(c),CR,Tales of Baghdad,
 pin-upsby TM,DMc,MK 5.00
50a Gold Ed. 22.00
51 BT,MBu(i),B:Inn at the end of
 the World,Gaheris' tale 4.00
52 BT,MBu(i),JWk,Cluracan's
 Story 4.00
53 BT,DG,MBu(i),MZi,Hob's
 Leviathan 4.00
54 BT,MiA,MBu(i),R:Prez 4.00
55 SAp,VcL,BT,MBu(i),F:Klaproth
 Cerements's Story 4.00
56 BT,MBu(i),DG(i),SLi(i),GyA,TyH(i),
 E:Inn at the end of the World,

 C:Endless 4.00
57 MaH,B:Kindly Ones,Inc.American
 Freak Preview 5.00
58 MaH,Kindly Ones,pt.2,
 A:Lucifer. 4.00
59 MaH,Kindly Ones,pt.3,R:Fury. . . 4.00
60 MaH,Kindly Ones,pt.4 . . . . 4.00
61 MaH,Kindly Ones,pt.5 . . . . 4.00
62 Kindly Ones,pt.6,Murder 4.00
63 MaH,Kindly Ones,pt.7,
 A:Rose Walker 4.00
64 Kindly Ones,pt.8 . . . . 4.00
65 MaH,Kindly Ones,pt.9,Dream
 Kingdom. 4.00
66 MaH,Kindly Ones,pt.10 . . . . . . 4.00
67 MaH,Kindly Ones,pt.11 . . . . . . 4.00
68 MaH,Kindly Ones,pt.12 . . . . . . 4.00
69 MaH,Kindly Ones finale 4.00
70 The Wake,pt.1 . . . . 4.00
71 The Wake,pt.2 . . . . 4.00
72 NGa,DMc,The Wake,pt.3 . . . . . 4.00
73 NGa,Sunday Mourning 4.00
74 NGa,V:Lord of Dreams 4.00
TPB Preludes & Nocturnes,
 rep. #1–#8 . . . . 20.00
TPB Doll's House, rep #8–#16 . . 18.00
TPB Dream Country,Rep.#17-#20 . 15.00
TPB Fables & Reflections,rep. . . 20.00
TPB Season of Mists,rep.#21-#28 . 20.00
TPB A Game of You,rep.#32–#37 . 20.00
TPB Brief Lives. 20.00
TPB The Wake, rep. #70–#75. . . 20.00
TPB World's End DMc(c) 20.00
Sandman Covers, 1989–96 . . . . 40.00
Spec.BT,Glow in the Dark(c),The
 Legend of Orpheus,
 (inc. Portrait Gallery) 6.00

SANDMAN MYSTERY THEATRE
DC/Vertigo, 1993–99
1 B:MWg(s),GyD,R:G.A.Sandman,
 B:Tarantula,I:Mr.Belmont,
 Dian Belmont 5.00
2 GyD,V:Tarantula 3.00
3 GyD,V:Tarantula 3.00
4 GyD,E:Tarantula 3.00
5 JWk,B:The Face 3.00
6 JWk,The Face #2 . . . . 3.00
7 JWk,The Face #3 . . . . 3.00
8 JWk,E:The Face 3.00
9 RGT,B:The Brute,I:Rocket
 Ramsey 3.00
10 RGT,The Brute#2. . . . . 3.00
11 RGT,The Brute#3 . . . . 3.00
12 RGT,E:The Brute 3.00
13 GyD,B:The Vamp 3.00
14 GyD,The Vamp#2 . . . . 3.00
15 GyD,The Vamp#3 . . . . 3.00
16 GyD,E:The Vamp. 3.00
17 GyD,B:The Scorpion 3.00
18 GyD,The Scorpion,pt.2 . . . . . . 3.00
19 GyD,The Scorpion,pt.3 . . . . . . 3.00
20 GyD,The Scorpion,pt.4 . . . . . . 3.00
21 Dr. Death. 3.00
22 Dr. Death,pt.2 . . . . 3.00
23 Dr. Death,pt.3 . . . . 3.00
24 Dr. Death,pt.4 . . . . 3.00
25 The Butcher,pt.1 . . . . 3.00
26 The Butcher,pt.2 . . . . 3.00
27 The Butcher,pt.3 . . . . 3.00
28 The Butcher,pt.4 . . . . 3.00
29 The Hourman,pt.1 . . . . 3.00
30 The Hourman,pt.2 . . . . 3.00
31 The Hourman,pt.3 . . . . 3.00
32 The Hourman,pt.4 . . . . 3.00
33 The Python,pt.1 . . . . 3.00
34 The Python,pt.2 . . . . 3.00
35 The Python,pt.3 . . . . 3.00
36 The Python,pt.4 . . . . 3.00

DC — Sandman–Secret

```
37 The Mist,pt.1 .............. 3.00
38 The Mist,pt.2 .............. 3.00
39 The Mist,pt.3 .............. 3.00
40 The Mist,pt.4 .............. 3.00
41 MWg&SSe(s),GyD,Phantom of
    the Fair,pt.1 .............. 2.50
42 MWg&SSe(s),GyD,Phantom of
    the Fair,pt.2 .............. 2.50
43 MWg&SSe(s),GyD,Phantom of
    the Fair, pt. 3. ............. 2.50
44 MWg&SSe(s),GyD,Phantom of
    the Fair, pt. 4. ............. 2.50
45 MWg&SSe(s),Blackhawk,pt.1. . . 2.50
46 MWg&SSe(s),Blackhawk,pt.2. . . 2.50
47 MWg&SSe(s),Blackhawk,pt.3. . . 2.50
48 MWg&SSe(s),RCa,Blackhawk . . 2.50
49 MWg&SSe(s),ScarletGhost,pt.1 2.50
50 MWg&SSe(s),The Scarlet
    Ghost, pt.2, 48pg .......... 4.50
51 MWg&SSe(s),ScarletGhost,pt.3 . 2.50
52 MWg&SSe(s),ScarletGhost,pt.4 . 2.50
53 MWg&SSe(s),The Crone,pt.1. . . 2.50
53 MWg&SSe(s),The Crone,pt.2. . . 2.50
54 SSe&MWg(s),The Crone,pt.3. . . 2.50
55 SSe&MWg(s),The Crone,pt.4. . . 2.50
56 SSe&MWg(s),The Crone, concl. 2.50
57 SSe&MWg(s),The Cannon,pt.1 . 2.50
58 SSe&MWg(s),The Cannon,pt.2 . 2.50
59 SSe&MWg(s),The Cannon,pt.3 . 2.50
60 SSe&MWg(s),The Cannon,pt.4 . 2.50
61 SSe(s),GyD,The City, pt.1 ..... 2.50
62 SSe(s),GyD,The City, pt.2 ..... 2.50
63 SSe(s),GyD,The City, pt.3 ..... 2.50
64 SSe(s),GyD,The City, pt.4 ..... 2.50
65 SSe,GyD,The Goblin, pt.1 ..... 2.50
66 SSe,GyD,The Goblin, pt.2 ..... 2.50
67 SSe,GyD,The Goblin, pt.3 ..... 2.50
68 SSe,GyD,The Goblin, pt.4 ..... 2.50
69 SSe,GyD................... 2.50
70 SSe,GyD,final issue.......... 2.50
Ann.#1 ....................... 3.95
TPB The Tarantula ............ 14.95
TPB The Dream Hunters ....... 19.95
TPB Season of the Mists ...... 19.95
TPB Sandman Companion ...... 14.95
```

SANDMAN PRESENTS:
LOVE STREET
DC/Vertigo, 1999
```
1 (of 3) MZi,VcL, ............. 3.00
2 MZi,VcL,F:John Constantine.... 3.00
3 MZi,VcL,Concl............... 3.00
```
LUCIFER
DC/Vertigo, 1999
```
1 (of 3) SHp, Morningstar Option .. 3.00
2 SHp ....................... 3.00
3 SHp, conclusion ............. 3.00
```
PETREFAX
DC/Vertigo, 2000
```
1 (of 4) SL................... 3.00
2 thru 4 SL................. @3.00
```
DEAD BOY DETECTIVES
DC/Vertigo, 2001
```
1 (of 4) ..................... 2.50
2 thru 4 SL................. @2.50
```
CORINTHIAN, THE
DC/Vertigo, 2001
```
1 (of 3) ..................... 2.50
2 thru 3 ................... @2.50
```
THESSALIAD, THE
DC/Vertigo, 2002
```
1 (of 4) ..................... 2.50
2 thru 4 DMc(s) ............ @2.50
```
BAST
DC/Vertigo, 2003
```
1 (of 3) F:Lady Bast........... 3.00
```

```
2 thru 3 ................... @3.00
Spec.1-Shot, Merv Pumpkinhead
    Agent of Dream,MBu ...... 6.00
Spec. Everything You've Ever
    Wanted to Know About Dreams
    But Were Afraid to Ask ..... 4.50
TPB The Furies (2003)........ 17.95
TPB Taller Tales (2003)........ 19.95
```

SCARAB
DC/Vertigo, 1993–94
```
1 GF(c),B:JnS(s),SEa,MkB(i),
    R&O:Scarab,V:Halaku-umid . . 2.25
2 GF(c),SEa,MkB(i),A:Phantom
    Stranger.................. 2.25
3 GF(c),SEa,MkB(i),in North
    Carolina ................. 2.25
4 GF(c),SEa,MkB(i),V:Rathoroch . 2.25
5 GF(c),SEa,MkB(i) ........... 2.25
6 GF(c),SEa,MkB(i),V:Gloryboys . 2.25
7 GF(c),SEa,MkB(i),V:Scientists . 2.25
8 GF(c),SEa,MkB(i),Final Issue . . 2.25
```

SCARE TACTICS
Oct., 1996
```
1 LKa(s),AWi,ALa,monsters of
    the MTV age ............. 2.25
2 LKa(s),AWi,ALa,I:Scaremobile . . 2.25
3 LKa(s),AWi,ALa, ............ 2.25
4 LKa(s),AWi,ALa, Big For His
    Age, O:Grossout .......... 2.25
5 LKa(s),AWi,ALa, Valentine's Day
    issue .................... 2.25
6 LKa(s),AWi,Ala, F:Fang ...... 2.25
7 LKa(s),AWi,ALa, F:The Children
    of the Beast ............. 2.25
8 LKa(s),AWi,ALa, Convergence,
    x-over, concl. ............ 2.25
9 LKa(s),AWi,ALa,Snake Oil,
    concl.................... 2.25
10 LKa(s),AWi,ALa,in Gotham ..... 2.25
11 LKa(s),AWi,ALa,A:Batman..... 2.25
```

Scarlett #3 © DC Comics, Inc.

SCARLETT
1993–94
```
1 I:Scarlett,Blood of the Innocent . . 3.50
2 Blood of the Innocent cont...... 2.25
3 Blood of the Innocent cont...... 2.25
4 V:The Nomads .............. 2.25
5 GM,O:Nomads .............. 2.25
6 thru 8 GM,Blood of the Damned . 2.25
9 GM,V:Undead............... 2.25
```

```
10 B:Blood of the City........... 2.25
11 I:Afterburn ................. 2.25
12 V:Sligoth .................. 2.25
13 V:Gearsman ............... 2.25
14 final issue ................. 2.25
```

SCENE OF THE CRIME
DC/Vertigo, 1999
```
1 (of 4) ..................... 2.50
2 thru 4 ................... @2.50
TPB A Little Piece of Goodnight . . 12.95
```

S.C.I.-SPY
DC/Vertigo, Feb., 2002
```
1 (of 6) DgM,PG,JP,F:Sebastian
    Starchild secret agent........ 2.50
2 DgM,PG,JP,V:Blackside ....... 2.50
3 DgM,PG,JP,Nano-tech bugs .... 2.50
4 DgM,PG,JP,Motherbank ....... 2.50
5 DgM,PG,JP,return to Earth ..... 2.50
6 DgM,PG,JP, concl............ 2.50
```

SCRIBBLY
Aug., 1948–Dec.–Jan., 1951–52
```
1 SM .................... 1,000.00
2 ........................ 650.00
3 ........................ 500.00
4 ........................ 500.00
5 ........................ 500.00
6 thru 10 ................ @350.00
11 thru 15 ............... @300.00
```

SCOOBY-DOO
Warner Bros./DC June, 1997
```
1 .......................... 5.00
2 thru 50 ................. @2.50
51 thru 78 ................ @2.25
Spooky Spectacular 2000........ 3.95
Spooky Summer Special #1 ..... 3.95
Spec. Super Scarefest #1 ....... 3.95
Spec. Dollar Comic, rep.#1...... 1.00
TPB Vol. 1,You Meddling Kids ... 6.95
TPB Vol. 2,Ruh Roh! .......... 6.95
```

SEA DEVILS
Sept.–Oct., 1961
```
1 RH...................... 900.00
2 RH ..................... 450.00
3 RH ..................... 250.00
4 RH ..................... 200.00
5 RH ..................... 200.00
6 thru 10 RH .............. @150.00
11 ........................ 100.00
12 ........................ 100.00
13 JKu,GC,RA .............. 100.00
14 thru 20 ................ @100.00
21 I:Capt X,Man Fish ......... 75.00
22 thru 35, May-June, 1967.... @75.00
```

SEBASTIAN O
DC/Vertigo, 1993
```
1 GMo(s),SY,I:Sebastian O,A:Lord
    Lavender,Roaring Boys ...... 2.50
2 GMo(s),SY,V:Roaring Boys,
    Assassins,A:Abbe ......... 2.50
3 GMo(s),SY,D:Lord Lavender.... 2.50
```

SECRET FILES & ORIGINS
2000
```
TPB DAn,ALa,guide to DCU...... 6.95
GN Secret Files Guide to DCU
    2001-2002 ............... 4.95
```

SECRET HEARTS
Sept.–Oct., 1949–July, 1971
1 `Make Believe Sweetheart' . . . 650.00
2 ATh,`Love Is Not A Dream' . . . 300.00
3 `Sing Me A Love Song' 250.00
4 ATh. 250.00
5 ATh. 250.00
6 . . . . 250.00
7 . . . . 450.00
8 . . . . 150.00
9 . . . . 150.00
10 thru 20 . . . . @150.00
21 thru 26 . . . . @125.00
27 B:Comics Code 100.00
28 thru 30 . . . . @100.00
31 thru 70 . . . . @75.00
71 thru 110 . . . . @50.00
111 thru 120 . . . . @30.00
121 thru 150 . . . . @20.00
151 thru 153 . . . . @15.00

SECRET ORIGINS
Feb., 1973–Oct., 1974
1 O:Superman,Batman,Ghost,
   Flash 50.00
2 O:Green Lantern,Atom,
   Supergirl 25.00
3 O:Wonder Woman,Wildcat 25.00
4 O:Vigilante by MMe 25.00
5 O:The Spectre 25.00
6 O:Blackhawk,Legion of Super
   Heroes 25.00
7 O:Robin, Aquaman 25.00

SECRET ORIGINS
April, 1986
1 JOy,WB,F:Superman 7.00
2 GK,F:Blue Beetle 4.00
3 JBi,F:Captain Marvel 4.00
4 GT,F:Firestorm 4.00
5 GC,F:Crimson Avenger. 4.00
6 DG,MR,F:Batman 5.00
7 F:Sandman,Guy Gardner 3.50
8 MA,F:Shadow Lass,Dollman . . . 2.50
9 GT,F:Skyman,Flash 2.50
10 JL,JO,JA,F:Phantom Stranger . . 2.50
11 LMc,TD,F:Hawkman,Powergirl . . 2.50
12 F:Challengers of the Unknown
   I:G.A. Fury 2.50
13 EL,F:Nightwing 3.00
14 F:Suicide Squad 2.50
15 KMo,DG,F:Deadman,Spectre. . . 2.50
16 AKu,F:Hourman,Warlord 2.50

Secret Origins #17 © DC Comics, Inc.

17 KGi,F:Green Lantern 2.75
18 . . . . 2.50
19 JM(c),MA. 2.50
20 RL,DG,F:Batgirl 3.00
21 GM,MA,F:Jonah Hex 2.50
22 F:Manhunter,Millennium tie-in . . 2.50
23 F:Manhunter,Millennium tie-in . . 2.50
24 F:Dr.Fate,Blue Devil. 2.50
25 F:The Legion 2.50
26 F:Black Lightning 2.50
27 F:Zatanna,Zatara. 2.50
28 RLd,GK,F:Nightshade,Midnight . 2.50
29 F:Atom,Red Tornado 2.50
30 F:Elongated Man 2.50
31 F:Justice Society of America. . . 2.50
32 F:Justice League America. 3.00
33 F:Justice League Inter. 2.50
34 F:Justice League Inter.. . . . . 2.50
35 KSu,F:Justice League Inter. 2.50
36 F:Green Lantern 3.00
37 F:Legion of Subst. Heroes 2.50
38 F:Green Arrow,Speedy. 2.50
39 F:Batman,Animal Man 3.50
40 F:Gorilla City 2.50
41 F:Flash Villains 2.75
42 DC,F:Phantom Girl 2.50
43 TVE,TT,F:Hawk & Dove 2.50
44 F:Batman,Clayface tie-in 3.00
45 F:Blackhawk,El Diablo 2.50
46 CS,F:All Headquarters 2.50
47 CS,F:The Legion 2.50
48 KG,F:Ambush Bug. 2.50
49 F: The Cadmus Project 2.50
50 GP,CI,DG,F:Batman,Robin,
   Flash,Black Canary 4.00
Ann.#1 JBy,F:Doom Patrol 3.00
Ann.#2 CI,MA,F:Flash 2.50
Ann.#3 F:The Teen Titans. 3.00
Spec.#1 SK,PB,DG,F:Batman's worst
   Villians,A:Penguin. 3.00
TPB DG,New Origin Batman. 4.50
GN rep of 1961 Annual 5.00
Replica Edition 80-page 5.00
Vol.3 Even More Secret Origins . . . 6.95

SECRET ORIGINS OF SUPER-VILLAINS
2000
1 80-pg. Giant 4.95

SECRET SOCIETY OF SUPER-HEROES
Aug., 2000
1 (of 2) HC,MMK,JP,Elseworlds . . . 5.95
2 HC,MMK,JP,concl. 5.95

SECRET SOCIETY OF SUPER-VILLAINS
May-June, 1976
1 A:Capt.Boomerang, Grodd,
   Sinestro 30.00
2 R:Capt.Comet,A:Green Lantern 15.00
3 A:Mantis, Darkseid 12.00
4 A:Kalibak,Darkseid,Gr.Lantern . 12.00
5 RB,D:Manhunter,A:JLA. 12.00
6 RB/BL,A:Black Canary 12.00
7 RB/BL,A:Hawkgirl,Lex Luthor . . 12.00
8 RB/BL,A:Kid Flash 12.00
9 RB/BMc,A:Kid Flash, Creeper. . 12.00
10 DAy/JAb,A:Creeper 12.00
11 JO,N:Wizard 12.00
12 BMc,A:Blockbuster. 12.00
13 A:Crime Syndicate of America . 12.00
14 A:Crime Syndicate of America . 12.00
15 A:G.A.Atom, Dr. Mid Nite 12.00

SECRETS OF HAUNTED HOUSE
April-May, 1975
1 LD(c),Dead Heat. 50.00
2 ECh(c),A Dead Man 25.00
3 ECh(c),Pathway To Purgatory . . 25.00
4 LD(c),The Face of Death 25.00
5 BWr(c),Gunslinger! 30.00
6 JAp(c),Deadly Allegiance 20.00
7 JAp(c),It'll Grow On You 20.00
8 MK(c),Raising The Devil 20.00
9 LD(c),The Man Who Didn't
   Believe in Ghosts 20.00
10 MK(c),Ask Me No Questions . . 20.00
11 MK(c),Picasso Fever! 20.00
12 JO&DG(c),Yorick's Skull. 20.00
13 JO&DG(c),The Cry of the
   Warewolf 20.00
14 MK(c),Selina 20.00
15 LD(c),Over Your Own Dead
   Body 15.00
16 MK(c),Water, Water Every Fear 15.00
17 LD(c),Papa Don. 15.00
18 LD(c),No Sleep For The Dying. 15.00
19 LD(c),The Manner of Execution 15.00
20 JO(c),The Talisman of the
   Serpent 15.00
21 LD(c),The Death's Head
   Scorpion. 15.00
22 LD(c),See How They Die 15.00
23 LD(c),The Creeping Red Death 15.00
24 LD(c),Second Chance To Die. . 15.00
25 LD(c),The Man Who Cheated
   Destiny. 15.00
26 MR(c),Elevator to Eternity 15.00
27 DH(c),Souls For the Master . . . 15.00
28 DH(c),Demon Rum 15.00
29 MK(c),Duel of Darkness. 15.00
30 JO(c),For the Love of Arlo 15.00
31 I:Mister E. 20.00
32 The Legend of the Tiger's Paw. 10.00
33 In The Attic Dwells Dark Seth. . 10.00
34 Double Your Pleasure 10.00
35 Deathwing, Lord of Darkness . . 10.00
36 RB&DG(c),Sister Sinister. 10.00
37 RB&DG(c),The Third Wish Is
   Death 10.00
38 RB&DG(c),Slaves of Satan . . . 10.00
39 RB&DG(c),The Witch-Hounds
   of Salem. 10.00
40 RB&DG(c),The Were-Witch
   of Boston 10.00
41 JKu(c),House at Devil's Tail . . . 10.00
42 JKu(c),Mystic Murder. 10.00
43 JO(c),Mother of Invention. 10.00
44 BWr(c),Halloween God 10.00
45 EC&JO(c),Star-Trakker 10.00
46 March, 1982 . . . . 10.00

SINISTER HOUSE OF SECRET LOVE
Oct.–Nov., 1971
1 . . . . 250.00
2 JJ(c) 100.00
3 ATh 125.00
4 April-May, 1972 . . . . 100.00
Becomes:

SECRETS OF SINISTER HOUSE
June-July, 1972
5 . . . . 50.00
6 . . . . 30.00
7 NR 30.00
8 . . . . 30.00
9 . . . . 30.00
10 NA(i) 35.00
11 . . . . 20.00

12 . . . . 20.00	6 Wonder Woman receives magic lasso,V:Baroness Gunther . 2,000.00	80 V:Don Enrago 450.00
13 . . . . 20.00	7 V:Baroness Gunther 1,400.00	81 V:Dr. Frenzi 500.00
14 . . . . 20.00	8 Meets Gloria Bullfinch 1,400.00	82 V:King Lunar 400.00
15 . . . . 20.00	9 A:The Real Diana Prince . . . 1,400.00	83 V:Prowd. 400.00
16 . . . . 20.00	10 V:Ishti 1,400.00	84 V:Duke Daxo 400.00
17 DBa 20.00	11 I:Queen Desira 1,400.00	85 Meets Leslie M. Gresham . . . 400.00
18 June-July, 1974 . . . . 20.00	12 V:Baroness Gunther 1,200.00	86 `Secret of the Amazing Bracelets' 400.00

SECRETS OF THE LEGION OF SUPER-HEROES
Jan., 1981

1 O:Legion 3.50	13 V:Olga,Hitler(c) 1,700.00
2 O:Brainiac 5 . . . . 3.50	14 . . . . 1,200.00
3 March, 1981,O:Karate Kid 3.50	15 V:Simon Slikery 1,200.00

87 In Twin Peaks(in Old West) . . 400.00
88 Wonder Woman in Holywood . 400.00
89 V:Abacus Rackeett gang 400.00
90 `The Secret of the Modern Sphinx' 400.00
91 . . . . 400.00
92 V:Duke of Deceptions 400.00
93 V:Talbot 400.00
94 Girl Isue. 550.00
95 . . . . 500.00
96 . . . . 500.00
97 . . . . 500.00
98 `Strange Mission'. 500.00
99 I:Astra 500.00
100 . . . . 650.00
101 `Battle for the Atom World' . . 500.00
102 `Queen of the South Seas' . . 500.00
103 V:Robot Archers. 500.00
104 `The End of Paradise Island' 500.00
105 `Secret of the Giant Forest' . 500.00
106 E:Wonder Woman 500.00
107 ATh,Mystery issue 800.00
108 ATh,GK,I:Johnny Peril 650.00
109 Ath,GK,A:Johnny Peril 800.00

Becomes:

SENSATION MYSTERY
1952–53

110 MA(c),B:Johnny Peril 550.00
111 GK,`Spectre in the Flame' . . 500.00
112 GK,`Death has 5 Guesses' . . 500.00
113 GK, ... 500.00
114 GK,GC,`The Haunted Diamond' 500.00
115 GK,`The Phantom Castle' . . . 500.00
116 `The Toy Assassins', July-Aug., 1953 . . . . 500.00

SEEKERS
DC/Vertigo
1 & 2 . . . . @2.50

SEEKERS INTO THE MYSTERY
1996

1 Pilgrimage of Lucas Hart,pt.1 . . . 2.50
2 Pilgrimage of Lucas Hart,pt.2 . . . 2.50
3 Pilgrimage of Lucas Hart,pt.3 . . . 2.50
4 Pilgrimage of Lucas Hart,pt.4 . . . 2.50
5 Pilgrimage of Lucas Hart,pt.5 . . . 2.50
6 Falling Down to Heaven,pt.1 . . . 2.50
7 Falling Down to Heaven,pt.2 . . . 2.50
8 Falling Down to Heaven,pt.3 . . . 2.50
9 JMD(s),MZi,Falling Down from Heaven,pt.4 concl. 2.50
10 JMD(s),JMu,F:Charlie Limbo . . 2.50
11 JMD(s),JIT,God's Shadow,pt.1 . 2.50
12 JMD(s),JIT,God's Shadow,pt.2 . 2.50
13 JMD(s),JIT,God's Shadow,pt.3 . 2.50
14 JMD(s),JIT,God's Shadow,pt.4 . . 2.50
15 JMD(s),JMu,Hart meets Magician, final issue 3.00

SENSATION COMICS
1942–52

1 I:Wonder Woman,Wildcat . . 38,000.00
2 I:Etta Candy & the Holiday Girls, Dr. Poison 6,500.00
3 Diana Price joins Military Intelligence 3,500.00
4 I:Baroness PaulaVonGunther 2,500.00
5 V:Axis Spies 2,000.00

16 V:Karl Schultz 1,200.00
17 V:Princess Yasmini 1,200.00
18 V:Quito 1,200.00
19 Wonder Woman goes berserk 1,200.00
20 V:Stoffer 1,200.00
21 V:American Adolf 1,000.00
22 V:Cheetah. 1,000.00
23 'War Laugh Mania' 1,000.00
24 I:Wonder Woman's mental radio 1,000.00
25 . . . . 1,000.00
26 A:Queen Hippolyte 1,000.00
27 V:Ely Close 1,000.00
28 V:Mayor Prude 1,000.00
29 V:Mimi Mendez 1,000.00
30 V:Anton Unreal 1,000.00
31 `Grow Down Land' 750.00
32 V:Crime Chief 750.00
33 Meets Percy Pringle. 750.00
34 I:Sargon 800.00
35 V:Sontag Henya in Atlantis . . . 600.00
36 V:Bedwin Footh 600.00
37 A:Mala((1st app. All-Star #8) . 600.00
38 V:The Gyp 600.00
39 V:Nero 600.00
40 I:Countess Draska Nishki 600.00
41 V:Creeper Jackson 550.00
42 V:Countess Nishki 550.00
43 Meets Joel Heyday 550.00
44 V:Lt. Sturm 550.00
45 V:Jose Perez 550.00
46 V:Lawbreakers Protective League 550.00
47 V:Unknown 550.00
48 V:Topso and Teena 550.00
49 V:Zavia 550.00
50 V:`Ears' Fellock 550.00
51 V:Boss Brekel 500.00
52 Meets Prof. Toxino 500.00
53 V:Wanta Wynn 500.00
54 V:Dr. Fiendo 500.00
55 V:Bughumans 500.00
56 V:Dr. Novel 500.00
57 V:Syonide 500.00
58 Meets Olive Norton 500.00
59 V:Snow Man 500.00
60 V:Bifton Jones 500.00
61 V:Bluff Robust 500.00
62 V:Black Robert of Dogwood . . 500.00
63 V:Prof. Vibrate 500.00
64 V:Cloudmen. 500.00
65 V:Lim Slait 500.00
66 V:Slick Skeener 500.00
67 V:Daredevil Dix 500.00
68 `Secret of the Menacing Octopus' 550.00
69 V:Darcy Wells 450.00
70 Unconquerable Woman of Cocha Bamba 450.00
71 V:Queen Flaming 450.00
72 V:Blue Seal Gang 450.00
73 Wonder Woman time travel story 450.00
74 V:Spug Spangle 450.00
75 V:Shark 450.00
76 V:King Diamond 450.00
77 V:Boss Brekel 450.00
78 V:Furiosa 450.00
79 Meets Leila and Solala 450.00

SENSATION COMICS
1999

1 JeR(s),ScB, F:Wonder Woman & Hawkgirl 2.25

SERGEANT BILKO
May-June, 1957

1 Based on TV show 850.00
2 . . . . 450.00
3 . . . . 350.00
4 . . . . 300.00
5 . . . . 300.00
6 thru 17 . . . . @275.00
18 March-April, 1960 . . . . 275.00

SERGEANT BILKO'S PVT. DOBERMAN
June-July, 1958

1 . . . . 500.00
2 . . . . 300.00
3 . . . . 200.00
4 . . . . 200.00
5 photo (c) 200.00
6 thru 10 . . . . @150.00
11 Feb.–March, 1960 . . . . 150.00

SGT. ROCK
See: OUR ARMY AT WAR

Sensation #24 © DC Comics Inc.

SGT. ROCK SPECIAL
Oct., 1988
#1 rep.Our Army at War#162-#63 . 12.00
#2 rep.Brave & Bold #52. . . . . 7.00
#3 rep.Showcase #45. . . . . 7.00
#4 thru #20 reprints. . . . . @7.00
Spec. #1 TT,MGo,JKu,CR,(new stories). 5.00

SGT. ROCK'S PRIZE BATTLE TALES
Winter, 1964
1 . . . . 450.00

SHADE
June-July, 1977
[1st Regular Series]
1 SD,I&O: Shade. 20.00
2 SD,V:Form 15.00
3 SD,V:The Cloak 12.00
4 SD,Return to Meta-Zone. 12.00
5 SD,V:Supreme Decider. 12.00
6 SD,V:Khaos 12.00
7 SD,V:Dr.Z.Z. 12.00
8 SD,last issue 12.00

SHADE, THE
Feb., 1997
1 (of 4) JeR(s),GeH,A:Ludlows . . . 3.00
2 JeR(s),JWi,MGy,poisoned by love of his life 3.00
3 JeR(s),BBl,Golden Age Flash Jay Garrick retiring 3.00
4 JeR(s),MZi,V:last of the Ludlows. 3.00

SHADE, THE CHANGING MAN
July, 1990
1 B:PrM(s),CBa,MPn,I:Kathy George, I&D:Troy Grezer 5.00
2 CBa,MPn,Who Shot JFK#1. . . . 4.00
3 CBa,MPn,Who Shot JFK#2. . . . 3.00
4 CBa,MPn,V:American Scream . . 3.00
5 CBa,MPn,V:Hollywood Monsters 3.00
6 CBa,MPn,V:Ed Loot 3.00
7 CBa,MPn,I:Arnold Major. 3.00
8 CBa,Mpn,I:Lenny 3.00
9 CBa,MPn,V:Arnold Major 3.00

Shade, The Changing Man 35 © DC Comics, Inc.

10 CBa,MPn,Paranoia 2.75
11 CBa,MPn,R:Troy Grezer 2.50
12 CBa,MPn,V:Troy Grezer 2.50
13 CBa,MPn,I:Fish Priest 2.50
14 CBa,MPn,V:Godfather of Guilt . . 2.50
15 CBa,MPn,I:Spirit 2.50
16 CBa,MPn,V:American Scream . . 2.50
17 RkB(i),V:Rohug 2.50
18 MPn,E:American Scream. 2.50
19 MPn,V:Dave Messiah Seeker. . . 2.50
20 JD,CBa,MPn,RkB,R:Roger 2.50
21 MPn,The Road,A:Stringer 2.25
22 The Road,Childhood 2.25
23 The Road 2.25
24 The Road 2.25
25 The Road 2.25
26 MPn(i),F:Lenny 2.25
27 MPn(i),Shade becomes female . 2.25
28 MPn(i),Changing Woman #2 . . . 2.25
29 MPn(i),Changing Woman #3 . . . 2.25
30 Another Life. 2.25
31 Ernest & Jim #1. . . . . 2.25
32 Ernest & Jim #2. . . . . 2.25

DC/Vertigo, 1993
33 CBa,B:Birth Pains 2.25
34 CBa,RkB(i),GID(i),A:Brian Juno, Garden of Pain. 2.25
35 CBa,RkB(i),E:Birth Pains, V:Juno. 2.25
36 CBa,PrG(i),RkB(i),B:Passion child, I:Miles Laimling 2.25
37 CBa,RkB(i),Shade/Kathy 2.25
38 CBa,RkB(i),Great American Novel 2.25
39 CBa,SEa,RkB(i),Pond Life 2.25
40 PBd,at Hotel Shade. 2.25
41 GID,Pandora's Story,Kathy is pregnant. 2.25
42 CBa,RkB(i),SY,B:History Lesson, A:John Constantine 2.50
43 CBa,RkB(i),PBd,Trial of William Matthieson,A:J.Constantine . . . 2.50
44 CBa,RkB(i),E:History Lesson, D:William Matthieson,A:John Constantine 2.50
45 CBa,B:A Season in Hell 2.25
46 CBa(c),GID,Season in Hell#2. . . 2.25
47 CBa(c),GID,A:Lenny 2.25
48 CBa(c),GID 2.25
49 CBa(c),GID,Kathy's Past 2.25
50 GID,BBl,MiA,pin-up gallery. 3.25
51 GID,BBl,MiA,Masks,pt.1. . . . . . 2.00
52 GID,BBl,MiA,Masks,pt.2. . . . . . 2.00
53 GID,BBl,MiA,Masks,pt.3. . . . . . 2.00
54 Meeting. 2.00
55 . . . . 2.00
56 . . . . 2.00
57 MBu,PrM,F:George 2.00
58 PrM,Michael Lark. 2.00
59 MBu,PrM,Nasty Infections,pt.1 . . 2.25
60 MBu,PrM,Nasty Infections,pt.2 . . 2.25
61 MBu,PrM,Nasty Infections,pt.3 . . 2.25
62 Nasty Infections,pt.4 . . . . 2.25
63 Nasty Infections,finale 2.25
64 The Madness. 2.25
65 The Roots of Madness,pt.1 . . . . 2.25
66 The Roots of Madness,pt.2 . . . . 2.25
67 The Roots of Madness,pt.3 . . . . 2.25
68 After Kathy,pt.1 . . . . 2.25
69 After Kathy,pt.2 . . . . 2.25
70 After Kathy,pt.3, final issue. 2.25
TPB The American Scream. 17.95

SHADO, SONG OF THE DRAGON
1992
1 GM(i),From G.A. Longbow Hunters 5.50
2 GM(i),V:Yakuza 5.00

3 GM(i),V:Yakuza 5.00
4 GM(i),V:Yakuza 5.00

SHADOW, THE
[1st Regular Series], 1973–75
1 MK,The Doom Puzzle. 50.00
2 MK,V:Freak Show Killer 25.00
3 MK,BWr 30.00
4 MK,HC,BWr,Ninja Story 25.00
5 FR 20.00
6 MK 22.00
7 FR 12.00
8 FR 12.00
9 FR 12.00
10 JCr 15.00
11 A:Avenger 12.00
12. . . . . 12.00

[Limited Series], 1986
1 HC,R:Shadow. 5.00
2 HC,O:Shadow 4.00
3 HC,V:Preston Mayrock 3.00
4 HC,V:Preston Mayrock 3.00
TPB rep. #1 thru #4 . . . . 12.95

[2nd Regular Series], 1987–89
1 BSz,Shadows & Light,pt.1 . . . . . 3.50
2 BSz,Shadows & Light,pt.2 . . . . . 3.50
3 BSz,Shadows & Light,pt.3 . . . . . 3.50
4 BSz,Shadows & Light,pt.4 . . . . . 3.50
5 BSz,Shadows & Light,pt.5 . . . . . 3.50
6 BSz,Shadows & Light,pt.6 . . . . . 3.50
7 MR,KB,Harold Goes to Washington 3.00
8 KB,Seven Deadly Finns,pt.1 . . . 3.00
9 KB,Seven Deadly Finns,pt.2 . . . 3.00
10 KB,Seven Deadly Finns,pt.3 . . . 3.00
11 KB,Seven Deadly Finns,pt.4. . . . 3.00
12 KB,Seven Deadly Finns,pt.5 . . . 3.00
13 KB,Seven Deadly Finns,pt.6 . . . 3.00
14 KB,Body And Soul,pt.1 . . . . 3.00
15 KB,Body And Soul,pt.2. . . . . . . 3.00
16 KB,Body And Soul,pt.3. . . . . . . 3.00
17 KB,Body And Soul,pt.4. . . . . . . 3.00
18 KB,Body And Soul,pt.5. . . . . . . 3.00
19 KB,Body And Soul,pt.6. . . . . . . 3.00
Ann.#1 JO,AA,Shadows & Light prologue. 4.00
Ann.#2 KB,Agents 3.50

SHADOW CABINET
Milestone, 1994–95
0 WS(c),3RL,Shadow War,Foil(c),A:All Milestone characters 3.00

Shadow Cabinet #6 © DC Comics Inc.

1 JBy(c),3RW,I&D:Corpsicle..... 2.50
2 3RW,V:Arcadian League....... 2.50
3 3RW,F:Sideshow 2.50
4 3RW,F:Sideshow 2.50
5 .... 2.50
6 .... 2.50
7 .... 2.50
8 New Cabinet................. 2.50
9 R:Old Cabinet................ 2.50
10 V:Red Dog.................. 2.50
11 Death Issue................. 2.50
12 SYSTEM.................... 2.50
13 A:Hardware,Starlight 2.50
14 Long Hot Summer, Iron Butterfly
   Starlight.................. 2.50
15 Long Hot Summer 2.50
16 Changing of the Guard 2.50
17 V:Dharma,final issue 2.50

SHADOWDRAGON ANNUAL
1995
Ann.#1 Year One Annual 3.50

SHADOW OF BATMAN
1 reprints of Detective Comics ... 10.00
2 thru 4 .... @7.50

SHADOW OF THE BATMAN
1985–86
1 WS,AM,MR,rep.............. 7.00
2 MR,TA,rep.A:Hugo Strange 5.00
3 MR,TA,rep.A:Penguin 5.00
4 MR,TA,rep.A:Joker 6.00
5 MR,DG,rep. 5.00

SHADOW'S FALL
1994–95
1 JVF,Voyage of self-discovery ... 3.00
2 JVF,More of tale 3.00
3 JVF,Shen confronts shadow 3.00
4 JVF,Gale wounded 3.00
5 JVF,Shadow goes Berserk 3.00
6 JVF,F:Warren Gale,final issue ... 3.00

SHADOW STRIKES!, THE
1989–92
1 EB,Death's Head 3.00
2 EB,EB,PoliticalKiller,V:Rasputin . 2.50
3 EB,V:Mad Monk,V:Rasputin 2.50
4 EB,D:Mad Monk,V:Rasputin 4.00
5 EB,Shadow & Doc Savage#1 ... 4.00
6 Shadow & Doc Savage #3 ..... 2.50
7 RM,A:Wunderkind,O:Shadow's
   Radio Show............... 2.50
8 EB,A:Shiwan Khan............ 2.50
9 Fireworks#2 .... 2.50
10 EB,Fireworks#3.............. 2.50
11 EB,O:Margo Lane 2.50
12 EB,V:Chicago Mob 2.50
13 EB,V:Chicago Mob 2.50
14 EB,V:Chicago Mob 2.50
15 EB,V:Chicago Mob 2.50
16 Assassins,pt.1............... 2.50
17 Assassins,pt.2............... 2.50
18 Shrevvie 2.50
19 NY,NJ Tunnel................ 2.50
20 Shadow+Margo Vs.Nazis...... 2.50
21 V:Shiwan Khan 2.50
22 V:Shiwan Khan 2.50
23 V:Shiwan Khan 2.50
24 Search for Margo Lane 2.50
25 In China.................... 2.50
26 V:Shiwan Khan 2.50
27 V:Shiwan Khan,Margo 2.50

Rescued................... 2.50
28 SL,In Hawaii 2.50
29 DSp,`Valhalla',V:Nazis........ 2.50
30 The Shadow Year One,pt.1 .... 2.50
31 The Shadow Year One,pt.2 .... 2.50
Ann.#1 DSp `Crimson Dreams'.... 4.00

SHADOW WAR OF HAWKMAN
May, 1985
1 AA,V:Thangarians............ 2.50
2 AA,V:Thangarians............ 2.50
3 AA,V:Thangarians,A:Aquaman,
   Elong.Man................ 2.50
4 AA,V:Thangarians............ 2.50
Spec.#1 V:Thangarians 2.50

SHAZAM!
1973–78
[1st Regular Series]
1 B:DON(s),CCB,O:Capt.Marvel . 30.00
2 CCB,A:Mr.Mind.............. 15.00
3 CCB,V:Shagg Naste.......... 15.00
4 E:DON(s),CCB,V:Ibac......... 15.00
5 B:ESM(s),CCB,A:Leprechaun .. 15.00
6 B:DON(s),CCB,Dr,Sivana 10.00
7 CCB,A:Capt Marvel Jr......... 10.00
8 CCB,O:Marvel Family......... 55.00
9 E:DON(S)DC,CCB,A:Mr.Mind,
   Captain Marvel Jr.......... 10.00
10 ESM(s)CCB,BO.............. 10.00
11 ViCKS,BO,rep............... 10.00
12 BO,DG 50.00
13 BO,KS,A:Luthor............. 50.00
14 KS,A:Monster Society 50.00
15 KS,BO,Luther 50.00
16 KS,BO..................... 50.00
17 KS,BO..................... 50.00
18 KS,BO..................... 50.00
19 KS,BO,Mary Marvel.......... 10.00
20 KS,A:Marvel Family.......... 10.00
21 reprint 10.00
22 reprint 10.00
23 reprint 10.00
24 reprint 10.00
25 KS,DG,I&O:Isis 15.00
26 KS....................... 10.00
27 KS,A:Kid Eternity 15.00
28 KS....................... 10.00
29 KS....................... 10.00
30 KS....................... 10.00
31 KS,A:Minute Man............ 10.00
32 KS....................... 10.00

Shazam #4 © DC Comics Inc.

33 KS....................... 10.00
34 O:Capt.Marvel Jr............ 10.00
35 DN,KS,A:Marvel Family 10.00
GN Power of Hope,64-page 9.95

SHAZAM! FAMILY
July, 2002
Annual #1 (1953, rep.) 80-pg...... 5.95

SHAZAM, THE NEW BEGINNING
April, 1987
1 O:Shazam & Capt.Marvel...... 2.50
2 V:Black Adam................ 2.50
3 V:Black Adam................ 2.50
4 V:Black Adam................ 2.50

SHERLOCK HOLMES
Sept.–Oct., 1975
1 ERc,WS................... 35.00

SHEVA'S WAR
DC/Helix, Aug., 1998
1 (of 5) CsM,Iron Empires 3.00
2 CsM,Iron Empires............ 3.00
3 CsM,Iron Empires............ 3.00
4 CsM,..................... 3.00
5 CsM..................... 3.00

SHOWCASE
1956–70, 1977–78
1 F:Fire Fighters 5,000.00
2 JKu,F:Kings of Wild 1,500.00
3 F:Frogmen................ 1,300.00
4 CI,JKu,I&O:S.A. Flash
   (Barry Allen)........... 40,000.00
5 F:Manhunters 1,400.00
6 JK,I&O:Challengers of the
   Unknown............... 5,500.00
7 JK,F:Challengers 2,500.00
8 CI,F:Flash,I:Capt.Cold 17,000.00
9 F:Lois Lane 10,000.00
10 F:Lois Lane............... 4,500.00
11 JK(c),F:Challengers........ 2,500.00
12 JK(c),F:Challengers 2,500.00
13 CI,F:Flash,Mr.Element...... 6,500.00
14 CI,F:Flash,Mr.Element...... 6,800.00
15 I:Space Ranger........... 3,000.00
16 F:Space Ranger 1,400.00
17 GK(c),I:Adam Strange..... 3,500.00
18 GK(c),F:Adam Strange 1,800.00
19 GK(c),F:Adam Strange 2,000.00
20 I:Rip Hunter 1,500.00
21 F:Rip Hunter 750.00
22 GK,I&O:S.A. Green Lantern
   (Hal Jordan) 6,800.00
23 GK,F:Green Lantern 2,200.00
24 GK,F:Green Lantern 2,200.00
25 JKu,F:Rip Hunter 500.00
26 JKu,F:Rip Hunter 500.00
27 RH,I:Sea Devils 1,300.00
28 RH,F:Sea Devils 550.00
29 RH,F:Sea Devils 550.00
30 O:Aquaman 1,200.00
31 GK(c),F:Aquaman 550.00
32 F:Aquaman............... 550.00
33 F:Aquaman............... 600.00
34 GK,MA,I&O:S.A. Atom..... 2,000.00
35 GK,MA,F:Atom 1,100.00
36 GK,MA,F:Atom............ 900.00
37 RA,I:Metal Man.......... 1,000.00
38 RA,F:Metal Man........... 650.00
39 RA,F:Metal Man........... 500.00
40 RA,F:Metal Man........... 400.00
41 F:Tommy Tomorrow 250.00
42 F:Tommy Tomorrow 250.00

Showcase–Sins — DC — Comics Values Annual

Showcase #41 © DC Comics, Inc.

43 F:Dr.No(James Bond 007) . . . 600.00
44 F:Tommy Tomorrow 200.00
45 JKu,O:Sgt.Rock 400.00
46 F:Tommy Tomorrow 150.00
47 F:Tommy Tomorrow 150.00
48 F:Cave Carson 150.00
49 F:Cave Carson 150.00
50 MA,CI,F:I Spy 125.00
51 MA,CI,F:I Spy 125.00
52 F:Cave Carson 100.00
53 JKu(c),RH,F:G.I.Joe 175.00
54 JKu(c),RH,F:G.I.Joe 175.00
55 MA,F:Dr.Fate,Spectre,1st S.A.
   Green Lantern,Solomon
   Grundy 350.00
56 MA,F:Dr.Fate 200.00
57 JKu,F:Enemy Ace 300.00
58 JKu,F:Enemy Ace 175.00
59 F:Teen Titans 175.00
60 MA,F:Spectre 400.00
61 MA,F:Spectre 200.00
62 JO,I:Inferior 5 . . . . 150.00
63 JO,F:Inferior 5 . . . . 75.00
64 MA,F:Spectre 200.00
65 F:Inferior 5 . . . . 75.00
66 I:B'wana Beast 50.00
67 F:B'wana Beast 50.00
68 I:Maniaks 50.00
69 F:Maniaks 50.00
70 I:Binky 50.00
71 F:Maniaks 50.00
72 JKu,ATh,F:Top Gun 60.00
73 SD,I&O:Creeper 200.00
74 I:Anthro 125.00
75 SD,I:Hawk & Dove 175.00
76 NC,I:Bat Lash 100.00
77 BO,I:Angel & Ape 100.00
78 I:Jonny Double 50.00
79 I:Dolphin 75.00
80 NA(c),F:Phantom Stranger . . 125.00
81 I:Windy & Willy 60.00
82 I:Nightmaster 125.00
83 BWr,MK,F:Nightmaster 100.00
84 BWr,MK,F:Nightmaster 100.00
85 JKu,F:Firehair 35.00
86 JKu,F:Firehair 35.00
87 JKu,F:Firehair 35.00
88 F:Jason's Quest 25.00
89 F:Jason's Quest 25.00
90 F:Manhunter 25.00
91 F:Manhunter 25.00
92 F:Manhunter 25.00
93 F:Manhunter (1970) 25.00

[Series Resumes], 1977
94 JA,JSon,I&O:2nd
   Doom Patrol 20.00
95 JA,JSon,F:2nd Doom Patrol . . . 12.00
96 JA,JSon,F:2nd Doom Patrol . . . 12.00
97 JO,JSon,O:Power Girl 12.00
98 JSon,DG,Power Girl 12.00
99 JSon,DG,Power Girl 12.00
100 JSon,all star issue 20.00
101 JKu(c),AM,MA,Hawkman 12.00
102 JKu(c),AM,MA,Hawkman 12.00
103 JKu(c),AM,MA,Hawkman 12.00
104 RE,OSS Spies 12.00
TPB Rep.1956–59 . . . . 20.00

SHOWCASE '93
1 AAd(c),EH,AV,F:Catwoman,
  Blue Devil,Cyborg 4.00
2 KM(c),EH,AV,F:Catwoman,
  Blue Devil,Cyborg 3.50
3 KM(c),EH,TC,F:Catwoman,
  Blue Devil,Flash 3.00
4 F:Catwoman,Blue Devil,
  Geo-Force 3.00
5 F:KD,DG,BHi,F:Robin,Blue
  Devil,Geo-Force 3.00
6 MZ(c),KD,DG,F:Robin,Blue
  Devil,Deathstroke 3.00
7 BSz(c),KJ,Knightfall#13,F:Two-
  Face,Jade&Obsidian 5.00
8 KJ,Knightfall#14,F:Two-Face,
  Peacemaker,Fire and Ice 4.00
9 F:Huntress,Peacemaker,Shining
  Knight 3.00
10 BWg,SI,F:Huntress,Batman,
   Dr.Light,Peacemaker,Deathstroke,
   Katana,M.Manhunter 3.00
11 GP(c),F:Robin,Nightwing,
   Peacemaker,Deathstroke,Deadshot,
   Katana,Dr.Light,Won.Woman . . 3.00
12 AD(c),BMc,F:Robin,Nightwing,
   Green Lantern,Creeper 3.00

SHOWCASE '94
1 KN,F:Joker,Gunfire,Orion,Metro . 3.00
2 KON(c),E:Joker,B:Blue Beetle . . . 3.00
3 MMi(c),B:Razorsharpe 3.00
4 AIG(s),DG,F:Arkham Asylum inmates
  E:Razorsharpe,Blue Bettle 3.00
5 WS(c),CDi(s),PJ,B:Robin&Huntress,
  F:Bloodwynd,Loose Cannon . . 3.00
6 PJ,KK(s),F:Robin & Huntress . . 3.00
7 JaL(c),PDd(s),F:Comm. Gordon . 3.00
8 AIG(s),O:Scarface,Ventriloquist,
  F:Monarch,1st Wildcat 3.25
9 AIG(s),DJ,O:Scarface,Ventriloquist,
  F:Monarch,Waverider 3.00
10 JQ(c),AIG(s),F:Azrael,Zero Hour,
   B:Black Condor 3.25
11 Black Condor, Man-Bat 3.00
12 Barbara Gordon 3.00

SHOWCASE '95
1 Supergirl 3.00
2 . . . . 3.00
3 F:Eradicator,Claw 3.00
4 A:Catwoman,Hawke 3.00
5 F:Thorne,Firehawk 3.00
6 DRo(c&a),F:Lobo,Bibbo 3.00
7 F:Mongul 3.00
8 . . . . 3.00
9 F:Lois Lane 3.00
10 F:Gangbuster 3.00
11 F:Agent Liberty 3.00
12 F:Supergirl,Maitresse 3.00

SHOWCASE '96
1 F:Steel & Warrior 3.00
2 F:Steel and Warrior 3.00

Showcase '94 #2 © DC Comics Inc.

3 . . . . 3.00
4 F:Firebrand 3.00
5 F:Green Arrow & Thorn 3.00
6 F:Superboy, Animated Series . . . 3.00
7 F:Mary Marvel 3.00
8 F:Superman, Superboy &
  Supergirl 4.00
9 F:Lady Shiva & Shadowdragon,
  Martian Manhunter 3.00
10 F:Ultra Boy, Captain Comet 3.00
11 Legion of Super-Heroes 3.00
12 10,000 Brainiacs 3.00

SILVER AGE DC CLASSICS
Action #252(rep) 3.00
Adventure #247(rep) 3.00
Brave and Bold #28 (rep) 3.00
Detective #225 (rep) 3.00
Detective #327 (rep) 3.00
Green Lantern #76 (rep) 3.00
House of Secrets #92 (rep) 3.00
Showcase #4 (rep) 3.00
Showcase #22 (rep) 3.00
Sugar & Spike #99(1st printing) . . . 3.00

SILVER AGE
May, 2000
Secret Files #1 . . . . 5.00
Justice League of America #1 . . . . 2.50
Challengers of the Unknown #1 . . . 2.50
Teen Titans #1 . . . . 2.50
Doom Patrol #1 . . . . 2.50
Dial "H" For Hero #1 . . . . 2.50
The Flash #1 . . . . 2.50
Green Lantern #1 . . . . 2.50
The Brave and the Bold #1 . . . . . . 2.50
Showcase #1 . . . . 2.50
80-Page Giant #1, 80-pg 6.50
Silver Age #1, 48-pg 3.95

SILVERBLADE
Sept., 1987
1 KJ,GC,maxi-series 2.25
2 thru 12 GC . . . . @2.25

SINS OF YOUTH
March, 2000
Aquaboy/Lagoon Man #1 x-over . . . 2.50
Batboy & Robin #1 x-over 2.50
JLA/Jr. #1 x-over 2.50
Kid Flash/Impulse #1 x-over 2.50

All comics prices listed are for *Near Mint* condition.

SKIN GRAFT
DC/Vertigo, 1993
1 B:JeP(s),WaP,I:John Oakes,
  A:Tattooed Man(Tarrant)...... 3.25
2 WaP,V:Assassins 3.00
3 WaP,In Kyoto,I:Mizoguchi Kenji.. 3.00
4 E:JeP(s),WaP,V:Tarrant,Kenji ... 3.00

SKREEMER
May, 1989
1 .... 2.25
2 thru 6 .... @2.25
TPB (2002)................... 19.95

SKULL AND BONES
1992
1 EH,I&O:Skull & Bones 5.00
2 EH,V:KGB 5.00
3 EH,V:KGB 5.00

SLASH MARAUD
Nov., 1987
1 PG........................ 2.25
2 PG........................ 2.25
3 thru 10 PG .... @2.25

SMALLVILLE
Sept., 2002
Spec. TV series 3.95

SMALLVILLE
March 2003
1 camping trip 3.95
2 Miss Smallville Pageant 3.50
3 F:Lex Luthor................ 3.50
4 F:Lex Luthor................ 3.50
5 .... 3.50

SMASH COMICS
1999
1 TPe(s),F:Doctor Mid-Nite
  & Hourman................ 2.25

SMAX
DC/Vertigo 2003
1 (of 5) AMo(s) 2.95
2 thru 4 AMo(s) 2.95

SONIC DISRUPTORS
1987–88
1 thru 10 .... @3.00

SON OF AMBUSH BUG
July, 1986
1 .... 2.25
2 thru 6 KG .... @2.25

SOVEREIGN SEVEN
1995–98
1 CCl(s),DT,I:Sovereign Seven,
  V:Female Furies,A:Darkseid ... 3.00
2 I:Nike,Kratos,Zelus,Bia 2.50
3 V:Nike,Kratos,Zelus,Bia 2.50
4 I:Skin Dance................ 2.50
5 CCl,DT,V:Skin Dance 2.50
6 CCl,DT,V:Force Majeure...... 2.50
7 CCl,DT,Wild Hunt,pt.2....... 2.50
8 CCl,DT,Clv,Wild Hunt,pt.3..... 2.50
9 CCl,DT,Clv................ 2.50
10 CCl,DT,Clv,Road Trip,pt.1 .... 2.50
11 CCl,DT,Clv,Road Trip,pt.2 (of 3). 2.50
12 CCl(s) 2.25
13 CCl(s) 2.25
14 CCl(s) 2.25
15 CCl,DT,Clv,Sovereign team
  betrayed................. 2.25
16 CCl,DT,Clv,Network betrays
  Sovereigns, Final Night tie-in .. 2.25
17 CCl(s),RLm,Clv,V:Network..... 2.25
18 CCl(s),RLm,Clv,V:Network and
  Kim 2.25
19 CCl(s) 2.25
20 CCl(s),VGi,Finale trapped in
  Forest Fire 2.25
21 CCl(s),RLm,DC,Clv,Danae's
  secret 2.25
22 CCl(s),RLm,DC,Clv,Indigo &
  Rampart fall 2.25
23 CCl(s),RLm,DC,Clv,Finale
  hallucinates 2.25
24 CCl(s),RLm,Clv,A:Superman .. 2.25
25 CCl(s),RLm,Clv,V:Power Girl .. 2.25
26 CCl(s),RLm,Clv,A:Hitman..... 2.25
27 CCl(s),RLm,Clv,Genesis tie-in . 2.25
28 CCl(s),RLm,Clv,A:Impulse 2.25
29 CCl(s),RLm,Clv,Sovereign dies . 2.25
30 CCl(s),RLm,Clv,revenge...... 2.25
31 CCl(s),RLm,Clv,F:Power Girl .. 2.25
32 CCl(s),RLm,Clv,F:Power Girl .. 2.25
33 CCl(s),RLm,Clv,F:Power Girl .. 2.25
34 CCl(s),RLm,Clv,in Kuristan ... 2.25
35 CCl(s),RLm,Clv,The Rapture .. 2.25
36 CCl(s),RLm,Clv,final issue 2.25
Ann.#1 CCl, Year One Annual..... 4.00
Ann.#2 CCl(s),RL,KJ,Legends of
  the Dead Earth............ 3.00
1-shot Sovereign Seven Plus
  (1977) 2.95
TPB CCl(s),DT, rep.#1–#5 ...... 12.95

SPACE JAM
Warner Bros./DC, Oct., 1996
one-shot comic adaptation of movie 5.95

SPANNER'S GALAXY
Dec., 1984
1 mini-series 2.25
2 thru 6 .... @2.25

SPECTRE, THE
1967–69
1 MA,V:Captain Skull.......... 200.00
2 NA,V:Dirk Rawley........... 125.00
3 NA,A:Wildcat 125.00
4 NA 125.00
5 NA 125.00
6 MA 75.00
7 MA,BU:Hourman 75.00
8 MA,Parchment of Power
  Perilous.................. 75.00
9 BWr(2nd BWr Art).......... 90.00
10 MA 75.00

[2nd Regular Series], 1987–89
1 GC,O:Spectre............... 5.00
2 GC,Cult of BRM 4.00
3 GC,Fashion Model Murders ... 3.00
4 GC....................... 3.00
5 GC,Spectre's Murderer....... 3.00
6 GC,Spectre/Corrigan separated . 3.00
7 A:Zatanna,Wotan 3.00
8 A:Zatanna,Wotan 3.00
9 GM,Spectre's Revenge....... 3.00
10 GM,A:Batman,Millennium...... 3.00
11 GM,Millennium.............. 3.00
12 GM,The Talisman,pt.1 .... 3.00
13 GM,The Talisman,pt.2 .... 3.00
14 GM,The Talisman,pt.3 .... 3.00
15 GM,The Talisman,pt.4 .... 3.00
16 Jim Corrigan Accused 3.00
17 New Direction,`Final Destiny' ... 3.00
18 Search for Host Body......... 3.00
19 `Dead Again' 3.00
20 Corrigan Detective Agency..... 3.00
21 A:Zoran 3.00
22 BS,Sea of Darkness,A:Zoran ... 3.00
23 A:Lords of Order,
  Invasion x-over............ 3.00
24 BWg,Ghosts i/t Machine#1..... 3.00
25 Ghosts in the Machine #2 .... 3.00
26 Ghosts in the Machine #3 .... 3.00
27 Ghosts in the Machine #4 .... 3.00
28 Ghosts in the Machine #5 .... 3.00
29 Ghosts in the Machine #6 .... 3.00
30 Possession 3.00
31 Spectre possessed, final issue.. 3.00
Ann.#1, A:Deadman 3.00

Spectre, 2nd Series Annual #1
© DC Comics Inc.

[3rd Regular Series], 1992–97
1 B:JOs(s),TMd,R:Spectre,
  Glow in the dark(c)......... 7.00
2 TMd,Murder Mystery.......... 6.00
3 TMd,O:Spectre 4.00
4 TMd,O:Spectre 4.00
5 TMd,BB(c),V:Kidnappers....... 3.50
6 TMd,Spectre prevents evil 3.50
7 TMd 3.50
8 TMd,Glow in the dark(c)...... 5.00
9 TMd,MWg(c),V:The Reaver 3.00
10 TMd,V:Michael.............. 3.00
11 TMd,V:Azmodeus............ 3.00
12 V:Reaver 3.00
13 TMd,V:Count Vertigo,
  Glow in the Dark(c)......... 4.00
14 JoP,A:Phantom Stranger 2.50
15 TMd,A:Phantom Stranger,Demon,
  Doctor Fate,John Constantine . 2.50
16 JAp,V:I.R.A................. 2.50
17 TT(c),TMd,V:Eclipso 2.50
18 TMd,D:Eclipso 2.50
19 TMd,V:Hate 2.50
20 A:Lucien 2.50
21 V:Naiad,C:Superman 3.00
22 A:Superman................. 2.50
23 Book of Judgment, pt.1 ...... 2.50
24 Book of Judgment, pt.2 ...... 2.50
25 Book of Judgment, pt.3 ...... 2.50

Spectre–Starman · DC · Comics Values Annual

26 . . . . 2.50
27 R:Azmodus 2.50
28 V:Azmodus 2.50
29 V:Azmodus 2.50
30 V:Azmodus 2.50
31 Descent into Pandemonium 2.50
32 V:Killo 2.50
33 . . . . 2.50
34 Power of the Undead 2.50
35 JOs,TMd,Underworld
  Unleashed tie-in 2.50
36 JOs,TMd,Underworld
  Unleashed tie-in 2.50
37 JOs,TMd,The Haunting of
  America,pt.1 . . . . 2.50
38 JOs,TMd,The Haunting of
  America,pt.2 . . . . 2.50
39 JOs,TMd,The Haunting of
  America,pt.3 . . . . 2.50
40 JOs,TMd,The Haunting of
  America,pt.4 . . . . 2.50
41 JOs,TMd,The Haunting of
  America,pt.5 . . . . 2.50
42 JOs,TMd,The Haunting of
  America,pt.6 . . . . 2.50
43 Witchcraft 2.50
44 Madame Xanadu 2.50
45 . . . . 2.50
46 JOs(s),TMd,discovery of the
  Spear of Destiny. 2.50
47 JOs(s),TMd,The Haunting of
  America, Final Night tie-in. 2.50
48 JOs(s),TMd,The Haunting of
  America 2.50
49 JOs(s),TMd,The Haunting of
  America 2.50
50 JOs(s),TMd, ... 2.50
51 JOs(s),TMd,A:Batman,Joker . . . 2.50
52 JOs(s),TMd,Nate Kane discovers
  murder evidence 2.50
53 JOs(s),TMd,Haunting of Jim
  Corrigan, cont. 2.50
54 JOs(s),TMd,hunt for murderer of
  Mister Terrific 2.50
55 JOs(s),TMd,Corrigan implicated
  in murder 2.50
56 JOs(s),TMd,JTo, Haunting of Jim
  Corrigan. 2.50
57 JOs(s),TMd,Spectre & Jim
  Corrigan in Heaven 2.50
58 JOs,TMd,Genesis tie-in 2.50
59 JOs,TMd,BWr(c), alien pod 2.50
60 JOs,TMd,Quest for God, cont. . . 2.50
61 JOs,TMd,Quest for God, concl. . 2.50
62 JOs,TMd,final issue 2.50
Ann.#1 JOs,TMd,Year One 4.00
TPB Punishment and Crimes 10.00
TPB Crimes & Punishments,
  JOs,TMd 10.00

SPECTRE, THE
Jan., 2001

1 JMD,F:Hal Jordan. 3.00
2 JMD,Redeeming the Demon,pt.1 2.50
3 JMD,Redeeming the Demon,pt.2 2.50
4 JMD,Redeeming the Demon,pt.3 2.50
5 JMD,F:Two-Face/Harvey Dent . . 2.50
6 JMD,The Redeemer,pt.1 . . . . 2.50
7 JMD,The Redeemer,pt.2 . . . . 2.50
8 JMD,The Redeemer,pt.3 . . . . 2.50
9 JMD,stolen soul 2.50
10 JMD,Joker:Last Laugh 2.50
11 JMD,F:Phantom Stranger 2.50
12 JMD,Spectre of Christmas 2.50
13 JMD,Eternity in an Hour. 2.50
14 JMD,vampire-lord 2.50
15 JMD,NBy,Mystery in Space,pt.1 . 2.50
16 JMD,NBy,Mystery in Space,pt.2 . 2.50
17 JMD,NBy,Mystery in Space,pt.3 . 2.50
18 JMD,NBy,Abin Sur, Materna. . . . 2.50

19 NBy,DJa,V:Darkseid. 2.50
20 NBy,DJa,magazine publisher . . 2.75
21 NBy,DJa,Stigmonus,C.Ferris . . 2.75
22 NBy,DJa,A:G.Arrow,
  M.Manhunter 2.75
23 JMD,NBy,DJa,Return of
  Sinestro,pt.3. . . . . 2.75
24 JMD,DJa,F:DCU characters 2.75
25 JMD,DJa,F:Rabid 2.75
26 JMD,DJa,terrorist. 2.75
27 JMD,DJa,final issue 2.75

SPEED FORCE
Sept., 1997

1 MWa,BAu,JBy,BML,JAp,BSn,
  Flash stories, 64pg. 4.00

Spelljammer #2 © DC Comics, Inc.

SPELLJAMMER
Sept., 1990

1 RogueShip#1 . . . . 3.00
2 RogueShip#2 . . . . 2.50
3 RogueShip#3 . . . . 2.25
4 RogueShip#4 . . . . 2.25
5 New Planet. 2.25
6 Tember, Planet contd 2.25
7 Planet contd 2.25
8 conclusion 2.25
9 Meredith Possessed 2.25
10 Tie-in w/Dragonlance #33&34 . . 2.25
11 Dwarf Citidel 2.25
12 Kirstig Vs. Meredith 2.25
13 Tember to the Rescue 2.25
14 Meredith's Son #1 . . . . 2.25
15 Meredith's Son #2 . . . . 2.25

STALKER
1975–1976

1 SD,WW,O&I:Stalker 25.00
2 thru 4 SD,WW. . . . . @15.00

STANLEY & HIS MONSTER
See: FOX AND THE CROW

STANLEY & HIS MONSTER
1993

1 R:Stanley 2.25

2 I:Demon Hunter 2.25
3 A:Ambrose Bierce 2.25
4 final issue 2.25

S.T.A.R. CORPS
1993

1 A:Superman 2.25
2 I:Fusion,A:Rampage 2.25
3 I:Brainstorm 2.25
4 I:Ndoki 2.25
5 I:Trauma. 2.25
6 I:Mindgame 2.25

STAR CROSSED
DC/Helix, April, 1997

1 (of 3) MHo,Dyltah's romance
  with Saa 2.50
2 MHo,Love During Wartime 2.50
3 concl. 2.50

[NEIL GAIMAN & CHARLES VESS'] STARDUST
DC/Vertigo, Oct., 1997

1 (of 4) NGa(s),CV 6.00
2 NGa(s),CV adult faerie tale 6.00
3 NGa(s),CV 6.00
4 NGa(s),CV 6.00

STARFIRE
1976–77

1 . . . . 20.00
2 thru 8 . . . . @12.00

STAR HUNTERS
Oct.–Nov., 1977

1 DN&BL 20.00
2 LH&BL 12.00
3 MN&BL,D:Donovan Flint 12.00
4 thru 7 . . . . @12.00

STARMAN
1988–92

1 TL,I&O:New Starman 4.00
2 TL,V:Serial Killer,C:Bolt. 3.00
3 TL,V:Bolt 3.00
4 TL,V:Power Elite. 2.50
5 TL,Invasion,A:PowerGirl,
  Firestorm 2.50
6 TL,Invasion,A:G.L.,Atom 2.50
7 TL,Soul Searching Issue 2.50
8 TL,V:LadyQuark 2.50
9 TL,A:Batman,V:Blockbuster 2.50
10 TL,A:Batman,V:Blockbuster . . . 2.50
11 TL,V:Power Elite 2.50
12 TL,V:Power Elite,A:Superman . . 2.50
13 TL,V:Rampage. 2.50
14 TL,A:A:Superman,V:Parasite . . 2.50
15 TL,V:Deadline 2.50
16 TL,O:Starman 2.50
17 TL,V:Dr.Polaris,A:PowerGirl . . . 2.50
18 TL,V:Dr.Polaris,A:PowerGirl . . . 2.50
19 TL,V:Artillery 2.50
20 TL,FireFighting 2.50
21 TL,Starman Quits 2.50
22 TL,V:Khunds 2.50
23 TL,A:Deadline 2.50
24 TL,A:Deadline 2.50
25 TL,V:Deadline 2.50
26 V:The Mist 6.00
27 V:The Mist. 5.00
28 A:Superman. 7.00
29 V:Plasmax 2.50
30 Seduction of Starman #1 . . . . . 2.50
31 Seduction of Starman #2 . . . . . 2.50

CVA Page 142 — All comics prices listed are for *Near Mint* condition.

Comics Values Annual — DC — Starman–Star Spangled

Starman #2 © DC Comics, Inc.

32 Seduction of Starman #3 . . . . . . 2.50
33 Seduction of Starman #4 . . . . . . 2.50
34 A:Batman. 2.50
35 A:Valor,Mr.Nebula,ScarletSkier. . 2.50
36 A:Les Mille Yeux 2.50
37 A:Les Mille Yeux 2.50
38 War of the Gods X-over. 2.50
39 V:Plasmax. 2.50
40 V:Las Vegas 2.50
41 V:Maaldor 2.50
42 Star Shadows,pt.1,A:Eclipso . . . 3.00
43 Star Shadows,pt.2,A:Lobo,
     Eclipso 2.50
44 Star Shadows,pt.3,A:Eclipso
     V:Lobo. 2.50
45 Star Shadows,pt.4, V:Eclipso . . . 2.50

[2nd Series], 1994
0 New Starman 8.00
1 Threat of the Mist 8.00
2 . . . . 7.00
3 V:Son of the Mist 6.00
4 . . . . 6.00
5 V:Starman 6.00
6 Times Past Features. 6.00
7 Sinister Circus 6.00
8 TyH(c),Sinister Circus. 5.00
9 TyH(c),Mist's daughter breaks
   out of prison. 5.00
10 Sins of the Chile,prelude 5.00
11 . . . . 5.00
12 JeR,TyH,Sins of the Child,pt.1 . . 5.00
13 JeR,TyH,Sins of the Child,pt.2 . . 5.00
14 JeR,TyH,Sins of the Child,pt.3 . . 5.00
15 JeR,TyH,Sins of the Child,pt.4 . . 5.00
16 JeR,TyH,Sins of the Child,pt.5 . . 5.00
17 JeR,TyH 5.00
18 JeR,TyH,Orig.Starman
    vs.The Mist 4.00
19 JeR,TyH,Talking with David 2. . . 4.00
20 JeR(s),TyH,GyD,Sand and
    Stars,pt.1. . . . . 4.00
21 JeR,TyH,GyD,Sand/Stars,pt.2 . . 3.00
22 JeR,TyH,GyD,Sand/Stars,pt.3 . . 3.00
23 JeR,TyH,GyD,Sand/Stars,pt.4 . . 3.00
24 JeR(s),TyH,Hell & Back,pt.1. . . . 3.00
25 JeR(s),TyH,Hell & Back,pt.2. . . . 3.00
26 JeR(s),TyH,Hell & Back,pt.3. . . . 3.00
27 . . . . 3.00
28 JeR(s)Superfreaks and
    Backstabbers 3.00
29 JeR(s),TyH,GyD,V:The Shade,
    Starman history 3.00
30 JeR(s),TyH,Infernal Devices
    pt.1 (of 6) 3.00

31 JeR(s),TyH,Devices,pt.2 . . . . . . 3.00
32 JeR(s),TyH,Devices,pt.3 . . . . . . 3.00
33 JeR(s),TyH,Infernal Devices
    pt.4,A:Batman, Sentinel 3.00
34 JeR(s),TyH,A:Batman, Sentinel,
    Floronic Man 3.00
35 JeR(s),TyH,A:Batman, Floronic
    Man, Sentinel. 3.00
36 JeR(s),TyH,F:Will Payton. 3.00
37 JeR(s),TyH,F:GoldenAgeHeroes 3.00
38 JeR(s),TyH,new JLE 2.50
39 JeR(s),TyH,Lightning &
    Stars, pt.1 x-over 2.50
40 JeR(s),TyH 2.50
41 JeR(s),GEr,TyH 2.50
42 JeR(s),MS,Nazis,Demon 2.50
43 JeR(s),TyH,help from JLA 2.50
44 JeR(s),times past story 2.50
45 JeR(s),search for Will Payton. . . 2.50
46 JeR(s),TyH,Bobo 2.50
47 JeR,SY,TyH, ... 2.50
48 JeR,SY,A:Swamp Thing 2.50
49 JeR,SY,Talking with David 2.50
50 JeR(s),PSj,48-page 5.00
51 JeR(s),PSj,to Krypton 2.50
52 JeR(s),PSj,A:Adam Strange . . . 2.50
53 JeR(s),PSj,A:Adam Strange. . . . 2.50
54 JeR(s),Times Past tale. 2.50
55 JeR(s),PSj,A:Space Cabby 2.50
56 JeR(s),PSj,A:ElongatedMan. . . . 2.50
57 JeR(s),PSj,TyH,AxR,A:Tigorr
    & Fastbak, pt.1. . . . . 2.50
58 JeR,TyH,AxR, pt.2. . . . . 2.50
59 JeR,TyH,AxR, pt.3. . . . . 2.50
60 JeR,TyH,AxR, concl. 2.50
61 JeR,TyH,AxR. 2.50
62 JeR,PSj,Grand Guignol,pt.1 . . . . 2.50
63 JeR,PSj,Grand Guignol,pt.2 . . . . 2.50
64 JeR,PSj,Grand Guignol,pt.3 . . . . 2.50
65 JeR,PSj,Grand Guignol,pt.4 . . . . 2.50
66 JeR,PSj,Grand Guignol,pt.5 . . . . 2.50
67 JeR,PSj,Grand Guignol,pt.6 . . . . 2.50
68 JeR,PSj,Grand Guignol,pt.7 . . . . 2.50
69 JeR,PSj,flashback 2.50
70 JeR,PSj,Grand Guignol,pt.8 . . . . 2.50
71 JeR,PSj,Grand Guignol,pt.9 . . . . 2.50
72 JeR,PSj,Grand Guignol, concl. . . 2.50
73 JeR,PSj,Grand Guignol,Eulogy . 2.50
74 JeR,RH,Times Past 2.50
75 JeR,A:Superman 2.50
76 JeR,Talking With David:2001 . . 2.50
77 JeR,1951,pt.1 . . . . 2.50
78 JeR,1951,pt.2 . . . . 2.50
79 JeR,1951,pt.3 . . . . 2.50
80 JeR,48-page final issue 4.50
Ann.#1 Legends o/t Dead Earth . . 4.00
Ann.#2 Pulp Heroes (Romance) . . 4.50
Spec.#1,000,000 JeR(s),PSj. 2.50
Secret Files #1,O:Starmen 5.00
Giant #1 80-page 5.00
Spec. Starman: The Mist, F:Mary
   Marvel, Girlfrenzy (1998) 2.50
TPB Sins of the Father,rep.#0–#5. 12.95
TPB Night and Day, rep. stories
   from #7–#16. . . . . 14.95
TPB A Wicked Inclination, rep. . . 18.00
TPB Times Past. 18.00
TPB Infernal Devices 17.95
TPB To Reach the Stars 17.95
TPB A Starry Knight (2002). 17.95

STARS AND S.T.R.I.P.E.
1999
0 LMd,DDv,I:Courtney Whitman . . . 3.00
1 LMd,DDv,O:Star-Spangled Kid . . 2.50
2 LMd,DDv,V:Paintball 2.50
3 LMd,DDv,V:Skeeter 2.50
4 LMd,DDv,Day of Judgment
   x-over. 2.50
5 LMd,DDv,F:Young Justice,pt.1 . . 2.50

6 . . . . 2.50
7 LMd,DDv,F:Mike Dugan 2.50
8 LMd,DDv 2.50
9 LMd,DDv,R:Nebula Man 2.50
10 LMd,DDv,cheating 2.50
11 DDv,V:Dr. Graft 2.50
12 DDv,V:Dragon King 2.50
13 DDv,V:Dragon King 2.50
14 LMd,DDv,final issue 2.50

STAR SPANGLED COMICS
Oct., 1941
1 O:Tarantula,B:Captain X of the
   R.A.F.,Star Spangled Kid,
   Armstrong of the Army. . . . 7,500.00
2 V:Dr. Weerd. 2,200.00
3 . . . . 1,400.00
4 V:The Needle. 1,400.00
5 V:Dr. Weerd 1,400.00
6 E:Armstrong 800.00
7 S&K,O&1st app:The Guardian,
   B:Robotman,The Newsboy
   Legion, TNT, ... 9,000.00
8 O:TNT & Dan the Dyna-Mite 3,000.00
9 . . . . 2,200.00
10 . . . . 2,200.00
11 . . . . 1,600.00
12 Newsboy Legion stories,
    `Prevue of Peril!' 1,600.00
13 `Kill Dat Story!' 1,600.00
14 `Meanest Man on Earth' . . 1,600.00
15 `Playmates of Peril' 1,600.00
16 `Playboy of Suicide Slum!'. 1,600.00
17 V:Rafferty Mob 1,600.00
18 O:Star Spangled Kid 2,200.00
19 E:Tarantula 1,600.00
20 B:Liberty Belle. 1,600.00
21 . . . . 1,400.00
22 `Brains for Sale' 1,400.00
23 `Art for Scrapper's Sake'. . 1,400.00
24 . . . . 1,400.00
25 `Victuals for Victory' 1,400.00
26 `Louie the Lug goes Literary' 1,400.00
27 `Turn on the Heat!' 1,400.00
28 `Poor Man's Rich Man' . . . 1,400.00
29 `Cabbages and Comics' . . 1,400.00
30 . . . . 750.00
31 `Questions Please!' 750.00
32 . . . . 750.00
33. . . . . 750.00
34 `From Rags to Run!' 750.00
35 `The Proud Poppas' 750.00
36 `Cowboy of Suicide Slum' . . 750.00

Star Spangled Comics #15 © DC Comics Inc.

All comics prices listed are for *Near Mint* condition.   CVA Page 143

Star Spangled

37	750.00
38	750.00
39 'Two Guardians are a Crowd'.	750.00
40	750.00
41 Back the 6th War Loan(c)	650.00
42	650.00
43 American Red Cross(c)	650.00
44	650.00
45 7th War Loan (c)	650.00
46	650.00
47	650.00
48	650.00
49	650.00
50	650.00
51 A:Robot Robber	650.00
52 'Rehearsal for Crime'	650.00
53 'The Poet of Suicide Slum'	650.00
54 'Dead-Shot Dade's Revenge'.	650.00
55 'Gabby Strikes a Gusher'	650.00
56 'The Treasuer of Araby'	650.00
57 'Recruit for the Legion'	650.00
58 'Matadors of Suicide Slum'	650.00
59	650.00
60	650.00
61	650.00
62 'Prevue of Tomorrow'	650.00
63	650.00
64 'Criminal Cruise'	650.00
65 B:Robin,(c) & stories	2,000.00
66 V:No Face	1,200.00
67 'The Castle of Doom'	900.00
68	900.00
69 'The Stolen Atom Bomb'	1,400.00
70 V:The Clock	900.00
71 'Perils of the Stone Age'	900.00
72 'Robin Crusoe'	900.00
73 V:The Black Magician	900.00
74 V:The Clock	900.00
75 The State vs. Robin	900.00
76 V:The Fence	900.00
77 'The Boy who Wanted Robin for Christmas'	900.00
78 ''Rajah Robin'	900.00
79 'V:The Clock,'The Tick-Tock Crimes'	900.00
80 'The Boy Disc Jockey'	900.00
81 'The Seeing-Eye Dog Crimes'	700.00
82 'The Boy who Hated Robin'	650.00
83 'Who is Mr. Mystery',B:Captain Compass backup story	650.00
84 How can we Fight Juvenile Delinquency?	1,100.00
85 'Peril at the Pole'	650.00
86	700.00
87 V:Sinister Knight	1,100.00

Star Spangled Comics #65
© DC Comics, Inc.

DC

88 Robin Declares War on Batman, B:Batman app.	750.00
89 'Batman's Utility Belt?'	750.00
90 'Rancho Fear!'	750.00
91 'Cops 'n' Robbers?'	750.00
92 'Movie Hero No. 1?'	750.00
93	750.00
94 'Underworld Playhouse'	800.00
95 'The Man with the Midas Touch', E:Robin(c),Batman story	800.00
96 B:Tomahawk(c) & stories	500.00
97 'The 4 Bold Warriors'	400.00
98	400.00
99 'The Second Pocahontas'	400.00
100 'The Frontier Phantom'	400.00
101 Peril on the High Seas	350.00
102	350.00
103 'Tomahawk's Death Duel!'	350.00
104 'Race with Death!'	350.00
105 'The Unhappy Hunting Grounds'	350.00
106 'Traitor in the War Paint'	350.00
107 'The Brave who Hunted Tomahawk'	350.00
108 'The Ghost called Moccasin Foot!'	350.00
109 'The Land Pirates of Jolly Roger Hill!'	350.00
110 'Sally Raines Frontier Girl'	350.00
111 'The Death Map of Thunder Hill'	350.00
112	350.00
113 FF,V:'The Black Cougar'	500.00
114 'Return of the Black Cougar'	500.00
115 'Journey of a Thousand Deaths'	400.00
116 'The Battle of Junction Fort'	400.00
117 'Siege?'	400.00
118 V:Outlaw Indians	375.00
119 'The Doomed Stockade?'	350.00
120 'Revenge of Raven Heart!'	400.00
121 'Adventure in New York!'	300.00
122 'I:Ghost Breaker,(c)& stories	500.00
123 'The Dolls of Doom'	350.00
124 'Suicide Tower'	350.00
125 The Hermit's Ghost Dog!'	350.00
126 'The Phantom of Paris!'	350.00
127 'The Supernatural Alibi!'	350.00
128 C:Batman,'The Girl who lived 5,000 Years!'	350.00
129 'The Human Orchids'	375.00
130 'The Haunted Town', July, 1952	400.00

Becomes:

STAR SPANGLED WAR STORIES
Aug., 1952

131 CS&StK(c),I Was A Jap Prisoner of War	1,300.00
132 CS&StK(c),The G.I. With The Million-Dollar Arm	800.00
133 CS&StK(c),Mission-San Marino	700.00
3 CS&StK(c),Hundred-Mission Mitchell	450.00
4 CS&StK(c),The Hot Rod Tank	450.00
5 LSt(c),Jet Pilot	450.00
6 CS(c),Operation Davy Jones	450.00
7 CS(c),Rookie Ranger,The	350.00
8 CS(c),I Was A Holywood Soldier	350.00
9 CS&StK(c),Sad Sack Squad	350.00
10 CS,The G.I. & The Gambler	350.00
11 LSt(c),The Lucky Squad	350.00
12 CS(c),The Four Horseman of Barricade Hill	350.00
13 No Escape	350.00
14 LSt(c),Pitchfork Army	350.00
15 The Big Fish	350.00
16 The Yellow Ribbon	350.00

Comics Values Annual

Star Spangled War Stories #15
© DC Comics, Inc.

17 IN(c),Prize Target	350.00
18 IN(c),The Gladiator	350.00
19 IN(c),The Big Lift	350.00
20 JGr(c),The Battle of the Frogmen	350.00
21 JGr(c),Dead Man's Bridge	250.00
22 JGr(c),Death Hurdle	250.00
23 JGr(c),The Silent Frogman	250.00
24 JGr(c),Death Slide	250.00
25 JGr(c),S.S. Liferaft	250.00
26 JGr(c),Bazooka Man	250.00
27 JGr(c),Taps for a Tail Gunner	250.00
28 JGr(c),Tank Duel	250.00
29 JGr(c),A Gun Called Slugger	250.00
30 JGr(c),The Thunderbolt Tank	250.00
31 IN(c),Tank Block	200.00
32 JGr(c),Bridge to Battle	200.00
33 JGr(c),Pocket War	200.00
34 JGr(c),Fighting...Snowbirds	200.00
35 JGr(c),Zero Hour	200.00
36 JGr(c),A G.I. Passed Here	200.00
37 JGr(c),A Handful of T.N.T.	200.00
38 RH(c),One-Man Army	200.00
39 JGr(c),Flying Cowboy	200.00
40 JGr(c),Desert Duel	200.00
41 IN(c),A Gunner's Hands	175.00
42 JGr(c),Sniper Alley	175.00
43 JGr(c),Top Kick Brother	175.00
44 JGr(c),Tank 711 Doesn't Answer	175.00
45 JGr(c),Flying Heels	175.00
46 JGr(c),Gunner's Seat	175.00
47 JGr(c),Sidekick	175.00
48 JGr(c),Battle Hills	175.00
49 JGr(c),Payload	175.00
50 JGr(c),Combat Dust	175.00
51 JGr(c),Battle Pigeon	125.00
52 JGr(c),Cannon-Man	125.00
53 JGr(c),Combat Close-Ups	125.00
54 JGr(c),Flying Exit	125.00
55 JKu(c),The Burning Desert	125.00
56 JKu(c),The Walking Sub	125.00
57 JGr(c),Call For a Frogman	125.00
58 JGr(c),MD,Waist Punch	125.00
59 JGr(c),Kick In The Door	125.00
60 JGr(c),Hotbox	125.00
61 JGr(c),MD,Tow Pilot	125.00
62 JGr(c),The Three GIs	125.00
63 JGr(c),Flying Range Rider	125.00
64 JGr(c),MD,Frogman Ambush	125.00
65 JGr(c),JSe,Frogman Block	125.00
66 JGr(c),Flattop Pigeon	125.00
67 RH(c),MD,Ashcan Alley	125.00
68 JGr(c),The Long Step	125.00
69 JKu(c),Floating Tank, The'	125.00

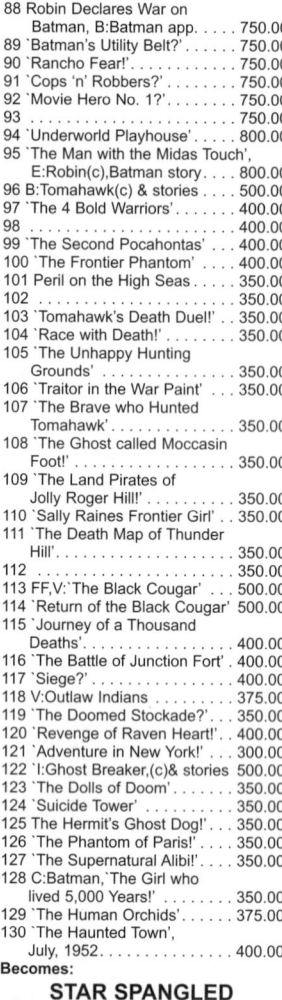

Comics Values Annual — DC — Star Spangled–Star Trek

70 JKu(c),No Medal For
    Frogman 110.00
71 JKu(c),Shooting Star 110.00
72 JGr(c),Silent Fish 110.00
73 JGr(c),MD,The Mouse &
    the Tiger 110.00
74 JGr(c),MD,Frogman Bait 110.00
75 JGr(c),MD,Paratroop
    Mousketeers 110.00
76 MD,JKu(c),Odd Man 110.00
77 MD,JKu(c),Room to Fight . . . 110.00
78 MD,JGr(c),Fighting Wingman . 110.00
79 MD,JKu(c),Zero Box. 110.00
80 MD,JGr(c),Top Gunner 110.00
81 MD,RH(c),Khaki Mosquito . . . 110.00
82 MD,JKu(c),Ground Flier 110.00
83 MD,JGr(c),Jet On
    My Shoulder 110.00
84 MD,IN(c),O:Mademoiselle
    Marie 250.00
85 IN(c),A Medal For Marie 150.00
86 JGr(c),A Medal For Marie 150.00
87 JGr(c),T.N.T. Spotlight 135.00
88 JGr(c),The Steel Trap 135.00
89 IN(c),Trail of the Terror 135.00
90 RA(c),Island of
    Armored Giants 550.00
91 JGr(c),The Train of Terror. . . . 125.00
92 Last Battle of the
    Dinosaur Age 200.00
93 Goliath of the Western Front . 125.00
94 JKu(c),The Frogman and
    the Dinosaur. 250.00
95 Guinea Pig Patrol,Dinosaurs . 200.00
96 Mission X,Dinosaur 200.00
97 The Sub-Crusher, Dinosaur . . 200.00
98 Island of Thunder, Dinosaur . . 200.00
99 The Circus of Monsters,
    Dinosaur 200.00
100 The Volcano of Monsters,
    Dinosaur 225.00
101 The Robot and the Dinosaur 150.00
102 Punchboard War,Dinosaur . . 150.00
103 Doom at Dinosaur Island,
    Dinosaur 150.00
104 The Tree of Terror,
    Dinosaurs. 150.00
105 The War of Dinosaur Island . 150.00
106 The Nightmare War,
    Dinosaurs. 150.00
107 Battle of the Dinosaur
    Aquarium 150.00
108 Dinosaur D-Day 150.00
109 The Last Soldiers 150.00
110 thru 133 . . . . @150.00
134 NA. 160.00
135 . . . . 150.00
136 . . . . 150.00
137 Dinosaur 150.00
138 Enemy Ace 175.00
139 O:Enemy Ace. 125.00
140 . . . . 85.00
141 . . . . 85.00
142 . . . . 85.00
143 . . . . 85.00
144 NA,JKu 100.00
145 . . . . 75.00
146 . . . . 75.00
147 . . . . 75.00
148 . . . . 75.00
149 . . . . 75.00
150 JKu,Viking Prince. 75.00
151 I:Unknown Soldier 75.00
152 . . . . 50.00
153 . . . . 50.00
154 O:Unknown Soldier 150.00
155. . . . . 50.00
156 I:Battle Album 40.00
157 thru 160 . . . . 30.00
161 E:Enemy Ace. 30.00
162 thru 170 . . . . @25.00

The Unknown Soldier #225
© DC Comics Inc.

171 thru 200 . . . . @15.00
201 thru 204 . . . . @10.00
Becomes:

UNKNOWN SOLDIER
April-May, 1977
205 thru 247 . . . . @15.00
248 and 249 O:Unknown Soldier @10.00
250 . . . . 10.00
251 B:Enemy Ace. 10.00
252 thru 268 . . . . @10.00

STAR SPANGLED COMICS
1999
1 CWn, F:Sandman & Star
    Spangled Kid 2.25

STAR TREK
1984-88
[1st Regular Series]
1 TS,The Wormhole Connection . 15.00
2 TS,The Only Good Klingon 8.00
3 TS,Errand of War 7.00
4 TS,Deadly Allies 7.00
5 TS,Mortal Gods 7.00
6 TS,Who is Enigma? 6.00
7 EB,O:Saavik. 6.00
8 TS,Blood Fever 6.00
9 TS,Mirror Universe Saga #1 . . . 6.00
10 TS,Mirror Universe Saga #2. . . 6.00
11 TS,Mirror Universe Saga #3 . . . 6.00
12 TS,Mirror Universe Saga #4. . . 6.00
13 TS,Mirror Universe Saga #5 . . . 5.00
14 TS,Mirror Universe Saga #6 . . . 5.00
15 TS,Mirror Universe Saga #7 . . . 5.00
16 TS,Mirror Universe Saga end. . . 5.00
17 TS,The D'Artagnan Three 5.00
18 TS,Rest & Recreation 5.00
19 DSp,W.Koenig story. 5.00
20 TS,Girl. 5.00
21 TS,Dreamworld 5.00
22 TS,The Wolf #1 . . . . 5.00
23 TS,The Wolf #2 . . . . 4.00
24 TS,Double Blind #1 . . . . 4.00
25 TS,Double Blind #2. . . . . 4.00
26 TSV:Romulans. 4.00
27 TS,Day in the Life 4.00
28 GM,The Last Word 4.00
29 Trouble with Bearclaw 4.00
30 CI,F:Uhura. 4.00
31 TS,Maggie's World. 4.00
32 TS,Judgment Day 4.00
33 TS,20th Anniv. 5.00
34 V:Romulans 3.00

Star Trek #45 © DC Comics, Inc.

35 GM,Excelsior. 3.00
36 GM,StarTrek IV tie-in 3.00
37 StarTrek IV tie-in 3.00
38 AKu,The Argon Affair 3.00
39 TS,A:Harry Mudd 3.00
40 TS,A:Harry Mudd 3.00
41 TS,V:Orions 3.00
42 TS,The Corbomite Effect 3.00
43 TS,Paradise Lost #1 . . . . 3.00
44 TS,Paradise Lost #2 . . . . 3.00
45 TS,Paradise Lost #3 . . . . 3.00
46 TS,Getaway. 3.00
47 TS,Idol Threats 3.00
48 TS,The Stars in Secret
    Influence 3.00
49 TS,Aspiring to be Angels 3.00
50 TS,Anniv. 4.00
51 TS,Haunted Honeymoon 3.00
52 TS,'Hell in a Hand Basket' 3.00
53 `You're Dead,Jim' 3.00
54 Old Loyalties 3.00
55 TS,Finnegan's Wake 3.00
56 GM, Took place during 5 year
    Mission 3.00
Ann.#1 All Those Years Ago 4.00
Ann.#2 DJw,The Final Voyage . . 3.00
Ann.#3 CS,F:Scotty 3.00
Star Trek III Adapt.TS 2.50
Star Trek IV Adapt. TS 2.50
StarTrek V Adapt. 2.50

[2nd Regular Series], 1989-96
1 The Return 9.00
2 The Sentence. 5.00
3 Death Before Dishonor 4.00
4 Reprocussions 4.00
5 Fast Friends 4.00
6 Cure All 4.00
7 Not Sweeney! 4.00
8 Going,Going 3.50
9 ...Gone 3.50
10 Trial of James Kirk #1 . . . . 3.50
11 Trial of James Kirk #2 . . . . 3.50
12 Trial of James Kirk #3 . . . . 3.50
13 Return of Worthy #1 . . . . 3.50
14 Return of Worthy #2 . . . . 3.50
15 Return of Worthy #3 . . . . 3.50
16 Worldsinger 3.00
17 Partners? #1 . . . . 3.00
18 Partners? #2 . . . . 3.00
19 Once A Hero 3.00
20 . . . . 3.00
21 Kirk Trapped 3.00
22 A:Harry Mudd 3.00
23 The Nasgul,A:Harry Mudd 3.00
24 25th Anniv.,A:Harry Mudd 4.00

All comics prices listed are for Near Mint condition.

Star Trek–Star Trek TNG — DC — Comics Values Annual

25 Starfleet Officers Reunion	2.50
26 Pilkor 3	2.50
27 Kirk Betrayed	2.50
28 V:Romulans	2.50
29 Mediators	2.50
30 Veritas #1	2.50
31 Veritas #2	2.50
32 Veritas #3	2.50
33 Veritas #4	2.50
34 JD,F:Kirk,Spock,McCoy	2.50
35 Tabukan Syndrome#1	2.50
36 Tabukan Syndrome#2	2.50
37 Tabukan Syndrome#3	2.50
38 Tabukan Syndrome#4	2.50
39 Tabukan Syndrome#5	2.50
40 Tabukan Syndrome#6	2.50
41 Runaway	2.50
42 Helping Hand	2.50
43 V:Binzalans	2.50
44 Acceptable Risk	2.50
45 V:Trelane	2.50
46 V:Captain Klaa	2.50
47 F:Spock & Saavik	2.50
48 The Neutral Zone	2.50
49 Weapon from Genesis	2.50
50 "The Peacemaker"	4.00
51 "The Price"	2.50
52 V:Klingons	2.50
53 Timecrime #1	2.50
54 Timecrime #2	2.50
55 Timecrime #3	2.50
56 Timecrime #4	2.50
57 Timecrime #5	2.50
58 F:Chekov	2.50
59 Uprising	2.50
60 Hostages	2.50
61 On Talos IV	2.50
62 Alone,pt.1, V:aliens	2.50
63 Alone,pt.2	2.50
64 Kirk	2.50
65 Kirk in Space	2.50
66 Spock	2.50
67 Ambassador Stonn	2.50
68	2.50
69 Wolf in Cheap Clothing,pt.1	2.50
70 Wolf in Cheap Clothing,pt.2	2.50
71 Wolf in Cheap Clothing,pt.3	2.75
72 Wolf in Cheap Clothing,pt.4	2.75
73 Star-crossed,pt.1	2.75
74 Star-crossed,pt.2	2.75
75 Star-crossed,pt.3	4.50
76 Tendar	2.50
77 to the Romulan Neutral Zone	2.50
78 The Chosen,pt.1 (of 3)	2.50
79 The Chosen,pt.2	2.50
80 The Chosen,pt.3	2.50
Ann.#1 GM,sty by G.Takei(Sulu)	4.00
Ann.#2 Kirks 1st Yr At Star Fleet Academy	4.00
Ann #3 KD,F:Ambassador Sarek	4.00
Ann.#4 F:Spock on Pike's ship	4.00
Ann.#6 Convergence,pt.1	4.50
Spec.#1 PDd(s),BSz	4.00
Spec.#2 The Defiant	4.50
Spec.#3 V:Orion pirates	4.50
Debt of Honor,AH,CCl(s),HC	27.00
Debt of Honor SC	14.95
Spec. 25th Anniv.	6.95
Star Trek VI,movie adapt(direct)	5.95
Star Trek VI,movie(newsstand)	4.00
TPB Best of Star Trek reps.	19.95
TPB Star Trek: Revisitations rep. #22–#24,F:Gary Seven, #49–#50,F:Harry Mudd, 176pg	19.95
TPB Who Killed Captain Kirk?, rep.Star Trek#49-#55	16.95
TPB The Ashes of Eden, Shatner novel adapt.	14.95

STAR TREK: THE MODALA IMPERATIVE
1991

1 Planet Modula	6.00
2 Modula's Rebels	4.50
3 Spock/McCoy rescue Attempt	4.00
4 Rebel Victory	4.00
TPB reprints both minis	19.95

STAR TREK: THE NEXT GENERATION
Feb., 1988

[1st Regular Series]

1 based on TV series,Where No Man Has Gone Before	10.00
2 Spirit in the Sky	8.00
3 Factor Q	5.00
4 Q's Day	5.00
5 Q's Effects	5.00
6 Here Today	5.00

[2nd Regular Series], 1989–95

1 Return to Raimon	15.00
2 Murder Most Foul	9.00
3 Derelict	7.50
4 The Hero Factor	7.50
5 Serafin's Survivors	6.00
6 Shadows in the Garden	6.00
7 The Pilot	5.00
8 The Battle Within	5.00
9 The Pay Off	5.00
10 The Noise of Justice	5.00
11 The Imposter	4.00
12 Whoever Fights Monsters	4.00
13 The Hand of the Assassin	4.00
14 Holiday on Ice	4.00
15 Prisoners of the Ferengi	3.50
16 I Have Heard the Mermaids Singing	3.50
17 The Weapon	3.50
18 MM,Forbidden Fruit	3.50
19 The Lesson	3.50
20 Lost Shuttle	3.50
21 Lost Shuttle cont.	3.50
22 Lost Shuttle cont.	3.50
23 Lost Shuttle cont.	3.50
24 Lost Shuttle conc.	3.50
25 Okona S.O.S.	3.50
26 Search for Okona	3.50
27 Worf,Data,Troi,Okona trapped on world	3.50
28 Worf/K'Ehleyr story	3.50
29 Rift,pt.1	3.50

Star Trek: The Next Generation #63
© DC Comics, Inc.

30 Rift,pt.2	3.50
31 Rift conclusion	3.50
32	3.50
33 R:Mischievous Q	3.50
34 V:Aliens,F:Mischievous Q	3.50
35 Way of the Warrior	3.50
36 Shore Leave in Shanzibar#1	3.25
37 Shore Leave in Shanzibar#2	3.25
38 Shore Leave in Shanzibar#3	3.25
39 Divergence #1	3.25
40 Divergence #2	3.25
41 V:Strazzan Warships	3.25
42 V:Strazzans	3.25
43 V:Strazzans	3.25
44 Disrupted Lives	3.25
45 F:Enterprise Surgical Team	3.25
46 Deadly Labyrinth	3.25
47 Worst of Both World's#1	3.00
48 Worst of Both World's#2	3.00
49 Worst of Both World's#3	3.00
50 Double Sized,V:Borg	4.00
51 V:Energy Beings	3.00
52 in the 1940's	3.00
53 F:Picard	3.00
54 F:Picard	3.00
55 Data on Trial	3.00
56 Abduction	3.00
57 Body Switch	3.00
58 Body Switch	3.00
59 B:Children in Chaos	3.00
60 Children in Chaos#2	3.00
61 E:Children in Chaos	3.00
62 V:Stalker	3.00
63 A:Romulans	3.00
64 Geordie	3.00
65 Geordie	3.00
66	3.00
67 Friends/Strangers	3.00
68 Friends/Strangers,pt.2	3.00
69 Friends/Strangers,pt.3	3.00
70 Friends/Strangers,pt.4	3.00
71 War of Madness,pt.1	3.00
72 War of Madness,pt.2	3.00
73 War of Madness,pt.3	3.00
74 War of Madness,pt.4	3.00
75 War of Madness,pt.5	4.50
76 F:Geordi	3.00
77 Gateway, pt.1	3.00
78 Gateway, pt.2	3.00
79 Crew transformed into androids	3.00
80 Mysterious illness	3.00
Ann.#1 A:Mischievous Q	4.50
Ann.#2 BP,V:Parasitic Creatures	4.00
Ann.#3	4.00
Ann.#4 MiB(s),F:Dr.Crusher	4.00
Ann.#6 Convergence,pt.2	4.50
Series Finale	4.25
Spec.#1	3.75
Spec.#2 CCl(s)	4.00
Star Trek N.G.:Sparticus	5.00
TPB Beginnings, BSz(c) rep.	19.95

STAR TREK: THE NEXT GENERATION DEEP SPACE NINE
1994–95

1 Crossover with Malibu	2.50
2	2.50

STAR TREK: THE NEXT GENERATION ILL WIND
1995–96

1 Solar-sailing race	2.50
2 Explosion Investigated	2.50
3 A bomb aboard ship	2.50
4 finale	2.50

All comics prices listed are for *Near Mint* condition.

STAR TREK THE NEXT GENERATION MODALA IMPERATIVE
1991
1 A:Spock,McCoy 6.00
2 Modula Overrun by Ferengi 5.00
3 Picard,Spock,McCoy & Troi
   trapped 4.00
4 final issue................ 4.00

STAR TREK THE NEXT GENERATION SHADOWHEART
1994–95
1 thru 3 .... @2.50
4 Worf Confront Nikolai 2.50

STATIC
Milestone, 1993–96
1 JPL,I:Static,Hotstreak,Frieda Goren,
   w/poster,card,D puzzle piece .. 4.00
1a Newstand Ed............. 2.50
1b Platinum Ed.............. 8.00
2 JPL,V:Hotstreak,I:Tarmack 2.50
3 JPL,V:Tarmack 2.50
4 JPL,A:Holocaust,I:Don Cornelius 2.50
5 JPL,I:Commando X 2.50
6 JPL,V:Commando X 2.50
7 3RW,V:Commando X 2.50
8 WS(c),3RW,Shadow War,I:Plus. . 2.50
9 3RW,I:Virus 2.50
10 3RW,I:Puff,Coil 2.50
11 3RW,V:Puff,Coil 2.50
12 3RW,I:Joyride 2.50
13 I:Shape Changer 2.50
14 Worlds Collide,V:Rift 3.00
15 V:Paris Bloods............. 2.50
16 Revelations 2.50
17 Palisade 2.50
18 Princess Nightmare 2.50
19 .... 2.50
20 .... 2.50
21 A:Blood Syndicate 2.50
22 V:Rabis 2.50
23 A:Boogieman.............. 2.50
24 A:Dusk................... 2.50
25 Long Hot Summer, V:Dusk,
   48pgs.................. 3.95
26 Long Hot Summer 2.50
27 .... 2.50
28 Drug Raid 2.50
29 HC(c), Friend Drug Dealer..... 2.50
30 Deals with Friend's Death 2.50
31 GK 2.50
32 V:Swarm 2.50
33 .... 2.50
34 V:Ruberband Man 2.50
35 new Prometheus 2.50
36 JP,V:Sinister Botanist......... 2.50
37 .... 2.50
38 .... 2.50
39 .... 2.50
40 JMr...................... 2.50
41 Virgil's relationship with Daisy . . 2.50
42 V:six enemies 2.50
43 A:Brickhouse, V:Frieda Goren . . 2.50
44 .... 2.50
45 MBr(s),JMr,Static lays a trap
   for Laserjet.............. 2.50
46 MBr(s),JMr 2.50
47 DMD(s),JMr, final issue 2.50

STATIC SHOCK
1999
TPB Static Shock: Trial by Fire . . . 10.00

STATIC SHOCK!: REBIRTH OF THE COOL
DC/Milestone, Nov., 2001
1 (of 4) DMD 2.50
2 DMD,F:Hardware 2.50
3 DMD,A:Hardware,Iron Butterfly. . 2.50
4 DMD,V:Power Junkie 2.50

Steel #14 © DC Comics Inc.

STEEL
1994–98
1 JBg(c),B:LSi(s),CsB,N:Steel 3.00
2 JBg(c),CsB,V:Toastmaster 2.50
3 JBg(c),CsB,V:Amertek 2.50
4 JBg(c),CsB................ 2.50
5 JBg(c),CsB,V:Sister's Attacker . . 2.50
6 JBg(c),CsB,Worlds Collide,pt.5 . . 2.50
7 Worlds Collide,pt.6 .... 2.50
8 Zero Hour,I:Hazard 2.50
9 F:Steel 2.50
10 F:Steel.................... 2.50
11 .... 2.50
12 .... 2.50
13 A:Maxima 2.50
14 A:Superman............... 2.50
15 R:White Rabbit 2.50
16 V:White Rabbit
   [new Miraweb format begins] . . 2.50
17 Steel controls armor powers ... 2.50
18 Abduction 2.50
19 .... 2.50
20 Body Rejects Armor......... 2.50
21 LSi,Underworld Unleashed tie-in 2.50
22 Steel separated from Superboy . 2.50
23 Steel attacked 2.50
24 V:Hazard's................ 2.50
25 .... 2.50
26 Natasha gains superpowers.... 2.50
27 LSi,V:Hazard 2.50
28 .... 2.50
29 .... 2.50
30 .... 2.50
31 LSi(s),V:Armorbeast.......... 2.50
32 V:Blockbuster 2.50
33 JAp,DG,Natasha's drug abuse. . 2.50
34 CPr(s),DCw,TP,A:Natasha, in
   Jersey City 2.50
35 CPr(s),DCw,TP, ... 2.50
36 CPr(s),DCw,TP,Combing the
   sewers of Jersey City 2.50
37 CPr(s),DCw,TP,John Irons,
   Amanda Quick & Skorpio a
   romantic triangle.......... 2.50
38 CPr(s),DCw,TP,A:The Question . 2.50
39 CPr(s),DCw,TP,V:Crash....... 2.50
40 CPr(s),VGi,Steel tries out
   new hammer 2.50
41 CPr(s),DCw,TMo, John Irons
   guilty of murder? 2.50
42 CPr(s),DCw,TP,Irons and
   Amanda assaulted 2.50
43 CPr(s),DCw,TP,to Metropolis . . 2.50
44 CPr(s),DCw,TP,Genesis tie-in . . 2.50
45 CPr(s),DCw,TP,seek policeman . 2.50
46 CPr(s),DCw,TP,F:Superboy ... 2.50
47 CPr(s),DCw,TP,F:Amanda..... 2.50
48 .... 2.50
49 CPr(s),DCw,TP,V:Deadline..... 2.50
50 CPr(s),DCw,TP,Millennium
   Giants 2.50
51 CPr(s),DCw,TP,bounty hunter . . 2.50
52 CPr(s),final issue 2.50
1-shot, movie adaptation......... 5.00
Ann.#1 Elseworlds story 2.95
TPB THe Forging of a Hero LSi(s) 19.95

STEEL, THE INDESTRUCTIBLE MAN
March, 1978
1 DH,I:Steel................. 12.00
2 DH...................... 8.00
3 DH...................... 8.00
4 DH...................... 8.00
5 Oct.–Nov., 1978 .... 12.00

STRANGE ADVENTURES
1950–74
1 The Menace of the Green
   Nebula................. 4,500.00
2 S&K,JM(c),Doom From
   Planet X 2,000.00
3 The Metal World 1,400.00
4 BP,The Invaders From the
   Nth Dimension.......... 1,400.00
5 The World Inside the Atom. . 1,200.00
6 Confessions of a Martian . . . 1,200.00
7 The World of Giant Ants..... 1,200.00
8 MA,ATh,Evolution Plus..... 1,200.00
9 MA,B:Captain Comet,The
   Origin of Captain Comet . . 2,800.00
10 MA,CI,The Air Bandits
   From Space............ 1,200.00
11 MA,CI,Day the Past
   Came Back 800.00
12 MA,CI,GK(c),The Girl From
   the Diamond Planet 800.00
13 MA,CI,GK(c),When the Earth
   was Kidnapped............ 800.00
14 MA,CI,GK(c),Destination
   Doom.................. 800.00
15 MA,CI,GK(c),Captain Comet-
   Enemy of Earth 750.00
16 MA,CI,GK(c),The Ghost of
   Captain Comet 750.00
17 MA,CI,GK(c),Beware the
   Synthetic Men 750.00
18 CI,MA(c),World of Flying Men 750.00
19 CI,MA(c),Secret of the
   Twelve Eternals 750.00
20 CI,Slaves of the Sea Master. . 750.00
21 CI,MA(c),Eyes of the
   Other Worlds 550.00
22 CI,The Guardians of the
   Clockwork Universe 550.00
23 CI,MA(c),The Brain Pirates
   of Planet X 550.00
24 CI,MA(c),Doomsday on Earth. 550.00
25 CI,GK(c),The Day
   That Vanished 550.00
26 CI,Captain Vs. Miss Universe. 550.00
27 CI,MA(c),The Counterfeit
   Captain Comet 550.00

Strange Adventures — DC — Comics Values Annual

Strange Adventures #3
© DC Comics, Inc.

28 CI,Devil's Island in Space ... 550.00
29 CI,The Time Capsule From
 1,000,000 B.C. 550.00
30 CI,MA(c),Menace From the
 World of Make-Believe 500.00
31 CI,Lights Camera Action 500.00
32 CI,MA(c),The Challenge of
 Man-Ape the Mighty 500.00
33 CI,MA(c),The Human Beehive 500.00
34 CI,MA(c) 500.00
35 CI,MA(c),Cosmic Chessboard 500.00
36 CI,MA(c),The Grab-Bag
 Planet................. 500.00
37 CI,MA(c),The Invaders From
 the Golden Atom.......... 500.00
38 CI,MA(c),Seeing-Eye Humans 500.00
39 CI,MA(c),The Guilty Gorilla .. 550.00
40 CI,MA(c),The Mind Monster .. 500.00
41 CI,MA(c),The Beast From Out
 of Time................. 500.00
42 CI,MD,MA(c),The Planet of
 Ancient Children.......... 500.00
43 CI,MD,MA(c),The Phantom
 Prize Fighter............. 500.00
44 CI,MA(c),The Planet That
 Plotted Murder 500.00
45 CI,MD,MA(c),Gorilla World... 500.00
46 CI,MA(c),E:Captain Comet
 Interplanetary War Base.... 500.00
47 CI,MA(c),The Man Who Sold
 the Earth 500.00
48 CI,MA(c),Human Phantom ... 500.00
49 CI,MA(c),The Invasion
 from Indiana............. 500.00
50 CI,MA(c),The World Wrecker . 350.00
51 CI,MA(c),The Man Who
 Stole Air 350.00
52 CI,MA(c),Prisoner of the
 Parakeets............... 350.00
53 CI,MA(c),The Human Icicle .. 350.00
54 CI,MA(c),The Electric Man ... 300.00
55 CI,MA(c),The Gorilla Who
 Challanged the World,pt.I ... 300.00
56 CI,The Jungle Emperor,pt.II .. 300.00
57 CI,The Spy from Saturn 300.00
58 CI,I Hunted the Radium Man . 300.00
59 CI,The Ark From Planet X ... 300.00
60 CI,Across the Ages 300.00
61 CI,The Mirages From Space . 300.00
62 CI,The Fireproof Man....... 300.00
63 CI,I Was the Man in the Moon 300.00
64 CI,GK(c),Gorillas In Space... 300.00
65 CI,GK(c),Prisoner From Pluto. 300.00

66 CI,GK(c),The Human Battery . 300.00
67 CI,GK(c),Martian Masquerader 300.00
68 CI,The Man Who Couldn't
 Drown 300.00
69 CI,Gorilla Conquest of Earth . 300.00
70 CI,Triple Life of Dr. Pluto 300.00
71 CI,MSy,Zero Hour For Earth.. 225.00
72 CI,The Skyscraper That Came
 to Life 225.00
73 CI,Amazing Rain of Gems ... 225.00
74 CI,The Invisible Invader
 From Dimension X 225.00
75 CI,Secret of the Man-Ape.... 225.00
76 CI,B:Darwin Jones,The Robot
 From Atlantis 225.00
77 CI,A:Darwin Jones,The World
 That Slipped Out of Space .. 225.00
78 CI,The Secret of the Tom
 Thumb Spaceman 225.00
79 CI,A:Darwin Jones,Invaders
 from the Ice World 225.00
80 CI,Mind Robbers of Venus ... 225.00
81 CI,The Secret of the
 Shrinking Twins 225.00
82 CI,Giants of the Cosmic Ray . 200.00
83 CI,Assignment in Eternity.... 200.00
84 CI,Prisoners of the Atom
 Universe................ 200.00
85 CI,The Amazing Human Race 200.00
86 CI,The Dog That Saved the
 Earth 200.00
87 CI,New Faces For Old 200.00
88 CI,A:Darwin Jones,The Gorilla
 War Against Earth......... 200.00
89 CI,Earth For Sale.......... 200.00
90 CI,The Day I Became a
 Martian 200.00
91 CI,Midget Earthmen of Jupiter 200.00
92 CI,GK(c),The Amazing Ray
 of Knowledge 200.00
93 CI,GK(c),A:Darwin Jones,
 Space-Rescue By Proxy.... 200.00
94 MA,CI,GK(c),Fisherman of
 Space................. 200.00
95 CI,The World at my Doorstep. 200.00
96 CI,MA(c),The Menace of
 Saturn's Rings 200.00
97 CI,MA(c),MSy,Secret of the
 Space-Giant............. 200.00
98 CI,GK(c),MSy,Attack on Fort
 Satellite 200.00
99 CI,MSy,GK(c),Big Jump Into
 Space................. 200.00
100 CI,MSy,The Amazing Trial
 of John (Gorilla) Doe 250.00
101 CI,MSy,GK(c),Giant From
 Beyond................ 150.00
102 MSy,GK(c),The Three Faces
 of Barry Morrell........... 150.00
103 GK(c),The Man Who
 Harpooned Worlds 150.00
104 MSy,GK(c),World of Doomed
 Spacemen 150.00
105 MSy,GK(c),Fisherman From
 the Sea 150.00
106 MSy,CI,GK(c),Genie in the
 Flying Saucer 150.00
107 MSy,CI,GK(c),War of the
 Jovian Bubble-Men........ 150.00
108 MSy,CI,GK(c),The Human
 Pet of Gorilla Land 150.00
109 MSy,CI,GK(c),The Man Who
 Weighted 100 Tons........ 150.00
110 MSy,CI,GK(c),Hand From
 Beyond................ 150.00
111 MSy,CI,GK(c),Secret of
 the Last Earth-Man........ 150.00
112 MSy,CI,GK(c),Menace of
 the Size-Changing Spaceman 150.00
113 MSy,CI,GK(c),Deluge From
 Space................. 150.00

114 MSy,CI,GK(c),Secret of the
 Flying Buzz Saw.......... 150.00
115 MSy,CI,GK(c),The Great
 Space-Tiger Hunt 150.00
116 MSy,CI,RH,GK(c),Invasion
 of the Water Warriors 150.00
117 MSy,CI,GK(c),I:Atomic
 Knights................. 800.00
118 MSy,CI,The Turtle-Men of
 Space................. 175.00
119 MSy,CI,MA(c),Raiders
 From the Giant World...... 150.00
120 MSy,CI,MA,Attack of the Oil
 Demons 350.00
121 MSy,CI,MA(c),Invasion of the
 Flying Reptiles 125.00
122 MSy,CI,MA(c),David and the
 Space-Goliath............ 125.00
123 MSy,CI,MA(c),Secret of the
 Rocket-Destroyer 225.00
124 MSy,CI,MA(c),The Face-Hunter
 From Saturn............. 150.00
125 MSy,CI,The Flying Gorilla
 Menace 125.00
126 MSy,CI,MA(c),Return of the
 Neanderthal Man 200.00
127 MSy,CI,MA(c),Menace
 From the Earth-Globe...... 125.00
128 MSy,CI,MA(c),The Man
 With the Electronic Brain ... 125.00
129 MSy,CI,MA(c),The Giant
 Who Stole Mountains 150.00
130 MSy,CI,MA.War With the
 Giant Frogs 125.00
131 MSy,CI,MA(c),Emperor
 of the Earth 125.00
132 MSy,CI,MA(c),The Dreams
 of Doom................ 150.00
133 MSy,CI,MA(c),The Invisible
 Dinosaur................ 125.00
134 MSy,CI,MA(c), The Aliens
 Who Raided New York 150.00
135 MSy,CI,MA(c),Fishing Hole
 in the Sky............... 125.00
136 MSy,CI,MA(c),The Robot
 Who Lost Its Head 100.00
137 MSy,CI,MA(c),Parade of the
 Space-Toys 100.00
138 MSy,CI,MA(c),Secret of the
 Dinosaur Skeleton 125.00
139 MSy,CI,MA(c),Space-Roots
 of Evil.................. 100.00
140 MSy,CI,MA(c),Prisoner of
 the Space-Patch.......... 100.00

Strange Adventures #231
© DC Comics Inc.

CVA Page 148 — All comics prices listed are for *Near Mint* condition.

141 MSy,CI,MA(c),Battle Between
   the Two Earths 125.00
142 MSy,CI,MA(c),The Return of
   the Faceless Creature 100.00
143 MSy,CI,MA(c),The Face in
   the Atom-Bomb Cloud. 100.00
144 MSy,CI,MA(c),A:Atomic
   Knights, When the Earth
   Blacked Out 175.00
145 MSy,CI,MA,The Man Who
   Lived Forever 100.00
146 MSy,CI,MA(c),Perilous Pet
   of Space. 100.00
147 MSy,CI,MA(c),The Dawn-
   World Menace 125.00
148 MSy,CI,MA(c),Earth Hero,
   Number One. 100.00
149 MSy,CI,MA(c),Raid of
   the Rogue Star. 100.00
150 MSy,CI,MA(c),When Earth
   Turned into a Comet. 125.00
151 MSy,CI,MA(c),Invasion Via
   Radio-Telescope. 100.00
152 MSy,MA(c),The Martian
   Emperor of Earth 100.00
153 MSy,MA(c),Threat of the
   Faceless Creature 100.00
154 CI,MSy,MA,GK(c),Earth's
   Friendly Invaders 100.00
155 MSy,MA,GK(c),Prisoner
   of the Undersea World 100.00
156 MSy,CI,MA(c),The Man
   With the Head of Saturn . . . 100.00
157 MSy,CI,MA(c),Plight of
   the Human Cocoons. 100.00
158 MSy,CI,MA(c),The Mind
   Masters of Space 100.00
159 MSy,CI,MA(c),The Maze
   of Time. 100.00
160 MSy,CI,MA(c),A:Atomic
   Knights, Here Comes the
   Wild Ones 100.00
161 MSy,CI,MA(c),Earth's Frozen
   Heat Wave,E:Space Museum . 75.00
162 CI,MA(c),Mystery of the
   12 O'Clock Man 75.00
163 MA(c),The Creature in
   the Black Light 75.00
164 DD&SMo(c),I Became
   a Robot 75.00
165 DD&SMo(c),I Broke the
   Supernatural Barrier. 75.00
166 DD&SMo(c),I Lived in
   Two Bodies 75.00
167 JkS(c),The Team That
   Conquered Time. 75.00
168 JkS(c),I Hunted Toki
   the Terrible 75.00
169 DD&SMo(c),The Prisoner
   of the Hour Glass 75.00
170 DD&SMo(c),The Creature
   From Strange Adventures. . . . 75.00
171 Diary of the 9-Planet Man? . . 75.00
172 DD&SMo(c),I Became
   the Juggernaut Man 75.00
173 The Secret of the
   Fantasy Films. 75.00
174 JkS(c),The Ten Ton Man 75.00
175 Danger: This Town is
   Shrinking 75.00
176 DD&SMo(c),The Case of
   the Cosmonik Quartet. 75.00
177 I Lived a Hundred Lives,
   O:Immortal Man 75.00
178 JkS(c),The Runaway Comet. . 75.00
179 JkS(c),I Buried Myself Alive . . 75.00
180 CI,I:Animal Man,`I Was the
   Man With Animal Powers' . . . 300.00
181 The Man of Two Worlds 50.00
182 JkS(c),The Case of the
   Blonde Bombshell 50.00
183 JM(c),The Plot to Destroy
   the Earth 50.00
184 GK(c),A:Animal Man,The
   Return of the Man With
   Animal Powers 175.00
185 JkS(c),Ilda-Gangsters Inc. . . . 50.00
186 Beware the Gorilla Witch 50.00
187 JkS(c),O:The Enchantress . . . 60.00
188 SD,JkS(c),I Was the
   Four Seasons. 50.00
189 SD,JkS(c),The Way-Out
   Worlds of Bertram Tilley 50.00
190 CI,A:Animal Man,A-Man-the
   Hero with Animal Powers . . . 200.00
191 JkS(c),Beauty vs. the Beast . . 50.00
192 Freak Island. 50.00
193 The Villian Maker. 50.00
194 JkS(c),The Menace of the
   Super- Gloves 50.00
195 JkS(c),Secret of the Three
   Earth Dooms,A:Animal Man . 125.00
196 JkS(c),Mystery of the
   Orbit Creatures. 50.00
197 The Hostile Hamlet 40.00
198 JkS(c),Danger! Earth
   is Doomed 40.00
199 Robots of the Round Table. . . 40.00
200 . . . . 40.00
201 JkS,Animal Man. 75.00
202 . . . . 40.00
203 . . . . 40.00
204 . . . . 40.00
205 CI,I&O:Deadman 175.00
206 NA,MSy. 125.00
207 NA. 100.00
208 NA. 100.00
209 NA. 100.00
210 NA. 100.00
211 NA. 100.00
212 NA. 100.00
213 NA. 100.00
214 NA. 100.00
215 NA. 100.00
216 NA. 100.00
217 MA,MSy,A:Adam Strange. . . . 25.00
218 MA,CI,MSy. 25.00
219 CI,JKu 25.00
220 CI,JKu 25.00
221 CI 25.00
222 MA,New Adam Strange 40.00
223 MA,CI 25.00
224 MA,CI 25.00
225 MA,JKu 25.00
226 MA,JKu,New Adam Strange. . 40.00
227 JKu 25.00
228 NA(c). 35.00
229 . . . . 30.00
230 GM(c) 25.00
231 E:Atomic Knights 25.00
232 JKu 25.00
233 JKu 25.00
234 JKu 25.00
235 NA(c). 30.00
236. . . . . 20.00
237. . . . . 15.00
238 MK(c) 15.00
239 . . . . 15.00
240 MK(c) 15.00
241 . . . . 15.00
242 MA 15.00
243 F:Adam Strange. 15.00
244 Oct.–Nov., 1974. . . . . 15.00

Strange Adventures #243
© *DC Comics, Inc.*

STRANGE ADVENTURES
DC/Vertigo, Sept., 1999
1 (of 4) BB,DGb. 2.50
2 KJ,Expiration Date 2.50
3 . . . . 2.50
4 concl. 2.50

STRANGE SPORTS STORIES
Sept.–Oct., 1973
1 CS,DG 40.00
2 thru 6 . . . . @25.00

STRAY
Homage/DC March, 2001
1 SLo,AdP,Stray dog, 48-page. . . . 5.95

STREETS
1993
1 Tenderloin 5.00
2 Procurement. 5.00
3 . . . . 5.00

SUGAR & SPIKE
April-May, 1956
1 SM 3,000.00
2 SM 1,000.00
3 SM 750.00
4 SM 750.00
5 SM 750.00
6 thru 10 SM . . . . @450.00
11 thru 20 SM . . . . @350.00
21 thru 29 SM . . . . @250.00
30 SM,A:Scribbly 250.00
31 thru 50 SM . . . . @200.00
51 thru 70 SM . . . . @125.00
71 thru 79 SM . . . . @100.00
80 SM,I:Bernie the Brain. 100.00
81 thru 97 SM . . . . @75.00
98 SM,Oct.–Nov., 1971. . . . . 75.00
1 Facsimile Edition,rep.(2002) 2.95

STUCK RUBBER BABY
DC/Paradox Press
GN by Howard Cruise. 20.00

SUICIDE SQUAD
1987–91
1 LMc,Legends,I:Jihad. 2.50
2 LMc,V:The Jihad. 2.25
3 LMc,V:Female Furies 2.25
4 LMc,V:William Hell 2.25
5 LM,A:Penguin. 2.50

Suicide–Superboy DC Comics Values Annual

Suicide Squad #27
© DC Comics, Inc.

6 LM,A:Penguin. 2.50
7 LMc,V:Peoples Hero. 2.25
8 LMc,O:SquadMembers. 2.25
9 LMc,Millennium 2.25
10 LMc,A:Batman 2.25
11 LMc,A:Vixen,Speedy 2.25
12 LMc,Enchantress,
  V:Nightshade 2.25
13 LMc,X-over,JLI#13. . . . . 2.25
14 Nightshade Odyssey #1. . . . . . . 2.25
15 Nightshade Odyssey #2. . . . . . . 2.25
16 R:Shade 3.25
17 LMc,V:The Jihad 2.25
18 LMc,V:Jihad. 2.25
19 LMc,Personal Files 1988 . . . . . . 2.25
20 LMc,V:Mirror Master 2.25
21 LMc,bonus book #10 . . . . 2.25
22 LMc,D:Senator Cray 2.25
23 LMc,Invasion 2.25
24 LMc,V:Guerillas 2.25
25 L:Nightshade 2.25
26 D:Rick Flag,Jihad 2.25
27 Janus Directive #2. . . . . 2.25
28 Janus Directive #4. . . . . 2.25
29 Janus Directive #8. . . . . 2.25
30 Janus Directive #10. . . . . 2.25
31 Personal Files 1989. . . . . 2.25
32 V:Female Furies 2.25
33 GI,V:Female Furies 2.25
34 GI,V:Granny Goodness 2.25
35 LMc,GI,V:Female Furies 2.25
36 GI,D:Original Dr.Light. 2.25
37 GI,A:Shade,The Changing
  Man,V:Loa 2.25
38 LMc,GI,O:Bronze Tiger 2.25
39 GI,D:Loa 2.25
40 Phoenix Gambit #1,A:Batman
  Int. Poster 2.25
41 Phoenix Gambit #2 . . . . 2.25
42 Phoenix Gambit,A:Batman. 2.25
43 Phoenix Gambit,A:Batman. 2.25
44 I:New Atom,O:Captain
  Boomerang 2.25
45 A:Kobra 2.25
46 A:Kobra 2.25
47 GI,A:Kobra,D:Ravan 2.25
48 GI,New Thinker 2.25
49 GI,New Thinker 2.25
50 GI,50 Years of S.Squad 2.25
51 A:Deadshot 2.25
52 R:Docter Light 2.25
53 GI,The Dragon's Horde #1. . . . . 2.25
54 GI,The Dragon's Horde #2. . . . . 2.25
55 GI,The Dragon's Horde #3. . . . . 2.25
56 GI,The Dragon's Horde #4. . . . . 2.25
57 GI,The Dragon's Horde conc.. . . 2.25
58 GI,War of the Gods x-over 2.25
59 GI,A:Superman, Batman,
  Aquaman,A:Jihad, Hayoth 2.25
60 GI,A:Superman,Batman,
  Aquaman,Jihad,The Hayoth . . . 2.25
61 GI,A:Superman,Batman,
  Aquaman,V:Jihad. 2.25
62 GI,R:Ray Palmer,A:Batman
  Superman,Aquaman. 2.25
63 GI,I:Gvede, Lord of Death 2.25
64 GI,A:Task Force X 2.25
65 GI,Bronze Tiger 2.25
66 GI,Final Iss.E:Suicide Squad . . . 2.25
Ann.#1 GN,V:Argent,A:Manhunter . 2.25

SUICIDE SQUAD
Sept., 2001

1 KG,R:Suicide Squad. 2.50
2 KG,F:Sgt. Rock 2.50
3 KG,Ants 2.50
4 KG,Need to Know. 2.50
5 KG,Deadshot 2.50
6 KG,new squad 2.50
7 KG,near KooeyKkooeykooey . . . 2.50
8 KG,Casualties of War 2.50
9 KG,Havana vs. the Wall 2.50
10 KG,JSe,back in time 2.50
11 KG,JSe,old foe 2.50
12 KG, F:JSA,final issue. 2.50

SUPERBOY
1949–76

1 Superman (c). 15,000.00
2 `Superboy Day' 3,000.00
3 . . . . 2,000.00
4 The Oracle of Smallville 1,500.00
5 Superboy meets Supergirl,
  Pre-Adventure #252. . . . . . 1,300.00
6 I:Humpty Dumpty,the Hobby
  Robber 1,200.00
7 WB,V:Humpty Dumpty 1,200.00
8 CS,I:Superbaby,V:Humpty
  Dumpty 1,000.00
9 V:Humpty Dumpty 1,000.00
10 CS,I:Lana Lang. 1,000.00
11 CS,2nd Lang,V:Humpty
  Dumpty 850.00
12 CS,The Heroes Club 850.00
13 CS,Scout of Smallville 850.00
14 CS,I:Marsboy. 850.00
15 CS,A:Superman. 850.00
16 CS,A:Marsboy. 550.00
17 CS,Superboy's Double. 550.00
18 CS,Lana Lang-Hollywood
  Star. 550.00
19 CS,The Death of Young
  Clark Kent 550.00
20 CS,The Ghost that Haunted
  Smallville 550.00
21 CS,Lana Lang-Magician. 450.00
22 CS,The New Clark Kent. 450.00
23 CS,The Super Superboy 450.00
24 CS,The Super Fat Boy of
  Steel 450.00
25 CS,Cinderella of Smallville . . . 450.00
26 CS,A:Superbaby 450.00
27 CS,Clark Kent-Runaway. 450.00
28 CS,The Man Who Defeated
  Superboy 450.00
29 CS,The Puppet Superboy . . . 450.00
30 CS,I:Tommy Tuttle 350.00
31 CS,The Amazing Elephant
  Boy From Smallville 350.00
32 CS,His Majesty King
  Superboy 350.00
33 CS,The Crazy Costumes of

Superboy #141
© DC Comics, Inc.

  the Boy of Steel 350.00
34 CS,Hep Cats o/Smallville. . . . 350.00
35 CS,The Five Superboys. 350.00
36 . . . . 350.00
37 CS,I:Thaddeus Lang 350.00
38 CS,A:Superman. 350.00
39 CS,Public Chimp #1. . . . . 350.00
40 CS,Boy w/Superboy Powers . 350.00
41 CS,The Magic Necklace. 300.00
42 CS,Superboy Meets
  Superbrave. 300.00
43 CS,Gaucho of Smallville 300.00
44 CS,Super-Farmer o/Smallville 300.00
45 The Amazing Adventure of
  Superboy's Costume 300.00
46 A Trap For Superboy 300.00
47 The Battle of Fort Smallville . . 300.00
48 CS,A:Superman. 300.00
49 CS,Boy Without Super-Suit . . 300.00
50 I:Metallo (Jor-El's Robot) 350.00
51 The Super-Giant of Smallville. 300.00
52 I:Krypto 200.00
53 CS,The Powerboy from Earth. 200.00
54 CS,A:Superman. 200.00
55 CS,The Silent Superboy. 200.00
56 CS,A:Jimmy Olson. 200.00
57 CS,A:Krypto. 200.00
58 CS,One-Man Baseball Team . 200.00
59 CS,The Great Kryptonite
  Mystery 200.00
60 CS,A:Superbaby 200.00
61 The 100,000 Cowboy. 200.00
62 The School For Superboys. . . 175.00
63 I:Gloria Kent 175.00
64 CS,The Two Boys of Steel . . . 175.00
65 CS,A:Krypto. 175.00
66 Superboy's Moonlight Spell . . 175.00
67 The Family with X-Ray Eyes . 175.00
68 I:Klax-Ar 175.00
69 O&I:Bizarro 650.00
70 How Superboy Learned
  To Fly 150.00
71 O:Superboy's Glasses 150.00
72 A:Superbaby 150.00
73 The Flying Girl of Smallville . . 150.00
74 CS,A:Superbaby 150.00
75 A:Jor-El & Lara 150.00
76 A:Superbaby 150.00
77 I:Super Monkey 150.00
78 Superboy's Best Friend 150.00
79 O:Mr.Mxyzptlk 250.00
80 A:Jar-El & Lara 150.00
81 Superboy meets Supergirl . . . 200.00
82 The Weakling From Earth . . . 125.00
83 A:Bizarro Krypto. 125.00

CVA Page 150   All comics prices listed are for *Near Mint* condition.

DC — Superboy

#	Description	Price
83	I:Kryptonite Kid	125.00
84	A:William Tell	125.00
85	Secret of Mighty Boy	125.00
86	I:PeteRoss,A:Legion	250.00
87	I:Scarlet Jungle of Krypton	125.00
88	The Invader from Earth	125.00
89	I:Mon-El	400.00
90	A:Pete Ross	125.00
91	CS,Superboy in Civil War	125.00
92	CS,I:Destructo,A:Lex Luthor	125.00
93	A:Legion	125.00
94	I:Superboy Revenge Squad, A:Pete Ross	100.00
95	Imaginary Story,The Super Family From Krypton	100.00
96	A:Pete Ross,Lex Luthor	100.00
97	Krypto Story	100.00
98	Legion,I&O:Ultraboy	150.00
99	O: The Kryptonite Kid	100.00
100	I:Phantom Zone	250.00
101	The Handsome Hound of Steel	90.00
102	O:Scarlet Jungle of Krypton	90.00
103	CS,A:King Arthur,Jesse James Red Kryptonite	90.00
104	O:Phantom Zone	90.00
105	CS,`The Simpleton of Steel'	90.00
106	CS,A:Brainiac	90.00
107	CS,I:Superboy Club of Smallville	100.00
108	The Kent's First Super Son	90.00
109	The Super Youth of Bronze	90.00
110	A:Jor-El	90.00
111	Red Kryptonite Story	90.00
112	CS,A:Superbaby	90.00
113	`The Boyhood of Dad Kent'	90.00
114	A:Phantom Zone, Mr.Mxyzptlk	90.00
115	A:Phantom Zone,Lex Luthor	90.00
116	`The Wolfboy of Smallville'	90.00
117	A:Legion	90.00
118	CS,`The War Between Superboy and Krypto'	90.00
119	V:Android Double	90.00
120	A:Mr.Mxyzptlk	90.00
121	CS,A:Jor-El,Lex Luthor	90.00
122	Red Kryptonite Story	90.00
123	CS,The Curse of the Superboy Mummy	90.00
124	I:Insect Queen	90.00
125	O:Kid Psycho	90.00
126	O:Krypto	90.00
127	A:Insect Queen	75.00
128	A:Phantom Zone,Kryptonite Kid,Dev En	75.00
129	rep.A:Mon-El,SuperBaby	100.00
130		75.00
131	A;Lex Luthor,Mr.Mxyzptlk,I:Space Canine Patrol Agents	75.00
132	CS,A:Space Canine Patrol Agents	75.00
133	A:Robin, repr.	75.00
134	`The Scoundrel of Steel'	75.00
135	A:Lex Luthor	75.00
136	A:Space Canine Agents	75.00
137	Mysterious Mighty Mites	75.00
138	giant, Superboy's Most Terrific Battles	90.00
139	`The Samson of Smallville'	60.00
140	V:The Gambler	50.00
141	No Mercy for a Hero	50.00
142	A:Super Monkey	50.00
143	NA(c),`The Big Fall'	50.00
144	`Superboy's Stolen Identity'	50.00
145	NA(c)Kents become young	50.00
146	NA(c),CS,`The Runaway'	50.00
147	giant O:Legion	55.00
148	NA(c),CS,C:PolarBoy	50.00
149	NA(c),A:Bonnie & Clyde	50.00
150	JAb,V:Mr.Cipher	50.00
151	NA(c),A:Kryptonite Kid	50.00
152	NA(c),WW	50.00
153	NA(c),WW,A;Prof Mesmer	50.00
154	WW(i),A:Jor-El & Lara `Blackout For Superboy'	50.00
155	NA(c),WW,`Revolt of the Teenage Robots'	50.00
156	giant	50.00
157	WW	50.00
158	WW,A:Jor-El & Lara	50.00
159	WW(i),A:Lex Luthor	50.00
160	WW,`I Chose Eternal Exile'	50.00
161	WW,`The Strange Death of Superboy'	50.00
162	A:Phantom Zone	50.00
163	NA(c),`Reform School Rebel'	50.00
164	NA(c),`Your Death Will Destroy Me'	50.00
165	giant	50.00
166	NA(c),A:Lex Luthor	25.00
167	NA(c),MA,A:Superbaby	25.00
168	NA(c),MA,Hitler	25.00
169	MA,A:Lex Luthor	25.00
170	MA,A:Genghis Khan	25.00
171	MA,A:Aquaboy	25.00
172	MA(i),GT,A:Legion, O:Lightning Lad,Yango	30.00
173	NA(c),GT,DG,O:CosmicBoy	25.00
174	giant	40.00
175	NA(c),MA,Rejuvenation of Ma & Pa Kent	25.00
176	NA(c),MA,GT,WW,A:Legion	25.00
177	MA,A:Lex Luthor	30.00
178	NA(c),MA,Legion Reprint	30.00
179	MA,A:Lex Luthor	30.00
180	MA,O:Bouncing Boy	30.00
181	MA	30.00
182	MA,A:Bruce Wayne	30.00
183	MA,GT,CS(rep),A:Legion	30.00
184	MA,WW,O:Dial H rep	30.00
185	A:Legion	20.00
186	MA	15.00
187	MA	15.00
188	MA,DC,O:Karkan,A:Legn	15.00
189	MA	15.00
190	MA,WW	15.00
191	MA,DC,O:SunBoy retold	15.00
192	MA	15.00
193	MA,WW,N:Chameleon Boy, Shrinking Violet	15.00
194	MA	15.00
195	MA,WW,I:Wildfire, N:Phantom Girl	15.00
196	last Superboy solo	30.00
197	DC,Legion begins, New Costumes,I:Tyr	30.00
198	DC,N:Element Lad, Princess Projects	20.00
199	DC,A:Tyr, Otto Orion	20.00
200	DC,M:Bouncing Boy & Duo Damsel	25.00
201	DC,Wildfire returns	18.00
202	N:Light Lass	60.00
203	MGr,D:Invisible Kid	25.00
204	MGr,A:Supergirl	15.00
205	MGr,CG,100 pages	50.00
206	MGr,A:Ferro Lad	25.00
207	MGr,O:Lightning Lad	25.00
208	MGr,CS,68pp,Legion of Super Villains	28.00
209	MGr,N:Karate Kid	20.00
210	MGr,O:Karate Kid	25.00
211	MGr	15.00
212	MGr,L:Matter Eater Lad	15.00
213	MGr,V:Benn Pares	15.00
214	MGr,V:Overseer	15.00
215	MGr,A:Emerald Empress	15.00
216	MGr,I:Tyroc	15.00
217	MGr,I:Laurel Kent	15.00
218	J:Tyroc,A:Fatal Five	15.00
219	MGr,A:Fatal Five	15.00
220	MGi,BWi	15.00
221	MGr,BWi,I:Grimbor	10.00
222	MGr,BWi,MN,BL,A:Tyroc	10.00
223	MGr,BWi	10.00
224	MGr,BWi,V:Pulsar Stargrave	10.00
225	MGr(c),BWi,JSh,MN	10.00
226	MGr(c),MN,JSh,JA,I:Dawnstar	10.00
227	MGr(c),JSon,JA,V:Stargrave	10.00
228	MGr(c),JSh,JA,D:Chemical King	10.00
229	MGr(c),JSh,JA,V:Deregon	10.00
230	MGr(c),JSh,V:Sden	10.00
Spec. #147 facsimile (2003)		6.95

Becomes:

SUPERBOY & THE LEGION OF SUPER-HEROES
1976–79

#	Description	Price
231	MGr(c),JSh,MN,JA,doub.size begins,V:Fatal Five	18.00
232	MGr(c),JSh,RE,JA,V:Dr.Regulus	18.00
233	MGr(c),JSh,BWi,MN,BL,I:Infinite Man	18.00
234	MGr(c),RE,JA,V:Composite Creature	18.00
235	MGr,GT	18.00
236	MGr(c),BMc,JSh,MN,JRu,V:Khunds	18.00
237	MGr(c),WS,JA	18.00
238	JSn(c),reprint	18.00
239	MGR(c),JSn,JRu,Ultra Boy accused	18.00
240	MGr(c),HC,BWi,JSh,BMc,O:Dawnstar;V:Grimbor	18.00
241	JSh,BMc,A:Ontir	18.00
242	JSh,BMc,E:Double Size	18.00
243	MGr(c),JA,JSon	18.00
244	JSon,V:Dark Circle	18.00
245	MA,JSon,V:Mordu	18.00
246	MGr(c),JSon,DG,MA,V:Fatal Five	15.00
247	JSon,JA,anniv.issue	15.00
248	JSon	15.00
249	JSon,JA	15.00
250	JSn,V:Omega	15.00
251	JSn,Brainiac 5 goes insane	15.00
252	JSon,V:Starburst bandits	10.00
253	JSon,I:Blok,League of Super Assassins	10.00
254	JSon,V:League of Super Assassins	10.00
255	JSon,A:Jor-El	10.00

Superboy #212 © DC Comics Inc.

All comics prices listed are for *Near Mint* condition.

Superboy–Superboy And

256 JSon 10.00
257 SD,JSon,DA,V:Psycho
   Warrior 10.00
258 JSon,V:Psycho Warrior 10.00
Becomes:

LEGION OF SUPER HEROES
[2nd Series]

[NEW ADVENTURES OF] SUPERBOY
Jan., 1980

1 KS 6.00
2 thru 6 KS . . . . @3.00
7 KS,JSa. 3.00
8 thru 33 KS . . . . @3.00
34 KS,I:Yellow Peri. 3.00
35 thru 44 KS . . . . @3.00
45 KS,I:Sunburst 3.00
46 KS,A:Sunburst. 3.00
47 KS,A:Sunburst. 3.00
48 KS. 3.00
49 KS,A:Zatara. 3.00
50 KS,KG,A:Legion 3.00
51 KS,FM(c)In Between Years 3.00
52 KS 3.00
53 KS. 3.00
54 KS. 3.00

SUPERBOY
1990–91

1 TV Tie-in,JM,photo(c) 5.00
2 JM,T.J.White Abducted 3.00
3 JM,`Fountain of Youth' 3.00
4 JM,`Big Man on Campus' 3.00
5 JM,Legion Homage 3.00
6 JM,Luthor. 3.00
7 JM,Super Boy Arrested. 3.00
8 JM,AAd(i),Bizarro 3.00
9 JM/CS,PhantomZone#1 . . . . . . 3.00
10 JM/CS,PhantomZone#2. . . . . . 3.00
11 CS. 3.00
12 CS,X-Mas in Smallville. 3.00
Becomes:

ADVENTURES OF SUPERBOY
1991

13 A:Mr.Mxyzptlk 3.50
14 CS,A:Brimstone. 3.00
15 CS,Legion Homage 3.00
16 CS,Into the Future 3.00
17 CS,A:Luthor. 3.00

Superboy #6 © DC Comics, Inc.

18 JM,`At the Movies'. 3.00
19 JM,Blood Transfusion 3.00
20 JM,O:Nicknack,(G.Gottfried
   script). 3.00
21 V:Frost Monster. 3.00
22 . . . . 3.00
Spec.#1 CS,A:Ma Kent. 2.50

SUPERBOY
[2nd Series]
1994

1 B:KK(s),TG,DHz,V:Sidearm 4.00
2 TG,DHz,I:Knockout. 2.50
3 TG,DHz,I:Scavenger. 2.50
4 TG,DHz,MeP,I:Lock n' Load . . . 2.50
5 TG,DHz,I:Silver Sword 2.50
6 TG,DHz,Worlds Collide,pt.3
   C:Rocket 2.50
7 Worlds Collide, pt.8,V:Rift. 2.50
8 Zero Hour,A:Superboy 2.50
9 Silican Dragon 2.50
10 Monster 2.50
11 Techno. 2.50
12 Copperhead. 2.50
13 Watery Grave,pt.1 . . . . 2.50
14 Watery Grave,pt.2 . . . . 2.50
15 Watery Grave,pt.3 . . . . 2.50
16 TG,DHz,KK,V:Loose Cannon
   [New Miraweb format begins] . . 2.50
17 TG,DHz,KK Looking for
   Roxy Leech 2.50
18 V:Valor. 2.50
19 . . . . 2.50
20 R:Scavenger 2.50
21 KK,TG,DHz,Future Tense,Pt.1 . . 2.50
22 KK,TG,DHz,Underworld
   Unleashed x-over. 2.50
23 KK,TG,DHz,V:Technician 2.50
24 KK,TG,DHz,V:Silversword 2.50
25 New Gods 3.00
26 KK,DHz,Losin'it,pt.2. . . . . 2.25
27 KK,DHz,Losin'it,pt.3. . . . . 2.25
28 KK,DHz,Losin'it,pt.4 (of 6) . . . 2.25
29 . . . . 2.25
30 . . . . 2.25
31 . . . . 2.25
32 RMz(s),RBe,DHz,V:King Shark . 2.25
33 RMz(s),RBe,DHz, survivors flee
   to Hawaii, Final Night tie-in . . . 2.25
34 RMz(s),RBe,DHz, V:Dubbilex. . . 2.25
35 RMz(s),RBe,DHz, Superboy
   abducted 2.25
36 RMz(s),RBe,DHz,V:King SHark . 2.25
37 RMz(s),SB,V:Sledge 2.25
38 RMz,RBe,DHz,Meltdown,pt.1 . . 2.25
39 RMz,RBe,DHz,Meltdown,pt.2 . . 2.25
40 RMz,RBe,DHz,Meltdown,pt.2,
   x-over. 2.25
41 RMz,RBe,DHz,Meltdown,pt.3 . . 2.25
42 SB, ... 2.25
43 SB,Lanie & Ken 2.25
44 SB,island of teenagers. 2.25
45 RMz,DHz,TGu,A:Legion. 2.25
46 RMz,DHz,TGu,V:Silver Sword . . 2.25
47 RMz,DHz,TGu,F:Green Lantern . 2.25
48 BKs,DHz,TGu,theme park 2.25
49 DHz. 2.25
50 KK,TGu,Last Boy on Earth pt.1 . 2.25
51 KK,TGu,Last Boy on Earth pt.2 . 2.25
52 KK,TGu,Last Boy on Earth pt.3 . 2.25
53 KK,TGu,Last Boy on Earth pt.4 . 2.25
54 KK,TGu,A:Wild Men. 2.25
55 KK,TGu,V:Grokk, Hex 2.25
56 KK,TGu,Project Cadmus 2.25
57 KK,TGu,Demolition Run,pt.1 . . 2.25
58 KK,TGu,Demolition Run,pt.2 . . 2.25
59 KK,DAb,A:Superman 2.25
60 KK,TGu,A:JLA,Hyper-
   Tension,pt.1 . . . . 2.25
61 KK,TGu,Hyper-Tension,pt.2 . . . 2.25

Superboy 2nd Series #9
© DC Comics, Inc.

62 KK,TGu,Hyper-Tension,pt.3 . . . 2.25
63 KK,TGu,Hyper-Tension,pt.4 . . . 2.25
64 KK,TGu,Hyper-Tension,pt.5 . . . 2.25
65 KK,TGu,guest-star packed 2.25
66 KK,TGu,Wild Lands 2.25
67 KK,AaL, in Wild Lands. 2.25
68 KK,TG,MM,Day of Judgment
   x-over, F:Demon. 2.25
69 KK,TG,return to Hawaii 2.25
70 KK,TG,Evil Factory,pt.1 . . . . . . 2.25
71 KK,TG,Evil Factory,pt.2 . . . . . . 2.25
72 KK,TG,Evil Factory,pt.3 . . . . . . 2.25
73 KK,TG,Evil Factory,pt.4 . . . . . . 2.25
74 KK,TG,Sins of Youth 2.25
75 KK,TG,as normal teenager 2.25
76 KK,TG,still Superboy 2.25
77 KK,TG,MBa,V:Kossak 2.25
78 KK,TG,prisoners 2.25
79 KK,TG,V:Kossak the Slaver . . . 2.25
80 BHr,F:The Titans,pt.1 . . . . 2.25
81 BHr,F:The Titans,pt.2 . . . . 2.25
82 JMz,V:Negative G 2.25
83 PFe,F:Young Justice 2.25
84 PFe,off to L.A. 2.25
85 PFe,A:Batman,Batgirl 2.25
86 PFe,shotgun wedding 2.25
87 V:Shrapnel,Deadman 2.25
88 PFe,V:DNAngels 2.25
89 PFe,Our Worlds at War, tie-in . 2.25
90 PFe,Our Worlds at War, tie-in . 2.25
91 PFe,Our Worlds at War, tie-in . 2.25
92 PFe,R:Doctor Sin. 2.25
93 PFe,Joker:Last Laugh, tie-in . . . 2.25
94 JMC,finding an apartment 2.25
95 JP,JMC,Slaughterhouse Six 2.25
96 JP,Trixie & Wipeout 2.25
97 JP,JMC,F:Wipeout 2.25
98 JP,JMC,F:Jimmy Olsen 2.25
99 WorldWithoutYoungJustice,pt.4 . 2.25
100 JP,KK,TG,48-pg. 3.50
Ann.#1 Elseworlds Story. 3.50
Ann.#2 KK,BKs, Year One 4.50
Ann.#3 Legends o/t Dead Earth . . . 3.50
Ann.#4 Pulp Heroes (High-
   Adventure). 4.50
Spec.#1,000,000 KK,TGu. 2.50

SUPERBOY & THE RAVERS
1996–98

1 KK&SMt(s),PaP,DDv, ... 2.50
2 KK&SMt(s),PaP,DDv,InterC.E.P.T.
   pursues Superboy and Kaliber . 2.50

Comics Values Annual — DC — Superboy–Supergirl

3 KK&SMT(s),PaP,DDv,teleported
  to Rann,V:Half-Life 2.50
4 KK&SMt(s),PaP,DDv,A:Adam
  Strange 2.50
5 KK&SMt(s),PaP,DDv,O:Hero 2.50
6 KK&SMt(s),PaP,DDv, ... 2.50
7 KK&SMt(s),PaP,DDv, Road Trip,
  pt.1,A:Impulse 2.50
8 KK&SMt(s),PaP,DDv, Road Trip,
  pt.2,A:Guy Gardner 2.50
9 KK&SMt(s),PaP,DDv, Road Trip,
  pt.3,A:Aura 2.50
10 KK&SMt(s),DDv,Meltdown,pt.4 . . 2.50
11 KK&SMt(s),PaP,DDv, Superboy
   presumed dead 2.50
12 KK(s),AaL, ... 2.50
13 KK(s),SMt,F:Hero,Sparx 2.50
14 KK&SMt(s),Genesis tie-in 2.50
15 KK&SMt(s),new Rave 2.50
16 KK&SMt(s),Half-Life. 2.50
17 KK&SMt(s),Kaliber. 2.50
18 KK&SMt(s),V:Qward 2.50
19 . . . . 2.50

SUPERBOY PLUS
Nov., 1996
1 RMz(s),ASm,F:Captain
  Marvel Jr. 3.50
2 LKa,AWi,ALa,F:Slither 3.00

SUPERBOY/RISK DOUBLE-SHOT
Dec., 1997
1 DJu,JoP,x-over 2.50

SUPERBOY'S LEGION
Feb., 2001
1 (of 2) Elseworlds, 48-page 5.95
2 MFm,AD, concl. 5.95

SUPER DC GIANT
1970–71, 1976
S-13 Binky 150.00
S-14 JKu,GK,Top Guns of
   the West. 75.00
S-15 JKu,GK,Western Comics . . 65.00
S-16 JKu,Best of the Brave
   & the Bold 50.00
S-17 Love 1970 . . . . 350.00
S-18 Three Mouseketeers. 150.00
S-19 NA,Jerry Lewis 175.00
S-20 NA,JK,House of Mystery. . . 100.00
S-21 Love 1971 . . . . 400.00
S-22 JKu,Top Guns of the West . . 40.00
S-23 The Unexpected. 50.00
S-24 Supergirl 50.00
S-25 Challengers of the Unknown. 50.00
S-26 Aquaman 40.00
S-27 GK,Strange Flying Saucer
   Adventures (1976) 35.00

SUPER FRIENDS
Nov., 1976
1 ECh(c),JO,RE,`Fury of the
  Superfoes',A:Penguin. 40.00
2 RE,A:Penguin. 20.00
3 RF(c),RF,A:JLA. 15.00
4 RF,V:Riddler,I:Skyrocket 15.00
5 RF(c),RF,V:Greenback 15.00
6 RF(c),RF,A:Atom 12.00
7 RF(c),RF,I:Zan & Jana,
  A:Seraph 12.00
8 RF(c),RF,A:JLA. 12.00
9 RF(c),RF,A:JLA,I:Iron Maiden . . 12.00
10 RF(c),RF`TheMonkeyMenace' . 12.00
11 RF(c),RF 10.00
12 RF(c),RF,A:TNT 10.00
13 RF(c),RF 10.00
14 RF(c),RF 10.00
15 RF(c),RF, A:The Elementals. . . 10.00
16 RF(c),RF,V:The Cvags. 10.00
17 RF(c),RF,A:Queen Hippolyte . . 10.00
18 KS(c),V:Tuantra,Time Trapper . 10.00
19 RF(c),RF,V:Menagerie Man . . . 10.00
20 KS(c),KS,V:Frownin' Fritz. 10.00
21 RF(c),RF,V:Evil Superfriends
   Doubles 9.00
22 RF(c),RF,V:Matador Mob 9.00
23 FR(c),RF,V:Mirror Master 9.00
24 RF(c),RF,V:Exorians 9.00
25 RF(c),RF,V:Overlord,
   A:Green Lantern, Mera. 9.00
26 RF(c),RF,A:Johnny Jones 9.00
27 RF(c),RF,`The Spaceman Who
   Stole the Stars 9.00
28 RF(c),RF,A:Felix Faust. 9.00
29 RF(c),RF,B.U.KS,`Scholar From
   the Stars 9.00
30 RF(c),RF,V:Grodd & Giganta . . 9.00
31 RF(c),RF,A:Black Orchid 10.00
32 KS(c),KS,A:Scarecrow. 8.00
33 RF(c),RF,V:Menagerie Man . . . 8.00
34 RF(c)RF,`The Creature That
   Slept a Million Years' 8.00
35 RT,`Circus o/t Super Stars 8.00
36 RF(c),RF,A:Plastic Man
   & Woozy 8.00
37 RF(c),RF,A:Supergirl;
   B.U. A:Jack O'Lantern 8.00
38 RF(c),RF,V:Grax;
   B.U. A:Serpah 8.00
39 RF(c),RF,A:Overlord;
   B.U. A:Wonder Twins 8.00
40 RF(c),RF,V:The Monacle;
   B.U. Jack O'Lantern 8.00
41 RF(c),RF,V:Toyman;
   B.U. A:Seraph 8.00
42 RT,A:Flora,V:Flame; B.U.Wonder
   Twins' Christmas Special 8.00
43 KS(c),RT,V:Futuro; B.U.JSon
   A:Plastic Man. 8.00
44 RF(c),RT,`Peril o/t Forgotten
   Identities'; B.U.Jack O'Lantern . 8.00
45 KS(c),RT,A:Bushmaster,
   Godiva, Rising Sun, Olympian,
   Little Mermaid, Wild Huntsman;
   B.U. Plastic Man,V: Sinestro. . . 8.00
46 RT,V:The Conqueror;
   B.U. BO,Seraph 8.00
47 KS(c),RT,A:Green Fury

Aug., 1981 . . . . 8.00
TPB Super Friends, 176-page. . . . 14.95
TPB Truth,Justice&Peace(2003) . . 14.95

SUPERGIRL
[1st Regular Series]
Nov., 1972—Sept., 1974
1 `Trail of the Madman';
  Superfashions From Fans;
  B:B.U. DG,Zatanna. 55.00
2 BO(c)A:Prof.Allan,Bottle
  City of Kandor 25.00
3 BO(c),`The Garden of Death' . . 20.00
4 V:Super Scavanger. 25.00
5 BO(c),A:Superman,V:Dax; B.U.
  MA:Rep.Hawkman #4 . . . . 30.00
6 BO(c),`Love & War' 25.00
7 BO(c),A:Zatanna. 25.00
8 BO(c),A:Superman,Green
  Lantern, Hawkman 30.00
9 BO(c),V:Sharkman 25.00
10 A:Prey,V:Master Killer 25.00

[DARING NEW ADVENTURES OF] SUPERGIRL
[2nd Regular Series]
Nov., 1982
1 CI,BO,I:Psi; B:B.U.Lois Lane . . . 3.00
2 CI,BO,C:Decay. 3.00
3 CI,BO,V:Decay,`Decay Day' 3.00
4 CI,BO,V:The Gang 3.00
5 CI,BO,V:The Gang 3.00
6 CI,BO,V:The Gang 3.00
7 CI,BO,V:The Gang 3.00
8 CI,BO,A:Doom Patrol 3.00
9 CI,BO,V:Reactron
  A:Doom Patrol 3.00
10 CI,BO,`Radiation Fever'. 3.00
11 CI,BO,V:Chairman 3.00
12 CI,BO,V:Chairman 3.00
13 CI,BO,N:Supergirl,A:Superman
   V:Blackstarr 3.00
Becomes:

SUPERGIRL
Dec., 1983–Sept., 1984
14 GK(c),CI,BO,V:Blackstarr
   A:Rabbi Nathan Zuber 3.00
15 CI,BO,V:Blackstarr,
   A:Blackstarr's Mom 3.00
16 KG/BO(c),CI,BO,
   A:Ambush Bug 3.00
17 CI/DG(c),CI,BO,V:Matrix
   Prime 3.00
18 DG(c),CI,BO, V:Kraken 3.00
19 EB/BO(c),CI,BO,`Who Stole
   Supergirl's Life'. 3.00
20 CI,BO,C:JLA,Teen Titans:
   Teh Parasite 3.00
21 EB/BO(c),EB,Kryptonite Man . . . 3.00
22 EB(c),CI,BO,`I Have Seen the
   Future & it is Me' 3.00
23 EB(c),CI,BO,`The Future
   Begins Today 3.00
Spec.#1 JL/DG(c),GM,MovieAdapt . 3.00
Spec.#1 AT,Honda give-away 3.00

[Limited Series], 1994
1 KGa(c),B:RSt(s),JBr,O:Supergirl . 5.00
2 KGa(c),JBr. 4.00
3 KGa(c),JBr,D:Clones 3.00
4 KGa(c),RSt(s),JBr,final Issue . . . 3.00

SUPERGIRL
Sept., 1996
1 PDd(s),GFr,CaS, ... 11.00
1a 2nd printing 3.00

Super DC Gian #S-15
© DC Comics Inc.

All comics prices listed are for *Near Mint* condition.

Supergirl–Superman — DC — Comics Values Annual

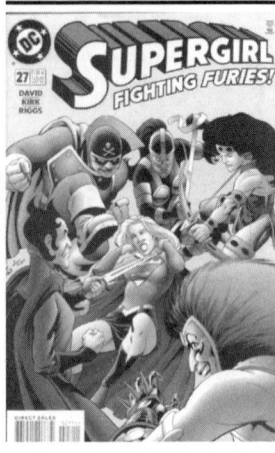

Supergirl #27 © DC Comics, Inc.

2 PDd(s),GFr,CaS,V:Chakat	5.00
3 PDd(s),GFr,CaS,V:Grodd, Final Night tie-in	5.00
4 PDd(s),GFr,CaS,transformed into savage	4.00
5 PDd(s),GFr,CaS,Supergirl visits the Kents,V:Chemo	4.00
6 PDd(s),GFr,CaS,	4.00
7 PDd(s),GFr,CaS,Supergirl learns about Linda Danvers	4.00
8 PDd(s),GFr,CaS,Buzz gets date with Supergirl	4.00
9 PDd(s),GFr,CaS,V:Tempus	4.00
10 PDd(s),Linda tries to relax	4.00
11 PDd(s),CaS,V:Silver Banshee	4.00
12 PDd(s),Mattie possessed by Silver Banshee	4.00
13 CaS, 3 girls dreams invaded by incubus	3.00
14 PDa,CaS,Genesis tie-in	3.00
15 PDa,CaS,V:Extremists	3.00
16 PDa,CaS,F:Power Girl	3.00
17 PDa,CaS,L-Ron, Despero	3.00
18 PDa,CaS,V:Despero	3.00
19	3.00
20 PDa,CaS,Millennium Giants	3.00
21 PDa,CaS,Comet	3.00
22 PDa,	3.00
23 PDa,A:Steel	3.00
24 PDa,Avenging Angels x-over	3.00
25 PDa,truth about Comet	3.00
26 PDd,truth discovered	3.00
27 PDd(s),V:Female Furies,pt.1	3.00
28 PDd(s),V:Female Furies,pt.2	3.00
29 PDd(s),V:Female Furies,pt.3	3.00
30 PDd(s),V:Matrix	3.00
31 PDd(s),A:Superman	3.00
32 PDd(s),SeP,V:Mr.Carnivean	3.00
33 PDd(s),V:Mr.Carnivean	3.00
34 PDd(s),V:Parasite	3.00
35 PDd(s),V:Parasite, concl.	3.00
36 PDd(s),Young Justice x-over,Hell's Angel's,pt.2	2.50
37 PDd(s),Hell's Angels,pt.4	2.50
38 PDd(s),Day of Judgment x-over	2.50
39 PDd(s),F:Comet	2.50
40 PDd(s)	2.50
41 PDd(s),F:Ember,V:Satan Girl	2.50
42 PDd(s),dates Dick Malverne	2.50
43 PDd(s),date become nightmare	2.50
44 PDd(s),F:Dick Malverne,dying	2.50
45 PDd(s),F:Comet,V:Carnivore	2.50
46 PDd(s),V:Comet,Carnivore	2.50
47 PDd(s),V:Carnivore	2.50
48 PDd(s),	2.50
49 PDd(s),V:Carnivore	2.50
50 PDd(s),48-pg.	4.00
51 PDd(s),to Metropolis, minus powers	2.50
52 PDd(s),V:Riot & Prankster	2.50
53 PDd(s),F:Green Lantern	2.50
54 PDd(s),F:Green Lantern	2.50
55 PDd(s),A:Lex Luthor	2.50
56 PDd(s),Buzz's daughter	2.50
57 PDd(s),Daddy's Little Girl	2.50
58 PDd(s),Buzz close to death	2.50
59 PDd(s),Our Worlds at War,tie-in	2.50
60 PDd(s),Our Worlds at War,tie-in	2.50
61 PDd(s),Our Worlds at War,tie-in	2.50
62 PDd(s),A:Two-Face	2.50
63 PDd(s),Joker:Last Laugh,tie-in	2.50
64 PDd(s),A:Lagoon Boy	2.50
65 PDd(s),hearing-impaired kids	2.25
66 PDd(s),F:Demon Etrigan	2.25
67 PDd(s),F:Demon Etrigan	2.25
68 PDd(s),F:Mary Marvel	2.25
69 PDd(s),F:Capt.Marvel,Jr.	2.25
70 PDd(s),F:Mary Marvel	2.25
71 PDd(s),V:Tara	2.25
72 PDd(s),V:Quetzlcoatl	2.25
73 PDd(s),Garden of Eden	2.50
74 PDd(s),Linda,Supergirl re-merge	2.50
75 PDd(s),EBe,spacecraft crashes	2.50
76 PDd(s),F:Superboy,Kara Zor-El	2.50
77 PDd(s),V:Fatalist	2.50
78 PDd(s),V:Fatalist	2.50
79 PDd(s),S.A.Supergirl	2.50
80 PDd(s),V:Kara & Xenon	2.50
Ann.#1 Legends o/t Dead Earth	3.00
Ann.#2 TPe,CDi,ACa, Pulp Heroes	4.00
Spec.#1,000,000 PDd(s),DAb.	2.00
GN Wings, Elseworlds, 48-page	5.95
TPB PDd(s),GFr,rep.#1-#9	15.00
TPB Many Happy Returns	14.95
Spec. Supergirl/Lex Luthor JBr, F:Lex Luthor (1993)	4.00
Spec. Supergirl/Prism Double-Shot DJu,TGb,Clv, x-over (1997)	2.00

SUPER HEROES BATTLE SUPER GORILLA
Winter, 1976

1 Superman Flash rep.	15.00

SUPERMAN
1939–86

1 JoS,O:Superman,reprints Action Comics #1-#4	250,000.00
2 JoS,I:George Taylor	18,000.00
3 JoS,V:Superintendent Lyman	11,000.00
4 JoS,V:Lex Luthor	11,000.00
5 JoS,V:Lex Luthor	8,000.00
6 JoS,V:'Brute' Bashby	4,000.00
7 JoS,I:Perry White	3,800.00
8 JoS,V:Jackal	3,600.00
9 JoS,V:Joe Gatson	3,600.00
10 JoS,V:Lex Luthor	3,500.00
11 JoS,V:Rolf Zimba	2,600.00
12 JoS,V:Lex Luthor	2,600.00
13 JoS,I:Jimmy Olsen,V:Lex Luthor,'The Archer'	2,600.00
14 JoS,I:Lightning Master	4,200.00
15 JoS,V:The Evolution King	2,600.00
16 JoS,V:Mr. Sinus	2,300.00
17 JoS,V:Lex Luthor,Lois Lane first suspects Clark is Superman	2,300.00
18 JoS,V:Lex Luthor	2,100.00
19 JoS,V:Funnyface, 1st Imaginary story	2,100.00
20 JoS,V:Puzzler,Leopard	2,100.00
21 JoS,V:Sir Gauntlet	1,600.00
22 JoS,V:Prankster	1,600.00
23 JoS,Propaganda story	1,600.00
24 V:Cobra King	2,500.00
25 Propaganda story	1,700.00
26 I:J.Wilbur Wolfingham, A:Mercury	1,700.00
27 V:Toyman	1,700.00
28 V:J.Wilbur Wolfingham, A:Hercules	1,700.00
29 V:Prankster	1,700.00
30 I&O:Mr. Mxyztplk	3,000.00
31 V:Lex Luthor	1,400.00
32 V:Toyman	1,400.00
33 V:Mr. Mxyzptlk	1,400.00
34 V:Lex Luthor	1,400.00
35 V:J.Wilbur Wolfingham	1,400.00
36 V:Mr. Mxyzptlk	1,400.00
37 V:Prankster,A:Sinbad	1,400.00
38 V:Lex Luthor	1,400.00
39 V:J.Wilbur Wolfingham	1,400.00
40 V:Mr. Mxyzptlk,A:Susie Thompkins	1,400.00
41 V:Prankster	1,000.00
42 V:J.Wilbur Wolfingham	1,000.00
43 V:Lex Luthor	1,000.00
44 V:Toyman,A:Shakespeare	1,000.00
45 A:Hocus & Pocus,Lois Lane as Superwoman	1,000.00
46 V:Mr. Mxyzptlk,Lex Luthor, Superboy flashback	1,000.00
47 V:Toyman	1,000.00
48 V:Lex Luthor	1,000.00
49 V:Toyman	1,000.00
50 V:Prankster	1,000.00
51 V:Mr. Mxyzptlk	900.00
52 V:Prankster	900.00
53 WB,O:Superman	3,500.00
54 V:Wrecker	900.00
55 V:Prankster	900.00
56 V:Prankster	900.00
57 V:Lex Luthor	900.00
58 V:Tiny Trix	900.00
59 V:Mr.Mxyzptlk	900.00
60 V:Toyman	900.00
61 I:Kryptonite,V:Prankster	1,800.00
62 V:Mr.Mxyzptlk,A:Orson Welles	900.00
63 V:Toyman	900.00
64 V:Prankster	900.00
65 V:Mala,Kizo and U-Ban	900.00
66 V:Prankster	900.00
67 A:Perry Como,I:Brane Taylor	900.00
68 V:Lex Luthor	900.00
69 V:Prankster,A:Inspector	

Superman #84 © DC Comics, Inc.

Comics Values Annual — DC — Superman

Erskine Hawkins 900.00	137 CS,I:Super-Menace 250.00	206 NA(c),F:The Day Superman
70 V:Prankster 900.00	138 A:Titano,Lori Lemaris 250.00	Became An Assistant 75.00
71 V:Lex Luthor 800.00	139 CS,O:Red Kryptonite 250.00	207 CS,F:The Case Of the
72 V:Prankster 800.00	140 WB,I:Bizarro Jr,Bizarro	Collared Crimefighter 90.00
72a giveaway 1,000.00	Supergirl,Blue Kryptonite 275.00	208 NA(c),CS 75.00
73 Flashback story 800.00	141 I:Lyla Lerrol,A:Jor-EL	209 CS,F:The Clark Kent Monster 75.00
74 V:Lex Luthor 800.00	& Lara 200.00	210 CS,F:Clark Kent's Last Rites . 75.00
75 V:Prankster 800.00	142 WB,CS,A:Al Capone 200.00	211 CS,RA 75.00
76 A:Batman (Superman &	143 WB,F:Bizarro meets	212 giant 90.00
Batman revel each other's	Frankenstein 200.00	213 CS,JA,V:Luthor,C:Brainiac 5 . . 75.00
identities) 2,200.00	144 O:Superboy's 1st Public	214 NA(c),CS,JA,F:The Ghosts
77 A:Pocahontas 750.00	Appearance 200.00	That Haunted Superman 75.00
78 V:Kryptonian snagriff,	145 F:April Fool's Issue 200.00	215 NA(c),CS,JA,V:Luthor,
A:Lana Lang 750.00	146 F:Superman's life story 250.00	Imaginary Story 75.00
79 V:Lex Luthor,A:Inspector	147 CS,I:Adult Legion 250.00	216 JKu(c),RA,Superman in Nam . 75.00
Erskine Hawkins 750.00	148 CS,V:Mxyzptlk 200.00	217 CS,A:Mr.Mxyzptlk 80.00
80 A:Halk Kar 750.00	149 CS:A:Luthor,C:JLA 200.00	218 CS,JA,A:Mr.Mxyzptlk 75.00
81 V:Lex Luthor 750.00	150 CS,KS,V:Mxyzptlk 150.00	219 CS,F:Clark Kent-Hero,
82 V:Mr. Mxyzptlk 650.00	151 CS 150.00	Superman Public Enemy 75.00
83 V:`The Brain' 650.00	152 A:Legion 150.00	220 CS,A:Flash 75.00
84 Time-travel story 650.00	153 CS 150.00	221 CS,F:The Two Ton Superman 75.00
85 V:Lex Luthor 650.00	154 CS,V:Mzyzptlk 150.00	222 giant 90.00
86 V:Mr.Mxyzptlk 650.00	155 WB,CS,V:Cosmic Man 150.00	223 CS,A:Supergirl 50.00
87 WB,V:The Thing from	156 CS,A:Legion,Batman 150.00	224 CS,Imaginary Story 50.00
40,000 AD' 650.00	157 CS,I:Gold kryptonite 165.00	225 CS,F:The Secret of the
88 WB,V:Lex Luthor,Toyman,	158 CS,I:Nightwing&Flamebird . . 150.00	Super Imposter 50.00
Prankster team 750.00	159 CS,Imaginary Tale	226 CS,F:When Superman Became
89 V:Lex Luthor 650.00	F:Lois Lane 150.00	King Kong 50.00
90 V:Lex Luthor 700.00	160 CS,F:Perry White 150.00	227 Krypton,(giant) 75.00
91 `The Superman Stamp' 650.00	161 D:Ma & Pa Kent 165.00	228 CS,DA 50.00
92 Goes back to 12th Century	162 A:Legion 165.00	229 WB,CS 50.00
England 650.00	163 CS 150.00	230 CS,DA,Luthor 50.00
93 V:`The Thinker' 650.00	164 CS,Luthor,I:Lexor 150.00	231 CS,DA,Luthor 50.00
94 `Clark Kent's Hillbilly Bride' . 650.00	165 CS,A:Saturn Woman 150.00	232 F:Krypton,(giant) 75.00
95 A:Susie Thompkins 650.00	166 CS 150.00	233 CS,MA,I:Quarrum 50.00
96 V:Mr. Mxyzptlk 450.00	167 CS,I:Ardora,Brainiac 165.00	234 NA(c),CS,MA 50.00
97 `Superboy's Last Day In	168 CS 100.00	235 CS,MA 50.00
Smallville' 450.00	169 Great DC Contest 100.00	236 CS,MA,DG,A:Green Arrow . . 50.00
98 `Clark Kent, Outlaw!' 450.00	170 CS,A:J.F.Kennedy,Luthor . . . 100.00	237 NA(c),CS,MA 50.00
99 V:Midnite gang 450.00	171 CS,Mxyzptlk 100.00	238 CS,MA,GM 50.00
100 F:Superman-Substitute	172 CS,Luthor,Brainiac 100.00	239 giant 75.00
Schoolteacher 2,400.00	173 CS,A:Batman 100.00	240 CS,DG,MK,A:I-Ching 35.00
101 A:Lex Luthor 450.00	174 Mxyzptlk 100.00	241 CS,MA,A:Wonder Woman . . 40.00
102 I:Superman Stock	175 CS,Luthor 100.00	242 CS,MA,A:Wonder Woman . . 40.00
Company 450.00	176 CS,Green Kryptonite 100.00	243 CS,MA 40.00
103 A:Mr.Mxyzptlk 450.00	177 Fortress of Solitude 100.00	244 CS,MA 40.00
104 F:Clark Kent,Jailbird 450.00	178 CS, Red Kryptonite 100.00	245 100 pg reprints 45.00
105 A:Mr.Mxyzptlk 450.00	179 CS,Clark Kent in Marines . . . 100.00	246 CS,MA,RB,I:S.T.A.R. Labs . . . 35.00
106 A:Lex Luthor 475.00	180 CS 100.00	247 CS,MA,Guardians o/Universe . 35.00
107 F:Superman In 30th century	181 Superman 2965 . . . . 100.00	248 CS,MA,A:Luthor,I:Galactic
(pre-Legion) 450.00	182 CS,Toyman 100.00	Golem 35.00
108 I:Perry White Jr 450.00	183 giant 100.00	249 CS,MA,DD,NA,I:Terra-Man . . 50.00
109 I:Abner Hokum 450.00	184 Secrets of the Fortress 90.00	250 CS,MA,Terraman 35.00
110 A:Lex Luthor 450.00	185 JM,Superman's Achilles	251 CS,MA,RB 35.00
111 Becomes Mysto the Great . . 375.00	Heel 90.00	
112 A:Lex Luthor 375.00	186 CS,The Two Ghosts of	
113 A:Jor-El 375.00	Superman 90.00	
114 V:The Great Mento 375.00	187 giant 90.00	
115 V:The Organizer 375.00	188 V:Zunial,The Murder Man . . . 90.00	
116 Return to Smallville 375.00	189 WB,The Mystery of Krypton's	
117 A:Lex Luthor 375.00	Second Doom 90.00	
118 F:Jimmy Olsen 375.00	190 WB,I:Amalak 90.00	
119 A:Zoll Orr 375.00	191 The Prisoner of Demon 90.00	
120 V:Gadget Grim 375.00	192 CS,Imaginary Story,	
121 I:XL-49 (Futureman) 325.00	I:Superman Jr. 90.00	
122 In the White House 325.00	193 giant 90.00	
123 CS,pre-Supergirl tryout	194 CS,Imaginary,A:Supes Jr. . . . 90.00	
A:Jor-El & Lara 350.00	195 CS,V:Amalak 90.00	
124 F:Lois Lane 325.00	196 WB,reprint 90.00	
125 F:Superman College Story . 325.00	197 giant 90.00	
126 F:Lois Lane 325.00	198 CS,F:The Real Clark Kent . . . 90.00	
127 WB,I&O:Titano 350.00	199 CS,F:Superman/Flash race,	
128 V:Vard & Boka 325.00	A:JLA 350.00	
129 WB,I&O:Lori Lemaris 350.00	200 WB,A:Brainiac 100.00	
130 A:Krypto,the Superdog 325.00	201 CS,F:Clark Kent Abandons	
131 A:Mr. Mxyzptlk 250.00	Superman 75.00	
132 A:Batman & Robin 250.00	202 A:Bizarro,(giant size) 90.00	
133 F:Superman Joins Army . . . 250.00	203 F:When Superman Killed His	
134 A:Supergirl & Krypto 250.00	Friends 75.00	
135 A:Lori Lemaris,Mr.Mxyzptlk . 250.00	204 NA(c),RA,A:Lori Lemaris 75.00	
136 O:Discovery Kryptonite 250.00	205 NA(c),I:Black Zero 75.00	

Superman #235 © DC Comics Inc.

All comics prices listed are for *Near Mint* condition.

Superman — DC — Comics Values Annual

Superman #256 © DC Comics, Inc.

Superman #299 © DC Comics, Inc.

#	Description	Price
252	NA(c),rep.100pgs.	45.00
253	CS,MA	35.00
254	CS,MA,NA	50.00
255	CS,MA,DG	20.00
256	CS,MA	20.00
257	CS,MA,DD,DG,A:Tomar-Re	20.00
258	CS,MA,DC	20.00
259	CS,MA,A:Terra-Man	20.00
260	CS,DC,I:Valdemar	20.00
261	CS,MA,V:Star Sapphire	20.00
262	CS,MA	20.00
263	CS,MA,DD,FMc	20.00
264	DC,CS,I:Steve Lombard	20.00
265	CS,MA	20.00
266	CS,MA,DD,V:Snowman	20.00
267	CS,MA,BO	20.00
268	CS,BO,DD,MA,A:Batgirl	20.00
269	CS,MA	20.00
270	CS,MA,V:Valdemar	20.00
271	CS,BO,DG,V:Brainiac	20.00
272	100pg.reprints	50.00
273	CS,DG	20.00
274	CS	20.00
275	CS,DG,FMc	20.00
276	CS,BO,I&O:Captain Thunder	20.00
277	CS	20.00
278	CS,BO,Terraman,100page	50.00
279	CS,Batgirl,Batman	20.00
280	CS,BO	20.00
281	CS,BO,I:Vartox	20.00
282	CS,KS,N:Luthor	20.00
283	CS,BO,Mxyzptlk	20.00
284	CS,BO,100p reprint	50.00
285	CS,BO	20.00
286	CS,BO	20.00
287	CS,BO,R:Krypto	20.00
288	CS,BO	20.00
289	CS,BO,JL	20.00
290	CS,V:Mxyzptlk	20.00
291	CS,BO	20.00
292	CS,BO,AM,O:Luthor	20.00
293	CS,BO	20.00
294	CS,JL,A:Brain Storm	20.00
295	CS,BO	20.00
296	CS,BO,Identity Crisis #1	20.00
297	CS,BO,Identity Crisis #2	20.00
298	CS,BO,Identity Crisis #3	20.00
299	CS,BO,Identity Crisis #4 A:Luthor,Brainiac,Bizarro	20.00
300	CS,BO,2001,anniversary	30.00
301	BO,JL,V:Solomon Grundy	10.00
302	JL,BO,V:Luthor,A:Atom	10.00
303	CS,BO,I:Thunder&Lightning	10.00
304	CS,BO,V:Parasite	10.00
305	CS,BO,V:Toyman	10.00
306	CS,BO,V:Bizarro	10.00
307	NA(c),JL,FS,A:Supergirl	10.00
308	NA(c),JL,FS,A:Supergirl	10.00
309	JL,FS,A:Supergirl	10.00
310	CS,V:Metallo	10.00
311	CS,FS,A:Flash	10.00
312	CS,FS,A:Supergirl	10.00
313	NA(c),CS,DA,A:Supergirl	10.00
314	NA(c),CS,DA,A:Gr.Lantern	10.00
315	CS,DA,V:Blackrock	10.00
316	CS,DA,V:Metallo	10.00
317	NA(c),CS,DA,V:Metallo	10.00
318	CS	10.00
319	CS,V:Solomon Grundy	10.00
320	CS,V:Solomon Grundy	10.00
321	CS,V:Parasite	9.00
322	CS,V:Solomon Grundy	9.00
323	CS,DA,I:Atomic Skull	9.00
324	CS,A:Atomic Skull	9.00
325	CS	9.00
326	CS,V:Blackrock	9.00
327	CS,KS,V:Kobra,C:JLA	9.00
328	CS,KS,V:Kobra	9.00
329	KS,CS	9.00
330	CS,F:glasses explained	9.00
331	CS,I:Master Jailer	9.00
332	CS,V:Master Jailer	9.00
333	CS,V:Bizarro	9.00
334	CS	6.00
335	CS,W:Mxyzptlk	6.00
336	CS,V:Rose And Thorn	6.00
337	CS,A:Brainiac,Bizarro	6.00
338	CS,F:Kandor enlarged	6.00
339	CS,I:N.R.G.X	6.00
340	CS,V:N.R.G.X	6.00
341	CS,F:Major Disaster	6.00
342	CS,V:Chemo	6.00
343	CS	6.00
344	CS,A:Phantom Stranger	6.00
345	CS,'When time ran backward'	6.00
346	CS,'Streak of Bad Luck'	6.00
347	JL	6.00
348	CS	6.00
349	CS,V:Mxyzptlk	6.00
350	CS,'Clark Kent's Vanishing Classmate'	5.00
351	CS,JL,A:Mxyzptlk	5.00
352	CS,RB	5.00
353	CS,origin	5.00
354	CS,JSon,I:Superman 2020	5.00
355	CS,JSon,F:Superman 2020	5.00
356	CS,V:Vartox	5.00
357	CS,DCw,F:Superman 2020	5.00
358	CS,DG,DCw	5.00
359	CS	5.00
360	CS,AS,F:World of Krypton	5.00
361	CS,AS	5.00
362	CS,KS,DA	5.00
363	CS,RB,C:Luthor	5.00
364	GP(c),RB,AS	5.00
365	CS,KS	5.00
366	CS,KS	5.00
367	CS,GK,F:World of Krypton	5.00
368	CS,AS	5.00
369	RB,FMc,V:Parasite	5.00
370	CS,KS,FMc,A:Chemo	5.00
371	CS	5.00
372	CS,GK,F:Superman 2021	5.00
373	CS,V:Vartox	5.00
374	GK(c),CS,DA,KS,V:Vartox	5.00
375	CS,DA,GK,V:Vartox	5.00
376	CS,DA,CI,BO,SupergirlPrev.	4.00
377	GK(c),CS,V:Terra-Man	4.00
378	CS	4.00
379	CS,V:Bizarro	4.00
380	CS	4.00
381	GK(c),CS	4.00
382	GK(c),CS	4.00
383	CS	4.00
384	CS	4.00
385	GK(c),CS,V:Luthor	4.00
386	GK(c),CS,V:Luthor	4.00
387	GK(c),CS	4.00
388	GK(c),CS	4.00
389	GK(c),CS	4.00
390	GK(c),CS,V:Vartox	4.00
391	GK(c),CS,V:Vartox	4.00
392	GK(c),CS,V:Vartox	4.00
393	IN,DG,V:Master Jailer	4.00
394	CS,V:Valdemar	4.00
395	CS,V:Valdemar	4.00
396	CS	4.00
397	EB,V:Kryptonite Man	4.00
398	CS,AS,DJ	4.00
399	CS,BO,EB	4.00
400	HC(c),FM,AW,JO,JSo,MR,TA,WP,MK,KJ,giant	8.00
401	CS,BO,V:Luthor	4.00
402	CS,BO,WB	4.00
403	CS,BO,AS	4.00
404	CI,BO,V:Luthor	4.00
405	KS,KK,AS,F:Super-Batman	4.00
406	IN,AS,KK	4.00
407	IN,V:Mxyzptlk	4.00
408	CS,AW,JRu,F:Nuclear Holocaust	4.00
409	CS,AW,KS	4.00
410	CS,AW,V:Luthor	4.00
411	CS,MA,F:End Earth-Prime	4.00
412	CS,AW,V:Luthor	4.00
413	CS,AW,V:Luthor	4.00
414	CS,AW,Crisis tie-in	5.00
415	CS,AW,Crisis,W:Super Girl	5.00
416	CS,AW,Luthor	4.00
417	CS,V:Martians	4.00
418	CS,V:Metallo	4.00
419	CS,V:Iago	4.00
420	CS,F:Nightmares	4.00
421	CS,V:Mxyzptlk	4.00
422	BB(c),CS,TY,LMa,V:Werewolf	4.00
423	AMo(c),CS,GP,F:Last Superman	9.00
Ann.#1	I:Supergirl Rep.	1,500.00
Ann.#2	I&O:Titano	600.00
Ann.#3	I:Legion	400.00
Ann.#4	O:Legion	350.00
Ann.#5	A:Krypton	250.00
Ann.#6	A:Legion	250.00
Ann.#7	O:Superman,Silver Anniv.	200.00
Ann.#8	F:Secret origins	150.00
Ann.#9	GK(c),ATh,TA,CS,A:Batman	7.00
Ann.#10	CS,MA,F:Sword of Superman	5.00
Ann.#11	AMo(s),DGb,A:Batman,Robin,Wonder Woman	6.00
Ann.#12	BB(c),AS,A:Lex Luthor,

CVA Page 156 — All comics prices listed are for *Near Mint* condition.

Comics Values Annual   DC   Superman

Last War Suit 4.00	476 DJu,BBr,Time & Time Again,pt.1,	Metropolis,Holografx(c). 3.00
Game Give-away 10.00	A:Booster Gold,Legion 3.00	505a Newstand Ed. 2.25
Giveaway CS,AT 2.25	477 DJu,BBr,T & T Again,pt.4,	506 TG,DHz,A:Guardian. 2.50
Pizza Hut 1977. . . . . 6.00	A:Legion. 3.00	507 Spilled Blood#1,V:Bloodsport . . 2.50
Radio Shack 1980 JSw,DG. 5.00	478 DJu,BBr,T & T Again,pt.7,	508 BKi,A:Challengers of the
Radio Shack 1981 CS 5.00	A:Legion,Linear Man 3.00	Unknown 2.50
Radio Shack 1982 CS 5.00	479 EH,Red Glass Trilogy#2. . . . . . 3.00	509 BKi,A:Auron. 2.50
Spec.#1 GK 3.50	480 JOy,DJu,BMc,TG,BBr,CS,	510 BKi,Bizarro's World #2,
Spec.#2 GK,V:Brainiac. 3.50	Revenge of the Krypton	V:Bizarro 2.50
Spec.#3 IN,V:Amazo 3.50	Man,pt.3. . . . . 3.00	511 BKi,A:Guardian 2.50
Superman III Movie,CS. 2.50	481 1st TG Supes,DHz,V:Parasite . 3.00	512 BKi,V:Parasite 2.50
Superman IV Movie,DH,DG,FMc . 2.50	482 TG,DHz,V:Parasite. 3.00	513 BKi,Battle for Metropolis #4 . . 2.50
Becomes:	483 TG,DHz,V:Blindspot. 3.00	514 BKi,Fall of Metropolis #4 . . . . 2.50
	484 TG,Blackout #1,V:Mr.Z. 3.00	515 BKi,Massacre in Metropolis . . . 2.50
ADVENTURES OF	485 TG,DHz,Blackout #5,A:Mr.Z . 3.00	516 BKi,Zero Hour,I:Alpha
SUPERMAN	486 TG,V:Purge. 3.00	Centurion 2.50
1987	487 TG,DHz,X-mas,A:Agent	517 BKi,deathtrap. 2.50
424 JOy,I:Man O'War 4.00	Liberty 3.00	518 BKi 2.50
425 JOy,Man O'War 3.00	488 TG,Panic in the Sky,pt.3,	519 KK,BKi,Secret of Superman's
426 JOy,Legends,V:Apokolips. . . . 3.00	V:Brainiac. 3.00	Tomb 2.50
427 JOy,V:Qurac 3.00	489 TG,Panic in the Sky,Epiloge. . 2.75	520 SI,KK,JMz,100 crimes at
428 JOy,V:Qurac,I:JerryWhite . . . 3.00	490 TG,A:Agent Liberty,Husque . . 3.00	midnight 2.50
429 JOy,V:Concussion 3.00	491 TG,DHz,V:Cerberus,Metallo . . 3.00	521 SI,KK,R:Thorn 2.50
430 JOy,V:Fearsome Five. 3.00	492 WS(c),V:Sons of Liberty,	522 SI,KKIdentity known. 2.50
431 JOy,A:Combattor 3.00	A:Agent Liberty. 3.00	523 SI,KK,Death of C.Kent,pt.2. . . 2.50
432 JOy,I:Jose Delgado 3.00	493 TG,Blaze/Satanus War,pt.1 . 3.00	524 SI,KK,Death of C.Kent,pt.6
433 JOy,V:Lex Luthor 3.00	494 TG,DHz,I:Kismet 3.00	[New Miraweb format begins] . . 2.50
434 JOy,KI:Gang Buster 3.00	495 TG,DHz,A:Forever People,	525 SI,KK. 2.50
435 JOy,A:Charger 3.00	Darkseid. 3.00	526 Bloodsport vs. Bloodsport . . . 2.50
436 JOy,Millennium x-over 5.00	496 V:Mr.Mxyzptlk,C:Doomsday . . 3.00	527 . . . . 2.50
437 JOy,Millennium X-over. 3.50	496a 2nd printing 2.50	528 Trial of Superman,prelude 2.50
438 JOy,N:Brainiac. 3.00	497 TG,Doomsday Pt.3,A:Maxima,	529 Trial of Superman 2.50
439 JOy,R:Superman Robot 3.00	Bloodwynd 5.00	530 KK,SI,JMz,Trial of Superman . . 2.50
440 JOy,A:Batman,Wond.Woman . 3.00	497a 2nd printing 2.50	531 KK,SI,JMz,Trial of Superman,
441 JOy,V:Mr.Mxyzptlk 3.00	498 TG,Funeral for a Friend#1 . . . 4.00	concl. 2.50
442 JOy,V:Dreadnaught,A:JLI . . . 3.00	498a 2nd Printing 2.50	532 KK,SI,JMz, return of Lori
443 JOy,DHz,I:Husque 3.00	499 TG,DHz,Funeral for a	Lemaris 2.50
444 JOy,Supergirl SagaPt.2 . . . . . 3.00	Friend#5. . . . . 3.50	533 KK,SI,JMz 2.50
445 JOy,V:Brainiac 3.00	500 JOy(c),B:KK(s),TG,DJu,JBg,JG,	534 KK,SI,JMz,V:Lord Satannus . . 2.50
446 JOy,A:Gangbuster,	BBr,Bagged,Superman in limbo,	535 KK,SI,JMz,Lois & LoriLemaris . 2.50
A:Luthor's Old Costume 3.00	I:Four Supermen,Direct Sales. . 3.50	536. . . . . 2.50
447 JOy,A:Gangbuster 3.00	500a Newsstand Ed. 2.25	537. . . . . 2.50
448 JOy,I:Dubbilex,A:Gangbuster . 3.00	500b Platinum Ed. 20.00	538. . . . . 2.50
449 JOy,Invasion X-over. 3.00	501 TG,Reign of Supermen#2,Direct	539 F:Guardian and the Newsboy
450 JOy,Invasion X-over. 3.00	Sales,Die-Cut(c),Mini-poster	Legion 2.50
451 JOy,`Superman in Space' . . . 3.00	F:Superboy 3.00	540 KK(s),TyD,KIS,A:Ferro, Final
452 DJu,V:Wordbringer. 3.00	501a Newstand Ed. 2.25	Night tie-in 2.50
453 JOy,DJu,A:Gangbuster 3.00	502 TG,A:Supergirl,V:Stinger 2.25	541 KK(s),SI,JMz,on Honeymoon,
454 JOy,DJu,I:New Mongul. 4.00	503 TG,Cyborg Superman Vs.	A:Superboy,Tana Moon,Kekona 2.50
455 DJu,ATb,A:Eradicator. 3.50	Superboy 2.50	542 KK&JOy(s),PR,JMz,V:Misa . . . 2.50
456 DJu,ATb,V:Turmoil 3.50	504 TG,DHz,A:All Supermen,	543 . . . . 2.50
457 DJu,V:Intergang. 3.50	V:Mongul 2.50	544 KK(s),SI,JMz,Who Killed Clark
458 DJu,KJ,R:Elastic Lad	505 TG,DHz,Superman returns to	Kent in broad daylight?. 2.50
(Jimmy Olsen) 3.50		545 KK(s),SEa,JMz,Return of the
459 DJu,V:Eradicator 3.50		Atomic Skull,new blue costume 2.50
460 DJu,NKu,V:Eradicator 3.50		546 KK(s),SI,JMz,V:Metallo, uses
461 DJu,GP,V:Eradicator 3.50		new powers 2.50
462 DJu,ATb,Homeless		547 KK(s),SI,JMz,Superman goes
Christmas Story 3.50		to Kandor,A:The Atom 2.50
463 DJu,ATb,Superman Races		548 KK(s),SI,JMz,V:Lex Luthor . . . 2.50
Flash 3.50		549 KK(s),SI,JMz,F:Jimmy Olsen . 2.50
464 DJu,ATb,Day of Krypton		550 KK(s),SI,TGu,JMz,DRo, 48pg . 3.50
Man #2,A:Lobo. 6.00		551 DJu,TGu,DRo,Genesis,
465 DJu,ATb,Day of Krypton		V:Cyborg 2.25
Man #5,V:Draaga. 3.00		552 KK,TGu,DRo,V:Parasite. 2.25
466 DJu,DG,V:Team Excalibur		553 KK,TGu,DRo,disappearances . 2.25
Astronauts,I:Hank Henshaw		554 KK,TGu,DRo,disappearances . 2.25
(becomes Cyborg Superman). . 4.50		555 KK,TRu,DRo,Red/Blue x-over . 2.25
467 DJu,ATb,A:Batman 3.00		556 KK,TRu,DRo,Red & Blue 2.25
468 DJu,ATb,Man Of Steel's		557 KK,VS,DRo,Millennium Giants
Journal,V:Hank Henshaw 3.00		x-over. 2.25
469 DJu,ATb,V:Dreadnaught. 3.00		558 KK,JOy,DRo,silver age?,pt.1 . 2.25
470 DJu,ATb,Soul Search #3,		559 KK,JOy,DRo,silver age?,pt.2 . 2.25
D:Jerry White 3.00		560 KK,JOy,DRo,silver age?,pt.3 . 2.25
471 CS,Sinbad Contract #2 . . . . . 3.00		561 KK,JOy,TGu,DRo,Waverider . . 2.25
472 DJu,ATb,Krisis of Krimson		562 KK(s),JOy,TGu,DRo,Lexcom . 2.25
Kryptonite #2 . . . . 3.00		563 RMz,TGb,TP,City of the
473 DJu,ATb,A:Green Lantern,		Future, pt.4 x-over 2.25
Guy Gardner 3.00		564 KK&JOy(s),TGu,DRo,
474 DJu,ATb,Drunk Driving issue . 3.00	*Adventures of Superman #485*	A:Geo-Force 2.25
475 DJu,ATb,V:Kilgrave,Sleez . . . 3.00	© DC Comics Inc.	565 KK&JOy(s),TGu,DRo,A:JLA. . . 2.25

All comics prices listed are for *Near Mint* condition.   CVA Page 157

Superman–Superman | DC | Comics Values Annual

Adventures of Superman #516
© DC Comics, Inc.

566 KK&JOy(s),TGu,DRo,V:Lex
  Luthor 2.25
567 KK&JOy(s),DRo,PR, ... 2.25
568 LSi(s),TMo,DRo,V:Metallo . . . 2.25
569 LSi(s),TMo,DRo,V:S.C.U. 2.25
570 RMz&TPe(s),TGb,TP,
  A:JLA,pt.2 x-over 2.25
571 LSi(s),DRo,V:Atomic Skull 2.25
572 RF,SB,Strange Visitor,pt.2 . . . . 2.25
573 SI,SEp,DRo,flashbacks 2.25
574 SI 2.25
575 SI,F:Lex Luthor 2.25
576 SI,V:Brainiac 13. . . . . 2.25
577 SI,JMz,A:Luthor. 2.25
578 JMD(s),JMz,alien utopia. 2.25
579 JMD(s),Lois has vanished . . . 2.25
580 JMD(s),CriticalCondition,pt.2 . . 2.25
581 JMD(s),V:Adversary,Lex Luthor 2.25
582 JMD(s),Arkham,pt.2. . . . . 2.25
583 JMD,JMz,Superman:Emperor . 2.25
584 JMD(s),JMz,V:Devouris 2.25
585 JMD,JMz,V:LexLuthor,Satanus. 2.25
586 JMD,JMz,V:Satanus. 2.25
587 JMD,JMz,V:Satanus. 2.25
588 JoC,JMz,V:Satanus 2.25
589 JoC,JMz,Return toKrypton,pt.2. 2.25
590 JoC,JMz,Luthor's Lackey? 2.25
591 MWm,Infestation x-over,pt.2. . . 2.25
592 JoC,JMz,F:Jimmy Olson 2.25
593 JoC,JMz,V:Manchester Black. . 2.25
594 JoC,MeW,All-Out War,x-over . . 2.25
595 JoC,MeW,Casualties of War. . . 2.25
596 JoC,MeW,No Superman's Job . 5.00
597 JoC,Joker:Last Laugh tie-in . . . 2.25
598 JoC,JMz,F:Perry White 2.25
599 JoC,JMz,Russian submarine . . 2.25
600 JoC,Lex Luthor, 64-pg.. . . . . . 5.00
601 JoC,Cult of Persuasion,pt.1 . . 2.25
602 JoC,Cult of Persuasion,pt.2 . . 2.25
603 JoC,F:Superbaby. 2.25
604 JoC,V:Ultra-Man 2.25
605 JoC,F:Superbaby, concl. 2.25
606 JoC,Return to KryptonII,pt.2. . . 2.25
607 F:Argent 2.25
608 JoC,Ending Battle,pt.2 . . . . . . 2.25
609 JoC,Ending Battle,pt.6 . . . . . . 2.25
610 JoC,in Guatemala 2.25
611 Lost Hearts,pt.2 x-over. 2.25
612 JoC,Hollow Man 2.25
613 JoC,Captain Cold. 2.25
614 JoC,Hollow Men 2.25
615 JoC,Hollow Men 2.25
616 JoC,Hollow Men 2.25
617 JoC,V:two Mr.Mxyzptlks. 2.25

618 JoC,CAd,Mxy Twins. 2.25
619 JoC,Lois and Clark 2.25
620 JoC,the Candidate 2.25
621 JoC,Minuteman 2.25
622 prophecy of the Minuteman . . . 2.25
Ann.#1 JSn(c),DJu,I:Word Bringer . 3.00
Ann.#2 CS/JBy,KGa/DG,BMc,
  A:L.E.G.I.O.N.'90 (Lobo). 4.00
Ann.#3 BHi,JRu,DG,
  Armageddon 2001. . . . . 3.00
Ann.#4 BMc,A:Lobo,Guy Gardner,
  Eclipso tie-in. 3.00
Ann.#5 TG,I:Sparx 2.75
Ann.#6 MMi(c),Elseworlds Story . . 3.00
Ann.#7 Year One Story. 4.00
Ann.#8 Legends o/t Dead Earth . . 2.95
Ann.#9 Pulp Heroes (Western) . . . 3.95
Spec.#1,000,000 ALa&DAn(s)LMa,
  A:Teen Titans, V:Solaris 3.00

SUPERMAN'S BUDDY
1954
1 w/costume 1,500.00
1 w/out costume 700.00

SUPERMAN'S CHRISTMAS ADVENTURE
1 (1940) 5,500.00
2 (1944) 1,200.00

SUPERMAN AND THE GREAT CLEVELAND FIRE
1948
1 for Hospital Fund 650.00

SUPERMAN (miniature)
1942
1 Py-Co-Pay Tooth Powder
  Give- Away. 800.00
2 CS,Superman Time Capsule. . 500.00
3 CS,Duel in Space 450.00
4 CS,Super Show in Metropolis. 450.00

SUPERMAN RECORD COMIC
1966
1 w/record 200.00
1 w/out record 100.00

SUPERMAN SPECTACULAR
1982
1 A:Luthor & Terra-Man 2.50

SUPERMAN-TIM STORE PAMPHLETS
1942
Superman-Tim store Monthly
  Membership Pamphlet, 16
  pages of stories, games,
  puzzles (1942), each 1,300.00
Superman-Tim store Monthly
  Membership Pamphlet, 16
  pages of stories, games,
  puzzles (1943), each 450.00
Superman-Tim store Monthly
  Membership Pamphlet, 16
  pages of stories, games,
  puzzles (1944), each 425.00
Superman-Tim store Monthly
  Membership Pamphlet, 16
  pages of stories, games,
  puzzles (1945), each 400.00

Superman-Tim store Monthly
  Membership Pamphlet, 14-16
  pages of stories, games,
  puzzles, 5"x8" color(c),
  (1946), each. 500.00
Superman-Tim stamp
  album, 1946 . . . . 350.00
Superman-Tim store Monthly
  Membership Pamphlet, 14-16
  pages of stories, games,
  puzzles, 5"x8" color(c),
  (1947), each. 300.00
Superman-Tim stamp album,
  Superman story, 1947. . . . . 450.00
Superman-Tim store Monthly
  Membership Pamphlet, 14-16
  pages of stories, games,
  puzzles, 5"x8" color(c),(1948),
  each 250.00
Superman-Tim stamp
  album, 1948 . . . . 350.00
Superman-Tim store Monthly
  Membership Pamphlet, 14-16
  pages of stories, games,
  puzzles, 5"x8" color(c),
  (1949), each. 250.00
Superman-Tim store Monthly
  Membership Pamphlet, 14-16
  pages of stories, games,
  puzzles, 5"x8" color(c)
  (1950), each. 300.00

SUPERMAN WORKBOOK
1945
1 rep. Superman #14 . . . . 1,200.00

SUPERMAN
[2nd Regular Series], 1987
1 JBy,TA,I:Metallo 5.00
2 JBy,TA,V:Luthor 3.00
3 JBy,TA,Legends tie-in. 3.00
4 JBy,KK,V:Bloodsport. 3.00
5 JBy,KK,V:Host 3.00
6 JBy,KK,V:Host 3.00
7 JBy,KK,V:Rampage 3.00
8 JBy,KK,A:Superboy,Legion 3.00
9 JBy,KK,V:Joker. 5.00
10 JBy,KK,V:Rampage 3.00
11 JBy,KK,V:Mr.Mxyzptlk 2.50
12 JBy,KK,A:Lori Lemerias 2.50
13 JBy,KK,Millennium 2.50
14 JBy,KK,A:Green Lantern 2.50

Superman 2nd Series #1
© DC Comics, Inc.

Comics Values Annual — DC — Superman

#	Description	Price
15	JBy,KK,I:New Prankster	2.50
16	JBy,KK,A:Prankster	4.00
17	JBy,KK,O:Silver Banshee	2.50
18	MMi,KK,A:Hawkman	2.50
19	JBy,V:Skyhook	2.50
20	JBy,KK,A:Doom Patrol	3.00
21	JBy,A:Supergirl	4.00
22	JBy,A:Supergirl	2.50
23	MMi,CR,O:Silver Banshee	2.50
24	KGa,V:Rampage	2.50
25	KGa,V:Brainiac	2.50
26	KGa,BBr,V:Baron Sunday	2.50
27	KGa,BBr,V:Guardian	2.50
28	KGa,BBr,Supes Leaves Earth	2.50
29	DJu,BBr,V:Word Bringer	2.50
30	KGa,DJu,A:Lex Luthor	2.50
31	DJu,PCu,V:Mxyzptlk	2.50
32	KGa,V:Mongul	2.50
33	KGa,A:Cleric	2.50
34	KGa,V:Skyhook	2.50
35	CS,KGa,A:Brainiac	2.50
36	JOy,V:Prankster	2.50
37	JOy,A:Guardian	2.50
38	JOy,Jimmy Olsen Vanished	2.50
39	JOy,KGa,V:Husque	2.50
40	JOy,V:Four Armed Terror	2.50
41	JOy,Day of Krypton Man #1, A:Lobo	3.50
42	JOy,Day of Krypton Man #4, V:Draaga	3.50
43	JOy,V:Krypton Man	3.50
44	JOy,A:Batman	2.50
45	JOy,F:Jimmy Olsen's Dairy	2.50
46	DJu,JOy,A:Jade,Obsidian, I:New Terra-Man	2.50
47	JOy,Soul Search #2,V:Blaze	2.50
48	CS,Sinbad Contract #1	2.50
49	JOy,Krisis of K.Kryptonite#1	3.00
50	JBy,KGa,DJu,JOy,BBr,CS,Krisis of Krimson Kryptonite #4, Clark Proposes To Lois	6.00
50a	2nd printing	2.50
51	JOy,I:Mr.Z	2.50
52	KGa,V:Terra-Man	2.50
53	JOy,Superman reveals i.d.	3.50
53a	2nd Printing	2.50
54	JOy,KK,Time & Time Again#3	2.50
55	JOy,KK,Time & Time Again#6	2.50
56	EH,KK,Red Glass Trilogy#1	2.50
57	JOy,DJu,BBr,ATi,JBg,BMc,TG, Revenge o/t Krypton Man #2	3.50
58	DJu,BBr,I:Bloodhounds	2.50
59	DJu,BBr,A:Linear Men	2.50
60	DJu,EB,I:Agent Liberty, V:Intergang	2.50
61	DJu,BBr,A:Waverider, V:Linear Men	2.50
62	DJu,BBr,Blackout #4,A:Mr.Z	2.50
63	DJu,A:Aquaman	2.50
64	JG,Christmas issue	2.50
65	DJu,Panic in the Sky#2, I:New Justice League	3.50
66	DJu,Panic in the Sky#6, V:Brainiac	8.00
67	DJu,Aftermath	2.50
68	DJu,V:Deathstroke	2.50
69	WS(c),DJu,A:Agent Liberty	2.50
70	DJu,BBr,A:Robin,V:Vampires	2.50
71	DJu,Blaze/Satanus War	2.50
72	DJu,Crisis at Hand#2	2.50
73	DJu,A:Waverider,V:Linear Men,C:Doomsday	5.00
73a	2nd printing	2.50
74	DJu,V:Doomsday,A:JLA	7.00
74a	2nd printing	2.00
75	DJu,V:Doomsday,D:Superman, Collectors Ed	20.00
75a	newstand Ed	9.00
75b	2nd printing	4.00
75c	3rd printing	2.50
75d	4th Printing	2.50
75e	Platinum Ed	45.00
76	DJu,BBr,Funeral for Friend#4	3.00
77	DJu,BBr,Funeral for Friend#8	3.00
78	DJu,BBr,Reign of Supermen#3, Die-Cut(c),Mini poster,F:Cyborg Supes,A:Doomsday	3.00
78a	Newsstand Ed	2.50
79	DJu,BBr,Memorial Service for Clark	3.00
80	DJu,BBr,Coast City Blows up, V:Mongul	4.00
81	DJu,O:Cyborg Superman	3.50
82	DJu,Chromium(c),A:All Supermen, V:Cyborg Superman	5.00
82a	Newstand Ed	2.50
83	DJu,A:Batman	3.00
84	DJu,V:Toyman	3.00
85	DJu,V:Toyman	3.00
86	DJu,A:Sun Devils	3.00
87	DJu(c&s),SI,JRu,Bizzaro's World#1, R:Bizarro	3.00
88	DJu(c&s),SI,JRu,Bizzaro's World#5, D:Bizarro	3.00
89	DJu(c&s),V:Cadmus Project	3.00
90	DJu(c&s),Battle for Metropolis#3	3.00
91	DJu(c&s),Fall of Metropolis#3	3.00
92	Massacre in Metropolis	3.00
93	Zero Hour,A:Batman	3.00
94	Conduit	3.00
95	Brainiac	3.00
96	Virtual Reality	3.00
97	Shadow Dragon	3.00
98	R:Shadow Strike	3.00
99	R:Agent Liberty	3.00
100	BBr,DJu,Death of C.Kent,pt.1	3.50
100a	Collectors Edition	4.00
101	Death of Clark Kent,pt.5 [New Miraweb format begins]	3.00
102	DJu,A:Captain Marvel	3.00
103	O:Arclight	3.00
104		3.00
105	A:Green Lantern	3.00
106	DJu,RF,The Trial of Superman	3.00
107	DJu,RF,The Trial of Superman	3.00
108	DJu,RF,The Trial of Superman	3.00
109	DJu,RF,V:Kill Fee	3.00
110		3.00
111	DJu,RF,Cat Grant in charge	3.00
112	DJu,RF,Lois & Clark	3.00
113	DJu(s),RF,JRu,	3.00
114	DJu(s),RF,JRu,A:Brainiac	3.00
115	DJu(s),RF,JRu,Lois leaves Metropolis	3.00
116	DJu(s),RF,JRu,battle city siga concl., V:Daxamite,B.U. Teen Titans preview	3.00
117	DJu(s),RF,JRu,V: his own robots, Final Night tie-in	3.00
118	DJu(s),RF,JRu,F:time-lost Legion of Super Heroes	3.00
119	DJu(s),RF,JRu,A:Legion of Super Heroes	3.00
120	DJu(s),RF,JRu,	3.00
121	DJu(s),RF,JRu,They Call it Suicide Slum	3.00
122	DJu(s),RF,JRu,Lois visits Fortress of Solitude	3.00
123	DJu(s),RF,Jru,Superman gets New Costume	4.00
123a	collector's edition, glow-in-the-dark cover	5.00
124	DJu(s),RF,JRu,A:Scorn, prince of Kandor	2.50
125	DJu(s),RF,JRu,Kandor and Metropolis,A:Atom	2.50
126	DJu(s),RF,JRu,A:Batman	2.50
127	DJu(s),RF,JRu,F:Jimmy Olsen	2.50
128	DJu(s),RF,JRu, Genesis tie-in	2.50
129	DJu(s),RF,JRu,A:Scorn	2.50
130	DJu(s),RF,JRu,dragon's tooth	2.50

Superman, 2nd Series #139
© DC Comics Inc.

#	Description	Price
131	DJu(s),RF,JRu,Luthor & Contessa's kid	2.50
132	DJu,RF,JRu,Red/Blue x-over	2.50
133		2.50
134	DJu,RF,JRu,Millennium Giants	2.50
135	DJu,RF,JRu,aftermath	2.50
136	DJu,PR,JRu,The Superman of 2999 A.D., pt.1	2.50
137	DJu,PR,JRu,2999 AD,pt.2	2.50
138	DJu,PR,JRu,2999 AD,pt.3	2.50
139	DJu(s),JSn,JRu,V:Dominus	2.50
140	RMz(s),TGb,TP,City of the Future, pt.3 x-over	2.50
141	DJu(s),SEa,JRu,I:Outburst	2.50
142	DJu(s),JRu,F:Outburst	2.50
143	DJu(s),SEp,JRu,	2.50
144	DJu(s),SEp,JRu,V:Lex Luthor	2.50
145	DJu(s),SEp,JRu,hate mail	2.50
146	DJu(s),SEp,JRu,V:Toyman	2.50
147	RMz(s),TGb,BAn,A:JLA,pt.1	2.50
148	DJu(s),SEp,JRu,	2.50
149	RF,SB,Strange Visitor,pt.1	2.50
150	DJu(s),SEp,JRu,48-pg.	3.50
150a	foil cover	4.50
151	JLb,MMK,Faster than a speeding bullet	3.00
152	JLb,MMK	2.50
153	JLb,MMK,V:Imperiex	2.50
154	JLb,CaS,V:Brainiac 13	2.50
155	JLb,CaS,F:Superboy	2.50
156	JLb,CaS,V:Parasite	2.50
157	JLb,CaS,Lois vs. Superman?	2.50
158	JLb,CaS,CriticalCondition,pt.1	2.50
159	JLb,CaS,F:Green Lantern	2.50
160	JLb,CaS,Arkham,pt.1	2.50
161	JLb,CaS,Superman:Emperor?	2.50
162	JLb,CaS,A:Aquaman,pt.1	2.50
163	JLb,PaP,CaS,F:Aquaman,pt.2	2.50
164	JLb,CaS,V:Bizarro	2.50
165	JLb,AAd,A:Linear Man	2.50
166	JLb,CaS,O:Superman(new)	4.00
166a	holofoil(c)	7.00
167	JLb,CaS,Return toKrypton,pt.1	2.50
168	JLb,CaS,Lord of the Ring,pt.1	2.50
169	MWm,Infestation x-over,pt.1	2.50
170	JLb,CaS,DK,V:Mogul	2.50
171	JLb,OurWorlds atWar,prelude	2.50
172	JLb,All-Out War	2.50
173	JLb,Casualties of War	2.50
174	JLb,CaS,War aftermath	2.50
175	JLb,CaS,Last Laugh,48-pg.	3.50
176	JLb,IaC,NRd,F:Dr. Foster	2.25
177	JLb,CaS,F:Toyman,Metallo	2.25

All comics prices listed are for *Near Mint* condition.

Superman–Superman

Superman 2nd Series Ann. #2
© DC Comics, Inc.

178 JLb,CaS,F:Uncle Sam 2.25
179 JLb,African-American hero 2.25
180 JLb,IaC,NRd,V:Dracula 2.25
181 JLb,CaS,F:Bizarro 2.25
182 JLb,CaS,F:Suicide Squad 2.25
183 JLb,CaS,Clarke fired from job . 2.25
184 PFe,CaS,Return to Krypton II. . 2.25
185 BA,PFe(c),baseball game 2.25
186 PFe,CaS,Ending Battle,pt.1 . . . 2.25
187 PFe,CaS,Ending Battle,pt.5 . . . 2.25
188 F:Lois Lane 2.25
189 PFe,Lost Hearts,pt.1 x-over . . . 2.25
190 SSe(c),SMc,rogue robot. 2.25
190a spec.newsstand ed.,56-pg. . . 3.95
191 F:The Flash 2.25
192 Supergirl vs. Radion 2.25
193 Supergirl vs. Radion 2.25
194 SMc,I:Ed 2.25
195 SMc,Futuresmiths 2.25
196 SMc,new adversary 2.25
197 SMc,deaf Superman,Krypto . . . 2.25
198 SMc,V:Bizarro 2.25
199 SMc,Supergirl origins. 2.25
Ann.#1 RF,BBr,A:Titano 4.00
Ann.#2 RF,BBr,R:Newsboy Legion
 & Guardian. 4.00
Ann.#3 DAb(1st Work),TA,DG,
 Armageddon 2001. . . . . 9.00
Ann.#3a 2nd printing(silver) 3.00
Ann.#4 Eclipso 3.00
Ann.#5 Bloodlines#6,DL,I:Myriad . 3.00
Ann.#6 Elseworlds Story. 3.50
Ann.#7 WS(c),Year One Annual
 A:Dr. Occult 4.50
Ann.#8 Legends o/t Dead Earth . . 3.00
Ann.#9 Pulp Heroes (High-
 Adventure) DJu 4.50
Ann.#10 DJu(s),PR,ClV,BWr,
 Ghosts 3.00
Ann.#11 JoP,AAd(c),JLApe:Gorilla
 Warfare 3.50
Ann.#12 Planet DC. 3.50
Spec.#1,000,000 DAn&ALa(s),NBy. 2.50
Giant Ann.#1 Replica edition. 5.00
Giant #1 80-page 5.00
Giant #2 80-page 5.00
Giant #3 80-page 5.95
Spec.#0 PeerPressure,pt.3 (1994) . 2.00
Spec.King of the World, foil. 5.00
Spec.King of the World, reg. 4.00
Spec. Superman: Lois Lane,
 Girlfrenzy (1998) 2.00
Spec.#1 WS,V:L.Luthor,`Sandman' . 6.00
Spec. Superman Plus One (1997) . 3.00
Spec.#1 Superman: The Earth
 Stealers, JBy,CS,JOy (1988) . . 3.50
 2nd printing 3.00
Spec. Superman:Emperor?(2000). . 3.50
Spec. Superman Forever, KK,DJu,LSi,
 JBy,SI,DG, Luthor's kidnapped
 daughter (1998) 5.00
 Deluxe ed.,AxR(c), lenticular . . 6.00
Spec.#1 Superman: The Legacy of
 Superman,WS,JG,F:Guardian,
 Waverider,Sinbad (1993) 4.00
Spec. Superman & Savage Dragon:
 Metropolis, KK,JBg,x-over 4.95
Spec. Superman/Toyman (1996). . 2.00
Spec. Team Superman, MMr(s),
 DHz,48-page,F:Superboy,
 Supergirl & Steel 3.00
Spec. 3-D #1 LSi,V:Mainframe . . . 4.00
Spec. Whatever Happened to the
 Man of Tomorrow 6.00
Spec. Superman Y2K,JBg (1999) . . 4.95
Newstime-The Life and Death of
 the Man of Steel-Magazine,
 DJu,BBr,JOy,JG,JBg. 3.25
Spec.#1 Superman Gallery (1993) . 2.95
Superman Secret Files, DJu,JOy,
 etc.,inc. O:Superman (1997). . 5.00
Secret Files #1 Superman Villains . 5.00
Secret Files #2. . . . . 5.00
Secret Files #1 Our Worlds at War . 5.95
Secret Files #1 President Luthor. . 4.95
Spec. Metropolis Secret Files #1. . 4.95
Spec. Team Superman Secret Files 5.00
Spec. 1-shot,Superman:Lex 2000,
 JLb,TyH,DoM,Vote for Lex . . . 3.50
Spec. 10-Cent Adventure,SMc . . . 0.10
Spec. Superman vs. Darkseid:
 Apokolips Now, MSh(s),48-pg. . 2.95
Spec. Blood of my Ancestors 6.95
GN Death of Superman rep.(1993) . 6.00
 Later printings 5.95
 Platinum Edition 15.00
GN Superman At Earth's End
 (Elseworlds 1995). 4.95
GN Superman: Distant Fires, HC,GK,
 nuclear winter (1997) 6.00
GN Superman: Earth Day 1991, KGa
 Metropolis `Clean-Up'. 5.50
GN Superman For Earth (1991) . . 4.95
GN Superman: Kal, Medieval
 Superman (Elseworlds 1995) . . 5.95
GN Superman: Last God of Krypton 5.00
GN Last Stand on Krypton (2003). . 6.95
GN Superman's Metropolis, RLo &
 RTs(s),TMK, in Fritz Lang's
 Metropolis (Elseworlds 1996) . . 5.95
GN The Superman Monster 7.00
GN A Nation Divided. 5.00
GN Superman: The Odyssey 5.00
GN Peace on Earth, oversized . . . 10.00
GN Superman Red/Superman Blue,
 V:Toyman, Cyborg, Superman
 split into two entities (1997) . . 4.00
 Deluxe, 3-D cover 5.00
GN Superman: Silver Banshee, 48pg,
 prestige format (1998) 5.00
GN Superman: Speeding Bullets,
 EB (Elseworlds 1993). 6.00
GN Superman, Under a Yellow Sun
 by Clark Kent,KGa,EB (1994). . 5.95
GN Superman: The Wedding Album,
 collector's edition, 96 pg.,
 cardstock cover 4.95
GN War of the Worlds,Elseworlds . 6.00
GN Superman, Inc. 6.95
GN Superman: Mann & Superman . 5.95
GN Superman:Where is thy Sting? . 6.95
GN Superman & Savage Dragon:
 Chicago, x-over, EL (2002) . . . 5.95
 Metropolis, x-over,KK,JBg. 4.95

Superman Special #1
© DC Comics Inc.

TPB Superman: Bizarro's World . . 10.00
TPB Tales of the Bizarro World . . . 14.95
TPB Critical Condition (2003) 14.95
TPB Day of Doom (2003) 9.95
TPB Superman: The Death of Clark
 Kent, rep. (1997) 20.00
TPB End of the Century (2003). . . 17.95
TPB Eradication 13.00
TPB Exile. 15.00
TPB Superman/Fantastic Four . . . 10.00
TPB Krisis of the Krimson Kryptonite
 rep. 12.95
TPB Panic in the Sky rep. 9.95
TPB President Lex (2003). 17.95
TPB Return of Superman rep. Reign
 of Superman 14.95
TPB The Revenge Squad (2000) . 12.95
TPB Son of Superman (2000). . . . 14.95
TPB Superman Vs. Revenge
 Squad 13.00
TPB They Saved Luthor's Brain . . 14.95
TPB Time and Time Again (1994) . . 7.50
TPB The Wedding and
 Beyond rep. 15.00
TPB World Without Superman 7.50
TPB Superman in the fifties 19.95
TPB Superman in the sixties. 20.00
TPB Superman in the seventies . . 20.00
TPB Sunday Classics 1939–1943. 19.95
TPB The Dailies,Vol.1. . . . . 14.95
TPB The Dailies,Vol.2. . . . . 14.95
TPB The Dailies,Vol.3. . . . . 14.95
TPB No Limits, 208-page 14.95
TPB Endgame, 176-page 14.95
TPB Superman/Gen 13, 80-page . . 9.95
TPB Superman Vs. Predator. 14.95
TPB Superman for All Seasons. . . 14.95
TPB Til Deat Do Us Part (2001) . . 17.95
TPB Our Worlds at War, Vol.1. . . . 19.95
TPB Our Worlds at War, Vol.2. . . . 19.95
TPB Greatest Superman Stories
 Ever Told 15.95

SUPERMAN ADVENTURES
Sept., 1996
1 PDi(s),RBr,TA, from animated
 TV show. 3.00
2 SMI,RBr,TA,V:Metallo 2.50
3 SMI(s),RBr,TA,V:Brainiac 2.50
4 SMI(s), ... 2.50
5 SMI(s),BBl,TA,V:Livewire 2.50

Superman–Superman Family

6 SMI(s),RBr,TA,Metropolis in ruins	2.50
7 SMI(s),RBr,TA,V:Jax-Ur, Mala	2.50
8 SMI(s),RBr,TA,V:Jax-Ur	2.50
9 SMI(s),MM,TA,Return of the Hero	2.50
10 SMI(s),RBr,TA,V:Toyman	2.50
11 SMI(s),RBr,TA,struck down by strange malady	2.50
12 SMI(s),RBr,TA,BB, Kryptonian virus, concl.	2.50
13 SMI(s),RBr,TA,BB, alien races	2.50
14 TA,Angela Chen	2.50
15 RBr,TA,Superman's pal Bibbo	2.50
16 MMr(s),TA, meets Man of Steel	2.50
17	2.50
18 TA,should Clark quit?	2.50
19 TA,V:Multi-Face	2.50
20 RBr,TA,V:MasterTrax	2.50
21 Supergirl Adventures, 64pg.	5.50
22 MMr,TA,RBr,War Games, pt.1	2.50
23 MMr,TA,RBr,War Games, pt.2	2.50
24 MMr,TA,RBr,V:Parasite	2.50
25 MMr,TA,RBr,F:Batgirl,C:Batman, Robin, Nightwing	2.50
26 MMr,TA,V:Mr.Mxyzptlk	2.50
27 MMr,TA,F:Lex Luthor	2.50
28 MMr,MM,TA,F:Jimmy Olsen	2.50
29 MMr,TA,A:Lobo, Bizarro	2.50
30 MMr,TA,A:Lara, pt.1	2.50
31 MMr,TA,A:Lara, pt.2	2.50
32 DvM(s),Lois Hypnotized	2.50
33 DvM(s),TA,Secret Identity	2.50
34 MMr(s),TA,MM,A:Dr.Fate	2.50
35 MMr(s),TA,A:Toyman	2.50
36 MMr(s),TA, many emergencies	2.50
37 MMr(s),TA,Clark Kent,Public Enemy Number One	2.50
38 MMr(s),TA,V:Parasite	2.50
39 TA	2.50
40 TTn(s),TA,F:Mxyzptlk	2.50
41 TTn,RBr,22 stories	2.50
42 TA,F:Mr. Miracle	2.50
43 TA,MM(c),Mother Box	2.50
44 TA,MM(c),F:The Commander	2.50
45 TA,MM(c),Three young sisters	2.50
46 TA,MM(c),Smallville	2.50
47 TA,MM(c),shrinking ray	2.50
48 TA,MM(c),alien abduction	2.50
49 TA,MM(c),powers lost	2.50
50 TA,MM(c),accused of murder	2.50
51 TA,MM(c),Lois & Lana	2.50
52 TA,MM(c),Death in the Family	2.50
53 TA,MM(c),F:Mister Miracle	2.50
54 TA,MM(c),Kryptonite No More	2.50
55 TA,MM(c),Kryptonite No More	2.50
56 TA,MM(c),Poker Face	2.50
57 TA,MM(c),Four-PointPerspective	2.50
58 TA,AxR(c),What Lurks Below	2.50
59 TA,MM(c),Ghost Flowers	2.50
60 TA,MM(c),F:Jimmy Olsen	2.50
61 TA,MM(c),V:Parasite	2.50
62 TA,MM(c),Heart of Stone	2.50
63 TA,MM(c),Magic Wand	2.50
64 TA,MM(c),F:Batman Beyond	2.50
65 TA,MM(c),Power Play,pt.1	2.50
66 TA,MM(c),Power Play,pt.2, final issue	2.50
Ann.#1 JoS,DDv,V:Akamin	4.50
TPB rep.#1–#6	8.00
Spec. #1 Superman vs. Lobo - Misery in Space, DvM,MM, A:Man of Tomorrow	4.00

SUPERMAN & BATMAN: GENERATIONS — AN IMAGINARY TALE
1998
1 (of 4) JBy, Elseworlds 5.00

2 JBy,V:Bat-Mite	5.00
3 JBy	5.00
4 JBy, conclusion	5.00
TPB, rep.	14.95

SUPERMAN & BATMAN: GENERATIONS II
Aug., 2001
1 (of 4) JBy,Elseworlds,48-page	5.95
2 JBy,48-page	5.95
3 JBy,48-page	5.95
4 JBy,48-page, concl.	5.95
TPB JBy	19.95

SUPERMAN & BATMAN: GENERATIONS III
Jan. 2003
1 (of 12) JBy,Elseworlds	3.00
2 JBy,Super Twins	3.00
3 JBy,22nd Century	3.00
4 JBy,23rd Century	3.00
5 JBy,24th Century	3.00
6 JBy,25th Century	3.00
7 JBy,26th Century	3.00
8 JBy,26th Century	3.00
9 JBy,27th Century	3.00
10 JBy,28th Century	3.00
11 JBy,29th century Superboy	3.00

SUPERMAN & BATMAN: WORLD'S FUNNEST
Nov., 2000
1-shot, Elseworlds 6.95

SUPERMAN & BUGS BUNNY
1999
1 (of 4) JSon,TP	2.50
2 thru 4 TP,JSon	@2.50

SUPERMAN/BATMAN
Aug. 2003
1 JLb,V:Metallo	4.00
2 JLb,both injured	4.00
3 JLb,V:Gorilla Grodd	2.95
4 F:Captain Atom,Luthor	2.95
Spec. Secret Files (2003)	4.95

SUPERMAN: BIRTHRIGHT
July 2003
1 (of 12) F:Jor-El,40-pg.	4.00
2 South Africa,40-pg.	3.50
3 O:retold	3.50
4 Job interview	3.50
5 anti-terrorism weapons	3.50

SUPERMAN: THE DARK SIDE
Elseworlds, Aug., 1998
1 JFM,KD,First Son of Apokolips	5.00
2	5.00
3 KD, conclusion	5.00
TPB Superman: The Dark Side	13.00

SUPERMAN: DAY OF DOOM
Nov., 2002
1 (of 4) DJu,BSz,F:Ty Duffy	2.95
2 thru 4 DJu,BSz	@2.95

Superman Doomsday Huntr/Prey #3
© DC Comics, Inc.

SUPERMAN/DOOMSDAY: HUNTER/PREY
1994
1 DJu(a&s),BBr,R:Doomsday,R:Cyborg Superman,A:Darkseid	5.50
2 DJu(a&s),BBr,V:Doomsday,Cyborg Superman,A:Darkseid	5.25
3 DJu(a&s),BBr,V:Doomsday	5.25
TPB Rep. #1-#3	14.95

SUPERMAN: THE DOOMSDAY WARS
1998
1 (of 3) DJu,BBr,R:Doomsday	5.00
2 DJu,V:Doomsday	5.00
3 DJu, conclusion	5.00

SUPERMAN FAMILY
Prev: Superman's Pal, Jimmy Olsen
1974–82
164 KS,NC(c),Jimmy Olsen:'Death Bites with Fangs of Stone'	50.00
165 KS,NC(c),Supergirl:'Princess of the Golden Sun'	40.00
166 KS,NC(c),Lois Lane:'The Murdering Arm of Metropolis'	35.00
167 KS,NC(c),Jimmy Olsen:'A Deep Death for Mr. Action'	35.00
168 NC(c),Supergirl:'The Girl with the See-Through Mind'	35.00
169 NC(c),Lois Lane:'Target of the Tarantula'	35.00
170 KS(c),Jimmy Olsen:'The Kid Who Adopted Jimmy Olsen'	25.00
171 ECh(c),Supergirl:'Cleopatra-Queen of America'	25.00
172 KS(c),Lois Lane:'The Cheat the Whole World Cheered'	25.00
173 KS(c),Jimmy Olsen:'Menace of the Micro-Monster'	25.00
174 KS(c),Supergirl:'Eyes of the Serpent'	25.00
175 KS(c),Lois Lane:'Fadeout For Lois'	25.00
176 KS(c),Jimmy Olsen:'Nashville, Super-Star'	25.00
177 KS(c),Supergirl:'Bride of the Stars'	20.00

All comics prices listed are for *Near Mint* condition.

Superman: Family–Man Of

178 KS(c),Lois Lane:'The Girl
 With the Heart of Steel'. 20.00
179 KS(c),Jimmy Olsen:'I Scared
 Superman to Death' 20.00
180 KS,Supergirl:'The Secret of
 the Spell-Bound Supergirl' . . . 20.00
181 ECh(c),Lois Lane:'The Secret
 Lois Lane Could Never Tell' . . 20.00
182 CS&NA(c),Jimmy Olsen:
 `Death on Ice'. 20.00
183 NA(c),Supergirl:'Shadows
 of Phantoms' 20.00
184 NA(c),Supergirl:'The
 Visitors From The Void'. 20.00
185 NA(c),Jimmy Olsen: The
 Fantastic Fists and Fury
 Feet of Jimmy Olsen' 20.00
186 JL&DG(c),Jimmy Olsen:
 `The Bug Lady'. 20.00
187 JL(c),Jimmy Olsen:'The
 Dealers of Death' 20.00
188 JL&DG(c),Jimmy Olsen:
 `Crisis in Kandor' 20.00
189 JL(c),Jimmy Olsen:'The
 Night of the Looter' 20.00
190 Jimmy Olsen:'Somebody
 Stole My Town' 20.00
191 Superboy:'The Incredible
 Shrinking Town' 20.00
192 RA&DG(c),Superboy:'This
 Town For Plunder' 20.00
193 RA&DG(c),Superboy:'Menace
 of the Mechanical Monster'. . . 20.00
194 MR,Superboy:'When
 the Sorcerer Strikes'. 20.00
195 RA&DG(c),Superboy:'The Curse
 of the Un-Secret Identity' 20.00
196 JL&DG(c),Superboy:'The
 Shadow of Jor-El' 20.00
197 JL(c),Superboy:'Superboy's
 Split Personality'. 20.00
198 JL(c),Superboy:'Challenge
 of the Green K-Tastrophe'. . . . 20.00
199 RA&DG(c),Supergirl:'The
 Case of Cape Caper' 20.00
200 RA&DG(c),Lois Lane:
 `Unhappy Anniversary' 22.00
201 RA&DG(c),Supergirl:'The
 Face on Cloud 9' 7.00
202 RA&DG(c),Supergirl:'The
 Dynamic Duel' 7.00
203 RA&DG(c),Supergirl:'The
 Supergirl From Planet Earth'. . . 7.00
204 RA&DG(c),Supergirl:'The
 Earth-quake Enchantment' 7.00
205 RA&DG(c),Supergirl:'Magic
 Over Miami' 7.00
206 RA&DG(c),Supergirl:'Strangers
 at the Heart's Core' 7.00
207 RA&DG(c),Supergirl:'Look
 Homeward, Argonian'. 7.00
208 RA&DG(c),Supergirl:'The
 Super-Switch to New York' 7.00
209 Supergirl:'Strike Three-
 You're Out'. 7.00
210 Supergirl:'The Spoil Sport
 of New York' 7.00
211 RA&DG(c),Supergirl:'The Man
 With the Explosive Mind' 7.00
212 RA&DG(c),Supergirl:'Payment
 on Demand' 7.00
213 thru 222 . . . . @7.00

SUPERMAN FOR ALL SEASONS
June, 1998

1 (of 4) JLb,TSe, from farmboy
 to superhero. 7.00
2 JLb,TSe,V:Lex Luthor 5.00
3 JLb,TSe,V:Lex Luthor 5.00

4 JLb,TSe, conclusion 5.00

SUPERMAN/GEN13
DC/Wildstorm April, 2000

1 (of 3) AH, x-over. 2.50
1a variant cover (1:4). 2.50
2 AH,x-over 2.50
2a variant cover (1:4). 2.50
3 AH, 40-pg. 3.50

SUPERMAN: LAST SON OF EARTH
July, 2000

1 (of 2) Elseworlds. 5.95
2 Green Lantern's powers 5.95

SUPERMAN: METROPOLIS
Feb. 2003

1 (of 12) F:Jimmy Olsen 2.95
2 Mystery of the Tech 2.95
3 Rebecca. 2.95
4 The Tech or the Devil 2.95
5 Jimmy and Lena 2.95
6 Jimmy and Lena 2.95
7 Lena lost 2.95
8 blackout 2.95
9 V:Creeper. 2.95
10 V:Killgrave,Creeper 2.95

SUPERMAN: THE MAN OF STEEL
1991–2003

1 B:LSi(s),DJu,BMc,JOy,BBr,TG,
 Revenge o/t Krypton Man#1 . . 5.00
2 JBg,V:Cerberus 4.00
3 JBg,War of the Gods X-over . . . 3.00
4 JBg,V:Angstrom 3.00
5 JBg,CS,V:Atomic Skull 3.00
6 JBg,Blackout#3,A:Mr.Z 3.00
7 JBg,V:Cerberus 3.00
8 KD,V:Jolt,Blockhouse 3.00
9 JBg,Panic in the Sky#1,
 V:Brainiac. 3.50
10 JBg,Panic in the Sky#5,
 D:Draaga 3.00
11 JBg,V:Flashpoint 3.00
12 JBg,V:Warwolves. 3.00

Superman: The Man of Steel #6
© DC Comics, Inc.

DC

Comics Values Annual

13 JBg,V:Cerberus 3.00
14 JBg,A:Robin,V:Vampires 3.00
15 KG,KGa,Blaze/Satanus War . . . 3.00
16 JBg,Crisis at Hand#1 . . . . 3.00
17 JBg,V:Underworld,
 C:Doomsday 8.00
17a 2nd printing 2.50
18 JBg,I:Doomsday,V:Underworld . 10.00
18a 2nd printing 4.00
18b 3rd printing 2.50
19 JBg,Doomsday,pt.5 . . . . 7.00
19a 2nd printing 2.50
20 JBg,Funeral for a Friend#3 . . . 3.00
21 JBg,Funeral for a Friend#7 . . . 3.00
22 JBg,Reign of Supermen#4,Direct
 Sales,Die-Cut(c),mini-poster,
 F:Man of Steel 2.50
22a Newsstand Ed. 2.50
23 JBg,V:Superboy. 2.50
24 JBg,V:White Rabbit,A:Mongul . . 2.50
25 JBg,A:Real Superman 3.00
26 JBg,A:All Supermen,V:Mongul,
 Cyborg Superman 2.75
27 JBg,A:Superboy,Lex Luthor . . . 2.50
28 JBg(c),A:Steel 2.50
29 LSi(s),JBg,Spilled Blood#3,
 V:Hi-Tech,Blood Thirst 2.50
30 LSi(s),JBg,V:Lobo,Vinyl(c) 3.50
30a Newstand Ed. 2.50
31 MBr,A:Guardian 2.50
32 MBr,Bizarro's World#4,
 V:Bizarro 2.50
33 MBr,V:Parasite. 2.50
34 JBg,A:Lex Men,Dubbie Men . . 2.50
35 JBg,Worlds Collide#1,
 I:Fred Bentson 2.50
36 JBf,Worlds Collide,pt.10,V:Rift
 A:Icon 2.50
37 JBg,Zero Hour,A:Batman 2.50
38 Mystery 2.50
39 JBg,Luthor. 2.50
40 . . . . 2.50
41 Locke 2.50
42 F:Locke 2.50
43 V:Deathtrap 2.50
44 Prologue to Death 2.50
45 JGb,DJa,Death of Clark Kent,pt.4
 [New Miraweb format begins] . . 2.50
46 JBg,DJa,A:Shadowdragon 2.50
47 O:Bloodsport 2.50
48 . . . . 2.50
49 Skyhook 2.50
50 JBg,DJa,The Trial of
 Superman, 48pg. 4.00
51 JBg,DJa,The Trial of Superman . 2.50
52 JBg,The Trial of Superman . . . 2.50
53 JBg,DRo,A:Lex Luthor,Contessa 2.50
54 JBg 2.50
55 JBg,DJa, Clark dates Lori
 Lemaris 2.50
56 JBg,DJa, manipulator revealed . 2.50
57 RSt,JBg,DJa, more twisters . . . 2.50
58 LSi(s),JBg,DJa,A:Supergirl. . . . 2.50
59 LSi(s),JBg,DJa,Parasite, Steel . . 2.50
60 LSi(s),JBg,DJa,R:Bottled City
 of Kandor. 2.50
61 LSi(s),JBg,DJa,V:Riot 2.50
62 LSi(s),JBg,DJa, Superman
 looses powers, Final Night tie-in 2.50
63 LSi(s),JBg,DJa,Clark is
 kidnapped & revealed identity. . 2.50
64 LSi(s),JBg,DJa,Superman tries to
 restore his powers 2.50
65 LSi(s),SB,DJa,V:Superman
 Revenge Squad 2.50
66 LSi(s),JBg,DJa,V:Rajiv. 2.50
67 LSi(s),JBg,DJa,New powers
 prequel. 3.00
68 LSi(s),JBg,DJa,V:Metallo 3.00
69 KK&LSi(s),SEa,DJa,A:Atom,
 in Kandor 2.50

Comics Values Annual — DC — Superman: Man Of–Superman's

70 LSi(s),SEa,DJa,V:Saviour 2.50
71 LSi(s),SEa,DJa,V:Mainframe,
   Superman Revenge Squad. . . . 2.50
72 LSi(s),SEa,JP,DJa,JBg,Genesis
   V:Mainframe. 2.50
73 LSi&MWa(s),SEa,DJa,V:Revenge
   Squad 2.50
74 LSi(s),SEa,DJa,dragon's tooth . . 2.50
75 LSi(s),DJa,JBg,Mr.Mxyzptlk dies
   parody of Superman #75 . . . . . 2.50
76 LSi(s),JBb,DJa,V:Mokkari 2.50
77 . . . . 2.50
78 JBg, Millennium Giants, pt.1
   x-over. 2.50
79 JBg, Millennium Giants 2.50
80 LSi,JBg,DJa,golden age?,pt.1 . . 2.50
81 LSi,JBg,DJa,golden age?,pt.2 . . 2.50
82 LSi,JBg,DJa,golden age?,pt.3 . . 2.50
83 LSi,SEa,DJa,Dominus 2.50
84 RMz(s),TGb,TP,City of the
   Future, pt.2 x-over 2.50
85 JBg,DJa,V:Simyan & Mokkari. . . 2.50
86 LSi(s),SEa,DJa,dreams
   of disasters 2.50
87 MSh(s),DoM,DJa,A:Steel,
   Superboy, Supergirl 2.50
88 MSh(s),DoM,DJa 2.50
89 MSh(s),DoM,V:Dominus. 2.50
90 MSh(s),V:Superman's Robot . . . 2.50
91 MSh(s),DoM,paranoia 2.50
92 TPe(s),TGb,TP,Secret
   origins,concl. 2.50
93 MSh,DoM 2.50
94 RF,SB,Strange Visitor,concl. . . . 2.50
95 MSh,DoM,Fortress of Solitude . . 2.50
96 MSh,DoM, ... 2.50
97 MSh,DoM,F:Eradicator. 2.50
98 MSh,DoM,V:Brainiac 13. . . . . . 2.50
99 MSh,DoM,new armor. 2.50
100 MSh,DoM,new Fortress of
    Solitude, 48-pg. 4.00
100a Collectors edition 4.25
101 MSh,DoM,growing sicker 2.50
102 MSh,DoM,Crit.Condition,pt.3 . . 2.50
103 MSh,DoM,A:Supergirl 2.25
104 MSh,DoM,Arkham,pt.3. . . . . . . 2.25
105 MSh,DoM,Superman:Emperor . 2.25
106 MSh,HuR,V:Kosnor,Netkon . . . 2.25
107 MSh,DoM, to Phantom Zone . . 2.25
108 MSh,DoM, from Phantom Zone 2.25
109 MSh,A:Linear Man. 2.25
110 MSh,DoM,A:Star-SpangledKid . 2.25
111 MSh,DoM,Return-Krypton,pt.3 . 2.25
112 MSh,A:Superdog 2.25
113 MWm,Infestation x-over,pt.3 . . . 2.25
114 MSh,DoM,R:Eradicator. 2.25
115 MSh,DoM,Metropolis abducted. 2.25
116 MSh,DoM,JMz,All-out War 2.25
117 MSh,DoM,Casualties of War . . 2.25
118 MSh,DoM,F:Spectre. 2.25
119 MSh,Joker:Last Laugh,tie-in . . . 2.25
120 MSh,V:LexCorp 2.25
121 TNu,Royal Flush Gang 2.25
122 MSh(s),Entropy Aegis Armor . . 2.25
123 MSh(s),Metropolis Gangs,pt.1 . 2.25
124 MSh(s),Metropolis Gangs,pt.2 . 2.25
125 MSh(s),Metropolis Gangs,pt.3 . 2.25
126 MSh(s),The Pantheon,pt.1 . . . . 2.25
127 MSh(s),The Pantheon,pt.2 . . . . 2.25
128 MSh(s),ReturntoKryptonII,pt.3 . 2.25
129 Bloodsport. 2.25
130 MSh(s),Ending Battle,pt.3 . . . . 2.25
131 MSh(s),Ending Battle,pt.7 . . . . 2.25
132 MSh,Parade, A:Mr.Mxyzptlk . . . 2.25
133 Lost Hearts,pt.3 x-over. 2.25
134 MSh,40-pg.,final issue 2.25
Ann.#1 Eclipso tie-in,A:Starman . . 3.00
Ann.#2 Bloodlines#2,I:Edge 3.00
Ann.#3 MBr,Elseworlds Story 3.50
Ann.#4 Year One Annual 3.50
Ann.#5 Legends o/t Dead Earth . . 3.50

Ann.#6 Pulp Heroes (Hard Boiled)
   LSi(s),DJa 4.50
Spec.#1,000,000 KK&JOy(s),
   AWi,DJa. 3.00
Gallery 1 . . . . 3.50
TPB 7.50
TPB The Man of Steel,Vol.1 . . . . . 9.95
TPB The Man of Steel,Vol.2 . . . . . 9.95

Superman The Man of Tomorrow #1
© *DC Comics, Inc.*

SUPERMAN: THE MAN OF TOMORROW
1995–96

1 TGu,BBr,RSt(s),V:Lex Luthor . . . 2.50
2 V:Parasite. 2.50
3 TG,BBr, The Trial of Superman. . 2.50
4 RSt(s),PR,BBr,A:Shazam 2.50
5 RSt(s),PR,BBr,Wedding of Lex
   Luthor 2.50
6 RSt(s),PR,BBr,Superman V:
   Jackal again. 2.50
7 RSt(s),PR,BBr, ... 2.50
8 RSt(s),PR,BBr,V:Carbide 2.50
9 RSt(s),PR,BBr,Ma and Pa Kent
   open their album 2.50
10 . . . . 2.50
11 LSi(s),PR,DJa,BBr 2.50
12 LSi(s),PR,DJa,. 2.50
13 LSi(s),PR,DJa,A:JLA 2.50
14 LSi(s),PR,DJa,V:Riot 2.50
15 Day of Judgment x-over,48-pg. . 3.00
Spec.#1,000,000 MSh(s),DRo . . . 2.00

SUPERMAN: RED SON
April 2003

1 (of 3) Elseworlds,MMr(s). 5.95
2 MMr(s). 5.95
3 MMr(s),concl. 5.95

SUPERMAN'S GIRL FRIEND, LOIS LANE
1958–74

1 CS,KS 5,500.00
2 CS,KS. 1,400.00
3 CS,KS,spanking panel 1,000.00
4 CS,KS 750.00
5 CS,KS 750.00
6 CS,KS 500.00
7 CS,KS 500.00
8 CS,KS 400.00
9 CS,KS, A:Pat Boone 400.00
10 CS,KS 400.00

11 CS,KS 250.00
12 CS,KS 250.00
13 CS,KS 250.00
14 KS,`Three Nights in the
   Fortress of Solitude' 250.00
15 KS,I:Van-Zee. 250.00
16 KS, Lois' Signal-Watch. 250.00
17 KS,CS,A:Brainiac. 250.00
18 KS,A:Astounding Man 250.00
19 KS,`Superman of the Past' . . . 250.00
20 KS,A:Superman. 275.00
21 KS,A:Van-Zee 225.00
22 KS,A:Robin Hood. 225.00
23 KS,A:Elastic Lass, Supergirl . . 225.00
24 KS,A:Van-Zee, Bizarro 225.00
25 KS,`Lois Lane's
   Darkest Secret'. 200.00
26 KS,A:Jor-El 200.00
27 KS,CS,A:Bizarro 200.00
28 KS,A:Luthor. 200.00
29 CS,A:Aquaman,Batman,Green
   Arrow 200.00
30 KS,A:Krypto,Aquaman 125.00
31 KS,A:Lori Lemaris 125.00
32 KS,CS,A:Bizarro 125.00
33 KS,CS,A:Phantom Zone,Lori
   Lemaris, Mon-El 125.00
34 KS,A:Luthor,Supergirl. 125.00
35 KS,CS,A:Supergirl 125.00
36 KS,CS,Red Kryptonite Story. . 125.00
37 KS,CS,`The Forbidden Box' . . 125.00
38 KS,CS,A:Prof.Potter,
   Supergirl. 125.00
39 KS,CS,A:Supergirl,Jor-El,
   Krypto, Lori Lemaris 125.00
40 KS,`Lois Lane, Hag!' 125.00
41 KS,CS,`The Devil and
   Lois Lane'. 125.00
42 KS,A:Lori Lemaris 125.00
43 KS,A:Luthor. 125.00
44 KS,A:Lori Lemaris,Braniac,
   Prof. Potter. 125.00
45 KS,CS,`The Superman-Lois
   Hit Record'. 125.00
46 KS,A:Luthor. 125.00
47 KS,`The Incredible Delusion' . 125.00
48 KS,A:Mr. Mxyzptlk 125.00
49 KS,The Unknown Superman . 125.00
50 KS,A:Legion. 135.00
51 KS,A:Van-Zee & Lori Lemaris. 100.00
52 KS,`Truce Between Lois
   Lane and Lana Lang' 100.00
53 KS,A:Lydia Lawrence. 100.00

Superman's Girl Friend Lois Lane #21 Ann. #6 © DC Comics Inc.

All comics prices listed are for *Near Mint* condition.

CVA Page 163

Superman's: Girl–Pal

Superman's Girl Friend Lois Lane #123
© DC Comics, Inc.

- 54 KS,CS,'The Monster That Loved Lois Lane' 100.00
- 55 KS,A:Supergirl 100.00
- 56 KS,'Lois Lane's Super-Gamble!' 100.00
- 57 KS,'The Camera From Outer Space' 100.00
- 58 KS,'The Captive Princess' . . . 100.00
- 59 KS,CS,A:Jor-El & Batman . . . 100.00
- 60 KS,'Get Lost, Superman!' 100.00
- 61 KS,A:Mxyzptlk 100.00
- 62 KS,A:Mxyzptlk 100.00
- 63 KS,'The Satanic Schemes of S.K.U.L.' 100.00
- 64 KS,A:Luthor 100.00
- 65 KS,A:Luthor 100.00
- 66 KS,'They Call Me the Cat!'. . . 100.00
- 67 KS,'The Bombshell of the Boulevards'. 100.00
- 68 giant size 125.00
- 69 KS,Lois Lane's Last Chance . 100.00
- 70 KS,I:Silver Age Catwoman, A:Batman,Robin,Penguin . . . 350.00
- 71 KS,A:Catwoman,Batman, Robin,Penguin 200.00
- 72 KS,CS,A:Ina Lemaris 75.00
- 73 KS,'The Dummy and the Damsell' 75.00
- 74 KS,A:Justice League & Bizarro World,I:Bizarro Flash 80.00
- 75 KS,'The Lady Dictator'. 75.00
- 76 KS,A:Hap-El 75.00
- 77 giant size 100.00
- 78 KS,Courtship,Kryptonian Style. 75.00
- 79 KS,B:NA(c) 75.00
- 80 KS,'Get Out of My Life, Superman' 75.00
- 81 KS,'No Witnesses in Outerspace' 75.00
- 82 GT,A:Brainiac&Justice League. 50.00
- 83 GT,'Witch on Wheels' 50.00
- 84 GT,KS,'Who is Lois Lane?' . . . 50.00
- 85 GT,KS,A:Kandorians 50.00
- 86 giant size 75.00
- 87 GT,KS,A:Cor-Lar 50.00
- 88 GT,KS,'Through a Murderer's Eyes' 50.00
- 89 CS,A:Batman & Batman Jr. . . 55.00
- 90 GT,A:Dahr-nel 50.00
- 91 GT,A:Superlass 50.00
- 92 GT,A:Superhorse 50.00
- 93 GT,A:Wonder Woman 50.00
- 94 GT,KS,A:Jor. 50.00
- 95 giant size 75.00
- 96 GT,A:Jor 40.00
- 97 GT,KS,A:Lori Lemaris, Luma Lynai,Lyla Lerrol 40.00
- 98 GT,A:Phantom Zone 40.00
- 99 GT,KS,A:Batman 40.00
- 100 GT,A:Batman 40.00
- 101 GT,KS,'The Super-Reckless Lois Lane' 40.00
- 102 GT,KS,When You're Dead, You're Dead 40.00
- 103 GT,KS,A:Supergirl 40.00
- 104 giant size 75.00
- 105 RA,I&O:Rose & Thorn 75.00
- 106 WR,'I am Curious Black!' . . . 50.00
- 107 WR,The Snow-Woman Wept. 40.00
- 108 WR,The Spectre Suitor 40.00
- 109 WR,'I'll Never Fall in Love Again'. 40.00
- 110 WR,'Indian Death Charge!' . . 40.00
- 111 WR,A:Justice League 40.00
- 112 WR,KS,A:Lori Lemaris 50.00
- 113 giant size 75.00
- 114 WR,KS,A:Rose & Thorn 40.00
- 115 WR,A:The Black Racer 40.00
- 116 WR,A:Darkseid & Desaad . . 40.00
- 117 WR,'S.O.S From Tomorrow!' . 40.00
- 118 WR,A:Darkseid & Desaad . . 40.00
- 119 WR,A:Darkseid & Lucy Lane . 40.00
- 120 WR,'Who Killed Lucy Lane?'. 40.00
- 121 WR,A:The Thorn 40.00
- 122 WR,A:The Thorn 40.00
- 123 JRo,'Ten Deadly Division of the 100' 40.00
- 124 JRo,'The Hunters' 25.00
- 125 JRo,'Death Rides Wheels!' . . 25.00
- 126 JRo,'The Brain Busters' 25.00
- 127 JRo,'Curse of the Flame' . . . 25.00
- 128 JRo,A:Batman & Aquaman . . 25.00
- 129 JRo,'Serpent in Paradise' . . . 25.00
- 130 JRo,'The Mental Murster'. . . 25.00
- 131 JRo,Superman–Marry Me!'. . 25.00
- 132 JRo,Zatanna B.U. 25.00
- 133 JRo,'The Lady is a Bomb' . . 25.00
- 134 JRo,A:Kandor 25.00
- 135 JRo,'Amazing After-Life of Lois Lane'. 25.00
- 136 JRo,A:Wonder Woman. 25.00
- 137 JRo,'The Stolen Subway'. . . 30.00
- Ann.#1 . . . . 300.00
- Ann.#2 . . . . 200.00

SUPERMAN: SILVER BANSHEE
1998
- 1 (of 2) DIB(s),ALa. 2.25
- 2 DIB(s),ALa, conclusion 2.25

SUPERMAN'S NEMESIS, LEX LUTHOR
1999
- 1 (of 4) VS,DJa,. 2.50
- 2 VS,DJa. 2.50
- 3 VS,DJa. 2.50
- 4 VS,DJa, conclusion 2.50

SUPERMAN'S PAL, JIMMY OLSEN
1954–74
- 1 CS,'The Boy of 100 Faces!' . 8,000.00
- 2 CS,The Flying Jimmy Olsen. 2,500.00
- 3 CS,'The Man Who Collected Excitement 1,200.00
- 4 CS,'King For A Day!'. 900.00
- 5 CS,'The Story of Superman's Souvenirs 900.00
- 6 CS,Kryptonite story. 600.00
- 7 CS,'The King of Marbles' 600.00
- 8 CS,'Jimmy Olsen, Crooner' . . 550.00

Superman's Pal Jimmy Olsen #70
© DC Comics, Inc.

- 9 CS,'The Missile of Steel'. 550.00
- 10 CS,'Jungle Jimmy Olsen'. . . . 550.00
- 11 CS,'TNT.Olsen,The Champ' . . 350.00
- 12 CS,'Invisible Jimmy Olsen'. . . 350.00
- 13 CS,'Jimmy Olsen's Super Issue' 350.00
- 14 CS,'The Boy Superman' 350.00
- 15 CS,'Jimmy Olsen,Speed Demon' 350.00
- 16 CS,'The Boy Superman' 350.00
- 17 CS,J.Olsen as cartoonist 350.00
- 18 CS,A:Superboy 350.00
- 19 CS,'Supermam's Kid Brother' 350.00
- 20 CS,'Merman of Metropolis'. . . 350.00
- 21 CS,'The Wedding of Jimmy Olsen'. 250.00
- 22 CS,'The Super Brain of Jimmy Olsen'. 250.00
- 23 CS,'The Adventure of Private Olsen'. 250.00
- 24 CS,'The Gorilla Reporter'. . . . 250.00
- 25 CS,'The Day There Was No Jimmy Olsen' 250.00
- 26 CS,'Bird Boy of Metropolis' . . 225.00
- 27 CS,'The Outlaw Jimmy Olsen' 225.00
- 28 CS,'The Boy Who Killed Superman' 225.00
- 29 CS,A:Krypto. 225.00
- 30 CS,'The Son of Superman' . . 225.00
- 31 CS,I:Elastic Lad 200.00
- 32 CS,A:Prof.Potter 200.00
- 33 CS,'Human Flame Thrower' . . 200.00
- 34 CS,'Superman's Pal of Steel'. 200.00
- 35 CS,'Superman's Enemy' 200.00
- 36 CS,I:Lois Lane,O:Jimmy Olsen as Superman's Pal 200.00
- 37 CS,O:Jimmy Olsen's SignalWatch, A:Elastic Lad(Jimmy Olsen) . 200.00
- 38 CS,'Olsen's Super-Supper' . . 200.00
- 39 CS,'The Super-Lad of Space' 200.00
- 40 CS,A:Supergirl,Hank White (Perry White's son). 200.00
- 41 CS,'The Human Octopus' . . . 150.00
- 42 CS,'Jimmy The Genie'. 150.00
- 43 WB,CS,'Jimmy Olsen's Private Monster'. 150.00
- 44 CS,'Miss Jimmy Olsen' 150.00
- 45 CS,A:Kandor 150.00
- 46 CS,A:Supergirl,Elastic Lad. . . 150.00
- 47 CS,'Monsters From Earth!'. . . 150.00
- 48 CS,I:Superman Emergency Squad 150.00
- 49 CS,A:Congorilla & Congo Bill. 150.00

Comics Values Annual — DC — Superman's Pal–Supermen

50 CS,A:Supergirl,Krypto,Bizarro 150.00
51 CS,A:Supergirl 125.00
52 CS,A:Mr. Mxyzptlk,
    Miss Gzptlsnz. 125.00
53 CS,A:Kandor,Lori Lemaris,
    Mr.Mxyztlk 125.00
54 CS,A:Elastic Lad 125.00
55 CS,A:Aquaman,Thor 125.00
56 KS,Imaginary story. 125.00
57 KS,A:Supergirl,Imaginary story. 75.00
58 CS,C:Batman. 75.00
59 CS,A:Titano. 75.00
60 CS,`The Fantastic Army of
    General Olsen'. 75.00
61 CS,Prof. Potter 75.00
62 CS,A:Elastic Lad,Phantom
    Zone 75.00
63 CS,A:Supergirl,Kandor. 100.00
64 CS,`Jimmy Olsen's
    Super-Romance' 75.00
65 CS,A:Miss Gzptlsnz 75.00
66 CS,KS,A:Mr. Mxyzptlk 75.00
67 CS,`The Dummy That Haunted
    Jimmy Olsen' 75.00
68 CS,`The Helmet of Hate' 75.00
69 CS,A:Nightwing,Flamebird . . . 75.00
70 A:Supergirl,Lori Lemaris,
    Element Lad 75.00
71 CS,A:Mr. Mxyzptlk 70.00
72 CS,A:Legion of Super-Heroes,
    Jimmy Olsen becomes honorary
    member. 75.00
73 A:Kandor 75.00
74 CS,A:Mr. Mxyzptlk,Lex Luthor . 70.00
75 CS,A:Supergirl. 70.00
76 CS,A:Legion of Super-Heroes . 70.00
77 CS,Jimmy Olsen becomes
    Colossal Boy, A:Titano 70.00
78 CS,A:Aqualad 70.00
79 CS,`The Red-Headed Beetle
    of 1,000 B.C.' 70.00
80 CS,A:Bizarro. 70.00
81 CS,KS,A:Lori Lemaris,I&O
    only A:Mighty Eagle 70.00
82 CS,`The Unbeatable Jimmy
    Olsen' 70.00
83 CS,A:Kandor 70.00
84 CS,A:Titano. 70.00
85 CS,C:Legion of Super-Heroes . 75.00
86 CS,A:Congorilla,Braniac. 70.00
87 A:Lex Luthor,Brainiac,Legion
    of Super-Villians 75.00
88 C:Legion of Super-Heroes . . . 70.00
89 I:Agent Double-Five,C:John F.
    Kennedy. 70.00
90 CS,A:Mr. Mxyzptlk 70.00
91 CS,C:Batman & Robin 70.00
92 JM,A:Batman,Robin,Supergirl . 70.00
93 `The Batman-Superman of
    Earth-X!' 70.00
94 O:Insect Queen retold 70.00
95 Giant 100.00
96 I:Tempus 50.00
97 A:Fortress of Solitude. 50.00
98 `The Bride of Jungle Jimmy'. . . 50.00
99 A:Legion of Super-Heroes . . . 50.00
100 A:Legion of Super-Heroes . . . 75.00
101 A:Jor-El and Lara 40.00
102 `Superman's Greatest Double
    Cross!' 40.00
103 `The Murder of Clark Kent!' . . 35.00
104 Giant 45.00
105 V:Tempus 30.00
106 CS,A:Legion of Super-Heroes 30.00
107 A:Krypto. 30.00
108 CS,`The Midas of Metropolis'. 30.00
109 A:Lex Luthor 30.00
110 CS,`Jimmy Olsen's Blackest
    Deeds!'. 30.00
111 . . . . 30.00
112 . . . . 30.00

Superman's Pal Jimmy Olsen #149
© DC Comics Inc.

113 V:Magnaman 75.00
114 `The Wrong Superman!' 30.00
115 A:Aquaman 30.00
116 A:Brainiac 30.00
117 `Planet of the Capes' 30.00
118 A:Lex Luthor 30.00
119 `Nine Lives Like a Cat!' 30.00
120 V:Climate King. 30.00
121 . . . . 30.00
122 . . . . 30.00
123 . . . . 30.00
124 . . . . 30.00
125 Superman's Saddest Day. . . . 30.00
126 CS,Riddle of Kryptonite Plus . 30.00
127 CS,Jimmy in Revolutionary
    War. 30.00
128 I:Mark Olsen(Jimmy'sFather) . 30.00
129 MA,A:Mark Olsen. 30.00
130 MA,A:Robin,Brainiac 30.00
131 . . . . 75.00
132 MA,When Olsen Sold out
    Superman 30.00
133 JK,B:New Newsboy Legion,
    I:Morgan Edge. 100.00
134 JK,I:Darkseid 125.00
135 JK,I:New Guardian. 75.00
136 JK,O:New Guardian,
    I:Dubbilex. 60.00
137 JK,I:Four Armed Terror. 45.00
138 JK,V:Four Armed Terror. 45.00
139 JK,A:Don Rickles,I:Ugly
    Mannheim 45.00
140 Rep. Jimmy Olsen #69, #72
    and Superman #158. . . . . . 45.00
141 JK,A:Don Rickles,Lightray
    B:Newsboy Legion rep 45.00
142 JK,I:Count Dragorian 45.00
143 JK,V:Count Dragorian 45.00
144 JK,A Big Thing in a Deep
    Scottish Lake 45.00
145 JK,Brigadoon. 45.00
146 JK,Homo Disastrous 45.00
147 JK,Superman on New
    Genesis,A:High Father,
    I:Victor Volcanium. 45.00
148 JK,V:Victor Volcanium,
    E:Newsboy Legion rep 45.00
149 BO(i),The Unseen Enemy,
    B:Plastic Man rep 25.00
150 BO(i) A Bad Act to Follow. . . . 25.00
151 BO(i),A:Green Lantern. 25.00
152 MSy,BO,I:Real Morgan Edge . 25.00
153 MSy,Murder in Metropolis. . . . 25.00

154 KS,The Girl Who Was Made
    of Money 25.00
155 KS,Downfall of Judas Olsen. . 25.00
156 KS,Last Jump for
    a Skyjacker 25.00
157 KS,Jimmy as Marco Polo. . . . 25.00
158 KS,A:Lena Lawrence
    (Lucy Lane) 25.00
159 KS,Jimmy as Spartacus. 25.00
160 KS,A:Lena Lawrence
    (Lucy Lane) 25.00
161 KS,V:Lucy Lane. 25.00
162 KS,A:Lex Luthor. 25.00
163 KS,Jimmy as Marco Polo. . . . 25.00

SUPERMAN: SAVE THE PLANET
Aug., 1998
1 LSi,SEa,DRo,JP,KN, last
    front page. 3.00
1 collector's edition 4.00

SUPERMAN: THE KANSAS SIGHTING
Nov. 2003
GN #1 F:Jor-El 6.95

SUPERMAN, THE SECRET YEARS
Feb., 1985
1 CS,KS,FM(c) 3.00
2 CS,KS,FM(c) 2.50
3 CS,KS,FM(c) 2.50
4 CS,KS,FM(c), May, 1985 . . . . . . 2.50

SUPERMAN VS. AMAZING SPIDER-MAN
DC/Marvel April, 1976
1 RA/DG,oversized 100.00
1a 2nd printing, signed 175.00

SUPERMAN VS. PREDATOR
DC/Dark Horse May, 2000
1 (of 3) weakened by virus. 5.00
2 . . . . 5.00
3 conclusion 5.00

SUPERMAN/ WONDER WOMAN: WHOM GODS DESTROY
Elseworlds Oct., 1996
Mini-series
1 CCI(s),DAb, Lois becomes the
    immortal Wonder Woman 5.00
2 CCI(s),DAb, search for Lana
    Lang 5.00
3 . . . . 5.00
4 CCI(s),DAb, romance of the
    century, concl. 5.00

SUPERMEN OF AMERICA
1999
GN with membership kit 5.00
GN standard edition 4.00
1 (of 6) FaN,DBw, ... 2.50
2 FaN,DBw,V:Lex Luthor 2.50
3 FaN,DBw,F:Brahma 2.50
4 FaN,DBw,F:White Lotus 2.50
5 FaN,F:The Loser 2.50
6 FaN,A:Superman,concl. 2.50

Super–Swamp DC Comics Values Annual

SUPER POWERS
1984
[Kenner Action Figures]
1 A:Batman & Joker............ 5.50
2 A:Batman & Joker............ 5.50
3 A:Batman & Joker............ 5.50
4 A:Batman & Joker............ 5.50
5 JK(c),JK,A:Batman & Joker..... 5.50

[2nd Series], 1985–86
1 JK,'Seeds of Doom' 4.00
2 JK,'When Past & Present Meet' . 4.00
3 JK,'Time Upon Time' 4.00
4 JK,'There's No Place Like Rome . 4.00
5 JK,'Once Upon a Tomorrow' 4.00
6 JK,'Darkkseid o/t Moon' 4.00

[3rd Series], 1986
1 Cl,'Threshold'................ 3.50
2 Cl,'Escape'.................. 3.50
3 Cl,'Machinations'............. 3.50
4 Cl,'A World Divided' 3.50

SUPER-TEAM FAMILY
1975–78
1 rep...................... 30.00
2 Creeper/Wildcat 15.00
3 RE/WW,Flash & Hawkman 15.00
4 .... 18.00
5 .... 18.00
6 .... 18.00
7 .... 18.00
8 JSh,Challengers 20.00
9 JSh,Challengers 20.00
10 JSh,Challengers 20.00
11 Supergirl,Flash,Atom 20.00
12 Green Lantern,Hawkman...... 20.00
13 Aquaman, Capt. Comet 20.00
14 Wonder Woman,Atom 20.00
15 Flash & New Gods.......... 22.00

SWAMP THING
[1st Regular Series]
Oct.–Nov., 1972
1 B:LWn(s),BWr,O:Swamp Thing 175.00
2 BWr,I:Arcane 75.00
3 BWr,I:Patchwork Man 60.00
4 BWr 50.00
5 BWr 50.00
6 BWr 50.00
7 BWr,A:Batman 55.00
8 BWr,Lurker in Tunnel 13 ...... 50.00
9 BWr 50.00
10 E:BWr,A:Arcane............ 50.00
11 thru 22 NR .... @20.00
23 NR,reverts to Dr.Holland 20.00
24 NR...................... 20.00
TPB rep.#1-#10,House of Secrets
  #92, Dark Genesis Saga..... 19.95

SWAMP THING
1986–96
Previously:
SAGA OF THE SWAMP THING
46 B:AMo(s) cont'd,SBi,JTo,Crisis,
  A:John Constantine,Phantom
  Stranger................... 4.00
47 SBi,Parliment of Trees,Full
  origin,A:Constantine 4.00
48 SBi,JTo,V:Brujeria,
  A:Constantine............. 4.00
49 SBi,AA,A:Constantine,Demon,Ph.
  Stranger,Spectre,Deadman... 4.00
50 SBi,RV,JTo,concl.American
  Gothic,D:Zatara&Sargon,
  Double Size 6.00
51 RV,AA,L:Constantine 4.00
52 RV,AA,Arkham Asylum,A:Flor.

Swamp Thing #66 © DC Comics, Inc.

  Man,Lex Luthor,C:Joker,
  2-Face,Batman............. 4.00
53 JTo,V:Batman,Swamp Thing
  Banished to Space 5.00
54 JTo script,RV,AA,C:Batman 4.00
55 RV,AA,JTo,A:Batman,........ 4.00
56 RV,AA,My Blue Heaven....... 4.00
57 RV,AA,A:Adam Strange 4.00
58 RV,AA,A:Adam Strange,GC,
  Spectre preview 4.00
59 JTo,RV,AA,D:Patchwork Man ... 4.00

Direct Sales Only
60 JTo,Loving the Alien.......... 4.00
61 RV,AA,All Flesh is Grass
  G.L.Corps X-over 4.00
62 RV(&script),AA,Wavelength,
  A:Metron,Darkseid 4.00
63 RV,AA,Loose Ends(reprise) 4.00
64 E:AMo(s),SBi,TY,RV,AA,
  Return of the Good Gumbo ... 4.00
65 RV,JTo,A:Constantine 3.50
66 RV,Elemental Energy......... 3.00
67 RV,V:Solomon Grundy,
  Hellblazer preview 4.00
68 RV,O:Swamp Thing 3.00
69 RV,O:Swamp Thing 3.00
70 RV,AA,Quest for SwampThing . 3.00
71 RV,AA,Fear of Flying 3.00
72 RV,AA,Creation 3.00
73 RV,AA,A:John Constantine..... 3.50
74 RV,AA,Abbys Secret 3.00
75 RV,AA,Plant Elementals....... 3.00
76 RV,AA,A:John Constantine..... 3.50
77 TMd,AA,A:John Constantine ... 3.50
78 TMd,AA,Phantom Pregnancy ... 3.00
79 RV,AA,A:Superman,Luthor..... 3.00
80 RV,AA,V:Aliends 3.00
81 RV,AA,Invasion x-over........ 3.00
82 RV,AA,A:Sgt.Rock & Easy Co... 3.00
83 RV,AA,A:Enemy Ace 3.00
84 RV,AA,A:Sandman........... 8.00
85 RV,TY,Time Travel contd....... 3.00
86 RV,TY,A:Tomahawk 3.00
87 RV,TY,Camelot,A:Demon 3.00
88 RV,TY,A:Demon,Golden
  Gladiator 3.00
89 MM,AA,The Dinosaur Age 3.00
90 BP,AA,Birth of Abbys Child
  (Tefe) 3.25
91 PB,AA,Abbys Child (New
  Elemental) 3.00
92 PB,AA,Ghosts of the Bayou.... 3.00
93 PB,AA,New Power........... 3.00
94 PB,AA,Ax-Murderer 3.00

95 PB,AA,Toxic Waste Dumpers... 3.00
96 PB,AA,Tefes Powers 3.00
97 PB,AA,Tefe,V:Nergal,
  A:Arcane 3.00
98 PB,AA,Tefe,in Hell........... 3.00
99 PB,AA,Tefe,A:Mantago,
  John Constantine........... 3.50
100 PB,AA,V:Angels of Eden,
  (48 pages)................. 4.00
101 AA,A:Tefe 3.00
102 V:Mantagos Zombies,inc. prev.
  of Worlds Without End 3.00
103 Green vs. Grey 3.00
104 Quest for Elementals,pt.1..... 3.00
105 Quest for Elementals,pt.2..... 3.00
106 Quest for Elementals,pt.3..... 3.00
107 Quest for Elementals,pt.4..... 3.00
108 Quest for Elementals,pt.5..... 3.00
109 Quest for Elementals,pt.6..... 3.00
110 TMd,A:Father Tocsin 3.00
111 V:Ghostly Zydeco Musician ... 3.00
112 TMd,B:Swamp Thing
  for Governor................ 3.00
113 E:Swamp Thing for Governor . 3.00
114 TMd,Hellblazer............. 3.25
115 TMd,A:Hellblazer,V:Dark
  Conrad 3.25
116 From Body of Swamp Thing... 3.00
117 JD,The Lord of Misrule,
  Mardi Gras 3.00
118 A Childs Garden,A:Matthew
  the Raven 3.00
119 A:Les Perdu 3.00
120 F:Lady Jane............... 3.00
121 V:Sunderland Corporation 3.00
122 I:The Needleman 3.00
123 V:The Needleman 3.00
124 In Central America 3.00
125 V:Anton Arcane,20th Anniv. ... 4.00
126 Mescalito 3.00
127 Project Proteus #1 .... 3.00
128 Project proteus #2 .... 3.00

DC/Vertigo, 1993
129 CV(c),B:NyC(s),SEa,KDM(i),
  Sw.Thing's Deterioration..... 3.00
130 CV(c),SEa,KDM(i),A:John
  Constantine,V:Doctor Polygon . 3.00
131 CV(c),SEa,KDM(i),I:Swamp
  Thing's,Doppleganger,
  F:The Folk 3.50
132 CV(c),SEa,KDM(i),
  V:Doppleganger 3.50
133 CV(c),SEa,KDM(i),R:General
  Sunderland,V:Thunder Petal... 3.50
134 CV(c),SEa,KDM(i),Abby Leaves,

Swamp Thing #86 © DC Comics, Inc.

CVA Page 166 — All comics prices listed are for *Near Mint* condition.

DC

Swamp–Tales Of

C:John Constantine 3.50
135 CV(c),SEa,KDM(i),A:J.Constantine,
Swamp Thing Lady Jane meld . 3.50
136 CV(c),RsB,KDM(i),A:Lady Jane,
Dr.Polygon,John Constantine . . 3.50
137 CV(c),E:NyC(s),RsB,KDM(i),
IR:Sunderland is Anton Arcane,
A:J.Constantine 3.50
138 CV(c),DiF(s),RGu,KDM,B:Mind
Fields 3.50
139 CV(c),DiF(s),RGu,KDM,A:Black
Orchid,In Swamp Thing's mind,
cont'd fr.Black Orchid #5. . . . . . 3.50
140 B:Bad Gumbo 3.50
140a Platinum Ed. 10.00
141 A:Abigail Arcane 3.00
142 Bad Gumbo#3 . . . . 3.00
143 E:Bad Gumbo 3.00
144 In New York City 3.00
145 In Amsterdam 3.00
146 V:Nelson Strong. 3.00
147 Hunter 3.00
148 Sargon 3.00
149 Sargon 3.00
150 V:Sargon 3.50
151 . . . . 2.50
152 River Run,pt.1 . . . . 2.50
153 River Run 2.50
154 River Run 2.50
155 River Run 2.50
156 PJ,River Run 2.50
157 . . . . 2.50
158 . . . . 2.50
159 Swamp Dog. 2.50
160 PhH,KDM,Atmospheres 2.50
161 Atmospheres 2.50
162 Atmospheres 2.50
163 Atmospheres 2.50
164 . . . . 2.50
165 CS,KDM,F:Chester Williams . . 2.50
166 PhH,KDM,Trial by Fire,pt.1 . . . 2.50
167 PhH,KDM, Trial by Fire,pt.2 . . . 2.50
168 MMr(s),PhH,KDM,Trial,pt.3 . . . 2.50
169 MMr(s),PhH,KDM,Trial,pt.4 . . . 2.50
170 MMr(s),PhH,KDM,Trial,pt.5 . . . 2.50
171 MMr(s),PhH,KDM,Trial by Fire,
pt.6, last issue 2.50
Ann.#3 AMo(s),Ape issue 4.00
Ann.#4 PB/AA,A:Batman 4.00
Ann.#5 A:BrotherPower Geek 4.00
Ann.#6 Houma 4.00
Ann.#7 CV(c),NyC(s),MBu(i),Childrens
Crusade,F:Tefe,A:Maxine,BU:
Beautyand the Beast 7.00

SWAMP THING
DC/Vertigo, March, 2000
1 JRu,F:Tefe Holland 4.00
2 JRu,new secrets. 3.00
3 JRu, ... 3.00
4 Killing Time,pt.1 . . . . 3.00
5 Killing Time,pt.2 . . . . 3.00
6 Killing Time,pt.3 . . . . 3.00
7 RM 3.00
8 RM. 3.00
9 RM. 3.00
10 RM 3.00
11 RM,Red Harvest, pt.1 . . . . 3.00
12 RM,Red Harvest, pt.2 . . . . 3.00
13 RM,Red Harvest, pt.3 . . . . 3.00
14 RM,Red Harvest, pt.4 . . . . 3.00
15 RM,Red Harvest, pt.5 . . . . 3.00
16 RM,Red Harvest, pt.6 . . . . 3.00
17 Red Harvest, pt.7. . . . . 3.00
18 R:Original Swamp Thing 3.00
19 The Tree of Knowledge 3.00
20 final issue 3.00
Secret Files #1, 64-pg. 4.95
TPB The Curse, AMo(s) 19.95
TPB A Murder of Crows 19.95

TPB Earth to Earth 17.95
TPB Dark Genesis (2003). 19.95
TPB Reunion (2003). 19.95

SWEATSHOP
April 2003
1 F:Mel Bowling. 2.95
2 A Traitor in Our Midst 2.95
3 Peerless Penciller. 2.95
4 Freddy Ferret 2.95
5 comic-book convention 2.95
6 I Have No Son 2.95

Sword of Sorcery #5
© DC Comics Inc.

SWORD OF SORCERY
Feb.–March, 1973
1 MK(c),HC 25.00
2 BWv,NA,Hc. 30.00
3 BWv,HC,MK,WS 25.00
4 HC,WS 10.00
5 Nov.–Dec., 1973. . . . . 10.50

SWORD OF THE ATOM
Sept., 1983
1 GK 3.00
2 thru 4 GK . . . . @3.00
Spec.#1 GK 2.50
Spec.#2 GK 2.50
Spec.#3 PB 2.50

SYSTEM, THE
DC/Vertigo, 1996
TPB by Peter Kuper 12.95

TAILGUNNER JO
Sept., 1988
1 . . . . 2.50
2 thru 6 . . . . @2.50

TAKION
1996
1 PuK,AaL,Josh Sanders
becomes Takion 2.50
2 thru 4 . . . . @2.50
5 PuK,AaL,Adventures of Source
Elemental, cont. 2.50
6 PuK,AaL,Final Night tie-in. 2.50
7 PuK,AaL,Arzaz trains Takion,
final issue 2.50

TALES OF THE GREEN LANTERN CORPS
May, 1981
1 JSon,FMc,O:Green Lantern 2.50
2 JSon,FMc. 2.50
3 JSon,FMc. 2.50

TALES OF THE LEGION OF SUPER HEROES
Aug., 1984
(Previously:
Legion of Super Heroes)
314 KG,V:Ontiir 2.50
315 KG(i),V:Dark Circle 2.50
316 KG(i),O:White Witch. 2.50
317 KG(i),V:Dream Demon 2.50
318 KG(i),V:Persuader 2.50
319 KG(i),V:Persuader,A:Superboy. 2.50
320 DJu,V:Magpie 2.50
321 DJu,Exile,V:Kol 2.50
322 DJu,Exile,V:Kol 2.50
323 DJu,Exile,V:Kol 2.50
324 DJu,EC,V:Dev-Em 2.50
325 DJu,V:Dark Circle 2.50
326 thru 354 rep. of Legion of Super
Heroes, 3rd Series #1–#29. . . . 2.50
Ann.#4 rep. Baxter Ann.#1 . . . . . . 2.50
Ann.#5 rep. Baxter Ann.#2 . . . . . . 2.50

TALES OF THE NEW TEEN TITANS
June, 1982
1 GP, O:Cyborg 3.50
2 GP, O:Raven 3.50
3 GD, O:Changling 3.50
4 GP/EC,O:Starfire 3.50

TALES OF THE TEEN TITANS
(see NEW TEEN TITANS)

TALES OF THE UNEXPECTED
1956–68
1 The Out-Of-The-World Club . 1,700.00
2 . . . . 750.00
3 . . . . 500.00
4 Seven Steps to the Unknown . 500.00
5 . . . . 500.00
6 `The Girl in the Bottle'. 400.00
7 NC(c),Pen That Never Lied . . . 400.00
8 . . . . 400.00
9 LSt(c),The Amazing Cube 400.00
10 MMe(c),The Strangest Show
On Earth 400.00
11 LSt(c),Who Am I? 250.00
12 JK,Four Threads of Doom . . . 350.00
13 JK(c),Weapons of Destiny . . . 350.00
14 SMo(c),The Forbidden Game. 250.00
15 JK,MMe,Three Wishes
to Doom 350.00
16 JK,The Magic Hammer 350.00
17 JK,Who Is Mr. Ashtar? 350.00
18 JK(c),MMe,A Man Without A
World 350.00
19 NC,Man From Two Worlds . . . 325.00
20 NC(c),The Earth Gladiator . . . 325.00
21 JK,The Living Phantoms 325.00
22 JK(c),The Man From Robot
Island 325.00
23 JK,The Invitation From Mars! . 325.00
24 LC,The Secret Of Planetoid
Zero! 325.00
25 The Sorcerer's Asteroid! 225.00

All comics prices listed are for *Near Mint* condition. CVA Page 167

Tales Of–Tales Of   DC   Comics Values Annual

Tales of the Unexpected #9
© DC Comics, Inc.

26 MMe,The Frozem City 225.00
27 MMe,The Prison In Space . . . 225.00
28 The Melting Planet 225.00
29 The Phantom Raider 225.00
30 The Jinxed Planet 225.00
31 RH,Keep Off Our Planet 200.00
32 Great Space Cruise Mystery . 200.00
33 The Man Of 1,000 Planets . . . 200.00
34 Ambush In Outer Space 200.00
35 MMe,I was a Space Refugee . 200.00
36 The Curse Of The
    Galactic Goodess 200.00
37 The Secret Prisoners
    Of Planet 13 . . . . 200.00
38 The Stunt Man Of Space 200.00
39 The Creatures From The
    Space Globe 200.00
40 B:Space Ranger,The Last
    Days Of Planet Mars! 1,600.00
41 SMo(c),The Destroyers From
    The Stars! 500.00
42 The Secret Of The
    Martian Helmet 500.00
43 The Riddle Of The Burning
    Treasures,I:Space Ranger . 1,100.00
44 DD&SMo(c),The Menace Of
    The Indian Aliens 350.00
45 DD&SMo(c),The Sheriff
    From Jupiter 350.00
46 DD&SMo(c),The
    Duplicate Doom! 350.00
47 DD(c),The Man Who Stole
    The Solar System 275.00
48 Bring 'Em Back Alive-
    From Space 275.00
49 RH,The Fantastic Lunar-Land 275.00
50 MA,King Barney The Ape 275.00
51 Planet Earth For Sale 275.00
52 Prisoner On Pluto 275.00
53 InterplanetaryTroubleShooter . 275.00
54 The Ugly Sleeper Of Klanth,
    Dinosaur 275.00
55 The Interplanetary
    Creature Trainer 275.00
56 B:Spaceman At Work,Invaders
    From Earth 275.00
57 The Jungle Beasts Of Jupiter . 275.00
58 The Boss Of The
    Saturnian Legion 275.00
59 The Man Who Won A World . . 275.00
60 School For Space Sleuths . . . 275.00
61 The Mystery Of The
    Mythical Monsters 225.00
62 The Menace Of The Red
    Snow Crystals 225.00

63 Death To Planet Earth 225.00
64 Boy Usurper Of Planet Zonn . 225.00
65 The Creature That
    Couldn't Exist 225.00
66 MMe,Trap Of The Space
    Convict 225.00
67 The Giant That
    Devoured A Village 225.00
68 Braggart From Planet Brax . . . 125.00
69 Doom On Holiday Asteroid . . . 125.00
70 The Hermit Of Planetoid X . . . 125.00
71 Manhunt In Galaxy G-2! 125.00
72 The Creature Of 1,000 Dooms 125.00
73 The Convict Defenders
    Of Space! 125.00
74 Prison Camp On Asteroid X-3! 125.00
75 The Hobo Jungle Of Space . . 125.00
76 The Warrior Of Two Worlds! . . 125.00
77 Dateline-Outer Space 125.00
78 The Siren Of Space 125.00
79 Big Show On Planet Earth! . . 125.00
80 The Creature Tamer! 125.00
81 His Alien Master! 125.00
82 Give Us Back Our Earth!,
    E:Space Ranger 125.00
83 DD&SMo(c),The Anti-Hex
    Merchant! 90.00
84 DD&SMo(c),The Menace Of
    The 50-Fathom Men 90.00
85 JkS(c),The Man Who Stole My
    Powers,B:Green Glob 90.00
86 DD&SMo(c),They'll Never
    Take Me Alive! 75.00
87 JkS(c),The Manhunt Through
    Two Worlds 75.00
88 DD&SMo(c),GK,The Fear
    Master 75.00
89 DD,SMo(c),Nightmare on Mars 75.00
90 JkS(c),The Hero Of 5,000 BC . 75.00
91 JkS(c),The Prophetic Mirages,
    I:Automan 90.00
92 The Man Who Dared To Die! . . 75.00
93 JkS(c),Prisoners Of Hate
    Island 75.00
94 The Monster Mayor - USA 75.00
95 The Secret Of Chameleo-Man . 75.00
96 Wanted For Murder...1966...
6966 . . . . 75.00
97 One Month To Die 75.00
98 Half-Man/Half Machine 75.00
99 JkS(c),Nuclear Super-Hero! . . . 75.00
100 Judy Blonde, Secret Agent! . . 90.00
101 The Man In The Liquid Mask! . 60.00
102 Bang!Bang! You're Dead 60.00
103 JA,ABC To Disaster 60.00
104 NA(c),Master Of The
    Voodoo Machine 60.00
Becomes:

UNEXPECTED, THE
1968–82

105 The Night I Watched
    Myself Die 75.00
106 B:Johnny Peril,The Doorway
    Into Time 50.00
107 MD,JkS(c),The Whip Of Fear! 50.00
108 JkS(c),Journey To
    A Nightmare 50.00
109 JkS(c),Baptism By Starfire! . . 50.00
110 NA(c),Death Town, U.S.A.! . . 50.00
111 NC(c),Mission Into Eternity . . 50.00
112 NA(c),The Brain Robbers! . . . 50.00
113 NA(c),The Shriek Of
    Vengeance 50.00
114 NA(c),My Self-My Enemy! . . . 40.00
115 BWr,NA(c),Diary Of
    A Madman 40.00
116 NC(c),Express Train
    To Nowhere! 35.00
117 NC(c),Midnight Summons
    The Executioner! 30.00

118 NA(c),A:Judge Gallows,Play
    A Tune For Treachery 30.00
119 BWr,NC(c),Mirror,Mirror
    On The Wall 55.00
120 NC(c),Rambeau's Revenge . . 35.00
121 BWr,NA(c),Daddy's
    Gone-A-Hunting 35.00
122 WW,DG(c),The Phantom
    Of The Woodstock Festival . . . 35.00
123 NC(c),Death Watch! 35.00
124 NA(c),These Walls Shall
    Be Your Grave 35.00
125 NC(c),Screech Of Guilt! 35.00
126 ATh,NC(c),You Are Cordially
    Invited To Die! 35.00
127 GT,JK,ATh,NC(c),Follow The
    Piper To Your Grave 35.00
128 DW,BWr,NC(c),Where Only
    The Dead Are Free! 50.00
129 NC(c),Farewell To A
    Fading Star 35.00
130 NC(c),One False Step 35.00
131 NC(c),Run For Your Death! . . 35.00
132 MD,GT,NC(c),The Edge Of
    Madness 40.00
133 WW,JkS(c),A:Judge Gallows,
    Agnes Doesn't Haunt Here
    Anymore! 35.00
134 GT,NC(c),The Restless Dead . 35.00
135 NC(c),Death, Come
    Walk With Me! 35.00
136 SMo,GT,NC(c),An Incident
    of Violence 35.00
137 WW,NC(c),Dark Vengeance! . 20.00
138 WW,NC(c),Strange Secret of
    the Huan Shan Idol 25.00
139 GT,NC(c),The 2 Brains of
    Beast Bracken! 20.00
140 JkS(c),The Anatomy of Hate . 20.00
141 NC(c),Just What Did Eric
    See? 20.00
142 NC(c),Let The Dead Sleep! . . 20.00
143 NC(c),Fear is a Nameless
    Voice 20.00
144 NC(c),The Dark Pit of
    Dr. Hanley 20.00
145 NC(c),Grave of Glass 20.00
146 NC(c),The Monstrosity! 20.00
147 NC(c),The Daughter of
    Dr. Jekyll 20.00
148 NC(c),Baby Wants Me Dead! . 20.00
149 NC(c),To Wake the Dead . . . 20.00
150 NC(c),No One Escapes From
    Gallows Island 20.00
151 NC(c),Sorry, I'm Not Ready
    To Die! 20.00
152 GT,NC(c),Death Wears Many
    Faces 20.00
153 NC(c),Who's That Sleeping
    In My Grave? 20.00
154 NC(c),Murder By Madness . . . 20.00
155 NC(c),Non-Stop Journey
    Into Fear 20.00
156 NC(c),A Lunatic Is Loose
    Among Us! 20.00
157 NC(c),The House of
    the Executioner 50.00
158 NC(c),Reserved for Madmen
    Only 50.00
159 NC(c),A Cry in the Night 50.00
160 NC(c),Death of an Exorcist . . 50.00
161 BWr,NC(c),Has Anyone
    Seen My Killer 50.00
162 JK,NC(c),I'll Bug You
    To Your Grave 50.00
163 DD,LD(c),Room For Dying . . . 15.00
164 House of the Sinister Sands . . 15.00
165 LD(c),Slayride in July 15.00
166 LD(c),The Evil Eyes of Night . 15.00
167 LD(c),Scared Stiff 15.00
168 LD(c),Freak Accident 15.00

DC

169 LD(c),What Can Be Worse
Than Dying?............. 15.00
170 LD(c),Flee To Your Grave.... 15.00
171 LD(c),I.O.U. One Corpse.... 15.00
172 LD(c),Strangler in Paradise.. 15.00
173 LD(c),What Scared Sally?... 15.00
174 LD(c),Gauntlet of Fear...... 15.00
175 LD(c),The Haunted Mountain. 15.00
176 JkS(c),Having A
Wonderful Crime.......... 15.00
177 ECh(c),Reward for the Wicked 15.00
178 LD(c),Fit To Kill!............ 15.00
179 LD(c),My Son, The Mortician.. 15.00
180 GT,LD(c),The Loathsome
Lodger of Nightmare Inn..... 18.00
181 LD(c),Hum of the Haunted... 15.00
182 LD(c),Sorry, This Coffin
is Occupied.............. 15.00
183 LD(c),The Dead Don't
Always Die................ 15.00
184 LD(c),Wheel of Misfortune!... 15.00
185 LD(c),Monsters from a
Thousand Fathoms......... 15.00
186 LD(c),To Catch a Corpse.... 15.00
187 LD(c),Mangled in Madness.. 15.00
188 LD(c),Verdict From The Grave 15.00
189 SD,LD(c),Escape From The
Grave..................... 16.00
190 LD(c),The Jigsaw Corpse.... 16.00
191 MR,JO(c),Night of the Voodoo
Curse..................... 18.00
192 LD(c),A Killer Cold & Clammy 15.00
193 DW,LD(c),Don't Monkey the
Murder.................... 15.00
194 LD(c),Have I Got a Ghoul
For You................... 15.00
195 JCr,LD(c),Whose Face is at
My Window................ 15.00
196 LD(c),The Fear of Number 13 10.00
197 LD(c),Last Laugh of a Corpse 10.00
198 JSn(c),Rage of the
Phantom Brain............ 10.00
199 LD(c),Dracula's Daughter.... 10.00
200 GT,RA&DG(c),A:Johnny Peril,
House on the Edge of Eternity 11.00
201 Do Unto Others............ 10.00
202 JO,LD(c),Death Trap........ 10.00
203 MK(c),Hang Down Your
Head, Joe Mundy........... 10.00
204 DN,JKu(c),Twinkle, Twinkle
Little Star................ 10.00
205 JkS,A:Johnny Peril,The Second
Possession of Angela Lake... 10.00
206 JkS,A:Johnny Peril,The
Ultimate Assassin........... 10.00
207 JkS,A:Johnny Peril,Secret of
the Second Star............ 10.00
208 JkS,A:Johnny Peril,Factory
of Fear................... 10.00
209 JkS,Game for the Ghastly... 10.00
210 Vampire of the Apes,Time
Warp..................... 10.00
211 A:Johnny Peril,The Temple
of the 7 Stars............ 10.00
212 JkS,MK(c),A:Johnny Peril,The
Adventure of the Angel's Smile 10.00
213 A:Johnny Peril,The Woman
Who Died Forever......... 10.00
214 JKu(c),Slaughterhouse Arena. 10.00
215 JKu(c),Is Someone
Stalking Sandra........... 10.00
216 GP,JKu(c), Samurai Nightmare 10.00
217 ShM,DSp,EC(c),Dear Senator 10.00
218 KG,ECh&DG(c),I'll Remember
You Yesterday............ 10.00
219 JKu(c),A Wild Tale......... 10.00
220 ShM,JKu(c),The Strange
Guide.................... 10.00
221 SD,ShM,JKu(c),Em the
Energy Monster.......... 10.00
222 KG,SD(c)................. 10.00

TALOS OF THE WILDERNESS SEA
Aug., 1987
1-shot GK..................... 2.25

TANGENT COMICS
(All Oct., 1997)
The Atom #1 DJu,PR,V:Fatal Five.. 3.00
The Flash #1, TDz,GFr,CaS...... 3.00
Doom Patrol #1 DJu,SCh,...... 3.00
Green Lantern #1 JeR,JWi,MGy... 3.00
The Joker #1 KK,MHy.......... 3.00
Metal Men #1 MRz,MkK......... 3.00
Nightwing #1 JOs,JD........... 3.00
Sea Devils #1 KBk,VGi,TP...... 3.00
The Secret Six #1 CDi,TG,...... 3.00

Tangent: Nightwing #1
© *DC Comics, Inc.*

TANGENT '98
(All June, 1998)
The Batman #1 DJu,KJ........ 2.25
JLA #1 DJu,DBk,V:UltraHumanites. 2.25
Joker's Wild #1 KK............ 2.25
Nightwing: Night Force #1 JOs.... 2.25
Powergirl #1 RMz.............. 2.25
The Superman #1 Harvey Dent... 2.25
Tales of the Green Lantern #1.... 2.25
The Trials of the Flash #1,
V:Plastic Man.............. 2.25
Wonder Woman #1 PDa,....... 2.25

TANK GIRL
1995
1 Movie Adaptation............ 6.00

TANK GIRL: APOCALYPSE
1995–96
1 AIG,BBo(c)................. 3.00
2 AIG,BBo(c)Tank Girl Pregnant... 3.00
3 AIG,BBo(c)................. 3.00
4 AIG, finale.................. 3.00

TANK GIRL: THE ODYSSEY
DC/Vertigo, 1995
1 New Limited Series........... 3.00
2 BBo(c),Land of Milk & Honey... 3.00
3 I:The Sirens................ 3.00

TARZAN
April, 1972
(Prev. published by Gold Key)
207 JKu,O:Tarzan,pt.1......... 75.00
208 thru 210 JKu,O:Tarzan,pt.2–4. 30.00
211 thru 229............... @20.00
230 RH...................... 40.00
231 thru 235................ @38.00
236 and 237................. @15.00
238 giant-size................ 25.00
239 thru 258 Feb., 1977..... @15.00

TARZAN FAMILY
Nov.–Dec., 1975
(Prev.: Korak, Son of Tarzan)
60 B:Korak................... 20.00
61 thru 66 Nov.–Dec.,1976.... @15.00

TATTERED BANNERS
1998
1 (of 4) AIG(s),MMc............ 3.00
2 AIG&KG(s),MMc.............. 3.00
3 AIG(s),MMc................. 3.00
4 AIG(s),MMc, conclusion....... 3.00

TEAM TITANS
1992–94
1 KM,Total Chaos#3,A:New Titans,
Deathstroke,V:Lord Chaos,
BU:KGa,Killowat........... 4.00
1a BU:AV(i),Mirage............ 2.50
1b BU:MN,GP,Nightrider........ 2.50
1c BU:AH,Redwing............ 2.50
1d BU:GP(i),Terra............. 2.50
2 KM,Total Chaos#6,A:New
Titans, V:Chaos,C:Battalion... 2.50
3 KM,Total Chaos#9,V:Lord
Chaos, A:New Titans......... 2.50
4 KM,Titans Sell-Out#4,
J:Battalion, Troia............ 2.50
5 KM,A:Battalion.............. 2.50
6 ANi,A:Battalion.............. 2.50
7 PJ,I:Nightwing of 2001........ 2.50
8 PJ,A:Raven................. 2.50
9 PJ,V:Bloodwing.............. 2.50
10 PJ,V:Vampiric Creatures..... 2.50
11 PJ,F:Battalion.............. 2.50
12 PJ,F:Battalion.............. 2.50
13 PJ,New Direction.......... 2.50
14 PJ,V:Clock King,Chronos,Calander
Man,Time Commander....... 2.50
15 PJ....................... 2.50
16 PJ,F:Nightrider............ 2.50
17 PJ,A:Deathwing............ 2.50
18 IR:Leader................. 2.50
19 V:Leader................. 2.50
20 PJ,V:Lazarium............. 2.50
21 PJ,V:US Government....... 2.50
22 PJ,A:Chimera............. 2.50
23 PJ,I:Warhawk(Redwing)..... 2.50
24 PJ,Zero Hour,R.Kole,last issue.. 2.50
Ann.#1 I:Chimera............. 3.50
Ann.#2 PJ,Elseworlds Story..... 3.75

TEEN BEAT
Nov.–Dec., 1967
1 Monkees photo........... 100.00
Becomes:

TEEN BEAM
2 Monkees................. 100.00

Teen Titans – Terminal / DC / Comics Values Annual

Teen Titans #9 © DC Comics, Inc.

TEEN TITANS
[1st Series]
Jan., 1966

1 NC,Titans join Peace Corps	350.00
2 NC,I:Garn Akaru	150.00
3 NC,I:Ding Dong Daddy	100.00
4 NC,A:Speedy	100.00
5 NC,I:Ant	100.00
6 NC,A:Beast Boy	75.00
7 NC,I:Mad Mod	75.00
8 IN/JAb,I:Titans Copter	75.00
9 NC,A:Teen Titan Sweatshirts	75.00
10 NC,I:Bat-Bike	75.00
11 IN/NC A:Speedy	60.00
12 NC,in Spaceville	75.00
13 NC,Christmas story	60.00
14 NC,I:Gargoyle	60.00
15 NC,I:Capt. Rumble	60.00
16 NC,I:Dimension X	60.00
17 NC,A:Mad Mod	60.00
18 NC,1:Starfire (Russian)	60.00
19 GK,WW,J:Speedy	60.00
20 NA,NC J:Joshua	75.00
21 NA,NC,A:Hawk,Dove	75.00
22 NA,NC,O:Wondergirl	75.00
23 GK,NC,N:Wondergirl	40.00
24 GK,NC	40.00
25 NC,I:Lilith,A:J.L.A.	40.00
26 NC,I:Mal	40.00
27 NC	40.00
28 NC,A:Ocean Master	40.00
29 NC,A:Ocean Master	40.00
30 NC,A:Aquagirl	40.00
31 NC,GT,A:Hawk,Dove	40.00
32 NC,I:Gnarrk	25.00
33 GT,NS,A:Gnarrk	25.00
34 GT,NC	25.00
35 GT,NC,O:Mal	25.00
36 GT,NC,JAp,V:Hunchback	25.00
37 GT,NC	25.00
38 GT,NC	25.00
39 GT,NC,Rep.Hawk & Dove	25.00
40 NC,A:Aqualad	25.00
41 NC,DC,Lilith Mystery	25.00
42 NC	25.00
43 NC,Inherit the Howling Night	25.00
44 C:Flash	25.00
45 IN,V:Fiddler	25.00
46 IN,A:Fiddler	25.00
47 C:Two-Face	15.00
48 I:Bumblebee,Harlequin, A:Two-Face	25.00
49 R:Mal As Guardian	15.00
50 DH,I:Teen Titans West	20.00
51 DH,A:Teen Titans West	15.00
52 DH,A:Teen Titans West	15.00
53 O:Teen Titans, A:JLA	15.00

TEEN TITANS, THE
Aug., 1996

1 DJu(s),GP,Titan's Children, pt.1 (of 3)	5.00
2 DJu(s),GP,Titan's Children, pt.2,V:Prysm	4.00
3 DJu(s),GP,Titan's Children, pt.3	4.00
4 DJu(s),GP,Coming Out,pt.1, A:Robin	3.00
5 DJu(s),GP,Coming Out,pt.2	3.00
6 DJu(s),DJu,GP,F:Risk	3.00
7 DJu(s),DJu,GP,The Atom quits team	3.00
8 DJu(s),DJu,GP,J:Atom,V:Dark Nemesis	3.00
9 DJu(s),DJu,GP,Lost World of Skartaris, pt.1	3.00
10 DJu(s),DJu,GP,Lost World of Skartaris, pt.2	3.00
11 DJu(s),DJu,GP,Lost World of Skartaris, concl.,A:Warlord,	3.00
12 DJu(s),DJu,GP,Original Titans, pt.1 (of 4) 48pg	4.00
13 DJu,GP,Original Titans, pt.2 Genesis tie-in	3.00
14 DJu,GP,Original Titans, pt.3	3.00
15 DJu,GP,Original Titans, pt.4	3.00
16 DJu,GP,aftermath	3.00
17 DJu,PJ,team reunites	3.00
18 DJu,PR	3.00
19 DJu,PJ,Millennium Giants, A:Superman Red	3.00
20 DJu, night with the Titans	3.00
21 DJu,Titans Hunt,pt.1	3.00
22 DJu,Titans Hunt,pt.2	3.00
23 DJu,Titans Hunt,pt.3	3.00
24 DJu,Titans Hunt,pt.4, final issue	3.00
Ann.#1 Pulp Heroes (High-Adventure)	4.50
Annual #1 (1967) 80-page, rep.	5.00

TEEN TITANS
July 2003

1 MMK	8.00
1a 2nd printing	3.50
2 MMK,Cyborg	2.50
3 MMK,	2.50
4 MMK,disobey order	2.50
5 MMk,Infighting	2.50
Spec. Swingin' Elseworlds Spec.	5.95

TEEN TITANS/OUTSIDERS
Oct. 2003

Spec. Secret Files ... 5.95

TEEN TITANS GO!
Nov. 2003

1 F:Robin,Cyborg,Beast Boy ... 2.50

TEEN TITANS SPOTLIGHT
Aug., 1986

1 DCw,DG,Starfire Apartheid	4.00
2 DCw,DG,Starfire Apartheid#2	3.00
3 RA,Jericho	3.00
4 RA,Jericho	3.00
5 RA,Jericho	3.00
6 RA,Jericho	3.00
7 JG,Hawk	4.00
8 JG,Hawk	3.00

Teen Titans Spotlight #9 © DC Comics, Inc.

9 Changeling	3.00
10 EL,Aqualad And Mento	3.00
11 JO,Brotherhood of Evil	3.00
12 EC,Wondergirl	3.00
13 Cyborg	3.00
14 1stNightwing/Batman Team-up	4.00
15 EL,Omega Men	3.00
16 Thunder And Lightning	3.00
17 DH,Magennta	3.00
18 ATi,Aqualad,A:Aquaman	3.00
19 Starfire,A:Harbinger,Millennium X-over	3.00
20 RT(i),Cyborg	3.00
21 DSp,Flashback sty w/orig.Teen Titans	3.00

TEMPEST
Mini-series Sept., 1996

1 (of 4) from Aquaman	2.25
2 new costume	2.25
3 O:Tempest	2.25
4 finale	2.25

TEMPUS FUGITIVE
1990

1 KSy,Time Travel,I:Ray 27	6.00
2 KSy,Viet Nam	6.00
3 KSy,World War I	6.00
4 KSy,final issue	6.00

TERMINAL CITY
DC/Vertigo, 1996–97

1 thru 3 DMt(s),MLr,	@2.50
4 DMt(s),MLr,I:Kid Gloves	2.50
5 DMt(s),MLr,Missing link on the loose	2.50
6 DMt(s),MLr,	2.50
7 DMt(s),MLr,A:Lady in Red	2.50
8 DMt(s),MLr,	2.50
9 (of 9) DMt(s),MLr,finale	2.50
TPB rep. mini-series	20.00

TERMINAL CITY: AERIAL GRAFFITI
DC/Vertigo, Sept., 1997

1 (of 5) DMt,MLr,MCo(c)	2.50
2 DMt,MLr,MCo(c),F:Cosmo Quinn	2.50
3 DMt,MLr,MCo(c)	2.50
4 DMt,MLr,MCo(c)	2.50

3-D BATMAN
1953, 1966
1 rep.Batman #42 & #48..... 1,400.00
1a A:Tommy Tomorrow (1966) .. 450.00

THRILLER
Nov., 1983
1 TVE 2.25
2 TVE,O:Thriller.............. 2.25
3 TVE 2.25
4 TVE 2.25
5 TVE,DG,Elvis satire 2.25
6 TVE,Elvis satire 2.25
7 TVE 2.25
8 TVE 2.25
9 TVE 2.25
10 TVE................... 2.25
11 AN.................... 2.25
12 AN.................... 2.25

THRILLING COMICS
1999
1 CDi(s),RH,F:Hawkman &
  Wildcat................. 2.25

THRILLKILLER
Elseworlds 1997
1 HC(s),DIB,F:Robin and Batgirl .. 3.50
2 HC(s),DIB................ 3.00
3 HC(s),DIB,conl............. 3.00

THRILLKILLERS '62
Feb., 1998
GN HC,DIB................. 5.00

TIMBER WOLF
1992–93
1 AG(i),V:Thrust.............. 2.25
2 V:Captain Flag 2.25
3 AG(i),V:Creeper 2.25
4 AG(i),V:Captain Flag......... 2.25
5 AG(i),V:Dominators,Capt.Flag... 2.25

TIME BREAKERS
DC/Helix, 1997
1 (of 5) RaP(s),CWn,time
  paradoxes created 2.50
2 RaP(s),CWn............... 2.50
3 RaP(s),CWn,expedition to 20th
  century England 2.50
4 RaP(s),CWn,Angela travels back
  in time 2.50
5 RaP(s),CWn,final issue....... 2.50

TIME MASTERS
Feb., 1990
1 ATi,O:Rip Hunter,A:JLA........ 2.50
2 ATi,A:Superman 2.25
3 ATi,A:Jonah Hex, Cave Carson.. 2.25
4 ATi,Animal Man #22 x-over 2.25
5 ATi,A:Viking Prince 2.25
6 ATi,A:Dr.Fate 2.25
7 ATi,A:GrLantern,Arion 2.25
8 ATi,V:Vandal Savage......... 2.25

TIME WARP
Oct.–Nov., 1979
1 JAp,RB,SD,MK(c),DN,TS 18.00
2 DN,JO,TS,HC,SD,MK(c),GK... 12.00
3 DN,SD,MK(c),TS 12.00
4 MN,SD,MK(c),DN 12.00
5 DN,MK(c),July, 1980......... 10.00

Titans #31
© *DC Comics Inc.*

TITANS
1999
1 MBu, new team, two covers 3.50
2 MBu,A:Superman 3.00
3 MBu.................... 3.00
4 MBu,V:Goth 3.00
5 MBu,A:Siren................ 3.00
6 MBu,A:Green Lantern......... 3.00
7 MBu,Velocity 10, pt.1 .... 3.00
8 MBu,Velocity 10, pt.2 .... 3.00
9 Day of Judgment x-over 3.00
10 MBu,F:Changeling
  & Deathstroke 3.00
11 MBu.................... 3.00
12 MBu,This Immortal Coil,pt.3.... 3.50
13 internal fight............... 3.00
14 to Scotland 3.00
15 MBu,pt.1 .... 3.00
16 MBu,V:Gargoyle 3.00
17 ALa,into space............. 3.00
18 ALa,into space,pt.2 .... 3.00
19 ALa,into space,pt.3 .... 3.00
20 ALa,end of Cyborg........... 3.00
21 PaP,Hangmen 3.00
22 PaP,Arsenal vs. Deathstroke ... 3.00
23 PaP,Who's Troia?,pt.1 .... 3.00
24 PaP,Who's Troia?,pt.2 .... 3.00
25 MWn,GP,48-page 4.00
26 PaP,V:Shockwave 3.00
27 PaP,F:Cheshire,Epsilon 3.00
28 PaP,The All-Nighter 3.00
29 PaP,tower of troublemakers ... 3.00
30 JP,Sins of the Past.......... 3.00
31 JP,V:Theta 3.00
32 V:Dakota Jameson 3.00
33 V:Theta 3.00
34 Cheshire Smile,Last Laugh ... 3.00
35 F:Beast Boy & Flamebird 3.00
36 V:Wildebeests 3.00
37 BKi,in the Orphanage 3.00
38 BKi,V:Epsilon,final stand 3.00
39 BKi,V:Dark Nemesis 3.00
40 BKi,F:The Favored.......... 3.00
41 PGr,F:Nikki 3.00
42 BKi,Chemical World,pt.1 ..... 3.00
43 BKi,Chemical World,pt.2 ..... 3.00
44 BKi,JmP,Chemical World,pt.3.. 3.00
45 BKi,JmP,F:Damage 3.00
46 BKi,JmP,F:Damag,Jesse 3.00
47 TPe,BKi,PGr,JmP 3.00
48 TPe,BKi,JmP,Murder,pt.1 .... 3.00
49 TPe,BKi,JmP,Murder,pt.2 .... 3.00
50 TPe,BKi,JmP,final issue 3.00

Ann.#1 Planet DC.............. 4.00
Spec. Secret Files #1 .... 5.50
Spec. Secret Files #2 .... 5.50
GN Scissors, Paper, Stone, manga
  style (1997) 5.50

TITANS SELL-OUT SPECIAL
1 SE,AV,I:Teeny Titans,
  w/Nightwing poster......... 3.75

TITANS, THE/LEGION OF SUPER-HEROES: UNIVERSE ABLAZE
Jan., 2000
1 (of 4) DJu,PJ 5.00
2 DJu,PJ................... 5.00
3 DJu,PJ................... 5.00
4 DJu,PJ, concl. 5.00

TITANS, THE/ YOUNG JUSTICE: GRADUATION DAY
May 2003
1 (of 3) 10.00
2 Indigo................... 7.00
3 Concl................... 6.00

TOMAHAWK
1950–72
1 Prisoner Called Tomahawk.. 2,000.00
2 FF(4pgs),Four Boys
  Against the Frontier 850.00
3 Warpath 450.00
4 Tomahawk Wanted: Dead
  or Alive................. 450.00
5 The Girl Who Was Chief..... 450.00
6 Tomahawk-King of the Aztecs . 350.00
7 Punishment of Tomahawk.... 350.00
8 The King's Messenger 350.00
9 The Five Doomed Men 350.00
10 Frontied Sabotage......... 350.00
11 Girl Who Hated Tomahawk... 250.00
12 Man From Magic Mountain... 250.00
13 Dan Hunter's Rival......... 250.00
14 The Frontier Tinker 250.00
15 The Wild Men of
  Wigwam Mountain 250.00
16 Treasure of the Angelique ... 250.00
17 Short-Cut to Danger........ 250.00
18 Bring In M'Sieur Pierre...... 250.00
19 The Lafayette Volunteers.... 250.00
20 NC(c),The Retreat of
  Tomahawk 250.00
21 NC(c),The Terror of the
  Wrathful Spirit........... 200.00
22 CS(c),Admiral Tomahawk.... 200.00
23 CS(c),The Indian Chief
  from Oxford 200.00
24 NC(c),Adventure In the
  Everglades.............. 200.00
25 NC(c),The Star-Gazer of
  Freemont 200.00
26 NC(c),Ten Wagons For
  Tomahawk 200.00
27 NC(c),Frontier Outcast...... 200.00
28 I:Lord Shilling............. 225.00
29 The Conspiracy of Wounded
  Bear................... 250.00
30 The King of the Thieves..... 200.00
31 NC(c),The Buffalo Brave
  From Misty Mountain 200.00
32 NC(c),The Clocks That
  Went to War 200.00
33 The Paleface Tribe......... 200.00
34 The Capture of General
  Washington 200.00
35 Frontier Feud............. 200.00

Tomahawk–Transmet. DC Comics Values Annual

36 NC(c),A Cannon for Fort
  Reckless 200.00
37 NC(c),Feathered Warriors . . . 200.00
38 The Frontier Zoo 200.00
39 The Redcoat Trickster 200.00
40 Fearless Fettle-Daredevil 200.00
41 The Captured Chieftain 200.00
42 The Prisoner Tribe 200.00
43 Tomahawk's Little Brother . . . 200.00
44 The Brave Named Tomahawk 200.00
45 The Last Days of Chief Tory . . 200.00
46 The Chief With 1,000 Faces . . 125.00
47 The Frontier Rain-Maker 125.00
48 Indian Twin Trouble 125.00
49 The Unknown Warrior 125.00
50 The Brave Who Was Jinxed . . 125.00
51 General Tomahawk 125.00
52 Tom Thumb of the Frontier . . . 125.00
53 The Four-Footed Renegade . . 125.00
54 Mystery of the 13th Arrows . . . 125.00
55 Prisoners of the Choctaw 125.00
56 The Riddle of the
  Five Little Indians 125.00
57 The Strange Fight
  at Fort Bravo 150.00
58 Track of the Mask 100.00
59 The Mystery Prisoner of
  Lost Island 100.00
60 The Amazing Walking Fort . . . 100.00
61 Tomahawk's Secret Weapons . 75.00
62 Strongest Man in the World . . . 75.00
63 The Frontier Super Men 75.00
64 The Outcast Brave 75.00
65 Boy Who Wouldn't Be Chief . . . 75.00
66 DD&SMo(c),A Trap For
  Tomahawk 75.00
67 DD&SMo(c),Frontier Sorcerer . 75.00
68 DD&SMo(c),Tomahawk's
  Strange Ally 75.00
69 DD&SMo(c),Tracker-King
  of the Wolves 75.00
70 DD&SMo(c),Three Tasks
  for Tomahawk 75.00
71 DD&SMo(c),The Boy Who
  Betrayed His Country 75.00
72 DD&SMo(c),The Frontier Pupil. 75.00
73 DD&SMo(c),The Secret of
  the Indian Sorceress 75.00
74 DD&SMo(c),The Great
  Paleface Masquerade 75.00
75 DD&SMo(c),The Ghost of
  Lord Shilling 75.00
76 DD&SMo(c),The Totem-Pole
  Trail 75.00
77 DD&SMo(c),The Raids of
  the One-Man Tribe 75.00
78 DD&SMo(c),The Menace
  of the Mask 75.00
79 DD&SMo(c),Eagle Eye's
  Debt of Honor 75.00
80 DD&SMo(c),The Adventures
  of Tracker 60.00
81 The Strange Omens of
  the Indian Seer 60.00
82 The Son of the Tracker 60.00
83 B:Tomahawk Rangers,
  Against the Tribe 60.00
84 There's a Coward Among
  the Rangers 60.00
85 The Wispering War 60.00
86 Rangers vs. King Colossus . . . 40.00
87 The Secrets of Sgt.
  Witch Doctor 40.00
88 The Rangers Who Held
  Back the Earth 40.00
89 The Terrible Tree-Man 40.00
90 The Prisoner In The Pit 40.00
91 The Tribe Below the Earth 40.00
92 The Petrified Sentry of
  Peaceful Valley 40.00
93 The Return of King Colosso . . . 40.00

94 Rip Van Ranger 40.00
95 The Tribe Beneath the Sea . . . 40.00
96 The Ranger Killers 40.00
97 The Prisoner Behind the
  Bull's-Eye 40.00
98 The Pied Piper Rangers 40.00
99 The Rangers vs.ChiefCobweb . 40.00
100 The Weird Water-Tomahawk . 50.00
101 Tomahawk, Enemy Spy 35.00
102 The Dragon Killers 35.00
103 The Frontier Frankenstein . . . 35.00
104 The Fearful Freak of
  Dunham's Dungeon 35.00
105 The Attack of the Gator God . 35.00
106 The Ghost of Tomahawk 35.00
107 Double-Cross of the
  Gorilla Ranger 35.00
108 New Boss For the Rangers . . 35.00
109 The Caveman Ranger 35.00
110 Tomahawk Must Die 35.00
111 Vengeance of the Devil-Dogs . 35.00
112 The Rangers vs. Tomahawk . . 35.00
113 The Mad Miser of
  Carlisle Castle 35.00
114 The Terrible Power of
  Chief Iron Hands 35.00
115 The Deadly Flaming Ranger . . 35.00
116 NA(c),The Last Mile of
  Massacre Trail 35.00
117 NA(c),Rangers'Last Stand . . . 35.00
118 NA(c),Tomahawk, Guilty
  of Murder 35.00
119 NA(c),Bait For a Buzzard 35.00
120 NC(c),The Coward Who
  Lived Forever 35.00
121 NA(c),To Kill a Ranger 35.00
122 IN(c),Must the Brave Die 35.00
123 NA(c),The Stallions of Death . 35.00
124 NA(c),The Valley of
  No Return 35.00
125 NA(c),A Chief's Feather
  For Little Bear 35.00
126 NA(c),The Baron of
  Gallows Hill 35.00
127 NA(c),The Devil is Waiting . . . 35.00
128 NA(c),Rangers-Your 9
  Lives For Mine 35.00
129 NA(c),Treachery at
  Thunder Ridge 35.00
130 NA(c),Deathwatch at
  Desolation Valley 35.00
131 JKu(c),B:Son of Tomahawk,
  Hang Him High 35.00
132 JKu(c),Small Eagle...Brother
  Hawk 25.00

Tor #5 © DC Comics, Inc.

133 JKu(c),Scalp Hunter 25.00
134 JKu(c),The Rusty Ranger . . . 25.00
135 JKu(c),Death on Ghost
  Mountain 25.00
136 JKu(c),A Piece of Sky 30.00
137 JKu(c),Night of the Knife 30.00
138 JKu(c),A Different Kind
  of Christmas 30.00
139 JKu(c),Death Council 35.00
140 Jku(c),The Rescue 30.00

TOR
May-June, 1975
1 JKu,O:Tor 15.00
2 thru 6, Tor reprints . . . . @10.00

TOTAL JUSTICE
Sept., 1996
1 thru 3 CPr(s),RBe,DG, toy
  line tie-in . . . . @2.25

TOTAL RECALL
1990
1 Movie Adaption 3.00

TOTEMS
DC/Vertigo, Dec., 1999
GN TPe,DFg 5.95

TOXIC GUMBO
DC/Vertigo, March, 1998
1-shot GN 6.00

TRANSMETROPOLITAN
DC/Helix, July, 1997
1 WEI,DaR,JeM, gonzo journalism
  in 21st century 10.00
2 WEI,DaR,Angels 8 district 6.00
3 WEI,DaR, riot in Angels 8 . . . . . 5.00
4 WEI,DaR, Vs President of US . . . 4.00
5 WEI,DaR, Watches TV 4.00
6 WEI,DaR,evangelicals 4.00
7 WEI,DaR 4.00
8 WEI,DaR,AnotherColdMorning . . 4.00
9 WEI,DaR,Wild in the Country . . . 3.00
10 WEI,DaR,Freeze Me with
  Your Kiss, pt.1 . . . . 3.00
11 WEI,DaR,Freeze Me, pt.2 . . . . 3.00
12 WEI,DaR,Freeze Me, pt.3 . . . . 3.00
13 WEI,DaR,JaL(c),Year of the
  Bastard, pt.1 . . . . 3.00
14 WEI,DaR,JaL(c),Bastard,pt.2 . . 3.00
15 WEI,DaR,JaL(c),Bastard,pt.3 . . 3.00
16 WEI,DaR,Bastard,pt.4 . . . . 3.00
17 WEI,DaR,Bastard,pt.5 . . . . 3.00
18 WEI,DaR,Bastard, concl. 3.00
19 WEI,DaR,New Scum,pt.1 . . . . 3.00
20 WEI,DaR,New Scum,pt.2 . . . . 3.00
21 WEI,DaR,New Scum,pt.3 . . . . 2.50
22 WEI,DaR,New Scum,pt.4 . . . . 2.50
23 WEI,DaR,New Scum,pt.5 . . . . 2.50
24 WEI,DaR,New Scum,pt.6 . . . . 2.50
25 WEI,DaR,JLe(c),Days in
  the City #1 . . . . 2.50
26 WEI,DaR,RyR,JLe(c),Days in
  the City #2 . . . . 2.50
27 WEI,DaR,RyR,JLe(c) 2.50
28 WEI,DaR,RyR,LonelyCity,pt.1 . 2.50
29 WEI,DaR,RyR,LonelyCity,pt.2 . 2.50
30 WEI,DaR,RyR,LonelyCity,pt.3 . 2.50
31 WEI,DaR,RyR,F:Spider 2.50
32 WEI,DaR,RyR, ... 2.50
33 WEI,DaR,RyR 2.50
34 WEI,DaR,RyR,Gouge Away,pt.1. 2.50
35 WEI,DaR,RyR,Gouge Away,pt.2. 2.50
36 WEI,DaR,RyR,Gouge Away,pt.3. 2.50

37 WEI,DaR,Back to Basics,pt.1 . . . 2.50
38 WEI,DaR,Back to Basics,pt.2 . . . 2.50
39 WEI,DaR,Back to Basics,pt.3 . . . 2.50
40 WEI,DaR,Streets atNight,pt.1 . . . 2.50
41 WEI,DaR,Streets atNight,pt.2 . . . 2.50
42 WEI,DaR,Streets atNight,pt.3 . . . 2.50
43 WEI,DaR,Dirge,pt.1 . . . . 2.50
44 WEI,DaR,Dirge,pt.2 . . . . 2.50
45 WEI,DaR,Dirge,pt.3 . . . . 2.50
46 WEI,DaR,Dirge aftermath. 2.50
47 WEI,DaR,A Disaster Zone 2.50
48 WEI,DaR,Year Four begins 2.50
49 WEI,DaR,rebuild Spider's case . 2.50
50 WEI,DaR,Filthy Assistants 2.50
51 WEI,DaR,F:Mitchell Royce. 2.50
52 WEI,DaR,The Cure,pt.1 . . . . 2.50
53 WEI,DaR,The Cure,pt.2 . . . . 2.50
54 WEI,DaR,The Cure,pt.3 . . . . 2.50
55 WEI,DaR,Vita Severn Zone 2.50
56 WEI,DaR,Martial law 2.50
57 WEI,DaR,White House siege . . . 2.50
58 WEI,DaR,martial law 2.50
59 WEI,DaR,final meeting 2.50
60 WEI,DaR,final issue 2.50
GN I Hate it Here 5.95
GN Filth of the City. 5.95
TPB Lust For Life 15.00
TPB Year of the Bastard 12.95
TPB Back on the Street 7.95
TPB New Scum, rep.#19–#24. . . . 12.95
TPB Lonely City 14.95
TPB Gouge Away (2002) 14.95
TPB Spider's Thrash (2002) 14.95
TPB The Cure (2003) 14.95
TPB Dirge (2003) 14.95

TRENCHCOAT BRIGADE
DC/Vertigo, 1999
1 (of 4) JNR(s),F:John Constantine,
  Mister E, Dr.Occult, Phantom
  Stranger 2.50
2 JNR 2.50
3 JNR 2.50
4 JNR, conclusion 2.50

TRIUMPH
[Mini-Series], 1995
1 From Zero Hour 2.25
2 Teamates Peril 2.25
3 V:Mind Readers 2.25

TROUBLE MAGNET
Dec., 1999
1 (of 4) KPI, F:robot whose mind
  has been stolen 2.50
2 KPI 2.50
3 KPI 2.50
4 KPI,concl. 2.50

TRUE FAITH
DC/Vertigo, Aug., 1997
TPB GEn,WaP, series rep. 25.00

TSR WORLDS
TSR 1990
1 I:SpellJammer 4.50

TV SCREEN CARTOONS
(see REAL SCREEN COMICS)

2020 VISIONS
DC/Vertigo, April, 1997
1 (of 12) the Disunited States
  of America 2.25
2 JaD(s), ... 2.25

3 JaD(s), ... 2.25
4 JaD(s),WaP,La Tormenta,pt.1 . . 2.25
5 JaD(s),WaP,La Tormenta,pt.2 . . 2.25
6 JaD(s),WaP,La Tormenta,pt.3 . . 2.25
7 JaD(s),Renegade,pt.1. . . . . 2.25
8 JaD(s),Renegade,pt.2. . . . . 2.25
9 JaD(s),Renegade,pt.3. . . . . 2.25
10 JaD(s),Repro-Man,pt.1. . . . . . . 2.25
11 JaD(s),Repro-Man,pt.2. . . . . . . 2.25
12 JaD(s),Repro-Man,pt.3. . . . . . . 2.25

Twilight #2
© DC Comics Inc.

TWILIGHT
1990–91
1 JL,Last Frontier 5.50
2 JL,K.SorensenVs.T.Tomorrow . . . 5.00
3 JL,K.SorensenVs.T.Tomorrow . . . 5.00

UNAUTHORIZED BIO OF LEX LUTHOR
1 EB 4.00

UNCLE SAM
DC/Vertigo, Nov, 1997
GN 1 (of 2) AxR 5.00
GN 2 AxR. 5.00
TPB 9.95

UNDERCOVER GENIE
DC/Vertigo June 2003
TPB 14.95

UNDERWORLD
Dec., 1987
1 EC,New Yorks Finest 2.50
2 EC,A:Black Racer. 2.50
3 EC,V:Black Racer. 2.50
4 EC,final issue 2.50

UNDERWORLD UNLEASHED
1995–96
1 PWa,F:Neron 5.00
2 PWa,Neron Vs.Green Lantern . . 4.00
3 PWa,conclusion 4.00
Abyss—Hell's Sentinel 1-shot . . . 3.00
Apokolips-Dark Uprising 1-shot. . . 3.00
Batman—Devil's Asylum 1-shot . . . . .

AIG,BSz 3.00
Patterns of Fear 1-shot 3.00

UNEXPECTED, THE
See: TALES OF THE UNEXPECTED

UNKNOWN SOLDIER
(see STAR SPANGLED)

UNKNOWN SOLDIER
April, 1988
1 True Origin revealed,Viet
  Nam 1970 . . . . 4.00
2 Origin contd.,Iran 1977 . . . . 3.00
3 Origin contd.Afghanistan1982. . . 3.00
4 Nicaragua. 3.00
5 Nicaragua contd. 3.00
6 . . . . 3.00
7 Libia 3.00
8 Siberia, U.S.S.R. 3.00
9 North Korea 1952 . . . . 3.00
10 C.I.A. 3.00
11 C.I.A., Army Intelligence 3.00
12 final issue,1989 . . . . 3.00

UNKNOWN SOLDIER
DC/Vertigo, Feb., 1997
1 (of 4) GEn(s),KPI,F:maverick
  CIA agent. 7.00
2 GEn(s),KPI,search for Unknown
  Soldier continues 5.00
3 GEn(s),KPI,search for Unknown
  Soldier continues 5.00
4 GEn(s),KPI,intrigue, finale 5.00
TPB series rep.. . . . . 13.00

UNTOLD LEGEND OF BATMAN
July, 1980
1 JA,JBy,(1st DC work)O:Batman . 6.00
2 JA,O:Joker&Robin 4.50
3 JA,O:Batgirl 4.50

USER
DC/Vertigo, Jan., 2001
1 (of 3) 48-page. 5.95
2 JBo,SeP,48-page 5.95
3 JBo,SeP,48-page 5.95

V
(TV Adaptation)
Feb., 1985
1 CI/TD 3.00
2 thru 5 CI/TD . . . . @2.25
6 thru 16 CI/TD . . . . @2.25
17 & 18 DG. . . . . @2.25

VALOR
1992–94
1 N:Valor,A:Lex Luthor Jr 3.00
2 MBr,AG,V:Supergirl 2.50
3 MBr,AG,V:Lobo. 2.50
4 MBr,AG,V:Lobo. 2.50
5 MBr,A:Blasters 2.50
6 A:Blasters,V:Kanjar Ru 2.50
7 A:Blasters. 2.50
8 AH(c),V:The Unimaginable 2.50
9 AH(c),PCu,A:Darkstar. 2.50
10 AH(c),V:Unimaginable 2.50
11 A:Legionnaires 2.50
12 AH(c),B:D.O.A. 2.50
13 AH(c),D:Valor's Mom 3.00

Valor–Vigilante — DC Comics Values Annual

Valor #10 © DC Comics, Inc.

14 AH(c),A:JLA,Legionnaires 2.50
15 SI(c),D.O.A #4. . . . . 2.50
16 CDo,D.O.A #5. . . . . 2.50
17 CDo,LMc,D:Valor. 2.50
18 A:Legionnaires. 2.50
19 CDo,A:Legionnaires,V:Glorith. . . 2.50
20 CDo,A:Wave Rider 2.50
21 . . . . 2.50
22 End of an Era,pt.2 . . . . 2.50
23 Zero Hour 2.50

VAMPS
DC/Vertigo, 1994–95
1 BB(c) 3.00
2 thru 6 BB(c) . . . . @3.00
TPB 10.00

VAMPS: HOLLYWOOD & VEIN
DC/Vertigo, 1996
1 F:Mink 2.50
2 . . . . 2.50
3 I:Maggot. 2.50
4 F:Mink,Screech 2.50
5 off to rescue Hugh Evans (of 6) . 2.50
6 . . . . 2.50

VAMPS: PUMPKIN TIME
DC/Vertigo, 1998
1 (of 3) Halloween mini-series 2.50
2 . . . . 2.50
3 . . . . 2.50

VERMILLION
DC/Helix, Aug., 1996
1 ADv,MKu(c) Lucius Shepard
   story. 2.50
2 ADv,MKu(c) Jonathan Cave's
   cover blown 2.50
3 ADv,riot aboard space ship,
   Ildiko's tale. 2.50
4 ADv,Starship's engines run wild . 2.50
5 ADv 2.50
6 ADv,Creation of Vermillion 2.50
7 ADv,Jonathan Cave discovers
   hiding place of enemy 2.50
8 ADv,Joyland 2.50
9 GEr, the library in Kaia Mortai. . . 2.50
10 GEr, Lord Iron and Lady
    Manganese, pt.2 . . . . 2.50
11 GEr,Lord Iron and Lady
    Manganese, concl. 2.50
12 final issue 2.50

VERTIGO GALLERY: DREAMS AND NIGHTMARES
1995
1 Various artists. 3.50

VERTIGO JAM
1993
1 GF(c),NGa(s),ANo(s),PrM(s),GEn(s),
   JaD(s),KN,SDi,SEa,NyC(s),EiS,PhH,
   KDM(i),SeP,MiA,RaP(s),MPn(i),
   Vertigo Short Stories 4.50

VERTIGO POP!: TOKYO
DC/Vertigo, July, 2002
1 (of 4) by Seth Fisher. 3.00
2 Steve, Maki 3.00
3 . . . . 3.00
4 . . . . 3.00

LONDON
DC/Vertigo, Nov., 2002
1 (of 4) PrM,PBd 3.00
2 thru 4 PrM,PBd . . . . @3.00

BANGKOK
DC Vertigo May 2003
1 (of 4) 3.00
2 thru 4 . . . . @3.00

VERTIGO PREVIEW
1992
Preview of new Vertigo titles,
   new Sandman story 2.25

VERTIGO VERITE: HELL ETERNAL
Feb., 1998
1-shot JaD,SeP 7.00

THE SYSTEM
1 thru 3 . . . . @3.00
GN Seven Miles a Second 8.00

THE UNSEEN HAND
DC/Vertigo, 1996
1 thru 3 TLa . . . . @2.50
4 TLa, final issue 2.50

VERTIGO VISIONS: DR. OCCULT
1 F:Dr. Occult 4.00

DR. THIRTEEN
July, 1998
GN evil artificial intelligence 6.00

THE GEEK
1993
1 RaP(s),MiA,V:Dr.Abuse. 4.25

PHANTOM STRANGER
1993
1 AaK(s),GyD,The Infernal House . 3.75

THE EATERS
1995
1 I:The Quills. 5.00

TOMAHAWK
DC/Vertigo, May, 1998
GN RaP,TY 5.00

VERTIGO: WINTER'S EDGE
DC/Vertigo, 1998
TPB BB(c) rep. 8.00
GN Winter's Edge II 7.00
GN Winter's Edge III 6.95

V FOR VENDETTA
Sept., 1988
1 Reps.Warrior Mag(U.K.),I:V,
   A:M.Storm (Moore scripts) 5.00
2 Murder Spree 3.50
3 Govt. Investigators close in. . . . 3.00
4 T.V. Broadcast take-over. 3.00
5 Govt.Corruption Expose 3.00
6 Evey in Prison 3.00
7 Evey released 3.00
8 Search for V,A:Finch. 3.00
9 V:Finch. 3.00
10 D:V 3.00
TPB 1990 . . . . 14.95

VEXT
1999
1 KG,MMK,MkM 2.50
2 KG,MMK,MkM 2.50
3 KG,MMK,MkM 2.50
4 KG,MMK,MkM 2.50
5 KG,MMK,MkM 2.50
6 KG,MMK,MkM, final issue. 2.50

VIGILANTE
Oct., 1983
1 KP,DG,F:Adrian Chase 3.50
2 KP 3.00
3 KP,Cyborg 2.50
4 DN,V:Exterminator 2.50
5 KP 2.50
6 O:Vigilante 3.00
7 O:Vigilante 3.00
8 RA,V:Electrocutioner. 2.50
9 RA,V:Electrocutioner. 2.50
10 RA,DG,avenges J.J. 2.50
11 RA,V:Controller 2.50
12 GK,"Journal" 2.50
13 GK,"Locke Room Murder" 2.50
14 RA,V:Hammer 2.50
15 RA,V:Electrocutioner 2.50
16 RA. 2.50
17 Moore 4.00
18 Moore 4.00
19 RA. 2.50
20 A:Nightwing 2.50
21 A:Nightwing 2.50
22 . . . . 2.50
23 V:Electrocutioner 2.50
24 "Mother's Day". 2.50
25 RM,V:Police Torturers 2.50
26 V:Electrocutioner 2.50
27 V:Electrocutioner 2.50
28 New Vigilante 2.50
29 RM,New Vigilante 2.50
30 RM,D:Glitz Jefferson 2.50
31 RM,New York Violence 2.50
32 RM,New York Violence 2.50
33 RM,V:Rapist 2.50
34 . . . . 2.50
35 JBy(c),O:MadBomber 2.50
36 MGr(c),V:Peacemaker 2.50
37 MGr,RM,V:Peacemaker 2.50
38 MGr,Peacemaker. 2.50
39 White Slavery 2.50
40 HC(c),White Slavery 2.50
41 . . . . 2.50
42 A:Peacemaker,V:Terrorists 2.50
43 V:PeaceMaker 2.50
44 DC,V:Qurac 2.50

DC

Vigilante–Warlord

Vigilante #33 © DC Comics, Inc.

45 I:Black Thorn 2.50
46 Viigilante in Jail 2.50
47 A:Batman 2.50
48 I:Homeless Avenger 2.50
49 . . . . 2.50
50 KSy(c)D:Vigilante 3.00
Ann.#1 . . . . 3.00
Ann.#2 V:Cannon 2.50

VIGILANTE: CITY LIGHTS, PRAIRIE JUSTICE
1995–96

1 JeR,MCo,(of 4) 2.50
2 JeR,V:Bugsy Siegel 2.50
3 JeR 2.50
4 finale 2.50

VIPER
1994

1 Based on the TV Show 2.25
2 . . . . 2.25
3 . . . . 2.25
4 final issue 2.25

WANDERERS
June, 1988

1 I:New Team 3.00
2 V:The Performer 3.00
3 A:Legion of Superheroes 3.00
4 V:Controller Hunters 3.00
5 O:Wanderers 3.00
6 V:Terrorists 3.00
7 V:Medtorians 3.00
8 O:Psyche 3.00
9 O:Psyche 3.00
10 F:Quantum Queen 3.00
11 F:Quantum Queen 3.00
12 V:Aliens 3.00
13 V:Dinosaurs 3.00

WANTED: THE WORLD'S MOST DANGEROUS VILLAINS
July-Aug., 1972

1 GK,rep. Batman,Green Lantern. 50.00
2 CI,Batman/Joker/Penguin 35.00
3 JK,MMe,Dr. Fate 30.00
4 Green Lantern 30.00

5 GK,Dollman/Green Lantern 30.00
6 JK,Starman 30.00
7 JK,MMe,Hawkman/Flash 30.00
8 Dr. Fate/Flash 30.00
9 Sandman/Superman 30.00

WARLORD
Jan., 1976

1 MGr,O:Warlord 30.00
2 MGr,I:Machiste 15.00
3 MGr,'War Gods of Skartaris' . . . 10.00
4 MGr,'Duel of the Titans' 10.00
5 MGr,'The Secret of Skartaris' . . 10.00
6 MGr,I:Mariah,Stryker 7.00
7 MGr,O:Machiste 7.00
8 MGr,A:Skyra 7.00
9 MGr,N:Warlord 7.00
10 MGr,I:Ashiya 7.00
11 MGr,rep.1st Issue special #8 . . . 5.00
12 MGr,I:Aton 5.00
13 MGr,D:Stryker 5.00
14 MGr,V:Death 5.00
15 MGr,I:Joshua 5.00
16 MGr,I:Saaba 5.00
17 MGr,'Citadel of Death' 5.00
18 MGr,I:Shadow 5.00
19 MGr,'Wolves of the Steppes' . . . 5.00
20 MGr,I:Joshua clone 7.00
21 MGr,D:Joshua clone,Shadow . . 4.00
22 MGr'Beast in the Tower' 4.00
23 MGr,'Children of Ba'al' 4.00
24 MGr,I:ligia 4.00
25 MGr,I:Ahir 4.00
26 MGr,'The Challenge' 4.00
27 MGr,'Atlantis Dying' 4.00
28 MGr,I:Wizard World' 4.00
29 MGr,I:Mongo Ironhand' 4.00
30 MGr,C:Joshua 4.00
31 MGr,'Wing over Shamballah' . . . 4.00
32 MGr,I:Shakira 4.00
33 MGr,Birds of Prey,A:Shakira . . . 4.00
34 MGr,Sword of the Sorcerer,
  I:Hellfire 4.00
35 MGr,C:Mike Grell 4.00
36 MGr,'Interlude' 4.00
37 MGr,JSn,I:Firewing,B:Omac . . . 6.00
38 MGr,I:Jennifer,A:Omac 4.00
39 MGr,JSn,'Feast of Agravar' 4.00
40 MGr,N:Warlord 4.00
41 MGr,A:Askir 4.00
42 MGr,JSn,A:Tara,Omac 4.00
43 MGr,JSn,'Berserk'A:Omac 4.00
44 MGr,'The Gamble' 4.00
45 MGr,'Nightmare in Vista
  Vision',A:Omac 4.00
46 MGr,D:Shakira 4.00
47 MGr,I:Mikola,E:Omac 4.00
48 MGr,EC,TY,I:Arak,Claw(B) 4.00
49 MGr,TY,A:Shakira,E:Claw 3.00
50 MGr,'By Fire and Ice' 3.00
51 MGr,TY,rep.#1,
  I(B):Dragonsword 3.00
52 MGr,TY,'Back in the U.S.S.R.' . . 3.00
53 MT,TY,'Sorcerer's Apprentice' . . 3.00
54 MT,'Sorceress Supreme',
  E:Dragonsword 3.00
55 MT,'Have a Nice Day' 3.00
56 MT,JD,I:Gregmore,(B:)Arion . . . 3.00
57 MT,'The Two Faces of
  Travis Morgan' 3.00
58 MT,O:Greamore 3.00
59 MGr,A:Joshua 3.00
60 JD,'Death Dual' 3.00
61 JD,A:Greamore 3.00
62 JD,TMd,A:Mikola,E:Arion 3.00
63 JD,RR,I(B):Barren Earth 4.00
64 DJu,RR'Elsewhere' 3.00
65 DJu,RR,A:Wizard World,
  No Barren Earth 3.00
66 DJu'Wizard World',

  No Barren Earth 3.00
67 DJu,RR,'The Mark' 3.00
68 DJu,RR 3.00
69 DJu,RR 3.00
70 DJu,'Outback' 3.00
71 DJu/DA,'The Journey Back'
  No Barren Earth 3.00
72 DJu,DA,I:Scarhart,No Barren
  Earth 3.00
73 DJ,DA,'Cry Plague' 3.00
74 DJu,No Barren Earth 3.00
75 DJu,'All Dreams Must Pass'
  No Barren Earth 3.00
76 DJu,DA,RR,A:Sarga 3.00
77 DJu,DA,RR,Let My People Go . 3.00
78 DJu,RR,'Doom's Mouth' 3.00
79 PB,RM,'Paradox',No Barren
  Earth 3.00
80 DJu,DA,RR,'Future Trek' 3.00
81 DJu,DA,RR,'Thief's Magic' 3.00
82 DJu,DA,RR,'Revolution' 3.00
83 DJu,RR,'All the President's
  Men' 3.00
84 DJu,DA,RR,'Hail to the Chief' . . 3.00
85 DJu,RR,'The Price of Change' . 3.00
86 DJ,DA,No Barren Earth 3.00
87 DJu,RB,RR,I:Hawk 3.00
88 DJu,RB,RR,I:Patch,E:Barren
  Earth 3.00
89 RB,I:Sabertooth 3.00
90 RB,'Demon's of the Past' 3.00
91 DJu,DA,I:Maddox,O:Warlord
  O:Jennifer 3.00
92 NKu,'Evil in Ebony' 3.00
93 RR,A:Sabertooth 3.00
94 'Assassin's Prey' 3.00
95 AKu,'Dragon's Doom' 3.00
96 'Nightmare Prelude' 3.00
97 RB,A:Saaba,D:Scarhart 3.00
98 NKu,Crisis tie-in 3.00
99 NKu'Fire and Sword' 3.00
100 AKu,D:Greamore,Sabertooth . 4.00
101 MGr,'Temple of Demi-god' 3.00
102 I:Zuppara,Error-Machiste
  with two hands 3.00
103 JBi,'Moon Beast' 3.00
104 RR,'Dragon Skinner' 3.00
105 RR,'Staliliers of Skinner' 3.00
106 RR,I:Daimon 3.00
107 RR,'Bride of Yano' 3.00
108 RR,I:Mortella 3.00
109 RR,A:Mortella 3.00
110 RR,A:Skyra III 3.00
111 RR,'Tearing o/t Island Sea' 3.00
112 RR,'Obsession' 3.00

Warlord #72 © DC Comics Inc.

All comics prices listed are for *Near Mint* condition.

CVA Page 175

Warlord–Weird | DC | Comics Values Annual

Warlord Ann. #6 © DC Comics, Inc.

113 RR,`Through Fiends
    Destroy Me' 3.00
114 RR,`Phenalegeno Dies' 3.00
115 RR,`Citadel of Fear' 3.00
116 RR,`Revenge of the Warlord' . . 3.00
117 RR,A:Power Girl 3.00
118 RR,A:Power Girl 3.00
119 RR,A:Power Girl 3.00
120 ATb,A:Power Girl 3.00
121 ATb,A:Power Girl 3.00
122 ATb,A:Power Girl 3.00
123 JD,TMd,N:Warlord 3.00
124 JD,TMd,I:Scavenger 3.00
125 JD,TMd,D:Tara 3.00
126 JD,TMd,A:Machiste 3.00
127 JD,`The Last Dragon'. 3.00
128 JD,I:Agife. 3.00
129 JD,Vision of Quest. 3.00
130 JD,A:Maddox. 3.00
131 JD,RLd,`Vengeful Legacies . . 5.00
132 `A New Beginning' 3.00
133 JD,final issue (44pg) 4.00
Ann.#1 MGr,A:Shakira 4.00
Ann.#2 I:Krystovar 3.00
Ann.#3 DJu,`Full Circle' 3.00
Ann.#4 A:New Gods,
    Legends tie-in 3.00
Ann.#5 AKu,Hellfire 3.00
Ann.#6 F:New Gods 3.00
TPB Warlord:Savage Empire,
    Rep.#1-#10,#12,Special #8. . . 19.95

[Limited Series], 1992
1 Travis Morgan retrospective 2.25
2 Fate of T. Morgan revealed. 2.25
3 Return of Deimos 2.25
4 V:Deimos 2.25
5 MGr(c),Skartaros at War. 2.25
6 finale 2.25

WAR OF THE GODS
1991
1 GP,A:Lobo,Misc.Heroes,Circe
    (direct) 2.25
2 GP,A:Misc.Heroes,V:Circe,
    w/poster 2.25
2a (Newsstand) 2.25
3 GP,A:Misc.Heroes,V:Circe,
    w/poster 2.25
3a Newsstand 2.25
4 GP,A:Misc.Heroes,V:Circe,
    w/poster 2.25
4a Newsstand 2.25

WAR STORY
DC/Vertigo, Sept., 2001
Spec. Johann's Tiger,GEn 4.95
Spec. D-Day Dodgers,GEn 4.95
Spec. Screaming Eagles,GEn. 4.95
Spec. The Reivers 4.95
Spec. Nightingale,GEn 4.95
Spec. J for Jenny 4.95
Spec. Condors 4.95
Spec. Archangel. 4.95
Spec. Johann's Tiger 4.95

WASTELAND
Dec., 1987
1 Selection of Horror stories 2.25
2 . . . . 2.25
3 . . . . 2.25
4 . . . . 2.25
5 `The big crossover story' 2.25
6 . . . . 2.25
7 `Great St.Louis Electrical
    Giraffe Caper'. 2.25
8 `Dead Detective'. 2.25
9 . . . . 2.25
10 TT,African Folk Tale 2.25
11 `Revenge o/t Swamp Creature' . 2.25
12 JO,`After the Dead Detective'. . 2.25
13 TT(c),JO 2.25
14 JO,RM,`Whistling Past the
    Graveyard' 2.25
15 JO,RM. 2.25
16 JO 2.25
17 JO 2.25
18 JO,RM,final issue 2.25

WATCHMEN
Sept., 1986
1 B:AMo,DGb,D:Comedian 8.00
2 DGb,Funeral for Comedian. 5.00
3 DGb,F:Dr.Manhattan. 5.00
4 DGb,O:Dr.Manhattan 5.00
5 DGb,F:Rorschach 5.00
6 DGb,O:Rorschach 5.00
7 DGb,F:Nite Owl 5.00
8 DGb,F:Silk Spectre. 5.00
9 DGb,O:Silk Spectre 5.00
10 DGb,A:Rorschach 5.00
11 DGb,O:Ozymandius 5.00
12 DGb,D:Rorsharch 5.00
TPB rep.#1-#12 . . . . 14.95
TPB 20.00

WEB, THE
DC/Impact, 1991–92
1 I:Gunny, Bill Grady, Templar 2.25
2 O:The Web, I:Brew, Jump,
    Sunshine Kid 2.25
3 Minions of Meridian, I:St.James . 2.25
4 Agent Jump vs. UFO 2.25
5 Agent Buster/Fly team-up
    V:Meridian 2.25
6 I:Posse,A:Templar 2.25
7 V:Meridian's Forces 2.25
8 R: Studs. 2.25
9 Earthquest,pt.1 . . . . 2.50
10 V:Templar 2.25
11 V:Templar 2.25
12 "The Gauntlet",A:Shield 2.25
13 Frenzy#1 . . . . 2.25
14 Frenzy#2 . . . . 2.25
Ann.#1 Earthquest,w/trading card . 2.50

WEIRD, THE
April, 1988
1 BWr,A:JLI 4.00
2 BWr,A:JLI 3.00
3 BWr,V:Jason. 3.00

Weird #2 © DC Comics, Inc.

4 final issue. 3.00

WEIRD
DC/Paradox Press, 1997
1 B&W magazine. 3.00
2 . . . . 3.00
3 . . . . 3.00

WEIRD WAR TALES
Sept.–Oct., 1971
1 JKu(c),JKu,RH,Fort which
    Did Not Return 350.00
2 JKu,MD,Military Madness 125.00
3 JKu(c),RA,The Pool 100.00
4 JKu(c),Ghost of Two Wars 75.00
5 JKu(c),RH,Slave 75.00
6 JKu(c),Pawns, The Sounds
    of War 50.00
7 JKu(c),JKu,RH,Flying Blind. . . . 50.00
8 NA(c),The Avenging Grave. . . . 75.00
9 NC(c),The Promise. 50.00
10 NC(c),Who is Haunting
    the Haunted Chateau 50.00
11 NC(c),ShM,Oct. 30, 1918:
    The German Trenches, WWI . 30.00
12 MK(c),God of Vengeance. 30.00
13 LD(c),The Die-Hards 30.00
14 LD(c),ShM,The Ghost of
    McBride's Woman 30.00
15 LD(c),Ace King Just Flew
    In From Hell 30.00
16 LD(c),More Dead Than Alive . . 30.00
17 GE(c),Dead Man's Hands 30.00
18 GE(c),Captain Dracula. 30.00
19 LD(c),The Platoon That
    Wouldn't Die. 30.00
20 LD(c),Operation Voodoo 30.00
21 LD(c),One Hour To Kill. 25.00
22 LD(c),Wings of Death. 25.00
23 LD(c),The Bird of Death 25.00
24 LD(c),The Invisible Enemy . . . 25.00
25 LD(c),Black Magic...White
    Death 25.00
26 LD(c),Jump Into Hell 25.00
27 LD(c),Survival of the
    Fittest. 25.00
28 LD(c),Isle of Forgotten
    Warriors 25.00
29 LD(c),Breaking Point 25.00
30 LD(c),The Elements of Death. . 25.00
31 LD(c),Death Waits Twice 25.00
32 LD(c),The Enemy, The Stars . . 25.00
33 LD(c),Pride of the Master

DC — Weird–Will Eisner

| Race.............25.00
34 LD(c),The Common Enemy...25.00
35 LD(c),The Invaders..........25.00
36 JKu(c),Escape..............30.00
37 LD(c),The Three Wars of
   Don Q...................10.00
38 JKu(c),Born To Die..........10.00
39 JKu(c),The Spoils of War....10.00
40 ECh(c),Back From The Dead..10.00
41 JL(c), The Dead Draftees of
   Regiment Six..............10.00
42 JKu(c),Old Soldiers Never
   Die.......................10.00
43 ECh(c),Bulletproof..........10.00
44 JKu(c),ShM,The Emperor
   Weehawken................10.00
45 JKu(c),The Battle of Bloody
   Valley....................10.00
46 Kill Or Be Killed..............10.00
47 JKu(c),Bloodbath of the Toy
   Soldiers..................10.00
48 JL(c),Ultimate Destiny......10.00
49 The Face Of The Enemy.....10.00
50 ECh(c),-An Appointment With
   Destiny...................10.00
51 JKu(c),Secret Weapon.......10.00
52 JKu(c),The Devil Is A
   Souvenir Hunter...........10.00
53 JAp(c), Deadly Dominoes....10.00
54 GM(c),Soldier of Satan......10.00
55 JKu(c),A Rebel Shall Rise
   From The Grave...........10.00
56 AM(c),The Headless Courier..10.00
57 RT(c), Trial By Combat......10.00
58 JKu(c),Death Has A Hundred
   Eyes......................10.00
59 The Old One..................10.00
60 JKu(c),Night Flight..........10.00
61 HC(c),Mind War...............7.00
62 JKu(c),The Grubbers..........7.00
63 JKu(c),Battleground..........7.00
64 JKu(c),Deliver Me For D-Day..7.00
65 JKu(c),The Last Cavalry
   Charge....................7.00
66 JKu(c),The Iron Star..........7.00
67 JKu(c),The Attack of the
   Undead...................7.00
68 FM,JKu(c),The Life and Death of
   Charlie Golem.............7.00
69 JKu(c),The Day After Doomsday 7.00
70 LD(c),The Blood Boat.........7.00
71 LD(c),False Prophet..........7.00
72 JKu(c),Death Camp............7.00
73 GE(c),The Curse of Zopyrus...7.00
74 GE(c),March of the Mammoth..7.00
75 JKu(c),The Forgery............7.00
76 JKu(c),The Fire Bug...........7.00
77 JKu(c),Triad..................7.00
78 JKu(c),Indian War In Space...7.00
79 JKu(c),The Gods Themselves..7.00
80 JKu(c),An Old Man's Profession.7.00
81 JKu(c),It Takes Brains To
   Be A Killer................7.00
82 GE(c),Funeral Fire............7.00
83 GE(c),Prison of the Mind.....7.00
84 JKu(c),Devil's Due............7.00
85 thru 124 June, 1983........@7.00

WEIRD WAR TALES
DC/Vertigo, April, 1997
1 (of 4) anthology.............3.00
2 MK(c)......................3.00
3..............................3.00
4 final issue.................3.00
Spec.#1 GEn (2000)............5.00

ALL-STAR WESTERN
Aug.–Sept., 1970
1 NA(c),CI..................75.00

2 NA(c),GM,B:Outlaw.........50.00
3 NA(c),GK,O:El Diablo......50.00
4 NA(c),GK,JKu,GM...........50.00
5 NA(c),JAp,E:Outlaw........50.00
6 GK,B:Billy the Kid.........50.00
7 JKu......................40.00
8 E:Billy the Kid...........40.00
9 FF........................40.00
10 GM,I:Jonah Hex..........550.00
11 GM,A:Jonah Hex..........250.00

Weird Western Tales #28
© DC Comics Inc.

Becomes:
WEIRD WESTERN TALES
June-July, 1972
12 NA,BWr,JKu.............150.00
13.........................100.00
14 ATh.....................75.00
15 NA(c),GK................50.00
16 thru 28..................@35.00
29 O:Jonah Hex.............50.00
30.........................25.00
31 thru 38.................@25.00
39 I&O:Scalphunter........25.00
40 thru 70................@15.00

WEIRD WESTERN TALES
DC/Vertigo, Feb., 2001
1 (of 4)....................2.50
2 thru 4...................@2.50

WEIRD WORLDS
Aug.–Sept., 1971
1 JO,MA,John Carter.........50.00
2 NA,JO(c),MA,BWr..........40.00
3 MA,NA....................25.00
4 MK(c),MK.................20.00
5 MK(c),MK.................20.00
6 MK(c),MK.................20.00
7 John Carter ends.........20.00
8 HC,I:Iron Wolf............20.00
9 and 10 HC...............@20.00

WESTERN COMICS
Jan.–Feb., 1948
1 MMe,B:Vigilante,Rodeo Rick,
   Wyoming Kid, Cowboy
   Marshal................1,000.00
2 MMe,Vigilante vs. Dirk Bigger.450.00
3 MMe,Vigilante vs. Pecos Kid..400.00
4 MMe,Vigilante as Pecos Kid..400.00
5 I:Nighthawk..............350.00

6 Wyoming Kid vs. 'The
   Murder Mustang'..........250.00
7 Wyoming Kid in 'The Town
   That Was Never Robbed...250.00
8 O:Wyoming Kid............400.00
9 Wyoming Kid vs. Jack
   Slaughter................250.00
10 Nighthawk in 'Tunnel ofTerror'250.00
11 Wyoming Kid vs. Mayor Brock 200.00
12 Wyoming Kid vs. Baldy Ryan.200.00
13 I:Running Eagle..........200.00
14 Wyoming Kid in 'The Siege
   of Prairie City'...........200.00
15 Nighthawk in 'Silver, Salt
   and Pepper'..............200.00
16 Wyoming Kid vs. Smilin' Jim.200.00
17 BP,Wyoming Kid vs. Prof.
   Penny....................200.00
18 LSt on Nighthawk,Wyoming Kid
   in 'Challenge of the Chiefs'..200.00
19 LSt,Nighthawk in 'The
   Invisible Rustlers'.........200.00
20 LSt,Nighthawk in 'The Mystery
   Mail From Defender Dip'..175.00
21 LSt,Nighthawk in 'Rattlesnake
   Hollow'..................175.00
22 LSt,I:Jim Pegton.........175.00
23 LSt,Nighthawk reveals
   ID to Jim................175.00
24 The $100,000 Impersonation.175.00
25 V:Souix Invaders.........175.00
26 The Storming of the Sante
   Fe Trail..................175.00
27 The Looters of Lost Valley..175.00
28 The Thunder Creek Rebellion 175.00
29 Six Guns of the Wyoming Kid.175.00
30 V:Green Haired Killer....175.00
31 The Sky Riding Lawman...175.00
32 Death Rides the Stage Coach 175.00
33.........................175.00
34 Prescription For Killers..175.00
35 The River of Rogues.....175.00
36 Nighthawk(c),Duel in the Dark 150.00
37 The Death Dancer........150.00
38 Warpath in the Sky......150.00
39 Death to Fort Danger....150.00
40 Blind Man's Bluff........150.00
41 thru 60.................@125.00
61 thru 85................@100.00

WHERE IN THE WORLD IS CARMEN SANDIEGO?
DC/Helix, 1996
1 thru 3...................@2.25
4..........................2.25

WHY I HATE SATURN
DC/Vertigo, Dec., 1999
TPB.......................17.95

WILL EISNER LIBRARY
April, 2000
TPB The Building............9.95
TPB City People Notebook....9.95
TPB A Contract with God....12.95
GN The Dreamer..............7.95
TPB Dropsie Avenue.........15.95
TPB A Family Matter........15.95
TPB Invisible People........12.95
TPB Life on Another Planet..12.95
TPB Minor Miracles.........13.00
TPB New York: The Big City.12.95
TPB To the Heart of the Storm.14.95
TPB Will Eisner Reader.....10.00

WHO'S WHO
1985–87
1 .... 5.00
2 thru 9 .... @4.00
10 inc. 4.00
11 inc. Infinity Inc. 4.00
12 inc. Kamandi 4.00
13 inc. Legion of Super Heroes/
  Villains 4.00
14 inc. 4.00
15 inc. Metal Men 4.00
16 inc. New Gods 4.00
17 inc. Outsiders 4.00
18 inc. Power Girl 4.00
19 inc. Robin 4.00
20 inc. 4.00
21 inc. The Spectre 4.00
22 inc. Superman 4.00
23 inc. Teen Titans 4.00
24 inc. Unknown Soldier .. 4.00
25 inc. 4.00
26 inc. 4.00

WHO'S WHO IN THE DC UNIVERSE
1990–92
1 inc. Superman 6.00
1a 2nd printing 5.50
2 inc. Flash 5.50
2a 2nd printing 5.00
3 inc. Green Lantern 5.50
4 inc. Wonder Woman 5.50
5 inc. Batman 5.50
6 inc. Hawkman 5.50
7 inc. Shade 5.50
8 inc. Lobo 6.00
9 inc. Legion of Super-Heroes . 5.50
10 inc. Robin 5.50
11 inc. L.E.G.I.O.N. '91 . 5.50
12 inc. Aquaman 5.50
13 Villains issue, inc. Joker . 6.00
14 inc. New Titans 5.50
15 inc. Doom Patrol 5.50
16 inc. Catwoman, final issue ... 5.50

WHO'S WHO IN IMPACT
1991
1 Shield 4.95
2 Black Hood 4.95

WHO'S WHO IN THE LEGION
1987–88
1 History/Bio of Legionnaires 3.50
2 inc. Dream Girl 3.50
3 inc. Karate Kid 3.50
4 inc. Lightning Lad 3.50
5 inc. Phantom Girl 3.50
6 inc. Timber Wolf 3.50
7 wraparound(c) 3.50

WHO'S WHO IN STAR TREK
1987
1 HC(c) 6.00
2 HC(c) 6.00

WHO'S WHO UPDATE '87
1 inc. Blue Beetle 3.00
2 inc. Catwoman 3.00
3 inc. Justice League 3.00
4 .... 3.00

5 inc. Superboy 3.00

WHO'S WHO UPDATE '88
1 inc. Brainiac 3.00
2 inc. JusticeLeagueInternational . . 3.00
3 inc. Shado 3.00
4 inc. Zatanna 3.00

WHO'S WHO UPDATE '93
1 F:Eclipso,Azrael 5.25

WILD DOG
Sept., 1987
1 mini series DG(i),I:Wild Dog ... 3.00
2 DG(i),V:Terrorists 2.50
3 DG(i) 2.50
4 DG(i),O:Wild Dog, final issue ... 2.50
Spec.#1 .... 2.50

WILD WILD WEST
1999
1-shot movie adaptation 5.00

WINDY & WILLY
May-June, 1969
1 .... 50.00
2 thru 4 .... @30.00

WISE SON: THE WHITE WOLF
DC/Milestone, Sept., 1996
1 by Ho Che Anderson 2.50
2 thru 4 .... @2.50

Witchcraft #1 © DC Comics, Inc.

WITCHCRAFT
DC/Vertigo, 1994
1 CV(c),Three Witches from
  Sandman 4.00
2 F:Mildred 3.50
3 Final issue 3.25
TPB rep. mini-series 14.95

WITCHCRAFT: LA TERREUR
Feb., 1998
1 (of 3) JeR, sequel 2.50
2 JeR 2.50

3 JeR 2.50

WITCHING HOUR
1969–78
1 NA,ATh 200.00
2 ATh 75.00
3 ATh,BWr 85.00
4 ATh 40.00
5 ATh,BWr 75.00
6 ATh 75.00
7 ATh 40.00
8 NA,ATh 40.00
9 ATh 40.00
10 ATh 40.00
11 ATh 40.00
12 ATh 40.00
13 NA 50.00
14 AW,CG,NA(c) 65.00
15 thru 20 .... @25.00
21 thru 30 .... @20.00
31 thru 37 .... @20.00
38 100-pg. 75.00
39 thru 60 .... @15.00
61 thru 85 .... @12.00

THE WITCHING HOUR
DC/Vertigo, Dec., 1999
1 (of 3) JLb,CBa,ATi 5.95
2 JLb,CBa,ATi 5.95
3 JLb,CBa,ATi, concl. 5.95
TPB 19.95

WONDER WOMAN
1942–86
1 O:Wonder Woman,A:Paula
  Von Gunther 35,000.00
2 I:Earl of Greed,Duke of
  Deception and Lord Conquest,
  A:Mars 5,200.00
3 Paula Von Gunther reforms . 2,800.00
4 A:Paula Von Gunther 2,200.00
5 I:Dr. Psycho,A:Mars 2,200.00
6 I:Cheetah 1,700.00
7 .... 1,700.00
8 I:Queen Clea 1,700.00
9 I:Giganto 1,700.00
10 I:Duke Mephisto Saturno ... 1,700.00
11 I:Hypnoto 1,400.00
12 I:Queen Desira 1,400.00
13 V:King Rigor & the Seal Men 1,400.00
14 I:Gentleman Killer 1,400.00
15 I:Solo 1,400.00
16 I:King Pluto 1,400.00
17 Wonder Woman goes to
  Ancient Rome 1,400.00
18 V:Dr. Psycho 1,400.00
19 V:Blitz 1,400.00
20 V:Nifty and the Air Pirates .. 1,400.00
21 I:Queen Atomia 1,100.00
22 V:Saturno 1,100.00
23 V:Odin and the Valkyries ... 1,100.00
24 I:Mask 1,100.00
25 V:Purple Priestess 1,100.00
26 I:Queen Celerita 1,100.00
27 V:Pik Socket 1,100.00
28 V:Cheetah,Clea,Dr. Poison,
  Giganta,Hypnata,Snowman,
  Zara (Villainy,Inc.) ... 800.00
29 V:Paddy Gypso 800.00
30 'The Secret of the
  Limestone Caves' 800.00
31 V:Solo 750.00
32 V:Uvo 750.00
33 V:Inventa 750.00
34 V:Duke of Deception ... 750.00
35 'Jaxo,Master of Thoughts' .. 750.00
36 V:Lord Cruello 750.00
37 A:Circe 750.00

Comics Values Annual — DC — Wonder Woman

Wonder Woman #17
© DC Comics, Inc.

Wonder Woman #176
© DC Comics Inc.

#	Description	Price
38	V:Brutex	750.00
39	`The Unmasking of Wonder Woman'	750.00
40	`Hollywood Goes To Paradise Island'	750.00
41	`Wonder Woman,Romance Editor'	600.00
42	V:General Vertigo	600.00
43	`The Amazing Spy Ring Mystery'	600.00
44	V:Master Destroyer	600.00
45	`The Amazon and the Leprachaun'	1,200.00
46	V:Prof. Turgo	575.00
47	V:Duke of Deception	575.00
48	V:Robot Woman	575.00
49	V:Boss	575.00
50	V:Gen. Voro	575.00
51	V:Garo	400.00
52	V:Stroggo	400.00
53	V:Crime Master of Time	400.00
54	A:Merlin	400.00
55	`The Chessmen of Doom'	400.00
56	V:Plotter Gang	400.00
57	V:Mole Men	400.00
58	V:Brain	400.00
59	V:Duke Dozan	400.00
60	A:Paula Von Gunther	400.00
61	`Earth's Last Hour'	350.00
62	V:Angles Andrews	350.00
63	V:Duke of Deception	350.00
64	V:Thought Master	350.00
65	V:Duke of Deception	350.00
66	V:Duke of Deception	350.00
67	`Confessions of a Spy'	350.00
68	`Landing of the Flying Saucers'	350.00
69	A:Johann Gutenberg,Chris. Columbus, Paul Revere and the Wright Brothers	350.00
70	I:Angle Man	350.00
71	`One-Woman Circus'	350.00
72	V:Mole Goldings	350.00
73	V:Prairie Pirates	350.00
74	`The Carnival of Peril'	300.00
75	V:Angler	300.00
76		300.00
77	V:Smokescreen gang	300.00
78	V:Angle Man	300.00
79	V:Spider	300.00
80	V:Machino	300.00
81	V:Duke of Deception, Angle Man	300.00
82	A:Robin Hood	300.00
83	`The Boy From Nowhere'	300.00
84	V:Duke of Deception, Angle Man	300.00
85	V:Capt. Virago	300.00
86	V:Snatcher	300.00
87	`The Day the Clocks Stopped'	300.00
88	V:Duke of Deception	300.00
89	`The Triple Heroine'	300.00
90	Wonder Woman on Jupiter	300.00
91	`The Interplanetary Olympics'	250.00
92	V:Angle Man	250.00
93	V:Duke of Deception	250.00
94	V:Duke of Deception, A:Robin Hood	250.00
95	O:Wonder Woman's tiara	250.00
96	V:Angle Man	250.00
97	`The Runaway Time Express'	250.00
98		250.00
99	V:Silicons	250.00
100	Anniversary Issue	275.00
101	V:Time Master	225.00
102	F:Steve Trevor	225.00
103	V:Gadget-Maker	225.00
104	A:Duke of Deception	225.00
105	O,I:Wonder Woman	1,200.00
106	W.Woman space adventure	225.00
107	Battles space cowboys	225.00
108	Honored by U.S. Post Off.	225.00
109	V:Slicker	225.00
110	I:Princess 1003	225.00
111	I:Prof. Menace	225.00
112	V:Chest of Monsters	175.00
113	A:Queen Mikra	175.00
114	V:Flying Saucers	175.00
115	A:Angle Man	175.00
116	A:Professor Andro	175.00
117	A:Etta Candy	175.00
118	A:Merman	175.00
119	A:Mer Boy	175.00
120	A:Hot & Cold Alien	175.00
121	A:Wonder Woman Family	150.00
122	I:Wonder Tot	150.00
123	A:Wonder Girl,Wonder Tot	150.00
124	A:Wonder Girl,Wonder Tot	150.00
125	WW-Battle Prize	150.00
126	I:Mr.Genie	150.00
127	Suprise Honeymoon	125.00
128	O:InvisiblePlane	125.00
129	A:WonderGirl,WonderTot	125.00
130	A:Angle Man	125.00
131		125.00
132	V:Flying Saucer	125.00
133	A:Miss X	125.00
134	V:Image-Maker	125.00
135	V:Multiple Man	125.00
136	V:Machine Men	125.00
137	V:Robot Wonder Woman	125.00
138	V:Multiple Man	125.00
139	Amnesia revels Identity	125.00
140	A:Morpheus,Mr.Genie	125.00
141	A:Angle Man	125.00
142	A:Mirage Giants	125.00
143	A:Queen Hippolyte	125.00
144	I:Bird Boy	125.00
145	V:Phantom Sea Beast	125.00
146	$1,000 Dollar Stories	125.00
147	Wonder Girl becomes Bird Girl and Fish Girl	125.00
148	A:Duke of Deception	125.00
149	Last Day of the Amazons	125.00
150	V:Phantome Fish Bird	125.00
151	F:1st Full Wonder Girl story	75.00
152	F:Wonder Girl	75.00
153	V:Duke of Deception	75.00
154	V:Boiling Man	75.00
155	I married a monster	75.00
156	V:Brain Pirate	75.00
157	A:Egg Fu,the First	75.00
158	A:Egg Fu,the First	75.00
159	Origin	125.00
160	A:Cheetah, Dr. Psycho	75.00
161	A:Angle Man	75.00
162	O:Diana Prince	75.00
163	A:Giganta	75.00
164	A:Angle Man	75.00
165	A:Paper Man,Dr.Psycho	75.00
166	A:Egg Fu,The Fifth	75.00
167	A:Crimson Centipede	75.00
168	RA,ME,V:Giganta	75.00
169	RA,ME,Crimson Centipede	75.00
170	RA,ME,V:Dr.Pyscho	75.00
171	A:Mouse Man	50.00
172	IN,A:Android Wonder Woman	50.00
173	A:Tonia	50.00
174	A:Angle Man	50.00
175	V:Evil Twin	50.00
176	A:Star Brothers	50.00
177	A:Super Girl	50.00
178	MSy,DG,I:New Wonder Woman	100.00
179	D:Steve Trevor,I:Ching	75.00
180	MSy,DG,wears no costume I:Tim Trench	40.00
181	MSy,DG,A:Dr.Cyber	35.00
182	MSy,DG	35.00
183	MSy,DG,V:War	35.00
184	MSy,DG,A:Queen Hippolyte	35.00
185	MSy,DG,V:Them	35.00
186	MSy,DG,I:Morgana	35.00
187	MSy,DG,A:Dr.Cyber	35.00
188	MSy,DG,A:Dr.Cyber	35.00
189	MSy,DG	35.00
190	MSy,DG	35.00
191	MSy,DG	35.00
192	MSy,DG	35.00
193	MSy,DG	35.00
194	MSy,DG	35.00
195	MSy,WW	40.00
196	MSy,DG,giant,Origin rep.	50.00
197	MSy,DG	50.00
198	MSy,DG	50.00
199	JJ(c),DG	60.00
200	JJ(c),DG	75.00
201	DG,A:Catwoman	35.00
202	DG,A:Catwoman,I:Fafhrd & the Gray Mouser	35.00
203	DG,Womens lib	25.00
204	DH,BO,rewears costume	50.00
205	DH,BO	25.00
206	DH,O:Wonder Woman	25.00
207	RE	25.00
208	RE	25.00
209	RE	25.00
210	RE	25.00
211	RE,giant	75.00
212	CS,A:Superman,tries to	

All comics prices listed are for *Near Mint* condition.

Wonder Woman — DC — Comics Values Annual

Wonder Woman #215
© DC Comics, Inc.

Wonder Woman 2nd Series #43
© DC Comics, Inc.

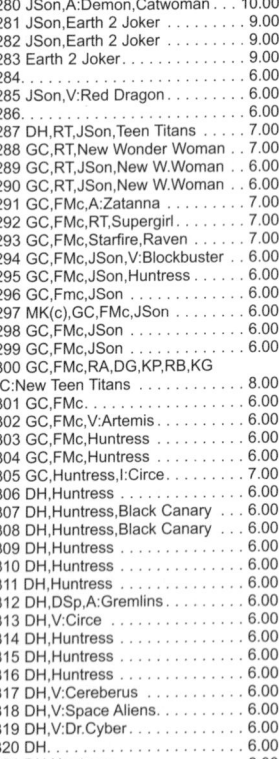

rejoin JLA	22.00
213 IN,A:Flash	22.00
214 CS,giant,A:Green Lantern	70.00
215 A:Aquaman	20.00
216 A:Black Canary	20.00
217 DD,A:Green Arrow,giant	32.00
218 KS,Red Tornado	15.00
219 CS,A:Elongated Man	15.00
220 DG,NA,A:Atom	15.00
221 CS,A:Hawkman	15.00
222 A:Batman	15.00
223 R:Steve Trevor	15.00
224	15.00
225	15.00
226	15.00
227	15.00
228 B:War stories	15.00
229	15.00
230 V:Cheetah	15.00
231	15.00
232 MN,A:JSA	15.00
233 GM	15.00
234	15.00
235	15.00
236	15.00
237 RB(c),O:Wonder Woman	20.00
238 RB(c)	15.00
239 RB(c)	15.00
240	15.00
241 JSon,DG,A:Spectre	18.00
242	12.00
243	12.00
244	12.00
245	12.00
246	12.00
247	12.00
248 D:Steve Trevor	15.00
249 A:Hawkgirl	12.00
250 I:Orana	12.00
251 O:Orana	12.00
252	15.00
253	12.00
254	12.00
255 V:Bushmaster	12.00
256 V:Royal Flush Gang	12.00
257	12.00
258	12.00
259	12.00
260	12.00
261	12.00
262 RE,A:Bushmaster	12.00
263	12.00
264	12.00
265	12.00
266	12.00
267 R:Animal Man	15.00
268 A:Animal Man	15.00
269 WW(i),Rebirth of Wonder Woman,pt.1	10.00
270 Rebirth,pt.2	10.00
271 JSon,B:Huntress,Rebirth,pt.3	10.00
272 JSon	10.00
273 JSon,A:Angle Man	10.00
274 JSon,I:Cheetah II	10.00
275 JSon,V:Cheetah II	10.00
276 JSon,V:Kobra	10.00
277 JSon,V:Kobra	10.00
278 JSon,V:Kobra	10.00
279 JSon,A:Demon,Catwoman	10.00
280 JSon,A:Demon,Catwoman	10.00
281 JSon,Earth 2 Joker	9.00
282 JSon,Earth 2 Joker	9.00
283 Earth 2 Joker	9.00
284	6.00
285 JSon,V:Red Dragon	6.00
286	6.00
287 DH,RT,JSon,Teen Titans	7.00
288 GC,RT,New Wonder Woman	7.00
289 GC,RT,JSon,New W.Woman	6.00
290 GC,RT,JSon,New W.Woman	6.00
291 GC,FMc,A:Zatanna	7.00
292 GC,FMc,RT,Supergirl	7.00
293 GC,FMc,Starfire,Raven	7.00
294 GC,FMc,JSon,V:Blockbuster	6.00
295 GC,FMc,JSon,Huntress	6.00
296 GC,Fmc,JSon	6.00
297 MK(c),GC,FMc,JSon	6.00
298 GC,FMc,JSon	6.00
299 GC,FMc,JSon	6.00
300 GC,FMc,RA,DG,KP,RB,KG C:New Teen Titans	8.00
301 GC,FMc	6.00
302 GC,FMc,V:Artemis	6.00
303 GC,FMc,Huntress	6.00
304 GC,FMc,Huntress	6.00
305 GC,Huntress,I:Circe	7.00
306 DH,Huntress	6.00
307 DH,Huntress,Black Canary	6.00
308 DH,Huntress,Black Canary	6.00
309 DH,Huntress	6.00
310 DH,Huntress	6.00
311 DH,Huntress	6.00
312 DH,DSp,A:Gremlins	6.00
313 DH,V:Circe	6.00
314 DH,Huntress	6.00
315 DH,Huntress	6.00
316 DH,Huntress	6.00
317 DH,V:Cereberus	6.00
318 DH,V:Space Aliens	6.00
319 DH,V:Dr.Cyber	6.00
320 DH	6.00
321 DH,Huntress	6.00
322 IN	6.00
323 DH,A:Cheetah, Angle Man	6.00
324 DH	6.00
325 DH	6.00
326 DH	6.00
327 DH,Crisis	6.00
328 DH,Crisis	6.00
329 DH,Crisis, giant	12.00

WONDER WOMAN
[2nd Regular Series], 1987

1 GP,O:Amazons,Wonder Woman	8.00
2 GP,I:Steve Trevor	6.00
3 GP,I:Julia Vanessa	6.00
4 GP,V:Decay	6.00
5 GP,V:Deimos,Phobos	6.00
6 GP,V:Ares	5.00
7 GP,I:Myndi Mayer	5.00
8 GP,O:Legends,A:JLA,Flash	5.00
9 GP,I:New Cheetah	5.00
10 GP,V:Seven Headed Hydra, Challenge of the Gods,pt.1, gatefold(c)	4.00
10a regular(c)	3.00
11 GP,V:Echidna,Challenge of the Gods,pt.3	4.00
12 GP,Millennium,V:Pan, Challenge of the Gods,pt.3, Millennium x-over	4.00
13 GP,Millennium,A:Ares,Challenge of the Gods,pt.4	4.00
14 GP,A:Hercules	4.00
15 GP,I:New Silver Swan	4.00
16 GP,V:Silver Swan	4.00
17 GP,DG,V:Circe	4.00
18 GP,DG,V:Circe,+Bonus bk#4	4.00
19 GP,FMc,V:Circe	4.00
20 GP,BMc,D:Myndi Mayer	4.00
21 GP,BMc,L:Greek Gods, Destruction of Olympus	3.00
22 GP,BMc,F:Julia, Vanessa	3.00
23 GP,R:Hermes,V:Phobos, Prelude to New Titans #50	3.00
24 GP,V:Ixion, Phobos	3.00
25 CMa,Invasion,A:JLA	3.00
26 CMa,Invasion,V:Capt.Atom	3.00
27 CMa,V:Khunds,A:Cheetah	3.00
28 CMa,V:Cheetah	3.00
29 CMa,V:Cheetah	3.00
30 CMa,V:Cheetah	3.00
31 CMa,V:Cheetah	3.00
32 TG,V:Amazons,A:Hermes	3.00
33 CMa,V:Amazons,Cheetah	3.00
34 CMa,I:Shim'Tar	3.00
35 CMa,V:Shim'Tar	3.00
36 CMa,A:Hermes	3.00
37 CMa,V:Discord,A:Superman	3.00
38 CMa,V:Eris	3.00
39 CMa,V:Eris,A:Lois Lane	3.00
40 CMa,V:Eris,A:Lois Lane	3.00
41 CMa,RT,F:Julia,Ties that Bind	3.00
42 CMa,RT,V:Silver Swan	3.00
43 CMA,RT,V:Silver Swan	3.00
44 CMa,RT,V:SilverSwan	3.00
45 CM,RT,Pandora's Box	3.00
46 RT,Suicide Issue,D:Lucy	3.00
47 RT,A:Troia	3.00
48 RTP,A:Troia	3.00
49 recap of 1st four years	3.00
50 RT,SA,BB,AH,CM,KN,PCR,MW A:JLA,Superman	4.00
51 RT,V:Mercury	3.00
52 CM,KN,Shards,V:Dr.Psycho	3.00
53 RT,A:Pariah	3.00
54 RT,V:Dr.Psycho	3.00
55 RT,V:Dr.Psycho	3.00

CVA Page 180 — All comics prices listed are for *Near Mint* condition.

Comics Values Annual — DC — Wonder Woman–World

#	Description	Price
56	RT,A:Comm.Gordon	3.00
57	RT,A:Clark Kent,Bruce Wayne	3.00
58	RT,War of the Gods,V:Atlas	3.50
59	RT,War of the Gods, A:Batman Robin	3.50
60	RT,War of the Gods, A:Batman, Lobo	3.50
61	RT,War of the Gods,V:Circe	3.50
62	War o/t Gods,Epilogue	3.00
63	BB(c)A:Deathstroke,Cheetah	5.00
64	BB(c),Kidnapped Child	2.50
65	BB(c),PCu,V:Dr.Psycho	2.50
66	BB(c),PCu,Exodus In Space#1	2.50
67	BB(c),PCu,Exodus In Space#2	2.50
68	BB(c),PCu,Exodus In Space#3	2.50
69	PCu, Exodus In Space#4	2.50
70	PCu,Exodus In Space#5	2.50
71	BB(c),DC,RT,Return fr.space	2.50
72	BB(c),O:retold	2.50
73	BB(c),Diana gets a job	2.50
74	BB(c),V:White Magician	2.50
75	BB(c),A:The White Magician	2.50
76	BB(c),A:Doctor Fate	2.50
77	BB(c)	2.50
78	BB(c),A:Flash	2.50
79	BB(c),V:Mayfly,A:Flash	2.50
80	BB(c),V:Ares Buchanan	2.50
81	BB(c),V:Ares Buchanan	2.50
82	BB(c),V:Ares Buchanan	2.50
83	BB(c),V:Ares Buchanan	2.50
84	BB(c),V:Ares Buchanan	2.50
85	BB(c)	15.00
86	BB(c),Turning Point	6.00
87	BB(c),No Quarter,NoSanctuary	6.00
88	BB(c),A:Superman	7.00
89	BB(c),A:Circle	6.00
90	New Direction	7.00
91	Choosing Wonder Woman	4.00
92	New Wonder Woman	4.00
93	New Wonder Woman	4.00
94		5.00
95	V:Cheetah	5.00
96	V:The Joker	5.00
97	V:The Joker	5.00
98	BB(c),F:Artemis	3.00
99	BB(c),A:White Magician	3.00
100	BB(c) White Magician defeats Artemis	5.00
100a	Collector's ed., holo(c)	6.00
101	V:White Magician	3.00
102	V:Metron,Darkseid	2.50
103	JBy,A:Darkseid	2.50
104	JBy,Diana takes crown?	2.50
105	JBy,Grecian artifact comes to life	2.50
106	JBy,A:The Demon,Phantom Stranger	2.50
107		2.50
108	JBy,F:The Demon,Arion,The Phantom Stranger	2.50
109	JBy,V:The Flash,I:Champion	2.50
110	JBy,V:Sinestro	2.50
111	JBy,I:New Wonder Girl, V:Doomsday	2.50
112	JBy,V:Doomsday,A:Superman	3.00
113	JBy,Wonder Girl vs. Decay	2.50
114	JBy,V:Doctor Psycho	2.50
115	JBy,beneath the Arctic ice	2.50
116	JBy,beneath the Arctic ice	2.50
117	JBy,V:Earth Moovers	2.50
118	JBy	2.50
119	JBy,fight to regain Cheetah's humanity, cont.	2.50
120	JBy,48pg., pin-ups	4.00
121	JBy, Wonder Woman reverting to clay	2.50
122	JBy,Gods of Olympus are back	2.50
123	JBy,R:Artemis	2.50
124	JBy,A:Demon	2.50
125	JBy,A:Donna Troy & JLA	2.50
126	JBy,JL,Genesis tie-in	2.50
127	JBy,JL(c),new era	2.50
128	JBy,JL,V:Egg Fu	2.50
129	JBy,JL,Hippolyta debuts as replacement Wonder Woman	2.50
130	JBy,JL,pt.1,A:Golden-age Flash	2.50
131	JBy,pt.2	2.50
132	JBy,pt.3,A:Justice Society	2.50
133		2.50
134	JBy,Who is Donna Troy?	2.50
135	JBy,secret revealed	2.50
136	JBy,back to Earth	2.50
137	CPr,V:Circe, pt.1	2.50
138	MBr,F:Hippolyta,V:Circe,pt.2	2.50
139	MBr,	2.50
140	BMc,A:Superman & Batman	2.50
141	BMc,A:Superman & Batman	2.50
142	BMc,The Wonder Dome	2.50
143	BMc,Devastation,pt.1	2.50
144	BMc,Devastation,pt.2	2.50
145	BMc,Devastation,pt.3	2.50
146	BMc,Devastation,pt.4	2.50
147	BMc,GodWar begins	2.50
148	BMc,GodWar,pt.2	2.50
149	RBr,BMc,GodWar,pt.3	2.50
150	GodWar, 48-pg	4.00
151	AH(c),V:Dr. Poison	2.50
152		2.50
153	MMr,F:Wonder Girl	2.50
154	Three Hearts,pt.1	2.50
155	Three Hearts,pt.2	2.50
156	Devastation Returns,pt.1	2.50
157	Devastation Returns,pt.2	2.50
158	Devastation Returns,concl.	2.50
159	WonderDome comes to Earth	2.50
160	A Piece of You,pt.1	2.50
161	A Piece of You,pt.2	2.50
162	GodComplex,pt.1,A:Aquaman	2.50
163	GodComplex,pt.2,A:Aquaman	2.50
164	Gods of Gotham,pt.1	6.00
165	Gods of Gotham,pt.2	2.25
166	Gods of Gotham,pt.3	2.25
167	Gods of Gotham,pt.4	2.25
168	GP,Paradise Island Lost,pt.1	2.25
169	GP,Paradise Island Lost,pt.2	2.25
170	PJ,ALa,Lois & Diana	2.25
171	Our Worlds at War, tie-in	2.25
172	Our Worlds at War, tie-in	2.25
173	Our Worlds at War, tie-in	2.25
174	PJ,ALa,Witch & Warrior,pt.1	2.25
175	PJ,ALa,Witch & Warrior,pt.2	3.50
176	PJ,ALa,Witch & Warrior,pt.3	2.25
177	PJ,ALa,Our Worlds at War	2.25
178	PJ,ALa,date with Trevor	2.25

Wonder Woman 2nd Series #139
© DC Comics Inc.

#	Description	Price
179	PJ,ALa,V:Villainy,Inc.	2.25
180	PJ,ALa,O:new Villainy, Inc.	2.25
181	PJ,ALa,prisoners of Skartaris	2.25
182	PJ,ALa,Shamballa	2.25
183	PJ,ALa,Skartaris mastermind	2.25
184	PJ,ALa,Diana,pt.1	2.25
185	PJ,ALa,Diana in '40s,pt.2	2.25
186	PJ,ALa,V:Barbara Minerva	2.25
187	PJ,ALa,Cat fight	2.25
188	PJ,ALa,Day in the Life	2.25
189	WS,JOy,CR,Game Gods,pt.1	2.25
190	WS,JOy,CR,Game Gods,pt.2	2.25
191	WS,JOy,CR,Game Gods,pt.3	2.25
192	WS,JOy,CR,Game Gods,pt.4	2.25
193	WS,JOy,CR,Game Gods,pt.5	2.25
194	WS,JOy,CR,Game Gods,pt.6	2.25
195	AH	2.25
196	Down to Earth,pt.1	2.25
197	Down to Earth,pt.2	2.25
198	Down to Earth,pt.3	2.25
Ann.#1	GP,AAd,RA,BB,JBo,JL,CS Tales of Paradise Island	4.00
Ann.#2	CM,F:Mayer Agency	4.00
Ann.#3	Eclipso tie-in	3.00
Ann.#4	Year One Annual	4.00
Ann.#5	JBy,DC,NBy,Legends of the Dead Earth	3.50
Ann.#6	Pulp Heroes (Macabre)	4.50
Ann.#7	Ghosts	3.50
Ann.#8	JLApe Gorilla Warfare	3.50
Annual #1 (1967) (rep.2003)		4.95
Spec.#1,000,000 CPr(s),MC,BMc		2.50
Spec #1 A:Deathstroke,Cheetah		2.25
Spec.#0 History of Amazons		7.00
Spec.#1 Our Worlds at War,48-pg		3.00
GN Amazonia, BML		8.00
GN The Once and Future Story		5.00
GN Amazonia, Elseworlds		8.00
GN The Gods of Gotham, rep.		5.95
Secret Files #2		5.00
Secret Files #3, 48-pg		4.95
Spec. Wonder Woman: Donna Troy Girlfrenzy (1998)		2.00
Spec. Wonder Woman Plus CPr(s), MC, TP,Jesse Quick & Wonder Woman (1996)		2.95
Spec. The Blue Amazon (2003)		6.95
TPB The Contest, rep. #90,#0 #91–#93		9.95
TPB The Challenge of Artemas		9.95
TPB Second Genesis JBy, rep. #101–#105		9.95
TPB Spirit of Truth, over-size		9.95
TPB Paradise Lost, rep.		14.95
TPB Paradist Found (2003)		14.95
TPB The Hiketeia (2003)		17.95

WORLD OF KRYPTON
July, 1979

#	Description	Price
1	HC/MA.O:Jor-El	10.00
2	HC/MA,A:Superman	6.00
3	HC	6.00

[2nd Series], 1987–88

#	Description	Price
1	MMi,John Byrne script	3.00
2	MMi,John Byrne script	3.00
3	MMi,John Byrne script	3.00
4	MMi,A:Superman	3.00

WORLD OF METROPOLIS
1988

#	Description	Price
1	DG(i),O:Perry White	2.50
2	DG(i),O:Lois Lane	2.50
3	DG(i),Clark Kent	2.50
4	DG(i),O:Jimmy Olsen	2.50

WORLD OF SMALLVILLE
1988

#	Description	Price
1	KS/AA,Secrets of Ma&Pa Kent	3.00

All comics prices listed are for Near Mint condition.

World–World's Finest DC Comics Values Annual

World of Smallville #3
© DC Comics, Inc.

2 KS/AA,`Stolen Moments' 3.00
3 KS/AA,Lana Lang/Manhunter ... 3.00
4 KS/AA,final issue 3.00

WORLDS COLLIDE
1994
1 MBr(c),3RW,CsB,Ccs,DCw,
 TG,A:Blood Syndicate,Icon,
 Hardware,Static,Superboy,
 Superman,Steel,Vinyl Cling(c) . 4.25
1a Newsstand Ed............. 2.75

WORLD'S BEST COMICS
Oct. 2003
Spec. G.A. DC Archives Sampler .. 0.99

WORLD'S BEST COMICS
Spring, 1941
1 Superman vs. the Rainmaker,
 Batman vs. Wright 22,000.00
Becomes:

WORLD'S FINEST COMICS
1941–86
2 Superman V:`The Unknown X',
 Batman V:Ambrose Taylor . 6,000.00
3 I&O:Scarecrow........... 4,500.00
4 Superman V:Dan Brandon,
 Batman V:Ghost Gang. . . . 3,200.00
5 Superman V:Lemuel P.Potts,
 Batman V:Brains Kelly 3,200.00
6 Superman V:Metalo,Batman
 meets Scoop Scanlon 2,500.00
7 Superman V:Jenkins,Batman
 V:Snow Man Bandits 2,500.00
8 Superman:`Talent Unlimited'
 Batman V:Little Nap Boyd,
 B:Boy Commandos 2,200.00
9 Superman:`One Second to
 Live',Batman V:Bramwell B.
 Bramwell 2,500.00
10 Superman V:The Insect Master,
 Batman reforms Oliver Hunt 2,000.00
11 Superman V:Charlie Frost,
 Batman V:Rob Calendar . . 1,700.00
12 Superman V:Lynx,Batman:
 `Alfred Gets His Man'. 1,700.00
13 Superman V:Dice Dimant,
 Batman,V:Swami Pravhoz . 1,700.00

14 Superman V:Al Bandar,Batman
 V:Jib Buckler 1,700.00
15 Superman V:Derby Bowser,
 Batman V:Mennekin...... 1,700.00
16 Superman:`Music for the Masses,
 Batman V:Nocky Johnson . 1,700.00
17 Superman:`The Great Godini',
 Batman V:Dr.Dreemo..... 1,500.00
18 Superman:`The Junior Reporters,
 Batman V:Prof.Brane 1,500.00
19 A:The Joker 1,500.00
20 A:Toyman 1,500.00
21 Superman:`Swindle in
 Sweethearts!'........... 1,100.00
22 Batman V:Nails Finney 1,100.00
23 Superman:`The Colossus
 of Metropolis'........... 1,100.00
24 .... 1,100.00
25 Superman V:Ed Rook,Batman:
 `The Famous First Crimes'. 1,100.00
26 `Confessions of Superman' . 1,100.00
27 `The Man Who Out-Supered
 Superman 1,100.00
28 A:Lex Luther,Batman V:Glass
 Man.................. 1,100.00
29 Superman:`The Books that
 couldn't be Bound'....... 1,100.00
30 Superman:`Sheriff Clark Kent`,
 Batman V:Joe Coyne..... 1,100.00
31 `Superman's Super-Rival`,Batman:
 `Man with the X-Ray Eyes'. 1,000.00
32 Superman visits
 Ancient Egypt 1,000.00
33 `Superman Press, Inc.',
 Batman V:James Harmon . 1,000.00
34 `The Un-Super Superman' . 1,000.00
35 Daddy Superman,A:Penguin 1,000.00
36 Lois Lane,Sleeping Beauty . 1,000.00
37 `The Superman Story`,Batman
 V:T-Gun Jones.......... 1,000.00
38 If There were No Superman 1,000.00
39 Superman V:Big Jim Martin,
 Batman V:J.J.Jason...... 1,000.00
40 Superman V:Check,Batman:`4
 Killers Against Fate!' 1,000.00
41 I:Supermanium,
 E:Boy Commandos....... 800.00
42 Superman goes to Uranus,
 A:Marco Polo & Kubla Khan . 800.00
43 A:J.Wilbur Wolfingham...... 800.00
44 Superman:`The Revolt of the
 Thought Machine'......... 800.00
45 Superman:`Lois Lane and Clark
 Kent,Private Detectives' 800.00
46 Superman V:Mr. 7 .... 800.00
47 Superman:`The Girl Who
 Hated Reporters' 800.00
48 A:Joker 800.00
49 Superman meets the
 Metropolis Shutterbug
 Society, A:Penguin 800.00
50 `Superman Super Wrecker' .. 800.00
51 Superman:`The Amazing
 Talents of Lois Lane'....... 800.00
52 A:J.Wilbur Wolfingham....... 800.00
53 Superman V:Elias Toomey ... 800.00
54 `The Superman Who Avoided
 Danger!'................. 800.00
55 A:Penguin 800.00
56 Superman V:Dr.Vallin,Batman
 V:Big Dan Hooker......... 800.00
57 `The Artificial Superman' 800.00
58 Superman V:Mr.Fenton 800.00
59 A:Lex Luthor,Joker......... 800.00
60 A:J.Wilbur Wolfingham....... 800.00
61 A:Joker,`Superman's
 Blackout' 700.00
62 A:Lex Luthor 700.00
63 Superman:`Clark Kent,
 Gangster' 700.00
64 Superman:`The Death of Lois

World's Finest #106
© DC Comics, Inc.

 Lane,Batman:`Bruce Wayne...
 Amateur Detective'........ 700.00
65 `The Confessions of Superman',
 Batman V:The Blaster 1,000.00
66 `Superman,Ex-Crimebuster;'
 Batman V:Brass Haley 700.00
67 Superman:`Metropolis-Crime
 Center!' 700.00
68 Batman V:The Crimesmith ... 700.00
69 A:Jor-El,Batman
 V:Tom Becket............ 700.00
70 `The Two Faces of Superman',
 Batman:`Crime Consultant' .. 700.00
71 B:Superman/Batman
 team-ups.............. 1,400.00
72 V:Heavy Weapon gang 1,000.00
73 V:Fang 1,000.00
74 `The Contest of Heroes'..... 800.00
75 V:The Purple Mask Mob..... 750.00
76 `When Gotham City
 Challenged Metropolis 600.00
77 V:Prof.Pender 600.00
78 V:Varrel mob 600.00
79 A:Aladdin 600.00
80 V:Mole.................. 600.00
81 Meet Ka Thar from future.... 450.00
82 A:Three Musketeers........ 450.00
83 `The Case of the Mother
 Goose Mystery' 450.00
84 V:Thad Linnis gang 450.00
85 Meet Princess Varina....... 450.00
86 V:Henry Bartle 450.00
87 V:Elton Craig 450.00
88 1st team-up Luthor & Joker .. 475.00
89 I:Club of Heroes........... 450.00
90 A:Batwoman 450.00
91 V:Rohtul,descendent of Lex
 Luthor.................. 300.00
92 1st & only A:Skyboy 300.00
93 V:Victor Danning 300.00
94 O:Superman/Batman team,
 A:Lex Luthor............. 900.00
95 `Battle o/t Super Heroes' 300.00
96 `Super-Foes from Planet X' .. 300.00
97 V:Condor Gang 300.00
98 I:Moonman 300.00
99 JK,V:Carl Verril 300.00
100 A:Kandor, Lex Luthor 550.00
101 A:Atom Master............ 225.00
102 V:Jo-Jo Groff gang,
 B:Tommy Tomorrow 225.00
103 `The Secrets of the
 Sorcerer's Treasure'....... 225.00
104 A:Lex Luthor 225.00
105 V:Khalex 225.00

CVA Page 182 All comics prices listed are for *Near Mint* condition.

Comics Values Annual — DC — World's Finest Comics

106 V:Duplicate Man 225.00
107 `The Secret of the Time Creature' 225.00
108 `The Star Creatures' 225.00
109 V:Fangan 225.00
110 `The Alien Who Doomed Robin!' 225.00
111 V:Floyd Frisby 225.00
112 . . . . 225.00
113 1st Bat-Mite/Mr.Mxyzptlk team-up 225.00
114 `Captives o/t Space Globes'. 225.00
115 The Curse That Doomed Superman 175.00
116 V:Vance Collins 175.00
117 A:Batwoman,Lex Luthor 175.00
118 V:Vath-Gar 175.00
119 V:General Grambly 175.00
120 V:Faceless Creature 175.00
121 I:Miss Arrowette 175.00
122 V:Klor 125.00
123 A:Bat-Mite & Mr. Mxyzptlk . . 125.00
124 V:Hroguth,E:Tommy Tomorrow 125.00
125 V:Jundy,B:Aquaman 125.00
126 A:Lex Luthor 125.00
127 V:Zerno 125.00
128 V:Moose Morans 125.00
129 Joker/Luthor T.U. 150.00
130 . . . . 125.00
131 V:Octopus 125.00
132 V:Denny Kale,Shorty Biggs . 125.00
133 . . . . 125.00
134 V:Band of Super-Villians 125.00
135 V:The Future Man 125.00
136 The Batman Nobody Remembered 125.00
137 A:Lex Luthor 125.00
138 V:General Grote 125.00
139 V:Sphinx Gang,E:Aquaman . 125.00
140 CS,V:Clayface 125.00
141 CS,A:Jimmy Olsen 125.00
142 CS,O:Composite Man 125.00
143 CS,A:Kandor,I:Mailbag 75.00
144 CS,A:Clayface,Brainiac 75.00
145 CS,Prison for Heroes 75.00
146 CS,Batman,Son of Krypton . . 75.00
147 CS,A:Jimmy Olsen 75.00
148 CS,A:Lex Luthor,Clayface . . . 75.00
149 CS,The Game of the Secret Identities 75.00
150 CS,V:Rokk and Sorban 60.00
151 CS,A:Krypto,B:Congorilla . . . 60.00
152 CS,A:The Colossal Kids,Bat-mite,V:Mr.Mxyzptlk 60.00
153 CS,V:Lex Luthor 60.00
154 CS,The Sons of Batman & Superman(Imaginary) 60.00
155 CS,The 1000th Exploit of Batman & Superman 60.00
156 CS,I:BizarroBatman,V:Joker. 150.00
157 CS,The Abominable Brats (Imaginary story) 60.00
158 CS,V:Brainiac 60.00
159 CS,A:Many Major villians,I:Jim Gordon as Anti-Batman & Perry White as Anti-Superman 60.00
160 V:Dr Zodiac 60.00
161 CS,80 page giant 75.00
162 V:The Jousting Master 50.00
163 CS,The Court of No Hope . . 50.00
164 CS,I:Genia,V:Brainiac 50.00
165 CS,The Crown of Crime 50.00
166 CS,V:Muto & Joker 60.00
167 CS,The New Superman & Batman(Imaginary) V:Luthor . . 50.00
168 CS,R:Composite Superman . . 50.00
169 The Supergirl/Batgirl Plot; V:Batmite,Mr.Mxyzptlk 50.00
170 80 page giant,reprint 50.00
171 CS,V:The Executioners 50.00

World's Finest #240
© DC Comics Inc.

172 CS,Superman & Batman Brothers (Imaginary) 50.00
173 CS,The Jekyll-Hyde Heroes . 125.00
174 CS,Secrets of the Double Death Wish 50.00
175 NA(1st Batman),C:Flash 50.00
176 NA,A:Supergirl & Batgirl 50.00
177 V:Joker & Luthor 50.00
178 CS,The Has-Been Superman . 40.00
179 CS,giant 50.00
180 RA,ME,Supermans Perfect Crime 40.00
181 RA,ME 40.00
182 RA,ME,The Mad Manhunter . . 40.00
183 RA,ME,Superman's Crimes of the Ages 40.00
184 RA,ME,A:JLA,Robin 40.00
185 CS,The Galactic Gamblers . . 40.00
186 RA,ME,The Bat Witch 40.00
187 RA,ME,Demon Superman . . . 40.00
188 giant,reprint 75.00
189 RA,ME,V:Lex Luthor 40.00
190 RA,V:Lex Luthor 30.00
191 RA,A:Jor-El,Lara 30.00
192 RA,The Prison of No Escape . 30.00
193 The Breaking of Batman and Superman 30.00
194 RA,ME,Inside the Mafia 30.00
195 RA,ME,Dig Now-Die Later . . . 30.00
196 CS,The Kryptonite Express, E:Batman 30.00
197 giant 60.00
198 DD,B:Superman T.U., A:Flash 125.00
199 DD,Superman & Flash race . 125.00
200 NA(c),DD,Prisoners of the Immortal World; A:Robin 40.00
201 NA(c),DD,A Prize of Peril, A:Green Lantern,Dr. Fate 25.00
202 NA(c),DD,Vengeance of the Tomb Thing,A:Batman 25.00
203 NA(c),DD,Who's Minding the Earth,A:Quamar 25.00
204 NA(c),DD,Journey to the End of Hope,A:Wonder Woman . . . 25.00
205 NA(c),DD,The Computer that Captured a Town,Frazetta Ad, A:Teen Titans 30.00
206 DD,giant reprint 65.00
207 DD,Superman,A:Batman, V:Dr.Light 35.00
208 NA(c),DD,A:Dr Fate 35.00
209 NA(c),DD,A:Green Arrow, Hawkman,I&V:The Temper . . 35.00

210 NA(c),DD,A:Batman 35.00
211 NA(c),DD,A:Batman 35.00
212 CS(c),And So My World Begins,A:Martian Manhunter. . 35.00
213 DD,Peril in a Very Small Place,A:The Atom 35.00
214 DD,A:Vigilante 35.00
215 DD,Saga of the Super Sons (Imaginary story) 40.00
216 DD,R:Super Sons,Little Town with a Big Secret 20.00
217 DD,MA,Heroes with Dirty Hands 20.00
218 DD,DC,A:Batman, BU:Metamorpho 20.00
219 DD,Prisoner of Rogues Rock; A:Batman 20.00
220 DD,MA,Let No Man Write My Epitaph,BU:Metamorpho 20.00
221 DD,Cry Not For My Forsaken Son; R:Super Sons 20.00
222 DD,Evil In Paradise 20.00
223 DD,giant,A:Deadman,Aquaman Robotman 50.00
224 DD,giant,A:Super Sons, Metamorpho,Johnny Quick . . . 50.00
225 giant,A:Rip Hunter,Vigilante, Black Canary,Robin 50.00
226 A:Sandman,Metamorpho, Deadman,Martian Manhunter . 50.00
227 MGr,BWi,A:The Demonic Duo, Vigilante,Rip Hunter,Deadman, I:Stargrave 50.00
228 ATh,A:Super Sons,Aquaman, Robin,Vigilante 50.00
229 I:Powerman,A:Metamorpho . . 30.00
230 A:Super-Sons,Deadman, Aquaman, giant-size 50.00
231 A:Green Arrow,Flash 18.00
232 DD,The Dream Bomb 18.00
233 A:Super-Sons 18.00
234 CS,Family That Fled Earth . . 18.00
235 DD,V:Sagitaurus 18.00
236 DD,A:The Atom 18.00
237 Intruder from a Dead World . . 18.00
238 DD,V:Luthor,A:Super-Sons . . 18.00
239 CS,A:Gold(from Metal Men) . . 18.00
240 DD,A:Kandor 15.00
241 Make Way For a New World . 15.00
242 EC,A:Super-Sons 15.00
243 CS,AM,A:Robin 15.00
244 NA(c),JL,MA,MN,TA,giant B:Green Arrow 20.00
245 NA(C),CS,MA,MN,TA, GM,JSh,BWi,giant 20.00
246 NA(c),KS,MA,MN,TA,GM, DH,A:JLA 20.00
247 KS,GM,giant 20.00
248 KS,GM,DG,TVE,A:Sgt.Rock . . 18.00
249 KS,SD,TVE,A:Phantom Stranger,B:Creeper 18.00
250 GT,SD,Superman,Batman, Wonder Woman,Green Arrow, Black Canary,team-up 15.00
251 GT,SD,JBi,BL,TVE,RE, JA,A:Poison Ivy,Speedy, I:CountVertigo 15.00
252 GT,TVE,SD,JA,giant 15.00
253 KS,DN,TVE,SD,B:Shazam . . 14.00
254 GT,DN,TVE,SD,giant 14.00
255 JL,DA,TVE,SD,DN,KS, E:Creeper 14.00
256 MA,DN,KS,DD,Hawkman,Black Lightning,giant 14.00
257 DD,FMc,DN,KS,GT,RB, RT,giant 14.00
258 NA(c),RB,JL,DG,DN,KS,RT, giant 15.00
259 RB,DG,MR,MN,DN,KS 14.00
260 RB,DG,MN,DN 14.00
261 RB,DG,AS,RT,EB,DN,

All comics prices listed are for *Near Mint* condition.

World's Finest–Yeah / DC / Comics Values Annual

World's Finest #303
© DC Comics, Inc.

302 DM,NA(rep) 5.00
303 Plague.................... 5.00
304 SLi,O:Null&Void 5.00
305 TVE,V:Null&Void 5.00
306 SLi,I:Swordfish & Barracuda .. 5.00
307 TVE,V:Null&Void 5.00
308 GT,Night and Day 5.00
309 MT,AA,V:Quantum 5.00
310 I:Sonik................... 5.00
311 A:Monitor 5.00
312 AA,I:Network 5.00
313 AA(i),V:Network 5.00
314 AA(i),V:Executrix 5.00
315 V:Cathode 5.00
316 LSn,I:Cheapjack 5.00
317 LSn,V:Cheapjack 5.00
318 AA(i),A:Sonik 5.00
319 AA(i),I:REM 5.00
320 AA(i),V:REM 5.00
321 AA,V:Chronos 5.00
322 KG,The Search 5.00
323 AA(i),final issue 5.00
Spec.#1 Our Worlds at War,48-pg. . 4.00

WORLD'S FINEST
[Limited Series], 1990
1 SR,KK,Worlds Apart 8.00
2 SR,KK,Worlds Collide........ 6.00
3 SR,KK,Worlds At War 6.00
TPB rep.#1–#3 .... 19.95

WORLD'S FINEST: SUPERBOY/ROBIN
Oct., 1996
1 (of 2) CDi&KK(s),TG,SHa,
    V:Poison Ivy, Metallo 5.00
2 CDi&KK(s),TG,SHa, V:Poison
    Ivy, Metallo................. 5.00

WORLD'S GREATEST SUPER-HEROES
1977
1 A:Batman,Robin 35.00

WORLD WITHOUT END
1990
1 The Host, I:Brother Bones 5.00
2 A:Brother Bones 3.50
3 .... 3.50
4 House of Fams................ 2.50
5 Female Fury.................. 2.50
6 conclusion 2.50

WRATH OF THE SPECTRE
May, 1988
1 JAp,rep.Adventure #431–#433 .. 4.00
2 JAp,rep.Adventure #434–#436 .. 4.00
3 JAp,rep.Adventure #437–#440 .. 4.00
4 JAp,reps.,final issue 5.00

XENOBROOD
1994–95
0 New team.................... 2.25
1 Battles 2.25
2 Bestiary 2.25
3 A:Superman 2.25
4 V:Bestiary.................. 2.25
5 V:Vimian.................... 2.25
6 final issue 2.25

XERO
March, 1997
1 Cpr(s),Ccs,Trane Walker/Xero .. 3.00
2 CPr(s),Ccs,The Rookie....... 2.50
3 Cpr(s),Ccs,The Beast........ 2.50
4 CPr(s) 2.50
6 CPr, Genesis tie-in 2.50
7 CPr(s),O:Zero, pt.1......... 2.50
8 CPr,O:Zero 2.25
9 CPr(s),...................... 2.25
10 CPr,a matter of ethics 2.25
11 .... 2.25
12 CPr, final issue, Xero dead ... 2.25

XOMBI
Milestone, 1994–96
0 WS(c),DCw,Shadow War,Foil(c),
    I:Xombi,Twilight 2.50
1 JBy(c),B:Silent Cathedrals ... 2.00
1a Platinum ed................ 7.00
2 I:Rabbi Simmowitz,Golms,Liam
    Knight of the Spoken Fire 2.50
3 A:Liam 2.00
4 Silent Cathedrals 2.00
5 Silent Cathedrals 2.50
6 Silent Cathedrals 2.50
7 School of Anguish........... 2.50
8 School of Anguish,pt.2 ..... 2.50
9 School of Anguish,pt.3 ..... 2.50
10 School of Anguish,pt.4..... 2.50
11 School of Anguish,pt.5..... 2.50
12 Truth and Surprises........ 2.50
13 V:Kinderessen 2.50
14 Long Hot Summer, A:Cheryl
    Saltz 2.50
15 Long Hot Summer 2.50
16 Long Hot Summer 2.50
17 Reader's Choice 2.50
18 Serpent's Tail............. 2.50
19 Mister Missy, Bellhop...... 2.50
20 .... 2.50
21 final issue 3.50

Y: THE LAST MAN
DC/Vertigo, July, 2002
1 JMz,UnManned,pt.1,40-pg..... 30.00
2 JMz,UnManned,pt.2 .... 25.00
3 JMz,UnManned,pt.3 .... 20.00
4 JMz,UnManned,pt.4 .... 15.00
5 JMz,UnManned,pt.5 .... 10.00
6 JMz,Cycles,pt.1 .... 7.00
7 JMz,Cycles,pt.2 .... 6.00
8 JMz,Cycles,pt.3 .... 5.00
9 JMz,Cycles,pt.4 .... 4.00
10 JMz,Cycles,pt.5............ 4.00
11 JMz,One Small Step,pt.1.... 3.50
12 JMz,One Small Step,pt.2.... 3.50
13 JMz,One Small Step,pt.3.... 3.50
14 JMz,One Small Step,pt.4.... 3.50
15 JMz,One Small Step,pt.5.... 3.50
16 JMz,Comedy&Tragedy,pt.1 ... 3.50
TPB Unmanned 12.95
TPB Cycles 12.95

YEAH!
Homage/DC, 1999
1 GHe 3.00
2 GHe 3.00
3 GHe 3.00
4 GHe,Origins of Yeah,pt.1 ... 3.00
5 GHe,Origins of Yeah,pt.2 ... 3.00
6 GHe, ... 3.00
7 GHe, ... 3.00
8 GHe, ... 3.00
9 GHe,final issue 3.00

A:Penguin, Terra Man........ 14.00
262 DG,DN,DA,JSon,RT,
    Aquaman 14.00
263 RB,DG,DN,TVE,JSh,Aquaman,
    Adam Strange 14.00
264 RB,DG,TVE,DN,Aquaman 14.00
265 RB,DN,RE,TVE 14.00
266 RB,TVE,DN 14.00
267 RB,DG,TVE,AS,DN,
    A:Challengers of the Unknown 14.00
268 DN,TVE,BBr,RT,AS 14.00
269 RB,FMc,TVE,BBr,AS,DN,DA . 14.00
270 NA(c),RB,RT,TVE,AS,
    DN,LMa 14.00
271 GP(c),RB,FMc,O:Superman/
    Batman T.U.................. 14.00
272 RB,DN,TVE,BBr,AS 12.00
273 TVE,LMa,JSon,AS,DN,
    A:Plastic Man 12.00
274 TVE,LMa,BBr,GC,AS,DN,
    Green Arrow 12.00
275 RB,FMc,TVE,LMa,DSp,AS,
    DN,DA,A:Mr.Freeze 12.00
276 GP(c),RB,TVE,LMa,DSp,CI,
    DN,DA 12.00
277 GP(c),RT,TVE,DSp,AS,DN,
    DH,V:Dr.Double X............. 12.00
278 GP(c),RB,TVE,LMa,DSp,DN . 12.00
279 KP,TVE,LMa,AS,DN,
    B:Kid Eternity............... 12.00
280 RB,TVE,LMa,AS,DN 12.00
281 GK(c),IN,TVE,LMa,AS,DN ... 12.00
282 IN,FMc,GK,CI,last giant
    E:Kid Eternity............... 12.00
283 GT,FMc,GK 12.00
284 GT,DSp,A:Legion,E:G.Arrow . 12.00
285 FM(c),RB,A:Zatanna 12.00
286 RB,A:Flash 12.00
287 TVE,A:Flash 12.00
288 A:JLA 12.00
289 GK(c),Kryll way of Dying 12.00
290 TD(i),I:Stalagron 12.00
291 WS(c),TD(i),V:Stalagron.... 12.00
292 .... 12.00
293 .... 12.00
294........................... 12.00
295 FMc(i) 12.00
296 RA........................ 12.00
297 GC,V:Pantheon 12.00
298 V:Pantheon 12.00
299 GC,V:Pantheon 12.00
300 RA,GP,KJ,MT,FMc,A:JLA 12.00
301 Rampage.................... 5.00

CVA Page 184   All comics prices listed are for *Near Mint* condition.

YOUNG ALL STARS
June, 1987
1 I:IronMunro&FlyingFox,D:TNT... 4.50
2 V:Axis Amerika 2.50
3 V:Axis Amerika 2.25
4 I:The Tigress 2.25
5 I:Dyna-mite,O:Iron Munro 2.25
6 .... 2.25
7 Baseball Game,A:Tigress 2.25
8 Millennium 2.25
9 Millennium 2.25
10 Hugo Danner 2.25
11 `Birth of Iron Munro'.......... 2.25
12 `Secret of Hugo Danner' 2.25
13 `V:Deathbolt,Ultra-Humanite ... 2.25
14 Fury+Ultra Humanite 2.25
15 IronMunro At high school 2.25
16 Ozyan Inheritance 2.25
17 Ozyan Inheritance 2.25
18 Ozyan Inheritance 2.25
19 Ozyan 2.25
20 O:Flying Fox 2.25
21 Atom & Evil#1 .... 2.25
22 Atom & Evil#2 .... 2.25
23 Atom & Evil#3 .... 2.25
24 Atom & Evil#4 .... 2.25
25 .... 2.25
26 End of the All Stars? 2.25
27 `Sons of Dawn' begins......... 2.25
28 Search for Hugo Danner 2.25
29 A:Hugo Danner 2.25
30 V:Sons of Dawn................ 2.25
31 V:Sons of Dawn,last issue 2.25
Ann.#1 MG,V:Mekanique 2.50

YOUNG HEROES IN LOVE
April, 1997
1 DeM,F:Hard Drive............. 3.00
2 DeM,sex, lies and superheroics . 2.50
3 A:Superman 2.50
4 F:Hard Drive.................. 2.50
5 Genesis tie-in 2.50
6 The Rat Pack 2.50
7 Secret Identity Issue......... 2.50
8 V:Scarecrow 2.50
9 F:Frostbite & Bonfire......... 2.50
10 V:Grundo'mu 2.50
11 V:Grundo'mu 2.50
12 Hard Drive dead? 2.50
13 New leader picked............. 2.50
14 Man of Inches vs. Man
    of Candles 2.50
15 Junior vs. Birthday Boy 2.50
16 DeM,Zip-Kid 2.50
17 DeM,Monstergirl's Uncle 2.50
Spec.#1,000,000 DeM final issue . . 3.00

YOUNG JUSTICE
July, 1998
1 PDd,TNu,Robin,Superboy,
  Impulse 4.50
2 PDd,TNu,V:Super-Cycle 3.00
3 PDd(s),TNu,V:Mr.Mxyzptlk 3.00
4 PDd(s),TNu,Girls join team ... 3.00
5 PDd(s),TNu,V:Harm 3.00
6 PDd(s),TNu,F:JLA 3.00
7 PDd(s),TNu,A:Nightwing........ 3.00
8 CDi(s),TNu,A:Razorsharp 3.00
9 PDd(s),V:Huggathugees......... 3.00
10 PDd(s),V:The Acolyte......... 3.00
11 PDd(s),Rescue Red Tornado ... 3.00
12 PDd(s),TNu,Supergirl x-over
   Hell's Angels,pt.1 .... 3.00
13 PDd(s), Hell's Angels,pt.3 ... 3.00

14 PDd(s),Day of Judgment x-over . 3.00
15 PDd(s),F:Arrowette 3.00
16 PDd(s)...................... 3.00
17 PDd(s),A:A.P.E.S. 3.00
18 PDd(s),Young Injustice....... 3.00
19 PDd(s),I:Empress 3.00
20 PDd(s),new team.............. 3.00
21 PDd(s),all new?.............. 2.75
22 Day in the life 2.75
23 PDd,TNu,AustraliaGames,pt.1 . 2.75
24 PDd,TNu,AustraliaGames,pt.2 . 2.75
25 PDd,TNu,Into space,pt.1 ..... 2.75
26 PDd,TNu,Into space,pt.2 ..... 2.75
27 PDd,TNu,Into space,pt.3 ..... 2.75
28 PDd,TNu,New Genesis 2.75
29 PDd,TNu,F:Forever People 2.75
30 PDd,TNu,Secret vs. Spoiler... 2.75
31 PDd,TNu,F:Empress 2.75
32 PDd,TNu,F:Empress 2.75
33 PDd,TNu,WendyWerewolfHunter 2.75
34 PDd,TNu,wolf bites 2.75
35 PDd,TNu,Worlds at War,tie-in . 2.75
36 PDd,TNu,Worlds at War,tie-in . 2.75
37 PDd,TNu,stuck in Hell 2.75
38 PDd,TNu,jokerized Match 2.75
39 PDd,TNu,V:New Genesis........ 2.75
40 PDd,TNu,Christmas Past...... 2.75
41 PDd,TNu,F:Ray................ 2.75
42 PDd,TNu,F:Hal Jordan......... 2.75
43 PDd,TNu,F:Traya.............. 2.75
44 PDd,TNu,WorldWithoutYJ,pt.1 2.75
45 PDd,TNu,WorldWithoutYJ,pt.5 2.75
46 PDd(s),TNu,election day at HQ 2.75
47 PDd,TNu,Fighting MAAD,pt.1. 2.75
48 PDd,TNu,Fighting MAAD,pt.2. 2.75
49 PDd,TNu,Fighting MAAD,pt.3. 2.75
50 PDd,TNu,F.MAAD,pg.4,48-pg. 3.95
51 PDd(s),TNu, on Zandia 2.75
52 PDd(s),TNu,Real World 2.75
53 PDd(s),TNu,V:Secret 2.75
54 PDd(s),TNu,V:Secret 2.75
55 PDd(s),TNu,final issue 2.75
Spec.#1,000,000 PDd(s),TNu..... 3.00
Giant#1 Secret Origins, 80-page... 5.00
Giant#1 80-page................. 5.00
Secret Files #1................. 5.00
Spec.#1 Young Justice in
   No Man's Land, CDi(s)....... 4.00

Spec.#1 Young Justice: The Secret
   Impulse,Superboy,Robin (1998) 2.50
Spec.#1 Our Worlds at War 2.95
TPB A League of Their Own 14.95

YOUNG JUSTICE: SINS OF YOUTH
March, 2000
1 (of 2) PDd,x-over 4.00
2 PDd,x-over................... 4.00
Secret Files #1 .... 5.00
TPB Sins of Youth 20.00

YOUNG LOVE
Sept.–Oct., 1963
39 .... 75.00
40 thru 50 .... @50.00
51 thru 60 .... @40.00
61 thru 68 .... @40.00
69 giant size................. 75.00
70 thru 80 .... @40.00
81 thru 99 giants, 52-page .. @30.00
100 .... 35.00
101 thru 106 .... @25.00
107 GC, Giant, 100-page 125.00
108 thru 114 Giant, 100-page . @100.00
115 thru 126 52-page .... @50.00

ZATANNA
1987
1 R:Zatanna 2.25
2 N:Zatanna 2.25
3 Come Together................ 2.25
4 V:Xaos 2.25

ZERO GIRL
DC/Homage Dec., 2000
1 (of 5) SK,F:Amy Snooster...... 3.00
2 SK,.......................... 3.00
3 SK,Vice Principal Hooly 3.00
4 SK,Mr. Foster 3.00
5 SK, concl.................... 3.00
TPB series rep. 144-page....... 13.00

ZERO GIRL: FULL CIRCLE
DC/Vertigo, Nov., 2002
1 (of 5) SK.................... 2.95

ZERO HOUR: CRISIS IN TIME
1994
4 DJu(a&s),JOy,A:All DC Heroes,
   D;2nd Flash 4.50
3 DJu(a&s),JOy,D:G.A.Sandman,
   G:A.Atom,Dr.Fate,1st Wildcat
   IR:Time Trapper is Rokk Krinn,
   Hawkman merged 2.50
2 DJu(a&s),Joy 2.50
1 DJu(a&s),JOy,b:Power Gir's
   Child 2.50
0 DJu(a&s),JOy,Gatefold(s),Extant
   vs. Spectre................. 2.50

Young Love #125 © DC Comics Inc.

Amazon–X-Patrol / Amalgam / Comics Values Annual

AMAZON
DC, 1996–97
1 JBy,TA 3.00
1 one-shot JBy,Princess Ororo
    is Wonder Woman 2.25

ASSASSINS
DC, 1996–97
1 DGC,SMc 3.00
1 one-shot DGC(s),SMc,F:Dare
    and Catsai 2.25

BAT-THING
DC, 1997
1 one-shot LHa(s),RDm,BSz,
    V:motorcycle gang 2.25

BRUCE WAYNE: AGENT OF S.H.I.E.L.D.
Marvel, 1996
1 CDi 3.00

BULLETS & BRACELETS
Marvel, 1996
1 JOs,GFr,CaS 3.00

CHALLENGERS OF THE FANTASTIC
Marvel, 1997
1 KK,TGu,AV 2.25

DARK CLAW ADVENTURES, THE
DC, 1997
1 one-shot TTy,RBr,V:Ladia Talia . 2.25

DC VERSUS MARVEL MARVEL VERSUS DC
1 (DC)DJu 6.00
1a 2nd printing 4.00
2 (Marvel)PDd,DJu 5.00
2a 2nd printing 4.00
3 (Marvel)DJu 4.00
4 (DC)PDd,DJu 4.00
TPB rep. mini series #1–#4 . . . . . 12.95

DOCTOR STRANGEFATE
DC, 1996–97
1 RMz,KN 3.00
1 one-shot RMz(s),JL,KN,Supreme
    Lord of Order 2.25

EXCITING X-PATROL
Marvel, 1997
1 BKs,BHi 2.25

GENERATION HEX
DC, 1997
1 one-shot,PrM(s),AdP,F:Jono Hex,
    Madam Banshee 2.25

IRON LANTERN
Marvel, 1997
1 KB,PSm,AW 2.25

JLX
DC Comics 1996–97
1 MWa,GJ 3.00
1 one-shot,MWa(s),GJ,HPo,JhD . . 2.25

JLX UNLEASHED
DC, 1997
1 one-shot, CPr,The Inextinguish-
    able Flame . . . .
    . . . . 2.25

LEGENDS OF THE DARK CLAW
DC, 1996–97
1 LHa,JBa 3.00
1 one-shot LHa(s),JBa 2.25
1 2nd printing 2.25

LOBO THE DUCK
DC, 1997
1 one-shot, AlG,VS 2.25

MAGNETO & THE MAGNETIC MEN
Marvel, 1996
1 MWa,GJ,JMs,ATi 3.00

MAGNETIC MEN FEATURING MAGNETO
Marvel, 1997
1 TPe,BKi,DPs 2.25

SPEED DEMON
Marvel, 1996
1 HMe,SvL,AM 3.00

SPIDER-BOY
Marvel, 1996
1 KK,MeW 3.00

SPIDER-BOY TEAM-UP
Marvel, 1997
1 KK,RSt 2.25

SUPER-SOLDIER
DC, 1996–97
1 MWa,DGb 3.00
1-shot MWa(s),DGb,V:Ultra-
    Metallo, Green Skull, Hydra . . . 2.25

SUPER SOLDIER: MAN OF WAR
DC, 1997
1 one-shot MWa(s),DGb,JP,
    V:Nazis 2.25

THORION OF THE NEW ASGODS
Marvel, 1997
1 KG,JR2 . . . . 2.25

X-PATROL
Marvel, 1996
1 KK,BKs 3.00
The Amalgam Age of Comics: The DC
    Comics Collection TPBs 12.95
The Amalgam Age of Comics: The
    Marvel Comics Collection TPBs . . . 12.95

Return to the Amalgam Age of Comics:
The DC Comics Collection TPB . . 13.00

Bat-Thing #1 © DC/Marvel

Iron Lantern #1 © DC/Marvel

X-Patrol #1 © DC/Marvel

MARVEL

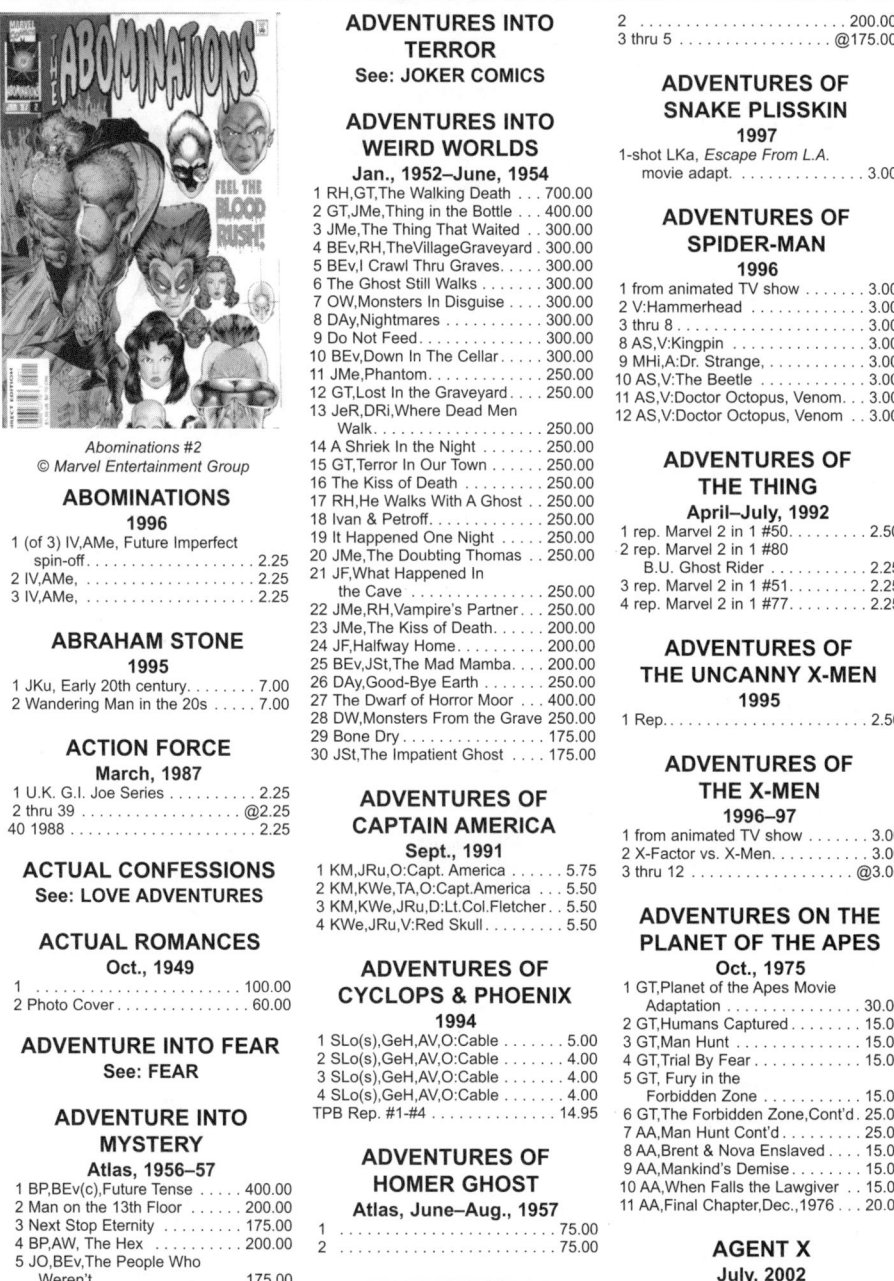

Abominations #2
© Marvel Entertainment Group

ABOMINATIONS
1996
1 (of 3) IV,AMe, Future Imperfect
 spin-off................... 2.25
2 IV,AMe,................... 2.25
3 IV,AMe,................... 2.25

ABRAHAM STONE
1995
1 JKu, Early 20th century........ 7.00
2 Wandering Man in the 20s..... 7.00

ACTION FORCE
March, 1987
1 U.K. G.I. Joe Series.......... 2.25
2 thru 39................. @2.25
40 1988..................... 2.25

ACTUAL CONFESSIONS
See: LOVE ADVENTURES

ACTUAL ROMANCES
Oct., 1949
1 .... 100.00
2 Photo Cover.............. 60.00

ADVENTURE INTO FEAR
See: FEAR

ADVENTURE INTO MYSTERY
Atlas, 1956–57
1 BP,BEv(c),Future Tense..... 400.00
2 Man on the 13th Floor...... 200.00
3 Next Stop Eternity......... 175.00
4 BP,AW, The Hex.......... 200.00
5 JO,BEv,The People Who
 Weren't................. 175.00
6 The Wax Man............. 175.00
7 AT,BEv(c)............... 175.00
8 AT,JWo,TSe............. 175.00

ADVENTURES INTO TERROR
See: JOKER COMICS

ADVENTURES INTO WEIRD WORLDS
Jan., 1952–June, 1954
1 RH,GT,The Walking Death... 700.00
2 GT,JMe,Thing in the Bottle... 400.00
3 JMe,The Thing That Waited.. 300.00
4 BEv,RH,TheVillageGraveyard. 300.00
5 BEv,I Crawl Thru Graves..... 300.00
6 The Ghost Still Walks....... 300.00
7 OW,Monsters In Disguise.... 300.00
8 DAy,Nightmares.......... 300.00
9 Do Not Feed.............. 300.00
10 BEv,Down In The Cellar.... 300.00
11 JMe,Phantom............ 250.00
12 GT,Lost In the Graveyard.... 250.00
13 JeR,DRi,Where Dead Men
 Walk................... 250.00
14 A Shriek In the Night...... 250.00
15 GT,Terror In Our Town..... 250.00
16 The Kiss of Death......... 250.00
17 RH,He Walks With A Ghost.. 250.00
18 Ivan & Petroff............ 250.00
19 It Happened One Night..... 250.00
20 JMe,The Doubting Thomas.. 250.00
21 JF,What Happened In
 the Cave................ 250.00
22 JMe,RH,Vampire's Partner... 250.00
23 JMe,The Kiss of Death...... 200.00
24 JF,Halfway Home.......... 200.00
25 BEv,JSt,The Mad Mamba.... 200.00
26 DAy,Good-Bye Earth....... 250.00
27 The Dwarf of Horror Moor... 400.00
28 DW,Monsters From the Grave 250.00
29 Bone Dry................ 175.00
30 JSt,The Impatient Ghost.... 175.00

ADVENTURES OF CAPTAIN AMERICA
Sept., 1991
1 KM,JRu,O:Capt. America..... 5.75
2 KM,KWe,TA,O:Capt.America... 5.50
3 KM,KWe,JRu,D:Lt.Col.Fletcher.. 5.50
4 KWe,JRu,V:Red Skull........ 5.50

ADVENTURES OF CYCLOPS & PHOENIX
1994
1 SLo(s),GeH,AV,O:Cable...... 5.00
2 SLo(s),GeH,AV,O:Cable...... 4.00
3 SLo(s),GeH,AV,O:Cable...... 4.00
4 SLo(s),GeH,AV,O:Cable...... 4.00
TPB Rep. #1-#4............. 14.95

ADVENTURES OF HOMER GHOST
Atlas, June–Aug., 1957
1 .... 75.00
2 .... 75.00

ADVENTURES OF PINKY LEE
Atlas, July, 1955
1 .... 300.00

2 .... 200.00
3 thru 5................. @175.00

ADVENTURES OF SNAKE PLISSKIN
1997
1-shot LKa, *Escape From L.A.*
 movie adapt............... 3.00

ADVENTURES OF SPIDER-MAN
1996
1 from animated TV show....... 3.00
2 V:Hammerhead............ 3.00
3 thru 8................... 3.00
8 AS,V:Kingpin.............. 3.00
9 MHi,A:Dr. Strange,......... 3.00
10 AS,V:The Beetle.......... 3.00
11 AS,V:Doctor Octopus, Venom. 3.00
12 AS,V:Doctor Octopus, Venom.. 3.00

ADVENTURES OF THE THING
April–July, 1992
1 rep. Marvel 2 in 1 #50........ 2.50
2 rep. Marvel 2 in 1 #80
 B.U. Ghost Rider.......... 2.25
3 rep. Marvel 2 in 1 #51........ 2.25
4 rep. Marvel 2 in 1 #77........ 2.25

ADVENTURES OF THE UNCANNY X-MEN
1995
1 Rep...................... 2.50

ADVENTURES OF THE X-MEN
1996–97
1 from animated TV show....... 3.00
2 X-Factor vs. X-Men........... 3.00
3 thru 12................. @3.00

ADVENTURES ON THE PLANET OF THE APES
Oct., 1975
1 GT,Planet of the Apes Movie
 Adaptation............... 30.00
2 GT,Humans Captured........ 15.00
3 GT,Man Hunt.............. 15.00
4 GT,Trial By Fear............ 15.00
5 GT, Fury in the
 Forbidden Zone........... 15.00
6 GT,The Forbidden Zone,Cont'd. 25.00
7 AA,Man Hunt Cont'd......... 25.00
8 AA,Brent & Nova Enslaved.... 15.00
9 AA,Mankind's Demise........ 15.00
10 AA,When Falls the Lawgiver.. 15.00
11 AA,Final Chapter,Dec.,1976... 20.00

AGENT X
July, 2002
1 Taskmaster trainee,40-pg...... 3.00
2 Hunts the Punisher.......... 2.25
3 V:Taskmaster.............. 2.25
4 Who is Mary Zero........... 2.25
5 .... 2.25

All comics prices listed are for *Near Mint* condition.

Agent X–Alien Legion — MARVEL

6	2.25
7	2.25
8 MkK,pt.1	2.25
9 MkK,pt.2	2.25
10 EDo(s)	3.00
11 EDo(s)	3.00
12 BSf(c)	3.00
13 Deadpool Walkin,pt.1	3.00
14 Deadpool Walkin,pt.2	3.00
15 Deadpool Walkin,pt.3	3.00

AGE OF INNOCENCE
1995

1-shot Timeslid aftermath	2.50

AIRTIGHT GARAGE
Epic, July–Oct., 1993

1 thru 4 rep.Moebius GNv	@3.50

AKIRA
Epic, Sept., 1988

1 The Highway,I:Kaneda,Tetsuo, Koy,Ryu,Colonel,Takaski	30.00
1a 2nd printing	4.00
2 Pursuit,I:Number27,(Masaru)	15.00
2a 2nd printing	3.50
3 Number 41,V:Clown Gang	10.00
4 King of Clowns,V:Colonel	10.00
5 Cycle Wars,V:Clown Gang	10.00
6 D:Yamagota	9.00
7 Prisoners and Players,I:Miyo	9.00
8 Weapon of Vengeance	9.00
9 Stalkers	9.00
10 The Awakening	9.00
11 Akira Rising	6.00
12 Enter Sakaki	6.00
13 Desperation	6.00
14 Caught in the Middle	6.00
15 Psychic Duel	6.00
16 Akira Unleashed	6.00
17 Emperor of Chaos	6.00
18 Amid the Ruins	5.00
19 To Save the Children	5.00
20 Revelations	5.00
21	5.00
22	5.00
23	5.00
24 Clown Gang	5.00
25 Search For Kay	5.00
26 Juvenile A Project	5.00
27 Kay and Kaneda	5.00
28 Tetsuo	5.00
29 Tetsuo	5.00
30 Tetsuo,Kay,Kaneda	5.00
31 D:Kaori,Kaneda,Vs.Tetsuo	5.00
32 Tetsuo'sForces vs.U.S.Forces	5.00
33 Tetsuo V:Kaneda	5.00
34 64pt. R:Otomo	11.00
35 Leads toward final battle	11.00
36 Lady Miyako	11.00
37 ghost of Tetsuo	11.00
38 conclusion	11.00
TPB Akira:Reprints#1-#3	13.95
TPB Akira:Reprints#4-#6	13.95
TPB Akira:Reprints#7-#9	13.95
TPB Akira:Reprints#10-#12	14.95
TPB Akira:Reprints#13-#15	14.95
TPB Akira:Reprints#16-#18	14.95
TPB Akira:Reprints#19-#21	16.95
TPB Akira:Reprints#22-#24	16.95
TPB Akira:Reprints#25-#27	16.95
TPB Akira:Reprints#28-#30	17.95

ALADDIN
1994

1 Aladdin's Quest	2.25
2 thru 12	@2.25

Alf #5
© Marvel Entertainment Group

ALF
Star, March, 1988

1 Photo Cover	4.00
1a 2nd printing	2.50
2 Alf Causes trouble	2.50
3 More adventures	2.50
4 Willie on Melmac	2.50
5 I:Alf's evil twin	2.50
6 Photo Cover	2.50
7 Pygm-Alien	2.50
8 Ochmoneks' Garage	2.50
9 Alf's Independence Day	2.50
10 Alf goes to College	2.50
11 Halloween special	2.50
12 Alf loses memory	2.50
13 Racetrack of my Tears	2.50
14 Night of the Living Bread	2.50
15 Alf on the Road	2.50
16 More Adventures	2.50
17 Future vision	2.50
18 More Adventures	2.50
19 The Alf-strologer	2.50
20 Alf the Baby Sitter,pt.1	3.00
21 Alf the Baby Sitter,pt.2	3.00
22 X-Men parody	3.00
23 Alf visits Australia	2.50
24 Rhonda visits Earth	2.50
25 More Adventures	2.50
26 Alf gets a job	2.50
27 Alf lost	2.50
28 Alf's Amnesia	2.50
29 Alf/Brian reporters	2.50
30 Shakespeare Baby	2.50
31 Alf's Summer Camp	3.00
32 Arnold Schwarzemeimac	3.00
33 Dungeons & Dragons Spoof	3.00
34 Alf-Red & Alf-Blue(2 Alfs)	3.00
35 Gone with the Wind	3.00
36 More Adventures	3.00
37 Melmacian Gothic	3.00
38 Boundtree Hunters	3.00
39 Pizarro Alf	3.00
40 A:Zoreo	3.00
41 TV	3.00
42 V:Alf	3.00
43 House Break-in	3.00
44 A:Fantastic Fur	4.00
45 Melmenopaus	4.00
46 Goes to Center of Earth	3.00
47 Meteor Bye-Products,pt.1	3.00
48 Meteor Bye-Products,pt.2	3.00
49 1st Rhonda solo story	3.00
50 Final Issue, giant size	4.00

Ann.#1 Evol.War	3.00
Ann.#2	3.00
Spring Spec.#1	3.00
Holiday Spec.#2	3.00

ALIAS
Marvel Max, Sept., 2001

1 BMB(s)	9.00
2 BMB(s), F:Jessica Jones	5.00
3 BMB(s)	5.00
4 BMB(s),DMk(c)	5.00
5 BMB(s),DMk(c)	3.00
6 BMB(s),DMk(c)	3.00
7 BMB(s),BSz	3.00
8 BMB(s),BSz	3.00
9 BMB(s),2nd story, concl	3.00
10 BMB(s),J.J.Jameson,Jessica	3.00
11 BMB(s),to small town	3.00
12 BMB(s),in small town	3.00
13 BMB(s)	3.00
14 BMB(s),DMk(c),case concludes	3.00
15 BMB(s),DMk(c),Cage again	3.00
16 BMB(s),DMk(c),Underneath	3.00
17 BMB(s),DMk(c),Underneath	3.00
18 BMB(s),DMk(c),Underneath	3.00
19 BMB(s),DMk(c),Underneath	3.00
20 BMB(s),DMk(c),Underneath	3.00
21 BMB(s),DMk(c),Underneath	3.00
22 BMB(s),DMk(c),Jessica Jones	3.00
23 BMB(s),DMk(c),Jessica Jones	3.00
24 BMB(s),DMk(c),Purple,pt.1	3.00
25 BMB(s),DMk(c),Purple,pt.2	3.00
26 BMB(s),DMk(c),Purple,pt.3	3.00
27 BMB(s),DMk(c),Purple,pt.4	3.00
28 BMB(s),DMk(c),Purple,pt.5	3.00
TPB Vol. 1	20.00
TPB Vol. 2: Come Home	14.00
TPB Vol. 3: Underneath	17.00

ALIEN LEGION
Epic, April, 1984

1 FC,TA,I:Sarigar,Montroc	4.00
2 FC,TA,CP,V:Harkilons	3.50
3 FC,TA,CW,V:Kroyzo	3.00
4 FC,TA,CW,F:Skob	3.00
5 FC,CW,D:Skob	3.00
6 FC,CW,WPo,V:Harkilons	3.00
7 CW,WPo,I:Lora	3.00
8 CW,WPo,V:Harkilons	3.00
9 CW,V:Harkilons	3.00
10 CW,LSn,V:Harkilons	3.00
11 CW,LSn,V:Harkilons	3.00
12 LSn,A:Aob-Sin	3.00
13 LSn,F:Montroc	3.00
14 LSn,V:Cordar	3.00
15 LSn,V:Alphor,Betro,&Gamoid	3.00
16 LSn,J:Tomaro	3.00
17 LSn,Durge on Drugs	3.00
18 LSn,V:Dun	3.00
19 LSn,A:GalarcyScientist	3.00
20 LSn,L:Skilene	3.00

[2nd Series], Aug., 1987

1 LSn,I:Guy Montroc	3.00
2 LSn,V:Quallians	2.50
3 LSn,Hellscope	2.50
4 LSn,V:Harkilons	2.50
5 LSn,F:JuggerGrimrod	2.50
6 LSn,F:JuggerGrimrod	2.50
7 LSn,A:Guy Montroc	2.50
8 LSn,I:Nakhira	2.50
9 LSn,V:Harkilons	2.50
10 LSn,V:Harkilons	2.50
11 LSn,V:Harkilons	2.50
12 LSn,Tamara Pregnant	2.50
13 LSn,V:MomojianKndrel	2.50
14 LSn,J:Saravil	2.50
15 LSn,J:Spellik	2.50
16 LSn,D:Jugger's Father	2.50
17 LSn,O:JuggerGrimrod	2.50

Comics Values Annual — MARVEL — Alien Legion–All Winners

18 LSn,O:JuggerGrimrod 2.50
GN Grimrod 5.95
1-shot Alien Legion: Binary Deep
   with trading card (1993) 3.50

ALIEN LEGION: JUGGER GRIMROD
Epic, Aug., 1992
Book One 6.00

ALIEN LEGION: ONE PLANET AT A TIME
Epic, Heavy Hitters May, 1993
1 HNg,CDi,One Planet at a Time . . 5.00
2 HNg,CDi. 5.00
3 HNg,CDi. 5.00

ALIEN LEGION: ON THE EDGE
Epic, Nov., 1990
1 LSn,V:B'Be No N'ngth 5.00
2 LSn,V:B'Be No N'ngth 5.00
3 LSn,V:B'Be No N'ngth 5.00
4 LSn,V:B'Be No N'ngth 5.00

ALIEN LEGION: TENANTS OF HELL
Epic, 1991
1 LSn,Nomad Squad On
   Combine IV 5.00
2 LSn,L:Torie Montroc,I:Stagg 5.00
TPB Alien Legion:Slaughterworld . 10.00

ALL-SELECT COMICS
Fall, 1943
Timely, (Daring Comics)
1 B:Capt.America,Sub-Mariner,
   Human Torch;WWII 16,000.00
2 A:Red Skull,V:Axis Powers. . 5,000.00
3 B:Whizzer,V:Axis 3,000.00
4 V: Axis 2,100.00
5 E:Sub-Mariner,V:Axis 2,100.00
6 A:The Destroyer,V:Axis 1,600.00
7 MSu,E:Whizzer,V:Axis 1,600.00
8 MSu,V:Axis Powers 1,600.00
9 V:Axis Powers 1,600.00
10 E:Capt.America,Human Torch;

All-Select Comics #4
© Marvel Entertainment Group

A:The Destroyer 1,600.00
11 I:Blonde Phantom,A:Miss
   America. 3,300.00
Becomes:

BLONDE PHANTOM
1946
12 B:Miss America;The Devil's
   Playground 1,900.00
13 B:Sub-Mariner;Horror In
   Hollywood 1,100.00
14 E:Miss America;Horror At
   Haunted Castle 1,000.00
15 The Man Who Deserved
   To Die 1,000.00
16 A:Capt.America,Bucky;
   Modeled For Murder 1,500.00
17 Torture & Rescue. 900.00
18 Jealously,Hate & Cruelty 900.00
19 Killer In the Hospital. 900.00
20 Blonde Phantom's Big Fall . . . 900.00
21 Murder At the Carnival 900.00
22 V: Crime Bosses 900.00
Becomes:

LOVERS
1949
23 Love Stories 150.00
24 My Dearly Beloved. 75.00
25 The Man I Love 60.00
26 thru 29 . . . . @40.00
30 MK 60.00
31 thru 36 . . . . @40.00
37 . . . . 60.00
38 BK. 60.00
39 . . . . 40.00
40 . . . . 40.00
41BEv 50.00
42 thru 65 . . . . @40.00
66 . . . . 35.00
67 ATh 50.00
68 thru 86 Aug., 1957 . . . . @35.00

ALL SURPRISE
Timely, Fall, 1943
1 (fa),F:Super Rabbit,Gandy,
   Sourpuss 250.00
2 . . . . 125.00
3 . . . . 100.00
4 thru 10 . . . . @100.00
11 HK 110.00
12 Winter, 1946 . . . . 75.00

ALL-TRUE CRIME
See: OFFICIAL TRUE CRIME CASES

ALL WINNERS COMICS
Summer, 1941
1 S&K,BEv,B:Capt.America & Bucky,
   Human Torch & Toro,Sub-Mariner
   A:The Angel,Black Marvel 30,000.00
2 S&K,B:Destroyer,Whizzer. . . 7,000.00
3 BEv,Bucky & Toro Captured 4,000.00
4 BEv,Battle For Victory
   For America 4,500.00
5 V:Nazi Invasion Fleet 2,800.00
6 V:Axis Powers,A:
   Black Avenger 3,200.00
7 V:Axis Powers 2,500.00
8 V:Axis Powers 2,200.00
9 V:Nazi Submarine Fleet . . . 2,200.00
10 V:Nazi Submarine Fleet . . . 2,500.00
11 V: Nazis 1,700.00
12 A:Red Skull,E:Destroyer;
   Jap P.O.W. Camp 1,800.00
13 V:Japanese Fleet 1,700.00
14 V:Japanese Fleet 1,700.00
15 Japanese Supply Train 1,700.00

All Winners Comics #1
© Marvel Entertainment Group

16 In Alaska V:Gangsters. 1,700.00
17 V:Gansters;Atomic
   Research Department 1,700.00
18 V:Robbers;Internal Revenue
   Department 2,000.00
19 I:All Winners Squad,
   Fall, 1946 . . . . 6,000.00
21 A:All-Winners Squad;Riddle
   of the Demented Dwarf . . . 4,500.00
Becomes:

ALL TEEN COMICS
1947
20 F:Georgie,Willie,
   Mitzi,Patsy Walker 150.00
Becomes:

TEEN COMICS
1947
21 HK,A:George,Willie,Mitzi,
   Patsy Walker, Hey Look 150.00
22 A:George,Willie,Margie,
   Patsy Walker 75.00
23 A:Patsy Walker,Cindy,George. . 75.00
24 . . . . 85.00
25 . . . . 75.00
26 . . . . 75.00
27 . . . . 75.00
28 . . . . 80.00
29 . . . . 75.00
30 HK, Hey Look 100.00
31 thru 34 . . . . @75.00
35 May, 1950 . . . . 75.00
Becomes:

JOURNEY INTO UNKNOWN WORLDS
Atlas, Sept., 1950
36(1) RH,End of the Earth. . . . 2,700.00
37(2) BEv,GC,When Worlds
   Collide. 1,200.00
38(3) GT,Land of Missing Men 1,100.00
4 MS,RH,Train to Nowhere 650.00
5 MS,Trapped in Space 650.00
6 GC,RH,World Below
   the Atlantic 650.00
7 BW,RH,JMn,House That
   Wasn't 1,100.00
8 RH,JMn,The Stone Thing 650.00
9 MS,JSt,The People Who
   Couldn't Exist 750.00
10 THe Undertaker 600.00
11 BEv,Frankie Was Afraid 500.00
12 BK,Last Voice You Hear. 500.00
13 The Witch Woman 400.00

All comics prices listed are for *Near Mint* condition.

All-Winners–Alpha Flight / MARVEL / Comics Values Annual

Journey Into Unknown Worlds #4
© Marvel Entertainment Group

14 BW,BEv,CondemnedBuilding . 800.00
15 JMn,They Crawl By Night. . . . 800.00
16 JMn,Scared to Death 400.00
17 BEv,GC,RH,The Ice
  Monster Cometh. 450.00
18 The Broth Needs Somebody . 450.00
19 MF,GC,The Long Wait 450.00
20 GC,RH,The Race That
  Vanished 350.00
21 MF,JMn,JSt,Decapitation 300.00
22 thru 32 . . . . @300.00
33 LO 300.00
34 MK,AT,DAy 250.00
35 AT,MD 250.00
36 thru 44 . . . . @200.00
45 AW,SD. 225.00
46 & 47. . . . . @200.00
48 GW,GM 200.00
49 JF,JMn. 200.00
50 JDa,RC 200.00
51 WW,SD,JSe. 200.00
52 . . . . 200.00
53 RC,BP 200.00
54 AT,BP 200.00
55 AW,RC,BEv 200.00
56 BEv 200.00
57 JO 150.00
58 MO,MD,JMn 150.00
59 AW,Aug., 1957 . . . . 175.00

ALL WINNERS COMICS
[2nd Series], Aug., 1948
1 F:Blonde Phantom,A:Capt.America
  Sub-Mariner,Human Torch 3,600.00
Becomes:

ALL WESTERN WINNERS
1948–49
2 B,I&O:Black Rider,B:Two-Gun
  Kid, Kid-Colt 1,000.00
3 Black Rider V: Satan. 450.00
4 Black Rider Unmasked 450.00
Becomes:

WESTERN WINNERS
1949
5 I Challenge the Army 350.00
6 The Mountain Mystery 300.00
7 Ph(c) Randolph Scott 300.00
Becomes:

BLACK RIDER
1950–55
8 Ph(c),B:Black Rider;Valley
  of Giants 500.00
9 Wrath of the Redskin 250.00
10 O:Black Rider 300.00
11 Redmen on the Warpath 175.00
12 GT,The Town That Vanished . 175.00
13 The Terrified Tribe 175.00
14 The Tyrant of Texas 175.00
15 Revolt of the Redskins. 150.00
16 . . . . 150.00
17 . . . . 150.00
18. . . . . 150.00
19 SSh,GT,A:Two-Gun Kid 150.00
20 GT. 175.00
21 SSh,GT,A:Two-Gun Kid 150.00
22 SSh,DAy(c),A:Two-Gun Kid . . 150.00
23 SSh,A:Two-Gun Kid 150.00
24 SSh,JSt 150.00
25 SSh,JSt,A:Arrowhead 150.00
26 SSh,A:Kid-Colt. 150.00
27 SSh,A:Kid-Colt. 175.00
Becomes:

WESTERN TALES OF BLACK RIDER
1955
28 JSe,D:Spider 125.00
29 . . . . 90.00
30 . . . . 90.00
31 . . . . 90.00
Becomes:

GUNSMOKE WESTERN
1955–63
32 MD,MB,F:Kid Colt,Billy
  Buckskin. 175.00
33 MD 150.00
34 MB 125.00
35 GC 150.00
36 AW,GC 150.00
37 JDa 125.00
38 . . . . 75.00
39 GC 75.00
40 AW 100.00
41 . . . . 50.00
42 . . . . 50.00
43 . . . . 50.00
44 AT 55.00
45 thru 55 . . . . @50.00
56 MB 55.00
57 thru 76 . . . . @50.00
77 July, 1963 . . . . 50.00

(TIMELY PRESENTS:) ALL-WINNERS
Oct., 1999
Spec. 48-pg. 4.00

ALPHA FLIGHT
Aug., 1983
1 JBy,I:Puck,Marrina,Tundra 4.00
2 JBy,I:Master,Vindicator Becomes
  Guardian,B:O:Marrina 2.50
3 JBy,O:Master,A:Namor,Invisible
  Girl, ... 2.50
4 JBy,A:Namor,Invisible Girl,
  E:O:Marrina,A:Master. 2.50
5 JBy,B:O:Shaman,F:Puck. 2.50
6 JBy,E:O:Shaman,I:Kolomag . . 2.50
7 JBy,B:O:Snowbird,I:Delphine
  Courtney & Deadly Ernest . . . 2.50
8 JBy,E:O:Snowbird,O:Deadly
  Ernest,I:Nemesis 2.50
9 JBy,O:Aurora,A:Wolverine,
  Super Skrull. 2.50
10 JBy,O:Northstar,V:SuperSkrull . . 2.50
11 JBy,I:Omega Flight,Wild Child
  O:Sasquatch 2.50
12 JBy,D:Guardian,V:Omega
  Flight 2.50
13 JBy,C:Wolverine,Nightmare 3.00
14 JBy,V:Genocide 2.50
15 JBy,R:Master. 2.50
16 JBy,BWi,V:Master,C:Wolverine
  I:Madison Jeffries 2.75
17 JBy,BWi,A:Wolverine,X-Men . . . 3.00
18 JBy,BWi,J:Heather,I:Ranaq . . 2.50
19 JBy,I:Talisman,V:Ranaq 2.50
20 JBy,I:Gilded Lily,N:Aurora. . . . 2.50
21 JBy,BWi,O:Gilded Lily,Diablo . . 2.50
22 JBy,BWi,I:Pink Pearl 2.50
23 JBy,BWi,D:Sasquatch,
  I:Tanaraq 2.50
24 JBy,BWi,V:Great Beasts,J:Box . . 2.50
25 JBy,BWi,V:Omega Flight
  I:Dark Guardian 2.50
26 JBy,BWi,A:Omega Flight,Dark
  Guardian 2.50
27 JBy,V:Omega Flight 2.50
28 JBy,Secret Wars II,V:Omega
  Flight,D:Dark Guardian 2.50
29 MMi,V:Hulk,A:Box 2.50
30 MMi,I&O:Scramble,R:Deadly
  Ernest 2.50
31 MMi,D:Deadly Ernest,
  O:Nemesis 2.50
32 MMi(c),JBg,O:Puck,I:2nd
  Vindicator. 2.50
33 MMi(c),SB,X-Men,I:Deathstrike . 3.00
34 MMi(c),SB,Wolverine,V:
  Deathstrike. 3.00
35 DR,R:Shaman 2.50
36 MMi(c),DR,A:Dr.Strange 2.50
37 DR,O:Pestilence,N:Aurora 2.50
38 DR,A:Namor,V:Pestilence . . . 2.50
39 MMi(c),DR,WPo,A:Avengers . . 2.75
40 DR,WPo,W:Namor & Marrina . . 2.75
41 DR,WPo,I:Purple Girl,
  J:Madison Jeffries 2.75
42 DR,WPo,I:Auctioneer,J:Purple
  Girl,A: Beta Flight. 2.75
43 DR,WPo,V:Mesmero,Sentinels . . 2.75
44 DR,WPo,D:Snowbird,
  A:Pestilence 2.75
45 JBr,WPo,R:Sasquatch,
  L:Shaman 2.75
46 JBr,WPo,I:2nd Box. 2.75
47 MMi,WPo,TA,Vindicator solo . . . 2.75
48 SL(i),I:Omega 2.75
49 JBr,WPo,I:Manikin,D:Omega . . 2.75
50 WS(c),JBr,WPo,L:Northstar,Puck,
  Aurora,A:Loki,Double size . . . 3.00
51 JLe(1st Marv),WPo(i),V:Cody . . . 5.00
52 JBr,WPo(i),I:Bedlam,
  A:Wolverine 3.00
53 JLe,WPo(i),I:Derangers,Goblyn
  D&V:Bedlam,A:Wolverine 3.00
54 WPo(i),O&J:Goblyn 2.50
55 JLe,TD,V:Tundra 2.75
56 JLe,TD,V:Bedlamites 2.75
57 JLe,TD,V:Crystals,
  C:Dreamqueen 2.75
58 JLe,AM,V:Dreamqueen 2.75
59 JLe,AM,I:Jade Dragon,R:Puck . . 2.75
60 JLe,AM,V:J.Dragon,D.Queen . . . 2.75
61 JLe,AM,on Trial
  (1st JLe X-Men) 2.75
62 JLe,AM,V:Purple Man 2.75
63 MG,V:U.S.Air Force 2.50
64 JLe,AM,V:Great Beasts 2.75
65 JLe(c),AM(i),Dream Issue 2.50
66 JLe(c),I:China Force 2.50
67 JLe(c),O:Dream Queen 2.50
68 JLe(c),V:Dream Queen 2.50
69 JLe(c),V:Dream Queen 2.50
70 MM(i),V:Dream Queen 2.50
71 MM(i),I:Sorcerer. 2.50

MARVEL

Alpha Flight–Amazing

Alpha Flight #48
© Marvel Entertainment Group

72 V:Sorcerer 2.50
73 MM(i),V:Sorcerer 2.50
74 MM(i),Alternate Earth 3.00
75 JLe(c),MMi(i),Double Size 3.00
76 MM(i),V:Sorcerer 2.25
77 MM(i),V:Kingpin 2.25
78 MM(i),A:Dr.Strange,Master ... 2.25
79 MM(i),AofV,V:Scorpion,Nekra . 2.25
80 MM(i),AofV,V:Scorpion,Nekra . 2.25
81 JBy(c),MM(i),B:R:Northstar .. 2.25
82 JBy(c),MM(i),E:R:Northstar .. 2.25
83 JSh 2.25
84 MM(i),Northstar 2.25
85 MM(i) 2.25
86 MBa,MM,V:Sorcerer 2.25
87 JLe(c),MM(i),A:Wolverine 3.00
88 JLe(c),MM(i),A:Wolverine 3.00
89 JLe(c),MM(i),R:Guardian,A:
    Wolverine 3.00
90 JLe(c),MM(i),A:Wolverine 3.00
91 MM(i),A:Dr.Doom 2.25
92 Guardian vs.Vindicator 2.25
93 MM(i),A:Fant.Four,I:Headlok . 2.25
94 MM(i),V:Fant.Four,Headlok ... 2.25
95 MM(i),Lifelines 2.25
96 MM(i),A:Master 2.25
97 B:Final Option,A:Her 2.25
98 A:Avengers 2.25
99 A:Avengers 2.25
100 JBr,TMo,DR,LMa,E:Final Option
    A:Galactus,Avengers,D:
    Guardian,G-Size 2.50
101 TMo,Final Option Epilogue,
    A:Dr.Strange,Avengers 2.25
102 TMo,I:Weapon Omega 2.25
103 TMo,V:Diablo,U.S.Agent 2.25
104 TMo,N:Alpha Flight,Weapon
    Omega is Wild Child 2.25
105 TMo,V:Pink Pearl 2.25
106 MPa,Aids issue,Northstar
    acknowledges homosexuality . 3.00
106a 2nd printing 2.50
107 A:X-Factor,V:Autopsy 2.25
108 A:Soviet Super Soldiers 2.25
109 V:Peoples Protectorate 2.25
110 PB,Infinity War,I:2nd Omega
    Flight,A:Wolverine 2.25
111 PB,Infinity War,V:Omega
    Flight,A:Wolverine 2.25
112 PB,Infinity War,V:Master ... 2.25
113 V:Mauler 2.25
114 A:Weapon X 2.25
115 PB,I:Wyre,A:Weapon X 2.25
116 PB,I:Rok,V:Wyre 2.25
117 PB,V:Wyre 2.25
118 PB,V:Thunderball 2.25
119 PB,V:Wrecking Crew 2.25
120 PB,10th Anniv.,V:Hardliners,
    w/poster 3.00
121 PCu,V:Brass Bishop,A:Spider-
    Man,Wolverine,C:X-Men 2.50
122 PB,BKi,Inf.Crusade 2.50
123 PB,BKi,Infinity Crusade ... 2.50
124 PB,BKi,Infinity Crusade ... 2.50
125 PB,V:Carcass 2.50
126 V:Carcass 2.50
127 SFu(s),Infinity Crusade ... 2.50
128 B:No Future 2.50
129 C:Omega Flight 2.50
130 E:No Future,last issue,
    Double Sized 3.00
Ann.#1 LSn,V:Diablo,Gilded Lily . 3.00
Ann.#2 JBr,BMc 2.50
Spec.#1 PB,A:Wolverine,
    O:First Team,V:Egghead 3.75
Spec.#1–#3 Newsstand versions
    of #97–#99 .... @2.50
Spec.#4 Newsstand ver.of #100 .. 2.50

ALPHA FLIGHT
1997
1 SSe,ScC, former team kidnapped,
    I:Murmur, Radius,Flex,Guardian 5.00
2 SSe,ScC 4.00
2 variant cover 3.50
3 SSe,ScC 3.50
4 SSe,ScC,V:Mesmero 3.00
5 SSe,ScC,A:Mesmero 3.00
6 SSe,What's up with Sasquatch? . 3.00
7 SSe,Evils explode 3.00
8 SSe,ScC,North & South prelude . 3.00
9 SSe,ScC,North & South pt.1,
    X-men x-over 3.00
10 SSe,Flung into Prometheus Pit . 3.00
11 SSe,race to save 2 worlds 3.00
12 SSe,Alphan dies,48pg. double
    size 3.50
13 SSe,F:Basil Killbrew 2.50
14 SSe,I:Brass Bishop 2.50
15 SSe 2.50
16 SSe,V:Brass Bishop 2.50
17 SSe,V:X the Unknown 2.50
18 SSe,Alpha:Omega:pt.1 .... 2.50
19 SSe,Alpha:Omega,pt.2 .... 2.50
20 SSe,Alpha:Omega,pt.3 .... 2.50
Spec. #1 SSe,îIn the Beginning,î
    Flashback, A:Wolverine 2.50
Ann.1998 Alpha Flight/Inhumans ... 3.50

ALPHA FLIGHT SPECIAL
1991
1 thru 4 reprints .... @2.25

AMAZING ADVENTURES
June, 1961
1 JK,SD,O&B:Dr.Droom;Torr . 2,000.00
2 JK,SD,This is Manoo 800.00
3 JK,SD,Trapped in the
    Twilight World 650.00
4 JK,SD, I Am X 600.00
5 JK,SD, Monsteroso 600.00
6 JK,SD,E:Dr.Droom; Sserpo .. 600.00
Becomes:

AMAZING ADULT FANTASY
Dec., 1961
7 SD,Last Man on Earth 800.00
8 SD,The Coming of the Krills . 600.00
9 SD,The Terror of Tim Boo Ba . 550.00
10 SD,Those Who Change 550.00
11 SD,In Human Form 550.00
12 SD,Living Statues 550.00
13 SD,At the Stroke of Midnight . 550.00
14 SD,Beware of the Giants 600.00
Becomes:

AMAZING FANTASY
Aug., 1962
15 JK(c),SD,I&O:Spider-Man,I:Aunt
    May, Flash Thompson, Burglar,
    I&D:Uncle Ben 50,000.00
Marvel Milestone rep.#15 (1992) .. 3.00

[Second Series], 1995
15a gold Rep. (1995) 25.00
16 KBk, O:Spider-Man,painted 4.00
17 KBk, More early adventures.... 4.00
18 KBk,conclusion 4.00

AMAZING ADVENTURES
Aug., 1970
[1st Regular Series]
1 JK,JB,B:Inhumans,Bl.Widow ... 75.00
2 JK,JB,A:Fantastic Four 30.00
3 JK,GC,BEv,V:Mandarin 30.00
4 JK,GC,BEv,V:Mandarin 30.00
5 NA,TP,DH,BEv,V:Astrologer ... 50.00
6 NA,DH,SB,V:Maximus 50.00
7 NA,DH,BEv 50.00
8 NA,DH,BEv,E:Black Widow,
    A:Thor,(see Avengers #95) .. 50.00
9 MSy,BEv,V:Magneto 30.00
10 GK(c),MSy,V:Magneto,
    E:Inhumans 30.00
11 GK(c),TS,B:O:New Beast,
    A:X-Men 175.00
12 GK(c),TS,MP,A:Iron Man 50.00
13 JR(c),TS,V:New Br'hood
    Evil Mutants,I:Buzz Baxter
    (Mad Dog) 50.00
14 GK(c),TS,JM,V:Quasimodo 50.00
15 JSn(c),TS,A:X-Men,V:Griffin . 50.00
16 JSn(c),FMc(i),V:Juggernaut .. 50.00
17 JSn,A:X-Men,E:Beast 50.00
18 HC,NA,B:Killraven 50.00
19 HC,Sirens on 7th Avenues 10.00
20 Coming of the Warlords 10.00
21 Cry Killraven 10.00
22 Killraven 10.00
23 Killraven 10.00
24 New Year Nightmare-2019AD .. 10.00
25 RB,V:Skar 10.00
26 GC,V:Ptson-Rage Vigilante ... 10.00
27 CR,JSn,V:Death Breeders 10.00

Amazing Adventures #14
© Marvel Entertainment Group

All comics prices listed are for *Near Mint* condition.   CVA Page 191

Amazing–Amazing / MARVEL / Comics Values Annual

28 JSn,CR,V:Death Breeders 10.00	14 Hands Off; Sept., 1952 ..... 300.00	Menace 450.00
29 CR,Killraven 10.00		23 SD,V:GreenGoblin(3rd App.) . 700.00
30 CR,Killraven 10.00	### AMAZING HIGH ADVENTURE	24 SD,V:Mysterio 400.00
31 CR,Killraven 10.00		25 SD,I:Spider Slayer,Spencer
32 CR,Killraven 10.00	**Aug., 1984**	Smythe,C:Mary Jane 450.00
33 CR,Killraven 10.00	1 BSz,JSo,JS 4.00	26 SD,I:CrimeMaster,V:Green
34 CR,D:Hawk 10.00	2 PS,AW,BSz,TA,MMi,BBl,CP,CW . 3.00	Goblin 500.00
35 KG,Killraven Continued 10.00	3 MMi,VM,JS................. 3.00	27 SD,V:CrimeMaster,
36 CR,Killraven Continued 10.00	4 JBo,JS,SBi................. 3.00	Green Goblin 500.00
37 CR,O:Old Skull 10.00	5 JBo; Oct., 1986 .... 3.00	28 SD,I:Molten Man,Peter Parker
38 CR,Killraven Continued....... 10.00		Graduates High School,rare
39 CR,E:Killraven.............. 10.00	### AMAZING SCARLET SPIDER	in near-mint condition 750.00
[2nd Regular Series], 1979		29 SD,V:Scorpion 350.00
1 rep.X-Men#1,38,Professor X... 10.00	**1995**	30 SD,I:Cat Burglar........... 350.00
2 rep.X-Men#1,39,O:Cyclops..... 7.00	1 MBa,LMa,VirtualMortality,pt.2 ... 2.50	31 SD,I:Gwen Stacy,Harry Osborn
3 rep.X-Men#2,40,O:Cyclops..... 7.00	2 TDF,MBa,CyberWar,pt.2 .... 2.50	Prof.Warren,V:Dr.Octopus... 350.00
4 rep.X-Men#2,41,O:Cyclops..... 7.00		32 SD,V:Dr.Octopus 300.00
5 rep.X-Men#3,42,O:Cyclops..... 7.00		33 SD,V:Dr.Octopus 300.00
6 JBy(c),rep.X-Men#3,43,Cyclops . 7.00		34 SD,V:Kraven 300.00
7 rep.X-Men#4,44,O:Iceman 7.00		35 SD,V:Molten Man.......... 300.00
8 rep.X-Men#4,45,O:Iceman 7.00		36 SD,I:The Looter........... 300.00
9 JBy(c),X-Men#5,46,O:Iceman ... 7.00		37 SD,V:Professor Stromm,
10 rep.X-Men#5,47,O:Iceman 7.00		I:Norman Osborn 300.00
11 rep.X-Men#6,48,Beast........ 7.00		38 SD,V:Joe Smith(Boxer) 300.00
12 rep.X-Men#6,Str.Tales#168 ... 7.00		39 JR,IR:Green Goblin is Norman
13 rep.X-Men #7............... 7.00		Osborn................ 400.00
14 rep.X-Men #8............... 7.00		40 JR,O:Green Goblin 550.00
		41 JR,I:Rhino,C:Mary Jane 300.00
		42 JR,V:John Jameson,I:Mary
		Jane (Face Revealed) 250.00
		43 JR,O:Rhino 200.00
		44 JR,V:Lizard(2nd App.) 200.00
		45 JR,V:Lizard 200.00
		46 JR,I&O:Shocker........... 225.00
		47 JR,V:Kraven 200.00
		48 JR,I:Fake Vulture,A:Vulture .. 200.00
		49 JR,V:Fake Vulture,Kraven ... 200.00
		50 JR,I:Kingpin,Spidey Quits,
		C:Johnny Carson 700.00
		51 JR,V:Kingpin 300.00
		52 JR,V:Kingpin,I:Robbie
		Robertson,D:Fred Foswell .. 150.00
		53 JR,V:Dr.Octopus 125.00
		54 JR,V:Dr.Octopus 125.00
		55 JR,V:Dr.Octopus 125.00
		56 JR,V:Dr.Octopus,I:Capt.Stacy. 125.00
		57 JR,DH,A:Ka-Zar........... 125.00
		58 JR,DH,V:Spencer Smythe,
	Amazing Spider-Man #3	Spider Slayer 125.00
	© Marvel Entertainment Group	59 JR,DH,V:Kingpin 125.00
		60 JR,DH,V:Kingpin 125.00
	### AMAZING SPIDER-MAN	61 JR,DH,V:Kingpin 125.00
	March, 1963	62 JR,DH,V:Medusa 100.00
	1 JK(c),SED,I:Chameleon,J.Jonah &	63 JR,DH,V:1st & 2nd
	John Jameson,A:F.Four .. 35,000.00	Vulture 100.00
	2 SD,I:Vulture,Tinkerer	64 JR,DH,V:Vulture........... 100.00
	C:Mysterio(disguised) 5,500.00	65 JR,JM,V:Prisoners 100.00
	3 SD,I&O:Dr.Octopus 5,000.00	66 JR,DH,V:Mysterio 100.00
Amazing Comics #1	4 SD,I&O:Sandman,I:Betty	67 JR,V:Mysterio,I:Randy
© Marvel Entertainment Group	Brant,Liz Allen 4,000.00	Robertson 100.00
	5 SD,V:Dr.Doom,C:Fant.Four .. 2,800.00	68 JR,JM,V:Kingpin 110.00
### AMAZING COMICS	6 SD,I&O:Lizard,The Connors. 2,500.00	69 JR,JM,V:Kingpin 110.00
Timely, Fall, 1944	7 SD,V:Vulture 1,700.00	70 JR,JM,V:Kingpin 110.00
1 F:Young Allies,Destroyer,	8 SD,JK,I:Big Brain,V:Human	71 JR,JM,V:Quicksilver,C:Scarlet
Whizzer, Sergeant Dix ... 2,500.00	Torch,A:Fantastic Four.... 1,600.00	Witch,Toad,A:Kingpin 100.00
Becomes:	9 SD,I&O:Electro 1,700.00	72 JR,JB,JM,V:Shocker........ 100.00
### COMPLETE COMICS	10 SD,I:Enforcers,Big Man.... 1,600.00	73 JR,JB,JM,I:Man Mountain Marko,
2 F:Young Allies,Destroyer,Whizzer	11 SD,V:Dr.Octopus,	Silverman.............. 100.00
Sergeant Dix; Winter '44-45 1,800.00	D:Bennett Brant 900.00	74 JR,JM,V:Silvermane......... 100.00
	12 SD,V:Dr.Octopus 900.00	75 JR,JM,V:Silvermane,A:Lizard . 90.00
### AMAZING DETECTIVE CASES	13 SD,I:Mysterio 1,200.00	76 JR,JM,V:Lizard,A:H.Torch ... 90.00
	14 SD,I:Green Goblin,	77 JR,JM,V:Lizard,A:H.Torch 90.00
Atlas, Nov., 1950	V:Enforcers, Hulk........ 3,000.00	78 JR,JM,I&O:Prowler 100.00
3 Detective/Horror Stories 300.00	15 SD,I:Kraven,A:Chameleon. 1,200.00	79 JR,JM,V:Prowler 75.00
4 Death of a Big Shot 175.00	16 SD,A:Daredevil,	80 JR,JB,JM,V:Chameleon 75.00
5 .... 175.00	V:Ringmaster 750.00	81 JR,JM,I:Kangaroo.......... 75.00
6 Danger in the City 175.00	17 SD,2nd A:Green Goblin,	82 JR,JM,V:Electro 75.00
7 .... 150.00	A:Human Torch......... 1,100.00	83 JR,I:Richard Fisk(as Schemer),
8 .... 150.00	18 SD,V:Sandman,Enforcers,	Vanessa(Kingpin's wife)
9 GC, The Man Who Wasn't ... 150.00	C:Avengers,F.F.,Daredevil... 700.00	V:Kingpin 75.00
10 GT...................... 150.00	19 SD,V:Sandman,I:Ned Leeds	84 JR,JB,JM,V:Schemer,Kingpin.. 75.00
11 The Black Shadow......... 300.00	A:Human Torch.......... 600.00	
12 MS,BK, Harrigan's Wake 300.00	20 SD,I&O:Scorpion 750.00	
13 BEv,JSt,................. 350.00	21 SD,A:Beetle,Human Torch .. 500.00	
	22 SD,V:The Clown,Masters of	

MARVEL

Amazing Spider-Man

Amazing Spider-Man #56
© Marvel Entertainment Group

Amazing Spider-Man #194
© Marvel Entertainment Group

85 JR,JB,JM,V:Schemer,Kingpin.. 75.00
86 JR,JM,V:Black Widow, C:Iron Man, Hawkeye 75.00
87 JR,JM,Reveals ID to his friends,changes mind 75.00
88 JR,JM,V:Dr.Octopus 75.00
89 GK,JR,V:Dr.Octopus 75.00
90 GK,JR,V:Dr.Octopus D:Capt.Stacy 125.00
91 GK,JR,I:Bullit 100.00
92 GK,JR,V:Bullit,A:Iceman..... 100.00
93 JR,V:Prowler 100.00
94 JR,SB,V:Beetle,O:Spider-Man 125.00
95 JR,SB,London,V:Terrorists ... 75.00
96 GK,JR,A:Green Goblin,Drug Mention,No Comic Code.... 165.00
97 GK,V:Green Goblin,Drugs ... 165.00
98 GK,V:Green Goblin,Drugs ... 165.00
99 GK,Prison Riot,A:Carson 100.00
100 JR(c),GK,Spidey gets four arms from serum 300.00
101 JR(c),GK,I:Morbius,the Living Vampire,A:Lizard ... 225.00
101a Reprint,Metallic ink.......... 5.00
102 JR(c),GK,O:Morbius, V:Lizard 150.00
103 GK,V:Kraven,A:Ka-Zar 75.00
104 GK,V:Kraven,A:Ka-Zar 75.00
105 GK,V:Spenser Smythe, Spider Slayer 75.00
106 JR,V:Spenser Smythe, Spider Slayer 75.00
107 JR,V:Spenser Smythe, Spider Slayer 75.00
108 JR,R:Flash Thompson, I:Sha-Shan,V:Vietnamese... 75.00
109 JR,A:Dr.Strange, V:Vietnamese.............. 75.00
110 JR,I:The Gibbon.............. 75.00
111 JR,V:The Gibbon,Kraven 75.00
112 JR,Spidey gets an Ulcer..... 75.00
113 JSn,JR,I:Hammerhead V:Dr.Octopus 75.00
114 JSn,JR,V:Hammerhead,Dr. Octopus,I:Jonas Harrow..... 75.00
115 JR,V:Hammerhead, Dr.Octopus 75.00
116 JR,JM,V:The Smasher 75.00
117 JR,JM,V:Smasher,Disruptor . 75.00
118 JR,JM,V:Smasher,Disruptor . 75.00
119 JR,A:Hulk................... 80.00
120 GK,JR,V:Hulk................ 80.00
121 GK,JR,V:Green Goblin

D:Gwen Stacy,Drugs 300.00
122 GK,JR,D:Green Goblin..... 275.00
123 GK,JR,A:Powerman........ 50.00
124 GK,JR,I:Man-Wolf 60.00
125 RA,JR,O:Man-Wolf 50.00
126 JM(c),RA,JM,V:Kangaroo, A: Human Torch 50.00
127 JR(c),RA,V:3rd Vulture, A:Human Torch............. 50.00
128 JR(c),RA,V:3rd Vulture...... 50.00
129 K&R(c),RA,I:Punisher, Jackal.................... 275.00
130 JR(c),RA,V:Hammerhead, Dr.Octopus,I:Spider-Mobile... 50.00
131 GK(c),RA,V:Hammerhead, Dr.Octopus................ 50.00
132 GK(c),JR,V:Molten Man 50.00
133 JR(c),RA,V:Molten Man 50.00
134 JR(c),RA,I:Tarantula,C: Punisher(2nd App.)......... 60.00
135 JR(c),RA,V:Tarantula, A:Punisher 100.00
136 JR(c),RA,I:2nd GreenGoblin.. 75.00
137 GK(c),RA,V:Green Goblin ... 75.00
138 K&R(c),RA,I:Mindworm 40.00
139 K&R(c),RA,I:Grizzly,V:Jackal. 40.00
140 GK(c),RA,I:Gloria Grant, V:Grizzly,Jackal 40.00
141 JR(c),RA,V:Mysterio......... 40.00
142 JR(c),RA,V:Mysterio......... 40.00
143 K&R(c),RA,I:Cyclone 40.00
144 K&R(c),RA,V:Cyclone 40.00
145 K&R(c),RA,V:Scorpion 40.00
146 RA,JR,V:Scorpion 40.00
147 JR(c),RA,V:Tarantula 40.00
148 GK(c),RA,V:Tarantula,IR:Jackal is Prof.Warren 50.00
149 K&R(c),RA,D:Jackal........ 75.00
150 GK(c),RA,V:Spenser Smythe . 50.00
151 RA,JR,V:Shocker 25.00
152 K&R(c),RA,V:Shocker 25.00
153 K&R(c),RA,V:Paine 25.00
154 JR(c),SB,V:Sandman 25.00
155 JR(c),SB,V:Computer....... 25.00
156 JR(c),RA,I:Mirage,W:Ned Leeds & Betty Brant 25.00
157 JR(c),RA,V:Dr.Octopus 25.00
158 JR(c),RA,V:Dr.Octopus 25.00
159 JR(c),RA,V:Dr.Octopus 25.00
160 K&R(c),RA,V:Tinkerer 25.00
161 K&R(c),RA,A:Nightcrawler, C:Punisher................ 35.00
162 JR(c),RA,Nightcrawler, Punisher,I:Jigsaw 35.00
163 JR(c),RA,Kingpin 20.00
164 JR(c),RA,Kingpin 20.00
165 JR(c),RA,Lizard 20.00
166 JR(c),RA,Lizard 20.00
167 JR(c),RA,V:Spiderslayer, I:Will-o-the Wisp.......... 20.00
168 JR(c),KP,V:Will-o-the Wisp ... 22.00
169 RA,V:Dr.Faustas 20.00
170 RA,V:Dr.Faustas 20.00
171 RA,A:Nova................ 22.00
172 RA,V:Molten Man.......... 20.00
173 JR(c),RA,JM,V:Molten Man . 20.00
174 RA,TD,JM,A:Punisher 25.00
175 RA,JM,A:Punisher,D:Hitman. 25.00
176 RA,TD,V:Green Goblin..... 22.00
177 RA,V:Green Goblin 22.00
178 RA,JM,V:Green Goblin 22.00
179 RA,V:Green Goblin 22.00
180 RA,IR&V:Green Goblin is Bart Hamilton)................. 22.00
181 GK(c),SB,O:Spider-Man.... 22.00
182 RA,A:Rocket Racer 20.00
183 RA,BMc,V:Rocket Racer ... 20.00
184 RA,V:White Tiger 20.00
185 RA,V:White Tiger 20.00
186 KP,A:Chameleon,Spidey cleared by police of charges. 20.00

187 JSn,BMc,A:Captain America,V:Electro........... 20.00
188 KP,A:Jigsaw............... 20.00
189 JBy,JM,A:Man-Wolf 25.00
190 JBy,JM,A:Man-Wolf 25.00
191 KP,V:Spiderslayer.......... 25.00
192 KP,JM,V:The Fly 25.00
193 KP,JM,V:The Fly 25.00
194 KP,I:Black Cat 35.00
195 KP,AM,JM,O:Black Cat 20.00
196 AM,JM,D:Aunt May,A:Kingpin. 15.00
197 KP,JM,V:Kingpin 15.00
198 SB,JM,V:Mysterio 15.00
199 SB,JM,V:Mysterio 15.00
200 JR(c),KP,JM,D:Burglar,Aunt May alive,O:Spider-Man......... 40.00
201 KP,JM,A:Punisher.......... 18.00
202 KP,JM,A:Punisher.......... 18.00
203 FM(c),KP,A:Dazzler 15.00
204 JR2(c),KP,V:Black Cat 15.00
205 KP,JM,V:Black Cat......... 15.00
206 JBy,GD,V:Jonas Harrow..... 15.00
207 JM,V:Mesmero............. 15.00
208 JR2,AM,BBr,V:Fusion(1stJR2 SpM art),I:Lance Bannon.... 15.00
209 KJ,BMc,JRu,BWi,AM, I:Calypso, V:Kraven 20.00
210 JR2,JSt,I:Madame Web 15.00
211 JR2,JM,A:Sub-mariner...... 15.00
212 JR2,JM,I:Hydro-Man 15.00
213 JR2,JM,V:Wizard 15.00
214 JR2,JM,V:Frightful Four, A: Namor,Llyra 15.00
215 JR2,JM,V:Frightful Four, A: Namor,Llyra 15.00
216 JR2,JM,A:Madame Web 15.00
217 JR2,JM,V:Sandman, Hydro-Man............... 15.00
218 FM(c),JR2,JM,AM,V:Sandman Hydro-Man............... 15.00
219 FM(c),LMc,JM,V:Grey Gargoyle,A:Matt Murdock... 15.00
220 BMc,A:Moon Knight......... 12.00
221 JM(i),A:Ramrod 12.00
222 WS(c),BH,JM,I:SpeedDemon. 12.00
223 JR2,AM,A:Red Ghost....... 12.00
224 JR2,V:Vulture.............. 12.00
225 JR2,BWi,V:Foolkiller 12.00
226 JR2,JM,A:Black Cat........ 12.00
227 JR2,JM,A:Black Cat........ 12.00
228 RL,Murder Mystery 12.00
229 JR2,JM,V:Juggernaut....... 12.00
230 JR2,JM,V:Juggernaut....... 12.00

Amazing Spider-Man — MARVEL — Comics Values Annual

Amazing Spider-Man #228
© Marvel Entertainment Group

231 JR2,AM,V:Cobra 12.00
232 JR2,JM,V:Mr.Hyde 12.00
233 JR2,JM,V:Tarantula 12.00
234 JR2,DGr,V:Tarantula 12.00
235 JR2,V:Tarantula,C:Deathlok
  O:Will-o-the Wisp 12.00
236 JR2,D:Tarantula 12.00
237 BH,A:Stilt Man 12.00
238 JR2,JR,I:Hobgoblin (inc.
  Tattoo transfer) 100.00
238a w/out Tattoo 12.00
239 JR2,V:Hobgoblin 50.00
240 JR2,BL,Vulture 12.00
241 JR2,O:Vulture 12.00
242 JR2,Mad Thinker 12.00
243 JR2,Peter Quits School 12.00
244 JR2,KJ,V:Hobgoblin 18.00
245 JR2,V:Hobgoblin 20.00
246 JR2,DGr,Daydreams issue . . 12.00
247 JR2,JR,V:Thunderball 12.00
248 JR2,BBr,RF,TA,V:Thunderball,
  Kid who Collects Spider-Man . 12.00
249 JR2,DGr,V:Hobgoblin,
  A:Kingpin 20.00
250 JR2,KJ,V:Hobgoblin 20.00
251 RF,KJ,V:Hobgoblin,Spidey
  Leaves for Secret Wars 20.00
252 RF,BBr,returns from Secret
  Wars,N:Spider-Man 50.00
253 RL,I:Rose 10.00
254 RL,JRu,V:Jack O'Lantern 10.00
255 RF,JRu,Red Ghost 10.00
256 RF,JRu,I:Puma,A:Black Cat . . 10.00
257 RF,JRu,V:Puma,
  A:Hobgoblin 10.00
258 RF,JRu,A:Black Cat,Fant.Four,
  Hobgoblin,V:Black Costume . 15.00
259 RF,JRu,A:Hobgoblin,O:
  Mary Jane 15.00
260 RF,JRu,BBr,V:Hobgoblin 12.00
261 CV(c),RF,JRu,V:Hobgoblin . . . 12.00
262 Ph(c),BL,Spidey Unmasked . . 13.00
263 RF,BBr,I:Spider-Kid 10.00
264 Paty,V:Red Nine 10.00
265 RF,JRu,V:Black Fox,
  I:Silver Sable 15.00
265a 2nd printing 3.00
266 RF,JRu,I:Misfits,Toad 10.00
267 BMc,PDd(s),Pulp(i):Human Torch . 10.00
268 JBy(c),RF,JRu,Secret WarsII . 10.00
269 RF,JRu,V:Firelord 10.00
270 RF,BMc,V:Firelord,
  A:Avengers,I:Kate Cushing . . 10.00
271 RF,JRu,A:Crusher Hogan,
  V:Manslaughter 10.00
272 SB,KB,I&O:Slyde 10.00
273 RF,JRu,Secret Wars II,
  A:Puma 10.00
274 TMo,JR,Secret Wars II,
  Beyonder V:Mephisto,A:1st
  Ghost Rider 10.00
275 RF,JRu,V:Hobgoblin,O:Spidey
  (From Amaz.Fantasy#15) . . . 20.00
276 RF,BBr,V:Hobgoblin 15.00
277 RF,BL,CV,A:Daredevil,
  Kingpin 10.00
278 A:Hobgoblin,V:Scourge,
  D:Wraith 10.00
279 RL,A:Jack O'Lantern,
  2nd A:Silver Sable 10.00
280 RF,BBr,V:Sinister Syndicate,
  A:Silver Sable,Hobgoblin,
  Jack O'Lantern 10.00
281 RF,BBr,V:Sinister Syndicate,
  A:Silver Sable,Hobgoblin,
  Jack O'Lantern 15.00
282 RL,BL,A:X-Factor 10.00
283 RF,BL,V:Titania,Absorbing
  Man,C:Mongoose 10.00
284 RF,BBr,JRu,B:Gang War,
  A: Punisher,Hobgoblin 15.00
285 MZ(c),A:Punisher,Hobgoblin . 15.00
286 ANi(i),V:Hobgoblin,A:Rose . . . 15.00
287 EL,ANi,A:Daredevil,Hobgoblin. 15.00
288 E:Gang War,A:Punisher,
  Falcon,Hobgoblin,Daredevil,
  Black Cat, Kingpin 15.00
289 TMo,IR:Hobgoblin is Ned Leeds,
  I:2nd Hobgoblin (Jack O'
  Lantern) 25.00
290 JR2,Peter Proposes 10.00
291 JR2,V:Spiderslayer 10.00
292 AS,V:Spiderslayer,Mary
  Jane Accepts proposal 10.00
293 MZ,BMc,V:Kraven 12.00
294 MZ,BMc,D:Kraven 12.00
295 BSz(c),KB(i),Mad Dog,pt.#2 . . 10.00
296 JBy(c),AS,V:Dr.Octopus 10.00
297 AS,V:Dr.Octopus 10.00
298 TM,BMc,V:Chance,C:Venom
  (not in costume) 50.00
299 TM,BMc,V:Chance,I:Venom . . 30.00
300 TM,O:Venom 100.00
301 TM,A:Silver Sable 20.00
302 TM,V:Nero,A:Silver Sable 20.00
303 TM,A:Silver Sable,Sandman . 20.00
304 TM,JRu,V:Black Fox,Prowler
  I:Jonathan Caesar 18.00
305 TM,JRu,V:BlackFox,Prowler . . 18.00
306 TM,V:Humbug,Chameleon . . . 15.00
307 TM,O:Chameleon 15.00
308 TM,V:Taskmaster,J.Caesar . . 15.00
309 TM,I:Styx & Stone 15.00
310 TM,V:Killershrike 15.00
311 TM,Inferno,V:Mysterio 15.00
312 TM,Inferno,Hobgoblin V:
  Green Goblin 20.00
313 TM,Inferno,V:Lizard 15.00
314 TM,X-mas issue,V:J.Caesar . . 15.00
315 TM,V:Venom,Hydro-Man 20.00
316 TM,V:Venom 20.00
317 TM,V:Venom,A:Thing 20.00
318 TM,V:Scorpion 20.00
319 TM,V:Scorpion,Rhino 15.00
320 TM,B:Assassin Nation Plot
  A:Paladin,Silver Sable 15.00
321 TM,A:Paladin,Silver Sable . . . 12.00
322 TM,A:Silver Sable,Paladin . . . 12.00
323 TM,A:Silver Sable,Paladin,
  Captain America 12.00
324 TM(c),EL,AG,V:Sabretooth,A:
  Capt.America,Silver Sable . . 12.00
325 TM,E:Assassin Nation Plot,
  V:Red Skull,Captain America,
  Silver Sable 12.00
326 V:Graviton,A of V. 7.00
327 EL,AG,V:Magneto,A of V. 7.00
328 TM,V:Hulk,A of V. 12.00
329 EL,V:Tri-Sentinel 7.00
330 EL,A:Punisher,Black Cat 7.00
331 EL,A:Punisher,C:Venom 6.00
332 EL,V:Venom,Styx & Stone . . . 7.00
333 EL,V:Venom,Styx & Stone . . . 7.00
334 EL,B:Sinister Six,A:Iron Man . . 5.00
335 EL,TA,A:Captain America 5.00
336 EL,D:Nathan Lubensky,
  A:Dr.Strange,Chance 5.00
337 WS(c),EL,TA,A:Nova 5.00
338 EL,A:Jonathan Caesar 5.00
339 EL,JR,E:Sinister Six,A:Thor
  D:Jonathan Caesar 5.00
340 EL,V:Femme Fatales 5.00
341 EL,V:Tarantula,Powers Lost . . . 5.00
342 EL,A:Blackcat,V:Scorpion 5.00
343 EL,Powers Restored,
  C:Cardiac,V:Chameleon 5.00
344 EL,V:Rhino,I:Cardiac,Cletus
  Kassady(Carnage),A:Venom . . 15.00
345 MBa,V:Boomerang,C:Venom,
  A:Cletus Kassady(infected
  with Venom-Spawn) 15.00
346 EL,V:Venom 10.00
347 EL,V:Venom 10.00
348 EL,A:Avengers 4.00
349 EL,A:Black Fox 4.00
350 EL,V:Doctor Doom,Black Fox . . 6.00
351 MBa,A:Nova,V:Tri-Sentinel 6.00
352 MBa,A:Nova,V:Tri-Sentinel 4.00
353 MBa,B:Round Robin:The Side
  Kick's Revenge,A:Punisher,
  Nova,Moon Knight,Darkhawk . 4.00
354 MBa,A:Nova,Punisher,
  Darkhawk,Moon Knight 4.00
355 MBa,A:Nova,Punisher,
  Darkhawk,Moon Knight 4.00
356 MBa,A:Moon Knight,
  Punisher,Nova 4.00
357 MBa,A:Moon Knight,
  Punisher,Darkhawk,Nova 4.00
358 MBa,E:Round Robin:The Side
  Kick's Revenge,A:Darkhawk,
  Moon Knight,Punisher,Nova,
  Gatefold(c) 4.00
359 CMa,A:Cardiac,C:Cletus
  Kasady (Carnage) 5.00
360 CMa,V:Cardiac,C:Carnage . . . 6.00
361 MBa,I:Carnage 9.00
361a 2nd printing 3.00

Amazing Spider-Man #266
© Marvel Entertainment Group

CVA Page 194 — All comics prices listed are for *Near Mint* condition.

Comics Values Annual — MARVEL — Amazing Spider-Man

#	Description	Price
362	MBa,V:Carnage,Venom	6.00
362a	2nd printing	3.00
363	MBa,V:Carnage,Venom,	6.00
364	MBa,V:Shocker	3.00
365	MBa,JR,V:Lizard,30th Anniv., Hologram(c),w/poster,Prev.of Spider-Man 2099 by RL	6.00
366	JBi,A:Red Skull,Taskmaster	3.00
367	JBi,A:Red Skull,Taskmaster	3.00
368	MBa,B:Invasion of the Spider Slayers #1,BU:Jonah Jameson	3.00
369	MBa,V:Electro,BU:Green Goblin	3.00
370	MBa,V:Scorpion,BU:A.May	3.00
371	MBa,V:Spider-Slayer, BU:Black Cat	3.00
372	MBa,V:Spider-Slayer	3.00
373	MBa,V:Sp.-Slayer,BU:Venom	4.00
374	MBa,V:Venom	5.00
375	MBa,V:Venom,30th Anniv.,Holographx(c)	6.00
376	V:Styx&Stone,A:Cardiac	2.50
377	V:Cardiac,O:Styx&Stone	2.50
378	MBa,Total Carnage#3,V:Shriek, Carnage,A:Venom,Cloak	3.00
379	MBa,Total Carnage#7, V:Carnage,A:Venom	3.00
380	MBa,Maximum Carnage#11	3.00
381	MBa,V:Dr.Samson,A:Hulk	2.50
382	MBa,V:Hulk,A:Dr.Samson	2.50
383	MBa,V:Jury	2.50
384	MBa,AM,V:Jury	3.00
385	B:DvM(s),MBa,RyE,V:Jury	2.50
386	MBa,RyE,B:Lifetheft,V:Vulture	3.00
387	MBa,RyE,V:Vulture	3.00
388	Blue Foil(c),MBa,RyE,RLm,TP, E:Lifetheft,D:Peter's Synthetic Parents,BU:Venom,Cardiac,Chance	5.00
388a	Newsstand Ed.	3.00
389	MBa,RyE,E:Pursuit, V:Chameleon,	2.50
390	MBa,RyE,B:Shrieking, A:Shriek,w/cel	4.00
390a	Newsstand Ed.	2.50
391	MBa,RyE,V:Shriek,Carrion	2.50
392	MBa,RyE,V:Shriek,Carrion	2.50
393	MBa,RyE,E:Shrieking, V:Shriek,Carrion	2.50
394	MBa,RyE,Power & Responsibility, pt.2,V:Judas Traveller,	4.00
394a	w/flip book,2 covers	3.00
395	MBa,RyE,R:Puma	2.50
396	MBa,RyE,A:Daredevil, V:Vulture, Owl	2.50
397	MBa,Web of Death,pt.1, V:Stunner,Doc Ock	3.00
398	MBa,Web of Death,pt.3	2.50
399	MBa,Smoke and Mirrors,pt.2	2.50
400	MBa,Death of a Parker	6.00
400a	die-cut cover	3.00
401	MBa,The Mark of Kaine,pt.2	2.50
402	MBa,R:Judas Travellor	2.50
403	MBa,JMD,LMa The Trial of Peter Parker,pt.2	2.50
404	Maximum Clonage	2.50
405	JMD,DaR,LMa,Exiled,pt.2,	2.50
406	I:New Doc Ock	2.50
407	TDF,MBa,LMa,Return of Spider-Man,pt.2	2.50
408	TDF,MBa,LMa,Media Blizzard,pt.2	2.50
409		2.50
410		2.50
411	TDF,MBa,LMa,Blood Brothers,pt.2	2.50
412		2.50
413		2.50
414	A:The Rose	2.50
415	Onslaught saga,V:Sentinels	2.50
416	Onslaught epilogue	3.00

Amazing Spider-Man #406
© Marvel Entertainment Group

#	Description	Price
417	TDF,RG,secrets of Scrier & Judas Traveler	2.50
418	Revelations,pt.3, R:Norman Osborn	2.50
419	TDF,SSr,V:Black Tarantula	2.50
420	TDF,SSr,X-Man x-over,pt.1	2.50
421	TDF,SSr,I:Dragonfly; Electro Kidnapped	2.50
422	TDF,SSr,V:Electro,Tarantula	2.50
423	TDF,V:Electro	2.50
424	TDF,JoB,V:Black Tarantula, The Hand, Dragonfly, Delilah, The Rose, Elektra	2.50
425	TDF,SSr, V:Electro,double size.	3.50
426	TDF,SSr,V:Doctor Octopus	2.50
427	TDF,SSr,JR gatefold cover, V:Doctor Octopus	2.50
428	TDF,SSr,V:Doctor Octopus	2.50
429	TDF,A:Daredevil, X-Man, Absorbing Man, Titania	2.50
430	TDF,SSr,V:Carnage,A:Silver Surfer	2.50
431	TDF,SSr,V:Carnage (with Silver Surfer's powers)	2.50
432	SSr,JR2,Spider-Hunt,pt.2 x-over	4.00
432a	variant cover	3.50
433	TDF,TL,Identity Crisis prelude, good-bye to Joe Robertson	2.50
434	TDF,JoB,Identity Crisis, as Ricochet vs. Black Tarantula	2.50
435	TDF,MD2,Ricochet,A:Delilah	2.50
436	TDF,JoB,V:Black Tarantula	2.50
437	TDF,JoB,F:Plant Man	2.50

Bi-weekly

#	Description	Price
438	TDF,V:Daredevil	2.50
439	TDF,future history chronicle	2.50
440	JBy,The Gathering of the Five, Pt.2 (of 5) x-over	2.50
441	JBy,V:Green Goblin, The Final Chapter, pt.1	5.00
Minus 1 Spec., TDF,JBe, flashback, early Kingpin		2.50
Ann.#1	SD,I:Sinister Six	1,400.00
Ann.#2	SD,A:Dr.Strange	500.00
Ann.#3	JR,DH,A:Avengers	200.00
Ann.#4	A:H.Torch,V:Mysterio, Wizard	175.00
Ann.#5	JR(c),A:Red Skull,I:Peter Parker's Parents	175.00
Ann.#6	JR(c),Rep.Ann.#1,Fant. Four Ann.#1,SpM #8	65.00
Ann.#7	JR(c),Rep.#1,#2,#38	65.00
Ann.#8	Rep.#46,#50	65.00
Ann.#9	JR(c),Rep.Spec.SpM #2	65.00
Ann.#10	JR(c),GK,V:Human Fly	30.00
Ann.#11	GK(c),DP,JM,JR2,AM,	20.00
Ann.#12	JBy(c),KP,Rep.#119,#120	25.00
Ann.#13	JBy,TA,V:Dr.Octopus	25.00
Ann.#14	FM,TP,A:Dr.Strange, V:Dr.Doom,Dormammu	25.00
Ann.#15	FM,KJ,BL,Punisher	25.00
Ann.#16	JR2,JR,I:New Captain Marvel,A:Thing	10.00
Ann.#17	EH,JM,V:Kingpin	10.00
Ann.#18	RF,BL,JG,V:Scorpion	10.00
Ann.#19	JR(c),MW,V:Spiderslayer	10.00
Ann.#20	BWi(i),V:Iron Man 2020	10.00
Ann.#21	JR(c),PR,W:SpM,direct	20.00
Ann.#21a	W:SpM,news stand	15.00
Ann.#22	JR(c),MBa(1stSpM),SD, JG,RLm,TD,Evolutionary War, I:Speedball,New Men	8.00
Ann.#23	JBy(c),RLd,MBa,RF, AtlantisAttacks#4,A:She-Hulk	7.00
Ann.#24	GK,SD,MZ,DGr, A:Ant Man	4.00
Ann.#25	EL(c),SB,PCu,SD, Vibranium Vendetta#1,Venom	6.00
Ann.#26	Hero Killers#1,A:New Warriors,BU:Venom,Solo	6.00
Ann.#27	TL,I:Annex,w/card	4.00
Ann.#28	SBt(s),V:Carnage,BU:Cloak & Dagger,Rhino	4.00
Ann. '96	two new stories, 48pg	3.50
Ann. '97	RSt,TL,RJn, 48pg	3.50
Ann. '98	TL,TDF,F:Spider-Man & Devil Dinosaur, 48pg	3.00
G-Size Superheroes #1	GK, A:Morbius,Man-Wolf	75.00
G-Size #1	JR(c),RA,DH, A:Dracula	40.00
G-Size #2	K&R(c),RA,AM, A:Master of Kung Fu	40.00
G-Size #3	GK(c),RA,DocSavage	40.00
G-Size #4	GK(c),RA,Punisher	75.00
G-Size #5	GK(c),RA,V:Magnum	30.00
G-Size #6	Rep.Ann.#4	30.00
G-Size Spec.#1	O:Symbiotes	5.00
Marvel Milestone rep. #1 (1993)		2.95
Marvel Milestone rep. #3 (1995)		2.95
Marvel Milestone rep. #129 (1992)		2.95
Marvel Milestone rep. #149 (1994)		2.95
GN Fear Itself RA,A:S.Sable		12.95
GN Spirits of the Earth CV,Scotland, V:Hellfire Club		25.00
TPB Assassination Plot, rep.#320-325		14.95
TPB Carnage,rep.#361-363		6.95
TPB Cosmic Adventures rep. Amaz.SpM #327-329,Web #59 61,Spec.SpM #158-160		19.95
TPB Kraven's Last Hunt, Reps. AS #293,294,Web.#31,32,P.Parker #131,132,SC		15.95
TPB Origin of the Hobgoblin rep.#238, 239,244,245,249-251		14.95
TPB Saga of the Alien Costume,reps. #252-259		9.95
TPB Spider-Man Vs. Venom,reps. A.SpM#298-300,315-317		10.00
TPB Venom Returns rep.Amaz.SpM. #331-333,344-347		12.95
TPB The Wedding,Reps.A.S. #290-292,Ann#21		12.95
Nothing Can Stop the Juggernaut, reps.#229,230		3.95
Sensational Spider-Man,reps. Ann.#14,15;		4.95
Skating on Thin Ice(Canadian)		15.00
Skating on Thin Ice(US)		2.00
Soul of the Hunter MZ,BMc, R:Kraven		7.00

All comics prices listed are for *Near Mint* condition.

CVA Page 195

Amazing–Archangel / MARVEL / Comics Values Annual

Unicef:Trial of Venom,
A:Daredevil,V:Venom 50.00
See Also:
PETER PARKER;
SPECTACULAR SPIDER-MAN;
WEB OF SPIDER-MAN

AMAZING SPIDER-MAN
Jan., 1999
1 HMe,JBy,DHz,V:Scorpion,48-page prismatic etched (c) 7.00
1a Dynamic Forces JR2 . . . . 15.00
2 HMe,JBy,DHz,I:Shadrac 5.00
2a variant BiT cover 6.00
3 HMe,JBy,DHz,V:Shadrac, A:Iceman 2.50
4 HMe,JBy,SHa,A:Fantastic Four. . 2.50
5 HMe,JBy,SHa,I:new Spider-Woman 2.50
6 JBy,HMe,SHa,F:Spider-Woman . 2.50
7 JBy,HMe,SHa,Reality Bent 2.50
8 JMy,HMe,SHa,JR2(c), Reality Bent x-over 2.50
9 JMy,HMe,SHa,JR2(c),V:Scorpion 2.50
10 JMy,HMe,SHa,JR2(c),Mary Jane 2.50
11 HMe,SHa,JBy,marital problems . 2.50
12 HMe,SHa,JBy,48-pg. 3.00
13 HMe,JBy 3.00
14 HMe,JBy,A:Sp.-Woman,x-over . . 2.50
15 HMe,JBy,DGr,x-over 2.50
16 HMe,JBy,DGr,Mary Jane gone . . 2.50
17 HMe,JBy,DGr,A:Sandman 2.50
18 HMe,JBy,JR,V:Green Goblin . . . 2.50
19 HMe,EL,DGr,Eddie Brock 2.50
20 HMe,EL,JBy,100-pg 3.00
21 HMe,EL,JhB,AlistairSmythe . . . 2.50
22 HMe,JR2,SHa,Senator Ward . . . 2.50
23 HMe,JR2,SHa,Ranger 2.50
24 HMe,JR2,SHa,Max.Security 2.50
25 HMe,JR2,SHa,A:Green Goblin . . 3.00
25a holographic foil(c) 6.00
26 HMe,JR2,SHa,F:Spidey's dad . . 2.50
27 HMe,JR2,SHa,V:A.I.M. 2.50
28 HMe,JR2,SHa,Enforcers 7.00
29 HMe,JR2,SHa,x-over 7.00
30 B:MSz(s),JR2,JSC(c) 15.00
31 MSz(s),JR2,JSC(c) 10.00
32 MSz(s),JR2,SHa,Ezekiel 9.00
33 MSz(s),JR2,SHa,Morlun 9.00
34 MSz(s),JR2,SHa,V:Morlun 6.00
35 MSz(s),JR2,SHa,pt.1 . . . . 6.00
36 MSz(s),JR2,SHa 15.00
37 MSz(s),JR2,SHa 5.00
38 MSz(s),JR2,SHa,'Nuff Said 3.00
39 MSz(s),JR2,SHa,Aunt May 2.50
40 MSz(s),JR2,SHa,Aunt May 2.50
41 MSz(s),JR2,SHa 2.50
42 MSz(s),JR2,SHa, ... 2.50
43 MSz(s),JR2,SHa 2.50
44 MSz(s),JR2,SHa 2.50
45 MSz(s),JR2,SHa 2.50
46 MSz(s),JR2,SHa 2.50
47 MSz(s),JR2,SHa 2.50
48 MSz(s),JR2,SHa 2.50
49 MSz(s),JR2,SHa 2.50
50 MSz(s),JR2,SHa,F:Mary Jane . . 4.50
51 MSz(s),JR2,SHa,F:Mary Jane . . 2.25
52 MSz(s),JR2,SHa,F:Mary Jane . . 2.25
53 MSz(s),JR2,SHa,F:Mary Jane . . 2.25
54 MSz(s),JR2,Digger 2.25
55 MSz(s),JR2,Consequences,pt.1 . 2.25
56 MSz(s),JR2,Consequences,pt.2 . 2.25
57 MSz(s),JR2,pt.1. . . . . 2.25
58 MSz(s),JR2,pt.2. . . . . 2.25
500 MSz(s),JR2,48-pg 3.50
501 . . . . 2.25
TPB Vol. 3 . . . . 13.00
TPB Vol. 4 . . . . 12.00
TPB Vol. 5 . . . . 13.00
Spec. Must Have,Rep. #30–#32 . . . 4.00
Ann.1999 JB,HMe, 48-page 4.00
Ann.2000 HMe,48-pg.. . . . . 4.00
Ann.2001 48-page 4.00
Giant Sized 80-pg. 4.50
Spec.Spider-Man/Sentry,PJe,RL,TA 3.00
Spec.Spider-Man/Marrow,SLo. 3.00
Spec.Coll. ed.,rep #30–#32 . . . . . . 4.00
Coll.Classics rep. #300. . . . . 2.50
Coll.Classics rep. #300 signed . . . 30.00
Coll.Classics rep. Sp-M #1 . . . . 2.50
Coll.Classics rep. Sp-M #1 signed. 30.00
TPB Revelations, 96-pg.. . . . . 9.00

AMAZING SPIDER-MAN INDEX
See: OFFICIAL MARVEL INDEX TO THE AMAZING SPIDER-MAN

AMAZING SPIDER-MAN COLLECTION
1 Mark Bagley card set 3.00
2 and 3 MBa, from card set . . . . @3.00

AMAZING X-MEN, THE
March–June, 1995
1 X-Men after Xavier 4.00
2 Exodus,Dazzler,V:Abyss 3.00
3 F:Bishop 3.00
4 V:Apocalypse 2.50
TPB Rep. #1–#4 . . . . 9.00

AMERICAN TAIL II
Dec., 1991
1 movie adaption 2.25
2 movie adaption 2.25

A-NEXT
Aug., 1998
1 TDF,RF,BBr,Next Generation of Avengers 3.00
2 TDF,RF,BBr,V:Kree & Sentry 2.25
2a variant cover 2.25
3 TDF,RF,BBr,Orig.Defenders vs. New Avengers 2.25
4 TDF,RF,BBr,turning points 2.25
5 TDF,RF,BBr,SB,Ghosts of the Past 2.25
6 TDF,RF,BBr,Majority Rules 2.25
7 TDF,RF,BBr,Last Days of the Avengers 2.25
8 TDF,RF,BBr,A:Ant-Man,Uneasy Allies 2.25
9 TDF,RF,BBr,Critical Choices . . . 2.25
10 TDF,RF,BBr,Incredible Journeys . 2.25
11 TDF,RF,BBr,A:Captain America & Doctor Doom 2.25
12 TDF,RF,BBr,I:Revengers 2.25

ANIMAX
Star, 1986–87
1 Based on Toy Line 3.00
2 thru 4 . . . . @3.00

ANNEX
Aug.–Nov., 1994
1 WMc,I:Brace, Crucible of Power . 2.25
2 WMc,V:Brace, Crucible,pt.2 . . . . 2.25
3 Crucible of Power, pt.3 . . . . 2.25
4 Crucible of Power, pt.4 . . . . 2.25

ANNIE
(Treasury Edition)
Oct., 1982
1 Movie Adaptation 3.00
2 Nov., 1982 . . . . 3.00

ANNIE OAKLEY
Atlas, Spring, 1948
1 A:Hedy Devine 500.00
2 CCB,I:Lana,A:Hedy Devine . . 275.00
3 . . . . 250.00
4 . . . . 250.00
5 . . . . 175.00
6 . . . . 125.00
7 . . . . 125.00
8 . . . . 125.00
9 AW, ... 135.00
10 . . . . 100.00
11 June, 1956 . . . . 100.00

ANT-MAN'S BIG CHRISTMAS
Dec., 1999
GN 48-pg. 6.00

A-1
1993
1 The Edge 8.00
2 Cheeky,Wee Budgie Boy 8.00
3 King Leon 8.00
4 King Leon 8.00

APACHE SKIES
July, 2002
1 (of 4) JOs,Apache Kid,wild west . 3.00
2 JOs 3.00
3 JOs 3.00
4 JOs, concl. 3.00
TPB 13.00

APOCALYPSE STRIKEFILES
1 After Xavier special 2.50

ARCHANGEL
1996
1-shot B&W 2.50

Amazing Spider-Man, Vol. 2 #1
© Marvel Entertainment Group

CVA Page 196   All comics prices listed are for *Near Mint* condition.

ARIZONA KID
Atlas, March, 1951
1 RH,Coming of the Arizons Kid. 250.00
2 RH,Code of the Gunman 125.00
3 RH(c) 100.00
4 PMo 100.00
5 PMo 100.00
6 PMo,JSt,Jan., 1952 .... 100.00

ARRGH!
Dec., 1974
Satire
1 MSy,TS,Vampire Rats 35.00
2 AA,TS. 25.00
3 TS,AA(c),Beauty and the
    Big Foot 25.00
4 The Night Gawker 25.00
5 Sept., 1975 .... 25.00

ARROWHEAD
April, 1954
1 JSt,Indian Warrior Stories ... 175.00
2 JSt 100.00
3 JSt 100.00
4 JSt,Nov., 1954 .... 100.00

ASTONISHING
See: MARVEL BOY

ASTONISHING TALES
Aug., 1970
1 BEv(c),JK,WW,Ka-Zar,Dr.Doom 75.00
2 JK,WW,Ka-Zar,Dr.Doom 40.00
3 BWS,WW,Ka-Zar,Dr.Doom ... 50.00
4 BWS,WW,Ka-Zar,Dr.Doom ... 50.00
5 BWS,GT,Ka-Zar,Dr.Doom ... 50.00
6 BWS,BEv,GT,I:Bobbi Morse ... 50.00
7 HT,GC,Ka-Zar,Dr.Doom 25.00
8 HT,TS,GT,GC,TP,Ka-Zar 25.00
9 GK(c),JB,Ka-Zar,Dr.Doom. ... 20.00
10 GK(c),BWS,SB,Ka-Zar. 25.00
11 GK,O:Ka-Zar 20.00
12 JB,DA,NA,V:Man Thing 40.00
13 JB,RB,DA,V:Man Thing 30.00
14 GK(c),rep. Ka-Zar 15.00
15 GK,TS,Ka-Zar 15.00
16 RB,AM,A:Ka-Zar 15.00
17 DA,V:Gemini 15.00
18 JR(c),DA,A:Ka-Zar. 15.00
19 JR(c),DA,JSn,JA,I:Victorious . . 15.00

Astonishing Tales #9
© *Marvel Entertainment Group*

20 JR(c),A:Ka-Zar. 15.00
21 RTs(s),DAy,B:It 35.00
22 RTs(s),DAy,V:Granitor 25.00
23 RTs(s),DAy,A:Fin Fang Foom. . 25.00
24 RTs(s),DAy,E:It 25.00
25 RB(a&s),B:I&O:Deathlok,
     GP(1st art) 50.00
26 RB(a&s),I:Warwolf 20.00
27 RB(a&s),V:Warwolf 20.00
28 RB(a&s),V:Warwolf 20.00
29 rep.Marv.Super Heroes #18 .. 15.00
30 RB(a&s),KP, ... 15.00
31 RB(a&s),BW,KP,V:Ryker 18.00
32 RB(a&s),KP,V:Ryker 18.00
33 RB(a&s),KJ,I:Hellinger 18.00
34 RB(a&s),KJ,V:Ryker. 18.00
35 RB(a&s),KJ,I:Doomsday-Mech. 18.00
36 RB(a&s),KP,E:Deathlok,
     I:Godwulf 25.00

ASTONISHING X-MEN
March–June, 1995
1 Uncanny X-Men 5.00
2 V:Holocaust 3.50
3 V:Abyss 3.00
4 V:Beast,Infinities. 3.00
TPB Rep. #1-#4 .... 8.95

ASTONISHING X-MEN
July, 1999
1 (of 3) BPe,HMe,new X-Men team 2.50
2 BPe,HMe,The Shattering x-over . 2.50
3 BPe,HMe,Shattering,concl 2.50
TPB 160-pg. 15.95

A-TEAM
March, 1984
1 .... 5.00
2 .... 5.00
3 May, 1984 .... 5.00

ATOMIC AGE
Epic, Nov., 1990
1 AW 4.50
2 AW 4.50
3 AW,Feb., 1991 .... 4.50

AVATAARS: COVENANT OF THE SHIELD
July, 2000
1 (of 3) LKa,Capt.Avalon 3.00
2 LKa,Dreadlord 3.00

AVENGERS
Sept., 1963
1 JK,O:Avengers,V:Loki 4,500.00
2 JK,V:Space Phantom 1,000.00
3 JK,V:Hulk,Sub-Mariner 600.00
4 JK,R&J:Captain America ... 3,200.00
5 JK,L:Hulk,V:Lava Men. 400.00
6 JK,I:Masters of Evil. 400.00
7 JK,V:BaronZemo,Enchantress 400.00
8 JK,I:Kang 300.00
9 JK(c),DH,I&D:Wonder Man .. 300.00
10 JK(c),DH,I:Immortus. 275.00
11 JK(c),DH,A:Spider-Man,
     V:Kang 400.00
12 JK(c),DH,V:Moleman,
     Red Ghost 300.00
13 JK(c),DH,I:Count Nefaria ... 300.00
14 JK,DH,V:Count Nefaria 300.00
15 JK,DH,D:Baron Zemo 200.00
16 JK,J:Hawkeye,Scarlet Witch,
     Quicksilver 250.00
17 JK(c),DH,V:Mole Man,A:Hulk . 200.00

18 JK(c),DH,V:The Commisar ... 200.00
19 JK(c),DH,I&O:Swordsman,
     O:Hawkeye. 150.00
20 JK(c),DH,WW,V:Swordsman,
     Mandarin 100.00
21 JK(c),DH,WW,V:Power Man
     (not L.Cage),Enchantress ... 100.00
22 JK(c),DH,WW,V:Power Man. . 100.00
23 JK(c),DH,JR,V:Kang 75.00
24 JK(c),DH,JR,V:Kang 75.00
25 JK(c),DH,V:Dr.Doom 75.00
26 DH,V:Attuma 75.00
27 DH,V:Attuma,Beetle. 75.00
28 JK(c),DH,I:1st Goliath,
     I:Collector. 75.00
29 DH,V:Power Man,Swordsman . 75.00
30 JK(c),DH,V:Swordsman 75.00
31 DH,V:Keeper of the Flame ... 75.00
32 DH,I:Bill Foster 65.00
33 DH,V:Sons of the Serpent
     A:Bill Foster 65.00
34 DH,V:Living Laser 65.00
35 DH,V:Mandarin 65.00
36 DH,V:The Ultroids 65.00
37 GK(c),DH,V:Ultroids. 65.00
38 GK(c),DH,V:Enchantress,
     Ares,J:Hercules 65.00
39 DH,V:Mad Thinker 65.00
40 DH,V:Sub-Mariner 65.00
41 JB,V:Dragon Man,Diablo 50.00
42 JB,V:Dragon Man,Diablo 50.00
43 JB,V:Red Guardian 50.00
44 JB,V:Red Guardian,
     O:Black.Widow. 50.00
45 JB,V:Super Adoptoid 50.00
46 JB,V:Whirlwind. 50.00
47 JB,GT,V:Magneto. 60.00
48 GT,I&O:New Black Knight 60.00
49 JB,V:Magneto 50.00
50 JB,V:Typhon 50.00
51 JB,GT,R:Iron Man,Thor,
     V:Collector 50.00
52 JB,J:Black Panther,
     I:Grim Reaper. 50.00
53 JB,GT,A:X-Men; x-over
     X-Men #45 .... 75.00
54 JB,GT,V:Masters of Evil
     I:Crimson Cowl(Ultron) ... 50.00
55 JB,I:Ultron,V:Masters of Evil. . 50.00
56 JB,D:Bucky retold,
     V:Baron Zemo 50.00
57 JB,I:Vision,V:Ultron 150.00
58 JB,O&J:Vision 100.00
59 JB,I:Yellowjacket 50.00

Avengers #58
© *Marvel Entertainment Group*

Avengers — MARVEL — Comics Values Annual

- 60 JB,W:Yellowjacket & Wasp.... 50.00
- 61 JB,A:Dr.Strange,x-over Dr. Strange #178 .... 50.00
- 62 JB,I:Man-Ape,A:Dr.Strange ... 50.00
- 63 GC,I&O:2nd Goliath(Hawkeye) V:Egghead 50.00
- 64 GC,V:Egghead,O:Hawkeye ... 50.00
- 65 GC,V:Swordsman,Egghead ... 50.00
- 66 BWS,I:Ultron 6,Adamantium... 55.00
- 67 BWS,V:Ultron 6 .... 55.00
- 68 SB,V:Ultron 40.00
- 69 SB,I:Nighthawk,Grandmaster, Squadron Supreme, V:Kang . 40.00
- 70 SB,O:Squadron Supreme V:Kang 40.00
- 71 SB,I:Invaders,V:Kang........ 75.00
- 72 SB,A:Captain Marvel, I:Zodiac 40.00
- 73 HT(i),V:Sons of Serpent 40.00
- 74 JB,TP,V:Sons of Serpent, IR:Black Panther on TV 40.00
- 75 JB,TP,I:Arkon............... 40.00
- 76 JB,TP,V:Arkon 40.00
- 77 JB,TP,V:Split-Second Squad .. 40.00
- 78 SB,TP,V:Lethal Legion 40.00
- 79 JB,TP,V:Lethal Legion 40.00
- 80 JB,TP,I&O:Red Wolf......... 45.00
- 81 JB,TP,A:Red Wolf 40.00
- 82 JB,TP,V:Ares,A:Daredevil..... 40.00
- 83 JB,TP,I:Valkyrie, V:Masters of Evil 50.00
- 84 JB,TP,V:Enchantress,Arkon ... 40.00
- 85 JB,V:Squadron Supreme 40.00
- 86 JB,JM,A:Squad Supreme..... 40.00
- 87 SB(i),O:Black Panther, V: A.I.M. 55.00
- 88 SB,JM,V:Psyklop,A:Hulk, Professor.X 45.00
- 88a 2nd Printing 10.00
- 89 SB,B:Kree/Skrull War........ 35.00
- 90 SB,V:Sentry #459,Ronan, Skrulls 35.00
- 91 SB,V:Sentry #459,Ronan, Skrulls 35.00
- 92 SB,V:Super Skrull,Ronan, ... 45.00
- 93 NA,TP,V:Super-Skrull,G-Size . 100.00
- 94 NA,JB,TP,V:Super-Skrull, I:Mandroids 65.00
- 95 NA,TP,V:Maximus,Skrulls, A:Inhumans,O:Black Bolt 60.00
- 96 NA,TP,V:Skrulls,Ronan 60.00
- 97 GK&BEv(c),JB,TP,E:Kree-Skrull War,V:Annihilus,Ronan,Skrulls, A:Golden Age Heroes....... 50.00
- 98 BWS,SB,V:Ares,R:Hercules, R&N:Hawkeye 50.00
- 99 BWS,TS,V:Ares 50.00
- 100 BWS,JSr,V:Ares & Kratos... 125.00
- 101 RB,DA,A:Watcher 30.00
- 102 RB,JSt,V:Grim Reaper, Sentinels 30.00
- 103 RB,JSt,V:Sentinels........... 30.00
- 104 RB,JSt,V:Sentinels........... 30.00
- 105 JB,JM,V:Savage Land Mutates; A:Black Panther 30.00
- 106 GT,DC,RB,V:Space Phantom. 30.00
- 107 GT,DC,JSn,V:Space Phantom, Grim Reaper...... 25.00
- 108 DH,DC,JSt,V:Space Phantom,Grim Reaper 30.00
- 109 DH,FMc,V:Champion, L:Hawkeye 30.00
- 110 DH,V:Magneto,A:X-Men 40.00
- 111 DH,J:Bl.Widow,A:Daredevil, X-Men,V:Magneto.......... 35.00
- 112 DH,I:Mantis,V:Lion-God, L:Black Widow 30.00
- 113 FBe(i),V:The Living Bombs... 20.00
- 114 JR(c),V:Lion-God,J:Mantis, Swordsman 20.00
- 115 JR(c),A:Defenders,V:Loki,

- Dormammu 20.00
- 116 JR(c),A:Defenders,S.Surfer V:Loki,Dormammu 20.00
- 117 JR(c),FMc(i),A:Defenders,Silv. Surfer,V:Loki,Dormammu 20.00
- 118 JR(c),A:Defenders,S.Surfer V:Loki,Dormammu 20.00
- 119 JR(c),DH(i),V:Collector 20.00
- 120 JSn(c),DH(i),V:Zodiac 20.00
- 121 JR&JSn(c),JB,DH,V:Zodiac .. 20.00
- 122 K&R(c),V:Zodiac 20.00
- 123 JR(c),DH(i),O:Mantis 20.00
- 124 JR(c),JB,DC,V:Kree,O:Mantis. 20.00
- 125 JR(c),JB,DC,V:Thanos 18.00
- 126 DC(i),V:Klaw,Solarr 18.00
- 127 GK(c),SB,JSon,A:Inhumans, V:Ultron,Maximus 18.00
- 128 K&R(c),SB,JSon,V:Kang 15.00
- 129 SB,JSon,V:Kang 15.00
- 130 GK(c),SB,JSon,V:Slasher, Titanic Three 15.00
- 131 GK(c),SB,JSon,V:Kang, Legion of the Unliving 15.00
- 132 SB,JSon,Kang,Legion of the Unliving 15.00
- 133 GK(c),SB,JSon,O:Vision 15.00
- 134 K&R(c),SB,JSon,O:Vision ... 15.00
- 135 JSn&JR(c),GT,O:Mantis, Vision,C:Thanos 20.00
- 136 K&R(c),rep Amazing Adv#12 . 18.00
- 137 JR(c),GT,J:Beast, Moondragon 18.00
- 138 GK(c),GT,V:Toad 15.00
- 139 K&R(c),GT,V:Whirlwind 15.00
- 140 K&R(c),GT,V:Whirlwind 15.00
- 141 GK(c),GP,V:Squad.Sinister ... 11.00
- 142 K&R(c),GP,V:Squadron Sinister,Kang 11.00
- 143 GK(c),GP,V:Squadron Sinister,Kang 11.00
- 144 GP,GK(c),V:Squad.Sinister, O&J:Hellcat,O:Buzz Baxter... 20.00
- 145 GK(c),DH,V:Assassin 10.00
- 146 GK(c),DH,KP,V:Assassin 10.00
- 147 GP,V:Squadron Supreme 10.00
- 148 JK(c),GP,V:Squad.Supreme .. 10.00
- 149 GP,V:Orka 12.00
- 150 GP,JK,rep.Avengers #16 .... 10.00
- 151 GP,new line-up, R:Wonder Man 12.00
- 152 JB,JSt,I:New Black Talon 12.00
- 153 JB,JSt,V:L.Laser,Whizzer.... 10.00
- 154 GP,V:Attuma 10.00

- 155 SB,V:Dr.Doom,Attuma 10.00
- 156 SB,I:Tyrak,V:Attuma........ 10.00
- 157 DH,V:Stone Black Knight 10.00
- 158 JK(c),SB,I&O:Graviton, ... 10.00
- 159 JK(c),SB,V:Graviton, ... 10.00
- 160 GP,V:Grim Reaper 10.00
- 161 GP,V:Ultron,A:Ant-Man...... 10.00
- 162 GP,V:Ultron,I:Jocasta 10.00
- 163 GT,A:Champions,V:Typhon .. 12.00
- 164 JBy,V:Lethal Legion 12.00
- 165 JBy,V:Count Nefario........ 10.00
- 166 JBy,V:Count Nefario........ 10.00
- 167 GP,A:Guardians,A:Nighthawk, Korvac,V:Porcupine 7.00
- 168 GP,A:Guardians,V:Korvac, I:Gyrich 7.00
- 169 SB,I:Eternity Man........... 7.00
- 170 GP,R:Jocasta,C:Ultron, A:Guardians 7.00
- 171 GP,V:Ultron,A:Guardians, Ms Marvel 7.00
- 172 SB,KJ,V:Tyrak 7.00
- 173 SB,V:Collector 7.00
- 174 GP(c),V:Collector........... 7.00
- 175 V&O:Korvac,A:Guardians.... 7.00
- 176 V:Korvac,A:Guardians 7.00
- 177 DC(c),D:Korvac,A:Guardians . 7.00
- 178 CI,V:Manipulator 7.00
- 179 JM,AG,V:Stinger,Bloodhawk. . 7.00
- 180 JM,V:Monolith,Stinger, D:Bloodhawk 7.00
- 181 JBy,GD,I:Scott Lang......... 9.00
- 182 JBy,KJ,V:Maximoff 9.00
- 183 JBy,KJ,J:Ms.Marvel 9.00
- 184 JBy,KJ,J:Falcon, V:Absorbing Man 9.00
- 185 JBy,DGr,O:Quicksilver & Scarlet Witch,I:Bova,V:Modred...... 9.00
- 186 JBy,DGr,V:Modred,Chthon ... 9.00
- 187 JBy,DGr,V:Chthon,Modred ... 9.00
- 188 JBy,DGr,V:The Elements..... 9.00
- 189 JBy,DGr,V:Deathbird 9.00
- 190 JBy,DGr,V:Grey Gargoyle, A:Daredevil 9.00
- 191 JBy,DGr,V:Grey Gargoyle, A:Daredevil 9.00
- 192 I:Inferno 7.00
- 193 FM(c),SB,DGr,O:Inferno..... 6.00
- 194 GP,JRu,J:Wonder Man...... 6.00
- 195 GP,JRu,A:Antman, I&C:Taskmaster............ 7.00
- 196 GP,JA,A:Antman, V:Taskmaster,............... 6.00
- 197 CI,JAb,V:Red Ronin 6.00
- 198 GP,DGr,V:Red Ronan 6.00
- 199 GP,DGr,V:Red Ronan 6.00
- 200 GP,DGr,V:Marcus, L:Ms.Marvel 9.00
- 201 GP,DGr,F:Jarvis 4.00
- 202 GP,V:Ultron 4.00
- 203 CI,V:Crawlers,F:Wonderman .. 4.00
- 204 DN,DGr,V:Yellow Claw...... 4.00
- 205 DGr,V:Yellow Claw......... 4.00
- 206 GC,DGr,V:Pyron 4.00
- 207 GC,DGr,V:Shadowlord...... 4.00
- 208 GC,DGr,V:Berserker 4.00
- 209 DGr,A:Mr.Fantastic,V:Skrull ... 4.00
- 210 GC,DGr,V:Weathermen 4.00
- 211 GC,DGr,Moon Knight,J:Tigra . 4.00
- 212 DGr,V:Elfqueen 4.00
- 213 BH,DGr,L:Yellowjacket...... 4.00
- 214 BH,DGr,V:Gh.Rider,A:Angel ... 7.00
- 215 DGr,A:Silver Surfer, V:Molecule Man 4.00
- 216 DGr,A:Silver Surfer, V:Molecule Man 4.00
- 217 BH,DGr,V:Egghead, R:Yellowjacket,Wasp3 .... 4.00
- 218 DP,V:M.Hardy 4.00
- 219 BH,A:Moondragon,Drax..... 4.00
- 220 BH,DGr,D:Drax,V:MnDragon .. 4.00

Avengers #133
© Marvel Entertainment Group

Comics Values Annual — MARVEL — Avengers

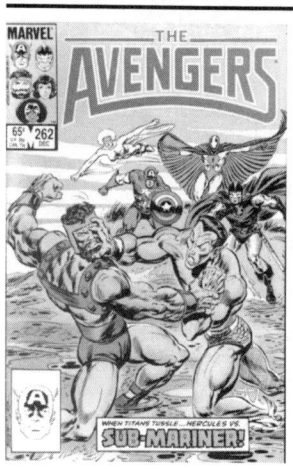

Avengers #262
© Marvel Entertainment Group

Avengers #400
© Marvel Entertainment Group

#	Description	Price
221	J:She Hulk	4.00
222	V:Masters of Evil	4.00
223	A:Antman	4.00
224	AM,A:Antman	4.00
225	A:Black Knight	4.00
226	A:Black Knight	4.00
227	J:2nd Captain Marvel, O:Avengers	4.00
228	V:Masters of Evil	4.00
229	JSt,V:Masters of Evil	4.00
230	A:Cap.Marvel,L:Yellowjacke	4.00
231	AM,JSi,J:2nd Captain Marvel, Starfox	4.00
232	AM,JSi	4.00
233	JBy,V:Annihilus	4.00
234	AM,JSi,O:ScarletWitch	4.00
235	AM,JSi,V:Wizard	4.00
236	AM,JSi,A:SpM,V:Lava Men	4.50
237	AM,JSi,A:SpM,V:Lava Men	4.50
238	AM,JSi,V:Moonstone, O:Blackout	4.00
239	AM,JSi,A:David Letterman	4.00
240	AM,JSi,A:Dr.Strange	4.00
241	AM,JSi,V:Morgan LeFey	4.00
242	AM,JSi,Secret Wars	4.00
243	AM,JSi,Secret Wars	4.00
244	AM,JSi,V:Dire Wraiths	4.00
245	AM,JSi,V:Dire Wraiths	4.00
246	AM,JSi,V:Eternals	4.00
247	AM,JSi,A:Eternals,V:Deviants	4.00
248	AM,JSi,A:Eternals,V:Deviants	4.00
249	AM,JSi,A:Maelstrom	4.00
250	AM,JSi,A:W.C.A. V:Maelstrom	5.00
251	BH,JSi,A:Paladin	4.00
252	BH,JSi,J:Hercules V:Blood Brothers	4.00
253	BH,JSi,J:Black Knight	4.00
254	BH,A:W.C.A.	4.00
255	TP,p(c),JB,Legacy of Thanos/Santuary II	4.00
256	JB,TP,A:Ka-Zar	4.00
257	JB,TP,D:Savage Land, I:Nebula	4.00
258	JB,TP,A:SpM,Firelord,Nebula	4.00
259	JB,TP,V:Nebula	4.00
260	JB,TP,SecretWarsII, IR:Nebula is Thanos' Granddaughter	4.00
261	JB,TP,Secret Wars II	4.00
262	JB,TP,J:Submariner	4.00
263	JB,TP,X-Factor tie-in, Rebirth,Marvel Girl,pt.1	6.00
264	JB,TP,I:2nd Yellow Jacket	4.00
265	JB,TP,Secret Wars II	3.00
266	JB,TP,Secret Wars II,A: Silver Surfer	3.00
267	JB,TP,V:Kang	3.00
268	JB,TP,V:Kang	3.00
269	JB,TP,V:Kang,A:Immortus	3.00
270	JB,TP,V:Moonstone	3.00
271	JB,TP,V:Masters of Evil	3.00
272	JB,TP,A:Alpha Flight	3.00
273	JB,TP,V:Masters of Evil	3.00
274	JB,TP,V:Masters of Evil	3.00
275	JB,TP,V:Masters of Evil	3.00
276	JB,TP,V:Masters of Evil	3.00
277	JB,TP,V:Masters of Evil	3.00
278	JB,TP,V:Tyrok,J:Dr.Druid	3.00
279	JB,TP,new leader	3.00
280	BH,KB,O:Jarvis	3.00
281	JB,TP,V:Olympian Gods	3.00
282	JB,TP,V:Cerberus	3.00
283	JB,TP,V:Olympian Gods	3.00
284	JB,TP,V:Olympian Gods	3.00
285	JB,TP,V:Zeus	3.00
286	JB,TP,V:Fixer	3.00
287	JB,TP,V:Fixer	3.00
288	JB,TP,V:Sentry 459	3.00
289	JB,TP,J:Marrina	3.00
290	JB,TP,V:Adaptoid	3.00
291	JB,TP,V:Marrina	3.00
292	JB,TP,V:Leviathon	3.00
293	JB,TP,V:Leviathon	3.00
294	JB,TP,V:Nebula	3.00
295	JB,TP,V:Nebula	3.00
296	JB,TP,V:Nebula	3.00
297	JB,TP,V:Nebula	3.00
298	JB,TP,Inferno,Edwin Jarvis	3.00
299	JB,TP,Inferno,V:Orphan Maker,R:Gilgemesh	3.00
300	JB,TP,WS,Inferno,V:Kang, O:Avengers,J:Gilgamesh, Mr.Fantastic,Invis.Woman	5.00
301	BH,DH,A:SuperNova	3.00
302	RB,TP,V:SuperNova, A:Quasar	3.00
303	RB,TP,V:SuperNova,A:FF	3.00
304	RB,TP,V:U-Foes,Puma	3.00
305	PR,TP,V:Lava Men	5.00
306	PR,TP,O:Lava Men	3.00
307	PR,TP,V:Lava Men	3.00
308	PR,TP,A:Eternals,J:Sersi	3.00
309	PR,TP,V:Blastaar	3.00
310	PR,TP,V:Blastaar	3.00
311	PR,TP,Acts of Veng.,V:Loki	3.00
312	PR,TP,Acts of Vengeance, V:Freedom Force	3.00
313	PR,TP,Acts of Vengeance, V:Mandarin,Wizard	3.00
314	PR,TP,J:Sersi,A:Spider-Man, V:Nebula	4.00
315	PR,TP,A:SpM,V:Nebula	4.00
316	PR,TP,J:Spider-Man	4.00
317	PR,TP,A:SpM,V:Nebula	4.00
318	PR,TP,A:SpM,V:Nebula	4.00
319	PR,B:Crossing Line	3.00
320	PR,TP,A:Alpha Flight	3.00
321	PR,Crossing Line#3	3.00
322	PR,TP,Crossing Line#4	3.00
323	PR,TP,Crossing Line#5	3.00
324	PR,TP,E:Crossing Line	3.00
325	V:MotherSuperior,3 Machinesmith	3.00
326	TP,I:Rage	5.00
327	TP,V:Monsters	3.00
328	TP,O:Rage	4.00
329	TP,J:Sandman,Rage	3.00
330	TP,V:Tetrarch of Entropy	3.00
331	TP,J:Rage,Sandman	3.00
332	TP,V:Dr.Doom	3.00
333	HT,V:Dr.Doom	3.00
334	NKu,TP,B:Collector, A:Inhumans	3.00
335	RLm(c),SEp,TP,V:Thane Ector,A:Collector	3.00
336	RLm(c),SEp,TP	3.00
337	RLm(c),SEp,TP,V:ThaneEctor	3.00
338	RLm(c),SEp,TP,A:Beast	3.00
339	RLm(c),SEp,TP,E:Collector	3.00
340	RLm(c),F:Capt.Amer.,Wasp	3.00
341	SEp,TP,A:New Warriors,V:Sons of Serpents	3.00
342	SEP,TP,A:New Warriors, V:Hatemonger	3.00
343	SEp,TP,J:Crystal,C&I:2nd Swordsman,Magdalene	3.00
344	SEp,TP,I:Proctor	3.00
345	SEp,TP,Oper. Galactic Storm Pt.5,V:Kree,Shiar	3.00
346	SEp,TP,Oper. Galactic Storm Pt.12,I:Star Force	3.00
347	SEp,TP,Oper. Galactic Storm Pt.19,D:Kree Race,Conclusion	3.00
348	SEp,TP,F:Vision	3.00
349	SEp,TP,V:Ares	3.00
350	SEp,TP,rep.Avengers#53,A:Prof. X,Cyclops,V:StarJammers	4.00
351	KWe,V:Star Jammers	3.00
352	V:Grim Reaper	3.00
353	V:Grim Reaper	3.00
354	V:Grim Reaper	3.00
355	BHs(s),SEp,I:Gatherers, Coal Tiger	3.00
356	B:BHs(s),SEp,TP,A:Bl.Panther D:Coal Tiger	3.00
357	SEp,TP,A:Watcher	3.00
358	SEp,TP,V:Arkon	3.00
359	SEp,TP,A:Arkon	3.00
360	SEp,TP,V:Proctor,double-size, bronze foil(c)	4.50
361	SEp,I:Alternate Vision	2.50
362	SEp,TP,V:Proctor	3.00
363	SEp,TP,V:Proctor,D:Alternate Vision,C:Deathcry,Silver Foil(c), 30th Anniv.	4.00
364	SEp,TP,I:Deathcry,V:Kree	3.00
365	SEp,TP,V:Kree	3.00
366	SEp,TP,V:Kree,N:Dr.Pym,Gold Foil(c)	5.00
367	F:Vision	3.00
368	SEp,TP,Bloodties#1, A:X-Men	4.00
369	SEp,TP,E:BHs(s),Bloodties#5, D:Cortez,V:Exodus,Platinum Foil(c)	4.00
370	SEp(c),TP(c),GI,V:Deviants, A:Kro,I:Delta Force	3.00
371	GM,TP,V:Deviants,A:Kro	3.00

All comics prices listed are for *Near Mint* condition.

CVA Page 199

Avengers–Avengers MARVEL Comics Values Annual

372 B:BHs(s),SEp,TP,I:2nd
    Gatherers,A:Proctor 3.00
373 SEp,TP,I:Alternate Jocasta,
    V:Sersi. 3.00
374 SEp,TP,O&IR:Proctor is Alternate
    Black Knight. 3.00
375 SEp,TP,Double Sized,D:Proctor,
    L:Sersi,Black Knight 3.50
376 F:Crystal,I:Terrigen. 3.00
377 F:Quicksilver 3.00
378 TP,I:Butcher. 3.00
379 TP,Hercules,V:Hera 3.00
379a Avengers Double Feature #1
    flip-book with Giant-Man #1 . . 3.50
380 Hera 6.00
380a Avengers Double Feature #2
    flip-book with Giant Man #2 . . 5.00
381 Quicksilvr, Scarlet Witch. 4.00
381a Avengers Double Feature #3
    flip-book with Giant Man #3 . . 3.00
382 Wundagore 2.50
382a Avengers Double Feature #4
    flip-book with Giant Man #4 . . 3.00
383 A:Fantastic Force,V:Arides. . . 3.00
384 Hercules Vs. Stepmom 4.00
385 V:Red Skull 3.00
386 F:Black Widow. 3.00
387 Taking A.I.M.,pt.2 . . . . 3.00
388 Taking A.I.M.,pt.4 . . . . 3.00
389 B:Mike Deodato 3.00
390 BHs,TP,The Crossing, prelude . 3.00
391 BHs,Cont. From Avg. Crossing. 3.00
392 BHs,TP,The Crossing. 3.00
393 BHs,TP,The Crossing. 3.00
394 BHs,TP,The Crossing. 3.00
395 BHs,TP,Timeslide concludes . . 3.00
396 . . . . 3.00
397 TP,Incred.Hulk #440 x-over . . 3.00
398 TP,V:Unknown foe 3.00
399 . . . . 3.00
400 MeW,MWa,double size 4.50
401 MeW,MWa,Onslaught saga . . 3.00
402 MWa,MD2,Onslaught, finale. . . 3.00
Ann.#1 DH,V:Mandarin,
    Masters of Evil 125.00
Ann.#2 DH,JB,V:Scar.Centurion . 75.00
Ann.#3 rep.#4,T.ofSusp.#66-68 . . 50.00
Ann.#4 rep.#5,#6 . . . . 30.00
Ann.#5 JK(c),rep.#8,#11 . . . . 25.00
Ann.#6 GP,HT,V:Laser,Nuklo,
    Whirlwind 20.00
Ann.#7 JSn,JRu,V:Thanos,A:Captain
    Marvel,D:Warlock(2nd) 40.00
Ann.#8 GP,V:Dr.Spectrum 15.00
Ann.#9 DN,V:Arsenal 10.00
Ann.#10 MGo,A:X-Men,Spid.Woman,
    I:Rogue,V:Br.o/Evil Mutants . . 40.00
Ann.#11 DP,V:Defenders 6.00
Ann.#12 JG,V:Inhumans,Maximus . 5.00
Ann.#13 JBy,V:Armin Zola 5.00
Ann.#14 JBy,KB,V:Skrulls 5.00
Ann.#15 SD,KJ,V:Freedom Force . 5.00
Ann.#16 RF,BH,TP,JR2,BSz,KP,AW,
    MR,BL,BWi,JG,KN,A:Silver
    Surfer,Rebirth Grandmaster . . 5.00
Ann.#17 MBr,MG,Evol.Wars,J:2nd
    Yellow Jacket 5.00
Ann.#18 MBa,MG,Atlan.Attack#8,
    J:Quasar 4.00
Ann.#19 HT,Terminus Factor. . . . 4.00
Ann.#20 Subterran.Odyssey#1 . . 4.00
Ann.#21 Citizen Kang#4 . . . . 4.00
Ann.#22 I:Bloodwraith,w/card . . . 4.00
Ann.#23 JB 4.00
G-Size#1 JR(c),RB,DA,I:Nuklo . . 15.00
G-Size#2 JR(c),DC,O.Kang,
    D:Swordsman,O:Rama-Tut . . 10.00
G-Size#3 GK(c),DC,V:Kang,Legion
    of the Unliving 8.00
G-Size#4 K&R(c),DH,W:Scarlet Witch
    &Vision,O:Mantis,Moondragon . 8.00

G-Size#5 rep,Annual #1. . . . . 7.00
GNv Death Trap:The Vault RLm,
    A:Venom 20.00
Marvel Milestone rep. #1 (1993) . . 2.95
Marvel Milestone rep. #4 (1995) . . 2.95
Marvel Milestone rep. #16 (1993) . . 2.95
TPB Greatest Battles of the
    Avengers 15.95
TPB Korvac Saga,rep.#167-177 . . 12.95
TPB Yesterday Quest,Rep.#181,182
    185-187 . . . . 6.95

Avengers Vol. 2, #7
© *Marvel Entertainment Group*

AVENGERS
Nov., 1996

1 RLd,JV,CYp,JSb,Heroes Reborn,
    F:Thor, Captain America,
    V:Loki. 6.00
1A Variant cover 8.00
1 gold signature edition, bagged . 20.00
2 RLd,JV,CYp,JSb,V:Kang 4.00
3 RLd,JV,CYp,JSb,V:Kang,A:Nick
    Fury 4.00
4 RLd,JLb,CYp,JSb, ... 4.00
4A variant cover 4.00
5 RLd,CYp,JSb,V:Hulk,concl. 3.50
6 RLd,JLb,CYp,JSb,Industrial
    Revolution,î pt.1 x-over. 3.50
7 RLd,JLb,IaC,JSb, ... 3.50
8 RLd,JLb,IaC,JSb,F:Simon
    Williams (Wonder Man),V:Ultron,
    Lethal Legion 3.50
9 JLb,RLd,IaC,F:Vision, Wonder
    Man 5.00
10 WS, ... 3.50
11 . . . . 3.50
12 WS,Galactus Saga, x-over. . . . 3.50
13 JeR, Wildstorm x-over. 3.50
Minus 1 Spec., JLb,RLd,IaC,JSb,
    flashback 2.50

AVENGERS
Dec., 1997

1 GP,KBk,AV,F:Everyone,48 pg. . . 7.00
1a Variant (c). 10.00
2 KBk,GP,AV,A:Scarlet Witch 5.00
3 KBk,GP,AV,trapped in midieval
    present. 4.00
4 KBk,GP,AV,who makes the
    team?. 5.00
5 KBk,GP,AV,Squadron Supreme . 5.00
6 KBk,GP,AV,V:SquadronSupreme. 5.00
7 KBk,GP,AV,Live Kree or Die,pt.4 . 2.50
8 KBk,GP,AV,I:Triathlon 2.50

9 KBk,GP,AV,V:Moses Magnum . . . 2.50
10 KBk,GP,AV,V:Grim Reaper. 2.50
11 KBk,GP,AV,V:Grim Reaper 2.50
12 KBk,GP,AV,V:Thunderbolts,
    48-page 40.00
12a Variant, white background 3.00
13 KBk,GP,AV,R:New Warriors . . . 2.50
14 KBk,GP,AV,R:Beast 2.50
15 KBk,GP,AV,A:Iron Man. 2.50
16 JOy,AG,R:Photon 5.00
16a variant JOy,GP cover 2.50
17 JOy,AG,A:Warbird &
    Black Knight. 2.50
18 JOy,AG,V:Wrecking Crew 2.50
19 KBk,GP,AV,Ultron,pt.1 . . . . 2.50
19a signed 30.00
20 KBk,GP,AV,Ultron,pt.2 . . . . 2.50
21 KBk,GP,AV,Ultron,pt.3 . . . . 2.50
22 KBk,GP,AV,Ultron,pt.4 . . . . 2.50
23 KBk,GP,AV,V:Wonder Man 2.50
24 KBk,GP,AV 2.50
25 KBk,GP,AV, 48-pg. 3.50
26 KBk,GP,AV,SI,V:Triune 2.50
27 KBk,GP,AV,100-pg. 3.50
28 KBk,GP,AV,Kulan Gath,pt.1 . . . 2.50
29 KBk,GP,AV,Kulan Gath,pt.2 . . . 2.50
30 KBk,GP,AV,Kulan Gath,pt.3 . . . 2.50
31 KBk,GP,AV,F:Vision 2.50
32 KBk,GP,AV,F:Black Widow 2.50
33 KBk,GP,AV,Thunderbolts 2.50
34 KBk,GP,AV,Thunderbolts 3.50
35 KBk,JR2,AV,MaximumSecurity . . 2.50
36 KBk,SEp,AV,A:Capt.Am.+poster. 2.50
37 KBk,SEp,AV,F:Capt.Am. 2.50
38 KBk,AD,MFm. 2.50
39 KBk,AD,MFm,F:Silverclaw 2.50
40 KBk,AD,MFm,F:Hulk,Silverclaw . 2.50
41 KBk,AD,MFm,A:Kang 2.50
42 KBk,AD,MFm,A:Kang 2.50
43 KBk,AD,MFm,V:Kang. 2.50
44 KBk,KK,V:Kang,Thor berserk . . 2.50
45 KBk,KK,V:Conqueror 2.50
46 KBk,Kang Dynasty 2.50
47 KBk,Kang Dynasty 2.50
48 KBk,KD,100-page 4.00
49 KBk,KD,F:Kang,'Nuff Said 2.50
50 KBk,KD,V:Kang, 48-pg. 4.00
51 KBk,KD,F:Wonder Man,
    Scarlet Witch 2.25
52 KBk,KD,Kang War 2.25
53 KBk,KD,Avengers Avenge 2.25
54 KBk,KD,Kang War,concl. 2.25
55 KBk,KD,Kang War,aftermath . . 2.25
56 KBk,F:Beast, She-Hulk,USAgent. 2.25
57 KD,World Trust, pt.1 . . . . 2.25
58 KD,World Trust, pt.2 . . . . 2.25
59 KD,World Trust, pt.3 . . . . 2.25
60 KD,World Trust, concl.,40-pg . . 4.00
61 GFr. 2.25
62 GFr. 2.25
63 AD,MFm,Standoff,pt.3,x-over . . 2.25
64 F:Falcon 2.25
65 ALa,Red Zone,pt.1 . . . . 2.25
66 ALa,Red Zone,pt.2 . . . . 2.25
67 ALa,Red Zone,pt.3 . . . . 2.25
68 ALa,Red Zone,pt.4 . . . . 2.25
69 ALa,Red Zone,pt.5 . . . . 2.25
70 ALa,Red Zone,pt.6 . . . . 2.25
71 V:Wasp, Yellowjacket 2.25
72 Sck,Search for She-Hulk,pt.1 . . 2.25
73 Sck,Search for She-Hulk,pt.2 . . 2.25
74 Sck,Search for She-Hulk,pt.3 . . 2.25
75 Sck,Search for She-Hulk,pt.4 . . 2.25
76 . . . . 2.25
Ann. '98 Avengers/Squadron Supreme
    KBk,CPa,GP, 48pg 2.50
Ann.1999 KBk,JFM, Why Avengers
    disbanded, 48-page 3.50
Ann.2000 KBk,NBy,48-pg. 3.50
Ann.2001 KBk,IaC,NRd 3.00

CVA Page 200   All comics prices listed are for *Near Mint* condition.

MARVEL

Comics Values Annual

Rough Cut Edition KBk,GP, 48pg,
  original pencils of #1, b&w 3.00
Spec. 1-1/2, 32-pg.RSt 2.50
Spec. Avengers: Year in Review ... 3.00
GN Ultron Imperative,BWS(c).... 6.00
TPB Avengers: Under Siege 16.95
TPB Avengers Visionaries:
  George Perez, 176-page 16.95
TPB The Morgan Conquest 14.95
TPB The Kree/Skrull War 24.95
TPB Ultron Unlimited,112-page ... 14.95
TPB Supreme Justice,304-page ... 17.95
TPB Clear & Present Danger 19.95
TPB Celestial Madonna, 224-pg... 19.95
TPB Avengers/Defenders War ... 17.95
TPB The Korvac Saga (2002).... 19.95
TPB The Kang Dynasty (2002) .. 30.00
TPB Vol.1: World Trust (2003) ... 15.00
TPB Vol.2: Red Zone (2003).... 15.00

AVENGERS: CELESTIAL QUEST
Sept., 2001
1 (of 8) SEt,SHa 2.50
2 SEt,SHa,F:Mantis............ 3.00
3 SEt,SHa,F:Quoi,Mantis....... 3.00
4 SEt,SHa,F:Quoi,Thanos 2.50
5 SEt,SHa,F:Thanos 2.50
6 SEt,SHa,F:Mantis & Vision ... 2.50
7 SEt,SHa,F:Mantis,Quoi,Vision. . 2.50
8 SEt,SHa,finale,48-pg.......... 3.50

AVENGERS FOREVER
Oct., 1998
1 (of 12) GP,KBk,CPa,Rick Jones
  radiation poisoning 4.00
2 GP,KBk,CPa,new Avengers 3.00
3 GP,KBk,CPa,Kang/Immortus.... 3.00
4 KBk,different eras............ 3.00
4a, b & c variant covers .... @3.00
5 KBk,RSt,A:1950s Avengers 3.00
6 KBk,RSt,V:Immortus.......... 3.00
7 KBk,RSt,reunited 3.00
8 KBk,Immortus' plan........... 3.00
9 KBk,RSt,Kang the Conqueror ... 3.00
10 KBk,RSt,V:Immortus 3.00
11 KBk,RSt,V:Avengers Battalion ... 3.00
12 KBk,RSt,concl.............. 3.00
TPB Avengers Forever,288-page . 24.95

AVENGERS ICONS: TIGRA
March, 2002
1 (of 4) MD2,................. 3.00
2 MD2,Brethren of the Blue Fist... 3.00
3 MD2,Brethren of the Blue Fist... 3.00
4 MD2,concl.................. 3.00

AVENGERS ICONS: THE VISION
Aug., 2002
1 (of 4) 3.00
2 .... 3.00
3 .... 3.00
4 concl....................... 3.00

AVENGERS INDEX
See: OFFICIAL MARVEL INDEX TO THE AVENGERS

AVENGERS INFINITY
July, 2000
1 (of 4) RSt,SCh,SHa 3.00
2 RSt,SCh,SHa,Servitors....... 3.00
3 RSt,SCh,SHa,Infinites........ 3.00
4 RSt,SCh,SHa,concl 3.00

AVENGERS LOG
1994
1 GP(c),History of the Avengers... 2.25

AVENGERS SPOTLIGHT
Aug., 1989
Formerly: Solo Avengers
21 AM,DH,TMo,JRu,Hawkeye,
  Starfox.................. 3.00
22 AM,DH,Hawkeye,O:Swordsman. 2.50
23 AM,DH,KD,Hawkeye,Vision 2.50
24 AM,DH,Hawkeye,O:Espirita ... 2.50
25 AM,TMo,Hawkeye,Rick Jones ... 2.50
26 A of V,Hawkeye,Iron Man...... 2.50
27 A of V,AM,DH,DT,Hawkeye
  Avengers 2.50
28 A of V,AM,DH,DT,Hawkeye,
  Wonder Man,Wasp.......... 2.50
29 A of V,DT,Hawkeye,Iron Man ... 2.50
30 AM,DH,Hawkeye,New Costume.. 2.50
31 AM,DH,KW,Hawkeye,US.Agent. 2.50
32 AM,KW,Hawkeye,U.S.Agent.... 2.50
33 AM,DH,KW,Hawkeye,US.Agent ... 2.50
34 AM,DH,KW,SLi(c),Hawkeye
  U.S.Agent................ 2.50
35 JV,Gilgamesh 2.50
36 AM,DH,Hawkeye 2.50
37 BH,Dr.Druid 2.50
38 JBr,Tigra 2.50
39 GCo,Black Knight 2.50
40 Vision,Last Issue 2.50

AVENGERS STRIKEFILE
1994
1 BHa(s),Avengers Pin-ups 2.25

AVENGERS: THE CROSSING
1995
1 BHs,Death of an Avenger,
  chromium cover,48pg........ 6.00

AVENGERS: THE TERMINATRIX OBJECTIVE
1993
1 B:MGu(s),MG,Holografx(c),
  V:Terminatrix 2.75
2 MG,V:Terminatrix,A:Kangs 2.25
3 MG,V:Terminatrix,A:Kangs 2.25
4 MG,Last issue 2.25

AVENGERS: TIMESLIDE
1996
1 BHs,TKa,End of the Crossing
  Megallic chrome cover 5.00

AVENGERS TWO: WONDER MAN & THE BEAST
Mar. 2000
1 (of 3) RSt,MBa,............. 3.00
2 RSt,MBa,.................. 3.00
3 RSt,MBa,concl.............. 3.00

AVENGERS/ULTRAFORCE
1995
1 V:Malibu's Ultraforce......... 4.00

Avengers–Avengers

AVENGERS: UNITED THEY STAND
Sept., 1999
1 TTn,RCa, Cartoon tie-in 3.00
2 TTn, ... 2.25
3 TTn, ... 2.25
4 TTn, ... 2.25
5 TTn,Hawkeye&Black Widow ... 2.25
6 TTn,A:Capt.America......... 2.25
7 TTn,F:Devil Dinosaur,Moonboy.. 3.25

AVENGERS UNIVERSE
June, 2000
1 rep. 3 stories, 80-pg.......... 5.00
2 rep. 3 stories, 80-pg.......... 5.00
3 rep. 3 stories, 80-pg.......... 5.00
4 rep. 3 stories, 80-pg.......... 4.25
5 rep. 3 stories, 80-pg.......... 4.25

AVENGERS UNLEASHED
1995
1 V:Count Nefarious 2.25

Avengers Unplugged #5
© Marvel Entertainment Group

Becomes:
AVENGERS UNPLUGGED
1996
2 Crushed by Graviton.......... 2.25
3 x-over with FF Unplugged..... 2.25
4 The Old Ball and Chain 2.25
5 A:Captain Marvel 2.25
6 final issue.................. 2.25

AVENGERS WEST COAST
Sept., 1989
Prev: West Coast Avengers
47 JBy,V:J.Random 3.00
48 JBy,V:J.Random 3.00
49 JBy,V:J.Random,W.Man...... 3.00
50 JBy,R:G.A.Human Torch 4.00
51 JBy,R:Iron Man 2.50
52 JBy,V:MasterPandmonum 2.50
53 JBy,Acts ofVeng.,V:U-Foes ... 2.50
54 JBy,Acts ofVeng.,V:MoleMan ... 2.50
55 JBy,Acts ofVeng.finale,V:Loki
  Magneto kidnaps Sc.Witch.... 2.50
56 JBy,V:Magneto............. 2.50
57 JBy,V:Magneto............. 2.50
58 V:Vibro.................... 2.50
59 TMo,V:Hydro-Man,A:Immortus . 2.50

All comics prices listed are for *Near Mint* condition.   CVA Page 201

Avengers–Battlefront — MARVEL — Comics Values Annual

60 PR,V:Immortus,	2.50
61 PR,V:Immortus	2.50
62 V:Immortus	2.50
63 PR,I:Living Lightning	2.50
64 F:G.A.Human Torch	2.50
65 PR,V:Ultron,Grim Reaper	2.50
66 PR,V:Ultron,Grim Reaper	2.50
67 PR,V:Ultron,Grim Reaper	2.50
68 PR,V:Ultron	2.50
69 PR,USAgent vs Hawkeye, I:Pacific Overlords	2.50
70 DR,V:Pacific Overlords	3.00
71 DR,V:Pacific Overlords	3.00
72 DR,V:Pacific Overlords	3.00
73 DR,V:Pacific Overlords	3.00
74 DR,J:Living Lightning,Spider Woman,V:Pacific Overlords	3.00
75 HT,A:F.F,V:Arkon,double	3.00
76 DR,Night Shift,I:Man-Demon	2.50
77 DR,A:Satannish & Nightshift	2.50
78 DR,V:Satannish & Nightshift	2.50
79 DR,A:Dr.Strange,V:Satannish.	2.50
80 DR,Galactic Storm,pt.2	2.50
81 DR,Galactic Storm,pt.9	2.50
82 DR,Galactic Storm,pt.16 A:Lilandra	2.50
83 V:Hyena	2.50
84 DR,I:Deathweb,A:SpM, O:Spider-Woman	3.00
85 DR,A:SpM,V:Death Web	2.50
86 DR,A:SpM,V:Death Web	2.50
87 DR,A:Wolverine,V:Bogatyri	3.00
88 DR,A:Wolverine,V:Bogatyri	2.50
89 DR,V:Ultron	2.50
90 DR,A:Vision,V:Ultron	2.50
91 DR,V:Ultron,I:War Toy	2.50
92 DR,V:Goliath(Power Man)	2.50
93 DR,V:Doctor Demonicus	2.50
94 DR,J:War Machine	2.50
95 DR,A:Darkhawk,V:Doctor Demonicus	2.50
96 DR,Inf.Crusade x-over	2.50
97 ACe,Inf.Crusade,V:Power Platoon	2.50
98 DR,I:4th Lethal Legion	2.50
99 DR,V:4th Lethal Legion	2.50
100 DR,D:Mockingbird,V:4th Lethal Legion,Red Foil(c)	4.50
101 DR,Bloodties#3,V:Exodus	4.00
102 DR,L:Iron Man,Spider-Woman, US Agent,Scarlet Witch,War Machine,last issue	4.00
Ann.#4 JBy,TA,MBa,Atlan.Attacks #12,V:Seven Brides of Set	4.00
Ann.#5 Terminus Factor	3.50
Ann.#6 Subterranean Odyssey#5	2.50
Ann.#7 Assault on Armor City#4	2.25
Ann.#8 DR,I:Raptor w/card	3.25

BACKPACK MARVELS:
Avengers (2001)	7.25
Spider-Man Vol. 1 (2001)	7.25
X-Men Vol.1 (2001)	7.25
X-Men Vol.2 (2000)	7.25

BALDER THE BRAVE
Nov., 1985

1 WS,SB,V:Frost Giants	3.00
2 WS,SB,V:Frost Giants	3.00
3 WS,SB,V:Frost Giants	3.00
4 WS,SB,V:Frost Giants;Feb,1986	3.00

BANNER
Startling Stories, July, 2001

1 (of 4) RCo, F:Hulk	3.00
2 RCo,	3.00
3 RCo,	3.00
4 RCo, concl.	3.00
TPB RCo(c) 96-page	12.95

Barbie #61
© Marvel Entertainment Group

BARBIE
Jan., 1991

1 polybagged with Credit Card	15.00
2 thru 49	@8.00
50 Anniv. issue, Disney World(c)	12.00
51 thru 66	@7.00

BARBIE FASHION
Jan., 1991

1 bagged with doorknob hanger	12.00
2 thru 63	@7.00

BATTLE
Atlas, March, 1951

1 They called Him a Coward	350.00
2 The War Department Secrets	175.00
3 The Beast of the Bataan	125.00
4 JMn,I:Buck Private O'Toole	125.00
5 Death Trap Of Gen. Wu.	125.00
6 RH, JMn	125.00
7 Enemy Sniper	125.00
8 A Time to Die	125.00
9 RH	100.00
10	100.00
11 SC	100.00
12 thru 20	@110.00
21	110.00
22	75.00
23 BK	75.00
24	75.00
25	75.00
26 JR	75.00
27	75.00
28 JSe	75.00
29	75.00
30	75.00
31 RH,JMn	75.00
32 JSe,GT	75.00
33 GC,JSe,JSt	75.00
34 JSe	75.00
35	75.00
36 BEv	75.00
37 RA,JSt	90.00
38	75.00
39	75.00
40	75.00
41	75.00
42 thru 46	@75.00
47 JO	75.00
48	75.00
49 JDa	85.00
50 BEv	75.00
51	75.00
52 GWb	75.00
53 BP	75.00
54	75.00
55 GC,AS,BP,AW,GWb	90.00
56	65.00
57	65.00
58	65.00
59 AT	65.00
60 A:Combat Kelly	65.00
61 JMn,A:Combat Kelly	65.00
62 A:Combat Kelly	65.00
63 SD	125.00
64 JK	125.00
65 JK	125.00
66 JSe,JK,JDa	125.00
67 JSe,JK,AS,JDa	125.00
68 JSe,JK,AW,SD	125.00
69 RH,JSe,JK,SW	135.00
70 BEv,SD; June, 1960	135.00

BATTLE ACTION
Atlas, Feb., 1952

1	250.00
2	150.00
3 JSt,RH	75.00
4	75.00
5	75.00
6 JeR	75.00
7 JeR	75.00
8 RH	85.00
9	75.00
10	75.00
11 thru 15	@70.00
16 thru 26	@65.00
27	65.00
28 GWb	65.00
29	65.00
30 GWb,Aug., 1957	65.00

BATTLEBOOKS
Nov., 1998

Captain America, BiT(c)	4.00
Citizen V, BiT(c)	4.00
Colossus, BiT(c)	4.00
Elektra, BiT(c)	4.00
Gambit, BiT(c)	4.00
Iron Man, BiT(c)	4.00
Rogue, BiT(c)	4.00
Spider-Girl, BiT(c)	4.00
Spider-Man, BiT(c)	4.00
Storm, BiT(c)	4.00
Thor, BiT(c)	4.00
Wolverine, BiT(c)	4.00

BATTLE BRADY
See: MEN IN ACTION

BATTLEFIELD
Atlas, April, 1952

1 RH, Slaughter on Suicide Ridge	250.00
2 RH	125.00
3 Ambush Patrol	125.00
4	125.00
5 Into the Jaws of Death	125.00
6 thru 10	@75.00
11 GC,May, 1953	75.00

BATTLEFRONT
Atlas, June, 1952

1 JeR,RH(c),Operation Killer	300.00
2 JeR	150.00
3 JeR,Spearhead	125.00
4 JeR,Death Trap of General Chun	125.00

All comics prices listed are for *Near Mint* condition.

Comics Values Annual — MARVEL — Battlefront–Beware

5 JeR,Terror of the Tank Men... 125.00
6 A:Combat Kelly............ 125.00
7 A:Combat Kelly............ 125.00
8 A:Combat Kelly............ 125.00
9 A:Combat Kelly............ 125.00
10 A:Combat Kelly........... 125.00
11 thru 20 .... @100.00
21 thru 39 .... @75.00
40 AW 100.00
41 .... 75.00
42 AW 90.00
43 thru 48 Aug.,1957....... @95.00

BATTLEGROUND
Atlas, Sept., 1954
1 .... 250.00
2 JKz. 125.00
3 thru 8 .... @75.00
9 BK 75.00
10 .... 75.00
11 AW,GC,GT............... 100.00
12 MD,JSe 65.00
13 AW 75.00
14 JD 100.00
15 .... 65.00
16 .... 65.00
17 .... 65.00
18 AS 100.00
19 JMn,JSe 65.00
20 Aug., 1957.............. 65.00

Battlestar Galactica #5
© Marvel Entertainment Group

BATTLESTAR GALACTICA
March, 1979
1 EC,B:TV Adaptation;
 Annihalation 10.00
2 EC,Exodus 8.00
3 EC,Deathtrap 8.00
4 WS,Dogfight 8.00
5 WS,E:TV Adaptation;Ambush .. 8.00
6 Nightmare 7.00
7 Commander Adama Trapped ... 7.00
8 Last Stand 7.00
9 Space Mimic 7.00
10 This Planet Hungers 7.00
11 WS,Starbbuck's Dilemma... 7.00
12 WS,Memory Ends 7.00
13 WS,All Out Attack 7.00
14 Radiation Threat 7.00
15 Ship of Crawling Death .. 7.00
16 .... 7.00

17 Animal on the Loose 7.00
18 Battle For the Forbidden Fruit .. 7.00
19 Starbuck's Back......... 7.00
20 Duel to the Death 7.00
21 To Slay a Monster..To Deatroy
 a World 7.00
22 WS,A Love Story?......... 7.00
23 Dec., 1981.............. 7.00

BATTLETIDE
1990
1 thru 4 F: Death's Head II and
 Killpower............... @2.25

BATTLETIDE II
1993
1 Foil embossed cover 3.25
2 thru 8 F: Death's Head II and
 Killpower............... @2.25

BEAST
March, 1997
1 (of 3) KG,CNn,F:Karma, Cannonball, V:Viper & Spiral..... 3.00
2 KG,CNn,V:Spiral........... 3.00
3 KG,CNn, concl............. 3.00

BEAUTY AND THE BEAST
Jan., 1985
1 DP,Beast & Dazzler,direct..... 3.00
1a DP,Beast & Dazzler,UPC 3.00
2 DP,Beast & Dazzler 3.00
3 DP,Beast & Dazzler 3.00
4 DP,Beast & Dazzler 3.00

BEAVIS & BUTT-HEAD
March, 1994
1 Based on the MTV Show 5.00
1a 2nd Printing 2.50
2 Dead from the Neck up...... 3.50
3 Break out at Burger World ... 3.00
4 Tattoo Parlor.............. 2.50
5 Field Day 2.50
6 Revulsion 2.50
7 Oldies bot................. 2.50
8 Be a clown 2.50
9 Makin' movies............ 2.50
10 Halloween 2.50
11 .... 2.50
12 .... 2.50
13 .... 2.50
14 Join Biker Gang........... 2.50
15 Spring Break 2.50
16 Capture The Flag.......... 2.50
17 with video camera 2.50
18 Woodsuck 2.50
19 break-up?................ 2.50
20 Solar Eclipse 2.50
21 Male Cheerleaders 2.50
22 Antics at theme park 2.50
23 Witless 2.50
24 Holiday suck-tacular 2.50
25 .... 2.50
26 .... 2.50
27 Easter spirit 2.50
28 .... 2.50
TPB Greatest Hits, rep.#1–#4.... 12.95
TPB Holidazed and Confused.... 12.95

BEFORE THE FANTASTIC 4: GRIMM AND LOGAN
May, 2000
1 (of 3) LHa,Wolverine&Thing 3.25
2 LHa,A:Carol Danvers 3.25
3 LHa,concl. 3.25

Before the Fantastic 4, Reed Richards #1 © Marvel Entertainment Group

BEFORE THE FANTASTIC 4: REED RICHARDS
July, 2000
1 (of 3) PDa,DFg,V:Dr.Doom 3.25
2 PDa,DFg.................... 3.25
3 PDa,DFg,concl............... 3.25

BEFORE THE FANTASTIC 4: THE STORMS
Oct., 2000
1 (of 3) TKa,CAd,F:Sue &
 Johnny Storm................ 3.25
2 V:St. Germaine.............. 3.25
3 TKa,CaD,concl............... 3.25

BEST OF MARVEL '96
TPB 224pg. 20.00

BEST WESTERN
June, 1949
58 A:KidColt,BlackRider,Two-Gun
 Kid; Million Dollar Train
 Robbery................. 225.00
59 A:BlackRider,KidColt,Two-Gun
 Kid;The Black Rider Strikes . 200.00
Becomes:

WESTERN OUTLAWS & SHERIFFS
1949
60 PH(c),Hawk Gaither........ 250.00
61 Ph(c),Pepper Lawson....... 200.00
62 Murder at Roaring
 House Bridge 200.00
63 thru 65 .... @200.00
66 Hanging 175.00
67 Cannibalism.............. 200.00
68 thru 72 .... @150.00
73 June, 1952. .... 150.00

BEWARE
March, 1973
1 Reprints 25.00
2 thru 8 .... @20.00
Becomes:

TOMB OF DARKNESS
1974
9 Reprints 30.00

All comics prices listed are for *Near Mint* condition.

Beware–Black — MARVEL — Comics Values Annual

10 thru 22 . . . . @20.00
23 November, 1976 . . . . 25.00

BIKER MICE FROM MARS
1993
1 I:Biker Mice 2.25
2 thru 3 . . . . 2.25

BILL & TED'S BOGUS JOURNEY
Nov., 1991
1 Movie Adaption 3.25

BILL & TED'S EXCELLENT COMICS
Dec., 1991
1 From Movie; Wedding Reception 2.25
2 Death Takes a Vacation 2.25
3 'Daze in the Lives' 2.25
4 Station Plague 2.25
5 Bill & Ted on Trial 2.25
6 Time Trial 2.25
7 Time Trial, Concl. 2.25
8 History Final 2.25
9 I:Morty(new Death) 2.25
10 'Hyperworld' 2.25
11 Lincoln assassination 2.25
12 Last issue 2.25

BILLY BUCKSKIN WESTERN
Atlas, Nov., 1955
1 MD,Tales of the Wild Frontier . 175.00
2 MD,Ambush 100.00
3 MD,AW, Thieves in the Night . 125.00
Becomes:

2-GUN KID
1956
4 SD,A: Apache Kid 125.00
Becomes:

TWO-GUN WESTERN
1956
5 B:Apache Kid,Doc Holiday,
  Kid Colt Outlaw 125.00
6 . . . . 65.00
7 . . . . 65.00
8 RC 75.00
9 AW 100.00
10 . . . . 65.00
11 AW 100.00
12 Sept., 1957,RC 65.00

BISHOP
1994
1 Mountjoy, foil cover 4.00
2 foil stamped cover 4.00
3 JOs 3.50
4 V:Mountjoy 3.50

BISHOP: THE LAST X-MAN
Aug., 1999
1 R:Bishop, 48-page debut 4.00
2A I:Nom,Link,Jinx & Scorch 2.50
2B variant (c) 2.50
3 V:Chronomancer 2.50
4 . . . . 2.50
5 V:The Kith 2.50
6 V:Chronomancer 2.50
7 ATi,A:Hellfire Club 2.50
8 ATi,V:GOL-19 . . . . 2.50
9 ATi,A:Trevor Fitzroy 2.50

Bishop #2
© Marvel Entertainment Group

10 ATi,Morlocks 2.50
11 ATi,A:Trevor Fitzroy 2.50
12 ATi,Chronowar,pt.1 . . . . 2.50
13 ATi,Chronowar,pt.2 . . . . 2.50
14 ATi,Chronowar,pt.3 . . . . 2.50
15 ATi,Maximum Security 2.50
16 NMa,Dream'sEnd,pt.3,x-over . . 2.50

BISHOP: XAVIER'S SECURITY ENFORCER
Nov., 1997
1 (of 3) JOs,SEp 3.00
2 JOs,SEp,hunted by X.S.E. 3.00
3 JOs,SEp,Bishop v. Rook, concl. . 3.00

BIZARRE ADVENTURES
See: MARVEL PREVIEW

BLACK AXE
1993
1 JR2(c),A:Death's Head II 3.00
2 JR2(2),A:Sunfire,V:The Hand . . 3.00
3 A:Death's Head II,V:Mesphisto . 3.00
4 in ancient Egypt 3.00
5 KJ(c),In Wakanda 3.00
6 KJ(c),A:Black Panther 3.00
7 KJ(c),A:Black Panther 3.00
8 thru 13 . . . . @3.00

BLACK CAT
[Limited Series]
1 Wld,A:Spider-Man,V:Cardiac,
  I:Faze 2.25
2 Wld,V:Faze 2.25
3 Wld,Cardiac 2.25
4 Wld,V:Scar 2.25

BLACK DRAGON
Epic, May, 1985
1 JBo 4.00
2 thru 6 JBo . . . . @3.00

BLACK GOLIATH
Feb., 1976—Nov., 1976
1 GT,O:Black Goliath,Cont's
  From Powerman #24 . . . . . . 30.00
2 GT,V:Warhawk 15.00
3 GT,D:Atom-Smasher 15.00

4 KP,V:Stilt-Man 15.00
5 D:Mortag 15.00

BLACK KNIGHT, THE
Atlas, May, 1955—April, 1956
1 JMn,O: Crusader;The Black
  Knight Rides 1,200.00
2 JMn,Siege on Camelot 750.00
3 JMn,Black Knight Unmasked . 550.00
4 JMn,Betrayed 550.00
5 JMn,SSh,The Invincible Tartar. 550.00

BLACK KNIGHT
June, 1990—Sept., 1990
1 TD,R:Original Black Knight 2.00
2 TD,A:Dreadknight 2.00
3 RB,A:Dr.Strange 2.00
4 RB,TD,A:Dr Strange, Valkyrie . . . 2.00

BLACK KNIGHT: EXODUS
1996
1-shot R:Black Knight,A:Sersi,
  O:Exodus 2.50

BLACK PANTHER
[1st Series]
Jan., 1977—May, 1979
1 JK,V:Collectors 30.00
2 JK,V:Six Million Year Man 20.00
3 JK,V:Ogar 20.00
4 JK,V:Collectors 20.00
5 JK,V:Yeti 20.00
6 JK,V:Ronin 20.00
7 JK,V:Mister Little 20.00
8 JK,D:Black Panther 20.00
9 JK,V:Jakarra 20.00
10 JK,V:Jakarra 20.00
11 JK,V:Kilber the Cruel 20.00
12 JK,V:Kilber the Cruel 20.00
13 JK,V:Kilber the Cruel 20.00
14 JK,A:Avengers,V:Klaw 25.00
15 JK,A:Avengers,V:Klaw 25.00

BLACK PANTHER
July, 1988—Oct., 1988
[1st Mini-Series]
1 I:Panther Spirit 2.50
2 V:Supremacists 2.50
3 A:Malaika 2.50
4 V:Panther Spirit 2.50

[2nd Mini-Series]
PANTHER'S PREY
May, 1991
1 DT,A:W'Kabi,V:Solomon Prey . . . 4.95
2 thru 4 DT,V:Solomon Prey . . . . @4.95

BLACK PANTHER
Sept., 1998
1 CPr,MT,A:T'Challa 5.00
2 CPr,MT,A:Mephisto 3.00
2a variant cover 3.00
3 CPr,MT,JQ,I:Achebe 3.00
4 CPr,MT,JQ,V:Mephisto 3.00
5 CPr,V:Mephisto 3.00
6 CPr,JJu,V:Kraven the Hunter . . . 2.50
7 CPr,JJu,V:Kraven, round 2 . . . . 2.50
8 CPr,JJu,A:Avengers 2.50
9 CPr,MM,A:Avengers 2.50
10 CPr,MM,political counter-
   attack 2.50
11 CPR,MBr,Enemy of
   the State,pt.3 . . . . 2.50
12 CPr,MBr,Enemy o/t State,pt.4 . . 2.50
13 CPr,A:T'Challa 2.50

CVA Page 204 — All comics prices listed are for *Near Mint* condition.

MARVEL

Black–Blaze

Black Panther #7
© Marvel Entertainment Group

14 CPr,	2.50
15 CPr,A:Hulk.	2.50
16 CPr,V:Killmonger	2.50
17 CPr,V:Killmonger	2.50
18 CPr,V:Killmonger,A:Nakia.	2.50
19 CPr,F:Queen Divine.	2.50
20 CPr,F:Moon Knight	2.50
21 CPr,F:Moon Knight	2.50
22 CPr,A:T'Challa.	2.50
23 CPr,Cat Trap,pt.2,x-over	2.50
24 CPr,MBr,Malice	2.50
25 CPr,Maximum Security	2.50
26 CPr,A:Storm	2.50
27 CPr,A:Storm,Avengers.	2.50
28 CPr,A:Lord Ghaur,Dr.Doom	2.50
29 CPr,V:Klaw	2.50
30 CPr,NBy,A:Capt.America	2.50
31 CPr,SaV,A:Dakota North	2.50
32 CPr,SaV,V:Malice.	2.50
33 CPr,SaV,V:Malice.	2.50
34 CPr,JCf,A:Man-Ape	2.50
35 CPr,JCf,Gorilla Warfare	2.50
36 CPr,SaV,100-page	3.50
37 CPr,SaV,Once & Future King	2.50
38 CPr,SaV,Return of the Dragon	2.50
39 CPr,SaV,V:Iron Fist,'Nuff Said	2.50
40 CPr,SaV,Return of the Dragon	2.50
41 CPr,SaV,Enemy of the State II	2.50
42 CPr,SaV,Enemy of the State II	2.50
43 CPr,SaV,Enemy of the State II	2.50
44 CPr,SaV,Enemy of the State II	2.50
45 CPr,SaV,Enemy of the State II	2.50
46 CPr,in Texas, in the past	2.50
47 CPr,trapped in the old west	2.50
48 CPr,Death of the Black Panther	2.50
49 CPr,Death of the Black Panther	2.50
50 CPr,NKu(c),T'Challa gone	2.50
51 CPr,DaF,Black & White,pt.1	2.50
52 CPr,Black & White,pt.2.	2.50
53 CPr,Black & White,pt.3.	2.50
54 NKu,Black & White,pt.4	2.50
55 NKu,Black & White,pt.5	2.50
56 NKu,Black & White,pt.6	2.50
57 F:T'Challa,pt.1	3.00
58 F:T'Challa,pt.2	3.00
59 NRd,Ascension,pt.1	3.00
60 NRd,Ascension,pt.2	3.00
61 NRd,Ascension,pt.3	3.00
62 NRd,Ascension,pt.4	3.00
63 NRd,Ascension,pt.5	3.00
TPB The Client, 128-page	14.95
TPB Enemy of the State, 224-pg.	16.95

BLACK RIDER
See: ALL WINNERS COMICS

BLACK RIDER RIDES AGAIN
Atlas, Sept., 1957
1 JK,Treachery at Hangman's Ridge	275.00

BLACKSTONE, THE MAGICIAN
May, 1948—Sept., 1948
2 B:Blonde Phantom	750.00
3	450.00
4 Bondage(c).	500.00

BLACK WIDOW
Apr. 1999
1 (of 3) Black Widow replaced?	5.00
1a variant cover (1:4).	6.00
2 A:Daredevil.	4.00
3 conclusion	4.00
TPB Web of Intrigue, rep. Marvel Fanfare #10–#13	4.00

BLACK WIDOW
Nov., 2000
1 (of 3) SHp,Natasha vs.Yelena	3.00
2 SHp,	3.00
3 SHp,concl.	3.00
TPB rep. 2 series, 144-page	15.95

BLACK WIDOW: PALE LITTLE SPIDER
Marvel Max, April, 2002
1 (of 3) F:Belova	3.25
2	3.25
3 concl.	3.25

BLACKWULF
1994–95
1 AMe,Embossied(c),I:Mammoth,Touchstone,Toxin,D:Pelops,V:Tantalus,	3.00
2 AMe,I:Sparrow,Wildwind	2.25
3 AMe,I:Scratch.	2.25
4 AMe,I:Giant-man.	2.25
5 AMe	2.25
6 AMe,Tantalus	2.25
7 AMe,V:Tantalus.	2.25
8 AMe	2.25
9 Seven Worlds of Tantalus,pt.1 A:Daredevil	2.25
10 Seven Worlds of Tantalus,pt.2, last issue	2.25

BLADE, THE VAMPIRE HUNTER
1994–95
1 Foil(c),Clv(i),R:Dracula	3.50
2 Clv(i),V:Dracula	2.50
3 Clv(i)	2.50
4 Clv(i)	2.50
5 Clv(i)	2.50
6 Clv(i)	2.50
7 Clv(i)	2.50
8 Bible John, Morbius	2.50
9	2.50
10 R:Dracula	2.50
11 Dracula Untombed,pt.2	2.50

BLADE
Sept., 1998
1 (of 6) DMG,40-page, photo(c)	3.50
1a variant cover (1:4).	3.50
2 DMG,A:Morbius,Dominique.	3.00
2a variant cover.	3.00
3 DMG,	3.00
4 DMG,F:Morbius	3.00
1-shot Blade: Crescent City Blues, MPe,V:Deacon Frost (1998)	3.50
1-shot DMG, movie tie-in (1998).	3.00
1-shot movie adaptation,48 pg	6.00
TPB Duel with Dracula (2002).	17.95

Blade, The Vampire Hunter #6
© Marvel Entertainment Group

BLADE: VAMPIRE HUNTER
Oct., 1999
1 (of 6) BS, 48-pg.	4.00
2 BS	3.00
3 BS,V:Reaper	3.00
4 BS,V:Hrolf	3.00
5 BS,V:Reaper	3.00
6 BS,V:Reaper, concl.	3.00

BLADE
Marvel Max, March, 2002
1 StP,V:Tryks.	3.25
2 StP,F:Tryks,Seven	3.25
3 StP,date with Susan	3.25
4 StP,Fofo's missing fingers	3.25
5 StP,V:Rowks.	3.25
6 horror hits home	3.25
GN Bloodhunt, movie adapt.	5.95

BLADE RUNNER
Oct., 1982
1 AW, Movie Adaption	4.00
2 AW,	4.00

BLAZE
[Limited Series], 1993–94
1 HMe(s),RoW,A:Clara Menninger.	2.50
2 HMe(s),RoW,I:Initiate	2.50
3 HMe(s),RoW,	2.50
4 HMe(s),RoW,D:Initiate	2.50

[Regular Series], Aug., 1994
1 HMz,LHa,foil (c)	3.50
2 HMz,LHa,I:Man-Thing.	2.50

All comics prices listed are for Near Mint condition.

Blaze–Cable

Blaze #7
© Marvel Entertainment Group

3 HMz,LHa,V:Ice Box Bob 2.50
4 HMz,LHa,Apache Autumn,pt.1 . . 2.50
5 HMz,LHa,Apache Autumn,pt.2 . . 2.50
6 Apache Autumn,pt.3 . . . . 2.50
7 Carnivale Quintano 2.50
8 A:Arcae 2.50
9 Clara's Eyeballs 2.50
10 Undead M.C. 2.50
11 A:Punisher 2.50
12 reunited with children 2.50

BLAZE CARSON
Sept., 1948
1 SSh(c),Fight,Lawman
  or Crawl 300.00
2 Guns Roar on Boot Hill 200.00
3 A:Tex Morgan 200.00
4 A:Two-Gun Kid 200.00
5 A:Tex Taylor 200.00
Becomes:

REX HART
1949
6 CCB,Ph(c),B:Rex Hart,
  A:Black Rider 300.00
7 Ph(c),Mystery at Bar-2 Ranch 200.00
8 Ph(c),The Hombre Who
  Killed His Friends 200.00
Becomes:

WHIP WILSON
1950
9 Ph(c),B:Whip Wilson,O:Bullet;
  Duel to the Death 700.00
10 Ph(c),Wanted for Murder 400.00
11 Ph(c) 400.00
Becomes:

GUNHAWK, THE
1950
12 The Redskin's Revenge 200.00
13 GT,The Man Who Murdered
  Gunhawk 150.00
14 . . . . 125.00
15 . . . . 125.00
16 EC 125.00
17 . . . . 125.00
18 JMn,Dec., 1951 . . . . 125.00

BLAZE OF GLORY
Dec., 1999
1 (of 4) JOs,F:John Woo 3.00

2 JOs, ... 3.00
3 JOs, ... 3.00
4 JOs,concl. 3.00
TPB westerns, 96-pg. (2002) 11.50

BLAZE, THE WONDER COLLIE
Oct., 1949
2 Ph(c),Blaze-Son of Fury 250.00
3 Ph(c), Lonely Boy;Feb.,1950. . 250.00

BLINK
Dec., 2000
1 (of 4) SLo,AKu(c) 3.25
2 SLo,Age of Apocalypse story . . . 3.25
3 SLo,AKu(c),in love 3.25
4 SLo,AKu(c),V:Blastaar 3.25

BLONDE PHANTOM
See: ALL-SELECT COMICS

BLOOD
Feb., 1988—April, 1988
1 . . . . 6.00
2 thru 4 . . . . @5.00

BLOOD & GLORY
1993
1 KJ Cap & the Punisher 6.00
2 KJ Cap & the Punisher 6.00
3 KJ Cap & the Punisher 6.00

BLOODLINES
Epic, 1992
1 F:Kathy Grant-Peace Corps 6.00

BLOODSEED
1993
1 LSh,I:Bloodseed 2.25
2 LSh,V:Female Bloodseed 2.25

BLOODSTONE
Oct., 2001
1 DAn,ALa,SHa,F:Elsa Bloodstone 3.25
2 DAn,ALa,SHa,F:Dracula 3.25
3 DAn,ALa,SHa,Living Mummy . . . 3.25
4 DAn,ALa,SHa, concl. 3.25

BOOK OF THE DEAD
1993–94
1 thru 4 Horror rep . . . . @4.00
5 . . . . @4.00

BORN
Marvel June 2003
1 (of 4) GEn(s),O:Punisher 3.50
2 GEn(s),Capt. Frank Castle 3.50
3 GEn(s),attacked 3.50
4 GEn(s),concl. 3.50

BOZZ CHRONICLES, THE
Epic, Dec., 1985
1 thru 5 . . . . @3.00
6 May, 1986 . . . . 3.00

BRATS BIZARRE
Epic, Heavy Hitters 1994
1 with trading card 3.25
2 thru 4 with trading card . . . . . . @2.75

BREAK THE CHAIN
1 KB,KRS-One,w/audio tape 7.00

BROTHERHOOD, THE
May, 2001
1 BSz(c),F:Magneto. 2.75
2A BSz(c), ... 2.50
2B variant cover 2.50
3 BSz(c) 2.50
4 JP,BWS(c) 2.50
5 JP,GF(c) 2.50
6 JP,GF(c) message to daddy 2.50
7 SeP,KW, X speaks out 2.50
8 SeP,KW, ... 2.50
9 SeP,KW, final issue. 2.50

BRUTE FORCE
Aug., 1990
1 JD/JSt 2.50
2 . . . . 2.50
3 . . . . 2.50
4 November, 1990 . . . . 2.50

B-SIDES
Sept., 2002
1 SK, super-team from New Jersey 3.00
2 SK, F:Fantastic Four. 3.00
3 SK, F:Fantastic Four. 3.00

BUCK DUCK
Atlas, June, 1953
1 (fa)stories 100.00
2 and 3 . . . . @50.00
4 Dec., 1953 . . . . 50.00

BUCKAROO BANZAI
Dec., 1984
1 Movie Adaption 3.00
2 Conclusion, Feb., 1985. . . . . 2.50

BUG
1997
1-shot 48pg 3.25

BULLWINKLE & ROCKY
Star, Nov., 1987
1 EC&AM,Based on 1960's TV
  Series 4.00
2 EC&AM, ... 3.00
3 EC&AM,Rumpled Mudluck
  Thyme Mag 3.00
4 EC&AM,Boris and Natasha. 3.00
5 EC&AM, ... 3.00
6 EC&AM,Wassamatta Me 3.00
7 EC&AM,Politics,Moose V:Boris . . 3.00
8 EC&AM,Superhero, March,1989 . 3.00
9 EC 3.00
TPB, Bullwinkle & Rocky Collection
  AM,early stories 4.95

CABLE
[Limited Series], 1992
1 JR2,DGr,V:Mutant Liberation
  Front,A:Weapon X 4.00
2 JR2,DGr,V:Stryfe,O:Weapon X . . 3.00
[Regular Series], 1993
1 B:FaN(s),ATi,O:Cable,V:New
  Canaanites,A:Stryfe,foil(c) 5.00
2 ATi,V:Stryfe. 4.00
3 ATi,A:Six Pack 4.00
4 ATi,A:Six Pack 4.00
5 DaR,V:Sinsear 4.00
6 DT,A:Tyler,Zero,Askani,

CVA Page 206 All comics prices listed are for *Near Mint* condition.

Comics Values Annual — MARVEL — Cable–Cage

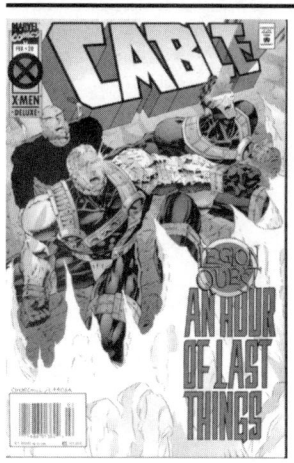

Cable #20
© Marvel Entertainment Group

Mr.Sinister,C:X-Men 4.00
7 V:Tyler,A:Askani,X-Men,Domino . 4.00
8 O:Cable,V:Tyler,A:X-Men,Cable is
   Nathan Summers 4.00
9 MCW,B:Killing Field,A:Excalibur,
   V:Omega Red 4.00
10 MCW,A:Acolytes,Omega Red . . 4.00
11 MCW,E:Killing Field,D:Katu 4.00
12 SLo(s),B:Fear & Loathing,
   V:Senyaka 4.00
13 V:D'Spayre 4.00
14 V:S'yM. 4.00
15 A:Thorn 4.00
16 Foil(c),Dbl-size,A:Jean,Scott
   Logan,V:Phalanx 9.00
16a Newsstand ed. 3.00
17 Deluxe ed. 3.00
17a Newsstand ed. 2.25
18 Deluxe ed. 3.00
18a Newsstand ed. 2.25
19 Deluxe ed. 3.00
19a Newsstand ed. 3.00
20 V:Legion, Deluxe ed. w/card . . . 5.00
20a Newsstand ed. 2.25
21 Cable makes tough decisions,
   A:Domino. 3.00
22 V:Fortress 3.00
23 IaC,A:Domino 3.00
24 F:Blaquesmith 3.00
25 IaC,SHa,F:Cable's Wife,foil(c) . . 5.00
26 Tries to return to X-Mansion . . . 3.00
27 IaC, A:Domino 3.00
28 IaC,SHa,concl. war in Genosha . 3.00
29 . . . . 3.00
30 . . . . 3.00
31 IaC, cont.X-Men/Cable war 3.00
32 Onslaught saga 3.50
33 Onslaught saga 3.00
34 Onslaught saga 3.00
35 Onslaught saga 3.00
36 . . . . 3.00
37 JLb,IaC,SHa,V:Askani'son,Kane 3.00
38 JLb,IaC,SHa,V:PSycho-Man,
   A:Kane. 3.00
39 JLb,IaC,SHa,V:Psycho-Man. . . . 3.00
40 TDz,IaC,SHa,A:Renee Majcomb 3.00
41 TDz,SHa,F:Bishop 3.00
42 TDz,RGr,SHa,ïThe Prophecy
   of the Twelveî. 3.00
43 TDz,RGr,Images of Nathan's
   past 3.00
44 TDz,RGr,SHa,A:Madelyne Pryor
   (Cable's mom) 3.00

45 JeR,RGr,Zero Tolerance,
   îNo Escape,îpt.2. . . . . 3.00
46 JeR,RGr,SHa,Zero Tolerance,
   îNo Escape,î pt.2 (of 3) 3.00
47 JeR,RGr,SHa, Operation Zero
   Tolerance, V:Batsion. 3.00
48 JeR,SHa,V:Hellfire Club. 3.00
49 JeR,SHa,V:Hellfire Club. 3.00
50 JeR,SHa,A:Cyclops, Phoenix,
   Union Jack, 48pg 4.00
51 JeR,Hellfire Hunt 2.50
52 JeR,Hellfire Hunt, pt.5 . . . . 2.50
53 JoC,Hellfire Hunt, concl. 2.50
54 JoC,A:Black Panther,V:Klaw . . . 2.50
55 JoC,A:Irene Merryweather,
   Domino 2.50
56 JoC,V:Stilt-Man & Hydro-Man . . 2.50
57 JoC,Cable powers altered by
   EMP wave 2.50
58 JoC,Persecution, pt.1. . . . . 2.50
59 JoC,I:Agent 18,V:Zzaxx 2.50
60 JoC,Nemesis Contract,pt.2 . . . . 2.50
61 JoC,Nemesis Contract,pt.3 . . . . 2.50
62 JoC,Nemesis Contract,pt.4 . . . . 2.50
63 JoC,Blood Brothers,pt.2,x-over . 2.50
64 JoC,O:Cable 2.50
65 JoC,Millennium countdown . . . 2.50
66 JoC,Sign of the End Times,pt.1 . 2.50
67 JoC,Sign of the End Times,pt.2 . 2.50
68 JoC,Sign of the End Times,pt.3 . 2.50
69 JoC,A:Blaquesmith,Archangel . . 2.50
70 JoC,A:Archangel 2.50
71 RLd,abandons his destiny,
   with RLd poster 2.50
72 RLd,reunited with X-force. 2.50
73 RLd,reunited 2.50
74 V:Caliban. 2.50
75 RLd,Apocalypse 3.50
76 Apocalypse The 12:pt.6 . . . . . . 3.00
77 Ages of Apocalypse,pt.2. . . . . . . 3.00
78 mutant no more 3.00
79 X-Men: Revolution 3.00
79a variant (c) 3.50
80 Apocalypse gone 2.50
81 The Undying 2.50
82 Nathan Summers, murderer?. . . 2.50
83 R:Domino 2.50
84 Phoenix & Beast 2.50
85 Mother Askani, Gaunt 2.50
86 Gaunt 2.50
87 Dream'sEnd,pt.2,x-over 2.50
88 F:Nightcrawler 2.50
89 in Washington DC 2.50
90 Dark Sisterhood. 2.50
91 Dark Sisterhood. 2.50
92 Cable quits X-Men? 2.50
93 V:Dark Sisterhood 2.50
94 V:Dark Sisterhood 2.50
95 V:Dark Sisterhood,concl. 2.50
96 Old Man Coll 2.50
97 Path of Most Resistance 2.50
98 Shining Path 2.50
99 V:Shining Path. 2.50
100 V: Techno-OrganicVirus,64-pg. . 4.50
101 Macedonian Plot 3.00
102 Albanians' deadly plan 2.50
103 shot in the head. 2.50
104 on the wrong side? 2.50
105 in Rio. 2.50
106 In Kazakhstan 2.50
107 final issue 2.50
Ann. '98 AOI(c) F:Cable vs. Machine
   Man, O:Bastion 3.00
Ann.1999 48-page 3.50
Minus 1 Spec., TDz,JeR, flashback. 2.00
GN Cable/Wolverine Guts 'N' Glory. 6.00
Cable: Second Genesis 4.00
TPB Cable,rep.New Mutants
   #87-94 . . . . 15.95
TPB The Shining Path, 144-pg. . . 15.95
TPB Vol.2 The End (2002) 15.00

CABLE & DEADPOOL
Marvel Nov. 2003
1 . . . . 2.50

CABLE & X-FORCE
1995–97
Cable & X-Force '95 Spec. 4.00
Cable & X-Force '96 Spec.48pg. . . 3.50
Cable & X-Force '97 Spec.#1
   JFM,CJ,V:Malekith,48pg. 3.50

CADILLACS & DINOSAURS
Epic, Nov., 1990
1 Rep.Xenozoic Tales 5.00
2 thru 6 Rep.Xenozoic Tales. . . . @3.00

CAGE
1992–93
1 DT,R:Luke Cage,I:Hardcore, ... 3.00
2 DT,V:Hammer. 2.50
3 DT,A:Punisher,V:Untouchables . . 2.50
4 DT,A:Punisher,V:Untouchables . . 2.50
5 DT,I:New Power Man 2.50
6 DT,V:New Power Man. 2.50
7 DT,A:Avengers West Coast. 2.50
8 DT,V:Steele,Wonder Man 2.50
9 V:Rhino,A:Hulk 2.50
10 DT,V:Hulk,Rhino 2.50
11 DT,V:Rapidfire 2.50
12 A:Iron Fist,double size 2.50
13 V:The Thinker 2.50
14 PCu,I:Coldfire 2.50
15 DT,For Love Nor Money#2,
   A:Silver Sable,Terror. 2.50
16 DT,For Love Nor Money#5,
   A:Silver Sable,Terror. 2.50
17 DT,Infinty Crusade 2.50
18 A:Dred,V:Creed 2.50
19 A:Dakota North 2.50
20 Last issue 2.50

CAGE
Marvel Max, Feb., 2002
1 (of 5) RCo,Justice isn't cheap . . . 3.25
2 RCo,teen-age girl murdered 3.25
3 RCo, ... 3.25
4 RCo,secret shame 3.25
5 RCo,Hammerhead 3.25

Cage #5
© Marvel Entertainment Group

All comics prices listed are for *Near Mint* condition.   CVA Page 207

Cage–Captain America   MARVEL   Comics Values Annual

TPB RCo 20.00
TPB 13.00

CALL, THE
Marvel April 2003
1 PO, everyday heroes 2.25
2 PO 2.25
3 PO 2.25
4 PO 2.25
TPB Vol. 1, series rep. 9.00

CALL OF DUTY, THE: THE BROTHER HOOD
June, 2002
1 (of 6) ATi,F:FDNY,48-pg. 4.00
2 ATi,F:FDNY 2.50
3 ATi, ... 2.50
4 ATi 2.50
5 ATi 2.50
6 ATi, concl. 2.50
The Call of Duty, Must Have ed. . . 3.00
TPB Vol. I. 15.00
TPB Vol. II: Precinct & Wagon . . 15.00

THE CALL OF DUTY: THE PRECINCT
July, 2002
1 (of 5) TMd,F:NYPD 3.00
2 TMd 2.50
3 TMd 2.50
4 TMd 2.50
5 TMd, concl. 2.50

THE CALL OF DUTY: THE WAGON
Marvel Aug., 2002
1 (of 4) F:NYC EMS 2.50
2 . . . . 2.50
3 . . . . 2.50
4 concl. 2.50

CAMP CANDY
May, 1990
1 thru 6, Oct., 1990 . . . . @4.00

CAPTAIN AMERICA COMICS
Timely/Atlas, May, 1941
1 S&K,Hitler(c),I&O:Capt.America & Bucky,A:Red Skull,B:Hurricane, Tuk the Caveboy 120,000.00
2 S&K,RC,AAv,Hitler(c), I:Circular Shield;Trapped in the Nazi Stronghold . . 19,000.00
3 S&K,RC,AAv,Stan Lee's 1st Text, A:Red Skull,Bondage(c) . 15,000.00
4 S&K,AAv,Horror Hospital . . 10,000.00
5 S&K,AAv,Ringmaster's Wheel of Death 9,000.00
6 S&K,AAv,O:Father Time, E:Tuk 8,000.00
7 S&K,A: Red Skull 9,000.00
8 S&K, The Tomb 6,000.00
9 S&K,RC,V:Black Talon 6,000.00
10 S&K,RC,Chamber of Horrors 6,000.00
11 AAv,E:Hurricane;Feuding Mountaneers 5,000.00
12 AAv,B:Imp,E:Father Time; Pygmie's Terror 4,700.00
13 AAv,O:Secret Stamp;All Out For America 5,000.00
14 AAv,V:Japs;Pearl Harbor Symbol cover. 5,000.00

Captain America #3
© Marvel Entertainment Group

15 AAv,Den of Doom 5,000.00
16 AAv,A:R.Skull;CapA Unmasked 6,000.00
17 AAv,I:Fighting Fool; Graveyard 4,000.00
18 AAv,V:Japanese 4,000.00
19 AAv,V:Ghouls, B:Human Torch 3,500.00
20 AAv,A:Sub-Mariner,V:Nazis . 3,500.00
21 SSh(c),Bucky Captured . . . 3,000.00
22 SSh(c),V:Japanese 3,000.00
23 SSh(c),V:Nazis 3,000.00
24 SSh(c),V:Black Dragon Society 3,000.00
25 SSh(c),V:Japs;Drug Story . . 3,000.00
26 SSh(c),V:Nazi Fleet 2,800.00
27 SSh(c)CapA&Russians V:Nazis, E:Secret Stamp . . 2,800.00
28 ASh(c),NaziTortureChamber 2,800.00
29 ASh(c),V:Nazis;French Underground 2,800.00
30 SSh(c),Bucky Captured . . . 2,800.00
31 ASh(c),Bondage(c) 2,500.00
32 SSh(c),V: Japanese Airforce 2,500.00
33 ASh(c),V:Nazis;BrennerPass 2,500.00
34 SSh(c),Bondage(c) 2,500.00
35 ASh(c),CapA in Japan 2,500.00
36 SSh(c),V:Nazis;Hitler(c) 3,800.00
37 ASh(c),CapA in Berlin, A:Red Skull 3,000.00
38 ASh(c),V:Japs;Bondage(c) . 2,200.00
39 ASh(c),V:Japs;Boulder Dam 2,200.00
40 SSh(c),V:Japs;Ammo Depot 2,200.00
41 ASh(c),FinalJapaneseWar(c) 2,100.00
42 ASh(c),V:Bank Robbers . . . 2,100.00
43 ASh(c),V:Gangsters 2,100.00
44 ASh(c),V:Gangsters 2,100.00
45 ASh(c),V:Bank Robbers . . . 2,100.00
46 ASh(c),Holocaust(c) 2,800.00
47 ASh(c),Final Nazi War(c) . . . 2,100.00
48 ASh(c),V:Robbers 1,800.00
49 ASh(c),V:Sabatuers 1,800.00
50 ASh(c),V:Gorilla Gang 1,800.00
51 ASh(c),V:Gangsters 1,800.00
52 ASh(c),V:AtomBombThieves 1,800.00
53 ASh(c),V:Burglars 1,800.00
54 ASh(c),TV Studio, V:Gangsters 1,800.00
55 V:Counterfeiters 1,800.00
56 SSh(c),V:Art Theives 1,800.00
57 Symbolic CapA(c) 1,800.00
58 ASh(c),V:Bank Robbers . . . 1,800.00
59 SSh(c)O:CapA Retold;Private Life of Captain America . . . 4,000.00

60 V:The Human Fly 1,800.00
61 SSh(c),V:Red Skull; Bondage(c) 4,000.00
62 SSh(c),Kingdom of Terror . . 2,200.00
63 SSh(c),I&O:Asbestos Lady; The Parrot Strikes 2,300.00
64 Diamonds Spell Doom 2,400.00
65 When Friends Turn Foes . . . 2,400.00
66 O:Golden Girl;Bucky Shot . . 2,500.00
67 E:Toro(in Human Torch); Golden Girl Team-Up 2,400.00
68 A:Golden Girl;Riddle of the Living Dolls 2,400.00
69 Weird Tales of the Wee Males, A:Sun Girl 2,400.00
70 A:Golden Girl,Sub-Mariner, Namora;Worlds at War 2,400.00
71 A:Golden Girl; Trapped 2,400.00
72 Murder in the Mind 2,400.00
73 The Outcast of Time 2,400.00
74 A:Red Skull;Capt.America's Weird Tales 7,500.00
75 Thing in the Chest 2,400.00
76 JR(c),Capt.America,Commie Smasher 2,400.00
77 Capt.A,Commie Smasher . . 1,300.00
78 JR(c),V:Communists; Sept.,1954 . . . . 1,300.00
Marvel Milestone rep. #1 (1995) . . . 3.95

CAPTAIN AMERICA
Prev: Tales of Suspense
April, 1968
100 JK,A:Avengers 600.00
101 JK,I:4th Sleeper 150.00
102 JK,V:Red Skull,4th Sleeper . . 80.00
103 JK,V:Red Skull 80.00
104 JK,DA,JSo,V:Red Skull 80.00
105 JK,DA,A:Batroc 70.00
106 JK,Cap.Goes Wild 70.00
107 JK,Red Skull 70.00
108 JK,Trapster 70.00
109 JK,O:Captain America 100.00
110 JSo,JSt,A:Hulk,Rick Jones in Bucky Costume 100.00
111 JSo,JSt,I:Man Killer 100.00
112 JK,GT,Album 50.00
113 JSo,TP,Avengers, D:Madame Hydra 100.00
114 JR,SB,C:Avengers 40.00
115 JB,SB,A:Red Skull 40.00
116 GC,JSt,A:Avengers 40.00
117 JR(c),GC,JSt,I:Falcon 100.00
118 JR(c),GC,JSt,A:Falcon 30.00
119 GC,JSt,O:Falcon 30.00
120 GC,JSt,A:Falcon 30.00
121 GC,JSt,V:Man Brute 22.00
122 GC,JSt,Scorpion 20.00
123 GC,JSt,A:NickFury, V:Suprema 20.00
124 GC,JSt,I:Cyborg 20.00
125 GC,Mandarin 20.00
126 JK&BEv(c),GC,A:Falcon 20.00
127 GC,WW,A:Nick Fury 20.00
128 GC,V:Satan's Angels 20.00
129 GC,Red Skull 20.00
130 GC,I:Batroc 20.00
131 GC,V:Hood 20.00
132 GC,A:Bucky Barnes 20.00
133 GC,O:Modok,B:Capt.America/ Falcon Partnership 20.00
134 GC,V:Stone Face 20.00
135 JR(c),GC,TP,A:Nick Fury 20.00
136 GC,BEv,V:Tyrannus 20.00
137 GC,BEv,A:Spider-Man 25.00
138 JR,A:Spider-Man 22.00
139 JR,Falcon solo 20.00
140 JR,O:Grey Gargoyle 20.00
141 JR,JSt,V:Grey Gargoyle 18.00
142 JR,JSt,Nick Fury 18.00

CVA Page 208   All comics prices listed are for *Near Mint* condition.

MARVEL — Captain America

Captain America #141
© Marvel Entertainment Group

Captain America #228
© Marvel Entertainment Group

#	Description	Price
143	JR,Red Skull	20.00
144	GM,JR,N:Falcon,V:Hydra	18.00
145	GK,JR,V:Hydra	18.00
146	JR(c),SB,V:Hydra	15.00
147	GK(c),SB,V:Hydra	15.00
148	SB,JR,Red Skull	15.00
149	GK(c),SB,JM,V:Batroc	15.00
150	K&R(c),SB,V:The Stranger	15.00
151	SB,V:Mr.Hyde	15.00
152	SB,V:Scorpion,Mr.Hyde	15.00
153	SB,JM,V:50's Cap	15.00
154	SB,V:50's Cap	15.00
155	SB,FMc,O:50's Cap	15.00
156	SB,FMc,V:50's Cap	15.00
157	SB,I:The Viper	15.00
158	SB,V:The Viper	15.00
159	SB,V:PlantMan,Porcupine	15.00
160	SB,FMc,V:Solarr	15.00
161	SB,V:Dr.Faustus	15.00
162	JSn(c),SB,V:Dr.Faustus	15.00
163	SB,I:Serpent Squad	15.00
164	JR(c),I:Nightshade	15.00
165	SB,FMc,V:Yellow Claw	15.00
166	SB,FMc,V:Yellow Claw	15.00
167	SB,V:Yellow Claw	15.00
168	SB,I&O:Phoenix (2nd Baron Zemo)	15.00
169	SB,FMc,C:Black Panther	15.00
170	K&R(c),SB,C:Black Panther	15.00
171	JR(c),SB,A:Black Panther	15.00
172	GK(c),SB,C:X-Men	20.00
173	GK(c),SB,A:X-Men	22.00
174	GK(c),SB,A:X-Men	22.00
175	SB,A:X-Men	22.00
176	JR(c),SB,O:Capt.America	15.00
177	JR(c),SB,A:Lucifer,Beast	12.00
178	SB,A:Lucifer	12.00
179	SB,A:Hawkeye	12.00
180	GK(c),SB,I:1st Nomad(Cap)	22.00
181	GK(c),SB,I&O:New Cap	18.00
182	FR,Madam Hydra	10.00
183	GK(c),FR,R:Cap,D:New Cap	12.00
184	K&R(c),HT,A:Red Skull	10.00
185	GK(c),SB,FR,V:Red Skull	10.00
186	GK(c),FR,O:Falcon	12.00
187	K&R(c),FR,V:Druid	10.00
188	GK(c),SB,V:Druid	10.00
189	GK(c),FR,V:Nightshade	10.00
190	GK(c),FR,A:Nightshade	10.00
191	FR,A:Stilt Man,N.Fury	10.00
192	JR(c),FR,A:Dr.Faustus	10.00
193	JR(c),JK,`Mad Bomb'	22.00
194	JK,I:Gen.Heshin	25.00
195	JK,1984	25.00
196	JK,Madbomb	25.00
197	JK,Madbomb	25.00
198	JK,Madbomb	25.00
199	JK,Madbomb	25.00
200	JK,Madbomb	22.00
201	JK,Epilogue	15.00
202	JK,Night People	15.00
203	JK,Night People	15.00
204	JK,I:Argon	15.00
205	JK,V:Argon	15.00
206	JK,I:Swine	15.00
207	JK,V:Swine	15.00
208	JK,I:Arnim Zola,D:Swine	15.00
209	JK,O:Arnim Zola,I:Primus	15.00
210	JK,A:Red Skull	15.00
211	JK,A:Red Skull	15.00
212	JK,A:Red Skull	15.00
213	JK,I:Night Flyer	15.00
214	JK,D:Night Flyer	15.00
215	GT,Redwing	10.00
216	Reprint,JK	10.00
217	JB, I:Quasar(Marvel Boy) I:Vamp	10.00
218	SB,A:Iron Man	6.00
219	SB,JSt,V:TheCorporation	6.00
220	SB,D:L.Dekker	6.00
221	SB,Ameridroid	6.00
222	SB,I:Animus(Vamp)	6.00
223	SB,Animus	6.00
224	MZ,V:Animus	6.00
225	SB,A:Nick Fury	6.00
226	SB,A:Nick Fury	6.00
227	SB,A:Nick Fury	6.00
228	SB,Constrictor	6.00
229	SB,R:SuperAgents of Shield	6.00
230	SB,A:Hulk	8.00
231	SB,DP,A:Grand Director	6.00
232	SB,DP,V:Grand Director	6.00
233	SB,DP,D:Sharon Carter	6.00
234	SB,DP,A:Daredevil	6.00
235	SB,FM,A:Daredevil	8.00
236	SB,V:Dr.Faustus	6.00
237	SB,`From the Ashes'	6.00
238	SB,V:Hawk Riders	6.00
239	JBy(c),SB,V:Hawk Riders	6.00
240	SB,V:A Guy Named Joe	6.00
241	A:Punisher	16.00
242	JSt,A:Avengers	6.00
243	GP(c),RB,V:Adonis	6.00
244	TS,`A Monster Berserk'	6.00
245	CI,JRn,Nazi Hunter	6.00
246	GP(c),JBi,V:Joe	6.00
247	JBy,V:BaronStrucker	8.00
248	JBy,JRu,Dragon Man	8.00
249	JBy,O:Machinesmith, A:Air-Walker	8.00
250	JBy,Cap for Pres	8.00
251	JBy,V:Mr.Hyde	8.00
252	JBy,V:Batrok	8.00
253	JBy,V:Baron Blood	8.00
254	JBy,D:B.Blood,UnionJack,I:3rd Union Jack	8.00
255	JBy,40th Anniv.,O:Cap	8.00
256	GC,V:Demon Druid	3.50
257	A:Hulk	3.50
258	MZ,V:Blockbuster	3.50
259	MZ,V:Dr. Octopus	3.50
260	AM,In Jail	3.50
261	MZ,A:Nomad	4.00
262	MZ,V:Ameridroid	3.50
263	MZ,V:Red Skull	3.50
264	MZ,X-Men	4.00
265	MZ,A:Spider-Man,N.Fury	3.50
266	MZ,A:Spider-Man	3.50
267	MZ,V:Everyman	3.00
268	MZ,A:Defenders(x-over from Def.#106)	3.00
269	MZ,A:Team America	3.00
270	MZ,V:Tess-One	3.00
271	MZ,V:Mr.X	3.00
272	MZ,I:Vermin	3.50
273	MZ,A:Nick Fury	3.00
274	MZ,D:SamSawyer	3.00
275	MZ,V:Neo-Nazis	3.00
276	MZ,V:Baron Zemo	3.00
277	MZ,V:Baron Zemo	3.00
278	MZ,V:Baron Zemo	3.00
279	MZ,V:Primus	3.00
280	MZ,V:Scarecrow	3.00
281	MZ,A:Spider Woman, R:'50's Bucky	3.00
282	MZ,I:2nd Nomad	6.00
282a	(second printing)	2.50
283	MZ,A:Viper	4.00
284	SB,Nomad	3.00
285	MZ,V:Porcupine	3.00
286	MZ,V:Deathlok	5.00
287	MZ,V:Deathlok	5.00
288	MZ,V:Deathlok,D:Hellinger	5.00
289	MZ,A:Red Skull	3.00
290	JBy(c),RF,A:Falcon	3.00
291	JBy(c),HT,V:Tumbler	3.00
292	I&O:Black Crow	3.00
293	V:Mother Superior	3.00
294	R:Nomad	3.00
295	V:Sisters of Sin	3.00
296	V:Baron Zemo	3.00
297	O:Red Skull	3.00
298	V:Red Skull	3.00
299	V:Red Skull	3.00
300	D:Red Skull	4.00
301	PNe,A:Avengers	3.00
302	PNe,I:Machete,V:Batroc	3.00
303	PNe,V:Batroc	3.00
304	PNe,V:Stane Armor	3.00
305	PNe,A:Capt.Britain,V:Modred	3.00
306	PNe,A:Capt.Britain,V:Modred	3.00
307	PNe,I:Madcap	3.00
308	PNe,I:Armadillo,Secret WarsII	3.00
309	PNe,V:Madcap	3.00
310	PNe,V:Serpent Society,I:Cotton Mouth,Diamondback	3.00
311	PNe,V:Awesome Android	3.00
312	PNe,I:Flag Smasher	3.00
313	PNe,D:Modok	3.00
314	PNe,V:Nighthawk	3.00
315	PNe,V:Serpent Society	3.00
316	PNe,A:Hawkeye	3.00
317	PNe,I:Death-Throws	3.00
318	PNe,V&D:Blue Streak	3.00
319	PNe,V:Scourge,D:Vamp	3.00
320	PNe,V:Scourge	3.00

All comics prices listed are for *Near Mint* condition.

Captain America

#	Description	Price
321	PNe,V:Flagsmasher, I:Ultimatum	3.00
322	PNe,V:Flagsmasher	3.00
323	PNe,I:Super Patriot (US Agent)	5.00
324	PNe,V:Whirlwind,Trapster	3.00
325	I:Slug,A:Nomad	3.00
326	V:Dr.Faustus	3.00
327	MZ(c)V:SuperPatriot	4.00
328	MZ(c),I:Demolition Man	3.00
329	MZ(c),A:Demolition Man	3.00
330	A:Night Shift,Shroud	3.00
331	A:Night Shift,Shroud	3.00
332	BMc,Rogers resigns	7.00
333	B:John Walker Becomes 6th Captain America	5.00
334	I:4th Bucky	5.00
335	V:Watchdogs	4.00
336	A:Falcon	3.00
337	TMo,I:The Captain	3.00
338	KD,AM,V:Professor Power	3.00
339	KD,TD,Fall of Mutants, V:Famine	3.00
340	KD,AM,A:Iron Man	3.00
341	KD,AM,I:Battlestar,A:Viper	3.00
342	KD,AM,A:D-Man,Falcon, Nomad,Viper	3.00
343	KD,AM,D-Man,Falcon, Nomad	3.00
344	KD,AM,A:D-Man,Nomad	3.50
345	KD,AM,V:Watchdogs	4.00
346	KD,AM,V:Resistants	4.00
347	KD,AM,V:RWinger&LWinger	4.00
348	KD,AM,V:Flag Smasher	4.00
349	KD,AM,V:Flag Smasher	4.00
350	KD,AM,doub-size,Rogers Ret, as Captain Am,V:Red Skull, E:6th Cap	5.00
351	KD,AM,A:Nick Fury	3.00
352	KD,AM,I:Supreme Soviets	3.00
353	KD,AM,V:Supreme Soviets	3.00
354	KD,AM,I:USAgent, V:Machinesmith	3.50
355	RB,AM,A:Falcon,Battlestar	3.00
356	AM,V:Sisters of Sin	3.00
357	KD,AM,V:Sisters of Sin Baron Zemo,Batroc	3.00
358	KD,B:Blood Stone Hunt	3.00
359	KD,V:Zemo,C:Crossbones	3.00
360	KD,I:Crossbones	3.00
361	KD,V:Zemo,Batroc	3.00
362	KD,V:Zemo,Crossbones	3.00
363	KD,E:Blood Stone Hunt, V:Crossbones,C:Wolverine	3.00
364	KD,V:Crossbones	3.00
365	KD,Acts of Vengeance, V:SubMariner,Red Skull	3.00
366	1st RLm Capt.Amer.,Acts of Vengeance,V:Controller	3.00
367	KD,Acts of Vengeance, Magneto Vs. Red Skull	3.00
368	RLm,V:Machinesmith	3.00
369	RLm,I:Skeleton Crew	3.00
370	RLm,V:Skeleton Crew	3.00
371	RLm,V:Trump,Poundcakes	3.00
372	RLm,B:Streets of Poison, Cap on Drugs,C:Bullseye	3.00
373	RLm,V:Bullseye,A:Bl.Widow	3.00
374	RLm,V:Bullseye,A:Daredevil	3.00
375	RLm,V:Daredevil	3.00
376	RLm,A:Daredevil	3.00
377	RLm,V:Crossbones,Bullseye	3.00
378	RLm,E:Streets of Poison,Red Skull vs Kingpin,V:Crossbones	3.00
379	RLm(c),V:Serpent Society	3.00
380	RLm,V:Serpent Society	3.00
381	RLm,V:Serpent Society	3.00
382	RLm,V:Serpent Society	3.00
383	RLm(c),RLm,50th Anniv. 64Pages	5.00
384	RLm,A:Jack Frost	2.50
385	RLm,A:USAgent	2.50
386	RLm,Cap./USAgent T.U.	2.50
387	B:Superia Strategem	2.50
388	A:Paladin	2.50
389	Superia Strategem #3	2.50
390	Superia Strategem #4	2.50
391	Superia Strategem #5	2.50
392	E:Superia Strategem	2.50
393	V:Captain Germany	2.50
394	A:Red Skull,Diamondback	2.50
395	A:Red Skull,Crossbones	2.50
396	I:2nd Jack O'Lantern	2.50
397	V:Red Skull,X-Bones,Viper	2.50
398	Operation:Galactic Storm Pt.1,V:Warstar	2.50
399	Operation Galactic Storm Pt.8,V:Kree Empire	2.50
400	Operation Galactic Storm Pt.15,BU:rep.Avengers #4	4.00
401	R:D-Man,A:Avengers	2.50
402	RLe,B:Man & Wolf, A:Wolverine	2.50
403	RLe,A:Wolverine	2.50
404	RLe,A:Wolverine	2.50
405	RLe,A:Wolverine	2.50
406	RLe,A:Wolverine	2.50
407	RLe,A:Wolverine,Cable	2.50
408	RLe,E:Man & Wolf	2.50
409	RLe,V:Skeleton Crew	2.50
410	RLe,V:Crossbones,Skel.Crew	2.50
411	RLe,V:Snapdragon	2.50
412	RLe,V:Batroc,A:Shang-Chi	2.50
413	A:Shang-Chi,V:Superia	2.50
414	RLe,V:Ka-Zar,Black Panther	2.50
415	Rle,A:Black Panther,Ka-Zar	2.50
416	RLe,Savage Land Mutates, A:Black.Panther,Ka-Zar	2.50
417	RLe,A:Black Panther,Ka-Zar, V:AIM	2.50
418	RLe,V:Night People	2.50
419	RLe,V:Viper	2.50
420	RLe,I:2nd Blazing Skull, A:Nightshift	3.00
421	RLe,V:Nomad	2.50
422	RLe,I:Blistik	2.50
423	RTs(s),MCW,V:Namor	2.50
424	MGv(s),A:Sidewinder	2.50
425	B:MGu(s),DHv,Embossed(c), I:2nd SuperPatriot,DeadRinger	4.00
426	DHv,A:Super Patriot,Dead Ringer,V:Resistants	2.50
427	DHv,V:Super Patriot,Dead Ringer	2.50
428	DHv,I:Americop	2.50
429	DHv,V:Kono	2.50
430	Daemon Dran, Americop	2.50
431	DHv,I:Free Spirit	2.50
432	DHv,Fighting Chance	2.50
433	DHv,Baron Zemo	2.50
434	DHv,A:Fighting Spirit, V:King Cobra	2.50
435	DHv,Fighting Chance	2.50
436	V:King Cobra, Mister Hyde, Fighting Chance conclusion	2.50
437	Cap in a Coma	2.50
438	I:New Body Armor	2.50
439	Dawn's Early Light,pt.2	2.50
440	Taking A.I.M.,pt.1	2.50
441	Taking A.I.M.,pt.3	2.50
442	Batroc, Cap,V:Zeitgeist	2.50
443	MGu,24 hours to live	2.50
444	MWa,RG,President Kidnapped	6.00
445	MWa,RG,R:Captain America	4.00
446	MWa,RG,Operation Rebirth,pt.2	3.50
447	MWa,RG,Op.Rebirth,pt.3	3.50
448	MWa,RG,Operation Rebirth,pt.4,double size	6.00
449	MWa,RG,A:Thor	2.50
450	MWa,RG,Man Without a Country, pt,1	2.50
450a	alternate cover	4.00
451	MWa,RG,DRo,Man Without A Country,pt.2,new costume	2.50
452	MWa,RG,Man Without a Country, pt.3	2.50
453	MWa,RG Man Without a Country, concl.,old costume	2.50
454	MWa,RG,A:Avengers	2.50
Ann.#1	rep	50.00
Ann.#2	rep	35.00
Ann.#3	JK	25.00
Ann.#4	JK,V:Magneto,I:Mutant Force	25.00
Ann.#5	'Deathwatcher'	6.00
Ann.#6	A:Contemplator	6.00
Ann.#7	O:Shaper of Worlds	6.00
Ann.#8	MZ,A:Wolverine	35.00
Ann.#9	MBa,SD,Terminus Factor #1,N:Nomad	4.50
Ann.#10	MM,Baron Strucker,pt.3 (see Punisher Ann.#4)	4.00
Ann.#11	Citizen Kang#1	4.00
Ann.#12	I:Bantam,w/card	4.00
Ann.#13	RTs(s),MCW, Drug Wars PDd(s),SaV,A:New Warriors	3.00
G-Size#1	GK(c),rep.O:Cap.Amer.	7.00
Medusa Effect RTs(s),MCW,RB, V:Master Man	3.50
Movie Adapt		3.00
Spec.#1 Rep.Cap.A #110,#111		2.00
Spec.#2 Rep.Cap.A.#113 & Strange Tales #169		2.00
TPB Bloodstone Hunt,rep. #357-364		15.95
TPB Captain America: Man Without a Country, MWa,RG,SK, rep. (1998)		15.00
TPB Streets of Poison, rep. #372–#377		12.95
TPB War and Remembrance, rep. #247–#255		12.95
Collector's Preview		1.95
Ashcan		.75

[2nd Series], Nov., 1996

#	Description	Price
1	RLd,CDi,JSb, Heroes Reborn, I:Nick Fury,48pg.	7.00
1A	Stars and stripes background variant cover	7.50
1b	gold signature edition, cardstock cover	18.00
1c	San Diego Con edition	25.00
2	RLd,JLb,JSb,Falcon & Red Skull	3.00

Captain America #403
© Marvel Entertainment Group

Captain America, 2nd Series #2
© Marvel Entertainment Group

3 RLd,JLb,JSb,A:Hulk,V:Red Skull
  & Master Man. 3.00
4 RLd,JLb,JSb,F:Prince Namor,. . . 3.00
5 RLd,JLb,JSb,V:Crossbones 3.00
6 RLd,JLb,JSb,iIndustrial
  Revolution,î epilogue,A:Cable. . 3.00
7 RLd,JLb,DaF, ... 3.00
8 JLb,RLd,SPa,A:Nick Fury,
  WWII story 3.00
9 JLb,RLd,SPa,WWII story. 3.00
10 JLb,RLd,SPa,WWII story, concl.. 3.00
11 JeR,JoB,Odyssey across
   America, pt.4, concl.. . . . . 3.00
12 JeR,JoB,Heroes Reborn, Galactus
   concl.. . . . . 4.00
13 JeR,RLm,Wildstorm x-over 3.00
Ashcan, ComicCon. 5.00

[3rd Series], Nov., 1997
1 MWa,RG,BWi,A:Lady Deathstrike,
  Red Skull, Sharon Carter, 48pg 4.00
1a variant cover. 10.00
2 MWa,RG,BWi,A devastating loss 5.00
2a variant cover. 4.00
3 MWa,RG,BWi,V:Hydra 3.00
4 MWa,RG,BWi,F:Batroc 3.00
5 MWa,RG,BWi,V:Hordes of Hydra 3.00
6 MWa,RG,V:Skrulls 3.00
7 MWa,NKu,Power & Glory concl. . 3.00
8 MWa,Nku,Live Kree or Die, pt.2
  x-over. 3.50
9 MWa,NKu,American Nightmare,
  pt.1 . . . . 3.00
10 MWa,NKu,American Nightmare,
   pt.2 . . . . 3.00
11 MWa,NKu,American
   Nightmare, pt.3. . . . . 3.00
12 MWa,NKu,American Night-
   mare, pt.4, 48-page 4.00
13 MWa,MFm,R:Red Skull 2.50
14 MWa,MFm,R:Red Skull 2.50
15 MWa,NKu,V:Red Skull 2.50
16 MWa,NKu,V:Red Skull 2.50
17 MWa,NKu,V:Red Skull 2.50
18 MWa,LW,RbC,V:Cosmic Cube
   double-size. 3.50
19 MWa,NKu,V:2 foes 2.50
20 MWa,NKu,Shield secrets 2.50
21 MWa,NKu,A:Black Panther . . . 2.50
22 MWa,NKu,A:Black Panther 2.50
23 MWa,Capt.America convict? . . 2.50
24 TDF,RF,V:Hydra 2.50
25 DJu,NKu,DGr,Twisted
   Tomorrows,pt.1. . . . . 4.00
26 DJu,NKu,DGr,Twisted,pt.2 . . . . 2.50
27 DJu,NKu,DGr,Twisted,pt.3 . . . . 2.50
28 DJu,NKu,DGr,V:CountNefaria . . 2.50
29 DJu,DGr,A:Ka-Zar 2.50
30 DJu,DGr,NKu,Savage Land . . . 2.50
31 DJu,NKu,DGr,F:Sharon Carter. . 2.50
32 DJu,JO,kidnapped 2.50
33 DJu,ATi,Protocide 2.50
34 DJu,ATi,Cache. 2.50
35 DJu,ATi,Protocide 2.50
36 DJu,ATi,Maximum Security . . . 2.50
37 DJu,ATi,V:Protocide 2.50
38 DJu,ATi,Capt.Am. unleashed . . 2.50
39 DJu,V:A.I.M. 2.50
40 DJu,V:A.I.M. 2.50
41 DJu,Batroc the Leaper. 2.50
42 DJu,BL,V:Crimson Dynamo . . . 2.50
43 DJu,DR,BL,A:David Ferrari 2.50
44 DJu,BL,A:Taskmaster 2.50
45 DJu,BL,America Lost,pt.1 . . . . . 2.50
46 DJu,BL,America Lost,pt.2 . . . . . 2.50
47 DJu,BL,America Lost,pt.3 . . . . . 2.50
48 DJu,BL,America Lost,pt.4 . . . . . 2.50
49 DJu,BL,F:Sam Wilson 2.50
50 96-page, last issue 6.50
Ann.1998 Captain America/
  Citizen V,KBk,KK, 48-page 4.00
Ann. 1999 JoC,V:Flag Smasher,
  48-page 4.00
Ann.2000 DJu,DGr,48-pg.. . . . . . . 4.00
Ann.2001 DJu,48-page 3.50
Spec.#1 Captain America (2000) . . 2.50
Spec.Cap: A Universe X Special. . . 4.00
GN Captain America/Nick Fury:
  The Otherworld War (2001) . . . 6.95
TPB The Classic Years,Vol.2 . . . 24.95
TPB To Serve and Protect 17.95

CAPTAIN AMERICA
April, 2002
1 JNR(s), terrorism, 48-pg. 4.00
2 JNR(s), terrorism,pt.2 . . . . 3.50
3 JNR(s), terrorism,pt.3 . . . . 3.50
4 JNR(s), terrorism,pt.4 . . . . 3.50
5 JNR(s), terrorism,pt.5 . . . . 3.50
6 JNR(s), terrorism,concl. 3.50
7 JNR(s) 3.50
8 JNR(s),Extremists,pt.2 . . . . 3.50
9 JNR(s),Extremists,pt.3 . . . . 3.50
10 JNR(s),Extremists,pt.4 . . . . . . 3.50
11 JNR(s),Extremists,pt.5 . . . . . . 3.50
12 JNR(s),JaL,Ice,pt.1 . . . . 3.50
13 JNR(s),JaL,Ice,pt.2 . . . . 3.50
14 JNR(s),JaL,Ice,pt.3 . . . . 3.50
15 JNR(s),JaL,Ice,pt.4 . . . . 3.50
16 JNR(s),JaL,Ice,pt.5 . . . . 3.50
17 LW,Cap.Am Lives Again,pt.1 . . 3.50
18 LW,Cap.Am Lives Again,pt.2 . . 3.50
19 LW,Cap.Am Lives Again,pt.3 . . 3.50
20 LW,Cap.Am Lives Again,pt.4 . . 3.50
TPB The New Deal. 17.00
TPB Vol. 2: Extremists 14.00
TPB Vol. 3: Ice 13.00

CAPTAIN AMERICA:
DEAD MAN RUNNING
Jan., 2002
1 (of 3) distress call 3.25
2 . . . . 3.25
3 concl. 3.25

CAPTAIN AMERICA:
SENTINEL OF LIBERTY
July, 1998
1 MWa,RG,new foe, in future. . . . 2.50
1 signed by MWa & RG 5.00
2A MWa,RG(c&a) F:Invaders,
  V:Nazis 2.25
2B variant JSm(c) 2.25
3 MWa,RG,DGr,A:Sub-Mariner . . . 2.25
4 MWa,RG,DGr,A:Human Torch. . . 2.25
5 MWa,RG,MFm,Tales of
  Suspense pt.1 . . . . 2.25
6 MWa,RG,MFm,Tales of
  Suspense pt.2 . . . . 3.50
7 RSt,RF,civil war tale concl. 2.25
8 MWa,R:Falcon 2.25
9 MWa,A:Falcon 2.25
10 psychedelic look back 2.25
11 MWa,A:Human Torch 2.25
12 MWa,DGr,F:Bucky,48-page . . . 3.50
Spec.RoughCut #1,MWa,RG,48-pg. 3.00

CAPTAIN AMERICA:
WHAT PRICE GLORY
Marvel March 2003
1 (of 4) SR 3.25
2 SR 3.25
3 SR 3.25
4 SR 3.25

CAPTAIN BRITAIN
Jan., 2002
TPB 208-pg.. . . . . 19.95

CAPTAIN BRITAIN
CLASSICS
1 AD rep.. . . . . 2.50

CAPTAIN CONFEDERACY
Epic, Nov., 1991
1 I:Capt.Confederacy,Kid Dixie . . . 2.25
2 Meeting of Superhero Reps 2.25
3 Framed for Murder 2.25
4 Superhero conference,final iss.. . 2.25

CAPTAIN JUSTICE
March, 1988
1 Based on TV Series 2.25
2 April, 1988 . . . . 2.25

CAPTAIN MARVEL
May, 1968
1 GC,O:retold,V:Sentry#459.. . . 165.00

Captain Marvel #22
© Marvel Entertainment Group

All comics prices listed are for *Near Mint* condition.

2 GC,V:Super Skrull 65.00
3 GC,V:Super Skrull 40.00
4 GC,Sub-Mariner 40.00
5 DH,I:Metazoid 40.00
6 DH,I:Solam 25.00
7 JR(c),DH,V:Quasimodo 25.00
8 DH,I:Cuberex 25.00
9 DH,D:Cuberex 25.00
10 DH,V:Number 1 . . . . 25.00
11 BWS(c),I:Z0 . . . . 25.00
12 K&R(c),I:Man-Slayer 20.00
13 FS,V:Man-Slayer 20.00
14 FS,Iron Man 20.00
15 TS,DA,Z0 . . . . 15.00
16 DH,Ronan 15.00
17 GK,DA,O:R.Jones ret,N:Capt.
    Marvel 20.00
18 GK,JB,DA,I:Mandroid 15.00
19 GK,DA,Master.of.MM 15.00
20 GK,DA,I:Rat Pack 15.00
21 GK,DA,Hulk 15.00
22 GK(c),WB,V:Megaton 15.00
23 GK(c),WB,FMc,V:Megaton 15.00
24 GK(c),WB,ECh,I:L.Mynde 15.00
25 1st JSn,Cap.Marvel,Cosmic
    Cube Saga Begins 30.00
26 JSn,DC,Thanos(2ndApp.)
    A:Thing 35.00
27 JSn,V:Thanos,A:Mentor,
    Starfox, I:Death 25.00
28 JSn,DGr,Thanos Vs.Drax,
    A:Avengers 25.00
29 JSn,AM,O:Zeus,C:Thanos
    I:Eon,O:Mentor 18.00
30 JSn,AM,Controller,C:Thanos . . 18.00
31 JSn,AM,Avengers,
    Thanos,Drax,Mentor 18.00
32 JSn,AM,DGr,O:Drax,
    Moondragon,A:Thanos 18.00
33 JSn,KJ,E:Cosmic Cube Saga
    1st D:Thanos 25.00
34 JSn,JA,V:Nitro(leads to
    his Death) 18.00
35 GK(c),AA,Ant Man 8.00
36 AM,Watcher,Rep.CM#1 . . . . . . 8.00
37 AM,KJ,Nimrod 8.00
38 AM,KJ,Watcher 8.00
39 AM,KJ,Watcher 8.00
40 AM,AMc,Watcher 8.00
41 AM,BWr,CR,BMc,TA,Kree 9.00
42 AM,V:Stranger,C:Drax 7.00
43 AM,V:Drax 7.00
44 GK(c),AM,V:Drax 10.00
45 AM,I:Rambu 10.00
46 AM,TA,D:Fawn 7.00
47 AM,TA,A:Human Torch 7.00
48 AM,TA,I:Chetah 7.00
49 AM,V:Ronan,A:Cheetah 7.00
50 AM,TA,Avengers,
    V:Super Adaptiod 8.00
51 AM,TA,V:Mercurio,4-D Man . . 10.00
52 AM,TA,V:Phae-dor 10.00
53 AM,TA,A:Inhumans 7.00
54 PB,V:Nitro 7.00
55 PB,V:Death-grip 7.00
56 PB,V:Death-grip 7.00
57 PB,V:Thor,A;Thanos 10.00
58 PB,Drax/Titan 7.00
59 PB,Drax/Titan,I:Stellarax 7.00
60 PB,Drax/Titan 7.00
61 PB,V:Chaos 7.00
62 PB,V:Stellarax 7.00
G-Size #1 reprints 8.00

CAPTAIN MARVEL
1989
1 MBr,I:Powerkeg,V:Moonstone . . . 3.00
1 DyM(s),MBr,V:Skinhead(1993) . . 2.50
PF Death of Captain Marvel 7.95
TPB Life of Captain Marvel,JSn . . 14.95

CAPTAIN MARVEL
1995
1 FaN,R:Captain Marvel(son of) . . . 4.00
2 FaN,V:X-Treme,Erik the Red . . . 3.00
3 FaN,V:X-treme 3.00
4 thru 6 FaN . . . . @3.00

CAPTAIN MARVEL
Jan., 2000
1A PDd,Ccs,A:Rick Jones 5.00
1B variant JOy (c) 5.50
2 PDd,Ccs 7.00
3 PDd,Ccs,V:Wendigo 3.00
4 PDd,Ccs,A:Moondragon 3.00
5 PDd,Ccs,V:Drax 3.00
6 PDd,Ccs,V:Marlo 3.00
7 PDd,Ccs,A:Comet Man 3.00
8 PDd,Ccs,V:Super-Skrull 3.00
9 PDd,Ccs,V:Hyssta 3.00
10 PDd,Ccs,V:Genis 3.00
11 PDd,JSn 3.00
12 PDd,Ccs,Maximum Security . . . 3.00
13 PDd,Ccs,V:kids of Yon-Rogg . . 3.00
14 PDd,Ccs,F:Psycho-Man 3.00
15 PDd,Ccs,F:Psycho-Man 3.00
16 PDd,Ccs,F:Psycho-Man 3.00
17 PDd,JSn,AM,V:Thanos 3.00
18 PDd,JSn,AM,A:Thor,Thanos . . 3.00
19 PDd,Ccs,A:Thor,Thanos 3.00
20 PDd,Ccs, ... 3.00
21 PDd,Ccs, ... 3.00
22 PDd,Ccs,Supreme Intelligence . 3.00
23 PDd,Ccs, ... 3.00
24 PDd,Ccs,Negative Zone 3.00
25 PDd,Ccs,V:Quasar, ... 3.00
26 PDd,F:Rick Jones,'Nuff Said . . 3.00
27 PDd,CCs,Time Flies,pt.1 . . . . . 3.00
28 PDd,Time Flies,pt.2 . . . . 3.00
29 PDd,Time Flies,pt.3 . . . . 3.00
30 PDd,Time Flies, pt.4 . . . . 3.00
31 PDd,Ccs,F:Marlo,V:Mephisto . . 3.00
32 PDd,Ccs,F:Moondragon 3.00
33 PDd,Ccs,V:Magus 3.50
34 PDd,Ccs,V:Magus,Rick Jones . . 3.00
35 PDd, last issue 3.00
TPB The Life and Death of
    Captain Marvel, 304-pg. 24.95
TPB First Contact (2002) 16.95

CAPTAIN MARVEL
Sept., 2002
1 PDd,Ccs, U-Decide 3.00
1b Variant JJu(c) 2.25
1c Variant AxR(c) 2.25
2 PDd,Ccs,F:Punisher 2.25
3 PDd,Ccs,AxR 2.25
3a Director's Cut, AxR, 40-pg . . . 3.50
4 PDd,CCs 2.25
5 PDd,CCs 2.25
6 PDd,CCs 2.25
7 PDd,A:Thor,pt.1 . . . . 2.25
8 PDd,A:Thor,pt.2 . . . . 3.00
9 PDd,Coven,pt.1 . . . . 3.00
10 PDd,Coven,pt.2 . . . . 3.00
11 PDd,Coven,pt.3 . . . . 3.00
12 PDd,Coven,pt.4 . . . . 3.00
13 PDd,Pop,V:Badoon 3.00
14 PDd,accidents do happen 3.00
15 PDd,NA(c),V:Kree 3.00
16 . . . . 3.00
TPB Vol. 1: Nothing to Lose 13.00
TPB Vol. 2: Coven 15.00

CAPTAIN PLANET
Oct., 1991
1 I&O:Captain Planet 5.00
2 thru 12 . . . . @3.00

CAPT. SAVAGE & HIS LEATHERNECK RAIDERS
Jan., 1968
1 SSh(c),C:Sgt Fury;The Last
    Bansai 60.00
2 SSh(c),O:Hydra;Return of Baron
    Strucker 25.00
3 SSh,Two Against Hydra 25.00
4 SSh,V:Hydra;The Fateful Finale 25.00
5 SSh,The Invincible Enemy 25.00
6 Mission;Save a Howler 25.00
7 SSh,Objective:Ben Grimm 28.00
8 Mission:Foul Ball 25.00
Becomes:

CAPT. SAVAGE & HIS BATTLEFIELD RAIDERS
1968
9 . . . . 25.00
10 To the Last Man 25.00
11 A:Sergeant Fury 25.00
12 V:The Japanese 25.00
13 The Junk Heap Juggernauts . . 25.00
14 Savage's First Mission 25.00
15 Within the Temple Waits Death 22.00
16 V:The Axis Powers 22.00
17 V:The Axis Powers 22.00
18 V:The Axis Powers 22.00
19 March, 1970 . . . . 22.00

CARE BEARS
Star, Nov., 1985
1 thru 14 . . . . @3.00
Marvel 1988
15 thru 20 . . . . @3.00

CARNAGE
1-shot Carnage: Its a Wonderful
    Life (1996) 3.00
1-shot Carnage: Mindbomb
    foil cover (1996) 3.50

CARTOON KIDS
Atlas, 1957
1 JMn,A:Dexter the Demon, Little
    Zelda,Willie,Wise Guy 100.00

Captain Marvel Giant-Size #1
© Marvel Entertainment Group

MARVEL

CAR WARRIORS
Epic, 1990
1 Based on Roll Playing Game ... 2.50
2 Big Race Preparations 2.50
3 Ft.Delorean-Lansing Race begin. 2.50
4 Race End, Final issue. 2.50

CASEY–CRIME PHOTOGRAPHER
Aug., 1949
1 Ph(c),Girl on the Docks. 250.00
2 Ph(c),Staats Cotsworth. 175.00
3 Ph(c),He Walked With Danger 175.00
4 Ph(c),Lend Me Your Life 175.00
Becomes:

TWO GUN WESTERN
[1st Series], 1950
5 JB,B,I&O:Apache Kid 275.00
6 JMn,The Outcast 200.00
7 Human Sacrifice 200.00
8 JR,DW,A:Kid Colt,Texas Kid,
  Doc Holiday 200.00
9 JMn,GM,A:Kid Colt,Marshall
  `Frosty' Bennet Texas Kid .. 200.00
10. .... 200.00
11 thru 14 JMn,June, 1952 ... @150.00

CASPER
1996
1 From Animated TV show 2.25
2 visit to Harvey Castle 2.25
3 and 4 .... @2.25

Cat #1
© Marvel Entertainment Group

CAT, THE
Nov., 1972—June, 1975
1 JM,I&O:The Cat 40.00
2 JM,V:The Owl 20.00
3 BEv,V:Kraken 20.00
4 JSn,V:Man-Bull 25.00

CENTURY: DISTANT SONS
1996
1-shot DAn,48pg. 3.25

CHAMBER OF CHILLS
Nov., 1972
1 SSh,A Dragon Stalks By
  Night,(H.Ellison Adapt.). 40.00
2 FB,BEv,SD,Monster From the
  Mound,(RE Howard Adapt.) .. 20.00
3 FB,BEv,SD, Thing on the Roof . 20.00
4 FB,BEv,SD, Opener of the
  Crypt,(J.Jakes,E.A.Poe Adapt) 20.00
5 FB,BEv,SD, Devils Dowry 20.00
6 FB,BEv,SD, Mud Monster 20.00
7 thru 24 FB,BEv,SD .... @20.00
25 FB,BEv,SD Nov., 1976. ...... 20.00

CHAMBER OF DARKNESS
Oct., 1969
1 JB, Tales of Maddening Magic . 75.00
2 NA(script),Enter the Red Death. 50.00
3 JK,BWS,JB, Something Lurks
  on Shadow Mountain 40.00
4 JK Monster Man Came Walking,
  BU:BWS. 65.00
5 JCr,JK,SD, And Fear Shall
  Follow, plus Lovecraft adapt. . 25.00
6 SD 25.00
7 SD,JK,BWr, Night of the
  Gargoyle 20.00
8 BWr(c),DA,BEv, Beast that Walks
  Like a Man Special, 5 Tales of
  Maddening Magic, Jan., 1972. 65.00
Becomes:

MONSTERS ON THE PROWL
1971
9 SAD,BWS,Monster Stories
  Inc,Gorgilla. 40.00
10 JK,Roc 20.00
11 JK,A Titan Walks the Land 20.00
12 HT,JK,Gomdulla The Living
  Pharoah 20.00
13 HT,JK,Tragg. 25.00
14 JK,SD,Return of the Titan 25.00
15 FrG,JK,The Thing Called It ... 20.00
16 JSe,SD,JK, Serpent God of
  Lost Swamp,A:King Kull 20.00
17 JK,SD,Coming of Colossus ... 20.00
18 JK,SD,Bruttu 20.00
19 JK,SD,Creature From the
  Black Bog. 20.00
20 JK,SD,Oog Lives Again 20.00
21 JK,SD,A Martian Stalks
  the City 20.00
22 JK,SD,Monster Runs Amok ... 15.00
23 JK,The Return of Grogg. 15.00
24 JK,SD, Magnetor 15.00
25 JK,Colossus Lives Again 15.00
26 JK,SD,The Two Headed Thing . 15.00
27 JK,Sserpo 15.00
28 JK,The Coming of Monsteroso . 15.00
29 JK,SD Monster at my Window . 15.00
30 JK,Diablo Demon from the 5th
  Dimension, Oct., 1974 ...... 15.00

CHAMPIONS
Oct., 1975
1 GK(c),DH,I&O:Champions 35.00
2 DH,O:Champions 15.00
3 GT,Assault on Olympus 13.00
4 GT,`Murder at Malibu' 12.00
5 DH,I:Rampage 12.00
6 JK(c),GT,V:Rampage 12.00
7 GT,O:Black Widow,I:Darkstar .. 12.00
8 BH,O:Black Widow 12.00
9 BH,BL,V:Crimson Dynamo ... 12.00
10 BH,BL,V:Crimson Dynamo. ... 12.00
11 JBy,A:Black Goliath,Hawkeye. . 13.00
12 JBy,BL,V:Stranger 13.00
13 JBy,BL,V:Kamo Tharn 13.00
14 JBy,I:Swarm 13.00
15 JBy,V:Swarm 13.00
16 BH,A:Magneto,Dr.Doom,
  Beast. 12.00
17 GT,JBy,V:Sentinels,last issue .. 13.00

CHILDREN OF THE VOYAGE
Frontier 1993
1 F:Sam Wantling 3.25
2 Counterfeit Man 2.25
3 V:Voyager. 2.25
4 Last Issue. 2.25

Chili #8
© Marvel Entertainment Group

CHILI
May, 1969
1 Millie's Rival 90.00
2 .... 50.00
3 .... 50.00
4 .... 50.00
5 .... 50.00
6 thru 15 .... @30.00
16 thru 20 .... @22.00
21 thru 25 .... @20.00
26 Dec., 1973 .... 20.00
Spec.#1, 1971 .... 45.00

CHUCK NORRIS
Star, Jan.–Sept., 1987
1 SD 4.00
2 thru 5 .... @5.00

CINDY COMICS
See: KRAZY COMICS

CITIZEN V
April, 2001
1 (of 3) FaN,F:V-Battalion 3.25
2 FaN, ... 3.25
3 FaN,F:Iron Cross 3.25

CITIZEN V & THE V BATTALION: THE EVERLASTING
Feb., 2002
1 (of 4) FaN, ... 3.25
2 FaN,Marduk 3.25

MARVEL

Citizen–Comet

Clandestine #1
© Marvel Entertainment Group

3 FaN, ... 3.25
4 FaN, concl. 3.25

CLANDESTINE
Oct., 1994–Sept., 1995

Preview issue, Intro (1994) 2.00
1 MFm,AD,foil(c) 3.25
2 Wraparound (c),A:Silver Surfer . . 2.75
3 I:Argent,Kimera,A:SilverSurfer . . 2.75
4 R:Adam 2.75
5 MFm,AD,O:Adam Destine. 2.75
6 A:Spider-Man 2.75
7 A:Spider-Man 2.75
8 A:Dr.Strange 2.75
9 Training Time 2.75
10 A:Britanic................. 2.75
11 V:Modan 2.75
12 Aftermath 2.75
13 Who Will Lead 2.75
14 Vincent Vs. Adam 2.75
TPB AD,MFm (1997) 12.00

CLASSIC CONAN
See: CONAN SAGA

CLASSIC X-MEN
See: X-MEN

CLIVE BARKER'S BOOK OF THE DAMNED
Epic, Nov., 1991

1 JBo,Hellraiser companion 5.00
2 MPa,Hellraiser Companion 5.00

CLIVE BARKER'S HELLRAISER
Epic, 1989–93

1 BWr,DSp 7.00
2 .... 6.00
3 .... 6.50
4 .... 4.50
5 .... 4.50
6 .... 7.00
7 The Devil's Brigade #1 .... 7.00
8 The Devil's Brigade #2&3 . . . . . 7.00
9 The Devil's Brigade #4&5 . . . . . 7.00
10 The Devil's Brigade #6&7
   foil Cover 5.00
11 The Devil's Brigade #8&9 . . . . . 4.50
12 The Devil's Brigade #10-12 . . 4.50
13 MMi,RH,Devil's Brigade #13 . . . 4.50
14 The Devil's Brigade #14. . . . . . . 5.00
15 The Devil's Brigade #15. . . . . . . 5.00
16 E:Devil's Brigade 5.00
17 BHa,DR,The Harrowing 10.00
18 O:Harrowers 5.00
19 A:Harrowers............... 5.00
20 NGa(s),DMc,Last Laugh 9.00
Dark Holiday Spec.#1 (1992) 5.00
Spring Slaughter Spec.#1 (1994) . . 7.00
Summer Spec.#1 (1992 .... 6.00

CLOAK & DAGGER
(Limited Series) Oct., 1983

1 RL,TA,I:Det.O'Reilly,
   Father Delgado 3.00
2 RL,TA,V:Duane Hellman....... 3.00
3 RL,TA,V:Street Gang 3.00
4 RL,TA,O:Cloak & Dagger,...... 3.00

CLOAK & DAGGER
[1st Regular Series], July, 1985

1 RL,Pornography 3.00
2 RL,Dagger's mother 2.50
3 RL,A:Spider-Man 2.50
4 RL,Secret Wars II 2.50
5 RL,I:Mayhem 2.50
6 RL,A:Mayhem. 2.50
7 RL,A:Mayhem. 2.50
8 TA, Drugs 2.50
9 AAd,TA,A:Mayhem 2.75
10 BBI,TA,V:Dr. Doom 2.50
11 BBI,TA,Last Issue 2.50

[Mutant Misadventures of] CLOAK & DAGGER
[2nd Regular Series] Oct., 1988

1 CR(i),A:X-Factor 3.00
2 CR(i),C:X-Factor,V:Gromitz. 2.50
3 SW(i),JLe(c),A:Gromitz....... 2.50
4 TA(i),Inferno,R:Mayhem 2.50
5 TA(i),R:Mayhem 2.50
6 TA(i),A:Mayhem 2.50
7 A:Crimson Daffodil,V:Ecstacy . . 2.50
8 Acts of Vengeance prelude 2.50
9 Acts of Vengeance 2.50
10 Acts of Vengeance,iX-Forceî
    name used,Dr.Doom......... 2.50
11 .... 2.50
12 A:Dr.Doom................ 2.50
13 A:Dr.Doom................ 2.50
14 & 15 RL.................. @2.50
16 RL,A:Spider-Man 2.50
17 A:Spider-Man, ... 2.50
18 Inf.Gauntlet X-over,
   A:Spider-Man, Ghost Rider. . . . 2.50
19 O:Cloak & Dagger,final issue . . . 2.50
GNv Predator and Prey 14.95

A CLUELESS VALENTINE
1 characters from movie, 48pg. . . . 2.50

CODENAME: GENETIX
1993

1 PGa,A:Wolverine 3.00
2 PGa,V:Prime EvilA:Wolverine . . . 3.00
3 .... 3.00
4 A:Wolverine,Ka-Zar........... 3.00

CODE OF HONOR
1996

1 (of 4) CDi,TnS,I:Jeff Piper,
   fully painted 5.95
2 thru 4 CDi, ... @5.95

CODE NAME: SPITFIRE
See: SPITFIRE AND THE TROUBLESHOOTERS

COLOSSUS
Aug., 1997

1-shot BRa,Colossus & Meggan
   V:Arcade, 48pg 3.50

COLOSSUS: GOD'S COUNTRY
PF V:Cold Warriors............. 7.00

COMBAT
Atlas, June, 1952

1 JMn,War Stories, Bare
   Bayonets 250.00
2 RH, Break Thru,(Dedicated to
   US Infantry) 125.00
3 JMn(c) 100.00
4 BK 120.00
5 thru 10 .... @100.00
11 April, 1953 .... 120.00

COMBAT CASEY
See: WAR COMBAT

COMBAT KELLY AND THE DEADLY DOZEN
Atlas, Nov., 1951

1 RH,Korean war stories 300.00
2 Big Push.................. 150.00
3 The Volunteer.............. 100.00
4 JMn,V:Communists.......... 100.00
5 JMn, OW,V:Communists 100.00
6 V:Communists 100.00
7 JMn,V:Communists.......... 100.00
8 JMn,Death to the Reds....... 100.00
9 .... 100.00
10 JMn(c)................... 100.00
11 .... 75.00
12 thru 16.................. @75.00
17 A:Combat Casey 100.00
18 A:Battle Brady 65.00
19 V:Communists 65.00
20 V:Communists 65.00
21 Transvestite Cover. 75.00
22 thru 40 .... @50.00
41 thru 44 Aug., 1957 .... @50.00

COMBAT KELLY
June, 1972

1 JM, Stop the Luftwaffe 30.00
2 The Big Breakout 15.00
3 O:Combat Kelly 20.00
4 Mutiny,A:Sgt.Fury and the
   Howling Commandoes 20.00
5 Escape or Die 15.00
6 The Fortress of Doom........ 15.00
7 Nun Hostage,V:Nazis........ 15.00
8 V:Nazis................... 15.00
9 Oct., 1973 .... 15.00

COMET MAN
Feb., 1987

1 BSz(c),I:Comet Man......... 2.50
2 BSz(c),A:Mr.Fantastic........ 2.50
3 BSz(c),A:Hulk.............. 2.50
4 BSz(c),A:Fantistic Four....... 2.50
5 BSz(c),A:Fantastic Four 2.50

CVA Page 214   All comics prices listed are for *Near Mint* condition.

MARVEL — Comet–Conan

6 BSz(c),Last issue, July,1987 . . . . 2.50

COMIX BOOK
(black & white magazine) 1974
1 BW. 65.00
2 BW 50.00
3 . . . . 35.00
4 . . . . 30.00
5 1976 . . . . 30.00

COMIX ZONE
1 video game tie-in 2.50
2 video game tie-in 2.50

Commando Adventures #2
© *Marvel Entertainment Group*

COMMANDO ADVENTURES
Atlas, June, 1957
1 Seek, Find and Destroy 125.00
2 MD, Hit 'em and Hit 'em Hard, Aug.,1957 . . . . 75.00

COMPLETE COMICS
See: AMAZING COMICS

COMPLETE MYSTERY
Aug., 1948
1 Seven Dead Men 550.00
2 Jigsaw of Doom 450.00
3 Fear in the Night. 450.00
4 A Squealer Dies Fast 450.00
Becomes:

TRUE COMPLETE MYSTERY
1949
5 Rice Mancini, The Deadly Dude 300.00
6 Ph(c),Frame-up that Failed . . 250.00
7 Ph(c),Caught 250.00
8 Ph(c),The Downfall of Mr. Anderson, Oct., 1949 . . . . . . 250.00

CONAN
1995–96
1 Pit Fighter. 3.00
2 LHa,Hyborean tortue factory . . . 3.00
3 V:Cannibals 3.00
4 LHa,JP,Rune Conan Prelude . . . 3.00
5 LHa,V:yeti. 3.00

6 LHa, the plague 3.00
7 LHa,BBl,V:The Iron Man 3.00
8 . . . . 3.00
9 . . . . 3.00
10 Conan kidnapped by Amazons. . 3.00
11 . . . . 3.00

CONAN: DEATH COVERED IN GOLD
July, 1999
1 (of 3) RTs 3.00
2 RTs 3.00
3 RTs,JB,concl. 3.00

CONAN THE ADVENTURER
1994–95
1 RT(s),RK,Red Foil(c) 3.00
2 RT(s),RK 2.50
3 RT(s),RK 2.50
4 thru 13 . . . . @2.50
14 RTs,Young Conan,last issue . . . 2.50

CONAN THE BARBARIAN
Oct., 1970
1 BWS/DA,O:Conan,A:Kull 350.00
2 BWS/SB,Lair o/t Beast-Men . . 125.00
3 BWS,SB,Grey God Passes. . . 200.00
4 BWS,SB,Tower o/t Elephant . . 85.00
5 BWS,Zukala's Daughter 85.00
6 BWS,SB,Devil Wings Over Shadizar. 65.00
7 BWS,SB,DA,C:Thoth-Amon, I:Set 65.00
8 BWS,TS,TP,Keepers o/t Crypt . 65.00
9 BWS,SB,Garden of Fear. 65.00
10 BWS,SB,JSe,Beware Wrath of Anu;BU:Kull 75.00
11 BWS,SB,Talons of Thak 75.00
12 BWS,GK,Dweller in the Dark, Blood of the Dragon B.U. 50.00
13 BWS,SB,Web o/t Spider-God . . 50.00
14 BWS,SB,Green Empress of Melnibone 65.00
15 BWS,SB 65.00
16 BWS,Frost Giant's Daughter . . 50.00
17 GK,Gods of Bal-Sagoth, A:Fafnir 35.00
18 GK,DA,Thing in the Temple, A:Fafnir 35.00
19 BWS,DA,Hawks from the Sea. 50.00
20 BWS,DA,Black Hound of Vengeance,A:Fafnir 50.00
21 BWS,CR,VM,DA,SB, Monster of the Monoliths 40.00
22 BWS,DA,rep.Conan #1 . . . . . . 50.00
23 BWS,DA,Shadow of the Vulture,I:Red Sonja 60.00
24 BWS,Song of Red Sonja 60.00
25 JB,SB,JSe,Mirrors of Kharam Akkad,A:Kull. 25.00
26 JB,Hour of the Griffin 20.00
27 JB,Blood of Bel-Hissar 15.00
28 JB,Moon of Zembabwei 15.00
29 JB,Two Against Turan 15.00
30 JB,The Hand of Nergal 15.00
31 JB,Shadow in the Tomb 12.00
32 JB,Flame Winds of Lost Khitai . 12.00
33 JB,Death & 7 Wizards 12.00
34 JB,Temptress in the Tower of Flame. 12.00
35 JB,Hell-Spawn of Kara-Shehr. . 12.00
36 JB,Beware of Hyrkanians bearing Gifts. 12.00
37 NA,Curse of the Golden Skull . 25.00
38 JB,Warrior & Were-Woman . . . 12.00

39 JB,Dragon from the Inland Sea. 12.00
40 RB,Fiend from Forgotten City. . 12.00
41 JB,Garden of Death & Life 15.00
42 JB,Night of the Gargoyle 15.00
43 JB,Tower o/Blood,A:RedSonja . 15.00
44 JB,Flame&Fiend,A:RedSonja. . 15.00
45 JB,NA,Last Ballad of Laza-Lanti 12.00
46 JB,NA,JSt,Curse of the Conjurer. 12.00
47 JB,DA,Goblins in the Moonlight 12.00
48 JB,DG,DA,Rats Dance at Ravengard,BU:Red Sonja. 12.00
49 JB,DG,Wolf-Woman. 12.00
50 JB,DG,Dweller in the Pool 12.00
51 JB,DG,Man Born of Demon 8.00
52 JB,TP,Altar and the Scorpion . . . 8.00
53 JB,FS,Brothers of the Blade 8.00
54 JB,TP,Oracle of Ophir 8.00
55 JB,TP,Shadow on the Land 8.00
56 JB,High Tower in the Mist 8.00
57 MP,Incident in Argos 8.00
58 JB,Queen o/tBlackCoast, 2nd A:Belit 10.00
59 JB,Ballad of Belit,O:Belit 7.00
60 JB,Riders o/t River Dragons. . . . 7.00
61 JB,She-Pirate,I:Amra 7.00
62 JB,Lord of the Lions,O:Amra . . . 7.00
63 JB,Death Among Ruins, V&D:Amra 7.00
64 JSon,AM,rep.Savage Tales#5 . . 7.00
65 JB,Fiend o/tFeatheredSerpent . . 7.00
66 JB,Daggers & Death Gods, C:Red Sonja. 6.00
67 JB,Talons of the Man-Tiger, A:Red Sonja. 6.00
68 JB,Of Once & Future Kings, V:KingKull,A:Belit,Red Sonja . . 6.00
69 VM,Demon Out of the Deep 6.00
70 JB,City in the Storm 6.00
71 JB,Secret of Ashtoreth 6.00
72 JB,Vengeance in Asgalun 6.00
73 JB,..In the Well of Skelos 6.00
74 JB,Battle at the Black Walls C:Thoth-Amon 6.00
75 JB,Hawk-Riders of Harakht 7.00
76 JB,Swordless in Stygia 7.00
77 JB,When Giants Walk the Earth 7.00
78 JB,rep.Savage Sword #1, A:Red Sonja 7.00
79 HC,Lost Valley of Iskander. 7.00

Conan the Barbarian #11
© *Marvel Entertainment Group*

All comics prices listed are for *Near Mint* condition.

Conan The Barbarian

- 80 HC,Trial By Combat......... 6.00
- 81 HC,The Eye of the Serpent.... 5.00
- 82 HC,The Sorceress o/t Swamp.. 5.00
- 83 HC,The Dance of the Skull.... 5.00
- 84 JB,Two Against the Hawk-City, I:Zula................... 5.00
- 85 JB,Of Swordsmen & Sorcerers, O:Zulu.................. 5.00
- 86 JB,Devourer of the Dead...... 5.00
- 87 TD, rep. Savage Sword #3..... 5.00
- 88 JB,Queen and the Corsairs.... 5.00
- 89 JB,Sword & the Serpent, A:Thoth-Amon............ 5.00
- 90 JB,Diadem of the Giant-Kings.. 5.00
- 91 JB,Savage Doings in Shem.... 5.00
- 92 JB,The Thing in the Crypt..... 5.00
- 93 JB,Of Rage & Revenge....... 5.00
- 94 JB,BeastKing ofAbombi,L:Zulu.. 5.00
- 95 JB,The Return of Amra....... 5.00
- 96 JB,Long Night of Fang & Talon,pt.1............... 5.00
- 97 JB,Long Night of Fang & Talon,pt.2............... 5.00
- 98 JB,Sea-Woman............ 5.00
- 99 JB,Devil Crabs o/t Dark Cliffs... 5.00
- 100 JB,Death on the Black Coast, D:Belit (double size)........ 7.00
- 101 JB,The Devil has many Legs.. 3.00
- 102 JB,The Men Who Drink Blood................ 3.00
- 103 JB,Bride of the Vampire...... 3.00
- 104 JB,The Vale of Lost Women... 3.00
- 105 JB,Whispering Shadows..... 3.00
- 106 JB,Chaos in Kush.......... 3.00
- 107 JB,Demon of the Night....... 3.00
- 108 JB,Moon-Eaters of Darfar.... 3.00
- 109 JB,Sons of the Bear God.... 3.00
- 110 JB,Beward the Bear of Heaven 3.00
- 111 JB,Cimmerian Against a City.. 3.00
- 112 JB,Buryat Besieged......... 3.00
- 113 JB,A Devil in the Family..... 3.00
- 114 JB,The Shadow of the Beast.. 3.00
- 115 JB,A War of Wizards, A:Red Sonja Double size 10th Anniv. (L:Roy Thomas script)....... 4.00
- 116 JB,NA,Crawler in the Mist.... 5.00
- 117 JB,Corridor of Mullah-Kajar... 3.00
- 118 JB,Valley of Forever Night.... 3.00
- 119 JB,Voice of One Long Gone... 3.00
- 120 JB,The Hand of Erlik........ 3.00
- 121 JB,BMc,Price of Perfection... 3.00
- 122 JB,BMc,The City Where Time Stood Still................. 3.00
- 123 JB,BMc,Horror Beneath the Hills..................... 3.00
- 124 JB,BMc,the Eternity War.... 3.00
- 125 JB,BMc,the Witches ofNexxx.. 3.00
- 126 JB,BMc,Blood Red Eye of Truth................... 3.00
- 127 GK,Snow Haired Woman of the Wastes............. 3.00
- 128 GK,And Life Sprang Forth From These............... 3.00
- 129 GK,The Creation Quest...... 3.00
- 130 GK,The Quest Ends......... 3.00
- 131 GK,The Ring of Rhax........ 3.00
- 132 GK,Games of Gharn........ 3.00
- 133 GK,The Witch of Windsor.... 3.00
- 134 GK,A Hitch in Time......... 3.00
- 135 MS,JRu,Forest of the Night... 3.00
- 136 JB,The River of Death....... 3.00
- 137 AA,Titans Gambit.......... 3.00
- 138 VM,Isle of the Dead........ 3.00
- 139 VM,In the Lair of the Damned............... 3.00
- 140 JB,Spider Isle............. 3.00
- 141 JB,The Web Tightens....... 3.00
- 142 JB,The Maze,the Man, the Monster............... 3.00
- 143 JB,Life Among the Dead..... 3.00
- 144 JB,The Blade & the Beast.... 3.00
- 145 Son of Cimmeria........... 3.00
- 146 JB,Night o/t Three Sisters.... 3.00
- 147 JB,Tower of Mitra........... 3.00
- 148 JB,The Plague of Forlek..... 3.00
- 149 JB,Deathmark.............. 3.00
- 150 JB,Tower of Flame.......... 3.00
- 151 JB,Vale of Death........... 3.00
- 152 JB,Dark Blade of Jergal Zadh................ 3.00
- 153 JB,Bird Men of Akah Ma'at... 3.00
- 154 JB,the Man-Bats of Ur-Xanarrh................ 3.00
- 155 JB,SL,The Anger of Conan... 3.00
- 156 JB,The Curse.............. 3.00
- 157 JB,The Wizard............. 3.00
- 158 JB,Night of the Wolf......... 3.00
- 159 JB,Cauldron of the Doomed... 3.00
- 160 Veil of Darkness............ 3.00
- 161 JB,House of Skulls,A:Fafnir.. 3.00
- 162 JB,Destroyer in the Flame, A:Fafnir................. 3.00
- 163 JB,Cavern of the Vines of Doom,A:Fafnir............ 3.00
- 164 The Jeweled Sword of Tem... 3.00
- 165 JB,V:Nadine............... 3.00
- 166 JB,GI,Blood o/t Titan,A:Fafnir.. 3.00
- 167 JB,Creature From Time's Dawn,A:Fafnir............. 3.00
- 168 JB,Bird Woman & the Beast... 3.00
- 169 JB,Tomb of the Scarlet Mage.. 3.00
- 170 JB,Dominion of the Dead, A&D:Fafnir................ 3.00
- 171 JB,Barbarian Death Song.... 3.00
- 172 JB,Reavers in Borderland.... 3.00
- 173 JB,Honor Among Thieves.... 3.00
- 174 JB,V:Tetra................ 3.00
- 175 JB,V:Spectre ofDeath....... 3.00
- 176 JB,Argos Rain............. 2.50
- 177 JB,V:Nostume............. 2.50
- 178 JB,A:Tetra,Well of Souls...... 2.50
- 179 JB,End of all there is,A:Kiev... 2.50
- 180 JBV:AnitRenrut............ 2.50
- 181 JB,V:KingMaddoc II......... 2.50
- 182 JB,V:King of Shem......... 2.50
- 183 JB,V:Imhotep............. 2.50
- 184 JB,V:Madoc............... 2.50
- 185 JB,R:Tetra................ 2.50
- 186 JB,The Crimson Brotherhood.. 2.50
- 187 JB,V:Council of Seven...... 2.50
- 188 JB,V:Devourer-Souls........ 2.50
- 189 JB,V:Devourer-Souls........ 2.50
- 190 JB,Devourer-Souls.......... 2.50
- 191 Deliverance................ 2.50
- 192 JB,V:TheKeeper........... 2.50
- 193 Devourer-Souls............ 2.50
- 194 V:Devourer-Souls........... 2.50
- 195 Blood of Ages............. 2.50
- 196 V:Beast.................. 2.50
- 197 A:Red Sonja.............. 2.50
- 198 A:Red Sonja.............. 2.50
- 199 O:Kaleb.................. 2.50
- 200 JB,D.sizeV:Dev-Souls....... 5.00
- 201 NKu,GI,Thulsa Doom....... 2.50
- 202 .... 2.50
- 203 V:Thulsa Doom............ 2.50
- 204 VS,GI,A:Red Sonja,I:Strakkus. 2.50
- 205 A:Red Sonja.............. 2.50
- 206 VS,GI,Heku trilogy,pt.1...... 2.50
- 207 VS,GI,Heku,pt.2,O:Kote..... 2.50
- 208 VS,GI,Heku,pt.3........... 2.50
- 209 VS,GI,Heku epilogue....... 2.50
- 210 VS,GI,V:Sevante.......... 2.50
- 211 VS,GI,V:Sevante.......... 2.50
- 212 EC,GI................... 2.50
- 213 V:Ghamud Assassins....... 2.50
- 214 AA..................... 2.50
- 215 VS,GI,Conan Enslaved..... 2.50
- 216 V:Blade of Zed............ 2.50
- 217 JLe(c),V:Blade of Zed...... 2.50
- 218 JLe(c),V:Picts............. 2.50
- 219 JLe(c),V:Forgotten Beasts... 2.50
- 220 Conan the Pirate.......... 2.50
- 221 Conan the Pirate.......... 2.50
- 222 AA,DP,Revenge........... 2.50
- 223 AA,Religious Cult.......... 2.50
- 224 AA,Cannibalism........... 2.50
- 225 AA,Conan Blinded......... 2.50
- 226 AA,Quest for Mystic Jewel... 2.50
- 227 AA,Mystic Jewel,pt.2....... 2.50
- 228 AA,Cannibalism,pt.1....... 2.50
- 229 AA,Cannibalism,pt.2....... 2.50
- 230 FS,SDr,Citadel,pt.1........ 2.50
- 231 FS,DP,Citadel,pt.2......... 2.50
- 232 RLm,Birth of Conan........ 3.00
- 233 RLm,DA,B:Conan as youth.. 2.50
- 234 RLm,DA................. 2.50
- 235 RLm,DA................. 2.50
- 236 RLm,DA................. 2.50
- 237 DA,V:Jorrma.............. 2.50
- 238 DA,D:Conan.............. 2.50
- 239 Conan Possessed......... 2.50
- 240 Conan Possessed......... 2.50
- 241 TM(c),R:RoyThomasScript... 3.50
- 242 JLe(c),A:Red Sonja........ 2.50
- 243 WPo(c),V:Zukala........... 2.50
- 244 A:Red Sonja,Zula.......... 2.50
- 245 A:Red Sonja,V:King of Vampires................ 2.50
- 246 A:Red Sonja,V:MistMonster... 2.50
- 247 A:Red Sonja,Zula.......... 2.50
- 248 V:Zulu................... 2.50
- 249 A:Red Sonja,Zula.......... 2.50
- 250 A:RedSonja,Zula,V:Zug double size................ 5.00
- 251 Cimmeria,V:Shumu Gorath... 3.00
- 252 ECh..................... 3.00
- 253 ECh,V:Kulan-Goth(X-Men Villain)................... 3.00
- 254 ECh,V:Shuma-Gorath (Dr. Strange Villain)............ 3.00
- 255 ECh,V:Shuma-Gorath....... 3.00
- 256 ECh,D:Nemedia's King..... 3.00
- 257 ECh,V:Queen Vammator.... 3.00
- 258 AA(i),A:Kulan Gath......... 3.00
- 259 V:Shuma-Gorath........... 3.00
- 260 AA(i),V:Queen Vammatar.... 3.00
- 261 V:Cult of the Death Goddess.. 3.00
- 262 V:The Panther............. 3.00
- 263 V:Malaq.................. 3.00
- 264 V:Kralic.................. 3.00
- 265 V:Karlik.................. 3.00
- 266 Conan the Renegade (adapt.). 3.00
- 267 adapt.,pt.2................ 3.00
- 268 adapt.,pt.3................ 3.00

Conan The Barbarian #163
© Marvel Entertainment Group

MARVEL

Conan–Conan

Conan The Barbarian Movie Special #2
© Marvel Entertainment Group

269 V:Agohoth,Prince Borin 3.00
270 Devourer of the Dead 3.00
271 V:Devourer of Souls 3.00
272 V:Devourer 3.00
273 V:Purple Lotus 3.00
274 V:She-Bat 3.00
275 RTs(s),Last Issue cont. in
  Savage Sword of Conan. 5.00
G-Size#1 GK,TS,Hour of the
  Dragon, inc.rep.Conan#3,
  I:Belit 25.00
G-Size#2 GK,TS,Conan Bound,
  inc. rep Conan #5 . . . . 11.00
G-Size#3 GK,TS,To Tarantia
  & the Tower,inc.rep.Conan#6 . . 8.00
G-Size#4,GK,FS,Swords of the
  South,inc.rep.Conan #7 . . . . . . 8.00
G-Size#5 rep.Conan #14,#15
  & Back-up story #12. . . . . 8.00
KingSz.#1 rep.Conan #2,#4 . . . . . 13.00
Ann.#2 BWS,Phoenix on the Sword
  A:Thoth-Amon 10.00
Ann.#3 JB,HC,Mountain of
  the Moon God, B.U.Kull story . . 8.00
Ann.#4 JB,Return of the
  Conqueror,A:Zenobia 8.00
Ann.#5 JB,W:Conan/Zenobia 5.00
Ann.#6 GK,King of the
  Forgotten People 5.00
Ann.#7 JB,Red Shadows
  & Black Kraken 4.00
Ann.#8 VM,Dark Night of the
  White Queen 4.00
Ann.#9 . . . . 4.00
Ann.#10 Scorched Earth
  (Conan #176 x-over) 4.00
Ann.#11 . . . . 4.00
Conan-Barbarian Movie Spec.#1 . . 3.00
Conan-Barbarian Movie Spec.#2 . . 3.00
Conan-Destroyer Movie Spec.#1 . . 3.00
Red Nails Special Ed.BWS 4.00
TPB Conan & Ravagers Out
  of Time 9.95
TPB Conan the Reaver 9.95
TPB Conan the Rogue,JB,V:Romm 9.95
TPB Horn of Azroth 9.95
TPB Skull of Set 9.95

CONAN: THE FLAME AND THE FIEND
June, 2000
1 (of 3) RTs,GI,V:Kulan Gath 3.00

2 RTs,GI,Bone Dragon. 3.00
3 RTs,GI,concl. 3.00

CLASSIC CONAN
June, 1987
1 BWS,rep. 7.00
2 BWS,rep. 5.00
3 BWS,rep. 5.00
Becomes:

CONAN SAGA
1987
4 thru 10 rep. . . . . @3.50
11 thru 98 rep. . . . . @3.00

CONAN CLASSICS
1994–95
1 rep. Conan #1 . . . . 2.25
2 thru 10 rep. . . . . @2.25

CONAN/RUNE
1995
1 BWS,Conan Vs. Rune 3.50

CONAN
1997
1 CCt, ... 2.00
2 CCt,V:Sorcerer 2.00
3 (of 3) CCt, ... 2.00

CONAN: RIVER OF BLOOD
April, 1998
1 (of 3) Valeria, vs. giant crocs. . . . 2.50
2 Caught in the middle of a war . . 2.50
3 Lord of the Crocodiles, concl. . . . 2.50

CONAN THE BARBARIAN VS. THE LORD OF THE SPIDERS
Jan., 1998
1 (of 3) RTs,V:Harpagus 2.50
2 RTs, ... 2.50
3 RTs,V:Harpagus 2.50

CONAN: THE RETURN OF STYRM
July, 1998
1 (of 3) V:Mecora. 2.50
2 (of 3) V:Mecora. 3.00
3 conclusion 3.00

CONAN: THE SCARLET SWORD
Oct., 1998
1 (of 3) RTs,V:Thun'da. 3.00
2 RTs,A:Helliana. 3.00
3 RTs,conclusion 3.00

CONAN: THE USURPER
Oct., 1997
1 (of 3) CDi,KJ,Conan attacks
  Cimmeria? 2.50
2 CDi,KJ, ... 2.50
3 CDi,KJ, concl.. . . . . 2.50

KING CONAN
March, 1980
1 JB,ECh,I:Conn,V:Thoth-Amon . . . 7.00
2 JB,Black Sphinx of Nebthu 4.00

3 JB,Dragon Wings Over
  Zembabwei 4.00
4 JB,V:Thoth-Amon 4.00
5 JB,The Sorcerer in the Realm
  of Madness 4.00
6 JB,The Lady's Name Is..Trouble . 4.00
7 PS,JB, ... 4.00
8 A:Queen Reclaimed 4.00
9 JB,V:Medusa Monster. 4.00
10 V:Sea Monster. 4.00
11 V:Giant Totem Monster. 4.00
12 V:Monster 4.00
13 V:Monster 4.00
14 V:Demon 4.00
15 V:Sea Monster. 4.00
16 Conan Into Battle. 4.00
17 A:Conn 4.00
18 King of the Freaks? 4.00
19 MK(c),Skull & X-Bones cover. . . 4.00
Becomes:

CONAN THE KING
1984
20 MS,The Prince is Dead 4.00
21 MS,Shadows 3.00
22 GI/MS,The Black Dragons,Prince
  Conan II back-up story begins . 3.00
23 MS/GI,Ordeal 3.00
24 GI/MS,Fragments:AWitch'sTale . 3.00
25 MS/GI,Daggers 3.00
26 MS/GI,PrinceConanII B.U.ends . 3.00
27 MS/GI,A Death in Stygia 3.00
28 MS/GI,Call of the Wild,
  A:Red Sonja. 3.00
29 MS,The Sleeping Lion 3.00
30 GI,Revenge on the Black River . 3.00
31 GI,Force of Arms 3.00
32 GI,Juggernaut 3.00
33 . . . . 3.00
34 . . . . 3.00
35 . . . . 3.00
36 . . . . 3.00
37 AW,Sack of Belverus 3.00
38 MM,A:Taurus,Leora 3.00
39 The Tower 3.00
40 . . . . 3.00
41 V:Leora 3.00
42 Thee Armada,A:Conn 3.00
43 . . . . 3.00
44 . . . . 3.00
45 V:Caliastros 3.00
46 V:Caliastros 3.00
47 TD,V:Caliastros 3.00
48 . . . . 3.00

Conan The King #21
© Marvel Entertainment Group

All comics prices listed are for *Near Mint* condition.

Conan–Crazy / MARVEL / Comics Values Annual

49 .... 3.00
50 GI,50th Anniversary issue 3.00
51 GI,Death of Prince Conn 3.00
52 GI,Prince Conn story contd 3.00
53 GI,A:Thoth-Amon............ 3.00
54 GI,V:Thoth-Amon............ 3.00
55 GI,Sorcerers Ring,final issue ... 3.00

CONAN THE SAVAGE
1995–96
(Black & White Magazine)
1 New Series................. 3.00
2 CDi,Conan a gladiator 3.00
3 V:Monster.................. 3.00
4 CDi,Conan vs. Rune.......... 3.00
5 MBn,VMk,Ice age tale......... 3.00
6 Bros.Hildebrandt(c),V:FallenIdol . 3.00
7 CDi,F:Iron Maidens........... 3.00
8 & 9 ....@3.00
10 JB story, 48pg.............. 3.00

Coneheads 32
© Marvel Entertainment Group

CONEHEADS
1994
1 Based Saturday Night Live 2.25
2 There Goes the Neighborhood .. 2.25
3 In Paris.................... 2.25

CONSPIRACY
Dec., 1997
1 (of 2) DAn,Were the origins of
  Marvel's superheroes really a
  conspiracy, not an accident?... 3.00
2 DAn,concl.................. 3.00

CONTEST OF CHAMPIONS
June, 1982
1 JR2,Grandmaster vs. Mistress
  Death, A:Alpha Flight 8.00
2 JR2,Grandmaster vs. Mistress
  Death, A:X-Men 7.00
3 JR2,D:Grandmaster, Rebirth
  Collector, A:X-Men 7.00

CONTEST OF CHAMPIONS II
July, 1999
1 (of 5) CCl,Marvel vs. Marvel 3.00
2 CCl,Atlas vs. Storm 3.00
3 CCl,super hero slugfest 3.00

4 CCl...................... 3.00
5 CCl, conclusion 3.00
TPB Contest of Champions,
  160-page, '70s rep......... 17.95

COPS: THE JOB
1992
1 MGo(c),V:Serial killer 2.25
2 MGo(c).................... 2.25
3 MGo(c),V:Eviscerator 2.25
4 MGo(c),D:Eviscerator,Nick 2.25

COSMIC POWERS
1994
1 RMz(s),RLm,JP,F:Thanos...... 2.75
2 RMz(s),JMr,F:Terrax.......... 2.75
3 RMz(s),F:Jack of Hearts....... 2.75
4 RMz(s),RLm,F:Legacy 2.75
5 RMz(s),F&O:Morg 2.75
6 RMz(s),F&O:Tyrant........... 2.75

COSMIC POWERS UNLIMITED
1995–96
1 Surfer vs. Thanos............ 4.25
2 Jack of Hearts vs. Jakar....... 4.25
3 GWt,JB,F:Lunatik,64pg........ 4.25
4 GWt,SEa,cont.StarMasters#3 .. 4.25
5 GWt,SEa,R:Captain Universe .. 4.25

COUNT DUCKULA
Star, Nov., 1988
1 O:CountDuckula,B:DangerMouse 4.00
2 A:Danger Mouse............. 3.00
3 thru 15 ....@3.00

COWBOY ACTION
See: WESTERN THRILLERS

COWBOY ROMANCES
Oct., 1949
1 Ph(c),Outlaw and the Lady ... 250.00
2 Ph(c),William Holden/Mona
  Freeman,Streets of Laredo.. 250.00
3 Phc,Romance in
  Roaring Valley 125.00
Becomes:

YOUNG MEN
1950
4 A Kid Names Shorty 200.00
5 Jaws of Death.............. 125.00
6 Man-Size 125.00
7 The Last Laugh 125.00
8 Adventure stories continued .. 125.00
9 Draft Dodging story.......... 125.00
10 JMn,US Draft Story 125.00
11 Adventure stories continued .. 125.00
12 JMn,B:On the Battlefield,
  inc.Spearhead 125.00
13 RH,Break-through 125.00
14 GC,RH,Fox Hole 125.00
15 GC,JMn,Battlefield stories
  cont.................... 125.00
16 Sniper Patrol 125.00
17 Battlefield stories cont,...... 125.00
18 BEv,Warlord.............. 125.00
19 BEv..................... 125.00
20 BEv,E:On the Battlefield 125.00
21 B:Flash Foster and his High
  Gear Hot Shots 125.00
22 Screaming Tires........... 125.00
23 E:Flash Foster and his High
  Gear Hot Shots 125.00

24 BEv,B:Capt. America,Human
  Torch,Sub-Mariner,O:Capt.
  America,Red Skull 3,500.00
25 BEv,JR, Human Torch,Capt.
  America,Sub-Mariner 1,400.00
26 BEv,Human Torch, Capt.
  America,Sub Mariner 1,500.00
27 Bev, Human Torch/Toro
  V:Hypnotist 1,400.00
28 E:Human Torch, Capt.America,
  Sub Mariner,June, 1954... 1,400.00

COWGIRL ROMANCES
See: DARING MYSTERY

COYOTE
Epic, June, 1983
1 SL,...................... 3.00
2 SL 2.50
3 BG 2.50
4 SL 2.50
5 SL 2.50
6 SL 2.50
7 SL,SD 2.50
8 SL 2.50
9 SL,SD 2.50
10 SL 2.50
11 FS,1st TM art,O:Slash 7.00
12 TM 4.00
13 TM 4.00
14 FS,TM,A:Badger 4.00
15 SL 3.00
16 SL,A:Reagan,Gorbachev..... 3.00

CRASH RYAN
Epic, Oct., 1984
1 War Story 2.25
2 Doomsday 2.25
3 Fortress Japan 2.25
4 Jan., 1985 .... 2.25

Crazy #3
© Marvel Entertainment Group

CRAZY
Atlas, Dec., 1953
1 JMn,BEv,satire, Frank N.
  Steins Castle 300.00
2 JMn,BEv,Beast from 1000
  Fathoms................ 200.00
3 JMn,BEv,RH,Madame Knock-
  wurst's Whacks Museum ... 160.00
4 JMn,BEv,DAv,I Love Lucy
  satire 160.00

5 JMn,BEv,Censorship satire ... 160.00
6 JMn,BEv,MD,satire 175.00
7 JMn,BEv,RH,satire,July, 1954 150.00

CRAZY
Feb., 1973–June, 1973
1 Not Brand Echh reps,
  Forbushman 30.00
2 Big,Batty Love & Hisses issue . 25.00
3 Stupor-Man,A:FantasticalFour.. 25.00

CREATURES ON THE LOOSE
See: TOWER OF SHADOWS

CREW
Marvel May 2003
1 JoB,DaM,Big Trouble,pt.1 .... 2.50
2 JoB,Big Trouble,pt.2 .... 2.50
3 JoB,Big Trouble,pt.3 .... 2.50
4 JoB,Big Trouble,pt.4 .... 2.50
5 JoB,Big Trouble,pt.5 .... 2.50
6 JoB,Big Trouble,pt.6 .... 2.50
7 JoB,Big Trouble,pt.7 .... 2.50

CRIME CAN'T WIN
See: KRAZY COMICS

CRIME FIGHTERS
April, 1948—Nov., 1949
1 Police Stories 250.00
2 Jewelry robbery 150.00
3 The Nine who were Doomed,
  addiction 165.00
4 Human Beast at Bay 125.00
5 V:Gangsters 125.00
6 Pickpockets 125.00
7 True Cases, Crime Can't Win . 125.00
8 True Cases, Crime Can't Win . 125.00
9 Ph(c),It Happened at Night ... 125.00
10 Ph(c),Killer at Large 125.00
Atlas, Sept., 1954—Jan., 1955
11 JMn,V:Gangsters 125.00
12 V:Gangsters 110.00
13 Clay Pidgeon 110.00

CRIMSON DYNAMO
Marvel Epic June 2003
1 high tech weapon 3.00
2 new cold war? 2.50
3 Dynamo's armor 2.50
4 .... 2.50

CRITICAL MASS
Epic, Jan.–July, 1990
1 KS,GM,BSzF:ShadowlineSaga .. 5.00
2 .... 5.00
3 GM,SDr,JRy 5.00
4 .... 5.00
5 JZ 5.00
6 .... 5.00
7 July, 1990 .... 5.00

CROSSOVER CLASSICS
TPB Marvel and D.C. GP(c),reprints
both Spider-Man/Superman,the
Batman/Hulk and the X-Men/New
Teen Titans Battles 18.00
TPB Vol.1 320-pg. (2001) 24.95

CRYPT OF SHADOWS
Jan., 1973–Nov. 1975
1 BW,RH,GK,Midnight on Black

Mountain 50.00
2 GT,BEv,JMn,Monster at
  the Door 35.00
3 Dead Man's Hand 25.00
4 CI,Secret in the Vault 25.00
5 JM,The Graveyard Ghoul 25.00
6 BEv,GK,Don't Bury Me Deep .. 35.00
7 JSt,The Haunting of Bluebeard. 35.00
8 How Deep my Grave 25.00
9 Beyond Death 25.00
10 A Scream in the Dark 25.00
11 The Ghouls in my Grave 20.00
12 BP,Behind the Locked Door .. 25.00
13 BEv,SD,Back From the Dead .. 25.00
14 The Thing that Creeps 20.00
15 My Coffin is Crowded 20.00
16 .... 20.00
17 In the Hands of Shandu 20.00
18 SD,Face of Fear 25.00
19 SD,Colossus that Challenged
  the World 25.00
20 A Monster walks Among Us .. 20.00
21 SD,Death Will Be Mine 25.00

CUPID
Dec., 1949–March, 1950
1 Ph(c),Cora Dod's Amazing
  Decision 150.00
2 Ph(c),BP,Betty Page 350.00

CURSE OF THE WEIRD
1993–94
1 thru 4 SD,rep. 50's Sci-Fi 2.25

CUTTING EDGE
1995
1 WML,F:Hulk,Ghosts of the
  Future tie-in 3.25

CYBERSPACE 3000
1993
1 A:Dark Angel,Galactus,V:Badoon,
  Glow in the dark(c) 3.25
2 SeT,A:Galactus,Dark Angel 2.25
3 SeT,A:Galactus,Keeper 2.25
4 SeT,A:Keeper 2.25
5 SeT,A:Keeper 2.25
6 SeT,A:Warlock 2.25
7 SeT,I:Gamble 2.25
8 SeT,A:Warlock 2.25
9 SeT 2.25
10 SeT 2.25
11 SeT 2.25

CYCLOPS
Aug., 2001
1 (of 4) MT,JP 2.75
2 MT,JP,I:Ulysses 2.75
3 MT,JP,in a savage land 2.75
4 MT,JP,V:Ulysses 2.75
TPB X-Men Icons: Cyclops 12.95

DAILY BUGLE
B&W 1996
1 (of 3) KIK,GA 2.75
2 KIK,GA 2.75
3 KIK,GA 2.75

DAKOTA NORTH
1986
1 (Now in Cage) 2.25
2 .... 2.25
3 .... 2.25
4 .... 2.25
5 Feb., 1987 .... 2.25

Damage Control #2
© Marvel Entertainment Group

DAMAGE CONTROL
May, 1989
1 EC/BWi;A:Spider-Man 3.00
2 EC/BWi;A:Fant.Four 2.50
3 EC/BWi;A:Iron Man 2.50
4 EC/BWi;A:X-Men 2.50
[2nd Series], 1989–90
1 EC,A:Capt.America&Thor 3.00
2 EC,A:Punisher 2.50
3 EC 2.50
4 EC,Punisher 2.50
[3rd Series], 1991
1 Clean-up Crew Returns 2.50
2 A:Hulk,New Warriors 2.50
3 A:Avengers W.C.,Wonder Man,
  Silver Surfer 2.50
4 A:SilverSurfer & others 2.50

DANCES WITH DEMONS
Frontier 1993
1 CAd 3.50
2 CAd,V:Manitou 2.50
3 CAd,V:Manitou 2.50
4 CAd,last issue 2.50
5 Okay, there's more! 2.50
6 .... 2.50

DAREDEVIL
April, 1964
1 B:StL(s),JK(c),BEv,I&O:Daredevil,
  I:Karen Page,Foggy Nelson 5,000.00
2 JK(c),JO,V:Electro 1,200.00
3 JK(c),JO,I&O:The Owl 800.00
4 JK(c),JO,I&O:Killgrave 700.00
5 JK(c),WW,V:Masked Matador . 400.00
6 WW,I&O Original Mr. Fear ... 300.00
7 WW,I:Red Costume,V:Namor . 600.00
8 WW,I&O:Stiltman 250.00
9 WW(i),Killers Castle 250.00
10 WW(i),V:Catman 250.00
11 WW(i),R:Cat 200.00
12 JK,JR,2nd A:Ka-Zar 200.00
13 JK,JR,O:Ka-Zar 200.00
14 JR,If This Be Justice 200.00
15 JR,A:Ox 200.00
16 JR,A:Spider-Man,
  I:Masked Marauder 300.00
17 JR,A:Spider-Man 300.00
18 DON(s),JR,I:Gladiator 200.00
19 JR,V:Gladiator 100.00

Daredevil — MARVEL — Comics Values Annual

#	Description	Price
20	JR(c),GC,V:Owl	100.00
21	GC,BEv,V:Owl	100.00
22	GC,V:Tri-man	100.00
23	GC,V:Tri-man	90.00
24	GC,A:Ka-Zar	125.00
25	GC,V:Leapfrog	100.00
26	GC,V:Stiltman	100.00
27	GC,Spider-Man	100.00
28	GC,V:Aliens	100.00
29	GC,V:The Boss	100.00
30	BEv(c),GC,A:Thor	100.00
31	GC,V:Cobra	75.00
32	GC,V:Cobra	75.00
33	GC,V:Beetle	75.00
34	BEv(c),GC,O:Beetle	75.00
35	BEv(c),GC,A:Susan Richards	75.00
36	GC,A:FF	75.00
37	GC,V:Dr.Doom	75.00
38	GC,A:FF	75.00
39	GC,GT,V:Unholy Three	75.00
40	GC,V:Unholy Three	75.00
41	GC,D:Mike Murdock	60.00
42	GC,DA,I:Jester	60.00
43	JK(c),GC,A:Capt.America	60.00
44	JSo(c),GC,V:Jester	50.00
45	GC,V:Jester	50.00
46	GC,V:Jester	50.00
47	GC,`Brother Take My Hand'	50.00
48	GC,V:Stiltman	50.00
49	GC,V:Robot,I:Starr Saxon	50.00
50	JR(c),BWS,JCr,V:Robot	65.00
51	B:RTs(s),BWS,V:Robot	65.00
52	BWS,JCr,A:Black Panther	65.00
53	GC,O:Daredevil	55.00
54	GC,V:Mr.Fear,A:Spidey	50.00
55	GC,V:Mr.Fear	40.00
56	GC,V:Death Head	40.00
57	GC,V:Death Head	40.00
58	GC,V:Stunt Master	40.00
59	GC,V:Torpedo	40.00
60	GC,V:Crime Wave	40.00
61	GC,V:Cobra	40.00
62	GC,O:Night Hawk	40.00
63	GC,V:Gladiator	40.00
64	GC,A:Stuntmaster	40.00
65	GC,V:BrotherBrimstone	40.00
66	GC,V:BrotherBrimstone	40.00
67	BEv(c),GC,V:Stiltman	40.00
68	AC,V:Kragg Blackmailer, a:Bl.Panther,DD'sID Rev.	40.00
69	E:RTs(s),GC,V:Thunderbolts, A:Bl.Panther(DD's ID Rev.)	40.00
70	GC,V:Terrorists	40.00
71	RTs(s),GC,V:Terrorists	40.00
72	GyC(s),GC,Tagak,V:Quother	40.00
73	GC,V:Zodiac	40.00
74	B:GyC(s),GC,I:Smasher	40.00
75	GC,V:El Condor	40.00
76	GC,TP,V:El Condor	40.00
77	GC,TP,V:Manbull	40.00
78	GC,TP,V:Manbull	40.00
79	GC,TP,V:Manbull	40.00
80	GK(c),GC,TP,V:Owl	40.00
81	GK(c),GC,JA,A:Black Widow	50.00
82	GK(c),GC,JA,V:Scorpion	25.00
83	JR(c),BWS,BEv,V:Mr.Hyde	28.00
84	GK(c),GC,A:Assassin	25.00
85	GK(c),GC,A:Black Widow	25.00
86	GC,TP,V:Ox	25.00
87	GC,TP,V:Electro	25.00
88	GK(c),GC,TP,O:Black Widow	25.00
89	GC,TP,A:Black Widow	25.00
90	E:StL(s),GK(c),GC,TP,V:Ox	25.00
91	GK(c),GC,TP,I:Mr. Fear III	25.00
92	GK(c),GC,TP,A:BlackPanther	25.00
93	GK(c),GC,TP,A:Black Widow	25.00
94	GK(c),GC,TP,V:Damon Dran	25.00
95	GK(c),GC,TP,V:Manbull	25.00
96	GK(c),GC,ECh,V:Manbull	25.00
97	GK(c),V:Dark Messiah	25.00
98	E:GyC(s),GC,ECh,V:Dark Messiah	25.00
99	B:SvG(s),JR(c),V:Hawkeye	25.00
100	GC,V:Angar the Screamer	40.00
101	RB,A:Angar the Screamer	20.00
102	A:Black Widow	20.00
103	JR(c),DH,A:Spider-Man	20.00
104	GK(c),DH,V:Kraven	20.00
105	DH,JSn,DP,C:Thanos	25.00
106	JR(c),DH,A:Black Widow	15.00
107	JSn(c),JB(i),A:Capt.Marvel	15.00
108	K&R(c),PG(i),V:Beetle	15.00
109	GK(c),DH(i),V:Beetle	15.00
110	JR(c),GC,A:Thing,O:Nekra	15.00
111	JM(i),I:Silver Samurai	20.00
112	GK(c),GC,V:Mandrill	15.00
113	JR(c),V:Gladiator	15.00
114	GK(c),I:Death Stalker	15.00
115	V:Death Stalker	14.00
116	GK(c),GC,V:Owl	15.00
117	E:SvG(s),K&R(c),V:Owl	14.00
118	JR(c),DH,I:Blackwing	14.00
119	GK(c),DH(i),V:Crusher	14.00
120	GK(c),V:Hydra,I:El Jaguar	14.00
121	GK(c),A:Shield	12.00
122	GK(c),V:Blackwing	12.00
123	V:Silvermane,I:Jackhammer	12.00
124	B:MWn(s),GK(c),GC,KJ, I:Copperhead	12.00
125	GK(c),KJ(i),V:Copperhead	12.00
126	GK(c),KJ(i),D: 2nd Torpedo	12.00
127	GK(c),KJ(i),V:3rd Torpedo	12.00
128	GK(c),KJ(i),V:Death Stalker	12.00
129	KJ(i),V:Man Bull	12.00
130	KJ(i),V:Brother Zed	12.00
131	KJ(i),I&O:2nd Bullseye	50.00
132	KJ(i),V:Bullseye	25.00
133	JM(i),GK(c),V:Jester	12.00
134	JM(i),V:Chameleon	12.00
135	JM(i),V:Jester	12.00
136	JB,JM,V:Jester	12.00
137	JB,V:Jester	12.00
138	JBy,A:Ghost Rider	15.00
139	SB,V:A Bomber	10.00
140	SB,V:Gladiator	10.00
141	GC,Bullseye	20.00
142	GC,V:Cobra	10.00
143	E:MWn(s),GC,V:Cobra	10.00
144	GT,V:Manbull	10.00
145	GT,V:Owl	10.00
146	GC,V:Bullseye	20.00
147	GC,V:Killgrave	10.00
148	GC,V:Deathstalker	10.00
149	KI,V:Smasher	10.00
150	GC,KJ,I:Paladin	10.00
151	GC,Daredevil Unmasked	10.00
152	KJ,V:Paladin	10.00
153	GC,V:Cobra	10.00
154	GC,V:Mr. Hyde	10.00
155	V:Avengers	10.00
156	GC,V:Death Stalker	10.00
157	GC,V:Death Stalker	10.00
158	FM,V:Death Stalker	75.00
159	FM,V:Bullseye	45.00
160	FM,Bullseye	35.00
161	FM,V:Bullseye	35.00
162	SD,JRu,`Requiem'	12.00
163	FM,V:Hulk,I:Ben Urich	25.00
164	FM,KJ,A:Avengers	25.00
165	FM,KJ,V:Dr.Octopus	25.00
166	FM,KJ,V:Gladiator	25.00
167	FM,KJ,V:Mauler	25.00
168	FM,KJ,I&O:Elektra	100.00
169	FM,KJ,V:Bullseye	35.00
170	FM,KJ,V:Bullseye	20.00
171	FM,KJ,V:Kingpin	15.00
172	FM,KJ,V:Bullseye	15.00
173	FM,KJ,V:Gliadator	15.00
174	FM,KJ,A:Gladiator	15.00
175	FM,KJ,A:Elektra,V:Hand	20.00
176	FM,KJ,A:Elektra	15.00
177	FM,KJ,A:Stick	20.00
178	FM,KJ,A:PowerMan&I.Fist	15.00
179	FM,KJ,V:Elektra	15.00
180	FM,KJ,V:Kingpin	15.00
181	FM,KJ,V:Bullseye,D:Elektra, A:Punisher	25.00
182	FM,KJ,A:Punisher	15.00
183	FM,KJ,V:PunisherDrug	15.00
184	FM,KJ,V:PunisherDrug	15.00
185	FM,KJ,V:King Pin	10.00
186	FM,KJ,V:Stiltman	10.00
187	FM,KJ,A:Stick	10.00
188	FM,KJ,A:Black Widow	10.00
189	FM,KJ,A:Stick,A:BlackWidow	10.00
190	FM,KJ,R:Elektra	10.00
191	FM,TA,A:Bullseye	10.00
192	KJ,V:Kingpin	5.00
193	KJ,Betsy	5.00
194	KJ,V:Kingpin	5.00
195	KJ,Tarkington Brown	5.00
196	KJ,A:Wolverine	15.00
197	V:Bullseye	5.00
198	V:Dark Wind	5.00
199	V:Dark Wind	5.00
200	JBy(c),V:Bullseye	7.00
201	JBy(c),A:Black Widow	5.00
202	I:Micah Synn	5.00
203	JBy(c),I:Trump	5.00
204	BSz(c),V:Micah Synn	5.00
205	I:Gael	5.00
206	V:Micah Synn	5.00
207	BSz(c),A:Black Widow	5.00
208	Harlan Ellison	6.00
209	Harlan Ellison	6.00
210	DM,V:Micah Synn	5.00
211	DM,V:Micah Synn	5.00
212	DM,V:Micah Synn	5.00
213	DM,V:Micah Synn	5.00
214	DM,V:Micah Synn	5.00
215	DM,A:Two-Gun Kid	5.00
216	DM,V:Gael	5.00
217	BS(c),V:Gael	5.00
218	KP,V:Jester	5.00
219	FM,JB	6.00
220	DM,D:Heather Glenn	5.00
221	DM,Venice	5.00
222	DM,A:Black Widow	5.00
223	DM,Secret Wars II	5.00
224	DM,V:Sunturion	5.00
225	DM,V:Vulture	5.00
226	FM(plot),V:Gladiator	5.00
227	FM,Kingpin,Kar.Page	12.00
228	FM,DM,V:Kingpin	10.00
229	FM,Kingpin,Turk	10.00

Daredevil #182
© Marvel Entertainment Group

Comics Values Annual — MARVEL — Daredevil

Daredevil #225
© Marvel Entertainment Group

Daredevil #358
© Marvel Entertainment Group

#	Description	Price
230	R:Matt's Mother	10.00
231	FM,DM,V:Kingpin	10.00
232	FM,V:Kingpin,Nuke	10.00
233	FM,Kingpin,Nuke,Capt.Am.	10.00
234	SD,KJ,V:Madcap	5.00
235	SD,KJ,V:Mr. Hyde	5.00
236	BWS,A:Black Widow	6.00
237	AW(i),V:Klaw	5.00
238	SB,SL,AAd(c),V:Sabretooth	7.00
239	AAd(c),AW,GI(i),V:Rotgut	5.00
240	AW,V:Rotgut	5.00
241	MZ(c),TM,V:Trixter	6.00
242	KP,V:Caviar Killer	5.00
243	AW,V:Nameless One	5.00
244	TD(i),V:Nameless One	5.00
245	TD(i),A:Black Panther	5.00
246	TD(i),V:Chance	5.00
247	KG,A:Black Widow	5.00
248	RL,AW,A:Wolverine,V:Bushwhacker	7.00
249	RL,AW,V:Wolverine,Bushwhacker	7.00
250	JR2,AW,I:Bullet	5.00
251	JR2,AW,V:Bullet	5.00
252	JR2,AW,Fall o/Mutants	6.00
253	JR2,AW,V:Kingpin	5.00
254	JR2,AW,I:Typhoid Mary	13.00
255	JR2,AW,A:Kingpin,TMary	6.00
256	JR2,AW,A:Kingpin,TMary	5.00
257	JR2,AW,A:Punisher	10.00
258	RLm,V:Bengal	6.00
259	JR2,AW,V:TyphoidMary	5.00
260	JR2,AW,V:T.Mary,K.pin	5.00
261	JR2,AW,HumanTorch	5.00
262	JR2,AW,Inferno	5.00
263	JR2,AW,Inferno	5.00
264	SD,AW,MM,V:The Owl	5.00
265	JR2,AW,Inferno	5.00
266	JR2,AW,V:Mephisto	5.00
267	JR2,AW,V:Bullet	5.00
268	JR2,AW,V:TheMob	5.00
269	JR2,AW,V:Pyro&Blob	5.00
270	JR2,AW,A:Spider-Man,I:Blackheart	5.00
271	JR2,AW,I:Number9	5.00
272	JR2,AW,I:Shotgun	5.50
273	JR2,AW,V:Shotgun	5.00
274	JR2,AW,V:Inhumans	5.00
275	JR2,AW,ActsOfVen.,V:Ultron	5.00
276	JR2,AW,ActsOfVen.,V:Ultron	5.00
277	RL,AW,Vivian's Story	5.00
278	JR2,AW,V:Blackheart,A:Inhumans	5.00
279	JR2,AW,V:Mephisto,A:Inhumans	5.00
280	JR2,AW,V:Mephisto,A:Inhumans	5.00
281	JR2,AW,V:Mephisto,A:Inhumans	5.00
282	JR2,AW,V:Mephisto,A:Silver Surfer, Inhumans	5.00
283	MBa,AW,A:Captain America	5.00
284	LW,AW,R:Bullseye	5.00
285	LW,AW,B:Bullseye become DD#1	5.00
286	LW,AW,GCa,Fake Daredevil #2	5.00
287	LW,AW,Fake Daredevil #3	5.00
288	LW,AW,A:Kingpin	5.00
289	LW,AW,A:Kingpin	5.00
290	LW,AW,E:Fake Daredevil	5.00
291	LW,AW,V:Bullet	5.00
292	LW,A:Punisher,V:Tombstone	5.00
293	LW,A:Punisher,V:Tombstone	5.00
294	LW,V:The Hand	5.00
295	LW,V:The Hand,A:GhostRider	5.00
296	LW,AW,V:The Hand	5.00
297	B:DGC(s),LW,AW,B:Last Rites,V:Typhoid Mary,A:Kingpin	5.00
298	LW,AW,A:Nick Fury,Kingpin	5.00
299	LW,AW,A:Nick Fury,Kingpin	5.00
300	LW,AW,E:Last Rites	8.00
301	V:The Owl	5.00
302	V:The Owl	5.00
303	V:The Owl	5.00
304	AW,Non-action issue	5.00
305	AW,A:Spider-Man	5.00
306	AW,A:Spider-Man	5.00
307	1st SMc DD,Dead Man's Hand #1,A:Nomad	6.00
308	SMc,Dead Man's Hand #5,A:Punisher,V:Silvermane	5.00
309	SMc,Dead Man's Hand#7,A:Nomad,Punisher	5.00
310	SMc,Inf.War,V:Calipso	5.00
311	SMc,V:Calypso	5.00
312	Firefighting issue	5.00
313	SMc,V:Pyromaniac	5.00
314	SMc,V:Mr.Fear,I:Shock.	5.00
315	SMc,V:Mr.Fear	5.00
316	Goes Underground	5.00
317	SMc,Comedy Issue	5.00
318	SMc,V:Taskmaster	5.00
319	SMc,Fall from Grace Prologue,A:Silver Sable,Garrett,Hand	7.00
319a	2nd Printing	3.00
320	SMc,B:Fall from Grace,V:Crippler,S.Sable,A:Stone	7.00
321	SMc,N:Daredevil,A:Venom,Garret, V:Hellspawn,Glow in the Dark(c)	6.00
321a	Newsstand Ed.	5.00
322	SMc,A:Venom,Garret,Siege	4.00
323	SMc,V:Venom,A:Siege,Garret,I:Erynys	4.00
324	SMc,A:Garret,R:Elektra,A:Stone, Morbius	4.00
325	SMc,E:Fall from Grace,A:Garret,Siege,Elektra,Morbius,V:Hand,D:Hellspawn,Double size	4.00
326	SMc,B:Tree of Knowledge,I:Killobyte,A:Capt.America	3.00
327	E:DGC(s),SMc,A:Capt.Amer.	3.00
328	GtW(s),V:Wirehead,A:Captain America,S.Sable,Wild Pack	3.00
329	B:DGC(s),SMc,A:Captain America, S.Sable,Iron Fist	3.00
330	SMc,A:Gambit	3.00
331	SMc,A:Captain America,VLHydra	3.00
332	A:Captain America,Gambit	3.00
333	TGb,GWt	3.00
334	TGb,GWt	3.00
335		3.00
336		3.00
337	V:Kingpin,A:Blackwulf	3.00
338	Wages of Sin,pt.1	3.00
339	Wages of Sin,pt.2	3.00
340	R:Kingpin	3.00
341	Kingpin	3.00
342	DGc,KP,V:Kingpin	3.00
343	Without Costume	3.00
344	Identity Crisis,pt.1	3.00
345	Identity Crisis,pt.2	3.00
346	V:Sir	3.00
347	V:mystery man	3.00
348	In NY City	3.00
349	Retreats to the Chaste	3.00
350	Double size	4.00
351		3.00
352	Return of Matt Murdock	3.00
353	KK,CNr,A:Mr. Hyde	3.00
354	KK,CNr,A:Spider-Man	3.00
355	KK,CNr,A:Pyro	3.00
356	KK,CNr,	3.00
357	KK,CNr,	3.00
358	KK,CNr,MRy,A:Mysterio	3.00
359	KK,CNr,A:Absorbing Man	3.00
360	KK,CNr,MRy,V:Onslaught	3.00
361	KK,CNr,MRy,A:Black Widow	3.00
362	KK,CNr,Romance	3.00
363	KK,GC,CaS,V:Insomnia	3.00
364	KK,CNr,MRy,V:Insomnia	3.00
365	CNr,MRy,V:Mr. Fear,A:Molten Man	3.00
366	GC,V:Gladiator	3.00
367	GC,V:Gladiator, concl.	3.00
368	GC,A:Black Widow and Omega Red	3.00
369	AOI,V:Soviet Super Soldiers	3.00
370	GC,Black Widow, concl.	3.00
371	AOI,Matt Murdock & Karen Page's relationship	3.00
372	AOI,Killers after Karen Page	3.00
373	AOI,V:The 3.	3.00
374	AOI,V:Mr. Fear	3.00
375	AOI,RL,V:Mr. Fear,double size	4.00
376	SLo,CHm,Daredevil deep undercover	3.00
377	SLo,TMo,SHa,Flying Blind,pt.2	3.00
378	SLo,TMo,SHa,Flying Blind,pt.3.	3.00
379	SLo,CHm,Flying Blind,concl.	3.00
380	DGC,LW,RbC, V:Bullseye,Bushwacker,Kingpin, double size	4.50
Minus 1 Spec., GC, flashback		3.00
Ann.#1 GC		60.00
Ann.#2 reprints		25.00

All comics prices listed are for *Near Mint* condition.

Daredevil–Daring   MARVEL   Comics Values Annual

| Ann.#3 reprints............... 25.00 |
| Ann.#4 (1976)GT,A:Black |
| Panther,Namor............. 7.00 |
| Ann.#5 (1989)MBa,JLe,JR2,KJ, |
| WPo,AM,Atlantis Attacks, |
| A:Spider-Man.............. 5.00 |
| Ann.#6 TS,Lifeform#2,A:Typhoid |
| Mary..................... 5.00 |
| Ann.#7 JG,JBr,Von Strucker |
| Gambit,pt.1,A:Nick Fury.... 5.00 |
| Ann.#8 Sys.Bytes#2,A:Deathlok... 5.00 |
| Ann.#9 MPa,I:Devourer,w/card,tie-in |
| to iFall From Gracei........ 5.00 |
| Ann.#10 I:Ghostmaker,A:Shang |
| Chi, Elektra............... 4.00 |
| G-Size #1 GK(c),reprints........ 12.00 |
| TPB Born Again,rep.#227-#233... 10.95 |
| TPB Fall of the Kingpin, |
| rep.#297-300............. 15.95 |
| TPB Gangwar,Reprints |
| #169-#172,#180........... 12.95 |
| TPB Marked for Death,reps#159- |
| 161,163,164............... 9.95 |
| Daredevil/Punisher:Child's Play |
| reprints#182-#184.......... 7.00 |
| TPB Daredevil: Man Without Fear. 15.95 |

Daredevil Vol. 2, #6
© *Marvel Entertainment Group*

DAREDEVIL
Sept., 1998
| 1 JP,JQ,F:Matt Murdock........ 32.00 |
| 1a Deluxe edition.............. 7.50 |
| 2 JP,JQ,blind faith dilemma..... 18.00 |
| 2a variant JSC cover.......... 15.00 |
| 3 JP,JQ,Guardian Devil,pt.3..... 12.00 |
| 4 JP,JQ,Guardian Devil,pt.4..... 12.00 |
| 5 JP,JQ,Guardian Devil,pt.5..... 20.00 |
| 5a Variant (c)................. 18.00 |
| 6 JP,JQ,Guardian Devil,pt.6..... 11.00 |
| 7 JP,JQ,Guardian Devil,pt.7..... 11.00 |
| 8 JP,JQ,Guardian Devil,concl.... 11.00 |
| 8a signed.................... 25.00 |
| 9 JP,JQ,DMk,V:Kingpin........ 5.00 |
| 9a signed.................... 25.00 |
| 10 JP,JQ,DMk,I:Echo.......... 5.00 |
| 11 JP,JQ,DMk,A:Kingpin....... 5.00 |
| 12 JP,JQ,DMk,V:Kingpin....... 5.00 |
| 13 JP,JQ,DMk,F:Ben........... 5.00 |
| 14 JQ,DMk,V:Kingpin.......... 6.00 |
| 15 JQ,DMk,V:Echo............. 5.00 |
| 16 BMB,DMk,................. 6.00 |
| 17 BMB,DMk,F:Ben Urich....... 6.00 |
| 18 BMB,DMk,F:Ben, Timmy..... 5.00 |
| 19 BMB,DMk,F:Ben, Timmy..... 5.00 |
| 20 40-page,BU:F:Spider-Man..... 6.00 |

| 21 A:Jester.................... 5.00 |
| 22 Matt Murdock vs. Daredevil.... 5.00 |
| 23 Matt Murdock vs. Daredevil.... 5.00 |
| 24 MPn,the trial begins......... 5.00 |
| 25 Playing to the Camera....... 5.00 |
| 26 BMB,V:Nitro............... 12.00 |
| 27 BMB,V:Silke,Kingpin........ 7.00 |
| 28 BMB,Elektra x-over,'Nuff Said... 7.00 |
| 29 BMB,Kingpin's Empire........ 7.00 |
| 30 BMB,Kingpin's Secrets....... 7.00 |
| 31 BMB,plot twist.............. 7.00 |
| 32 BMB,Kingpin's Empire........ 10.00 |
| 33 BMB,F:Matt Murdock........ 6.00 |
| 34 BMB, anger's terms......... 5.00 |
| 35 BMB,V:Mr. Hyde............ 5.00 |
| 36 BMB,F:Luke Cage........... 5.00 |
| 37 BMB,F:Elektra............... 5.00 |
| 38 BMB,Trial of White Tiger,pt.1... 5.00 |
| 39 BMB,Trial of White Tiger,pt.2... 5.00 |
| 40 BMB,Trial of the Century..... 5.00 |
| 41 BMB,Lowlife,pt.1............ 0.50 |
| 42 BMB,Lowlife,pt.2............ 3.00 |
| 43 BMB,Lowlife,pt.3............ 3.00 |
| 44 BMB,Lowlife,pt.4............ 3.00 |
| 45 BMB,Lowlife,concl........... 3.00 |
| 46 BMB,Hardcore,pt.1.......... 3.00 |
| 47 BMB,Hardcore,pt.2.......... 3.00 |
| 48 BMB,Hardcore,pt.3.......... 3.00 |
| 49 BMB,Hardcore,pt.4.......... 3.00 |
| 50 BMB,Hardcore,pt.5.......... 3.00 |
| 51 DMk,R:Echo,pt.1............ 3.00 |
| 52 DMk,V:Echo,pt.2............ 3.00 |
| 53 DMk,V:Echo,pt.3............ 3.00 |
| 54 .... 3.00 |
| Spec.Daredevil vs. Punisher..... 3.50 |
| Spec. Daredevil/Deadpool, BCh, JHo, |
| Two annuals in one,48pg.(1997) 5.00 |
| Spec. Daredevil/Batman, DGC, |
| SMc, 48pg. (1997)........... 6.00 |
| Spec.#1 Daredevil (2000)....... 2.25 |
| Spec. Daredevil Movie adapt..... 3.00 |
| TPB rep. #1–#3................ 9.95 |
| TPB Gang War,FM,KJ.......... 15.95 |
| TPB Daredevil: Born Again...... 17.95 |
| TPB Visionaries: Frank Miller.... 24.95 |
| TPB Visionaries: Kevin Smith.... 19.95 |
| TPB Parts of a Hole, 160-pg..... 16.95 |
| TPB Wake Up (2002)........... 10.00 |
| TPB Underboss, 144-pg. (2002).. 15.00 |
| TPB Love's Labor Lost (2002).... 20.00 |
| TPB Daredevil Movie adapt...... 13.00 |
| TPB Legends Vol.4:Typhoid Mary. 20.00 |
| TPB Vol. 4: Hardcore........... 14.00 |
| TPB Vol. 5: Out................ 20.00 |
| TPB Vol. 6: Lowlife............. 14.00 |

DAREDEVIL: THE MAN WITHOUT FEAR
1993–94
| 1 B:FM(s),JR2,AW,O:Daredevil, |
| A:Stick,D:Daredevil's Father... 7.00 |
| 2 JR2,AW,A:Stick,Stone,Elektra... 6.00 |
| 3 JR2,AW,A:Elektra,Kingpin...... 6.00 |
| 4 JR2,AW,A:Kingpin,I:Mickey.... 6.00 |
| 5 JR2,AW,A:Mickey,Last Issue.... 6.00 |
| TPB rep.#1#5................. 15.95 |

DAREDEVIL: NINJA
Oct., 2000
| 1 (of 3) BMB,Stick.............. 5.00 |
| 2 BMB,V:Hand................. 4.00 |
| 3 BMB,concl................... 4.00 |
| TPB rep. 80-page.............. 8.95 |

DAREDEVIL/SHI SHI/DAREDEVIL
Marvel/Crusade 1996
| 1 (Daredevil/Shi) TSg,AW, |
| x-over,pt.1................. 5.00 |
| 1 (Shi/Daredevil) x-over, pt.2..... 5.00 |

DAREDEVIL/SPIDER-MAN
Nov., 2000
| 1 (of 4) AxR,PJe,............... 4.00 |
| 2 AxR,PJe,Gladiator,Stilt-Man.... 4.00 |
| 3 AxR,PJe,Owl,Copperhead...... 4.00 |
| 4 AxR,PJe,TP,concl............. 4.00 |

DAREDEVIL: THE TARGET
Nov., 2002
| 1 (of 4) KSm,GF,V:Bullseye...... 3.50 |

DAREDEVIL: YELLOW
March, 2001
| 1 (of 6) JLb,TSe,O:Daredevil.... 10.00 |
| 2 JLb,TSe,Vengeance.......... 6.00 |
| 3 JLb,TSe,F:Fantastic Four...... 6.00 |
| 4 JLb,TSe,V:Electro............ 6.00 |
| 5 JLb,TSe,V:Owl............... 6.00 |
| 6 JLb,TSe,last yellow costume.... 6.00 |
| TPB series rep................ 15.00 |

DARING MYSTERY COMICS
Timely, Jan., 1940
| 1 ASh(c),JSm,O:Fiery Mask, |
| A:Monako John Steele,Doc Doyle, |
| Flash FosterBarney Mullen, |
| Sea Rover, Bondage (c).. 30,000.00 |
| 2 ASh(c),JSm,O:Phantom Bullet |
| A:Zephyr Jones & K4,Laughing |
| Mask Mr.E,B:Trojak...... 12,000.00 |
| 3 ASh(c),JSm,A:Phantom |
| Reporter,Marvex,Breeze |
| Barton, B:Purple Mask.... 7,000.00 |
| 4 ASh(c),A:G-Man Ace,K4, |
| Monako,Marvex,E:Purple |
| Mask,B:Whirlwind Carter.. 4,500.00 |
| 5 JSm,B:Falcon,A:Fiery Mask,K4, |
| Little Hercules,Bondage(c) 4,500.00 |
| 6 S&K,O:Marvel Boy,A:Fiery |
| Mask, Flying Fame,Dynaman, |

Daring #10
© *Marvel Entertainment Group*

CVA Page 222   All comics prices listed are for *Near Mint* condition.

MARVEL

Daring–Dazzler

```
           Stuporman,E:Trojak . . . . . 5,500.00
 7 S&K,O:Blue Diamond,A:The Fin,
   Challenger,Captain Daring,
   Silver Scorpion,Thunderer . 4,500.00
 8 S&K,O:Citizen V,A:Thunderer,
   Fin Silver Scorpion,Captain
   Daring Blue Diamond. . . . . 3,500.00
 Becomes:
```

DARING COMICS
1944

```
 9 A:Sh(c),B:Human Torch,Toro,
   Sub Mariner . . . . . . . . . . . 1,500.00
10 A:Sh(c),A;The Angel. . . . . . . 1,200.00
11 A:Sh(c),A:The Destroyer. . . . 1,200.00
12 E:Human Torch,Toro,Sub-
   Mariner, Fall, 1945. . . . . . . 1,200.00
Becomes:
```

JEANIE COMICS
1947

```
13 B:Jeanie,Queen of the
   Teens Mitzi,Willie . . . . . . . . 200.00
14 Baseball(c) . . . . . . . . . . . . . . 150.00
15 Schoolbus(c) . . . . . . . . . . . . . 150.00
16 Swimsuit(c) . . . . . . . . . . . . . 165.00
17 HK,Fancy dress party(c),
   Hey Look . . . . . . . . . . . . . . 125.00
18 HK,Jeanie'sDate(c),Hey Look. 100.00
19 Ice-Boat(c),Hey Look . . . . . . 125.00
20 Jukebox(c). . . . . . . . . . . . . . 100.00
21 . . . . . . . . . . . . . . . . . . . . . . 100.00
22 HK,Hey Look . . . . . . . . . . . . 125.00
23 . . . . . . . . . . . . . . . . . . . . . . 100.00
24 . . . . . . . . . . . . . . . . . . . . . . 100.00
25 . . . . . . . . . . . . . . . . . . . . . . 100.00
26 . . . . . . . . . . . . . . . . . . . . . . 100.00
27 E:Jeanie,Queen of Teens. . . . 100.00
Becomes:
```

COWGIRL ROMANCES
1950

```
28 Ph(c),Mona Freeman/MacDonald
   Carey,Copper Canyon . . . . . 225.00
```

DARK ANGEL
See: HELL'S ANGEL

DARK CRYSTAL
April, 1983

```
1 movie adaption . . . . . . . . . . . . . 3.00
2 movie adaption,May, 1983 . . . . 3.00
```

DARK GUARD
1993–94

```
1 A:All UK Heroes . . . . . . . . . . . . 3.00
2 A:All UK Heroes . . . . . . . . . . . . 2.25
3 V:Leader,MyS-Tech . . . . . . . . . 2.25
4 V:MyS-Tech . . . . . . . . . . . . . . . 2.25
5 . . . . . . . . . . . . . . . . . . . . . . . . . 2.25
6 and 7 . . . . . . . . . . . . . . . . . . @2.25
```

DARKHAWK
March, 1991

```
 1 MM,I&O:Darkhawk,
   A:Hobgoblin . . . . . . . . . . . . . . 5.00
 2 MM,A:Spider-Man,V:Hobgoblin . . 3.00
 3 MM,A:Spider-Man,V:Hobgoblin . . 3.00
 4 MM,I:Savage Steel . . . . . . . . . . 3.00
 5 MM,I:Portal. . . . . . . . . . . . . . . . 3.00
 6 MM,A:Cap.Am,D.D.,Portal,
   V:U-Foes . . . . . . . . . . . . . . . . 3.00
 7 MM,I:Lodestone . . . . . . . . . . . . 2.50
 8 MM,V:Lodestone . . . . . . . . . . . 2.50
 9 MM,A:Punisher,V:Savage Steel . 2.50
10 MM,A&N:Tombstone . . . . . . . . 2.50
11 MM,V:Tombstone . . . . . . . . . . . 2.50
12 MM,V:Tombstone,R:Dark
```

Darkhawk #43
© Marvel Entertainment Group

```
   Hawks'Father. . . . . . . . . . . . . 2.50
13 MM,V:Venom. . . . . . . . . . . . . . 3.00
14 MM,V:Venom,D:Dark
   Hawks Father. . . . . . . . . . . . . 3.00
15 MM,Heart of the Hawk,concl . . . 2.25
16 MM,V:Terrorists . . . . . . . . . . . . 2.25
17 MM,I:Peristrike Force. . . . . . . . 2.25
18 MM,V:Mindwolf . . . . . . . . . . . . 2.25
19 MM,R:Portal,A:Spider-Man,V:The
   Brotherhood of Evil Mutants . . . 2.25
20 MM,A:Spider-Man,Sleepwalker,
   V:Brotherhood of Evil Mutants . 2.25
21 MM,B:Return to Forever . . . . . 2.25
22 MM,A:Ghost Rider . . . . . . . . . . 2.25
23 MM,I:Evilhawk . . . . . . . . . . . . . 2.25
24 V:Evilhawk. . . . . . . . . . . . . . . . 2.25
25 MM,O:Darkhawk,V:Evilhawk,
   Holo-graphx(c) . . . . . . . . . . . . 3.50
26 A:New Warriors . . . . . . . . . . . . 2.25
27 A:New Warriors,V:Zarrko . . . . . 2.25
28 A:New Warriors,Zarrko . . . . . . . 2.25
29 A:New Warriors . . . . . . . . . . . . 2.25
30 I:Purity. . . . . . . . . . . . . . . . . . . 2.25
31 Infinity Crusade . . . . . . . . . . . . 2.25
32 R:Savage Steel . . . . . . . . . . . . 2.25
33 I:Cuda . . . . . . . . . . . . . . . . . . . 2.25
34 V:Cuda . . . . . . . . . . . . . . . . . . 2.25
35 DFr(s),V:Venom . . . . . . . . . . . 2.25
36 DFr(s),V:Scokers,A:Venom . . . 2.25
37 DFr(s),V:Venom. . . . . . . . . . . . 2.25
38 DFr(s),N:Darkhawk . . . . . . . . . 2.25
39 DFr(s) . . . . . . . . . . . . . . . . . . . 2.25
40 DFr(s) . . . . . . . . . . . . . . . . . . . 2.25
41 DFr(s) . . . . . . . . . . . . . . . . . . . 2.25
42 DFr(s), V:Portal,I:Shaper . . . . . 2.25
43 DFr(s) . . . . . . . . . . . . . . . . . . . 2.25
44 DFr(s) . . . . . . . . . . . . . . . . . . . 2.25
45 DFr(s),A:Portal. . . . . . . . . . . . . 2.25
46 DFr(s) . . . . . . . . . . . . . . . . . . . 2.25
47 . . . . . . . . . . . . . . . . . . . . . . . . 2.25
48 R:Darkhawk,V:Mahari . . . . . . . 2.25
49 V:Overhawk. . . . . . . . . . . . . . . 2.25
50 V:Overhawk. . . . . . . . . . . . . . . 2.25
Ann.#1 MM,Assault on ArmorCity . . 3.00
Ann.#2 GC,AW,I:Dreamkiller,
   w/Trading card . . . . . . . . . . . 3.00
Ann.#3 I:Damek . . . . . . . . . . . . . . 3.00
```

DARKHOLD
1992–94

```
1 RCa,I:Redeemers,Polybagged
  w/poster,A:Gh.Rider,Blaze . . . . 3.00
2 RCa,R:Modred . . . . . . . . . . . . . 2.50
3 A:Modred,Scarlet Witch . . . . . . 2.25
4 V:Sabretooth,N'Garai . . . . . . . . 2.25
5 A:Punisher, Ghost Rider . . . . . . 2.25
6 RCa,V:Dr.Strange. . . . . . . . . . . 2.25
7 A:Dr.Strange,V:Japanese Army . . 2.25
8 Betrayal #1. . . . . . . . . . . . . . . . 2.25
9 Diabolique . . . . . . . . . . . . . . . . 2.25
10 V:Darkholders . . . . . . . . . . . . . 2.25
11 Midnight Massacre#3,D:Modred,
   Vicki . . . . . . . . . . . . . . . . . . . 2.50
12 V:Chthon . . . . . . . . . . . . . . . . . 2.25
13 V:Missing Link . . . . . . . . . . . . . 2.25
14 Vicki's Secret revealed. . . . . . . 2.25
15 Siege of Darkness,pt.#4. . . . . . 2.25
16 Siege of Darkness,pt.#12. . . . . 2.25
```

DARK MAN
MOVIE ADAPTION
Sept., 1990

```
1 BH/MT/TD . . . . . . . . . . . . . . . . 3.00
2 BH/TD . . . . . . . . . . . . . . . . . . . 2.50
3 BH/TD,final issue . . . . . . . . . . . 2.50
```

DARKMAN
Sept., 1990

```
1 JS,R:Darkman . . . . . . . . . . . . . 4.50
2 JS,V:Witchfinder . . . . . . . . . . . . 3.00
3 JS,Witchfinder . . . . . . . . . . . . . 3.00
4 JS,V:Dr.West . . . . . . . . . . . . . . 3.00
5 JS,Durant . . . . . . . . . . . . . . . . 3.00
6 JS,V:Durant . . . . . . . . . . . . . . . 3.00
```

DATE WITH MILLIE
Atlas, Oct., 1956
[1st Series]

```
1 . . . . . . . . . . . . . . . . . . . . . . . 275.00
2 . . . . . . . . . . . . . . . . . . . . . . . 150.00
3 thru 7 . . . . . . . . . . . . . . . . . @100.00
```

[2nd Series], Oct., 1959

```
1 . . . . . . . . . . . . . . . . . . . . . . . 150.00
2 thru 7 . . . . . . . . . . . . . . . . . @100.00
Becomes:
```

LIFE WITH MILLIE
1960

```
8 . . . . . . . . . . . . . . . . . . . . . . . 100.00
9 & 10 . . . . . . . . . . . . . . . . . . . @75.00
11 thru 20 . . . . . . . . . . . . . . . . . @50.00
Becomes:
```

MODELING WITH MILLIE
1963

```
21 . . . . . . . . . . . . . . . . . . . . . . . 75.00
22 thru 54 June, 1967 . . . . . . . . @50.00
```

DATE WITH PATSY
Sept., 1957

```
1 A:Patsy Walker . . . . . . . . . . . 125.00
```

DAYDREAMERS
Aug., 1997

```
1 (of 3) JMD,MEg,HSm . . . . . . . . 2.75
2 JMD,MEg,HSm . . . . . . . . . . . . 2.75
3 JMD,TDz,MEg,HSm,concl. . . . . 2.75
```

DAZZLER
March, 1981

```
1 AA,JR2,A:X-Men,Spm,
  O:Dazzler. . . . . . . . . . . . . . . . 5.00
2 WS,JR2,AA,X-Men,A:SpM . . . . 3.00
3 JR2,Dr.Doom . . . . . . . . . . . . . . 3.00
4 FS,Dr.Doom . . . . . . . . . . . . . . . 3.00
5 FS,I:Blue Shield . . . . . . . . . . . . 3.00
6 FS,Hulk . . . . . . . . . . . . . . . . . . 3.00
7 FS,Hulk . . . . . . . . . . . . . . . . . . 3.00
```

Dazzler–Deadpool

8 FS,Quasar	3.00
9 FS,D:Klaw	3.00
10 FS,Galactus	3.00
11 FS,Galactus	3.00
12 FS,The Light That Failed	3.00
13 FS,V:Grapplers	3.00
14 FS,She Hulk	3.00
15 FS,BSz,Spider Women	3.00
16 FS,BSz,Enchantress	3.00
17 FS,Angel,V:Doc Octopus	3.00
18 FS,BSz,A:Fantastic Four,Angel, V:Absorbing Man	3.00
19 FS,Blue Bolt,V:Absorbing Man	3.00
20 FS,V:Jazz and Horn	3.00
21 FS,A:Avengers,F.F.,C:X-Men, (double size)	3.00

Dazzler #20
© Marvel Entertainment Group

22 FS,V:Rogue,Mystique	4.00
23 FS,V:Rogue,A:Powerman, Iron Fist	3.00
24 FS,V:Rogue,A:Powerman, Iron Fist	4.00
25 FS,`The Jagged Edge'	3.00
26 FS,Lois London	3.00
27 FS,Fugitive	3.50
28 FS,V:Rogue	4.00
29 FS,Roman Nekoboh	3.00
30 FS,Moves to California	3.00
31 FS,The Last Wave	3.00
32 FS,A:Inhumans	3.00
33 Chiller	3.50
34 FS,Disappearance	3.00
35 FS,V:Racine Ramjets	3.00
36 JBy(c),FS,V:Tatterdemalion	3.00
37 JBy(c),FS	3.00
38 PC,JG,X-Men	5.00
39 PC,JG,Caught in the grip of death	3.00
40 PC,JG,Secret Wars II	3.50
41 PC,JG,A:Beast	3.50
42 PC,JG,A:Beast,last issue	3.50

DEADLIEST HEROES OF KUNG FU
Summer, 1975

1 Magazine size	30.00

DEADLINE
April, 2002

1 (of 4) GyD, F:Katherine Farrell Daily Bugle reporter	3.25

MARVEL

2 GyD,The Judge	3.25
3 GyD,The Judge	3.25
4 GyD,finale	3.25
TPB series rep	10.00

DEADLY FOES OF SPIDER-MAN
May, 1991

1 AM,KGa,V:Sinister Syndicate	4.00
2 AM,Boomerang on Trial	3.00
3 AM,Deadly Foes Split	3.00
4 AM,Conclusion	3.00
TPB rep. #1–#4	12.95

DEADLY HANDS OF KUNG FU
April, 1974

1 NA(c),JSa,JSon,O:Sons of the Tiger, B:Shang-Chi, Bruce Lee Pin-up	50.00
2 NA(c),JSa	35.00
3 NA(c),JSon,A:Sons of the Tiger	25.00
4 NA(Bruce Lee)(c),JSon,Bruce Lee biography	25.00
5 BWS,PG	22.00
6 GP,JSon,A:Sons of the Tiger	22.00
7 GP,JSon,A:Sons of the Tiger	25.00
8 GP,JSon,A:Sons of the Tiger	20.00
9 GP,JSon,A:Sons of the Tiger	20.00
10 GP,JSon,A:Sons of the Tiger	25.00
11 NA(c),GP,JSon,A:Sons of the Tiger	20.00
12 NA(c),GP,JSon,A:Sons of the Tiger	20.00
13 GP,JSon,A:Sons of the Tiger	20.00
14 NA(c),GP,HC,JSon,A:Sons of the Tiger	65.00
15 JS.PG,JSn,,Annual #1	22.00
16 JSn,A:Sons of the Tiger	20.00
17 NA(c),JSn,KG,A:Sons of the Tiger	20.00
18 JSn,A:Sons of the Tiger	20.00
19 JSn,I:White Tiger	22.00
20 GP,O:White Tiger	20.00
21	20.00
22 KG,C:Jack of Hearts	20.00
23 GK,Jack of Hearts	25.00
24 KG,Ironfist	25.00
25 I:Shimaru	25.00
26	25.00
27	20.00
28 Bruce Lee Special	75.00
29 Ironfist vs. Shang Chi	25.00
30 Swordquest	20.00
31 JSon, Jack of Hearts	20.00
32 MR,JSon,Daughters of the Dragon	20.00
33 MR,Feb., 1977	22.00
Spec. Album Ed.,NA, Sum.,1974	25.00

DEAD OF NIGHT
Dec., 1973–Aug., 1975

1 JSt,Horror reprints,A Haunted House is not a Home	30.00
2 BEv(c),House that Fear Built	15.00
3 They Lurk Below	15.00
4 Warewolf Beware	15.00
5 Deep Down	15.00
6 Jack the Ripper	15.00
7 SD,The Thirteenth Floor	15.00
8 Midnight Brings Dark Madness	15.00
9 Deathride	15.00
10 SD,I Dream of Doom	15.00
11 GK/BWr(c),I:Scarecrow, Fires of Rebirth,Fires of Death	35.00

Comics Values Annual

DEADPOOL
1993

1 B:FaN(s),JMd,MFm(i), V:Slayback,Nyko	5.00
2 JMd,MFm(i),V:Black Tom Cassidy,Juggernaut	4.00
3 JMd,MFm(i),I:Comcast, Makeshift,Rive,A:Slayback	4.00
4 E:FaN(s),JMd,MFm(i), A:Slayback,Kane	4.00

[2nd Limited Series], 1994

1 A:Banshee,Syrin,Juggernaut Black Tom	4.00
2 A:Banshee,Syrin,V:Juggernaut	4.00
3 A:Syrin,Juggernaut	4.00
4 Final issue	4.00

DEADPOOL
1996

1 NMa,V:Sasquatch,48pg	7.00
2 NMa,A:Copycat	4.00
3 NMa,A:Siryn	3.00
4 NMa,Will Hulk cure him?	3.00
5 NMa,A:Siryn,T-Ray	3.00
6 NMa,I:	3.00
7 AaL,A:Typhoid Mary	3.00
8 NMa, cont. from Daredevil/ Deadpool '97,A:Gerry	3.00
9 NMa, new villain	3.00
10 NMa,A:Great Lake Avengers	3.00
11 NMa,Fall through time, A:Alfred	5.00
12 NMa,Typhoid Mary, Zoe Culldoon & Siryn return	2.50
13 NMa,V:T-Ray	2.50
14 WMc,Deal of a Lifetime	2.50
15 WMc,A:Landau, Luckman & Lake	2.50
16 WMc, in middle east	2.50
17 WMc, Landau, Luckman & Lake's plan	2.50
18 WMc,V:Ajax	2.50
19 WMc,more secrets of blind Al	2.50
20 Cosmic Messiah	2.50
21	2.50
22 WMc,A:Cable	2.50
23 WMc,Dead Reckoning,pt.1 48-page	3.00
24 WMc,Dead Reckoning,pt.2	2.50
25 WMc,Dead Reckoning,pt.3	3.00
26 Dead Reckoning, aftermath	2.50
27 V:A.I.M. concl	2.50
28 R:Weasel	2.50
29 V:Bullseye	2.50
30 A:Mercedes,T-Ray	2.50
31 V:T-Ray	2.50
32 V:T-Ray,A:Mercedes	2.50
33 V:T-Ray	2.50
34 CPr,Chapter Pt.1	2.50
35 CPr	2.50
36 CPr	2.50
37 CPr,Chapter X,Addendum	2.50
38 CPr,F:Taskmaster	2.50
39 CPr,F:Taskmaster	2.50
40 CPr,space station	2.50
41 CPr,V:Dirty Wolf	2.25
42 V:Humbug	2.25
43 CPr,JCf,V:Rasputin	2.25
44 CPr,JCf,CatTrap,pt.1,x-over	2.25
45 CPr,JCf,Constrictor	2.25
46 JJu,JP,PC,CruelSummer,pt.1	2.25
47 JP,PC,CruelSummer,pt.2	2.25
48 JP,PC,CruelSummer,pt.3	2.25
49 JP,dating?	2.25
50 AAd,JP,DaR,I:Kid Deadpool	2.25
51 JP,DaR,F:Kid Deadpool	2.25
52 JP,AWi,ALa,V:Mercy Sisters	2.25
53 JP,AWi,ALa,V:Mercy Sisters	2.25
54 JP,V:Punisher	2.25
55 JP,V:Punisher, round two	2.25

MARVEL

Deadpool–Death's

Deadpool #5
© Marvel Entertainment Group

56 F:Siryn	2.25
57 JHo,BWS(c),Agent of Weapon X	3.00
58 JHo,BWS(c),Agent of Weapon X	3.00
59 JHo,BWS(c),Agent of Weapon X	3.00
60 JHo,BWS(c),Agent of Weapon X	3.00
61 Funeral For a Freak 1	2.50
62 Funeral For a Freak 2	2.50
63 Funeral For a Freak 3	2.50
64 Funeral For a Freak 4	2.50
65 Did Deadpool survive.	2.25
66 steal from Rhino?	2.25
67 R:Dazzler	2.25
68 V:Black Swan, insanity	2.25
69 V:Black Swan	2.25
Ann. '98 BCh(c) F:Deadpool & Death, 48pg	3.00
Minus 1 Spec., ALo, flashback, O:Deadpool	2.00
Spec. Deadpool Team-Up,2 Deadpools,F:Widdle Wade	3.00
Spec. Baby's First Deadpool Book	3.00
Spec. Encyclopedia Deadpoolica	3.00
TPB Circle Chase,FaN,JMd,MFm,	12.95
TPB Mission Improbable	14.95
TPB MWa,IaC,Sins of the Past, rep. limited series	6.00

DEATH3
1993
1 I:Death Metal,Death Wreck	3.00
2 V:Ghost Rider	2.50
3 A:Hulk,Cable,Storm,Thing	2.50
4 Last issue	2.50

DEATHLOK
[Limited Series], July, 1990
1 JC,SW,I:Michael Colins (2nd Deathlok)	4.00
2 JC,SW,V:Wajler	3.50
3 DCw,SW,V:Cyberants	3.50
4 DCw,SW,V:Sunfire,final issue	3.50

[Regular Series], 1991–94
1 DCw,MM,V:Warwolf	2.50
2 DCw,MM,A:Dr.Doom,Machine Man,Forge	2.50
3 DCw,MM,V:Dr.Doom, A:Mr.Fantastic	2.50
4 DCw,MM,A:X-Men,F.F.,Vision, O:Mechadoom	2.50
5 DCw,MM,V:Mechadoom, A:X-Men,Fantastic Four	2.50
6 DCw,MM,A:Punisher, V:Silvermane	2.50
7 DCw,MM,A:Punisher, V:Silvermane	2.50
8 A:Main Frame,Ben Jacobs	2.00
9 DCw,MM,A:Ghost Rider, V:Nightmare	2.50
10 DCw,MM,A:GhR,V:Nightmare	2.50
11 DCw,MM,V:Moses Magnum	2.50
12 DCw,MM,Biohazard Agenda	2.50
13 DCw,MM,Biohazard Agenda	2.50
14 DCw,MM,Biohazard Agenda	2.50
15 DCw,MM,Biohazard Agenda	2.50
16 DCw,MM,Inf.War,V:Evilok.	2.50
17 WMc,MM,B:Cyberwar	2.50
18 WMc,A:Silver Sable	2.50
18a Newstand Ed.	2.50
19 SMc,Cyberwar#3	3.50
20 SMc,Cyberwar#4	2.50
21 E:Cyberwar,A:Cold Blood Nick Fury	2.50
22 V:MosesMagnum,A:Bl.Panther	2.50
23 A:Bl.Panther,V:Phreak,Stroke	2.50
24 V:MosesMagnum,A:Bl.Panther	2.50
25 WMc,V:MosesMagnum,A:Black Panther,holo-grafx(c)	3.50
26 V:Hobogoblin	2.50
27 R:Siege	2.50
28 Infnty Crusade	2.50
29 Inner Fears	2.50
30 KHd,V:Hydra	2.50
31 GWt(s),KoK,B:Cyberstrike, R:1st Deathlok	2.50
32 GWt(s),KoK,A:Siege	2.50
33 GWt(s),KoK,V:Justice Peace	2.50
34 GWt(s),KoK,E:Cyberstrike,V:Justice Peace,final issue	2.50
Ann.#1 JG,I:Timestream	3.00
Ann.#2 I:Tracer,w/card	3.25

DEATHLOK
July, 1999
1 JoC,JQ&JaL(c),Marvel Tech	2.50
2 JoC,A:Nick Fury	2.25
2a variant cover	2.25
3 JoC,I:Billy Bailey	2.25
4 JoC,R:Clown	2.25
5 JoC,I:Jack Truman	2.25
6 JoC,	2.25
7 JoC,V:Serpent Society	2.25
8 JoC,Nick Fury	2.50
9 JoC,V:Ringmaster	2.50
10 JoC,V:Clown	2.50
11 JoC,V:Clown	2.50

DEATHLOK SPECIAL
1991
1 Rep.Mini Series	2.50
2 Rep.Mini Series	2.50
3 Rep.Mini Series	2.50
4 Rep.Mini Series, final issue	2.50

DEATH METAL
Marvel UK, 1994
1 JRe,I:Argon,C:Alpha Flight	2.25
2 JRe,V:Alpha Flight	2.25
3 JRe,I:Soulslug	2.25
4 Re,Last Issue	2.25

DEATH METAL VS. GENETIX
Marvel UK, 1993–94
1 PaD,w/card	3.00
2 PaD,w/card	3.00

DEATH'S HEAD
Marvel UK, Dec., 1988
1 V:Backbreaker	5.00
2 A:Dragons Claws	4.00
3	4.00
4 V:Plague Dog	3.00
5 V:Big Shot	3.00
6 V:Big Shot	3.00
7 & 8	@3.00
9 A:Fantastic Four	3.50
10 A:Iron Man	3.50
TPB Reprints#1-#10	12.95

DEATH'S HEAD
[Limited Series]
1 A:`Old' Death's Head	2.00

Death's Head II #10
© Marvel Entertainment Group

DEATH'S HEAD II
Marvel UK, March, 1992
[Limited Series]
1 LSh,I:2nd Death's Head, D:1st Death's Head	4.00
1a 2nd printing,Silver	2.50
2 LSh,A:Fantastic Four	3.00
2a 2nd printing,Silver	3.00
3 LSh,I:Tuck	3.50
4 LSh,A:Wolverine,Spider-Man, Punisher	3.50

[Regular Series], 1992
1 LSh,A:X-Men,I:Wraithchilde	3.00
2 LSh,A:X-Men	2.25
3 LSh,A:X-Men,V:Raptors	2.25
4 LSh,A:X-Men,V:Wraithchilde	2.25
5 V:UnDeath's Head II, A:Warheads	2.25
6 R:Tuck,V:Major Oak	2.25
7 V:Major Oak	2.25
8 V:Wizard Methinx	2.25
9 BHi,V:Cybernetic Centaurs	2.25
10 DBw,A:Necker	2.25
11 SCy,R:Charnel	2.25
12 DAn(s),SvL,V:Charnel	2.25
13 SvL,A:Liger	2.25
14 SvL,Brain Dead Cold,Blue Foil(c)	3.25
15 SvL,V:Duplicates	2.25
16 SvL,DAn	2.25
17 SvL,DAn	2.00
18 SvL,DAn	2.00
Spec. Gold Ed. LSh(a&s)	3.95

Death's–Defenders / MARVEL / Comics Values Annual

DEATH'S HEAD II/DIE CUT
Marvel UK, 1993
1 I:Die Cut................. 3.25
2 O:Die Cut................ 2.25

DEATH'S HEAD II/ KILLPOWER: BATTLETIDE
[1st Limited Series]
1 GSr,A:Wolverine........... 2.50
2 thru 4 GSr,A:Wolverine..... @2.25

[2nd Limited Series]
1 A:Hulk.................. 3.25
2 V:Hulk.................. 2.25
3 A:Hulk.................. 2.25
4 last issue................ 2.25

DEATH-WRECK
Marvel UK, 1994
1 A:Death's Head II.......... 2.25
2 V:Gangsters.............. 2.25
3 A:Dr.Necker.............. 2.25
4 last issue................ 2.25

DEEP, THE
Nov., 1977
1 CI,Movie Adaption.......... 8.00

DEFENDERS
Aug., 1972
1 SB,I&D:Necrodames....... 135.00
2 SB,V:Calizuma............ 60.00
3 GK(c),SB,JM,V:UndyingOne... 40.00
4 SB,FMc,Bl.Knight,V:Valkyrie... 40.00
5 SB,FMc,D:Omegatron....... 40.00
6 SB,FMc,V:Cyrus Black...... 35.00
7 SB,FBe,A:Hawkeye......... 30.00
8 SB,FBe,Avengers,SilverSurfer. 40.00
9 SB,FMc,Avengers.......... 40.00
10 SB,FBe,Thor vs. Hulk...... 50.00
11 SB,FBe,A:Avengers....... 35.00
12 SB,JA,Xemnu............ 20.00
13 GK(c),SB,KJ,J:Night Hawk... 20.00
14 SB,DGr,O:Hyperion....... 20.00
15 SB,KJ,A:Professor X,V:Magneto,
   Savage Land Mutates....... 25.00
16 GK(c),SB,Professor X,V:Magneto,
   Savage Land Mutates....... 25.00
17 SB,DGr,Power Man......... 12.00
18 GK(c),SB,DGr,A:Power Man.. 12.00
19 GK(c),SB,KJ,A:Power Man.. 12.00
20 K&R(c),SB,A:Thing........ 12.00
21 GK(c),SB,O:Valkyrie....... 7.00
22 GK(c),SB,V:Sons o/t Serpent.. 7.00
23 GK(c),SB,A:Yellow Jacket... 7.00
24 GK(c),SB,BMc,A:Daredevil.... 7.00
25 GK(c),SB,JA,A:Daredevil..... 7.00
26 K&R(c),SB,A:Guardians... 10.00
27 K&R(c),SB,A:Guardians
   C:Starhawk.............. 10.00
28 K&R(c),SB,A:Guardians
   I:Starhawk............... 8.00
29 K&R(c),SB,A:Guardians..... 8.00
30 JA(i),A:Wong............. 6.00
31 GK(c),SB,JM,Nighthawk..... 6.00
32 GK(c),SB,JM,O:Nighthawk.... 6.00
33 GK(c),SB,JM,V:Headmen..... 6.00
34 SB,JM,V:Nebulon.......... 6.00
35 GK(c),SB,KJ,I:Red Guardian.. 6.00
36 GK(c),SB,KJ,A:Red Guardian. 12.00
37 GK(c),SB,KJ,J:Luke Cage.... 7.00
38 SB,KJ,V:Nebulon.......... 12.00
39 SB,KJ,V:Felicia............ 5.00
40 SB,KJ,V:Assassin.......... 5.00
41 KG,KJ,Nighthawk.......... 5.00
42 KG,KJ,V:Rhino............ 5.00
43 KG,KJ,Cobalt Man,Egghead.. 5.00
44 KG,KJ,J:Hellcat,V:Red Rajah... 5.00
45 KG,KJ,Valkyrie V:Hulk...... 5.00
46 KG,KJ,L:DrStrange,LukeCage.. 5.00
47 KG,KJ,Moon Knight........ 5.00
48 KG,A:Wonder Man......... 5.00
49 KG,O:Scorpio............. 5.00
50 KG,Zodiac,D:Scorpio....... 5.00
51 KG,Moon Knight.......... 5.00
52 KG,Hulk,V:Sub Mariner..... 5.00
53 KG,DC,MG,TA,C&I:Lunatik... 4.00
54 MG,Nigh Fury............. 4.00
55 CI,O:Red Guardian......... 4.00
56 CI,KJ,Hellcat,V:Lunatik..... 4.00
57 DC,Ms.Marvel............ 4.00
58 Return of Dr.Strange....... 4.00
59 I:Belathauzer............. 4.00
60 V:Vera Gemini............ 4.00
61 Spider-Man,A:Lunatik...... 5.00
62 Hercules,C:Polaris......... 3.00
63 Mutli Heroes.............. 3.00
64 Mutli Heroes.............. 3.00

Defenders #64
© Marvel Entertainment Group

65 Red Guardian............. 3.00
66 JB,Valkyrie I.............. 3.00
67 Valkryie II................ 3.00
68 HT,When Falls the Mountain.. 3.00
69 HT,A:The Anything Man..... 3.00
70 HT,A:Lunatik.............. 3.00
71 HT,O:Lunatik.............. 3.00
72 HT,V:Lunatik.............. 3.00
73 HT,Foolkiller,V:WizardKing... 5.00
74 HT,Foolkiller,L:Nighthawk... 5.00
75 HT,Foolkiller.............. 4.00
76 HT,O:Omega.............. 2.50
77 HT,Moon Dragon.......... 2.50
78 HT,Yellow Jacket.......... 2.50
79 HT,Tunnel World.......... 2.50
80 HT,DGr,Nighthawk......... 2.50
81 HT,Tunnel World.......... 2.50
82 DP,JSt,Tunnel World....... 2.50
83 DP,JSt,Tunnel World....... 2.50
84 DP,JSt,Black Panther....... 2.50
85 DP,JSt,Black Panther....... 2.50
86 DP,JSt,Black Panther....... 2.50
87 DP,JSt,V:Mutant Force..... 2.50
88 DP,JSt,Matt Mardock...... 2.50
89 DP,JSt,D:Hellcat's
   Mother, O:Mad-Dog....... 2.50
90 DP,JSt,Daredevil.......... 2.50
91 DP,JSt,Daredevil.......... 2.50
92 DP,JSt,A:Eternity,
   Son of Satan............. 3.00
93 DP,JSt,Son of Satan....... 3.00
94 DP,JSt,I:Gargoyle......... 2.50
95 DP,JSt,V:Dracula,O:Gargoyle.. 2.50
96 DP,JSt,Ghost Rider........ 3.00
97 DP,JSt,False Messiah...... 2.50
98 DP,JSt,A:Man Thing....... 2.50
99 DP,JSt,Conflict............ 2.50
100 DP,JSt,DoubleSize,V:Satan... 6.00
101 DP,JSt,Silver Surfer....... 2.50
102 DP,JSt,Nighthawk......... 2.50
103 DP,JSt,I:Null............. 2.50
104 DP,JSt,Devilslayer,J:Beast... 2.50
105 DP,JSt,V:Satan........... 2.50
106 DP,Daredevil,D:Nighthawk... 2.50
107 DP,JSt,Enchantress,A:D.D... 2.50
108 DP,A:Enchantress......... 2.50
109 DP,A:Spider-Man......... 3.00
110 DP,A:Devilslayer......... 2.50
111 DP,A:Hellcat............. 2.50
112 DP,A:SquadronSupreme... 2.50
113 DP,A:SquadronSupreme... 2.50
114 DP,A:SquadronSupreme... 2.50
115 DP,A:Submariner......... 2.50
116 DP,Gargoyle............. 2.50
117 DP,Valkyrie.............. 2.50
118 DP,V:Miracleman........ 2.50
119 DP,V:Miracleman........ 2.50
120 DP,V:Miracleman........ 2.50
121 DP,V:Miracleman........ 2.50
122 DP,A:Iceman............ 2.50
123 DP,I:Cloud,V:Secret Empire.. 2.50
124 DP,V:Elf................ 2.50
125 DP,New Line-up:Gargoyle,Moon
   dragon,Valkyrie,Iceman,Beast,
   Angel,W:Son of Satan & Hellcat
   I:Mad Dog............... 5.00
126 DP,A:Nick Fury.......... 2.50
127 DP,V:Professor Power.... 2.50
128 DP,V:Professor Power.... 2.50
129 DP,V:Professor Power,New
   Mutants X-over........... 2.50
130 DP,V:Professor Power.... 2.50
131 DP,V:Walrus,A:Frogman... 2.50
132 DP,V:Spore Monster...... 2.50
133 DP,V:Spore Monster...... 2.50
134 DP,I:Manslaughter....... 2.50
135 DP,V:Blowtorch Brand.... 2.50
136 DP,V:Gargoyle........... 2.50
137 DP,V:Gargoyle........... 2.50
138 DP,O:Moondragon....... 2.50
139 DP,A:Red Wolf,V:Trolls... 2.50
140 DP,V:Asgardian Trolls.... 2.50
141 DP,All Flesh is Grass..... 2.50
142 DP,V:M.O.N.S.T.E.R....... 2.50
143 DP,I:Andromeda,Runner.. 2.50
144 DP,A:Moondragon........ 2.50
145 DP,V:Moondragon........ 2.50
146 DP,Cloud............... 2.50
147 DP,A:Andromeda,I:Interloper.. 2.50
148 DP,A:Nick Fury.......... 2.50
149 DP,V:Manslaughter,O:Cloud.. 2.50
150 DP,O:Cloud,double-size... 5.00
151 DP,A:Interloper.......... 2.50
152 DP,Secret Wars II,D:Moon-
   dragon,Valkyrie,Gargoyle... 5.00
G-Size#1 GK(c),JSn,AM,O:Hulk.. 22.00
G-Size#2 GK,KJ,Son of Satan... 15.00
G-Size#3 JSn,DA,JM,DN,A:D.D... 10.00
G-Size#4 GK(c),DH,A:YellowJack. 20.00
G-Size#5 K&R(c),DH,A:Guardians 25.00
Ann.#1 SB,KJ................ 7.00

DEFENDERS
Jan., 2001
1 EL,KBk,KJ,48-page......... 6.00
2A EL,KBk,KJ................ 3.00
2B variant AAd(c)............. 3.50
3 EL,KBk,KJ,V:Pluto.......... 2.50
4 EL,KBk,KJ,V:Pluto.......... 2.50
5 EL,KBk,KJ,A:Dr.Strange..... 2.50
6 EL,KBk,KJ,A:Red Raven..... 2.50
7 EL,KBk,KJ,A:Red Raven..... 2.50

| 8 EL,KBk,AG,V:Headmen 2.50
9 EL,KBk,RF,V:Headmen 2.50
10 EL,KBk,SB,V:Headmen 2.50
11 EL,KBk,SB,V:Attuma,DeepSix . . 2.50
12 EL,'KBk,'Nuff Said,48-pg. 3.50
Spec.Day of the Defenders, mag. . . 3.50

DEFENDERS OF DYNATRON CITY
1992
1 FC,I:Defenders of Dynatron City
  (from video game & TV ser.) . . . 3.00
2 FC,O:Defender of D.City 3.00
3 FC,A:Dr Mayhem 3.00
4 FC 3.00
5 FC,V:Intelligent Fleas 3.00
6 FC,V:Dr.Mayhem 3.00

DEFENDERS OF THE EARTH
Jan., 1987—Sept., 1984
1 AS,Flash Gordon & Mandrake . . 5.00
2 AS,Flash Gordon & Mandrake . . 4.00
3 AS,O:Phantom 4.00
4 AS,O:Mandrake 4.00

DELLA VISION
Atlas, April, 1955
1 The Television Queen 175.00
2 . . . . 125.00
3 . . . . 125.00
Becomes:

PATTY POWERS
1955
4 . . . . 100.00
5 . . . . 50.00
6 . . . . 50.00
7 Oct., 1956 . . . . 50.00

DENNIS THE MENACE
Nov., 1981–Nov., 1982
1 . . . . 12.00
2 thru 13 . . . . @7.00

DESTROYER, THE
Nov., 1989
1 Black & White Mag. 3.50

Dennis The Menace #1
© Marvel Entertainment Group

MARVEL

2 thru 9 . . . . @2.50
10 June, 1990 . . . . 2.50
TPB rep. B/w mag(color) 9.95

THE DESTROYER: TERROR
Dec., 1991
1 V:Nuihc 2.50
2 V:Nuihc 2.25
3 GM,V:Nuihc 2.25
4 DC,`The Last Dinosaur' 2.25

DEVIL DINOSAUR
April, 1978—Dec., 1978
1 JK,I:Devil Dinosaur,Moon Boy . 25.00
2 JK,War With the Spider God . . . 15.00
3 JK,Giant 15.00
4 JK,Objects From the Sky 15.00
5 JK,The Kingdom of the Ants . . 15.00
6 JK.The Fall 15.00
7 JK,Prisoner of the Demon Tree 15.00
8 JK,V:Dino Riders 15.00
9 JK,Lizards That Stand 15.00

DEVIL DINOSAUR SPRING FLING
1997
Spec. F:Devil Dinosaur,
  Moon-Boy, 48pg 3.00

DEVIL-DOG DUGAN
Atlas, July, 1956
1 War Stories 125.00
2 JSe(c) 75.00
3 . . . . 50.00
Becomes:

TALE OF THE MARINES
4 BP,War Stories 60.00
Becomes:

MARINES AT WAR
5 War Stories 50.00
6 . . . . 50.00
7 The Big Push, Aug., 1957 . . . . 50.00

DEXTER THE DEMON
See: MELVIN THE MONSTER

DIE-CUT
Marvel UK, 1993–94
1 A:Beast 2.50
2 V:X-Beast 2.25
3 A:Beast,Prof.X 2.25
4 V:Red Skull 2.25

DIE-CUT VS. G-FORCE
Marvel UK, 1993
1 SFr(s),LSh(c),I:G-Force 3.00
2 SFr(s),LSh(c),Last issue 3.00

DIGITEK
Marvel UK, 1992–93
1 DPw,I:Digitek,C:Deathlok 2.25
2 DPw,A:Deathlok,V:Bacillicons . . 2.25
3 DPw,A:Deathlok,V:Bacillicons . . 2.25
4 DPw,V:Bacillicons 2.25

DINO RIDERS
Feb., 1989
1 Based on Toys 3.00
2 & 3 . . . . @3.00

Defenders–Doc Savage

DINOSAURS: A CELEBRATION
Epic, 1992
Horns and Heavy Armor 5.00
Bone-Heads and Duck-Bills 5.00
Terrible Claws and Tyrants 5.00
Egg Stealers and Earth Shakers . . 5.00
TPB 192pg 12.95

DISNEY AFTERNOON
1994–95
1 DarkwingDuck vs.FearsomeFive. 3.50
2 thru 10 . . . . @3.00

Disney Comi Hits 36
© Marvel Entertainment Group

DISNEY COMIC HITS
1995
1 . . . . 5.00
2 thru 9 . . . . @4.00
10 Hunchback of Notre Dame 5.00
11 thru 17 . . . . @4.00

DISNEY PRESENTS
1 F:Aladdin 2.50
2 F:Timon & Pummba 2.50
3 . . . . 2.50

DOC OCK VS. SPIDER-MAN
Marvel Nov. 2003
1 . . . . 2.50

DOC SAMSON
1996
1 From The Incredible Hulk 2.25
2 A:She-Hulk 2.25
3 . . . . 2.25
4 . . . . 2.25

DOC SAVAGE
Oct., 1972
1 JM,Pulp Adapts,Death Eighty
  Stories High 30.00
2 JSo(c),The Feathered Serpent
  Strikes 20.00
3 JSo(c),Silver Death's Head 20.00
4 JSo(c),The Hell Diver 15.00
5 GK(c),Night of the Monsters . . . 15.00
6 JSo(c),Where Giants Walk 15.00

All comics prices listed are for *Near Mint* condition.

Doc Savage–Dr. Strange — MARVEL — Comics Values Annual

7 JSo(c),Brand of the Werewolfs . 15.00
8 In the Lair of the Werewolf
 Jan., 1974 .... 15.00
G-Size#1 thru #2 Reprints 12.00

DOC SAVAGE
Aug., 1975
(black & white magazine)
1 JB,Ph(c),Ron Ely 20.00
2 JB 15.00
3 JB 15.00
4 .... 15.00
5 thru 7 .... @15.00
8 Spring 1977 .... 15.00

DOCTOR OCTOPUS: NEGATIVE EXPOSUER
Marvel Oct. 2003
1 (of 5) 2.50
2 .... 2.50

DR. STRANGE
[1st Series], June, 1968
Prev: Strange Tales
169 DA,O:Dr.Strange 225.00
170 DA,A:Ancient One 75.00
171 TP,DA,V:Dormammu 50.00
172 GC,TP,V:Dormammu 50.00
173 GC,TP,V:Dormammu 50.00
174 GC,TP,I:Satannish 50.00
175 GC,TP,I:Asmodeus 50.00
176 GC,TP,V:Asmodeus 50.00
177 GC,TP,D:Asmodeus,
 N:Dr.Strange 50.00
178 GC,TP,A:Black Knight 50.00
179 BWS(c),rep.Amazing Spider-
 Man Ann.#2 .... 50.00
180 GC,TP,V:Nightmare 50.00
181 FB(c),GC,TP,I:Demons of
 Despair 50.00
182 GC,TP,V:Juggernaut 60.00
183 BEv(c),GC,TP,
 I:Undying Ones 60.00

[2nd Regular Series], 1974–87
1 FB,DG,I:Silver Dagger 75.00
2 FB,DG,I:Soul Eater 35.00
3 FB,A:Dormammu 20.00
4 FB,DG,V:Death 20.00
5 FB,DG,A:Silver Dagger 20.00
6 FB(c),GC,KJ,A:Umar,I:Gaea ... 12.00
7 GC,JR,A:Dormammu 12.00
8 GK(c),GC,TP,O:Clea 12.00
9 GK(c),GC,A:Dormammu,O:Clea 12.00
10 B:MWn(s),GK(c),GC,A:Eternity 12.00
11 JR(c),GC,TP,A:Eternity 7.00
12 GC,TP,A:Eternity 7.00
13 GC,TP,A:Eternity 7.00
14 GC,TP,A:Dracula 7.00
15 GC,TP,A:Devil 7.00
16 GC,TP,A:Devil 7.00
17 GC,TP,A:Styggro 7.00
18 GC,A:Styggro 7.00
19 GC,AA,I:Xander 7.00
20 A:Xander 7.00
21 DA,O:Dr.Strange 8.00
22 I:Apalla 8.00
23 E:MWn(s),JSn,A:Wormworld .. 8.00
24 JSn,A:Apalla,I:Visamajoris ... 8.00
25 AM,V:Dr.Strange Yet 8.00
26 JSn,A:The Ancient One 8.00
27 TS,A:Stygyro,Sphinx 8.00
28 TS,A:Ghost Rider,
 V:In-Betweener 5.00
29 TS,A:Nighthawk 4.00
30 I:Dweller 4.00
31 TS,A:Sub Mariner 4.00
32 A:Sub Mariner 4.00
33 TS,A:The Dreamweaver 4.00
34 TS,A:Nightmare,D:CyrusBlack . 4.00
35 TS,V:Dweller,I:Ludi 4.00
36 Thunder of the Soul 4.00
37 Fear,the Final Victor 4.00
38 GC,DG,A:Baron Mordo 4.00
39 GC,DG,A:Baron Mordo 4.00
40 GC,A:Asrael 4.00
41 GC,A:Man Thing 3.50
42 GC,A:Black Mirror 3.50
43 V:Shadow Queen 3.50
44 GC,A:Princess Shialmar 3.50
45 GC,A:Demon in the Dark 3.50
46 FM,A:Sibylis 3.50
47 MR,TA,I:Ikonn 3.50
48 MR,TA,Brother Voodoo 3.50
49 MR,TA,A:Baron Mordo 3.50
50 MR,TA,A:Baron Mordo 3.50
51 MR,TA,A:Sgt. Fury,
 V:Baron Mordo 3.50
52 MR,TA,A:Nightmare 4.00
53 MR,TA,A:Nightmare,Fantastic
 Four,V:Rama-Tut 4.00
54 PS,V:Tiboro 4.00
55 MGo,TA,V:Madness 4.00
56 PS,TA,O:Dr.Strange 5.00
57 KN,TA,A:Dr.Doom 4.00
58 DGr,TA,V:Dracula 4.00
59 DGr,TA,V:Dracula 5.00
60 DGr,TA,Scarlet Witch 5.00
61 DGr,TA,V:Dracula 5.00
62 SL,V:Dracula 5.00
63 CP,V:Topaz 4.00
64 TSa,`Art Rage' 4.00
65 PS,Charlatan 4.00
66 PS,`The Cosen One' 4.00
67 SL,A:Jessica Drew,Shroud .. 4.00
68 PS,A:Black Knight 4.00
69 PS,A:Black Knight 4.00
70 BBI,V:Umar 4.00
71 DGr,O:Dormammu 4.00
72 PS,V:Umar 4.00
73 PS,V:Umar 4.00
74 MBg,Secret Wars II 4.00
75 A:Fantastic Four 4.00
76 A:Fantastic Four 4.00
77 A:Topaz 4.00
78 A:Cloak,I:Ecstacy 3.50
79 A:Morganna 3.00
80 A:Morganna,C:Rintah 3.00
81 V:Urthona,I:Rintah 3.00
Ann.#1 CR,`Doomworld' 15.00
G-Size#1 K&R(c),reps Strange
 Tales#164-#168 .... 10.00
GN Dr.Strange: What is it that
 Distrubs you, Stephen?, CR,
 revised from Dr.Strange Ann.#1,
 48pg bookshelf (Aug., 1997) .. 10.00

[3rd Regular Series], 1988–96
1 V:Dorammu 4.00
2 V:Dorammu 3.00
3 I:Dragon Force 3.00
4 EL(c),A:Dragon Force 3.00
5 JG,V:Baron Mordo 3.50
6 JG,I:Mephista 3.00
7 JG,V:Agamotto,Mephisto 3.00
8 JG,V:Mephisto & Satanish 3.00
9 JG,O:Dr.Strange 3.00
10 JG,V:Morbius 3.50
11 JG,A of V,V:Hobgoblin,
 C:Morbius 4.00
12 JG,A of V,V:Enchantress 2.75
13 JG,A of V,V:Arkon 2.75
14 JG,B:Vampiric Verses,
 A:Morbius 3.50
15 JG,A:Morbius,Amy Grant(C) .. 5.00
16 JG,A:Morbius,Brother Voodoo . 3.50
17 JV,TD,A:Morbius,Br.Voodoo .. 3.50
18 JG,E:Vampiric Verses,A:Morbius,
 Brother Voodoo,R:Varnae ... 3.50
19 GC,A:Azrael 2.50

Doctor Strange 3rd Series, #78
© Marvel Entertainment Group

20 JG,TD,A:Morbius,V:Zom 3.50
21 JG,TD,B:Dark Wars,
 R:Dormammu 2.50
22 JG,TD,LW,V:Dormammu 2.50
23 JG,LW,V:Dormammu 2.50
24 JG,E:Dark Wars,V:Dormammu . 2.50
25 RLm,A:Red Wolf, Black Crow . 2.50
26 GI,V:Werewolf By Night 2.50
27 GI,V:Werewolf By Night 2.50
28 X-over Ghost Rider #12,
 V:Zodiac 3.00
29 A:Baron Blood 2.50
30 Topaz' Fate 2.50
31 TD,Inf.Gauntlet,A:Silver Surfer . 3.00
32 Inf.Gauntlet,A:Warlock,Silver
 Surfer,V:Silver Dagger 2.50
33 Inf.Gauntlet,V:Thanos,
 Zota,A:Pip 2.50
34 Inf.Gauntlet,V:Dr.Doom,
 A:Pip,Scarlet Witch 2.50
35 Inf.Gauntlet,A:Thor,Pip,
 Scarlet Witch 2.50
36 Inf.Gauntlet,A:Warlock(leads
 into Warlock&Inf.Watch#1) .. 3.00
37 GI,V:Frankensurfer 2.50
38 GI,Great Fear #1 .... 2.50
39 GI,Great Fear #2 .... 2.50
40 GI,Great Fear #3,A:Daredevil .. 2.50
41 GI,A:Wolverine 3.00
42 GI,Infinity War,V:Galactus,A:
 Silver Surfer 2.50
43 GI,Infinity War,Galactus Vs.
 Agamotto,A:Silver Surfer ... 2.50
44 GI,Infinity War,V:Juggernaut .. 2.50
45 GI,Inf.War,O:Doctor Strange .. 2.50
46 GI,Inf.War,R:old costume 2.50
47 GI,Inf.War,V:doppleganger ... 2.50
48 GI,V:The Vishanti 2.50
49 GI,R:Dormammu 2.50
50 GI,A:Hulk,Ghost Rider,Silver
 Surfer,V:Dormammu(leads into
 Secret Defenders)holo-grafx(c) . 3.50
51 GI,V:Religious Cult 2.50
52 GI,A:Morbius 2.50
53 GI,Closes Mansion,L:Wong ... 2.50
54 GI,Infinity Crusade 2.50
55 GI,Inf.Crusade 2.50
56 GI,Inf.Crusade 2.50
57 A:Kyllian,Urthona 2.50
58 V:Urthona 2.50
59 GI,V:Iskelior 2.50
60 B:DQ(s),Siege of
 Darkness,pt.#7 .... 4.00

CVA Page 228 — All comics prices listed are for *Near Mint* condition.

MARVEL — Doctor-Doom

61 Siege of Darkness,pt.#15 . . . . . . 3.25
62 V:Dr.Doom 2.50
63 JJ(c),V:Morbius 2.50
64 MvR,V:Namor 2.50
65 MvR,V:Namor,Vengeance 2.75
66 A:Wong 2.75
67 R:Clea 2.75
68 MvR 2.50
69 MvR 2.50
70 A:Hulk 2.50
71 V:Hulk 2.50
72 Metallic(c),Last Rites,pt.1 . . . . . . 2.50
73 Last Rites,pt.2 . . . . 2.50
74 SY,DQ,Last Rites,pt.3 . . . . 2.50
75 Prismatic cover 4.00
76 I:New Costume 2.50
77 Mob Clean-up 2.50
78 R:Chton 2.50
79 Doc's new Asylum 2.50
80 Missing for four months? 2.50
81 A:Nick Fury 2.50
82 A:Hellstorm 2.50
83 V:Tempo Mob,Dormammu 2.50
84 The Homecoming,pt.1 . . . . 2.50
85 The Homecoming,pt.2 . . . . 2.50
86 The Homecoming,pt.3 . . . . 2.50
87 The Homecoming,pt.4 . . . . 2.50
88 The Fall of the Tempo,pt.1 . . . . 2.50
89 The Fall of the Tempo,pt.2 . . . . 2.50
90 final issue 2.50
Ann #2 Return of Defenders,Pt4 . . . 5.00
Ann #3 GI,I:Killiam,w/card 3.50
Ann.#4 V:Salome 3.50
Spec. Dr. Strange/Ghost Rider#1
  Newsstand vers. of Dr.
  Strange #28 (1991) 6.00
Spec.#1 Dr. Strange vs. Dracula
  rep. MWn(s),GC (1994) 2.50
GNv Triumph and Torment MBg,
  F:Dr. Strange & Dr.Doom 9.95
  HC 14.95
Ashcan 75
TPB A Separate Reality, 224-pg . . . 19.95

DOCTOR STRANGE
Dec., 1998
1 (of 4) TyH,killer pursued 3.00
2 TyH,secrets in Topaz 3.00
3 TyH,magic in Manhattan 3.00
4 TyH,PC,conclusion 3.00

DR. STRANGE CLASSICS
March, 1984
1 SD,Reprints 3.50
2 . . . . 3.50
3 . . . . 3.50
4 June, 1984 . . . . 3.50

DOCTOR WHO
1984–86
1 BBC TV Series,UK reprints,
  Return of the Daleks 7.00
2 Star Beast 6.00
3 Transformation 5.00
4 A:K-9,Daleks 5.00
5 V:Time Witch,Colin Baker
  interview 5.00
6 B:Ancient Claw saga 5.00
7 . . . . 5.00
8 The Collector 5.00
9 The Life Bringer 5.00
10 This is your Life 5.00
11 The Deal 5.00
12 End of the Line 5.00
13 V:The Cybermen 5.00
14 Clash of the Neutron Knight . . . 5.00
15 B:Peter Davison-Dr. Who 5.00
16 Into the Realm of Satan, ... 5.00

Doctor Who #5
© Marvel Entertainment Group

17 Peter Davison Interview 5.00
18 A:Four Dr.Who's 5.00
19 A:The Sontarans 5.00
20 The Stockbridge Horror 5.00
21 The Stockbridge Horror 5.00
22 The Stockbridge Horror 5.00
23 The Unearthly Child 5.00

DR. ZERO
Epic, April, 1988
1 BSz,DCw,I:Dr.Zero 2.50
2 BSz,DCw 2.25
3 BSz,DCw 2.25
4 thru 6 . . . . @2.25
7 DSp 2.25
8 End series, Aug., 1989 . . . . 2.25

DOLLY DILL
1945
1 Newsstand 165.00

DOMINATION FACTOR
Sept., 1999
1.1 Fantastic Four (of 4) DJu,
  JOy,BMc,x-over 2.50
1.2 Avengers, DJu,JO,
  DJa, x-over 2.50
2.3 Fantastic Four, DJu,BMc 2.50
2.4 Avengers, DJu,JOy,DJa 2.50
3.5 Fantastic Four, DJu,BMc 2.50
3.6 Avengers, JOy,DJa 2.50
4.7 Fantastic Four, DJu,BMc 2.50
4.8 Avengers, DJa,JOy,concl 2.50

DOMINO
1996
1 thru 3 . . . . @2.25

DOMINO
Marvel May 2003
1 (of 4) BSf 2.50
2 BSf 2.50
3 BSf,Florida Everglades 2.50
4 BSf, concl 2.50

DOOM 2099
1993–96
1 PB,I:Doom 2099,V:Tiger Wylde,
  foil(c) 3.00

Doom 2099 #2
© Marvel Entertainment Group

2 I:Rook Seven 2.50
3 PB,V:Tiger Wylde 2.50
4 PB,V:Tiger Wylde 2.50
5 PB,I:Fever 2.50
6 I:Duke Stratosphear 2.50
7 PB,I:Paloma,V:Duke,Fever Haze 2.50
8 PB,C:Ravage 2.50
9 EC,V:Jack the Ripper 2.50
10 PB,w/Poster 2.50
11 PB,I:Thandaza 2.50
12 PB,V:Thandaza 2.50
13 PB(c),JFm(s),V:Necrotek 2.50
14 RLm(c),PB,Fall o/t Hammer#4 . 2.50
15 PB,I:Radian 2.50
16 EC(a&s), ... 2.50
17 PB,V:Radian,w/card 2.50
18 PB, ... 2.50
19 PB,C:Bloodhawk 2.50
20 PB,A:Bloodhawk 2.50
21 PB,Shadow King 2.50
22 PB,R:Duke Stratosphere 2.50
23 PB,R:Tyger Wylde 2.50
24 PB 2.50
25 PB 3.50
25a foil cover 4.00
26 . . . . 2.50
27 Revolution 2.50
28 Prologue to D-Day 2.50
Becomes:

DOOM 2099 A.D.
1995
29 Doom Invades America 4.00
29a Chromium Cover 4.00
30 D:Corporate Head 2.50
31 PB,One Nation Under Doom . . 2.50
32 Ravage Aftermath 2.50
33 . . . . 2.50
34 I:Anthony Herod 2.50
35 E:One Nation Under Doom . . . 2.50
36 . . . . 2.50
37 . . . . 2.50
38 . . . . 2.50
39 . . . . 2.50
40 Rage Against Time,pt.1 . . . . . 2.50
41 Rage Against Time,pt.2 . . . . . 2.50
TPB Villainy of Doctor Doom 17.95

DOOM
Aug., 2000
1 (of 3) CDi,F:Dr.Doom 3.00
2 CDi,Al Khalad 3.00
3 CDi,concl 3.00

All comics prices listed are for Near Mint condition.

Doom–Dune — MARVEL — Comics Values Annual

DOOM: THE EMPEROR RETURNS
Nov., 2001
1 CDi,F:Dr. Doom 2.50
2 CDi,center of Counter-Earth 2.50
3 CDi, ... 2.50
TPB Doom, rep. 144-pg. 15.95

DOPEY DUCK COMICS
Timely, Fall, 1945
1 A:Casper Cat,Krazy Krow . . . 250.00
2 A:Casper Cat,Krazy Krow . . . 225.00
Becomes:

WACKY DUCK
1946
3 Paperchase(c) 225.00
4 Wacky Duck(c) 200.00
5 Duck & Devil(c) 150.00
6 Cliffhanger(c) 125.00
1 Baketball(c) 60.00
2 Traffic Light(c) 60.00
Becomes:
JUSTICE COMICS

DOUBLE DRAGON
July, 1991
1 I:Billy&Jimmy Lee 2.50
2 Dragon Statue Stolen,V:Stelth . . 2.50
3 Billy Vs. Jimmy 2.50
4 Dragon Force out of control 2.50
5 V:Stealth 2.50
6 V:Nightfall, final issue 2.50

DOUBLE EDGE
1995
Alpha Punisher vs. Nick Fury 5.00
Omega D:Major Character 5.00

D.P. 7
Nov., 1986
1 O:DP7 . . . . 2.50
2 V:Headhunter 2.50
3 RT,Headhunters 2.50
4 RT,V:Wompus. 2.50
5 RT,Exorcist. 2.50
6 RT,I:The Sweat Shop 2.50
7 RT,V:Clinic 2.50
8 RT,V:Clinic 2.50
9 RT,AW,I:New Paranormals 2.50
10 RT,I:Mysterious People 2.50
11 AW(i)V:Regulator 2.50
12 O:Randy 2.50
13 O:Charly 2.50
14 AW 2.50
15 . . . . 2.50
16 V:BlackPower 2.50
17 . . . . 2.50
18 Pitt tie-in 2.50
19 . . . . 2.50
20 Spitfire. 2.50
21 . . . . 3.00
22 . . . . 3.00
23 A:PsiForce 3.00
24 A:Mastodon 3.00
25 V:Familee ch 3.00
26 V:Familee ch 3.00
27 The Pitt 3.00
28 V:The Candidate 3.00
29 Deadweight 3.00
30 V:Para-troop 3.00
31 A:Chrome 3.00
32 I:The Cure,last issue,
  June, 1989. . . . . 3.00
Ann.#1,I:Witness 3.00

DRACULA LIVES
B&W Magazine, 1973—75
1 GC. 65.00
2 NA,GC,JSn,O:Dracula 50.00
3 NA,JB, ... 40.00
4 MP 30.00
5 GC 30.00
6 JB,GC 30.00
7 GE 30.00
8 GC 30.00
9 AA,RG 30.00
10 . . . . 40.00
11 thru 13 . . . . @35.00

DRACULA: LORD OF THE UNDEAD
Oct., 1998
1 (of 3) PO,TP,R:Dracula 3.00
2 PO,TP,V:Seward. 3.00
3 PO,TP,conclusion 3.00

DRAFT, THE
1988
1 Sequel to The Pit 3.75

DRAGON LINES
Epic, Heavy Hitters 1993
[1st Limited Series]
1 RLm,V:Terrorist on Moon,
  Embossed(c) 3.00
2 RLm,V:Kuei Emperor 2.25
3 RLm,V:Spirit Boxer 2.25
4 RLm,K:Kuei Emperor 2.25
[Regular Series]
1 B:PQ(s),RLm,I:Tao 2.50
2 RLm, ... 2.50

DRAGONSLAYER
Oct.–Nov., 1981
1 Movie adapt. 3.00
2 Movie adapt.. . . . . 3.00

DRAGON STRIKE
1994
1 Based on TSR Game 2.25

DRAGON'S TEETH/ DRAGON'S CLAWS
July, 1988
1 GSr,I:Mercy Dragon,
  Scavenger,Digit Steel 2.25
2 GSr,V:Evil Dead 2.25
3 GSr,Go Home. 2.25
4 GSr 2.25
5 GSr,I:Death's Head. 18.00
6 thru 10 GSr. . . . . @2.00

DREADLANDS
Epic, 1992
1 Post-Apocalyptic Mini-series 4.00
2 Trapped in Prehistoric Past. 4.00
3 V:Alien Time Travelers 4.00
4 Final Issue 4.00

DREADSTAR
Epic, Nov., 1982
1 JSn,I:Lord Papal. 5.00
2 JSn,O:Willow 3.50
3 JSn,V:Lord Papal 3.50
4 JSn,I:Z 3.50
5 JSn,V:Teutun 3.50
6 JSn,BWr,Interstellar Toybox . . . 4.00

Dragon Claws #2
© Marvel Entertainment Group

7 JSn,BWr,V:Dr.Mezlo 4.00
8 JSn,V:Z 3.00
9 JSn,V:Z 3.00
10 JSn,V:Z 3.00
11 JSn,O:Lord Papal 3.00
12 JSn,I:Dr.Delphi. 3.00
13 JSn,V:Infra Red & Ultra Violet . . 3.00
14 JSn,V:Lord Papal. 3.00
15 JSn,new powers 3.00
16 JSn,V:Lord Papal. 3.00
17 JSn,V:Willows father 3.00
18 JSn,V:Dr.Mezlo 3.00
19 JSn,V:Dr Mezlo 3.00
20 JSn,D:Oedi 3.00
21 JSn,D:Dr.Delphi. 3.00
22 JSn,V:Lord Papal. 3.00
23 JSn,V:Lord Papal. 3.00
24 JSn,JS,V:Lord Papal 3.00
25 JSn,V:Lord Papal. 3.00
26 JSn,R:Oedi 3.00
Ann.#1 JSn,The Price. 3.00
See COLOR COMICS section

DREADSTAR & COMPANY
July, 1985
1 thru 5 JSo,reprint . . . . @2.25

DROIDS
Star, April, 1986
1 JR 25.00
2 AW. 15.00
3 JR/AW 15.00
4 AW. 15.00
5 AW 15.00
6 EC/AW,A:Luke Skywalker. . . . 15.00
7 EC/AW,A:Luke Skywalker. . . . 15.00
8 EC/AW,A:Luke Skywalker. . . . 15.00

DRUID
1995
1 R:Dr. Druid Surprise!!! 3.50
2 F:Nekra 3.00
3 deranged canibal wisemen 3.00
4 Why Must He Die? 3.00

DUNE
April–June, 1985
1 Movie Adapt,Rep. Marvel
  Super Spec,BSz 3.50
2 Movie Adapt,BSz 3.50
3 Movie Adapt,BSz, ... 3.50

MARVEL

Dune #1
© Marvel Entertainment Group

Elektra #13
© Marvel Entertainment Group

DYNOMUTT
Nov., 1977
1 Based on TV series 50.00
2 thru 5 .... @25.00
6 Sept., 1978 .... 25.00

EARTHWORM JIM
1995–96
1 I:Earthworm Jim 3.00
2 Cow tipping 3.00
3 V:Lawyers,conclusion 3.00

EARTH X
Jan., 1999
0 (of 14) AxR,JPL,Machine Man & Watcher 6.00
0a signed 25.00
1 AxR,JPL,V:Inhumans,32-page .. 8.00
1a signed 30.00
2 AxR,JPL,fate of Fant.Four 4.00
3 AxR,JPL,World Super Powers ... 4.00
4 JPL,AxR(c),A:new Hulk 4.00
5 JPL,AxR(c),V:Doombots 4.00
6 JPL,AxR(c),different X-Men 4.00
7 JPL,AxR(c),A:Hulk 4.00
8 JPL,AxR(c),A:Venom 4.00
9 JPL,AxR(c),Revelations 4.00
10 JPL,AxR(c) 4.00
11 JPL,AxR(c),V:Skull 4.00
12 JPL,AxR(c),concl 4.00
Spec.X AxR(c) concl.,48-pg 6.00
Sketchbook 6.00
TPB 464-page, rep. 24.95

ECTOKID
Razorline 1993–94
1 I:Dex Mungo,BU:Hokum & Hex. . 3.50
2 O:Dex 2.50
3 I:Ectosphere 2.50
4 I:Brothers Augustine 2.50
5 A:Saint Sinner 2.50
6 Highway 61 Revisited 2.50
7 .... 2.50
8 V:Ice Augustine 2.50
9 Love is like a Bullet 2.50
10 .... 2.50
Ectokid Unleashed 3.25

EDEN'S TRAIL
Nov., 2002
1 (of 6) western 3.00
2 .... 3.00
3 .... 3.00
4 .... 3.00
5 concl 3.00

ELECTRIC UNDERTOW
Dec., 1989
1 MBa,Strike Force 4.00
2 MBa, Will Deguchis 4.00
3 MBa, Alien Invaders 4.00
4 MBa,Attack on Beijing 4.00
5 MBa, Morituri defeated,March, 1990 .... 4.00

ELEKTRA
Nov., 1996
1 PrM,MD2, ... 3.50
1A variant (c) 4.50
2 PrM,MD2,V:Bullseye, round two . 3.00
3 PrM,MD2, ... 3.00
4 PrM,MD2 .... 3.00
5 PrM,MD2, ... 3.00
6 PrM,MD2 .... 3.00
7 PrM,MD2,A:Konrad,The Architect 3.00
8 PrM,MD2,V:The Architect 3.00
9 PrM,MD2,V:The Four Winds 3.00
10 PrM,MD2,V:Daredevil,¡American Samurai,¡ pt.1 .... 3.00
11 PrM,MD2,F:Daredevil 3.00
12 PrM,MD2,F:Daredevil,V:American Samuri 3.00
13 PrM,MD2,F:Daredevil, concl. ... 3.00
14 LHa,MD2,A:Wolverine 3.00
15 LHa,MD2,A:Silver Samurai 3.00
16 LHa,MD2,A Hole in the Soul ... 3.00
17 LHa,MD2,V:The Hand 3.00
18 LHa,MD2,A:Shang-Chi&Kingpin. 3.00
19 LHa,MD2,last issue 3.00
Minus 1 Spec.,PMg,MD2,flashback. 3.00

ELEKTRA
July, 2001
1 BMB,non-comics code series ... 4.00
2A BMB,A:S.H.I.E.L.D. 3.00
2B variant BSz(c) 3.00
3 BMB,A:Hydra 3.00
4 BMB,A:Nick Fury 3.00
5 BMB,concl 3.00
6 BMB,F:Daredevil,'Nuff Said 3.00
7 Hubris, pt.1 .... 3.00
8 Hubris, pt.2 .... 3.00
9 Hubris, pt.3 .... 3.00
10 Hubris, concl 3.00
11 Elektra between jobs 3.00
12 F:Mr. Locke 3.00
13 DaM 3.00
14 DaM,Elektra fights back 3.00
15 DaM 3.00
16 DaM 3.00
17 DaM 3.00
18 DaM 3.00
19 DaM 3.00
20 DaM,V:The Hand 3.00
21 V:The Hand 3.00
22 V:The Hand, concl. 3.00
23 BSz(c),pt.1 .... 3.00
24 BSz(c),pt.2 .... 3.00
25 BSz(c),How to,pt.1 .... 3.00
26 How to,pt.2 .... 3.00
27 How to,pt.3,concl. 3.00
28 .... 3.00
29 .... 3.00
TPB Vol. 1: Introspect 17.00
TPB Vol. 2: Everything Old 17.00
TPB Elektra Lives Again, FM 25.00

ELEKTRA: ASSASSIN
Aug., 1986
1 FM,BSz,V:Shield 8.00
2 FM,BSz,I:Garrett 5.00
3 FM,BSz,V:Shield,A:Garrett 5.00
4 FM,BSz,V:Shield,A:Garrett 5.00
5 FM,BSz,I:Chastity,A:Garrett 5.00
6 FM,BSz,A:Nick Fury,Garrett ... 5.00
7 FM,BSz,V:Ken Wind,A:Garrett .. 5.00
8 FM,BSz,V:Ken Wind,A:Garrett .. 6.00
TPB Rep #1-8 .... 13.00

ELEKTRA: GLIMPSE & ECHO
July, 2002
1 (of 4) F:The Hand 3.50
2 .... 3.50
3 .... 3.50
4 concl 3.50

ELEKTRA LIVES AGAIN
1991
Graphic Novel FM,R:Elektra,A:Matt Murdock,V:The Hand 30.00
TPB FM, rep. of HC, 80pg 7.00

ELEKTRA: ROOT OF EVIL
1 V:Snakeroot 3.00
2 V:Snakeroot 3.00
3 Elektra's Brother 3.00
4 V:The Hand 3.00

ELEKTRA: SAGA
Feb., 1984
1 FM,rep.Daredevil 7.00
2 FM,rep.Daredevil 7.00
3 FM,rep.Daredevil 7.00
4 FM,rep.Daredevil 7.00
TPB Reprints#1-#4 .... 17.00
GN Book One FM,KJ, rep. from Daredevil, 96pg 4.00
GN Book Two FM,KJ, rep. from Daredevil, 96pg 4.00

ELEKTRA & WOLVERINE: THE REDEEMER
Nov., 2001
GN#1 painted, 48-page 6.50

Elektra–Ewoks

GN#2 48-page 6.50
GN#3 concl., 48-page 6.50

ELEKTRA/WITCHBLADE
1-shot ìDevil's Reign,î
    pt.6, x-over. 3.00

ELFQUEST
Aug., 1985
1 WP,reprints. 4.00
2 WP. 2.50
3 WP. 2.50
4 WP. 2.50
5 WP. 2.50
6 WP,Young Cutter V:Mad Coil . . . 2.50
7 WP,Young Cutter V:Mad Coil . . . 2.50
8 WP. 2.50
9 WP. 2.50
10 WP,A:Cutter, Skywise 2.50
11 WP,I:Two Edge 2.50
12 WP,The Mysterious Forest 2.50
13 WP,The Forest, A:Leetah 2.50
14 WP,A:The Bone Woman 2.50
15 WP,The Forest, continued 2.50
16 WP,Forbidden Grove 2.50
17 WP,Blue Mountain 2.50
18 WP,Secrets 2.50
19 WP,Twisted Gifts 2.50
20 WP,Twisted Gifts 2.50
21 WP 2.50
22 WP,A:Winnowill 2.50
23 WP,Blue Mountain,A:Winnowill. . 2.50
24 WP,The Quest Usurped 2.50
25 WP,Northern Wastelands 2.50
26 WP,Rayeks Story 2.50
27 WP,Battle Preparations 2.50
28 WP,Elves vs. Trolls 2.50
29 WP,Battle Beneath Blue
    Mountain 2.50
30 and 31 WP . . . . @2.50
32 WP,Conclusion, March, 1988 . . . 2.50

ELSEWHERE PRINCE
Epic, May–Oct., 1990
1 thru 6 . . . . @3.00

ELVIRA
Oct., 1988
Spec.B&W, Movie Adapt. 3.00

Elsewhere Prince #1
© Marvel Entertainment Group

MARVEL

EMMA FROST
Marvel July 2003
1 RGr,Higher Learning,pt.1 . . . . . . 4.00
2 RGr,Higher Learning,pt.2 . . . . . . 4.00
3 RGr,Higher Learning,pt.3 . . . . . . 4.00
4 RGr,Higher Learning,pt.4 . . . . . . 4.00
5 RGr,Higher Learning,pt.5 . . . . . . 4.00

EPIC
1992
1 Wildcards,Hellraiser 6.00
2 Nightbreed,Wildcards 6.00
3 DBw,MFm,Alien Legion, ... 6.00
4 Stalkers,Metropol,Wildcards 6.00

EPIC, GRAPHIC NOVEL
Moebius 1: Upon a Star 10.00
Moebius 2: Arzach 10.00
Moebius 3: Airtight Garage 10.00
Moebius 4: Long Tomorrow 10.00
Moebius 5: 10.00
Moebius 6: Pharadonesia 10.00
Last of Dragons 7.00
The Incal 1 Moebius 11.00
The Incal 2 Moebius 11.00
The Incal 3 Moebius 11.00
JBo,Someplace Strange 7.00
MZ,Punisher 16.95

EPIC, ILLUSTRATED
Spring, 1980
1 Black and White/Color Mag. . . . 14.00
2 thru 10 . . . . @8.00
11 thru 20 . . . . @10.00
21 thru 25 . . . . @12.00
26 thru 34, March, 1986 . . . . . . @14.00

EPIC, LITE
Epic, Nov., 1991
One-shot short stories 4.00

ESSENTIALS
1999–2003
(528 pages, B&W reprints)
TPB Ant-Man, 576-pg. (2002) 16.00
TPB Avengers,Vol.1 . . . . 16.00
TPB Avengers,Vol.2, ... 16.00
TPB Avengers,Vol.3,rep.#47–#68 . 16.00
TPB Avengers (2003) 17.00
TPB Captain America,Vol.1 . . . . . 16.00
TPB Captain America,Vol.2 (2002) 16.00
TPB Conan,Vol.1 . . . . 17.00
TPB Daredevil, Vol.1 (2002) 17.00
TPB Fantastic Four,Vol.1 . . . . . . 16.00
TPB Fantastic Four,Vol.2(2000) . . 16.00
TPB Fantastic Four,Vol.3(2001) . . 16.00
TPB Howard the Duck (2002) . . . 16.00
TPB Hulk, Vol.1 (2002) 17.00
TPB Human Torch, Vol. 1 . . . . . . 17.00
TPB Incredible Hulk,Vol.1 . . . . . . 16.00
TPB Incredible Hulk,Vol.2(2001) . . 16.00
TPB Iron Man, Vol.1 (2002) 17.00
TPB Marvel Team-Up (2002) . . . 17.00
TPB Silver Surfer,Vol.1 . . . . 16.00
TPB Spider-Man,Vol.1 (1997) . . . 17.00
TPB Spider-Man,Vol.2 (1997) . . . 17.00
TPB Spider-Man,Vol.3 . . . . 16.00
TPB Spider-Man,Vol.4 . . . . 16.00
TPB Spider-Man,Vol.5 (2002) . . . 16.00
TPB Thor,Vol.1 . . . . 16.00
TPB Tomb of Dracula (2002) 17.00
TPB Wolverine,Vol.1 . . . . 16.00
TPB Wolverine,Vol.2 . . . . 16.00
TPB Wolverine,Vol.3 (1998) 17.00
TPB Uncanny X-Men, Vol.1 (2002) 17.00
TPB X-Men,Vol.1 . . . . 16.00

Comics Values Annual

TPB X-Men,Vol.2 . . . . 16.00
TPB X-Men,Vol.3 . . . . 16.00
TPB X-Men,Vol.4 . . . . 16.00

ETERNAL
Marvel Max June 2003
1 Gift of the Gods,pt.1 . . . . 3.00
2 Gift of the Gods,pt.2 . . . . 3.00
3 Gift of the Gods,pt.3 . . . . 3.00
4 Gift of the Gods,pt.4 . . . . 3.00
5 Gift of the Gods,pt.5 . . . . 3.00
6 Gift of the Gods,pt.6 . . . . 3.00

ETERNALS
[1st Series], July, 1976
1 JK,I:Ikaris,25 cent edition 20.00
2 JK,I:Ajak,25 cent edition 15.00
3 JK,I:Sersi 10.00
4 JK,Night of the Demons 10.00
5 JK,I:Makarri,Zuras Thena,Domo 10.00
6 JK,Gods & Men at City College. 10.00
7 JK,V:Celestials 10.00
8 JK,I:Karkas, Reject. 10.00
9 JK,I:Sprite,Reject vs. Karkas . . . 10.00
10 JK,V:Celestials. 10.00
11 JK,I:Kingo Sunen 10.00
12 JK,I:Uni-Mind 10.00
13 JK,I:ForgottenOne(Gilgamesh). 10.00
14 JK,V:Hulk 10.00
15 JK,V:Hulk 10.00
16 JK,I:Dromedan 10.00
17 JK,I:Sigmar 10.00
18 JK,I:Nerve Beast 10.00
19 JK,Secret o/t Pyramid 10.00
Ann.#1 JK,V:Timekillers 12.00

[2nd Series], Oct., 1985
1 SB,I:Cybele 3.00
2 SB,V:Deviants 2.50
3 SB,V:Deviants 2.50
4 SB,V:Deviants 2.50
5 SB,V:Deviants 2.50
6 SB,V:Deviants 2.50
7 SB,V:Deviants 2.50
8 WS,SB,V:Deviants 2.50
9 WS,SB,V:Deviants 2.50
10 WS,SB,V:Deviants 2.50
11 WS,KP,V:Deviants 2.50
12 WS,KP,V:Deviants 2.50

ETERNALS: HEROD FACTOR
Nov., 1991
1 MT/BMc,A:Sersi (giant size) 2.50

EVERYMAN
Epic, 1991
1-shot Supernatural Story
    (Animated Cel Artwork) 8.00

EWOKS
Star, June, 1985—Sept., 1987
1 Based on TV Series 18.00
2 . . . . 15.00
3 . . . . 15.00
4 A:Foonars. 15.00
5 Wicket vs. Ice Demon 15.00
6 Mount Sorrow, A:Teebo 15.00
7 A:Logray,V:Morag 15.00
8 . . . . 15.00
9 Lost in Time 15.00
10 AW,Lost in Time. 18.00
11 Kneesaa Shrunk,A:Fleebogs . . 15.00
12 . . . . 15.00
13 . . . . 15.00
14 Teebo- King for a Day 15.00
15 . . . . 15.00

CVA Page 232   All comics prices listed are for *Near Mint* condition.

MARVEL

Excalibur–Exiles

Excalibur #17
© Marvel Entertainment Group

EXCALIBUR
April, 1988

1 AD,Special,O:Excalibur,
  V:Technet. 5.00
1a 2nd Printing 2.50
1b 3rd Printing. 2.00
2 AAd,Mojo Mayhem,A:X-Babies . . 4.00
3 Air Apparent Spec.RLm,KJ,JG,TP,
  RL,EL,JRu,A:Coldblood 4.00

[Regular Series]
1 B:CCI(s),AD,V:Warwolves,
  I:Widget. 6.00
2 AD,V:Warwolves,I:Kylun 5.00
3 AD,V:Juggernaut 4.00
4 AD,V:Arcade,Crazy Gang 4.00
5 AD,V:Arcade. 3.00
6 AD,Inferno,I:Alistaire Stuart. 3.00
7 AD,Inferno 3.00
8 RLm,JRu,A:New Mutants 3.00
9 AD,I:Nazi-Excalibur. 3.00
10 MR,V:Nazi-Excalibur 3.00
11 MR,V:Nazi-Excalibur 3.00
12 AD,Fairy Tale Dimension 3.00
13 AD,The Prince,N:Capt.Britian . . . 3.00
14 AD,Too Many Heroes. 2.50
15 AD,I:US James Braddock. 2.50
16 AD,V:Anjulie 2.50
17 AD,C:Prof.X,Starjammers. 2.50
18 DJ,DA,V:Jamie Braddock. 2.50
19 RL,TA,AM,V:Jamie Braddock . . . 2.50
20 RLm,JRu,V:Demon Druid. 2.50
21 I:Crusader X 2.50
22 V:Crusader X 2.50
23 AD,V:Magik 2.50
24 AD,Return Home,C:Galactus . . . 2.50
25 E:CCI(s),AM,A:Galactus,Death,
  Watcher 2.50
26 RLm,JRu,V:Mastermind 2.50
27 BWS,BSz,A:Nth Man. 3.00
28 BBI,Night at Bar. 2.50
29 JRu,V:Nightmare,A:PowerPack . 2.50
30 DR,AM,A:Doctor Strange. 2.50
31 DR,AM,V:Son of Krakoa 2.50
32 V:Mesmero 2.50
33 V:Mesmero 2.50
34 V:Mesmero 2.50
35 AM,Missing Child 2.50
36 AM,V:Silv.Sable,Sandman 2.50
37 A:Avengers W.C.,Dr.Doom. 2.50
38 A:Avengers W.C.,Dr.Doom. 2.50
39 A:Avengers W.C.,Dr.Doom. 2.50
40 O:Excalibur,Trial-Lockheed 2.50

41 V:Warwolves,C:Cable 3.00
42 AD,Team Broken Up 3.50
43 AD,Nightcrawler,V:Capt.Brit. . . . 3.00
44 AD,Capt.Britain On Trial. 3.00
45 AD,I:N-Men, ... 3.00
46 AD,Return of Kylun,C:Cerise . . . 3.00
47 AD,I:Cerise 3.00
48 AD,A:Anti-Phoenix 3.00
49 AD,MFm,V:Necrom,R:Merlyn . . . 3.00
50 AD,Phoenix,V:Necrom,Merlyn . . 5.00
51 V:Giant Dinosaurs 2.50
52 O:Phoenix,A:Prof X,MarvGirl . . . 2.50
53 A:Spider-Man,V:The Litter 2.50
54 AD,MFm,V:Crazy Gang 2.50
55 AD,MFm,A:Psylocke 2.50
56 AD,MFm,A:Psylocke,
  V:Saturyne,Jamie Braddock . . . 2.50
57 A:X-Men,Alchemy,V:Trolls 2.75
58 A:X-Men,Alchemy,V:Trolls 2.75
59 A:Avengers 2.50
60 A:Avengers 2.50
61 AD,MFm,Phoenix Vs.Galactus . . 2.50
62 AD,MFm,A:Galactus 2.50
63 AD,MFm,V:Warpies 2.50
64 AD,MFm,V:RCX,R:Rachel 2.50
65 AD,MFm,R:Dark Phoenix. 2.50
66 AD,MFm,V:Ahab,Sentinels,
  O:Widget 2.50
67 AD,MFm,V:Ahab,Sentinels 2.50
68 V:Starjammers. 2.50
69 A:Starjammers 2.50
70 A:Starjammers 2.50
71 DaR,Hologram(c),N:Excalibur . . 5.00
72 KeL,V:Siena Blaze 2.50
73 TSr,V:Siena Blaze 2.50
74 InC,A:Mr.Sinster,Siena Blaze . . . 2.50
75 SLo(s),KeL,I:Daytripper(Amanda
  Sefton),Britannic(Capt.Britain),
  BU:Nightcrawler 4.00
75a Newstand Ed. 2.25
76 KeL,V:D'spayre 2.50
77 KeL,R:Doug Ramsey. 2.50
78 A:Zero,Doug Ramsey. 2.50
79 A:Zero,Doug Ramsey. 2.50
80 A:Zero,Doug Ramsey. 2.50
81 Doug Ramsey 2.50
82 . . . . 3.00
82a foil(c) 3.50
83 regular ed. 2.25
83a Deluxe ed. Kitty,Nightcrawler . . 2.50
84 regular ed. 2.25
84a Deluxe ed. 2.50
85 regular ed. 2.25
85a Deluxe ed. 2.50
86 regular ed. 2.25
86a Deluxe ed. 2.50
87 KeL,Secrets of the Genoshan
  Mutate Technology 2.50
88 Dream Nails,pt.1 . . . . 2.50
89 Dream Nails,pt.2 . . . . 2.50
90 Between Uncreated,Phalanx . . . 4.00
91 F:Colossus 2.50
92 F:Colossus 2.50
93 F:Wolfsbane 2.50
94 A:Karma & Psylocke 2.50
95 . . . . 2.50
96 . . . . 2.50
97 BWi,B.Braddock's secrets told . . 2.50
98 . . . . 2.50
99 European Hellfire Club,
  Onslaught 2.50
100 Onslaught saga, double size . . 4.00
101 . . . . 2.50
102 . . . . 2.50
103 WEl,F:Colossus,Kitty &
  Nichtcrawler. 2.50
104 JAr,BHi,PNe,Douglock's
  dark side 2.50
105 JAr,BHi,PNe,V:Moonstar, ... 2.50
106 . . . . 2.50
107 SvL,New direction 2.50

Excalibur #99
© Marvel Entertainment Group

108 Dragons of the Crimson Dawn . 2.50
109 V:Spiral,A:Captain Britain 2.50
110 V:The Dragons of the
  Crimson Dawn 2.50
111 F:Shadowcat,R:Rory Cambell
  (Ahab?) 2.50
112 Quicksilver tie-in 2.50
113 BRa,Colossus & Meggan 2.50
114 BRa,Vanisher. 2.50
115 BRa,Quarantine,F:GenerationX 2.50
116 BRa,Legacy Virus, cont. 2.50
117 BRa,F:Kitty Pryde, Colossus &
  Nightcrawler 2.50
118 BRa,V:Creatures from the
  Shadows 2.50
119 BRa,V:Nightmare 2.50
120 BRa,F:Kitty Pryde & Pete
  Wisdom 2.50
121 BRa,to Egypt 2.50
122 BRa,V:Original X-Men? 2.50
123 BRa,V:Mimic 2.50
124 BBr,Captain Britain's bachelor
  party 2.50
125 TvS,SHa, W:Captain Britain &
  Meggan, final issue 4.00
Minus 1 Spec., flashback,
  F:Nightcrawler 2.50
Ann.#1 I:Khaos,w/card 3.25
Spec #1 The Possession 4.00
Spec #2 RLm,DT,JG,RL,
  A:Original X-Men 3.00
PF Cold Blood 4.95
GN Weird War III 9.95
TPB Wild, Wild Life. 5.95

EXCALIBUR:
SWORD OF POWER
Dec., 2000

1 (of 4) IaC,BRa,F:Capt.Britain . . . 3.00
2 BRa, ... 3.00
3 BRa,V:Roma 3.00
4 BRa, concl 3.00

EXILES
June, 2001

1 MkK,F:Blink, 48-page 11.00
2A MkK, ... 5.00
2B variant JWi(c). 5.00
3 MkK,trial of Phoenix 4.00
4 MkK,trial of Phoenix 4.00
5 MkK,JCf,F:Hulk 4.00
6 MkK,JCf,F:Alpha Flight 4.00

FANTASTIC FIRSTS
Marvel Dec., 2001
TPB Superhero origins, 428-pg. . . 29.95

FANTASTIC FIVE
Aug., 1999
1 TDF,PR,AM,New Team:Human Torch Thing,Ms.Fantastic,Psilord & Big Brain.	2.25
2A TDF,PR,AM,Bloody Reunions x-over.	2.25
2B variant MSh(c).	2.25
3 TDF,PR,AM,A:Spider-Girl.	2.25
4 TDF,PR,AM.	2.25
5 TDF,PR,AM,A:Kristoff.	2.25

FANTASTIC FORCE
1994–96
1 Foil stamped cover.	3.00
2 Moses.	2.25
3	2.25
4 A:Captain America.	2.25
5 I:Dreadface.	2.25
6 F:Vibraxis.	2.25
7 V:Doom.	2.25
8 V:Crimson Cadre.	2.25
9 Atlantis Rising.	2.25
10 A:Human Torch.	2.25
11 A:Black Panther.	2.25
12 V:Vanguard.	2.25
13 J:She-Hulk.	2.25
14 V:Wakanda.	2.25
15 End of the Fantastic Force?.	2.25
16 End of the Fantastic Force?.	2.25
17	2.25
18	2.25

FANTASTIC FOUR
Nov., 1961
1 JK,I&O:Mr.Fantastic,Thing Invisible Girl,Human Torch Mole Man	35,000.00
2 JK,I:Skrulls.	7,000.00
3 JK,I:Miracleman.	4,500.00
4 JK,R:Submariner.	5,000.00
5 JK,JSt,I&O:Doctor Doom.	6,500.00
6 JK,V:Doctor Doom.	2,500.00
7 JK,I:Kurrgo.	2,000.00
8 JK,I:Alicia Masters,I&O: Puppet Master.	2,000.00

Fantastic Four #12
© Marvel Entertainment Group

Exiles–Fantastic Four

7 MkK,'Nuff Said (no words)	4.00
8 MkK,A World Apart,pt.1.	4.00
9 MkK,A World Apart,pt.2.	4.00
10 MkK,A World Apart,pt.3	4.00
11 MkK,F:Morph.	3.00
12 MkK,New team	3.00
13 MkK,team must kill	3.00
14 MkK,V:Dr. Doom	3.00
15 MkK,Mimic vs. Namor	3.00
16 MkK,	3.00
17 world gone reptile	2.50
18 MkK,F:Morph.	2.50
19 MkK,JHo	2.50
20 JCf,V:Legacy Virus,pt.1	2.50
21 JCf,V:Legacy Virus,pt.2	2.50
22 JCf,One goew down	2.50
23 With an Iron Fist,pt.1	2.50
24 With an Iron Fist,pt.2	2.50
25 With an Iron Fist,pt.3	3.50
26 Hard Choices,pt.1	3.00
27 Hard Choices,pt.2	3.00
28 Unnatural Selection,pt.1.	3.00
29 Unnatural Selection,pt.2.	3.00
30 Unnatural Selection,pt.3.	3.00
31 Avengers Forever,pt.1	3.00
32 Avengers Forever,pt.2	3.00
33 A Second Farewell,pt.1	3.00
34 A Second Farewell,pt.2	3.00
35 Fantastic Voyage,pt.1	3.00
36 Fantastic Voyage,pt.2	3.00
37 Fantastic Voyage,pt.3	3.00
TPB rep. #1-#4.	12.95
TPB Vol.1 A World Apart.	15.00
TPB Vol. 3: Out of Time	18.00
TPB Vol. 4: Legacy.	13.00
TPB Vol. 5: Unnatural Instinct	15.00

FACTOR X
1995
1 After Xavier	4.00
2 Scott vs. Alex Summers	3.00
3 Cyclops vs. Havok	3.00
4 Jean & Scott.	3.00
TPB Rep. #1-#4	8.95

FAFHRD AND THE GRAY MOUSER
Epic, Oct., 1990
1 MMi,Fritz Leiber adapt.	5.00
2 & 3 MMi	@5.00
4 MMi, Feb., 1991.	5.00

FAITHFUL
Nov., 1949
1 Ph(c),I Take This Man.	100.00
2 Ph(c),Love Thief,Feb.,1950.	100.00

FALCON
Nov., 1983
1 PS,V:Nemesis.	3.00
2 V:Sentinels.	3.00
3 V:Electro	3.00
4 A:Capt.America, Feb., 1984	3.00

FALLEN ANGELS
April, 1987
1 KGa,TP,A:Sunspot,Warlock.	3.00
2 KGa,TP,I:Gomi,Fallen Angels	2.50
3 KGa,TP,A:X-Factor	2.50
4 KGa,TP,A:Moon Boy, Devil Dinosaur	2.50
5 JSon,D:Angel,Don	2.50
6 JSon,Coconut Grove	2.50
7 KGa,Captured in CoconutGrove	2.50
8 KGa,L:Sunspot,Warlock	2.50

Comics Values Annual

9 JK,V:Submariner	2,000.00
10 JK,V:Doctor Doom,I:Ovoids.	2,000.00
11 JK,I:Impossible Man	1,200.00
12 JK,V:Hulk	2,500.00
13 JK,SD,I&O:Red Ghost, I:Watcher	750.00
14 JK,SD,V:Submariner	500.00
15 JK,I:Mad Thinker	500.00
16 JK,V:Doctor Doom	500.00
17 JK,V:Doctor Doom	500.00
18 JK,V:Super Skrull	500.00
19 JK,I&O:Rama Tut.	500.00
20 JK,I:Molecule Man	525.00
21 JK,I:Hate Monger.	350.00
22 JK,V:Mole Man	250.00
23 JK,V:Doctor Doom	250.00
24 JK,I:Infant Terrible	250.00
25 JK,Thing vs.Hulk	600.00
26 JK,V:Hulk,A:Avengers	600.00
27 JK,A:Doctor Strange	275.00
28 JK,1st X-Men x-over	650.00
29 JK,V:Red Ghost.	300.00
30 JK,I&O:Diablo	300.00
31 JK,V:Mole Man	275.00
32 JK,V:Superskrull	275.00
33 JK,I:Attuma	275.00
34 JK,I:Gideon	275.00
35 JK,I:Dragon Man,A:Diablo	275.00
36 JK,I:Medusa,Frightful Four	275.00
37 JK,V:Skrulls.	250.00
38 JK,V:Frightful Four,I:Trapster	250.00
39 JK,WW,A:Daredevil	250.00
40 JK,A:Daredevil,Dr.Doom	250.00
41 JK,V:Fright.Four,A:Medusa.	200.00
42 JK,V:Frightful Four	200.00
43 JK,V:Frightful Four	200.00
44 JK,JSt,I:Gorgon, V:Dragon Man	135.00
45 JK,JSt,I:Inhumans(Black Bolt, Triton,Lockjaw,Crystal, Karnak)	150.00
46 JK,JSt,V:Seeker.	150.00
47 JK,JSt,I:Maximus,Attilan, Alpha Primitives	150.00
48 JK,JSt,I:Silver Surfer, C:Galactus	1,500.00
49 JK,JSt,A:Silver Surfer, V:Galactus	400.00
50 JK,JSt,V:Galactus,Silver Surfer,I:Wyatt Wingfoot.	700.00
51 JK,JSt,I:Negative Zone	100.00
52 JK,JSt,I:Black Panther	250.00
53 JK,JSt,I:Klaw,Vibranium	200.00
54 JK,JSt,I:Prester John	100.00
55 JK,JSt,A:Silver Surfer.	250.00
56 JK,JSt,O:Klaw,A:Inhumans, C:Silver Surfer	125.00
57 JK,JSt,V:Doc Doom, A:Silver Surfer.	125.00
58 JK,JSt,V:Doc Doom, A:Silver Surfer.	125.00
59 JK,JSt,V:Doc Doom, A:Silver Surfer.	125.00
60 JK,JSt,V:Doc Doom, A:Silver Surfer.	125.00
61 JK,JSt,V:Sandman, A:Silver Surfer.	125.00
62 JK,JSt,I:Blastaar	90.00
63 JK,JSt,V:Blastaar.	90.00
64 JK,JSt,I:The Kree,Sentry	90.00
65 JK,JSt,I:Ronan,Supreme Intelligence.	90.00
66 JK,JSt,O:Him,A:Crystal	150.00
67 JK,JSt,I:Him.	200.00
68 JK,JSt,V:Mad Thinker	75.00
69 JK,JSt,V:Mad Thinker	90.00
70 JK,JSt,V:Mad Thinker	75.00
71 JK,JSt,V:Mad Thinker	75.00
72 JK,JSt,A:Watcher,S.Surfer.	150.00
73 JK,JSt,A:SpM,DD,Thor.	100.00
74 JK,JSt,A:Silver Surfer.	120.00

Comics Values Annual   **MARVEL**   Fantastic Four

Fantastic Four #133
© Marvel Entertainment Group

Fantastic Four #219
© Marvel Entertainment Group

#	Description	Price
75	JK,JSt,A:Silver Surfer	120.00
76	JK,JSt,V:Psycho Man,S.Surf	75.00
77	JK,JSt,V:Galactus,S.Surfer	75.00
78	JK,JSt,V:Wizard	75.00
79	JK,JSt,A:Crystall,V:Mad Thinker	75.00
80	JK,JSt,A:Crystal	75.00
81	JK,JSt,J:Crystal,V:Wizard	75.00
82	JK,JSt,V:Maximus	75.00
83	JK,JSt,V:Maximus	75.00
84	JK,JSt,V:Doctor Doom	75.00
85	JK,JSt,V:Doctor Doom	60.00
86	JK,JSt,V:Doctor Doom	60.00
87	JK,JSt,V:Doctor Doom	60.00
88	JK,JSt,V:Mole Man	60.00
89	JK,JSt,V:Mole Man	60.00
90	JK,JSt,V:Skrulls	50.00
91	JK,JSt,V:Skrulls,I:Torgo	50.00
92	JK,JSt,V:Torgo,Skrulls	50.00
93	JK,V:Torgo,Skrulls	50.00
94	JK,JSt,I:Agatha Harkness	50.00
95	JK,JSt,I:Monocle	50.00
96	JK,JSt,V:Mad Thinker	50.00
97	JK,JSt,V:Monster from Lost Lagoon	50.00
98	JK,JSt,V:Kree Sentry	50.00
99	JK,JSt,A:Inhumans	50.00
100	JK,JSt,V:Puppetmaster	135.00
101	JK,V:Maggia	50.00
102	JK,JSt,V:Magneto	50.00
103	JR,V:Magneto	50.00
104	JR,V:Magneto	50.00
105	JR,L:Crystal	50.00
106	JR,JSt,'Monster's Secret'	50.00
107	JR,JSt,V:Annihilus	50.00
108	JK,JB,JR,JSt, V:Annihilus	50.00
109	JR,JSt,V:Annihilus	50.00
110	JB,JSt,V:Annihilus	45.00
111	JB,JSt,A:Hulk	40.00
112	JB,JSt,Thing vs. Hulk	135.00
113	JB,JSt,I:Overmind	35.00
114	JR(c),JB,V:Overmind	35.00
115	JR(c),JB,JSt,I:Eternals	35.00
116	JB,JSt,O:Stranger	45.00
117	JB,JSt,V:Diablo	30.00
118	JR(c),JB,JM,V:Diablo	30.00
119	JB,JSt,V:Klaw	30.00
120	JB,JSt,I:Gabriel(Airwalker) (Robot)	30.00
121	JB,JSt,V:Silver Surfer,D: Gabriel Destroyer	35.00
122	JR(c),JB,JSt,V:Galactus, A:Silver Surfer	35.00
123	JB,JSt,V:Galactus, A:Silver Surfer	35.00
124	JB,JSt,V:Monster	30.00
125	E:StL(s),JB,JSt,V:Monster	30.00
126	B:RTs(s),JB,JSt, O:FF,MoleMan	30.00
127	JB,JSt,V:Mole Man	30.00
128	JB,JSt,V:Mole Man	30.00
129	JB,JSt,I:Thundra, V:Frightful Four	30.00
130	JSo(c),JB,JSt,V:Frightful Four	30.00
131	JSo(c),JB,JSt,V:QuickSilver	30.00
132	JB,JSt,J:Medusa	30.00
133	JSt(i),V:Thundra	30.00
134	JSt,JSt,V:Dragon Man	30.00
135	JB,JSt,V:Gideon	30.00
136	JB,JSt,A:Shaper	30.00
137	JB,JSt,A:Shaper	30.00
138	JB,JSt,O:Miracle Man	30.00
139	JB,V:Miracle Man	30.00
140	JB,JSt,O:Annihilus	30.00
141	JR(c),JB,JSt,V:Annihilus	30.00
142	RB,JSt,A:Doc Doom	30.00
143	GK(c),RB,V:Doc Doom	30.00
144	RB,JSt,V:Doc Doom	30.00
145	JSt&GK(c),RA,I:Ternak	30.00
146	RA,JSt,V:Ternak	30.00
147	RB,JSt,V:Subby	30.00
148	RB,JSt,V:Frightful Four	30.00
149	RB,JSt,V:Sub-Mariner	30.00
150	GK(c),RB,JSt,W:Crystal & Quicksilver,V:Ultron	35.00
151	RB,JSt,O:Thundra	15.00
152	JR(c),RB,JM,A:Thundra	15.00
153	GK(c),RB,JSt,A:Thundra	15.00
154	GK(c),rep.Str.Tales #127	15.00
155	RB,JSt,A:Surfer	20.00
156	RB,JSt,A:Surfer,V:Doom	20.00
157	RB,JSt,A:Surfer	20.00
158	RB,JSt,V:Xemu	15.00
159	RB,JSt,V:Xemu	15.00
160	K&R(c),JB,V:Arkon	15.00
161	RB,JSt,V:Arkon	10.00
162	RB,DA,JSt,V:Arkon	10.00
163	RB,JSt,V:Arkon	10.00
164	JK(c),GP,JSt,V:Crusader,R: Marvel Boy,I:Frankie Raye	10.00
165	GP,JSt,O:Crusader, O&D:Marvel Boy	10.00
166	GP,V:Hulk	15.00
167	JK(c),GP,JSt,V:Hulk	15.00
168	RB,JSt,J:Luke Cage	10.00
169	RB,JSt,V:Puppetmaster	10.00
170	GP,JSt,L:Luke Cage	10.00
171	JK(c),RB,GP,JSt,I:Gor	10.00
172	JK(c),GP,JSt,V:Destroyer	10.00
173	JB,JSt,V:Galactus,O:Heralds	10.00
174	JB,V:Galactus	10.00
175	JB,A:High Evolutionary	10.00
176	GP,JSt,V:Impossible Man	10.00
177	JP,JS,A:Frightful Four I:Texas Twister,Capt.Ultra	10.00
178	GP,V:Frightful Four,Brute	10.00
179	JSt,V:Annihilus	10.00
180	reprint #101	10.00
181	E:RTs(s),JSt,V:Brute, Annihilus	10.00
182	SB,JSt,V:Brute,Annihilus	10.00
183	SB,JSt,V:Brute,Annihilus	10.00
184	GP,JSt,V:Eliminator	10.00
185	GP,JSt,V:Nich.Scratch	10.00
186	GP,JSi,I:Salem's Seven	10.00
187	GP,JSt,V:Klaw,Molecule Man	10.00
188	GP,JSt,V:Molecule Man	10.00
189	reprint FF Annual #4	10.00
190	SB,O:Fantastic Four	11.00
191	GP,JSt,V:Plunderer, Team Breaks Up	10.00
192	GP,JSt,V:Texas Twister	10.00
193	KP,JSt,V:Darkoth,Diablo	10.00
194	KP,V:Darkoth,Diablo	10.00
195	KP,A:Sub-Mariner	10.00
196	KP,V:Invincible Man (Reed), A:Dr.Doom,Team Reunited	10.00
197	KP,JSt,Red Ghost	10.00
198	KP,JSt,V:Doc Doom	10.00
199	KP,JSt,V:Doc Doom	10.00
200	KP,JSt,V:Doc Doom	15.00
201	KP,JSt,FF's Machinery	7.00
202	KP,JSt,V:Quasimodo	7.00
203	KP,JSt,V:Mutant	7.00
204	KP,JSt,V:Skrulls	7.00
205	KP,JSt,V:Skrulls	7.00
206	KP,JSt,V:Skrulls,A:Nova	7.00
207	SB,JSt,V:Monocle,A:SpM	7.00
208	SB,V:Sphinx,A:Nova	7.00
209	JBy,JSt,I:Herbie,A:Nova	8.00
210	JBy,JS,A:Galactus	7.00
211	JBy,JS,I:Terrax,A:Galactus	8.00
212	JBy,JSt,V:Galactus,Sphinx	7.00
213	JBy,JSt,V:Terrax,Galactus Sphinx	7.00
214	JBy,JSt,V:Skrull	7.00
215	JBy,JSt,V:Blastaar	7.00
216	JBy,V:Blastaar	7.00
217	JBy,JSt,A:Dazzler	7.00
218	JBy,JSt,V:FrightfulFour, A:Spider-Man	7.00
219	BSz,JSt,A:Sub-Mariner	6.00
220	JBy,JSt,A:Vindicator	6.00
221	JBy,JSt,V:Vindicator	6.00
222	BSz,JSt,V:Nicholas Scratch	6.00
223	BSz,JSt,V:Salem's Seven	6.00
224	BSz,A:Thor	6.00
225	BSz,A:Thor	6.00
226	BSz,A:Shogun	6.00
227	BSz,JSt,V:Ego-Spawn	6.00
228	BSz,JSt,V:Ego-Spawn	6.00
229	BSz,JSt,I:Firefrost,Ebon Seeker	6.00
230	BSz,JSt,A:Avengers, O:Firefrost & Ebon Seeker	6.00
231	BSz,JSt,V:Stygorr	6.00
232	JBy,New Direction,V:Diablo	7.00
233	JBy,V:Hammerhead	6.00
234	JBy,V:Ego	6.00
235	JBy,O:Ego	6.00
236	JBy,V:Dr.Doom,A:Puppet Master, 20th Anniv.	6.00
237	JBy,V:Solons	5.00
238	JBy,O:Frankie Raye, new Torch	5.00
239	JBy,I:Aunt Petunia, Uncle Jake	6.00

All comics prices listed are for *Near Mint* condition.   CVA Page 235

Fantastic Four — MARVEL — Comics Values Annual

- 240 JBy,A:Inhumans,b:Luna 5.00
- 241 JBy,A:Black Panther 5.00
- 242 JBy,A:Daredevil,Thor,Iron Man
  Spider-Man,V:Terrax. 5.00
- 243 JBy,A:Daredevil,Dr.Strange,
  Spider-Man,Avengers,V:Galactus,
  Terrax. 5.00
- 244 JBy,A:Avengers,Dr.Strange,
  Galactus, Frankie Raye
  Becomes Nova. 5.00
- 245 JBy,V:Franklin Richards 5.00
- 246 JBy,V:Dr.Doom,
  A:Puppet Master 5.00
- 247 JBy,A:Dr.Doom,I:Kristoff,
  D:Zorba 5.00
- 248 JBy,A:Inhumans. 5.00
- 249 JBy,V:Gladiator 5.00
- 250 JBy,A:Capt.America,SpM
  V:Gladiator................ 5.00
- 251 JBy,A:Annihilus 5.00
- 252 JBy,1st sideways issue,V:
  Ootah,A:Annihilus,w/tattoo ... 5.00
- 252a w/o tattoo................ 5.00
- 253 JBy,V:Kestorans,A:Annihilus .. 5.00
- 254 JBy,V:Mantracora,
  A:She-Hulk,Wasp........... 5.00
- 255 JBy,A:Daredevil,Annihilus,
  V:Mantracora 5.00
- 256 JBy,A:Avengers,Galactus,
  V:Annihilus,New Costumes.... 5.00
- 257 JBy,A:Galactus,Death,Nova,
  Scarlet Witch 4.50
- 258 JBy,A:Dr.Doom,D:Hauptmann . 4.50
- 259 JBy,V:Terrax,Dr.Doom,
  C:Silver Silver 4.50
- 260 JBy,V:Terrax, Dr.Doom,
  A:Silver Surfer,Sub-Mariner ... 5.00
- 261 JBy,A:Sub-Mariner,Marrina,
  Silver Surfer,Sc.Witch,Lilandra . 5.00
- 262 JBy,O:Galactus,A:Odin,
  (J.Byrne in story) 4.00
- 263 JBy,V:Messiah,A:Mole Man ... 4.00
- 264 JBy,V:Messiah,A:Mole Man ... 4.00
- 265 JBy,A:Trapster,Avengers,
  J:She-Hulk,Secret Wars 4.00
- 266 KGa,JBy,A:Hulk,Sasquatch,
  V:Karisma 4.00
- 267 JBy,A:Hulk,Sasquatch,Morbius,
  V:Dr.Octopus,Sue miscarries .. 4.00
- 268 JBy,V:Doom's Mask 4.00
- 269 JBy,R:Wyatt Wingfoot,
  I:Terminus 4.00
- 270 JBy,V:Terminus 4.00
- 271 JBy,V:Gormuu............. 4.00
- 272 JBy,I:Warlord (Nathaniel
  Richards) 4.00
- 273 JBy,V:Warlord 4.00
- 274 JBy,AG,cont.from Thing#19,
  A:Spider-Man's Black Costume. 4.00
- 275 JBy,AG,V:T.J.Vance 4.00
- 276 JBy,JOy,V:Mephisto,
  A:Dr.Strange 4.00
- 277 JBy,JOy,V:Mephisto,
  A:Dr.Strange,R:Thing 4.00
- 278 JBy,JOy,O:Dr.Doom,A:Kristoff
  (as Doom) 4.00
- 279 JBy,JOy,V:Dr.Doom(Kristoff),
  I:New Hate-Monger 4.00
- 280 JBy,JOy,I:Malice,
  V:Hate-Monger 4.00
- 281 JBy,JOy,A:Daredevil,V:Hate
  Monger,Malice 4.00
- 282 JBy,JOy,A:Power Pack,Psycho
  Man,Secret Wars II. 4.00
- 283 JBy,JOy,V:Psycho-Man 4.00
- 284 JBy,JOy,V:Psycho-Man 4.00
- 285 JBy,JOy,Secret Wars II
  A:Beyonder 4.00
- 286 JBy,TA,R:Jean Grey,
  A:Hercules Capt.America 5.00
- 287 JBy,JSt,A:Wasp,V:Dr.Doom ... 4.00

- 288 JBy,JSt,V:Dr.Doom,Secret
  Wars II 5.00
- 289 JBy,AG,D:Basilisk,V:Blastaar,
  R:Annihilus................ 4.00
- 290 JBy,AG,V:Annihilus 4.00
- 291 JBy,CR,A:Nick Fury......... 4.00
- 292 JBy,AG,A:Nick Fury,V:Hitler ... 4.00
- 293 JBy,AG,A:Avengers.W.C...... 4.00
- 294 JOy,AG,V:FutureCentralCity... 3.00
- 295 JOy,AG,V:Fut.Central City 3.00
- 296 BWS,KGa,RF,BWi,AM,KJ,JB,
  SL,MS,JRu,JOy,JSt,25th
  Anniv.,V:MoleMan........... 5.00
- 297 JB,SB,V:Umbra-Sprite 3.00
- 298 JB,SB,V:Umbra-Sprite 2.50
- 299 JB,SB,She-Hulk,V:Thing,
  A:Spider-Man,L:She-Hulk 3.00
- 300 JB,SB,W:Torch & Fake Alicia
  (Lyja),A:Puppet-Master,Wizard,
  Mad Thinker,Dr.Doom........ 4.00
- 301 JB,SB,V:Wizard,MadThinker .. 3.00
- 302 JB,SB,V:Project Survival 3.00
- 303 JB,RT,A:Thundra,V:Machus ... 3.00
- 304 JB,JSt,V:Quicksilver,
  A:Kristoff 3.00
- 305 JB,JSt,V:Quicksilver,
  J:Crystal,A:Dr.Doom......... 3.00
- 306 JB,JSt,A:Capt.America,
  J:Ms.Marvel,V:Diablo 3.00
- 307 JB,JSt,L:Reed&Sue,V:Diablo .. 3.00
- 308 JB,JSt,I:Fasaud 3.00
- 309 JB,JSt,I:Fasaud 3.00
- 310 KP,JSt,V:Fasaud,N:Thing
  & Ms.Marvel............... 3.00
- 311 KP,JSt,A:Black Panther,
  Dr.Doom,V:THRob.......... 3.00
- 312 KP,JSt,A:Black Panther,
  Dr.Doom,X-Factor 3.00
- 313 SB,JSt,V:Lava Men,
  A:Moleman................ 3.00
- 314 KP,JSt,V:Belasco 3.00
- 315 KP,JSt,V:Mast.Pandem. 3.00
- 316 KP,JSt,A:CometMan 3.00
- 317 KP,JSt,L:Crystal........... 3.00
- 318 KP,JSt,V:Dr.Doom 3.00
- 319 KP,JSt,G-Size,O:Beyonder.... 3.00
- 320 KP,JSt,Hulk vs Thing 3.00
- 321 RLm,RT,A:She-Hulk......... 3.00
- 322 KP,JSt,Inferno,V:Graviton..... 3.00
- 323 KP,JSt,RT,Inferno A:Mantis. .. 3.00
- 324 KP,JSt,RT,A:Mantis 3.00
- 325 RB,RT,A:Silver Surfer,
  D:Mantis. 3.00

- 326 KP,RT,I:New Frightful Four.... 3.00
- 327 KP,RT,V:Frightful Four 3.00
- 328 KP,RT,V:Frightful Four 3.00
- 329 RB,RT,V:Mole Man 3.00
- 330 RB,RT,V:Dr.Doom 3.00
- 331 RB,RT,V:Ultron 3.00
- 332 RB,RT,V:Aron 3.00
- 333 RB,RT,V:Aron,Frightful Four... 3.00
- 334 RB,Acts of Vengeance 3.00
- 335 RB,RT,Acts of Vengeance 3.00
- 336 RLm,Acts of Vengeance..... 3.00
- 337 WS,A:Thor,Iron Man,
  B:Timestream saga 4.00
- 338 WS,V:Deathshead,A:Thor,
  Iron Man 3.00
- 339 WS,V:Gladiator 3.00
- 340 WS,V:Black Celestial 3.00
- 341 WS,A:Thor,Iron Man 3.00
- 342 A:Rusty,C:Spider-Man 3.00
- 343 WS,V:Stalin 3.00
- 344 WS,V:Stalin 3.00
- 345 WS,V:Dinosaurs 3.00
- 346 WS,V:Dinosaurs 3.00
- 347 AAd,ATi(i)A:Spider-Man,
  GhostRider,Wolverine,Hulk.... 4.00
- 347a 2nd printing 3.00
- 348 AAd,ATi(i)A:Spider-Man,
  GhostRider,Wolverine,Hulk.... 4.00
- 348a 2nd printing 3.00
- 349 AAd,ATi(i),AM(i)A:Spider-Man,
  Wolverine,GhostRider,Hulk,
  C:Punisher 3.50
- 350 WS,Am(i),R:Bon Grimm as
  Thing,(48p)................ 3.50
- 351 MBa,Kubic................ 3.00
- 352 WS,Reed Vs.Dr.Doom 3.00
- 353 WS,E:Timestream Saga,
  A:Avengers................ 3.00
- 354 WS,Secrets of the Time
  Variance Authority 3.00
- 355 AM,V:Wrecking Crew 3.00
- 356 B:TDF(s),PR,A:New Warriors,
  V:Puppet Master............ 3.00
- 357 PR,V:Mad Thinker,
  Puppetmaster.............. 3.00
- 358 PR,AAd,30th Anniv.,1st Marv.
  Die Cut(c),D:Lyja,V:Paibok,
  BU:Dr.Doom............... 3.50
- 359 PR,I:Devos the Devastator.... 3.00
- 360 PR,V:Dreadface............ 3.00
- 361 PR,V:Dr.Doom,X-masIssue ... 3.00
- 362 PR,A:Spider-Man,
  I:WildBlood................ 3.00
- 363 PR,I:Occulus,A:Devos 3.00
- 364 PR,V:Occulus 3.00
- 365 PR,V:Occulus 3.00
- 366 PR,Infinity War,R:Lyja 3.00
- 367 PR,Inf.War,A:Wolverine 3.00
- 368 PR,V:Infinity War X-Men 3.00
- 369 PR,Inf.War,R:Malice,
  A:Thanos 3.00
- 370 PR,Inf.War,V:Mr.Fantastic
  Doppleganger. 3.00
- 371 PR,V:Lyja,foil(c)............ 4.00
- 371a 2nd Printing 3.00
- 372 PR,A:Spider-Man,Silver
  Sable 3.00
- 373 PR,V:Aron,Silver sable....... 3.00
- 374 PR,V:Secret Defenders 3.00
- 375 V:Dr.Doom,A:Inhumans,Lyja,
  Holo-Grafix(c).............. 3.50
- 376 PR,A:Nathan Richards,V:Paibok,
  Devos,w/Dirt Magazine....... 3.50
- 376a w/out Dirt Magazine........ 2.50
- 377 PR,V:Paibok,Devos,Klaw,
  I:Huntara.................. 2.50
- 378 PR,A:Sandman,SpM,DD 2.50
- 379 PR,V:Ms.Marvel............ 2.50
- 380 PR,A:Dr.Doom,V:Hunger 2.50
- 381 PR,D:Dr.Doom,Mr.Fantastic,
  V:Hunger 5.00

Fantastic Four #367
© Marvel Entertainment Group

Comics Values Annual — MARVEL — Fantastic Four

Fantastic Four #404
© Marvel Entertainment Group

382 PR,V:Paibok,Devos,Huntara . . 3.00
383 PR,V:Paibok,Devos,Huntara . . 2.50
384 PR,A:Ant-Man,V:Franklin
   Richards. 2.50
385 PR,A:Triton,Tiger Shark,
   Starblast#7. . . . . 2.50
386 PR,Starblast#11,A:Namor,Triton,
   b:Johnny & Lyja child 2.50
387 Die-Cut & Foil (c),PR,N:Invisible
   Woman,J:Ant-Man,A:Namor . . . 4.00
387a Newsstand Ed. 2.50
388 PR,I:Dark Raider,V:FF,
   Avengers,w/cards. 2.50
389 PR,I:Raphael Suarez,A:Watcher,
   V:Collector 2.50
390 PR,A:Galactus. 2.50
391 PR,I:Vibraxas. 2.50
392 Dark Raider. 2.50
393 . . . . 2.50
394 Neon(c) w/insert print. 3.00
394a Newsstand ed.,no bag/inserts 2.50
395 Thing V:Wolverine 2.50
396 . . . . 2.50
397 Resurrection,pt.1 . . . . 2.50
398 regular edition 2.50
398a Enhanced cover. 3.00
399 Watcher's Lie. 3.00
399a Foil stamped cover 3.00
400 Watcher's Lie,pt.3 . . . . 5.00
401 V:Tantalus 2.50
402 Atlantis Rising,Namor
   vs. Black Bolt. 2.50
403 TDF,PR,DBi,F:Thing,Medusa . . 2.50
404 R:Namor,I:New Villian 2.50
405 J:Namor. 2.50
406 TDF,PR,DBI,R:Dr. Doom,
   I:Hyperstorm 2.50
407 TDF,PR,DBi,Return of
   Reed Richards. 2.50
408 TDF,PR,DBi,Original FF unite. . 2.50
409 TDF,PR,DBi,All new line-up . . . 2.50
410 . . . . 2.50
411 . . . . 2.50
412 TDF,PR,DBi,Mr.Fantastic
   vs. Sub-Mariner 2.50
413 . . . . 2.50
414 Galactus vs. Hyperstorm 2.50
415 Onslaught saga, A:X-Men 4.00
416 Onslaught saga, A:Dr. Doom,
   double size, finale 5.00
Ann.#1 JK,SD,I:Atlantis,Dorma,
   Krang,V:Namor,O:FF 1,200.00
Ann.#2 JK,JSt,O:Dr.Doom. 600.00

Ann.#3 JK,W:Reed and Sue 250.00
Ann.#4 JK,JSt,I:Quasimodo 150.00
Ann.#5 JK,JSt,A:Inhumans,Silver
   Surfer,Black Panther,
   I:Psycho Man 160.00
Ann.#6 JK,JSt,I:Annihilus,
   Franklin Richards 100.00
Ann.#7 JK(c),reprints 50.00
Ann.#8 JR(c),reprints 30.00
Ann.#9 JK(c),reprints. 30.00
Ann.#10 reprints Ann.#3 . . . . 30.00
Ann.#11 JK(c),JB,A:The Invaders . 12.00
Ann.#12 A:The Invaders 12.00
Ann.#13 V:The Mole Man 12.00
Ann.#14 GP,V:Salem's Seven . . . 12.00
Ann.#15 GP,V:Dr.Doom,Skrulls . . 10.00
Ann.#16 V:Dragonlord 10.00
Ann.#17 JBy,V:Skrulls. 10.00
Ann.#18 KGa,V:Skrulls,W:Black
   Bolt and Medusa,A:Inhumans . 10.00
Ann.#19 JBy,V:Skrulls. 10.00
Ann.#20 TD(i),V:Dr.Doom 4.00
Ann.#21 JG,JSt,Evol.Wars 4.00
Ann.#22 RB,Atlantis Attacks,
   A:Avengers 4.00
Ann.#23 JG,GCa,Days of Future
   Present #1 . . . . 5.00
Ann.#24 JG,AM,Korvac Quest #1,
   A:Guardians of the Galaxy 3.00
Ann.#25 Citizen Kang #3 . . . . 3.00
Ann.#26 HT,I:Wildstreak,
   V:Dreadface,w/card 3.50
Ann.#27 MGu,V:Justice Peace . . . 3.50
G-Size#1 RB,Thing/Hulk. 17.00
G-Size#2 K&R(c),JB,Time to Kill . . 15.00
G-Size#3 RB,JSt,Four Horseman . 15.00
G-Size#4 JB,JSt,I:Madrox. 15.00
G-Size#5 JK(c),V:Psycho Man,
   Molecule Man. 12.00
G-Size#6 V:Annihilus 12.00
Spec.#1 Rep.Ann.#1 JBy(c) 2.50
TPB Rep.#347-349. . . . . 5.95
TPB Nobody Gets Out Alive, rep.
   Fant.Four #387–#392 + new. . 15.95
TPB Trial of Galactus,reprints
   #242-244,#257-262 . . . . 9.95
Marvel Milestone rep. #1 (1991) . . 2.95
Marvel Milestone rep. #5 (1992) . . 2.95
Ashcan. 75
Spec. The Origin of Galactus 2.50

[2nd Series], Nov., 1996
1 JLe,BCi,SW, 48pg 5.00
1A Mole Man cover 12.00
1B Gold signature, bagged,
   limited 25.00
2 JLe,BCi,V:Namor 5.00
3 JLe,BCi,SW,A:Avengers 4.00
4 JLe,BCi,SW,I:Black Panther 4.00
4A x-mas cover 5.00
5 JLe,BCi,SW,V:Dr. Doom 4.00
6 JLe,BCi,SW,Industrial Revolution
   prologue. 3.00
7 JLe,BCi,BBh,V:Blastaar 3.00
8 JLe,BCi,BBh,V:Inhumans 3.00
9 JLe,BCi,BBh,V:Inhumans 3.00
10 JLe,BCi,BBh,A:Silver Surfer,
   Tyrax 3.00
11 JLe,BCi,BBh,A:Silver Surfer,
   Firelord, Terrax. 3.00
12 JLe,BCi,BBh,GalactusSaga,pt.1,
   reunited 5.00
13 JeR,Wildstorm x-over. 3.00
Ashcan, signed, numbered 10.00

[3rd Series], Nov., 1997
1 SLo,AD,MFm, The Ruined, 48pg
   debut 5.00
2 SLo,AD,MFm,A:Iconoclast 4.00
3 SLo,AD,MFm,V:Red Ghost 4.00
4 SLo,SvL,ATi,A:Silver Surfer,
   double size. 4.00

Fantastic Four 2nd Series #7
© Marvel Entertainment Group

4 signed by SLo, (500 copies) . . . 20.00
5 SLo,SvL,ATi,V:The Crucible 3.00
6 CCl,SvL, new villains 3.00
7 CCl,SvL,ATi,V:Technet 3.00
8 CCl,SvL,V:Captain Britain corp. . . 3.00
9 CCl,SvL,A:Spider-Man 3.00
10 CCl,SvL,ATi. 3.00
11 CCl,SvL,ATi,Crucible—unleashed
   in Genosha 3.00
12 CCl,SvL,ATi,V:Fantastic Four
   double-size. 4.50
13 CCl,SvL,A:Ronan the Accuser . . 2.50
14 CCl,SvL,V:Ronan. 2.50
15 CCl,SvL,ATi,Iron Man x-over . . . 2.50
16 CCl,SvL,ATi,V:Kree Avengers. . . 2.50
17 CCl,SvL,ATi,I:Lockdown. 2.50
18 CCl,SvL,ATi,Jail Break 2.50
19 CCl,SvL,ATi,V:Annihilus 2.50
20 CCl,SvL,ATi,V:Ruined 2.50
21 CCl,SvL,ATi,V:Hades 2.50
22 CCl,SvL,ATi,V:Valeria
   Von Doom 2.50
23 CCl,SvL,ATi,A:She-Hulk 2.50
24 CCl,SvL,ATi,F:FranklinRichards . 2.50
25 CCl,SvL,ATi,V:Dr.Doom 3.50
26 CCl,SvL,ATi,F:ValeriaVonDoom . 3.00
27 CCl,SvL,F:Invisible Woman 3.00
28 CCl,SvL,ATi,Planet Doom 3.00
29 CCl,SvL,ATi,Frightful Four 2.50
30 CCl,SvL,ATi,Castle Doom 2.25
31 CCl,SvL,ATi,InvisibleWoman . . . 2.25
32 CCl,SvL,ATi,InvisibleWoman . . . 2.25
33 JFM,SvL,ATi,Kid Colt 2.25
34 JFM,SvL,ATi,aliens 2.25
35A CPa,Diablo,foil (c) 5.00
35B painted (c). 2.25
36 CPa,Diablo triumphant. 2.25
37 CPa,F:Johnny Storm 2.25
38 CPa,JLb,V:Grey Gargoyle 2.25
39 CPa,JLb,V:Grey Gargoyle 2.25
40 CPa,JLb,Negative Zone. 2.25
41 CPa,JLb,Hellscout 2.25
42 CPa,JLb,SI,V:Namor 2.25
43 CPa,JLb,JoB,new Fant.Four . . . 2.25
44 CPa,JLb,Negative Zone,concl.. . 2.25
45 CPa,JLb,one new costume . . . 2.25
46 CPa,JLb,Abraxas Saga 2.25
47 CPa,JLb,Abraxas,pt.3 . . . . 2.25
48 CPa,JLb,Abraxas,pt.4 . . . . 2.25
49 CPa,JLb,Abraxas,pt.5 . . . . 2.25
50 Four new stories,BWS(c),64-pg. 5.00
51 MBa,KK,F:Inhumans 3.50
52 MBa,KK,F:Dr. Doom 2.25

All comics prices listed are for *Near Mint* condition.

Fantastic Four–Fear / MARVEL / Comics Values Annual

Fantastic Four 3rd Series 31
© Marvel Entertainment Group

53 MBa,KK,Inhumans 2.25
54 MBa,KK,Inhumans, 100-pg. 4.00
55 KK,SI,Thing,Human Torch 2.25
56 F:Thing 2.25
57 AWa,F:Thing,pt.1 . . . . 2.25
58 AWa,F:Thing,pt.2 . . . . 2.25
59 AWa,F:Thing,pt.3 . . . . 2.25
60 MWa,KK 0.09
61 MWa,KK 2.25
62 MWa,KK,Sentient,pt.1, 48-pg. 2.25
63 MWa,KK,Sentient,pt.2 . . . . 2.25
64 MWa,KK,Sentient,pt.3 . . . . 2.25
65 MWa,MBu,Small Stuff/Big Stuff . 2.25
66 MWa,MBu,Small Stuff/Big Stuff . 2.25
67 MWa,KK,Unthinkable 5.00
68 MWa,KK,Unthinkable 3.00
69 MWa,KK,Unthinkable 3.00
70 MWa,Unthinkable 3.00
500 MWa,Unthinkable,48-pg. 5.00
500a Director's Cut, foil 5.00
501 MWa,CJ,Fifth Wheel,pt.1 . . . . 2.25
502 MWa,CJ,Fifth Wheel,pt.2 . . . . 2.25
503 MWa,Authoritative Action,pt.1. . 2.25
504 MWa,Authoritative Action,pt.2. . 2.25
505 MWa,Authoritative Action,pt.3. . 2.25
506 MWa,Authoritative Action,pt.4. . 2.25
507 MWa,Authoritative Action,pt.5. . 2.25
Ann.1998 Fant.Four & Fant.Four . . 4.00
Ann.1999 CCI,I:Mechamage 4.00
Ann.2000 LSi,SvL,48-pg. 4.00
Ann.2001 Galactus,48-page 3.50
Spec.#1 KIK FantasticFour (2000) . 2.25
Spec. Fantastic Four/Sentry 3.00
Spec. Fantastic Fourth Voyage
  of Sinbad, 48-page (2001) . . . 5.95
TPB Heroes Return, 96-page 10.95
TPB Heroes Reborn, 176-pg. 17.95
TPB Into the Breach, 144-pg. 15.95
TPB (Vol.3) Flesh & Stone (2002). 12.95
TPB (Vol.1) Visionaries (2002) . . . 19.95
TPB Vol. 1: Imaginauts (2003) . . 18.00
TPB Legends, Vol. 1 (2003) 14.00
TPB Vol. 2: Unthinkable (2003). . . 18.00

FANTASTIC FOUR: ATLANTIS RISING
1995
1 B:Atlantis Rising 5.00
2 TDF,MCW,finale, acetate(c) 5.00

FANTASTIC FOUR INDEX
See: OFFICIAL MARVEL INDEX TO THE FANTASTIC FOUR

FANTASTIC FOUR: 1 2 3 4
June, 2001
1 (of 4) GMo,JaL,F:Thing. 3.00
2 GMo,JaL,F:Invisible Woman . . . 3.00
3 GMo,JaL,F:Human Torch 3.00
4 GMo,JaL,F:Mr. Fantastic. 3.00
TPB JaL,GMo. 10.00

FANTASTIC FOUR ROAST
May, 1982
1 FH/MG/FM/JB/MA/TA 5.00

FANTASTIC FOUR'S BIG TOWN
Nov., 2000
1 (of 4) SEt,MMK,MkK,48-page . . . 3.50
2 SEt,MMK,MkK 3.00
3 SEt,MMK,MkK 3.00
4 SEt,MMK,MkK,48-page 3.50

FANTASTIC FOUR 2099
1996
1 Cont. from 2099 Genesis 4.00
2 V:Stark/Fujikawa elite guard . . . 2.25
3 . . . . 2.25
4 . . . . 2.25
5 A:Spider-Man 2099. . . . . 2.25

FANTASTIC FOUR UNLIMITED
1993–96
1 HT,A:Bl.Panther,V:Klaw. 4.50
2 HT,JQ(c),A:Inhumans 4.25
3 HT,V:Blastaar,Annihilus. 4.25
4 RTs(s),HT,V:Mole Man,A:Hulk . 4.25
5 RTs(s),HT,V:Frightful Four. 4.25
6 RTs(s),HT,V:Namor. 4.00
7 HT,V:Monsters 4.00
8 . . . . 4.00
9 A:Antman 4.00
10 RTs,HT,V:Maelstrom,A:Eternals. 4.00
11 RTs,HT,Atlantis Rising fallout . . 4.00
12 RTs,TDF,V:Hyperstorm. 4.00
13 . . . . 4.00

FANTASTIC FOUR UNPLUGGED
1995–96
1 comic for a buck. 2.25
2 Reed Richard's Will 2.25
3 F:Mr. Fantastic 2.25
4 . . . . 2.25
5 Back in NY,V:Blastaar. 2.25

FANTASTIC FOUR: UNSTABLE MOLECULES
Marvel Jan. 2003
1 (of 4) GyD 3.00
2 GyD 3.00
3 GyD 3.00

FANTASTIC FOUR VS. X-MEN
Feb., 1987
1 JBg,TA,V:Dr.Doom 5.00
2 JBg,TA,V:Dr.Doom 4.00
3 JBg,TA,V:Dr.Doom 4.00
4 JBg,TA,V:Dr.Doom, June, 1987. . 4.00
TPB Reprints Mini-series 12.95

FANTASTIC FOUR THE WORLD'S GREATEST COMIC MAGAZINE
Dec., 2000
1 (of 12) EL,ErS,V:Dr.Doom. 3.00
2 F:Dr.Doom,Crystal 3.00
3 A:X-Men,Spider-Man 3.00
4 A:X-Men,Capt.America 3.00
5 EL(c),Hulk vs. Thing 3.00
6 MGo(c),A:Silver Surfer 3.00
7 KG(c),A:Dr.Doom,Inhumans . . . 3.00
8 KG(c),F:Avengers. 3.00
9 EL,KG,A:Dr.Doom 3.00
10 EL,KG,Cosmic Cube 3.00
11 RF,Planet Doom. 3.00
12 StL,EL,JSt, concl. 3.00

FANTASTIC WORLD OF HANNA-BARBERA
Dec., 1977
1 . . . . 30.00
2 . . . . 20.00
3 June, 1978 . . . . 20.00

FANTASY MASTERPIECES
Feb., 1966
1 JK/DH/SD,reprints 85.00
2 JK,SD,DH,Fin Fang Foom 50.00
3 GC,DH,JK,SD,Capt.A rep. 60.00
4 JK,Capt.America rep. 60.00
5 JK,Capt.America rep. 60.00
6 JK,Capt.America rep. 60.00
7 SD,Sub Mariner rep. 60.00
8 H.Torch & Sub M.rep. 60.00
9 SD,MF,O:Human Torch Rep . . 65.00
10 rep.All Winners #19 . . . . 50.00
11 JK,(rep),O:Toro 50.00

Becomes:

MARVEL SUPER-HEROES

FANTASY MASTERPIECES
[Volume 2], Dec., 1979
1 JB,JSt,Silver Surfer rep. 5.00
2 JB,JSt,Silver Surfer rep. 5.00
3 JB,JSt,Silver Surfer rep. 5.00
4 JB,JSt,Silver Surfer rep. 5.00
5 JB,JSt,Silver Surfer rep. 5.00
6 JB,JSt,Silver Surfer rep. 5.00
7 JB,JSt,Silver Surfer rep. 5.00
8 JB/JSn,Warlock rep.Strange
   Tales #178 . . . . 4.00
9 JB,JSn,rep.StrangeTales#179. . . 4.00
10 JB,JSn,rep.StrangeTales#180 . . 4.00
11 JB,JSn,rep.StrangeTales#181 . . 4.00
12 JB,JSn,rep.Warlock #9. . . . . . . 4.00
13 JB,JSn,rep.Warlock #10. . . . . . 4.00
14 JB,JSn,rep.Warlock #11. . . . . . 4.00

FAREWELL TO WEAPONS
1 DirtBag,W/Nirvana Tape 3.50

FEAR
Nov., 1970
1 JK,1950's Monster rep.B:I
  Found Monstrum,The Dweller
  in the Black Swamp 50.00
2 JK,X The Thing That Lived . . . 30.00
3 JK,Zzutak, The Thing That
  Shouldn't Exist 30.00
4 JK,I Turned Into a Martian. . . . 30.00

CVA Page 238   All comics prices listed are for *Near Mint* condition.

MARVEL

Comics Values Annual — Fear–Frontier

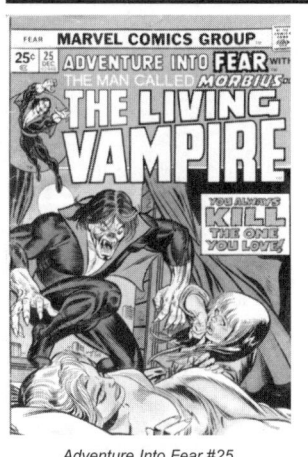

Adventure Into Fear #25
© Marvel Entertainment Group

5 JK,I Am the Gorilla Man	30.00
6 JK,SD,The Midnight Monster	30.00
7 JK,SD,I Dream of Doom	20.00
8 JK,SD,It Crawls By Night!	20.00
9 JK,Dead Man's Escape	20.00

Becomes:

ADVENTURE INTO FEAR
1972

10 HC,GM,B:Man-Thing	40.00
11 RB,I:Jennifer Kale,Thog	20.00
12 JSn,RB	20.00
13 VM,Where World's Collide	15.00
14 VM,Plague o/t Demon Cult.	15.00
15 VM,Lord o/t Dark Domain.	15.00
16 VM,ManThing in Everglades	15.00
17 VM,I:Wundarr(Aquarian)	15.00
18 VM	15.00
19 VM,FMc,I:Howard the Duck, E:Man-Thing	50.00
20 PG,GK,B:Morbius	50.00
21 GK,V:Uncanny Caretaker	15.00
22 RB,V:Cat-Demond	15.00
23 GC,GK,1st CR art,A World He Never Made	15.00
24 CR,SMn,V:Blade, The Vampire Slayer	35.00
25 FR,GK,You Always Kill the One You Love	12.00
26 FR,GK,V:Uncanny Caretaker	12.00
27 FR,GK,V:Simon Stroud	12.00
28 GK,Doorway Down into Hell	12.00
29 Death has a Thousand Eyes	12.00
30 Bloody Sacrifice	12.00
31 FR,GK,last issue,Dec., 1975	12.00

FEUD
Epic, 1993

1 I:Skids,Stokes,Kite	3.00
2 V:Grunts,Skide,Stockers	2.25
3	2.25
4	2.25

FIGHT MAN
1993

1 I:Fight Man 2.25

FIRESTAR
March, 1986

1 MW,SL,O:Firestar,A:X-Men, New Mutants	5.00
2 MW,BWI,A:New Mutants	4.00

3 AAd&BSz(c),MW,SL, A:White Queen	4.00
4 MW,SL,V:White Queen	4.00

FISH POLICE
1992–93

1 V:S.Q.U.I.D,Hook	2.50
2 V:Hook	2.50
3 V:Hook	2.50
4 V:Hook	2.50
5 V:Goldie Prawn	2.50
6 Shark Bait #1	2.50

FLASH GORDON
1995

1 R:Flash Gordon	3.00
2 AW,V:Ming, final issue	3.00

FLINTSTONE KIDS
Star, Aug., 1987

1 thru 10	@3.00
11 April, 1989	3.00

FLINTSTONES
Oct., 1977–Feb., 1979

1 From TV Series	50.00
2	50.00
3	30.00
4 A:Jetsons	30.00
5 thru 7	@35.00

FLYING HERO BARBIE

1 Super Hero Barbie 2.25

FOOFUR
Star, Aug., 1987

1 thru 6 .... @3.00

FOOLKILLER
Oct., 1990

1 I:Kurt Gerhardt (Foolkiller III)	3.50
2 O:Foolkiller I & II	3.00
3 Old Costume	3.00
4 N:Foolkiller	2.50
5 Body Count	2.50
6 Fools Paradise	2.25

Foolkiller #4
© Marvel Entertainment Group

7 Who the Fools Are	2.25
8 Sane Must Inherit Earth,A:SpM.	2.25
9 D:Darren Waite	2.25
10 New Identity, July, 1991	2.25

FORCE WORKS
1994–96

1 TmT,Pop-up(c),I:Century,V:Kree, N:US Agent	4.00
2 TmT,V:Scatter	2.25
3 TmT,V:Scatter	2.25
4 Civil War	2.25
5 regular cover	2.25
5a Neon(c),bagged w/print	3.25
6 Hands of the Mandarin,pt.1	2.25
7 Hands of the Mandarin,pt.2	2.25
8 DAn,ALa,Christmas Party	2.25
9 I:Dream Guard	2.25
10 V:Dream Guard	2.25
11 F:War Machine	2.25
12 V:Recorder	3.00
13 DAn,ALa,A:Avengers	2.25
14	2.25
15 DAn,ALa,O:Century	2.25
16	2.25
17 DAn,ALa,The Crossing	2.25
18 DAn,ALa,The Crossing	2.25
19 DAn,ALa,The Crossing	2.25
20 DAn,cont.Avengers:Timeslide	2.25

411
Marvel April 2003

1 (of 3) peacemakers	3.50
2	3.50
3	3.50

FOR YOUR EYES ONLY

1 HC,James Bond rep.	3.00
2 HC,James Bond rep.	3.00

FRAGGLE ROCK
1985

1 thru 8 .... @5.00

[Volume 2], April, 1988

1 thru 5 rep.	@2.50
6 Sept., 1988	2.50

FRANCIS, BROTHER OF THE UNIVERSE
1980

1-shot SB 5.00

FRANKENSTEIN
See: MONSTER OF FRANKENSTEIN

FRED HEMBECK

1-shot Destroys the Marvel Universe, parody (1989)	2.25
1-shot Sells the Marvel Universe parody (1990)	2.25

FRIGHT
June, 1975

1 Son of Dracula 15.00

FRONTIER WESTERN
Feb., 1956

1 RH,	200.00
2 AW,GT,GC,JMn	150.00
3 MD	150.00
4 MD,Ringo Kid	100.00
5 RC,DW,JDa	150.00

All comics prices listed are for *Near Mint* condition.   CVA Page 239

Frontier–Generation X

6 AW,GC 125.00
7 JR,JMn 100.00
8 RC,DW 100.00
9 JMn 100.00
10 SC,Aug., 1957 . . . . 100.00

FUNNY FROLICS
Summer, 1945
1 Shardy Fox,KrazyKroid,(fa) . . . 250.00
2 . . . . 125.00
3 . . . . 100.00
4 . . . . 100.00
5 HK 125.00

FURTHER ADVENTURES OF CYCLOPS AND PHOENIX
1996
1 thru 4 . . . . @3.00
TPB PrM,JPL, O:Mr. Sinister, . . . 12.00

FURY
1994
1 MCW,O:Fury,A:S.A. Heroes 3.25

FURY
Marvel Max, Sept., 2001
1 (of 6) GEn,DaR,JP,F:Nick Fury . . 3.00
2 GEn,DaR,JP,F:Rudi Gagarin 3.00
3 GEn,DaR,JP, ... 3.00
4 GEn,DaR,JP. 3.00
5 GEn,DaR,JP. 3.00
6 GEn,DaR,JP. 3.00
TPB GEn,DaR, 144-pg. 15.95

FURY/AGENT 13
March, 1998
1 (of 2) TKa,is Nick Fury alive? . . . 3.00
2 TKa,MZ(c),Sharon Carter's searches
  for Nick 3.00

FURY OF S.H.I.E.L.D.
1995
1 Foil etched cover 3.00
2 A:Iron Man 2.50
3 J:Hydra 2.50
4 w/decoder kit 3.00

GALACTIC GUARDIANS
1994
1 KWe,C:Woden 2.25
2 KWe,I:Hazmat,Savant,Ganglia . . 2.25
3 KWe, ... 2.25
4 KWe,final issue. 2.25

GALACTUS THE DEVOURER
April, 1999
1 (of 6) JMu,LSi,A:Silver Surfer,
  Fant.Four & Avengers,48-page . 4.00
2 LSi,JB,BSz. 2.50
3 LSi,JB,BSz. 2.50
4 LSi,JB,BSz,A:Silver Surfer 2.50
5 LSi,JB,BSz. 2.50
6 LSi,JB,BSz,concl 3.50

GAMBIT
1997
1 HMe(c),LW,KJ,V:Assassin'sGuild,
  D:Henri LeBeau,Embossed(c) . 5.00
1a Gold Ed. 15.00

MARVEL

2 LW,KJ,C:Gideon,A:Rogue 3.00
3 LW,KJ,A:Candra,Rogue,
  D:Gambit's Father 3.00
4 LW,KJ,A:Candra,Rogue,D:Tithe
  Collector. 3.00
TPB Rep.#1-#4. . . . . 8.95

GAMBIT
1997
1 (of 4) HMe,KJ,In Miami 3.50
2 thru 4 HMe,KJ, ... @3.00

Gambit #6
© Marvel Entertainment Group

GAMBIT
Dec., 1998
1 FaN,SSr,O:Gambit,48-page 4.00
1a signed 24.95
2 FaN,SSr,V:Storm 3.00
2a variant cover. 3.00
3 FaN,SSr,V:Mengo Brothers. 2.50
4 FaN,SSr,A:Blade 2.50
5 FaN,SSr,R:Rogue. 2.50
6 FaN,SSr,I:The Pig. 2.50
7 FaN,SSr, ... 2.50
8 FaN,A:Sinister,Sabretooth. 2.50
9 FaN,The Shattering,x-over 2.50
10 FaN,V:Candra & Fenris 2.50
11 FaN,A:Daredevil 2.50
12 FaN. 2.50
13 FaN,Black Womb. 2.50
14 FaN,ALa,A:Mr. Sinister 2.50
15 FaN,F:Rogue. 2.50
16 FaN,X-Men: Revolution 2.50
16a variant (c) 2.50
17 FaN,AssassinationGame,pt.1 . . 2.25
18 FaN,AssassinationGame,pt.2 . . 2.25
19 FaN,AssassinationGame,pt.3 . . 2.25
20 FaN,Fontanelle 2.25
21 FaN,Remy LeBeau 2.25
22 FaN,Neo,Remy LeBeau,Rax . . . 2.25
23 FaN,X-Cutioner 2.25
24 FaN,V:New Son 2.25
25 SLo, 48-page. 3.50
Ann.1999 48-page 3.50
Ann.2000 FaN,F:X-Men 3.50
Giant Sized Gambit, 96-page, rep. . 4.00

GAMBIT & BISHOP: SONS OF THE ATOM
Jan., 2001
1 SLo,Bishop captured 2.25

Comics Values Annual

2 SLo,on the run 2.25
3 SLo,common enemy. 2.25
4 SLo, ... 2.25
5 SLo,Ultimate sacrifice. 2.25
6 SLo,finale 2.25
Spec. Alpha, SLo,CNr. 2.25
Spec. Genesis,CCl 3.50

GAMBIT AND THE X-TERNALS
1995
1 X-Force after Xavier 3.50
2 V:Deathbird,Starjammers 2.50
3 V:Imperial Guard 2.50
4 Charles Kidnapped. 2.50

GARGOYLE
June, 1985
1 BWr(c),from 'Defenders' 4.00
2 thru 4 . . . . @3.00

GARGOYLES
1995–96
1 TV Series 4.00
2 TV Series 3.00
3 F:Broadway 3.00
4 V:Statues 3.00
5 Humanoid Gargoyles 3.00
6 Medusa Project concl. 3.00
7 Demona & Triad 3.00
8 I:The Pack 3.00
9 V:Demonia,Triad. 3.00
10 Demonia gains magical powers . 3.00
11 Elisa turns to Xanatos 3.00
12 Sorceress traps Gargoyles. 3.00
13 Behind Enemy Lines 3.00
14 . . . . 3.00
15 . . . . 3.00
16 Hammer of Fear 3.00

GENE DOGS
Marvel UK, 1993–94
1 I:Gene DOGS,w/cards 3.00
2 V:Genetix 2.25
3 V:Hurricane 2.25
4 last issue 2.25

GENERATION NEXT
1995
1 Generation X AX. 3.50
2 Genetic Slave Pens 2.50
3 V:Sugar Man 2.50
4 V:Sugar Man 2.50

GENERATION X
Oct., 1994
1 CBa,Banshee & White Queen. . . 7.00
2 CBa,SLo. 4.00
2a Deluxe edition. 4.00
3 CBa 3.00
3a Deluxe edition. 4.00
4 CBa,V:Nanny,Orphanmaker 3.00
4a Deluxe edition. 4.00
5 SLo,CBa,MBu,two new young
  mutants at the Academy 3.50
6 A:Wolverine 3.50
7 SLo,F:Banshee,A:White Queen . 3.50
8 F:Banshee 3.50
9 SLo,TG,Chamber in a kilt 3.50
10 SLo,TG,MBu,Banshee vs.
  OmegaRed. 3.50
11 SLo,TG,V:Omega Red 3.00
12 SLo,TG,V:Emplate. 3.00
13 . . . . 3.00
14 . . . . 3.00

CVA Page 240   All comics prices listed are for *Near Mint* condition.

MARVEL

Generation X–Ghost Rider

15 SLo,MBu,Synch goes psycho . . 3.00
16 . . . . 3.00
17 SLo,CBa,Onslaught saga,
   X-Cutioner vs. Skin. 3.00
18 SLo,CBa,Onslaught saga. 3.00
19 SLo,CBa,. 3.00
20 SLo,CBa,. 3.00
21 SLo,CBa,MBu,F:Skin & Chamber,
   A:Beverly Switzer, Howard
   the Duck 3.00
22 SLo,CBa,. 3.00
23 SLo,CBa,V:Black Tom Cassidy. . 3.00
24 SLo,MBy,F:Monet,Emplate. 3.00
25 SLo,CBa,double size 4.00
26 SLo,CBa,Shot down over the
   Atlantic. 3.00
27 SLo,CBa,on nuclear sub. 3.00
28 SLo,CBa,No Exit prelude 3.00
29 JeR,CBa, V:Sentinels 3.00
30 JeR,CBa, V:Zero Tolerance . . . 3.00
31 JeR,CBa, ... 3.00
32 TDF,MBu,F:Banshee, Moira
   McTaggert 3.00
33 LHa,MBu,new direction 3.00
34 LHa,Truth behind M 3.00
35 LHa,Jubilee,V:Emplate. 3.00
36 LHa,Final Fate of M 3.00
37 LHa,Final Fate of M 3.00

Generation X #45
© Marvel Entertainment Group

38 LHa,TyD,kids save universe. . . . 2.50
39 LHa,TyD, multi-dimensional trip . 2.50
40 LHa,TyD,Penance mystery
   revealed. 2.50
41 LHa,TyD,Jubilee,V:Bastion,
   Omega Red, Sabretooth. 2.50
42 LHa,TyD,results of EMP wave . . 2.50
43 LHa,TyD,V:Bianca LaNiege 2.50
44 LHa,TyD,V:White Queen 2.50
45 LHa,TyD,F:Banshee. 2.50
46 LHa,TyD,F: Forge 2.50
47 LHa,TyD,Danger Room 2.50
48 TyD,Jubilee vs. M 2.50
49 TyD,V:Maggott. 2.50
50 TyD,War of the Mutants,pt.1 . . . 3.50
50a signed 20.00
51 V:Hunter Brawn 2.50
52 TyD,blackmail 2.50
53 TyD,V:Rising Sons,A:Paladin . . 2.50
54 TyD,A:Paladin 2.50
55 TyD,in bodies of Hellions 2.50
56 TyD,A:X-Men of past 2.50
57 TyD, double sized 3.50
58 TyD, new Penance 2.50

59 TyD, ... 2.50
60 TyD,F:Siryn 2.50
61 TyD,ATi,R:Mondo. 2.50
62 TyD,F:Monet St. Croix 2.50
63 WEI,X-Men Revolution. 2.50
63a variant (c) 2.50
64 WEI,Correction,pt.2 . . . . 2.25
65 WEI,Correction,pt.3 . . . . 2.25
66 WEI,Correction,pt.4 . . . . 2.25
67 WEI,Come On Die Young,pt.1 . . 2.25
68 WEI,Come On Die Young,pt.2 . . 2.25
69 WEI,Come On Die Young,pt.3 . . 2.25
70 WEI,Come On Die Young,pt.4 . . 2.25
71 WEI,Four Days,pt.1 . . . . 2.25
72 AAd(c),StP,Four Days,pt.2 . . . . . 2.25
73 AAd(c),StP,Four Days,pt.3 . . . . . 2.25
74 AAd(c),StP,Four Days,pt.4 . . . . . 2.25
75 AAd(c),StP,final issue. 3.50
Minus 1 Spec., JeR,CBa, flashback,
   F:Banshee 2.50
Ann. '95 SLo,J:Mondo,
   V:Hellfire Club 4.50
Ann. '96 GN MGo,JJ,DPs,V:Fenris . 3.50
Ann. '97, Haunted by Ghosts
   of Hellions 3.50
Ann.1998 Generation X/Dracula . . 4.00
Ann.1999 48-pg. 4.00
Holliday Spec. 48-page 1-shot 4.00

GENERATION X/GEN 13
Dec., 1997
1-shot JeR,SvL,V:Mr. Pretorious . . . 4.00
1a variant cover CBa (1:4) 4.00

GENERATION X: UNDERGROUND
March, 1998
1-shot by Jim Mahfood, b&w. 2.50

GENERIC COMIC
1 . . . . 2.25

GENETIX
Marvel UK, 1993–94
1 B:ALa(s),w/cards 3.00
2 I:Tektos 2.25
3 V:Tektos 2.25
4 PGa,V:MyS-Tech 2.25
5 PGa,V:MyS-Tech 2.25
6 V:Tektos 2.25

GEORGIE COMICS
Spring, 1945
1 Georgie stories begin 250.00
2 Pet Shop (c) 250.00
3 Georgie/Judy(c) 125.00
4 Wedding Dress(c) 125.00
5 Monty/Policeman(c) 125.00
6 Classroom(c) 125.00
7 Fishing(c) 135.00
8 Soda Jerk(c) 135.00
9 Georgie/Judy(c),HK,Hey Look 135.00
10 Georgie/Girls(c),HK,Hey Look 135.00
11 Table Tennis(c),A:Margie,Millie . 75.00
12 Camping(c). 75.00
13 Life Guard(c),HK,Hey Look . . 100.00
14 Classroom(c),HK,Hey Look . . 100.00
15 Winter Sports(c). 75.00
16 . . . . 75.00
17 HK,Hey Look 75.00
18 . . . . 75.00
19 Baseball(c) 75.00
Becomes:

GEORGIE & JUDY COMICS
20 . . . . 75.00
21 . . . . 50.00

Becomes:
GEORGIE COMICS
22 Georgie comics 50.00
23 . . . . 50.00
24 . . . . 50.00
25 Driben painted (c) 100.00
26 . . . . 50.00
27 . . . . 50.00
28 . . . . 50.00
29 . . . . 75.00
30 thru 38 . . . . @50.00
39 Oct., 1952 . . . . 50.00

GETALONG GANG
May, 1985—March, 1986
1 thru 6 . . . . @3.50

Ghost Rider #4
© Marvel Entertainment Group

GHOST RIDER
1967
1 O&I:Ghost Rider (western) . . . 125.00
2 V:Tarantula. 75.00
3 Cougar's Circus of Fear 50.00
4 Sting Ray 50.00
5 Tarantula Strikes Back 50.00
6 Behold a Falling Star 50.00
7 Mystery of Massacre Mountain . 50.00

GHOST RIDER
[1st Regular Series], Sept., 1973
1 GK,JSt,C:Son of Satan 100.00
2 GK,I:Son of Satan,A:Witch
   Woman 50.00
3 JR,D:Big Daddy Dawson,
   new Cycle 35.00
4 GK,A:Dude Jensen. 35.00
5 GK,JR,I:Roulette. 35.00
6 JR,O:Ghost Rider 25.00
7 JR,A:Stunt Master 25.00
8 GK,A:Satan,I:Inferno. 25.00
9 GK,TP,O:Johnny Blaze 25.00
10 JSt,A:Hulk 25.00
11 GK,KJ,SB,A:Hulk 25.00
12 GK,KJ,FR,A:Phantom Eagle . . 15.00
13 GK,JS,GT,A:Trapster 15.00
14 GT,A:The Orb 15.00
15 SB,O:The Orb 15.00
16 DC,GT,Blood in the Water 15.00
17 RB,FR,I:Challenger 15.00
18 RB,FR,A:Challenger,
   Spider-Man 15.00

All comics prices listed are for *Near Mint* condition.

Ghost Rider–Ghost Rider — MARVEL — Comics Values Annual

19 GK,FR,A:Challenger	15.00
20 GK,KJ,JBy,A:Daredevil	22.00
21 A:Gladiator,D:Eel	10.00
22 AM,DH,KP,JR,A:Enforcer	10.00
23 JK,DH,DN,I:Water Wiz.	10.00
24 GK,DC,DH,A:Enforcer	10.00
25 GK,DH,A:Stunt Master	10.00
26 GK,DP,A:Dr. Druid	10.00
27 SB,DP,A:Hawkeye	10.00
28 DP,A:The Orb	10.00
29 RB,DP,A:Dormammu	10.00
30 DP,A:Dr.Strange	10.00
31 FR,DP,BL,A:Bounty Hunt.	10.00
32 KP,BL,DP,A:Bounty Hunt.	10.00
33 DP,I:Dark Riders	10.00
34 DP,C:Cyclops	10.00
35 JSn,AM,A:Death	15.00
36 DP,Drug Mention	10.00
37 DP,I:Dick Varden	10.00
38 DP,A:Death Cult	10.00
39 DP,A:Death Cult	10.00
40 DP,I:Nuclear Man	10.00
41 DP,A:Jackal Gang	10.00
42 DP,A:Jackal Gang	10.00
43 CI:Crimson Mage	10.00
44 JAb,CI,A:Crimson Mage	10.00
45 DP,I:Flagg Fargo	10.00
46 DP,A:Flagg Fargo	10.00
47 AM,DP	10.00
48 BMc,DP	10.00
49 DP,I:The Manitou	10.00
50 DP,A:Night Rider	15.00
51 AM,PD,A:Cycle Gang	6.00
52 AM,DP	6.00
53 DP,I:Lord Asmodeus	6.00
54 DP,A:The Orb	6.00
55 DP,A:Werewolf By Night	6.00
56 DP,A:Moondark,I:Night Rider	6.00
57 AM,DP,I:The Apparition	6.00
58 DP,FM,A:Water Wizard	6.00
59 V:Water Wizard,Moon Dark	6.00
60 DP,HT,A:Black Juju	6.00
61 A:Arabian Knight	6.00
62 KJ,A:Arabian Knight	6.00
63 LMc,A:The Orb	6.00
64 BA,V:Azmodeus	6.00
65 A:Fowler	6.00
66 BL,A:Clothilde	6.00
67 DP,A:Sally Stantop	6.00
68 O:Ghost Rider	6.00
69	6.00
70 I:Jeremy	6.00
71 DP,I:Adam Henderson	6.00
72 A:Circus of Crime	6.00
73 A:Circus of Crime	6.00
74 A:Centurions	6.00
75 I:Steel Wind	6.00
76 DP,A:Mephisto,I:Saturnine	6.00
77 O:Ghost Rider's Dream	6.00
78 A:Nightmare	6.00
79 A:Man Cycles	6.00
80 A:Centurions	6.00
81 D:Ghost Rider	15.00

[2nd Regular Series], 1990–98
1 JS,MT,I:2nd Ghost Rider, Deathwatch	6.00
1a 2nd printing	3.00
2 JS,MT,I:Blackout	3.00
3 JS,MT,A:Kingpin,V:Blackout, Deathwatch	3.00
4 JS,MT,V:Mr.Hyde	3.00
5 JLe(c),JS,MT,A:Punisher	3.00
5a rep.Gold	2.50
6 JS,MT,A:Punisher	3.00
7 MT,V:Scarecrow	3.00
8 JS,MT,V:H.E.A.R.T.	3.00
9 JS,MT,A:Morlocks,X-Factor	2.50
10 JS,MT,V:Zodiac	2.50
11 LSn,MT,V:Nightmare, A:Dr.Strange	2.50
12 JS,MT,A:Dr.Strange	2.50
13 MT,V:Snow Blind,R:J.Blaze	2.50
14 MT,Blaze Vs.Ghost Rider	2.50
15 MT,A:Blaze,V:Blackout Glow in Dark(c)	3.00
15a 2nd printing (gold)	2.50
16 MT,A:Blaze,Spider-Man, V:Hobgoblin	2.50
17 MT,A:Spider-Man,Blaze, V:Hobgoblin	2.50
18 MT,V:Reverend Styge	2.50
19 MT,A:Mephisto	2.50
20 MT(i),O:Zodiac	2.50
21 MT(i),V:Snowblind, A:Deathwatch	2.50
22 MT,A:Deathwatch,Ninjas	2.50
23 MT,I:Hag & Troll,A:Deathwatch	2.50
24 MT,V:Deathwatch,D:Snowblind, C:Johnny Blaze	2.50
25 V:Blackout (w/Center spread pop-up)	3.00
26 A:X-Men,V:The Brood	3.00
27 A:X-Men,V:The Brood	3.00
28 NKu,JKu,Rise of the Midnight Sons#1,V:Lilith,w/poster	3.00
29 NKu,JKu,A:Wolverine,Beast	2.50
30 NKu,JKu,V:Nightmare	2.50
31 NKu,JKu,Rise o/t Midnight Sons#6, A:Dr.Strange,Morbius, Nightstalkers,Redeemers, V:Lilith,w/poster	3.00
32 BBi,A:Dr.Strange	2.50
33 BBi,AW,V:Madcap (inc.Superman tribute on letters page)	2.50
34 BBi,V:Deathwatchs' ninja	2.50
35 BBi,AW,A:Heart Attack	2.50
36 BBi,V:Mr.Hyde,A:Daredevil	2.50
37 BBi,A:Archangel,V:HeartAttack	2.50
38 MM,V:Scarecrow	2.50
39 V:Vengeance	2.50
40 Midnight Massacre#2, D:Demogblin	3.00
41 Road to Vengeance#1	2.25
42 Road to Vengeance#2	2.25
43 Road to Vengeance#3	2.25
44 Siege of Darkness,pt.#2	2.25
45 Siege of Darkness,pt.#10	2.25
46 HMe(s),New Beginning	2.25
47 HMe(s),RG,	2.25
48 HMe(s),RG,A:Spider-Man	2.25
49 HMe(s),RG,A:Hulk,w/card	2.25
50 Red Foil(c),AKu,SMc,A:Blaze, R:2nd Ghost Rider	3.25
50a Newsstand Ed.	2.75
51 SvL	2.25
52 SvL	2.25
53 SvL,V:Blackout	2.25
54 SvL,V:Blackout	2.25
55 V:Mr. Hyde	2.25
56 The Next Wave	2.25
57 A:Wolverine	2.25
58 HMe,SvL,Betrayal,pt.1	2.25
59 Betrayal,pt.2	2.25
60 Betrayal,pt.3	2.25
61 Betrayal,pt.4	3.00
62 EventInChains,pt.1,A:Fury	2.25
63 EventInChains,pt.2	2.25
64 EventInChains,pt.3	2.25
65 EventInChains,pt.4,R:Blackout	2.25
66 V:Blackout	2.25
67 A:Gambit,V:Brood	2.25
68 A:Gambit,Wolverine,V:Brood	2.25
69 Domestic Violence	2.25
70 New Home in Bronx	2.25
71	2.25
72	2.25
73 John Blaze is back	2.25
74 A:Blaze, Vengeance	2.25
75	2.25
76 V:Vengeance	2.25
77 A:Dr. Strange	2.25
78 new costume, A:Dr. Strange	2.25
79 IV,New costume, A:Valkyrie	2.25
80 IV,V:Furies,Valkyrie A:Black Rose	2.25
81 IV,A:Howard the Duck, Devil Dinosaur	2.25
82 IV,A:Devil Dinosaur	2.25
83 IV,A:Scarecrow,Lilith	2.25
84 IV,A:Scarecrow, Lilith	2.25
85 IV,V:Lilith, Scarecrow	2.25
86 IV,rampage through the Bronx	2.25
87 IV,KIK,AM,	2.25
88 IV, V:Pao Fu,Blackheart	2.25
89 IV,JS,	2.25
90 IV,JS,Last Temptation,pt.1	2.25
91 IV,JS,A:Blackheart	2.25
92 IV,JS,Journey into the past	2.25
93 IV,JS,MT,Last Temptation concl., double sized	3.00
94 IV,JS,MT,Becomes Lord of the Underworld, last issue	2.00
Ann.#1 I:Night Terror,w/card	3.25
Ann.#2 F:Scarecrow	2.95
GN Ghost Rider/Captain America: Fear, AW, V:Scarecrow (1992)	6.25
GN Ghost Rider/Wolverine/Punisher: Dark Design (1994)	5.95
GN Ghost Rider/Wolverine/Punisher: Hearts of Darkness, JR2/KJ,V: Blackheart, gatefold(c) (1991)	5.50
TPB Midnight Sons,rep.GhR#28,31, Morbius#1,Darkhold#1,Spirirts of Vengeance#1,Nightstalkers#1	19.95
TPB Resurrected rep.#1-#7	12.95
TPB Resurrected (2000)	12.95
Poster Book	4.95
Spec. Crossroads	3.95
Minus 1 Spec., IV,JS, flashback	2.00

GHOST RIDER/BALLISTIC
Marvel/Top Cow 1996
1-shot WEl,BTn,iDevil's Reign,î pt.3, x-over 3.00

GHOST RIDER/BLAZE SPIRITS OF VENGEANCE
1992–94
1 AKu,polybagged w/poster,V:Lilith, Rise of the Midnight Sons#2 .. 3.50
2 AKu,V:Steel Wind 3.00
3 AKu,CW,V:The Lilin 3.00
4 AKu,V:Hag & Troll,C:Venom ... 3.00

Ghost Rider #23
© Marvel Entertainment Group

CVA Page 242 — All comics prices listed are for *Near Mint* condition.

Comics Values Annual — MARVEL — Ghost–G.I. Joe

Ghost Rider/Blaze Spirits of Vengeance #2 © Marvel Entertainment Group

5 AKu,BR,Spirits of Venom#2,
   A:Venom,Spidey,Hobgoblin.... 5.00
6 AKu,Spirits of Venom#4,A:Venom,
   Spider-Man,Hobgoblin...... 3.50
7 AKu,V:Steel Vengeance 2.25
8 V:Mephisto................. 2.25
9 I:Brimstone................. 2.25
10 AKu,V:Vengeance 2.25
11 V:Human Spider Creature 2.25
12 AKu,BR, Vengeance,glow in the
   dark(c).................. 3.25
13 AKu,Midnight Massacre#5 .... 2.50
14 Missing Link#2............ 2.25
15 Missing Link#3............ 2.25
16 V:Zarathos,Lilith........... 2.25
17 HMe(s),Siege/Darkness,pt.8 .. 2.25
18 HMe(s),Siege/Darkness,pt.13 . 2.25
19 HMe(s),HMz,V;Vampire 2.25
20 HMe(s),A:Steel Wind 2.25
21 HMe(s),HMz,V:Werewolves ... 2.25
22 HMe(s),HMz,V:Cardiac 2.25
23 HMe(s),HMz,A:Steel Wind 2.25

GHOST RIDER/CYBLADE
Marvel/Top Cow 1996
1-shot IV,ACh,iDevil's Reign,î
   pt.2, x-over................. 3.25

GHOST RIDER:
THE HAMMER LANE
June, 2001
1 (of 6) TKn.................. 3.00
2 TKn,DaM................... 3.00
3 TKn,DaM,Gunmetal Gray 3.00
4 TKn,DaM,Gunmetal Gray 3.00
5 TKn,DaM,Gunmetal Gray 3.00
6 TKn,DaM,Gunmetal Gray 3.00
TPB series rep. 144-pg. 15.95

GHOST RIDER:
HIGHWAY TO HELL
June, 2001
Spec. 64-pages 3.50

GHOST RIDER 2099
1994–96
1 Holografx(c),LKa,CBa,MBu,I:Ghost
   Rider 2099,w/card 3.00
1a Newsstand Ed............. 2.25
2 LKa,CBa,MBu,............. 2.25

3 LKa,CBa,MBu,I:Warewolf 2.25
4 LKa,CBa,MBu,V:Warewolf 2.25
5 LKa,CBa,MBu............... 2.25
6 LKa,CBa,MBu............... 2.25
7 LKa,CBa,MBu............... 2.25
8 LKa,CBa,MBu............... 2.25
9 .... 2.25
10 .... 2.25
11 V:Bloodsport Society 2.25
12 I:Coda.................... 2.25
Becomes:

GHOST RIDER 2099 A.D.
1995
13 F:Doom................... 2.25
14 Deputized by Doom......... 2.25
15 One Nation Under Doom 2.25
16 V:Max Synergy 2.25
17 .... 2.25
18 V:L-Cipher 2.25
19 V:L-Cipher 2.25
20 .... 2.25
21 V:Vengeance 2099 .... 2.25
22 V:Vengeance 2099 .... 2.25
23 .... 2.25
24 .... 2.25
25 Double size final issue....... 3.50

GIANT-SIZE CHILLERS
1975
1 AA,....................... 30.00
2 .... 20.00
3 BWr,Night of the Gargoyle ... 25.00

GIANT-SIZE CHILLERS
1974
1 I&O:Lilith,F:Curse of Dracula... 30.00
Becomes:

GIANT-SIZE DRACULA
2 Vengeance of the Elder Gods .. 20.00
3 rep. Uncanny Tales #6 .... 15.00
4 SD,Demon of Devil's Lake 15.00
5 JBy, 1st Marvel art 25.00

GIANT-SIZE
MINI-MARVELS:
STARRING SPIDEY
Dec., 2001
1 F:Hawkeye, 48-pg............ 3.50

G.I. JOE:
A REAL AMERICAN HERO
June, 1982
1 HT,BMc,Baxter paper 25.00
2 DP,JAb,North Pole 20.00
3 HT,JAb,Trojan Robot......... 15.00
4 HT,JAb,Wingfield 15.00
5 DP,Central Park 15.00
6 HT,V:Cobra................ 15.00
7 HT,Walls of Death........... 15.00
8 HT,Sea Strike 15.00
9 The Diplomat 15.00
10 Springfield 15.00
11 Alaska Pipeline 12.00
12 V:Snake Eyes 12.00
13 Rio Lindo................. 12.00
14 V:Destro 12.00
15 A:Red Eye 12.00
16 V:Cobra 12.00
17 Loose Ends 12.00
18 V:Destro 12.00
19 D:General Kwinn........... 12.00
20 JBy(c),GI,Clutch............ 12.00
21 SL(i),Silent Interlude 35.00
22 V:Destro 7.00
23 I:Duke.................... 7.00

*G.I. Joe #52
© Marvel Entertainment Group*

24 RH,I:Storm Shadow......... 7.00
25 FS,I:Zartan 7.00
26 SL(i),O:Snake Eyes 9.00
27 FS,O:Snake Eyes 9.00
28 Swampfire................ 7.00
29 FS,V:Destro 7.00
30 JBy(c),FS,V:Dreddnoks 7.00
31 V:Destro 3.00
32 FS,V:Dreddnoks 3.00
33 FS,Celebration............. 3.00
34 Shakedown 3.00
35 JBy(c),MBr,V:Dreddnoks 3.00
36 MBr,Shipwar 3.00
2a to 36a 2nd printings ...... @2.00
37 FS,Twin Brothers,I:Flint 3.00
38 V:Destro 3.00
39 Jungle.................... 3.00
40 Hydrofoil 3.00
41 .... 3.00
42 A:Stormsshadow 3.00
43 Death Issue,New Joe........ 3.00
44 V:Cobra................... 3.00
45 V:Cobra................... 3.00
46 V:Cobra................... 3.00
47 V:Cobra,D:Stormshadow 3.00
48 V:Cobra................... 3.00
49 V:Cobra,I:Serpentor......... 3.00
50 I:G.I.Joe Missions,R:S'shadow.. 3.00
51 V:Cobra Emperor........... 3.00
52 V:Stormshadow 3.00
53 Hawk V:Cobra 3.00
54 V:Destro 3.00
55 The Pit 3.00
56 V:Serpentor 3.00
57 V:Destro 3.00
58 V:Cobra................... 3.00
59 Armor 3.00
60 TM,I:Zanzibar 5.00
61 MR,D:Cobra Commander 3.00
62 Trial...................... 3.00
63 A:GI Joe Snow Job 3.00
64 V:Baroness 3.00
65 V:Cobra................... 3.00
66 Stalker Rescued 3.00
67 .... 3.00
68 I:Battleforce 2000 .... 3.00
69 TSa...................... 3.00
70 V:Destro 3.00
71 .... 3.00
72 .... 3.00
73 .... 3.00
74 .... 3.00
75 MR 3.00

All comics prices listed are for *Near Mint* condition.

G.I. Joe–Godzilla — MARVEL — Comics Values Annual

#	Price
76 D:Serpentor	3.00
77 MR,V:Cobra	3.00
78 V:Cobra	3.00
79 MR,V:Dreadnoks	3.00
80 V:Cobra	3.00
81 MR,V:Dreadnoks	3.00
82 MR,V:Cobra	3.00
83 I:RoadPig	3.00
84 MR,O:Zartan	3.00
85 Storm Shadow,Vs.Zartan	3.00
86 MR,25th Anniv.	3.00
87 TSa,V:Cobra	3.00
88 TSa,V:Python Patrol	3.00
89 MBr,V:Road Pig	3.00
90 MBr,R:Red Ninjas	3.00
91 TSa,V:Red Ninjas,D:Blind Masters	4.00
92 MBr,V:Cobra Condor	4.00
93 MBr,V:Baroness	15.00
94 MBr,A:Snake Eyes	6.00
95 MBr,A:Snake Eyes	6.00
96 MBr,A:Snake Eyes	6.00
97	4.00
98 MBr,R:Cobra Commander	4.00
99 HT	4.00
100 MBr	4.00
101 MBr	4.00
102 MBr	4.00
103 MBr,A:Snake Eyes	4.00
104 MBr,A:Snake Eyes	4.00
105 MBr,A:Snake Eyes	4.00
106 MBr,StormShadowStalker	4.00
107	4.00
108 I:G.I.Joe Dossiers	4.00
109 Death Issue	4.00
110 Mid-East Crisis	5.00
111 A:Team Ninjas	4.00
112 A:Team Ninjas	4.00
113 V:Cobra	4.00
114 V:Cobra	4.00
115 Story Concl.Dusty Dossier	4.00
116 Destro:Search&Destroy #1	4.00
117 Destro:Search&Destroy #2	4.00
118 Destro:Search&Destroy #3	4.00
119 HT,Android Dopplegangers	4.00
120 V:Red Ninjas,Slice & Dice	6.00
121 V:Slice & Dice	4.00
122 V:Slice & Dice	4.00
123 I:Eco-Warriors,A:Big Man	4.00
124 V:Headman	4.00
125 V:Headhunters	4.00
126 R:Firefly	4.00
127 R:Original G.I.Joe	4.00
128 V:Firefly	4.00
129 V:Cobra Commander	4.00
130 V:Cobra Commander	4.00
131 V:Cobra Commander	4.00
132 V:Cobra	4.00
133 V:Cobra	4.00
134 V:Red Ninjas, Firefly, Hostilities	4.00
135 V:Cobra Ninja w/card	5.00
136 w/Trading Card	5.00
137 V:Night Creepers,w/card	5.00
138 V:Night Creepers,w/card	5.00
139 R:Transformers,V:Cobra	5.00
140 A:Transformers	5.00
141 A:Transformers	5.00
142 A:Transformers	5.00
143 F:Scarlet	5.00
144 O:Snake Eyes	5.00
145 V:Cobra	5.00
146 F:Star Brigade	5.00
147 F:Star Brigade	5.00
148 F:Star Brigade	5.00
149	5.00
150 Cobra Commander vs. Snake Eyes	15.00
151 V:Cobra	10.00
152 First G.I. Joe	10.00
153 V:Cobra	10.00
154	20.00
155 final issue	25.00
SC GI Joe and the Transformers	4.95
Spec. TM rep.#61	4.00
Ann.#1	4.00
Ann.#2	4.00
Ann.#3	4.00
Ann.#4	4.00
Ann.#5	4.00
Yearbook #1 (1985)	4.00
Yearbook #2 (1986)	4.00
Yearbook #3 (1987)	4.00
Yearbook #4 (1988)	4.00
TPB Vol.1, 240-pg. (2002)	24.95
TPB Vol.2, 240-pg. (2002)	24.95
TPB Vol.3, 240-pg. (2002)	24.95
TPB Vol.4 (2002)	26.00
TPB Vol 5 (2003)	25.00

G.I. JOE EUROPEAN MISSIONS
June, 1988

#	Price
1 British rep.	7.00
2	5.00
3	7.00
4 thru 15	@5.00

G.I. JOE SPECIAL MISSIONS
Oct., 1986

#	Price
1 HT,New G.I. Joe	4.00
2 thru 9 HT	@4.00
10 thru 20 HT	@4.00
21 & 22	@5.00
23 HT	5.00
24	5.00
25 HT	5.00
26 HT	5.00
27	5.00
28 HT,final	5.00

G.I. JOE AND THE TRANSFORMERS
1987

#	Price
1 HT,mini-series	3.00
2 HT,Cobra	3.00
3 HT,Cobra,Deceptions	3.00
4 HT,Cobra,Deceptions	3.00

G.I. JOE UNIVERSE

#	Price
1 Biographies rep.#1	3.50
2	2.50
3 MZ(c)	2.50
4	2.50

G.I. TALES
See: SERGEANT BARNEY BARKER

GIRL COMICS
Atlas, Nov., 1949

#	Price
1 Ph(c),True love stories,I Could Escape From Love	250.00
2 Ph(c),JKu,Blind Date	135.00
3 BEv,Ph(c),Liz Taylor	225.00
4 PH(c),Borrowed Love	100.00
5 Love stories	100.00
6 same	100.00
7 same	100.00
8 same	100.00
9 same	100.00
10 The Deadly Double-Cross	100.00
11 Love stories	100.00
12 BK,The Dark Hallway	125.00
Becomes:	

GIRL CONFESSIONS
1952

#	Price
13	125.00
14	75.00
15	75.00
16 BEv	100.00
17 BEv	100.00
18 BEv	100.00
19	75.00
20	75.00
21 thru 34	@60.00
35 Aug., 1954	60.00

GIRLS' LIFE
Atlas, Jan., 1954

#	Price
1	125.00
2	75.00
3	50.00
4	50.00
5	50.00
6 November, 1954	50.00

GLADIATOR/SUPREME
1997

#	Price
1 KG,ASm,x-over	5.00

GODZILLA
Aug., 1977

#	Price
1 HT,JM,Based on Movie Series	30.00
2 HT,FrG,GT,Seattle Under Seige	12.00
3 HT,TD,A;Champions	20.00
4 TS,TD,V;Batragon	10.00
5 TS,KJ,Isle of the Living Demons	10.00
6 HT,A Monster Enslaved	10.00
7 V:Red Ronin	10.00
8 V:Red Ronin	10.00
9 Las Gamble in Las Vegas	10.00
10 V:Yetrigar	10.00
11 V;Red Ronin,Yetrigar	8.00
12 Star Sinister	8.00
13 V:Mega-Monster	8.00
14 V:Super-Beasts	8.00
15 Stampede	8.00
16 Jaws of Fear	8.00
17 Godzilla Shrunk	8.00
18 Battle Beneath Eighth Avenue	8.00
19 Panic on the Pier	8.00
20 A;Fantastic Four	10.00
21 V;Devil Dinosaur	8.00

Godzilla #22
© Marvel Entertainment Group

CVA Page 244 — All comics prices listed are for *Near Mint* condition.

MARVEL

Godzilla–Guardians

22 V:Devil Dinosaur 8.00
23 A;Avengers 10.00
24 July, 1979 . . . . 8.00

GOLDEN AGE OF MARVEL
TPB RyL 10.00
Vol.1, 176-page 20.00
Vol.2, 176-page 20.00

GREATEST SPIDER-MAN & DAREDEVIL TEAM-UPS
TPB 175pg 10.00

GREEN GOBLIN
1995–96
1 I:New Green Goblin 4.00
2 TDF,SMc,V:Rhino 2.25
3 TDF,SMc,CyberWar tie-in 2.25
4 TDF,SMc,V:Hobgoblin 2.25
5 TDF,V:Hobgoblin 2.25
6 . . . . 2.25
7 . . . . 2.25
8 TDF,SMc,I:Angelface 2.25
9 . . . . 2.25
10 . . . . 2.25
11 . . . . 2.25
12 Onslaught saga 2.25
13 Onslaught saga 2.25

GROO CHRONICLES
Epic, 1989
1 SA 5.00
2 thru 6 SA . . . . @4.00

[SERGIO ARAGONE'S] GROO, THE WANDERER
(see Pacific, Eclipse)
Epic, 1985–95
1 SA,I:Minstrel 15.00
2 SA,A:Minstrel 6.00
3 SA,Medallions 5.00
4 SA,Airship 5.00
5 SA,Slavers 5.00
6 SA,The Eye of the Kabala 5.00
7 SA,A:Sage 5.00
8 SA,A:Taranto 5.00
9 SA,A:Sage 5.00

Groo, The Wanderer #41
© Marvel Entertainment Group

10 SA,I:Arcadio 5.00
11 SA,A:Arcadio 4.00
12 SA,Groo Meets the Thespians . . 4.00
13 SA,A:Sage 4.00
14 SA 4.00
15 SA,Monks 4.00
16 SA,A:Taranto 4.00
17 SA,Pirannas 4.00
18 SA,I:Groo Ella 4.00
19 SA,A:Groo Ella 3.00
20 SA,A:Groo Ella 3.00
21 SA,I:Arba,Dakarba 3.00
22 SA,Ambassador 3.00
23 SA,I:Pal,Drumm 3.00
24 SA,Arcadio's 3.00
25 SA,Taranto 3.00
26 SA,A:Arba,Taranto 3.00
27 SA,A:Minstrel,Sage 3.00
28 SA 3.00
29 SA,I:Ruferto 4.00
30 SA,A:Ruferto 3.00
31 SA,A:Pal,Drumm 3.00
32 SA,C:Sage 3.00
33 SA,Pirates 3.00
34 SA,Wizard's amulet 3.00
35 SA,A:Everybody 3.00
36 SA,A:Everybody 3.00
37 SA,A:Ruferto 3.00
38 SA,Dognappers 3.00
39 SA,A:Pal,Drumm 3.00
40 SA 3.00
41 SA,I:Granny Groo 3.00
42 SA,A:Granny Groo 3.00
43 SA,A:Granny Groo 3.00
44 SA,A:Ruferto 3.00
45 SA 3.00
46 SA,New Clothes 3.00
47 SA,A:Everybody 3.00
48 SA,A:Ruferto 3.00
49 SA,C:Chakaal 3.00
50 SA,double size 4.00
51 SA,A:Chakaal 2.50
52 SA,A:Chakaal 2.50
53 SA,A:Chakaal 2.50
54 SA,A:Ahak 2.50
55 SA,A:Ruferto 2.50
56 SA,A:Minstrael 2.50
57 SA,A:Ruferto 2.50
58 SA,A:Idol 2.50
59 SA 2.50
60 SA,A:Ruferto 2.50
61 SA,A:Horse 2.50
62 SA,A:Horse 2.50
63 SA,A:Drumm 2.50
64 SA,A:Artist 2.50
65 SA 2.50
66 SA 2.50
67 SA 2.50
68 SA 2.50
69 SA 2.50
70 SA 2.50
71 SA 2.50
72 SA 2.50
73 SA,Amnesia,pt1 . . . . 2.50
74 SA,Amnesia,pt2 . . . . 2.50
75 SA,Memory Returns 2.50
76 SA 2.50
77 SA 2.50
78 SA,R:Weaver,Scribe 2.50
79 SA,Groo the Assassin 2.50
80 SA,I:Thaiis,pt.1 . . . . 2.50
81 SA,Thaiis,pt.2 . . . . 2.50
82 SA,Thaiis,pt.3 . . . . 2.50
83 SA,Thaiis,pt.4 . . . . 2.50
84 SA,Thaiis Conclusion 2.50
85 SA,Groo turns invisible 2.50
86 SA,Invisible Groo 2.50
87 SA,Groo's Army 2.50
88 SA,V:Cattlemen,B.U. Sage . . . 3.00
89 SA,New Deluxe Format 2.50
90 SA,Worlds 1st Lawyers 2.50

91 SA,Bonus Pages 2.50
92 SA,Groo Becomes Kid Groo . . . 2.50
93 SA,Groo destroys glacier 2.50
94 SA 2.50
95 SA,Endangered Species 2.50
96 SA,Wager of the Gods#1 . . . . . 2.50
97 SA,Wager of the Gods#2 . . . . . 2.50
98 SA,Wager of the Gods#3 . . . . . 2.50
99 SA,E:Wager of the Gods 2.50
100 SA,Groo gets extra IQ points . . 8.00
101 SA,Groo loses intelligence 2.50
102 SA,F:Newly literate Groo 2.50
103 SA,General Monk 2.50
104 SA,F:Oso,Ruferto 2.50
105 SA,V:Minotaurs 2.50
106 SA,B:Man of the People 2.50
107 SA,Man of the People#2 . . . . . 2.50
108 SA,Man of the People#3 . . . . . 2.50
109 SA,E:Man of the People 2.50
110 SA,Mummies 2.50
111 SA,The Man who Killed Groo . . 2.50
112 SA,Rufferto Avenged 2.50
113 SA 2.50
114 SA,V:Vultures 2.50
115 SA 2.50
116 SA,Early unto Morning 2.50
117 SA 2.50
118 SA 2.50
119 SA 2.50
120 Groo hangs up swords 2.50
GNv Death of Groo 15.00
GNv 2nd print 8.00
TPB Groo Adventures 8.95
TPB Groo Carnival 8.95
TPB Groo Expose 8.95
TPB GRoo Festival 8.95
TPB Groo Garden 10.95

GROOVY
March, 1968—July, 1968
1 Monkeys,Ringo Starr,Photos . . 100.00
2 Cartoons,Gags,Jokes 65.00
3 . . . . 65.00

GUARDIANS OF THE GALAXY
June, 1990
1 B:JV(a&s),I:Taserface,R:Aleta . . . 4.00
2 MZ(c),JV,V:Stark,C:Firelord 3.00
3 JV,V:Stark,I:Force,C:Firelord 3.00
4 JV,V:Stark,A:Force,Firelord 3.00

Guardians of the Galaxy #19
© Marvel Entertainment Group

All comics prices listed are for *Near Mint* condition.

Guardians–Heathcliff — MARVEL — Comics Values Annual

5 JV,TM(c),V:Force,I:Mainprofile
  (Vision). 3.00
6 JV,V:Force,Vance Possesses
  Capt.America Shield. 3.00
7 GP(c),JV,I:Malevolence,
  O:Starhawk 3.00
8 SLi(c),JV,V:Yondu,C:Rancor 3.00
9 RLd(c),JV,I:Replica,Rancor 3.00
10 JLe(c),JV,V:Rancor,The Nine
  I&C:Overkill(Taserface). 3.00
11 BWi(c),JV,V:Rancor,I:Phoenix. . . 3.00
12 ATb(c),JV,V:Overkill
  A:Firelord 3.00
13 JV,A:Ghost Rider,Force,
  Malevolence 3.00
14 JS(c),JV,A:Ghost Rider,Force,
  Malevolence 3.00
15 JSn(c),JV,I:Protege,V:Force 3.00
16 JV,V:Force,A:Protege,
  Malevolence,L:Vance Astro. . . . 3.00
17 JV,V:Punishers(Street Army),
  L:Martinex,N:Charlie-27, ... 2.50
18 JV,V:Punishers,I&C:Talon,A:
  Crazy Nate 3.00
19 JV,V:Punishers,A:Talon 2.50
20 JV,I:Major Victory (Vance Astro)
  J:Talon & Krugarr 2.50
21 JV,V:Rancor. 2.50
22 JV,V:Rancor. 2.50
23 MT,V:Rancor,C:Silver Surfer. . . . 2.50
24 JV,A:Silver Surfer. 3.00
25 JV, Prismatic Foil(c)
  V:Galactus,A:SilverSurfer 3.50
25a 2nd printing,Silver 2.50
26 JV,O:Guardians(retold) 2.25
27 JV,Infinity War,O:Talon,
  A:Inhumans 2.25
28 JV,Inf.War,V:Various Villians. . . . 2.25
29 HT,Inf.War,V:Various Villians . . . 2.25
30 KWe,A:Captain America. 2.25
31 KWe,V:Badoon,A:Capt.A. 2.25
32 KWe,V:Badoon Gladiator 2.25
33 KWe,A:Dr.Strange,R:Aleta 2.25
34 KWe,J:Yellowjacket II. 2.25
35 KWe,A:Galatic Guardians,
  V:Bubonicus. 2.25
36 KWe,A:Galatic Guardians,
  V:Dormammu 2.25
37 KWe,V:Dormammu,A:Galatic
  Guardians 2.25
38 KWe,N:Yjacket,A:Beyonder 2.25
39 KWe,Rancor Vs. Dr.Doom,Holo-
  grafx(c) 3.25
40 KWe,V:Loki,Composite 2.25
41 KWe,V:Loki,A:Thor 2.25
42 KWe,I:Woden 2.25
43 KWe,A:Woden,V:Loki. 2.25
44 KWe,R:Yondu 2.25
45 KWe,O:Starhawk 2.25
46 KWe,N:Major Victory 2.25
47 KWe,A:Beyonder,Protoge,
  Overkill. 2.25
48 KWe,V:Overkill. 2.25
49 KWe,A:Celestial. 2.25
50 Foil(c),R:Yondu,Starhawk sep-
  arated,BU:O:Guardians 3.25
51 KWe,A:Irish Wolfhound 2.25
52 KWe,A:Drax. 2.25
53 KWe,V:Drax. 2.25
54 KWe,V:Sentinels 2.25
55 KWe,Ripjack 2.25
56 Ripjack 2.25
57 R:Keeper. 2.25
58 . . . . 2.25
59 A:Keeper. 2.25
60 F:Starhawk 2.25
61 F:Starhawk 2.25
62 Guardians Stop War of the Worlds
  last issue 2.25
Ann.#1 Korvac Quest #4,I:Krugarr . 3.25
Ann.#2 HT,I:Galactic Guardians,
  System Bytes #4 . . . . 3.25
Ann.#3 CDo,I:Irish Wolfhound,
  w/Trading card 3.25
Ann.#4 V:Nine 3.25
TPB rep #1 thru #6. . . . . 12.95

GUNHAWK, THE
See: BLAZE CARSON

Gunhawks #1
© Marvel Entertainment Group

GUNHAWKS
Oct., 1972
1 SSh,B:Reno Jones & Kid
  Cassidy Two Rode Together . . 25.00
2 Ride out for Revenge 20.00
3 Indian Massacre. 20.00
4 Trial by Ordeal 20.00
5 The Reverend Mr. Graves. 20.00
6 E:Reno Jones & Kid Cassidy
  D:Kid Cassidy. 20.00
7 A Gunhawks Last Stand
  A;Reno Jones, Oct., 1973 . . . 20.00

GUNRUNNER
Marvel UK, 1993–94
1 I:Gunrunner,w/trading cards 3.00
2 A:Ghost Rider. 2.25
3 V:Cynodd 2.25
4 . . . . 2.25
5 A:Enhanced 2.25
6 final issue. 2.25

GUNSLINGERS
Dec., 1999
1-shot 64-pg. 3.00

GUNSLINGER
See: TEX DAWSON, GUNSLINGER

GUNSMOKE WESTERN
See: ALL WINNERS COMICS

GUN THEORY
Marvel Epic Aug. 2003
1 (of 4) 2.50
2 . . . . 2.50
3 . . . . 2.50

4 concl. 2.50

HARROWERS
1993–94
1 MSt(s),GC,F:Pinhead 3.50
2 GC,AW(i), ... 3.00
3 GC,AW(i), ... 3.00
4 GC,AW(i), ... 3.00
5 GC,AW(i),Devil's Pawn#1 . . . . . . 3.00
6 GC,AW(i),Devil's Pawn#2 . . . . . . 3.00

HARVEY
Oct., 1970–Dec., 1972
1 . . . . 100.00
2 thru 6 . . . . @65.00

HARVEY PRESENTS: CASPER
1 . . . . 2.25

HAVOK & WOLVERINE
Epic, March, 1988
1 JMu,KW,V:KGB,Dr.Neutron. 5.00
2 JMu,KW,V:KGB,Dr.Neutron. 4.00
3 JMu,KW,V:Meltdown. 4.00
4 JMu,KW,V:Meltdown,Oct.1989 . . 4.00
TPB rep.#1-4 . . . . 16.95

HAWKEYE
[1st Limited Series], Sept., 1983
1 A:Mockingbird. 3.00
2 I:Silencer. 3.00
3 I:Bombshell,Oddball 3.00
4 V:Crossfire,W:Hawkeye &
  Mockingbird, Dec., 1983 . . . . . . 3.00
[2nd Limited Series], 1994
1 B:CDi(s),ScK,V:Trickshot,
  I:Javelynn,Rover. 2.25
2 ScK,V:Viper 2.25
3 ScK,A:War Machine,N:Hawkeye,
  V:Secret Empire 2.25
4 E:CDi(s),ScK,V:Trickshot,Viper,
  Javelynn. 2.25

HAWKEYE
Marvel Oct. 2003
1 FaN(s),High,Hard Shaft,pt.1 . . . 3.00
2 FaN(s),High,Hard Shaft,pt.2 . . . 3.00

HAWKEYE: EARTH'S MIGHTIEST MARKSMAN
Aug., 1998
1-shot TDF,MBa,JJ,DR,AM 48pg . . 3.00

HEADMASTERS
Star, July, 1987
1 FS,Transformers. 2.25
2 and 3 . . . . @2.25
4 Jan., 1988 . . . . 2.25

HEATHCLIFF
Star, April, 1985
1 . . . . 7.00
2 thru 10 . . . . @4.00
11 thru 16 . . . . @3.00
17 Masked Moocher. 5.00
18 thru 49 . . . . @3.00
50 Double-size 4.00
51 thru 55 . . . . @3.00

CVA Page 246 — All comics prices listed are for *Near Mint* condition.

HEATHCLIFF'S FUNHOUSE
Star, May, 1987
1 thru 10 . . . . @3.00

HEAVY HITTERS
Ann.#1 (1993) 4.00

HEDY DEVINE COMICS
Aug., 1947—Sept., 1952
22 I:Hedy Devine 250.00
23 BW,Beauty and the Beach,
  HK,Hey Look 175.00
24 High Jinx in Hollywood,
  HK, Hey Look. 175.00
25 Hedy/Bull(c),HK,Hey Look . . . 175.00
26 Skating(c),HK,Giggles&Grins . 150.00
27 Hedy at Show(c),HK,Hey Look 110.00
28 Hedy/Charlie(c),HK,Hey Look. 110.00
29 Tennis(c),HK,Hey Look. 110.00
30 . . . . 110.00
31 thru 50 . . . . @100.00

HEDY WOLFE
Atlas, Aug., 1957
1 Patsy Walker's Rival 125.00

HELLCAT
July, 2000
1 (of 3) SEt,NBy,F:PatsyWalker . . . 3.00
2 SEt,NBy, ... 3.00
3 SEt,NBy,Concl. 3.00

HELLHOUND
1993–94
1 Hellhound on my Trial. 3.00
2 Love in Vain 3.00
3 Last Fair Deal Gone Down 3.00

HELLRAISER
See: CLIVE BARKER'S HELLRAISER

HELLRAISER III HELL ON EARTH
1 Movie Adaptation,(prestige) 5.00
1a Movie Adapt.(magazine) 3.00

HELLSTORM, PRINCE OF LIES
1993
1 R:Daimon Hellstrom,
  Parchment(c) 3.50
2 A:Dr.Strange,Gargoyle 3.00
3 O:Hellstorm. 2.75
4 V:Ghost Rider 2.75
5 MB, ... 2.50
6 MB,V:Dead Daughter 2.50
7 A:Armaziel 2.50
8 Hell is where the heart is 2.50
9 LKa(s),Highway to Heaven 2.50
10 LKa(s),Heaven's Gate 2.50
11 LKa(s),PrG,Life in Hell 2.50
12 Red Miracles 2.50
13 Red Miracles Sidewalking 2.50
14 Red Miracles Murder is Easy . . . 2.50
15 Cigarette Dawn 3.00
16 Down Here 2.50
17 The Saint of the Pit 2.50
18 . . . . 2.50
19 . . . . 2.50
20 . . . . 2.50
21 final issue 2.50

Hell's Angel #2
© Marvel Entertainment Group

HELL'S ANGEL
1992
1 GSr,A:X-Men,O:Hell's Angel 3.00
2 GSr,A:X-Men,V:Psycho Warriors . 2.50
3 GSr,A:X-Men,V:MyS-Tech. 2.25
4 GSr,A:X-Men,V:MyS-Tech. 2.25
5 GSr,A:X-Men,V:MyS-Tech. 2.25
6 Gfr,A:X-Men,V:MyS-Tech 2.25
Becomes:

DARK ANGEL
1992
7 DMn,A:Psylocke,V:MyS-Tech . . . 2.25
8 DMn,A:Psylocke 2.25
9 A:Punisher 2.25
10 MyS-Tech Wars tie-in 2.25
11 A:X-Men,MyS-Tech wars tie-in . 2.25
12 A:X-Men 2.25
13 A:X-Men,Death's Head II 2.25
14 Afthermath#2 . . . . 2.25
15 Afthermath#3 . . . . 2.25
16 SvL,E:Afthermath,last issue 2.25

HERCULES AND THE HEART OF CHAOS
Limited Series Aug., 1997
1 (of 3) TDF,RF,PO, ... 2.50
2 TDF,RF,PO, ... 2.50
3 TDF,RF,PO,V:Ares, concl. 2.25

HERCULES PRINCE OF POWER
Sept., 1982
1 BL,I:Recorder 5.00
2 BL,I:Layana Sweetwater 3.00
3 BL,V:The Brothers,C:Galactus . . 3.00
4 BL,A:Galactus 3.00
[2nd Series], March, 1984
1 BL,I:Skyypi. 3.00
2 BL,A:Red Wolf 2.50
3 BL,A:Starfox 2.50
4 BL,D:Zeus, June, 1984 . . . . 2.50
TPB BL rep. Vol.1 #1–#4 and
  Vol.2 #1–#4 . . . . 6.00

HERO
May, 1990
1 . . . . 2.50
2 . . . . 2.25
3 . . . . 2.25

4 RH 2.25
5 RH 2.25
6 Oct., 1990 . . . . 2.25

HERO FOR HIRE
June, 1972
1 GT,JR,I&O:Power Man 75.00
2 GT,A:Diamond Back 35.00
3 GT,I:Mace. 25.00
4 V:Phantom of 42nd St. 25.00
5 GT,A:Black Mariah 25.00
6 V:Assassin 15.00
7 GT,Nuclear Bomb issue 15.00
8 GT,A:Dr.Doom 15.00
9 GT,A:Dr.Doom,Fant.Four 15.00
10 GT,A:Dr.Death,Fant.Four 15.00
11 GT,A:Dr.Death 12.00
12 GT,C:Spider-Man 12.00
13 A:Lion Fang 12.00
14 V:Big Ben 12.00
15 Cage Goes Wild 12.00
16 O:Stilletto,D:Rackham 12.00
Becomes:

POWER MAN

Hero For Hire #15
© Marvel Entertainment Group

HEROES FOR HIRE
July, 1997
1 JOs,PFe,F:Iron Fist 5.00
2 JOs,PFe,V:Nitro 3.00
2A Variant PFe cover. 3.00
3 JOs,PFe,V:Nitro 3.00
4 JOs,Power Man vs. Iron Fist. . . . 3.00
5 JOs,V:Sersi, Diabolical Deviants . 3.00
6 JOs,PFe, Deviants 3.00
7 JOs V:Thunderbolts 3.00
8 JOs,Iron Fist's agenda revealed . 3.00
9 JOs,Search for Punisher. 3.00
10 JOs,Deadpool hired. 3.00
11 JOs,PFe,A:Deadpool, V:Silver
  Sable and Wild Pack 3.00
12 JOs,PFe,Traitor revealed, 48pg . 3.50
13 JOs,PFe,V:Master 3.00
14 JOs,F:Black Knight 3.00
15 JOs,PFe,Siege of Wundagore,
  pt.1 (of 5) 3.00
16 JOs,PFe,Siege of Wundagore,
  pt.3 . . . . 3.00
17 JOs,DBw,F:Luke Cage
  & She-Hulk. 3.00
18 JOs,PFe,A:Wolverine 3.00
19 JOs,PFe,F:Wolverine 3.00

Heroes–Hulk / MARVEL / Comics Values Annual

Ann.'98 JOs,BWi,PFe,Heroes For
 Hire/Quicksilver, The Siege of
 Wundagore, pt.5 (of 5) 48pg ... 3.00

HEROES FOR HOPE
1985
1 TA/JBy/HC/RCo/BWr,A:XMen ... 7.00

HEROES REBORN: THE RETURN
Oct., 1997
? Heroes Reborn prequel, (Marvel/
 Wizard 1996) 7.50
1 (of 4) PDd,ATi,SvL,F:Franklin
 Richards. 4.00
2 PDd,ATi,SvL, F:Spider-Man,
 Thunderbolts & Doctor Strange. 4.00
3 PDd,SvL,ATi,A UniverseMayDie . 4.00
4 PDd,SvL,ATi, crossover to Marvel
 Universe?. 4.00
TPB Return of the Heroes. 14.95

HOKUM & HEX
Razorline 1993–94
1 BU:Saint Sinner 3.00
2 I:Analyzer 2.25
3 I:Wrath 2.25
4 I:Z-Man 2.25
5 V:Hyperkind 2.25
6 B:Bloodshed. 2.25
7 V:Bloodshed. 2.25
8 V:Bloodshed. 2.25
9 E:Bloodshed,final issue. 2.25

HOLIDAY COMICS
Jan., 1951
1 LbC(c),Christmas(c) 400.00
2 LbC(c),Easter Parade(c) 400.00
3 LbC(c),4th of July(c) 275.00
4 LbC(c),Summer Vacation 250.00
5 LbC(c),Christmas(c) 250.00
6 LbC(c),Birthday(c). 250.00
7 LbC(c),Rodeo (c) 250.00
8 LbC(c),Xmas(c) Oct., 1952 . . 250.00

HOLLYWOOD SUPERSTARS
Epic, Nov., 1990
1 DSp 3.00
2 thru 5 DSp, March, 1991 . . . . . @2.50

HOMER, THE HAPPY GHOST
March, 1955
1 . . . . 250.00
2 . . . . 125.00
3 . . . . 100.00
4 thru 15 . . . . @100.00
16 thru 22 . . . . @75.00
[2nd Series], Nov., 1969
1 . . . . 150.00
2 thru 5 . . . . @100.00

HOOD, THE
Marvel Max, May, 2002
1 (of 6) F:Parker Robbins,40-pg. . . 3.00
2 FBI attention. 3.00
3 diamond heist. 3.00
4 . . . . 3.00
5 . . . . 3.00
6 concl. 3.00
TPB Vol. 1: Blood From Stones . . 15.00

HOOK
1992
1 JRy,GM,movie adaption 2.25
2 JRy,Return to Never Land. 2.25
3 Peter Pans Magic. 2.25
4 conclusion 2.25
Hook Super Spec.#1 . . . . 3.00

HORRORS, THE
Jan., 1953—April, 1954
11 LbC(c),The Spirit of War. 325.00
12 LbC(c),Under Fire 300.00
13 LbC(c),Terror Castle. 300.00
14 LbC(c),Underworld Terror. . . . 300.00
15 LbC(c),The Mad Bandit 300.00

HOT SHOTS AVENGERS
1 Painted Pin-ups (1995). 3.00
SPIDER-MAN
1 Painted pin-ups 3.00
X-MEN
1 Painted pin-ups 3.00

HOUSE II
1 1987, Movie Adapt. 2.00

HOWARD THE DUCK
Jan., 1976
1 FB,SL,A:Spider-Man,I:Beverly. . 25.00
2 FB,V:TurnipMan&Kidney Lady . 10.00
3 JB,Learns Quack Fu. 10.00
4 GC,V:Winky Man 10.00
5 GC,Becomes Wrestler 9.00
6 GC,V:Gingerbread Man 6.00
7 GC,V:Gingerbread Man 6.00
8 GC,A:Dr.Strange,ran for Pres. . . 6.00
9 GC,V:Le Beaver 6.00
10 GC,A:Spider-Man 6.00
11 GC,V:Kidney Lady 6.00
12 GC,I:Kiss 25.00
13 GC,A:Kiss 30.00
14 GC,Howard as Son of Satan . . 4.00
15 GC,A:Dr.Strange,A:Dr.Bong. . . 4.00
16 GC,DC,JB,DG,TA,
 V:Incredible Creator 4.00
17 GC,D:Dr.Bong 4.00
18 GC,Howard the Human #1. . . . 4.00
19 GC,Howard the Human #2. . . . 4.00
20 GC,V:Sudd 4.00
21 GC,V:Soofi 4.00
22 A:ManThing,StarWars Parody . 4.00
23 A:ManThing,StarWars Parody . . 4.00
24 GC,NightAfter..SavedUniverse . 4.00
25 GC,V:Circus of Crime 4.00
26 GC,V:Circus of Crime 4.00
27 GC,V:Circus of Crime 4.00
28 GC,Cooking With Gas 4.00
29 Duck-Itis Poster Child 1978 . . . 4.00
30 Iron Duck,V:Dr. Bong 4.00
31 Iron Duck,V:Dr. Bong 4.00
32 V:Gopher. 4.00
33 BB(c),The Material Duck 6.00
Ann.#1, V:Caliph of Bagmom 3.00
Holiday Spec. LHa,ATi,PFe (1996) . 3.50

HOWARD THE DUCK
Marvel Max, Jan., 2002
1 (of 6) SvG,Making the Band 4.00
2 SvG,Beverly's ex 3.00
3 SvG,GF,The former Duck 3.00
4 SvG,GF,House of Mystery 3.00
5 SvG,GF,House of Mystery,pt.2 . . 3.00
6 SvG,GF,Duck or Mouse 3.00
TPB series rep. 15.00

HOWARD THE DUCK MAGAZINE
(B&W) Oct., 1979–March, 1981
1 . . . . 6.00
2 & 3 . . . . @5.00
4 Beatles,Elvis,Kiss 6.00
5 thru 9 . . . . @5.00

HUGGA BUNCH
Star, Oct., 1986—Aug., 1987
1 . . . . 4.00
2 thru 6 . . . . @3.00

HULK, THE
Feb., 1999
1 JBy,RG,DGr,48-page 4.00
1a signed 20.00
1b gold foil cover 10.00
2 JBy,RG,DGr,Hulk unleashed. . . 2.50
2a variant AdP cover 2.50
3 JBy,RG,DGr,Hulk berserk 2.50
4 JBy,RG,DGr,old foe 2.50
5 JBy,RG,DGr,V:Man-Thing 2.50
6 JBy,RG,DGr,V:Man-Thing 2.50
7 JBy,RG,DGr,A:Avengers 2.50
8 JBy,RG,DGr,V:Wolverine 2.50
9 RG,V:Thing 2.50
10 RG 2.50
11 PJe,RG,SB,A:DocSamson 2.50
Becomes:

INCREDIBLE HULK
2000
12 PJe,RG,SB,48-page 3.00
13 PJe,RG,SB,new Hulk 2.50
14 PJe,RG,SB,V:Ryker. 2.50
15 PJe,RG,SB,Dogs of War,pt.2 . . 2.50
16 PJe,RG,SB,Dogs of War,pt.3 . . 2.50
17 PJe,RG,SB,Dogs of War,pt.4 . . 2.50
18 PJe,RG,SB,Dogs of War,pt.5 . . 2.50
19 PJe,RG,SB,Dogs of War,pt.6 . . 2.50
20 PJe,RG,SB,Dogs of War,pt.7 . . 2.50
21 PJe,Maximum Security 2.50
22 PJe,Joe Fixit's Money 2.50
23 PJe,Nobby Stiles 2.50
24 PJe,JR2,V:Abomination 2.50
25 PJe,JR2,V:Abomination 3.50
26 Psyche of child-like Hulk 2.50
27 PJe,JR2,TP 2.50
28 PJe,JR2,TP,V:Devil Hulk 2.50

Howard the Duck #27
© Marvel Entertainment Group

MARVEL

Hulk–Human

29 FaN,A:Angela,Doc Samson 2.50
30 PJe,JoB,TP, ... 2.50
31 PJe,JoB,TP,Banner gone 2.50
32 PJe,JoB,TP,Ant-Man inside 2.50
33 CPr,JBg,100-page 4.00
34 JR2,TP,The beast within 2.50
35 JR2,TP,crosses the line? 2.50
36 JR2,TP,Gangs All Here,pt.1 ... 2.50
37 JR2,TP,Remember This,pt.2 ... 2.50
38 JR2,TP, ... 2.50
39 JR2,TP,Tag-You're Dead 2.50
40 LW,TP,madman with gun 2.50
41 JR2,TP,madman with gun 2.50
42 LW,TP,hostage crisis 2.50
43 JR2,TP,hostage crisis,concl. ... 2.50
44 SI 2.50
45 SI,dream lover 2.50
46 SI 2.50
47 SI 2.50
48 SI 2.50
49 SI 2.50
50 MD2,R:Abomination,pt.1 .... 4.00
51 MD2,R:Abomination,pt.2 .... 2.50
52 MD2,R:Abomination,pt.3 .... 2.50
53 MD2,R:Abomination,pt.4 .... 2.50
54 MD2,R:Abomination,pt.5 .... 2.50
55 Hide in Plain Sight,pt.1 ..... 0.50
56 Hide in Plain Sight,pt.2 ..... 2.50
57 Hide in Plain Sight,pt.3 ..... 2.50
58 Hide in Plain Sight,pt.4 ..... 2.50
59 Hide in Plain Sight,pt.5 ..... 2.50
60 MD2,Split Decisions,pt.1 .... 2.50
61 MD2,Split Decisions,pt.2 .... 2.50
62 MD2,Split Decisions,pt.3 .... 2.50
63 MD2,Split Decisions,pt.4 .... 2.50
Ann. 1999 JBy,DGr,48-page 4.00
Ann. 2001 EL,V:Thor 3.50
Spec. Hulk/Sentry 3.50
GN The End, DK, ... 5.95
TPB Transformations 17.95
TPB Ground Zero 17.95
TPB The Dogs of War,224-page .. 19.95
TPB Vol.1,Return of the Monster.. 13.00
TPB Vol.2, The Morning After 9.00
TPB Vol. 3: Transfer of Power. ... 13.00
TPB Vol. 4: Abominable 12.00
TPB Vol. 5: Hide in Plain Sight ... 12.00
Spec. Must Have, rep. #34–#36 .. 4.00

HULK: GREY
Marvel Oct. 2003
1 JLb,TSe 3.50
2 JLb,TSe 3.50
3 JLb,TSe 3.50

HULK: THE MOVIE ADAPTATION
Marvel June 2003
Spec. 48-pg. 3.50
TPB Movie 13.00

HULK: NIGHTMERICA
Marvel June 2003
1 (of 6) 3.00
2 Chrissie Cutler 3.00
3 within the citadel. 3.00
4 Mrs. Grey 3.00
5 .... 3.00
6 .... 3.00

HULK SMASH
Jan., 2001
1 (of 2) GEn,JMC 3.00
2 GEn,JMC 3.00

Hulk 2099 #1
© Marvel Entertainment Group

HULK 2099
1994–95
1 GJ,Foil(c),V:Draco 3.00
2 GJ,V:Draco 2.25
3 I:Golden Boy 2.25
4 .... 2.25
5 Ultra Hulk 2.25
Becomes:

HULK 2099 A.D.
1995
6 Gamma Ray Scientist 2.25
7 A:Doom,Dr.Apollo 2.25
8 One Nation Under Doom 2.25
9 California Quake 2.25

HULK/WOLVERINE: 6 HOURS
Marvel Jan. 2003
1 (of 4) ScK,SBs(c),rescue 3.00
2 ScK,SBs(c). 3.00
3 ScK,SBs(c). 3.00
4 ScK,SBs(c),concl. 3.00
TPB Hulk Legends, Vol. 1, rep. ... 14.00

HUMAN FLY
July, 1987
1 I&O:Human Fly,A:Spider-Man . 10.00
2 A:Ghost Rider 15.00
3 DC,JSt(c),DP,`Fortress of Fear'.. 5.00
4 JB/TA(c),`David Drier' 5.00
5 V:Makik 5.00
6 Fear in Funland 5.00
7 ME,Fury in the Wind 5.00
8 V:White Tiger 5.00
9 JB/TA(c),ME,V:Copperhead,A:
  White Tiger,Daredevil 5.00
10 ME,Dark as a Dungeon 5.00
11 ME,A:Daredevil 5.00
12 ME,Suicide Sky-Dive 5.00
13 BLb/BMc(c),FS,V:Carl Braden .. 5.00
14 BLb/BMc(c),SL,Fear Over
  Fifth Avenue 5.00
15 BLb/BMc(c),War in the
  Washington Monument 5.00
16 BLb/BMc(c),V:Blaze Kendall ... 5.00
17 BLb,DP,Murder on the Midway.. 5.00
18 V:Harmony Whyte 5.00
19 BL(c),V:Jacopo Belbo
  March, 1979 .... 5.00

RED RAVEN COMICS
Timely Comics Aug., 1940
1 JK,O:Red Raven,I:Magar,A:Comet
  Pierce & Mercury,Human Top,
  Eternal Brain 16,000.00
Becomes:

HUMAN TORCH
Fall, 1940–Aug., 1954
2 (#1)ASh(c),BEv,B:Sub-Mariner
  A:Fiery Mask,Falcon,Mantor,
  Microman 45,000.00
3 (#2)Ash(c),BEv,V:Sub-
  Mariner,Bondage(c) 7,200.00
4 (#3)ASh(c),BEv,O:Patriot ... 5,500.00
5 (#4)V:Nazis,A:Patriot,Angel
  crossover 4,500.00
5a(#5)ASh(c),V:Sub-Mariner .. 7,000.00
6 ASh(c),Doom Dungeon 3,000.00
7 ASh(c),V:Japanese 3,200.00
8 ASh(c),BW,V:Sub-Mariner .. 4,500.00
9 ASh(c),V:General Rommel .. 3,500.00
10 ASh(c),BW,V:Sub-Mariner .. 3,600.00
11 ASh(c),Nazi Oil Refinery ... 2,200.00
12 ASh(c),V:Japanese,
  Bondage(c) 3,700.00
13 ASh(c),V:Japanese,
  Bondage(c) 2,200.00
14 ASh(c),V:Nazis 2,200.00
15 ASh(c),Toro Trapped 2,200.00
16 ASh(c),V:Japanese 1,500.00
17 ASh(c),V:Japanese 1,500.00
18 ASh(c),V:Japanese,
  MacArthurs HQ 1,500.00
19 ASh(c),Bondage(c) 1,500.00
20 ASh(c),Last War Issue 1,500.00
21 ASh(c),V:Organized Crime . 1,500.00
22 ASh(c),V:Smugglers 1,500.00
23 ASh(c),V:Giant Robot 1,600.00
24 V:Mobsters 1,400.00
25 The Masked Monster 1,400.00
26 Her Diary of Terror 1,400.00
27 SSh(c),BEv,V:The Asbestos
  Lady 1,400.00
28 BEv,The Twins Who Weren't 1,400.00
29 You'll Die Laughing 1,400.00
30 BEv,The Stranger,
  A:Namora 1,300.00
31 A:Namora 1,200.00
32 A:Sungirl,Namora 1,200.00
33 Capt.America crossover ... 1,250.00
34 The Flat of the Land 1,200.00
35 A;Captain America,Sungirl.. 1,250.00
36 A:Submariner 1,200.00

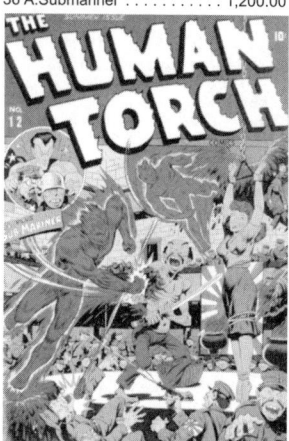

The Human Torch #12
© Marvel Entertainment Group

Human–Incredible Hulk / MARVEL / Comics Values Annual

37 BEv,A:Submariner........ 1,200.00
38 BEv,A:Submariner........ 1,200.00

HUMAN TORCH
Sept., 1974
1 JK,rep.StrangeTales #101..... 25.00
2 thru 8 rep.Strange Tales .... @15.00

HUMAN TORCH
Marvel April 2003
1 KK(s),Burn,pt.1............. 2.50
2 KK(s),Burn,pt.2............. 2.50
3 KK(s),Burn,pt.3............. 2.50
4 KK(s),Burn,pt.4............. 2.50
5 KK(s),Burn,concl............ 2.50
6 KK(s),Burn,concl............ 2.50
7 KK(s),Out,pt.1.............. 2.50
8 KK(s),Out,pt.2.............. 2.50
TPB Human Torch: Burn, Vol.1 ....

HUMAN TORCH COMICS
Feb., 1999
1-shot V:Sub-Mariner, 48-page 4.00

Hyperkind #7
© Marvel Entertainment Group

HYPERKIND
Marvel/Razorline 1993
1 I:Hyperkind,BU:EctoKid 3.00
2 I:Bliss..................... 2.25
3 V:Living Void 2.25
4 FBk(s),I:Paragon John 2.25
5 V:Paragon John 2.25
6 Vetus Unleashed 2.25
7 Ambertrance................ 2.25
8 I:Tempest 2.25
9 I:Lazurex,w/card 2.25

HYPERKIND UNLEASHED
1994
1 BU,V:Thermakk 3.25

ICEMAN
Dec., 1984
1 DP,mini-series 3.00
2 DP,V:Kali 3.00
3 DP,A;Original X-Men,Defenders
   Champions................ 3.00
4 DP,Oblivion,June, 1985...... 4.00

ICEMAN
Oct., 2001
1 (of 4) DAn,ALa,KIK........... 3.00
2 DAn,ALa,KIK,A:Augmen 3.00
3 DAn,ALa,KIK,F:Foe-Dog,Augmen 3.00
4 DAn,ALa, concl.............. 3.00

IDEAL
Timely, July, 1948
1 Antony and Cleopatra 400.00
2 The Corpses of Dr.Sacotti ... 325.00
3 Joan of Arc 300.00
4 Richard the Lionhearted
   A:The Witness 450.00
5 Phc,Love and Romance 200.00
Becomes:

LOVE ROMANCES
6 Ph(c),I Loved a Scoundrel ... 150.00
7 Ph(c)..................... 75.00
8 Ph(c)..................... 80.00
9 thru 12 Ph(c)............. @75.00
13 thru 20................. @75.00
21 BK..................... 100.00
22 .... 75.00
23 .... 75.00
24 BK..................... 100.00
25 .... 75.00
26 thru 35................. @75.00
36 BK..................... 75.00
37 .... 60.00
38 BK..................... 75.00
39 thru 44................. @60.00
45 MB..................... 65.00
46 .... 65.00
47 .... 65.00
48 .... 50.00
49 ATh.................... 60.00
50 .... 50.00
51 .... 50.00
52 .... 50.00
53 ATh.................... 65.00
54 .... 50.00
55 .... 50.00
56 .... 50.00
57 MB..................... 80.00
58 thru 74................. @50.00
75 MB..................... 75.00
76 .... 50.00
77 MB..................... 75.00
78 .... 50.00
79 .... 50.00
80 RH(c).................. 50.00
81 .... 50.00
82 MB,JK(c)............... 75.00
83 JSe,JK(c).............. 75.00
84 JK..................... 75.00
85 JK..................... 75.00
86 thru 95................ @50.00
96 JK..................... 100.00
97 .... 75.00
98 JK..................... 100.00
99 JK..................... 100.00
100 thru 104.............. @100.00
105 JK.................... 100.00
106 JK,July, 1963......... 100.00

IDEAL COMICS
Timely, Fall, 1944
1 B:Super Rabbit,Giant Super
   Rabbit V:Axis(c) 250.00
2 Super Rabbit at Fair(c) 150.00
3 Beach Party(c) 135.00
4 How to Catch Robbers 135.00
Becomes:

WILLIE COMICS
1946
5 B:Willie,George,Margie,Nellie
   Football(c) 200.00

6 Record Player(c) 125.00
7 Soda Fountain(c),HK,HeyLook 125.00
8 Fancy Dress(c) 100.00
9 .... 100.00
10 HK,Hey Look 100.00
11 HK,Hey Look 100.00
12 .... 75.00
13 .... 75.00
14 thru 18 .... @60.00
19 .... 100.00
20 Li'L Willie Comics 75.00
21 Li'L Willie Comics........ 75.00
22 .... 75.00
23 May, 1950 .... 75.00

IDOL
Epic, 1992
1 I:Idol..................... 3.25
2 Phantom of the Set......... 3.25
3 Conclusion................ 3.25

ILLUMINATOR
1993
1 .... 5.50
2 .... 5.50
3 .... 3.25
4 .... 3.25

IMMORTALIS
1 A:Dr.Strange............... 2.25
2 A:Dr.Strange............... 2.25
3 A:Dr.Strange,V:Vampires..... 2.25
4 Mephisto, final issue......... 2.25

IMPERIAL GUARD
[Limited Series], 1997
1 (of 3) BAu,Woj,............. 2.25
2 and 3 BAu,Woj .... @2.25

IMPOSSIBLE MAN SUMMER VACATION
1990–91
1 GCa,DP................... 2.50
2 .... 2.50
Summer Fun Spec. TPe, Vacation
   on Earth................. 2.50

INCAL, THE
Epic, Nov., 1988
1 Moebius,Adult 12.00
2 Moebius,Adult 12.00
3 Moebius,Adult, Jan., 1989 .... 12.00

INCOMPLETE DEATH'S HEAD
1993
1 .... 3.50
2 thru 11 rep.Death's Head #1
   thru #11 .... @2.25

INCREDIBLE HULK
May, 1962
1 JK,I:Hulk(Grey Skin),Rick Jones,
   Thunderbolt Ross,Betty Ross,
   Gremlin,Gamma Base ... 20,000.00
2 JK,SD,O:Hulk,(Green skin). . 4,500.00
3 JK,O:rtd.,I:Ring Master,
   Circus of Crime 2,700.00
4 JK,V:Mongu 2,500.00
5 JK,I:General Fang 2,500.00
6 SD,I:Metal Master 3,200.00
See: Tales to Astonish #59-#101

CVA Page 250 — All comics prices listed are for *Near Mint* condition.

Comics Values Annual — MARVEL — Incredible Hulk

Incredible Hulk #116
© Marvel Entertainment Group

April, 1968
102 MSe,GT,O:Retold......... 350.00
103 MSe,I:Space Parasite..... 200.00
104 MSe,O&N:Rhino.......... 175.00
105 MSe,GT,I:Missing Link..... 125.00
106 MSe,HT,GT 125.00
107 HT,V:Mandarin........... 125.00
108 HT,JMe,A:Nick Fury....... 125.00
109 HT,JMe,A:Ka-Zar......... 100.00
110 HT,JMe,A:Ka-Zar......... 100.00
111 HT,DA,I:Galaxy Master..... 80.00
112 HT,DA,O:Galaxy Master..... 80.00
113 HT,DA,V:Sandman......... 80.00
114 HT,DA 80.00
115 HT,DA,A:Leader 80.00
116 HT,DA,V:Super Humanoid .. 80.00
117 HT,DA,A:Leader 80.00
118 HT,V:Sub-Mariner......... 80.00
119 HT,V:Maximus 60.00
120 HT,V:Maximus 60.00
121 HT,I:The Glob 60.00
122 HT,V:Thing 110.00
123 HT,V:Leader............. 50.00
124 HT,SB,V:Rhino,Leader..... 50.00
125 HT,V:Absorbing Man 50.00
126 HT,A:Dr.Strange........... 50.00
127 HT,Moleman vs.Tyrannus
I:Mogol.................. 45.00
128 HT,A:Avengers............. 45.00
129 HT,V:Glob 45.00
130 HT,Banner vs. Hulk........ 45.00
131 HT,A:Iron Man 40.00
132 HT,JSe,V:Hydra 40.00
133 HT,JSe,I:Draxon.......... 40.00
134 HT,SB,I:Golem 40.00
135 HT,SB,V:Kang 40.00
136 HT,SB,I:Xeron 40.00
137 HT,V:Abomination 40.00
138 HT,V:Sandman 40.00
139 HT,V:Leader............. 40.00
140 HT,V:Psyklop 40.00
141 HT,JSe,I&O:Doc.Samson ... 100.00
142 HT,JSe,V:Valkyrie,A:Doc
Samson 50.00
143 DA,JSe,V:Dr.Doom 50.00
144 DA,JSe,V:Dr.Doom 50.00
145 HT,JSe,O:Retold 55.00
146 HT,JSe,Leader............ 40.00
147 HT,JSe,Doc.Samson loses
Powers.................. 40.00
148 HT,JSe,I:Fialan 40.00
149 HT,JSe,I:Inheritor......... 40.00
150 HT,JSe,I:Viking,A:Havoc ... 40.00
151 HT,JSe,C:Ant Man 40.00
152 HT,DA,Many Cameos....... 40.00
153 HT,JSe,C:Capt.America..... 40.00
154 HT,JSe,A:Ant Man,
V:Chameleon 40.00
155 HT,JSe,I:Shaper of Worlds... 40.00
156 HT,V:Hulk 40.00
157 HT,I:Omnivac,Rhino........ 40.00
158 HT,C:Warlock,V:Rhino...... 40.00
159 HT,V:Abomination,Rhino 40.00
160 HT,V:Tiger Shark 40.00
161 HT,V:Beast............... 35.00
162 HT,I:Wendigo I 40.00
163 HT,I:Gremlin.............. 30.00
164 HT,I:Capt.Omen.......... 30.00
165 HT,I:Aquon............... 30.00
166 HT,I:Zzzax 30.00
167 HT,JAb,V:Modok 30.00
168 HT,JAb,I:Harpy........... 30.00
169 HT,JAb,I:Bi-Beast......... 30.00
170 HT,JAb,V:Volcano 30.00
171 HT,JAb,A:Abomination,Rhino . 30.00
172 HT,JAb,X:X-Men 50.00
173 HT,V:Cobolt Man 20.00
174 HT,V:Cobolt Man 20.00
175 JAb,V:Inhumans........... 20.00
176 HT,JAb,A:Man-Beast,C:Warlock
Crisis on Counter-Earth..... 25.00
177 HT,JAb,D:Warlock 25.00
178 HT,JAb,Warlock Lives 25.00
179 HT,JAb.................. 20.00
180 HT,JAb,I:Wolverine
V:Wendigo I 300.00
181 HT,JAb,A:Wolverine (1st
Full Story),V:Wendigo II ... 1,300.00
182 HT,JAb,I&D:Crackajack
Jackson,C:Wolverine 140.00
183 HT,V:Zzzax 20.00
184 HT,V:Living Shadow........ 20.00
185 HT,V:General Ross 20.00
186 HT,I:Devastator 20.00
187 HT,JSt,V:Gremlin 20.00
188 HT,JSt,I:Droog............ 20.00
189 HT,JSt,I:Datrine 20.00
190 HT,MSe,Toadman 20.00
191 HT,JSt,Toadman,I:Glorian... 20.00
192 HT,V:The Lurker.......... 20.00
193 HT,JSt,Doc.Samson regains
Powers.................. 20.00
194 SB,JSt,V:Locust........... 20.00
195 SB,JSt,V:Abomination 20.00
196 SB,JSt,V:Army 20.00
197 BWr(c),SB,JSt,A:Man-Thing . 20.00
198 SB,JSt,A:Man-Thing....... 20.00
199 SB,JSt,V:Shield,Doc.Samson . 20.00
200 SB,JSt,Multi,Hulk in Glenn
Talbots Brain 30.00
201 SB,JSt,V:Fake Conan 8.00
202 SB,JSt,A:Jarella........... 8.00
203 SB,JSt,A:Jarella........... 8.00
204 SB,JStI:Kronus 8.00
205 SB,JSt,D:Jarella.......... 8.00
206 SB,JSt,C:Dr.Strange 8.00
207 SB,JSt,A:Dr.Strange 8.00
208 SB,JSt,V:Absorbing Man 8.00
209 SB,JSt,V:Absorbing Man 8.00
210 SB,A:Dr.Druid,O:Merlin II 8.00
211 SB,A:Dr.Druid 8.00
212 SB,I:Constrictor 9.00
213 SB,TP,I:Quintronic Man 8.00
214 SB,Jack of Hearts 8.00
215 SB,V:Bi-Beast 7.00
216 SB,Gen.Ross............. 7.00
217 SB,I:Stilts,A:Ringmaster..... 7.00
218 SB,KP,Doc.Samson versus
Rhino................... 7.00
219 SB,V:Capt.Barravuda....... 7.00
220 SB,Robinson Crusoe 7.00
221 SB,AA,A:Sting Ray 7.00
222 JSn,AA,Cavern of Bones 7.00
223 SB,V:Leader 7.00
224 SB,V:The Leader.......... 7.00

Incredible Hulk #212
© Marvel Entertainment Group

225 SB,V:Leader,A:Doc.Samson... 7.00
226 SB,JSt,A:Doc.Samson....... 7.00
227 SB,JK,A:Doc.Samson 7.00
228 SB,BMc,I:Moonstone,V:Doc
Samson 10.00
229 SB,O:Moonstone,V:Doc
Samson 7.00
230 JM,BL,A:Bug Thing 7.00
231 SB,I:Fred Sloan 7.00
232 SB,A:Capt.America 7.00
233 SB,A:Marvel Man......... 7.00
234 SB,Marvel Man Changes name
to Quasar............... 7.00
235 SB,A:Machine Man 7.00
236 SB,A:Machine Man 7.00
237 SB,A:Machine Man 7.00
238 SB,JAb,Jimmy Carter....... 7.00
239 SB,I:Gold Bug 7.00
240 SB,Eldorado 7.00
241 SB,A:Tyrannus........... 7.00
242 SB,Eldorado 7.00
243 SB,A:Gammernon 7.00
244 SB,A:It................. 7.00
245 SB,A:Super Mandroid 7.00
246 SB,V:Capt.Marvel 7.00
247 SB,A:Bat Dragon 7.00
248 SB,V:Gardener 7.00
249 SD,R:Jack Frost 7.00
250 SB,A:Silver Surfer........ 12.00
251 MG,A,3-D Man........... 5.00
252 SB,A:Woodgod 5.00
253 SB,A:Woodgod 5.00
254 SB,I:U-Foes............. 5.00
255 SB,V:Thor 5.00
256 SB,I&O:Sabra 5.00
257 SB,I&O:Arabian Knight..... 5.00
258 I:Soviet Super Soldiers 5.00
259 SB,A:Soviet Super-Soldiers,
O:Darkstar 5.00
260 SB,Sugata 5.00
261 SB,V:Absorbing Man 5.00
262 SB,I:Glazer.............. 5.00
263 SB,Avalanche 5.00
264 SB,A:Corruptor 5.00
265 SB,I:Rangers 5.00
266 SB,V:High Evolutionary 5.00
267 SB,V:Rainbow,O:Glorian.... 5.00
268 SB,I:Pariah 5.00
269 SB,I:Bereet 5.00
270 SB,A:Abomination 5.00
271 SB,I:Rocket Raccoon,
20th Anniv............... 5.00
272 SB,C:X-Men,I:Wendigo III 6.00

All comics prices listed are for *Near Mint* condition.

Incredible Hulk

273 SB,A:Alpha Flight............ 5.00
274 SB,Beroct 5.00
275 SB,JSt,I:Megalith 5.00
276 SB,JSt,V:U-Foes 5.00
277 SB,JSt,V:U-Foes............. 5.00
278 SB,JSt,C:X-Men,
    Avengers,Fantastic Four...... 6.00
279 SB,JSt,C:X-Men,
    Avengers,Fantastic Four...... 6.00
280 SB,JSt,Jack Daw............ 5.00
281 SB,JSt,Trapped in Space..... 5.00
282 SB,JSt,A:She Hulk.......... 5.00
283 SB,JSt,A:Avengers 5.00
284 SB,JSt,A:Avengers 5.00
285 SB,JSt,Northwind,V:Zzzax ... 5.00
286 SB,JSt,V:Soldier 5.00
287 SB,JSt,V:Soldier 5.00
288 SB,JSt,V:Abomination 5.00
289 SB,JSt,V:Modok............. 5.00
290 SB,JSt,V:Modok............. 5.00
291 SB,JSt,V:Thunderbolt Ross ... 5.00
292 SB,JSt,V:Dragon Man 5.00
293 SB,V:Nightmare............. 5.00
294 SB,V:Boomerang............ 5.00
295 SB,V:Boomerang............ 5.00
296 SB,A:Rom 5.00
297 SB,V:Nightmare............. 5.00
298 KN(c),SB,V:Nightmare........ 5.00
299 SB,A:Shield 5.00
300 SB,A:Spider-Man,Avengers
    Doctor Strange............. 8.00
301 SB,Crossroads 4.00
302 SB,Crossroads 4.00
303 SB,V:The Knights 4.00
304 SB,V:U-Foes 4.00
305 SB,V:U-Foes 4.00
306 SB,V:Klaatu................. 4.00
307 SB,V:Klaatu................. 4.00
308 SB,V:Puffball Collective 4.00
309 SB,V:Goblin & Glow......... 4.00
310 Crossroads 4.00
311 Crossroads 4.00
312 Secret Wars II,O:Bruce 4.50
313 A:Alpha Flight 4.00
314 JBy,V:Doc.Samson 6.00
315 JBy,A:Doc.Samson,Banner
    & Hulk Separated............ 4.00
316 JBy,A:Avengers,N:Doc
    Samson 4.00
317 JBy,I:Hulkbusters,A:Doc
    Samson 4.00
318 JBy,A:Doc.Samson 4.00
319 JBy,W:Bruce & Betty 6.00
320 AM,A:Doc.Samson........... 3.00
321 AM,A:Avengers 3.00
322 AM,A:Avengers 3.00
323 AM,A:Avengers 3.00
324 AM,R:Grey Hulk(1st since #1),
    A:Doc.Samson............. 15.00
325 AM,Rick Jones as Hulk 6.00
326 A:Rick Jones,New Hulk 7.00
327 AM,F:General Ross 3.00
328 AM,1st PDd(s),Outcasts...... 7.00
329 AM,V:Enigma............... 5.00
330 1st TM Hulk,D:T-bolt Ross ... 20.00
331 TM,V:Leader 18.00
332 TM,V:Leader 15.00
333 TM,V:Leader 15.00
334 TM,I:Half-life 15.00
335 Horror Issue................. 5.00
336 TM,A:X-Factor 15.00
337 TM,A:X-Factor,
    A:Doc.Samson............. 15.00
338 TM,I:Mercy,V:Shield 15.00
339 TM,A:RickJones............ 15.00
340 TM,Hulk vs Wolverine 45.00
341 TM,V:Man Bull 8.00
342 TM,V:Leader 8.00
343 TM,V:Leader 8.00
344 TM,V:Leader 8.00
345 TM,V:Leader,Double-Size 9.00
346 TM,EL,L:Rick Jones......... 8.00
347 In Las Vegas,I:Marlo Chandler,
    V:Absorbing Man 4.00
348 V:Absorbing Man 4.00
349 A:Spider-Man............... 4.00
350 Hulk vs Thing,A:Beast
    V:Dr.Doom 5.00
351 R:Jarella's World 3.00
352 V:Inquisitor 3.00
353 R:Bruce Banner............. 3.00
354 V:Maggia 3.00
355 V:Glorian 3.00
356 V:Glorian,Cloot 3.00
357 V:Glorian,Cloot 3.00
358 V:Glorian,Cloot 3.00
359 JBy(c),C:Wolverine(illusion) ... 4.00
360 V:Nightmare & Dyspare 3.00
361 A:Iron Man,V:Maggia 3.00
362 V:Werewolf By Night 3.00
363 Acts of Vengeance........... 3.00
364 A:Abomination,B:Countdown . 3.00
365 A:Fantastic Four 3.00
366 A:Leader,I:Riot Squad 3.00
367 1st DK Hulk,I:Madman(Leader's
    brother),E:Countdown....... 10.00
368 SK,V:Mr.Hyde 5.00
369 DK,V:Freedom Force 3.00

Incredible Hulk #369
© Marvel Entertainment Group

370 DK,R:Original Defenders 3.00
371 DK,BMc,A:Orig.Defenders 3.00
372 DK,R:Green Hulk........... 10.00
373 DK,Green Hulk & Grey Hulk... 4.00
374 DK,BMc,Skrulls,
    R:Rick Jones 4.00
375 DK,BMc,V:Super Skrull 4.00
376 DK,BMc,Green Hulk,Grey
    Hulk & Banner fight 5.00
377 DK,BMc,New Green Hulk,
    combination of green, grey, and
    Bruce Banner,A:Ringmaster .. 12.00
377a 2nd printing (gold) 5.00
378 V:Rhino,Christmas Issue 3.00
379 DK,MFm,I:Pantheon 4.00
380 A:Nick Fury,D:Crazy-8 .... 3.00
381 DK,MFm,Hulk,J:Pantheon 4.00
382 DK,MFm,A:Pantheon........ 4.00
383 DK,MFm,Infinity Gauntlet 4.00
384 DK,MFm,Infinity Gauntlet 4.00
385 DK,MFm,Infinity Gauntlet..... 4.00
386 DK,MFm,V:Sabra,A:Achilles... 4.00
387 DK,MFm,V:Sabra,A:Achilles... 4.00
388 DK,MFm,I:Speed Freak,Jim
    Wilson,revealed to have AIDS . 5.00
389 1st Comic art By Gary Barker
    (Garfield),A:Man-Thing,Glob... 4.00
390 DK,MFm,B:War & Pieces,
    C:X-Factor 4.00
391 DK,MFm,V:X-Factor.......... 4.00
392 DK,MFm,E:War & Pieces,
    A:X-Factor 4.00
393 DK,MFm,R:Igor,A:Soviet Super
    Soldiers,30th Ann.,Green foil(c) 6.00
393a 2nd printing,Silver 2.50
394 MFm(i),F:Atalanta,I:Trauma ... 3.00
395 DK,MFm,A:Punisher,
    I:Mr.Frost 3.00
396 DK,MFm,A:Punisher,
    V:Mr.Frost 3.00
397 DK,MFm,B:Ghost of the
    Past,V:U-Foes,A:Leader...... 3.00
398 DK,MFm,D:Marlo,V:Leader ... 3.00
399 JD,A:FF,Dr.Strange 3.00
400 JD,MFm,E:Ghost of the Past,
    V:Leader,1st Holo-grafx(c),1st
    GFr Hulk(pin-up) 3.50
400a 2nd Printing 3.00
401 JDu,O:Agememnon 3.00
402 JDu,V:Juggernaut 3.00
403 GFr,V:Red Skull,A:Avengers .. 3.00
404 GFr,V:Red Skull,Juggernaut,
    A:Avengers 3.50
405 GFr,Ajax vs. Achilles 3.00
406 GFr,V:Captain America 3.00
407 GFr,I:Piecemeal,A:Madman,
    B:O:Ulysses 3.00
408 GFr,V:Madman,Piecemeal,
    D:Perseus,A:Motormouth,
    Killpower 3.00
409 GFr,A:Motormouth,Killpower,
    V:Madman 3.00
410 GFr,A:Nick Fury,S.H.I.E.L.D.,
    Margo agrees to marry Rick ... 3.00
411 GFr,V:Nick Fury,S.H.I.E.L.D.... 3.00
412 PaP,V:Bi-Beast,A:She-Hulk ... 3.00
413 GFr,CaS,B:Troyjan War,
    I:Cassiopea,Armageddon,
    V:Trauma 3.00
414 GFr,CaS,V:Trauma,C:S.Surfer . 3.00
415 GFr,CaS,V:Trauma,A:Silver
    Surfer,Starjammers.......... 3.00
416 GFr,CaS,E:Troyjan War,D:Trauma,
    A:S.Surfer,Starjammers 3.00
417 GFr,CaS,Rick's/Marlo's Bachelor/
    Bachelorette Party 3.00
418 GFr,CaS,W:Rick & Marlo,
    A:Various Marvel persons,
    Die Cut(c)................. 3.00
418a Newsstand ed.............. 2.50
419 CaS,V:Talos................. 3.00
420 GFr,CaS,AIDS Story,
    D:Jim Wilson 3.00
421 CaS,B:Myth Conceptions 3.00
422 GFr,Myth Conceptions,pt.2.... 3.00
423 GFr,CaS,Myth Concept.,pt.3 ... 3.00
424 B:Fall of the Hammer......... 3.00
425 Regular edition 3.00
425a Enhanced cover............ 4.00
426 PDa,LSh,R:Mercy........... 3.00
426a Deluxe edition 3.00
427 A:Man-Thing 3.00
427a Deluxe edition 3.00
428 Suffer The Children 3.00
429 Abortion Issue 3.00
430 A:Speed Freak.............. 3.00
431 PDa,LSh R:Abomination 3.00
432 V:Abomination 3.00
433 PDd,V:Abomination 3.00
434 Funeral of the Year 3.00
435 Hulk vs. Rhino baseball 3.50
436 PDd,AMe,Ghosts of the
    Future,pt.1................. 3.00
437 PDd,AMe,Ghosts of the
    Future,pt.2................. 3.00
438 PDd,AMe,Ghosts of the
    Future,pt.3................. 3.00
439 PDd,AMe,Ghosts of the

CVA Page 252   All comics prices listed are for *Near Mint* condition.

MARVEL

Incredible Hulk–Infinity

Future,pt.4 .... 3.00
440 PDd,AMe. 3.00
441 PDd,AMe,A:She-Hulk. 3.00
442 A:Molecule Man, She-Hulk. ... 3.00
443 Janis 3.00
444 Onslaught saga, V:Cable 4.50
445 Onslaught saga 4.00
446 Blamed for loss of Fantastic
    Four and Avengers 3.00
447 PDd,MD2,F:The Unleashed
    Hulk 4.00
447a Variant Tank Smashing cover . 7.50
448 PDd,MD2,V:The Pantheon 3.00
449 PDd,MD2,I:Thunderbolts 10.00
450 PDd,MD2,F:Doctor Strange,
    56pg. 6.00
451 PDd,MD2, ... 3.00
452 PDd,MD2, ... 3.00
453 PDd,MD2,V:Future Hulk. 3.00
454 PDd,AKu,MFm,A God,
    In Savage Land 3.00
455 PDd,AKu,MFm,in X-Mansion .. 3.00
456 PDd,AKu,MFm,A:Apocalypse. .. 3.00
457 PDd,Hulk vs. Juggernaut 3.00
458 PDd,AKu,MFm,V:Mercy 3.00
459 PDd,AKu,MFm,V:Abomination . 3.00
460 PDa,AKu,MFm, Return of Bruce
    Banner 3.00
461 PDa,V:Thunderbolt Ross 3.00
462 PDa,AKu,MFm,V:Thunderbolt
    Ross 3.00
463 PDa,AKu,MFm,V:Thunderbolt
    Ross 3.00
464 PDa,AKu,MFm,V:Troygens
    & Silver Surfer 3.00
465 PDa,MFm,Poker game. 3.00
466 PDa,AKu,MFm,tragic loss 5.00
467 PDa,AKu,MFm,Hulk attempts
    suicide 5.00
468 JoC,new direction 2.50
469 JoC,LMa,F:Super-Adaptoid ... 3.00
470 JoC,NMa,V:Ringmaster
    & Circus of Crime 2.50
471 JoC,NMa,Circus of
    Crime,concl. 2.50
472 JoC,Great Astonishment,pt.1 . 2.50
473 JoC,Great Astonishment,pt.2 . 2.50
474 JoC,Great Astonishment,pt.3 . 4.00
Spec.#1 A:Inhumans (1968) ... 125.00
Spec.#2 rep.O:Hulk,A:Leader
    (1969) 75.00
Spec.#3 rep.A:Leader (1971) ... 25.00
Spec.#4 IR:Hulk/Banner (1972). . 20.00
Ann.#5 V:Xemnu,Diablo (1976)... 12.00

Incredible Hulk King Size Ann. #5
© Marvel Entertainment Group

Ann.#6 HT,A:Dr.Strange,I:Paragon
    (Her) (1977) 12.00
Ann.#7 JBy,BL,A:Angel,Iceman
    A:Doc.Samson (1978) 12.00
Ann.#8 Alpha Flight (1979) 12.00
Ann.#9 Checkmate (1980) 6.00
Ann.#10 A:Captain Universe (1981) 6.00
Ann.#11 RB,JSt,A:Spider-Man,
    Avengers,V:Unis (1982) 5.00
Ann.#12 (1983). 4.00
Ann.#13 (1984). 4.00
Ann.#14 JBy,SB (1985) 4.00
Ann.#15 V:Abomination (1986) ... 4.00
Ann.#16 HT,Life Form #3,
    A:Mercy (1990). 4.00
Ann.#17 Subterran.Odyssey #2
    (1991) 4.00
Ann #18 KM,TA,TC(1st Work),Return
    of the Defenders,Pt.1 (1992). . 7.00
Ann.#19 I:Lazarus,w/card (1993) . 4.00
Ann.#20 SvL,SI (1994) 4.00
Ann.'98 F:Hulk&Sub-Mariner, 48pg. 3.00
Ann. Hulk 1999. .... 3.50
Marvel Milestone rep. #1 (1991) . . 3.00
G-Size#1 rep. Greatest Foes 10.00
Minus 1 Spec., PDd,AKu,MFm,
    flashback 3.00
Spec. '97 Onslaught aftermath 3.00
Spec. Incredible Hulk
    vs. Superman, 48-pg. 6.00
Spec. Hulk vs. Superman, signed . 20.00
Milestone #181, F:Wolverine. 3.00
Hulk vs. Thing, rep. 4.00
TPB Ground Zero rep.#340-#345 . 12.95
TPB Future Imperfect, PDd,GP,
    96pg. 12.00
TPB Ghosts of the Past,
    rep. #396–#400 .... 12.00
TPB Transformations, 176pg. 12.00
TPB Beauty and the Beast 17.00

INCREDIBLE HULK: FUTURE IMPERFECT
1993
1 GP,V:Maestro 10.00
2 GP,V:Maestro 8.00
TPB Rep. 12.95

INCREDIBLE HULK MEGAZINE
TPB six stories, 96pg. 4.00

INCREDIBLE HULK/PITT
1997
Spec. PDd,DK,x-over 6.00

INCREDIBLE HULK VS. WOLVERINE
Oct., 1986
1 HT,rep. #181 B:,V:Wolverine. . . 12.00
1a 2nd printing 4.00

INDEPENDENCE DAY
1996
0 .... 5.00
1 .... 2.50
2 .... 2.50
TPB rep. #0–#2, 96pg 6.95

[Further Adventures of] INDIANA JONES
Jan., 1983
1 JBy/TA 3.00
2 JBy/TA 2.50

Indiana Jones #5
© Marvel Entertainment Group

3 .... 2.50
4 KGa 2.50
5 KGa 2.50
6 HC/TA 2.50
7 thru 24 KGa .... @2.50
25 SD,What Lurks Within the Tomb 2.50
26 SD. 2.50
27 SD. 2.50
28 SD. 2.50
29 SD. 2.50
30 SD. 2.50
31 SD,The Summit Meeting 2.50
32 SD,Fly the Friendly Skies. ... 2.50
33 SD. 2.50
34 SD, March, 1986 .... 2.50

INDIANA JONES AND THE LAST CRUSADE
1 B&W,Mag.,movie adapt, 1989. . . 3.00
[Mini-Series], 1989
1 Rep., Movie adapt., 1989. ..... 3.50
2 Rep., Movie adapt. 3.50
3 Rep., Movie adapt. 3.50
4 Rep., Movie adapt. 3.50

INDIANA JONES AND THE TEMPLE OF DOOM
1984
1 Movie adapt. 3.00
2 Movie adapt. 3.00
3 Movie adapt. 3.00

INFINITY ABYSS
June, 2002
1 (of 6) JSn,AM,V:Thanos 3.00
2 JSn,AM,F:Adam Warlock 3.00
3 JSn,AM,Spider-Man,Capt.Marvel 3.00
4 JSn,AM,Eternity & Infinity 3.00
5 JSn,AM 3.00
6 48-pg. 3.50
TPB JSn, rep. 18.00

INFINITY CRUSADE
1993
1 RLm,AM,I:Goddess,A:Marvel
    Heroes,foil(c) 4.00
2 RLm,AM,V:Goddess 3.00
3 RLm,AM,V:Goddess,Mephisto . . 3.00
4 RLm,AM,V:Goddess,A:Magnus . 3.00

Infinity–Iron Man / MARVEL / Comics Values Annual

5 RLm,AM,V:Goddess 3.00
6 RLm,AM,V:Goddess 3.00

INFINITY GAUNTLET
July, 1991
1 GP,O:Infinity Gauntlet 5.00
2 GP,JRu,2nd Rebirth:Warlock . . . 4.00
3 GP,JRu,I:Terraxia 4.00
4 GP,JRu,RLm,V:Thanos 4.00
5 JRu,RLm,V:Thanos,D:Terraxia . 4.00
6 RLm,JRu,V:Nebula 4.00
TPB rep. #1 thru #6 . . . . 24.95
TPB GP,rep. #1-#6 (2002) 24.95

INFINITY WAR
1992
1 RLm,AM,R:Magus,Thanos 5.00
2 RLm,AM,V:Magus,A:Everyone . . 3.00
3 RLm,AM,V:Magus,A:Everyone . . 2.50
4 RLm,AM,Magus gets Gauntlet . 2.50
5 RLm,AM,V:Magus 2.50
6 RLm,AM,V:Magus 2.50

INHUMANOIDS
Star, Jan.–July, 1987
1 Hasbro Toy 3.00
2 O:Inhumanoids 3.00
3 V:D'Compose 3.00
4 A:Sandra Shore 3.00

INHUMANS
Oct., 1975
1 GP,V:Blastaar 20.00
2 GP,V:Blastaar 10.00
3 GP,I:Kree S 15.00
4 GK,Maximus 15.00
5 GK,V:Maximus 15.00
6 GK,Maximus 15.00
7 GK,DP,I:Skorrn 15.00
8 GP,DP,Skorrn 15.00
9 rep., V:Mor-Tog 15.00
10 KP,D:Warkon 15.00
11 KP,JM,I:Pursuer 15.00
12 KP,Hulk 15.00
Spec.#1(The Untold Saga),
 O:Inhumans 4.00
Spec. Atlantis Rising story 2.95

INHUMANS
Sept., 1998
1 (of 12) PJe,JaL,F:Black Bolt,
 Medusa, Karnak, Triton, Gorgon,
 Crystal, Lockjaw 9.00
2 PJe,JaL,F:Tonaje 4.00
2a Variant cover 3.00
3 PJe,JaL,Attilan's dark side 3.00
4 PJe,JaL,War against Attilan . . . 3.00
5 PJe,JaL,Earth vs. Attilan 3.00
6 PJe,JaL,V:Maximus 3.00
7 PJe,JaL,F:Black Bolt 3.00
8 PJe,JaL,F:Lockjaw 3.00
9 PJe,JaL,F:Triton 3.00
10 PJe,JaL,F:Woz & Medusa . . . 3.00
11 PJe,JaL,F:Black Bolt 3.00
12 PJe,JaL,concl. 3.00
TPB 264pg. 24.95

INHUMANS
Apr. 2000
1 (of 4) V:Ronan the Accuser 3.00
2 A:Kree 3.00
3 Maximus the Mad 3.00
4 concl. 3.00

INHUMANS
Marvel May 2003
1 Lunar,pt.1 . . . . 2.50
2 Lunar,pt.2 . . . . 2.50
3 Lunar,pt.3 . . . . 2.50
4 Culture Shock,pt.1 . . . . 2.50
5 Culture Shock,pt.2 . . . . 2.50
6 Culture Shock,pt.3 . . . . 2.50
7 . . . . 2.50

INTERFACE
Epic, Dec., 1989
1 ESP 2.50
2 thru 7 . . . . @2.25
8 . . . . 2.25

INVADERS
Aug., 1975
1 FR,JR(c),A:Invaders,
 A:Mastermind 50.00
2 FR,JR(c),I:Brain Drain 20.00
3 FR,JR(c),I:U-Man 20.00
4 FR,O&V:U-Man 20.00
5 RB,JM,V:Red Skull 20.00
6 FR,V:Liberty Legion 15.00
7 FR,I:Baron Blood,
 1st Union Jack 15.00
8 FR,FS,J:Union Jack 15.00
9 FR,FS,O:Baron Blood 15.00
10 FR,FS,rep.Captain
 America Comics #22 . . . . . . 15.00
11 FR,FS,I:Blue Bullet 10.00
12 FR,FS,I:Spitfire 10.00
13 FR,FS,GK(c),I:Golem,
 Half Face 10.00
14 FR,FS,JK(c),I:Crusaders 10.00
15 FR,FS,JK(c),V:Crusaders . . . 10.00
16 FR,JK(c),V:Master Man 10.00
17 FR,FS,GK(c),I:Warrior Woman . 10.00
18 FR,FS,GK(c),R:1st Destroyer . . 10.00
19 FR,FS,V:Adolph Hitler 10.00
20 FR,FS,GK(c),I&J:2nd Union Jack,
 BU:rep.Marvel Comics #1 . . . 15.00
21 FR,FS,GK(c),BU:rep.Marvel
 Mystery #10 . . . . 9.00
22 FR,FS,GK(c),O:Toro 8.00
23 FR,FS,GK(c),I:Scarlet Scarab . 8.00
24 FR,FS,GK(c),rep.Marvel
 Mystery #17 . . . . 9.00
25 FR,FS,GK(c),V:Scarlet Scarab . 8.00
26 FR,FS,GK(c),V:Axis Agent 8.00
27 FR,FS,GK(c),V:Axis Agent 8.00
28 FR,FS,I:2nd Human Top,
 Golden Girl,Kid Commandos . . 8.00
29 FR,FS,I:Teutonic Knight 8.00
30 FR,FS,V:Teutonic Knight 8.00
31 FR,FS,V:Frankenstein 8.00
32 FR,FS,JK(c),A:Thor 10.00
33 FR,FS,JK(c),A:Thor 10.00
34 FR,FS,V:Master Man 8.00
35 FR,FS,I:Iron Cross 8.00
36 FR,FS,O:Iron Cross 8.00
37 FR,FS,V:Iron Cross 8.00
38 FR,FS,V:Lady Lotus 8.00
39 FR,FS,O:Lady Lotus 8.00
40 FR,FS,V:Baron Blood 8.00
41 E:RTs(s)FR,FS,V:Super Axis,
 double-size 10.00
Ann.#1 A:Avengers,R:Shark 10.00
G-Size#1 FR,rep.Submariner #1 . . 10.00

[Limited Series], 1993
1 R:Invaders 2.50
2 V:Battle Axis 2.50
3 R:Original Vison (1950's) 2.50
4 V:The Axis 2.50

IRON FIST
Nov., 1975
1 JBy,A:Iron Man 50.00
2 JBy,V:H'rythl 30.00
3 JBy,KP,KJ,V:Ravager 20.00
4 JBy,V:Radion 20.00
5 JBy,V:Scimitar 20.00
6 JBy,O:Misty Knight 20.00
7 JBy,V:Khimbala Bey 20.00
8 JBy,V:Chaka 20.00
9 JBy,V:Chaka 20.00
10 JBy,DGr,A:Chaka 20.00
11 JBy,V:Wrecking Crew 20.00
12 JBy,DGr,V:Captain America . . 20.00
13 JBy,A:Boomerang 20.00
14 JBy,I:Sabretooth 150.00
15 JBy,A&N:Wolverine,A:X-Men
 Sept., 1977 . . . . 60.00
Marvel Milestone rep. #14 (1992) . . 4.00

IRON FIST
May, 1998
1 (of 3) DJu,JG, from Heroes For
 Hire 2.50
2 DJu,JG,search for Scorpio Key,
 V:S.H.I.E.L.D. 2.50
3 DJu,JG,concl. 2.50

IRON FIST/WOLVERINE
Sept., 2000
1 (of 4) F:DannyRand,Junzo Moto . 3.00
2 K'un L'un 3.00
3 A:Capt.America,Dragon Kings . . . 3.00
4 concl. 3.00

IRON MAN
May, 1968
1 B:StL,AGw(s),JCr,GC,
 I:Mordius 600.00
2 JCr,I:Demolisher 200.00
3 JCr,V:The Freak 125.00
4 JCr,A:Unicorn 100.00
5 JCr,GT,I:Cerebos 90.00
6 JCr,GT,V:Crusher 75.00
7 JCr,GT,V:Gladiator 75.00
8 JCr,GT,O:Whitney Frost 75.00
9 JCr,GT,A:Mandarin 75.00
10 JCr,GT,V:Mandarin 75.00
11 JCr,GT,V:Mandarin 60.00
12 JCr,GT,I:Controller 60.00
13 JCr,GT,A:Nick Fury 60.00
14 JCr,V:Night Phantom 60.00

Invaders #17
© Marvel Entertainment Group

CVA Page 254 — All comics prices listed are for *Near Mint* condition.

MARVEL — Iron Man

Iron Man #11
© Marvel Entertainment Group

Iron Man #126
© Marvel Entertainment Group

#	Description	Price
15	JCr,GT,A:Red Ghost	60.00
16	JCr,GT,V:Unicorn	50.00
17	JCr,GT,I:Madam Masque, Midas	50.00
18	JCr,GT,V:Madame Masque	50.00
19	JCr,GT,V:Madame Masque	50.00
20	JCr,I:Charlie Gray	50.00
21	JCr,I:Eddie	35.00
22	JCr,D:Janice Cord	35.00
23	JCr,I:Mercenary	38.00
24	JCr,GT,V:Madame Masque	35.00
25	JCr,A:Sub-Mariner	38.00
26	JCr,DH,J:Val-Larr	35.00
27	JCr,DH,I:Firebrand	35.00
28	E:AGw(s),JCr,DH,V:Controller	35.00
29	B:StL,AyB(s),DH,V:Myrmidon	35.00
30	DH,I:Monster Master	35.00
31	DH,I:Mastermind	35.00
32	GT,I:Mechanoid	35.00
33	DH,I:Spy Master	35.00
34	DH,A:Spy Master	35.00
35	DH,A:Daredevil,Spy Master	35.00
36	E:AyB(s),DH,I:Ramrod	35.00
37	DH,A:Ramrod	35.00
38	GT,Jonah	35.00
39	HT,I:White Dragon	30.00
40	GT,A:White Dragon	30.00
41	GT,JM,I:Slasher	30.00
42	GT,I:Mikas	30.00
43	GT,JM,A:Mikas,I:Guardsmen	30.00
44	GT,A:Capt.America	30.00
45	GT,A:Guardsman	30.00
46	GT,D:Guardsman	30.00
47	BS,JM,O:Iron Man	35.00
48	GT,V:Firebrand	20.00
49	GT,V:Adaptoid	20.00
50	B:RTs(s),GT,V:Prin.Python	20.00
51	GT,C:Capt.America	20.00
52	GT,I:Raga	20.00
53	GT,JSn,I:Black Lama	20.00
54	GT,BEv,Sub-Mariner,I:Madame MacEvil (Moondragon)	40.00
55	JSn,I:Destroyer,Thanos,Mentor Starfox(Eros),Blood Bros.	125.00
56	JSn,I:Fangor	30.00
57	GT,R:Mandarin	20.00
58	GT,V:Mandarin	20.00
59	GT,A:Firebrand	20.00
60	GT,C:Daredevil	20.00
61	GT,Marauder	20.00
62	whiplash	20.00
63	GT,A:Dr.Spectrum	20.00
64	GT,I:Rokk	20.00
65	GT,O:Dr.Spectrum	20.00
66	GT,V:Thor	20.00
67	GT,V:Freak	20.00
68	GT,O:Iron Man	16.00
69	GT,V:Mandarin	14.00
70	GT,A:Sunfire	14.00
71	GT,V:Yellow Claw	12.00
72	E:RTs(s),GT,V:Black Lama	12.00
73	B:LWn(s),KP,JM,V:Titanic Three	12.00
74	KP,V:Modok	12.00
75	V:Black Lama	12.00
76	Rep., A:Hulk	12.00
77	V:Thinker	12.00
78	GT,V:Viet Cong	12.00
79	GT,I:Quasar(not Current one)	12.00
80	JK(c),O:Black Lama	12.00
81	A:Black Lama	11.00
82	MSe,A:Red Ghost	11.00
83	E:LWn(s),HT,MSe,Red Ghost	11.00
84	HT,A:Dr.Ritter	11.00
85	HT,MSe,A:Freak	11.00
86	B:MWn(s),GT,I:Blizzard	11.00
87	GT,V:Blizzard	11.00
88	E:MWn(s),GT,V:Blood Brothers	11.00
89	GT,A:D.D.,Blood Bros.	11.00
90	JK(c),GT,Controller,A:Thanos	12.00
91	GT,BL,A:Controller	10.00
92	JK(c),GT,V:Melter	10.00
93	JK(c),HT,V:Kraken	10.00
94	JK(c),HT,V:Kraken	10.00
95	JK(c),GT,PP,V:Ultimo	10.00
96	GT,DP,V:Ultimo	10.00
97	GT,DP,I:Guardsman II	10.00
98	GT,DP,A:Sunfire	10.00
99	GT,V:Mandarin	10.00
100	JSn(c),GT,V:Mandarin	25.00
101	GT,I:Dread Knight	14.00
102	GT,O:Dread Knight	14.00
103	GT,V:Jack of Hearts	14.00
104	GT,V:Midas	9.00
105	GT,V:Midas	9.00
106	GT,V:Midas	9.00
107	KP,V:Midas	9.00
108	CI,A:Growing Man	9.00
109	JBy(c),CI,V:Van Guard	9.00
110	KP,I:C.Arcturus	9.00
111	KP,O:Rigellians	9.00
112	AA,KP,V:Punisher from Beyond	9.00
113	KP,HT,V:Unicorn,Spy Master	10.00
114	KG,I:Arsenal	9.00
115	JR2,O:Unicorn,V:Ani-men	9.00
116	JR2,BL,V:Madame Masque	9.00
117	BL,JR2,1st Romita Jr	10.00
118	JBy,BL,A:Nick Fury	10.00
119	BL,JR2,Alcoholic Plot	10.00
120	JR2,BL,A:Sub-Mariner,I:Rhodey(becomes War Machine),Justin Hammer	10.00
121	BL,JR2,A:Submariner	9.00
122	DC,CI,BL,O:Iron Man	9.00
123	BL,JR2,V:Blizzard	9.00
124	BL,JR2,A:Capt.America	7.00
125	BL,JR2,A:Ant-Man	7.00
126	BL,JR2,V:Hammer	7.00
127	BL,JR2,Battlefield	7.00
128	BL,JR2,Alcohol	9.00
129	SB,A:Dread Night	7.00
130	BL,V:Digital Devil	7.00
131	BL,V:Hulk	7.00
132	BL,V:Hulk	7.00
133	BL,A:Hulk,Ant-Man	7.00
134	BL,V:Titanium Man	7.00
135	BL,V:Titanium Man	7.00
136	V:Endotherm	7.00
137	BL,Fights oil rig fire	7.00
138	BL,Dreadnought,Spymaster	7.00
139	BL,Dreadnought,Spymaster	7.00
140	BL,V:Force	7.00
141	BL,JR2,V:Force	7.00
142	BL,JR2,Space Armor	7.00
143	BL,JR2,V:Sunturion	7.00
144	BL,JR2,Sunturion,O:Rhodey	7.00
145	BL,JR2,A:Raiders	7.00
146	BL,JR2,I:Black Lash	7.00
147	BL,JR2,V:Black Lash	6.00
148	BL,JR2,V:Terrorists	6.00
149	BL,JR2,V:Dr.Doom	6.00
150	BL,JR2,V:Dr.Doom,Dble	8.00
151	TA,BL,A:Ant-Man	4.00
152	BL,JR2,New Armor	4.00
153	BL,JR2,V:Living Laser	4.00
154	BL,JR2,V:Unicorn	4.00
155	JR2,V:Back-Getters	4.00
156	JR2,I:Mauler	4.00
157	V:Spores	4.00
158	CI,AM,Iron Man Drowning	4.00
159	PS,V:Diablo	4.00
160	SD,V:Serpent'sSquad	4.00
161	A:Moon Knight	4.00
162	V:Space Ships	4.00
163	V:Chessmen	4.00
164	LMc,A:Bishop	4.00
165	LMc,Meltdown	4.00
166	LMc,V:Melter	4.00
167	LMc,Alcoholic Issue	4.00
168	LMc,A:Machine Man	4.00
169	LMc,B:Rhodey as 2nd Iron Man	10.00
170	LMc,2nd Iron Man	8.00
171	LMc,2nd Iron Man	3.00
172	LMc,V:Firebrand	3.00
173	LMc,Stane International	3.00
174	LMc,Alcoholism	3.50
175	LMc,Alcoholism	3.50
176	LMc,Alcoholism	3.50
177	LMc,Alcoholism	3.00
178	LMc,V:Wizard	3.00
179	LMc,V:Mandarin	3.00
180	LMc,V:Mandarin	3.00
181	LMc,V:Mandarin	3.00
182	LMc,Secret Wars	3.00
183	LMc,Turning Point	3.00
184	LMc,Moves to California	3.00
185	LMc,V:Zodiac Field	3.00
186	LMc,I:Vibro	3.00
187	LMc,V:Vibro	3.00
188	LMc,I:New Brother's Grimm	3.00
189	LMc,I:Termite	3.00
190	LMc,O:Termite,A:Scar.Witch	3.00
191	LMc,New Grey Armor	5.00

All comics prices listed are for Near Mint condition.

Iron Man — MARVEL — Comics Values Annual

- 192 LMc,V:Iron Man(Tony Stark)... 5.00
- 193 LMc,V:Dr.Demonicus 3.00
- 194 LMc,I:Scourge,A:West Coast Avengers 3.00
- 195 LMc,A:Shaman 3.00
- 196 LMc,V:Dr.Demonicus 3.00
- 197 LMc,Secret Wars II 3.00
- 198 SB,V:Circuit Breaker 3.00
- 199 LMc,E:Rhodey as 2nd Iron Man, V:Obadiah Stone 3.00
- 200 LMc,D:Obadiah Stone 6.00
- 201 MBr,V:Madam Masque........ 3.00
- 202 A:Ka-Zar 3.00
- 203 MBr,A:Hank Pym 3.00
- 204 MBr,V:Madame Masque 3.00
- 205 MBr,V:A.I.M. 3.00
- 206 MBr,V:Goliath 3.00
- 207 MBr,When the Sky Rains Fire . 3.00
- 208 MBr,V:A.I.M. 3.00
- 209 V:Living Laser 3.00
- 210 MBr,V:Morgan LeFey 3.00
- 211 AS,V:Living Laser............ 3.00
- 212 DT,V:Iron Monger............ 3.00
- 213 A:Dominic Fortune 3.00
- 214 A:Spider-Woman 3.00
- 215 BL,A.I.M. 3.00
- 216 BL,MBr,D:Clymenstra. 3.00
- 217 BL,MRr,V:Hammer........... 3.00
- 218 BL,MBr,Titanic 3.00
- 219 BL,V:The Ghost.............. 3.00
- 220 BL,MBr,V:The Ghost, D:Spymaster 3.00
- 221 BL,MBr,V:The Ghost 3.00
- 222 BL,MBr,R:Abrogast 3.00
- 223 BL,MBr,V:Blizzard,Beetle.... 3.00
- 224 BL,V:Justin Hammer,Force... 3.00
- 225 BL,MBr,B:Armor Wars 5.00
- 226 BL,MBr,V:Stingray 4.50
- 227 BL,MBr,V:Mandroids, ... 4.00
- 228 BL,MBr,V:Guardsmen 4.00
- 229 BL,D:Titanium Man 4.00
- 230 V:Firepower................... 4.00
- 231 V:Firepower,N:Iron Man 4.00
- 232 BWS,Nightmares,E:Armor Wars 4.50
- 233 JG,BL,A:Ant-Man. 2.50
- 234 JG,BL,A:Spider-Man 3.00
- 235 JG,BL,V:Grey Gargoyle 2.50
- 236 JG,BL,V:Grey Gargoyle 2.50
- 237 JG,BL,V:SDI Monster........ 2.50
- 238 JG,BL,V:Rhino,D:M.Masque.. 2.50
- 239 JG,BL,R:Ghost 2.50
- 240 JG,BL,V:Ghost............... 2.50
- 241 BL,V:Mandarin 2.50
- 242 BL,BWS,V:Mandarin 3.00
- 243 BL,BWS,Stark Paralyzed 3.00
- 244 BL,V:Fixer,A:Force,double-size 5.00
- 245 BL(c),V:Dreadnaughts 2.50
- 246 BL,HT,V:A.I.M.,Maggia 2.50
- 247 BL,A:Hulk 2.50
- 248 BL,Tony Stark Cured 2.50
- 249 BL,V:Dr.Doom 2.50
- 250 BL,V:Dr.Doom,A of V 3.00
- 251 HT,AM,V:Wrecker,A of V ... 2.50
- 252 HT,AM,V:Chemistro,A of V .. 2.50
- 253 BL,V:Slagmire 2.50
- 254 BL,V:Spymaster.............. 2.50
- 255 HT,V:Devestator I:2nd Spymaster............. 2.50
- 256 JR2,V:Space Station 2.50
- 257 V:Samurai Steel............... 2.50
- 258 JR2,BWi,B:Armor Wars II,V: Titanium Man 2.50
- 259 JR2,BWi,V:Titanium Man 2.50
- 260 JR2,BWi,V:Living Laser 2.50
- 261 JR2,BWi,V:Mandarin 2.50
- 262 JR2,BWi,A:Mandarin 2.50
- 263 JR2,BWi,A:Wonderman, V:Living Laser 2.50
- 264 JR2,BWi,V:Mandarin 2.50
- 265 JR2,BWi,V:Dewitt............. 2.50

Iron Man #328
© Marvel Entertainment Group

- 266 JR2,BWi,E:Armor Wars II..... 2.50
- 267 PR,BWi,B:New O:Iron Man, Mandarin,V:Vibro 2.50
- 268 PR,BWi,E:New O:Iron Man... 2.50
- 269 PR,BWi,A:Black Widow 2.50
- 270 PR,BWi,V:Fin Fang Foom ... 2.50
- 271 PR,BWi,V:Fin Fang Foom ... 2.50
- 272 PR,BWi,O:Mandarin.......... 2.50
- 273 PR,BWi,V:Mandarin 2.50
- 274 MBr,BWi,V:Mandarin 2.50
- 275 PR,BWi,A:Mandarin,Fin Fang Foom, double-size 4.00
- 276 PR,BWi,A:Black Widow 2.50
- 277 PR,BWi,A:Black Widow 2.50
- 278 BWi,Galactic Storm,pt.6 A:Capt.America,V:Shatterax .. 2.50
- 279 BWi,Galactic Storm,pt.13, V:Ronan,A:Avengers 2.50
- 280 KHd,V:The Stark 2.50
- 281 KHd,I&V:Masters of Silence, C:War Machine Armor 4.00
- 282 KHd,I:War Machine Armor, V:Masters of Silence......... 4.00
- 283 KHd,V:Masters of Silence ... 2.50
- 284 KHd,Stark put under Cryogenic Freeze,B:Rhodey as Iron Man . 3.50
- 285 KHd,BWi(i),Tony's Funeral ... 2.50
- 286 KHd,V:Avengers West Coast .. 2.50
- 287 KHd,I:New Atom Smasher ... 2.50
- 288 KHd,30th Anniv.,V:Atom Smasher,foil(c)............... 4.50
- 289 KHd,V:Living Laser, R:Tony Stark 2.50
- 290 KHd,30th Anniv.,N:Iron Man, Gold foil(c).................. 5.00
- 291 KHd,E:Rhodey as Iron Man, Becomes War Machine....... 2.50
- 292 KHd,Tony reveals he is alive .. 2.50
- 293 KHd,V:Controller 2.50
- 294 KHd,Infinity Crusade 2.50
- 295 KHd,Infinity Crusade 2.50
- 296 KHd,V:Modam,A:Omega Red.. 2.50
- 297 KHd,V:Modam,Omega Red ... 2.50
- 298 KHd(c),I:Earth Mover 2.50
- 299 KHd(c),R:Ultimo.............. 2.50
- 300 KHd,TMo,N:Iron Man,I:Iron Legion, A:War Machine,V:Ultimo Foil(c) 5.00
- 300a Newsstand ed................ 2.75
- 301 KHd,B:Crash and Burn, A:Deathlok,C:Venom 2.50
- 302 KHd,V:Venom 2.50
- 303 KHd,V:New Warriors, C:Thundrstrike 2.50
- 304 KHd,C:Hulk,V:New Warriors, Thundrstrike,N:Iron Man...... 2.50
- 305 KHd,V:Hulk,................... 2.50
- 306 KHd,E:Stark Enterprise 2.50
- 307 TMo,I:Vor/Tex,R:Mandarin ... 2.50
- 308 TMo,Vor/Tex 2.50
- 309 TMo,Vor/Tex 2.50
- 310 regular...................... 3.00
- 310a Neon(c),with insert print..... 3.50
- 311 V:Mandarin 2.50
- 312 double-size 3.00
- 313 LKa,TMo,AA Meeting........ 2.50
- 314 LKa,TMo,new villain......... 2.50
- 315 A:Black Widow............... 2.50
- 316 I:Slag,A:Crimson Dynamo ... 2.50
- 317 In Dynamos Armor........... 3.00
- 318 LKa,TMo,V:Slag.............. 2.50
- 319 LKa,TMo,New Space Armor... 2.50
- 320 F:Hawkeye 2.50
- 321 Cont. From Avg. Crossing ... 2.50
- 322 TKa,TheCrossing,V:JackFrost . 2.50
- 323 TKa,V:Avengers............... 2.50
- 324 TKa,The Crossing 2.50
- 325 TKa,Avengers:Timeslide after . 3.50
- 326 First Sign,pt.3 .... 2.50
- 327 Frostbite..................... 2.50
- 328 TKa,Tony Stark at ColumbiaU . 2.50
- 329 Stark Enterprises taken over .. 2.50
- 330 .... 2.50
- 331 .... 2.50
- 332 final issue 4.00
- Ann.#1 rep.Iron Man #25 .... 45.00
- Ann.#2 rep.Iron Man #6 .... 25.00
- Ann.#3 SB,Manthing........... 15.00
- Ann.#4 DP,GT,V:Modok, A:Champions 10.00
- Ann.#5 JBr,A:Black Panther 6.00
- Ann.#6 A:Eternals,V:Brother Tode........................ 6.00
- Ann.#7 LMc,A:West Coast Avengers, I:New Goliath....... 6.00
- Ann.#8 A:X-Factor 6.00
- Ann.#9 V:Stratosfire,A:Sunturion... 5.00
- Ann.#10 PS,BL,Atlantis Attacks #2 A:Sub-Mariner 4.00
- Ann.#11 SD,Terminus Factor #2 ... 4.00
- Ann.#12 Subterran.Odyssey #4 ... 4.00
- Ann.#13 GC,AW,Assault on Armor City,A:Darkhawk............. 4.00
- Ann.#14 TMo,I:Face Theif,w/card, BU:War Machine 4.00
- Ann.#15 GC,V:Controller 4.00
- Spec.#1 rep.Sub-Mariner x-over .. 40.00
- Spec.#2 rep.(1971)............. 20.00
- Marvel Milestone rep. #55 (1992) .. 2.95
- G-Size#1 Reprints 15.00
- 1-shot Iron Man/Force Works Collectors' Preview, Neon wrap-around cover, double size, X-over 2.50
- 1-shot Iron Manual, BSz(c),Guide to Iron Man's technology..... 2.50
- GN Iron Man 2020 .... 5.95
- TPB Armor Wars rep.#225-#232 .. 12.95
- TPB Many Armors of Iron Man ... 15.95
- TPB Power of Iron Man 9.95
- TPB JR2,BL,Iron Man vs. Dr. Doom rep. #149-#150,#249-#250 ... 12.95
- Iron Manual BSz(c),guide to Iron Man's technology............. 2.50

[2nd Series], Nov., 1996

- 1 JLe,SLo,WPo,SW,A:Bruce Banner, New O:Hulk,48pg.... 4.00
- 1A variant Hulk showing cover.... 5.00
- 1 gold signature ed., bagged ... 18.00
- 2 JLe,SLo,WPo,SW. 4.00
- 3 JLe,SLo,WPo,SW,Heroes brawl . 3.00
- 4 JLe,SLo,WPo,SW,V:Laser 3.00
- 4A X-mas cover................. 5.00
- 5 JLe,SLo,WPo,SW, Whirlwind .. 3.00
- 6 JLe,SLo,WPo,SW,Industrial Revolution,¡ pt.2 x-over....... 3.00

MARVEL — Iron Man–John Carter

Iron Man Vol. 2 #1
© Marvel Entertainment Group

7 JLe,SLo,WPo,SW,A:Pepper
  Potts,Villain revealed 3.00
8 JLe,SLo,RBn,fate of Rebel 3.00
9 JLe,SLo,RBn,V:Mandarin 3.00
10 JLe,SLo,RBn,F:The Hulk 3.00
11 JLb,RBn,V:Dr. Doom,A:Hydra... 3.00
12 WPo,JLe,JLb,F:Dr. Doom,
   Galactus.................... 3.00
13 JeR,LSn,Wildstorm x-over 3.00

[3rd Series], 1997
1 SCh,KBk,V:Mastermind,48-pg. .. 5.00
2 KBk,SCh,in Switzerland 3.50
3 KBk,SCh,V:Hydra Dreadnought
  Robot....................... 3.00
4 KBk,SCh,R:Firebrand 3.00
5 KBk,SCh,V:Firebrand 3.00
6 KBk,F:Black Widow 3.00
7 KBk,SCh,Live Kree or Die,pt.1
  x-over....................... 3.00
8 KBk,SCh,secret identity out ... 3.00
9 KBk,SCh,A:Black Widow 3.00
10 KBk,SCh,A:Avengers........... 3.00
11 KBk,SCh,A:Warbird &
   War Machine 3.00
12 KBk,V:War Machine........... 3.00
13 KBk,SCh,V:Controller,48-pg. .. 4.00
13a signed 20.00
14 KBk,SCh,Fant.Four x-over..... 3.00
15 KBk,SCh,V:Nitro 3.00
16 KBk,RSt,V:Dragon Lord 3.00
17 KBk,RSt,SCh,V:Fin Fang Foom . 3.00
18 KBk,RSt,SCh,V:War Machine.... 3.00
19 KBk,RSt,V:War Machine....... 3.00
20 KBk,RSt,SCh,V:War Machine... 3.00
21 KBk,RSt,TGu,MBa,
   Eighth Day prologue......... 3.00
22 KBk,RSt,Eighth Day,pt.2,
   I:Carnivore 3.00
23 KBk,RSt,UltimateDanger,pt.1 .. 3.00
24 KBk,RSt,UltimateDanger,pt.2 .. 2.50
25 KBk,RSt,Ultimate
   Danger,pt.3, 48-pg.......... 3.50
26 JQ,Mask of Iron Man,pt.1..... 2.50
27 JQ,Mask of Iron Man,pt.2..... 2.50
28 JQ,Mask of Iron Man,pt.3..... 2.50
29 JQ,Mask of Iron Man,pt.4..... 2.50
30 JQ,Mask of Iron Man,pt.5..... 2.50
31 JQ,Sons of Yinsen,pt.1 ...... 2.50
32 JQ,Sons of Yinsen,pt.2 ...... 2.50
33 JQ,Sons of Yinsen,pt.3 ...... 2.50
34 JQ,Dr. Power................ 2.50
35 JQ,Maximum Security 2.50
36 CDi,PR 2.50
37 JQ,F:Tyberius Stone 2.50
38 R:classic foe 2.50
39 MPn,Remote Control 2.50
40 MPn,Remote Control 2.50
41 new art team............... 2.50
42 Big Bang Theory,pt.1 .... 2.50
43 Big Bang Theory,pt.2 .... 2.50
44 Big Bang,pt.3,new armor 2.50
45 Big Bang Theory,pt.4 .... 2.50
46 Frankenstein Syndrome,pt.1
   100-pages 4.00
47 IaC,Frankenstein Syndrome... 2.25
48 IaC,Frankenstein Syndrome... 2.25
49 CsB,V:Titanium Man 2.25
50 MGr,48-pg. 4.00
51 MGr,Jane Doe,pt.1........... 2.25
52 MGr,Jane Doe,pt.2........... 2.25
53 MGr,Book of Ten Rings 2.25
54 MGr,Temugin................ 2.25
55 MGr,would be #400 issue,54-pg. 4.00
56 MGr,fall-out begins......... 2.25
57 MGr,fight on, fight on 2.25
58 MGr......................... 2.25
59 MGr,In Shining Armor 2.25
60 MGr,In Shining Armor,pt.2 .. 2.25
61 MGr,In Shining Armor,pt.3 .. 2.25
62 MGr,You Can't Always Get,pt.1 . 2.25
63 MGr,You Can't Always Get,pt.2 . 2.25
64 AD,MFm,MGr,Standoff,pt.1 ... 2.25
65 MGr,Manhunt,pt.1 .... 2.25
66 MGr,Manhunt,pt.2 .... 2.25
67 MGr,Manhunt,pt.3 .... 3.00
68 MGr,Manhunt,pt.4 .... 3.00
69 MGr,Manhunt,pt.5 .... 3.00
70 Vegal Bleeds Neon,pt.1...... 3.00
71 Vegas Bleeds Neon,pt.2 ..... 3.00
72 Vegas Bleeds Neon,pt.3 ..... 3.00
73 The Best Defense,pt.1 ...... 3.00
74 The Best Defense,pt.2....... 3.00
Ann.1998 Iron Man/Captain
   America, KBk,MWa, 48-pg..... 3.50
Ann.1999 KBk,JoC,48-pg........ 3.50
Ann.2000 Sons of Yin-Sen,pt.3 .. 3.50
Ann.2001 CCI,48-pg............ 3.00
Spec.#1 Age of Innocence, Avengers:
   Timeslide 2.50
TPB The Mask in the Iron Man .. 14.95

IRON MAN & SUBMARINER
April, 1968
1 GC, 2 stories 200.00

IRON MAN: BAD BLOOD
July, 2000
1 (of 4) BL,DvM,V:JustinHammer.. 3.00
2 BL,DvM,Spymaster............ 3.00
3 BL,DvM,James Rhodes 3.00
4 BL,DvM,Justin Hammer 3.00

IRON MAN: THE IRON AGE
June, 1998
1 (of 2) KBk,48pg bookshelf..... 6.00
2 KBk,48pg bookshelf, concl..... 6.00

ISLAND OF DR. MOREAU
Oct., 1977
1 GK(c),movie adapt............ 7.50

IT'S A DUCK'S LIFE
Feb., 1950
1 F:Buck Duck,Super Rabbit ... 150.00
2 .... 60.00
3 thru 10 .... @50.00
11 Feb., 1952 .... 50.00

JACK OF HEARTS
Jan., 1984
1 Mini series 2.50
2 thru 4 .... @2.50

JAMES BOND JR.
1992
1 I&O:JamesBondJr.(TVseries) ... 3.00
2 Adventures Contd. 2.25
3 V:Goldfinger,Odd Job 2.25
4 thru 6 .... @2.25
V:Scumlord 2.25
8 V:Goldfinger,Walter D.Plank ... 2.25
9 V:Dr.No in Switzerland 2.25
10 V:Robot,Dr.DeRange 2.25
11 V:S.C.U.M.................. 2.25
12 V:Goldfinger,Jaws 2.25

JANN OF THE JUNGLE
See: JUNGLE TALES

JEANIE COMICS
See: DARING MYSTERY

JIHAD
Epic
1 Cenobites vs. Nightbreed 4.50
2 E:Cenobites vs. Nightbreed ... 4.50

JLA/AVENGERS
Marvel/DC Sept. 2003
1 KBk,GP(c),x-over,48-pg....... 5.95
3 .... 5.95

JOHN CARTER, WARLORD OF MARS
June, 1977–Aug. 1979
1 GK,DC,O:John Carter,Created
  by Edgar Rice Burroughs 12.00
2 GK/DC(c),GK,RN, White Apes
  of Mars..................... 7.00
3 GK,RN,Requiem for a Warlord .. 7.00
4 GK,RN, Raiding Party......... 7.00
5 GK,RN,Giant Battle Issue..... 7.00
6 GK/DC(c),GK,Alone Against a
  World 7.00
7 GK,TS,Showdown 7.00
8 GK,RN,Beast With Touch of

John Carter, Warlord of Mars #2
© Marvel Entertainment Group

All comics prices listed are for *Near Mint* condition.

John Carter–Journey — MARVEL — Comics Values Annual

Stone 7.00	44(2)AH,`Won't You Step Into	14 DAy,RH,`The Man Who
9 GK,RN,Giant Battle Issue 7.00	My Palor' 500.00	Owned A World' 500.00
10 GK,The Death of Barsoom?. . . . 7.00	3 GC,`I Stalk By Night' 300.00	15 RH(c),`Till Death Do
11 RN,O:Dejah Thoris. 7.00	4 DR,`The Torture Room' 300.00	Us Part' 500.00
12 RN,City of the Dead. 7.00	5 GC,DR,`The Hitchhiker' 300.00	16 DW,`Vampire Tale' 500.00
13 RN,March of the Dead. 7.00	6 RH,`The Dark Room' 325.00	17 SC,`Midnight On Black
14 RN,The Day Helium Died. 7.00	7 GT(c),BW,JMn,`Where Monsters	Mountain' 500.00
15 RN,GK,Prince of Helium	Dwell' 700.00	18 `He Wouldn't Stay Dead' 500.00
Returns 7.00	8 JSt,`Enter... the Lizard' 275.00	19 JF,`The Little Things' 500.00
16 RN,John Carters Dilemna 7.00	9 RH(c),JSt,`The Dark	20 BEv,BP,`After Man, What'. . . . 500.00
17 BL,What Price Victory 10.00	Dungeon' 250.00	21 JKu,`The Man With No Past' . 500.00
18 FM,Tars Tarkas Battles Alone. . . 7.00	10 JMn,`When the Vampire Calls' 250.00	22 `Haunted House' 500.00
19 RN(c),War With the Wing Men . . 7.00	11 JMn,JSt,`Dead Man's Escape' 225.00	23 GC,`Gone, But Not Forgotten' 300.00
20 RN(c),Battle at the Bottom	12 BK,`The Man Who Cried	24 `The Locked Drawer' 300.00
of the World 7.00	Ghost' 235.00	25 `The Man Who Lost Himself' . 300.00
21 RN(c),The Claws of the Banth . 7.00	13 BEv(c),`The Hands of Death' . 235.00	26 `The Man From Out There' . . 300.00
22 RN(c),The Canyon of Death. . . . 7.00	14 GC,GT,`The Hands' 200.00	27 `BP,JSe,`Masterpiece' 300.00
23 Murder on Mars. 7.00	15 `Trapped by the Tarantula' . . . 200.00	28 `The Survivor' 300.00
24 GP/TA(c),Betrayal 7.00	16 RH(c),`Her Name Is Death' . . . 200.00	29 `Three Frightened People' . . . 300.00
25 Inferno. 7.00	17 `I Die Too Often',Bondage(c) . 200.00	30 JO,`The Lady Who Vanished'. 300.00
26 Death Cries the Guild of	18 `He's Trying To Kill Me' 200.00	31 `The Man Who Had No Fear'. 300.00
Assassins 7.00	19 `The Girl Who Couldn't Die' . . 225.00	32 `Elevator In The Sky' 300.00
27 Death Marathon. 7.00	20 . . . . 225.00	33 SD,AW,`There'll Be Some
28 Guardians of the Lost City 7.00	21 GC,JMn 200.00	Changes Made' 350.00
Ann.#1 RN(c),GK,Battle story 7.00	22 JMn 200.00	34 BP,BK,`The Of The
Ann.#2 RN(c),GK,Outnumbered . . . 7.00	23 . . . . 200.00	Mystic Ring' 300.00
Ann.#3 RN(c),GK,Battle story 7.00	24 MF,GC. 200.00	35 LC,JF,`Turn Back The Clock' . 300.00
	25 MF. 250.00	36 `I, The Pharaoh' 300.00
JOKER COMICS	26 GC 200.00	37 BEv(c),`The Volcano' 300.00
Timely, April, 1942	27 . . . . 200.00	38 SD,`Those Who Vanish' 300.00
1 BW,I&B:Powerhouse Pepper,	28 GC 200.00	39 BEv(c),DAy,WW,`The
A:Stuporman 3,500.00	29 GC,JMn. 200.00	Forbidden Room' 300.00
2 BW,I:Tessie the Typist 1,200.00	30 . . . . 200.00	40 BEv(c),JF,`The Strange
3 BW,A:Tessie the Typist,	31 May, 1954 . . . . 200.00	Secret Of Henry Hill' 300.00
Squat Car Squad 650.00		41 BEv(c),GM,RC,`I Switched
4 BW,Squat Car only 650.00	**JOURNEY INTO MYSTERY**	Bodies' 275.00
5 BW,same 650.00	**June, 1952**	42 BEv(c),GM,`What Was
6 BW, ... 450.00	1 RH(c),B:Mystery/Horror	Farley's Other Face 275.00
7 BW 450.00	stories 4,000.00	43 AW,`Ghost Ship'. 300.00
8 BW 450.00	2 `Don't Look' 1,400.00	44 SD,JK,BEv. 300.00
9 BW 450.00	3 `I Didn't See Anything' 1,000.00	45 BEv,JO 250.00
10 BW,Shooting Gallery (c). 450.00	4 RH,BEv(c),`I'm Drowning,'	46 . . . . 250.00
11 BW 350.00	severed hand (c) 1,000.00	47 BEv 250.00
12 BW 350.00	5 RH,BEv(c),`Fright' 650.00	48 . . . . 250.00
13 BW 350.00	6 BEv(c),`Till Death Do	49 . . . . 250.00
14 BW 350.00	Us Part' 650.00	50 SD 250.00
15 BW 350.00	7 BEv(c),`Ghost Guard' 650.00	51 SD,JK 300.00
16 BW 350.00	8 `He Who Hesitates' 650.00	52 JK 250.00
17 BW 350.00	9 BEv(c),`I Made A Monster' . . 650.00	53 DH. 250.00
18 BW 350.00	10 `The Assassin of Paris' 650.00	54 AW 275.00
19 BW 350.00	11 RH,GT,`Meet the Dead' 600.00	55 . . . . 250.00
20 BW 350.00	12 `A Night At Dragmoor Castle' . 500.00	56 thru 61 SD,JK. . . . . @250.00
21 BW 300.00	13 `The Living and the Dead' . . . 500.00	62 SD,JK,I:Xemnu 400.00
22 BW 300.00		63 SD,JK 250.00
23 BW,HK,`Hey Look'. 300.00		64 SD,JK 250.00
24 BW,HK,`Laff Favorites' 300.00		65 SD,JK 250.00
25 BW,HK,same 300.00		66 Hulk Type 400.00
26 BW,HK,same 300.00		67 SD,JK 275.00
27 BW 300.00		68 SD,JK 275.00
28 . . . . 100.00		69 SD,JK 275.00
29 BW 250.00		70 Sandman Type 350.00
30 BW 250.00		71 JK,SD 275.00
31 BW 250.00		72 JK,SD 275.00
32 B:Millie,Hedy 100.00		73 JK,DH,Spider-Man type 550.00
33 HK 125.00		74 . . . . 275.00
34 . . . . 100.00		75 JK,DH 275.00
35 HK 125.00		76 JK,DH 550.00
36 HK 100.00		77 DH,SD,JK 225.00
37 . . . . 100.00		78 DH,Dr.Strange Type. 300.00
38 . . . . 100.00		79 JK,DH,SD 350.00
39 . . . . 100.00		80 JK,DH,SD 225.00
40 . . . . 100.00		81 JK,DH,SD 225.00
41 A:Nellie the Nurse 100.00		82 JK,DH,SD 225.00
42 I:Patty Pin-up. 125.00		83 JK,SD,I&O:Thor 7,500.00
Becomes:		84 JK,SD,DH,I:Executioner . . . 1,500.00
ADVENTURES INTO		85 JK,SD,I:Loki,Heimdall,Balder,
TERROR		Tyr,Odin,Asgard. 1,000.00
1950		86 JK,SD,DH,V:Tomorrow Man . . 700.00
43(1)AH,B:Horror Stories 800.00		87 JK,SD,V:Communists. 500.00
	Journey Into Mystery #86	88 JK,SD,V:Loki 500.00
	© Marvel Entertainment Group	89 JK,SD,O:Thor(rep) 500.00

CVA Page 258   All comics prices listed are for *Near Mint* condition.

MARVEL

Journey–Justice

Journey Into Mystery #96
© Marvel Entertainment Group

Jungle Action #5
© Marvel Entertainment Group

90 SD,I:Carbon Copy 300.00
91 JSt,SD,I:Sandu 250.00
92 JSt,SD,V:Loki,I:Frigga 250.00
93 DAy,JK,SD,I:Radioactive
 Man 300.00
94 JSt,SD,V:Loki 250.00
95 JSt,SD,I:Duplicator 250.00
96 JSt,SD,I:Merlin II 250.00
97 JK,I:Lava Man,O:Odin 300.00
98 DH,JK,I&O:Cobra 225.00
99 DH,JK,I:Mr.Hyde,Surtur 225.00
100 DH,JK,V:Mr.Hyde 225.00
101 JK,V:Tomorrow Man 150.00
102 JK,I:Sif,Hela 150.00
103 JK,I:Enchantress,
 Executioner 150.00
104 JK,Giants 150.00
105 JK,V:Hyde,Cobra 150.00
106 JK,O:Balder 150.00
107 JK,I:Grey Gargoyle,Karnilla . 150.00
108 JK,A:Dr.Strange 150.00
109 JK,V:Magneto 175.00
110 JK,V:Hyde,Cobra,Loki 150.00
111 JK,V:Hyde,Cobra,Loki 150.00
112 JK,V:Hulk,O:Loki 350.00
113 JK,V:Grey Gargoyle 125.00
114 JK,I&O:Absorbing Man 125.00
115 JK,O:Loki,V:Absorbing Man . 175.00
116 JK,V:Loki,C:Daredevil 125.00
117 JK,V:Loki 125.00
118 JK,I:Destroyer 125.00
119 JK,V:Destroyer,I:Hogun,
 Fandrall,Volstagg 125.00
120 JK,A:Avengers,Absorbing
 Man 125.00
121 JK,V:Absorbing Man 125.00
122 JK,V:Absorbing Man 125.00
123 JK,V:Absorbing Man 125.00
124 JK,A:Hercules 150.00
125 JK,A:Hercules 125.00
Annual #1, JK,I:Hercules 300.00
Becomes:

THOR

JOURNEY INTO MYSTERY
[2nd series], Oct., 1972
1 GK,TP,MP,`Dig Me No Grave' . 35.00
2 GK,`Jack the Ripper' 25.00
3 JSn,TP,`Shambler From
 the Stars' 25.00
4 GC,DA,`Haunter of the Dark',

 H.P. Lovecraft adaptation 25.00
5 RB,FrG,`Shadow From the
 Steeple',R. Bloch adaptation . 25.00
6 Mystery Stories 20.00
7 thru 19 . . . . @20.00

JOURNEY INTO UNKNOWN WORLDS
See: ALL WINNERS COMICS

J-2
Aug., 1998
1 TDF,RLm,AM,F:J2 with the powers
 of Juggernaut 2.25
2 TDF,RLm,AM,V:Buffer Zone,
 Enthralla & Uncanny X-People . 2.25
2a variant cover 2.25
3 TDF,RLm,AM,V:Hulk 2.25
4 TDF,RLm,AM,turning points . . . 2.25
5 TDF,RLm,AM,Ghosts of the Past 2.25
6 TDF,RLm,AM,Majority Rules . . . 2.25
7 TDF,RLm,AM,Last Days of
 the Original Juggernaut 2.25
8 TDF,RLm,AM,Uneasy Allies . . . 2.25
9 TDF,RLm,AM,Critical Choices . . 2.25
10 TDF,RLm,AM,Incredible
 Journeys 2.25
11 TDF,RLm,AM,Master of Jug-Fu . 2.25
12 TDF,RLm,AM,A:Juggernaut,
 last issue 2.25

JUGGERNAUT
1997
1-shot 48pg. 3.00

JUGGERNAUT: THE EIGHTH DAY
Sept., 1999
1-shot JoC,TSr,AKu(c),x-over,pt.4 . . 3.00

JUNGLE ACTION
Atlas, Oct., 1954
1 JMn,JMn(c),B:Leopard Girl . . 400.00
2 JMn,JMn(c) 425.00
3 JMn,JMn(c) 250.00
4 JMn,JMn(c) 250.00
5 JMn,JMn(c) 250.00
6 JMn,JMn(c),Aug., 1955 . . . . . 250.00

JUNGLE ACTION
Oct., 1972—Nov., 1976
1 JB(c),Lorna,Tharn,Jann
 reprints 25.00
2 GK(c),same 15.00
3 JSn(c),same 15.00
4 GK(c),same 15.00
5 JR(c),JB,B:Black Panther,
 V:Man-Ape 30.00
6 RB/FrG(c),RB,V:Kill-Monger . . 25.00
7 RB/KJ(c),RB,V:Venomn 15.00
8 RB/KJ(c),RB,GK,
 O:Black Panther 20.00
9 GK/KJ(c),RB,V:Baron Macabre 15.00
10 GK/FrG(c),V:King Cadaver 15.00
11 GK(c),V:Baron Macabre,Lord
 Karnaj 15.00
12 RB/KJ(c),V:Kill Monger 10.00
13 GK/JK(c),V:White Gorilla,
 Sombre 10.00
14 GK(c),V:Prehistoric
 Monsters 10.00
15 GK(c),V:Prehistoric
 Monsters 10.00
16 GK(c),V:Venomm 10.00
17 GK(c),V:Kill Monger 10.00

18 JKu(c),V:Madame Slay 10.00
19 GK(c),V:KKK,`Sacrifice
 of Blood' 10.00
20 V:KKK,`Slaughter In The
 Streets' 10.00
21 V:KKK,`Cross Of Fire, Cross
 Of Death' 9.00
22 JB(c),V:KKK,Soul Stranger . . . 9.00
23 JBy(c),V:KKK 9.00
24 GK(c),I:Wind Eagle 9.00

JUNGLE TALES
Atlas, Sept., 1954
1 B:Jann of the Jungle,Cliff
 Mason,Waku 400.00
2 GT,Jann Stories cont. 275.00
3 Cliff Mason,White Hunter,
 Waku Unknown Jungle 275.00
4 Cliff Mason,Waku,Unknown
 Jungle 275.00
5 RH,SSh,Cliff Mason,Waku,
 Unknown Jungle 275.00
6 DH,SSh,Cliff Mason,Waku,
 Unknown Jungle 275.00
7 DH,SSh,Cliff Mason,Waku,
 Unknown Jungle 275.00
Becomes:

JANN OF THE JUNGLE
1955
8 SH,SSh,`The Jungle Outlaw' . 300.00
9 `With Fang and Talons' 200.00
10 AW,`The Jackal's Lair' 200.00
11 `Bottomless Pit' 200.00
12 `The Lost Safari' 200.00
13 `When the Trap Closed' 200.00
14 V:Hunters 200.00
15 BEv(c),DH,V:Hunters 200.00
16 BEv(c),AW,JungleVengeance . 225.00
17 BEv(c),DH,AW,June, 1957 . . 225.00

JUSTICE
Nov., 1986
1 I:Justice 2.25
2 . . . . 2.25
3 Yakuza Assassin 2.25
4 thru 8 . . . . @2.25
9 KG 2.25
10 thru 18 . . . . @2.25
19 thru 31 . . . . @2.25
32 Last issue,A:Joker 2.25

All comics prices listed are for *Near Mint* condition.

Justice–Kid Colt — MARVEL — Comics Values Annual

JUSTICE COMICS
Atlas, Fall, 1947
- 7(1) B:FBI in Action,`Mystery of White Death'. 300.00
- 8(2),HK,`Crime is For Suckers' . . 200.00
- 9(3),FBI Raid 175.00
- 4 Bank Robbery 175.00
- 5 Subway(c) 165.00
- 6 E:FBI In Action 165.00
- 7 Symbolic(c) 165.00
- 8 Funeral(c) 165.00
- 9 B:`True Cases Proving Crime Can't Win'. 165.00
- 10 Ph(c),Bank Hold Up 165.00
- 11 Ph(c),Behind Bars 165.00
- 12 Ph(c),The Crime of Martin Blaine 125.00
- 13 Ph(c),The Cautiouc Crook . . . 125.00
- 14 Ph(c) 125.00
- 15 Ph(c) 125.00
- 16 F:"Ears"Karpik-Mobster 100.00
- 17 `The Ragged Stranger' 100.00
- 18 `Criss-Cross' 100.00
- 19 `Death Of A Spy' 100.00
- 20 `Miami Mob'. 100.00
- 21 `Trap' 100.00
- 22 `The Big Break' 100.00
- 23 thru 40 . . . . @75.00
- 41 Electrocution cover 125.00
- 42 thru 51 . . . . @75.00
- 52 `Flare Up' 75.00

Becomes:

TALES OF JUSTICE
May, 1955—Aug., 1957
- 53 BEv,`Keeper Of The Keys' . . . 175.00
- 54 thru 57 . . . . @100.00
- 58 BK 125.00
- 59 BK 125.00
- 60 thru 63 . . . . @75.00
- 64 RC,DW,JSe 100.00
- 65 RC 100.00
- 66 JO,AT 100.00
- 67 DW 100.00

JUSTICE: FOUR BALANCE
1994
- 1 A:Thing, Yancy Street Gang 2.25
- 2 V:Hate Monger 2.25
- 3 the story continues... . . . . 2.25
- 4 ...to its conclusion. 2.25

KATHY
Atlas, Oct., 1959—Feb., 1964
- 1 `Teenage Tornado' 100.00
- 2 . . . . 50.00
- 3 thru 15 . . . . @35.00
- 16 thru 27 . . . . @25.00

KA-ZAR
[Reprint Series], Aug., 1970
- 1 X-Men ID 35.00
- 2 Daredevil 12, 13 . . . . 25.00
- 3 DDH,Spider-Man,March, 1971 . 25.00

[1st Series], Jan., 1974
- 1 O:Savage Land 20.00
- 2 DH,JA,A:Shanna The She-Devil 10.00
- 3 DH,V:Man-God,A:El Tigre 10.00
- 4 DH,V:Man-God 10.00
- 5 DH,D:El-Tigre 6.00
- 6 JB,AA,V:Bahemoth 6.00
- 7 JB/BMc`Revenge of the River-Gods' 6.00
- 8 JB/AA,`Volcano of Molten Death'. 6.00
- 9 JB,`Man Who Hunted Dinosaur' . 6.00
- 10 JB,`Dark City of Death' 6.00
- 11 DH/FS,`Devil-God of Sylitha' . . . 5.00
- 12 RH,`Wizard of Forgotten Death' 5.00
- 13 V:Lizard Men 5.00
- 14 JAb,V:Klaw 5.00
- 15 VM,V:Klaw,`Hellbird' 5.00
- 16 VM,V:Klaw. 5.00
- 17 VM,V:Klaw. 5.00
- 18 VM,V:Klaw,Makrum 5.00
- 19 VM,V:Klaw,Raknor the Slayer . . 5.00
- 20 VM,V:Klaw,`Fortress of Fear' . . . 5.00

[2nd Series], Apr. 1981
- 1 BA,O:Ka-Zar. 4.00
- 2 thru 7 BA . . . . @3.00
- 8 BA,Ka-Zar Father 2.50
- 9 BA 2.50
- 10 BA,Direct D 2.50
- 11 BA/GK,Zabu 2.50
- 12 BA,Panel Missing 2.50
- 12a Scarce Reprint. 2.50
- 13 BA. 2.50
- 14 BA/GK,Zabu 2.50
- 15 BA. 2.50
- 16 . . . . 2.50
- 17 Detective 2.50
- 18 . . . . 2.50
- 19 . . . . 2.50
- 20 A:Spider-Man. 3.00
- 21 . . . . 3.00
- 22 A:Spider-Man. 3.00
- 23 A:Spider-Man. 3.00
- 24 A:Spider-Man. 3.00
- 25 A:Spider-Man. 3.00
- 26 A:Spider-Man. 3.00
- 27 A:Buth 3.00
- 28 Pangea 3.00
- 29 W:Ka-Zar & Shanna, Doub.Size. 3.00
- 30 V:Pterons 3.00
- 31 PangeaWarII 3.00
- 32 V:Plunderer 3.00
- 33 V:Plunderer 3.00
- 34 Last Issue Doub.Size. 3.00

[3rd Series], 1997
- 1 MWa,NKu,Ka-Zar, Shanna, Zabu, V:Gregor, 40pg. 5.00
- 1a 2nd printing 2.50
- 2 MWa,NKu,V:Gregor 4.00
- 2A NKu variant cover. 3.00
- 3 MWa,NKu,Ka-Zar's son dead? . . 3.00
- 4 MWa,NKu,in New York City. 3.00
- 5 MWa,NKu, ... 2.50
- 6 MWa,V:Rampaging Rhino. 2.25
- 7 MWa,NKu,F:Shanna the She-Devil 2.25
- 8 MWa,NKu, Urban Jungle, pt.1. . . 2.25
- 9 MWa,NKu, Urban Jungle, pt.2. . . 2.25
- 10 MWa,NKu, Urban Jungle, pt.3 . . 2.25
- 11 MWa,NKu, Urban Jungle, pt.4, concl. 2.25
- 12 MWa,A:High Evolutionary 2.25
- 13 MWa,A:High Evolutionary 2.25
- 14 MWa,NKu,end old & begin new storyline, double size 3.50
- 15 A:Punisher. 3.00
- 16 A:Punisher. 2.25
- 17 Ka-Zar clears his name, A:Jameka. 2.25
- 18 People of the Savage Land revolt 2.25
- 19 V:Gregor 2.25
- 20 A:Gregor,Zira, final issue 2.25
- Ann. '97 V:Garrok, the Petrified Man 2.50
- Ann. '98 Ka-Zar/Daredevil heroes unite. 3.00
- 1-shot Ka-Zar of the Savage Land, CDi,V:Sauron, 48-pg., prelude to 3rd series (1996) 3.00
- 1-shot Ka-Zar: Sibling Rivalry, MWa,TDz,Flashback (1997) . . 2.00

KELLYS, THE
See: KID KOMICS

KENT BLAKE OF THE SECRET SERVICE
May, 1951—July, 1953
- 1 U.S. Govt. Secret Agent stories,Bondage cover 225.00
- 2 JSt,Drug issue,`Man with out A Face 150.00
- 3 JMn,`Trapped By The Chinese Reds' 100.00
- 4 Secret Service Stories 100.00
- 5 RH(c),`Condemned To Death' 100.00
- 6 Cases from Kent Blake files . . 100.00
- 7 RH(c),Behind Enemy Lines . . 100.00
- 8 GT,V:Communists 100.00
- 9 thru 14 . . . . @100.00

KICKERS INC.
Nov., 1986
- 1 SB,O:Kickers 2.50
- 2 SB 2.50
- 3 RF,Witches. 2.50
- 4 RF,FIST 2.50
- 5 RF,A:D.P.7 . . . . 2.50
- 6 thru 8 RF . . . . @2.50
- 9 . . . . 2.50
- 10 TD 2.50
- 11 . . . . 2.50
- 12 Oct., 1987 . . . . 2.50

KID & PLAY
- 1 Based on Rap Group 2.25
- 2 Drug Issue 2.25
- 3 At your Friends Expense. 2.25
- 4 . . . . 2.25
- 5 . . . . 2.25
- 6 Record Contract 2.25
- 7 Fraternity Pledging 2.25
- 8 Kid and Cindy become an item . . 2.25
- 9 C:Marvel Heroes 2.25

KID COLT OUTLAW
Atlas, Aug., 1948
- 1 B:Kid Colt,A:Two-Gun Kid . . 1,200.00
- 2 `Gun-Fighter and the Girl' 600.00

Kazar 3rd Series #2
© Marvel Entertainment Group

MARVEL

Kid Colt–King Arthur

#	Description	Price
3	`Colt-Quick Killers For Hire'.	500.00
4	`Wanted',A:Tex Taylor	500.00
5	`Mystery of the Misssing Mine',A:Blaze Carson	500.00
6	A:Tex Taylor,`Valley of the Warewolf'	300.00
7	B:Nimo the Lion	300.00
8		300.00
9		300.00
10	`The Whip Strikes',E:Nimo the Lion'	300.00
11	O:Kid Colt	350.00
12		225.00
13	DRi	225.00
14		225.00
15	`Gun Whipped in Shotgun City'	225.00
16		225.00
17		225.00
18	DRi	225.00
19		200.00
20	`The Outlaw'	200.00
21 thru 30		@200.00
31		200.00
32		200.00
33 thru 45	A:Black Rider	@150.00
46	RH(c)	125.00
47	DW	125.00
48	RH(c),JKu	125.00
49		125.00
50		125.00
51 thru 56		@100.00
57	AW	100.00
58	AW	100.00
59	AW	100.00
60	AW	100.00
61		65.00
62		65.00
63		65.00
64		70.00
65		70.00
66 thru 78		@60.00
79	Origin Retold	65.00
80 thru 86		@60.00
87	JDa(reprint)	65.00
88	AW	75.00
89	AW,Matt Slade	75.00
90 thru 99		@60.00
100		65.00
101		60.00
102		55.00
103	`The Great Train Robbery'	55.00
104	JKu(c),DH,`Trail of Kid Colt'	55.00
105	DH,V:Dakota Dixon	55.00
106	JKu(c),`The Circus of Crime'	55.00
107		55.00
108	BEv	55.00
109	DAy,V:The Barracuda	55.00
110	GC,V:Iron Mask	55.00
111	JKu(c),V:Sam Hawk, The Man Hunter	55.00
112	JKu(c),V:Mr. Brown	55.00
113	JKu(c),GC,V:Bull Barton	55.00
114	JKu(c),Return of Iron Mask	55.00
115	JKu(c),V:The Scorpion	55.00
116	JKu(c),GC,V:Dr. Danger & Invisible Gunman	55.00
117	JKu(c),GC,V:The Fatman & His Boomerang	55.00
118	V:Scorpion,Bull Barton, Dr. Danger	55.00
119	DAy(c),JK,V:Bassett The Badman	55.00
120	`Cragsons Ride Again'	55.00
121	A:Rawhide Kid,Iron Mask	35.00
122	V:Rattler Ruxton	35.00
123	V:Ringo Barker	35.00
124	A:Phantom Raider	35.00
125	A:Two-Gun Kid	35.00
126	V:Wes Hardin	30.00
127 thru 129		@30.00
130	O:Kid Colt	30.00
131 thru 150		@30.00
151 thru 200 reprints		@25.00
201 thru 228 reprints		@20.00
229	April, 1979	20.00

KID FROM DODGE CITY
Atlas, July, 1957—Sept., 1957

#	Price
1	100.00
2	65.00

KID FROM TEXAS
Atlas, June, 1957—Aug., 1957

#	Price
1	100.00
2	65.00

KID KOMICS
Timely, Feb., 1943

#	Description	Price
1	SSh(c),BW,O:Captain Wonder & Tim Mulrooney I:Whitewash, Knuckles,Trixie Trouble, Pinto Pete Subbie	5,500.00
2	AsH(c),F:Captain Wonder Subbie, B:Young Allies, B:Red Hawk,Tommy Tyme	2,300.00
3	ASh(c),A:The Vision & Daredevils	1,800.00
4	ASh(c),B:Destroyer,A:Sub-Mariner, E:Red Hawk,Tommy Tyme	1,500.00
5	ASh(c),V:Nazis	1,200.00
6	ASh(c),V:Japanese	1,200.00
7	ASh(c),B;Whizzer	1,000.00
8	ASh(c),V:Train Robbers	1,000.00
9	ASh(c),V:Elves	1,000.00
10	ASh(c),E:Young Allies, The Destoyer,The Whizzer	1,000.00

Becomes:

KID MOVIE KOMICS
1946

#	Description	Price
11	F:Silly Seal,Ziggy Pig HK,Hey Look	300.00

Becomes:

RUSTY COMICS
1947

#	Description	Price
12	F:Rusty,A:Mitzi	225.00
13	Do not Disturb(c)	100.00
14	Beach(c),BW,HK,Hey Look	225.00
15	Picnic(c),HK,Hey Look	150.00
16	Juniors Grades,HK,HeyLook	150.00
17	John in Trouble,HK,HeyLook	150.00
18	John Fired	100.00
19	Fridge raid(c),HK	100.00
20	And Her Family,HK	200.00
21	And Her Family,HK	225.00
22	HK	225.00

Becomes:

KELLYS, THE
1950

#	Description	Price
23	F:The Kelly Family(Pop, Mom,Mike,Pat & Goliath)	125.00
24	Mike's Date,A;Margie	75.00
25	Wrestling(c)	75.00

Becomes:

SPY CASES
1950

#	Description	Price
26(#1)	Spy stories	250.00
27(#2)	BEv,Bondage(c)	150.00
28(#3)	Sabotage,A:Douglas Grant Secret Agent	150.00
4	The Secret Invasion	125.00
5	The Vengeance of Comrade de Casto	125.00
6	A:Secret Agent Doug Grant	125.00
7	GT,A:Doug Grant	125.00
8	Atom Bomb(c),Frozen Horror	125.00
9	Undeclared War	100.00
10	Battlefield Adventures	100.00
11	Battlefield Adventures	100.00
12	Battlefield Adventures	100.00
13	Battlefield Adventures	100.00
14	Battlefield Adventures	100.00
15	Doug Grant	100.00
16	Doug Grant	100.00
17	Doug Grant	100.00
18	Contact in Ankara	100.00
19	Final Issue,Oct., 1953	100.00

KID SLADE GUNFIGHTER
See: MATT SLADE

KILLFRENZY

#	Description	Price
1		2.25
2	Castle Madspike	2.25

KILLPOWER: THE EARLY YEARS
1993

#	Description	Price
1	B:MiB,Goes on Rampage	3.25
2 thru 3	O:Killpower	@2.25
4	E:MiB,last issue	2.25

KILLRAVEN
Dec., 2000

Spec. JLi,R:Killraven 3.00

KILLRAVEN
Oct., 2002

#	Description	Price
1 (of 6)	AD,MFm,V:Martians	3.00
2	AD,MFm	3.00
3	AD,MFm	3.00
4	AD,MFm	3.00
5	AD,MFm	3.00
6	AD,MFm	3.00

KING ARTHUR & THE KNIGHTS OF JUSTICE
1993–94

#	Description	Price
1	Based on Cartoon	2.25
2	Based on Cartoon	2.25
3	Based on Cartoon	2.25

Kid Colt Outlaw #103
© Marvel Entertainment Group

All comics prices listed are for *Near Mint* condition.

KING CONAN:
See: CONAN THE KING

KINGPIN
Nov., 1997
1-shot StL,JR, bookshelf 48pg 6.00

KINGPIN
Marvel June 2003
1 SeP,KJ,Wilson Fixk........... 2.50
2 thru 6 SeP,KJ .... @2.50

KISSNATION
1997
1 Rock & Roll, A:X-Men........ 10.00

KITTY PRYDE:
AGENT OF S.H.I.E.L.D.
Oct., 1997
1 (of 3) LHa,V:Ogun 2.50
2 LHa,V:Ogun 2.50
3 LHa,Ogun's Slave?........... 2.50

KITTY PRYDE
& WOLVERINE
Nov., 1984
1 AM,V:Ogun................. 6.00
2 AM,V:Ogun................. 5.00
3 thru 5 AM,V:Ogun .... @5.00
6 AM,D:Ogun, April, 1985 ...... 5.00

Knights of Pendragon #6
© Marvel Entertainment Group

KNIGHTS OF
PENDRAGON
[1st Regular Series], July, 1990
1 GEr 2.75
2 thru 7 .... @2.25
8 inc.SBi Poster............... 2.25
9 V:Bane Fisherman 2.25
10 Cap.Britain/Union Jack 2.25
11 A:Iron Man................. 2.25
12 A:Iron Man,Union Jack....... 2.25
13 O:Pendragon 2.25
14 A:Mr.Fantastic,Invisible Woman
   Black Panther.............. 2.25
15 BlackPanther/Union Jack T.U. .. 2.25

16 A:Black Panther............. 2.25
17 D:Albion, Union Jack,
   A:Black Panther 2.25
18 A:Iron Man,Black Panther 2.25

[2nd Regular Series], 1992
1 GEr,A:Iron Man,R:Knights of
   Pendragon,V:MyS-TECH 2.25
2 A:Iron Man,Black Knight 2.25
3 PGa,A:Iron Man,Black Knight ... 2.25
4 Gawain Vs. Bane 2.25
5 JRe,V:Magpie................ 2.25
6 A:Spider-Man................ 2.25
7 A:Spider-Man,V:Warheads 2.25
8 JRe,A:Spider-Man 2.25
9 A:Spider-Man,Warheads....... 2.25
10 V:Baron Blood 2.25
11........................... 2.25
12 MyS-TECH Wars,V:Skire 2.25
13 A:Death's Head II............ 2.25
14 A:Death's Head II............ 2.25
15 D:Adam,A:Death's Head II..... 2.25

KRAZY KOMICS
Timely, July, 1942
1 B:Ziggy Pig,Silly Seal 700.00
2 Toughy Tomcat(c) 300.00
3 Toughy Tomcat/Bunny(c) 200.00
4 Toughy Tomcat/Ziggy(c) 200.00
5 Ziggy/Buzz Saw(c) 200.00
6 Toughy/Cannon(c) 200.00
7 Cigar Store Indian(c) 200.00
8 Toughy/Hammock(c) 200.00
9 Hitler(c) 225.00
10 Newspaper(c) 200.00
11 Canoe(c)................. 200.00
12 Circus(c) 275.00
13 Pirate Treasure(c) 200.00
14 Fishing(c)................. 200.00
15 Ski-Jump(c) 150.00
16 Airplane(c)................ 100.00
17 Street corner(c) 100.00
18 Mallet/Bell(c) 100.00
19 Bicycle(c)................. 100.00
20 Ziggy(c) 100.00
21 Toughy's date(c) 100.00
22 Crystal Ball(c) 100.00
23 Sharks in bathtub(c)........ 150.00
24 Baseball(c) 100.00
25 HK,Krazy Krow(c) 150.00
26 Super Rabbit(c) 100.00
Becomes:

CINDY COMICS
1947
27 HK,B:Margie,Oscar 200.00
28 HK,Snow sled(c) 125.00
29 .... 125.00
30 .... 125.00
31 HK...................... 125.00
32 .... 100.00
33 A;Georgie 100.00
34 thru 40 .... @100.00
Becomes:

CRIME CAN'T WIN
1950
41 Crime stories 275.00
42 .... 150.00
43 GT,Horror story 175.00
4 thru 11 .... @125.00
12 Sept., 1953 .... 100.00

KRAZY KOMICS
Timely
[2nd Series], Aug., 1948
1 BW,HK,B:Eustice Hayseed .. 500.00
2 BW,O:Powerhouse Pepper
   November, 1948 .... 350.00

KRAZY KROW
Summer, 1945
1 B:Krazy Krow 250.00
2 .... 150.00
3 Winter, 1945-46 .... 150.00

KREE-SKRULL WAR
Sept.–Oct., 1983
1 & 2 JB,NA,reprints .... @5.00

KRULL
Nov.–Dec., 1983
1 Ph(c),BBI,movie adapt 2.50
2 BBI,rep.,Marvel Super Spec..... 2.50

KULL THE CONQUEROR
[1st Series], June, 1971
1 MSe,RA,WW,A King Comes
   Riding,O:Kull 40.00
2 MSe,JSe,Shadow Kingdom.... 15.00
3 MSe,JSe,Death Dance of
   Thulsa Doom 15.00
4 MSe,JSe,Night o/t Red Slayers. 10.00
5 MSe,JSe,Kingdom By the Sea .. 8.00
6 MSe,JSe,Lurker Beneath
   the Sea 8.00
7 MSe,JSe,Delcardes'Cat,
   A:Thulsa Doom 8.00
8 MSe,JSe,Wolfshead 8.00
9 MSe,JSe,The Scorpion God 8.00
10 MSe,Swords o/t White Queen .. 8.00
11 MP,King Kull Must Die, O:Kull
   cont.,A:Thulsa Doom 7.00
12 MP,SB,Moon of Blood,V:Thulsa
   Doom,B:SD,B.U.stories 7.00
13 MP,AM, Torches From Hell,
   V:Thulsa Doom 7.00
14 MP,JA,The Black Belfry,
   A:Thulsa Doom 7.00
15 MP,Wings o/t Night-Beast,
   E:SD,B.U.stories 7.00
16 EH,Tiger in the Moon,
   A:Thulsa Doom 10.00
17 AA,EH,Thing from Emerald
   Darkness 6.00
18 EH,AA,Keeper of Flame
   & Frost................... 6.00
19 EH,AA,The Crystal Menace 6.00
20 EH,AA,Hell Beneath Atlantis .. 6.00
21 City of the Crawling Dead 6.00

Kull the Conqueror #5
© Marvel Entertainment Group

MARVEL

22 Talons of the Devil-Birds 6.00
23 Demon Shade 6.00
24 Screams in the Dark 9.00
25 A Lizard's Throne............. 9.00
26 Into Death's Dimension 9.00
27 The World Within............. 9.00
28 Creature and the Crown,
 A:Thulsa Doom 9.00
29 To Sit the Topaz Throne,
 V:Thulsa Doom, final issue.... 9.00

[2nd Series], 1982
1 JB,Brule 4.00
2 Misareenia 3.00

[3rd Series], 1983–85
1 JB,BWi,DG,Iraina 3.50
2 JB,Battle to the Death........ 3.00
3 JB 3.00
4 JB 3.00
5 JB 3.00
6 JB 3.00
7 JB,Masquerade Death 3.00
8 JB 3.00
9 JB 3.00
10 JB 3.00

KULL AND THE BARBARIANS
May, 1975
1 NA,GK,reprint Kull #1 .... 20.00
2 BBI,reprint,Dec., 1983....... 13.00
3 NA,HC,O:Red Sonja.......... 15.00

LABRYNTH
1986–87
1 Movie adapt 3.00
2 and 3 .... @3.00

LAFF-A-LYMPICS
1978–79
1 F;Hanna Barbera 30.00
2 thru 5 .... @20.00
6 thru 13 .... @25.00

LANA
Aug., 1948
1 F:Lana Lane The Show Girl,
 A:Rusty,B:Millie 225.00
2 HK,Hey Look,A:Rusty 125.00
3 Show(c),B:Nellie 100.00
4 Ship(c) 100.00
5 Audition(c) 100.00
6 Stop sign(c) 100.00
7 Beach(c) 100.00
Becomes:

LITTLE LANA
1949
8 Little Lana(c) 90.00
9 Final Issue,March, 1950 ..... 90.00

LANCE BARNES: POST NUKE DICK
Epic, 1993
1 I:Lance Barnes.............. 2.50
2 Cigarettes................... 2.50
3 Warring Mall Tribe 2.50
4 V:Ex-bankers,last issue 2.50

LAST AMERICAN
Epic, 1990–91
1 .... 3.50
2 .... 3.00
3 .... 2.50
4 Final issue.................. 2.25

THE LAST AVENGERS STORY
1995
1 PDd, Alterverse,Future world ... 6.00
2 PDd, Final fate,fully painted 6.00
TPB PDd,AOl, rep. Alternviverse
 story, 96pg. 12.95

The Last Starfighter #1
© Marvel Entertainment Group

LAST STARFIGHTER, THE
Oct.–Dec., 1984
1 JG(c),BBI,Movie adapt........ 2.25
2 Movie adapt 2.25
3 BBI 2.25

LAWBREAKERS ALWAYS LOSE!
Spring, 1948–Oct., 1949
1 Partial Ph(c),Adam and Eve,
 HK,Giggles and Grins 400.00
2 FBI V:Fur Theives 250.00
3 .... 175.00
4 Asylum(c) 200.00
5 .... 200.00
6 Pawnbroker(c) 200.00
7 Crime at Midnight 250.00
8 Prison Break 150.00
9 Ph(c),He Prowled at Night ... 150.00
10 Phc(c),I Met My Murderer ... 150.00

LAWDOG
1993
1 B:CDi(s),FH,I:Lawdog......... 2.50
2 FH,V:Vocal-yokel Cultist 2.25
3 FH,Manical Nazis 2.25
4 FH,V:Zombies 2.25
5 FH 2.25
6 FH 2.25
7 FH,V:Zombies 2.25
8 FH,w/card................... 2.25
9 FH,w/card................... 2.25
10 last issue, w/card........... 2.25

LAWDOG & GRIMROD: TERROR AT THE CROSSROADS
1993
1 .... 3.50

LEGION OF MONSTERS
Sept., 1975
(black & white magazine)
1 NA(c),GM,I&O:Legion of
 Monsters,O:Manphibian 35.00

LEGION OF NIGHT
Oct., 1991
1 WPo/SW,A:Fin Fang Foom..... 5.50
2 WPo,V:Fin Fang Foom 5.50

LETHAL FOES OF SPIDER-MAN
1993
1 B:DFr(s),SMc,R:Stegron 3.00
2 SMc,A:Stegron............... 3.00
3 SMc,V:Spider-Man 3.00
4 E:DFr(s),SMc,Last Issue....... 3.00

LIFE OF CAPTAIN MARVEL
Aug., 1985
1 rep.Iron Man #55,
 Capt.Marvel #25,26 .... 9.00
2 rep.Capt.Marvel#26-28 .... 6.50
3 rep.Capt.Marvel#28-30
 Marvel Feature #12 .... 6.00
4 rep.Marvel Feature #12,Capt.
 Marvel #31,32,Daredevil#105 .. 6.00
5 rep.Capt.Marvel #32-#34 ...... 6.00

LIFE OF CHRIST
1993
1 Birth of Christ............... 5.00
2 MW,The Easter Story 5.00

LIFE OF POPE JOHN-PAUL II
1983
1 JSt, Jan., 1983............... 6.00
1a Special reprint 4.00

LIFE WITH MILLIE
See: DATE WITH MILLIE

LIGHT AND DARKNESS WAR
Epic, Oct., 1988
1 .... 4.00
2 .... 3.00
3 thru 6 Dec., 1989 .... @2.50

LINDA CARTER, STUDENT NURSE
Atlas, Sept., 1961
1 .... 75.00
2 thru 9, Jan., 1963 .... @50.00

LION KING
1 based on Movie 2.75

LI'L KIDS
Aug., 1970–June, 1973
1 .... 75.00
2 thru 12 .... @50.00

All comics prices listed are for Near Mint condition.

Li'l Pals–Mad Dog · MARVEL · Comics Values Annual

LI'L PALS
Sept., 1972
1 .... 75.00
2 thru 5, May, 1973 .... @50.00

LITTLE ASPRIN
July, 1949
1 HK,A;Oscar 175.00
2 HK 100.00
3 Dec., 1949 .... 50.00

LITTLE LANA
See: LANA

LITTLE LENNY
June, 1949
1 .... 125.00
2 .... 60.00
3 November, 1949 .... 60.00

LITTLE LIZZIE
June, 1949
1 Roller Skating(c) 125.00
2 Soda(c) 75.00
3 Movies(c) 75.00
4 Lizzie(c) 75.00
5 Lizzie/Swing(c) April,1950 .. 75.00
[2nd Series], Sept., 1953
1 .... 75.00
2 .... 50.00
3 Jan., 1954 .... 50.00

LITTLE MERMAID, THE
1993
1 .... 3.50
2 Reception for Pacifica royalty .. 2.50
3 TrR,Ariel joins fish club 2.50
4 .... 2.50
5 .... 2.50
6 TrR,Ariel decorates coral"tree" .. 2.50
7 TrR,Flogglefish banished 2.50
8 .... 2.50
9 Annual Sea Horse Tournament .. 2.50
10 TrR,AnnualBlowfishTournament . 2.50
11 TrR,Sharkeena,King Triton 2.50
12 .... 2.50
13 Lobster Monster 2.50

LOGAN
1-shot HMe,48pg 6.00
1-shot Logan: Path of the
  Warrior (1996) 5.00
1-shot Logan: Shadow Society,
  HMe,TCk Early life of
  Wolverine (1996) 5.00

LOGAN'S RUN
Jan., 1977
1 GP,From Movie 15.00
2 GP,Cathedral Kill 7.00
3 GP,Lair of Laser Death 7.00
4 GP,Dread Sanctuary 7.00
5 GP,End Run 7.00
6 MZ,B.U.Thanos/Drax 20.00
7 TS,Cathedral Prime 7.00

LONGSHOT
Sept., 1985
1 AAd,WPo(i),BA,I:Longshot 8.00
2 AAd,WPo(i),I:RicoshetRita 6.00
3 AAd,WPo(i),I:Mojo,Spiral 6.00
4 AAd,WPo(i),A:Spider-Man 6.00
5 AAd,WPo(i),A:Dr. Strange 6.00

6 AAd,WPo(i),A:Dr. Strange 6.00
TPB Reprints #1-#6 .... 16.95
1-shot, JMD,MZi,AW, 48pg
  (Dec., 1997) 4.00

LOOSE CANNONS
1 and 2 DAn .... @2.50
3 DAn 2.75

LORNA, THE JUNGLE GIRL
Atlas, 1953–57
1 Terrors of the Jungle,O:Lorna . 400.00
2 Headhunter's Strike
  I:Greg Knight 200.00
3 .... 175.00
4 .... 175.00
5 .... 175.00
6 RH(c),GT 135.00
7 RH(c) 135.00
8 Jungle Queen Strikes Again .. 135.00
9 .... 135.00
10 White Fang 135.00
11 Death From the Skies 135.00
12 Day of Doom 100.00
13 thru 17 .... @100.00
18 AW(c) 125.00
19 thru 26 .... @75.00

LOVE ADVENTURES
Atlas, Oct., 1949
1 Ph(c) 175.00
2 BP,Ph(c),Tyrone Power/
  Gene Tierney 150.00
3 thru 12 .... @75.00
Becomes:

ACTUAL CONFESSIONS
1952
13 .... 65.00
14 Dec., 1952 .... 65.00

LOVE DRAMAS
Oct., 1949
1 Ph(c),JKa 200.00
2 Jan., 1950 .... 125.00

LOVE ROMANCES
See: IDEAL

LOVERS
See: ALL-SELECT COMICS

LOVE SECRETS
Oct., 1949
1 .... 150.00
2 Jan., 1950 .... 100.00

LUNATIK
1995
1 KG 2.25
2 V:The Avengers 2.25
3 conclusion 2.25

MACHINE MAN
April, 1978
1 JK,From 2001 .... 20.00
2 JK 10.00
3 JK,V:Ten-For,The Mean
  Machine 10.00
4 JK,V;Ten-For,Battle on A
  Busy Street 10.00
5 JK,V;Ten-For,Day of the

Machine Man #15
© Marvel Entertainment Group

  Non-Hero 10.00
6 JK,V;Ten-For 10.00
7 JK,With A Nation Against Him .. 10.00
8 JK,Escape:Impossible 10.00
9 JK,In Final Battle 10.00
10 SD,Birth of A Super-Hero .. 6.00
11 SD,V;Binary Bug 6.00
12 SD,`Where walk the Gods' .. 6.00
13 SD,Xanadu 6.00
14 SD,V:Machine Man 6.00
15 SD,A:Thing,Human Torch .. 6.00
16 SD,I:Baron Brimstone And the
  Satan Squad 6.00
17 SD,Madam Menace 6.00
18 A:Alpha Flight 20.00
19 I:Jack o'Lantern 20.00

MACHINE MAN
[Limited-Series]
Oct., 1984
1 HT,BWS,V:Baintronics 4.00
2 HT,BWS,C:Iron Man of 2020 .. 4.00
3 HT,BWS,I:Iron Man of 2020 .. 4.00
4 HT,BWS,V:Iron Man of 2020 .. 4.00
TPB rep.#1-4 .... 5.95

MACHINE MAN 2020
1994
1 rep. limited series #1–#2 ... 2.25
2 rep. limited series #3–#4 ... 2.25

MAD ABOUT MILLIE
April, 1969
1 .... 100.00
2 thru 3 .... @60.00
4 thru 10 .... @35.00
11 thru 16 .... @30.00
17 Dec., 1970 .... 30.00
Ann.#1 .... 35.00

MADBALLS
Star, Sept., 1986
1 Based on Toys 4.00
2 thru 9 .... @4.00
10 June, 1988 .... 4.00

MAD DOG
1 from Bob TV Show 2.50
2 V:Trans World Trust Corp. .. 2.50

CVA Page 264 · All comics prices listed are for *Near Mint* condition.

MARVEL

Mad Dog–Marines

3 V:Cigarette Criminals 2.50
4 V:Dogs of War 2.50
5 thru 6 . . . . @2.50

MADE MEN
May, 1998
1-shot HMe gangster epic 6.00

Magik #4
© Marvel Entertainment Group

MAGIK
Dec., 1983
1 JB,TP,F:Storm and Illyana 4.00
2 JB,TP,A:Belasco,Sym 3.00
3 TP,A:New Mutants,Belasco 3.00
4 TP,V:Belasco,A:Sym 3.00

MAGNETO
1993
0 JD,JBo,rep. origin stories 6.00
0a Gold ed. 8.00
0b Platinum ed. 10.00

MAGNETO
1996
1 (of 4) PrM,KJo,JhB, Joseph 2.50
2 PrM,KJo,JhB, Joseph's search
 for his past life 2.50
3 PrM,KJo,JhB 2.50
4 PrM,KJo,JhB, concl. 2.50
TPB 192-pg. 19.95

MAGNETO: DARK SEDUCTION
April, 2000
1 (of 4) FaN,X-Men: Revolution . . . 3.00
2 FaN,Scarlet Witch. 3.00
3 FaN,RCz,V:Scarlet Witch 3.00
4 FaN,RCz,concl. 3.00

MAGNETO REX
March, 1999
1 (of 3) BPe,takes over Genosha . . 2.50
1a signed 19.95
2 BPe,V:Rogue 2.50
3 BPe,A:Rogue,Quicksilver 2.50
GN Magneto Ascendant,
 96-page rep. 4.00

MAN COMICS
Atlas, 1949–53
1 GT, Revenge 250.00
2 GT, Fury in his Fists 150.00
3 Mantrap 100.00
4 The Fallen Hero 100.00
5 Laugh,Fool,Laugh 100.00
6 Black Hate 100.00
7 The Killer 100.00
8 BEv,An Eye For an Eye 100.00
9 B:War Issues,Here Comes
 Sergeant Smith 75.00
10 Korean Communism 75.00
11 RH,Cannon Fodder 75.00
12 The Black Hate 75.00
13 GC,RH,Beach Head. 75.00
14 GT,No Prisoners 85.00
15 . . . . 75.00
16 . . . . 60.00
17 RH. 60.00
18 thru 20 . . . . @60.00
21 GC 60.00
22 BEv,BK,JSt 75.00
23 thru 26 . . . . @60.00
27 E:War Issues 60.00
28 Where Mummies Prowl 60.00

MANDRAKE
1995
1 fully painted series 3.25
2 V:Octon 3.25
3 final issue 3.25

MAN FROM ATLANTIS
Feb., 1978–Aug., 1978
1 TS,From TV Series,O:Mark
 Harris 20.00
2 FR,FS,The Bermuda Triangle
 Trap 12.00
3 FR,FS,Undersea Shadow 12.00
4 FR,FS,Beware the Killer
 Spores 12.00
5 FR,FS,The Ray of the
 Red Death 12.00
6 FR,FS,Bait for the Behemoth . . 12.00
7 FR,FS,Behold the Land
 Forgotten 12.00

MAN-THING
[1st Series] Jan., 1974
1 FB,JM,A:Howard the Duck 50.00
2 VM,ST,Hell Hath No Fury 25.00
3 VM,JA,I:Original Foolkiller. 20.00
4 VM,JA,O&D:Foolkiller 15.00
5 MP,Night o/t Laughing Dead . . 15.00
6 MP,V:Soul-Slayers,Drug Issue. . 15.00
7 MP,A Monster Stalks Swamp . . 15.00
8 MP,Man Into Monster 15.00
9 MP,Deathwatch. 15.00
10 MP,Nobody Dies Forever 15.00
11 MP,Dance to the Murder. 15.00
12 KJ,Death-Cry of a Dead Man . . 10.00
13 TS,V:Captain Fate 10.00
14 AA,V:Captain Fate 10.00
15 A Candle for Saint Cloud 10.00
16 JB,TP,Death of a Legend 10.00
17 JM,Book Burns in Citrusville. . . 10.00
18 JM,Chaos on the Campus 10.00
19 JM,FS,I:Scavenger 10.00
20 JM,A:Spider-Man,Daredevil,
 Shang-Chi,Thing. 11.00
21 JM,O:Scavenger,Man Thing . . 10.00
22 JM,C:Howard the Duck 10.00
G-Size #1 MP,SD,JK,rep.TheGlob . 5.00
G-Size #2 JB,KJ,The
 Monster Runs Wild 4.00
G-Size #3 AA,A World He
 Never Made 4.00

Man-Thing #19
© Marvel Entertainment Group

G-Size #4 FS,EH,inc.Howard the
 Duck vs.Gorko 4.00
G-Size #5 DA,EH,inc.Howard the
 Duck vs.Vampire 6.00

[2nd Series] 1979–1981
1 JM,BWi. 11.00
2 BWi,JM,Himalayan Nightmare. . 10.00
3 BWi.JM,V:Snowman 10.00
4 BWi,DP,V:Mordo,A:Dr Strange . 10.00
5 DP,BWi,This Girl is Terrified . . . 10.00
6 DP,BWi,Fraternity Rites 10.00
7 BWi,DP Return of Captain Fate 10.00
8 BWi,DP,V:Captain Fate. 10.00
9 BWi(c),Save the Life of My
 Own Child 10.00
10 BWi,DP,Swampfire. 10.00
11 Final issue 10.00

[3rd Series] Oct., 1997
1 JMD,LSh, non-code 3.00
2 JMD,LSh, reunion with ex-wife,
 A:Dr. Strange 3.00
3 JMD,LSh, visit to Devil Slayer . . 3.00
4 JMD,LSh, V:Devil-Slayer. 3.00
5 JMD,LSh, new abilities revealed . 3.00
6 JMD,LSh, V:Cult of Entropy . . . 3.00
7 JMD,LSh, Muck Monster, Namor 3.00
8 JMD,LSh, Muck Monster turned
 back into Ted Sallis. 3.00
Storyline continues in Strange Tales

MARINES AT WAR
See: DEVIL-DOG DUGAN

MARINES IN ACTION
Atlas, June, 1955
1 B:Rock Murdock,Boot Camp
 Brady 125.00
2 thru 13 . . . . @100.00
14 Sept., 1957 . . . . 100.00

MARINES IN BATTLE
Atlas, Aug., 1954
1 RH,B:Iron Mike McGraw 250.00
2 . . . . 125.00
3 thru 6 . . . . @100.00
7 . . . . 100.00
8 . . . . 100.00
9 . . . . 100.00
10 . . . . 100.00
11 thru 16 . . . . @100.00

All comics prices listed are for *Near Mint* condition.

Marines–Marvel | MARVEL | Comics Values Annual

17 . . . . 100.00
18 thru 22 . . . . @75.00
23 . . . . 100.00
24 . . . . 75.00
25 Sept., 1958 . . . . 100.00

MARK HAZZARD: MERC
Nov., 1986–Oct., 1987

1 GM,O:Mark Hazzard 2.25
2 GM 2.25
3 M,Arab Terrorists 2.25
4 GM 2.25
5 GM 2.25
6 GM 2.25
7 GM 2.25
8 GM 2.25
9 NKu/AKu 2.25
10 thru 12 . . . . @2.25
Ann.#1 D:Merc 2.25

MARSHALL LAW
Epic, 1987–89

1 . . . . 4.50
2 . . . . 3.00
3 thru 6 . . . . @2.50

MARVEL ACTION HOUR: FANTASTIC FOUR
1994–95

1 regular 2.25
1a bagged with insert print from
  animated series 3.00
2 V:Puppet Master 2.25
3 . . . . 2.25
4 V:Sub-Mariner 2.25
5 . . . . 2.25
6 R:Skrulls 2.25
7 V:Doctor Doom 2.25
8 Wanted by the Law 2.25

MARVEL ACTION HOUR: IRON MAN
1994–95

1 regular 2.25
1a bagged with insert print from
  animated series 3.25
2 V:War Machine 2.25
3 V:Ultimo 2.25
4 A:Force Works, Hawkeye,
  War Machine 2.25

Marvel Action Hour: Fantastic Four #3
© Marvel Entertainment Group

5 O:Iron Man 2.25
6 V:Fing Fang Foom 2.25
7 V:Mandarin 2.25
8 V:Robots 2.25

MARVEL ACTION UNIVERSE
TV Tie-in, Jan., 1989

1 Rep.Spider-Man & Friends 4.00

MARVEL ADVENTURES STARRING DAREDEVIL
Dec., 1975–Oct., 1976

1 Rep,Daredevil #22 . . . . 15.00
2 thru 5, Rep,Daredevil #23-26 . @7.00
6 DD #27 . . . . 7.00

MARVEL ADVENTURES
Feb., 1997

1 RMc,F:The Hulk 2.25
2 RMc,F:Spider-Man 2.25
3 RMc,F:Quicksilver & Scarlet
  Witch 2.25
4 RMc,BHr,F:Hulk,V:Brotherhood
  of Evil Mutants 2.25
5 RMc,BHr,F:Spider-Man, The
  X-Men 2.25
6 RMc,BHr,A:Spider-Man,Invisible
  Woman, Human Torch 2.25
7 RMc,F:Hulk,V:Tyrannus 2.25
8 RMc,V:Molto 2.25
9 RMc,F:Fantastic Four,
  Subterranean War, concl. 2.25
10 RMc,Sky-Rider vs. Gladiator . . . 2.25
11 RMc,F:Spider-Man,Sandman . . 2.25
12 RMc,F:Fantastic Four,V:Frightful
  Four 2.25
13 AM,F:Spider-Man, Silver Surfer . 2.25
14 RMc,F:The Hulk,A:Dr. Strange,
  Juggernaut 2.25
15 RMc,F:X-Men,V:Beast's army . . 2.25
16 RMc,F:Silver Surfer 2.25
17 RMc,F:Spider-Man, Iron Man . . . 2.25
18 RMc,F:Sentinel of Liberty 2.25
19 RMc,F:The Avengers 2.25
20 RMc,F:Iron Man 2.25

MARVEL & DC PRESENTS
Nov., 1982

1 WS,TA,X-Men & Titans,A:Darkseid,
  Deathstroke(3rd App.), ... 25.00

MARVEL BOY
Dec., 1950

1 RH,O:Marvel Boy,Lost World 1,400.00
2 BEv,The Zero Hour 1,000.00
Becomes:

ASTONISHING
1951

3 BEv,Marvel Boy,V:Mr Death . 1,100.00
4 BEv,Stan Lee,The
  Screaming Tomb 800.00
5 BEv,Horro in the Caves of
  Doom 800.00
6 BEv,My Coffin is Waiting
  E:Marvel Boy 800.00
7 JR,JMn,Nightmare 350.00
8 RH,Behind the Wall 350.00
9 RH(c),The Little Black Box . . . 350.00
10 BEv,Walking Dead 350.00
11 BF,JSt.Mr Mordeau 300.00
12 GC,BEv,Horror Show 300.00
13 BK,MSy,Ghouls Gold 350.00

14 BK,The Long Jump Down . . . 350.00
15 BEv(c),Grounds for Death . . . 300.00
16 BEv(c),DAy,SSh,Don't Make
  a Ghoul of Yourself 300.00
17 Who Was the Wilmach
  Werewolf? 300.00
18 BEv(c),JR,Vampire at my
  Window 300.00
19 BK,Back From the Grave 300.00
20 GC,Mystery at Midnight 300.00
21 Manhunter 250.00
22 RH(c),Man Against Werewolf . 250.00
23 The Woman in Black 275.00
24 JR,The Stone Face 275.00
25 RC,I Married a Zombie 275.00
26 RH(c),I Died Too Often 250.00
27 . . . . 250.00
28 TLw,No Evidence 250.00
29 BEv(c),GC,Decapitation(c) . . . 250.00
30 Tentacled eyeball story 300.00
31 JMn 200.00
32 A Vampire Takes a Wife 200.00
33 SMo,JMn 200.00
34 JMn,Transformation 200.00
35 . . . . 200.00
36 Pithecanthrope Giant 200.00
37 BEv,TLw,Poor Pierre 200.00
38 The Man Who Didn't Belong . 150.00
39 . . . . 150.00
40 . . . . 150.00
41 MD 150.00
42 TLw 150.00
43 BP,JR 150.00
44 RC,BP 165.00
45 BK 165.00
46 . . . . 150.00
47 BK,JO 165.00
48 BP 150.00
49 . . . . 150.00
50 DCn 150.00
51 . . . . 150.00
52 GM 150.00
53 SD,JF 165.00
54 . . . . 165.00
55 . . . . 175.00
56 JMn,JK 150.00
57 JR 175.00
58 JF,JO 150.00
59 . . . . 150.00
60 JF 150.00
61 GM,JO,JR 150.00
62 MD 150.00
63 August, 1957 . . . . 150.00

MARVEL BOY
June, 2000

1 (of 6) GMo,F:Noh-Varr 3.00
2 GMo,V:Human Race 3.00
3 GMo,Hexus 3.00
4 GMo,Exterminatrix 3.00
5 GMo,Oubliette 3.00
6 GMo,V:Dr. Midas,concl. 3.00
TPB rep.,144-page 15.95

MARVEL CHILLERS
Oct., 1975

1 GK(c),I:Mordred the Mystic . . . 20.00
2 E:Mordred 12.00
3 HC/BWr(c),B:Tigra,The Were
  Woman 12.00
4 V:Kraven The Hunter 12.00
5 V:Rat Pack,A:Red Wolf 12.00
6 RB(c),JBy,V:Red Wolf 12.00
7 JK(c),GT,V:Super Skrull
  E:Tigra,Oct., 1976 . . . . 12.00
GN MGu(s),LSh,F:The Hulk 10.00
GN LHa(s) F:Wolverine 10.00

MARVEL

MARVEL COLLECTORS ITEM CLASSICS
Feb., 1965
1 SD,JK,reprint FF #2 . . . . 125.00
2 SD,JK,reprint FF #3 . . . . 65.00
3 SD,JK,reprint FF #4 . . . . 65.00
4 SD,JK,reprint FF #7 . . . . 65.00
5 SD,JK,reprint FF #8 . . . . 50.00
6 SD,JK,reprint FF #9 . . . . 50.00
7 SD,JK,reprint FF #13 . . . . 50.00
8 SD,JK,reprint FF #10 . . . . 50.00
9 SD,JK,reprint FF #14 . . . . 50.00
10 SD,JK,reprint FF #15 . . . . 50.00
11 thru 22 SD,JK,reprint FF. . . . @35.00
Becomes:

MARVEL'S GREATEST COMICS
1969
23 thru 34 SD,JK,reprint FF. . . . @25.00
35 thru 37 JK,reprint FF . . . . . . @15.00
38 thru 50 JK,reprint FF . . . . . . @10.00
51 thru 75 JK,reprint FF . . . . @7.00
76 thru 82 JK,reprint FF . . . . @6.00
83 thru 95 Reprint FF . . . . @6.00
96 Reprint FF#, Jan., 1981 . . . . . 6.00

MARVEL COMICS
Oct.-Nov., 1939
1 FP(c),BEv,CBu,O:Sub-Mariner
 I&B:The Angel,A:Human Torch,
 Ka-Zar,Jungle Terror,
 B:The Masked Raider . . 350,000.00
Becomes:

MARVEL MYSTERY COMICS
2 CSM(c),BEv,CBu,PGn,
 B:American, Ace,Human
 Torch,Sub-Mariner,Ka-Zar 37,000.00
3 ASh(c),BEv,CBu,PGn,
 E:American Ace 18,000.00
4 ASh(c),BEv,CBu,PGn,
 I&B:Electro,The Ferret,
 Mystery Detective 16,000.00
5 ASh(c),BEv,CBu,PGn,
 Human Torch(c) 30,000.00
6 ASh(c),BEv,CBu,PGn,
 Angel(c) 9,000.00
7 ASh(c),BEv,CBu,PGn,
 Bondage(c) 9,000.00
8 ASh(c),BEv,CBu,PGn,Human
 TorchV:Sub-Mariner 15,000.00
9 ASh(c),BEv,CBu,PGn,Human
 Torch V:Sub-Mariner(c) . . 35,000.00
10 ASh(c),BEv,CBu,PGn,B:Terry
 Vance Boy Detective 9,000.00
11 ASh(c),BEv,CBu,PGn,
 Human Torch V:Nazis(c) . . 4,500.00
12 ASh(c),BEv,CBu,
 PGn,Angel(c). 5,000.00
13 ASh(c),BEv,CBu,PGn,S&K,
 I&B:The Vision. 6,500.00
14 ASh(c),BEv,CBu,PGn,S&K,
 Sub-Mariner V:Nazis 3,000.00
15 ASh(c),BEv,CBu,PGn,S&K,
 Sub-Mariner(c). 3,000.00
16 ASh(c),BEv,CBu,PGn,S&K,
 HumanTorch/NaziAirbase. . 3,000.00
17 ASh(c),BEv,CBu,PGn,S&K
 Human Torch/Sub-Mariner 3,500.00
18 ASh(c),BEv,CBu,PGn,S&K,
 Human Torch & Toro(c) . . . 2,800.00
19 ASh(c),BEv,CBu,PGn,S&K,
 O:Toro,E:Electro 2,800.00
20 ASh(c),BEv,CBu,PGn,S&K,
 O:The Angel 2,800.00
21 ASh(c),BEv,CBu,PGn,S&K,
 I&B:The Patriot 2,700.00

Marvel Chillers #1
© Marvel Entertainment Group

MARVEL CHRISTMAS SPECIAL
1 DC/AAd/KJ/SB/RLm,A:Ghost Rider
 X-Men,Spider-Man 2.25

MARVEL CLASSICS COMICS
1976-78
1 GK/DA(c),B:Reprints from
 Pendulum Illustrated Comics
 Dr.Jekyll & Mr. Hyde 25.00
2 GK(c),AN,Time Machine 15.00
3 GK/KJ(c) The Hunchback of
 Notre Dame 15.00
4 GK/DA(c),20,000 Leagues-
 Beneath the Sea by Verne. . . 15.00
5 GK(c),RN,Black Beauty 15.00
6 GK(c),Gullivers Travels 15.00
7 GK(c),Tom Sawyer 15.00
8 GK(c),AN,Moby Dick 15.00
9 GK(c),NR,Dracula. 15.00
10 GK(c),Red Badge of Courage . 15.00
11 GK(c),Mysterious Island. 12.00
12 GK/DA(c),AN,3 Musketeers . . 12.00
13 GK(c),Last of the Mohicans . . 12.00
14 GK(c),War of the Worlds 12.00
15 GK(c),Treasure Island 12.00
16 GK(c),Ivanhoe 10.00
17 JB/ECh(c),The Count of
 Monte Cristo 10.00
18 ECh(c),The Odsyssey 10.00
19 JB(c),Robinson Crusoe 10.00
20 Frankenstein 10.00
21 GK(c),Master of the World . . . 10.00
22 GK(c),Food of the Gods. 10.00
23 Moonstone by Wilkie Collins . . 10.00
24 GK/RN(c),She 10.00
25 The Invisible Man by H.G.Wells 10.00
26 JB(c),The Illiad by Homer. . . . 10.00
27 Kidnapped 10.00
28 MGo(1st art) The Pit and
 the Pendulum. 12.00
29 The Prisoner of Zenda. 10.00
30 The Arabian Nights 10.00
31 The First Men in the Moon. . . . 10.00
32 GK(c),White Fang 10.00
33 The Prince and the Pauper . . . 10.00
34 AA,Robin Hood 10.00
35 FBe,Alice in Wonderland 10.00
36 A Christmas Carol 10.00

Marvel Mystery Comics #9
© Marvel Entertainment Group

22 ASh(c),BEv,CBu,PGn,S&K,
 Toro/Bomb(c). 2,500.00
23 ASh(c),BEv,CBu,PGn,S&K,
 O:Vision,E:The Angel. . . . 2,500.00
24 ASh(c),BEv,CBu,S&K,
 Human Torch(c). 2,500.00
25 BEv,CBu,S&K,ASh Nazi(c) . 2,500.00
26 ASh(c),BEv,CBu,S&K,
 Sub-Mariner(c). 2,200.00
27 ASh(c),BEv,CBu,
 S&K,E:Ka-Zar 2,200.00
28 ASh(c),BEv,CBu,S&K,Bondage
 (c),B:Jimmy Jupiter. 2,200.00
29 ASh(c),BEv,CBu,Bondage(c) 2,200.00
30 BEv,CBu,Pearl Harbor(c) . . 2,200.00
31 BEv,CBu,Human Torch(c) . . 2,000.00
32 CBu,I:The Boboes. 2,000.00
33 ASHc(c),CBu,Japanese(c). . 2,000.00
34 ASh(c),CBu,V:Hitler. 2,200.00
35 ASh(c),Beach Assault(c) . . . 2,000.00
36 ASh(c),Nazi Invasion of
 New York(c). 2,000.00
37 SSh(c),Nazi(c) 2,000.00
38 SSh(c),Battlefield(c). 2,000.00
39 ASh(c),Nazis/U.S(c) 2,000.00
40 ASh(c),Zeppelin(c) 2,000.00
41 ASh(c),Jap. Command(c) . . 1,800.00
42 ASh(c),Japanese Sub(c) . . . 1,800.00
43 ASh(c),Destroyed Bridge(c). 1,800.00
44 ASh(c),Nazi Super Plane(c). 1,800.00
45 ASh(c),Nazi(c). 1,800.00
46 ASh(c),Hitler Bondage(c). . . 1,800.00
47 ASh(c),Ruhr Valley Dam(c) . 1,800.00
48 ASh(c),E:Jimmy Jupiter,
 Vision,Allied Invasion(c). . . 1,800.00
49 SSh(c),O:Miss America,
 Bondage(c) 2,200.00
50 ASh(c),Bondage(c),Miss
 Patriot 1,900.00
51 ASh(c),Nazi Torture(c). 1,600.00
52 ASh(c),Bondage(c) 1,600.00
53 ASh(c),Bondage(c) 1,600.00
54 ASh(c),Bondage(c) 1,600.00
55 ASh(c),Bondage(c) 1,600.00
56 ASh(c),Bondage(c) 1,600.00
57 ASh(c),Torture/Bondage(c) . 1,600.00
58 ASH(c),Torture(c) 1,600.00
59 ASh(c),Testing Room(c) . . . 1,600.00
60 ASh(c),Japanese Gun(c) . . . 1,600.00
61 Torturer Chamber(c) 1,600.00
62 ASh(c),Violent(c). 1,600.00
63 ASh(c),Nazi High
 Command(c). 1,600.00
64 ASh(c),Last Nazi(c). 1,600.00

Marvel: Comics–Comics

65 ASh(c),Bondage(c)	1,600.00
66 ASh(c),Last Japanese(c)	1,600.00
67 ASh(c),Treasury raid(c)	1,500.00
68 ASh(c),Torture Chamber(c)	1,500.00
69 ASh(c),Torture Chamber(c)	1,500.00
70 Cops & Robbers(c)	1,500.00
71 ASh(c),Egyptian(c)	1,500.00
72 Police(c)	1,500.00
73 Werewolf Headlines(c)	1,500.00
74 ASh(c),Robbery(c),E:The Patriot	1,500.00
75 Tavern(c),B:Young Allies	1,500.00
76 ASh(c),Shoot-out(c),B:Miss America	1,500.00
77 Human Torch/Sub-Mariner(c)	1,500.00
78 Safe Robbery(c)	1,500.00
79 Super Villians(c),E:The Angel	1,300.00
80 I:Capt.America(in Marvel)	1,700.00
81 Mystery o/t Crimson Terror	1,300.00
82 I:Sub-Mariner/Namora Team-up O:Namora,A:Capt.America	3,500.00
83 The Photo Phantom,E;Young Allies	1,200.00
84 BEv,B:The Blonde Phantom	1,700.00
85 BEv,A:Blonde Phantom, E;Miss America	1,200.00
86 BEv,Blonde Phantom ID Revealed,E:Bucky	1,300.00
87 BEv,I:Capt.America/Golden Girl Team-up	1,500.00
88 BEv,E:Toro	1,300.00
89 BEv,I:Human Torch/Sun Girl Team-up	1,300.00
90 BEv,Giant of the Mountains	1,300.00
91 BEv,I:Venus,E:Blonde Phantom,Sub-Mariner	1,300.00
92 BEv,How the Human Torch was Born,D:Professor Horton,I:The Witness,A:Capt.America	3,500.00
92a Marvel #33(c)rare,reprints	30,000.00

Becomes:

MARVEL TALES
Aug., 1949

93 The Ghoul Strikes	1,800.00
94 BEv,The Haunted Love	1,200.00
95 The Living Death	750.00
96 MSy,The Monster Returns	750.00
97 DRi,MSy,The Wooden Horror	1,000.00
98 BEv,BK,MSy,The Curse of the Black Cat	800.00
99 DRi,The Secret of the Wax Museum	800.00
100 The Eyes of Doom	800.00
101 The Man Who Died Twice	800.00
102 BW,A Witch Among Us	1,100.00
103 RA,A Touch of Death	850.00
104 RH(c),BW,BEv,The Thing in the Mirror	1,200.00
105 RH(c),GC,JSt,The Spider	750.00
106 RH(c),BK,BEv,In The Dead of the Night	600.00
107 GC,OW,BK,The Thing in the Sewer	600.00
108 RH(c),BEv,JR,Horror in the Moonlight	450.00
109 BEv(c),Sight for Sore Eyes	450.00
110 RH,SSh,A Coffin for Carlos	450.00
111 BEv,Horror Under the Earth	450.00
112 The House That Death Built	450.00
113 RH,Terror Tale	450.00
114 BEv,GT,JM,2 for Zombie	450.00
115 The Man With No Face	450.00
116 JSt	450.00
117 BEv(c),GK,Terror in the North	450.00
118 RH,DBr,GC,A World Goes Mad	450.00

MARVEL

119 RH,They Gave Him A Grave	450.00
120 GC,Graveyard(c)	450.00
121 GC,Graveyard(c)	350.00
122 JKu,Missing One Body	350.00
123 No Way Out	350.00
124 He Waits at the Tombstone	350.00
125 JF,Horror House	350.00
126 DW,It Came From Nowhere	250.00
127 BEv(c),GC,MD,Gone is the Gargoyle	250.00
128 Emily,Flying Saucer(c)	250.00
129 You Can't Touch Bottom	250.00
130 RH(c),JF,The Giant Killer	250.00
131 GC,BEv,Five Fingers	250.00
132	225.00
133	225.00
134 BK,JKu,Flying Saucer(c)	225.00
135 thru 143	@200.00
144	225.00
145	200.00
146	175.00
147	200.00
148 thru 151	@175.00
152	200.00
153	225.00
154 thru 158	@175.00
159 Aug., 1957	200.00

MARVEL COMICS PRESENTS
Sept., 1988

1 WS(c),B:Wolverine(JB,KJ),Master of Kung Fu(TS),Man-Thing(TGr,DC) F:Silver Surfer(AM)	10.00
2 F:The Captain(AM)	5.00
3 JR2(c),F:The Thing(AM)	4.00
4 F:Thor(AM)	4.00
5 F:Daredevil(DT,MG)	4.00
6 F:Hulk	4.00
7 F:Submariner(SD)	4.00
8 CV(c),E:Master of Kung Fu,F: Iron Man(JS)	4.00
9 F:Cloak,El Aquila	4.00
10 E:Wolverine,B:Colossus(RL,CR), F:Machine Man(SD,DC)	4.00
11 F:Ant-Man(BL),Slag(RWi)	3.00
12 E:Man-Thing,F:Hercules(DH), Namorita(FS)	3.00
13 B:Black Panther(GC,TP),F: Shanna,Mr.Fantastic & Invisible Woman	3.00
14 F:Nomad(CP),Speedball(SD)	3.00

Marvel Comics Presents #1
© Marvel Entertainment Group

Comics Values Annual

15 F:Marvel Girl(DT,MG),Red Wolf(JS)	3.00
16 F:Ka-Zar(JM),Longshot(AA)	3.00
17 E:Colossus,B:Cyclops(RLm), F:Watcher(TS)	4.00
18 F:She-Hulk(JBy,BWi),Willie Lumpkin(JSt)	3.00
19 RLd(c)B:Dr.Strange(MBg), I:Damage Control(EC,AW)	3.00
20 E:Dr.Strange,F:Clea(RLm)	3.00
21 F:Thing,Paladin(RWi,DA)	3.00
22 F:Starfox(DC),Wolfsbane & Mirage	3.00
23 F:Falcon(DC),Wheels(RWi)	3.00
24 E:Cyclops,B:Havok(RB,JRu), F:Shamrock(DJ,DA)	3.00
25 F:Ursa Major,I:Nth Man	4.00
26 B&I:Coldblood(PG),F:Hulk	2.50
27 American Eagle(RWi)	2.50
28 F:Triton(JS)	2.50
29 F:Quasar(PR)	2.50
30 F:Leir(TMo)	2.50
31 EL,E:Havok,B:Excalibur (EL,TA)	4.00
32 TM(c),F:Sunfire(DH,DC)	3.00
33 F:Namor(JLe)	4.00
34 F:Captain America(JsP)	3.00
35 E:Coldblood,F:Her(EL,AG)	4.00
36 BSz(c),F:Hellcat(JBr)	4.00
37 E:Bl.Panther,F:Devil-Slayer	3.00
38 E:Excalibur,B:Wonderman(JS), Wolverine(JB),F:Hulk(MR,DA)	4.00
39 F:Hercules(BL),Spider-Man	3.50
40 F:Hercules(BL),Overmind(DH)	3.50
41 F:Daughters of the Dragon(DA), Union Jack(KD)	3.50
42 F:Iron Man(MBa),Siryn(LSn)	3.50
43 F:Iron Man(MBa),Siryn(LSn)	3.50
44 F:Puma(BWi),Dr.Strange	3.50
45 E:Wonderman,F:Hulk(HT), Shooting Star	3.50
46 RLd(c),B:Devil-Slayer,F:Namor, Aquarian	3.50
47 JBy(c),E:Wolverine,F:Captain America,Arabian Knight(DP)	3.50
48 B:Wolverine&Spider-Man(EL), F:Wasp,Storm&Dr.Doom	5.00
49 E:Devil-Slayer,F:Daredevil(RWi), Gladiator(DH)	4.50
50 F:Wolverine&Spider-Man,B:Comet Man(KJo),F:Captain Ultra(DJ), Silver Surfer(JkS)	4.50
51 B:Wolverine(RLd),F:Iron Man (MBr,DH),Le Peregrine	4.00
52 F:Rick Jones,Hulk(RWi,TMo)	4.00
53 E:Wolverine,Comet Man,F: Silver Sable&Black Widow (RLd,BWi),B:Stingray	4.00
54 B:Wolverine&Hulk(DR), Werewolf,F:Shroud(SD,BWi)	6.00
55 F:Collective Man(GLa)	6.00
56 E:Stingray,F:Speedball(SD)	6.00
57 DK(c),B:Submariner(MC,MFm), Black Cat(JRu)	6.00
58 F:Iron Man(SD)	6.00
59 E:Submariner,Werewolf, F:Punisher	6.00
60 B:Poison,Scarlet Witch, F:Captain America(TL)	6.00
61 E:Wolverine&Hulk, F:Dr.Strange	6.00
62 F:Wolverine(PR),Deathlok(JG)	6.00
63 F:Wolverine(PR),E:Scarlet Witch,Thor(DH)	4.00
64 B:Wolverine&Ghost Rider(MT), Fantastic Four(TMo),F:Blade	4.00
65 F:Starfox(ECh)	3.50
66 F:Volstagg	3.50
67 E:Poison,F:Spider-Man(MG)	3.50
68 B:Shanna(PG),E:Fantastic Four F:Lockjaw(JA,AM)	3.50

Comics Values Annual — MARVEL — Marvel: Comics–Comics

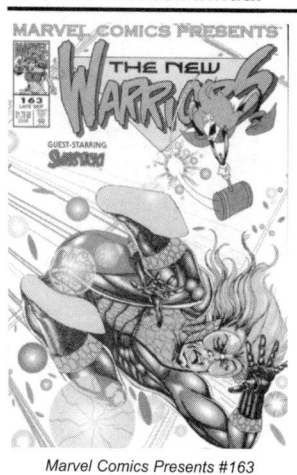

Marvel Comics Presents #163
© Marvel Entertainment Group

69 B:Daredevil(DT),F:Silver Surfer . 3.50
70 F:BlackWidow&Darkstar(AM) . . . 3.50
71 F:Wolverine&Ghost Rider,F:
    Warlock(New Mutants)(SMc) . . 3.50
72 B:Weapon X(BWS),E:Daredevil,
    F:Red Wolf(JS) 7.00
73 F:Black Knight(DC),
    Namor(JM) 5.00
74 F:Constrictor(SMc),Iceman &
    Human Torch(JSon,DA) 5.00
75 F:Meggan & Shadowcat,
    Dr.Doom(DC) 5.00
76 F:Death's Head(BHi,MFm),
    A:Woodgod(DC) 5.00
77 E:Shanna,B:Sgt.Fury&Dracula
    (TL,JRu),F:Namor 4.50
78 F:Iron Man(KSy),Hulk&Selene . . 4.50
79 F:Sgt.Fury&Dracula,F:Dr.Strange,
    Sunspot(JBy) 4.50
80 F:Daughters of the Dragon,Mister
    Fantastic(DJ),Captain America
    (SD,TA) 4.50
81 F:Captain America(SD,TA),
    Daredevil(MR,AW),Ant-Man . . . 4.00
82 B:Firestar(DT),F:Iron Man(SL),
    Power Man 4.00
83 F:Hawkeye,Hum.Torch(SD,EL) . 4.00
84 F:Weapon X 4.00
85 B:Wolverine(SK),Beast(RLd,JaL-
    1st Work),F:Speedball(RWi),
    I:Cyber 7.00
86 F:PaladinE:RLd on Beast 5.00
87 E:Firestar,F:Shroud(RWi) 5.00
88 F:Solo,Volcana(RWi) 5.00
89 F:Spitfire(JSn),Mojo(JMa) 5.00
90 B:Ghost Rider & Cable,F:
    Nightmare 4.50
91 F:Impossible Man 3.50
92 E:Wolverine,Beast,
    F:Northstar(JMa) 3.50
93 SK(c),B:Wolverine,Nova,
    F:Daredevil 3.00
94 F:Gabriel 3.00
95 SK(c),E:Wolverine,F:Hulk 3.00
96 F:Wolverine(TT),E:Nova,
    F:Speedball 3.00
97 F:Chameleon,Two-Gun Kid,
    E:Ghost Rider/Cable 3.00
98 F:Wolverine,F:Ghost Rider,
    Werewolf by Night 2.50
99 F:Wolverine,Ghost Rider,
    Mary Jane,Captain America . . . 2.50
100 SK,F:Ghost Rider,Wolverine,
    Dr.Doom,Nightmare 3.00
101 SK(c),B:Ghost Rider&Doctor
    Strange,Young Gods,Wolverine
    &Nightcrawler,F:Bar With
    No Name 2.50
102 RL,GC,AW,F:Speedball 2.50
103 RL,GC,AW,F:Puck 2.50
104 RL,GC,AW,F:Lockheed 2.50
105 RL,GC,AW,F:Nightmare 2.50
106 RL,GC,AW,F:Gabriel,E:Ghost
    Rider&Dr.Strange 2.50
107 GC,AW,TS,B:Ghost Rider&
    Werewolf 2.50
108 GC,AW,TS,SMc,E:Wolverine&
    Nightcrawler,B:Thanos 2.50
109 SLi,TS,SMc,B:Wolverine&
    Typhoid Mary,E:Young Gods . . 2.50
110 SLi,SMc,F:Nightcrawler 2.50
111 SK(c),SLi,RWi,F:Dr.Strange,
    E:Thanos 2.50
112 SK(c),SLi,F:Pip,Wonder Man,
    E:Ghost Rider&Werewolf 2.50
113 SK(c),SLi,B:Giant Man,
    Ghost Rider&Iron Fist 2.50
114 SK(c),SLi,F:Arabian Knight 2.50
115 SK(c),SLi,F:Cloak&Dagger 2.50
116 SK(c),SLi,E:Wolverine &
    Typhoid Mary 2.50
117 SK,PR,B:Wolverine&Venom,
    I:Ravage 2099 . . . . 4.00
118 SK,PB,RWi,E:Giant Man,
    I:Doom 2099 . . . . 3.00
119 SK,GC,B:Constrictor,E:Ghost
    Rider&Iron Fist,F:Wonder Man . 3.00
120 SK,GC,E:Constrictor,B:Ghost
    Rider/Cloak & Dagger,
    F:Spider-Man 2.50
121 SK,GC,F:Mirage,Andromeda . . 2.50
122 SK(c),GK,E:Wolverine&Venom,
    Ghost Rider&Cloak&Dagger,F:
    Speedball&Rage,Two-Gun Kid . 2.50
123 SK(c),DJ,SLi,B:Wolverine&Lynx,
    Ghost Rider&Typhoid Mary,
    She-Hulk,F:Master Man 2.50
124 SK(c),DJ,MBa,SLi,F:Solo 2.50
125 SLi,SMc,DJ,B:Iron Fist 2.50
126 SLi,DJ,E:She-Hulk 2.50
127 SLi,DJ,DP,F:Speedball 2.50
128 SLi,DJ,RWi,F:American Eagle . 2.50
129 SLi,DJ,F:Ant Man 2.50
130 DJ,SLi,RWi,E:Wolverine&Lynx,
    Ghost Rider&Typhoid Mary,Iron
    Fist,F:American Eagle 2.50
131 MFm,B:Wolverine,Ghost Rider&
    Cage,Iron Fist&Sabretooth,
    F:Shadowcat 2.50
132 KM(c),F:Iron Man 2.50
133 F:Cloak & Dagger 2.50
134 SLi,F:Vance Astro 2.50
135 SLi,F:Daredevil 2.50
136 B:Gh.Rider&Masters of Silence,
    F:Iron Fist,Daredevil 2.50
137 F:Ant Man 2.50
138 B:Wolverine,Spellbound 2.50
139 F:Foreigner 2.50
140 F:Captain Universe 2.50
141 BCe(s),F:Iron Fist 2.50
142 E:Gh.Rider&Masters of Silence,
    F:Mr.Fantastic 2.50
143 Siege of Darkness,pt.#3,
    B:Werewolf,Scarlet Witch,
    E:Spellbound 2.50
144 Siege of Darkness,pt.#6,
    B:Morbius 2.50
145 Siege of Darkness,pt.#11 . . . . . 2.50
146 Siege of Darkness,pt.#14 . . . . . 2.50
147 B:Vengeance,F:Falcon,Masters of
    Silence,American Eagle 2.50
148 E:Vengeance,F:Capt.Universe,
    Black Panther 2.50
149 F:Daughter o/t Dragon,Namor,
    Vengeance,Starjammers 2.50
150 ANo(s),SLi,F:Typhoid Mary,DD,
    Vengeance,Wolverine 2.50
151 ANo(s),F:Typhoid Mary,DD,
    Vengeance 2.50
152 CDi(s),PR,B:Vengeance,Wolverine,
    War Machine,Moon Knight . . . 2.50
153 CDi(s),A:Vengeance,Wolverine,
    War Machine,Moon Knight . . . 2.50
154 CDi(s),E:Vengeance,Wolverine,
    War Machine,Moon Knight . . . 2.50
155 CDi(s),B:Vengeance,Wolverine,
    War Machine,Kymaera 2.50
156 B:Shang Chi,F:Destroyer 2.50
157 F:Nick Fury 2.50
158 AD,I:Clan Destine,E:Kymaera,
    Shang Chi,Vengeance 2.50
159 B:Hawkeye, New Warriors,
    F:Fun,E:Vengeance 2.50
160 B:Vengeance,Mace 2.50
161 E:Hawkeye 2.50
162 B:Tigra,E:Mace 2.50
163 E:New Warriors 2.50
164 Tigra, Vengeance 2.50
165 Tigra, Vengeance 2.50
166 Turbo, Vengeance 2.50
167 Turbo, Vengeance 2.50
168 Thing, Vengeance 2.50
169 Mandarin, Vengeance 2.50
170 Force, Vengeance 2.50
171 Nick Fury 2.50
172 Lunatik 2.50
173 . . . . 2.50
174 . . . . 2.50
175 . . . . 2.50
TPB Ghost Rider & Cable,rep
    #90-97 . . . . 3.95
TPB Save the Tyger,rep.Wolverine
    story from #1-10 . . . . 3.95

MARVEL COMICS SUPER SPECIAL
[Magazine, 1977]
1 JB,WS,Kiss,Features &Photos 175.00
2 JB,Conan(1978) 20.00
3 WS,Close Encounters 15.00
4 GP,KJ,Beatles story 50.00
Becomes:

MARVEL SUPER SPECIAL
5 Kiss 1978 . . . . 150.00
6 GC,Jaws II 12.00
7 Does Not Exist
8 Battlestar Galactica(Tabloid) . . 20.00
9 Conan 15.00
10 GC,Starlord 10.00
11 JB,RN,Weirdworld, ... 10.00
12 JB,Weirdworld 10.00
13 JB,Weirdworld 10.00
14 GC,Meteor,adapt 10.00
15 Star Trek 10.00
15a Star Trek 12.00
16 AW,B:Movie Adapts,Empire
    Strikes Back 10.00
17 Xanadu 7.00
18 HC(c),JB,Raiders of the Lost
    Ark 7.00
19 HC,For Your Eyes Only 9.00
20 Dragonslayer 7.00
21 JB,Conan 7.00
22 JSo(c),AW,Bladerunner 9.00
23 Annie 9.00
24 Dark Crystal 9.00
25 Rock and Rule 9.00
26 Octopussy 8.00
27 AW,Return of the Jedi 9.00
28 PH(c),Krull 8.00
29 DSp,Tarzan of the Apes 8.00
30 Indiana Jones and the Temple
    of Doom 9.00
31 The Last Star Fighter 9.00

All comics prices listed are for Near Mint condition.

Marvel Comics–Graphic

32 Muppets Take Manhattan...... 9.00
33 Buckaroo Banzai............. 9.00
34 GM,Sheena................. 9.00
35 JB,Conan The Destroyer...... 9.00
36 Dune...................... 9.00
37 2010...................... 9.00
38 Red Sonja.................. 9.00
39 Santa Claus................. 9.00
40 JB,Labrynth................ 9.00
41 Howard the Duck,Nov.,1986.... 9.00

Marvel Double Feature #5
© *Marvel Entertainment Group*

MARVEL DOUBLE FEATURE
Dec., 1973

1 JK,GC,B:Tales of Suspense
  Reprints,Capt.America,
  Iron-Man 15.00
2 JK,GC ,A:Nick Fury 10.00
3 JK,GC 10.00
4 JK,GC,Cosmic Cube 10.00
5 JK,GC,V:Red Skull 10.00
6 JK,GC,V:Adaptoid 10.00
7 JK,GC,V:Tumbler 10.00
8 JK,GC,V:Super Adaptoid..... 10.00
9 GC,V:Batroc 10.00
10 GC 10.00
11 GC,Capt.America Wanted 8.00
12 GC,V:Powerman,Swordsman... 8.00
13 GC,A:Bucky................ 8.00
14 GC,V:Red Skull............. 8.00
15 GK,GC,V:Red Skull 8.00
16 GC,V:Assassin 8.00
17 JK,GC,V:Aim,Iron Man &
   Sub-Mariner #1 .... 8.00
18 JK,GC,V:Modok,Iron Man #1 .. 8.00
19 JK,GC,E:Capt.America 8.00
20 JK(c) 7.00
21 Capt.America,Black Panther
   March, 1977.............. 7.00

MARVEL DOUBLE-SHOT
Nov., 2002

1 JJu(c),Hulk, Thor............. 3.00
2 JJu(c),Doom & Avengers 3.00
3 JJu(c),F:Mr. Fantastic 3.00
4 JJu(c),F:Iron Man 3.00

MARVEL FANFARE
March, 1972

1 MG,TA,PS,F:Spider-Man,
  Daredevil,Angel 7.00

MARVEL

2 MG,SM,FF,TVe,F:SpM,Ka-Zar .. 5.00
3 DC,F:X-Men............... 5.00
4 PS,TA,MG,F:X-Men,Deathlok .. 5.00
5 MR,F:Dr.Strange............ 4.00
6 F:Spider-Man,Scarlet Witch ... 4.50
7 F:Hulk/Daredevil............ 3.00
8 CI,TA,GK,F:Dr.Strange 3.00
9 GM,F:Man Thing 3.00
10 GP,B:Black Widow........... 3.50
11 GP,D:M.Corcoran........... 3.50
12 GP,V:Snapdragon 3.50
13 GP,E:B.Widow,V:Snapdragon .. 3.50
14 F:Fantastic Four,Vision 2.75
15 BWS,F:Thing,Human Torch ... 3.00
16 DC,JSt,F:Skywolf............ 2.50
17 DC,JSt,F:Skywolf............ 2.50
18 FM,JRu,F:Captain America ... 3.00
19 RL,F:Cloak and Dagger 2.50
20 JSn,F:Thing&Dr.Strange 3.00
21 JSn,F:Thing And Hulk 3.00
22 KSy,F:Iron Man 2.50
23 KSy,F:Iron Man 2.50
24 F:Weird World 3.00
25 F:Weird World 2.50
26 F:Weird World 2.50
27 F:Daredevil 2.50
28 KSy,F:Alpha Flight 2.50
29 JBy,F:Hulk................. 3.00
30 BA,AW,F:Moon Knight 2.50
31 KGa,F:Capt.America,
   Yellow Claw 2.50
32 KGa,PS,F:Capt.America,
   Yellow Claw 2.50
33 JBr,F:X-Men................ 5.00
34 CV,F:Warriors Three 2.50
35 CV,F:Warriors Three 2.50
36 CV,F:Warriors Three 2.50
37 CV,F:Warriors Three 2.50
38 F:Captain America 2.50
39 JSon,F:Hawkeye,Moon Knight .. 2.50
40 DM,F:Angel,Storm,Mystique... 3.00
41 DGb,F:Dr.Strange 2.50
42 F:Spider-Man............... 3.00
43 F:Sub-Mariner,Human Torch .. 2.50
44 KSy,F:Iron Man vs.Dr.Doom... 2.50
45 All Pin-up Issue,WS,AAd,MZ,
   JOy,BSz,KJ,HC,PS,JBy 3.00
46 F:Fantastic Four 2.50
47 MG,F:Spider-Man,Hulk 3.00
48 KGa,F:She-Hulk 2.50
49 F:Dr.Strange 2.50
50 JSon,JRu,F:Angel 3.00
51 JB,JA,GC,AW,F:Silver Surfer... 4.00
52 F:Fantastic Four 2.50
53 GC,AW,F:Bl.Knight,Dr.Strange.. 2.50
54 F:Black Knight,Wolverine 3.50
55 F:Powerpack,Wolverine 3.50
56 CI,DH,F:Shanna t/She-Devil ... 2.50
57 BBI,AM,F:Shanna,Cap.Marvel .. 2.50
58 BBI,F:Shanna,Vision/Sc.Witch .. 2.50
59 BBI,F:Shanna,Hellcat......... 2.50
60 PS,F:Daredevil,Capt.Marvel.... 2.50

MARVEL FANFARE
Second Series 1996

1 Captain America, Falcon....... 2.25
2 New Fantastic Four 2.25
3 BbB,F:Spider-Man, Ghost Rider,. 2.25
4 F:Longshot................. 2.25
5 F:Longshot................. 2.25
6 F:Power Man & Iron Fist V:
  Sabretooth 2.25

MARVEL FEATURE
[1st Regular Series]
Dec., 1971

1 RA,BE,NA,I&O:Defenders &
  Omegatron 225.00
2 BEv,F:The Defenders 100.00

Comics Values Annual

Marvel Feature #5
© *Marvel Entertainment Group*

3 BEv,F:The Defenders 75.00
4 F:Ant-Man 35.00
5 F:Ant-Man 20.00
6 F:Ant-Man 15.00
7 CR,F:Ant-Man 15.00
8 JSc,CR,F:Ant-Man,O:Wasp.... 15.00
9 CR,F:Ant-Man 15.00
10 CR,F:Ant-Man 15.00
11 JSn,JSt,F:Thing & Hulk 65.00
12 JSn,JSt,F:Thing,Iron Man,
   Thanos,Blood Brothers...... 30.00

[2nd Regular Series]
(All issues feature Red Sonja)

1 DG,The Temple of Abomination 12.00
2 FT,Blood of the Hunter 7.00
3 FT,Balek Lives 7.00
4 FT,Eyes of the Gorgon 8.00
5 FT,The Bear God Walks 8.00
6 FT,C:Conan,Belit............. 8.00
7 FT,V:Conan,A:Belit,Conan#68... 12.00

MARVEL FRONTIER COMICS SPECIAL

1 All Frontier Characters 3.25
1994 .... 2.95

MARVEL FUMETTI BOOK
April, 1984

1 NA(c),Stan Lee, All photos 5.00

MARVEL GRAPHIC NOVEL
1982

1 JSn,D:Captain Marvel,A:Most
  Marvel Characters 30.00
1a 2nd printing 10.00
1b 3rd-5th printing 8.00
2 F:Elric,Dreaming City 12.00
2a 2nd printing 7.00
3 JSn,F:Dreadstar............. 15.00
3a 2nd-3rd printing 7.00
4 BMc,I:New Mutants,Cannonball
  Sunspot,Psyche,Wolfsbane .. 22.00
4a 2nd printing 10.00
4b 3rd-4th printing 8.00
5 BA,F:X-Men 20.00
5a 2nd printing 9.00
5b 3rd-5th printing 7.00
6 WS,F:Starslammers 10.00
6a 2nd printing 7.00
7 CR,F:Killraven 10.00

CVA Page 270   All comics prices listed are for *Near Mint* condition.

Marvel Graphic Novel #1
© Marvel Entertainment Group

MARVEL HALLOWEEN: THE SUPERNATURALS TOUR BOOK
Sept., 1999
1-shot, 16-page, cardstock cov 3.00

MARVEL HEROES
1 StL,FaN,Mega-Jam,48-pg. 3.00

MARVEL: HEROES AND LEGENDS 1997
Aug., 1997
1-shot, Stan Lee, JR(c) 6.00

MARVEL HOLIDAY SPECIAL
1 StG(s),PDd(s),SLo(s),RLm,PB, . . 3.25
1-shot MWa,KK 2.95

MARVEL KIDS
1999
Fantastic Four: Franklin's Adventures 3.50
Incredible Hulk: Project Hide 3.50
Spider-Man Mysteries 3.50
X-Men: Mutant Search R.U.1 . . . . . 3.50

MARVEL KNIGHTS
May, 2000
1 JQ,JP,KJ 3.50
2A JQ,KJ,CDi,EB,V:Ulik 3.00
2B variant EB(c) 3.00
3 JQ,KJ,CDi,EB,V:Ulik 3.00
4 JQ,KJ,CDi,EB,Zaran 3.00
5 JQ,KJ,CDi,EB,DaddyWronglegs . 3.00
6 JQ,KJ,CDi,EB,MaximumSecurity . 3.00
7 JQ,KJ,CDi,EB,F:Dr.Strange 3.00
8 JQ,CDi,EB,V:Cloak 3.00
9 JQ,CDi,EB,Dagger vs. Cloak . . . 3.00
10 JQ,CDi,EB,Punisher 3.00
11 CDi,EB,Luke Cage, Power Man . 3.00
12 CDi,EB,A:Cloak 3.00
13 CDi,EB,A:Black Widow,Dagger . 3.00
14 CDi,EB,one quits 3.00
15 CDi,EB,V:S.H.I.E.L.D. 3.00
GN Millennial Visions,TyH,48-pg. . . 4.00

MARVEL KNIGHTS
March, 2002
1 Punisher,Daredevil,Black Widow . 3.00
2 F:The Brothers Grace, Mr. Tune . 3.00
3 F:Brothers Grace 3.00
4 F:Brothers Grace 3.00
5 F:Mr. Tune 3.00
6 . . . . 3.00

MARVEL KNIGHTS: DOUBLE-SHOT
Oct., 2001
1 GEn,JQ,Daredevil & Punisher. . . 3.00
2 GEn,Nick Fury & Man-Thing 3.00
3 GF(c),Elektra & Cloak&Daggar . . 3.00
4 GeH,GF(c),Iron Fist 3.00
5 GeH,GF(c),Daredevil 3.00

MARVEL KNIGHTS MAGAZINE
May, 2001
2 thru 7, 80-page, rep. . . . . @4.00

MARVEL KNIGHTS TOUR BOOK
Aug., 1998
1-shot, cardstock cover 3.00

MARVEL: THE LOST GENERATION
Jan., 2000
12 (of 12) JBy,AM,Fireball, Flatiron, Cassandra, Oxbow, etc 3.00
11 JBy,AM,F:Justice 3.00
10 JBy,AM,O:Walkabout 3.00
9 JBy,AM,Effigy,Black Fox 3.00
8 JBy,AM,Nocturne 3.00
7 JBy,AM,Knight Templar 3.00
6 JBy,AM,First Line 3.00
5 JBy,AM,F:Thor 3.00
4 JBy,AM,Yankee Clipper 3.00
3 JBy,AM,Liberty Girl 3.00
2 JBy,AM,V:Yankee Clipper 3.00
1 JBy,AM,concl. 3.00

MARVEL MANGAVERSE
Jan., 2002
New Dawn #1 BDn 3.00
Avengers #1 . . . . 2.25
Fantastic Four #1 AWa 2.25
Ghost Rider #1 . . . . 2.25
Punisher #1 PDd(s) 2.25
Spider-Man #1 . . . . 2.25
X-Men #1 JMs 2.25
Eternal Twilight #1 BDn 3.00
TPB series rep. 224-pg.(2002) . . . 24.95
TPB Vol. 2 (2002) 13.00

MARVEL MANGAVERSE
April, 2002
1 BDn, F:Marvin Elwood 3.00
2 BDn, Inhumans 2.25
3 BDn, V:Galactus 2.25
4 BDn, UN held hostage 2.25
5 BDn 2.25
6 BDd, only Doom knows 2.25
TPB Vol. 3: Spider-Man 12.00
TPB Vol. 4: X-Men – Ronin 14.00

MARVEL MASTERPIECES COLLECTION
1993
1 Joe Jusko Masterpiece Cards . . . 3.25
2 F:Wolverine,Thanos,Apocalypse . 3.00
3 F:Gambit,Venom,Hulk 3.00
4 F:Wolverine Vs. Sabretooth 3.00

MARVEL MASTERPIECES II COLLECTION
1994
1 thru 3 w/cards . . . . @3.00

MARVEL MILESTONE EDITIONS 1991–95
See: ORIGINAL TITLES

MARVEL MINI-BOOKS
1966
(black & white)
1 F:Capt.America,Spider-Man,Hulk Thor,Sgt.Fury 75.00
2 F:Capt.America,Spider-Man,Hulk Thor,Sgt.Fury 75.00
3 F:Capt.America,Spider-Man,Hulk

---

8 RWi,AG,F:Super Boxers 10.00
8a 2nd printing 7.00
9 DC,F:Futurians 12.00
9a 2nd printing 7.00
10 RV,F:Heartburst 10.00
10a 2nd printing 6.00
11 VM,F:Void Indigo 12.00
12 F:Dazzler the Movie 10.00
12a 2nd printing 6.00
13 MK,F:Starstruck 10.00
14 JG,F:SwordsofSwashbucklers . 10.00
15 CV,F:Raven Banner 10.00
16 GLa,F:Alladin Effect 10.00
17 MS,F:Living Monolith 10.00
18 JBy,F:She-Hulk 15.00
18 later printings 14.00
19 F:Conan 15.00
20 F:Greenberg the Vampire 10.00
21 JBo,F:Marada the She-wolf . . . 10.00
22 BWr,Hooky,F:Spider-Man 16.00
23 DGr,F:Dr.Strange 10.00
24 FM,BSz,F:Daredevil 15.00
25 F:Dracula 10.00
26 FC,TA,F:Alien Legion 15.00
27 BH,F:Avengers 15.00
28 JSe,F:Conan the Reaver 16.00
29 BWr,F:Thing & Hulk 10.00
30 F:A Sailor's Story 10.00
31 F:Wolf Pack 10.00
32 SA,F:Death of Groo 17.00
33 F:Thor 10.00
34 AW,F:Cloak & Dagger 10.00
35 MK/RH,F:The Shadow 18.00
36 F:Willow movie adaption 10.00
37 BL,F:Hercules 15.00
38 JB,F:Silver Surfer 20.00
39 F:Iron Man,Crash 14.50
40 JZ,F:The Punisher 12.00
41 F:Roger Rabbit 10.00
42 F:Conan of the Isles 15.00
43 EC,F:Ax 12.00
44 BJ,F:Arena 10.00
45 JRy,F:Dr.Who 12.00
46 TD,F:Kull 10.00
47 GM,F:Dreamwalker 10.00
48 F:Sailor's Storm II 10.00
49 MBd,F:Dr.Strange&Dr.Doom . . 25.00
50 F:Spider-Man,Parallel Lives . . . 12.00
51 F:Punisher,Intruder 14.00
52 DSp,F:Roger Rabbit 12.00
53 PG,F:Conan 12.00
54 HC,F:Wolverine & Nick Fury . . 20.00

Marvel: Mini–Preview

Thor,Sgt.Fury 75.00
4 thru 6 F:Capt.America,Spider-Man,
Hulk,Thor,Sgt.Fury . . . . @75.00

MARVEL MOVIE PREMIERE
B&W Magazine, 1975
1 Land That Time Forgot,
Burroughs adapt. 20.00

MARVEL MOVIE SHOWCASE FEATURING STAR WARS
Nov., 1982
1 Rep,Stars Wars #1-6 . . . . 5.00
2 Dec., 1982 . . . . 5.00

MARVEL MOVIE SPOTLIGHT FEATURING RAIDERS OF THE LOST ARK
Nov., 1982
1 Rep,Raiders of Lost Ark#1-3 . . . 3.00

MARVEL MYSTERY COMICS
See: MARVEL COMICS

MARVEL MYSTERY COMICS
Oct., 1999
Spec. 80-pg. 4.00

MARVEL NO-PRIZE BOOK
Jan., 1983
1 MGo(c),Stan Lee as
Dr.Doom(c). 4.00

MARVEL: PORTRAITS OF A UNIVERSE
1 Fully painted moments 3.00
2 Fully painted moments 3.00
3 F:Death of Elektra 3.00
4 final issue. 3.00

Marvel Premier #57
© Marvel Entertainment Group

MARVEL

MARVEL POSTER BOOK
June, 2001
Summer 2001, 64-page 3.50
Winter 2001, 64-page 3.50

MARVEL PREMIERE
April, 1972
1 GK,O:Warlock,Receives Soul Gem,
Creation of Counter Earth. . . . 75.00
2 GK,JK,F:Warlock 35.00
3 BWS,F:Dr.Strange 65.00
4 FB,BWS,F:Dr.Strange. 25.00
5 MP,CR,F:Dr.Strange,I:Sligguth . 20.00
6 MP,FB,F:Dr.Strange 15.00
7 MP,CR,F:Dr.Strange,I:Dagoth . 15.00
8 JSn,F:Dr.Strange 15.00
9 NA,FB,F:Dr.Strange 15.00
10 FB,F:Dr.Strange,
D:Ancient One 25.00
11 NA,FB,F:Dr.Strange,I:Shuma . 15.00
12 NA,FB,F:Dr.Strange 15.00
13 NA,FB,F:Dr.Strange 15.00
14 NA,FB,F:Dr.Strange 15.00
15 GK,DG,I&O:Iron Fist,pt.1 . . . 100.00
16 DG,O:Iron Fist,pt.2,V:Scythe . 35.00
17 DG,`Citadel on the
Edge of Vengeance' 20.00
18 DG,V:Triple Irons 20.00
19 DG,A:Ninja 20.00
20 I:Misty Knight. 20.00
21 V:Living Goddess. 20.00
22 V:Ninja. 20.00
23 PB,V:Warhawk. 20.00
24 PB,V:Monstroid 20.00
25 1st JBy,AMc,E:Iron Fist 35.00
26 JK,GT,F:Hercules. 8.00
27 F:Satana 8.00
28 F:Legion Of Monsters,A:Ghost
Rider,Morbius,Werewolf. 20.00
29 JK,I:Liberty Legion,
O:Red Raven 6.00
30 JK,F:Liberty Legion 6.00
31 JK,I:Woodgod 6.00
32 HC,F:Monark 5.00
33 HC,F:Solomon Kane 5.00
34 HC,F:Solomon Kane 5.00
35 I&O:Silver Age 3-D Man. 5.00
36 F:3-D Man 5.00
37 F:3-D Man 5.00
38 AN,MP,I:Weird World 5.00
39 AM,I:Torpedo(1st solo) 5.00
40 AM,F:Torpedo 5.00
41 TS,F:Seeker 3000 . . . . 5.00
42 F:Tigra. 5.00
43 F:Paladin. 5.00
44 KG,F:Jack of Hearts(1stSolo). . 5.00
45 GP,F:Manwolf 5.00
46 GP,F:Manwolf 5.00
47 JBy,I:2nd Antman(Scott Lang) . . 6.00
48 JBy,F:2nd Antman 5.00
49 F:The Falcon 4.00
50 TS,TA,F:Alice Cooper 20.00
51 JBi,F:Black Panther,V:Klan . . . 3.00
52 JBi,F:B.Panther,V:Klan. 3.00
53 JBi,F:B.Panther,V:Klan. 3.00
54 GD,TD,I:Hammer. 3.00
55 JSt,F:Wonderman(1st solo) . . . 4.00
56 HC,TA,F:Dominic Fortune 3.00
57 WS(c),I:Dr.Who 5.00
58 TA(c),FM,F:Dr.Who 3.00
59 F:Dr.Who. 3.00
60 WS(c),DGb,F:Dr.Who 3.00
61 TS,F:Starlord 3.00

MARVEL PRESENTS
Oct., 1975
1 BMc,F:Bloodstone 15.00
2 BMc,O:Bloodstone 9.00
3 AM,B:Guardians/Galaxy 16.00

Marvel Presents #10
© Marvel Entertainment Group

4 AM,I:Nikki 12.00
5 AM,`Planet o/t Absurd' 12.00
6 AM,V:Karanada 12.00
7 AM,`Embrace the Void' 12.00
8 AM,JB,JSt,reprint.S.Surfer#2. . 15.00
9 AM,O:Starhawk. 12.00
10 AM,O:Starhawk 12.00
11 AM,D:Starhawk's Children . . . 12.00
12 AM,E:Guardians o/t Galaxy . . 12.00

MARVEL PREVIEW
B&W Mag, Feb., 1975
1 NA,AN,Man Gods From
Beyond the Stars 15.00
2 GM(c),O:Punisher 100.00
3 GM(c),Blade the Vampire Slayer 20.00
4 GM(c),I&O:Starlord 15.00
5 Sherlock Holmes 15.00
6 Sherlock Holmes 15.00
7 KG,Satana,A:Sword in the Star. 15.00
8 GM,MP,Legion of Monsters. . . . 20.00
9 Man-God,O:Starhawk. 10.00
10 JSn,Thor the Mighty. 20.00
11 JBy,I:Starlord 10.00
12 MK,Haunt of Horror 6.00
13 JSn(c),Starhawk 6.00
14 JSn(c),Starhawk 6.00
15 MK(c),Starhawk 6.00
16 GC,Detectives 6.00
17 GK,Black Mask 5.00
18 GC,Starlord 5.00
19 Kull 5.00
20 HC,NA,GP,Bizarre Adventures . . 6.00
21 SD,Moonlight. 6.00
22 JB,King Arthur 5.00
23 JB,GC,FM,Bizarre Adventures . . 6.00
24 Debut Paradox 5.00
Becomes:

BIZARRE ADVENTURES
1981
25 MG,TA,MR,Lethal Ladies 10.00
26 JB(c),King Kull. 10.00
27 JB,AA,GP,Phoenix,A:Ice-Man. . 15.00
28 MG,TA,FM,NA,The Unlikely
Heroes,Elektra 15.00
29 JB,WS,Horror 10.00
30 JB,Tomorrow 10.00
31 JBy,After the Violence Stops . . 10.00
32 Gods 10.00
33 Ph(c),Horror. 10.00
34 PS,Christmas Spec,Son of Santa
Howard the Duck,Feb.,1983 . . 8.00

CVA Page 272   All comics prices listed are for *Near Mint* condition.

MARVEL PREVIEW
1993
Preview of 1993 . . . . 4.00

MARVEL REMIX
Nov., 1998
1 (of 3) Fantastic Four 3.00
1a signed 20.00
2 Fantastic Four:Fireworks 3.00
3 Fantastic Four:Fireworks 3.00

MARVELS
1994
1 B:KBk(s),AxR,I:Phil Sheldon,
  A:G.A.Heroes,Human Torch Vs
  Namor 10.00
2 AxR,A:S.A.Avengers,FF,X-Men . . 8.00
3 AxR,FF vs Galactus 8.00
4 AxR,Final issue 8.00

MARVEL SAGA
Dec., 1985
1 JBy,Fantastic Four,Wolv 3.00
2 Hulk 2.50
3 Spider-Man 3.00
4 X-Men 3.00
5 Thor 2.50
6 Fantastic Four 2.50
7 Avengers 2.50
8 X-Men 2.50
9 Angel 2.50
10 X-Men 2.50
11 X-Men 2.50
12 O:Capt. America 2.50
13 O:Daredevil,Elektra 2.50
14 O:Green Goblin 2.50
15 Avengers 2.50
16 Daredevil,X-Men 2.50
17 Ka-Zar,X-Men 2.50
18 Hawkeye-Quicksilver 2.50
19 SpM,Thor,Daredevil 2.50
20 Daredevil,Giant Man 2.50
21 FF,V:Frightful Four 2.50
22 Wedding 2.50
23 . . . . 2.50
24 . . . . 2.50
25 O:Silver Surfer,Dec.,1987 . . . . . 2.75

MARVEL SELECTS: FANTASTIC FOUR
Nov., 1999
1 (of 12) 2.75
2 rep. Vol. 1, #108, AD(c) 2.75
3 rep. Vol. 1, #109, AD(c) 2.75
4 rep. Vol. 1, #110, AD(c) 2.75
5 rep. Vol. 1, #111, AD(c) 2.75
6 rep. Vol. 1, #112, AD(c) 2.75

MARVEL SELECTS: SPIDER-MAN
Nov., 1999
1 (of 12) 2.75
2 rep. Amaz.Sp-M #101 . . . . 2.75
3 rep. Amaz.Sp-M #102 . . . . 2.75
4 rep. Amaz.Sp-M #103 . . . . 2.75
5 rep. Amaz.Sp-M #104 . . . . 2.75
6 rep. Amaz.Sp-M #105 . . . . 2.75

MARVEL: SHADOWS & LIGHT
B&W 1996
1-shot MGo,JPL,KJ,48-pg 3.00

MARVEL 1602
Marvel Aug. 2003
1 (of 8) NGa(s),NKu 3.50
2 NGa(s),NKu 3.50
3 NGa(s),NKu 3.50
4 NGa(s),NKu 3.50

MARVEL SPECTACULAR
Aug., 1973–Nov., 1975
1 JK,rep Thor #128 . . . . 15.00
2 thru 10 JK,rep Thor #129–#139 @7.00
11 thru 19 JK,rep Thor#140–#148 @6.00

MARVEL SPOTLIGHT
[1st Regular Series] Nov., 1971
1 NA(c)WW,F:Red Wolf 50.00
2 MP,BEv,NA,I&O:Werewolf 225.00
3 MP,F:Werewolf 75.00
4 SD,MP,F:Werewolf 75.00
5 SD,MP,I&O:Ghost Rider 200.00
6 MP,TS,F:Ghost Rider 50.00
7 MP,TS,F:Ghost Rider 50.00
8 JM,MB,F:Ghost Rider 50.00
9 TA,F:Ghost Rider 45.00
10 SD,JM,F:Ghost Rider 45.00
11 SD,F:Ghost Rider 45.00
12 SD,2nd A:Son of Satan 45.00
13 F:Son of Satan 18.00
14 JM,F:Son of Satan,I:Ikthalon . . 18.00
15 JM, F:Son of Satan,
   I:Baphomet 15.00
16 JM,F:Son of Satan 15.00
17 JM,F:Son of Satan 15.00
18 F:Son of Satan, I:Allatou 15.00
19 F:Son of Satan 15.00
20 F:Son of Satan 15.00
21 F:Son of Satan 15.00
22 F:Son of Satan, Ghost Rider . . 18.00
23 F:Son of Satan 15.00
24 JM,F:Son of Satan 15.00
25 GT,F:Sinbad 12.00
26 F:The Scarecrow 12.00
27 F:The Sub-Mariner 20.00
28 F:Moon Knight (1st full solo) . . 35.00
29 F:Moon Knight 40.00
30 JSt,JB,F:Warriors Three 20.00
31 HC,JSn,F:Nick Fury 20.00
32 I:Spiderwoman, Jessica Drew . 20.00
33 F:Deathlok, I:Devilslayer 10.00

[2nd Regualar Series] 1979
1 PB,F:Captain Marvel 4.00
1a No`1' on Cover 12.00
2 FM(c),F:Captain Marvel,A:Eon . . 3.00
3 PB,F:Captain Marvel 3.00
4 PB,F:Captain Marvel 3.00
5 FM(c),SD,F:Dragon Lord 3.00
6 F:Star Lord 3.00
7 FM(c),F:StarLord 3.00
8 FM,F:Captain Marvel 7.00
9 FM(c),SD,F:Captain Universe . . . 3.00
10 SD,F:Captain Universe 3.00
11 SD,F:Captain Universe 3.00

MARVEL SPOTLIGHT ON CAPTAIN AMERICA
1 thru 4, Captain America rep . . . @3.00

MARVEL SPOTLIGHT ON DR. STRANGE
1 thru 4, Dr. Strange, rep . . . . . . @3.00

MARVEL SPOTLIGHT ON SILVER SURFER
1 thru 4, Silver Surfer, rep . . . . . . @3.00

MARVEL SUPER ACTION
Jan., 1976
1-shot TD,GE,FS,MP,HC,F:Punisher,
  Weirdworld,Dominic Fortune,
  I:Huntress(Mockingbird) 65.00

Marvel Super Action #24
© Marvel Entertainment Group

MARVEL SUPER ACTION
May, 1977–Nov., 1981
1 JK,reprint,Capt.America #100 . . 15.00
2 JK,reprint,Capt.America #101 . . 10.00
3 JK,reprint,Capt.America #102 . . 10.00
4 BEv,RH,reprint,Marvel Boy #1 . . 10.00
5 JK,reprint,Capt.America #103 . . 10.00
6 JK,reprint,Capt.America #104 . . . 8.00
7 JK,reprint,Capt.America #105 . . . 8.00
8 JK,reprint,Capt.America #106 . . . 8.00
9 JK,reprint,Capt.America #107 . . . 8.00
10 JK,reprint,Capt.America #108 . . 8.00
11 JK,reprint,Capt.America #109 . . 8.00
12 JSo,reprint,Capt.America #110 . . 8.00
13 JSo,reprint,Capt.America #111 . . 8.00
14 JB,reprint,Avengers #55 . . . . . . 8.00
15 JB,reprint,Avengers #56 . . . . . . 8.00
16 Reprint,Avengers,annual #2 . . . 5.00
17 Reprint,Avengers # 5.00
18 JB(c),reprint,Avengers #57 . . . . 5.00
19 JB(c),reprint,Avengers #58 . . . . 5.00
20 JB(c),reprint,Avengers #59 . . . . 5.00
21 Reprint,Avengers #60 . . . . 4.00
22 JB(c),reprint,Avengers #61 . . . . 4.00
23 Reprint,Avengers #63 . . . . 4.00
24 Reprint,Avengers #64 . . . . 4.00
25 Reprint,Avengers #65 . . . . 4.00
26 Reprint,Avengers #66 . . . . 4.00
27 BWS,Reprint,Avengers #67 . . . 4.00
28 BWS,Reprint,Avengers #68 . . . 4.00
29 Reprint,Avengers #69 . . . . 4.00
30 Reprint,Avengers #70 . . . . 4.00
31 Reprint,Avengers #71 . . . . 4.00
32 Reprint,Avengers #72 . . . . 4.00
33 Reprint,Avengers #73 . . . . 4.00
34 Reprint,Avengers #74 . . . . 4.00
35 JB(c),Reprint,Avengers #75 . . . 4.00
36 JB(c),Reprint,Avengers #75 . . . 4.00
37 JB(c),Reprint,Avengers #76 . . . 4.00

MARVEL SUPERHEROES
Oct., 1966
1-shot Rep. D.D. #1, Avengers #2,
  Marvel Mystery #8 . . . . 150.00

Marvel: Super–Tales

Marvel Super-Heroes #16
© Marvel Entertainment Group

MARVEL SUPER-HEROES
[1st Regular Series] 1967–71
(Prev.: Fantasy Masterpieces)
12 GC,I&O:Captain Marvel 175.00
13 GC,2nd A:Captain Marvel 75.00
14 F:Spider-Man 125.00
15 GC,F:Medusa 50.00
16 I:Phantom Eagle 50.00
17 O:Black Knight 50.00
18 GC,I:Guardians o/t Galaxy ... 65.00
19 F:Ka-Zar 30.00
20 F:Dr.Doom,Diablo 30.00
21 thru 31 reprints .... @20.00
32 thru 55 rep. Hulk/Submariner
    from Tales to Astonish ..... @7.00
56 reprints Hulk #102 .... 5.00
57 thru 105 reps.Hulk issues ... @5.00

MARVEL SUPERHEROES
[2nd Regular Series] May, 1990
1 RLm,F:Hercules,Moon Knight,
   Magik,Bl.Panther,Speedball ... 4.00
2 .... 3.50
3 F:Captain America,Hulk,Wasp... 4.00
4 AD,F:SpM,N.Fury,D.D.,Speedball
   Wond.Man,Spitfire,Bl.Knight ... 3.50
5 F:Thor,Thing,Speedball,
   Dr.Strange 3.50
6 RB,SD,F:X-Men,Power Pack,
   Speedball,Sabra 3.00
7 RB,F:X-Men,Cloak & Dagger ... 2.75
8 F:X-Men,Iron Man,Namor 2.75
9 F:Avengers W.C,Thor,Iron Man.. 3.00
10 DH,F:Namor,Fantastic Four,
    Ms.Marvel#24 .... 3.50
11 F:Namor,Ms.Marvel#25 .... 3.00
12 F:Dr.Strange,Falcon,Iron Man . 3.00
13 F:Iron Man 3.00
14 BMc,RWi,F:Iron Man,
    Speedball, Dr.Strange 3.00
15 KP,DH,F:Thor,Iron Man,Hulk ... 3.00
Holiday Spec.#1 AAd,DC,JRu,F:FF,
    X-Men,Spider-Man,Punisher... 3.25
Holiday Spec.#2 AAd(c),SK,MGo,
    RLm,SLi,F:Hulk,Wolverine,
    Thanos,Spider-Man 3.25
Fall Spec.RB,A:X-Men,Shroud,
    Marvel Boy,Cloak & Dagger .. 3.00

MARVEL

MARVEL SUPERHEROES MEGAZINE
1 thru 6 rep .... @3.00

MARVEL SUPER SPECIAL
See: MARVEL COMICS

MARVEL SWIMSUIT
1992
1 Schwing Break 10.00

MARVEL TAILS
Nov., 1983
1 ST,Peter Porker 5.00

MARVEL TALES
1964
1 All reprints,O:Spider-Man 400.00
2 rep.Avengers #1,X-Men #1,
   Hulk #3 .... 150.00
3 rep.Amaz.SpM.#6 .... 75.00
4 rep.Amaz.SpM.#7 .... 50.00
5 rep.Amaz.SpM.#8 .... 50.00
6 rep.Amaz.SpM.#9 .... 50.00
7 rep.Amaz.SpM.#10 .... 50.00
8 rep.Amaz.SpM.#13 .... 35.00
9 rep.Amaz.SpM.#14 .... 35.00
10 rep.Amaz.SpM.#15 .... 35.00
11 rep.Amaz.SpM.#16 .... 35.00
12 rep.Amaz.SpM.#17 .... 35.00
13 rep.Amaz.SpM.#18
    rep.1950's Marvel Boy 35.00
14 rep.Amaz.SpM.#19,
    reps.Marvel Boy 25.00
15 rep.Amaz.SpM.#20,
    reps.Marvel Boy 25.00
16 rep.Amaz.SpM.#21,
    reps.Marvel Boy 25.00
17 thru 22 rep.Amaz.SpM.
    #22-#27 .... @25.00
23 thru 27 rep.Amaz.SpM.
    #30-#34 .... @25.00
28 rep.Amaz.SpM.#35&36 ...... 25.00
29 rep.Amaz.SpM.#39&40 ...... 25.00
30 rep.Amaz.SpM.#58&41 ...... 25.00
31 rep.Amaz.SpM.#42 .... 25.00
32 rep.Amaz.SpM.#43&44 ...... 25.00
33 rep.Amaz.SpM.#45&47 ...... 25.00
34 rep.Amaz.SpM.#48 .... 10.00
35 rep.Amaz.SpM.#49 .... 10.00
36 thru 41 rep.
    Amaz.SpM.#51-#56 .... @10.00
42 thru 53 rep.
    Amaz.SpM.#59-#70 .... @10.00
54 thru 80 rep.
    Amaz.SpM.#73-#99 .... @10.00
81 rep.Amaz.SpM.#103 .... 10.00
82 rep.Amaz.SpM.#103-4 ...... 10.00
83 thru 97 rep.
    Amaz.SpM.#104-#118 ...... @10.00
98 rep.Amaz.SpM.#121 .... 10.00
99 rep.Amaz.SpM.#122 .... 10.00
100 rep.Amaz.SpM.#123,BU:Two
    Gun Kid,Giant-Size 4.00
101 thru 105 rep.Amaz.
    SpM.#124-#128 .... @4.00
106 rep.Amaz.SpM.#129,
    (I:Punisher) 4.00
107 thru 110 rep.Amaz.
    SpM.#130-133 .... @4.00
111 Amaz.SpM.#134,A:Punisher ... 4.00
112 Amaz.SpM.#135,A:Punisher ... 4.00
113 thru 125 rep.Amaz.Spider
    Man #136-#148 .... @4.00
126 rep.Amaz.Spider-Man#149 .... 4.00
127 rep.Amaz.Spider-Man#150 .... 4.00
128 rep.Amaz.Spider-Man#151 .... 4.00

Comics Values Annual

Marvel Tales #39
© Marvel Entertainment Group

129 thru 136 rep.Amaz.Spider
    Man #152-#159 .... @4.00
137 rep.Amaz.Fantasy#15 ...... 7.00
138 rep.Amaz.SpM.#1 .... 7.00
139 thru 149 rep.
    AmazSpM#2-#12 .... @4.00
150 rep.AmazSpM Ann#1 .... 4.00
151 rep.AmazSpM#13 .... 4.00
152 rep.AmazSpM#14 .... 4.00
153 thru 190
    rep.AmazSpM#15-52 ...... @2.50
191 rep. #96-98 .... 2.50
192 rep. #121-122 .... 2.50
193 thru 198 rep.Marv.Team
    Up#59-64 .... @2.50
199 .... 2.50
200 rep. SpM Annual 14 .... 2.50
201 thru 206 rep.Marv.
    Team Up#65-70 .... @2.50
207 .... 2.50
208 .... 2.50
209 MZ(c),rep.SpM#129,Punisher.. 3.00
210 MZ(c),rep.SpM#134 .... 4.00
211 MZ(c),rep.SpM#135 .... 4.00
212 MZ(c),rep.Giant-Size#4 .... 4.00
213 MZ(c),rep.Giant-Size#4 .... 4.00
214 MZ(c),rep.SpM#161 .... 4.00
215 MZ(c),rep.SpM#162 .... 3.00
216 MZ(c),rep.SpM#174 .... 3.00
217 MZ(c),rep.SpM#175 .... 3.00
218 MZ(c),rep.SpM#201 .... 3.00
219 MZ(c),rep.SpM#202 .... 3.00
220 MZ(c),rep.Spec.SpM #81 ... 3.00
221 MZ(c),rep.Spec.SpM #82 ... 3.00
222 MZ(c),rep.Spec.SpM #83 ... 2.25
223 thru 227 TM(c),rep.
    SpM #88-92 .... @2.50
228 TM(c),rep.Spec.SpM.#17 ... 2.25
229 TM(c),rep.Spec.SpM.#18 ... 2.25
230 TM(c),rep.SpM #203 .... 2.25
231 TM(c),rep.Team-Up#108 .... 2.25
232 TM(c),rep 2.25
233 thru 236 TM(c),rep. X-Men .. @2.25
237 TM(c),rep 2.25
238 TM(c),rep 2.25
239 TM(c),rep.SpM,Beast 2.25
240 rep.SpM,Beast,MTU#90 ..... 2.25
241 rep.MTU#124 .... 2.25
242 rep.MTU#89,Nightcrawler .. 2.25
243 rep.MTU#117,SpM,Wolverine. 2.25
244 MR(c),rep 2.25
245 MR(c),rep 2.25
246 MR(c),rep 2.25

Comics Values Annual — MARVEL — Marvel: Tales–Team

247 MR(c),rep.MTU Annual #6 .... 2.25
248 MR(c),rep. 2.25
249 MR(c),rep.MTU #14 .... 2.25
250 MR(c),rep.MTU #100 .... 2.25
251 rep.Amaz.SpM.#100 .... 2.25
252 rep.Amaz.SpM.#101 .... 3.50
253 rep.Amaz.SpM.#102 .... 3.00
254 rep.MTU #15,inc.2 Ghost
    Rider pin-ups by JaL 3.00
255 SK(c),rep.MTU #58,
    BU:Ghost Rider 2.25
256 rep. MTU 2.25
257 rep.Amaz.SpM.#238 .... 2.25
258 rep.Amaz.SpM.#239 .... 2.25
259 thru 261 rep.Amaz.SpM#249
    thru #251 .... @2.25
262 rep Marvel Team-Up #53 .... 2.25
263 rep Marvel Team-Up #54 .... 2.25
264 rep.B:Amaz.SpM.Ann.#5 ..... 2.25
265 rep.E:Amaz.SpM.Ann.#5 ..... 2.25
266 thru 275 rep.Amaz.SpM#252
    thru #261 .... @2.25
276 rep Amaz.SpM#263 .... 2.25
277 rep.Amaz.SpM#265 .... 2.25
278 thru 282 rep.Amaz.SpM # 268
    thru #272 .... @2.25
283 rep.Amaz.SpM#273 .... 2.25
284 thru 287 rep.Amaz.SpM#275
    thru #278 .... @2.25
288 rep.Amaz.SpM#280 .... 2.25
289 rep.Amaz.SpM#281 .... 2.25
290 & 291 rep.Amaz.SpM 2.25

MARVEL TALES
See: MARVEL COMICS

MARVEL TEAM-UP
March, 1972
(Spider-Man in all, unless *)

1 RA,F:Hum.Torch,V:Sandman . 200.00
2 RA,F:Hum.Torch,V:Sandman ... 60.00
3 F:Human Torch,V:Morbius. 75.00
4 GK,F:X-Men,A:Morbius 75.00
5 GK,F:Vision 25.00
6 GK,F:Thing,O:Puppet Master,
    V:Mad Thinker 25.00
7 RA,F:Thor 25.00
8 JM,F:The Cat 25.00
9 RA,F:Iron Man 25.00
10 JM,F:Human Torch 25.00
11 JM,F:The Inhumans 18.00
12 RA,F:Werewolf 25.00
13 GK,F:Captain America 25.00

Marvel Team-Up #1
© Marvel Entertainment Group

14 GK,F:Sub-Mariner 15.00
15 RA,F:Ghostrider 30.00
16 GK,JM,F:Captain Marvel 14.00
17 GK,F:Mr.Fantastic,
    A:Capt.Marvel 14.00
18 *F:Hulk,Human Torch 14.00
19 SB,F:Ka-Zar 14.00
20 SB,F:Black Panther 17.00
21 SB,F:Dr.Strange 10.00
22 SB,F:Hawkeye 12.00
23 *F:Human Torch,Iceman,
    C:Spider-Man,X-Men 12.00
24 JM,F:Brother Voodoo 12.00
25 JM,F:Daredevil 12.00
26 *F:H.Torch,Thor,V:Lavamen . 12.00
27 JM,F:The Hulk 12.00
28 JM,F:Hercules 12.00
29 *F:Human Torch,Iron Man ... 12.00
30 JM,F:The Falcon 12.00
31 JM,F:Iron Fist 12.00
32 *F:Hum.Torch,Son of Satan . 12.00
33 SB,F:Nighthawk 12.00
34 SB,F:Valkyrie 12.00
35 SB,*F:H.Torch,Dr.Strange .. 12.00
36 SB,F:Frankenstein 10.00
37 SB,F:Man-Wolf 10.00
38 SB,F:Beast 10.00
39 SB,F:H.Torch,I:Jean Dewolff . 10.00
40 SB,F:Sons of the Tiger 10.00
41 SB,F:Scarlet Witch 10.00
42 SB,F:Scarlet Witch,Vision . 10.00
43 SB,F:Dr.Doom 10.00
44 SB,F:Moon Dragon 10.00
45 SB,F:Killraven 10.00
46 SB,F:Deathlok 7.00
47 F:The Thing 6.00
48 SB,F:Iron Man,I:Wraith 6.00
49 SB,F:Iron Man 6.00
50 SB,F:Dr.Strange 6.00
51 SB,F:Iron Man 6.00
52 SB,F:Captain America 6.00
53 1st JBy New X-Men,F:Hulk .. 30.00
54 JBy,F:Hulk,V:Woodgod 7.00
55 JBy,F:Warlock,I:Gardener ... 9.00
56 SB,F:Daredevil 7.00
57 SB,F:Black Widow 7.00
58 SB,F:Ghost Rider,V:Trapster . 7.00
59 JBy,F:Yellowjacket,V:Equinox ... 7.00
60 JBy,F:Wasp,V:Equinox 7.00
61 JBy,F:Human Torch 7.00
62 JBy,F:Ms.Marvel 7.00
63 JBy,F:Iron Fist 7.00
64 JBy,F:Daughters o/t Dragon . 7.00
65 JBy,I:Captain Britain(U.S.)
    I:Arcade 7.50
66 JBy,F:Captain Britain 7.00
67 JBy,F:Tigra,V:Kraven 7.00
68 JBy,F:Man-Thing,I:D'Spayre . 7.00
69 JBy,F:Havok 7.00
70 JBy,F:Thor 7.00
71 F:The Falcon,V:Plantman 5.00
72 F:Iron Man 5.00
73 F:Daredevil 5.00
74 BH,F:Not ready for prime time
    players(Saturday Night Live) ... 5.00
75 JBy,F:Power Man 6.00
76 HC,F:Dr.Strange 5.00
77 HC,F:Ms.Marvel 5.00
78 DP,F:Wonderman 5.00
79 JBy,TA,F:Red Sonja 6.00
80 SpM,F:Dr.Strange,Clea 5.00
81 F:Satana 5.00
82 SB,F:Black Widow 6.00
83 SB,F:Nick Fury 5.00
84 SB,F:Master of Kung Fu 5.00
85 SB,F:Bl.Widow,Nick Fury 5.00
86 BMc,F:Guardians o/t Galaxy . 4.00
87 GC,F:Black Panther 4.00
88 SB,F:Invisible Girl 4.00
89 RB,F:Nightcrawler 4.50
90 BMc,F:The Beast 4.00

Marvel Team-Up #113
© Marvel Entertainment Group

91 F:Ghost Rider 4.00
92 CI,F:Hawkeye,I:Mr.Fear IV .. 3.50
93 CI,F:Werewolf
    I:Tatterdemalion (named) .. 4.00
94 MZ,F:Shroud 3.50
95 I:Mockingbird(Huntress) 4.00
96 F:Howard the Duck 3.50
97 *F:Hulk,Spider-Woman 3.50
98 F:Black Widow 3.50
99 F:Machine Man 3.50
100 FM,JBy,F:F.F.,I:Karma,
    BU:Storm & Bl.Panther 8.00
101 F:Nighthawk 3.00
102 F:Doc Samson,Rhino 3.00
103 F:Antman 3.00
104 *F:Hulk,Ka-zar 3.00
105 *F:Powerman,Iron Fist,Hulk . 3.00
106 HT,F:Captain America 3.00
107 HT,F:She-Hulk 3.50
108 HT,F:Paladin 3.00
109 HT,F:Dazzler 3.00
110 HT,F:Iron Man 3.00
111 HT,F:Devil Slayer 3.00
112 HT,F:King Kull 3.00
113 HT,F:Quasar,V:Lightmaster . 3.00
114 HT,F:Falcon 3.00
115 HT,F:Thor 3.00
116 HT,F:Valkyrie 3.00
117 HT,F:Wolv,V:Prof Power ... 12.00
118 HT,F:Professor X 4.00
119 KGa,F:Gargoyle 3.00
120 KGa,F:Dominic Fortune 3.00
121 KGa,F:Human Torch,I:Leap
    Frog(Frog Man) 3.00
122 KGa,F:Man-Thing 3.00
123 KGa,F:Daredevil 3.00
124 KGa,F:Beast 3.50
125 KGa,F:Tigra 3.00
126 BH,F:Hulk 3.00
127 KGa,F:Watcher,X-mass issue . 3.00
128 Ph(c)KGa,F:Capt.America ... 3.00
129 KGa,F:The Vision 3.00
130 KGa,F:The Scarlet Witch ... 3.00
131 KGa,F:Leap Frog 3.00
132 KGa,F:Mr.Fantastic 3.00
133 KGa,F:Fantastic Four 3.00
134 F:Jack of Hearts 3.00
135 F:Kitty Pryde 3.00
136 F:Wonder Man 3.00
137 *F:Aunt May & F.Richards .. 3.00
138 F:Sandman,I:New Enforcers . 3.00
139 F:Sandman,Nick Fury 3.00
140 F:Black Widow 3.00

All comics prices listed are for *Near Mint* condition. CVA Page 275

Marvel: Team–Two / MARVEL / Comics Values Annual

141 SpM(2nd App Black Costume) F:Daredevil 4.00
142 F:Captain Marvel(2nd one). . . . 3.00
143 F:Starfox 3.00
144 F:M.Knight,V:WhiteDragon . . . 3.00
145 F:Iron Man. 3.00
146 F:Nomad 3.50
147 F:Human Torch 3.00
148 F:Thor 3.00
149 F:Cannonball 3.50
150 F:X-Men,V:Juggernaut 5.50
Ann.#1 SB,F:New X-Men 30.00
Ann.#2 F:The Hulk 10.00
Ann.#3 F:Hulk,PowerMan 6.00
Ann.#4 F:Daredevil,Moon Knight. . . 5.00
Ann.#5 F:Thing,Scarlet Witch, Quasar,Dr.Strange 5.00
Ann.#6 F:New Mutants,Cloak & Dagger(cont.New Mutants#22) . 5.00
Ann.#7 F:Alpha Flight 3.00

MARVEL TEAM-UP INDEX
See: OFFICIAL MARVEL INDEX TO MARVEL TEAM-UP

MARVEL TEAM-UP
1997
1 TPe,PO,AW, F:Spider-Man, Generation X 2.25
2 TPe,PO,AW, F:Spider-Man & Hercules. 2.25
3 TPe,DaR,AW, F:Spider-Man & Sandman 2.25
4 TPe,DaR,F:Spider-Man & Man-Thing 2.25
5 TPe,DaR,F:Spider-Man & Mystery guest. 2.25
6 TPe,F:Spider-Man & Sub-Mariner 2.25
7 MWn,TPe,F:Spider-Man & Blade 2.25
8 TPe,F:Sub-Mariner & Doctor Strange 2.25
9 TPe,F:Sub-Mariner & Captain America 2.25
10 TPe,AW,F:Sub Mariner & Thing . 2.25
11 TPe,AW,PO,F:Sub-Mariner & Iron Man, final issue 2.25

MARVEL Treasury Edition
Sept., 1974
1 SD,Spider-Man,I:Contemplator . 75.00
2 JK,F:Fant.Four,Silver Surfer . . . 30.00
3 F:Thor 25.00
4 BWS,F:Conan 25.00
5 O:Hulk 25.00
6 GC,FB,SD,F:Dr.Strange 25.00
7 JB,JK,F:The Avengers 25.00
8 F:X-Mass stories. 25.00
9 F:Super-Hero Team-Up. 25.00
10 F:Thor 25.00
11 F:Fantastic Four. 20.00
12 F:Howard the Duck 20.00
13 F:X-Mas stories 20.00
14 F:Spider-Man 20.00
15 BWS,F:Conan,Red Sonja. 22.00
16 F:Defenders. 20.00
17 F:The Hulk. 20.00
18 F:Spider Man,X-Men 22.00
19 F:Conan 22.00
20 F:Hulk 22.00
21 F:Fantastic Four 22.00
22 F:Spider-Man. 22.00
23 F:Conan 22.00
24 F:The Hulk. 22.00
25 F:Spider-Man,Hulk. 22.00
26 GP,F:Hulk,Wolverine,Hercules . 25.00
27 HT,F:Hulk,Spider-Man 22.00
28 JB,JSt,F:SpM/Superman 50.00

MARVEL TREASURY OF OZ
(oversized) 1975
1 JB,movie adapt. 30.00

MARVEL TREASURY SPECIAL
Vol. I Spider-Man, 1974 . . . . 25.00
Vol. II Capt. America, 1976 . . . . . 30.00

MARVEL TRIPLE ACTION
Feb., 1972
1 Rep. 25.00
2 thru 5 rep. . . . . @15.00
6 thru 10 rep. . . . . @10.00
11 thru 47 rep. . . . . @5.00
G-Size#1 F:Avengers 7.00
G-Size#2 F:Avengers 7.00

MARVEL TWO-IN-ONE
Jan., 1974
(Thing in all, unless *)
1 GK,F:Man-Thing 75.00
2 GK,JBy,F:Namor Namorita. . . . 20.00
3 F:Daredevil 16.00
4 F:Capt.America,Namorita 20.00
5 F:Guardians of the Galaxy . . . 20.00
6 F:Dr.Strange 22.00
7 F:Valkyrie 12.00
8 F:Ghost Rider 20.00
9 F:Thor 12.00
10 KJ,F:Black Widow 12.00
11 F:Golem 7.00
12 F:Iron Man. 7.00
13 F:Power Man 7.00
14 F:Son of Satan 8.00
15 F:Morbius 8.00
16 F:Ka-Zar 7.00
17 F:Spider-Man. 7.00
18 F:Spider-Man 7.00
19 F:Tigra 7.00
20 F:The Liberty Legion 7.00
21 F:Doc Savage 5.00
22 F:Thor,Human Torch 5.00
23 F:Thor,Human Torch 5.00
24 SB,F:Black Goliath. 5.00
25 F:Iron Fist 5.00
26 F:Nick Fury 5.00
27 F:Deathlok 5.00

Marvel Two-In-One #84
© Marvel Entertainment Group

28 F:Sub-Mariner 7.00
29 F:Master of Kung Fu 5.00
30 JB,F:Spiderwoman 6.00
31 F:Spiderwoman 5.00
32 F:Invisible girl 5.00
33 F:Modred the Mystic 5.00
34 F:Nighthawk,C:Deathlok 5.00
35 F:Skull the Slayer 5.00
36 F:Mr.Fantastic 5.00
37 F:Matt Murdock 5.00
38 F:Daredevil 5.00
39 F:The Vision 5.00
40 F:Black Panther. 5.00
41 F:Brother Voodoo 5.00
42 F:Captain America 5.00
43 JBy,F:Man-Thing 6.00
44 GD,F:Hercules 4.00
45 GD,F:Captain Marvel 5.00
46 F:The Hulk. 8.00
47 GD,F:Yancy Street Gang, I:Machinesmith 4.00
48 F:Jack of Hearts 4.00
49 GD,F:Dr.Strange 4.00
50 JBy,JS,F:Thing & Thing 4.00
51 FM,BMc,F:Wonderman,Nick Fury, Ms.Marvel 5.00
52 F:Moon Knight,I:Crossfire 4.00
53 JBy,JS,F:Quasar,C:Deathlok . . 4.00
54 JBy,JS,D:Deathlok, I:Grapplers 10.00
55 JBy,JS,I:New Giant Man 4.00
56 GP,GD,F:Thundra 3.00
57 GP,GD,F:Wundarr 3.00
58 GP,GD,I:Aquarian,A:Quasar . . . 3.00
59 F:Human Torch 3.00
60 GP,GD,F:Impossible Man, I:Impossible Woman. 3.00
61 GD,F:Starhawk,I&O:Her. 4.00
62 GD,F:Moondragon 4.00
63 GD,F:Warlock 4.00
64 DP,GD,F:Stingray, I:Serpent Squad 3.00
65 GP,GD,F:Triton 3.00
66 GD,F:Scarlet Witch, V:Arcade 3.00
67 F:Hyperion,Thundra 3.00
68 F:Angel,V:Arcade. 3.00
69 GD,F:Guardians o/t Galaxy . . . 3.00
70 F:The Inhumans 3.00
71 F:Mr.Fantastic,I:Deathurge, Maelstrom 3.00
72 F:Stingray 3.00
73 F:Quasar. 3.00
74 F:Puppet Master,Modred 3.00
75 F:The Avengers,O:Blastaar . . . 4.00
76 F:Iceman,O:Ringmaster. 3.00
77 F:Man-Thing 3.00
78 F:Wonder Man. 3.00
79 F:Blue Diamond,I:Star Dancer . 3.00
80 F:Ghost Rider 3.50
81 F:Sub-Mariner 2.50
82 F:Captain America 2.50
83 F:Sasquatch 3.50
84 F:Alpha Flight 3.50
85 F:Giant-Man 3.00
86 O:Sandman 3.00
87 F:Ant-Man 3.00
88 F:She-Hulk 3.00
89 F:Human Torch 3.00
90 F:Spider-Man. 4.00
91 V:Sphinx 3.00
92 F:Jocasta,V:Ultron 3.00
93 F:Machine Man,D:Jocasta 3.00
94 F:Power Man,Iron Fist 3.00
95 F:Living Mummy 3.00
96 F:Sandman,C:Marvel Heroes . . 3.00
97 F:Iron Man. 3.00
98 F:Franklin Richards 3.00
99 JBy(c),F:Rom 3.00
100 F:Ben Grimm 4.00
Ann.#1 SB,F:Liberty Legion 7.00

CVA Page 276 — All comics prices listed are for *Near Mint* condition.

Ann.#2 JSn,2nd D:Thanos,A:Spider
  Man,Avengers,Capt.Marvel,
  I:Lord Chaos,Master Order ... 22.00
Ann.#3 F:Nova 5.00
Ann.#4 F:Black Bolt 4.00
Ann.#5 F:Hulk,V:Pluto 4.00
Ann.#6 I:American Eagle 4.00
Ann.#7 I:Champion,A:Hulk,Thor,
  DocSamson,Colossus,Sasquatch,
  Wonder Man 4.00

OFFICIAL HANDBOOK OF THE MARVEL UNIVERSE
Jan., 1983
1 Abomination-Avengers'
  Quintet.................... 7.50
2 BaronMordo-Collect.Man 6.00
3 Collector-Dracula 5.00
4 Dragon Man-Gypsy Moth 5.00
5 Hangman-Juggernaut......... 5.00
6 K-L......................... 4.00
7 Mandarin-Mystique........... 4.00
8 Na,oria-Pyro 4.00
9 Quasar to She-Hulk 4.00
10 Shiar-Sub-Mariner 4.00
11 Subteraneans-Ursa Major 4.00
12 Valkyrie-Zzzax............... 4.00
13 Book of the Dead............. 4.00
14 Book of the Dead............. 4.00
15 Weaponry 4.00

[2nd Series] 1985
1 Abomination-Batroc 5.00
2 Beast-Clea 4.00
3 Cloak & D.-Dr.Strange 4.00
4 Dr.Strange-Galactus 4.00
5 Gardener-Hulk 4.00
6 Human Torch-Ka-Zar 3.25
7 Kraven-Magneto.............. 3.25
8 Magneto-Moleman 3.25
9 Moleman-Owl................ 3.25
10 .... 3.25
11 .... 3.00
12 S-T 3.00
13 .... 3.00
14 V-Z 3.00
15 .... 3.00
16 Book of the Dead............. 3.00
17 Handbook of the Dead,inc.
  JLe illus. 3.00
18 .... 3.00
19 .... 3.00
20 Inc.RLd illus. 3.00

Official Handbook of the Marvel
Universe #1 © Marvel Ent. Group

MARVEL

Marvel Universe Update
1 thru 8 .... @3.00
Marvel Universe Packet
1 inc. Spider-Man 5.50
2 inc. Captain America......... 4.50
3 inc. Ghost Rider 5.00
4 inc. Wolverine............... 4.50
5 inc. Punisher 4.25
6 inc. She-Hulk 4.00
7 inc. Daredevil 4.00
8 inc. Hulk.................... 4.00
9 inc. Moon Knight............. 4.00
10 inc. Captain Britain 4.00
11 inc. Storm 4.00
12 inc. Silver Surfer 4.00
13 inc. Ice Man................. 4.50
14 inc. Thor 4.50
15 thru 22 .... @4.50
23 inc. Cage................... 4.50
24 inc. Iron Fist................ 4.50
25 inc.Deadpool,Night Thrasher . 4.50
26 inc. Wonder Man 5.00
27 inc.Beta Ray Bill,Pip 5.00
28 inc.X-Men 5.00
29 inc.Carnage................. 5.00
30 thru 36................... @5.00

MARVEL UNIVERSE
1996
1 Post Onslaught.............. 3.25

MARVEL UNIVERSE
April, 1998
1 CPa(c),RSt,SEp,AW,F:Human
  Torch,Capt.Am.,Namor,48-pg... 3.00
2A JBy(c),RSt,SEp,AW,V:Hydra,
  Baron Strucker............. 2.25
2B DGb(c).................... 2.25
3 RSt,SEp,AW,V:Hydra 2.25
4 RSt,MM, all-star jam cover,
  F:Monster Hunters 2.25
5 MM,RSt,F:The Monster Hunters . 2.25
6 MM,RSt,F:Monster Hunters,pt.3 . 2.25
7 MM,RSt,F:Monster Hunters,pt.4 . 2.25
TPB Vol. 1: Thanos 18.00

MARVEL UNIVERSE: MILLENNIAL VISIONS
Dec., 2001
Spec.2001 48-page 4.00

MARVEL UNIVERSE: THE END
Marvel March 2003
1 (of 6) JSn,AM................ 2.25
2 JSn,AM 2.25
3 JSn,AM 3.00
4 JSn,AM 3.00
5 JSn,AM 3.00
6 JSn,AM 3.00

MARVEL VALENTINE'S SPECIAL
1997
1-shot MWa,TDF, 48-pg. 3.00

MARVEL VISIONARIES
July, 2002
TPB Gil Kane,256-pg........... 30.00
TPB Jim Steranko, ... 15.00

Marvel Valentine Special #1
© Marvel Entertainment Group

MARVEL X-MEN COLLECTION
1994
1 thru 3 JL from the 1st series
  X-Men Cards .... @3.25

MARVELOUS ADVENTURES OF GUS BEEZER
Marvel April 2003
Spec. F:Spider-Man 3.00
Spec. F:X-Men 3.00
Spec. F:The Hulk 3.00

MARVILLE
Sept., 2002
1 U-Decide 3.00
1b foil (c) 40-pg. 4.00
1c variant foil (c) 4.00
2 thru 6 .... @2.25
5a thru 6a MBr,variant (c)..... @2.25
7 .... 3.00
TPB Vol. 1 .... 13.00

MARVIN MOUSE
Atlas, Sept., 1957
1 BEv,F:Marvin Mouse 125.00

MASTER OF KUNG FU, SPECIAL MARVEL ED.
April, 1974
Prev: Special Marvel Edition
17 JSn,I:Black Jack Tarr........ 25.00
18 PG,1st Gulacy Art 15.00
19 PG,A:Man-Thing 18.00
20 GK(c),PG,AM,V:Samurai 15.00
21 AM,Season of Vengeance..
  Moment of Death 9.00
22 PG,DA,Death................ 9.00
23 AM,KJ,River of Death 9.00
24 JSn,WS,AM,ST,Night of the
  Assassin 10.00
25 JSt(c),PG,ST,Fists Fury...
  Rites of Death 9.00
26 KP,ST,A:Daughter of
  Fu Manchu................ 8.00
27 SB,FS,A:Fu Manchu 8.00

Master–Menace / MARVEL / Comics Values Annual

28 EH,ST,Death of a Spirit 8.00	72 V:Shockwave. 4.50	Movie #1 GT 2.00
29 PG,V:Razor-Fist. 8.00	73 RN(c),V:Behemoths 4.50	
30 PG,DA,Pit of Lions. 8.00	74 TA(c),A:Shockwave 4.50	## MATT SLADE, GUNFIGHTER
31 GK&DA(c),PG,DA,Snowbuster. . 8.00	75 Where Monsters Dwell. 4.50	
32 GK&ME(c),SB,ME,Assault on an Angry Sea 8.00	76 GD,Battle on the Waterfront. . . . 4.00	### Atlas, May, 1956
	77 GD,I:Zaran 4.00	1 AW,AT,F:Matt Slade,Crimson Avenger 225.00
33 PG,Messenger of Madness, I:Leiko Wu 8.00	78 GD,Moving Targets 4.00	
	79 GD,This Side of Death. 4.00	2 AW,A:Crimson Avenger 175.00
34 PG,Captive in A Madman's Crown 8.00	80 GD,V:Leopard Men 4.00	3 A:Crimson Avenger 150.00
	81 GD,V:Leopard Men 4.00	4 A:Crimson Avenger 125.00
35 PG,V:Death Hand 8.00	82 GD,Flight into Fear 4.00	Becomes:
36 The Night of the Ninja's 8.00	83 GD, ... 4.00	## KID SLADE GUNFIGHTER
37 V:Darkstrider & Warlords of the Web 5.00	84 GD,V:Fu Manchu 4.00	
	85 GD,V:Fu Manchu. 4.00	5 F:Kid Slade 125.00
38 GK(c),PG,A:The Cat 5.00	86 GD,V:Fu Manchu 4.00	6 . . . . 100.00
39 GK(c),PG,A:The Cat 5.00	87 GD,V:Zaran, ... 4.00	7 AW,Duel in the Night 110.00
40 PG,The Murder Agency 5.00	88 GD,V:Fu Manchu. 4.00	8 July, 1957 . . . . 100.00
41 . . . . 5.00	89 GD,D:Fu Manchu. 4.00	
42 GK(c),PG,TS,V:Shockwave . . . 5.00	90 MZ,Death in Chinatown 4.00	## MAVERICK
43 PG,V:Shockwave. 5.00	91 GD,Gang War,drugs 5.00	### 1997
44 SB(c),PG,V:Fu Manchu 5.00	92 GD,Shadows of the Past 4.00	1 JGz,F:Christopher Nord/David North/Maverick, 48-pg. 3.50
45 GK(c),PG,Death Seed 5.00	93 GD,Cult of Death 4.00	
46 PG,V:Sumo 5.00	94 GD,V:Agent Synergon 4.00	2 JGz,A:Victor Creed and Logan . . 3.00
47 PG,The Cold White Mantle of Death 5.00	95 GD,Raid 4.00	2a variant cover. 3.00
	96 GD,I:Rufus Carter 4.00	3 JGz,V:Puck & Vindicator. 3.00
48 PG,Bridge of a 1,000 Dooms . . . 5.00	97 GD,V:Kung Fu's Dark Side. 4.00	4 JGz,A:Wolverine. 3.00
49 PG,V:Shaka III..., The Demon Warrior. 5.00	98 GD,Fight to the Finish 4.00	5 JGz,A:The Blob 3.00
	99 GD,Death Dept 4.00	6 JGz,V:Sabretooth 3.00
50 PG,V:Fu Manchu. 5.00	100 GD,Doublesize 6.00	7 JGz,V:Sabretooth 3.00
51 PG(c),To End...To Begin 5.00	101 GD,Not Smoke,Nor Beads, Nor Blood. 3.75	8 JGz,V:The Confessor 3.00
52 Mayhem in Morocco 5.00		9 JGz,Maverick's secrets 3.00
53 . . . . 5.00	102 GD,Assassins,1st GD(p) 4.00	10 JGz,V:Ivan the Terrible, Chris Bradley becomes Bolt. 3.00
54 JSn(c),Death Wears Three Faces. 5.00	103 GD,V:Assassins. 3.75	
	104 GD,Fight without Reason, C:Cerberus. 3.75	11 JGz,A:Darkstar,Vanguard, Ursa Major 3.00
55 PG(c),The Ages of Death. 5.00		
56 V:The Black Ninja 5.00	105 GD,I:Razor Fist 3.75	12 JGz, double sized last issue. . . . 3.50
57 V:Red Baron 5.00	106 GD,C:Velcro 3.75	1-shot LHa, V:Sabretooth,48-pg. . . . 2.95
58 Behold the Final Mask 5.00	107 GD,A:Sata 3.75	
59 GK(c),B:Phoenix Gambit, Behold the Angel of Doom 5.00	108 GD 3.75	## MAXIMUM SECURITY
	109 GD,Death is a Dark Agent 3.75	### Oct., 2000
60 A:Dr.Doom,Doom Came. 5.00	110 GD,Perilous Reign 3.75	1 (of 3) KBk,JOy,x-over 3.00
61 V:Skull Crusher 4.50	111 GD. 3.75	2 KBk,JOy,x-over. 3.00
62 Coast of Death 4.50	112 GD(c),Commit and Destroy . . . 3.75	3 KBk,JOy,x-over,concl. 3.00
63 GK&TA(c),Doom Wears Three Faces. 4.50	113 GD(c),V:Panthers. 3.75	Spec. Thor vs. Ego, 64-pg.,SL,JK . . 3.00
	114 Fantasy o/t Autumn Moon 3.75	Spec. Dangerous Planet. 3.00
64 PG(c),To Challenge a Dragon . . 4.50	115 GD. 3.75	
65 V:Pavane. 4.50	116 GD. 3.75	## MEKANIX
66 V:Kogar 4.50	117 GD,Devil Deeds Done in Darkness 3.75	### Oct., 2002
67 PG(c),Dark Encounters 4.50		1 (of 6) CCl,F:Kitty Pryde. 3.00
68 Final Combats,V:The Cat. 4.50	118 GD,D:Fu Manchu,double 4.50	2 CCl,back in school 3.00
69 . . . . 4.50	119 GD. 3.75	3 CCl. 3.00
70 A:Black Jack Tarr,Murder Mansion 4.50	120 GD,Dweller o/t Dark Stream. . . 3.75	4 CCl. 3.00
	121 Death in the City of Lights' . . . 3.00	5 CCl. 3.00
71 PG(c),Ying & Yang (c) 4.50	122 . . . . 3.00	6 CCl, concl. 3.00
	123 V:Ninjas. 3.00	
	124 . . . . 3.00	## MELVIN THE MONSTER
	125 double-size 6.00	### Atlas, July, 1956
	G-Size#1,CR,PG 20.00	1 JMn 150.00
	G-Size#2 PG,V:Yellow Claw 3.00	2 thru 6 . . . . @100.00
	G-Size#3 . . . . 3.00	Becomes:
	G-Size#4 JK,V:Yellow Claw 3.00	## DEXTER THE DEMON
	Spec.#1 Bleeding Black 3.00	### Sept., 1957
	## MASTER OF KUNG FU: BLEEDING BLACK	7 . . . . 60.00
	1 V:ShadowHand, 1991. . . . . 3.00	## MEMORIES
	## MASTERS OF TERROR	### Epic
	### July–Sept., 1975	1 Space Adventures 2.50
	1 GM(c),FB,BWS,JSn,NA 20.00	
	2 JSn(c),GK,VM, ... 15.00	## MENACE
		### Atlas, May, 1953
	## MASTERS OF THE UNIVERSE	1 RH,BEv,GT,One Head Too Many 800.00
	### Star, May, 1986—March, 1988	2 RH,BEv,GT,JSt,Burton'sBlood . 600.00
	1 I:Hordak 7.00	3 BEv,RH,JR,The Werewolf . . . 400.00
	2 thru 11 . . . . @4.00	
	12 D:Skeletor 8.00	

Master of Kung Fu #84
© Marvel Entertainment Group

CVA Page 278 — All comics prices listed are for *Near Mint* condition.

4 BEv,RH,The Four Armed Man. 400.00
5 BEv,RH,GC,GT,I&O:Zombie . . 700.00
6 BEv,RH,JR,The Graymoor
    Ghost 400.00
7 JSt,RH,Fresh out of Flesh. . . . 300.00
8 RH,The Lizard Man 300.00
9 BEv,The Walking Dead 350.00
10 RH(c),Half Man,Half... . . . . . 300.00
11 JKz,JR,Locked In,May, 1954 . 300.00

MEN IN ACTION
Atlas, April, 1952
1 Sweating it Out 200.00
2 US Infantry stories 100.00
3 RH 75.00
4 War stories 75.00
5 JMn,Squad Charge 75.00
6 War stories 75.00
7 RH(c),BK,No Risk Too Great . 100.00
8 JRo(c),They Strike By Night . . 75.00
9 SSh(c),Rangers Strike Back . . 75.00
Becomes:

BATTLE BRADY
10 SSh(c),F:Battle Brady 150.00
11 SSh(c) 100.00
12 SSh(c),Death to the Reds 75.00
13 . . . . 75.00
14 Final Issue,June, 1953. . . . . . . 75.00

MEN IN BLACK
1 ANi, prequel to movie (1997) . . . 4.00
Spec. Movie Adaptation (1997). . . . 4.00

MEN IN BLACK: RETRIBUTION
Aug., 1997
1 continuation from movie 4.00

MEN'S ADVENTURES
See: TRUE WESTERN

MEPHISTO vs. FOUR HEROES
April–July, 1987
1 JB,BWi,A:Fantastic Four. 3.50
2 JB,BWi,A:X-Factor 3.00
3 JB,AM,A:X-Men 3.00
4 JB,BWi,A:Avengers 3.00

METEOR MAN
1993–94
1 R:Meteor Man 2.25
2 V:GhostStrike,Malefactor,Simon . 2.25
3 A:Spider-Man 2.25
4 A:Night Thrasher 2.25
5 Exocet 2.25
6 final issue. 2.25

[TED McKEEVER'S} METROPOL
Epic, 1991–92
1 Ted McKeever 3.00
2 . . . . 3.00
3 . . . . 3.00
4 . . . . 3.00
5 . . . . 3.00
6 . . . . 3.00
7 . . . . 3.00
8 Return of Eddy Current. 3.00
9 `Wings of Silence'. 3.00
10 `Rotting Metal,Rusted Flesh' . . 3.00
11 `Diagram of the Heart' 3.00
12 . . . . 3.00

METROPOL A.D.
Epic, 1992
1 R:The Angels 3.50
2 V:Demons 3.50
3 V:Nuclear Arsenal. 3.50

MICRONAUTS
[1st Series] Jan., 1979
1 MGo,JRu,O:Micronauts 5.00
2 MGo,JRu,Earth. 3.00
3 MGo,JRu 3.00
4 MGo. 3.00
5 MGo,V:Prometheus 3.00
6 MGo. 3.00
7 MGo,A:Man Thing 3.00
8 MGo,BMc,I:Capt. Univ. 3.00
9 MGo,I:Cilicia. 3.00
10 MGo 3.00
11 MGo 3.00
12 MGo 3.00
13 HC,F:Bug 3.00
14 HC,V:Wartstaff. 3.00
15 HC,AM,A:Fantastic Four 3.00
16 HC,AM,A:Fantastic Four 3.00
17 HC,AM,A:Fantastic Four 3.00
18 HC,Haunted House Issue 3.00
19 PB,V:Odd John 3.00
20 PB,A:Antman 3.00
21 PB,I:Microverse 3.00
22 PB. 3.00
23 PB,V:Molecule Man 3.00
24 MGo,V:Computrex 3.00
25 PB,A:Mentallo 3.00
26 PB,A:Baronkarza 3.00
27 PB,V:Hydra,A:Shield 3.00
28 PB,V:Hydra,A:Shield 3.00
29 PB,Doc Samson 3.00
30 PB,A:Shield 3.00
31 PB,A:Dr.Strange 3.00
32 PB,A:Dr.Strange 3.00
33 PB,A:Devil of Tropica. 3.00
34 PB,A:Dr.Strange 3.00
35 O:Microverse 3.00
36 KG,Dr.Strange 3.00
37 KG,Nightcrawler 4.00
38 GK,1st direct 2.50
39 SD. 2.50
40 GK,A:FF 2.50
41 GK,Dr.Doom 2.50
42 GK 2.50
43 . . . . 2.50
44 . . . . 2.50
45 Arcade. 2.50
46 . . . . 2.50
47 . . . . 2.50
48 JG 2.75
49 JG,V:Baron Karza 2.50
50 JG,V:Baron Karza 2.50
51 JG 2.50
52 JG 2.50
53 JG,V:Untouchables 2.50
54 JG,V:Tribunal 2.50
55 JG,V:Karza World 2.50
56 JG,Kaliklak 2.50
57 JG,V:Baron Karza 2.50
58 JG,V:Baron Karza 2.50
59 JG,V:The Makers. 2.50
Ann.#1,SD 2.50
#2 SD. 2.50

[2nd Series] 1984
1 V:The Makers. 2.50
2 AAd(c),V:The Makers 2.50
3 Huntarr'sEgg 2.50
4 V:The Makers. 2.50
5 The Spiral Path 2.50
6 L:Bug 2.50
7 Acroyear. 2.50
8 V:Scion 2.50
9 R:Devil 2.50

Micronauts 2nd Series #1
© Marvel Entertainment Group

10 V:Enigma Force. 2.50
11 V:Scion 2.50
12 V:Scion 2.50
13 V:Dark Armada 2.50
14 V:Keys of the Zodiac 2.50
15 O:Marionette 2.50
16 Secret Wars II 3.00
17 V:Scion 2.50
18 Acroyear 2.50
19 R:Baron Karza 2.50
20 Last Issue 2.50

MICRONAUTS
(Special Edition) Dec., 1983
1 MGo/JRu,rep. 3.00
2 MGo/JRu,rep. 3.00
3 Rep.MG/JRu 3.00
4 Rep.MG/JRu 3.00
5 Rep.MG/JRu,April, 1984. . . . . . 3.00

MIDNIGHT MEN
Epic *Heavy Hitters*, 1993
1 HC,I:Midnight Men 3.00
2 HC,J:Barnett. 2.25
3 HC,Pasternak is Midnight Man . 2.25
4 HC,Last issue. 2.25

MIDNIGHT SONS UNLIMITED
1993–95
1 JQ,JBi,MT(c),A:Midnight Sons . . 4.25
2 BSz(c),F:Midnight Sons 4.25
3 JR2(c),JS,A:Spider-Man 4.25
4 Siege of Darkness #17,
    D:2nd Ghost Rider 4.25
5 DQ(s),F:Mordred,Vengeance,
    Morbius,Werewolf,Blaze,
    I:Wildpride 4.25
6 DQ(s),F:Dr.Strange. 3.95
7 DQ(s),F:Man-Thing. 3.95
8 . . . . 3.95
9 J:Mighty Destroyer 3.95

MIGHTY MARVEL WESTERN
Oct., 1968
1 JK,All reprints,B:Rawhide Kid
    Kid Colt,Two-Gun Kids 75.00
2 JK,DAy,Beware of the Barker
    Brothers 50.00

Mighty–Moebius / MARVEL / Comics Values Annual

3 HT(c),JK,DAy,Walking Death . . 50.00
4 HT(c),DAy 50.00
5 HT(c),DAy,Ambush 50.00
6 HT(c),DAy Doom in the Desert . 50.00
7 DAy,V:MurderousMasquerader 50.00
8 HT(c),DAy,Rustler's on the
 Range 50.00
9 JSe(c),JK,DAy,V:Dr Danger . . . 50.00
10 OW,DH,Cougar 50.00
11 V:The Enforcers 30.00
12 JK,V:Blackjack Bordon 30.00
13 V:Grizzly 30.00
14 JK.V:The Enforcers 30.00
15 Massacre at Medicine Bend . . . 30.00
16 JK,Mine of Death 30.00
17 Ambush at Blacksnake Mesa . . 25.00
18 Six-Gun Thunderer 25.00
19 Reprints cont 25.00
20 same 25.00
21 same 20.00
22 . . . . 20.00
23 same 20.00
24 JDa,E:Kid Colt 20.00
25 B:Matt Slade 20.00
26 thru 31 Reprints . . . . @20.00
32 JK,AW,Ringo Kid #23 . . . . 15.00
33 thru 36 Reprints . . . . @15.00
37 JK,AW Two-Gun #51 . . . . 15.00
38 thru 45 Reprints . . . . @15.00
46 same,Sept., 1976 . . . . 15.00

MIGHTY HEROES
Nov., 1997
1-shot SLo, Diaper Man, Rope Man,
 Cuckoo Man, Tornado Man, Strong
 Man, etc. 3.00

[SABAN'S] MIGHTY MORPHIN POWER RANGERS
1 SLo,FaN,New ongoing series . . . 2.25
2 FaN,RLm,JP,more 2.25
3 FaN,RLm,JP,more adventures . . 2.25
4 LSn,JP,V:Glob monster 2.25
5 . . . . 2.25
6 . . . . 2.25
7 Close Encounter with Alien 2.25
Photo Adaptation 2.95

[SABAN'S] MIGHTY MORPHIN POWER RANGERS: NINJA RANGERS/ VR TROOPERS
1 FaN,RLm,JP,flip book 2.25
2 JP,flip book 2.25
3 New outfits 2.25
4 . . . . 2.25
5 . . . . 2.25
6 . . . . 2.25

MIGHTY MOUSE
[1st Series] Fall, 1946
1 Terytoons Presents 1,500.00
2 . . . . 700.00
3 . . . . 450.00
4 Summer, 1947 . . . . 450.00

MIGHTY MOUSE
Oct., 1990
1 EC,Dark Mite Returns 3.00
2 EC,V:The Glove 2.25
3 EC/JBr(c)Prince Say More 2.25
4 EC/GP(c)Alt.Universe #1 . . . . . . 2.25

Mighty Mouse #3
© Marvel Entertainment Group

5 EC,Alt.Universe #2 . . . . 2.25
6 `Ferment',A:MacFurline' 2.25
7 EC,V:Viral Worm 2.25
8 EC,BAT-BAT:Year One,
 O:Bug Wonder 2.25
9 EC,BAT-BAT:Year One,
 V:Smoker 2.25
10 `Night o/t Rating Lunatics' 2.25

MILLIE THE MODEL
Winter, 1945
1 O:Millie the Model,
 Bowling(c) 1,000.00
2 Totem Pole(c) 450.00
3 Anti-Noise(c) 300.00
4 Bathing Suit(c) 300.00
5 Blame it on Fame 300.00
6 Beauty and the Beast 300.00
7 Bathing Suit(c) 300.00
8 Fancy Dress(c),HK,Hey Look . 300.00
9 Paris(c),BW 350.00
10 Jewelry(c),HK,Hey Look 300.00
11 HK,Giggles and Grins 225.00
12 A;Rusty,Hedy Devine 150.00
13 A;Hedy Devine,HK,Hey Look . 175.00
14 HK,Hey Look 175.00
15 HK,Hey Look 150.00
16 HK,Hey Look 125.00
17 thru 20 . . . . @150.00
21 thru 30 . . . . @100.00
31 thru 75 . . . . @100.00
76 thru 99 . . . . @50.00
100 . . . . 75.00
101 thru 126 . . . . @50.00
127 Millie/Clicker 55.00
128 A:Scarlet Mayfair 35.00
129 The Truth about Agnes 35.00
130 thru 153 . . . . @35.00
154 B:New Millie 35.00
155 thru 206 . . . . @35.00
207 Dec., 1973 . . . . 35.00
Ann.#1 How Millie Became
 a Model 250.00
Ann.#2 Millies Guide to
 the world of Modeling 150.00
Ann.#3 Many Lives of Millie 100.00
Ann.#4 Many Lives of Millie 50.00

MISS AMERICA COMICS
1944
1 Miss America(c),pin-ups . . . 2,000.00

MISS AMERICA MAGAZINE
Nov., 1944—Nov., 1958
2 Ph(c),Miss America costume
 I;Patsy Walker,Buzz Baxter,
 Hedy Wolfe 1,500.00
3 Ph(c),A:Patsy Walker,Miss
 America 600.00
4 Ph(c),Betty Page,A:Patsy
 Walker,Miss America 600.00
5 Ph(c),A:Patsy Walker,Miss
 America 600.00
6 Ph(c),A:Patsy Walker 125.00
7 Patsy Walker stories 100.00
8 same 100.00
9 same 100.00
10 same 100.00
11 same 100.00
12 same 100.00
13 thru 18 . . . . @100.00
21 . . . . 125.00
22 thru 45 . . . . @75.00
46 thru 93 . . . . @75.00

MISS FURY COMICS
Timely, Winter, 1942-43
1 Newspaper strip reprints,
 ASh(c) O:Miss Fury 5,000.00
2 V:Nazis(c) 2,400.00
3 Hitler/Nazi Flag(c) 2,000.00
4 ASh(c),Japanese(c) 1,400.00
5 ASh(c),Gangster(c) 1,300.00
6 Gangster(c) 1,200.00
7 Gangster(c) 1,100.00
8 Atom-Bomb Secrets(c)
 Winter, 1946 . . . . 1,100.00

MISSION: IMPOSSIBLE
May, 1996
1 RLd,MWn(s),Movie adapt. 3.00

MISTY
Star, Dec., 1985
1 F:Millie the Models Niece 3.50
2 thru 5 . . . . @3.50
6 May, 1986 . . . . 3.50

MITZI COMICS
Timely, Spring, 1948
1 HK:Hey Look,Giggles
 and Grins 250.00
Becomes:

MITZI'S BOYFRIEND
2 F:Chip,Mitzi/Chip(c) 125.00
3 Chips adventures 100.00
4 thru 7 same . . . . @100.00
Becomes:

MITZI'S ROMANCES
8 Mitzi/Chip(c) 100.00
9 . . . . 75.00
10 Dec., 1949 . . . . 75.00

MODELING WITH MILLIE
See: DATE WITH MILLIE

MOEBIUS
Epic, Oct., 1987
1 . . . . 12.00
2 . . . . 12.00
3 . . . . 15.00
4 . . . . 12.00
5 . . . . 12.00
6 1988 . . . . 12.00

MARVEL

MOEBIUS: FUSION
1 128-pg. Sketchbook 19.95

MOLLY MANTON'S ROMANCES
Sept., 1949
1 Ph(c),Dare Not Marry 150.00
2 Ph(c),Romances of 125.00
Becomes:

ROMANTIC AFFAIRS
3 Ph(c) 100.00

MOMENT OF SILENCE
Dec., 2001
Spec. 9-11-01 tribute issue 3.50

MONSTER MENACE
1 thru 4 SD,rep. .... @3.00

MONSTER OF FRANKENSTEIN
Jan., 1973
1 MP,Frankenstein's Monster 60.00
2 MP,Bride of the Monster 35.00
3 MP,Revenge 35.00
4 MP,Monster's Death 35.00
5 MP,The Monster Walks
　 Among Us 35.00
Becomes:

FRANKENSTEIN
1973–75
6 MP,Last of the Frankensteins . . 25.00
7 JB,The Fiend and the Fury . . 25.00
8 JB,A:Dracula 40.00
9 JB,A:Dracula 40.00
10 JB,Death Strikes Frankenstein . 20.00
11 Carnage at CastleFrankenstein 15.00
12 Frankenstein's Monster today . 15.00
13 Undying Fiend 15.00
14 Fury of the Night Creature 15.00
15 Trapped in a Nightmare 15.00
16 The Brute and the Berserker . . 15.00
17 Phoenix Aflame 15.00
18 Children of the Damned
　 Sept., 1975. .... 15.00

MONSTERS ON THE PROWL
See: CHAMBER OF DARKNESS

MONSTERS UNLEASHED
July, 1973
1 GM(c),GC,DW,B&W Mag 40.00
2 JB,FB,BEv,B:Frankenstein 35.00
3 NA(c),GK,GM,GT,B:Man-Thing 35.00
4 JB,GC,BK,I:Satana 35.00
5 JB 25.00
6 MP 25.00
7 AW 25.00
8 GP,NA 30.00
9 A:Wendigo 30.00
10 O:Tigra 30.00
11 FB(C),April, 1975 .... 30.00
Ann.#1 GK 30.00

MOON KNIGHT
[1st Regular Series] Nov., 1980
1 BSz,O:Moon Knight 5.00
2 BSz,V:Slasher 3.50
3 BSz,V:Midnight Man 3.50
4 BSz,V:Committee of 5 .... 3.50
5 BSz,V:Red Hunter 3.50
6 BSz,V:White Angels 3.50
7 BSz,V:Moon Kings 3.50
8 BSz,V:Moon Kings, Drug 3.00
9 BSz,V:Midnight Man 3.00
10 BSz,V:Midnight Man 3.00
11 BSz,V:Creed (Angel Dust) 3.00
12 BSz,V:Morpheus 3.00
13 BSz,A:Daredevil & Jester..... 3.00
14 BSz,V:Stained Glass Scarlet . . 3.00
15 FM(c),BSz, 1st Direct 4.00
16 V:Blacksmith 3.00
17 BSz,V:Master Sniper 3.00
18 BSz,V:Slayers Elite 3.00
19 BSz,V:Arsenal 3.00
20 BSz,V:Arsenal 3.00
21 A:Bother Voodoo 2.50
22 BSz,V:Morpheus 2.50
23 BSz,V:Morpheus 2.50
24 BSz,V:Stained Glass Scarlet . . 2.50
25 BSz,Black Specter 2.50
26 KP,V:Cabbie Killer 2.50
27 A:Kingpin 2.50
28 BSz, `Spirits in the Sands' 2.50
29 BSz,V:Werewolf 2.50
30 BSz,V:Werewolf 2.50
31 TA,V:Savage Studs 2.50
32 KN,Druid Walsh 2.50
33 KN,V:Druid Walsh 2.50
34 KN,Marc Spector 2.50
35 KN,X-Men,FF,V:The Fly
　 DoubleSized 3.00
36 A:Dr.Strange 2.50
37 V:Zohar 2.50
38 V:Zohar 2.50
[2nd Regular Series] 1985
1 O:Moon Knight,DoubleSize..... 2.50
2 Yucatan 2.50
3 V:Morpheus 2.50
4 A:Countess............... 2.50
5 V:Lt.Flint 2.50
6 GI,LastIssue 2.50
[3rd Regular Series] 1989–94
1 V:Bushmaster............. 4.00
2 A:Spider-Man 3.00
3 V:Bushmaster............. 2.50
4 RH,A:Midnight,Black Cat 2.50
5 V:Midnight,BlackCat 2.50
6 A:BrotherVoodoo 2.50
7 A:BrotherVoodoo 2.50

8 TP,A:Punisher,A of V. 3.00
9 TP,A:Punisher,A of V. 3.00
10 V:Killer Shrike,A of V 2.00
11 TP,V:Arsenal 2.00
12 TP,V:Bushman,A:Arsenal 2.50
13 TP,V:Bushman. 2.50
14 TP,V:Bushman. 2.50
15 TP,Trial o/Marc Spector #1,A:
　 Silv.Sable,Sandman,Paladin . . 3.00
16 TP,Trial o/Marc Spector #2,A:
　 Silv.Sable,Sandman,Paladin . . 3.00
17 TP,Trial o/Marc Spector #3. . . 3.00
18 TP,Trial o/Marc Spector #4. . . 3.00
19 RLd(c),TP,SpM,Punisher 3.00
20 TP,A:Spider-Man,Punisher 3.00
21 TP,Spider-Man,Punisher 3.00
22 I:Harbinger 2.50
23 Confrontation. 2.50
24 A:Midnight. 2.50
25 MBa,TP,A:Ghost Rider. 3.00
26 BSz(c),TP,B:Scarlet Redemption
　 V:Stained Glass Scarlet 2.50
27 TP,V:Stained Glass Scarlet . . . 2.50
28 TP,V:Stained Glass Scarlet . . . 2.50
29 TP,V:Stained Glass Scarlet . . . 2.50
30 TP,V:Stained Glass Scarlet . . . 2.50
31 TP,E:Scarlet Redemption,
　 A:Hobgoblin 2.75
32 TP,V:Hobgoblin,SpM(in Black) . 3.00
33 TP,V:Hobgoblin,A:Spider-Man . . 3.00
34 V:Killer Shrike 2.50
35 TP,Return of Randall Spector
　 Pt.1,A:Punisher 2.50
36 TP,A:Punisher,Randall. 2.50
37 TP,A:Punisher,Randall 2.50
38 TP,A:Punisher,Randall 2.50
39 TP,N:Moon Knight,A:Dr.Doom . . 2.50
40 TP,V:Dr.Doom 2.50
41 TP,Infinity War,I:Moonshade. . . . 2.50
42 TP,Infinity War,V:Moonshade . . . 2.50
43 TP(i),Infinity War 2.50
Inf.War,A:Dr.Strange.FF. 2.50
45 V:Demogoblin 2.50
46 V:Demogoblin 2.50
47 Legacy Quest Scenario 2.50
48 I:Deadzone 2.50
49 V:Deadzone. 2.50
50 A:Avengers,I:Hellbent,
　 Die-cut(c)................ 3.50
51 A:Gambit,V:Hellbent. 2.50
52 A:Gambit,Werewolf 2.50
53 `Pang' 2.50
54 .... 2.50

Frankenstein #7
© Marvel Entertainment Group

Mioon Knight #26
© Marvel Entertainment Group

Moon Knight–Mutant

MARVEL

55 SPa,V:Sunstreak 6.00
56 SPa,V:Seth 6.00
57 SPa,Inf.Crusade 4.00
58 SPa(c),A:Hellbent 3.00
59 SPa(c), ... 3.00
60 E:TKa(s),SPa,D:Moonknight . . . 4.00
Spec.#1 ANi,A:Shang-Chi 2.50
1-shot Moon Knight: Divided We Fall
   DCw,V:Bushman (1992) 4.95

MOON KNIGHT
(Special Edition) Nov., 1983
1 BSz,reprints 2.50
2 BSz,reprints 2.50
3 BSz,reprints,Jan., 1984. . . . . 2.50

MOON KNIGHT
Nov., 1997–Feb., 1998
1 (of 4) DgM, Moon Knight returns . 2.50
1A signed by Tommy Lee Edwards
   (250 copies) 20.00
2 DgM,A:Scarlet 2.50
3 DgM,Resurrection War,V:Black
   Spectre 2.50
4 DgM,Resurrecton War, concl. . . . 2.50

MOON KNIGHT
Dec., 1998
1 (of 4) DgM,MT,A:Marlene 3.00
2 DgM,MT 3.00
3 DgM,MT 3.00
4 DgM,MT,concl. 3.00

MOONSHADOW
Epic, May, 1985
1 JMu,O:Moonshadow 6.00
2 JMu,Into Space 4.00
3 JMu,The Looney Bin. 4.00
4 JMu,Fights Ira 4.00
5 JMu,Prisoner 4.00
6 JMu,Hero of War 4.00
7 JMu,UnkshussFamily 4.00
8 JMu,Social Outcast. 4.00
9 JMu,Search For Ira. 4.00
10 JMu,Internat.House of T 4.00
11 JMu,UnkshussFamily 4.00
12 JMu,UnkshussFamily,Feb.1987 . 4.00

MORBIUS
1992–95
1 V:Lilith,Lilin,A:Blaze,Gh.Rider,
   Rise o/t Midnight Sons #3,
   polybagged w/poster 3.00
2 V:Simon Stroud 2.50
3 A:Spider-Man 2.25
4 I:Dr.Paine, C:Spider-Man 2.25
5 V:Basilisk,(inc Superman tribute
   on letters page) 2.25
6 V:Basilisk 2.25
7 V:Vic Slaughter. 2.25
8 V:Nightmare 2.25
9 V:Nightmare 2.25
10 Two Tales 2.25
11 A:Nightstalkers. 2.25
12 Midnight Massacre#4. . . . . 2.50
13 R:Martine,A:Lilith 2.25
14 RoW,V:Nightmare,A:Werewolf . 2.25
15 A:Ghost Rider,Werewolf 2.25
16 GWt(s),Siege of Darkness#5 . . 2.25
17 GWt(s),Siege of Darkness#17 . 2.25
18 GWt(s),A:Deathlok 2.25
19 GWt(s),A:Deathlok. 2.25
20 GWt(s),I:Bloodthirst 2.25
21 B:Dance of the Hunter,A:SpM . 2.25
22 A:Spider-Man. 2.25
23 E:Dance of the Hunter,A:SpM . 2.25
24 Return of the Dragon 2.25

MARVEL

Morbius #31
© Marvel Entertainment Group

25 RoW 2.50
26 . . . . 2.00
27 . . . . 2.00
28 A:Werewolf 2.00
29 . . . . 2.00
30 New Morbius 2.00
31 A:Mortine. 2.00
32 Another Kill 2.00

MORBIUS REVISITED
1993
1 WMc,rep.Fear #20 . . . . 2.25
2 WMc,rep.Fear #28 . . . . 2.25
3 WMc,rep.Fear #29 . . . . 2.25
4 WMc,rep.Fear #30 . . . . 2.25
5 WMc,rep.Fear #31 . . . . 2.25

MORLOCKS
April, 2002
1 (of 4) SMa, outsiders 2.50
2 SMa,mutants stay hidden 2.50
3 SMa,where lurk the Morlocks . . . 2.50
4 SMa,concl 2.50

MORT THE DEAD TEENAGER
1993–94
1 LHa(s),I:Mort 2.25
2 thru 4 LHa(s), ... @2.25

MOTHER TERESA
1984
1 Mother Teresa Story 5.00

MOTOR MOUTH & KILLPOWER
Marvel UK, 1992–93
1 GFr,A:Nick Fury,I:Motor
   Mouth,Killpower 2.50
2 GFr,A:Nick Fury, ... 2.25
3 GFr,V:Killpower,A:Punisher. 2.25
4 GFr,A:Nick Fury,Warheads,
   Hell's Angel,O:Killpower 2.25
5 GFr,A:Excalibur,Archangel 2.25
6 GFr,A:Cable,Punisher. 2.25
7 EP,A:Cable,Nick Fury 2.25
8 JFr,A:Cable,Nick Fury. 2.25
9 JFr,A:Cable,N.Fury,V:Harpies . . . 2.25

Comics Values Annual

10 V:Red Sonja 2.25
11 V:Zachary Sorrow 2.25
12 A:Death's Head II. 2.25
13 A:Death's Head II. 2.25

MS. MARVEL
Jan., 1977
1 JB,O:Ms Marvel 15.00
2 JB,JSt,V:Scorpion 7.00
3 JB,JSt,V:Doomsday Man 7.00
4 JM,JSt,V:Destructor 7.00
5 JM,JSt,A:V:Vision 7.00
6 JM,JSt,V:Grotesk 7.00
7 JM,JSt,V:Modok 7.00
8 JM,JSt,GF(c),V:Grotesk 7.00
9 KP,JSt,I:Deathbird 8.00
10 JB,TP,V:Deathbird,Modok 6.00
11 V:Elementals 5.00
12 JSn(c),V:Hecate 5.00
13 Bedlam in Boston 5.00
14 CI,TA(c),V:Steeplejack 5.00
15 V:Tigershark 5.00
16 TA,V:Tigershark,A:Beast 12.00
17 TA,C:Mystique 10.00
18 I:Mystique,A;Avengers 20.00
19 A:Captain Marvel 5.00
20 V:Lethal Lizards,N;Ms.Marvel . 5.00
21 V:Lethal Lizards. 5.00
22 TA,V:Deathbirds. 5.00
23 The Woman who Fell to Earth
   April, 1979 . . . . 5.00

MUPPET BABIES
Star, Aug., 1984
1 thru 10 . . . . @2.25
11 thru 20 . . . . @2.25
21 thru 25 July, 1989 . . . . @2.25

MUPPETS TAKE MANHATTAN
1 movie adapt,November, 1984 . . . 3.00
2 movie adapt 3.00
3 movie adapt,Jan., 1985 . . . . 3.00

MUTANTS: THE AMAZING X-MEN
1 X-Men After Xavier 3.50
2 Exodus, Dazzler,V:Abyss 2.25
3 F:Bishop 2.25
4 V:Apocalypse 2.25

MUTANTS: THE ASTONISHING X-MEN
1 Uncanny X-Men 3.50
2 V:Holocaust 2.25
3 V:Abyss 2.25
4 V:Beast,Infinities. 2.25

MUTANTS: GENERATION NEXT
1 Generation X Ax 3.50
2 Genetic Slave Pens 2.25
3 V:Sugar Man 2.25
4 V:Sugar Man 2.25

MUTANT X
Aug., 1998
1 HMe,TR,F:Havok, 48-pg. 3.00
2 HMe,TR,F:Havok 2.50
2a variant cover. 2.50
3 HMe,TR,V:Pack 2.50
4 HMe,TR,V:Goblin Queen 2.50
5 HMe,F:Brute, Fallen 2.50
6 HMe,A:Mutant-X Spider-Man . . . 2.50

MARVEL

Mutant–Mystical

Mutant X #4
© Marvel Entertainment Group

7 HMe,Trial of the Brute......... 2.50
8 HMe,V:Goblin Queen 2.50
9 HMe,V:Sentinels.............. 2.50
10 HMe,V:The Six 2.50
11 HMe,Bloodstorm vs. Havok 2.50
12 HMe,O:Goblin Queen,Havok,
    48-page 3.50
13 O:Bloodstorm 2.50
14 HMe,CNr,I:Cyclops 2.50
15 HMe,F:Havok 2.50
16 HMe 2.50
17 HMe,CNr,V:Cyclops........... 2.50
18 HMe,CNr,A:Punisher 2.50
19 HMe,A:Professor X 2.50
20 HMe,A:Havok 2.50
21 HMe,BS,Prof.X & Apocalypse .. 2.50
22 HMe,BS,Galactus 2.50
23 HMe,TL,Apocalypse........... 2.50
24 HMe,TL,Master Planner 2.50
25 HMe,TL,The Six,48-pg........ 3.50
26 HMe,TL,The Six,Bloodstorm ... 2.50
27 HMe,TL,Dagger,Outcasts...... 2.50
28 HMe,TL,F:Wolverine 2.50
29 HMe,TL,F:Wolverine 2.50
30 HMe,RLm,F:Capt.America 2.50
31 HMe,RLm,F:Capt.America 2.50
32 HMe,RLm,48-page, final 3.00
GN Mutant X, rep.#1 & #2 .... 6.00
Ann.1999, 48-page.............. 3.50
Ann.2000 HMe,secrets 3.50
Ann.2001 HMe,48-page 3.00

MUTANT X
Oct., 2001
1 HC,JHo, TV show tie-in 3.00
2 HC,JHo, ... 2.50
Spec.#1 48-pg.,photo(c) (2002) ... 3.50
Spec.Dangerous Discoveries (2002)3.50

MUTANT X: FUTURE SHOCK
May, 2002
1 CCl,F:Shalimar,54-pg.......... 3.50

MUTATIS
Epic
1 I:Mutatis..................... 2.50
2 O:Mutatis 2.50
3 A:Mutatis 2.50

MUTIES
Feb., 2002
1 (of 6) F:Jared 2.50
2 in Japan, I:Seiji.............. 2.50
3 F:Riek Bukenya 2.50
4 .... 2.50
5 .... 2.50
6 concl 2.50

MY DIARY
Dec., 1949–March, 1950
1 Ph(c),The Man I Love 150.00
2 Ph(c),I Was Anybody's Girl ... 125.00

MY LOVE
July, 1949
1 Ph(c),One Heart to Give 150.00
2 Ph(c),Hate in My Heart 100.00
3 Ph(c), ... 100.00
4 Ph(c),Betty Page, April,1950 .. 350.00

MY LOVE
Sept., 1969
1 Love story reprints 75.00
2 thru 9 .... @40.00
10 .... 50.00
11 thru 38 .... @25.00
39 March, 1976 .... 25.00

MY ROMANCE
Sept., 1948
1 Romance Stories 150.00
2 .... 100.00
3 .... 100.00
Becomes:

MY OWN ROMANCE
4 Romance Stories Continue . . . 150.00
5 thru 10 .... @100.00
11 thru 20 .... @100.00
21 thru 50 .... @75.00
51 thru 54 .... @50.00
55 ATh 75.00
56 thru 60 .... @50.00
61 thru 70 .... @40.00
71 AW 100.00
72 thru 76 .... @40.00
Becomes:

TEENAGE ROMANCE
77 Romance Stories Continue ... 40.00
78 thru 85 .... @40.00
86 March, 1962 .... 40.00

MYS-TECH WARS
Marvel UK, 1993
1 BHi,A:FF,X-Men,Avengers 2.25
2 A:FF,X-Men,X-Force 2.25
3 BHi,A:X-Men,X-Force 2.25
4 A:Death's Head II............ 2.25

MYSTERY TALES
Atlas, March, 1952
1 GC,Horror Strikes at
    Midnight 1,100.00
2 BK,BEv,OW,The Corpse
    is Mine 550.00
3 RH,GC,JM, The Vampire
    Strikes 400.00
4 Funeral of Horror 400.00
5 Blackout at Midnight 400.00
6 .... 400.00
7 JRo,The Ghost Hunter 400.00
8 BEv 400.00
9 BEv(c),the Man in the Morgue 400.00
10 BEV(c),GT,What Happened

to Harry 400.00
11 BEv(c) 300.00
12 GT,MF 325.00
13 .... 300.00
14 BEv(c),GT 300.00
15 RH(c),EK 300.00
16 .... 300.00
17 RH(c). 300.00
18 AW,DAy,GC 325.00
19 .... 300.00
20 Electric Chair 300.00
21 JF,MF,BP,Decapitation 300.00
22 JF,MF 300.00
23 thru 27 .... @250.00
28 .... 225.00
29 thru 32 .... @235.00
33 BEv 225.00
34 .... 225.00
35 BEv,GC 225.00
36 .... 235.00
37 DW,BP,JR 225.00
38 BP 225.00
39 BK 235.00
40 .... 235.00
41 MD,BEv................... 225.00
42 .... 225.00
41 GC 225.00
44 AW 200.00
45 SD 175.00
46 RC,SD,JP 200.00
47 DAy,BP 200.00
48 .... 175.00
49 GM,AT,DAy 175.00
50 JO,AW,GM. 200.00
51 DAy,JO 200.00
52 .... 175.00
53 .... 175.00
54 RC,Aug., 1957 .... 200.00

MYSTICAL TALES
Atlas, June, 1956
1 BEv,BP,JO,Say the Magical
    Words 600.00
2 BEv(c),JO,Black Blob 300.00
3 BEv(c),RC,Four Doors To ... 275.00
4 BEv(c).The Condemned 275.00
5 AW,Meeting at Midnight 300.00
6 BK,AT,He Hides in the Tower . 250.00
7 BEv,JF,JO,AT,FBe,The
    Haunted Tower.......... 250.00
8 BK,SC, Stone Walls Can't
    Stop Him,Aug., 1957 ..... 250.00

Mystic Comics #3
© Marvel Entertainment Group

All comics prices listed are for *Near Mint* condition.

MYSTIC COMICS
Timely, March, 1940
[1st Series]
1 ASh(c),O;The Blue Blaze,Dynamic Man,Flexo,B:Dakor the Magician A:Zephyr Jones,3X's,Deep Sea Demon,Bondage(c) 20,000.00
2 ASh(c),B:The Invisible Man Mastermind,Blue Blaze ... 6,000.00
3 ASh(c),O:Hercules 4,000.00
4 ASh(c),O:Thin Man,Black Widow E:Hercules,Blue Blazes,Dynamic Man,Flexo,Invisible Man .. 4,300.00
5 ASh(c)O:The Black Marvel, Blazing Skull,Super Slave Terror,Sub-Earth Man .. 4,000.00
6 ASh(c),O:The Challenger, B:The Destroyer 5,000.00
7 S&K(c),B:The Witness,O:Davey and the Demon,E;The Black Widow,Hitler(c) 5,200.00
8 Bondage(c) 2,600.00
9 MSy,DRi,Hitler/Bondage(c) . 2,600.00
10 E:Challenger,Terror 2,600.00

[2nd Series] Oct., 1944
1 B:The Angel,Human Torch, Destroyer,Terry Vance, Tommy Tyme,Bondage(c) . 3,000.00
2 E:Human Torch,Terry Vance,Bondage(c) 1,500.00
3 E:The Angel,Tommy Tyme Bondage(c) 1,400.00
4 ASh(c),A:Young Allies Winter, 1944-45 .... 1,300.00

MYSTIC
[3rd Series] March, 1951
1 MSy,Strange Tree 1,200.00
2 MSy,Dark Dungeon 600.00
3 GC,Jaws of Creeping Death . 500.00
4 BW,MSy,The Den of the Devil Bird 1,000.00
5 MSy,Face 350.00
6 BW,She Wouldn't Stay Dead 1,000.00
7 GC,Untold Horror waits in the Tomb 350.00
8 DAy(c),BEv,GK,A Monster Among Us 350.00
9 BEv 350.00
10 GC 350.00
11 JR,The Black Gloves 300.00
12 GC 300.00
13 In the Dark............... 300.00
14 The Corpse and I.......... 300.00
15 GT,JR,House of Horror..... 300.00
16 A Scream in the Dark...... 300.00
17 BEv,Behold the Vampire..... 300.00
18 BEv(c),The Russian Devil ... 300.00
19 Swamp Girl 300.00
20 RH(c).................... 300.00
21 BEv(c),GC................ 250.00
22 RH(c).................... 250.00
23 RH(c),RA,RMn,Chilling Tales . 250.00
24 GK,RMn,How Many Times Can You Die 250.00
25 RH(c),RA,E.C.Swipe 250.00
26 Severed Head(c) 250.00
27 Who Walks with a Zombie ... 225.00
28 DW,RMn(c),Not Enough Dead 225.00
29 SMo,RMn(c),The Unseen.... 225.00
30 RH(c),DW 225.00
31 SC,JKz,RMn(c) 225.00
32 The Survivor 225.00
33 thru 36 ....@225.00
37 thru 51 ....@200.00
52 WW,RC 225.00
53 thru 57 ....@200.00
58 thru 60 ....@225.00
61........................ 200.00

MYSTIQUE
Marvel April 2003
1 JLi(c),Drop Dead Gorgeous,pt.1 . 3.00
2 JLi(c),Drop Dead Gorgeous,pt.2 . 3.00
3 JLi(c),Drop Dead Gorgeous,pt.3 . 3.00
4 JLi(c),Drop Dead Gorgeous,pt.4 . 3.00
5 JLi(c),Drop Dead Gorgeous,pt.5 . 3.00
6 JLi(c),Drop Dead Gorgeous,pt.6 . 3.00
7 Tinker,Tailor,Mutant,Spy,pt.1 ... 3.00
8 Tinker,Tailor,Mutant,Spy,pt.2 ... 3.00
TPB Dead Drop Gorgeous 19.95

'NAM, THE
Dec., 1986
1 MGo,Vietnam War 3.00
1a 2nd printing 2.50
2 MGo,Dust Off 2.50
3 MGo,Three Day Pass........ 2.25
4 MGo,TV newscrew 2.25
5 MGo,Top Sgt............... 2.25
6 MGo,Monsoon 2.25
7 MGo,Cedar Falls 2.25
8 MGo,5th to the 1st 2.25
9 MGo,Action Issue,Tunnel Rat ... 3.50
10 MGo,Saigon 2.25
11 MGo,Christmas 2.25
12 MGo,AgentOrange........... 2.25
13 MGo 2.25
14 .... 2.25
15 ReturningVets 2.25
16 .... 2.25
17 Vietcong 2.25
18 .... 2.25
19 .... 2.25
20 .... 2.25
21 .... 2.25
22 Thanksgiving 2.25
23 XmasTruce of'67 .... 2.25
24 TetOffensive 2.25
25 TetOffensive-KheSanh 2.25
26 HomefrontIssue 2.25
27 Candle in the Wind 2.25
28 Borderline 2.25
29 PeaceTalks 2.25
30 TheBunker................. 2.25
31 Fire and Ice 2.25
32 Nam in America 2.25
33 SpecialistDaniels 2.25
34 OperationPhoenix 2.25
35 Xmas-BobHope 2.25
36 RacialTension 2.25
37 Colorblind 2.25
38 Minefields 2.25
39 .... 2.25
40 .... 2.25
41 ,A:Thor,Iron Man, Cap.Am 2.25
42 .... 2.25
43 .... 2.25
44 SDr 2.25
45 .... 2.25
46 .... 2.25
47 TD 2.25
48 TD 2.25
49 Donut Dolly #1............. 2.25
50 HT,Donut Dolly #2 DoubSz ... 2.50
51 HT,Donut Dolly #3 .... 2.25
52 Frank Castle(Punisher)#1 ..... 3.00
52a 2nd printing 2.25
53 Punisher #2................ 2.50
54 Death of Joe Hallen #1 ..... 2.25
55 TD,Death of Joe Hallen #2.... 2.25
56 TD,Death of Joe Hallen #3..... 2.25
57 TD,Death of Joe Hallen #4..... 2.25
58 TD,Death of Joe Hallen #5..... 2.25
59 P.O.W. Story #1............ 2.25
60 P.O.W. Story #2............ 2.25
61 P.O.W. Story #3............ 2.25
62 Speed & Ice,pt.1 .... 2.25
63 Speed & Ice,pt.2 .... 2.25
64 Speed & Ice,pt.3 .... 2.25
65 Speed & Ice,pt.4 .... 2.25
66 RH,Speed & Ice,pt.5 .... 2.25
67 thru 69 A:Punisher .... @2.25
70 Don Lomax writes 2.25
71 Vietnamese Point of View 2.25
72 The trials of war............. 2.25
73 War on the Homefront 2.25
74 Seige at An Loc............. 2.25
75 My Lai Massacre 2.50
76 R:Rob Little 2.25
77 Stateside.................. 2.25
78 .... 2.25
79 Beginning of the End#1 ..... 2.25
80 MGo(c),'68 Tet Offensive 2.25
81 MGo(c),TET Offensive ends.... 2.25
82 TET Offensive 2.25
83 thru 84 Last issue......... @2.25
TPB rep. #1–#4 (1999)......... 14.95

'NAM MAGAZINE, THE
(B&W) Aug., 1988–May, 1989
1 Reprints 3.00
2 thru 10 .... @2.50

NAMOR
Marvel April 2003
1 MiS,manga 0.25
2 MiS 2.25
3 SvL 2.25
4 SvL,F:Sandy................ 2.25
5 SvL,F:Sandy................ 2.25
6 SvL,Namor's choice 2.25
7 PO 2.25
8 PO 2.25
9 .... 2.25
TPB Vol. 1 .... 19.95

NAMORA
Fall, 1948–Dec., 1948
1 BEv,DR 3,000.00
2 BEv,A:Sub-Mariner,Blonde Phantom 1,600.00
3 BEv,A:Sub-Mariner 1,700.00

NAMOR THE SUB-MARINER
April, 1990
1 JBy,BWi,I:Desmond & Phoebe Marrs............ 5.00
2 JBy,BWi,V:Griffin 3.00

MARVEL

Namor–New Mutants

3 JBy,BWi,V:Griffin	3.00	
4 JBy,A:Reed & Sue Richards, Tony Stark	3.00	
5 JBy,A:FF,IronMan,C:Speedball	3.00	
6 JBy,V:Sluj	3.00	
7 JBy,V:Sluj	3.00	
8 JBy,V:Headhunter,R:D.Rand	3.00	
9 JBy,V:Headhunter	3.00	
10 JBy,V:Master Man,Warrior Woman	2.50	
11 JBy,V:Mast.Man,War.Woman	3.00	
12 JBy,R:Invaders,Spitfire	2.50	
13 JBy,Namor on Trial,A:Fantastic Four,Captain America,Thor	2.50	
14 JBy,R:Lady Dorma,A:Ka-Zar Griffin	2.50	
15 JBy,A:Iron Fist	2.50	
16 JBy,A:Punisher,V:Iron Fist	2.50	
17 JBy,V:Super Skrull(Iron Fist)	2.50	
18 JBy,V:SuperSkrull,A:Punisher	2.50	
19 JBy,V:Super Skrull,D:D.Marrs.	2.50	
20 JBy,Search for Iron Fist, O:Namorita	2.50	
21 JBy,Visit to K'un Lun	2.50	
22 JBy,Fate of Iron Fist, C:Wolverine	2.50	
23 JBy,BWi,Iron Fist Contd., C:Wolverine	2.50	
24 JBy,BWi,V:Wolverine	3.00	
25 JBy,BWi,V:Master Khan	2.50	
26 JaL,BWi,Search For Namor	5.00	
27 JaL,BWi,V:Namorita	4.00	
28 JaL,BWi,A:Iron Fist	3.00	
29 JaL,BWi,After explosion	3.00	
30 JaL,A:Doctor Doom	3.00	
31 JaL,V:Doctor Doom	3.00	
32 JaL,V:Doctor Doom, Namor regains memory	3.00	
33 JaL,V:Master Khan	2.50	
34 JaL,R:Atlantis	2.50	
35 JaL,V:Tiger Shark	2.50	
36 JaL,I:Suma-Ket,A:Tiger Shark	2.50	
37 JaL,Blue Holo-Grafix,Altantean Civil War,N:Namor	2.75	
38 JaL,O:Suma-Ket	2.50	
39 A:Tigershark,V:Suma-Ket	2.50	
40 V:Suma-Ket	2.50	
41 V:War Machine	2.50	
42 MCW,A:Stingray,V:Dorcas	2.50	
43 MCW,V:Orka,Dorcas	2.50	
44 I:Albatross	2.50	
45 GI,A:Sunfire,V:Attuma	2.50	
46 GI,	2.50	
47 GI,Starblast #2	2.50	
48 GI,Starblast #9,A:FF	2.50	
49 GI,A:Ms. Marrs	2.50	
50 GI,Holo-grafx(c),A:FF.	4.00	
50a Newsstand Ed.	2.50	
51 AaL,,	2.50	
52 GI,I:Sea Leopard	2.50	
53 GI,V:Sea Leopard	2.50	
54 GI,I:Llyron	2.50	
55 GI,V:Llyron	2.50	
56 GI,V:Llyron	2.50	
57 A:Capt. America, V:Llyron	2.50	
58	2.50	
59 GI,V:Abomination.	2.50	
60 A:Morgan Le Fay	2.50	
61 Atlantis Rising	2.50	
62 V:Triton	2.50	
Ann.#1 Subterran.Odyssey #3	3.00	
Ann.#2 Return o/Defenders,pt.3	4.00	
Ann.#3 I:Assassin,A:Iron Fist, w/Trading card	3.25	
Ann.#4 V:Hydra	3.25	

NAVY ACTION
Aug., 1954

1 BP,US Navy War Stories	200.00
2 TLn,Navy(c)	100.00
3 BEv	75.00
4 and 5	@75.00
6 JH(c)	75.00
7 MD,JMn	75.00
8 JMn,GC	75.00
9 thru 15	@75.00
16 BEv(c)	75.00
17 MD,BEv(c)	75.00
18 Aug., 1957	75.00

NAVY COMBAT
Atlas, June, 1955

1 DH,JMn(c),B:Torpedo Taylor	200.00
2 DH	100.00
3 DH,BEv	75.00
4 DH	75.00
5 DH	75.00
6 JMn,A:Battleship Burke	75.00
7 thru 10	@75.00
11 MD,GC,JMn	75.00
12 RC	100.00
13 GT	75.00
14 AT,GT	75.00
15 GT	75.00
16	75.00
17 AW,AT,JMn	85.00
18	75.00
19	75.00
20 BEv,BP,AW,Oct., 1958	80.00

NAVY TALES
Atlas, Jan., 1957

1 BEv(c),BP,Torpedoes	175.00
2 AW,RC,JMn(c),One Hour to Live	175.00
3 JSe(c)	150.00
4 JSe(c),GC,JSt,RC,July, 1957	150.00

NELLIE THE NURSE
Atlas, 1945

1 Beach(c)	350.00
2 Nellie's Date(c)	200.00
3 Swimming Pool(c)	125.00
4 Roller Coaster(c)	125.00
5 Hospital(c),HK,Hey Look	125.00
6 Bedside Manner(c)	125.00
7 Comic book(c)A:Georgie	125.00
8 Hospital(c),A:Georgie	125.00
9 BW,Nellie/Swing(c)A:Millie	125.00
10 Bathing Suit(c),A:Millie	125.00
11 HK,Hey Look	150.00
12 HK, Giggles `n' Grins	125.00
13 HK	100.00
14 HK	125.00
15 HK	125.00
16 HK	125.00
17 HK.A:Annie Oakley	125.00
18 HK	125.00
19	100.00
20	100.00
21	75.00
22	75.00
23	75.00
24	75.00
25	75.00
26	75.00
27	75.00
28 HK,Rusty Reprint	75.00
29 thru 35	@60.00
36 Oct., 1952	60.00

NEW ADVENTURES OF CHOLLY & FLYTRAP
Epic

1	4.95
2	3.95
3	3.95

NEW ETERNALS: APOCALYPSE NOW
Dec., 1999

1-shot JoB,SHa,64-pg.	4.00

NEW MUTANTS, THE
March, 1983

1 BMc,MG,O:New Mutants	5.00
2 BMc,MG,V:Sentinels	4.00
3 BMc,MG,V:Brood Alien	3.50
4 SB,BMc,A:Peter Bristow	3.50
5 SB,BMc,A:Dark Rider	3.50
6 SB,AG,V:Viper	3.50
7 SB,BMc,V:Axe	3.50
8 SB,BMc,I:Amara Aquilla	3.50
9 SB,TMd,I:Selene	3.50
10 SB,BMc,C:Magma	3.50
11 SB,TMd,I:Magma	3.50
12 SB,TMd,J:Magma	3.50
13 SB,TMd,I:Cypher(Doug Ramsey) A:Kitty Pryde,Lilandra	4.00
14 SB,TMd,J:Magik,A:X-Men	3.00
15 SB,TMd,Mass.Academy	3.00
16 SB,TMd,V:Hellions,I:Warpath I:Jetstream	4.00
17 SB,TMd,V:Hellions,A:Warpath	4.00
18 BSz,V:Demon Bear,I:New Warlock,Magus	5.00
19 BSz,V:Demon Bear	3.00
20 BSz,V:Demon Bear	3.00
21 BSz,O&J:Warlock,doub.sz	5.00
22 BSz,A:X-Men	3.50
23 BSz,Sunspot,Cloak & Dagger	3.00
24 BSz,A:Cloak & Dagger	3.00
25 BSz,A:Cloak & Dagger	6.00
26 BSz,I:Legion(Prof.X's son)	7.00
27 BSz,V:Legion	4.00
28 BSz,O:Legion	4.00
29 BSz,V:Gladiators,I:Guido (Strong Guy)	3.00
30 BSz,A:Dazzler	3.00
31 BSz,A:Shadowcat	3.00
32 SL,V:Karma	3.00
33 SL,V:Karma	3.00
34 SL,V:Amahl Farouk	3.00
35 BSz,J:Magneto	3.00
36 BSz,A:Beyonder	3.00
37 BSz,D:New Mutants	3.00
38 BSz,A:Hellions	3.00
39 BSz,A:White Queen	3.00
40 JG,KB,V:Avengers	3.00
41 JG,TA,Mirage	3.00

New Mutants #42
© Marvel Entertainment Group

All comics prices listed are for *Near Mint* condition.

New: Mutants–Warriors — MARVEL — Comics Values Annual

42 JG,KB,A:Dazzler 3.00
43 SP,V:Empath,A:Warpath 3.00
44 JG,V:Legion 5.00
45 JG,A:Larry Bodine 3.00
46 JG,KB,Mutant Massacre 3.50
47 JG,KB,V:Magnus 3.00
48 JG,CR,Future 3.00
49 VM,Future 3.00
50 JG,V:Magus,R:Prof.X 4.00
51 KN,A:Star Jammers 3.00
52 RL,DGr,Limbo 3.00
53 RL,TA,V:Hellions 3.00
54 SB,TA,N:New Mutants 3.00
55 BBI,TA,V:Aliens 3.00
56 JBr,TA,V:Hellions,A:Warpath . 3.00
57 BBI,TA,I&J:Bird-Boy 3.00
58 BBI,TA,Bird-Boy 3.00
59 BBI,TA,Fall of Mutants,
    V:Dr.Animus 3.00
60 BBI,TA,F.of M.,D:Cypher 2.50
61 BBI,TA,Fall of Mutants 2.50
62 JMu,A:Magma,Hellions 2.50
63 BHa,JRu,Magik 2.50
64 BBI,TA,R:Cypher 2.50
65 BBI,TA,V:FreedomForce 2.50
66 BBI,TA,V:Forge 2.50
67 BBI,I:Gosamyr 2.50
68 BBI,V:Gosamyr 2.50
69 BBI,AW,I:Spyder 2.50
70 TSh,AM,V:Spyder 2.50
71 BBI,AW,V:N'Astirh 2.50
72 BBI,A,Inferno 2.50
73 BBI,W,A:Colossus 3.00
74 BBI,W,A:X-Terminators 2.50
75 JBy,Mc,Black King,V:Magneto . 3.50
76 RB,TP,J:X-Terminators 2.50
77 RB,V:Mirage 2.50
78 RL,AW,V:FreedomForce 2.50
79 BBI,AW,V:Hela 2.50
80 BBI,AW,Asgard 2.50
81 LW,TSh,JRu,A:Hercules 2.50
82 BBI,AW,Asgard 2.50
83 BBI,Asgard 2.50
84 TSh,AM,A:QueenUla 2.50
85 RLd&TMc(c),BBI,V:Mirage ... 5.00
86 RLd,BWi,V:Vulture,C:Cable . 6.00
87 RLd,BWi,I:Mutant Liberation
    Front,Cable 16.00
87a 2nd Printing 2.00
88 RLd,2nd Cable,V:Freedom
    Force 7.50
89 RLd,V:Freedom Force 6.00
90 RLd,A:Caliban,V:Sabretooth . 6.00
91 RLd,A:Caliban,Masque,
    V:Sabretooth 6.00
92 RLd(c),BH,V:Skrulls 4.00
93 RLd,A:Wolverine,Sunfire,
    V:Mutant Liberation Front .. 6.00
94 RLd,A:Wolverine,Sunfire,
    V:Mutant Liberation Front .. 5.00
95 RLd,Extinction Agenda,V:Hodge
    A:X-Men,X-Factor,C:Warlock . 5.00
95a 2nd printing(gold) 5.00
96 RLd,ATb,JRu,Extinction Agenda
    V:Hodge,A:X-Men,X-Factor . 5.00
97 E:LSi(s),RLd(c),JRu,Extinction
    Agenda,V:Hodge 5.00
98 FaN(s),RLd,I:Deadpool,Domino,
    Gideon,L:Rictor 9.00
99 FaN(s),RLd,I:Feral,Shatterstar,
    L:Sunspot,J:Warpath 5.00
100 FaN(s),RLd,J:Feral,Shatterstar,
    I:X-Force,V:Masque,Imperial
    Protectorate,A:MLF 6.00
100a 2nd Printing(Gold) 4.00
100b 3rd Printing(Silver) 3.50
Ann.#1 BMc,TP,L.Cheney 7.00
Ann.#2 AD,V:Mojo,I:Psylocke,Meggan
    (American App.) 10.00
Ann.#3 AD,PN,V:Impossible Man . 4.00
Ann.#4 JBr,BMc,Evol.Wars 6.00

Ann.#5 RLd,JBg,MBa,KWi,Atlantis
    Attacks,A:Namorita,I:Surf 8.00
Ann.#6 RLd(c),Days o/Future Present
    V:FranklinRichards,(Pin-ups) . 6.00
Ann.#7 JRu,RLd,Kings of Pain,
    I:Piecemeal & Harness,
    Pin-ups X-Force 5.00
Spec #1,AAd,TA,Asgard War 6.00
Summer Spec.#1 BBI,Megapolis . 3.50
TPB New Mutants: Demon Bear,
    CCI/BSz,Rep #18–#21 .... 8.95

NEW MUTANTS
Sept., 1997
1 (of 3) BRa,BCh,F:Cannonball,
    Moonstar, Wolfsbane,Karma &
    Sunspot 2.50
2 BRa,BCh,meeting with mutants
    of the past 2.50
3 BRa,BCh, will Magik return
    for good? 2.50

NEW MUTANTS
Marvel May 2003
1 R:Original New Mutants 2.50
2 F:Dani Moonstar 2.50
3 new student 2.50
4 F:Karma 2.50
5 mutant teens 2.50
6 V:Reavers 2.50
7 .... 2.50
8 .... 2.50

NEW WARRIORS
July, 1990
1 B:FaN(s),MBa,AW,V:Terrax,
    O:New Warriors 5.00
1a Gold rep. 2.50
2 FaN(s),MBa,AW,I:Midnight's Fire,
    Silhouette 3.50
3 MBa,LMa(i),V:Mad Thinker 3.50
4 MBa,LMa(i),I:Psionex 3.50
5 MBa,LMa(i),V:Star Thief,
    C:White Queen 3.50
6 MBa,LMa(i),V:StarThief,
    A:Inhumans 3.50
7 MBa,LMa(i),V:Bengal,
    C:Punisher 3.50
8 MBa,LMa(i),V:Punisher,
    I:Force of Nature 3.50

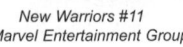

New Warriors #11
© *Marvel Entertainment Group*

9 MBa,LMa(i),V:Punisher,Bengal,
    Force of Nature 3.50
10 MBa,LMa(i),V:Hellions,White
    Queen,I:New Sphinx 3.50
11 MBa,LMa(i),V:Sphinx,
    B:Forever Yesterday 2.50
12 MBa,LMa(i),V:Sphinx 2.50
13 MBa,LMa(i),V:Sphinx,
    E:Forever Yesterday 2.50
14 MBa,LMa(i),A:Namor,
    Darkhawk 2.50
15 MBa,LMa(i),V:Psionex,
    R:Terrax,N:Nova 2.50
16 MBa,LMa(i),A:Psionex,
    V:Terrax 2.50
17 MBa,LMa(i),A:Silver Surfer,Fant.
    Four,V:Terrax,I:Left Hand 2.50
18 MBa,LMa(i),O:Night Thrasher . 2.50
19 MBa,LMa(i),V:Gideon 2.50
20 MBa,LMa(i),V:Clan Yashida,
    Marvel Boy kills his father 2.50
21 MBa,LMa(i),I:Folding Circle ... 2.50
22 MBa,LMa(i),A:Darkhawk,Rage . 2.50
23 MBa,LMa(i),V:Folding Circle .. 2.50
24 LMa(i),V:Folding Circle 2.50
25 MBa,LMa(i),Die-Cut(c),Marvel Boy
    found guilty of murder,D:Tai,
    O:Folding Circle 2.50
26 DaR,LMa(i),V:Guardsmen 2.50
27 DaR,LMa(i),Inf.War,Speedball Vs.
    his doppelganger,N:Rage 2.50
28 DaR,LMa(i),I:Turbo,Cardinal .. 2.50
29 DaR,LMa(i),V:Trans-Sabal 2.50
30 DaR,LMa(i),V:Trans Sabal 2.50
31 DaR,LMa(i)A:Cannonball,Warpath,
    Magma,O&N:Firestar 2.50
32 DaR,LMa(i),B:Forces of Darkness,
    Forces of Light,A:Spider-Man,
    Archangel,Dr.Strange 2.50
33 DaR,LMa(i),A:Cloak & Dagger,
    Turbo,Darkhawk 2.50
34 DaR,LMa(i),A:Avengers,SpM,
    Thing,Torch,Darkhawk,
    C:Darkling 2.50
35 DaR,LMa(i),A:Turbo 2.50
36 DaR,LMa(i),A:Turbo 2.50
37 F:Marvel Boy,V:Wizard 2.50
38 DaR,LMa(i),D:Rage's granny,
    V:Poison Memories 2.50
39 DaR,LMa(i),L:Namorita 2.50
40 DaR,LMa(i),B:Starlost,
    V:Supernova 2.50
40a Newsstand Ed. 2.50
41 DaR,LMa(i),V:Supernova 2.50
42 DaR,LMa(i),E:Starlost,N:Nova,
    V:Supernova 2.50
43 DaR,LMa(i),N&I:Justice
    (Marvel Boy) 2.50
44 Ph(c),DaR,LMa(i),N&I:Kymaera
    (Namorita) 2.50
45 DaR,LMa(i),Child's Play#2,
    N:Silhouette,Speedball,
    V:Upstarts 2.50
46 DaR,LMa(i),Child's Play#4,
    V:Upstarts 2.50
47 DaR,LMa(i),Time&TimeAgain,pt.1,
    A:Sphinx,I:Powerpax 2.50
48 DaR,LMa(i),Time&TimeAgain,pt.4,
    J:Cloak&Dagger,Darkhawk,Turbo,
    Powerpax,Bandit 2.50
49 DaR,LMa(i),Time&TimeAgain,pt.8
    V:Sphinx 2.50
50 reg. (c) 2.25
50a Glow-in-the-dark(c),V:Sphinx . 3.25
51 revamp 2.25
52 R:Psionex 2.25
53 V:Psionex 2.25
54 V:Speedball 2.25
55 V:Soldiers of Misfortune 2.25
56 V:Soldiers 2.25
57 A:Namor 2.25

All comics prices listed are for Near Mint condition.

MARVEL

New Warriors–Nighthawk

58 F:Sabra 2.25
59 F:Speedball 2.25
60 Nova Omega,pt.2 . . . . 2.50
61 J:Scarlet Spider,Maximum
　　Clonage prologue. 2.25
62 F:Scarlet Spider,Maximum
　　Clonage tie-in. 2.25
63 F:Firestar. 2.25
64 I:Psionix 2.25
65 F:Scarlet Spider,V:Kymaera 2.25
66 F:Speedball 2.25
67 Nightmare in Scarlet,pt.2 . . . . . . 2.25
68 Future Shock,pt.1 . . . . 2.25
69 . . . . 2.25
70 . . . . 2.25
71 Future Shock,pt.4 . . . . 2.25
Ann.#1 MBa,A:X-Force,V:Harness,
　　Piecemeal,Kings of Pain #2 . . . 4.00
Ann.#2 Hero Killers #4,V:Sphinx . . . 2.75
Ann.#3 LMa(i),E:Forces of Light,
　　Forces of Darkness,I:Darkling
　　w/card 3.25
Ann.#4 DaR(s),V:Psionex 3.25
TPB New Beginnings rep.Thor #411,
　　412,New Warriors #1-#4 . . . . 12.95

NEW WARRIORS
Aug., 1999
1 F:Speedball,48-page 3.00
2A DaR 2.50
2B variant Steve Scott (c) 2.50
3 . . . . 2.50
4 . . . . 2.50
5 F:Generation X. 2.50
6 F:Night Thrasher, Nova. 2.50
7 F:Turbo 2.50
8 A:Iron Fist & Night Thrasher 2.50
9 Iron Man #29 x-over 2.50
10 A:Hercules 2.50

NEW X-MEN
See: X-MEN

NFL SUPERPRO
1 . . . . 7.00
Spec.#1 reprints 2.50

[Regular Series] Oct., 1991
1 A:Spider-Man,I:Sanzionaire. 2.50
2 V:Quickkick 2.50
3 I:Instant Replay 2.50
4 V:Sanction 2.50
5 A:Real NFL Player 2.50
6 Racism Iss.,recalled by Marvel . . 6.00
7 thru 11 . . . . @2.50
12 V:Nefarious forces of evil 2.50

NICK FURY, AGENT OF S.H.I.E.L.D.
[1st Regular Series] June, 1968
1 JSo/JSt,I:Scorpio 175.00
2 JSo,A:Centaurius 75.00
3 JSo,DA,V:Hell Hounds 75.00
4 FS,O:Nick Fury. 75.00
5 JSo,V:Scorpio. 90.00
6 FS,'Doom must Fall'. 50.00
7 FS,V:S.H.I.E.L.D. 50.00
8 FS,Hate Monger 35.00
9 FS,Hate Monger 35.00
10 FS,JCr,Hate Monger 35.00
11 BS(c),FS,Hate Monger 35.00
12 BS 40.00
13 . . . . 35.00
14 . . . . 35.00
15 I:Bullseye. 90.00
16 JK,rep. 25.00
17 JK,rep. 25.00
18 JK,rep.. . . . . 25.00

Nick Future Agent of S.H.I.E.L.D. #39
© Marvel Entertainment Group

[Limited Series] 1983–94
1 JSo,rep. 4.00
2 JSo,rep. 3.50

[2nd Regular Series] 1989–93
1 BH,I:New Shield,V:Death's
　　Head(not British hero) 3.00
2 KP,V:Death's Head 2.25
3 KP,V:Death's Head 2.25
4 KP,V:Death's Head 2.25
5 KP,V:Death's Head 2.25
6 KP,V:Death's Head 2.25
7 KP,Chaos Serpent #1 . . . . 2.25
8 KP,Chaos Serpent #2 . . . . 2.25
9 KP,Chaos Serpent #3 . . . . 2.25
10 KP,Chaos Serpent ends,
　　A:Capt.America 2.25
11 D:Murdo MacKay 2.25
12 Hydra Affair #1. . . . . 2.25
13 Hydra Affair #2. . . . . 2.25
14 Hydra Affair #3. . . . . 2.25
15 Apogee of Disaster #1 . . . . . . 2.25
16 Apogee of Disaster #2 . . . . . . 2.25
17 Apogee of Disaster #3 . . . . . . 2.25
18 Apogee of Disaster #4 . . . . . . 2.25
19 Apogee of Disaster #5 . . . . . . 2.25
20 JG,A:Red Skull 2.50
21 JG,R:Baron Strucker 2.25
22 JG,A:Baron Strucker,R:Hydra. . . 2.25
23 JG,V:Hydra 2.25
24 A:Capt.Am,Thing,V:Mandarin . . . 2.25
25 JG,Shield Vs. Hydra 2.25
26 JG,A:Baron Strucker,
　　C:Wolverine 2.50
27 JG,V:Hydra,A:Wolverine 2.50
28 V:Hydra,A:Wolverine 2.50
29 V:Hydra,A:Wolverine 2.50
30 R:Leviathan,A:Deathlok 2.25
31 A:Deathlok,V:Leviathan 2.25
32 V:Leviathan 2.25
33 Super-Powered Agents 2.25
34 A:Bridge(X-Force),V:Balance
　　of Terror 2.25
35 A:Cage,V:Constrictor 2.25
36 . . . . 2.25
37 . . . . 2.25
38 Cold War of Nick Fury #1 . . . . 2.25
39 Cold War of Nick Fury #2. . . . 2.25
40 Cold War of Nick Fury #3. . . . 2.25
41 Cold War of Nick Fury #4. . . . 2.25
42 I:Strike Force Shield 2.25
43 R:Clay Quatermain 2.25
44 A:Captain America 2.25
45 A:Bridge 2.25

46 V:Gideon,Hydra 2.25
47 V:Baron Strucker,last issue . . . 2.25
TPB Death Duty V:Night Raven . . . 5.95
TPB Captain America 5.95
TPB Scorpion Connection. 7.95
TPB JSo, 248-pg 19.95
TPB Scorpio 14.95
Ashcan. 75

NICK FURY, VERSUS S.H.I.E.L.D.
June, 1988
1 JSo(c),D:Quartermail 6.00
2 BSz(c),Into The Depths 5.00
3 Uneasy Allies 4.00
4 V:Hydra 4.00
5 V:Hydra 4.00
6 V:Hydra, Dec., 1988 . . . . 4.00
TPB Reprints #1-#6 . . . . 15.95

NIGHTBREED
Epic, April, 1990
1 . . . . 4.00
2 . . . . 3.00
3 . . . . 2.50
4 . . . . 2.50
5 JG 2.50
6 BBI,Blasphemers,pt.1 . . . . 2.50
7 JG,Blasphemers,pt.2 . . . . 2.50
8 BBI,MM,Blasphemers,pt.3. . . . . 2.50
9 BBI,Blasphemers,pt.4 . . . . 2.50
10 BBI,Blasphemers,pt.5 . . . . 2.50
11 South America,pt.1. . . . . 2.25
12 South America,pt.2 . . . . 2.25
13 Emissaries o/Algernon Kinder . . 2.25
14 Rawhead Rex Story. 2.25
15 Rawhead Rex 2.25
16 Rawhead Rex 2.25
17 KN(i),V:Werewolves. 2.25
18 V:Werewolves 2.25
19 V:Werewolves 2.25
20 Trapped in the Forest. 2.25
21 V:Ozymandias 2.50
22 V:Ozymandias 2.50
23 F:Peloquin 2.50
24 Search for New Midian 2.50
25 Search for New Midian 2.50
Nightbreed:Genesis, Rep.#1-#4 . . . 9.95

NIGHTCAT
1 DCw,I&O:Night Cat. 4.50

NIGHTCRAWLER
Nov., 1985
1 DC,A;Bamfs 4.00
2 DC 3.50
3 DC,A:Other Dimensional X-Men . 3.50
4 DC,A:Lockheed,V:Dark Bamf
　　Feb., 1986 . . . . 3.50

NIGHTCRAWLER
Nov., 2001
1 (of 4) Passion Play 2.50
2 . . . . 2.50
3 . . . . 2.50
4 finale 2.50

NIGHTHAWK
July, 1998
1 (of 3) RCa,BWi,Nighthawk shake
　　off coma. 3.00
2 (of 3) RCa,BWi,V:Mephisto 3.00
3 RCa,BWi,conclusion 3.00

All comics prices listed are for Near Mint condition.

Nightmare–Not Brand   MARVEL   Comics Values Annual

NIGHTMARE
1994
1 ANo	2.25
2 ANo	2.25
3 ANo	2.25

NIGHTMARE CIRCUS
1 video-game tie-in	2.50
2 video-game tie-in	2.50

NIGHTMARE ON ELM STREET
Oct., 1989
1 RB/TD/AA.,Movie adapt	3.00
2 AA,Movie adapt,Dec., 1989.	2.25

NIGHTMASK
Nov., 1986
1 O:Night Mask	2.50
2 V:Gnome	2.50
3 V:Mistress Twilight	2.50
4 EC,D:Mistress Twilight	2.50
5 EC,Nightmare	2.50
6 EC	2.50
7 EC	2.50
8 EC	2.50
9	2.50
10 Lucian	2.50
11	2.50
12 Oct., 1987	2.50

NIGHT NURSE
Nov., 1972
1 The Making of a Nurse	150.00
2 Moment of Truth	100.00
3	100.00
4 Final Issue,May, 1973	100.00

NIGHT RIDER
Oct., 1974–Aug., 1975
1 Reprint Ghost Rider #1	20.00
2 Reprint Ghost Rider #2	12.00
3 Reprint Ghost Rider #3	12.00
4 Reprint Ghost Rider #4	12.00
5 Reprint Ghost Rider #5	12.00
6 Reprint Ghost Rider #6	12.00

NIGHTSIDE
Oct., 2001
1 (of 4) TDr,The OThers	3.00
2 TDr,The Others	3.00
3 TDr,Sydney Taine	3.00
4 TDr,Black Dragons	3.00

NIGHTSTALKERS
1992–94
1 TP(i),Rise o/t Midnight Sons#5 A:GR,J.Blaze,I:Meatmarket, polybagged w/poster	3.00
2 TP(i),V:Hydra	2.50
3 TP(i),V:Dead on Arrival	2.50
4 TP(i),V:Hydra	2.50
5 TP(i),A:Punisher	2.50
6 TP(i),A:Punisher	2.50
7 TP(i),A:Ghost Rider	2.50
8 Hannibal King vs Morbius	2.50
9 MPa,A:Morbius	2.50
10 Midnight Massacre#1,D:Johnny Blaze, Hannibal King	2.50
11 O:Blade	2.50
12 V:Vampires	2.50
13 V:Vampires	2.50
14 Wld,Siege of Darkness#1	2.50
15 Wld,Siege of Darkness#9	2.50

Nightstalkers #3
© Marvel Entertainment Group

16 V:Dreadnought	2.50
17 F:Blade	2.50
18 D:Hannibal King,Frank Drake, last issue	2.50

NIGHT THRASHER
[Limited Series] 1992–93
1 B:FaN(s),DHv,N:Night Thrasher, V:Bengal	2.50
2 DHv,I:Tantrium	2.25
3 DHv,V:Gideon	2.25
4 E:FaN(s),DHv,A:Silhoutte	2.25

[Regular Series] 1993–95
1 B:FaN(s),MBa,JS,V:Poison Memories	3.50
2 JS,V:Concrete Dragons	2.25
3 JS(c),I:Aardwolf,A:Folding Circle	2.25
4 JS(c),V:Aardwolf,I:Air Force	2.25
5 JS,V:Air Force	2.25
6 Face Value,A:Rage	2.25
7 DdB,V:Bandit	2.25
8 DdB,V:Bandit	2.25
9 DdB,A:Tantrum	2.25
10 DdB,A:Iron Man,w/card	2.25
11 DdB,Time & Time Again,pt.2	2.25
12 DdB,Time & Time Again,pt.5	2.25
13 Lost in the Shadows,pt.1	2.25
14 Lost in the Shadows,pt.2	2.25
15 Money Don't Buy,pt.1	2.25
16 A:Prowler	2.25
17	2.25
18	2.25
19 V:Tantrum	2.25
20	2.25
21 Rage vs. Grind	2.25

NIGHTWATCH
1994–95
1 RLm,I:Salvo,Warforce Holo(c)	3.00
1a Newsstand ed.	2.25
2 RLm,AM,I:Flashpoint	2.25
3 RLm,AM,V:Flashpoint	2.25
4 RLm,A:Warrent,V:Gauntlet	2.25
5 I:Sunstreak,A:Venom	2.25
6 V:Venom	2.25
7 I:Cardiaxe	2.25
8 V:Cardiaxe	2.25
9 origins	2.25
10	2.25
11	2.25
12	2.25

NOCTURNE
1995
1 DAn, in London	2.25
2 DAn,O:Nocturne	2.25
3 Interview with Amy	2.25
4 V:Dragon	2.25

NO ESCAPE
1994
1 & 2 Movie adaptation	@2.25

NOMAD
[Limited Series] Nov., 1990
1 B:FaN(s),A:Capt.America	3.00
2 A:Capt.America	2.50
3 A:Capt.America	2.50
4 A:Capt.America, final issue, Feb., 1989	2.50

[Regular Series] 1992–94
1 B:FaN(s),R:Nomad,[Gatetfold(c), map]	3.00
2 V:Road Kill Club	2.50
3 V:U.S.Agent	2.25
4 DeadMan's Hand#2,V:Deadpool	2.25
5 DeadMan's Hand#4,V:Punisher	2.25
6 DeadMan's Hand#8,A:Punisher, Daredevil	2.25
7 Infinity War,V:Gambit, Doppleganger	2.25
8 L.A.Riots	2.25
9 I:Ebbtide	2.25
10 A:Red Wolf	2.25
11 in Albuquerque	2.25
12 In Texas	2.25
13 AIDS issue	2.25
14 Hidden in View	2.25
15 Hidden in View	2.25
16 A:Gambit	2.25
17 Bucky Kidnapped	2.25
18 A:Captain America,Slug	2.25
19 FaN(s),Faustus Affair	2.25
20 A:Six Pack	2.25
21 A:Man-Thing	2.25
22 American Dreamers#1,V:Zaran	2.25
23 American Dreamers#2	2.25
24 American Dreamers#3	2.25
25 American Dreamers#4, finale	2.25

NORTHSTAR
1994
1 SFr,DoC,V:Weapon:P.R.I.M.E.	2.25
2 SFr,DoC,V:Arcade	2.25
3 SFr,DoC,V:Arcade	2.25
4 SFr,DoC,final issue	2.25
N Presents James O'Barr	2.50

NOT BRAND ECHH
Aug., 1967
1 JK(c),BEv,Forbush Man(c)	75.00
2 MSe,FrG,Spidey-Man,Gnat-Man & Rotten	40.00
3 MSe(C),TS,JK,FrG,O:Charlie America	40.00
4 GC,JTg,TS,Scaredevil, ECHHs-Men	40.00
5 JK,TS,GC,I&O:Forbush Man	40.00
6 MSe(c),GC,TS,W:Human Torch	40.00
7 MSe(c),JK,GC,TS,O:Fantastical Four,Stupor Man	40.00
8 MSe(c),GC,TS,C:Beatles	45.00
9 MSe,GC,TS,Bulk V:Sunk-Mariner	50.00
10 JK,TS,MSe,The Worst of...	50.00
11 King Konk	50.00
12 MSe,Frankenstein,A:Revengers	50.00
13 GC,MSe,Stamp Out Trading Cards(c)	50.00

CVA Page 288 All comics prices listed are for *Near Mint* condition.

NOTHING CAN STOP THE JUGGERNAUT
1989
1 JR2,rep.SpM#229&#230 . . . . 4.00

Nova #1
© Marvel Entertainment Group

NOVA
[1st Regular Series] Sept., 1976
1 B:MWn(s),JB,JSt,I&O:Nova . . . 20.00
2 JB,JSt,I:Condor,Powerhouse . . . 8.00
3 JB,JSt,I:Diamondhead 8.00
4 SB,TP,A:Thor,I:Corruptor 8.00
5 SB,V:Earthshaker 7.00
6 SB,V:Condor,Powerhouse,
  Diamondhead,I:Sphinx 7.00
7 SB,War in Space,O:Sphinx 7.00
8 V:Megaman 7.00
9 V:Megaman 7.00
10 V:Condor,Powerhouse,
   Diamond-head Sphinx 7.00
11 V:Sphinx 8.00
12 A:Spider-Man 6.00
13 I:Crimebuster,A:Sandman 6.00
14 A:Sandman 6.00
15 CI,C:Spider-Man, Hulk 6.00
16 CI,A:Yellow Claw 6.00
17 A:Yellow Claw 6.00
18 A:Yellow Claw, Nick Fury 6.00
19 CI,TP,I:Blackout 6.00
20 What is Project X? 6.00
21 JB,BMc,JRu 6.00
22 CI,I:Comet 6.00
23 CI,V:Dr.Sun 6.00
24 CI,I:New Champions,V:Sphinx . . 6.00
25 E:MWn(s),CI,A:Champions,
   V:Sphinx 6.00
[2nd Regular Series] 1994–95
1 B:FaN(s),ChM,V:Gladiator,Foil
  Embossed(c) 3.50
2 ChM,V:Tail Hook Rape 2.25
3 ChM,A:Spider-Man,Corruptor . . . 2.25
4 ChM,I:NovaO:O 2.25
5 ChM,R:Condor,w/card 2.25
6 ChM,Time & Time Again,pt.3 . . . 2.25
7 ChM,Time & Time Again,pt.6 . . . 2.25
8 ChM,I:Shatterforce 2.25
9 ChM,V:Shatterforce 2.25
10 ChM,V:Diamondhead 2.25
11 ChM,V:Diamondhead 2.25
12 ChM,A:Inhumans 2.25
13 ChM,A:Inhumans 2.25
14 A:Condor 2.25
15 V:Brethren of Zorr 2.25

16 Countdown Conclusion 2.25
17 Nova Loses Powers 2.25
18 Nova Omega,pt.1 . . . . 2.25

NOVA
March, 1999
1 EL,JoB,F:Rich Rider,48-page . . . 3.00
2 EL,JoB,A:Capt.America 2.25
2a variant JoB cover 2.25
3 EL,JoB,A:Capt.America & Hulk . . 2.25
4 EL,JoB,A:Mr.Fantastic 2.25
5 EL,JoB,A:Spider-Man 2.25
6 EL,JoB,V:Sphinx 2.25
7 EL,JoB, final issue 2.25

Nth MAN
Aug., 1989
1 . . . . 2.25
2 thru 7 . . . . @2.25
8 DK 2.25
9 thru 16, finale, Sept., 1990 . . . @2.25

'NUFF SAID
Aug., 2002
TPB 240-pg., silent stories 22.00

NYX
Marvel Oct. 2003
1 JQ,gutterpunks 3.00
2 . . . . 3.00

OBNOXIO THE CLOWN
April, 1983
1 X-Men 3.50

OFFCASTES
Epic *Heavy Hitters,* 1993
1 MV,I:Offcastes 2.50
2 MV,V:Kaoro 2.25
3 MV,Last Issue 2.25

OFFICIAL MARVEL INDEX:
1985–88
TO THE AMAZING SPIDER-MAN
Index 1 . . . . 3.00
Index 2 thru 9 . . . . @2.50
TO THE AVENGERS
Index 1 thru 7 . . . . @2.50
TO THE FANTASTIC FOUR
Index 1 thru 12 . . . . @2.25
TO MARVEL TEAM-UP
Index 1 thru 6 . . . . @2.25
TO THE X-MEN
Index 1 thru 7 . . . . @2.95
[Vol. 2] 1994
Index 1 thru 5 . . . . @2.25

OFFICIAL MARVEL TIMELINE
1-shot, 48-pg. 5.95

OFFICIAL TRUE CRIME CASES
Fall, 1947
24 (1)SSh(c),The Grinning Killer . 250.00
25 (2)She Made Me a Killer,HK . . 200.00
Becomes:

ALL-TRUE CRIME
26 SSh(c),The True Story of Wilbur
   Underhill 350.00
27 Electric Chair(c),Robert Mais . 275.00
28 Cops V:Gangsters(c) 125.00
29 Cops V:Gangsters(c) 125.00
30 He Picked a Murderous Mind 125.00
31 Hitchiking Thugs(c) 125.00
32 Jewel Thieves(c) 125.00
33 The True Story of Dinton
   Phillips 125.00
34 Case of the Killers Revenge . . 125.00
35 Ph(c),Date with Danger 125.00
36 Ph(c) 125.00
37 Ph(c),Story of Robert Marone . 125.00
38 Murder Weapon,Nick Maxim . 125.00
39 Story of Vince Vanderee 125.00
40 . . . . 125.00
41 Lou 'Lucky' Raven 125.00
42 BK,Baby Face Nelson 150.00
43 Doc Channing Paulson 100.00
44 Murder in the Big House 100.00
45 While the City Sleeps 100.00
46 . . . . 100.00
47 Gangster Terry Craig 100.00
48 GT,They Vanish By Night 100.00
49 BK,Squeeze Play 125.00
50 Shoot to Kill 100.00
51 Panic in the Big House 100.00
52 Prison Break, Sept., 1952 . . . 100.00

OLYMPIANS
Epic, July, 1991
1 Spoof Series 3.95
2 Conclusion 3.95

OMEGA THE UNKNOWN
March, 1976
1 JM,I:Omega 12.00
2 JM,A:Hulk 7.00
3 JM,A:Electro 7.00
4 JM,V:Yellow Claw 6.00
5 JM,V:The Wrench 6.00
6 JM,V:Blockbuster 6.00
7 JM,V:Blockbuster 6.00
8 JM,C:New Foolkiller,V:Nitro 7.00
9 JM,A:New Foolkiller,
  D:Blockbuster 10.00
10 JM,D:Omega the Unknown 5.00

Omega the Unknown #8
© Marvel Entertainment Group

ONE, THE
Epic, July, 1985
1 thru 5 .... @2.50
6 Feb., 1986 .... 2.50

100 GREATEST MARVELS
Sept., 2001
1 (of 5) weekly, 112-pages 8.00
2 thru 5 112-pages .... @8.00
5 Top 5 #5, 32-pages 4.00
4 Top 5 #4, 32-pages 4.00
3 Top 5 #3, 48-pages 4.00
2 Top 5 #2, 48-pages 4.00
1 Top 5 #1, 48-pages 4.00

101 WAYS TO END THE CLONE SAGA
1-shot (1997) 2.50

ONSLAUGHT
1996–97
Marvel Universe: AKu,SLo,MWd,
   Marvel Heroes vs. Onslaught .. 7.00
Marvel Universe: Gold edition 15.00
X-Men: AKu,SLo,MWd (1996) 6.00
X-Men: Gold editon 15.00
Onslaught: Epilogue (1997) 3.00
TPB Book 1, rep. X-Men #53 & #54,
   Uncanny X-Men 322 & 334
   and Onslaught X-Men 12.95
TPB Book 2, rep. X-Man #18 & #19
   and X-Force #57 & 58 .... 9.95
TPB Book 3, rep. Uncanny X-Men
   #335, Avengers #401, FF #315,
   X-Men #55 .... 9.95
TPB Book 4, rep. Inc.Hulk #444
   & #445, Cable #34 & #35 .... 9.95
TPB Book 5, rep. X-Factor #125,
   Punisher #11, Green Goblin #12,
   Amaz. Sp.-M. #415, Sp.-M. #72 9.95
TPB Book 6, rep. Uncanny X-Men
   #336, X-Men #56, Avengers #402,
   FF #416 & Onslaught: Marvel
   Universe 12.95

ONYX OVERLORD
Epic, 1992–93
1 JBi,Sequel to Airtight Garage 3.00
2 JBi,The Joule 3.00
3 JBi,V:Overlord 3.00
4 V:Starbilliard 3.00

OPEN SPACE
Dec., 1989–Aug., 1990
1 .... 6.00
2 thru 4 .... @5.25

ORDER, THE
Feb., 2002
1 (of 6) KBk,JDy,MHy,F:Hulk, Namor,
   Dr. Strange, & Silver Surfer ... 2.25
2 KBk,JDy,MHy,A:Avengers 2.25
3 KBk,JDy,MHy,DPs,V:Avengers .. 2.25
4 KBk,JDy,DPs,Hulk,Nighthawk .. 2.25
5 KBk,JDy,DPs,F:Nighthawk 2.25
6 KBk,JDy,DPs,V:everybody 2.25

ORIGIN
Aug., 2001
1 (of 6) PJe,NKu,F:Wolverine 3.50
2 PJe,NKu,JQ(c) 3.50
3 PJe,NKu,JQ(c) 3.50
4 PJe,NKu,JQ(c) 3.50
5 PJe,NKu,JQ(c) 3.50

6 PJe,NKu,final part 3.50
TPB JQ(c) 15.00

ORIGINAL GHOST RIDER
1992–94
1 MT(c),rep 2.25
2 thru 23 rep .... @2.25

ORIGINAL GHOST RIDER RIDES AGAIN
July, 1991
1 rep.GR#68+#69(O:JohnnyBlaze) 3.00
2 thru 7 rep.G.R. .... @2.25

ORIGINS OF MARVEL COMICS
TPB StL,JK,SD reprinting, 260-pg. 25.00

OSBORN JOURNALS, THE
1997
1-shot KHt,F:Norman Osborn 3.00

OUR LOVE
Sept., 1949
1 Ph(c),Guilt of Nancy Crane .. 150.00
2 Ph(c),My Kisses Were Cheap 100.00
Becomes:

TRUE SECRETS
3 Love Stories,continued 125.00
4 .... 75.00
5 .... 75.00
6 BEv 100.00
7 .... 75.00
8 .... 75.00
9 .... 75.00
10 .... 75.00
11 thru 21 .... @65.00
22 BEv 75.00
23 thru 39 .... @50.00
40 Sept., 1956 .... 50.00

OUR LOVE STORY
Oct., 1969
1 JB 75.00
2 JB 35.00
3 JB 35.00
4 .... 35.00
5 JSo,JB 125.00
6 thru 13 .... @45.00
14 Gary Friedman &Tarpe Mills .. 50.00
15 thru 37 .... @25.00
38 Feb., 1976 .... 25.00

OUTLAW FIGHTERS
Atlas, Aug., 1954
1 GT,Western Tales 150.00
2 GT ,JMn(c) 100.00
3 .... 100.00
4 A;Patch Hawk 100.00
5 RH, Final Issue,April, 1955 .. 100.00

OUTLAW KID
Atlas, Sept., 1954
1 SSh,DW,JMn(c),B&O:Outlaw Kid,
   A;Black Rider 300.00
2 DW,JMn(c),A:Black Rider ... 175.00
3 DW,AW,GWb,JMN(c) 175.00
4 DW(c),Death Rattle 150.00
5 JMn 150.00
6 JMn 150.00
7 JMn 150.00
8 AW,DW,JMn 150.00
9 .... 125.00

Outlaw Kid #2
© Marvel Entertainment Group

10 JSe 125.00
11 thru 17 .... @100.00
18 AW,JMn 100.00
19 JSe,Sept., 1957 .... 100.00

[2nd series] Aug., 1970
1 JSe(c),DW,Jo,Showdown,rep .. 40.00
2 DW,One Kid Too Many 25.00
3 HT(c),DW,Six Gun Double
   Cross 25.00
4 DW 20.00
5 DW 20.00
6 DW 20.00
7 HT(c),DW,Treachery on
   the Trail 20.00
8 HT(c),DW,RC,Six Gun Pay Off . 30.00
9 JSe(c),DW,GWb,The Kids
   Last Stand 20.00
10 GK(c),DAy,NewO:Outlaw Kid .. 40.00
11 GK(c),Thunder Along the
   Big Iron 20.00
12 The Man Called Bounty Hawk . 20.00
13 The Last Rebel 20.00
14 The Kid Gunslingers of
   Calibre City 20.00
15 GK(c),V:Madman of Monster
   Mountain 20.00
16 The End of the Trail 20.00
17 thru 29 .... @20.00
30 Oct., 1975 .... 20.00

OVER THE EDGE AND UNDER A BUCK
1995–96
1 F:Daredevil vs. Mr. Fear 2.25
2 F:Doctor Strange 2.25
3 F:Hulk 2.25
4 in Cypress Hills 2.25
5 .... 2.25
6 F:Daredevil 2.25
7 Doc & Nightmare 2.25

PARADISE X: THE HERALDS
Oct., 2001
1 (of 3) AxR, Earth X trilogy 3.50
2 AxR, ... 3.50
3 AxR,StP,concl. 3.50

PARADISE X
Feb., 2002
1 (of 13) AxR,Earth X trilogy 3.50
2 AxR,DBw,F:Captain Mar-Vell. ... 3.50
3 AxR,DBw,King Britain,Medusa .. 3.00
4 AxR,DBw,nature of new Paradise 3.00
5 AxR,DBw 3.00
6 AxR,DBw,the new Death 3.00
7 AxR,DBw 3.00
8 AxR,DBw 3.00
9 AxR,DBw,O:Ghost Rider 3.00
10 AxR,DBw,F:Matt Murcock 3.00
11 AxR,DBw,F:Harry Pym 3.00
12 AxR,DBw,concl. 3.00
Spec.#0, AxR, prologue to series .. 3.50
Special A DBw 3.00
Special 1-shot, Earth X 3.00
GN Paradise X:Xen, 56-pg 4.50
GN Devils AxR, 48-pg. 4.50

PARADISE X/RAGNAROK
Marvel Jan. 2003
1 (of 2) AxR 3.00
2 AxR 3.00

PARAGON
1 I:Paragon,Nightfire 5.00

PATSY & HEDY
Atlas, Feb., 1952
1 AJ(c),B:Patsy Walker &
 Hedy Wolfe 225.00
2 Skating(c) 125.00
3 Boyfriend Trouble 100.00
4 Swimsuit(c) 100.00
5 Patsy's Date(c) 100.00
6 Swimsuit/Picnic(c) 100.00
7 Double-Date(c) 100.00
8 AJ(c),The Dance 100.00
9 .... 100.00
10 .... 100.00
11 thru 25 .... @75.00
26 thru 50 .... @50.00
51 thru 60 .... @40.00
61 thru 109 .... @35.00
110 Feb., 1967 .... 35.00

PATSY & HER PALS
May, 1953
1 MWs(c),F:Patsy Walker 200.00
2 MWs(c),Swimsuit(c) 125.00
3 MWs(c),Classroom(c) 90.00
4 MWs(c),Golfcourse(c) 90.00
5 MWs(c).Patsy/Buzz(c) 90.00
6 thru 10 .... @90.00
11 thru 28 .... @60.00
29 Aug., 1957 .... 60.00

PATSY WALKER
1945–Dec., 1965
1 F:Patsy Walker Adventures .. 600.00
2 Patsy/Car(c) 275.00
3 Skating(c) 200.00
4 Perfume(c) 200.00
5 Archery Lesson, Eye Injury(c) 200.00
6 Bus(c) 200.00
7 Charity Drive(c) 200.00
8 Organ Driver Monkey(c) 200.00
9 Date(c) 200.00
10 Skating(c),Wedding Bells,
 A:Millie 200.00
11 Date with a Dream,A:Mitzi ... 135.00
12 Love in Bloom,Artist(c),
 A:Rusty 135.00
13 Swimsuit(c),There Goes My
 Heart;HK,Hey Look 135.00

14 An Affair of the Heart,
 HK,Hey Look 135.00
15 Dance(c) 125.00
16 Skating(c) 125.00
17 Patsy's Diary(c),HK,Hey Look 135.00
18 Autograph(c) 125.00
19 HK,Hey Look 135.00
20 HK,Hey Look 135.00
21 HK,Hey Look 135.00
22 HK,Hey Look 135.00
23 .... 100.00
24 .... 100.00
25 HK,Rusty 150.00
26 .... 100.00
27 .... 100.00
28 .... 100.00
29 .... 100.00
30 HK,Egghead Double 100.00
31 .... 75.00
32 thru 56 .... @65.00
57 thru 58 AJ(c) .... @75.00
59 thru 99 .... @45.00
100 .... 40.00
101 thru 124 .... @35.00
Fashion Parade #1 .... 125.00

Peter Parker #20
© Marvel Entertainment Group

PETER PARKER, THE SPECTACULAR SPIDER-MAN
Dec., 1976
1 SB,V:Tarantula 60.00
2 SB,V:Kraven, Tarantula 20.00
3 SB,I:Lightmaster 15.00
4 SB,V:Vulture,Hitman 15.00
5 SB,V:Hitman,Vulture 15.00
6 SB,V:Morbius,rep.M.T.U.#3 .... 16.00
7 SB,V:Morbius,A:Human Torch .. 18.00
8 SB,V:Morbius 16.00
9 SB,I:White Tiger 15.00
10 SB,A:White Tiger 12.00
11 JM,V:Medusa 10.00
12 SB,V:Brother Power. 10.00
13 SB,V:Brother Power. 10.00
14 SB,V:Brother Power. 10.00
15 SB,V:Brother Power. 10.00
16 SB,V:The Beetle 10.00
17 SB,A:Angel & Iceman
 Champions disbanded 10.00
18 SB,A:Angel & Iceman 10.00
19 SB,V:The Enforcers 9.00
20 SB,V:Lightmaster 9.00
21 JM,V:Scorpion 9.00
22 MZ,A:Moon Knight,V:Cyclone .. 9.00

23 A:Moon Knight,V:Cyclone. 9.00
24 FS,A:Hypno-Hustler 8.00
25 JM,FS,I:Carrion 9.00
26 JM,A:Daredevil,V:Carrion 8.00
27 DC,FM,I:Miller Daredevil,
 V:Carrion 25.00
28 FM,A:Daredevil,V:Carrion ... 20.00
29 JM,FS,V:Carrion 7.00
30 JM,FS,V:Carrion 7.00
31 JM,FS,D:Carrion 7.00
32 BL,JM,FS,V:Iguana 7.00
33 JM,FS,O:Iguana 7.00
34 JM,FS,V:Iguana,Lizard. 7.00
35 V:Mutant Mindworm 7.00
36 JM,V:Swarm 7.00
37 DC,MN,V:Swarm 7.00
38 SB,V:Morbius. 7.00
39 JM,JR2,V:Schizoid Man 8.00
40 FS,V:Schizoid Man 7.00
41 JM,V:Meteor Man,A:GiantMan . 7.00
42 JM,A:Fant.Four,V:Frightful 4. ... 7.00
43 JBy(c),MZ,V:The Ringer,
 V:Belladonna 7.00
44 JM,V:The Vulture 7.00
45 MSe,V:The Vulture. 7.00
46 FM(c),MZ,V:Cobra 7.00
47 MSe,A:Prowler II 7.00
48 MSe,A:Prowler II 7.00
49 MSe,I:Smuggler 7.00
50 JR2,JM,V:Mysterio. 7.00
51 MSe&FM(c),V:Mysterio 7.00
52 FM(c),D:White Tiger. 7.00
53 JM,FS,V:Terrible Tinkerer. 7.00
54 FM,WS,MSe,V:Silver Samurai .. 7.00
55 LMc,JM,V:Nitro 7.00
56 FM,JM,V:Jack-o-lantern 12.00
57 JM,V:Will-o-the Wisp 6.00
58 JBy,V:Ringer,A:Beetle 7.00
59 JM,V:Beetle 6.00
60 JM&FM(c),O:Spider-Man,
 V:Beetle 7.00
61 JM,V:Moonstone 5.00
62 JM,V:Goldbug 5.00
63 JM,V:Molten Man 5.00
64 JM,I:Cloak & Dagger 12.00
65 BH,JM,V:Kraven,Calypso. 5.00
66 JM,V:Electro 5.00
67 AMb,V:Boomerang. 5.00
68 LMc,JM,V:Robot of Mendell
 Stromm 5.00
69 AM,A:Cloak & Dagger 6.00
70 A:Cloak & Dagger 6.00
71 JM,Gun Control issue 5.00
72 AM,V:Dr.Octopus 5.00
73 AM,JM,V:Dr.Octopus,A:Owl ... 5.00
74 AM,JM,V:Dr.Octopus,R:Bl.Cat . 5.00
75 AM,JM,V:Owl,Dr.Octopus 6.00
76 AM,Black Cat on deathbed. ... 5.00
77 AM,V:Gladiator,Dr.Octopus. ... 5.00
78 AM,V:Dr.Octopus,C:Punisher ... 5.00
79 AM,V:Dr.Octopus,A:Punisher ... 5.00
80 AM,F:J.Jonah Jameson 5.00
81 A:Punisher. 6.00
82 A:Punisher. 6.00
83 A:Punisher. 8.00
84 AM,F:Black Cat 4.00
85 AM,O:Hobgoblin powers
 (Ned Leeds) 10.00
86 FH,V:Fly 4.00
87 AM,Reveals I.D.to Black Cat ... 4.00
88 AM,V:Cobra,Mr.Hyde 4.00
89 AM,Secret Wars,A:Kingpin..... 5.00
90 AM,Secret Wars. 6.00
91 AM,V:Blob 4.00
92 AM,I:Answer 4.00
93 AM,V:Answer. 4.00
94 AM,A:Cloak & Dagger,V:
 Silver Mane 4.00
95 AM,A:Cloak & Dagger,V:
 Silvermane. 4.00
96 AM,A:Cloak & Dagger,V:

Peter Parker–Pint-Sized   MARVEL   Comics Values Annual

Peter Parker King Size Ann. #3
© *Marvel Entertainment Group*

Silvermane	4.00
97 HT,JM,A:Black Cat	4.00
98 HT,JM,I:Spot	4.00
99 HT,JM,V:Spot	4.00
100 AM,V:Kingpin,C:Bl.Costume	6.00
101 JBy(c),AM,V:Killer Shrike	3.00
102 JBy(c),AM,V:Backlash	3.00
103 AM,V:Blaze;Not John Blaze	3.00
104 JBy(c),AM,V:Rocket Racer	3.00
105 AM,A:Wasp	3.00
106 AM,A:Wasp	3.00
107 RB,D:Jean DeWolf,I:SinEater	4.00
108 RB,A:Daredevil,V:Sin-Eater	3.00
109 RB,A:Daredevil,V:Sin-Eater	3.00
110 RB,A:Daredevil,V:Sin-Eater	3.00
111 RB,Secret Wars II	3.00
112 RB,A:Santa Claus,Black Cat	3.00
113 RB,Burglars,A:Black Cat	3.00
114 BMc,V:Lock Picker	3.00
115 BMc,A:Black Cat,Dr.Strange, I:Foreigner	4.00
116 A:Dr.Strange, Foreigner, Black Cat, Sabretooth	5.00
117 DT,C:Sabretooth,A:Foreigner, Black Cat,Dr.Strange	4.00
118 MZ,D:Alexander,V:SHIELD	3.00
119 RB,BMc,V:Sabretooth, A:Foreigner,Black Cat	5.00
120 KG	3.00
121 RB,BMc,V:Mauler	3.00
122 V:Mauler	3.00
123 V:Foreigner,Black Cat	3.00
124 V:Dr.Octopus	3.00
125 V:Wr.Crew,A:Spiderwoman	3.00
126 JM,A:Sp.woman,V:Wrecker	3.00
127 AM,V:Lizard	3.00
128 C:DDevil,A:Bl.Cat,Foreigner	3.50
129 A:Black Cat,V:Foreigner	3.00
130 A:Hobgoblin	6.00
131 MZ,BMc,V:Kraven	7.00
132 MZ,BMc,V:Kraven	7.00
133 BSz(c),Mad Dog,pt.3	5.00
Ann.#1 RB,JM,V:Dr.Octopus	10.00
Ann.#2 JM,I&O:Rapier	7.00
Ann.#3 JM,V:Manwolf	5.00
Ann.#4 AM,O:Aunt May,A:Bl.Cat	5.00
Ann.#5 I:Ace,Joy Mercado	5.00
Ann.#6 V:Ace	4.50
Ann.#7 Honeymoon iss,A:Puma	4.50

Becomes:

SPECTACULAR SPIDER-MAN

PETER PARKER: SPIDER-MAN
Nov., 1998

1 JR2,HMe,SHa,A:new Spider-Man, V:Ranger,48-page	3.00
1a signed	15.00
2 JR2,HMe,SHa,A:Thor	2.25
2a variant cover	2.00
3 HMe,JR2,SHa,A:Iceman,V:Shadrac	2.25
4 HMe,JR2,SHa,V:Marrow	2.25
5 HMe,SHa,BS,JBy(c),F:Spider-Woman,Aunt May,Black Cat	2.25
6 HMe,SHa,RJ2,JBy(c),V:Kingpin	2.25
7 JR2,HMe,SHa,Reality Bent	2.25
8 JR2,HMe,SHa,V:Bullseye	2.25
9 JR2,HMe,SHa,R:Venom	2.25
10 JR2,HMe,SHa,R:Carnage	2.25
11 JR2,HMe,SHa,Eighth Day,pt.3 x-over	2.25
12 JR2,HMe,SHa, 48-pg.	3.50
13 JR2,HMe	2.25
14 JR2,HMe,A:Hulk	2.25
15 JR2,HMe,x-over	2.25
16 JR2,HMe,V:Sinister Six	2.25
17 JR2,HMe,SHa,V:Kraven	2.25
18 HMe,JR2,SHa,V:Green Goblin	2.50
19 HMe,JR2,SHa,Mary Jane dies	2.50
20 PJe,MBu,DGr,Mary Jane dead	2.50
21 PJe,MBu,DGr,HumanTorch	2.50
22 PJe,MBu,DGr,FlintMarko	2.50
23 PJe,MBu,DGr,Type Face	2.50
24 PJe,MBu,DGr,Max.Security	2.50
25 PJe,MBu,DGr,V:Green Goblin	3.50
26 PJe,JoB,DGr,F:NYPD	2.50
27 PJe,MBu,DGr,F:NYPD	2.50
28 PJe,MBu,DGr,	2.50
29 PJe,CAd,DGr,x-over	2.50
30 PJe,MBu,HuR(c),I:Terminal	2.50
31 PJe,MBu,HuR(c),I:Fusion	2.50
32 PJe,MBu,HuR(c),V:Fusion	2.50
33 PJe,MBu,HuR(c),ballpark	2.50
34 PJe,MBu,cleanse the city	2.50
35 PJe,MBu,Jamal	2.50
36 PJe,MBu,private-eye	2.50
37 PJe,slice-of-life	2.50
38 PJe,MBu,V:Mimes,'Nuff Said	2.50
39 PJe,MBu,return of Dr. Octopus	2.50
40 PJe,MBu,Doc Octopus,pt.2	2.50
41 PJe,MBu,Doc Octopus,pt.3	2.50
42 Spring Break,pt.1	2.50
43 Spring Break,pt.2	2.50
44 PJe,HuR,R:Green Goblin	2.50
45 PJe,HuR,R:Green Goblin,pt.2	2.50
46 PJe,HuR,R:Green Goblin,pt.3	2.50
47 PJe,HuR,R:Green Goblin,pt.4	2.50
48 PJe,MBu	2.50
49 PJe,MBu	2.50
50 PJe,MBu	2.50
51 pt.1	2.50
52 pt.2	2.50
53 pt.1	2.50
54 pt.2	2.50
55 pt.3	2.50
56 SK,Reborn,pt.1,F:Sandman	2.50
57 SK,Reborn,pt.2,F:Sandman	2.50
Ann.1999,CCs, 48-pg.	4.00
Ann.2000 CCl,JoB,80-pg.	4.00
Ann.2001 South America, 28-pg.	3.50
Spec. Peter Parker, Spider-Man 2000	4.00
TPB Peter Parker:Spider-Man.	14.95
TPB One Small Break, 160-pg.	16.95
TPB Return of the Goblin	9.00
TPB Trials & Tribulations	12.00
TPB Vol. 5: Senseless Violence	15.00

PETER PORKER
Star, May, 1985

1 Parody	4.50
2	3.00
3	3.00
4	3.00
5 V:Senior Simians	3.00
6 A Blitz in Time	3.00
7	3.00
8 Kimono My House	3.00
9 Uncouth my Tooth	3.00
10 Lost Temple of the Golden Retriever	3.00
11 Dog Dame Afternoon	3.00
12 The Gouda,Bad & Ugly	3.00
13 Halloween issue	3.00
14 Heavy Metal Issue	3.00
15	3.00
16 Porker Fried Rice,Final Issue	3.00
17 Sept., 1987	3.00

PETER, THE LITTLE PEST
Nov., 1969–May, 1970

1 F:Peter	75.00
2 Rep,Dexter & Melvin	50.00
3 Rep,Dexter & Melvin	50.00
4 Rep,Dexter & Melvin	50.00

PHANTOM

1 Lee Falk's Phantom	4.00
2 V:General Babalar	4.00
3 final issue	4.00

PHANTOM 2040

1 Based on cartoon	2.50
2 V:Alloy	2.50
3 MPa,V:Crime Syndicate	2.50
4 Vision Quest	2.50

PHOENIX (UNTOLD STORY)
April, 1984

1 JBy,O:Phoenix (R.Summers)	12.00

PILGRIM'S PROGRESS

1 adapts John Bunyans novel	10.00

PINHEAD
1993–94

1 Red Foil(c),from Hellraiser	3.00
2 DGC(s),V:Cenobites	2.50
3 DGC(s),V:Cenobites	2.50
4 DGC(s),V:Cenobites	2.50
5 DGC(s),Devil in Disguise	2.50
6 DGC(s)	2.50

PINHEAD VS. MARSHALL LAW
1993

1 KON,In Hell	3.00
2 KON	3.00

PINOCCHIO & THE EMPEROR OF THE NIGHT
March, 1988

1 Movie adapt	3.00

PINT-SIZED X-BABIES: MURDERAMA
June, 1998

1-shot, Mojo, Arcade, 48-pg.	3.00

CVA Page 292   All comics prices listed are for *Near Mint* condition.

PIRATES OF DARK WATERS
Nov., 1991
1 based on T.V. series 2.00
2 Search for 13 Treasures 2.00
3 V:Albino Warriors,Konk 2.00
4 A:Monkey Birds 2.00
5 Tula Steals 1st Treasuer 2.00
6 thru 9 .... @2.00

PITT, THE
March, 1988
1 SB,SDr,A:Spitfire 4.00

PLANET OF THE APES
Aug., 1974–Feb., 1977
(black & white magazine)
1 MP 45.00
2 MP 25.00
3 .... 20.00
4 .... 20.00
5 .... 20.00
6 thru 10 .... @20.00
11 thru 20 .... @25.00
21 thru 29 .... @55.00

Planet Terry #12
Man #12 © Marvel Ent.Group

PLANET TERRY
Star, April, 1985
1 thru 11 .... @3.00
12 March, 1986 .... 3.00

PLASMER
Marvel UK, 1993–94
1 A:Captain America 3.50
2 A:Captain Britain,Black Knight. . . 2.25
3 A:Captain Britain............ 2.25
4 A:Captain Britain............ 2.25
5 thru 7 .... @2.00

PLASTIC FORKS
Epic, 1990
1 .... 6.00
2 thru 5 .... @5.50

POLICE ACADEMY
Nov., 1989
1 Based on TV Cartoon 2.25
2 thru 5 .... @2.25
6 Feb., 1990 .... 2.25

POLICE ACTION
Jan., 1954
1 JF,GC,JMn(c),Riot Squad ... 225.00
2 JF,Over the Wall 150.00
3 JMn 125.00
4 DAy 125.00
5 DAy,JMn 125.00
6 .... 125.00
7 BPNov., 1954 .... 125.00

POLICE BADGE
See: SPY THRILLERS

POPPLES
Star, Dec., 1986
1 Based on Toys 3.00
2 .... 3.00
3 .... 3.00
4 .... 3.00
5 Aug., 1987 .... 3.00

POWDERED TOAST-MAN
Spec. F:Powder Toast-Man 3.25

POWERHOUSE PEPPER COMICS
1943—Nov., 1948
1 BW,Movie Auditions(c) 2,200.00
2 BW,Dinner(c) 1,100.00
3 BW,Boxing Ring(c) 1,000.00
4 BW,Subway(c) 1,000.00
5 BW,Bankrobbers(c) 1,200.00

POWER LINE
Epic, May, 1988
1 BMc(i) 2.25
2 Aw(i) 2.25
3 A:Dr Zero 2.25
4 .... 2.25
5 thru 7 GM .... @2.25
8 GM Sept., 1989 .... 2.25

POWER MAN
Prev: Hero for Hire
Feb., 1974
17 GT,A:Iron Man 15.00
18 GT,V:Steeplejack 10.00
19 GT,V:Cottonmouth 10.00
20 GT,Heroin Story............ 10.00
21 V:Original Power Man 8.00
22 V:Stiletto & Discus......... 8.00
23 V:Security City............. 8.00
24 GT,I:BlackGoliath(BillFoster) ... 8.00
25 A:Circus of Crime........... 8.00
26 GT,V:Night Shocker 8.00
27 GP,AMc,V:Man Called X 8.00
28 V:Cockroach 8.00
29 V:Mr.Fish................. 8.00
30 RB,KJ,KP,I:Piranha 8.00
31 SB,NA(i),V:Piranha 8.00
32 JSt,FR,A:Wildfire 7.00
33 FR,A:Spear 7.00
34 FR,A:Spear,Mangler 7.00
35 DA,A:Spear,Mangler 7.00
36 V:Chemistro............... 7.00
37 V:Chemistro............... 7.00
38 V:Chemistro............... 7.00
39 KJ,V:Chemistro,Baron 7.00

Powerman & Iron Fist #50-
© Marvel Ent.Group

40 V:Baron 7.00
41 TP,V:Thunderbolt,Goldbug 7.00
42 V:Thunderbolt,Goldbug 7.00
43 AN,V:Mace 7.00
44 TP,A:Mace 7.00
45 JSn,A:Mace................ 7.00
46 GT,I:Zzzax(recreated) 7.00
47 BS,A:Zzzax 9.00
48 JBy,A:Iron Fist 12.00
49 JBy,A:Iron Fist 12.00
Becomes:

POWER MAN & IRON FIST
1978
50 JBy,I:Team-up with Iron Fist ... 11.00
51 MZ,Night on the Town 4.00
52 MZ,V:Death Machines 4.00
53 SB,O:Nightshade............. 4.00
54 TR,O:Iron Fist 4.00
55 Chaos at the Coliseum 4.00
56 Mayhem in the Museum........ 4.00
57 X-Men,V:Living Monolith 25.00
58 1st El Aguila(Drug)........... 4.00
59 BL(c),TVE,V:Big Apple
   Bomber................... 4.00
60 BL(c),V:Terrorists............ 4.00
61 BL(c),V:The Maggia.......... 4.00
62 BL(c),KGa,V:Man Mountain
   D:Thunerbolt.............. 4.00
63 BL(c),Cage Fights Fire........ 4.00
64 DGr&BL(c),V:Suetre,Muertre ... 4.00
65 BL(c),A:El Aguila,........... 4.00
66 FM(c),Sabretooth(2nd App.)... 35.00
67 V:Bushmaster 4.00
68 FM(c),V:Athur Nagan 4.00
69 V:Soldier 4.00
70 FM(c)V:El Supremo 4.00
71 FM(c),I:Montenegro 4.00
72 FM(c),V:Chako 4.00
73 FM(c),V:Rom 4.00
74 FM(c),V:Ninja 4.00
75 KGa,O:IronFist.............. 4.00
76 KGa,V:Warhawk 4.00
77 KGa,A:Daredevil 4.00
78 KGa,A:El Aguila,Sabretooth
   (Slasher)(3rd App.)......... 20.00
79 V:Dredlox 3.00
80 KJ(c),V:Montenegro 3.00
81 V:Black Tiger............... 3.00
82 V:Black Tiger............... 3.00
83 V:Warhawk 3.00
84 V:Constrictor,A:Sabertooth
   (4th App.)................ 20.00
85 KP,V:Mole Man 3.00

Power–Psi Force / MARVEL / Comics Values Annual

86 A:Moon Knight 3.00
87 A:Moon Knight 3.00
88 V:Scimtar 3.00
89 V:Terrorists 3.00
90 V:Unus BS(c) 3.00
91 `Paths and Angles'. 3.00
92 V:Hammeread,I:New Eel 3.00
93 A:Chemistro 3.00
94 V:Chemistro 3.00
95 Danny Rand 3.00
96 V,Chemistro 3.00
97 K'unlun,A:Fera 3.00
98 V:Shades & Commanche 3.00
99 R:Daught.of Dragon 3.00
100 O:K'unlun,DoubleSize 3.00
101 A:Karnak 3.00
102 V:Doombringer 3.00
103 O:Doombringer 3.00
104 V:Dr.Octopus,Lizard 3.00
105 F:Crime Buster 3.00
106 Luke Gets Shot 3.00
107 JBy(c),Terror issue 3.00
108 V:Inhuman Monster 3.00
109 V:The Reaper 3.00
110 V:Nightshade,Eel 3.00
111 I:Captain Hero 3.00
112 JBy(c),V:Control7 . . . . 3.00
113 JBy(c),A:Capt.Hero 3.00
114 JBy(c),V:Control7 . . . . 3.00
115 JBy(c),V:Stanley 3.00
116 JBy(c),V:Stanley 3.00
117 R:K'unlun 3.00
118 A:Colleen Wing 3.00
119 A:Daught.of Dragon 3.00
120 V:Chiantang 3.00
121 Secret Wars II 3.00
122 V:Dragonkin 3.00
123 V:Race Killer 3.00
124 V:Yellowclaw 3.00
125 MBr,LastIssue;D:Iron Fist. 3.00
G-Size#1 reprints 4.00
Ann.#1 Earth Shock 5.00

POWER PACHYDERMS
Sept., 1989
1 Elephant Superheroes 2.50

POWER PACK
Aug., 1984
1 JBr,BWi,I&O:Power Pack,
  I:Snarks 2.50
2 JBr,BWi,V:Snarks 2.25
3 JBr,BWi,V:Snarks 2.25
4 JBr,BWi,V:Snarks 2.25
5 JBr,BWi,V:Bogeyman 2.25
6 JBr,BWi,A:Spider-Man 2.25
7 JBr,BWi,A:Cloak & Dagger 2.25
8 JBr,BWi,A:Cloak & Dagger 2.25
9 BA,BWi,A:Marrina 2.25
10 BA,BWi,A:Marrina 2.25
11 JBr,BWi,V:Morlocks 2.25
12 JBr,BWi,A:X-Men,V:Morlocks . . 3.00
13 BA,BWi,Baseball issue 2.25
14 JBr,BWi,V:Bogeyman 2.25
15 JBr,BWi,A:Beta Ray Bill 2.25
16 JBr,BWi,I&O:Kofi,J:Tattletale
  (Franklin Richards) 2.25
17 JBr,BWi,V:Snarks 2.25
18 BA,SW,Secret Wars II,
  V:Kurse 2.25
19 BA,SW,Doub.size,Wolverine . . . 4.00
20 BMc,A:NewMutants 2.25
21 BA,TA,C:Spider-Man 2.25
22 JBg,BWi,V:Snarks 2.25
23 JBg,BWi,V:Snarks,C:FF 2.25
24 JBg,BWi,V:Snarks,C:Cloak 2.25
25 JBg,BWi,A:FF,V:Snarks 2.25
26 JBg,BWi,A:Cloak & Dagger 2.25
27 JBg,AG,A:Wolverine,X-Factor,

Power Pack #15
© Marvel Entertainment Group

  V:Sabretooth 5.00
28 A:Fantastic Four,Hercules 2.25
29 JBg,DGr,A:SpM,V:Hobgoblin . . . 2.50
30 VM,Crack 2.25
31 JBg,I:Trash 2.25
32 JBg,V:Trash 2.25
33 JBg,A:Sunspot,Warlock,
  C:Spider-Man 2.25
34 TD,V:Madcap 2.25
35 JBg,A:X-Factor,D:Plague 2.25
36 JBg,V:Master Mold 2.25
37 SDr(i),I:Light-Tracker 2.25
38 SDr(i),V:Molecula 2.25
39 V:Bogeyman 2.25
40 A:New Mutants,V:Bogeyman . . . 2.25
41 SDr(i),V:The Gunrunners 2.25
42 JBg,SDr,Inferno,V:Bogeyman . . . 2.25
43 JBg,SDr,AW,Inferno,
  V:Bogeyman 2.25
44 JBr,Inferno,A:New Mutants 2.25
45 JBr,End battle w/Bogeyman 2.25
46 WPo,A:Punisher,Dakota North . . 2.50
47 JBg,I:Bossko 2.25
48 JBg,Toxic Waste #1 . . . . 2.25
49 JBg,JSh,Toxic Waste #2 . . . . . . 2.25
50 AW(i),V:Snarks 2.25
51 GM,I:Numinus 2.25
52 AW(i),V:Snarks,A:Numinus 2.25
53 EC,A of V,A:Typhoid Mary 2.25
54 JBg,V:Mad Thinker 2.25
55 DSp,V:Mysterio 2.25
56 TMo,A:Fant.Four,Nova 2.25
57 TMo,A:Nova,V:Star Stalker 2.25
58 TMo,A:Galactus,Mr.Fantastic . . . 2.25
59 TMo,V:Ringmaster 2.25
60 TMo,V:Puppetmaster 2.25
61 TMo,V:Red Ghost & Apes 2.25
62 V:Red Ghost & Apes
  (last issue) 2.25
Holiday Spec.JBr,Small Changes . . 2.25

POWER PACK: PEER PRESSURE
June, 2000
1 (of 4) TA,CDo 3.00
2 TA,CDo,V:Snarks 3.00
3 TA,CDo, ... 3.00
4 Ta,CDo,concl 3.00

PRINCE NAMOR, THE SUB-MARINER
Sept., 1984
1 I:Dragonrider, Dara 3.00
2 I:Proteus 2.50
3 . . . . 2.50
4 Dec., 1984 . . . . 2.50

PRINCE VALIANT
1994–95
1 JRy,CV,Thule, Camelot
  and the Misty Isles 4.00
2 JRy,CV 4.00
3 JRy,CV 4.00
4 JRy,CV, final issue 4.00

PRIVATE EYE
Atlas, Jan., 1951
1 . . . . 225.00
2 . . . . 150.00
3 GT 150.00
4 . . . . 100.00
5 . . . . 100.00
6 JSt 100.00
7 . . . . 100.00
8 March, 1952 . . . . 100.00

PROFESSOR XAVIER AND THE X-MEN
1995
1 1st Year Together 3.00
2 V:The Vanisher 2.50
3 FaN,F:The Blob 2.50
4 V:Magneto & Brotherhood 2.50
5 . . . . 2.50
6 . . . . 2.50
7 FdS,Sub-Mariner 2.50
8 thru 12 . . . . @2.50
13 AHo,F:Juggernaut 2.50
14 JGz,V:Juggernaut, ... 2.50
15 JGz,F:Quicksilver & Scarlet
  Witch 2.50
16 . . . . 2.50
17 JGz,V:Sentinels,F:Beast 2.50
18 JGz,X-Men vs. Sentinels,
  final issue 2.50

PROWLER, THE
1994
1 Creatures of the Night, pt.1 . . . . . 2.25
2 V:Nightcreeper, Creatures, pt.2 . . 2.25
3 Creatures of the Night, pt.3 . . . . . 2.25
4 V:Vulture, Creatures, pt.4 . . . . . . 2.25

PSI FORCE
Nov., 1986–June, 1989
1 MT,O:PSI Force 2.50
2 MT 2.50
3 MT,CIA 2.50
4 MT,J:Network 2.50
5 MT 2.50
6 MT(c) 2.50
7 MT(c) 2.50
8 MT 2.50
9 MT(c) 2.50
10 PSI Hawk 2.50
11 . . . . 2.50
12 MT(c) 2.50
13 . . . . 2.50
14 AW 2.50
15 . . . . 2.50
16 RLm 2.50
17 RLm 2.50
18 RLm 2.50
19 RLm 2.50

Comics Values Annual — MARVEL — Psi Force–Punisher

Psi Force #9
© Marvel Entertainment Group

20 RLm,V:Medusa Web;Rodstvow . 2.50
21 RLm 2.50
22 RLm,A:Nightmask 2.50
23 A:D.P.7 . . . . 2.50
24 thru 32 . . . . @2.50
Ann.#1 . . . . 2.50

PSYCHONAUTS
Epic, 1993–94
1 thru 4 War in the Future . . . . . @5.50

PSYLOCKE & ANGEL: CRIMSON DAWN
1997
1 SvL,ATi,V:Obsideon 3.00
2 SvL,ATi, ... 3.00
3 BRa,SvL,ATi 3.00
4 (of 4) BRa,SvL,ATi 3.00

PUNISHER
[Limited Series] Jan., 1986
1 MZ,Circle of Blood,double size . 20.00
2 MZ,Back to the War 10.00
3 MZ,V:The Right 10.00
4 MZ,V:The Right 10.00
5 V:Jigsaw,end Mini-Series 10.00

[Regular Series] 1987–95
1 KJ,V:Wilfred Sobel,Drugs 10.00
2 KJ,V:General Trahn,Bolivia 6.00
3 KJ,V:Colonel Fryer 5.00
4 KJ,I:The Rev,Microchip Jr. 5.00
5 KJ,V:The Rev. 5.00
6 DR,KN,V:The Rosettis 5.00
7 DR,V:Ahmad,D:Rose 5.00
8 WPo,SW(1st Punisher),
    V:Sigo & Roky 4.00
9 WPo,SW,D:MicrochipJr,V:Sigo . . 4.00
10 WPo,SW,A:Daredevil (x-over
    w/Daredevil #257) 7.00
11 WPo,SW,O:Punisher 5.00
12 WPo,SW,V:Gary Saunders 2.50
13 WPo,SW,V:Lydia Spoto 2.50
14 WPo,SW,I:McDowell,Brooks . . . 2.50
15 WPo,SW,V:Kingpin 2.50
16 WPo,SW,V:Kingpin 2.50
17 WPo,SW,V:Kingpin 2.50
18 WPo,SW,V:Kingpin,C:X-Men . . 2.50
19 LSn,In Australia 2.50
20 WPo(c),In Las Vegas 2.50
21 EL,SW,Boxing Issue 2.50
22 EL,SW,I:Saracen 2.50
23 EL,SW,V:Scully 2.50
24 EL,SW,A:Shadowmasters 2.50
25 EL,AW,A:Shadowmasters 2.50
26 RH,Oper.Whistle Blower#1 . . . . 2.50
27 RH,Oper.Whistle Blower#2 . . . . 2.50
28 BR,A:Dr.Doom,A of Veng. 2.50
29 BR,A:Dr.Doom,A of Veng. 2.50
30 BR,V:Geltrate 2.50
31 BR,V:Bikers #1 . . . . 2.50
32 BR,V:Bikers #2 . . . . 2.50
33 BR,V:The Reavers 2.50
34 BR,V:The Reavers 2.50
35 BR,MF,Jigsaw Puzzle #1 . . . . . . 2.50
36 MT,MF,Jigsaw Puzzle #2 . . . . . . 2.50
37 MT,Jigsaw Puzzle #3 . . . . 2.50
38 BR,MF,Jigsaw Puzzle #4 . . . . . . 2.50
39 JSh,Jigsaw Puzzle #5 . . . . 2.50
40 BR,JSh,Jigsaw Puzzle #6 . . . . . 2.50
41 BR,TD,V:Terrorists 2.50
42 MT,V:Corrupt Mili. School 2.50
43 BR,Border Run 2.50
44 Flag Burner 2.50
45 One Way Fare 2.50
46 HH,Cold Cache 2.50
47 HH,Middle East #1 . . . . 2.50
48 HH,Mid.East #2,V:Saracen 2.50
49 HH,Punisher Hunted 2.50
50 HH,MGo(c),I:Yo Yo Ng 2.50
51 Chinese Mafia 2.50
52 Baby Snatchers 2.50
53 HH,in Prison 2.50
54 HH,in Prison 2.50
55 HH,in Prison 2.50
56 HH,in Prison 2.50
57 HH,in Prison 2.50
58 V:Kingpin's Gang,A:Micro 2.50
59 MT(c),V:Kingpin 2.50
60 VM,AW,Black Punisher,
    A:Luke Cage 2.50
61 VM,A:Luke Cage 2.50
62 VM,AW,A:Luke Cage 2.50
63 MT(c),VM,V:Thieves 2.50
64 Eurohit #1 . . . . 2.50
65 thru 70 Eurohit . . . . @2.50
71 AW(i) 2.50
72 AW(i) 2.50
73 AW(i),Police Action #1 . . . . 2.50
74 AW(i),Police Action #2 . . . . 2.50
75 AW(i),Police Action #3,foil(c),
    double size 3.00
76 LSn,in Hawaii 2.50
77 VM,Survive#1 . . . . 2.50
78 VM,Survive#2 . . . . 2.50
79 VM,Survive#3 . . . . 2.50
80 Goes to Church 2.50
81 V:Crooked Cops 2.50
82 B:Firefight 2.50
83 Firefight#2 . . . . 2.50
84 E:Firefight 2.50
85 Suicide Run 2.25
86 Suicide Run#3,Foil(c), ... 2.25
87 Suicide Run#6 . . . . 2.25
88 LSh(c),Suicide Run #9 . . . . 2.25
89 . . . . 2.25
90 Hammered 2.25
91 Silk Noose 2.25
92 Razor's Edge 2.25
93 Killing Streets 2.25
94 B:No Rules 2.25
95 No Rules 2.25
96 . . . . 2.25
97 CDi 2.25
98 . . . . 2.25
99 . . . . 2.25
100 New Punisher 4.00
100a Enhanced ed. 5.00
101 CC,Raid's Franks Tomb 2.25
102 A:Bullseye 2.25
103 Countdown 4 . . . . 2.25
104 CDi,Countdown 1, V:Kingpin,

Punisher #99
© Marvel Entertainment Group

    final issue 2.25
Ann.#1 MT,A:Eliminators,
    Evolutionary War. 4.00
Ann.#2 JLe,Atlantis Attacks #5,
    A:Moon Knight 3.50
Ann.#3 LS,MT,Lifeform #1 . . . . . . 3.50
Ann.#4 Baron Strucker,pt.2
    (see D.D.Annual #7) 3.50
Ann.#5 System Bytes #1 . . . . 3.50
Ann.#6 I:Eradikator,w/card 3.50
GNv 5.00
Summer Spec.#1 VM,MT 3.50
Summer Spec.#2 SBs(c) 2.50
Summer Spec.#3 V:Carjackers . . . 2.50
Summer Spec.#4 . . . . 3.25
Spec. Punisher/Batman,CDi,JR2,
    48-pg. (1994) 5.00
Spec.#1 Punisher/Daredevil, rep.
    Daredevil 6.00
Punisher:No Escape A:USAgent,
    Paladin (1990) 5.50
Punisher Movie Spec.BA (1989) . . 5.95
GNv Punisher: The Prize (1990) . . 5.50
Punisher:Bloodlines DC 6.25
Punisher:Blood on the Moors . . . 16.95
Punisher:G-Force 5.25
Punisher:Origin of Mirco Chip #1,
    O:Mirco Chip 2.50
Punisher:Origin of Mirco Chip #2
    V:The Professor 2.50
Classic Punisher rep early
    B&W magazines. 7.00
Punisher:Back To School Spec.
    #1 JRy,short stories 3.25
    #2 BSz 2.95
Punisher:Die Hard in the Big
    Easy Mardi Gras 5.25
Holiday Spec.#1 V:Young
    Mob Capo 3.25
Holiday Spec #2 . . . . 2.95
Punisher:Ghosts of the Innocent#1
    TGr, V:Kingpin's Dead Men . . 5.95
Punisher:Ghosts of the Innocent#2
    TGr, V:Kingpin,Snake 5.95
TPB Punisher: Eye For An Eye . . . 9.95

[2nd Regular Series] 1995
1 JOs,TL,Clv,Punisher sent to
    the Electric Chair, foil(c) 3.00
2 JOs,TL,Clv,Crime family boss . . . 2.50
3 JOs,TL,Clv,V:Hatchetman 2.50
4 JOs,TL,Clv,A:Daredevil, Jigsaw . . 2.50
5 . . . . 2.50
6 . . . . 2.50

All comics prices listed are for *Near Mint* condition.

CVA Page 295

Punisher–Punisher

7 JOs,TL,Clv,V:Son of Nick Fury . . 2.50
8 . . . . 2.50
9 . . . . 2.50
10 . . . . 2.50
11 Onslaught saga 2.50
12 A:X-Cutioner 3.00
13 JOs,TL, Working for S.H.I.E.L.D.?,
   A:X-Cutioner 2.50
14 . . . . 2.50
15 JOs,TL, X-Cutioner 2.50
16 JOS,TL, concl.? 2.50
17 JOS,TL,A:Daredevil,Doc Samson,
   Spider-Man 2.50
18 JOS,TL,Frank Castle amnesia? . 2.50
19 JOS,TL,V:Taskmaster 2.50
20 JOS,TL, fugitive Punisher 2.50

PUNISHER
Sept., 1998
1 (of 4) BWr,JP,TSg,F:Frank
   Castle 3.00
2 BWr,JJu,JP,A:Hellstrom 3.00
3 BWr,JJu,TSg,JP,A:Gadriel 3.00
4 BWr,JJu,TSg,JP,Hell on Earth . . . 3.00

PUNISHER
Jan., 2000
1 (of 12) JP,GEn,SDi,R:Punisher . . 3.00
2A JP,GEn,SDi,V:Ma Gnucci 3.00
2B variant SDi(c) 3.00
3 GEn,JP,SDi,polybaged 7.00
4 GEn,JP,SDi,Gnuccis 3.00
5 GEn,JP,SDi,Mr.Payback 3.00
6 GEn,JP,SDi,Elite 3.00
7 GEn,JP,SDi,Mr.Payback 3.00
8 GEn,JP,SDi,Gnuccis 3.00
9 GEn,JP,SDi,Russian 3.00
10 GEn,JP,SDi,Russian 3.00
11 GEn,JP,SDi,Russian 3.00
12 GEn,JP,SDi,concl. 3.00
Spec. Punisher/Painkiller Jane 3.50
GN Punisher Kills the Marvel
   Universe, 48-pg. GEn,DBw . . . 5.95
TPB Welcome Back, Frank 24.95
TPB Circle of Blood 12.95

PUNISHER
June, 2001
1 GEn,JP,SDi,pt.1 . . . . 4.00
2A GEn,JP,SDi,pt.2 . . . . 3.00
2B variant SDi(c) 3.00
3 GEn,JP,SDi,Grand Nixon Island . 3.00
4 GEn,JP,SDi,Survivor 3.00
5 GEn,JP,SDi,V:Kriegkopf 3.00
6 GEn,JP,Viet Nam 3.00
7 SDi,JP,'Nuff Said 3.00
8 TPe,Taxi Wars 3.00
9 TPe,Taxi Wars 3.00
10 TPe,Taxi Wars 3.00
11 TPe,Taxi Wars, Medallion. 3.00
12 TPE,Taxi Wars, concl. 3.00
13 GeN,SDi, to South America 3.00
14 GeN,SDi, in Columbia 3.00
15 GeN,SDi,F:Wolverine 3.00
16 GeN,SDi,F:Wolverine 3.00
17 GeN,DaR,F:Wolverine 3.00
18 GeN,SDi,Northern Ireland 3.00
19 GeN,SDi, ... 3.00
20 GeN,SDi,Brotherhood,pt.1 . . . . . 3.00
21 GeN,SDi,Brotherhood,pt.2 . . . . . 3.00
22 GEn,SDi 3.00
23 GEn,SDi,Giant Squid 3.00
24 GEn,TMd,Hidden,pt.1 . . . . 3.00
25 GEn,TMd,Hidden,pt.2 . . . . 3.00
26 GEn,TMd,Hidden,pt.3 . . . . 3.00
27 GEn,SDi,F:Elektra 3.00
28 GEn,CK,Streets of Loredo,pt.1. . 3.00
29 GEn,CK,Streets of Loredo,pt.2. . 3.00

30 GEn,CK,Streets of Loredo,pt.3. . 3.00
31 GEn,CK,Streets of Loredo,pt.4. . 3.00
32 GEn,CK,Streets of Loredo,pt.5. . 3.00
33 GEn,JMC,Dunces,pt.1 . . . . 3.00
34 GEn,JMC,Dunces,pt.2 . . . . 3.00
35 GEn,JMC,Dunces,pt.3 . . . . 3.00
36 GEn,JMC,Dunces,pt.4 . . . . 3.00
TPB Army of One, rep. 144-pg. . . . 15.95
TPB Vol. 3: Business as Usual . . . 15.00
TPB Vol. 4: Full Auto 18.00
TPB Streets of Laredo, Vol.5 . . . . . 18.00

PUNISHER ARMORY
July, 1990
1 JLe(c) 3.00
2 JLe(c) 2.50
3 . . . . 2.50
4 thru 6 . . . . @2.50
7 thru 10 . . . . @2.50

PUNISHER/CAPTAIN AMERICA: BLOOD AND GLORY
1 thru 3 KJ,V:Drug Dealers . . . . . @6.25

CLASSIC PUNISHER
1 TDz 4.95

PUNISHER KILLS THE MARVEL UNIVERSE
1995
1-shot Alterniverse 5.95

PUNISHER MAGAZINE
Oct., 1989
1 MZ,rep.,Punisher #1 . . . . 3.00
2 MZ,rep 2.50
3 thru 13 KJ,rep . . . . @2.50
14 rep. PWJ #1&#2 . . . . 2.50
15 rep. PWJ 2.50
16 rep.,1990 . . . . 2.50

PUNISHER MEETS ARCHIE
1994
1 JB 4.25
1a newsstand ed. 3.25

PUNISHER MOVIE COMIC
Nov., 1989
1 Movie adapt. 2.25
2 Movie adapt.. . . . . 2.25
3 Movie adapt,Dec., 1989 . . . . . . 2.25

PUNISHER P.O.V.
July, 1991
1 BWr,Punisher/Nick Fury 5.50
2 BWr,A:Nick Fury,Kingpin 5.50
3 BWr,V:Mutant Monster,
   A:Vampire Slayer 5.50
4 BWr,A:Nick Fury 5.25

PUNISHER 2099
1993–95
1 TMo,Jake Gallows family
   Killed, foil(c) 2.50
2 TMo,I:Fearmaster,Kron,Multi
   Factor 2.25
3 TMo,V:Frightening Cult 2.25
4 TMo,V:Cyber Nostra 2.25
5 TMo,V:Cyber Nostra,Fearmaster. 2.25
6 TMo,V:Multi-Factor 2.25

7 TMo,Love and Bullets#1 . . . . . . 2.25
8 TMo,Love and Bullets#2 . . . . . . 2.25
9 TMo,Love and Bullets#3 . . . . . . 2.25
10 TMo,I:Jigsaw 2.25
11 TMo,V:Jigsaw 2.25
12 TMo,A:Spider-Man 2099 . . . . . . 2.25
13 TMo,Fall of the Hammer#5 . . . . 2.25
14 WSm, ... 2.25
15 TMo,V:Fearmaster,
   I:Public Enemy 2.25
16 TMo,V:Fearmaster,
   Public Enemy 2.25
17 TMo,V:Public Enemy 2.25
18 TMo,I:Goldheart 2.25
19 TMo,I:Vendetta 2.25
20 . . . . 2.25
21 . . . . 2.25
22 V:Hotwire 2.25
23 I:Synchron,V:Hotwire 2.25
24 V:Synchron 2.25
25 Enhanced cover 3.50
25a newsstand ed 2.25
26 V:Techno-Shaman 2.25
27 R:Blue Max 2.25
Becomes:

PUNISHER 2099 A.D.
28 Minister of Punishment 2.25
29 Minister of Punishment 2.25
30 One Nation Under Doom 2.25
31 . . . . 2.25
32 Out of Ammo 2.25
33 Counddown to final issue 2.25
34 final issue 2.25

PUNISHER WAR JOURNAL
Nov., 1988
1 CP,JLe,O:Punisher 5.00
2 CP,JLe,A:Daredevil 4.00
3 CP,JLe,A:Daredevil 4.00
4 CP,JLeV:The Sniper 4.00
5 CP,JLe,V:The Sniper 4.00
6 CP,JLe,A:Wolverine 4.00
7 CP,JLe,A:Wolverine 4.00
8 JLe,I:Shadowmasters 4.00
9 JLe,A:Black Widow 4.00
10 JLe,V:Sniper 4.00
11 JLe,Shock Treatment 3.00
12 JLe,AM,V:Bushwacker 3.00
13 JLe(c),V:Bushwacker 3.00
14 JLe(c),DR,RH,A:Spider-Man . . . 3.00
15 JLe(c),DR,RH,A:Spider-Man . . . 3.00

Punisher 2099 #12
© Marvel Entertainment Group

CVA Page 296 — All comics prices listed are for *Near Mint* condition.

MARVEL

Punisher–Quasar

Punisher War Journal #75
© Marvel Entertainment Group

16 MT(i),Texas Massacre 3.00
17 JLe,AM,Hawaii. 3.00
18 JLe,AM,Kahuna,Hawaii 3.00
19 JLe,AM,Traume in Paradise. . . . 3.00
20 AM 3.00
21 TSm,AM 3.00
22 TSm,AM,Ruins #1 . . . . 3.00
23 TSm,AM,Ruins #2 . . . . 3.00
24 . . . . 3.00
25 MT 3.00
26 MT,A:Saracen 3.00
27 MT,A:Saracen 3.00
28 MT 3.00
29 MT,A:Ghostrider. 3.00
30 MT,A:Ghostrider. 3.00
31 NKu,Kamchatkan
  Konspiracy#1 . . . . 3.00
32 Kamchatkan Konspiracy #2 . . . . 3.00
33 Kamchatkan Konspiracy #3 . . . . 3.00
34 V:Psycho 3.00
35 Movie Stuntman. 3.00
36 Radio Talk Show #1 . . . . 3.00
37 Radio Talk Show #2 . . . . 3.00
38 . . . . 3.00
39 DGr,V:Serial Killer 3.00
40 MWg 3.00
41 Armageddon Express. 3.00
42 Mob run-out. 3.00
43 JR2(c). 3.00
44 Organ Donor Crimes 3.00
45 Dead Man's Hand #3,V:Viper . . . 3.00
46 Dead Man's Hand #6,V:Chainsaw
  and the Praetorians 3.00
47 Dead Man's Hand #7,A:Nomad,
  D.D,V:Hydra,Secret Empire . . . 3.00
48 B:Payback 3.00
49 JR2(c),V:Corrupt Cop 3.00
50 MT,V:Highjackers,I:Punisher
  2099 . . . . 3.00
51 E:Payback. 3.00
52 A:Ice(from The'Nam) 3.00
53 A:Ice(from the Nam). 3.00
54 Hyper#1 . . . . 3.00
55 Hyper#2 . . . . 3.00
56 Hyper#3 . . . . 3.00
57 A:Ghost Rider,Daredevil. 3.00
58 A:Ghost Rider,Daredevil. 3.00
59 F:Max the Dog. 3.00
60 CDi(s),F:Max the Dog 3.00
61 CDi(s),Suicide Run#1,Foil(c) . . . 3.00
62 CDi(s),Suicide Run#2 . . . . 2.50
63 CDi(s),Suicide Run#7 . . . . 2.50
64 CDi(s),Suicide Run#10 . . . . 3.00

64a Newsstand Ed. 2.50
65 B:Pariah 2.50
66 A:Captain America 2.50
67 Pariah#3 . . . . 2.50
68 A:Spider-Man. 2.50
69 E:Pariah 2.50
70 . . . . 2.50
71 . . . . 2.50
72 V:Fake Punisher 2.50
73 E:Frank Castle. 2.50
74 . . . . 2.50
75 MT(c) 3.00
76 First Entry 2.50
77 R:Stone COld 2.50
78 V:Payback,Heathen 2.50
79 Countdown 3. . . . . 2.50
80 Countdown 0, A:Nick Fury,
  V:Bullseye, final issue. 2.50
TPB reprints #6,7 . . . . 4.95

PUNISHER WAR ZONE
1992

1 JR2,KJ,Punisher As Johnny Tower
  Die-Cut Bullet Hole(c). 3.00
2 JR2,KJ,Mafia Career 2.25
3 JR2,KJ,Punisher/Mafia,contd . . 2.25
4 JR2,KJ,Cover gets Blown 2.25
5 JR2,KJ,A:Shotgun 2.25
6 JR2,KJ,A:Shotgun 2.25
7 JR2,V:Rapist in Central Park . . . 2.25
8 JR2,V:Rapist in Central Park . . . 2.25
9 JR2,V:Magnificent Seven 2.25
10 JR2,V:Magnificent Seven 2.25
11 JR2,MM,V:Magnificent Seven. . 2.25
12 Punisher Married 2.25
13 Self-Realization 2.25
14 Psychoville#3 . . . . 2.25
15 Psychoville#4 . . . . 2.25
16 Psychoville#5 . . . . 2.25
17 Industrial Esponiage 2.25
18 Jerico Syndrome#2 . . . . 2.25
19 Jerico Syndrome#3 . . . . 2.25
20 B:2 Mean 2 Die 2.25
21 2 Mean 2 Die#2. . . . . 2.25
22 A:Tyger Tyger 2.25
23 Suicide Run#2,Foil(c). 3.25
24 Suicide Run#5, ... 2.25
25 Suicide Run#8, ... 2.50
26 CDi(s),JB,Pirates 2.25
27 CDi(s),JB, ... 2.25
28 CDi(s),JB,Sweet Revenge 2.25
29 CDi(s),JB,The Swine 2.25
30 CDi(s),JB. 2.25
31 CDi(s),JB,River of Blood,pt.1 . . 2.25
32 CDi(s),JB,River of Blood,pt.2 . . 2.25
33 CDi(s),JB,River of Blood,pt.3 . . 2.25
34 CDi(s),JB,River of Blood,pt.4 . . 2.25
35 River of Blood,pt.5. . . . . 2.25
36 River of Blood,pt.6. . . . . 2.25
37 O:Max 2.25
38 Dark Judgment,pt.1 . . . . 2.25
39 Dark Judgment,pt.2 . . . . 2.25
40 In Court 2.25
41 CDi,Countdown 2, final issue . . 2.25
Ann.#1 Jb,MGo,(c),I:Phalanx,
  w/Trading card 3.25
Ann.#2 CDi(s),DR. 2.95
TPB CDi,JR2, rep. #1-#6 . . . . 16.00

PUNISHER: YEAR ONE
1994

1 O:Punisher 2.50
2 O:Punisher 2.50
3 O:Punisher 2.50
4 finale 2.50

PUSSYCAT
(B&W Magazine) Oct., 1968
1 BEv,BWa,WW 250.00

QUASAR
Oct., 1989

1 O:Quasar 3.00
2 V:Deathurge,A:Eon. 2.50
3 A:Human Torch,V:The Angler . . 2.50
4 Acts of Vengeance,A:Aquarian . . 2.50
5 A of Veng,V:Absorbing Man 2.50
6 V:Klaw,Living Laser,Venom,
  Red Ghost 3.00
7 MM,A:Cosmic SpM,V:Terminus. . 2.50
8 MM,A:New Mutants,BlueShield . . 2.25
9 MM,A:Modam. 2.25
10 MM,A:Dr.Minerva 2.25
11 MM,A:Excalibur,A:Modred 2.25
12 MM,A:Makhari,Blood Bros.. . . . 2.25
13 JLe(c)MM,J.into Mystery #1 . . . 2.25
14 TM(c)MM,J.into Mystery #2 . . . 2.25
15 MM,Journey into Mystery #3 . . 2.25
16 MM,Double sized. 2.25
17 MM,Race,A:Makkari,Whizzer,
  Quicksilver,Capt.Marv,Super
  Sabre,Barry Allen Spoof 2.25
18 GCa,N:Quasar. 2.25
19 GCa,B:Cosmos in Collision,
  C:Thanos. 2.25
20 GCa,A:Fantastic Four 2.25
21 GCa,V:Jack of Hearts 2.25
22 GCa,D:Quasar,A:Ghost Rider . . 2.25
23 GCa,A:Ghost Rider 2.25
24 GCa,A:Thanos,Galactus,
  D:Maelstrom. 2.25
25 GCa,A:Eternity & Infinity,N:Quasar,
  E:Cosmos Collision 2.25
26 GCa,Inf.Gauntlet,A:Thanos 2.50
27 GCa,Infinity Gauntlet,I:Epoch . . 2.25
28 GCa,A:Moondragon,Her,
  X-Men 2.25
29 GCa,A:Moondragon,Her 2.25
30 GCa,What If? tie-in 2.25
31 GCa,R:New Universe. 2.25
32 GCa,Op.GalacticStorm,pt.3 . . . 2.25
33 GCa,Op.GalacticStorm,pt.10 . . 2.25
34 GCa,Op.GalacticStorm,pt.17 . . 2.25
35 GCa,Binary V:Her 2.25
36 GCa,V:Soul Eater 2.25
37 GCa,V:Soul Eater 2.25
38 GCa,Inf.War,V:Warlock 2.25
39 SLi,Inf.War,V:Deathurge. 2.25

Quasar #41
© Marvel Entertainment Group

All comics prices listed are for *Near Mint* condition.

CVA Page 297

Quasar–Rawhide — MARVEL — Comics Values Annual

40 SLi,Inf.War,V:Deathurge 2.25
41 R:Marvel Boy 2.25
42 V:Blue Marvel 2.25
43 V:Blue Marvel 2.25
44 V:Quagmire 2.25
45 V:Quagmire,Antibody 2.25
46 Neutron,Presence 2.25
47 1st Full Thunderstrike Story 2.25
48 A:Thunderstrike 2.25
49 Kalya Vs. Kismet 2.25
50 A:Man-Thing,Prism(c) 3.50
51 V:Angler,A:S.Supreme 2.25
52 V:Geometer 2.25
53 . . . . 2.25
54 MGu(s),Starblast #2 . . . . 2.25
55 MGu(s),A:Stranger 2.25
56 MGu(s),Starblast #10 . . . . 2.25
57 MGu(s),A:Kismet 2.25
58 . . . . 2.25
59 A:Thanos,Starfox 2.25
60 final issue 2.25

QUEST
Marvel June 2003
1 (of 6) Manga,F:Katherine West . . 2.50
2 Quest & Kaori 2.50

QUESTPROBE
Aug., 1984
1 JR,A:Hulk,I:Chief Examiner 3.00
2 AM,JM,A:Spider-Man 3.00
3 JSt,A:Thing & Torch 3.00

QUICKSILVER
Sept., 1997
1 CJ,TPe, V:Exodus, cont. from
   Excalibur #113 . . . . 3.00
2 TPe,CJ,A:Knights of Wundagore. 2.25
3 TPe,CJ,V:Arkon 2.25
4 TPe, Crystal returns 2.25
5 TPe,V:Inhumans 2.25
6 TPe,Inhumands trilogy concl. . . . 2.25
7 JOs,F:The Black Knight 2.25
8 JOs,F:Pietro,V:Pyro 2.25
9 JOs,Savage Land concl.,A:High
   Evolutionary 2.25
10 JOS,Live Kree or Die, pt.3,
   x-over. 2.25
11 JOs,The Seige of Wundagore,
   pt.2 (of 5) 2.25
12 JOs,The Seige of Wundagore,
   pt.4 (of 5) 48-pg. 3.00
13 JOs,Seige of Wundagore,pt.5,
   final issue. 2.25

QUICK-TRIGGER WESTERN
See: WESTERN THRILLERS

RAIDERS OF THE LOST ARK
Sept., 1981
1 JB/KJ,movie adaption 3.00
2 JB/KJ, ... 3.00
3 JB/KJ,Nov.,1981 . . . . 3.00

RAMPAGING HULK, THE
May, 1998
1 RL,double size, savage Hulk era. 3.00
2A RL,DGr,I:Ravage 2.25
2B JQ,JP,variant cover 2.25
3 RL,DGr,V:Ravage, concl. 2.25
4 DR, Trapped by an Avalanche . . . 2.25
5 RL,F:Fantastic Four 2.25
6 RL,DGr,V:Puma 2.25

Ravage 2099 #20
© Marvel Entertainment Group

RAVAGE 2099
1992–95
1 PR,I:Ravage 3.00
2 PR,V:Deathstryk 2.25
3 PR,V:Mutroids 2.25
4 PR,V:Mutroids 2.25
5 PR,Hellrock 2.25
6 PR,N:Ravage 2.25
7 PR,New powers 2.25
8 V:Deathstyke. 2.25
9 PR,N:Ravage 2.25
10 V:Alchemax 2.25
11 A:Avatarr 2.25
12 Ravage Transforms 2.25
13 V:Fearmaster. 2.25
14 V:Punisher 2099 . . . . 2.25
15 Fall of the Hammer #2 . . . . 2.25
16 I:Throwback 2.25
17 GtM,V:Throwback,O:X-11. . . . . . 2.25
18 GtM,w/card 2.25
19 GtM, ... 2.25
20 GtM,V:Hunter. 2.25
21 Savage on the Loose. 2.25
22 Exodus 2.25
23 Blind Justice 2.25
24 Unleashed 2.25
25 Flame Bearer. 2.25
25a Deluxe ed.. . . . . 3.00
26 V:Megastruck. 2.25
27 V:Deathstryke 2.25
28 R:Hela 2.25
29 V:Deathstryke 2.25
30 King Ravage 2.25
Becomes:

RAVAGE 2099 A.D.
31 V:Doom. 2.25
32 One Nation Under Doom 2.25
33 Final issue. 2.25

RAWHIDE KID
Atlas, March, 1955—May, 1979
1 JMn,B:Rawhide Kid & Randy,
   A:Wyatt Earp 1,200.00
2 JMn,Shoot-out(c) 500.00
3 V:Hustler 350.00
4 Rh(c) 350.00
5 GC,JMn 350.00
6 JMn,Six-Gun Lesson 250.00
7 AW 250.00
8 . . . . 250.00
9 . . . . 250.00

10 thru 16 . . . . @225.00
17 JK,O:Rawhide Kid 225.00
18 thru 20 . . . . @225.00
21 . . . . 225.00
22 . . . . 225.00
23 JK,O:Rawhide Kid Retold. . . . 275.00
24 thru 30 . . . . @200.00
31 JK,DAy,No Law in Mesa. 200.00
32 JK,DAy,Beware of the
   Parker Brothers 200.00
33 JK(c),JDa,V:Jesse James . . . 200.00
34 JDa,JK,V:Mister Lightning . . . 200.00
35 JK(c),GC,JDa,I&D:The Raven 200.00
36 DAy,A Prisoner in
   Outlaw Town. 125.00
37 JK(c),DAy,GC,V:The Rattler . . 125.00
38 DAy.V:The Red Raven 125.00
39 DAy. 125.00
40 JK(c),DAy,A:Two Gun Kid . . . 125.00
41 JK(c),The Tyrant of
   Tombstone Valley 125.00
42 JK 125.00
43 JK 125.00
44 JK(c),V:The Masked Maverick 125.00
45 JK(c),O:Rawhide Kid Retold . . 150.00
46 JK(c),ATh 125.00
47 JK(c),The Riverboat Raiders . . 75.00
48 GC,V:Marko the Manhunter . . . 65.00
49 The Masquerader 65.00
50 A;Kid Colt,V:Masquerader 65.00
51 DAy,Trapped in the
   Valley of Doom 65.00
52 DAy,Revenge at
   Rustler's Roost. 65.00
53 Guns of the Wild North 55.00
54 DH,BEv,The Last Showdown . . 55.00
55 . . . . 55.00
56 DH,JTgV:The Peacemaker. . . . 55.00
57 V:The Scorpion 55.00
58 DAy. 55.00
59 V:Drako. 55.00
60 DAy,HT,Massacre at Medicine
   Bend 55.00
61 DAy,TS,A:Wild Bill Hickok 50.00
62 Gun Town,V:Drako. 50.00
63 Shootout at Mesa City 50.00
64 HT,Duel of the Desparadoes . . 50.00
65 JTg,HT,BE 50.00
66 JTg,BEv,Death of a Gunfighter. 50.00
67 Hostage of Hungry Hills 50.00
68 JB,V:The Cougar 50.00
69 JTg,The Executioner 50.00
70 JTg,The Night of the Betrayers 40.00
71 JTg,The Last Warrior 40.00
72 JTg,The Menace of Mystery
   Valley 40.00
73 JTg,The Manhunt. 40.00
74 JTg,The Apaches Attack 40.00
75 JTg,The Man Who Killed
   The Kid 40.00
76 JTg,V:The Lynx 40.00
77 JTg,The Reckoning 40.00
78 JTg 40.00
79 JTg,AW,The Legion of the Lost 40.00
80 Fall of a Hero 40.00
81 thru 85 . . . . @40.00
86 JK,O:Rawhide Kid retold 40.00
87 thru 99 . . . . @25.00
100 O:Rawhide Kid retold 30.00
101 thru 124 . . . . @25.00
125 JDa 30.00
126 thru 151 . . . . @25.00

RAWHIDE KID
Aug., 1985
1 JSe,mini-series 4.00
2 thru 4 . . . . @4.00

CVA Page 298 — All comics prices listed are for *Near Mint* condition.

RAWHIDE KID
Marvel Max Feb. 2003
1 (of 5) JSe 3.00
2 JSe 3.00
3 JSe 3.00
4 JSe 3.00
5 JSe,concl. 3.00
TPB 13.00

RAZORLINE FIRST CUT
1993
1 Intro Razorline 2.25

REAL EXPERIENCES
See: TESSIE THE TYPIST

RED RAVEN
See: HUMAN TORCH

Red Sonja #1
© *Marvel Entertainment Group*

RED SONJA
[1st Series] Jan., 1977
1 FT,O:Red Sonja,`Blood of the
   Unicorn' 15.00
2 FT,`Demon of the Maze' 8.00
3 FT,`The Games of Gita' 8.00
4 FT,`The Lake of the Unknown' . . 8.00
5 FT,`Master of the Bells' 8.00
6 FT,`The Singing Tower' 8.00
7 FT,`Throne of Blood' 8.00
8 FT,Vengeance o/t Golden Circle . 8.00
9 FT,`Chariot o/t Fire-Stallions' 8.00
10 FT,Red Lace,pt.1 . . . . 8.00
11 FT,Red Lace,pt.2 . . . . 7.00
12 JB/JRu,`Ashes & Emblems' 7.00
13 JB/AM,`Shall Skranos Fall' 7.00
14 SB/AM,`Evening on the Border' . 7.00
15 JB/TD,`Tomb of 3 Dead Kings'
   May, 1979 . . . . 7.00

[2nd Series] Feb., 1983
1 TD,GC, The Blood That Binds . . 4.00
2 GC, March,1983 . . . . 4.00

[3rd Series] Aug., 1983
1 . . . . 3.00
2 thru 13 . . . . @3.00
1 movie adaption, 1985 . . . . 2.50
2 movie adaption, 1985 . . . . 2.50

RED SONJA
1-shot Bros.Hildebrandt(c),48-pg. . . 2.95

RED WARRIOR
Atlas, Jan.–Dec., 1951
1 GT,Indian Tales 200.00
2 GT(c),The Trail of the Outcast 125.00
3 The Great Spirit Speaks 100.00
4 O:White Wing 100.00
5 . . . . 100.00
6 JMn(c) final issue 100.00

RED WOLF
May, 1972–Sept., 1973
1 SSh(c),GK,JSe,F:Red Wolf
   & Lobo 35.00
2 GK(c),SSh,Day of the Dynamite
   Doom 20.00
3 SSh,War of the Wolf Brothers . 20.00
4 SSh,V:Man-Bear 20.00
5 GK(c),SSh 20.00
6 SSh,JA,V;Devil Rider 20.00
7 SSh,JA,Echoes from a Golden
   Grave 20.00
8 SSh,Hell on Wheels 20.00
9 DAy,To Die Again,O:Lobo 20.00

REN AND STIMPY SHOW
1992–96
1 Polybagged w/Air Fowlers,
   Ren(c) 5.00
1a Stimpy(c) 4.00
1b 2nd Printing 3.00
1c 3rd Printing 2.00
2 Frankenstimpy 3.00
2a 2nd Printing 2.00
3 Christmas issue 3.00
3a 2nd Printing 2.00
4 thru 12 . . . . @3.00
13 Halloween issue 2.50
14 Mars needs Vecro 2.50
15 thru 24 . . . . @2.25
25 regular (c) 2.25
25a die-cut(c),A new addition 3.00
26 thru 42 . . . . @2.25
Spec.#1 . . . . 3.25
Spec.#2 . . . . 3.25
Spec.#3 Powder Toast Man 3.25
Spec.#4 . . . . 3.25
Spec.#5 Virtual Stupidity 3.25
Spec.#6 History of Music 3.25
Holiday Special 3.00
Spec. Radio Dazed & Confused . . 2.50
Spec. Around the World in a Daze . 3.00
TPB Running Joke,rep.#1-4,w/new
   material 13.25
TPB Pick of the Litter 13.25
TPB Tastes Like Chicken 13.25
TPB Your Pals 12.95
TPB Seech Little Monkeys 12.95

RETURN OF THE JEDI
1 AW,movie adapt 3.00
2 AW,movie adapt 3.00
3 AW,movie adapt 3.00
4 AW,movie adapt 3.00

REX HART
See: BLAZE CARSON

RICHIE RICH
1 Movie Adaptation 2.95

RINGO KID
[2nd Series] Jan., 1970
1 AW,Reprints 35.00
2 JSe,Man Trap 20.00
3 JR,Man from the Panhandle . . 20.00
4 HT(c),The Golden Spur 20.00
5 JMn,Ambush 20.00
6 Capture or Death 20.00
7 HT(c),JSe,JA,Terrible Treasure
   of Vista Del Oro 20.00
8 The End of the Trail 20.00
9 JSe,Mystery of the Black
   Sunset 20.00
10 Bad day at Black Creek 20.00
11 Bullet for a Bandit 20.00
12 A Badge to Die For 30.00
13 DW,Hostage at Fort Cheyenne. 15.00
14 Showdown in the Silver
   Cartwheel 15.00
15 Fang,Claw, and Six-Gun 15.00
16 Battle of Cattleman's Bank . . . 15.00
17 Gundown at the Hacienda . . . 15.00
18 . . . . 15.00
19 Thunder From the West 15.00
20 AW 15.00
21 thru 29 . . . . @15.00
30 Nov., 1973 . . . . 15.00

RINGO KID WESTERN
Atlas, Aug., 1954
1 JMn,JSt,O:Ringo Kid,
   B:Ringo Kid 325.00
2 JMn,I&O:Arab,A:Black Rider . 200.00
3 JMn 125.00
4 JMn 125.00
5 JMn 125.00
6 . . . . 125.00
7 . . . . 125.00
8 JSe 125.00
9 . . . . 100.00
10 JSe(c),AW 100.00
11 JSe(c) 100.00
12 JO 100.00
13 AW 100.00
14 thru 20 . . . . @100.00
21 Sept., 1957 . . . . 100.00

ROBOCOP
March, 1990
1 LS,I:Nixcops 6.00
2 LS,V:Nixcops 4.00

Robocop #1
© *Marvel Entertainment Group*

All comics prices listed are for *Near Mint* condition.

Robocop–Runaways

3 LS	3.00
4 LS	3.00
5 LS,WarzonePt1	3.00
6 LS,WarzonePt2	3.00
7 LS	2.50
8 LS,V:Gang-5.	2.50
9 LS,V:Vigilantes	2.50
10 LS	2.50
11 HT	2.50
12 LS,Robocop Army #1	2.50
13 LS,Robocop Army #2	2.50
14 LS,Robocop Army #3	2.50
15 LS,Robocop Army #4	2.50
16 TV take over	2.50
17 LS,V:The Wraith	2.50
18 LS,Mindbomb #1	2.50
19 LS,Mindbomb #2	2.50
20 In Detroit	2.50
21 LS,Beyond the Law,pt.1	2.50
22 LS,Beyond the Law,pt.2	2.50
23 LS,Beyond the Law,pt.3,final	2.50
Robocop Movie Adapt.	4.95
Robocop II Movie Adapt	4.95

ROBOCOP II
Aug., 1990

1 MBa,rep.Movie Adapt	2.50
2 and 3 MBa,rep.Movie adapt	@2.50

ROBOTIX
Feb., 1986

1 Based on toys	3.00

ROCKET RACCOON
May, 1985—Aug., 1985

1 thru 4 MM	@3.00

ROCKO'S MODERN LIFE
1994

1 and 2	@2.25
3 and 4	@2.25

ROGUE
1995

1 Enhanced cover	4.50
2 A:Gambit	4.00
3 Gamtit or Rogue?	3.00
4 final issue	3.00

ROGUE
Aug., 2001

1 (of 4) AaL,RyE,	2.50
2 AaL,RyE	2.50
3 AaL,RyE, leaves school	2.50
4 AaL,RyE,JuB(c)	2.50

ROM
Dec., 1979

1 SB,I&O:Rom	10.00
2 FM(c),SB,V:Dire Wraiths	4.00
3 FM(c),SB,I:Firefall	4.00
4 SB,A:Firefall	4.00
5 SB,A:Dr.Strange	4.00
6 SB,V:Black Nebula	4.00
7 SB,V:Dark Nebula	4.00
8 SB,V:Dire Wraiths	4.00
9 SB,V:Serpentine	4.00
10 SB,V:U.S.Air Force	4.00
11 SB,V:Dire Wraiths	4.00
12 SB,A:Jack O' Hearts	4.00
13 SB,V:Plunderer	4.00
14 SB,V:Mad Thinker	4.00
15 SB,W:Brandy and Dire Wraith	4.00
16 SB,V:Watchwraith	4.00
17 SB,A:X-Men	9.00
18 SB,A:X-Men	9.00
19 SB,JSt,C:X-Men	4.00
20 SB,JSt,A:Starshine	4.00
21 SB,JSt,A:Torpedo	4.00
22 SB,JSt,A:Torpedo	4.00
23 SB,JSt,A:Powerman,Iron Fist.	4.00
24 SB,JSt,A:Nova	6.00
25 SB,JSt,Double-Sized	6.00
26 SB,JSt,V:Galactus	6.00
27 SB,JSt,V:Galactus	6.00
28 SB,JSt,D:Starshine	3.00
29 SB,Down in the Mines	3.00
30 SB,JSt,A:Torpedo	3.00
31 SB,JSt,V:Evil Mutants,Rogue	2.50
32 SB,JSt,V:Evil Mutants	2.50
33 SB,V:Sybil	2.50
34 SB,A:Sub-Mariner	2.50
35 SB,A:Sub-Mariner	2.50
36 SB,V:Scarecrow	2.50
37 SB,A:Starshine	2.50
38 SB,A:Master of Kung Fu	2.50
39 SB,A:Master of Kung Fu	2.50
40 SB,A:Torpedo	2.50
41 SB,A:Dr.Strange	2.50
42 SB,A:Dr.Strange	2.50
43 SB,Rom Becomes Human	2.50
44 SB,A:Starshine,O:Gremlin	2.50
45 SB,V:Soviet Super Soldiers	2.50
46 SB,V:Direwraiths	2.50
47 SB,New Look for Wraiths	2.50
48 SB,V:Dire Wraiths	2.50
49 SB,V:Dire Wraiths	2.50
50 SB,D:Torpedo,V:Skrulls	4.00
51 SB,F:Starshine	2.50
52 BSz(c),SB,V:Dire Wraiths.	2.50
53 SB,BSz,V:Dire Wraiths.	2.50
54 V:Dire Wraiths	2.50
55 V:Dire Wraihs	2.50
56 A:Alpha Flight	3.00
57 A:Alpha Flight	3.00
58 JG(c),A:Antman	2.50
59 SD,BL,V:Microbe Menace	2.50
60 SD,TP,V:Dire Wraiths.	5.00
61 SD,V:Wraith-Realm	2.50
62 SD,A:Forge	2.50
63 SD,V:Dire Wraiths	2.50
64 SD,V:Dire Wraiths	2.50
65 SD,A:X-Men,Avengers	2.50
66 SD,Rom leaves Earth	2.50
67 SD,V:Scorpion	2.50
68 BSz(c)SD,Man & Machine	2.50
69 SD,V:Ego	2.50
70 SD	2.50
71 SD,V:Raak	2.50
72 SD,Secret Wars II	2.50
73 SD,JSt	2.50
74 SD,JBy,Code of Honor	2.50
75 SD,CR,Doublesize,last issue	7.00
Ann.#1 PB,A:Stardust	3.00
Ann.#2 I:Knights of Galador	3.00
Ann.#3 A:New Mutants	3.00
Ann.#4 V:Gladiator	3.00

Rom #21
© Marvel Entertainment Group

ROMANCE DIARY
Dec., 1949

1	150.00
2 March, 1950	125.00

ROMANCES OF THE WEST
Nov., 1949

1 Ph(c),Calamity Jane, Sam Bass	250.00
2 March, 1950	175.00

ROMANCE TALES
Oct., 1949
(no #1 thru 6)

7	150.00
8	100.00
9 March, 1950	100.00

ROMANTIC AFFAIRS
See: **MOLLY MANTON'S ROMANCES**

ROYAL ROY
Star, May, 1985

1 thru 5	@3.00
6 March, 1986	3.00

RUGGED ACTION
Atlas, Dec., 1954

1 AyB,Man-Eater	150.00
2 JSe,DAy,JMn(c),Manta-Ray	100.00
3 DAy,JMn(c)	100.00
4	100.00

Becomes:

STRANGE STORIES OF SUSPENSE

5 RH,JMn(c),Little Black Box	400.00
6 BEv,The Illusion	250.00
7 JSe(c),BEv,Old John's House	265.00
8 AW,BP,TYhumbs Down	265.00
9 BEv(c),Nightmare	250.00
10 RC,MME,AT	250.00
11 BEv(c)	200.00
12 AT	200.00
13 BEv,GM	200.00
14 AW	225.00
15 BK	225.00
16 MF,BP, Aug., 1957	225.00

RUINS
1995

1 Marvel's Alterverse	5.00
2 Fully painted, 32-pg.	5.00

RUNAWAYS
Marvel April 2003

1 Pride & Joy, pt.1	2.50
2 Pride & Joy, pt.2	2.50
3 Pride & Joy, pt.3	2.50
4 Pride & Joy, pt.4	2.50
5 Pride & Joy, pt.5	2.50

All comics prices listed are for *Near Mint* condition.

MARVEL

6 Pride & Joy, pt.6 . . . . 2.50
7 Teenage Wasteland,pt.1 . . . . 2.50
8 Teenage Wasteland,pt.2 . . . . 2.50
TPB Runaways: Pride & Joy 19.95
Spec Runaways/Sentinel flip book . 4.00

RUSTY COMICS
See: KID KOMICS

SABRETOOTH
[Limited Series] 1993
1 B:LHa(s),MT,A:Wolverine 5.00
2 MT,A:Mystique,C:Wolverine 4.00
3 MT,A:Mystique,Wolverine 4.00
4 E:LHa(s),MT,D:Birdy 4.00
TPB rep. #1-#4 . . . . 12.95

SABRETOOTH CLASSICS
1994–95
1 rep. Power Man/Iron Fist #66 . . . 4.00
2 rep. Power Man/Iron Fist #78 . . . 3.00
3 rep. Power Man/Iron Fist #84 . . . 3.00
4 rep. Spider-Man #116 . . . . 3.00
5 rep. Spider-Man #119 . . . . 3.00
6 reprints 3.00
7 reprints 3.00
8 reprints 3.00
9 reprints 3.00
10 Morlock Massacre 3.00
11 rep. Daredevil #238 . . . . 3.00
12 rep. V:Wolverine 3.00
13 rep 3.00
14 A:Maurauders 3.00
15 Mutant Massacre, rep.
    Uncanny X-Men #221 . . . . 3.00

SABRETOOTH
Spec.#1 FaN, cont.from X-Men#48 . 4.95

SABRETOOTH
Oct., 1997
1-shot,F:Wildchild 2.50

SABRETOOTH & MYSTIQUE
1 JGz,AOl, ... 2.50
2 thru 4 JGz,AOl . . . . @2.50

SABRETOOTH: MARY SHELLEY OVERDRIVE
June, 2002
1 (of 4) F:Creed 3.00
2 TyH 3.00
3 . . . . 3.00
4 TyH 3.00

SACHS & VIOLENS
Epic, 1993–94
1 GP,PDd(s) 3.00
2 GP,PDd(s),V:Killer 2.50
3 GP,PDd(s),V:White Slavers 2.50
4 GP,PDd(s),D:Moloch 2.50

SAGA OF CRYSTAR
May, 1983
1 O:Crystar 5.00
2 A:Ika 4.00
3 A:Dr.Strange 4.00
4 . . . . 4.00
5 . . . . 4.00
6 A:Nightcrawler 4.00
7 I:Malachon 4.00
8 . . . . 4.00

9 . . . . 4.00
10 Chaos 4.00
11 Alpha Flight,Feb., 1985 . . . . 4.00

SAGA OF ORIGINAL HUMAN TORCH
1 RB,O:Original Human Torch 3.00
2 RB,A:Toro 2.50
3 RB,V:Adolph Hitler 2.50
4 RB,Torch vs. Toro 2.50

ST. GEORGE
Epic, June, 1988
1 KJ,Shadow Line 2.25
2 KJ,I:Shrek 2.25
3 KJ 2.25
4 KJ 2.25
5 . . . . 2.25
6 . . . . 2.25
7 DSp 2.25
8 Oct., 1989 . . . . 2.25

SAINT SINNER
Razorline 1993–94
1 I:Phillip Fetter 2.75
2 F:Phillip Fetter 2.25
3 in Vertesque 2.25
4 . . . . 2.25
5 Arcadia 2.25
6 . . . . 2.25
7 The Child Stealer 2.25
8 . . . . 2.25

SAM & MAX GO TO THE MOON
1 Dirtbag Special,w/Nirvana Tape . 4.00
[Regular Series]
1 MMi,AAd,F:Skull Boy 3.25
2 AAd,MMi 3.25
3 . . . . 3.25

SAMURAI CAT
Epic, 1991
1 I:MiaowaraTomokato 2.25
2 I:Con-Ed,V:Thpaghetti-Thoth 2.25
3 EmpireStateStrikesBack 2.25

SATANA
Nov., 1997
1 JaL,WEI,AOl,V:Doctor Strange,
   non-code series 3.00
2 WEI,AOl,to the gates of Hell 3.00

SAVAGE SWORD OF CONAN
Aug., 1974
(black & white magazine)
1 BWS,JB,NA,GK,O:Blackmark,
   3rdA:Red Sonja,Boris(c) 120.00
2 NA(c),HC,GK,`Black Colossus,'
   B.U.King Kull;B.U.Blackmark . 50.00
3 JB,BWS,GK,`At The Mountain
   of the Moon God';B.U.s:
   Kull;Blackmark 30.00
4 JB,RCo,GKIron Shadows in the
   Moon B.U.Blackmark,Boris(c) . 25.00
5 JB,A WitchShall beBorn,Boris(c) 20.00
6 AN,`Sleeper `Neath the Sands' . 20.00
7 JB,Citadel at the Center
   of Time Boris(c) 20.00
8 inc.GK,`Corsairs against Stygia. 20.00
9 Curse of the Cat-Goddess,
   Boris(c),B.U.King Kull 20.00

Savage Sword of Conan #7
© Marvel Entertainment Group

10 JB,`Sacred Serpent of Set'
   Boris(c) 20.00
11 JB,`The Abode of the Damned' 18.00
12 JB,Haunters of Castle Crimson
   Boris(c) 18.00
13 GK,The Thing in the Temple,
   B.U. Solomon Kane 18.00
14 NA,Shadow of Zamboula,
   B.U.Solomon Kane 18.00
15 JB,Boris(c),`Devil in Iron' 18.00
16 JB,BWS,People of the Black
   Circle,B.U.Bran Mak Morn . . . 18.00
17 JB,`On to Yimsha!,'
   B.U.Bran Mak Morn 18.00
18 JB,`The Battle of the Towers'
   B.U. Solomon Kane 18.00
19 JB,`Vengeance in Vendhya'
   B.U. Solomon Kane 18.00
20 JB,`The Slithering Shadow'
   B.U. Solomon Kane 12.00
21 JB,`Horror in the Red Tower' . . 12.00
22 JB,`Pool o/t Black One'
   B.U. Solomon Kane 12.00
23 JB,FT,`Torrent of Doom'
   B.U. Solomon Kane 12.00
24 JB,BWS,`Tower of the
   Elephant,'B.U.Cimmeria 12.00
25 DG,SG,Jewels of Gwahlur,
   B.U.Solomon Kane 12.00
26 JB,TD,Beyond the Black River,
   B.U.Solomon Kane 12.00
27 JB/TD,Children of Jhebbal Sag 12.00
28 JB/AA,Blood of the Gods 12.00
29 ECh,FT,Child of Sorcery,
   B.U. Red Sonja 12.00
30 FB,The Scarlet Citadel 12.00
31 JB/TD,The Flaming Knife,pt.1 . 12.00
32 JB/TD,Ghouls of Yanaldar,pt.2 . 12.00
33 GC,Curse of the Monolith,
   B.U.Solomon Kane 12.00
34 Cl/AA,MP,Lair o/t Ice Worm;B.U.
   Solomon Kane,B.U.King Kull . 12.00
35 ECh,Black Tears 12.00
36 JB,AA,Hawks over Shem 12.00
37 SB,Sons of the White Wolf
   B.U. Solomon Kane 12.00
38 JB/TD,The Road of the Eagles. 12.00
39 SB/TD,The Legions of the Dead,
   B.U.Solomon Kane concl 12.00
40 JB/TD,A Dream of Blood 12.00
41 JB/TD,Quest for the Cobra Crown
   A:Thoth-Amon,B.U.Sol.Kane . 12.00
42 JB/TD,Devil-Tree of Gamburu,
   A:Thoth-Amon,B.U.Sol.Kane . 12.00
43 JB/TD,King Thoth-Amon,
   B.U.King Kull 12.00

Savage Sword of Conan — MARVEL — Comics Values Annual

#	Title	Price
44	SB/TD,The Star of Khorala	12.00
45	JB/TD,The Gem in the Tower, B.U. Red Sonja	12.00
46	EC/TD,Moon of Blood, B.U. Hyborian Tale	12.00
47	GK/JB/JRu,Treasure of Tranicos C:Thoth-Amon	12.00
48	JB/KJ,A Wind Blows from Stygia C:Thoth-Amon	12.00
49	JB/TD,When Madness Wears the Crown, B.U.Hyborian Tale	12.00
50	JB/TD,Swords Across the Alimane	15.00
51	JB/TD,Satyrs' Blood	8.00
52	JB/TD,Conan the Liberator	8.00
53	JB,The Sorcerer and the Soul, B.U. Solomon Kane	8.00
54	JB,The Stalker Amid the Sands, B.U. Solomon Kane	8.00
55	JB,Black Lotus & Yellow Death B.U. King Kull	8.00
56	JB/TD,The Sword of Skelos	8.00
57	JB/TD,Zamboula	8.00
58	JB/TD,KGa,For the Throne of Zamboula,B.U.OlgerdVladislav	8.00
59	AA,ECh,City ofSkulls,B.U.Gault	8.00
60	JB,The Ivory Goddess	8.00
61	JB,Wizard Fiend of Zingara	8.00
62	JB/ECh,Temple of the Tiger, B.U. Solomon Kane	8.00
63	JB/ECh,TP/BMc,GK,Moat of Blood I:Chane of the Elder Earth	8.00
64	JB/ECh,GK,Children of Rhan, B.U. Chane	8.00
65	GK,JB,Fangs of the Serpent, B.U. Bront	8.00
66 thru 75		@8.00
76 thru 80		@8.00
81	JB/ECh,Palace of Pleasure, B.U. Bront	8.00
82	AA,BWS,Devil in the Dark.Pt.1 B.U.repConan#24,Swamp Gas	8.00
83	AA,MW,NA,ECh,Devil in the Dark Pt.2,B.U. Red Sonja,Sol.Kane	8.00
84	VM,Darksome Demon of Rabba Than	8.00
85	GK,Daughter of the God King	8.00
86	GK,Revenge of the Sorcerer	8.00
87		8.00
88	JB,Isle of the Hunter	8.00
89	AA,MW,Gamesman of Asgalun, B.U. Rite of Blood	8.00
90	JB,Devourer of Souls	8.00
91	JB,VM,Forest of Friends, B.U. The Beast,The Chain	8.00

Savage Sword of Conan #90
© Marvel Entertainment Group

#	Title	Price
92	JB,The Jeweled Bird	8.00
93	JB/ECh,WorldBeyond the Mists	8.00
94 thru 101		@8.00
102	GD,B.U.Bran Mac Morn	6.00
103	GD,White Tiger of Vendhya, B.U. Bran Mac Morn	6.00
104		6.00
105		6.00
106	Feud of Blood	6.00
107 thru 118		@6.00
119	ECh,A:Conan's Sister	6.00
120	Star of Thama-Zhu	6.00
121		6.00
122		6.00
123	ECh,Secret of the GreatStone	6.00
124	ECh,Secret of the Stone	6.00
125	Altar of the Goat God	6.00
126	The Mercenary	6.00
127	Reunion in Scarlet,Return of Valeria	6.00
128		6.00
129		6.00
130	Reavers of the Steppes	6.00
131	GI,Autumn of the Witch	6.00
132	ECh,Masters o/t Broadsword	6.00
133		6.00
134	Conan the Pirate	6.00
135	Conan the Pirate	6.00
136	NKu,Stranded on DesertIsland	6.00
137	ECh,The Lost Legion	6.00
138	ECh,Clan o/t Lizard God	6.00
139	ECh,A:Valeria	6.00
140	ECh,The Ghost's Revenge	6.00
141	ECh	6.00
142	ECh,V:Warlord	6.00
143	ECh	6.00
144	ECh	6.00
145	ECh	6.00
146	ECh	6.00
147	ECh	6.00
148	BMc	6.00
149	TGr,BMc,Conan Enslaved	6.00
150	ECh	6.00
151	ECh	6.00
152	ECh,Valley Beyond the Stars	6.00
153	Blood on the Sand,Pt.1	6.00
154	Blood on the Sand,Pt.2	6.00
155	ECh,V:Vampires	6.00
156	V:Corinthian Army	6.00
157	V:Hyborians	6.00
158	ECh,The Talisman-Gem	6.00
159	Conan Enslaved	6.00
160		6.00
161	V:Magician/Monsters	6.00
162	AW,Horned God,B.U.Sol.Kane	5.00
163	V:Picts	5.00
164	Conan's Revenge	5.00
165	B.U. King Kull	5.00
166	ECh,Conan in New World,Pt.1	5.00
167	ECh,Conan in New World,Pt.2	5.00
168	ECh,Conan in New World,concl	5.00
169		5.00
170	AW,A:Red Sonja,Valeria B.U. Solomon Kane	5.00
171	TD,Conan Youth Story	5.00
172	JS,JRu,Haunted Swamp, B.U.King Kull,Valeria, Red Sonja	5.00
173	ECh,Under Siege	5.00
174	AA,Red Stones of Rantha Karn	5.00
175	The Demonslayer Sword	5.00
176	FH,TT,V:Wizard,B.U. Witch Queen,Dagon,Ghouls	4.00
177	LMc,TD,ECh,Conan the Prey, B.U.King Conan,Red Sonja	4.00
178	AA,The Dinosaur God	4.00
179	ECh,A:Red Sonja,Valeria, B.U.Conan	4.00
180	ECh,Sky-God Bardisattva,	

#	Title	Price
	B.U. King Kull	4.00
181	TD,Conan the Pagan God?, B.U. Voodoo Tribe	4.00
182	RB/RT,V:Killer Ants	4.00
183	ECh,V:Kah-Tah-Dhen, B.U.King Kull	4.00
184	AA,Return of Sennan	4.00
185	The Ring of Molub	4.00
186	AW,A:Thulsa Doom	4.00
187	ECh,A:Conan's Brother?	4.00
188	V:Kharban the Sorcerer	4.00
189	A:Search Zukala for Gem	4.00
190	JB/TD,Skull on the Seas,pt.1	4.00
191	JB/ECh,Skull on the Seas,pt.2 Thulsa Doom Vs.Thoth-Amon	4.00
192	JB/ECh,Skull on the Seas,pt.3 B.U. King Kull	4.00
193	JB/ECh,Skull on the Seas concl. V:Thulsa Doom & Thoth-Amon	4.00
194	JB/ECh,Wanted for Murder, B.U. Li-Zya	4.00
195	JB/ECh,V:Yamatains, Giant Tortoise	4.00
196	JB/ECh,Treasure of the Stygian Prince-Toth-Mekri,A:Valeria	4.00
197	RTs,JB,EC,Red Hand	4.00
198	RTs,JB,EC,Red Hand	4.00
199	RTs,JB,EC,V:Black Zarona	4.00
200	RTs,JB,ECh,JJu(c),The Barbarian from Cross Plains	4.00
201	RTs,MCW,return to Tarantia	4.00
202	RTs,JB,ECh,Conan in the City City of Magicians,pt.1	4.00
203	RTs,JB,ECh,Conan in the City City of Magicians,pt.2	4.00
204	RTs,JB,ECh,Conan in the City City of Magicians,pt.3	4.00
205	RTs,JB,ECh,Conan in the City City of Magicians,pt.4	4.00
206	RTs,JB,ECh,BLr(c),Conan in the City of Magicians,concl.	4.00
207	RTs,JB,ECh,MK(c), Conan and the Spider God, pt.1	4.00
208	RTs,JB,ECh, Conan and the Spider God, pt.2	4.00
209	RTs,JB,Conan and the Spider God,pt.3	4.00
210	RTs,Conan and the Spider God,pt.4	4.00
211	RTs,Conan and the Gods of the Mountain,pt.1	4.00
212	RTs,Conan and the Gods of the Mountain,pt.2	4.00
213	RTs,Conan and the Gods of the Mountain,pt.3	4.00
214	RTs,Conan and the Gods of	

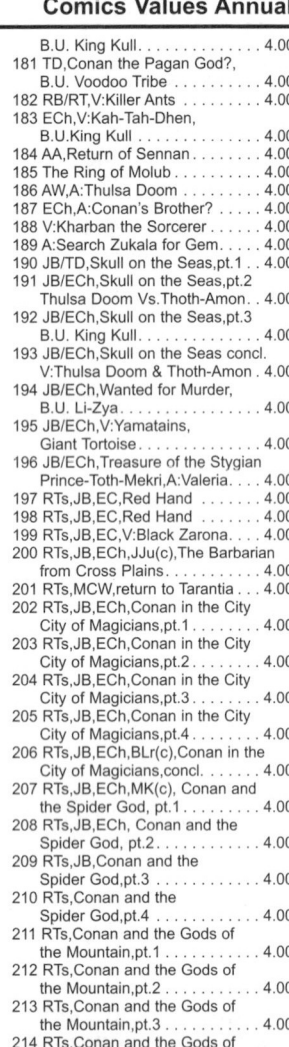

Savage Sword of Conan Ann. #1
© Marvel Entertainment Group

All comics prices listed are for *Near Mint* condition.

Comics Values Annual — MARVEL — Savage–Sensational

the Mountain,pt.4 .... 4.00
215 RTs,JuB(c),Conan and the Gods of the Mountain,concl......... 4.00
216 RTs,AA,Vengeance of Nitocris . 4.00
217 RTs,Conan theMercenary,pt.1 . 4.00
218 RTs,Conan theMercenary,pt.2 . 4.00
219 RTs,A:Solomon Kane........ 4.00
220 RTs,V:Skull Out of Time 4.00
221 RTs,C.L.Moore story adapt.... 4.00
222 RTs,The Haunter of the Towers B.U.JB,Conan Barbarian #1 ... 4.00
223 RTs,A:Tuzune Thune 4.00
224 RTs,JWk,The Dwellers Under the Tombs,adapt. B.U.V:Dinosaurs . 4.00
225 .... 4.00
226 RTs,EN(c),The Four Ages of Conan, A:Red Sonja....... 4.00
227 RTs,JBu, besieged in a lost city, B.U. Kull,Red Sonja...... 4.00
228 RTs,AN,Conan in chains!..... 4.00
229 RTs 4.00
230 RTs, Acheron falls, Ring of Tkrubu,pt.2, R:Kull 4.00
231 RTs, V:Tuzoun Thune, B.U. EM,Red Sonja 4.00
232 RTs 4.00
233 RTs,A:Juma the Black, Kull 4.00
234 RTs,JBu, A:Nefartari; A:Red Sonja, Zula 4.00
235 RTs,JBu,The Daughter of Raktauanishi, final issue...... 4.00
Ann.#1 SB,BWS,inc.'Beware the Wrath of Anu',B.U. King Kull Vs.Thulsa Doom 4.00

SAVAGE TALES
May, 1971
(black & white magazine)
1 GM,BWS,JR,I&O:Man-Thing, B:Conan,Femizons,A:Ka-Zar 200.00
2 GM,FB,BWS,AW,BWr,A:King Kull rep,Creatures on the Loose #10 .... 60.00
3 FB,BWS,AW,JSo 35.00
4 NA(c),E:Conan 30.00
5 JSn,JB,B:Brak the Barbarian .. 30.00
6 NA(c),JB,AW,B:Ka-Zar 20.00
7 GM,NA 15.00
8 JB,A:Shanna,E:Brak 15.00
9 MK,A:Shanna 15.00
10 RH,NA,AW,A:Shanna........ 15.00
11 RH..................... 15.00
12 Summer, 1975........... 15.00
Ann.#1 GM,GK,BWS,O:Ka-Zar ... 15.00

SAVAGE TALES
Nov., 1985–March, 1987
(black & white magazine)
1 MGo,I:The `Nam 6.00
2 thru 9 MGo .... @4.00

SCARLET SPIDER
1995–96
1 HMe,GK,TP,VirtualMortality,pt.3 . 2.25
2 HMe,JR2,AW,CyberWar,pt.3 .... 2.25
3 and 4 HMe .... @2.25

SCARLET SPIDER UNLIMITED
1995
1 True Origin,64-pg........... 4.50

SCARLET WITCH
1994
1 ALa(s),DAn(s),JH,I:Gargan,

C:Master Pandemonium 2.25
2 C:Avengers West Coast 2.25
3 A:Avengers West Coast 2.25
4 V:Lore,last issue........... 2.25

SCOOBY-DOO
Oct., 1977
1 B:DynoMutt 30.00
2 thru 5 .... @25.00
6 thru 9 Feb., 1979 .... @25.00

Secret Defenders #6
© Marvel Entertainment Group

SECRET DEFENDERS
1993–95
1 F:Dr.Strange(in all),Spider Woman,Nomad,Darkhawk, Wolverine,V:Macabre 3.25
2 F:Spider Woman,Nomad,Darkhawk, Wolverine,V:Macabre....... 2.50
3 F:Spider Woman,Nomad,Darkhawk, Wolverine,V:Macabre....... 2.25
4 F:Namorita,Punisher, Sleepwalker,V:Roadkill 2.25
5 F:Naromita,Punisher, Sleepwalker, V:Roadkill 2.25
6 F:Spider-Man,Scarlet Witch,Captain America,V:Suicide Pack 2.25
7 F:Captain America,Scarlet Witch, Spider-Man 2.25
8 F:Captain America,Scarlet Witch, Spider-Man 2.25
9 F:War Machine,Thunderstrike, Silver Surfer.............. 2.25
10 F:War Machine,Thunderstrike, Silver Surfer.............. 2.25
11 TGb,F:Hulk,Nova,Northstar 2.25
12 RMz(s),TGb,F:Thanos 2.75
13 RMz(s),TGb,F:Thanos,Super Skrull, Rhino,Nitro,Titanium Man 2.25
14 RMz(s),TGb,F:Thanos,Super Skrull, Rhino,Nitro, Titanium Man, A:Silver Surfer 2.25
15 F:Dr.Druid,Cage,Deadpool..... 2.25
16 F:Dr.Druid,Cage,Deadpool..... 2.25
17 F:Dr.Druid,Cage,Deadpool..... 2.25
18 F:Iron Fist,Giant Man......... 2.25
19 F:Dr.Druid,Cadaver, Shadowoman............ 2.25
20 V:Venom 2.25
21 V:Slaymaker 2.25
22 Final Defense,pt.1 .... 2.25
23 Final Defense,pt.2 .... 2.25

24 Final Defense,pt.3 .... 2.25
25 V:Dr.Druid 2.25

SECRET WARS
May, 1984
1 MZ,A:X-Men,Fant.Four,Avengers, Hulk,SpM in All,I:Beyonder 7.00
2 MZ,V:Magneto 6.00
3 MZ,I:Titania & Volcana 6.00
4 BL,V:Molecule Man........... 6.00
5 BL,F:X-Men 6.00
6 MZ,V:Doctor Doom........... 6.00
7 MZ,I:New Spiderwoman 7.00
8 MZ,I:Alien Black Costume (for Spider-Man) 25.00
9 MZ,V:Galactus 5.00
10 MZ,V:Dr.Doom.............. 5.00
11 MZ,V:Dr.Doom.............. 5.00
12 MZ,Beyonder Vs. Dr.Doom 7.00
TPB rep #1-#12 .... 19.95
TPB rep. 12 issues, 336-pg..... 24.95

SECRET WARS II
July, 1985
1 AM,SL,A:X-Men,New Mutants... 5.00
2 AM,SL,A:Fantastic Four 3.00
3 AM,SL,A:Daredevil 3.00
4 AM,I:Kurse 3.00
5 AM,SL,I:Boom Boom 3.50
6 AM,SL,A:Mephisto 3.00
7 AM,SL,A:Thing 3.00
8 AM,SL,A:Hulk 3.00
9 AM,SL,A:Everyone,double-size.. 5.00

SECTAURS
June, 1985
1 Based on toys 3.00
2 .... 3.00
3 .... 3.00
4 .... 3.00
5 thru 10 1986 .... @3.00

SEEKER 3000
April, 1998
1 (of 4) DAn,IEd,sci-fi adventure, 48-pg................... 3.00
2 DAn,IEd,encounter with aliens .. 3.00
3 DAn,IEd,V:Hkkkt............ 3.00
4 DAn,IEd,V:Hkkkt, concl........ 3.00

SEMPER FI
Dec., 1988
1 JSe 2.50
2 JSe 2.50
3 JSe 2.50
4 JSe 2.50
5 JSe 2.50
6 .... 2.50
7 and 8 .... @2.50
9 Aug., 1989,final issue 2.50

SENSATIONAL SPIDER-MAN
1 KM/TP/KJ,rep. (1989)......... 6.00

SENSATIONAL SPIDER-MAN
Jan., 1996
0 DJu,KJ,Return of Spider-Man,pt.1 Lenticular cover 6.00
1 DJu,KJ,Media Blizzard,pt.1, V:New Mysterio 5.00
2 DJu,KJ,Return of Kaine,pt.2 .... 4.00
3 DJu,KJ,Web of Carnage,pt.1 ... 4.00

All comics prices listed are for *Near Mint* condition.

Sensational–Sgt. Fury — MARVEL — Comics Values Annual

#	Title	Price
4	DJu,KJ,Blood Brothers,pt.1	4.00
5	DJu	4.00
6	DJu	3.00
7	TDz,A:Onslaught	3.00
8	TDz,The Looter	3.00
9	TDz,Onslaught tie-in	3.00
10	TDz,RCa,V:Swarm	3.00
11	TDz,Revelations, pt.2	3.00
11A	bagged with card, etc.	5.00
12	TDz,SwM, V:Trapster	3.00
13	TDz,RCa,A:Ka-Zar, Shanna	3.00
14	TDz,RCa,Savage Land saga	3.00
15	TDz,RCa,Savage Land saga	3.00
16	TDz,RCa,R:Black Cat, V:Prowler,Vulture	3.00
17	TDz,RCa,V:Black Cat, Prowler,Vulture	3.00
18	TDz,RCa,V:Vulture	3.00
19	TDz,RCa,R:Living Monolith	2.50
20	TDz,RCa,Living Pharoah, concl.	2.50
21	TDz,RCa,Techomancers	2.50
22	TDz,RCa,A:Doctor Strange	2.50
23	TDz,RCa,A:Doctor Strange	2.50
24	TDz,RCa,A:S.H.I.E.L.D., Looter	3.00
25	TDz,RCa,Spider-Hunt,pt1 x-over	4.00
26	TDz,RCa,JoB,Identity Crisis prelude	2.50
27	TDz,RCa,MeW,Identity Crisis, as Hornet V:Phaeton	2.50
28	TDz,RCa,as Hornet, V:Vulture	2.50
29	TDz,RCa,V:Arcade, Black Cat	2.50
30	TDz,A:Black Cat,V:Arcade	2.50
31	TDz,MeW,RCa,V:Rhino	2.50
32	TDz,JoB,The Gathering of the Five, pt.1 (of 5)	2.50
33	TDz,JoB,Gathering of the Five,pt.5	2.50
	Minus 1 Spec.,TDz,RCa, flashback	3.00
	TPB In the Savage Land rep.#13-#15	6.00
	TPB Sensational Spider-Man '96 JMD,SwM, seq. to Kraven's Last Hunt, 64-pg.	3.00

SENTINEL
Marvel April 2003

#	Title	Price
1	Salvage,pt.1	3.00
2	Salvage,pt.2	3.00
3	Salvage,pt.3	3.00
4	Salvage,pt.4	3.00
5	Salvage,pt.5	2.50
6	Salvage,pt.6	2.50
7	No Hero,pt.1	2.50
8	No Hero,pt.2	2.50
9	No Hero,pt.3	2.50
	TPB Sentinel: Salvage, Vol. 1	19.95

SENTRY
July, 2000

#	Title	Price
1	(of 5) PJe,JaL	3.00
2	PJe,JaL,Unicorn	3.00
3	PJe,JaL,Hulk,Spider-Man	3.00
4	PJe,JaL,Prof.X	3.00
5	PJe,JaL	3.00
	TPB The Sentry, JaL	24.95
	Spec.#1 Sentry vs. The Void, JaL,PJe (2001)	3.00

SERGEANT BARNEY BARKER
Aug., 1956

#	Title	Price
1	JSe,Comedy	200.00
2	JSe,Army Inspection(c)	150.00
3	JSe,Tank(c)	150.00

Becomes:

G.I. TALES
| 4 | JSe,At Grips with the Enemy | 60.00 |

#	Title	Price
5		50.00
6	JO,BP,GWb, July, 1957	55.00

SGT. FURY & HIS HOWLING COMMANDOS
May, 1963–Dec., 1981

#	Title	Price
1	Seven Against the Nazis	2,200.00
2	JK,Seven Doomed Men	600.00
3	JK,Midnight on Massacre Mountain	300.00
4	JK,V:Lord Ha-Ha,D:Junior Juniper	300.00
5	JK,V:Baron Strucker	300.00
6	JK,The Fangs of the Fox	200.00
7	JK,Fury Court Martial	200.00
8	JK,V:Dr Zemo,I:Percival Pinkerton	200.00
9	DAy,V:Hitler	200.00
10	DAy,On to Okinwawa,I:Capt. Savage	200.00
11	DAy,V:Capt.Flint	100.00
12	DAy,Howler deserts	100.00
13	DAy,JK,A;Capt.America	500.00
14	DAy,V:Baron Strucker	100.00
15	DAy,SD,Too Small to Fight Too Young to Die	100.00
16	DAy,In The Desert a Fortress Stands	100.00
17	DAy,While the Jungle Sleeps	100.00
18	DAy,Killed in Action	100.00
19	DAy,An Eye for an Eye	100.00
20	DAy,V:the Blitz Squad	100.00
21	DAy,To Free a Hostage	75.00
22	DAy,V:Bull McGiveney	75.00
23	DAy,The Man who Failed	75.00
24	DAy,When the Howlers Hit the Home Front	75.00
25	DAy,Every Man my Enemy	75.00
26	DAy,Dum Dum Does it the Hard Way	75.00
27	DAy,O:Fury's Eyepatch	75.00
28	DAy,Not a Man Shall Remain Alive	75.00
29	DAy,V:Baron Strucker	75.00
30	DAy,Incident in Italy	75.00
31	DAy,Into the Jaws of Death	50.00
32	DAy,A Traitor in Our Midst	50.00
33	DAy,The Grandeur That was Greece	50.00
34	DAy,O:Howling Commandoes	50.00
35	DAy,Berlin Breakout,J:Eric Koenig	50.00
36	DAy,My Brother My Enemy	50.00
37	DAy,In the Desert to Die	50.00

Sgt. Fury and His Howling Commandos #18 © Marvel Entertainment Group

---

#	Title	Price
38	This Ones For Dino	50.00
39	Into the Fortress of Fear	50.00
40	That France Might be Free	50.00
41	V:The Blitzers	50.00
42	Three Were AWOL	50.00
43	Scourge of the Sahara,A:Bob Hope,Glen Miller	50.00
44	JSe,The Howlers First Mission	50.00
45	JSe,I:The War Lover	50.00
46	JSe,They Also Serve	50.00
47	Tea and Sabotage	50.00
48	A:Blitz Squad	50.00
49	On to Tarawa	50.00
50	The Invasion Begins	50.00
51	The Assassin	50.00
52	Triumph at Treblinka	50.00
53	To the Bastions of Bavaria	50.00
54	Izzy Shoots the Works	50.00
55	Cry of Battle, Kiss of Death	35.00
56	Gabriel Blow Your Horn	35.00
57	TS,The Informer	35.00
58	Second Front	35.00
59	D-Day for Dum Dum	35.00
60	Authorised Personnel Only	35.00
61	The Big Breakout	35.00
62	The Basic Training of Fury	35.00
63	V:Nazi Tanks	35.00
64	The Peacemonger,A:Capt Savage	35.00
65	Eric Koenig,Traitor	35.00
66	Liberty Rides the Underground	35.00
67	With a Little Help From My Friends	50.00
68	Welcome Home Soldier	35.00
69	While the City Sleeps	35.00
70	The Missouri Marauders	35.00
71	Burn,Bridge,Burn	35.00
72	Battle in the Sahara	35.00
73	Rampage on the Russian Front	35.00
74	Each Man Alone	35.00
75	The Deserter	35.00
76	He Fought the Red Baron	25.00
77	A Traitor's Trap,A:Eric Koenig	25.00
78	Escape or Die	25.00
79	Death in the High Castle	25.00
80	To Free a Hostage	25.00
81	The All American	25.00
82	Howlers Hit The Home Front,rep	25.00
83	Dum DumV:Man-Mountain McCoy	25.00
84	The Devil's Disciple	25.00
85	Fury V:The Howlers	25.00
86	Germ Warfare	25.00
87	Dum Dum does it...rep	25.00
88	Save General Patton	25.00
89	O:Fury's eyepatch,rep	25.00
90	The Chain That Binds	25.00
91	Not A Man...rep	25.00
92	Some Die Slowly	20.00
93	A Traitor...rep	20.00
94	GK(c),Who'll Stop the Bombs	20.00
95	7 Doomed Men, rep	20.00
96	GK(c),Dum-Dum Sees it Through	20.00
97	Till the Last Man Shall Fail	20.00
98	A:Deadly Dozen	20.00
99	Guerillas in Greece	20.00
100	When a Howler Falls	25.00
101	Pearl Harbor	15.00
102	Death For A Dollar	15.00
103	Berlin Breakout	15.00
104	The Tanks Are Coming	15.00
105	My Brother,My Enemy	15.00
106	Death on the Rhine	15.00
107	Death-Duel in the Desert	15.00
108	Slaughter From the Skies	15.00
109	This Ones For Dino,rep	15.00
110	JSe(c),The Reserve	15.00
111	V:Colonel Klaw	15.00

CVA Page 304 — All comics prices listed are for *Near Mint* condition.

MARVEL

Sgt. Fury and his Howling Commandos #136 © Marvel EntertainmEnt Group

112 V:Baron Strucker	15.00
113 That France Might Be Free,rep	15.00
114 Jungle Bust Out	15.00
115 V:Baron Strucker	15.00
116 End of the Road	15.00
117 Blitz Over Britain	15.00
118 War Machine	15.00
118 War Machine	15.00
119 They Strike by Machine	15.00
120 Trapped in the Compound of Death	15.00
121 An Eye for an Eye	10.00
122 A;The Blitz Squad	10.00
123 To Free a Hostage	10.00
124 A:Bull McGiveney	10.00
125 The Man Who Failed	10.00
126 When the Howlers Hit Home	10.00
127 Everyman My Enemy,rep	10.00
128 Dum Dum does it...rep	10.00
129 O:Fury's Eyepatch	10.00
130 A:Baron Strucker	10.00
131 Armageddon	10.00
132 Incident in Italy	10.00
133 thru 140	@10.00
141 thru 150	@10.00
151 thru 160	@10.00
161 thru 167	@10.00
Ann.#1 Korea #4,#5	150.00
Ann.#2 This was D-Day	50.00
Ann.#3 Vietnam	30.00
Ann.#4 Battle of the Bulge	25.00
Ann.#5 Desert Fox	15.00
Ann.#6 Blaze of Battle	15.00
Ann.#7 Armageddon	15.00

SERGIO ARAGONES MASSACRES MARVEL
1996
1-shot Parody.................. 5.00

SEVEN BLOCK
Epic, 1990
1 .... 2.50

SHADOWMASTERS
Oct., 1989–Jan., 1990
1 RH	7.00
2	5.00
3 and 4	@4.00

SHADOWRIDERS
1993
1 I:Shadowriders,A:Cable, Ghost Rider	3.00
2 A:Ghost Rider	2.50
3 A:Cable	2.50
4 A:Cable	2.50

SHADOWS & LIGHT
Dec., 1997
1 BSf,RMz,LWn,BWr,GeH,SD,B&W anthology series	3.00
2 JSn,LW,LSh,GK	3.00
3 BL,JSn	3.00
4 three new tales	3.00

SHANG-CHI: MASTER OF KUNG FU
Marvel Max, Sept., 2002
1 (of 6) DgM,PG	3.00
2 DgM,PG,JP	3.00
3 PG,JP	3.00
4 PG,JP	3.00
5 PG,JP	3.00
6 PG,JP	3.00
TPB Vol. 1: Hellfire Apocalypse	16.00

SHANNA, THE SHE-DEVIL
Dec., 1972–Aug., 1973
1 GT,F:Shanna	35.00
2 RA,The Dungeon of Doom	20.00
3 RA,The Hour of the Bull	15.00
4 RA,Mandrill	15.00
5 JR(c),RA,V:Nekra	15.00

SHEENA
Dec., 1984–Feb., 1985
1 and 2 Movie adapt .... @3.00

SHE-HULK
[1st Regular Series] Feb., 1980
1 JB,BWi,I&O:She-Hulk	15.00
2 BWi,D:She-Hulk's best friend	7.00
3 BWi,Wanted for Murder	7.00
4 BWi,V:Her Father	7.00
5 BWi,V:Silver Serpent	7.00
6 A:Iron Man	5.00
7 BWi,A:Manthing	5.00
8 BWi,A:Manthing	5.00
9 BWi,Identity Crisis	5.00
10 V:The Word	5.00
11 BWi,V:Dr.Morbius	5.00
12 V:Gemini	5.00
13 V:Man-Wolf	5.00
14 V:Hellcat	5.00
15 V:Lady Kills	5.00
16 She Hulk Goes Berserk	5.00
17 V:Man-Elephant	5.00
18 V:Grappler	5.00
19 V:Her Father	5.00
20 A:Zapper	5.00
21 V:Seeker	5.00
22 V:Radius	5.00
23 V:Radius	5.00
24 V:Zapper	5.00
25 Double-sized,last issue	5.00

[2nd Regular Series] 1989–94
1 JBy,V:Ringmaster	4.00
2 JBy	2.50
3 JBy,A:Spider-Man	2.50
4 JBy,I:Blond Phantom	3.00
5 JBy	2.50
6 JBy,A:U.S.1,Razorback	2.50
7 JBy,A:U.S.1,Razorback	2.50
8 JBy,A:Saint Nicholas	2.50
9 AM(i)	2.50
10 AM(i)	2.50
11	2.50
12	2.50
13 SK(c)	2.50
14 MT(c),A:Howard the Duck	3.00
15 SK(c)	3.00
16 SK(c)	3.00
17 SK(c),V:Dr.Angst	3.00
18 SK(c)	2.50
19 SK(c),V:Nosferata	2.50
20 SK(c),Darkham Asylum	2.50
21 SK(c),V:Blonde Phantom	3.00
22 SK(c),V:Blonde Phantom,A:All Winners Squad	3.00
23 V:Blonde Phantom	3.00
24 V:Deaths'Head	4.00
25 A:Hercules,Thor	2.50
26 A:Excalibur	2.50
27 Cartoons in N.Y.	2.50
28 Game Hunter Stalks She-Hulk	2.50
29 A:Wolv.,Hulk,SpM,Venom	2.50
30 MZ(c),A:Silver Surfer,Thor Human Torch	2.25
31 JBy,V:Spragg the Living Hill	2.50
32 JBy,A:Moleman,V:Spragg	2.50
33 JBy,A:Moleman,V:Spragg	2.50
34 JBy,Returns to New York	2.50
35 JBy,V:X-Humed Men	2.50
36 JBy,X-mas issue (#8 tie-in)	2.50
37 JBy,V:Living Eraser	2.50
38 JBy,V:Mahkizmo	2.50
39 JBy,V:Mahkizmo	2.50
40 JBy,V:Spraggs,Xemnu	2.50
41 JBy,V:Xemnu	2.50
42 JBy,V:USArcher	2.50
43 JBy,V:Xemnu	2.50
44 JBy,R:Rocket Raccoon	2.50
45 JBy,A:Razorback	2.50
46 JBy,A:Rocket Raccoon	2.50
47 V:D'Bari	2.50
48 JBy,A:Rocket Raccoon	2.50
49 V:Skrulls,D'Bari	2.50
50 JBy,WS,TA,DGb,AH,HC, D:She-Hulk	4.00
51 TMo,V:Savage She-Hulk	2.50
52 D:She-Hulk,A:Thing,Mr.Fantastic, I:Rumbler,V:Titania	2.50
53 AH(c),A:Zapper	2.50
54 MGo(c),A:Wonder Man	2.50
55 V:Rumbler	2.50
56 A:War Zone	2.50
57 A:Hulk	2.50
58 V:Electro	2.50

She-Hulk #24 © Marvel Entertainment Group

She Hulk–Silver / MARVEL / Comics Values Annual

59 V:Various Villains............ 2.50
60 last issue 2.50
TPB rep. #1-#8............... 12.95

SHE HULK: CEREMONY
1989
1 JBr/SDr 4.00
2 JBr/FS 4.00

Shield #1
© Marvel Entertainment Group

SHIELD
Feb., 1973
1 JSo 20.00
2 JSo 15.00
3 JB,JSo,JK................. 15.00
4 JSo 15.00
5 JSo,Oct., 1973 .... 15.00

SHOGUN WARRIORS
Feb., 1979
1 HT,DGr,F:Raydeen,Combatra,
   Dangard Ace 15.00
2 HT,DGr,V:Elementals of Evil.... 8.00
3 AM(c),HT,DGr,V:Elementals
   of Evil 8.00
4 HT,DGr,`Menace of the
   Mech Monsters' 8.00
5 HT,DGr,`Into The Lair
   of Demons' 8.00
6 HT,ME 8.00
7 HT,ME 8.00
8 HT,ME 8.00
9 `War Beneath The Waves'..... 8.00
10 `Five Heads of Doom' 8.00
11 TA(c) 7.00
12 WS(c) 7.00
13 `Demons on the Moon' 7.00
14 V:Dr. Demonicus 7.00
15 .... 7.00
16 .... 7.00
17 .... 7.00
18 .... 7.00
19 A:Fantastic Four 7.00
20 Sept., 1980 .... 7.00

SHROUD
Limited Series 1994
1 B:MiB(s),MCW,A:Spider-Man,
   V:Scorpion 2.25
2 MCW,A:Spider-Man,V:Scorpion . 2.25
3 MCW,I:Kali 2.25
4 MCW,Final Issue 2.25

SILVERHAWKS
Aug., 1987
1 thru 5 .... @3.00
6 June, 1988 .... 3.00

SILVER SABLE
1992–95
1 Foil stamped(c),A:Sandman,
   Spider-Man 3.00
2 I:Gattling.................. 2.50
3 V:Gattling,Foreigner 2.50
4 Infinity War,V:Doctor Doom..... 2.50
5 Infinity War,V:Doctor Doom..... 2.50
6 A:Deathlok 2.50
7 A:Deathlok 2.50
8 V:Hydra 2.50
9 O:Silver Sable 2.50
10 A:Punisher,Leviathan....... 2.50
11 Cyber Warriors,Hydra....... 2.25
12 V:Cyberwarriorss,R:Sandman. 2.25
13 For Love Nor Money#3,
   A:Cage,Terror........... 2.25
14 For Love Nor Money#6,
   A:Cage,Terror........... 2.25
15 V:Viper,A:Captain America 2.25
16 SBt,Infinity Crusade 2.25
17 Infinity Crusade 2.25
18 A:Venom 2.25
19 Siege of Darkness x-over..... 2.25
20 GWt(s),StB,BU:Sandman,Fin .. 2.25
21 Gang War 2.25
22 .... 2.25
23 GWt(s),A:Deadpool,Daredevil,
   BU:Sandman 2.25
24 GWt(s),BU:Crippler,w/card... 2.25
25 V:Hydra 2.50
26 F:Sandman 2.25
27 A:Code Blue 2.25
28 F:Chen 2.25
29 A:Wild Pack............... 2.25
30 problems with law 2.25
31 V:terrorists................ 2.25
32 A:The Foreigner........... 2.25
33 V:Hammerhead 2.25
34 .... 2.25
35 Li'l Silvie Tale............. 2.25

SILVER SURFER
[1st Series] Aug., 1968
1 B:StL(s),JB,JSr,GC,O:Silver Surfer,
   O:Watcher,I:Shala Bal...... 700.00
2 JB,JSr,GC,A:Watcher 300.00
3 JB,JSr,GC,I:Mephisto 250.00
4 JB,A:Thor,low distribution
   scarce 600.00
5 JB,A:Fant.Four,V:Stranger ... 150.00
6 JB,FB,A:Watcher 165.00
7 JB,A:Watcher,I:Frankenstein's
   Monster 165.00
8 JB,DA,A:Mephisto,I:Ghost..... 150.00
9 JB,DA,A:Mephisto,A:Ghost..... 150.00
10 JB,DA,South America....... 150.00
11 JB,DA 100.00
12 JB,DA,V:The Abomination ... 100.00
13 JB,DA,V:Doomsday Man 100.00
14 JB,DA,A:Spider-Man 125.00
15 JB,DA,A:Human Torch 100.00
16 JB,V:Mephisto 100.00
17 JB,V:Mephisto 100.00
18 E:StL(s),JK,V:Inhumans..... 100.00

[2nd Regular Series] 1982
1 JBy,TP,Direct Only,V:Mephisto . 12.00

[3rd Regular Series] July, 1987
1 MR,JRu,A:Fantastic Four,
   Galactus,V:Champion...... 12.00
2 MR,V:Shalla Bal,V:Skrulls..... 6.00
3 MR,V:Collector & Runner..... 5.00
4 MR,JRu,A:Elders,I:Obliterator ... 5.00
5 MR,JRu,V:Obliterator 5.00
6 MR,JRu,O:Obliterator,A:Kree,
   Skrulls 5.00
7 MR,JRu,V:Supremor,Elders/
   Soul Gems............... 5.00
8 MR,JRu,V:Supremor......... 5.00
9 MR,Elders Vs.Galactus....... 5.00
10 MR,A:Galactus,Eternity 5.00
11 JSon,JRu,V:Reptyl.......... 4.50
12 MR,JRu,V:Reptyl,A:Nova..... 4.50
13 JSon,DC,V:Ronan 4.50
14 JSon,JRu,V:Skrull Surfer...... 4.50
15 RLm,JRu,A:Fantastic Four..... 6.00
16 RLm,Inbetweener possesses
   Soul Gem,A:Fantastic Four.... 4.00
17 RLm,A:Inbetweener,Galactus,
   Fantastic Four,D:Trader,
   Possessor,Astronomer 4.00
18 RLm,Galactus V:Inbetweener... 4.00
19 RLm,MR,V:Firelord 4.00
20 RLm,A:Superskrull,Galactus .. 4.00
21 MR,DC,V:Obliterator 4.00
22 RLm,V:Ego 4.00
23 RLm,V:Dragon............. 4.00
24 RLm,V:G.I.G.O. 4.00
25 RLm,V:Ronan,Kree Skrull War.. 4.00
26 RLm,V:Nenora.............. 4.00
27 RLm,V:Stranger............ 4.00
28 RLm,D:Super Skrull,V:Reptyl ... 4.00
29 RLm,V:Midnight Sun 4.00
30 RLm,V:Midnight Sun 4.00
31 RLm,O:Living Tribunal &
   Stranger (double size) 4.50
32 RF,JSt,A:Mephisto 4.00
33 Rlm,V:Impossible Man....... 4.00
34 RLm,(1stJSn),2nd R:Thanos ... 5.00
35 RLm,A:Thanos,R:Drax....... 4.00
36 RLm,V:Impossible Man,A:Warlock
   Capt.Marvel,C:Thanos 4.00
37 RLm,V:Drax,A:Mentor 4.00
38 RLm,V:Thanos(continued in
   Thanos Quest)............ 4.00
39 JSh,V:Algol 3.00
40 RLm,V:Dynamo City 3.00
41 RLm,V:Dynamo City,A:Thanos.. 4.00
42 RLm,V:Dynamo City,A:Drax.... 3.00
43 RLm,V:DynamoCity 3.00
44 RLm,R:Thanos,Drax,
   O:Inf.Gems............... 4.00
45 RLm,Thanos vs. Mephisto 4.00
46 RLm,R:Warlock,A:Thanos 4.00
47 RLm,Warlock V:Drax,
   A:Thanos 4.00
48 RLm,A:Galactus,Thanos 4.00
49 RLm,V:Thanos Monster 4.00
50 RLm,Silver Stamp(D.size),
   V:Thanos Monster 8.00
50a 2nd printing 3.00
50b 3rd printing 3.00
51 RLm,Infinity Gauntlet x-over.... 3.00
52 RLm,Infinity Gauntlet x-over.... 3.00
53 RLm,Infinity Gauntlet x-over.... 3.00
54 RLm,I.Gauntlet x-over,V:Rhino .. 3.00
55 RLm,I.Gauntlet x-over,Universe
   According to Thanos,pt.1 ..... 3.00
56 RLm,I.Gauntlet x-over,Universe
   According to Thanos,pt.2 ..... 3.00
57 RLm,Infinity Gauntlet x-over.... 3.00
58 RLm(c),Infinity Gauntlet x-over,
   A:Hulk,Namor,Dr.Strange ... 3.00
59 RLm(c),TR,Infinity Gauntlet,
   Thanos:Silver Surfer....... 3.00
60 RLm,V:Midnight Sun,
   A:Inhumans............... 2.50
61 RLm,I:Collection.Agency 2.50
62 RLm,O:Collection Agency 2.50
63 RLm,A:Captain Marvel......... 2.50
64 RLm,V:Dark Silver Surfer...... 2.50
65 RLm,R:Reptyl,I:Princess
   Alaisa.................... 2.50
66 RLm,I:Avatar,Love & Hate 2.50

CVA Page 306   All comics prices listed are for *Near Mint* condition.

Comics Values Annual — MARVEL — Silver–Sisterhood

Silver Surfer #2
© Marvel Entertainment Group

67 RLm(c),KWe,Inf.War,V:Galactus A:DrStrange 2.50
68 RLm(c),KWe,Inf.War,O:Nova . . . 2.50
69 RLm(c),KWe,Infinity War, A:Galactus 2.50
70 RLm(c),Herald War#1,I:Morg . . 2.50
71 RLm(c),Herald War#2,V:Morg . . 2.50
72 RLm(c),Herald War#3,R:Nova . . 2.50
73 RLm,R:Airwalker 2.50
74 RLm,V:Terrax. 2.50
75 RLm,E:Herald Ordeal,V:Morg, D:Nova. 3.00
76 RLm,A:Jack of Hearts 2.50
77 RLm,A:Jack of Hearts 2.50
78 RLm,R:Morg,V:Nebula 2.50
79 RLm,V:Captain Atlas 2.50
80 RLm,I:Ganymede,Terrax Vs.Morg 2.50
81 RLm,O:Ganymede!:Tyrant 2.50
82 RLm,V:Tyrant,double sized 2.50
83 Infinity Crusade 2.50
84 RLm(c),Infinity Crusade 2.50
85 RLm(c),Infinity Crusade 2.50
86 RLm(c), Blood & Thunder,pt.2 V:Thor,A:Beta Ray Bill 2.50
87 RLm(c),Blood & Thunder,pt.7 . . . 2.50
88 RLm(c),Blood & Thunder,pt.10 . . 2.50
89 RLm(c),CDo,C:Legacy. 2.50
90 RLm(c),A:Legacy,C:Avatar. 2.50
91 RLm 2.50
92 RLm,V:Avatar 2.50
93 V:Human Torch 2.50
94 A:Fantastic Four, Warlock 2.50
95 SEa,A:Fantastic Four. 2.50
96 A:Fantastic Four,Hulk. 2.50
97 A:Fantastic Four,R:Nova 2.50
98 R:Champion 2.50
99 A:Nova 2.50
100 V:Mephisto 2.50
100a enhanced ed. 5.00
101 RMz,JoP,A:Shalla Bal 2.25
102 V:Galactus. 2.25
103 I:Death quad 2.25
104 Surfer Rampage 2.25
105 V:Super Skrull 2.25
106 A:Legacy,Morg. 2.25
107 TGb,BAn,A:Galactus,Morg, Tyrant. 2.25
108 Galactus Vs. Tyrant. 2.25
109 Morg has Ultimate Nulifier 2.25
110 JB,F:Nebula. 2.25
111 GP,TGb,BAn,to Other Side of Galaxy 2.25
112 GP,TGb,BAn,. 2.25

113 GP,TGb,BAn,V:Blackbody 2.25
114 . . . . 2.25
115 GP,TGb,BAn,Surfer in pieces . . 2.25
116 GP,TGb,BAn,Pieces cause trouble 2.25
117 . . . . 2.25
118 . . . . 2.25
119 . . . . 2.25
120 . . . . 2.25
121 A:Quasar, Beta Ray Bill 2.25
122 GP,SEa, returns to Marvel Universe. 2.25
123 GP,RG 2.25
124 GP,RG. 2.25
125 RG,V:Hulk, double size 3.50
126 JMD,RG,BWi,A:Dr. Strange . . . 2.25
127 JMD,RG,BWi,A:Alicia Masters . 2.25
128 JMD,RG,BWi,V:Puppet Master. 2.25
129 JMD,RG,BWi,back in time, late 1940s 2.25
130 JMD,CNr,BWi, trapped in past . 2.25
131 JMD,RG,BWi, ... 2.25
132 JMD,PaP,Puppet Master missing 2.25
133 JMD,MRy,PaP,V:PuppetMaster 2.25
134 JMD,TGm,MRy,Regains his memories, pt.1 (of 4) 2.25
135 JMD,TGm,MRy,Alicia summons Scrier. 2.25
136 JMD,TGm,MRy, ... 2.25
137 JMD,TGm,MRy,Mephisto v. Scrier. 2.25
138 JMD,RCz,MRy,A:The Thing, tie-in. 2.25
139 JMD,RCz,MRy,V:Gargoyle 2.25
140 JMD,JMu,on Zenn-La untouched by Galactus 2.25
141 JMD,JMu,A:Sama-D,Alicia Masters 2.25
142 JMD,JMu,Tenebrae,The Union, Cipher 2.25
143 JMD,DCw,Tenebrae,V:Psycho Man 2.25

Bi-Weekly Issues
144 JMD,JMu,V:Psycho-Man, A:Tenebrae. 2.25
145 JMD,JMu,A:Psycho-Man, Tenebrae,Cypphyrr. 2.25
146 TDF,DCw,V:Firelord 2.25
Minus 1 Spec., JMD,RG,BWi, flashback, first human contact . 2.25
Spec. Silver Surfer: Dangerous Artifacts,RMz, Galactus,Thanos (1996) 4.00
Spec. Silver Surfer: Inner Demons, rep. JMD,RGa,BWi (1998) 3.00
Ann.#1 RLm,JSon,Evolution War . . 7.00
Ann.#2 RLm,Atlantis Attacks. 5.00
Ann.#3 RLm,Lifeform #4 . . . . 4.00
Ann.#4 RLm,Korvac Quest #3,A: Guardians of Galaxy. 3.00
Ann.#5 RLm,Ret.o/Defenders #3 . . 2.50
Ann.#6 RLm(c),I:Legacy,w/card . . . 3.75
Ann.'97 1 JMD,VS,KJ,V:Scrier, 48-pg. 2.25
Ann.'98 MPe,RBe,TDF,F:Thor, 48-pg. 3.00
TPB Silver Surger, The Enslavers, KP 16.95
TPB Homecoming,A:Moondragon . 12.95
TPB Silver Surfer: Parable, StL,Moe, rep. of hc, 64-pg. (1998). 6.00
TPB Rebirth of Thanos,reprints #34-38 . . . . 12.95
TPB StL,JK, new origin. 13.00
Ashcan. 75

SILVER SURFER
Epic, Dec., 1988
1 Moebius,V:Galactus 5.00

Silver Surfer #1 (Epic)
© Marvel Entertainment Group

2 Moebius,V:Galactus 5.00
Graphic Novel. 14.95

SILVER SURFER
Marvel July 2003
1 JJu(c),children disappear 2.50
2 JaL(c),Denise Waters 2.50
3 Denise Waters 2.50
4 Communion,pt.4 . . . . 2.25
HC Silver Surfer Masterworks 2 . . 50.00

SILVER SURFER: LOFTIER THAN MORTALS
Aug., 1999
1 MFr,V:Dr. Doom 2.50
2 MFr,V:Dr. Doom, concl. 2.50

SILVER SURFER/ SUPERMAN
Marvel/DC 1996
Spec. GP,RLm,TA, x-over 6.00

SILVER SURFER VS. DRACULA
1994
1 rep,MWn(s),GC,TP 2.50

SILVER SURFER/ WARLOCK: RESURRECTION
1993
1 JSn,V:Mephisto,Death 3.50
2 JSn,TA,V:Death 3.00
3 JSn,TA,V:Mephisto 3.00
4 JSn,TA,V:Mephisto 3.00

SILVER SURFER/ WEAPON ZERO
Marvel/Top Cow 1997
1-shot Devil's Reign, pt.8 . . . . 4.00

SISTERHOOD OF STEEL
Epic, Dec., 1984
1 I:Sisterhood 4.00

Sisterhood–Solo Avengers

2 .... 3.00
3 .... 3.00
4 thru 8 .... @3.00

SIX FROM SIRIUS
Epic, July, 1984
1 PG,limited series 3.00
2 PG 2.25
3 PG 2.25
4 PG 2.25

SIX FROM SIRIUS II
Epic, Feb., 1986
1 PG 2.25

SIX-GUN WESTERN
Atlas, Jan., 1957
1 JSe(c),RC,JR,'Kid Yukon
  Gunslinger' 225.00
2 SSh,AW,DAy,JO,'His Guns
  Hang Low' 150.00
3 AW,BP,DAy 150.00
4 JSe(c),JR,GWb 125.00

SKELETON WARRIORS
1995
1 based on cartoon 2.25
2 Legion of Light 2.25
3 V:Grimstar 2.25
4 Grimskull abandons Legion
  of Light 2.25

SKRULL KILL CREW
1995
1 I:Kill Crew 3.00
2 V:Hydra 2.25
3 V:Captain America 3.00
4 V:Fantastic Four 3.00
5 Conclusion 3.00

SKULL, THE SLAYER
Aug., 1975
1 GK(c),O:Skull the Slayer 15.00
2 GK(c),'Man Against Gods' 10.00
3 'Trapped in the Tower
  of Time' 10.00
4 'Peril of the Pyramids',
  A:Black Knight 10.00
5 A:Black Knight 10.00
6 'The Savage Sea' 10.00
7 'Dungeon of Blood' 10.00
8 JK(c),Nov., 1976 .... 10.00

SLAPSTICK
1992–93
1 TA(i),I:Slapstick 2.25
2 TA(i),A:Spider-Man,V:Overkill . 2.25
3 V:Dr.Denton 2.25
4 A:GR,DD,FF,Cap.America 2.25

SLEDGE HAMMER
Feb., 1988
1 .... 5.00
2 March, 1988 .... 3.00

SLEEPWALKER
June, 1991
1 BBl,I:Rick Sheridan,C:8-Ball ... 3.00
2 BBl,V:8-Ball 2.25
3 BBl,A:Avengers,X-Men,X-Factor,
  FF,I:Cobweb,O:Sleepwalker . 2.25
4 RL,I:Bookworm 2.25
5 BBl,A:SpM,K.Pin,V:Ringleader . 2.25
6 BBl,A:SpM,Inf.Gauntlet x-over . 2.25
7 BBl,Infinity Gauntlet x-over,
  V:Chain Gang 2.25
8 BBl,A:Deathlok 2.25
9 BBl,I:Lullabye 2.25
10 BBl,MM,I:Dream-Team 2.25
11 BBl,V:Ghost Rider 2.25
12 JQ,A:Nightmare 3.00
13 BBl,MM,I:Spectra 2.25
14 BBl,MM,V:Spectra 2.25
15 BBl,MM,I:Thought Police 2.25
16 BBl,MM,A:Mr.Fantastic,Thing . 2.25
17 BBl,A:Spider-Man,Darkhawk,
   V:Brotherhood o/Evil Mutants . 2.25
18 JQ(c),Inf.War,A:Prof.X 2.25
19 V:Cobweb,w/pop out Halloween
   Mask 2.50
20 V:Chain Gang,Cobweb 2.25
21 V:Hobgoblin 2.25
22 V:Hobgoblin,8-Ball 2.25
23 V:Cobweb,Chain Gang 2.25
24 Mindfield#6 .... 2.25
25 O:Sleepwalker,Holo-grafx(c) . 3.50
26 V:Mindspawn 2.25
27 A:Avengers 2.25
28 I:Psyko 2.25
29 DG,V:Psyko 2.25
30 V:Psyko 2.25
31 DG(ci),A:Spectra 2.25
32 V:Psyko 2.25
33 V:Mindspawn,Last issue 2.25
Holiday Spec.#1 JQ(c) 2.50

SLEEZE BROTHERS
Aug., 1989
1 Private Eyes 2.25
2 thru 6 .... @2.25

SLINGERS
Oct., 1998
1 Ccs,F:Ricochet, Hornet,
  Prodigy & Dusk, 48-page:
1a Ricochet edition 3.00
1b Hornet edition 3.00
1c Prodigy edition 3.00
1d Dusk edition 3.00
2 CCs,V:Maggia 2.50
2a variant cover 2.25
3 CCs,F:Prodigy 2.25
4 CCs,F:Prodigy 2.25
5 CCs,F:Black Marvel 2.25
6 CCs,Truth or Dare 2.25
7 CCs,V:The Griz 2.25
8 CCs,V:The Griz 2.25
9 CCs,A:Ricochet 2.25
10 CCs,Raising Hell'sChildren,pt.1 . 2.25
11 CCs,Raising Hell'sChildren,pt.2 . 2.25
12 CCs,Hell's Children,pt.3 final . . . 2.25

SMURFS
Dec., 1982
1 .... 10.00
2 .... 7.00
3 .... 7.00
Treasury Edition 30.00

SOLARMAN
Jan., 1989
1 JM 3.00
2 MZ/NR,A:Dr.Doom, May, 1990 . . 3.00

SOLDIER X
July, 2002
1 Cable's future, 40-pg 3.00
2 .... 2.25
3 to Russia without love 2.25
4 Geo debuts 2.25
5 .... 2.25
6 .... 2.25
7 .... 2.25
8 Askani religion 2.25
9 V:Racist militia group 2.25
10 V:Racism 3.00
11 SEa,Dead Ends,pt.1 .... 3.00
12 SEa,Dead Ends,pt.2 .... 3.00

SOLO
[Limited Series] 1994
1 RoR,I:Cygnus 2.25
2 RoR,V.A.R.E.S. 2.25
3 RoR,V:Spidey 2.25
4 final issue 2.25

SOLO AVENGERS
Dec., 1987
1 MBr,JRu,JLe,AW,Hawkey;
  Mockingbird 4.00
2 MBr,JRu,KD,BMc,Hawkey;
  Capt.Marvel 2.50
3 MBr,JRu,BH,SDr,Hawkey;
  Moon Knight 2.50
4 RLm,JRu,PR,BL,Hawkey;
  Black Knight 2.50
5 MBr,JRu,JRy,Hawkey;
  Scarlet Witch 2.50
6 MBr,JRu,TGr,Hawkey;Falcon . . 2.50
7 MBr,JG,BL,Hawkey;Bl.Widow . 2.50
8 MBr,Hawkey;Dr.Pym 2.50
9 MBr,JBr,SDr,Hawkey;Hellcat . . 2.50
10 MBr,LW,Hawkey;Dr.Druid . . . 2.50
11 MBr,JG,BL,Hawkey;Hercules . 2.50
12 RLm,SDr,Hawkey; New
   Yellow Jacket 2.50
13 RLm,JG,Hawkey;WonderMan . 2.50
14 AM,AD,JRu,Hawkey;She-Hulk . 2.50
15 AM,Hawkey;Wasp 2.50
16 AM,DP,JA,Hawkey;
   Moondragon 2.50
17 AM,DH,DC,Hawkey;
   Sub-Mariner 2.50
18 RW,DH,Hawkey;Moondragon . 2.50
19 RW,DH,Hawkey;BlackPanther . 2.50
20 RW,DH,Hawkey;Moondragon . 2.50
Becomes:

AVENGERS SPOTLIGHT

Sleepwalker #31
© Marvel Entertainment Group

Solomon Kane #1
© Marvel Entertainment Group

SOLOMON KANE
Sept., 1985
1 F:Solomon Kane 3.00
2 .... 3.00
3 BBl,`Blades of the Brotherhood' . 3.00
4 MMi 3.00
5 `Hills of the Dead' 3.00
6 .... 3.00

SON OF SATAN
Dec., 1975–Feb., 1977
1 GK(c),JM,F:Daimon Hellstrom. . 30.00
2 Demon War,O:Possessor 20.00
3 .... 20.00
4 The Faces of Fear 15.00
5 V:Mind Star 15.00
6 A World Gone Mad 15.00
7 Mirror of Judgement 15.00
8 RH,To End in Nightmare 15.00

SOVIET SUPER SOLDIERS
1 AMe,JS,I:Redmont 4 .... 2.25

SPACEKNIGHTS
Aug., 2000
1 (of 5) JSn,R:Spaceknights 3.00
2 JSn,Terminator 3.00
3 JSn,Deathwings 3.00
4 JSn,Wraith Knights 3.00
5 JSn,concl. 3.00

SPACEMAN
Atlas, Sept., 1953
1 BEv(c),F:Speed Carter and
 the Space Sentinals 800.00
2 JMn,`Trapped in Space' 500.00
3 BEv(c),JMn,V:Ice Monster 400.00
4 JMn, A-Bomb 450.00
5 GT 400.00
6 JMn,`The Thing From Outer
 Space',Oct., 1954 .... 400.00

SPACE SQUADRON
Atlas, June, 1951
1 AyB,F:Capt. Jet Dixon,Blast,
 Dawn,Revere,Rusty Blake . . 800.00
2 GT(c), ... 650.00
3 `Planet of Madness',GT 550.00
4 .... 550.00

5 AyB 550.00
Becomes:

SPACE WORLDS
April, 1952
6 `Midnight Horror' 500.00

SPECIAL COLLECTOR'S EDITION
Dec., 1975
1 Kung-Fu,Iron Fist 10.00

SPECIAL MARVEL EDITION
Jan., 1971
1 JK,B:Thor,B:Reprints 45.00
2 JK,V:Absorbing Man 20.00
3 JK,`While a Universe
 Trembles' 20.00
4 JK,`Hammer and the Holocaust',
 E:Thor 20.00
5 JSe(c),JK,DAy,B:Sgt. Fury 20.00
6 HT(c),DAy,`Death Ray of
 Dr. Zemo' 12.00
7 DAy,V:Baron Strucker 12.00
8 JSe(c),DAy`On To Okinawa' . . 12.00
9 DAy,`Crackdown of
 Captain Flint 12.00
10 DAy 12.00
11 JK,DAy,A:Captain
 America & Bucky 12.00
12 DAy,V:Baron Strucker 12.00
13 JK/DAy(c),DAy,SD,`Too Small
 to Fight, Too Young To Die' . . 12.00
14 DAy,E:Reprints,Sgt. Fury 12.00
15 JSn,AM,I:Shang-Chi & Master of
 Kung Fu,I&O:Nayland Smith,
 Dr. Petrie 100.00
16 JSn,AM,I&O:Midnight 40.00
KingSz.Ann.#1 A:Iron Fist 18.00
Becomes:

MASTER OF KUNG FU

SPECTACULAR SCARLET SPIDER
1995
1 SB,BSz,Virtual Morality,pt.4 .... 2.25
2 SB,BSz,CyberWar,pt.4 .... 2.25

SPECTACULAR SPIDER-MAN
(Magazine) July, 1968
1 JR,JM. 125.00
2 JR,JM,V:Green Goblin 150.00

SPECTACULAR SPIDER-MAN
Dec., 1976
Prev: Peter Parker
134 SB,A:Sin-Eater,V:Electro 4.00
135 SB,A:Sin-Eater,V:Electro 3.00
136 SB,D:Sin-Eater,V:Electro 3.00
137 SB,I:Tarantula II 3.00
138 SB,A:Capt.A.,V:TarantulaII 3.00
139 SB,O:Tombstone 4.00
140 SB,A:Punisher,V:Tombstone. . . 3.50
141 SB,A:Punisher,V:Tombstone. . . 4.00
142 SB,A:Punisher,V:Tombstone. . . 4.00
143 SB,A:Punisher,D:Persuader,
 I:Lobo Brothers 4.00
144 SB,V:Boomerang 3.00
145 SB,A:Boomerang 3.00
146 SB,R:Green Goblin 5.00
147 SB,V:Hobgoblin (Demonic

Power) 12.00
148 SB,Inferno 3.00
149 SB,V:Carrion II. 5.00
150 SB,A:Tombstone,Trial
 J.Robertson 3.00
151 SB,V:Tombstone 3.00
152 SB,O:Lobo Bros.,A:Punisher,
 Tombstone 4.00
153 SB,V:Hammerhead,A:
 Tombstone 3.00
154 SB,V:Lobo Bros.,Puma 3.00
155 SB,V:Tombstone 3.00
156 SB,V:Banjo,A:Tombstone 3.00
157 SB,V:Shocker,Electro,
 A:Tombstone 3.00
158 SB,Super Spider Spec.,
 I:Cosmic Spider-Man 10.00
159 Cosmic Powers,V:Brothers
 Grimm 5.00
160 SB,A:Hydro Man,Shocker,
 Rhino,Dr.Doom 4.00
161 SB,V:Hobgoblin,Hammerhead,
 Tombstone 3.00
162 SB,V:Hobgoblin,Carrion II 3.00
163 SB,V:Hobgoblin,D:Carrion II. . . 3.00
164 SB,V:Beetle 3.00
165 SB,SDr,D:Arranger,I:Knight
 & Fogg 3.00
166 SB,O:Knight & Fogg 3.00
167 SB,D:Knight & Fogg 3.00
168 SB,A:Kingpin,Puma,
 Avengers 3.00
169 SB,I:Outlaws,A:R.Racer,
 Prowler,Puma,Sandman 3.00
170 SB,A:Avengers,Outlaws 3.00
171 SB,V:Puma 2.50
172 SB,V:Puma 2.50
173 SB,V:Puma 2.50
174 SB,A:Dr.Octopus 2.50
175 SB,A:Dr.Octopus 2.50
176 SB,I:Karona 2.50
177 SB,V:Karona,A:Mr.Fantastic . . 2.50
178 SB,B:Child Within,V:Green
 Goblin, A:Vermin 2.50
179 SB,V:Green Goblin,Vermin. . . . 2.50
180 SB,V:Green Goblin,Vermin. . . . 2.50
181 SB,V:Green Goblin 2.50
182 SB,V:Green Goblin 2.50
183 SB,V:Green Goblin 2.50
184 SB,E:Child Within,V:Green
 Goblin 2.50
185 SB,A:Frogman,White Rabbit . . 2.50
186 SB,B:FuneralArrangements
 V:Vulture 2.50

Spectacular Spider-Man #138
© Marvel Entertainment Group

Spectacular–Spellbound MARVEL Comics Values Annual

Spectacular Spider-Man #263
© Marvel Entertainment Group

187 SB,V:Vulture 2.50
188 SB,E:Funeral Arrangements
     V:Vulture 2.50
189 SB,30th Ann.,Hologram(c),
     V:Green Goblin 6.00
189a Gold 2nd printing 3.00
190 SB,V:Rhino,Harry Osborn 2.50
191 SB,Eye of the Puma 2.50
192 SB,Eye of the Puma 2.50
193 SB,Eye of the Puma 2.50
194 SB,Death of Vermin#1 . . . . 2.50
195 SB,Death of Vermin#2 . . . . 4.00
195a Dirtbag Spec,w/Dirt#2 tape . . 2.50
196 SB,Death of Vermin#3 . . . . 2.50
197 SB,A:X-Men,V:Prof.Power 2.50
198 SB,A:X-Men,V:Prof.Power 2.50
199 SB,A:X-Men,Green Goblin . . . 2.50
200 SB,V:Green Goblin,D:Harry
     Osborn,Holografx(c) 4.00
201 SB, Total Carnage,V:Carnage,
     Shriek,A:Black Cat,Venom . . . 2.00
202 SB, Total Carnage#9,A:Venom,
     V:Carnage 2.00
203 SB,Maximum Carnage#13 . . . . 2.00
204 SB,A:Tombstone 2.00
205 StG(s),SB,V:Tombstone,
     A:Black Cat 2.00
206 SB,V:Tombstone 2.00
207 SB,A:The Shroud 2.00
208 SB,A:The Shroud 2.00
209 StB,SB,I:Dead Aim,
     BU:Black Cat 2.00
210 StB,SB, V:Dead Aim,
     BU:Black Cat 2.00
211 Pursuit#2,V:Tracer 2.00
212 . . . . 2.00
213 ANo(s),V:Typhiod Mary,w/cel . 3.50
213a Newsstand Ed. 2.00
214 V:Bloody Mary 2.00
215 V:Scorpion 2.00
216 V:Scorpion. 2.00
217 V:Judas Traveller,clone 3.00
217a Foil(c),bonus stuff 5.00
218 V:Puma 2.00
219 Back from the Edge,pt.2 . . . . 3.00
220 Web of Death,pt.3 . . . . 3.00
221 Web of Death,finale 3.00
222 The Price of Truth 2.00
223 Aftershocks,pt.4 . . . . 3.00
223a enhanced cover 3.00
224 The Mark of Kaine,pt.4. . . . . . 2.50
225 SB,TDF,BSz,I:New Green
     Goblin, 48-pg. 3.00
225a 3-D HoloDisk Cover 5.00
226 SB,BSz,The Trial of Peter
     Parker,pt.4, identity revealed . . 3.00
227 TDF,SB,BSz,Maximum
     Clonage,pt.5. . . . . 2.50
228 Timebomb,pt.1 . . . . 2.50
229 Greatest Responsibility,pt.3 . . . 3.00
229a Special cover. 5.00
230 SB,Return of Spider-Man,pt.4 . 2.50
231 SB,Return of Kaine,pt.1 . . . . . . 2.50
232 . . . . 2.50
233 SB,JP,Web of Carnage,pt.4 . . . 2.50
234 SB,Blood Brothers,pt.4. . . . . . . 2.50
235 . . . . 2.50
236 . . . . 2.50
237 V:Lizard 2.50
238 V:Lizard 2.50
239 V:Lizard 2.50
240 TDz,LRs,ïBook of Revelations,î
     pt.1 (of 4) 3.00
241 Revelations epilogue 2.50
242 JMD,LRs,R:Chameleon,
     A:Kangaroo 2.50
243 JMD,LRs,R:Chameleon 2.50
244 JMD,LRs,V:Chameleon 2.50
245 JMD,LRs,V:Chameleon,
     A:Kangaroo 2.50
246 JMD,LRs,V:Kangaroo,Grizzly . . 2.50
247 JMD,LRs,F:JackO'Lantern,pt.1 . 2.50
248 JMD,LRs,DGr,F:Jack O'
     Lantern, pt.2 . . . . 2.50
249 JMD,LRs,DGr, Last Temptation
     of Flash Thompson. 2.50
250 JR, V:Original Green Goblin,
     double gatefold cover 3.50
251 JMD,LRs,DGr,V:Kraven the
     Hunter 2.50
252 JMD,LRs,DGr,V:Norman
     Osborn. 2.50
253 JMD,LRs,DGr,V:Norman Osborn,
     Gibbon, Grizzly. 2.50
254 JMD,LRs,DGr,V:Prof.Angst . . . 2.50
255 JMD,LRs,DGr,Spider-Hunt,pt.4
     x-over, double size 3.00
256 JMD,LRs,DGr,Identity Crisis
     prelude, A:Prodigy 2.50
257 JMD,LRs,DGr,Identity Crisis,
     as Prodigy, V:Conundrum. 2.50
258 JMD,LRs,DGa,as Prodigy 2.50
259 RSt,LRs,DGa,V:Hobgoblin 2.50
260 JR, RSt,LRs,DGa,Green Goblin
     vs. Hobgoblin 2.50
261 RSt,LRs,AM,Goblins at the
     Gate,pt.3 . . . . 2.50
262 JBy, AM, LRs, The Gathering of
     the Five, pt.4 (of 5) x-over 2.50
263 JBy,AM,LRs,The Final
     Chapter,pt.3 x-over. 2.50
Ann.#8 MBa,RLm, TD, Evolutionary
     Wars,O:Gwen Stacy Clone 7.00
Ann.#9 DR,MG,DJu,MBa,Atlantis
     Attacks. 4.00
Ann.#10 SLi(c),RB,MM,TM,RA . . . 6.00
Ann.#11 EL(c),RWi,Vib.Vendetta . . . 3.00
Ann.#12 Hero Killers#2,A:New
     Warriors,BU:Venom 4.50
Ann.#13 I:Noctune,w/Card 3.25
Ann.#14 V:Green Goblin. 2.95
Super-Size Spec.#1 Planet of the
     Symbiotes,pt.4,64-pg.flip-book . 3.95
Minus 1 Spec., JMD,LRs,DGr,
     flashback, F:Flash Thompson . . 2.00
TPB rep. 80-pg. (2002) 12.95

SPECTACULAR SPIDER-MAN
Marvel June 2003
1 HuR,V:Venom,pt.1 . . . . 2.25
2 HuR,V:Venom,pt.2 . . . . 2.25
3 HuR,V:Venom,pt.3 . . . . 2.25
4 HuR,V:Venom,pt.4 . . . . 2.25
5 HuR,V:Venom,pt.5 . . . . 2.25
6 HuR,Should Venom live? 2.25
7 . . . . 2.25

SPEEDBALL
Sept., 1988
1 SD,JG,O:Speedball 2.50
2 SD,JG,V:Sticker,GraffitiGorillas . . 2.50
3 SD,V:Leaper Logan 2.50
4 SD,DA,Ghost Springdale High . . 2.50
5 SD,V:Basher. 2.50
6 SD,V:Bug-Eyed Voice 2.50
7 SD,V:Harlequin Hit Man 2.50
8 SD,V:Bonehead Gang 2.50
9 SD,V:Nathan Boder 2.50
10 SD,V:Mutated Pigs,Killer
    Chickens, last issue 2.50

SPELLBOUND
Atlas, March, 1952
1 AyB(c),'Step into my Coffin' . . 800.00
2 BEv,RH,'Horror Story',
   A:Edgar A. Poe 500.00
3 RH(c),OW 400.00
4 RH,Decapitation story 400.00
5 AyB,BEv,JM,'Its in the Bag' . . 400.00
6 AyB,BK,'The Man Who Couldn't
   be Killed' 400.00
7 AyB,BEv,JMn,'Don't Close
   the Door' 300.00
8 BEv(c),RH,JSt,DAy,
   'The Operation' 300.00
9 BEv(c),RH,'The Death of
   Agatha Slurl' 300.00
10 AyB,BEv,RH,JMn(c),'The Living
   Mummy'. 300.00
11 'The Empty Coffin' 250.00
12 RH,'My Friend the Ghost' . . . 250.00
13 JM,AyB,'The Dead Men' 250.00
14 BEv(c),RH,JMn,'Close Shave' 250.00
15 AyB,CI,'Get Out of my
   Graveyard'. 250.00
16 RH,BEv,JF,JSt,'Behind
   the Door' 250.00
17 BEv(c),GC,BK,'Goodbye
   Forever' 250.00
18 BEv(c),JM 250.00
19 BEv(c),BP,'Witch Doctor' . . . 250.00
20 RH(c),BP 250.00
21 RH(c) 200.00
22 . . . . 200.00
23 . . . . 200.00

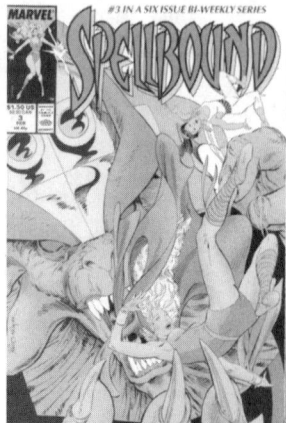

Spellbound #3
© Marvel Entertainment Group

CVA Page 310   All comics prices listed are for *Near Mint* condition.

Comics Values Annual — MARVEL — Spellbound–Spider-Man

24 JMn(c),JR 175.00	
25 JO,AyB,`Look into my Eyes'. . 175.00	
26 JR,AyB,`The Things in the Box' 175.00	
27 JMn,JR,AyB,`Trap in the Mirage'. 175.00	
28 BEv 175.00	
29 JSe(c),SD 200.00	
30 BEv(c) 175.00	
31 . . . . 175.00	
32 BP,AyB,`Almost Human'. 175.00	
33 AT 175.00	
34 June, 1957. . . . . 175.00	

SPELLBOUND
Jan., 1988

1 thru 5 . . . . @2.50
6 double-size. 3.00

SPIDER-GIRL
Aug., 1998

0 TDF,RF,BSz, cont. from What-If? #105, Peter & Mary Jane's daughter. 5.00
1 TDF,PO,AW, F:Mayday Parker, V:Mr. Nobody 8.00
2 TDF,PO,AW,V:Crazy Eight & Darkdevil 4.00
2a variant cover. 4.00
3 TDF,PO,AW,A:Fantastic Five . . 2.50
4 TDF,PO,AW,turning points 2.50
5 TDF,PO.AW,Ghosts of the Past. . 2.50
6 TDF,PO,AW,Majority Rules 2.50
7 TDF,PO,AW,Last Days of Spider-Man 2.50
8 TDF,PO,AW,A:Spider-Man, Uneasy Allies 2.50
8a autographed 20.00
9 TDF,PO,AW,Critical Choices . . . 2.50
10 TDF,PO,AW,Incredible Journeys 2.50
11 TDF,PO.AW,V:Spider-Man 2.50
12 TDF,PO,AW,A:Darkdevil 2.50
13 TDF,Po,AW,Joins A-Next 2.50
14 TDF,PO,AW,Bloody Reunions x-over. 2.50
15 TDF,PO,AW,A:Speedball 2.50
16 TDF,PO,AW 2.50
17 TDF,PO,AW,48-pg. 3.00
18 TDF,SB,RF,A:Buzz. 2.50
19 TDF,AW,PO,V:A-Next foes 2.50
20 TDF,AW,PO,V:Green Goblin 2.50
21 TDF,AW,PO,V:Earthshaker. 2.25
22 TDF,AW,PO,Darkdevil 2.25
23 TDF,AW,PO,Basketball 2.25
24 TDF,AW,PO,Dragonfist. 2.25
25 TDF,AW,PO,Savage Six. 3.50
26 TDF,AW,PO,Phil Urich 2.25
27 TDF,AW, PO,Parker/Osborn war concl.. . . . . 2.25
28 TDF,AW,PO,V:Raptor. 2.25
29 TDF,AW,PO,A:Nova 2.25
30 TDF,AW,PO,V:Avengers. 2.25
31 TDF,AW,PO,V:Avengers. 2.25
32 TDF,PO,Steel Spider 2.25
33 TDF,AW,PO,A:Spider-Man 2.25
34 TDF,AW,PO,A:Fant.Five. 2.25
35 TDF,AW,PO,V:Canis 2.25
36 TDF,AW,PO,V:Canis 2.25
37 TDF,AW,PO,V:Green Goblin. . . . 2.25
38 TDF,AW,PO,V:Green Goblin. . . . 2.25
39 TDF,AW,PO,Green Goblin 2.25
40 TDF,AW,PO,Death in the family . 2.25
41 TDF,AW,PO,V:Canis,'Nuff Said . . 2.25
42 TDF,RF,mothers. 2.25
43 TDF,AW,PO,original Spider-Man 2.25
44 TDF,AW,PO,F:Ben Reilly 2.25
45 TDF,AW,PO,A:Big Brain,H.Torch 2.25
46 TDF,AW,PO,F:Fantastic Five . . . 2.25
47 TDF,RF,V:Apox,+ Chapter 1 . . . . 2.25
48 TDF,AW,PO,Spider-Man,Kaine. . 2.25
49 TDF,AW,PO,V:Green Goblin. . . . 2.25
50 TDF,AW,PO,48-pg. 4.00
51 CJ, ... 2.25
52 TDF,AW,RF 2.25
53 TDF,AW,PO 2.25
54 TDF,AW,PO,Serpent,pt.1 . . . . . . 2.25
55 TDF,AW,PO,Serpent,pt.2 . . . . . . 2.25
56 TDF,AW,PO,Serpent,pt.3 . . . . . . 2.25
57 TDF,AW,PO,Serpent,pt.4 . . . . . . 2.25
58 TDF,AW,PO,Serpent,pt.5 . . . . . . 2.25
59 TDF,RF,Serpent,pt.6 . . . . 3.00
60 TDF,RF,finale. 3.00
61 TDF,RF,Marked for Death,pt.1 . . 3.00
62 TDF,RF,Marked for Death,pt.2 . . 3.00
63 TDF,RF,Marked for Death,pt.3 . . 3.00
64 TDF,RF,Marked for Death,pt.4 . . 3.00
65 TDF,RF,Marked for Death,pt.5 . . 3.00
66 TDF,RF,Marked for Death,pt.6 . . 3.00
Ann.#1 TDF,PO,AW,A:Green Goblin 6.00
TPB rep. #1 & #2 . . . . 9.95
TPB Spider-Girl,208-page. 19.95

SPIDER-GIRL PRESENTS: THE BUZZ
May, 2000

1 (of 3) TDF,RF,SB 3.00
2 TDF,RF,SB,A:Spider-Girl. 3.00
3 TDF,RF,SB,Dr.Jade. 3.00

SPIDER-GIRL PRESENTS: DARKDEVIL
Sept., 2000

1 (of 3) TDF,RF,AM,Kingpin 3.00
2 TDF,RF,AM,O:Darkdevil 3.00
3 TDF,RF,AM, concl. 3.00

SPIDER-MAN
Aug., 1990

1 TM Purple Web(c),V:Lizard, A:Calypso,B:Torment 5.00
1a Silver Web(c) 6.00
1b Bag,Purple Web 9.00
1c Bag,Silver Web 20.00
1d 2nd print,Gold(c). 5.00
1e 2nd print Gold UPC(rare) . . . 150.00
1f Platinum Ed. 135.00
2 TM,V:Lizard,A:Calypso 6.00
3 TM,V:Lizard,A:Calypso 6.00
4 TM,V:Lizard,A:Calypso 6.00
5 TM,V:Lizard,A:Calypso, E:Torment 6.00
6 TM,A:Ghost Rider,V:Hobgoblin . . 6.00
7 TM,A:Ghost Rider,V:Hobgoblin . . 6.00
8 TM,B:Perceptions,A:Wolverine I:Wendigo IV 6.00
9 TM,A:Wolverine,Wendigo 6.00
10 TM,RLd,SW,JLe(i),A:Wolv. 6.00
11 TM,A:Wolverine, Wendigo. 6.00
12 TM,E:Perceptions,A:Wolv. 6.00
13 TM,V:Morbius,R:Black Cost. . . . 6.00
14 TM,V:Morbius,A:Black Cost. 6.00
15 EL,A:Beast 6.00
16 TM,RLd,A:X-Force,V:Juggernaut, Black Tom,cont.in X-Force#4 . . 6.00
17 RL,AW,A:Thanos,Death 4.00
18 EL,B:Return of the Sinister Six, A:Hulk 3.50
19 EL,A:Hulk,Deathlok 3.50
20 EL,A:Nova 3.50
21 EL,A:Hulk,Deathlok,Solo 3.50
22 EL,A:Ghost Rider,Hulk 3.00
23 EL,E:Return of the Sinister Six, A:Hulk, G.Rider,Deathlok,FF . . . 4.00
24 Infinity War,V:Hobgoblin, Demogoblin 3.00
25 CMa,A:Excalibur,V:Arcade 3.00
26 RF,MBa,Hologram(c),30th Anniv. I:New Burglar 5.00
27 MR,Handgun issue 3.00
28 MR,Handgun issue 3.00
29 CMa,Ret.to Mad Dog Ward#1 . . 3.00
30 CMa,Ret.to Mad Dog Ward#2 . . 3.00
31 CMa,Ret.to Mad Dog Ward#3 . . 3.00
32 BMc,A:Punisher,V:Master of Vengeance. 3.00
33 BMc,A:Punisher,V:Master of Vengeance. 3.00
34 BMc,A:Punisher,V:Master of Vengeance. 3.00
35 TL,Total Carnage#4,V:Carnage, Shriek,A:Venom,Black Cat 3.00
36 TL,Total Carnage#8,V:Carnage, A:Venom,Morbius 3.00
37 TL,Total Carnage#12, V:Carnage 3.00
38 thru 40 KJ,V:Electro 3.00
41 TKa(s),JaL,I:Platoon, A:Iron Fist 3.00
42 TKa(s),JaL,V:Platoon, A:Iron Fist 3.00
43 TKa(s),JaL,V:Platoon, A:Iron Fist 3.00
44 HMe(s),TL,V:Hobgoblin 3.00
45 HMe(s),TL,SHa,Pursuit#1, V:Chameleon 2.50
46 HMe(s),TL,V:Hobgoblin,w/cel . . . 3.25
46a Newsstand Ed. 2.00
47 TL,SHa,V:Demogoblin 2.50
48 TL,SHa,V:Hobgoblin, D:Demogoblin 2.50
49 TL,SHa,I:Coldheart 2.50
50 TL,SHa,I:Grim Hunter,foil(c) 5.00
50a newsstand ed. 2.50
51 TL,SHa,Power,pt.3,foil(c) 4.00
51a newsstand ed. 2.50
52 TL,SHa,Spide-clone,V:Venom . . 2.50
53 TL,SHa,Clone,V:Venom 2.50
54 Web of Life,pt.3 . . . . 3.00
55 Web of Life,finale. 2.50
56 Smoke and Mirrors 2.50
57 Aftershocks,pt.1 . . . . 2.50
57a enhanced cover. 3.00
58 The Mark of Kaine,pt.3 . . . . 2.50
59 F:Travellor,Host 2.50
60 TL,SHa,HMa,The Trial of Peter Parker,pt.3 . . . . 2.50
61 TL,Maximum Clonage,pt.4 . . . . . 2.50
62 HMe,TL,Exiled,pt.3 . . . . 2.50
63 HMe,TL,Greatest

Spider-Man #57
© Marvel Entertainment Group

CVA Page 311

All comics prices listed are for *Near Mint* condition.

Spider-Man–Spider-Man / MARVEL / Comics Values Annual

Responsibility,pt.2........... 2.50
64 HMe,JR2,Return of
   Spider-Man,pt.3............ 2.50
65 HMe,JR2,AW,Media
   Blizzard,pt.3............... 2.50
66 HMe,JR2,Return of Kaine,pt.4 . 2.50
67 HMe,JR2,Web of Carnage,pt.3 . 2.50
68 HMe,JR2,AW,Blood
   Brothers,pt.3 .... 2.50
69 HMe,JR2,Blood Brothers
   aftermath 2.50
70 HMe,JR2,A:Onslaught 3.00
71 HMe,JR2,.................... 3.00
72 HMe,JR2,Onslaught saga 3.00
73 HMe,JR2 .... 3.00
74 HMe,JR2,AW,A:Daredevil,
   V:Fortunato 3.00
75 HMe,JR2,Revelations, pt.4 .... 3.50
76 HMe,JR2,SHa,Post-Onslaught
   world,I:Shoc 2.50
77 HMe,JR2,SHa,V:Morbius 2.50
Becomes:

PETER PARKER, SPIDER-MAN
78 HMe,JR2,SHa,F:Mary Jane
   Parker 2.50
79 HMe,JR2,SHa,V:Hydra,A:Captain
   Arthur Stacy................ 2.50
80 HMe,JR2,SHa,V:S.H.O.C. 2.50
81 HMe,JR2,SHa,V:Shang-Chi,pt.1. 2.50
82 HMe,JR2,SHa,Anti-Mutant
   Movement 2.50
83 HMe,JR2,SHa,V:Morbius 2.50
85 HMe,JR2,SHa,V:Friends of
   Humanity 2.50
86 HMe,JR2,SHa,F:Jimmy Six,
   Hammerhead 2.50
87 HMe,JR2,SHa,A:Trapster &
   Shocker 2.50
88 HMe,JR2,SHa,Spider-Man is
   Public Enemy #1 .... 2.50
89 HMe,JR2,SHa,Spider-Hunt,pt.3
   x-over..................... 3.00
90 HMe,JR2,SHa,Identity Crisis
   prelude.................... 2.50
91 HMe,JR2,SHa,Identity Crisis,
   as Dusk 2.50
92 HMe,JR2,as Dusk,V:Trapster .. 2.50
93 HMe,JR2,JS,R:Ghost Rider 2.50
94 HMe,JR2,SHa,Who wasJoeyZ?. 2.50
95 HMe,JR2,SHa,Trapped in
   elevator shaft 2.50
96 HMe,JR2,SHa,The Gathering of
   the Five (pt. 3 of 5)x-over 2.50
97 HMe,JR2,SHa,JBy(c),The Final
   Chapter,pt.2 x-over.......... 2.50
98 HMe,JR2,SHa,JBy(c),The Final
   Chapter,pt.4 x-over.......... 2.50
98a alternate JBy(c) (1:2) 2.50
Minus 1 Spec., HMe,JR2,SHa,
   flashback, A:Stacys 2.50
Ann.'97 Simon Garth—Zombie 3.50
Ann.'98 HMe, Spider-Man/Elektra,
   V:The Silencer, 48-pg. 3.00
Spec. Chaos in Calgary 2.50
Spec. Double Trouble........... 2.50
Spec. Hit and Run, Canadian 2.50
Spec. Skating on Thin Ice....... 2.50
Spec. Trial of Venom,UNICEF.... 15.00
Spec.#1 Spider-Man (2000) 2.50
Spec. Spider-Man vs. Punisher.... 3.00
Spec. Year in Review(1999)48-pg. . 3.00
Holiday Spec.'95 .... 3.50
Sup.Sz.Spec#1 Planet of the
   Symbiotes, pt.2;
   flipbook F:Scarlet Spider...... 4.00
Giant-Sized CCI,JBy............ 4.00
1-shot Spider-Man Startling Stories:
   Megalomaniacal Spider-Man .. 3.00
Spec.#1 Spider-Man/Daredevil 3.00

GN Fear Itself................. 12.95
GN Nothing Stops Juggernaut 4.00
GN Parallel Lives 9.00
GN JMD,MZ,Soul of the Hunter ... 6.00
GN Spider-Man: Made Men
   HMe,gangster epic (1998) 6.00
GN Spider-Man ParallelLives(2002) 5.95
GN Sweet Charity,Scorpion,64-pg. . 4.95
TPB Assasination Plot 15.00
TPB Carnage 7.00
TPB Cosmic Adventures........ 20.00
TPB Death of Gwen Stacy 15.00
TPB Hooky.................... 7.00
TPB Identity Crisis 20.00
TPB Maximum Carnage 25.00
TPB Origin of the Hobgoblin 15.00
TPB Return of the Sinister Six ... 16.00
TPB Spider-Man: Revelations,JR2,
   rep. +14 new pages (1997)... 12.00
TPB Round Robin.............. 16.00
TPB Saga of the Alien Costume .. 14.00
   2nd printing 13.00
TPB Spider-Man vs. Venom 10.00
TPB Torment Rep.#1-#5 .... 13.00
TPB Venom Returns............ 13.00
TPB Very Best of Spider-Man.... 16.00
TPB The Wedding 13.00
TPB Invasion Spider Slayers 16.00
TPB Clone Genesis 17.00
TPB V:Green Goblin 16.00
TPB Spider-Man'sGreatestVillains. 16.00
TPB Spider-Man vs.DocOc,
   176-pg.................... 18.00
TPB Kraven's Last Hunt (2001).. 16.00
TPB Torment,128-page (2001) ... 16.00
TPB Death of Gwen Stacy (2001). 15.00
TPB Visionaries: Todd McFarlane . 20.00
TPB Revenge of the Green Goblin 16.95
TPB Spider-Man: The Wedding... 15.95
TPB Kraven's Last Hunt 15.95
TPB Death of Gwen Stacy, rep. .. 13.00
TPB Legends (2003)........... 20.00

SPIDER-MAN ADVENTURES
1994–96
1 From animated series......... 2.25
1a foil (c)..................... 3.00
2 Animated Adventures 2.25
3 V:Spider-Slayer 2.25
4 Animated Adventures 2.25
5 V:Mysterio 2.25
6 V:Kraven 2.25
7 V:Doctor Octopus 2.25
8 O:Venom,pt.1 .... 2.25
9 O:Venom,pt.2 .... 2.25
10 V:Venom 2.25
11 V:Hobgoblin................. 2.25
12 V:Hobgoblin................. 2.25
13 V:Chameleon................ 2.25
14 V:Doc Octopus 2.25
15 Doc Conners 2.25
TPB Rep.#1-#5, 112-pg......... 8.95

SPIDER-MAN & AMAZING FRIENDS
Dec., 1981
1 DSp,A:Iceman,I:Firestar 10.00

SPIDER-MAN & WOLVERINE
Marvel June 2003
1 (of 4) Stuff of Legends 3.00
2 .... 3.00
3 .... 3.00
4 concl........................ 3.00

SPIDER-MAN/BADROCK
Marvel/Maximum Press 1997
1 x-over, pt.1.................. 3.00
2 x-over, pt. 2 .... 3.00

SPIDER-MAN/BATMAN
1995
1 JMD,MBa,MFm,V:Carnage,Joker 6.00

Spider-Man/Black Cat #1
© Marvel Entertainment Group

SPIDER-MAN/BLACK CAT: THE EVIL THAT MEN DO
June, 2002
1 (of 5) KSm,TyD............... 3.00
2 KSm,TyD 3.00
3 KSm,TyD 3.00
4 KSm,TyD,concl............... 3.00
5 KSm,TyD,concl.,pt.2.......... 3.00

SPIDER-MAN: BLUE
May, 2002
1 (of 6) JLb,TSe,Green Goblin.... 3.50
2 JLb,TSe,Gwen Stacy,Rhino 3.50
3 JLb,TSe,Gwen & Mary Jane.... 3.50
4 JLb,TSe,college years 3.50
5 JLb,TSe,..................... 3.50
6 JLb,TSe,concl................ 3.50

SPIDER-MAN, CHAPTER 1
Oct., 1998
1 (of 13) JBy,formative years..... 2.50
1a signed 20.00
2 JBy,A:Fantastic Four.......... 2.50
2a variant JBy cover 5.00
2b signed, both covers......... 30.00
3 JBy,V:J.Jonah Jameson 2.50
4 JBy,V:Dr.Octopus & Dr.Doom ... 2.50
5 JBy,V:Lizard 2.50
6 JBy,V:Electro 2.50
7 JBy,V:Mysterio 2.50
8 JBy,V:Green Goblin 2.50
9 JBy,V:Circus of Crime......... 2.50
10 JBy,V:Green Goblin 2.50
11 JBy,V:Giant-Man 2.50
12 JBy,V:Sandman, double size
   final issue................. 4.00
Spec.#0 JBy,O:Sandman,Vulture
   & Lizard 2.50

SPIDER-MAN CLASSICS
1993–94
1 rep.Amazing Fantasy#15 ...... 2.50
2 thru 11 rep.Amaz.SpM#1-#10 . @2.50
12 rep.Amaz.SpM#11 .... 2.50
13 rep.Amaz.SpM#12 .... 2.50
14 rep.Amaz.SpM#13 .... 2.50
15 rep.Amaz.SpM#14,w/cel 3.25
15a Newsstand Ed. 2.50

SPIDER-MAN COMICS MAGAZINE
Jan., 1987
1 .... 7.00
2 thru 13 .... @6.00

SPIDER-MAN: DEAD MAN'S HAND
1997
1-shot, RSt,DaR,JeM,V:Carrion ... 3.00

SPIDER-MAN: DEATH & DESTINY
June, 2000
1 (of 3) LW,RCa,F:Gwen Stacy ... 3.00
2 LW,RCa,Doctor Octopus........ 3.00
3 LW,RCa,concl. 3.00
Spec.Death of Gwen Stacy,64-pg.
  rep. of Amaz.Sp-M #88-#90 ... 3.50

SPIDER-MAN: THE FINAL ADVENTURE
1995–96
1 FaN,DaR,Clv,I:Tendril 3.00
2 FaN,DaR,JAl,V:Tendril 3.00
3 FaN,DaR,JAl,V:Tendril 3.00
4 FaN,DaR,JAl,V:Tendril,concl. .. 3.00

SPIDER-MAN: FRIENDS AND ENEMIES
1995
1 V:Metahumes 2.00
2 A:Nova,Darkhawk,Speedball.... 2.00
3 V:Metahumes 2.00
4 F:Metahumes 2.00

SPIDER-MEN: FUNERAL FOR AN OCTOPUS
1995
1 Doc Oc Dead 2.50
2 A:Sinister Six 2.00
3 Final Issue 2.00

SPIDER-MAN/GEN13
Marvel/Wildstorm 1996
1-shot PDd,SI,CaS x-over 5.00

SPIDER-MAN: HOBGOBLIN LIVES
1997
1 (of 3) RSt,RF,GP 2.50
2 RSt,RF,GP,Who was the original
  Hobgoblin?.................. 2.50
3 RSt,RF,GP,Original identity
  revealed.................... 2.50
TPB RF(c), series rep. 15.00

MARVEL

Spider-Man Hobgoblin Lives #3
© Marvel Entertainment Group

SPIDER-MAN: GET KRAVEN
June, 2002
1 (of 7) F:Alyosha Kravinoff 3.00
2 wants to make a movie........ 2.25
3 thru 6 JQ(c) .... @2.25

SPIDER-MAN: LEGEND OF THE SPIDER-CLAN
Marvel Mangaverse Oct., 2002
1 (of 3) 2.25
2 F:Manga Daredevil............ 2.25
3 F:Manga Green Govlin 2.25
4 .... 2.25
5 concl. 2.25

SPIDER-MAN: LIFELINE
Feb., 2001
1 (of 3) FaN,SR,BWi, ... 3.00
2 FaN,SR,BWi,V:Hammerhead ... 3.00
3 FaN,SR,BWi,concl............ 3.00

SPIDER-MAN: THE MANGA
Black & White, Oct., 1997
Bi-weekly
1 imported, translated 4.00
2 .... 3.00
3 V:Elektro 3.00
4 V:Lizard 3.00
5 V:Lizard 3.00
6 V:Lizard, concl.............. 3.00
7 V:Kangaroo 3.00
8 V:Kangaroo 3.00
9 V:Kangaroo 3.00
10 Imposter Spider-Man 3.00
11 Real Spider-Man returns 3.00
12 Name dragged through the mud 3.00
13 V:Mysterio.................. 3.00
14 V:Mysterio.................. 3.00
15 V:Mysterio, double size 4.00
16 Human side of Japanese
  Spider-Man 3.00
17 Human side concl............ 3.00
18 Human side concl............ 3.00
19 Spidey's vacation........... 3.00
20 and 21 .... @3.00
22 Woman who creates blizzards .. 3.00
23 Secrets of the Ice Woman 3.00

Spider-Man: Class.–Power

24 Blood donated 3.00
25 V:Mitsuo Kitano 3.00
26 Mitsuo Kitano insane 3.00
27 Yu refuses costume 3.00
28 JMd(c), Yu puts on costume.... 3.00
29 JMd(c), Yu vs. Kitano....... 3.00
30 Yu vs. Kitano 3.00
31 .... 3.00
32 Yu escapes 3.00
33 V:Motorcyclists 3.00
34 thru 37 .... @3.00

SPIDER-MAN: MAXIMUM CLONAGE
1995
Alpha Maximum Clonage,pt.1 ..... 5.50
Omega TL,Maximum Clonage,pt.6 . 4.95

SPIDER-MAN MEGAZINE
1994–95
1 thru 4 rep.................. @3.00
5 Vision rep. 3.00
6 V:Thing & Torch, rep. 3.00

SPIDER-MAN: THE MOVIE
April, 2002
GN StL,AD,photo(c), 48-pg. 5.95
TPB movie + stories, 112-pg. 12.95

Spider-Man Mutant Agenda #1
© Marvel Entertainment Group

SPIDER-MAN: MUTANT AGENDA
0 thru 2 Paste in Book .... @2.25
3 Paste in Book............... 2.25

SPIDER-MAN: THE MYSTERIO MANIFESTO
Nov., 2000
1 (of 3) TDF,BMc,LW 3.00
2 TDF,BMc,LW 3.00
3 TDF,BMc,LW,concl............. 3.00

SPIDER-MAN: POWER OF TERROR
1995
1 R:Silvermane,A:Deathlok 2.25
2 V:Silvermane 2.25

All comics prices listed are for *Near Mint* condition.

Spider-Man: Power–Vs.

3 New Scorpion 2.25
4 V:Silvermane 2.25

SPIDER-MAN/PUNISHER
Part 1 TL,A:Tombstone 3.00
Part 2 TL,A:Tombstone 3.00

SPIDER-MAN/PUNISHER/ SABERTOOTH: DESIGNER GENES
1 SMc,Foil(c) 9.50

SPIDER-MAN: QUALITY OF LIFE
May, 2002
1 (of 4) V:The Lizard, 40-pg. 3.00
2 the Yith. 3.00
3 V:The Lizard 3.00
4 concl 3.00
TPB series rep 13.00

SPIDER-MAN: REDEMPTION
1996
1 thru 4 JMD,MZ,BMc, Mary Jane arrested for Murder . . . . @2.25

SPIDER-MAN: REVENGE OF THE GREEN GOBLIN
Aug., 2000
1 (of 3) RCa,LW,RSt, R:Norman Osborn 3.00
2 LW,RSt,F:Norman Osborn 3.00
3 RSt,RF,PO, concl 3.00

SPIDER-MAN SAGA
Nov., 1991
1 SLi(c),History from Amazing Fantasy #15-Amaz.SpM #100. . 3.25
2 SLi(c),Amaz.SpM #101-#175 . . . 3.25
3 Amaz.SpM #176-#238 . . . . 3.25
4 Amaz.SpM #239-#300 . . . . 3.25

SPIDER-MAN SUPER SIZE SPECIAL
1 Planet of the Symbiotes,pt.2 . . . 3.95

SPIDER-MAN TEAM-UP
1995–96
1 MWa,KeL,V:Hellfire Club 3.00
2 thru 4 . . . . @3.00
5 SvG,DaR,JFr,F:Gambit, Howard the Duck 3.00
6 JMD,LHa,F:Hulk & Doctor Strange 3.00
7 KBk,SB,F:Thunderbolts 3.00

SPIDER-MAN: THE ARACHNIS PROJECT
1984–95
1 Wld, beginnings 2.25
2 Wld,V:Diggers 2.25
3 Wld,V:Jury 2.25
4 Wld,V:Life Foundation 2.25
5 Wld,V:Jury 2.25

SPIDER-MAN: THE CLONE JOURNALS
1-shot (1995) 2.25

MARVEL

SPIDER-MAN: THE JACKAL FILES
1 Files of the Jackal (1995) 2.25

SPIDER-MAN: THE LOST YEARS
1995
0 JMD,JR2,LSh,64-pg.,rep. 4.00
1 History of Kaine,Ben. 3.00
2 JMD,JR2,KJ,Kaine & Ben 3.00
3 Ben vs. Kaine 3.00

SPIDER-MAN: THE PARKER YEARS
1995
1 JR2,JPi,F:The Real Clone 2.50

Spider-Man 2099 #25
© Marvel Entertainment Group

SPIDER-MAN 2099
1992–96
1 RL,AW,I:Spider-Man 2099 . . . . . 4.00
2 RL,AW,O:Spider-Man 2099 . . . . . 3.00
3 RL,AW,V:Venture 2.50
4 RL,AW,I:Specialist, A:Doom 2099 . . . . 2.25
5 RL,AW,V:Specialist 2.25
6 RL,AW,I:New Vulture 2.25
7 RL,AW,Vulture of 2099 . . . . 2.25
8 RL,AW,V:New Vulture 2.25
9 KJo,V:Alchemax 2.25
10 RL,AW,O:Wellvale Home 2.25
11 RL,AW,V:S.I.E.G.E. 2.25
12 RL,AW,w/poster 2.25
13 RL,AW,V:Thanatos 2.25
14 PDd(s),RL(c),TGb,Downtown . . 2.25
15 PDd(s),RL,I:Thor 2099, Heimdall 2099 . . . . 2.25
16 PDd(s),RL,Fall of the Hammer #1 . . . . 2.25
17 PDd(s),RL,V:Bloodsword 2.25
18 PDd(s),RLm,V:Lyla 2.25
19 PDd(s),RL,w/card 2.25
20 PDd(s),RL,Crash & Burn 2.25
21 V:Gangs 2.25
22 V:Gangs 2.25
23 RL,I:Risque 3.00
24 Kasey 2.25
25 A:Hulk 2099, dbl-size,foil(c) . . . 4.00
25a Newsstand ed. 2.50
26 V:Headhunter, Travesty 2.25
27 V:Travesty 2.25

Comics Values Annual

28 V:Travesty 2.25
29 V:Foragers 2.25
30 V:Flipside 2.25
31 I:Dash 2.25
Becomes:

SPIDER-MAN 2099 A.D.
32 I:Morgue 2.25
33 One Nation Under Doom 2.25
34 V:Alchemex 2.25
35 . . . . 2.25
36a Spider-Man 2099(c) 2.25
36b Venom 2099(c) 2.25
37a Venom 2099 . . . . 2.25
37b variant cover 2.25
38 . . . . 2.25
39 A:Venom 2099 . . . . 2.25
40 V:Goblin 2099 . . . . 2.25
41 and 42 . . . . @2.25
43 V:Sub-Mariner 2099 . . . . 2.25
Ann.#1 PDd(s),RL 3.00
Spec.#1 I:3 new villains 4.00

SPIDER-MAN UNLIMITED
1993
1 RLm,Maximun Carnage #1, I:Shriek,R:Carnage 5.00
2 RLm,Maximum Carnage #14 . . . 4.50
3 RLm,O:Doctor Octopus. 4.50
4 RLm,V:Mystrerio,Rhino 4.25
5 RLm,A:Human Torch, I:Steel Spider 4.25
6 RLm,A:Thunderstrike 4.25
7 RLm,A:Clone 4.25
8 Tom Lyle 4.25
9 The Mark of Kaine,pt.5 . . . . 4.25
10 SwM,Exiled,pt.4 . . . . 4.25
11 FaN,V:Black Cat 4.25
12 Blood Brother,tie-in 4.25
13 . . . . 3.25
14 JoB, an ally dies 3.25
15 TDF,JoB,F:Puma 3.25
16 cont. from X-Force #64 . . . . . . 3.25
17 JoB, Revelations, sequel 3.25
18 TDF,JoB,F:Doctor Octopus . . . 3.25
19 JoB,F:Lizard 3.25
20 JoB,A:Hannibal King, V:Lilith . . . 3.25
21 MD2,Frankenstein Monster Lives 3.25
22 MD2,V:The Scorpion 3.25

SPIDER-MAN UNIVERSE
Jan., 2000
1 rep. 3 stories, 80-pg. 5.00
2 rep. 3 stories, 80-pg. 5.00
3 rep. 3 stories, 80-pg. 5.00
4 rep. 3 stories, 80-pg. 5.00
5 rep. 3 stories, 80-pg. 5.00
6 rep. 3 stories, 80-pg 5.00
7 thru 9 rep. 3 stories, 80-pg . . . @4.00

SPIDER-MAN UNLIMITED
Nov., 1999
1 cartoon, tie-in 2.25
2 cartoon, tie-in 2.25
3 cartoon, tie-in 2.25
4 Counter-Earth 2.25
5 F:Wolverine 2.25

SPIDER-MAN UNMASKED
1996
1-shot 64-pg. information source . . 6.00

SPIDER-MAN VS. DRACULA
1994
1 rep. 2.25

MARVEL

Spider-Man–Spidey

SPIDER-MAN VS. VENOM
1990
1 TM(c) 8.95

SPIDER-MAN: THE VENOM AGENDA
Nov., 1997
1-shot LHa,TL, J. Jonah Jameson,
V:Venom 3.00

SPIDER-MAN VS. WOLVERINE
1990
1 MBr,AW,D:Ned Leeds(the original Hobgoblin),V:Charlie....... 25.00
1a reprint................... 5.00

SPIDER-MAN: WEB OF DOOM
1994
1 3-part series............... 2.25
2 Spidey falsely accused...... 2.25
3 conclusion 2.25

SPIDER-MAN & X-FACTOR: SHADOW GAMES
1 PB,I:Shadowforce........... 2.25
2 PB,V:Shadowforce 2.25
3 PB,V:Shadowforce, final issue . 2.25

SPIDER-WOMAN
April, 1978
1 CI,TD,O:Spider-Woman 25.00
2 CI,TD,I:Morgan LeFey 6.00

Spider-Woman #25
© Marvel Entertainment Group

3 CI,TD,I:Brothers Grimm 6.00
4 CI,TD,V:Hangman 6.00
5 CI,TD,Nightmares............ 6.00
6 CI,A:Werewolf By Night 7.00
7 CI,SL,AG,V:Magnus 6.00
8 CI,AG,'Man Who Would Not Die' 6.00
9 CI,AG,A:Needle,Magnus....... 6.00
10 CI,AG,I:Gypsy Moth......... 6.00
11 CI,AG,V:Brothers Grimm 6.00
12 CI,AG,V:Brothers Grimm 6.00
13 CI,AG,A:Shroud............. 6.00
14 BSz(c),CI,AG,A:Shroud 6.00
15 BSz(c),CI,AG,A:Shroud 6.00
16 BSz(c),CI,AG,V:Nekra 6.00
17 CI,Death Plunge 6.00
18 CI,A:Flesh................. 6.00
19 CI,A:Werewolf By Night,
V:Enforcer 7.00
20 FS,A:Spider-Man............ 7.00
21 FS,A:Bounty Hunter......... 6.00
22 FS,A:Killer Clown........... 6.00
23 TVE,V:The Gamesmen 6.00
24 TVE,V:The Gamesmen 6.00
25 SL,Two Spider-Women 6.00
26 JBy(c),SL,V:White Gardenia... 6.00
27 BSz(c),JBi,A:Enforcer 6.00
28 BSz(c),SL,A:Enforcer,Spidey .. 7.00
29 JR2(c),ECh,FS,A:Enforcer,
Spider-Man 7.00
30 FM(c),SL,JM,I:Dr.Karl Malus .. 6.00
31 FM(c),SL,JM,A:Hornet 6.00
32 FM(c),SL,JM,A:Werewolf 6.00
33 SL,V:Yesterday's Villain 6.00
34 SL,AM,V:Hammer and Anvil.... 6.00
35 SL,AG,V:Angar the Screamer .. 6.00
36 SL,Spider-Woman Shot 6.00
37 SL,TA,BWi,AM,FS,A:X-Men,I:
Siryn,V:Black Tom 8.00
38 SL,BWi,A:X-Men,Siryn........ 8.00
39 SL,BWi,Shadows............ 5.00
40 SL,BWi,V:The Flying Tiger 5.00
41 SL,BWi,V:Morgan LeFay 5.00
42 SL,BWi,V:Silver Samurai...... 5.00
43 SL,V:Silver Samurai.......... 5.00
44 SL,V:Morgan LeFay.......... 5.00
45 SL,Spider-Man Thief cover ... 5.00
46 SL,V:Mandroids,A:Kingpin 5.00
47 V:Daddy Longlegs 5.00
48 O:Gypsy Moth 5.00
49 A:Tigra.................... 5.00
50 PH(c),D:Spider-Woman 3.50

[Limited Series] 1993–94
1 V:Therak 2.25
2 O:Spider-Woman 2.25
3 V:Deathweb 2.25
4 V:Deathweb, last issue 2.25

SPIDER-WOMAN
May, 1999
1 JBy,BS,48-pg................ 3.00
1a signed 20.00
2 BS,JBy,A:Dr. Octopus........ 2.00
2a variant JR2 cover 2.00
3 BS,JBy,V:Flesh & Bones....... 2.00
4 BS,JBy,V:Flesh & Bones....... 2.00
5 BS,JBy,I:Shadowcaster........ 2.00
6 BS,JBy,V:Shadowcaster 2.00
7 BS,JBy.................... 2.00
8 BS,JBy,A:Cluster,x-over 2.00
9 BS,JBy,A:Mattie 2.00
10 BS,JBy,A:Rhino 2.00
11 BS,JBy,V:Exomorph......... 2.00
12 BS,JBy,F:J.Jonah Jameson ... 2.25
13 BS,JBy,V:Werewolf 2.25
14 JBy,GN,BS(c),V:Nighteyes.... 2.25
15 JBy,BS,Itch & Scratch 2.25
16 JBy,BS,Flesh............... 2.25
17 JBy,BS,Flesh & Bones....... 2.25
18 JBy,BS,final issue 2.25

SPIDEY AND THE MINI MARVELS
Marvel April 2003
Spec. Bullpen bits, 40-pg........ 3.50

Spidey Super Stories #7
© Marvel Entertainment Group

SPIDEY SUPER STORIES
Oct., 1974
1 Younger reader's series in
association with the Electric
Company,O:Spider-Man 50.00
2 A:Kraven 25.00
3 A:Ringleader 20.00
4 A:Medusa 20.00
5 A:Shocker 20.00
6 A:Iceman 20.00
7 A:Lizard, Vanisher 20.00
8 A:Dr. Octopus 20.00
9 A:Dr. Doom 20.00
10 A:Green Goblin 15.00
11 A:Dr. Octopus 15.00
12 A:The Cat,V:The Owl....... 15.00
13 A:Falcon 15.00
14 A:Shanna................. 15.00
15 A:Storm.................. 20.00
16 .... 15.00
17 A:Captain America 15.00
18 A:Kingpin 15.00
19 A:Silver Surfer,Dr. Doom 15.00
20 A:Human Torch,Invisible Girl . 15.00
21 A:Dr. Octopus 12.00
22 A:Ms. Marvel,The Beetle 12.00
23 A:Green Goblin 12.00
24 A:Thundra................ 12.00
25 A:Dr. Doom 12.00
26 A:Sandman 12.00
27 A:Thor,Loki 12.00
28 A:Medusa 12.00
29 A:Kingpin 12.00
30 A:Kang 12.00
31 A:Moondragon,Dr. Doom 10.00
32 A:Spider-Woman,Dr. Octopus . 10.00
33 .... 10.00
34 A:Sub-Mariner 10.00
35 .... 10.00
36 A:Lizard.................. 10.00
37 A:White Tiger............. 10.00
38 A:Fantastic Four 10.00
39 A:Hellcat,Thanos 15.00
40 A:Hawkeye 10.00
41 A:Nova,Dr. Octopus 10.00
42 A:Kingpin 10.00
43 A:Daredevil,Ringmaster 10.00
44 A:Vision 10.00
45 A:Silver Surfer,Dr. Doom 15.00
46 A:Mysterio 10.00
47 A:Spider-Woman,Stilt-Man ... 10.00

Spidey–Starriors / MARVEL / Comics Values Annual

48 A:Green Goblin 10.00
49 Spidey for President 10.00
50 A:She-Hulk 10.00
51 and 52 . . . . @10.00
53 A:Dr. Doom 10.00
54 'Attack of the Bird-Man' 10.00
55 A:Kingpin 10.00
56 A:Captain Britain,
   Jack O'Lantern 10.00
57 March, 1982 . . . . 10.00

SPITFIRE AND THE TROUBLESHOOTERS
Oct., 1986

1 HT/JSt 2.50
2 HT 2.50
3 HT,Macs Armor 2.50
4 TM/BMc(Early TM work) 3.50
5 HT/TD,A:Star Brand 2.50
6 HT,Trial 2.50
7 HT 2.50
8 HT,New Armor 2.50
9 . . . . 2.50
Becomes:

CODE NAME: SPITFIRE
10 MR/TD 2.25
11 thru 13 . . . . @2.25

SPOOF
Oct., 1970

1 MSe 25.00
2 MSe,'Brawl in the Family' 15.00
3 MSe,Richard Nixon cover 15.00
4 MSe,'Blechhula' 15.00
5 MSe,May, 1973 . . . . 20.00

SPORT STARS
Nov., 1949

1 The Life of Knute Rockne . . . 500.00
Becomes:

SPORTS ACTION
2 BP(c),Life of George Gipp 500.00
3 BEv,Hack Wilson 250.00
4 Art Houtteman 225.00
5 Nile Kinnick 225.00
6 Warren Gun 225.00
7 Jim Konstanty 225.00
8 Ralph Kiner 250.00
9 Ed 'Strangler' Lewis 225.00
10 JMn,'The Yella-Belly' 225.00
11 'The Killers' 225.00
12 BEv,'Man Behind the Mask' . . 225.00
13 BEv,Lew Andrews 235.00
14 MWs,Ken Roper,Sept.,1952 . . 235.00

SPOTLIGHT
Sept., 1978

1 F:Huckleberry Hound,Yogi Bear 40.00
2 Quick Draw McGraw 35.00
3 The Jetsons 35.00
4 Magilla Gorilla, March, 1979 . . 25.00

SPUMCO COMIC BOOK
1 I:Jimmy the Hapless Boy 7.00
2 . . . . 7.00
3 64-pgs. of sick humor 7.00
4 More sick humor 7.00
TPB 24.95

SPY CASES
See: KID KOMICS

Spy Fighters 6
© Marvel Entertainment Group

SPY FIGHTERS
March, 1951

1 GT 250.00
2 GT 150.00
3 . . . . 125.00
4 thru 13 . . . . @125.00
14 thru 15 July, 1953 . . . . @135.00

SPYKE
Epic *Heavy Hitters*, 1993

1 MBn,BR,I:Spyke 2.75
2 MBn,BR,V:Conita 2.75
3 thru 4 MBn,BR . . . . @2.00

SPY THRILLERS
Atlas, Nov., 1954

1 AyB(c),'The Tickling Death' . . 250.00
2 V:Communists 150.00
3 . . . . 100.00
4 . . . . 100.00
Becomes:

POLICE BADGE
5 Sept., 1955 . . . . 125.00

SQUADRON SUPREME
Sept., 1985

1 BH,L:Nighthawk 3.00
2 BH,F:Nuke,A:Scarlet Centurion . . 2.50
3 BH,D:Nuke 2.50
4 BH,L:Archer 2.25
5 BH,L:Amphibian 2.25
6 PR,J:Institute of Evil 2.25
7 JB,JG,V:Hyperion 2.25
8 BH,V:Hyperion 2.25
9 BSz(c),PR,D:Tom Thumb 2.25
10 PR,V:Quagmire 2.25
11 PR,V:Redeemers 2.25
12 PR,D:Nighthawk,Foxfire,
   Black Archer 2.50
GN Death of a Universe 9.95
TPB 352 pages 15.00

STALKERS
Epic, 1990–91

1 MT 2.25
2 MT 2.25
3 MT 2.25
4 MT 2.25
5 MT 2.25

6 VM,MT 2.25
7 VM,MT 2.25
8 VM,MT 2.25
9 thru 12 VM . . . . @2.25

STARBLAST
1994

1 MGu(s),HT,After the Starbrand . . 2.25
2 MGu(s),HT,After the Starbrand . . 2.25
3 MGu(s),HT,After the Starbrand . . 2.25
4 MGu(s),HT,final issue 2.25

STARBRAND
Oct., 1986

1 JR2,O:Starbrand 2.50
2 JR2/AW 2.50
3 JR2/AW 2.50
4 JR2/AW 2.50
5 JR2/AW 2.50
6 JR2/AW 2.50
7 JR2/AW 2.50
8 JR2/AW 2.50
9 KG/BWi,A:Nightmask 2.50
10 . . . . 2.50
11 JR2,TP 2.50
12 JR2,TP,X-Men x-over 2.50
13 JR2,TP 2.50
14 JR2,TP 2.50
15 . . . . 2.50
16 . . . . 2.50
17 JBy,TP,New Starbrand 3.00
18 JBy,TP 3.00
19 JBy,TP 3.00
Ann.#1 . . . . 2.50

STAR COMICS MAGAZINE
Dec., 1986 (digest size)

1 F:Heathcliff,Muppet Babies,
   Ewoks 2.25
2 thru 13 1988 . . . . @2.25

STARJAMMERS
1995–96

1 I:The Uncreated 3.00
2 War For the Shi'ar 3.00
3 Stuck in deep space 3.00
4 Conclusion 3.00

STAR-LORD, SPECIAL EDITION
Feb., 1982

1 JBy reprints 6.00

STARLORD
Mini-Series 1996

1 (of 3) DLw 2.50
2 DLw 2.50
3 DLw,V:Damyish 2.50

STARLORD MEGAZINE
TPB CCl,JBy,TA, rep., 64-pg. 2.95

STAR MASTER
1 MGu,Cosmic Avengers assemble 2.25
2 MGu,World Engine saga 2.25
3 MGu,Cauldron of Conversion . . . 2.25

STARRIORS
Aug., 1984

1 . . . . 4.00
2 . . . . 3.00
3 . . . . 3.00

CVA Page 316   All comics prices listed are for *Near Mint* condition.

4 Feb., 1982 . . . . 3.00

STARSTRUCK
March, 1985
1 MK 3.00
2 MK 3.00
3 thru 8 MK, Feb., 1986 . . . . . . @3.00

STARTLING STORIES: THE THING–NIGHT FALLS ON YANCY ST.
Marvel May 2003
1 (of 4) EDo(s),40-pg. 3.50
2 EDo(s),40-pg. 3.50
3 EDo(s),40-pg. 3.50
4 EDo(s),concl. 3.50
Spec. Last Line of Defense. 3.50

STAR TREK
April, 1980
1 DC,KJ,rep.1st movie adapt. . . . 15.00
2 DC,KJ,rep.1st movie adapt. 8.00
3 DC,KJ,rep.1st movie adapt. 8.00
4 DC,KJ,The Weirdest Voyage . . . 8.00
5 DC,KJ,Dr.McCoy...Killer 8.00
6 DC,KJ,A:Ambassador Phlu. 8.00
7 MN,KJ,Kirk/Spock(c). 8.00
8 DC(p),F:Spock 8.00
9 DC,FS,Trapped in a Web of
 Ghostly Vengeance 8.00
10 KJ(i),Spock the Barbarian 8.00
11 TP(i),Like A Woman Scorned . . . 8.00
12 TP(i),Trapped in a Starship
 Gone Mad 8.00
13 TP(i),A:Barbara McCoy 8.00
14 LM,GD,We Are Dying,
 Egypt,Dying 8.00
15 GK,The Quality of Mercy 8.00
16 LM,There's no Space
 like Gnomes. 8.00
17 EH,TP,The Long Nights Dawn . 15.00
18 A Thousand Deaths,last issue . 20.00

STAR TREK: DEEP SPACE NINE
1996
1 HWe(s),TGb,AM,DS9 in the
 Gamma Quadrant,pt.1 (of 2). . . 3.00
2 DS9 in Gamma Quadrant,pt.2. . . 2.50
3 TGb,AM,pt.1 (of 2) 2.50
4 TGb,AM,pt.2. . . . . 2.50
5 AM,terrorist attack. 2.50
6 HWe(s),TGb,AM,Shirn sentence
 Sisko to Death, iRisk,î pt.1 . . . . 2.50
7 HWe(s),TGb,iRisk,î pt.2 . . . . 2.50
8 TGb,AM,V:Maquis & Romulans. . 2.50
9 TGb,AM,V:Maquis & Romulans,
 pt.2 . . . . 2.50
10 HWe,TGb, trapped in the
 holosuite 2.50
11 HWe,TGb 2.50
12 Telepathy War x-over 2.50
13 Jem'Hadar Battle 2.50
14 Why Do Klingons Hate Tribbles? 2.50
15 The Tailor's deeds 2.50

STAR TREK: EARLY VOYAGES
Dec., 1996
1 DAn,IEd,Captain Pike's crew,
 double size premier 4.00
2 DAn,IEd,distress signal. 2.50
3 DAn,IEd,on Rigel 7, prologue to
 "The Cage". 2.50
4 DAn,IEd, prologue to "The Cage" 2.50

Star Trek Early Voyages #6
© Marvel Entertainment Group

5 DAn,IEd, V:Vulcans 2.50
6 DAn,IEd, Cloak & Dagger concl. . 2.50
7 DAn,IEd, The wrath of Kaaj 2.50
8 DAn,IEd,F:Dr. Boyce. 2.50
9 DAn,IEd,F:Nano 2.50
10 DAn,V:Chakuun, Tholians 2.50
11 DAn,IEd,The Fallen, pt. 2. . . . . . 2.50
12 DAn,IEd, ... 2.50
13 DAn,IEd,F:Yeoman Colt. 2.50
14 DAn,IEd,Pike vs. Kirk. 2.50
15 DAn,IEd,F:Yeoman Colt 2.50
16 . . . . 2.50
17 DAn,IEd, Pike & Kaaj. 2.50

STAR TREK: FIRST CONTACT
GN Movie adapt. 6.00

STAR TREK: MIRROR, MIRROR
1996
1-shot continuation of famous
 classic episode. 4.00

STAR TREK: THE NEXT GENERATION— RIKER SPECIAL
May, 1998
1-shot, DAn,IEd,Riker photo cover . 3.50

STAR TREK: THE NEXT GENERATION/X-MEN: SECOND CONTACT
March, 1998
1-shot, DAn,IEd,64-pg. 5.00
1-shot, variant CNr cover (1:5) 5.00

STAR TREK: OPERATION ASSIMILATION
1-shot Borg story. 3.00

STAR TREK: STARFLEET ACADEMY
1996
1 Cadets vs. Gorns 2.50

2 ALa, R&R in Australia 2.50
3 F:Decker 2.50
4 V:Klingon Bird-of-prey 2.50
5 V:Klingons 2.50
6 Funeral of Kamilah
 Goldstein,I:Edam Astrun 2.50
7 ALa,F:Edam Astrun,Nog 2.50
8 ALa, Return of Charlie X. 2.50
9 ALa, on Talos, V:Jem'Hadar . . . 2.50
10 ALa,F:Captain Pike, Jem'Hadar . 2.50
11 F:Christopher Pike 2.50
12 ALa, Telepathy War x-over 2.50
13 Parent's Day 2.50
14 T'Priell revealed, pt.1 (of 3) 2.50
15 T'Priell dead?, pt.2. . . . . 2.50
16 T'Priell Revealed, pt3. . . . . 2.50
17 Battle for T'Priell's Mind 2.50
18 Entirely in Klingon language. . . . 2.50
19 Pava vs. Kovold. 2.50

STAR TREK: TELEPATHY WAR
Sept., 1997
1-shot Telepathy War, pt.4
 x-over, 48-pg. 3.00

STAR TREK: UNLIMITED
1996
1 DAn,IEd,MBu,JeM,AW, Classic
 series & TNG 5.00
2 DAn,IEd,MBu 4.00
3 DAn,IEd,MBu 4.00
4 DAn,IEd,MBu,AW, 2 tales 4.00
5 DAn,IEd,TMo,RoR,AW,ANi,48-pg.4.00
6 DAn, Telepathy War x-over 4.00
7 DAn,IEd,F:Q & Trelane 4.00
8 DAn,IEd,Day of Honor tie-in 4.00
9 DAn,IEd,V:Klingons 4.00
10 A Piece of the Action,
 conclusion of series. 4.00

STAR TREK: THE UNTOLD VOYAGES
Jan., 1998
1 (of 5) Star Trek 2nd Five Year
 Mission 3.00
2 Spock, Savik, Dr. McCoy 3.00
3 F:McCoy, McCoy's Daughter. . . . 3.00
4 F:Sulu 3.00
5 48-pg. finale 3.50

Star Trek Voyager #8
© Marvel Entertainment Group

STAR TREK: VOYAGER
1996
1 F:Neelix & Talaxians, pt.1 . . . . . . 3.00
2 F:Neelix & Talaxians, pt.2 . . . . . . 3.00
3 F:Neelix & Talaxians, pt.3 . . . . . . 3.00
4 HWe(s),Homeostasis, pt.1 . . . . . 3.00
5 HWe(s),Homeostasis, pt.2 . . . . . 3.00
6 HWe(s),Homeostasis, pt.3 . . . . . 3.00
7 Ancient Relic 3.00
8 Mysterious relic encountered . . . 3.00
9 DAn,IEd,AM, rescue mission . . . 3.00
10 The Borg Are Back 3.00
11 Zoological Experiment 3.00
12 Zoological Experiment 3.00
13 Crew loses a member 3.00
14 Distress Call 3.00
15 Tuvok Trapped. 3.00

STAR TREK: VOYAGER: SPLASHDOWN
Jan., 1998
1 (of 4) AM,Crash landing on
  water planet 3.00
2 AM,The ship may sink 3.00
3 AM,adventure undersea 3.00
4 AM,escape from sea creatures . . 3.00

STAR TREK/X-MEN
1-shot SLo,MS, 64-pg.. . . . . 5.00
1a rep. of STAR TREK/X-MEN . . . 5.00

STAR WARS
July, 1977
1 HC,30 Cent,movie adaption. . . . 65.00
1a HC,35 Cent(square Box). . . . 725.00
1b "Reprint". 7.50
2 HC,movie adaptation 30.00
2b "Reprint" 4.00
3 HC,movie adaptation 25.00
3b "Reprint" 4.00
4 HC,SL,movie adapt.(low dist.). . 22.00
4b "Reprint" 4.00
5 HC,SL,movie adaptation 22.00
5b "Reprint" 3.00
6 HC,DSt,E:movie adaption 22.00
6b "Reprint" 3.00
7 HC,FS,F:Luke & Chewbacca . . 20.00
7b "Reprint" 2.50
8 HC,TD,Eight against a World . . 20.00
8b "Reprint" 2.50
9 HC,TP,V:Cloud Riders. 20.00
9b "Reprint" 2.50
10 HC,TP,Behemoth From Below . 22.00
11 CI,TP,Fate of Luke Skywalker. . 20.00
12 TA,CI,Doomworld. 20.00
13 TA,JBy,CI,Deadly Reunion 20.00
14 TA,CI 20.00
15 CI,V:Crimson Jack 20.00
16 WS,V:The Hunter. 20.00
17 Crucible, low dist. 20.00
18 CI,Empire Strikes,low dist. 20.00
19 CI,Ultimate Gamble,low dist. . . 20.00
20 CI,Death Game, scarce 20.00
21 TA,CI,Shadow of a Dark
  Lord(Scarce) 20.00
22 CI,Han Solo vs.Chewbacca . . . 15.00
23 CI,Flight Into Fury 15.00
24 CI,Ben Kenobi Story 15.00
25 CI,Siege at Yavin 15.00
26 CI,Doom Mission 15.00
27 CI,V:The Hunter. 15.00
28 CI,Cavern o/t Crawling Death. . 15.00
29 CI,Dark Encounter 15.00
30 CI,A Princess Alone 15.00
31 CI,Return to Tatooine 15.00
32 CI,The Jawa Express. 15.00
33 CI,GD,V:Baron Tagge 15.00
34 CI,Thunder in the Stars 15.00

Star Wars #12
© *Marvel Entertainment Group*

35 CI,V:Darth Vader 15.00
36 CI,V:Darth Vader 15.00
37 CI,V:Darth Vader 15.00
38 TA,MG,Riders in the Void. 15.00
39 AW,B:Empire Strikes Back 25.00
40 AW,Battleground Hoth 25.00
41 AW,Imperial Pursuit 25.00
42 AW,Bounty Hunters 25.00
43 AW,Betrayal at Bespin 25.00
44 AW,E:Empire Strikes Back 25.00
45 CI,GD,Death Probe 15.00
46 DI,TP,V:Dreamnaut Devourer . . 15.00
47 CI,GD,Droid World. 15.00
48 CI,Leia vs.Darth Vader. 15.00
49 SW,TP,The Last Jedi 15.00
50 WS,AW,TP,G-Size issue 15.00
51 WS,TP,Resurrection of Evil . . . 12.00
52 WS,TP,D:Death Star II 12.00
53 CI,WS,Gift of Alderaan. 12.00
54 CI,WS,Starfire Rising 12.00
55 thru 66 WS,TP . . . . @12.00
67 TP, The Darker 12.00
68 GD,TP,O:Boba Fett 20.00
69 GD,TP,Death in City of Bone . . 20.00
70 A:Han Solo 20.00
71 A:Han Solo 20.00
72 Fool's Boontu 20.00
73 Secret of Planet Lansbane. . . . 20.00
74 thru 91. . . . . @20.00
92 BSz(c),The Dream 22.00
93 thru 97 . . . . @20.00
98 AW,Supply & Demand 20.00
99 Touch of Goddess 20.00
100 Painted(c),double-size 22.00
101 BSz, Far,Far Away 22.00
102 KRo's Back 15.00
103 thru 106 . . . . @15.00
107 WPo(i),last issue 90.00
Ann.#1 WS(c),V:Winged Warlords 100.00
Ann.#2 RN 15.00
Ann.#3 RN,Darth Vader(c) 15.00

STEELGRIP STARKEY
Epic, July, 1986
1 . . . . 2.50
2 thru 6 June, 1987 . . . . @2.50

STEELTOWN ROCKERS
April, 1990—Sept., 1990
1 SL 2.25
2 thru 6 SL. . . . . @2.25

STORM
1 TyD,KIS,V:Candra. 4.00
2 . . . . 4.00
3 . . . . 4.00
4 TyD,KIS, conclusion,foil cover . . . 4.00

STRANGE COMBAT TALES
1 and 2 . . . . @2.75
3 Tiger by the Tail 2.50
4 Midnight Crusade 2.50

STRANGE STORIES OF SUSPENSE
See: RUGGED ACTION

STRANGE TALES
[1st Regular Series] June, 1951
1 'The Room' 4,000.00
2 'Trapped In A Tomb' 1,300.00
3 JMn,'Man Who Never Was' . 1,000.00
4 BEv,'Terror in the Morgue' . . 1,100.00
5 'A Room Without A Door' . . 1,000.00
6 RH(c),'The Ugly Man' 700.00
7 'Who Stands Alone' 700.00
8 BEv(c),'Something in the Fog' 700.00
9 'Drink Deep Vampire' 700.00
10 BK,'Hidden Head' 800.00
11 BEv(c),GC,'O'Malley's Friend' 500.00
12 'Graveyard At Midnight' 500.00
13 BEv(c),'Death Makes A Deal' . 500.00
14 GT,'Horrible Herman' 500.00
15 BK,'Don't Look Down' 550.00
16 Decapitation cover 500.00
17 DBr,JRo,'Death Feud' 500.00
18 'Witch Hunt' 500.00
19 RH(c),'The Rag Doll' 500.00
20 RH(c),GC,SMo,'Lost World' . 500.00
21 BEv 400.00
22 BK,JF 400.00
23 'The Strangest Tale in
  the World' 400.00
24 'The Thing in the Coffin' 400.00
25 . . . . 400.00
26 . . . . 400.00
27 JF,'The Garden of Death' 400.00
28 'Come into my Coffin' 400.00
29 'Witch-Craft'. 350.00
30 'The Thing in the Box' 350.00
31 'The Man Who Played
  with Blocks' 350.00
32 . . . . 350.00
33 JMn(c),'Step Lively Please' . . 350.00
34 'Flesh and Blood' 300.00
35 'The Man in the Bottle' 300.00
36 . . . . 300.00
37 'Out of the Storm' 300.00
38 . . . . 300.00
39 'Karnoff's Plan' 300.00
40 BEv,'The Man Who Caught a
  Mermaid' 300.00
41 BEv,'Riddle of the Skull' 325.00
42 DW,BEv,JMn,'Faceless One' . 325.00
43 JF,'The Mysterious Machine' . 300.00
44 . . . . 300.00
45 JKa,'Land of the
  Vanishing Men'. 325.00
46 thru 57 . . . . @300.00
58 AW 300.00
59 BK 300.00
60 . . . . 250.00
61 BK. 300.00
62 . . . . 250.00
63 . . . . 300.00
64 AW 300.00
65 . . . . 250.00
66 . . . . 250.00
67 thru 78 . . . . @350.00

Comics Values Annual — MARVEL — Strange Tales

Strange Tales #72
© Marvel Entertainment Group

79 SD,JK,Dr.Strange Prototype. . 350.00
80 thru 83 SD,JK . . . . @250.00
84 SD,JK,Magneto Prototype . . . 250.00
85 SD,JK 225.00
86 SD,JK,`I Who
 Created Mechano' 225.00
87 SD,JK,`Return of Grogg' 225.00
88 SD,JK,`Zzutak'. 225.00
89 SD,JK,`Fin Fang Foom' 700.00
90 SD,JK,`Orrgo the
 Unconquerable' 225.00
91 SD,JK,`The Sacrifice'. 225.00
92 SD,JK,`The Thing That Waits
 For Me'. 225.00
93 SD,JK,`The Wax People' 225.00
94 SD,JK,`Pildorr the Plunderer' . 225.00
95 SD,JK,`Two-Headed Thing' . . 225.00
96 SD,JK,`I Dream of Doom'. . . . 225.00
97 SD,JK,`When A Planet Dies' . 600.00
98 SD,JK,`No Human Can
 Beat Me'. 200.00
99 SD,JK,`Mister Morgan's
 Monster'. 200.00
100 SD,JK,`I Was Trapped
 in the Crazy Maze' 200.00
101 B:StL(s),SD,JK,
 B:Human Torch 1,500.00
102 SD,JK,I:Wizard 500.00
103 SD,JK,I:Zemu 400.00
104 SD,JK,I:The Trapster 400.00
105 SD,JK,V:Wizard 400.00
106 SD,A:Fantastic Four. 250.00
107 SD,V:Sub-Mariner 300.00
108 SD,JK,A:FF,I:The Painter . . . 250.00
109 SD,JK,I:Sorcerer 250.00
110 SD,I&B:Dr.Strange,
 Nightmare 1,900.00
111 SD,I:Asbestos,
 Baron Mordo 500.00
112 SD,I:The Eel 200.00
113 SD,I:Plant Man. 200.00
114 SD,JK,A:Captain America. . . 650.00
115 SD,O:Dr.Strange 700.00
116 SD,V:Thing. 200.00
117 SD,V:The Eel 150.00
118 SD,V:The Wizard 200.00
119 SD,C:Spider-Man 200.00
120 SD,1st Iceman/Torch T.U. . . . 225.00
121 SD,V:Plant Man 125.00
122 SD,V:Dr.Doom 100.00
123 SD,A:Thor,I:Beetle 125.00
124 SD,I:Zota 100.00
125 SD,V:Sub-Mariner 125.00
126 SD,I:Dormammu,Clea 100.00
127 SD,V:Dormammu. 90.00

128 SD,I:Demon. 90.00
129 SD,I:Tiboro 90.00
130 SD,C:Beatles 100.00
131 SD,I:Dr.Vega 90.00
132 SD,I:Orini 90.00
133 SD,I:Shazana 90.00
134 SD,E:Torch,I:Merlin 90.00
135 SD,JK:I:Shield & Hydra
 B:Nick Fury 250.00
136 SD,JK,V:Dormammu 75.00
137 SD,JK,A:Ancient One. 90.00
138 SD,JK,I:Eternity 85.00
139 SD,JK,V:Dormammu 85.00
140 SD,JK,V:Dormammu 85.00
141 SD,JK,I:Fixer,Mentallo 85.00
142 SD,JK,I:THEM,V:Hydra 85.00
143 SD,JK,V:Hydra. 85.00
144 SD,JK,V:Druid,I:Jasper
 Sitwell 85.00
145 SD,JK,I:Mr.Rasputin. 85.00
146 SD,JK,V:Dormammu,I:A.I.M. . 85.00
147 BEv,JK,F:Wong 85.00
148 BEv,JK,O:Ancient One 100.00
149 BEv,JK,V:Kaluu 75.00
150 BEv,JK,JB(1st Marvel Art)
 I:Baron Strucker,Umar 75.00
151 JK,JSo(1st Marvel Art),
 I:Umar 100.00
152 BEv,JK,JSo,V:Umar 75.00
153 JK,JSo,MSe,V:Hydra 75.00
154 JSo,MSe,I:Dreadnought. 75.00
155 JSo,MSe,A:L.B.Johnson 75.00
156 JSo,MSe,I:Zom 75.00
157 JSo,MSe,A:Zom,C:Living
 Tribunal 75.00
158 JSo,MSe,A:Zom,I:Living
 Tribunal(full story). 75.00
159 JSo,MSe,O:Nick Fury,A:Capt.
 America,I:Val Fontaine 85.00
160 JSo,MSe,A:Captain America,
 I:Jimmy Woo. 75.00
161 JSo,I:Yellow Claw 75.00
162 JSo,DA,A:Captain America. . . 75.00
163 JSo,DA,V:Yellow Claw 60.00
164 JSo,DA,V:Yellow Claw 60.00
165 JSo,DA,V:Yellow Claw 60.00
166 DA,GT,JSo,A:AncientOne. . . . 60.00
167 JSo,DA,V:Doctor Doom 100.00
168 JSo,DA,E:Doctor Strange,Nick
 Fury,V:Yandroth 60.00
169 JSo,I&O:Brother Voodoo 20.00
170 JSo,O:Brother Voodoo 15.00
171 GC,V:Baron Samed 15.00
172 GC,DG,V:Dark Lord 15.00
173 GC,DG,I:Black Talon 15.00
174 JB,JM,O:Golem 12.00
175 SD,R:Torr. 12.00
176 F:Golem 12.00
177 FB,F:Golem 12.00
178 JSn,B&O:Warlock,I:Magus . . . 40.00
179 JSn,I:Pip,I&D:Capt.Autolycus . 35.00
180 JSn,I:Gamora,Kray-tor 35.00
181 JSn,E:Warlock 35.00
182 SD,GK,rep. Str.Tales
 #123,124 . . . . 10.00
183 SD,rep.Str.Tales #130,131 . . . 10.00
184 SD,rep.Str.Tales #132,133 . . . 10.00
185 SD,rep.Str.Tales #134,135 . . . 10.00
186 SD,rep.Str.Tales #136,137 . . . 10.00
187 SD,rep.Str.Tales #138,139 . . . 10.00
188 SD,rep.Str.Tales #140,141 . . . 10.00
Ann.#1 V:Grottu,Diablo 750.00
Ann.#2 A:Spider-Man 1,200.00
Marvel Milestone rep. stories from
 #110–#111, #114–#115 (1995) . 2.95

[2nd Regular Series] 1987–88
1 BBI,CW,B:Cloak&Dagger,Dr.
 Strange,V:Lord of Light. 3.00
2 BBI,CW,V:Lord of Light,Demon . 2.50
3 BBI,AW,CW,A:Nightmare,Khat . 2.50
4 BBI,CW,V:Nightmare. 2.50

Strange Tales #170
© Marvel Entertainment Group

5 BBI,V:Rodent,A:Defenders 2.50
6 BBI,BWi,V:Erlik Khan,
 A:Defenders. 2.50
7 V:Nightmare,A:Defenders 2.50
8 BBI,BWi,V:Kaluu. 2.50
9 BBI,BWi,A:Dazzler,I:Mr.Jip,
 V:Kaluu 2.50
10 BBI,BWi,RCa,A:Black Cat,
 V:Mr.Jip,Kaluu 2.50
11 RCa,BWi,V:Mr.Jip,Kaluu. 2.50
12 WPo,BWi,A:Punisher,V:Mr.Jip . 2.50
13 JBr,BWi,RCa,Punisher,
 Power Pack 2.50
14 JBr,BWi,RCa,Punisher,P.Pack . 2.50
15 RCa,BMc,A:Mayhem 2.50
16 RCa,BWi,V:Mr.Jip 2.50
17 RCa,BWi,V:Night 2.50
18 RCa,KN,A:X-Factor,V:Night . . . 2.50
19 MMi(c),EL,TA,RCa,A:Thing 2.50
TPB Fully painted 6.95

STRANGE TALES
June, 1998
1 JMD,PJe,LSh,Man-Thing, 64-pg. 5.00
2A JMD,PJe,LSh,Man-Thing,
 Werewolf, 64-pg. 5.00
2B variant cover 5.00
3 JMD,PJe,NA(c),Man-Thing,
 Werewolf, 64-pg. 5.00
4 JMD,PJe,LSh,F:Man-Thing
 final issue. 5.00

STRANGE TALES:
DARK CORNERS
March, 1998
1-shot JEs, three stories, 48-pg. . . . 4.00

STRANGE TALES
OF THE UNUSUAL
Dec., 1955—Aug., 1957
1 JMn(c),BP,DH,JR,`Man Lost' . 600.00
2 BEv,`Man Afraid' 300.00
3 AW,`The Invaders' 325.00
4 `The Long Wait' 225.00
5 RC,SD,`The Threat' 275.00
6 BEv 225.00
7 JK,JO 225.00
8 . . . . 225.00
9 BEv(c),BK 250.00
10 GM,AT. 225.00
11 BEv(c),Aug., 1957 . . . . 225.00

All comics prices listed are for *Near Mint* condition.   CVA Page 319

Strange–Sub-Mariner — MARVEL — Comics Values Annual

STRANGE WORLDS
Dec., 1958
- 1 JK,SD,Flying Saucer 1,100.00
- 2 SD 650.00
- 3 JK 500.00
- 4 AW 450.00
- 5 SD 350.00

STRAWBERRY SHORTCAKE
Star, June, 1985—April, 1986
- 1 .... 3.00
- 2 thru 7 .... @3.00

STRAY TOASTERS
Epic, Jan., 1988
- 1 BSz 5.00
- 2 BSz 4.50
- 3 and 4 BSz .... @4.00

STRIKEFORCE MORITURI
Dec., 1986
- 1 BA,SW,WPo(1st pencils-3 pages),I:Blackwatch 3.00
- 2 BA,SW,V:The Horde 2.50
- 3 BA,SW,V:The Horde 2.50
- 4 BA,SW,WPo,V:The Horde 2.50
- 5 BA,SW,V:The Horde 2.50
- 6 BA,SW,V:The Horde 2.50
- 7 BA,SW,V:The Horde 2.50
- 8 BA,SW,V:The Horde 2.50
- 9 BA,SW,V:THe Horde 2.50
- 10 WPo(1st pencils-full story), SW,R:Black Watch,O:Horde ... 3.00
- 11 BA,SW,V:The Horde 2.50
- 12 BA,SW,D:Jelene 2.50
- 13 BA,SW,Old vs. NewTeam 2.50
- 14 BA,AW,V:The Horde 2.50
- 15 BA,AW,V:The Horde 2.50
- 16 WPo,SW,V:The Horde 2.50
- 17 WPo(c),SW,V:The Horde 2.50
- 18 BA,SW,V:Hammersmith 2.50
- 19 BA,SW,V:THe Horde,D:Pilar . 2.50
- 20 BA,SW,V:The Horde 2.50
- 21 MMi(c),TD(i),V:The Horde .. 2.50
- 22 TD(i),V:The Horde 2.50
- 23 MBa,VM,V:The Horde 2.50
- 24 VM(i),I:Vax,V:The Horde ... 2.50
- 25 TD(i),V:The Horde 3.00
- 26 MBa,VM,V:The Horde 3.00
- 27 MBa,VM,O:Morituri Master .. 3.00
- 28 MBa,V:The Tiger 3.00
- 29 MBa,V:Zakir Shastri 3.00
- 30 MBa,V:Andre Lamont,The Wind . 3.00
- 31 MBa(c),V:The Wind,last issue . 3.00

STRONG GUY REBORN
Spec. TDz,ASm,ATi (1997) 3.00

STRYFE'S STRIKE FILE
- 1 LSn,NKu,GCa,BP,C:Siena Blaze,Holocaust (1993) 4.00
- 1a 2nd printing 2.25

SUB-MARINER
May, 1968
- 1 JB,O:Sub-Mariner 350.00
- 2 JB,A:Triton 150.00
- 3 JB,A:Triton 100.00
- 4 JB,V:Attuma 100.00
- 5 JB,I&O:Tiger Shark 100.00
- 6 JB,DA,V:Tiger Shark 125.00
- 7 JB,I:Ikthon 100.00
- 8 JB,V:Thing 100.00
- 9 MSe,DA,A:Lady Dorma 100.00
- 10 GC,DA,O:Lemuria 100.00
- 11 GC,V:Capt.Barracuda 50.00
- 12 MSe,I:Lyna 50.00
- 13 MSe,JS,A:Lady Dorma 50.00
- 14 MSe,V:Fake Human Torch 55.00
- 15 MSe,V:Dragon Man 50.00
- 16 MSe,I:Nekaret,Thakos 55.00
- 17 MSe,I:Stalker,Kormok 50.00
- 18 MSe,A:Triton 30.00
- 19 MSe,I:Stingray 30.00
- 20 JB,V:Dr.Doom 30.00
- 21 MSe,D:Lord Seth 30.00
- 22 MSe,A:Dr.Strange 30.00
- 23 MSe,I:Orka 30.00
- 24 JB,JM,V:Tiger Shark 30.00
- 25 SB,JM,O:Atlantis 25.00
- 26 SB,A:Red Raven 25.00
- 27 SB,I:Commander Kraken 25.00
- 28 SB,V:Brutivae 25.00
- 29 SB,V:Hercules 20.00
- 30 SB,A:Captain Marvel 22.00
- 31 SB,A:Triton 20.00
- 32 SB,JM,I&O:Llyra 22.00
- 33 SB,JM,I:Namora 25.00
- 34 SB,JM,AK,1st Defenders ... 100.00
- 35 SB,JM,A:Silver Surfer 100.00
- 36 BWr,SB,W:Lady Dorma 35.00
- 37 RA,D:Lady Dorma 35.00
- 38 RA,JSe,O:Rec,I:Thakorr,Fen . 35.00
- 39 RA,JM,V:Llyra 35.00
- 40 GC,I:Turalla,A:Spidey 25.00
- 41 GT,V:Rock 20.00
- 42 GT,JM,V:House Named Death . 20.00
- 43 GC,V:Tunal 18.00
- 44 MSe,JM,V:Human Torch 20.00
- 45 MSe,JM,V:Tiger Shark 20.00
- 46 GC,D:Namor's Father 20.00
- 47 GC,A:Stingray,V:Dr.Doom ... 20.00
- 48 GC,V:Dr.Doom 20.00
- 49 GC,V:Dr.Doom 20.00
- 50 BEv,I:Namorita 20.00
- 51 BEv,O:Namorita,C:Namora ... 20.00
- 52 GK,V:Sunfire 20.00
- 53 BEv,V:Sunfire 18.00
- 54 BEv,AW,V:Sunfire,I:Lorvex . 18.00
- 55 BEv,V:Torg 18.00
- 56 DA,I:Coral 18.00
- 57 BEv,I:Venus 18.00
- 58 BEv,I:Tamara 18.00
- 59 BEv,V:Tamara 25.00
- 60 BEv,V:Tamara 15.00
- 61 BEv,JM,V:Dr.Hydro 15.00
- 62 HC,JSt,I:Tales of Atlantis . 15.00
- 63 HC,JSt,V:Dr.Hydro,I:Arkus . 15.00
- 64 HC,JSe,I:Maddox 15.00
- 65 DH,DP,V:She-Devil,inc.BEv Eulogy pin-up 15.00
- 66 DH,V:Orka,I:Raman 15.00
- 67 DH,A:FF,V:Triton,N:Namor I&O:Force 15.00
- 68 DH,O:Force 15.00
- 69 GT,V:Spider-Man 18.00
- 70 GT,I:Piranha 15.00
- 71 GT,V:Piranha 15.00
- 72 DA,V:Slime/Thing 15.00
- Spec.#1 rep. Tales to Astonish #70-#73 .... 25.00
- Spec.#2 rep. Tales to Astonish ... 20.00

[Limited Series]
- 1 RB,BMc,Namor's Birth 2.50
- 2 RB,BMc,Namor Kills Humans .. 2.25
- 3 RB,BMc,V:Surface Dwellers .. 2.25
- 4 RB,BMc,V:Human Torch 2.25
- 5 RB,BMc,A:Invaders 2.25
- 6 RB,BMc,V:Destiny 2.25
- 7 RB,BMc,A:Fantastic Four 2.25
- 8 RB,BMc,A:Hulk,Avengers 2.25
- 9 RB,BMc,A:X-Men,Magneto 2.25
- 10 RB,BMc,V:Thing 2.25
- 11 RB,BMc,A:Namorita,Defenders . 2.25
- 12 RB,BMc,A:Dr.Doom, Alpha Flight 2.25

(SAGA OF THE) SUB-MARINER
[Mini-Series] Nov., 1988
- 1 RB,BMc,Namor's Birth 3.00
- 2 RB,BMc,Namor Kills Humans .. 3.00
- 3 RB,BMc,V:Surface Dwellers .. 3.00
- 4 RB,BMc,V:Human Torch 3.00
- 5 RB,BMc,A:Invaders 3.00
- 6 RB,BMc,V:Destiny 3.00
- 7 RB,BMc,A:Fantastic Four 3.00
- 8 RB,BMc,A:Hulk,Avengers 3.00
- 9 RB,BMc,A:X-Men,Magneto 3.50
- 10 RB,BMc,V:Thing 3.00
- 11 RB,BMc,A:Namorita,Defenders . 3.00
- 12 RB,BMc,A:Dr.Doom,Alp.Flight . 3.00

SUB-MARINER COMICS
Timely, Spring, 1941
- 1 ASh(c),BEv,PGn,B:Sub-Mariner, The Angel 45,000.00
- 2 ASh(c),BEv,Nazi Submarine (c) 7,500.00
- 3 ASh(c),BEv,Churchill 6,000.00
- 4 ASh(c),BEv,BW 4,500.00
- 5 .... 3,500.00
- 6 ASh(c) 3,000.00
- 7 .... 3,000.00
- 8 ASh(c) 3,000.00
- 9 ASh(c),BW,Flag(c) 3,000.00
- 10 ASh(c) 3,000.00
- 11 ASh(c) 2,700.00
- 12 ASh(c) 2,000.00
- 13 ASh(c) 2,000.00
- 14 ASh(c) 2,000.00
- 15 ASh(c) 2,000.00
- 16 ASh(c) 2,000.00
- 17 ASh(c) 2,000.00
- 18 ASh(c) 2,000.00
- 19 .... 2,000.00
- 20 ASh(c) 2,000.00
- 21 SSh(c),BEv,Last Angel ... 1,500.00
- 22 SSh(c),BEv,A:Young Allies . 1,500.00
- 23 SSh(c),BEv,Human Torch .. 1,500.00
- 24 MSy(c),BEv,A:Namora, bondage cover 1,500.00
- 25 MSy(c),HK,B:The Blonde Phantom, A:Namora, bondage(c) 1,800.00

Sub-Mariner #40
© Marvel Entertainment Group

Comics Values Annual — MARVEL — Sub-Mariner–Tale Of

26 BEv,A:Namora 1,300.00
27 DRi(c),BEv,A:Namora 1,300.00
28 DRi(c),BEv,A:Namora 1,300.00
29 BEv,A:Namora,Human Torch 1,300.00
30 DRi(c),BEv,`Slaves Under
   the Sea' 1,300.00
31 BEv,`The Man Who Grew',
   A:Capt. America,E:Blonde
   Phantom 1,300.00
32 BEv,O:Sub-Mariner 2,000.00
33 BEv,O:Sub-Mariner,A:Human
   Torch,B:Namora. 1,500.00
34 BEv,A:Human Torch,bondage
   cover 1,000.00
35 BEv,A:Human Torch 1,000.00
36 BEv,Hidden World 1,000.00
37 JMn(c),BEv 1,000.00
38 SSh(c),BEv,JMn,O:Sub-
   Mariner 1,100.00
39 JMn(c),BEv,Commie
   Frogman 1,000.00
40 JMn(c),BEv,Secret Tunnel . . 1,000.00
41 JMn(c),BEv,A:namora 1,000.00
42 BEv,Oct., 1955 . . . . 1,200.00

SUBURBAN JERSEY NINJA SHE-DEVILS
1 I:Ninja She-Devils 2.25

SUNFIRE & BIG HERO 6
July, 1998
1 (of 3) SLo,from Alpha Flight 2.50
2 SLo,V:Everwraith 2.50
3 SLO,conclusion 2.50

SUPERNATURALS
Oct., 1998
1 (of 4) BnP,JBa(c),F:Brother
   Voodoo, V:Jack O'Lantern, with
   mask 4.00
1a signed 30.00
2 BnP,JBa(c), with mask 4.00
3 BnP,JBa(c), with mask 4.00
4 BnP,JBa(c), with mask, concl. . . . 4.00

SUPERNATURAL THRILLERS
Dec., 1972
1 JSo(c),JSe,FrG,IT! 50.00
2 VM,DA,The Invisible Man 30.00

Supernatural Thrillers #6
© Marvel Entertainment Group

3 GK,The Valley of the Worm . . 30.00
4 Dr. Jekyll and Mr. Hyde 30.00
5 RB,The Living Mummy 75.00
6 GT,JA,The Headless Horseman 40.00
7 VM,B:The Living Mummy,
   `Back From The Tomb' 40.00
8 VM,`He Stalks Two Worlds' . . . 40.00
9 GK/AM(c),VM,DA,`Pyramid of
   the Watery Doom' 40.00
10 VM,`A Choice of Dooms' 40.00
11 VM,`When Strikes the ASP' . . . 40.00
12 VM,KJ,`The War That Shook
   the World' 40.00
13 VM,DGr,`The Tomb of the
   Stalking Dead' 40.00
14 VM,AMc,`All These Deadly
   Pawns' 40.00
15 TS, E:The Living Mummy,`Night
   of Armageddon', Oct.,1975 . . . 40.00

SUPER SOLDIERS
Marvel UK, 1993
1 I:Super Soldier,A:USAgent 2.75
2 A:USAgent 2.25
3 A:USAgent 2.25
4 A:USAgent,Avengers 2.25
5 A:Captain America,AWC 2.25
6 O:Super Soldiers 2.25
7 in Savage Land 2.25

SUPER-VILLAIN CLASSICS
May, 1983
1 O:Galactus 6.00

SUPER-VILLAIN TEAM-UP
Aug., 1975
1 GT/BEv(c),B:Dr.Doom/Sub-
   Mariner,A:Attuma,Tiger Shark 35.00
2 SB,A:Tiger Shark, Attuma 15.00
3 EH(c),JA,V:Attuma 15.00
4 HT,JM,Dr.Doom vs. Namor 15.00
5 RB/JSt(c),HT,DP,A:Fantastic
   Four,I:Shroud 15.00
6 HT,JA,A:Shroud,Fantastic Four. 12.00
7 RB/KJ(c),HT,O:Shroud 12.00
8 KG,V:Ringmaster 12.00
9 ST,A:Avengers,Iron Man 12.00
10 BH,DP,A:Capt.America,
   V:Attuma,Red Skull 12.00
11 DC/JSt(c),BH,DP,B:Dr. Doom,
   Red Skull,A:Capt. America . . . 12.00
12 DC/AM(c),BH,DP,Dr.Doom vs.
   Red Skull 12.00
13 KG,DP,Namor vs. Krang 12.00
14 JBy/TA(c),BH,DP,V:Magneto,
   x-over with Champions #15 . . 12.00
15 GT,ME,A:Red Skull 12.00
16 CI,A:Dr. Doom 12.00
17 KP(c),Red Skull Vs.Hatemonger
   June, 1976 . . . . 12.00
G-Size#1 F:Namor, Dr.Doom . . . 12.00
G-Size#2 F:Namor, Dr.Doom . . . 12.00

SUPREME POWER
Marvel Max July 2003
1 MSz(s),GFr. 3.00
1a special edition, JQ(c) 5.00
2 MSz(s),GFr. 3.00
3 MSz(s),GFr. 3.00
4 . . . . 3.00

SUSPENSE
Atlas, Dec., 1949
1 BP,Ph(c),Sidney Greenstreet/

Peter Lorne (Maltese Falcon) 750.00
2 Ph(c),Dennis O'Keefe/Gale
   Storm (Abandoned) 400.00
3 B:Horror stories,`The Black
   Pit' 400.00
4 `Thing In Black' 300.00
5 BEv,GT,RH,BK,DBr,
   `Hangman's House' 325.00
6 BEv,GT,PAM,RH,`Madness
   of Scott Mannion' 325.00
7 DBr,GT,DR,`Murder' 300.00
8 GC,DRi,RH,`Don't Open
   the Door' 300.00
9 GC,DRi,Back From The Dead. 300.00
10 JMn(c),WIP,RH,`Trapped
   In Time' 300.00
11 MSy,`The Suitcase' 250.00
12 GT,`Dark Road' 250.00
13 JMn(c),`Strange Man',
   bondage cover 250.00
14 RH,Death And Doctor Parker . 350.00
15 JMn(c),OW,`The Machine' . . 250.00
16 OW,`Horror Backstage' 250.00
17 `Night Of Terror' 250.00
18 BK,`The Cozy Coffin' 275.00
19 BEv,RH 250.00
20 . . . . 250.00
21 BEv(c) 250.00
22 BEv(c),BK,OW 250.00
23 BEv 250.00
24 RH,GT 275.00
25 `I Died At Midnight' 350.00
26 BEv(c) 225.00
27 DBr 250.00
28 BEv 250.00
29 JMn,BF,JRo,April, 1953 . . . . 250.00

Swords of the Swashbucklers 310
© Marvel Entertainment Group

SWORDS OF THE SWASHBUCKLERS
Epic, 1985–87
1 JG,Adult theme 3.00
2 JG 2.50
3 JG 2.50
4 JG 2.50
5 JG 2.50
6 JG 2.50
7 JG 2.50
8 thru 12, June, 1987 . . . . @2.50

TALE OF THE MARINES
See: DEVIL-DOG DUGAN

TALES OF ASGARD
Oct., 1968
1 .... 50.00
Vol.2 #1 Feb,1984 .... 4.00

TALES OF G.I. JOE
Jan., 1988
1 reprints,#1 .... 3.00
2 thru 7 rep. .... @2.50

TALES OF JUSTICE
See: JUSTICE COMICS

TALES OF THE AGE OF APOCALYPSE
1996
1-shot SLo,JoB,Age of Apocalypse stories 5.00
GN, rep. 6.00

TALES OF THE AGE OF APOCALYPSE: SINISTER BLOODLINE
Dec., 1997
GN JFM,SEp, 48-pg. bookshelf. ... 6.00

TALES OF THE MARVELS: BLOCKBUSTER
Fully painted (1995) 6.00

TALES OF THE MARVELS: INNER DEMONS
Fully painted, 48-pg. (1996) 6.00

TALES OF THE MARVELS: WONDER YEARS
1 & 2 DAb (1995) .... @5.00

TALES OF SUSPENSE
Jan., 1959
1 DH(c),AW,'The Unknown Emptiness' 2,500.00
2 SK,JH,'Robot in Hiding' 900.00
3 SD,JK,'The Aliens Who Captured Earth' 800.00
4 JK,AW,'One Of Us Is A Martian' 750.00
5 JF,'Trapped in the Tunnel To Nowhere' 500.00
6 JK(c),'Howl in the Swamp' ... 500.00
7 SD,JK,Molten Man-Thing 550.00
8 BEv,'Monstro' 500.00
9 JK(c),JF,'Diablo' 600.00
10 RH,'I Brought Cyclops Back To Life' 500.00
11 JK(c),'I Created Sporr' 400.00
12 RC,'Gorkill The Living Demon' 400.00
13 'Elektro' 400.00
14 JK(c),'I Created Colossus' ... 400.00
15 JK/DAy(c),'Behold...Goom' .. 400.00
16 JK/DAy(c),'The Thing Called Metallo' 500.00
17 JK/DAy(c),'Goo Gam, Son of Goom' 400.00
18 JK/DAy(c),'Kraa the Inhuman' 400.00
19 JK/DAy,SD,'The Green Thing' 400.00
20 JK,DAy,SD,'Colossus Lives Again' 400.00
21 JK/DAy(c),SD,'This Is Klagg' . 325.00
22 JK/DAy(c),SD,'Beware Of Bruttu' 325.00

23 JK,DAy,SD,'The Creature in the Black Bog' 325.00
24 JK,DAy,SD,'Insect Man' 325.00
25 JK,DAy,SD,'The Death of Monstrollo' 325.00
26 JK,DAy,SD,'The Thing That Crawled By Night' 300.00
27 JK,DAy,SD,'When Oog Lives Again' 300.00
28 JK,DAy,SD,'Back From the Dead' 300.00
29 JK,DAy,SD,DH,'The Martian Who Stole A City' 275.00
30 JK,DAy,SD,DH,'The Haunted Roller Coaster' 300.00
31 JK,DAy,SD,DH,'The Monster in the Iron Mask' 325.00
32 JK,DAy,SD,DH,'The Man in the Bee-Hive' 500.00
33 JK,DAy,SD,DH,'Chamber of Fear' 275.00
34 JK,DAy,SD,DH,'Inside The Blue Glass Bottle' 275.00
35 JK,DAy,SD,DH,'The Challenge of Zarkorr' 325.00
36 SD,'Meet Mr. Meek' 275.00
37 DH,SD,'Hagg' 275.00
38 JDa,'The Teenager Who Ruled the World' 275.00
39 JK,O&I:Iron Man 7,000.00
40 JK,C:Iron Man. 2,000.00
41 JK,A:Iron Man,V:Dr.Strange 1,100.00
42 DH,SD,I:Red Pharoah 500.00
43 JK,DH,I:Kala,A:Iron Man ... 500.00
44 DH,SD,V:Mad Pharoah 500.00
45 DH,V:Jack Frost 500.00
46 DH,CR,I:Crimson Dynamo . 350.00
47 SD,V:Melter 300.00
48 SD,N:Iron Man 350.00
49 SD,A:Angel 300.00
50 DH,I:Mandarin 250.00
51 DH,I:Scarecrow 225.00
52 DH,I:Black Widow 350.00
53 DH,O:Watcher 235.00
54 DH,V:Mandarin 150.00
55 DH,V:Mandarin 150.00
56 DH,I:Unicorn 150.00
57 DH,I&O:Hawkeye 275.00
58 DH,GT,B:Captain America . 400.00
59 DH,1st S.A. Solo Captain America,I:Jarvis 400.00
60 DH,JK,V:Assassins 200.00
61 DH,JK,V:Mandarin 125.00
62 DH,JK,O:Mandarin 125.00

Tales of Suspense #71
© Marvel Entertainment Group

63 JK,O:Captain America 325.00
64 DH,JK,A:Black Widow, Hawkeye 125.00
65 DH,JK,I:Red Skull 200.00
66 DH,JK,O:Red Skull 200.00
67 DH,JK,V:Adolph Hitler 75.00
68 DH,JK,V:Red Skull 75.00
69 DH,JK,I:Titanium Man 75.00
70 DH,JK,GT,V:Titanium Man ... 75.00
71 DH,JK,WW,GT,V:Titanium Man 80.00
72 DH,JK,GT,V:The Sleeper 75.00
73 JA,JK,GT,A:Black Knight 75.00
74 JA,JK,GT,V:The Sleeper 75.00
75 JA,JK,I:Batroc,Sharon Carter . 75.00
76 JA,JR,V:Mandarin 75.00
77 JA,JK,JR,V:Ultimo,I:Peggy Carter 70.00
78 JA,GC,JK,V:Ultimo 70.00
79 JA,GC,JK,V:Red Skull, I:Cosmic Cube 125.00
80 JA,GC,JK,V:Red Skull 135.00
81 JA,GC,JK,V:Red Skull 75.00
82 GC,JK,V:The Adaptoid 75.00
83 GC,JK,V:The Adaptoid 75.00
84 GC,JK,V:Mandarin 75.00
85 GC,JK,V:Batroc 75.00
86 GC,JK,V:Mandarin 75.00
87 GC,V:Mole Man 75.00
88 GK,JK,GC,V:Power Man 75.00
89 GK,JK,GC,V:Red Skull 75.00
90 GK,JK,GC,V:Red Skull 75.00
91 GK,GC,JK,V:Crusher 75.00
92 GC,JK,A:Nick Fury 75.00
93 GC,JK,V:Titanium Man 75.00
94 GC,JK,I:Modok 75.00
95 GC,JK,V:Grey Gargoyle, IR:Captain America 75.00
96 GC,JK,V:Grey Gargoyle 75.00
97 GC,JK,I:Whiplash, A:Black Panther 75.00
98 GC,JK,I:Whitney Frost A:Black Panther 125.00
99 GC,JK,A:Black Panther 150.00
Marvel Milestone rep. #39 (1993) .. 2.95
Becomes:

CAPTAIN AMERICA

TALES OF THE ZOMBIE
Aug., 1973
(Black & White Magazine)
1 Reprint Menace #5,O:Zombie . 40.00
2 GC,GT 30.00
3 .... 30.00
4 'Live and Let Die' 30.00
5 BH 30.00
6 .... 30.00
7 thru 9 AA .... @30.00
10 March, 1975 .... 30.00

TALES TO ASTONISH
[1st Series] Jan., 1959
1 JDa,'Ninth Wonder of the World' 2,500.00
2 SD,'Capture A Martian' ... 1,000.00
3 SD,JK,'The Giant From Outer Space' 700.00
4 SD,JK,'The Day The Martians Struck' 700.00
5 SD,AW,'The Things on Easter Island' 750.00
6 SD,JK,'Invasion of the Stone Men' 600.00
7 SD,JK,'The Thing on Bald Mountain' 600.00
8 DAy,SD,JK,'Mummex, King of the Mummies' 600.00
9 DAy,JK(c),SD,'Droom, the Living Lizard' 600.00
10 DAy,JK,SD,'Titano' 600.00

MARVEL

Comics Values Annual — Tales To–Tarzan

11 DAy,JK,SD,`Monstrom, the Dweller in the Black Swamp'...... 400.00	53 DH,V:Porcupine........... 150.00	10 Impact on Kids............. 3.00
12 JK/DAy(c),SD,`Gorgilla'..... 400.00	54 DH,I:El Toro.............. 150.00	11 Open All Night, 48-pg....... 3.50
13 JK,SD,`Groot, the Monster From Planet X'........... 400.00	55 V:Human Top............. 150.00	12 I Was A Teenaged Frog-Man... 3.00
14 JK,SD,`Krang'............ 400.00	56 V:The Magician........... 200.00	13 SeP,Double Shots........... 3.00
15 JK/DAy,`The Blip'........ 550.00	57 A:Spider-Man............. 250.00	14 The Last Shoot............. 3.00
16 DAy,JK,SD,`Thorr'....... 450.00	58 V:Colossus(not X-Men one).. 150.00	15 The Collaborator........... 3.00
17 JK,SD,`Vandoom'........ 400.00	59 V:Hulk,Black Knight........ 250.00	16 F:Tombstone, Kangaroo...... 3.00
18 DAy,JK,SD,`Gorgilla Strikes Again'................ 400.00	60 SD,B:Hulk,Giant Man....... 275.00	17 Tombstone in jail........... 3.00
19 DAy,JK,SD,`Rommbu'..... 400.00	61 SD,I:Glenn Talbot, V:Egghead............ 125.00	18 TMK..................... 3.00
20 JK,SD,`X, The Thing That Lived'............. 400.00	62 I:Leader,N:Wasp.......... 125.00	19 F:Grizzly & Rhino........... 3.00
21 JK,SD,`Trull the Inhuman'... 400.00	63 SD,O:Leader(1st full story)... 125.00	20 J.Jonah Jameson........... 3.00
22 JK,SD,`The Crawling Creature'.............. 300.00	64 SD,V:Leader............. 125.00	21........................ 3.00
23 JK,SD,`Moomba is Here!'... 300.00	65 BP,DH,SD,N:Giant-Man,.... 125.00	22 The System............... 3.00
24 JK,SD,`The Abominable Snowman'.............. 300.00	66 BP,JK,SD,V:Leader, Chameleon............. 125.00	TPB Spider-Man: Tangled Web... 15.95
25 JK,SD,`The Creature From Krogarr'............... 300.00	67 BP,JK,SD,I:Kanga Khan..... 125.00	TPB Spider-Man: Tangled Web 2. 14.95
26 JK,SD,`Four-Armed Things'.. 300.00	68 BP,JK,N:Human Top,V:Leader 125.00	TPB Spider-Man: Tangled Web 3. 16.00
27 StL(s),SD,JK,I:Ant-Man.... 5,500.00	69 BP,JK,V:Human Top,Leader, E:Giant-Man........... 125.00	**TARZAN**
28 JK,SD,I Am the Gorilla Man.. 300.00	70 GC,JK,B:Sub-Mariner/Hulk,I: Neptune............... 150.00	**June, 1977**
29 JK,SD,When the Space Beasts Attack.......... 300.00	71 GC,JK,V:Leader,I:Vashti..... 90.00	1 JB,Edgar Rice Burroughs Adapt.25.00
30 JK,SD,Thing From the Hidden Swamp........... 300.00	72 GC,JK,V:Leader............ 90.00	2 JB,O:Tarzan................ 18.00
31 JK,SD,The Mummy's Secret. 300.00	73 GC,JK,V:Leader,A:Watcher... 90.00	3 JB,`The Alter of the Flaming God',I:LA............... 18.00
32 JK,SD,Quicksand........ 300.00	74 GC,JK,V:Leader,A:Watcher... 90.00	4 JB,TD,V:Leopards........... 18.00
33 JK,SD,Dead Storage...... 300.00	75 GC,JK,A:Watcher........... 90.00	5 JB,TD,`Vengeance',A:LA..... 10.00
34 JK,SD,Monster at Window... 300.00	76 GC,GK,JK,Atlantis........... 90.00	6 JB,TD,`Rage of Tantor',A:LA... 10.00
35 StL(s),JK,SD, B:Ant-Man (2nd App.)............. 2,200.00	77 JK,V:Executioner........... 90.00	7 JB,TD,`Tarzan Rescues The Moon'................. 10.00
36 JK,SD,V:Comrade X...... 1,000.00	78 BEv,GC,JK,Prince and the Puppet............ 90.00	8 JB,`Battle For The Jewel Of Opar'................. 10.00
37 JK,SD,V:The Protector...... 700.00	79 BEv,GC,JK,Hulk vs.Hercules.. 90.00	9 JB,`Histah, the Serpent'...... 10.00
38 JK,SD,Betrayed By the Ants.. 700.00	80 BEv,GC,JK,Moleman vs. Tyrannus.............. 90.00	10 JB,`The Deadly Peril of Jane Clayton'............ 10.00
39 JK,DH,V:Scarlet Beetle..... 700.00	81 BEv,GC,JK,I:Boomerang,Secret Empire,Moleman vs. Tyrannus 90.00	11 JB...................... 10.00
40 JK,SD,DH,The Day Ant-Man Failed................. 700.00	82 BEv,GC,JK,V:Iron Man....... 100.00	12 JB,`Fangs of Death'......... 10.00
41 DH,St,SD,V:Kulla......... 400.00	83 BEv,JK,V:Boomerang........ 90.00	13 JB,`Lion-God'............. 10.00
42 DH,JSe,SD,Voice of Doom... 400.00	84 BEv,GC,JK,Like a Beast at Bay 90.00	14 JB,`The Fury of Fang and Claw'10.00
43 DH,SD,Master of Time...... 400.00	85 BEv,GC,JB,Missile & the Monster........... 90.00	15 JB,`Sword of the Slaver'..... 10.00
44 JK,SD,I&O:Wasp......... 400.00	86 BEv,JB,V:Warlord Krang..... 90.00	16 JB,`Death Rides the Jungle Winds'................ 10.00
45 DH,SD,V:Egghead......... 300.00	87 BEv,JB,IR:Hulk............. 90.00	17 JB,`The Entrance to the Earths Core'............ 10.00
46 DH,SD,V:Cyclops(robot)..... 300.00	88 BEv,GK,V:Boomerang....... 90.00	18 JB,`Corsairs of the Earth's Core'.... 10.00
47 DH,SD,V:Trago........... 300.00	89 BEv,GK,V:Stranger.......... 90.00	19 `Pursuit'.................. 10.00
48 DH,SD,I:Porcupine......... 300.00	90 JK,GK,BEv,I:Abomination..... 90.00	20 `Blood Bond'.............. 10.00
49 JK,DH,AM,Ant-Man Becomes Giant-Man.............. 325.00	91 GK,BEv,DA,V:Abomination... 90.00	21 `Dark and Bloody Sky'....... 8.00
50 JK,SD,I&O:Human Top..... 200.00	92 MSe,C:Silver Surfer x-over... 100.00	22 JM,RN,`War In Pellucidar'.... 8.00
51 JK,V:Human Top......... 200.00	93 MSe,Silver Surfer x-over.... 125.00	23 `To the Death'............. 8.00
52 I&O:Black Knight......... 200.00	94 BEv,MSe,V:Dragorr,High Evolutionary............ 90.00	24 `The Jungle Lord Returns'.... 8.00
	95 BEv,MSe,V:High Evolutionary. 90.00	25 RB(c),V:Poachers.......... 8.00
	96 MSe,Skull Island,High Evol.... 90.00	26 RB(c),`Caged'............. 8.00
	97 MSe,C:Ka-Zar,X-Men....... 100.00	27 RB(c),`Chaos in the Caberet'... 8.00
	98 DA,MSe,I:Legion of the Living Lightning,I:Seth.......... 90.00	
	99 DA,MSe,V:Legion of the Living Lighting............... 90.00	
	100 MSe,DA,Hulk vs.Sub-Mariner 125.00	
	101 MSe,GC,V:Loki........... 125.00	
	Becomes:	
	INCREDIBLE HULK	
	TALES TO ASTONISH	
	[2nd Series] Dec., 1979	
	1 JB,rep.Sub-Mariner#1........ 5.00	
	2 thru 14 JB,rep.Sub-Mariner... @3.00	
	TANGLED WEB	
	April, 2001	
	1 GEn,JMC,The Thousand...... 3.00	
	2 GEn,JMC,The Thousand...... 3.00	
	3 GEn,JMC,V:The Thousand..... 3.00	
	4 Severance Package.......... 3.00	
	5 PrM,DFg,Flowers for Rhino..... 3.00	
	6 PrM,DFg,Flowers/Rhino,pt.2.... 3.00	
	7 Gentlemen's Agreement...... 3.00	
	8 Gentlemen's Agreement...... 3.00	
	9 LW,Gentlemen's Agreement,pt.3. 3.00	

Tales To Astonish #23
© Marvel Entertainment Group

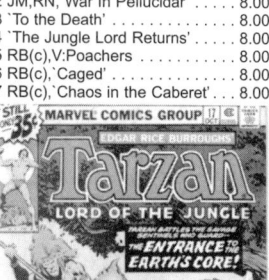

Tarzan #17
© Marvel Entertainment Group

All comics prices listed are for *Near Mint* condition.

CVA Page 323

Tarzan–Thanos — MARVEL — Comics Values Annual

28 `A Savage Against A City'...... 8.00
29 Oct., 1979 .... 8.00
Ann.#1 JB 7.00
Ann.#2 `Drums of the
  Death-Dancers' 7.00
Ann.#3 `Ant-Men and the
  She-Devils 7.00

TARZAN OF THE APES
July, 1984
1 (movie adapt.) 4.00
2 .... 4.00

TASKMASTER
Feb., 2002
1 (of 4) F:Iron Man 3.00
2 crime syndicates............. 3.00
3 syndicates catch on 3.00
4 concl..................... 3.00

TEAM AMERICA
June, 1982
1 O:Team America............. 2.50
2 V:Marauder 2.50
3 LMc,V:Mr.Mayhem 2.50
4 LMc,V:Arcade Assassins. 2.50
5 A:Marauder................ 2.50
6 A:R.U. Ready 2.50
7 LMc,V:Emperor of Texas...... 2.50
8 DP,V:Hydra................. 2.50
9 A:Iron Man 2.50
10 V:Minister Ashe 2.50
11 A:Marauder,V:Ghost Rider ... 3.00
12 DP,Marauder unmasked,
  May, 1983 .... 2.50

TEAM HELIX
1993
1 A:Wolverine 2.25
2 A:Wolverine 2.25

TEAM X/TEAM 7
1996
1-shot LHa,SEp,MRy 4.95

TEAM X 2000
Dec., 1998
1-shot, 48-page............... 3.50

TEEN COMICS
See: **ALL WINNERS COMICS**

TEENAGE ROMANCE
See: **MY ROMANCE**

TEK WORLD
See: **WILLIAM SHATNER'S TEK WORLD**

TERMINATOR 2
Sept., 1991
1 KJ,movie adaption 3.00
2 KJ,movie adaption 3.00
3 KJ,movie adaption 3.00
Terminator II (bookshelf format) .. 5.00
Terminator II (B&W mag. size) ... 2.25

TERRARISTS
Epic, 1993–94
1 thru 4 w/card............... @2.50
5 thru 7 .... @2.50

Terror, Inc. #1
© Marvel Entertainment Group

TERROR INC.
1992–93
1 JZ,I:Hellfire................. 3.00
2 JZ,I:Bezeel,Hellfire 2.50
3 JZ,A:Hellfire 2.25
4 JZ,A:Hellfire,V:Barbados...... 2.25
5 JZ,V:Hellfire,A:Dr. Strange ... 2.25
6 JZ,MT,A:Punisher............ 2.25
7 JZ,V:Punisher.............. 2.25
8 Christmas issue 2.25
9 JZ,V:Wolverine 2.25
10 V:Wolverine............... 2.25
11 A:Silver Sable,Cage 2.25
12 For Love Nor Money#4,A:Cage,
  Silver Sable 2.25
13 Inf.Crusade,A:Gh.Rider 2.25

TESSIE THE TYPIST
Timely, Summer, 1944
1 BW,`Doc Rockblock' 750.00
2 BW,`Powerhouse Pepper' ... 400.00
3 Football cover 150.00
4 BW 300.00
5 BW 300.00
6 BW,HK,`Hey Look' 300.00
7 BW 300.00
8 BW 300.00
9 BW,HK,`Powerhouse Pepper' 325.00
10 BW,A:Rusty............. 325.00
11 BW,A:Rusty............. 325.00
12 BW,HK................. 325.00
13 BW,A:Millie The Model,Rusty . 275.00
14 BW 275.00
15 HK,A:Millie,Rusty......... 275.00
16 HK..................... 150.00
17 HK,A:Millie, Rusty 150.00
18 HK..................... 150.00
19 Annie Oakley story........ 100.00
20 .... 100.00
21 A:Lana, Millie 100.00
22 .... 100.00
23 .... 100.00
Becomes:

TINY TESSIE
24 .... 100.00
Becomes:

REAL EXPERIENCES
25 Ph(c),Jan., 1950 .... 100.00

TEXAS KID
Atlas, Jan., 1951
1 GT,JMn,O:Texas Kid 275.00
2 JMn 150.00
3 JMn,`Man Who Didn't Exist' .. 125.00
4 JMn 125.00
5 JMn 125.00
6 JMn 125.00
7 JMn 125.00
8 JMn 125.00
9 JMn 125.00
10 JMn,July, 1952........... 125.00

TEX DAWSON, GUNSLINGER
Jan., 1973
1 JSo(c) 35.00
Becomes:

GUNSLINGER
2 .... 25.00
3 June, 1973 .... 25.00

TEX MORGAN
Aug., 1948
1 .... 300.00
2 `Boot Hill Welcome For A
  Bad Man' 200.00
3 .... 125.00
4 `Trapped in the Outlaw's Den',
  A:Arizona Annie 125.00
5 `Valley of Missing Cowboys' .. 125.00
6 `Never Say Murder',
  A:Tex Taylor 125.00
7 CCB,Ph(c),`Captain Tootsie',
  A:Tex Taylor 200.00
8 Ph(c),`Terror Of Rimrock
  Valley', A:Diablo 200.00
9 Ph(c),`Death to Tex Taylor',
  Feb., 1950 .... 200.00

TEX TAYLOR
Sept., 1948
1 `Boot Hill Showdown' 325.00
2 `When Two-Gun Terror Rides
  the Range' 175.00
3 `Thundering Hooves and
  Blazing Guns' 150.00
4 Ph(c),`Draw or Die Cowpoke' . 175.00
5 Ph(c),`The Juggler of Yellow
  Valley',A:Blaze Carson 175.00
6 Ph(c),`Mystery of Howling Gap' 175.00
7 Ph(c),`Trapped in Time's Lost
  Land',A:Diablo 225.00
8 Ph(c),`The Mystery of Devil-
  Tree Plateau',A:Diablo 225.00
9 Ph(c),`Guns Along the Border',
  A:Nimo,March, 1950 ...... 225.00

THANOS
Marvel Oct. 2003
1 JSn 3.00
2 JSn 3.00
TPB The End, Vol.3 .... 19.95

THANOS QUEST
1990
1 JSn,RLm,V:Elders,
  for Soul Gems 8.00
1a 2nd printing 4.00
2 JSn,RLm,O:SoulGems,I:
  Infinity Gauntlet (story
  cont.in Silver Surfer #44) 8.00
2a 2nd printing 4.00

CVA Page 324 — All comics prices listed are for *Near Mint* condition.

MARVEL

THANOS QUEST
Jan., 2000
GN JSn,RLm,96-pg............ 4.00

THING, THE
July, 1983
1 JBy,O:Thing................ 3.50
2 JBy,Woman from past......... 2.50
3 JBy,A:Inhumans.............. 2.50
4 JBy,A:Lockjaw............... 2.50
5 JBy,A:Spider-Man,She-Hulk... 2.50
6 JBy,V:Puppet Master......... 2.50
7 JBy,V:Goody Two Shoes....... 2.50
8 JBy,V:Egyptian Curse........ 2.50
9 JBy,F:Alicia Masters........ 2.50
10 JBy,Secret Wars............ 2.50
11 JBy,B:Rocky Grimm.......... 2.50
12 JBy,F:Rocky Grimm.......... 2.50
13 JBy,F:Rocky Grimm.......... 2.50
14 F:Rocky Grimm.............. 2.50
15 F:Rocky Grimm.............. 2.50
16 F:Rocky Grimm.............. 2.50
17 F:Rocky Grimm.............. 2.50
18 F:Rocky Grimm.............. 2.50
19 F:Rocky Grimm.............. 2.50
20 F:Rocky Grimm.............. 2.50
21 V:Ultron................... 2.50
22 V:Ultron................... 2.50
23 R:Thing to Earth,A:Fant. Four.. 2.50
24 V:Rhino,A:Miracle Man...... 2.50
25 V:Shamrock................. 2.50
26 A:Vance Astro.............. 2.50
27 I:Sharon Ventura........... 2.50
28 A:Vance Astro.............. 2.50
29 A:Vance Astro.............. 2.50
30 Secret Wars II,A:Vance Astro.. 2.50
31 A:Vance Astro.............. 2.50
32 A:Vance Astro.............. 2.50
33 A:Vance Astro,I:New Grapplers. 2.50
34 V:Titania,Sphinx........... 2.50
35 I:New Ms.Marvel,Power Broker. 2.50
36 Last Issue,A:She-Hulk...... 2.50

[Mini-Series]
1 rep.Marvel Two-in-One #50..... 2.50
2 rep Marvel Two-in-One,V:GR... 2.50
3 rep Marvel Two-in-One #51.... 2.00
4 rep Marvel Two-in-One #43.... 2.00

THING/SHE-HULK
March, 1998
1-shot TDz,V:Dragon Man, 48-pg.. 3.00
1-shot The Long Night, 48-pg..... 3.00

THING, THE: FREAKSHOW
June, 2002
1 (of 4) ALa,grumpiest super-hero. 3.00
2 ALa,people are enthralled........ 3.00
3 ALa,ScK...................... 3.00
4 ALa,ScK,concl................ 3.00

THOR, THE MIGHTY
Prev: Journey Into Mystery
March, 1966
126 JK,V:Hercules............ 225.00
127 JK,I:Pluto,Volla.......... 125.00
128 JK,V:Pluto,A:Hercules..... 125.00
129 JK,V:Pluto,I:Ares......... 125.00
130 JK,V:Pluto,A:Hercules..... 125.00
131 JK,I:Colonizers........... 125.00
132 JK,A:Colonizers,I:Ego..... 125.00
133 JK,A:Colonizers,A:Ego..... 125.00
134 JK,I:High Evolutionary,
    Man-Beast................ 175.00
135 JK,O:High Evolutionary..... 90.00
136 JK,F:Odin................. 70.00
137 JK,I:Ulik................. 70.00
138 JK,V:Ulik,A:Sif........... 70.00
139 JK,V:Ulik................. 70.00
140 JK,V:Growing Man.......... 70.00
141 JK,V:Replicus............. 60.00
142 JK,V:Super Skrull......... 60.00
143 JK,BEv,V:Talisman......... 60.00
144 JK,V:Talisman............. 60.00
145 JK,V:Ringmaster........... 60.00
146 JK,O:Inhumans Part 1..... 100.00
147 JK,O:Inhumans Part 2..... 100.00
148 JK,I:Wrecker,O:Black Bolt. 100.00
149 JK,O:Black Bolt,Medusa... 100.00
150 JK,V:Triton............... 90.00
151 JK,V:Destroyer............ 90.00
152 JK,V:Destroyer............ 90.00
153 JK,F:Dr.Blake............. 90.00
154 JK,I:Mangog............... 90.00
155 JK,V:Mangog............... 90.00
156 JK,V:Mangog............... 90.00
157 JK,D:Mangog............... 90.00
158 JK,O:Don Blake Part 1.... 150.00
159 JK,O:Don Blake Part 2..... 90.00
160 JK,I:Travrians............ 65.00
161 JK,Shall a God Prevail.... 65.00
162 JK,O:Galactus............. 80.00
163 JK,I:Mutates,A:Pluto...... 50.00
164 JK,A:Pluto,V:Greek Gods... 50.00
165 JK,V:Him/Warlock......... 150.00
166 JK,V:Him/Warlock......... 125.00
167 JK,F:Sif.................. 50.00
168 JK,O:Galactus............. 75.00
169 JK,O:Galactus............. 75.00
170 JK,BEv,V:Thermal Man...... 50.00
171 JK,BEv,V:Wrecker.......... 50.00
172 JK,BEv,V:Ulik............. 50.00
173 JK,BEv,V:Ulik,Ringmaster.. 50.00
174 JK,BEv,V:Crypto-Man....... 50.00
175 JK,Fall of Asgard,V:Surtur. 50.00
176 JK,V:Surtur............... 50.00
177 JK,I:Igon,V:Surtur........ 50.00
178 JK,C:Silver Surfer........ 60.00
179 JK,MSe,C:Galactus......... 50.00
180 NA,JSi,V:Loki............. 60.00
181 NA,JSi,V:Loki............. 60.00
182 JB,V:Dr.Doom.............. 50.00
183 JB,V:Dr.Doom.............. 50.00
184 JB,I:The Guardian......... 50.00
185 JB,JSt,V:Silent One....... 50.00
186 JB,JSt,V:Hela............. 50.00
187 JB,JSt,V:Odin............. 50.00
188 JB,JM,F:Odin.............. 50.00
189 JB,JSt,V:Hela............. 50.00
190 JB,I:Durok................ 50.00
191 JB,JSt,V:Loki............. 50.00
192 JB........................ 50.00
193 JB,SB,V:Silver Surfer..... 75.00
194 JB,SB,V:Loki.............. 50.00
195 JB,JR,V:Mangog............ 50.00
196 JB,NR,V:Kartag............ 50.00
197 JB,V:Mangog............... 50.00
198 JB,V:Pluto................ 50.00
199 JB,V:Pluto,Hela........... 50.00
200 JB,Ragnarok............... 60.00
201 JB,JM,Odin resurrected.... 40.00
202 JB,V:Ego-Prime............ 40.00
203 JB,V:Ego-Prime............ 40.00
204 JB,JM,Demon from t/Depths. 40.00
205 JB,V:Mephisto............. 40.00
206 JB,V:Absorbing Man........ 30.00
207 JB,V:Absorbing Man........ 30.00
208 JB,V:Mercurio............. 30.00
209 JB,I:Druid................ 30.00
210 JB,DP,I:Ulla,V:Ulik....... 30.00
211 JB,DP,V:Ulik.............. 30.00
212 JB,JSt,V:Sssthgar......... 30.00
213 JB,DP,I:Gregor............ 30.00
214 SB,JM,V:Dark Nebula....... 30.00
215 JB,JM,J:Xorr.............. 30.00
216 JB,JM,V:4D-Man............ 30.00
217 JB,SB,I:Krista,V:Odin..... 30.00
218 JB,JM,A:Colonizers........ 30.00
219 JB,I:Protector............ 30.00
220 JB,V:Avalon............... 30.00
221 JB,V:Olympus.............. 30.00
222 JB,JSe,A:Hercules,V:Pluto. 30.00
223 JB,A:Hercules,V:Pluto..... 30.00
224 JB,V:Destroyer............ 30.00
225 JB,JSi,I:Fire Lord........ 35.00
226 JB,A:Watcher,Galactus..... 25.00
227 JB,JSi,V:Ego.............. 25.00
228 JB,JSi,A:Galactus,D:Ego... 25.00
229 JB,JSi,A:Hercules,I:Dweller. 25.00
230 JB,A:Hercules............. 25.00
231 JB,DG,V:Armak............. 25.00
232 JB,JSi,A:Firelord......... 25.00
233 JB,Asgard Invades Earth... 25.00
234 JB,V:Loki................. 25.00
235 JB,JSi,I:Possessor
    (Kamo Tharnn)........... 25.00
236 JB,JSi,V:Absorbing Man.... 25.00
237 JB,JSi,V:Ulik............. 25.00
238 JB,JSi,V:Ulik............. 25.00
239 JB,JSi,V:Ulik............. 25.00
240 SB,KJ,V:Seth.............. 25.00
241 JB,JGi,I:Geb.............. 25.00
242 JB,JSi,V:Servitor......... 25.00
243 JB,JSt,V:Servitor......... 25.00
244 JB,JSt,V:Servitor......... 25.00
245 JB,JSt,V:Servitor......... 25.00
246 JB,JSt,A:Firelord......... 25.00
247 JB,JSt,A:Firelord......... 25.00
248 JB,V:Storm Giant.......... 25.00
249 JB,V:Odin................. 25.00
250 JB,D:Igron,V:Mangog....... 25.00
251 JB,A:Sif.................. 20.00
252 JB,V:Ulik................. 20.00
253 JB,I:Trogg................ 20.00
254 JK,O:Dr.Blake rep......... 20.00
255 Stone Men of Saturn rep... 20.00
256 JB,I:Sporr................ 20.00
257 JK,JB,I:Fee-Lon........... 20.00
258 JK,JB,V:Grey Gargoyle..... 20.00
259 JB,A:Spider-Man........... 20.00
260 WS,I:Doomsday Star........ 20.00
261 WS,I:Soul Survivors....... 20.00
262 WS,Odin Found,I:Odin Force. 20.00
263 WS,V:Loki................. 20.00
264 WS,V:Loki................. 20.00
265 WS,V:Destroyer............ 20.00
266 WS,Odin Quest............. 20.00
267 WS,F:Odin................. 20.00
268 WS,V:Damocles............. 20.00
269 WS,V:Stilt-Man............ 20.00
270 WS,V:Blastaar............. 20.00
271 Avengers,Iron Man x-over.. 20.00
272 JB,Day the Thunder Failed. 20.00

Thor #195
© Marvel Entertainment Group

Thor — MARVEL — Comics Values Annual

#	Entry	Price
273	JB,V:Midgard Serpent	20.00
274	JB,D:Balder,I:Hermod,Hoder	20.00
275	JB,V:Loki,I:Sigyn	20.00
276	JB,Trial of Loki	20.00
277	JB,V:Fake Thor	20.00
278	JB,V:Fake Thor	20.00
279	A:Pluto,V:Ulik	20.00
280	V:Hyperion	20.00
281	O:Space Phantom	15.00
282	V:Immortus,I:Tempus	15.00
283	JB,V:Celestials	15.00
284	JB,V:Gammenon	15.00
285	JB,R:Karkas	15.00
286	KP,KRo,D:Kro,I:Dragona	15.00
287	KP,2nd App. & O:Forgotten One(Hero)	15.00
288	KP,V:Forgotten One	15.00
289	KP,V:Destroyer	15.00
290	I:Red Bull(Toro Rojo)	15.00
291	KP,A:Eternals,Zeus	15.00
292	KP,V:Odin	15.00
293	KP,Door to Mind's Eye	15.00
294	KP,O:Odin & Asgard,I:Frey	15.00
295	KP,I:Fafnir,V:Storm Giants	15.00
296	KP,D:Siegmund	15.00
297	KP,V:Sword of Siegfried	15.00
298	KP,V:Dragon(Fafnir)	15.00
299	KP,A:Valkyrie,I:Hagen	15.00
300	KP,giant,O:Odin & Destroyer, Rindgold Ring Quest ends,D:Uni-Mind,I:Mother Earth	25.00
301	KP,O:Mother Earth,V:Apollo	15.00
302	KP,V:Locus	15.00
303	Whatever Gods There Be	15.00
304	KP,V:Wrecker	15.00
305	KP,R:Gabriel(Air Walker)	15.00
306	KP,O&V:Firelord,O:Air Walker	15.00
307	KP,I:Dream Demon	15.00
308	KP,V:Snow Giants	15.00
309	V:Bomnardiers	15.00
310	KP,V:Mephisto	15.00
311	KP,GD,A:Valkyrie	15.00
312	KP,V:Tyr	15.00
313	KP,Thor Trial	15.00
314	KP,A:Drax,Moondragon	15.00
315	KP,O:Bi-Beast	15.00
316	KP,A:Iron Man,Man Thing, V:Man-Beast	15.00
317	KP,V:Man-Beast	15.00
318	GK,V:Fafnir	15.00
319	KP,I&D:Zaniac	15.00
320	KP,V:Rimthursar	15.00
321	I:Menagerie	15.00
322	V:Heimdall	15.00
323	V:Death	15.00
324	V:Graviton	15.00
325	JM,O:Darkoth,V:Mephisto	15.00
326	I:New Scarlet Scarab	15.00
327	V:Loki & Tyr	15.00
328	I:Megatak	15.00
329	HT,V:Hrungnir	15.00
330	BH,I:Crusader	15.00
331	Threshold of Death	15.00
332	V:Dracula	15.00
333	BH,V:Dracula	15.00
334	Quest For Rune Staff	15.00
335	V:Possessor	15.00
336	A:Captain Ultra	15.00
337	WS,I:Beta Ray Bill,A:Surtur	25.00
338	WS,O:Beta Ray Bill,I:Lorelei	20.00
339	WS,V:Beta Ray Bill	15.00
340	WS,A:Beta Ray Bill	15.00
341	WS,V:Fafnir	15.00
342	WS,V:Fafnir,I:Eilif	15.00
343	WS,V:Fafnir	15.00
344	WS,Balder vs. Loki,I:Malekith	15.00
345	WS,V:Malekith	15.00
346	WS,V:Malekith	15.00
347	WS,V:Malekith,I:Algrim (Kurse)	15.00
348	WS,V:Malekith	15.00
349	WS,R:Beta Ray Bill,O:Odin, I&O:Vili & Ve(Odin's brothers)	15.00
350	WS,V:Surtur	15.00
351	WS,V:Surtur	15.00
352	WS,V:Surtur	15.00
353	WS,V:Surtur,D:Odin	10.00
354	WS,V:Hela	10.00
355	WS,SB,A:Thor's Great Grandfather	10.00
356	BL,BG,V:Hercules	10.00
357	WS,A:Beta Ray Bill	10.00
358	WS,A:Beta Ray Bill	10.00
359	WS,V:Loki	10.00
360	WS,V:Hela	10.00
361	WS,V:Hela	10.00
362	WS,V:Hela	10.00
363	WS,Secret Wars II,V:Kurse	10.00
364	WS,I:Thunder Frog	10.00
365	WS,A:Thunder Frog	10.00
366	WS,A:Thunder Frog	10.00
367	WS,D:Malekith,A:Kurse	10.00
368	WS,F:Balder t/Brave,Kurse	10.00
369	WS,F:Balder the Brave	10.00
370	JB,V:Loki	10.00
371	SB,I:Justice Peace,V:Zaniac	10.00
372	SB,V:Justice Peace	10.00
373	SB,A:X-Factor,(Mut.Mass)	12.00
374	WS,SB,A:X-Factor,(Mut.Mass) A:Sabretooth	15.00
375	WS,SB,N:Thor(Exoskeleton)	10.00
376	WS,SB,V:Absorbing Man	10.00
377	WS,SB,N:Thor,A:Ice Man	10.00
378	WS,SB,V:Frost Giants	10.00
379	WS,V:Midgard Serpent	10.00
380	WS,V:Midgard Serpent	10.00
381	WE,SB,A:Avengers	10.00
382	WS,SB,V:Frost Giants,Loki	12.00
383	BBr,Secret Wars story	10.00
384	RF,BBr,I:Future Thor(Dargo)	15.00
385	EL,V:Hulk	10.00
386	RF,BBr,I:Leir	10.00
387	RF,BBr,V:Celestials	10.00
388	RF,BBr,V:Celestials	10.00
389	RF,BBr,V:Celestials	10.00
390	RF,BBr,A:Avengers,V:Seth	10.00
391	RF,BBr,I:Mongoose,Eric Masterson,A:Spider-Man	15.00
392	RF,I:Quicksand	12.00
393	RF,BBr,V:Quicksand,A:DD	12.00
394	RF,BBr,V:Earth Force	12.00
395	RF,V:Earth Force	12.00
396	RF,A:Black Knight	12.00
397	RF,A:Loki	12.00
398	RF,DH,R:Odin,V:Seth	12.00
399	RF,RT,R:Surtur,V:Seth	12.00
400	RF,JSt,CV,V:Surtur,Seth	15.00
401	V:Loki	8.00
402	RF,JSt,V:Quicksand	8.00
403	RF,JSt,V:Executioner	8.00
404	RF,JSt,TD,V:Annihilus	8.00
405	RF,JSt,TD,V:Annihilus	8.00
406	RF,JSt,TD,V:Wundagore	8.00
407	RF,JSt,R:Hercules,High Evol.	8.00
408	RF,JSt,I:Eric Masterson/Thor, V:Mongoose	10.00
409	RF,JSt,V:Dr.Doom	8.00
410	RF,JSt,V:Dr.Doom,She-Hulk.	8.00
411	RF,JSt,C:New Warriors V:Juggernaut,A of V	6.00
412	RF,JSt,I:New Warriors V:Juggernaut,A of V	7.00
413	RF,JSt,A:Dr.Strange	5.00
414	RF,JSt,V:Ulik	5.00
415	HT,O:Thor	5.00
416	RF,JSt,A:Hercules	5.00
417	RF,JSt,A:High Evolutionary	5.00
418	RF,JSt,V:Wrecking Crew	5.00
419	RF,JSt,B:Black Galaxy Saga,I:Stellaris	5.00
420	RF,JSt,A:Avengers,V:Stellaris	5.00
421	RF,JSt,V:Stellaris	5.00
422	RF,JSt,V:High Evol.,Nobilus	5.00
423	RF,JSt,A:High Evol.,Celestials Count Tagar	5.00
424	RF,JSt,V:Celestials,E:Black Galaxy Saga	5.00
425	RF,AM,V:Surtur,Ymir	5.00
426	RF,JSt,HT,O:Earth Force	5.00
427	RF,JSt,A:Drago	5.00
428	RF,JSt,A:Excalibur	5.00
429	RF,JSt,A:Ghost Rider	5.00
430	RF,AM,A:Mephisto,Gh.Rider	5.00
431	HT,AM,V:Ulik,Loki	5.00
432	RF,D:Loki,Thor Banished,Eric Masterson becomes 2nd Thor	6.00
433	RF,V:Ulik	7.00
434	RF,AM,V:Warriors Three	5.00
435	RF,AM,V:Annihilus	5.00
436	RF,AM,V:Titania,Absorbing Man,A:Hercules	5.00
437	RF,AM,V:Quasar	5.00
438	RF,JSt,A:Future Thor(Drago)	5.00
439	RF,JSt,A:Drago	5.00
440	RF,AM,I:Thor Corps	6.00
441	RF,AM,Celestials vs.Ego	6.00
442	RF,AM,Don Blake,Beta Ray Bill,Mephisto	4.00
443	RF,AM,A:Dr.Strange,Silver Surfer,V:Mephisto	4.00
444	RF,AM,Special X-mas tale	4.00
445	AM,Galactic Storm,pt.7, V:Gladiator	4.00
446	AM,Galactic Storm,pt.14, A:Avengers	4.00
447	RF,AM,V:Absorbing Man, A:Spider-Man	4.00
448	RF,AM,V:Titania,A:SpM	4.00
449	RF,AM,V:Ulik	4.00
450	RF,AM,V:Heimdall,A:Code Blue Double-Sized,Gatefold(c),rep. Journey Into Mystery#87	4.00
451	RF,AM,I:Bloodaxe	4.00
452	RF,AM,V:Bloodaxe	4.00
453	RF,AM,V:Mephisto	4.00
454	RF,AM,V:Mephisto,Loki, Karnilla	4.00
455	AM(i),V:Loki,Karnilla,R:Odin, A:Dr.Strange	4.00
456	RF,AM,V:Bloodaxe	4.00
457	RF,AM,R:1st Thor	4.00
458	RF,AM,Thor vs. Eric	4.00
459	RF,AM,C&I:Thunderstrike(Eric Masterson)	3.00
460	I:New Valkyrie	3.00

Thor #391
© Marvel Entertainment Group

MARVEL

461 V:Beta Ray Bill............ 3.00
462 A:New Valkyrie............ 3.00
463 Infinity Crusade........... 3.00
464 Infinity Crusade,V:Loki...... 3.00
465 Infinity Crusade........... 3.00
466 Infinity Crusade........... 3.00
467 Infinity Crusade........... 3.00
468 RMz(s),Blood & Thunder#1 .. 3.00
469 RMz(s),Blood & Thunder#5 .. 3.00
470 MCW,Blood & Thunder#9 .... 3.00
471 MCW,E:Blood & Thunder..... 3.00
472 B:RTs(s),MCW,I:Godling,C:High
    Evolutionary 3.00
473 MCW,V:Godling,High Evolutionary,
    I&C:Karnivore(Man-Beast).... 3.00
474 MCW,C:High Evolutionary 3.00
475 MCW,Foil(c),A:Donald Blake,
    N:Thor.................... 3.50
475a Newsstand ed............. 3.00
476 V:Destroyer 3.00
477 V:Destroyer,A:Thunderstrike... 3.00
478 V:Norvell Thor 3.00
479 V:Norvell Thor 3.00
480 V:High Evolutionary 3.00
481 V:Grotesk 3.00
482 Don Blake construct......... 3.00
483 RTs,MCW,V:Loki 3.00
484 Badoy and Soul 3.00
485 V:The Thing................ 3.00
486 High Evolutionary,Godpack ... 3.00
487 V:Kurse................... 3.00
488 RTs,MCW,Kurse Saga concl... 3.00
489 RTs,V:Kurse,A:Hulk 3.00
490 TDF,after Thunderstrike 3.00
491 N:Thor.................... 7.50
492 Worldengine's Secrets 5.00
493 Worldengine trigers Ragnarok . 3.00
494 Worldengine saga conclusion. . 3.00
495 BML,Avengers:Timeslide 3.00
496 MD2,BML,A:Capt.America 3.00
497 MD2,BML,Thor Must Die 3.00
498 BML,V:Absorbing Man 3.00
499 MD2,BML 3.00
500 MD2,BML,double size,A:Dr.
    Strange 3.50
501 MD2,BML,I:Red Norvell 3.00
502 MD2,BML,Onslaught tie-in, A:Red
    Norvell, Jane Foster, Hela 3.00
Becomes:

JOURNEY INTO MYSTERY
[Third Series] Nov., 1996
503 TDF,MD2, The Lost Gods, New
    Norse gods?............... 2.50

Journey Into Mystery #503
© Marvel Entertainment Group

Thor King-Size Ann. #7
© Marvel Entertainment Group

504 TDF,Golden Realm in ruins,
    V:Ulik the Troll 2.50
505 TDF,MD2, V:Wrecker,
    A:Spider-Man 2.50
506 TDF,MD2, R:Heimdall 2.50
507 TDF,Odin kidnapped 2.50
508 TDF...................... 2.50
509 TDF,Battle for the Future
    of Asgard 2.50
510 TDF,Return of Loki,A:Seth 2.50
511 TDF,EBe,Lost Gods reunited
    with Odin 2.50
512 EBe, Odin vs. Seth 2.50
513 TDF,SB,AM, Odin vs.
    Seth, concl............... 2.50
514 BRa,VRu,F:Shang Chi, Master
    of Kung Fu 2.50
515 BRa,VRu,F:Shang Chi, Master
    of Kung Fu, pt.2 .... 2.50
516 BRa,VRu,F:Shang Chi, Master
    of Kung Fu, pt.3 .... 2.50
517 SLo,RGr,F:Black Widow...... 2.50
518 SLo,RGr,F:Black Widow...... 2.50
519 SLo,RGr,F:Black Widow, concl. 2.50
520 MWn,F:Hannibal King, pt.1 ... 2.50
521 MWn,F:Hannibal King, pt.2 ... 2.50
Ann.#2 JK,V:Destroyer 75.00
Ann.#3 JK,rep,Grey Gargoyle. .. 30.00
Ann.#4 JK,rep,TheLivingPlanet. .. 25.00
Ann.#5 JK,JB,Hercules,O:Odin ... 25.00
Ann.#6 JK,JB,A:Guardians of the
    Galaxy,V:Korvac........... 25.00
Ann.#7 WS,Eternals 20.00
Ann.#8 JB,V:Zeus............. 20.00
Ann.#9 LMc,Dormammu......... 20.00
Ann.#10 O:Chthon,Gaea,A:Pluto... 15.00
Ann.#11 O:Odin 15.00
Ann.#12 BH,I:Vidar(Odin's son) .. 15.00
Ann.#13 JB,V:Mephisto......... 15.00
Ann.#14 AM,DH,Atlantis Attacks ... 7.00
Ann.#15 HT,Terminus Factor #3 ... 5.00
Ann.#16 Korvac Quest,pt.2,
    Guardians of Galaxy........ 3.00
Ann.#17 Citizen Kang#2 .... 3.00
Ann.#18 TGr,I:The Flame,w/card .. 3.50
Ann.#19 V:Flame 3.50
G-Size.#1 Battles,A:Hercules ... 14.00
TPB Alone Against the Celestials,
    rep.Thor#387-389.......... 5.95
TPB Ballad of Beta Ray Bill,rep.
    Thor #337-340 .... 8.95
Minus 1 Spec., TDF,EBe,flashback . 2.00
1-shot, Rough Cut, DJu,JR,original
    pencils, b&w 48-pg. 3.00

THOR
May, 1998
1 JR2,KJ,DJu,The hero returns,
    48-pg.................... 6.00
2A JR2,KJ,DJu,V:Destroyer,A:Hela,
    Marnot................... 3.50
2B JR2,KJ variant cover 3.50
3 DJu,JR2,KJ,A:Marnot,V:Sedna .. 3.00
4 DJu,JR2,KJ,A:Namor,Sedna 3.00
5 DJu,JR2,KJ,V:Charles Diamond . 3.00
6 DJu,JR2,KJ,V:Hercules........ 3.00
7 DJu,JR2,KJ,V:Zeus 3.00
8 DJu,JR2,KJ,PeterParker x-over . 3.00
9 DJu,JB, JOy,War on
    Asgard,prelude............ 3.00
10 DJu,JR2,KJ,War on Asgard,pt.1 . 3.00
11 DJu,JR2,KJ,War on Asgard,pt.2 . 3.00
12 DJu,JR2,KJ,War on
    Asgard,concl. 48-page 3.50
12a signed 20.00
13 DJu,JR2,KJ,A:Marnot........ 2.25
14 DJu,Hammer secret.......... 2.25
15 DJu,KJ,JR2(c),A:Warriors 3 ... 2.25
16 DJu,KJ,JR2,A:Warriors 3 ..... 2.25
17 DJu,KJ,JR2,Eighth
    Day,pt.1, x-over 2.25
18 DJu,KJ,JR2,V:Enrakt......... 2.25
19 DJu 2.25
20 DJu,V:Loki................. 2.25
21 DJu,JR2,KJ,R:Thanos 2.25
22 DJu,JR2,KJ,V:Thanos 2.25
23 DJu,JR2,DG,V:Thanos........ 2.25
24 DJu,JR2,DG,V:Thanos........ 2.25
25A DJu,JR2,DG,48-pg.,foil(c) ... 6.00
25B variant (c) 3.00
26 DJu,EL,KJ,V:AbsorbingMan.... 2.25
27 DJu,EL,KJ,Dr.Jane Foster 2.25
28 DJu,EL,KJ,WarriorsThree 2.25
29 DJu,NKu,SHa,Jagrfelm 2.25
30 DJu,NKu,SHa,MaxSecurity 2.25
31 DJu,NKu,SHa,V:Malekith 2.25
32 DJu,NKu,SHa,100-page....... 4.00
33 DJu,SI,I:new 2.25
34 DJu,NKu,SHa 2.25
35 DJu,NKu,SHa,V:Gladiator,
    48-page 3.00
36 DJu,R:Loki,A:Destroyer 2.25
37 DJu,JSn,AM,A:Watcher 2.25
38 DJu,SI,BWS(c),V:Destroyer 2.25
39 DJu,SI,BWS(c),V:Surtur 2.25
40 DJu,SI,V:Surtur.............. 2.25
41 DJu,SI,V:Surtur,concl......... 2.25
42 DJu,SI,Asgard,Midgard....... 2.25
43 DJu,JoB,Thor:King of Asgard .. 2.25
44 DJu,SI,Odin funeral,'Nuff Said .. 2.25
45 TR,new King in Asgard 2.25
46 DJu,SHa,TR,F:Thor-Girl....... 2.25
47 DJu,SHa,TR,Enchantress 2.25
48 DJu,JoB,TP,V:Desak 2.25
49 DJu,TR,SHa,V:Desak 2.25
50 DJu,TR,SHa,proclaimation,
    64-pg.................... 6.00
51 DJu,TR,SHa,F:Spider-Man 2.25
52 DJu,TP 2.25
53 DJu 2.25
54 DJu,TR,SHa 2.25
55 DJu,TR,SHa 2.25
56 DJu,TR,................... 2.25
57 DJu,JoB 2.25
58 DJu,AD,Standoff,pt.1,x-over.... 2.50
59 CPr(s) 2.25
60 DJu,JoB,Spiral,pt.1 .... 2.25
61 DJu,Spiral,pt.2.............. 2.25
62 DJu,Spiral,pt.3.............. 3.00
63 DJu,Spiral,pt.4.............. 3.00
64 DJu,Spiral,pt.5.............. 3.00
65 DJu,Spiral,pt.6.............. 3.00
66 DJu,Spiral,pt.7.............. 3.00
67 DJu,Spiral,concl............. 3.00
68 DJu,SEa,The Reigning,prologue 3.00
69 DJu,SEa,The Reigning,pt.1 .... 3.00

All comics prices listed are for *Near Mint* condition. CVA Page 327

Thor–Thunderstrike — MARVEL — Comics Values Annual

70 DJu,SEa,The Reigning,pt.2 .... 3.00	2 rep. 4.50	74 FaN 2.25
71 .... 3.00	3 KBk,MBa,VRu,Headquarters at Freedom's Plaza 4.50	75 FaN,48-pg. 3.50
Ann.1999 DJu,KJ, 48-page 3.50	4 KBk,MBa,VRu,I:Jolt 4.50	76 Fight club 2.25
Ann.1999 signed. 20.00	5 KBk,MBa,VRu,V:Elements of Doom 4.50	77 JAr(s) 2.25
Ann.2000, 48-pg. 3.50	6 KBk,MBa,VRu,V:Elements of Doom 4.50	78 JAr(s) 3.00
Ann.2001 TG,DJu,48-page 3.50	7 KBk,MBa,VRu,F:Citizen V. 4.00	79 JAr(s) 3.00
Spec.#1 Thor (2000). 2.25	8 KBk,MBa,VRu,Songbird fights alone 4.00	80 JAr(s),F:Spider-Man,pt.1 .... 2.25
Spec. rep.#1 & #2. .... 6.00	9 KBk,MBa,VRu,Black Widow 4.00	81 JAr(s),F:Spider-Man,pt.2 .... 2.25
TPB The Dark Gods, 128-pg. 15.95	10 KBk,MBa,VRu,Secret Identities discovered 4.00	Ann. '97 KBk,MBa,TGu,GP, O:Thunderbolts, 48-pg. 2.95
TPB Across All Worlds 16.95	11 KBk,MBa,VRu,V:Citizen V 4.00	Ann.2000 FaN,NBy, 48-pg. 3.50
TPB Thor Visionaries:Walt Simonson, 288-page 24.95	12 KBk,MBa,VRu,A:Fantastic Four, Avengers 10.00	Spec.#0 Wizard Nov., 1998 ...... 5.00
TPB The Death of Odin 13.00	13 KBk,MBa,SHa,on trial 3.00	Spec.First Strikes, rep.#1 & #2 .... 5.00
TPB Lord of Asgard 16.00	14 KBk,MBa,VRu,V:Citizen V, Meteorite 3.00	Spec #1 Distant Rumblings KBk, SEp,Flashback,F:Citizen V 2.50
TPB Vol. 2: Legends (2003) 25.00	15 KBk,MBa,VRu,V:S.H.I.E.L.D. 3.00	Spec.Life Sentences (2001) 3.50
TPB Vol. 3: Gods on Earth 22.00	16 KBk,MBa,SHa,V:Lightningrods. . 3.00	TPB 176-pg., secret history. 12.00
TPB Vol. 4: Spiral (2003) 20.00	17 KBk,MBa,SHa,V:Graviton 3.00	TPB Vol. 1: How to Lose. 15.00

THOR CORPS
[Limited Series]
1 TDF(s),PO,V:Demonstaff 2.25
2 TDF(s),PO,A:Invaders 2.25
3 TDF(s),PO,A:Spider-Man 2099 .. 2.25
4 TDF(s),PO,last issue 2.25

THOR: GODSTORM
Sept., 2001
1 (of 3) KBk,SR 3.50
2 KBk,SR,V:Loki 3.50
3 KBk,SR,V:Loki,concl. 3.50

THOR: VIKINGS
Marvel Max July 2003
1 GEn(s),GF,Zombie Vikings 3.50
2 GEn(s),GF,F:Doctor Strange 3.50
3 GEn(s),GF 3.50
4 GEn(s),GF,back in time 3.50
5 .... 3.50

THREE MUSKETEERS
1 thru 2 movie adapt. 2.25

THUNDERBOLTS
Feb., 1997
1 KBk,MBa,VRu,Post-onslaught new team:Citizen V, Meteroite, Techno, Songbird, Atlas & Mach-1 .... 10.00
1 rep. 3.00
2 KBk,MBa,VRu,V:Mad Thinker ... 6.00
2a variant cover by MBa&VRu 6.00

Thunderbolts #1
© Marvel Entertainment Group

18 KBk,MBa,SHa,villains once again? 3.00
19 KBk,MBa,SHa 3.00
20 KBk,MBa,SHa,V:Masters of Evil. 3.00
21 KBk,MBa,SHa,F:Songbird 3.00
22 KBk,MBa,SHa,A:Hercules 3.00
23 KBk,MBa,SHa,V:U.S.Agent 3.00
24 KBk,MBa,SHa,R:Citizen V 3.00
25 KBk,MBa,SHa, 48-page 3.50
25a signed 20.00
26 KBk,MBa,SHa,JoC,A:Mach-1... 2.50
27 KBk,MBa,SHa,A:Archangel 2.50
28 KBk,MBa,SHa,V:Graviton 2.50
29 KBk,MBa,SHa,V:Graviton 2.50
30 KBk,MBa,SHa,V:Graviton 2.50
31 KBk,MBa,SHa,R:Citizen V 2.50
32 KBk,MBa,SHa,V:Citizen V 2.50
33 KBk,MBa,SHa,F:Jolt 2.50
34 MBa,SHa 2.50
35 FaN,MBa,SHa 2.50
36 FaN,MBa,SHa,V:Beetle 2.50
37 FaN,MBa,SHa,A:Hawkeye 2.50
38 FaN,MBa,SHa,V:Citizen V 2.50
39 FaN,MBa,SHa,100-pg. 3.00
40 FaN,MBa,SHa,V:Citizen V 2.25
41 FaN,MBa,Sandman 2.25
42 FaN,MBa,Avengers x-over 2.25
43 FaN,MBa,Avengers x-over 2.25
44 FaN,MBa,Avengers x-over 2.25
45 FaN,MBa,Maximum Security ... 2.25
46 FaN,MBa,V:Scourge 2.25
47 FaN,MBa,A:Songbird 2.25
48 FaN,MBa,V:Scourge,pt.1 ...... 2.25
49 FaN,V:Scourge,face shown 2.25
50 FaN,MBa,48-page 4.00
51 FaN,AV,rescue mission 2.25
52 FaN,AV,V:Dr.Doom 2.25
53 FaN,AV,F:Charcoal 2.25
54 FaN,AV,F:Fixer 2.25
55 FaN,AV,V:Redeemers 2.25
56 FaN,AV,V:Graviton 2.25
57 FaN,AV,V:Graviton 2.25
58 FaN,AV,V:Graviton 2.25
59 FaN,MBa,AV,Songbird,'NuffSaid 2.25
60 FaN,MBa,AV,Chain Gang. 2.25
61 FaN,Heroes Return,pt.2 .... 2.25
62 FaN,Heroes Return,pt.3 .... 2.25
63 FaN,Hawkeye,Screaming Mimi . 2.25
64 FaN,F:Zemo 2.25
65 FaN,V:Masters of Evil 2.25
66 FaN,F:Baron Zemo,Jolt 2.25
67 FaN,F:Harrier, Hawkeye. 2.25
68 FaN,F:Moonstone,PhantomEagle 2.25
69 FaN,AV 2.25
70 FaN, ... 2.25
71 FaN. 2.25
72 FaN. 2.25
73 Fan,AV 2.25

Thundercats #1
© Marvel Entertainment Group

THUNDERCATS
Star, Dec., 1985
1 JM,TV tie-in 10.00
1a 2nd printing 7.00
2 JM,A:Berbils,V:Mumm-Ra 7.00
3 .... 7.00
4 JM,I:Lynxana 7.00
5 JM 7.00
6 JM 7.00
7 Return to Thundera 7.00
8 V:Monkiang 7.00
9 V:Pekmen. 7.00
10 .... 7.00
11 I:The Molemen. 5.00
12 `The Protectors'. 5.00
13 EC/AW,V:Safari Joe. 5.00
14 V:Snaf 5.00
15 JM,A:Spidera 5.00
16 `Time Capsule' 5.00
17 .... 5.00
18 EC/AW,`Doom Gaze' 5.00
19 .... 5.00
20 EC/AW 5.00
21 JM,A:Hercules Baby 5.00
22 I:Devious Duploids. 5.00
23 V:Devious Duploids 5.00
24 June, 1988 .... 5.00

THUNDERSTRIKE
1993–95
1 B:TDF(s),RF,Holografx(c), V:Bloodaxe,I:Car Jack 3.25

MARVEL

Thunderstrike #1
© Marvel Entertainment Group

TIMESPIRITS
Epic, Jan., 1985
1 TY 3.00
2 .... 2.25
3 .... 2.25
4 AW 2.25
5 .... 2.25
6 .... 2.25
7 .... 2.25
8 March, 1986 .... 2.25

TIMESTRYKE
1 .... 2.25
2 .... 2.25

TINY TESSIE
See: TESSIE THE TYPIST

TOMB OF DARKNESS
See: BEWARE

TOMB OF DRACULA
April, 1972
1 GC,Night of the Vampire 300.00
2 GC,Who Stole My Coffin? 100.00
3 GC,TP,I:Rachel Van Helsing ... 75.00
4 GC,TP,Bride of Dracula! 75.00
5 GC,TP,To Slay A Vampire 75.00
6 GC,TP,Monster of the Moors ... 60.00
7 GC,TP,Child is Slayer of
   the Man 60.00
8 GC(p),The Hell-Crawlers 60.00
9 The Fire Cross 60.00
10 GC,I:Blade Vampire Slayer .. 125.00
11 GC,TP,Master of the Undead
   Strikes Again! 30.00
12 GC,TP,House that Screams ... 30.00
13 GC,TP,O:Blade 50.00
14 GC,TP,Vampire has Risen
   from the Grave 30.00
15 GC,TP,Stay Dead 30.00
16 GC,TP,Back from the Grave .. 30.00
17 GC,TP,A Vampire Rides This
   Train! 30.00
18 GC,TP,A:Werewolf By Night .. 32.00
19 GC,TP,Snowbound in Hell 30.00
20 GC,TP,Manhunt For A Vampire 30.00
21 GC,TP,A:Blade 25.00
22 GC,TP,V:Gorna 25.00
23 GC,TP,Shadow over Haunted
   Castle 25.00
24 GC,TP,I am your Death 25.00
25 GC,TP,Blood Stalkers of Count
   Dracula 25.00
26 GC,TP,A Vampire Stalks the
   Night 25.00
27 GC,TP,..And the Moon Spews
   Death! 25.00
28 GC,TP,Five came to Kill a
   Vampire' 25.00
29 GC,TP,Vampire goes Mad? ... 25.00
30 GC,TP,A:Blade 25.00
31 GC,TP,Child of Blood 25.00
32 GC,TP,The Vampire Walks
   Among Us 25.00
33 GC,TP,Blood on My Hands ... 25.00
34 GC,TP,Bloody Showdown 25.00
35 GC,TP,A:Brother Voodoo 25.00
36 GC,TP,Dracula in America ... 25.00
37 GC,TP,The Vampire Walks
   Among Us 25.00
38 GC,TP,Bloodlust for a Dying
   Vampire 25.00
39 GC,TP,Final Death of Dracula 25.00
40 GC,TP,Triumph of Dr.Sun 25.00
41 GC,TP,A:Blade 20.00
42 GC,TP,V:Dr.Sun 20.00

Tomb of Dracula #23
© Marvel Entertainment Group

2 RF,V:Juggernaut 2.25
3 RF,I:Sangre 2.25
4 RF,A:Spider-Man,I:Pandora ... 2.25
5 RF,A:Spider-Man,V:Pandora ... 2.25
6 RF,I:Blackwulf,Bristle,Schizo,Lord
   Lucian,A:SpM,Code:Blue,Stellaris,
   V:SHIELD,Pandora,C:Tantalus . 2.25
7 KP,V:Tantalus,D:Jackson 2.25
8 RF,I&V:Officer ZERO 2.25
9 RF,V:Bloodaxe 2.25
10 RF,A:Thor 2.25
11 RF,A:Wildstreak 2.25
12 RF,A:Whyte Out 2.25
13 RF,Inferno 42 .... 2.25
13a Double Feature flip book
   with Code Blue #1 .... 2.50
14 RF, Inferno 42 .... 2.25
14a Double Feature flip book
   with Code Blue #2 .... 2.50
15 RF,V:Methisto 2.25
15a Double Feature flip book
   with Code Blue #3 .... 2.50
16 .... 2.25
17 V:Bloodaxe 2.25
18 V:New Villain 2.25
19 Shopping Network 2.25
20 A:Black Panther 2.25
21 A:War Machine,V:Loki 2.25
22 TDF,AM,RF,Mystery of Bloodaxe
   blows open 2.25
23 TDF,A:Avengers 2.25
24 TDF,V:Bloodaxe, final issue . 2.25

TIMELY PRESENTS: HUMAN TORCH COMICS
Aug., 1998
1-shot GN 6.00

TIMESLIP COLLECTION
Sept., 1998
1-shot, 48-page 3.00

TIMESLIP: THE COMING OF THE AVENGERS
Aug., 1998
1-shot GN 6.00

43 GC,TP,A:NewYear'sNightmare . 20.00
44 GC,TP,A:Dr.Strange 20.00
45 GC,TP,A:Hannibal King 20.00
46 GC,TP,W:Dracula & Domini ... 20.00
47 GC,TP,Death-Bites 20.00
48 GC,TP,A:Hannibal King 20.00
49 GC,TP,A:Robin Hood,
   Frankenstein's Monster 20.00
50 GC,TP,A:Silver Surfer 30.00
51 GC,TP,A:Blade 15.00
52 GC,TP,V:Demon 15.00
53 GC,TP,A:Hannibal King,Blade . 15.00
54 GC,TP,Twas the Night Before
   Christmas 15.00
55 GC,TP,Requiem for a Vampire . 15.00
56 GC,TP,A:Harold H. Harold ... 15.00
57 GC,TP,The Forever Man 15.00
58 GC,TP,A:Blade 15.00
59 GC,TP,The Last Traitor 15.00
60 GC,TP,The Wrath of Dracula . 15.00
61 GC,TP,Resurrection 15.00
62 GC,TP,What Lurks Beneath ... 15.00
63 GC,TP,A:Janus 15.00
64 GC,TP,A:Satan 15.00
65 GC,TP,Where No Vampire
   Has Gone Before 15.00
66 GC,TP,Marked for Death 15.00
67 GC,TP,A:Lilith 15.00
68 GC,TP,Dracula Turns Human .. 15.00
69 GC,TP,Cross of Fire 15.00
70 GC,TP,double size,last issue . 20.00
Savage Return of Dracula. rep.
   Tomb of Dracula #1,#2 ...... 2.50
Wedding of Dracula. rep.Tomb
   of Dracula #30,#45,#46 ..... 2.50
Requiem for Dracula. rep.Tomb
   of Dracula #69,#70 .... 2.50

TOMB OF DRACULA
[Mini-Series] Nov., 1991
1 GC,AW,Day of Blood 6.00
2 GC,AW,Dracula in D.C 5.50
3 GC,AW,A:Blade 5.50
4 GC,AW,D:Dracula 5.50

TOMB OF DRACULA
(B&W Mag.) Nov., 1979
1 .... 20.00
2 SD 15.00
3 FM 15.00
4 .... 12.00
5 .... 12.00
6 Sept., 1980 .... 12.00

MARVEL

TOMB OF DRACULA MEGAZINE
TPB Halloween, MWn,GC,TP 3.95

TOMORROW KNIGHTS
Epic, June, 1990
1 .... 2.25
2 .... 2.25
3 .... 2.25
4 Origin 2.25
5 .... 2.25
6 .... 2.25

TOP DOG
Star, April, 1985
1 .... 3.00
2 thru 14, June, 1987 .... @3.00

TOR
Epic *Heavy Hitters*, 1993
1 JKu,R:Tor,magazine format 6.25
2 JKu 6.25
3 JKu,V:The Iduard Ring 6.25

TOUGH KID SQUAD COMICS
Timely, March, 1942
1 O:The Human Top,Tough Kid Squad,A:The Flying Flame, V:Doctor Klutch 13,000.00

TOWER OF SHADOWS
Sept., 1969
1 JR(c),JSo,JCr,`At The Stroke of Midnight' 85.00
2 JR(c),DH,DA,NA,`The Hungry One' 50.00
3 GC,BWs,GT,`Midnight in the Wax Museum' 50.00
4 DH,Within The Witching Circle . 40.00
5 DA,BWS,WW,`Demon That Stalks Hollywood' 50.00
6 WW,SD,`Pray For the Man in the Rat-Hole 50.00
7 BWS,WW,`Titano' 50.00
8 WW,SD,`Demons of Dragon-Henge' 50.00
9 BWr(c),TP,Lovecraft story 50.00
Becomes:

CREATURES ON THE LOOSE
March, 1971
10 BWr,A:King Kull 75.00
11 DAy,rep. Moomba is Here 25.00
12 JK,`I Was Captured By Korilla'. 25.00
13 RC,`The Creature From Krogarr' 25.00
14 MSe,`Dead Storage' 25.00
15 SD,Spragg the Living Mountain 25.00
16 GK,BEv,GK,B&O:Gulliver Jones, Warrior of Mars 20.00
17 GK,`Slaves o/t Spider Swarm' . 20.00
18 RA,`The Fury of Phra' 20.00
19 WB,JM,GK,`Red Barbarian of Mars' 20.00
20 GK(c),GM,SD,`The Monster... And the Maiden 20.00
21 JSo(c),GM,`Two Worlds To Win',E:Guilliver 20.00
22 JSo(c),SD,VM,B:Thongor, Warrior of Lost Lemuria 22.00
23 VM,`The Man-Monster Strikes'. 12.00
24 VM,Attack of the Lizard-Hawks 12.00
25 VM,GK(c),Wizard of Lemuria .. 12.00

Creatures on the Loose #16
© Marvel Entertainment Group

26 VM,Doom of the Serpent Gods 12.00
27 VM,SD,`Demons Dwell in the Crypts of Yamath' 12.00
28 SD,`The Hordes of Hell' 12.00
29 GK(c),`Day of the Dragon Wings', E:Thongor,Warrior of Lost Lemuria 12.00
30 B:Man-Wolf,`Full Moon, Dark Fear' 20.00
31 GT,`The Beast Within' 15.00
32 GT,V:Kraven the Hunter 15.00
33 GK(c),GP,`The Name of the Game is Death' 15.00
34 GP,`Nightflight to Fear' 12.00
35 GK(c),GP 12.00
36 GK(c),GP,`Murder by Moonlight'12.00
37 GP,Sept., 1975 .... 12.00

TOXIC AVENGER
March, 1991
1 VM(i),I&O:Toxic Avenger 2.25
2 VM(i) 2.25
3 VM(i),Night of Living H.bodies... 2.25
4 Legend of Sludgeface 2.25
5 I:Biohazard 2.25
6 V:Biohazard 2.25
7 `Sewer of Souviaki' 2.25
8 `Sewer of Souviaki' conc. 2.25
9 Abducted by Aliens 2.25
10 `Die,Yuppie Scum',pt.1 .... 2.25

TOXIC CRUSADERS
1992
1 F:Toxic Avengers & Crusaders .. 2.25
2 SK(c),V:Custard-Thing 2.25
3 SK(c),V:Custard-Thing 2.25
4 V:Giant Mutant Rats 2.25
5 V:Dr.Killemoff 2.25
6 V:Dr.Killemoff 2.25
7 F:Yvonne 2.25
8 V:Psycho 2.25

[2nd Series]
1 .... 2.25
2 .... 2.25

TRANSFORMERS
[1st Regular Series] Sept., 1984
1 FS,Toy Comic 18.00
2 FS,OptimusPrime V:Megatron .. 11.00
3 FS.A:Spider-Man 11.00
4 MT(c),FS 6.00
5 Transformers Dead? 6.00

6 Autobots vs.Decepticons 6.00
7 KB,V:Megatron 6.00
8 KB,A:Dinobots 6.00
9 MM,A:Circuit Breaker 6.00
10 Dawn of the Devastator 6.00
11 HT 4.00
12 HT,V:Shockwave 4.00
13 DP,Return of Megatron 4.00
14 DP,V:Decepticons 4.00
15 DP 4.00
16 KN,A:Bumblebee 4.00
17 DP,I:New Transformers,pt.1 .. 4.00
18 DP,I:New Transformers,pt.2 .. 4.00
19 DP,I:Omega Supreme 4.00
20 HT,Skid vs.Ravage 4.00
21 DP,I:Aerialbots 4.00
22 DP,I:Stuntacons(Menasor) ... 4.00
23 DP,Return of Circuit Breaker . 4.00
24 DP,D:Optimus Prime 4.00
25 DP,Decpticons (full story) ... 4.00
26 DP 4.00
27 DP,V:Head Hunter 4.00
28 DP 4.00
29 DP,I:Scraplets, Triplechangers . 4.00
30 DP,V:Scraplets 4.00
31 DP,Humans vs. Decepticons .. 4.00
32 DP,`Autobots for Sale' 4.00
33 DP,Autobots vs.Decepticons .. 4.00
34 V:Sky Lynx 4.00
35 JRy,I:U.K.version Transformers . 4.00
36 .... 4.00
37 .... 4.00
38 .... 4.00
39 .... 4.00
40 Autobots' New Leader 4.00
41 .... 4.00
42 Return of Optimus Prime 4.00
43 Optimus Prime,Goldbug 4.00
44 FF,Return of Circuit Breaker .. 4.00
45 V:The Jammers 4.00
46 I:New Transformers 4.00
47 B:Underbase saga,I:Seacons .. 4.00
48 Optimus Prime/Megatron (past story) 4.00
49 Underbase saga cont. 4.00
50 E:Underbase saga,I:new characters 5.00
51 I:Pretender Decepticon Beasts.. 5.00
52 I:Mecannibals,pt.1 .... 5.00
53 Mecannibals,pt.2 .... 5.00
54 I:Micromasters 5.00
55 MG 5.00
56 Return of Megatron 5.00
57 Optimus Prime vs.Scraponok .. 5.00
58 V:Megatron 5.00
59 A:Megatron,D:Ratchet 5.00
60 Battle on Cybertron 9.00
61 O:Transformers 9.00
62 B:Matrix Quest,pt.1 .... 9.00
63 .... 9.00
64 I:The Klud 9.00
65 GSr 15.00
66 E:Matrix Quest,pt.5 .... 15.00
67 V:Unicorn,also Alternative World 15.00
68 I:Neoknights 15.00
69 Fate of Ratchet & Megatron revealed 15.00
70 Megatron/Ratchet fused together 15.00
71 Autobots Surrender to Decepticons 20.00
72 Decepticon Civil War, I:Gravitron 20.00
73 I:Unicorn,A:Neoknights 20.00
74 A:Unicorn & Brothers of Chaos 20.00
75 V:Thunderwing & Dark Matrix.. 20.00
76 Aftermath of War 20.00
77 Unholy Alliance 20.00
78 Galvatron vs.Megatron 25.00
79 Decepticons Invade Earth 25.00

Comics Values Annual — MARVEL — Transformers–Two-Gun

80 Return of Optimus Prime,final . 35.00
[2nd Regular Series]
1 Split Foil(c),A:Dinobots 3.00
2 A:G.I.Joe,Cobra 2.25
3 . . . . 2.25
4 MaG,V:Jhiaxus 2.25
5 . . . . 2.25
6 V:Megatron. 2.25
7 V:Darkwing. 2.25
8 V:Darkwing. 2.25
9 . . . . 2.25
10 Total War. 2.25
11 . . . . 2.25

TRANSFORMERS COMICS MAGAZINE
1986–88
1 Digest-size 2.25
2 thru 11 . . . . @2.25

TRANSFORMERS, THE MOVIE
Dec., 1986–Feb., 1987
1 thru 3 Animated movie adapt. . @2.25

TRANSFORMERS UNIVERSE
Dec., 1986
1 . . . . 3.00
2 . . . . 3.00
3 . . . . 3.00
4 March, 1987 . . . . 3.00

TRANSMUTATION OF IKE GARUDA
Epic, 1991
1 JSh,I:Ike Garuda 3.95
2 JSh,conclusion 3.95

TROUBLE
Marvel Epic June 2003
1 MMr(s),Tyd,Teenage Romance . . 3.00
2 MMr(s),Tyd,photo (c) 3.00
3 MMr(s),Tyd,consequences 3.00
4 MMr(s),TyD,consequences 3.00
5 . . . . 3.00

The Trouble With Girls #3
© Marvel Entertainment Group

TROUBLE WITH GIRLS: NIGHT OF THE LIZARD
Epic *Heavy Hitters*, 1993
1 BBI,AW,R:Lester Girls. 2.75
2 BBI,AW,V:Lizard Lady. 2.25
3 BBI,AW,V:Lizard Lady. 2.25
4 BBI,AW,last issue 2.25

TRUE COMPLETE MYSTERY
See: COMPLETE MYSTERY

TRUE SECRETS
See: OUR LOVE

TRUE WESTERN
Dec., 1949
1 Ph(c),Billy the Kid 175.00
2 Ph(c),Alan Ladd,Badmen vs. Lawmen 250.00
Becomes:

TRUE ADVENTURES
3 BP,MSy,Boss of Black Devil . . 175.00
Becomes:

MEN'S ADVENTURES
4 AvB,He Called me a Coward . 350.00
5 AvB,Brother Act 225.00
6 AvB,Heat of Battle 200.00
7 AvB,The Walking Death 200.00
8 AvB,RH,Journey Into Death . . 200.00
9 AvB,Bullets,Blades and Death 125.00
10 BEv,The Education of Thomas Dillon 125.00
11 Death of A Soldier 125.00
12 Firing Squad 125.00
13 RH(c),The Three Stripes 125.00
14 GC,BEv,Steel Coffin. 125.00
15 JMn(c). 125.00
16 . . . . 125.00
17 . . . . 125.00
18 . . . . 125.00
19 JRo 125.00
20 GC,RH(c) 125.00
21 BEv(c),JSt,The Eye of Man . . 200.00
22 BEv,JR,Mark of the Witch . . . 200.00
23 BEv(c),RC,The Wrong Body. . 200.00
24 RH,JMn,GT,Torture Master. . . 200.00
25 SSh(c),Who Shrinks My Head 200.00
26 Midnight in the Morgue 200.00
27 BP,CBu(c),A:Capt.America, Human Torch,Sub-Mariner . . 1,300.00
28 BEv,A:Capt.America,Human Torch, Sub-Mariner,July, 1954 . . . 1,200.00

TRUTH: RED WHITE BLACK
Nov., 2002
1 (of 7) untold Capt. America. 3.50
2 KB 3.50
3 KB 3.50
4 KB 3.50
5 KB 3.50
6 KB 3.50
7 KB,A:Steve Rogers. 3.50
GN Truth, Red White & Black 4.00

TRY-OUT WINNER BOOK
March, 1988
1 Spider-Man vs. Doc Octopus . . 15.00

TV STARS
Aug., 1978
1 A:Great Grape Ape 35.00

2 . . . . 25.00
3 ATh,DSt 30.00
4 A:Top Cat,Feb., 1979 . . . . 25.00

2099: MANIFEST DESTINY
March, 1998
GN LKa,MMK,F:Miguel O'Hara, 48-pg. 6.00

2-GUN KID
See: BILLY BUCKSKIN

Two-Gun Kid #109
© Marvel Entertainment Group

TWO-GUN KID
Atlas, March, 1948—April, 1977
1 B:Two-Gun Kid,The Sheriff . 1,300.00
2 Killers of Outlaw City 600.00
3 RH,A:Annie Oakley 400.00
4 RH,A:Black Rider 400.00
5 RH 500.00
6 . . . . 400.00
7 RH,Brand of a Killer 400.00
8 The Secret of the Castle of Slaves 400.00
9 JSe,Trapped in Hidden Valley, A:Black Rider 400.00
10 JK(c),The Horrible Hermit of Hidden Mesa 400.00
11 JMn(c),GT,A:Black Rider 250.00
12 JMn(c),GT,A:Black Rider 250.00
13 thru 24 . . . . @225.00
25 AW,JMn 225.00
26 DAy,JMn 150.00
27 DAy,JMn 150.00
28 JMn 150.00
29 . . . . 150.00
30 AW 150.00
31 thru 44. . . . . 125.00
45 JDa 100.00
46 JDa 100.00
47 JDa 100.00
48 . . . . 100.00
49 JMn 100.00
50 . . . . 75.00
51 AW 75.00
52 thru 59. . . . . @75.00
60 DAy,New O:Two-Gun Kid . . . 100.00
61 JK,DAy,The Killer and The Kid . 75.00
62 JK,DAy,At the Mercy of Moose Morgan. 75.00
63 DAy,The Guns of Wild Bill Taggert. 50.00

All comics prices listed are for *Near Mint* condition.

Two-Gun–Ultimates / MARVEL / Comics Values Annual

64 DAy,Trapped by Grizzly
   Gordon. 50.00
65 DAy,Nothing Can Save Fort
   Henry. 50.00
66 DAy,Ringo's Raiders 50.00
67 DAy,The Fangs of the Fox 50.00
68 DAy,The Purple Phantom. 50.00
69 DAy,Badman Called Goliath. . . 50.00
70 DAy,Hurricane 50.00
71 DAy,V:Jesse James. 50.00
72 DAy,V:Geronimo 50.00
73 Guns of the Galloway Gang. . . 50.00
74 Dakota Thompson 50.00
75 JK,Remember the Alamo 50.00
76 JK,Trapped on the Doom 50.00
77 JK,V:The Panther 50.00
78 V:Jesse James 50.00
79 The River Rats 50.00
80 V:The Billy Kid 50.00
81 The Hidden Gun 40.00
82 BEv,Here Comes the Conchos. 40.00
83 Durango,Two-Gun
   Kid Unmasked 40.00
84 Gunslammer 40.00
85 Fury at Falcon Flats,
   A:Rawhide Kids 40.00
86 V:Cole Younger 40.00
87 OW,The Sidewinder and the
   Stallion. 40.00
88 thru 100 . . . . @40.00
101 . . . . 40.00
102 thru 136 . . . . @30.00

TWO-GUN KID: SUNSET RIDERS
1995
1 FaN,R:Two-Gun Kid,64-pg. 6.95
2 FaN,concl. 64-pg. 6.95

TWO GUN WESTERN
See: CASEY–CRIME PHOTOGRAPHER

TWO-GUN WESTERN
See: BILLY BUCKSKIN

2001: A SPACE ODYSSEY
Oct., 1976
1 JK,FRg,Based on Movie 10.00

2001: A SPACE ODYSSEY
Dec., 1976—Sept., 1977
1 JK,Based on Movie 25.00
2 JK,Vira the She-Demon 15.00
3 JK,Marak the Merciless 15.00
4 JK,Wheels of Death 15.00
5 JK,Norton of New York 15.00
6 JK,Immortality ...Death 15.00
7 JK,The New Seed 15.00
8 JK,Capture of X-51,I&O:Mr.
   Machine(Machine-Man) 20.00
9 JK,A:Mr Machine 15.00
10 Hotline to Hades,A:Mr Machine 15.00

2010
April, 1985
1 TP,movie adapt. 2.25
2 TP,movie adapt,May, 1985 . . . . 2.25

2099 A.D.
1995
1 Chromium cover. 4.00

2099 APOCALYPSE
1995
1 . . . . 5.00

2099 GENESIS
1996
1 Chromium Cover 4.00

2099 SPECIAL: THE WORLD OF DOOM
1995
1 The World of Doom 2.25

2099 UNLIMITED
1993–96
1 DT,I:Hulk 2099,A:Spider-Man 2099,
   I:Mutagen. 4.50
2 DT,F:Hulk 2099, Spider-Man 2099,
   I:R-Gang 4.25
3 GJ(s),JJB,F:Hulk & SpM 2099 . . 4.25
4 PR(c),GJ(s),JJB,I:Metalscream
   2099,Lachryma 2099 . . . . 4.25
5 GJ(s),I:Vulx,F:Hazarrd 2099 . . . 4.25
6 . . . . 4.25
Becomes:

2099 A.D. UNLIMITED
7 . . . . 4.25
8 F:Public Enemy 4.25
9 One Nation Under Doom 4.25
10 V:Chameleon 2099 . . . . 4.25
Spec. #1 The World of Doom 2.25

2099 World of Tomorrow #2
© Marvel Entertainment Group

2099: WORLD OF TOMORROW
1996–97
1 . . . . 2.50
2 . . . . 2.50
3 MMk,MsM,ATi,F:Spider-Man,
   X-Men 2.50
4 ATi,X-Men 2099 discover secret . 2.50
5 ATi 2.50
6 PFe&ATi(c),Phalanx's final
   assault. 2.50
7 Spider-Man 2099 searches for his
   brother: Green Goblin. 2.50
8 Phalanx invasion aftermath. . . . 2.50
9 Humanity vs. Lunatika 2.50

TYPHOID
1995–96
1 ANo,JVF,Painted series 3.95
2 ANo,JVF,Hunt for serial killer. . . 3.95
3 ANo,JVF,sex,blood & videotapes. 3.95
4 ANo,JVF,conclusion 3.95

ULTIMATE ADVENTURES (OF HAWK-OWL & ZIPPY)
Sept., 2002
1 JQ designs,U-Decide 2.25
2 DFg 2.25
3 DFg 2.25
4 DFg,Hawk-Owl & Zippy 2.25
5 DFg 2.25
6 DFg 3.00

ULTIMATE AGE OF APOCALYPSE
Rep. #1-#4 Age of Apocalypse stories:
Ultimate Amazing X-Men 8.95
Ultimate Astonishing X-Men 8.95
Ultimate Factor X 8.95
Ultimate Gambit and the X-Ternals . 8.95
Ultimate Generation Next 8.95
Ultimate Weapon X. 8.95
Ultimate X-Calibre 8.95
Ultimate X-Man. 8.95

ULTIMATE DAREDEVIL & ELEKTRA
Nov., 2002
1 (of 4) DaM, at Columbia U 5.00
2 SvL,DaM 3.00
3 SvL,DaM 3.00
4 SvL,concl. 3.00
TPB Series rep. 12.00

ULTIMATE MARVEL TEAM-UP
Feb., 2001
1 Spider-Man & Wolverine. 5.00
2 Spider-Man & The Hulk 4.00
3 Spider-Man & The Hulk 4.00
4 Spider-Man & Iron Man. 4.00
5 Spider-Man & Iron Man,MiA . . . 4.00
6 Spider-Man & Punisher,BSz . . . 3.00
7 Spider-Man & Daredevil,BSz . . . 3.00
8 Spider-Man,Daredevil,Punisher. . 3.00
9 Spider-Man & Fantastic Four . . . 3.00
10 Spider-Man & Man-Thing. 3.00
11 BMB(s),Spider-Man & X-Men . . 3.00
12 Spider-Man & Dr. Strange 3.00
13 Spider-Man & Dr. Strange 3.00
14 Spider-Man & Black Widow . . . 3.00
15 Spider-Man & Shang-Chi. 3.00
16 Spider-Man & Shang-Chi. 3.00
TPB Vol. 1 . . . . 14.95
TPB Vol. 2 . . . . 12.00
TPB Vol. 3 . . . . 13.00

ULTIMATE MARVEL MAGAZINE
May, 2001
5 thru 11, 80-page, rep. . . . . . . @4.00

ULTIMATES, THE
Jan., 2002
1 MMr,BHi,Nick Fury, heroes 6.00
2 MMr,BHi,Search forCap.America 10.00
3 MMr,BHi,Cap.America lives 8.00
4 MMr,BHi,no one to fight 8.00
5 MMr,BHi, ... 8.00

Comics Values Annual — MARVEL — Ultimates–Uncanny

```
6 MMr,BHi,celebrities. . . . . . . . . . 5.00
7 MMr,BHi,new additions . . . . . . . 5.00
8 MMr,Quicksilver & ScarletWitch . 3.00
9 MMr,BHi. . . . . . . . . . . . . . . . . . . 3.00
10 MMr,BHi,F:Hawkeye . . . . . . . . . 3.00
11 BHi,PNe . . . . . . . . . . . . . . . . . . 3.00
12 BHi,PNe . . . . . . . . . . . . . . . . . . 3.00
13 . . . . . . . . . . . . . . . . . . . . . . . . . 3.00
Spec. Must Have rep. #1–#3 . . . . . 4.00
TPB Vol.1, 160-pg. . . . . . . . . . . . . 13.00
```

ULTIMATE SIX
Marvel Sept. 2003
```
1 BMB,JQ,F:Villains. . . . . . . . . . . . 3.00
2 BMB,Sinister Six. . . . . . . . . . . . . 3.00
3 BMB,Ultimate Spidey . . . . . . . . . 3.00
4    . . . . . . . . . . . . . . . . . . . . . . . . 3.00
```

ULTIMATE SPIDER-MAN
Sept., 2000
```
1 BMB,JQ,MBa,ATi,A:Mary Jane
   48-pg.red card(c) . . . . . . . . 100.00
1A variant white (c) . . . . . . . . . . 150.00
1B Dynamic Forces (c) . . . . . . . . 65.00
2A BMB,MBa,ATi,Dr.Otto Octopus,
   car. . . . . . . . . . . . . . . . . . . . . 50.00
2B Dynamic Forces JaL(c),
   Spider-Man swinging . . . . . . . 35.00
3 BMB,ATi,MBa,A:Mary Jane . . . 40.00
4 BMB,ATi,MBa,D:Uncle Ben. . . . 40.00
5 BMB,ATi,MBa,hand of fate,
   scarce . . . . . . . . . . . . . . . . . . 80.00
6 BMB,ATi,MBa,V:Green Goblin . . 50.00
7 BMB,ATi,MBa,V:Green Goblin . . 35.00
8 BMB,ATi,MBa,V:Shocker. . . . . . 20.00
9 BMB,ATi,MBa,V:Kingpin . . . . . . 10.00
10 BMB,ATi,MBa,V:Kingpin. . . . . . 10.00
11 BMB,ATi,MBa,V:Kingpin. . . . . . 10.00
12 BMB,ATi,MBa,V:Kingpin. . . . . . 10.00
13 BMB,ATi,MBa,Mary Jane . . . . . 12.00
14 BMB,MBa,ATi,Doctor Octopus . 10.00
15 BMB,MBa,ATi,Doctor Octopus . . 9.00
16 BMB,MBa,ATi,F:Ock,Kraven . . . 9.00
17 BMB,MBa,ATi,F:Justin Hammer . 8.00
18 BMB,MBa,ATi,Doc kicks butt . 8.00
19 BMB,MBa,ATi,Justin Hammer . . 8.00
20 BMB,MBa,ATi,Doc Oc,Kraven . . 8.00
21 BMB,MBa,ATi,vs. the press . . . . 8.00
22 BMB,MBa,ATi,R:Green Goblin
   + Chapter 1, 54-pg. . . . . . . . . 8.00
23 BMB,MBa,ATi,G.Goblin,G.Stacy. 8.00
24 BMB,MBa,ATi,Green Goblin deal 4.00
25 BMB,MBa,ATi . . . . . . . . . . . . . . 4.00
26 BMB,MBa,ATi,S.H.I.E.L.D. . . . . 3.00
27 BMB,MBa,ATi . . . . . . . . . . . . . . 3.00
28 BMB,MBa,ATi . . . . . . . . . . . . . . 3.00
29 BMB,MBa,ATi . . . . . . . . . . . . . . 3.00
30 BMB,MBa,ATi . . . . . . . . . . . . . . 3.00
31 BMB,MBa,ATi . . . . . . . . . . . . . . 3.00
32 BMB,MBa,ATi . . . . . . . . . . . . . . 3.00
33 BMB,MBa,ATi,V:Venom . . . . . . 9.00
34 BMB,MBa,ATi,V:Venom . . . . . . 8.00
35 BMB,MBa,ATi,V:Venom . . . . . . 8.00
36 BMB,MBa,ATi,V:Venom . . . . . . 5.00
37 BMB,MBa,ATi,V:Venom . . . . . . 4.00
38 BMB,MBa,ATi,V:Venom,concl. . 3.00
39 BMB,MBa,ATi,F:Nick Fury . . . . 2.50
40 BMB,MBa,Irresponsible,pt.1. . . 2.50
41 BMB,MBa,Irresponsible,pt.2. . . 2.25
42 BMB,MBa,Irresponsible,pt.3. . . 2.25
43 BMB,MBa,Irresponsible,pt.4. . . 2.25
44 BMB,MBa,Irresponsible,pt.5. . . 2.25
45 BMB,MBa,Irresponsible,pt.6. . . 2.25
46 BMB,MBa,F:S.H.I.E.L.D.,40-pg . 3.00
47 BMB,MBa,Unfair,pt.1 . . . . . . . . 2.25
48 BMB,MBa,Unfair,pt.2 . . . . . . . . 2.25
49 BMB,MBa,Unfair,pt.3 . . . . . . . . 2.25
Spec.1 Collected, rep.#1–#3. . . . . 4.00
Spec.#1-#2-#3, 96-pg. . . . . . . . . . 4.00
```

```
Spec.#1 all-star artists, 54-pg. . . . . 3.50
TPB Vol.3, 176-pg. . . . . . . . . . . . 17.95
TPB Vol 4, . . . . . . . . . . . . . . . . . 15.00
TPB Power & Responsibility . . . . 14.95
TPB Vol. 5: Public Scutiny . . . . . 12.00
TPB Vol. 6: Venom . . . . . . . . . . . 16.00
TPB Vol. 7: Irresponsible . . . . . . 13.00
Spec. Must Have, rep. . . . . . . . . . 4.00
```

ULTIMATE WAR
Marvel Dec. 2002
```
1 (of 4) CBa,X-Men vs. Ultimates. . 2.25
2 CBa . . . . . . . . . . . . . . . . . . . . . 2.25
3 CBa . . . . . . . . . . . . . . . . . . . . . 2.25
4 CBa,concl. . . . . . . . . . . . . . . . . 2.25
```

Ultimate X-Men #3
© *Marvel Entertainment Group*

ULTIMATE X-MEN
Dec., 2000
```
1 AKu,ATi,MMr,48-page, card (c) . 17.00
1A Dynamic Forces (c) . . . . . . . . 30.00
1B Preview . . . . . . . . . . . . . . . . . 30.00
2 AKu,ATi,MMr,F:Wolverine . . . . . 17.00
3 AKu,ATi,MMr,V:Magneto . . . . . 12.00
4 AKu,ATi,MMr,V:Magneto . . . . . 12.00
5 AKu,ATi,MMr,One traitor? . . . . . 7.00
6 AKu,ATi,MMr,V:Magneto . . . . . . 7.00
7 AKu,ATi,MMr,Weapon X,pt.1 . . . 7.00
8 AKu,ATi,MMr,Weapon X,pt.2. . . 7.00
9 MMr,TR,SHa,Weapon X,pt.3. . . 7.00
10 MMr,TR,SHa,Weapon X,pt.4 . . 7.00
11 MMr,AKu,ATi,Weapon X,pt.5 . . 4.00
12 MMr,AKu,Weapon X,pt.6 . . . . . 4.00
13 AKu(c),F:Gambit . . . . . . . . . . . 4.00
14 AKu(c),F:Gambit,pt.2 . . . . . . . . 3.50
15 AKu,MMr,Xavier's teachings. . . 3.50
16 AKu, MMr,to Scotland . . . . . . . 3.50
17 AKu,MMr,Proteus Saga,pt.2 . . . 3.50
18 AKu,MMr,World Tour . . . . . . . . 3.50
19 AKu,MMr,World Tour,concl. . . . 3.50
20 AKu,MMr,World Tour,epilogue . 3.50
21 MMr,DaM,Hellfire & Brimstone . 3.50
22 MMr,DaM,Hellfire & Brimstone . 3.50
23 MMr,DaM,Hellfire & Brimstone . 3.50
24 MMr,DaM,Hellfire&Brimstone . . 3.50
25 MMr,DaM,AKu(c), Hellfire &
   Brimstone, 48-pg. . . . . . . . . . 4.00
26 MMr,AKu,Professor-X . . . . . . . 3.00
27 MMr,AKu,V:Brotherhood . . . . . 3.00
28 MMr,AKu,V:Brotherhood . . . . . 3.00
29 MMr,AKu,Missing X-Man . . . . . 3.00
30 MMr,AKu,Storm's gang . . . . . . 3.00
31 MMr,AKu,V:Magneto . . . . . . . . 3.00
32 MMr,AKu,Ultimate fate . . . . . . . 3.00
```

```
33 MMr,AKu,Return of the King . . . 3.00
34 BMB,Blockbuster,pt.1. . . . . . . . 4.00
35 BMB,Blockbuster,pt.2. . . . . . . . 3.00
36 BMB,Blockbuster,pt.3. . . . . . . . 2.25
37 BMB,Blockbuster,pt.4. . . . . . . . 2.25
38 BMB,Blockbuster,pt.5. . . . . . . . 2.25
39 BMB,Blockbuster,pt.6. . . . . . . . 2.25
Spec. #1-#2-#3, 96-pg. . . . . . . . . . 4.00
TPB rep.#1–#6, 160-pg. . . . . . . . 14.95
TPB Ultimate X-Men, Weapon X . . 14.95
TPB Vol.3, World Tour . . . . . . . . 18.00
TPB Vol.4, Hellfire & Brimstone. . 13.00
TPB Vol.5: Ultimate War . . . . . . . 11.00
TPB Vol.6: Return of the King . . . 17.00
Spec. rep. Must Have #1–#3 . . . . 4.00
```

ULTRAFORCE/AVENGERS
```
1 V:Loki,A:Malibu's Ultraforce . . . 3.95
```

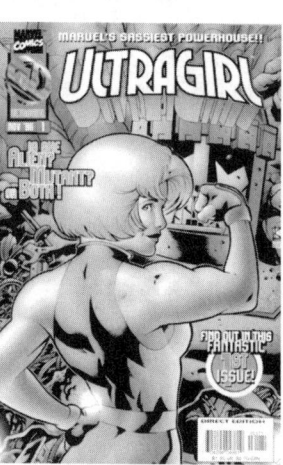

Ultragirl #1
© *Marvel Entertainment Group*

ULTRA GIRL
[Mini-series] 1996
```
1 BKs,I&O:Ultra Girl. . . . . . . . . . . 2.25
2 BKs, . . . . . . . . . . . . . . . . . . . . . 2.25
3 BKs,R:New Warriors. . . . . . . . . 2.25
```

ULTRA X-MEN COLLECTION
```
1 Metallic(c), art from cards . . . . . 3.00
2 thru 5 art from cards . . . . . . . @3.00
```

ULTRA X-MEN III
```
Preview . . . . . . . . . . . . . . . . . . . . 3.00
```

ULTRON
June, 1999
```
1-shot Ultron Unleashed, rep. . . . . 3.50
```

UNCANNY ORIGINS
Sept., 1996
```
1 F:Cyclops. . . . . . . . . . . . . . . . . 2.25
2 F:Quicksilver . . . . . . . . . . . . . . 2.25
3 DHv,BAn,F:Archangel. . . . . . . . 2.25
4 F:Firelord . . . . . . . . . . . . . . . . . 2.25
5 MHi,F:Hulk . . . . . . . . . . . . . . . . 2.25
6 F:Beast . . . . . . . . . . . . . . . . . . 2.25
7 F:Venom. . . . . . . . . . . . . . . . . . 2.25
8 F:Nightcrawler . . . . . . . . . . . . . 2.25
9 F:Storm . . . . . . . . . . . . . . . . . . 2.25
```

All comics prices listed are for Near Mint condition.

CVA Page 333

Uncanny–Untold · MARVEL · Comics Values Annual

Uncanny Origins #2
© Marvel Entertainment Group

10 F:Black Cat	2.25
11 F:Luke Cage	2.25
12 F:Black Knight	2.25
13 LWn,MCa,F:Doctor Strange	2.25
14 LWn,MCW,F:Iron Fist	2.25

UNCANNY TALES
Atlas, June, 1952
1 RH,While the City Sleeps . . 1,100.00
2 JMn,BEv 600.00
3 Escape to What 500.00
4 JMn,Nobody's Fool 500.00
5 Fear 500.00
6 He Lurks in the Shadows 550.00
7 BEv,Kill,Clown,Kill 550.00
8 JMn,Bring Back My Face 400.00
9 BEv,RC,The Executioner 400.00
10 JMn,RH(c),JR,The Man Who Came Back To Life 400.00
11 GC,The Man Who Changed . . 300.00
12 BP,BEv,Bertha Gets Buried . . 300.00
13 RH,Scared Out of His Skin. . . 300.00
14 RH,TLw,Victims of Vonntor. . . 300.00
15 RA,JSt,The Man Who Saw Death 300.00
16 JMn,GC,Zombie at Large 300.00
17 GC,TLw,I Live With Corpses . 300.00
18 JF,BP,Clock Face(c) 300.00
19 DBr,RKr,TLw,The Man Who Died Again 300.00
20 DBr,Ted's Head 300.00
21 . . . . 250.00
22 DAy 250.00
23 TLw 250.00
24 . . . . 250.00
25 MSy 250.00
26 Spider-Man prototype story . . 400.00
27 RA,TLw 250.00
28 TLw 250.00
29 JMn 200.00
30 . . . . 200.00
31 . . . . 200.00
32 BEv 200.00
33 . . . . 200.00
34 BP 200.00
35 TLw,JMn 200.00
36 BP,BEv 200.00
37 MD 200.00
38 BP 200.00
39 BEv 200.00
40 . . . . 200.00
41 . . . . 200.00
42 MD 225.00
43 . . . . 200.00
44 . . . . 200.00
45 MD 200.00
46 GM 200.00
47 TSe 200.00
48 BEv 200.00
49 JO 200.00
50 JO 200.00
51 GM 225.00
52 GC 200.00
53 JO,AT 200.00
54 . . . . 220.00
55 . . . . 200.00
56 Sept., 1957 . . . . 225.00

UNCANNY TALES FROM THE GRAVE
Dec., 1973—Oct., 1975
1 RC,Room of no Return 30.00
2 DAy,Out of the Swamp 20.00
3 No Way Out 20.00
4 JR,SD,Vampire 20.00
5 GK,GT,Don't Go in the Cellar . . 20.00
6 JR,SD,The Last Kkrul 20.00
7 RH,SD,Never Dance With a Vampire 20.00
8 SD,Escape Into Hell 20.00
9 JA,The Nightmare Men 20.00
10 SD,DH,Beware the Power of Khan 20.00
11 SD,JF,RH,Dead Don't Sleep. . 20.00
12 SD,Final Issue 20.00

UNCANNY X-MEN
See: X-MEN

UNKNOWN WORLDS OF SCIENCE FICTION
Jan., 1975
(Black & White Magazine)
1 AW,RKr,AT,FF,GC 25.00
2 FB,GP 20.00
3 GM,AN,GP,GC 20.00
4 . . . . 20.00
5 GM,NC,GC 20.00
6 FB,AN,GC,Nov., 1975 . . . . . . 20.00
Spec.#1 AN,NR,JB 25.00

UNION JACK
Oct., 1998
1 (of 3) BRa,F:Joey Chapman 3.00
2 BRa,V:Baroness 3.00
3 BRa,conclusion 3.00
TPB 96-pg. (2002) 11.50

U.S.A. COMICS
Timely, Aug., 1941
1 S&K(c),BW,Bondage(c),The Defender(c) 17,000.00
2 S&K(c),BW,Capt.Terror(c) . . 5,000.00
3 S&K(c),Capt.Terror(c). 4,000.00
4 Major Liberty 3,500.00
5 Hitler(c),O:AmericanAvenger 3,800.00
6 ASh(c),Capt.America(c) . . . 4,000.00
7 BW,O:Marvel Boy 3,800.00
8 Capt.America (c) 3,500.00
9 Bondage(c), Capt.America . . 3,500.00
10 SSh(c),Bondage(c), Capt. America 3,500.00
11 SSh(c),Bondage(c), Capt. America 2,000.00
12 ASh(c),Capt.America 2,000.00
13 ASh(c),Capt.America 2,000.00
14 AyB(c),Capt.America 1,500.00
15 Capt.America 1,500.00
16 ASh(c),Bondage(c), Capt.America 1,500.00
17 Bondage(c),Capt.America . . 1,500.00

U.S. 1
May, 1983–Oct., 1984
1 AM(c),HT,Trucking Down the Highway 3.00
2 HT,Midnight 3.00
3 FS,ME,Rhyme of the Ancient Highwayman 3.00
4 FS,ME 3.00
5 FS,ME,Facing The Maze 3.00
6 FS,ME 3.00
7 FS,ME 3.00
8 FS,ME 3.00
9 FS,ME,Iron Mike-King of the Bike 3.00
10 thru 12 FS,ME . . . . @3.00

U.S. AGENT
June–Dec., 1993
1 V:Scourge,O:U.S.Agent 2.25
2 thru 4 . . . . @2.25

U.S. AGENT
May, 2001
1 (of 3) JOy,KK,Maximum Security 3.00
2 JOy,KK, ... 3.00
3 JOy,KK,A:Capt.America 3.00

U.S. WAR MACHINE
Marvel Max, Sept., 2001
1 (of 12) Weekly series,24-page . . 2.25
2 thru 12 . . . . @2.25
TPB rep., 288-page 14.95

UNIVERSE X
July, 2000
0 AxR,DBw,48-pg. 4.00
1 (of 12) AxR,DBw,Capt.MarVell . . 3.50
2 AxR,DBw, ... 3.50
3 AxR,DBw, ... 3.50
4 AxR,DBw,Cap.Am vs. Hydra . . . 3.50
5 AxR,DBw,Mar-Vell vs.Death . . . 3.50
6 AxR,DBw,Moonknight 3.50
7 AxR,DBw,Supreme Intelligence. . 3.50
8 AxR,DBw,Monster Generation . . 3.50
9 AxR,DBw,Supreme Intelligence. . 3.50
10 AxR,DBw,V:Mephisto 3.50
11 AxR,DBw,A:Belasco 3.50
12 AxR,DBw,V:Absorbing Man . . . 3.50
Spec."4",F:Fantastic Four 4.00
Spec. Spidey,AxR,JG,JR,48-page . . 4.00
Spec. Beasts,AxR,48-page 4.00
Spec. Omnibus,AxR 4.00
Spec. Iron Men, 48-page 4.00
Spec. Universe X:X 48-page. 4.00
TPB Vol.1 384-pg. 24.95
TPB Vol.2 336-pg. 29.95

UNTAMED
Epic *Heavy Hitters*, 1993
1 I:Griffen Palmer 2.75
2 V:Kosansui 2.25
3 V:Kosansui 2.25

UNTOLD LEGEND OF CAPTAIN MARVEL, THE
1997
1 (of 3) Early days of Captain Marvel 2.50

MARVEL

Untold–Venom

Untold Legend of Captain Marvel #1
© Marvel Entertainment Group

2 Early days of Captain Marvel . . . 2.50
3 V:Kree 2.50

UNTOLD TALES OF SPIDER-MAN
Sept., 1995 – Sept., 1997
1 F:Young Spider-Man. 3.00
2 V:Batwing. 2.25
3 V:Sandman 2.25
4 V:J.Jonah Jameson 2.25
5 V:Vulture 2.25
6 A:Human Torch. 2.25
7 . . . . 2.25
8 . . . . 2.25
9 A:Batwing,Lizard. 2.25
10 KBk,PO,I:Commanda. 2.25
11 KBk,PO, ... 2.25
12 KBk,PO, ... 2.25
13 KBk,PO, ... 2.25
14 KBk,PO, ... 2.25
15 KBk,PO,AV, Gordon's plan to
  control the Bugle 2.25
16 Re-I:Mary Jane Watson 2.25
17 KBk,PO,AV,V:Hawkeye 2.25
18 KBk,PO,AV,A:Green Goblin,
  Headsman 2.25
19 KBk,PO,AW,F:Doctor Octopus . . 2.25
20 KBk,PO,AW,V:Vulture 2.25
21 KBk,PO,AW,V:Menace,A:Original
  X-Men 2.25
22 KBk,PO,AW,V:Scarecrow, ... 2.25
23 KBk,PO,AW,V:Crime Master,
  A:Green Goblin 2.25
24 KBk,PO,BMc, Fate of Batwing . . 2.25
25 LBl,PO,BMc, V:Green Goblin,
  final issue. 2.25
Minus 1 Spec., RSt,JR, flashback,
  Peter's parents. 2.25
Ann.'96 1 KBk,MiA,JSt,A date with
  Invisible Girl? 2.25
Ann.'97 KBk,TL,A:everyone, 48-pg. 2.95
TPB rep. #1–#8 . . . . 17.00
one-shot GN KBk,SL,Encounter,
  A:Dr. Strange 48-pg. 6.00

US WAR MACHINE 2.0
Marvel June 2003
1 (of 3) V:Iron Man 3.00
2 . . . . 3.00
3 concl. 3.00

VALKYRIE
1996
1-shot JMD 2.50

VAMPIRE TALES
Aug., 1973
(black & white magazine)
1 BEv,B:Morbius the Living
  Vampire. 60.00
2 JSo,I:Satana 40.00
3 A:Satana 30.00
4 GK 30.00
5 GK,O:Morbius The Living
  Vampire 40.00
6 AA,I:Lilith 35.00
7 HC,PG 35.00
8 AA,A:Blade The Vampire
  Slayer 35.00
9 RH,AA 35.00
10 . . . . 35.00
11 June, 1975. . . . . 35.00
Ann.#1 . . . . 25.00

Vault of Evil #6
© Marvel Entertainment Group

VAULT OF EVIL
Feb., 1973—Nov., 1975
1 GK,B:1950's reps,Come
  Midnight,Come Monster 30.00
2 The Hour of the Witch 20.00
3 The Woman Who Wasn't 20.00
4 Face that Follows 20.00
5 Ghost 20.00
6 GT,The Thing at the Window . . 20.00
7 Monsters 20.00
8 The Vampire is my Brother . . . 20.00
9 Giant Killer 20.00
10 MD,The Lurkers in the Caves. . 20.00
11 JK,BEv,Two Feasts For
  a Vampire. 20.00
12 Midnight in the
  Haunted Mansion 20.00
13 Hot as the Devil. 20.00
14 SD,Midnight in the Haunted
  Manor 20.00
15 SD,Don't Shake Hands with
  the Devil. 20.00
16 A Grave Honeymoon 20.00
17 Grave Undertaking. 20.00
18 The Deadly Edge. 20.00
19 Vengeance of Ahman Ra 20.00
20 SD. 20.00
21 Victim of Valotorr 20.00
22 SD. 20.00
23 Black Magician Lives Again . . . 20.00

VENOM
Marvel April 2003
1 SK(c),Shiver,pt.1. . . . . 3.00
2 Shiver,pt.2 . . . . 2.25
3 SK(c),Shiver,pt.3. . . . . 2.25
4 SK(c),Shiver,pt.4. . . . . 2.25
5 SK(c),Shiver,pt.5. . . . . 2.25
6 . . . . 2.25
7 SK(c) 2.25
8 . . . . 2.25
TPB Shiver, Vol. 1 . . . . 19.95

VENOM: ALONG CAME A SPIDER
1996
1 LHA,GLz,V:New Spider-Man. . . . 3.00
2 LHa,JPi,V:New Spider-Man. 3.00
3 . . . . 3.00
4 conclusion, 48-pg 3.00

VENOM: CARNAGE UNLEASHED
1995
1 Venom vs. Carnage 3.00
2 Venom vs. Carnage 3.00
3 No Spider-Help. 3.00
4 JRu,Wld,LHa,cardstock(c) 3.00

VENOM: THE ENEMY WITHIN
1994
1 BMc,Glow-in-the-dark(C),
  A:Demogoblin,Morbius 3.25
2 BMc,A:Demogoblin,Morbius . . . 3.25
3 BMc,V:Demogoblin,A:Morbius. . . 3.25

VENOM: FINALE
1997–98
1 (of 3) LHa, ... 3.00
2 LJa, ... 3.00
3 LHa, finale 3.00

VENOM: FUNERAL PYRE
1993
1 TL,JRu,A:Punisher 3.50
2 TL,JRu,AM,V:Gangs 3.50
3 TL,JRu,Last issue. 3.50

VENOM: THE HUNGER
1996
1 thru 4 LKa,TeH,V:Dr. Paine . . . @2.25

VENOM: THE HUNTED
1996
1 LHa,3 part mini-series. 3.00

VENOM: LETHAL PROTECTOR
1993
1 MBa,A:Spider-Man.holo-grafx(c) . 7.00
1a Gold Ed.. . . . . 25.00
2 MBa,A:Spider-Man. 3.50
3 MBa,Families of Venom's
  victims 3.50
4 RLm,A:Spider-Man,V:Life
  Foundation. 3.50
5 RLm,V:Five Symbiotes,A:SpM . . 3.50

All comics prices listed are for *Near Mint* condition.

CVA Page 335

Venom–War Adventures   MARVEL   Comics Values Annual

6 RLm,V:Spider-Man 3.50
Super Size Spec.#1 Planet of
   the Symbiotes,pt.3 . . . . 3.95
Venom:Deathtrap:The Vault,RLm,
   A:Avengers,Freedom Force . . . 6.95
TPB Lethal Protector RLm,DvM . . 15.95

VENOM: LICENSE TO KILL
1997
1 (of 3) LHa,KHt, sequel to Venom
   on trial 2.25
2 LHa,V:Dr. Yes 2.25
3 LHa,V:Dr. Yes 2.25

VENOM: THE MACE
1994
1 Embossed(c),CP(s),LSh,I:Mace . 3.25
2 CP(s),LSh,V:Mace 3.25
3 CP(s),LSh,V:Mace,final issue . . . 3.25

VENOM: THE MADNESS
1993–94
1 B:ANi(s),KJo,V:Juggernaut 3.50
2 KJo,V:Juggernaut 3.25
3 E:ANi(s),KJo,V:Juggernaut 3.25

VENOM: NIGHTS OF VENGEANCE
1994
1 RLm,I:Stalkers,A:Vengeance . . . 3.25
2 RLm,A:Vengeance,V:Stalkers . . . 3.25
3 RLm,V:Stalkers 3.25
4 RLm,final issue 3.25

VENOM: ON TRIAL
Jan.–May, 1997
1 LHa,Tries to break out 2.25
2 LHa,Defended by Matt Murdock
   (Daredevil),A:Spider-Man 2.25
3 LHa,A:Spider-Man, Carnage,
   Daredevil 2.25

VENOM: SEED OF DARKNESS
1997
1 LKa,JFy,Flashback, early Eddie
   Brock 2.25

VENOM: SEPARATION ANXIETY
1994–95
1 Embossed(c) 3.00
2 V:Symbiotes 3.00
3 . . . . 3.00
4 . . . . 3.00
TPB Rep.#1-#4 HMe,RoR,SDR . . . 9.95

VENOM: SIGN OF THE BOSS
1997
1 (of 2) IV,TDr,V:Ghost Rider 2.25
2 (of 2) IV,TDr,conclusion. 2.25

VENOM: SINNER TAKES ALL
1995
1 LHa,GLz,I:New Sin-Eater 3.00
2 V:Sineater 3.00
3 Wrong Man 3.00
4 LHa,GLz,V:Sin-Eater 3.00

5 LHa, finale 3.00

VENOM: TOOTH AND CLAW
1996–97
1 (of 3) LHa,JPi,AM, Dirtnap usurps
   Venom's body. 2.25
2 LHa,JPi,AM,V:Wolverine 2.25
3 LHa,JPi,AM,V:Wolverine,
   Chimera 2.25

VENUS
Atlas, Aug., 1948
1 B:Venus,Hedy Devine,HK,Hey
   Look 1,500.00
2 Venus(c) 900.00
3 Carnival(c) 750.00
4 Cupid(c).HK,Hey Look 750.00
5 Serenade(c) 750.00
6 Wrath of a Goddess,A:Loki . . . 650.00
7 The Romance That Could
   Not Be 650.00
8 The Love Trap 650.00
9 Whom the Gods Destroy 650.00
10 JMn,B:Science Fiction/Horror,
   Trapped On the Moon. 900.00
11 RH,The End of the World . . 1,100.00
12 GC,The Lost World 600.00
13 BEv,King of the Living Dead. . 900.00
14 BEv,The Fountain of Death . . 900.00
15 BEv,The Empty Grave 900.00
16 BEv,Where Gargoyles Dwell . 900.00
17 BEv,Tower of Death,
   Bondage(c). 900.00
18 BEv,Terror in the Tunnel. 900.00
19 BEv,PMo,The Kiss Of Death . 900.00

VERY BEST OF MARVEL COMICS
1-shot reps Marvel Artists
   Favorite Stories 12.95

VIDEO JACK
Nov., 1987
1 KGi,O:Video Jack 3.00
2 KGi. 2.50
3 KGi. 2.50
4 KGi. 2.50
5 KGi. 2.50
6 KGi,NA,BWr,AW 2.50

VISION, THE
1994–95
1 BHs,mini-series 2.25
2 BHs 2.25
3 BHs 2.25
4 BHs 2.25

VISION & SCARLET WITCH
[1st Series] Nov., 1982
1 RL,V:Halloween 3.00
2 RL,V:Isbisa,D:Whizzer 3.00
3 RL,A:Wonderman,V:GrimReaper 3.00
4 RL,A:Magneto,Inhumans 3.00
[2nd Series] 1985–86
1 V:Grim Reaper 2.50
2 V:Lethal Legion,D:Grim Reaper . 2.50
3 V:Salem's Seven 2.50
4 I:Glamor & Illusion 2.50
5 A:Glamor & Illusion 2.50
6 A:Magneto 2.50
7 V:Toad 2.50
8 A:Powerman 2.50

*Vision and Scarlet Witch, 2nd Series
#10 © Marvel Entertainment Group*

9 V:Enchantress 2.50
10 A:Inhumans 2.50
11 A:Spider-Man. 2.50
12 Birth of V&S's Child 2.50

VISIONARIES
Star, Nov., 1987
1 thru 5 . . . . @2.50
6 Sept., 1988 . . . . 2.50

VOID INDIGO
Epic, Nov., 1984
1 VM,Epic Comics 2.50
2 VM,Epic Comics,March, 1985 . . . 2.50

WACKY DUCK
See: DOPEY DUCK

WALLY THE WIZARD
Star, April, 1985
1 . . . . 4.00
2 thru 11 . . . . @4.00
12 March, 1986 . . . . 4.00

WAR, THE
1989
1 Sequel to The Draft & The Pit . . 4.00
2 . . . . 4.00
3 . . . . 4.00
4 1990. . . . . 4.00

WAR ACTION
Atlas, April, 1952
1 JMn,RH,War Stories, Six Dead
   Men 225.00
2 GT 125.00
3 Invasion in Korea 90.00
4 thru 10 . . . . @90.00
11 . . . . 100.00
12 . . . . 100.00
13 BK 100.00
14 Rangers Strike,June, 1953. . . . 90.00

WAR ADVENTURES
Atlas, Jan., 1952
1 GT,Battle Fatigue 175.00
2 The Story of a Slaughter 100.00

Comics Values Annual — MARVEL — War–Warlock

3 JRo 75.00	13 Xenophiles Reptiles 2.25	2 JSn,rep.Strange Tales #180
4 RH(c) 75.00	14 last issue 2.25	& Warlock #9 . . . . 4.00
5 RH,Violent(c) 75.00		3 JSn,rep.Warlock #10–#12 . . . . . 4.00
6 Stand or Die 75.00	### WARHEADS: BLACK DAWN	4 JSn,rep.Warlock #13–#15 . . . . . 4.00
7 JMn(c) 75.00		5 JSn,rep.Warlock #15 . . . . 4.00
8 BK 100.00	1 A:Gh.Rider,Morbius. 3.25	6 JSn,rep. 4.00
9 RH(c) 75.00	2 V:Dracula 2.25	
10 JRo(c),Attack at Dawn 75.00		### WARLOCK [Limited Series]
11 Red Trap 75.00	### WAR IS HELL Jan., 1973—Oct., 1975	1 Rep.Warlock Series 3.50
12 . . . . 75.00		2 Rep.Warlock Series 3.00
13 RH(c),The Commies Strike Feb., 1953 . . . . 75.00	1 BP,B:reps.,Decision at Dawn . . 35.00	3 Rep.Warlock Series 3.00
	2 Anytime,Anyplace,War is Hell . 20.00	4 Rep.Warlock Series 3.00
### WAR COMBAT Atlas, March, 1952	3 Retreat or Die 20.00	5 Rep.Warlock Series 3.00
	4 Live Grenade 20.00	6 Rep.Warlock Series 3.00
1 JMn,Death of Platoon Leader . 175.00	5 Trapped Platoon 20.00	
2 . . . . 100.00	6 We Die at Dawn 20.00	### WARLOCK Sept., 1998
3 JMn(c) 75.00	7 While the Jungle Sleeps,A:Sgt Fury 20.00	
4 JMn(c) 75.00		1 (of 4) TL,RJn,R:Adam Warlock . . 3.00
5 The Red Hordes 75.00	8 Killed in Action,A;Sgt Fury . . . 20.00	2 TL,murderer revealed 3.00
Becomes:	9 B:Supernatural,War Stories . . . 55.00	3 TL,V:Drax 3.00
### COMBAT CASEY	10 Death is a 30 Ton Tank 20.00	4 TL,Concl. 3.00
	11 thru 15 . . . . @20.00	
6 BEv,Combat Casey cont 150.00		### WARLOCK Aug., 1999
7 . . . . 100.00		
8 JMn(c) 90.00		1 LSi,PFe,Marvel Tech. 3.00
9 . . . . 75.00		2 LSi,PFe,A:Iron Man 2.50
10 RH(c). 125.00		2a variant PFe cover 2.50
11 . . . . 60.00		3 LSi,PFe,MMo,F:Psiren 2.50
12 . . . . 60.00		4 LSi,PFe,MMo,V:Mole Man 2.50
13 thru 19 . . . . @125.00		5 LSi,PFe,MMo 2.50
20 . . . . 60.00		6 LSi,PFe,MMo,A:Kitty Pryde 2.50
21 thru 33 . . . . @55.00		7 LSi,PFe,MMo,R:Wolfsbane, Magus 2.50
34 July, 1957 . . . . 55.00		
		8 LSi,PFe,MMo,V:Bastion 2.50
### WAR COMICS Atlas, Dec., 1950		9 LSi,PFe,MMo,F:Bastion 2.50
		### WARLOCK AND THE INFINITY WATCH 1992–95
1 You Only Die Twice 300.00		
2 Infantry's War 150.00		
3 . . . . 125.00		1 AMe,Trial of the Gods(from Infinity Gauntlet) 3.00
4 GC,The General Said Nuts . . 125.00		
5 . . . . 125.00		2 AMe,I:Infinity Watch(Gamora,Pip, Moondragon,Drax & 1 other) . . 2.75
6 The Deadly Decision of General Kwang 125.00		
7 RH,JMn 125.00	*Warlock #1* © Marvel Entertainment Group	3 RL,TA,A:High Evolutionary, Nobilus,I:Omega. 2.75
8 RH,No Survivors 125.00		4 RL,TA,V:Omega 2.50
9 RH,JMn 125.00	### WARLOCK [1st Regular Series] Aug., 1972	5 AMe,TA,V:Omega 2.50
10 . . . . 125.00		6 AMe,V:Omega(Man-Beast) 2.50
11 Flame thrower 135.00		7 TR,TA,V:Mole Man,A:Thanos . . . 2.50
12 thru 21 . . . . @100.00	1 MGr,GK,I:Counter Earth, A:High Evolutionary 60.00	8 TR,TA,Infinity War,A:Thanos . . . 2.25
22 . . . . 100.00		9 AMe,TA,Inf.War,O:Gamora 2.25
23 thru 37 . . . . @75.00	2 MGr,JB,TS,V:Man Beast 35.00	10 AMe,Inf.War,Thanos vs Doppleganger. 2.50
38 JKu 80.00	3 MGr,GK,TS,V:Apollo 35.00	
39 . . . . 75.00	4 MGr,JK,TS,V:Triax 20.00	11 O:Pip,Gamora,Drax,M'dragon . . 2.25
40 . . . . 75.00	5 MGr,GK,TS,V:Dr.Doom 20.00	12 TR,Drax Vs.Hulk 2.25
41 . . . . 75.00	6 MGr,TS(i),O:Brute. 20.00	13 TR,Drax vs Hulk 2.25
42 JO 75.00	7 MGr,TS(i),V:Brute,D:Dr.Doom . . 20.00	14 AMe,V:United Nations 2.25
43 AT,MD 80.00	8 MGr,TS(i),R:Man-Beast(cont. in Hulk #176) 20.00	15 AMe,Magnus,Him 2.25
44 . . . . 75.00		16 TGr,I:Count Abyss 2.25
45 . . . . 75.00	9 MGr,JSn,1st'Rebirth'Thanos, O:Magnus,N:Warlock, I:In-Betweener 30.00	17 TGr,I:Maxam 2.25
46 RC. 85.00		18 AMe,Inf.Crusade,N:Pip. 2.25
47 . . . . 75.00		19 TGr,A:Hulk,Wolverine,Infinity Crusade 2.25
48 MD,JO. 75.00	10 MGr,JSn,SL,O:Thanos,V:Magus, A:In-Betweener. 35.00	
49 Sept., 1957 . . . . 85.00		20 AMe,Inf.Crusade 2.25
	11 MGr,JSn,SL,D:Magus,A:Thanos, In-Betweener 30.00	21 V:Thor 2.25
### WARHEADS Marvel UK, 1992–93		22 AMe, Infinity Crusade 2.25
	12 MGr,JSn,SL,O:Pip,V:Pro-Boscis A:Starfox 20.00	23 JSn(s),TGb,Blood & Thunder#4 . . . . 2.25
1 GEr,I:Warheads,A:Wolverine, . . . 2.25		
2 GEr,V:Nick Fury 2.25	13 MGr,JSn,SL,I&O:Star-Thief . . . 20.00	24 JSn(s),TGb,V:Geirrodur 2.25
3 DTy,A:Iron Man. 2.25	14 MGr,JSn,SL,V:Star-Thief 20.00	25 JSn(s),AMe,Die-Cut(c),Blood & Thunder #12. . . . . 3.50
4 SCy,A:X-Force 2.25	15 MGr,JSn,A:Thanos,V:Soul-Gem 30.00	
5 A:X-Force,C:Deaths'Head II . . . 2.25		26 A:Avengers 2.25
6 SCy,A:Death's Head II 2.25	### [2nd Regular Series] 1992	27 TGb,V:Avengers 2.25
7 SCy,A:Death's Head II,S.Surfer. . 2.25		28 TGb,V:Man-Beast 2.25
8 SCy,V:Mephisto 2.25	1 JSn,rep.Strange Tales #178-180 Baxter Paper 5.00	29 A:Maya 2.25
9 SCy,V:Mephisto 2.25		30 PO 2.25
10 JCz,V:Mephisto 2.25		
11 A:Death's Head II. 2.25		
12 V:Mechanix 2.25		

All comics prices listed are for Near Mint condition.

Warlock–Web Of   MARVEL   Comics Values Annual

31 . . . . 2.00	1-shot Marrow #1, JWi, ... 2.25	12 BMc,SB,V:Thugs 10.00
32 Heart & Soul 2.00	1-shot Agent Zero #1, JWi 2.25	13 BMc,V:J.JonahJameson. 10.00
33 V:Count Abyss 2.00	1 . . . . 2.25	14 KB,V:Black Fox 10.00
34 V:Count Abyss 2.00	2 F:Marrow 2.25	15 V:Black Fox,I:Chance 7.00
35 V:Tyrannus 2.00	3 . . . . 2.25	16 MS,KB,V:Magma 7.00
36 . . . . 2.00	4 Hunt for Sabretooth 2.25	17 MS,V:Magma 7.00
37 A:Zaharius 2.00	5 Evil plans 2.25	18 MS,KB,Where is Spider-Man? . . 7.00
38 . . . . 2.00	6 NRd,special mission 2.25	19 MS,BMc,I:Solo,Humbug. 7.00
39 V:Domitron 2.00	7 The Underground,pt.1 . . . . 2.25	20 MS,V:Terrorists 7.00
40 A:Thanos. 2.00	8 The Underground,pt.2 . . . . 3.00	21 V:Fake Spider-Man 7.00
41 Monster Island 2.00	9 The Underground,pt.3 . . . . 3.00	22 MS,V:Terrorists 7.00
42 Warlock vs. Maxam, Atlantis Rising, final issue 2.00	10 The Underground,pt.4 . . . . 3.00	23 V:Slyde 7.00
	11 The Underground,pt.5 . . . . 3.00	24 SB,V:Vulture,Hobgoblin 7.00
	12 The Underground,pt.6 . . . . 3.00	25 V:Aliens 7.00
	13 The Underground,concl.. . . . . . 3.00	26 V:Thugs 7.00
WARLOCK CHRONICLES	14 R:Mr. Sinister 3.00	27 V:Headhunter 7.00
1993–94	15 X-Man 3.00	28 BL,V:Thugs 7.00
1 TR,F:Adam Warlock,holo-grafx(c), I:Darklore,Meer'lyn 3.25	16 . . . . 3.00	29 A:Wolverine,2nd App:New Hobgoblin. 20.00
2 TR,Infinity Crusade,Thanos revealed to have the Reality Gem 2.25	TPB Vol. 1 . . . . 22.00	30 KB,O:Rose,C:Daredevil,Capt. America,Wolverine,Punisher . . 10.00
3 TR,A:Mephisto 2.25	TPB The Underground	31 MZ,BMc,V:Kraven 9.00
4 TR,A:Magnus 2.25	**WEAVEWORLD**	32 MZ,BMc,V:Kraven 9.00
5 TR(c),Inf.Crusade 2.25	**Epic, 1991–92**	33 BSz(c),SL,V:Kingpin,Mad Dog Ward,pt.#1 . . . . 6.00
6 TR,Blood & Thunder,pt.#3 . . . . 2.25	1 MM, Clive Barker adaptation. . . . 5.00	34 SB,A:Watcher 6.00
7 TR,Blood & Thunder,pt.#7 . . . . 2.25	2 MM,`Into the Weave' 5.00	35 AS,V:Living Brain. 6.00
8 TR,Blood & Thunder,pt.#11 . . . 2.25	3 MM. 5.00	36 AS,V:Phreak Out,I:Tombstone . . 7.00
9 TR 2.25		37 V:Slasher 7.00
10 TR. 2.25	**WEB OF SCARLET SPIDER**	38 AS,A:Tombstone,V:Hobgoblin. . . 7.00
11 TR. 2.25	**1995–96**	39 AS,V:Looter(Meteor Man). 6.00
	1 TDF,Virtual Mortality,pt.1 . . . . 2.00	40 AS,V:Cult of Love 6.00
WAR MACHINE	2 TDF,CyberWar,pt.2 . . . . 2.00	41 AS,V:Cult of Love 6.00
1994–96	3 Nightmare in Scarlet,pt.1 . . . . . . 2.00	42 AS,V:Cult of Love 6.00
1 GG,Foil Embossed(c),B:LKa&StB, O:War Machine,V:Cable, C:Deathlok 3.25	4 Nightmare in Scarlet,pt.3 . . . . . . 2.00	43 AS,V:Cult of Love 6.00
		44 AS,V:Warzone,A:Hulk 5.00
	WEB OF SPIDER-MAN	45 AS,V:Vulture 5.00
1a Newstand Ed. 2.25	**April, 1985**	46 A:Dr.Pym,V:Nekra 5.00
2 GG,V:Cable,Deathlok,w/card . . . 3.25	1 JM,V:New Costume 25.00	47 AS,V:Hobgoblin 6.00
3 GG,V:Cable,Deathlok 2.25	2 JM,V:Vulture. 15.00	48 AS,O:New Hobgoblin's Demonic Power 15.00
4 GG,C:Force Works 3.25	3 JM,V:Vulture. 15.00	49 VM,V:Drugs 5.00
5 GG,I:Deachtoll 3.25	4 JM,JBy,V:Dr.Octopus 10.00	50 AS,V:Chameleon(double size) . . 7.00
6 GG,V:Deathtoll 3.25	5 JM,JBy,V:Dr.Octopus 10.00	51 MBa,V:Chameleon,Lobo Bros. . . 5.00
7 GG,A:Hawkeye 3.25	6 MZ,BL,JM,Secret Wars II 10.00	52 FS,JR,O:J Jonah Jameson V:Chameleon 5.00
8 reg ed. 2.25	7 SB,A:Hulk,V:Nightmare, C:Wolverine 10.00	53 MBa,V:Lobo Bros.,C:Punisher A:Chameleon 5.00
8a neon(c),w/insert print 3.00	8 V:Smithville Thunder 10.00	54 AS,V:Chameleon,V:Lobo Bros. . 5.00
9 Hands of Mandarin,pt.2 . . . . 2.25	9 V:Smithville Thunder 10.00	55 AS,V:Chameleon,Hammerhead, V:Lobo Bros. 5.00
10 Hands of Mandarin,pt.5 . . . . . . 2.25	10 JM,A:Dominic Fortune, V:Shocker 10.00	56 AS,I&O:Skin Head, A:Rocket Racer 5.00
11 X-Mas Party. 2.25	11 BMc,V:Thugs 10.00	57 AS,D:SkinHead, A:Rocket Racer 5.00
12 V:Terror Device 2.25		58 AS,V:Grizzly 5.00
13 V:The Rush Team 2.25		59 AS,Acts of Vengeance,V:Titania A:Puma,Cosmic Spider-Man. . . 7.00
14 A:Force Works 2.25		60 AS,A of V,V:Goliath 5.00
15 In The Past of WWII 2.25		61 AS,A of V,V:Dragon Man 5.00
16 DAn,A:Rick Fury,Cap.America . . 2.25		62 AS,V:Molten Man. 3.00
17 The Man Who Won WWII 2.25		63 AS,V:Mister Fear 3.00
18 DAn,N:War Machine 2.25		64 AS,V:Graviton,Titania,Trapster . . 3.00
19 DAn,A:Hawkeye 2.25		65 AS,V:Goliath,Trapster,Graviton. . 3.00
20 DAn,The Crossing 2.25		66 AS,V:Tombstone,A:G.Goblin . . . 3.00
21 DAn,The Crossing 2.25		67 AS,A:GreenGoblin, V:Tombstone 3.00
22 DAn,V:Iron Man 2.25		68 AS,A:GreenGoblin, V:Tombstone 3.00
23 DAn,Avengers:Timeslide 2.25		69 AS,V:Hulk 3.00
		70 AS,I:The Spider/Hulk 3.00
WAR MAN		71 A:Silver Sable 3.00
Epic, 1993		72 AM,A:Silver Sable 3.00
1 thru 2 CDi(s). 2.50		73 AS,A:Human Torch, Colossus,Namor. 3.00
		74 AS,I:Spark,V:Bora 3.00
WEAPON X		75 AS,C:New Warriors 3.00
1995		76 AS,Spidey in Ice 3.00
1 Wolverine After Xavier 4.00		77 AS,V:Firebrand,Inheritor. 3.00
2 Full Scale War 2.25		78 AS,A:Firebrand,Cloak&Dagger. . 3.00
3 Jean Leaves. 2.25		79 AS,V:Silvermane 3.00
4 F:Gateway 2.25		
TPB Rep.#1–#4. . . . . 8.95		

WEAPON X
Aug., 2002
1-shot Wild Child #1, JWi 2.25
1-shot Sauron #1, JWi,KIK 2.25
1-shot Kane #1, JWi 2.25

Web of Spider-Man #2
© Marvel Entertainment Group

Comics Values Annual — MARVEL — Web Of–Werewolf

Web of Spider-Man #121
© Marvel Entertainment Group

80 AS,V:Silvermane 3.00
81 I:Bloodshed 3.00
82 V:Man Mountain Marko 3.00
83 V:A.I.M. Supersuit 3.00
84 AS,B:Name of the Rose 3.00
85 AS,Name of the Rose 3.00
86 AS,I:Demogoblin 3.00
87 AS,I:Praetorian Guard 3.00
88 AS,Name of the Rose 3.00
89 AS,E:Name of the Rose,
  I:Bloodrose. 3.00
90 AS,30th Ann.,w/hologram,
  polybagged,V:Mysterio 3.50
90a Gold 2nd printing 3.00
91 AS,V:Whisper And Pulse 3.00
92 AS,V:Foreigner 3.00
93 AS,BMc,V:Hobgoblin,A:Moon
  Knight,Foreigner. 3.00
94 AS,V:Hobgoblin,A:MoonKnight. . . 3.00
95 AS,Spirits of Venom#1,A:Venom,
  J.Blaze,GR,V:Hag & Troll 3.00
96 AS,Spirits of Venom#3, A:G.R.,
  J.Blaze,Venom,Hobgoblin. 3.00
97 AS,I:Dr.Trench,V:Bloodrose 3.00
98 AS,V:Bloodrose,Foreigner 3.00
99 I:Night Watch,V:New Enforcer . . 3.00
100 AS,JRu,V:Enforcers,Bloodrose,
  Kingpin(Alfredo),I:Spider Armor,
  O:Night Watch,Holografx(c) . . 4.00
101 AS,Total Carnage,V:Carnage,
  Shriek,A:Cloak and Dagger,
  Venom 2.50
102 Total Carnage#6,V:Carnage,
  A:Venom,Morbius 2.50
103 AS,Maximum Carnage#10,
  V:Carnage 2.50
104 AS,Infinity Crusade 2.50
105 AS,Infinity Crusade 2.50
106 AS,Infinity Crusade 2.50
107 AS,A:Sandman,Quicksand 2.50
108 B:TKa(s),AS,I:Sandstorm,
  BU:Cardiac. 2.50
109 AS,V:Shocker,A:Night Thrasher,
  BU:D:Calypso. 2.50
110 AS,I:Warrant,A:Lizard. 2.50
111 AS,V:Warrant,Lizard 2.50
112 AS,Pursuit#3,V:Chameleon,
  w/card 2.50
113 AS,A:Gambit,Black Cat,w/cel . . 3.50
113a Newsstand Ed.. . . . . 2.50
114 AS 2.50
115 AS,V:Facade 2.50
116 AS,V:Facade 2.50

117 Foil(c), flip book with
  Power & Responsibility #1 . . . . 5.00
117a Newsstand ed.. . . . . 2.50
118 Spider-clone, V:Venom. 3.00
119 Clone,V:Venom 3.00
119a bagged with Milestone rep.
  Amazing Sp-Man #150,checklist 7.50
120 Web of Life,pt.1 . . . . 2.50
121 Web of Life,pt.3 . . . . 2.50
122 Smoke and Mirrors,pt.1 . . . . . . 2.50
123 The Price of Truth,pt.2 . . . . 2.25
124 The Mark of Kaine,pt.1. . . . . . . 2.00
125 R:Gwen Stacy 3.00
125a 3-D Holodisk cover 4.25
126 The Trial of Peter Parker,pt.1 . . 2.25
127 Maximum Clonage,pt.2 . . . . . . 2.25
128 TDF,Exiled,pt.1 . . . . 2.25
129 Timebomb,pt.2. . . . . 2.25
Ann.#1 V:Future Max 7.00
Ann.#2 AAd,MMi,A:Warlock 10.00
Ann.#3 AS,DP,JRu,JM,BL 4.50
Ann.#4 AS,TM,RLm,Evolutionary
  Wars,A:Man Thing,V:Slug 5.00
Ann.#5 AS,SD,JS,Atlantis
  Attacks,A:Fantastic Four. 4.00
Ann.#6 SD,JBr,SB,A:Punisher 4.50
Ann.#7 Vibranium Vendetta #3 . . . . 3.50
Ann.#8 Hero Killers#3,A:New
  Warriors,BU:Venom,Black Cat . 3.50
Ann.#9 CMa,I:Cadre,w/card 3.50
Ann.#10 V:Shriek 4.00
Super Size Spec.#1 Planet of
  the Symbiotes,pt.5 . . . . 3.95

WEBSPINNERS: TALES OF SPIDER-MAN
Nov., 1998

1 JMD,JR,MZi,A:Mysterio,seq.to
  Amaz.Sp-M#38, 48-page 3.00
1a signed 19.63
2 JMD,JR,V:J.Jonah Jameson. . . . 2.50
2a variant SR cover 2.50
3 JMD,V:Mysterio, concl.. . . . . 2.50
4 KG,ErS,seq.to Silver Surfer#18. . 2.50
5 KG,ErS,A:Silver Surfer 2.50
6 KG,ErS,F:Silver Surfer,
  Psycho-Man & Annihilus. 2.50
7 BS,MPn,V:Sandman. 2.50
8 BS,MPn,V:Sandman. 2.50
9 V:Sandman 2.50
10 V:Chameleon, pt.1 . . . . 2.50
11 V:Chameleon, pt.2 . . . . 2.50
12 conclusion, 48-pg. 3.50
13 . . . . 2.50
14 HMe,BS,A:Carnage 2.50
15 V:Vulture 2.50
16 V:Vulture 2.50
17 TDF, black costume 2.50
18 TDF, Silversable 2.50

WEIRD WONDERTALES
Dec., 1973

1 B:Reprints 45.00
2 I Was Kidnapped by a Flying
  Saucer 25.00
3 BP,The Thing in the Bog 25.00
4 SD,SK,It Lurks Behind
  the Wall 25.00
5 SD 25.00
6 The Man Who Owned a Ghost . 25.00
7 BP,The Apes That Walked
  like Men 25.00
8 JMn,Reap A Deadly Harvest . . 25.00
9 The Murder Mirror 25.00
10 SD,SK,Mister Morgan's
  Monster 25.00
11 SD,SK,Slaughter in
  Shrangri-La 20.00
12 SD,MD,The Stars Scream

  Murder 20.00
13 SD,The Totem Strikes 20.00
14 Witching Circle. 20.00
15 . . . . 20.00
16 GC,The Shark 20.00
17 Creature From Krogarr. 20.00
18 Krang 20.00
19 SD,A:Dr Druid 20.00
20 SD,MD,The Madness. 20.00
21 SD,A:Dr Druid 20.00
22 The World Below,May, 1975. . . 20.00

Werewolf by Night #25
© Marvel Entertainment Group

WEREWOLF BY NIGHT
Sept., 1972

1 MP,(cont from Marvel Spotlight)
  FullMoonRise..WerewolfKill. . 200.00
2 MP,Like a Wild Beast at Bay . . . 75.00
3 MP,Mystery of the Mad Monk . . 50.00
4 MP,The Danger Game 50.00
5 MP,A Life for a Death 50.00
6 MP,Carnival of Fear 40.00
7 MP,JM,Ritual of Blood. 40.00
8 MP,Krogg,Lurker from Beyond . 40.00
9 TS,V:Tatterdemalion 40.00
10 TS,bondage cover 40.00
11 GK,TS,Full Moon..Fear Moon. . 30.00
12 GK,Cry Monster. 30.00
13 MP,ManMonsterCalledTaboo . . 25.00
14 MP,Lo,the Monster Strikes 25.00
15 MP,(new)O:Werewolf,
  V:Dracula. 50.00
16 MP,TS,A:Hunchback of Notre
  Dame. 35.00
17 Behold the Behemoth 35.00
18 War of the Werewolves 35.00
19 V:Dracula. 32.00
20 The Monster Breaks Free 30.00
21 GK(c),To Cure a Werewolf 15.00
22 GK(c),Face of a Friend 15.00
23 Silver Bullet for a Werewolf . . . 15.00
24 GK(c),V:The Brute 15.00
25 GK(c),Eclipse of Evil 15.00
26 GK(c),A Crusade of Murder . . 15.00
27 GK(c),Scourge o/t Soul-Beast . 15.00
28 GK(c),V:Dr.Glitternight 15.00
29 GK(c),V:Dr.Glitternight 15.00
30 GK(c),Red Slash across
  Midnight 15.00
31 Death in White. 15.00
32 I&O:Moon Knight 160.00
33 Were-Beast..Moon Knight
  A:Moon Knight(2nd App). . . . 160.00
34 GK(c),TS,House of Evil..House
  of Death 15.00

All comics prices listed are for *Near Mint* condition.

Werewolf–Western — MARVEL — Comics Values Annual

35 TS,JS,BWi,Jack Russell vs.
  Werewolf 15.00
36 Images of Death 15.00
37 BWr(c),BW,A:Moon Knight,
  Hangman,Dr.Glitternight 20.00
38 . . . . 22.00
39 V:Brother Voodoo 22.00
40 A:Brother Voodoo,V:Dr.
  Glitternight 15.00
41 V:Fire Eyes 15.00
42 A:IronMan,Birth of a Monster . . 15.00
43 Tri-Animal Lives,A:Iron Man . . . 15.00
G-Size#2,SD,A:Frankenstein
  Monster (reprint). 15.00
G-Size#3 GK(c),Transylvania 15.00
G-Size#4 GK(c),A:Morbius 15.00
G-Size#5 GK(c),Peril of
  Paingloss 10.00

WEREWOLF BY NIGHT
Dec., 1997
1 PJe,F:Jack Russell returns 3.00
2 PJe,Search for wolf Amulet. 3.00
3 PJe,Stuck between man & wolf. . 3.00
4 PJe,to the depths of hell 3.00
5 PJe, confronts demon. 3.00
6 PJe, visit Underworld nightclub . . 3.00
Storyline continues in Strange Tales

WEST COAST AVENGERS
[Limited Series] Sept., 1984
1 BH,A:Shroud,J:Hawkeye,IronMan,
  WonderMan,Mockingbird,Tigra . 4.00
2 BH,V:Blank. 3.00
3 BH,V:Graviton 3.00
4 BH,V:Graviton 3.00

[Regular Series] 1985–89
1 AM,JSt,V:Lethal Legion. 4.00
2 AM,JSt,V:Lethal Legion. 3.00
3 AM,JSt,V:Kraven 3.00
4 AM,JSt,A:Firebird,Thing,I:Master
  Pandemonium 3.00
5 AM,JSt,A:Werewolf,Thing 3.00
6 AM,KB,A:Thing. 3.00
7 AM,JSt,V:Ultron 3.00
8 AM,JSt,V:Rangers,A:Thing 3.00
9 AM,JSt,V:Master Pandemonium . 3.00
10 AM,JSt,V:Headlok,Griffen. 3.00
11 AM,JSt,A:Nick Fury 2.50
12 AM,JSt,V:Graviton 2.50
13 AM,JSt,V:Graviton 2.50

West Coast Avengers #1
© *Marvel Entertainment Group*

14 AM,JSt,V:Pandemonium 2.50
15 AM,JSt,A:Hellcat 2.50
16 AM,JSt,V:Tiger Shark,
  Whirlwind. 2.50
17 AM,JSt,V:Dominus' Minions 2.50
18 AM,JSt,V:The Wild West 2.50
19 AM,JSt,A:Two Gun Kid. 2.50
20 AM,JSt,A:Rawhide Kid. 2.50
21 AM,JSt,A:Dr.Pym,Moon Knight . . 2.50
22 AM,JSt,A:Fant.Four,Dr.Strange,
  Night Rider. 2.50
23 AM,RT,A:Phantom Rider 2.50
24 AM,V:Dominus. 2.50
25 AM,V:Abomination 2.50
26 AM,V:Zodiac 2.50
27 AM,V:Zodiac 2.50
28 AM,V:Zodiac 2.50
29 AM,V:Taurus,A:Shroud. 2.50
30 AM,C:Composite Avenger 2.50
31 AM,V:Arkon 2.50
32 AM,TD,V:Yetrigar,J:Wasp 2.50
33 AM,O:Ant-Man,Wasp;
  V:Madam X,El Toro. 2.50
34 AM,V:Quicksilver,J:Vision &
  Scarlet Witch 2.50
35 AM,V:Dr.Doom,Quicksilver 2.50
36 AM,V:The Voice 2.50
37 V:The Voice,A:Mantis. 2.50
38 AM,TMo,V:Defiler. 2.50
39 AM,V:Swordsman 2.50
40 AM,MGu,V:NightShift,
  A:Shroud 2.50
41 TMo,I:New Phantom Rider,
  L:Moon Knight 2.50
42 JBy,Visionquest#1,V:Ultron 2.75
43 JBy,Visionquest#2,. 2.50
44 JBy,Visionquest#3,J:USAgent . . 2.50
45 JBy,Visionquest#4,
  I:New Vision. 2.75
46 JBy,I:Great Lakes Avengers 2.50
Ann. #1 MBr,GI,V:Zodiak 2.75
Ann. #2 AM,A:SilverSurfer,V:Death,
  Collector,R:Grandmaster 2.00
Ann. #3 AM,RLm,TD,Evolutionary
  Wars,R:Giant Man 3.50
Becomes:

AVENGERS WEST COAST

WESTERN GUNFIGHTERS
[2nd series] Aug., 1970
1 JK,JB,DAy,B:Ghost Rider
  A:Fort Rango,The Renegades
  Gunhawk 65.00
2 HT(c),DAy,JMn,O:Nightwind,
  V:Tarantula 35.00
3 DAy,MD,V:Hurricane, rep. 35.00
4 HT(c),DAy,TS,B:Gunhawk,
  Apache Kid,A:Renegades . . . 35.00
5 DAy,FrG,A:Renegades 35.00
6 HT(c),DAy,SSh,Death of
  Ghost Rider 30.00
7 HT(c),DAy,SSh,O:Ghost Rider
  retold,E:Ghost Rider,Gunhawk 30.00
8 DAy,SSh,B:Black Rider,Outlaw
  Kid(rep) 25.00
9 DW,Revenge rides the Range. . 25.00
10 JK,JMn,O:Black Rider,B:Matt
  Slade,E:Outlaw Kid. 25.00
11 JK,Duel at Dawn 25.00
12 JMn,O:Matt Slade 30.00
13 Save the Gold Coast Expires . . 25.00
14 JSo(c),Outlaw Town. 25.00
15 E:Matt Slade,Showdown in
  Outlaw Canyon. 25.00
16 B:Kid Colt,Shoot-out in Silver
  City 25.00
17 thru 20 . . . . @25.00
21 thru 24 . . . . @15.00
25 . . . . 15.00
26 F:Kid Colt,Gun-Slinger,

Western Kid #3
© *Marvel Entertainment Group*

Apache Kid. 15.00
27 thru 32 . . . . @15.00
33 Nov., 1975. . . . . 15.00

WESTERN KID
[1st Series] Dec., 1954
1 JR,B:Western Kid,O:Western Kid
  (Tex Dawson). 250.00
2 JMn,JR,Western Adventure. . . 125.00
3 JMn(c),JR,Gunfight(c) 100.00
4 JMn(c),JR,The Badlands 100.00
5 JR 100.00
6 JR 100.00
7 JR 100.00
8 JR 100.00
9 JR,AW 125.00
10 JR,AW,Man in the Middle 125.00
11 thru 16 . . . . @75.00
17 Aug., 1957. . . . . 75.00

[2nd Series]
Dec., 1971–Aug., 1972
1 Reprints 35.00
2 . . . . 20.00
3 AW 25.00
4 . . . . 20.00
5 . . . . 20.00

WESTERN OUTLAWS
Atlas, Feb., 1954—Aug., 1957
1 JMn(c),RH,BP,The Greenville
  Gallows,Hanging(c) 250.00
2 . . . . 125.00
3 thru 10 . . . . @100.00
11 AW,MD. 125.00
12 JMn 75.00
13 MB,JMn. 100.00
14 AW 100.00
15 AT,GT 75.00
16 BP,JMn,JSe. 75.00
17 JMn. 75.00
18 JSe 75.00
19 JMn,JSe 100.00
20 and 21 JSe . . . . @75.00

WESTERN OUTLAWS & SHERIFFS
See: **BEST WESTERN**

CVA Page 340 — All comics prices listed are for *Near Mint* condition.

WESTERN TALES OF BLACK RIDER
See: ALL WINNERS COMICS

WESTERN TEAM-UP
Nov., 1973
1 Rawhide Kid/Dakota Kid 50.00

WESTERN THRILLERS
Nov., 1954
1 JMn,Western tales 150.00
2 .... 100.00
3 .... 100.00
4 .... 100.00
Becomes:

COWBOY ACTION
March, 1955–March, 1956
5 JMn(c),The Prairie Kid 100.00
6 .... 75.00
7 .... 75.00
9 .... 75.00
10 .... 75.00
11 MN,AW,The Manhunter, ... 100.00
Becomes:

QUICK-TRIGGER WESTERN
May, 1956–Sept., 1957
12 Bill Larson Strikes 100.00
13 The Man From Cheyenne ... 125.00
14 BEv,RH(c) 75.00
15 AT 60.00
16 JK 55.00
17 GT 45.00
18 GM 55.00
19 JSe 50.00

WESTERN WINNERS
See: ALL WINNERS COMICS

WHAT IF?
[1st Regular Series] Feb., 1977
1 Spider-Man joined Fant.Four... 30.00
2 GK(c),Hulk had Banner brain .. 15.00
3 GK,KJ,F:Avengers 12.00
4 GK(c),F:Invaders 12.00
5 F:Captain America 12.00
6 F:Fantastic Four 12.00

What If #13
© Marvel Entertainment Group

7 GK(c),F:Spider-Man 10.00
8 GK(c),F:Daredevil 10.00
9 JK(c),F:Avengers of the '50s... 10.00
10 JB,F:Thor 10.00
11 JK,F:FantasticFour 8.00
12 F:Hulk 8.00
13 JB,Conan Alive Today 8.00
14 F:Sgt. Fury 6.00
15 CI,F:Nova 6.00
16 F:Master of Kung Fu 6.00
17 CI,F:Ghost Rider 6.00
18 TS,F:Dr.Strange 5.00
19 PB,F:Spider-Man 6.00
20 F:Avengers 5.00
21 GC,F:Sub-Mariner 5.00
22 F:Dr.Doom 5.00
23 JB,F:Hulk 5.00
24 GK,RB,Gwen Stacy had lived .. 6.00
25 F:Thor,Avengers,O:Mentor..... 5.00
26 JBy(c),F:Captain America 5.00
27 FM(c),Phoenix hadn't died 18.00
28 FM,F:Daredevil,Ghost Rider... 15.00
29 MG(c),F:Avengers 5.00
30 RB,F:Spider-Man 10.00
31 Wolverine killed the Hulk 20.00
32 Avengers lost to Korvac 5.00
33 BL,Dazzler herald of Galactus .. 5.00
34 FH,FM,JBy,BSz:Humor issue... 5.00
35 FM,Elektra had lived 6.00
36 JBy,Fant.Four had no powers .. 5.00
37 F:Thing,Beast,Silver Surfer 5.00
38 F:Daredevil,Captain America ... 5.00
39 Thor had fought Conan 5.00
40 F:Dr.Strange 5.00
41 F:Sub-Mariner 5.00
42 F:Fantastic Four 5.00
43 F:Conan 5.00
44 F:Captain America 5.00
45 F:Hulk, Berserk 5.00
46 Uncle Ben had lived 7.00
47 F:Thor,Loki 5.00
Spec.#1 F:Iron Man,Avengers..... 6.00
Best of What IF? rep.#1,#24,
  #27,#28 .... 12.95

[2nd Regular Series]
1 RWi,MG,The Avengers had lost
  the Evolutionary War 5.00
2 GCa,Daredevil Killed Kingpin,
  A:Hobgoblin, The Rose......... 4.00
3 Capt.America Hadn't Given Up
  Costume,A:Avengers 3.50
4 MBa,Spider-Man kept Black
  Costume,A:Avengers,Hulk 4.50
5 Vision Destroyed Avengers,
  A:Wonder Man 3.50
6 RLm,X-Men Lost Inferno,
  A:Dr.Strange 6.00
7 RLd,Wolverine Joined Shield,
  A:Nick Fury,Black Widow 7.00
8 Iron Man Lost The Armor Wars,
  A:Ant Man 3.50
9 RB,New X-Men Died 6.00
10 MZ(c),BMc,Punisher's Family
  Didn't Die,A:Kingpin 3.00
11 TM(c),JV,SM,Fant.Four had the
  Same Powers,A:Nick Fury 3.50
12 JV,X-Men Stayed in Asgard,
  A:Thor,Hela 5.00
13 JLe(c),Prof.X Became
  Juggernaut,A:X-Men........... 3.50
14 RLm(c),Capt.Marvel didn't die
  A:Silver Surfer 3.50
15 GCa,Fant.Four Lost Trial of
  Galactus,A:Gladiator 3.00
16 Wolverine Battled Conan,
  A:X-Men,Red Sonja 5.00
17 Kraven Killed Spider-Man,
  A:Daredevil,Captain America ... 3.00
18 LMc,Fant.Four fought Dr.Doom
  before they gained powers 3.00
19 RW,Vision took over Earth,

What If, Vol. 2 #27
© Marvel Entertainment Group

  A:Avengers,Dr.Doom 3.00
20 Spider-Man didn't marry Mary
  Jane,A:Venom,Kraven 3.00
21 Spider-Man married Black Cat,
  A:Vulture,Silver Sable.......... 3.00
22 RLm,Silver Surfer didn't escape
  Earth,A:F.F,Mephisto,Thanos .. 4.00
23 New X-Men never existed,
  A:Eric the Red,Lilandra 3.00
24 Wolverine Became Lord of
  Vampires,A:Punisher 3.00
25 Marvel Heroes lost Atlantis
  Attacks,double size 3.50
26 LMc,Punisher Killed Daredevil,
  A:Spider-Man 3.00
27 Submariner Joined Fantastic
  Four,A:Dr. Doom 3.00
28 RW,Capt.America led Army of
  Super-Soldiers,A:Submariner .. 3.00
29 RW,Capt.America formed the
  Avengers 3.00
30 Inv.Woman's 2nd Child had
  lived,A:Fantastic Four 3.00
31 Spider-Man/Captain Universe
  Powers 3.00
32 Phoenix Rose Again,pt.1 ...... 3.00
33 Phoenix Rose Again,pt.2 ...... 3.00
34 Humor Issue 3.00
35 B:Time Quake,F.F. vs.Dr. Doom
  & Annihilus 3.00
36 Cosmic Avengers,V:Guardians
  of the Galaxy 3.00
37 X-Vampires,V:Dormammu 3.00
38 Thor was prisoner of Set 3.00
39 E:Time Quake,Watcher saved the
  Universe 3.00
40 Storm remained A thief? 3.00
41 JV,Avengers fought Galactus ... 3.00
42 KWe,Spidey kept extra arms ... 3.00
43 Wolverine married Mariko 3.50
44 Punisher possessed by Venom .. 3.00
45 Barbara Ketch became G.R. ... 3.00
46 Cable Killed Prof.X,Cyclops &
  Jean Grey 3.00
47 Magneto took over USA 3.00
48 Daredevil Saved Nuke 3.00
49 Silver Surfer had Inf.Gauntlet? .. 3.50
50 Hulk killed Wolverine 4.00
51 PCu,Punisher is Capt.America... 3.00
52 BHi,Wolverine led Alpha Flight .. 3.50
53 F:Iron Man,Hulk 3.00
54 F:Death's Head 3.00
55 LKa(s),Avengers lose G.Storm... 3.00
56 Avengers lose G.Storm#2 ..... 3.00

MARVEL

What If–Wild

57 Punisher a member of SHIELD . 3.00
58 Punisher kills SpM. 3.00
59 Wolverine lead Alpha Flight 3.50
60 RoR,Scott & Jean's Wedding . . . 3.00
61 Spider-Man's Parents 3.00
62 Woverine vs Weapon X 3.50
63 F:War Machine,Iron Man 3.00
64 Iron Man sold out. 3.00
65 Archangel fell from Grace 3.00
66 Rogue and Thor 3.00
67 Cap.America returns 3.00
68 Captain America story 3.00
69 Stryfe Killed X-Men 3.00
70 Silver Surfer 3.50
71 The Hulk 3.00
72 Parker Killed Burglar 3.00
73 Daredevil,Kingpin. 3.00
74 Sinister Formed X-Men 3.00
75 Gen-X's Blink had lived 3.00
76 Flash Thompson Spider-Man. . . 3.00
77 Legion had killed Magneto 3.00
78 FF had stayed together 3.00
79 Storm had Phoenix's Power. . . . 3.00
80 KGa,Hulk was Cured 3.00
81 Age of Apocalypse didn't end. . . 3.00
82 WML,J. JonahJameson
 adopted Spider-Man. 3.00
83 Daredevil. 3.00
84 Shard 3.00
85 Magneto Ruled all mutants 3.00
86 Scarlet Spider vs. Spider-Man . . 3.00
87 Sabretooth. 3.00
88 Spider-Man 3.00
89 Fantastic Four 3.00
90 Cyclops & Havok 3.00
91 F:Hulk, nice guy, Banner violent. 3.00
92 F:Cannonball,Husk 3.00
93 F:Wolverine. 3.50
94 JGz,F:Juggernaut 3.00
95 IV,F:Ghost Rider 3.00
96 CWo,F:Quicksilver, ... 3.00
97 F:Black Knight. 3.00
98 F:Nightcrawler & Rogue. 3.00
99 F:Black Cat 3.00
100 IV,KJ,F:Gambit &
 Rogue, 48-pg. 3.50
101 ATi,F:Archangel 3.00
102 F:Daredevil's Dad 3.00
103 DaF,F:Captain America 3.00
104 F:Silver Surver,ImpossibleMan . 3.00
105 TDF,RF,F:Spider-Man and
 Mary Jane's Daughter. 25.00
106 TDF,F:X-Men,Gambit
 sentenced to death. 3.00
107 TDF,RF,BSz,F:Thor 3.00
108 TDF,F:The Avengers 3.00
109 TA,F:Fantastic Four 3.00
110 TDF,F:Wolverine 3.00
111 TDF,F:Wolverine. 3.00
112 F:Ka-Zar 3.00
113 F:Iron Man, Dr. Strange, ... 3.00
114 F:Secret Wars, 32-page,
 final issue. 3.50
Minus 1 Spec., AOI, flashback,
 F:Bishop. 3.00
TPB Best of What If? 12.95

WHAT THE -?!
[Parodies]
Aug., 1988
1 . . . . 5.00
2 JBy,JOy,AW, ... 4.00
3 TM, ... 5.00
4 . . . . 3.00
5 EL,JLe,WPo,Wolverine. 5.00
6 Wolverine,Punisher. 3.00
7 . . . . 2.50
8 DK 2.50
9 . . . . 2.50
10 JBy,X-Men,Dr.Doom, Cap.

America 2.50
11 DK,RLd(part) 2.50
12 Conan, F.F.,Wolverine. 2.50
13 Silver Burper,F.F.,Wolverine. . . 2.50
14 Spittle-Man 2.50
15 Capt.Ultra,Wolverina 2.50
16 Ant Man,Watcher 2.50
17 Wulverean/Pulverizer,Hoagg/
 Spider-Ham,Sleep Gawker,F.F. . 2.50
18 . . . . 2.50
19 . . . . 2.50
20 Infinity Wart Crossover. 2.50
21 Weapon XX,Toast Rider. 2.50
22 F:Echs Farce. 2.50
23 . . . . 2.50
24 Halloween issue 2.50
25 . . . . 2.50
26 Spider-Ham 2099 . . . . 2.50
Summer Spec. 2.50
Fall Spec. 2.50

WHERE CREATURES ROAM
July, 1970—Sept., 1971
1 JK,SD,DAy,B:Reprints
 The Brute That Walks 40.00
2 JK,SD,Midnight/Monster 25.00
3 JK,SD,DAy,Thorg 25.00
4 JK,SD,Vandoom 25.00
5 JK,SD,Gorgilla 25.00
6 JK,SD,Zog 25.00
7 SD 25.00
8 The Mummy's Secret,E:Reprints 25.00

WHERE MONSTERS DWELL
Jan., 1970
1 JK,SD,B:Reprints,Cyclops 40.00
2 JK,Sporr 25.00
3 JK,Grottu 25.00
4 . . . . 25.00
5 JK,Taboo 25.00
6 JK,Groot 25.00
7 JK,Rommbu 25.00
8 JK,SD,The Four-Armed Men . . 25.00
9 JK,Bumbu 25.00
10 JK,SD,Monster That Walks
 Like A Man 25.00
11 JK,Gruto 20.00
12 JK,GC,SD,Orogo,giant-size . . 35.00
13 JK,The Thing That Crawl 20.00

Where Monsters Dwell #31
© *Marvel Entertainment Group*

Comics Values Annual

14 JK,The Green Thing 20.00
15 JK,JSe,Kraa- The Inhuman . . . 20.00
16 JK,Beware the Son Of Goom. . 20.00
17 SD,The Hidden Vampires. 20.00
18 SD,The Mask of Morghum 20.00
19 SD,The Insect Man 20.00
20 Klagg 20.00
21 Fin Fang Foom 20.00
22 Elektro 20.00
23 SD,The Monster Waits For Me . 20.00
24 SD,The Things on Easter Island 20.00
25 SD,The Ruler of the Earth 20.00
26 . . . . 20.00
27 . . . . 20.00
28 Droom,The Living Lizard 20.00
29 thru 37 Reprints . . . . @20.00
38 AW,reprints, Oct., 1975 . . . . . 20.00

WHIP WILSON
See: BLAZE CARSON

WILD
Atlas, Feb., 1954
1 BEv,JMn,Charlie Chan
 Parody 300.00
2 BEv,RH,JMn,Witches(c) . . . 175.00
3 CBu(c),BEv,RH,JMn, ... 150.00
4 GC,Didja Ever See a Cannon
 Brawl. 150.00
5 RH,JMn,Aug., 1954 . . . . 150.00

WILD CARDS
Epic, Sept., 1990
1 JG 5.50
2 JG,V:Jokers 4.50
3 A:Turtle. 4.50

WILDC.A.T.S/X-MEN: THE DARK AGE
Dec., 1997
1-shot MtB,WEI,V:Daemonites
 & Sentinels, 48-pg. 4.50
1a variant cover MGo 4.50

WILD THING
Marvel UK, 1993
1 A:Virtual Reality Venom and
 Carnage 3.00
2 A:VR Venom and Carnage 2.25
3 A:Shield 2.25
4 . . . . 2.25
5 Virtual Reality Gangs 2.25
6 Virtual Reality Villians 2.25
7 V:Trask. 2.25
8 . . . . 2.25
9 . . . . 2.25
10 . . . . 2.25
11 . . . . 2.25
12 . . . . 2.25
13 . . . . 2.25

WILD THING
Aug., 1999
1 RLm,AM,LHa,F:Wolverine's
 daughter Rina 2.25
2A RLm,AM,LHa,Bloody
 Reunions 2.25
2B variant AW (c) 2.25
3 RLm,AM,LHa,A:Rina 2.25
4 RLm,AM,LHa 2.25
5 RLm,AM,LHa,V:Robot monster . . 2.25

CVA Page 342   All comics prices listed are for *Near Mint* condition.

Comics Values Annual | **MARVEL** | Wild–Wolverine

WILD WEST
Spring, 1948
1 SSh(c),B:Two Gun Kids,Tex
  Taylor,Arizona Annie 400.00
2 SSh(c),CCb, Captain Tootsie . 250.00
Becomes:

WILD WESTERN
3 SSh(c),B:Tex Morgan,Two Gun
  Kid,Tex Taylor,Arizona Annie 300.00
4 RH,SSh,CCB, Capt. Tootsie.
  A:Kid Colt,E:Arizona Annie . . 250.00
5 RH,CCB,Captain Tootsie
  A;Black Rider,Blaze Carson . 250.00
6 A:Blaze Carson,Kid Colt 150.00
7 Two-Gun Kid. 150.00
8 RH 150.00
9 Ph(c),B:Black Rider,
  Tex Morgan 200.00
10 Ph(c), Black Rider 250.00
11 Black Rider 150.00
12 Black Rider 150.00
13 Black Rider 150.00
14 Prairie Kid,Black Rider...... 150.00
15 Black Rider 150.00
16 thru 18 Black Rider....... @150.00
19 Black Rider 160.00
20 thru 29 Kid Colt .... @125.00
30 JKa, Kid Colt 125.00
31 thru 40 .... @100.00
41 thru 47 .... @100.00
48 AW 125.00
49 thru 53 .... @100.00
54 AW 125.00
55 AW 125.00
56 and 57 Sept., 1957....... @100.00

WILLIAM SHATNER'S TEK WORLD
1992–94
1 LS,Novel adapt. 2.25
2 LS,Novel adapt.cont. 2.25
3 LS,Novel adapt.cont. 2.25
4 LS,Novel adapt.cont. 2.25
5 LS,Novel adapt.concludes 2.25
6 LS,V:TekLords 2.25
7 E:The Angel 2.25
8 .... 2.25
9 .... 2.25
10 .... 2.25
11 thru 17 .... @2.25
18 .... 2.25

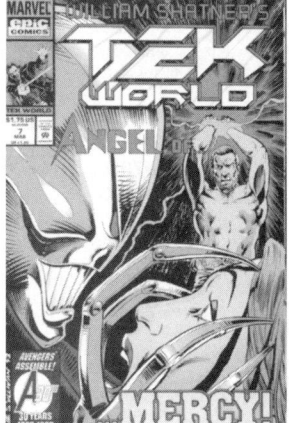

*William Shatner's Tek World #7
© Marvel Entertainment Group*

19 Sims of the Father#1 .... 2.25
20 Sims of the Father#2 .... 2.25
21 Who aren't in Heaven 2.25
22 Father and Guns 2.25
23 We'll be Right Back 2.25
24 .... 2.25

WILLIE COMICS
See: IDEAL COMICS

WILLOW
Aug., 1988
1 Movie adapt. 3.00
2 Movie adapt. 3.00
3 Movie adapt,Oct., 1988. ...... 3.00

WITNESS, THE
Sept., 1948
1 .... 2,000.00

WOLFPACK
Aug., 1988
1 I:Wolfpack 2.00
2 thru 11 .... @2.00
12 July, 1988 .... 2.00

WOLVERINE
[Limited Series] Sept., 1982
1 B:CCl(s),FM,JRu,A:Mariko,
  I:Shingen 50.00
2 FM,JRu,A:Mariko,I:Yukio. 40.00
3 FM,JRu,A:Mariko,Yukio. 40.00
4 B:CCl(s),FM,JRu,A:Mariko,
  D:Shingen 45.00
[Regular Series] 1988
1 JB,AW,V:Banipur 50.00
2 JB,KJ,V:Silver Samurai 25.00
3 JB,AW,V:Silver Samurai 15.00
4 JB,AW,I:Roughouse,
  Bloodsport 15.00
5 JB,AW,V:Roughouse,
  Bloodsport 15.00
6 JB,AW,V:Roughouse,
  Bloodsport 15.00
7 JB,A:Hulk 15.00
8 JB,A:Hulk 15.00
9 GC,Old Wolverine Story 15.00
10 JB,BSz,V:Sabretooth
  (1st battle) 35.00
11 JB,BSz,B:Gehenna Stone ... 10.00
12 JB,BSz,Gehenna Stone 10.00
13 JB,BSz,Gehenna Stone 10.00
14 JB,BSz,Gehenna Stone 10.00
15 JB,BSz,Gehenna Stone 10.00
16 JB,BSz,E:Gehenna Stone ... 10.00
17 JBy,KJ,V:Roughouse 10.00
18 JBy,KJ,V:Roughouse 10.00
19 JBy,KJ,A of V,I:La Bandera .. 10.00
20 JBy,KJ,A of V,V:Tigershark... 7.00
21 JBy,KJ,V:Geist 7.00
22 JBy,KJ,V:Geist,Spore 7.00
23 JBy,KJ,V:Geist,Spore. 7.00
24 GC,`Snow Blind' 5.00
25 JB,O:Wolverine(part) 5.00
26 KJ,Return to Japan 5.00
27 thru 30 Lazarus Project 5.00
31 MS,DGr,A:Prince o'Mandripoor . 5.00
32 MS,DGr,V:Ninjas 5.00
33 MS,Wolverine in Japan 5.00
34 MS,DGr,Wolverine in Canada . 5.00
35 MS,DGr,A:Puck 5.00
36 MS,DGr,A:Puck,Lady D'strike. . 5.00
37 MS,DGr,V:Lady Deathstrike . . 5.00
38 MS,DGr,A:Storm,I:Elsie Dee . 5.00
39 MS,DGr,Wolverine Vs. Clone . . 5.00
40 MS,DGr,Wolverine Vs. Clone . . 5.00

*Wolverine #9
© Marvel Entertainment Group*

41 MS,DGr,R:Sabretooth,
  A:Cable 8.00
41a 2nd printing 2.25
42 MS,DGr,A:Sabretooth,Cable ... 7.00
42a 2nd printing 2.00
43 MS,DGr,A:Sabretooth,C:Cable ... 7.00
44 LSn,DGr 6.00
45 MS,DGr,A:Sabretooth 7.00
46 MS,DGr,A:Sabretooth 7.00
47 V:Tracy 6.00
48 LHa(s),MS,DGr,B:Shiva
  Scenario. 6.00
49 LHa(s),MS,DGr, ... 6.00
50 LHa(s),MS,DGr,A:X-Men,Nick Fury,
  I:Shiva,Slash-Die Cut(c) ... 7.00
51 MS,DGr,A:Mystique,X-Men 5.00
52 MS,DGr,A:Mystique,V:Spiral ... 5.00
53 MS,A:Mystique,V:Spiral,Mojo ... 5.00
54 A:Shatterstar 5.00
55 MS,V:Cylla,A:Gambit,Sunfire ... 5.00
56 MS,A:Gambit,Sunfire,V:Hand,
  Hydra 5.00
57 MS,D:Lady Mariko,A:Gambit .. 5.50
58 A:Terror 5.00
59 A:Terror 5.00
60 Sabretooth vs.Shiva,
  I:John Wraith 5.00
61 MT,History of Wolverine and
  Sabretooth,A:John Wraith.... 5.00
62 MT,A:Sabretooth,Silver Fox ... 5.00
63 MT,V:Ferro,D:Silver Fox. 5.00
64 MPa,V:Ferro,Sabretooth 5.00
65 MT,A:Professor X. 5.00
66 MT,A:X-Men. 5.00
67 MT,A:X-Men. 5.00
68 MT,V:Epsilon Red 5.00
69 DT,A:Rogue,V:Sauron,tie-in to
  X-Men#300 .... 5.00
70 DT,Sauron,A:Rogue,Jubilee.... 5.00
71 DT,V:Sauron,Brain Child,
  A:Rogue, Jubilee 5.00
72 DT,Sentinels 5.00
73 DT,V:Sentinels 5.00
74 ANi,V:Sentinels 5.00
75 AKu,Hologram(c),Wolv.has
  Bone Claws,leaves X-Men ... 10.00
76 DT(c),B:LHa(s),A:Deathstrike,
  Vindicator,C:Puck 5.00
77 AKu,A:Vindicator,Puck,V:Lady
  Deathstrike. 5.00
78 AKu,V:Cylla,Bloodscream ... 5.00
79 AKu,V:Cyber,I:Zoe Culloden... 5.00
80 IaC,V:Cyber, ... 5.00

All comics prices listed are for Near Mint condition.

Wolverine–Wolverine — MARVEL — Comics Values Annual

#	Description	Price
81	IaC,V:Cyber,A:Excalibur	5.00
82	AKu,BMc,A:Yukio,Silver Samurai	5.00
83	AKu,A:Alpha Flight	5.00
84	A:Alpha Flight	5.00
85	Phalanx Covenant, Final Sanction, V:Phalanx,holografx(c)	5.50
85a	newsstand ed.	5.00
86	AKu,V:Bloodscream	3.00
87	AKu,deluxe,V:Juggernaut	3.00
87a	newsstand ed.	3.00
88	AKu,deluxe ed.	3.00
88a	newsstand ed.	3.00
89	deluxe ed.	3.00
89a	newsstand ed.	2.00
90	V:Sabretooth, deluxe ed.	4.00
90a	newsstand ed.	2.00
91	LHa,Logan's future unravels	3.00
92	LHa,AKu,DGr,A:Sabretooth	3.00
93	R:Cyber	3.00
94	Feral Wolverine	3.00
95	LHa,AKu,DGr,V:Dark Riders	3.00
96	LHa,Aku,DGr,Death of Cyber	3.00
97	LHa,AKu,DGr,A:Genesis	3.00
98	LHa,AKu,F:Genesis	3.00
99		3.00
100	LHa,AKu,DG,A:Elektra;double-size, Foil Hologram cover	12.00
100a	regular edition	4.00
101	LHa,AKu,A:Elektra	3.00
102	LHa	3.00
103	LHa,Elektra,A:Onslaught	3.00
104	LHa,Gateway, Onslaught	3.00
105	LHa,Gateway, Elektra	3.00
106	LHa	3.00
107	LHa,VS,prologue to Elektra#1	3.00
108	LHa,back to Tokyo,A:Yukio	3.00
109	LHa,DG	3.00
110	LHa,DG,Who's spying on Logan	3.00
111	LHa,DG,Logan moves to NYC	3.00
112	LHa,DG,Logan in NYC	3.00
113	LHa,R:Ogun,A:Lady Deathstrike & Spiral	3.00
114	LHa,back in costume,V:Cyborg Donald Pierce	3.00
115	LHa,Zero Tolerance,V:Bastion	3.00
116	LHa,Zero Tolerance,	3.00
117	LHa,Zero Tolerance, V:Prime Sentinels	3.00
118	LHa,Zero Tolerance aftermath	3.00
119	WEI,Pt.1 (of 4)	3.00
120	WEI,The White Ghost	3.00
121	WEI,Not Yet Dead, pt.3	3.00
122	WEI,Not Yet Dead, pt.4	3.00
123	TDF,DCw,R:Roughouse, Bloodscream	3.00
124	TDF,DCw,A:Captain America, V:Rascal	3.00
125	CCl,V:Viper,48-pg.	5.00
125a	Dynamic Forces (c)	6.50
126	CCl,V:Sabretooth	3.50
127	CCl,Sabretooth takes over	3.00
128	CCl,V:Hydra, The Hand	3.00
129	TDz,A:Wendigo	3.00
130	TDz,V:Viper	3.00
131	TDz,V:Viper	3.00
131a	Uncensored	12.00
132	TDz,Halloween in SalemCenter	3.00
133	EL,JMs,F:Warbird	3.00
133a	variant EL cover (1:4)	6.00
134	EL,JMs,V:Big Apple heroes	3.00
135	EL,JMs,Joins Starjammers	3.00
136	EL,JMs,on prison planet.	3.00
137	EL,JMs,V:The Collector	3.00
138	EL,JMs,Great Escape concl.	3.00
139	EL,A:Cable	3.00
140	EL,Xavier paranoid	3.00
141	EL,Wolverine paranoid	3.00
142	EL,R:Alpha Flight	3.00
143	EL,A:Alpha Flight	3.00
144	EL,A:Hercules,V:Leader	3.00
145	EL,25th Anniv. 48-pg.	3.00
145A	Foil Stamped (c)	10.00
146	EL	5.00
147	FaN	5.00
148	EL,Ages of Apocalypse,pt.3	3.00
149	EL,mutant no more?	3.00
150	X-Men: Revolution	4.00
150a	variant (c)	7.00
151	SSr,V:Lord Haan	3.00
152	SSr,Lord Haan, Gom	3.00
153	SSr,Kia	3.00
154	RLd,ErS,Deadpool	3.00
155	RLd,Watchtower,Siryn	3.00
156	RLd,IaC,F:Spider-Man	3.00
157	RLd,IaC,F:Spider-Man	3.00
158	RLd,IaC,V:Administrator	3.00
159	SCh,V:Mr.X	3.00
160	SCh,V:Lady Killers,Mr.X	3.00
161	SCh,V:Mr.X	3.00
162	SCh,A:Sabretooth	3.00
163	SCh,F:Beast	3.00
164	SCh,F:Beast	3.00
165	SCh,NRd,trapped	3.00
166	SCh,NRd,BWS,48-pag.	8.00
167	DaF,NRd,BWS(c),V:Viper	2.25
168	DaF,NRd,F:Patch	2.25
169	DaF,NRd,Bloodsport,concl.	2.25
170	SCh,NRd,Stay Alive,pt.1	2.25
171	SCh,NRd,V:Wendigo,'Nuff Said	2.25
172	SCh,NRd,Stay Alive,pt.3	2.25
173	SCh,NRd,in Las Vegas	2.25
174	SCh,NRd,Amiko & Yukio	2.25
175	SCh,NRd,Omega Red,48-pg.	3.50
176	SCh,NRd,	2.25
177	SCh,DaF,Shadow Pulpit,pt.1	2.25
178	SCh,DaF,Shadow Pulpit,pt.2	2.25
179	SCh&MRd(c),R:Alpha Flight	2.25
180	AKu(c)	2.25
181	SCh, new direction.	2.25
182	SCh, TP	2.25
183	SCh,, 48-pg.	3.50
184	SCh,When Animals Attack	2.25
185	SCh,When Animals Attack	2.25
186	SCh,V:Punisher, Round 2	3.00
187	JMC	2.25
188	pt.1	2.25
189	pt.2	2.25
Ann. '97	JOs,V:Volk	3.00
Ann. 1999	F:Deadpool, 48-pg.	3.50
Ann. 2000	48-page	3.00
Ann. 2001	48-page	3.00
Spec. '95	LHa,F:Nightcrawler	3.95
Spec. Minus 1	LHa,CNn, flashback, F:Weapon X	2.25
Spec. Global Jeapordy,PDd(s)		2.95
Spec. Save the Tiger,rep.		2.95
Spec. Winter Spec. MWa B&W		3.00
Spec. Jungle Adventure,MMi,deluxe		5.50
1-shot Bloodlust,AD,V:Siberian Were-Creatures		6.00
GN Acts of Vengeance, rep.		6.95
GN Black Rio, 48-page		6.00
GN Bloody Choices JB,A:N.Fury		12.95
GN Inner Fury,BSz,V:Nanotech Machines		6.25
GN Killing, KSW,JNR		5.95
GN Rahne of Terror, C:Cable		8.00
GN Scorpio Rising, T.U.Fury		5.95
GN Typhoid's Kiss,rep.		6.95
GN Bloodhungry SK		6.95
TPB Wolverine rep. Marvel Comics Presents #1-#10		12.95
TPB Triumphs & Tragedies		16.95
TPB Not Dead Yet		14.95
TPB Wolverine:Weapon X,BWS		15.95
TPB Blood Debt, 112-page		12.95
TPB Wolverine/Gambit: Victims		12.95
TPB Wolverine/Deadpool:WeaponX		22.00
TPB The Best There Is		13.00
TPB Legends, Vol. 3		13.00
TPB Legends, Vol. 4:Xisle		14.00
TPB Snikt, Vol. 5		15.00

WOLVERINE
Marvel May 2003

#	Description	Price
1	DaR,Brothers,pt.1, relaunch	2.25
2	DaR,Brothers,pt.2	2.25
3	DaR,Brothers,pt.3	2.25
4	DaR,Brothers,pt.4	2.25
5	DaR,Brothers,pt.5	2.25
6	DaR,F:Nightcrawler	2.25
7		2.25
8		2.25

WOLVERINE & PUNISHER: DAMAGING EVIDENCE
1993

#	Description	Price
1	B:CP(s),GEr,A:Kingpin	2.50
2	GEr,A:Kingpin,Sniper	2.50
3	GEr,Last issue	2.50

WOLVERINE: DAYS OF FUTURE PAST
Oct., 1997

#	Description	Price
1 (of 3)	JFM,JoB,JHo, Logan & Magneto in far future	2.50
2	JFM,JoB,JHo,with Jubilee	2.50
3	JFM,JoB,JHo,V:Council of the Chosen, concl.	2.50

WOLVERINE: DOOMBRINGER
Nov., 1997

1-shot DgM,JP,F:Silver Samurai . . . 3.00

WOLVERINE/DOOP
Marvel May 2003

#	Price
1 (of 2)	3.00
2	3.00

WOLVERINE ENCYCLOPEDIA

Vol.	Price
Vol. 1 AKu(c) 48-pg.	8.50
Vol. 2 48-pg.	6.50
Vol. 3 48-pg.	6.50

Wolverine #125
© Marvel Entertainment Group

CVA Page 344 — All comics prices listed are for *Near Mint* condition.

MARVEL

WOLVERINE/GAMBIT: VICTIMS
1995
1 Takes Place in London 3.00
2 Is Wolverine the Killer? 3.00
3 V:Mastermind 3.00
4 conclusion 3.00

WOLVERINE/HULK
Feb., 2002
1 (of 4) SK, and a girl named Po . . 3.50
2 SK,snowy wasteland. 3.50
3 SK,ghostly little girl. 3.50
4 SK,concl. 3.50
TPB series rep.. . . . . 10.00

WOLVERINE/NETSUKE
Sept., 2002
1 (of 4) GgP, Wolverine Samurai . . 3.00
2 GgP . . . .,. . . 4.00
3 GgP 4.00
4 GgP, concl. 4.00

WOLVERINE/PUNISHER: REVELATION
Apr. 1999
1 (of 4) TSg,PtL,Revelation 3.00
1a signed 30.00
2 TSg,PtL,V:Revelation 3.00
3 TSg,PtL,V:Revelation 3.00
4 TsG,PtL,V:Revelation,concl. 3.00
TPB rep. 14.95

WOLVERINE SAGA
Sept., 1989
1 RLd(c), ... 6.50
2 . . . . 5.50
3 . . . . 5.50
4 Dec., 1989 . . . . 5.50

WOLVERINE: SNIKT!
Marvel May 2003
1 (of 5) 3.00
2 alien landscape 3.00
3 . . . . 3.00
4 V:Mandate aliens 3.00
5 Concl. 3.00

WOLVERINE: THE END
Marvel Nov. 2003
1 . . . . 2.50

WOLVERINE: X-ISLE
Marvel April 2003
1 (of 5) A:Amiko. 2.50
2 . . . . 2.50
3 . . . . 2.50
4 . . . . 2.50
5 . . . . 2.50

WONDER DUCK
Sept., 1949
1 Whale(c) 150.00
2 . . . . 100.00
3 March, 1950 . . . . 100.00

WONDERMAN
March, 1986
1 KGa,one-shot special 3.00

Wonder Man #3
© Marvel Entertainment Group

WONDER MAN
Sept., 1991
1 B:GJ(s),JJ,V:Goliath 2.50
2 JJ,A:West Coast Avengers 2.25
3 JJ,V:Abominatrix,I:Spider 2.25
4 JJ,I:Splice,A:Spider. 2.25
5 JJ,A:Beast,V:Rampage. 2.25
6 JJ,A:Beast,V:Rampage. 2.25
7 JJ,Galactic Storm,pt.4,
  A:Hulk & Rich Jones. 2.25
8 JJ,GalacticStorm,pt.11,A:Vision. . 2.25
9 JJ,GalacticStorm,pt.18,A:Vision 2.25
10 JJ,V:Khmer Rouge. 2.25
11 V:Angkor 2.25
12 V:Angkor 2.25
13 Infinity War 2.25
14 Infinity War,V:Warlock 2.25
15 Inf.War,V:Doppleganger 2.25
16 JJ,I:Armed Response,
  A:Avengers West Coast 2.25
17 JJ,A:Avengers West Coast. . . . 2.25
18 V:Avengers West Coast 2.25
19 . . . . 2.25
20 V:Splice,Rampage. 2.25
21 V:Splice, Rampage 2.25
22 JJ,V:Realm of Death 2.25
23 JJ,A:Grim Reaper,Mephisto . . . 2.25
24 JJ,V:Grim Reaper,Goliath. 2.25
25 JJ,N:Wonder Man,D:Grim Reaper,
  V:Mephisto 3.25
26 A:Hulk,C:Furor,Plan Master . . . 2.25
27 A:Hulk 2.25
28 RoR,A:Spider-Man. 2.25
29 RoR,A:Spider-Man. 2.25
30 V:Hate Monger 2.25
31 . . . . 2.25
32 . . . . 2.25
33 . . . . 2.25
Spec.#1 (1985),KGa. 3.00
Ann.#1 System Bytes #3 . . . . 2.25
Ann.#2 I:Hit-Maker,w/card. 2.95

WORLD CHAMPIONSHIP WRESTLING
1 F:Lex Luger,Sting 2.25
2 . . . . 2.25
3 . . . . 2.25
4 Luger Vs El Gigante 2.25
5 Rick Rude Vs. Sting 2.25
6 F:Dangerous Alliance,R.Rude . . 2.25
7 F:Steiner Brothers 2.25
8 F:Sting,Dangerous Alliance. . . . 2.25

9 Bunkhouse Brawl 2.25
10 Halloween Havoc. 2.25
11 Sting vs Grapplers 2.25
12 F:Ron Simmons. 2.25

World of Fantasy #8
© Marvel Entertainment Group

WORLD OF FANTASY
Atlas, May, 1956
1 The Secret of the Mountain. . . 550.00
2 JMn,AW,Inside the Tunnel. . . . 350.00
3 DAy,SC, The Man in the Cave 300.00
4 BEv(c),BP,JF,Back to the
  Lost City. 250.00
5 BEv(c),BP,In the Swamp 250.00
6 BEv(c),BP,The Strange Wife
  of Henry Johnson 250.00
7 BEv(c),GM,Man in Grey 250.00
8 GM,JO,MF,The Secret of the
  Black Cloud 275.00
9 BEv,BK. 250.00
10 . . . . 200.00
11 AT 200.00
12 BEv(c). 200.00
13 BEv,JO. 200.00
14 JMn(c),GM,JO,CI,JM 200.00
15 JK(c) 200.00
16 AW,SD,JK 250.00
17 JK(c),SD 225.00
18 JK(c) 225.00
19 JK(c),SD,Aug., 1959 . . . . 225.00

WORLD OF MYSTERY
Atlas, June, 1956
1 BEv(c),AT,JO,The Long Wait . 550.00
2 BEv(c),The Man From
  Nowhere 225.00
3 SD,AT,JDa, The Bugs 250.00
4 SD(c),BP,What Happened in
  the Basement 250.00
5 JO,She Stands in Shadows . . 200.00
6 AW,SD,GC,Sinking Man 225.00
7 GC,JSe,Pick A Door,
  July, 1957 . . . . 200.00

WORLD OF SUSPENSE
Atlas, April, 1956
1 JO,BEv,MO,JMn,A Stranger
  Among Us 450.00
2 SD,LC,JMN(c),When Walks
  the Scarecrow 250.00
3 AW,JMN(c),The Man Who
  Couldn't Be Touched. 250.00
4 Something is in This House . . 200.00

All comics prices listed are for Near Mint condition.

CVA Page 345

MARVEL

World–X-Factor

5 BEv,DH,JO 200.00
6 BEv(c),BP 200.00
7 AW,The Face 250.00
8 Prisoner of the Ghost Ship . . . 200.00

WORLDS UNKNOWN
May, 1973

1 GK,AT,The Coming of the
  Martians,Reprints 30.00
2 GK,TS,A Gun For A Dinosaur . . 20.00
3 The Day the Earth Stood
  Still. 20.00
4 JB,Arena 20.00
5 DA,JM,Black Destroyer. 20.00
6 GK(c),The Thing Called It 20.00
7 GT,The Golden Voyage of
  Sinbad,Part 1 . . . . 20.00
8 The Golden Voyage of
  Sinbad,Part 2, Aug., 1974 . . . 20.00

WYATT EARP
Atlas, Nov., 1955

1 JMn,F:Wyatt Earp 250.00
2 AW,Saloon(c) 150.00
3 JMn(c),The Showdown,
  A:Black Bart 100.00
4 Ph(c),Hugh O'Brian,JSe,
  India Sundown 100.00
5 Ph(c),Hugh O'Brian,DW,
  Gun Wild Fever 100.00
6 BEv(c) 100.00
7 AW 100.00
8 JMn,Wild Bill Hickok 100.00
9 and 10 . . . . @100.00
11 . . . . 100.00
12 AW,JMn 100.00
13 thru 20 . . . . @75.00
21 JDa(c) 75.00
22 thru 29 . . . . @60.00
30 Reprints 25.00
31 thru 33 Reprints . . . . @20.00
34 June, 1973 . . . . 20.00

XAVIER INSTITUTE ALUMNI YEARBOOK
GN 48-pg. (1996) 5.95

X-CALIBRE
1995

1 Excaliber After Xavier 4.00
2 V:Callisto & Morlock Crew 3.00
3 D:Juggernaut 3.00
4 Secret Weapon 3.00
TPB Rep.#1-#4 . . . . 8.95

X-FACTOR
Feb., 1986

1 WS(c),JG,BL,JRu,I:X-Factor,
  Rusty 10.00
2 JG,BL,I:Tower 5.00
3 JG,BL,V:Tower 4.00
4 KP,JRu,V:Frenzy 4.00
5 JG,JRu,I:Alliance of Evil,
  C:Apocalypse 5.00
6 JG,BMc,I:Apocalypse 15.00
7 JG,JRu,V:Morlocks,I:Skids 4.00
8 MS,JRu,I:Freedom Force 4.00
9 JRu(i),V:Freedom Force
  (Mutant Massacre) 5.00
10 WS,BWi,V:Marauders(Mut.Mass),
   A:Sabretooth 6.00
11 WS,BWi,A:Thor(Mutant Mass) . . 5.00
12 MS,BWi,V:Vanisher 4.00
13 WS,DGr,V:Mastermold 4.00
14 WS,BWi,V:Mastermold 4.00
15 WS,BWi,D:Angel 5.00
16 DM,JRu,V:Masque 4.00
17 WS,BWi,I:Rictor 5.00
18 WS,BWi,V:Apocalypse 4.00
19 WS,BWi,V:Horsemen of
   Apocalypse 3.00
20 JBr,A:X-Terminators 3.00
21 WS,BWi,V:The Right 3.00
22 SB,BWi,V:The Right 3.00
23 WS,BWi,C:Archangel 8.00
24 WS,BWi,Fall of Mutants,
   I:Archangel 10.00
25 WS,BWi,Fall of Mutants 3.50
26 WS,BWi,Fall of Mutants,
   N:X-Factor 3.50
27 WS,BWi,Christmas Issue 3.00
28 WS,BWi,V:Ship 3.00
29 WS,BWi,V:Infectia 3.00
30 WS,BWi,V:Infectia,Free.Force . . 3.00
31 WS,BWi,V:Infectia,Free.Force . . 3.00
32 SLi,A:Avengers 3.00
33 WS,BWi,V:Tower & Frenzy,
   R:Furry Beast 3.00
34 WS,BWi,I:Nanny,
   Orphan Maker 3.00
35 JRu(i),WS(c),V:Nanny,
   Orphan Maker 3.00
36 WS,BWi,Inferno,V:Nastirh 3.00
37 WS,BWi,Inferno,V:Gob.Queen . 3.00
38 WS,AM,Inferno,A:X-Men,D:
   MadelynePryor(GoblinQueen) . 3.00
39 WS,AM,Inferno,A:X-Men,
   V:Mr.Sinister 3.00
40 RLd,AM,O:Nanny,Orphan Maker
   1st Liefeld Marvel work 6.00
41 AAd,AM,I:Alchemy 3.00
42 AAd,AM,A:Alchemy 3.00
43 PS,AM,V:Celestials 3.00
44 PS,AM,V:Rejects 3.00
45 PS,AM,V:Rask 3.00
46 PS,AM,V:Rejects 3.00
47 KD,AM,V:Father 3.00
48 thru 49 PS,AM,V:Rejects 3.00
50 RLd&TM(c),RB,AM,A:Prof.X
   (double sized),BU:Apocalypse . 4.00
51 AM,V:Sabretooth,Caliban 4.00
52 RLd(c),AM,V:Sabretooth,
   Caliban 3.00
53 AM,V:Sabretooth,Caliban 3.00
54 MS,AM,A:Colossus,I:Crimson . . 3.00
55 MMi(c),CDo,AM,V:Mesmero . . . 3.00
56 AM,V:Crimson 3.00
57 NKu,V:Crimson 3.00
58 JBg,AM,V:Crimson 3.00
59 AM,V:Press Gang 3.00

X-Factor #18
© Marvel Entertainment Group

Comics Values Annual

60 JBg,AM,X-Tinction Agenda#3 . . . 3.50
60a 2nd printing(gold) 2.50
61 JBg,AM,X-Tinction Agenda#6 . . . 3.00
62 JBg,AM,JLe(c),E:X-Agenda 3.00
63 WPo,I:Cyberpunks 3.00
64 WPo,ATb,V:Cyberpunks 3.00
65 WPo,ATb,V:Apocalypse 3.00
66 WPo,ATb,I:Askani,
   V:Apocalypse 3.00
67 WPo,ATb,V:Apocalypse,I:Shinobi
   Shaw,D:Sebastian Shaw 3.00
68 WPo,ATb,JLe(c),V:Apocalypse,
   L:Nathan,(taken into future) . . 3.00
69 WPo,V:Shadow King 3.00
70 MMi(c),JRu,Last old team 3.00
71 LSn,AM,New Team 4.00
71a 2nd printing 2.50
72 LSn,AM,Who shot Madrox
   revealed 3.00
73 LSn,AM,Mob Chaos in D.C. . . . 3.00
74 LSn,AM,I:Slab 3.00
75 LSn,AM,I:Nasty Boys(doub.sz) . 3.50
76 LSn,AM,A:Hulk,Pantheon 3.25
77 LSn,AM,V:Mutant Lib. Front . . . 3.25
78 LSn,AM,V:Mutant Lib. Front . . . 3.25
79 LSn,AM,V:Helle's Belles 3.25
80 LSn,AM,V:Helle's Belles,
   C:Cyber 3.25
81 LSn,AM,V:Helle's Belles,Cyber . 3.25
82 JQ(c),LSn,V:Brotherhood of Evil
   Mutants,I:X-iles 3.25
83 MPa,A:X-Force,X-iles 3.25
84 JaL,X-Cutioners Song #2,
   V:X-Force,A:X-Men 3.25
85 JaL,X-Cutioners Song #6,
   Wolv.& Bishop,V:Cable 3.25
86 JaL,AM,X-Cutioner's Song#10,
   A:X-Men,X-Force,V:Stryfe . . . 3.25
87 JQ,X-Cutioners Song
   Aftermath 3.00
88 JQ,AM,V:2nd Genegineer,
   I:Random 4.00
89 JQ,V:Mutates,Genosha 3.00
90 JQ,AM,Genosha vs. Aznia 3.00
91 AM,V:Armageddon 3.00
92 JQ,AM,V:Fabian Cortez,
   Acolytes,hologram(c) 6.00
93 Magneto Protocols 3.00
94 PR,J:Forge 3.00
95 B:JMD(s),AM,Polaris
   Vs. Random 3.00
96 A:Random 3.00
97 JD,I:Haven,A:Random 3.00
98 GLz,A:Haven,A:Random 3.00
99 JD,A:Haven,Wolfsbane returns
   to human 3.00
100 JD,Red Foil(c),V:Haven,
   D:Madrox 5.00
100a Newstand Ed 5.00
101 JD,AM,Aftermath 2.50
102 JD,AM,V:Crimson Commando,
   Avalanche 2.50
103 JD,AM,A:Malice 2.50
104 JD,AM,V:Malice,
   C:Mr. Sinister 2.50
105 JD,AM,V:Malice 2.50
106 Phalanx Covenant,Life Signs
   Holografx(c) 3.50
106a newsstand ed 2.50
107 A:Strong Guy 2.50
108 A:Mystique, deluxe ed. 2.50
108a newsstand ed 2.00
109 A:Mystique,V:Legion, deluxe . 2.50
109a newsstand ed 2.25
110 Invasion 2.50
110a deluxe ed 2.25
111 Invasion 2.50
111a deluxe ed 2.25
112 AM,JFM,SEp,F:Guido,Havok . . 2.50
113 A:Mystique 2.50
114 AM,Wild Child & Mystique . . . 2.50

CVA Page 346   All comics prices listed are for *Near Mint* condition.

Comics Values Annual — MARVEL — X-Factor–X-Force

X-Factor #103
© Marvel Entertainment Group

115 F:Wild Child,Havok 2.50
116 F:Wild Child 2.50
117 HMe,AM,F:Cyclops 2.50
118 HMe,AM,A:Random,Shard . . . 2.50
119 HMe,AM,F:Sabretooth 2.50
120 A:Sabretooth 2.50
121 A:Sabretooth 2.50
122 HMe,SEp,AM,J:Sabretooth . . . 2.50
123 A:Hound 2.50
124 A:Onslaught. 3.50
125 Onslaught saga, double size . . 4.00
126 Beast vs. Dark Beast. 2.50
127 Mystique 2.50
128 HMe,JMs,AM,Hound Program . 2.50
129 HMe,JMs,AM,Graydon Creed's
    campaign 2.50
130 HMe,JMs,AM,Assassination of
    Graydon Creed. 2.50
131 HMe,JMs,ATi,Havok strikes
    back. 2.50
132 HMe,JMs,ATi,Break away from
    government 2.50
133 HMe,JMs,ATi,A:Multiple Man &
    Strong Guy. 2.50
134 HMe,JMs,Ati,`Operation X-Factor
    Underground,' cont. 2.50
135 HMe,JMs,Strong Guy awakes . 2.50
136 HMe,JMs,ATi, A:Sabretooth . . . 2.50
137 HMe,JMs,ATi, Final fate of
    Shard and Polaris. 2.50
138 HMe,JMs,ATi, Sabretooth,
    V:Maberick. 2.50
139 HMe,ATi,Who killed Graydon
    Creed. 2.50
140 HMe,ATi,Who killed Graydon
    Creed, A:Mystique 2.50
141 HMe,ATi,Shard's Plan 2.50
142 ATi,F:Wild Child 2.50
143 HMe,ATi,Havok vs.DarkBeast . 2.50
144 HMe,ATi,V:Brotherhood,
    Dark Beast. 2.50
145 HMe,ATi,Havok vs. X.U.E. 2.50
146 HMe,ATi, Havok, Multiple
    Man,V:Polaris. 2.50
147 HMe,Havok v. Mandroids. 2.50
148 F:Shard 2.50
149 HMe,Polaris & Madrox rejoin . . 3.00
Spec #1 JG,Prisoner of Love 5.00
Ann.#1 BL,BBr,V:CrimsonDynamo . 5.00
Ann.#2 TGr,JRu,A:Inhumans 4.00
Ann.#3 WS(c),AM,JRu,PC,TD,
    Evolutionary War 3.50
Ann.#4 JBy,WS,JRu,MBa,Atlantis
    Attacks,BU:Doom & Magneto . . 3.50

Ann.#5 JBg,AM,DR,GI,Days of Future
    Present,A:Fant.Four,V:Ahab . . 4.00
Ann.#6 Flesh Tears Saga,pt.4,
    A:X-Force, New Warriors 4.00
Ann #7 JQ,JRu,Shattershot,pt.3 . . . 4.00
Ann.#8 I:Charon,w/card 3.25
Ann.#9 JMD(s),MtB,V:Prof.Power,
    A:Prof.X,O:Haven. 3.25
Minus 1 Spec., HMe,JMs,ATi,
    flashback,F:Havok 2.50
GN X-Men: Wrath of Apocalypse,
    rep.X-Factor#65-#68 . . . . 4.95

X-FACTOR
April, 2002
1 (of 4) When will it stop 2.50
2 FBI agents 2.50
3 in San Francisco. 2.50
4 Concl.. . . . . 2.50
TPB Vol. 1 . . . . 10.00

X-51
July, 1999
1 JQ&JP(c) Marvel Tech 2.00
2 JoB,V:Brotherhood of Mutants . . 2.00
2a variant cover. 2.00
3 JoB,A:X.E.R.O. 2.00
4 JoB,A:Avengers 2.00
5 JoB,V:Vision. 2.00
6 JoB 2.00
7 JoB,A:Sebastian Shaw 2.00
8 JoB,F:X-Men 2.50
9 JoB, ... 2.50
10 JoB,F:Machine Man. 2.50
11 JoB,F:Celestial. 2.50
12 JoB,final issue 2.50

X-FORCE
Aug., 1991
1 RLd,V:Stryfe,Mutant Liberation
    Front,bagged, white on black
    graphics with X-Force Card . . . 4.00
1a with Shatterstar Card 4.00
1b with Deadpool Card 4.00
1c with Sunspot & Gideon Card . . . 4.00
1d with Cable Card 5.00
1e Unbagged Copy 2.75
1f 2nd Printing 2.00
2 RLd,I:New Weapon X,V:
    Deadpool 3.00
3 RLd,C:Spider-Man,
    V:Juggernaut,Black Tom 3.00
4 RLd,SpM/X-Force team-up,
    V:Juggernaut(cont.from SpM#16)
    Sideways format. 3.00
5 RLd,A:Brotherhood Evil Mutants . 3.00
6 RLd,V:Bro'hood Evil Mutants . . . 3.00
7 RLd,V:Bro'hood Evil Mutants . . . 3.00
8 MMi,O:Cable(Part) 3.00
9 RLd,D:Sauron,Masque 3.00
10 MPa,V:Mutant Liberation Front. . 3.00
11 MPa,Deadpool Vs Domino. 2.50
12 MPa,A:Weapon Prime,Gideon . . 2.50
13 MPa,V:Weapon Prime 2.50
14 TSr,V:Weapon Prime,Krule 2.50
15 GCa,V:Krule,Deadpool. 2.50
16 GCa,X-Cutioners Song #4,
    X-Factor V:X-Force. 3.00
17 GCa,X-Cutioners Song#8,
    Apocalypse V:Stryfe 3.00
18 GCa,X-Cutioners Song#12,
    Cable vs Stryfe. 3.00
19 GCa,X-Cutioners Song
    Aftermath,N:X-Force. 2.50
20 GCa,O:Graymalkin 2.50
21 GCa,V:War Machine,SHIELD. . . 2.50
22 GCa,V:Externals 2.50
23 GCa,V:Saul,Gigeon,A:Six Pack . . 2.50

24 GCa,A:Six Pack,A:Deadpool . . . 2.50
25 GCa,A:Magneto,Exodus,
    R:Cable 5.00
26 GCa(c),MtB,I:Reignfire. 2.50
27 GCa(c),MtB,V:Reignfire,MLF,
    I:Moonstar,Locus 2.50
28 MtB,V:Reignfire,MLF 2.50
29 MtB,V:Arcade,C:X-Treme. 2.50
30 TnD,V:Arcade,A:X-Treme. 2.50
31 F:Siryn. 2.50
32 Child's Play#1,A:New Warriors. . 2.50
33 Child's Play#3,A:New Warriors,
    V:Upstarts 2.50
34 F:Rictor,Domino,Cable 3.00
35 TnD,R:Nimrod 2.50
36 TnD,V:Nimrod 2.50
37 PaP,I&D:Absalom 2.50
38 TaD,Life Signs,pt.2,
    I:Generation X, foil(c) 5.00
38a newsstand ed. 2.50
39 TaD 2.50
40 TaD, deluxe 2.50
40a newsstand ed. 2.25
41 TaD,O:feral,deluxe 2.50
41a newsstand ed. 2.25
42 Emma Frost, deluxe. 2.50
42a newsstand ed. 2.25
43 Home is Where Heart 2.50
43a deluxe ed. 2.50
44 AdP,Prof.X,X-Mansion 2.50
45 AdP,Caliban vs. Sabretooth 2.50
46 R:The Mimic 2.50
47 A:Deadpool 2.50
48 AdP,Siryn Takes Charge. 2.50
49 ADp,MBu,Holocaust is here 2.50
50 AdP,MPn,F:Sebastian Shaw. . . . 2.50
50a prismatic foil cover. 4.50
50b variant RLd(c) 6.00
51 AdP,MPn,V:Risque. 2.50
52 A:Onslaught. 3.50
53 . . . . 2.50
54 AdP, Can X-Force
    protect X-Ternals? 2.50
55 V:S.H.I.E.L.D. 2.50
56 Deadpool, A:Onslaught 3.50
57 Onslaught saga 2.50
58 Onslaught saga 2.50
59 Longshot, with card 2.50
60 JLb,,F:Shatterstar,A:Long Shot . 2.50
61 JLb,R:Longshot,O:Shatterstar . . 2.50
62 JLb,F:Sunspot 2.50
63 JFM,AdP,F:Risque,Cannonball. . 2.50
64 JFM,AdP,In Latveria, searching
    for Doctor Doom's weapons . . . 2.50

X-Force #62
© Marvel Entertainment Group

All comics prices listed are for *Near Mint* condition. CVA Page 347

X-Force–X-Man — MARVEL — Comics Values Annual

X-Force Ann. #2
© Marvel Entertainment Group

65 JFM,AdP,Warpath follows Risque
  to Florida 2.50
66 JFM,AdP,A:Risque,James
  Proudstar 2.50
67 JFM,AdP,F:Warpath, Risque . . . 2.50
68 JFM,AdP,Sunfire & Meltdown . . 2.50
69 JFM,AdP,Zero Tolerance
  aftermath 2.50
70 JFM,AdP,new direction starts . . 2.50
71 JFM,AdP,new direction 2.50
72 JFM,AdP,on the road 2.50
73 JFM,AdP,in New Orleans 2.50
74 JFM,ASm,Skids is back 2.50
75 JFM,AdP,A:Reignfire,
  double size, ... 3.00
76 JFM,AdP,F:Shatterstar 2.50
77 JFM,AdP,F:Sunfire & Meltdown . 2.50
78 JFM,AdP,Reignfire makes his
  move 2.50
79 JFM,AdP,O:Reignfire 2.50
80 JFM,AdP,V:Reignfire 2.50
81 JFM,AdP,trip to Hawaii,
  V:Lava Men, AdP Poster. 2.50
82 JFM,V:Griffin, Damocles
  Foundation. 2.50
83 JFM,F:Cannonball 2.50
84 JFM,V:Deviants 2.50
85 JFM,Return of Skids 2.50
86 JFM,A:Hulk 2.50
87 JFM,V:new Hellions 2.50
88 JFM,V:new Hellions 2.50
89 JFM,prisoners of the Hellions. . 2.50
90 JFM,Hellion War, concl. 2.50
91 JFM,home to San Francisco . . 2.50
92 JFM,F:Domino 2.50
93 JFM,Domino returns 2.50
94 JFM,destination Genosha 2.50
95 JFM,F:Magneto 2.50
96 JFM,A:Selene 2.50
97 JFM,V:Reignfire 2.50
98 . . . . 2.50
99 JFM,F:Dani Moonstar 2.50
100 JFM,Four Personas,48-pg. . . . 3.00
101 new members,some gone . . . 2.50
102 WPo,X-Men: Revolution. 2.50
102a variant (c) 5.00
103 WPo,WEl,Games Without
  Frontiers,pt.2 . . . . 2.50
104 WPo,WEl,Games,pt.3 . . . . 2.50
105 WPo,WEl,Games,pt.4 . . . . 2.50
106 WEl,IEd,WPo,Murder
  Ballads,pt.1 . . . . 2.50
107 WEl,IEd,MurderBallads,pt.2 . . 2.50

108 WEl,IEd,Ballads,pt.3 . . . . 2.50
109 WEl,IEd,Ballads,pt.4 . . . . 2.50
110 WEl,IEd,Rage War,pt.1. . . . . . . 2.50
111 WEl,IEd,Rage War,pt.2. . . . . . . 2.50
112 WEl,IEd,Rage War,pt.3. . . . . . . 2.50
113 WEl,IEd,Rage War,pt.4. . . . . . . 2.50
114 . . . . 2.50
115 IEd,final issue? 2.50
116 PrM,MiA,new team. 5.00
117 PrM,MiA,new members 5.00
118 PrM,MiA,F:U-Go Girl 2.25
119 PrM,MiA,F:U-Go Girl 2.25
120 PrM,MiA,A:Wolverine. 2.25
121 PrM,MiA,I:Lacuna 2.25
122 PrM,MiA,F:Lacuna 2.25
123 PrM,MiA,'Nuff Said 2.25
124 PrM,Orphan & U-Go Girl . . . 2.25
125 PrM,Anarchist, Doop 2.25
126 PrM,MiA,one won't come home 2.25
127 PrM,MiA,who won't come home 2.25
128 PrM,MiA,body bag time 2.25
129 PrM,DFg,something
  even worse 2.25
Ann.#1 Shattershot,pt1 . . . . 3.00
Ann.#2 JaL,LSn,I:X-Treme,w/card. . 3.25
Ann.#3 . . . . 3.50
Ann.1998 X-Force/Champions . . . 6.00
Ann.1999 R:Shatterstar & Rictor . . 3.50
Spec.#102 Rough cut edition 3.00
Minus 1 Spec., JFM,AdP, flashback,
  F:John Proudstar 2.50
TPB X-Force & Spider-Man: Sabotage,
  rep.X-Force #3 & #4 and
  Spider-Man #16 . . . . 6.95
TPB New Beginnings 12.95
TPB Vol.2 (2002) 20.00

X-FORCE MEGAZINE
TPB LSi,RLd, rep. New Mutants
  #99–#100 . . . . 4.00

X-MAN
March, 1995
1 Cable after Xavier. 5.00
2 Sinister's Plan 4.00
3 V:Domino 3.00
4 V:Sinister 3.00
5 Into this World 3.00
6 V:X-Men 2.50
7 Evil from Age of Apocalypse . . . 2.50
8 Crossover Adventure 2.50
9 F:Nate's Past 2.50
10 Nate's Past 2.50
11 Young Nate seeks out X-Men. . . 2.50
12 F:Excalibur 2.50
13 . . . . 2.50
14 . . . . 2.50
15 JOs,X-Men/Cable war aftermath 3.00
16 Holocaust,A:Onslaught 2.50
17 Holocaust,Quicksilver,Scarlet
  Witch, A:Onslaught. 2.50
18 Onslaught saga 2.50
19 Onslaught saga 2.50
20 . . . . 2.50
21 TKa,RCz,F:Nate 2.50
22 TKa,RCz,F:Threnody,A:Madelyne
  Pryor 2.50
23 TKa,RCz,F:Bishop 2.50
24 TKa,RCz,Spider-Man vs. Nate . . 2.50
25 TKa,RCz,Madelyne Pryor,
  double size, ... 4.00
26 TKa,RCz,Nate limps to Muir
  Isle,A:Moira Mactaggert 2.50
27 TKa,RCz,Hellfire Club, concl. . . . 2.50
28 TKa,RCz,Dark Beast's offer . . . 2.50
29 TKa,RCz,Back in New York, . . . 2.50
30 TKa,RCz,F:Nate Grey 2.50
31 RL,DGr,F:Nate Grey 2.50
32 TKa,V:Jacknife. 2.50
33 TKa,V:Jacknife. 2.50

34 TKa,Secret of Nate's popularity . 2.50
35 TKa,Terrorists Strike 2.50
36 TKa,V:Purple Man 2.50
37 TKa,Nate leaves N.Y.,
  A:Spider-Man 2.50
38 TKa,A:Spider-Man, Gwen Stacy. 2.50
39 TKa,AOl,Nate & Madeline Pryor. 2.50
40 TKa,RPc,V:Great Beasts 2.50
41 TKa,RCz,Madelyne Pryor 2.50
42 TKa,RCz,hunted by leprechauns 2.50
43 TKa,RCz,Nate Grey–murderer?! 2.50
44 TKa,RCz,F:Nate Grey,Gauntlet . 2.50
45 TKa,prelude to X-Man/Cable
  x-over. 2.50
46 TKa,Cable x-over. 2.50
47 TKa,Blood Brothers,pt.3. . . . . . 2.50
48 LRs,V:Crusader 2.50
49 LRs,TKa,F:Nate. 2.50
50 TKa,LRs,War of the
  Mutants,pt.2, 48-page. 3.50
51 TKa,LRs,V:Psi-Ops 2.50
52 TKa,LRs,V:Psi-Ops 2.50
53 TKa,Strange Relations,pt.1 . . . 2.50
54 TKa,Strange Relations,pt.2 . . . 2.50
55 TKa,M'Kraan Crystal 2.50
56 TKa,Nate in Greyville. 2.50
57 TKa,V:Mysterio 2.50
58 TKa,V:Threnody. 2.50
59 TKa, ... 2.50
60 TKa, ... 2.50
61 TKa, ... 2.50
62 TKa,trapped. 2.50
63 WEl,X-Men: Revolution. 2.25
63a variant(c) 2.25
64 WEl,No Direction Home,pt.2 . . . 2.25
65 WEl,No Direction Home,pt.3 . . . 2.25
66 WEl,No Direction Home,pt.4 . . . 2.25
67 WEl,Down the Spiral,pt.1 . . . . . 2.25
68 WEl,Down the Spiral,pt.2 . . . . . 2.25
69 WEl,Down the Spiral,pt.3 . . . . . 2.25
70 WEl,Down the Spiral,pt.4 . . . . . 2.25
71 AOl,StG,Fearful
  Symmetries,pt.1 . . . . 2.25
72 AOl,StG,Symmetries,pt.2 . . . . . 2.25
73 AOl,StG,Symmetries,pt.3 . . . . . 2.25
74 AOl,StG,Symmetries,pt.4 . . . . . 2.25
75 Anti-Man, final issue. 3.00
Minus 1 Spec., TKa,RCz,
  flashback,O:Nate Grey 2.00
Spec.#1 X-Man '96. . . . . 3.50
Ann. '97 RBe, Nate, Sugar Man,
  Dark Beast, Holocaust 3.00
Ann. '98 X-Man, The Hulk, Thanos,

X-Man #51
© Marvel Entertainment Group

CVA Page 348 — All comics prices listed are for *Near Mint* condition.

48-pg. 3.00
GNv X-Man,BRa,TyD, 48-pg. 6.00

X-MEN
Sept., 1963

1 JK,O:X-Men,I:Professor X,Beast Cyclops,Marvel Girl,Iceman Angel,Magneto 14,000.00
2 JK,I:Vanisher 4,000.00
3 JK,I:Blob 1,500.00
4 JK,I:Quicksilver,Scarlet Witch Mastermind,Toad 2,000.00
5 JK,V:Broth. of Evil Mutants. . 1,500.00
6 JK,V:Sub-Mariner 800.00
7 JK,V:Broth. of Evil Mutants, Blob 800.00
8 JK,I:Unus,1st Ice covered Iceman 800.00
9 JK,A:Avengers,I:Lucifer...... 800.00
10 JK,I:Modern Ka-Zar 800.00
11 JK,I:Stranger 500.00
12 JK,O:Prof.X,I:Juggernaut. . . 1,000.00
13 JK,JSt,V:Juggernaut 500.00
14 JK,I:Sentinels............ 500.00
15 JK,O:Beast,V:Sentinels 500.00
16 JK,V:Mastermold,Sentinels. . . 500.00
17 JK,V:Magneto 350.00
18 V:Magneto................ 350.00
19 I:Mimic.................... 350.00
20 V:Lucifer 350.00
21 V:Lucifer,Dominus 300.00
22 V:Maggia 300.00
23 V:Maggia 300.00
24 I:Locust(Prof.Hopper)....... 300.00
25 JK,I:El Tigre 300.00
26 V:El Tigre................ 275.00
27 C:Fant.Four,V:Puppet Master. 275.00
28 I:Banshee................ 450.00
29 V:Super-Apaptoid.......... 300.00
30 JK,I:The Warlock 175.00
31 JK,I:Cobalt Man 150.00
32 V:Juggernaut 150.00
33 GK,A:Dr.Strange,Juggernaut . 150.00
34 V:Tyrannus,Mole Man 150.00
35 JK,A:Spider-Man,Banshee... 150.00
36 V:Mekano 150.00
37 DH,V:Blob,Unus............ 150.00
38 DH,A:Banshee,O:Cyclops ... 250.00
39 DH,GT,A:Banshee,V:Mutant Master,O:Cyclops......... 350.00
40 DH,GT,V:Frankenstein, O:Cyclops 250.00
41 DH,GT,I:Grotesk,O:Cyclops .. 250.00

X-Men #6
© Marvel Entertainment Group

42 DH,GT,JB,V:Grotesk, O:Cyclops,D:Prof.X........ 135.00
43 GT,JB,V:Magneto,Quicksilver, Scarlet Witch,C:Avengers . . . 250.00
44 V:Magneto,Quicksilver,Sc.Witch, R:Red Raven,O:Iceman 200.00
45 PH,JB,V:Magneto,Quicksilver, Scarlet Witch,O:Iceman 200.00
46 DH,V:Juggernaut,O:Iceman . . 125.00
47 DH,I:Maha Yogi 125.00
48 DH,JR,V:Quasimodo 125.00
49 JSo,DH,C:Magneto,I:Polaris, Mesmero,O:Beast.......... 125.00
50 JSo,V:Magneto,O:Beast..... 150.00
51 JSo,V:Magneto,Polaris, Erik the Red,O:Beast 150.00
52 DH,MSe,JSt,O:Lorna Dane V:Magneto,O:Beast 100.00
53 1st BWS,O:Beast........... 125.00
54 BWS,DH,I:Havok,O:Angel . . . 125.00
55 BWS,DH,O:Havok,Angel 125.00
56 NA,V:LivingMonolith,O:Angel . 125.00
57 NA,V:Sentinels,A:Havok..... 125.00
58 NA,A:Havoc,V:Sentinels..... 150.00
59 NA,V:Sentinels,A:Havoc..... 125.00
60 NA,I:Sauron................ 125.00
61 NA,V:Sauron 125.00
62 NA,A:Ka-Zar,Sauron,Magneto 125.00
63 A:Ka-Zar,V:Magneto 110.00
64 DH,A:Havok,I:Sunfire....... 125.00
65 NA,MSe,A:Havok,Shield, Return of Prof.X 125.00
66 SB,MSe,V:Hulk,A:Havok 125.00
67 rep.X-Men #12,#13 .... 100.00
68 rep.X-Men #14,#15 .... 100.00
69 rep.X-Men #16,#19 .... 100.00
70 rep.X-Men #17,#18 .... 100.00
71 rep.X-Men #20............ 100.00
72 rep.X-Men #21,#24 .... 100.00
73 thru 93 rep.X-Men #25-45 . . @75.00
94 GK(c),B:CCl(s),DC,BMc,B:2nd X-Men,V:Count Nefaria . . . 1,500.00
95 GK(c),DC,V:Count Nefaria, Ani-Men,D:Thunderbird..... 300.00
96 DC,I:Moira McTaggert, Kierrok 200.00
97 DC,V:Havok,Polaris,Eric the Red,I:Lilandra 200.00
98 DC,V:Sentinels,Stephen Lang 150.00
99 DC,V:Sentinels,S.Lang....... 150.00
100 DC,V:Stephen Lang 200.00
101 DC,I:Phoenix,Black Tom, A:Juggernaut 200.00
102 DC,O:Storm,V:Juggernaut, Black Tom 125.00
103 DC,V:Juggernaut,Bl.Tom . . . 125.00
104 DC,V:Magneto,I:Star Jammers,A:Lilandra 100.00
105 DC,BL,V:Firelord 90.00
106 DC,TS,V:Firelord 90.00
107 DC,DGr,I:Imperial Guard,Star Jammers,Gladiator,Corsair . . 100.00
108 JBy,TA,A:Star Jammers, C:Fantastic Four,Avengers.. 125.00
109 JBy,TA,I:Vindicator 110.00
110 TD,DC,V:Warhawk 75.00
111 JBy,TA,V:Mesmero,A:Beast, Magneto 75.00
112 GP(c),JBy,TA,V:Magneto, A:Beast 75.00
113 JBy,TA,V:Magneto,A:Beast... 75.00
114 JBy,TA,A:Beast,R:Sauron..... 90.00
115 JBy,TA,V:Sauron,Garokk, A:Ka-Zar,I:Zaladane 75.00
116 JBy,TA,V:Sauron,Garokk, A:Ka-Zar 65.00
117 JBy,TA,O:Prof.X,I:Amahl Farouk (Shadow King) 65.00
118 JBy,I:Moses Magnum,A:Sunfire C:Iron Fist,I:Mariko 60.00
119 JBy,TA,V:Moses Magnum,

X-Men #73
© Marvel Entertainment Group

A:Sunfire 60.00
120 JBy,TA,I:AlphaFlight (Shaman, Sasquatch,Northstar,Snowbird, Aurora).................. 125.00
121 JBy,TA,V:Alpha Flight....... 100.00
122 JBy,TA,A:Juggernaut,Black Tom,Arcade,Power Man 60.00
123 JBy,TA,V:Arcade,A:SpM...... 50.00
124 JBy,TA,V:Arcade 50.00
125 JBy,TA,A:Beast,Madrox the Multiple Man,Havok,Polaris... 50.00
126 JBy,TA,I:Proteus, A:Havok,Madrox........... 50.00
127 JBy,TA,V:Proteus,A:Havok, Madrox.................. 50.00
128 GP(c),JBy,TA,V:Proteus, A:Havok,Madrox........... 50.00
129 JBy,TA,I:Shadow Cat,White Queen,C:Hellfire Club........ 60.00
130 JR2(c),JBy,TA,I:Dazzler V:White Queen............. 55.00
131 JBy,TA,V:White Queen, A:Dazzler 50.00
132 JBy,TA,I:Hellfire Club, V:Mastermind 50.00
133 JBy,TA,V:Hellfire Club, Mastermind,F:Wolverine..... 50.00
134 JBy,TA,V:Hellfire Club,Master mind,I:Dark Phoenix,A:Beast . 45.00
135 JBy,TA,V:Dark Phoenix,C:SpM, Fant.Four,Silver Surfer 45.00
136 JBy,TA,V:Dark Phoenix, A:Beast 40.00
137 JBy,TA,D:Phoenix,V:Imperial Guard,A:Beast 50.00
138 JBy,TA,History of X-Men, L:Cyclops,C:Shadow Cat 40.00
139 JBy,TA,A:Alpha Flight,R:Wendigo, N:Wolverine,J:Shadowcat.... 45.00
140 JBy,TA,V:Wendigo,A:Alpha Flight 40.00
141 JBy,TA,I:2nd Brotherhood of Evil Mutants,I:Rachel (Phoenix II) . 55.00
Becomes:

UNCANNY X-MEN

142 JBy,TA,V:Evil Mutants, A:Rachel (Phoenix II) 45.00
143 JBy,TA,V:N'Garai,I:Lee Forrester 30.00
144 BA,JRu,A:Man-Thing, O:Havok, V:D'Spayre 20.00
145 DC,JRu,V:Arcade,A:DrDoom . 20.00
146 DC,JRu,V:Dr.Doom,Arcade .. 20.00
147 DC,JRu,V:Dr.Doom,Arcade .. 20.00

X-Men   MARVEL   Comics Values Annual

Uncanny X-Men #150
© Marvel Entertainment Group

148 DC,JRu,I:Caliban,A:Dazzler
  Spiderwoman 15.00
149 DC,JRu,A:Magneto 15.00
150 DC,JRu,BWi,V:Magneto 20.00
151 JSh,BMc,JRu,V:Sentinels 15.00
152 BMc,JRu,V:White Queen 15.00
153 DC,JRu,I:Bamf 15.00
154 DC,JRu,BWi,I:Sidrian Hunters
  A:Corsair,O:Cyclops(part) 15.00
155 DC,BWi,V:Deathbird,I:Brood . 15.00
156 DC,BWi,V:Death Bird,
  A:Tigra, Star Jammers 15.00
157 DC,BWi,V:Deathbird 15.00
158 DC,BWi,2nd A:Rogue,
  Mystique 25.00
159 BSz,BWi,V:Dracula 15.00
160 BA,BWi,V:Belasco,I:Magik . . . 15.00
161 DC,BWi,I:Gabrielle Haller,
  O:Magneto,Professor X 16.00
162 DC,BWi,V:Brood 18.00
163 DC,BWi,V:Brood 15.00
164 DC,BWi,V:Brood,I:Binary 15.00
165 PS,BWi,V:Brood. 20.00
166 PS,BWi,V:Brood,A:Binary,
  I:Lockheed 15.00
167 PS,BWi,V:Brood,A:N.Mutants. 15.00
168 PS,BWi,I:Madelyne Pryor. . . . 12.00
169 PS,BWi,I:Morlocks. 12.00
170 PS,BWi,A:Angel,V:Morlocks . . 12.00
171 WS,BWi,J:Rogue,V:Binary . . . 20.00
172 PS,BWi,V:Viper,Silver
  Samurai. 18.00
173 PS,BWi,V:Viper,Silver
  Samurai. 12.00
174 PS,BWi,A:Mastermind 12.00
175 PS,JR2,BWi,W:Cyclops and
  Madelyne,V:Mastermind 18.00
176 JR2,BWi,I:Val Cooper 12.00
177 JR2,JR,V:Brotherhood of
  Evil Mutants 12.00
178 JR2,BWi,BBr,V:Brotherhood
  of Evil Mutants 12.00
179 JR2,DGr,V:Morlocks. 12.00
180 JR2,DGr,BWi,Secret Wars . . . 12.00
181 JR2,DGr,A:Sunfire 12.00
182 JR2,DGr,V:S.H.I.E.L.D. 12.00
183 JR2,DGr,V:Juggernaut 12.00
184 JR2,DGr,V:Selene,I:Forge . . . 15.00
185 JR2,DGr,V:Shield,U.S.
  Govt.,Storm loses powers. . . . 12.00
186 BWS,TA,Lifedeath,
  V:Dire Wraiths 14.00
187 JR2,DGr,V:Dire Wraiths 12.00
188 JR2,DGr,V:Dire Wraiths 12.00

189 JR2,SL,V:Selene,A:Magma . . 12.00
190 JR2,DGr,V:Kulan Gath,A:SpM,
  Avengers,New Mutants. 12.00
191 JR2,DGr,A:Avengers,Spider-Man,
  New Mutants,I:Nimrod 12.00
192 JR2,DGr,V:Magus 12.00
193 JR2,DGr,V:Hellions,I:Firestar
  Warpath,20th Anniv. 20.00
194 JR2,DGr,SL,V:Nimrod 12.00
195 BSz(c),JR2,DGr,A:Power
  Pack,V:Morlocks. 12.00
196 JR2,DGr,J:Magneto 15.00
197 JR2,DGr,V:Arcade 12.00
198 BWS,F:Storm,'Lifedeath II' . . . 12.00
199 JR2,DGr,I:Freedom Force,
  Rachel becomes 2nd Phoenix 12.00
200 JR2,DGr,A:Magneto,I:Fenris. . 15.00
201 RL,WPo(i),I:Nathan
  Christopher (Cyclops son) . . . 20.00
202 JR2,AW,Secret Wars II. 12.00
203 JR2,AW,Secret Wars II. 12.00
204 JBr,WPo,V:Arcade 12.00
205 BWS,A:Lady Deathstrike 17.00
206 JR2,DGr,V:Freedom Force. . . 12.00
207 JR2,DGr,V:Selene 12.00
208 JR2,DGr,V:Nimrod,
  A:Hellfire Club 12.00
209 JR2,CR,V:Nimrod,A:Spiral . . . 12.00
210 JR2,DGr,I:Marauders,
  (Mutant Massacre) 25.00
211 JR2,BBI,AW,V:Marauders,
  (Mutant Massacre) 25.00
212 RL,DGr,V:Sabretooth,
  (Mutant Massacre) 30.00
213 AD,V:Sabretooth (Mut.Mass) . 30.00
214 BWS,BWi,V:Malice,A:Dazzler. 12.00
215 AD,DGr,I:Stonewall,Super
  Sabre,Crimson Commando. . . 12.00
216 BWS(c),JG,DGr,V:Stonewall . 12.00
217 WS(c),JG,SL,V:Juggernaut . . 12.00
218 AAD(c),MS,DGr,V:Juggernaut 12.00
219 BBI,DGr,V:Marauders,Polaris
  becomes Malice,A:Sabertooth 12.00
220 MS,DGr,A:Naze 12.00
221 MS,DGr,I:Mr.Sinister,
  V:Maruaders. 20.00
222 MS,DGr,V:Marauders,Eye
  Killers,A:Sabertooth 18.00
223 KGa,DGr,A:Freedom Force . . 12.00
224 MS,DGr,V:Adversary 12.00
225 MS,DGr,Fall of Mutants
  I:1st US App Roma. 15.00
226 MS,DGr,Fall of Mutants 15.00
227 MS,DGr,Fall of Mutants 15.00
228 RL,TA,A:OZ Chase 12.00
229 MS,DGr,I:Reavers,Gateway . . 12.00
230 RL,DGr,Xmas Issue 12.00
231 RL,DGr,V:Limbo. 12.00
232 MS,DGr,V:Brood. 12.00
233 MS,DGr,V:Brood 12.00
234 MS,JRu,V:Brood 12.00
235 RL,CR,V:Magistrates 12.00
236 MS,DGr,V:Magistrates 12.00
237 RL,TA,V:Magistrates 12.00
238 MS,DGr,V:Magistrates 12.00
239 MS,DGr,Inferno,A:Mr.Sinister . 12.00
240 MS,DGr,Inferno,V:Marauders . 12.00
241 MS,DGr,Inferno,O:Madeline
  Pryor,V:Marauders 12.00
242 MS,DGr,Inferno,D:N'Astirh,
  A:X-Factor,Double-sized 12.00
243 MS,Inferno,A:X-Factor. 12.00
244 MS,DGr,I:Jubilee 22.00
245 RLd,DGr,Invasion Parody. . . . 10.00
246 MS,DGr,V:Mastermold,
  A:Nimrod 10.00
247 MS,DGr,V:Mastermold 10.00
248 JLe(1st X-Men Art),DGr,
  V:Nanny & Orphan Maker. . . . 30.00
248a 2nd printing 3.00
249 MS,DGr,C:Zaladane,

  V:Savage Land Mutates. 8.00
250 MS,SL,I:Zaladane. 8.00
251 MS,DGr,V:Reavers 8.00
252 JLe,BSz(c),RL,SW,V:Reavers . 8.00
253 MS,SL,V:Amahl Farouk 8.00
254 JLe(c),MS,DGr,V:Reavers . . . 8.00
255 MS,DGr,V:Reavers,D:Destiny. . 8.00
256 JLe,SW,Acts of Vengeance,
  V:Manderin,A:Psylocke 15.00
257 JLe,JRu,AofV,V:Manderin. . . . 15.00
258 JLe,SW,AofV,V:Manderin . . . 15.00
259 MS,DGr,V:Magistrates, ... 8.00
260 JLe(c),MS,DGr,A:Dazzler 8.00
261 JLe(c),MS,DGr,V:Hardcase &
  Harriers 8.00
262 KD,JRu,V:Masque,Morlocks . . 8.00
263 JRu(i),O:Forge,V:Morlocks . . . 8.00
264 JLe(c),MC,JRu,V:Magistrate. . . 8.00
265 JRu(i),V:Shadowking 8.00
266 NKu(c),MC,JRu,I:Gambit 50.00
267 JLe,WPo,SW,V:Shadowking. . 25.00
268 JLe,SW,A:Captain America,
  Black Widow,V:The Hand,
  Baron Strucker 25.00
269 JLe,ATi,Rogue V:Ms.Marvel . . 10.00
270 JLe,ATi,SW,X-Tinction Agenda
  #1, A:Cable,New Mutants 12.00
270a 2nd printing(Gold) 4.00
271 JLe,SW,X-Tinction Agenda
  #4,A:Cable,New Mutants 10.00
272 JLe,SW,X-Tinction Agenda
  #7,A:Cable,New Mutants 10.00
273 JLe,WPo,JBy,KJ,RL,MS,MGo,
  LSn,SW,A:Cable,N.Mutants . . 10.00
274 JLe,SW,V:Zaladane,A:Magneto,
  Nick Fury,Ka-Zar 10.00
275 JLe,SW,R:Professor X,A:Star
  Jammers,Imperial Guard 8.00
275a 2nd Printing (Gold) 3.00
276 JLe,SW,V:Skrulls,Shi'ar 10.00
277 JLe,SW,V:Skrulls,Shi'ar 10.00
278 PS,Professor X Returns to
  Earth,V:Shadowking 7.00
279 NKu,SW,V:Shadowking 7.00
280 E:CCl(s),NKu,A:X-Factor,
  D:Shadowking,Prof.X Crippled . 7.00
281 WPo,ATi,new team (From X-Men
  #1),D:Pierce,Hellions,V:Sentinels,
  I:Trevor Fitzroy,Upstarts 7.00
281a 2nd printing,red(c) 3.00
282 WPo,ATi,V:Fitzroy,C:Bishop . . 15.00
282a 2nd printing,gold(c) of #281
  inside 3.00
283 WPo,ATi,I:Bishop,Malcolm,

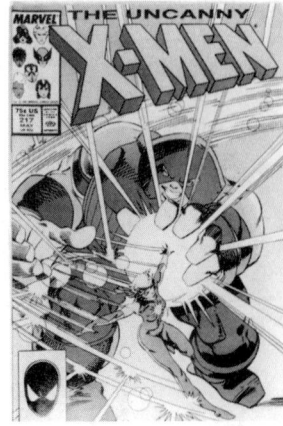

Uncanny X-Men #217
© Marvel Entertainment Group

CVA Page 350   All comics prices listed are for *Near Mint* condition.

Comics Values Annual — MARVEL — X-Men (Uncanny)

Randall. 15.00
284 WPo,ATi,SOS from USSR. 5.00
285 WPo,I:Mikhail(Colossus'
  brother from Russia) 5.00
286 JLe,WPo,ATi,A:Mikhail. 5.00
287 JR2,O:Bishop,
  D:Malcolm,Randall 5.00
288 NKu,BSz,A:Bishop. 5.00
289 WPo,ATi,Forge proposes
  to Storm. 5.00
290 WPo,SW,V:Cyberpunks,
  L:Forge 5.00
291 TR,V:Morlocks. 5.00
292 TR,V:Morlocks. 5.00
293 TR,D:Morlocks,Mikhail. 5.00
294 BP,TA,X-Cutioner's Song#1,
  Stryfe shoots Prof X,A:X-Force,
  X-Factor,polybag.w/ProfX card . 5.00
295 BP,TA,X-Cutioners Song #5,
  V:Apocalypse 5.00
296 BP,TA,X-Cutioners Song #9,
  A:X-Force,X-Factor,V:Stryfe . . . 5.00
297 BP,X-Cutioners Song
  Aftermath 5.00
298 BP,TA,V:Acolytes 5.00
299 BP,A:Forge,Acolytes,I:Graydon
  Creed (Sabretooth's son) 5.00
300 JR2,DGr,BP,V:Acolytes,A:Forge,
  Nightcrawler,Holografx(c) 10.00
301 JR2,DGr,I:Sienna Blaze,
  V:Fitzroy. 5.00
302 JR2,V:Fitzroy. 5.00
303 JR2,V:Upstarts,D:Illyana 6.00
304 JR2,JaL,PS,L:Colossus,
  V:Magneto,Holo-grafx(c) 8.00
305 JD,F:Rogue,Bishop 5.00
306 JR2,V:Hodge 5.00
307 JR2,Bloodties#4,A:Avengers,
  V:Exodus,Cortez 6.00
308 JR2,Scott & Jean announce
  impending marriage 5.00
309 JR2,O:Professor X & Amelia . . 5.00
310 JR2,DG,A:Cable,V:X-Cutioner,
  w/card 5.00
311 JR2,DG,AV,V:Sabretooth,
  C:Phalanx 5.00
312 JMd,DG,A:Yukio,I:Phalanx,
  w/card 5.00
313 JMd,DG,V:Phalanx 5.00
314 LW,BSz,R:White Queen. 5.00
315 F:Acolytes 5.00
316 V:Phalanx,I:M,Phalanx Covenant
  Generation Next,pt.1, holo(c) . . 5.00

Uncanny X-Men #296
© Marvel Entertainment Group

316a newsstand ed. 3.00
317 JMd,V:Phalanx,prism(c). 5.00
317a newsstand ed. 3.00
318 JMd,L:Jubilee, deluxe 5.00
318a newsstand ed. 3.00
319 R:Legion, deluxe 5.00
319a newsstand ed. 3.00
320 deluxe ed. 5.00
320 newsstand ed. 3.00
321 R:Lilandra, deluxe ed. 5.00
321 newsstand ed. 3.00
322 SLo,TGu,Rogue,Iceman run from
  Gambit's Secret 8.00
323 I:Onslaught 5.00
324 SLo,F:Cannonball 5.00
325 R:Colossus 7.00
326 SLo,JMd,F:Gambit,Sabretooth . 4.00
327 SLo,JMd,Magneto's Fate 4.00
328 SLo,JMd,Sabretooth freed 4.00
329 SLo,JMd,A:Doctor Strange. . . . 4.00
330 Dr.Strange 4.00
331 White Queen 4.00
332 SLo,JMd, cont from
  Wolverine #100 . . . . 4.00
333 SLo,JMd, Operation: Zero
  Tolerance, Onslaught saga . . . 4.00
334 SLo,JMd, Onslaught saga 4.00
335 SLo,JMd, Onslaught saga 4.00
336 Apocalypse vs. Onslaught 4.00
337 Operation: Zero Tolerance 4.00
338 SLo,JMd,R:Angel. 4.00
339 SLo,JMd,F:Cyclops, J.J.
  Jameson, Havok 4.00
340 SLo,JMd,F:Iceman. 4.00
341 SLo,JMd,Rogue gets gift 4.00
342 SLo,JMd, Shi'ar Empire, pt.1 . . 5.00
342a Rogue cover 15.00
343 SLo,JMd, Shi'ar Empire, pt.2 . . 4.00
344 SLo,JMd, Shi'ar Empire, pt.3 . . 4.00
345 SLo,JMd, trip home, A:Akron . . 5.00
346 SLo,JMd,Zero Tolerance,
  A:Spider-Man. 4.00
347 SLo,JMd,Zero Tolerance 4.00
348 SLo,JMd,at Magneto's base . . . 4.00
349 SLo,JMd,Maggot vs. Psylocke
  & Archangel 4.00
350 SSe,JMd,Trial of Gambit,
  double-sized. 4.00
350a Gambit (c) 10.00
351 SSe,JMd,Dr. Cecilia Reyes . . . 3.00
352 SSe,EBe,Cyclops & Phoenix
  leave, Facade arrives 3.00
353 SSe,CBa,Rogues Anguish 3.00
354 SSe,CBa,F:Rogue 3.00
354a Jean Gray (c). 6.00
355 SSe,CBa, North & South
  pt.2 x-over 5.00
356 SSe,CBa, originals V:Phoenix . 3.00
357 SSe,Cyclops & Phoenix. 3.00
358 SSe,CBa,Phoenix collapses. . . 3.00
359 SSe,CBa, Rogue 3.00
360A SSe,CBa, I:New X-Men, foil
  etched cover 5.00
360B regular cover 4.00
361 SSe,SSr,R:Gambit 3.00
362 SSe,CBa,Hunt for Xavier,pt.1 . . 3.00
363 SSe,CBa,Hunt for Xavier,pt.3 . . 3.00
364 SSe,Hunt for Xavier,pt.5 . . . . . 3.00
365 SSe,CBa,A:Professor X 3.00
366 AD,BPe,Magneto War,pt.1 . . . . 3.00
367 AD,Magneto War,pt.3 . . . . 3.00
368 AD,AKu,Requiem for an X-Man 3.00
368a signed 20.00
369 AD,AKu,V:Juggernaut 3.00
370 AD,AKu,in the past. 3.00
371 AD,AKu(c),Rage Against
  the Machine, pt.1 x-over. 3.00
371a signed 20.00
372 AKu,AD,The Shattering,pt.1 . . . 3.00
373 AKu,AD,The Shattering,pt.2 . . . 3.00
374 AKu,AD,The Shattering 3.00

Uncanny X-Men #374
© Marvel Entertainment Group

375 AKu,AD,48-pg. 5.00
376 AKu,AD 3.00
377 AKu,AD,Apocalypse12,pt.5 . . . 3.00
378 AKu,AD,TTn,Ages of
  Apocalypse,pt.1,x-over 3.00
379 AKu,AD,TTn,mutants no more . 3.00
380 AD,TR,poly-bagged w/Genesis. 4.00
381 CCl,AKu,TTn,X-Men:
  Revolution 10.00
381a foil (c) 15.00
382 CCl,TTn,Shockwave Riders . . . 3.00
383 CCl,AKu,TTn,48-pg. 3.50
384 CCl,AKu,TTn,I:Killion 3.00
385 CCl,TR,Red Pirates 3.00
386 CCl,TR,Phoenix 3.00
387 CCl,TTn,Maximum Security . . . 3.00
388 CCl,SvL,Dream's End,pt.1 . . . . 4.00
389 CCl,SvL,F:Cecilia Reyes 3.00
390 CCl,SvL,Legacy Virus,
  D:Colossus. 7.00
391 SLo,SvL,return. 3.00
392 SLo,SvL,Eve of Destruction . . . 3.00
393 SLo,SvL,Eve of Destruction . . . 5.00
394 JoC,IaC,F:Warp Savant 5.00
395A JoC,IaC,Poptopia,pt.1 . . . . . . 3.00
395B variant BWS(c) 5.00
396 JoC,IaC,Poptopia,pt.2 . . . . 3.00
397 JoC,IaC,Poptopia,pt.3 . . . . 3.00
398 JoC,IaC,Poptopia,pt.4 . . . . 3.00
399 JoC,SHa,X-Ranch 3.00
400 F:XStacy,48-page 4.00
401 JoC,RG,F:Banshee,'Nuff Said . 3.50
402 JoC,RG,vs.X-Corp. 2.50
403 JoC,AaL,DaM,X-Corp's secret . 2.50
404 JoC,RG,V:Multiple Men 2.50
405 JoC,SeP,V:Banshee. 2.50
406 JoC,AaL,X-Corps,concl. 2.50
407 JoC,SeP,Nightcrawler 2.50
408 JoC,SeP,V:Vanisher. 2.50
409 JoC,SeP,V:Vanisher. 2.50
410 RG,Hope 2.50
411 RG,Hope,pt.2. . . . . 2.50
412 RG,Hope,pt.3. . . . . 2.50
413 RG,Annie's Moving 2.50
414 Northstar Joins team 2.50
415 SeP,F:Nightcrawler 2.50
416 KiA,F:Juggernaut. 4.00
417 KiA,Dominant Species 3.00
418 KiA,Dominant Species 3.00
419 KiA,Archangel and Husk 2.25
420 KiA,Dominant Species,concl. . . 2.25
421 RG,V:Alpha Flight,pt.1 . . . . 2.25
422 RG,V:Alpha Flight,pt.2,48-pg. . . 3.50

All comics prices listed are for *Near Mint* condition.

CVA Page 351

X-Men (Uncanny)–X-Men — MARVEL — Comics Values Annual

423 RG,Holy War,pt.1 . . . . 0.25
424 RG,Holy War,pt.2 . . . . 2.25
425 Sacred Vows,pt.1 . . . . 2.25
426 Sacred Vows,pt.2 . . . . 2.25
427 F:Jubilee, Angel, Husk 2.25
428 O:Nightcrawler,F:Mystique 2.25
429 Draco,pt.1 . . . . 2.25
430 Draco,pt.2 . . . . 2.25
431 Draco,pt.3 . . . . 2.25
432 Draco,pt.4 . . . . 2.25
433 Draco,pt.5 . . . . 2.25
434 Draco,pt.6 . . . . 2.25
Ann.#1 rep.#9,#11 . . . . 200.00
Ann.#2 rep.#22,#23 . . . . 100.00
Ann.#3 GK(c),GP,TA,A:Arkon . . . 40.00
Ann.#4 JR2,BMc,A:Dr.Strange . . . 25.00
Ann.#5 BA,BMc,A:F.F. 20.00
Ann.#6 BSz,BWi,Dracula 20.00
Ann.#7 MGo,TMd,BWi,TA,BBr,
   BA,JRu,BBl,SL,AM,
   V:Impossible Man 15.00
Ann.#8 SL,Kitty's story 15.00
Ann.#9 AAd,AG,MMi,Asgard,V:Loki,
   Enchantress,A:New Mutants . . 20.00
Ann.#10 AAd,TA,V:Mojo,
   J:Longshot,A:New Mutants . . . 18.00
Ann.#11 AD,V:Horde,A:CaptBrit . . 7.00
Ann.#12 AAd,BWi,RLm,TD,Evol.
   War,V:Terminus,Savage Land . . 7.00
Ann.#13 MBa,JRu,Atlantis Attacks . 6.00
Ann.#14 AAd,DGr,BWi,AM,ATi,
   V:Ahab,A:X-Factor. 10.00
Ann.#15,TR,JRu,MMi(c),Flesh Tears,
   Pt.3,A:X-Force,New Warriors . . 6.00
Ann.#16 JaL,JRu,Shattershot
   Part.2. . . . . 5.00
Ann.#17 JPe,MFm,I:X-Cutioner,
   D:Mastermind,w/card 5.00
Ann.#18 JR2,V:Caliban,
   BU:Bishop 4.00
Ann.1999 AD 3.50
Ann.2000 SLo,F:Professor X 3.50
Ann.2001 JoC,48-pg. 3.50
Marvel Milestone rep. #1 (1991) . . 2.95
Marvel Milestone rep. #9 (1993) . . 2.95
Marvel Milestone rep. #28 (1994) . . 2.95
G-Size #1,GK,DC,I:New X-Men
   (Colossus,Storm,Nightcrawler,
   Thunderbird,3rd A:Wolv.) . . 1,000.00
G-Size #2,rep.#57-59 . . . . 100.00
Marvel Milestone rep. Giant
   Size #1 (1991) 4.00
Spec.#1 X-Men: Earth Fall,
   rep. #232–#234 (1996) 3.00
Spec.#1 X-Men vs. Dracula, rep.
   X-Men Ann.#6 (1993) 2.00
GN X-Men: Days of Future Past
   rep. X-Men #141-142 . . . . 5.00
GN Pryde of the X-Men. 11.00
GN God Loves,Man Kills,
   (1994) prestige 7.00
GN X-Men Firsts,I:Wolverine,Rogue,
   Gambit & Mr. Sinister, rep. Avengers
   Ann.#10, Uncanny X-Men
   #221/#266
   & Incredible Hulk #181 (1996) . 5.00
GN X-Men Rarities,F:Classic
   Stories (1995) 5.95
TPB Asgardian Wars 15.95
TPB Bloodties V:Exodus 15.95
TPB The Coming of Bishop, rep.
   #282–#285,#287–#288 (1995) 12.95
TPB Dark Phoenix Saga 12.95
TPB Dark Phoenix, 192-pg.(2001) 19.95
TPB X-Men: Days of Future Present,
   MMi(c),Rep.F.F.Ann.#23,X-Men
   Ann.#14,X-Factor Ann.#5,
   New Mutant Ann.#10 . . . . . . 14.95
TPB Fall of the Mutants, 272-pg.. . 24.95
TPB Fatal Attractions (1994). . . . 17.95
TPB From the Ashes 16.95
TPB Greatest Battles 15.95
TPB X-Men: Poptopia (2001) 16.95
TPB X-Men: Inferno, 352-pg. 19.95
TPB X-Men Megazine, CCl,JLe, rep.
   Uncanny X-Men #273–#275 . . . 3.95
TPB X-Men: Mutant Massacre,
   rep. 256-pg. 24.95
TPB Savage Land 9.95
TPB X-Cutioner's Song. 24.95
TPB X-Tinction Agenda, rep.X-Men
   #270-272,X-Factor #60-62,
   New Mutants #95-97 . . . . 19.95
X-Men Survival Guide to the
   Mansion, NKu(c) (1993) 6.95
TPB Vol. 1: Hope 13.00
TPB Vol. 2: Dominant Species . . 12.00
TPB Vol. 3: Holy War 18.00

X-MEN
[2nd Regular Series] Oct., 1991

1A(c);Storm,Beast,B:CCl(s),JLe,SW
   I:Fabian Cortez,Acolytes,
   V:Magneto 4.00
1B(c);Colossus,Psylocke 5.00
1C(c);Cyclops,Wolverine 5.00
1D(c);Magneto. 5.00
1E(c);Gatefold w/ pin-ups 7.00
2 JLe,SW,V:Magneto Contd. 6.00
3 E:CCl(s),JLe,SW,V:Magneto . . . 6.00
4 JBy(s),JLe,SW,I:Omega Red,
   V:Hand. 5.00
5 B:SLo(s),JLe,SW,V:Hand,
   Omega Red,I:Maverick 5.00
6 JLe,SW,V:Omega Red, Hand,
   Sabretooth 5.00
7 JLe,SW,V:Omega Red,Hand,
   Sabretooth 5.00
8 JLe,SW,Bishop vs. Gambit 4.00
9 JLe,SW,A:Ghost Rider,V:Brood . 4.00
10 JLe,SW,MT,Longshot Vs. Mojo,
   BU:Maverick. 4.00
11 E:SLo(s)JLe,MT,V:Mojo,
   BU:Maverick. 3.00
12 B:FaN(s),ATb,BWi,I:Hazard . . . 3.00
13 ATb,BWi,V:Hazard 3.00
14 NKu,X-Cutioners Song#3,A:X-Fact.
   X-Force,V:Four Horsemen 3.00
15 NKu,X-Cutioners Song #7,
   V:Mutant Liberation Front 3.00
16 NKu,MPn,X-Cutioners Song #11,
   A:X-Force,X-Factor,V:Dark Riders,
   Apocalypse Vs.Archangel,IR:Stryfe
   is Nathan Summers 3.00
17 NKu,MPn,R:Illyana,A:Darkstar . . 3.00
18 NKu,MPn,R:Omega Red,V:Soul
   Skinner 3.00
19 NKu,MPn,V:Soul Skinner,
   Omega Red 3.00
20 NKu,MPn,J.Grey vs Psylocke . . 3.00
21 NKu,V:Silver Samurai,Shinobi . . 3.00
22 BPe,V:Silver Samurai,Shinobi . . 3.00
23 NKu,MPn,V:Dark Riders,
   Mr.Sinister 3.00
24 NKu,BSz,A Day in the Life 3.00
25 NKu,Hologram(c),V:Magneto,
   Wolverine's Adamantium skeleton
   pulled out 15.00
25a Gold Edition. 38.00
25b B&W cover 30.00
26 NKu,Bloodties#2,A:Avengers,
   I:Unforgiven 3.00
27 RiB,I:Threnody. 3.00
28 NKu,MRy,F:Sabretooth 3.00
29 NKu,MRy,V:Shinobi 3.00
30 NKu,MRy,W:Cyclops&Jean Grey,
   w/card 5.00
31 NKu,MRy,A:Spiral,Matsuo,
   D:Kwannon 3.00
32 NKu,MRy,A:Spiral,Matsuo 3.00
33 NKu,MRy,F:Gambit &
Sabretooth 3.00
34 NKu,MRy,A:Riptide 3.00
35 LSh,A:Nick Fury. 3.00
36 NKu,MRy,I:Synch,PhalanxCovenant
   Generation Next,pt.2, deluxe . . 5.00
36a Newsstand ed. 2.25
37 NKu,MRy,Generation Next,pt.3
   foil(c) 5.00
37a newsstand ed. 2.50
38 NKu,MRy,F:Psylocke 3.00
38a newsstand ed. 2.50
39 X-Treme, deluxe 3.00
39a newsstand ed. 2.50
40 deluxe 3.00
40a newsstand ed. 2.50
41 V:Legion, deluxe 3.50
41a newsstand ed. 2.50
42 PS,PaN,Mysterious Visitor 3.00
43 Rogue and Iceman 3.00
44 FaN,Mystery of Magneto 3.00
45 20th Anniv.pt.2 . . . . 5.00
46 FaN,Aku,V:Comcast 3.00
47 SLo,AKu,CaS,F:Dazzler 3.00
48 SLo,AKu,CaS,F:Sabretooth . . . 3.00
49 SLo,AKu,Bishop wanted 3.00
50 Onslaught(c) 6.00
50a regular edition 5.00
51 MWa,Onslaught. 3.00

X-Men 2nd Series #30
© Marvel Entertainment Group

52 MWa,AKu,CaS,V:Sinister 3.00
53 Onslaught saga 6.00
54 Onslaught saga 5.00
54a Foil cover. 22.00
55 Onslaught saga 3.00
56 Onslaught saga 3.00
57 Operation: Zero Tolerance 3.00
58 SLo,NKu 3.00
59 . . . . 3.00
60 SLo,NKu,F:Ororo, V:Candra . . . 3.00
61 SLo,CNn,F:Storm, V:Candra . . 3.00
62 SLo,CPa,F:Sebastian Shaw,
   Shang Chi 3.00
62A variant Storm/Wolverine(c) . . 13.00
63 SLo,CPa,ATi,A:Sebastian Shaw,
   Inner Circle 3.00
64 SLo,CPa,ATi,V:Hellfire Club . . . 3.00
65 SLo,CPa,ATi, No Exit prelude . . 3.00
66 SLo,CPa,ATi, Zero Tolerance,
   A:Bastion 3.00
67 SLo,CPa,ATi, Zero Tolerance,
   F:Iceman, Cecilia Reyes 3.00
68 SLo,CPa,ATi, Operation: Zero
   Tolerance 3.00

MARVEL

X-Men–X-Men Adv.

X-Men 2nd Series #78
© *Marvel Entertainment Group*

69 SLo,CPa, Operation: Zero Tolerance, concl. 3.00
70 ATi,Who will join X-Men?, double-sized. 5.00
71 ATi,Cyclops banished. 4.00
72 ATi,Professor Logan's School of Hard Knocks 3.00
73 ATi,Marrow visits Callisto 3.00
74 ATi, Terror in Morlock Tunnels . . 3.00
75 ATi,V'N'Garai, double size 3.00
76 CCI,V:Sabretooth, 35th anniv kickoff 3.00
77 ATi,A:Black Panther,Maggott . . . 3.00
78 Return of Professor X 3.00
79 ATi,Cannonball must leave team 3.00
80A BPe, ATi, cont. from Uncanny X-Men #360, etched foil (c). . . . 7.50
80B regular cover. 4.00
81 AKu,MFm,Search for Prof.X . . . 3.00
82 AKu,MFm,Hunt for Xavier 3.00
83 AKu,MFm,Hunt for Xavier,pt.4 . . 3.00
84 AJu,Hunt for Xavier,concl. 3.50
85 AD,MFm,R:Magneto 3.00
85a signed 30.00
86 AD,MFm,Magneto War,pt.2, O:Joseph 3.00
87 AD,MFm,Magneto War,pt.4 . . . . 3.00
88 AD,MFm,R:Juggernaut. 3.00
89 AD,MFm,In the past. 3.00
90 AD,MFm,In the past,concl. 3.00
91 AD,AKu,Rage Against the Machine, pt.2 x-over 3.00
91a signed 30.00
92 AD,MFm,The Shattering x-over . 3.00
93 AD,MFm,The Shattering x-over . 3.00
94 AD,MFm,Shattering,x-over 4.00
95 AD,TR,A:Death, ... 3.00
96 AD. 3.00
97 AD,MFm,Apocalypse12,pt.7 . . . 3.00
97a variant (c) 4.00
98 AD,MFm,Ages of Apocalypse,pt.5 . . . . 3.00
99 AD,BBh,mutants no more?. 3.00
100 CCI,X-Men:Revolution,48-pg. . . 4.00
100a variant covers 6.00
101 CCI,X-Men:Revolution 3.00
102 CCI,R:Wolverine 3.00
103 CCI,Wolverine v. Rogue. 3.00
104 CCI,V:Killion. 3.00
105 CCI,Archangel,Psylocke. 3.00
106 CCI,Neo,Cecelia Reyes 3.50
107 CCI,Cadre K 3.00
108 CCI,Dream'sEnd,pt.4,x-over. . . 5.00

109 CCI,at X-Mansion, 100-page . . 4.00
110 SLo,F:Kitty Pryde. 4.00
111 SLo,F:Trish Tilby 3.00
112 SLo,Eve of Destruction,pt.2 . . 2.50
113 SLo,Eve of Destruction,pt.4 . . . 2.50
Becomes:

NEW X-MEN

114 GMo,E is for Extinction,pt.1 . . . 8.00
115A GMo,E for Extinction,pt.2 . . . . 6.00
115B variant BWS(c) 4.00
116 GMo,E for Extinction,pt.3 . . . . . 3.50
117 GMo,F:Beast 3.50
118 GMo,GermFreeGeneration,pt.1 3.50
119 GMo,Germ Free Gen.,pt.2 . . . . 3.50
120 GMo,Germ Free Gen.,concl. . . 3.50
121 GMo,Xavier's mind,'Nuff Said. . 3.00
122 GMo,Imperial,pt.1 . . . . 3.00
123 GMo,Imperial,pt.2 . . . . 2.50
124 GMo,Imperial,pt.3 . . . . 2.50
125 GMo,Imperial,pt.4 . . . . 2.50
126 GMo,Imperial,pt.5 . . . . 3.50
127 GMo,F:Xorn. 3.00
128 GMo,Jean Grey, Emma Frost. . 3.00
129 GMo,Weapon XII 2.50
130 GMo 2.50
131 GMo,JPL,BSz 2.50
132 GMo,PJ,F:Storm 2.25
133 . . . . 2.25
134 GMo,NRd,no Magneto 2.25
135 GMo,Riot At Xavier's 2.25
136 GMo,Riot At Xavier's 2.25
137 GMo,Riot At Xavier's 2.25
138 GMo,Riot At Xavier's,concl. . . . 2.25
139 GMo,PJ,Murder at Mansion . . 2.25
140 GMo,PJ,Murder at Mansion . . 2.25
141 GMo,PJ,Murder at Mansion . . 2.25
142 GMo,CBa,Weapon Plus,pt.1 . . 2.25
143 GMo,CBa,Weapon Plus,pt.2 . . 2.25
144 GMo,CBa,Weapon Plus,pt.3 . . 2.25
145 GMo,CBa,Weapon Plus,pt.4 . . 2.25
146 PJ,Planet X,pt.1. . . . . 2.25
147 PJ,Planet X,pt.2. . . . . 2.25
148 PJ,Planet X,pt.3. . . . . 2.25
149 PJ,Planet X,pt.4. . . . . 2.25
Ann.#1 JLe,Shattershot,pt.1, I:Mojo II 4.00
Ann.#2 I:Empyrean,w/card 4.00
Ann.#3 F:Storm 4.00
Ann. Uncanny X-Men '97, V:Brotherhood, 48-pg. 3.50
Ann. '98 RMz, F:X-Men & Doctor Doom. 3.50
Ann. '98 X-Men/Fantastic Four, JoC, PaP, 48-pg. 3.50
Ann.1999 Rage Against the Machine, pt.3 x-over, 48-pg. . . . 3.50
Ann.2000 CCI,SHa,SEa,48-pg. . . . 4.00
Ann. 2001 GMo,Marvelscope 7.50
Uncanny X-Men'95 Spec. F:Husk . . 4.00
Spec.X-Men'95, F:Mr.Sinister 3.00
Spec.X-Men'96 LHa, 64-pg., F:Gambit, Rogue, Magneto, Jubilee & Wolverine 4.00
Spec. X-Men'97,JFM,SEp,F:Gambit, Joesph & Phoenix 3.00
Minus 1 Spec., SLo,JMd,, flashback, discovery of mutants 2.00
Spec.#1 X-Men: Road to Onslaught (1996) 2.50
Spec. X-Men Universe: Past, Present and Future. 3.00
Spec. X-Men:Year in Review 3.00
Spec.#1 X-Men (2000) 3.50
Spec. Millennial Visions 4.00
Spec.2001, Millennial Vision 48-page 3.50
Spec. X-Men:Declassified,48-pg . . 3.50
Spec. Unearthed Archives Sketchbook 3.00
Spec. X-Men/Sentry, PJe,MT . . . 3.00
Spec. God Loves, Man Kills 5.00

Spec. rep. Must Have #114–#116 . . 4.00
Chrom.Classics, Vol.2,#1,signed. . 30.00
GN TKa,AD,MFm, Age of Apocalypse 2.95
TPB Dark Phoenix Saga. 15.95
TPB Dawn of the Age of Apocalypse, gold foil cover. . . . 8.95
TPB Twilight of the Age of Apocalypse, gold foil cover. . . . 8.95
TPB Legion Quest 8.95
TPB Magneto Returns 15.95
TPB Rise of Apocalypse 9.00
TPB Crossroads 15.95
TPB Phoenix Rising 14.95
TPB Road Trippin 20.00
TPB Zero Tolerance, 336-pg. 24.95
TPB The Origin of Generation X . . 24.95
TPB X-Men: Vignettes 16.95
TPB Visionaries Joe Madureira. . . 17.95
TPB Visionaries Neal Adams 24.95
TPB Jim Lee, 288-pg. (2002) 23.00
TPB Jim Lee (2002) 30.00
TPB Mutant Genesis (2002) 17.95
TPB Vol. 2, Imperial (2002). 20.00
TPB X-Men/Spider-Man: The Savage Land, rep. #1–#4, 80-pg. 9.95
TPB Vol. 3: New Worlds 15.00
TPB Vol. 4: Riot at Xaviers 12.00
TPB Vol. 5: Weapon Plus 15.00
TPB Evolution Vol. 2. . . . . 12.00
TPB X-Men Legends,Vol.1 . . . . . 17.95
TPB X-Men Legends,Vol.2 . . . . . 20.00
TPB X-Men Legends,Vol.3 . . . . . 25.00

X-MEN ADVENTURES
[1st Season] 1992–94

1 V:Sentinals, Based on TV Cartoon 6.00
2 V:Sentinals,D:Morph. 5.00
3 V:Magneto,A:Sabretooth. 4.00
4 V:Magneto 4.00
5 V:Morlocks 4.00
6 V:Sabretooth 3.50
7 V:Cable,Genosha,Sentinels 3.00
8 A:Colossus,A:Juggernaut 3.00
9 I:Colussus(on cartoon), V:Juggernaut 3.00
10 A:Angel,V:Mystique 3.00
11 I:Archangel(on cartoon) 2.50
12 V:Horsemen of Apocalypse . . . 2.50
13 RMc(s),I:Bishop(on cartoon) . . . 2.50
14 V:Brotherhood of Evil Mutants . . 2.50
15 . . . . 2.50

X-Men Adventures 1st Season, #12
© *Marvel Entertainment Group*

All comics prices listed are for *Near Mint* condition.

CVA Page 353

X-Men: Adv.–Classics

TPB Vol.1	4.95
TPB Vol.2	4.95
TPB Vol.3	5.95
TPB Vol.4 rep. Days of Future Past and Final Conflict	6.95

[2nd Season] 1994–95

1 R:Morph,I:Mr. Sinister (on cartoon)	3.00
2 I:Nasty Boys (on cartoon)	2.50
3 I:Shadow King (on cartoon)	2.50
4 I:Omega Red (on cartoon)	2.50
5 I:Alpha Flight (on cartoon)	2.50
6 F:Gambit	2.50
7 A:Cable,Bishop,Apocalypse	2.50
8 A:Cable,Biship,Apocalypse	2.50
9 O:Rogue	2.50
10	2.50
11 F:Mojo,Longshot	2.50
12 Reunions,pt.1	2.50
13 Reunions,pt.1	2.50

[3rd Season] 1995–96

1 Out of the Past,pt.1	3.00
2 V:Spirit Drinker	2.50
3 Phoenix Saga,pt.1	2.50
4 Phoenix Saga,pt.2	2.50
5 Phoenix Saga,pt.3	2.50
6 Phoenix Saga,pt.4	2.50
7 Phoenix Saga,pt.5	2.50
8 War in The Savage Land	2.50
9 F:Ka-Zar	2.50
10 Dark Phoenix,Saga,pt.1	2.50
11 Dark Phoenix Saga,pt.2	2.50
12 Dark Phoenix Saga,pt.3	2.50
13 Dark Phoenix Saga,pt.4	2.50

X-MEN: ALPHA
1994

1 Age of Apocalypse, double size	9.00
1a gold edition, 48pp	50.00

X-MEN/ALPHA FLIGHT
Jan., 1986

1 PS,BWi,V:Loki	5.00
2 PS,BWi,V:Loki	5.00

X-MEN/ALPHA FLIGHT: THE GIFT
Jan., 1998

1-shot CCl,PS, rep. of limited series	6.00

X-Men Archives #3
© Marvel Entertainment Group

X-MEN/ ANIMATION SPECIAL

TV Screenplay Adapt	10.95

X-MEN ARCHIVES: CAPTAIN BRITAIN
1995

1 AMo,AD,Secret History	3.00
2 AMo,AD,F:Captain Britain	3.00
3 AMo,AD,Trial of Captain Britain	3.00
4 AMo,AD,Trial cont.	3.00
5 AD,AMo,F:Captain Britain	3.00
6 AMo,AD,Final Apocalypse?	3.00
7 AMo,AD,conclusion	3.00

X-MEN: ASKANI'SON

1 SLo,GeH,sequel to Adventures of Cyclops & Phoenix	3.00
2 SLo,GeH,A:Stryfe	3.00
3 SLo,GeH	3.00
4 SLo,GeH,conclusion	3.00
Books of Askani, portraits (1995)	3.00

X-MEN AT STATE FAIR

1 KGa,Dallas Times Herald	65.00

X-MEN: BLACK SUN
Sept., 2000

1 (of 5) CCl,New X-Men	3.00
2 CCl,Storm	3.00
3 CCl,RT,Banshee & Sunfire	3.00
4 CCl,LSi,Colossus&Nightcrawler	3.00
5 CCl,Wolverine & Thunderbird	3.00

X-MEN: CHILDREN OF THE ATOM
Jan., 2000

1 (of 6) JoC,SR,O:X-Men	3.00
2 JoC,SR,F:Professor X	3.00
3 JoC,SR	3.00
4 JoC,SR	3.00
5 JoC,SR,	3.00
6 JoC,SR,concl.	3.00

X-MEN CHRONICLES
1995

1 X-Men Unlimited AX	5.00
2 V:Abbatoir	5.00

X-MEN/CLANDESTINE
1996

1 & 2 AD,MFm,48-pg.	@3.00

X-MEN CLASSICS
Dec., 1983

1 NA,rep.	7.00
2 NA,rep.	7.00
3 NA,rep.	7.00

CLASSIC X-MEN
Sept., 1986

1 AAd(c),JBo,New stories, rep. giant size X-Men 1	9.00
2 rep.#94,JBo/AAd(c),BU: Storm & Marvel Girl	6.00
3 rep.#95,JBo/AAd(c),BU: I:Thunderbird II	4.00
4 rep.#96,JBo/AAd(c),BU: Wolverine & N.Crawler	4.00
5 rep.#97,JBo/AAd(c),BU: Colossus	4.00
6 rep.#98,JBo/AAd(c),BU: JeanGrey,I:Seb.Shaw	4.00
7 rep.#99,JBo/AAd(c),BU: HellfireClub,W.Queen	4.00
8 rep.#100,JBo/AAd(c),BU: O:Jean Grey/Phoenix	4.00
9 rep.#101,JBo/AAd(c),BU: Nightcrawler	4.00
10 rep.#102,JBo/AAd(c),BU: Wolverine,A:Sabretooth	8.00
11 rep.#103,JBo/BL(c),BU:Storm	3.00
12 rep.#104,JBo/AAd(c),BU: O:Magneto	7.00
13 rep.#105,JBo/AAd(c),BU: JeanGrey & Misty Knight	3.00
14 rep.#107,JBo/AAd(c),BU: Lilandra	3.00
15 rep.#108,JBo/AAd(c),BU: O:Starjammers	3.00
16 rep.#109,JBo/AAd(c),BU: Banshee	3.00
17 rep.#111,JBo/TA(c),BU: Mesmero	5.00
18 rep.#112,JBo/AAd(c),BU: Phoenix	4.00
19 rep.#113,JBo/AAd(c),BU: Magnetoo	4.00
20 rep.#114,JBo/AAd(c), BU:Storm	3.00
21 rep.#115,JBo/AAd(c), BU:Colossus	3.00
22 rep.#116,JBo/AAd(c), BU:Storm	3.00
23 rep.#117,JBo/KGa(c),BU: Nightcrawler	3.00
24 rep.#118,JBo/KGa(c),BU: Phoenix	3.00
25 rep.#119,JBo/KGa(c),BU:Wolv.	3.00
26 rep.#120,JBo/KGa(c),BU:Wolv.	4.00
27 rep.#121,JBo/KD(c),BU: Wolverine & Phoenix	3.00
28 rep.#122,JBo/KD(c),BU:X-Men.	3.00
29 rep.#123,JBo/KD(c),BU: Colossus	3.00
30 rep.#124,JBo/SLi(c),BU: O:Arcade	3.00
31 rep.#125,JBo/SLi(c),BU: Professor.X	3.00
32 rep.#126,JBo/SLi(c),BU: Wolverine	3.00
33 rep.#127,JBo/SLi(c),BU: Havok	3.00
34 rep.#128,JBo/SLi(c),BU: W.Queen,M.Mind	3.00
35 rep.#129,JBo/SLi(c),BU: K.Pryde	3.00
36 rep.#130,JBo/MBr/SLi(c),BU: Banshee & Moira	3.00
37 rep.#131,RL/SLi(c),BU: Dazzler	3.00
38 rep.#132,KB/SLi(c),BU: Dazzler	3.00
39 rep.#133,2nd JLe X-Men/SLi(c), BU:Storm	11.00
40 rep.#134,SLi(c),BU:N.Crawler	3.00
41 rep.#135,SLi(c),BU: Mr. Sinister,Cyclops	3.00
42 rep.#136,SLi(c),BU: Mr. Sinister,Cyclops	3.00
43 rep.#137,JBy(c),BU: Phoenix,Death	3.00

Becomes:

X-MEN CLASSICS
1990

44 rep.#138,KD/SLi(c)	3.00
45 thru 49 rep.#139–#145,SLi(c)	@3.00
50 thru 69 rep.#146–#165	@3.00
70 rep.#166	2.50
71 thru 99 rep.#167–#195	@2.50
100 thru 105 rep. #196–#201	@2.50
106 Phoenix vs. Beyonder	2.50

All comics prices listed are for Near Mint condition.

MARVEL

X-Men: Classics–Phoenix

X-Men Classics #93
© Marvel Entertainment Group

107 F:Rogue 2.50
108 F:Nightcrawler 2.50
109 Rep. Uncanny X-Men #205 ... 2.50
110 Rep. Uncanny X-Men #206 ... 2.50

X-MEN: EARLY YEARS
1 rep. X-Men (first series) #1 .... 2.50
2 rep. X-Men (first series) #2 .... 2.50
3 rep. X-Men (first series) #3 .... 2.50
4 thru 16 rep. X-Men (first series)
    #4 to #16 .... @2.50
17 Rep. X-Men #17 & #18 .... 2.50

X-MEN EVOLUTION
Nov., 2001
1 cartoon series tie-in 2.25
2 F:Cyclops 2.25
3 F:Jean Grey 2.25
4 F:Nigntcrawler, Shadowcat,
    Spyke, Rogue 2.25
5 F:Mystique, Rogue 2.25
6 I:Mimic 2.25
7 new recruits, Beast.......... 2.25
8 F:Angel, Storm 2.25
9 F:Professor X, Brotherhood ... 2.25
10 .... 2.25
TPB Vol.1, 96-pg............... 9.00

X-MEN FOREVER
Nov., 2000
1 (of 6) FaN,KM, ... 3.50
2 FaN,KM,displaced in time 3.50
3 FaN,KM, crucial points 3.50
4 FaN,KM,Toad 3.50
5 FaN,KM,Prosh 3.50
6 FaN,KM, concl............... 3.50

X-MEN: HELLFIRE CLUB
Nov., 1999
1 (of 4) AKu,BRa,CAd 2.50
2 AKu,BRa,CAd,O:Inner Circle... 2.50
3 AKu,BRa,CAd,O:cont.......... 2.50
4 AKu,BRa,O:Concl. 2.50

X-MEN: THE HIDDEN YEARS
Oct., 1999
1 JBy,TP,Original team,48-pg. ... 4.00
2 JBy,TP 3.00

3 JBy,TP, ... 3.00
4 JBy,TP,Savage Land concl. 3.00
5 JBy,TP,A:Candy Southern 3.00
6 JBy,TP,F:Storm 3.00
7 JBy,TP,V:Deluge 3.00
8 JBy,TP,Fant.Four 3.00
9 JBy,TP,Phoenix 3.00
10 JBy,TP,Candy Southern 3.00
11 JBy,TP,Beast 3.00
12 JBy,TP,48-pg. 4.00
13 JBy,TP,Beast 3.00
14 JBy,TP,Beast,Angel 3.00
15 JBy,X-Mansion.............. 3.00
16 JBy,return, to new conflicts 3.00
17 JBy,Kraven,Beast 3.00
18 JBy,Tad Carter,Lorna Dane ... 3.00
19 JBy,TP,Lorna,Angel,Promise .. 3.00
20 JBy,TP,Sub-Mariner,Magneto .. 3.00
21 JBy,TP,Namor,Magneto 3.00
22 JBy,TP,X-Men & Fant.Four.... 3.00

X-MEN ICONS: CHAMBER
Aug., 2002
1 (of 4) NRd 3.00
2 NRd 3.00
3 NRd 3.00
4 NRd, concl 3.00

X-MEN INDEX
See: OFFICIAL MARVEL INDEX TO THE X-MEN

X-MEN: LIBERATORS
Sept., 1999
1 (of 4) PJ,F:Wolverine,Nightcrawler
    & Colossus................ 3.00
2 PJ,V:Russian army 3.00
3 PJ,V:Nikolas................ 3.00
4 PJ,V:Omega Red 3.00

X-MEN: LOST TALES
1997
1 CCl,JBo,rep. from Classic X-Men 3.00
2 CCl,JBo,rep. from Classic X-Men 3.00

X-MEN: MAGIK
Oct., 2000
1 (of 4) DAn,ALa,LSh 3.00
2 DAn,ALa,LSh,V:Mephisto 3.00
3 DAn,ALa,LSh,F:Limbo 3.00
4 DAn,ALa,LSh,concl. 3.00

X-MEN/MICRONAUTS
Jan., 1984
1 JG,BWi,Limited Series 4.00
2 JG,BWi,KJo,V:Baron Karza..... 3.00
3 JG,BWi,V:Baron Karza 3.00
4 JG,BWi,V:Baron Karza,Apr.1984. 3.00

X-MEN: THE MANGA
Jan., 1998
1 b&w,translated,F:Jubilee....... 4.00
2 Jubilee joins, V:Sentinels 3.00
3 Agent Gyrich strikes 3.00
4 Beast captured, morph dead.... 3.00
5 Magneto attempts to rescue
    Beast..................... 3.00
6 Beast on trial, A:Sabretooth 3.00
7 V:Magneto 3.00
8 V:Magneto 3.00
9 V:Morlocks 3.00
10 V:Morlocks, 40-pg. finale 3.00
11 Wolverine vs. Sabretooth 3.00
12 Wolverine vs. Sabretooth 3.00
13 F:Storm, Jubilee & Gambit..... 3.00

X-Men Manga #15
© Marvel Entertainment Group

14 .... 3.00
15 .... 3.00
16 A:Colossus,V:Juggernaut,
    double-size................ 4.00
17 F:Cable & Angel 3.00
18 Angel becomes Archangel 3.00
19 Angel becomes Death 3.00
20 Rogue vs. Apocalypse 3.00
21 V:Four Horsemen 3.00
22 V:Sentinels 3.00
23 RGr(c),F:Bishop............. 3.00
24 RGr(c),V:Nimrod 3.00
25 Bishop vs. Gambit 3.00
26 V:Brotherhood of Evil Mutants .. 3.00
27 Magneto Returns............ 3.00
28 V:Master Mold,A:Magneto 3.00
29 .... 3.00
30 .... 3.00
31 .... 3.00
31 .... 3.00

X-MEN: THE MOVIE
June, 2000
Magneto, photo(c) 6.00
Rogue, photo(c) 6.00
Wolverine, photo(c) 6.00
X-Men The Movie, photo(c) 6.00
TPB Beginnings, 144-pg. 15.00
TPB X-Men The Movie, 4 diff.
    photo(c)s .... @15.00

X-MEN OMEGA
1995
1 FaN,Slo,After Xavier, concl. ... 10.00
1a Gold ed. Chromium(c) 48-pg. .. 50.00

X-MEN: PHOENIX
Oct., 1999
1 (of 3) JFM,F:Rachel Summers .. 3.00
2 JFM 3.00
3 JFM,concl.................. 3.00

X-MEN: PHOENIX
Marvel May 2003
1 (of 3) Legacy of Fire 3.00
2 Sword of Limbo 3.00
3 Concl..................... 3.00

All comics prices listed are for *Near Mint* condition.

X-MEN PRIME
1995
1 SLo,FaN,BHi,major plotlines for all X books begin, chromium(c) 10.00

X-MEN: PRYDE & WISDOM
1 WEl,TyD,KIS 3.00
2 & 3 WEl,TyD,KIS . . . . @3.00

X-MEN: RONIN
Marvel March 2003
1 (of 5) manga mania 3.00
2 . . . . 3.00
3 . . . . 3.00
4 . . . . 3.00
5 . . . . 3.00

X-MEN: THE MAGNETO WAR
Jan., 1999
1-shot AD, Joseph vs. Magneto . . . 3.00
1a signed 20.00

X-MEN: THE RISE OF APOCALYPSE
1 TKa,AdP, ancient history of X-Men 3.00
2 thru 4 TKa,AdP, ... @3.00
TPB 10.00

X-MEN: THE SEARCH FOR CYCLOPS
Oct., 2000
1A (of 4) TR,SHa, ... 3.00
1B variant AdP (c) 3.00
2A TR,SHa,Scott alive? 3.00
2B variant AdP(c) 3.00
3A TR,SHa, ... 3.00
3B variant AdP(c) 3.00
4A TR,SHa, concl. 3.00

X-MEN SPOTLIGHT ON STARJAMMERS
1990
1 DC,F:Starjammers,A:Prof.X 5.00
2 DC,F:Starjammers,A:Prof.X 5.00

X-MEN: TRUE FRIENDS
July, 1999
1 (of 3) CCl,RL,JP,F:Shadowcat. . . 3.00
2 CCl,RL,JP,A:Kitty Pryde 3.00
3 CCl,RL,JP,A:Wolverine,concl. . . . 3.00

X-MEN 2099
1993–96
1 B:JFM(s),RLm,JP,I:X-Men 2099 . 4.00
1a Gold Ed. 5.00
2 RLm,JP,V:Rat Pack 3.00
3 RLm,JP,D:Serpentina 3.00
4 RLm,JP,I:Theatre of Pain 3.00
5 RLm,JP,Fall of the Hammer#3 . . 3.00
6 RLm,JP,I:Freakshow. 3.00
7 RLm,JP,V:Freakshow 3.00
8 RLm(c),JS3,JP,N;Metalhead, I:2nd X-Men 2099. . . . . 3.00
9 RLm,JP,V:2nd X-Men 2099. . . . . 3.00
10 RLm,JP,A:La Lunatica 3.00
11 RLm,JP,V:2nd X-Men 2099 . . . . 3.00
12 RLm,JP,A:Junkpile 3.00
13 RLm,JP 3.00
14 RLm,JP,R:Loki 3.00
15 RLm,JP,F:Loki,I:Haloween Jack . 3.00

16 . . . . 3.00
17 X'ian 3.00
18 Haloween Jack 3.00
19 Conclusion Halloween Jack 3.00
Becomes:

X-MEN 2099 A.D.
20 F:Bloodhawk 3.00
21 Doom Factor 3.00
22 One Nation Under Doom 3.00
23 V:Junkpile 3.00
24 . . . . 3.00
25 X-Men Reunited. 3.00
25a variant cover 4.25
26 V:Graverobber 3.00
27 . . . . 3.00
28 X-Nation x-over 3.00
29 X-Nation x-over 3.00
30 . . . . 3.00
31 . . . . 3.00
32 V:Foolkiller. 3.00
Spec.#1 Bros.Hildebrandt(c) 4.50
GN X-Men 2099: Oasis, rep., Greg Hildebrandt(c) 64-pg., (1998) . . 6.00

X-MEN 2: THE MOVIE
Marvel March 2003
Prequel Wolverine, TMd 3.50
Prequel Nightcrawler 3.50
Spec. Movie Adapt., 48-pg. 3.50
TPB The Movie. 13.00

X-MEN UNIVERSE
Oct., 1999
1 rep. July 99 stories,80-pg. 5.00
2 rep. Aug.99 stories,80-pg. 5.00
3 rep. Sept.99 stories,80-pg. 5.00
4 rep. Oct.99 stories,80-pg. 5.00
5 rep. Nov.99 stories,80-pg. 5.00
6 rep. Dec.99 stories,80-pg. 5.00
7 rep. Jan.00 stories,80-pg. 5.00
8 rep. Feb.00 stories,80-pg. 5.00
9 rep. Mar.00 stories,80-pg. 5.00
10 rep. Apr.00 stories,80-pg. 5.00
11 rep. May 00 stories,80-pg. 5.00
12 rep. June 00 stories,80-pg 4.00
13 rep. July 00 stories,80-pg. 4.00
14 thru 17,rep., 80-pg.. . . . . @4.00

X-Men 2099 #5
© Marvel Entertainment Group

X-MEN UNLIMITED
1993
1 CBa,BP,O:Siena Blaze 7.00
2 JD,O:Magneto 6.00
3 FaN(s),BSz(c),MMK,Sabretooth joins X-Men,A:Maverick 7.00
4 SLo(s),RiB,O:Nightcrawler,Rogue, Mystique,IR:Mystique is Nightcrawler's mother. 5.00
5 JFM(s),LSh,After Shi'ar/ Kree War 4.50
6 JFM(s),PS,Sauron 4.50
7 JR2,HMe,O:Storm 4.50
8 Legacy Virus Victim 4.50
9 LHa,Wolverine & Psylocke 4.50
10 MWa,Dark Beast,Beast, double-size. 8.00
11 Rogue & Magneto, double-size . 8.00
12 Onslaught x-over,A:Juggernaut . 3.00
13 GP,Binary gone berserk 3.00
14 TKa, Onslaught fallout 3.00
15 HMe,F:Wolverine, Iceman & Maverick 3.00
16 MvR,F:Banshee, White Queen, I:Primal 3.00
17 TKa,Wolverine vs. Sabretooth, minds are switched. 3.00
18 TDF,V:Hydro Man 3.00
19 BRa,Nightcrawler v. Belasco . . . 3.00
20 F:Generation X 3.00
21 TDz,Strong Guy returns 3.00
22 into Marrow's World 3.00
23 F:Professor X 3.00
24 F:Wolverine & Cecilia Reyes . . . 3.00
25 BBh,48-pg. 3.00
26 BBh,Ages of Apocalypse,pt.4 . . . 3.00
27 BBh,X-Men: Revolution 3.00
28 BBh,Russia 3.00
29 BBh,Maximum Security 3.00
30 BBh, ... 3.00
31 MGo(c) three stories 3.00
32 JIT(c). 3.00
33 MK(c),Sabretooth,Blob. 3.00
34 Marvel Girl vs. Sabretooth 3.50
35 F:Emma Frost, Jubilee. 3.50
36 three stories 3.50
37 multiple dimensions, 48-pg. 3.50
38 DaR,F:Colossus 2.25
39 KIS,48-pg. 3.50
40 All evil issue, 48-pg. 3.50
41 I:MC Mystik,48-pg. 3.50
42 F:Prof. X, Jean Grey,48-pg. 3.50
43 CCl,BSz 2.50
44 animal cruelty 2.50
45 V:Alpha Flight 2.50
46 SB,F:Wolverine 2.50
47 Return of Psylocke 2.50
48 Mystique returns 2.50
49 F:Nightcrawler 2.50
50 PS,Japan connections 2.50

X-MEN VS. AVENGERS
April, 1987
1 MS,JRu,V:Soviet SuperSoldiers . 5.00
2 MS,JRu,V:Sov.Super Soldiers . . 3.50
3 MS,JRu,V:Sov.Super Soldiers . . 3.50
4 KP,JRu,BMc,AW,AM,V:Magneto July, 1987 . . . . 3.50
TPB 12.95

X-MEN VS. THE BROOD
1996
1 and 2 Day of Wrath. . . . . @3.00
TPB rep. #1,#2 and Unc.X-Men #232–#234 . . . . 17.00

MARVEL

X-NATION 2099
1996
1 .... 4.00
2 .... 2.50
3 At Herod's Themepark 2.50

X.S.E.
Mini-Series 1996
1 (of 4) JOs,Bishop & Shard's secrets 2.25
2 JOs, How did Shard die 2.25
3 JOs, How Shard died 2.25
4 JOs, conclusion 2.25

X-STATIX
July, 2002
1 PrM,MiA,super-team, 40-pg..... 3.00
2 PrM,MiA, ... 2.25
3 PrM,MiA.................. 2.25
4 PrM,MiA, sex = death? 2.25
5 PrM,PPo. 2.25
6 PrM,MiA,pt.1 .... 2.25
7 PrM,MiA.................. 2.25
8 PrM,MiA,Orphan's New Love .. 2.25
9 PrM,MiA, ... 2.25
10 PrM,Diaries of Edie Sawyer ... 3.00
11 PrM,F:Latino 2.25
12 PrM,If You Think I'm Sexy 2.25
13 PrM,MiA,Di Another Day,pt.1 .. 2.25
14 PrM,MiA,Di Another Day,pt.2 .. 2.25
15 PrM,MiA,Di Another Day,pt.3 .. 2.25
16 PrM,MiA,Di Another Day,pt.4 .. 2.25
TPB Vol. 1 .... 12.00
TPB Vol. 2: GoodGuys & BadGuys 16.00

X-Terminators #1
© Marvel Entertainment Group

X-TERMINATORS
Oct., 1988—Jan., 1989
1 JBg,AW,AM,I:N'astirh 4.00
2 JBg,AM,V:N'astirh........... 3.50
3 JBg,AM,V:N'astirh............ 3.00
4 JBg,AM,A:New Mutants 3.00

X-TREME X-MEN
June, 2001
1 CCI,SvL,Destiny,48-page 4.50
2A CCI,SvL,Guardia,Vargas..... 3.00
2B variant CPa(c) 3.00
3 CCI,SvL,V:Vargas........... 3.00
4 CCI,SvL,V:Vargas........... 3.00
5 CCI,SvL,F:Gambit 3.00

6 CCI,SvL,F:Gambit,Rogue 3.00
7 CCI,SvL.................... 3.00
8 CCI,SvL,concl.'Nuff Said....... 3.00
9 CCI,SvL,V:Lady Mastermind.... 3.00
10 CCI,SvL,Dimension X,pt.1 ..... 3.00
11 CCI,SvL,Dimension X,pt.2 ..... 3.00
12 CCI,SvL,V:Shaitan,Khan 3.00
13 CCI,SvL,F:Gambit,Lifeguard.... 3.00
14 CCI,SvL,F:Storm, Sage 3.00
15 CCI,SvL,F:Storm,Rogue....... 3.00
16 CCI,SvL,F:Rogue, Gambit 3.00
17 CCI,SvL................... 3.00
18 CCI,SvL,F:Jean Grey,Beast, Nightcrawler................ 3.00
19 CCI,F:Jean Grey 3.00
20 CCI,SvL,Scism,pt.1 .... 3.00
21 CCI,SvL,Scism,pt.2 .... 3.00
22 CCI,SvL,Scism,pt.3 .... 3.00
23 CCI,SvL,Scism,pt.4 .... 3.00
24 CCI,SvL,R:Cannonball....... 3.00
25 CCI,SvL,God Loves,Man Kills2 . 3.00
26 CCI,SvL,God Loves,Man Kills2 . 3.00
27 CCI,SvL,God Loves,Man Kills2 . 3.00
28 CCI,SvL,God Loves,Man Kills2 . 3.00
29 CCI,SvL,God Loves,Man Kills2 . 3.00
30 CCI,SvL,God Loves,Man Kills2 . 3.00
31 CCI,SHa,Intifada,pt.1......... 3.00
32 CCI,SHa,Intifada,pt.2......... 3.00
33 CCI,SHa,Intifada,pt.3......... 3.00
34 CCI,SHa,Intifada,pt.4......... 3.00
35 CCI,SHa,Intifada,pt.5......... 3.00
Ann.2001 CCI,SvL,64-pg........ 4.95
TPB rep.#1-#4, 192-pg. (2002) .. 18.95
TPB Vol. 2: Invasion 20.00
TPB Vol. 3: Schism 17.00
TPB Vol. 4: Mekanix 17.00
TPB Vol. 5: God Loves, Man Kills . 20.00

X-TREME X-MEN: SAVAGE LAND
July, 2001
1 (of 4) CCI,F:Rogue 3.00
2 CCI,Velociraptors & T-Rexes.... 3.00
3 CCI...................... 3.00
4 CCI,concl................. 3.00
TPB 96-pg.................. 12.95

X-TREME X-MEN: X-POSE
Nov., 2002
1 (of 2) Ccl, two reporters 3.00
2 CCI,Forbidden Mutant Love ... 3.00

X-UNIVERSE
1995
1 The Other Heroes............ 5.00
2 F:Ben Grimm,Tony Stark....... 5.00

YOGI BEAR
Nov., 1977
1 A:Flintstones 30.00
2 .... 20.00
3 .... 20.00
4 .... 20.00
5 .... 20.00
6 .... 20.00
7 .... 20.00
8 .... 20.00
9 March, 1979 .... 20.00

YOUNG ALLIES COMICS
Timely,
Summer, 1941—Oct., 1946
1 S&K,Hitler(c),I&O:Young Allies 1st meeting Capt. America &

Young Allies Comics #8
© Marvel Entertainment Group

Human Torch,A:Red Skull 20,000.00
2 S&K,A;Capt.America,Human Torch................... 5,000.00
3 Remember Pearl Harbor(c) . 3,500.00
4 A;Capt. America,Torch,Red Skull ASh(c),Horror In Hollywood A:Capt.America,Torch 5,000.00
5 ASh(c),Capt.America 2,500.00
6 ASh(c) 1,600.00
7 ASh(c) 1,600.00
8 ASh(c) 1,600.00
9 ASh(c),Axis leaders(c), B:Tommy Type.......... 1,800.00
10 ASh(c),O:Tommy Type 1,600.00
11 ASh(c)................. 1,200.00
12 ASh(c),Decapitation 1,200.00
13 ASh(c) 1,200.00
14 .... 1,200.00
15 AxB,ASh(c)............. 1,200.00
16 ASh(c) 1,200.00
17 ASh(c) 1,200.00
18 ASh(c) 1,200.00
19 ASh(c),E:Tommy Type..... 1,200.00
20 .... 1,200.00

YOUNG HEARTS
Nov., 1949—Feb., 1950
1 .... 125.00
2 Feb., 1950 .... 75.00

YOUNG MEN
See: COWBOY ROMANCES

YUPPIES FROM HELL
1989
1 Satire 3.00
2 .... 3.00
3 .... 3.00

ZORRO
Marvel UK, 1990
1 Don Diego 3.00
2 thru 12 .... @3.00

All comics prices listed are for Near Mint condition.

GOLDEN AGE

A-1 COMICS
Magazine Enterprises, 1944
N# F:Kerry Drake,BU:Johnny
  Devildog & Streamer Kelly . . 200.00
1 A:Dotty Driple,Mr. EX,Bush
  Berry and Lew Loyal 100.00
2 A:Texas Slim & Dirty Dalton,
  The Corsair,Teddy Rich, Dotty
  Dripple,Inca Dinca,Tommy Tinker
  Little Mexico and Tugboat. . . . 75.00
3 same 50.00
4 same 50.00
5 same 50.00
6 same 50.00
7 same 50.00
8 same 50.00
9 Texas Slim Issue 75.00
10 Same characters as
   issues #2–#8 . . . . 50.00
11 Teena 75.00
12 Teena 50.00
13 JCr,Guns of Fact and Fiction,
   narcotics & junkies featured . 300.00
14 Tim Holt WesternAdventures . 750.00
15 Teena 50.00
16 Vacation Comics 50.00
17 Tim Holt #2, E:A-1 on cover . . 400.00
18 Jimmy Durante, Ph(c) 500.00
19 Tim Holt #3 . . . . 300.00
20 Jimmy Durante Ph(c) 500.00
21 OW,Joan of Arc movie adapt. . 300.00
22 Dick Powell (1949) 250.00
23 Cowboys N' Indians #6 . . . . . 100.00
24 FF(c),LbC,Trail Colt #2 . . . . . . 425.00
25 Fibber McGee & Molly (1949) 100.00
26 LbC, Trail Colt #2 . . . . 350.00
27 GhostRider#1,O:GhostRider 1,100.00
28 Christmas (Koko & Kola) 30.00
29 FF(c), Ghost Rider #2 . . . . . . 900.00
30 BP, Jet Powers #1 . . . . 350.00
31 FF,Ghost Rider#3,O:Ghost
   Rider 800.00
32 AW,GE,Jet Powers #2 . . . . . . 300.00
33 Muggsy Mouse #2 . . . . 60.00
34 FF(c),Ghost Rider #4 . . . . 800.00
35 AW,Jet Powers. 425.00
36 Muggsy Mouse 100.00
37 FF(c),Ghost Rider 800.00
38 AW,WW,Jet Powers, Drugs . . 450.00
39 Muggsy Mouse 50.00
40 Dogface Dooley 50.00
41 Cowboys 'N' Indians 75.00
42 BP,Best of the West 500.00
43 Dogface Dooley 40.00
44 Ghost Rider 300.00
45 American Air Forces 65.00
46 Best of the West 250.00
47 FF,Thunda King of the
   Congo 1,700.00
48 Cowboys N' Indians 60.00
49 Dogface Dooley 40.00
50 BP,Danger Is Their Busines . . 150.00
51 Ghost Rider 300.00
52 Best of the West 225.00
53 Dogface Dooley 40.00
54 BP,American Air Forces 65.00
55 BP,U.S. Marines 40.00
56 BP,Thunda King of the Congo 250.00
57 Ghost Rider, Drugs 350.00
58 American Air Forces 65.00
59 Best of the West 250.00
60 The U.S. Marines. 50.00
61 Space Ace 600.00
62 Starr Flagg–Undercover Girl. . 500.00
63 FF,Manhunt 425.00
64 Dogface Dooley 40.00
65 BP,American Air Forces 65.00
66 Best of the West 250.00
67 American Air Forces 65.00
68 U.S. Marines 40.00
69 Ghost Rider, Drugs 350.00
70 Best of the West 250.00
71 Ghost Rider, A:Frankenstein. . 300.00
72 U.S. Marines 40.00
73 BP,Thunda. 175.00
74 BP,American Air Forces 65.00
75 Ghost Rider 225.00
76 Best of the West 150.00
77 LbC,Grl,Manhunt 350.00
78 BP,Thunda. 175.00
79 American Air Forces. 65.00
80 Ghost Rider, Bondage(c) 225.00
81 Best of the West 150.00
82 BP,Cave Girl 550.00
83 BP,Thunda King of the Congo 150.00
84 Ghost Rider 225.00
85 Best of the West 150.00
86 BP,Thunda King of the Congo 150.00
87 Best of the West 150.00
88 Bobby Benson's B-Bar-B . . . 125.00
89 BP,Home Run,Stan Musial . . . 175.00
90 Red Hawk 125.00
91 BP,American Air Forces 50.00
92 Dream Book of Romance. . . . 125.00
93 BP,Great Western 225.00
94 FF,White Indian 250.00
95 BP,Muggsy Mouse. 30.00
96 BP,Cave Girl 375.00
97 Best of the West 150.00
98 Starr Flagg–Undercover Girl. . 400.00
99 Muggsy Mouse 30.00
100 Badmen of the West 250.00
101 FF,White Indian 235.00
101(a) BP(c),FG, Dream Book of
   Romance, Marlon Brando. . . 225.00
103 BP,Best of the West 150.00
104 FF,White Indian 235.00
105 Great Western 150.00
106 BP,Dream Book of Love 125.00
107 Hot Dog. 75.00
108 BP,BC,Red Fox 200.00
109 BP,Dream Book of Romance . 80.00
110 Dream Book of Romance. . . . 80.00
111 BP,I'm a Cop 150.00
112 Ghost Rider 225.00
113 BP,Great Western. 125.00
114 Dream Book of Love 100.00
115 Hot Dog. 50.00
116 BP,Cave Girl 350.00
117 White Indian. 125.00
118 BP(c),Starr Flagg–
   Undercover Girl 400.00
119 Straight Arrow's Fury 165.00
120 Badmen of the West 150.00
121 Mysteries of the
   Scotland Yard. 175.00
122 Black Phantom. 425.00
123 Dream Book of Love 75.00
124 Hot Dog. 50.00
125 BP,Cave Girl 350.00
126 BP,I'm a Cop. 100.00
127 BP,Great Western 200.00
128 BP,I'm a Cop 150.00
129 The Avenger 425.00
130 BP,Strongman 250.00
131 BP,The Avenger 300.00
132 Strongman 200.00
133 BP,The Avenger 300.00
134 Strongman 200.00
135 White Indian. 125.00
136 Hot Dog. 50.00
137 BP,Africa 200.00
138 BP,Avenger 300.00
139 BP,Strongman, 1955 . . . . . . 200.00

ABBIE AN' SLATS
**United Features Syndicate
March–Aug., 1948**
1 RvB(c) 200.00
2 RvB(c) 175.00
3 RvB(c) 100.00
4 Aug., 1948 . . . . 100.00
N# 1940,Earlier Issue 400.00
N# 350.00

ABBOTT AND COSTELLO
**St. John Publishing Co.
Feb., 1948**
1 PP(c), Waltz Time 700.00
2 Jungle Girl and Snake(c) 325.00
3 Outer Space (c) 225.00
4 MD, Circus (c) 200.00
5 MD,Bull Fighting (c) 200.00
6 MD,Harem (c) 200.00
7 MD,Opera (c) 200.00
8 MD,Pirates (c) 200.00
9 MD,Polar Bear (c). 200.00
10 MD,PP(c),Son of Sinbad tale . 250.00
11 MD 150.00
12 PP(c), Movie issue 175.00
13 Fire fighters (c) 150.00
14 Bomb (c) 150.00
15 Bubble Bath (c) 150.00
16 thru 29 MD. . . . . @125.00
30 thru 39 MD. . . . .@80.00
40 MD,Sept., 1956 . . . . 80.00
3-D #1, Nov., 1953 . . . . 400.00

ACE COMICS
**David McKay Publications
April, 1937**
1 JM, F:Katzenjammer Kids . . 4,500.00
2 JM, A:Blondie. 1,200.00
3 JM, A:Believe It Or Not 850.00

A-1 Comics #83
© Magazine Enterprises

GOLDEN AGE

Ace–Air Ace

4 JM, F:Katzenjammer Kids.... 800.00
5 JM, A:Believe It Or Not 800.00
6 JM, A:Blondie 600.00
7 JM, A:Believe It Or Not 600.00
8 JM, A:Jungle Jim 600.00
9 JM, A:Blondie 600.00
10 JM, F:Katzenjammer Kids ... 550.00
11 I:The Phantom series 1,000.00
12 A:Blondie, Jungle Jim....... 450.00
13 A:Ripley's Believe It Or Not . 425.00
14 A:Blondie, Jungle Jim....... 425.00
15 A:Blondie 400.00
16 F:Katzenjammer Kids....... 400.00
17 A:Blondie 400.00
18 A:Ripley's Believe It Or Not .. 400.00
19 F:Katzenjammer Kids....... 400.00
20 A:Jungle Jim 400.00
21 A:Blondie 375.00
22 A:Jungle Jim 375.00
23 F:Katzenjammer Kids....... 375.00
24 A:Blondie 375.00
25 .... 375.00
26 O:Prince Valiant 1,200.00
27 thru 36 ....@375.00
37 Krazy Kat Ends 250.00
38 thru 49 ....@200.00
50 thru 59 ....@175.00
60 thru 69 ....@150.00
70 thru 79 ....@125.00
80 thru 89 ....@125.00
90 thru 99 ....@100.00
100 .... 125.00
101 thru 109 ....@100.00
110 thru 119 ....@75.00
120 thru 143 ....@75.00
144 Phantom covers begin 100.00
145 thru 150 ....@75.00
151 Oct.–Nov., 1949.......... 100.00

ACES HIGH
E.C. Comics, March–April, 1955

1 GE(a&c),JDa,WW,BK 300.00
2 GE(a&c),JDa,WW,BK 165.00
3 GE(a&c),JDa,WW,BK 150.00
4 GE(a&c),JDa,WW,BK 150.00
5 GE(c),JDa,WW,BK,
  Nov.–Dec., 1955.......... 150.00

ADVENTURES INTO DARKNESS
Standard Publications
Aug., 1952

5 JK(c), ATh................. 425.00
6 GT, JK 250.00
7 JK(c) 250.00
8 ATh...................... 275.00
9 JK,ATh 275.00
10 JK,ATh,MSy............... 250.00
11 JK,ATh,MSy............... 250.00
12 JK,ATh,MYs............... 250.00
13 Cannibalism feature........ 275.00
14 .... 175.00

ADVENTURES INTO THE UNKNOWN!
American Comics Group
Fall 1948

1 FG, Haunted House (c) 2,500.00
2 Haunted Island (c) 1,000.00
3 AF, Sarcophagus (c)....... 1,000.00
4 Monsters (c) 500.00
5 Monsters (c) 500.00
6 Giant Hands (c) 350.00
7 Skeleton Pirate (c) 350.00
8 Horror.................... 350.00
9 Snow Monster 350.00
10 Red Bats 350.00

Adventures Into the Unknown #13
© American Comics Group

11 Death Shadow............ 350.00
12 OW(c)................... 350.00
13 OW(c),Dinosaur........... 300.00
14 OW(c),Cave............... 300.00
15 Red Demons 300.00
16 .... 300.00
17 OW(c),The Thing Type...... 350.00
18 OW(c),Wolves............ 275.00
19 OW(c),Graveyard.......... 250.00
20 OW(c),Graveyard.......... 250.00
21 Bats and Dracula 250.00
22 Death 250.00
23 Bats..................... 250.00
24 .... 250.00
25 .... 250.00
26 .... 250.00
27 AW 325.00
28 thru 37 ....@200.00
38 A-Bomb 200.00
39 thru 49 ....@175.00
50 .... 175.00
51 Lazarus 375.00
52 Lazarus, 3-Dish 350.00
53 thru 55 ....@350.00
56 Lazarus 350.00
57 .... 350.00
58 Lazarus 350.00
59 3-Dish 300.00
60 .... 135.00
61 .... 135.00
62 thru 69 ....@100.00
70 thru 79 ....@85.00
80 thru 90 ....@75.00
91 AW 100.00
92 thru 95 ....@65.00
96 AW 100.00
97 thru 99 ....@60.00
100 JB 75.00
101 thru 106 ....@60.00
107 AW 100.00
108 thru 115 ....@60.00
116 AW,AT 50.00
117 thru 127 ....@45.00
128 AW,Forbidden Worlds....... 50.00
129 thru 151 ....@45.00
152 JCr 50.00
153 A:Magic Agent 45.00
154 O:Nemesis................ 65.00
155 Nemesis 45.00
156 A:Magic Agent 45.00
157 thru 167 ....@50.00
168 JB,SD, Nemesis 65.00
169 Nemesis vs. Hitler 75.00
170 thru 174, Aug., 1967......@60.00

ADVENTURES IN WONDERLAND
Lev Gleason Publications
April, 1955

1 .... 100.00
2 .... 60.00
3 .... 50.00
4 .... 50.00
5 Christmas................. 50.00

ADVENTURES OF MIGHTY MOUSE
St. John Publishing Co.
Nov., 1951

1 Mighty Mouse Adventures.... 350.00
2 Menace of the Deep 250.00
3 Storm Clouds of Mystery..... 150.00
4 Thought Control Machine 150.00
5 Jungle Peril 150.00
6 'The Vine of Destruction'..... 100.00
7 Space Ship(c).............. 100.00
8 Charging Alien(c) 100.00
9 Meteor(c) 90.00
10 'Revolt at the Zoo' 90.00
11 Jungle(c) 90.00
12 A:Freezing Terror........... 90.00
13 A:Visitor from Outer Space.... 90.00
14 V:Cat.................... 85.00
15 .... 85.00
16 .... 85.00
17 .... 85.00
18 May, 1955 .... 85.00

AGGIE MACK
Four Star Comics/
Superior Comics, Jan., 1948

1 AF,HR(c),Johnny Prep 350.00
2 JK(c) 200.00
3 AF,JK(c) 200.00
4 AF, Johnny Prep 250.00
5 AF,JK(c) 200.00
6 AF,JK(c) 190.00
7 AF,Burt Lancaster on cover ... 200.00
8 AF,JK(c), Aug., 1949 .... 190.00

BILL BARNES, AMERICA'S AIR ACE
Street and Smith Publications
July, 1940

1 (Bill Barnes Comics) 1,000.00
2 Second Battle Valley Forge... 600.00
3 A:Aviation Cadets 400.00
4 Shotdown(c).............. 400.00
5 A:Air Warden, Danny Hawk... 400.00
6 A:Danny Hawk,RocketRodney 350.00
7 How to defeat the Japanese .. 350.00
8 Ghost Ship 350.00
9 Flying Tigers, John Wayne ... 375.00
10 I:Roane Waring 350.00
11 Flying Tigers 350.00
12 War Workers 350.00
Becomes:

AIR ACE
Jan., 1944

2-1 Invades Germany 400.00
2-2 Jungle Warfare 350.00
2-3 A:The Four Musketeers 175.00
2-4 A:Russell Swann 175.00
2-5 A:The Four Musketeers 175.00
2-6 Raft(c).................. 150.00
2-7 BP, What's New In Science . 150.00
2-8 XP-59 .... 150.00
2-9 The Northrop P-61 .... 150.00
2-10 NCG-14................ 150.00
2-11 Whip Lanch 150.00

All comics prices listed are for Near Mint condition.

GOLDEN AGE

Air Ace–All Good

2-12 PP(c)	150.00
3-1	125.00
3-2 Atom and It's Future	125.00
3-3 Flying in the Future	125.00
3-4 How Fast Can We Fly	125.00
3-5 REv(c)	125.00
3-6 V:Wolves	125.00
3-7 BP(c), Vortex of Atom Bomb	250.00
3-8 BP,Feb.–March, 1947	150.00

AIRBOY
See: AIR FIGHTERS COMICS

Airfighters #5
© Hillman Periodicals

AIR FIGHTERS COMICS
Hillman Periodicals, Nov., 1941

1 I:Black Commander (only App)	2,700.00
2 O:Airboy A:Sky Wolf	4,500.00
3 O:Sky Wolf and Heap	2,500.00
4 A:Black Angel, Iron Ace	1,600.00
5 A:Sky Wolf and Iron Ace	1,300.00
6 Airboy's Bird Plane	1,500.00
7 Airboy battles Kultur	1,300.00
8 A:Skinny McGinty	1,000.00
9 A:Black Prince, Hatchet Man	1,000.00
10 I:The Stinger	1,000.00
11 Kida(c)	1,000.00
12 A:Misery	1,000.00
2-1 A:Flying Dutchman	1,100.00
2-2 I:Valkyrie	1,300.00
2-3 Story Panels (c)	800.00
2-4 V:Japanese	800.00
2-5 Air Boy in Tokyo	800.00
2-6 'Dance of Death'	800.00
2-7 A:Valkyrie	800.00
2-8 Airboy Battles Japanese	800.00
2-9 Airboy Battles Japanese	800.00
2-10 O:Skywolf	900.00

Becomes:

AIRBOY
Dec., 1945

2-11	900.00
2-12 A:Valykrie	600.00
3-1	400.00
3-2	400.00
3-3 Never published	
3-4 I:The Heap	350.00
3-5 Airboy	325.00
3-6 A:Valykrie	325.00
3-7 AMc,Witch Hunt	325.00
3-8 A:Condor	335.00
3-9 O:The Heap	350.00
3-10	300.00
3-11	300.00
3-12 Airboy missing	350.00
4-1 Elephant in chains (c)	335.00
4-2 I:Rackman	250.00
4-3 Airboy profits on name	250.00
4-4 S&K	300.00
4-5 S&K,The American Miracle	250.00
4-6 S&K,A:Heap and Flying Fool	250.00
4-7 S&K	250.00
4-8 S&K,Girlfriend captured	250.00
4-9 S&K,Airboy in quick sand	250.00
4-10 S&K,A:Valkyrie	250.00
4-11 S&K,A:Frenchy	250.00
4-12 FBe	275.00
5-1 LSt	175.00
5-2 I:Wild Horse of Calabra	175.00
5-3	175.00
5-4 Cl	175.00
5-5 Skull on cover	175.00
5-6	175.00
5-7	175.00
5-8 Bondage (c)	175.00
5-9 Zoi,Row	175.00
5-10 A:Valykrie,O:The Heap	200.00
5-11 Airboy vs. The Rats	175.00
5-12 BK,Rat Army captures Airboy	175.00
6-1	175.00
6-2	175.00
6-3	175.00
6-4 Airboy boxes	225.00
6-5 A:The Ice People	175.00
6-6	175.00
6-7 Airboy vs. Chemical Giant	175.00
6-8 O:The Heap	200.00
6-9	175.00
6-10	175.00
6-11	175.00
6-12	175.00
7-1	165.00
7-2 BP	165.00
7-3 BP	165.00
7-4 I:Monsters of the Ice	165.00
7-5 V:Monsters of the Ice	165.00
7-6	165.00
7-7 Mystery of the Sargasso Sea	165.00
7-8 A:Centaur	165.00
7-9 I:Men of the StarlightRobot	165.00
7-10 O:The Heap	165.00
7-11	165.00
7-12 Airboy visits India	165.00
8-1 BP,A:Outcast and Polo Bandits	150.00
8-2 BP,Suicide Dive (c)	150.00
8-3 BK, I:The Living Fuse	150.00
8-4 Death Merchants of the Air	165.00
8-5 A:Great Plane from Nowhere	150.00
8-6	150.00
8-7	150.00
8-8	150.00
8-9	150.00
8-10 A:Mystery Walkers	150.00
8-11	150.00
8-12	175.00
9-1	150.00
9-2 A:Valykrie	125.00
9-3 A:Heap (c)	125.00
9-4 A:Water Beast, Frog Headed Riders	125.00
9-5 A:Heap vs.Man of Moonlight	125.00
9-6 Heap (c)	125.00
9-7 Heap (c)	125.00
9-8 Heap (c)	150.00
9-9	150.00
9-10 Space (c)	150.00
9-11	125.00
9-12 Heap (c)	125.00
10-1 Heap (c)	125.00
10-2 Ships on Space	115.00
10-3	125.00
10-4 May, 1953	125.00

AL CAPP'S DOG PATCH COMICS
Toby Press, June, 1949

1	250.00
2 A:Daisy	175.00
3	150.00
4 Dec., 1949	150.00

AL CAPP'S SHMOO
Toby Press, July, 1949

1 100 Trillion Schmoos	400.00
2 Super Shmoo(c)	300.00
3	300.00
4	275.00
5 April, 1950	275.00

AL CAPP'S WOLF GAL
Toby Press, 1951

1 Pin-Up	375.00
2 1952	350.00

ALL-FAMOUS CRIME
Star Publications, May, 1951

4 LbC(c)	300.00
5 LbC(c)	225.00
8 LbC(c)	175.00
9 LbC(c)	400.00
10 LbC(c)	150.00

Becomes:

ALL-FAMOUS POLICE CASES
Feb., 1952

6 LbC(c)	200.00
7 LbC(c)	175.00
8 LbC(c)	175.00
9 LbC(c)	150.00
10 thru 15 LbC(c)	@150.00
16 Sept., 1954	150.00

ALL GOOD COMICS
R. W. Voight/Fox Publ./ St. John Publ.

1 1944	300.00
1 1946	250.00
N# 1949	800.00

All-Humor Comics #2
© Quality Comics

All comics prices listed are for *Near Mint* condition.

GOLDEN AGE

ALL GREAT COMICS
See: **DAGAR, DESERT HAWK**

ALL HERO COMICS
Fawcett Publications March, 1943
1 A:Capt. Marvel Jr.,Capt. Midnight,Ibis, Golden Arrow and Spy Smasher 2,000.00

ALL HUMOR COMICS
Comic Favorites, Inc. (Quality Comics), Spring 1946
1 . . . . 200.00
2 PG 100.00
3 I:Kelly Poole 60.00
4 thru 7 . . . . @50.00
8 PG 60.00
9 . . . . 60.00
10 . . . . 60.00
11 thru 17 . . . . @50.00

ALL LOVE ROMANCES
See: **SCREAM COMICS**

ALL NEGRO COMICS
June, 1947
1 . . . . 6,500.00

All-New Comics #8
© Family Comics/Harvey Publications

ALL-NEW COMICS
Family Comics (Harvey Publ.), Jan., 1943
1 A:Steve Case, Johnny Rebel I:Detective Shane 3,700.00
2 JKu,O:Scarlet Phantom 1,400.00
3 . . . . 1,000.00
4 AdH 1,000.00
5 Flash Gordon 1,000.00
6 I:Boy Heroes and Red Blazer 1,000.00
7 JKu,AS(c),A:Black Cat & Zebra 1,000.00
8 JKu,A:Shock Gibson 1,000.00
9 JKu,A:Black Cat. 1,000.00
10 JKu,A:Zebra. 950.00
11 BP,A:Man in Black, Girl Commandos 950.00

12 JKu 800.00
13 Stuntman by S&K, A:Green Hornet&(c) 900.00
14 BP,A:Green Hornet 800.00
15 Smaller size, Distributed by Mail, March–April, 1947 . . 900.00

ALL TOP COMICS
William H. Wise Co., 1944
N# 132pgs.,A:Capt. V,Red Robbins 350.00

ALL TOP COMICS
Fox Features Syndicate Spring 1946
1 A:Cosmo Cat, Flash Rabbit. . . 225.00
2 . . . . 100.00
3 . . . . 75.00
4 . . . . 75.00
5 . . . . 75.00
6 . . . . 75.00
7 . . . . 75.00
7a 75.00
8 JKa(c),I:Blue Beetle 3,200.00
9 JKa(c),A:Rulah. 1,600.00
10 JKa(c),A:Rulah 1,700.00
11 A:Rulah,Blue Beetle 1,400.00
12 A:Rulah,Jo Jo,Blue Beetle. . 1,400.00
13 A:Rulah. 1,400.00
14 A:Rulah,Blue Beetle 1,700.00
15 A:Rulah. 1,400.00
16 A:Rulah,Blue Beetle 1,400.00
17 A:Rulah,Blue Beetle 1,400.00
18 A:Dagar,Jo Jo 900.00

Green Publ.
6 1957 . . . . 50.00
6 1958 . . . . 50.00
6 1959 . . . . 50.00
6 1959 . . . . 50.00
6 Supermouse (c). 50.00

ALLEY OOP
Argo Publications Nov., 1955
1 . . . . 175.00
2 . . . . 150.00
3 March, 1956 . . . . 150.00

AMAZING ADVENTURE FUNNIES
Centaur Publ. 1940
1 BEv,The Fantom of the Fair . 2,500.00
2 rep. 1,500.00
Becomes:

FANTOMAN
Aug., 1940
2 The Fantom of the Fair 1,500.00
3 . . . . 1,200.00
4 Red Blaze 1,200.00

AMAZING ADVENTURES
Ziff-Davis Publ. Co., 1950
1 MA,WW, Asteroid Witch 1,000.00
2 MA,Masters of Living Flame . . 400.00
3 Ma,The Evil Men Do 400.00
4 Invasion of the Love Robots . . 400.00
5 MA,Secret of the Crater-Men . 400.00
6 BK,Man Who Killed a World . . 450.00

AMAZING GHOST STORIES
See: **WEIRD HORRORS**

AMAZING-MAN COMICS
Centaur Publications Sept., 1939–Feb., 1942
5 BEv,O:Amazing Man 21,000.00
6 BEv,FT,B:The Shark. 4,000.00
7 BEv,I:Magician From Mars . . 3,000.00
8 BEv 2,000.00
9 BEv,FT 2,000.00
10 BEv,FT 1,500.00
11 BEv,I:Zardi 1,500.00
12 SG(c) 1,400.00
13 SG(c) 1,400.00
14 FT,B:Reef Kinkaid, Dr. Hypo 1,200.00
15 FT,A:Zardi. 1,000.00
16 Mighty Man's powers revealed 1,200.00
17 FT,A:Dr. Hypo 1,000.00
18 FT,BLb(a),SG(c) 1,000.00
19 FT,BLb(a),SG(c) 1,000.00
20 FT,BLb(a),SG(c) 1,000.00
21 FT,O:Dash Dartwell. 1,100.00
22 A:Silver Streak, The Voice. . 1,000.00
23 I&O:Tommy the AmazingKid 1,000.00
24 B:King of Darkness,Blue Lady 950.00
25 A:Meteor Marvin 1,500.00
26 A:Meteor Marvin,ElectricRay 1,400.00

AMAZING MYSTERY FUNNIES
Centaur Publications, 1938
1 Skyrocket Steele in Year X . . 4,500.00
2 WE,Skyrocket Steele 2,500.00
3 . . . . 1,200.00
(#4) WE,bondage (c). 1,300.00
2-1(#5). 1,100.00
2-2(#6) Drug use 1,000.00
2-3(#7) Air Sub DX 1,000.00
2-4(#8). 1,000.00
2-5(#9). 1,500.00
2-6(#10). 1,000.00
2-7(#11) scarce 4,500.00
2-8(#12) Speed Centaur 1,700.00
2-9(#13). 1,100.00
2-10(#14). 1,100.00
2-11(#15). 1,100.00
2-12(#16) BW,I:Space Patrol . 2,500.00
3-1(#17) I:Bullet 1,100.00
18 . . . . 1,100.00
19 BW,Space Patrol. 1,300.00
20 . . . . 1,000.00
21 BW,Space Patrol. 1,100.00
22 BW,Space Patrol. 1,100.00
23 BW,Space Patrol. 1,100.00
24 BW,Space Patrol. 1,100.00

AMAZING WILLIE MAYS
Famous Funnies, 1954
1 Willie Mays(c) 1,000.00

AMERICAN LIBRARY
David McKay Publ., 1943
(#1) Thirty Seconds Over Tokyo, movie adapt. 400.00
(#2) Guadalcanal Diary 300.00
3 Look to the Mountain 125.00
4 The Case of the Crooked Candle (Perry Mason). 125.00
5 Duel in the Sun. 125.00
6 Wingate's Raiders 125.00

AMERICA'S BEST COMICS
Nedor/Better/Standard Publications, Feb., 1942
1 B:Black Terror, Captain Future, The Liberator,Doc Strange . 3,000.00

All comics prices listed are for *Near Mint* condition.

America's–Archie's   GOLDEN AGE   Comics Values Annual

2 O:American Eagle 1,300.00
3 B:Pyroman 900.00
4 A:Doc Strange, Jimmy Cole . . 700.00
5 A:Lone Eagle, Capt. Future . . . 700.00
6 American Crusader 675.00
7 A:Hitler,Hirohito 1,100.00
8 The Liberator ends 600.00
9 ASh(c),Fighting Yank 700.00
10 ASh(c),American Eagle 550.00
11 ASh(c) Hirihito & Tojo(c) 700.00
12 Red Cross (c) 550.00
13 Fighting Yank. 550.00
14 Last American Eagle app 550.00
15 ASh(c),Fighting Yank 550.00
16 ASh(c),Fighting Yank 550.00
17 Doc Strange carries football . . 550.00
18 Fighting Yank,Bondage(c) . . . 550.00
19 ASh(c),Fighting Yank 550.00
20 vs. the Black Market 550.00
21 Infinity (c). 550.00
22 A:Captain Future 500.00
23 B:Miss Masque 650.00
24 Miss Masque,Bondage (c) . . . 650.00
25 A:Sea Eagle. 450.00
26 A:The Phantom Detective. . . . 450.00
27 Pyroman,ASh(c) 450.00
28 A:Commando Cubs,
    Black Terror 450.00
29 A:Doc Strange 450.00
30 ASh(c).Xela 450.00
31 ASh(c),Xela,July, 1949 . . . . . . 450.00

AMERICA'S BIGGEST COMICS BOOK
William H. Wise, 1944
1 196 pgs. A:Grim Reaper, Zudo,
  Silver Knight, Thunderhoof,
  Jocko and Socko,Barnaby
  Beep,Commando Cubs. 450.00

AMERICA'S GREATEST COMICS
Fawcett Publications, Fall 1941
1 MRa(c),A:Capt. Marvel,
  Bulletman,Spy Smasher and
  Minute Man 4,000.00
2 F:Capt. Marvel 1,800.00
3 F:Capt. Marvel. 1,300.00
4 B:Commando Yank 1,000.00
5 Capt.Marvel in 'Lost Lighting' 1,000.00
6 Capt.Marvel fires MachineGun 850.00
7 A:Balbo the Boy Magician 850.00
8 A:Capt. Marvel Jr.,Golden
  Arrow, Summer 1943 . . . . . . 850.00

AMERICA IN ACTION
Dell Publishing Co., 1942
1 . . . . 200.00

ANDY COMICS
See: SCREAM COMICS

ANGEL
Dell Publishing Co., Aug., 1954
(1) see Dell Four Color #576
2 . . . . 30.00
3 thru 16 . . . . @20.00

ANIMAL ANTICS
Dell Publishing Co., 1946
1 B:Racoon Kids 500.00
2 . . . . 250.00
3 thru 10 . . . . @150.00
11 thru 23 . . . . @100.00

ANIMAL COMICS
Dell Publishing Co., 1942
1 WK,Pogo 1,200.00
2 Uncle Wiggily(c),A:Pogo 600.00
3 Muggin's Mouse(c),A:Pogo . . . 450.00
4 Uncle Wiggily(c) 300.00
5 Uncle Wiggily(c) 450.00
6 Uncle Wiggily 250.00
7 Uncle Wiggily 250.00
8 WK,Pogo 300.00
9 WK,War Bonds(c),A:Pogo. . . . 325.00
10 WK,Pogo 300.00
11 WK,Pogo 200.00
12 WK,Pogo 200.00
13 WK,Pogo 200.00
14 WK,Pogo 200.00
15 WK,Pogo 200.00

Animal Comics #11
© Dell Publishing Co.

16 Uncle Wiggily 125.00
17 WK,Pogo(c) 150.00
18 WK,Pogo(c) 150.00
19 WK,Pogo(c) 150.00
20 WK,Pogo 125.00
21 WK,Pogo(c) 150.00
22 WK,Pogo 100.00
23 WK,Pogo 100.00
24 WK,Pogo(c) 110.00
25 WK,Pogo(c) 110.00
26 WK,Pogo(c) 110.00
27 thru 30 WK,Pogo(c) . . . . . . @100.00

ANIMAL FABLES
E.C. Comics, July–Aug., 1946
1 B:Korky Kangaroo,Freddy Firefly
  Petey Pig & Danny Demon . 500.00
2 B:Aesop Fables 300.00
3 . . . . 250.00
4 . . . . 250.00
5 Firefly vs. Red Ants 250.00
6 . . . . 250.00
7 O:Moon Girls,Nov.–Dec.1947 . 750.00

ANIMAL FAIR
Fawcett Publications, March, 1946
1 B:Captain Marvel Bunny,
  Sir Spot 275.00
2 A:Droopy, Colonel Walrus . . . 125.00
3 . . . . 75.00
4 A:Kid Gloves, Cub Reporter . . . 75.00
5 thru 7 . . . . @75.00

8 . . . . 65.00
9 . . . . 65.00
10 . . . . 65.00
11 Feb., 1947 . . . . 65.00

ANNIE OAKLEY & TAGG
Dell Publishing Co., 1953
(1) see Dell Four Color #438
(2) see Dell Four Color #481
(3) see Dell Four Color #575
4 . . . . 250.00
5 . . . . 200.00
6 thru 10 . . . . @125.00
11 thru 18 . . . . @100.00

ARCHIE COMICS
**MLJ Magazines
Winter, 1942-43**
1 I:Jughead & Veronica 19,000.00
2 . . . . 3,500.00
3 . . . . 3,000.00
4 . . . . 1,500.00
5 . . . . 1,500.00
6 Christmas issue 1,000.00
7 thru 11 . . . . @1,100.00
12 thru 15 . . . . @750.00
16 thru 19 . . . . @650.00
Archie Publications, 1946
20 . . . . 750.00
21 . . . . 500.00
22 thru 31 . . . . @450.00
32 thru 42 . . . . @275.00
43 thru 50 . . . . @175.00
51 A:Katy Keene 150.00
52 thru 64 . . . . 125.00
65 thru 70 A:Katy Keene . . . . . @125.00
71 . . . . 75.00
72 thru 74 A:Katy Keene . . . . . @100.00
75 thru 99 . . . . @60.00
100 . . . . 75.00
101 thru 122 . . . . @40.00
123 UFO,Vampire 30.00
124 thru 130 . . . . @35.00
131 thru 145 . . . . @25.00
146 thru 182 . . . . @20.00
183 Caveman Archie 22.00
184 . . . . 20.00
185 I:The Archies Band 30.00
186 thru 195 . . . . 18.00
196 I:Cricket O'Dell 35.00
197 thru 200 . . . . @20.00
201 thru 228 . . . . @15.00
229 Lost Child 18.00
230 thru 260 . . . . 12.00
261 thru 300 . . . . @10.00

ARCHIE'S GIANT SERIES MAGAZINE
Archie Publications, 1954
1 . . . . 1,500.00
2 . . . . 850.00
3 . . . . 600.00
4 . . . . 550.00
5 . . . . 550.00
6 thru 10 . . . . @400.00
11 thru 20 . . . . @250.00
21 thru 29 . . . . @135.00
30 thru 35 . . . . @100.00
136 thru 141 . . . . @100.00
142 . . . . 100.00
143 thru 160 . . . . @50.00
161 thru 199 . . . . @40.00
200 . . . . 35.00
201 thru 250 . . . . @15.00
251 thru 299 . . . . @12.00
300 thru 500 . . . . @12.00

GOLDEN AGE

ARCHIE'S GIRLS BETTY AND VERONICA
Archie Publications, 1950
1 . . . . 2,200.00
2 . . . . 1,000.00
3 . . . . 500.00
4 . . . . 450.00
5 . . . . 450.00
6 thru 10 . . . . @400.00
11 thru 15 . . . . @300.00
16 thru 20 . . . . @275.00
21 . . . . 250.00
22 thru 29 . . . . @225.00
30 thru 40 . . . . @150.00
41 thru 50 . . . . @135.00
51 thru 60 . . . . @100.00
61 thru 70 . . . . @85.00
71 thru 74 . . . . @75.00
75 Devil 150.00
76 thru 90 . . . . @60.00
91 thru 99 . . . . @55.00
100 . . . . 65.00
101 thru 120 . . . . @35.00
121 thru 140 . . . . @25.00
141 thru 160 . . . . @20.00
161 thru 180 . . . . @15.00
181 thru 199 . . . . @15.00
200 . . . . 18.00
201 thru 220 . . . . @10.00
221 thru 240 . . . . @12.00
241 thru 347 . . . . @10.00

ARCHIE'S JOKE BOOK MAGAZINE
Archie Publications, 1953
1 . . . . 1,000.00
2 . . . . 500.00
3 . . . . 400.00
15 thru 19 . . . . @250.00
20 thru 25 . . . . @150.00
26 thru 35 . . . . @125.00
36 thru 40 . . . . @100.00
41 1st NA art 250.00
42 & 43 TV Personalities 125.00
44 thru 48 NA . . . . @135.00
49 thru 60 . . . . @50.00
61 thru 70 . . . . @30.00
71 thru 80 . . . . @25.00
81 thru 100 . . . . @25.00
101 thru 200 . . . . @15.00
201 thru 288 . . . . @10.00

ARCHIE'S MECHANICS
Archie Publications, 1954
1 . . . . 1,200.00
2 . . . . 600.00
3 . . . . 500.00

ARCHIE'S PAL, JUGHEAD
Archie Publications, 1949
1 . . . . 1,700.00
2 . . . . 750.00
3 . . . . 500.00
4 . . . . 400.00
5 . . . . 400.00
6 . . . . 300.00
7 thru 10 . . . . @300.00
11 thru 15 . . . . @200.00
16 thru 20 . . . . @175.00
21 thru 30 . . . . @125.00
31 thru 39 . . . . @75.00
40 thru 50 . . . . @65.00
51 thru 60 . . . . @50.00
61 thru 70 . . . . @45.00
71 thru 80 . . . . @35.00

81 thru 99 . . . . @30.00
100 . . . . 30.00
101 thru 126 . . . . @25.00

Archie's Pals 'N' Gals #4
© Archie Publications

ARCHIE'S PALS 'N' GALS
Archie Publications 1952–53
1 . . . . 900.00
2 . . . . 500.00
3 . . . . 300.00
4 . . . . 225.00
5 . . . . 225.00
6 . . . . 200.00
7 . . . . 200.00
8 thru 10 . . . . @175.00
11 thru 15 . . . . @125.00
16 thru 20 . . . . @100.00
21 thru 30 . . . . @75.00
31 thru 40 . . . . @65.00
41 thru 50 . . . . @50.00
51 thru 60 . . . . @30.00
61 thru 70 . . . . @25.00
71 thru 80 . . . . @20.00
81 thru 99 . . . . @18.00
100 . . . . 15.00
101 thru 120 . . . . @10.00
121 thru 160 . . . . @8.00
161 thru 224 . . . . @10.00

ARCHIE'S RIVAL REGGIE
Archie Publications, 1950
1 . . . . 1,000.00
2 . . . . 500.00
3 . . . . 350.00
4 . . . . 300.00
5 . . . . 300.00
6 . . . . 250.00
7 thru 9 . . . . @200.00
10 thru 14 A: Katy Keen . . . . . @150.00
15 . . . . 125.00
16 Aug., 1954 . . . . 140.00

ARMY & NAVY COMICS
See: SUPERSNIPE COMICS

ARROW, THE
Centaur Publications Oct., 1940–Oct., 1941
1 B:Arrow 4,000.00
2 BLB(c) 1,700.00
3 O:Dash Dartwell,Human Meteor,
  Rainbow, Bondage(c) 1,600.00

ATOMAN
Spark Publications, Feb., 1946
1 JRo,MMe,O:Atoman,A:Kid
  Crusaders 800.00
2 JRo,MMe 500.00

ATOMIC COMICS
Green Publishing Co. Jan., 1946
1 S&S,A:Radio Squad, Barry
  O'Neal 1,800.00
2 MB,A:Inspector Dayton, Kid
  Kane 750.00
3 MB,A:Zero Ghost Detective . . 500.00
4 JKa(c), July–Aug., 1946 . . . . . 500.00

ATOMIC COMICS
Daniels Publications 1946 (Reprints)
1 A:Rocketman,Yankee Boy,
  Bondage (c),rep 450.00

ATOMIC MOUSE
Capital Stories/ Charlton Comics, March, 1953
1 AFa,O:Atomic Mouse 350.00
2 AFa,Ice Cream (c) 125.00
3 AFa,Genie and Magic
  Carpet (c) 100.00
4 AFa 100.00
5 AFa,A:Timmy the Timid Ghost 100.00
6 thru 10 Funny Animal . . . . . . @75.00
11 thru 14 Funny Animal . . . . . @50.00
15 A:Happy the Marvel Bunny. . . . 60.00
16 Funny Animal,Giant 45.00
17 thru 30 Funny Animal . . . . . @35.00
31 thru 36 Funny Animal . . . . . @30.00
37 A:Atom the Cat 30.00
38 thru 40 Funny Animal . . . . . @25.00
41 thru 53 Funny Animal . . . . . @20.00
54 June, 1963 . . . . 20.00

ATOMIC THUNDER BOLT, THE
Regor Company, Feb., 1946
1 I:Atomic Thunderbolt,
  Mr. Murdo 800.00

AUTHENTIC POLICE CASES
St. John Publ. Co., 1948
1 Hale the Magician 500.00
2 Lady Satan, Johnny Rebel . . . 300.00
3 A:Avenger 500.00
4 Masked Black Jack 300.00
5 JCo 300.00
6 JCo,MB(c) 600.00
7 thru 10 . . . . @250.00
11 thru 15 . . . . @250.00
16 thru 23 . . . . @150.00
24 thru 28 Giants . . . . @300.00
29 thru 38 . . . . @100.00

All comics prices listed are for *Near Mint* condition.

GOLDEN AGE

AVIATION AND MODEL BUILDING
See: TRUE AVIATION PICTURE STORIES

AVON ONE-SHOTS
Avon Periodicals, 1949-1953
{Listed in Alphabetical Order}
1 Atomic Spy Cases 350.00
N# WW,Attack on Planet Mars . 1,000.00
1 Batchelor's Diary 400.00
1 Badmen of the West 400.00
N# Badmen of Tombstone 150.00
1 EK,Behind Prison Bars 300.00
2 Betty and Her Steady 100.00
N# EK,Blackhawk Indian
  Tomahawk War 150.00
1 EK,Blazing Sixguns 150.00
1 EK,Butch Cassidy 200.00
N# Chief Crazy Horse 200.00
N# FF,AW,EK,Chief Victorio's
  Apache Massacre 500.00
N# City of the Living Dead 500.00
1 Complete Romance 400.00
N# Custer's Last Fight 200.00
1 EK(c),Dalton Boys 175.00
N# GT(c),Davy Crockett 200.00
N# The Dead Who Walk 600.00
1 Diary of Horror,Bondage(c) . . . 400.00
N# WW,Earth Man on Venus . 1,600.00
1 Eerie, bondage (c) 800.00
1 EK,Escape from Devil's Island 400.00
N# EK,Fighting Daniel Boone . . . 200.00
N# EK(c),For a Night of Love . . 300.00
1 WW,Flying Saucers 1,000.00
N# Flying Saucers 600.00
1 Going Steady with Betty 150.00
N# Hooded Menace 600.00
N# EK,King of the Badmen
  of Deadwood 175.00
1 King Solomon's Mines 400.00
N# EK(c),Kit Carson &
  Blackfeet Warriors 100.00
N# EK,Last of the Comanches . . 175.00
N# EK,Masked Bandit 175.00
1 WW,Mask of Dr. Fu Manchu. 1,100.00
N# EK,Night of Mystery 500.00
1 WW,JKu,Outlaws of the
  Wild West 350.00
1 JKu,Out of this World 800.00
N# EK,Pancho Villa 250.00
1 EK,Phantom Witch Doctor . . . 500.00

Avon One-Shot: Out of the World
© *Avon Periodicals*

1 Pixie Puzzle Rocket
  to Adventureland 125.00
1 EK,Prison Riot,drugs 300.00
N# EK,Red Mountain Featuring
  Quantrell's Raiders 300.00
N# Reform School Girl 1,800.00
1 Robotmen of the Lost Planet 1,200.00
N# JO,WW(c),Rocket to
  the Moon 1,250.00
N# JKu,Secret Diary of
  Eerie Adventures 2,200.00
1 EK,Sheriff Bob Dixon's
  Chuck Wagon 150.00
1 Sideshow 350.00
1 JKu,Sparkling Love 250.00
N# Speedy Meteor 65.00
1 EK(c)Teddy Roosevelt &
  His Rough Riders 200.00
N# The Underworld Story 300.00
N# EK(c),The Unknown Man . . . 350.00
1 EK,War Dogs of the U.S. Army 150.00
N# EK(c),White Chief of the
  Pawnee Indians 175.00
N# Women to Love 400.00

BABE
Prize/Headline Feature
June—July, 1948
1 BRo,A;Boddy Rogers 250.00
2 BRo,same 150.00
3 Bro,same 125.00
4 thru 9 BRo,same . . . . @100.00

BABE RUTH SPORTS COMICS
Harvey Publications, April, 1949
1 BP 500.00
2 BP,Baseball 300.00
3 BP,Joe DiMaggio(c) 400.00
4 BP,Bob Feller(c) 325.00
5 BP,Football(c) 325.00
6 BP,Basketball(c) 325.00
7 BP 250.00
8 BP,Yogi Berra 325.00
9 BP,Stan Musial(c) 300.00
10 . . . . 300.00
11 Feb., 1951 . . . . 250.00

BANG-UP COMICS
Progressive Publ. 1941
1 CosmoMan, Lady Fairplay,
  O:Buzz Balmer 1,200.00
2 Buzz Balmer 550.00
3 Buzz Balmer 550.00

BANNER COMICS
Ace Magazines, Sept., 1941
3 B:Captain Courageous,
  Lone Warrior 1,300.00
4 JM(c),Flag(c) 800.00
5 . . . . 700.00
Becomes:

CAPTAIN COURAGEOUS COMICS
March, 1942
6 I:The Sword 1,000.00

BARNYARD COMICS
Animated Cartoons, June, 1944
1 (fa) 200.00
2 (fa) 100.00
3 (fa) 55.00
4 (fa) 55.00
5 (fa) 55.00

6 thru 12 (fa) . . . . @40.00
13 FF(ti) 60.00
14 FF(ti) 60.00
15 FF(ti) 60.00
16 . . . . 50.00
17 FF(ti) 45.00
18 FF,FF(ti) 100.00
19 FF,FF(ti) 100.00
20 FF,FF(ti) 100.00
21 FF(ti) 50.00
22 FF,FF(ti) 100.00
23 FF(ti) 50.00
24 FF,FF(ti) 100.00
25 FF,FF(ti) 100.00
26 FF(ti) 50.00
27 FF(ti) 50.00
28 . . . . 30.00
29 FF(ti) 50.00
30 and 31 . . . . @30.00
Becomes:

DIZZY DUCK
32 thru 39 . . . . @25.00

BASEBALL COMICS
Will Eisner Productions Spring, 1949
1 WE,A:Rube Rocky 900.00

BASEBALL HEROS
Fawcett Publications, 1952
N# Babe Ruth (c) 1,100.00

BASEBALL THRILLS
Ziff-Davis Publ. Co., 1951
10 Bob Feller Predicts Pennant
  Winners 500.00
2 BP, Yogi Berra story 350.00
3 EK, Joe DiMaggio story,
  Summer 1952 . . . . 450.00

BATTLEFIELD ACTION
See: DYNAMITE

BEANY & CECIL
Dell Publishing Co., Jan., 1952
1 . . . . 250.00
2 . . . . 150.00
3 . . . . 150.00
4 . . . . 150.00
5 . . . . 150.00

BEN BOWIE & HIS MOUNTAIN MEN
Dell Publishing Co., 1952
(1) *see Dell Four Color #443*
(2 thru 6) *see Dell Four Color*
7 . . . . 100.00
8 thru 10 . . . . @50.00
11 I:Yellow Hair 55.00
12 . . . . 35.00
13 . . . . 35.00
14 . . . . 35.00
15 thru 17 . . . . @35.00

BEST COMICS
Better Publications, Nov., 1939
1 B:Red Mask 1,000.00
2 A:Red Mask, Silly Willie 650.00
3 A:Red Mask 650.00
4 Cannibalism story,
  Feb., 1940 . . . . 750.00

GOLDEN AGE

BEWARE
See: CAPTAIN SCIENCE

BIG CHIEF WAHOO
Eastern Color Printing
July, 1942
1 .... 500.00
2 BWa(c),Three Ring Circus ... 250.00
3 BWa(c) 200.00
4 BWa(c) 200.00
5 BWa(c),Wild West Rodeo 200.00
6 A:Minnie-Ha-Cha 150.00
7 .... 125.00
8 .... 100.00
9 .... 100.00
10 .... 125.00
11 thru 22 .... @100.00
23 1943 .... 100.00

Big Shot Comics #17
© Columbia Comics

BIG SHOT COMICS
Columbia Comics Group
May, 1940
1 MBI,OW,Skyman,B:The Face,
  Joe Palooka, Rocky Ryan . 3,000.00
2 MBi,OW,Marvelo (c)....... 1,200.00
3 MBi,Skyman (c) 1,000.00
4 MBi,OW,Joe Palooka (c) 700.00
5 MBi,Joe Palooka (c) 650.00
6 MBi,Joe Palooka (c) 600.00
7 MBi,Elect Joe Palooka
  and Skyman 500.00
8 MBi,Joe Palooka and Skyman
  dress as Santa 500.00
9 MBi,Skyman 500.00
10 MBi,Skyman 500.00
11 MBi 475.00
12 MBi,OW 475.00
13 MBi,OW 475.00
14 MBi,OW,O:Sparky Watts ... 475.00
15 MBi,OW,O:The Cloak....... 500.00
16 MBi,OW 400.00
17 MBi(c),OW 400.00
18 MBi,OW 400.00
19 MBi,OW,The Face (c) 350.00
20 MBi,OW,OW(c),Skyman cov. . 350.00
21 MBi,OW,A:Raja the Arabian
  Knight. 300.00
22 MBi,OW,Joe Palooka (c) ... 300.00
23 MBi,OW,Sparky Watts (c).. . 275.00
24 MBi,OW,Uncle Sam (c) 300.00
25 MBi,OW,Hitler,Sparky Watts(c) 275.00
26 MBi,OW,Hitler,Devildog (c)... 300.00
27 MBi,OW,Skyman (c)........ 300.00
28 MBi,OW,Hitler (c).......... 400.00
29 MBi,OW,I:Captain Yank 300.00
30 MBi,OW,Santa (c) 275.00
31 MBi,OW,Sparky Watts (c)... 250.00
32 MBi,OW,B:Vic Jordan
  newspaper reps 275.00
33 MBi,OW,Sparky Watts (c)... 250.00
34 MBi,OW 250.00
35 MBi,OW 250.00
36 MBi,OW,Sparky Watts (c)... 225.00
37 MBi,OW 225.00
38 MBi,Uncle Slap Happy (c) .. 225.00
39 MBi,Uncle Slap Happy (c) .. 225.00
40 MBi,Joe Palooka Happy (c) . 225.00
41 MBi,Joe Palooka 200.00
42 MBi,Joe Palooka parachutes . 200.00
43 MBi,V:Hitler 300.00
44 MBi,Slap Happy (c) 200.00
45 MBi,Slap Happy (c) 200.00
46 MBi,Uncle Sam (c),V:Hitler.. 275.00
47 MBi,Uncle Slap Happy (c) .. 200.00
48 MBi 200.00
49 MBi 175.00
50 MBi,O:The Face 175.00
51 MBi 175.00
52 MBi,E:Vic Jordan (Hitler cov)
  newspaper reps 275.00
53 MBi,Uncle Slap Happy (c) .. 175.00
54 MBi,Uncle Slap Happy (c) .. 175.00
55 MBi,Happy Easter (c)....... 175.00
56 MBi 175.00
57 MBi 175.00
58 MBi 175.00
59 MBi,Slap Happy 175.00
60 MBi,Joe Palooka 150.00
61 MBi 125.00
62 MBi 125.00
63 MBi 125.00
64 MBi,Slap Happy............ 125.00
65 MBi,Slap Happy............ 125.00
66 MBi,Slap Happy............ 125.00
67 MBi 125.00
68 MBi,Joe Palooka 125.00
69 MBi 125.00
70 MBi,OW,Joe Palooka (c) ... 125.00
71 MBi,OW 135.00
72 MBi,OW 135.00
73 MBi,OW,The Face (c) 135.00
74 MBi,OW 135.00
75 MBi,OW,Polar Bear swim
  club (c)..................... 135.00
76 thru 80 MBi,OW .... @110.00
81 thru 84 MBi,OW .... @100.00
85 MBi,OW,Dixie Dugan (c) ... 100.00
86 thru 95 MBi,OW .... @90.00
96 MBi,OW,X-Mas (c)........... 90.00
97 thru 99 MBi,OW .... @90.00
100 MBi,OW,Special issue 100.00
101 thru 103 MBi,OW .... @90.00
104 MBi, Aug., 1949 .... 100.00

BIG-3
Fox Features Syndicate
Fall 1940
1 B:BlueBeetle,Flame,Samson 3,000.00
2 A:BlueBeetle,Flame,Samson 1,200.00
3 same 900.00
4 same 800.00
5 same 800.00
6 E:Samson, bondage (c) 700.00
7 A:V-Man, Jan., 1942 .... 600.00

BILL BARNES,
AMERICA'S AIR ACE
See: AIR ACE

BILL BOYD WESTERN
Fawcett Publications, 1950
1 B:Bill Boyd, Midnite,Ph(c) 600.00
2 P(c) 300.00
3 B:Ph(c)....................... 250.00
4 .... 200.00
5 .... 200.00
6 .... 200.00
7 .... 150.00
8 .... 150.00
9 .... 150.00
10 .... 150.00
11 .... 150.00
12 .... 125.00
13 .... 125.00
14 .... 125.00
15 thru 21 .... @125.00
22 E:Ph(c) 125.00
23 June, 1952................. 150.00

BILL STERN'S
SPORTS BOOK
Approved Comics
Spring-Summer, 1951
1 Ewell Blackwell.............. 250.00
2 .... 200.00
2-2 EK Giant 250.00

BILLY THE KID
ADVENTURE MAGAZINE
Toby Press, Oct., 1950
1 AW(a&c),FF(a&c) 300.00
2 Photo (c) 125.00
3 AW,FF 400.00
4 .... 75.00
5 .... 75.00
6 FF,Photo (c) 150.00
7 Photo (c) 75.00
8 .... 75.00
9 HK Pot-Shot Pete 125.00
10 .... 75.00
11 .... 60.00
12 .... 60.00
13 HK 60.00
14 AW,FF 100.00
15 thru 21 .... @50.00
22 AW,FF 65.00
23 thru 29 .... @45.00
30 1955 .... 50.00

BINGO COMICS
Howard Publications, 1945
1 LbC,Drug 500.00

BLACK CAT COMICS
Harvey Publications
(Home Comics),
June–July, 1946
1 JKu 900.00
2 JKu,JSm(c) 400.00
3 JSm(c) 300.00
4 B:Red Demon 300.00
5 S&K 400.00
6 S&K,A:Scarlet Arrow,
  O:Red Demon 400.00
7 S&K 400.00
8 S&K,B:Kerry Drake 350.00
9 S&K,O:Stuntman 400.00
10 JK,JSm 275.00
11 .... 275.00
12 'Ghost Town Terror' 275.00
13 thru 16 LEI .... @250.00
17 A:Mary Worth, Invisible
  Scarlet 250.00
18 LEI......................... 250.00
19 LEI......................... 250.00

All comics prices listed are for *Near Mint* condition.

GOLDEN AGE

Black Cat–Blackhawk / Comics Values Annual

Black Cat Mystery #32
© Harvey Publications

20 A:Invisible Scarlet 250.00
21 LEI 250.00
22 LEI thru 26 . . . . @250.00
27 X-Mas issue 275.00
28 I:Kit,A:Crimson Raider 275.00
29 Black Cat bondage (c) 260.00
Becomes:

BLACK CAT MYSTERY
Aug., 1951
30 RP,Black Cat(c) 300.00
31 RP 250.00
32 BP,RP,Bondage (c) 275.00
33 BP,RP,Electrocution (c) 300.00
34 BP,RP 225.00
35 BP,RP,OK, Atomic Storm . . . 300.00
36 RP 325.00
37 RP 260.00
38 RP 260.00
39 RP 275.00
40 RP 260.00
41 . . . . 260.00
42 . . . . 260.00
43 BP 260.00
44 BP,HN,JkS,Oil Burning (c) . . 275.00
45 BP,HN,Classic (c) 300.00
46 BP,HN 250.00
47 BP,HN 250.00
48 BP,HN 250.00
49 BP,HN 250.00
50 BP,Rotting Face 900.00
51 BP,HN,MMe 250.00
52 BP 150.00
53 BP 150.00
Becomes:

BLACK CAT WESTERN
Feb., 1955
54 A:Black Cat & Story 275.00
55 A:Black Cat 150.00
56 same 150.00
Becomes:

BLACK CAT MYSTIC
Sept., 1956
58 JK,Starts Comic Code 250.00
59 KB 200.00
60 JK 250.00
61 HN 200.00
62 . . . . 150.00
63 JK 150.00
64 JK 200.00
65 April, 1963 . . . . 200.00

BLACK DIAMOND WESTERN
See: DESPERADO

UNCLE SAM QUARTERLY
Quality Comics Group
Fall, 1941
1 BE,LF(c),JCo,O:Uncle Sam . 5,000.00
2 LG(c),BE,Ray,Black Condor . 1,300.00
3 GT(a&c) 1,100.00
4 GT,GF(c) 1,000.00
5 RC,GT 1,200.00
6 GT 1,000.00
7 Hitler, Tojo, Mussolini 1,300.00
8 GT 1,000.00
Becomes:

BLACKHAWK
Comic Magazines, Winter, 1944
9 Bait for a Death Trap 5,000.00
10 RC 1,500.00
11 RC 1,000.00
12 Flies to thrilling adventure . . . 950.00
13 Blackhawk Stalks Danger 950.00
14 BWa 1,000.00
15 Patrols the Universe 950.00
16 RC,BWa,Huddles for Action . . 800.00
17 BWa,Prepares for Action 800.00
18 RC(a&c),BWa,One for All
 and All for One 750.00
19 RC(a&c),BWa,Calls
 for Action 750.00
20 RC(a&c),BWa,Smashes
 Rugoth the ruthless God 750.00
21 BWa,Battles Destiny
 Written n Blood 600.00
22 RC(a&c),BWa,Fear battles
 Death and Destruction 600.00
23 RC(a&c),BWa,Batters
 Down Oppression 600.00
24 RC(a&c),BWa 600.00
25 RC(a&c),BWa,V:The Evil
 of Mung 600.00
26 RC(a&c),V:Menace of a
 Sunken World 550.00
27 BWa,Destroys a War-Mad
 Munitions Magnate 550.00
28 BWa,Defies Destruction in the
 Battle of the Test Tube 550.00
29 BWa,Tale of the Basilisk
 Supreme Chief 550.00
30 BWa,RC(a&c),The Menace
 of the Meteors 550.00
31 BWa,RC(a&c),JCo,Treachery
 among the Blackhawks 500.00
32 BWa,RC(a&c),A:Delya,
 Flying Fish 500.00
33 RC(a&c),BWa,A:The Mockers 500.00
34 BWa,A:Tana,Mavis 500.00
35 BWa,I:Atlo,Strongest Man
 on Earth 500.00
36 RC(a&c),BWa,V:Tarya 450.00
37 RC(a&c),BWa,V:Sari,The
 Rajah of Ramastan 450.00
38 BWa 450.00
39 RC(a&c),BWa,V:Lilith 450.00
40 RC(a&c),BWa,Valley of
 Yesterday 450.00
41 RC(a&c),BWa 400.00
42 RC(a&c),BWa,V:Iron Emperor 400.00
43 RC(a&c),BWa,Terror
 from the Catacombs 400.00
44 RC(a&c),BWa,The King
 of Winds 400.00
45 BWa,The Island of Death 400.00
46 RC(a&c),BWa,V:DeathPatrol . 400.00
47 RC(a&c),BWa,War! 400.00
48 RC(a&c),BWa,A:Hawks of
 Horror,Port of Missing Ships . 400.00

Blackhawk #14
© Comic Magazines

49 RC(a&c),BWa,A:Valkyrie,
 Waters of Terrible Peace 400.00
50 RC(a&c),BWa,I:Killer Shark,
 Flying Octopus 425.00
51 RC(a&c),BWa,V:The Whip, Whip of
 Nontelon 400.00
52 RC(a&c),BWa,Traitor in
 the Ranks 400.00
53 RC(a&c),BWa,V:Golden
 Mummy 400.00
54 RC(a&c),BWa,V:Dr. Deroski,
 Circles of Suicide 400.00
55 RC(a&c),BWa,V:Rocketmen . . 400.00
56 RC(a&c),BWa,V:The Instructor,
 School for Sabotage 400.00
57 RC(a&c),BWa,Paralyzed City
 of Armored Men 400.00
58 RC(a&c),BWa,V:King Cobra,
 The Spider of Delanza 400.00
59 BWa,V:Sea Devil 400.00
60 RC(a&c),BWa,V:Dr. Mole and
 His Devils Squadron 400.00
61 V:John Smith, Stalin's
 Ambassador of Murder 325.00
62 V:General X, Return of
 Genghis Kahn 325.00
63 RC(a&c),The Flying
 Buzz-Saws 325.00
64 RC(a&c),V:Zoltan Korvas,
 Legion of the Damned 325.00
65 Olaf as a Prisoner in Dungeon
 of Fear 325.00
66 RC(a&c),V:The Red
 Executioner, Crawler 325.00
67 RC(a&c),V:Future Fuehrer . . . 325.00
68 V:Killers of the Kremlin 300.00
69 V:King of the Iron Men,
 Conference of the Dictators . 300.00
70 V:Killer Shark 300.00
71 V:Von Tepp, The Man Who
 could Defeat Blackhawk
 O:Blackhawk 350.00
72 V:Death Legion 300.00
73 V:Hangman,The Tyrannical
 Freaks 250.00
74 Plan of Death 250.00
75 V:The Mad Doctor Baroc,
 The Z Bomb Menace 250.00
76 The King of Blackhawk Island 250.00
77 V:The Fiendish
 Electronic Brain 250.00
78 V:The Killer Vulture,
 Phantom Raider 250.00
79 V:Herman Goering, The
 Human Bomb 250.00

CVA Page 366 All comics prices listed are for *Near Mint* condition.

GOLDEN AGE

Blackhawk–Blue Beetle

80 V:Fang, the Merciless, Dr. Death	250.00
81 A:Killer Shark, The Sea Monsters of Killer Shark	250.00
82 V:Sabo Teur, the Ruthless Commie Agent	250.00
83 I:Hammer & Sickle, V:Madam Double Cross	250.00
84 V:Death Eye,Dr. Genius, The Dreaded Brain Beam	250.00
85 V:The Fiendish Impersonator	250.00
86 V:The Human Torpedoes	250.00
87 A:Red Agent Sovietta,V:Sea Wolf, Le Sabre,Comics Code	200.00
88 V:Thunder the Indestructible, The Phantom Sniper	200.00
89 V:The Super Communists	225.00
90 V:The Storm King, Villainess who smashed the Blackhawk team	225.00
91 Treason in the Underground	225.00
92 V:The World Traitor	225.00
93 V:Garg the Destroyer, O:Blackhawk	250.00
94 V:Black Widow, Darkk the Destroyer	225.00
95 V:Madam Fury, Queen of the Pirates	225.00
96 Doom in the Deep	225.00
97 Revolt of the Slave Workers	225.00
98 Temple of Doom	225.00
99 The War That Never Ended	225.00
100 The Delphian Machine	250.00
101 Satan's Paymaster	200.00
102 The Doom Cloud	200.00
103 The Super Race	200.00
104 The Jet Menace	200.00
105 The Red Kamikaze Terror	200.00
106 The Flying Tank Platoon	200.00
107 The Winged Menace	200.00

(Please see DC Listings)

BLACK HOOD
See: LAUGH COMICS

BLACK TERROR
Better Publications/ Standard, Winter, 1942-43

1 Bombing (c)	4,000.00
2 V:Arabs,Bondage(c)	1,500.00
3 V:Nazis,Bondage(c)	1,000.00
4 V:Sub Nazis	800.00
5 V:Japanese	800.00
6 Air Battle	750.00
7 Air Battle,V:Japanese, A:Ghost	750.00
8 V:Nazis	750.00
9 V:Japanese,Bondage(c)	800.00
10 V:Nazis	700.00
11 thru 16	@700.00
17 Bondage(c)	700.00
18 ASh	600.00
19 ASh	600.00
20 ASh	600.00
21 ASh	700.00
22 FF,ASh	600.00
23 ASh	600.00
24 Bondage(c)	700.00
25 ASh	550.00
26 GT,ASh	550.00
27 MME,GT,ASh	550.00

BLAZING COMICS
Enwil Associates/Rural Home June, 1944

1 B:Green Turtle, Red Hawk, Black Buccaneer	600.00
2 Green Turtle (c)	400.00

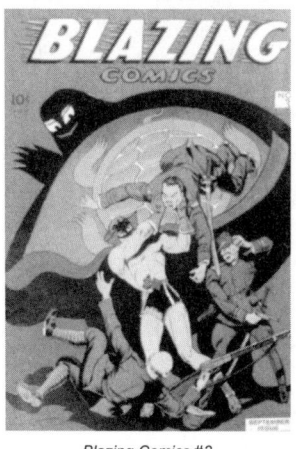

Blazing Comics #3
© Enwil Associates

3 Green Turtle (c)	350.00
4 Green Turtle (c)	350.00
5 March, 1945	350.00
5a Black Buccaneer(c),1955	200.00
6 Indian-Japanese(c), 1955	200.00

BLONDIE COMICS
David McKay, Spring, 1947

1	275.00
2	150.00
3	100.00
4	100.00
5	100.00
6 thru 10	@75.00
11 thru 15	@50.00

Harvey Publications

16	75.00
17 thru 20	@50.00
21 thru 30	@35.00
31 thru 50	@25.00
51 thru 80	@20.00
81 thru 99	@15.00
100	20.00
101 thru 124	@15.00
125 Giant	20.00
126 thru 135	@15.00
136 thru 140	@15.00
141 thru 163	@20.00

King Publications

164 thru 167	@20.00
168 thru 174	@10.00

Charlton Comics

175 thru 200	@10.00
201 thru 220	@10.00

BLUE BEETLE, THE
Fox Features Syndicate/ Holyoke Publ., Winter 1939

1 O:Blue Beetle,A:Master Magician	7,000.00
2 BP,Wonder World	2,000.00
3 JSm(c)	1,500.00
4 Mentions marijuana	1,200.00
5 GT,A:Zanzibar the Magician	1,000.00
6 B:Dynamite Thor, O:Blue Beetle	1,000.00
7 A:Dynamo	900.00
8 E:Thor,A:Dynamo	900.00
9 BP(c),A:Black Bird,Gorilla	900.00
10 BP(c),A:BlackBird,bondage(c)	900.00
11 BP(c),A:Gladiator	750.00
12 A:Black Fury	750.00
13 B:V-Man	800.00
14 JKu,I:Sparky	750.00
15 JKu	750.00
16	600.00
17 AyB,A:Mimic	550.00
18 JKu,E:V-Man,A:Red Knight	550.00
19 JKu,A:Dascomb Dinsmore	600.00
20 I&O:The Flying Tiger Squadron	650.00
21	400.00
22 A:Ali-Baba	400.00
23 A:Jimmy DooLittle	400.00
24 I:The Halo	400.00
25	400.00
26 General Patton story	425.00
27 A:Tamoa	400.00
28	350.00
29	350.00
30 L:Holyoke	350.00
31 F:Fox	300.00
32 Hitler (c)	500.00
33 Fight for Freedom	300.00
34 A:Black Terror,Menace of K-4	300.00
35 Threat From Saturn	300.00
36 The Runaway House	300.00
37 Inside the House	300.00
38 Revolt of the Zombies	300.00
39	300.00
40	300.00
41 A:O'Brine Twins	250.00
42	250.00
43	250.00
44	250.00
45	250.00
46 BP,A:Puppeteer	300.00
47 JKa,V:Junior Crime Club	1,500.00
48 JKa,A:Black Lace	1,200.00
49 JKa	1,200.00
50 JKa,The Ambitious Bride	1,000.00
51 JKa, Shady Lady	900.00
52 BP,JKa(c),Bondage (c)	1,500.00
53 JKa,A:Jack "Legs" Diamond,Bondage(c)	1,000.00
54 JKa,The Vanishing Nude	1,600.00
55 JKa	950.00
56 JKa,Tri-State Terror	950.00
57 JKa,The Feagle Bros.	950.00
58	200.00
59	175.00
60 Aug., 1960	200.00

BLUE BEETLE
See: THING!, THE

Blue Beetle #10
© Fox Features Syndicate

Blue Bolt–Bomber

GOLDEN AGE

Comics Values Annual

Blue Bolt #18
© Star Publications

BLUE BOLT
**Funnies, Inc./Novelty Press/
Premium Service Co, 1940**
1 JSm,PG,O:Blue Bolt 5,000.00
2 JSm,S&K 2,500.00
3 S&K,A:Space Hawk 2,000.00
4 PG,S&K 1,800.00
5 BEv,B:Sub Zero 1,800.00
6 JK,JSm 1,500.00
7 S&K,BEv 1,500.00
8 S&K(c) 1,500.00
9 . . . . 1,400.00
10 S&K(c) 1,400.00
11 BEv(c) 1,500.00
12 . . . . 1,500.00
2-1 BEv(c),PG,O:Dick Cole &
V:Simba 500.00
2-2 BEv(c),PG,O:Twister 400.00
2-3 PG,Cole vs Simba 300.00
2-4 BD 300.00
2-5 I:Freezum 300.00
2-6 O:Sgt.Spook, Dick Cole . . . 250.00
2-7 BD,Lois Blake 200.00
2-8 BD 200.00
2-9 JW 200.00
2-10 JW 200.00
2-11 JW 200.00
2-12 E:Twister 200.00
3-1 A:115th Infantry 200.00
3-2 A:Phantom Sub 200.00
3-3 . . . . 200.00
3-4 JW(c) 175.00
3-5 Jor 175.00
3-6 Jor 175.00
3-7 X-Mas (c) 175.00
3-8 . . . . 175.00
3-9 A:Phantom Sub 175.00
3-10 DBa 175.00
3-11 April Fools (c) 175.00
3-12 . . . . 175.00
4-1 Hitler,Tojo,Mussolini (c) . . . 350.00
4-2 Liberty Bell (c) 125.00
4-3 What are You Doing for Your
Country 125.00
4-4 I Fly for Vengence 125.00
4-5 TFH(c) 125.00
4-6 HcK 125.00
4-7 JWi(c) 125.00
4-8 E:Sub Zero 125.00
4-9 . . . . 125.00
4-10 . . . . 125.00
4-11 . . . . 125.00
4-12 . . . . 125.00
5-1 thru 5-12 . . . . @100.00

6-1 . . . . 100.00
6-2 War Bonds (c) 100.00
6-3 . . . . 100.00
6-4 Racist(c) 165.00
6-5 Soccer (c) 100.00
6-6 thru 6-12 . . . . @100.00
7-1 thru 7-12 . . . . @100.00
8-1 Baseball (c) 100.00
8-2 JHa 100.00
8-3 JHe 100.00
8-4 JHa 100.00
8-5 JHe 100.00
8-6 JDo 100.00
8-7 LbC(c) 225.00
8-8 . . . . 100.00
8-9 AMc(c) 100.00
8-10 . . . . 100.00
8-11 Basketball (c) 125.00
8-12 . . . . 100.00
9-1 AMc,Baseball (c) 100.00
9-2 AMc 100.00
9-3 . . . . 100.00
9-4 JHe 100.00
9-5 JHe 100.00
9-6 LbC(c),Football (c) 225.00
9-7 JHe 100.00
9-8 Hockey (c) 125.00
9-9 LbC(c),3-D effect 200.00
9-10 . . . . 100.00
9-11 . . . . 100.00
9-12 . . . . 100.00
10-1 Baseball (c),3-D effect . . . 125.00
10-2 3-D effect 110.00

Star Publications
102 LbC(c),Chameleon 400.00
103 LbC(c),same 300.00
104 LbC(c),same 300.00
105 LbC(c),O:Blue Bolt Space,
Drug Story 600.00
106 S&K,LbC(c),A:Space Hawk . 550.00
107 S&K,LbC(c),A:Space Hawk . 550.00
108 S&K,LbC(c),A:Blue Bolt 550.00
109 BW,LbC(c) 550.00
110 B:Horror (c)s,A:Target 550.00
111 Weird Tales of Horror,
A:Red Rocket 550.00
112 JyD,WiP 500.00
113 BW,JyD,A:Space Hawk 550.00
114 LbC(c),JyD 500.00
115 LbC(c),JyD,A:Sgt.Spook 550.00
116 LbC(c),JyD,A:Jungle Joe . . . 550.00
117 LbC(c),A:Blue Bolt,Jo-Jo . . . 550.00
118 WW,LbC(c),A:White Spirit . . . 550.00
119 LbC(c) 550.00
Becomes:

GHOSTLY WEIRD STORIES
Star Publications, Sept., 1953
120 LbC,A:Jo-Jo 500.00
121 LbC,A:Jo-Jo 450.00
122 LbC,A:The Mask,Sci-Fi 500.00
123 LbC,A:Jo-Jo 450.00
124 LbC, Sept., 1954 . . . . 450.00

BLUE CIRCLE COMICS
**Enwil Associates/
Rural Home, June, 1944**
1 B:Blue Circle,O:Steel Fist 350.00
2 . . . . 250.00
3 Hitler parody (c) 300.00
4 . . . . 200.00
5 E:Steel Fist,A:DriftwoodDavey 200.00
6 . . . . 200.00

BLUE RIBBON COMICS
MLJ Magazines, Nov., 1939
1 JCo,B:Dan Hastings,
Richy-Amazing Boy 5,000.00

2 JCo,B:Bob Phantom,
Silver Fox 2,000.00
3 JCo,A:Phantom,Silver Fox . . 1,500.00
4 O:Fox,Ty Gor,B:Doc Strong,
Hercules 1,600.00
5 Gattling Gun (c) 900.00
6 Amazing Boy Richy (c) 800.00
7 A:Fox (c),Corporal Collins
V:Nazis 800.00
8 E:Hercules 800.00
9 O&I:Mr. Justice 4,000.00
10 Mr. Justice (c) 1,500.00
11 SCp(c) 1,500.00
12 E:Doc Strong 1,500.00
13 B:Inferno 1,500.00
14 A:Inferno 1,200.00
15 A:Inferno,E:Green Falcon . . 1,200.00
16 O:Captain Flag 2,500.00
17 Captain Flag V:Black Hand . 1,200.00
18 Captain Flag-Black Hand . . 1,000.00
19 Captain Flag (c) 1,000.00
20 Captain Flag V:Nazis (c) . . 1,200.00
21 Captain Flag V:Death 1,000.00
22 Circus (c), March, 1942 . . . . 1,000.00

BLUE RIBBON COMICS
**St. John Publications
Feb., 1949**
1 Heckle & Jeckle 100.00
2 MB(c),Diary Secrets 250.00
3 MB,MB(c),Heckle & Jeckle . . . 100.00
4 Teen-age Diary Secrets 250.00
5 MB,Teen-age Diary Secrets . . 300.00
6 Dinky Duck 50.00

BO
Charlton Comics, June, 1955
1 . . . . 75.00
2 . . . . 75.00
3 Oct., 1955 . . . . 75.00

BOB COLT
**Fawcett Publications
Nov., 1950**
1 B:Bob Colt,Buck Skin 500.00
2 Death Round Train 250.00
3 Mysterious Black Knight of the
Prairie 200.00
4 Death Goes Downstream . . . 200.00
5 The Mesa of Mystery 200.00
6 The Mysterious Visitors 200.00
7 Dragon of Disaster 175.00
8 Redman's Revenge 175.00
9 Hidden Hacienda 175.00
10 Fiend from Vulture
Mountain 175.00

BOLD STORIES
Kirby Publishing Co., 1950
1 WW,Near nudity (c) 2,000.00
2 GI,Cobra's Kiss 1,500.00
3 WW,Orge of Paris 1,200.00
4 Case of the Winking Buddha . 500.00
5 It Rhymes with Lust 500.00
6 Candid Tales, April, 1950 . . . . 500.00

BOMBER COMICS
Elliot Publishing Co., 1944
1 B:Wonder Boy,Kismet,
Eagle Evans 900.00
2 Wonder Boy(c) Hitler 600.00
3 Wonder Boy-Kismet (c) 500.00
4 Hitler,Tojo, Mussolini (c) 700.00

Comics Values Annual — GOLDEN AGE — Book–Buck Rogers

BOOK OF ALL COMICS
William H. Wise, 1945
1 A:Green Mask,Puppeteer 500.00

BOOK OF COMICS, THE
William H. Wise, 1945
N# A:Captain V 500.00

BOY COMICS
**Comic House, Inc.
(Lev Gleason Publ.), April, 1942**
3 O:Crimebuster,Bombshell,Young
  Robin, B:Yankee Longago,
  Swoop Storm 5,000.00
4 Hitler,Tojo,Mussolini (c) 2,000.00
5 Crimebuster saves day (c) . 1,500.00
6 O:Iron Jaw & Death of Son,
  B:Little Dynamite 4,000.00
7 Hitler,Tojo,Mussolini (c) 1,500.00
8 D:Iron Jaw 1,600.00
9 I:He-She 1,500.00
10 Iron Jaw returns 1,800.00
11 Iron Jaw falls in love 1,200.00
12 Crimebuster V:Japanese 700.00
13 V:New,more terrible
  Iron Jaw............... 700.00
14 V:Iron Jaw 700.00
15 I:Rodent,D:Iron Jaw........ 800.00
16 Crimebuster V:Knight 450.00
17 Flag (c),Crimebuster
  V:Moth 500.00
18 Smashed car (c) 450.00
19 Express train (c) 450.00
20 Coffin (c) 450.00
21 Boxing (c) 300.00
22 Under Sea (c) 300.00
23 Golf (c) 300.00
24 County insane asylum (c).... 300.00
25 52 pgs 300.00
26 68 pgs 300.00
27 Express train (c) 325.00
28 E:Yankee Longago.......... 325.00
29 Prison break (c) 325.00
30 O:Crimebuster,Murder (c) ... 400.00
31 68 pgs 300.00
32 E:Young Robin Hood 300.00
33 .... 300.00
34 Suicide (c) & story 250.00
35 .... 200.00
36 .... 200.00
37 .... 200.00
38 .... 200.00

Boy Comics #11
© Lev Gleason Publications

39 E:Little Dynamite 200.00
40 .... 200.00
41 thru 50 .... @175.00
51 thru 56................ @150.00
57 B:Dilly Duncan............ 200.00
58 .... 150.00
59 .... 150.00
60 Iron Jaw returns 175.00
61 O:Iron Jaw,Crimebuster 200.00
62 A:Iron Jaw 175.00
63 thru 70 .... @150.00
71 E:Dilly Duncan............ 150.00
72 .... 150.00
73 .... 150.00
74 thru 79 .... @150.00
80 I:Rocky X 100.00
81 thru 88 .... @100.00
89 A:The Claw 120.00
90 same................... 120.00
91 same................... 120.00
92 same................... 120.00
93 The Claw(c),A:Rocky X 120.00
94 .... 75.00
95 .... 75.00
96 .... 75.00
97 .... 75.00
98 A:Rocky X 75.00
99 .... 75.00
100 .... 125.00
101 .... 125.00
102 .... 125.00
103 thru 118 .... @125.00
119 March, 1956............. 125.00

BOY EXPLORERS
See: TERRY AND THE PIRATES

BRENDA STARR
**Four Star Comics Corp./
Superior Comics Ltd.,
Sept., 1947**
13(1) 1,100.00
14(2) JKa,Bondage (c) 1,200.00
2-3 .... 900.00
2-4 JKa,Operating table (c) ... 1,000.00
2-5 Swimsuit (c) 800.00
2-6 .... 800.00
2-7 .... 800.00
2-8 Cosmetic (c) 800.00
2-9 Giant Starr (c) 800.00
2-10 Wedding (c) 800.00
2-11 .... 800.00
2-12 .... 800.00

BRICK BRADFORD
**Best Books
(Standard Comics),
July, 1949**
5 .... 250.00
6 Robot (c) 300.00
7 AS 150.00
8 .... 150.00

BROADWAY ROMANCES
Quality Comics Group, 1950
1 PG,BWa(a&c)............. 375.00
2 BWa,Glittering Desire 275.00
3 BL,Stole My Love 125.00
4 Enslaved by My Past 125.00
5 Flame of Passion,Sept.,1950 . 125.00

BRONCHO BILL
**Visual Editions
(Standard Comics), Jan., 1948**
5 .... 150.00

6 AS(c) 75.00
7 AS(c) 55.00
8 ASh 55.00
9 AS(c) 55.00
10 AS(c) 55.00
11 AS(c) 50.00
12 AS(c) 50.00
13 AS(c) 50.00
14 ASh 50.00
15 ASh 50.00
16 AS(c) 50.00

BRUCE GENTRY
**Four Star Publ./
Visual Editions/
Superior, Jan., 1948**
1 B:Ray Bailey reprints 550.00
2 Plane crash (c) 400.00
3 E:Ray Bailey reprints 300.00
4 Tiger attack (c) 250.00
5 .... 250.00
6 Help message (c).......... 250.00
7 .... 250.00
8 End of Marriage (c),July, 1949 250.00

BUCCANEERS
See: KID ETERNITY

Buck Jones
© Dell Publishing Co.

BUCK JONES
Dell Publishing Co., 1950
1 .... 200.00
2 .... 100.00
3 .... 75.00
4 .... 75.00
5 .... 75.00
6 .... 75.00
7 .... 75.00
8 .... 75.00

BUCK ROGERS
**Eastern Color Printing
Winter 1940**
1 Partial Painted(c) 5,000.00
2 .... 2,000.00
3 Living Corpse from Crimson
  Coffin................. 1,500.00
4 One man army of greased
  lightning.............. 1,400.00
5 Sky Roads 1,300.00
6 Sept., 1943 .... 1,300.00

All comics prices listed are for Near Mint condition.

Buck Rogers–Captain Aero GOLDEN AGE Comics Values Annual

Toby Press
100 Flying Saucers 300.00
101 . . . . 250.00
9 MA 250.00

BUG MOVIES
Dell Publishing Co., 1931
1 . . . . 400.00

BUGS BUNNY
DELL GIANT EDITIONS
Dell Publishing Co.
Christmas
1 Christmas Funnies (1950) 350.00
2 Christmas Funnies (1951) 300.00
3 Christmas Funnies (1952) 250.00
4 Christmas Funnies (1953) 200.00
5 Christmas Funnies (1954) 200.00
6 Christmas Party (1955) 175.00
7 Christmas Party (1956) 185.00
8 Christmas Funnies (1957) 185.00
9 Christmas Funnies (1958) 185.00
1 County Fair (1957) 200.00

Halloween
1 Halloween Parade (1953) 200.00
2 Halloween Parade (1954) 175.00
3 Trick 'N' Treat
  Halloween Fun (1955) 185.00
4 Trick 'N' Treat
  Halloween Fun (1956) 185.00

Vacation
1 Vacation Funnies (1951) 300.00
2 Vacation Funnies (1952) 275.00
3 Vacation Funnies (1953) 250.00
4 Vacation Funnies (1954) 200.00
5 Vacation Funnies (1955) 200.00
6 Vacation Funnies (1956) 175.00
7 Vacation Funnies (1957) 175.00
8 Vacation Funnies (1958) 175.00
9 Vacation Funnies (1959) 175.00

BUGS BUNNY
Dell Publishing Co., 1942
see Four Color for early years
28 thru 30 . . . . @75.00
31 thru 50 . . . . @50.00
51 thru 70 . . . . @35.00
71 thru 85 . . . . @30.00
86 Giant-Show Time 100.00
87 thru 100 . . . . @30.00
101 thru 120 . . . . @25.00
121 thru 140 . . . . @18.00
141 thru 190 . . . . @15.00
191 thru 245 . . . . @10.00

BULLETMAN
Fawcett Publications
Summer, 1941
1 I:Bulletman & Bulletgirl 5,500.00
2 MRa(c) 2,200.00
3 MRa(c) 1,600.00
4 V:Headless Horror,
  Guillotine (c) 1,500.00
5 Riddle of Dr. Riddle 1,500.00
6 V:Japanese 1,000.00
7 V:Revenge Syndicate 1,000.00
8 V:Mr. Ego 1,000.00
9 V:Canine Criminals 1,000.00
10 I:Bullet Dog 1,100.00
11 V:Fiendish Fiddler 800.00
12 . . . . 750.00
13 . . . . 750.00
14 V:Death the Comedian 750.00
15 V:Professor D 750.00
16 Vanishing Elephant, Fall 1946 . 750.00

Buster Crabbe #6
© *Famous Funnies*

BUSTER CRABBE
Famous Funnies, Nov., 1951
1 The Arrow of Death 500.00
2 AW&GE(c) 550.00
3 AW&GE(c) 600.00
4 FF(c) 650.00
5 AW,FF(a&c) 1,500.00
6 Sharks (c) 200.00
7 FF 250.00
8 Gorilla (c) 200.00
9 FF 250.00
10 . . . . 225.00
11 Snakes (c) 150.00
12 Sept., 1953 . . . . 150.00

BUSTER CRABBE
Lev Gleason Pub., 1953
1 Ph(c) 250.00
2 ATh 200.00
3 ATh 200.00
4 F. Gordon(c) 200.00

BUZ SAWYER
Standard Comics, June, 1948
1 . . . . 250.00
2 I:Sweeney 150.00
3 . . . . 100.00
4 . . . . 100.00
5 June, 1949 . . . . 100.00

CALLING ALL BOYS
Parents Magazine Institute
Jan., 1946
1 Skiing 125.00
2 . . . . 60.00
3 Peril Out Post 75.00
4 Model Airplane 75.00
5 Fishing 75.00
6 Swimming 75.00
7 Baseball 85.00
8 School 75.00
9 The Miracle Quarterback 75.00
10 Gary Cooper (c) 100.00
11 Rin-Tin-Tin (c) 75.00
12 Bob Hope (c) 150.00
13 Bing Cosby (c) 125.00
14 J. Edgar Hoover (c) 75.00
15 Tex Granger (c) 50.00
16 . . . . 50.00
17 Tex Granger (c), May, 1948 . . . 50.00
Becomes:

TEX GRANGER
June, 1948
18 Bandits of the Badlands 75.00
19 The Seven Secret Cities 65.00
20 Davey Crockett's Last Fight . . 50.00
21 Canyon Ambush 50.00
22 V:Hooded Terror 50.00
23 V:Billy the Kid 50.00
24 A:Hector, Sept., 1949 . . . . 60.00

CALLING ALL GIRLS
Parent Magazine Press, Inc.
Sept., 1941
1 . . . . 150.00
2 Virginia Weidler (c) 75.00
3 Shirley Temple (c) 100.00
4 Darla Hood (c) 50.00
5 Gloria Hood (c) 50.00
6 . . . . 50.00
7 . . . . 50.00
8 . . . . 50.00
9 Flag (c) 50.00
10 . . . . 50.00
11 Gary Cooper as Lou Gerrig . . . 75.00
12 thru 20 . . . . @50.00
21 thru 39 . . . . @35.00
40 Liz Taylor 150.00
41 . . . . 30.00
42 . . . . 30.00
43 Oct., 1945 . . . . 30.00

CALLING ALL KIDS
Quality Comics, Inc.
Dec./Jan., 1946
1 Funny Animal stories 125.00
2 . . . . 50.00
3 . . . . 35.00
4 . . . . 35.00
5 . . . . 35.00
6 . . . . 35.00
7 . . . . 35.00
8 . . . . 35.00
9 . . . . 35.00
10 . . . . 35.00
11 thru 25 . . . . @30.00
26 Aug., 1949 . . . . 30.00

CAMERA COMICS
U.S. Camera Publishing Corp.
July–Sept., 1944
1 Airfighter, Grey Comet 250.00
2 How to Set Up a Darkroom . . 150.00
3 Linda Lens V:Nazi (c) 125.00
4 Linda Lens (c) 110.00
5 Diving (c) 110.00
6 Jim Lane (c) 110.00
7 Linda Lens (c) 110.00
8 Linda Lens (c) 110.00
9 Summer, 1946 . . . . 110.00

CAMP COMICS
Dell Publishing Co., 1942
1 Ph(c),WK,A:Bugs Bunny . . . 1,000.00
2 Ph(c),WK,A:Bugs Bunny 800.00
3 Ph(c),Wk 750.00

CAPTAIN AERO COMICS
Holyoke Publishing Co., 1941
1 B:Flag-Man&Solar, Master
  of Magic Captain Aero,
  Captain Stone 2,500.00
2 A:Pals of Freedom 1,000.00
3 JKu,B:Alias X,A:Pals of
  Freedom 1,000.00
4 JKu,O:Gargoyle,
  Parachute jump 1,000.00

CVA Page 370   All comics prices listed are for *Near Mint* condition.

GOLDEN AGE

Captain: Aero–Marvel

Captain Aero #6
© Holyoke Pub. Col

CAPTAIN FEARLESS COMICS
Helnit Publishing Co., 1941
1 O:Mr. Miracle,Alias X,Captain Fearless Citizen Smith,
  A:Miss Victory 1,200.00
2 A:Border Patrol, Sept.,1941. . . 750.00

CAPTAIN FLASH
Sterling Comics, Nov., 1954
1 O:Captain Flash 500.00
2 V:Black Knight 250.00
3 Beasts from 1,000,000 BC . . . 250.00
4 Flying Saucer Invasion 250.00

CAPTAIN FLEET
Approved Comics, Fall, 1952
1 Storm and Mutiny ...Typhoon . 175.00

CAPTAIN FLIGHT COMICS
Four Star Publications March, 1944–Feb.-March, 1947
N# B:Captain Flight,Ace Reynolds Dashthe Avenger,Professor X 600.00
2 . . . . 300.00
3 . . . . 250.00
4 B:Rock Raymond Salutes America's Wartime Heroines. 300.00
5 Bondage (c),B:Red Rocket
  A:The Grenade 1,400.00
6 Girl tied at the stake 250.00
7 LbC(c),Dog Fight (c) 600.00
8 LbC(c),B:Yankee Girl,
  A:Torpedoman 600.00
9 LbC(c),Dog Fight (c) 600.00
10 LbC(c),Bondage (c) 600.00
11 LbC(c),Future(c) 1,300.00

CAPTAIN GALLANT
Charlton Comics, 1955
1 Ph(c),Buster Crabbe 100.00
2 . . . . 75.00
3 . . . . 75.00
4 Sept., 1956 . . . . 75.00

CAPTAIN JET
Four Star Publ., May, 1952
1 Factory bombing (c) 225.00
2 Parachute jump (c) 125.00
3 Tank bombing (c) 100.00
4 Parachute (c) 100.00
5 . . . . 100.00

CAPTAIN KIDD
See: ALL GREAT COMICS

CAPTAIN MARVEL ADVENTURES
Fawcett Publications, 1941
N# JK, B:Captain Marvel & Sivana 40,000.00
2 GT,JK(c),Billy Batson (c) . . . 6,000.00
3 JK(c),Thunderbolt (c) 3,500.00
4 Shazam(c) 2,500.00
5 V:Nazis 2,000.00
6 Solomon, Hercules, Atlas, Zeus, Achilles & Mercury (c) 1,500.00
7 Ghost of the White Room. . . 1,500.00
8 Forward America 1,500.00
9 A:Ibac the Monster, Nippo the Nipponese, Realm of the Subconscious 1,500.00
10 V:Japanese 1,500.00
11 V:Japanese and Nazis. 1,500.00
12 Joins the Army 1,200.00
13 V:Diamond-Eyed Idol of Doom 1,200.00
14 Nippo meets his Nemesis . . 1,200.00
15 Big "Paste the Axis" contest 1,200.00
16 Uncle Sam (c), Paste the Axis 1,200.00
17 P(c), Paste the Axis 1,100.00
18 P(c), O:Mary Marvel 2,700.00
19 Mary Marvel & Santa (c) 900.00
20 Mark of the Black Swastika 5,000.00
21 Hitler (c) 1,000.00
22 B:Mr. Mind serial, Shipyard Sabotage 1,100.00
23 A:Steamboat 900.00
24 Minneapolis Mystery 900.00
25 Sinister Faces (c) 900.00
26 Flag (c) 900.00
27 Joins Navy 750.00
28 Uncle Sam (c) 750.00
29 Battle at the China Wall 750.00
30 Modern Robinson Crusoe . . . 750.00
31 Fights his own Conscience. . . 750.00
32 V:Mole Men, Dallas 750.00
33 Mt. Rushmore parody (c), Omaha 600.00
34 Oklahoma City 600.00
35 O:Radar the International Policeman, Indianapolis 550.00
36 Missing face contest, St. Louis 550.00
37 V:Block Busting Bubbles, Cincinnati 550.00
38 V:Chattanooga Ghost, Rock Garden City 550.00
39 V:Mr. Mind's Death Ray, Pittsburgh 550.00
40 V:Ghost of the Tower,Boston . 550.00
41 Runs for President, Dayton . . 450.00
42 Christmas special, St. Paul . . 450.00
43 V:Mr. Mind,I:Uncle Marvel, Chicago 450.00
44 OtherWorlds,Washington,D.C. 450.00
45 V:Blood Bank Robbers 450.00
46 E: Mr. Mind Serial, Tall Stories of Jonah Joggins . . . 450.00
47 . . . . 400.00
48 Signs Autographs (c) 400.00
49 V: An Unknown Killer 400.00
50 Twisted Powers 400.00
51 Last of the Batsons 350.00

Captain Marvel Adventures #21
© Fawcett Publications

Comics Values Annual

5 JKu 900.00
6 JKu,Flagman,A:Miss Victory . . 800.00
7 Alias X 500.00
8 O:Red Cross,A:Miss Victory . . 500.00
9 A:Miss Victory,Alias X 375.00
10 A:Miss Victory,Red Cross 350.00
11 A:Miss Victory 250.00
12 A:Miss Victory 250.00
13 A:Miss Victory 250.00
14 A:Miss Victory 250.00
15 AS(c),A:Miss Liberty. 250.00
16 AS(c),Leather Face 225.00
17 LbC(c) 550.00
21 LbC(c) 550.00
22 LbC(c),I:Mighty Mite 550.00
23 LbC(c) 550.00
24 LbC(c) American Planes Dive Bomb Japan 900.00
25 LbC(c),Science Fiction(c) 550.00
26 LbC(c) 1,200.00

CAPTAIN BATTLE
New Friday Publ./ Magazine Press, Summer, 1941
1 B:Captain Battle,O:Blackout 2,000.00
2 Pirate Ship (c) 1,000.00
3 Dungeon (c) 900.00
4 *.may not exist*
5 V:Japanese, Summer, 1943 . . 650.00

CAPTAIN BATTLE, Jr.
Comic House, Fall, 1943
1 Claw V:Ghost, A:Sniffer 1,300.00
2 Man who didn't believe in Ghosts 1,000.00

CAPTAIN COURAGEOUS
See: BANNER COMICS

CAPTAIN EASY
Standard Comics, 1939
N# Swash Buckler 1,500.00
10 . . . . 200.00
11 . . . . 150.00
12 . . . . 150.00
13 ASh(c) 150.00
14 . . . . 150.00
15 . . . . 150.00
16 ASh(c) 150.00
17 Sept., 1949 . . . . 150.00

All comics prices listed are for *Near Mint* condition.

Captain: Marvel–Midnight — GOLDEN AGE — Comics Values Annual

52 O&I:Sivana Jr.,V:Giant Earth Dreamer 350.00	126 thru 130 . . . . @250.00	23 MRa(c) 600.00
53 Gets promoted. 350.00	131 . . . . 250.00	24 MRa(c),V:Weather Man 600.00
54 Marooned in the Future, Kansas City 350.00	132 V:Flood 250.00	25 MRa(c),Flag (c) 600.00
55 Endless String, Columbus . . . 350.00	133 . . . . 250.00	26 MRa(c),Happy New Year 600.00
56 Goes Crazy, Mobile 350.00	134 . . . . 250.00	27 MRa(c),Jungle Thrills 600.00
57 A:Haunted Girl, Rochester . . . 350.00	135 Perplexing Past Puzzle 250.00	28 MRa(c),V:Sivana's Crumbling Crimes 600.00
58 V:Sivana 350.00	136 . . . . 250.00	29 MRa(c),Blazes a Wilderness Trail 600.00
59 . . . . 350.00	137 . . . . 250.00	30 MRa(c) 600.00
60 Man who made Earthquakes . 350.00	138 V:Haunted Horror. 275.00	31 MRa(c) 400.00
61 I&V: Oggar, the Worlds Mightiest Immortal 375.00	139 . . . . 250.00	32 Keeper of the Lonely Rock. . . 400.00
62 The Great Harness Race 350.00	140 Hand of Horror 250.00	33 . . . . 400.00
63 Stuntman. 350.00	141 Horror 250.00	34/35 I&O:Sivana Jr.. . . . . 400.00
64 . . . . 350.00	142 . . . . 250.00	36 Underworld Tournament. 400.00
65 V:Invaders from Outer Space. 350.00	143 Great Stone Face on the Moon. 250.00	37 FreddyFreeman'sNews-stand. 400.00
66 Atomic War (c). 350.00	144 thru 147 . . . . @250.00	38 A:Arabian Knight 400.00
67 Hartford 300.00	148 V:The World. 250.00	39 V:Sivana Jr., Headline Stealer 400.00
68 Scenes from the Past, Baltimore 300.00	149 . . . . 250.00	40 Faces Grave Situation 400.00
69 Gets Knighted 300.00	150 Captains Marvel's Wedding, Nov., 1953 . . . . 500.00	41 I:The Acrobat. 300.00
70 Horror in the Box 300.00		42 V:Sivana Jr. 300.00
71 Wheel of Death 300.00		43 V:Beasts on Broadway. 300.00
72 . . . . 300.00	**CAPTAIN MARVEL JR.**	44 Key to the Mystery. 300.00
73 Becomes a Petrophile 300.00	**Fawcett Publications, 1942**	45 A:Icy Fingers 300.00
74 Who is the 13th Guest 300.00	1 MRa(c),O:Captain Marvel, Jr., A:Capt. Nazi 7,500.00	46 . . . . 300.00
75 V:Astonishing Yeast Menace . 300.00	2 MRa(c),O:Capt.Nippon, V:Capt. Nazi 2,500.00	47 V:Giant of the Beanstalk 300.00
76 A:Atom Ambassador 300.00	3 MRa(c),Parade to Excitement 1,500.00	48 Whale of a Fish Story 300.00
77 The Secret Life 300.00	4 MRa(c),V:Invisible Nazi 1,500.00	49 V:Dream Recorder. 300.00
78 O:Mr. Tawny 350.00	5 MRa(c),V:Capt. Nazi 1,200.00	50 Wanted: Freddy Freeman . . . 300.00
79 O:Atom,A:World's Worst Actor 400.00	6 MRa(c),Adventure of Sabbac 1,000.00	51 The Island Riddle. 275.00
80 Twice told story 750.00	7 MRa(c),City under the Sea . 1,000.00	52 A:Flying Postman. 275.00
81 A:Mr. Atom. 275.00	8 MRa(c),Dangerous Double . 1,000.00	53 Atomic Bomb on the Loose . . 300.00
82 A:Mr. Tawny 275.00	9 MRa(c),Independence (c) . . 1,100.00	54 V:Man with 100 Heads 275.00
83 Indian Chief. 275.00	10 Hitler (c) 1,050.00	55 Pyramid of Eternity 275.00
84 V:Surrealist Imp 275.00	11 MRa(c). 800.00	56 Blue Boy's Black Eye 275.00
85 Freedom Train 325.00	12 MRa(c),Scuttles the Axis Isle in the Sky. 850.00	57 MRa(c),Magic Ladder. 275.00
86 A:Mr. Tawny 275.00	13 MRa(c),V:The Axis,Hitler,(c) 1,000.00	58 Amazing Mirror Maze. 275.00
87 V:Electron Thief 275.00	14 MRa(c),X-Mas (c), Santa wears Capt. Marvel uniform 750.00	59 MRa(c) 275.00
88 Billy Batson's Boyhood. 275.00	15 MRa(c),V:Capt. Nazi 800.00	60 V:Space Menace 275.00
89 V:Sivana 275.00	16 MRa(c),A:Capt. Marvel, Sivana, Pogo 750.00	61 V:Himself. 250.00
90 A:Mr. Tawny 275.00	17 MRa(c),Meets his Future self 750.00	62 . . . . 250.00
91 A:Chameleon Stone. 275.00	18 MRa(c),V:Birds of Doom . . . 750.00	63 V:Witch of Winter. 250.00
92 The Land of Limbo. 275.00	19 MRa(c),A:Capt. Nazi & Capt. Nippon 750.00	64 thru 70 . . . . @250.00
93 Book of all Knowledge 275.00	20 MRa(c),Goes on the Warpath 700.00	71 thru 74. . . . . @250.00
94 Battle of Electricity 275.00	21 MRa(c),Buy War Stamps . . . 600.00	75 V:Outlaw of Crooked Creek . . 250.00
95 The Great Ice Cap 275.00	22 MRa(c),Rides World's oldest steamboat 600.00	76 thru 85 . . . . @250.00
96 V:Automatic Weapon 275.00		86 Defenders of time 250.00
97 Wiped Out 275.00		87 thru 89. . . . . @250.00
98 United Worlds 275.00		90 The Magic Trunk 200.00
99 Rain of Terror. 275.00		91 thru 99 . . . . @200.00
100 V:Sivana,Plot against the Universe. 600.00		100 V:Sivana Jr 250.00
101 Invisibility Trap 250.00		101 thru 106 . . . . @200.00
102 Magic Mix-up. 250.00		107 The Horror Dimension 200.00
103 Ice Covered World of 1,000,000 AD 250.00		108 thru 118 . . . . @200.00
104 Mr. Tawny's Masquerade . . . 250.00		119 Condemned to Die, Electric Chair, June, 1953 . . . . 200.00
105 The Dog Catcher 250.00		
106 V:Menace of the Moon. 250.00		**CAPTAIN MIDNIGHT**
107 V:Space Hunter 250.00		**Fawcett Publications, 1942**
108 V:Terrible Termites 250.00		1 O:Captain Midnight, Capt. Marvel (c) 5,000.00
109 The Invention Inventor 250.00		2 Smashes Jap Juggernaut. . . 2,000.00
110 V:Sivana 250.00		3 Battles the Phantom Bomber 1,500.00
111 The Eighth Sea 250.00		4 Grapples the Gremlins . . . 1,400.00
112 . . . . 250.00		5 Double Trouble in Tokyo . . . 1,400.00
113 Captain Marvel's Feud 250.00		6 Blasts the Black Mikado . . . 1,000.00
114 V:The Ogre 250.00		7 Newspaper headline (c) . . . 1,000.00
115 . . . . 250.00		8 Flying Torpedoes Berlin-Bound 950.00
116 Flying Saucer. 300.00		9 MRa(c), Subs in Mississippi . 950.00
117 . . . . 250.00		10 MRa(c), Flag (c). 950.00
118 V:Weird Water Man 250.00		11 MRa(c), Murder in Mexico . . 750.00
119 . . . . 250.00		12 V:Sinister Angels 750.00
120 . . . . 250.00		13 Non-stop Flight around the World 750.00
121 . . . . 250.00		14 V:King of the Villains 750.00
122 . . . . 250.00		15 V:Kimberley Killer. 750.00
123 . . . . 250.00		16 Hitler's Fortress Breached . . 750.00
124 V:Discarded Instincts 250.00	*Captain Marvel Jr. #3*	
125 V:Ancient Villain. 250.00	*© Fawcett Publications*	

GOLDEN AGE

Captain Midnight–Cat Man

Captain Midnight #1
© *Fawcett Publications*

17 MRa(c), Hello Adolf 700.00
18 Death from the Skies 700.00
19 Hour of Doom for the Axis . . . 700.00
20 Brain and Brawn against Axis 700.00
21 Trades with Japanese 600.00
22 Plea for War Stamps 600.00
23 Japanese Prison (c). 600.00
24 Rising Sun Flag (c) 600.00
25 Amusement Park Murder 600.00
26 Hotel of Horror. 600.00
27 Death Knell for Tyranny 600.00
28 Gliderchuting to Glory 600.00
29 Bomb over Nippon. 600.00
30 . . . . 600.00
31 . . . . 450.00
32 . . . . 450.00
33 V:Shark 450.00
34 thru 40 . . . . @450.00
41 thru 50 . . . . @350.00
51 thru 63 . . . . @350.00
64 V:XOG, Ruler of Saturn 350.00
65 . . . . 350.00
66 V:XOG. 350.00
67 Fall, 1948 . . . . 350.00
Becomes:

SWEETHEARTS
Oct., 1948
68 Robert Mitchum 150.00
69 thru 110 . . . . @100.00
111 Ronald Reagan story 175.00
112 thru 118 . . . . @100.00
119 WW,Marilyn Monroe. 500.00
120 Atomic Bomb story . . . . . . @100.00
121 Liz Taylor. 125.00
122 Marjuana,1954. . . . . 100.00

CAPTAIN SCIENCE
Youthful Magazines, 1950
1 WW,O:Captain Science,
   V:Monster God of Rogor . . 1,300.00
2 WW,V:Cat Men of Phoebus,
   Space Pirates. 600.00
3 Ghosts from the Underworld . 600.00
4 WW,Vampires 1,000.00
5 WW,V:Shark Pirates of
   Pisces 1,000.00
6 WW,V:Invisible Tyrants,
   bondage (c) 700.00
7 WW,Bondage(c) Dec., 1951 . . 700.00
Becomes:

FANTASTIC
Feb., 1952
8 Isle of Madness 500.00
9 Octopus (c) 400.00
Becomes:

BEWARE
June, 1952
10 SHn,Doll of Death 500.00
11 SHn,Horror Head. 400.00
12 SHn,Body Snatchers 400.00
Becomes:

CHILLING TALES
Dec., 1952
13 MF,Screaming Skull 700.00
14 SHn,Smell of Death 450.00
15 SHn,Curse of the Tomb 550.00
16 HcK,Mark of the Beast
   Bondage(c) 450.00
17 MFc(c),Wandering Willie,
   Oct.,1953 . . . . 550.00

CAPTAIN STEVE SAVAGE
Avon Periodicals
[1st Series] 1950
N# WW 500.00
2 EK(c),The Death Gamble 165.00
3 EK(c),Crash Landing in
   Manchuria 100.00
4 EK(c),V:Red Raiders from
   Siang-Po 75.00
5 EK(c),Rockets of Death 75.00
6 Operation Destruction 75.00
7 EK(c),Flight to Kill 75.00
8 EK(c),V:Red Mystery Jet 75.00
9 EK(c) 75.00
10 . . . . 75.00
11 EK(c) 80.00
12 WW 150.00
13 ThW 75.00
[2nd Series] Sept./Oct., 1954
5 . . . . 75.00
6 WW 100.00
7 thru 13 . . . . @50.00

CAPTAIN VIDEO
Fawcett Publications, 1951
1 GE,Ph(c) From TV series. . . 1,500.00
2 Time when Men could not
   Walk 1,000.00
3 GE,Indestructible Antagonist . 800.00
4 GE,School of Spies 800.00
5 GE,Missiles of Doom,
   photo (c). 800.00
6 GE,Island of Conquerors,
   Photo (c); Dec., 1951 . . . . . . 800.00

CAPTAIN WIZARD
Rural Home 1946
1 Impossible Man 250.00

CASPER, THE FRIENDLY GHOST
St. John Publishing, 1949
1 O:Baby Huey 2,200.00
2 . . . . 900.00
3 . . . . 600.00
4 . . . . 600.00
5 . . . . 650.00
Harvey Publications
7 Baby Huey 500.00
8 thru 9 Baby Huey . . . . @275.00
10 I:Spooky 300.00
11 A:Spooky 150.00
12 thru 18 . . . . @150.00

19 I:Nightmare 250.00
20 I:Wendy the Witch 300.00
21 thru 30 . . . . @125.00
31 thru 40. . . . . @100.00
41 thru 50 . . . . @75.00
51 thru 60 . . . . @75.00
61 thru 69 . . . . @75.00
70 July, 1958 . . . . 75.00

CATMAN COMICS
**Helnit Publ. Co./
Holyoke Publ. Co./
Continental Magazine, 1941**
1 O:Deacon&Sidekick Mickey,
   Dr. Diamond & Ragman,A:Black
   Widow, B:Blaze Baylor. . . . 5,000.00
2 Ragman. 2,000.00
3 B:Pied Piper 1,800.00
4 CQ 1,500.00

Cat Man Comics #8
© *Continental Magazine*

5 I&O: The Kitten 1,000.00
6 CQ 1,000.00
7 CQ 1,000.00
8 JKa, I:Volton 1,200.00
9 JKa 850.00
10 JKa,O:Blackout,
   B:Phantom Falcon 850.00
11 JKa,DRi,BF,PzF 850.00
12 . . . . 600.00
13 . . . . 700.00
14 CQ 600.00
15 Rajah of Destruction 600.00
16 Bye-Bye Axis, Hitler 900.00
17 Buy Bonds and Stamps 600.00
18 Buy Bonds and Stamps 600.00
19 CQ,Hitler,Tojo and
   Mussolini (c) 1,000.00
20 CQ,Hitler,Tojo and
   Mussolini (c) 1,000.00
21 CQ 600.00
22 CQ 600.00
23 CQ 600.00
N# DRiV:Japanese,Bondage(c). . 650.00
N# V:Demon. 600.00
N# LbC(c),A:Leather Face 600.00
27 LbC(c),Flag (c),O:Kitten . . . 1,100.00
28 LbC(c),Horror (c). 1,100.00
29 LbC(c),BF,RP 1,000.00
30 LbC(c),BF,Bondage(c). . . . 1,050.00
31 LbC(c) 1,000.00
32 LbC(c),RP,Aug., 1946 . . . . 1,000.00

GOLDEN AGE

CHALLENGER, THE
Interfaith Publications, 1945
- N# O:The Challenger Club 500.00
- 2 JKa 350.00
- 3 JKa 350.00
- 4 JKa,BF 350.00

CHAMBER OF CHILLS
Harvey Publications/ Witches Tales, June, 1951
- 21 (1)..................... 550.00
- 22 (2)..................... 325.00
- 23 (3) Eyes Ripped Out 325.00
- 24 (4) LE,Bondage (c) 350.00
- 5 LE,Shrunken Skull,
  Operation Monster 350.00
- 6 LE,Seven Skulls of Magondi . 325.00
- 7 LE,Pit of the Damned 300.00
- 8 LE,Formula for Death 325.00
- 9 LE,Bondage (c) 275.00
- 10 LE,Cave of Death 275.00
- 11 Curse of Morgan Kilgane .. 200.00
- 12 Swamp Monster........... 200.00
- 13 The Lost Race........... 250.00
- 14 LE,Down to Death 200.00
- 15 LE,Nightmare of Doom. ... 250.00
- 16 LE,Cycle of Horror 250.00
- 17 LE,Amnesia.............. 250.00
- 18 LE,Hair cut-Atom Bomb 300.00
- 19 LE,Happy Anniversary 250.00
- 20 Shock is Struck 250.00
- 21 LE,BP,RP,Nose for News ... 275.00
- 22 LE,Is Death the End?..... 200.00
- 23 LE,BP,RP,Heartline 200.00
- 24 LE,BP,Bondage(c)......... 300.00
- 25 LE, ... 165.00
- 26 LE,HN,Captains Return ... 165.00

Becomes:

CHAMBER OF CLUES
Feb., 1955
- 27 BP,A:Kerry Drake......... 125.00
- 28 A:Kerry Drake 75.00

CHAMPION COMICS
Worth Publishing Co., 1939
- 2 B:Champ, Blazing Scarab, Neptina,
  Liberty Lads, Jingleman... 2,500.00
- 3 .... 1,000.00
- 4 Bailout(c)............... 1,000.00
- 5 Jungleman(c) 1,000.00
- 6 MNe 1,000.00
- 7 MNe,Human Meteor 1,000.00

Champion Comics #9
© Worth Publishing Co.

- 8 JK 2,000.00
- 9 JK,S&K 2,000.00
- 10 JK,Bondage (c).......... 2,000.00

Becomes:

CHAMP COMICS
Oct. 1940
- 11 Human Meteor 1,200.00
- 12 Human Heteor 1,000.00
- 13 Dragon's Teeth........... 900.00
- 14 Liberty Lads.............. 900.00
- 15 RC,Liberty Lads........... 900.00
- 16 Liberty Lads.............. 900.00
- 17 Liberty Lads.............. 900.00
- 18 Liberty Lads 1,200.00
- 19 JSm,A:The Wasp 1,300.00
- 20 S&K,A:The Green Ghost 900.00
- 21 S&K..................... 700.00
- 22 A:White Mask............. 750.00
- 23 Flag (c) 750.00
- 24 Hitler,Tojo & Mussolini 700.00
- 25 .... 700.00
- 26 thru 29................. @700.00

CHARLIE McCARTHY
Dell Publishing Co., 1947
- 1 Ph(c) 250.00
- 2 .... 125.00
- 3 .... 125.00
- 1 .... 125.00
- 2 .... 125.00
- 3 .... 125.00
- 4 .... 125.00
- 5 .... 125.00
- 6 .... 125.00
- 7 .... 125.00
- 8 .... 125.00
- 9 .... 125.00

CHIEF, THE
Dell Publishing Co., 1950
(1) see Dell Four Color #290
- 2 .... 75.00

CHILLING TALES
See: CAPTAIN SCIENCE

CHOICE
Great Comics 1941
- 1 O:Secret Circle 2,200.00
- 2 .... 1,200.00
- 3 The Lost City 1,500.00

CHUCKLE THE GIGGLY BOOK OF COMIC ANIMALS
R. B. Leffing Well Co., 1944
- 1 .... 200.00

CINEMA COMICS HERALD
Paramount/Universal/RKO/ 20th Century Fox Giveaways 1941-43
- N# Mr. Bug Goes to Town 150.00
- N# Bedtime Story 100.00
- N# Lady for a Night,J.Wayne ... 200.00
- N# Reap the Wild Wind 100.00
- N# Thunderbirds 75.00
- N# They All Kissed Me 75.00
- N# Bombardier 90.00
- N# Crash Dive 90.00
- N# Arabian Nights 75.00

CIRCUS THE COMIC RIOT
Globe Syndicate, June, 1938
- 1 BKa,WE,BW 8,000.00
- 2 BKa,WE,BW 5,000.00
- 3 BKa,WE,BW, Aug., 1938 .. 4,500.00

CISCO KID, THE
Dell Publishing Co.
(1) See Dell Four Color #292
- 2 Jan., 1951 .... 175.00
- 3 thru 5 .... @150.00
- 6 thru 10 .... @125.00
- 11 thru 20 .... @100.00
- 21 thru 36 .... @80.00
- 37 thru 41 Ph(c)'s .... @150.00

CLAIRE VOYANT
Leader Publ./Visual Ed./ Pentagon Publ., 1946-47
- N# 900.00
- 2 JKa(c).................... 600.00
- 3 Case of the Kidnapped Bride . 750.00
- 4 Bondage (c) 550.00

CLOAK AND DAGGER
Approved Comics (Ziff-Davis), Fall, 1952
- 1 NS(c),Al Kennedy of the Secret
  Service 300.00

CLUE COMICS
Hillman Periodicals, 1943
- 1 O:Boy King,Nightmare,Micro-Face,
  Twilight,Zippo.......... 1,500.00
- 2 .... 750.00
- 3 Boy King V:The Crane 750.00
- 4 V:The Crane 500.00
- 5 V:The Crane 500.00
- 6 Hells Kitchen 350.00
- 7 V:Dr. Plasma,Torture(c) 375.00
- 8 RP,A:The Gold Mummy King . 350.00
- 9 I:Paris 300.00
- 10 O:Gun Master 300.00
- 11 A:Gun Master............. 300.00
- 12 O:Rackman............... 300.00
- 2-1 S&K,O:Nightro,A:Iron Lady .. 600.00
- 2-2 S&K,Bondage(c).......... 800.00
- 2-3 S&K 600.00

Becomes:

REAL CLUE CRIME STORIES
June, 1947
- 2-4 DBw,S&K,True Story of
  Ma Barker 600.00
- 2-5 S&K, Newface surgery(c) ... 500.00
- 2-6 S&K, Breakout (c)........ 450.00
- 2-7 S&K, Stick up (c) 450.00
- 2-8 Kidnapping (c) 100.00
- 2-9 DBa,Boxing fix (c)........ 100.00
- 2-10 DBa,Murder (c)......... 100.00
- 2-11 Attempted bankrobbery (c) . 100.00
- 2-12 Murder (c)............. 100.00
- 3-1 thru 3-12............... @75.00
- 4-1 thru 4-12.............. @100.00
- 5-1 thru 5-12............... @75.00
- 6-1 thru 6-12............... @75.00
- 6-10 Bondage(c)............ 100.00
- 7-1 thru 7-12............... @65.00
- 8-1 thru 8-5, May, 1953 ..... @65.00

C-M-O COMICS
Comic Corp. of America (Centaur), May, 1942
- 1 Invisible Terror 1,500.00

GOLDEN AGE

2 Super Ann 1,000.00

COCOMALT BIG BOOK OF COMICS
Harry A. Chesler, 1938
1 BoW,PGn,FG,JCo,(Give away)
  Little Nemo 2,500.00

COLOSSUS COMICS
Sun Publications March, 1940
1 A:Colossus 7,500.00

COLUMBIA COMICS
William H. Wise Co., 1944
1 Joe Palooka,Charlie Chan . . . 350.00

COMICS, THE
Dell Publishing Co. March, 1937
1 I:Tom Mix & Arizona Kid 2,500.00
2 A:Tom Mix & Tom Beaty 1,200.00
3 A:Alley Oop 1,000.00
4 same 1,000.00
5 same 1,000.00
6 thru 11 same . . . . @1,000.00

COMICS ON PARADE
United Features Syndicate April, 1938–Feb., 1955
1 B:Tarzan,Captain and the Kids,
  Little Mary, Mixup,Abbie & Slats,
  Broncho Bill,Li'l Abner 5,000.00
2 Circus Parade of all 1,800.00
3 . . . . 1,300.00
4 On Rocket 1,000.00
5 All at the Store 1,000.00
6 All at Picnic 700.00
7 Li'l Abner(c) 700.00
8 same 700.00
9 same 700.00
10 same 700.00
11 same 600.00
12 same 600.00
13 same 600.00
14 Abbie n' Slats (c) 600.00
15 Li'l Abner(c) 600.00
16 Abbie n' Slats(c) 600.00
17 Tarzan,Abbie n' Slats(c) 650.00
18 Li'l Abner(c) 600.00
19 same 600.00
20 same 500.00
21 Li'l Abner(c) 500.00
22 Tail Spin Tommy(c) 500.00
23 Abbie n' Slats(c) 500.00
24 Tail Spin Tommy(c) 500.00
25 Li'l Abner(c) 500.00
26 Abbie n' Slats(c) 500.00
27 Li'l Abner(c) 500.00
28 Tail Spin Tommy(c) 500.00
29 Abbie n' Slats(c) 500.00
30 Li'l Abner(c) 300.00
31 The Captain & the Kids(c) . . . 175.00
32 Nancy and Fritzi Ritz(c) 150.00
33 Li'l Abner(c) 200.00
34 The Captain & the Kids(c) . . . 150.00
35 Nancy and Fritzi Ritz(c) 150.00
36 Li'l Abner(c) 200.00
37 The Captain & the Kids(c) . . . 150.00
38 Nancy and Fritzi Ritz(c) 125.00
39 Li'l Abner(c) 200.00
40 The Captain & the Kids(c) . . . 150.00
41 Nancy and Fritzi Ritz(c) 100.00
42 Li'l Abner(c) 200.00
43 The Captain & the Kids(c) . . . 150.00
44 Nancy and Fritzi Ritz(c) 100.00

Comics on Parade #10
© United Features Syndicate

45 Li'l Abner(c) 150.00
46 The Captain & the Kids(c) . . . 100.00
47 Nancy and Fritzi Ritz(c) 100.00
48 Li'l Abner(c) 150.00
49 The Captain & the Kids(c) . . . 100.00
50 Nancy and Fritzi Ritz(c) 100.00
51 Li'l Abner(c) 150.00
52 The Captain & the Kids(c) . . . 100.00
53 Nancy and Fritzi Ritz(c) 100.00
54 Li'l Abner(c) 150.00
55 Nancy and Fritzi Ritz(c) 100.00
56 The Captain & the Kids(c) . . . 100.00
57 Nancy and Fritzi Ritz(c) 100.00
58 Li'l Abner(c) 150.00
59 The Captain & the Kids(c) . . . 100.00
60 Nancy and Fritzi Ritz(c) 75.00
61 thru 76 Nancy & Fritzi Ritz(c) @75.00
77 Nancy & Sluggo(c) 60.00
78 thru 104 Nancy & Sluggo(c) . @60.00

COMPLETE BOOK OF COMICS AND FUNNIES
William H. Wise & Co., 1945
1 Wonderman-Magnet 500.00

COMPLETE BOOK OF TRUE CRIME COMICS
William H. Wise & Co., 1945
1 rep. Crime Does Not Pay . . . 1,300.00

CONFESSIONS OF LOVE
Artful Publications April, 1950
1 . . . . 300.00
2 July, 1950 . . . . 175.00

CONFESSIONS OF LOVE
Star Publications, July, 1952
11 AW,LbC(c)Intimate Secrets of
  Daring Romance 150.00
12 AW,LbC(c),I Couldn't Say No 150.00
13 AW,LbC(c),Heart Break 150.00
14 AW,LbC(c),My Fateful Love . 125.00
4 JyD,AW,LbC(c),The Longing
  Heart 125.00
5 AW,LbC(c),I Wanted Love 125.00
6 AW,LbC(c),My Jealous Heart . 125.00
Becomes:

CONFESSIONS OF ROMANCE
Nov., 1953
7 LbC(c)Too Good 150.00
8 AW,LbC(c),I Lied About Love . 125.00
9 WW,AW,LbC(c),I Paid
  Love's Price 150.00
10 JyD,AW,LbC(c),My Heart Cries
  for Love 125.00
11 JyD,AW,LbC(c),Intimate
  Confessions, Nov., 1954 . . . . 125.00

CONFESSIONS OF LOVELORN
See: LOVELORN

CONQUEROR COMICS
Albrecht Publications Winter, 1945
1 . . . . 250.00

CONTACT COMICS
Aviation Press, July, 1944
N# LbC(c),B:Black Venus,
  Golden Eagle 650.00
2 LbC(c),Peace Jet 500.00
3 LbC(c),LbC,E:Flamingo 450.00
4 LbC(c),LbC 450.00
5 LbC(c),A:Phantom Flyer 500.00
6 LbC(c),HK 600.00
7 LbC(c),Flying Tigers 400.00
8 LbC(c),Peace Jet 400.00
9 LbC(c),LbC,A:Marine Flyers . . 400.00
10 LbC(c),A:Bombers of the AAF 400.00
11 LbC(c),HK,AF,Salutes Naval
  Aviation 600.00
12 LbC(c),A:Sky Rangers, Air Kids,
  May, 1946 . . . . 1,000.00

COO COO COMICS
Nedor/Animated Cartoons (Standard), Oct., 1942
1 O&I:Super Mouse 300.00
2 . . . . 150.00
3 . . . . 75.00
4 . . . . 100.00
5 . . . . 100.00
6 . . . . 75.00
7 thru 10 . . . . @70.00
11 thru 33 . . . . @70.00
34 thru 40 FF illustration . . . . @100.00
41 FF 200.00
42 FF 200.00
43 FF illustration 100.00
44 FF illustration 100.00
45 FF illustration 100.00
46 FF illustration 100.00
47 FF 150.00
48 FF illustration 100.00
49 FF illustration 100.00
50 FF illustration 100.00
51 thru 61 . . . . @50.00
62 April, 1952 . . . . 50.00

"COOKIE"
Michel Publ./Regis Publ. (American Comics Group) April, 1946
1 . . . . 200.00
2 . . . . 100.00
3 . . . . 75.00
4 . . . . 75.00
5 . . . . 75.00
6 thru 20 . . . . @50.00
21 thru 30 . . . . @40.00

GOLDEN AGE

Cookie–Crackajack | Comics Values Annual

31 thru 54 . . . . @35.00
55 Aug., 1955 . . . . 35.00

COSMO CAT
Fox Features Syndicate, 1946
1 . . . . 300.00
2 . . . . 150.00
3 O:Cosmo Cat 200.00
4 thru 10 . . . . @75.00

COURAGE COMICS
J. Edward Slavin, 1945
1 . . . . 100.00
2 Boxing (c) 100.00
77 Naval rescue, PT99 (c) 100.00

COWBOY COMICS
See: STAR RANGER

COWBOYS 'N' INJUNS
Compix
(M.E. Enterprises), 1946-47
1 Funny Animal Western 100.00
2 thru 8 . . . . @75.00

COWBOY WESTERN COMICS/HEROES
See: YELLOWJACKET

COWGIRL ROMANCES
Fiction House Magazine, 1952
1 The Range of Singing Guns . . 375.00
2 The Lady of Lawless Range . . 200.00
3 Daughter of the
  Devil's Band 150.00
4 Bride Wore Buckskin 150.00
5 Taming of Lone-Star Lou. 150.00
6 Rose of Mustang Mesa 125.00
7 Nobody Loves a Gun Man . . . 125.00
8 Wild Beauty 125.00
9 Gun-Feud Sweethearts 125.00
10 JKa,AW,No Girl of Stampede
  Valley 200.00
11 Love is Where You Find It . . . 125.00
12 Dec., 1952 . . . . 125.00

COW PUNCHER
Avon Periodicals/
Realistic Publ., Jan., 1947
1 JKu 450.00
2 JKu,JKa(c),Bondage (c) 350.00
3 AU(c) 250.00
4 . . . . 250.00
5 . . . . 250.00
6 WJo(c),Drug story 300.00
7 . . . . 250.00
1 JKu 250.00

CRACK COMICS
Comic Magazines
(Quality Comics Group)
May, 1940
1 LF,O:Black Condor,Madame
  Fatal, Red Torpedo, Rock
  Bradden, Space Legion,
  B:The Clock,Wizard Wells . 7,000.00
2 Black Condor (c) 3,000.00
3 The Clock (c) 2,200.00
4 Black Condor (c) 2,000.00
5 LF,The Clock (c) 1,500.00
6 PG,Black Condor (c) 1,400.00
7 Clock (c) 1,400.00
8 Black Condor (c) 1,400.00

Crack Comics #5
© Quality Comics Group

9 Clock (c) 1,400.00
10 Black Condor (c) 1,400.00
11 LF,PG,Clock (c) 1,200.00
12 LF,PG,Black Condor (c) . . . 1,200.00
13 LF,PG,Clock (c) 1,200.00
14 AMc,LF,PG,Clack Condor(c) 1,200.00
15 AMc,LF,PG,Clock (c) 1,200.00
16 AMc,LF,PG,Black Condor (c) 1,200.00
17 FG,AMc,LF,PG,Clock (c) . . . 1,200.00
18 AMc,LF,PG,Black Condor(c) 1,200.00
19 AMc,LF,PG,Clock (c) 1,200.00
20 AMc,LF,PG,BlackCondor(c) 1,200.00
21 AMc,LF,PG,same 900.00
22 LF,PG,same 900.00
23 AMc,LF,PG,same 900.00
24 AMc,LF,PG,same 900.00
25 AMc,same 750.00
26 AMc,same 750.00
27 AMc,I&O:Captain Triumph . 1,300.00
28 Captain Triumph (c) 750.00
29 A:Spade the Ruthless 750.00
30 I:Biff 600.00
31 Helps Spade Dig His Own
  Grave 350.00
32 Newspaper (c) 350.00
33 V:Men of Darkness 350.00
34 . . . . 350.00
35 V:The Man Who Conquered
  Flame 350.00
36 Good Neighbor Tour 350.00
37 V:The Tyrant of Toar Valley . . 350.00
38 Castle of Shadows 350.00
39 V:Crime over the City 350.00
40 Thrilling Murder Mystery . . . 250.00
41 . . . . 250.00
42 All that Glitters is Not Gold . . . 250.00
43 Smashes the Evil Spell of
  Silent 250.00
44 V:Silver Tip 250.00
45 V:King-The Jack of all Trades. 250.00
46 V:Mr. Weary 250.00
47 V:Hypnotic Eyes Khor 275.00
48 Murder in the Sky 275.00
49 . . . . 275.00
50 A Key to Trouble 275.00
51 V:Werewolf 275.00
52 V:Porcupine 275.00
53 V:Man Who Robbed the Dead 275.00
54 Shoulders the Troubles
  of the World 275.00
55 Brain against Brawn 275.00
56 Gossip leads to Murder 275.00
57 V:Sitok–Green God of Evil . . 275.00
58 V:Targets 200.00
59 A Cargo of Mystery 200.00

60 Trouble is no Picnic 200.00
61 V:Mr. Pointer-Finger of Fear . . 200.00
62 V:The Vanishing Vandals 200.00
Becomes:

CRACK WESTERN
Nov., 1949–May, 1951
63 PG, I&O:Two-Gun Lil, B:Frontier
  Marshal,Arizona Ames, ... 250.00
64 RC,Arizona AmesV:Two-
  Legged Coyote 200.00
65 RC,Ames Tramples on
  Trouble 200.00
66 Arizona Ames Arizona Raines,
  Tim Holt,Ph(c) 150.00
67 RC, Ph(c),Randolph Scott . . . 200.00
68 . . . . 150.00
69 RC 150.00
70 O&I:Whip and Diablo 175.00
71 RC(c) 200.00
72 RC,Tim Holt,Ph(c) 150.00
73 Tim Holt,Ph(c) 100.00
74 RC(c) 125.00
75 RC(c) 125.00
76 RC(c),Stage Coach to
  Oblivion 125.00
77 RC(c),Comanche Terror 125.00
78 RC(c),Killers of Laurel Ridge . 125.00
79 RC(c),Fires of Revenge 125.00
80 RC(c),Mexican Massacre . . . 125.00
81 RC(c),Secrets of Terror
  Canyon 125.00
82 The Killer with a Thousand
  Faces 75.00
83 Rattlesnake Pete's Revenge . . 75.00
84 PG(c),Revolt at Broke Creek . . 75.00

CRACKAJACK FUNNIES
Dell Publishing Co.
June, 1938
1 AMc,A:Dan Dunn,The Nebbs,
  Don Winslow 3,000.00
2 AMc,same 1,300.00
3 AMc,same 950.00
4 AMc,same 650.00
5 AMc,Naked Women(c) 750.00
6 AMc,same 500.00
7 AMc,same 500.00
8 AMc,same 500.00
9 AMc,A:Red Ryder 2,000.00
10 AMc,A:Red Ryder 500.00
11 AMc,A:Red Ryder 450.00
12 AMc,A:Red Ryder 450.00
13 AMc,A:Red Ryder 450.00
14 AMc,A:Red Ryder 450.00
15 AMc,A:Tarzan 500.00
16 AMc 350.00
17 AMc 350.00
18 AMc,A:Stratosphere Jim 350.00
19 AMc 350.00
20 AMc 350.00
21 AMc 350.00
22 AMc 350.00
23 AMc,A:Ellery Queen 350.00
24 AMc 350.00
25 AMc,I:The Owl 1,000.00
26 AMc 650.00
27 AMc 650.00
28 AMc,A:The Owl 650.00
29 AMc,A:Ellery Queen 650.00
30 AMc,A:Tarzan 650.00
31 AMc,A:Tarzan 650.00
32 AMc,O:Owl Girl 700.00
33 AMc,A:Tarzan 600.00
34 AMc,same 600.00
35 AMc,same 600.00
36 AMc,same 600.00
37 AMc 600.00
38 AMc 600.00
39 AMc,I:Andy Panada 700.00

All comics prices listed are for Near Mint condition.

GOLDEN AGE

Crackajack–Crime

Crackajack Funnies #24
© Dell Pub. Co.

40 AMc,A:Owl(c).	450.00
41 AMc.	450.00
42 AMc.	450.00
43 AMc,Terry & The Pirates, A:Owl(c).	400.00

CRASH COMICS
Tem Publishing Co.
May, 1940

1 S&K,O:Strongman, B:Blue Streak, Perfect Human, Shangra	4,000.00
2 S&K	2,000.00
3 S&K	1,800.00
4 S&K,O&I:Catman	4,000.00
5 S&K, Nov., 1940	1,800.00

CRIME AND PUNISHMENT
Lev Gleason Publications
April, 1948

1 CBi(c),Mr.Crime(c)	350.00
2 CBi(c)	175.00
3 CBi(c),BF	200.00
4 CBi(c),BF	125.00
5 CBi(c)	125.00
6 thru 10 CBi(c)	@100.00
11 thru 15 CBi(c)	@75.00
16 thru 27 CBi(c)	@70.00
28 thru 38	@65.00
39 Drug issue	100.00
40 thru 44	@65.00
45 Drug issue	75.00
46 thru 73	@65.00
66 ATh	400.00
67 Drug Storm	350.00
68 ATh(c)	300.00
69 Drug issue	100.00
74 Aug., 1955	65.00

CRIME DETECTIVE COMICS
Hillman Publications
March–April, 1948

1 BFc(c),A:Invisible 6	300.00
2 Jewel Robbery (c)	125.00
3 Stolen cash (c)	100.00
4 Crime Boss Murder (c)	100.00
5 BK,Maestro (c)	100.00
6 AMc,Gorilla (c)	90.00
7 GMc,Wedding (c)	90.00
8	85.00
9 Safe Robbery (c) (a classic)	350.00
10	90.00
11 BP	90.00
12 BK	90.00
2-1 Bluebird captured	125.00
2-2	75.00
2-3	75.00
2-4 BK	85.00
2-5	75.00
2-6	75.00
2-7 BK,GMc.	85.00
2-8	75.00
2-9	75.00
2-10	75.00
2-11	75.00
2-12	75.00
3-1 Drug Story	75.00
3-2 thru 3-7	@75.00
3-8 May/June, 1953	60.00

CRIME DOES NOT PAY
See: **SILVER STREAK COMICS**

CRIME ILLUSTRATED
E.C. Comics, Nov.–Dec., 1955

1 Grl,RC,GE,JO.	175.00
2 Grl,RC,JCr,JDa,JO	150.00

CRIME MUST STOP
Hillman Periodicals, Oct., 1952

1 BK	900.00

CRIME MYSTERIES
Ribage Publishing Corp.
May, 1952

1 Transvestism,Bondage(c)	750.00
2 A:Manhunter, Lance Storm, Drug.	500.00
3 FF-one page, A:Dr. Foo	400.00
4 A:Queenie Star, BondageStar	700.00
5 Claws of the Green Girl	350.00
6	350.00
7 Sons of Satan	350.00
8 Death Stalks the Crown, Bondage(c)	350.00
9 You are the Murderer	325.00
10 The Hoax of the Death.	325.00
11 The Strangler	325.00
12 Bondage(c)	350.00
13 AT,6 lives for one	375.00
14 Painted in Blood	325.00
15 Feast of the Dead,Acid Face	500.00
Becomes:	

SECRET MYSTERIES
Nov., 1954

16 Hiding Place,Horror	300.00
17 The Deadly Diamond,Horror.	200.00
18 Horror	250.00
19 Horror,July, 1955	250.00

INTERNATIONAL COMICS
E.C. Publ. Co., Spring, 1947

1 KS,I:Manhattan's Files	700.00
2 KS,A: Van Manhattan & Madelon	550.00
3 KS,same	350.00
4 KS,same	350.00
5 I:International Crime-Busting Patrol	350.00
Becomes:	

INTERNATIONAL CRIME PATROL
Spring, 1948

6 A:Moon Girl & The Prince	650.00
Becomes:	

CRIME PATROL
Summer, 1948

7 SMo,A:Capt. Crime Jr.,Field Marshall of Murder	800.00
8 JCr,State Prison (c)	700.00
9 AF,JCr,Bank Robbery	700.00
10 AF,JCr,Wanted:James Dore	700.00
11 AF,JCr	700.00
12 AF,Grl,JCr,Interrogation(c)	700.00
13 AF,JCr	700.00
14 AF,JCr,Smugglers (c)	700.00
15 AF,JCr,Crypt of Terror	4,000.00
16 AF,JCr,Crypt of Terror	2,500.00
Becomes:	

CRYPT OF TERROR
E.C. Comics, April, 1950

17 JCr(a&c),AF,'Werewolf Strikes Again'.	4,000.00
18 JCr(a&c),AF,WW,HK 'The Living Corpse'	2,500.00
19 JCr(a&c),AF,Grl, 'Voodoo Drums'	2,400.00
Becomes:	

TALES FROM THE CRYPT
Oct., 1950

20 JCr(a&c),AF,GI,JKa 'Day of Death'	1,800.00
21 AF(a&c),WW,HK,Gl,'Cooper Dies in the Electric Chair .	1,500.00
22 AF, JCr(c)	1,000.00
23 AF(a&c),JCr,JDa,Grl 'Locked in a Mauseleum'	800.00
24 AF(c),WW,JDa,JCr,Grl 'Danger...Quicksand'.	800.00
25 AF(c),WW,JDa,JKa,Grl 'Mataud Waxworks'.	800.00
26 WW(c),JDa,Grl, 'Scared Graveyard'.	650.00
27 JKa, WW(c), Guillotine (c)	650.00
28 AF(c),JDa,JKa,Grl,JO 'Buried Alive'.	650.00
29 JDa(a&c),JKa,Grl,JO 'Coffin Burier'	650.00
30 JDa(a&c),JO,JKa,Grl 'Underwater Death'	650.00

Tales From the Crypt #43
© E.C. Comics

Crime–Crusader — GOLDEN AGE — Comics Values Annual

31 JDa(a&c),JKa,Grl,AW
   'Hand Chopper' 700.00
32 JDa(a&c),GE,Grl,'Woman
   Crushed by Elephant' 700.00
33 JDa(a&c),GE,JKa,Grl,'Lower
   Berth',O:Crypt Keeper 1,000.00
34 JDa(a&c),JKa,GE,Grl,'Jack the
   Ripper,'Ray Bradbury adapt.. 650.00
35 JDa(a&c),JKa,JO,Grl,
   'Werewolf' 700.00
36 JDa(a&c),JKa,GE,Grl, Ray
   Bradbury adaptation 700.00
37 JDa(c),JO,BE............ 700.00
38 JDa(c),BE,RC,Grl,'Axe Man' . 700.00
39 JDa(a&c),JKa,JO,Grl,'Children
   in the Graveyard' 700.00
40 JDa(a&c),GE,BK,Grl,
   'Underwater Monster' 600.00
41 JDa(a&c),JKa,GE,Grl,
   'Knife Thrower' 550.00
42 JDa(c),JO,Vampire (c) 550.00
43 JDa(c),JO,GE 550.00
44 JO,RC,Guillotine (c)........ 550.00
45 JDa(a&c),JKa,BK,Gl,'Rat
   Takes Over His Life' 550.00
46 JDa(a&c),GE,JO,Gl,Werewolf
   man being hunted,Feb.1955 . 650.00

CRIME REPORTER
St. John Publishing Co.
Aug., 1948
1 Death Makes a Deadline 650.00
2 GT,MB(c),Matinee Murders . 1,000.00
3 GT,MB(c),Dec., 1948 .... 500.00

CRIMES BY WOMEN
Fox Features Syndicate
June, 1948
1 Bonnie Parker 1,700.00
2 Vicious Female 900.00
3 Prison break (c) 800.00
4 Murder (c) 800.00
5 .... 800.00
6 Girl Fight (c) 850.00
7 .... 700.00
8 .... 700.00
9 .... 700.00
10 Girl Fight (c)............ 700.00
11 .... 700.00
12 .... 700.00
13 ACME jewelry robbery (c) ... 700.00
14 Prison break (c).......... 700.00
15 Aug., 1951.............. 700.00

CRIME SMASHER
Fawcett Publications
Summer, 1948
1 The Unlucky Rabbit's Foot ... 600.00

CRIME SMASHERS
Ribage Publishing Corp.
Oct., 1950
1 Girl Rape............. 1,200.00
2 JKu,A:Sally the Sleuth, Dan
   Turner, Girl Friday, Rat Hale . 600.00
3 MFa 450.00
4 Zak(c) 450.00
5 WW 500.00
6 .... 350.00
7 Bondage (c),Drugs 400.00
8 .... 350.00
9 Bondage (c) 400.00
10 .... 350.00
11 .... 350.00
12 FF, Eye Ingury 400.00
13 .... 400.00
14 .... 350.00
15 .... 350.00

GOLDEN AGE

CRIMES ON THE WATERFRONT
See: FAMOUS GANGSTERS

Crime SuspenStories #22
© E.C. Comics

CRIME SUSPENSTORIES
L.L. Publishing Co.
(E.C. Comics), Oct.–Nov., 1950
1a JCr,Grl 2,000.00
1 JCr,WW,Grl 1,500.00
2 JCr,JKa,Grl 800.00
3 JCr,WW,Grl,Poe Story 600.00
4 JCr,Gln,Grl,JDa 550.00
5 JCr,JKa,Grl,JDa 550.00
6 JCr,JDa,Grl 500.00
7 JCr,Grl 500.00
8 JCr,Grl 500.00
9 JCr,Grl 500.00
10 JCr,Grl................ 500.00
11 JCr,Grl................ 400.00
12 JCr,Grl................ 400.00
13 JCr,AW 425.00
14 JCr 400.00
15 JCr,Old Witch........... 400.00
16 JCr,AW 425.00
17 JCr,FF,AW, Ray Bradbury ... 500.00
18 JCr,RC,BE.............. 425.00
19 JCr,RC,GE,AF(c)......... 425.00
20 RC,JCr, Hanging (c) 450.00
21 JCr 250.00
22 RC,JO,JCr(c),
   Severed head (c) 400.00
23 JKa,RC,GE 400.00
24 BK,RC,JO 250.00
25 JKa,(c),RC.............. 250.00
26 JKa,(c),RC,JO 250.00
27 JKa,(c),GE,Grl,March, 1955 .. 250.00

CRIMINALS ON THE RUN
Premium Group of Comics
Aug., 1948
4-1 LbC(c) 350.00
4-2 LbC(c), A:Young King Cole . 300.00
4-3 LbC(c), Rip Roaring Action
   in Alps 300.00
4-4 LbC(c), Shark (c) 300.00
4-5 AMc 300.00
4-6 LbC,Dr. Doom 275.00
4-7 LbC 700.00
5-1 LbC 250.00
5-2 LbC 250.00
10 LbC 250.00
Becomes:

CRIME-FIGHTING DETECTIVE
April–May, 1950
11 LbC, Brodie Gang Captured.. 250.00
12 LbC(c), Jail Break Genius ... 252.00
13 .... 200.00
14 LbC(c), A Night of Horror 250.00
15 LbC(c)................ 250.00
16 LbC(c), Wanton Murder 250.00
17 LbC(c), The Framer
   was Framed 250.00
18 LbC(c), A Web of Evil....... 250.00
19 LbC(c), Lesson of the Law ... 250.00
Becomes:

SHOCK DETECTIVE CASES
Sept., 1952
20 LbC(c), The Strangler 250.00
21 LbC(c), Death Ride 250.00
Becomes:

SPOOK DETECTIVE CASES
Jan., 1953
22 Headless Horror........... 300.00
Becomes:

SPOOK SUSPENSE AND MYSTERY
23 LbC,Weird Picture of Murder . 250.00
24 LbC(c),Mummy's Case...... 300.00
25 LbC(c),Horror Beyond Door .. 250.00
26 LbC(c),JyD,Face of Death ... 250.00
27 LbC(c),Ship of the Dead...... 250.00
28 LbC(c),JyD,Creeping Death .. 250.00
29 LbC(c), Solo for Death 250.00
30 LbC(c),JyD,Nightmare,
   Oct.,1954.............. 250.00

CROWN COMICS
Golfing/McCombs Publ.
Winter 1944
1 Edgar Allen Poe adapt....... 400.00
2 MB,I:Mickey Magic 300.00
3 MB,Jungle adventure (c) 300.00
4 MB(c),A:Voodah........... 300.00
5 MB(c),Jungle adventure (c) .. 300.00
6 MB(c),Jungle adventure (c) .. 300.00
7 JKa,AF,MB(c),Race Car (c) .. 300.00
8 MB................... 250.00
9 .... 200.00
10 Plane crash (c),A:Voodah.... 200.00
11 LSt,A:Voodah............ 150.00
12 LSt,AF,Master Marvin....... 150.00
13 LSt,AF,A:Voodah 150.00
14 A:Voodah............... 200.00
15 FBe,A:Voodah 150.00
16 FBe,A:Voodah,Jungle
   adventure(c)............ 150.00
17 FBe,A:Voodah 150.00
18 FBe,A:Voodah 150.00
19 BP,A:Voodah,July, 1949 ..... 150.00

CRUSADER FROM MARS
Approved Publ.
(Ziff-Davis), Jan.–March, 1952
1 Mission Thru Space, Death in
   the Sai............... 1,100.00
2 Beachhead on Saturn's Ring,
   Bondage(c),Fall, 1952 ..... 750.00

CVA Page 378 — All comics prices listed are for *Near Mint* condition.

GOLDEN AGE

Cryin'–Daredevil

CRYIN' LION, THE
William H. Wise Co.
Fall, 1944
1 . . . . 150.00
2 . . . . 125.00
3 Spring, 1945 . . . . 100.00

CRYPT OF TERROR
See: CRIME PATROL

CYCLONE COMICS
Bibara Publ. Co., June, 1940
1 O:Tornado Tom 2,400.00
2 . . . . 1,000.00
3 . . . . 1,300.00
4 Voltron 750.00
5 A:Mr. Q,Oct., 1940 . . . . 1,000.00

ALL GREAT COMICS
Fox Features Syndicate
Oct., 1947
12 A:Brenda Starr 750.00
13 JKa,O:Dagar, Desert Hawk . . 900.00

Dagar, Desert Hawk #21
© *Fox Features Syndicate*

Becomes:
DAGAR, DESERT HAWK
Feb., 1948
14 JKa,Monster of Mura. 1,000.00
15 JKa,Curse of the Lost
  Pharaoh 600.00
16 JKa,Wretched Antmen 550.00
19 Pyramid of Doom 500.00
20 . . . . 500.00
21 JKa(c),The Ghost of Fate 550.00
22 . . . . 500.00
23 Bondage (c) 550.00
Becomes:
CAPTAIN KIDD
June, 1949
24 Blackbeard the Pirate 150.00
25 Sorceress of the Deep 150.00
Becomes:
MY SECRET STORY
Oct., 1949
26 He Wanted More Than Love . 125.00
27 My Husband Hated Me 75.00
28 I Become a Marked Women . . . 75.00
29 My Forbidden Rapture,
  April, 1950 . . . . 75.00

DAFFY
Dell Publishing Co.,
March, 1953
(1) see *Dell Four Color #457*
(2) see *Dell Four Color #536*
(3) see *Dell Four Color #615*
4 thru 7 . . . . @50.00
8 thru 11 . . . . @35.00
12 thru 17 . . . . @30.00
Becomes:
DAFFY DUCK
July, 1959
18 . . . . 30.00
19 . . . . 30.00
20 . . . . 30.00
21 thru 30 . . . . @25.00
Gold Key, 1962
31 thru 40 . . . . @25.00
41 thru 59 . . . . @15.00
60 B&A:Road Runner 10.00
61 thru 90 same . . . . @10.00
91 thru 127 . . . . @8.00
Whitman, 1980
128 thru 145 . . . . @7.00

DAGWOOD
Harvey Publications, 1950
1 . . . . 200.00
2 . . . . 100.00
3 thru 10 . . . . @75.00
11 thru 20 . . . . @60.00
21 thru 30 . . . . @50.00
31 thru 50 . . . . @40.00
51 thru 70 . . . . @35.00
71 thru 109 . . . . @25.00
110 thru 140 . . . . @25.00

DANGER AND ADVENTURE
See: THIS MAGAZINE IS HAUNTED

DANGER IS OUR BUSINESS
Toby Press/
I.W. Enterprises, 1953
1 AW,FF,Men who Defy Death
  for a Living 550.00
2 Death Crowds the Cockpit . . . 150.00
3 Killer Mountain 125.00
4 . . . . 125.00
5 thru 9 . . . . @100.00
10 June, 1955 . . . . 125.00

DAREDEVIL COMICS
Lev Gleason Publications
July, 1941
1 Daredevil Battles Hitler, A:Silver
  Streak, Lance Hale, Dickey Dean,
  Cloud Curtis,V:The Claw,
  O:Hitler 18,000.00
2 I:The Pioneer, Champion of
  American,B:London,Pat
  Patriot,Pirate Prince 4,500.00
3 CBi(c),O:Thirteen 2,500.00
4 CBi(c),Death is the Refere . . 2,000.00
5 CBi(c),I:Sniffer&Jinx, Claw
  V:Ghost,Lottery of Doom . . 1,800.00
6 CBi(c) 1,500.00
7 CBi(c), What Ghastly Sight Lies
  within the Mysterious Trunk 1,400.00
8 V:Nazis (c), E:Nightro 1,300.00
9 V:Double 1,300.00

Daredevil Comics #6
© *Lev Gleason*

10 America will Remember
  Pearl Harbor 1,300.00
11 Bondage (c), E:Pat
  Patriot, London 1,500.00
12 BW,CBi(c), O:The Law 2,000.00
13 BW,I:Little Wise Guys 1,500.00
14 BW,CBi(c) 900.00
15 BW,CBi(c), D:Meatball 1,200.00
16 BW,CBi(c) 800.00
17 BW,CBi(c), Into the Valley
  of Death 800.00
18 BW,CBi(c), O:Daredevil,
  double length story 1,500.00
19 BW,CBi(c), Buried Alive 700.00
20 BW,CBi(c), Boxing (c) 700.00
21 CBi(c), Can Little Wise Guys
  Survive Blast of Dynamite? 1,100.00
22 CBi(c) 500.00
23 CBi(c), I:Pshyco 500.00
24 CBi(c), Punch and Judy
  Murders 500.00
25 CBi(c), baseball (c) 500.00
26 CBi(c) 450.00
27 CBi(c), Bondage (c) 500.00
28 CBi(c) 450.00
29 CBi(c) 450.00
30 CBi(c), Ann Hubbard White
  1922-1943 . . . . 450.00
31 CBi(c), D:The Claw 1,000.00
32 V:Blackmarketeers 300.00
33 CBi(c) 300.00
34 CBi(c) 300.00
35 B:Two Daredevil stories
  every issue 325.00
36 CBi(c) 325.00
37 CBi(c) 325.00
38 CBi(c), O:Daredevil 600.00
39 CBi(c) 350.00
40 CBi(c) 350.00
41 . . . . 300.00
42 thru 50 CBi(c) . . . . @300.00
51 CBi(c) 250.00
52 CBi(c),Football (c) 275.00
53 thru 57 . . . . @250.00
58 Football (c) 275.00
59 . . . . 250.00
60 . . . . 250.00
61 thru 68 . . . . @250.00
69 E:Daredevil 250.00
70 . . . . 150.00
71 thru 78 . . . . @100.00
79 B:Daredevil 150.00
80 . . . . 135.00
81 . . . . 75.00
82 . . . . 75.00

All comics prices listed are for *Near Mint* condition.

Daredevil–Dell Giant / GOLDEN AGE / Comics Values Annual

83 thru 99 . . . . @75.00
100 . . . . 100.00
101 thru 133 . . . . @75.00
134 Sept., 1956 . . . . 75.00

DARING CONFESSIONS
See: YOUTHFUL HEART

DARING LOVE
See: YOUTHFUL ROMANCES

Dark Mysteries #24
© Merit Publications

DARK MYSTERIES
Merit Publications
June–July, 1951
1 WW(a&c), Curse of the
　Sea Witch 1,500.00
2 WW(a&c), Vampire Fangs
　of Doom 1,000.00
3 Terror of the Unwilling
　Witch 600.00
4 Corpse that Came Alive 600.00
5 Horror of the Ghostly Crew . . 500.00
6 If the Noose Fits Wear It! 500.00
7 Terror of the Cards of Death . 500.00
8 Terror of the Ghostly Trail 500.00
9 Witch's Feast at Dawn 500.00
10 Terror of the Burning Witch . . 500.00
11 The River of Blood 400.00
12 Horror of the Talking Dead . . . 400.00
13 Terror of the Hungry Cats 400.00
14 Horror of the Fingers of Doom 450.00
15 Terror of the Vampires Teeth . 350.00
16 Horror of the Walking Dead . . 350.00
17 Terror of the Mask of Death . . 350.00
18 Terror of the Burning Corpse . 350.00
19 The Rack of Terror 550.00
20 Burning Executioner 500.00
21 The Sinister Secret 300.00
22 The Hand of Destiny 300.00
23 The Mardenburg Curse 250.00
24 Give A Man enough Rope,
　July, 1955 . . . . 250.00

DAVY CROCKETT
Avon Periodicals, 1951
1 . . . . 200.00

GOLDEN AGE

DEAD END CRIME STORIES
Kirby Publishing Co.
April, 1949
N# BP 600.00

DEAD-EYE WESTERN COMICS
Hillman Periodicals
Nov.–Dec., 1948
1 BK 250.00
2 . . . . 100.00
3 . . . . 75.00
4 thru 12 . . . . @50.00
2-1 . . . . 45.00
2-2 . . . . 45.00
2-3 . . . . 60.00
2-4 . . . . 60.00
2-5 thru 2-12 . . . . @35.00
3-1 . . . . 35.00

DEADWOOD GULCH
Dell Publishing Co., 1931
1 . . . . 450.00

DEAR BEATRICE FAIRFAX
Best Books
(Standard Comics), Nov., 1950
5 . . . . 100.00
6 thru 9 . . . . @50.00

DEAR LONELY HEART
Artful Publications
March, 1951
1 . . . . 200.00
2 . . . . 75.00
3 MB, Jungle Girl 200.00
4 . . . . 75.00
5 thru 8 . . . . @65.00

DEAR LONELY HEARTS
Comic Media, Aug., 1953
1 Six Months to Live 100.00
2 Date Hungry, Price of Passion . 50.00
3 thru 8 . . . . @60.00

DEARLY BELOVED
Approved Comics
(Ziff-Davis), Fall, 1952
1 Ph(c) 200.00

DEBBIE DEAN, CAREER GIRL
Civil Service Publishing
April, 1945
1 . . . . 150.00
2 . . . . 125.00

DELL GIANT EDITIONS
Dell Publishing Co.
1953-58
Abe Lincoln Life Story 125.00
Cadet Gray of West Point 125.00
Golden West Rodeo Treasury . . . 175.00
Life Stories of
　American Presidents 100.00
Lone Ranger Golden West 350.00
Lone Ranger Movie Story 750.00
Lone Ranger Western
　Treasury('53) 350.00

Lone Ranger Western
　Treasury('54) 450.00
Moses & Ten Commandments . . 100.00
Nancy & Sluggo Travel Time 150.00
Pogo Parade 600.00
Raggedy Ann & Andy 300.00
Santa Claus Funnies 175.00
Tarzan's Jungle Annual #1 . . . . . 250.00
Tarzan's Jungle Annual #2 . . . . . 200.00
Tarzan's Jungle Annual #3 . . . . . 175.00
Tarzan's Jungle Annual #4 . . . . . 175.00
Tarzan's Jungle Annual #5 . . . . . 175.00
Tarzan's Jungle Annual #6 . . . . . 175.00
Tarzan's Jungle Annual #7 . . . . . 175.00
Treasury of Dogs 125.00
Treasury of Horses 125.00
Universal Presents-Dracula-
　The Mummy & Other Stories 400.00
Western Roundup #1 . . . . 450.00
Western Roundup #2 . . . . 250.00
Western Roundup #3 . . . . 200.00
Western Roundup #4 thru #5 . . @175.00
Western Roundup #6 thru #10 . @150.00
Western Roundup #11 thru #17 @150.00
Western Roundup #18 . . . . 135.00
Western Roundup #19 thru #25 . 135.00
Woody Woodpecker Back
　to School #1 . . . . 200.00
Woody Woodpecker Back
　to School #2 . . . . 150.00
Woody Woodpecker Back
　to School #3 . . . . 150.00
Woody Woodpecker Back
　to School #4 . . . . 150.00
Woody Woodpecker County
　Fair #5 . . . . 150.00
Woody Woodpecker Back
　to School #6 . . . . 175.00
Woody Woodpecker County
　Fair #2 . . . . 150.00
Also See: Bugs Bunny; Marge's Little
Lulu; Tom and Jerry, and Walt Disney
Dell Giant Editions

DELL GIANT COMICS
Dell Publishing Co.
Sept., 1959
21 M.G.M. Tom & Jerry
　Picnic Time 200.00
22 W.Disney's Huey, Dewey & Louie
　Back to School (Oct 1959) . . 150.00
23 Marge's Little Lulu &
　Tubby Halloween Fun 200.00
24 Woody Woodpeckers
　Family Fun 150.00
25 Tarzan's Jungle World 200.00
26 W.Disney's Christmas
　Parade,CB 400.00
27 W.Disney's Man in
　Space (1960) 200.00
28 Bugs Bunny's Winter Fun 200.00
29 Marge's Little Lulu &
　Tubby in Hawaii 200.00
30 W.Disney's DisneylandU.S.A. . 175.00
31 Huckleberry Hound
　Summer Fun 250.00
32 Bugs Bunny Beach Party . . . 125.00
33 W.Disney's Daisy Duck &
　Uncle Scrooge Picnic Time . . . 175.00
34 Nancy&SluggoSummerCamp. 150.00
35 W.Disney's Huey, Dewey &
　Louie Back to School 200.00
36 Marge's Little Lulu & Witch
　Hazel Halloween Fun 225.00
37 Tarzan, King of the Jungle . . . 200.00
38 W.Disney's Uncle Donald and
　his Nephews Family Fun . . . 250.00
39 W.Disney's Merry Christmas . 250.00
40 Woody Woodpecker
　Christmas Parade 125.00

CVA Page 380　All comics prices listed are for *Near Mint* condition.

Comics Values Annual — GOLDEN AGE — Dell Giant–Dickie Dare

41 Yogi Bear's Winter Sports . . . 250.00
42 Marge's Little Lulu &
  Tubby in Australia 225.00
43 Mighty Mouse in OuterSpace . 400.00
44 Around the World with
  Huckleberry & His Friends . . 250.00
45 Nancy&SluggoSummerCamp. 125.00
46 Bugs Bunny Beach Party 125.00
47 W.Disney's Mickey and
  Donald in Vacationland 175.00
48 The Flintstones #1
  (Bedrock Bedlam) 350.00
49 W.Disney's Huey, Dewey &
  Louie Back to School 150.00
50 Marge's Little Lulu &
  Witch Hazel Trick 'N' Treat . . 225.00
51 Tarzan, King of the Jungle . . . 150.00
52 W.Disney's Uncle Donald &
  his Nephews Dude Ranch . . 150.00
53 W.Disney's Donald Duck
  Merry Christmas 150.00
54 Woody Woodpecker
  Christmas Party 150.00
55 W.Disney's Daisy Duck & Uncle
  Scrooge Show Boat (1961). . 175.00

DELL JUNIOR TREASURY
Dell Publishing Co.
June, 1955
1 Alice in Wonderland 150.00
2 Aladdin 100.00
3 Gulliver's Travels 75.00
4 Adventures of Mr. Frog 100.00
5 Wizard of Oz 100.00
6 Heidi 110.00
7 Santa & the Angel 110.00
8 Raggedy Ann 110.00
9 Clementina the Flying Pig 100.00
10 Adventures of Tom Sawyer . . . 100.00

DENNIS THE MENACE
Visual Editions/Literary Ent.
(Standard, Pines)
Aug., 1953
1 . . . . 600.00
2 . . . . 250.00
3 . . . . 150.00
4 . . . . 150.00
5 thru 10 . . . . @125.00
11 thru 20 . . . . @110.00
21 thru 31 . . . . @75.00
Hallden (Fawcett Publications)
32 thru 40 . . . . @50.00
41 thru 50 . . . . @40.00
51 thru 60 . . . . @35.00
61 thru 70 . . . . @30.00
71 thru 90 . . . . @25.00
91 thru 140 . . . . @10.00
141 thru 166 . . . . @8.00

DESPERADO
Lev Gleason Publications
June, 1948
1 CBi(c) 150.00
2 CBi(c) 75.00
3 CBi(c) 100.00
4 CBi(c) 65.00
5 CBi(c) 65.00
6 CBi(c) 65.00
7 CBi(c) 65.00
8 CBi(c) 65.00
Becomes:
BLACK DIAMOND WESTERN
March, 1949
9 CBi(c) 250.00
10 CBi(c) 125.00

---

11 CBi(c) 75.00
12 CBi(c) 75.00
13 CBi(c) 75.00
14 CBi(c) 75.00
15 CBi(c) 75.00
16 thru 28 BW,Big Bang Buster @100.00
29 thru 40 . . . . @50.00
41 thru 52 . . . . @35.00
53 3-D 75.00
54 3-D 65.00
55 thru 60 . . . . @50.00

DETECTIVE EYE
Centaur Publications
Nov., 1940
1 B:Air Man, The Eye Sees,
  A:Masked Marvel 2,900.00
2 O:Don Rance, Mysticape,
  Dec., 1940 . . . . 1,800.00

DETECTIVE PICTURE STORIES
Comics Magazine Co.
Dec., 1936
1 The Phantom Killer 5,000.00
2 . . . . 2,500.00
3 . . . . 1,500.00
4 WE, Muss Em Up 1,400.00
5 Trouble, April, 1937 . . . . 1,700.00

Detective Picture Stories #1
© Comics Magazine Co.

DEVIL DOGS
Street and Smith 1942
1 U.S. Marines 250.00

DEXTER COMICS
Dearfield Publications
Summer, 1948–July, 1949
1 . . . . 90.00
2 . . . . 75.00
3 . . . . 50.00
4 . . . . 50.00
5 . . . . 50.00

DIARY CONFESSIONS
See: TENDER ROMANCE

DIARY LOVES
Comic Magazines
(Quality Comics Group)
Sept., 1949
1 BWa Love Diary 200.00
2 BWa 175.00
3 . . . . 75.00
4 RC 85.00
5 . . . . 60.00
6 . . . . 60.00
7 . . . . 60.00
8 BWa 100.00
9 BWa 100.00
10 BWa 100.00
11 . . . . 50.00
12 . . . . 50.00
13 . . . . 50.00
14 . . . . 50.00
15 BWa 100.00
16 BWa 100.00
17 . . . . 50.00
18 . . . . 50.00
19 . . . . 50.00
20 . . . . 50.00
21 BWa 75.00
22 thru 31 . . . . @30.00
Becomes:
G.I. SWEETHEARTS
June, 1953
32 Love Under Fire 65.00
33 . . . . 50.00
34 . . . . 50.00
35 . . . . 50.00
36 Lend Lease Love Affair 50.00
37 thru 45 . . . . @50.00
Becomes:
GIRLS IN LOVE
Sept., 1955
46 Somewhere I'll Find You 55.00
47 thru 56 . . . . @40.00
57 MB(a&c), Can Love Really
  Change Him, Dec., 1956 . . . . 75.00

DIARY SECRETS
See: TEEN-AGE DIARY SECRETS

DICK COLE
Curtis Publ./
Star Publications
Dec.–Jan., 1949
1 LbC(a&c),CS,All sports(c) 350.00
2 LbC 150.00
3 LbC(a&c) 200.00
4 LbC(a&c),Rowing (c) 200.00
5 LbC(a&c) 200.00
6 LbC(a&c), Rodeo (c) 200.00
7 LbC(a&c) 200.00
8 LbC(a&c), Football (c) 200.00
9 LbC(a&c), Basketball (c) . . . 200.00
10 Joe Louis 200.00
Becomes:
SPORTS THRILLS
Nov., 1950–Nov., 1951
11 Ted Williams & Ty Cobb 350.00
12 LbC, Joe DiMaggio & Phil
  Rizzuto, Boxing (c) 300.00
13 LbC(c),Basketball (c) 250.00
14 LbC(c),Baseball (c) 250.00
15 LbC(c),Baseball (c) 250.00

DICKIE DARE
Eastern Color Printing Co.
1941–42
1 BEv(c),M.Caniff 650.00

Dickie Dare–Dick Tracy

2 . . . . 350.00
3 . . . . 350.00
4 H. Scorcery Smith. 400.00

DICK TRACY MONTHLY
Dell Publishing Co.
Jan., 1948

1 ChG,Dick Tracy & the Mad
  Doctor' 600.00
2 ChG,A:MarySteele,BorisArson 350.00
3 ChG,A:Spaldoni,Big Boy 350.00
4 ChG,A:Alderman Zeld 350.00
5 ChG,A:Spaldoni,Mrs.Spaldoni 300.00
6 ChG,A:Steve the Tramp 300.00
7 ChG,A:Boris Arson,Mary
  Steele 300.00
8 ChG,A:Boris & Zora Arson . . . 300.00
9 ChG,A:Chief Yellowpony 300.00
10 ChG,A:Cutie Diamond 300.00
11 ChG,A:Toby Townly,
  Bookie Joe 250.00
12 ChG,A:Toby Townly,
  Bookie Joe 250.00
13 ChG,A:Toby Townly, Blake . . . 275.00
14 ChG,A:Mayor Waite Wright . . . 250.00
15 ChG,A:Bowman Basil. 250.00
16 ChG,A:Maw,'Muscle'
  & 'Cut' Famon 250.00
17 ChG,A:Jim Trailer,
  Mary Steele 250.00
18 ChG,A:Lips Manlis,
  Anthel Jones 250.00
19 'Golden Heart Mystery'. 275.00
20 'Black Cat Mystery' 275.00
21 'Tracy Meets Number One' . . 275.00
22 'Tracy and the Alibi Maker' . . . 225.00
23 'Dick Tracy Meets Jukebox' . . 225.00
24 'Dick Tracy and Bubbles' 225.00
Becomes:

DICK TRACY COMICS MONTHLY
Harvey, May, 1950

25 ChG,A:Flattop 250.00
26 ChG,A:Vitamin Flinthirt 200.00
27 ChG,'Flattop Escapes Prision' 200.00
28 ChG,'Case o/t Torture
  Chamber' 200.00
29 ChG,A:Brow,Gravel Gertie . . . 250.00
30 ChG,'Blackmail Racket' 175.00
31 ChG,A:Snowflake Falls 150.00
32 ChG,A:Shaky,Snowflake Falls 150.00
33 ChG,'Strange Case
  of Measles'. 200.00
34 ChG,A:Measles,Paprika 175.00
35 ChG,'Case of Stolen $50,000' 175.00
36 ChG,'Case of the
  Runaway Blonde' 200.00
37 ChG,'Case of Stolen Money' . . 175.00
38 ChG,A:Breathless Mahoney. . 175.00
39 ChG,A:Itchy,B.O.Pleanty 175.00
40 ChG,'Case of Atomic Killer' . . . 175.00
41 ChG,Pt.1'Murder by Mail' 150.00
42 ChG,Pt.2'Murder by Mail' 150.00
43 ChG,'Case of the
  Underworld Brat'. 150.00
44 ChG,'Case of the Mouthwash
  Murder'. 150.00
45 ChG,'Case of the Evil Eyes' . . 150.00
46 ChG,'Case of the
  Camera Killers'. 150.00
47 ChG,'Case of the
  Bloodthirsty Blonde' 150.00
48 ChG,'Case of the
  Murderous Minstrel' 150.00
49 ChG,Pt.1'Killer Who Returned
  From the Dead 150.00

GOLDEN AGE

Dick Tracy Monthly #5
© Dell Publishing Co.

50 ChG,Pt.2'Killer Who
  Returned From the Dead' . . . 150.00
51 ChG,'Case of the
  High Tension Hijackers'. 125.00
52 ChG,'Case of the
  Pipe-Stem Killer' 125.00
53 ChG,Pt.1'Dick Tracy Meets
  the Murderous Midget' 125.00
54 ChG,Pt.2'Dick Tracy Meets
  the Murderous Midget' 125.00
55 ChG,Pt.3'Dick Tracy Meets
  the Murderous Midget' 125.00
56 ChG,'Case of the
  Teleguard Terror' 125.00
57 ChG,Pt.1'Case of the
  Ice Cold Killer' 150.00
58 ChG,Pt.2'Case of the
  Ice Cold Killer' 125.00
59 ChG,Pt.1'Case of the
  Million Dollar Murder' 125.00
60 ChG,Pt.2'Case of the
  Million Dollar Murder' 110.00
61 ChG,'Case of the
  Murderers Mask'. 110.00
62 ChG,Pt.1'Case of the
  White Rat Robbers'. 110.00
63 ChG,Pt.2'Case of the
  White Rat Robbers' 110.00
64 ChG,Pt.1'Case of the
  Interrupted Honeymoon' 110.00
65 ChG,Pt.2'Case of the
  Interrupted Honeymoon' 110.00
66 ChG,Pt.1'Case of the
  Killer's Revenge' 110.00
67 ChG,Pt.2'Case of the
  Killer's Revenge' 110.00
68 ChG,Pt.1'Case o-t TV Terror' . 110.00
69 ChG,Pt.2'Case o-t TV Terror' . 110.00
70 ChG,Pt.3'Case o-t TV Terror' . 100.00
71 ChG,A:Mrs. Forchune,Opal . . 100.00
72 ChG,A:Empty Wiliams,Bonny. 100.00
73 ChG,A:Bonny Braids 100.00
74 ChG,A:Mr. & Mrs.
  Fortson Knox 100.00
75 ChG,A:Crewy Lou, Sphinx . . . 100.00
76 ChG,A:Diet Smith,Brainerd. . . 100.00
77 ChG,A:Crewy Lou,
  Bonny Braids 100.00
78 ChG,A:Spinner Records. 100.00
79 ChG,A:Model Jones,
  Larry Jones 100.00
80 ChG,A:Tonsils,Dot View 100.00
81 ChG,A:Edward Moppet,Tonsils100.00
82 ChG,A:Dot View,Mr. Crime. . . 100.00
83 ChG,A:RifleRuby,NewsuitNan 100.00

Comics Values Annual

84 ChG,A:Mr.Crime,NewsuitNan . 100.00
85 ChG,A:NewsuitNan, Mrs.Lava 100.00
86 ChG,A:Mr. Crime,Odds Zonn . 100.00
87 ChG,A:Odds Zonn,Wingy. . . . 100.00
88 ChG,A:Odds Zonn,Wingy. . . . 100.00
89 ChG,Pt.1'Canhead' 100.00
90 ChG,Pt.2'Canhead' 100.00
91 ChG,Pt.3'Canhead' 100.00
92 ChG,Pt.4'Canhead' 100.00
93 ChG,Pt.5'Canhead' 100.00
94 ChG,Pt.6'Canhead' 100.00
95 ChG,A:Mrs. Green,Dewdrop . 100.00
96 ChG,A:Dewdrop,Sticks. 100.00
97 ChG,A:Dewdrop,Sticks. 100.00
98 ChG,A:Open-Mind Monty,
  Sticks. 100.00
99 ChG,A:Open-Mind Monty,
  Sticks. 125.00
100 ChG,A:Half-Pint,Dewdrop. . . 150.00
101 ChG,A:Open-Mind Monty . . . 100.00
102 ChG,A:Rainbow Reiley,
  Wingy. 100.00
103 ChG,A:Happy,Rughead 100.00
104 ChG,A:Rainbow Reiley,
  Happy 100.00
105 ChG,A:Happy,Rughead 100.00
106 ChG,A:Fence,Corny,Happy . 100.00
107 ChG,A:Rainbow Reiley. 100.00
108 ChG,A:Rughead,Corny,
  Fence. 100.00
109 ChG,A:Rughead,Mimi,Herky 100.00
110 ChG,A:Vitamin Flintheart . . . 100.00
111 ChG,A:Shoulders,Roach. . . . 100.00
112 ChG,A:Brilliant,Diet Smith. . . 100.00
113 ChG,A:Snowflake Falls. 100.00
114 ChG,A:'Sketch'Paree,. 100.00
115 ChG,A:Rod & Nylon Hoze . . 100.00
116 ChG,A:Empty Williams 100.00
117 ChG,A:Spinner Records. . . . 100.00
118 ChG,A:Sleet. 100.00
119 ChG,A:Coffyhead 100.00
120 ChG,'Case Against
  Mumbles Quartet'. 100.00
121 ChG,'Case of the Wild Boys' 100.00
122 ChG,'Case of the
  Poisoned Pellet' 100.00
123 ChG,'Case of the Deadly
  Treasure Hunt' 100.00
124 ChG,'Case of Oodles
  Hears Only Evil 100.00
125 ChG,'Case of the Desparate
  Widow' 100.00
126 ChG,'Case of Oodles'
  Hideout' 100.00
127 ChG,'Case Against
  Joe Period' 100.00
128 ChG,'Case Against Juvenile
  Delinquent' 100.00
129 ChG,'Case of Son of Flattop' 100.00
130 ChG,'Case of Great
  Gang Roundup' 100.00
131 ChG,'Strange Case of
  Flattop's Conscience' 100.00
132 ChG,'Case of Flattop's
  Big Show'. 100.00
133 ChG,'Dick Tracy Follows Trail
  of Jewel Thief Gang'. 100.00
134 ChG,'Last Stand of
  Jewel Thieves' 100.00
135 ChG,'Case of the
  Rooftop Sniper' 100.00
136 ChG,'Mystery of the
  Iron Room' 100.00
137 ChG,'Law Versus Dick Tracy' 100.00
138 ChG,'Mystery of Mary X' . . . 100.00
139 ChG,'Yogee the Merciless' . . 100.00
140 ChG,'The Tunnel Trap'. 100.00
141 ChG,'Case of Wormy &
  His Deadly Wagon 100.00
142 ChG,'Case of the
  Killer's Revenge'. 100.00

GOLDEN AGE

143 ChG,'Strange Case of
   Measles'................ 100.00
144 ChG,'Strange Case of
   Shoulders'.............. 100.00
145 ChG,'Case of the Feindish
   Photo-graphers';April, 1961 . 100.00

Dime Comics #1
© *Newsbrook Publ. Co.*

DIME COMICS
Newsbook Publ. Corp., 1945
1 LbC,A:Silver Streak 900.00

DING DONG
**Compix
(Magazine Enterprises), 1947**
1 (fa)..................... 225.00
2 (fa)..................... 100.00
3 thru 5 (fa) .... @75.00

DINKY DUCK
**St. John Publ. Co./Pines
Nov., 1951**
1 .... 100.00
2 .... 50.00
3 thru 10 .... @35.00
11 thru 15 .... @30.00
16 thru 18 .... @25.00
19 Summer, 1958............ 25.00

DIXIE DUGAN
**Columbia Publ./
Publication Enterprises
July, 1942**
1 Boxing (c),Joe Palooka...... 300.00
2 .... 175.00
3 .... 125.00
4 & 5..................... @75.00
6 thru 12 .... @60.00
13 1949 .... 60.00

DIZZY DAMES
**B&M Distribution Co.
(American Comics)
Sept.–Oct., 1952**
1 .... 150.00
2 .... 100.00
3 thru 6 July–Aug., 1953 ..... @75.00

DIZZY DON COMICS
**Howard Publications/
Dizzy Dean Ent., 1943**
1 B&W interior.............. 125.00
2 B&W Interior............... 75.00
3 B&W Interior............... 60.00
4 B&W Interior............... 60.00
5 thru 21 .... @60.00
22 Oct., 1946 .... 125.00
1a thru 3a .... @100.00

DIZZY DUCK
See: BARNYARD COMICS

DOC CARTER
**V.D. COMICS
Health Publ. Inst., 1949**
N# 250.00
N# 150.00

DOC SAVAGE COMICS
Street & Smith, May, 1940
1 B:Doc Savage, Capt. Fury, Danny
   Garrett, Mark Mallory, Whisperer,
   Capt. Death, Treasure
   Island, A: The Magician ... 7,500.00
2 O:Ajax,The Sun Man,E:The
   Whisperer 2,400.00
3 Artic Ice Wastes 1,600.00
4 E:Treasure Island, Saves
   U.S. Navy 1,100.00
5 O:Astron, the Crocodile
   Queen, Sacred Ruby 1,000.00
6 E: Capt. Fury, O:Red Falcon,
   Murderous Peace Clan 800.00
7 V:Zoombas 800.00
8 Finds the Long Lost Treasure . 800.00
9 Smashes Japan's Secret Oil
   Supply 800.00
10 O:Thunder Bolt, The Living
   Dead A:Lord Manhattan ... 800.00
11 V:Giants of Destruction...... 600.00
12 Saves Merchant Fleet from
   Complete Destruction...... 600.00
2-1 The Living Evil 600.00
2-2 V:Beggar King 600.00
2-3 .... 600.00
2-4 Fight to Death............. 600.00
2-5 Saves Panama Canal from
   Blood Raider 600.00
2-6 .... 600.00
2-7 V:Black Knight 600.00
2-8 Oct., 1943 .... 600.00

DR. ANTHONY KING
**HOLLYWOOD LOVE
DOCTOR
Harvey, Publ., 1952**
1 .... 125.00
2 .... 75.00
3 .... 75.00
4 BP,May, 1954 .... 75.00

DOLL MAN
**Comic Favorites
(Quality Comics Group)
Fall, 1941–Oct., 1953**
1 RC,B:Doll Man & Justine
   Wright 5,000.00
2 B:Dragon 1,800.00
3 Five stories 1,500.00
4 Dolls of Death, Wanted:
   The Doll Man........... 1,300.00
5 RC,Four stories 1,000.00

Doll Man #3
© *Quality Comics Group*

6 Buy War Stamps (c) 750.00
7 Four stories 750.00
8 BWa,Three stories,A:Torchy . 2,200.00
9 .... 750.00
10 RC,V:Murder Marionettes,
   Grim, The Good Sport 600.00
11 Shocks Crime Square in the
   Eye 600.00
12 .... 600.00
13 RC,Blows Crime Sky High ... 600.00
14 Spotlight on Comics......... 600.00
15 Faces Danger 600.00
16 .... 550.00
17 Deals out Punishment for
   Crime................... 550.00
18 Redskins Scalp Crime 550.00
19 Fitted for a Cement Coffin ... 550.00
20 Destroys the Black Heart of
   Nemo Black 550.00
21 Problem of a Poison Pistol... 500.00
22 V:Tom Thumb 500.00
23 V:Minstrel, musician
   of menace 500.00
24 V:Elixir of Youth 500.00
25 V:Thrawn, Lord of Lightning.. 500.00
26 V:Sultan of Satarr &
   Wonderous Runt.......... 500.00
27 Space Conquest 500.00
28 V:The Flame 500.00
29 V:Queen MAB 500.00
30 V:Lord Damion 500.00
31 I:Elmo, the Wonder Dog..... 400.00
32 A:Jeb Rivers 400.00
33 & 34................... @400.00
35 Prophet of Doom 400.00
36 Death Trap in the Deep 400.00
37 V:The Skull,B:Doll Girl,
   Bondage(c)............... 500.00
38 The Cult of Death 400.00
39 V:The Death Drug 300.00
40 Giants of Crime 250.00
41 The Headless Horseman 250.00
42 Tale of the Mind Monster 250.00
43 The Thing that Kills 250.00
44 V:Radioactive Man......... 250.00
45 What was in the Doom Box? . 250.00
46 Monster from Tomorrow..... 250.00
47 V:Mad Hypnotist 250.00

FAMOUS GANG,
BOOK OF COMICS
**Firestone Tire & Rubber Co.
1942**
N# 1,200.00

GOLDEN AGE

Donald–Double / Comics Values Annual

DONALD AND MICKEY MERRY CHRISTMAS
N# (2),CB, 1943 . . . . 1,000.00
N# (3),CB, 1944 . . . . 900.00
N# (4),CB, 1945 . . . . 1,400.00
N# (5),CB, 1946 . . . . 1,000.00
N# (6),CB, 1947 . . . . 1,000.00
N# (7),CB, 1948 . . . . 1,000.00
N# (8),CB, 1949 . . . . 850.00

DONALD DUCK
Whitman
W.Disney's Donald Duck ('35) . 3,000.00
W.Disney's Donald Duck ('36) . 3,000.00
W.Disney's Donald Duck ('38) . 3,000.00

DONALD DUCK GIVEAWAYS
Donald Duck Surprise Party (Icy Frost Ice Cream 1948)WK . 3,000.00
Donald Duck (Xmas Giveaway 1944). 1,000.00
Donald Duck Tells About Kites (P.G.&E., Florida 1954) . . . 2,500.00
Donald Duck Tells About Kites (S.C.Edison 1954). 2,200.00
Donald Duck and the Boys (Whitman 1948) 750.00
Donald Ducks Atom Bomb (Cherrios 1947) 750.00

(WALT DISNEY'S) DONALD DUCK
Dell Publishing Co. Nov., 1952
(#1-#25) See *Dell Four Color*
26 CB;"Trick or Treat" (1952) . . . 500.00
27 CB(c);"Flying Horse"('53) . . . 200.00
28 CB(c); Robert the Robot. 150.00
29 CB(c). 150.00
30 CB(c). 150.00
31 thru 39. . . . . @75.00
40 thru 44. . . . . @70.00
45 CB 200.00
46 CB; "Secret of Hondorica" . . . 300.00
47 thru 51 . . . . @75.00
52 CB; "Lost Peg-Leg Mine" . . . 200.00
53 . . . . 75.00
54 CB; "Forbidden Valley". 200.00
55 thru 59 . . . . @75.00
60 CB; "Donald Duck & the Titanic Ants" 200.00
61 thru 67 . . . . @60.00
68 CB 150.00
69 thru 78 . . . . @50.00
79 CB (1 page). 75.00
80 . . . . 50.00
81 CB (1 page). 60.00
82 . . . . 50.00
83 . . . . 50.00
84 . . . . 50.00
See: Independent Color Listings

DON FORTUNE MAGAZINE
Don Fortune Publ. Co. Aug., 1946
1 CCB 250.00
2 CCB 150.00
3 CCB,Bondage(c) 125.00
4 CCB 125.00
5 CCB 125.00
6 CCB, Jan., 1947 . . . . 125.00

DON NEWCOMBE
Fawcett Publications, 1950
1 Baseball Star 500.00

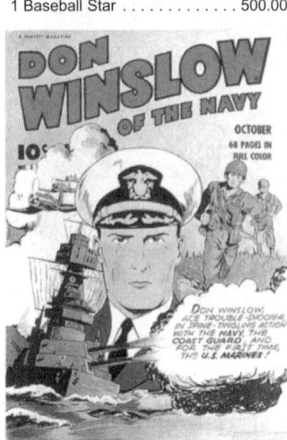

Don Winslow of the Navy #8
© *Fawcett Publications*

DON WINSLOW OF THE NAVY
Fawcett Publ./ Charlton Comics, Feb., 1943
1 Captain Marvel (c) 1,500.00
2 Nips the Nipponese in the Solomons 700.00
3 Single-Handed invasion of the Philippines 500.00
4 Undermines the Nazis! 350.00
5 Stolen Battleship Mystery . . . 350.00
6 War Stamps for Victory (c) . . . 350.00
7 Coast Guard 250.00
8 U.S. Marines 250.00
9 Fighting Marines 250.00
10 Fighting Seabees. 250.00
11 . . . . 225.00
12 Tuned for Death. 225.00
13 Hirohito's Hospitality 225.00
14 Catapults against the Axis . . 225.00
15 Fighting Merchant Marine. . . 200.00
16 V:The Most Diabolical Villain of all Time 200.00
17 Buy War Stamps (c). 200.00
18 The First Underwater Convoy. 200.00
19 Bonape Excersion 200.00
20 The Nazi Prison Ship 200.00
21 Prisoner of the Nazis 150.00
22 Suicide Football 150.00
23 Peril on the High Seas 150.00
24 Adventures on the High Seas. 150.00
25 Shanghaied Red Cross Ship . 150.00
26 V:The Scorpion 150.00
27 Buy War Stamps 150.00
28 . . . . 150.00
29 Invitation to Trouble 150.00
30 . . . . 150.00
31 Man or Myth? 125.00
32 Return of the Renegade. 125.00
33 Service Ribbons. 125.00
34 Log Book. 125.00
35 . . . . 125.00
36 . . . . 125.00
37 V: Sea Serpent 125.00
38 Climbs Mt. Everest. 125.00
39 Scorpion's Death Ledger 125.00
40 Kick Off! 125.00
41 Rides the Skis!. 100.00
42 Amazon Island. 100.00
43 Ghastly Doll Murder Case . . . 100.00
44 The Scorpions Web 100.00
45 V:Highwaymen of the Seas . . 100.00
46 Renegades Jailbreak 100.00
47 The Artic Expedition. 100.00
48 Maelstrom of the Deep. 100.00
49 The Vanishing Ship! 100.00
50 V:The Snake 100.00
51 A:Singapore Sal. 100.00
52 Ghost of the Fishing Ships . . . 100.00
53 . . . . 100.00
54 . . . . 100.00
55 . . . . 100.00
56 Far East. 100.00
57 A:Singapore Sal. 100.00
58 . . . . 100.00
59 . . . . 100.00
60 thru 63 . . . . @100.00
64 MB 125.00
65 Ph(c) 135.00
66 Ph(c) 135.00
67 Ph(c) 135.00
68 Ph(c) 135.00
69 Ph(c), Jaws of Destruction . . . 135.00
70 . . . . 90.00
71 . . . . 90.00
72 . . . . 90.00
73 Sept., 1955 . . . . 90.00

DOPEY DUCK
Non-Pareil Publ. Corp. Fall, 1945
1 A:Krazy Krow,Casper Cat 225.00
2 same 200.00
Becomes:

WACKY DUCK
Fall, 1946
3 . . . . 75.00
4 . . . . 60.00
5 . . . . 60.00
6 Summer, 1947 . . . . 60.00

DOROTHY LAMOUR
See: JUNGLE LIL

DOTTY DRIPPLE
Magazine Enterprises/ Harvey Publications, 1946
1 . . . . 75.00
2 . . . . 50.00
3 thru 10 . . . . @35.00
11 thru 20 . . . . @20.00
21 thru 23 . . . . @15.00
24 June, 1952 . . . . 15.00
Becomes:

HORACE & DOTTY DRIPPLE
Aug., 1952
25 thru 42 . . . . @15.00
43 Oct., 1955 . . . . 15.00

DOUBLE COMICS
Elliot Publications
1 ('40),Masked Marvel 3,000.00
2 ('41),Tornado Tim 2,000.00
3 ('42) 1,500.00
4 ('43) 1,100.00
5 ('44) 1,100.00

DOUBLE UP
Elliot Publications, 1941
1 . . . . 1,000.00

CVA Page 384 — All comics prices listed are for *Near Mint* condition.

GOLDEN AGE

DOWN WITH CRIME
Fawcett Publications
Nov., 1951
1 A:Desarro 400.00
2 BP, A:Scanlon Gang 200.00
3 H-is for Heroin 150.00
4 BP, A:Desarro 125.00
5 No Jail Can Hold Me 150.00
6 The Puncture-Proof Assassin . 125.00
7 The Payoff, Nov., 1952 . . . . . 125.00

DUDLEY
Prize Publications
Nov.–Dec., 1952
1 . . . . 150.00
2 . . . . 100.00
3 March–April, 1950 . . . . 85.00

DUMBO WEEKLY
The Walt Disney Co., 1942
1 Gas giveaways 900.00
2 . . . . 275.00
3 . . . . 275.00
4 . . . . 275.00
5 thru 16 . . . . @275.00

DURANGO KID
Magazine Enterprises
Oct.–Nov., 1949
1 FF, Charles Starrett photo (c)
  B:Durango Kid & Raider . . 1,000.00
2 FF, Charles Starrett Ph(c) . . . 450.00
3 FF, Charles Starrett Ph(c) . . . 400.00
4 FF, Charles Starrett Ph(c),
  Two-Timing Guns 350.00
5 FF, Charles Starrett Ph(c),
  Tracks Across the Trail 350.00
6 FF 200.00
7 FF,Atomic(c) 225.00
8 FF thru 10 . . . . @200.00
11 FF 150.00
12 FF 150.00
13 FF 150.00
14 thru 16 FF . . . . @150.00
17 O:Durango Kid. 200.00
18 FMe,DAy(c) 125.00
19 FMe,FG 100.00
20 FMe,FG 100.00
21 FMe,FG 100.00
22 FMe,FG 110.00
23 FMe,FG,I:Red Scorpion 110.00
24 thru 30 FMe,FG . . . . @110.00
31 FMe,FG 110.00
32 thru 40 FG . . . . @100.00
41 FG,Oct., 1941 . . . . 110.00

DYNAMIC COMICS
Dynamic Publications
(Harry 'A' Chesler)
Oct., 1941
1 EK,O:Major Victory, Dynamic Man,
  Hale the Magician, A:Black
  Cobra 2,400.00
2 O:Dynamic Boy & Lady
  Satan,I:Green Knight,
  Lance Cooper 1,000.00
3 GT 900.00
8 Horror (c). 1,000.00
9 MRa,GT,B:Mr.E 900.00
10 . . . . 700.00
11 GT. 600.00
12 GT. 500.00
13 GT. 600.00
14 . . . . 500.00
15 Sky Chief. 500.00
16 GT,Bondage(c),Marijuana. . . 850.00
17 . . . . 750.00

Dynamic Comics #18
© Harry A Chesler

18 Ric. 400.00
19 A:Dynamic Man 375.00
20 same,Nude Woman 900.00
21 same,Dinosaur(c). 375.00
22 same 375.00
23 A:Yankee Girl,1.0948 . . . . . . 375.00

DYNAMITE
Comic Media/Allen Hardy Publ.
May, 1953
1 DH(c),A:Danger#6 . . . . 250.00
2 . . . . 150.00
3 PAM(a&c),B:Johnny
  Dynamite,Drug 175.00
4 PAM(a&c),Prostitution 200.00
5 PAM(a&c) 125.00
6 PAM(a&c) 125.00
7 PAM(a&c) 125.00
8 PAM(a&c) 125.00
9 PAM(a&c) 125.00
Becomes:

JOHNNY DYNAMITE
Charlton Comics, June, 1955
10 PAM(c) 100.00
11 . . . . 75.00
12 . . . . 75.00
Becomes:

FOREIGN INTRIGUES
1956
13 A:Johnny Dynamite 90.00
14 same 60.00
15 same 60.00
Becomes:

BATTLEFIELD ACTION
Nov., 1957
16 . . . . 50.00
17 . . . . 30.00
18 . . . . 30.00
19 . . . . 30.00
20 . . . . 30.00
21 thru 30 . . . . @25.00
31 thru 70 . . . . @10.00
71 thru 84 Oct., 1984 . . . . @8.00

EAGLE, THE
Fox Features Syndicate
July, 1941
1 B:The Eagle,A:Rex Dexter
  of Mars 2,500.00
2 B:Spider Queen 1,100.00

3 B:Joe Spook 825.00
4 Jan., 1942 . . . . 800.00

EAGLE, THE
Rural Home Publ.
Feb.–March, 1945
1 LbC 600.00
2 LbC,April–May, 1945 . . . . 300.00

EAT RIGHT
TO WORK AND WIN
Swift Co., 1942
N# Flash Gordon,Popeye 500.00

EDDIE STANKY
Fawcett Publications, 1951
N# New York Giants 400.00

Eerie #17
© Avon Periodicals

EERIE
Avon Periodicals
May–June, 1951–
Aug.–Sept., 1954
1 JKa,Horror from the Pit,
  Bondage(c) 5,000.00
2,WW(a&c), Chamber of Death . 900.00
3 WW(a&c),JKa,JO
  Monster of the Storm 1,100.00
4 WW(c),Phantom of Reality . 1,000.00
5 WW(c), Operation Horror 800.00
6 Devil Keeps a Date 400.00
7 WW(c),JKa,JO,Blood for
  the Vampire 700.00
8 EK, Song of the Undead 400.00
9 JKa, Hands of Death 400.00
10 Castle of Terror 400.00
11 Anatomical Monster 400.00
12 Dracula 500.00
13 . . . . 350.00
14 Master of the Dead 350.00
15 . . . . 250.00
16 WW, Chamber of Death 250.00
17 WW(c),JO,JKa, ... 300.00

EERIE ADVENTURES
Approved Comics
(Ziff-Davis), Winter, 1951
1 BP,JKa,Bondage 450.00

All comics prices listed are for Near Mint condition.

EGBERT
**Arnold Publications/
Comic Magazine
Spring, 1946**
1 I:Egbert & The Count 200.00
2 . . . . 100.00
3 . . . . 50.00
4 . . . . 50.00
5 . . . . 50.00
6 . . . . 60.00
7 . . . . 50.00
8 . . . . 50.00
9 . . . . 50.00
10 . . . . 50.00
11 thru 17 . . . . @35.00
18 1950 . . . . 35.00

EH!
**Charlton Comics
Dec., 1953–Nov., 1954**
1 DAy(c),DG,Atomic Mouse 400.00
2 DAy(c) 250.00
3 DAy(c) 200.00
4 DAy(c),Sexual 225.00
5 DAy(c) 200.00
6 DAy(c),Sexual. 225.00
7 DAy(c) 200.00

EL BOMBO COMICS
Frances M. McQueeny, 1945
1 . . . . 125.00

ELLERY QUEEN
**Superior Comics
May–Nov., 1949**
1 LbC(c),JKa,Horror. 600.00
2 . . . . 450.00
3 Drug issue 400.00
4 The Crooked Mile 500.00

ELLERY QUEEN
**Approved Comics
(Ziff-Davis)
Jan.–March, 1952**
1 NS(c),The Corpse the Killed . . 500.00
2 NS,Killer's Revenge,
 Summer, 1952 . . . . 400.00

ELSIE THE COW
**D.S. Publishing Co.
Oct.–Nov., 1949**
1 P(c) 250.00
2 Bondage(c). 225.00
3 July–Aug., 1950 . . . . 175.00

ENCHANTING LOVE
**Kirby Publishing Co.
Oct., 1949**
1 Branded Guilty, Ph(c) 125.00
2 Ph(c),BP. 75.00
3 Ph(c),Utter Defeat was our
 Victory; Jimmy Stewart. 65.00
4 thru 6 . . . . @75.00

ETTA KETT
**Best Books, Inc.
(Standard Comics)
Dec., 1948**
11 . . . . 75.00
12 . . . . 50.00
13 . . . . 50.00
14 Sept., 1949 . . . . 50.00

ERNIE COMICS
See: SCREAM COMICS

EXCITING COMICS
**Better Publ./Visual Editions
(Standard Comics)
April, 1940**
1 O:Mask, Jim Hatfield,
 Dan Williams 5,200.00
2 B:Sphinx 2,500.00
3 V;Robot 1,500.00
4 V:Sea Monster 1,000.00
5 V:Gargoyle 1,000.00
6 . . . . 1,100.00
7 AS(c) 750.00
8 . . . . 750.00
9 O:Black Terror & Tim,
 Bondage(c) 13,000.00
10 A:Black Terror 3,500.00
11 same. 1,800.00
12 Bondage(c). 1,200.00
13 Bondage(c). 1,200.00
14 O:Sphinx 700.00
15 O:Liberator 750.00
16 Black Terror 650.00
17 same 650.00
18 same 650.00
19 same 650.00
20 E:Mask,Bondage(c) 600.00
21 A:Liberator 600.00
22 O:The Eaglet,B:American
 Eagle 650.00
23 Black Terror 550.00
24 Black Terror 550.00
25 Bondage(c) 575.00
26 ASh(c). 550.00
27 ASh(c). 550.00
28 ASh(c),B:Crime Crusader. . . 850.00
29 ASh(c) 700.00
30 ASh(c),Bondage(c). 750.00
31 ASh(c) 600.00
32 ASh(c) 600.00
33 ASh(c) 600.00
34 ASh(c) 600.00
35 ASh(c),E:Liberator 600.00
36 ASh(c) 600.00
37 ASh(c) 600.00
38 ASh(c) 600.00
39 ASh(c)O:Kara, Jungle
 Princess 650.00
40 ASh(c) 675.00
41 ASh(c) 675.00
42 ASh(c),B:Scarab 700.00
43 ASh(c). 650.00
44 ASh(c). 650.00
45 ASh(c),V:Robot 650.00
46 ASh(c). 650.00
47 ASh(c). 650.00
48 ASh(c). 650.00
49 ASh(c),E:Kara &
 American Eagle 650.00
50 ASh(c),E:American Eagle. . . . 650.00
51 ASh(c),B:Miss Masque. 800.00
52 ASh(c),Miss Masque 625.00
53 ASh(c),Miss Masque 625.00
54 ASh(c),E:Miss Masque. 625.00
55 ASh(c),O&B:Judy o/t Jungle. . 650.00
56 ASh(c) 625.00
57 ASh(c). 625.00
58 ASh(c). 625.00
59 ASh(c),FF,Bondage(c) 650.00
60 ASh(c),The Mystery Rider . . . 625.00
61 ASh(c). 625.00
62 ASh(c). 625.00
63 ASh(c). 625.00
64 ASh(c). 625.00
65 ASh(c). 625.00
66 . . . . 625.00
67 GT. 625.00
68 . . . . 625.00
69 Sept., 1949 . . . . 625.00

EXCITING ROMANCES
Fawcett Publications, 1949
1 Ph(c) 125.00
2 . . . . 75.00
3 . . . . 75.00
4 Ph(c) 75.00
5 thru 14 . . . . @60.00

EXOTIC ROMANCE
**See: TRUE WAR
ROMANCES**

EXPLORER JOE
**Approved Comics
(Ziff-Davis), Winter, 1951**
1 NS,The Fire Opal
 of Madagscar 125.00
2 BK, Oct.–Nov., 1952 . . . . 150.00

EXPOSED
**D.S. Publishing Co.
March–April, 1948**
1 Corpses Cash and Carry 250.00
2 Giggling Killer 300.00
3 One Bloody Night 125.00
4 JO,Deadly Dummy 125.00
5 Body on the Beach 125.00
6 Grl,The Secret in the Snow . . 400.00
7 The Gypsy Baron,
 July–Aug., 1949 . . . . 400.00

EXTRA
Magazine Enterprises, 1947
1 . . . . 500.00

EXTRA!
**E.C. Comics,
March–April, 1955**
1 JCr,RC,JSe 250.00
2 JCr,RC,JSe 200.00
3 JCr,RC,JSe 200.00
4 JCr,RC,JSe 200.00
5 Nov.–Dec., 1955 . . . . 200.00

*Exciting Comics #9
© Standard Comics*

All comics prices listed are for *Near Mint* condition.

GOLDEN AGE

FACE, THE
Publication Enterprises (Columbia Comics), 1942
1 MBi(c),The Face 1,200.00
2 MBi(c) 750.00
Becomes:

TONY TRENT
1948
3 MBi,A:The Face 150.00
4 1949 . . . . 100.00

FAIRY TALE PARADE
Dell Publishing Co., 1942
1 WK,Giant. 1,900.00
2 WK,Flying Horse. 750.00
3 WK. 550.00
4 WK. 500.00
5 WK. 500.00
6 WK. 400.00
7 WK. 400.00
8 WK. 400.00
9 WK,Reluctant Dragon 400.00

FAMOUS COMICS
Zain-Eppy Publ.
N# Joe Palooka 500.00

FAMOUS CRIMES
Fox Features Syndicate June, 1948
1 Cold Blooded Killer 600.00
2 Near Nudity (c) 500.00
3 Crime Never Pays 600.00
4 . . . . 250.00
5 . . . . 250.00
6 . . . . 250.00
7 Drug issue 550.00
8 thru 19 . . . . @200.00
20 Aug., 1951 . . . . 200.00
51 1952 . . . . 125.00

FAMOUS FAIRY TALES
K.K. Publication Co., 1942
N# WK, Giveaway 450.00
N# WK, Giveaway 350.00
N# WK, Giveaway 350.00

FAMOUS FEATURE STORIES
Dell Publishing Co., 1938
1A:Tarzan, Terry and the Pirates
  Dick Tracy,Smilin' Jack. . . . 1,000.00

FAMOUS FUNNIES
Eastern Color Printing Co. 1933
N# A Carnival of Comics 13,000.00
N# Feb., 1934,
  1st 10-cent comic 35,000.00
1 July, 1934 . . . . 25,000.00
2 . . . . 5,000.00
3 B:Buck Rogers 7,500.00
4 Football (c) 2,500.00
5 Christmas 2,000.00
6 . . . . 1,200.00
7 . . . . 1,200.00
8 . . . . 1,200.00
9 . . . . 1,200.00
10 . . . . 1,200.00
11 Four pages of Buck Rogers. 1,100.00
12 Four pages of Buck Rogers. 1,100.00
13 . . . . 800.00
14 . . . . 800.00
15 Football (c) 800.00

Famous Funnies #85
© Eastern Color Printing

16 . . . . 800.00
17 Christmas (c) 800.00
18 Four pages of Buck Rogers. 1,100.00
19 . . . . 800.00
20 . . . . 800.00
21 Baseball 600.00
22 Buck Rogers 650.00
23 . . . . 575.00
24 B: War on Crime 575.00
25 . . . . 575.00
26 . . . . 575.00
27 G-Men (c) 575.00
28 . . . . 575.00
29 Christmas 575.00
30 . . . . 575.00
31 . . . . 400.00
32 Phantom Magician 600.00
33 A:Baby Face Nelson &
  John Dillinger 450.00
34 . . . . 400.00
35 Buck Rogers 475.00
36 . . . . 400.00
37 . . . . 400.00
38 Portrait,Buck Rogers 475.00
39 . . . . 400.00
40 . . . . 400.00
41 thru 50 . . . . @350.00
51 thru 57 . . . . @300.00
58 Baseball (c) 300.00
59 . . . . 300.00
60 . . . . 300.00
61 . . . . 250.00
62 . . . . 250.00
63 . . . . 250.00
64 . . . . 250.00
65 JK 250.00
66 . . . . 250.00
67 . . . . 250.00
68 JK 250.00
69 . . . . 250.00
70 . . . . 250.00
71 BEv 200.00
72 BEv,B:Speed Spaulding . . . 200.00
73 BEv 200.00
74 BEv 200.00
75 BEv 200.00
76 BEv 200.00
77 BEv,Merry Christmas (c) . . . 200.00
78 BEv 200.00
79 BEv 200.00
80 BEv,Buck Rogers 200.00
81 O:Invisible Scarlet O'Neil . . . 200.00
82 Buck Rogers (c) 200.00
83 Dickie Dare 150.00
84 Scotty Smith 150.00

85 Eagle Scout,Roy Rogers 150.00
86 Moon Monsters 150.00
87 Scarlet O'Neil 150.00
88 Dickie Dare 150.00
89 O:Fearless Flint 150.00
90 Bondage (c) 175.00
91 . . . . 150.00
92 . . . . 150.00
93 . . . . 150.00
94 War Bonds. 175.00
95 Invisible Scarlet O'Neil 150.00
96 . . . . 150.00
97 War Bonds Promo 150.00
98 . . . . 150.00
99 . . . . 150.00
100 Anniversary issue. 150.00
101 thru 110 . . . . @150.00
111 thru 130 . . . . @100.00
131 thru 150 . . . . @75.00
151 thru 162 . . . . @75.00
163 Valentine's Day (c) 75.00
164 . . . . 65.00
165 . . . . 65.00
166 . . . . 65.00
167 . . . . 65.00
168 . . . . 65.00
169 AW 100.00
170 AW 100.00
171 thru 190 . . . . @60.00
191 thru 203 . . . . @50.00
204 War (c) 60.00
205 thru 208 . . . . @55.00
209 FF(c),Buck Rogers 1,500.00
210 FF(c),Buck Rogers 1,500.00
211 FF(c),Buck Rogers 1,500.00
212 FF(c),Buck Rogers 1,500.00
213 FF(c),Buck Rogers 1,500.00
214 FF(c),Buck Rogers 1,500.00
215 FF(c),Buck Rogers 1,500.00
216 FF(c),Buck Rogers 1,500.00
217 . . . . 65.00
218 July, 1955 . . . . 65.00

FAMOUS GANG, BOOK OF COMICS
See: DONALD AND MICKEY MERRY CHRISTMAS

FAMOUS GANGSTERS
Avon Periodicals, 1951
1 Al Capone, Dillinger,
  Luciano & Shultz 450.00
2 WW(c),Dillinger Machine-
  Gun Killer 400.00
3 Lucky Luciano & Murder Inc. . . 400.00
Becomes:

CRIME ON THE WATERFRONT
May, 1952
4 Underworld Gangsters who
  Control the Shipment of
  Drugs! 400.00

FAMOUS STARS
Ziff-Davis Publ. Co., 1950
1 OW,Shelley Winter,Susan
  Peters & Shirley Temple . . . 375.00
2 BEv,Betty Hutton, Bing Crosby 300.00
3 OW,Judy Garland, Alan Ladd . 325.00
4 RC,Jolson, Bob Mitchum 250.00
5 BK,Elizabeth Taylor,
  Esther Williams. 350.00
6 Gene Kelly, Spring, 1952 . . . . 250.00

All comics prices listed are for Near Mint condition.

GOLDEN AGE

Famous–Feature | Comics Values Annual

FAMOUS STORIES
Dell Publishing Co., 1942
1 Treasure Island 350.00
2 Tom Sawyer 325.00

FAMOUS WESTERN BADMEN
See: REDSKIN

FANTASTIC
See: CAPTAIN SCIENCE

FANTASTIC COMICS
Fox Features Syndicate, 1939
1 LF(c),I&O:Samson,B:Star Dust, Super Wizard, Space Smith & Capt. Kid 7,000.00
2 BP,LF(c),Samson destroyed the Battery & Routed the Foe . 3,000.00
3 BP,LF(c),Slays the Iron Monster 8,000.00
4 GT,LF(c), Demolishes the Closing Torture Walls 2,500.00
5 GT,LF(c),Crumbles the Mighty War Machine 2,300.00
6 JSm(c),Bondage(c) 1,800.00
7 JSm(c) 1,800.00
8 GT,Destroys the Mask of Fire,Bondage(c). 1,200.00
9 Mighty Muscles saved the Drowning Girl 1,200.00
10 I&O:David. 1,200.00
11 Wrecks the Torture Machine to save his fellow American 1,000.00
12 Heaved the Huge Ship high into the Air. 1,000.00
13 Samson(c) 1,000.00
14 Samson(c) 1,000.00
15 Samson(c) 1,000.00
16 E:Stardust. 1,000.00
17 Samson(c) 1,000.00
18 I:Black Fury & Chuck 1,000.00
19 Samson(c) 900.00
20 Samson(c) 900.00
21 B&I: The Banshee,Hittler(c) . 1,100.00
22 Hittler & Samson(c). 1,000.00
23 O:The Gladiator, Hitler (c) Nov., 1941. . . . . 1,100.00

Fantastic Comics #3
© Fox Features Syndicate

FARGO KID
See: JUSTICE TRAPS OF THE GUILTY

FAST FICTION
Seaboard Publ./ Famous Author Illustrated
Oct., 1949
1 Scarlet Pimpernel 400.00
2 HcK,Captain Blood 375.00
3 She 500.00
4 The 39 Steps 300.00
5 HcK,Beau Geste 300.00
Becomes:

STORIES BY FAMOUS AUTHORS ILLUSTRATED
Aug., 1950
1a Scarlet Pimpernel 350.00
2a Captain Blood. 350.00
3a She 400.00
4a The 39 Steps 300.00
5a Beau Geste 275.00
6 HcK,MacBeth 300.00
7 HcK,Window. 250.00
8 HcK,Hamlet 275.00
9 Nicholas Nickleby 250.00
10 HcK,Romeo & Juliet. 250.00
11 GS,Ben Hur 260.00
12 GS,La Svengali 265.00
13 HcK,Scaramouche. 265.00

FAWCETT FUNNY ANIMALS
Fawcett Publications
Dec., 1942
1 I:Hoppy the Marvel Bunny, Captain Marvel (c) 650.00
2 X-Mas Issue 350.00
3 Spirit of '43 . . . . 200.00
4 and 5 . . . . @200.00
6 Buy War Bonds and Stamps . 150.00
7 . . . . 150.00
8 Flag (c). 150.00
9 and 10 . . . . @150.00
11 thru 20 . . . . @100.00
21 thru 30 . . . . @75.00
31 thru 40 . . . . @50.00
41 thru 83 . . . . @50.00
Charlton Comics
84 . . . . 50.00
85 thru 91 Feb., 1956 . . . . . . @35.00

FAWCETT MOVIE COMICS
Fawcett Publications, 1949
N# Dakota Lil 350.00
N#a Copper Canyon 250.00
N# Destination the Moon 1,000.00
N# Montana 250.00
N# Pioneer Marshal 250.00
N# Powder River Rustlers 300.00
N# Singing Guns 250.00
7 Gunmen of Abilene 275.00
8 King of the Bull Whip 400.00
9 BP,The Old Frontier 250.00
10 The Missourians 250.00
11 The Thundering Trail 350.00
12 Rustlers on Horseback. . . . 275.00
13 Warpath. 200.00
14 Last Outpost,RonaldReagan . 500.00
15 The Man from Planet-X 3,000.00
16 10 Tall Men 150.00
17 Rose Cimarron 125.00
18 The Brigand. 150.00
19 Carbine Williams 150.00
20 Ivanhoe, Dec., 1952 . . . . . . 250.00

FEATURE BOOKS
David McKay Publications
May, 1937
N# Dick Tracy 10,000.00
N# Popeye 8,500.00
1 Zane Grey's King of the Royal Mounted 800.00
2 Popeye 1,000.00
3 Popeye and the "Jeep" . . . 900.00
4 Dick Tracy 1,500.00
5 Popeye and his Poppa 800.00
6 Dick Tracy 1,100.00
7 Little Orphan Annie 1,200.00
8 Secret Agent X-9 . . . . 600.00
9 Tracy & the Famon Boys . . . 1,100.00
10 Popeye & Susan 800.00
11 Annie Rooney 350.00
12 Blondie 1,000.00
13 Inspector Wade 300.00
14 Popeye in Wild Oats 1,000.00
15 Barney Baxter in the Air 400.00
16 Red Eagle 400.00
17 Gang Busters 750.00
18 Mandrake the Magician . . . 700.00
19 Mandrake 700.00
20 The Phantom 1,100.00
21 Lone Ranger. 1,000.00
22 The Phantom 900.00
23 Mandrake in Teibe Castle. . . 700.00

Feature Books #3
© David McKay Publications

24 Lone Ranger. 1,000.00
25 Flash Gordon on the Planet Mongo 1,400.00
26 Prince Valiant 1,200.00
27 Blondie 200.00
28 Blondie and Dagwood 200.00
29 Blondie at the Home Sweet Home. 200.00
30 Katzenjammer Kids 200.00
31 Blondie Keeps the Home Fires Burning 200.00
32 Katzenjammer Kids 150.00
33 Romance of Flying. 150.00
34 Blondie Home is Our Castle. . 200.00
35 Katzenjammer Kids 175.00
36 Blondie on the Home Front . . 175.00
37 Katzenjammer Kids 175.00
38 Blondie the ModelHomemaker 125.00
39 The Phantom 650.00
40 Blondie 175.00

CVA Page 388 | All comics prices listed are for *Near Mint* condition.

GOLDEN AGE

41 Katzenjammer Kids 175.00
42 Blondie in Home-Spun Yarns . 175.00
43 Blondie Home-Cooked Scraps 175.00
44 Katzenjammer Kids in
  Monkey Business 175.00
45 Blondie in Home of the Free
  and the Brave 175.00
46 Blondie in Fire World 500.00
47 Blondie in Eaten out of
  House and Home 175.00
48 The Maltese Falcon 1,000.00
49 Perry Mason - The Case of
  the Lucky Legs 300.00
50 The Shoplifters Shoe,
  P. Mason 300.00
51 Rip Kirby - Mystery of
  the Mangler 350.00
52 Mandrake in the Land of X . . . 400.00
53 Phantom in Safari Suspense . 500.00
54 Rip Kirby - Case of the
  Master Menace 350.00
55 Mandrake in 5-numbers
  Treasue Hunt 400.00
56 Phantom Destroys the
  Sky Band 450.00
57 Phantom in the Blue Gang,
  1948 . . . . 450.00

FEATURE FUNNIES
Harry A. Chesler Publ./
Comic Favorites, Oct., 1937
1 RuG(a&c),A:Joe Palooka,
  Mickey Finn, Bungles, Dixie
  Dugan, Big Top, Strange as
  It Seems, Off the Record . . 3,500.00
2 A: The Hawk 1,500.00
3 WE,Joe Palooka,The Clock . 1,100.00
4 RuG,WE,RuG(c),JoePalooka 1,000.00
5 WE, Joe Palooka drawing . . 1,000.00
6 WE, Joe Palooka (c) 1,000.00
7 WE,LLe, Gallant Knight story
  by Vernon Henkel 650.00
8 WE 600.00
9 WE, Joe Palooka story 1,000.00
10 WE,Micky Finn(c) 575.00
11 WE,LLe,The Bungles(c) 575.00
12 WE, Joe Palooka(c) 500.00
13 WE,LLe, World Series(c) 750.00
14 WE,Ned Brant(c) 500.00
15 WE,Joe Palooka(c) 525.00
16 Mickey Finn(c) 500.00
17 WE 500.00
18 Joe Palooka (c) 525.00
19 WE,LLe,Mickey Finn(c) 500.00
20 WE,LLe 500.00
Becomes:

FEATURE COMICS
Quality Comics Group
June. 1939–May, 1950
21 Joe Palooka(c). 750.00
22 LLe(c),Mickey Finn(c). 450.00
23 B:Charlie Chan 500.00
24 AAr,Joe Palooka(c) 425.00
25 AAr,The Clock(c) 425.00
26 AAr,The Bundles(c) 425.00
27 WE,AAr,I:Doll Man 6,000.00
28 LF,AAr,The Clock(c) 2,400.00
29 LF,AAr,The Clock(c) 1,200.00
30 LF,AAr,Doll Man(c) 1,200.00
31 LF,AAr,Mickey Finn(c) 1,000.00
32 PGv,LF,GFx,Doll Man(c). . . . 750.00
33 PGv,LF,GFx,Bundles(c) 650.00
34 PGv,LF,GFx,Doll Man(c). . . . 750.00
35 PGv,LF,GFx,Bundles(c) 650.00
36 PGv,LF,GFx,Doll Man(c). . . . 750.00
37 PGv,LF,GFx,Bundles(c) 650.00
38 PGv,GFx,Doll Man(c) 500.00
39 PGv,GFx,Bundles(c) 500.00
40 PGv,GFx,WE(c),Doll Man(c) . 500.00
41 PGv,GFx,WE(c),Bundles(c) . 500.00
42 GFx,Doll Man(c). 400.00
43 RC,GFx,Bundles(c) 375.00
44 RC,GFx,Doll Man(c). 550.00
45 RC,GFx,Bundles(c) 350.00
46 RC,PGv,GFx,Doll Man(c) . . . 500.00
47 RC,GFx,Bundles(c) 350.00
48 RC,GFx,Doll Man(c) 500.00
49 RC,GFx,Bundles(c) 350.00
50 RC,GFx,Doll Man(c) 500.00
51 RC,GFx,Bundles(c) 350.00
52 RC,GFx,Doll Man(c) 400.00
53 RC,GFx,Bundles(c) 300.00
54 RC,GFx,Doll Man(c) 400.00
55 RC,GFx,Bundles(c) 300.00
56 RC,GFx,Doll Man(c) 400.00
57 RC,GFx,Bundles(c) 300.00
58 RC,GFx,Doll Man (c) 400.00
59 RC,GFx,Mickey Finn(c) 300.00
60 RC,GFx,Bundles(c) 400.00
61 RC,GFx,Bundles(c) 250.00
62 RC,GFx,Doll Man(c). 350.00
63 RC,GFx,Bundles(c) 250.00
64 BP,GFx,Doll Man(c) 350.00
65 BP,GFx(c),Bundles(c). 250.00
66 BP,GFx,Doll Man(c) 350.00
67 BP 250.00
68 BP,Doll Man vs.BeardedLady . 300.00
69 BP,GFx(c),Devil (c) 250.00
70 BP,Doll Man(c) 350.00
71 BP,GFx(c) 250.00
72 BP,Doll Man(c). 250.00
73 BP,GFx(c),Bundles(c). 200.00
74 Doll Man(c) 250.00
75 GFx(c) 200.00
76 GFx(c) 200.00
77 Doll Man (c) until #140. . . . . 200.00
78 Knows no Fear but the
  Knife Does 200.00
79 Little Luck God. 200.00
80 . . . . 200.00
81 Wanted for Murder. 175.00
82 V:Shawunkas the Shaman . . . 175.00
83 V:Mechanical Man 175.00
84 V:Masked Rider, Death
  Goes to the Rodeo 175.00
85 V:King of Beasts 175.00
86 Is He A Killer? 175.00
87 The Maze of Murder 175.00
88 V:The Phantom Killer. 175.00
89 Crook's Goose. 175.00
90 V:Whispering Corpse 175.00
91 V:The Undertaker. 175.00
92 V:The Image 175.00
93 . . . . 175.00
94 V:The Undertaker. 175.00
95 Flatten's the Peacock's Pride . 175.00
96 Doll Man Proves
  Justice is Blind 175.00
97 V:Peacock 175.00
98 V:Master Diablo 175.00
99 On the Warpath Again! 175.00
100 Crushes the City of Crime . . 200.00
101 Land of the Midget Men! . . . 150.00
102 The Angle 150.00
103 V:The Queen of Ants 150.00
104 V:The Botanist. 150.00
105 Dream of Death 150.00
106 V:The Sword Fish 150.00
107 Hand of Horror! 150.00
108 V:Cateye 150.00
109 V:The Brain 150.00
110 V:Fat Cat 150.00
111 V:The Undertaker. 150.00
112 I:Mr. Curio & His Miniatures . 150.00
113 V:Highwayman. 150.00
114 V:Tom Thumb. 150.00
115 V:The Sphinx 150.00
116 V:Elbows 150.00
117 Polka Dot on the Spot 150.00
118 thru 144 . . . . @150.00

FEDERAL MEN COMICS
Gerard Publ. Co., 1942
2 S&S,Spanking 500.00

FELIX THE CAT
Dell Publishing Co.
Feb.–March, 1948
1 . . . . 400.00
2 . . . . 300.00
3 . . . . 200.00
4 . . . . 200.00
5 . . . . 200.00
6 . . . . 150.00
7 . . . . 150.00
8 . . . . 150.00
9 . . . . 150.00
10 . . . . 150.00
11 thru 19 . . . . @125.00
Toby Press
20 thru 30 . . . . @350.00
31 . . . . 150.00
32 . . . . 350.00
33 . . . . 350.00
34 . . . . 150.00
35 . . . . 150.00

Feature Comics #34
© Quality Comics Group

Felix the Cat #36
© Dell Publishing Co./Toby Press

All comics prices listed are for *Near Mint* condition.

GOLDEN AGE

Felix–Fighting

36 thru 59	@300.00
60	275.00
61	275.00

Harvey
62 thru 80	@60.00
81 thru 99	@50.00
100	45.00
101 thru 118	@30.00
Spec., 100 pgs, 1952	300.00
Summer Ann., 100 pgs. 1953	400.00
Winter Ann.,#2 100 pgs, 1954	400.00

FERDINAND THE BULL
Dell Publishing Co., 1938
1 .... 250.00

FIGHT AGAINST CRIME
Story Comics May, 1951
- 1 Scorpion of Crime Inspector "Brains" Carroway 400.00
- 2 Ganglands Double Cross ... 250.00
- 3 Killer Dolan's Double Cross .. 200.00
- 4 Hopped Up Killers - The Con's Slaughter,Drug issue . 250.00
- 5 FF,Horror o-t Avenging Corpse 225.00
- 6 Terror of the Crazy Killer 200.00
- 7 .... 200.00
- 8 Killer with the Two-bladed Knife 150.00
- 9 Rats Die by Gas,Horror..... 400.00
- 10 Horror of the Con's Revenge . 400.00
- 11 Case of the Crazy Killer 400.00
- 12 Horror,Drug issue......... 450.00
- 13 The Bloodless Killer........ 400.00
- 14 Electric Chair (c) 450.00
- 15 .... 400.00
- 16 RA,Bondage(c) 500.00
- 17 Knife in Neck(c)........... 500.00
- 18 Attempted hanging (c) 500.00
- 19 Bondage(c) 500.00
- 20 Severed Head (c) 750.00
- 21 .... 350.00

Becomes:

FIGHT AGAINST THE GUILTY
Dec., 1954
- 22 RA,Electric Chair.......... 375.00
- 23 March, 1955 .... 250.00

FIGHT COMICS
Fight Comics Inc. (Fiction House Magazines) Jan., 1940
- 1 LF,GT,WE(c),O:Spy Fighter . 4,200.00
- 2 GT,WE(c),Joe Lewis 1,500.00
- 3 WE(c),GT,B:Rip Regan, The Powerman 1,200.00
- 4 GT,LF(c)................. 900.00
- 5 WE(c) 900.00
- 6 GT,BP(c)................. 650.00
- 7 GT,BP(c),Powerman-Blood Money 650.00
- 8 GT,Chip Collins-Lair of the Vulture 650.00
- 9 GT,Chip Collins-Prey of the War Eagle 650.00
- 10 GT,Wolves of the Yukon..... 650.00
- 11 .... 600.00
- 12 RA,Powerman-Monster of Madness 600.00
- 13 Shark Broodie-Legion of Satan 600.00
- 14 Shark Broodie-Lagoon of Death 600.00
- 15 Super-American-Hordes of the Secret Dictator....... 750.00
- 16 B:Capt.Fight,SwastikaPlague . 750.00

Fight Comics #38
© Fiction House Magazines

- 17 Super-American-Blaster of the Pig-Boat Pirates 650.00
- 18 Shark Broodie-Plague of the Yellow Devils 650.00
- 19 E:Capt. Fight............. 650.00
- 20 .... 550.00
- 21 Rip Carson-Hell's Sky-Riders . 400.00
- 22 Rip Carson-Sky Devil's Mission 400.00
- 23 Rip Carson-Angels of Vengeance 400.00
- 24 Baynonets for the Banzai Breed! Bondage(c)....... 375.00
- 25 Rip Carson-Samurai Showdown 375.00
- 26 Rip Carson-Fury of the Sky-Brigade 375.00
- 27 War-Loot for the Mikado Bondage(c)............. 375.00
- 28 Rip Carson 375.00
- 29 Rip Carson-Charge of the Lost Region 375.00
- 30 Rip Carson-Jeep-Raiders of the Torture Jungle 375.00
- 31 Gangway for the Gyrenes, Decapitation (c) 390.00
- 32 Vengeance of the Hun-Hunters,Bondage(c) 390.00
- 33 B:Tiger Girl 300.00
- 34 Bondage(c) 300.00
- 35 MB 300.00
- 36 MB 300.00
- 37 MB 300.00
- 38 MB,Bondage(c).......... 325.00
- 39 MB,Senorita Rio-Slave Brand of the Spider Cult 300.00
- 40 MB,Bondage (c) 350.00
- 41 MB,Bondage (c)........... 350.00
- 42 MB 250.00
- 43 MB,Senorita Rio-The Fire-Brides of the Lost Atlantis, Bondage(c).............. 300.00
- 44 MB,R:Capt. Fight......... 250.00
- 45 MB,Tonight Don Diablo Rides. 250.00
- 46 MB 250.00
- 47 MB,SenoritaRio-Horror's Hacienda 250.00
- 48 MB 250.00
- 49 MB,JKa,B:Tiger Girl(c) 250.00
- 50 MB 250.00
- 51 MB,O:Tiger Girl 450.00
- 52 MB,Winged Demons of Doom 225.00
- 53 MB,Shadowland Shrine 225.00
- 54 MB,Flee the Cobra Fury..... 225.00
- 55 MB,Jungle Juggernaut..... 225.00
- 56 MB 225.00
- 57 MB,Jewels of Jeopardy 225.00
- 58 MB 225.00
- 59 MB,Vampires ofCrystalCavern 225.00
- 60 MB,Kraal of DeadlyDiamonds 225.00
- 61 MB,Seekers of the Sphinx, O:Tiger Girl............. 300.00
- 62 MB,Graveyard if the Tree Tribe.............. 225.00
- 63 MB 225.00
- 64 MB,DawnBeast from Karama-Zan! 225.00
- 65 Beware the Congo Girl..... 200.00
- 66 Man or Ape!............. 200.00
- 67 Head-Hunters of Taboo Trek . 200.00
- 68 Fangs of Dr. Voodoo 200.00
- 69 Cage of the Congo Fury.... 200.00
- 70 Kraal of Traitor Tusks 200.00
- 71 Captives for the Golden Crocodile 200.00
- 72 Land of the Lost Safaris.... 200.00
- 73 War-Gods of the Jungle.... 200.00
- 74 Advengers of the Jungle.... 200.00
- 75 Perils of Momba-Kzar 200.00
- 76 Kraal of Zombi-Zaro....... 200.00
- 77 Slave-Queen of the Ape Man . 200.00
- 78 Great Congo Diamond Robbery 225.00
- 79 A:Space Rangers.......... 225.00
- 80 .... 200.00
- 81 E:Tiger Girl(c) 200.00
- 82 RipCarson-CommandoStrike . 200.00
- 83 NobodyLoves a Minesweeper 200.00
- 84 Rip Carson-Suicide Patrol ... 200.00
- 85 .... 200.00
- 86 GE,Tigerman,Summer,1954 . . 225.00

FIGHTING AMERICAN
Headline Publications (Prize), April–May, 1954
- 1 S&K,O:Fighting American & Speedboy 2,500.00
- 2 S&K(a&c) 1,000.00
- 3 S&K(a&c) 800.00
- 4 S&K(a&c) 800.00
- 5 S&K(a&c) 800.00
- 6 S&K(a&c),O:Fighting American 750.00
- 7 S&K(a&c), April–May, 1955 .. 650.00

FIGHTING DAVY CROCKETT
See: KIT CARSON

FIGHTING INDIANS OF THE WILD WEST
Avon Periodicals March, 1952
- 1 EK,EL,Geronimo, Crazy Horse, Chief Victorio 175.00
- 2 EK,Same, Nov., 1952 ..... 125.00

FIGHTING LEATHERNECKS
Toby Press, Feb., 1952
- 1 JkS,Duke's Diary 150.00
- 2 .... 100.00
- 3 .... 75.00
- 4 .... 75.00
- 5 .... 60.00
- 6 Dec., 1952 .... 60.00

FIGHTIN' TEXAN
See: TEXAN, THE

CVA Page 390 — All comics prices listed are for *Near Mint* condition.

GOLDEN AGE

FIGHTING YANK
**Nedor Publ./Better Publ.
(Standard Comics) Sept., 1942**
1 B:Fighting Yank, A:Wonder Man, Mystico, Bondage (c) 3,500.00
2 JaB 1,400.00
3 . . . . 1,000.00
4 AS(c) 1,000.00
5 AS(c) 750.00
6 AS(c) 750.00
7 AS(c),A:Fighting Yank 700.00
8 AS(c) 700.00
9 AS(c) 700.00
10 AS(c) 700.00
11 AS(c), A:Grim Reaper, Nazis bomb Washington (c) 600.00
12 AS(c), Hirohito bondage (c) . . 600.00
13 AS(c) 550.00
14 AS(c) 550.00
15 AS(c) 550.00
16 AS(c) 550.00
17 AS(c) 550.00
18 AS(c), A:American Eagle 550.00
19 AS(c) 550.00
20 AS(c) 550.00
21 AS(c) A:Kara,Jungle Princess 550.00
22 AS(c) A:Miss Masque- (c) story 600.00
23 AS(c) Klu Klux Klan parody (c) 700.00
24 A:Miss Masque 500.00
25 JRo,MMe,A:Cavalier 650.00
26 JRo,MMe,A:Cavalier 500.00
27 JRo,MMe,A:Cavalier 500.00
28 JRo,MMe,AW,A:Cavalier 550.00
29 JRo,MMe,Aug., 1949 . . . . 550.00

FILM STAR ROMANCES
Star Publications, 1950
1 LbC(c), Rudy Valentino story . 500.00
2 Liz Taylor & Robert Taylor, photo (c) 400.00
3 May–June, 1950, photo(c) . . . 300.00

FIREHAIR COMICS
**Flying Stories, Inc.
(Fiction House Magazine)
Winter, 1948–Spring, 1952**
1 I:Firehair, Riders on the Pony Express 750.00
2 Bride of the Outlaw Guns 350.00

*The Flame #1
© Fox Feature Syndicate*

3 Kiss of the Six-Gun Siren! . . . 250.00
4 & 5 . . . . @250.00
6 . . . . 200.00
7 War Drums at Buffalo Bend . . 200.00
8 Raid on the Red Arrows 200.00
9 French Flags and Tomahawks 200.00
10 Slave Maiden of the Crees. . . 200.00
11 Wolves of the Overland Trail . 200.00

FLAME, THE
**Fox Feature Syndicate
Summer, 1940**
1 LF,O:The Flame 4,500.00
2 GT,LF,Wing Turner 2,000.00
3 BP,Wonderworld 1,300.00
4 . . . . 1,200.00
5 GT 1,200.00
6 GT 1,200.00
7 A:The Yank 1,200.00
8 The Finger of the Frozen Death!, Jan., 1942 . . . . . . 1,200.00

FLAMING LOVE
**Comic Magazines
(Quality Comics Group)
Dec., 1949**
1 BWa,BWa(c),The Temptress I Feared in His Arms 500.00
2 Torrid Tales of Turbulent Passion 200.00
3 BWa,RC,My Heart's at Sea . . 300.00
4 One Women who made a Mockery of Love, Ph(c) 150.00
5 Bridge of Longing, Ph(c) 150.00
6 Men both Loved & Feared Me, Oct., 1950 . . . . 150.00

FLASH GORDON
**Harvey Publications
Oct., 1950**
1 AR,Bondage(c) 400.00
2 AR 250.00
3 AR Bondage(c) 225.00
4 AR, April, 1951 . . . . 225.00

FLIP
**Harvey Publications
April, 1954**
1 HN 250.00
2 HN,BP,June, 1954 . . . . 250.00

FLY BOY
**Approved Comics
(Ziff-Davis) Spring, 1952**
1 NS(c),Angels without Wings . . 250.00
2 NS(c),Flyboy's Flame-Out, Oct.–Nov., 1952 . . . . 150.00

THE FLYING A'S RANGE RIDER
**Dell Publishing Co.
June–Aug., 1953**
(1) = *Dell Four Color #404*
2 Ph(c) all 150.00
3 . . . . 100.00
4 . . . . 75.00
5 . . . . 75.00
6 . . . . 75.00
7 . . . . 75.00
8 . . . . 75.00
9 . . . . 75.00
10 . . . . 75.00
11 . . . . 60.00
12 . . . . 60.00
13 . . . . 60.00

14 . . . . 60.00
15 . . . . 60.00
16 . . . . 60.00
17 ATh 100.00
19 . . . . 60.00
20 . . . . 60.00
21 . . . . 60.00
22 . . . . 60.00
23 . . . . 60.00
24 . . . . 60.00

FOODINI
**Continental Publications
March, 1950**
1 TV Puppet 250.00
2 Jingle Dingle 125.00
3 . . . . 75.00
4 Aug., 1950 . . . . 75.00

FOOTBALL THRILLS
**Approved Comics
(Ziff-Davis)
Fall-Winter, 1952**
1 BP,NS(c),Red Grange story . . 350.00
2 NS(c),Bronko Nagurski, Spring,1952 . . . . 250.00

FORBIDDEN LOVE
**Comic Magazine
(Quality Comics Group)
March, 1950**
1 RC,Ph(c),Heartbreak Road . 1,000.00
2 Ph(c),I loved a Gigolo 750.00
3 Kissless Bride 500.00
4 BWa,Brimstone Kisses, Sept., 1950 . . . . 500.00

FORBIDDEN WORLDS
**American Comics Group
July–Aug., 1951**
1 AW,FF 2,000.00
2 . . . . 900.00
3 AW,WW,JD 1,000.00
4 Werewolf (c) 500.00
5 AW 650.00
6 AW,King Kong (c) 600.00
7 . . . . 350.00
8 . . . . 350.00
9 Atomic Bomb 400.00
10 JyD 300.00
11 The Mummy's Treasure 250.00
12 Chest of Death 250.00
13 Invasion from Hades 250.00
14 Million-Year Monster 250.00
15 The Vampire Cat 250.00
16 The Doll 250.00
17 . . . . 250.00
18 The Mummy 250.00
19 Pirate and the Voodoo Queen 250.00
20 Terror Island 250.00
21 The Ant Master 200.00
22 The Cursed Casket 200.00
23 Nightmare for Two 200.00
24 . . . . 200.00
25 Hallahan's Head 200.00
26 The Champ 200.00
27 SMo,The Thing with the Golden Hair 200.00
28 Portrait of Carlotta 200.00
29 The Frogman 200.00
30 The Things on the Beach . . . 200.00
31 SMo,The Circle of the Doomed 175.00
32 The Invasion of the Dead Things 175.00
33 . . . . 175.00
34 Atomic Bomb 200.00

GOLDEN AGE

Forbidden–Four Color — Comics Values Annual

Forbidden Worlds #14
© American Comics Group

35 Comics Code	175.00
36 thru 62	@100.00
63 AW	100.00
64	75.00
65	75.00
66	75.00
67	75.00
68 OW(c)	75.00
69 AW	100.00
70	75.00
71	75.00
72	75.00
73 OW,I:Herbie	400.00
74	75.00
75 JB	75.00
76 AW	100.00
77	75.00
78 AW,OW(c)	100.00
79 thru 85 JB	@75.00
86 Flying Saucer	85.00
87	75.00
88	75.00
89	75.00
90	75.00
91	75.00
92	75.00
93	75.00
94 OW(c),A:Herbie	125.00
95	60.00
96 AW	75.00
97 thru 115	@50.00
116 OW(c)A:Herbie	85.00
117	50.00
118	50.00
119	50.00
120 thru 124	@50.00
125 I:O:Magic Man	75.00
126 A:Magic Man	45.00
127 same	45.00
128 same	45.00
129 same	45.00
130 same	45.00
131 same	45.00
132 same	45.00
133 I:O:Dragona	45.00
134 A:Magic Man	45.00
135 A:Magic Man	45.00
136 A:Nemesis	45.00
137 A:Magic Man	45.00
138 A:Magic Man	45.00
139 A:Magic Man	45.00
140 SD,A:Mark Midnight	50.00
141 thru 145	@35.00

FOREIGN INTRIGUES
See: DYNAMITE

FOUR COLOR
Dell Publishing Co., 1939

N# Dick Tracy	9,000.00
N# Don Winslow of the Navy	2,500.00
N# Myra North	1,200.00
4 Disney's Donald Duck (1940)	15,000.00
5 Smilin' Jack	1,000.00
6 Dick Tracy	2,200.00
7 Gang Busters	600.00
8 Dick Tracy	1,200.00
9 Terry and the Pirates	1,000.00
10 Smilin' Jack	900.00
11 Smitty	600.00
12 Little Orphan Annie	750.00
13 Walt Disney's Reluctant Dragon (1941)	2,500.00
14 Moon Mullins	600.00
15 Tillie the Toiler	600.00
16 W.Disney's Mickey Mouse Outwits the Phantom Blob (1941)	15,000.00
17 W.Disney's Dumbo the Flying Elephant (1941)	3,000.00
18 Jiggs and Maggie	600.00
19 Barney Google and Snuffy Smith	600.00
20 Tiny Tim	500.00
21 Dick Tracy	950.00
22 Don Winslow	500.00
23 Gang Busters	450.00
24 Captain Easy	700.00
25 Popeye	1,100.00

[Second Series]

1 Little Joe	750.00
2 Harold Teen	400.00
3 Alley Oop	750.00
4 Smilin' Jack	650.00
5 Raggedy Ann and Andy	750.00
6 Smitty	350.00
7 Smokey Stover	500.00
8 Tillie the Toiler	400.00
9 Donald Duck finds Pirate Gold!	12,500.00
10 Flash Gordon	1,500.00
11 Wash Tubs	500.00
12 Bambi	900.00
13 Mr. District Attorney	500.00
14 Smilin' Jack	600.00
15 Felix the Cat	1,200.00
16 Porky Pig	1,300.00
17 Popeye	800.00
18 Little Orphan Annie's Junior Commandos	650.00
19 W.Disney's Thumper meets the Seven Dwarfs	900.00
20 Barney Baxter	500.00
21 Oswald the Rabbit	750.00
22 Tillie the Toiler	250.00
23 Raggedy Ann and Andy	600.00
24 Gang Busters	500.00
25 Andy Panda	900.00
26 Popeye	800.00
27 Mickey Mouse and the Seven Colored Terror	1,300.00
28 Wash Tubbs	350.00
29 CB,Donald Duck and the Mummy's Ring	9,000.00
30 Bambi's Children	900.00
31 Moon Mullins	300.00
32 Smitty	250.00
33 Bugs Bunny	1,800.00
34 Dick Tracy	650.00
35 Smokey Stover	250.00
36 Smilin' Jack	375.00
37 Bringing Up Father	300.00
38 Roy Rogers	3,500.00

Four Color 1st Series #9
© Dell Publishing Co.

39 Oswald the Rabbit	600.00
40 Barney Google and Snuffy Smith	350.00
41 WK,Mother Goose	350.00
42 Tiny Tim	250.00
43 Popeye	550.00
44 Terry and the Pirates	600.00
45 Raggedy Ann	500.00
46 Felix the Cat and the Haunted House	600.00
47 Gene Autry	650.00
48 CB,Porky Pig of the Mounties	1,400.00
49 W.Disney's Snow White and the Seven Dwarfs	1,000.00
50 WK,Fairy Tale Parade	450.00
51 Bugs Bunny Finds the Lost Treasure	600.00
52 Little Orphan Annie	500.00
53 Wash Tubbs	250.00
54 Andy Panda	400.00
55 Tillie the Toiler	250.00
56 Dick Tracy	600.00
57 Gene Autry	600.00
58 Smilin' Jack	350.00
59 WK,Mother Goose	300.00
60 Tiny Folks Funnies	250.00
61 Santa Claus Funnies	350.00
62 CB,Donald Duck in Frozen Gold	2,800.00
63 Roy Rogers-photo (c)	750.00
64 Smokey Stover	200.00
65 Smitty	165.00
66 Gene Autry	600.00
67 Oswald the Rabbit	250.00
68 WK,Mother Goose	250.00
69 WK,Fairy Tale Parade	350.00
70 Popeye and Wimpy	400.00
71 WK,Walt Disney's Three Caballeros	1,200.00
72 Raggedy Ann	400.00
73 The Grumps	200.00
74 Marge's Little Lulu	1,800.00
75 Gene Autry and the Wildcat	500.00
76 Little Orphan Annie	400.00
77 Felix the Cat	600.00
78 Porky Pig & the Bandit Twins	400.00
79 Mickey Mouse in the Riddle of the Red Hat	1,800.00
80 Smilin' Jack	300.00
81 Moon Mullins	200.00
82 Lone Ranger	750.00
83 Gene Autry in Outlaw Trail	500.00
84 Flash Gordon	750.00
85 Andy Panda and the Mad Dog Mystery	300.00

All comics prices listed are for *Near Mint* condition.

Comics Values Annual — GOLDEN AGE — Four Color

Four Color #84
© Dell Publishing Co.

86 Roy Rogers-photo (c) 600.00
87 WK,Fairy Tale Parade 400.00
88 Bugs Bunny. 350.00
89 Tillie the Toiler 250.00
90 WK,Christmas with
  Mother Goose 300.00
91 WK,Santa Claus Funnies. . . . 300.00
92 WK,W.Disney's Pinocchio . . . 900.00
93 Gene Autry 500.00
94 Winnie Winkle 200.00
95 Roy Rogers,Ph(c) 600.00
96 Dick Tracy 500.00
97 Marge's Little Lulu 800.00
98 Lone Ranger 600.00
99 Smitty 200.00
100 Gene Autry Comics-photo(c) 500.00
101 Terry and the Pirates 500.00
102 WK,Oswald the Rabbit. 250.00
103 WK,Easter with
  Mother Goose 300.00
104 WK,Fairy Tale Parade 325.00
105 WK,Albert the Aligator 1,100.00
106 Tillie the Toiler 150.00
107 Little Orphan Annie 350.00
108 Donald Duck in the
  Terror of the River 2,200.00
109 Roy Rogers Comics. 450.00
110 Marge's Little Lulu 500.00
111 Captain Easy 250.00
112 Porky Pig's Adventure in
  Gopher Gulch. 250.00
113 Popeye 250.00
114 WK,Fairy Tale Parade 300.00
115 Marge's Little Lulu 500.00
116 Mickey Mouse and the
  House of Many Mysteries . . . 400.00
117 Roy Rogers Comics, Ph(c). . 350.00
118 Lone Ranger 500.00
119 Felix the Cat 450.00
120 Marge's Little Lulu 450.00
121 Fairy Tale Parade. 200.00
122 Henry. 250.00
123 Bugs Bunny's Dangerous
  Venture 275.00
124 Roy Rogers Comics,Ph(c) . . 350.00
125 Lone Ranger 350.00
126 WK,Christmas with
  Mother Goose 250.00
127 Popeye 200.00
128 WK,Santa Claus Funnies . . . 200.00
129 W.Disney's Uncle Remus
  & his tales of Brer Rabbit . . . 500.00
130 Andy Panda 200.00
131 Marge's Little Lulu 500.00

132 Tillie the Toiler 150.00
133 Dick Tracy 300.00
134 Tarzan and the Devil Ogre. 1,000.00
135 Felix the Cat 350.00
136 Lone Ranger 325.00
137 Roy Rogers Comics. 350.00
138 Smitty 150.00
139 Marge's Little Lulu 500.00
140 WK,Easter with
  Mother Goose 250.00
141 Mickey Mouse and the
  Submarine Pirates 325.00
142 Bugs Bunny and the
  Haunted Mountain 250.00
143 Oswald the Rabbit &
  the Prehistoric Egg. 150.00
144 Poy Rogers Comics,Ph(c) . . 325.00
145 Popeye 200.00
146 Marge's Little Lulu 450.00
147 W.Disney's Donald Duck
  in Volcano Valley 1,450.00
148 WK,Albert the Aligator
  and Pogo Possum 900.00
149 Smilin' Jack 150.00
150 Tillie the Toiler 125.00
151 Lone Ranger 300.00
152 Little Orphan Annie 250.00
153 Roy Rogers Comics. 300.00
154 Andy Panda. 200.00
155 Henry. 150.00
156 Porky Pig and the Phantom . 175.00
157 W.Disney's Mickey Mouse
  and the Beanstalk. 325.00
158 Marge's Little Lulu 500.00
159 CB,W.Disney's Donald Duck
  in the Ghost of the Grotto . 1,250.00
160 Roy Rogers Comics,Ph(c) . . 300.00
161 Tarzan & the Fires of Tohr . . 900.00
162 Felix the Cat 300.00
163 Dick Tracy 275.00
164 Bugs Bunny Finds the
  Frozen Kingdom. 250.00
165 Marge's Little Lulu 500.00
166 Roy Rogers Comics,Ph(c) . . 300.00
167 Lone Ranger 300.00
168 Popeye 200.00
169 Woody Woodpecker,Drug. . . 225.00
170 W.Disney's Mickey Mouse
  on Spook's Island 300.00
171 Charlie McCarthy 350.00
172 WK,Christmas with
  Mother Goose 200.00
173 Flash Gordon. 200.00
174 Winnie Winkle 150.00
175 WK,Santa Claus Funnies . . . 200.00
176 Tillie the Toiler 100.00
177 Roy Rogers Comics,Ph(c) . . 300.00
178 CB,W.Disney's Donald
  Duck Christmas on Bear
  Mountain 1,800.00
179 WK,Uncle Wiggily 250.00
180 Ozark the Ike 150.00
181 W.Disney's Mickey Mouse
  in Jungle Magic 300.00
182 Porky Pig in Never-
  Never Land 175.00
183 Oswald the Rabbit 150.00
184 Tillie the Toiler 150.00
185 WK,Easter with
  Mother Goose 250.00
186 W.Disney's Bambi 275.00
187 Bugs Bunny and the
  Dreadful Bunny 175.00
188 Woody Woodpecker. 175.00
189 W.Disney's Donald Duck in
  The Old Castle's Secret. . . 1,100.00
190 Flash Gordon 275.00
191 Porky Pig to the Rescue. . . . 175.00
192 WK,The Brownies 185.00
193 Tom and Jerry 225.00

Four Color #162
© Dell Publishing Co.

194 W.Disney's Mickey Mouse
  in the World Under the Sea. . 250.00
195 Tillie the Toiler 100.00
196 Charlie McCarthy in The
  Haunted Hide-Out. 275.00
197 Spirit of the Border. 175.00
198 Andy Panda 175.00
199 W.Disney's Donald Duck in
  Sheriff of Bullet Valley 1,200.00
200 Bugs Bunny, Super Sleuth . 200.00
201 WK,Christmas with
  Mother Goose 175.00
202 Woody Woodpecker. 100.00
203 CB,W.Disney's Donald Duck in
  The Golden Christmas Tree . 800.00
204 Flash Gordon. 200.00
205 WK,Santa Claus Funnies . . . 225.00
206 Little Orphan Funnies. 200.00
207 King of the Royal Mounted . 250.00
208 W.Disney's Brer Rabbit
  Does It Again 175.00
209 Harold Teen 65.00
210 Tippe and Cap Stubbs 60.00
211 Little Beaver. 125.00
212 Dr. Bobbs 55.00
213 Tillie the Toiler 70.00
214 W.Disney's Mickey Mouse
  and his Sky Adventure 250.00
215 Sparkle Plenty 150.00
216 Andy Panda and the
  Police Pup 100.00
217 Bugs Bunny in Court Jester . 150.00
218 W.Disney's 3 Little Pigs 175.00
219 Swee'pea. 150.00
220 WK,Easter with
  Mother Goose 200.00
221 WK,Uncle Wiggily 175.00
222 West of the Pecos 100.00
223 CB,W.Disney's Donald Duck in
  Lost in the Andes. 1,200.00
224 Little Iodine 75.00
225 Oswald the Rabbit 60.00
226 Porky Pig and Spoofy 125.00
227 W.Disney's Seven Dwarfs . . 150.00
228 The Mark of Zorro 350.00
229 Smokey Stover 80.00
230 Sunset Press 75.00
231 W.Disney's Mickey Mouse
  and the Rajah's Treasure . . . 250.00
232 Woody Woodpecker. 125.00
233 Bugs Bunny. 150.00
234 W.Disney's Dumbo in Sky
  Voyage. 175.00
235 Tiny Tim. 60.00
236 Heritage of the Desert 100.00

All comics prices listed are for *Near Mint* condition.

CVA Page 393

Four Color / GOLDEN AGE / Comics Values Annual

Four Color

- 237 Tillie the Toiler 75.00
- 238 CB,W.Disney's Donald Duck in Voodoo Hoodoo 850.00
- 239 Adventure Bound 60.00
- 240 Andy Panda 75.00
- 241 Porky Pig 100.00
- 242 Tippie and Cap Stubbs 50.00
- 243 W.Disney's Thumper Follows His Nose 150.00
- 244 WK,The Brownies 150.00
- 245 Dick's Adventures in Dreamland 75.00
- 246 Thunder Mountain 60.00
- 247 Flash Gordon 175.00
- 248 W.Disney's Mickey Mouse and the Black Sorcerer 200.00
- 249 Woody Woodpecker 100.00
- 250 Bugs Bunny in Diamond Daze 175.00
- 251 Hubert at Camp Moonbeam .. 65.00
- 252 W.Disney's Pinocchio 175.00
- 253 WK,Christmas with Mother Goose 175.00
- 254 WK,Santa Claus Funnies, A:Pogo 200.00
- 255 The Ranger 60.00
- 256 CB,W.Disney's Donald Duck in Luck of the North 650.00
- 257 Little Iodine 125.00
- 258 Andy Panda and the Ballon Race 125.00
- 259 Santa and the Angel 75.00
- 260 Porky Pig, Hero of the Wild West 125.00
- 261 W.Disney's Mickey Mouse and the Missing Key 225.00
- 262 Raggedy Ann and Andy 125.00
- 263 CB,W.Disney's Donald Duck in Land of the Totem Poles 600.00
- 264 Woody Woodpecker in the Magic Lantern 125.00
- 265 King of the Royal Mountain . 125.00
- 266 Bugs Bunny on the Isle of Hercules 135.00
- 267 Little Beaver 60.00
- 268 W.Disney's Mickey Mouse's Surprise Visitor 250.00
- 269 Johnny Mack Brown,Ph(c) .. 350.00
- 270 Drift Fence 60.00
- 271 Porky Pig 125.00
- 272 W.Disney's Cinderella 175.00
- 273 Oswald the Rabbit 80.00
- 274 Bugs Bunny 135.00
- 275 CB,W.Disney's Donald Duck in Ancient Persia 600.00
- 276 Uncle Wiggly 125.00
- 277 PorkyPig in DesertAdventure 125.00
- 278 Bill Elliot Comics,Ph(c) 225.00
- 279 W.Disney's Mickey Mouse & Pluto Battle the Giant Ants .. 150.00
- 280 Andy Panda in the Isle of the Mechanical Men 125.00
- 281 Bugs Bunny in The Great Circus Mystery 135.00
- 282 CB,W.Disney's Donald Duck in The Pixilated Parrot 600.00
- 283 King of the Royal Mounted .. 125.00
- 284 Porky Pig in the Kingdom of Nowhere 125.00
- 285 Bozo the Clown 300.00
- 286 W.Disney's Mickey Mouse and the Uninvited Guest 150.00
- 287 Gene Autry's Champion in the Ghost of BlackMountain,Ph(c)175.00
- 288 Woody Woodpecker 100.00
- 289 BugsBunny in IndianTrouble. 135.00
- 290 The Chief 100.00
- 291 CB,W.Disney's Donald Duck in The Magic Hourglass 600.00
- 292 The Cisco Kid Comics 350.00
- 293 WK,The Brownies 150.00
- 294 Little Beaver 60.00
- 295 Porky Pig in President Pig .. 100.00
- 296 W.Disney's Mickey Mouse Private Eye for Hire 150.00
- 297 Andy Panda in The Haunted Inn 100.00
- 298 Bugs Bunny in Sheik for a Day 150.00
- 299 Buck Jones & the Iron Trail . 250.00
- 300 CB,W.Disney's Donald Duck in Big-Top Bedlam 600.00
- 301 The Mysterious Rider 75.00
- 302 Santa Claus Funnies 75.00
- 303 Porky Pig in The Land of the Monstrous Flies 100.00
- 304 W.Disney's Mickey Mouse in Tom-Tom Island 125.00
- 305 Woody Woodpecker 75.00
- 306 Raggedy Ann 75.00
- 307 Bugs Bunny in Lumber Jack Rabbit 125.00
- 308 CB,W.Disney's Donald Duck in Dangerous Disguise 500.00
- 309 Dollface and Her Gang 75.00
- 310 King of the Rotal Mounted .. 100.00
- 311 Porky Pig in Midget Horses of Hidden Valley 75.00
- 312 Tonto 150.00
- 313 W.Disney's Mickey Mouse in the Mystery of the Double-Cross Ranch 125.00
- 314 Ambush 60.00
- 315 Oswald Rabbit 75.00
- 316 Rex Allen,Ph(c) 200.00
- 317 Bugs Bunny in Hare Today Gone Tomorrow 125.00
- 318 CB,W.Disney's Donald Duck in No Such Varmint 500.00
- 319 Gene Autry's Champion 75.00
- 320 Uncle Wiggly 125.00
- 321 Little Scouts 50.00
- 322 Porky Pig in Roaring Rockies . 150.00
- 323 Susie Q. Smith 50.00
- 324 I Met a Handsome Cowboy . 125.00
- 325 W.Disney's Mickey Mouse in the Haunted Castle 150.00
- 326 Andy Panda 60.00
- 327 Bugs Bunny and the Rajah's Treasure 125.00
- 328 CB,W.Disney's Donald Duck in Old California 525.00
- 329 Roy Roger's Trigger,Ph(c) .. 200.00
- 330 Porky Pig meets the Bristled Bruiser 75.00
- 331 Disney's Alice in Wonderland 250.00
- 332 Little Beaver 60.00
- 333 Wilderness Trek 60.00
- 334 W.Disney's Mickey Mouse and Yukon Gold 150.00
- 335 Francis the Famous Talking Mule 150.00
- 336 Woody Woodpecker 75.00
- 337 The Brownies 60.00
- 338 Bugs Bunny and the Rocking Horse Thieves 150.00
- 339 W.Disney's Donald Duck and the Magic Fountain 135.00
- 340 King of the Royal Mountain . 125.00
- 341 W.Disney's Unbirthday Party with Alice in Wonderland 225.00
- 342 Porky Pig the Lucky Peppermint Mine 65.00
- 343 W.Disney's Mickey Mouse in Ruby Eye of Homar-Guy-Am 100.00
- 344 Sergeant Preston from Challenge of the Yukon 175.00
- 345 Andy Panda in Scotland Yard . 65.00
- 346 Hideout 60.00
- 347 Bugs Bunny the Frigid Hare . 125.00
- 348 CB,W.Disney's Donald Duck The Crocodile Collector 275.00
- 349 Uncle Wiggly 125.00
- 350 Woody Woodpecker 75.00
- 351 Porky Pig and the Grand Canyon Giant 75.00
- 352 W.Disney's Mickey Mouse Mystery of Painted Valley ... 125.00
- 353 CB(c),W.Disney'sDuckAlbum 150.00
- 354 Raggedy Ann & Andy 75.00
- 355 Bugs Bunny Hot-Rod Hair . 125.00
- 356 CB(c),W.Disney's Donald Duck in Rags to Riches 275.00
- 357 Comeback 50.00
- 358 Andy Panada 75.00
- 359 Frosty the Snowman 125.00
- 360 Porky Pig in Tree Fortune ... 60.00
- 361 Santa Claus Funnies 75.00
- 362 W.Disney's Mickey Mouse & the Smuggled Diamonds 100.00
- 363 King of the Royal Mounted ... 85.00
- 364 Woody Woodpecker 65.00
- 365 The Brownies 60.00
- 366 Bugs Bunny Uncle Buckskin Comes to Town ... 125.00
- 367 CB,W.Disney's Donald Duck in A Christmas for Shacktown .. 500.00
- 368 Bob Clampett's Beany and Cecil 400.00
- 369 Lone Ranger's Famous Horse Hi-Yo Silver 150.00
- 370 Porky Pig in Trouble in the Big Trees 75.00
- 371 W.Disney's Mickey Mouse the Inca Idol Case 125.00
- 372 Riders of the Purple Sage ... 50.00
- 373 Sergeant Preston 125.00
- 374 Woody Woodpecker 60.00
- 375 John Carter of Mars 400.00
- 376 Bugs Bunny 125.00
- 377 Susie Q. Smith 50.00
- 378 Tom Corbett, Space Cadet . . 250.00
- 379 W.Disney's Donald Duck in Southern Hospitality 125.00
- 380 Raggedy Ann & Andy 75.00
- 381 Marge's Tubby 325.00
- 382 W.Disney's Show White and the Seven Dwarfs 175.00
- 383 Andy Panda 50.00
- 384 King of the Royal Mounted ... 75.00
- 385 Porky Pig 60.00
- 386 CB,W.Disney's Uncle Scrooge in Only A Poor Old Man ... 1,500.00
- 387 W.Disney's Mickey Mouse in High Tibet 125.00

Four Color #355
© Dell Publishing Co.

CVA Page 394 — All comics prices listed are for *Near Mint* condition.

Four Color

#	Title	Price
388	Oswald the Rabbit	75.00
389	Andy Hardy Comics	55.00
390	Woody Woodpecker	60.00
391	Uncle Wiggly	100.00
392	Hi-Yo Silver	75.00
393	Bugs Bunny	125.00
394	CB(c),W.Disney's Donald Duck in Malayalaya	275.00
395	Forlorn River	50.00
396	Tales of the Texas Rangers, Ph(c)	165.00
397	Sergeant Preston o/t Yukon	125.00
398	The Brownies	60.00
399	Porky Pig in the Lost Gold Mine	60.00
400	AMc,Tom Corbett	150.00
401	W.Disney's Mickey Mouse & Goofy's Mechanical Wizard	75.00
402	Mary Jane and Sniffles	75.00
403	W.Disney's Li'l Bad Wolf	125.00
404	The Ranger Rider,Ph(c)	175.00
405	Woody Woodpecker	60.00
406	Tweety and Sylvester	100.00
407	Bugs Bunny, Foreign-Legion Hare	100.00
408	CB,W.Disney's Donald Duck and the Golden Helmet	475.00
409	Andy Panda	50.00
410	Porky Pig in the Water Wizard	60.00
411	W.Disney's Mickey Mouse and the Old Sea Dog	75.00
412	Nevada	50.00
413	Disney's Robin Hood(movie), Ph(c)	150.00
414	Bob Clampett's Beany and Cecil	225.00
415	Rootie Kazootie	150.00
416	Woody Woodpecker	60.00
417	Double Trouble with Goober	50.00
418	Rusty Riley	60.00
419	Sergeant Preston	125.00
420	Bugs Bunny	100.00
421	AMc,Tom Corbett	150.00
422	CB,W.Disney's Donald Duck and the Gilded Man	500.00
423	Rhubarb	75.00
424	Flash Gordon	150.00
425	Zorro	175.00
426	Porky Pig	60.00
427	W.Disney's Mickey Mouse & the Wonderful Whizzix	75.00
428	Uncle Wiggily	75.00
429	W.Disney's Pluto in Why Dogs Leave Home	125.00
430	Marge's Tubby	175.00
431	Woody Woodpecker	75.00
432	Bugs Bunny and the Rabbit Olympics	100.00
433	Wildfire	50.00
434	Rin Tin Tin,Ph(c)	225.00
435	Frosty the Snowman	75.00
436	The Brownies	50.00
437	John Carter of Mars	250.00
438	W.Disney's Annie Oakley (TV)	225.00
439	Little Hiawatha	75.00
440	Black Beauty	50.00
441	Fearless Fagan	50.00
442	W.Disney's Peter Pan	150.00
443	Ben Bowie and His Mountain Men	100.00
444	Marge's Tubby	150.00
445	Charlie McCarthy	75.00
446	Captain Hook and Peter Pan	125.00
447	Andy Hardy Comics	50.00
448	Beany and Cecil	225.00
449	Tappan's Burro	50.00
450	CB(c),W.Disney's Duck Album	100.00
451	Rusty Riley	50.00
452	Raggedy Ann and Andy	75.00
453	Susie Q. Smith	50.00
454	Krazy Kat Comics	50.00
455	Johnny Mack Brown Comics, Ph(c)	100.00
456	W.Disney's Uncle Scrooge Back to the Klondike	1,000.00
457	Daffy	125.00
458	Oswald the Rabbit	50.00
459	Rootie Kazootie	125.00
460	Buck Jones	100.00
461	Marge's Tubby	125.00
462	Little Scouts	25.00
463	Petunia	45.00
464	Bozo	125.00
465	Francis the Talking Mule	75.00
466	Rhubarb, the Millionaire Cat	60.00
467	Desert Gold	50.00
468	W.Disney's Goofy	175.00
469	Beetle Bailey	150.00
470	Elmer Fudd	75.00
471	Double Trouble with Goober	25.00
472	Wild Bill Elliot,Ph(c)	65.00
473	W.Disney's Li'l Bad Wolf	65.00
474	Mary Jane and Sniffles	125.00
475	M.G.M.'s the Two Mouseketeers	125.00
476	Rin Tin,Ph(c)	125.00
477	Bob Clampett's Beany and Cecil	225.00
478	Charlie McCarthy	75.00
479	Queen o/t West Dale Evans	350.00
480	Andy Hardy Comics	40.00
481	Annie Oakley and Tagg	125.00
482	Brownies	50.00
483	Little Beaver	50.00
484	River Feud	50.00
485	The Little People	100.00
486	Rusty Riley	50.00
487	Mowgli, the Jungle Book	75.00
488	John Carter of Mars	250.00
489	Tweety and Sylvester	75.00
490	Jungle Jim	100.00
491	EK,Silvertip	125.00
492	W.Disney's Duck Album	100.00
493	Johnny Mack Brown,Ph(c)	100.00
494	The Little King	150.00
495	CB, W.Disney's Uncle Scrooge	750.00
496	The Green Hornet	400.00
497	Zorro, (Sword of)	200.00
498	Bugs Bunny's Album	75.00
499	M.G.M.'s Spike and Tyke	65.00
500	Buck Jones	75.00
501	Francis the Famous Talking Mule	60.00
502	Rootie Kazootie	125.00
503	Uncle Wiggily	65.00
504	Krazy Kat	50.00
505	W.Disney's the Sword and the Rose (TV),Ph(c)	125.00
506	The Little Scouts	30.00
507	Oswald the Rabbit	50.00
508	Bozo	125.00
509	W.Disney's Pluto	75.00
510	Son of Black Beauty	50.00
511	EK,Outlaw Trail	50.00
512	Flash Gordon	100.00
513	Ben Bowie and His Mountain Men	50.00
514	Frosty the Snowman	75.00
515	Andy Hardy	40.00
516	Double Trouble With Goober	25.00
517	Walt Disney's Chip 'N' Dale	150.00
518	Rivets	40.00
519	Steve Canyon	125.00
520	Wild Bill Elliot,Ph(c)	75.00
521	Beetle Bailey	75.00
522	The Brownies	50.00
523	Rin Tin Tin,Ph(c)	125.00
524	Tweety and Sylvester	60.00
525	Santa Claus Funnies	75.00
526	Napoleon	30.00
527	Charlie McCarthy	75.00
528	Queen o/t West Dale Evans, Ph(c)	150.00
529	Little Beaver	50.00
530	Bob Clampett's Beany and Cecil	250.00
531	W.Disney's Duck Album	75.00
532	The Rustlers	50.00
533	Raggedy Ann and Andy	75.00
534	EK,Western Marshal	100.00
535	I Love Lucy,Ph(c)	800.00
536	Daffy	75.00
537	Stormy, the Thoroughbred	50.00
538	EK,The Mask of Zorro	200.00
539	Ben and Me	50.00
540	Knights of the Round Table, Ph(c)	125.00
541	Johnny Mack Brown,Ph(c)	100.00
542	Super Circus Featuring Mary Hartline	100.00
543	Uncle Wiggly	75.00
544	W.Disney's Rob Roy(Movie), Ph(c)	125.00
545	The Wonderful Adventures of Pinocchio	125.00
546	Buck Jones	75.00
547	Francis the Famous Talking Mule	60.00
548	Krazy Kat	50.00
549	Oswald the Rabbit	50.00
550	The Little Scouts	25.00
551	Bozo	125.00
552	Beetle Bailey	75.00
553	Susie Q. Smith	40.00
554	Rusty Riley	45.00
555	Range War	45.00
556	Double Trouble with Goober	25.00
557	Ben Bowie and His Mountain Men	50.00
558	Elmer Fudd	50.00
559	I Love Lucy,Ph(c)	500.00
560	W.Disney's Duck Album	75.00
561	Mr. Magoo	175.00
562	W.Disney's Goofy	125.00
563	Rhubarb, the Millionaire Cat	75.00
564	W.Disney's Li'l Bad Wolf	75.00
565	Jungle Jim	50.00
566	Son of Black Beauty	50.00
567	BF,Prince Valiant,Ph(c)	175.00
568	Gypsy Cat	60.00
569	Priscilla's Pop	50.00
570	Bob Clampett's Beany and Cecil	225.00

Four Color #462
© Dell Publishing Co.

All comics prices listed are for *Near Mint* condition.

GOLDEN AGE

Four Color

#	Title	Price
571	Charlie McCarthy	75.00
572	EK,Silvertip	60.00
573	The Little People	65.00
574	The Hand of Zorro	200.00
575	Annie and Oakley and Tagg, Ph(c)	150.00
576	Angel	30.00
577	M.G.M.'s Spike and Tyke	40.00
578	Steve Canyon	65.00
579	Francis the Talking Mule	50.00
580	Six Gun Ranch	50.00
581	Chip 'N' Dale	75.00
582	Mowgli, the Jungle Book	65.00
583	The Lost Wagon Train	50.00
584	Johnny Mack Brown,Ph(c)	100.00
585	Bugs Bunny's Album	75.00
586	W.Disney's Duck Album	110.00
587	The Little Scouts	30.00
588	MB,King Richard and the Crusaders,Ph(c)	150.00
589	Buck Jones	75.00
590	Hansel and Gretel	100.00
591	EK,Western Marshal	75.00
592	Super Circus	100.00
593	Oswald the Rabbit	50.00
594	Bozo	125.00
595	Pluto	50.00
596	Turok, Son of Stone	900.00
597	The Little King	75.00
598	Captain Davy Jones	60.00
599	Ben Bowie and His Mountain Men	50.00
600	Daisy Duck's Diary	100.00
601	Frosty the Snowman	75.00
602	Mr. Magoo and the Gerald McBoing-Boing	175.00
603	M.G.M.'s The Two Mouseketeers	60.00
604	Shadow on the Trail	50.00
605	The Brownies	50.00
606	Sir Lancelot	125.00
607	Santa Claus Funnies	75.00
608	EK,Silver Tip	60.00
609	The Littlest Outlaw,Ph(c)	100.00
610	Drum Beat,Ph(c)	135.00
611	W.Disney's Duck Album	75.00
612	Little Beaver	50.00
613	EK,Western Marshal	75.00
614	W.Disney's 20,000 Leagues Under the Sea (Movie)	150.00
615	Daffy	75.00
616	To The Last Man	50.00
617	The Quest of Zorro	175.00
618	Johnny Mack Brown,Ph(c)	100.00
619	Krazy Kat	50.00
620	Mowgli, Jungle Book	65.00
621	Francis the Famous Talking Mule	50.00
622	Beetle Bailey	75.00
623	Oswald the Rabbit	50.00
624	Treasure Island,Ph(c)	125.00
625	Beaver Valley	100.00
626	Ben Bowie and His Mountain Men	50.00
627	Goofy	125.00
628	Elmer Fudd	50.00
629	Lady & The Tramp with Jock	125.00
630	Priscilla's Pop	50.00
631	W.Disney's Davy Crockett Indian Fighter (TV),Ph(c)	300.00
632	Fighting Caravans	50.00
633	The Little People	50.00
634	Lady and the Tramp Album	75.00
635	Bob Clampett's Beany and Cecil	250.00
636	Chip 'N' Dale	75.00
637	EK,Silvertip	60.00
638	M.G.M.'s Spike and Tyke	40.00
639	W.Disney's Davy Crockett at the Alamo (TV),Ph(c)	250.00
640	EK,Western Marshal	75.00
641	Steve Canyon	85.00
642	M.G.M.'s The Two Mouseketeers	60.00
643	Wild Bill Elliott,Ph(c)	50.00
644	Sir Walter Raleigh,Ph(c)	100.00
645	Johnny Mack Brown,Ph(c)	100.00
646	Dotty Dripple and Taffy	50.00
647	Bugs Bunny's Album	75.00
648	Jace Pearson of the Texas Rangers,Ph(c)	75.00
649	Duck Album	75.00
650	BF,Prince Valiant	100.00
651	EK,King Colt	50.00
652	Buck Jones	50.00
653	Smokey the Bear	150.00
654	Pluto	60.00
655	Francis the Famous Talking Mule	50.00
656	Turok, Son of Stone	500.00
657	Ben Bowie and His Mountain Men	50.00
658	Goofy	125.00
659	Daisy Duck's Diary	85.00
660	Little Beaver	50.00
661	Frosty the Snowman	75.00
662	Zoo Parade	75.00
663	Winky Dink	125.00
664	W.Disney's Davy Crockett in the Great Keelboat Race (TV),Ph(c)	250.00
665	The African Lion	85.00
666	Santa Claus Funnies	75.00
667	EK,Silvertip and the Stolen Stallion	75.00
668	W.Disney's Dumbo	150.00
668a	W.Disney's Dumbo	125.00
669	W.Disney's Robin Hood (Movie),Ph(c)	75.00
670	M.G.M.'s Mouse Musketeers	60.00
671	W.Disney's Davey Crockett & the River Pirates(TV),Ph(c)	250.00
672	Quentin Durward,Ph(c)	100.00
673	Buffalo Bill Jr.,Ph(c)	100.00
674	The Little Rascals	100.00
675	EK,Steve Donovan,Ph(c)	125.00
676	Will-Yum!	40.00
677	Little King	75.00
678	The Last Hunt,Ph(c)	125.00
679	Gunsmoke	275.00
680	Out Our Way with the Worry Wart	40.00
681	Forever, Darling,Lucile Ball Ph(c)	200.00
682	When Knighthood Was in Flower,Ph(c)	125.00
683	Hi and Lois	50.00
684	SB,Helen of Troy,Ph(c)	150.00
685	Johnny Mack Brown,Ph(c)	125.00
686	Duck Album	75.00
687	The Indian Fighter,Ph(c)	125.00
688	SB,Alexander the Great, Ph(c)	125.00
689	Elmer Fudd	50.00
690	The Conqueror, John Wayne Ph(c)	275.00
691	Dotty Dripple and Taffy	40.00
692	The Little People	50.00
693	W.Disney's Brer Rabbit Song of the South	150.00
694	Super Circus,Ph(c)	100.00
695	Little Beaver	50.00
696	Krazy Kat	50.00
697	Oswald the Rabbit	50.00
698	Francis the Famous Talking Mule	50.00
699	BA,Prince Valiant	120.00
700	Water Birds and the Olympic Elk	75.00
701	Jimmy Cricket	125.00
702	The Goofy Success Story	125.00
703	Scamp	150.00
704	Priscilla's Pop	50.00
705	Brave Eagle,Ph(c)	100.00
706	Bongo and Lumpjaw	75.00
707	Corky and White Shadow, Ph(c)	125.00
708	Smokey the Bear	75.00
709	The Searchers,John Wayne Ph(c)	400.00
710	Francis the Famous Talking Mule	50.00
711	M.G.M.'s Mouse Musketeers	40.00
712	The Great Locomotive Chase, Ph(c)	125.00
713	The Animal World	50.00
714	W.Disney's Spin & Marty (TV)	175.00
715	Timmy	50.00
716	Man in Space	125.00
717	Moby Dick,Ph(c)	125.00
718	Dotty Dripple and Taffy	35.00
719	BF,Prince Valiant	100.00
720	Gunsmoke,Ph(c)	150.00
721	Captain Kangaroo,Ph(c)	250.00
722	Johnny Mack Brown,Ph(c)	100.00
723	EK,Santiago	150.00
724	Bugs Bunny's Album	60.00
725	Elmer Fudd	40.00
726	Duck Album	75.00
727	The Nature of Things	85.00
728	M.G.M.'s Mouse Musketeers	40.00
729	Bob Son of Battle	50.00
730	Smokey Stover	60.00
731	EK,Silvertip and The Fighting Pony	60.00
732	Zorro, (the Challenge of)	200.00
733	Buck Rogers	50.00
734	Cheyenne,C.Walker Ph(c)	250.00
735	Crusader Rabbit	500.00
736	Pluto	50.00
737	Steve Canyon	75.00
738	Westward Ho, the Wagons, Ph(c)	150.00
739	MD,Bounty Guns	50.00
740	Chilly Willy	75.00
741	The Fastest Gun Alive,Ph(c)	125.00
742	Buffalo Bill Jr.,Ph(c)	75.00
743	Daisy Duck's Diary	80.00
744	Little Beaver	50.00
745	Francis the Famous Talking Mule	50.00
746	Dotty Dripple and Taffy	40.00
747	Goofy	125.00
748	Frosty the Snowman	75.00

Four Color #666
© Dell Publishing Co.

GOLDEN AGE — Four Color

749 Secrets of Life,Ph(c) 75.00
750 The Great Cat 100.00
751 Our Miss Brooks,Ph(c) 125.00
752 Mandrake, the Magician 150.00
753 Walt Scott's Little People . . . 60.00
754 Smokey the Bear 75.00
755 The Littlest Snowman 60.00
756 Santa Claus Funnies 75.00
757 The True Story of
     Jesse James,Ph(c) 150.00
758 Bear Country 75.00
759 Circus Boy,Ph(c) 200.00
760 W.Disney's Hardy Boys(TV). 200.00
761 Howdy Doody 200.00
762 SB,The Sharkfighters,Ph(c) . 125.00
763 GrandmaDuck'sFarmFriends 125.00
764 M.G.M.'s Mouse Musketeers . 40.00
765 Will-Yum! 40.00
766 Buffalo Bill,Ph(c) 75.00
767 Spin and Marty 150.00
768 EK,Steve Donovan, Western
     Marshal,Ph(c) 100.00
769 Gunsmoke 135.00
770 Brave Eagle,Ph(c) 50.00
771 MD,Brand of Empire 50.00
772 Cheyenne,C.Walker Ph(c) . . 125.00
773 The Brave One,Ph(c) 75.00
774 Hi and Lois 35.00
775 SB,Sir Lancelot and
     Brian,Ph(c) 150.00
776 Johnny Mack Brown,Ph(c) . . 100.00
777 Scamp 110.00
778 The Little Rascals 75.00
779 Lee Hunter, Indian Fighter . . 75.00
780 Captain Kangaroo,Ph(c) 200.00
781 Fury,Ph(c) 125.00
782 Duck Album 75.00
783 Elmer Fudd 40.00
784 Around the World in 80
     Days,Ph(c) 100.00
785 Circus Boys,Ph(c) 200.00
786 Cinderella 100.00
787 Little Hiawatha 75.00
788 BF,Prince Valiant 100.00
789 EK,Silvertip-Valley Thieves. . . 75.00
790 ATh,The Wings of Eagles,
     J.Wayne Ph(c) 250.00
791 The 77th Bengal Lancers,
     Ph(c) 125.00
792 Oswald the Rabbit 50.00
793 Morty Meekle 40.00
794 SB,The Count of Monte
     Cristo 125.00
795 Jiminy Cricket 100.00
796 Ludwig Bemelman's
     Madeleine and Genevieve . . 50.00
797 Gunsmoke,Ph(c) 150.00
798 Buffalo Bill,Ph(c) 75.00
799 Priscilla's Pop 50.00
800 The Buccaneers,Ph(c) 125.00
801 Dotty Dripple and Taffy 35.00
802 Goofy 125.00
803 Cheyenne,C.Walker Ph(c) . . 125.00
804 Steve Canyon 75.00
805 Crusader Rabbit 375.00
806 Scamp 100.00
807 MB,Savage Range 50.00
808 Spin and Marty,Ph(c) 150.00
809 The Little People 60.00
810 Francis the Famous
     Talking Mule 50.00
811 Howdy Doody 150.00
812 The Big Land,A.Ladd Ph(c) . 150.00
813 Circus Boy,Ph(c) 175.00
814 Covered Wagon,A:Mickey
     Mouse 100.00
815 Dragoon Wells Massacre . . 125.00
816 Brave Eagle,Ph(c) 50.00
817 Little Beaver 50.00
818 Smokey the Bear. 75.00
819 Mickey Mouse in Magicland . . 60.00
820 The Oklahoman,Ph(c) 150.00
821 Wringle Wrangle,Ph(c) 125.00
822 ATh,W.Disney's Paul Revere's
     Ride (TV) 150.00
823 Timmy 40.00
824 The Pride and the Passion,
     Ph(c) 125.00
825 The Little Rascals 75.00
826 Spin and Marty and Annette,
     Ph(c) 350.00
827 Smokey Stover 75.00
828 Buffalo Bill, Jr,Ph(c).. . . . . . . 75.00
829 Tales of the Pony Express,
     Ph(c) 75.00
830 The Hardy Boys,Ph(c) 150.00
831 No Sleep 'Til Dawn,Ph(c) . . 100.00
832 Lolly and Pepper 50.00
833 Scamp 100.00
834 Johnny Mack Brown,Ph(c) . . 100.00
835 Silvertip- The Fake Rider 75.00
836 Man in Fight 125.00
837 All-American Athlete
     Cotton Woods 50.00
838 Bugs Bunny's Life
     Story Album 75.00
839 The Vigilantes 125.00
840 Duck Album 75.00
841 Elmer Fudd 40.00
842 The Nature of Things 80.00
843 The First Americans 125.00
844 Gunsmoke,Ph(c) 125.00
845 ATh,The Land Unknown 200.00
846 ATh,Gun Glory 150.00
847 Perri 75.00
848 Marauder's Moon 50.00
849 BF,Prince Valiant 100.00
850 Buck Jones 50.00
851 The Story of Mankind,
     V.Price Ph(c) 125.00
852 Chilly Willy 50.00
853 Pluto 60.00
854 Hunchback of Notre Dame,
     Ph(c) 200.00
855 Broken Arrow,Ph(c) 75.00
856 Buffalo Bill, Jr.,Ph(c). 75.00
857 The Goofy Adventure Story . 125.00
858 Daisy Duck's Diary 75.00
859 Topper and Neil 70.00
860 Wyatt Earp,Ph(c) 150.00
861 Frosty the Snowman 65.00
862 Truth About Mother Goose . 125.00
863 Francis the Famous
     Talking Mule 50.00
864 The Littlest Snowman 60.00
865 Andy Burnett,Ph(c). 150.00
866 Mars and Beyond 125.00
867 Santa Claus Funnies 75.00
868 The Little People 60.00
869 Old Yeller,Ph(c) 85.00
870 Little Beaver 50.00
871 Curly Kayoe 40.00
872 Captain Kangaroo,Ph(c) 200.00
873 Grandma Duck's
     Farm Friends 75.00
874 Old Ironsides 100.00
875 Trumpets West 50.00
876 Tales of Wells Fargo,Ph(c) . . 150.00
877 ATh,Frontier Doctor,Ph(c) . . 150.00
878 Peanuts 250.00
879 Brave Eagle,Ph(c) 50.00
880 MD,Steve Donovan,Ph(c). . . . 60.00
881 The Captain and the Kids 50.00
882 ATh,W.DisneyPresentsZorro. 250.00
883 The Little Rascals 75.00
884 Hawkeye and the Last
     of the Mohicans,Ph(c). 125.00
885 Fury,Ph(c) 100.00
886 Bongo and Lumpjaw 75.00
887 The Hardy Boys,Ph(c) 150.00
888 Elmer Fudd 40.00
889 ATh,W.Disney's Clint
     & Mac(TV),Ph(c) 200.00
890 Wyatt Earp,Ph(c) 125.00
891 Light in the Forest,
     C.Parker Ph(c) 125.00
892 Maverick,J.Garner Ph(c) . . . 400.00
893 Jim Bowie,Ph(c) 75.00
894 Oswald the Rabbit 50.00
895 Wagon Train,Ph(c). 175.00
896 Adventures of Tinker Bell . . . 125.00
897 Jiminy Cricket 100.00
898 EK,Silvertip 65.00
899 Goofy 75.00
900 BF,Prince Valiant 100.00
901 Little Hiawatha 75.00
902 Will-Yum! 40.00
903 Dotty Dripple and Taffy. 35.00
904 Lee Hunter, Indian Fighter . . 50.00
905 W.Disney's Annette (TV),
     Ph(c) 425.00
906 Francis the Famous
     Talking Mule 50.00
907 Ath,Sugarfoot,Ph(c) 200.00
908 The Little People
     and the Giant 60.00
909 Smitty 45.00
910 ATh,The Vikings,
     K.Douglas Ph(c) 125.00
911 The Gray Ghost,Ph(c) 125.00
912 Leave it to Beaver,Ph(c). . . . 250.00
913 The Left-Handed Gun,
     Paul Newman Ph(c) 150.00
914 ATh,No Time for Sergeants,
     Ph(c) 150.00
915 Casey Jones,Ph(c). 75.00
916 Red Ryder Ranch Comics . . . 60.00
917 The Life of Riley,Ph(c) 175.00
918 Beep Beep, the Roadrunner. 150.00
919 Boots and Saddles,Ph(c) . . . 125.00
920 Ath,Zorro,Ph(c) 200.00
921 Wyatt Earp,Ph(c) 125.00
922 Johnny Mack Brown,Ph(c) . . 125.00
923 Timmy 40.00
924 Colt .45,Ph(c). 150.00
925 Last of the Fast Guns,Ph(c) . 125.00
926 Peter Pan 60.00
927 SB,Top Gun 50.00
928 Sea Hunt,L.Bridges Ph(c) . . 200.00
929 Brave Eagle,Ph(c) 50.00
930 Maverick,J. Garner Ph(c) . . 175.00
931 Have Gun, Will Travel,Ph(c). 225.00
932 Smokey the Bear 75.00
933 ATh,W.Disney's Zorro 200.00
934 Restless Gun 200.00
935 King of the Royal Mounted . . 50.00
936 The Little Rascals 75.00

Four Color #805
© Dell Publishing Co.

GOLDEN AGE

Four Color

937 Ruff and Ready 200.00
938 Elmer Fudd 50.00
939 Steve Canyon 75.00
940 Lolly and Pepper 40.00
941 Pluto 50.00
942 Pony Express 75.00
943 White Wilderness 100.00
944 SB,7th Voyage of Sinbad . . 200.00
945 Maverick,J.Garner Ph(c) . . 200.00
946 The Big Country,Ph(c) ... 125.00
947 Broken Arrow,Ph(c) 75.00
948 Daisy Duck's Diary 75.00
949 High Adventure,Ph(c)...... 75.00
950 Frosty the Snowman 60.00
951 ATh,Lennon Sisters
    Life Story,Ph(c).......... 225.00
952 Goofy 75.00
953 Francis the Famous
    Talking Mule 45.00
954 Man in Space............ 125.00
955 Hi and Lois 35.00
956 Ricky Nelson,Ph(c) 300.00
957 Buffalo Bee 150.00
958 Santa Claus Funnies 75.00
959 Christmas Stories 60.00
960 ATh,W.Disney's Zorro..... 175.00
961 Jace Pearson's Tales of
    Texas Rangers,Ph(c) 75.00
962 Maverick,J.Garner Ph(c) ... 175.00
963 Johnny Mack Brown,Ph(c) . 100.00
964 The Hardy Boys,Ph(c) 150.00
965 GrandmaDuck'sFarmFriends . 75.00
966 Tonka,Ph(c) 125.00
967 Chilly Willy 50.00
968 Tales of Wells Fargo,Ph(c). 125.00
969 Peanuts................ 175.00
970 Lawman,Ph(c).......... 200.00
971 Wagon Train,Ph(c)....... 100.00
972 Tom Thumb 150.00
973 SleepingBeauty & the Prince 175.00
974 The Little Rascals 100.00
975 Fury,Ph(c) 100.00
976 ATh,W.Disney's Zorro,Ph(c) . 175.00
977 Elmer Fudd 40.00
978 Lolly and Pepper 40.00
979 Oswald the Rabbit 50.00
980 Maverick,J.Garner Ph(c) ... 175.00
981 Ruff and Ready 125.00
982 The New Adventures of
    Tinker Bell 125.00
983 Have Gun, Will Travel,Ph(c). 150.00
984 Sleeping Beauty's Fairy
    Godmothers 135.00
985 Shaggy Dog,Ph(c) 125.00
986 Restless Gun,Ph(c) 125.00
987 Goofy 75.00
988 Little Hiawatha.......... 75.00
989 Jimmy Cricket 100.00
990 Huckleberry Hound 200.00
991 Francis the Famous
    Talking Mule............. 50.00
992 ATh,Sugarfoot,Ph(c) 175.00
993 Jim Bowie,Ph(c).......... 75.00
994 Sea HuntL.Bridges Ph(c) . . 125.00
995 Donald Duck Album 100.00
996 Nevada 50.00
997 Walt Disney Presents,Ph(c) . 125.00
998 Ricky Nelson,Ph(c) 300.00
999 Leave It To Beaver,Ph(c) . . 250.00
1000 The Gray Ghost,Ph(c) 135.00
1001 Lowell Thomas' High
    Adventure,Ph(c) 75.00
1002 Buffalo Bee 100.00
1003 ATh,W.Disney's Zorro,Ph(c) 175.00
1004 Colt .45,Ph(c). 125.00
1005 Maverick,J.Garner Ph(c) . . 175.00
1006 SB,Hercules 150.00
1007 John Paul Jones,Ph(c) 75.00
1008 Beep, Beep, the
    Road Runner 75.00
1009 CB,The Rifleman,Ph(c) . . . 400.00

1010 Grandma Duck's Farm
    Friends................ 200.00
1011 Buckskin,Ph(c).......... 125.00
1012 Last Train from Gun
    Hill,Ph(c) 135.00
1013 Bat Masterson,Ph(c) 200.00
1014 ATh,The Lennon Sisters,
    Ph(c) 200.00
1015 Peanuts............... 150.00
1016 Smokey the Bear......... 60.00
1017 Chilly Willy 50.00
1018 Rio Bravo,J.Wayne Ph(c) . 350.00
1019 Wagoon Train,Ph(c)...... 100.00
1020 Jungle 50.00
1021 Jace Pearson's Tales of
    the Texas Rangers,Ph(c) ... 75.00
1022 Timmy 40.00
1023 Tales of Wells Fargo,Ph(c) . 125.00
1024 ATh,Darby O'Gill and
    the Little People,Ph(c) 150.00
1025 CB,W.Disney's Vacation in
    Disneyland 300.00
1026 Spin and Marty,Ph(c) 125.00
1027 The Texan,Ph(c). 135.00
1028 Rawhide,
    Clint Eastwood Ph(c) 375.00
1029 Boots and Saddles,Ph(c) . . . 75.00
1030 Spanky and Alfalfa, the
    Little Rascals 75.00
1031 Fury,Ph(c) 100.00
1032 Elmer Fudd 40.00
1033 Steve Canyon,Ph(c)....... 75.00
1034 Nancy and Sluggo
    Summer Camp.......... 60.00
1035 Lawman,Ph(c) 125.00
1036 The Big Circus,Ph(c) 100.00
1037 Zorro,Ph(c) 250.00
1038 Ruff and Ready 125.00
1039 Pluto 60.00
1040 Quick Draw McGraw 225.00
1041 ATh,Sea Hunt,
    L.Bridges Ph(c)........... 135.00
1042 The Three Chipmunks 90.00
1043 The Three Stooges,Ph(c) . .350.00
1044 Have Gun,Will Travel,Ph(c) 150.00
1045 Restless Gun,Ph(c) 125.00
1046 Beep Beep, the
    Road Runner 75.00
1047 CB,W.Disney's
    GyroGearloose.......... 275.00
1048 The Horse Soldiers
    J.Wayne Ph(c) 200.00
1049 Don't Give Up the Ship
    J.Lewis Ph(c) 125.00
1050 Huckleberry Hound 125.00

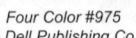

Four Color #975
© Dell Publishing Co.

Comics Values Annual

1051 Donald in Mathmagic Land. 125.00
1052 RsM,Ben-Hur............ 150.00
1053 Goofy................... 75.00
1054 Huckleberry Hound
    Winter Fun 125.00
1055 CB,Daisy Duck's Diary 150.00
1056 Yellowstone Kelly,
    C.Walker Ph(c)........... 90.00
1057 Mickey Mouse Album...... 50.00
1058 Colt .45,Ph(c)............ 125.00
1059 Sugarfoot.............. 135.00
1060 Journey to the Center of the
    Earth, P.Boone Ph(c) 175.00
1061 Buffalo Bill 100.00
1062 Christmas Stories......... 60.00
1063 Santa Claus Funnies 75.00
1064 Bugs Bunny's Merry
    Christmas............... 75.00
1065 Frosty the Snowman 65.00
1066 ATh,77 Sunset Strip,Ph(c) . 200.00
1067 Yogi Bear 175.00
1068 Francis the Famous
    Talking Mule 50.00
1069 ATh,The FBI Story,Ph(c)... 150.00
1070 Soloman and Sheba,Ph(c) . 140.00
1071 ATh,TheRealMcCoys,Ph(c) 150.00
1072 Blythe 75.00
1073 CB,Grandma Duck's Farm
    Friends................ 200.00
1074 Chilly Willy 50.00
1075 Tales of Wells Fargo,Ph(c) . 135.00
1076 MSy,The Rebel,Ph(c)...... 150.00
1077 SB,The Deputy,
    H.Fonda Ph(c) 200.00
1078 The Three Stooges,Ph(c). . 200.00
1079 The Little Rascals 75.00
1080 Fury,Ph(c) 100.00
1081 Elmer Fudd 40.00
1082 Spin and Marty.......... 125.00
1083 Men into Space,Ph(c)..... 125.00
1084 Speedy Gonzales......... 75.00
1085 ATh,The Time Machine.... 250.00
1086 Lolly and Pepper 40.00
1087 Peter Gunn,Ph(c)......... 150.00
1088 A Dog of Flanders,Ph(c)... 65.00
1089 Restless Gun,Ph(c) 125.00
1090 Francis the Famous
    Talking Mule 50.00
1091 Jacky's Diary 65.00
1092 Toby Tyler,Ph(c)......... 100.00
1093 MacKenzie's Raiders,Ph(c) 100.00
1094 Goofy.................. 75.00
1095 CB,W.Disney's
    GyroGearloose.......... 150.00
1096 The Texan,Ph(c). 125.00
1097 Rawhide,C.Eastwood Ph(c) 250.00
1098 Sugarfoot,Ph(c) 125.00
1099 CB(c),Donald Duck Album . 100.00
1100 W.Disney's Annette's
    Life Story (TV),Ph(c)...... 350.00
1101 Robert Louis Stevenson's
    Kidnapped,Ph(c)......... 100.00
1102 Wanted: Dead or Alive,
    Ph(c) 200.00
1103 Leave It To Beaver,Ph(c) . . 250.00
1104 Yogi Bear Goes to College . 125.00
1105 ATh,Gale Storm,Ph(c)..... 200.00
1106 ATh,77 Sunset Strip,Ph(c) . 150.00
1107 Buckskin,Ph(c).......... 100.00
1108 The Troubleshooters,Ph(c). . 75.00
1109 This Is Your Life, Donald
    Duck,O:Donald Duck 225.00
1110 Bonanza,Ph(c) 550.00
1111 Shotgun Slade 100.00
1112 Pixie and Dixie
    and Mr. Jinks 125.00
1113 Tales of Wells Fargo,Ph(c) . 135.00
1114 Huckleberry Finn,Ph(c)..... 75.00
1115 Ricky Nelson,Ph(c)....... 250.00
1116 Boots and Saddles,Ph(c) . . . 75.00
1117 Boy and the Pirate,Ph(c). . . 100.00

GOLDEN AGE

1118 Sword and the Dragon,Ph(c) 125.00
1119 Smokey and the Bear
  Nature Stories 50.00
1120 Dinosaurus,Ph(c) 125.00
1121 RC,GE,HerculesUnchained 150.00
1122 Chilly Willy 50.00
1123 Tombstone Territory,Ph(c) . . 150.00
1124 Whirlybirds,Ph(c) 135.00
1125 GK,RH,Laramie,Ph(c). 150.00
1126 Sundance,Ph(c) 100.00
1127 The Three Stooges,Ph(c) . . 200.00
1128 Rocky and His Friends 550.00
1129 Pollyanna,H.Mills Ph(c) . . . 125.00
1130 SB,The Deputy,
  H.Fonda Ph(c) 150.00
1131 Elmer Fudd 40.00
1132 Space Mouse. 60.00
1133 Fury,Ph(c) 100.00
1134 ATh,Real McCoys,Ph(c) . . . 150.00
1135 M.G.M.'s Mouse Musketeers 75.00
1136 Jungle Cat,Ph(c) 100.00
1137 The Little Rascals. 75.00
1138 The Rebel,Ph(c). 135.00
1139 SB,Spartacus,Ph(c) 200.00
1140 Donald Duck Album 100.00
1141 Huckleberry Hound for
  President 125.00
1142 Johnny Ringo,Ph(c) 125.00
1143 Pluto 50.00
1144 The Story of Ruth,Ph(c) . . . 135.00
1145 GK,The Lost World,Ph(c) . . 150.00
1146 Restless Gun,Ph(c) 125.00
1147 Sugarfoot,Ph(c) 135.00
1148 I aim at the Stars,Ph(c). . . . 125.00
1149 Goofy. 75.00
1150 CB,Daisy Duck's Diary 150.00
1151 Mickey Mouse Album 50.00
1152 Rocky and His Friends 350.00
1153 Frosty the Snowman 75.00
1154 Santa Claus Funnies 75.00
1155 North to Alaska. 250.00
1156 Walt Disney Swiss
  Family Robinson. 125.00
1157 Master of the World 75.00
1158 Three Worlds of Gulliver. . . 100.00
1159 ATh,77 Sunset Strip 150.00
1160 Rawhide 225.00
1161 CB,Grandma Duck's
  Farm Friends 200.00
1162 Yogi Bera joins the Marines 125.00
1163 Daniel Boone 75.00
1164 Wanted: Dead or Alive 150.00
1165 Ellery Queen 175.00
1166 Rocky and His Friends 350.00
1167 Tales of Wells Fargo,Ph(c) . 125.00
1168 The Detectives,
  R.Taylor Ph(c) 150.00
1169 New Adventures of
  Sherlock Holmes 250.00
1170 The Three Stooges,Ph(c) . 200.00
1171 Elmer Fudd 40.00
1172 Fury,Ph(c) 100.00
1173 The Twilight Zone. 350.00
1174 The Little Rascals. 60.00
1175 M.G.M.'s Mouse Musketeers 40.00
1176 Dondi,Ph(c) 60.00
1177 Chilly Willy 50.00
1178 Ten Who Dared 125.00
1179 The Swamp Fox,
  L.Nielson Ph(c). 135.00
1180 The Danny Thomas Show . 250.00
1181 Texas John Slaughter,Ph(c) 125.00
1182 Donald Duck Album 150.00
1183 101 Dalmatians 150.00
1184 CB,W.Disney's
  Gyro Gearloose 150.00
1185 Sweetie Pie 60.00
1186 JDa,Yak Yak. 135.00
1187 The Three Stooges,Ph(c) . . 175.00
1188 Atlantis the Lost
  Continent,Ph(c) 175.00

1189 Greyfriars Bobby,Ph(c) 125.00
1190 CB(c),Donald and
  the Wheel 125.00
1191 Leave It to Beaver,Ph(c) . . . 235.00
1192 Rocky Nelson,Ph(c) 250.00
1193 The Real McCoys,Ph(c) . . . 135.00
1194 Pepe,Ph(c). 50.00
1195 National Velvet,Ph(c) 100.00
1196 Pixie and Dixie
  and Mr. Jinks 75.00
1197 The Aquanauts,Ph(c) 125.00
1198 Donald in Mathmagic Land. 125.00
1199 Absent-Minded Professor,
  Ph(c) 125.00
1200 Hennessey,Ph(c) 125.00
1201 Goofy 75.00
1202 Rawhide,C.Eastwood Ph(c) 250.00
1203 Pinocchio. 75.00
1204 Scamp. 60.00
1205 David & Goliath,Ph(c). 100.00
1206 Lolly and Pepper 40.00
1207 MSy,The Rebel,Ph(c). 125.00
1208 Rocky and His Friends 350.00
1209 Sugarfoot,Ph(c) 125.00
1210 The Parent Trap,
  H.Mills Ph(c) 150.00
1211 RsM,77 Sunset Strip,Ph(c) . 135.00
1212 Chilly Willy 50.00
1213 Mysterious Island,Ph(c) . . . 125.00
1214 Smokey the Bear 55.00
1215 Tales of Wells Fargo,Ph(c) . 125.00
1216 Whirlybirds,Ph(c) 125.00
1218 Fury,Ph(c) 100.00
1219 The Detectives,
  Robert Taylor Ph(c). 135.00
1220 Gunslinger,Ph(c) 135.00
1221 Bonanza,Ph(c). 275.00
1222 Elmer Fudd 40.00
1223 GK,Laramie,Ph(c) 100.00
1224 The Little Rascals 60.00
1225 The Deputy,H.Fonda Ph(c). 150.00
1226 Nikki, Wild Dog of the North . 75.00
1227 Morgan the Pirate,Ph(c). . . 125.00
1229 Thief of Bagdad,Ph(c) 100.00
1230 Voyage to the Bottom
  of the Sea,Ph(c) 175.00
1231 Danger Man,Ph(c) 175.00
1232 On the Double 75.00
1233 Tammy Tell Me True 100.00
1234 The Phantom Planet 125.00
1235 Mister Magoo 150.00
1236 King of Kings,Ph(c) 125.00
1237 ATh,The Untouchables,
  Ph(c). 350.00
1238 Deputy Dawg 175.00

1239 CB(c),Donald Duck Album . 100.00
1240 The Detectives,
  R.Taylor Ph(c) 135.00
1241 Sweetie Pies 50.00
1242 King Leonardo and
  His Short Subjects 200.00
1243 Ellery Queen 135.00
1244 Space Mouse. 75.00
1245 New Adventures of
  Sherlock Holmes 225.00
1246 Mickey Mouse Album. 50.00
1247 Daisy Duck's Diary. 75.00
1248 Pluto 50.00
1249 The Danny Thomas Show,
  Ph(c). 250.00
1250 Four Horseman of the
  Apocalypse,Ph(c) 120.00
1251 Everything's Ducky 65.00
1252 The Andy Griffith Show,
  Ph(c). 550.00
1253 Spaceman 125.00
1254 'Diver Dan'. 75.00
1255 The Wonders of Aladdin . . . 100.00
1256 Kona, Monarch of
  Monster Isle 125.00
1257 Car 54, Where Are You?,
  Ph(c). 125.00
1258 GE,The Frogmen 125.00
1259 El Cid,Ph(c) 125.00
1260 The Horsemasters,Ph(c) . . 200.00
1261 Rawhide,C.Eastwood Ph(c) 235.00
1262 The Rebel,Ph(c). 135.00
1263 RsM,77 Sinset Strip,Ph(c) . 135.00
1264 Pixie & Dixie & Mr.Jinks 80.00
1265 The Real McCoys,Ph(c) . . . 135.00
1266 M.G.M.'s Spike and Tyke . . . 35.00
1267 CB,GyroGearloose. 125.00
1268 Oswald the Rabbit 50.00
1269 Rawhide,C.Eastwood Ph(c) 225.00
1270 Bullwinkle and Rocky 300.00
1271 Yogi Bear Birthday Party . . . 80.00
1272 Frosty the Snowman 75.00
1273 Hans Brinker,Ph(c). 100.00
1274 Santa Claus Funnies 75.00
1275 Rocky and His Friends 350.00
1276 Dondi 40.00
1278 King Leonardo and
  His Short Subjects 200.00
1279 Grandma Duck's Farm
  Friends. 75.00
1280 Hennessey,Ph(c) 100.00
1281 Chilly Willy 50.00
1282 Babes in Toyland,Ph(c) . . . 200.00
1283 Bonanza,Ph(c). 275.00
1284 RH,Laramie,Ph(c) 100.00
1285 Leave It to Beaver,Ph(c). . . 250.00
1286 The Untouchables,Ph(c). . . 250.00
1287 Man from Wells Fargo,Ph(c). 80.00
1288 RC,GE,The Twilight Zone. . 200.00
1289 Ellery Queen 135.00
1290 M.G.M.'s Mouse
  Musketeers 40.00
1291 RsM,77 Sunset Strip,Ph(c) . 135.00
1293 Elmer Fudd 40.00
1294 Ripcord 125.00
1295 Mr. Ed, the Talking Horse,
  Ph(c). 200.00
1296 Fury,Ph(c) 100.00
1297 Spanky, Alfalfa and the
  Little Rascals 60.00
1298 The Hathaways,Ph(c). 75.00
1299 Deputy Dawg 175.00
1300 The Comancheros 250.00
1301 Adventures in Paradise 80.00
1302 JohnnyJason,TeenReporter . 50.00
1303 Lad: A Dog,Ph(c) 60.00
1304 Nellie the Nurse 125.00
1305 Mister Magoo 135.00
1306 Target: The Corruptors,
  Ph(c). 80.00
1307 Margie 75.00

Four Color #1120
© Dell Publishing Co.

All comics prices listed are for *Near Mint* condition.

Four Color–Fritzi GOLDEN AGE

1308 Tales of the Wizard of Oz	175.00
1309 BK,87th Precinct,Ph(c)	150.00
1310 Huck and Yogi Winter Sports	135.00
1311 Rocky and His Friends	350.00
1312 National Velvet,Ph(c)	50.00
1313 Moon Pilot,Ph(c)	125.00
1328 GE,The Underwater City,Ph(c)	125.00
1330 GK,Brain Boy	200.00
1332 Bachelor Father	125.00
1333 Short Ribs	75.00
1335 Aggie Mack	50.00
1336 On Stage	65.00
1337 Dr. Kildare,Ph(c)	135.00
1341 The Andy Griffith Show, Ph(c)	500.00
1348 JDa,Yak Yak	135.00
1349 Yogi Berra Visits the U.N.	150.00
1350 Commanche,Ph(c)	75.00
1354 Calvin and the Colonel	135.00

Four Favorites #4
© *Ace Magazines*

FOUR FAVORITES
Ace Magazines
Sept., 1941

1 B:Vulcan, Lash Lighting, Magno the Magnetic Man, Raven, Flag (c),Hitler.	2,000.00
2 A: Black Ace	750.00
3 E:Vulcan	650.00
4 E:Raven,B:Unknown Soldiers	550.00
5 B:Captain Courageous	550.00
6 A: The Flag, B: Mr. Risk	500.00
7 JM	475.00
8	475.00
9 RP,HK	550.00
10 HK	600.00
11 HK,LbC,UnKnown Soldier	700.00
12 LbC	400.00
13 LbC	350.00
14 Fer	350.00
15 Fer	350.00
16 Bondage(c)	375.00
17 Magno Lighting	325.00
18 Magno Lighting	325.00
19 RP(a&c)	325.00
20 RP(a&c)	325.00
21 RP(a&c)	250.00
22 RP(c)	250.00
23 RP(c)	250.00
24 RP(c)	250.00
25 RP(c)	250.00
26 RP(c)	250.00
27 RP(c)	175.00
28 thru 32	@175.00

4MOST
Novelty Publ./Star Publ.
Winter 1941

1 The Target, The Cadet	1,800.00
2 The Target	700.00
3 Dan'l Flannel, Flag(c)	500.00
4 Dr. Seuss (1pg.)	400.00
2-1	175.00
2-2	175.00
2-3	175.00
2-4 Hitler,Tojo,Mussolini (c)	300.00
3-1	135.00
3-2	135.00
3-3	135.00
3-4	135.00
4-1	125.00
4-2 Walter Johnson(c)	125.00
4-3	125.00
4-4	125.00
5-1 The Target, Football(c)	100.00
5-2	100.00
5-3	100.00
5-4 Football(c)	100.00
6-1 Skiing(c)	100.00
6-2 LbC(c)	100.00
6-3 Tennis(c)	100.00
6-4 Football(c)	100.00
6-5	250.00
7-1 Basketball(c)	90.00
7-2 LbC(c)	250.00
7-3	125.00
7-4 LbC(c)	250.00
7-5	125.00
7-6 LbC(c)	250.00

Becomes:

FOREMOST BOYS
Jan., 1949

8-1	75.00
8-2 LbC(c),Surfing(c)	250.00
8-3 LbC(c)	250.00
8-4 LbC	200.00
8-5 LbC(c)	250.00
8-6 LbC	200.00
38 LbC(c), Johnny Weismuller	250.00
39 LbC(c), Johnny Weismuller	250.00
40 LbC(c), White Rider	250.00

Becomes:

THRILLING CRIME CASES

FRANKENSTEIN COMICS
Crestwood Publications
(Prize Publ.)
Summer, 1945

1 B:Frankenstein,DBr(a&c)	1,400.00
2 DBr(a&c)	750.00
3 DBr(a&c)	500.00
4 DBr(a&c)	500.00
5 DBr(a&c)	500.00
6 DBr(a&c),S&K	400.00
7 DBr(a&c),S&K	400.00
8 DBr(a&c),S&K	400.00
9 DBr(a&c),S&K	400.00
10 DBr(a&c),S&K	400.00
11 DBr(a&c)A:Boris Karloff	350.00
12 DBr(a&c)	350.00
13 DBr(a&c)	350.00
14 DBr(a&c)	350.00
15 DBr(a&c)	350.00
16 DBr(a&c)	350.00
17 DBr(a&c)	350.00
18 DBr,B:Horror	500.00
19 DBr	300.00
3-4 DBr	225.00
3-5 DBr	225.00
3-6 DBr	225.00
4-1 thru 4-6 DBr	@225.00
5-1 thru 5-4 DBr	@225.00
5-5 DBr, Oct.–Nov., 1954	225.00

FRISKY FABLES
Novelty Press/Premium Group
Spring, 1945

1 AFa	175.00
2 AFa	75.00
3 AFa	50.00
4 AFa	40.00
5 AFa	40.00
6 AFa	40.00
7 AFa,Flag (c)	45.00
2-1 AFa,Rainbow(c)	50.00
2-2 AFa	45.00
2-3 AFa	45.00
2-4 AFa	45.00
2-5 AFa	45.00
2-6 AFa	45.00
2-7 AFa	45.00
2-8 AFa,Halloween (c)	45.00
2-9 AFa,Thanksgiving(c)	40.00
2-10 AFa,Christman (c)	45.00
2-11 AFa	45.00
2-12 AFa,Valentines Day (c)	40.00
3-1 AFa	40.00
3-2 AFa	40.00
3-3 AFa	45.00
3-4 AFa	40.00
3-5 AFa	40.00
3-6 AFa	40.00
3-7 AFa	40.00
3-8 AFa,Turkey (c)	40.00
3-9 AFa	40.00
3-10 AFa	40.00
3-11 AFa,1948(c)	40.00
3-12 AFa	40.00
4-1 thru 4-7 AFa	@40.00
5-1 AFa	40.00
5-2 AFa	40.00
5-3	40.00
5-4 Star Publications	40.00
39 LbC(c)	250.00
40 LbC(c), Christmas	250.00
41 LbC(c)	250.00
42 LbC(c)	250.00
43 LbC(c)	40.00

Becomes:

FRISKY ANIMALS
Star Publications
Jan., 1951

44 LbC, Super Cat	250.00
45 LbC	300.00
46 LbC,Baseball	250.00
47 LbC	250.00
48 LbC	250.00
49 LbC	250.00
50 LbC	250.00
51 LbC(c)	250.00
52 LbC(c), Christmas	275.00
53 LbC(c)	250.00
54 LbC(c),Supercat(c)	250.00
55 LbC(c),same	250.00
56 LbC(c),same	250.00
57 LbC(c),same	250.00
58 LbC(c),same,July, 1954	250.00

FRITZI RITZ
United Features Syndicate/
St. John Publications
Fall, 1948

N# Special issue	150.00
2	100.00
3	75.00
4 thru 7	@65.00
6 A:Abbie & Slats	70.00
8 thru 11 1958	@40.00

All comics prices listed are for Near Mint condition.

Comics Values Annual — GOLDEN AGE — Frogman–Funny Funnies

FROGMAN COMICS
Hillman Periodicals
Jan.–Feb., 1952–May, 1953
1 .... 150.00
2 .... 75.00
3 .... 75.00
4 MMe. 50.00
5 BK,AT 55.00
6 .... 40.00
7 .... 40.00
8 thru 11 .... @40.00

FRONTIER ROMANCES
Avon Periodicals
Nov.–Dec., 1949
1 She Learned to Ride and Shoot, and Kissing Came Natural .. 600.00
2 Bronc-Busters Sweetheart, Jan.–Feb., 1950 .... 400.00

FRONTLINE COMBAT
Tiny Tot Publications (E.C. Comics), July–Aug., 1951
1 HK(c),WW, JSe,JDa,Hanhung Changjn (c) 900.00
2 HK(c),WW,Tank Battle (c) ... 500.00
3 HK(c),WW,Naval Battleship fire (c) 400.00
4 HK(c),WW, Bazooka (c) 375.00
5 HK(c),JSe 300.00
6 HK(c),WW,JSe 250.00
7 HK(c),WW,JSe,Document of the Action at Iwo Jima 250.00
8 HK(c),WW,ATh 250.00
9 HK(c),WW,JSe,Civil War iss. 250.00
10 GE,HK(c),WW, Crying Child (c) 275.00
11 GE 200.00
12 GE,Air Force issue 200.00
13 JSe,GE,WW(c), Bi-Planes (c) 200.00
14 JKu,GE,WW(c) 200.00
15 JSe,GE,WW(c), Jan., 1954 .. 200.00

FRONT PAGE COMIC BOOK
Front Page Comics, 1945
1 JKu,BP,BF(c),I:Man in Black . 500.00

Funnies #26
© Dell Publishing Co.

FUGITIVES FROM JUSTICE
St. John Publishing Co.
Feb., 1952
1 .... 250.00
2 MB, Killer Boomerang 275.00
3 GT 250.00
4 .... 100.00
5 Bondage (c), Oct., 1952 ..... 125.00

FUNNIES, THE (1ST SERIES)
Dell Publishing Co.
1929-30
1 B:Foxy Grandpa, Sniffy 1,500.00
2 thru 21 .... @500.00
N#(22) 400.00
N#(23) thru (36) .... @400.00

FUNNIES, THE (2ND SERIES)
Dell Publishing Co.
Oct., 1936
1 Tailspin Tommy,Mutt & Jeff, Capt. Easy,D.Dixon 3,800.00
2 Scribbly 2,000.00
3 .... 1,200.00
4 Christmas issue 1,000.00
5 .... 1,000.00
6 thru 10 .... @750.00
11 thru 22 .... 650.00
23 thru 29 .... @500.00
30 B:John Carter of Mars 1,800.00
31 inc. Dick Tracy 1,000.00
32 .... 1,000.00
33 .... 1,000.00
34 .... 1,000.00
35 John Carter (c) 1,000.00
36 John Carter (c) 1,000.00
37 John Carter (c) 1,000.00
38 Rex King of the Deep (c) . 1,000.00
39 Rex King (c) 1,000.00
40 John Carter (c) 1,000.00
41 Sky Ranger (c) 1,000.00
42 Rex King (c) 1,000.00
43 Rex King (c) 1,000.00
44 Rex King (c) 1,000.00
45 I&O:Phantasmo:Master of the World 1,200.00
46 Phantasmo (c) 700.00
47 Phantasmo (c) 650.00
48 Phantasmo (c) 650.00
49 Phantasmo (c) 650.00
50 Phantasmo (c) 650.00
51 Phantasmo (c) 650.00
52 Phantasmo (c) 550.00
53 Phantasmo (c) 550.00
54 Phantasmo (c) 550.00
55 Phantasmo (c) 550.00
56 Phantasmo (c) E:John Carter
57 I&O:Captain Midnight 4,500.00
58 Captain Midnight (c) 1,200.00
59 Captain Midnight (c) 1,200.00
60 Captain Midnight (c) 1,200.00
61 Captain Midnight (c) 900.00
62 Captain Midnight (c) 850.00
63 Captain Midnight (c) 850.00
64 B: Woody Woodpecker 1,500.00
Becomes:

NEW FUNNIES
Dell Publishing Co. July, 1942
65 Andy Panda, Ragady Ann & Andy, Peter Rabbit 1,200.00
66 same 500.00
67 Felix the Cat 500.00
68 .... 500.00

69 WK, The Brownies 500.00
70 .... 500.00
71 .... 300.00
72 WK 300.00
73 .... 300.00
74 .... 300.00
75 WK,Brownies 300.00
76 CB,Andy Panda, Woody Woodpecker 1,500.00
77 same 300.00
78 Andy Panda 300.00
79 .... 250.00
80 .... 250.00
81 .... 250.00
82 WK,Brownies 265.00
83 WK,Brownies 265.00
84 WK,Brownies 265.00
85 WK,Brownies 265.00
86 .... 200.00
87 Woody Woodpecker 175.00
88 same 175.00
89 same 175.00
90 same 175.00
91 thru 99 .... @125.00
100 .... 135.00
101 thru 110 .... @80.00
111 thru 118 .... @75.00
119 Christmas 75.00
120 thru 142 .... @75.00
143 Christmas (c) 80.00
144 thru 149 .... @75.00
150 thru 154 .... @60.00
155 Christmas 75.00
156 thru 167 .... @60.00
168 Christmas (c) 75.00
169 thru 181 .... @60.00
182 I&O:Knothead & Splinter ... 60.00
183 thru 200 .... @60.00
201 thru 240 .... @50.00
241 thru 288 .... @40.00

FUNNY BOOK
Funny Book Publ. Corp.
(Parents Magazine) Dec., 1952
1 Alec, the Funny Bunny, Alice in Wonderland 150.00
2 Gulliver in Giant-Land 75.00
3 .... 60.00
4 Adventures of Robin Hood . 50.00
5 .... 50.00
6 .... 50.00
7 .... 50.00
8 .... 50.00
9 .... 50.00

FUNNY FILMS
Best Syndicated Features (American Comics Group) Sept.–Oct., 1949
1 B:Puss An' Boots, Blunderbunny 200.00
2 .... 100.00
3 .... 65.00
4 .... 50.00
5 .... 50.00
6 .... 50.00
7 .... 50.00
8 .... 50.00
9 .... 50.00
10 .... 50.00
11 thru 20 .... @45.00
21 thru 28 .... @40.00
29 May–June, 1954 .... 40.00

FUNNY FUNNIES
Nedor Publ. Co.
April, 1943
1 Funny Animals 200.00

All comics prices listed are for *Near Mint* condition.

CVA Page 401

GOLDEN AGE

Funny Pages–Gene Autry

Funny Pages #34
© Comics Magazine/Centaur

COMICS MAGAZINE
Comics Magazine/Centaur
May, 1936
1 S&S, Dr. Mystic 15,000.00
2 S&S, Federal Agent 3,000.00
3 . . . . 2,500.00
4 . . . . 2,500.00
5 . . . . 2,500.00
Becomes:

FUNNY PAGES
Nov., 1936
6 I:The Clock, 1st masked hero 3,000.00
7 WE 1,200.00
8 WE 1,200.00
9 . . . . 1,200.00
10 WE 1,200.00
11 . . . . 1,200.00
12 . . . . 800.00
13 FG,BoW 800.00
14 JCo,FG,BoW 800.00
15 JCo 800.00
16 JCo,FG 800.00
17 Centaur 1,200.00
18 . . . . 800.00
19 . . . . 800.00
20 . . . . 800.00
21 B:The Arrow 4,000.00
22 BEv,GFx 1,700.00
23 . . . . 1,700.00
24 BKa,B.Wayne prototype . . . 1,900.00
25 JCo. 1,400.00
26 . . . . 1,400.00
27 . . . . 1,400.00
28 . . . . 1,400.00
29 JCo,BoW 1,400.00
30 BoW,The Arrow(c). 3,000.00
31 . . . . 1,500.00
32 JCo,BoW 1,500.00
33 JCo,BoW,The Arrow(c) 2,500.00
34 JCo,The Arrow(c) 2,800.00
35 BoW,The Arrow(c). 2,800.00
36 Mad Ming (c). 1,500.00
37 JCo,Mad Ming (c) 1,500.00
38 Mad Ming(c) 1,500.00
39 The Arrow(c) 2,400.00
40 BoW,The Arrow(c). 2,400.00
41 BoW,The Arrow(c). 2,400.00
42 BoW,The Arrow(c). 2,400.00

FUNNY PICTURE STORIES
Comics Magazine/Centaur
Publ., Nov., 1936
1 B:The Clock. 4,500.00
2 The Spinner Talks 1,600.00
3 Tyrant Gold 1,000.00
4 WE,The Brothers Three 1,000.00
5 Timber Terror. 1,000.00
6 War in Asia (c). 1,000.00
7 Racist Humor (c) 1,000.00
Vol 2
#1(10) 650.00
#2 (11) BoW 600.00
#3 (12)BoW 600.00
#4 (13) Christmas (c) 700.00
#5 (14) BoW 600.00
#6 (15) Centaur 1,000.00
#7 (16) 500.00
#8 (17) 500.00
#9 (18) 500.00
#10 (19) 500.00
#11 (20) 500.00
Vol 3
#1 . . . . 500.00
#2 . . . . 500.00
#3 . . . . 500.00
Becomes:

COMIC PAGES
July, 1939
4 BoW. 800.00
5 . . . . 600.00
6 . . . . 600.00

FUNNYMAN
Magazine Enterprises
of Canada, Dec., 1947
1 S&K(a&c) 600.00
2 S&K(a&c) 300.00
3 S&K(a&c) 250.00
4 S&K(a&c) 250.00
5 S&K(a&c) 250.00
6 S&K(a&c), Aug., 1948 . . . . . 250.00

FUNNY TUNES
Avon Periodicals
July, 1953
1 (fa),Space Mouse, Peter Rabbit
   Merry Mouse,Cicero the Cat. 100.00
2 same 75.00
3 same 75.00
Becomes:

SPACE COMICS
Avon Periodicals
March–April, 1954
4 (fa),F:Space Mouse 50.00
5 (fa),F:Space Mouse 40.00

FUTURE COMICS
David McKay Publications
June, 1940
1 Lone Ranger,Phantom 3,500.00
2 Lone Ranger 1,600.00
3 Lone Ranger. 1,400.00
4 Lone Ranger,Sept. 1940 . . 1,300.00

FUTURE WORLD COMICS
George W. Dougherty
Summer, 1946
1 . . . . 400.00
2 Fall, 1946 . . . . 350.00

GABBY HAYES WESTERN
Fawcett Publ./Charlton Comics
Nov., 1948
1 Ph(c) 600.00
2 Ph(c) 250.00
3 The Rage of the Purple Sage,
   Ph(c) 175.00
4 Ph(c) 175.00
5 Ph(c) 150.00
6 Ph(c) 150.00
7 Ph(c) 135.00
8 Ph(c) 135.00
9 Ph(c),V:The Kangaroo Crook . 135.00
10 Ph(c) 135.00
11 Ph(c), Chariot Race 135.00
12 V:Beaver Ben, The Biting
   Bandit,Ph(c) 100.00
13 thru 15 . . . . @100.00
16 . . . . 90.00
17 . . . . 90.00
18 thru 20 . . . . @90.00
21 thru 51 . . . . @75.00
51 thru 59 Dec., 1954 . . . . . . @50.00

GANGSTERS AND GUN MOLLS
Realistic Comics
(Avon) Sept., 1951
1 WW,A:Big Jim Colosimo,
   Evelyn Ellis 600.00
2 JKa, A:Bonnie Parker, The
   Kissing Bandit 500.00
3 EK, A:Juanita Perez, Crimes
   Homicide Squad 400.00
4 A:Mara Hite, Elkins Boys,
   June, 1952 . . . . 350.00

GANGSTERS CAN'T WIN
D.S. Publishing Co.
Feb.–March, 1948
1 Shot Cop (c) 400.00
2 A:Eddie Bentz 200.00
3 Twin Trouble Trigger Man . . . 175.00
4 Suicide on SoundStageSeven 200.00
5 Trail of Terror 150.00
6 Mystery at the Circus 150.00
7 Talisman Trail 125.00
8 . . . . 125.00
9 Suprise at Buoy 13,
   June–July, 1949 . . . . 125.00

GANG WORLD
Literary Enterprises
(Standard Comics)
Oct., 1952
5 Bondage (c) 225.00
6 Mob Payoff, Jan., 1953 . . . . . 150.00

GASOLINE ALLEY
Star Publications
Oct., 1950
1 . . . . 250.00
2 LBc 250.00
3 LBc(c), April, 1950 . . . . 250.00

GEM COMICS
Spotlight Publ. April, 1945
1 A:Steve Strong,Bondage(c) . . 600.00

GENE AUTRY COMICS
Fawcett Publications
Jan., 1942
1 The Mark of Cloven Hoof . 11,000.00

CVA Page 402 — All comics prices listed are for *Near Mint* condition.

GOLDEN AGE

GEORGE PAL'S PUPPETOON'S
Fawcett Publications
Dec., 1945
1 Captain Marvel (c) 500.00
2 .... 250.00
3 .... 150.00
4 thru 17 .... @150.00
18 Dec., 1947................. 125.00

GERALD McBOING-BOING AND THE NEARSIGHTED MR. MAGOO
Dell Publishing Co.
Aug.–Oct., 1952
1 .... 200.00
2 thru 5 .... @150.00

GERONIMO
Avon Periodicals, 1950
1 Massacre at San Pedro Pass . 200.00
2 EK(c), Murderous Battle
   at Kiskayah 125.00
3 EK(c) 125.00
4 EK(c),Apache Death Trap,
   Feb., 1952 .... 100.00

GET LOST
Mikeross Publications
Feb.–March, 1954
1 .... 350.00
2 .... 200.00
3 June–July, 1954 .... 175.00

GHOST
Fiction House Magazine
Winter, 1951–Summer, 1954
1 The Banshee Bells 900.00
2 I Woke In Terror 450.00
3 The Haunted Hand of X 350.00
4 Flee the Mad Furies 350.00
5 The Hex of Ruby Eye 350.00
6 The Sleepers in the Crypt .. 350.00
7 When Dead Rogues Ride ... 350.00
8 Curse of the Mist-Thing 350.00
9 It Crawls by Night,Bondage(c). 375.00
10 Halfway to Hades.......... 350.00
11 GE, The Witch's Doll 350.00

GHOST BREAKERS
Street & Smith, Sept., 1948
1 BP(a&c), A:Dr. Neff 500.00
2 BP(a&c), Breaks the Voodoo
   Hoodoo,Dec., 1948........ 400.00

GHOSTLY WEIRD STORIES
See: BLUE BOLT

GIANT BOY BOOK OF COMICS
Newsbook Publ.
(Lev Gleason), 1945
1 A:Crime Buster & Young
   Robin Hood 1,200.00

GIANT COMICS EDITION
St. John Publ., 1948
1 Mighty Mouse 600.00
2 Abbie and Slats 300.00
3 Terry Toons 500.00

4 Crime Comics 750.00
5 MB, Police Case Book 750.00
6 MB(a&c), Western
   Picture Story.............. 650.00
7 Mopsy 400.00
8 Adventures of Mighty Mouse.. 450.00
9 JKu,MB,Romance & Confession
   Stories,Ph(c) 750.00
10 Terry Toons 450.00
11 MB(a&c),JKu,Western
   Picture Stories 600.00
12 MB(a&c),Diary Secrets,
   Prostitute.................. 1,300.00
13 MB,JKu, Romances 600.00
14 Mighty Mouse Album 450.00
15 MB(c),Romance............ 750.00
16 Little Audrey............... 450.00
N#, Mighty Mouse Album ... 450.00

GIANT COMICS EDITION
United Features Syndicate
1945
1 A:Abbie & Slats, Jim Hardy,
   Ella Cinders,Iron Vic 500.00
2 Elmo, Jim Hardy, Abbie &
   Slats, 1945................ 350.00

G.I. COMBAT
Quality Comics Group, 1952
1 RC(c), Beyond the Call
   of Duty 850.00
2 RC(c), Operation Massacre .. 350.00
3 An Indestructible Marine 300.00
4 Bridge to Blood Hill 300.00
5 Hell Breaks loose on
   Suicide Hill................ 300.00
6 Beachhead Inferno 275.00
7 Fire Power Assault 250.00
8 RC(c),Death-trap Hill 250.00
9 Devil Riders 250.00
10 RC(c), Two-Ton Booby Trap . 275.00
11 Hell's Heroes 200.00
12 Hand Grenade Hero....... 200.00
13 Commando Assault 200.00
14 Spear Head Assault....... 200.00
15 Vengeance Assault 200.00
16 Trapped Under Fire 175.00
17 Attack on Death Mountain .. 175.00
18 Red Battle Ground........ 175.00
19 Death on Helicopter Hill.... 175.00
20 Doomed Legion-Death Trap . 175.00
21 Red Sneak Attack 150.00
22 Vengeance Raid 150.00

G. I. Combat #2
© *Quality Comics Group*

Gene Autry
© *Dell Publishing Co.*

2 .... 2,000.00
3 Secret o/t Aztec Treasure .. 1,500.00
4 .... 1,200.00
5 Mystery of Paint Rock
   Canyon 1,200.00
6 Outlaw Round-up 1,000.00
7 Border Bullets 1,000.00
8 Blazing Guns 1,000.00
9 Range Robbers 1,000.00
10 Fightin' Buckaroo, Danger's
   Trail, Sept., 1943......... 1,000.00
11 .... 900.00
12 .... 900.00

GENE AUTRY COMICS
Dell Publishing Co.
May/June, 1946
1 .... 650.00
2 Ph(c) 350.00
3 Ph(c) 250.00
4 Ph(c),I:Flap Jack............ 250.00
5 Ph(c), all.................... 250.00
6 thru 10 .... @225.00
11 thru 19 .... @225.00
20 .... 235.00
21 thru 29 .... @150.00
30 thru 40, B:Giants .... @125.00
41 thru 56 E:Giants.......... @100.00
57 .... 90.00
58 Christmas (c)............... 80.00
59 thru 66 .... @75.00
67 thru 80, B:Giant .... @85.00
81 thru 90, E:Giant .... @65.00
91 thru 93 .... @60.00
94 Christmas (c)............... 65.00
95 thru 99................... @60.00
100 .... 75.00
101 thru 111 .... @50.00
112 thru 121 .... @50.00

GENE AUTRY'S CHAMPION
Dell Publishing Co.
Aug., 1950
(1) see Dell Four Color #287
(2) see Dell Four Color #319
3 .... 65.00
4 thru 19 .... @50.00

All comics prices listed are for *Near Mint* condition.   CVA Page 403

G.I. Combat–Goofy / GOLDEN AGE / Comics Values Annual

G.I. Combat (cont.)
- 23 No Grandstand in Hell 150.00
- 24 Operation Steel Trap, Comics Code 150.00
- 25 Charge of the CommieBrigade 150.00
- 26 Red Guerrilla Trap 150.00
- 27 Trapped Behind Commie Lines 150.00
- 28 Atomic Battleground........ 150.00
- 29 Patrol Ambush............. 150.00
- 30 Operation Booby Trap 150.00
- 31 Human Fly on Heartbreak Hill 150.00
- 32 Atomic Rocket Assault 175.00
- 33 Bridge to Oblivion 150.00
- 34 RC, Desperate Mission...... 175.00
- 35 Doom Patrol 150.00
- 36 Fire Power Assault......... 150.00
- 37 Attack at Dawn............ 150.00
- 38 Get That Tank 150.00
- 39 Mystery of No Man's Land ... 150.00
- 40 Maneuver Battleground 150.00
- 41 Trumpet of Doom.......... 150.00
- 42 March of Doom 150.00
- 43 Operation Showdown....... 150.00
- See DC Comics for 44–120

GIFT COMICS
Fawcett Publications
March, 1942
- 1 A:Captain Marvel, Bulletman, Golden Arrow, Ibis, the Invincible, Spy Smasher .. 3,500.00
- 2 .... 2,000.00
- 3 .... 1,400.00
- 4 A:Marvel Family, 1949 .... 850.00

GIGGLE COMICS
Creston Publ./ American Comics Group
Oct., 1943
- 1 (fa)same................. 350.00
- 2 KHu 150.00
- 3 KHu 125.00
- 4 KHu 100.00
- 5 KHu 100.00
- 6 KHu 75.00
- 7 KHu 75.00
- 8 KHu 75.00
- 9 I:Super Katt 85.00
- 10 KHu 50.00
- 11 thru 20 KHu .... @45.00
- 21 thru 30 KHu .... @40.00
- 31 thru 40 KHu .... @30.00
- 41 thru 94 KHu .... @35.00

Giggle Comics #49
© American Comics Group

- 95 A:Spencer Spook........... 30.00
- 96 KHu..................... 30.00
- 97 KHu..................... 30.00
- 98 KHu..................... 30.00
- 99 KHu..................... 30.00
- 100 and 101 March–April,1955 . @30.00

G.I. JANE
Stanhall Publ.
May, 1953
- 1 .... 125.00
- 2 thru 6 .... @75.00
- 7 thru 9 .... @60.00
- 10 Dec., 1954............... 50.00

G.I. JOE
Ziff-Davis Publication Co.
1950
- 10 NS(c),Red Devils of Korea, V:Seoul City Lou........... 150.00
- 11 NS(c),The Guerrilla's Lair.... 125.00
- 12 NS(c)................... 125.00
- 13 NS(c),Attack at Dawn....... 125.00
- 14 NS(c),Temple of Terror, A:Peanuts the Great........ 100.00
- 2-6 It's a Foot Soldiers Job, I:Frankie of the Pump...... 100.00
- 2-7 BP,NS(c),The Rout at Sugar Creek 100.00
- 8 BP,NS(c),Waldo'sSqueezeBox 100.00
- 9 NS(c),Dear John........... 100.00
- 10 NS(c),Joe Flies the Payroll .. 100.00
- 11 NS(c),For the Love of Benny . 100.00
- 12 NS(c),Patch work Quilt...... 100.00
- 13 NS(c).................... 100.00
- 14 NS(c),The Wedding Ring.... 100.00
- 15 The Lacrosse Whoopee..... 100.00
- 16 Mamie's Mortar 100.00
- 17 A Time for Waiting 100.00
- 18 Giant 250.00
- 19 Old Army Game..Buck Passer . 75.00
- 20 General Confusion 75.00
- 21 Save 'Im for Brooklyn....... 75.00
- 22 Portrait of a Lady........... 75.00
- 23 Take Care of My Little Wagon . 75.00
- 24 Operation 'Operation'....... 75.00
- 25 The Two-Leaf Clover 75.00
- 26 NS(c),Nobody Flies Alone Mud & Wings 75.00
- 27 'Dear Son...Come Home'.... 75.00
- 28 They Alway's Come Back Bondage (c).............. 75.00
- 29 What a Picnic 60.00
- 30 NS(c),The One-Sleeved Kimono 60.00
- 31 NS(c),Get a Horse.......... 55.00
- 32 thru 47 .... @55.00
- 48 Atom Bomb............... 60.00
- 49 thru 51 June, 1957........ @55.00

GINGER
Close-Up Publ. (Archie Publications)
Jan., 1951
- 1 GFs 150.00
- 2 .... 75.00
- 3 .... 60.00
- 4 .... 60.00
- 5 .... 50.00
- 6 .... 50.00
- 7 thru 9 .... @75.00
- 10 A:Katy Keene,Summer,1954 .. 75.00

GIRLS IN LOVE
Fawcett Publications
May, 1950
- 1 .... 125.00

- 2 Ph(c),July, 1950 .... 100.00

GIRLS IN LOVE
See: DIARY LOVES

G.I. SWEETHEARTS
See: DIARY LOVES

G.I. WAR BRIDES
Superior Publ. Ltd.
April, 1954
- 1 .... 75.00
- 2 .... 50.00
- 3 thru 7 .... @40.00
- 8 June, 1955 .... 40.00

GOING STEADY
See: TEEN-AGE TEMPTATIONS

GOLDEN ARROW
Fawcett Publications
Spring, 1942
- 1 B:Golden Arrow 1,100.00
- 2 .... 550.00
- 3 .... 400.00
- 4 .... 350.00
- 5 Spring, 1947 .... 350.00
- 6 BK 400.00
- 6a 1944 Well Known Comics (Giveaway) 450.00

GOLDEN LAD
Spark Publications
July, 1945–June, 1946
- 1 MMe(a&c),A:Kid Wizards, Swift Arrow,B:Golden Ladd 1,000.00
- 2 MMe(a&c) 450.00
- 3 MMe(a&c) 450.00
- 4 MMe(a&c), The Menace of the Minstrel 450.00
- 5 MMe(a&c),O:Golden Girl..... 450.00

GOLDEN WEST LOVE
Kirby Publishing Co.
Sept.–Oct., 1949
- 1 BP,I Rode Heartbreak Hill, Ph(c) 250.00
- 2 BP 150.00
- 3 BP,Ph(c) 150.00
- 4 BP,April, 1950 .... 150.00

GOLD MEDAL COMICS
Cambridge House, 1945
- N# Captain Truth 350.00

GOOFY COMICS
Nedor Publ. Co./ Animated Cartoons (Standard Comics)
June, 1943
- 1 (fa)..................... 300.00
- 2 .... 150.00
- 3 VP 125.00
- 4 VP 110.00
- 5 VP 110.00
- 6 thru 10 VP............... @110.00
- 11 thru 15 .... @100.00
- 15 thru 19 .... @100.00
- 20 thru 35 FF .... @125.00
- 36 thru 48 .... @75.00

CVA Page 404 — All comics prices listed are for *Near Mint* condition.

GOLDEN AGE

GREAT AMERICAN COMICS PRESENTS– THE SECRET VOICE
4 Star Publ., 1944
1 Hitler,Secret Weapon 400.00

GREAT COMICS
Novak Publ. Co., 1945
1 LbC(c) 500.00

GREAT COMICS
Great Comics Publications Nov., 1941
1 I:The Great Zorro 1,700.00
2 Buck Johnson 850.00
3 The Lost City, Jan., 1942 . . 3,000.00

GREAT LOVER ROMANCES
Toby Press, March, 1951
1 Jon Juan,A:Dr. King 200.00
2 Hollywood Girl 100.00
3 Love in a Taxi 60.00
4 The Experimental Kiss 60.00
5 After the Honeymoon 60.00
6 HK,The Kid Sister Falls
   in Love 100.00
7 Man Crazy 60.00
8 Stand-in Boyfriend 60.00
9 The Cheat 60.00
10 Heart Breaker 60.00
11 . . . . 60.00
12 . . . . 60.00
13 Powerhouse of Deceit 60.00
14 . . . . 60.00
15 Ph(c),Still Undecided,
   Liz Taylor 175.00
16 thru 21 . . . . @50.00
22 May, 1955 . . . . 50.00

GREEN GIANT COMICS
Pelican Publications, 1941
1 Black Arrow, Dr. Nerod
   O:Colossus 16,000.00

GREEN HORNET COMICS
Helnit Publ. Co./ Family Comics (Harvey Publ.), Dec., 1940
1 B:Green Hornet,P(c) 7,500.00
2 . . . . 2,500.00
3 BWh(c) 1,900.00
4 BWh(c) 1,500.00
5 BWh(c) 1,500.00
6 . . . . 1,500.00
7 BP, O:Zebra, B:Robin
   Hood & Spirit of 76 . . . . . 1,200.00
8 BP,Bondage (c) 1,000.00
9 BP,JK(c),Behind the (c) . . . 1,200.00
10 BP 1,000.00
11 Who is Mr. Q? 1,000.00
12 BP,A:Mr.Q. 1,000.00
13 Hitler (c) 1,100.00
14 BP,Spirit of 76-Twinkle
   Twins, Bondage(c) 800.00
15 ASh(c),Nazi Ghost Ship 800.00
16 BP,Prisoner of War 800.00
17 BP,ASh(c),Nazis' Last Stand . 800.00
18 BP,ASh(c),Jap's Treacherous
   Plot,Bondage (c) 800.00
19 BP,ASh(c),Clash with the
   Rampaging Japs 800.00
20 BP,ASh(c),Tojo's
   Propaganda Hoax 800.00
21 BP,ASh(c),Unwelcome Cargo . 600.00
22 ASh(c),Rendezvous with
   Jap Saboteurs 600.00
23 BF,ASh(c),Jap's Diabolical
   Plot #B2978 . . . . 600.00
24 BF,Science Fiction (c) 650.00
25 thru 29 . . . . @600.00
30 BP,JKu 600.00
31 BP,JKu 650.00
32 BP,JKu 500.00
33 BP,JKu 500.00
34 BP,JKu 500.00
35 BP,JKu 500.00
36 BP,JKu,Bondage (c) 550.00
37 BP,JKu 500.00
38 BP,JKu 500.00
39 S&K 575.00
40 thru 45 . . . . @400.00
46 Drug 425.00
47 Sept., 1949 . . . . 400.00

GREEN LAMA
Spark Publications/Prize Publ. Dec., 1944
1 I:Green Lama, Lt. Hercules
   & Boy Champions 1,700.00
2 MRa,Forward to Victory
   in 1945 . . . . 1,000.00
3 MRa,The Riddles of Toys 800.00
4 MRa,Dive Bombs Japan 750.00
5 MRa(a&c),Fights for
   the Four Freedoms 750.00
6 MRa,Smashes a Plot
   against America 750.00
7 MRa,Merry X-Mas 450.00
8 MRa,Smashes Toy Master
   of Crime, March, 1946 . . . . . 450.00

GREEN MASK, THE
Fox Features Syndicate Summer, 1940
1 O:Green Mask & Domino . . 5,500.00
2 A:Zanzibar 1,900.00
3 BP 1,200.00
4 B:Navy Jones 900.00
5 . . . . 750.00
6 B:Nightbird,E:Navy Jones,
   Bondage (c) 600.00
7 B:Timothy Smith &
   The Tumbler 500.00

Green Mask #11
© Fox Features Syndicate

8 JSs 400.00
9 E:Nightbird, Death Wields
   a Scalpel! 450.00
10 . . . . 375.00
11 The Banshee of Dead
   Man's Hill 375.00
2-1 Election of Skulls 300.00
2-2 Pigeons of Death 300.00
2-3 Wandering Gold Brick 250.00
2-4 Time on His Hands 250.00
2-5 JFe,SFd 300.00
2-6 Adventure of the Disappearing
   Trains, Oct.–Nov., 1946 . . . . 300.00

GUMPS, THE
Dell Publishing Co., 1945
1 . . . . 200.00
2 . . . . 175.00
3 . . . . 125.00
4 . . . . 125.00
5 . . . . 125.00

GUNS AGAINST GANGSTERS
Curtis Publ./Novelty Press Sept.–Oct., 1948
1 LbC(a&c),B:Toni Gayle 500.00
2 LbC(a&c) 350.00
3 LbC(a&c) 300.00
4 LbC(a&c) 300.00
5 LbC(a&c) 300.00
6 LbC(a&c),Shark 300.00
2-1 LbC(a&c),Sept.–Oct., 1949 . 300.00

GUNSMOKE
Western Comics, Inc. April–May, 1949
1 GRi(a&c),Gunsmoke & Masked
   Marvel,Bondage (c) 500.00
2 GRi(a&c) 350.00
3 GRi(a&c) 250.00
4 GRi(c),Bondage(c) 250.00
5 GRi(c) 250.00
6 . . . . 125.00
7 . . . . 125.00
8 . . . . 125.00
9 . . . . 125.00
10 . . . . 125.00
11 thru 15 . . . . @100.00
16 Jan., 1952 . . . . 100.00

HA HA COMICS
Creston Publ. (American Comics Group) Oct., 1943
1 Funny Animal, all 350.00
2 . . . . 150.00
3 . . . . 125.00
4 . . . . 125.00
5 . . . . 125.00
6 thru 10 . . . . @100.00
11 . . . . 75.00
12 thru 15 KHu . . . . @75.00
16 thru 20 KHu . . . . @75.00
21 thru 30 KHu . . . . @60.00
31 thru 101 . . . . @50.00
102 Feb.–March, 1955 . . . . 50.00

MISTER RISK
Humor Publ. Oct., 1950
1 (7) B:Mr. Risk 75.00
2 . . . . 50.00
Becomes:

MEN AGAINST CRIME
Feb., 1951
3 A:Mr. Risk, Case of the Carnival
   Killer 100.00
4 Murder-And the Crowd Roars . 60.00
5 . . . . 60.00
6 . . . . 60.00
7 Get Them! 60.00
Becomes:

HAND OF FATE
Ace Magazines, Dec., 1951
8 . . . . 500.00
9 LC 250.00
10 LC 225.00
11 Genie(c) 200.00
12 . . . . 200.00
13 Hanging(c) 225.00
14 . . . . 225.00
15 . . . . 225.00
16 . . . . 200.00
17 . . . . 200.00
18 . . . . 200.00
19 Drug issue,Quicksand(c) 225.00
20 . . . . 200.00
21 Drug issue 225.00
22 . . . . 200.00
23 Graveyard(c) 200.00
24 LC,Electric Chair 325.00
25 Nov., 1954 . . . . 150.00
25a Dec., 1954 . . . . 200.00

HANGMAN COMICS
See: LAUGH COMICS

HAP HAZARD COMICS
**A.A. Wyn/Red Seal Publ./
Readers Research
Summer, 1944**
1 Funny Teen 150.00
2 Dog Show 75.00
3 Sgr, ... 60.00
4 Sgr, ... 60.00
5 thru 10 Sgr, ... @50.00
11 thru 13 Sgr, ... @45.00
14 AF(c) 75.00
15 . . . . 45.00
16 thru 24 . . . . @45.00
Becomes:

REAL LOVE
April, 1949
25 Dangerous Dates 75.00
26 . . . . 60.00
27 LbC(c), Revenge Conquest . . . 65.00
28 thru 40 . . . . @50.00
41 thru 66 . . . . @45.00
67 Comics code 30.00
68 thru 76, Nov., 1956 . . . . . . @30.00

HAPPY COMICS
**Nedor Publications/
Animated Cartoons
Aug., 1943**
1 Funny Animal in all 275.00
2 . . . . 150.00
3 . . . . 100.00
4 . . . . 100.00
5 thru 10 . . . . @100.00
11 thru 20 . . . . @75.00
21 thru 31 . . . . @75.00
32 FF 200.00
33 FF 300.00
34 thru 37 FF . . . . @100.00
38 thru 40 . . . . @50.00
Becomes:

HAPPY RABBIT
Standard Comics, Feb., 1951
41 Funny Animal in all 50.00
42 thru 50 . . . . @40.00
Becomes:

HARVEY COMIC HITS
Harvey Publications, Oct., 1951
51 Phantom 350.00
52 Steve Canyon's Air Power . . . 150.00
53 Mandrake 250.00
54 Tim Tyler's Tales of Jungle
   Terror 150.00
55 Love Stories of Mary Worth . . . 75.00
56 Phantom, Bondage (c) 275.00
57 AR,Kidnap Racket 175.00
58 Girls in White 75.00
59 Tales of the Invisible 150.00
60 Paramount Animated Comics 400.00
61 Casper the Friendly Ghost . . 500.00
62 Paramount Animated Comics,
   April, 1953 . . . . 150.00

HAPPY HOULIHANS
See: SADDLE JUSTICE

*Haunted Thrills 316
© Four Star Publ.*

HAUNTED THRILLS
**Four Star Publ.
(Ajax/Farrell) June, 1952**
1 Ellery Queen 600.00
2 LbC,Ellery Queen 450.00
3 Drug Story 400.00
4 Ghouls Castle 350.00
5 Fatal Scapel 350.00
6 Pit of Horror 300.00
7 Trail to a Tomb 300.00
8 Vanishing Skull 300.00
9 Madness of Terror 300.00
10 . . . . 300.00
11 Nazi Concentration Camp . . . 325.00
12 RWb 225.00
13 . . . . 225.00
14 RWb 250.00
15 The Devil Collects 225.00
16 . . . . 225.00
17 Mirror of Madness 225.00
18 No Place to Go,
   Nov.–Dec., 1954 . . . . 250.00

HAUNT OF FEAR
**Fables Publ. (E.C. Comics)
May–June, 1950**
15 JCr(a&c),AF,WW 3,700.00
16 JCr(a&c),AF,WW 1,800.00
17 JCr(a&c),AF,WW,O:Crypt
   of Terror,Vault of Horror
   & Haunt of Fear 1,700.00
4 AF(c),WW,JDa 1,000.00
5 JCr(a&c),WW,JDa,Eye Injury . 800.00
6 JCr(a&c),WW,JDa 600.00
7 JCr(a&c),WW,JDa 600.00
8 AF(c),JKa,JDa,
   Shrunken Head 600.00
9 AF(c),JCr,JDa 600.00
10 AF(c),Grl,JDa 575.00
11 JKa,Grl,JDa 500.00
12 JCr,Grl,JDa 500.00
13 Grl,JDa 500.00
14 Grl(a&c),JDa,O:Old Witch . . . 750.00
15 JDa 500.00
16 GRi(c),JDa,Ray Bradbury
   adaptation 500.00
17 JDa,Grl(c),Classic
   Ghastly (c) 500.00
18 JDa,Grl(c),JKa,Ray Bradbury
   adaptation 550.00
19 JDa,Guillotine (c),
   Bondage (c) 600.00
20 RC,JDa,Grl(a&c) 425.00
21 JDa,Grl(a&c) 325.00
22 JDa,Grl(a&c) 325.00
23 JDa,Grl(a&c) 325.00
22 JDa,Grl(a&c) 325.00
23 JDa,Grl(a&c) 325.00
24 JDa,Grl(a&c) 325.00
25 JDa,Grl(a&c) 325.00
26 RC,JDa,Grl(a&c) 350.00
27 JDa,Grl(a&c), Cannibalism . . . 325.00
28 Dec., 1954 . . . . 350.00

HAWK, THE
**Approved Comics
(Ziff-Davis)
Winter, 1951**
1 MA,The Law of the Colt,P(c) . 250.00
2 JKu,Iron Caravan of the
   Mojave, P(c) 125.00
3 Leverett's Last Stand,P(c) . . . 110.00
4 Killer's Town,P(c) 100.00
5 . . . . 100.00
6 . . . . 100.00
7 . . . . 100.00
8 MB(c),Dry River Rampage . . . 135.00
9 MB(a&c),JKu 135.00
10 MB(c) 135.00
11 MB(c) 135.00
12 MB(a&c), May, 1955 . . . . . . 135.00

HEADLINE COMICS
**American Boys Comics/
Headline Publ. (Prize Publ.)
Feb., 1943**
1 B:Jr. Rangers 650.00
2 JaB(a&c) 250.00
3 JaB(a&c) 200.00
4 . . . . 200.00
5 HcK 200.00
6 HcK 200.00
7 HcK,Jr. Rangers 200.00
8 HcK,Hitler (c) 600.00
9 HcK 200.00
10 HcK,Hitler story,Wizard(c) . . 250.00
11 . . . . 150.00
12 HcK,Heroes of Yesterday . . . 150.00
13 HcK,A:Blue Streak 150.00
14 HcK,A:Blue Streak 150.00
15 HcK,A:Blue Streak 150.00
16 HcK,O:Atomic Man 300.00
17 Atomic Man(c) 150.00
18 Atomic Man(c) 150.00

GOLDEN AGE

Headline–Heroic

Headline Comics #19
© Prize Publications

19 S&K,Atomic Man(c)	300.00
20 Atomic Man(c)	150.00
21 E:Atomic Man	150.00
22 HcK	125.00
23 S&K(a&c),Valentines Day Massacre	325.00
24 S&K(a&c),You can't Forget a Killer	300.00
25 S&K(a&c),Crime Never Pays	300.00
26 S&K(a&c),Crime Never Pays	300.00
27 S&K(a&c),Crime Never Pays	300.00
28 S&K(a&c),Crime Never Pays	300.00
29 S&K(a&c),Crime Never Pays	300.00
30 S&K(a&c),Crime Never Pays	300.00
31 S&K(a&c),Crime Never Pays	300.00
32 S&K(a&c),Crime Never Pays	300.00
33 S&K(a&c),Police and FBI Heroes	300.00
34 S&K(a&c),same	300.00
35 S&K(a&c),same	300.00
36 S&K,same,Ph(c)	250.00
37 S&K,MvS,same,Ph(c)	275.00
38 S&K,same,Ph(c)	75.00
39 S&K,same,Ph(c)	75.00
40 S&K,Ph(c)Violent Crime	75.00
41 Ph(c),J.Edgar Hoover(c)	75.00
42 Ph(c)	60.00
43 Ph(c)	60.00
44 MMe,MvS,WE,S&K	85.00
45 JK	100.00
46	75.00
47	75.00
48	75.00
49 MMe	75.00
50	75.00
51 JK	80.00
52	75.00
53	75.00
54	75.00
55	75.00
56 S&K	150.00
57	50.00
58	50.00
59	50.00
60 MvS(c)	50.00
61 MMe,MvS(c)	50.00
62 MMe(a&c)	50.00
63 MMe(a&c)	50.00
64 MMe(a&c)	50.00
65 MMe(a&c)	50.00
66 MMe(a&c)	50.00
67 MMe(a&c)	50.00
68 MMe(a&c)	50.00
69 MMe(a&c)	50.00
70 MMe(a&c)	50.00
71 MMe(a&c)	50.00
72 MMe(a&c)	50.00
73 MMe(a&c)	50.00
74 MMe(a&c)	50.00
75 MMe(a&c)	50.00
76 MMe(a&c)	50.00
77 MMe(a&c),Oct., 1956	50.00

HEART THROBS
Comics Magazines (Quality)
Aug., 1949

1 BWa(c),PG,Spoiled Brat	500.00
2 BWa(c),PG,Siren of the Tropics	300.00
3 PG	100.00
4 BWa(c),Greed Turned Me into a Scheming Vixen,Ph(c)	150.00
5 Ph(c)	75.00
6 BWa	150.00
7	75.00
8 BWa	150.00
9 I Hated Men,Ph(c)	125.00
10 BWa,My Secret Fears	135.00
11	60.00
12	60.00
13	60.00
14 BWa	60.00
15 My Right to Happiness,Ph(c)	100.00
16	50.00
17	50.00
18	50.00
19	50.00
20	50.00
21 BWa	100.00
22 BWa	90.00
23 BWa	90.00
24 thru 30	@50.00
31 thru 33	@50.00
34 thru 39	@50.00
40 BWa	75.00
41	50.00
42	50.00
43 thru 45	@50.00

(Please see DC listings)

HECKLE AND JECKLE
St. John Publ./Pines
Nov., 1951

1 Blue Ribbon Comics	250.00
2 Blue Ribbon Comics	125.00
3	85.00
4	75.00
5	75.00
6	75.00
7	65.00
8	60.00
9	60.00
10	60.00
11	50.00
12	50.00
13	50.00
14	50.00
15	50.00
16 thru 20	@45.00
21 thru 33	@40.00
34 June, 1959	40.00

HELLO PAL COMICS
Harvey Publications
Jan., 1943

1 B:Rocketman & Rocket Girl, Mickey Rooney (c), Ph(c) all	900.00
2 Charlie McCarthy (c)	750.00
3 Bob Hope (c), May, 1943	850.00

HENRY
Dell Publishing Co.
Oct., 1946

1	125.00
2	75.00
3 thru 10	@60.00
11 thru 20	@40.00
21 thru 30	@35.00
31 thru 40	@30.00
41 thru 50	@20.00
51 thru 65	@15.00

HENRY ALDRICH COMICS
Dell Publishing Co.
Aug.–Sept., 1950

1	125.00
2	75.00
3	50.00
4	50.00
5	50.00
6 thru 10	@45.00
11 thru 22	@35.00

HEROIC COMICS
Eastern Color Printing Co./
Famous Funnies Aug., 1940

1 BEv(a&c),O:Hydroman,Purple Zombie, B:Man of India	2,500.00
2 BEv(a&c),B:Hydroman (c)s	1,000.00
3 BEv(a&c)	650.00
4 BEv(a&c)	600.00
5 BEv(a&c)	550.00
6 BEv(a&c)	500.00
7 BEv(a&c),O:Man O'Metal	600.00
8 BEv(a&c)	400.00
9 BEv	400.00
10 BEv	400.00
11 BEv,E:Hydroman (c)s	400.00
12 BEv,B&0:Music Master	425.00
13 BEv,RC,LF	400.00
14 BEv	425.00
15 BEv,I:Downbeat	425.00
16 BEv,CCB(c),A:Lieut Nininger, Major Heidger,Lieut Welch,B:P(c)	300.00
17 BEv,A:JohnJames Powers,Hewitt T.Wheless, Irving Strobing	300.00
18 HcK,BEv,Pass the Ammunition	300.00
19 HcK,BEv,A:Barney Ross	300.00
20 HcK,BEv	250.00
21 HcK,BEv	200.00

Heroic Comics #4
© Eastern Color Printing

All comics prices listed are for *Near Mint* condition.

Heroic–Holiday

GOLDEN AGE

Comics Values Annual

#	Description	Price
22	HcK,BEv,Howard Gilmore	200.00
23	HcK,BEv	200.00
24	HcK,BEv	200.00
25	HcK,BEv	200.00
26	HcK,BEv	200.00
27	HcK,BEv	200.00
28	HcK,BEv,E:Man O'Metal	200.00
29	HcK,BEv,E:Hydroman	200.00
30	BEv	200.00
31	BEv,CCB,Capt. Tootsie	65.00
32	ATh,CCB,WWII(c), Capt. Tootsie	75.00
33	ATh,	75.00
34	WWII(c)	65.00
35	Ath,B:Rescue(c)	75.00
36	HcK,ATh	75.00
37	same	75.00
38	ATh	75.00
39	HcK,ATh	75.00
40	ATh,Boxing	75.00
41	Grl(c),ATh	75.00
42	ATh	75.00
43	ATh	65.00
44	HcK,ATh	65.00
45	HcK	65.00
46	HcK	65.00
47	HcK	65.00
48	HcK	65.00
49	HcK	65.00
50	HcK	65.00
51	HcK,ATh,AW	75.00
52	HcK,AW	75.00
53	HcK	70.00
54		55.00
55	ATh	55.00
56	ATh(c)	60.00
57	ATh(c)	60.00
58	ATh(c)	60.00
59	ATh(c)	60.00
60	ATh(c)	60.00
61	BEv(c)	55.00
62	BEv(c)	65.00
63	BEv(c)	65.00
64	GE,BEv(c)	60.00
65	HcK(c),FF,ATh,AW,GE	100.00
66	HcK(c),FF	70.00
67	HcK(c),FF,Korean War(c)	80.00
68	HcK(c),Korean War(c)	70.00
69	HcK(c),FF	100.00
70	HcK(c),FF,B:Korean War(c)	70.00
71	HcK(c),FF	70.00
72	HcK(c),FF	100.00
73	HcK(c),FF	75.00
74	HcK(c)	60.00
75	HcK(c),FF	70.00
76	HcK(c),HcK(c)	40.00
77	same	40.00
78	same	40.00
79	same	40.00
80	same	40.00
81	FF,HcK(c)	40.00
82	FF,HcK(c)	55.00
83	FF,HcK(c)	55.00
84	HcK(c)	55.00
85	HcK(c)	55.00
86	FF,HcK(c)	70.00
87	FF,HcK(c)	70.00
88	HcK(c),E:Korean War (c)s	40.00
89	HcK(c)	40.00
90	HcK(c)	40.00
91	HcK(c)	40.00
92	HcK(c)	40.00
93	HcK(c)	40.00
94	HcK(c)	65.00
95	HcK(c)	40.00
96	HcK(c)	40.00
97	HcK(c),E:P(c),June, 1955	40.00

HICKORY
Comic Magazine
(Quality Comics Group)
Oct., 1949

#	Description	Price
1	ASa,	175.00
2	ASa,	100.00
3	ASa,	75.00
4	ASa,	75.00
5	ASa,	75.00
6	ASa,Aug., 1950	75.00

HI-HO COMICS
Four Star Publications, 1946

#	Description	Price
1	LbC(c)	400.00
2	LbC(c)	250.00
3	1946	220.00

HI-JINX
B & I Publ. Co.
(American Comics Group)
July–Aug., 1947

#	Description	Price
1	(fa) all	225.00
2		175.00
3		100.00
4 thru 7		@75.00
N#		125.00

HI-LITE COMICS
E.R. Ross Publ. Fall, 1945

#	Description	Price
1		200.00

HIT COMICS
Comics Magazine
(Quality Comics Group)
July 1940

#	Description	Price
1	LF(c),O:Neon,Hercules,I:The Red Bee, B:Bob & Swab, Blaze Barton Strange Twins,X-5 Super Agent Casey Jones,Jack & Jill	9,000.00
2	GT,LF(c),B:Old Witch	3,500.00
3	GT,LF(c),E:Casey Jones	3,000.00
4	GT,LF(c),B:Super Agent & Betty Bates,E:X-5	2,700.00
5	GT,LF(c),B:Red Bee (c)	7,500.00
6	GT,LF(c)	2,500.00
7	GT,LF(c),E:Red Bee (c)	2,500.00
8	GT,LF(c),B:Neon (c)	2,500.00
9	JCo,LF(c),E:Neon (c)	2,500.00
10	JCo,RC,LF(c),B:Hercules(c)	2,500.00
11	JCo,RC,LF(c),A:Hercules	2,200.00
12	JCo,RC,LF(c),A:Hercules	2,200.00
13	JCo,RC,LF(c),A:Hercules	2,200.00
14	JCo,RC,LF(c),A:Hercules	2,200.00
15	JCo,RC,A:Hercules	1,500.00
16	JCo,RC,LF(c),A:Hercules	1,500.00
17	JCo,RC,LF(c),E:Hercules(c)	1,500.00
18	JCo,RC(a&c),O:Stormy Foster,B:Ghost of Flanders	1,600.00
19	JCo,RC(c),B:Stormy Foster(c)	1,300.00
20	JCo,RC(c),A:Stormy Foster.	1,400.00
21	JCo,RC(c)	1,350.00
22	JCo.	1,350.00
23	JCo,RC(a&c)	1,300.00
24	JCo,E:Stormy Foster (c)	1,300.00
25	JCo,RP,O:Kid Eternity	2,500.00
26	JCo,RP,A:Black Hawk	1,400.00
27	JCo,RP,B:Kid Eternity (c)s	700.00
28	JCo,RP,A:Her Highness	700.00
29	JCo,RP	700.00
30	JCo,RP,HK,V:Julius Caesar and his Legion of Warriors	600.00
31	JCo,RP	600.00
32	JCo,RP,V:Merlin the Wizard	350.00
33	JCo,RP	300.00
34	JCo,RP,E:Stormy Foster	300.00
35	JCo,Kid Eternity accused of Murder	300.00
36	JCo,The Witch's Curse	300.00
37	JCo,V:Mr. Silence	300.00
38	JCo	300.00
39	JCo,Runaway River Boat	300.00
40	PG,V:Monster from the Past	300.00
41	PG,Did Kid Eternity Lose His Power?	250.00
42	PG,Kid Eternity Loses Killer Cronson	250.00
43	JCo,PG,V:Modern Bluebeard	250.00
44	JCo,PG,Trips up the Shoe	250.00
45	JCo,PG,Pancho Villa against Don Pablo	250.00
46	JCo,V:Mr. Hardeel	250.00
47	A Polished Diamond can be Rough on Rats	250.00
48	EhH,A Treasure Chest of Trouble	250.00
49	EhH,V:Monsters from the Mirror	250.00
50	EhH,Heads for Trouble	250.00
51	EhH,Enters the Forgotten World	225.00
52	EhH,Heroes out of the Past	225.00
53	EhH,V:Mr. Puny	225.00
54	V:Ghost Town Killer	225.00
55	V:The Brute	225.00
56	V:Big Odds	225.00
57	Solves the Picture in a Frame	225.00
58	Destroys Oppression!	225.00
59	Battles Tomorrow's Crimes Today!	225.00
60	E:Kid Eternity (c)s, V:The Mummy	225.00
61	RC(a&c),I:Jeb Rivers	250.00
62	RC(c)	200.00
63	RC(c),A:Jeb Rivers	250.00
64	RC,A:Jeb Rivers	250.00
65	Bondage (c),RC,July, 1950	275.00

HOLIDAY COMICS
Fawcett Publ., Nov., 1942

#	Description	Price
1	Captain Marvel (c)	2,000.00

HOLIDAY COMICS
Star Publ., Jan., 1951

#	Description	Price
1	LbC(c),(fa),Christmas (c)	400.00
2	LbC(c),Parade(c)	450.00
3	LbC(c),July 4th(c)	250.00

Hit Comics #9
© Quality Comics Group

GOLDEN AGE

Holiday–Horse

4 LbC(c),Vacation(c) 250.00
5 LbC(c),Christmas(c) 250.00
6 LbC(c),Birthday(c). 250.00
7 LbC(c) 225.00
8 LbC(c),Christmas(c) 250.00

HOLLYWOOD COMICS
New Age Publishers
Winter, 1944
1 (fa) 175.00

HOLLYWOOD CONFESSIONS
St. John Publ. Co.
Oct., 1949
1 JKu(a&c) 300.00
2 JKu(a&c), Dec., 1949 . . . . 350.00

HOLLYWOOD DIARY
Comics Magazine
(Quality Comics), Dec., 1949
1 . . . . 200.00
2 Photo (c) 125.00
3 Photo (c) 100.00
4 . . . . 100.00
5 Photo (c), Aug., 1950 . . . . 100.00

HOLLYWOOD FILM STORIES
Feature Publications
(Prize) April, 1950
1 June Allison,Ph(c). 200.00
2 Lizabeth Scott,Ph(c) 150.00
3 Barbara Stanwick,Ph(c) 150.00
4 Beth Hutton, Aug., 1950 . . . . . 150.00

HOLLYWOOD SECRETS
Comics Magazine
(Quality Comics Group)
Nov., 1949
1 BWa,BWa(c) 350.00
2 BWa,BWa(c),RC 250.00
3 Ph(c) 125.00
4 Ph(c),May, 1950 . . . . 125.00
5 Ph(c) 125.00
6 Ph(c) 125.00

HOLYOKE ONE-SHOT
Tem Publ.
(Holyoke Publ. Co.), 1944
1 Grit Grady 150.00
2 Rusty Dugan 150.00
3 JK,Miss Victory,O:Cat Woman. 350.00
4 Mr. Miracle 125.00
5 U.S. Border Patrol 150.00
6 Capt. Fearless 125.00
7 Strong Man 150.00
8 Blue Streak 125.00
9 S&K, Citizen Smith 200.00
10 S&K, Capt. Stone. 225.00

HONEYMOON ROMANCE
Artful Publications
(Digest Size) April, 1950
1 . . . . 400.00
2 July, 1950 . . . . 375.00

HOODED HORSEMAN
See: OUT OF THE NIGHT

HOPALONG CASSIDY
Fawcett Publications
Feb., 1943
1 B:Hopalong Cassidy & Topper,
  Captain Marvel (c) 7,000.00
2 . . . . 1,000.00
3 Blazing Trails 500.00
4 5-full length story 400.00
5 Death in the Saddle, Ph(c) . . . 350.00
6 . . . . 300.00
7 . . . . 300.00
8 Phantom Stage Coach 300.00
9 The Last Stockade 300.00
10 4-spine tingling adventures . . 300.00
11 Desperate Jetters! Ph(c) 200.00
12 The Mysterious Message 200.00
13 The Human Target, Ph(c) 200.00
14 Land of the Lawless, Ph(c). . . 200.00
15 Death holds the Reins, Ph(c) . 200.00
16 Webfoot's Revenge, Ph(c) . . . 200.00
17 The Hangman's Noose, Ph(c) 200.00
18 The Ghost of Dude Ranch,
  Ph(c) 200.00
19 A:William Boyd,Ph(c) 200.00
20 The Notorious Nellie Blaine!,
  B:P(c). 175.00
21 V:Arizona Kid. 175.00
22 V:Arizona Kid. 175.00
23 Hayride Horror 175.00
24 Twin River Giant 175.00
25 On the Trails of the Wild
  and Wooly West 175.00
26 thru 30 . . . . @150.00
31 52 pages 125.00
32 36 pages 125.00
33 52 pages 125.00
34 52 pages 125.00
35 52 pages 125.00
36 36 pages 100.00
37 thru 40, 52 pages . . . . @125.00
40 36 pages 125.00
41 E:P(c). 125.00
42 B:Ph(c) 100.00
43 . . . . 100.00
44 . . . . 75.00
45 . . . . 90.00
46 thru 51 . . . . @75.00
52 . . . . 70.00
53 . . . . 75.00
54 . . . . 75.00
55 . . . . 70.00
56 . . . . 75.00
57 thru 70 . . . . @75.00
71 thru 84 . . . . @60.00

Hopalong Cassidy #5
© *Fawcett Publications*

85 E:Ph(c),Jan., 1954 . . . . 75.00
(See also: DC listings)

HOPPY THE MARVEL BUNNY
Fawcett Publications
Dec., 1945
1 A:Marvel Bunny 300.00
2 . . . . 150.00
3 . . . . 125.00
4 . . . . 125.00
5 . . . . 125.00
6 thru 14 . . . . @100.00
15 Sept., 1947 . . . . 100.00

HORRIFIC
Artful/Comic Media/
Harwell Publ./Mystery
Sept., 1952
1 Conductor in Flames(c). 550.00
2 Human Puppets(c) 300.00
3 DH(c),Bullet hole in
  head(c) 600.00
4 DH(c),head on a stick (c) 250.00
5 DH(c) 250.00
6 DH(c),Jack the Ripper 225.00
7 DH(c),Shrunken Skulls 225.00
8 DH(c),I:The Teller 250.00
9 DH(c),Claws of Horror, Wolves
  of Midnight 225.00
10 DH(c),The Teller-four
  eerie tales of Horror 225.00
11 DH(c),A:Gary Ghoul,Freddie,
  Demon,Victor Vampire
  Walter Werewolf 200.00
12 DH(c),A:Gary Ghoul,Freddie
  Demon,Victor Vampire,
  Walter Werewolf 200.00
13 DH(c),A:Gary Ghoul,Freddie
  Demom,Victor Vampire,
  Walter Werewolf 200.00
Becomes:

TERRIFIC COMICS
Dec., 1954
14 . . . . 350.00
15 . . . . 300.00
16 B:Wonderboy. 300.00
Becomes:

WONDERBOY
Ajax/Farrell Publ., May, 1955
17 The Enemy's Enemy 500.00
18 Success is No Accident,
  July, 1955. . . . . 450.00

HORROR FROM THE TOMB
See: MYSTERIOUS STORIES

HORRORS, THE
Star Publications
Jan., 1953–April, 1954
11 LbC(c),JyD,of War 350.00
12 LbC(c),of War 350.00
13 LbC(c),of Mystery 300.00
14 LbC(c),of the Underworld. . . . 350.00
15 LbC(c),of the Underworld. . . . 350.00

HORSE FEATHER COMICS
Lev Gleason Publications
Nov., 1947
1 BW 225.00

All comics prices listed are for Near Mint condition.

GOLDEN AGE

Horse–Indian

2 .... 100.00
3 .... 75.00
4 Summer, 1948 .... 75.00

HOT ROD AND SPEEDWAY COMICS
Hillman Periodicals Feb.–March, 1952

1 .... 350.00
2 BK 200.00
3 .... 125.00
4 .... 125.00
5 April–May, 1953 .... 125.00

HOT ROD COMICS
Fawcett Publications Feb., 1952–53

N# BP,BP(c),F:Clint Curtis 350.00
2 BP,BP(c),Safety comes First .. 200.00
3 BP,BP(c),The Racing Game .. 150.00
4 BP,BP(c),Bonneville National
  Championships 150.00
5 BP,BP(c), ... 150.00
6 BP,BP(c),Race to Death 150.00

HOT ROD KING
Approved Comics (Ziff-Davis), Fall, 1952

1 P(c) 300.00

HOWDY DOODY
Dell Publishing Co. Jan., 1950

1 Ph(c) 1,500.00
2 Ph(c) 600.00
3 Ph(c) 325.00
4 Ph(c) 325.00
5 Ph(c) 325.00
6 P(c) 350.00
7 .... 225.00
8 .... 225.00
9 .... 225.00
10 .... 225.00
11 .... 200.00
12 .... 200.00
13 Christmas (c) 200.00
14 thru 20 .... @200.00
21 thru 38 .... @150.00

HOW STALIN HOPES WE WILL DESTROY AMERICA
Pictorial News, 1951

N# (Giveaway) 550.00

HUMBUG
Harvey Kurtzman, 1957

1 JDa,WW,WE,End of the World 350.00
2 JDa,WE,Radiator 150.00
3 JDa,WE 125.00
4 JDa,WE,Queen Victoria(c) ... 125.00
5 JDa,WE 125.00
6 JDa,WE 125.00
7 JDa,WE,Sputnik(c) 135.00
8 JDa,WE,Elvis/George
  Washington(c) 125.00
9 JDa,WE 125.00
10 JDa,Magazine 150.00
11 JDw,WE,HK,Magazine 150.00

HUMDINGER
Novelty Press/Premium Service May–June, 1946

1 B:Jerkwater Line,Dink,
  Mickey Starlight 400.00
2 .... 150.00
3 .... 125.00
4 .... 125.00
5 .... 125.00
6 .... 125.00
2-1 .... 100.00
2-2 July–Aug., 1947 .... 100.00

HUMPHREY COMICS
Harvey Publications Oct., 1948

1 BP,Joe Palooka 125.00
2 BP 75.00
3 BP 60.00
4 BP,A:Boy Heroes 75.00
5 BP 50.00
6 BP 50.00
7 BP,A:Little Dot 50.00
8 BP,O:Humphrey 55.00
9 BP 35.00
10 BP 35.00
11 thru 21 .... @35.00
22 April, 1952 .... 35.00

HYPER MYSTERY COMICS
Hyper Publications, May, 1940

1 B:Hyper 2,600.00
2 June, 1940 .... 1,300.00

Ibis The Invincible #5
© Hyper Publications

IBIS, THE INVINCIBLE
Fawcett Publications Jan., 1942–Spring, 1948

1 MRa(c),O:Ibis 2,500.00
2 Bondage (c) 1,200.00
3 BW 1,000.00
4 BW,A:Mystic Snake People .. 600.00
5 BW,Bondage (c),The
  Devil's Ibistick 650.00
6 BW, The Book of Evil 650.00

IDEAL ROMANCE
See: TENDER ROMANCE

Comics Values Annual

IF THE DEVIL WOULD TALK
Catechetical Guild, 1950

N# Rare 800.00
N#, 1958 Very Rare 600.00

ILLUSTRATED STORIES OF THE OPERA
B. Bailey Publ. Co., 1943

N# Faust 800.00
N# Aida 750.00
N# Carman 750.00
N# Rigoletto 750.00

I LOVED
See: ZOOT COMICS

I LOVE LUCY COMICS
Dell Publishing Co., 1954

(1) see Dell Four Color #535
(2) see Dell Four Color #559
3 Lucile Ball Ph(c) all 325.00
4 .... 300.00
5 .... 300.00
6 thru 10 .... @250.00
11 thru 20 .... @175.00
21 thru 35 .... @150.00

IMPACT
E.C. Comics March–April, 1955

1 RC,GE,BK,Grl 250.00
2 RC,JDu,Grl,BK,JO 150.00
3 JO,RC,JDU,Grl,JKa,BK 125.00
4 RC,JO,JDa,GE,Grl,BK 125.00
5 Nov.–Dec., 1955 .... 125.00

INCREDIBLE SCIENCE FANTASY
See: WEIRD SCIENCE

INCREDIBLE SCIENCE FICTION
E.C. Comics, July–Aug., 1955

30 JDa,BK,JO,WW 600.00
31 AW,WW,BK 550.00
32 AW,JDa,BK,JO 550.00
33 JDa,BK,JO,WW 550.00

INDIAN CHIEF
Dell Publishing Co. July–Sept., 1951

3 P(c) all 60.00
4 .... 50.00
5 .... 50.00
6 A:White Eagle 50.00
7 .... 50.00
8 .... 50.00
9 .... 50.00
10 .... 50.00
11 .... 50.00
12 I:White Eagle 55.00
13 thru 29 .... @40.00
30 SB 45.00
31 thru 33 SB .... @45.00

INDIAN FIGHTER
Youthful Magazines May, 1950

1 Revenge of Chief Crazy Horse 125.00
2 Bondage (c) 80.00

CVA Page 410 — All comics prices listed are for *Near Mint* condition.

GOLDEN AGE

3 . . . . 50.00
4 Cheyenne Warpath 50.00
5 . . . . 50.00
6 Davy Crockett in Death Stalks
 the Alamo 50.00
7 Tom Horn-Bloodshed at
 Massacre Valley 50.00
8 Tales of Wild Bill Hickory,
 Jan., 1952 . . . . 50.00

INDIANS
**Wings Publ. Co.
(Fiction House) Spring, 1950**
1 B:Long Bow, Manzar, White
 Indian & Orphan 300.00
2 B:Starlight 150.00
3 Longbow(c). 125.00
4 Longbow(c). 100.00
5 Manzar(c). 125.00
6 Captive of the Semecas 100.00
7 Longbow(c). 100.00
8 A:Long Bow 100.00
9 A:Long Bow 100.00
10 Manzar(c) 100.00
11 thru 16 . . . . @75.00
17 Spring, 1953,Longbow(c). 75.00

Indians on the Warpath
© *St. John Publ. Co.*

INDIANS ON THE WARPATH
St. John Publ. Co., 1950
N# MB(c). 350.00

INFORMER, THE
**Feature Television
Productions, April, 1954**
1 MSy,The Greatest Social
 Menace of our Time! 125.00
2 MSy 75.00
3 MSy 60.00
4 MSy 60.00
5 Dec., 1954 . . . . 60.00

IN LOVE
Mainline, Aug., 1954
1 S&K,Bride of the Star 400.00
2 S&K,Marilyn's Men 250.00
3 S&K 250.00
4 S&K,Comics Code 200.00
5 S&K(c) 100.00
6 . . . . 75.00

Becomes:
I LOVE YOU
Charlton Comics, Sept., 1955
7 JK(c),BP 125.00
8 . . . . 50.00
9 . . . . 50.00
10 . . . . 50.00
11 thru 16 . . . . @40.00
17 . . . . 35.00
18 . . . . 25.00
19 . . . . 25.00
20 . . . . 25.00
21 thru 50 . . . . @20.00
51 thru 59 . . . . @15.00
60 Elvis 225.00
61 thru 100 . . . . @8.00
101 thru 130 . . . . @8.00

INTERNATIONAL COMICS
See: CRIME PATROL

INTERNATIONAL CRIME PATROL
See: CRIME PATROL

INTIMATE CONFESSIONS
**Fawcett Publ./
Realistic Comics, 1951**
1a P(c) all, Unmarried Bride . . . 850.00
1 EK,EK(c),Days of Temptation...
 Nights of Desire 250.00
2 Doomed to Silence 225.00
3 EK(c), The Only Man For Me . 250.00
3a Robert Briffault 225.00
4 EK(c),Tormented Love 225.00
5 Her Secret Sin 225.00
6 Reckless Pick-up 225.00
7 A Love Like Ours,Spanking . . . 250.00
8 Fatal Woman, March, 1953 . . 225.00

INTIMATE LOVE
**Standard Magazines
Jan., 1950**
5 Wings on My Heart,Ph(c) 75.00
6 WE,JSe,Ph(c). 100.00
7 WE,JSe,Ph(c),I Toyed
 with Love 100.00
8 WE,JSe,Ph(c). 100.00
9 Ph(c) 50.00
10 Ph(c),My Hopeless Heart. 75.00
11 . . . . 40.00
12 . . . . 40.00
13 thru 18 . . . . @40.00
19 ATh 75.00
20 . . . . 30.00
21 ATh 75.00
22 ATh 75.00
23 ATh 30.00
24 ATh 75.00
25 ATh 30.00
26 ATh 75.00
27 ATh 30.00
28 ATh,Aug., 1954 . . . . 30.00

INTIMATE SECRETS OF ROMANCE
**Star Publications
Sept., 1953**
1 LbC(c) 225.00
2 LbC(c) 200.00

INVISIBLE SCARLET O'NEIL
**Harvey Publications
Dec., 1950**
1 . . . . 150.00
2 . . . . 100.00
3 April, 1951 . . . . 100.00

IRON VIC
**United Features Syndicate/
St. John Publ. Co., 1940**
1-shot 300.00

IT REALLY HAPPENED
**William H. Wise/
Visual Editions, 1945**
1 Benjamin Franklin, Kit Carson 250.00
2 The Terrible Tiddlers 125.00
3 Maid of the Margiris 100.00
4 Chaplain Albert J. Hoffman . . 100.00
5 AS(c),Monarchs of the Sea,Lou
 Gehrig, Amelia Earhart 200.00
6 AS(c),Ernie Pyle 100.00
7 FG,Teddy Roosevelt,Jefferson
 Davis,Story of the Helicopter. 100.00
8 FG,Man O' War,Roy Rogers . . 200.00
9 AS(c),The Story of
 Old Ironsides 100.00
10 AS(c),Honus Wagner, The
 Story of Mark Twain 150.00
11 AS(c),MB,Queen of the Spanish
 Main, Oct., 1947. . . . . 125.00

JACE PEARSON OF THE TEXAS RANGERS
**Dell Publishing Co.
May, 1952**
(1) see Dell Four Color #396
2 Ph(c),Joel McRae 75.00
3 Ph(c),Joel McRae 75.00
4 Ph(c),Joel McRae 75.00
5 Ph(c),Joel McRae 75.00
6 Ph(c),Joel McRae 75.00
7 Ph(c),Joel McRae 75.00
8 Ph(c),Joel McRae 75.00
9 Ph(c),Joel McRae 75.00
(10) see Dell Four Color #648
Becomes:
TALES OF JACE PEARSON OF THE TEXAS RANGERS
Feb., 1955
11 . . . . 50.00
12 . . . . 50.00
13 . . . . 50.00
14 . . . . 50.00
15 ATh 60.00
16 ATh 60.00
17 thru 20 . . . . @50.00

JACK ARMSTRONG
**Parents' Institute
Nov., 1947**
1 Artic Mystery 500.00
2 Den of the Golden Dragon . . . 225.00
3 Lost Valley of Ice 150.00
4 Land of the Leopard Men 150.00
5 Fight against Racketeers of
 the Ring 150.00
6 . . . . 125.00
7 Baffling Mystery on the
 Diamond 125.00
8 . . . . 125.00

GOLDEN AGE

Jack–Joe College

9 Mystery of the Midgets 125.00
10 Secret Cargo 125.00
11 .... 125.00
12 Madman's Island, rare 150.00
13 Sept., 1949 .... 125.00

JACKIE GLEASON
**St. John Publishing Co.
Sept., 1955**
1 Ph(c) 750.00
2 .... 500.00
3 .... 450.00
4 Dec., 1955 .... 450.00

JACKIE ROBINSON
**Fawcett Publications
May, 1950**
N# Ph(c) all issues 1,200.00
2 .... 750.00
3 thru 5 .... @600.00
6 May, 1952 .... 550.00

JACK IN THE BOX
See: YELLOW JACKET COMICS

JACKPOT COMICS
MLJ Magazines, Spring, 1941
1 CBi(c),B:Black Hood,Mr.Justice,
  Steel Sterling,Sgt.Boyle .. 4,000.00
2 SCp(c), ... 2,000.00
3 Bondage (c) 1,500.00
4 First Archie 5,000.00
5 Hitler(c) 2,000.00
6 Son of the Skull v:Black
  Hood, Bondage(c) 1,400.00
7 Bondage (c) 1,400.00
8 Sal(c), ... 1,400.00
9 Sal(c), ... 1,400.00
Becomes:

JOLLY JINGLES
Summer, 1943
10 Super Duck,(fa) 400.00
11 Super Duck 200.00
12 Hitler parody (c),A:Woody
   Woodpecker 150.00
13 thru 15 Super Duck ..... @100.00
16 Dec., 1944 .... 100.00

JACK THE GIANT KILLER
**Bimfort & Co.
Aug.–Sept., 1953**
1 HcK,HcK(c). 250.00

JAMBOREE
**Round Publishing Co.
Feb., 1946**
1 .... 300.00
2 March, 1946 .... 175.00

JANE ARDEN
**St. John Publ. Co.
March, 1948**
1 .... 200.00
2 June, 1948 .... 150.00

JEEP COMICS
**R.B. Leffingwell & Co.
Winter, 1944**
1 B;Captain Power. 650.00
2 .... 350.00

3 LbC(c),March–April, 1948 ... 600.00

JEFF JORDAN, U.S. AGENT
D.S. Publ. Co., Dec., 1947
1 .... 150.00

JESSE JAMES
**Avon Periodicals/
Realistic Publ., Aug., 1950**
1 JKu,The San Antonio Stage
  Robbery 200.00
2 JKu,The Daring Liberty Bank
  Robbery 150.00
3 JKu,The California Stagecoach
  Robberies 125.00
4 EK(c),Deadliest Deed! 60.00
5 JKu,WW,Great Prison Break . 125.00
6 JKu,Wanted Dead or Alive ... 125.00
7 JKu,Six-Gun Slaughter at
  San Romano!............. 100.00
8 EK,Daring Train Robbery! ... 75.00
9 EK 60.00
10 thru 14 {Do not exist}
15 EK 75.00
16 EK, Butch Cassidy......... 50.00
17 EK, Jessie James 45.00
18 JKu 45.00
19 JKu 45.00
20 AW,FF,A:Chief Vic,Kit West .. 150.00
21 EK, Two Jessie James...... 45.00
22 EK, Chuck Wagon 45.00
23 EK. 45.00
24 EK,B:New McCarty 45.00
25 EK. 45.00
26 EK. 45.00
27 EK,E:New McCarty 45.00
28 Quantrells Raiders........ 45.00
29 Aug., 1956............... 45.00

JEST
Harry 'A' Chesler, 1944
10 J. Rebel,Yankee Boy 200.00
11 1944,Little Nemo 225.00

JET ACES
**Real Adventure Publ. Co.
(Fiction House), 1952**
1 Set 'em up in MIG Alley 150.00
2 Kiss-Off for Moscow Molly ... 75.00
3 Red Task Force Sighted 75.00
4 Death-Date at 40,000, 1953 ... 75.00

JET FIGHTERS
**Standard Magazines
Nov., 1953**
5 ATh,Korean War Stories 125.00
6 Circus Pilot 50.00
7 ATh, Iron Curtains for Ivan,
  March, 1953 .... 75.00

JETTA OF THE 21st CENTURY
Standard Comics, Dec., 1952
5 Teen Stories 235.00
6 Robot (c) 150.00
7 April, 1953 .... 150.00

JIGGS AND MAGGIE
**Best Books (Standard)/
Harvey Publ., June, 1949**
11 .... 125.00
12 thru 21 .... @75.00
22 thru 26................. @50.00

27 Feb.–March, 1954 .... 50.00

JIM HARDY
Spotlight Publ., 1944
N# Dynamite Jim,Mirror Man ... 500.00

JIM RAY'S AVIATION SKETCH BOOK
Vital Publishers, Feb., 1946
1 Radar, the Invisible eye 400.00
2 Gen.Hap Arnold, May, 1946 .. 300.00

*Jingle Jangle Comics #15
© Eastern Color Printing*

JINGLE JANGLE COMICS
**Eastern Color Printing Co.
Feb., 1942**
1 B:Benny Bear,Pie Face Prince,
  Jingle Jangle Tales,Hortense 500.00
2 GCn 250.00
3 GCn 225.00
4 GCn,Pie Face (c) 225.00
5 GCn,B:Pie Face 225.00
6 GCn, ... 175.00
7 .... 175.00
8 .... 175.00
9 .... 175.00
10 .... 175.00
11 thru 15 E:Pie Face ...... @150.00
16 thru 20 .... @125.00
21 thru 25 .... @100.00
26 thru 30 .... @100.00
31 thru 41 .... @75.00
42 Dec., 1949............... 75.00

JING PALS
**Victory Publ. Corp.
Feb., 1946**
1 Johnny Rabbit 150.00
2 .... 75.00
3 .... 75.00
4 Aug., 1948 .... 75.00

JOE COLLEGE
**Hillman Periodicals
Fall, 1949**
1 BP,DPr 125.00
2 BP, Winter, 1949 .... 100.00

CVA Page 412   All comics prices listed are for *Near Mint* condition.

GOLDEN AGE

JOE LOUIS
Fawcett Periodicals
Sept., 1950
1 Ph(c),Life Story........... 750.00
2 Ph(c),Nov., 1950 .... 500.00

JOE PALOOKA
Publication Enterprises
(Columbia Comics Group) 1943
1 Lost in the Desert 1,200.00
2 Hitler (c) 750.00
3 KO's the Nazis! 400.00
4 Eiffel tower (c), 1944 .... 350.00

JOE PALOOKA
Harvey Publications
Nov., 1954–March, 1961
1 Joe Tells How he became
   World Champ 600.00
2 Skiing (c) 250.00
3 .... 165.00
4 Welcome Home Pals! 165.00
5 S&K,The Great Carnival
   Murder Mystery 250.00
6 Classic Joe Palooka (c) .. 165.00
7 BP,V:Grumpopski 165.00
8 BP,Mystery of the Ghost Ship 125.00
9 Drooten Island Mystery ... 125.00
10 BP..................... 125.00
11 .... 100.00
12 BP,Boxing Course 100.00
13 .... 110.00
14 BP,Palooka's Toughest Fight . 110.00
15 BP,O:Humphrey.......... 165.00
16 BP,A:Humphrey 110.00
17 BP,A:Humphrey 110.00
18 .... 110.00
19 BP,Freedom Train(c) 125.00
20 Punch Out(c) 110.00
21 .... 75.00
22 V:Assassin.............. 75.00
23 Big Bathing Beauty Issue. 75.00
24 .... 75.00
25 .... 75.00
26 BP,Big Prize Fight Robberies .. 75.00
27 BP,Mystery of Bal
   Eagle Cabin 75.00
28 BP,Fights out West 75.00
29 BP,Joe Busts Crime
   Wide Open 75.00
30 BP,V:Hoodlums 70.00
31 BP...................... 70.00
32 BP,Fight Palooka was sure
   to Lose................ 70.00
33 BP,Joe finds Ann 70.00
34 BP,How to Box like a Champ .. 70.00
35 BP,More Adventures of Little
   Max 70.00
36 BP...................... 70.00
37 BP,Joe as a Boy 70.00
38 BP...................... 70.00
39 BP,Original Hillbillies with
   Big Leviticus.......... 70.00
40 BP,Joe's Toughest Fight .. 70.00
41 BP,Humphrey's Grudge Fight. 70.00
42 BP...................... 70.00
43 BP...................... 70.00
44 BP,M:Ann Howe.......... 75.00
45 BP...................... 60.00
46 Champ of Champs......... 60.00
47 BP,BreathtakingUnderwaterBattle . 60.00
48 BP,Exciting Indian Adventure . 60.00
49 BP...................... 60.00
50 BP,Bondage(c) 60.00
51 BP...................... 60.00
52 BP,V:Balonki 60.00
53 BP...................... 60.00
54 V:Bad Man Trigger McGehee. 60.00
55 .... 60.00

Joe Palooka #1
© Harvey Publications

56 Foul Play on the High Seas ... 60.00
57 Curtains for the Champ 60.00
58 V:The Man-Eating Swamp
   Terror................. 60.00
59 The Enemy Attacks 60.00
60 Joe Fights Escaped Convict .. 60.00
61 .... 50.00
62 S&K..................... 75.00
63 .... 50.00
64 .... 50.00
65 .... 50.00
66 .... 50.00
67 .... 50.00
68 .... 50.00
69 A Package from Home..... 50.00
70 BP...................... 50.00
71 .... 50.00
72 .... 50.00
73 BP...................... 50.00
74 thru 118 .... @50.00
Giant 1 Body Building........ 100.00
Giant 2 Fights His Way Back .. 150.00
Giant 3 Visits Lost City 80.00
Giant 4 All in Family 100.00

JOE YANK
Visual Editions
(Standard Comics)
March, 1952
5 ATh,WE,Korean Jackpot! 75.00
6 Bacon and Bullets,
   G.I.Renegade 100.00
7 Two-Man War,A:Sgt. Glamour . 50.00
8 ATh(c),Miss Foxhole of 1952, . 50.00
9 G.I.'s and Dolls,Colonel Blood . 40.00
10 A Good Way to Die,
   A:General Joe 40.00
11 .... 40.00
12 RA..................... 40.00
13 .... 40.00
14 .... 40.00
15 .... 40.00
16 July, 1954 .... 40.00

JOHN HIX SCRAPBOOK
Eastern Color Printing Co.
1937
1 Strange as It Seems 450.00
2 Strange as It Seems 350.00

JOHNNY DANGER
Toby Press, Aug., 1954
1 Ph(c),Private Detective 200.00

JOHNNY DYNAMITE
See: DYNAMITE

JOHNNY HAZARD
Best Books
(Standard Comics)
Aug., 1948
5 FR...................... 200.00
6 FR,FR(c) 175.00
7 FR(c).................... 100.00
8 FR,FR(c), May, 1949 ..... 100.00

JOHNNY LAW,
SKY RANGER
Good Comics (Lev Gleason)
April, 1955
1 .... 100.00
2 .... 50.00
3 .... 50.00
4 Nov., 1955 .... 50.00

JOHN WAYNE
ADVENTURE COMICS
Toby Press, Winter, 1949
1 Ph(c),The Mysterious Valley
   of Violence 2,000.00
2 AW,FF,Ph(c) 900.00
3 AW,FF,Flying Sheriff 900.00
4 AW,FF,Double-Danger,Ph(c) . 900.00
5 Volcano of Death,Ph(c) ... 600.00
6 AW,FF,Caravan of Doom,
   Ph(c) 800.00
7 AW,FF,Ph(c) 600.00
8 AW,FF,Duel of Death,Ph(c) . 900.00
9 Ghost Guns,Ph(c) 450.00
10 Dangerous Journey,Ph(c)... 400.00
11 Manhunt!,Ph(c) 400.00
12 HK,Joins the Marines,Ph(c) . 400.00
13 V:Frank Stacy 350.00
14 Operation Peeping John ... 350.00
15 Bridge Head 350.00
16 AW,FF,Golden Double-Cross . 350.00
17 Murderer's Music......... 350.00
18 AW,FF,Larson's Folly 400.00
19 .... 300.00
20 Whale (c)................ 300.00
21 .... 300.00
22 Flash Flood!............. 300.00
23 Death on Two Wheels 300.00
24 Desert 300.00
25 AW,FF,Hondo!,Ph(c)...... 450.00
26 Ph(c).................... 375.00
27 Ph(c).................... 375.00
28 Dead Man's Boots! 375.00
29 AW,FF,Ph(c),Crash in
   California Desert....... 450.00
30 The Wild One, Ph(c) 375.00
31 AW,FF,May, 1955.......... 450.00

JO-JO COMICS
Fox Features Syndicate
Spring, 1946
N# (fa) 200.00
2 (fa) 100.00
3 (fa).................... 100.00
4 (fa) 100.00
5 (fa) 100.00
6 (fa).................... 100.00
7 B:Jo-Jo Congo King....... 1,200.00
8 (7)B:Tanee,V:The
   Giant Queen........... 750.00

All comics prices listed are for *Near Mint* condition.

9 (8)The Mountain of Skulls.... 700.00
10 (9)Death of the Fanged Lady . 650.00
11 (10) 650.00
12 (11)Bondage(c),
 Water Warriors 625.00
13 (12) Jade Juggernaut....... 600.00
14 The Leopards of Learda..... 600.00
15 The Flaming Fiend......... 600.00
16 Golden Gorilla,bondage(c)... 600.00
17 Stark-Mad Thespian,
 bondage(c)................ 675.00
18 The Death Traveler 600.00
19 Gladiator of Gore 600.00
20 .... 600.00
21 .... 600.00
22 .... 600.00
23 .... 600.00
24 .... 600.00
25 Bondage(c) 675.00
26 .... 600.00
27 .... 600.00
28 .... 600.00
29 July, 1949 .... 650.00

JOURNEY INTO FEAR
Superior Publications
May, 1951–Sept., 1954
1 MB,Preview of Chaos....... 850.00
2 Debt to the Devil........... 600.00
3 Midnight Prowler 500.00
4 Invisible Terror 500.00
5 Devil Cat 350.00
6 Partners in Blood 350.00
7 The Werewolf Lurks 350.00
8 Bells of the Damned........ 350.00
9 Masked Death 350.00
10 Gallery of the Dead 350.00
11 Beast of Bedlam 300.00
12 No Rest for the Dead....... 300.00
13 Cult of the Dead........... 300.00
14 Jury of the Undead 300.00
15 Corpse in Make-up 350.00
16 Death by Invitation......... 275.00
17 Deadline for Death......... 275.00
18 Here's to Horror........... 275.00
19 This Body is Mine!......... 275.00
20 Masters of the Dead 275.00
21 Horror in the Clock........ 275.00

JUDO JOE
Jay-Jay Corp.
Aug., 1952
1 Drug..................... 100.00
2 .... 50.00
3 Drug, Dec., 1953 .... 60.00

JUDY CANOVA
Fox Features Syndicate
May, 1950–Sept., 1950
23 (1)WW(a&c).............. 250.00
24 (2)WW(a&c).............. 235.00
3 JO,WW(a&c) 275.00

JUKE BOX
Famous Funnies
March, 1948
1 ATh(c),Spike Jones......... 500.00
2 Dinah Shore,Transvestitism .. 300.00
3 Vic Damone, Peggie Lee 250.00
4 Jimmy Durante............. 250.00
5 .... 250.00
6 Jan., 1949,Desi Arnaz 300.00

Jumbo Comics #27
© Fiction House

JUMBO COMICS
Real Adventure Publ. Co.
(Fiction House)
Sept., 1938
1 LF,BKa,JK,WE(a&c),B:Sheena
 Queen of the Jungle,The Hawk
 The Hunchback 27,000.00
2 LF,JK,WE,BKa,BP,
 O:Sheena 9,000.00
3 JK,WE(a&c),BP,LF,BKa ... 6,000.00
4 WE(a&c),MMe,LF,BKa,
 O:The Hawk 5,800.00
5 WE(a&c),BP,BKa 5,000.00
6 WE(a&c),BP,BKa 4,500.00
7 WE,BKa,BP 4,400.00
8 LF(c),BP,BKa,World of
 Tomorrow............ 4,400.00
9 LF(c),BP 3,500.00
10 WE,LF(c),BKa,Regular size
 issues begin 2,500.00
11 LF(c),WE&BP,War of the
 Emerald Gas 2,000.00
12 WE(c),WE&BP,Hawk in Buccaneer
 Vengeance,Bondage(c) ... 2,100.00
13 WE(c),BP,Sheena in The
 Thundering Herds 2,000.00
14 WE(c),LF,BP,Hawk in Siege
 of Thunder Isle,B:Lightning 2,100.00
15 BP(a&c),Sheena(c)....... 1,000.00
16 BP(a&c),The Lightning
 Strikes Twice.......... 1,500.00
17 BP(c), B:Sheena covers
 and lead stories......... 1,000.00
18 BP 1,000.00
19 BP(c),BKa,Warriors of
 the Bush 1,000.00
20 BP,BKa,Spoilers of the Wild 1,000.00
21 BP,BKa,Prey of the
 Giant Killers 800.00
22 BP,BKa,Victims of the
 Super-Ape,O:Hawk....... 900.00
23 BP,BKa,Swamp of the
 Green Terror............ 900.00
24 BP,BKa,Curse of the Black
 Venom 900.00
25 BP,BKa,Bait for the Beast ... 800.00
26 BP,BKa,Tiger-Man Terror 800.00
27 BP,BKa,Sabre-Tooth Terror .. 800.00
28 BKa,RWd,The Devil of
 the Congo 800.00
29 BKa,RWd,Elephant-Scourge . 800.00
30 BKa,RWd,Slashing Fangs ... 800.00
31 BKa,RWd,Voodoo Treasure
 of Black Slave Lake 750.00

32 BKa,RWd,AB,Captives of
 the Gorilla-Men.......... 750.00
33 BKa,RWd,AB,Stampede
 Tusks................. 750.00
34 BKa,RWd,AB,Claws of the
 Devil-Cat 750.00
35 BKa,RWd,AB,Hostage of the
 Devil Apes 750.00
36 BKa,RWd,AB,Voodoo Flames 750.00
37 BKa,RWd,AB,Congo Terror .. 750.00
38 BKa,RWd,ABDeath-Trap of
 the River Demons........ 750.00
39 BKa,RWd,AB,Cannibal Bait .. 750.00
40 BKa,RWd,AB,
 Assagai Poison 750.00
41 BKa,RWd,AB,Killer's Kraal,
 Bondage(c)............. 600.00
42 BKa,RWd,AB,Plague of
 Spotted Killers 600.00
43 BKa,RWd,AB,Beasts of the
 Devil Queen 600.00
44 BKa,RWd,AB,Blood-Cult of
 K'Douma 600.00
45 BKa,RWd,AB,Fanged
 Keeper of the Fire-Gem ... 600.00
46 BKa,RWd,AB,Lair of the
 Armored Monsters 600.00
47 BKa,RWd,AB,The Bantu
 Blood-Monster 600.00
48 BKa,RWd,AB,Red Meat for
 the Cat-Pack 600.00
49 BKa,RWd,AB,Empire of the
 Hairy Ones............. 600.00
50 BKa,RWd,AB,Eyrie of the
 Leopard Birds 600.00
51 BKa,RWd.AB,Monsters with
 Wings................. 500.00
52 BKa,RWd,AB,Man-Eaters
 Paradise............... 500.00
53 RWd,AB,Slaves of the
 Blood Moon 500.00
54 RWd,AB,Congo Kill 500.00
55 RWd,AB,Bait for the Silver
 King Cat............... 500.00
56 RWd,AB,Sabre Monsters of
 the Aba-Zanzi,Bondage(c) .. 500.00
57 RWd,AB,Arena of Beasts.... 500.00
58 RWd,AB,Sky-Atlas of the
 Thunder-Birds........... 500.00
59 RWd,AB,Kraal of Shrunken
 Heads 500.00
60 RWd,AB,Land of the
 Stalking Death 350.00
61 RWd,AB,King-Beast of
 the Masai.............. 350.00
62 RWd,AB,Valley of Golden
 Death................. 350.00
63 RWd,AB,The Dwarf Makers .. 350.00
64 RWd,The Slave-Brand of Ibn
 Ben Satan,Male Bondage... 350.00
65 RWd,The Man-Eaters of
 Linpopo 350.00
66 RWd,Valley of Monsters..... 350.00
67 RWd,Land of Feathered Evil . 350.00
68 RWd,Spear of Blood Ju-Ju... 350.00
69 RWd,AB,Slaves for the
 White Sheik 350.00
70 RWd,AB,MB,The Rogue
 Beast's Prey............ 350.00
71 RWd,AB,MB,The Serpent-
 God Speaks............ 250.00
72 RWd,AB,MB,Curse of the
 Half-Dead.............. 250.00
73 RWd,AB,MB,War Apes of
 the T'Kanis............. 250.00
74 RWd,AB,MB,Drums of the
 Voodoo God............ 250.00
75 RWd,AB,MB,Terror Trail of
 the Devil's Horn 250.00
76 RWd,AB,MB,Fire Gems of
 Skull Valley............. 250.00

GOLDEN AGE — Jumbo–Jungle

Jumbo Comics #82
© Fiction House

77 RWd,AB,MB,Blood Dragons
   from Fire Valley 250.00
78 RWd,AB,MB,Veldt of the
   Vampire Apes 250.00
79 RWd,AB,MB,Dancing
   Skeletons 250.00
80 RWd,AB,MB,Banshee Cats . . 250.00
81 RWd,MB,AB,JKa,Heads for
   King' Hondo's Harem 225.00
82 RWd,MB,AB,JKa,Ghost Riders
   of the Golden Tuskers 225.00
83 RWd,MB,AB,JKa,Charge of
   the Condo Juggernauts 225.00
84 RWd,AB,MB,JKa,Valley of
   the Whispering Fangs. 225.00
85 RWd,MB,AB,JKa,Red Tusks
   of Zulu-Za'an 225.00
86 RWd,MB,AB,JKa,Witch-Maiden
   of the Burning Blade. 225.00
87 RWd,AB,MB,JKa,Sargasso of
   Lost Safaris 225.00
88 RWd,AB,MB,JKa,Kill-Quest
   of the Ju-Ju Tusks 225.00
89 RWd,AB,MB,JKa,Ghost Slaves
   of Bwana Rojo 225.00
90 RWd,AB,MB,JKa,Death Kraal
   of the Mastadons 225.00
91 RWd,AB,MB,JKa,Spoor of
   the Sabre-Horn Tiger 200.00
92 RWd,MB,JKa,Pied Piper
   of the Congo 200.00
93 RWd,MB,JKa,The Beasts
   that Dawn Begot. 200.00
94 RWd,MB,JKa,Wheel of a
   Thousand Deaths 200.00
95 RWd,MB,JKa,Flame Dance
   of the Ju-Ju Witch. 200.00
96 RWd,MB,JKa,Ghost Safari. . . 200.00
97 RWd,MB,JKa,Banshee Wail
   of the Undead,Bondage(c) . . 200.00
98 RWd,MB,JKa,Seekers of
   the Terror Fangs. 200.00
99 RWd,MB,JKa,Shrine of
   the Seven Souls. 200.00
100 RWd,MB,Slave Brand
    of Hassan Bey 250.00
101 RWd,MB,Quest of the
    Two-Face Ju Ju 200.00
102 RWd,MB,Viper Gods of
    Vengeance Veldt 200.00
103 RWd,MB,Blood for the
    Idol of Blades 200.00
104 RWd,MB,Valley of Eternal
    Sleep 200.00

105 RWd,MB,Man Cubs from
    Momba-Zu 300.00
106 RWd,MB,The River of
    No-Return 300.00
107 RWd,MB,Vandals of
    the Veldt. 200.00
108 RWd,MB,The Orphan of
    Vengeance Vale 200.00
109 RWd,MB,The Pygmy's Hiss
    is Poison 200.00
110 RWd,MB,Death Guards the
    Congo Keep 200.00
111 RWd,MB,Beware of the
    Witch-Man's Brew. 200.00
112 RWd,MB,The Blood-Mask
    from G'Shinis Grave. 175.00
113 RWd,MB,The Mask's of
    Zombi-Zan 175.00
114 RWd,MB 175.00
115 RWd,MB,Svengali of
    the Apes. 175.00
116 RWd,MB,The Vessel of
    Marbel Monsters. 175.00
117 RWd,MB,Lair of the Half-
    Man King 175.00
118 RWd,MB,Quest of the
    Congo Dwarflings 175.00
119 RWd,MB,King Crocodile's
    Domain 175.00
120 RWd,MB,The Beast-Pack
    Howls the Moon 175.00
121 RWd,MB,The Kraal of
    Evil Ivory 175.00
122 RWd,MB,Castaways of
    the Congo 175.00
123 RWd,MB, ... 175.00
124 RWd,MB,The Voodoo Beasts
    of Changra-Lo 175.00
125 RWd,MB,JKa(c),The Beast-
    Pack Strikes at Dawn 175.00
126 RWd,MB,JKa(c),Lair of the
    Swamp Beast. 175.00
127 RWd,MB,JKa(c),The Phantom
    of Lost Lagoon 175.00
128 RWd,MB,JKa(c),Mad Mistress
    of the Congo-Tuskers 175.00
129 RWd,MB,JKa(c),Slaves of
    King Simbas Kraal 175.00
130 RWd,MB,JKa(c),Quest of
    the Pharaoh's Idol 175.00
131 RWd,JKa(c),Congo Giants
    at Bay 175.00
132 RWd,JKa(c),The Doom of
    the Devil's Gorge 175.00
133 RWd,JKa(c),Blaze the
    Pitfall Trail 175.00
134 RWd,JKa(c),Catacombs of
    the Jackal-Men. 175.00
135 RWd,JKa(c),The 40 Thieves
    of Ankar-Lo. 175.00
136 RWd,JKa(c),The Perils of
    Paradise Lost 175.00
137 RWd,JKa(c),The Kraal of
    Missing Men 175.00
138 RWd,JKa(c),The Panthers
    of Kajo-Kazar 175.00
139 RWd,JKa(c),Stampede of
    the Congo Lancers 175.00
140 RWd,JKa(c),The Moon
    Beasts from Vulture Valley . 175.00
141 RWd,JKa(c),B:Long Bow . . . 200.00
142 RWd,JKa(c),Man-Eaters
    of N'Gamba 175.00
143 RWd,JKa(c),The Curse of
    the Cannibal Drum 175.00
144 RWd,JKa(c),The Secrets of
    Killers Cave 175.00
145 RWd,JKa(c),Killers of
    the Crypt 175.00
146 RWd,JKa(c),Sinbad of the
    Lost Lagoon 175.00

147 RWd,JKa(c),The Wizard of
    Gorilla Glade 175.00
148 RWd,JKa(c),Derelict of
    the Slave King 175.00
149 RWd,JKa(c),Lash Lord of
    the Elephants 175.00
150 RWd,JKa(c),Queen of
    the Pharaoh's Idol 165.00
151 RWd,The Voodoo Claws
    of Doomsday Trek 165.00
152 RWd,Red Blades of Africa . . 165.00
153 RWd,Lost Legions of the Nile 165.00
154 RWd,The Track of the
    Black Devil 165.00
155 RWd,The Ghosts of
    Blow-Gun Trail. 165.00
156 RWd,The Slave-Runners
    of Bambaru 165.00
157 RWd,Cave of the
    Golden Skull 165.00
158 RWd,Gun Trek to
    Panther Valley 165.00
159 RWd,A:Space Scout 160.00
160 RWd,Savage Cargo,
    E:Sheena covers 160.00
161 RWd,Dawns of the Pit 160.00
162 RWd,Hangman's Haunt 160.00
163 RWd,Cagliostro Cursed Thee 160.00
164 RWd,Death Bars the Door . . 160.00
165 RWd,Day off from a Corpse . 160.00
166 RWd,The Gallows Bird 160.00
167 RWd,Cult of the Clawmen,
    March, 1953. . . . . 160.00

JUNGLE COMICS
Glen Kel Publ./Fiction House
Jan., 1940

1 HcK,DBr,LF(c),O:The White
  Panther,Kaanga,Tabu, B:The
  Jungle Boy,Camilla, all
  Kaanga covers & stories . . 6,500.00
2 HcK,DBr,WE(c),B:Fantomah 2,300.00
3 HcK,DBr,GT,The Crocodiles
  of Death River 1,900.00
4 HcK,DBr,Wambi in
  Thundering Herds 1,700.00
5 WE(c),GT,HcK,DBr,Empire
  of the Ape Men 1,900.00
6 WE(c),GT,DBr,HcK,Tigress
  of the Deep Jungle Swamp 1,100.00
7 BP(c),DBr,GT,HcK,Live
  Sacrifice,Bondage(c) 1,000.00
8 BP(c),GT,HcK,Safari into
  Shadowland. 1,000.00

Jungle Comics #34
© Fiction House

All comics prices listed are for *Near Mint* condition.

Jungle Comics

9 GT,HcK,Captive of the
  Voodoo Master 1,000.00
10 GT,HcK,BP,Lair of the
  Renegade Killer......... 1,000.00
11 GT,HcK,V:Beasts of Africa's Ancient
  Primieval Swamp Land..... 750.00
12 GT,HcK,The Devil's
  Death-Trap.............. 750.00
13 GT(c),GT,HcK,Stalker of
  the Beasts 800.00
14 HcK,Vengeance of the
  Gorilla Hordes 750.00
15 HcK,Terror of the Voodoo
  Cauldron 750.00
16 HcK,Caveman Killers....... 750.00
17 HcK,Valley of the Killer-Birds . 750.00
18 HcK,Trap of the Tawny
  Killer, Bondage(c)......... 800.00
19 HcK,Revolt of the Man-Apes . 750.00
20 HcK,One-offering to
  Ju-Ju Demon 750.00
21 HcK,Monster of the Dismal
  Swamp, Bondage(c)....... 600.00
22 HcK,Lair o/t Winged Fiend ... 550.00
23 HcK,Man-Eater Jaws 550.00
24 HcK,Battle of the Beasts 550.00
25 HcK,Kaghis the Blood God,
  Bondage(c).............. 600.00
26 HcK,Gorillas of the
  Witch-Queen 550.00
27 HcK,Spore o/t Gold-Raiders . . 550.00
28 HcK,Vengeance of the Flame
  God, Bondage(c) 600.00
29 HcK,Juggernaut of Doom.... 550.00
30 HcK,Claws o/t Black Terror .. 500.00
31 HcK,Land of Shrunken Skulls. 500.00
32 HcK,Curse of the King-Beast . 500.00
33 HcK,Scaly Guardians of
  Massacre Pool,Bondage(c).. 500.00
34 HcK,Bait of the Spotted
  Fury,Bondage(c)......... 500.00
35 HcK,Stampede of the
  Slave-Masters 500.00
36 HcK,GT,The Flame-Death of
  Ju Ju Mountain........... 500.00
37 HcK,GT,Scaly Sentinel of
  Taboo Swamp 500.00
38 HcK,GT,Duel of the Congo
  Destroyers 500.00
39 HcK,Land of Laughing Bones. 500.00
40 HcK,Killer Plague 500.00
41 Hck,The King Ape
  Feeds at Dawn........... 400.00
42 Hck,RC,Master of the
  Moon-Beasts 400.00
43 HcK,The White Shiek....... 400.00
44 HcK,Monster of the
  Boiling Pool 400.00
45 HcK,The Bone-Grinders of
  B'Zambi, Bondage(c)...... 400.00
46 HcK,Blood Raiders of
  Tree Trail 400.00
47 HcK,GT,Monsters of the Man
  Pool, Bondage(c) 400.00
48 HcK,GT,Strangest Congo
  Adventure............... 350.00
49 HcK,GT,Lair of the King
  -Serpent................ 350.00
50 HcK,GT,Juggernaut of
  the Bush................ 350.00
51 HcK,GT,The Golden Lion of
  Genghis Kahn 350.00
52 HcK,Feast for the River
  Devils, Bondage(c)........ 375.00
53 HcK,GT,Slaves for Horrors
  Harem 375.00
54 HcK,GT,Blood Bride of
  the Crocodile 350.00
55 HcK,GT,The Tree Devil 350.00
56 HcK,Bride for the
  Rainmaker Raj........... 350.00

GOLDEN AGE

Jungle Comics #84
© Fiction House

57 HcK,Fire Gems of T'ulaki 350.00
58 HcK,Land of the
  Cannibal God............ 350.00
59 HcK,Dwellers of the Mist
  Bondage(c).............. 375.00
60 HcK,Bush Devil's Spoor 350.00
61 HcK,Curse of the Blood
  Madness 350.00
62 Bondage(c) 375.00
63 HcK,Fire-Birds for the
  Cliff Dwellers 300.00
64 Valley of the Ju-Ju Idols..... 300.00
65 Shrine of the Seven Ju Jus,
  Bondage(c).............. 325.00
66 Spoor of the Purple Skulls ... 300.00
67 Devil Beasts of the Golden
  Temple 300.00
68 Satan's Safari 300.00
69 Brides for the Serpent King .. 300.00
70 Brides for the King Beast,
  Bondage(c).............. 325.00
71 Congo Prey,Bondage(c)..... 325.00
72 Blood-Brand o/t Veldt Cats ... 250.00
73 The Killer of M'omba Raj,
  Bondage(c).............. 275.00
74 AgF,GoldenJaws,Bondage(c) . 275.00
75 AgF,Congo Kill............ 250.00
76 AgF,Blood Thrist of the
  Golden Tusk............. 250.00
77 AgF,The Golden Gourds
  Shriek Blood,Bondage(c) ... 275.00
78 AgF,Bondage(c)........... 275.00
79 AgF,Death has a
  Thousand Fangs 250.00
80 AgF,Salome of the
  Devil-Cats Bondage(c) 275.00
81 AgF,Colossus of the Congo .. 250.00
82 AgF,Blood Jewels of the
  Fire-Bird 250.00
83 AgF,Vampire Veldt,
  Bondage(c).............. 275.00
84 AgF,Blood Spoor of the
  Faceless Monster........ 250.00
85 AgF,Brides for the Man-Apes
  Bondage(c).............. 275.00
86 AgF,Firegems of L'hama
  Lost, Bondage(c) 275.00
87 AgF,Horror Kraal of the
  Legless One,Bondage(c) ... 250.00
88 AgF,Beyond the Ju-Ju Mists.. 265.00
89 AgF,Blood-Moon over the
  Whispering Veldt 250.00
90 AgF,The Skulls for the
  Altar of Doom,Bondage(c) .. 265.00

Comics Values Annual

91 AgF,Monsters from the Mist
  Lands, Bondage(c)........ 265.00
92 AgF,Vendetta of the
  Tree Tribes.............. 250.00
93 AgF,Witch Queen of the
  Hairy Ones.............. 250.00
94 AgF,Terror Raid of
  the Congo Caesar 250.00
95 Agf,Flame-Tongues of the
  Sky Gods 250.00
96 AgF,Phantom Guardians of the
  Enchanted Lake,Bondage(c). 200.00
97 AgF,Wizard of the Whirling
  Doom,Bondage(c) 275.00
98 AgF,Ten Tusks of Zulu Ivory . . 350.00
99 AgF,Cannibal Caravan,
  Bondage(c).............. 250.00
100 AgF,Hate has a
  Thousand Claws......... 250.00
101 AgF,The Blade of
  Buddha, Bondage(c)...... 250.00
102 AgF,Queen of the
  Amazon Lancers 200.00
103 AgF,The Phantoms of
  Lost Lagoon 200.00
104 AgF 200.00
105 AgF,The Red Witch
  of Ubangi-Shan 200.00
106 AgF,Bondage(c).......... 250.00
107 Banshee Valley 250.00
108 HcK,Merchants of Murder . 250.00
109 HcK,Caravan of the
  Golden Bones 200.00
110 HcK,Raid of the Fire-Fangs . 200.00
111 HcK,The Trek of the
  Terror-Paws 200.00
112 HcK,Morass of the
  Mammoths 200.00
113 HcK,Two-Tusked Terror 200.00
114 HcK,Mad Jackals Hunt
  by Night 200.00
115 HcK,Treasure Trove in
  Vulture Sky............. 200.00
116 HcK,The Banshees of
  Voodoo Veldt 200.00
117 HcK,The Fangs of the
  Hooded Scorpion 200.00
118 HcK,The Muffled Drums
  of Doom............... 200.00
119 HcK,Fury of the Golden
  Doom.................. 200.00
120 HcK,Killer King Domain 200.00
121 HcK,Wolves of the
  Desert Night............ 200.00
122 HcK,The Veldt of
  Phantom Fangs 200.00
123 HcK,The Ark of the
  Mist-Maids 200.00
124 HcK,The Trail of the
  Pharaoh's Eye 200.00
125 HcK,Skulls for Sale on
  Dismal River............ 200.00
126 HcK,Safari Sinister......... 250.00
127 HcK,Bondage(c).......... 175.00
128 HcK,Dawn-Men of the
  Congo 175.00
129 HcK,The Captives of
  Crocodile Swamp 175.00
130 HcK,Phantoms of the Congo 175.00
131 HcK,Treasure-Tomb of the
  Ape-King 175.00
132 HcK,Bondage(c). 200.00
133 HcK,Scourge of the Sudan
  Bondage(c)............. 200.00
134 HcK,The Black Avengers of
  Kaffir Pass 175.00
135 HcK 175.00
136 HcK,The Death Kraals
  of Kongola 175.00
137 BWg(c),HcK,The Safari of
  Golden Ghosts 175.00

CVA Page 416 — All comics prices listed are for *Near Mint* condition.

GOLDEN AGE

138 BWg(c),HcK,Track of the
  Black Terror Bondage(c) 175.00
139 BWg(c),HcK,Captain Kidd
  of the Congo 175.00
140 BWg(c),HcK,The Monsters
  of Kilmanjaro 175.00
141 BWg(c)HcK,The Death Hunt
  of the Man Cubs.......... 175.00
142 BWg(c),Hck,Sheba of the
  Terror Claws,Bondage(c) ... 225.00
143 BWg(c)Hck,The Moon of
  Devil Drums 225.00
144 BWg(c)Hck,Quest of the
  Dragon's Claw 225.00
145 BWg(c)Hck,Spawn of the
  Devil's Moon............. 225.00
146 BWg(c),HcK, Orphans of
  the Congo 225.00
147 BWg(c),HcK,The Treasure
  of Tembo Wanculu 225.00
148 BWg(c),HcK,Caged Beasts
  of Plunder-Men,Bondage(c) . 225.00
149 BWg(c),HcK............. 175.00
150 BWg(c),HcK,Rhino Rampage,
  Bondage(c) 225.00
151 BWg(c),HcK............. 175.00
152 BWg(c),HcK,The Rogue of
  Kopje Kull............... 175.00
153 BWg(c),HcK,The Wild Men
  of N'Gara 175.00
154 BWg(c),HcK,The Fire Wizard 175.00
155 BWg(c),HcK,Swamp of
  the Shrieking Dead........ 175.00
156 BWg(c),HcK............. 175.00
157 BWg(c),HcK............. 175.00
158 BWg(c),HcK,A:Sheena.... 175.00
159 BWg(c),HcK,The Blow-Gun
  Kill 175.00
160 BWg,HcK,King Fang 175.00
161 BWg(c),HcK,The Barbarizi
  Man-Eaters 175.00
162 BWg(c) 175.00
163 BWg(c),Jackals at the
  Kill, Summer,1954 .... 175.00

JUNGLE JIM
**Best Books
(Standard Comics) Jan., 1949**
11 .... 100.00
12 Mystery Island 50.00
13 Flowers of Peril 50.00
14 .... 50.00
15 .... 50.00
16 .... 50.00
17 .... 50.00
18 .... 50.00
19 .... 50.00
20 1951 .... 50.00

JUNGLE JIM
Dell Publishing Co., Aug., 1953
(1) see Dell Four Color #490
(1) see Dell Four Color #565
3 P(c) all 50.00
4 .... 50.00
5 .... 50.00
6 .... 40.00
7 .... 40.00
8 thru 12 .... @40.00
13 'Mystery Island' 40.00
14 'Flowers of Peril' 40.00
15 thru 20 .... @40.00

JUNGLE JO
**Hero Books
(Fox Features Syndicate)
March, 1950**
N# Congo King 550.00

1 WW,Mystery of Doc Jungle .. 600.00
2 Tangl 450.00
3 The Secret of Youth,
  Sept., 1950 .... 400.00

JUNGLE LIL
Hero Books, April, 1950
1 Betrayer of the Kombe Dead.. 450.00
Becomes:

DOROTHY LAMOUR
**Fox Features Syndicate,
June 1950**
2 WW,Ph(c)The Lost Safari 350.00
3 WW,Ph(c), Aug., 1950 ...... 300.00

JUNGLE THRILLS
**See: TERRORS OF
THE JUNGLE**

JUNIE PROM
**Dearfield Publishing Co.
Winter, 1947**
1 Teenage Stories 125.00
2 .... 75.00
3 thru 5 .... @50.00
6 June, 1949 .... 50.00

Junior #14
© Fox Features Syndicate

JUNIOR COMICS
**Fox Features Syndicate
Sept., 1947**
9 AF(a&c),Teenage Stories .. 1,000.00
10 AF(a&c)................. 900.00
11 AF(a&c)................. 900.00
12 AF(a&c)................. 900.00
13 AF(a&c)................. 900.00
14 AF(a&c)................. 900.00
15 AF(a&c)................. 900.00
16 AF(a&c),July,1948 .... 900.00

JUNIOR HOOP COMICS
**Stanmor Publications
Jan., 1952**
1 .... 100.00
2 .... 50.00
3 July, 1952 .... 50.00

JUSTICE TRAPS
THE GUILTY
**Headline Publications
(Prize) Oct.–Nov., 1947**
2-1 S&K(a&c),Electric chair (c) . 700.00
2 S&K(a&c) 450.00
3 S&K(a&c) 400.00
4 S&K(a&c),True Confession
  of a Girl Gangleader 400.00
5 S&K(a&c) 400.00
6 S&K(a&c) 400.00
7 S&K(a&c) 400.00
8 S&K(a&c) 400.00
9 S&K(a&c) 400.00
10 S&K(a&c)................ 400.00
11 S&K(a&c)................ 150.00
12 .... 75.00
13 .... 100.00
14 .... 75.00
15 .... 75.00
16 .... 75.00
17 .... 75.00
18 S&K(a&c) 75.00
19 S&K(a&c) 75.00
20 .... 70.00
21 S&K..................... 125.00
22 S&K(c).................. 125.00
23 S&K(c).................. 125.00
24 .... 60.00
25 .... 60.00
26 .... 60.00
27 S&K(c).................. 75.00
28 .... 60.00
29 .... 60.00
30 S&K.................... 100.00
31 thru 50 .... @60.00
51 thru 54................. @50.00
55 .... 50.00
56 .... 50.00
57 .... 50.00
58 Drug 300.00
59 thru 92................ @50.00
Becomes:

FARGO KID
**Headline Publications
(Prize) June–July. 1958**
93 AW,JSe,O:Kid Fargo 175.00
94 JSe 125.00
95 June–July, 1958,JSe 125.00

KA'A'NGA COMICS
**Glen-Kel Publ.
(Fiction House)
Spring, 1949–Summer, 1954**
1 Phantoms of the Congo 700.00
2 V:The Jungle Octopus 350.00
3 .... 250.00
4 The Wizard Apes of
  Inkosi-Khan 235.00
5 .... 225.00
6 Captive of the Devil Apes ... 175.00
7 GT,Beast-Men of Mombassa . 200.00
8 The Congo Kill-Cry 175.00
9 .... 175.00
10 Stampede for Congo Gold ... 175.00
11 Claws of the Roaring Congo.. 125.00
12 Bondage(c) 150.00
13 Death Web of the Amazons . 125.00
14 Slave Galley of the Lost
  Nile Bondage(c).......... 150.00
15 Crocodile Moon,Bondage(c).. 150.00
16 Valley of Devil-Dwarfs 150.00
17 Tembu of the Elephants 125.00
18 The Red Claw of Vengeance . 125.00
19 The Devil-Devil Trail........ 125.00
20 The Cult of the Killer Claws .. 125.00

All comics prices listed are for Near Mint condition.

GOLDEN AGE

KASCO COMICS
Kasco Grainfeed (Giveaway), 1945
1 BWo 200.00
2 1949,BWo 150.00

KATHY
Standard Comics Sept., 1949
1 Teen-Age Stories 100.00
2 ASh 75.00
3 thru 6 . . . . @40.00
7 thru 17 . . . . @30.00

KATY KEENE
Archie Publications/Close-Up Radio Comics, 1949
1 BWo 1,300.00
2 BWo 700.00
3 BWo 500.00
4 BWo 500.00
5 BWo 450.00
6 BWo 350.00
7 BWo 350.00
8 thru 12 BWo . . . . @325.00
13 thru 20 BWo. . . . . @300.00
21 thru 29 BWo. . . . . @250.00
30 thru 38 BWo. . . . . @235.00
39 thru 62 BWo. . . . . @225.00
Ann.#1 . . . . 600.00
Ann.#2 thru #6 . . . . 350.00

KEEN DETECTIVE FUNNIES
Centaur Publications July, 1938
1-8 B:The Clock, ... 2,900.00
1-9 WE 1,200.00
1-10 . . . . 1,000.00
1-11 Dean Denton 1,000.00
2-1 The Eye Sees 900.00
2-2 JCo 900.00
2-3 TNT. 900.00
2-4 Gabby Flynn 900.00
5 . . . . 1,000.00
6 . . . . 900.00
7 Masked Marvel 3,000.00
8 PGn,Gabby Flynn,Nudity
   Expanded 16 pages. 1,200.00
9 Dean Denton 1,000.00
10 . . . . 1,000.00

Keen Detective Funnies Vol. 2, #1
© *Centaur Publications*

11 BEv,Sidekick 1,000.00
12 Masked Marvel(c) 1,200.00
3-1 Masked Marvel(c) 1,000.00
3-2 Masked Marvel(c) 1,000.00
3-3 BEv 1,000.00
16 BEv 1,000.00
17 JSm 1,000.00
18 The Eye Sees,Bondage(c) . 1,000.00
19 LFe 950.00
20 BEv,The Eye Sees 1,200.00
21 Masked Marvel(c) 950.00
22 Masked Marvel(c) 950.00
23 B:Airman. 1,200.00
24 Airman 1,300.00

KEEN KOMICS
Centaur Publications May, 1939
1 Teenage Stories 1,300.00
2 PGn,JaB,CBu,Cut Carson. . . . 800.00
3 JCo,Saddle Sniffl 800.00

KEEN TEENS
Life's Romances Publ./Leader/ Magazine Enterprises, 1945
N# P(c),Claire Voyant 400.00
N# Ph(c),Van Johnson 350.00
3 Ph(c), ... 100.00
4 Ph(c),Glenn Ford 125.00
5 Ph(c),Perry Como 125.00
6 . . . . 100.00

KEN MAYNARD WESTERN
Fawcett Publications Sept., 1950–Feb., 1952
1 B:Ken Maynard & Tarzan (horse)
   The Outlaw Treasure Trail . . 750.00
2 Invasion of the Badmen 450.00
3 Pied Piper of the West 350.00
4 Outlaw Hoax 350.00
5 Mystery of Badman City 350.00
6 Redwood Robbery 350.00
7 Seven Wonders of the West . . 350.00
8 Mighty Mountain Menace 350.00

KEN SHANNON
Quality Comics Group Oct., 1951–April, 1953
1 RC, Evil Eye of Count Ducrie . 500.00
2 RC, Cut Rate Corpses 350.00
3 RC, Corpse that Wouldn't
   Sleep 250.00
4 RC, Stone Hatchet Murder . . . 225.00
5 RC, Case of the Carney Killer 225.00
6 Weird Vampire Mob 250.00
7 RC,Ugliest Man in the World . 225.00
8 Chinatown Murders,Drug 250.00
9 RC, Necklace of Blood 200.00
10 RC, Shadow of the Chair 200.00

KERRY DRAKE DETECTIVE CASES
Life's Romances/M.E., 1944
(1) *see N# A-1 Comics* 350.00
2 A:The Faceless Horror 200.00
3 . . . . 150.00
4 A:Squirrel, Dr. Zero, Caresse . 150.00
5 Bondage (c) 175.00
Harvey Publ., Jan., 1952
6 A:Stitches 125.00
7 A:Shuteye 135.00
8 Bondage (c) 150.00
9 Drug 200.00
10 BP,A:Meatball,Drug 200.00

11 BP,I:Kid Gloves 100.00
12 BP 100.00
13 BP,A:Torso 75.00
14 BP,Bullseye Murder Syndicate . 75.00
15 BP,Fake Mystic Racket 90.00
16 BP,A:Vixen. 60.00
17 BP,Case of the $50,000
   Robbery 60.00
18 BP,A:Vixen 60.00
19 BP,Case of the Dope
   Smugglers 75.00
20 BP,Secret Treasury Agent 60.00
21 BP,Murder on Record 50.00
22 BP,Death Rides the Air Waves . 50.00
23 BP,Blackmailer's Secret
   Weapon 50.00
24 Blackmailer's Trap 50.00
25 Pretty Boy Killer 50.00
26 . . . . 50.00
27 . . . . 50.00
28 BP 50.00
29 BP 50.00
30 Mystery Mine,Bondage(c) 50.00
31 . . . . 50.00
32 . . . . 50.00
33 Aug., 1952 . . . . 50.00

KEWPIES
Will Eisner Publications Spring, 1949
1 . . . . 600.00

KEY COMICS
Consolidated Magazines Jan., 1944
1 B:The Key, Will-O-The-Wisp . 550.00
2 . . . . 300.00
3 . . . . 250.00
4 O:John Quincy,B:The Atom . . 275.00
5 HoK,Aug., 1946 . . . . 300.00

KID COWBOY
Approved Comics/ St. John Publ. Co., 1950
1 B:Lucy Belle & Red Feather . . 200.00
2 Six-Gun Justice 100.00
3 Shadow on Hangman's Bridge . 90.00
4 Red Feather V:Eagle of Doom . 80.00
5 Killers on the Rampage 80.00
6 The Stovepipe Hat 80.00
7 Ghost Town of Twin Buttes . . . 80.00
8 Thundering Hoofs 80.00
9 Terror on the Salt Flats 80.00
10 Valley of Death 80.00
11 Vanished Herds,Bondage(c) . . . 90.00
12 . . . . 80.00
13 . . . . 80.00
14 1954 . . . . 80.00

KIDDIE KARNIVAL
Approved Comics, 1952
N# 450.00

KID ETERNITY
Comics Magazine Spring, 1946
1 . . . . 1,200.00
2 . . . . 500.00
3 Follow Him Out of This World 550.00
4 Great Heroes of the Past . . . 350.00
5 Don't Kid with Crime 300.00
6 Busy Battling Crime 300.00
7 Protects the World 300.00
8 Fly to the Rescue 300.00
9 Swoop Down on Crime 300.00
10 Golden Touch from Mr. Midas 300.00

11 Aid the Living by Calling
  the Dead 250.00
12 Finds Death 250.00
13 Invades General Poschka ... 250.00
14 Battles Double 250.00
15 A: Master Man 250.00
16 Balance Scales of Justice ... 200.00
17 A:Baron Roxx........... 200.00
18 A:Man with Two Faces..... 200.00
Becomes:

BUCCANEERS
Quality Comics Group
Jan., 1950
19 RC,Sword Fight(c)........ 550.00
20 RC,Treasure Chest 450.00
21 RC,Death Trap........... 500.00
22 A:Lady Dolores,Snuff,
  Bondage(c)............ 350.00
23 RC,V:Treasure Hungry
  Plunderers of the Sea..... 375.00
24 A:Adam Peril,Black Roger,
  Eric Falcon............ 250.00
25 V:Clews 250.00
26 V:Admiral Blood.......... 250.00
27 RC(a&c)May, 1951........ 450.00

KID ZOO COMICS
Street & Smith, July, 1948
1 (fa) 275.00

KILLERS, THE
Magazine Enterprises, 1947
1 LbC(c),Thou Shall Not Kill .. 1,350.00
2 Grl,OW,Assassins Mad Slayers
  of the East,Hanging(c),Drug 1,200.00

Kilroys #2
© B&L Publishing

KILROYS, THE
B&L Publishing Co./
American Comics
June–July, 1947
1 Three Girls in Love(c)....... 275.00
2 Flat Tire(c).............. 125.00
3 Right to Swear(c) 75.00
4 Kissing Booth(c) 75.00
5 Skiing(c) 75.00
6 Prom(c) 60.00
7 To School 60.00
8 .... 60.00
9 .... 60.00
10 B:Solid Jackson solo 60.00
11 .... 50.00

12 Life Guard(c).............. 50.00
13 thru 21................. @50.00
22 thru 30................. @40.00
31 thru 40................. @35.00
41 thru 47................. @30.00
48 3-D effect.............. 200.00
49 3-D effect.............. 200.00
50 thru 54, July, 1954 .... @35.00

KING COMICS
David McKay Publications
April, 1936
(all have Popeye covers)
1 AR,EC,B:Popeye,Flash Gordon,B:
  Henry,Mandrake 15,000.00
2 AR,EC,Flash Gordon 3,500.00
3 AR,EC,Flash Gordon 2,500.00
4 AR,EC,Flash Gordon 2,000.00
5 AR,EC,Flash Gordon 1,500.00
6 AR,EC,Flash Gordon 1,100.00
7 AR,EC,King Royal Mounties 1,050.00
8 AR,EC,Thanksgiving(c).... 1,000.00
9 AR,EC,Christmas(c) 1,000.00
10 AR,EC,Flash Gordon...... 1,000.00
11 AR,EC,Flash Gordon 750.00
12 AR,EC,Flash Gordon 750.00
13 AR,EC,Flash Gordon 750.00
14 AR,EC,Flash Gordon 750.00
15 AR,EC,Flash Gordon 750.00
16 AR,EC,Flash Gordon 750.00
17 AR,EC,Flash Gordon 700.00
18 AR,EC,Flash Gordon 700.00
Covers say: "Starring Popeye"
19 AR,EC,Flash Gordon 700.00
20 AR,EC,Football(c) 700.00
21 AR,EC,Flash Gordon 600.00
22 AR,EC,Flash Gordon 600.00
23 AR,EC,Flash Gordon 600.00
24 AR,EC,Flash Gordon 600.00
25 AR,EC,Flash Gordon 600.00
26 AR,EC,Flash Gordon 550.00
27 AR,EC,Flash Gordon 550.00
28 AR,EC,Flash Gordon 550.00
29 AR,EC,Flash Gordon 550.00
30 AR,EC,Flash Gordon 550.00
31 AR,EC,Flash Gordon 550.00
32 AR,EC,Flash Gordon 550.00
33 AR,EC,Skiing(c) 550.00
34 AR,Ping Pong(c) 450.00
35 AR,Flash Gordon 450.00
36 AR,Flash Gordon 450.00
37 AR,Flash Gordon 450.00
38 AR,Flash Gordon 450.00
39 AR,Baseball(c)........... 450.00
40 AR,Flash Gordon 450.00
41 AR,Flash Gordon 400.00
42 AR,Flash Gordon 400.00
43 AR,Flash Gordon 400.00
44 AR,Popeye golf(c) 400.00
45 AR,Flash Gordon 400.00
46 AR,B:Little Lulu 400.00
47 AR,Flash Gordon 400.00
48 AR,Flash Gordon 400.00
49 AR,Weather Vane 400.00
50 AR,B:Love Ranger 400.00
51 AR,Flash Gordon 300.00
52 AR,Flash Gordon 300.00
53 AR,Flash Gordon 300.00
54 AR,Flash Gordon 300.00
55 AR,Magic Carpet 300.00
56 AR,Flash Gordon 300.00
57 AR,Cows Over Moon(c) ... 300.00
58 AR,Flash Gordon 300.00
59 AR,Flash Gordon 300.00
60 AR,Flash Gordon 300.00
61 AR,B:Phantom,Baseball(c)... 300.00
62 AR,Flash Gordon 300.00
63 AR,Flash Gordon 300.00
64 AR,Flash Gordon 200.00
65 AR,Flash Gordon 200.00

66 AR,Flash Gordon 200.00
67 AR,Sweet Pea 200.00
68 AR,Flash Gordon 200.00
69 AR,Flash Gordon 200.00
70 AR,Flash Gordon 200.00
71 AR,Flash Gordon 200.00
72 AR,Flash Gordon 175.00
73 AR,Flash Gordon 175.00
74 AR,Flash Gordon 175.00
75 AR,Flash Godron 175.00
76 AR,Flag(c) 200.00
77 AR,Flash Gordon 175.00
78 AR,Popeye,Olive Oil(c) 175.00
79 AR,Sweet Pea 175.00
80 AR,Wimpy(c) 175.00
81 AR,B:Blondie(c) 175.00
82 thru 91 AR .... @150.00
92 thru 98 AR .... @150.00
99 AR,Olive Oil(c) 150.00
100 .... 175.00
101 thru 116 AR .... @165.00
117 O:Phantom............. 150.00
118 Flash Gordon............ 175.00
119 Flash Gordon............ 150.00
120 Wimpy(c)............... 100.00
121 thru 140 .... @100.00
141 Flash Gordon............ 100.00
142 Flash Gordon............ 100.00
143 Flash Gordon............ 100.00
144 Flash Gordon............ 100.00
145 Prince Valiant........... 75.00
146 Prince Valiant........... 75.00
147 Prince Valiant........... 75.00
148 thru 154 .... @60.00
155 E:Flash Gordon 60.00
156 Baseball(c) 60.00
157 thru 159 .... @55.00

KING OF THE
ROYAL MOUNTED
Dell Publishing Co.
Dec., 1948–1958
(1) see Dell Four Color #207
(2) see Dell Four Color #265
(3) see Dell Four Color #283
(4) see Dell Four Color #310
(5) see Dell Four Color #340
(6) see Dell Four Color #363
(7) see Dell Four Color #384
8 Zane Grey adapt. 75.00
9 .... 75.00
10 .... 75.00
11 thru 28 .... @50.00

KIT CARSON
Avon Periodicals, 1950
N# EK(c) Indian Scout 150.00
2 EK(c),Kit Carson's Revenge,
  Doom Trail 100.00
3 EK(c),V:Comanche Raiders ... 75.00
4 .... 75.00
5 EK(c),Trail of Doom 75.00
6 EK(c) 75.00
7 EK(c) 75.00
8 EK(c) 75.00
Becomes:

FIGHTING DAVY
CROCKETT
Oct.–Nov, 1955
9 EK(c) 75.00

KOKO AND KOLA
Compix/Magazine Enterprises
Fall, 1946
1 (fa) 100.00
2 X-Mas Issue 75.00
3 .... 50.00

Koko–Laugh

4 . . . . 50.00
5 . . . . 50.00
6 May, 1947 . . . . 50.00

KO KOMICS
Gerona Publications
Oct., 1945
1 . . . . 900.00

KRAZY KAT COMICS
Dell Publishing Co.
May–June, 1951
1 . . . . 125.00
2 . . . . 75.00
3 . . . . 75.00
4 . . . . 75.00
5 . . . . 75.00

KRAZY LIFE
See: PHANTOM LADY

LABOR IS A PARTNER
Catechetical Guild
Educational Society, 1949
1 . . . . 250.00

LAFFY-DAFFY COMICS
Rural Home Publ. Co.
Feb., 1945
1 (fa) 100.00
2 . . . . 100.00

LANCE O'CASEY
Fawcett, 1946–47
1 High Seas Adventure
 from Whiz comics 400.00
2 thru 4 . . . . @250.00

LAND OF THE LOST
EC Comics
July–Aug., 1946–Spring 1948
1 Radio show adapt. 400.00
2 . . . . 250.00
3 thru 9 . . . . @200.00

LARGE FEATURE COMICS
Dell Publishing Co., 1939
1 Dick Tracy vs. the Blank 2,100.00
2 Terry and the Pirates 1,100.00
3 Heigh-Yo Silver!
 the Lone Ranger 1,700.00
4 Dick Tracy gets his man 1,200.00
5 Tarzan of the Apes 2,000.00
6 Terry and the Pirates 1,200.00
7 Lone Ranger to the rescue . . 1,500.00
8 Dick Tracy, Racket Buster . . 1,200.00
9 King of the Royal Mounted . . . 700.00
10 Gang Busters 800.00
11 Dick Tracy, Mad Doc Hump . 1,200.00
12 Smilin' Jack 750.00
13 Dick Tracy and Scottie
 of Scotland Yard 1,200.00
14 Smilin' Jack helps G-Men . . . 750.00
15 Dick Tracy and
 the kidnapped princes . . . 1,200.00
16 Donald Duck, 1st Daisy 7,000.00
17 Gang Busters 600.00
18 Phantasmo The Master
 of the World 500.00
19 Walt Disney's Dumbo 4,000.00
20 Donald Duck 7,500.00
21 Private Buck 150.00

GOLDEN AGE

22 Nuts and Jolts 150.00
23 The Nebbs 200.00
24 Popeye in 'Thimble Theatre' . . 900.00

Large Feature #13
© Dell Publishing Co.

25 Smilin' Jack 700.00
26 Smitty 300.00
27 Terry and the Pirates 750.00
28 Grin and Bear It 100.00
29 Moon Mullins 300.00
30 Tillie the Toiler 275.00

[Series 2]
1 Peter Rabbit 500.00
2 Winnie Winkle 250.00
3 Dick Tracy 1,000.00
4 Tiny Tim 300.00
5 Toots and Casper 150.00
6 Terry and the Pirates 750.00
7 Pluto saves the Ship 2,000.00
8 Bugs Bunny 2,000.00
9 Bringing Up Father 250.00
10 Popeye 650.00
11 Barney Google&SnuffySmith . 300.00
12 Private Buck 150.00
13 1001 Hours of Fun 200.00

LARRY DOBY, BASEBALL HERO
Fawcett Publications, 1950
1 Ph(c),BW 1,100.00

LARS OF MARS
Ziff-Davis Publishing Co.
April–May, 1951
10 MA,'Terror from the Sky' . . . 1,100.00
11 GC, The Terror Weapon 900.00

LASH LARUE WESTERN
Fawcett Publications
Summer, 1949
1 Ph(c),The Fatal Roundups . . 1,300.00
2 Ph(c),Perfect Hide Out 600.00
3 Ph(c),The Suspect 500.00
4 Ph(c),Death on Stage 500.00
5 Ph(c),Rustler's Haven 500.00
6 Ph(c) 400.00
7 Ph(c),Shadow of the Noose . . 350.00
8 Ph(c),Double Deadline 350.00
9 Ph(c),Generals Last Stand . . . 350.00
10 Ph(c) 350.00
11 Ph(c) 300.00

Comics Values Annual

12 thru 20 Ph(c) . . . . @250.00
21 thru 29 Ph(c) . . . . @200.00
30 thru 46 Ph(c) . . . . @150.00
46 Ph(c),Lost Chance 150.00

LASSIE
(& SEVERAL SPECIAL ISSUES)
Dell Publishing Co.
Oct.–Dec., 1950
1 Ph(c) all 225.00
2 . . . . 100.00
3 . . . . 75.00
4 . . . . 75.00
5 . . . . 75.00
6 . . . . 75.00
7 . . . . 75.00
8 . . . . 75.00
9 . . . . 75.00
10 . . . . 75.00
11 . . . . 50.00
12 Rocky Langford 55.00
13 . . . . 50.00
14 . . . . 50.00
15 I:Timbu 55.00
16 . . . . 50.00
17 . . . . 50.00
18 . . . . 50.00
19 . . . . 50.00
20 MB 60.00
21 MB 60.00
22 MB 60.00
23 thru 38 . . . . @45.00
39 I:Timmy 50.00
40 thru 62 . . . . @40.00
63 E:Timmy 35.00
64 thru 70 . . . . @25.00

LATEST COMICS
Spotlight Publ./
Palace Promotions
March, 1945
1 Funny Animal-Super Duper . . . 150.00
2 . . . . 100.00

SPECIAL COMICS
MLJ Magazines
Winter, 1941
1 O:Boy Buddies & Hangman,
 D:The Comet 3,500.00
Becomes:

HANGMAN COMICS
Spring, 1942
2 B:Hangman & Boy Buddies . 2,700.00
3 V:Nazis (c),Bondage(c) 1,800.00
4 V:Nazis (c) 1,500.00
5 Bondage (c) 1,500.00
6 . . . . 1,500.00
7 BF,Graveyard (c) 1,500.00
8 BF 1,500.00
Becomes:

BLACK HOOD
Winter, 1943–44
9 BF, Hang Man 1,500.00
10 BF,A:Dusty, the Boy Detective 750.00
11 Here lies the Black Hood 600.00
12 . . . . 500.00
13 EK(c) 500.00
14 EK(c) 500.00
15 EK 500.00
16 EK(c) 500.00
17 Bondage (c) 550.00
18 . . . . 500.00
19 I.D. Revealed 700.00
Becomes:

CVA Page 420   All comics prices listed are for *Near Mint* condition.

LAUGH COMICS
Archie Comics, Fall, 1946
20 BWo,B:Archie,Katy Keene . . . 750.00
21 BWo 350.00
22 BWo 350.00
23 Bwo. 350.00
24 BWo,JK,Pipsy 375.00
25 BWo 350.00
26 BWo 200.00
27 BWo 200.00
28 BWo 200.00
29 BWo 200.00
30 BWo 200.00
31 thru 40 BWo. . . . . @150.00
41 thru 50 BWo. . . . . @125.00
51 thru 60 BWo. . . . . @110.00
61 thru 80 BWo. . . . . @75.00
81 thru 99 BWo. . . . . @60.00
100 BWo 75.00
101 thru 126 BWo . . . . @50.00
127 A:Jaguar 60.00
128 A:The Fly 60.00
129 A:The Fly 60.00
130 A:Jaguar 60.00
131 A:Jaguar 60.00
132 A:The Fly 60.00
133 A:Jaguar 60.00
134 A:The Fly 60.00
135 A:Jaguar 60.00
136 A:Fly Girl 60.00
137 A:Fly Girl 60.00
138 A:The Fly 60.00
139 A:The Fly 60.00
140 A:Jaguar 60.00
141 A:Jaguar 60.00
142 thru 144 . . . . @60.00
145 A:Josie. 35.00
146 thru 165 . . . . @25.00
166 Beatles (c) 35.00
167 thru 220 . . . . @20.00
221 thru 250 . . . . @15.00
251 thru 300 . . . . @15.00
301 thru 400 . . . . @8.00

LAUGH COMIX
See: TOP-NOTCH COMICS

LAUREL AND HARDY
**St. John Publishing Co.
March, 1949**
1 . . . . 900.00
2 . . . . 500.00
3 . . . . 350.00
26 Rep #1 . . . . 200.00
27 Rep #2 . . . . 200.00
28 Rep #3 . . . . 200.00

LAWBREAKERS
**Law & Order Magazines
(Charlton) March, 1951**
1 . . . . 500.00
2 . . . . 250.00
3 . . . . 150.00
4 Drug 225.00
5 . . . . 150.00
6 LM(c) 175.00
7 Drug 225.00
8 . . . . 150.00
9 StC(c) 150.00
Becomes:

LAWBREAKERS SUSPENSE STORIES
Jan., 1953
10 StC(c) 500.00
11 LM(c), Negligee(c) 1,200.00
12 LM(c). 250.00

*Law Breakers Suspense Stories #11
© Charlton Comics*

13 DG(c) 250.00
14 DG(c),Sharks. 250.00
15 DG(c),Acid in Face(c) 600.00
Becomes:

STRANGE SUSPENSE STORIES
Jan., 1954
16 DG(c) 400.00
17 DG(c) 300.00
18 SD,SD(c). 450.00
19 SD,SD(c),Electric Chair 600.00
20 SD,SD(c). 500.00
21 SD,SD(c). 300.00
22 SD,SD(c). 450.00
Becomes:

THIS IS SUSPENSE
Feb., 1955
23 WW; Comics Code 250.00
24 GE,DG(c). 150.00
25 DG(c) 125.00
26 DG(c) 125.00
Becomes:

STRANGE SUSPENSE STORIES
Oct., 1955
27 . . . . 150.00
28 . . . . 125.00
29 . . . . 125.00
30 . . . . 125.00
31 SD. 250.00
32 SD. 250.00
33 SD. 250.00
34 SD. 550.00
35 SD. 250.00
36 SD. 250.00
37 SD. 250.00
38 . . . . 125.00
39 SD 200.00
40 SD 225.00
41 SD 200.00
42 . . . . 75.00
43 . . . . 75.00
44 . . . . 75.00
45 . . . . 75.00
46 . . . . 75.00
47 SD. 225.00
48 SD. 225.00
49 . . . . 75.00
50 SD. 225.00
51 SD. 225.00
52 SD. 225.00
53 SD. 225.00
54 thru 60 . . . . @50.00
61 thru 74 . . . . @40.00
75 SD,SD(c). 200.00
77 Oct 1965 . . . . 75.00

LAWBREAKERS ALWAYS LOSE
**Crime Bureau Stories
Spring, 1948**
1 HK; FBI Reward Poster Photo. 500.00
2 . . . . 200.00
3 . . . . 150.00
4 AyB(c),Vampire 150.00
5 AyB(c) 125.00
6 Anti Wertham Edition 125.00
7 Drug 350.00
8 . . . . 125.00
9 Ph(c) 125.00
10 Ph(c), Oct., 1949 . . . . 125.00

LAW-CRIME
**Essenkay Publications
April, 1948**
1 LbC,LbC-(c);Raymond Hamilton
    Dies In The Chair 1,000.00
2 LbC,LbC-(c);Strangled
    Beauty Puzzles Police 750.00
3 LbC,LbC-(c);Lipstick Slayer
    Sought; Aug., 1943. . . . . 900.00

LEROY
**Visual Editions
(Standard Comics) Nov., 1949**
1 FunniestTeenager of them All . . 75.00
2 . . . . 50.00
3 thru 6 . . . . @40.00

LET'S PRETEND
**D.S. Publishing Company
May–June, 1950**
1 From Radio Nursery Tales . . . 200.00
2 . . . . 150.00
3 Nov., 1950 . . . . 150.00

MISS LIBERTY
Burten Publishing, circa 1944
1 Reprints-Shield,Wizard 550.00
Becomes:

LIBERTY COMICS
Green Publishing, May, 1946
10 Reprints,Hangman. 250.00
11 Wilbur in women's clothes . . . 200.00
12 Black Hood 250.00
14 Patty of Airliner 150.00
15 Patty of Airliner 125.00

LIBERTY GUARDS
**Chicago Mail Order
(Comic Corp of America)
Circa 1942**
1 PG(c),Liberty Scouts. 500.00
Becomes:

LIBERTY SCOUTS
June, 1941–Aug., 1941
PG(a&c)O:Fireman,Liberty
    Scouts 1,800.00
3 PG,PG(c),O:Sentinel 1,200.00

LIFE STORY
**Fawcett Publications
April, 1949**
1 Ph(c) 150.00

Life–Little Giant

GOLDEN AGE

Comics Values Annual

2 Ph(c)	75.00
3 Ph(c)	60.00
4 Ph(c)	60.00
5 Ph(c)	60.00
6 Ph(c)	60.00
7 Ph(c)	50.00
8 Ph(c)	50.00
9 Ph(c)	50.00
10 Ph(c)	50.00
11	45.00
12	45.00
13 WW,Drug	150.00
14 thru 21	@45.00
22 Drug	75.00
23 thru 35	@50.00
36 Drug	60.00
37 thru 42	@45.00
43 GE	60.00
44	45.00
45 1952	45.00

LIFE WITH SNARKY PARKER
Fox Feature Syndicate
Aug., 1950

1	300.00

Lightning Comics #8
© Ace Magazines

SURE-FIRE
Ace Magazines 1940

1 O:Flash Lightning	2,200.00
2 Whiz Wilson	1,000.00
3 The Raven, Sept., 1940	750.00
3a Ace McCoy, Oct., 1940	750.00

Becomes:

LIGHTNING COMICS
Dec., 1940

4 Sure-Fire Stories	1,400.00
5 JM	900.00
6 JM, Dr. Nemesis	900.00
Vol. 2	
1 JM	750.00
2 JM, Flash Lightning	750.00
3 JM	750.00
4 JM	750.00
5 JM	750.00
6 JM, bondage(c)	750.00
Vol. 3	
1 I:Lightning Girl	750.00

LI'L ABNER
Harvey Publications
Dec., 1947

61 BP,BW,Sadie Hawkins Day	400.00
62	250.00
63	250.00
64	250.00
65 BP	250.00
66	200.00
67	200.00
68 FearlessFosdick V:Any Face	275.00
69	275.00
70	175.00

Toby Press

71	175.00
72	175.00
73	175.00
74	175.00
75 HK	200.00
76	175.00
77 HK	200.00
78 HK	200.00
79 HK	200.00
80	175.00
81	150.00
82	150.00
83 Baseball	175.00
84	150.00
85	150.00
86 HK	250.00
87	150.00
88	150.00
89	150.00
90	150.00
91 Rep. #77	165.00
92	150.00
93 Rep. #71	165.00
94	150.00
95 Fearless Fosdick	175.00
96 and 97 Jan., 1955	@150.00

LI'L GENIUS
Charlton Comics, 1955

1	125.00
2	50.00
3 thru 15	@40.00
16 Giants	60.00
17 Giants	60.00
18 Giants,100 pages	100.00
19 thru 40	@30.00
41 thru 54	@25.00
55 1965	25.00

LI'L PAN
Fox Features Syndicate
Dec.–Jan., 1946-47

6	100.00
7	75.00
8 April–May, 1947	75.00

LINDA
See: **PHANTOM LADY**

LITTLE AUDREY
St. John Publ. Co./
Harvey Comics, April, 1948

1	450.00
2	225.00
3 thru 6	@150.00
7 thru 10	@100.00
11 thru 20	@75.00
21 thru 24	@60.00
25 B:Harvey Comics	200.00
26 A: Casper	100.00
27 A: Casper	100.00
28 A: Casper	100.00
29 thru 31	@85.00
32 A: Casper	75.00
33 A: Casper	75.00
34 A: Casper	75.00
35 A: Casper	75.00
36 thru 53	@50.00

LITTLE BIT
Jubilee Publishing Company
March, 1949

1	75.00
2 June, 1949	60.00

LITTLE DOT
Harvey Publications
Sept., 1953

1 I: Richie Rich & Little Lotta	1,800.00
2	650.00
3	450.00
4	350.00
5 O:Dots on Little Dot's Dress	450.00
6 1st Richie Rich(c)	350.00
7	250.00
8	225.00
9	225.00
10	225.00
11 thru 20	@150.00
21 thru 30	@100.00
31 thru 39	@75.00
40 thru 50	@50.00
51 thru 60	@45.00
61 thru 70	@35.00
71 thru 80	@35.00
81 thru 100	@30.00
101 thru 130	@20.00
131 thru 140	@20.00
141 thru 145, 52 pages	@25.00
146 thru 163	@10.00

LITTLE EVA
St. John Publishing Co.
May, 1952

1	175.00
2	100.00
3	75.00
4	75.00
5 thru 10	@50.00
11 thru 30	@50.00
31 Nov., 1956	50.00

LITTLE GIANT COMICS
Centaur Publications
July, 1938

1 PG, B&W with Color(c)	900.00
2 B&W with Color(c)	750.00
3 B&W with Color(c)	750.00
4 B&W with Color(c)	750.00

LITTLE GIANT DETECTIVE FUNNIES
Centaur Publications
Oct., 1938–Jan., 1939

1 B&W	1,000.00
2 B&W	750.00
3 B&W	750.00
4 WE	750.00

LITTLE GIANT MOVIE FUNNIES
Centaur Publications
Aug., 1938

1 Ed Wheelan-a	1,000.00
2 Ed Wheelan-a, Oct., 1938	750.00

CVA Page 422   All comics prices listed are for *Near Mint* condition.

GOLDEN AGE

LITTLE IKE
**St. John Publishing Co.
April, 1953**
1 .... 100.00
2 .... 50.00
3 .... 40.00
4 Oct., 1953 .... 40.00

LITTLE IODINE
**Dell Publishing Co.
April, 1949**
1 .... 135.00
2 .... 60.00
3 .... 60.00
4 .... 60.00
5 .... 60.00
6 thru 10 .... @40.00
11 thru 30 .... @30.00
31 thru 50 .... @25.00
51 thru 56 .... @25.00

LITTLE JACK FROST
Avon Periodicals, 1951
1 .... 100.00

LITTLE LULU
See: MARGE'S LITTLE LULU

LITTLE MAX COMICS
**Harvey Publications
Oct., 1949**
1 I: Little Dot, Joe Palooka(c) ... 200.00
2 A: Little Dot, Joe Palooka(c) ... 125.00
3 A: Little Dot, Joe Palooka(c) 75.00
4 .... 60.00
5 C: Little Dot 60.00
6 thru 10 .... @50.00
11 thru 22 .... @50.00
23 A: Little Dot 40.00
24 thru 37 .... @30.00
38 Rep. #20 .... 30.00
39 thru 72 .... @30.00
73 A: Richie Rich; Nov.'61 ...... 30.00

LITTLE MISS MUFFET
**Best Books
(Standard Comics)
Dec., 1948**
11 Strip Reprints 75.00
12 Strip Reprints 50.00
13 Strip Reprints; Mar.'49 ...... 50.00

LITTLE MISS SUNBEAM COMICS
**Magazine Enterprises
June–July, 1950**
1 .... 175.00
2 .... 100.00
3 .... 100.00
4 Dec.–Jan., 1951 .... 100.00

LITTLE ORPHAN ANNIE
Dell Publishing Co., 1941
1 .... 250.00
2 Orphan Annie and the Rescue 150.00
3 .... 150.00

LITTLE ROQUEFORT
**St. John Publishing Co.
June, 1952**
1 .... 100.00

2 .... 60.00
3 thru 9 .... @50.00

Pines
10 Summer 1958 .... 50.00

LITTLE SCOUTS
**Dell Publishing Co.
March, 1951**
(1) see Dell Four Color #321
2 .... 35.00
3 .... 30.00
4 .... 30.00
5 .... 30.00
6 .... 30.00

LITTLEST SNOWMAN
**Dell Publishing Co.
Dec., 1956**
1 .... 60.00

LIVING BIBLE, THE
**Living Bible Corp.
Autumn, 1945**
1 LbC-(c) Life of Paul 500.00
2 LbC-(c) Joseph & His Brethern 400.00
3 LbC-(c) Chaplains At War .. 450.00

LONE EAGLE
**Ajax/Farrell
April–May, 1954**
1 .... 125.00
2 .... 75.00
3 Bondage(c) 100.00
4 Oct.–Nov., 1954 .... 75.00

LONE RANGER
**Dell Publishing Co.
Jan.–Feb., 1948**
1 B: Lone Ranger & Tonto
   B: Strip Reprint 1,000.00
2 .... 500.00
3 .... 350.00
4 .... 350.00
5 .... 350.00
6 .... 300.00
7 .... 300.00
8 O: Retold 350.00
9 .... 300.00
10 .... 300.00

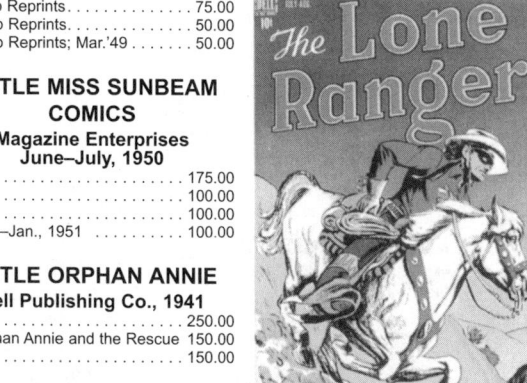

*The Lone Ranger #4
© Dell Publishing Co.*

11 B: Young Hawk 200.00
12 thru 20 .... @200.00
21 .... 150.00
22 .... 150.00
23 O: Retold 200.00
24 thru 30 .... @150.00
31 (1st Mask Logo) 175.00
32 thru 36 .... @125.00
37 (E: Strip reprints) 125.00
38 thru 50 .... @100.00
51 thru 75 .... @100.00
76 thru 99 .... @75.00
100 .... 100.00
101 thru 111 .... @100.00
112 B: Clayton Moore Ph(c) 275.00
113 thru 117 .... @150.00
118 O: Lone Ranger & Tonto
   retold, Anniv. issue 350.00
119 thru 144 .... @150.00
145 final issue, May/July, 1962 .. 150.00

THE LONE RANGER'S COMPANION TONTO
Dell Publishing Co., Jan., 1951
(1) see Dell Four Color #312
2 P(c) all 165.00
3 .... 80.00
4 .... 60.00
5 .... 60.00
6 thru 10 .... @60.00
11 thru 20 .... @50.00
21 thru 25 .... @40.00
26 thru 33 .... @40.00

THE LONE RANGER'S FAMOUS HORSE HI-YO SILVER
Dell Publishing Co., Jan., 1952
(1) see Dell Four Color #369
(1) see Dell Four Color #392
3 P(c) all 60.00
4 .... 60.00
5 .... 60.00
6 thru 10 .... @60.00
11 thru 36 .... @50.00

LONE RIDER
Farrell (Superior Comics) April, 1951
1 .... 300.00

*The Lone Rider
© Superior Comics*

Lone Rider–Love Diary GOLDEN AGE Comics Values Annual

2 I&O: Golden Arrow; 52 pgs. . . 165.00
3 . . . . 140.00
4 . . . . 140.00
5 . . . . 140.00
6 E: Golden Arrow 145.00
7 G.Arrow Becomes Swift Arrow 145.00
8 O: Swift Arrow 165.00
9 thru 14 . . . . @75.00
15 O: Golden Arrow Rep. #2. . . . . 85.00
16 thru 19 . . . . @60.00
20 . . . . 60.00
21 3-D (c). 150.00
22 . . . . 60.00
23 A: Apache Kid 60.00
24 . . . . 60.00
25 . . . . 60.00
26 July, 1955 . . . . 60.00

LONG BOW
**Real Adventures Publ.
(Fiction House) Winter, 1950**
1 . . . . 175.00
2 . . . . 100.00
3 'Red Arrows Means War' 85.00
4 'Trial of Tomahawk' 85.00
5 . . . . 85.00
6 'Rattlesnake Raiders' 75.00
7 . . . . 75.00
8 . . . . 75.00
9 Spring, 1953 . . . . 75.00

LOONEY TUNES AND MERRIE MELODIES
Dell Publishing Co., 1941
1 B:&1st Comic App. Bugs Bunny
   Daffy Duck,Elmer Fudd . . 16,000.00
2 Bugs/Porky(c) 3,000.00
3 Bugs/Porky(c) B:WK,
   Kandi the Cave 2,000.00
4 Bugs/Porky(c),WK 2,000.00
5 Bugs/Porky(c),WK,
   A:Super Rabbit 1,500.00
6 Bugs/Porky/Elmer(c),E:WK,
   Kandi the Cave 1,400.00
7 Bugs/Porky(c). 900.00
8 Bugs/Porky swimming(c),F:WK,
   Kandi the Cave 1,200.00
9 Porky/Elmer car painted(c) . . . 900.00
10 Porky/Bugs/Elmer Parade(c) . 900.00
11 Bugs/Porky(c),F:WK,
   Kandi the Cave. 900.00
12 Bugs/Porky rollerskating(c). . . 600.00

*Looney Tunes and Merrie Melodies #3
© Dell PublishingCo.*

13 Bugs/Porky(c) 600.00
14 Bugs/Porky(c) 600.00
15 Bugs/Porky X-Mas(c),F:WK
   Kandi the Cave. 550.00
16 Bugs/Porky ice-skating(c). . . . 550.00
17 Bugs/Petunia Valentines(c) . . 550.00
18 Sgt.Bugs Marine(c) 550.00
19 Bugs/Painting(c) 550.00
20 Bugs/Porky/ElmerWarBonds(c),
   B:WK,Pat,Patsy&Pete. 550.00
21 Bugs/Porky 4th July(c). 550.00
22 Porky(c). 550.00
23 Bugs/Porky Fishing(c) 550.00
24 Bugs/Porky Football(c). 550.00
25 Bugs/Porky/Petunia Halloween
   (c),E:WK,Pat, Patsy & Pete . 550.00
26 Bugs Thanksgiving(c). 400.00
27 Bugs/Porky New Years(c). . . . 400.00
28 Bugs/Porky Ice-Skating(c) . . . 400.00
29 Bugs Valentine(c). 400.00
30 Bugs(c) 400.00
31 Bugs(c) 300.00
32 Bugs/Porky Hot Dogs(c). 300.00
33 Bugs/Porky War Bonds(c) . . . 325.00
34 Bugs/Porky Fishing(c) 300.00
35 Bugs/Porky Swimming(c). . . . 300.00
36 Bugs/Porky(c) 300.00
37 Bugs Halloween(c). 300.00
38 Bugs Thanksgiving(c). 300.00
39 Bugs X-Mas(c). 300.00
40 Bugs(c) 300.00
41 Bugs Washington's
   Birthday(c) 250.00
42 Bugs Magician(c). 250.00
43 Bugs Dream(c). 250.00
44 Bugs/Porky(c). 250.00
45 Bugs War Bonds(c) 250.00
46 Bugs/Porky(c). 225.00
47 Bugs Beach(c). 225.00
48 Bugs/Porky Picnic(c) 225.00
49 Bugs(c) 225.00
50 Bugs(c) 225.00
51 thru 60 . . . . @175.00
61 thru 80 . . . . @150.00
81 thru 86 . . . . @100.00
87 Bugs X-Mas(c). 125.00
88 thru 99 . . . . @100.00
100. . . . . 125.00
101 thru 110 . . . . @75.00
111 thru 125 . . . . @70.00
126 thru 150 . . . . @60.00
151 thru 165 . . . . @50.00
Becomes:

LOONEY TUNES
Aug., 1955
166 thru 200 . . . . @50.00
201 thru 245 . . . . @45.00
246 final issue,Sept.1962 . . . . . . 50.00

LOST WORLD
**Literacy Enterprises
(Standard Comics)
Oct., 1952**
5 ATh, Alice in Terrorland 600.00
6 ATh 450.00

LOVE AND MARRIAGE
**Superior Comics Ltd.
March, 1952**
1 . . . . 135.00
2 . . . . 75.00
3 . . . . 50.00
4 . . . . 50.00
5 . . . . 50.00
6 . . . . 50.00
7 . . . . 50.00
8 thru 15 . . . . @50.00
16 Sept., 1954 . . . . 50.00

*Looney Tunes and Merrie Melodies
© Dell Publishing Co.*

LOVE AT FIRST SIGHT
**Periodical House
(Ace Magazines)
Oct., 1949**
1 P(c) 150.00
2 P(c) 75.00
3 . . . . 50.00
4 P(c) 50.00
5 thru 10 . . . . @50.00
11 thru 33 . . . . @40.00
34 1st Edition Under Code 35.00
35 thru 41 . . . . @35.00
42 1956 . . . . 35.00

LOVE CONFESSIONS
**Comics Magazine
(Quality Comics Group)
Oct., 1949**
1 PG,BWa(c)& Some-a 350.00
2 PG,BWa(c) 200.00
3 . . . . 75.00
4 RC 100.00
5 BWa 150.00
6 Ph(c) 60.00
7 Ph(c) Van Johnson 75.00
8 BWa,Robert Mitchum 75.00
9 Ph(c)Jane Russell/Robert
   Mitchum 75.00
10 BWa 125.00
11 thru 18 Ph(c) . . . . @100.00
19 . . . . 100.00
20 BWa 100.00
21 . . . . 40.00
22 BWa 75.00
23 thru 28 . . . . @40.00
29 BWa 100.00
30 thru 38 . . . . @40.00
39 MB 75.00
40 thru 42 . . . . @40.00
43 1st Edition Under Code 40.00
44 . . . . 40.00
45 BWa(a) 65.00
46 . . . . 40.00
47 BWa(c) 75.00
48 . . . . 40.00
49 MB 75.00
50 thru 54 Dec., 1956 . . . . @40.00

LOVE DIARY
**Our Publishing Co./Toytown
July, 1949–Oct., 1955**
1 BK,Ph(c) 200.00
2 BK,Ph(c) 150.00

CVA Page 424 All comics prices listed are for *Near Mint* condition.

GOLDEN AGE — Love Diary–Love Stories

3 BK,Ph(c) 150.00	17 BWa, Ph(c) of Jane Russell . . 125.00	8 BP 50.00
4 thru 9 Ph(c) . . . . @60.00	18 thru 28 Ph(c) . . . . @30.00	9 BP 50.00
10 BEv, Ph(c) 60.00	29 . . . . 45.00	10 BP 50.00
11 thru 24 Ph(c) . . . . @50.00	30 & 31 BWa. . . . . @75.00	11 BP 45.00
25 . . . . 40.00	Becomes:	12 BP 45.00
26 . . . . 40.00	**LOVE SECRETS**	13 BP 45.00
27 Ph(c) 45.00	Aug., 1953	14 BP 45.00
28 . . . . 40.00	32 . . . . 100.00	15 . . . . 40.00
29 Ph(c). 40.00	33 . . . . 50.00	16 . . . . 40.00
30 . . . . 40.00	34 BWa 125.00	17 thru 23 BP . . . . @40.00
31 JB(c) 40.00	35 thru 39 . . . . @50.00	24 BP, Rape Scene 50.00
32 thru 41 . . . . @40.00	40 MB(c)1st Edition Under Code . 75.00	25 BP 35.00
42 MB(c) 40.00	41 thru 48 . . . . @50.00	26 . . . . 35.00
43 thru 47 . . . . @40.00	49 MB 75.00	27 . . . . 35.00
48 1st Edition Under Code 40.00	50 MB 75.00	28 BP 35.00
	51 MB(c) 85.00	29 BP 35.00
LOVE DIARY	52 thru 56 . . . . @40.00	30 . . . . 35.00
Quality Comics Group		31 . . . . 35.00
Sept., 1949	**LOVELORN**	32 Comics Code. 25.00
1 BWa(c) 350.00	Best Syndicated/Michel Publ.	33 BP 25.00
	(American Comics Group)	34 . . . . 25.00
LOVE LESSONS	Aug.–Sept., 1949	35 . . . . 25.00
Harvey Publications	1 . . . . 175.00	36 . . . . 25.00
Oct., 1949	2 . . . . 100.00	37 . . . . 25.00
1 Silver(c) 150.00	3 thru 10 . . . . @75.00	38 S&K (c) 25.00
2 BP 75.00	11 thru 17 . . . . @50.00	39 . . . . 25.00
3 Ph(c) 50.00	18 2pgs. MD-a 50.00	40 BP 25.00
4 . . . . 50.00	19 . . . . 50.00	41 BP 25.00
5 June, 1950 . . . . 50.00	20 . . . . 50.00	42 . . . . 25.00
	21 Prostitution Story 60.00	43 . . . . 25.00
LOVE LETTERS	22 thru 50 . . . . @50.00	44 March, 1957 . . . . 25.00
Comic Magazines	51 July, 1954, 3-D 150.00	
(Quality Comics Group)	Becomes:	**LOVERS LANE**
Nov., 1949	**CONFESSIONS OF**	Lev Gleason Publications
1 PG,BWa(c) 250.00	**THE LOVELORN**	Oct., 1949
2 PG,BWa(c) 200.00	Aug., 1954	1 CBi (c),FG-a 125.00
3 PG,Ph(c) 150.00	52 3-D 165.00	2 P(c) 60.00
4 BWa,Ph(c) 200.00	53 . . . . 50.00	3 P(c) 45.00
5 Ph(c) 75.00	54 3-D 150.00	4 P(c) 45.00
6 Ph(c) 75.00	55 . . . . 40.00	5 P(c) 45.00
7 Ph(c) 75.00	56 Communist Story 60.00	6 GT,P(c), ... 45.00
8 Ph(c) 75.00	57 Comics Code. 25.00	7 P(c), ... 45.00
9 Ph(c) of Robert Mitchum 90.00	58 thru 90 . . . . @25.00	8 P(c), ... 45.00
10 Ph(c) 65.00	91 AW 50.00	9 P(c), ... 45.00
11 BWa,Ph(c) Broadway	92 thru 105 . . . . @25.00	10 P(c) 45.00
Romances 100.00	106 P(c) 25.00	11 thru 19 P(c) . . . . @40.00
12 Ph(c) 50.00	107 P(c) 25.00	20 Ph(c); FF 1 page Ad, ... 45.00
13 Ph(c) 50.00	108 thru 114 . . . . @25.00	21 Ph(c) 35.00
14 Ph(c) 50.00		22 Ph(c) 35.00
15 Ph(c) 50.00	**LOVE MEMORIES**	23 . . . . 35.00
16 Ph(c) of Anthony Quinn 125.00	Fawcett Publications	24 . . . . 35.00
	Autumn, 1949	25 . . . . 35.00
	1 Ph(c) 150.00	26 Ph(c) 35.00
	2 Ph(c) 85.00	27 Ph(c) 35.00
	3 Ph(c) 85.00	28 Ph(c) 35.00
	4 Ph(c) 85.00	29 thru 38 . . . . @35.00
		39 Story Narrated by
	LOVE MYSTERY	Frank Sinatra 60.00
	Fawcett Publications	40 . . . . 35.00
	June, 1950	41 June, 1954 . . . . 35.00
	1 GE, Ph(c) 250.00	
	2 GE, Ph(c) 200.00	**LOVE SCANDALS**
	3 GE & BP, Ph(c); Oct., 1950 . . . 200.00	Comic Magazines
		(Quality Comics Group)
	LOVE PROBLEMS AND	Feb., 1950
	ADVICE ILLUSTRATED	1 BW(a&c) 275.00
	McCombs/Harvey Publications	2 PG-a, Ph(c) 125.00
	Home Comics, June, 1949	3 PG-a, Ph(c) 125.00
	1 BP 175.00	4 BWa(a&c) 18Pgs.; GFx-a 250.00
	2 BP 100.00	5 Ph(c), Oct., 1950 . . . . 100.00
	3 . . . . 75.00	
	4 . . . . 75.00	**LOVE STORIES**
	5 L. Elias(c) 50.00	**OF MARY WORTH**
	6 . . . . 50.00	Harvey Publications
	7 BP 50.00	Sept., 1949
		1 Newspaper Reprints 75.00
		2 Newspaper Reprints 60.00
		3 Newspaper Reprints 50.00

Love Letters #2
© Quality Comics Group

All comics prices listed are for *Near Mint* condition.

GOLDEN AGE

Love–Mad Magazine

4 Newspaper Reprints, ... 50.00
5 May, 1950 . . . . 50.00

LUCKY COMICS
Consolidated Magazines
Jan., 1944–Summer 1946
1 Lucky Star 250.00
2 Henry C. Kiefer(c) 150.00
3 . . . . 150.00
4 . . . . 150.00
5 Devil(c) 150.00

LUCKY DUCK
Standard Comics
(Literary Enterprises)
Jan.–Sept., 1953
5 IS(a&c) 125.00
6 IS(a&c) 100.00
7 IS(a&c) 100.00
8 IS(a&c) 100.00

LUCKY FIGHTS IT THROUGH
Educational Comics, 1949
N# HK-a, V.D. Prevention . . . 1,500.00

LUCKY "7" COMICS
Howard Publications, 1944
1 Bondage(c) Pioneer 500.00

LUCKY STAR
Nationwide Publications 1950
1 JDa,B:52 pages western 200.00
2 JDa 100.00
3 JDa 100.00
4 JDa 90.00
5 JDa 90.00
6 JDa 90.00
7 JDa 90.00
8 thru 13 . . . . @65.00
14 1955,E:52 pages western 65.00

LUCY, THE REAL GONE GAL
St. John Publishing Co.
June, 1953
1 Negligee Panels,Teenage 125.00
2 . . . . 75.00
3 MD-a 60.00
4 Feb., 1954 . . . . 60.00
Becomes:

MEET MISS PEPPER
April, 1954
5 JKu-a 150.00
6 JKu (a&c), June,1954 . . . . . . 125.00

MAD
E.C. Comics
Oct.–Nov., 1952
1 JSe,HK(c),JDa,WW 10,000.00
2 JSe,JDa(c),JDa,WW 3,000.00
3 JSe,HK(c),JDa,WW 2,700.00
4 JSe,HK(c),JDa-Flob Was A Slob,JDa,WW 2,700.00
5 JSe,BE(c).JDa,WW 3,000.00
6 JSe,HK(c),Jda,WW 1,200.00
7 HK(c),JDa,WW 1,200.00
8 HK(c),JDa,WW 1,200.00
9 JSe,HK(c),JDa,WW 1,200.00
10 JSe,HK(c),JDa,WW. 1,300.00
11 BW,BW(c),JDa,WW,Life(c) 1,200.00
12 BK,JDa,WW 1,000.00

Mad #9
© E.C. Comics

13 HK(c),JDa,WW,Red(c) 1,000.00
14 RH,HK(c),JDa,WW, Mona Lisa(c) 1,000.00
15 JDa,WW,Alice in Wonderland(c). 1,000.00
16 HK(c),JDa,WW, Newspaper(c) 1,000.00
17 BK,BW,JDa,WW 1,000.00
18 HK(c),JDa,WW 1,000.00
19 JDa,WW,Racing Form(c) 900.00
20 JDa,WW,Composition(c) 900.00
21 JDa,WW,1st A.E.Neuman(c) . 900.00
22 BE,JDa,WW,Picasso(c) 900.00
23 Last Comic Format Edition, JDa,WW Think(c) 900.00
24 BK,WW, HK Logo & Border; 1st Magazine Format 1,800.00
25 WW,AlJaffee Becomes Reg. 1,000.00
26 BK,WW,WW(c) 500.00
27 WWa,RH,JDa(c) 400.00
28 WW,BE(c),RH Back(c) 400.00
29 JKa,BW,WW,WW(c); 1st Don Martin Artwork 400.00
30 BE,WW,RC; 1st A.E. Neuman(c) By Mingo 600.00
31 JDa,WW,BW,Mingo(c) 350.00
32 MD,JO 1st as reg.;Mingo(c); WW-Back(c) 350.00
33 WWa,Mingo(c);JO-Back(c) . . . 350.00
34 WWa,Mingo(c);1st Berg as Reg. 250.00
35 WW,RC,Mingo Wraparound(c) 225.00
36 WW,BW,Mingo(c),JO,MD 200.00
37 WW,Mingo(c)JO,MD 200.00
38 WW,JO,MD 200.00
39 WW,JO,MD 200.00
40 WW,BW,JO,MD 200.00
41 WW,JO,MD 150.00
42 WW,JO,MD 150.00
43 WW,JO,MD 150.00
44 WW,JO,MD 150.00
45 WW,JO,MD 150.00
46 JO,MD. 150.00
47 JO,MD. 150.00
48 JO,MD. 150.00
49 JO,MD. 150.00
50 JO,MD. 150.00
51 JO,MD. 125.00
52 JO,MD. 125.00
53 JO,MD. 125.00
54 JO,MD. 125.00
55 JO,MD. 125.00
56 JO,MD. 125.00
57 JO,MD. 125.00

58 JO,MD. 125.00
59 WW,JO,MD 150.00
60 JO,MD. 150.00
61 JO,MD. 85.00
62 JO,MD. 85.00
63 JO,MD. 85.00
64 JO,MD. 85.00
65 JO,MD. 85.00
66 JO,MD. 75.00
67 JO,MD. 75.00
68 Don Martin(c),JO,MD. 75.00
69 JO,MD. 75.00
70 JO,MD. 75.00
71 JO,MD. 75.00
72 JO,MD. 75.00
73 JO,MD. 75.00
74 JO,MD. 75.00
75 Mingo(c),JO,MD. 70.00
76 Mingo(c),SA,JO,MD. 90.00
77 Mingo(c),SA,JO,MD. 60.00
78 Mingo(c),SA,JO,MD. 60.00
79 Mingo(c),SA,JO,MD 60.00
80 Mingo(c),SA,JO,MD 60.00
81 Mingo(c),SA,JO,MD 60.00
82 BW,Mingo(c),SA,JO,MD. 60.00
83 Mingo(c),SA,JO,MD 60.00
84 Mingo(c),SA,JO,MD 60.00
85 Mingo(c)SA,JO,MD 60.00
86 Mingo(c);1st Fold-in Back(c), SA,JO,MD 65.00
87 Mingo(c),JO,MD 55.00
88 Mingo(c),JO,MD. 55.00
89 WK,Mingo(c),JO,MD 60.00
90 Mingo(c); FF-Back(c),JO,MD . . 55.00
91 Mingo(c),JO,MD. 50.00
92 Mingo(c),JO,MD. 50.00
93 Mingo(c),JO,MD. 50.00
94 Mingo(c),JO,MD. 50.00
95 Mingo(c),JO,MD. 50.00
96 Mingo(c),JO,MD. 50.00
97 Mingo(c),JO,MD. 50.00
98 Mingo(c),JO,MD. 50.00
99 JDa,Mingo(c),JO,MD 60.00
100 Mingo(c),JO,MD. 50.00
101 Infinity(c) by Mingo,JO,MD . . . 40.00
102 Mingo(c)JO,MD 35.00
103 Mingo(c)JO,MD 35.00
104 Mingo(c)JO,MD 35.00
105 Mingo(c);Batman TV Spoof ,JO,MD. 40.00
106 Mingo(c);FF-Back(c),JO,MD. . 40.00
107 Mingo(c),JO,MD. 35.00
108 Mingo(c),JO,MD. 35.00
109 Mingo(c),JO,MD. 35.00
110 Mingo(c),JO,MD. 35.00
111 Mingo(c),JO,MD. 35.00
112 JO,MD. 35.00
113 JO,MD. 35.00
114 JO,MD. 35.00
115 JO,MD. 35.00
116 JO,MD. 35.00
117 JO,MD. 35.00
118 JO,MD. 35.00
119 JO,MD. 35.00
120 JO,MD. 35.00
121 Beatles,JO,MD. 35.00
122 MD & Mingo(c),JO,MD, Reagan 30.00
123 JO,MD. 25.00
124 JO,MD. 25.00
125 JO,MD. 25.00
126 JO,MD. 25.00
127 JO,MD. 25.00
128 Last JO;MD. 25.00
129 MD 25.00
130 MD 25.00
131 MD 25.00
132 MD 25.00
133 MD 25.00
134 MD 25.00
135 JDa(c),MD 30.00

GOLDEN AGE

MAD HATTER, THE
O.W. Comics, 1946
1 Freddy the Firefly	1,000.00
2 V:Humpty Dumpty	500.00

MAGIC COMICS
David McKay Publications
Aug., 1939–Nov.-Dec., 1949
1 Mandrake the Magician, Henry, Popeye,Blondie, Barney Baxter, Secret Agent X-9, Bunky, Henry on(c)	3,600.00
2 Henry on(c)	1,400.00
3 Henry on(c)	1,000.00
4 Henry on(c),Mandrake-Logo	850.00
5 Henry on(c),Mandrake-Logo	750.00
6 Henry on(c),Mandrake-Logo	500.00
7 Henry on(c),Mandrake-Logo	500.00
8 B:Inspector Wade,Tippie	450.00
9 Henry-Mandrake Interact(c)	450.00
10 Henry-Mandrake Interact(c)	450.00
11 Henry-Mandrake Interact(c)	425.00
12 Mandrake on(c)	425.00
13 Mandrake on(c)	425.00
14 Mandrake on(c)	425.00
15 Mandrake on(c)	425.00
16 Mandrake on(c)	425.00
17 B:Lone Ranger	500.00
18 Mandrake/Robot on(c)	400.00
19 Mandrake on(c)	500.00
20 Mandrake on(c)	400.00
21 Mandrake on(c)	300.00
22 Mandrake on(c)	300.00
23 Mandrake on(c)	300.00
24 Mandrake on(c)	300.00
25 B:Blondie; Mandrake in Logo for Duration	300.00
26 Blondie (c)	250.00
27 Blondie(c); HighSchoolHeroes	250.00
28 Blondie(c); HighSchoolHeroes	250.00
29 Blondie(c); HighSchoolHeroes	250.00
30 Blondie (c)	250.00
31 Blondie(c);High School Sports Page	225.00
32 Blondie (c);Secret Agent X-9	225.00
33 C.Knight's-Romance of Flying	225.00
34 ClaytonKnight's-War in the Air	225.00
35 Blondie (c)	225.00
36 July'42; Patriotic-(c)	225.00
37 Blondie (c)	225.00
38 ClaytonKnight's-Flying Tigers	225.00
39 Blondie (c)	225.00
40 Jimmie Doolittle bombs Tokyo	225.00
41 How German Became British Censor	200.00
42 Joe Musial's-Dollar-a-Dither	200.00
43 Clay Knight's-War in the Air	200.00
44 Flying Fortress in Action	200.00
45 Clayton Knight's-Gremlins	200.00
46 Adventures of Aladdin Jr.	200.00
47 Secret Agent X-9	200.00
48 General Arnold U.S.A.F.	200.00
49 Joe Musial's-Dollar-a-Dither	200.00
50 The Lone Ranger	200.00
51 Joe Musial's-Dollar-a-Dither	150.00
52 C. Knights-Heroes on Wings	150.00
53 C. Knights-Heroes on Wings	150.00
54 High School Heroes	150.00
55 Blondie (c)	175.00
56 High School Heroes	150.00
57 Joe Musial's-Dollar-a-Dither	150.00
58 Private Breger Abroad	150.00
59	150.00
60	150.00
61 Joe Musial's-Dollar-a-Dither	125.00
62	125.00
63 B:Buz Sawyer, Naval Pilot	125.00
64 thru 70	@125.00
71 thru 80	@125.00
81 thru 90	@100.00
91 thru 99	@100.00
100	125.00
101 thru 108	@75.00
108 Flash Gordon	100.00
109 Flash Gordon	100.00
110 thru 113	@100.00
114 The Lone Ranger	100.00
115 thru 119	@100.00
120 Secret Agent X-9	120.00
121 Secret Agent X-9	120.00
122 Secret Agent X-9	120.00
123 Sec. Agent X-9	120.00

MAJOR HOOPLE COMICS
Nedor Publications, 1942
1 Mary Worth,Phantom Soldier; Buy War Bonds On(c)	500.00

MAJOR VICTORY COMICS
H. Clay Glover Svcs./ Harry A. Chestler, 1944
1 O:Major Victory,I:Spider Woman	850.00
2 A: Dynamic Boy	500.00
3 A: Rocket Boy	450.00

MAN HUNT!
Magazine Enterprises, 1953
1 LbC,FG,OW(c);B:Red Fox, Undercover Girl, Space Ace	650.00
2 LbC,FG,OW(c); Electrocution(c)	500.00
3 LbC,FG,OW,OW(c)	400.00
4 LbC,FG,OW,OW(c)	400.00
5 LbC,FG,OW,OW(c)	400.00
6 LbC,OW,OW(c)	350.00
7 LbC,OW; E:Space Ace	350.00
8 LbC,OW,FG(c);B:Trail Colt	350.00
9 LbC,OW	350.00
10 LbC,OW,OW(c),Gwl	350.00
11 LbC,FF,OW;B:The Duke, Scotland Yard	500.00
12 LbC,OW	300.00
13 LbC,FF,OW;Rep.Trail Colt #1	350.00
14 LbC,OW;Bondage, Hypo-(c);1953	350.00

Comics Values Annual — left column:
136 MD	25.00
137 BW,MD	25.00
138 MD	25.00
139 JDa(c),MD	25.00
140 thru 149 MD	@25.00
150	30.00
151 thru 153	@20.00
154 Mineo(c),MD	20.00
155 thru 159	@20.00
160 Mingo(c),JDa,AT	20.00
161	18.00
162 Mingo(c),MD,AT	18.00
163	18.00
164 Mingo,PaperMoon(c),AT, MD,SA	18.00
165 Don Martin(c),At,MD	18.00
166	18.00
167	18.00
168 Mingo(c),AT,MD	18.00
169 MD(c)	18.00
170	18.00
171 Mingo(c)	15.00
172 Mingo(c)	15.00
173 JDa(c)	15.00
174	15.00
175	15.00
176 MD(c)	15.00
177	15.00
178 JDa(c)	15.00
179	15.00
180 Jaws(c),SA,MD,JDA,AT	15.00
181 G.Washington(c),JDa	15.00
182	15.00
183 Mingo(c),AT,SA,MD	15.00
184 Mingo(c),Md,AT	15.00
185	15.00
186 Star Trek Spoof	20.00
187	15.00
188	20.00
189	15.00
190	15.00
191 Clark(c),JDa,MD,AT	15.00
192	15.00
193 Charlies Angels(c), Rickart,JDa,SA,MD	15.00
194 Rocky(c),Rickart,AT,MD	15.00
195	15.00
196 Star Wars Spoof, Rickart,AT,JDa	25.00
197	20.00
198 UPC(c),AT,MD	15.00
199 Jaffee(c),AT,JDa,SA,MD	15.00
200 Rickart(c),Close Encounters	20.00
201 Rickart(c),Sat.Night Fever	15.00
202	15.00
203 Star Wars Spoof,Rickart(c)	10.00
204 Hulk TV Spoof,JawsII(c)	10.00
205 Rickart(c),Grease	10.00
206 Mingo,(c),AT,JDa,Md	10.00
207 Jones(c),Animal House(c)	10.00
208 Superman Movie Spoof, Rickart(c)	15.00
209 Mingo(c),AT,MD	10.00
210 Mingo,Lawn Mower,AT, JDa,MD	10.00
211 Mingo(c)	10.00
212 Jda(c),AT,MD	10.00
213 JDa(c),SA,AT,JDa	10.00
214	10.00
215 Jones(c),MD,AT,JDa	10.00
216	10.00
217 Jaffee(c),For Pres,AT,MD	10.00
218 Martin(c),AT,MD	10.00
219 thru 250	@10.00
251 thru 260	@8.00
261 thru 299	@6.00
300 thru 303	@8.00
304 thru 330	@5.00
331 thru 350	@4.00
350 thru 390	@3.00

Magic Comics #8
© David McKay Publications

All comics prices listed are for *Near Mint* condition.

CVA Page 427

MAN OF WAR
Comic Corp. of America (Centaur Publ.), Nov., 1941
1 PG,PG(c);Flag(c);B:The Fire-Man,Man of War,The Sentinel, Liberty Guards,Vapoman . . 2,500.00
2 PG,PG(c);I: The Ferret 1,800.00

MAN O'MARS
Fiction House/ I.W. Enterprises, 1953
1 MA, Space Rangers 500.00
1 MA, Rep. Space Rangers . . . 100.00

MARCH OF COMICS
K.K. Publications/ Western Publ., 1946 (All were Giveaways)
N# WK back(c),Goldilocks . . . 300.00
N# WK,How Santa got His Red Suit 300.00
N# WK,Our Gang 400.00
N# CB,Donald Duck; 'Maharajah Donald' 8,500.00
5 Andy Panda 200.00
6 WK,Fairy Tales 250.00
7 Oswald the Lucky Rabbit . . . 200.00
8 Mickey Mouse 600.00
9 Gloomey Bunny 100.00
10 Santa Claus 100.00
11 Santa Claus 75.00
12 Santa's Toys 75.00
13 Santa's Suprise 75.00
14 Santa's Kitchen 75.00
15 Hip-It-Ty Hop 75.00
16 Woody Woodpecker 150.00
17 Roy Rogers 260.00
18 Fairy Tales 125.00
19 Uncle Wiggily 100.00
20 CB, Donald Duck 5,000.00
21 Tom and Jerry 125.00
22 Andy Panda 100.00
23 Raggedy Ann and Andy 125.00
24 Felix the Cat; By Otto Messmer 250.00
25 Gene Autrey 250.00
26 Our Gang 275.00
27 Mickey Mouse 450.00
28 Gene Autry 250.00
29 Easter 50.00
30 Santa 50.00
31 Santa 50.00
32 Does Not Exist
33 A Christmas Carol 50.00
34 Woody Woodpecker 100.00
35 Roy Rogers 250.00
36 Felix the Cat 200.00
37 Popeye 150.00
38 Oswald the Lucky Rabbit 75.00
39 Gene Autry 250.00
40 Andy and Woody 75.00
41 CB,DonaldDuck,SouthSeas . 4,500.00
42 Porky Pig 80.00
43 Henry 75.00
44 Bugs Bunny 100.00
45 Mickey Mouse 350.00
46 Tom and Jerry 100.00
47 Roy Rogers 250.00
48 Santa 35.00
49 Santa 35.00
50 Santa 35.00
51 Felix the Cat 175.00
52 Popeye 150.00
53 Oswald the Lucky Rabbit 75.00
54 Gene Autrey 250.00
55 Andy and Woody 75.00
56 CB back(c),Donald Duck 350.00
57 Porky Pig 75.00
58 Henry 50.00
59 Bugs Bunny 75.00
60 Mickey Mouse 300.00
61 Tom and Jerry 75.00
62 Roy Rogers 250.00
63 Santa 40.00
64 Santa 40.00
65 Jingle Bells 40.00
66 Popeye 125.00
67 Oswald the Lucky Rabbit 75.00
68 Roy Rogers 225.00
69 Donald Duck 300.00
70 Tom and Jerry 60.00
71 Porky Pig 75.00
72 Krazy Kat 75.00
73 Roy Rogers 200.00
74 Mickey Mouse 300.00
75 Bugs Bunny 75.00
76 Andy and Woody 65.00
77 Roy Rogers 175.00
78 Gene Autrey; last regular sized issue 175.00
79 Andy Panda,5"x7" format 50.00
80 Popeye 100.00
81 Oswald the Lucky Rabbit 35.00
82 Tarzan 200.00
83 Bugs Bunny 50.00
84 Henry 35.00
85 Woody Woodpecker 35.00
86 Roy Rogers 150.00
87 Krazy Kat 65.00
88 Tom and Jerry 50.00
89 Porky Pig 40.00
90 Gene Autrey 125.00
91 Roy Rogers and Santa 150.00
92 Christmas w/Santa 30.00
93 Woody Woodpecker 30.00
94 Indian Chief 100.00
95 Oswald the Lucky Rabbit 30.00
96 Popeye 75.00
97 Bugs Bunny 50.00
98 Tarzan,Lex Barker Ph(c) 200.00
99 Porky Pig 30.00
100 Roy Rogers 125.00
101 Henry 30.00
102 Tom Corbet,P(c) 150.00
103 Tom and Jerry 30.00
104 Gene Autrey 100.00
105 Roy Rogers 125.00
106 Santa's Helpers 30.00
107 Not Published
108 Fun with Santa 30.00
109 Woody Woodpecker 30.00
110 Indian Chief 45.00
111 Oswald the Lucky Rabbit 30.00
112 Henry 25.00
113 Porky Pig 30.00
114 Tarzan,RsM 175.00
115 Bugs Bunny 50.00
116 Roy Rogers 125.00
117 Popeye 75.00
118 Flash Gordon, P(c) 150.00
119 Tom and Jerry 25.00
120 Gene Autrey 100.00
121 Roy Rogers 125.00
122 Santa's Suprise 25.00
123 Santa's Christmas Book 25.00
124 Woody Woodpecker 25.00
125 Tarzan, Lex Barker Ph(c) . . . 175.00
126 Oswald the Lucky Rabbit 30.00
127 Indian Chief 35.00
128 Tom and Jerry 30.00
129 Henry 25.00
130 Porky Pig 30.00
131 Roy Rogers 125.00
132 Bugs Bunny 35.00
133 Flash Gordon,Ph(c) 125.00
134 Popeye 75.00
135 Gene Autrey 75.00
136 Roy Rogers 100.00
137 Gifts from Santa 20.00
138 Fun at Christmas 20.00
139 Woody Woodpecker 25.00
140 Indian Chief 35.00
141 Oswald the Lucky Rabbit 25.00
142 Flash Gordon 100.00
143 Porky Pig 25.00
144 RsM,Ph(c),Tarzan 150.00
145 Tom and Jerry 25.00
146 Roy Rogers,Ph(c) 125.00
147 Henry 20.00
148 Popeye 60.00
149 Bugs Bunny 30.00
150 Gene Autrey 100.00
151 Roy Rogers 100.00
152 The Night Before Christmas . . 20.00
153 Merry Christmas 20.00
154 Tom and Jerry 25.00
155 Tarzan,Ph(c) 150.00
156 Oswald the Lucky Rabbit 20.00
157 Popeye 50.00
158 Woody Woodpecker 25.00
159 Indian Chief 25.00
160 Bugs Bunny 25.00
161 Roy Rogers 100.00
162 Henry 20.00
163 Rin Tin Tin 65.00
164 Porky Pig 25.00
165 The Lone Ranger 100.00
166 Santa & His Reindeer 20.00
167 Roy Rogers and Santa 100.00
168 Santa Claus' Workshop 20.00
169 Popeye 50.00
170 Indian Chief 35.00
171 Oswald the Lucky Rabbit 25.00
172 Tarzan 150.00
173 Tom and Jerry 20.00
174 The Lone Ranger 100.00
175 Porky Pig 25.00
176 Roy Rogers 75.00
177 Woody Woodpecker 20.00
178 Henry 20.00
179 Bugs Bunny 25.00
180 Rin Tin Tin 75.00
181 Happy Holiday 20.00
182 Happi Tim 20.00
183 Welcome Santa 20.00
184 Woody Woodpecker 20.00
185 Tarzan, Ph(c) 125.00
186 Oswald the Lucky Rabbit 20.00
187 Indian Chief 35.00
188 Bugs Bunny 30.00
189 Henry 20.00
190 Tom and Jerry 22.00
191 Roy Rogers 75.00
192 Porky Pig 25.00
193 The Lone Ranger 100.00

March of Comics #41
© Walt Disney

Comics Values Annual — GOLDEN AGE — March of Comics

#	Title	Price
194	Popeye	45.00
195	Rin Tin Tin	75.00
196	Not Published	
197	Santa is Coming	25.00
198	Santa's Helper	25.00
199	Huckleberry Hound	75.00
200	Fury	40.00
201	Bugs Bunny	30.00
202	Space Explorer	75.00
203	Woody Woodpecker	20.00
204	Tarzan	100.00
205	Mighty Mouse	40.00
206	Roy Rogers, Ph(c)	75.00
207	Tom and Jerry	20.00
208	The Lone Ranger, Ph(c)	125.00
209	Porky Pig	20.00
210	Lassie	35.00
211	Not Published	
212	Christmas Eve	20.00
213	Here Comes Santa	20.00
214	Huckleberry Hound	65.00
215	Hi Yo Silver	50.00
216	Rocky & His Friends	100.00
217	Lassie	25.00
218	Porky Pig	25.00
219	Journey to the Sun	50.00
220	Bugs Bunny	25.00
221	Roy and Dale, Ph(c)	75.00
222	Woody Woodpecker	20.00
223	Tarzan	100.00
224	Tom and Jerry	20.00
225	The Lone Ranger	75.00
226	Christmas Treasury	20.00
227	Not Published	
228	Letters to Santa	20.00
229	The Flintstones	125.00
230	Lassie	25.00
231	Bugs Bunny	25.00
232	The Three Stooges	125.00
233	Bullwinkle	100.00
234	Smokey the Bear	25.00
235	Huckleberry Hound	50.00
236	Roy and Dale	75.00
237	Mighty Mouse	25.00
238	The Lone Ranger	75.00
239	Woody Woodpecker	20.00
240	Tarzan	100.00
241	Santa Around the World	15.00
242	Santa Toyland	15.00
243	The Flintstones	125.00
244	Mr.Ed, Ph(c)	50.00
245	Bugs Bunny	25.00
246	Popeye	30.00
247	Mighty Mouse	20.00
248	The Three Stooges	100.00
249	Woody Woodpecker	15.00
250	Roy and Dale	65.00
251	Little Lulu & Witch Hazel	135.00
252	P(c), Tarzan	80.00
253	Yogi Bear	30.00
254	Lassie	40.00
255	Santa's Christmas List	15.00
256	Christmas Party	15.00
257	Mighty Mouse	25.00
258	The Sword in the Stone (Disney Version)	75.00
259	Bugs Bunny	25.00
260	Mr. Ed	35.00
261	Woody Woodpecker	20.00
262	Tarzan	70.00
263	Donald Duck	90.00
264	Popeye	30.00
265	Yogi Bear	35.00
266	Lassie	35.00
267	Little Lulu	100.00
268	The Three Stooges	90.00
269	A Jolly Christmas	15.00
270	Santa's Little Helpers	15.00
271	The Flintstones	90.00
272	Tarzan	75.00
273	Bugs Bunny	25.00
274	Popeye	25.00
275	Little Lulu	90.00
276	The Jetsons	150.00
277	Daffy Duck	20.00
278	Lassie	25.00
279	Yogi Bear	35.00
280	Ph(c), The Three Stooges	90.00
281	Tom & Jerry	20.00
282	Mr. Ed	25.00
283	Santa's Visit	15.00
284	Christmas Parade	15.00
285	Astro Boy	350.00
286	Tarzan	45.00
287	Bugs Bunny	25.00
288	Daffy Duck	20.00
289	The Flintstones	75.00
290	Ph(c), Mr. Ed	22.00
291	Yogi Bear	30.00
292	Ph(c), The Three Stooges	90.00
293	Little Lulu	65.00
294	Popeye	25.00
295	Tom & Jerry	20.00
296	Lassie	25.00
297	Christmas Bells	15.00
298	Santa's Sleigh	15.00
299	The Flintstones	75.00
300	Tarzan	60.00
301	Bugs Bunny	20.00
302	Ph(c), Laurel & Hardy	35.00
303	Daffy Duck	15.00
304	Ph(c), The Three Stooges	75.00
305	Tom & Jerry	15.00
306	Ph(c), Daniel Boone	60.00
307	Little Lulu	50.00
308	Ph(c), Lassie	20.00
309	Yogi Bear	30.00
310	Ph(c) of Clayton Moore; The Lone Ranger	85.00
311	Santa's Show	15.00
312	Christmas Album	15.00
313	Daffy Duck	18.00
314	Laurel & Hardy	35.00
315	Bugs Bunny	20.00
316	The Three Stooges	60.00
317	The Flintstones	35.00
318	Tarzan	50.00
319	Yogi Bear	25.00
320	Space Family Robinson	135.00
321	Tom & Jerry	18.00
322	The Lone Ranger	55.00
323	Little Lulu	35.00
324	Ph(c), Lassie	18.00
325	Fun With Santa	15.00
326	Christmas Story	15.00
327	The Flintstones	75.00
328	Space Family Robinson	125.00
329	Bugs Bunny	20.00
330	The Jetsons	90.00
331	Daffy Duck	18.00
332	Tarzan	60.00
333	Tom & Jerry	18.00
334	Lassie	20.00
335	Little Lulu	30.00
336	The Three Stooges	60.00
337	Yogi Bear	25.00
338	The Lone Ranger	60.00
339	Not Published	
340	Here Comes Santa	15.00
341	The Flintstones	65.00
342	Tarzan	50.00
343	Bugs Bunny	25.00
344	Yogi Bear	28.00
345	Tom & Jerry	18.00
346	Lassie	20.00
347	Daffy Duck	18.00
348	The Jetsons	80.00
349	Little Lulu	30.00
350	The Lone Ranger	40.00
351	Beep-Beep, The Road Runner	25.00
352	Space Family Robinson	120.00
353	Beep-Beep, The Road Runner	25.00
354	Tarzan	35.00
355	Little Lulu	30.00
356	Scooby Doo, Where Are You	60.00
357	Daffy Duck & Porky Pig	18.00
358	Lassie	20.00
359	Baby Snoots	18.00
360	Ph(c), H.R. Pufnstuf	65.00
361	Tom & Jerry	18.00
362	Smokey the Bear	20.00
363	Bugs Bunny & Yosemite Sam	20.00
364	Ph(c), The Banana Splits	60.00
365	Tom & Jerry	18.00
366	Tarzan	35.00
367	Bugs Bunny & Porky Pig	20.00
368	Scooby Doo	55.00
369	Little Lulu	25.00
370	Ph(c), Lassie	18.00
371	Baby Snoots	15.00
372	Smokey The Bear	20.00
373	The Three Stooges	60.00
374	Wacky Witch	15.00
375	Beep-Beep & Daffy Duck	18.00
376	The Pink Panther	25.00
377	Baby Snoots	15.00
378	Turok, Son of Stone	135.00
379	Heckle & Jeckle	15.00
380	Bugs Bunny & Yosemite Sam	20.00
381	Lassie	18.00
382	Scooby Doo	22.00
383	Smokey the Bear	18.00
384	The Pink Panther	25.00
385	Little Lulu	20.00
386	Wacky Witch	20.00
387	Beep-Beep & Daffy Duck	15.00
388	Tom & Jerry	15.00
389	Little Lulu	20.00
390	The Pink Panther	25.00
391	Scooby Doo	22.00
392	Bugs Bunny & Yosemite Sam	20.00
393	Heckle & Jeckle	15.00
394	Lassie	15.00
395	Woodsy the Owl	15.00
396	Baby Snoots	15.00
397	Beep-Beep & Daffy Duck	15.00
398	Wacky Witch	15.00
399	Turok, Son of Stone	120.00
400	Tom & Jerry	15.00
401	Baby Snoots	15.00
402	Daffy Duck	15.00
403	Bugs Bunny	15.00
404	Space Family Robinson	75.00
405	Cracky	10.00
406	Little Lulu	20.00
407	Smokey the Bear	10.00
408	Turok, Son of Stone	75.00

March of Comics #70
© M. G. M.

All comics prices listed are for *Near Mint* condition.

GOLDEN AGE

March of–Marvel Family / Comics Values Annual

#	Title	Price
409	The Pink Panther	20.00
410	Wacky Witch	10.00
411	Lassie	15.00
412	New Terrytoons	8.00
413	Daffy Duck	8.00
414	Space Family Robinson	80.00
415	Bugs Bunny	15.00
416	The Road Runner	20.00
417	Little Lulu	20.00
418	The Pink Panther	20.00
419	Baby Snoots	8.00
420	Woody Woodpecker	8.00
421	Tweety & Sylvester	8.00
422	Wacky Witch	8.00
423	Little Monsters	8.00
424	Cracky	8.00
425	Daffy Duck	8.00
426	Underdog	40.00
427	Little Lulu	15.00
428	Bugs Bunny	10.00
429	The Pink Panther	11.00
430	The Road Runner	11.00
431	Baby Snoots	8.00
432	Lassie	9.00
433	Tweety & Sylvester	8.00
434	Wacky Witch	8.00
435	New Terrytoons	8.00
436	Cracky	8.00
437	Daffy Duck	8.00
438	Underdog	35.00
439	Little Lulu	15.00
440	Bugs Bunny	10.00
441	The Pink Panther	15.00
442	The Road Runner	7.00
443	Baby Snoots	6.00
444	Tom & Jerry	6.00
445	Tweety & Sylvester	6.00
446	Wacky Witch	6.00
447	Mighty Mouse	7.00
448	Cracky	6.00
449	The Pink Panther	8.00
450	Baby Snoots	6.00
451	Tom & Jerry	6.00
452	Bugs Bunny	6.00
453	Popeye	5.00
454	Woody Woodpecker	6.00
455	The Road Runner	7.00
456	Little Lulu	5.00
457	Tweety & Sylvester	5.00
458	Wacky Witch	5.00
459	Mighty Mouse	7.00
460	Daffy Duck	5.00
461	The Pink Panther	9.00
462	Baby Snoots	5.00
463	Tom & Jerry	6.00
464	Bugs Bunny	7.00
465	Popeye	6.00
466	Woody Woodpecker	6.00
467	Underdog	35.00
468	Little Lulu	6.00
469	Tweety & Sylvester	6.00
470	Wacky Witch	6.00
471	Mighty Mouse	7.00
472	Heckle & Jeckle	6.00
473	The Pink Panther	6.00
474	Baby Snoots	6.00
475	Little Lulu	6.00
476	Bugs Bunny	7.00
477	Popeye	6.00
478	Woody Woodpecker	7.00
479	Underdog	30.00
480	Tom & Jerry	10.00
481	Tweety & Sylvster	6.00
482	Wacky Witch	6.00
483	Mighty Mouse	7.00
484	Heckle & Jeckle	6.00
485	Baby Snoots	6.00
486	The Pink Panther	9.00
487	Bugs Bunny	8.00
488	April, 1982; Little Lulu	10.00

MARGE'S LITTLE LULU
Dell Publishing Co.

#	Title	Price
1	B:Lulu's Diary	1,000.00
2	I:Gloria,Miss Feeny	500.00
3		450.00
4		450.00
5		450.00
6		350.00
7	I:Annie,X-Mas (c)	350.00
8		350.00
9		350.00
10		350.00
11 thru 18		@300.00
19	I:Wilbur	300.00
20	I:Mr.McNabbem	300.00
21 thru 25		@250.00
26	rep.Four Color#110	250.00
27 thru 29		@250.00
30	Christmas (c)	250.00
31 thru 34		@225.00
35	B:Mumday Story	225.00
36 thru 38		@225.00
39	I:Witch Hazel	250.00
40	Halloween (c)	175.00
41		175.00
42	Christmas (c)	175.00
43	Skiing (c)	175.00
44	Valentines Day (c)	175.00
45	2nd A:Witch Hazel	175.00
46 thru 60		@175.00
61		150.00
62		150.00
63	I:Chubby	150.00
64 thru 67		@150.00
68	I:Professor Cleff	150.00
69 thru 77		@150.00
78	Christmas (c)	150.00
79		150.00
80		150.00
81 thru 89		@100.00
90	Christmas (c)	100.00
91 thru 99		@100.00
100		150.00
101 thru 122		@100.00
123	I:Fifi	85.00
124 thru 164		@75.00
165	giant sized	200.00
166	giant sized	200.00
167 thru 169		@60.00
170		30.00
171		30.00
172		35.00
173		30.00
174		30.00
175		35.00
176		35.00
177		30.00
178 thru 196		@30.00
197		30.00
198 thru 200		@35.00
201		20.00
202		25.00
203		20.00
204		25.00
205		25.00
206		20.00

MARMADUKE MOUSE
Quality Comics Group (Arnold Publications), 1946

#	Title	Price
1	Funny Animal	175.00
2	Funny Animal	100.00
3 thru 8	Funny Animal	@75.00
9	Funny Animal	50.00
10	Funny Animal	50.00
11 thru 20	Funny Animal	@40.00
21 thru 30	Funny Animal	@30.00
31 thru 40	Funny Animal	@30.00
41 thru 50	Funny Animal	@30.00
51 thru 65	Funny Animal	@30.00

MARTIN KANE
Hero Books (Fox Features Syndicate) June, 1950

#	Title	Price
1	WW,WW-(c)	350.00
2	WW,JO, Auguat, 1950	250.00

Marvel Family #9
© Fawcett Publications

MARVEL FAMILY, THE
Fawcett Publications Dec., 1945–Jan., 1954

#	Title	Price
1	O:Captain Marvel,Captain Marvel Jr., Mary Marvel,Uncle Marvel; V:Black Adam	2,400.00
2	Uncle Marvel	1,000.00
3		750.00
4	The Witch's Tale	600.00
5	Civilization of a Prehistoric Race	550.00
6		500.00
7	The Rock of Eternity	450.00
8	The Marvel Family Round Table	450.00
9	V: The Last Vikings	450.00
10	V: The Sivana Family	450.00
11	V: The Well of Evil	350.00
12	V: The Iron Horseman	350.00
13		350.00
14	Captain Marvel Invalid	350.00
15	V: Mr. Triangle	325.00
16	World's Mightiest Quarrell	325.00
17		325.00
18		325.00
19	V: The Monster Menace	325.00
20	The Marvel Family Feud	325.00
21	V: The Trio of Terror	300.00
22	V: The Triple Threat	300.00
23	March of Independence (c)	325.00
24	V: The Fighting Xergos	300.00
25	Trial of the Marvel Family	300.00
26	V: Mr. Power	300.00
27	V: The Amoeba Men	300.00
28		300.00
29	V: The Monarch of Money	300.00
30	A:World's Greatest Magician	300.00
31	V:Sivana & The Great Hunger	250.00
32	The Marvel Family Goes Into Buisness	250.00
33	I: The Hermit Family	250.00
34	V: Sivana's Miniature Menace	250.00
35	V: The Berzerk Machines	250.00
36	V: The Invaders From Infinity	250.00
37	V: The Earth Changer	250.00
38	V: Sivana's Instinct Exterminator Gun	250.00

CVA Page 430 — All comics prices listed are for *Near Mint* condition.

GOLDEN AGE — Marvel–Master Comics

#	Title	Price
39	The Legend of Atlantis	250.00
40	Seven Wonders of the Modern World	250.00
41	The Great Oxygen Theft	250.00
42	V: The Endless Menace	200.00
43		200.00
44	V: The Rust That Menaced the World	200.00
45	The Hoax City	200.00
46	The Day Civilization Vanished	200.00
47	V: The Interplanetary Thieves	300.00
48	V: The Four Horsemen	200.00
49	...Proves Human Hardness	200.00
50	The Speech Scrambler Machine	200.00
51	The Living Statues	210.00
52	The School of Witches	200.00
53	V: The Man Who Changed the World	200.00
54		200.00
55		200.00
56	The World's Mightiest Project	200.00
57		200.00
58	The Triple Time Plot	200.00
59		200.00
60		200.00
61		200.00
62		200.00
63	V: The Pirate Planet	200.00
64		200.00
65		200.00
66	The Miracle Stone	200.00
67		200.00
68		200.00
69	V: The Menace of Old Age	200.00
70	V: The Crusade of Evil	200.00
71		200.00
72		200.00
73		200.00
74		200.00
75	The Great Space Struggle	200.00
76		225.00
77	Anti-Communist	275.00
78	V: The Red Vulture	200.00
79		175.00
80		175.00
81		175.00
82		175.00
83	V: The Flying Skull	175.00
84 thru 87		@175.00
88	Jokes of Jeopardy	175.00
89	And Then There Were None	175.00

MARVELS OF SCIENCE
Charlton Comics, 1946

#	Title	Price
1	1st Charlton Book; Atomic Bomb Story	250.00
2		150.00
3		150.00
4	President Truman(c); Jun.'6	150.00

MARY MARVEL COMICS
Fawcett Publications/Charlton Comics, Dec., 1945

#	Title	Price
1	Intro: Mary Marvel	2,500.00
2		1,000.00
3		750.00
4	On a Leave of Absence	700.00
5	Butterfly (c)	500.00
6	A:Freckles,Teenager of Mischief	500.00
7	The Kingdom Undersea	500.00
8	Holiday Special Issue	500.00
9	Air Race (c)	400.00
10	A: Freckles	400.00
11	A: The Sad Dryads	300.00
12	Red Cross Appeal on(c)	300.00
13	Keep the Homefires Burning	300.00
14	Meets Ghosts (c)	300.00

Mary Marvel #1
© Fawcet Publications

#	Title	Price
15	A: Freckles	300.00
16	The Jukebox Menace	250.00
17	Aunt Agatha's Adventures	250.00
18		250.00
19	Witch (c)	250.00
20		250.00
21	V: Dice Head	225.00
22	The Silver Slippers	225.00
23	The Pendulum Strikes	225.00
24	V: The Nightowl	225.00
25	A: Freckles	225.00
26	A:Freckles dressed as Clown	225.00
27	The Floating Oceanliner	225.00
28	Sept., 1948	225.00

Becomes:

MONTE HALE WESTERN
Oct., 1948

#	Title	Price
29	Ph(c),B:Monte Hale & His Horse Pardner	550.00
30	Ph(c),B:Big Bow-Little Arrow; CCB,Captain Tootsie	300.00
31	Ph(c),Giant	250.00
32	Ph(c),Giant	250.00
33	Ph(c),Giant	250.00
34	Ph(c),E:Big Bow-Little Arrow;B:Gabby Hayes,Giant	250.00
35	Ph(c),Gabby Hayes, Giant	250.00
36	Ph(c),Gabby Hayes, Giant	250.00
37	Ph(c),Gabby Hayes	150.00
38	Ph(c),Gabby Hayes, Giant	200.00
39	Ph(c);CCB, Captain Tootsie; Gabby Hayes, Giant	200.00
40	Ph(c),Gabby Hayes, Giant	200.00
41	Ph(c),Gabby Hayes	150.00
42	Ph(c),Gabby Hayes, Giant	175.00
43	Ph(c),Gabby Hayes, Giant	175.00
44	Ph(c),Gabby Hayes, Giant	175.00
45	Ph(c),Gabby Hayes	150.00
46	Ph(c),Gabby Hayes, Giant	150.00
47	Ph(c),A:Big Bow-Little Arrow; Gabby Hayes, Giant	150.00
48	Ph(c),Gabby Hayes, Giant	150.00
49	Ph(c),Gabby Hayes	150.00
50	Ph(c),Gabby Hayes, Giant	150.00
51	Ph(c),Gabby Hayes, Giant	125.00
52	Ph(c),Gabby Hayes, Giant	125.00
53	Ph(c),A:Slim Pickens; Gabby Hayes	100.00
54	Ph(c),Gabby Hayes, Giant	110.00
55	Ph(c),Gabby Hayes, Giant	110.00
56	Ph(c),Gabby Hayes, Giant	110.00
57	Ph(c),Gabby Hayes	75.00
58	Ph(c),Gabby Hayes, Giant	100.00
59	Ph(c),Gabby Hayes, Giant	100.00
60 thru 79	Ph(c),Gabby Hayes	@90.00
80	Ph(c),E: Gabby Hayes	90.00
81	Ph(c)	90.00
82	Final Ph(c)	75.00

Charlton Comics, Feb., 1955

#	Title	Price
83	R:G. Hayes Back B&W Ph(c)	75.00
84		75.00
85		75.00
86	E: Gabby Hayes	75.00
87		75.00
88	Jan., 1956	75.00

MASK COMICS
Rural Home Publications Feb.–March, 1945

#	Title	Price
1	LbC,LbC-(c), Evil (c)	4,000.00
2	LbC-(c),A:Black Rider,The Collector The Boy Magician; Apr-May'45, Devil (c)	2,500.00

MASKED MARVEL
Centaur Publications Sept., 1940

#	Title	Price
1	I: The Masked Marvel	2,400.00
2	PG,	1,500.00
3	Dec., 1940	1,400.00

MASKED RANGER
Premier Magazines April, 1954

#	Title	Price
1	FF,O&B:The Masked Ranger, Streak the Horse,The Crimson Avenger	500.00
2		175.00
3		175.00
4	B: Jessie James,Billy the Kid, Wild Bill Hickok, Jim Bowie's Life Story	200.00
5		200.00
6		200.00
7		200.00
8		200.00
9	AT,E:All Features; A:Wyatt Earp Aug., 1955	225.00

MASTER COMICS
Fawcett Publications March, 1940
1-6 Oversized, 7-Normal Format

#	Title	Price
1	O:Master Man; B:The Devil's Dagger, El Carin-Master of Magic, Rick O'Say, Morton Murch, White Rajah, Shipwreck Roberts, Frontier Marshall, Mr. Clue, Streak Sloan	12,000.00
2	Master Man (c)	3,000.00
3	Master Man (c) Bondage	2,500.00
4	Master Man (c)	2,400.00
5	Master Man (c)	2,400.00
6	E: All Above Features	2,500.00
7	B:Bulletman,Zorro,The Mystery Man, Lee Granger, Jungle King,Buck Jones	4,000.00
8	B:The Red Gaucho,Captain Venture, Planet Princess	2,000.00
9	Bulletman & Steam Roller	1,800.00
10	E: Lee Granger	1,800.00
11	O: Minute Man	3,500.00
12	Minute Man (c)	1,800.00
13	O:Bulletgirl; E:Red Gaucho	2,600.00
14	B: The Companions Three	1,500.00
15	MRa, Bulletman & Girl (c)	1,500.00
16	MRa, Minute Man (c)	1,500.00
17	B:MRa on Bulletman	1,400.00
18	MRa,	1,400.00
19	MRa, Bulletman & Girl (c)	1,400.00

All comics prices listed are for Near Mint condition.

GOLDEN AGE

Master–Meet

20 MRa,C:Cap.Marvel-
Bulletman 1,400.00
21 MRa-(c),Capt. Marvel in
Bulletman,I&O:CaptainNazi 7,500.00
22 MRa-(c),E:Mystery Man,Captain
Venture; Bondage(c);Capt.
Marvel Jr. X-Over In
Bulletman; A:Capt. Nazi . . . 6,500.00
23 MRa(a&c),B:Capt. Marvel Jr.
V:Capt. Nazi 3,800.00
24 MRa(a&c),Death By Radio . 1,400.00
25 MRa(a&c),The Jap Invasion 1,400.00
26 MRa(a&c),Capt. Marvel Jr.
Avenges Pearl Harbor 1,300.00
27 MRa(a&c),V For Victory(c) . 1,300.00
28 MRa(a&c),Liberty Bell(c) . . . 1,300.00
29 MRa(a&c),Hitler &
Hirohito(c) 1,300.00
30 MRa(a&c),Flag (c);Capt.
Marvel Jr, V: Capt. Nazi . . 1,300.00
31 MRa(a&c),E:Companions
Three,Capt.Marvel Jr,
V:Mad Dr. Macabre. 900.00
32 MRa(a&c),E: Buck Jones;
CMJr Strikes Terror Castle . . 900.00
33 MRa(a&c),B:Balbo the Boy
Magician,Hopalong Cassidy . 900.00
34 MRa(a&c),Capt.Marvel Jr
V: Capt.Nazi 1,100.00
35 MRa(a&c),CMJr Defies
the Flame. 900.00
36 MRa(a&c),Statue Of
Liberty(c) 900.00
37 MRa(a&c),CMJr Blasts
the Nazi Raiders. 800.00
38 MRa(a&c),CMJr V:the Japs . . 800.00
39 MRa(a&c),CMJr Blasts
Nazi Slave Ship 800.00
40 MRa(a&c),Flag (c) 800.00
41 MRa(a&c),Bulletman,Bulletgirl,
CMJr X-over In Minuteman . . 900.00
42 MRa(a&c),CMJr V: Hitler's
Dream Soldier 500.00
43 MRa(c),CMJr Battles For
Stalingrad. 500.00
44 MRa(c),CMJr In Crystal City
of the Peculiar Penguins. . . . 500.00
45 MRa(c), ... 500.00
46 MRa(c) 500.00
47 MRa(c),A:Hitler; E: Balbo 550.00
48 MRa(c),I:Bulletboy;Capt.
Marvel A: in Minuteman 600.00
49 MRa(c),E: Hopalong Cassidy,
Minuteman 500.00

Master Comics #21
© Fawcett Publications

50 I&O: Radar,A:Capt. Marvel,
B:Nyoka the Jungle Girl 500.00
51 MRa(c),CMJr V: Japanese . . . 300.00
52 MRa(c),CMJr & Radar Pitch
War Stamps on (c) 300.00
53 CMJR V: Dr. Sivana. 300.00
54 MRa(c),Capt.Marvel Jr
Your Pin-Up Buddy. 300.00
55 . . . . 300.00
56 MRa(c) 250.00
57 CMJr V: Dr. Sivana 250.00
58 MRa(a&c), ... 250.00
59 MRa(c),A:The Upside
Downies. 300.00
60 MRa(c) 300.00
61 CMJr Meets Uncle Marvel . . . 300.00
62 Uncle Sam on (c). 300.00
63 W/ Radar (c) 250.00
64 W/ Radar (c) 250.00
65 . . . . 250.00
66 CMJr & Secret Of the Sphinx. 250.00
67 Knight (c). 250.00
68 CMJr in the Range of
the Beasts 250.00
69 . . . . 250.00
70 . . . . 250.00
71 CMJr,V:Man in Metal Mask . . 200.00
72 CMJr V: Sivana & The Whistle
That Wouldn't Stop. 200.00
73 CMJr V: The Ghost of Evil . . . 200.00
74 CMJr & The Fountain of Age . 200.00
75 CMJr V: The Zombie Master . 200.00
76 . . . . 200.00
77 Pirate Treasure (c) 200.00
78 CMJr in Death on the Scenic
Railway 200.00
79 CMJr V: The Black Shroud. . . 200.00
80 CMJr-The Land of Backwards 200.00
81 CMJr & The Voyage 'Round
the Horn 175.00
82 CMJr,IN,Death at the
Launching 175.00
83 . . . . 175.00
84 CMJr V: The Human Magnet . 175.00
85 CMJr-Crime on the Campus . 175.00
86 CMJr & The City of Machines. 175.00
87 CMJr & The Root of Evil 175.00
88 CMJr V: The Wreckers;
B: Hopalong Cassidy 175.00
89 . . . . 175.00
90 CMJr V: The Caveman 175.00
91 CMJr V: The Blockmen 175.00
92 CMJr V: The Space Slavers . . 175.00
93 BK,CMJr,V:TheGrowingGiant . 175.00
94 E: Hopalong Cassidy 175.00
95 B: Tom Mix; CMJr Meets
the Skyhawk. 175.00
96 CMJr Meets the Worlds
Mightiest Horse 175.00
97 CMJr Faces the Doubting
Thomas 175.00
98 KKK Type 175.00
99 Witch (c) 175.00
100 CMJr V: The Ghost Ship . . . 200.00
101 thru 105 . . . . @175.00
106 E: Bulletman 175.00
107 CMJr Faces the Disappearance
of the Statue of Liberty 175.00
108 . . . . 175.00
109 . . . . 175.00
110 CMJr & The Hidden Death . 175.00
111 thru 122 . . . . @175.00
123 CMJr V: The Flying
Desperado 175.00
124 . . . . 175.00
125 CMJr & The Bed of Mystery . 175.00
126 thru 131 . . . . @175.00
132 V: Migs 190.00
133 E: Tom Mix; April, 1953 . . . . 200.00

MD #4
© E.C. Publications

MD
E.C. Comics
April, 1955–Jan., 1956
1 RC,GE,GrI,JO,JCr(c) 200.00
2 thru 5 RC,GE,GrI,JO,JCr(c). @150.00

MEDAL OF HONOR COMICS
Stafford Publication
Spring, 1947
1 True Stories of Medal of Honor
Recipants 125.00

MEET CORLISS ARCHER
Fox Features Syndicate
March, 1948
1 AF,AF(c), Teenage 1,300.00
2 AF(c) 750.00
3 . . . . 600.00
Becomes:

MY LIFE
Sept., 1948
4 JKa,AF, ... 500.00
5 JKa, ... 250.00
6 JKa,AF, ... 250.00
7 Watercolor&Ink Drawing on(c) 150.00
8 . . . . 125.00
9 . . . . 125.00
10 WW, July, 1950 . . . . 175.00

MEET MERTON
Toby Press, Dec., 1953
1 Dave Berg-a,Teen Stories. 75.00
2 Dave Berg-a 50.00
3 Dave Berg-a 50.00
4 Dave Berg-a; June, 1954 . . . . 50.00

MEET THE NEW POST GAZETTE SUNDAY FUNNIES
Pitsberg Post Gazette
N# One Shot Insert F: Several
Syndicated Characters in Stories
Exclusive to This Edition . . 1,500.00

MEL ALLEN SPORTS COMICS
Visual Editions, 1949
1 GT 250.00
2 Lou Gehrig 200.00

MEN AGAINST CRIME
See: HAND OF FATE

MERRY-GO-ROUND COMICS
LaSalle/Croyden/Rotary Litho., 1944
1 LaSalle Publications Edition . . 200.00
1a 1946, Croyden Edition 75.00
1b Sept-Oct.'47,Rotary Litho Ed. 100.00
2 . . . . 100.00

MERRY MOUSE
Avon Periodicals June, 1953
1 (fa),F. Carin (a&c) 100.00
2 (fa),F. Carin (a&c) 50.00
3 (fa),F. Carin (a&c) 50.00
4 (fa),F. Carin (a&c);Jan.'54 . . . . 50.00

METEOR COMICS
Croyden Publications Nov., 1945
1 Captain Wizard & Baldy Bean . 500.00

MICKEY FINN
Eastern Color/Columbia Comics Group, 1942
1 . . . . 350.00
2 . . . . 200.00
3 A: Charlie Chan 150.00
4 . . . . 100.00
5 thru 9 . . . . @75.00
10 thru 15 . . . . @50.00

(WALT DISNEY'S) MICKEY MOUSE
Dell Publishing Co. Dec., 1952
#1-#27 Dell Four Color
28 . . . . 60.00
29 . . . . 55.00
30 . . . . 55.00
31 . . . . 55.00
32 thru 34 . . . . @55.00
35 thru 50 . . . . @50.00
51 thru 73 . . . . @40.00
74 . . . . 50.00
75 thru 99 . . . . @35.00
100 thru 105 rep. . . . . @50.00
106 thru 120 . . . . @40.00
121 thru 130 . . . . @25.00
131 thru 146 . . . . @25.00
147 rep,Phantom Fires 30.00
148 rep. 30.00
149 thru 158 . . . . @15.00
159 rep. 18.00
160 thru 170 . . . . @10.00
171 thru 199 . . . . @8.00
200 rep. 10.00
201 thru 218 . . . . @8.00
See: Color Comics section

GOLDEN AGE

Mickey Mouse Magazine Vol. 1, #7
© Dell Publishing Co.

MICKEY MOUSE MAGAZINE
Kay Kamen
1 (1933) scarce. 8,000.00
2 . . . . 1,600.00
3 thru 8 . . . . @1,500.00
9 . . . . 1,500.00

MICKEY MOUSE MAGAZINE
Kay Kamen
1 digest size (1933) 2,500.00
2 dairy give-away promo(1933) 1,000.00
3 dairy give-away promo(1934) . 900.00
4 dairy give-away promo(1934) . 900.00
5 dairy give-away promo(1934) . 900.00
6 dairy give-away promo(1934) . 900.00
7 dairy give-away promo(1934) . 900.00
8 dairy give-away promo(1934) . 900.00
9 dairy give-away promo(1934) . 900.00
10 dairy give-awaypromo(1934) . 900.00
11 dairy give-awaypromo(1934) . 900.00
12 dairy give-awaypromo(1934) . 900.00

Volume II
1 dairy give-awaypromo(1934) . 750.00
2 dairy give-away promo(1934) . 750.00
3 dairy give-away promo(1935) . 750.00
4 dairy give-away promo(1935) . 750.00
5 dairy give-away promo(1935) . 750.00
6 dairy give-away promo(1935) . 750.00
7 dairy give-away promo(1935) . 750.00
8 dairy give-away promo(1935) . 750.00
9 dairy give-away promo(1935) . 750.00
10 dairy give-awaypromo(1935) . 750.00
11 dairy give-awaypromo(1935) . 750.00
12 dairy give-awaypromo(1935) . 750.00

MICKEY MOUSE MAGAZINE
K.K. Pub./Westen Pub
1 (1935) 13″x10″ 17,000.00
2 . . . . 1,600.00
3 . . . . 1,100.00
4 . . . . 1,100.00
5 (1936) Donald Duck solo . . . 1,200.00
6 Donald Duck editor 1,000.00
7 . . . . 1,000.00
8 Donald Duck solo. 1,000.00
9 . . . . 1,000.00
10 . . . . 1,000.00
11 Mickey Mouse, editor 900.00
12 . . . . 900.00

Volume II
1 . . . . 900.00
2 . . . . 900.00
3 Christmas issue, 100pg 3,500.00
4 (1937) Roy Ranger adv.strip . . 800.00
5 Ted True strip 750.00

6 Mickey Mouse cut-outs 700.00
7 Mickey Mouse cut-outs 700.00
8 Mickey Mouse cut-outs 700.00
9 Mickey Mouse cut-outs 700.00
10 Full color. 1,100.00
11 . . . . 700.00
12 Hiawatha 700.00
13 . . . . 700.00

Volume III
2 Big Bad Wolf (c) 800.00
3 First Snow White 2,500.00
4 (1938) Snow White 900.00
5 Snow White (c) 1,000.00
6 Snow White ends 750.00
7 7 Dwarfs Easter (c). 600.00
8 . . . . 600.00
9 Dopey(c). 600.00
10 Goofy(c) 600.00
11 Mickey Mouse Sheriff. 600.00
12 A:Snow White 600.00

Volume IV
1 Practile Pig. 600.00
2 I:Huey,Louis & Dewey(c). 700.00
3 Ferdinand the Bull 650.00
4 (1939),B:Spotty. 550.00
5 Pluto solo 650.00
7 Ugly Duckling 600.00
7a Goofy & Wilber 600.00
8 Big Bad Wolf(c) 600.00
9 The Pointer. 600.00
10 July 4th 750.00
11 . . . . 550.00
12 Donald's Penguin. 650.00

Volume V
1 Black Pete 650.00
2 Goofy(c) 800.00
3 Pinocchio 900.00
4 (1940). 600.00
5 Jiminy Cricket(c) 600.00
6 Tugboat Mickey 600.00
7 Huey, Louis & Dewey(c) 600.00
8 Figaro & Cleo 600.00
9 Donald(c),J.Cricket 700.00
10 July 4th 700.00
11 Mickey's Tailor 700.00
12 Change of format 6,500.00
becomes:

WALT DISNEY COMICS & STORIES

MICKEY MOUSE
Whitman
904 W.Disney's Mickey Mouse
and his friends (1934) 1,500.00
948 Disney'sMickeyMouse('34) 1,500.00

MIDGET COMICS
St. John Publishing Co. Feb., 1950
1 MB(c),Fighting Indian Stories . 200.00
2 April, 1950;Tex West-Cowboy
Marshall 100.00

MIGHTY ATOM, THE
See: PIXIES

MIGHTY MIDGET COMICS
Samuel E. Lowe & Co., 1942-43 4″x5″ Format
1 Bulletman 300.00
2 Captain Marvel 300.00
3 Captain Marvel Jr. 300.00
4 Golden Arrow 250.00

Mighty–Minute Man

GOLDEN AGE

Comics Values Annual

5 Ibis the Invincible	300.00
6 Spy Smasher	300.00
7 Balbo, The Boy Magician	150.00
8 Bulletman	200.00
9 Commando Yank	150.00
10 Dr. Voltz, The Human Generator	135.00
11 Lance O'Casey	135.00
12 Leatherneck the Marine	135.00
13 Minute Man	200.00
14 Mister Q.	150.00
15 Mr. Scarlet & Pinky	135.00
16 Pat Wilson & His Flying Fortress	125.00
17 Phantom Eagle	150.00
18 State Trooper Stops Crime	125.00
19 Tornado Tom	125.00

MIGHTY MOUSE
[1st Series] Fall, 1946

1 Terytoons Presents	1,500.00
2	750.00
3	500.00
4 Summer, 1947	500.00

St. John Publishing, Aug., 1947

5	500.00
6 thru 10	@250.00
11 thru 20	@150.00
21 thru 25	@125.00
26 thru 30	@100.00
31 thru 34	@75.00
35 Flying Saucer	125.00
36	75.00
37	75.00
38 thru 45 Giant 100 pgs	@200.00
46 thru 66	@75.00
67 P(c),	75.00

Pines

68 thru 81 Funny Animal	@60.00
82 Infinity (c).	60.00
83 June, 1959	60.00

MIGHTY MOUSE ADVENTURE STORIES
St. John Publishing Co., 1953

N# 384 Pages,Rebound	500.00

MIKE BARNETT, MAN AGAINST CRIME
Fawcett Publications Dec., 1951

1 The Mint of Dionysosi	250.00
2 Mystery of the Blue Madonna	135.00
3 Revenge Holds the Torch	125.00
4 Special Delivery	125.00
5 Market For Morphine	150.00
6 Oct., 1952	125.00

MILITARY COMICS
Comics Magazines (Quality Comics Group) Aug., 1941

1 JCo,CCu,FG,BP,WE(c),O:Blackhawk, Miss America, Death Patrol, Blue Tracer; B:X of the Underground, Yankee Eagle,Q-Boat, Shot & Shell, Archie Atkins, Loops & Banks	14,000.00
2 JCo,FG,BP,CCu,CCu(c),B: Secret War News	3,700.00
3 JCo,FG,BP,AMc,CCu,CCu(c), I&O:Chop Chop	3,000.00
4 FG,BP,AMc,CCu,CCu(c),	2,600.00
5 FG,BP,AMc,CCu,CCu(c), B: The Sniper	2,000.00
6 FG,BP,AMc,CCu,CCu(c)	1,500.00

Military Comics #11
© Quality Comics Group

7 FG,BP,AMc,CCu,CCu(c) E:Death Patrol	1,500.00
8 FG,BP,AMc,CCu,CCu(c)	1,500.00
9 FG,BP,AMc,CCu,CCu(c), B: The Phantom Clipper	1,500.00
10 FG,BP,CCu,AMc,WE(c)	1,600.00
11 FG,BP,CCu,AMc, WE(c),Flag(c)	1,400.00
12 FG,BP,AMc,RC(a&c)	1,500.00
13 FG,BP,AMc,RC(a&c),E:X of the Underground	1,400.00
14 FG,AMc,RC(a&c),B:Private Dogtag	1,400.00
15 FG,AMc,RC(a&c),	1,400.00
16 FG,AMc,RC(a&c),E:The Phantom Clipper,Blue Tracer	1,100.00
17 FG,AMc,RC(a&c), B:P.T. Boat	1,100.00
18 FG,AMc,RC(a&c), V: The Thunderer	1,100.00
19 FG,RC(a&c), V:King Cobra	1,100.00
20 GFx,RC(a&c), Death Patrol	1,100.00
21 FG,GFx	1,000.00
22 FG,GFx	1,000.00
23 FG,GFx	1,000.00
24 FG,GFx,V: Man-Heavy Glasses	1,000.00
25 FG,GFx,V: Wang The Tiger	1,000.00
26 FG,GFx,V: Skull	900.00
27 FG,JCo,R:The Death Patrol	900.00
28 FG,JCo, Dungeon of Doom	900.00
29 FG,JCo,V: Xanukhara	900.00
30 FG,JCo,BWa(a&c),B.Hwk V: Dr. Koro	900.00
31 FG,JCo,BWa,E:Death Patrol; I: Captain Hitsu	900.00
32 JCo,A: Captain Hitsu	800.00
33 W/ Civil War Veteran	800.00
34 A: Eve Rice	800.00
35 Shipwreck Island	800.00
36 Cult of the Wailing Tiger	800.00
37 Pass of Bloody Peace	800.00
38 B.Hwk Faces Bloody Death	800.00
39 A: Kwan Yin	800.00
40 V: Ratru	750.00
41 W/ Chop Chop (c)	750.00
42 V: Jap Mata Hari	750.00
43	750.00

Becomes:

MODERN COMICS
Nov., 1945

44 Duel of Honor	750.00
45 V: Sakyo the Madman	500.00
46 RC, Soldiers of Fortune	500.00
47 RC,PG,V:Count Hokoy	500.00
48 RC,PG,V:Pirates of Perool	500.00
49 RC,PG,I:Fear,Lady Adventuress	500.00
50 RC,PG	500.00
51 RC,PG, Ancient City of Evil	400.00
52 PG,BWa,V: The Vulture	400.00
53 PG,BWa,B: Torchy	600.00
54 PG,RC,RC/CCu,BWa	350.00
55 PG,RC,RC/CCu,BWa	350.00
56 PG,RC/CCu,BWa	350.00
57 PG,RC/CCu,BWa	350.00
58 PG,RC,RC/CCu,BWa, V:The Grabber	350.00
59 PG,RC/CCu,BWa	350.00
60 PG,RC/CCu,BWa,RC(c), V:Green Plague	350.00
61 PG,RC/CCu,BWa,RC(c)	350.00
62 PG,RC/CCu,BWa,RC(c)	350.00
63 PG,RC/CCu,BWa,RC(c)	335.00
64 PG,RC/CCu,BWa,RC(c)	335.00
65 PG,RC/CCu,BWa,RC(c)	335.00
66 PG,RC/CCu,BWa	335.00
67 PG,RC/CCu,BWa,RC(c)	335.00
68 PG,RC/CCu,BWa,RC(c); I:Madame Butterfly	335.00
69 PG,RC/CCu,BWa,RC(c)	335.00
70 PG,RC/CCu,BWa,RC(c)	335.00
71 PG,RC/CCu,BWa,RC(c)	335.00
72 PG,RC/CCu,BWa,RC(c)	325.00
73 PG,RC/CCu,BWa,RC(c)	325.00
74 PG,RC/CCu,BWa,RC(c)	325.00
75 PG,RC/CCu,BWa,RC(c)	325.00
76 PG,RC/CCu,BWa,RC(c)	325.00
77 PG,RC/CCu,BWa,RC(c)	325.00
78 PG,RC/CCu,BWa,JCo,RC(c)	350.00
79 PG,RC/CCu,BWa,JCo,RC(c)	325.00
80 PG,RC/CCu,BWa,JCo,RC(c)	325.00
81 PG,RC/CCu,BWa,JCo,RC(c)	325.00
82 PG,RC/CCu,BWa,JCo,RC(c)	325.00
83 PG,RC/CCu,BWa,JCo,RC(c); E: Private Dogtag	325.00
84 PG,RC/CCu,BWa,RC(c)	325.00
85 PG,RC/CCu,BWa,RC(c)	325.00
86 PG,RC/CCu,BWa,RC(c)	325.00
87 PG,RC/CCu,BWa,RC(c)	325.00
88 PG,RC/CCu,BWa,RC(c)	325.00
89 PG,RC/CCu,BWa,RC(c)	325.00
90 PG,RC/CCu,GFx,RC(c)	325.00
91 RC/CCu,GFx,RC(c)	325.00
92 RC/CCu,GFx,RC(c)	325.00
93 RC/CCu,GFx,RC(c)	325.00
94 RC/CCu,GFx,RC(c)	325.00
95 RC/CCu,GFx,RC(c)	325.00
96 RC/CCu,GFx,RC/CCu(c)	325.00
97 RC/CCu,GFx,RC/CCu(c)	325.00
98 RC/CCu,GFx,RC/CCu(c)	325.00
99 RC/CCu,GFx,JCo,RC/CCu(c)	325.00
100 GFx,JCo,RC/CCu(c)	325.00
101 GFx,JCo,RC/CCu(c)	325.00
102 GFx,JCo,WE,BWa, RC/CCu(c)	400.00

MILT GROSS FUNNIES
Milt Gross, Inc. Aug., 1947

1 Gag Oriented Caricature	200.00
2 Gag Oriented Caricature	150.00

MINUTE MAN
Fawcett Publications Summer, 1941

1 V: The Nazis	2,500.00
2 V: The Mongol Horde	1,500.00
3 V: The Black Poet;Spr'42	1,500.00

CVA Page 434 — All comics prices listed are for *Near Mint* condition.

GOLDEN AGE

Miracle–Mopsy

Miracle Comics #4
© E.C. Comics

MIRACLE COMICS
E.C. Comics
Feb.,1940
1 B:Sky Wizard,Master of Space,
 Dash Dixon,Man of Might,Dusty
 Doyle,Pinkie Parker, The Kid
 Cop,K-7 Secret Agent,Scorpion
 & Blandu,Jungle Queen .. 2,500.00
2 .... 1,400.00
3 B:Bill Colt,The Ghost Rider .. 1,400.00
4 A:The Veiled Prophet,
 Bullet Bob; Mar'41 ...... 1,100.00

MISS CAIRO JONES
Croyden Publishers, 1944
1 BO,Rep. Newspaper Strip ... 250.00

MR. ANTHONY'S LOVE CLINIC
Hillman Periodicals, 1945
1 Ph(c) 150.00
2 .... 100.00
3 .... 75.00
4 .... 75.00
5 Ph(c),Apr/May'50 .... 75.00

MR. MUSCLES
See: THING, THE

MISTER MYSTERY
Media Publ./SPM Publ./
Aragon Publ. Sept., 1951
1 HK,RA,Horror 1,400.00
2 RA,RA(c) 800.00
3 RA(c) 800.00
4 Bondage(c) 900.00
5 Lingerie(c) 800.00
6 Bondage(c) 800.00
7 BW,Bondage(c);The Brain
 Bats of Venus 1,500.00
8 Lingerie(c) 750.00
9 HN 750.00
10 .... 750.00
11 BW,Robot Woman 1,000.00
12 Flaming Object to Eye (c) .. 1,600.00
13 .... 500.00
14 .... 500.00
15 The Coffin & Medusa's Head . 450.00
16 Bondage(c) 450.00
17 .... 450.00
18 BW,Bondage(c) 750.00

MISTER RISK
See: HAND OF FATE

MISTER UNIVERSE
Mr. Publ./Media Publ./
Stanmore, July, 1951
1 .... 250.00
2 RA(c);Jungle That time Forgot 150.00
3 Marijuana Story 125.00
4 Mr. Universe Goes to War.... 100.00
5 Mr. Universe Goes to War;
 April, 1952 .... 100.00

MODERN COMICS
See: MILITARY COMICS

MODERN LOVE
Tiny Tot Comics
(E.C. Comics)
June–July, 1949
1 Stolen Romance 900.00
2 JcR,AF(c),I Craved
 Excitement 600.00
3 AF(c);Our Families Clashed .. 500.00
4 AF(c);I Was a B Girl 700.00
5 AF(c);Saved From Shame ... 700.00
6 AF(c);The Love That
 Might Have Been 700.00
7 AF(c);They Won't Let Me
 Love Him 500.00
8 AF(c);Aug-Sept'50 .... 550.00

MOE & SHMOE COMICS
O.S. Publishing Co.
Spring, 1948
1 Gag Oriented Caricature 100.00
2 Gag Oriented Caricature 60.00

MOLLY O'DAY
Avon Periodicals
Feb., 1945
1 GT;The Enchanted Dagger .. 700.00

MONKEYSHINES COMICS
Publ. Specialists/Ace/
Summer, 1944
1 (fa),Several Short Features .. 125.00
2 (fa),Same Format Throughout
 Entire Run 75.00
3 thru 16 Funny Animal ..... @50.00
Ace
17 Funny Animal............. 70.00
18 thru 21 .... @50.00
Unity Publ.
22 (fa) 50.00
23 (fa) 50.00
24 (fa),AFa,AFa(c) 50.00
25 (fa) 50.00
26 (fa) 50.00
27 (fa),July, 1949 .... 50.00

MONSTER
Fiction House Magazines, 1953
1 Dr. Drew 750.00
2 .... 500.00

MONSTER CRIME COMICS
Hillman Periodicals
Oct., 1952
1 52 Pgs,15 Cent (c) Price ... 1,400.00

MONTE HALL WESTERN
See: MARY MARVEL COMICS

MONTY HALL OF THE U.S. MARINES
Toby Press, Aug., 1951
1 B:Monty Hall,Pin-Up Pete;
 (All Issues) 125.00
2 .... 75.00
3 thru 5 .... @50.00
6 .... 50.00
7 The Fireball Express 50.00
8 .... 50.00
9 .... 50.00
10 The Vial of Death.......... 50.00
11 Monju Island Prison Break ... 50.00

MOON GIRL AND THE PRINCE
E.C. Comics, Autumn, 1947
1 JCr(c),O:Moon Girl 1,400.00
2 JCr(c),Battle of the Congo ... 800.00
3 .... 750.00
4 V: A Vampire 750.00
5 1st E.C. Horror-Zombie
 Terror 1,500.00
6 .... 700.00
7 O:Star;The Fient Who
 Fights With Fire 700.00
8 True Crime Feature 700.00
Becomes:

A MOON, A GIRL ...ROMANCE
Sept.–Oct., 1949
9 AF,Grl,AF(c),C:Moon Girl;
 Spanking Panels 1,000.00
10 AF,Grl,WW,AF(c),Suspicious
 of His Intentions 800.00
11 AF,Grl,WW,AF(c),Hearts
 Along the Ski Trail 800.00
12 AF,Grl,AF(c),
 March–April, 1950 ...... 1,100.00
Becomes:

WEIRD FANTASY

MOPSY
St. John Publishing Co.
Feb., 1948
1 Paper Dolls Enclosed 200.00
2 .... 100.00
3 .... 80.00
4 Paper Dolls Enclosed 80.00
5 Paper Dolls Enclosed 80.00
6 Paper Dolls Enclosed 80.00
7 .... 75.00
8 Paper Dolls Enclosed;
 Lingerie Panels 80.00
9 .... 75.00
10 .... 75.00
11 & 12 .... @60.00
13 Paper Dolls Enclosed........ 65.00
14 thru 18 .... @60.00
19 Lingerie(c);Paper
 Dolls Enclosed 65.00

Mortie–Murderous **GOLDEN AGE** Comics Values Annual

MORTIE
Magazine Publishers
Dec., 1952
1 ...Mazie's Friend 75.00
2 . . . . 50.00
3 . . . . 45.00

MOTION PICTURE COMICS
Fawcett Publications
Nov., 1950
101 Ph(c),Monte Hale's-
   Vanishing Westerner. 350.00
102 Ph(c),Rocky Lane's-Code
   of the Silver Sage. 325.00
103 Ph(c),Rocky Lane's-Covered
   Wagon Raid 325.00
104 BP,Ph(c),Rocky Lane's-
   Vigilante Hideout 325.00
105 BP,Ph(c),Audie Murphy's-
   Red Badge of Courage. 400.00
106 Ph(c),George Montgomery's-
   The Texas Rangers 350.00
107 Ph(c),Rocky Lane's-Frisco
   Tornado 325.00
108 Ph(c),John Derek's-Mask
   of the Avenger 250.00
109 Ph(c),Rocky Lane's-Rough
   Rider of Durango 325.00
110 GE,Ph(c), When Worlds
   Collide 1,400.00
111 Ph(c),Lash LaRue's-The
   Vanishing Outpost 400.00
112 Ph(c),Jay Silverheels'-
   Brave Warrior 200.00
113 KS,Ph(c),George Murphy's-
   Walk East on Beacon 150.00
114 Ph(c),George Montgomery's-
   Cripple Creek;Jan, 1953 . . . . 150.00

MOTION PICTURES FUNNIES WEEKLY
1st Funnies Incorporated, 1939
1 BEv,1st Sub-Mariner 30,000.00
2 Cover Only 1,500.00
3 Cover Only 1,500.00
4 Cover Only 1,500.00

MOVIE CLASSICS
(NO #S)
Dell Publishing Co. Jan., 1953
1 Around the World Under
   the Sea 40.00
2 Bambi 45.00
3 Battle of the Buldge 40.00
4 Ph(c),Beach Blanket Bingo . . 100.00
5 Ph(c),Bon Voyage 45.00
6 Castilian 40.00
7 Cat 35.00
8 Cheyenne Autumn 75.00
9 Ph(c),Circus World,
   John Wayne (c) 150.00
10 Ph(c),Countdown,J.Caan(c) . . . 40.00
11 Creature 100.00
12 Ph(c),David Ladd's Life Story . 125.00
13 Ph(c),Die Monster Die 75.00
14 Dirty Dozen 50.00
15 Ph(c),Dr. Who & the Daleks . . 165.00
16 Dracula 100.00
17 El Dorado,J.WaynePh(c) 165.00
18 Ensign Pulver 40.00
19 Frankenstein 100.00
20 Ph(c),Great Race. 50.00
21 B.LancasterPh(c) 55.00
22 Hatari 125.00
23 Horizontal Lieutenant 35.00
24 Ph(c) Mr. Limpet 45.00
25 Jack the Giant Killer. 120.00
26 Ph(c),Jason & the Argonauts . 135.00
27 Lancelot & Guinevere 65.00
28 Lawrence. 75.00
29 Lion of Sparta 45.00
30 Mad Monster Party 80.00
31 Magic Sword 70.00
32 Ph(c),Masque of Red Death. . . 70.00
33 Maya. 50.00
34 McHale's Navy. 60.00
35 Ph(c) Merrills' Marauders 35.00
36 Ph(c),Mouse on the Moon 45.00
37 Mummy 100.00
38 Music Man. 40.00
39 Ph(c),Naked Prey 65.00
40 Ph(c),Night of the Grizzly 45.00
41 None but the Brave 65.00
42 Ph(c),Operation Bikini 40.00
43 Operation Cross Bold. 40.00
44 Prince & the Pauper. 40.00
45 Raven,V.Price(c) 55.00
46 Ring of Bright Water 45.00
47 Runaway 35.00
48 Ph(c),Santa Claus Conquers
   the Martians 100.00
49 Ph(c),Six Black Horses 40.00
50 Sky Party 45.00
51 Smoky. 35.00
52 Ph(c),Sons of Katie Elder. . . . 175.00
53 GE,Tales of Terror 60.00
54 Ph(c),3 Stooges-Hercules . . . 135.00
55 Tomb of Legeia 60.00
56 Treasure Island 40.00
57 Twice Told Tales(V.Price) 60.00
58 Two on a Guillotine 50.00
59 Valley of Gwangi 65.00
60 War Gods of the Deep. 40.00
61 War Wagon (John Wayne) . . . 125.00
62 Who's Minding the Mint 35.00
63 Wolfman 100.00
64 Ph(c),Zulu 125.00
65 . . . . 40.00

MOVIE COMICS
Fiction House Magazines
Dec., 1946
1 Big Town on(c) 700.00
2 MB,White Tie & Tails 500.00
3 MB,Andy Hardy Laugh Hit . . . 500.00
4 MB,Slave Girl 650.00

MOVIE LOVE
Famous Funnies Publications
Feb., 1950
1 Ph(c),Dick Powell(c) 150.00
2 Ph(c),Myrna Loy(c) 75.00
3 Ph(c),Cornell Wilde(c) 60.00
4 Ph(c),Paulette Goddard(c) 60.00
5 Ph(c),Joan Fontaine(c) 60.00
6 Ph(c),Ricardo Montalban(c) . . . 60.00
7 Ph(c),Fred Astaire(c) 75.00
8 AW,FF,Ph(c),Corinne
   Calvert(c) 500.00
9 Ph(c),John Lund(c) 50.00
10 Ph(c),Mona Freeman(c) 500.00
11 Ph(c),James Mason(c) 75.00
12 Ph(c),Jerry Lewis &
   Dean Martin(c) 85.00
13 Ph(c),Ronald Reagan(c). 250.00
14 Ph(c),Janet Leigh,Gene Kelly. . 75.00
15 Ph(c), ... 50.00
16 Ph(c),Angela Lansbury. 100.00
17 FF,Ph(c),Leslie Caron 50.00
18 Ph(c),Cornel Wilde. 50.00
19 Ph(c),John Derek. 50.00
20 Ph(c),Debbie Reynolds 75.00
21 Ph(c),Patricia Medina. 50.00
22 Ph(c),John Payne 50.00

MOVIE THRILLERS
Magazine Enterprises 1949
1 Ph(c),Burt Lancaster's-
   Rope of Sand 375.00

MR. MUSCLES
See: THING!, THE

MUGGY-DOO, BOY CAT
Stanhall Publications
July, 1953
1 . . . . 75.00
2 and 3 . . . . @50.00
4 Jan., 1954 . . . . 50.00

Murder Incorporated #4
© Fox Features Inc.

MURDER, INCORPORATED
Fox Features Incorporated
Jan., 1948–Aug., 1951
1 For Adults Only-on(c) 750.00
2 For Adults Only(c);Male
   Bondage(c),Electrocution sty. 500.00
3 Dutch Schultz-Beast of Evil . . 275.00
4 The Ray Hamilton Case,
   Lingerie(c) 275.00
5 thru 8 . . . . @275.00
9 Bathrobe (c) 250.00
9a Lingerie (c) 275.00
10 . . . . 250.00
11 . . . . 250.00
12 . . . . 250.00
13 . . . . 275.00
14 Bill Hale-King o/t Murderers . 250.00
15 . . . . 250.00
16(5),Second Series 200.00
17(2) 200.00
18(3), Bondage(c) w/Lingerie . . 225.00

MURDEROUS GANGSTERS
Avon Periodicals/Realistic
July, 1951
1 WW,Pretty Boy Floyd,
   Leggs Diamond 550.00
2 WW,Baby Face Nelson,Mad
   Dog Esposito 350.00

GOLDEN AGE

MY LOVE STORY
Fox Features Syndicate
Sept., 1949
1 Men Gave Me Jewels 150.00
2 He Dared Me 100.00
3 WW,I Made Love a Plaything . 250.00
4 WW,I Tried to Be Good 250.00

MY PAST CONFESSIONS
See: WESTERN THRILLERS

MY PRIVATE LIFE
Fox Features Syndicate
Feb., 1950
16 My Friendship Club Affair.... 135.00
17 My Guilty Kisses;April'50 .... 125.00

MY SECRET
Superior Comics
Aug., 1949
1 True Love Stories 135.00
2 I Was Guilty of Being a
   Cheating Wife 125.00
3 Was I His Second Love?; 125.00
Becomes:

OUR SECRET
Nov., 1949–June, 1950
4 JKa,She Loves Me,She Loves
   Me Not................. 200.00
5 .... 125.00
6 .... 125.00
7 How Do You Fall In Love?.... 135.00
8 His Kiss Tore At My Heart.... 125.00

MY SECRET AFFAIR
Hero Books
(Fox Features Syndicate)
Dec., 1949
1 WW,SHn,My Stormy
   Love Affair 250.00
2 WW,I Loved a Weakling 200.00
3 WW, April, 1950 .... 235.00

MY SECRET LIFE
Fox Features Syndicate
July, 1949
22 I Loved More Than Once.... 150.00
23 WW...................... 200.00
24 Love Was a Habit 100.00
25 .... 100.00
Becomes:

ROMEO TUBBS
Dec., 1952
26 WW,That Lovable Teen-ager . 250.00

MY SECRET LOVE
See: PHANTOM LADY

MY SECRET MARRIAGE
Superior Comics
May, 1953
1 I Was a Cheat 125.00
2 .... 75.00
3 We Couldn't Wait 50.00
4 .... 50.00
5 .... 50.00
6 .... 50.00
7 thru 23 .... @50.00
24 1956 .... 50.00

Comics Values Annual
3 P(c),Tony & Bud Fenner,
   Jed Hawkins 300.00
4 EK(c),Murder By Needle-
   Drug Story, June, 1952..... 300.00

MUTINY
Aragon Magazines
Oct., 1954
1 AH(c),Stormy Tales of the
   Seven Seas 200.00
2 AH(c) 150.00
3 Bondage(c),Feb., '55 .... 150.00

MY CONFESSIONS
See: WESTERN TRUE CRIME

MY DATE COMICS
Hillman Periodicals
July, 1944
1 S&K,S&K (c), Teenage 400.00
2 S&K,DB,S&K(c) 300.00
3 S&K,DB,S&K(c) 300.00
4 S&K,DB,S&K(c) 300.00

MY DESIRE
Fox Features Syndicate
Oct., 1949
1 Intimate Confessions 150.00
2 WW,They Called Me Wayward 125.00
3 I Hid My Lover 125.00
4 WW, April, 1950 .... 250.00

MY GREAT LOVE
Fox Features Syndicate
Oct., 1949
1 Reunion In a Shack 100.00
2 My Crazy Dreams 50.00
3 He Was Ashamed of Me 45.00
4 My Two Wedding Rings;Apr'50 50.00

MY INTIMATE AFFAIR
Fox Features Syndicate
March, 1950
1 I Sold My Love 175.00
2 I Married a Jailbird;May'50 ... 100.00

MY LIFE
See: MEET CORLISS ARCHER

MY LOVE AFFAIR
Fox Features Syndicate
July, 1949
1 Truck Driver's Sweetheart ... 175.00
2 My Dreadful Secret 100.00
3 WW,I'll Make Him Marry Me .. 200.00
4 WW,They Called Me Wild ... 200.00
5 WW,Beauty Was My Bait 200.00
6 WW,The Man Downstairs 200.00

MY LOVE MEMORIES
See: WOMEN OUTLAWS

MY LOVE LIFE
See: TEGRA, JUNGLE EMPRESS

Murderous–Mysterious

MY SECRET ROMANCE
Hero Books
(Fox Features Syndicate)
Jan., 1950
1 WW,They Called Me 'That'
   Woman 150.00
2 WW,They Called Me Cheap .. 175.00

MYSTERIES WEIRD AND STRANGE
Superior Comics/
Dynamic Publ., May, 1953
1 The Stolen Brain 500.00
2 The Screaming Room,
   Atomic Bomb 250.00
3 SD,The Avenging Corpse 300.00
4 SD,Ghost on the Gallows 300.00
5 SD,Horror a la Mode 300.00
6 SD,Howling Horror 300.00
7 SD,Demon in Disguise 200.00
8 SD,The Devil's Birthmark 200.00
9 SD 200.00
10 SD 300.00
11 SD 300.00

MYSTERIOUS ADVENTURES
Story Comics
March, 1951
1 Wild Terror of the
   Vampire Flag 750.00
2 Terror of the Ghoul's Corpse . 350.00
3 Terror of the Witche's Curse .. 325.00

Mysterious Adventures #5
© *Story Comics*

4 The Little Coffin That Grew .. 325.00
5 LC,Curse of the Jungle,
   Bondage(c)............. 350.00
6 LC,Ghostly Terror in the
   Cave 325.00
7 LC,Terror of the Ghostly
   Castle 450.00
8 Terror of the Flowers of Deat.. 500.00
9 The Ghostly Ghouls-
   Extreme Violence 350.00
10 Extreme Violence.......... 325.00
11 The Trap of Terror 350.00
12 SHn, Vultures of Death-
   Extreme Violence 350.00
13 Extreme Violence.......... 350.00
14 Horror of the Flame Thrower
   Extreme Violence 350.00
15 DW,Ghoul Crazy 450.00

All comics prices listed are for *Near Mint* condition.

CVA Page 437

Mysterious–National GOLDEN AGE Comics Values Annual

16 Chilling Tales of Horror 450.00
17 DW,Bride of the Dead 450.00
18 Extreme Violence 450.00
19 The Coffin 450.00
20 Horror o/t Avenging Corpse . . 450.00
21 Mother Ghoul's Nursery
   Tales, Bondage (c) 450.00
22 RA,Insane 350.00
23 RA,Extreme Violence 350.00
24 KS, ... 300.00
25 KS,Aug., 1955 . . . . 300.00

HORROR FROM THE TOMB
Premier Magazines
Sept., 1954
1 AT,GWb,The Corpse Returns . 500.00
Becomes:

MYSTERIOUS STORIES
Dec., 1954–Jan., 1955
2 GWb(c),Eternal Life 600.00
3 GWb,The Witch Doctor 350.00
4 That's the Spirit 300.00
5 King Barbarossa 300.00
6 GWb,Strangers in the Night . . 325.00
7 KS,The Pipes of Pan;Dec'55 . . 300.00

MYSTERIOUS TRAVELER COMICS
Trans-World Publications
Nov., 1948
1 BP,BP(c),Five Miles Down . . . 700.00

MYSTERY COMICS
William H. Wise & Co., 1944
1 AS(c),B:Brad Spencer-Wonderman,
   King of Futeria,The Magnet, Zudo-
   Jungle Boy,Silver Knight . . 1,500.00
2 AS(c),Bondage (c) 900.00
3 AS(c),Robot(c),LanceLewis,B . 750.00
4 AS(c),E:All Features,
   KKK Type(c) 750.00

MYSTERY MEN COMICS
Fox Features Syndicate
Aug., 1939
1 GT,DBr,LF(c),Bondage(c);I:Blue
   Beetle,Green Mask,Rex Dexter
   of Mars,Zanzibar,Lt.Drake,D-13
   Secret Agent,Chen Chang,
   Wing Turner,Capt. Denny 15,000.00
2 GT,BP,DBr,LF(c),
   Rex Dexter (c) 4,500.00
3 LF(c) 6,000.00
4 LF(c),B:Captain Savage 3,500.00
5 GT,BP,LF(c),Green Mask (c) 3,500.00
6 GT,BP 3,000.00
7 GT,BP,Bondage(c),
   Blue Beetle(c) 3,500.00
8 GT,BP,LF(c),Bondage(c),
   Blue Beetle 3,200.00
9 GT,BP,DBr(c),B:The Moth . . 1,500.00
10 GT,BP,JSm(c),A:Wing
   Turner; Bondage(c) 1,400.00
11 GT,BP,JSm(c),I:The Domino 1,400.00
12 GT,BP,JSm(c),BlueBeetle(c) 1,400.00
13 GT,I:The Lynx & Blackie . . . 1,000.00
14 GT,Male Bondage (c) 950.00
15 GT,Blue Beetle (c) 900.00
16 GT,Hypo(c),MaleBondage(c) . 950.00
17 GT,BP,Blue Beetle (c) 900.00
18 GT,Blue Beetle (c) 900.00
19 GT,I&B:Miss X 1,000.00
20 GT,DBr,Blue Beetle (c) 900.00
21 GT,E:Miss X 900.00
22 GT,CCu(c),Blue Beetle (c) . . . 900.00

Mystery Men Comics #29
© *Fox Features Syndicate*

23 GT,Blue Beetle (c) 900.00
24 GT,BP,DBr, Blue Beetle (c) . . . 900.00
25 GT,Bondage(c);
   A:Private O'Hara 950.00
26 GT,Bondage(c);B:The Wraith . 950.00
27 GT,Bondage(c),BlueBeetle(c) . 950.00
28 GT,Bondage(c);Satan's
   Private Needlewoman 950.00
29 GT,Bondage(c),Blue
   Beetle (c) 950.00
30 Holiday of Death 900.00
31 Bondage(c);Feb'42 . . . . 950.00

MY STORY
See: ZAGO, JUNGLE PRINCE

NATIONAL COMICS
Comics Magazines
(Quality Comics Group)
July, 1940
1 GT,HcK,LF(c),B:Uncle Sam,Wonder
   Boy,Merlin the Magician,Cyclone,
   Kid Patrol,Sally O'Neil-Police-
   woman, Pen Miller,Prop
   Powers, Paul Bunyan 8,000.00
2 WE,GT,HcK,LF&RC(c) 3,200.00
3 GT,HcK,WE&RC(c) 2,400.00
4 GT,HcK,LF&RC(c),E:Cyclone;
   Torpedo Islands of Death . . 1,900.00
5 GT,LF&RC(c),B:Quicksilver;
   O:Uncle Sam 2,500.00
6 GT,LF&RC(c) 1,800.00
7 GT,LF&RC(c) 2,900.00
8 GT,LF&RC(c) 1,800.00
9 JCo,LF&RC(c) 1,800.00
10 RC,JCo,LF&RC(c) 1,800.00
11 RC,JCo,LF&RC(c) 1,800.00
12 RC,JCo,LF&RC(c) 1,500.00
13 RC,JCo,LF,LF&RC(c) 1,400.00
14 RC,JCo,LF,PG,LF&RC(c) . . 1,400.00
15 RC,JCo,LF,PG,LF&RC(c) . . 1,400.00
16 RC,JCo,LF,PG,LF&RC(c) . . 1,400.00
17 RC,JCo,LF,PG,LF&RC(c) . . 1,000.00
18 JCo,LF,PG,LF&RC(c),
   Pearl Harbor 1,700.00
19 JCo,LF,PG,RC(c),The Black
   Fog Mystery 1,000.00
20 JCo,LF,PG,LF&RC(c) 1,000.00
21 LF,JCo,PG,LF(c) 1,000.00
22 JCo,LF,PG,FG,GFx,LF(c),
   E:Jack & Jill,Pen Miller,
   Paul Bunyan 1,000.00

23 JCo,PG,FG,GFx,AMc,LF
   & GFx(c),B:The Unknown,
   Destroyer 171 . . . . 1,100.00
24 JCo,PG,RC,AMc,FG,
   GFx,RC(c) 1,100.00
25 AMc,RC,JCo,PG,FG,
   GFx,RC(c) 750.00
26 AMc,Jco,RC,PG,RC(c),
   E:Prop Powers,WonderBoy . . 750.00
27 JCo,AMc 750.00
28 JCo,AMc 750.00
29 JCo,O:The Unknown;U.Sam
   V:Dr. Dirge 775.00
30 JCo,RC(c) 750.00
31 JCo,RC(c) 600.00
32 JCo,RC(c) 600.00
33 JCo,GFx,RC(c),B:Chic Carter;
   U.Sam V:Boss Spring 600.00
34 JCo,GFx,U.Sam V:Big John
   Fales 600.00
35 JCo,GFx,E:Kid Patrol 500.00
36 JCo 500.00
37 JCo,FG,A:The Vagabond 500.00
38 JCo,FG,Boat of the Dead 500.00
39 JCo,FG,Hitler(c);U.Sam
   V:The Black Market 600.00
40 JCo,FG,U.Sam V:The
   Syndicate of Crime 450.00
41 JCo,FG 450.00
42 JCo,FG,JCo(c),B:The Barker . 300.00
43 JCo,FG,JCo(c) 300.00
44 JCo,FG 300.00
45 JCo,FG,E:Merlin the Magician 300.00
46 JCo,JCo(c),Murder is no Joke 300.00
47 JCo,JCo(c),E:Chic Carter 300.00
48 JCo,O:The Whistler 300.00
49 JCo,JCo(c),A Corpse
   for a Cannonball 300.00
50 JCo,JCo(c),V:Rocks Myzer . . 300.00
51 JCo,BWa,JCo(c),
   A:Sally O'Neil 350.00
52 JCo,A Carnival of Laughs 250.00
53 PG,V:Scramolo 250.00
54 PG,V:Raz-Ma-Taz 250.00
55 JCo,AMc,V:The Hawk 250.00
56 GFx,JCo,AMc,V:The Grifter . . 250.00
57 GFX,JCo,AMc,V:Witch Doctor 250.00
58 GFz,JCo,AMc,Talking Animals 250.00
59 GFx,JCo,AMc,V:The Birdman 250.00
60 GFx,JCo,AMc,V:Big Ed Grew 250.00
61 GFx,AMc,Trouble Comes in
   Small Packages 200.00
62 GFx,AMc,V:Crocodile Man . . . 200.00
63 GFx,AMc,V:Bearded Lady . . . 200.00
64 GFx,V:The Human Fly 200.00

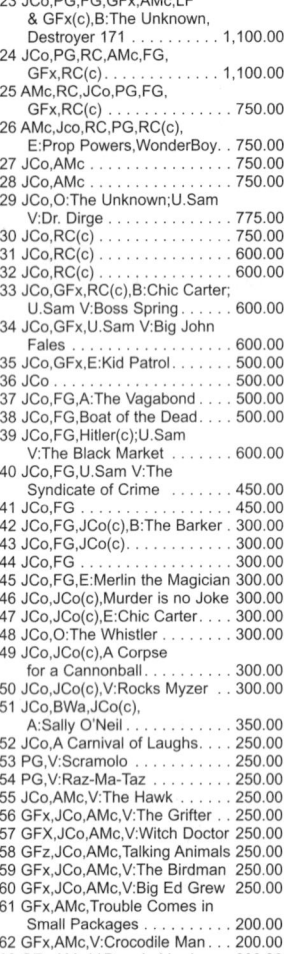

National Comics #8
© *Quality Comics Group*

CVA Page 438   All comics prices listed are for *Near Mint* condition.

Comics Values Annual

65 GFx,GFx(c)V:The King......200.00
66 GFx,GFx(c)V:THe Man Who
   Hates the Circus..........200.00
67 GFx,Gfx(c),A:Quicksilver;
   V:Ali Ben Riff Raff........200.00
68 GFx,GFx(c),V:Leo theLionMan 200.00
69 GFx,Gfx(c),A:Percy the
   Powerful..................200.00
70 GFx,GFx(c),Barker Tires
   of the Big Top............200.00
71 PG,GFx(c),V:SpellbinderSmith 200.00
72 PG,GFx(c),The Oldest Man
   in the World..............200.00
73 PG,GFx(c),V:A CountrySlicker 200.00
74 PG,GFx(c),V:Snake Oil Sam . 200.00
75 PG,GFx(c),Barker Breakes the
   Bank at Monte Marlo;Nov'49. 200.00

NEBBS, THE
Dell Publishing Co., 1941
1 rep......................150.00

NEGRO ROMANCE
**Fawcett Publications
June, 1950**
1 GE,Ph(c), Love's Decoy....1,600.00
2 GE,Ph(c), A Tragic Vow 1,200.00
3 GE,Ph(c), My Love
  Betrayed Me 1,200.00
Charlton Comics
4 Rep.FawcettEd.#2;May,1955 1,000.00

NEW ROMANCES
**Standard Comics
May, 1951**
5 Ph(c), The Blame I Bore 125.00
6 Ph(c), No Wife Was I 75.00
7 Ph(c), My Runaway Heart,
  Ray Miland...............60.00
8 Ph(c) 60.00
9 Ph(c) 60.00
10 ATh,Ph(c) 85.00
11 ATh,Ph(c) of Elizabeth Taylor . 200.00
12 Ph(c) 55.00
13 Ph(c) 55.00
14 ATh,Ph(c) 75.00
15 Ph(c) 55.00
16 ATh,Ph(c) 75.00
17 Ath, ...75.00
18 and 19..................@55.00
20 GT, ...60.00
21 April, 1954..............55.00

NICKEL COMICS
Dell Publishing Co., 1938
1 Bobby & Chip 1,000.00

NICKEL COMICS
**Fawcett Publications
May, 1940**
1 JaB(c),O&I: Bulletman.....6,000.00
2 JaB(c), ...1,800.00
3 JaB(c), ...1,400.00
4 JaB(c), B: Red Gaucho 1,300.00
5 CCB(c),Bondage(c) 1,300.00
6 and 7 CCB(c) ....@1,200.00
8 CCB(c),Aug. 23, 1940,
  World's Fair.............1,300.00

NIGHTMARE
See: WEIRD HORRORS

GOLDEN AGE

NIGHTMARE
Ziff-Davis Publishing Co.
1 EK,GT,P(c),The Corpse That
  Wouldn't Stay Dead 750.00
2 EK,P(c),Vampire Mermaid ...500.00
St. John Publishing Co.
3 EK,P(c),The Quivering Brain . 400.00
4 P(c),1953 ....350.00

NORTHWEST MOUNTIES
**Jubilee Publications/
St. John Publ. Co.
Oct., 1948**
1 MB,BLb(c),Rose of the Yukon 600.00
2 MB,BLb(c),A:Ventrilo.......500.00
3 MB, Bondage(c) 550.00
4 MB(c),A:Blue Monk,July'49 ..450.00

NURSERY RHYMES
Ziff-Davis Publishing Co., 1950
1 How John Came Clean 150.00
2 The Old Woman Who
  Lived in a Shoe 135.00

NUTS!
**Premere Comics Group
March, 1954**
1 ....350.00
2 ....250.00
3 Mention of "Reefers".......275.00
4 ....250.00
5 Captain Marvel Spoof;Nov.'54 250.00

NUTTY COMICS
**Fawcett Publications
Winter, 1946**
1 (fa),F:Capt. Kid,Richard Richard,
  Joe Miller...Among others ..150.00

NUTTY LIFE
See: PHANTOM LADY

NYOKA THE JUNGLE GIRL
**Fawcett Publications
Winter, 1945**
1 Bondage(c);Partial Ph(c) of
  Kay Aldridge as Nyoka 750.00

*Nyoka The Jungle Girl #3
© Fawcett Publications*

National–One Hundred

2 ....350.00
3 ....350.00
4 Bondage(c) 350.00
5 Barbacosi Madness;
  Bondage(c) 350.00
6 ....275.00
7 North Pole Jungle;Bondage(c) 250.00
8 Bondage(c) 250.00
9 ....225.00
10 ....225.00
11 Danger! Death! in an
   Unexplored Jungle 200.00
12 ....200.00
13 The Human Leopards 200.00
14 The Mad Witch Doctor;
   Bondage(c)..............200.00
15 Sacred Goat of Kristan.....200.00
16 BK,The Vultures of Kalahari . . 225.00
17 BK......................225.00
18 BK,The Art of Murder 225.00
19 The Elephant Battle 225.00
20 Explosive Volcano Action ...225.00
21 ....125.00
22 The Weird Monsters.......125.00
23 Danger in Duplicate.......125.00
24 The Human Jaguar;
   Bondage(c)..............120.00
25 Hand Colored Ph(c) 110.00
26 A Jungle Stampede 110.00
27 Adventure Laden 110.00
28 The Human Statues of
   the Jungle...............110.00
29 Ph(c) 110.00
30 Ph(c) 110.00
31 thru 40 Ph(c) ....@100.00
41 thru 50 Ph(c) ....@110.00
51 thru 59 Ph(c) ....@75.00
60 Ph(c) 60.00
61 Ph(c),The Sacred Sword of
   the Jungle...............60.00
62 & 63 Ph(c) ....@60.00
64 Ph(c), The Jungle Idol 60.00
65 Ph(c) 60.00
66 Ph(c) 60.00
67 Ph(c), The Sky Man.......60.00
68 thru 74 Ph(c) ....@60.00
75 Ph(c), The Jungle Myth
   of Terror.................60.00
76 Ph(c) 60.00
77 Ph(c),The Phantoms of the
   Elephant Graveyard;Jun'53...60.00

OAKY DOAKS
**Eastern Color Printing Co.
July, 1942**
1 Humor Oriented 450.00

OH, BROTHER!
**Stanhall Publications
Jan., 1953**
1 Bill Williams-a 75.00
2 thru 5 ....@50.00

OK COMICS
**United Features Syndicate
July, 1940**
1 B:Pal Peyton,Little Giant, Phantom
  Knight,Sunset Smith,Teller Twins,
  Don Ramon, Jerrry Sly,Kip Jaxon,
  Leatherneck,Ulysses 1,000.00
2 Oct., 1940 ....1,100.00

100 PAGES OF COMICS
Dell Publishing Co., 1937
101 Alley Oop,OG, Wash Tubbs,
    Tom Mix,Dan Dunn 2,000.00

All comics prices listed are for Near Mint condition.

On the–Out of

ON THE AIR
NBC Network Comics, 1947
1 Giveaway, no cover 250.00

ON THE SPOT
Fawcett Publications
Autumn, 1948
N# Bondage(c),PrettyBoyFloyd . . 450.00

OPERATION PERIL
American Comics Group
(Michel Publ.)
Oct.–Nov., 1950
1 LSt,OW,OW(c),B:TyphoonTyler,
  DannyDanger,TimeTravellers 450.00
2 OW,OW(c),War (c) 275.00
3 OW,OW(c),Horror 250.00
4 OW,OW(c), Flying Saucers . . . 250.00
5 OW,OW(c), Science Fiction. . . 250.00
6 OW, Tyr. Rex 250.00
7 OW,OW(c),Sabretooth 250.00
8 OW,OW(c) 200.00
9 OW,OW(c) 200.00
10 OW,OW(c),science fiction . . . 200.00
11 OW,OW(c), War 200.00

Operation Peril #2
© American Comics Group

12 OW,OW(c),E:Time Travellers . 200.00
13 OW,OW(c),War Stories 100.00
14 OW,OW(c),War Stories 100.00
15 OW,OW(c),War Stories 100.00
16 OW,OW(c),April–May,1953,
   War Stories 100.00

OUR FLAG COMICS
Ace Magazines
Aug., 1941–April, 1942
1 MA,JM,B:Capt.Victory,Unknown
  Soldier,The Three Cheers . 3,700.00
2 JM,JM(c),O:The Flag 1,500.00
3 Tank Battle (c) 1,200.00
4 MA 1,200.00
5 I:Mr. Risk, Male Bondage . . 1,200.00

OUR GANG COMICS
Dell Publishing Co.
Sept.–Oct., 1942
1 WK,Barney Bear, Tom &
  Jerry 1,500.00
2 WK 750.00
3 WK,Benny Burro 500.00

GOLDEN AGE

Our Gang #3
© Dell Publishing Co.

4 WK 500.00
5 WK 500.00
6 WK 750.00
7 WK 350.00
8 WK,CB,Benny Burro 900.00
9 WK,CB,Benny Burro 850.00
10 WK,CB,Benny Burro 600.00
11 WK,I:Benny Bear 850.00
12 thru 20 WK . . . . @400.00
21 thru 29 WK . . . . @300.00
30 WK,Christmas(c) 250.00
31 thru 34 WK . . . . @200.00
35 WK,CB 200.00
36 WK,CB 200.00
37 thru 40 WK . . . . @125.00
41 thru 50 WK . . . . @75.00
51 thru 56 WK . . . . @75.00
57 . . . . 50.00
58 Our Gang 50.00
59 Our Gang 50.00
Becomes:

TOM AND JERRY
July, 1949
60 . . . . 150.00
61 . . . . 100.00
62 . . . . 75.00
63 . . . . 75.00
64 . . . . 75.00
65 . . . . 75.00
66 Christmas (c) 90.00
67 thru 70 . . . . @75.00
71 thru 76 . . . . @70.00
77 Christmas (c) 75.00
78 thru 80 . . . . @70.00
81 thru 89 . . . . @60.00
90 Christmas (c) 70.00
91 thru 99 . . . . @60.00
100 . . . . 70.00
101 thru 120 . . . . @50.00
121 thru 150 . . . . @40.00
151 thru 212 . . . . @35.00

OUR SECRET
See: MY SECRET

OUTLAWS
D.S. Publishing Co.
Feb.–March, 1948
1 HcK,Western Crime Stories . . 400.00
2 Grl,Doc Dawson's Dilema . . . 400.00
3 Cougar City Cleanup 175.00
4 JO,Death Stakes A Claim 200.00

Comics Values Annual

5 RJ,RJ(c),Man Who Wanted
  Mexico 175.00
6 AMc,RJ,RJ(c),The Ghosts of
  Crackerbox Hill 175.00
7 Grl,Dynamite For Boss Cavitt . 300.00
8 Grl,The Gun & the Pen 300.00
9 FF,Shoot to Kill;June–
  July, 1949 . . . . 600.00

WHITE RIDER AND SUPER HORSE
Star Publications
Sept., 1950
1 LbC(c) 150.00
2 LbC(c) 100.00
3 LbC(c) 100.00
4 LbC(c) 100.00
5 LbC(c),Stampede of Hard
  Riding Thrills 125.00
6 LbC(c),Drums of the Sioux . . . 125.00
Becomes:

INDIAN WARRIORS
June, 1951
7 LbC(c),Winter on the Great
  Plains 125.00
8 LbC(c) 100.00
Becomes:

WESTERN CRIME CASES
Dec., 1951
9 LbC(c),The Card Sharp Killer . 150.00
Becomes:

OUTLAWS, THE
May, 1952
10 LbC(c),Federated Express . . 250.00
11 LbC(c),Frontier Terror!!! 200.00
12 LbC(c),Ruthless Killer!!! 200.00
13 LbC(c),The Grim Avengers. . . 200.00
14 AF,JKa,LbC(c), Trouble in
   Dark Canyon,April, 1954. . . . 200.00

OUT OF THE NIGHT
American Comics Group/
Best Synd. Feature
Feb.–March, 1952
1 AW 800.00
2 AW 600.00
3 . . . . 300.00
4 AW 500.00
5 . . . . 300.00
6 The Ghoul's Revenge 300.00
7 . . . . 300.00
8 The Frozen Ghost 300.00
9 Death Has Wings,
  Science Fiction. 300.00
10 Ship of Death 300.00
11 . . . . 275.00
12 Music for the Dead 275.00
13 HN,From the Bottom of
   the Well 275.00
14 Out of the Screen 275.00
15 The Little Furry Thing 250.00
16 Nightmare From the Past . . . 250.00
17 The Terror of the Labyrinth . . 250.00
Becomes:

HOODED HORSEMAN
Dec., 1954–Jan., 1955
18 B: The Hooded Horseman . . 100.00
19 The Horseman's Strangest
   Adventure 150.00
20 OW,O:Johnny Injun 90.00
21 OW,OW(c) 150.00
22 OW 100.00
23 . . . . 100.00
24 . . . . 100.00

GOLDEN AGE

25 .... 80.00
26 O&I:Cowboy Sahib. 100.00
27 Jan.–Feb., 1953. .... 90.00

OUT OF THE SHADOWS
Visual Editions (Standard Comics) July, 1952–Aug., 1954
5 ATh,GT,The Shoremouth Horror 750.00
6 ATh,JKz,Salesman of Death .. 500.00
7 JK,Plant of Death 350.00
8 Mask of Death 625.00
9 RC,Till Death Do Us Part 350.00
10 MS,We Vowed,Till Death Do Us Part 350.00
11 ATh,Fountain of Fear 300.00
12 ATh,Hand of Death 500.00
13 MS,The Cannibal 300.00
14 ATh,The Werewolf 300.00

OXYDOL-DREFT
Giveaways, 1950
The Set is More Valuable if the Original Envelope is Present
1 L'il Abner 150.00
2 Daisy Mae 150.00
3 Shmoo 175.00
4 AW&FF(c),John Wayne 200.00
5 Archie 150.00
6 Terry Toons Comics 125.00

OZZIE AND BABS
Fawcett Publications Winter, 1946
1 Humor Oriented, Teenage..... 90.00
2 Humor Oriented 50.00
3 Humor Oriented 40.00
4 Humor Oriented 40.00
5 Humor Oriented 40.00
6 Humor Oriented 40.00
7 Humor Oriented 40.00
8 Humor Oriented 40.00
9 Humor Oriented 40.00
10 Humor Oriented 40.00
11 Humor Oriented 40.00
12 Humor Oriented 40.00
13 Humor Oriented;1949 ...... 40.00

PAGEANT OF COMICS
St. John Publishing Co. Sept., 1947
1 Rep. Mopsy 100.00
2 Rep. Jane Arden,Crime Reporter................ 100.00

PANHANDLE PETE AND JENNIFER
J. Charles Lave Publishing Co., July, 1951
1 (fa) 100.00
2 (fa) 60.00
3 (fa),Nov.'51 .... 60.00

PANIC
Tiny Tot Publications (E.C. Comics), March, 1954 "Humor in a Jugular Vein"
1 BE,JKa,JO,JDa,AF(c) 500.00
2 BE,JO,WW,JDa,A:Bomb..... 250.00
3 BE,JO,BW,WW,JDa,AF(c) ... 200.00
4 BE,JO,WW,JDa,BW(c), Infinity(c) 200.00
5 BE,JO,WW,JDa,AF(c) 150.00
6 BE,JO,WW,JDa,Blank (c) 150.00

7 BE,JO,WW,JDa 150.00
8 BE,JO,WW,JDa,Eye Chart (c). 150.00
9 BE,JO,WW,JDa,Ph(c), Confidential(c) 150.00
10 BE,JDa, Postal Package(c) .. 150.00
11 BE,WW,JDa,Wheaties parody as Weedies (c) 150.00
12 BE,WW,JDa,JDa(c); Dec.–Jan., 1955–56 ...... 200.00

PARAMOUNT ANIMATED COMICS
Family Publications (Harvey Publ.) June, 1953
1 (fa),B:Baby Herman & Katnip, Baby Huey,Buzzy the Crow . 275.00
2 (fa) 125.00
3 (fa) 100.00
4 (fa) 100.00
5 (fa) 100.00
6 (fa) 100.00
7 (fa), Baby Huey (c) 250.00
8 (fa), Baby Huey (c) 75.00
9 (fa), Infinity(c),Baby Huey (c) . 75.00
10 thru 21 (fa),Baby Huey(c)... @60.00
22 (fa), July, 1956, Baby Huey (c). 60.00

PAROLE BREAKERS
Avon Periodicals/Realistic Dec., 1951–July, 1952
1 P(c),Hellen Willis,Gun Crazed Gun Moll 550.00
2 JKu,P(c),Vinnie Sherwood, The Racket King 400.00
3 EK(c),John "Slicer" Berry, Hatchetman of Crime 350.00

PATCHES
Rural Home Publ./ Patches Publ. March–April, 1945
1 LbC(c),Imagination In Bed(c) . 500.00
2 Dance (c) 200.00
3 Rocking Horse (c).......... 150.00
4 Music Band (c) 150.00
5 LbC(c),A:Danny Kaye,Football 250.00
6 A: Jackie Kelk 150.00
7 A: Hopalong Cassidy 225.00
8 A: Smiley Burnettte 150.00
9 BK,A: Senator Claghorn 150.00
10 A: Jack Carson 150.00
11 A: Red Skeleton; Dec'47 .... 200.00

PAWNEE BILL
Story Comics Feb.–July, 1951
1 A:Bat Masterson,Wyatt Earp, Indian Massacre at Devil's Gulch 125.00
2 Blood in Coffin Canyon 75.00
3 LC,O:Golden Warrior,Fiery Arrows at Apache Pass 75.00

PAY-OFF
D.S. Publishing Co. July–Aug., 1948– March–April, 1949
1 True Crime 1 & 2 .... 300.00
2 The Pennsylvania Blue-Beard 175.00
3 The Forgetful Forger 150.00
4 RJ(c),Lady and the Jewels ... 150.00
5 The Beautiful Embezzeler.... 150.00

PEDRO
Fox Features Syndicate Jan., 1950
1 WW,WW(c),Humor Oriented . 250.00
2 Aug., 1950 .... 175.00

PENNY
Avon Publications, 1947
1 The Slickest Chick of 'em All . 125.00
2 .... 75.00
3 America's Teen-age Sweetheart 75.00
4 .... 75.00
5 .... 75.00
6 Perry Como Ph(c),Sept.– Oct., 1949 .... 90.00

PEP COMICS
MJL Magazines/ Archie Publications Jan., 1940
1 IN,JCo,MMe,IN(c),I:Shield, O:Comet,Queen of Diamonds, B:The Rocket,Press Guardian, Sergeant Boyle Chang,Bently of Scotland Yard 13,000.00
2 CBi,JCo,IN,IN(c),O:Rocket.. 3,500.00
3 JCo,IN,IN(c),Shield (c) 2,500.00
4 Cbi,JCo,MMe,IN,IN(c), C:Wizard(not Gareb) 2,000.00
5 Cbi,JCo,MMe,IN,IN(c), C:Wizard 2,000.00
6 IN,IN(c), Shield (c) 1,500.00
7 IN,IN(c),Bondage(c),Shield(c)1,500.00
8 JCo,IN, Shield (c)......... 1,500.00
9 IN, Shield (c) 1,500.00
10 IN,IN(c), Shield (c) 1,500.00
11 MMe,IN,IN(c),I:Dusty, Boy Detective 1,600.00
12 IN,IN(c),O:Fireball Bondage(c), E:Rocket, Queen of Diamonds...... 1,800.00
13 IN,IN(c),Bondage(c) 1,200.00
14 IN,IN(c).................. 1,200.00
15 IN,Bondage(c) 1,200.00
16 IN,O:Madam Satan 1,800.00
17 IN,IN(c),O:Hangman, D:Comet 4,800.00
18 IN,IN(c),Bondage(c) 1,200.00
19 IN..................... 1,200.00
20 IN,IN(c),E:Fireball 1,200.00
21 IN,IN(c),Bondage(c), E: Madam Satan 1,200.00

Pep #27
© Archie Publications

Pep–Phantom Lady

Pep Comics #61
© Archie Publications

22 IN,IN(c)I:Archie,
  Jughead, Betty........ 21,000.00
23 IN,IN(c)................ 2,000.00
24 IN,IN(c)................ 1,500.00
25 IN,IN(c)................ 1,500.00
26 IN,IN(c),I:Veronica....... 2,100.00
27 IN,IN(c),Bill of Rights (c)... 1,500.00
28 IN,IN(c), V:Capt. Swastika.. 1,500.00
29 ASH (c)................. 1,500.00
30 B:Capt.Commando........ 1,500.00
31 Bondage(c).............. 1,500.00
32 Bondage(c).............. 1,100.00
33 .... 1,100.00
34 Bondage(c).............. 1,100.00
35 .... 1,100.00
36 1st Archie(c)............ 2,500.00
37 Bondage(c)................ 750.00
38 ASH(c).................... 700.00
39 ASH(c), Human Shield...... 700.00
40 .... 700.00
41 2nd Archie; I:Jughead...... 500.00
42 F:Archie & Jughead........ 500.00
43 F:Archie & Jughead........ 500.00
44 .... 500.00
45 .... 500.00
46 .... 500.00
47 E:Hangman,Infinity(c)..... 500.00
48 B:Black Hood............. 500.00
49 .... 500.00
50 .... 500.00
51 .... 350.00
52 B:Suzie.................. 350.00
53 .... 350.00
54 E:Captain Commando...... 350.00
55 .... 350.00
56 thru 58................ @300.00
59 E:Suzie.................. 300.00
60 B:Katy Keene............. 300.00
61 .... 250.00
62 I L'il Jinx............... 250.00
63 .... 250.00
64 .... 250.00
65 E:Shield.................. 250.00
66 thru 71................ @150.00
72 thru 80................ @125.00
81 thru 90................ @100.00
91 thru 99................ @100.00
100......................... 150.00
101 thru 110.............. @100.00
111 thru 120............... @75.00
121 thru 130............... @60.00
131 thru 140............... @50.00
141 thru 150............... @40.00
151 thru 160,A:Super Heroes.. @40.00
161 thru 200............... @35.00
201 thru 250............... @20.00

GOLDEN AGE

251 thru 300.............. @20.00
301 thru 350.............. @20.00
351 thru 411.............. @10.00

PERFECT CRIME, THE
Cross Publications
Oct., 1949
1 BP,DW................... 400.00
2 BP....................... 200.00
3 .... 150.00
4 BP....................... 150.00
5 DW...................... 150.00
6 .... 150.00
7 B:Steve Duncan........... 150.00
8 Drug Story............... 200.00
9 .... 150.00
10........................ 150.00
11 Bondage (c)............. 200.00
12........................ 150.00
13........................ 150.00
14 Poisoning (c)............ 150.00
15 'The Most Terrible Menace',
  Drug..................... 200.00
16........................ 150.00
17........................ 150.00
18 Drug (c)................. 250.00
19........................ 150.00
20 thru 25................ @125.00
26 Drug w/ Hypodermic (c).... 250.00
27........................ 150.00
28........................ 150.00
29........................ 150.00
30 E:Steve Duncan, Rope
  Strangulation (c).......... 300.00
31........................ 100.00
32........................ 100.00
33........................ 100.00

PERFECT LOVE
Approved Comics(Ziff-Davis)/
St. John Publ. Co.
Aug.–Sept., 1951
1 (10),P(c),Our Kiss was a
  Prelude to Love Adrift...... 250.00
2 .... 150.00
3 P(c)..................... 100.00
4 .... 100.00
5 .... 100.00
6 .... 100.00
7 .... 100.00
8 EK....................... 125.00
9 EK,P(c).................. 75.00
10 Ph(c), Dec '53............ 75.00

PERSONAL LOVE
Famous Funnies, Jan., 1950
1 Ph(c) Are You in Love...... 200.00
2 Ph(c) Serenade for Suzette
  Mario Lanzo.............. 100.00
3 Ph(c).................... 75.00
4 Ph(c).................... 75.00
5 Ph(c).................... 75.00
6 Ph(c) Be Mine Forever..... 90.00
7 Ph(c) You'll Always Be
  Mine, Robert Walker....... 90.00
8 EK,Ph(c),Esther Williams &
  Howard Keel.............. 100.00
9 EK,Ph(c),Debra Paget & Louis
  Jordan.................... 100.00
10 Ph(c),Loretta Young
  Joseph Cotton............. 75.00
11 ATh, Ph(c),Gene Tierney &
  Glenn Ford................ 150.00
12 Ph(c) Jane Greer &
  William Lundigan.......... 75.00
13 Ph(c) Debra Paget &
  Louis Jordan.............. 70.00

Comics Values Annual

14 Ph(c) Kirk Douglas &
  Patrice Wymore........... 80.00
15 Ph(c) Dale Robertson &
  Joanne Dru............... 65.00
16 Ph(c) Take Back Your Love... 65.00
17 Ph(c) My Cruel Deception.... 65.00
18 Ph(c) Gregory Peck &
  Susan Hayward........... 75.00
19 Ph(c) Anthony Quinn....... 75.00
20 Ph(c) The Couple in the
  Next Apartment, Bob Wagner. 70.00
21 Ph(c) I'll Make You Care.... 65.00
22 Ph(c) Doorway To Heartbreak. 65.00
23 Ph(c) SaveMe from that Man.. 70.00
24 FF, Ph(c) Tyrone Power..... 500.00
25 FF, Ph(c) The Dark Light.... 500.00
26 Ph(c) Love Needs A Break... 65.00
27 FF, Ph(c) Champ or Chump?. 500.00
28 FF, Ph(c) A Past to Forget... 500.00
29 Ph(c) Charlton Heston...... 75.00
30 Ph(c) The Lady is Lost...... 65.00
31 Ph(c) Marlon Brando....... 100.00
32 FF, Ph(c) The Torment,
  Kirk Douglas.............. 650.00
33 Ph(c) June, 1955........... 65.00

PETER COTTONTAIL
Key Publications
Jan., 1954
1 No 3-D (fa)................ 80.00
1 Feb '54 3-D (fa)............ 250.00
2 Rep of 3-D #1,not in 3-D..... 50.00

PETER PAUL'S 4 IN 1 JUMBO COMIC BOOK
Capitol Stories, 1953
1 F: Racket Squad in Action,
  Space Adventures,Crime &
  Justice,Space Western.... 500.00

PETER PENNY AND HIS MAGIC DOLLAR
American Bakers Assn., 1947
1 History from Colonial
  America to the 1950's...... 200.00
2 .... 125.00

PETER RABBIT
Avon Periodicals, 1947
1 H. Cady art............... 450.00
2 H. Cady art............... 275.00
3 H. Cady art............... 250.00
4 H. Cady art............... 250.00
5 H. Cady art............... 250.00
6 H. Cady art............... 250.00
7 thru 10.................. @60.00
11......................... 60.00

KRAZY LIFE
Fox Features Syndicate, 1945
1 (fa)..................... 100.00
Becomes:

NUTTY LIFE
Summer, 1946
2 (fa)..................... 75.00
Becomes:

WOTALIFE
Fox Features Synd./
Green Publ., Aug.–Sept., 1946
3 (fa)B:L'il Pan,Cosmo Cat.... 65.00
4 .... 50.00
5 thru 11.................. @35.00
12 July, 1947............... 35.00
Becomes:

CVA Page 442   All comics prices listed are for *Near Mint* condition.

GOLDEN AGE

PHANTOM LADY
Fox Features Syndicate
Aug., 1947
- 13(#1) MB,MB(c) Knights of the Crooked Cross 5,500.00
- 14(#2) MB,MB(c) Scoundrels and Scandals.......... 3,200.00
- 15 MB,MB(c) The Meanest Crook In the World....... 3,000.00
- 16 MB,MB(c) Claa Peete The Beautiful Beast, Negligee.. 3,000.00
- 17 MB.MB(c) The Soda Mint Killer, Bondage (c)....... 7,500.00
- 18 MB,MB(c) The Case of Irene Shroeder 2,500.00
- 19 MB,MB(c) The Case of the Murderous Model 2,500.00
- 20 MB,MB(c) Ace of Spades .. 2,000.00
- 21 MB,MB(c) 1,700.00
- 22 MB,JKa................ 1,700.00
- 23 MB,JKa Bondage (c)...... 2,000.00

Phantom Lady #17
© Fox Feature Syndicate

Becomes:

MY LOVE SECRET
June, 1949
- 24 JKa, My Love Was For Sale.. 150.00
- 25 Second Hand Love 100.00
- 26 WW I Wanted Both Men..... 250.00
- 27 I Was a Love Cheat........ 75.00
- 28 WW, I Gave Him Love 200.00
- 29.......................... 75.00
- 30 Ph(c) 75.00

LINDA
Ajax/Farrell, April–May, 1954
- 1 .... 125.00
- 2 Lingerie section 75.00
- 3 .... 60.00
- 4 Oct.–Nov.,1954 .... 60.00

Becomes:

PHANTOM LADY
Dec., 1954–Jan., 1955
- 5(1) MB 1,500.00
- 2 Last Pre-Code Edition 1,250.00
- 3 Comics Code 1,000.00
- 4 Red Rocket,June, 1955 .... 1,000.00

PHIL RIZZUTO
Fawcett Publications, 1951
Ph(c) The Sensational Story of The American Leagues MVP 950.00

PICTORIAL CONFESSIONS
St. John Publishing Co.
Sept., 1949
- 1 MB,MB(c),I Threw Away My Reputation on a Worthless Love . 350.00
- 2 MB,Ph(c) I Tried to be a Hollywood Glamour Girl 250.00
- 3 JKY,MB,MB(c),They Caught Me Cheating............. 300.00

Becomes:

PICTORIAL ROMANCES
Jan., 1950
- 4 Ph(c) MB, Trapped By Kisses I Couldn't Resist.......... 350.00
- 5 MB,MB(c).................. 300.00
- 6 MB,MB(c) I Was Too Free With Boys 250.00
- 7 MB,MB(c) 250.00
- 8 MB,MB(c) I Made a Sinful Bargain............. 250.00
- 9 MB,MB(c) Dishonest Love ... 250.00
- 10 MB,MB(c) I Was The Other Woman............. 200.00
- 11 MB,MB(c) The Worst Mistake A Wife Can Make... 225.00
- 12 MB,MB(c) Love Urchin...... 200.00
- 13 MB,MB(c) Temptations of a Hatcheck Girl 200.00
- 14 MB,MB(c) I Was A Gamblers Wife 200.00
- 15 MB,MB(c) Wife Without Pride or Principles 200.00
- 16 MB,MB(c) The Truth of My Affair With a Farm Boy .. 200.00
- 17 MB,MB(c) True Confessions of a Girl in Love 300.00
- 18 MB,MB(c) 300.00
- 20 MB,MB(c) 300.00
- 21 MB,MB(c) 175.00
- 22 MB,MB(c) 175.00
- 23 MB,MB(c) 175.00
- 24 MB,MB(c) March,1954...... 175.00

PICTORIAL LOVE STORIES
St. John Publishing Co.
Oct., 1952
- 1 MB,MB(c) I Lost My Head, My Heart and My Resistance ... 350.00

PICTURE NEWS
299 Lafayette Street Corp.
Jan., 1946–Jan.-Feb., 1947
- 1 Will The Atom Blow The World Apart 500.00
- 2 Meet America's 1st Girl Boxing Expert,Atomic Bomb........ 250.00
- 3 Hollywood's June Allison Shows You How to be Beautiful, Atomic Bomb 200.00
- 4 Amazing Marine Who Became King of 10,000 Voodoos, Atomic Bomb 225.00
- 5 G.I.Babies,Hank Greenberg .. 200.00
- 6 Joe Louis(c).............. 225.00
- 7 Lovely Lady, Englands Future Queen........... 175.00
- 8 Champion of them All 175.00
- 9 Bikini Atom Bomb, Joe DiMaggio............. 200.00
- 10 Dick Quick, Ace Reporter, Atomic Bomb 200.00

PICTURE STORIES FROM SCIENCE
Educational Comics
Spring, 1947
- 1 Understanding Air and Water . 350.00
- 2 Fall '47 Amazing Discoveries About Food & Health 300.00

PICTURE STORIES FROM WORLD HISTORY
E.C. Comics, Spring, 1947
- 1 Ancient World to the Fall of Rome.............. 350.00
- 2 Europes Struggle for Civilization 300.00

PINHEAD AND FOODINI
Fawcett Publications
July, 1951–Jan., 1952
- 1 Ph(c) 350.00
- 2 Ph(c) 200.00
- 3 Ph(c) Too Many Pinheads.... 150.00
- 4 Foodini's Talking Camel 150.00

PIN-UP PETE
Minoan Magazine Publishers
1952
- 1 Loves of a GI Casanova..... 250.00

PIONEER PICTURE STORIES
Street & Smith,
Dec., 1941
- 1 Red Warriors in Blackface.... 350.00
- 2 Life Story Of Errol Flynn 200.00
- 3 Success Stories of Brain Muscle in Action 150.00
- 4 Legless Ace & Boy Commando Raid Occupied France 150.00
- 5 How to Tell Uniform and Rank of Any Navy Man..... 150.00
- 6 General Jimmy Doolittle 165.00
- 7 Life Story of Admiral Halsey .. 165.00
- 8 Life Story of Timoshenko 150.00
- 9 Dec., '43,Man Who Conquered The Wild Frozen North 150.00

PIRACY
E.C. Comics, Oct.–Nov., 1954
- 1 WW,JDa,AW,WW(c),RC,AT . 400.00
- 2 RC,JDa(c),WW,AW,AT 250.00
- 3 RC,GE, RC(c),Grl 225.00
- 4 RC,GE,RC(c),Grl 200.00
- 5 RC,GE,BK(c),Grl 200.00
- 6 JDa,RC,GE,BK(c),Grl 200.00
- 7 Oct Nov GE(c),RC,GE,Grl ... 200.00

PIRATES COMICS
Hillman Periodicals, Feb., 1950
- 1 .... 300.00
- 2 .... 200.00
- 3 .... 175.00
- 4 Aug–Sept., 1950........... 175.00

PIXIES, THE
Magazine Enterprises
Winter, 1946
- 1 Mighty Atom.............. 100.00
- 2 .... 50.00
- 3 .... 35.00
- 4 .... 35.00

Pixies–Plastic Man — GOLDEN AGE — Comics Values Annual

5 . . . . 40.00
Becomes:

MIGHTY ATOM, THE
1949

6 . . . . 40.00

PLANET COMICS
**Love Romance Publ.
(Fiction House Magazines)
Jan., 1940–Winter, 1953**

1 AB,DBR,HCk, Planet Comics,
WE&LF,O:Aura,B:Flint Baker,
Red Comet,Spurt Hammond,
Capt. Nelson Cole 16,000.00
2 HcK,LF(c) 6,500.00
3 WE(c),HcK. 4,000.00
4 HcK,B:Gale Allan and
the Girl Squad 3,500.00
5 BP,HcK 3,200.00
6 BP,HcK,BP(c),The Ray
Pirates of Venus 3,400.00
7 BP,AB,HcK,BP(c) B:Buzz
Crandall Planet Payson . . 3,000.00
8 BP,AB HcK 3,000.00
9 BP,AB,GT,HcK,B:Don
Granville Cosmo Corrigan . 3,000.00
10 BP,AB,GT HcK 3,000.00
11 HcK, B:Crash Parker. 3,000.00
12 Dri,B:Star Fighter 3,000.00
13 Dri,B:Reef Ryan 2,000.00
14 Dri B:Norge Benson 1,800.00
15 B: Mars,God of War 3,600.00
16 Invasion From The Void . . . 1,800.00
17 Warrior Maid of Mercury . . 1,800.00
18 Bondage(c). 2,000.00
19 Monsters of the Inner World 1,800.00
20 RP, Winged Man Eaters
of the Exile Star. 1,800.00
21 RP,B:Lost World
Hunt Bowman 2,000.00
22 Inferno on the Fifth Moon . . 1,800.00
23 GT,Lizard Tyrant of
the Twilight World 1,700.00
24 GT,Grl Raiders From
The Red Moon. 1,700.00
25 Grl,B:Norge Benson 1,700.00
26 Grl,B:The Space Rangers
Bondage(c) 1,800.00
27 Grl, The Fire Eaters of
Asteroid Z 1,500.00
28 Grl, Bondage (c) 1,700.00
29 Grl,Dragon Raiders of Aztla. 1,500.00
30 GT,Grl City of Lost Souls. . . 1,500.00
31 Grl,Fire Priests of Orbit6X . . 1,200.00
32 Slaver's Planetoid 1,300.00
33 MA 1,200.00
34 MA,Bondage 1,300.00
35 MA B:Mysta of The Moon . . 1,100.00
36 MA Collosus of the
Blood Moon. 1,100.00
37 MA, Behemoths of the
Purple Void 1,100.00
38 MA 1,000.00
39 MA.Death Webs Of Zenith 3 1,000.00
40 Chameleon Men from
Galaxy 9 . . . . 1,000.00
41 MA,Aaf,New O: Auro
Bondage (c). 1,050.00
42 MA,AaF,E:Gale Allan. 1,000.00
43 MA,AaF Death Rays
From the Sun. 1,000.00
44 MA,Bbl,B:Futura 1,000.00
45 Ma,Bbl,Her Evilness
from Xanado 1,000.00
46 MA,Bbl,GE The Mecho-Men
From Mars. 1,000.00
47 MA,Bbl,GE,The Great
Green Spawn 900.00
48 MA,GE. 900.00

Planet Comics #31
© *Fiction House Magazines*

49 MA,GE, Werewolves From
Hydra Hell 900.00
50 MA,GE,The Things of Xeves . 900.00
51 MA,GE, Mad Mute X-Adapts . 750.00
52 GE,Mystery of the Time
Chamber 750.00
53 MB,GE,Bondage(c)
Dwarflings From Oceania . . 750.00
54 MB,GE,Robots From Inferno . 750.00
55 MB,GE,Giants of the
Golden Atom 750.00
56 MB,GE,Grl. 600.00
57 MB,GE,Grl. 600.00
58 MB,GE,Grl. 600.00
59 MB,GE,Grl,LSe 600.00
60 GE,Grl,Vassals of Volta 600.00
61 GE,Grl, The Brute in the
Bubble 550.00
62 GE,Musta,Moon Goddess . . . 550.00
63 GE,Paradise or Inferno 550.00
64 GE,Monkeys From the Blue . . 550.00
65 The Lost World 550.00
66 The Plague of the
Locust Men 550.00
67 The Nymphs of Neptune 550.00
68 Synthoids of the 9th Moon . . 550.00
69 The Mentalists of Mars. 550.00
70 Cargo For Amazonia 550.00
71 Sandhogs of Mars 500.00
72 Last Ship to Paradise. 500.00
73 The Martian Plague 500.00

PLASTIC MAN
**Comics Magazines
(Quality Comics Group)
Summer, 1943–Nov., 1956**

1 JCo(a&c)Game of Death . . . 5,500.00
2 JCo(a&c)The Gay Nineties
Nightmare 2,500.00
3 JCo(a&c) 1,500.00
4 JCo(a&c) 1,300.00
5 JCo(a&c) 1,200.00
6 JCo(a&c) 800.00
7 JCo(a&c) 800.00
8 JCo(a&c) 800.00
9 JCo(a&c) 800.00
10 JCo(a&c) 800.00
11 JCo(a&c) 600.00
12 JCo(a&c),V:Spadehead 600.00
13 JCo(a&c),V:Mr.Hazard 600.00
14 JCo(a&c),Words,Symbol
of Crime 600.00
15 JCo(a&c),V:BeauBrummel . . . 600.00
16 JCo(a&c),Money
Means Trouble 600.00
17 JCo(a&c),A:The Last
Man on Earth 600.00
18 JCo(a&c),Goes Back
to the Farm. 600.00
19 JCo(a&c),V;Prehistoric
Plunder 600.00
20 JCo(a&c),A:Sadly,Sadly 600.00
21 JCo(a&c),V:Crime Minded
Mind Reader. 500.00
22 JCo(a&c), Which Twin
is the Phony 500.00
23 JCo(a&c),The Fountain
of Age 500.00
24 JCo(a&c),The Black Box
of Terror 500.00
25 JCo(a&c),A:Angus
MacWhangus 500.00
26 JCo(a&c),On the Wrong
Side of the Law? 500.00
27 JCo(a&c),V:The Leader 500.00
28 JCo(a&c),V:Shasta. 500.00
29 JCo(a&c),V:Tricky Toledo 500.00
30 JCo(a&c),V:Weightless
Wiggins 500.00
31 JCo(a&c),V:Raka the
Witch Doctor. 400.00
32 JCo(a&c),V:Mr.Fission 400.00
33 JCo(a&c),V:The Mad
Professor 400.00
34 JCo(a&c),Smuggler'sHaven . . 400.00
35 JCo(a&c),V:The Hypnotist . . . 400.00
36 JCo(a&c),The Uranium
Underground 400.00
37 JCo(a&c),V:Gigantic Ants 400.00
38 JCo(a&c),The Curse of
Monk Mauley 400.00
39 JCo(a&c),The Stairway
to Madness 400.00
40 JCo(a&c),The Ghoul of
Ghost Swamp. 400.00
41 JCo(a&c),The Beast with
the Bloody Claws 350.00
42 JCo(a&c),The King of
Thunderbolts 350.00
43 JCo(a&c),The Evil Terror 350.00
44 JCo(a&c),The Magic Cup 350.00
45 The Invisible Raiders 350.00
46 V:The Spider 350.00
47 The Fiend of a
Thousand Faces. 350.00
48 Killer Crossbones. 350.00
49 JCo,The Weapon for Evil 350.00

Plastic Man #17
© *Quality Comics Group*

CVA Page 444 — All comics prices listed are for *Near Mint* condition.

GOLDEN AGE

Comics Values Annual — Plastic Man–Police Comics

50 V:Iron Fist	350.00
51 Incredible Sleep Weapon	300.00
52 V:Indestructible Wizard	350.00
53 V:Dazzia,Daughter of Darkness	350.00
54 V:Dr.Quomquat	350.00
55 The Man Below Zero	350.00
56 JCo, The Man Who Broke the Law of Gravity	350.00
57 The Chemist's Cauldron	350.00
58 JCo,The Amazing Duplicating Machine	350.00
59 JCo,V:The Super Spy	350.00
60 The Man in the Fiery Disguise	325.00
61 V:King of the Thunderbolts	325.00
62 V:The Smokeweapon	325.00
63 V:Reflecto	325.00
64 The Invisible Raiders	325.00

POCAHONTAS
Pocahontas Fuel Co.
Oct., 1941

N#	250.00
2	225.00

POCKET COMICS
Harvey Publications,
Aug., 1941

1 100 pages,O:Black Cat,Spirit of '76,Red Blazer Phantom Sphinx & Zebra,B:Phantom Ranger,British Agent #99, Spin Hawkins,Satan	1,400.00
2	900.00
3	650.00
4 Jan.'42,All Features End	600.00

POGO POSSUM
Dell Publishing Co.

1 WK,A:Swamp Land Band	750.00
2 WK	600.00
3 WK	450.00
4 WK	450.00
5 WK	450.00
6 thru 10 WK	@350.00
11 WK, Christmas (c)	@375.00
12 thru 16 WK	@300.00

POLICE COMICS
Comic Magazines
(Quality Comics Group)
Aug., 1941

1 JCo,WE,PGn,RC,FG,AB, GFx(a&c),B&O:Plastic Man The Human Bomb,#711,I&B, Chic Canter,The Firebrand Mouthpiece,Phantom Lady The Sword	11,000.00
2 JCo,PGn,WE,RC,FG, GFx(a&c)	5,000.00
3 JCo,PGn,WE,RC,FG, GFx(a&c)	2,800.00
4 JCo,GFx,PGn,WE,RC,FG, GFx&WEC(c)	2,500.00
5 JCo,PGn,WE,RC,FG, GFx(a&c)	2,200.00
6 JCo,PGn,WE,RC,FG, GFx(a&c)	2,000.00
7 JCo,PGn,WE,RC,FG, GFx(a&c)	1,900.00
8 JCo,PGn,WE,RC,FG, GFx(a&c),B&O:Manhunter	2,500.00
9 JCo,PGn,WE,RC,FG, GFx(a&c)	1,800.00
10 JCo,PGn,WE,RC,FG, GFx(a&c)	1,700.00

Pocket Comics #2
© *Harvey Publications*

11 JCo,PGn,WE,RC,FG,GFx(a&c), B:Rep:Rep.Spirit Strips	2,800.00
12 JCo,GFX,PGn,WE,FG,AB, RC(c) I:Ebony	1,700.00
13 JCo,GFx,PGn,WE,FG,AB,RC(c) E:Firebrand,I:Woozy Winks	1,700.00
14 JCo,PGn,WE,Jku,GFX(a&c)	1,500.00
15 JCo,PGn,WE,Jku,GFX(a&c) E#711,B:Destiny	1,500.00
16 JCo,PGn,WE,JKu	1,500.00
17 PGn,WE,JKu,JCo(a&c)	1,500.00
18 PGn,WE,JCo(a&c)	1,500.00
19 PGn,WE,JCo(a&c)	1,500.00
20 PGn,WE,JCo(a&c),A:Jack Cole in Phantom Lady	1,500.00
21 PGn,WE,JCo(a&c)	1,100.00
22 PGn,WE,RP,JCo(a&c) The Eyes Have it	1,100.00
23 WE,RP,JCo(a&c),E:Phantom Lady	1,000.00
24 WE,HK,JCo(a&c),B:Flatfoot Burns	1,000.00
25 WE,HK,RP,JCo(a&c),The Bookstore Mysrery	1,000.00
26 WE,Hk,JCo(a&c)E:Flatfoot Burns	1,000.00
27 WE,JCo(a&c)	1,000.00
28 WE,JCo(a&c)	1,000.00
29 WE,JCo(a&c)	1,000.00
30 WE,JCo(a&c),A Slippery Racket	1,000.00
31 WE,JCo(a&c),Is Plastic Man Washed Up?	700.00
32 WE,JCo(a&c),Fiesta Turns Into a Fracas	700.00
33 JCo,WE	700.00
34 WE,JCo(a&c)	700.00
35 WE,JCo(a&c)	700.00
36 WE,JCo(a&c),Rest In Peace	700.00
37 WE,PGn,JCo(a&c),Love Comes to Woozy	700.00
38 WE,PGn,JCo(a&c)	700.00
39 WE,PGn,JCo(a&c)	700.00
40 WE,PGn,JCo(a&c)	700.00
41 WE,PGn,JCo(a&c),E:Reps. of Spirit Strip	700.00
42 LF&WE,PGn,JCo(a&c), Woozy Cooks with Gas	600.00
43 LF&WE,PGn,JCo(a&c)	600.00
44 PGn,LF,JCo(a&c)	550.00
45 PGn,LF,JCo(a&c)	550.00
46 PGn,LF,JCo(a&c)	550.00
47 PGn,LF,JCo(a&c),V:Dr.Slicer	550.00
48 PGn,LF,JCo(a&c),V:Big Beaver	550.00
49 PGn,LF,JCo(a&c),V:Thelma Twittle	550.00
50 PGn,LF,JCo(a&c)	550.00
51 PGn,LF,JCo(a&c),V:The Granite Lady	400.00
52 PGn,LF,JCo(a&c)	400.00
53 PGn,LF,JCo(a&c),V:Dr.Erudite	400.00
54 PGn,LF,JCo(a&c)	400.00
55 PGn,LF,JCo(a&c),V:The Sleepy Eyes	400.00
56 PGn,LF,JCo(a&c),V:The Yes Man	400.00
57 PGn,LF,JCo(a&c),V:Mr.Misfit	400.00
58 PGn,LF,JCo(a&c),E:The Human Bomb	400.00
59 PGn,LF,JCo(a&c),A:Mr. Happiness	400.00
60 PGn,LF,JCo(a&c)	350.00
61 PGn,LF,JCo(a&c)	350.00
62 PGn,LF,JCo(a&c)	350.00
63 PGn,LF,JCo(a&c),V:The Crab	350.00
64 PGn,LF,HK,JCo(a&c)	350.00
65 PGn,LF,JCo(a&c)	350.00
66 PGn,LF,JCo(a&c) Love Can Mean Trouble	350.00
67 LF,JCo(a&c), V:The Gag Man	350.00
68 LF,JCo(a&c)	350.00
69 LF,JCo(a&c),V:Strecho	350.00
70 LF,JCo(a&c)	350.00
71 LF,JCo(a&c)	300.00
72 LF,JCo(a&c),V:Mr.Cat	300.00
73 LF,JCo(a&c)	300.00
74 LF,JCo(a&c),V:Prof.Dimwit	300.00
75 LF,JCo(a&c)	300.00
76 LF,JCo(a&c),V:Mr.Morbid	300.00
77 LF,JCo(a&c),V:Skull Face & Eloc	300.00
78 LF,JCo(a&c),A Hot Time In Dreamland	300.00
79 LF,JCo(a&c),V:Eaglebeak	300.00
80 LF,JCo(a&c),V:Penetro	300.00
81 LF,JCo(a&c),V:A Gorilla	300.00
82 LF,JCo(a&c)	300.00
83 LF,JCo(a&c)	300.00
84 LF,JCo(a&c)	300.00
85 LF,JCo(a&c),V:Lucky 7	300.00
86 LF,JCo(a&c),V:The Baker	300.00
87 LF,JCo(a&c)	300.00
88 LF,JCo(a&c),V:The Seen	300.00
89 JCo(a&c),V:The Vanishers	275.00
90 LF,JCo(a&c),V:Capt.Rivers	275.00
91 JCo(a&c),The Forest Primeval	300.00
92 LF,JCo(a&c),V:Closets Kennedy	300.00
93 JCo(a&c),V:The Twinning Terror	275.00
94 JCo(a&c),WE	400.00
95 JCo(a&c),WE,V:Scowls	400.00
96 JCo(a&c),WE,V:Black Widow	400.00
97 JCo(a&c),WE,V:The Mime	400.00
98 JCo(a&c),WE	400.00
99 JCo(a&c),WE	400.00
100 JCo(a&c)	500.00
101 JCo(a&c)	500.00
102 JCo(a&c),E:Plastic Man	500.00
103 JCo,LF,B&I:Ken Shannon; Bondage(c)	325.00
104 The Handsome of Homocide	250.00
105 Invisible Hands of Murder	250.00
106 Museum of Murder	250.00
107 Man with the ShrunkenHead	250.00
108 The Headless Horse Player	250.00
109 LF,Bondage(c),Blood on the Chinese Fan	250.00
110 Murder with a Bang	250.00
111 Diana, Homocidal Huntress	250.00
112 RC,The Corpse on the Sidewalk	275.00

All comics prices listed are for *Near Mint* condition.

GOLDEN AGE

Police–Popular

113 RC(a&c), The Dead Man
  with the Size 13 Shoe 275.00
114 The Terrifying Secret of
  the Black Bear 250.00
115 Don't Let Them Kill Me..... 250.00
116 Stage Was Set For Murder.. 250.00
117 Bullet Riddled Bookkeeper.. 250.00
118 Case of the Absent Corpse.. 250.00
119 A Fast & Bloody Buck...... 250.00
120 Death & The Derelict 250.00
121 Curse of the Clawed Killer.. 250.00
122 The Lonely Hearts Killer.... 250.00
123 Death Came Screaming.... 250.00
124 Masin Murder............. 250.00
125 Bondage(c),The Killer of
  King Arthur's Court........ 275.00
126 Hit & Run Murders......... 250.00
127 Oct'53,Death Drivers 250.00

POLICE LINE-UP
**Avon Periodicals/
Realistic Comics, Aug., 1951**
1 WW,P(c)................. 500.00
2 P(c),Drugs 300.00
3 JKu,EK,P(c) 250.00
4 July, '52;EK 250.00

POLICE TRAP
Mainline, Sept., 1954
1 S&K(c).................. 350.00
2 S&K(c).................. 200.00
3 S&K(c).................. 200.00
4 S&K(c).................. 200.00

Charlton Comics, July, 1955
5 S&K,S&K(c) 300.00
6 S&K,S&K(c) 300.00
Becomes:

PUBLIC DEFENDER IN ACTION
March, 1956
7 .... 100.00
8 thru 12, Oct., 1957 .... @75.00

POLLY PIGTAILS
**Parents' Magazine Institute
Jan., 1946**
1 Ph(c) 125.00
2 Ph(c) 75.00
3 Ph(c) 50.00
4 Ph(c) 50.00
5 Ph(c) 50.00
6 Ph(c) 50.00
7 Ph(c) 40.00
8 .... 40.00
9 .... 40.00
10 .... 40.00
11 thru 22 .... @35.00
22 Ph(c) 35.00
23 Ph(c).................... 35.00
34 thru 43 .... @35.00

POPEYE
Dell Publishing Co., 1948
1 .... 450.00
2 .... 250.00
3 'Welcome to Ghost Island' ... 225.00
4 .... 225.00
5 .... 225.00
6 .... 225.00
7 .... 225.00
8 .... 225.00
9 .... 225.00
10 .... 225.00
11 .... 200.00
12 .... 200.00
13 .... 200.00

14 thru 20 .... @200.00
21 thru 30 .... @150.00
31 thru 40 .... @125.00
41 thru 45 .... @100.00
46 O:Swee' Pea 125.00
47 thru 50 .... @75.00
51 thru 60 .... @60.00
61 thru 65 .... @50.00

POPULAR COMICS
**Dell Publishing Co.
Feb., 1936**
1 Dick Tracy, Little Orphan
  Annie................. 9,000.00
2 Terry Pirates 4,000.00
3 Terry,Annie,Dick Tracy 3,000.00
4 .... 2,000.00
5 B:Tom Mix 2,000.00
6 I:Scribbu 1,800.00
7 .... 1,500.00
8 Scribbu & Reg Fellers 1,500.00
9 .... 1,500.00
10 Terry,Annie,Tracy 1,500.00
11 Terry,Annie,Tracy........ 1,000.00
12 Christmas(c)........... 1,000.00
13 Terry,Annie,Tracy 1,000.00
14 Terry,Annie,Tracy 1,000.00
15 Terry,Annie,Tracy 1,000.00
16 Terry,Annie,Tracy 1,000.00
17 Terry,Annie,Tracy 1,000.00
18 Terry,Annie,Tracy 1,000.00
19 Terry,Annie,Tracy 1,000.00
20 Terry,Annie,Tracy 1,000.00
21 Terry,Annie,Tracy 750.00
22 Terry,Annie,Tracy 750.00
23 Terry,Annie,Tracy 750.00
24 Terry,Annie,Tracy 750.00
25 Terry,Annie,Tracy 750.00
26 Terry,Annie,Tracy 750.00
27 E:Terry,Annie,Tracy 750.00
28 A:Gene Autry 500.00
29 .... 500.00
30 .... 500.00
31 A:Jim McCoy 500.00
32 A:Jim McCoy 500.00
33 .... 500.00
34 .... 500.00
35 Christmas(c),Tex Ritter..... 500.00
36 .... 500.00
37 .... 500.00
38 B:Gang Busters 550.00
39 .... 500.00
40 .... 500.00
41 .... 500.00
42 .... 500.00
43 F:Gang Busters 550.00
44 .... 400.00
45 Tarzan(c).............. 400.00
46 O:Martan the Marvel Man ... 500.00
47 F:Martan the Marvel Man.... 350.00
48 F:Martan the Marvel Man.... 350.00
49 F:Martan the Marvel Man.... 350.00
50 .... 350.00
51 B&O:Voice.............. 350.00
52 A:Voice 300.00
53 F:The Voice 300.00
54 F:Gang Busters,A:Voice..... 300.00
55 F:Gang Busters 325.00
56 F:Gang Busters 300.00
57 F:The Marvel Man 300.00
58 F:The Marvel Man 300.00
59 F:The Marvel Man 300.00
60 O:Prof. Supermind........ 325.00
61 Prof. Supermind & Son 250.00
62 Supermind & Son......... 250.00
63 B:Smilin' Jack............ 250.00
64 Smilin'Jack,Supermind...... 250.00
65 Professor Supermind 250.00
66 .... 250.00
67 Gasoline Alley 250.00

*Popular Comics #53
© Dell Publishing Co.*

68 F:Smilin' Jack 250.00
69 F:Smilin' Jack 250.00
70 F:Smilin' Jack Publications .. 250.00
71 F:Smilin' Jack 250.00
72 B:Owl,Terry & the Pirates.... 500.00
73 F:Terry and the Pirates..... 300.00
74 F:Smilin' Jack 300.00
75 F:Smilin'Jack,A:Owl 300.00
76 Captain Midnight 425.00
77 Captain Midnight 425.00
78 Captain Midnight 425.00
79 A:Owl.................. 300.00
80 F:Smilin' Jack,A:Owl 300.00
81 F: Terry&thePirates,A:Owl ... 300.00
82 F:Smilin' Jack,A:Owl 300.00
83 F:Smilin' Jack,A:Owl 300.00
84 F:Smilin' Jack,A:Owl 300.00
85 F:ThreeLittleGremlins,A:Owl.. 300.00
86 F:Three Little Gremlins...... 200.00
87 F:Smilin' Jack 200.00
88 F:Smilin' Jack 200.00
89 F:Smokey Stover......... 200.00
90 F:Terry and the Pirates..... 200.00
91 F:Smokey Stover......... 200.00
92 F:Terry and the Pirates..... 200.00
93 F:Smilin' Jack 200.00
94 F:Terry and the Pirates..... 200.00
95 F:Smilin' Jack 200.00
96 F:Gang Busters 200.00
97 F:Smilin' Jack 200.00
98 B:Felix Cat............... 225.00
99 F:Bang Busters 200.00
100 .... 250.00
101 thru 141 .... @175.00
142 E:Terry & the Pirates 100.00
143 .... 100.00
144 .... 100.00
145 F:Harold Teen 100.00

POPULAR ROMANCES
**Better Publications
(Standard Comics), Dec., 1949**
5 B:Ph(c) 100.00
6 Ph(c) 75.00
7 RP 75.00
8 Ph(c) 75.00
9 Ph(c) 75.00
10 WW..................... 85.00
11 thru 16 .... @50.00
17 WE 60.00
18 thru 21 .... @60.00
22 thru 27 ATh,Ph(c).........@90.00

SCHOOL DAY ROMANCES
Star Publications
Nov.–Dec., 1949
1 LbC(c),Teen-Age 375.00
2 LbC(c) 350.00
3 LbC(c),Ph(c) 350.00
4 LbC(c),JyD,RonaldReagan . . 400.00
Becomes:

POPULAR TEEN-AGERS
Sept., 1950
5 LbC(c),Toni Gay, Eve Adams . 400.00
6 LbC(c),Ginger Bunny,
   Midge Martin 350.00
7 LbC(c) 350.00
8 LbC(c) 350.00
9 LbC(c) 250.00
10 LbC(c) 225.00
11 LbC(c) 225.00
12 LbC(c) 225.00
13 LbC(c),JyD 225.00
14 LbC,WW,Spanking 300.00
15 LbC(c),JyD 225.00
16 . . . . 200.00
17 LbC(c),JyD 200.00
18 LbC(c) 200.00
19 LbC(c) 200.00
20 LbC(c),JyD 225.00
21 LbC(c),JyD 225.00
22 LbC(c) 200.00
23 LbC(c) 200.00

POWER COMICS
Holyoke/Narrative Publ., 1944
1 LbC(c) 2,000.00
2 B:Dr.Mephisto,Hitler(c) . . . 2,100.00
3 LbC(c) 2,400.00
4 LbC(c) 2,000.00

PRIDE OF THE YANKEES
Magazine Enterprises, 1949
1 N#,OW,Ph(c),The Life
   of Lou Gehrig 1,100.00

PRISON BREAK
Avon Periodicals/Realistic
Sept., 1951
1 WW(c),WW 550.00
2 WW(c),WW,JKu 350.00
3 JD,JO 300.00
4 EK 250.00
5 EK,CI 250.00

PRIZE COMICS
Feature Publications
(Prize Publ.), March, 1940
1 O&B:Power Nelson,Jupiter.
   B:Ted O'Neil,Jaxon of
   the Jungle,Bucky Brady,
   Storm Curtis, Rocket(c) . . . 3,000.00
2 B:The Owl 1,500.00
3 Power Nelson(c) 1,400.00
4 Power Nelson(c) 1,400.00
5 A:Dr.Dekkar 1,200.00
6 A:Dr.Dekkar 1,200.00
7 S&K,DBr,JK(c),O&B DR Frost,
   Frankenstein,B:GreenLama,
   Capt Gallant,Voodini
   Twist Turner 2,500.00
8 S&K,DBr 1,400.00
9 S&K,DBr,Black Owl(c) 1,300.00
10 DBr,Black Owl(c) 1,000.00
11 DBr,O:Bulldog Denny 900.00
12 DBr 900.00
13 DBR,O&B:Yank and
   Doodle,Bondage(c) 1,000.00
14 DBr,Black Owl(c) 900.00
15 DBr,Black Owl(c) 900.00
16 DBr,JaB,B:Spike Mason 900.00
17 DBr,Black Owl(c) 900.00
18 DBr,Black Owl(c) 900.00
19 DBr,Yank&Doodle(c) 900.00
20 DBr,Yank&Doodle(c) 900.00
21 DBr,JaB(c),Yank&Doodle(c) . . 600.00
22 DBr,Yank&Doodle(c) 600.00
23 DBr,Uncle Sam(c) 600.00
24 DBr,Abe Lincoln(c) 600.00
25 DBr,JaB,Yank&Doodle(c) . . . 600.00
26 DBr,JaB,JaB(c),Liberty
   Bell(c) 600.00
27 DBr,Yank&Doodle(c) 400.00
28 DBr,Yank&Doodle(c) 350.00
29 DBr,JaB(c)Yank&Doodle(c) . . 350.00
30 DBr,Yank&Doodle(c) 400.00
31 DBr,Yank&Doodle(c) 350.00
32 DBr,Yank&Doodle(c) 350.00
33 DBr,Bondage(c),Yank
   & Doodle 400.00
34 DBr,O:Airmale;New
   Black Owl 400.00

Prize Comics #11
© Prize Publications

35 DBr,B:Flying Fist & Bingo . . . 300.00
36 DBr,Yank&Doodle(c) 300.00
37 DBr,I:Stampy,Hitler(c) 350.00
38 DBr,B.Owl,Yank&Doodle(c) . . 300.00
39 DBr,B.Owl,Yank&Doodle(c) . . 300.00
40 DBr,B.Owl,Yank&Doodle(c) . . 300.00
41 DBr,B.Owl,Yank&Doodle(c) . . 300.00
42 DBr,B.Owl,Yank&Doodle(c) . . 250.00
43 DBr,B.Owl,Yank&Doodle(c) . . 250.00
44 DBr, B&I:Boom Boom
   Brannigan 250.00
45 DBr 250.00
46 DBr 250.00
47 DBr 250.00
48 DBr,B:Prince Ra;Bondage(c) . 275.00
49 DBr,Boom Boom(c) 250.00
50 DBr,Frankenstein(c) 250.00
51 DBr 250.00
52 DBr, B:Sir Prize(c) 250.00
53 DBr, The Man Who Could
   Read Features 250.00
54 DBr 250.00
55 DBr,Yank&Doodle(c) 250.00
56 DBr,Boom Boom (c) 250.00
57 DBr,Santa Claus(c) 250.00
58 DBr,The Poisoned Punch . . . 250.00
59 DBr,Boom Boom(c) 250.00
60 DBr,Sir Prise(c) 250.00
61 DBr,The Man wih the
   Fighting Feet 250.00
62 DBr,Hck(c),Yank&Doodle(c) . . 250.00
63 DBr,S&K,S&K(c),Boom
   Boom(c) 275.00
64 DBr,Blackowl Retires 200.00
65 DBr,DBr(c),Frankenstein 200.00
66 DBr,DBr(c),Frankenstein 200.00
67 DBr,B:Brothers in Crime 200.00
68 DBr,RP(c) 200.00
Becomes:

PRIZE COMICS WESTERN
April–May, 1948
69 ACa(c),B:Dusty Ballew 150.00
70 ACa(c) 100.00
71 ACa(c) 100.00
72 ACa(c),JSe 100.00
73 ACa(c) 100.00
74 ACa(c) 100.00
75 JSe,S&K(c),6-Gun Showdown
   at Rattlesnake Gulch 110.00
76 Ph(c),Randolph Scott 150.00
77 Ph(c),JSe,Streets of
   Laredo,movie 100.00
78 Ph(c),JSe,HK,Bullet
   Code, movie 175.00
79 Ph(c),JSe,Stage to
   China, movie 175.00
80 Ph(c),Gunsmoke Justice 125.00
81 Ph(c),The Man Who Shot
   Billy The Kid 125.00
82 Ph(c),MBi,JSe&BE,Death
   Draws a Circle 125.00
83 JSe,S&K(c) 90.00
84 JSe 75.00
85 JSe,B:American Eagle 300.00
86 JSe 125.00
87 JSe&BE 80.00
88 JSe&BE 80.00
89 JSe&BE 80.00
90 JSe&Be 80.00
91 JSe&BE,JSe&BE(c) 80.00
92 JSe,JSe&BE(c) 80.00
93 JSe,JSe&BE(c) 80.00
94 JSe&BE,JSe&BE(c) 80.00
95 JSe,JSe&BE(c) 80.00
96 JSe,JSe&BE,JSe&BE(c) 80.00
97 JSe,JSe&BE,JSeBE(c) 80.00
98 JSe&BE,JSe&BE(c) 80.00
99 JSe&BE,JSe&BE(c) 80.00
100 JSe,JSe(c) 150.00
101 JSe 125.00
102 JSe 125.00
103 JSe 125.00
104 JSe 125.00
105 JSe 125.00
106 JSe 75.00
107 JSe 75.00
108 JSe 90.00
109 JSe&AW 100.00
110 JSe&BE 100.00
111 JSe&BE 100.00
112 . . . . 75.00
113 AW&JSe 100.00
114 MMe,B:The Drifter 75.00
115 MMe 75.00
116 MMe 75.00
117 MMe 75.00
118 MMe,E:The Drifter 75.00
119 Nov/Dec'56 . . . . 75.00

PSYCHOANALYSIS
E.C. Comics
March–April, 1955
1 JKa,JKa(c) 250.00
2 JKa,JKa(c) 200.00
3 JKa,JKa(c) 200.00
4 JKa,JKa(c) Sept.–Oct., 1955 . . 200.00

Public–Rangers   **GOLDEN AGE**   Comics Values Annual

PUBLIC ENEMIES
D.S. Publishing Co., 1948
1 AMc	300.00
2 AMc	250.00
3 AMc	200.00
4 AMc	200.00
5 AMc	200.00
6 AMc	150.00
7 AMc,Eye Injury	200.00
8	150.00
9	150.00

PUNCH AND JUDY COMICS
Hillman Periodicals, 1944
1 (fa)	250.00
2	150.00
3	100.00
4 thru 12	@90.00
2-1	75.00
2-2 JK	250.00
2-3	75.00
2-4	75.00
2-5	75.00
2-6	75.00
2-7	75.00
2-8	75.00
2-9	75.00
2-10 JK	250.00
2-11 JK	250.00
2-12 JK	250.00
3-1 JK	250.00
3-2	200.00
3-3	75.00
3-4	75.00
3-5	75.00
3-6	75.00
3-7	75.00
3-8	75.00
3-9	75.00

PUNCH COMICS
Harry 'A' Chesler, Dec., 1941
1 B:Mr.E,The Sky Chief,Hale the Magician,Kitty Kelly	1,700.00
2 A:Capt.Glory	1,100.00
3-8 Do Not Exist	
9 B:Rocket Man & Rocket girl,Master Ken	1,000.00
10 JCo,A:Sky Chief	900.00

Punch Comics #9
© Harry A Chesler

11 JCo,O:Master Key,A:Little Nemo	900.00
12 A:Rocket Boy,Capt.Glory	2,800.00
13 Ric(c)	900.00
14 GT	750.00
15 FSm(c)	750.00
16	750.00
17	750.00
18 FSm(c),Bondage(c),Drug	1,000.00
19 FSm(c)	900.00
20 Women semi-nude(c)	1,200.00
21 Drug	750.00
22 I:Baxter,Little Nemo	350.00
23 A:Little Nemo	350.00

PUPPET COMICS
Dougherty, Co., Spring, 1946
1 Funny Animal	125.00
2	125.00

PURPLE CLAW, THE
Minoan Publishing Co./ Toby Press, Jan., 1953
1 O:Purple Claw	350.00
2 and 3	@250.00

PUZZLE FUN COMICS
George W. Dougherty Co. Spring, 1946
1 PGn	250.00
2	200.00

QUEEN OF THE WEST, DALE EVANS
Dell Publishing Co. July, 1953
(1) see Dell Four Color #479	
(1) see Dell Four Color #528	
3 ATh, Ph(c) all	125.00
4 ATh,RsM	110.00
5 RsM	100.00
6 RsM	100.00
7 RsM	100.00
8 RsM	100.00
9 RsM	100.00
10 RsM	100.00
11	75.00
12 RsM	85.00
13 RsM	85.00
14 RsM	85.00
15 RsM	85.00
16 RsM	85.00
17 RsM	85.00
18 RsM	85.00
19	75.00
20 RsM	85.00
21	75.00
22 RsM	85.00

RACKET SQUAD IN ACTION
Capitol Stories/ Charlton Comics May–June, 1952
1 Carnival(c)	350.00
2	150.00
3 Roulette	150.00
4 FFr(c)	150.00
5 Just off the Boat	250.00
6 The Kidnap Racket	175.00
7	150.00
8	150.00
9 2 Fisted fix	150.00
10 Explosion Blast (c)	175.00
11 SD(a&c),Racing(c)	350.00

12 JoS,SD(c),Explosion(c)	750.00
13 JoS(c),The Notorious Modelling Agency Racket,Acid	125.00
14 DG(c),Drug	150.00
15 Photo Extortion Racket	125.00
16 thru 28	@125.00
29,March, 1958	125.00

RAGGEDY ANN AND ANDY
Dell Publishing Co., 1942
1 Billy & Bonnie Bee	450.00
2	250.00
3 DNo,B:Egbert Elephant	250.00
4 DNo,WK	300.00
5 DNo	250.00
6 DNo	250.00
7 Little Black Sambo	250.00
8	250.00
9	250.00
10	250.00
11	200.00
12	200.00
13	200.00
14	200.00
15	200.00
16 thru 20	@200.00
21 Alice in Wonderland	175.00
22 thru 27	@125.00
28 WK	150.00
29 thru 39	@125.00

RALPH KINER HOME RUN KING
Fawcett Publications, 1950
1 N#, Life Story of the Famous Pittsburgh Slugger	800.00

RAMAR OF THE JUNGLE
Toby Press/ Charlton Comics, 1954
1 Ph(c),TV Show	250.00
2 Ph(c)	200.00
3	200.00
4	200.00
5 Sept '56	200.00

RANGE ROMANCES
Comics Magazines (Quality Comics), Dec., 1949
1 PGn(a&c)	300.00
2 RC(a&c)	350.00
3 RC,Ph(c)	275.00
4 RC,Ph(c)	250.00
5 RC,PGn,Ph(c)	250.00

RANGERS OF FREEDOM
Flying Stories, Inc. (Fiction House), Oct., 1941
1 I:Ranger Girl & Rangers of Freedom;V:Super-Brain	3,500.00
2 V:Super -Brain	1,200.00
3 Bondage(c) The Headsman of Hate	1,000.00
4 Hawaiian Inferno	800.00
5 RP,V:Super-Brain	800.00
6 RP,Bondage(c);Bugles of the Damned	800.00
7 RP,Death to Tojo's Butchers	600.00

Becomes:

RANGERS COMICS
Dec., 1942
8 RP,B:US Rangers	600.00

CVA Page 448   All comics prices listed are for *Near Mint* condition.

GOLDEN AGE — Range–Real Love

9 GT,BLb,Commando Steel
  for Slant Eyes. 600.00
10 BLb,Bondage (c) 650.00
11 Raiders of the
  Purple Death 500.00
12 A:Commando Rangers. 500.00
13 Grl,B:Commando Ranger. . . . 500.00
14 Grl,Bondage(c) 500.00
15 GT,Grl,Bondage(c). 500.00
16 Grl,GT;Burma Raid 550.00
17 GT,GT,Bondage(c),Raiders
  of the Red Dawn 550.00
18 GT. 550.00
19 GE,Blb,GT,Bondage(c). 450.00
20 GT. 400.00
21 GT,Bondage(c). 450.00
22 GT,B&O:Firehair 350.00

Rangers of Freedom #3
© Fiction House

23 GT,BLb,B:Kazanda 300.00
24 Bondage(c) 350.00
25 Bondage(c) 350.00
26 Angels From Hell 300.00
27 Bondage(c) 350.00
28 BLb,E:Kazanda;B&O Tiger
  Man 350.00
29 Bondage(c) 350.00
30 BLb,B:Crusoe Island 375.00
31 BLb,Bondage(c). 300.00
32 BLb 275.00
33 BLb,Drug 275.00
34 BLb 275.00
35 BLB,Bondage(c) 300.00
36 BLb,MB 275.00
37 BLb,Mb 275.00
38 BLb,MB,GE,Bondage(c). 300.00
39 BLb,GE 250.00
40 BLb,GE,BLb(c). 250.00
41 BLb,GE 225.00
42 BLb,GE 225.00
43 BLb,GE 225.00
44 BLb,GE 225.00
45 BLb,GEl 225.00
46 BLb,GE 200.00
47 BLb,JGr. 200.00
48 BLb,JGr. 200.00
49 BLb,JGr. 200.00
50 BLb,JGr,Bondage(c). 225.00
51 BLb,JGr. 200.00
52 BLb,JGr,Bondage(c). 225.00
53 BLb,JGr,Prisoners of
  Devil Pass 200.00
54 JGr,When The Wild
  Commanches Ride 200.00
55 JGr,Massacre Guns at
  Pawnee Pass 200.00

56 JGr, Gun Smuggler of
  Apache Mesa. 200.00
57 JGr,Redskins to the
  Rescue. 200.00
58 JGr,Brides of the
  Buffalo Men 200.00
59 JGr,Plunder Portage 200.00
60 JGr, Buzzards of
  Bushwack Trail 200.00
61 BWh(c)Devil Smoke at
  Apache Basin 150.00
62 BWh(c)B:Cowboy Bob 150.00
63 BWh(c) 150.00
64 BWh(c)B:Suicide Smith 150.00
65 BWh(c):Wolves of the
  Overland Trail,Bondage(c) . . 165.00
66 BWh(c) 150.00
67 BWh(c)B:Space Rangers. . . . 150.00
68 BWh(c);Cargo for Coje. 150.00
69 BWh(c);Great Red Death Ray 150.00

REAL CLUE CRIME STORIES
See: CLUE COMICS

REAL FUNNIES
Nedor Publishing Co. Jan., 1943
1 (fa) 350.00
2 and 3 (fa) . . . . @200.00

REAL HEROES COMICS
Parents' Magazine Institiute Sept., 1941
1 HcK,Franklin Roosevelt. 400.00
2 J, Edgar Hoover 200.00
3 General Wavell 150.00
4 Chiang Kai Shek, Churchill . . . 175.00
5 Stonewall Jackson 150.00
6 Lou Gehrig. 250.00
7 Chennault and his
  Flying Tigers. 100.00
8 Admiral Nimitz 100.00
9 The Panda Man 75.00
10 Carl Akeley-Jungle
  Adventurer 75.00
11 Wild Jack Howard 75.00
12 General Robert L
  Eichelberger. 60.00
13 HcK,Victory at Climback. 60.00
14 Pete Gray 60.00
15 Alexander Mackenzie. 60.00
16 Balto of Nome Oct '46 . . . . . . 60.00

REAL LIFE STORY OF FESS PARKER
Dell Publishing Co., 1955
1 . . . . 125.00

REALISTIC ROMANCES
Avon Periodicals/ Realistic Comics July–Aug., 1951
1 EK,Ph(c) 250.00
2 Ph(c) 125.00
3 P(c) 100.00
4 P(c) 95.00
5 . . . . 100.00
6 EK 125.00
7 GE, Avon (c). 125.00
8 EK 110.00
9 thru 14 . . . . @100.00
15 . . . . 75.00
16 EK,Drug. 125.00
17 EK. 100.00

REAL LIFE COMICS
Visual Editions/Better/ Standard/Nedor, Sept., 1941
1 ASh(c),Lawrence of
  Arabia,Uncle Sam(c). 750.00
2 ASh(c),Liberty(c) 300.00
3 Adolph Hitler(c) 1,000.00
4 ASh(c)Robert Fulton,
  Charles DeGaulle. 200.00
5 ASh(c)Alexander the Great . . . 200.00
6 ASh(c)John Paul Jones,CDR . 175.00
7 ASh(c)Thomas Jefferson. 175.00
8 Leonardo Da Vinci 175.00
9 US Coast Guard Issue 175.00
10 Sir Hubert Wilkens. 175.00
11 Odyssey on a Raft 150.00
12 ImpossibleLeatherneck 150.00
13 ASh(c)The Eternal Yank. 150.00
14 Sir Isaac Newton 150.00
15 William Tell 150.00
16 Marco Polo 150.00
17 Albert Einstein 175.00
18 Ponce De Leon 150.00
19 The Fighting Seabees 150.00
20 Joseph Pulitzer 150.00
21 Admiral Farragut 125.00
22 Thomas Paine 125.00
23 Pedro Menendez 125.00
24 Babe Ruth 250.00
25 Marcus Whitman 125.00
26 Benvenuto Cellini. 125.00
27 A Bomb Story. 175.00
28 Robert Blake 125.00
29 Daniel DeFoe, A Bomb. 150.00
30 Baron Robert Clive 125.00
31 Anthony Wayne 125.00
32 Frank Sinatra. 150.00
33 Frederick Douglass 125.00
34 Paul Revere,Jimmy Stewart . . 150.00
35 Rudyard Kipling 125.00
36 Story of the Automobile 125.00
37 Francis Manion, Motion
  Picture 125.00
38 Richard Henry Dana 100.00
39 Samuel FB Morse 100.00
40 FG,ASh(c),Hans Christian
  Anderson, Bob Feller 125.00
41 Abraham Lincoln,Jimmy Foxx. 125.00
42 Joseph Conrad,Fred Allen . . . 100.00
43 Louis Braille,O.W.Holmes. . . . 75.00
44 Citizens of Tomorrow 75.00
45 ASh(c),FrancoisVillon,
  Olympics 135.00
46 The Pony Express 135.00
47 ASh(c),Montezuma 125.00
48 . . . . 125.00
49 ASh(c),Gene Bearden,
  Baseball. 125.00
50 FF,ASh(c),Lewis & Clark 350.00
51 GE,ASh(c),Sam Houston 250.00
52 GE,FF,ASh(c),JSe&BE
  Leif Erickson. 375.00
53 GT,JSe&BE,Henry Wells &
  William Fargo. 150.00
54 GT,Alexander Graham Bell. . . 150.00
55 ASh(c),JSe&BE, The James
  Brothers 150.00
56 JSe&BE. 150.00
57 JSe&BE. 150.00
58 JSe&BE,Jim Reaves 175.00
59 FF,JSe&BE,Battle Orphan
  Sept '52 . . . . 150.00

REAL LOVE
See: HAP HAZARD COMICS

All comics prices listed are for Near Mint condition.

GOLDEN AGE

REAL WEST ROMANCES
Crestwoood Publishing Co./ Prize Publ., April–May, 1949
1 S&K,Ph(c) 275.00
2 Ph(c),Spanking 150.00
3 JSe,BE,Ph(c) 150.00
4 S&K,JSe,BE,Ph(c) 250.00
5 S&K,MMe,JSe,Audie
  Murphy Ph(c) 225.00
6 S&K,JSe,BE,Ph(c) 100.00

RECORD BOOK OF FAMOUS POLICE CASES
St. John Publishing Co., 1949
1 N#,JKu,MB(c) 450.00

RED ARROW
P.L. Publishing Co. May, 1951
1 Bondage(c) 125.00
2 . . . . 100.00
3 P(c) 100.00

RED BAND COMICS
Enwil Associates Nov., 1944
1 The Bogeyman 500.00
2 O:Bogeyman,same(c)as#1 . . 350.00
3 A:Captain Wizard 300.00
4 May, '45,Repof#3,Same(c) . . 300.00

RED CIRCLE COMICS
Enwil Associates (Rural Home Public) Jan., 1945
1 B:Red Riot,The Prankster 500.00
2 LSt,A:The Judge 400.00
3 LSt(A&c) 250.00
4 LSt(a&c) covers of #4
  stapled over other comics . . . 250.00

TRAIL BLAZERS
Street & Smith, Jan., 1942
1 Wright Brothers 350.00
2 Benjamin Franklin,Dodgers . . . 400.00
3 Red Barber,Yankees 500.00
4 Famous War song 250.00
Becomes:

Red Dragon #4
© Street & Smith

RED DRAGON COMICS
Jan., 1943
5 JaB(c),B&O:Red Rover:
  B:Capt.Jack Comkmando
  Rex King&Jet,Minute Man . 1,400.00
6 O:Red Dragon 2,700.00
7 The Curse of the
  Boneless Men 2,400.00
8 China V:Japan 1,000.00
9 The Reducing Ray,Jan '44 . . 1,000.00
(2nd Series) Nov., 1947
1 B:Red Dragon 1,200.00
2 BP 900.00
3 BP,BP(c),I:Dr Neff 750.00
4 BP,BP(c) 850.00
5 BP,BP(c) 550.00
6 BP,BP(c) 550.00
7 BP,BP(c),May, 49 . . . . 550.00

RED MASK
See: TIM HOLT

RED RABBIT
Dearfield/ J. Charles Lave Publ. Co. Jan., 1941
1 (fa) 150.00
2 . . . . 75.00
3 thru 10 . . . . @60.00
11 thru 22 . . . . @50.00

RED SEAL COMICS
See: SCOOP

REDSKIN
Youthful Magazines Sept., 1950
1 Redskin,Bondage(c) 200.00
2 Apache Dance of Death 125.00
3 Daniel Boone 100.00
4 Sitting Bull- Red Devil
  of the Black Hills 100.00
5 . . . . 100.00
6 Geronimo- Terror of the
  Desert,Bondage 125.00
7 Firebrand of the Sioux 100.00
8 . . . . 100.00
9 . . . . 100.00
10 Dead Man's Magic 100.00
11 . . . . 100.00
12 Quanah Parker,Bondage(c) . . 125.00
Becomes:

FAMOUS WESTERN BADMEN
Dec., 1952
13 Redskin- Last of the
  Comanches 75.00
14 . . . . 60.00
15 The Dalton Boys Apr '52 . . . . 60.00

REMEMBER PEARL HARBOR
Street & Smith, 1942
1 N# JaB,Battle of the
  Pacific,Uncle Sam(c) 600.00

RETURN OF THE OUTLAW
Minoan Publishing Co. Feb., 1953
1 Billy The Kid 125.00

2 . . . . 60.00
3 thru 11 . . . . @50.00

REVEALING ROMANCES
A.A. Wyn (Ace Magazines), Sept., 1949
1 . . . . 100.00
2 . . . . 75.00
3 thru 6 . . . . @50.00

REX ALLEN COMICS
Dell Publishing Co. Feb., 1951
(1) see Dell Four Color #316
2 Ph(c) all 200.00
3 thru 10 . . . . @125.00
11 thru 23 . . . . @100.00
24 ATh 110.00
25 thru 31 . . . . @100.00

REX DEXTER OF MARS
Fox Features Syndicate Autumn, 1940
1 DBr,DBr(c) Battle ofKooba . . 2,800.00

RIBTICKLER
Fox Features Syndicate, 1945
1 . . . . 200.00
2 . . . . 100.00
3 Cosmo Cat 75.00
4 thru 6 . . . . @60.00
7 Cosmo Cat 60.00
8 thru 9 . . . . @60.00

RIN TIN TIN
Dell Publishing Co. Nov., 1952
(1) see Dell Four Color #434
(1) see Dell Four Color #476
(1) see Dell Four Color #523
4 thru 10 Ph(c) all . . . . @100.00
11 thru 20 . . . . @125.00

ROCKET COMICS
Hillman Periodicals March, 1940
1 O:Red Roberts;B:Rocket
  Riley,Phantom Ranger,Steel
  Shank,Buzzard Baynes,Lefty
  Larson,The Defender,Man
  with 1,000 Faces 3,500.00
2 . . . . 1,500.00
3 May, '40 E:All Features 1,700.00

ROCKET KELLY
Fox Features Syndicate Autumn, 1945–Oct., Nov., 1946
N# 400.00
1 . . . . 300.00
2 A:The Puppeteer 275.00
3 thru 6 . . . . @250.00

ROCKETMAN
Ajax/Farrell Publications June, 1952
1 Space Stories of the Future . . 500.00

ROCKET SHIP X
Fox Features Syndicate Sept., 1951
1 . . . . 900.00
2 N# Variant of Original 500.00

GOLDEN AGE

Rocket–Romeo

Rocket Comics #2
© Hillman Periodicals

ROCKY LANE WESTERN
Fawcett/Charlton Comics
May, 1949
1 Ph(c)B:Rocky Lane,Slim Pickins 1,200.00
2 Ph(c) 600.00
3 Ph(c) 500.00
4 Ph(c)CCB,Rail Riders Rampage,F Capt Tootsie . . . 500.00
5 Ph(c)The Missing Stagecoaches 450.00
6 Ph(c)Ghost Town Showdown . 300.00
7 Ph(c)The Border Revolt 350.00
8 Ph(c)The Sunset Feud 350.00
9 Ph(c)Hermit of the Hills 350.00
10 Ph(c)Badman's Reward 300.00
11 Ph(c)Fool's Gold Fiasco 250.00
12 Ph(c),CCB,Coyote Breed F:Capt Tootsie,Giant 250.00
13 Ph(c),Giant 250.00
14 Ph(c) 200.00
15 Ph(c)B:Black Jacks Hitching Post,Giant 225.00
16 Ph(c),Giant 200.00
17 Ph(c),Giant 200.00
18 Ph(c) 225.00
19 Ph(c),Giant 235.00
20 Ph(c)The Rodeo Rustler E:Slim Pickens 235.00
21 Ph(c)B: Dee Dickens 200.00
22 Ph(c) 175.00
23 thru 30 . . . . @200.00
31 thru 40 . . . . @175.00
41 thru 55 . . . . @175.00
56 thru 60 . . . . @150.00
61 thru 70 . . . . @150.00
71 thru 87 . . . . @150.00

ROD CAMERON WESTERN
Fawcett Publications
Feb., 1950
1 Ph(c) 750.00
2 Ph(c) 350.00
3 Ph(c),Seven Cities of Cipiola . 300.00
4 Ph(c),Rip-Roaring Wild West . 250.00
5 Ph(c),Six Gun Sabotage 250.00
6 Ph(c),Medicine Bead Murders 250.00
7 Ph(c),Wagon Train Of Death . 250.00
8 Ph(c),Bayou Badman 250.00
9 Ph(c),Rustlers Ruse 250.00
10 Ph(c),White Buffalo Trail 250.00
11 Ph(c),Lead Poison 225.00

12 thru 19 Ph(c) . . . . @225.00
20 Phc(c),Great Army Hoax 225.00

ROLY-POLY COMICS
Green Publishing Co., 1945
1 B:Red Rube&Steel Sterling . . 400.00
6 A:Blue Cycle 250.00
10 A:Red Rube 250.00
11 . . . . 250.00
12 Black Hood 250.00
13 . . . . 250.00
14 A:Black Hood 250.00
15 A:Steel Fist;1946 . . . . 450.00

ROMANCE AND CONFESSION STORIES
St. John Publishing Co., 1949
1 MB(c),MB 500.00

ROMANTIC LOVE
Avon Periodicals/Realistic Sept.–Oct., 1949
1 P(c) 275.00
2 P(c) 200.00
3 P(c) 200.00
4 Ph(c) 200.00
5 P(c) 200.00
6 Ph(c),Drug,Thrill Crazy 250.00
7 P(c) 200.00
8 P(c) 200.00
9 EK,P(c) 225.00
10 thru 11 P(c) . . . . @225.00
12 EK 225.00
20 . . . . 200.00
21 . . . . 200.00
22 EK 200.00
23 EK 200.00

ROMANTIC MARRIAGE
Ziff-Davis/ St. John Publishing Co.
Nov.–Dec., 1950
1 Ph(c),Selfish wife 250.00
2 P(c),Mother's Boy 150.00
3 P(c),Hen Peck House 135.00
4 P(c) 135.00
5 Ph(c) 135.00
6 Ph(c) 125.00
7 Ph(c) 125.00
8 P(c) 125.00
9 P(c) 125.00
10 P/PH(c) 250.00
11 . . . . 100.00
12 . . . . 100.00
13 Ph(c) 100.00
14 thru 20 . . . . @100.00
20 Ph(c) 100.00
21 . . . . 100.00
22 . . . . 100.00
23 MB 125.00
24 . . . . 100.00

ROMANTIC PICTURE NOVELETTES
Magazine Enterprises, 1946
1 Mary Worth adventure 200.00

ROMANTIC SECRETS
Fawcett Publ./Charlton Comics
Sept., 1949
1 Ph(c) 200.00
2 MSy(c) 100.00
3 MSy(c) 100.00

4 GE 125.00
5 BP 90.00
6 . . . . 75.00
7 BP 75.00
8 . . . . 75.00
9 GE 80.00
10 BP 75.00
11 . . . . 50.00
12 BP 75.00
13 . . . . 50.00
14 . . . . 50.00
15 . . . . 50.00
16 BP,MSy 75.00
17 BP 75.00
18 . . . . 50.00
19 . . . . 50.00
20 BP,MBi 75.00
21 . . . . 50.00
22 . . . . 50.00
23 . . . . 50.00
24 GE 75.00
25 MSy 40.00
26 BP,MSy 40.00
27 MSy 40.00
28 . . . . 40.00
29 BP 35.00
30 thru 32 . . . . @35.00
33 MSy 35.00
34 BP 35.00
35 . . . . 35.00
36 BP 35.00
37 BP 35.00
38 thru 52 . . . . @35.00

ROMANTIC STORY
Fawcett Publ./Charlton Comics
Nov., 1949
1 Ph(c) 200.00
2 Ph(c) 100.00
3 Ph(c) 75.00
4 Ph(c) 75.00
5 Ph(c) 75.00
6 Ph(c) 75.00
7 BP,Ph(c) 60.00
8 BP,Ph(c) 50.00
9 Ph(c) 50.00
10 Ph(c) 50.00
11 Ph(c) 50.00
12 Ph(c) 50.00
13 Ph(c) 50.00
14 Ph(c) 50.00
15 GE,Ph(c) 75.00
16 BP,Ph(c) 55.00
17 Ph(c) 50.00
18 Ph(c) 50.00
19 Ph(c) 50.00
20 BP,Ph(c) 50.00
22 ATh,Ph(c) 50.00

Charlton Comics
23 . . . . 20.00
24 Ph(c) 20.00
25 thru 29 . . . . @20.00
30 BP 35.00
31 thru 39 . . . . @20.00

ROMANTIC WESTERN
Fawcett Publications
Winter, 1949
1 Ph(c) 300.00
2 Ph(c),AW,AMc 325.00
3 Ph(c) 250.00

ROMEO TUBBS
See: MY SECRET LIFE

ROUNDUP
D.S. Publishing Co.
July–Aug., 1948
1 HcK 250.00
2 Drug 150.00
3 . . . . 125.00
4 . . . . 125.00
5 Male Bondage 135.00

ROY CAMPANELLA, BASEBALL HERO
Fawcett Publications, 1950
N# Ph(c),Life Story of the
  Battling Dodgers Catcher . . 1,000.00

ROY ROGERS
Dell Publishing Co.
1 photo (c) 1,300.00
2 . . . . 500.00
3 . . . . 300.00
4 . . . . 300.00
5 . . . . 300.00
6 thru 10 . . . . @250.00
11 thru 20 . . . . @225.00
21 thru 30 . . . . @200.00
31 thru 46 . . . . @150.00
47 thru 50 . . . . @125.00
51 thru 56 . . . . @110.00
57 Drug 125.00
58 thru 70 . . . . @110.00
71 thru 80 . . . . @100.00
81 thru 91 . . . . @80.00
Becomes:

ROY ROGERS AND TRIGGER
Aug., 1955
92 thru 99 . . . . @75.00
100 . . . . 100.00
101 thru 118 . . . . @75.00
119 thru 125 ATn . . . . @150.00
126 thru 131 . . . . @90.00
132 thru 144 RsM . . . . @110.00
145 . . . . 150.00

ROY ROGER'S TRIGGER
Dell Publishing Co.
May, 1951
(1) see Dell Four Color #329
2 Ph(c) 200.00
3 P(c) 75.00

Roy Rogers
© Dell Publishing Co.

GOLDEN AGE

4 P(c) 75.00
5 P(c) 75.00
6 thru 17 P(c) . . . . @60.00

RULAH, JUNGLE GODDESS
See: ZOOT COMICS

SAARI, THE JUNGLE GODDESS
P.L. Publishing Co.
Nov., 1951
1 The Bantu Blood Curse 600.00

SABU, ELEPHANT BOY
Fox Features Syndicate
June, 1950
1(30) WW,Ph(c) 300.00
2 JKa,Ph(c),Aug.'50 . . . . 250.00

HAPPY HOULIHANS
Fables Publications
(E.C. Comics), Autumn, 1947
1 O:Moon Girl 600.00
2 . . . . 350.00
Becomes:

SADDLE JUSTICE
Spring, 1948
3 HcK,JCr,AF 700.00
4 AF,JCr, Grl 600.00
5 AF,Grl,WI 500.00
6 AF,Grl 450.00
7 AF,Grl 450.00
8 AF,Grl,WI 500.00
Becomes:

SADDLE ROMANCES
Nov., 1949
9 Grl(c),Grl 600.00
10 AF(c),WW,Grl 550.00
11 AF(c),Grl 600.00

SAD SACK
Harvey Publications
Sept., 1949
1 I:Little Dot 750.00
2 . . . . 350.00
3 . . . . 200.00
4 thru 10 . . . . @100.00
11 thru 21 . . . . @75.00
22 Back in the Army Again,
  The Specialist 50.00
23 thru 50 . . . . @35.00
51 thru 100 . . . . @25.00
101 thru 150 . . . . @18.00
151 thru 200 . . . . @12.00
200 thru 287 . . . . @10.00
See also Other Pub. (Color)

SAINT, THE
Avon Periodicals
Aug., 1947
1 JKa,JKa(c),Bondage(c) 1,000.00
2 . . . . 500.00
3 Rolled Stocking Leg(c) 400.00
4 MB(c) Longerie 400.00
5 Spanking Panel 450.00
6 B:Miss Fury 550.00
7 P(c),Detective Cases(c) 350.00
8 P(c),Detective Cases(c) 300.00
9 EK(c),The Notorious
  Murder Mob 300.00
10 WW,P(c),V:The Communist
  Menace 350.00

The Saint #1
© Avon Periodicals

11 P(c),Wanted For Robbery 250.00
12 P(c),The Blowpipe Murders
  March, 1952 . . . . 250.00

SAM HILL PRIVATE EYE
Close-Up Publications, 1950
1 The Double Trouble Caper . . . 200.00
2 . . . . 150.00
3 . . . . 125.00
4 Negligee panels 150.00
5 thru 7 . . . . @100.00

SAMSON
Fox Features Syndicate
Autumn, 1940
1 BP,GT,A:Wing Turner 3,500.00
2 BP,A:Dr. Fung 1,400.00
3 JSh(c),A:Navy Jones 900.00
4 WE,B:Yarko 800.00
5 WE 750.00
6 WE,O:The Topper;Sept'41 . . . 750.00

SAMSON
Ajax Farrell Publ
(Four Star) April, 1955
12 The Electric Curtain 350.00
13 Assignment Danger . . . 300.00
14 The Red Raider;Aug'55 . . . . . 300.00

SANDS OF THE SOUTH PACIFIC
Toby Press, Jan., 1953
1 2-Fisted Romantic Adventure . 250.00

SCHOOL DAY ROMANCES
See: POPULAR TEEN-AGERS

SCIENCE COMICS
Fox Features Syndicate
Feb., 1940
1 GT,LF(c),O&B:Electro,Perisphere
  Payne,The Eagle,Navy Jones;
  B:Marga,Cosmic Carson,
  Dr. Doom; Bondage(c) . . 6,000.00
2 GT,LF(c) 2,700.00
3 GT,LF(c),Dynamo 2,500.00

Comics Values Annual — GOLDEN AGE — Science–Shadow

Science Comics #8
© Fox Features Syndicate

4 JK,Cosmic Carson........ 2,200.00
5 Giant Comiscope Offer
    Eagle(c)................. 1,200.00
6 Dynamop(c) 1,200.00
7 Bondage(c),Dynamo 1,200.00
8 Sept., 1940 Eagle(c) 1,100.00

SCIENCE COMICS
Humor Publications
Jan., 1946
1 RP(c),Story of the A-Bomb ... 250.00
2 RP(c),How Museum Pieces
    Are Assembled 100.00
3 AF,RP(c),How Underwater
    Tunnels Are Made 175.00
4 RP(c),Behind the Scenes at
    A TV Broadcast 75.00
5 The Story of the World's
    Bridges; Sept., 1946 ...... 90.00

SCIENCE COMICS
Ziff-Davis Publ. Co.
May, 1946
N# Used For A Mail Order
    Test Market 500.00

SCIENCE COMICS
Export Publication Enterprises
March, 1951
1 How to resurrect a dead rat .. 125.00

SCOOP COMICS
Harry 'A' Chesler Jr.
Nov., 1941
1 I&B:Rocketman&Rocketgirl;B:Dan
    Hastings;O&B:Master Key . 1,800.00
2 A:Rocketboy,Eye Injury 2,000.00
3 Partial rep. of #2 .... 900.00
4 thru 7 do not exist
8 1945 .... 600.00
Becomes:

SNAP
1944
N# Humorous 150.00
Becomes:

KOMIK PAGES
1944
1(10) JK,Duke of Darkness 450.00
Becomes:

BULLS-EYE
1944
11 Green Knight, Skull (c)...... 500.00
Becomes:

KAYO
1945
12 Green Knight............. 200.00
Becomes:

CARNIVAL
1945
(13) Guardineer 225.00
Becomes:

RED SEAL COMICS
Harry 'A' Chesler, Jr./Superior
Oct., 1945
14 GT,Bondage(c),Black Dwarf 1,000.00
15 GT,Torture 650.00
16 GT...................... 800.00
17 GT,Lady Satan,Sky Chief.... 700.00
18 Lady Satan,Sky Chief 700.00
19 Lady Satan,Sky Chief 600.00
20 Lady Satan,Sky Chief 600.00
21 Lady Satan,Sky Chief 550.00
22 Rocketman 400.00

SCREAM COMICS
Humor Publ./Current Books
(Ace Magazines)
Autumn, 1944
1 .... 200.00
2 .... 100.00
3 .... 75.00
4 thru 15 .... @75.00
16 I:Lily Belle 80.00
17 .... 60.00
18 Drug 75.00
19 .... 60.00
Becomes:

ANDY COMICS
June, 1948
20 Teenage 50.00
21 .... 50.00
Becomes:

ERNIE COMICS
Sept., 1948
22 Teenage 55.00
23 thru 25................. @40.00
Becomes:

ALL LOVE ROMANCES
May, 1949
26 Ernie.................... 55.00
27 LbC..................... 60.00
28 thru 32................. @40.00

(Capt. Silvers Log of...)
SEA HOUND, THE
Avon Periodicals, 1945
N# The Esmerelda's Treasure .. 250.00
2 Adventures in Brazil 150.00
3 Louie the Llama 150.00
4 In Greed & Vengence;
    Jan-Feb, 1946 .... 150.00

SECRET LOVES
Comics Magazines
(Quality Comics)
Nov., 1949
1 BWa(c)................... 250.00
2 BWa(c),Lingerie(c) 225.00
3 RC 200.00
4 .... 150.00
5 Boom Town Babe 200.00
6 .... 150.00

SECRET MYSTERIES
See: CRIME MYSTERIES

SELECT DETECTIVE
D.S. Publishing Co.
Aug.–Sept., 1948
1 MB,Exciting New Mystery
    Cases.................. 300.00
2 MB,AMc,Dead Men......... 200.00
3 Face in theFrame;Dec-Jan'48 . 175.00

SERGEANT PRESTON
OF THE YUKON
Dell Publishing Co., Aug., 1951
(1 thru 4) see Dell Four Color #344;
    #373, 397, 419
5 thru 10 P(c)............. @75.00
11 P(c) 60.00
12 P(c) 60.00
13 P(c),O:Sergeant Preston 75.00
14 thru 17 P(c) .... @60.00
18 P(c).................... 75.00
19 thru 29 Ph(c)........... @75.00

Seven Seas Comics #5
© Universal Phoenix

SEVEN SEAS COMICS
Universal Phoenix Features/
Leader Publ., April, 1946
1 MB,RWb(c),B:South Sea
    Girl, Captain Cutlass 1,200.00
2 MB,RWb(c) 1,000.00
3 MB,AF,MB(c) 900.00
4 MB,MB(c) 1,000.00
5 MB,MB(c),Hangman's Noose . 900.00
6 MB,MB(c);1947 .... 900.00

SHADOW COMICS
Street & Smith, March, 1940
1-1 P(c),B:Shadow,Doc Savage,
    Bill Barnes,Nick Carter,
    Frank Merriwell,Iron Munro 6,500.00
1-2 P(c),B: The Avenger 2,500.00
1-3 P(c),A: Norgill the
    Magician............... 2,000.00
1-4 P(c),B:The Three
    Musketeers 1,500.00
1-5 P(c),E: Doc Savage 1,500.00
1-6 A: Captain Fury 1,200.00

All comics prices listed are for *Near Mint* condition.

Shadow–Shocking

GOLDEN AGE

Comics Values Annual

- 1-7 O&B: The Wasp 1,300.00
- 1-8 A:Doc Savage 1,200.00
- 1-9 A:Norgill the Magician 1,200.00
- 1-10 O:Iron Ghost;B:The Dead End Kids 1,200.00
- 1-11 O:Hooded Wasp. 1,200.00
- 1-12 Crime Does Not pay. 1,100.00
- 2-1 . . . . 1,200.00
- 2-2 Shadow Becomes Invisible 1,500.00
- 2-3 O&B:supersnipe; F:Little Nemo 1,300.00
- 2-4 F:Little Nemo 900.00
- 2-5 V:The Ghost Faker 900.00
- 2-6 A:Blackstone the Magician . . 750.00
- 2-7 V:The White Dragon 750.00
- 2-8 A:Little Nemo 750.00
- 2-9 The Hand of Death 750.00
- 2-10 A:Beebo the WonderHorse . 750.00
- 2-11 V:Devil Kyoti 750.00
- 2-12 V:Devil Kyoti 700.00
- 3-1 JaB(c),V:Devil Kyoti 700.00
- 3-2 Red Skeleton Life Story 700.00
- 3-3 V:Monstrodamus 700.00
- 3-4 V:Monstrodamus 700.00
- 3-5 V:Monstrodamus 700.00
- 3-6 V:Devil's of the Deep 700.00
- 3-7 V: Monstrodamus 700.00
- 3-8 E: The Wasp 700.00
- 3-9 The Stolen Lighthouse 700.00
- 3-10 A:Doc Savage. 700.00
- 3-11 P(c),V: Thade 700.00
- 3-12 V: Thade. 700.00
- 4-1 Red Cross Appeal on (c) . . . 600.00
- 4-2 V:The Brain of Nippon 600.00
- 4-3 Little Men in Space 600.00
- 4-4 ...Mystifies Berlin 600.00
- 4-5 ...Brings Terror to Tokio 600.00
- 4-6 V:The Tarantula 600.00
- 4-7 Crypt of the Seven Skulls . . . 600.00
- 4-8 V:the Indigo Mob 600.00
- 4-9 Ghost Guarded Treasure of the Haunted Glen 600.00
- 4-10 V:The Hydra 600.00
- 4-11 V:The Seven Sinners 600.00
- 4-12 Club Curio 550.00
- 5-1 A:Flatty Foote 550.00
- 5-2 Bells of Doom 550.00
- 5-3 The Circle of Death. 550.00
- 5-4 The Empty Safe Riddle. 550.00
- 5-5 The Mighty Master Nomad . . 550.00
- 5-6 ...Fights Piracy Among the Golden Isles 550.00
- 5-7 V:The Talon 550.00
- 5-8 V:The Talon 550.00
- 5-9 V:The Talon 550.00
- 5-10 V:The Crime Master 550.00
- 5-11 The Clutch of the Talon 550.00
- 5-12 Most Dangerous Criminal . . 550.00
- 6-1 Double Z 500.00
- 6-2 Riddle of Prof.Mentalo 500.00
- 6-3 V:Judge Lawless 500.00
- 6-4 V:Dr. Zenith 500.00
- 6-5 . . . . 500.00
- 6-6 ...Invades the Crucible of Death 500.00
- 6-7 Four Panel (c). 500.00
- 6-8 Crime Among the Aztecs . . . 500.00
- 6-9 I:Shadow Jr. 500.00
- 6-10 Devil's Passage 500.00
- 6-11 The Black Pagoda. 500.00
- 6-12 BP,BP(c),Atomic Bomb Secrets Stolen 550.00
- 7-1 The Yellow Band 550.00
- 7-2 A:Shadow Jr. 550.00
- 7-3 BP,BP(c),Crime Under the Border 700.00
- 7-4 BP,BP(c),One Tree Island, Atomic Bomb 750.00
- 7-5 A:Shadow Jr. 550.00
- 7-6 BP,BP(c),The Sacred Sword of Sanjorojo 700.00
- 7-7 Crime K.O. 550.00
- 7-8 ...Raids Crime Harbor 550.00
- 7-9 BP,BP(c),Kilroy Was Here . . 700.00
- 7-10 BP,BP(c),The Riddle of the Flying Saucer 800.00
- 7-11 BP,BP(c),Crime Doesn't Pay 700.00
- 7-12 BP,BP(c)Back From the Grave. 700.00
- 8-1 BP,BP(c),Curse of the Cat . . 700.00
- 8-2 BP,BP(c),Decay,Vermin & Murder in the Bayou 700.00
- 8-3 BP,BP(c),The Spider Boy . . . 700.00
- 8-4 BP,BP(c),Death Rises Out of the Sea 700.00
- 8-5 BP,BP(c),Jekyll- Hyde Murders. 700.00
- 8-6 Secret of Valhalla Hall 700.00
- 8-7 BP,BP(c),Shadow in Danger 700.00
- 8-8 BP,BP(c),...Solves a Twenty Year Old Crime 700.00
- 8-9 BP,BP(c),3-D Effect(c). 700.00
- 8-10 BP,BP(c),Up&Down(c) 700.00
- 8-11 BP,BP(c). 700.00
- 8-12 BP,BP(c),Arabs,Boat(c). . . . 700.00
- 9-1 Airport(c) 700.00
- 9-2 BP,BP(c),Flying Cannon(c) . . 700.00
- 9-3 BP,BP(c),Shadow's Shadow . 700.00
- 9-4 BP,BP(c) 700.00
- 9-5 Death in the Stars;Aug'49 . . 700.00

SHARP COMICS
H.C. Blackerby
Winter, 1945
- 1 O:Planetarian(c) 550.00
- 2 O:The Pioneer 400.00

SHEENA, QUEEN OF THE JUNGLE
Real Adventures (Fiction House)
Spring, 1942–Winter, 1952
- 1 Blood Hunger 3,500.00
- 2 Black Orchid of Death 1,500.00
- 3 Harem Shackles 1,100.00
- 4 The Zebra Raiders 700.00
- 5 War of the Golden Apes 650.00
- 6 . . . . 625.00
- 7 They Claw By Night 600.00
- 8 The Congo Colossus 600.00
- 9 and 10 . . . . @550.00
- 11 Red Fangs of the Tree Tribe. . 550.00
- 12 . . . . 450.00
- 13 Veldt o/t Voo Doo Lions 450.00
- 14 The Hoo Doo Beasts of Mozambique. 450.00
- 15 . . . . 450.00
- 16 Black Ivory. 450.00
- 17 Great Congo Treasure Trek . . 450.00
- 18 Doom of the Elephant Drum. . 450.00

SHIELD-WIZARD COMICS
MLJ Magazines
Summer, 1940
- 1 IN,EA,O:Shield. 7,000.00
- 2 O:Shield;I:Roy 3,000.00
- 3 Roy,Child Bondage(c) 2,000.00
- 4 Shield,Roy,Wizard 1,800.00
- 5 B:Dusty-Boy Dectective,Child Bondage 1,700.00
- 6 B:Roy the Super Boy,Child Bondage 1,500.00
- 7 Shield(c),Roy Bondage(c) . . 1,600.00
- 8 Bondage(c) 1,500.00
- 9 Shield/Roy(c) 1,200.00
- 10 Shield/Roy(c) 1,200.00
- 11 Shield/Roy(c) 1,200.00
- 12 Shield/Roy(c) 1,200.00
- 13 Bondage (c);Spring'44. . . . . 1,300.00

SHIP AHOY
Spotlight Publishers
Nov., 1944
- 1 LbC(c) 250.00

SHOCK DETECTIVE CASE(S)
See: CRIMINALS ON THE RUN

Shock SuspenStories #13
© EC Comics

SHOCK SUSPENSTORIES
Tiny Tot Comics (E.C. Comics)
Feb.–March, 1952
- 1 JDa,JKa,AF(c),ElectricChair. 1,200.00
- 2 WW,JDa,Grl,JKa,WW(c). 750.00
- 3 WW,JDa,JKa,WW(c). 500.00
- 4 WW,JDa,JKa,WW(c). 500.00
- 5 WW,JDa,JKa,WW(c),Hanging 550.00
- 6 WW,AF,JKa,WW(c), Bondage(c). 600.00
- 7 JKa,WW,GE,AF(c),Face Melting 600.00
- 8 JKa,AF,AW,GE,WW,AF(c). . . . 500.00
- 9 JKa,AF,RC,WW,AF(c) 450.00
- 10 JKa,WW,RC,JKa(c),Drug . . . 450.00
- 11 JCr,JKa,WW,RC,JCr(c) 400.00
- 12 AF,JKa,WW,RC,AF(c)Drug(c). 450.00
- 13 JKa,WW,FF,JKa(c). 600.00
- 14 JKa,WW,BK,WW(c) 400.00
- 15 JKa,WW,RC,JDa(c) Strangulation 350.00
- 16 GE,RC,JKa,GE(c),Rape. 350.00
- 17 GE,RC,JKa,GE(c) 300.00
- 18 GE,RC,JKa,GE(c);Jan'55. . . . 300.00

SHOCKING MYSTERY CASES
See: THRILLING CRIME CASES

CVA Page 454   All comics prices listed are for *Near Mint* condition.

GOLDEN AGE

Silver Streak Comics #12
© Lev Gleason

SILVER STREAK COMICS
Your Guide/New Friday/ Comic House/Newsbrook Publications/Lev Gleason Dec., 1939

1 JCo(a&c),I&B:The Claw,Red Reeves Capt.Fearless;B:Mr.Midnight,Wasp;A:Spiritman .. 15,000.00
2 JSm,JCo,JSm(c) 6,000.00
3 JaB(c),I&O:Silver Streak; B:Dickie Dean,Lance Hale, Ace Powers,Bill Wayne, Planet Patrol 5,000.00
4 JCo,JaB(c)B:Sky Wolf; N:Silver Streak,I:Lance Hale's Sidekick-Jackie 2,500.00
5 JCo(a&c),Dickie Dean V:The Raging Flood 3,000.00
6 JCo,JaB,JCo(a&c),O&I:Daredevil [Blue & Yellow Costume]; R:The Claw 20,000.00
7 JCo,N: Daredevil 15,000.00
8 JCo(a&c) 5,000.00
9 JCo,BoW(c) 3,000.00
10 BoW,BoW(c)........... 2,500.00
11 DRi(c) I:Mercury 2,000.00
12 DRi(c)................ 1,500.00
13 JaB,JaB(c),O:Thun-Dohr... 1,500.00
14 JaB,JaB(c),A:Nazi Skull Men 1,500.00
15 JaB,DBr,JaB(c), B:Bingham Boys 1,200.00
16 DBr,BoW(c),Hitler(c) 1,600.00
17 DBr,JaB(c),E:Daredevil ... 1,200.00
18 DBr,JaB(c),B:The Saint.... 1,100.00
19 DBr,EA 900.00
20 BW,BEv,EA 900.00
21 BW,BEv................. 900.00
Becomes:

CRIME DOES NOT PAY
June 1942

22(23) CBi(c),The Mad Musician & Tunes of Doom 3,500.00
23 CBi(c),John Dillinger-One Man Underworld 1,900.00
24 CBi(c),The Mystery of the Indian Dick 1,500.00
25 CBi(c),Dutch Shultz-King of the Underworld...... 800.00
26 CBi(c),Lucky Luciano-The Deadliest of Crime Rats ... 800.00
27 CBi(c),Pretty Boy Floyd 800.00
28 CBi(c),................ 800.00
29 CBi(c),Two-Gun Crowley-The Bad Kid with the Itchy Trigger Finger.......... 750.00
30 CBi(c),"Monk"Eastman V:Thompson's Mob........ 750.00
31 CBi(c) The Million Dollar Bank Robbery 500.00
32 CBi(c),Seniorita of Sin 500.00
33 CBi(c),Meat Cleaver Murder.. 550.00
34 CBi(c),Elevator Shaft 500.00
35 CBi(c),Case o/t MissingToe . 500.00
36 CBi(c) 450.00
37 CBi(c) 400.00
38 CBi(c) 400.00
39 FG,CBi(c) 400.00
40 FG,CBi(c) 450.00
41 FG,RP,CBi(c),The Cocksure Counterfeiter 350.00
42 FG,RP,CBi(c)............ 350.00
43 FG,RP,CBi(c)Electrocution... 500.00
44 FG,CBi(c),The Most Shot At Gangster 250.00
45 FG,CBi(c) 250.00
46 FG,CBi(c),ChildKidnapping(c) 300.00
47 FG,CBi(c),ElectricChair 400.00
48 FG,CBi(c) 250.00
49 FG,CBi(c) 250.00
50 FG,CBi(c) 250.00
51 FG,GT,CBi(c),1st Monthly Iss. 200.00
52 FG,GT,CBi(c) 200.00
53 FG,CBi(c) 200.00
54 FG,CBi(c) 200.00
55 FG,CBi(c) 200.00
56 FG,GT,CBi(c)............ 200.00
57 FG,CBi(c) 200.00
58 FG,CBi(c) 200.00
59 FG,Cbi(c) 200.00
60 FG,CBi(c) 200.00
61 FG,GT,CBi(c) 200.00
62 FG,CBi(c),Bondage(c) 200.00
63 FG,GT,CBi(c)............ 175.00
64 FG,GT,CBi(c)............ 175.00
65 FG,CBi(c) 175.00
66 FG,GT,CBi(c)............ 175.00
67 FG,GT,CBi(c)............ 175.00
68 FG,CBi(c) 175.00
69 FG,CBi(c) 175.00
70 FG,Cbi(c)............... 175.00
71 FG,CBi(c) 150.00
72 FG,CBi(c) 150.00
73 FG,CBi(c) 150.00
74 FG,CBi(c) 150.00
75 FG,CBi(c) 150.00
76 FG,CBi(c) 150.00
77 FG,CBi(c),Electrified Safe ... 175.00
78 FG,CBi(c) 150.00
79 FG.................... 150.00
80 FG.................... 150.00
81 FG.................... 150.00
82 FG.................... 150.00
83 FG.................... 150.00
84 FG.................... 150.00
85 FG.................... 150.00
86 FG.................... 150.00
87 FG,P(c),The Rock-A-Bye Baby Murder........... 150.00
88 FG,P(c),Death Carries a Torch 150.00
89 FG,BF,BF P(c),The Escort Murder Case 150.00
90 FG,BF P(c),The Alhambra Club Murders 150.00
91 FG,AMc,BF P(c),Death Watches The Clock 150.00
92 BF,FG,BF P(c)........... 150.00
93 BF,FG,AMc,BF P(c) 150.00
94 BF,FG,BF P(c)........... 150.00
95 FG,AMc,BF P(c) 150.00
96 BF,FG,BF P(c),The Case of the Movie Star's Double 150.00
97 FG,BF P(c) 150.00
98 BF,FG,BF P(c),Bondage(c)... 150.00
99 BF,FG,BF P(c)........... 150.00
100 FG,BF,AMc,P(c),The Case of the Jittery Patient 150.00
101 FG,BF,AMc,P(c).......... 125.00
102 FG,BF,AMc,BF P(c) 125.00
103 FG,BF,AMc,BF P(c) 125.00
104 thru 110 FG .... @125.00
111 thru 120 .... @125.00
121 thru 140 .... @100.00
141 JKu 100.00
142 JKu,CBi(c).............. 100.00
143 JKu,Comic Code 100.00
144 I Helped Capture"Fat Face" George Klinerz........... 75.00
145 RP,Double Barrelled Menace . 75.00
146 BP,The Con & The Canary... 75.00
147 JKu,BP,A Long Shoe On the Highway;July, 1955........... 125.00

SINGLE SERIES
United Features Syndicate 1938

1 Captain & The Kids 1,200.00
2 Bronco Bill 600.00
3 Ella Cinders 500.00
4 Li'l Abner 850.00
5 Fritzi Ritz 300.00
6 Jim Hardy 500.00
7 Frankie Doodle 300.00
8 Peter Pat 300.00
9 Strange As it Seems 350.00
10 Little Mary Mixup 300.00
11 Mr. & Mrs. Beans 300.00
12 Joe Jinx................. 300.00
13 Looy Dot Dope........... 300.00
14 Billy Make Believe 300.00
15 How It Began............ 300.00
16 Illustrated Gags 250.00
17 Danny Dingle............ 250.00
18 Li'l Abner 800.00
19 Broncho Bill.............. 500.00
20 Tarzan 1,500.00
21 Ella Cinders 400.00
22 Iron Vic 300.00
23 Tailspin Tommy 500.00
24 Alice In Wonderland........ 450.00
25 Abbie an' Slats........... 375.00
26 Little Mary Mixup 300.00
27 Jim Hardy 400.00
28 Ella Cinders & Abbie AN' Slats 1942 .... 400.00

SKELETON HAND
American Comics Group Sept.–Oct., 1952

1 .... 600.00
2 The Were-Serpent of Karnak . 350.00
3 Waters of Doom 300.00
4 Black Dust 300.00
5 The Rise & Fall of the Bogey Man.............. 300.00
6 July–Aug., 1953 .... 300.00

SKY BLAZERS
Hawley Publications Sept., 1940

1 Flying Aces,Sky Pirates 800.00
2 Nov., 1940 .... 600.00

SKYMAN
Columbia Comics Group, 1941

1 OW,OW(c),O:Skyman,Face . 1,500.00
2 OW,OW(c),Yankee Doodle ... 800.00
3 OW,OW(c) 500.00
4 OW,OW(c),Statue of Liberty(c) 1948 .... 500.00

GOLDEN AGE

Sky Pilot–Smilin' — Comics Values Annual

Skyman #4
© Columbia Comics Group

SKY PILOT
Ziff-Davis Publishing Co.
1950
10 NS P(c),Lumber Pirates 150.00
11 Ns P(c),The 2.00 Foot Drop;
April–May, 1951 . . . . 125.00

SKY ROCKET
Home Guide Publ.
(Harry 'A' Chesler), 1944
1 Alias the Dragon,Skyrocket . . . 400.00

SKY SHERIFF
D.S. Publishing
Summer, 1948
1 I:Breeze Lawson & the Prowl
Plane Patrol 150.00

SLAM BANG COMICS
Fawcett Publications
Jan., 1940
1 B:Diamond Jack,Mark Swift,
Lee Granger,Jungle King . . 2,800.00
2 F:Jim Dolan Two-Fisted
Crime Buster 1,200.00
3 A: Eric the Talking Lion 1,900.00
4 F: Hurricane Hansen-Sea
Adventurer 1,000.00
5 . . . . 1,000.00
6 I: Zoro the Mystery Man;
Bondage(c) 1,000.00
7 Bondage(c);Sept., 1940 . . . 1,000.00

SLAPSTICK COMICS
Comic Magazine Distrib., Inc.
1945
N# Humorous Parody 300.00

SLAVE GIRL COMICS
Avon Periodicals
Feb., 1949
1 . . . . 1,200.00
2 April, 1949 . . . . 900.00

SLICK CHICK COMICS
Leader Enterprises, Inc., 1947
1 Teen-Aged Humor 125.00
2 Teen-Aged Humor 100.00

3 1947 . . . . 100.00

SMASH COMICS
Comics Magazine, Inc.
(Quality Comics Group)
Aug., 1939
1 WE,O&B:Hugh Hazard, Bozo
the Robot,Black X, Invisible
Justice: B:Wings Wendall,
Chic Carter 4,000.00
2 WE,A:Lone Star Rider 1,500.00
3 WE,B:Captain Cook,JohnLaw 900.00
4 WE,PGn,B:Flash Fulton 800.00
5 WE,PGn,Bozo Robot 800.00
6 WE,PGn,GFx,Black X(c) 800.00
7 WE,PGn,GFx,Wings
Wendell(c) 750.00
8 WE,PGn,GFx,Bozo Robot 750.00
9 WE,PGn,GFx,Black X(c) 750.00
10 WE,PGn,GFx,Bozo robot(c) . . . 750.00
11 WE,PGn,GFx,BP,Black X(c) . . 750.00
12 WE,PGn,GFx,BP,Bozo(c) 750.00
13 WE,PGn,GFx,AB,BP,B:Mango,
Purple Trio,BlackX(c) 750.00
14 BP,LF,AB,PGn,I:The Ray . . . 3,700.00
15 BP,LF,AB,PGn,The Ram(c) . 1,500.00
16 BP,LF,AB,PGn,Bozo(c) 1,500.00
17 BP,LF,AB,PGn,JCo,
The Ram(c) 1,600.00
18 BP,LF,AB,JCo,PGn,
B&O:Midnight 2,000.00
19 BP,LF,AB,JCo,PGn,Bozo(c) . 1,100.00
20 BP,LF,AB,JCo,PGn,
The Ram(c) 1,000.00
21 BP,LF,AB,JCo,PGn 1,000.00
22 BP,LF,AB,JCo,PGn,
B:The Jester 1,000.00
23 BP,AB,JCo,RC,PGn,
The Ram(c) 1,100.00
24 BP,AB,JCo,RC,PGn,A:Sword,
E:ChicCarter,
N:WingsWendall 1,100.00
25 AB,JCo,RC,PGn,O:Wildfire . 1,000.00
26 AB,JCo,RC,PGn,Bozo(c) 850.00
27 AB,JCo,RC,PGn,The Ram(c) . 850.00
28 AB,JCo,RC,PGn,
1st Midnight (c) 850.00
29 AB,JCo,Rc,PGn,B;Midnight(c) 850.00
30 AB,JCo,PGn 850.00
31 AB,JCo,PGn 750.00
32 AB,JCo,PGn 750.00
33 AB,JCo,PGn,O:Marksman . . . 800.00
34 AB,JCo,PGn 750.00
35 AB,JCo,RC,PGn 750.00
36 AB,JCo,RC,PGn,E:Midnight(c) 750.00
37 AB,JCo,RC,PGn,Doc Wacky
becomes Fastest Human
on Earth 750.00
38 JCo,RC,PGn,B:YankeeEagle 1,200.00
39 PGn,B:Midnight(c) 700.00
40 PGn,E:Ray 700.00
41 PGn 500.00
42 PGn,B:Lady Luck 1,500.00
43 PGn 500.00
44 PGn 500.00
45 PGn,E:Midnight(c) 500.00
46 RC,Twelve Hours to Live 500.00
47 Wanted Midnight,
Dead or Alive 500.00
48 Midnight Meets the
Menace from Mars 500.00
49 PGn,FG,Mass of Muscle 500.00
50 I:Hyram the Hermit 500.00
51 A:Wild Bill Hiccup 300.00
52 PGn,FG,Did Ancient Rome Fall,
or was it Pushed? 300.00
53 Is ThereHonorAmongThieves. 300.00
54 A:Smear-Faced Schmaltz . . . 300.00
55 Never Trouble Trouble until
Trouble Troubles You 300.00

Smash Comics #37
© Quality Comics Group

56 The Laughing Killer 300.00
57 A Dummy that Turns Into
A Curse 300.00
58 . . . . 300.00
59 A Corpse that Comes Alive . . . 300.00
60 The Swooner & the Trush . . . 300.00
61 . . . . 250.00
62 V:The Lorelet 250.00
63 PGn 250.00
64 PGn,In Search of King Zoris . . 250.00
65 PGn,V:Cyanide Cindy 250.00
66 Under Circle's Spell 250.00
67 A Living Clue 250.00
68 JCo,Atomic Dice 250.00
69 JCo,V:Sir Nuts 250.00
70 . . . . 250.00
71 . . . . 225.00
72 JCo,Angela,the Beautiful
Bovine 225.00
73 . . . . 225.00
74 . . . . 225.00
75 The Revolution 225.00
76 Bowl Over Crime 225.00
77 Who is Lilli Dilli? 225.00
78 JCo,Win Over Crime 225.00
79 V:The Men From Mars 225.00
80 JCo,V:Big Hearted Bosco 225.00
81 V:Willie the Kid 225.00
82 V:Woodland Boy 225.00
83 JCo,Quizmaster 225.00
84 A Date With Father Time 225.00
85 JCo,A Singing Swindle 225.00

SMASH HITS SPORTS COMICS
Essankay Publications
Jan., 1949
1 LbC,LbC(c) 350.00

SMILEY BURNETTE WESTERN
Fawcett Publications
March, 1950
1 Ph(c),B:Red Eagle 550.00
2 Ph(c) 400.00
3 Ph(c) 400.00
4 Ph(c) 400.00

SMILIN' JACK
Dell Publishing Co., 1948
1 . . . . 150.00

All comics prices listed are for *Near Mint* condition.

GOLDEN AGE — Smilin'–Sparkler

2 .... 100.00
3 thru 8 .... @75.00

SMITTY
Dell Publishing Co., 1948
1 .... 125.00
2 .... 75.00
3 .... 50.00
4 thru 7 .... @40.00

SNAPPY COMICS
Cima Publications (Prize), 1945
1 A:Animale 350.00

SNIFFY THE PUP
Animated Cartoons (Standard Comics) Nov., 1949
5 FF,Funny Animal 100.00
6 thru 9 Funny Animal .... @50.00
10 thru 17 Funny Animal ... @40.00
18 Sept., 1953 .... 40.00

SOLDIER COMICS
Fawcett Publications Jan., 1952
1 Fighting Yanks on Flaming Battlefronts 150.00
2 Blazing Battles Exploding with Combat 75.00
3 .... 60.00
4 A Blow for Freedom 50.00
5 Only The Dead Are Free ... 50.00
6 Blood & Guts 45.00
7 The Phantom Sub 45.00
8 More Plasma! 45.00
9 Red Artillery 45.00
10 .... 45.00
11 Sept., 1953 .... 45.00

SOLDIERS OF FORTUNE
Creston Publications (American Comics Group) Feb.–March, 1952
1 OW(c),B:Ace Carter, Crossbones, Lance Larson . 300.00
2 OW(c) 175.00
3 OW(c) 125.00
4 .... 125.00
5 OW(c) 125.00

Space Adventures #3 © Charlton Comics

6 OW(c),OW,Bondage(c) 150.00
7 .... 125.00
8 OW thru 10 .... @125.00
11 OW,Format Change to War ... 75.00
12 .... 75.00
13 OW,Feb.–March, 1953 ...... 75.00

SON OF SINBAD
St. John Publishing Co. Feb., 1950
1 JKu,JKu(c),The Curse of the Caliph's Dancer 500.00

SPACE ACTION
Junior Books (Ace Magazines) June, 1952–Oct., 1952
1 Invaders from a Lost Galaxy 1,000.00
2 The Silicon Monster from Galaxy X 750.00
3 Attack on Ishtar 750.00

SPACE ADVENTURES
Capitol Stories/ Charlton Comics July, 1952
1 AFa&LM(c) 650.00
2 .... 300.00
3 DG(c) 250.00
4 DG(c) 250.00
5 StC(c) 250.00
6 StC(c),Two Worlds 200.00
7 DG(c),Transformation 250.00
8 DG(c),All For Love 200.00
9 DG(c) 200.00
10 SD,SD(c) 650.00
11 SD,JoS 750.00
12 SD(c) 750.00
13 A:Blue Beetle 250.00
14 A:Blue Beetle 250.00
15 Ph(c) of Rocky Jones 250.00
16 BKa,A:Rocky Jones 250.00
17 A:Rocky Jones 225.00
18 A:Rocky Jones 225.00
19 .... 200.00
20 First Trip to the Moon ... 350.00
21 .... 200.00
22 Does Not Exist
23 SD,Space Trip to the Moon . 300.00
24 .... 225.00
25 Brontosaurus 225.00
26 SD,Flying Saucers 300.00
27 SD,Flying Saucers 300.00
28 Moon Trap 100.00
29 Captive From Space 100.00
30 Peril in the Sky 100.00
31 SD,SD(c),Enchanted Planet . 250.00
32 SD,SD(c),Last Ship from Earth 250.00
33 Galactic Scourge, I&O:Captain Atom 650.00
34 SD,SD(c),A:Captain Atom ... 275.00
35 thru 40 SD,SD(c), A:Captain Atom .... @275.00
41 .... 75.00
42 SD,A:Captain Atom 75.00
43 .... 75.00
44 A:Mercury Man 75.00
45 A:Mercury Man 75.00
46 thru 58 .... @75.00
59 Nov., 1964 .... 75.00

SPACE BUSTERS
Ziff-Davis Publishing Co. Spring, 1952
1 BK,NS(c),Ph(c),Charge of the Battle Women 1,000.00

2 EK,BK,MA,NS(c), Bondage(c),Ph(c) 800.00
3 Autumn, 1952 .... 750.00

SPACE COMICS
See: FUNNY TUNES

SPACE DETECTIVE
Avon Periodicals July, 1951
1 WW,WW(c),Opium Smugglers of Venus 1,500.00
2 WW,WW(c),Batwomen of Mercury 1,000.00
3 EK(c),SeaNymphs ofNeptune 600.00
4 EK,Flame Women of Vulcan, Bondage(c) 650.00

SPACE MOUSE
Avon Periodicals April, 1953
1 Funny Animal 100.00
2 Funny Animal 75.00
3 thru 5 Funny Animal ..... @50.00

SPACE PATROL
Approved Comics (Ziff-Davis) Summer, 1952
1 BK,NS,Ph(c), The Lady of Diamonds 1,400.00
2 BK,NS,Ph(c),Slave King of Pluto,Oct.–Nov., 1952 ..... 850.00

SPACE THRILLERS
Avon Periodicals, 1954
N# Contents May Vary 1,500.00

SPACE WESTERN COMICS
See: YELLOWJACKET COMICS

SPARKLER COMICS
United Features Syndicate July, 1940
1 Jim Handy 500.00
2 Frankie Doodle,Aug., 1940 .. 400.00

SPARKLER COMICS
United Features Syndicate July, 1941
1 BHg,O:Sparkman;B:Tarzan,Captain & the Kids,Ella Cinders,Danny Dingle,Dynamite Dunn, Nancy, Abbie an' Slats, Frankie Doodle,Broncho Bill 3,000.00
2 BHg, The Case of Poisoned Fruit 1,200.00
3 BHg 1,000.00
4 BHg,Case of Sparkman & the Firefly 1,000.00
5 BHg,Sparkman,Natch 800.00
6 BHg,Case o/t Bronze Bees .. 800.00
7 BHg,Case o/t Green Raiders . 800.00
8 BHg,V:River Fiddler 800.00
9 BHg,N:Sparkman 800.00
10 BHg,B:Hap Hopper, Sparkman's ID revealed ... 800.00
11 BHg,V:Japanese 600.00
12 BHg,Another N:Sparkman ... 600.00

Sparkler–Spirit GOLDEN AGE Comics Values Annual

13 BHg,Hap Hopper Rides
   For Freedom 600.00
14 BHg,BHg(c),Tarzan
   V:Yellow Killer. 750.00
15 BHg. 500.00
16 BHg,Sparkman V:Japanese . . 500.00
17 BHg,Nancy(c) 500.00
18 BHg,Sparkman in Crete 500.00
19 BHg,I&B:Race Riley,
   Commandos. 500.00
20 BHg,Nancy(c) 500.00
21 BHg,Tarzan(c) 550.00
22 BHg,Nancy(c) 400.00
23 BHg,Capt&Kids(c) 400.00
24 BHg,Nancy(c) 400.00
25 BHg,BHg(c),Tarzan(c) 550.00
26 BHg,Capt&Kids(c) 400.00
27 BHg,Nancy(c) 400.00
28 BHg,BHg(c),Tarzan(c) 550.00
29 BHg,Capt&Kids(c) 400.00
30 BHg,Nancy(c) 400.00
31 BHg,BHg(c),Tarzan(c) 550.00
32 BHg,Capt&Kids(c) 250.00
33 BHg,Nancy(c) 250.00
34 BHg,BHg(c),Tarzan(c) 550.00
35 BHg,Capt&Kids(c) 250.00
36 BHg,Nancy(c) 250.00
37 BHg,BHg(c),Tarzan(c) 550.00
38 BHg,Capt&Kids(c) 225.00
39 BHg,BHg(c),Tarzan(c) 550.00
40 BHg,Nancy(c) 225.00
41 BHg,Capt&Kids(c) 175.00
42 BHg,BHg,Tarzan(c) 350.00
43 BHg,Nancy(c) 175.00
44 BHg,Tarzan(c) 350.00
45 BHg,Capt&Kids(c) 175.00
46 BHg,Nancy(c) 175.00
47 BHg,Tarzan(c) 350.00
48 BHg,Nancy(c) 175.00
49 BHg,Capt&Kids(c) 175.00
50 BHg,BHg(c),Tarzan(c) 350.00
51 BHg,Capt&Kids(c) 175.00
52 BHg,Nancy(c) 175.00
53 BHg,BHg(c),Tarzan(c) 350.00
54 BHg,Capt&Kids(c) 150.00
55 BHg,Nancy(c) 150.00
56 BHg,Capt&Kids(c) 150.00
57 BHg,F:Li'l Abner. 150.00
58 BHg,A:Fearless Fosdick. 175.00
59 BHg,B:Li'l Abner. 175.00
60 BHg,Nancy(c) 150.00
61 BHg,Capt&Kids(c) 150.00
62 BHg,Li'l Abner(c). 150.00
63 BHg,Capt&Kids(c) 150.00
64 BHg,Valentines (c) 150.00
65 BHg,Nancy(c) 150.00
66 BHg,Capt&Kids(c) 150.00
67 BHg,Nancy(c) 150.00
68 BHg, ... 150.00
69 BHg,B:Nancy (c) 150.00
70 BHg. 150.00
71 thru 80 BHg . . . . @100.00
81 BHg,E:Nancy(c). 100.00
82 BHg. 100.00
83 BHg,Tarzan(c) 175.00
84 BHg. 75.00
85 BHg,E:Li'l Abner 75.00
86 BHg. 75.00
87 BHg,Nancy(c) 75.00
88 thru 96 BHg . . . . @75.00
97 BHg,O:Lady Ruggles. 175.00
98 BHg. 75.00
99 BHg,Nancy(c) 75.00
100 BHg,Nancy(c) 90.00
101 thru 107 BHg . . . . @60.00
108 & 109 BHg,ATh 100.00
110 BHg. 60.00
111 BHg. 60.00
112 BHg. 60.00
113 BHg,ATh 100.00
114 thru 120 BHg . . . . @75.00

SPARKLING STARS
Holyoke Publishing Co.
June, 1944
1 B:Hell's Angels,Ali Baba,FBI,
   Boxie Weaver,Petey & Pop . 250.00
2 Speed Spaulding 150.00
3 FBI. 100.00
4 thru 12 . . . . @100.00
13 O&I:Jungo, The Man-Beast . . 110.00
14 thru 19. . . . . @100.00
20 I:Fangs the Wolfboy. 100.00
21 thru 28 . . . . @100.00
29 Bondage(c). 110.00
30 thru 32. . . . . @75.00
33 March, 1948 . . . . 75.00

SPARKMAN
Frances M. McQueeny, 1944
1 O:Sparkman 375.00

SPARKY WATTS
Columbia Comics Group, 1942
1 A:Skyman,Hitler(c) 900.00
2 . . . . 350.00
3 . . . . 250.00
4 O:Skyman 250.00
5 A:Skyman 225.00
6 . . . . 100.00
7 . . . . 100.00
8 . . . . 150.00
9 . . . . 100.00
10 1949 . . . . 100.00

[STEVE SAUNDERS] SPECIAL AGENT
Parents Magazine/ Commended Comics, Dec., 1947
1 J. Edgar Hoover, Ph(c) 125.00
2 . . . . 75.00
3 thru 7 . . . . @60.00
8 Sept., 1949. . . . . 60.00

SPECIAL COMICS
See: LAUGH COMICS

SPECIAL EDITION COMICS
Fawcett Publications Aug., 1940
1 CCB,CCB(c),F:Captain
   Marvel 14,000.00

SPEED COMICS
Brookwood/Speed Publ. Harvey Publications Oct., 1939
1 BP,B&O:Shock Gibson,B:Spike
   Marlin,Biff Bannon 5,000.00
2 BP,B:Shock Gibson(c) 1,500.00
3 BP,GT 900.00
4 BP 750.00
5 BP,DBr 750.00
6 BP,GT 700.00
7 GT,JKu,B:Mars Mason 700.00
8 JKu 650.00
9 JKu 650.00
10 JKu,E:Shock Gibson(c) 650.00
11 JKu,E:Mars Mason. 650.00
12 B:The Wasp. 750.00
13 I:Captain Freedom;B:Girls
   Commandos,Pat Parker 800.00
14 Pocket sized format-100pgs. . 900.00
15 Pocket size 900.00
16 JKu,Pocket size 900.00
17 O:Black Cat 1,000.00
18 B:Capt.Freedom,Bondage(c) . 800.00
19 S&K. 750.00
20 . . . . 750.00
21 JKu(c). 750.00
22 JKu(c) 750.00
23 JKu(c),O:Girl Commandos . . . 800.00
24 Hitler,Tojo & Mussilini(c). 750.00
25 . . . . 550.00
26 Flag (c) 550.00
27 . . . . 550.00
28 E:Capt Freedom 550.00
29 Case o/t Black Marketeers . . . 550.00
30 POW Death Chambers 550.00
31 ASh(c),Nazi Thrashing(c) 850.00
32 ASh(c) 700.00
33 ASh(c) 700.00
34 ASh(c) 700.00
35 ASh(c),BlackCat'sDeathTrap . 725.00
36 ASh(c) 700.00
37 RP(c) 700.00
38 RP(c),War Bond Plea with Iwo
   Jima flag allusion(c) 700.00
39 RP(c),B:Capt Freedom(c). . . . 500.00
40 RP(c) 500.00
41 RP(c) 500.00
42 JKu,RP(c) 500.00
43 JKu,E:Capt Freedom(c) 550.00
44 BP,JKu,Four Kids on a raft,
   Jan.–Feb., 1947 . . . . 600.00

SPEED SMITH THE HOT ROD KING
Ziff-Davis Publishing Co.
Spring, 1952
1 INS,Ph(c),A:Roscoe
   the Rascal 250.00

SPIRIT, THE
Will Eisner (Weekly Coverless Comic Book), June, 1940
WE,O:SPirit 1,000.00
6/9/40 WE 600.00
6/16/40 WE,Black Queen . . . 300.00
6/23/40 WE,Mr Mystic. 250.00
6/30/40 WE 250.00
7/7/40 WE,Black Queen 250.00
7/14/40 WE 200.00
7/21/40 WE 200.00
7/28/40 WE 200.00

Sparky Watts #2
© Columbia Comics Group

GOLDEN AGE

8/4/40 WE 200.00
7/7/40-11/24/40,WE 165.00
11/10/40 WE,Black Queen . . 150.00
12/1/40 WE,Ellen
  Spanking(c) 225.00
12/8/40-12/29/40 . . . . 125.00
1941 WE Each 125.00
3/16 WE I:Silk Satin 200.00
6/15 WE I Twilight 125.00
6/22 WE Hitler 125.00
1942 WE Each 100.00
2-1 Duchess 125.00
2-15 . . . . 100.00
2-23 . . . . 150.00
1943 WE Each,LF,WE scripts 50.00
1944 JCo,LF, ... 30.00
1945 LF Each, ... 30.00
1946 WE Each 50.00
1/13 WE,O:The Spirit 75.00
1/20 WE,Satin 75.00
3/17 WE,I:Nylon 75.00
4/21 WE,I:Mr.Carrion 85.00
7/7 WE,I:Dulcet Tone&Skinny . 75.00
10/6 WE,I:F:Gell. 100.00
1947 WE Each 50.00
7/13.,WE,Hansel &Gretel 70.00
7/20,WE,A:Bomb 75.00
9/28,WE,Flying Saucers . . . 100.00
10/5,WE, Cinderella 70.00
12/7,WE,I:Power Puff 75.00
1948 WE Each 50.00
1/11,WE,Sparrow Fallon 60.00
1/25,WE,I:Last A Net 65.00
3/14,WE,A:Kretuama 60.00
4/4,WE,A:Wildrice. 60.00
7/25,The Thing 100.00
8/22,Poe Tale,Horror. 125.00
9/18, A:Lorelei 60.00
11/7,WE,A:Plaster of Paris . . . 65.00
1949 WE Each 50.00
1/23 WE,I:Thorne 65.00
8/21 WE,I:Monica Veto 65.00
9/25 WE,A;Ice 65.00
12/4 WE,I:Flaxen 60.00
1950 WE Each 50.00
1/8 WE,I:Sand Saref. 150.00
2/10, Horror Issue. 60.00
1951 WE(Last WE 8/12/51) . . . @50.00
Non-Eisners . . . . @25.00
1952 Non-Eisners . . . . @25.00
7/27 WW,Denny Colt 500.00
8/3 WW,Moon. 500.00
8/10 WW.Moon. 500.00
8/17 WW,WE,Heart 400.00
8/24 WW,Rescue 400.00
8/31 WW,Last Man 400.00
9/7 WW,Man Moon. 550.00
9/14 WE. 150.00
9/21 WE Space 350.00
9/28 WE Moon 400.00
10/5 WE Last Story 250.00

SPIRIT, THE
**Quality Comics Group/
Vital Publ., 1944**
N# Wanted Dead or Alive! . . . 1,000.00
N# ...in Crime Doesn't Pay. . . . 600.00
N# ...In Murder Runs Wild 500.00
4 ...Flirts with Death. 400.00
5 ...Wanted Dead or Alive . . . 300.00
6 ...Gives You Triple Value . . . 250.00
7 ...Rocks the Underworld . . . 250.00
8 . . . . 250.00
9 ...Throws Fear Into the
  Heart of Crime 250.00
10 ...Stalks Crime. 250.00
11 ...America's Greatest
  Crime Buster 250.00
12 WE(c),...The Famous Outlaw
  Who Smashes Crime 400.00

13 WE(c),...and Ebony Cleans Out
  the Underworld;Bondage(c) . 400.00
14 WE(c) 400.00
15 WE(c),Bank Robber at Large . 400.00
16 WE(c),The Caase of the
  Uncanny Cat 400.00
17 WE(c),The Organ Grinding
  Bank Robber 400.00
18 WE,WE(c),'The Bucket
  of Blood 450.00
19 WE,WE(c),'The Man Who
  Murdered the Spirit' 450.00
20 WE,WE(c),'The Vortex' 450.00
21 WE,WE(c),'P'Gell of Paris' . . . 450.00
22 WE(c),TheOctopus,Aug.1950 . 800.00

SPIRIT, THE
**Fiction House Magazines
1952**
1 Curse of Claymore Castle . . . 500.00
2 WE,WE(c),Who Says Crime
  Doesn't Pay 450.00
3 WE/JGr(c),League of Lions . . 400.00
4 WE,WE&JGr(c),Last Prowl of
  Mr. Mephisto;Bondage (c) . . 450.00
5 WE,WE(c),Ph(c)1954 . . . . . . 450.00

SPIRITMAN
Will Eisner, 1944
1 3 Spirit Sections from
  1944 Bound Together 250.00
2 LF, 2 Spirit Sections
  from 1944 Bound Together . 200.00

SPITFIRE COMICS
Harvey Publ., Aug., 1941
1 MKd(c),100-pgs.,Pocket-size 1,000.00
2 100-pgs.,Pocket-size,
  Oct., 1941 . . . . 900.00

SPOOK COMICS
Baily Publications, 1946
1 A:Mr. Lucifer 400.00

SPOOK DETECTIVE CASES
See: CRIMINALS ON THE RUN

SPOOKY
**Harvey Publications
Nov., 1955**
1 Funny Apparition 500.00
2 same 300.00
3 thru 10 same . . . . @150.00
11 thru 20 same . . . . @75.00
21 thru 30 same . . . . @60.00
31 thru 40 same . . . . @50.00
41 thru 70 same . . . . @35.00
71 thru 90 same . . . . @30.00
91 thru 120 same . . . . @18.00
121 thru 160 same . . . . @8.00
161 same,Sept., 1980. . . . . . . 8.00

SPOOKY MYSTERIES
**Your Guide Publishing Co.
1946**
1 Rib-Tickling Horror 250.00

SPORT COMICS
See: TRUE SPORT PICTURE STORIES

SPORTS THRILLS
See: DICK COLE

*Spotlight Comics #1
© Harry A Chesler*

SPOTLIGHT COMICS
**Harry 'A' Chesler Jr.
Publications
Nov., 1944**
1 GT,GT(c),B:Veiled Avenger,
  Black Dwarf,Barry Kuda 900.00
2 . . . . 750.00
3 1945,Eye Injury. 800.00

SPUNKY
**Standard Comics
April, 1949**
1 FF,Adventures of a Junior
  Cowboy 125.00
2 FF 100.00
3 . . . . 75.00
4 . . . . 75.00
5 . . . . 75.00
6 . . . . 75.00
7 Nov., 1951 . . . . 75.00

SPY AND COUNTER SPY
**Best Syndicated Features
(American Comics Group)
Aug.–Sept., 1949**
1 I&O:Jonathan Kent 350.00
2 . . . . 200.00
Becomes:

SPY HUNTERS
Dec., 1949–Jan., 1950
3 Jonathan Kent 300.00
4 J.Kent 150.00
5 J.Kent 150.00
6 J.Kent 150.00
7 OW(c),J.Kent 150.00
8 OW(c),J.Kent 150.00
9 OW(c),J.Kent 150.00
10 OW(c),J.Kent 150.00
11 . . . . 125.00
12 OW(c),MD 125.00
13 and 14 . . . . @100.00
15 OW(c) 125.00
16 AW 175.00
17 . . . . 75.00
18 War (c) 100.00

Spy Hunters–Startling

19 and 20 . . . . @100.00
21 B:War Content 100.00
22 . . . . 100.00
23 Torture 250.00
24 'BlackmailBrigade',July,1953 . 100.00

SPY SMASHER
Fawcett Publications
Autumn, 1941
1 B;Spy Smasher 5,000.00
2 Mra(c) 2,500.00
3 Bondage (c) 1,500.00
4 . . . . 1,400.00
5 Mra,Mt. Rushmore(c) 1,400.00
6 MRa(a&c),V:The Sharks
   of Steel 1,200.00
7 Mra 1,200.00
8 AB 1,000.00
9 AB,Hitler,Tojo, Mussolini(c) . . 1,200.00
10 AB,Did Spy Smasher
   Kill Hitler? 1,200.00
11 AB,Feb., 1943 . . . . 1,000.00

SQUEEKS
Lev Gleason Publications
Oct., 1953
1 CBi(c),(fa) 75.00
2 CBi(c),(fa) 35.00
3 CBi(c),(fa) 35.00
4 (fa) 35.00
5 (fa),Jan., 1954 . . . . 35.00

STAMP COMICS
Youthful Magazines/Stamp
Comics, Inc.
Oct., 1951
1 HcK,Birth of Liberty 350.00
2 HcK,RP,Battle of White Plains 200.00
3 HcK,DW,RP,Iwo Jima 150.00
4 HcK,DW,RP 150.00
5 HcK,Von Hindenberg disaster . 175.00
6 HcK,The Immortal Chaplains . 150.00
7 HcK,RKr,RP,B&O:Railroad . . . 250.00
Becomes:

THRILLING ADVENTURES IN STAMPS
Jan., 1953
8 HcK, 100 Pgs. 700.00

STAR COMICS
Comic Magazines/Ultem
Publ./Chesler
Centaur Publications
Feb., 1937
1 B:Dan Hastings 2,500.00
2 . . . . 1,000.00
3 . . . . 900.00
4 WMc(c) 900.00
5 WMc(c),A:Little Nemo 900.00
6 CBi(c),FG 850.00
7 FG 800.00
8 BoW,BoW(c),FG,A:Little
   Nemo,Horror 850.00
9 FG,CBi(c) 800.00
10 FG,CBi(c),BoW,A:Impyk . . 1,100.00
11 FG,BoW,JCo 850.00
12 FG,BoW,B:Riders of the
   Golden West 750.00
13 FG,BoW 750.00
14 FG,GFx(c) 750.00
15 CBu,B:The Last Pirate 750.00
16 CBu,B:Phantom Rider 750.00
2-1 CBu,B:Phantom Rider(c) . . . 800.00
2-2 CBu,A:Diana Deane 750.00
2-3 GFx(c),CBu 700.00
2-4 CBu 700.00

GOLDEN AGE

2-5 CBu 700.00
2-6 CBu,E:Phantom Rider 700.00
2-7 CBu,Aug., 1939 . . . . 700.00

STARLET O'HARA IN HOLLYWOOD
Standard Comics
Dec., 1948
1 The Terrific Tee-Age Comic . . . 250.00
2 Her Romantic Adventures in
   Movie land 150.00
3 and 4, Sept., 1949 . . . . . . @125.00

STAR RANGER
Comics Magazines/Ultem/
Centaur Publ.
Feb., 1937
1 FG,I:Western Comic 2,500.00
2 . . . . 1,300.00
3 FG 1,100.00
4 . . . . 1,100.00
5 . . . . 1,100.00
6 FG 1,000.00
7 FG 900.00
8 GFx,FG,PGn,BoW 900.00
9 GFx,FG,PGn,BoW 900.00
10 JCo,GFx,FG,PGn,BoW 1,300.00
11 . . . . 850.00
12 JCo(a&c),FG,PGn 850.00
Becomes:

COWBOY COMICS
July, 1938
13 FG,PGn 1,000.00
14 FG,PGn 900.00
Becomes:

STAR RANGER FUNNIES
Oct., 1938
15 WE,PGn 1,200.00
2-1(16) JCo(a&c) 1,000.00
2-2(17) PGn,JCo,A:Night Hawk. . 900.00
2-3(18) JCo,FG 750.00
2-4(19) A:Kit Carson 750.00
2-5(20) Oct., 1939 . . . . 750.00

STARS AND STRIPES COMICS
Comic Corp of America
(Centaur Publications)
May, 1941
2 PGn,PGn(c),'Called to Colors',
   The Shark,The Voice 3,000.00
3 PGn,PGn(c),O:Dr.Synthe . . 1,700.00
4 PGn,PGn(c),I:The Stars
   & Stripes 1,500.00
5 . . . . 1,000.00
6(5), Dec., 1941 . . . . 1,000.00

STAR STUDDED
Cambridge House, 1945
N# 25 cents (c) price;128 pgs.;
   32 F:stories 400.00
N# The Cadet,Hoot Gibson,
   Blue Beetle 350.00

STARTLING COMICS
Better Publ./Nedor Publ.
June, 1940
1 WE,LF,B&O:Captain Future,
   Mystico, Wonder Man;
   B:Masked Rider 3,500.00
2 Captain Future(c) 1,200.00
3 same 1,000.00

Comics Values Annual

Star Comics #1
© Comic Magazines

4 same 800.00
5 same 750.00
6 same 700.00
7 same 700.00
8 ASh(c),Captain Future 700.00
9 Bondage(c) 700.00
10 O:Fighting Yank 5,000.00
11 Fighting Yank(c) 1,300.00
12 Hitler,Mussolini,Tojo (c) . . . 1,100.00
13 JBi 800.00
14 JBi 800.00
15 Fighting Yank (c) 800.00
16 Bondage(c),O:FourComrades 900.00
17 Fighting Yank (c),
   E:Masked Rider 700.00
18 JBi,B&O:Pyroman 1,200.00
19 Pyroman(c) 600.00
20 Pyroman(c),B:Oracle 600.00
21 HcK,ASh(c)Bondage(c)O:Ape 750.00
22 HcK,ASh(c),Fighting Yank(c) . 600.00
23 HcK,BEv,ASh(c),Pyroman(c) . 600.00
24 HcK,BEv,ASh(c),Fighting
   Yank(c) 600.00
25 HcK,BEv,ASh(c),Pyroman(c) . 600.00
26 BEv,ASh(c),Fighting Yank(c) . 600.00
27 BEv,ASh(c),Pyroman(c) . . . 600.00
28 BEv,ASh(c),Fighting Yank(c) . 600.00
29 BEv,ASh(c),Pyroman(c) . . . 600.00
30 ASh(c),Fighting Yank(c) . . . 600.00
31 ASh(c),Pyroman(c) 600.00
32 ASh(c),Fighting Yank(c) . . . 600.00
33 ASh(c),Pyroman(c) 600.00
34 ASh(c),Fighting Yank(c),
   O:Scarab 600.00
35 ASh(c),Pyroman(c) 650.00
36 ASh(c),Fighting Yank(c) . . . 500.00
37 ASh(c),Bondage (c) 500.00
38 ASh(c),Bondage(c) 500.00
39 ASh(c),Pyroman(c) 500.00
40 ASh(c),E:Captain Future . . . 500.00
41 ASh(c),Pyroman(c) 500.00
42 ASh(c),Fighting Yank(c) . . . 500.00
43 ASh(c),Pyroman(c),
   E:Pyroman 500.00
44 Grl(c),Lance Lewis(c). 900.00
45 Grl(c),I:Tygra 750.00
46 Grl,Grl(c),Bondage(c) 1,200.00
47 ASh(c),Bondage(c). 800.00
48 ASh(c),Lance Lewis(c) 800.00
49 ASh(c),Bondage(c),
   E:Fighting Yank 5,000.00
50 ASh(c),Lance Lewis(c),
   Sea Eagle 800.00
51 ASh(c),Sea Eagle 800.00

GOLDEN AGE

Comics Values Annual — Startling–Strange

Startling Comics #49
© Nedor Publications

52 ASh(c) 800.00
53 ASh(c),Sept., 1948 . . . . 800.00

STARTLING TERROR TALES
Star Publications
May, 1952
10 WW,LbC(c),The Story Starts 1,000.00
11 LbC(c),The Ghost Spider
 of Death 1,500.00
12 LbC(c),White Hand Horror . . . 350.00
13 JyD,LbC(c),Love From
 a Gorgor 375.00
14 LbC(c),Trapped by the
 Color of Blood 350.00
4 LbC(c),Crime at the Carnival . 300.00
5 LbC(c),The Gruesome
 Demon of Terror 300.00
6 LbC(c),Footprints of Death . . 300.00
7 LbC(c),The Case of the
 Strange Murder 300.00
8 RP,LbC(c),Phantom Brigade . . 300.00
9 LbC(c),The Forbidden Tomb . 250.00
10 LbC(c),The Horrible Entity . . . 325.00
11 RP,LbC(c),The Law Will
 Win, July, 1954 . . . . 300.00

STEVE CANYON COMICS
Harvey Publications
Feb., 1948–Dec., 1948
1 MC,BP,O:Steve Canyon 275.00
2 MC,BP 175.00
3 MC,BP,Canyon's Crew 150.00
4 MC,BP,Chase of Death 150.00
5 MC,BP,A:Happy Easter 150.00
6 MC,BP,A:Madame Lynx 165.00

STEVE ROPER
Famous Funnies
April, 1948
1 Reprints newspaper strips . . . 150.00
2 . . . . 75.00
3 . . . . 60.00
4 . . . . 60.00
5 Dec., 1948 . . . . 60.00

STORIES BY FAMOUS AUTHORS ILLUSTRATED
See: FAST FICTION

STORY OF HARRY S. TRUMAN, THE
Democratic National Committee, 1948
N# Giveaway-The Life of Our
 33rd President 200.00

STRAIGHT ARROW
Magazine Enterprises
Feb.–March, 1950
1 OW,B:Straight Arrow & his
 Horse Fury 600.00
2 BP,B&O:Red Hawk 275.00
3 BP,FF(c) 350.00
4 BP,Cave(c) 250.00
5 BP,StraightArrow'sGreatLeap . 250.00
6 BP 225.00
7 BP,The Railroad Invades
 Comanche Country 225.00
8 BP 225.00
9 BP 225.00
10 BP 225.00
11 BP,The Valley of Time 250.00
12 thru 19 BP . . . . @200.00
20 BP,Straight Arrow's
 Great War Shield 225.00
21 BP,O:Fury 250.00
22 BP,FF(c) 275.00
23 BP 150.00
24 BP,The Dragons of Doom . . . 200.00
25 BP 150.00
26 BP 150.00
27 BP 125.00
28 BP,Red Hawk 125.00
29 thru 35 BP . . . . @100.00
36 BP Drug 110.00
37 BP 110.00
38 BP 110.00
39 BP,The Canyon Beasts 125.00
40 BP,Secret of the
 Spanish Specters 125.00
41 BP 100.00
42 BP 100.00
43 BP,I:Blaze 120.00
44 BP 100.00
45 BP 100.00

Straight Arrow #24
© Magazine Enterprises

46 thru 53 BP . . . . @100.00
54 BP,March, 1956 . . . . 100.00

STRANGE CONFESSIONS
Approved Publications (Ziff-Davis)
Spring, 1952
1 EK,Ph(c) 650.00
2 . . . . 400.00
3 EK,Ph(c),Girls reformatory . . . 400.00
4 Girls reformatory 400.00

STRANGE FANTASY
Farrell Publications/ Ajax Comics
Aug., 1952
(2)1 Jungle Princess 600.00
2 . . . . 500.00
3 The Dancing Ghost 500.00
4 Demon in the Dungeon,
 A:Rocketman 500.00
5 Visiting Corpse 300.00
6 . . . . 300.00
7 A:Madam Satan 400.00
8 A:Black Cat 275.00
9 S&K,SD 300.00
10 . . . . 275.00
11 Fearful Things Can Happen
 in a Lonely Place 400.00
12 The Undying Fiend 275.00
13 Terror in the Attic,
 Bondage(c) 400.00
14 Monster in the Building,
 Oct.–Nov., 1954 . . . . 275.00

UNKNOWN WORLD
Fawcett Publications
June, 1952
1 NS(c),Ph(c),Will You Venture
 to Meet the Unknown 800.00
Becomes:

STRANGE STORIES FROM ANOTHER WORLD
Aug., 1952
2 NS(c),Ph(c),Will You?
 Dare You 750.00
3 NS(c),Ph(c),The Dark Mirror . 500.00
4 NS(c),Ph(c),Monsters of
 the Mind 500.00
5 NS(c),Ph(c),Dance of the
 Doomed Feb., 1953 . . . . . . 500.00

STRANGE SUSPENSE STORIES
Fawcett Publications
June, 1952
1 BP,MSy,MBi 1,000.00
2 MBi,GE 550.00
3 MBi,GE(c) 500.00
4 BP 500.00
5 MBi(c),Voodoo(c) 500.00
6 BEv 250.00
7 BEv 275.00
8 AW 275.00
9 . . . . 250.00
10 . . . . 350.00
11 . . . . 200.00
12 . . . . 200.00
13 . . . . 200.00
14 . . . . 250.00
15 AW,BEv(c) 250.00
Charlton Comics
16 . . . . 350.00
17 . . . . 300.00

All comics prices listed are for *Near Mint* condition.

Strange–Super / GOLDEN AGE / Comics Values Annual

18 SD,SD(c) 500.00
19 SD,SD(c) 700.00
20 SD,SD(c) 500.00
21 . . . . 250.00
22 SD(c) 450.00
Becomes:

THIS IS SUSPENSE!
Feb., 1955

23 WW 400.00
24 . . . . 150.00
25 . . . . 100.00
26 . . . . 100.00
Becomes:

STRANGE SUSPENSE STORIES
Oct., 1955

27 . . . . 200.00
28 . . . . 150.00
29 . . . . 150.00
30 . . . . 150.00
31 SD(c) 300.00
32 SD 300.00
33 SD 300.00
34 SD,SD(c) 600.00
35 SD 300.00
36 SD,SD(c) 300.00
37 SD 375.00
38 . . . . 300.00
39 SD 400.00
40 SD 300.00
41 SD 300.00
42 . . . . 90.00
43 . . . . 90.00
44 . . . . 90.00
45 SD 250.00
46 . . . . 90.00
47 SD 250.00
48 SD 250.00
49 . . . . 90.00
50 SD 250.00
51 thru 53 SD . . . . @150.00
54 thru 60 . . . . @75.00
61 thru 74 . . . . @50.00
75 . . . . 250.00
76 . . . . 75.00
77 . . . . 75.00

STRANGE SUSPENSE STORIES
See: LAWBREAKERS

STRANGE TERRORS
**St. John Publishing Co.
June, 1952**

1 The Ghost of Castle
   Karloff, Bondage(c) 700.00
2 Unshackled,Flight intoNowhere 400.00
3 JKu,Ph(c),The Ghost Who
   Ruled Crazy Heights 500.00
4 JKu,Ph(c),Terror from
   the Tombs 700.00
5 JKu,Ph(c),No Escaping
   the Pool of Death 500.00
6 LC,PAM,Bondage(c),Giant . . . 700.00
7 JKu,JKu(c),Cat's Death,Giant . 750.00

STRANGE WORLD OF YOUR DREAMS
**Prize Group
Aug., 1952**

1 S&K(c),What Do They Mean–
   Messages Rec'd in Sleep . . 800.00
2 MMe,S&K(c),Why did I Dream
   That I Was Being Married
   to a Man without a Face? . . . 700.00

GOLDEN AGE

3 S&K(c) 500.00
4 MMe,S&K(c),The Story of
   a Man Who Dreamed a Murder
   that Happened 450.00

Strange Worlds #4
© Avon Periodicals

STRANGE WORLDS
**Avon Periodicals
Nov., 1950**

1 JKu,Spider God of Akka . . . 1,500.00
2 WW,Dara of the Vikings . . . 1,400.00
3 AW&FF,EK(c),WW,JO 2,500.00
4 JO,WW,WW(c),The
   Enchanted Dagger 1,400.00
5 WW,WW(c),JO,Bondage(c);
   Sirens of Space 900.00
6 EK,WW(c),JO,SC,
   Maid o/t Mist 600.00
7 EK, Sabotage on
   Space Station 1 . . . . 500.00
8 JKu,EK,The Metal Murderer . . 500.00
9 The Radium Monsters 500.00
18 JKu 400.00
19 Astounding Super
   Science Fantasies 400.00
20 WW(c),Fighting War Stories . . 125.00
21 EK(c) 75.00
22 EK(c),Sept.–Oct., 1955 . . . . . . 75.00

STRICTLY PRIVATE
**Eastern Color Printing
July, 1942**

1 You're in theArmyNow-Humor . 275.00
2 F:Peter Plink, 1942 . . . . 250.00

STUNTMAN COMICS
**Harvey Publications
April–May, 1946**

1 S&K,O:Stuntman 1,500.00
2 S&K,New Champ of Split-
   Second Action 900.00
3 S&K,Digest sized,Mail Order
   Only, B&W interior,
   Oct.–Nov., 1946 . . . . 1,000.00

SUGAR BOWL COMICS
**Famous Funnies
May, 1948**

1 ATh,ATh(c),The Newest in
   Teen Age! 175.00
2 . . . . 75.00
3 ATh 100.00

4 . . . . 50.00
5 Jan., 1949 . . . . 50.00

SUN FUN KOMIKS
Sun Publications, 1939

1 F:Spineless Sam the
   Sweetheart 400.00

SUNNY, AMERICA'S SWEETHEART
**Fox Features Syndicate
Dec., 1947**

11 AF,AF(c) 1,000.00
12 AF,AF(c) 750.00
13 AF,AF(c) 750.00
14 AF,AF(c) 750.00

SUNSET CARSON
**Charlton Comics
Feb., 1951–Aug., 1951**

1 Painted, Ph(c);Wyoming
   Mail 1,200.00
2 Kit Carson-Pioneer 800.00
3 . . . . 700.00
4 Panhandle Trouble 700.00

SUPER BOOK OF COMICS
Western Publishing Co. 1943

N# Dick Tracy 500.00
1 Dick Tracy, Smuggling 500.00
1a Smilin' Jack 250.00
2 Smitty,Magic Morro 250.00
3 Capt. Midnight 500.00
3a Moon Mullins 200.00
4 Red Ryder,Magic Morro 250.00
4a Smitty 200.00
5 Don Winslow,Magic Morro . . . 250.00
5a DonWinslow,StratosphereJim 250.00
5a Terry & the Pirates 300.00
6 Don Winslow 300.00
6a King of the Royal Mounties . 300.00
7 Little Orphan Annie 200.00
7a Dick Tracy 400.00
8 Dick Tracy 300.00
8a Dan Dunn 200.00
9 Terry & the Pirates 350.00
10 Red Ryder, Magic Morro 250.00

SUPER-BOOK OF COMICS
Western Publishing Co., 1944

1 Dick Tracy (Omar) 250.00
1 Dick Tracy (Hancock) 175.00
2 Bugs Bunny (Omar) 75.00
2 Bugs Bunny (Hancock) 50.00
3 Terry & the Pirates (Omar) . . . 125.00
3 Terry & the Pirates (Hancock) . 100.00
4 Andy Panda (Omar) 75.00
4 Andy Panda (Hancock) 60.00
5 Smokey Stover (Omar) 75.00
5 Smokey Stover (Hancock) 60.00
6 Porky Pig (Omar) 75.00
6 Porky Pig (Hancock) 50.00
7 Smilin' Jack (Omar) 75.00
7 Smilin' Jack (Hancock) 75.00
8 Oswald the Rabbit (Omar) . . . 75.00
8 Oswald the Rabbit (Hancock) . 60.00
9 Alley Oop (Omar) 150.00
9 Alley Oop (Hancock) 135.00
10 Elmer Fudd (Omar) 75.00
10 Elmer Fudd (Hancock) 50.00
11 Little Orphan Annie (Omar) . . 75.00
11 Little Orphan Annie (Hancock) . 75.00
12 Woody Woodpecker (Omar) . . 75.00

Comics Values Annual — GOLDEN AGE — Super: Book–Magician

12 WoodyWoodpecker(Hancock) . 50.00	27 Magic Morro(c) 400.00	116 Smokey Stover(c) 75.00
13 Dick Tracy (Omar) 150.00	28 Jim Ellis(c). 450.00	117 Gasoline Alley(c) 75.00
13 Dick Tracy (Hancock) 125.00	29 Smilin'Jack(c) 400.00	118 Smokey Stover(c) 75.00
14 Bugs Bunny (Omar) 75.00	30 inc.The Sea Hawk 450.00	119 Terry and the Pirates(c) 80.00
14 Bugs Bunny (Hancock) 50.00	31 Dick Tracy(c) 350.00	120 . . . . 75.00
15 Andy Panda (Omar) 60.00	32 Smilin' Jack(c) 365.00	121 . . . . 75.00
15 Andy Panda (Hancock) 50.00	33 Jim Ellis(c). 350.00	
16 Terry & the Pirates (Omar) . . . 150.00	34 Magic Morro(c) 350.00	**SUPER-DOOPER**
16 Terry & the Pirates (Hancock) 125.00	35 thru 40 Dick Tracy(c) . . . . . @350.00	**COMICS**
17 Smokey Stover (Omar) 75.00	41 B:Lightning Jim 300.00	**Able Manufacturing Co., 1946**
17 Smokey Stover (Hancock) 60.00	42 thru 50 Dick Tracy(c) . . . . . @300.00	1 A:Gangbuster 250.00
18 Porky Pig (Omar) 60.00	51 thru 54 Dick Tracy(c) . . . . . @250.00	2 . . . . 200.00
18 Smokey Stover (Hancock) 35.00	55 . . . . 250.00	3 & 4 . . . . @150.00
19 Smilin' Jack (Omar) 75.00	56 . . . . 250.00	5 A:Captain Freedom,Shock
N# Smilin' Jack (Hancock) 60.00	57 Dick Tracy(c) 250.00	Gibson 150.00
20 Oswald the Rabbit (Omar) 35.00	58 Smitty(c) 250.00	6 & 7 same . . . . @150.00
N# Oswald the Rabbit (Hancock) . 20.00	59 . . . . 250.00	8 A:Shock Gibson, 1946 . . . . . . 150.00
21 Gasoline Alley (Omar) 75.00	60 Dick Tracy(c) 275.00	
N# Gasoline Alley (Hancock) 60.00	61 . . . . 235.00	**SUPER DUCK COMICS**
22 Elmer Fudd (Omar) 50.00	62 Flag(c). 235.00	**MLJ Magazines/Close-Up**
N# Elmer Fudd (Hancock) 40.00	63 Dick Tracy(c) 235.00	**(Archie Publ.) Autumn, 1944**
23 Little Orphan Annie (Omar) . . . 75.00	64 Smitty(c) 225.00	1 O:Super Duck, Hitler. 750.00
N# Little Orphan Annie (Hancock) . 60.00	65 Dick Tracy(c) 235.00	2 . . . . 300.00
24 Woody Woodpecker (Omar). . . 50.00	66 Dick Tracy(c) 235.00	3 I:Mr. Monster 250.00
N# WoodyWoodpecker(Hancock) . 40.00	67 Christmas(c) 235.00	4 & 5 . . . . @225.00
25 Dick Tracy (Omar) 135.00	68 Dick Tracy(c) 235.00	6 thru 10 . . . . @200.00
N# Dick Tracy (Hancock) 125.00	69 Dick Tracy(c) 235.00	11 thru 20 . . . . @150.00
26 Bugs Bunny (Omar). 50.00	70 Dick Tracy(c) 235.00	21 thru 40 . . . . @125.00
N# Bugs Bunny (Hancock) 40.00	71 Dick Tracy(c) 200.00	41 thru 60 . . . . @100.00
27 Andy Panda (Omar). 50.00	72 Dick Tracy(c) 200.00	61 thru 94 . . . . @72.00
27 Andy Panda (Hancock) 40.00	73 Smitty(c) 200.00	
28 Terry & the Pirates (Omar) . . . 150.00	74 War Bond(c) 200.00	**SUPER FUNNIES**
28 Terry & the Pirates (Hancock) 125.00	75 Dick Tracy(c) 200.00	**Superior Comics Publishers**
29 Smokey Stover (Omar) 50.00	76 Dick Tracy(c) 200.00	**March, 1954**
29 Smokey Stover (Hancock) 40.00	77 Dick Tracy(c) 200.00	1 Dopey Duck 500.00
30 Porky Pig (Omar). 50.00	78 Smitty(c) 150.00	2 Out of the Booby-Hatch 200.00
30 Porky Pig (Hancock) 40.00	79 Dick Tracy(c) 150.00	Becomes:
N# Bugs Bunny (Hancock) 30.00	80 Smitty(c) 150.00	**SUPER WESTERN**
	81 Dick Tracy(c) 150.00	**FUNNIES**
SUPER CIRCUS	82 Dick Tracy(c) 150.00	**1954**
Cross Publishing Co.	83 Smitty(c) 135.00	3 F:Phantom Ranger 100.00
Jan., 1951	84 Dick Tracy(c) 150.00	4 F:Phantom Ranger,Sept., 1954 100.00
1 Partial Ph(c) 75.00	85 Smitty(c) 135.00	
2 . . . . 60.00	86 All on cover 150.00	**SUPER MAGICIAN**
3 . . . . 50.00	87 All on cover 150.00	**COMICS**
4 . . . . 50.00	88 Dick Tracy(c) 150.00	**Street & Smith, May, 1941**
5 1951 . . . . 50.00	89 Smitty(c) 125.00	1 B:The Mysterious Blackstone . 800.00
	90 Dick Tracy(c) 135.00	2 V:Wild Tribes of Africa 500.00
SUPER COMICS	91 Smitty(c) 125.00	3 V:Oriental Wizard 500.00
Dell Publishing Co.	92 Dick Tracy(c) 135.00	4 V:Quetzal Wizard,O:Transo. . . 475.00
May, 1938	93 Dick Tracy(c) 135.00	5 A:The Moylan Sisters 475.00
1 Dick Tracy,Terry and the	94 Dick Tracy(c) 135.00	6 JaB,JaB(c),The Eddie
Pirates,Smilin'Jack,Smokey	95 thru 99 . . . . @125.00	Cantor story 475.00
Stover,Orphan Annie,etc. . . 3,000.00	100 . . . . 150.00	7 In the House of Skulls 500.00
2 . . . . 1,400.00	101 thru 115 . . . . @120.00	8 A:Abbott & Costello 500.00
3 . . . . 1,200.00		9 V:Duneen the Man-Ape 500.00
4 . . . . 1,100.00		10 V:Pirates o/t Sargasso Sea . . 500.00
5 Gumps(c). 1,000.00		11 JaB(c),V:Fire Wizards. 500.00
6 . . . . 750.00		12 V:Baal 500.00
7 Smokey Stover(c). 750.00		2-1 A:The Shadow 500.00
8 Dick Tracy(c) 750.00		2-2 In the Temple of the
9 . . . . 750.00		10,000 Idols 250.00
10 Dick Tracy(c) 750.00		2-3 Optical Illusion on (c)–
11 . . . . 500.00		turn Jap into Monkey 250.00
12 . . . . 500.00		2-4 V:Cannibal Killers 250.00
13 . . . . 500.00		2-5 V:The Pygmies of Lemuria . 250.00
14 . . . . 500.00		2-6 V;Pirates & Indians 250.00
15 . . . . 500.00		2-7 Can Blackstone Catch the
16 Terry & the Pirates 450.00		Cannonball? 250.00
17 Dick Tracy(c) 450.00		2-8 V:Marabout,B:Red Dragon . . 250.00
18 . . . . 450.00		2-9 . . . . 250.00
19 . . . . 450.00		2-10 Pearl Dives Swallowed By
20 Smilin'Jack(c) 500.00		Sea Demons 250.00
21 B:Magic Morro 400.00		2-11 Blackstone Invades
22 Magic Morro(c) 450.00		Pelican Islands 250.00
23 all star(c) 400.00		
24 Dick Tracy(c) 450.00		
25 Magic Morro(c) 400.00	Super Comics #27	
26 . . . . 400.00	© Cross Publishing Co.	

All comics prices listed are for Near Mint condition.

Super: Magician–Spy

2-12 V:Bubbles of Death	250.00
3-1	275.00
3-2 Bondage(c),Midsummers Eve	250.00
3-3 The Enchanted Garden	250.00
3-4 Fabulous Aztec Treasure	250.00
3-5 A:Buffalo Bill	250.00
3-6 Magic Tricks to Mystify	250.00
3-7 V:Guy Fawkes	250.00
3-8 V:Hindu Spook Maker	250.00
3-9	250.00
3-10 V:The Water Wizards	250.00
3-11 V:The Green Goliath	250.00
3-12 Lady in White	250.00
4-1 Cannibal of Crime	225.00
4-2 The Devil's Castle	225.00
4-3 V:Demons of Golden River	225.00
4-4 V:Dr. Zero	225.00
4-5 Bondage(c)	225.00
4-6 V:A Terror Gang	225.00
4-7	225.00
4-8 Mystery of the Disappearing Horse	225.00
4-9 A Floating Light?	225.00
4-10 Levitation	225.00
4-11 Lost, Strange Land of Shangri	225.00
4-12 I:Nigel Elliman	225.00
5-1 V:Voodoo Wizards of the Everglades,Bondage (c)	225.00
5-2 Treasure of the Florida Keys; Bondage (c)	225.00
5-3 Elliman Battles Triple Crime	225.00
5-4 Can A Human Being Really Become Invisible	225.00
5-5 Mystery of the Twin Pools	225.00
5-6 A:Houdini	225.00
5-7 F:Red Dragon	500.00
5-8 F:Red Dragon, Feb.–March, 1947	500.00

SUPERMOUSE
Standard Comics/Pines Dec., 1948

1 FF,(fa)	350.00
2 FF,(fa)	150.00
3 FF,(fa)	100.00
4 FF,(fa)	100.00
5 FF,(fa)	100.00
6 FF,(fa)	100.00
7 thru 10 (fa)	@50.00
11 thru 20 (fa)	@40.00
21 thru 44 (fa)	@35.00

Super-Mystery Comics Vol. 3 #1
© Street & Smith

GOLDEN AGE

45 (fa),Autumn, 1958	35.00

SUPER-MYSTERY COMICS
Periodical House (Ace Magazines) July, 1940

1 B:Magno,Vulcan,Q-13,Flint of the Mountes	3,600.00
2 Bondage (c)	1,300.00
3 JaB,B:Black Spider	1,000.00
4 O:Davy;A:Captain Gallant	750.00
5 JaB,JM(c),I&B:The Clown	750.00
6 JM,JM(c),V:The Clown	600.00
2-1 JM,JM(c),O:Buckskin, Bondage(c)	600.00
2-2 JM,JM(c),V:The Clown	500.00
2-3 JM,JM(c),V:The Clown	500.00
2-4 JM,JM(c),V:The Nazis	500.00
2-5 JM,JM(c),Bondage(c)	500.00
2-6 JM,JM(c),Bondage(c), 'Foreign Correspondent'	500.00
3-1 B:Black Ace	600.00
3-2 A:Mr, Risk, Bondage(c)	600.00
3-3 HK,HK(c),I:Lancer;B:Dr. Nemesis, The Sword	650.00
3-4 HK	600.00
3-5 HK,LbC,A:Mr. Risk	600.00
3-6 HK,LbC,A:Paul Revere Jr.	600.00
4-1 HK,LbC,A:Twin Must Die	500.00
4-2 A:Mr. Risk	350.00
4-3 Mango out to Kill Davey!	350.00
4-4 Danger Laughs at Mr. Risk	350.00
4-5 A:Mr. Risk	350.00
4-6 RP,A:Mr. Risk	350.00
5-1 RP	350.00
5-2 RP,RP(c),The Riddle of the Swamp-Land Spirit	350.00
5-3 RP,RP(c),The Case of the Whispering Death	350.00
5-4 RP,RP(c)	350.00
5-5 RP,Harry the Hack	350.00
5-6	350.00
6-1	275.00
6-2 RP,A:Mr. Risk	275.00
6-3 Bondage (c)	275.00
6-4 E:Mango;A:Mr. Risk	275.00
6-5 Bondage(c)	275.00
6-6 A:Mr. Risk	275.00
7-1	275.00
7-2 KBa(c)	275.00
7-3 Bondage(c)	275.00
7-4	275.00
7-5	275.00
7-6	275.00
8-1 The Riddle of the Rowboat	275.00
8-2 Death Meets a Train	275.00
8-3 The Man Who Couldn't Die	275.00
8-4 RP(c)	275.00
8-5 GT,MMe,Staged for Murder	275.00
8-6 Unlucky Seven,July, 1949	275.00

ARMY AND NAVY COMICS
Street & Smith, May, 1941

1 Hawaii is Calling You,Capt. Fury,Nick Carter	750.00
2 Private Rock V;Hitler	600.00
3 The Fighting Fourth	600.00
4 The Fighting Irish	600.00
5 I:Super Snipe	700.00

Becomes:

SUPERSNIPE COMICS
Oct., 1942

6 A "Comic" With A Sense of Humor	1,300.00
7 A:Wacky, Rex King	700.00
8 Axis Powers & Satan(c),Hitler(c)	1,000.00

Comics Values Annual

9 Hitler Voodoo Doll (c)	1,100.00
10 Lighting (c)	700.00
11 A:Little Nemo	700.00
12 Football(c)	700.00
2-1 B:Huck Finn	900.00
2-2 Battles Shark	500.00
2-3 Battles Dinosaur	500.00
2-4 Baseball(c)	500.00
2-5 Battles Dinosaur	500.00
2-6 A:Pochontas	500.00
2-7 A:Wing Woo Woo	500.00
2-8 A:Huck Finn	500.00
2-9 Dotty Loves Trouble	500.00
2-10 Assists Farm Labor Shortage	500.00
2-11 Dotty & the Jelly Beans	500.00
2-12 Statue of Liberty	500.00
3-1 Ice Skating(c)	400.00
3-2 V:Pirates(c)	400.00
3-3 Baseball(c)	400.00
3-4 Jungle(c)	400.00
3-5 Learn Piglatin	400.00
3-6 Football Hero	400.00
3-7 Saves Girl From Grisley	400.00
3-8 Rides a Wild Horse	400.00
3-9 Powers Santa's Sleigh	400.00
3-10 Plays Basketball	400.00
3-11 Is A Baseball Pitcher	400.00
3-12 Flies with the Birds	400.00
4-1 Catches A Whale	300.00
4-2 Track & Field Athlete	300.00
4-3 Think Machine(c)	300.00
4-4 Alpine Skiier	300.00
4-5 Becomes a Boxer	300.00
4-6 Race Car Driver	300.00
4-7 Bomber(c)	300.00
4-8 Baseball Star	300.00
4-9 Football Hero	300.00
4-10 Christmas(c)	300.00
4-11 Artic Adventure	300.00
4-12 The Ghost Remover	300.00
5-1 Aug.–Sept., 1949	300.00

SUPER SPY
Centaur Publications Oct.–Nov., 1940

1 O:Sparkler	1,500.00
2 A:Night Hawk, Drew Ghost, Tim Blain, S.S. Swanson the Inner Circle, Duke Collins, Gentlemen of Misfortune	900.00

Superworld Comics #1
© Hugo Gernsback

CVA Page 464 — All comics prices listed are for *Near Mint* condition.

GOLDEN AGE

SUPER WESTERN COMICS
Youthful Magazines Aug., 1950
1 BP,BP,(c),B;Buffalo Bill,Wyatt
 Earp,CalamityJane,SamSlade 150.00
2 thru 4 March, 1951 ...... @100.00

SUPER WESTERN FUNNIES
See: SUPER FUNNIES

SUPERWORLD COMICS
Komos Publications (Hugo Gernsback) April, 1940
1 FP,FP(c),B:MilitaryPowers,BuzzAllen
 Smarty Artie, Alibi Alige .. 10,000.00
2 FP,FP(c),A:Mario 6,000.00
3 FP,FP(c),V:Vest Wearing
 Giant Grasshoppers 4,000.00

SUSPENSE COMICS
Et Es Go Mag. Inc. (Continental Magazines) Dec., 1945
1 LbC, Bondage(c),B:Grey
 Mask 6,500.00
2 DRi,I:The Mask 4,000.00
3 LbC,ASh(c),Bondage(c) .. 20,000.00
4 LbC,LbC(c),Bondage(c) ... 3,000.00
5 LbC,LbC(c) 3,000.00
6 LbC,LbC(c),The End of
 the Road 3,000.00
7 LbC,LbC(c) 2,500.00
8 LbC,LbC(c) 6,500.00
9 LbC,LbC(c) 2,500.00
10 RP,LbC,LbC(c) 2,500.00
11 RP,LbC,LbC(c),Satan(c) .. 5,000.00
12 LbC,LbC(c),Dec., 1946 ... 2,500.00

SUSPENSE DETECTIVE
Fawcett Publications June, 1952
1 GE,MBi,MBi(c),Death Poised
 to Strike 650.00
2 GE,MSy 400.00
3 A Furtive Footstep 350.00
4 MBi,MSy,Bondage(c),A Blood
 Chilling Scream 350.00
5 MSy,MSy(c),MBi,A Hair-Trigger
 from Death, March, 1953 ... 350.00

SUZIE COMICS
See: TOP-NOTCH COMICS

SWEENEY
Standard Comics June, 1949
4 Buzz Sawyer's Pal 100.00
5 Sept., 1949 .... 80.00

SWEETHEART DIARY
Fawcett Winter, 1949
1 .... 200.00
2 .... 100.00
3 WW 250.00
4 WW 250.00
5 thru 10 .... @75.00
11 thru 14 .... @50.00

SWEETHEART DIARY
Charlton Comics Jan., 1953
32 .... 60.00
33 thru 40 .... @50.00
41 thru 65 .... @30.00

SWEET HEART
See: CAPTAIN MIDNIGHT

SWEET LOVE
Harvey Publications (Home Comics) Sept., 1949
1 Ph(c) 125.00
2 Ph(c) 60.00
3 BP 50.00
4 Ph(c) 40.00
5 BP,JKa,Ph(c) 100.00

SWEET SIXTEEN
Parents' Magazine Group Aug.–Sept., 1946
1 Van Johnson story 250.00
2 Alan Ladd story 200.00
3 Rip Taylor 150.00
4 Elizabeth Taylor ph(c) 250.00
5 Gregory Peck story (c) 150.00
6 Dick Haymes(c) 150.00
7 Ronald Reagan(c) & story .. 300.00
8 Shirley Jones(c) 125.00
9 William Holden(c) 100.00
10 James Stewart(c) 150.00
11 .... 100.00
12 Bob Cummings(c) 100.00
13 Robert Mitchum(c) 150.00

SWIFT ARROW
Farrell Publications(Ajax) Feb.–March, 1954
1 Lone Rider's Redskin Brother 175.00
2 .... 100.00
3 .... 75.00
4 .... 75.00
5 Oct.–Nov., 1954 .... 75.00

(2nd Series) April, 1957
1 .... 90.00
2 B:Lone Rider 60.00
3 Sept., 1957 .... 50.00

TAFFY
Orbit Publications/Rural Home/ Taffy Publications March–April, 1945
1 LbC(c),(fa),Bondage(c) 800.00
2 LbC(c),(fa) 350.00
3 (fa) 150.00
4 (fa) 150.00
5 LbC(c),A:Van Johnson 250.00
6 A:Perry Como 150.00
7 A:Dave Clark 150.00
8 A:Glen Ford 150.00
9 A:Lon McCallister 150.00
10 A:John Hodiak 150.00
11 A:Mickey Rooney 165.00
12 Feb., 1948 .... 150.00

TAILSPIN
Spotlight Publications Nov., 1944
N# LbC(c),A:Firebird 350.00

TALES FROM THE CRYPT
See: CRIME PATROL

TALES FROM THE TOMB
See: DELL GIANTS

TALES OF HORROR
Toby Press/Minoan Publ. Corp June, 1952–Oct., 1954
1 Demons of the Underworld ... 500.00
2 What was the Thing in
 the Pool?,Torture 400.00
3 The Big Snake 300.00
4 The Curse of King Kala! 300.00
5 Hand of Fate 300.00
6 The Fiend of Flame 300.00
7 Beast From The Deep 300.00
8 The Snake that Held A
 City Captive 300.00
9 It Came From the Bottom
 of the World 350.00
10 The Serpent Strikes 300.00
11 Death Flower? 350.00
12 Guaranteed to Make Your
 Hair Stand on End,Torture . 350.00
13 Ghost with a Torch 350.00

TALES OF TERROR
Toby Press, 1952
1 Just A Bunch of Hokey
 Hogwash 300.00

Tales of Terror Annual #2
© E.C. Comics

TALES OF TERROR ANNUAL
E.C. Comics 1951
N# AF 6,000.00
2 AF 3,000.00
3 .... 2,700.00

TALLY-HO COMICS
Baily Publishing Co. Dec., 1944
N# FF,A:Snowman 500.00

GOLDEN AGE

Target–Teen-Age

Target Comics Vol. 3 #4
© Star Publications

TARGET COMICS
**Funnnies Inc./Novelty Publ./
Premium Group/Curtis
Circulation Co./Star
Publications, Feb., 1940**
1 BEv,JCo,CBu,JSm;B,O&I:Manowar,
White Streak,Bull's-Eye;B:City
Editor,High Grass Twins,T-Men,
Rip Rory,Fantastic Feature
Films, Calling 2-R 7,500.00
2 BEv,JSm,JCo,CBu,White
Streak(c) 4,000.00
3 BEv,JSm,JCo,CBu 2,500.00
4 JSm,JCo 2,500.00
5 CBu,BW,O:White Streak .. 6,500.00
6 CBu,BW,White Streak(c) .. 2,700.00
7 CBu,BW,BW(c),V:Planetoid
Stories,Space Hawk(c) .. 7,500.00
8 CBu,BW,White Shark(c) ... 1,900.00
9 CBu,BW,White Shark(c) ... 1,900.00
10 CBu,BW,JK(c),The
Target(c) 2,500.00
11 BW,The Target(c) 2,100.00
12 BW,same 2,000.00
2-1 BW,CBu 1,400.00
2-2 BW,BoW(c) 1,200.00
2-3 BW,BoW(c),The Target(c) . 800.00
2-4 BW,B:Cadet 800.00
2-5 BW,BoW(c),The Target(c) . 800.00
2-6 BW,The Target(c) 750.00
2-7 BW,The Cadet(c) 750.00
2-8 BW,same 750.00
2-9 BW,The Target(c) 750.00
2-10 BW,same 1,300.00
2-11 BW,The Cadet(c) 800.00
2-12 BW,same 800.00
3-1 BW,same 800.00
3-2 BW 800.00
3-3 BW,The Target(c) 800.00
3-4 BW,The Cadet(c) 800.00
3-5 BW 800.00
3-6 BW,War Bonds(c) 800.00
3-7 BW 800.00
3-8 BW,War Bonds(c) 800.00
3-9 BW 800.00
3-10 BW 800.00
3-11 .... 200.00
3-12 .... 200.00
4-1 JJo(c) 135.00
4-2 ERy(c) 135.00
4-3 AVi 135.00
4-4 .... 135.00
4-5 APl(c),Statue of Liberty(c)... 150.00
4-6 BW 135.00
4-7 AVi 135.00
4-8,Christmas(c) 135.00
4-9 .... 135.00
4-10 .... 135.00
4-11 .... 135.00
4-12 .... 135.00
5-1 .... 125.00
5-2 The Target 125.00
5-3 Savings Checkers(c) 125.00
5-4 War Bonds Ph(c) 125.00
5-5 thru 5-12 .... @125.00
6-1 The Target(c) 125.00
6-2 .... 125.00
6-3 Red Cross(c) 125.00
6-4 .... 125.00
6-5 Savings Bonds(c) 150.00
6-6 The Target(c) 125.00
6-7 The Cadet(c) 125.00
6-8 AFa 125.00
6-9 The Target(c) 125.00
6-10 .... 125.00
6-11 .... 125.00
6-12 .... 125.00
7-1 .... 125.00
7-2 Bondage(c) 150.00
7-3 The Target(c) 125.00
7-4 DRi,The Cadet(c) 125.00
7-5 .... 125.00
7-6 DRi(c) 125.00
7-7 The Cadet(c) 125.00
7-8 DRi(c) 125.00
7-9 The Cadet(c) 125.00
7-10 DRi,DRi(c) 125.00
7-11 .... 125.00
7-12 JH(c) 125.00
8-1 .... 110.00
8-2 DRi,DRi(c),BK 110.00
8-3 DRi,The Cadet(c) 110.00
8-4 DRi,DRi(c) 110.00
8-5 DRi,The Cadet(c) 110.00
8-6 DRi,DRi(c) 110.00
8-7 BK,DRi,DRi(c) 110.00
8-8 DRi,The Cadet(c) 110.00
8-9 DRi,The Cadet(c) 110.00
8-10 DRi,KBa,LbC(c) 400.00
8-11 DRi,The Cadet 125.00
8-12 DRi,The Cadet 125.00
9-1 DRi,LbC(c) 400.00
9-2 DRi 125.00
9-3 DRi,Bondage(c),The Cadet(c) 150.00
9-4 DRi,LbC(c) 400.00
9-5 DRi,Baseball(c) 125.00
9-6 DRi,LbC(c) 400.00
9-7 DRi 125.00
9-8 DRi,LbC(c) 400.00
9-9 DRi,Football(c) 125.00
9-10 DRi,LbC(c) 400.00
9-11,The Cadet 125.00
9-12 LbC(c),Gems(c) 450.00
10-1,The Cadet 125.00
10-2 LbC(c) 400.00
10-3 LbC(c) 400.00
Becomes:

TARGET WESTERN ROMANCES
**Star Publications
Oct.–Nov., 1949**
106 LbC(c),The Beauty Scar.... 500.00
107 LbC(c),The Brand Upon His
Heart 450.00

TARZAN
**Dell Publishing Co.
Jan.–Feb., 1948**
1 V:White Savages of Vari.... 1,900.00
2 Captives of Thunder Valley ... 900.00
3 Dwarfs of Didona 600.00
4 The Lone Hunter 600.00

Tarzan #8
© Dell Publishing Co.

5 The Men of Greed 600.00
6 Outlaws of Pal-ul-Don 500.00
7 Valley of the Monsters 500.00
8 The White Pygmies 500.00
9 The Men of A-Lur 500.00
10 Treasure of the Bolgani 500.00
11 The Sable Lion 400.00
12 The Price of Peace 400.00
13 B:Lex Barker photo(c) 350.00
14 Lex Barker ph(c) 350.00
15 Lex Barker ph(c) 350.00
16 Lex Barker ph(c) 300.00
17 Lex Barker ph(c) 300.00
18 Lex Barker ph(c) 300.00
19 Lex Barker ph(c) 300.00
20 Lex Barker ph(c) 300.00
21 thru 30 Lex Barker ph(c)... @250.00
31 thru 54 E:L.Barker ph(c)... @200.00
55 thru 70 .... @150.00
71 thru 79 .... @100.00
80 thru 90 B:ScottGordonPh(c) . @75.00
91 thru 99 .... @65.00
100 .... 75.00
101 thru 110 E:S.GordonPh(c).. @65.00
111 thru 120 .... @50.00
121 thru 131 .... @50.00

TEENA
Standard Comics, 1949
20 .... 60.00
21 .... 60.00
22 .... 60.00

TEEN-AGE DIARY SECRETS
**St. John Publishing Co.
Oct., 1949**
6 MB,PH(c) 350.00
7 MB,PH(c) 300.00
8 MB,PH(c) 250.00
9 MB,PH(c) 300.00
Becomes:

DIARY SECRETS
Feb., 1952
10 MB 250.00
11 MB 200.00
12 thru 19 MB .... @150.00
20 MB,JKu 200.00
21 thru 28 MB .... @100.00
29 MB,Comics Code 75.00
30 MB 75.00

GOLDEN AGE

Teen-Age–Terrors

Teena #21
© *Standard Comics*

TEGRA, JUNGLE EMPRESS
See: ZEGRA, JUNGLE EMPRESS

TELEVISION COMICS
Animated Cartoons (Standard Comics), Feb., 1950
5 Humorous Format,I:Willie Nilly 100.00
6 . . . . 75.00
7 . . . . 75.00
8 May, 1950 . . . . 75.00

TELEVISION PUPPET SHOW
Avon Periodicals, 1950
1 F:Sparky Smith,Spotty, Cheeta, Speedy 250.00
2 Nov., 1950 . . . . 150.00

TELL IT TO THE MARINES
Toby Press, March, 1952
1 I:Spike & Pat 250.00
2 A:Madame Cobra 150.00
3 Spike & Bat on a Commando Raid! 100.00
4 Veil Dancing(c) 75.00
5 . . . . 75.00
6 To Paris 60.00
7 Ph(c),The Chinese Bugle 60.00
8 Ph(c),V:Communists in South Korea 60.00
9 Ph(c) 60.00
10 . . . . 60.00
11 . . . . 60.00
12 . . . . 60.00
13 John Wayne Ph(c) 135.00
14 Ph(c) 60.00
15 Ph(c),July, 1955 . . . . 60.00

TENDER ROMANCE
Key Publications Dec., 1953
1 . . . . 200.00
2 . . . . 125.00
Becomes:

IDEAL ROMANCE
April, 1954
3 . . . . 75.00
4 thru 8 . . . . @50.00
Becomes:

DIARY CONFESSIONS
May, 1955
9 . . . . 60.00
10 . . . . 40.00

TERRIFIC COMICS
See: HORRIFIC

TERRIFIC COMICS
Et Es Go Mag. Inc./ Continental Magazines Jan., 1944
1 LbC,DRi(c),F:Kid Terrific Drug 5,000.00
2 LcC,ASh(c),B:Boomerang, 'Comics' McCormic 3,500.00
3 LbC,LbC(c) 3,500.00
4 LbC,RP(c) 6,000.00
5 LbC,BF,ASh(c),Bondage(c) . 8,000.00
6 LbC,LbC(c),BF,Nov.,1944 . . 3,200.00

TERROR ILLUSTRATED
E.C. Comics Nov.–Dec., 1955
1 JCr,GE,Grl,JO,RC(c) 250.00
2 Spring, 1956 . . . . 150.00

TERRIFYING TALES
Star Publications Jan., 1953
11 LbC,LbC(c),'TyrantsofTerror' . . 700.00
12 LbC,LbC(c),'Bondage(c), 'Jungle Mystery' 600.00
13 LbC(c),Bondage(c),'The Death-Fire,Devil Head(c) . . . 750.00
14 LbC(c),Bondage(c),'The Weird Idol' 500.00
15 LbC(c),'The Grim Secret', April, 1954 . . . . 500.00
Becomes:

JUNGLE THRILLS
Star Publications Feb., 1952
16 LbC(c),'Kingdom of Unseen Terror' 550.00
Becomes:

TERRORS OF THE JUNGLE
May, 1952
17 LbC(c),Bondage(c) 700.00
18 LbC(c),Strange Monsters 400.00
19 JyD,LbC(c),Bondage(c),The Golden Ghost Gorilla 400.00
20 JyD,LbC(c),The Creeping Scourge 400.00
21 LbC(c),Evil Eyes of Death! . . . 450.00
4 JyD,LbC(c),Morass of Death . 400.00
5 JyD,LbC(c),Bondage(c), Savage Train 425.00
6 JyD,LbC(c),Revolt of the Jungle Monsters 425.00
7 JyD,LbC(c) 450.00
8 JyD,LbC(c),Death's Grim Reflection 450.00
9 JyD,LbC(c),Doom to Evil-Doers 450.00
10 JyD,LbC(c),Black Magic, Sept., 1954 . . . . 450.00

TEEN-AGE ROMANCES
St. John Publishing Co. Jan., 1949
1 MB(c),MB 500.00
2 MB(c),MB 300.00
3 MB(c),MB 350.00
4 Ph(c) 300.00
5 MB,Ph(c) 300.00
6 MB,Ph(c) 300.00
7 MB,Ph(c) 300.00
8 MB,Ph(c) 300.00
9 MB,MB(c),JKu 325.00
10 thru 27 MB,MB(c),JKu . . . . @250.00
28 thru 30 . . . . @100.00
31 thru 34 MB(c) . . . . @100.00
35 thru 42 MB(c),MB . . . . . . @125.00
43 MB(c),MB,Comics Code 150.00
44 MB(c),MB 150.00
45 MB(c),MB 150.00

TEEN-AGE TEMPTATIONS
St. John Publishing Co. Oct., 1952
1 MB(c),MB 600.00
2 MB(c),MB 200.00
3 MB(c),MB 250.00
4 MB(c),MB 250.00
5 MB(c),MB 250.00
6 MB(c),MB 250.00
7 MB(c),MB 250.00
8 MB(c),MB,Drug 275.00
9 MB(c),MB 250.00
Becomes:

GOING STEADY
Dec., 1954
10 MB(c),MB 150.00
11 MB(c),MB 125.00
12 MB(c),MB 125.00
13 MB(c),MB 125.00
14 MB(c),MB 125.00

TEENIE WEENIES, THE
Ziff-Davis Publishing Co. 1951
10 . . . . 250.00
11 . . . . 250.00

TEEN LIFE
See: YOUNG LIFE

Terrors of the Jungle #4
© *Star Publications*

All comics prices listed are for *Near Mint* condition.

CVA Page 467

GOLDEN AGE

Terry–This Magazine — Comics Values Annual

BOY EXPLORERS
1 S&K(c),S&K,The Cadet 1,000.00
2 S&K(c),S&K............. 1,200.00
Becomes:

TERRY AND THE PIRATES
April, 1947
3 S&K,MC(c),MC,Terry and
  Dragon Lady......... 500.00
4 S&K,MC(c),MC............ 300.00
5 S&K,MC(c),MC,BP,
  Chop-Chop(c)........... 175.00
6 S&K,.MC(c),MC 175.00
7 S&K,MC(c),MC,BP.......... 175.00
8 S&K,MC(c),MC,BP 175.00
9 S&K,MC(c),MC,BP.......... 175.00
10 S&K,MC(c),MC,BP......... 175.00
11 S&K,MC(c),MC,BP,
   A:Man in Black.......... 150.00
12 S&K,MC(c),MC,BP......... 150.00
13 S&K,MC(c),MC,Belly Dancers 150.00
14 thru 20 S&K,MC(c),MC.... @125.00
21 thru 26 S&K,MC(c),MC.... @110.00
27 Charlton Comics 100.00
28....................... 100.00

TERRY-BEARS COMICS
**St. John Publishing Co.
June, 1952**
1 .... 100.00
2 & 3 .... @50.00

TERRY-TOONS COMICS
**Select, Timely, Marvel,
St. Johns, 1942**
1 Paul Terry (fa) 2,500.00
2 .... 800.00
3 thru 6 .... @500.00
7 Hitler,Hirohito,Mussolini(c) 700.00
8 thru 20 .... @400.00
21 thru 37 .... @300.00
38 I&(c):Mighty Mouse..... 1,600.00
39 Mighty Mouse 450.00
40 thru 49 All Mighty Mouse .. @250.00
50 I:Heckle & Jeckle....... 600.00
51 thru 60 .... @150.00
61 thru 70 .... @100.00
71 thru 86 .... @100.00

TEXAN, THE
**St. John Publishing Co.
Aug., 1948**
1 GT,F:Buckskin Belle,The Gay
  Buckaroo,Mustang Jack 200.00
2 GT 125.00
3 BLb(c) 100.00
4 MB,MB(c) 175.00
5 MB,MB(c),Mystery Rustlers
  of the Rio Grande 175.00
6 MB(c),Death Valley
  Double-Cross 125.00
7 MB,MB(c),Comanche Justice
  Strikes at Midnight 175.00
8 MB,MB(c),Scalp Hunters
  Hide their Tracks 175.00
9 MB(c),Ghost Terror of
  the Blackfeet 175.00
10 MB,MB(c),Treason Rides
   the Warpath 125.00
11 MB,MB(c),Hawk Knife 175.00
12 MB 250.00
13 MB,Doublecross at Devil'sDen 175.00
14 MB,Ambush at Buffalo Trail .. 175.00
15 MB,Twirling Blades Tame
   Treachery 175.00
Becomes:

FIGHTIN' TEXAN
Sept., 1952
16 GT,Wanted Dead or Alive ... 125.00
17 LC,LC(c);Killers Trail,
   Dec., 1952 .... 100.00

TEX FARRELL
**D.S. Publishing Co.
March–April, 1948**
1 Pride of the Wild West 175.00

TEX GRANGER
See: CALLING ALL BOYS

TEX RITTER WESTERN
**Fawcett Publications/
Charlton Comics
Oct., 1950–May, 1959**
1 Ph(c),B:Tex Ritter, his Horse
  White Flash, his dog Fury, and
  his mom Nancy 900.00
2 Ph(c),Vanishing Varmints 400.00
3 Ph(c),Blazing Six-Guns 300.00
4 Ph(c),The Jaws of Terror ... 225.00
5 Ph(c),Bullet Trail 225.00
6 Ph(c),Killer Bait 225.00
7 Ph(c),Gunsmoke Revenge ... 200.00
8 Ph(c),Lawless Furnace Valley 200.00
9 Ph(c),The Spider's Web 200.00
10 Ph(c),The Ghost Town..... 200.00
11 Ph(c),Saddle Conquest 200.00
12 Ph(c),Prairie Inferno....... 175.00
13 Ph(c)................. 175.00
14 Ph(c)................. 175.00
15 Ph(c)................. 175.00
16 thru 19 Ph(c)........... @175.00
20 Ph(c),Stagecoach To Danger . 175.00
21 Ph(c),................. 200.00
22 Panic at Diamond B....... 150.00
23 A:Young Falcon 125.00
24 A:Young Falcon 125.00
25 A:Young Falcon 125.00
26 thru 38 .... @100.00
39 AW,AW(c).............. 100.00
40 thru 46 .... @90.00

THING!, THE
**Song Hits/Capitol Stories/
Charlton Comics, Feb., 1952**
1 Horror 1,300.00

*The Thing! #2
© Charlton Comics*

2 Crazy King(c) 750.00
3 .... 750.00
4 AFa(c),I Was A Zombie 600.00
5 LM(c),Severed Head(c)..... 650.00
6 .... 600.00
7 Fingenail to Eye(c) 850.00
8 .... 650.00
9 Severe cruelty 1,000.00
10 Devil(c) 600.00
11 SC,Cleaver, eye injury 800.00
12 SD,SD(c),Neck Blood
   Sucking 1,200.00
13 SD,SD(c) 1,200.00
14 SD,SD(c) torture 1,200.00
15 SD,SD(c).............. 1,200.00
16 Eye Torture 550.00
17 BP,SD(c).............. 1,000.00
Becomes:

BLUE BEETLE
Feb., 1955
18 America's Fastest Moving
   Crusader Against Crime.... 250.00
19 JKa,Lightning Fast........ 275.00
20 JKa 275.00
21 The Invincible 200.00
Becomes:

MR. MUSCLES
March, 1956
22 World's Most Perfect Man 75.00
23 Aug., 1956.............. 50.00

THIS IS SUSPENSE
See: LAWBREAKERS

THIS IS WAR
**Standard Comics
July, 1952**
5 ATh,Show Them How To Die . 150.00
6 ATh,Make Him A Soldier 125.00
7 One Man For Himself 75.00
8 Miracle on Massacre Hill 75.00
9 ATh,May, 1953 .... 125.00

THIS IS SUSPENSE!
See: STRANGE
SUSPENSE STORIES

THIS MAGAZINE IS
HAUNTED
**Fawcett Publications/
Charlton Comics
Oct., 1951**
1 MBi,F:Doctor Death 850.00
2 GE 650.00
3 MBi,Quest of the Vampire ... 400.00
4 BP,The Blind, The Doomed
  and the Dead 400.00
5 BP,GE,The Slithering Horror
  of Skontong Swamp! 650.00
6 Secret of the Walking Dead .. 300.00
7 The Man Who Saw Too Much . 300.00
8 The House in the Web 300.00
9 The Witch of Tarlo........ 300.00
10 I Am Dr Death,
   Severed Head(c) 500.00
11 BP,Touch of Death 300.00
12 BP................... 300.00
13 BP,Severed Head(c) 500.00
14 BP,Horrors of the Damned ... 300.00
15 DG(c) 250.00
16 SD(c) 500.00
17 SD,SD(c).............. 550.00
18 SD,SD(c).............. 500.00
19 SD(c)................. 450.00
20 SMz(c)................ 265.00

CVA Page 468 — All comics prices listed are for *Near Mint* condition.

GOLDEN AGE

21 SD(c). 400.00
Becomes:
DANGER AND ADVENTURE
Feb., 1955
22 The Viking King,F:Ibis the
    Invincible 150.00
23 F:Nyoka the Jungle Girl
    Comics Code 125.00
24 DG&AA(c) 100.00
25 thru 27 . . . . @60.00
Becomes:
ROBIN HOOD AND HIS MERRY MEN
April, 1956
28 . . . . 75.00
29 thru 37 . . . . @60.00
38 SD,Aug., 1958 . . . . 125.00

3-D-ELL
Dell Publishing Co., 1953
1 Rootie Kazootie 500.00
2 Rootie Kazootie 450.00
3 Flunkey Louise 450.00

THREE RING COMICS
**Spotlight Publishers
March, 1945**
1 Funny Animal 200.00

THREE STOOGES
**Jubilee Publ.
Feb., 1949**
1 JKu,Infinity(c) 1,500.00
2 JKu,On the Set of the
    'The Gorilla Girl' 1,000.00
St. John Publishing Co.
1JKu,'Bell Bent for
    Treasure, Sept., 1953 . . . . . . 900.00
2 JKu. 650.00
3 JKu,3D 650.00
4 JKu,Medical Mayhem 500.00
5 JKu,Shempador-Matador
    Supreme 500.00
6 JKu, ... 500.00
7 JKu,Ocotber, 1954 . . . . 500.00

THRILLING COMICS
**Better Publ./Nedor/
Standard Comics
Feb., 1940**
1 B&O:Doc Strange,B:Nickie
    Norton 4,000.00
2 B:Rio Kid,Woman in Red
    Pinocchio 1,800.00
3 B:Lone Eagle,The Ghost . . . 1,000.00
4 Dr Strange(c) 800.00
5 Bondage(c) 775.00
6 Dr Strange(c) 750.00
7 Dr Strange(c). 1,000.00
8 V:Pirates 750.00
9 ASh,Bondage(c) 750.00
10 V:Nazis 750.00
11 ASh(c),V:Nazis. 650.00
12 ASh(c). 600.00
13 ASh(c),Bondage(c). 700.00
14 ASh(c). 650.00
15 ASh(c),V:Nazis. 650.00
16 Bondage(c) 700.00
17 Dr Strange(c). 700.00
18 Dr Strange(c). 700.00
19 I&O:American Crusader. . . . 750.00
20 Bondage(c) 700.00
21 American Crusader(c) 550.00
22 Bondage(c) 575.00

*Thrilling Comics #19
© Fawcett Publications*

23 American Crusader 550.00
24 I:Mike in Doc Strange. 550.00
25 DR Strange(c) 550.00
26 Dr Strange(c). 550.00
27 Bondage(c) 575.00
28 Bondage(c) 575.00
29 E:Rio Kid;Bondage(c). 575.00
30 Bondage(c) 575.00
31 Dr Strange(c). 500.00
32 Dr Strange(c). 500.00
33 Dr Strange(c). 500.00
34 Dr Strange(c). 500.00
35 Dr Strange. 500.00
36 ASh(c),B:Commando 525.00
37 BO,ASh(c) 500.00
38 ASh(c) 500.00
39 ASh(c),E:American Crusader . 500.00
40 ASh(c) 500.00
41 ASh(c),F:American Crusader,
    Hitler 1,000.00
42 ASh(c) 400.00
43 ASh(c) 400.00
44 ASh(c),Hitler(c) 900.00
45 EK,ASh(c) 400.00
46 ASh(c) 400.00
47 ASh(c) 400.00
48 EK,ASh(c) 400.00
49 ASh(c) 400.00
50 ASh(c) 400.00
51 ASh(c) 400.00
52 ASh(c),E:Th Ghost;
    Peto-Bondage(c) 450.00
53 ASh(c),B:Phantom Detective . 400.00
54 ASh(c),Bondage(c). 400.00
55 ASh(c),E:Lone Eagle 350.00
56 ASh(c),B:Princess Pantha . . . 550.00
57 ASh(c) 450.00
58 ASh(c) 450.00
59 ASh(c) 450.00
60 ASh(c) 450.00
61 ASh(c),GRi,A:Lone Eagle. . . . 450.00
62 ASh(c) 450.00
63 ASh(c),GT 450.00
64 ASh(c) 450.00
65 ASh(c),E:Commando Cubs,
    Phantom Detective 450.00
66 ASh(c) 450.00
67 FF,ASh(c) 550.00
68 FF,ASh(c) 550.00
69 FF,ASh(c) 550.00
70 FF,ASh(c) 550.00
71 FF,ASh(c) 550.00
72 FF,ASh(c),Sea Eagle 550.00
73 FF,ASh(c) 550.00

74 E:Princess Pantha;
    B:Buck Ranger. 350.00
75 B:Western Front. 200.00
76 Western. 200.00
77 ASh(c) 200.00
78 Bondage(c) 225.00
79 BK. 200.00
80 JSe,BE,April, 1951. . . . . 200.00

*Thrilling Crime Cases #49
© Standard Comics*

THRILLING CRIME CASES
**Star Publications
June–July, 1950**
41 LbC(c),The Unknowns 350.00
42 LbC(c),The Gunmaster 325.00
43 LbC,LbC(c),The Chameleon. . 350.00
44 LbC(c),Sugar Bowl Murder. . . 350.00
45 LbC(c),Maze of Murder 350.00
46 LbC,LbC(c),Modern
    Communications 300.00
47 LbC(c),The Careless Killer . . . 300.00
48 LbC(c),Road Black. 300.00
49 LbC(c),The Poisoner 500.00
Becomes:
SHOCKING MYSTERY CASES
Sept., 1952–Oct., 1954
50 JyD,LbC(c),Dead Man's
    Revenge. 500.00
51 JyD,LbC(c),A Murderer's
    Reward 350.00
52 LbC(c),The Carnival Killer . . . 350.00
53 LbC(c),The Long Shot of Evil . 350.00
54 LbC(c),Double-Cross of Death 350.00
55 LbC(c),Return from Death . . . 350.00
56 LbC(c),The Chase 375.00
57 LbC(c),Thrilling Cases 350.00
58 LbC(c),Killer at Large. 350.00
59 LbC(c),Relentless Huntdown. . 350.00
60 LbC(c),Lesson of the Law . . . 350.00

THRILLING ROMANCES
**Standard Comics
Dec., 1949**
5 Ph(c) 125.00
6 Ph(c) 75.00
7 Ph(c),JSe,BE 85.00
8 Ph(c) 75.00
9 Ph(c),GT 90.00
10 Ph(c),JSe,BE 90.00
11 Ph(c),JSe,BE 90.00

All comics prices listed are for Near Mint condition.

Thrilling–Tip Top

GOLDEN AGE

Comics Values Annual

12 Ph(c),WW	125.00
13 Ph(c),JSe	80.00
14 Ph(c),Danny Kaye	50.00
15 Ph(c),Tony Martin,Ph(c)	50.00
16 Ph(c)	50.00
17 Ph(c)	50.00
18 Ph(c)	50.00
19 Ph(c)	50.00
20 Ph(c)	50.00
21 Ph(c)	50.00
22 Ph(c),ATn	100.00
23 Ph(c),ATn	100.00
24 Ph(c),ATn3	100.00
25 Ph(c),ATn	100.00

THRILLING TRUE STORY OF THE BASEBALL GIANTS
Fawcett Publications, 1952
N# Partial Ph(c),Famous Giants of the Past, Willie Mays 900.00
2 Yankees Ph(c),Joe DiMaggio, Yogi Berra,Mickey Mantle, Casey Stengel 850.00

TICK TOCK TALES
Magazine Enterprises Jan., 1946
1 (fa) Koko & Kola	150.00
2 (fa) Calender	100.00
3 thru 10 (fa)	@75.00
11 thru 18 (fa)	@60.00
19 (fa),Flag(c)	60.00
20 (fa)	60.00
21 (fa)	60.00
22 (fa)	60.00
23 (fa),Mugsy Mouse	60.00
24 thru 33 (fa)	@60.00
34 (fa), 1951	60.00

TIM HOLT
Magazine Enterprises Jan.–Feb., 1949
4 FBe,Ph(c)	900.00
5 FBe,Ph(c)	500.00
6 FBe,Ph(c),I:Calico Kid	400.00
7 FBe,Ph(c),Man-Killer Mustang	350.00
8 FBe,Ph(c)	350.00
9 FBe,DAy(c),TerribleTenderfoot	350.00
10 FBe,DAy(c),The Devil Horse	350.00
11 FBe,DAy(c),O&I:Ghost Rider	600.00
12 FBe,DAy(c),Battle at Bullock Gap	150.00
13 FBe,DAy(c),Ph(c)	150.00
14 FBe,DAy(c),Ph(c),The Honest Bandits	150.00
15 FBe,DAy,Ph(c)	150.00
16 FBe,DAy,Ph(c)	150.00
17 FBe,DAy,Ph(c)	500.00
18 FBe,DAy(c),Ph(c)	140.00
19 FBe,DAy,They Dig By Night	125.00
20 FBe,DAy,O:Red Mask	150.00
21 FBe,DAy,FF(c)	400.00
22 FBe,DAy	125.00
23 FF,FBe,DAy	350.00
24 FBe,DAy,FBe(c)	125.00
25 FBe,DAy,FBe(c)	250.00
26 FBe,DAy,FBe(c)	125.00
27 FBe,DAy,FBe(c),V:Straw Man	125.00
28 FBe,DAy,FBe(c),Ph(c)	125.00
29 FBe,DAy,FBe,Ph(c),	125.00
30 FBe,DAy,FBe(c),Lady Doom & The Death Wheel	110.00
31 FBe,DAy,FBe(c)	110.00
32 FBe,DAy,FBe(c)	110.00
33 FBe,DAy,FBe(c)	110.00
34 FBe,DAy,FBe(c)	125.00

35 FBe,DAy,FBe(c)	125.00
36 FBe,DAy,FBe(c),Drugs	135.00
37 FBe,DAy,FBe(c)	125.00
38 FBe,DAy,FBe(c)	125.00
39 FBe,DAy,FBe(c),3D Effect	150.00
40 FBe,DAy,FBe(c)	150.00
41 FBe,DAy,FBe(c)	150.00

Becomes:
RED MASK
June–July, 1954
42 FBe,DAy,FBe(c),3D	250.00
43 FBe,DAy,FBe(c),3D	225.00
44 FBe,DAy,FBe(c),Death at Split Mesa,3D	225.00
45 FBe,DAy,FBe(c),V:False Red Mask	225.00
46 FBe,DAy,FBe(c)	225.00
47 FBe,DAy,FBe(c)	225.00
48 FBe,DAy,FBe(c),Comics Code	200.00
49 FBe,DAy,FBe(c)	200.00
50 FBe,DAy	200.00
51 FBe,DAy,The Magic of 'The Presto Kid'	200.00
52 FBe,DAy,O:Presto Kid	225.00
53 FBe,DAy	150.00
54 FBe,DAy,Sept., 1957	225.00

TIM TYLER COWBOY
Standard Comics Nov., 1948
11	100.00
12	75.00
13 The Doll Told the Secret	75.00
14 Danger at Devil's Acres	75.00
15 Secret Treasure	75.00
16	75.00
17	75.00
18 1950	75.00

TINY TOTS COMICS
Dell Publishing Co., 1943
1 .... 500.00

TINY TOTS COMICS
E.C. Comics, March, 1946
N# Your First Comic Book B:Burton Geller(c) and art ... 500.00
2	275.00
3 Celebrate the 4th	200.00
4 Go Back to School	250.00
5 Celebrate the Winter	200.00
6 Do Their Spring Gardening	200.00
7 On a Thrilling Ride	200.00
8 On a Summer Vacation	200.00
9 On a Plane Ride	200.00
10 Merry X-Mas Tiny Tots E:Burton Geller(c)and art	200.00

TIP TOP COMICS
United Features,St. John,Dell 1930
1 HF,Li'l Abner	10,000.00
2 HF	2,600.00
3 HF,Tarzan(c)	2,400.00
4 HF,Li'l Abner(c)	1,500.00
5 HF,Capt&Kids(c)	1,000.00
6 HF	900.00
7 HF	900.00
8 HF,Li'l Abner(c)	900.00
9 HF,Tarzan(c)	1,200.00
10 HF,Li'L Abner(c)	900.00
11 HF,Tarzan(c)	850.00
12 HF,Li'l Abner	800.00
13 HF,Tarzan(c)	850.00
14 HF,Li'l Abner(c)	800.00
15 HF,Capt&kids(c)	800.00

Tip Top #55
© Dell Publishing Co.

16 HF,Tarzan(c)	850.00
17 HF,Li'L Abner(c)	800.00
18 HF,Tarzan(c)	850.00
19 HF,Football(c)	750.00
20 HF,Capt&Kids(c)	750.00
21 HF,Tarzan(c)	750.00
22 HF,Li'l Abner(c)	500.00
23 HF,Capt&Kids(c)	500.00
24 HF,Tarzan(c)	750.00
25 HF,Capt&Kids(c)	500.00
26 HF,Li'l Abner(c)	500.00
27 HF,Tarzan(c)	750.00
28 HF,Li'l Abner(c)	500.00
29 HF,Capt&Kids(c)	500.00
30 HF,Tarzan(c)	750.00
31 HFCapt&Kids(c)	500.00
32 HF,Tarzan(c)	600.00
33 HF,Tarzan(c)	750.00
34 HF,Capt&Kids(c)	750.00
35 HF	450.00
36 HF,HK,Tarzan(c)	750.00
37 HF,Tarzan	750.00
38 HF	450.00
39 HF,Tarzan	700.00
40 HF	450.00
41 Tarzan(c)	750.00
42	450.00
43 Tarzan(c)	400.00
44 HF	450.00
45 HF,Tarzan(c)	400.00
46 HF	450.00
47 HF,Tarzan(c)	400.00
48 HF	450.00
49 HF	450.00
50 HF,Tarzan(c)	400.00
51	350.00
52 Tarzan(c)	450.00
53	350.00
54	475.00
55	350.00
56	350.00
57 BHg	350.00
58	300.00
59 BHg	350.00
60	300.00
61 and 62 BHg	@350.00
63 thru 90	@200.00
91 thru 99	@150.00
100	175.00
101 thru 150	@125.00
151 thru 188	@100.00
189 thru 225	@75.00

CVA Page 470 All comics prices listed are for *Near Mint* condition.

GOLDEN AGE

T-Man–Tom Mix

T-Man #21
© *Quality Comics Group*

T-MAN
**Comics Magazines
(Quality Comics Group)
Sept., 1951**
1 JCo,Pete Trask-the
　Treasury Man 450.00
2 RC(c),The Girl with Death
　in Her Hands 250.00
3 RC(a&c),Death Trap in Iran . . 225.00
4 RC(a&c),Panama Peril 225.00
5 RC(a&c),Violence in Venice . . 225.00
6 RC(c),The Man Who
　Could Be Hitler 225.00
7 RC(c),Mr. Murder & The
　Black Hand 200.00
8 RC(c),Red Ticket to Hell 200.00
9 RC(c),Trial By Terror 200.00
10 . . . . 200.00
11 The Voice of Russia 175.00
12 Terror in Tokyo 175.00
13 Mind Assassins 175.00
14 Trouble in Bavaria, Hitler . . . 200.00
15 The Traitor,Bondage(c) 175.00
16 Hunt For a Hatchetman 175.00
17 Red Triggerman 175.00
18 Death Rides the Rails 175.00
19 Death Ambush 175.00
20 The Fantastic H-Bomb Plot . . 200.00
21 The Return of Mussolini 150.00
22 Propaganda for Doom 165.00
23 Red Intrigue in Parid,H-Bomb. 150.00
24 Red Sabotage 150.00
25 RC,The Ingenious Red Trap. . 150.00
26 . . . . 125.00
27 . . . . 125.00
28 . . . . 125.00
29 . . . . 125.00
30 thru 37 . . . . @125.00
38 Dec., 1956 . . . . 125.00

TNT COMICS
**Charles Publishing Co.
Feb., 1946**
1 FBI story,YellowJacket 400.00

TODAY'S BRIDES
**Ajax/Farrell Publishing Co.
Nov., 1955**
1 . . . . 75.00
2 . . . . 50.00
3 . . . . 50.00
4 Nov., 1956 . . . . 50.00

TODAY'S ROMANCE
**Standard Comics
March, 1952**
5 . . . . 75.00
6 ATh. 100.00
7 . . . . 50.00
8 . . . . 50.00

TOM AND JERRY
**DELL GIANT EDITIONS
Dell Publishing Co.
1952–58**
Back to School 300.00
Picnic Time 250.00
Summer Fun 1 . . . . 350.00
Summer Fun 2 . . . . 200.00
Winter Carnival 1 . . . . 500.00
Winter Carnival 2 . . . . 350.00
Winter Fun 3 . . . . 200.00
Winter Fun 4 . . . . 175.00
Winter Fun 5 . . . . 150.00
Winter Fun 6 . . . . 150.00
Winter Fun 7 . . . . 150.00

TOMB OF TERROR
**Harvey Publications
June, 1952**
1 BP,The Thing From the
　Center of the Earth 500.00
2 RP,The Quagmire Beast 350.00
3 BP,RP,Caravan of the
　Doomed, Bondage(c) 350.00
4 RP,I'm Going to Kill You,
　Torture 300.00
5 RP 300.00
6 RP,Return From the Grave . . . 300.00
7 RP,Shadow of Death 300.00
8 HN,The Hive 300.00
9 BP,HN,The Tunnel 300.00
10 BP,HN,The Trial 300.00
11 BP,HN,The Closet 300.00
12 BP,HN,Tale of Cain 325.00
13 BP,What Was Out There . . . 400.00
14 BP,SC,End Result 400.00
15 BP,HN,Break-up, Exploding
　Head 750.00
16 BP,Going,Going,Gone 350.00
Becomes:

THRILLS OF TOMORROW
Oct., 1954
17 RP,BP,The World of Mr. Chatt 100.00
18 RP,BP,The Dead Awaken 75.00
19 S&K,S&K(c),A:Stuntman 450.00
20 S&K,S&K(c),A:Stuntman 400.00

TOM CORBETT SPACE CADET
**Dell Publishing Co.
Jan., 1952**
See also Dell Four Color
4 based on TV show 150.00
5 . . . . 125.00
6 . . . . 100.00
7 . . . . 100.00
8 . . . . 100.00
9 . . . . 100.00
10 and 11 . . . . @100.00

TOM CORBETT SPACE CADET
**Prize Publications
May–June, 1955**
1 Robot(c) 400.00

Tom Corbett Space Cadet #2
© *Prize Publications*

2 . . . . 300.00
3 Sept.–Oct., 1955 . . . . 300.00

TOM MIX
**Ralston-Purina Co.
Sept., 1940**
1 O:Tom Mix 4,500.00
2 . . . . 1,500.00
3 . . . . 800.00
4 thru 9 . . . . @750.00
Becomes:

TOM MIX COMMANDOS COMICS
Nov., 1942
10 . . . . 700.00
11 Invisible Invaders 700.00
12 Terrible Talons Of Tokyo 700.00

TOM MIX WESTERN
**Fawcett Publications
Jan., 1948**
1 Ph(c),Two-Fisted
　Adventures 1,500.00
2 Ph(c),Hair-Triggered Action . . 600.00
3 Ph(c),Double Barreled Action . 500.00
4 Ph(c),Cowpunching 500.00
5 Ph(c),Two Gun Action 500.00
6 CCB,Most Famous Cowboy . . 350.00
7 CCB,A Tattoo of Thrills 350.00
8 EK,Ph(c),Gallant Guns 300.00
9 CCB,Song o/t Deadly Spurs . . 300.00
10 CCB,Crack Shot Western 300.00
11 CCB,EK(C),Triple Revenge . . 300.00
12 King of the Cowboys 250.00
13 Ph(c),Leather Burns 250.00
14 Ph(c),Brand of Death 250.00
15 Ph(c),Masked Treachery 250.00
16 Ph(c),Death Sputring Guns . . 250.00
17 Ph(c),Trail of Doom 250.00
18 Ph(c),Reign of Terror 200.00
19 Hand Colored Ph(c) 225.00
20 Ph(c),CCB,F:Capt Tootsie . . 200.00
21 Ph(c) 200.00
22 Ph(c),The Human Beast 200.00
23 Ph(c),Return of the Past 200.00
24 Hand Colored Ph(c),
　The Lawless City 200.00
25 Hand Colored Ph(c),
　The Signed Death Warrant . . 200.00
26 Hand Colored Ph(c),
　Dangerous Escape 200.00

Tom Mix–Top Secrets   GOLDEN AGE   Comics Values Annual

27 Hand Colored Ph(c),
   Hero Without Glory 200.00
28 Ph(c),The Storm Kings 200.00
29 Hand Colored Ph(c),The
   Case of the Rustling Rose . . 200.00
30 Ph(c),Disappearance
   in the Hills 200.00
31 Ph(c) 175.00
32 Hand Colored Ph(c),
   Mystery of Tremble Mountain 175.00
33 . . . . 175.00
34 . . . . 175.00
35 Partial Ph(c),The Hanging
   at Hollow Creek 175.00
36 Ph(c) 175.00
37 Ph(c) 175.00
38 Ph(c),36 pages 150.00
39 Ph(c) 175.00
40 Ph(c) 175.00
41 Ph(c) 175.00
42 Ph(c) 175.00
43 Ph(c) 150.00
44 Ph(c) 150.00
45 Partial Ph(c),The Secret
   Letter 150.00
46 Ph(c) 150.00
47 Ph(c) 150.00
48 Ph(c) 150.00
49 Partial Ph(c),Blind Date
   With Death 150.00
50 Ph(c) 150.00
51 Ph(c) 150.00
52 Ph(c) 150.00
53 Ph(c) 150.00
54 Ph(c) 150.00
55 Ph(c) 150.00
56 Partial Ph(c),Deadly Spurs . . . 150.00
57 Ph(c)5 . . . . 150.00
58 Ph(c) 150.00
59 Ph(c) 150.00
60 Ph(c) 150.00
61 Partial Ph(c),Lost in the
   Night,May, 1953 . . . . 175.00

TOMMY OF THE BIG TOP
King Features/ Standard Comics, 1948
10 Thrilling Circus Adventures 75.00
11 . . . . 50.00
12 March, 1949 . . . . 50.00

TOM-TOM THE JUNGLE BOY
Magazine Enterprises, 1946
1 (fa) 125.00
2 (fa) 100.00
3 Winter 1947,(fa),X-mas issue . . 50.00
1 . . . . 50.00

TONTO
See: LONE RANGER'S COMPANION TONTO

TONY TRENT
See: FACE, THE

TOP FLIGHT COMICS
Four Star/St. John Publ. Co. July, 1949
1 . . . . 125.00
1 Hector the Inspector 75.00

TOP LOVE STORIES
Star Publications May, 1951
3 LbC(c) 300.00
4 LbC(c) 200.00
5 LbC(c) 200.00
6 LbC(c),WW 300.00
7 LbC(c) 250.00
8 LbC(c), WW Story 275.00
9 LbC(c) 250.00
10 thru 16 LbC(c) . . . . @250.00
17 LbC(c),WW 275.00
18 LbC(c) 250.00
19 LbC(c),JyD 250.00

Top-Notch Comics #4
© MLJ Magazines

TOP-NOTCH COMICS
MLJ Magazines Dec., 1939
1 JaB,JCo,B&O:The Wizard,
   B:Kandak,Swift of the Secret
   Service,The Westpointer,
   Mystic, Air Patrol,Scott
   Rand, Manhunter 9,000.00
2 JaB,JCo,B:Dick Storm,
   E:Mystic, B:Stacy Knight . . 3,500.00
3 JaB,JCo,EA(c),E:Swift of the
   Secret Service,Scott Rand 2,500.00
4 JCo,EA(c),MMe,O&I:Streak,
   Chandler 2,000.00
5 Ea(c),MMe,O&I:Galahad,
   B:Shanghai Sheridan 2,000.00
6 Ea(c),MMe,A:The Sheild . . . 1,500.00
7 Ea(c),MMe,N:The Wizard . 2,000.00
8 E:Dick Sorm,B&O:Roy The1
   Super Boy,The Firefly 2,000.00
9 O&I:Black Hood,
   B:Fran Frazier 8,000.00
10 A:Black Hood 2,500.00
11 . . . . 1,300.00
12 . . . . 1,300.00
13 . . . . 1,300.00
14 Bondage(c) 1,300.00
15 MMe 1,300.00
16 . . . . 1,200.00
17 Bondage(c) 1,250.00
18 . . . . 1,200.00
19 Bondage(c) 1,150.00
20 . . . . 1,200.00
21 . . . . 1,000.00
22 . . . . 1,000.00
23 Bondage(c) 1,050.00
24 Black Hood Smashes
   Murder Ring 1,000.00
25 E:Bob Phantom 1,000.00
26 . . . . 1,000.00
27 E:The Firefly 1,000.00
28 B:Suzie,Pokey Okay,
   Gag Oriented 1,000.00
29 E:Kandak 1,000.00
30 . . . . 1,000.00
31 . . . . 500.00
32 . . . . 500.00
33 BWo,B:Dotty&Ditto 500.00
34 BWo 500.00
35 BWo 500.00
36 BWo 500.00
37 thru 40 BWo . . . . @500.00
41 . . . . 500.00
42 BWo 500.00
43 . . . . 500.00
44 EW:Black Hood,I:Suzie 500.00
45 Suzie(c) 600.00
Becomes:

LAUGH COMIX
Summer, 1944
46 Suzie & Wilbur 250.00
47 Suzie & Wilbur 200.00
48 Suzie & Wilbur 200.00
Becomes:

SUZIE COMICS
Spring, 1945
49 B:Ginger 325.00
50 AFy(c) 200.00
51 AFy(c) 200.00
52 AFy(c) 200.00
53 AFy(c) 200.00
54 AFy(c) 250.00
55 AFy(c) 250.00
56 BWo,B;Katie Keene 150.00
57 thru 70 BWo . . . . @150.00
71 thru 79 BWo . . . . @100.00
80 thru 99 BWo . . . . @90.00
100 Aug., 1954, BWo 90.00

TOPS
Tops Mag. Inc. (Lev Gleason), July, 1949
1 RC&Lb,GT,DBa,CBi(c),I'll Buy
   That Girl,Our Explosive
   Children 1,500.00
2 FG,BF,CBi(c),RC&BLb 1,400.00

TOPS COMICS
Consolidated Book Publishers 1944
2000 Don on the Farm 300.00
2001 The Jack of Spades
   V:The Hawkman 200.00
2002 Rip Raiders 150.00
2003 Red Birch 50.00

TOP SECRET
Hillman Publications Jan., 1952
1 The Tricks of the Secret
   Agent Revealed 250.00

TOP SECRETS
Street & Smith, Nov., 1947
1 BP,BP(c),Of the Men Who
   Guard the U.S. Mail 400.00
2 BP,BP(c),True Story of Jim
   the Penman 350.00
3 BP,BP(c),Crime Solved by
   Mental Telepathy 300.00
4 Highway Pirates 300.00
5 BP,BP(c),Can Music Kill 300.00
6 BP,BP(c),The Clue of the
   Forgotten Film 300.00

CVA Page 472   All comics prices listed are for *Near Mint* condition.

GOLDEN AGE

7 BP,BP(c),Train For Sale 375.00
8 BP,BP(c) 300.00
9 BP,BP(c) 300.00
10 BP,BP(c),July–Aug., 1949 ... 375.00

TOPS IN ADVENTURE
Approved Comics (Ziff-Davis)
Autumn, 1952
1 BP,Crusaders From Mars 600.00

TOP SPOT COMICS
Top Spot Publishing Co.
1945
1 The Duke Of Darkness 450.00

TOPSY-TURVY
R.B. Leffingwell Publ.
April, 1945
1 I:Cookie 125.00

TOR
St. John Publishing Co.
Sept., 1953
1 JKu,JKu(c),O;Tor,One Million Years Ago 150.00
2 JKu,JKu(c),3-D Issue 100.00
3 JKu,JKu(c),ATh,historic Life .. 125.00
4 JKu,JKu(c),ATh 125.00
5 JKu,JKu(c),ATh,Oct., 1954 ... 125.00

TORCHY
Quality Comics Group
Nov., 1949
1 GFx,BWa(c),The Blonde Bombshell 2,000.00
2 GFx,GFx(c),Beauty at its' Best 900.00
3 GFX,GFx(c),You Can't Beat Nature 900.00
4 GFx,GFx(c),The Girl to Keep Your Eye On 1,000.00
5 BWa,GFx,BWa(c),At the Masquerade Party 1,500.00
6 Sept., 1950,BWa,GFx, BWa(c),The Libido Driven Boy Scout 1,500.00

TORMENTED, THE
Sterling Comics
July, 1954
1 Buried Alive 300.00
2 Sept., 1954,The Devils Circus 250.00

TOYLAND COMICS
Fiction House Magazines
Jan., 1947
1 Wizard of the Moon 400.00
2 Buddy Bruin & Stu Rabbit ... 200.00
3 GT,The Candy Maker 250.00
4 July, 1947 .... 200.00

TOY TOWN COMICS
Toytown Publ./Orbit Publ.
Feb., 1945
1 LbC,LbC(c)(fa) 500.00
2 LbC,(fa) 300.00
3 LbC,LbC(c),(fa) 250.00
4 LbC,(fa) 250.00
5 LbC,(fa) 250.00
6 LbC,(fa) 250.00
7 LbC,(fa),May, 1947 .... 250.00

TRAIL BLAZERS
See: RED DRAGON COMICS

TREASURE COMICS
Prize Comics Group, 1943
1 S&K,Reprints of Prize Comics #7 through #11 .... 2,700.00

Treasure Comics #4
© *Quality Comics Group*

TREASURE COMICS
American Boys Comics (Prize Publications)
June–July, 1945
1 HcK,B:PaulBunyan,MarcoPolo 450.00
2 HcK(a&c),B:Arabian Knight, Gorilla King,Dr.Styx 250.00
3 HcK 175.00
4 HcK 175.00
5 HcK,JK, Marco Polo 250.00
6 BK,HcK(a&c) 200.00
7 FF,HcK(a&c),Capt.Kidd, Jr. .. 450.00
8 HcK,FF 450.00
9 HcK,DBa 160.00
10 JK,DBa,JK(c)............. 400.00
11 BK,HcK,DBa,The Weird Adventures of Mr. Bottle 250.00
12 DBa,DBa(c),Autumn, 1947... 160.00

TREASURY OF COMICS
St. John Publishing Co., 1947
1 RvB,RvB(c),Abbie an' Slats .. 150.00
2 Jim Hardy 125.00
3 Bill Bimlin 125.00
4 RvB,RvB(c),Abbie an' Slats .. 125.00
5 Jim Hardy,Jan., 1948 ...... 100.00

TRIPLE THREAT
Gerona Publications
Winter, 1945
1 F:King O'Leary,The Duke of Darkness,Beau Brummell .. 350.00

TRUE AVIATION PICTURE STORIES
Parents' Institute/P.M.I.
Aug., 1942
1 How Jimmy Doolittle Bombed Tokyo 200.00

Top Secrets–True Comics
2 Knight of the Air Mail 150.00
3 The Amazing One-Man Air Force 125.00
4 Joe Foss America's No. 1 Air Force 125.00
5 Bombs over Germany 125.00
6 Flight Lt. Richard Hillary R.A.F............ 125.00
7 "Fatty" Chow China's Sky Champ 125.00
8 Blitz over Burma 125.00
9 Off the Beam 125.00
10 "Pappy" Boyington........ 125.00
11 Ph(c).................... 125.00
12 .... 125.00
13 Ph(c),Flying Facts 125.00
14 .... 125.00
15 True Aviation Adventures ... 125.00
Becomes:

AVIATION AND MODEL BUILDING
Dec., 1946
16 .... 75.00
17 Feb., 1947.............. 100.00

TRUE COMICS
True Comics/Parents' Magazine Press
April, 1941–Aug., 1950
1 My Greatest Adventure-by Lowell Thomas 450.00
2 BEv,The Story of the Red Cross 200.00
3 Baseball Hall of Fame....... 225.00
4 Danger in the Artic 150.00
5 Father Duffy-the Fighting Chaplain 165.00
6 The Capture of Aquinaldo ... 175.00
7 JKa,Wilderness Adventures of George Washington 165.00
8 U.S. Army Wings 125.00
9 A Pig that Made History 125.00
10 Adrift on an Ice Pan 125.00
11 Gen. Douglas MacArthur ... 110.00
12 Mackenzie-King of Cananda. 110.00
13 The Real Robinson Crusoe .. 110.00
14 Australia war base of the South Pacific.......... 110.00
15 The Story of West Point..... 125.00
16 How Jimmy Doolittle Bombed Tokyo 120.00
17 The Ghost of Captain Blig, B.Feller 125.00
18 Battling Bill of the Merchant Marine 135.00
19 Secret Message Codes 110.00
20 The Story of India 100.00
21 Timoshenko the Blitz Buster.. 110.00
22 Gen. Bernard L. Montgomery. 100.00
23 The Story of Steel 100.00
24 Gen. Henri Giraud-Master of Escape 100.00
25 Medicine's Miracle Men 100.00
26 Hero of the Bismarck Sea ... 100.00
27 Leathernecks have Landed .. 110.00
28 The Story of Radar 100.00
29 The Fighting Seabees 100.00
30 Dr. Norman Bethune-Blood Bank Founder. 100.00
31 Our Good Neighbor Bolivia, Red Grange 110.00
32 Men against the Desert 75.00
33 Gen. Clark and his Fighting 5th 80.00
34 Angel of the Battlefield...... 75.00
35 Carlson's Marine Raiders..... 75.00
36 Canada's Sub-Busters....... 75.00
37 Commander of the Crocodile Fleet................... 75.00

All comics prices listed are for Near Mint condition.

True: Comics–Sweatheart — GOLDEN AGE — Comics Values Annual

38 Oregon Trailblazer 75.00
39 Saved by Sub 75.00
40 Sea Furies. 75.00
41 Cavalcade of England 50.00
42 Gen. Jaques Le Clerc-Hero
   of Paris 50.00
43 Unsinkable Ship. 55.00
44 El Senor Goofy 50.00
45 Tokyo Express 50.00
46 The Magnificent Runt. 50.00
47 Atoms Unleashed,
   Atomic Bomb 125.00
48 Pirate Patriot 50.00
49 Smiking Fists 50.00
50 Lumber Pirates 50.00
51 Exercise Musk-Ox 50.00
52 King of the Buckaneers 50.00
53 Baseline Booby 50.00
54 Santa Fe Sailor 50.00
55 Sea Going Santa 50.00
56 End of a Terror. 50.00
57 Newfangled Machines 50.00
58 Leonardo da Vinci-500 years
   too Soon 50.00
59 Pursuit of the Pirates 55.00
60 Emmett Kelly-The World's
   Funniest Clown 50.00
61 Peter Le Grand-
   Bold Buckaneer 50.00
62 Sutter's Gold 50.00
63 Outboard Outcome 50.00
64 Man-Eater at Large 50.00
65 The Story of Scotland Yard . . . 50.00
66 Easy Guide to Football
   Formations 55.00
67 The Changing Zebra 50.00
68 Admiral Byrd 50.00
69 FBI Special Agent Steve
   Saunders 55.00
70 The Case of the Seven
   Hunted Men 50.00
71 Story of Joe DiMaggio 150.00
72 FBI,Jackie Robinson 100.00
73 The 26 Mile Dash-Story of
   the Marathon, Walt Disney . . . 75.00
74 A Famous Coach's Special
   Football Tips. 55.00
75 King of Reporters. 55.00
76 Story of a Buried Treasure 55.00
77 France's Greatest Detective. . . 55.00
78 Cagliostro-Master Rogue 75.00
79 Ralph Bunche-Hero of Peace. . 55.00
80 Rocket Trip to the Moon. 200.00
81 Red Grange 200.00
82 Marie Celeste Ship of
   Mystery 175.00
83 Bullfighter from Brooklyn 175.00
84 King of the Buckaneers 175.00

TRUE CONFIDENCES
**Fawcett Publications
Autumn, 1949**
1 . . . . 200.00
2 and 3 . . . . @125.00
4 DP 125.00

TRUE CRIME COMICS
**Magazine Village, Inc.
May, 1947**
2 JCo(c),James Kent-Crook,
   Murderer,Escaped Convict;
   Drug 2,000.00
3 JCo(a&c),Benny Dickson-
   Killer;Drug 1,500.00
4 JCo(a&c),Little Jake-
   Big Shot 1,400.00
5 JCo(c),The Rat & the Blond
   Gun Moll;Drug 1,000.00

*True Crime #3
© Magazine Village*

6 Joseph Metley-Swindler,
   Jailbird, Killer 800.00
2-1(7) ATh,WW,Ph(c),Phil
   Coppolla,Sept., 1949 . . . . 1,200.00

TRUE LIFE SECRETS
**Romantic Love Stories/
Charlton Comics
March–April, 1951**
1 . . . . 125.00
2 . . . . 75.00
3 . . . . 50.00
4 . . . . 50.00
5 thru 20 . . . . @50.00
21 thru 25 . . . . @40.00
26 Comics Code 35.00
27 thru 29 . . . . @35.00

TRUE LIFE ROMANCES
**Ajax/Farrell Publications
Dec., 1955**
1 . . . . 100.00
2 . . . . 60.00
3 Aug., 1956 . . . . 75.00

TRUE LOVE PICTORIAL
St. John Publishing Co., 1952
1 Ph(c) 200.00
2 MB 250.00
3 MB(c),MB,JKu 400.00
4 MB(c),MB,JKu 400.00
5 MB(c),MB,JKu 400.00
6 MB(c) 200.00
7 MB(c) 200.00
8 MB(c) 150.00
9 MB(c). 150.00
10 MB(c),MB 150.00
11 MB(c),MB. 150.00

TRUE MOVIE AND TELEVISION
Toby Press, Aug., 1950
1 Liz Taylor, Ph(c) 600.00
2 FF,Ph(c),John Wayne,
   L.Taylor 400.00
3 June Allyson,Ph(c) 350.00
4 Jane Powell,Ph(c),Jan.,1951 . 200.00

SPORT COMICS
Street & Smith, Oct., 1940
1 F:Lou Gehrig 700.00
2 F:Gene Tunney 400.00
3 F:Phil Rizzuto 450.00
4 F:Frank Leahy 300.00
Becomes:

TRUE SPORT PICTURE STORIES
Feb., 1942–July-Aug., 1949
5 Joe DiMaggio 400.00
6 Billy Confidence 250.00
7 Mel Ott 275.00
8 Lou Ambers 250.00
9 Pete Reiser 250.00
10 Frankie Sinkwich 250.00
11 Marty Serfo 250.00
12 JaB(c),Jack Dempsey 265.00
2-1 JaB(c),Willie Pep 250.00
2-2 JaB(c). 250.00
2-3 JaB(c),Carl Hubbell. 265.00
2-4 Advs. in Football & Battle . . 275.00
2-5 Don Hutson 250.00
2-6 Dixie Walker 275.00
2-7 Stan Musial 300.00
2-8 Famous Ring Champions
   of All Time 275.00
2-9 List of War Year Rookies . . . 300.00
2-10 Connie Mack 275.00
2-11 Winning Basketball Plays . . 250.00
2-12 Eddie Gottlieb. 250.00
3-1 Bill Conn 250.00
3-2 Philadelphia Athletics 200.00
3-3 Leo Durocher 250.00
3-4 Rudy Dusek 200.00
3-5 Ernie Pyle 200.00
3-6 Bowling with Ned Day 200.00
3-7 Return of the Mighty (Home
   from War);Joe DiMaggio(c) . . 400.00
3-8 Conn V:Louis 300.00
3-9 Reuben Shark 200.00
3-10 BP,BP(c),Don "Dopey"
   Dillock 200.00
3-11 BP,BP(c),Death
   Scores a Touchdown 200.00
3-12 Red Sox V:Senators 200.00
4-1 Spring Training in
   Full Spring 200.00
4-2 BP,BP(c),How to Pitch 'Em
   Where They Can't Hit 'Em . . 200.00
4-3 BP,BP(c),1947 Super Stars . 235.00
4-4 BP,BP(c),Get Ready for
   the Olympics 235.00
4-5 BP,BP,(c),Hugh Casey 200.00
4-6 BP,BP(c),Phantom Phil
   Hergesheimer 200.00
4-7 BP,BP(c),How to Bowl Better 200.00
4-8 Tips on the Big Fight 235.00
4-9 BP,BP(c),Bill McCahan 200.00
4-10 BP,BP(c),Great Football
   Plays 200.00
4-11 BP,BP(c),Football 200.00
4-12 BP,BP(c),Basketball 200.00
5-1 Satchel Paige 250.00
5-2 History of Boxing 200.00

TRUE SWEETHEART SECRETS
**Fawcett Publications
May, 1950**
1 Ph(c) 150.00
2 WW 250.00
3 BD 100.00
4 BD 100.00
5 BD 100.00
6 thru 11 . . . . @80.00

TRUE-TO-LIFE ROMANCES
Star Publications
Nov.–Dec., 1949
3 LbC(c),GlennFord/JanetLeigh . 300.00
4 LbC(c) 200.00
5 LbC(c) 200.00
6 LbC(c) 200.00
7 LbC(c) 200.00
8 LbC(c) 200.00
9 LbC(c) 200.00
10 LbC(c) 200.00
11 LbC(c) 200.00
12 LbC(c) 200.00
13 LbC(c),JyD 200.00
14 LbC(c),JyD 200.00
15 LbC(c),WW,JyD 250.00
16 LbC(c),WW,JyD 250.00
17 LbC(c),JyD 175.00
18 LbC(c),JyD 175.00
19 LbC(c),JyD 175.00
20 LbC(c),JyD 175.00
21 LbC(c),JyD 175.00
22 LbC(c) 175.00
23 LbC(c) 175.00

TRUE WAR ROMANCES
Comic Magazines, Inc. (Quality Comics)
Sept., 1952
1 Ph(c) 150.00
2 .... 75.00
3 thru 10 .... @60.00
11 thru 20 .... @50.00
21 Comics Code 50.00
Becomes:

EXOTIC ROMANCES
Oct., 1955
22 .... 60.00
23 thru 26 .... @40.00
27 MB 60.00
28 MB 60.00
29 .... 40.00
30 MB 60.00
31 MB 60.00

TUROK, SON OF STONE
Dell Publishing Co.
Dec., 1954
(1) see Dell Four Color #596
(2) see Dell Four Color #656
3 .... 350.00
4 and 5 .... @300.00
6 thru 10 .... @250.00
11 thru 20 .... @150.00
21 thru 29 .... @125.00
See Color Pub. section

TWEETY AND SYLVESTER
Dell Publishing Co.
June, 1952
(1) see Dell Four Color #406
(2) see Dell Four Color #489
(3) see Dell Four Color #524
4 thru 20 .... @50.00
21 thru 37 .... @40.00

TWINKLE COMICS
Spotlight Publications
May, 1945
1 Humor Format 300.00

GOLDEN AGE

TWO-FISTED TALES
Fables Publications (E.C. Comics)
Nov.–Dec., 1950–March, 1955
18 JCr,WW,JSe,HK(a&c) 1,500.00
19 JCr,WW,JSe,HK(a&c) 1,200.00
20 JDa,WW,JSe,HK(a&c) 750.00
21 JDa,WW,JSe,HK(a&c) 600.00
22 JDa,WW,JSe,HK(a&c) 600.00
23 JDa,WW,JSe,HK(a&c) 450.00
24 JDa,WW,JSe,HK(a&c) 400.00
25 JDa,WW,JSe,HK(a&c) 400.00
26 JDa,JSe,HK(c),Action at
   the Changing Reservoir 300.00
27 JDa,JSe,HK(c) 300.00
28 JDa,JSe,HK(c) 300.00
29 JDa,JSe,HK(c) 350.00
30 JSe,JDa(a&c) 350.00
31 JDa,JSe,HK(c),Civil
   War Story 300.00
32 JDa,JKu,WW(c) 300.00
33 JDa,JKu,WW(c) 300.00
34 JSe,JDa(a&c) 300.00
35 JSe,JDa(a&c),Civil
   War Story 300.00
36 JDa,JSe(a&c),A
   Difference of Opinion 250.00
37 JSe(a&c),Bugles &
   Battle Cries 250.00
38 JSe(a&c) 250.00
39 JSe(a&c) 250.00
40 JDa,JSe,GE(a&c) 300.00
41 JSe,GE,JDa(c) 250.00

UNCLE CHARLIE'S FABLES
Lev Gleason Publications
Jan., 1952
1 CBi(c),Ph(c) 200.00
2 BF,CBi(c),Ph(c) 125.00
3 CBi(c),Ph(c) 135.00
4 CBi(c),Ph(c) 135.00
5 CBi,Ph(c),Sept., 1952 ..... 135.00

UNCLE SAM
See: BLACKHAWK

UNCLE SCROOGE
Dell Publishing Co.
March, 1952
(1) see Dell Four Color #386
(2) see Dell Four Color #456
(3) see Dell Four Color #495
4 .... 600.00
5 .... 450.00
6 .... 350.00
7 CB 325.00
8 .... 300.00
9 .... 300.00
10 .... 300.00
11 thru 20 .... @275.00
21 thru 30 .... @250.00
31 thru 39 .... @200.00
See Color Pub. section

UNDERWORLD
D.S. Publishing Co.
Feb.–March, 1948
1 SMo(c),Violence 600.00
2 SMo(c),Electrocution 600.00
3 AMc,AMc(c),The Ancient Club 500.00
4 Grl,The Beer Baron Murder .. 450.00
5 Grl,The Postal Clue 300.00
6 The Polka Dot Gang 250.00

Underworld #9
© D.S. Publishing Co.

7 Mono-The Master 250.00
8 The Double Tenth 250.00
9 Thrilling Stories of the Fight
   against Crime,June, 1953 .. 250.00

UNDERWORLD CRIME
Fawcett Publications
June, 1952
1 The Crime Army 400.00
2 Jailbreak 250.00
3 Microscope Murder 200.00
4 Death on the Docks 200.00
5 River of Blood 200.00
6 The Sky Pirates 200.00
7 Bondage & Torture(c) 400.00
8 .... 200.00
9 June, 1953 .... 200.00

UNITED COMICS
United Features Syndicate
1950
8 thru 26 Bushmiller(c),
   Fritzi Ritz .... @60.00

UNITED STATES FIGHTING AIR FORCE
Superior Comics, Ltd.
Sept., 1952
1 Coward's Courage 125.00
2 Clouds that Killed 60.00
3 Operation Decoy 50.00
4 thru 28 .... @50.00
29 Oct., 1959 .... 50.00

UNITED STATES MARINES
Wm. H. Wise/Magazine Ent/ Toby Press, 1943
N# MBi,MBi(c),Hellcat out
   of Heaven 175.00
2 MBi,Drama of Wake Island .. 400.00
3 A Leatherneck Flame Thrower 300.00
4 MBi 125.00
5 BP 75.00
6 BP 75.00
7 BP 60.00
8 thru 10 .... @60.00
11 1952 .... 60.00

Unkept–Voodoo / GOLDEN AGE / Comics Values Annual

UNKEPT PROMISE
Legion of Truth, 1949
1 Anti:Alcoholic Drinking 100.00

UNKNOWN WORLDS
See: STRANGE STORIES FROM ANOTHER WORLD

UNSEEN, THE
Visual Editions (Standard Comics), 1952
5 ATh,The Hungry Lodger 500.00
6 JKa,MSy,Bayou Vengeance . . 350.00
7 JKz,MSy,Time is the Killer 350.00
8 JKz,MSy,The Vengance Vat . . 300.00
9 JKz,MSy,Your Grave is Ready 350.00
10 JKz,MSy 350.00
11 JKz,MSy 300.00
12 ATh,GT,Till Death Do Us Part . 350.00
13 . . . . 250.00
14 . . . . 250.00
15 ATh,The Curse of the Undead!, July, 1954 . . . . 350.00

UNTAMED LOVE
Comic Magazines (Quality Comics Group) Jan., 1950
1 BWa(c),PGn 275.00
2 Ph(c) 175.00
3 PGn 200.00
4 . . . . 175.00
5 PGn 200.00

USA IS READY
Dell Publishing Co., 1941
1 Propaganda WWII 500.00

U.S. JONES
Fox Features Syndicate Nov., 1941
1 Death Over the Airways . . . 1,900.00
2 Nazi (c),Jan., 1942. . . . . 1,400.00

U.S. Jones 32
© Fox Features Syndicate

GOLDEN AGE

U.S. MARINES IN ACTION!
Avon Periodicals Aug.–Dec., 1952
1 On Land,Sea & in the Air 100.00
2 The Killer Patrol 50.00
3 EK(c),Death Ridge 55.00

U.S. TANK COMMANDOS
Avon Periodicals June, 1952
1 EK(c),Fighting Daredevils of the USA 100.00
2 EK(c) 60.00
3 EK,EK(c),Robot Armanda 60.00
4 EK,EK(c),March, 1953 . . . . 60.00

VALOR
E.C. Comics, March, 1955
1 AW,AT,WW,WW(c),Grl,BK 400.00
2 AW(c),AW,WWGrl,BK 300.00
3 AW,RC,BK,JOc(c). 250.00
4 WW(c),RC,Grl,BK,JO 250.00
5 WW(c),WW,AW,GE,Grl,BK . . . 225.00

VARIETY COMICS
Rural Home Publ./ Croyden Publ. Co., 1944
1 MvS,MvS(c),O:Capt, Valiant . . 300.00
2 MvS,MvS(c) 200.00
3 MvS,MvS(c) 150.00
4 . . . . 125.00
5 1946 . . . . 110.00

VAULT OF HORROR
See: WAR AGAINST CRIME

V...COMICS
Fox Features Syndicate Jan., 1942
1 V:V-Man 1,800.00
2 The Horror of the Dungeons, March, 1942 . . 1,400.00

VERI BEST SURE SHOT COMICS
Holyoke Publishing Co. 1945
1 reprint Holyoke One-Shots . . . 500.00

VIC FLINT
St. John Publishing Co. Aug., 1948
1 ...Crime Buster 150.00
2 . . . . 125.00
3 . . . . 75.00
4 . . . . 75.00
5 April, 1949 . . . . 75.00

VIC JORDAN
Civil Service Publications April, 1945
1 Escape From a Nazi Prison . . 150.00

VIC TORRY AND HIS FLYING SAUCER
Fawcett Publications, 1950
1 Ph(c),Revealed at Last. 1,000.00

Victory Comics #1
© Hillman Periodicals

VICTORY COMICS
Hillman Periodicals Aug., 1941
1 BEv,BEv(c),F:TheConqueror 4,200.00
2 BEv,BEv(c) 1,900.00
3 The Conqueror(c) 1,200.00
4 Dec., 1941 . . . . 1,100.00

VIC VERITY MAGAZINE
Vic Verity Publications 1945
1 CCB,CCB(c),B:Vic Verity,Hot-Shot Galvan, Tom Travis . . . 250.00
2 CCB,CCB(c),Annual Classic Dance Recital 150.00
3 CCB 125.00
4 CCB,I:Boomer Young;The Bee-U-TiFul Weekend 125.00
5 CCB,Championship Baseball Game 125.00
6 CCB,High School Hero 125.00
7 CCB,CCB(c),F:Rocket Rex . . 125.00

VOODA
April, 1955
20 MB,MB(c),Echoes of an A-Bomb 500.00
21 MB,MB(c),Trek of Danger . . 400.00
22 MB,MB(c),The Sun Blew Away, Aug., 1955 . . . . 400.00

VOODOO
Four Star Publ./Farrell/ Ajax Comics May, 1952
1 MB,South Sea Girl 800.00
2 MB 600.00
3 Face Stabbing 500.00
4 MB,Rendezvous 500.00
5 Ghoul For A Day,Nazi 350.00
6 The Weird Dead, Severed Head 400.00
7 Goodbye World 350.00
8 MB, Revenge 450.00
9 Will this thing Never Stew? . . 350.00
10 Land of Shadows & Screams. 350.00
11 Human Harvest 300.00
12 The Wazen Taper. 300.00
13 Bondage(c),Caskets to Fit Everybody 325.00
14 Death Judges the Beauty Contest. 300.00

CVA Page 476 — All comics prices listed are for *Near Mint* condition.

GOLDEN AGE

Voodoo–Walt Disney

15 Loose their Heads 325.00
16 Fog Was Her Shroud 300.00
17 Apes Laughter,Electric Chair . 325.00
18 Astounding Fantasy 300.00
19 MB,Bondage(c);
  Destination Congo 450.00
Ann.#1 . . . . 1,250.00
Becomes:

WACKY DUCK
See: DOPEY DUCK

WALT DISNEY'S COMICS & STORIES
Dell Publishing Co.
N# 1943 dpt.store giveaway. 750.00
N# 1945 X-mas giveaway 350.00

WALT DISNEY'S COMICS & STORIES
Dell Publishing Co.
Oct., 1940
1 (1940)FG,Donald Duck &
  Mickey Mouse 25,000.00
2 . . . . 9,000.00
3 . . . . 3,000.00
4 1st Huey, Dewey & Louie
  Christmas(c) 2,000.00
4a Promo issue. 3,000.00
5 Goofy(c) 1,700.00
6 . . . . 1,500.00
7 . . . . 1,500.00
8 Clarabelle Cow(c) 1,500.00
9 . . . . 1,500.00
10 . . . . 1,500.00
11 2nd Huey,Louie,Dewey(c) . . 1,100.00
12 . . . . 1,200.00
13 . . . . 1,100.00
14 . . . . 1,100.00
15 3 Little Kittens. 1,000.00
16 3 Little Pigs 950.00
17 The Ugly Ducklings. 1,000.00
18 . . . . 800.00
19 . . . . 750.00
20 . . . . 750.00
21 . . . . 800.00
22 . . . . 750.00
23 . . . . 750.00
24 Flying Gauchito 700.00
25 . . . . 700.00
26 . . . . 700.00
27 Jose Carioca 700.00
28 . . . . 750.00
29 . . . . 700.00
30 . . . . 700.00
31 CB; Donald Duck 4,000.00
32 CB 1,900.00
33 CB 1,500.00
34 CB;WK; Gremlins 1,200.00
35 CB;WK; Gremlins. 1,200.00
36 CB;WK; Gremlins 1,200.00
37 CB;WK; Gremlins. 600.00
38 CB;WK; Gremlins. 750.00
39 CB;WK; Gremlins. 750.00
40 CB;WK; Gremlins. 750.00
41 CB;WK; Gremlins 650.00
42 CB. 600.00
43 CB,Seven Dwarfs 600.00
44 CB. 600.00
45 CB,Nazis in stories 600.00
46 CB,Nazis in stories 600.00
47 CB,Nazis in stories 600.00
48 CB,Nazis in stories 600.00
49 CB,Nazis in stories 600.00
50 CB,Nazis in stories 600.00
51 CB,Christmas 450.00
52 CB; Li'l Bad Wolf begins 450.00

Walt Disney's Comics & Stories #114
© *Walt Disney*

53 CB. 450.00
54 CB. 450.00
55 CB. 450.00
56 CB. 450.00
57 CB. 450.00
58 CB. 450.00
59 CB. 450.00
60 CB. 450.00
61 CB; Dumbo 350.00
62 CB. 350.00
63 CB; Pinocchio 350.00
64 CB; Pinocchio 350.00
65 CB; Pluto. 350.00
66 CB. 350.00
67 CB. 350.00
68 CB. 350.00
69 CB. 350.00
70 CB. 350.00
71 CB. 300.00
72 CB. 300.00
73 CB. 300.00
74 CB. 300.00
75 CB; Brer Rabbit 300.00
76 CB; Brer Rabbit 300.00
77 CB; Brer Rabbit 300.00
78 CB. 300.00
79 CB. 300.00
80 CB. 300.00
81 CB. 300.00
82 CB;Bongo,Googy 300.00
83 CB;Bongo 300.00
84 CB;Bongo 300.00
85 CB. 300.00
86 CB;Goofy & Agnes. 300.00
87 CB;Goofy & Agnes. 275.00
88 CB;Goofy & Agnes,
  I:Gladstone Gander 350.00
89 CB;Goofy&Agnes,Chip'n'Dale 275.00
90 CB;Goofy & Agnes. 275.00
91 CB. 250.00
92 CB. 250.00
93 CB. 250.00
94 CB. 250.00
95 CB(c). 250.00
96 Little Toot. 250.00
97 CB; Little Toot 250.00
98 CB; Uncle Scrooge 400.00
99 CB. 250.00
100 CB. 300.00
101 CB. 250.00
102 CB. 250.00
103 CB. 200.00
104 . . . . 200.00
105 CB. 250.00

106 CB. 250.00
107 CB. 250.00
108 . . . . 200.00
109. . . . . 200.00
110 CB. 250.00
111 CB. 250.00
112 CB; drugs. 250.00
113 CB. 250.00
114 CB. 250.00
115 . . . . 100.00
116 Dumbo. 100.00
117 . . . . 100.00
118 . . . . 100.00
119 . . . . 100.00
120 . . . . 100.00
121 Grandma Duck begins 100.00
122 . . . . 100.00
123 . . . . 100.00
124 CB,Christmas. 150.00
125 CB;I:Junior Woodchucks . . . 200.00
126 CB. 125.00
127 CB. 125.00
128 CB. 125.00
129 CB. 125.00
130 CB. 125.00
131 CB. 125.00
132 CB A:Grandma Duck 125.00
133 CB. 125.00
134 I:The Beagle Boys 250.00
135 CB. 125.00
136 CB. 125.00
137 CB. 125.00
138 CB. 125.00
139 CB. 125.00
140 CB; I:Gyro Gearloose. 250.00
141 CB. 100.00
142 CB. 100.00
143 CB; Little Hiawatha 100.00
144 CB; Little Hiawatha 100.00
145 CB; Little Hiawatha 100.00
146 CB; Little Hiawatha 100.00
147 CB; Little Hiawatha 100.00
148 CB; Little Hiawatha 100.00
149 CB; Little Hiawatha 100.00
150 CB; Little Hiawatha 100.00
151 CB; Little Hiawatha 100.00
152 thru 200 CB . . . . @75.00
201 CB. 60.00
202 CB. 60.00
203 CB. 60.00
204 CB, Chip 'n' Dale & Scamp . . 60.00
205 thru 240 CB . . . . @60.00
241 CB; Dumbo x-over 50.00
242 CB. 50.00
243 CB. 50.00
244 CB. 50.00
245 CB. 50.00
246 CB. 50.00
247 thru 255 CB;GyroGearloose @50.00
256 thru 263 CB;Ludwig Von
  Drake & Gearloose . . . . . . @50.00
See: Independent Color Comics

WALT DISNEY ANNUALS
Walt Disney's Autumn Adventure . . 4.00
Walt Disney's Holiday Parade. 3.50
Walt Disney's Spring Fever. 3.25
Walt Disney's Summer Fun. 3.25

WALT DISNEY DELL GIANT EDITIONS
Dell Publishing Co.
1 CB,W.Disney'sXmas
  Parade('49) 1,200.00
2 CB,W.Disney'sXmas
  Parade('50) 1,000.00
3 W.Disney'sXmas Parade('51) . 300.00
4 W.Disney'sXmas Parade('52) . 250.00
5 W.Disney'sXmas Parade('53) . 250.00

All comics prices listed are for Near Mint condition.

GOLDEN AGE

Walt Disney–War Against

6 W.Disney'sXmas Parade('54) . 250.00
7 W.Disney'sXmas Parade('55) . 250.00
8 CB,W.Disney'sXmas
  Parade('56) 500.00
9 CB,W.Disney'sXmas
  Parade('57) 450.00
1 CB,W.Disney's Christmas in
  Disneyland (1957) 600.00
1 CB,W.Disney's Disneyland
  Birthday Party (1958) 600.00
1 W.Disney's Donald and Mickey
  in Disneyland (1958)....... 250.00
1 W.Disney's Donald Duck
  Beach Party (1954)........ 300.00
2 W.Disney's Donald Duck
  Beach Party (1955)........ 250.00
3 W.Disney's Donald Duck
  Beach Party (1956)........ 250.00
4 W.Disney's Donald Duck
  Beach Party (1957)........ 250.00
5 W.Disney's Donald Duck
  Beach Party (1958)........ 250.00
6 W.Disney's Donald Duck
  Beach Party (1959)........ 250.00
1 W.Disney's Donald Duck
  Fun Book (1954) 1,200.00
2 W.Disney's Donald Duck
  Fun Book (1954) 1,100.00
1 W.Disney's Donald Duck
  in Disneyland (1955)....... 275.00
1 W.Disney's Huey, Dewey
  and Louie (1958) 175.00
1 W.Disney's DavyCrockett('55) . 350.00
1 W.Disney's Lady and the
  Tramp (1955) 400.00
1 CB,W.Disney's Mickey Mouse
  Almanac (1957) 600.00
1 W.Disney's Mickey Mouse
  Birthday Party (1953) 700.00
1 W.Disney's Mickey Mouse
  Club Parade (1955) 600.00
1 W.Disney's Mickey Mouse
  in Fantasyland (1957)...... 275.00
1 W.Disney's Mickey Mouse
  in Frontierland (1956) 275.00
1 W.Disney's Summer Fun('58) . 275.00
2 CB,W.Disney'sSummer
  Fun('59) 275.00
1 W.Disney's Peter Pan
  Treasure Chest (1953).... 2,200.00
1 Disney Silly Symphonies('52) . 600.00
2 Disney Silly Symphonies('53) . 500.00
3 Disney Silly Symphonies('54) . 450.00
4 Disney Silly Symphonies('54) . 450.00
5 Disney Silly Symphonies('55) . 400.00
6 Disney Silly Symphonies('56) . 400.00
7 Disney Silly Symphonies('57) . 400.00
8 Disney Silly Symphonies('58) . 400.00
9 Disney Silly Symphonies('59) . 400.00
1 Disney SleepingBeauty('59) . . 600.00
1 CB,W.Disney's Uncle Scrooge
  Goes to Disneyland (1957).. 550.00
1 W.Disney's Vacation in
  Disneyland (1958) 250.00
1 CB,Disney's Vacation
  Parade('50)............. 1,700.00
2 Disney'sVacation Parade('51) . 600.00
3 Disney'sVacation Parade('52) . 300.00
4 Disney'sVacation Parade('53) . 300.00
5 Disney'sVacation Parade('54) . 300.00
6 Disney's Picnic Party (1955) . . 250.00
7 Disney's Picnic Party (1956) . . 250.00
8 CB,Disney's Picnic
  Party (1957) 500.00

DELL JUNIOR TREASURY

1 W.Disney's Alice in Wonderland
  (1955) 150.00

WALT DISNEY PRESENTS
**Dell Publishing Co.
June–Aug., 1952**

1 Ph(c), Four Color 125.00
2 Ph(c) 75.00
3 Ph(c) 75.00
4 Ph(c) 75.00
5 and 6 Ph(c)............... @75.00

WAMBI JUNGLE BOY
**Fiction House Magazines
Spring, 1942–Winter, 1952**

1 HcK,HcK(c),Vengence of
  the Beasts 1,200.00
2 HcK,HcK(c),Lair of the
  Killer Rajah 600.00
3 HcK,HcK(c) 500.00
4 HcK,HcK(c),The Valley of
  the Whispering Drums 250.00
5 HcK,HcK(c),SwamplandSafari. 250.00
6 Taming of the Tigress 225.00
7 Duel of the Congo Kings 225.00
8 AB(c),Friend of the Animals .. 225.00
9 Quest of the Devils Juju 225.00
10 Friend of the Animals....... 200.00
11 .... 200.00
12 Curse of the Jungle Jewels .. 200.00
13 New Adventures of Wambi .. 175.00
14 .... 175.00
15 The Leopard Legions 175.00
16 .... 175.00
17 Beware Bwana!........... 175.00
18 Ogg the Great Bull Ape 175.00

WANTED COMICS
**Toytown Comics/
Orbit Publications
Sept.–Oct., 1947**

9 Victor Everhart 250.00
10 Carlo Banone............. 150.00
11 Dwight Band 150.00
12 Ralph Roe 165.00
13 James Spencer;Drug....... 165.00
14 John "Jiggs" Sullivan;Drug . . 165.00
15 Harry Dunlap;Drug........ 100.00
16 Jack Parisi;Drug........... 110.00
17 Herber Ayers;Drug......... 110.00
18 Satan's Cigarettes;Drug 250.00
19 Jackson Stringer 100.00
20 George Morgan........... 100.00
21 BK,Paul Wilson 110.00
22......................... 110.00
23 George Elmo Wells 75.00
24 BK,Bruce Cornett;Drug...... 110.00
25 Henry Anger 75.00
26 John Wormly 75.00
27 Death Always Knocks Twice... 75.00
28 Paul H. Payton 75.00
29 Hangmans Holiday 75.00
30 George Lee 75.00
31 M Consolo................. 75.00
32 William Davis............... 75.00
33 The Web of Davis 75.00
34 Dead End 75.00
35 Glen Roy Wright 100.00
36 SSh,SSh(c),Bernard Lee
  Thomas 75.00
37 SSh,SSh(c),Joseph M. Moore . 75.00
38 SSh,SSh(c)................. 75.00
39 The Horror Weed;Drug....... 150.00
40.......................... 75.00
41.......................... 75.00
42.......................... 75.00
43.......................... 75.00
44.......................... 75.00
45 Killers on the Loose;Drug.... 100.00

*The Vault of Horror #35
and the Tramp © Walt Disney*

46 Chalres Edward Crews 75.00
47 .... 75.00
48 SSh,SSh(c) 75.00
49 .... 90.00
50 JB(c),Make Way for Murder .. 150.00
51 JB(c),Dope Addict on a
  Holiday of Murder;Drug..... 125.00
52 The Cult of Killers;
  Classic Drug.............. 125.00
53 April, 1953................ 75.00

WAR AGAINST CRIME
**L.L. Publishing Co.
(E.C. Comics), Spring, 1948**

1 Grl..................... 1,000.00
2 Grl,Guilty of Murder 600.00
3 JCr(c) 600.00
4 AF,JCr(c) 500.00
5 JCr(c) 500.00
6 AF,JCr(c) 500.00
7 AF,JCr(c) 500.00
8 AF,JCr(c) 500.00
9 AF,JCr(c),The Kid 500.00
10 JCr(c),I:Vault Keeper 2,800.00
11 JCr(c) 1,600.00
Becomes:

VAULT OF HORROR
April–May, 1950–Jan., 1955

12 AF,JCr(a&c),Wax Museum. . 6,000.00
13 AF,WW,JCr(c),Grl,Drug 1,400.00
14 AF,WW,JCr(c),Grl 1,200.00
15 AF,JCr(a&c),Grl,JKa 1,200.00
16 Grl,JKa,JCr(a&c) 850.00
17 JDa,Grl,JKa,JCr(a&c) 800.00
18 JDa,Grl,JKa,JCr(a&c) 800.00
19 JDa,Grl,JKa,JCr(a&c) 800.00
20 JDa,Grl,JKa,JCr(a&c) 750.00
21 JDa,Grl,JKa,JCr(a&c) 750.00
22 JDa,JKa,JCr(a&c) 750.00
23 JDa,Grl,JCr(a&c).......... 750.00
24 JDa,Grl,JO,JCr(a&c) 750.00
25 JDa,Grl,JKa,JCr(a&c) 750.00
26 JDa,Grl,JCr(a&c).......... 750.00
27 JDa,Grl,GE,JCr(a&c) 700.00
28 JDa,Grl,JCr(a&c).......... 700.00
29 JDa,Grl,JKa,JCr(a&c),
  Bradbury Adapt........... 700.00
30 JDa,Grl,JCr(a&c).......... 700.00
31 JDa,Grl,JCr(a&c),
  Bradbury Adapt........... 500.00
32 JDa,Grl,JCr(a&c).......... 500.00
33 JDa,Grl,RC,JCr(c) 500.00
34 JDa,Grl,RC,JCr(a&c) 500.00

GOLDEN AGE

35 JDa,Grl,JCr(a&c) 500.00
36 JDa,Grl,BK,JCr(a&c),Drug . . . 500.00
37 JDa,Grl,AW,JCr(a&c)
  Hanging 500.00
38 JDa,Grl,BK,JCr(a&c) 500.00
39 GRi,BK,RC,JCr(a&c)
  Bondage(c). 500.00
40 Grl,BK,JO,JCr(a&c) 700.00

WAR BATTLES
**Harvey Publications
Feb., 1952**
1 BP,Devils of the Deep 150.00
2 BP,A Present From Benny 75.00
3 BP 60.00
4 . . . . 60.00
5 . . . . 60.00
6 HN 60.00
7 BP 75.00
8 . . . . 60.00
9 Dec., 1953 . . . . 60.00

WAR BIRDS
Fiction House Magazines, 1952
1 Willie the Washout 150.00
2 Mystery MIGs of Kwanjuman . . 85.00
3 thru 6 . . . . @75.00
7 Winter, 1953,Across the
  Wild Yalu 75.00

WAR COMICS
**Dell Publishing Co.
May, 1940**
1 AMc,Sky Hawk 800.00
2 O:Greg Gildam 450.00
3 . . . . 350.00
4 O:Night Devils 400.00

WAR HEROES
**Dell Publishing Co.
July–Sept., 1942**
1 Gen. Douglas MacArthur (c) . . 350.00
2 . . . . 200.00
3 . . . . 150.00
4 A:Gremlins 250.00
5 . . . . 125.00
6 thru 11 . . . . @100.00

WAR HEROES
**Ace Magazines
May, 1952**
1 Always Comin' 125.00
2 LC,The Last Red Tank 75.00
3 You Got it 50.00
4 A Red Patrol 50.00
5 Hustle it Up 50.00
6 LC,Hang on Pal 75.00
7 . . . . 75.00
8 LC,April, 1953 . . . . 75.00

WARPATH
**Key Publications/
Stanmore
Nov., 1954**
1 Red Men Raid 125.00
2 AH(c),Braves Battle 75.00
3 April, 1955 . . . . 75.00

WARRIOR COMICS
H.C. Blackerby, 1944
1 Ironman wing Brady 300.00

*War Stories #8
© Dell Publishing Co.*

WAR SHIPS
Dell Publishing Co., 1942
1 AMc 200.00

WAR STORIES
Dell Publishing Co., 1942
5 O:The Whistler 300.00
6 A:Night Devils 250.00
7 A:Night Devils 250.00
8 A:Night Devils 250.00

WARTIME ROMANCES
**St. John Publishing Co.
July, 1951**
1 MB(c),MB 400.00
2 MB(c),MB 300.00
3 MB(c),MB 250.00
4 MB(c),MB 250.00
5 MB(c),MB 225.00
6 MB(c),MB 250.00
7 MB(c),MB 225.00
8 MB(c),MB 225.00
9 MB(c),MB 200.00
10 MB(c),MB 200.00
11 MB(c),MB. 200.00
12 MB(c),MB 200.00
13 MB(c) 100.00
14 MB(c) 100.00
15 MB(c) 100.00
16 MB(c),MB 100.00
17 MB(c) 100.00
18 MB(c),MB 100.00

WAR VICTORY COMICS
**U.S. Treasury/War Victory/
Harvey Publ.
Summer, 1942**
1 Savings Bond Promo with
  Top Syndicated Cartoonists,
  benefit USO 500.00
Becomes:

WAR VICTORY ADVENTURES
Summer, 1942
2 BP,2nd Front Comics 300.00
3 BP,F:Capt Cross of the
  Red Cross 250.00

WEB OF EVIL
**Comic Magazines, Inc.
(Quality Comics Group)
Nov., 1952**
1 Custodian of the Dead 750.00
2 JCo,Hangmans Horror 500.00
3 JCo 500.00
4 JCo(a&c),Monsters of
  the Mist 500.00
5 JCo(a&c),The Man who Died
  Twice,Electric Chair(c) 600.00
6 JCo(a&c),Orgy of Death 500.00
7 JCo(a&c),The Strangling
  Hands 500.00
8 JCo,Flaming Vengeance 450.00
9 JCo,The Monster in Flesh . . . 450.00
10 JCo,Brain that Wouldn't Die . . 450.00
11 JCo,Buried Alive. 450.00
12 Phantom Killer. 300.00
13 Demon Inferno. 300.00
14 RC(c),The Monster Genie . . . 300.00
15 Crypts of Horror. 300.00
16 Hamlet of Horror 300.00
17 Terror in Chinatown 250.00
18 Scared to Death,Acid Face . . 300.00
19 Demon of the Pit 250.00
20 Man Made Terror 250.00
21 Dec., 1954, Death's Ambush . 250.00

WEB OF MYSTERY
**A.A. Wyn Publ.
(Ace Magazines), Feb., 1951**
1 MSy,Venom of the Vampires . 700.00
2 MSy,Legacy of the Accursed . 350.00
3 MSy,The Violin Curse 300.00
4 GC 300.00
5 . . . . 300.00
6 LC 300.00
7 MSy 300.00
8 LC,LC(c),MSy,The Haunt of
  Death Lake 300.00
9 LC,LC(c) 300.00
10 . . . . 300.00
11 MSy. 300.00
12 LC 250.00
13 LC,LC(c) 250.00
14 MSy. 250.00
15 . . . . 250.00
16 . . . . 250.00
17 LC,LC(c) 250.00
18 LC. 250.00
19 LC 250.00
20 LC. 250.00

*Web of Evil #4
© Quality Comics Group*

GOLDEN AGE

Web of–Weird

```
21 MSy..................... 250.00
22 ........................ 250.00
23 ........................ 250.00
24 LC....................... 250.00
25 LC....................... 250.00
26 ........................ 250.00
27 LC....................... 250.00
28 RP,1st Issue under Comics
   Code Authority........... 200.00
29 MSy,Sept., 1955.......... 200.00
```

WEDDING BELLS
Quality Comics Group
Feb., 1954
```
1 OW........................ 150.00
2 .......................... 100.00
3 ........................... 60.00
4 ........................... 60.00
5 ........................... 60.00
6 ........................... 60.00
7 ........................... 60.00
8 ........................... 60.00
9 Comics Code................ 60.00
10 BWa...................... 150.00
11 .......................... 50.00
12 .......................... 45.00
13 .......................... 45.00
14 .......................... 45.00
15 MB(c).................... 50.00
16 MB(c),MB................. 100.00
17 .......................... 45.00
18 MB....................... 50.00
19 MB....................... 50.00
```

WEEKENDER, THE
Rucker Publishing Co.
Sept., 1945
```
1-1 rep.(c)................. 150.00
1-2 thru -4............... @150.00
2-1 rep.(c)................. 200.00
2-2 JCo,rep.(c)............. 150.00
2-3 WMc,Jan., 1946.......... 150.00
```

WEIRD ADVENTURES
P.L. Publishing
May, 1951–Oct., 1951
```
1 MB,Missing Diamonds....... 650.00
2 Puppet Peril.............. 500.00
3 Blood Vengeance........... 500.00
```

WEIRD ADVENTURES
Approved Comics
(Ziff-Davis)
July–Aug., 1951
```
10 P(c),Seeker from Beyond... 500.00
```

WEIRD CHILLS
Key Publications
July, 1954
```
1 MBi(c),BW............... 1,100.00
2 Eye Torture(c).......... 1,000.00
3 Bondage(c),Nov., 1954..... 600.00
```

WEIRD COMICS
Fox Features Syndicate
April, 1940
```
1 LF(c),Bondage(c),B:Birdman,
   Thor,Sorceress of Doom,
   BlastBennett,Typhon,Voodoo
   Man, Dr.Mortal.......... 6,500.00
2 LF(c),Mummy(c).......... 3,000.00
3 JSm(c).................. 1,500.00
4 JSm(c).................. 1,500.00
```

Weird Comics #9
© Fox Features Syndicate

```
5 Bondage(c),I:Dart,Ace;
   E:Thor................. 1,500.00
6 Dart & Ace(c)........... 1,400.00
7 Battle of Kooba......... 1,400.00
8 B:Panther Woman,Dynamo,
   The Eagle.............. 1,400.00
9 V:Pirates............... 1,000.00
10 A:Navy Jones........... 1,000.00
11 Dart & Ace(c)............ 800.00
12 Dart & Ace(c)............ 800.00
13 Dart & Ace(c)............ 800.00
14 The Rage(c).............. 800.00
15 Dart & Ace (c)............ 800.00
16 Flag,The Encore(c)....... 800.00
17 O:Black Rider............ 775.00
18 .......................... 750.00
19 .......................... 750.00
20 Jan., 1941,I'm The Master
    of Life and Death........ 900.00
```

WEIRD FANTASY
I.C. Publishing Co.
(E.C. Comics)
May–June, 1950
```
13(1)AF,HK,JKa,WW,AF(c),
    Roger Harvey's Brain... 2,800.00
14(2)AF,HK,JKa,WW,AF(c),Cosmic
    Ray Brain Explosion.... 1,300.00
15(3)AF,HK,JKa,WW,AF(c),Your
    Destination is the Moon... 900.00
16(4)AF,HK,JKa,WW,AF(c)..... 900.00
17(5)AF,HK,JKa,WW,AF(c),Not
    Made by Human Hands..... 750.00
6 AF,HK,JKa,WW,AF(c)........ 700.00
7 AF,JKa,WW,AF(c)........... 700.00
8 AF,JKa,WW,AF(c)........... 700.00
9 AF,Jka,WW,JO,AF(c)........ 700.00
10 AF,Jka,WW,JO,AF(c)....... 800.00
11 AF,Jka,WW,JO,AF(c)....... 550.00
12 AF,Jka,WW,JO,AF(c)....... 550.00
13 AF,Jka,WW,JO,AF(c)....... 550.00
14 AF,Jka,WW,JO,AW&FF,AF(c). 800.00
15 AF,JKa,JO,AW&RKr,AF(c),
    Bondage(c)............... 500.00
16 AF,Jka,JO,AW&RKr,AF(c)... 500.00
17 AF,JOP,JKa,AF(c),Bradbury. 500.00
18 AF,JO,JKa,AF(c),Bradbury.. 500.00
19 JO,JKa,JO(c),Bradbury.... 500.00
20 JO,JKa,FF,AF(c).......... 500.00
21 JO,JKa,AW&FF(c).......... 750.00
22 JO,JKa,JO(c),Nov.,1953... 400.00
```

Comics Values Annual

WEIRD HORRORS
St. John Publishing Co.
June, 1952
```
1 GT,Dungeon of the Doomed.. 750.00
2 Strangest Music Ever...... 400.00
3 PAM,Strange Fakir From
   the Orient.............. 400.00
4 Murderers Knoll........... 350.00
5 Phantom Bowman........... 350.00
6 Monsters from Outer Space. 600.00
7 LC,Deadly Double.......... 700.00
8 JKu,JKu(c),Bloody Yesterday. 500.00
9 JKu,JKu(c),Map Of Doom.... 500.00
```
Becomes:

NIGHTMARE
Dec., 1953
```
10 JKu(c),The Murderer's Mask. 800.00
11 BK,Ph(c),Fangs of Death... 600.00
12 JKu(c),The Forgotten Mask. 500.00
13 BP,Princess of the Sea.... 350.00
```
Becomes:

AMAZING GHOST STORIES
Oct., 1954
```
14 EK,MB(c),................. 300.00
15 BP........................ 250.00
16 Feb., 1955, EK,JKu........ 350.00
```

WEIRD MYSTERIES
Gilmore Publications
Oct., 1952
```
1 BW(c)................... 1,000.00
2 BWi..................... 1,500.00
3 Severed Heads(c).......... 750.00
4 BW,Human headed ants(c). 1,300.00
5 BW,Brains From Head(c).. 1,300.00
6 Severed Head(c)............ 750.00
7 Used in "Seduction"...... 1,000.00
8 The One That Got Away..... 800.00
9 Epitaph,Cyclops............ 750.00
10 The Ruby................. 600.00
11 Voodoo Dolls.............. 500.00
12 Sept., 1954............... 500.00
```

WEIRD SCIENCE
E.C. Comics, 1950
```
1 AF(a&c),JKu,HK,WW...... 2,900.00
2 AF(a&c),JKu,HK,WW,Flying
   Saucers(c)............. 1,500.00
3 AF(a&c),JKu,HK.......... 1,400.00
4 AF(a&c),JKu,HK.......... 1,400.00
5 AF(a&c),JKu,HK,WW,
   Atomic Bomb(c)........... 850.00
6 AF(a&c),JKu,HK............ 750.00
7 AF(a&c),JKu,HK,Classic(c). 750.00
8 AF(a&c),JKu............... 750.00
9 WW(c),JKu,Classic(c)...... 750.00
10 WW(c),JKu,JO,Classic(c).. 750.00
11 AF,JKu,Space war......... 600.00
12 WW(c),JKu,JO,Classic(c).. 600.00
13 WW(c),JKu,JO,............ 600.00
14 WW(a&c),JO............... 700.00
15 WW(a&c),JO,GRi,AW,
    RKr,JKa................. 700.00
16 WW(a&c),JO,AW,RKr,Jka... 700.00
17 WW(a&c),JO,AW,RKr,JKa... 700.00
18 WW(a&c),JO,AW,RKr,
    JKa,Atomic Bomb......... 700.00
19 WW(a&c),AW,
    FF,Horror(c)............ 750.00
20 WW(a&c),JO,AW,FF,JKa.... 750.00
21 WW(a&c),JO,AW,FF,JKa.... 750.00
22 WW(a&c),JO,AW,FF........ 750.00
```
Becomes:

CVA Page 480   All comics prices listed are for *Near Mint* condition.

GOLDEN AGE — Weird–Western

Weird Science-#17
© E.C. Comics

WEIRD SCIENCE FANTASY
March, 1954
23 WW(a&c),AW,BK 550.00
24 WW,AW,BK,Classic(c) 550.00
25 WW,AW,BK,Classic(c) 600.00
26 AF(c),WW,RC,
  Flying Saucer(c) 500.00
27 WW(a&c),RC 450.00
28 AF(c),WW 600.00
29 AF(c),WW,Classic(c) 800.00
Becomes:

INCREDIBLE SCIENCE FANTASY
July–Aug., 1955
30 WW,JDa(c),BK,AW,RKr,JO . . 600.00
31 WW,JDa(c),BK,AW,RKr 750.00
32 JDa(c),BK,WW,JO 750.00
33 WW(c),BK,WW,JO 750.00

WEIRD TALES OF THE FUTURE
S.P.M. Publ./ Aragon Publications March, 1952
1 RA 1,200.00
2 BW,BW(c) 1,800.00
3 BW,BW(c) 1,800.00
4 BW,BW(c) 1,400.00
5 BW,BW(c),Jumpin' Jupiter
  Lingerie(c) 1,800.00
6 Bondage(c) 750.00
7 BW,Devil(c) 1,500.00
8 July–Aug., 1953 . . . . 1,000.00

WEIRD TERROR
Allen Hardy Associates (Comic Media), Sept., 1952
1 RP,DH,BP,DH(c),Dungeon of the
  Doomed;Hitler 750.00
2 HcK(c),PAM 600.00
3 PAM,DH,DH(c) 600.00
4 PAM,DH,DH(c) 600.00
5 PAM,DH,RP,DH(c),Hanging(c) 500.00
6 DH,RP,DH(c),Step into
  My Parlour 500.00
7 PAM,DH,PAM,DH(c),Blood o/t Bats . 450.00
8 DH,RP,DH(c),Step into
  My Parlour 500.00
9 DH,PAM,DH(c),The Fleabite . 450.00

10 DH,BP,RP,DH(c) 450.00
11 DH,DH(c),Satan's Love Call . . 500.00
12 DH,DH(c),King Whitey 400.00
13 DH,DH(c),Sept., 1954,
  Wings of Death 400.00

WEIRD THRILLERS
Approved Comics (Ziff-Davis) Sept.–Oct., 1951
1 Ph(c),Monsters & The Model 1,200.00
2 AW,P(c),The Last Man 800.00
3 AW,P(c),Princess o/t Sea . . 1,100.00
4 AW,P(c),The Widows Lover. . . 750.00
5 BP,Oct., 1952,AW,P(c),
  Wings of Death 800.00

WESTERN ACTION THRILLERS
Dell Publishing Co. April, 1937
1 . . . . 1,200.00

WESTERN ADVENTURES COMICS
A.A. Wyn, Inc. (Ace Magazines), Oct., 1948
N#(1)Injun Gun Bait 275.00
N#(2)Cross-Draw Kid 150.00
N#(3)Outlaw Mesa 150.00
4 Sheriff 125.00
5 . . . . 125.00
6 Rip Roaring Adventure 125.00
Becomes:

WESTERN LOVE TRAILS
Nov., 1949
7 . . . . 150.00
8 Maverick Love 125.00
9 March, 1950 . . . . 100.00

WESTERN BANDIT TRAILS
St. John Publishing Co. Jan., 1949
1 GT,MB(c) 300.00
2 GT,MB(c) 250.00
3 GT,MB,MB(c),Gingham Fury . 275.00

WESTERN CRIME-BUSTERS
Trojan Magazines Sept., 1950–April, 1952
1 Gunslingin' Galoots 400.00
2 K-Bar Kate 250.00
3 Wilma West 250.00
4 Bob Dale 250.00
5 Six-Gun Smith 250.00
6 WW 400.00
7 WW,Wells Fargo Robbery . . . 400.00
8 . . . . 250.00
9 WW,Lariat Lucy 400.00
10 WW,Tex Gordon. 400.00

WESTERN CRIME CASES
See: WHITE RIDER

WESTERNER, THE
Wanted Comics Group/ Toytown Publ. June, 1948
14 F:Jack McCall 150.00
15 F:Bill Jamett. 75.00

16 F:Tom McLowery 75.00
17 F:Black Bill Desmond. 75.00
18 BK,F:Silver Dollar Dalton 100.00
19 MMe,F:Jess Meeton 60.00
20 . . . . 60.00
21 BK,MMe 100.00
22 BK,MMe 100.00
23 BK,MMe 100.00
24 BK,MMe 100.00
25 O,I,B:Calamity Jane. 100.00
26 BK,F:The Widowmaker 125.00
27 BK. 150.00
28 thru 31 . . . . @50.00
32 E:Calamity Jane 50.00
33 A:Quest 50.00
34 . . . . 50.00
35 SSh(c) 50.00
36 . . . . 50.00
37 Lobo-Wolf Boy 50.00
38 . . . . 50.00
39 . . . . 50.00
40 SSh(c) 50.00
41 Dec., 1951. . . . . 50.00

WESTERN FIGHTERS
Hillman Periodicals April–May, 1948
1 S&K(c) 450.00
2 BF(c) 125.00
3 BF(c) 100.00
4 BK,BF 125.00
5 . . . . 75.00
6 . . . . 75.00
7 BK 100.00
8 . . . . 75.00
9 . . . . 75.00
10 BK. 100.00
11 AMC&FF 400.00
2-1 BK 100.00
2-2 BP 60.00
2-3 thru 2-12 . . . . @50.00
3-1 thru 3-11 . . . . @50.00
3-12 BK 100.00
4-1 . . . . 50.00
4-2 BK 100.00
4-3 BK 100.00
4-4 BK 100.00
4-5 BK 100.00
4-6 BK 100.00
4-7 March–April, 1953 . . . . 50.00

WESTERN FRONTIER
P.L. Publishers (Approved Comics) May, 1951
1 Flaming Vengeance 125.00
2 . . . . 75.00
3 Death Rides the Iron Horse . . . 50.00
4 thru 6 . . . . @50.00
7 1952. . . . . 50.00

WESTERN HEARTS
Standard Magazine, Inc. Dec., 1949
1 Ph(c),JSe 250.00
2 Ph(c),AW,FF 275.00
3 Ph(c) 125.00
4 Ph(c),JSe,BE 125.00
5 Ph(c),JSe,BE 125.00
6 Ph(c),JSe,BE 125.00
7 Ph(c),JSe,BE 125.00
8 Ph(c) 150.00
9 Ph(c),JSe,BE 150.00
10 Ph(c),JSe,BE 100.00

All comics prices listed are for Near Mint condition.

GOLDEN AGE

WESTERN LOVE
Feature Publications (Prize Comics Group)
July–Aug., 1949
1 S&K 350.00
2 S&K 250.00
3 JSE,BE. 200.00
4 JSE,BE. 200.00
5 JSE,BE. 200.00

WESTERN PICTURE STORIES
Comics Magazine Co.
Feb., 1937–June, 1937
1 WE,Treachery Trail, 1st Western 2,500.00
2 WE,Weapons of the West . . 1,500.00
3 WE,Dragon Pass 1,000.00
4 CavemanCowboy 1,000.00

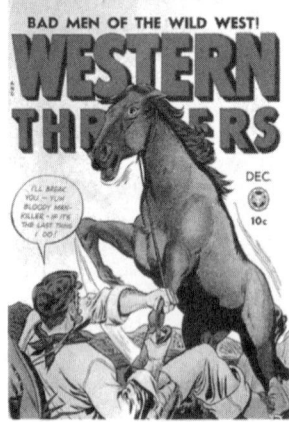

Western Thrillers #3
© Fox Features Syndicate

WESTERN THRILLERS
Fox Features Syndicate
Aug., 1948
1 . . . . 600.00
2 . . . . 250.00
3 GT,RH(c) 225.00
4 . . . . 250.00
5 . . . . 250.00
6 June, 1949 . . . . 225.00
Becomes:

MY PAST CONFESSIONS
Aug., 1949
7 . . . . 150.00
8 . . . . 75.00
9 . . . . 75.00
10 . . . . 75.00
11 . . . . 125.00
12 . . . . 50.00

WESTERN TRUE CRIME
Fox Features Syndicate
Aug., 1948
1 . . . . 450.00
2 . . . . 300.00
3 . . . . 250.00
4 JCr 300.00
5 . . . . 200.00
6 . . . . 200.00
Becomes:

MY CONFESSION
Aug., 1949–Feb., 1950
7 WW 400.00
8 WW,My Tarnished Reputation 350.00
9 I:Tormented Men 150.00
10 I Am Damaged Goods 150.00

WHACK
St. John Publishing Co.
Dec., 1953
1 Steve Crevice,Flush Jordan V:Bing(Crosby)The Merciful . 400.00
2 . . . . 200.00
3 F:Little Awful Fannie 200.00

WHAM COMICS
Centaur Publications
Nov., 1940
1 PG,The Sparkler & His Disappearing Suit 2,400.00
2 Dec., 1940,PG,PG(C), Men Turn into Icicles 1,500.00

WHIRLWIND COMICS
Nita Publications
June, 1940
1 F:The Cyclone 2.400.00
2 A:Scoops Hanlon,Cyclone(c) 1,500.00
3 Sept., 1940,A:Magic Mandarin,Cyclone(c) 1,400.00

WHITE PRINCESS OF THE JUNGLE
Avon Periodicals July, 1951
1 EK(c),Terror Fangs 750.00
2 EK,EK(c),Jungle Vengeance . 500.00
3 EK,EK(c),The Blue Gorilla . . 450.00
4 Fangs of the Swamp Beast . . 400.00
5 EK,Coils of the Tree Snake Nov., 1952 . . . . 400.00

WHIZ COMICS
Fawcett Publications
Feb., 1940
1 O:Captain Marvel,B:Spy Smasher,Golden Arrow,Dan Dare, Scoop Smith, Ibis the Invincible, Sivana . . . 85,000.00
2 . . . . 7,500.00
3 Make way for Captain Marvel 5,000.00
4 Captain Marvel Crashes Through 3,500.00
5 Captain Marvel Scores Again! 3,000.00
6 Circus of Death 2,400.00
7 B:Dr Voodoo,Squadron of Death 2,400.00
8 Saved by Captain Marvel! . . 2,400.00
9 MRa,Captain Marvel on the Job 2,400.00
10 Battles the Winged Death . . 2,400.00
11 Hurray for Captain Marvel . . 1,600.00
12 Captain Marvel rides the Engine of Doom. 1,600.00
13 Worlds Most Powerful Man!. 1,600.00
14 Boomerangs the Torpedo . . 1,600.00
15 O:Sivana. 1,800.00
16 . . . . 1,800.00
17 Knocks out a Tank 1,800.00
18 V:Spy Smasher. 1,800.00
19 Crushes the Tiger Shark . . . 1,200.00
20 V:Sivana 1,200.00
21 O:Lt. Marvels 1,300.00
22 Mayan Temple 900.00
23 GT,A:Dr. Voodoo 900.00
24 . . . . 900.00
25 O&I:Captain Marvel Jr., Stops the Turbine of Death 8,500.00
26 . . . . 800.00
27 V:Death God of the Katonkas. 900.00
28 V:Mad Dervish of Ank-Har . . . 900.00
29 Three Lt. Marvels (c), Pan American Olympics. 900.00
30 . . . . 800.00
31 Douglass MacArthur&Spy Smasher(c). 750.00
32 Spy Smasher(c). 750.00
33 Spy Smasher(c). 800.00
34 Three Lt. Marvels (c) 500.00
35 Capt. Marvel and the Three Fates 700.00
36 Haunted Hallowe'en Hotel . . . 500.00
37 Return of the Trolls 500.00
38 Grand Steeplechase 500.00
39 A Nazi Utopia. 500.00
40 A:Three Lt. Marvels, The Earth's 4 Corners 500.00
41 Captain Marvel 1,000 years from Now 400.00
42 Returns in Time Chair 400.00
43 V:Sinister Spies, Spy Smasher(c) 400.00
44 Life Story of Captain Marvel. . 450.00
45 Cures His Critics 400.00
46. . . . . 400.00
47 Captain Marvel needs a Birthday. 400.00
48. . . . . 400.00
49 Writes a Victory song 400.00
50 Captain Marvel's most embarrassing moment 400.00
51 Judges the Ugly- Beauty Contest. 350.00
52 V:Sivana, Chooses His Birthday 350.00
53 Captain Marvel fights Billy Batson 350.00
54 Jack of all Trades. 350.00
55 Family Tree 350.00
56 Tells what the Future Will Be . 350.00
57 A:Spy Smasher,Golden Arrow, Ibis. 350.00
58 . . . . 350.00
59 V:Sivana's Twin 350.00
60 Missing Person's Machine . . . 350.00
61 Gets a first name 300.00
62 Plays in a Band 300.00
63 Great Indian Rope Trick 300.00
64 Suspected of Murder 300.00
65 Lamp of Diogenes 300.00
66 The Trial of Mr. Morris! 300.00
67 . . . . 300.00
68 Laugh Lotion, V:Sivana 300.00
69 Mission to Mercury. 300.00
70 Climbs the World's Mightiest Mountain 300.00
71 Strange Magician. 250.00
72 V:The Man of the Future 250.00
73 In Ogre Land 250.00
74 Old Man River 250.00
75 The City Olympics 250.00
76 Spy Smasher become Crime Smasher 250.00
77 . . . . 250.00
78 . . . . 250.00
79 . . . . 250.00
80 . . . . 250.00
81. . . . . 250.00
82 The Atomic Ship 250.00
83 Magic Locket 250.00
84 . . . . 250.00
85 The Clock of San Lojardo. . . . 250.00
86 V:Sinister Sivanas 250.00
87 The War on Olympia 250.00
88 The Wonderful Magic Carpet . 250.00

All comics prices listed are for Near Mint condition.

GOLDEN AGE

Whiz Comics #4
© Fawcett Publications

WHODUNIT?
D.S. Publishing Co.
Aug.–Sept., 1948
1 MB,Weeping Widow 300.00
2 Diploma For Death 150.00
3 Dec.–Jan., 1949 . . . . 150.00

WHO IS NEXT?
Standard Comics
Jan., 1953
5 ATh,RA,Don't Let Me Kill 250.00

WILD BILL ELLIOT
Dell Publishing Co.
May, 1950
(1) see Dell Four Color #278
2 . . . . 125.00
3 thru 5 . . . . @75.00
6 thru 10 . . . . @75.00
(11-12) see Four Color #472, 520
13 thru 17 . . . . @60.00

WILD BILL HICKOK AND JINGLES
See: YELLOWJACKET COMICS

WILBUR COMICS
MLJ Magazines
(Archie Publications)
Summer, 1944
1 F:Wilbur Wilkin-America's Song
  of Fun 700.00
2 . . . . 350.00
3 . . . . 250.00
4 . . . . 200.00
5 I:Katy Keene 1,000.00
6 . . . . 200.00
7 . . . . 200.00
8 . . . . 200.00
9 . . . . 200.00
10 . . . . 200.00
11 thru 20 . . . . @150.00
21 thru 30 . . . . @100.00
31 thru 40 . . . . @75.00
41 thru 50 . . . . @60.00
51 thru 89 . . . . @50.00
90 Oct., 1965 . . . . 50.00

WILD BILL HICKOK
Avon Periodicals
Sept.–Oct., 1949
1 GRI(c),Frontier Fighter 275.00
2 Ph(c),Gambler's Guns 150.00
3 Ph(c),Great Stage Robbery . . 80.00
4 Ph(c),Guerilla Gunmen 80.00
5 Ph(c),Return of the Renegade . 80.00
6 EK,EK(c),Along the Apache
  Trail 80.00
7 EK,EK(c)Outlaws of
  Hell's Bend 80.00
8 Ph(c),The Border Outlaws . . . 80.00
9 PH(c),Killers From Texas 80.00
10 Ph(c) 80.00
11 EK,EK(c),The Hell Riders . . . 80.00
12 EK,EK(c),The Lost Gold Mine 100.00
13 EK,EK(c),Bloody Canyon
  Massacre 100.00
14 . . . . 100.00
15 . . . . 60.00
16 JKa 80.00
17 thru 23 . . . . @60.00
24 EK,EK(c) 80.00
25 EK,EK(c) 80.00
26 EK,EK(c) 80.00
27 EK,EK(c) 80.00
28 EK,EK(c),May–June, 1956 . . . 80.00

WILD BOY OF THE CONGO
Approved(Ziff-Davis)/
St. John Publ. Co.
Feb.–March, 1951
10(1)NS,PH(c),Bondage(c),The
  Gorilla God 275.00
11(2)NS,Ph(c),Star of the Jungle. 150.00
12(3)NS,Ph(c),Ice-Age Men . . . 150.00
4 NS.Ph(c),Tyrant of the Jungle 175.00
5 NS,Ph(c),The White Robe
  of Courage 125.00
6 NS,Ph(c) 125.00
7 MB,EK.Ph(c) 150.00
8 Ph(c),Man-Eater 125.00
9 Ph(c),Killer Leopard 125.00
10 . . . . 125.00
11 MB(c) 150.00
12 MB(c) 150.00
13 MB(c) 150.00
14 MB(c) 150.00
15 June, 1955 . . . . 100.00

WINGS COMICS
Wings Publ.
(Fiction House Magazines)
Sept., 1940
1 HcK,AB,GT,Ph(c),B:Skull Squad,
  Clipper Kirk,Suicide Smith,
  War Nurse,Phantom Falcons,
  GreasemonkeyGriffin,Parachute
  Patrol,Powder Burns 3,500.00
2 HcK,AB,GT,Bomber Patrol . . 1,500.00
3 HcK,AB,GT. 850.00
4 HcK,AB,GT,B:Spitfire Ace . . . 850.00
5 HcK,AB,GT,Torpedo Patrol . . 850.00
6 HcK,AB,GT,Bombs for Berlin . 750.00
7 HcK,AB 750.00
8 HcK,AB,The Wings of Doom . 750.00
9 Sky-Wolf 700.00
10 The Upside Down 700.00
11 . . . . 650.00
12 Fury of the fire Boards 650.00
13 Coffin Slugs For The
  Luftwaffe 650.00
14 Stuka Buster 650.00
15 Boomerang Blitz 650.00
16 O:Capt.Wings 750.00
17 Skyway to Death 600.00
18 Horsemen of the Sky 600.00
19 Nazi Spy Trap 600.00
20 The One Eyed Devil 600.00
21 Chute Troop Tornado 500.00
22 TNT for Tokyo 500.00
23 RP,Battling Eagles of Bataan . 500.00
24 RP,The Death of a Hero 500.00
25 RP,Suicide Squeeze 500.00
26 Tojo's Eagle Trap 500.00
27 Blb,Mile High Gauntlet 500.00
28 Blb,Tail Gun Tornado 500.00
29 Blb,Buzzards from Berlin . . . 500.00
30 Blb,Monsters of the
  Stratosphere 450.00
31 BLb,Sea Hawks away 450.00
32 BLb,Sky Mammoth 450.00
33 BLb,Roll Call of the Yankee
  Eagles 450.00
34 BLb,So Sorry,Mr Tojo 450.00
35 BLb,RWb,Hell's Lightning . . 450.00
36 RWb,The Crash-Master 450.00
37 RWb,Sneak Blitz 450.00
38 RWb,Rescue Raid of the
  Yank Eagle 450.00
39 RWb,Sky Hell/Pigboat Patrol . 450.00
40 RWb,Luftwaffe Gamble 450.00
41 RWb,.50 Caliber Justice 400.00

89 Webs of Crime 250.00
90 . . . . 250.00
91 Infinity (c) 250.00
92 . . . . 250.00
93 Captain America become
  a Hobo? 250.00
94 V:Sivana 250.00
95 Captain Marvel is grounded . . 250.00
96 The Battle Between Buildings. 250.00
97 Visits Mirage City 250.00
98 . . . . 250.00
99 V:Menace in the Mountains . . 250.00
100 . . . . 350.00
101 . . . . 235.00
102 A:Commando Yank 235.00
103 . . . . 235.00
104 . . . . 235.00
105 . . . . 235.00
106 A:Bulletman 235.00
107 The Great Experiment 300.00
108 thru 114 . . . . @235.00
115 The Marine Invasion 235.00
116 . . . . 235.00
117 V:Sivana 235.00
118 . . . . 235.00
119 . . . . 235.00
120 . . . . 235.00
121 . . . . 235.00
122 V:Sivana 235.00
123 . . . . 235.00
124 . . . . 235.00
125 Olympic Games of the Gods 235.00
126 . . . . 235.00
127 . . . . 235.00
128 . . . . 235.00
129 . . . . 235.00
130 . . . . 235.00
131 The Television Trap 235.00
132 thru 142 . . . . @235.00
143 Mystery of the Flying Studio. 235.00
144 V:The Disaster Master 235.00
145 . . . . 235.00
146 . . . . 235.00
147 . . . . 235.00
148 . . . . 235.00
149 . . . . 235.00
150 V:Bug Bombs 235.00
151 . . . . 235.00
152 . . . . 235.00
153 V:The Death Horror 350.00
154 Horror Tale, I:Dr.Death 350.00
155 V:Legend Horror,Dr.Death . . 400.00

GOLDEN AGE

Wings–Women

42 RWb,PanzerMeat forMosquito 400.00
43 RWb,Suicide Sentinels...... 400.00
44 RWb,Berlin Bombs Away.... 400.00
45 RWb,Hells Cargo........... 400.00
46 RWb,Sea-Hawk Patrol...... 400.00
47 RWb,Tojo's Tin Gibraltar..... 400.00
48 RWb...................... 400.00
49 RWb,Rockets Away......... 400.00
50 RWb,Mission For a Madman . 400.00
51 RWb,Toll for a Typhoon..... 300.00
52 MB,Madam Marauder....... 300.00
53 MB,Robot Death Over
   Manhattan................ 300.00
54 MB,Juggernauts of Death.... 300.00
55 MB........................ 300.00
56 MB,Sea Raiders Grave...... 300.00
57 MB,Yankee Warbirds over
   Tokyo.................... 300.00
58 MB........................ 300.00
59 MB,Prey of the Night Hawks . 300.00
60 MB,E:Skull Squad,
   Hell's Eyes............... 300.00
61 MB,Raiders o/t Purple Dawn . 250.00
62 Twilight of the Gods......... 250.00
63 Hara Kiri Rides the Skyways . 250.00
64 Taps For Tokyo............. 250.00
65 AB,Warhawk for the Kill..... 250.00
66 AB,B:Ghost Patrol.......... 250.00
67 AB........................ 250.00
68 AB,ClipperKirkBecomesPhantom
   Falcon;O:Phantom Falcon .. 250.00
69 AB,O:cont,Phantom Falcon .. 250.00
70 AB,N:Phantom Falcon;
   O:Final Phantom Falcon.... 250.00
71 Ghost Patrol becomes
   Ghost Squadron........... 250.00
72 V:Capt. Kamikaze........... 250.00
73 Hell & Stormoviks.......... 250.00
74 BLb(c),Loot is What She
   Lived For................. 250.00
75 BLb(c),The Sky Hag......... 250.00
76 BLb(c),Temple of the Dead... 250.00
77 BLb(c),Sky Express to Hell... 250.00
78 BLb(c),Loot Queen of
   Satan's Skyway........... 250.00
79 BLb(c),Buzzards of
   Plunder Sky.............. 250.00
80 BLb(c),Port of Missing Pilots . 250.00
81 BLb(c),Sky Trail of the
   Terror Tong............... 250.00
82 BLb(c),Bondage(c),Spider &
   The Fly Guy............... 265.00
83 BLb(c),GE,Deep Six For
   Capt. Wings............... 250.00
84 BLb(c),GE,Sky Sharks to
   the Kill................... 250.00
85 BLb(c),GE................. 250.00
86 BLb(c),GE,Moon Raiders.... 250.00
87 BLb(c),GE................. 250.00
88 BLb(c),GE,Madmans Mission. 250.00
89 BLb(c),GE,Bondage(c),
   Rockets Away............. 265.00
90 BLb(c),GE,Bondage(c),The
   Radar Rocketeers......... 265.00
91 BLb(c),GE,Bondage(c),V-9 for
   Vengeance............... 265.00
92 BLb(c),GE,Death's red Rocket 250.00
93 BLb(c),GE,Kidnap Cargo.... 250.00
94 BLb(c),GE,Bondage(c),Ace
   of the A-Bomb Patrol...... 265.00
95 BLb(c),GE,The Ace of
   the Assassins............. 250.00
96 BLb(c),GE................. 250.00
97 BLb(c),GE,The Sky Octopus . 250.00
98 BLb(c),GE,The Witch Queen
   of Satan's Skyways........ 250.00
99 BLb(c),GE,The Spy Circus... 250.00
100 BLb(c),GE,King o/t Congo . 265.00
101 BLb(c),GE,Trator of
   the Cockpit............... 250.00
102 BLb(c),GE,Doves of Doom.. 250.00

FIGHTING ACES OF WAR SKIES

Wings Comics #33
© Fiction House

103 BLb(c),GE............... 250.00
104 BLb(c),GE,Fireflies of Fury.. 250.00
105 BLb(c),GE............... 250.00
106 BLb(c),GE,Six Aces & A
   Firing Squad.............. 250.00
107 BLb(c),GE,Operation Satan . 250.00
108 BLb(c),GE,The Phantom
   of Berlin................. 250.00
109 GE,Vultures of
   Vengeance Sky........... 250.00
110 GE,The Red Ray Vortex.... 250.00
111 GE,E:Jane Martin........ 200.00
112 The Flight of the
   Silver Saucers............ 200.00
113 Suicide Skyways.......... 200.00
114 D-Day for Death Rays..... 200.00
115 Ace of Space............. 200.00
116 Jet Aces of Korea......... 200.00
117 Reap the Red Wind....... 200.00
118 Vengeance Flies Blind..... 200.00
119 The Whistling Death....... 200.00
120 Doomsday Mission........ 200.00
121 Ace of the Spyways....... 200.00
122 Last Kill Korea............ 200.00
123 The Cat & the Canaries.... 200.00
124 Summer, 1954, Death
   Below Zero............... 200.00

WINNIE WINKLE
Dell Publishing Co., 1941

1 .... 100.00
2 .... 75.00
3 thru 7 ....@60.00

WITCHCRAFT
Avon Periodicals March–April, 1952

1 SC,JKu,Heritage of Horror ... 900.00
2 SC,JKu,The Death Tattoo ... 700.00
3 EK,Better off Dead.......... 500.00
4 Claws of the Cat,
   Boiling Humans........... 525.00
5 Ph(c),Where Zombies Walk .. 550.00
6 March, 1953 Mysteries of the
   Moaning Statue.......... 450.00

WITCHES TALES
Harvey Publications Jan., 1951

1 RP,Bondage(c),Weird Yarns
   of Unseen Terror......... 700.00
2 RP,We Dare You.......... 400.00
3 RP,Bondage(c)Forest of
   Skeletons................ 250.00
4 BP....................... 250.00
5 BP,Bondage(c),Share
   My Coffin................ 300.00
6 BP,Bondage(c),Servants of
   the Tomb................ 250.00
7 BP,Screaming City......... 250.00
8 Bondage(c)................ 300.00
9 Fatal Steps................ 225.00
10 BP,.....,IT!............... 225.00
11 BP,Monster Maker......... 210.00
12 Bondage(c);The Web
   of the Spider............. 225.00
13 The Torture Jar........... 210.00
14 Transformation........... 225.00
15 Drooling Zombie.......... 210.00
16 Revenge of a Witch....... 210.00
17 Dimension IV............. 250.00
18 HN,Bird of Prey........... 225.00
19 HN,The Pact............. 225.00
20 HN,Kiss & Tell............ 225.00
21 HN,The Invasion.......... 225.00
22 HN,A Day of Panic........ 225.00
23 HN,The Wig Maker........ 225.00
24 HN,The Undertaker........ 325.00
25 What Happens at 8:30 PM?
   Severed Heads(c)......... 350.00
26 Up There................ 210.00
27 The Thing That Grew...... 210.00
28 Demon Flies.............. 210.00
Becomes:

WITCHES WESTERN TALES
Feb., 1955

29 S&K(a&c),F:Davy Crockett... 275.00
30 S&K(a&c).................. 300.00
Becomes:

WESTERN TALES
Oct., 1955

31 S&K(a&c),F:Davy Crockett... 250.00
32 S&K(a&c).................. 250.00
33 S&K(a&c),July–Sept.,1956... 250.00

WITH THE MARINES ON THE BATTLEFRONTS OF THE WORLD
Toby Press, June, 1953

1 Ph(c),Flaming Soul 325.00
2 Ph(c),March, 1954 .... 100.00

WITTY COMICS
Irwin H. Rubin/Chicago Nite Life News, 1945

1 .... 300.00
2 1945..................... 150.00
3 thru 7 ....@125.00

WOMEN IN LOVE
Fox Features Synd./ Hero Books/ Ziff-Davis, Aug., 1949

1 .... 700.00

WOMEN OUTLAWS
Fox Features Syndicate July, 1948

1 .... 1,000.00
2 .... 800.00
3 .... 800.00
4 .... 700.00
5 thru 8 ....@550.00

CVA Page 484   All comics prices listed are for *Near Mint* condition.

Comics Values Annual — GOLDEN AGE — Women–Wow Comics

Becomes:
MY LOVE MEMORIES
Nov., 1949
9 . . . . 150.00
10 . . . . 100.00
11 . . . . 125.00
12 WW 150.00

WONDERBOY
See: HORRIFIC

WONDER COMICS
**Great Publ./Nedor/
Better Publications
May, 1944**
1 SSh(c),B:Grim Reaper,
 Spectro Hitler(c) 1,900.00
2 ASh(c),O:Grim Reaper,B:Super
 Sleuths,Grim Reaper(c) . . . 1,000.00
3 ASh(c),Grim Reaper(c) 900.00
4 ASh(c),Grim Reaper(c) 850.00
5 ASh(c),Grim Reaper(c) 850.00
6 ASh(c),Grim Reaper(c) 750.00
7 ASh(c),Grim Reaper(c) 750.00
8 ASh(c),E:Super Sleuths,
 Spectro 750.00
9 ASh(c),B:Wonderman 750.00
10 ASh(c),Wonderman(c) 800.00
11 Grl(c),B:Dick Devins 850.00
12 Grl(c),Bondage(c) 850.00
13 ASh(c),Bondage(c) 850.00
14 ASh(c),Bondage(c)
 E:Dick Devins 850.00

Wonder Comics #20
© *Better Publications*

15 ASh(c),Bondage(c),B:Tara . . 1,000.00
16 ASh(c),A:Spectro,
 E:Grim Reaper 850.00
17 FF,ASh(c),A:Super Sleuth . . . 900.00
18 ASh(c),B:Silver Knight 850.00
19 ASh(c),FF 850.00
20 FF,Oct., 1948 . . . . 1,000.00

WONDERLAND COMICS
**Feature Publications
(Prize Comics Group)
Summer, 1945**
1 (fa),B:Alex in Wonderland . . . 200.00
2 . . . . 100.00
3 thru 8 . . . . @75.00
9 1947 . . . . 75.00

WONDER COMICS
**Fox Features Syndicate
May, 1939**
1 BKa,WE,WE(c),B:Wonderman,
 DR.Kung,K-51 . . . . 24,000.00
2 WE,BKa,LF(c),B:Yarko the
 Great,A:Spark Stevens . . . 7,500.00
Becomes:
WONDERWORLD COMICS
July, 1939–Jan., 1942
3 WE,LF,BP,LF&WE,I:Flame . 10,000.00
4 WE,LF,BP,LF(c) 5,000.00
5 WE,LF,BP,GT,LF(c),Flame . 2,500.00
6 WE,LF,BP,GT,LF(c),Flame . 2,400.00
7 WE,LF,BP,GT,LF(c),Flame . . 4,000.00
8 WE,LF,BP,GT,LF(c),Flame . . 3,400.00
9 WE,LF,BP,GT,LF(c),Flame . . 1,900.00
10 WE,LF,BP,LF(c),Flame 1,900.00
11 WE,LF,BP,LF(c),O:Flame . . 1,800.00
12 BP,LF(c),Bondage(c),Flame 1,600.00
13 E:Dr Fung,Flame 1,500.00
14 JoS,Bondage(c),Flame 1,600.00
15 JoS&LF(c),Flame 1,500.00
16 Flame(c) 1,200.00
17 Flame(c) 1,200.00
18 Flame(c) 1,200.00
19 Male Bondage(c),Flame . . . 1,300.00
20 Flame(c) 1,200.00
21 O:Black Club &Lion,Flame . 1,100.00
22 Flame(c) 950.00
23 Flame(c) 800.00
24 Flame(c) 800.00
25 A:Dr Fung,Flame 800.00
26 Flame(c) 800.00
27 Flame(c) 800.00
28 Bondage(c)I&O:US Jones,
 B:Lu-nar,Flame 1,200.00
29 Bondage(c),Flame 700.00
30 O:Flame(c),Flame 1,300.00
31 Bondage(c),Flame 700.00
32 Hitler(c),Flame 850.00
33 Male Bondage(c) 700.00

WORLD FAMOUS HEROES MAGAZINE
**Comic Corp. of America
(Centaur)
Oct., 1941**
1 BLb,Paul Revere 1,500.00
2 BLb,Andrew Jackson,V:
 Dickinson 750.00
3 BLb,Juarez-Mexican patriot . . 600.00
4 BLb,Canadian Mounties 600.00

WORLD'S GREATEST STORIES
**Jubilee Publications
Jan., 1949**
1 F:Alice in Wonderland 400.00
2 F:Pinocchio 350.00

WORLD WAR III
**Ace Periodicals
March–May, 1953**
1 Atomic Bomb (c) 1,000.00
2 The War That Will Never
 Happen 750.00

WOTALIFE COMICS
See: PHANTOM LADY

WOW COMICS
**David McKay/Henle Publ.
July, 1936–Nov., 1936**
1 WE,DBr(c),Fu Manchu,
 Buck Jones 3,500.00
2 WE,Little King 2,800.00
3 WE,WE(c) 2,500.00
4 WE,BKa,AR,DBr(c),Popeye,
 Flash Gordon 3,000.00

WOW COMICS
**Fawcett Publications
Winter, 1940**
N#(1)S&K,CCB(c),B&O:Mr Scarlett;
 B:Atom Blake,Jim Dolan,Rick
 O'Shay,Bondage(c) 24,000.00
2 B:Hunchback 3,500.00
3 V:Mummy Ray Gun 1,800.00
4 O:Pinky 2,000.00
5 F:Pinky the Whiz Kid 1,000.00
6 O:Phantom Eagle;
 B:Commando Yank 1,000.00
7 Spearhead of Invasion 800.00
8 All Three Heroes 800.00
9 A:Capt Marvel,Capt MarvelJr.
 Shazam,B:Mary Marvel . . 1,800.00
10 The Sinister Secret of
 Hotel Hideaway 800.00
11 . . . . 750.00
12 Rocketing adventures 750.00

Wow Comics #7
© *Fawcett Publications*

13 Thrill Show 750.00
14 V:Mr Night 750.00
15 The Shazam Girl of America . 700.00
16 Ride to the Moon 700.00
17 V:Mary Batson,Alter Ego
 Goes Berserk 700.00
18 I:Uncle Marvel,Infinity(c)
 V is For Victory 700.00
19 A Whirlwind Fantasy 700.00
20 Mary Marvel's Magic Carpet . . 700.00
21 Word That Shook the World . . 350.00
22 Come on Boys-
 Everybody Sing 350.00
23 Trapped by the Terror of
 the Future 350.00
24 Mary Marvel 350.00
25 Mary Marvel Crushes Crime . . 350.00
26 Smashing Star-
 Studded Stories 300.00
27 War Stamp Plea(c) 300.00
28 . . . . 300.00
29 . . . . 300.00

All comics prices listed are for *Near Mint* condition.

GOLDEN AGE

Wow–Young

30 In Mirror Land	300.00
31 Stars of Action	250.00
32 The Millinery Marauders	250.00
33 Mary Marvel(c)	250.00
34 A:Uncle Marvel	250.00
35 I:Freckles Marvel	250.00
36 Secret of the Buried City	250.00
37 7th War loan plea	250.00
38 Pictures That Came to Life	250.00
39 The Perilous Packages	250.00
40 The Quarrel of the Gnomes	250.00
41 Hazardous Adventures	200.00
42	200.00
43 Curtain Time	200.00
44 Volcanic Adventure	200.00
45	200.00
46	200.00
47	200.00
48	200.00
49	200.00
50 Mary Marvel/Commando Yank	200.00
51	175.00
52	175.00
53 Murder in the Tall Timbers	175.00
54 Flaming Adventure	175.00
55 Earthquake!	175.00
56 Sacred Pearls of Comatesh	175.00
57	175.00
58 E:Mary Marvel;The Curse of the Keys	175.00
59 B:Ozzie the Hilarious Teenager	175.00
60 thru 64	@175.00
65 A:Tom Mix	175.00
66 A:Tom Mix	175.00
67 A:Tom Mix	175.00
68 A:Tom Mix	175.00
69 A:Tom Mix,Baseball	175.00

Becomes:

REAL WESTERN HERO
Sept., 1948

70 It's Round-up Time	350.00
71 CCB,P(c),A Rip Roaring Rodeo	250.00
72 w/Gabby Hayes	250.00
73 thru 75	@250.00

Becomes:

WESTERN HERO
March, 1949

76 Partial Ph(c)&P(c)	350.00
77 Partial Ph(c)&P(c)	200.00
78 Partial Ph(c)&P(c)	200.00
79 Partial Ph(c)&P(c), Shadow of Death	175.00
80 Partial Ph(c)&P(c)	200.00
81 CCB,Partial Ph(c)&P(c), F:Tootsie	200.00
82 Partial Ph(c)&P(c), A:Hopalong Cassidy	200.00
83 Partial Ph(c)&P(c)	200.00
84 Ph(c)	175.00
85 Ph(c)	175.00
86 Ph(c),The Case of the Extra Buddy, giant	175.00
87 Ph(c),The Strange Lands	175.00
88 Ph(c),A:Senor Diablo	175.00
89 Ph(c),The Hypnotist	175.00
90 Ph(c),The Menace of the Cougar, giant	150.00
91 Ph(c),Song of Death	150.00
92 Ph(c),The Fatal Hide-out, giant	150.00
93 Ph(c),Treachery at Triple T, giant	150.00
94 Ph(c),Bank Busters,giant	150.00
95 Ph(c),Rampaging River	150.00
96 Ph(c),Range Robbers,giant	150.00
97 Ph(c),Death on the Hook,giant	150.00
98 Ph(c),Web of Death,giant	150.00
99 Ph(c),The Hidden Evidence	150.00
100 Ph(c),A:Red Eagle,Giant	150.00
101 Ph(c)	150.00
102 thru 111 Ph(c)	@150.00
112 Ph(c),March, 1952	175.00

Yankee Comics #2
© *Charlton Comics*

YANKEE COMICS
**Chesler Publications
(Harry A. Chesler)
Sept., 1941–March, 1942**

1 F:Yankee Doodle Jones	2,400.00
2 The Spirit of '41	1,100.00
3 Yankee Doodle Jones	800.00
4 JCo,Yankee Doodle Jones	800.00

YELLOWJACKET COMICS
**Levy Publ./Frank Comunale/Charlton
Sept., 1944**

1 O&B:Yellowjackets,B:Diana the Huntress	1,000.00
2 Rosita &The Filipino Kid	500.00
3	450.00
4 Fall of the House of Usher	500.00
5 King of Beasts	500.00
6	550.00
7 I:Diane Carter;The Lonely Guy	1,200.00
8 The Buzzing Bee Code	600.00
9	500.00
10 Capt Grim V:The Salvage Pirates	600.00

Becomes:

JACK IN THE BOX
Feb., 1946

11 Funny Animal,Yellow Jacket	125.00
12 Funny Animal	75.00
13 BW,Funny Animal	150.00
14 thru 16 Funny Animal	@60.00

Becomes:

COWBOY WESTERN COMICS
July, 1948

17 Annie Oakley,Jesse James	250.00
18 JO,JO(c)	200.00
19 JO,JO(c),Legends of Paul Bunyan	200.00
20 JO(c),Jesse James	100.00
21 Annie Oakley VisitsDryGulch	100.00
22 Story of the Texas Rangers	100.00
23	100.00
24 Ph(c),F:James Craig	100.00
25 Ph(c),F:Sunset Carson	100.00
26 Ph(c)	150.00
27 Ph(c),Sunset Carson movie	600.00
28 Ph(c),Sunset Carson movie	300.00
29 Ph(c),Sunset Carson movie	300.00
30 Ph(c),Sunset Carson movie	300.00
31 Ph(c)	100.00
32 thru 34 Ph(c)	@90.00
35 thru 37 Sunset Carson	@275.00
38 and 39	@50.00

Becomes:

SPACE WESTERN COMICS
Charlton Comics, Oct., 1952

40 Spurs Jackson,V:The Saucer Men	1,100.00
41 StC(c),Space Vigilantes	750.00
42 StC(c),Aomic Bomb	900.00
43 StC(c),Battle of Spacemans Gulch	800.00
44 StC(c),The Madman of Mars	750.00
45 StC(c),The Moon Bat,Hitler	775.00

Becomes:

COWBOY WESTERN COMICS
Oct., 1953

46	200.00

Becomes:

COWBOY WESTERN HEROES
Dec., 1953

47	50.00
48	50.00

Becomes:

COWBOY WESTERN
May–June, 1954

49	50.00
50 F:Jesse James	40.00
51 thru 56	@40.00
58, giant	50.00
59 thru 66	@40.00
67 AW&AT	125.00

Becomes:

WILD BILL HICKOK AND JINGLES
Aug., 1958

68 AW	125.00
69 AW	100.00
70 AW	75.00
71 thru 73	@60.00
74 1960	60.00

YOGI BERRA
Fawcett 1957

1 Ph(c)	1,000.00

YOUNG BRIDES
**Feature Publications
(Prize Comics) Sept.–Oct., 1952**

1 S&K,Ph(c)	400.00
2 S&K,Ph(c)	225.00
3 S&K,Ph(c)	200.00
4 S&K	200.00
5 S&K	200.00
6 S&K	200.00
2-1 S&K	175.00
2-2 S&K	100.00
2-3 S&K	175.00

All comics prices listed are for *Near Mint* condition.

GOLDEN AGE

Young–Zago

2-4 S&K	125.00
2-5 S&K	125.00
2-6 S&K	125.00
2-7 S&K	175.00
2-8 S&K	75.00
2-9 S&K	75.00
2-10 S&K	175.00
2-11 S&K	175.00
2-12 S&K	175.00
3-1	60.00
3-2	60.00
3-3	60.00
3-4	60.00
3-5	60.00
3-6	60.00
4-1	60.00
4-2 S&K	150.00
4-3	60.00
4-4 S&K	150.00
4-5	60.00

YOUNG EAGLE
Fawcett Publications/ Charlton Comics, Dec., 1950

1 Ph(c)	200.00
2 Ph(c),Mystery of Thunder Canyon	125.00
3 Ph(c),Death at Dawn	100.00
4 Ph(c)	100.00
5 Ph(c),The Golden Flood	100.00
6 Ph(c),The Nightmare Empire	100.00
7 Ph(c),Vigilante Veangeance	100.00
8 Ph(c),The Rogues Rodeo	100.00
9 Ph(c),The Great Railroad Swindle	100.00
10 June, 1952, Ph(c),Thunder Rides the Trail,O:Thunder	80.00

YOUNG KING COLE
Novelty Press/Premium Svcs. Co., Autumn, 1945

1-1 Detective Toni Gayle	350.00
1-2	200.00
1-3	175.00
1-4	135.00
2-1	135.00
2-2	135.00
2-3	135.00
2-4	135.00
2-5	135.00
2-6	135.00
2-7	135.00
3-1	125.00

Young King Cole #3-1
© *Novelty Press*

3-2 LbC	200.00
3-3 The Killer With The Hat	125.00
3-4 The Fierce Tiger	125.00
3-5 AMc	125.00
3-6	135.00
3-7 LbC(c),Case of the Devil's Twin	250.00
3-8	125.00
3-9 The Crime Fighting King	125.00
3-10 LbC(c)	200.00
3-11 LbC(c)	200.00
3-12 July, 1948,AMc(c)	120.00

YOUNG LIFE
New Age Publications Summer, 1945

1 Partial Ph(c),Louis Prima	175.00
2 Partial Ph(c),Frank Sinatra	200.00

Becomes:

TEEN LIFE
Winter, 1945

3 Partial Ph(c),Croon without Tricks,June Allyson(c)	150.00
4 Partial Ph(c),Atom Smasher Blueprints,Duke Ellington(c)	100.00
5 Partial Ph(c), Build Your Own Pocket Radio, Jackie Robinson(c)	150.00

YOUNG LOVE
Feature Publ. (Prize Comics Group) Feb.–March, 1949

1 S&K,S&K(c)	600.00
2 S&K,Ph(c)	300.00
3 S&K,JSe,BE,Ph(c)	250.00
4 S&K,Ph(c)	150.00
5 S&K,Ph(c)	150.00
2-1 S&K,Ph(c)	250.00
2-2 Ph(c)	135.00
2-3 Ph(c)	135.00
2-4 Ph(c)	135.00
2-5 Ph(c)	135.00
2-6 S&K(c)	200.00
2-7 S&K(c),S&K	200.00
2-8 S&K	200.00
2-9 S&K(c),S&K	200.00
2-10 S&K(c),S&K	200.00
2-11 S&K(c),S&K	200.00
2-12 S&K(c),S&K	200.00
3-1 S&K(c),S&K	200.00
3-2 S&K(c),S&K	200.00
3-3 S&K(c),S&K	200.00
3-4 S&K(c),S&K	200.00
3-5 Ph(c)	150.00
3-6 BP,Ph(c)	150.00
3-7 Ph(c)	150.00
3-8 Ph(c)	150.00
3-9 MMe,Ph(c)	150.00
3-10 Ph(c)	150.00
3-11 Ph(c)	150.00
3-12 Ph(c)	150.00
4-1 S&K	150.00
4-2 Ph(c)	125.00
4-3 Ph(c)	125.00
4-4 Ph(c)	125.00
4-5 Ph(c)	125.00
4-6 S&K,Ph(c)	125.00
4-7 thru 4-12 Ph(c)	@100.00
5-1 thru 5-12 Ph(c)	@60.00
6-1 thru 6-9	@50.00
6-10 thru 6-12	@50.00
7-1 thru 7-7	@40.00
7-8 thru 7-11	@40.00
7-12 thru 8-5	@40.00
8-6 thru 8-12	@50.00

YOUNG ROMANCE COMICS
Feature Publ./Headline/ Prize Publ., Sept.–Oct., 1947

1 S&K(c),S&K	600.00
2 S&K(c),S&K	350.00
3 S&K(c),S&K	300.00
4 S&K(c),S&K	300.00
5 S&K(c),S&K	300.00
6 S&K(c),S&K	300.00
2-1 S&K(c),S&K	275.00
2-2 S&K(c),S&K	275.00
2-3 S&K(c),S&K	275.00
2-4 S&K(c),S&K	275.00
2-5 S&K(c),S&K	275.00
2-6 S&K(c),S&K	275.00
3-1 thru 3-12 S&K(c),S&K	@250.00
4-1 thru 4-12 S&K	@250.00
5-1 ATh,S&K	250.00
2	250.00
3	250.00
5-4 thru 5-12 S&K	@250.00
6-1 thru 6-3	@100.00

YOUR UNITED STATES
Lloyd Jacquet Studios, 1946

1N# Teeming nation of Nations	250.00

YOUTHFUL HEART
Youthful Magazines May, 1952

1 Frankie Lane(c)	350.00
2 Vic Damone	250.00
3 Johnnie Ray	250.00

Becomes:

DARING CONFESSIONS
Nov., 1952

4 DW,Tony Curtis	150.00
5	125.00
6 DW	135.00
7	125.00
8 DW	125.00

YOUTHFUL ROMANCES
Pix Parade/Ribage/ Trojan, Aug.–Sept., 1949

1	300.00
2	200.00
3 Tex Beneke	150.00
4	150.00
5	125.00
6	125.00
7 Tony Martin(c)	150.00
8 WW(c), Frank Sinatra	250.00
9 thru 14	@75.00

Becomes:

DARLING LOVE
Oct.–Nov., 1949

15 WD	100.00
16	75.00
17 DW,Ph(c)	75.00

ZAGO, JUNGLE PRINCE
Fox Features Syndicate Sept., 1948

1 A:Blue Beetle	900.00
2 JKa	750.00
3 JKa	600.00
4 MB(c)	600.00

Becomes:

MY STORY
May, 1949

5 JKa,Too Young To Fall in Love	250.00
6 I Was A She-Wolf	100.00

All comics prices listed are for Near Mint condition.

Zago–Zoot

GOLDEN AGE

Comics Values Annual

7 I Lost My Reputation	100.00
8 My Words Condemned Me	100.00
9 WW,Wayward Bride	225.00
10 WW,March, 1950,Second Rate Girl	225.00
11	100.00
12	100.00

TEGRA, JUNGLE EMPRESS
Fox Features Syndicate
Aug., 1948

1 Blue Bettle,Rocket Kelly	750.00

Becomes:

ZEGRA, JUNGLE EMPRESS
Oct., 1948

2 JKa	750.00
3	600.00
4	600.00
5	600.00

Becomes:

MY LOVE LIFE
June, 1949–Aug., 1950

6 I Put A Price Tag On Love	175.00
7 An Old Man's Fancy	125.00
8 My Forbidden Affair	125.00
9 I Loved too Often	125.00
10 My Secret Torture	125.00
11 I Broke My Own Heart	125.00
12 I Was An Untamed Filly	125.00
13 I Can Never Marry You	100.00

ZIP COMICS
MLJ Magazines
Feb., 1940–Summer, 1944

1 MMe,O&B:Kalathar,The Scarlet Avenger,Steel Sterling,B:Mr Satan,Nevada Jones,War Eagle Captain Valor	7,500.00
2 MMe,CBi(c)B:Steel Sterling(c)	3,000.00
3 MMe,CBi(a&c)	2,500.00
4 MMe,CBi(a&c)	2,000.00
5 MMe,CBi(a&c)	2,000.00
6 MMe,CBi(a&c)	1,600.00
7 MMe,CBi(a&c)	1,600.00
8 MMe,CBi(a&c),Bondage(c)	1,600.00
9 CMMe,CBi(a&c),E:Kalathar, Mr Satan;Bondage(c)	2,000.00
10 MMe,CBi(a&c),B:Inferno	1,800.00
11 MMe,CBi(a&c)	1,500.00
12 MMe,CBi(a&c),Bondage(c)	1,500.00
13 MMe,CBi(a&c),E:Inferno, Bondage(c),Woman in Electric Chair	1,600.00
14 MMe,CBi(a&c),Bondage(c)	1,500.00
15 MMe,CBi(a&c),Bondage(c)	1,500.00
16 MMe,CBi(a&c),Bondage(c)	1,500.00
17 CBI(a&c),E:Scarlet Avenger Bondage(c)	1,500.00
18 IN(c),B:Wilbur	1,500.00
19 IN(c),Steel Sterling(c)	1,500.00
20 IN(c),O&I:Black Jack Hitler(c)	2,400.00
21 IN(c),V:Nazis	1,200.00
22 IN(c)	1,200.00
23 IN(c),Flying Fortress	1,200.00
24 IN(c),China Town Exploit	1,200.00
25 IN(c),E:Nevada Jones	1,200.00
26 IN(c),B:Black Witch, E:Capt Valor	1,200.00
27 IN(c),I:Web,V:Japanese	2,000.00
28 IN(C),O:Web,Bondage(c)	1,600.00
29 Steel Sterling & Web	750.00
30 V:Nazis	750.00
31 IN(c)	650.00
32	650.00
33 Bondage(c)	700.00
34 I:Applejack;Bondage(c)	700.00
35 E:Zambini	650.00
36 I:Senor Banana	650.00
37	650.00
38 E:Web	650.00
39 O&B:Red Rule	650.00
40	500.00
41	500.00
42	500.00
43	500.00
44	500.00
45 E:Wilbur	500.00
46	500.00
47 Crooks Can't Win	500.00

ZIP-JET
St. John Publishing Co.
Feb., 1953

1 Rocketman	1,000.00
2 April–May, 1953, Assassin of the Airlanes	650.00

ZOOM COMICS
Carlton Publishing Co.
Dec., 1945

N# O:Captain Milksop	600.00

ZOOT COMICS
Fox Features Syndicate
Spring, 1946

N#(1)(fa)	250.00
2 A:Jaguar(fa)	250.00
3 (fa)	150.00
4 (fa)	150.00
5 (fa)	100.00
6 (fa)	100.00
7 B:Rulah	1,200.00
8 JKa(c),Fangs of Stone	850.00
9 JKa(c),Fangs of Black Fury	850.00
10 JKa(c),Inferno Land	850.00
11 JKa,The Purple Plague, Bondage(c)	800.00
12 JKa(c),The Thirsty Stone, Bondage(c)	650.00
13 Bloody Moon	650.00
14 Pearls of Pathos,Woman Carried off by Bird	750.00
15 Death Dancers	650.00
16	650.00

Becomes:

RULAH, JUNGLE GODDESS
Aug., 1948

17 JKa(c),Wolf Doctor	1,300.00
18 JKa(c),Vampire Garden	900.00
19 JKa(c)	850.00
20	850.00
21 JKa(c)	850.00
22 JKa(c)	850.00
23	750.00
24	650.00
25	650.00
26	650.00
27	700.00

Becomes:

I LOVED
July, 1949–March, 1950

28	150.00
29 thru 31	@100.00
32 My Poison Love	100.00

Zip Comics #9
© MLJ Magazines

Zoot #9
© Fox Features Syndicate

Rulah, Jungle Goddess #17
© Fox Features Syndicate

All comics prices listed are for *Near Mint* condition.

DARK HORSE

ABE SAPIEN: DRUMS OF THE DEAD
March, 1998
1-shot Hellboy spin-off 3.00

ABYSS, THE
1989
1 MK,Movie Adaptation 2.50
2 MK,Movie Adaptation 2.50

ACCIDENT MAN
(B&W) 1993
1 I:Accident Man 2.50
2 . . . . 2.50
3 . . . . 2.50

ADRENALYNN: WEAPON OF WAR
Aug., 2001
TPB TnD 12.95

ADVENTURES OF LUTHER ARKWRIGHT
Valkyrie Press/Dark Horse
(B&W) 1987–89
1 thru 9 . . . . @2.00
(B&W) 1990
1 thru 9 Rep. . . . . @1.95
TPB 14.95
TPB rep. 16.95

ADVENTURES OF THE MASK
1996
1 thru 12 by Michael Eury & Marc Campos, TV cartoon adapt. . @2.50
Ash can (1995). 3.00

AGENTS OF LAW
Comics' Greatest World 1995
1 KG, I:Law 2.50
2 A:Barb Wire 2.50
3 KG,DLw,The Judgment Gate . . . 2.50
4 Open Golden City 2.50
5 Who is the Mystery figure 2.50
6 V:Predator 2.50

AGE OF REPTILES
1993–94
1 DRd,Story on Dinosaurs 3.00
2 DRd,Story on Dinosaurs 3.00
3 DRd,Story on Dinosaurs 3.00
4 DRd,Story on Dinosaurs 3.00
TPB Tribal Warfare 14.95

AGE OF REPTILES: THE HUNT
1996
1 thru 5 by Ricardo Delgado. . . . @3.00
TPB The Hunt 17.95

AKIRA
TPB #1, 364-pg.,B&W 24.95
TPB #2, 304-pg.,B&W 24.95
TPB #3, 288-pg.,B&W 24.95
TPB #4, 400-pg.,B&W 27.95
TPB #5, 416-pg.,B&W 27.95
TPB #6, 440-pg.,B&W 29.95

AL CAPP'S LI'L ABNER: THE FRAZETTA SUNDAYS
May 2003
TPB Vol. 1 1954–55 . . . . 18.95
TPB Vol. 2 1956–57 . . . . 18.95
TPB Vol. 3 1958–59 . . . . 18.95

ALIEN RESURRECTION
Oct., 1997
1 (of 2) movie adaptation 2.50
2 DMc(c) 2.50

ALIENS
(B&W) 1988
1 Movie Sequel,R:Hicks,Newt . . . 20.00
1a 2nd printing 3.00
1b 3rd printing 2.25
1c 4th printing 2.25
2 Hicks raids Mental Hospital. 8.00
2a 2nd printing 2.50
2a 3rd printing 2.25
3 Realize Queen is on Earth 7.00
3a 2nd printing 2.25
4 Queen is freed, Newton on Aliens World 5.00
5 All out war on Aliens World 5.00
6 Hicks & Newt return to Earth. . . . 5.00
TPB rep.#1–#6 & DHP #24 . . . . . 11.00
TPB 2nd printing, DvD(c) 11.00

ALIENS (II)
[Mini-Series] 1989
1 DB,Hicks,Newt hijack ship 5.00
1a 2nd Printing 3.00
2 DB,Crazed general trains aliens . 3.00
2a 2nd Printing 3.00
3 DB,HicksV:General Spears 3.00
3a 2nd Printing 2.50
4 DB,Heroes reclaim earth from aliens 3.00

ALIENS
1-shot Earth Angel, JBy (1994) 3.00
TPB rep. Earth Angel (1991) 15.00
1-shot Glass Corridor, DvL 3.00
1-shot Mondo Heat, I:Herk Mondo . 2.50
1-shot Mondo Pest (1995) 3.00
1-shot Purge, IEd,PhH 3.00
1-shot Pig, CDi,FH 3.00
1-shot Sacrifice, rep.Aliens UK (1993) 4.95
1-shot Salvation DGb,MMi,KN, F:Selkirk (1993) 4.95
1-shot Special 2.50
1-shot Stalker 2.50
1-shot Wraith 3.00
GN Female War, remastered 16.95
GN Genocide, remastered 16.95
GN Labyrinth, remastered 17.95
GN Nightmare Asylum, remaster. . 16.95
GN Outbreak, remastered 17.95
GN Rogue, Remastered 16.95

ALIENS: ALCHEMY
Sept., 1997
1 (of 3) JAr,RCo 3.00
2 thru 3 . . . . @3.00

ALIENS: APOCALYPSE — DESTROYING ANGELS
Jan., 1999
1 (of 4) MSh 3.00
2 thru 4 MSh . . . . @3.00
TPB 10.95
TPB Salvation and Sacrifice 12.95

ALIENS: BERSERKER
1995
1 I:Crew of the Nemesis 2.50
2 Terminall 949 . . . . 2.50
3 Traitor 2.50
4 Finale 2.50

ALIENS: COLONIAL MARINES
1993
1 I: Lt. Joseph Henry 3.00
2 I: Pvt. Carmen Vasquez 2.75
3 V:Aliens 2.75
4 F:Lt.Henry 2.75
5 V:Aliens 2.75
6 F:Herk Mondo 2.75
7 A:Belliveau 2.75
8 F:Lt.Joseph Henry 2.75
9 F:Lt.Joseph Henry 2.75
10 final issue 2.50

ALIENS: EARTH WAR
1991
1 SK,JBo(c),Alien's War renewed . . 4.00
1a 2nd Printing 2.50
2 SK,JBo(c),To trap the Queen . . . 4.00
3 SK,JBo(c) Stranded on Alien's planet 3.00

Aliens: Pig
© Dark Horse Comics

All comics prices listed are for *Near Mint* condition.

CVA Page 489

Aliens–American / DARK HORSE / Comics Values Annual

4 SK,JBo(c),Resolution,final 5.00

ALIENS: GENOCIDE
1991
1 Aliens vs. Aliens. 3.50
2 Alien Homeworld 3.00
3 Search for Alien Queen. 3.00
4 Conclusion, inc. poster 3.00
TPB Genocide rep. #1–#4 . . . . . . 13.95

ALIENS: HIVE
1992
1 KJo,I:Stanislaw Mayakovsky. . . . 4.00
2 KJo,A:Norbert. 3.50
3 KJo,A:Julie,Gill 3.25
4 KJo,A:Stan,Final. 3.00
TPB Hive rep. #1–#4 . . . . 14.00

ALIENS: HAVOC
1 (of 2) 'over 40 creators'. 3.00
2 . . . . 3.00

ALIENS: KIDNAPPED
Dec., 1997–Feb., 1998
1 (of 3) 3.00
2 thru 3 . . . . @3.00
TPB Aliens:Kidnapped 9.95

ALIENS: LABYRINTH
1993
1 F:Captured Alien. 3.00
2 . . . . 3.00
3 O:Dr.Church 3.00
4 D:Everyone 3.00
TPB rep. #1–#4 . . . . 17.95
TPB remastered 17.95

ALIENS: MUSIC OF THE SPEARS
1994
1 I:Damon Eddington. 3.00
2 TBd(c),A:Damon Eddington . . . 3.00
3 TBd(c),A:Damon Eddington . . . 3.00
4 TBd(c),last issue. 3.00

ALIENS: NEWT'S TALE
1992
1 How Newt Survived 5.50
2 JBo(c),Newt's point of view
 on how 'Aliens' ended. 5.50

ALIENS: ROGUE
1993
1 F:Mr.Kay. 3.00
2 V:Aliens 3.00
3 V:Aliens 3.00
4 V:Aliens King 3.00
TPB Nel(c),rep.#1–#4 . . . . 14.95

ALIENS: STRONGHOLD
1994
1 DoM,JP 3.00
2 thru 4 DoM,JP. . . . . @3.00
TPB 16.95

ALIENS: SURVIVAL
Feb.–Apr. 1998
1 (of 3) TyH(c). 3.00
2 thru 3 . . . . @3.00

ALIENS: TRIBES
TPB 11.95

ALIENS/PREDATOR: DEADLIEST OF THE SPECIES
1993
1 B:CCl(s),JG,F:Caryn Delacroix . . 3.75
2 JG,V:Predator. 3.00
3 JG,F:Caryn Delacroix 3.00
4 JG,V:Predator. 3.00
5 JG,Roadtrip 3.00
6 JG,in Space Station 3.00
7 JG,EB 3.00
8 JG,EB 3.00
9 JG,EB 3.00
10 CCl(s), Human Predators. 3.00
11 CCl,EB,JBo(c),Delacroix vs.
 DeMatier 3.00
12 Caryn's Fate 3.00
TPB 29.95

ALIENS VS. PREDATOR
1996
0 PN,KS,Rep.DHP#34-36,(B&W) . . 9.00
1 Duel to the Death 9.00
1a 2nd Printing 3.00
2 Dr. Revna missing 5.00
3 Predators attack Aliens 5.00
4 CW,F:Machiko & Predator 5.00
TPB Rep.#1–#4 . . . . 19.95
TPB PN,KS,rep.DHP#34-36 . . . . 19.95
HC PN,KS,rep.DHP#34-36 . . . . . 79.95
Ann.#1 (1999) 4.95
1-shot Booty, rep. *Previews* 3.00

ALIENS VS. PREDATOR: DUEL
1995
1 Trap, JS 3.00
2 War 3.00

ALIENS VS. PREDATOR: ETERNAL
June, 1998
1 (of 4) IEd,GF(c) 3.00
2 thru 4 IEd,GF(c) . . . . @3.00

Aliens Vs. Predator: Eternal #4
Comics © Dark Horse Comics

TPB 9.95

ALIENS VS. PREDATOR: WAR
1995
0 Prelude to New Series 3.00
1 RSd,MM,RCo(c) F:Machiko 3.00
2 I:Machiko Naguchi 3.00
3 F:Machiko Naguchi. 3.00
4 final issue. 3.00
TPB 19.95

ALIENS VS. PREDATOR: XENOGENESIS
Dec., 1999
1 (of 4) MvR 3.50
2 MvR,trapped. 3.50
3 MvR,trapped. 3.50
4 MvR,battle for survival 3.50

ALIENS VS. PREDATOR VS. THE TERMINATOR
April, 2000
1 (of 4) MSh,MvR 3.50
2 MSh,MvR,V:Terminator-Alien
 hybrid. 3.50
3 MSh,MvR,on Predator ship 3.50
4 MSh,MvR,concl. 3.50
TPB 96-pg. series rep. 11.95

ALIENS: XENOGENESIS
Aug., 1999
1 (of 4) 3.50
2 DR 3.50
3 DR 3.50
4 . . . . 3.50

ALIEN 3
1992
1 Movie Adaptation 3.00
2 Movie Adaptation 3.00
3 Movie Adaptation 3.00

AL WILLIAMSON: HIDDEN LANDS
(B&W) Nov., 2002
TPB AW,224-pg. 22.95

AMAZING SCREW-ON HEAD, THE
May, 2002
1-shot MMi 3.00

AMERICAN, THE
(B&W) 1987
1 CW,'Chinese Boxes,'D:Gleason . 5.00
2 CW,'Nightmares 4.00
3 CW,Secrets of the American 4.00
4 CW,American vs.Kid America . . . 4.00
5 A:Kiki the Gorilla. 4.00
6 Rashomon-like plot. 3.50
7 Pornography business issue 3.50
8 Deals with violence issue 3.50
9 American Falls into a cult 3.50
Spec. (1990). 4.00

THE AMERICAN: LOST IN AMERICA
1992
1 CMa, American joins a cult 2.50

CVA Page 490 — All comics prices listed are for *Near Mint* condition.

DARK HORSE

American Splendor, Music Comics
© Dark Horse Comics

2 CMa, V:'Feel-Good' cult 2.50
3 CMa, 'ApeMask' cult 2.50
4 CMa, Final issue 2.50
ColorSpec.#1 . . . . 2.95

AMERICAN SPLENDOR
1993
1-shot Letterman by Harvey Pekar . 3.50
1-shot A Step Out of the Nest 3.50
1-shot On the Job 3.50
1-shot Comics Con, JZe 3.50
1-shot Music Comics 3.50
1-shot Odds & Ends 3.50
1-shot Transatlantic Comics 3.50
1-shot Terminal 3.50
1-shot Bedtime Stories 4.50
TPB (2002) 11.95

AMERICAN SPLENDOR: UNSUNG HERO
DH Maverick Aug., 2002
1 (of 3) b&w 4.00
2 . . . . 4.00
3 . . . . 4.00

AMERICAN SPLENDOR WINDFALL
(B&W) 1995
1 Windfall Gained,pt.1 . . . . 4.25
2 Windfall Lost 4.25
1-shot Portrait of The Artist
  in his declining years 4.00

ANCIENT JOE
DH Maverick, Oct., 2001
1 (of 3) B&W 3.00
2 . . . . 3.50
3 concl 3.50
TPB 12.95

ANGEL
Oct., 1999
1 Buffy spin-off 3.00
2 . . . . 3.00
3 . . . . 3.00
4 in Los Angeles 3.00
5 V:Demons,pt.1 . . . . 3.00
6 V:Demons,pt.2 . . . . 3.00
7 V:Demons,pt.3 . . . . 3.00
8 . . . . 3.00
9 . . . . 3.00
10 TSg 3.00
11 TSg 3.00
12 TSg,MMi(c) 3.00
13 TSg,demonic rats 3.00
14 TSg,Little Girl Lost 3.00
15 TSg,Past Lives,Buffy x-over . . . 4.00
16 TSg,Past Lives,Buffy x-over . . . 4.00
17 The Cordelia Special 3.00
1–17a newsstand photo(c) . . . . @4.00
TPB Surrogates 9.95
TPB Earthly Possessions 9.95
TPB Hunting Ground 9.95
TPB Angel Autumnal 9.95
TPB The Hollower 9.95
TPB Strange Bedfellows, rep . . . 12.95

ANGEL
Sept., 2001
1 (of 4) 3.00
1a photo (c) 3.00
1b gold-foil (c) 13.00
1c gold-foil (c) signed 20.00
2 . . . . 3.00
2a photo(c) 3.00
3 . . . . 3.00
3a photo(c) 3.00
4 MvR, conclusion 3.00
4a photo (c) 3.00
TPB Long Night's Journey 12.95

ANOTHER CHANCE TO GET IT RIGHT
1995
1 B&W 14.95
TPB AVs, GfD(c) 9.95
TPB 3rd printing (2002) 11.95

APPLESEED
(B&W) Manga
TPB Book One: The Promethean
  Challenge 14.95
TPB Book Two: Prometheus
  Unbound 14.95
TPB Book Three: The Scales of
  Prometheus 14.95
TPB Book Four: The Promethean
  Balance 14.95

APPLESEED DATABOOK
(B&W) Manga 1994
1 Flip Book, by Masamune Shirow. 5.00
1a 2nd printing 3.50
2 Flip Book 3.50
TPB Rep. #1–#2 (1995) 12.95

ARZACH
1996
TPB by Moebius 6.95

A SMALL KILLING
GN by Alan Moore & Oscar Zarate 11.95

ASTRO BOY
(B&W) March, 2002
TPB Vol.1 224-pg.Osamu Tezuka . 9.95
TPB Vol.2 208-pg. 9.95
TPB Vol.3 208-pg. 9.95
TPB Vol.4 216-pg. 9.95
TPB Vol.5 216-pg. 9.95
TPB Vol.6 thru Vol. 22 . . . . @9.95

ATLAS
1994
1 BZ,I:Atlas 2.75
2 BZ,V:Sh'en Chui 2.75
3 BZ,V:Sh'en Chui 2.50
4 BZ, final issue 2.50

AUTOBIOGRAPHIX
Nov. 2003
TPB 14.95

Babe #1
© Dark Horse Comics

BABE
Legend 1994
1 JBy(a&s) 3.00
2 thru 4 JBy(a&s) . . . . @2.50

BABE 2
Legend 1995
1 V:Shrewmanoid 2.50
2 A:Abe Sapien 2.50

BACCHUS COLOR SPECIAL
1995
1 A:Thor 2.95
2 A:Abe Sapien 2.50

BADGER: SHATTERED MIRROR
1994
1 R:Badger 3.00
2 R:Badger 3.00
3 Badger 3.00
4 Phantom, final issue 3.00

BADGER: ZEN POP FUNNY ANIMAL VERSION
1 MBn,R:Badger (1994) 3.00
2 Ham 3.00

BADLANDS
(B&W) 1991
1 I:Connie Bremen 3.50
2 Anne Peck, C.I.A. 3.00
3 Assassination Rumor 2.50

DARK HORSE

Badlands–Blade		Comics Values Annual

4 Connie heads South 2.50
5 November 22, 1963, Dallas 2.25
6 . . . . 2.25

BARB WIRE
Comics' Greatest World 1994
1 Foil(c),I:Deathcard 2.25
2 DLw,I:Hurricane Max 2.25
3 V:Mace Blitzkrieg 2.25
4 Ghost,pt.1 . . . . 2.25
5 Ghost,pt.2 . . . . 2.25
6 Hardhide, Ignition 2.50
7 A:Motorhead 2.50
8 V:Ignition 2.50
9 A:Mecha, V:Ignition 2.50
Movie Spec 3.95
TPB 8.95

BARB WIRE: ACE OF SPADES
1996
1 CW,TBd & DoM 2.95
2 CW,TBd & DoM 2.95
3 CW,TBd & DoM 2.95
4 CW,TBd & DoM 2.95

BARRY WINDSOR-SMITH: STORYTELLER
Oct., 1996
TPBs 1 thru 9 9'x12fi' . . . . @4.95

BASEBALL GREATS
1 Jimmy Piersall story 3.25

BASIL WOLVERTON'S FANTASIC FABLES
(B&W) Oct. 1993
1 BW 2.50
2 BW 2.50

BASIL WOLVERTON'S
GN Gateway to Horror (1988) 5.00
TPB In Space, 240-pg. (1999) . . . 16.95
GN Planet of Terror (1987) 5.00

BATMAN/ALIENS
Dark Horse/DC March, 1997
1 (of 2) RMz,BWr. 4.95
2 conclusion 4.95
TPB RMz,BWr 14.95

BATMAN/TARZAN: CLAWS OF THE CATWOMAN
1999
1 (of 4) RMz,DvD(c),V:Dent,x-over. 2.95
2 RMz,DvD(c) 2.95
3 RMz,DvD(c) 2.95
4 RMz,DvD(c) concl. 2.95
TPB 96-pg.,DvD(c) 10.95

BATTLE GODS: WARRIORS OF THE CHAAK
April, 2000
1 (of 9) by Francisco Ruiz
  Velasco 3.00
2 the Lucha Libre 3.00
3 F:Takan, El Charro 3.00
4 another tournament 3.00
5 The Chaak begins 3.00
6 Deathmatch: Takan vs. Chilbacan 3.00

7 sleeping god awakens 3.00
8 Hell breaks loose 3.00
9 concl. 3.00
TPB 240-pg. 19.95

BERSERK
Oct. 2003
TPB Vol. 1 The Black Swordsman 12.95

BETTIE PAGE COMICS
1996–97
1-shot, some nudity (1996) 3.95
1-shot Bettie Page Comics: Spicy
  Adventure, by Jim Silke (1997) . 2.95
1 Queen of Hearts, movie adapt. . . 2.00
TPB Queen of Hearts 19.95

BETTIE PAGE: QUEEN OF THE NILE
Dec., 1999
1 (of 3) low-budget time machine . . 2.95
2 . . . . 2.95
3 concl. 2.95
TPB, series rep. 12.95

BIG
1989
1 Movie Adaptation 2.00

BIG BLOWN BABY
(B&W) Aug., 1996
1 thru 4 by Bill Wray . . . . @2.95

BIG GUY AND RUSTY THE ROBOT BOY
1995
1 V:Monster 4.95
2 V:Monster 4.95
TPB FM & GfD 14.95
TPB King Size 29.95

BIG HOAX
Dark Horse Venture 2001
TPB B&W 128-pg. 10.95

BILLI 99
(B&W) 1991
1 'Pray for us Sinners' 4.50
2 'Trespasses' 4.00
3 'Daily Bread' 4.00
TPB TSe,200-pg. B&W (2002) . . . 14.95

BIRD: THE TATTOO
Nov., 2001
TPB color, 48-pg. 14.95

BLACKBURNE COVENANT, THE
Apr. 2003
1 (of 4) FaN 3.00
2 thru 4 . . . . @3.00
TPB FaN 12.95

BLACK CROSS: DIRTY WORK
April, 1997
1-shot by Chris Warner 2.95

BLACK DRAGON, THE
(B&W) Apr., 1996
TPB C. Claremont & J. Bolton 17.95

BLACK MAGIC
B&W 1998
TPB 16.95

The Black Pearl #2 photo cover © Dark Horse Comics

BLACK PEARL, THE
Sept., 1996
1 by Mark Hamill 2.95
2 thru 5 . . . . @2.95
TPB by Mark Hamill 16.95

BLADE OF THE IMMORTAL
(B&W) Manga July, 1996
Conquest
1 by Hiroaki Samura 11.00
2 thru 4 pt. 2 thru pt.4 . . . . @6.00
Genius, Oct., 1996
5 by Hiroaki Samura 6.00
6 . . . . 6.00
Fanatic, 1997
7 . . . . 6.00
8 . . . . 6.00
Call of the Worm, April, 1997
9 48-pg. 6.00
10 48-pg. 6.00
11 48-pg. 6.00
TPB Cry of the Worm 12.95
Dreamsong, July, 1997
12 (of 7) by Hiroaki Samura 3.50
13 thru 18 . . . . @3.50
TPB Dreamsong 12.95
Rin's Bane, March, 1998
19 48-pg. 4.50
20 48-pg. 4.50
On Silent Wings, May, 1998
21 (of 8) 3.50
22 thru 25 . . . . @3.50
26 48-pg. 4.50
27 thru 28 . . . . @3.50
TPB Blood of a Thousand 12.95
TPB On Silent Wings 14.95
TPB On Silent Wings II 14.95
Dark Shadows, Jan., 1999
29 thru 33 . . . . @3.50
TPB Dark Shadows 14.95

CVA Page 492 — All comics prices listed are for *Near Mint* condition.

DARK HORSE

Blade of the Immortal #23
© *Dark Horse Comics*

Food, June, 1999
34 48-pg. 4.50
Heart of Darkness
35 (of 8) 3.50
36 thru 42 . . . . @3.50
TPB Heart of Darkness. 16.95
The Gathering
43 (of 15) by Hiroaki Samura 3.50
44 thru 49 . . . . @3.50
50 thru 57 . . . . @3.50
TPB The Gathering. 15.95
TPB The Gathering, Vol.2. . . . . . . 15.95
Secrets
58 thru 61, pt.1 thru pt.4 . . . . . . @3.50
62 Stigmata 3.50
63 Husk 3.50
64 Skin,pt.1 . . . . 3.50
65 Skin,pt.2 . . . . 3.50
TPB Secrets, 232-pg. b&w 16.95
Beasts
66 thru 72 Beasta pt.1 thru pt. 7 . @3.50
Fall Frost, 2002
73 thru 78 pt.1 thru pt. 6 . . . . . . @3.50
TPB Fall Frost 16.95
79 The Wind and the Crane 3.50
80 Petals on the Wind 3.50
81 Shadows 3.50
82 Mourning Shadows 3.50
83 Path of Shadows 3.50
84 Thorns. 3.50

BLAIR WHICH?
Dec., 1999
1-shot SA, Scary as heck 3.50

BLANCHE GOES TO NEW YORK
1 Turn of the Century N.Y. 2.95

BLAST CORPS
Sept., 1998
1-shot F:demolition experts 2.50

BLOOD TIES
Nov., 2000
GN 14.95

BLOOD WORLD
March 2003
1 (of 3) 3.00
2 . . . . 3.00

BLUE LILY
1993
1 thru 3 . . . . @4.00

BODY BAGS
Aug., 1996
1 (of 4) by Jason Pearson and
   Ken Bruzinak 3.00
2 and 3 . . . . @3.00
TPB 12.95

BOOK OF NIGHT
(B&W) 1987
1 CV 2.50
2 CV 2.25
TPB Children of the Stars 12.95

BORIS THE BEAR
(B&W) 1986
1 V:Funny Animals. 3.00
1a 2nd printing 2.25
2 V:Robots 2.25
3 V:Super Heroes 2.25
4 Bear of Steel 2.25
5 Dump Thing 2.25
6 Bat Bear. 2.25
7 Elves 2.25
8 LargeSize. 2.50
9 Awol 2.25
10 thru 12 . . . . @2.25
See: B & W Pub. section

BORIS THE BEAR
Color Classics 1987
1 thru 7 . . . . @2.25

BRAVE
March, 1997
1 by Cully Hamner & Jason Martin. 2.95

BUBBLE GUM CRISIS: GRAND MAL
Manga 1994
1 . . . . 2.75
2 and 3 . . . . @2.75
4 final issue. 2.50
TPB Rep.#1–#4 . . . . 14.95

BUFFY THE VAMPIRE SLAYER
Sept., 1998
1 JoB,AAd(c) Wu-Tang Fang 10.00
1a 2nd printing 4.00
2 JoB, Halloween 6.00
3 JoB, Cold Turkey 6.00
4 White Christmas 6.00
5 Happy New Year. 6.00
6 New Kid on the Block,pt.1. . . . . 6.00
7 JoB, New Kid on the Block,pt.2. . 6.00
8 The Final Cut 6.00
9 Hey, Good Looking,pt.1 . . . . . . 6.00
10 Hey, Good Looking,pt.2 . . . . . . 6.00
11 A Boy Named Sue 6.00
12 A Nice Girl Like You 6.00
12a gold foil (c). 13.00
13 F:Cordelia Chase. 5.00
14 Bad Blood,pt.5 . . . . 5.00
15 Bad Blood,pt.6 . . . . 5.00
16 Food Chain 5.00
17 Bad Blood,pt.7 . . . . 3.00
18 Mardi Gras 3.00
19 Bad Blood, concl. 3.00
20 Angel heads to L.A. 3.00
21 Blood of Carthage,pt.1 . . . . . . 3.00
22 Blood of Carthage,pt.2 . . . . . . 3.00
23 Blood of Carthage,pt.3 . . . . . . 3.00
24 Blood of Carthage,pt.4 . . . . . . 3.00
25 Blood of Carthage,concl. 3.00
26 Heart of the Slayer,pt.1 . . . . . . 3.00
27 Heart of the Slayer,pt.2 . . . . . . 3.00
28 revenge 3.00
29 Past Lives,pt.2,Angel x-over. . . . 4.00
30 Past Lives,pt.4,Angel x-over. . . . 4.00
31 Lost and Found 4.00
32 hobo ghost 3.00
33 Demonic Entomology. 3.00
34 Bug hunt, concl. 3.00
35 False Memories,pt.1 . . . . 3.00
36 False Memories,pt.2 . . . . 3.00
37 False Memories,pt.3 . . . . 3.00
38 False Memories,pt.4 . . . . 3.00
39 Night of a Thousand Vampires. . 3.00
40 JmP,Ugly Little Monsters,pt.1. . . 3.00
41 JmP,Ugly Little Monsters,pt.2. . . 3.00
42 JmP,Ugly Little Monsters,pt.3 . . 3.00
43 JmP,Death of Buffy,pt.1 . . . . . . 3.00
44 JmP,Death of Buffy,pt.2 . . . . . . 3.00
45 JmP,Death of Buffy,pt.3 . . . . . . 3.00
46 JmP,Withdrawal 3.00
47 Hellmouth to Mouth,pt.1. . . . . 3.00
48 Hellmouth to Mouth,pt.2. . . . . 3.00
49 Hellmouth to Mouth,pt.3. . . . . 3.00
50 Hellmouth to Mouth,pt.4. . . . . 3.50
51 SLo,FaN,Viva Las Buffy,pt.1. . . 3.00
52 SLo,Viva Las Buffy, pt.2 . . . . . . 3.00
53 SLo,Viva Las Buffy, pt.3 . . . . . . 3.00
54 SLo,Viva Las Buffy, pt.4 . . . . . . 3.00
55 Dawn and Hoopy the Bear. . . . 3.00
56 Slayer, Interrupted,pt.1 . . . . . . 3.00
57 Slayer, Interrupted,pt.2 . . . . . . 3.00
58 Slayer, Interrupted,pt.3 . . . . . . 3.00
59 Slayer, Interrupted,pt.4 . . . . . . 3.00
60 FaN,A Stake to the Heart,pt.1 . 3.00
61 FaN,A Stake to the Heart,pt.2 . 3.00
62 FaN,A Stake to the Heart,pt.3 . . 3.00
63 FaN,A Stake to the Heart,pt.4 . . 3.00
2a–63a newsstand photo(c) . . . . @3.00
Ann. 1999, 64-pg. 4.95
Spec. 1-shot Spike and Dru 3.00
Spec. 1-shot Giles 3.00

Buffy the Vampire Slayer #8
© *Dark Horse Comics*

Buffy–Chronowar / DARK HORSE / Comics Values Annual

Spec. 1-shot Giles, photo(c) . . . 3.00
Spec. 1-shot Jonathan 3.00
   Spec. 1-shotA photo (c) 3.00
Spec. 1-shot Lovers' Walk 3.00
   Spec. 1-shotA photo (c) 3.00
Spec. 1-shot Spike & Dru—The
   Queen of Hearts, photo (c) 2.95
Spec. 1-shot Spike & Dru—All'sFair 3.00
   Spec. 1-shot Spike & Dru, ph(c) 3.00
Spec. 1-shot Willow & Tara 3.00
   Spec. 1-shotA photo(c) 3.00
   Spec. 1-shotB foil photo (c) . . . 10.00
   Spec. 1-shotC foil photo(c) sgn 20.00
   Spec. 1-shotD red foil 16.95
Spec.1-shot Lost & Found, FaN . . . 3.00
   Spec. 1-shotA photo (c) 3.00
Spec.1-shot Buffy the Vampire
   Slayer/Angel: Reunion (2002) . . 3.00
   Spec. 1-shotA photo (c). 3.00
Spec.1-shot Tales of the Slayers
   Broken Bottle of Djinn (2002) . . 3.50
   Spec. 1-shotA photo (c). 3.50
Spec. 1-shot Chaos Bleeds 3.00
   Spec. Chaos Bleeds, photo(c) . 3.00
GN Ring of Fire, photo(c) 9.95
TPB The Dust Waltz 10.00
TPB The Remaining Sunlight 10.00
TPB Uninvited Guests 10.95
TPB The Origin 9.95
TPB Bad Blood. 9.95
TPB Crash Test Demons,
   rep.#9–#11. . . . . 9.95
TPB Pale Reflections, rep.#17–#19 9.95
TPB The Blood of Carthage 10.95
TPB Spike and Dru. 11.95
TPB Food Chain, 168-pg. 16.95
TPB Past Lives. 12.95
TPB Autumnal 9.95
TPB Tales of the Slayer 14.95
TPB Creatures of Habit (2002) . . 17.95
TPB Out of the Woodwork (2002) . 12.95
TPB False Memories (2002). 12.95
TPB Ugly Little Monsters (2002) . 12.95
TPB The Death of Buffy (2002). . 15.95
TPB Note From the Underground . 12.95
TPB Willow and Tara 9.95
TPB Viva Las Buffy. 12.95
TPB Slayer, Interrupted. 14.95

BUFFY THE VAMPIRE SLAYER: ANGEL
May, 1999

1 (of 3) 3.00
2 & 3. . . . . @3.00
1a thru 3a newsstand, photo(c) . @3.00

BUFFY THE VAMPIRE SLAYER: HAUNTED
Dec., 2001

1 (of 4) deceased enemy's ghost . . 3.00
2 thru 4 . . . . @3.00
1a thru 4a photo (c) . . . . @3.00
TPB 96-pg. 12.95

BUFFY THE VAMPIRE SLAYER: THE ORIGIN
Feb., 1999

1 (of 3) DIB, JoB. 3.00
2 & 3 . . . . @3.00
2a & 3a newsstand, photo(c) . . . @3.00
TPB rep. 9.95

BUFFY THE VAMPIRE SLAYER: OZ
July, 2001

1 (of 3) 3.00
1a photo(c) 3.00
1b gold foil photo (c) 12.95
1c gold foil photo(c) signed 25.00
1d fiery red foil photo(c). 17.00
2 . . . . 3.00
2a photo (c). 3.00
3 . . . . 3.00
3a photo (c) 3.00
TPB 80-pg. 9.95

BUFFY THE VAMPIRE SLAYER: WILLOW AND TARA — WILDERNESS
July, 2002

1 (of 2) 3.00
1a photo (c). 3.00
2 (of 2) 3.00
2a photo (c). 3.00

BY BIZARRE HANDS
(B&W) 1994

1 JLd(s). 2.50
2 JLd(s). 2.50
3 JLd(s). 2.50

CAIN
Nov., 2002

TPB 96-pg. B&W 9.95

CANNON GOD EXAAXION
Manga, Nov., 2001

1 Stage 1, part 1 (of 8) 3.00
2 Stage One,pt.2. . . . . 3.00
3 Stage One,pt.3. . . . . 3.00
4 Stage One,pt.4. . . . . 3.00
5 Stage One,pt.5. . . . . 3.00
6 Stage One,pt.6. . . . . 3.00
7 Stage One,pt.7. . . . . 3.00
8 Stage One,pt.8. . . . . 3.00
9 Stage Two,pt.1. . . . . 3.00
10 Stage Two,pt.2 . . . . 3.50
11 Stage Two,pt.3. . . . . 3.50
13 thru 15 . . . . @3.50
16 thru 19 . . . . @3.00
TPB Stage One, rep. 208-pg. b&w 15.95
TPB Stage 2. . . . . 14.95

CARAVAN KIDD
(B&W) Manga 1992

1 thru 10 by Johji Manabe . . . . . @2.50

[2nd Series] 1993

1 thru 10 F:Miam . . . . @2.50
TPB Rep. #1–#10. . . . . 19.95
Holiday Spec. 2.50
Valentine's Day Spec. 2.50

[3rd Series] 1994

1 thru 8 . . . . @2.50
Christmas Special. 2.50
TPB Vol. 2 . . . . 19.95
TPB Vol. 3 . . . . 19.95

CATALYST: AGENTS OF CHANGE
Comics' Greatest World 1994

1 JPn(c),V:US Army. 2.25
2 JPn(c),I:Grenade 2.25
3 JPn(c),Rebel vs. Titan. 2.25

Caravan Kidd, Vol. 3, #1
© Dark Horse Comics

4 JPn(c),Titan vs. Grace 2.25
5 JPn(c),V:Ape 2.25
6 and 7 . . . . @2.25

CHEVAL NOIR
(B&W) 1989

1 DSt(c). 4.00
2 thru 6 . . . . @3.50
7 DSt(c). 3.50
8 . . . . 3.50
9 . . . . 3.50
10 80 pg. 4.50
11 80 pg. 4.50
12 MM(c). 4.50
13 thru 15. . . . . @4.50
16 thru 19 with 2-card strip . . . . @4.50
20 Great Power o/t Chninkel. 4.50
21 Great Power o/t Chninkel. 4.50
22 Great Power o/t Chninkel,concl. . 4.50
23 inc.'Rork','Forever War' concl. . . 4.50
24 In Dreams,pt.1 . . . . 4.50
25 In Dreams,pt.2. . . . . 4.50
26 In Dreams,pt.3. . . . . 4.50
27 I:The Man From Ciguri (Airtight
   Garage sequel) Dreams,pt.4. . . 3.50
28 Ciguri cont. 3.50
29 Ciguri cont. 3.50
30 Ciguri,cont. 3.50
31 Angriest Dog in the World 3.50
32 thru 38. . . . . @3.50
39 In Search of Peter Pan 3.50
40 . . . . 3.50
41 F:Demon 3.50
42 F:Demon 3.50
43 F:Demon 3.50
44 F:Demon 3.50
45 thru 47 . . . . @3.50
48 SwM(c) 3.50
49 F:Rork 3.50
50 F:Rork 3.50

CHRONICLES OF CONAN
Sept. 2003

TPB Vol. 1 RTs,BWS reprints 15.95
TPB Vol. 2 Tower of the Elephant . 15.95

CHRONOWAR
(B&W) Aug., 1996

1 (of 9) by Kazumasa Takayama . . 2.95
2 thru 9 . . . . @2.95

CVA Page 494   All comics prices listed are for *Near Mint* condition.

DARK HORSE

Classic—Comics

Classic Star Wars 320
© Dark Horse Comics

CLASSIC STAR WARS
1992
1 AW,newspaper strip reps. 6.00
2 AW,newspaper strip reps. 4.00
3 AW,newspaper strip reps. 4.00
4 AW,newspaper strip reps. 4.00
5 AW,newspaper strip reps. 4.00
6 AW,newspaper strip reps. 4.00
7 AW,newspaper reps. 4.00
8 AW,newspaper reps. w/card 4.00
9 AW,newspaper reps. 3.50
10 AW,newspaper reps. 3.50
11 thru 19 AW,newspaper reps. . . @3.00
20 AW,newspaper strip reps., with
 trading card, final issue. 4.00
TPB Vol. 1, 'In Deadly Pursuit,'
 rep.#1–#7. . . . . 15.99
TPB Vol. 1, rep. 2nd edition 16.95
TPB Vol. 2, 'Rebel Storm,'
 rep. #8–#14 . . . . 16.95
TPB Vol. 3, 'Escape to Hoth,'
 rep. #15–#20 . . . . 16.95

CLASSIC STAR WARS:
A LONG TIME AGO
June, 2002
TPB Vol. 1, 336-pg. 29.95
TPB Vol. 2, 336-pg. 29.95
TPB Vol. 3, 344-pg. 29.95
TPB Vol. 4 Screams in the Void . . 29.95
TPB Vol. 5 Fool's Bounty 29.95
TPB Vol. 6 Wookiee World 29.95
TPB Vol. 7 Far, Far Away 29.95

CLASSIC STAR WARS:
A NEW HOPE
1994
1 AAd(c), rep. 4.25
2 AH(c), rep. 3.95
TPB Rep. #1–#2. . . . . 9.95

CLASSIC STAR WARS:
DEVILWORLDS
Aug., 1996
1 (of 2) by Alan Moore. 2.50
2 . . . . 2.50

CLASSIC STAR WARS:
EARLY ADVENTURES
Aug., 1994–April, 1995
1 MiA(c), Gambler's World. 3.00
2 RHo&MGr(c),Blackhole. 2.50
3 EiS(c),Rebels of Vorzyd-5. . . . . . 2.50
3 bagged with trading card DH2. . . 5.00
4 RHo(c),Tatooine 2.50
5 RHo(c),A:Lady Tarkin 2.50
6 Weather Dominator 2.50
7 RHo(c),V:Darth Vader. 2.50
8 KPl(c),X-Wing Secrets 2.50
9 KPl(c),A:Boba Fett 2.50
TPB RsM & AGw, AW(c). 19.95

CLASSIC STAR WARS:
EMPIRE STRIKES BACK
1994
1 and 2 Movie Adaptation. . . . . . @4.00
TPB Rep.#1–#2 AW&CG(c) 9.95
TPB reprint, Hildebrandt(c) 9.95

CLASSIC STAR WARS:
HAN SOLO
AT STAR'S END
March, 1997
1 (of 3) by Alfredo Alcala 3.00
2 . . . . 3.00
3 . . . . 3.00
TPB rep. AW(c) 6.95

CLASSIC STAR WARS:
A LONG TIME AGO
(B&W) March, 1999
1 (of 6) rep. Marvel comics 6.00
2 thru 6. @6.00

CLASSIC STAR WARS:
RETURN OF THE JEDI
1994
1 Movie Adaptation 4.00
2 Movie Adaptation 3.50
TPB Rep.#1–#2 . . . . 9.95
TPB rep. Hildebrandt(c) 9.95

CLASSIC STAR WARS:
VANDELHELM MISSION
1995
1-shot F:Han Solo, Lando. 3.95

CLONEZONE
(B&W) 1989
Spec #1 . . . . 2.00

CLOWNS, THE
(PAGLIACCI)
April, 1998
1-shot B&W, CR. 2.95

CLUB 9
Feb. 2003
TPB B&W. 15.95
TPB Vol. 2 . . . . 15.95

COLORS IN BLACK
Comics From Spike 1995
1 B:Passion Play. 2.95
2 Images. 2.95

3 Back on the Bus. 2.95
4 final issue. 2.95

COMIC BOOK
1 thru 4 9'x12' John Kricfalusi. . . @5.95

COMICS & STORIES
1996
1 (of 4) by Martin & Millionaire 2.95
2 thru 4 . . . . @2.95

Comics Greatest World, Steel Harbor
#4 © Dark Horse Comics

COMICS' GREATEST
WORLD
1993
(Arcadia)
1 B:MRi(s),FM(c),B:LW,B:O:Vortex,
 F:X,I:Seekers 3.00
1a B&W proof ed. (1,500 made) . . 9.00
1b Hologram(c), with cards 7.00
2 JoP,I:Pit Bulls 2.00
3 AH,I:Ghost 5.00
4 I:Monster 2.25
TPB Arcadia. 25.00
(Golden City)
1 B:BKs(s),JOy(c),I:Rebel,
 Amaz.Grace,V:WarMaker 2.25
1a Gold Ed. 5.00
2 I:Mecha 2.25
3 WS(c),I:Titan 2.25
4 E:BKs(s),GP(c),JD,I:Catalyst . . . 2.25
TPB Golden City. 11.00
(Steel Harbor)
1 B:CW(s),PG,I:Barb Wire,
 V:Ignition 2.25
2 MMi(c),TNa,I:Machine. 2.25
3 CW(a&s),I:Wolf Gang 2.25
4 E:CW(s),VGi,I:Motorhead 2.25
TPB Steel Harbor 11.00
(Vortex)
1 B:RSd(s),LW,DoM,I:Division 13. . 2.25
2 I:Hero Zero. 2.25
3 PC,I:King Tiger 2.25
4 B:RSd(s),E:MRi(s)BMc,E:LW,
 E:O:Vortex,C:Vortex 2.25
TPB Vortex. 11.00
Sourcebook 10.00

All comics prices listed are for Near Mint condition.

DARK HORSE

COMPLETELY PIP AND NORTON
DH Maverick Sept., 2002
TPB 72-pg. 9.95

CONAN THE LEGEND
Nov. 2003
1-shot KBk, CNr prologue. 0.25

CONCRETE
(B&W) 1987
1 PC,R:Concrete, A Stone among Stones 11.00
1a 2nd printing 3.00
2 PC,'Transatlantic Swim' 7.00
3 PC 5.00
4 PC 4.00
5 PC,'An Armchair Stuffed with Dynamite'. 4.00
6 PC,Concrete works on farm 4.00
7 PC,Concrete grows horns. 4.00
8 PC,Climbs Mount Everest. 4.00
9 PC,Mount Everest,pt.2 . . . . 4.00
10 PC,last Issue 4.00
TPB The Complete Concrete 25.00
Spec. #1 Concrete ColorSpec.,PC (1989) 4.00
Spec. Concrete Celebrates Earth Day PC,Moebius (1990) 2.50
Spec. 1 A New Life, B&W rep., O: Concrete (1989). 3.50
Spec. Concrete: Land & Sea, rep. #1 & #2 (1989) 3.25
Spec. Concrete: Odd Jobs, rep. #5 & #6 (1990) 3.50

CONCRETE: ECLECTICA
1993
1 PC,The Ugly Boy 3.25
2 PC 3.25

CONCRETE: FRAGILE CREATURE
1991
1 PC,'Rulers o/t Omniverse'Pt.1. . . 4.00
2 PC,'Rulers o/t Omniverse'Pt.2. . . 3.00
3 PC,'Rulers o/t Omniverse'Pt.3. . . 3.00
4 PC,'Rulers o/t Omniverse'Pt.3. . . 3.00
TPB 15.95

CONCRETE: KILLER SMILE
Dark Horse-Legend 1994
1 PC 3.50
2 thru 4 PC . . . . @3.00
TPB Rep.#1–#4 . . . . 16.95

CONCRETE: STRANGE ARMOR
Dec., 1997–Apr. 1998
1 (of 5) 3.00
2 thru 5 . . . . @3.00
TPB Strange Armor 17.00

CONCRETE: THINK LIKE A MOUNTAIN
(B&W) 1996
1 thru 6 PC,GfD(c) . . . . @3.00
TPB PC,GfD(c). 17.95

CORMAC MAC ART
July, 1989
1 Robert E. Howard adapt. 3.00
2 . . . . 3.00
3 . . . . 3.00

CORNY'S FETISH
April, 1998
GN by Renee French, 64-pg... . . . 4.95

COUTOO
(B&W)
1 Lt. Joe Kraft 3.50

CREEPY
(B&W) 1992
1 KD,TS,GC,SL,Horror 3.95
2 TS,CI,DC,Demonic Baby 3.95
3 JM,TS,JG,V:Killer Clown. 3.95
4 TS,Final issue 3.95

CREATURE FROM THE BLACK LAGOON
1 Movie Adaptation 4.95

CRIMINAL MACABRE
May 2003
1 (of 5) F:Cal McDonald 4.00
2 thru 5 . . . . @3.00

CRITICAL ERROR
1992
1 rep.Classic JBy story 2.75

[ANDREW VACHSS'] CROSS
1995
0 GfD(c),I:Cross,Rhino,Princess . . 2.50
1 thru 7 . . . . @2.95

CRUSH
DH Rocket Comics Oct. 2003
1 . . . . 3.00
2 . . . . 3.00

Cud Comics #5
© Dark Horse Comics

CUD COMICS
(B&W) 1996
1 thru 8 by Terry LaBan . . . . @3.00

THE CURSE OF DRACULA
July, 1998
1 (of 3) MWn,GC. 3.00
2 thru 3 . . . . @3.00

DANGER UNLIMITED
Dark Horse-Legend 1994
1 JBy(a&s),KD,I:Danger Unlimited, B:BU:Torch of Liberty 2.50
2 JBy(a&s),KD,O:DangerUnlimited. 2.50
3 JBy(a&s),KD,O: Torch of Liberty . 2.50
4 JBy(a&s),KD,Final Issue. 2.50
TPB rep. #1–#4 . . . . 14.95

DARK HORSE CLASSICS
(B&W) 1992
1 Last of the Mohicans 4.50
2 20,000 Leagues Under the Sea . 4.50

DARK HORSE CLASSICS: ALIENS VS. PREDATOR
Feb., 1997
1 thru 6 Rep. . . . . @3.00

DARK HORSE CLASSICS: GODZILLA, KING OF THE MONSTERS
July, 1998
1 RSd,SBi,now color 3.00
2 rep. from 1995 . . . . 3.00
3 rep. from 1995 . . . . 3.00
4 rep. Godzilla #2, from 1995. . . . . 3.00
5 . . . . 3.00
6 V:Bagorah 3.00

DARK HORSE CLASSICS: PREDATOR: JUNGLE TALES
1-shot Rep. 3.00

DARK HORSE CLASSICS: STAR WARS— DARK EMPIRE
1997
1 rep. by Tom Veitch,CK,DvD(c) . . 3.00
2 thru 6 rep., DvD(c) . . . . @3.00

DARK HORSE CLASSICS: TERROR OF GODZILLA
Aug., 1998
1 by Kazuhisa Iwata, AAd(c) 3.00
2 & 2 . . . . @3.00
4 rep. of 1988 B&W. 3.00
5 AAd(c) 3.00
6 AAd(c) 3.00

DARK HORSE COMICS
1992
1 RL,CW,F:Predator,Robocop, I:Renegade,Time Cop,(double gatefold cover) 4.00
2 RL,CW,F:Predator,Robocop, Renegade,Time Cop 3.00
3 CW,F:Robocop,Time Cop,Aliens, Indiana Jones. 3.00

DARK HORSE

4 F:Predator,Aliens,Ind.Jones 3.00
5 F:Predator,E:Aliens............ 3.00
6 F:Robocop,Predator, E:Indiana
  Jones 3.00
7 F:Robocop,Predator,B:StarWars . 6.00
8 B&I:X,Robocop................ 8.00
9 F:Robocop,E:Star Wars 4.00
10 E:X,B:Godzilla,Predator,
   James Bond.................. 3.50
11 F:Godzilla,Predator,James
   Bond,B:Aliens............... 2.75
12 F:Predator.................... 2.75
13 F:Predator,B:Thing............ 2.75
14 MiB(s),B:The Mark............ 2.75
15 MiB(s),E:The Mark,B:Aliens.... 2.75

Dark Horse Comics #9
© Dark Horse Comics

16 B:Predator,E:Thing,Aliens 2.75
17 B:Aliens,Star Wars:Droids 2.75
18 E:Predator.................... 2.75
19 RL(c),B:X,E:Star Wars:Droids,
   Aliens..................... 2.75
20 B:Predator.................... 2.75
21 F:Mecha 2.75
22 B:Aliens, E:Mecha 2.75
23 B:The Machine 2.75
24 The Machine 2.75
25 Final issue................... 2.75

DARK HORSE DOWNUNDER
(B&W) 1994
1 F:Australian Writers 2.50
2 Australian Writers 2.50
3 Australian Writers, finale...... 2.50

DARK HORSE MAVERICK
Ann.2000 48-pg. B&W 5.00
Ann.2001 48-pg. B&W 5.00

DARK HORSE MONSTERS
Feb., 1997
1-shot...................... 3.00

DARK HORSE PRESENTS
(B&W) 1986
1 PC,I:Concrete............... 15.00

1a 2nd printing 2.50
2 PC,Concrete................. 6.00
3 Boris theBear,Concrete....... 5.00
4 PC,Concrete................. 5.00
5 PC,Concrete................. 5.00
6 PC,Concrete................. 5.00
7 I:MONQ 5.00
8 PC,Concrete................. 5.00
9 .... 5.00
10 PC,Concrete, I:Masque 10.00
11 Masque 6.00
12 PC,Concrete, Masque 5.00
13 Masque 5.00
14 PC,Concrete, Masque 5.00
15 Masque 5.00
16 PC,Concrete, Masque 5.00
17 .... 5.00
18 PC,Concrete, Mask 5.00
19 Masque 5.00
20 double,Flaming Carrot 9.00
21 Masque 5.00
22 I:Duckman.................. 5.00
23 .... 5.00
24 PC,I:Aliens................. 20.00
25 thru 31 .... @3.00
32 A:Concrete 4.00
33 .... 3.00
34 Aliens 4.00
35 Predator 4.00
36 Aliens vs.Predator 4.00
36a painted cover.............. 5.00
37 .... 3.00
38 A:Concrete 3.00
39 .... 3.00
40 I:The Aerialist............... 3.00
41 .... 3.00
42 Aliens 5.00
43 Aliens 4.00
44 .... 3.00
45 .... 3.00
46 Predator 4.00
47 Monkers 3.00
48 with 2-card strip............. 3.00
49 with 2-card strip............. 3.00
50 inc.'Heartbreakers', with
   2-card strip................ 4.00
51 FM(c),inc.'Sin City'.......... 4.00
52 FM,inc. 'Sin City' 4.00
53 FM,inc. 'Sin City' 4.00
54 FM,Sin City;JBy Preview of
   Next Men,pt.1............. 5.00
55 FM,Sin City;JBy Preview of
   Next Men (JBy),pt.2 .... 6.00
56 FM,Sin City,JBy,Next MenPt.3
   Aliens Genocide(prologue).... 5.00
57 FM,SinCity;JBy Next Men,pt.4 .. 5.00
58 FM,Sin City,Alien Fire 5.00
59 FM,Sin City,Alien Fire 5.00
60 FM,Sin City 5.00
61 FM,Sin City 5.00
62 FM,E:Sin City 5.00
63 Moe,Marie Dakar............ 3.00
64 MWg,R:The Aerialist 3.00
65 B:Accidental Death 3.00
66 PC,inc.Dr.Giggles 3.00
67 B:Predator story (lead in to
   'Race War'),double size 4.50
68 F:Predator,Swimming Lessons
   (Nestrobber tie-in) 3.00
69 F:Predator 3.00
70 F:Alec 3.00
71 F:Madwoman............... 3.00
72 F:Eudaemon 3.00
73 F:Eudaemon 3.00
74 F:Eudaemon 3.00
75 F:Chairman 3.00
76 F:Hermes Vs.the Eye,Ball Kid . 2.50
77 F:Hermes Vs.the Eye,Ball Kid . 2.50
78 F:Hermes Vs.the Eye,Ball Kid . 2.50
79 B:Shadow Empires Slaves..... 2.50
80 AAd,I:Monkey Man & O'Brien... 5.00

81 B:Buoy 3.00
82 B:Just Folks................. 3.00
83 Last Impression 3.00
84 MBn,F:Nexus,E:Hermes Vs. the
   Eye Ball Kid 3.00
85 Winner Circle, Eighth Woman .. 3.00
86 Eighth Woman.............. 3.00
87 F:Concrete 4.00
88 Hellboy 3.00
89 Hellboy 3.00
90 Hellboy 3.00
91 Blackheart, Baden 3.00
92 Too Much Coffee Man 6.00
93 Cud, Blackheart,Coffee Man .. 8.00
94 A:Eyeball Kid,Coffee Man 6.00
95 Too Much Coffee Man 7.00
96 Kabuli Kid 3.00
97 F:Kabuki Kid 3.00
98 Pot Full of Noodles 3.00
99 Anthology title 3.00
100–#1 Lance Blastoff 3.00
100–#2 Hellboy 3.00
100–#3 Concrete 3.00
100–#4 Black Cross 3.00
100–#5 Pan Fried Girl 3.00
101 BW,F:Aliens................ 3.00
102 F:Mr. Painter 3.00

Dark Horse Presents #124
© Dark Horse Comics

103 F:The Pink Tornado 3.00
104 F:The Pink Tornado 3.00
105 F:The Pink Tornado 3.00
106 F:Godzilla 3.00
107 F:Rusty Razorclam 3.00
108............................ 3.00
109............................ 3.00
110 F:Egg..................... 3.00
111 Ninth Gland 3.00
112 three stories, concl. 3.00
113 Trypto the Acid Dog 3.00
114 F:Star Slammers/Lance Blastoff 3.00
115 flip-book Dr. Spin/The Creep .. 3.00
116 Fat Dog Mendoza 3.00
117 F:Aliens 3.00
118 Monkeyman O'Brien........ 3.00
119 Trout 3.00
120 'One Last Job' 3.00
121 F: Imago 3.00
122 'Lords of Misrule' 3.00
123 F: Jack Zero 3.00
124 F:Predator................. 3.00
125 F:Nocturnals 3.00
126 flip book, 48-pg............. 4.50
127 F:The Nocturnals 3.00

All comics prices listed are for *Near Mint* condition.

Dark Horse–Division

128 F:Dan & Larry 3.00
129 F:Hammer 3.00
130 F:Wanted Man 3.00
131 F:Girl Crazy 3.00
132 flip book 3.00
133 F:Tarzan 3.00
134 F:The Dirty Pair 3.00
135 F:The Fall, concl. 3.00
136 The Ark 3.00
137 Predator 3.00
138 F:Terminators. 3.00
139 F:Roachmill 3.00
140 F:Aliens 3.00
141 F:Buffy the Vampire Slayer. . . . 3.00
142 F:Lovecraftian tales 3.00
143 F:Tarzan tales 3.00
144 F:Vortex. 3.00
145 F:Burglar Girls 3.00
146 F:Aliens vs. Predator 3.00
147 F:Ragnok. 3.00
148 . . . . 3.00
149 Wunderkind 3.00
150 F:Buffy, 48-pg. 4.50
151 F:Hellboy 3.00
152 It! The Beast from Twenty
   Billion Years Beyond Earth 3.00
153 Helm of Harxis. 3.00
154 Iron Reich 3000, flip-book 3.00
155 Angel, flip-book 3.00
156 Witch's Son, flip-book 3.00
157 F:Witch's Son, final issue 3.00
Fifth Anniv. Special DGi,PC,
   SBi,CW,MW,FM,Sin City,
   Aliens,Give Me Liberty 8.00
Ann. 1997 F:Body Bags 4.95
Ann. 1998 F:Hellboy 4.95
Ann. 1999 DHP, JR. 4.95
Ann.2000 Girls Rule, 64-pg. 4.95
Milestone Ed.#1,rep.DHP#1 . . . . . . 2.25
TPB rep.Sin City. 6.00
TPB Best of DHP #1–#20 . . . . 9.95
TPB Best of DHP #1–#20 2nd ed. . 9.95
TPB Best of DHP #21–#30 . . . . 8.95
TPB Best of DHP #31–#50 . . . . 8.95
TPB Best of Dark Horse
   Presents Two 8.95
TPB Best of Dark Horse
   Presents Three. 12.95

DARK HORSE PRESENTS: ALIENS

1 Rep. 4.95
1a Platinum Edition 8.00

DARKNESS FALLS: THE TOOTH FAIRY— THE TRAGIC LIFE OF MATILDA DIXON
Jan. 2003

1-shot CAd. 3.00

DEADFACE: DOING ISLANDS WITH BACCHUS
(B&W) 1991

1 rep. Bacchus apps. 2.95
2 rep. inc.'Book-Keeper of Atlantis . 2.95

DEADFACE: EARTH, WATER, AIR & FIRE
(B&W) 1992

1 Bacchus & Simpson in Sicily. . . . 2.50
2 A:Don Skylla. 2.50
3 Mafia/Kabeirol-War prep. 2.50
4 Last issue. 2.50

DARK HORSE

DEAD IN THE WEST
(B&W) 1993

1 TT,Joe Landsdale adapt. 5.00
2 TT,adapt. 5.00
Spec. #1 TT(c) 3.95

DEAD OR ALIVE— A CYBERPUNK WESTERN
April, 1998

1 (of 4) by Tatjana and Alberto
   Ponticelli 2.50
2 thru 4 . . . . @2.50

DEADLINE USA
(B&W) 1991

1 rep. Deadline UK,Inc. Tank Girl
   Johnny Nemo. 9.95
2 inc. Tank Girl,Johnny Nemo 9.95

DEAD TO RIGHTS
Oct., 2002

1-shot 64-pg. 5.95

DECADE OF DARK HORSE, A
1996

1 (of 4) inc. Star Wars, Nexus,
   Ghost. 2.95
2 thru 4 . . . . @2.95

[RANDY BOWEN'S] DECAPITATOR
June, 1998

1 (of 4) GEr,DoM. 3.00
2 GEr 3.00
3 MMi,KJo,AAl. 3.00
4 MMi, conclusion 3.00

DEVIL CHEF
1994

1 I:Devil Chef 2.50

DEVIL'S FOOTPRINTS
March 2003

1 (of 4) 3.00
2 thru 4 . . . . @3.00
TPB 14.95

DIABLO: TALES OF SANCTUARY
Nov., 2001

1-shot 64-pg. 5.95

DIGIMON
June, 2000, Bi-weekly

1 . . . . 2.95
2 thru 6 . . . . @2.95
7 thru 12 ND(c) 3.00
TPB Digital Monsters 10.00

DIRTY PAIR
(B&W) Manga 1999

TPB Book 3 A Plague of Angels . . 12.95
TPB Dangerous Acquaintances. . . 12.95
TPB Biohazards 12.95
1-shot Start the Violence, AWa(c) . 2.95
1-shot Start the Violence, JPn(c). . . 2.95

Comics Values Annual

DIRTY PAIR: FATAL BUT NOT SERIOUS
Manga 1995

1 R:Kei,Yuri 2.95
2 V:Kevin Sleet,Yuri 2.95
3 Anti Yuri 2.95
4 V:Terrorists 2.95
5 conclusion 2.95

DIRTY PAIR: RUN FROM THE FUTURE
Jan., 2000

1 (of 4) AWa(c) 2.95
1a AH(c) 2.95
2 AWa(c) 2.95
2a BSf(c). 2.95
3 AWa(c) 2.95
3a Bruce Timm(c) 2.95
4 AWa(c) 2.95
4a HuR(c) 2.95
TPB series rep.. . . . . 14.95

DIRTY PAIR: SIM HELL
(B&W) Manga 1993

1 thru 4 by Adam Warren . . . . . . @3.25
TPB rep. #1–#4 . . . . 13.95

DIRTY PAIR: SIM HELL: REMASTERED
May, 2001

1 (of 4) full color, AWa 3.00
2 thru 4 AWa . . . . @3.00
TPB 3rd. ed. 14.95

DISNEY'S ATLANTIS THE LOST EMPIRE
June, 2001

GN 56-pg. color 6.95

DISNEY'S TARZAN
June, 1999

1 and 2 Animated movie adapt. . @2.95

DIVISION 13

1 & 2 . . . . @2.50
3 A:Payback 2.50

Disney's Tarzen #2
© Dark Horse Comics

DARK HORSE

4 Carnal Genesis............ 2.50

DOC SAVAGE: CURSE OF THE FIRE GOD
1 R:Man of Bronze............ 2.95
2 Exploding Plane............ 2.95
3 & 4 .... @2.95

DR. GIGGLES
1 Horror movie adapt.......... 2.50
2 Movie adapt.contd........... 2.50

DR. ROBOT
April, 2000
1-shot, by Bernie E. Mireault...... 2.95

DOMINION
(B&W) Manga
TPB 1 by Masamune Shirow..... 15.00
TPB 2nd printing.............. 14.95
TPB 3rd edition............... 16.95

Dominion: Conflict 1, #5
© Dark Horse Comics

DOMINION: CONFLICT 1 — NO MORE NOISE
(B&W) Manga 1996
1 thru 6 by Masamune Shirow .. @2.95
TPB series rep................ 14.95

DOMINION SPECIAL: PHANTOM OF THE AUDIENCE
(B&W) Manga
1-shot by Masamune Shirow...... 2.50

DOMU: A CHILD'S DREAMS
(B&W) Manga
1 Psychic Warfare............. 5.95
2 Murders Continue............ 5.95
3 Psychic war conclusion....... 5.95
TPB by Katsuhiro Otomo........ 17.95
TPB 2nd edition.............. 17.95

DRACULA
1 Movie Adaptation........... 4.95

DRAKUUN
(B&W) Feb., 1997
Rise of the Dragon Princess
1 (of 6) by Johji Manabe........ 3.00
2 thru 6 .... @3.00
TPB rep.................... 12.95
The Revenge of Gustav (Aug., 1997)
7 (1 of 6) by Johji Manabe....... 3.00
8 thru 12 pt.2 thru pt.6 .... @3.00
TPB, rep................... 14.95
Shadow of the Warlock (Feb., 1998)
13 (1 of 6) by Johji Manabe..... 3.00
14 thru 18 pt.2 thru pt.6....... @3.00
TPB rep.................... 14.95
The Hidden War (Sept., 1998)
19 (1 of 6) by Johji Manabe..... 3.00
20 thru 24 pt.2 thru pt.6....... @3.00
Flames of Empire (1999)
25 Flames of Empire (1 of 6) 3.00

DRAWING ON YOUR NIGHTMARES
Oct. 2003
1-shot Halloween 2003 Special.... 3.00

DYLAN DOG
(B&W) Bonelli March, 1999
1 (of 6) by Tiziano Di Sclavi & Angelo Stano, MMi(c), 96-pg........ 4.95
2 thru 6 .... @4.95
TPB Zed 96-pg. b&w.......... 5.95

EDGAR RICE BURROUGHS' RETURN OF TARZAN
April, 1997
1 adapted by Thomas Yeates & John Totleben........... 3.00
2 thru 3 .... @3.00

EDGAR RICE BURROUGHS' TARZAN
1996
Mugambi
1 by Bruce Jones, Christopher Schenck & TY, Betrayed by 3 man-beasts 3.00
2 'Tarzan's Jungle Fury'....... 3.00
3 'Tarzan's Jungle Fury'....... 3.00
4 vs. the Tara virus.......... 3.00
5 Cure to the Tara virus....... 3.00
6 .... 3.00
Tarzan and the Legion of Hate
7 by Allan Gross, Christopher Schenck, George Freeman 3.00
8 pt.2..................... 3.00
9 pt.3..................... 3.00
10 pt.4, concl............... 3.00
Le Monstre, June, 1997
11 pt.1 .... 3.00
12 pt.2 Bernie Wrightson(c) 3.00
Modern Prometheus, Aug., 1997
13 pt.1 MK(c) in New York 3.00
14 pt.2 MK(c)............... 3.00
Tooth and Nail, Oct., 1997
15 pt.1 MSh(c).............. 3.00
16 pt.2 .... 3.00
TPB adapts #11–#16 .... 16.95
Tarzan vs. the Moon Men
17 TT,AW,TY 3.00
18 TT,AW,TY 3.00

Edgar Rice Burroughs' Tarzan #5
© Dark Horse Comics

19 TT,AW,TY 3.00
20 TT,AW,TY 3.00
Primeval
21 MGr.................... 3.00
22 MGr.................... 3.00
23 MGr.................... 3.00
24 MGr.................... 3.00
TPB RsM,The Land That Time Forgot 12.95
TPB Tarzan of the Apes 12.95
TPB The Jewls of Opar........ 10.95

EDGAR RICE BURROUGHS' TARZAN: CARSON OF VENUS
May, 1998
1 (of 4) by Darko Macan and Igor Kordey, F:Carson Napier .. 3.00
2 thru 4 novels adapt. .... @3.00
TPB Carson of Venus.......... 12.95

EDGAR RICE BURROUGHS' TARZAN: THE LOST ADVENTURE
1995
1 Lost Manuscript............ 3.00
2 V:Gorgo the Buffalo......... 3.00
3 V:Bandits................. 3.00
4 V:Bandits................. 3.00

EDGAR RICE BURROUGHS' TARZAN: THE RIVERS OF BLOOD
Nov., 1999
1 .... 3.00
2 thru 8 .... @3.00

EDGAR RICE BURROUGHS' TARZAN— THE SAVAGE HEART
Apr. 1999
1 (of 4) MGr Jane is dead 3.00
2 thru 4 .... @3.00

DARK HORSE

EGON
Jan.–Feb., 1998
1 and 2 . . . . @2.95

EIGHTH WONDER, THE
Nov., 1997
1-shot by P. Janes & K. Plunkett. . . 2.95

ELRIC: STORMBRINGER
Dark Horse/Topps 1996
1 by Michael Moorcock & CR. 3.00
2 thru 7 (of 7). . . . . @3.00
TPB rep. series. 17.95

ENEMY
1 MZ(c),StG(s),I:Enemy 2.75
2 MZ(c),StG(s),F:Heller 2.75
3 MZ(c),StG(s),A:Heller 2.50
4 . . . . 2.50
5 final issue 2.95
TPB 14.95

ENO AND PLUM
Sept., 1997
TPB 12.95

EUDAEMON, THE
1 Nel,I:New Eudaemon 3.00
2 Nel,V:Mordare 2.75
3 Nel,V:Mordare 2.75

EVIL DEAD III: ARMY OF DARKNESS
1 JBo,Movie adaptation 4.00
2 JBo,Movie adaptation 3.50
3 JBo,Movie adaptation 3.00

EXOTICS, THE
TPB by Moebius 7.95

EYEBALL KID
(B&W)
1 I:Eyeball Kid 2.25
2 V:Stygian Leech 2.25
3 V:Telchines Brothers,last iss. . . . 2.25

FAT DOG MENDOZA
(B&W) 1992
1 I&O:Fat Dog Mendoza 2.50

FAX FROM SARAJEVO
Oct., 1996
GN JKu, 224 pg. 24.95

FEEDERS
Oct., 1999
1-shot MiA, prequel to Eyes
  to Heaven 2.95

FELIX THE CAT'S GREATEST HITS
Sept., 2002
TPB 96-pg. 9.95

F5 ORIGIN
1-shot, rep. 3.00

FLAMING CARROT
(B&W) 2001
Previous issues: see B&W section
18 . . . . 4.00
18a Ash-Can-Limited 4.00
19 . . . . 4.00
20 . . . . 4.00
21 . . . . 3.00
22 . . . . 3.00

Flaming Carrot #25
© Dark Horse Comics

23 . . . . 3.00
24 . . . . 4.00
25 F:TMNT,Mysterymen, with
  2-card strip. 3.00
26 A:TMNT. 3.00
27 TM(c),A:TMNT conclusion 3.00
28 . . . . 3.00
29 Man in the Moon,Iron City . . . 3.00
30 V:Man in the Moon 3.00
31 A:Fat Fury 3.00
Ann. 1 by Bob Burden 5.00
TPB Man of Mystery, B&W 12.95
TPB The Wild Shall Wild Remain
  rep. #4–#11 . . . . 17.95
TPB Flaming Carrot's Greatest Hits,
  rep. #12–#18 . . . . 17.95
TPB Fortune Favors the Bold,
  rep.#19–#24 . . . . 16.95

FLAXEN
1 Based on Model,w/poster 2.95

FLOATERS
(B&W) 1993–94
1 thru 6 From Spike Lee . . . . . @2.50

FLOOD!
DH Maverick 2002
TPB 160-pg. 14.95

FOOT SOLDIERS, THE
1 thru 4 by Jim Krueger 2.95
TPB 14.95
See also Image Comics

FORT: PROPHET OF THE UNEXPLAINED
June, 2002
1 (of 4) F:Charles Fort 3.00
2 thru 4 . . . . @3.00
TPB 96-pg. B&W 9.95

FRANKENSTEIN
1 Movie Adaptation 3.95

FREAKSHOW
1 JBo,DMc,KB, 'Wanda the Worm
  Woman,' 'Lillie' 9.95

FUTURE WORLD
Sept. 2003
TPB Vol. 1 b&w,160-pg. 13.95
TPB Vol. 2 . . . . 13.95

GALACTIC
DH Rocket Comics Aug. 2003
1 . . . . 3.00
2 . . . . 3.00
3 . . . . 3.00

GAMERA
Aug., 1996
1 (of 4) by Dave Chipps &
  Mozart Couto 2.95
2 thru 4 . . . . @2.95

GARY GIANNI'S MONSTERMEN
Aug., 1999
1-shot 2.95

GHOST
Comics' Greatest World
Spec. AH(c) 3.95

GHOST
1995
1 by Eric Luke, R:Ghost 7.00
2 AH,MfM,Arcadia Nocturne,pt.2 . . 4.00
3 Arcadia Nocturn,pt.3 . . . . 4.00
4 . . . . 3.00
5 V:Predator 3.00
6 . . . . 3.00
7 Hell Night 3.00
8 thru 20 . . . . @3.00
21 Two heroes, one room. 3.00
22 'The key is forever beyond
  your reach' 3.00
23 I: The Goblins 3.00
24 X is dead. 3.00
25 double size 4.00
26 Fairytale version 3.50
27 . . . . 3.50
28 CW(c),Painful Music,pt.1 . . . . 3.50
29 CW(c),Painful Music,pt.2 . . . . 3.50
30 CW(c),Painful Music,pt.3 . . . . 3.50
31 CW(c),Painful Music,pt.4 . . . . 3.50
32 A Pathless Land. 3.50
33 Jade Cathedral,pt.1 . . . . 3.50
34 Jade Cathedral,pt.2 . . . . 3.50
35 Jade Cathedral,pt.3 . . . . 3.50
36 Jade Cathedral,pt.4 . . . . 3.50
Spec.#2 Immortal Coil 4.50
Spec.#3 Scary Monsters 4.50
TPB Ghost Stories 8.95
TPB Ghost: Nocturnes 9.95
TPB Exhuming Elisa 17.95

DARK HORSE

Ghost Series 2, #1
#2 © Dark Horse Comics

GHOST
Sept., 1998
1 CW,O:Ghost. 3.00
2 CW,V:Dr.Trouvaille 3.00
3 CW,V:Silhouette 3.00
4 CW,The Devil Inside,O:pt.1. . . . 3.00
5 CW,Stare at the Sun,O:pt.2 . . . . 3.00
6 CW,Stare at the Sun,O:pt.3 . . . . 3.00
7 CW,Shifter,pt.1,F:King Tiger 3.00
8 CW,Shifter,pt.2 . . . . 3.00
9 CW,Shifter,pt.3 . . . . 3.00
10 CW,Shifter,pt.4. . . . . 3.00
11 CW,back in Arcadia 3.00
12 Red Shadows,pt.1 (of 4) 3.00
13 Red Shadows,pt.2. . . . . 3.00
14 Red Shadows,pt.3 . . . . 3.00
15 Red Shadows,pt.4 . . . . 3.00
16 When the Devil Daydreams,pt.1. 3.00
17 When the Devil Daydreams,pt.2. 3.00
18 rogue agent. 3.00
19 Arcadia in chaos 3.00
20 F:Chris 3.00
21 F:Malcolm Greymater 3.00
22 final issue 3.00
TPB Black October. 14.95
TPB Painful Music 9.95
TPB No World So Dark. 14.95
Spec. Handbook #1 . . . . 2.95

GHOST/BATGIRL
Aug., 2000
1 (of 4) RBn,A:oracle 3.00
2 RBn,V:Two-Face 3.00
3 RBn,V:Carver, Greymater 3.00
4 RBn,concl. 3.00
TPB 96-pg. 11.95

GHOST/HELLBOY COLLECTION
TPB MMi 4.95

GHOST AND THE SHADOW
1995
Spec. 1-shot. 2.95

GHOST IN THE SHELL
Manga 1995
1 Manga Style 25.00
2 Wetware Virus 20.00
3 Killer Robots. 10.00
4 Rookie Cop Killed. 8.00
5 F:Major Kusanagi. 8.00
6 . . . . 8.00
7 Kusanagi in Jail 8.00
8 final issue. 8.00
TPB by Masamune Shirow 24.95

GHOST IN THE SHELL 2: MAN-MACHINE INTERFACE
Oct., 2002
1 40-pg.by Masamune Shirow . . . 4.00
2 32-pg.. . . . . 3.50
3 thru 10 . . . . @3.50
Spec. #1 Holographic Edition 5.00

G.I. JOE
1995
1 by Mike Barr & Tatsuya Ishida . . 3.00
2 thru 4 . . . . @3.00
Vol. 2 1996
1 . . . . 3.00
2 thru 4 . . . . @3.00

GIRL CRAZY
TPB by GHe, rep.#1–#3 . . . . 9.95

GIVE ME LIBERTY
1990
1 FM/DGb, Homes & Gardens. . . . 6.00
2 FM/DGb 5.00
3 and 4 FM/DGb . . . . @5.00
TPB 16.00
TPB Dell edition 16.00

GO BOY 7: HUMAN ACTION MACHINE
DH Rocket Comics July 2003
1 TPe 3.00
2 thru 7 . . . . @3.00

GODZILLA
(B&W) 1988
1 Japanese Manga 5.00
2 thru 6 . . . . @4.00
Spec #1 . . . . 2.25
TPB 2nd printing. 17.95

GODZILLA COLOR SPECIAL
1992
1 AAd,R:Godzilla,V:Gekido-Jin. . . . 3.50
1a rep (1998) 3.00
Spec.1 Godzilla vs. Barkley MBn(s),
JBt,DvD (1993). 3.50

GODZILLA
1995
0 RSd,The King of Monsters
is back! 4.00
1 R:Godzill 4.00
2 V:Cybersaur. 4.00
3 I:Bagorah the Bat Creature. 4.00
4 V:Bagorah,Cybersaur 4.00
5 V:U.S. Army 4.00
6 thru 14 . . . . @4.00

Godzilla #13
© Dark Horse Comics

15 'Thunder Downunder' 4.00
16 'Thunder in the Past' 4.00
TPB Past, Present, Future 17.95
TPB Godzilla: Age of Monsters . . . 17.95
Spec.1 Godzilla vs. Hero Zero
Tatsuya Ishida (1995). 2.50

GO GIRL!
Oct., 2002
TPB TrR 88-pg. b&w. 11.95

GOON, THE
June 2003
1 . . . . 3.00
2 . . . . 3.00
3 . . . . 3.00
TPB Nothin' But Misery 15.95

GREEN LANTERN VS. ALIENS
Aug., 2000
1 RMz,RL,F:Hal Jordan, x-over . . . 3.00
2 (of 4) RMz,RL,F:Kyle Rayner . . . 3.00
3 RMz,RL, without ring 3.00
4 RMz,RL, V:Alien Queen 3.00
TPB RMz,RL 12.95

GRENDEL
TPB Past Prime,MWg. 14.95
Spec.1 Grendel Cycle, Grendel
History (1995) 5.95

GRENDEL: BLACK, WHITE, AND RED
(B&W&R) Nov., 1998
1 (of 4) MWa, 48-pg. 5.00
2 thru 4 MWa, 48-pg. . . . . @4.00
TPB Black, White & Red, MWg. . . 18.95

GRENDEL CLASSICS
1995
1 Rep.#18–#19 Comico series. . . . 4.00
2 Rep. 4.00

All comics prices listed are for *Near Mint* condition.

GRENDEL: DEVIL BY THE DEED
1993
1 MWg,RRa 4.00
1 representation (1997) 4.00
TPB Devil Tales 9.95

GRENDEL: DEVIL CHILD
June, 1999
1 (of 2) MWg 3.00
2 conclusion 3.00

GRENDEL: THE DEVIL INSIDE
DH Maverick, Sept., 2001
1 (of 3) MWg 3.00
2 . . . . 3.00
3 concl. 3.00

GRENDEL: DEVIL'S LEGACY
Aug., 1996
1 (of 12) by Matt Wagner 3.00
2 thru 3 . . . . @3.00
TPB Devils and Deaths 16.95

GRENDEL: DEVIL'S LEGACY
DH/Maverick, March, 2000
1 (of 12) MWg, rep. from 1986 . . . 3.00
2 thru 6 MWg. . . . . @3.00
7 MWg,V:Tujiro XIV 3.00
8 MWg,back to N.Y. 3.00
9 MWg,F:Dominic Riley 3.00
10 MWg 3.00
11 MWg 3.00
12 MWg, concl. 3.00
TPB 328-pg 29.95

GRENDEL: GOD AND THE DEVIL
Jan. 2003
0 MWg,TSe 3.50
1 MWg (of 10) 3.50
2 thru 9 MWg. . . . . @3.50
10 MWg, concl., 48-pg 5.00
TPB The Devil Inside 12.95

GRENDEL: RED, WHITE, & BLACK
DH Maverick Sept., 2002
1 (of 4) 48-pg. B&W 5.00
2 MWg,KJo,DlB 5.00
3 . . . . 5.00
4 MWg 5.00

GRENDEL TALES: DEVIL'S APPRENTICE
Sept., 1997
1 (of 3) 3.00
2 thru 3 . . . . @3.00

GRENDEL TALES: DEVILS AND DEATHS
1994
1 . . . . 3.00
2 . . . . 3.00
TPB rep. Devils and Deaths plus Devil's Choices 16.95

Grendel Tales, The Devil's Apprentice #2 © Dark Horse Comics

GRENDEL TALES: DEVIL'S CHOICES
1995
1 F:Goran 3.00
2 Marica 3.00
3 Marica vs. Goran 3.00
4 conclusion 3.00

GRENDEL TALES: FOUR DEVILS, ONE HELL
1 MWg(c),F:Four Grendels 3.50
2 MWg(c),F:Four Grendels 3.50
3 MWg(c),F:Four Grendels 3.50
4 MWg(c),F:Four Grendels 3.50
5 MWg(c),F:Four Grendels 3.50
6 MWg(c),last issue 3.25
TPB Rep. #1–#6 . . . . 17.95

GRENDEL TALES: HOMECOMING
1994
1 Babylon Crash 3.00
2 Babylon Crash,pt. 2 . . . . 3.00
3 Too Dead To Die 3.00
TPB Homecoming 7.95

GRENDEL TALES: THE DEVIL IN OUR MIDST
1994
1 MWg(c) 3.50
2 MWg(c) 3.25
3 MWg(c) 3.00
4 & 5 . . . . @3.00
TPB series rep 15.95

GRENDEL TALES: THE DEVIL MAY CARE
1995
1 thru 6 mini-series 3.00
TPB The Devil May, Care (2002) . 19.95

GRENDEL TALES: THE DEVIL'S HAMMER
1994
1 MWg(a&s),I:Petrus Christus 3.50
2 MWg(a&s),A:P.Christus 3.25
3 MWg(a&s),last issue. 3.25

GRENDEL: WAR CHILD
1992
1 MWg 4.00
2 thru 9 MWg 3.00
10 MWg, final issue, dbl.size 4.00
TPB 18.95
TPB War Child, 304-pg. (2002) . . . 24.95

GRIFTER AND THE MASK
Sept., 1996
1 by Seagle, Lima & Pimentel 2.50
2 . . . . 2.50

GROO: DEATH AND TAXES
DH Maverick Dec., 2002
1 (of 4) SA. 3.00
2 no more killing? 3.00
3 village goes to war 3.00
4 concl. 3.00
TPB series rep. 112-pg. 12.95

GUFF
April, 1998
1-shot by Sergio Aragones, flip book, with Meanie Babies card, B&W 2.25

GUNSMITH CATS
(B&W) Manga 1995
1 I:Rally & Mini May 3.00
2 Revolver Freak 3.00
3 . . . . 3.00
4 V:Bonnie and Clyde 3.00
5 V:Bonnie and Clyde 3.00
6 Hostage Situation 3.00
7 thru 10 (10 part series) 3.00
TPB Misfire rep. #7–#10 & Return of Gray #1–#3 . . . . 12.95
TPB Misty's Run (2002) 14.95

GUNSMITH CATS: BAD TRIP
(B&W) June, 1998
1 (of 6) by Kenichi Sonoda 3.00
2 thru 4 . . . . @3.00
TPB Bad Trip 13.95

GUNSMITH CATS: BEAN BANDIT
(B&W) June, 1998
1 (of 9) by Kenichi Sonoda 3.00
2 thru 9 . . . . @3.00
TPB Bean Bandit, 224-pg. 16.95

GUNSMITH CATS: BONNIE & CLYDE
TPB by Kenichi Sonoda 12.95

GUNSMITH CATS: GOLDIE VS. MISTY
(B&W) Nov., 1997
1 (of 7) by Kenichi Sonoda 3.00

2 thru 7 . . . . @3.00
TPB Goldie vs. Misty 12.95

GUNSMITH CATS: KIDNAPPED
November 1999
1 (of 10) by Kenichi Sonoda 3.00
2 thru 10 . . . . @3.00
TPB Bad Trip 13.95

GUNSMITH CATS: MISTER V
B&W, October 2000
1 (of 11) by Kenichi Sonoda. 3.50
2 thru 11 . . . . @3.50
TPB Mister V, 224-pg.. . . . . 18.95
TPB Kidnapped 16.95
Spec. 3.00

GUNSMITH CATS: SHADES OF GRAY
(B&W) May, 1997
1 (of 5) by Kenichi Sonoda 3.00
2 thru 5 (of 5). . . . . @3.00

Gunsmith Cats, The Return of Gray #3 Atlantis #1 © Dark Horse Comics

GUNSMITH CATS: THE RETURN OF GRAY
(B&W) Aug., 1996
1 thru 7 by Kenichi Sonoda . . . . @3.00
TPB rep. series. 17.95

HAMMER OF GOD: BUTCH
1994
1 MBn. 2.50
2 and 3 MBn . . . . @2.50

HAMMER OF GOD: PENTATHLON
1994
1 MiB(s),NV. 2.50

DARK HORSE

THE HAMMER: UNCLE ALEX
Aug., 1998
1-shot KJo. 2.95

HAPPY BIRTHDAY MARTHA WASHINGTON
1995
1 Frank Miller 2.95

HAPPY ENDINGS
DH Maverick Sept., 2002
TPB 96-pg. B&W 9.95

HARD BOILED
1990
1 GfD 7.00
2 and 3 . . . . @6.00
TPB 14.95
TPB Big Damn Hard Boiled 29.95

HARD LOOKS
(B&W) 1992
1 thru 10 AVs Adaptations . . . . . @2.50
Book One. 14.95
TPB AVs. 17.95
TPB 3rd printing 19.95

HARLAN ELLISON'S DREAM CORRIDOR
1995
1 Various stories 3.00
2 Various stories 3.00
3 JBy, I Have No Mouth and I
  Must Scream & other stories . . 3.00
4 Catman 3.00
5 . . . . 3.00
6 Opposites Attract 3.00
Spec.#1 Various stories 4.95
TPB 18.95

HARLAN ELLISON'S DREAM CORRIDOR QUARTERLY
Aug., 1996
1 & 2 . . . . @6.00

HAUNTED MAN, THE
March, 2000
1 (of 3) GJ,MBg. 2.95
2 GJ,MBg 2.95
3 . . . . 2.95

HEARTBREAKERS
1996
1 . . . . 2.95
2 thru 4 . . . . @2.95

HEART OF EMPIRE: THE LEGACY OF LUTHER ARKWRIGHT
April, 1999
1 (of 9) BT. 3.00
2 thru 5 . . . . @3.00
6 plot against royal family 3.50
7 countdown to cataclysm 3.50
8 . . . . 3.50
9 conclusion 2.95
TPB series rep.. . . . . 29.95

HELL
DH Rocket Comics July 2003
1 BAu 3.00
2 thru 4 BAu . . . . @3.00

HELLBOY
Christmas Special (1997) MMi,
  48-pg.. . . . . 4.00
Hellboy Junior Halloween Special. . 4.00
Hellboy Junior Lurid Easter Special. 4.00
TPB The Lost Army 14.95
TPB The Chained Coffin & Others 17.95
TPB The Right Hand of Doom,
  MMi. 17.95
TPB The Bones of the Giants
  200-pg.. . . . . 14.95

Hellboy: Almost Colossus #2 © Dark Horse Comics

HELLBOY: ALMOST COLOSSUS
Legend 1997
1 (of 2) MMi, sequel to Wake the
  Devil 3.00
2 (of 2) 3.00

HELLBOY: BOX FULL OF EVIL
Aug., 1999
1 (of 2) MMi. 3.00
2 MMi, conclusion 3.00

HELLBOY: CONQUEROR WORM
May, 2001
1 (of 4) MMi. 3.00
2 thru 4 . . . . @3.00
TPB series rep. 144-pg. 17.95

HELLBOY: SEEDS OF DESTRUCTION
Legend/Dark Horse
1 JBy,MMi,AAd,V:Vampire Frog,
  BU:Monkeyman & O'Brien 3.50
2 MMi(c),JBy,AAd,BU:Monkeyman
  & O'Brien 3.00
3 MMi(c),JBy,AAd,BU:Monkeyman
  & O'Brien 3.00

All comics prices listed are for Near Mint condition.

DARK HORSE

Hellboy–Invincible

4 MMi(c),JBy,AAd,BU:Monkeyman
   & O'Brien 3.00
TPB Seed of Destruction 17.95

HELLBOY: THE THIRD WISH
July, 2002
1 (of 2) MMi 3.00
2 . . . . 3.00

HELLBOY: WAKE THE DEVIL
Legend 1996
1 (of 5) MMi 3.00
2 thru 5 . . . . @3.00
TPB Wake The Devil 17.95

HELLBOY: WEIRD TALES
Feb. 2003
1 FaN 3.00
2 thru 5 . . . . @3.00
TPB Weird Tales Vol. 1 . . . . 17.95

HELLBOY JR.
October 1999
1 (of 2) MMi 3.00
2 . . . . 3.00

HELLHOUNDS
(B&W) 1994
1 I:Hellhounds 3.00
2 and 3 . . . . @3.00
Becomes:

HELLHOUNDS: PANZER CORPS
3 thru 6 . . . . @3.00
TPB 14.95

HELLSING
2003
TPB Vol. 1 b&w 13.95

HERBIE
1992
1 JBy,reps.& new material 3.00
2 Reps.& new material 2.50

HERETIC, THE
Nov., 1996
1 (of 4) by Rich DiLeonardo, Joe
   Phillips & Dexter Vines 2.95
2 thru 4 . . . . @2.95

HERMES VS. THE EYEBALL KID
1994
1 thru 3 Symphony of Blood 2.95

HERO ZERO
1994
1 First and last issue 2.50

HIEROGLYPH
Nov., 1999
1 RdD,F:Francisco Chavez 2.95
2 thru 4 RdD . . . . @2.95

THE HORROR OF COLLIER COUNTY
Oct., 1999
1 (of 5) Halloween special 2.95
2 thru 5 concl. . . . . @2.95
TPB 12.95

H.P.'S ROCK CITY
TPB by Moebius 7.95

Hypersonic #4
© *Dark Horse Comics*

HYPERSONIC
Nov., 1997
1 (of 4) DAn,GEr 2.95
2 thru 4 . . . . @2.95

IGUANA, THE
DH Venture Feb., 2002
TPB 88-pg. 10.95

ILLEGAL ALIEN
June 2003
TPB b&w 10.95

INDIANA JONES AND THE ARMS OF GOLD
1994
1 In South America 2.75
2 In South America 2.75
3 V:Incan Gods 2.75
4 . . . . 2.50

INDIANA JONES AND THE FATE OF ATLANTIS
1991
1 DBa,Search for S.Hapgood with
   2-card strip 4.00
1a 2nd printing 3.00
2 DBa,Lost Dialogue of Plato with
   2-card strip 3.00
3 Map Room of Atlantis 3.00
4 Atlantis, Last issue 3.00
TPB 13.95

INDIANA JONES AND THE GOLDEN FLEECE
1994
1 SnW 2.75
2 SnW 2.50

INDIANA JONES AND THE IRON PHOENIX
1994
1 . . . . 2.50
2 V:Nazis 2.50
3 A:Nadia Kirov 2.50
4 V:Undead 2.50

INDIANA JONES AND THE SARGASSO PIRATES
1995
1 thru 4 . . . . @2.50

INDIANA JONES AND THE SHRINE OF THE SEA DEVIL
199
1 . . . . 2.50

INDIANA JONES AND THE SPEAR OF DESTINY
1995
1 I:Spear T/Pierced Christ 2.50
2 DSp, with Henry Jones 2.50
3 Search for the Shaft 2.50

INDIANA JONES: THUNDER IN THE ORIENT
1993
1 DBa(a&s),in Tripoli 2.75
2 DBa(a&s),Muzzad Ram 2.75
3 DBa(a&s),V:Sgt.Itaki 2.75
4 DBa(a&s),In Hindu Kush 2.75
5 DBa(a&s),V:Japanese Army . . . 2.75
6 DBa(a&s),last issue 2.75

INSTANT PIANO
(B&W) 1994
1 Offbeat humor 3.95
2 . . . . 3.95
3 Various stories 3.95
4 Devil Puppet 3.95

INTRON DEPOT
Nov., 1998
TPB Intron Depot 40.00
TPB Intron Depot 2: Blades 37.95

INTRON DEPOT
Feb. 2003
TPB Vol. 1 . . . . 44.95
TPB Vol. 2 Blades 44.95
TPB Vol. 3 Ballistics 44.95

INVINCIBLE ED:
2003
1 The Beating of Ed 3.50
2 I'm Too Sexy 3.95
3 Lance Lundgrin Unleashes 3.00

All comics prices listed are for *Near Mint* condition.

IRONHAND OF ALMURIC
(B&W) 1991
1 Robert E. Howard adaption 2.25
2 A:Cairn,V:Yagas 2.25
3 V:Yasmeena,The Hive Queen... 2.25
4 Conclusion 2.25
GN 10.95

JAMES BOND 007: QUASIMODO GAMBIT
1995
1 I:Maximillion Quasimodo....... 3.95
2 V:Fanatical Soldiers 3.95
3 V:Steel 3.95

JAMES BOND 007: SERPENT'S TOOTH
1992
1 PG,DgM,V:Indigo 5.50
2 PG,DgM,V:Indigo 5.00
3 PG,DgM 5.25
TPB 15.95

JAMES BOND 007: SHATTERED HELIX
1994
1 V:Cerberus 3.00
2 V:Cerberus 3.00

JAMES BOND 007: A SILENT ARMAGEDDON
1993
1 V:Troy 3.25
2 V:Omega 3.25
3 V:Omega 3.25

JOHN BOLTON'S STRANGE WINK
March, 1998
1 (of 3) 2.95
2 thru 3 .... @2.95

JOHNNY DYNAMITE
1994
1 .... 2.95
2 .... 2.95
3 V:Faust 2.95
4 Last issue 2.95

JOKER/MASK
May, 2000
1 (of 4) Batman x-over 2.95
2 Joker becomes Joker/Mask 2.95
3 A:Harley Quinn, Poison Ivy 2.95
4 three nuclear bombs, concl. ... 2.95
TPB 96-pg 11.95

JONNY DEMON
1994
1 SL(c),KBk,NV 2.75
2 SL(c),KBk,NV 2.75
3 SL(c),KBk,NV, final issue 2.50

JOSS WHEDON'S FRAY
June, 2001
1 (of 8) 3.00
1a gold foil (c) 10.00
1b gold foil (c) signed 25.00
2 thru 8 .... @3.00
TPB Future Slayer 19.95

DARK HORSE

JUDGE DREDD VS. ALIENS: INCUBUS
March 2003
1 (of 4) 3.00
2 thru 4 .... @3.00

JUNIOR CARROT PATROL
(B&W) 1989
1 and 2 .... @2.25

KELLEY JONES' THE HAMMER
Sept., 1997
1 (of 4) KJo, horror series 2.95
2 thru 4 KJo .... @2.95
TPB 12.95

KELLEY JONES' THE HAMMER: THE OUTSIDER
Feb., 1999
1 (of 3) KJo 2.95
2 and 3 .... @2.95

KINGS OF THE NIGHT
1990
1 Robert E. Howard adapt. 2.25
2 end Mini-Series 2.25

King Tiger & Motorhead #2
© *Dark Horse Comics*

KING TIGER/MOTORHEAD
1996
1 (of 2) by D.G. Chichester, Karl
   Waller & Eric Shanower 2.95
2 .... 2.95

KISS
July, 2002
1 JoC 4.00
2 JoC 3.00
3 JoC 3.00
4 JoC 3.00
5 .... 3.00
5a photo (c) 3.00
6 .... 3.00
6a photo (c) 3.00

Ironhand–Legend

7 SLo 3.00
8 SLo 3.00
9 SLo 3.00
10 SLo 3.00
11 .... 3.00
12 .... 3.00
13 MBn 3.00
1a thru 13a photo (c) ...... @3.00
TPB Rediscovery 10.95
TPB Return of the Phantom 9.95
TPB Men and Monsters 12.95

KLING KLANG KLATCH
GN 11.95

Land of Nod #1
© *Dark Horse Comics*

LAND OF NOD
(B&W) July, 1997
1 (of 4) by Jay Stephens 3.00
2 thru 4 .... @3.00
TPB Rockabye Book 13.95

LAST DAY IN VIETNAM
GN by Will Eisner 10.95
GN rep 10.95

LAST TEMPTATION, THE
DH Maverick, Nov., 2000
TPB NGa,MZi,6'x9' 9.95

THE LEGEND OF MOTHER SARAH
B&W, Manga 1995
1 I:Mother Sarah 4.00
2 Sarah and Tsutsu 4.00
3 Firing Squad 4.00
4 F:Toki 4.00
5 Yunnel Town 4.00
6 Kill or Be Killed 4.00
7 Firing Squad 4.00
8 Conclusion 4.00
TPB The Tunnel Town 18.95

THE LEGEND OF MOTHER SARAH: CITY OF THE ANGELS
B&W, Manga Oct., 1996
1 (of 9) by Katsuhiro Otomo and
   Takumi Nagayasu, 48-pg 4.25

All comics prices listed are for Near Mint condition.

Legend–Marshall

DARK HORSE

1 rep. (1997) 4.25
2 thru 4 . . . . 4.25
2 thru 4 rep. (1997) 4.25
5 Tsue a victim 4.25
6 Mother Teres questioned 4.25
7 put in front trenches 4.25
8 Teres suicide run 4.25
9 concl., 32-pg. 3.25

THE LEGEND OF MOTHER SARAH: CITY OF THE CHILDREN
B&W, Manga 1996
1 thru 4 (7 part mini-series) . . . . @4.25

LITTLE ANNIE FANNY
1962–70
October 2000
TPB cartoons from playboy 25.00
TPB Vol. 2 . . . . 24.95

LONE
DH Rocket Comics Sept. 2003
1 . . . . 3.00
2 . . . . 3.00
3 . . . . 3.00

LONE GUNMEN, THE
June, 2001
1-shot 3.00
1-shot photo(c) 3.00
1-shot photo (c) lim ed. 7.00
1-shot photo (c) lim ed. signed . . . 20.00

LONE WOLF AND CUB
TPB Vol 1. . . . . 20.00
TPB Vol 2. . . . . 12.00
TPB Vol 3 Flute of the Fallen Tiger 12.00
TPB Vol.4 Shishogan Eyes 10.00
TPB Vol.5 Black Wind. 10.00
TPB Vol.6 Lanterns For The Dead 10.00
TPB Vol.7 DragonCloud,WindTiger 10.00
TPB Vol.8 Chains of the Kurokuwa 10.00
TPB Vol.9 Shadows, Echoes 10.00
TPB Vol.10 Separate Paths 10.00
TPB Vol.11 Talisman of Hades . . . 10.00
TPB Vol.12 Shattered Stones 10.00
TPB Vol.13 The Moon in the East, The Sun in the West. 10.00
TPB Vol.14 Day of the Demons . . 10.00
TPB Vol.15 Brothers of the Grass . 10.00
TPB Vol.16 Gateway Into Winter. . 10.00
TPB Vol.17 The Will of the Fang . . 10.00
TPB Vol.18 The Last Kurokuwa . . 10.00
TPB Vol.19 Moon in Our Hearts . . 10.00
TPB Vol.20 A Taste of Poison 10.00
TPB Vol.21 Fragrance of Death . . 10.00
TPB Vol.22 Heaven and Earth . . . 10.00
TPB Vol.23 Tears of Ice 10.00
TPB Vol.24 In These Small Hands 10.00
TPB Vol.25 Perhaps in Death 10.00
TPB Vol.26 Battle in the Dark 10.00
TPB Vol.27 Battle's Eve 10.00
TPB Vol.28 Falling Tree 10.00

LONE WOLF 2100
May, 2002
1 (of 4) War Spore. 4.00
2 thru 4 War Spore. . . . . @3.00
5 thru 9 . . . . @3.00
10 Pattern Storm, concl. 3.00
1-shot The Red File 3.00
TPB Shadows on Saplings 12.95
TPB Vol. 2 . . . . 14.95

LORDS OF MISRULE
(B&W) Jan., 1997
1 by DAn, PSj 3.00
2 thru 6 . . . . @3.00
TPB The Lords of Misrule 17.95

LOST IN SPACE
April, 1998
1 (of 3) sequel to film. 3.00
2 thru 3 GEr(c). . . . . @3.00
TPB rep. series, GEr(c) 7.95

LOST WORLD
July 2003
TPB b&w 17.95

THE LUCK IN THE HEAD
TPB 11.95

THE MACHINE
Comics Greatest World 1994
1 (a) The Barb Wire spin 2.50
2 V:Salvage. 2.50
3 Freak Show 2.50
4 I:Skion 2.50

MAC RAYBOY'S FLASH GORDON
Jan. 2003
TPB b&w 19.95
TPB Vol. 2 . . . . 19.95
TPB Vol. 3 . . . . 19.95
TPB Vol. 4 . . . . 19.95

MADMAN
Legend 1994
1 MiA(s) 8.00
2 MiA(s) 6.00
3 MiA(s) 5.00
4 MiA(s),Muscleman 5.00
5 MiA(s),I:The Blast. 4.00
6 MiA(s),A:Big Guy, Big Brain-o-rama,pt.1 . . . . 12.00
7 MiA(s),FM,A:Big Guy, Big Brain-o-rama,pt.2 . . . . 6.00
8 MiA(s) 4.00
9 Micro Madman 4.00
10 . . . . 4.00
11 . . . . 4.00
Yearbook '95 TPB. 17.95

Lords of Misrule #4
© *Dark Horse Comics*

Comics Values Annual

Yearbook '96 TPB. 17.95
Yearbook '95 new printing (2003) . 17.95
Apr. 1999
12 MiA 3.00
13 MiA 3.00
14 MiA 3.00
15 MiA 3.00
16 MiA 3.00
TPB Boogaloo 8.95
TPB The Exit of Dr. Boiffard 17.95
TPB Vol. 4 Heaven and Hell 17.95
G-Men From Hell (Aug., 2000)
17 Pt.1 MiA 3.00
18 Pt.2 MiA, Is Frank Einstein dead?. 3.00
19 Pt.3 MiA 3.00
20 Pt.4 MiA, V:Mr.Monstadt 3.00

MADMAN/THE JAM
July, 1998
1 (of 2) MiA 3.00
2 MiA 3.00

MADWOMAN OF THE SACRED HEART, THE
(B&W)
TPB by Alex Jodorowsky & Moe . . 12.95

MAGIC: THE GATHERING
March, 1998
1 (of 4) MGr,Initiation. 2.95
2 MGr, Legacy. 2.95
3 MGr, Crucible 2.95
4 MGr, Destiny 2.95
TPB Gerrard's Quest 11.95

MAGNUS/NEXUS
Dark Horse/Valiant
1 MBn(s), SR 3.25
2 MBn(s), SR 3.25

MAN FROM THE CIGUIRI
TPB by Moebius. 7.95

MARK, THE
1987–89
1 LSn 2.25
2 LSn 2.25
3 LSn 2.25
4 thru 6. . . . . @2.25
[Second Series] 1993
1 MiB(s),in America,V:Archon . . . 2.75
2 MiB(s),V:Archon 2.75
3 MiB(s),V:Archon,A:Pierce 2.75
4 MiB(s),last issue. 2.75

MARSHALL LAW
GN Super Babylon, KON (1992). . . 4.95
TPB Blood Sweat and Fears (1998) 15.95

MARSHALL LAW: CAPE FEAR
1 KON. 2.95

MARSHALL LAW: SECRET TRIBUNAL
1993
1 KON. 2.95
2 KON. 2.95

All comics prices listed are for *Near Mint* condition.

DARK HORSE
Martha–Minotaur

Martha Washington Goes To War #3
© Dark Horse Comics

MARTHA WASHINGTON GOES TO WAR
Dark Horse-Legends 1994
1 FM(s),DGb, V:Fat Boys Corp. . . . 3.25
2 FM(s),DGb, V:Fat Boys Corp. . . . 3.25
3 FM(s),DGb, V:Fat Boys Corp. . . . 3.25
4 FM(s),DGb, V:Fat Boys Corp. . . . 3.25
5 FM(s),DBb, final issue 3.25
TPB Rep.#1–#5 . . . . 17.95

MARTHA WASHINGTON SAVES THE WORLD
Dec., 1997
1 (of 3) FM,DGb 3.25
2 thru 3 . . . . @3.25
TPB rep. 12.95

MARTHA WASHINGTON STRANDED IN SPACE
1995
1 . . . . 3.25

MARTIN MYSTRY
(B&W) DH/Bonelli Mar. 1999
1 by Alfredo Castelli & Giancarlo Alessandrini, DGb(c) 92-pg. . . . 4.95
2 thru 6 . . . . @4.35

MASAKAZU KATSURA'S SHADOW LADY
Manga (B&W) Oct., 1998
Dangerous Love
1 (of 7) Masakazu Katsura. 2.50
2 thru 7 . . . . @2.50
The Eyes of a Stranger, May, 1999
8 thru 12, pt.1–pt.5. . . . . @2.50
The Awakening
13 thru 19, pt.1–pt.7 . . . . @2.50
Sudden Death
20 thru 24, pt.1–pt.5 . . . . @2.50
Spec.48-pg. final issue 4.00
TPB Dangerous Love 17.95
TPB The Awakening 15.95
TPB Sudden Death. 14.95

MASK, THE
1991
0 'Who's Laughing Now' (B&W) . . . 6.00
1 I:Lt.Kellaway Mask 5.00
2 V:Rapaz & Walter. 5.00
3 O:Mask 5.00
4 final issue. 5.00
TPB 14.95

MASK, THE
1994
1 Movie Adaptation 3.00
2 Movie Adaptation 2.50

MASK , THE
[Mini-series] 1995
The Mask Strikes Back (1995)
1 Mask Strikes Back,pt.1 . . . . 2.50
2 Mask Strikes Back,pt.2 . . . . 2.50
3 Mask Strikes Back,pt.3 . . . . 2.50
4 DoM,Mask Strikes Back,pt.4 . . . . 2.50
5 Mask Strikes Back,pt.5 . . . . 2.50
TPB by John Arcudi, Doug Mahnke & Keith Williams 14.95
The Hunt for Green October (1995)
6 Pt.1 . . . . 2.50
7 Pt.2 Kellaway vs. Ray Tuttle 2.50
8 Pt.3 F:Emily Tuttle 2.50
9 Pt.4 final issue 2.50
World Tour (1995)
10 Pt.1 . . . . 2.50
11 Pt.2 . . . . 2.50
12 Pt.3 . . . . 2.50
13 Pt.4 . . . . 2.50
Southern Discomfort (1996)
14 Pt.1 Mardi Gras time 2.50
15 Pt.2 . . . . 2.50
16 Pt.3 . . . . 2.50
17 Pt.4 . . . . 2.50

MASK/MARSHALL LAW
Feb., 1998
1 (of 2) by Pat Mills and Kevin O'Neill 2.95
2 concl. 2.95

MASK RETURNS, THE
1992
1 inc.cut-out Mask 5.00
2 Mask's crime spree. 4.00
3 . . . . 4.00
4 . . . . 4.00
TPB by John Arcudi & Doug Mahnke 14.95

MASK: TOYS IN THE ATTIC
Aug., 1998
1 (of 4) 2.95
2 thru 4 . . . . @2.95

MASK, THE: VIRTUAL SURREALITY
1997
1-shot F: MMi,SA 2.95

MAXIMUM OVERLOAD
1 Masque (Mask). 12.00
2 thru 4 Mask. . . . . @8.00

MAXIMUM OVERLOAD
1 thru 5 . . . . @3.95

The Mask: Virtual Surreality
© Dark Horse Comics

MAYHEM
1989
1 F:The Mask, The Mark 5.00
2 thru 4 . . . . @4.00

MECHA
Comics Greatest World 1995
1 color. 3.00
2 color. 3.00
3 thru 6 B&W . . . . @3.00
Spec.(#1) CW(c),color 3.00

MEDAL OF HONOR
1994
1 Ace of Aces 2.50
2 . . . . 2.50
3 Andrew's Raid 2.50
4 Frank Miller(c) 2.50
5 final issue. 2.50
Spec. #1 JKu (1994). 2.50

METROPOLIS
Apr. 2003
TPB by Oxamu Tezuka, b&w 13.95

MEZZ GALACTIC TOUR 2494
1994
1 MBn,MV. 2.50

MIKE MIGNOLA'S B.P.R.D.: HOLLOW EARTH
Jan., 2002
1 (of 3) 3.00
2 . . . . 3.00
3 . . . . 3.00
TPB 120-pg. 17.95
1-shot Something Under My Bed . . 3.00
1-shot The Soul of Venice. 3.00
1-shot Dark Waters. 3.00
1-shot Night Train 3.00

THE MINOTAUR'S TALE
TPB by Al Davison 11.95

MR. MONSTER
(B&W) 1988

1 .... 3.50
2 .... 3.00
3 Alan Moore story 3.00
4 .... 3.00
5 I:Monster Boy 3.00
6 .... 3.00
7 .... 3.00
8 V:Vampires (giant size) 4.95

MONKEYMAN & O'BRIEN
Legend 1996

1 by Arthur Adams 3.00
2 and 3 .... @3.00
Spec 3.00
TPB 16.95

MONSTERS, INC.
Oct., 2001

1-shot 56-pg., Disney-Pixar 4.95

MORPHOS THE SHAPE CHANGER
July, 1996

1-shot BHg 4.95

MOTHER, COME HOME
Nov. 2003

TPB 14.95

MOTORHEAD
Comics Greatest World 1995

1 V:Predator 2.50
2 Laughing Wolf Carnival 2.50
3 V:Jackboot 2.50
Spec.#1 JLe(c),V:Mace Blitzkrieg
  (1994) 3.95

[BOB BURDEN'S ORIGINAL] MYSTERYMEN
July, 1999

1 .... 3.00
2 The Amazing Disc Man 3.00
3 F:Screwball 3.00
4 All Villain Comics #1 .... 3.50

MYSTERY MEN
July, 1999

1 (of 2) Movie adapt. 3.00
2 movie adaptation, concl. 3.00

MYST: THE BOOK OF THE BLACK SHIPS
Aug., 1997

1 (of 4) from CD-Rom game 2.95
2 thru 4 .... @2.95

NATHAN NEVER
(B&W) DH/Bonelli Mar., 1999

1 (of 6) by Michele Medda & Nicola
  Mari, AAd(c) 102-pg. 4.95
2 thru 6 .... @4.95

NEVERMEN, THE
May, 2000

1 (of 4) GyD, V:Clockwork 3.00
2 GyD,V:Honshu 3.00

3 GyD,V:Clockwork 3.00
4 GyD,V:League of Crows 3.00
TPB 128-pg. 14.95

NEVERMEN, THE: STREETS OF BLOOD
Jan. 2003

1 (of 3) GyD 3.00
2 .... 3.00
3 concl. 3.00
TPB 9.95

NEW FRONTIER
(B&W) 1992

1 From series in Heavy Metal .. 2.75
2 Who Killed Ruby Fields? 2.75
3 Conclusion 2.75

NEW TWO FISTED TALES: VOL II
1993

1 War stories 4.95

[JOHN BYRNE'S] NEXT MEN
1992

0 Rep Next Men from Dark Horse
  Presents 3.00
1 JBy,'Breakout'inc.trading card
  certificate 5.00
1a 2nd Printing Blue 3.00
2 JBy,World View 4.00
3 JBy,A:Sathanis 4.00
4 JBy,A:Sathanis 4.00
5 JBy,A:Sathanis 4.00
6 JBy,O:Senator Hilltop,
  Sathanis,Project Next Men .. 3.50
7 JBy,I:M-4,Next Men Powers
  explained 3.50
8 JBy,I:Omega Project,A:M-4 .. 3.00
9 JBy,A:Omega Project,A:M-4 .. 3.00
10 JBy,V:OmegaProject,A:M-4 .. 3.00
11 JBy,V:OmegaProject,A:M-4 .. 3.00
12 JBy,V:Dr.Jorgenson 3.00
13 JBy,Nathan vs Jack 3.00
14 JBy,I:Speedboy 3.00
15 JBy,in New York 3.00
16 JBy,Jasmine's Pregnant 3.00
17 FM(c),JBy,Arrested 3.00
18 JBy,On Trial 3.00

Next Men: Faith (1993)
19 Faith, pt.1 JBy(a&s),V:Dr.
  Trogg, Blue Dahila 3.25
20 Faith, pt.2 JBy,(a&s),F:Jack .. 3.00
21 Faith,pt.3 MMi(c),JBy(a&s),
  I:Hellboy 18.00
22 Faith,pt.4 JBy(a&s),Last issue .. 3.00
Next Men: Power (1994)
23 Power,pt.1, JBy(a&s) 2.75
24 Power,pt.2, JBy(a&s) 2.75
25 Power,pt.3, JBy(a&s) 2.75
26 Power,pt.4, JBy(a&s) concl. .. 2.50
Next Men: Lies (1994)
27 Lies,pt.1,JBy 2.50
28 Lies,pt.2,JBy 2.50
29 Lies,pt.3,JBy 2.50
30 Lies,pt.4, JBy 2.50
TPB rep.#1-6 .... 16.95
TPB Book 2, rep. #7–#12 ..... 16.95
TPB Book 3, rep. #13–#18 .... 16.95
TPB Book 4, rep. #19–#22 .... 14.95
TPB Book 5, rep. #23–#26 .... 14.95
TPB Book 6, rep. #27–#30 .... 16.95

NEXUS: ALIEN JUSTICE
1992

1 .... 4.25
2 .... 4.25
3 .... 3.95
TPB series rep. (1996) 16.95

NEXUS: EXECUTIONER'S SONG
1996

1 (of 4) by Mike Baron, Steve
  Rude & Gary Martin 3.00
2 thru 4 .... @3.00

NEXUS: GOD CON
April, 1997

1 (of 2) by Mike Baron, Steve
  Rude & Gary Martin 3.00
2 .... 3.00

NEXUS: THE LIBERATOR
1992

1 'Waking Dreams' 3.00
2 Civil War,D:Gigo 3.00
3 Civil War contd. 3.00
4 Last issue 3.00

NEXUS MEETS MADMAN
1996

1-shot 3.00

NEXUS: NIGHTMARE IN BLUE
(B&W) July, 1997

1 (of 4) MBn,SR,GyM 3.00
2 thru 4 .... @3.00

NEXUS: THE ORIGIN
1995

1 SR,O:Nexus 5.00

NEXUS: OUT OF THE VORTEX
1 R:Nexus 3.00
2 Zolot & Nexus Together 3.00
3 O:Vortex 3.00

DARK HORSE

Nexus: Nightmare in Blue #2
© Dark Horse Comics

NEXUS: THE WAGES OF SIN
1995
1 The Client 3.00
2 V:Munson 3.00
3 SR(c&a) Murders in New Eden . . 3.00

NIGHT BEFORE CHRISTMASK
1 Rick Geary 9.95

NINA'S NEW AND IMPROVED ALL-TIME GREATEST
1994
1 Anthology: Nina Paley 2.50

NINTH GLAND, THE
(B&W) March, 1997
1-shot by Renee French 3.95

NOCTURNALS: WITCHING HOUR
May, 1998
1-shot by Dan Brereton 4.95

NOSFERATU
(B&W) 1991
1 The Last Vampire 3.95
2 . . . . 2.95

OH MY GODDESS!
(B&W) Manga 1994
1 by Kosuke Fujishima 5.00
2 & 3 . . . . @4.00
4 thru 6 . . . . @3.00
TPB 1-555-Goddess 12.95
TPB Vol.1 Wrong Number 13.95
TPB Vol.2 Leader of the Pack . . . 13.95
TPB Vol.3 Final Exam 13.95

Part II, 1995
1 F:Keiichi 4.00
2 thru 9 . . . . @3.00
TPB Sympathy for the Devil 12.95

Part III, 1996
1 Wishes are Granted 3.00
2 Love Potion Number 9 . . . . 3.00
3 thru 5 . . . . @3.00
6 thru 11 Terrible Master Urd,
 pt.1 thru pt.6 . . . . @3.00
TPB Love Potion Number 9 . . . . 12.95
TPB Terrible Master Urd 12.95

Part IV, 1996–97
1 Robot Wars 3.00
2 The Trials of Morisato,pt.1 . . . . 3.00
3 The Trials of Morisato,pt.2 . . . . 3.00
4 The Trials of Morisato,pt.3 . . . . 3.00
5 The Queen of Vengeance 3.00
6 Mara Strikes Back,pt.1,48-pg . . 4.00
7 Mara Strikes Back,pt.2 . . . . 3.00
8 Mara Strikes Back,pt.3 . . . . 3.00

Part V, 1997–98
1 The Forgotten Promise 3.00
2 The Lunch Box of Love 3.00
3 Meet Me by the Seashore, 48-pg. 4.00
4 You're So Bad, 48-pg 4.00
5 Ninja Master,pt.1 . . . . 3.00
6 Ninja Master,pt.2, 48-pg. 4.00
7 Miss Keiichi,pt.1, 48-pg. 4.00
7 & 8 Miss Keiichi,pt.2 . . . . 3.00
9 It's Lonely at the Top 3.50
10 Fallen Angel, 48-pg 4.00
11 Play the Game, 48-pg 4.00
12 Sorrow, Fear Not 4.00

Part VI, 1998–99
1 Devil in Miss Urd,pt.1, 40-pg. . . 3.50
2 Devil in Miss Urd,pt.2 . . . . 3.00
3 Devil in Miss Urd,pt.3 . . . . 3.00
4 Devil in Miss Urd,pt.4 . . . . 3.00
5 Devil in Miss Urd,pt.5 . . . . 3.00
6 SuperUrd 3.00

Part VII, 1999
1 (of 8)The Fourth Goddess,pt.1 . . 3.00
2 The Fourth Goddess,pt.2 . . . . . 3.00
3 The Fourth Goddess,pt.3 . . . . . 3.00
4 The Fourth Goddess,pt.4,40-pg. 3.50
5 The Fourth Goddess,pt.5,40-pg. 3.50
TPB The Adventures of the
 Mini-Goddesses 9.95

Part VIII, 1999
1 (of 2) Childhood's End,
 by Kosuke Fujishima 3.50
2 Childhood's End,pt.2 . . . . 3.50
3 The Queen and the Goddess . . 3.50
4 Hail to the Chief,pt.1 . . . . 3.50
5 Hail to the Chief,pt.2 . . . . 3.50
6 Hail to the Chief,pt.3 . . . . 3.50
TPB Childhood's End 216-pg . . . 15.95

Part IX, 2000
1 Pretty in Scarlet 3.00
2 The Goddess's Apprentice 3.00
3 Queen Sayoko,pt.1 . . . . 3.00
4 Queen Sayoko,pt.2 . . . . 3.50
5 Queen Sayoko,pt.3 (of 5) 3.00
6 Queen Sayoko,pt.4 . . . . 3.00
7 Queen Sayoko,pt.5 . . . . 3.50
TPB Ninja Master 13.95
TPB Queen of Vengeance 13.95
TPB Mara Strikes Back 14.95
TPB Miss Keiichi 16.95
TPB The Devil in Miss URD 14.95
TPB The Fourth Goddess 18.95
TPB Queen Sayoko, 240-pg. . . . 16.95

PART X Feb., 2001
1 The Secret of Speed 3.00
2 The Secret of Speed,concl 3.00
3 one-shot 3.50
4 Hand in Hand,pt.1 . . . . 3.50
5 Hand in Hand,pt.2 . . . . 3.50

PART XI Aug., 2001
1 Banpei in Love,pt.1 (of 2) 3.50
2 Banpei in Love,pt.2 . . . . 3.50

Oh My Goddess, Vol. 6, #3
© Dark Horse Comics

3 Mystery Child,pt.1 (of 8) 3.00
4 Mystery Child,pt.2 . . . . 3.00
5 Mystery Child,pt.3 . . . . 3.00
6 Mystery Child,pt.4 . . . . 3.00
7 Mystery Child,pt.5 . . . . 3.50
8 Mystery Child,pt.6 . . . . 3.50
9 Mystery Child,pt.7 . . . . 3.00
10 Mystery Child,pt.8, 48-pg. . . . 4.00
TPB series rep 18.95

PART XII July, 2002
1 (of 3) Learning to Love,pt.1 . . . 3.50
2 Learning to Love,pt.2 . . . . 3.50
3 Learning to Love,pt.3 . . . . 3.50

Continuing series (Oct., 2002)
91 Traveler,pt.1 (of 5) 3.00
92 Traveler,pt.2 . . . . 3.00
93 Traveler, pt.3 . . . . 3.00
94 Traveler, pt.4 . . . . 3.00
95 Traveler, pt.5 . . . . 3.50
96 The Phantom Racer, pt.1 . . . . 3.00
97 The Phantom Racer, pt.2 . . . . 3.00
98 The Phantom Racer, pt.3 . . . . 3.00
99 The Phantom Racer, pt.4 . . . . 3.00
100 Dr. Moreau, pt.1 . . . . 3.00
101 Dr. Moreau, pt.2 . . . . 3.00
102 Dr. Moreau, pt.3 . . . . 3.00
103 Dr. Moreau, pt.4 . . . . 3.00
TPB Hand in Hand 17.95
TPB Traveler 17.95

OKTANE
1995
1 R:Oktane 2.50
2 V:God Zero 2.50
3 V:God Zero 2.50
4 conclusion 2.50

ONE BAD RAT
1 BT 2.95
2 thru 4 . . . . @2.95

ONE-TRICK RIP-OFF
1997
TPB by Paul Pope 12.95

ORION
(B&W) Manga 1993
1 SF by Masamune Shirow 2.50
2 F:Yamata Empire 2.95

Orion–Predator — DARK HORSE — Comics Values Annual

3 thru 6 . . . . @2.95
TPB 15.95
TPB 3rd edition. 19.95

OTIS GOES HOLLYWOOD
(B&W) April, 1997
1 (of 2) by Bob Fingerman 2.95
2 . . . . 2.95

OTTO PORFIRI:
Oct., 2001
TPB Drama on the Cliff. 9.95
TPB Red Moon 88-pg. (2002). . . . 9.95

OUT FOR BLOOD
B&W 1999
1 (of 4) GEr,F:Dan Sanger 3.00
2 The Wings; The Claws 3.00
3 . . . . 3.00
4 concl. 3.00

OUTLANDERS
(B&W) Manga 1988
1 . . . . 3.00
2 . . . . 2.50
3 thru 7 . . . . @2.50
8 thru 20 . . . . @2.50
21 Operation Phoenix 2.50
22 thru 24 . . . . @2.50
25 thru 29 with 2-card strip . . . . @2.50
30 . . . . 2.50
31 Tetsua dying 2.50
32 D:The Emperor 2.50
33 Story finale 2.50
#0 The Key of Graciale 2.75
TPB Vol. 1 by Johji Manabe 13.95
TPB Vol. 1 2nd edition 13.95
TPB Vol. 2 . . . . 13.95
TPB Vol. 2 2nd edition 13.95
TPB Vol. 3 . . . . 13.95
TPB Vol. 4 . . . . 12.95
TPB Vol. 5 thru Vol. 8 . . . . . . @14.95

OUTLANDERS: EPILOGUE
(B&W) 1994
1 . . . . 2.75

OUTLAW 7
Aug., 2001
1 (of 4) 3.00
2 thru 4 . . . . @3.00

OUT OF THE VORTEX
Comics' Greatest World 1993
1 B:JOs(s),V:Seekers 2.25
2 MMi(c),DaW,A:Seekers 2.25
3 WS(c),E:JOs(s),DaW,A:Seeker,
C:Hero Zero 2.25
4 DaW,A:Catalyst 2.25
5 V:Destroyers,A:Grace 2.25
6 V:Destroyers,A:Hero Zero 2.25
7 AAd(c),DaW,V:Destroyers,
A:Mecha 2.25
8 DaW,A:Motorhead 2.25
9 DaW,V:Motorhead 2.25
10 MZ(c), A:Division 13. . . . . 2.25
11 V:Reaver Swarm 2.50
12 Final issue 2.50

OZ
by Eric Shanower
TPB The Blue Witch of Oz 9.95
TPB The Forgotten Forest of Oz. . 8.95
TPB The Ice King of Oz 8.95

TPB The Secret Island of Oz 8.95

PETE VON SHOLLY'S MORBID
Oct. 2003
TPB 14.95

PI: THE BOOK OF ANTS
Artisan Entertainment, 1998
1-shot, movie adapt. 2.95

PLANET OF THE APES: THE HUMAN WAR
June, 2001
1 (of 3) IEd,with trading card 3.00
1a photo (c) 3.00
2 IEd,JSC 3.00
2a photo (c) 3.00
3 IEd,JSC 3.00
3a photo (c) 3.00

PLANET OF THE APES
Sept., 2001
1 IEd,MWg 3.00
1a photo(c) 3.00
1b gold foil photo(c) 13.00
1c gold foil photo(c) signed 30.00
2 IEd 3.00
2a photo(c) 3.00
3 IEd 3.00
3a photo(c) 3.00
4 DAn,IEd,Bloodlines,pt.1 (of 3) . . 3.00
4a photo (c) 3.00
5 DAn,IEd,Bloodlines,pt.2 . . . . . . 3.00
5a photo (c) 3.00
6 DAn,IEd,Bloodlines,pt.3 . . . . . . 3.00
6a photo (c) 3.00
TPB Vol. 1 80-pg 9.95
TPB Vol. 2 Bloodlines 9.95

PLANET OF THE APES (MOVIE)
1-shot Movie adaptation 6.95
1-shotA Movie adapt, foil (c) . . . 10.00
1-shotB Movie, foil(c) signed . . . 30.00
TPB 9.95

Planet of the Apes 36
© *Dark Horse Comics*

POP GUN WAR
June 2003
TPB b&w 13.95

PREDATOR
1989
1 CW,Mini Series 6.00
1a 2ndPrinting 3.00
2 CW 5.00
3 CW 4.00
4 CW 3.00
1 thru 4 later printings . . . . @2.50

PREDATOR
1-shot Predator: Invaders from the
Fourth Dimension (1994) 4.00
1-shot Predator Jungle Tales,
Rite of Passage (1995) 3.00
1-shot Predator: Strange Roux
(1995) 3.00
1-shot Predator: Captive (1998) . . 3.00
TPB Predator: Concrete Jungle . . 14.95

PREDATOR: BAD BLOOD
1993
1 CW,I:John Pulnick 3.00
2 CW,V:Predator 3.00
3 CW,V:Predator,C.I.A. 3.00
4 Last issue 3.00

PREDATOR: BIG GAME
1991
1 Corp.Nakai Meets Predator 3.50
2 Army Base Destroyed, with
2-card strip 3.50
3 Corp.Nakai Arrested, with
2-card strip 3.50
4 Nakai vs. Predator 3.50
TPB rep. #1–#4 . . . . 13.95
TPB rep. #1–#4, 2nd edition 14.95

PREDATOR: BLOODY SANDS OF TIME
1992
1 DBa,CW,Predator in WWI 3.50
2 DBa,CW, WWII cont'd. 3.25

PREDATOR: COLD WAR
1991
1 Predator in Siberia 3.50
2 U.S. Elite Squad in Siberia 3.25
3 U.S. vs. USSR commandos 3.25
4 U.S. vs. USSR in Siberia 3.00
TPB 13.95
TPB 2nd printing 13.95

PREDATOR: DARK RIVER
1996
1 thru 4 by Verheiden,RoR,RM. . @3.00

PREDATOR: HELL & HOT WATER
1997
1 thru 3 MSh, GC & GWt . . . . . @3.00
TPB rep. 9.95

CVA Page 510 — All comics prices listed are for *Near Mint* condition.

DARK HORSE

Predator: Hell Come A Walkin' #1
© Dark Horse Comics

PREDATOR: HELL COME A WALKIN'
Feb., 1998
1 (of 2) by Nancy Collins, Dean Ormston 3.00
2 concl. 3.00

PREDATOR: HOMEWORLD
Mar. 1999
1 (of 4) 3.00
2 thru 4 .... @3.00

PREDATOR: KINDRED
1996
1 .... 3.00
2 thru 4 .... @3.00
TPB Predator: Kindred 14.95

PREDATOR: NEMESIS
Dec., 1997
1 (of 2) TTg(c) 3.00
2 .... 3.00

PREDATOR: PRIMAL
1997
1 (of 2) Kevin J. Anderson(s), ScK,Low. 3.00
2 (of 2) 3.00

PREDATOR: RACE WAR
1993
0 F:Serial Killer 3.00
1 V:Serial Killer 3.00
2 D:Serial Killer 3.00
3 in Prison. 3.00
4 Last Issue. 3.00
TPB Race War, series rep. 17.95

PREDATOR 2
1991
1 DBy, Movie Adapt,pt1 .... 3.50
2 MBr, Movie Adapt.,pt2 with 2-card strip. 3.00

PREDATOR VS. JUDGE DREDD
Sept., 1997
1 (of 3) by John Wagner and Enrique Alcatena 3.00
2 thru 3 .... @3.00
TPB Predator vs. Judge Dredd ... 8.95

PREDATOR VS. MAGNUS ROBOT FIGHTER
Valiant/Dark Horse 1992
1 LW,A:Tekla 3.00
1a Platinum Ed. 5.00
1b Gold Ed. 3.00
2 LW,Magnus Vs. Predator, with 2-card strip. 3.00
TPB Rep. #1–#2. .... 7.95

PREDATOR: XENOGENESIS
Aug., 1999
1 (of 4) 3.00
2 IEd. 3.00
3 IEd. 3.00
4 .... 3.00

PRIMAL
1 Contd.from Primal:from the Cradle to the Grave 2.95
2 A:TJ Cyrus 2.50
GN Primal From the Cradle to the Grave. 9.95

PROPELLER MAN
1993
1 I:Propeller Man. 2.95
2 O:Propeller Man,w/2 card strip .. 2.95
3 V:Manipulator 2.95
4 V:State Police,w/2 card strip 2.95
5 V:Manipulator 2.95
6 V:Thing, w/2 card strip 2.95
7 .... 2.95
8 Last issue,w/2 card strip 2.95

PUBO
DH Maverick, Nov., 2002
1 (of 3) by Leland Purvis, B&W ... 3.50
2 .... 3.50
3 .... 3.50
TPB 96-pg. 9.95

PUMPKINHEAD: THE RITES OF EXORCISM
1992
1 Based on the movie 2.50
2 thru 4 .... @2.50

RACE OF SCORPIONS
(B&W) 1990
Book 1 short stories 5.00
Book 2 .... 4.95

RACE OF SCORPIONS
(B&W) 1991
1 A:Argos,Dito,Alma,Ka 2.25
2 thru 4 .... @2.50

RACK & PAIN
1994
1 GCa(c),I:Rack,Pain. 3.00

2 GCa(c),V:Web 3.00
3 GCa(c),V:Web 3.00
4 GCa(c),Final Issue 3.00

RASCALS IN PARADISE
1994
1 I:Spicy Sanders 3.95
2 .... 3.95
3 last issue 3.95
TPB Rep.#1–#3 .... 16.95

Real Adventures of Jonny Quest #1
© Dark Horse Comics

REAL ADVENTURES OF JONNY QUEST, THE
Sept., 1996
1 .... 3.00
2 .... 3.00
3 thru 12 .... @3.00

REBEL SWORD
(B&W) Manga 1994
1 by Yoshikazu Yashiko 2.50
2 .... 2.50
3 .... 2.50
4 V:Ruken 2.50
5 Choice of Jiro 2.50
6 R:Ruken. 2.50

REDBLADE
1993
1 V:Demons 3.00
2 V:Tull 3.00
3 Last Issue. 3.00

RED ROCKET 7
Aug., 1997
1 (of 7) MiA 3.95
2 thru 7 .... @3.95
TPB rep. series, 208 pg 29.95

REID FLEMING/ FLAMING CARROT
B&W Jan. 2003
1-Shot Reid Fleming/Flaming Carrot 4.00

All comics prices listed are for *Near Mint* condition.

DARK HORSE

REVEAL
Oct., 2002
1 64-pg................. 6.95

RING OF ROSES
(B&W) 1991
1 Alternate world,1991......... 2.50
2 Plague in London.......... 2.50
3 Plague cont.A:Secret Brotherhood of the Rosy Cross...... 2.50
4 Conclusion................ 2.50

R.I.P.D.
November 1999
1 (of 4) F:Rest in Peace Dept..... 2.95
2 thru 4.................@2.95
TPB Rest in Peace Department . . 12.95

RING OF THE NIEBELUNG, THE:
DH Maverick 2000
RHINEGOLD, Feb., 2000
1 (of 4) CR................ 3.00
2 CR...................... 3.00
3 CR...................... 3.00
4 CR, concl................ 3.00
VALKYRIE Aug., 2000
1 (of 3) CR................ 3.00
2 CR...................... 3.00
3 CR, concl................ 3.00
SIEGFRIED, Dec., 2000
1 (of 3) CR................ 3.00
2 CR...................... 3.00
3 CR, concl................ 3.00
GOTTERDAMMERUNG June, 2001
1 (of 4) CR................ 3.00
2 .... 3.00
3 .... 3.00
4 finale, 64-pg............. 6.00
TPB Vol. 1 Rhinegold & Valkyrie . 21.95
TPB Vol. 2 Siegfried and Gotterdammerung, 224-pg.(2002) .. 21.95

RING, THE
Nov. 2003
TPB Vol. 1................. 14.95

RIO AT BAY
1992
1 F:Doug Wildey art........... 3.00
2 F:Doug Wildey art........... 3.00
TPB....................... 6.95

RIPLEY'S BELIEVE IT OR NOT
June, 2002
1 (of 4) Into Thin Air.......... 3.00
2 Grim Reaping.............. 3.00
3 Human Wonders............ 3.00
4 Strange Invaders........... 3.00
TPB....................... 9.95

ROACHMILL
(B&W) 1988
1 thru 8.................@3.50
9 and 10................@2.00

ROBOCOP: MORTAL COILS
1993
1 V:Gangs................. 2.75
2 V:Gangs................. 2.75
3 V:Coffin,V:Gangs........... 2.75

ROBOCOP VERSUS TERMINATOR
1992
1 FM(s),WS,w/Robocop cut-out. . . 3.50
2 FM(s),WS,w/Terminator cut-out. . 3.00
3 FM(s),WS,w/cut-out......... 3.00
4 FM(s),WS,Conclusion........ 3.00

ROBOCOP: PRIME SUSPECT
1992
1 Robocop framed............ 2.75
2 thru 4 V:ZED-309s........@2.50
TPB series rep.............. 13.95

ROBOCOP: ROULETTE
1993
1 V:ED-309s................ 2.75
2 I:Philo Drut............... 2.75
3 V:Stealthbot.............. 2.75
4 last issue................ 2.75

ROBOCOP 3
1993
1 B:StG(s),Movie Adapt........ 2.75
2 V:Aliens,OCP.............. 2.75
3 HNg,ANi(i)................ 2.75

Rocketeer Adventure Magazine 33
© Dark Horse Comics

ROCKETEER ADVENTURE MAGAZINE
1988–95
1 and 2..................@4.00
3 .... 3.00
TPB Cliff's New York Adventure by Dave Stevens........... 9.95

ROCKSTAR GAMES' ONI
Feb., 2001
1 video-game tie-in........... 3.00
1a gold foil (c)............. 7.00
2 .... 3.00
3 concl.................... 3.00

THE SAFEST PLACE
SC, SD.................... 2.50

SCATTERBRAIN
June, 1998
1 (of 4) MMi................ 2.95
2 thru 4.................@2.95

SCORPION KING, THE
March, 2002
1 (of 2) movie adapt.......... 3.00
1a photo (c)................ 3.00
2 (of 2) movie adapt.......... 3.00
2a photo (c)................ 3.00

SECRET OF THE SALAMANDER
(B&W)
1 Jacquestardi, rep........... 2.95

SERAPHIC FEATHER
Nov., 2001
TPB....................... 16.95
TPB Seeds of Chaos.......... 17.95
TPB Target Zone............. 17.95
TPB Vol. 3 Dark Angel........ 17.95

SERGIO ARAGONES ACTIONS SPEAK
Jan., 2001
1 (of 6)................... 3.00
2 .... 3.00
3 thru 6.................@3.00
TPB 160-pg................ 13.95

SERGIO ARAGONES' BOOGEYMAN
(B&W) June, 1998
1 (of 4)................... 3.00
2 thru 4.................@3.00
TPB, rep................... 9.95

SERGIO ARAGONES' DAY OF THE DEAD
Oct., 1998
1-shot..................... 3.00

SERGIO ARAGONES' GROO
Jan.–April, 1998
1 (of 4)................... 3.00
2 thru 4.................@3.00
TPB The Most Intelligent Man in the World............. 9.95
TPB Houndbook............. 9.95
TPB Inferno................ 9.95
TPB Jamboree.............. 9.95
TPB Library................ 9.95
TPB Kingdom............... 9.95
TPB Groo Odyssey........... 12.95
TPB Mightier Than the Sword.... 13.95
TPB Groo Maiden 96-pg....... 12.95
TPB The Groo Nursery........ 11.95

SERGIO ARAGONES' GROO & RUFFERTO
Dec., 1998
1 (of 4)................... 3.00
2 thru 4.................@3.00
TPB....................... 9.95

DARK HORSE

Sergio–Sin

Sergio Aragonés' Louder Than Words #1 © Dark Horse Comics

SERGIO ARAGONES' GROO: MIGHTIER THAN THE SWORD
Jan., 2000
1 (of 4) SA. 3.00
2 SA,V:Pipil Khan 3.00
3 SA,V:Relmihio 3.00
4 SA,concl. 3.00

SERGIO ARAGONES' LOUDER THAN WORDS
(B&W) July–Dec., 1997
1 (of 6) SA. 3.00
2 thru 6 . . . . @3.00
TPB rep. series. 12.95

SERGIO STOMPS STAR WARS
1-shot SA, parody 3.00

SEX WARRIORS
1 I:Dakini. 2.50
2 V:Steroids. 2.50

THE SHADOW
1994
1 MK. 3.00
2 MK. 3.00

THE SHADOW AND DOC SAVAGE
1995
1 . . . . 3.50
2 The Shrieking Skeletons. 3.50

THE SHADOW: HELL'S HEAT WAVE
1995
1 Racial War 3.00
2 MK,V:Ghost 3.00
3 Final issue 3.00

THE SHADOW: IN THE COILS OF LEVIATHAN
1993
1 MK,V:Monster. 3.25
2 MK. 3.25
3 MK,w/ GfD poster. 3.25
4 MK,Final issue 3.25
TPB, reprints #1–#4 . . . . 13.95

THE SHADOW AND THE MYSTERIOUS 3
1994
1 Three stories 3.00

SHADOW EMPIRES: FAITH CONQURES
1994
1 CsM. 3.00
2 CsM,V:Vaylen. 3.00
3 CsM 3.00
4 CsM, final issue 3.00

SHADOW STAR
Sept., 2001
TPB 15.95
TPB Darkness Visible 14.95
TPB Shadows of the Past. 13.95
TPB Nothing But the Truth 14.95

SHINOBI
Nov., 2002
Spec.1-shot The Rise of Hotsuma . 3.00

SHREK
Apr. 2003
1 (of 4) 3.00
2 . . . . 3.00
TPB 96-pg. 12.95

SIGNAL TO NOISE
April, 1999
TPB NGa,DMc 14.95

SILKE
Jan., 2001
1 TnD,F:Sandra Silke 3.00
1a variant(c) 3.00
2 TnD 3.00
3 TnD, The Hunt is on 3.00
4 TnD 3.00
4a variant(c) 3.00
TPB series rep. 96-pg. 12.95

SIN CITY:
Dark Horse-Legend
GN A Small Killing 14.00
GN Family Values (1997) 10.00
1-shot The Babe Wore Red (1994) . 3.50
1-shot The Babe Wore Red and
 other stories (1996) nudity 3.00
1-shot Lost Lonely, and Lethal,
 two-color 3.00
1-shot Sex and Violence. 3.00
1-shot Silent Night (1995). 2.95
TPB, 10th Anniv. edition,
 with print & sketchbook. 175.00
HC The Art of Sin City (2002) . . . 39.95

SIN CITY: A DAME TO KILL FOR
Dark Horse-Legend (B&W) 1993
1 FM(a&s),I:Dwight,Ava. 6.00
2 FM(a&s),A:Ava. 4.00
3 FM(a&s),D:Ava's Husband 4.00
1a thru 3a 2nd printings . . . . . . @3.00
4 thru 6 FM(a&s) . . . . @4.00
TPB rep. #1–#6, new pages 15.00

Sin City: Hell and Back #3 © Dark Horse Comics

SIN CITY: HELL AND BACK
July, 1999
1 (of 9) FM 3.00
2 . . . . 3.00
3 . . . . 3.00
4 Five Foot Two, Eyes of Blue 3.00
5 . . . . 3.00
6 quest for Esther 3.00
7 . . . . 3.00
8 . . . . 3.00
9 56-pg. 5.00
TPB FM 25.00

SIN CITY: JUST ANOTHER SATURDAY NIGHT
Dark Horse/Wizard
1/2 (Wizard, 24-pg.). 7.00
1/2 rep., Dark Horse, new (c). . . . 3.00

SIN CITY: THAT YELLOW BASTARD
(B&W) 1996
1 F.Miller 5.00
2 thru 6 . . . . @5.00
TPB by Frank Miller 15.00

SIN CITY: THE BIG FAT KILL
Dark Horse-Legend 1994
1 FM 5.00
2 FM 5.00
3 FM, Dump the Stiffs 5.00
4 FM, Town Without Pity 5.00
5 FM, final issue 5.00
TPB 15.00

All comics prices listed are for Near Mint condition.

DARK HORSE

Sock Monkey, Vol. 2, #2
© Dark Horse Comics

SOCK MONKEY
(B&W) Sept., 1998
1 by Tony Millionaire 2.95
2 F:Uncle Gabby 2.95
VOLUME 2
1 and 2 . . . . @2.95
DH Maverick Sept. 2002
Spec. #1 (of 2) 3.00
Spec. #2 . . . . 3.00

SOLO
1996
1 and 2 . . . . @1.00

SPACE CIRCUS
DH Maverick, July, 2000
1 (of 4) SA. 2.95
2 thru 4 SA . . . . @2.95

SPACEHAWK
(B&W) 1989
1 BW reps. 3.50
2 thru 5 BW . . . . @3.50

SPACE USAGI
[Vol. 3] 1996
1 thru 3 Stan Sakai . . . . @3.00
TPB 16.95

SPECIES
1995
1 Alien Human Hybrid 3.00
2 thru 4 SIL . . . . @3.00

SPECIES: HUMAN RACE
1996
1 PhH 3.00
2 . . . . 3.00
3 SBi 3.00
4 . . . . 3.00
TPB 11.95

SPIRIT OF WONDER
(B&W) 1996
1 thru 5 by Kenji Tsuruia . . . . . . @2.95
TPB 12.95

SPYBOY
Oct., 1999
1 PDd,F:Alex Fleming 3.00
2 PDd 3.00
3 PDd,F:Bombshell 3.00
4 PDd,F:Judge and Jury 3.00
5 PDd,V:Judge and Jury 3.00
6 PDd,V:Barbie Q 3.00
7 PDd,V:Madam Imadam. 3.00
8 PDd,V:Madam Imadam. 3.00
9 PDd,V:Madam Imadam
  & Barbie Q 3.00
10 PDd,death-defying action 3.00
11 PDd,V:Slackjaw 3.00
12 PDd,V:Slackjaw 3.00
13 PDd. 3.00
14 PDd,F:SpyGirl 3.00
15 PDd. 3.00
15a variant TnD (c). 3.00
16 PDd. 3.00
17 PDd. 3.00
TPB Deadly Gourmet Affair, PDd . . 8.95
TPB Trial and Terror 9.95
TPB Bet Your Life. 9.95
TPB Vol.4 Undercover, Underwear . 9.95
TPB Vol.5 Spy-School Confidential 12.95
Spec. 1-shot 48-pg. 5.00

SPYBOY 13: THE M.A.N.G.A. AFFAIR
Apr. 2003
1 (of 3) PDd(s) 3.00
2 and 3 . . . . @3.00
TPB 9.95

SPYBOY/YOUNG JUSTICE
Feb., 2002
1 PDd, x-over 3.00
2 and 3 . . . . @3.00
TPB PDd(s) 10.00

STAN SHAW'S BEAUTY & THE BEAST
1 Based on the book 4.95

STARSHIP TROOPERS
Sept., 1997
1 (of 2) movie adaptation. 3.00
2 movie adaptation, concl. 3.00
TPB rep., inc. Brute Creations,
  Insect Touch, & movie 152 pg. 14.95

STARSHIP TROOPERS: BRUTE CREATIONS
1997
1-shot RbC. 3.00

STARSHIP TROOPERS: DOMINANT SPECIES
Aug., 1998
1 (of 4) 3.00
2 JoB,RyE. 3.00
3 & 4 . . . . @3.00

STARSHIP TROOPERS: INSECT TOUCH
1997
1 by Warren Ellis & Paolo Parente . 3.00
2 and 3 (of 3). . . . . @3.00

STARSTRUCK: THE EXPANDING UNIVERSE
(B&W) 1990
1 Part 1 . . . . 3.00
2 Part 2, with 2-card strip. 3.00

Star Wars #5
© Dark Horse Comics

STAR WARS
Dec., 1998
1 F:Ki-Adi-Mundi 5.00
2 F:Ki-Adi-Mundi 4.00
3 F:Ki-Adi-Mundi 3.50
4 F:Sylvn. 3.50
5 V:Ephant Mon. 5.00
6 V:Jabba the Hutt. 5.00
7 Outlander 3.00
8 A:Jabba the Hutt. 3.00
9 A:Tusken Raiders 3.00
10 TT,RL,F:Ki-Adi-Mundi. 3.00
11 TT,RL,F:Aurra Sing 3.00
12 TT 3.00
13 TT,TL,A'Sharad Hett 3.00
14 TT,TL,on Malastare 3.00
15 TT,TL,Podracing 3.00
16 TT,TL,V:Lannik terrorists 3.00
17 TT,TL,V:Red Iaro terrorists 3.00
18 TT,TL,Smugglers Moon 3.00
19 JOs,JD,Twilight,pt.1 . . . . 3.00
20 JOs,JD,Twilight,pt.2 . . . . 3.00
21 JOs,JD,Twilight,pt.3 . . . . 3.00
22 JOs,JD,Twilight,pt.4 . . . . 3.00
23 Infinity's End,pt.1 . . . . 3.00
24 Infinity's End,pt.2 . . . . 3.00
25 Infinity's End,pt.3 . . . . 3.00
26 Infinity's End,pt.4 . . . . 3.00
27 Star Crash one-shot. 3.00
28 Hunt for Aurra Sing,pt.1 . . . . . . 3.00
29 Hunt for Aurra Sing,pt.2 . . . . . . 3.00
30 Hunt for Aurra Sing,pt.3 . . . . . . 3.00
31 Hunt for Aurra Sing,pt.4 . . . . . . 3.00
32 Darkness,pt.1, JOs,JD. 3.00
33 Darkness,pt.2, JOs,JD. 3.00
34 Darkness,pt.3, JOs,JD. 3.00
35 Darkness,pt.4, JOs,JD. 3.00
36 Stark Hyperspace War,pt.1 . . . . 3.00
37 Stark Hyperspace War,pt.2 . . . . 3.00
38 Stark Hyperspace War,pt.3 . . . . 3.00
39 Stark Hyperspace War,pt.4 . . . . 3.00
40 The Devaronian Version,pt.1 . . . 3.00
41 The Devaronian Version,pt.2 . . . 3.00
42 Rite of Passage,pt.1 . . . . 3.00
43 Rite of Passage,pt.2 . . . . 3.00

Comics Values Annual — DARK HORSE — Star Wars–Star Wars

44 Rite of Passage,pt.3 . . . . 3.00
45 Rite of Passage,pt.4 . . . . 3.00
46 Republic,pt.1 . . . . 3.00
47 Republic,pt.2 . . . . 3.00
48 Republic,pt.3 . . . . 3.00
49 Republic,pt.5 . . . . 3.00
50 Republic,pt.6, 64-page. 6.00
51 Republic,pt.7 . . . . 3.00
52 Republic,pt.8 . . . . 3.00
53 Republic: Blast Radius. 3.00
54 Republic 3.00
55 Republic:Battle of Jabiim,pt.1 . . . 3.00
56 Republic:Battle of Jabiim,pt.2 . . . 3.00
57 Republic:Battle of Jabiim,pt.3 . . . 3.00
58 Republic:Battle of Jabiim,pt.4 . . . 3.00
59 Republic: Enemy Lines 3.00
60 Republic 3.00
TPB Prelude to Rebellion 14.95
TPB Darkness (2002) 12.95

STAR WARS: A NEW HOPE— SPECIAL EDITION
Jan.–April, 1997
1 EB, AW 6.00
2 thru 4 . . . . @5.00
TPB Rep. #1–#4 Hildebrandt(c) . . . 9.95
Spec. Edition boxed set 30.00

STAR WARS: A NEW HOPE
(B&W) Manga July, 1998
1 (of 4) by Tamaki Hisao, 96-pg... 9.95
2 thru 4 . . . . @9.95

STAR WARS: A NEW HOPE—MANGA
November 1999
1 (of 4) by Kia Asamiya,96-pg. 9.95
2 thru 4, 88-pg. . . . . @9.95

STAR WARS: BATTLE OF THE BOUNTY HUNTERS
July, 1996
Pop-up Comic. 17.95

STAR WARS: BOBA FETT—
1-shot Bounty on Bar-Kooda, 48-pg. 11.00
1-shot When the Fat Lady Swings . 7.00
1-shot Murder Most Foul. 7.00
1-shot Twin Engins of Destruction. . 6.00
1-shot Agent of Doom, CK 3.00
TPB Death, Lies & Treachery 12.95

STAR WARS: BOBA FETT— ENEMY OF THE EMPIRE
Jan., 1999
1 (of 4) V:Dark Lord of the Sith . . . 3.00
2 thru 4 IG . . . . @3.00
TPB rep., includes #1/2 . . . . 16.95

STAR WARS: BOUNTY HUNTERS
Aug., 1999
1-shot Aurra Sing, TT 3.00
1-shot Kir Kanos, MRi,RSd. 3.00
1-shot Scoundrel's Wages,

Star Wars: Crimson Empire II #3
© Dark Horse Comics

F:Dengar, 4-LOM & Bossk 3.00
TPB Star Wars: Bounty Hunters. . 12.95

STAR WARS: CHEWBACCA
Jan., 2000
1 (of 4) various tales 4.00
1 gold foil (c) 13.00
2 thru 4 . . . . @3.50
TPB 12.95

STAR WARS: CLONE WARS
June 2003
TPB Vol.1 Defense of Kamino. . . . 14.95
TPB Vol.2 Victories and Sacrifices 14.95

STAR WARS: CRIMSON EMPIRE
Dec., 1997–May, 1998
1 PG,CR,DvD(c) 10.00
3 PG,CR,DvD(c) 8.00
3 thru 5 PG,CR,DvD(c) . . . . @5.00
TPB Crimson Empire 17.95

VOL II: COUNCIL OF BLOOD
1998
1 MRi,RSd,PG,DvD(c) 4.00
2 thru 6 RSd,PG,DvD(c). . . . . . . @3.00
TPB Council of Blood 17.95

STAR WARS: DARK EMPIRE
Dec., 1991
1 CK,Destiny of a Jedi. 14.00
1a 2nd Printing 5.00
1b Gold Ed. 15.00
2 CK,Destroyer of worlds, very
  low print run 12.00
2a 2nd Printing 5.00
2b Gold Ed. 15.00
3 CK,V:The Emperor 8.00
3a 2nd printing 4.00
3b Gold Ed. 10.00
4 CK,V:The Emperor 5.00
4a Gold Ed. 5.00

5 CK,V:The Emperor 5.00
5a Gold Ed. 10.00
6 CK,V:Emperor,last issue 5.00
6a Gold Ed. 9.00
Gold editions, foil logo set. 50.00
Platinum editions, embossed set. 100.00
TPB Preview 32pg. 1.00
TPB rep.#1–#6 . . . . 19.95
TPB CK & Tom Veitch 2nd ed. . . . 17.95

STAR WARS DARK EMPIRE II
1994
1 2nd chapter 6.00
2 F:Boba Fett 5.00
3 V:Darksiders. 5.00
4 Luke Vs. Darksiders 5.00
5 Creatures 5.00
6 CK,DvD(c), save the twins 5.00
Platinum editions, set 50.00
TPB CK & Tom Veitch rep.#1–#6 . 17.95

STAR WARS: DARK FORCE RISING
May–Oct., 1997
1 thru 6 (of 6) MBn,TyD,KN . . . . @5.00
TPB series rep 17.95

STAR WARS: DARK FORCES
TPB Jedi Knight (Sept., 1998). . . . 14.95
TPB Rebel Agent (March, 1998) . . 14.95
TPB Soldier for the Empire 14.95

STAR WARS: DARTH MAUL
Sept., 2000
1 (of 4) RMz,JD,Struzan(c) 3.00
1 photo (c). 5.00
2 Struzan(c),V:Black Sun. 3.00
3 RMz,JD,Struzan(c) 3.00
4 RMz,JD,Struzan(c) 3.00
2 thru 4 photo(c) . . . . @3.00
TPB RMz,JD,Struzan(c) 12.95

STAR WARS: DROIDS
April–Sept., 1994
1 F:C-3PO,R2-D2 . . . . 5.00
2 V:Thieves. 3.00
3 on the Hosk moon 3.00
4 . . . . 3.00
5 A meeting 3.00
6 final issue 3.00
Spec.#1 I:Olag Greck 3.00
TPB The Kalarba Adventures, rep. 17.95

[2nd Series] April, 1995
1 Deputized Droids 3.00
2 Marooned on Nar Shaddaa. 3.00
3 C-3PO to the Rescue 3.00
4 . . . . 3.00
5 Caretaker virus. 3.00
6 Revolution 3.00
7 & 8 . . . . @3.00
TPB Droids—Rebellion, rep. 17.95

STAR WARS: EMPIRE'S END
Oct.–Nov., 1995
1 R:Emperor Palpatine 3.50
2 conclusion 3.50
TPB rep. 6.00

All comics prices listed are for *Near Mint* condition.

STAR WARS: THE EMPIRE STRIKES BACK
TPB Hildebrandt(c)............ 10.00

STAR WARS: THE EMPIRE STRIKES BACK
(B&W) Manga Dec., 1998
1 (of 4) by Toshiki Dudo, 96-pg.. . 10.00
2 thru 4 .... @10.00

STAR WARS: EMISSARIES TO MALASTARE
Aug., 2001
TPB TT,TL,JD............... 15.95

STAR WARS: EMPIRE
Sept., 2002
1 .... 3.00
2 .... 3.00
2 Betrayal.................... 3.00
3 Betrayal.................... 3.00
4 .... 3.00
5 National Public Radio adapt..... 3.00
6 .... 3.00
7 .... 3.00
8 Darklighter,pt.1.............. 3.00
9 Darklighter,pt.2.............. 3.00
10 Yavin Base,pt.1............. 3.00
11 Yavin Base,pt.2............. 3.00
12 Darklighter,pt.3............. 3.00
13 Darklighter,pt.4............. 3.00
14 Soldier's perspective 3.00
15 .... 3.00
TPB Vol. 1 .... 12.95

STAR WARS: EPISODE I THE PHANTOM MENACE
Apr. 1999
1 RdM,AW.................. 3.00
1a newsstand edition, photo (c)... 3.00
2 RdM,AW.................. 3.00
2a newsstand edition, photo (c)... 3.00
3 RdM,AW.................. 3.00
3a newsstand edition, photo (c)... 3.00
4 RdM,AW.................. 3.00
4a newsstand edition, photo (c)... 3.00
GN Phantom Menace RdM,AW .. 12.95
Spec. Anakin Skywalker 3.00
Spec. Anakin Skywalker, newsstand 3.00
Spec. Obi-Wan Kenobi 3.00
Spec. Obi-Wan Kenobi, newsstand. 3.00
Spec. Queen Amidala........... 3.00
Spec. Qui-Gon Jinn 3.00
TPB 12.95
TPB Adventures, rep........... 12.95

STAR WARS: EPISODE I THE PHANTOM MENACE—MANGA
Dec., 1999
1 (of 2) 88-pg.................. 9.95

STAR WARS EPISODE II— ATTACK OF THE CLONES
April, 2002
1 (of 4) 48-pg................. 4.00
2 thru 4 48-pg................ @4.00
1A thru 4A photo (c).......... @4.00
TPB 144-pg.................. 17.95

STAR WARS HANDBOOK
July, 1998
1 X-Wing Rogue Squadron 3.50
2 Crimson Empire 3.00
Dark Empire 3.00

STAR WARS: HEIR TO THE EMPIRE
Oct., 1995–April, 1996
1 I:Grand Admiral Thrawn 4.00
2 thru 6 .... @3.50
TPB from novel by Timothy Zahn . 19.95

STAR WARS: THE HUNT FOR AURRA SING
July, 2002
TPB 96-pg. TT 12.95

STAR WARS: INFINITIES — A NEW HOPE
May, 2001
1 (of 4) CW,TyH,Luke's attack fails,
 Death Star survives 3.00
1a gold foil photo (c) 13.00
2 CW,TyH 3.00
3 CW,TyH 3.00
4 CW,TyH, concl.............. 3.00
TPB series rep. 96-pg.......... 12.95

STAR WARS: INFINITIES — THE EMPIRE STRIKES BACK
July, 2002
1 (of 4) 3.00
2 thru 4 .... @3.00
TPB 12.95

STAR WARS: INFINITIES — RETURN OF THE JEDI
Nov. 2003
1 (of 4) 3.00

STAR WARS: JABBA THE HUTT—
1995–1996
1-shot The Garr Suppoon Hit 3.00
1-shot Hunger of Princess Nampi.. 3.00
1-shot The Dynasty Trap 3.00
1-shot Betrayal............... 3.00
1-shot The Jabba Tape.......... 3.00

STAR WARS: JANGO FETT
Dec., 2001
TPB 64-pg..,RMz 5.95

STAR WARS: JANGO FETT—OPEN SEASONS
April, 2002
1 (of 4) 3.00
2 thru 4 .... @3.00
TPB 96-pg................... 12.95

STAR WARS: JEDI
Feb. 2003
Spec. Mace Windu, JOs,JD,48-pg . 5.00
Spec. Shaak Ti, JOs,JD, 48-pg ... 5.00
Spec. Aayla Secura, JOs,JD,48-pg. 5.00
Spec. Dooku,JOs,JD,48-pg....... 5.00

STAR WARS: JEDI ACADEMY LEVIATHAN
Oct., 1998
1 (of 4) by Kevin J. Anderson..... 3.00
2 thru 4 .... @3.00
TPB 11.95

STAR WARS: JEDI COUNCIL — ACTS OF WAR
June, 2000
1 (of 4) RSd, V;Yinchorri 3.00
1b gold foil (c) 10.00
2 thru 4 RSd .... @3.00
TPB 96-pg. rep.............. 12.95

DARK HORSE

STAR WARS: JEDI QUEST
Sept., 2001
1	3.00
1a ruby red foil	13.00
1b ruby red foil, signed	30.00
2 thru 4	@3.00

STAR WARS: JEDI VS. SITH
April, 2001
1 (of 6)	3.00
1a gold foil, lim.e.	10.00
2 V:Darth Bane	3.00
3 thru 6	@3.00
TPB 144-pg.	17.95

STAR WARS: THE LAST COMMAND
Nov., 1997–July, 1998
1 thru 6 MBn.	@3.50
TPB, rep.	17.95

STAR WARS: MARA JADE— BY THE EMPEROR'S HAND
Aug., 1998
1 (of 6) by Timothy Zahn	5.00
2 thru 6	@4.00
TPB rep.	15.95

STAR WARS: OUTLANDER
March, 2001
TPB F:Ki-Adi-Mundi	12.95

STAR WARS: THE PROTOCOL OFFENSIVE
Sept., 1997
1-shot written by Anthony Daniels . . 4.95

STAR WARS: QUI-GON & OBI-WAN—LAST STAND ON ORD MANTELL
Jan., 2001
1	3.00
1a variant TnD (c)	3.00
1c gold foil (c)	15.00
2	3.00
3	3.00
1a thru 3a photo(c)	@3.00

STAR WARS: QUI-GON & OBI-WAN—THE AURORIENT EXPRESS
Feb., 2002
1 (of 2)	3.00
2	3.00

STAR WARS: RETURN OF THE JEDI—SPECIAL EDITION
TPB Hildebrandt(c) 9.95

STAR WARS: THE RETURN OF THE JEDI
(B&W) Manga June, 1999
1 (of 4) Shin-ichi Hiromoto, 96-pg.	9.95
2 thru 4	@9.95

STAR WARS: RIVER OF CHAOS
May–Nov., 1995
1 LSi,JBr,Emperor sends spies	3.00
2 Imperial in Allies Clothing	3.00
3	3.00
4 F:Ranulf	3.00

STAR WARS: SHADOWS OF THE EMPIRE
May, 1996
1 (of 6) by John Wagner, Kilian Plunkett & P. Craig Russell	3.50
2 thru 6	@3.50
TPB	17.95

STAR WARS: SHADOWS OF THE EMPIRE — EVOLUTION
Feb.–June, 1998
1 thru 5	@3.50
TPB Steve Perry(s)	14.95

STAR WARS: SHADOW STALKER
Nov., 1997
1-shot from Star Wars Galaxy Mag. 3.50

STAR WARS: SPLINTER OF THE MIND'S EYE
Dec., 1995–June, 1996
1 thru 4 A.D.Foster novel adapt.	@3.50
TPB	14.95

STAR WARS: STARFIGHTER— CROSSBONES
Jan., 2002
1 (of 3) F:Nym, pirate captain	3.00
2 from video game	3.00
3	3.00

STAR WARS: TAG & BINK ARE DEAD
Oct., 2001
1 (of 2)	3.00
2	3.00

STAR WARS TALES
Sept., 1999
1 various authors, 64-pg.	10.00
2 thru 4, 64-pg.	@6.00
5 F:Lando's Commandos	6.00
6 thru 9	@6.00
10 thru 17	@6.00
5a thru 17a photo(c)	@6.00
TPB Vol. 1	19.95
TPB Vol. 2	19.95
TPB Vol. 3	19.95

Star Wars: Tales of the Jedi #4
© Dark Horse Comics

STAR WARS: TALES FROM MOS EISLEY
1-shot, from Star Wars Galaxy Mag. #2–#4 . . . . 3.50

STAR WARS: TALES OF THE JEDI
Oct. 1993
1 RV,I:Ulic Qel-Droma	6.00
2 RV,A:Ulic Qel-Droma	5.00
3 RV,D:Andur	5.00
4 RV,A:Jabba the Hut	4.00
5 RV,last issue	4.00
TPB	14.95
TPB 2nd printing	14.95
TPB Redemption, 112-pg.	14.95

STAR WARS: TALES OF THE JEDI: DARK LORDS OF THE SITH
Oct., 1994–March, 1995
1 Bagged with card	3.00
2	3.00
3 Krath Attack	3.00
4 F:Exar Kun	3.00
5 V:TehKrath	3.00
6 Final battle	3.00
TPB	17.95

STAR WARS: TALES OF THE JEDI: THE FREEDON NADD UPRISING
Aug.–Sept., 1997
1 and 2	@3.00
2	3.00
TPB series rep.	5.95

STAR WARS: TALES OF THE JEDI: THE SITH WAR
Aug., 1995–Jan., 1996
1 F:Exar Kun	3.00
2 F:Ulic Oel-Droma	3.00
3 F:Exar Kun	3.00
4 thru 6 (6 part mini-series)	@3.00
TPB	17.95

DARK HORSE

*Star Wars: Tales of the Jedi–
The Golden Age of the Sith #2
© Dark Horse Comics*

STAR WARS: TALES OF THE JEDI—THE FALL OF THE SITH EMPIRE
June–Oct., 1997
1 (of 5) 3.50
2 thru 5 . . . . @3.00

STAR WARS: TALES OF THE JEDI—THE GOLDEN AGE OF THE SITH
Oct., 1996–Feb., 1997
1 thru 5 . . . . @3.50
TPB 16.95

STAR WARS: TALES OF THE JEDI—THE REDEMPTION OF ULIC QEL-DROMA
July, 1998
1 (of 5) by Kevin J. Anderson. 3.50
2 thru 5 . . . . @3.50

STAR WARS: THE STARK HYPERSPACE WAR
Nov. 2003
TPB JOs. 12.95

STAR WARS: TWILIGHT
Nov., 2001
TPB JOs,JD 12.95

STAR WARS: UNDERWORLD—THE YAVIN VASSILIKA
Dec., 2000
1 (of 5) F:Han Solo 3.00
2 thru 5 . . . . @3.00
1a thru 5a photo (c) . . . . @3.00
TPB 120-pg. 14.95

STAR WARS: UNION
Nov., 1999
1 (of 4) by Stackpole 3.00
1a gold foil (c) 10.00
2 the wedding approaches 3.00
3 almost there 3.00
4 wedding day 3.00
TPB Luke & Mara Jade 12.95

STAR WARS: VADER'S QUEST
Feb., 1999
1 (of 4) DGb,AMK 3.00
2 thru 4 . . . . @3.00
TPB with poster 11.95

STAR WARS: A VALENTINE STORY
Feb. 2003
1-shot PC 3.50

STAR WARS: X-WING ROGUE SQUADRON
July, 1995
The Rebel Opposition
1 F:Wedge Antilles 5.00
2 . . . . 3.50
3 F:Tycho Clehu 3.50
4 F:Tycho Clehu 3.50
fi Wizard limited exclusive 6.00
The Phantom Affair
5 thru 8 . . . . @3.50
TPB rep 12.95
Battleground Tatooine
9 thru 12 . . . . @3.50
TPB rep 12.95
The Warrior Princess
13 thru 16 . . . . @3.50
TPB rep 13.95
Requiem for a Rogue
17 thru 20 . . . . @3.50
TPB rep 12.95
In the Empire's Service
21 thru 24 . . . . @3.50
TPB rep 12.95
Making of Baron Fell
25 . . . . 5.00
Family Ties
26 thru 27 . . . . @3.50
Masquerade
28 thru 31 . . . . @3.50
TPB Masquerade, rep. 12.95
Mandatory Retirement
32 thru 35 . . . . @3.50
TPB Blood and Honor 12.95
TPB Mandatory Retirement 12.95

STAR WARS: ZAM WESELL
Feb., 2002
TPB RMz, 64-pg. 5.95

SUBHUMAN
Nov., 1998
1 (of 4) MSh 3.00
2 thru 4 MSh . . . . @3.00

SUPERMAN/MADMAN HULLABALOO
June–Aug., 1997
1 (of 3) MiA 3.00
2 and 3 (of 3) . . . . @3.00

*SubHuman #2
© Dark Horse Comics*

SUPERMAN/TARZAN: SONS OF THE JUNGLE
Oct., 2001
1 (of 3) CDi,HuR 3.00
2 CDi,HuR 3.00
3 CDi,HuR(c) 3.00
TPB 80-pg. 9.95

SUPERMAN VS. ALIENS
DC/Dark Horse 1995
1 DJu,KN 6.00
2 V:Queen Alien 5.00
TPB 14.95

SUPERMAN VS. ALIENS II
May, 2002
1 (of 4) CDi,JBg,KN, x-over 3.00
2 CDi,JBg,KN 3.00
3 CDi,JBg,KN 3.00
4 CDi,JBg,KN 3.00
TPB God War 12.95

SUPERMAN VS. THE TERMINATOR: DEATH TO THE FUTURE
Dec., 1999
1 (of 4) AIG,StP,x-over 3.00
2 AIG,StP,into the future 3.00
3 AIG,StP,A:Supergirl 3.00
4 AIG,StP,concl 3.00
TPB AIG,StP,series rep. 10.95

SUPER MANGA BLAST
March, 2000
1 128-pg. 4.95
2 thru 6 128-pg. . . . . @4.95
7 F:Oh My Goddess 5.00
8 F:Oh My Goddess 5.00
9 F:3x3 Eyes 5.00
10 F:Seraphic Feather 5.00
11 F:Oh My Goddess 5.00
12 F:Oh My Goddess 5.00
13 F:Club 9 . . . . 5.00
14 F:Club 9 . . . . 5.00
15 F:Club 9, 50-pg. 6.00
16 F:3x3 Eyes 6.00
17 F:Club 9 . . . . 6.00

DARK HORSE

18 F:Club 9 .... 6.00
19 Seraphic Feather 6.00
20 What's Michael? 6.00
21 F:Club 9 .... 6.00
22 Club 9, 3x3 Eyes 6.00
23 Club 9, What's Michael? ... 6.00
24 F:Seraphic Feather 6.00
25 F:Appleseed 6.00
26 F:Shadow Star 6.00
27 F:What's Michael? 6.00
28 thru 37 .... @6.00
TPB Vol.5 What's Michael's
  Favorite Spot 8.95

SYN
Rocket Comics Aug. 2003
1 KG 3.00
2 thru 4 .... @3.00

TALE OF ONE BAD RAT
1994
1 BT 3.00
2 thru 4 .... @3.00
TPB Rep.#1–#4 .... 14.95

TALES OF ORDINARY MADNESS
(B&W)
1 JBo(c),Paranoid 3.00
2 JBo(c),Mood 2.50
3 JBo(c),A Little Bit of Neurosis ... 2.50

TALES TO OFFEND
July, 1997
1-shot by Frank Miller 2.95

TANK GIRL
(B&W) 1991
1 Rep. from U.K.Deadline Mag.
  with 2-card strip 4.50
2 V:Indiana Potato Jones 4.00
3 On the Run 4.00
4 .... 4.00
TPB colorized 14.95
[2nd Series] 1993
1 .... 3.50
2 thru 4 .... @3.00

TARZAN
TPB The Untamed 11.95

TARZAN/JOHN CARTER: WARLORDS OF MARS
1996
1 (of 4) E.R.Burroughs adapt. 3.00
2 thru 4 .... @3.00

TARZAN VS. PREDATOR AT THE EARTH'S CORE
1996
1 Tarzan vs. Predator 3.00
2 V:Predator 3.00
3 Tarzan on the Hunt 3.00
4 .... 3.00
TPB series rep. 12.95

TENTH, THE: NIGHTWALKER
April, 2002
1 (of 4) TnD 3.00

2 thru 4 .... @3.00
1a thru 4a variant (c) ...... @3.00
TPB No Sweets After Dark 9.95

TENTH, THE: RESURRECTED
April, 2001
1 TnD 3.00
1a variant(c) 6.95
1b variant(c) signed 20.00
2 TnD 3.00
3 TnD 3.00
3a variant (c) 3.00
4 TnD 3.00
4a variant (c) 3.00
TPB Blackout, rep.#1-#5 .... 14.95

TERMINAL POINT
1993
1 .... 2.50
2 .... 2.50

TERMINATOR
1990
1 CW,Tempest 4.00
2 CW,Tempest 3.00
3 CW 3.00
4 CW, conclusion 3.00

TERMINATOR
1-shot MW,3-D const(c2,
  pop-up inside (1991) 5.00
Spec. AlG,GyD,GeD(1998) 3.00

TERMINATOR, THE
Sept., 1998
1 AlG,StP 3.00
2 F:Sarah Connor 3.00
3 F:Killerman 3.00
4 F:D-800L & D-810X 3.00
TPB Death Valley 14.95

TERMINATOR, THE: THE DARK YEARS
Sept., 1999
1 (of 4) AlG,MvR,BWi 3.00
2 AlG,MvR,BWi,F:Jon Norden ... 3.00
3 .... 3.00
4 AlG,MvR,concl. 3.00

TERMINATOR: END GAME
1992
1 JG,Final Terminator series ... 3.00
2 JG,Cont.last Term.story 3.00
3 JG, Concl. 3.00
TPB Endgame 9.95

TERMINATOR: ENEMY WITHIN
1991
1 cont. from Sec.Objectives 4.00
2 C890.L.threat contd. 3.00
3 Secrets of Cyberdyne 3.00
4 Conclusion 3.00
SC rep #1–#4 .... 13.95

TERMINATOR: HUNTERS & KILLERS
1992
1 V:Russians 3.00

2 V:Russians 3.00
3 V:Russians 3.00

TERMINATOR: SECONDARY OBJECTIVES
1991
1 cont. 1st DH mini-series 4.00
2 PG,A:New Female Terminator ... 3.00
3 PG,Terminators in L.A.&Mexico .. 3.00
4 PG,Terminator vs Terminator 3.00

Territory #1
© Dark Horse Comics

TERRITORY, THE
Jan., 1999
1 (of 4) JaD,DvL,F:Ishmael 3.00
2 thru 4 .... @3.00

TEX AVERY'S DROOPY
1 Dr. Droopenstein 2.50
2 and 3 .... @2.50

TEX AVERY'S SCREWBALL SQUIRREL
1 I:Screwball Squirrel 2.50
2 Cleaning House 2.50
3 School of Hard Rocks 2.50

THING, THE
1991
1 JHi, Movie adaptation 4.00
2 JHi, Movie adaptation 3.50

THING FROM ANOTHER WORLD: CLIMATE OF FEAR
1994
1 Argentinian Military Base
  (Bahiathetis) 2.75
2 Thing on Base 2.75
3 Thing/takeover 2.75
4 Conclusion 2.75
TPB 15.95

All comics prices listed are for Near Mint condition.

DARK HORSE

Thing–Usagi

*Tongue*Lash #2*
© Dark Horse Comics

THING FROM ANOTHER WORLD: ETERNAL VOWS
1993
1 PG,I:Sgt. Rowan............ 2.75
2 PG.................... 2.75
3 PG,in New Zealand.......... 2.75
4 PG,Last issue............. 2.75

THIRTEEN O'CLOCK
(B&W)
1 Mr.Murmer,from Deadline USA.. 2.95

3 X 3 EYES: CURSE OF THE GESU
(B&W) Manga 1995
1 I:Pai,Yakumo.............. 2.95
2 thru 5................ @2.95
TPB Curse of the Gesu, by Yuzo
  Takada................ 12.95
TPB House of Demons......... 12.95
TPB 208-pg................ 16.95
TPB Blood of the Sacred Demon. 13.95
TPB Summoning the Beast (2002) 14.95
TPB Key to the Sacred Land... 13.95
TPB House of Demons, 2nd ed... 14.95
TPB Curse of the Gesu, 2nd ed... 14.95
TPB Shadow of the Kunlun...... 17.95

300
May, 1998
1 (of 5) FM & Lynn Varley....... 2.95
2 F:Spartans............... 2.95
3 thru 5................ @2.95

TIME COP
1994
1 Movie Adaptation........... 2.75
2 Movie Adaptation........... 2.50

TITAN
1994
Spec.#1 BS(c),I:Inhibitors....... 4.25

TITAN A.E.
May, 2000
1 (of 3) film prequel,pt.1........ 2.95
2 thru 3 prequel,pt.2–pt.3...... @2.95

TONGUE*LASH
Aug., 1996
1 by Randy and Jean-Marc
  Lofficier & Dave Taylor....... 2.95
2...................... 2.95
[VOL. II] 1999
1 (of 2).................. 2.95
2...................... 2.95

TONY DANIEL'S F5
May, 2002
TPB Color, 128-pg........... 14.95

TONY MILLIONAIRE'S SOCK MONKEY
TPB..................... 9.95
VOL. 3
1 (of 2).................. 3.00
2 concl................... 3.00
TPB A Children's Book........ 9.95

TOO MUCH COFFEE MAN
(B&W) July, 1997
1-shot by Shannon Wheeler...... 3.00
TPB Guide for the Perplexed.... 10.95
TPB Parade of Tirade......... 12.95
TPB Amusing Musings......... 12.95

TREKKER
(B&W) 1987
1 thru 4................ @2.25
5 thru 7................ @2.25
8 O:Trekker................ 2.25
9...................... 2.25
Spec.#1 Sins of the Fathers..... 2.95

TRIGUN
Nov. 2003
TPB Vol. 1 b&w............. 14.95

TRIPLE X
(B&W) 1994
TPB by Arnold & Jacob Pander... 24.95

TWO FACES OF TOMORROW, THE
(B&W) Manga Aug., 1997
1 (of 13) from James P. Hogan
  novel, by Yukinobu Hoshino... 3.00
2 thru 4................ @3.00
5 thru 13............... @4.00

TWO FISTED TALES
Spec. WW,WiS............. 4.95

2112
GN JBy,A:Next Men........... 2.00
2nd Printing............... 5.00
TPB GNv, JBy,A:Next Men...... 10.00
2nd & 3rd printing........... 9.95

ULTRAMAN TIGA
Aug. 2003
1 (of 10)................. 4.00
2 thru 4................ @4.00

[ANDREW VACHSS'] UNDERGROUND
(B&W) 1993
1 AVs(s)................. 4.25
2 thru 5 AVs(s)............ @3.95

UNIVERSAL MONSTERS
1991
1 AAd,Creature From The
  Black Lagoon............. 5.50
1 Dracula................. 5.50
1 Frankenstein............. 5.50
1 The Mummy............... 5.50

USAGI YOJIMBO
(B&W) 1996
1 by Stan Sakai............. 8.00
2 thru 9................ @4.00
10 with Sergio Aragones........ 5.00
11 'The Lord of Owls'.......... 5.00
12 'Vampire Cat of the Geishu'... 3.00
13 thru 22 'Grasscutter,',pt.1
  thru pt. #10........... @3.00
23 My Father's Sword.......... 3.00
24 The Demon Flute.......... 3.00
25 Momo-Usagi-Taro.......... 3.00
26 The Hairpin Murders,pt.1..... 3.00
27 The Hairpin Murders,pt.2..... 3.00
28 Courtesan conspiracy,pt.1.... 3.00
29 Courtesan conspiracy,pt.2.... 3.00
30 Inspector Ishida mystery..... 3.00
31 The Haunted Inn of Moon
  Shadow Hill............. 3.00
32 Two stories............. 3.00
33...................... 3.00
34 Demon Mask,pt.1.......... 3.00
35 Demon Mask,pt.2.......... 3.00
36 Demon Mask,pt.3.......... 3.00
37 F:Sasuke the Demon Queller... 3.00
38 Priest Sanshobo's temple..... 3.00
39 Grasscutter II,pt.1......... 3.00
40 V:Captain Quark........... 3.00
41 V:Neko Ninja............. 3.00
42 Grasscutter II,pt.4......... 3.00
43 Grasscutter II............ 3.00
44 Grasscutter II............ 3.00
45 Grasscutter II............ 3.00
46 wraparound(c),pt.1......... 3.00
47 wraparound(c),pt.2......... 3.00
48...................... 3.00

Usagi Yojimbo #7
© Dark Horse Comics

CVA Page 520 — All comics prices listed are for *Near Mint* condition.

DARK HORSE

49 Three seasons	3.00
50 Usagi dead?	3.00
51 The Shrouded Moon	3.00
52 Kitsune's youth	3.00
53 hunt for four ronin	3.00
54 Lone Goat and Kid	3.00
55 Lord Yoshikawa is dying	3.00
56 Katsuichi vs. Nakamura Joji	3.00
57 Crows,pt.1, renegade ronin	3.00
58 Crows,pt.2	3.00
59 Crows,pt.3	3.00
60 duel at Kitanoji	3.00
61 F:Chizu	3.00
62 Cursed woods	3.00
63 SS, return of Kitsune	3.00
64 SS, Tomago	3.00
65 SS	3.00
66 SS,giant monsters,pt.1	3.00
67 SS,giant monsters,pt.2	3.00
68 SS,giant monsters,pt.3	3.00
69 SS,Fathers and Sons,pt.1	3.00
70 SS,Fathers and Sons,pt.2	3.00
71 SS	3.00
TPB Demon Mask	15.95
TPB Shades of Death, rep. of Mirage series	14.95
TPB Daisho, rep. Mirage	14.95
TPB The Brink of Life & Death	14.95
TPB Seasons	14.95
TPB Grasscutter	16.95
TPB Grasscutter	16.95
TPB Grey Shadows	14.95
TPB Grasscutter II	15.95
TPB SS, Shrouded Moon, 184-pg.	15.95
TPB Duel at Kitanoji	16.95

USAGI YOJIMBO
1996
1 SS,color spec	4.00
2 SS,color spec	3.00
3 SS,color spec	3.00
4 thru 6	@3.00

USAGI YOJIMBO COLOR SPECIAL: GREEN PERSIMMON
1-shot by Stan Sakai ... 2.95

VAMPIRELLA
(B&W)
1 'The Lion and the Lizard'Pt.1	4.50
2 'The Lion and the Lizard'Pt.2	3.95
3 'The Lion and the Lizard'Pt.3	3.95
4 'The Lion and the Lizard'Pt.3	3.95

VENUS WARS
(B&W) Manga 1991
1 Aphrodia V:Ishtar, with 2-card strip	3.00
2 I: Ken Seno	2.50
3 Aphrodia V:Ishtar	2.50
4 Seno Joins Hound Corps	2.50
5 SenoV:Octopus Supertanks	2.50
6 Chaos in Aphrodia	2.50
7 All Out Ground War	2.50
8 Ishtar V:Aphrodia contd	2.50
9 Ishtar V:Aphrodia contd	2.50
10 Supertanks of Ishtar Advance	2.50
11 Aphrodia Captured	2.50
12 A:Miranda,48-pg.	2.75
13 Hound Brigade-Suicide Assault	2.25
14 V:Army	2.50
15	2.50
TPB Vol. 1	13.95

VENUS WARS II
1992
1 V:Security Police	2.75
2 Political Unrest	2.25
3 Conspiracy	2.25
4 A:Lupica	2.25
5 Love Hotel	2.25
6 Terran Consulate	2.25
7 Doublecross	2.25
8 D:Lupisa	2.95
9 A:Matthew	2.95
10 A:Mad Scientist	2.95
11 thru 15 V:Troopers	@2.95

VERSION
(B&W) Manga
1.1 by Hisashi Sakaguchi	2.50
1.2 thru 1.8	@2.50

VERSION II
(B&W) Manga
1.1 by Hisashi Sakaguchi	2.50
1.2 thru 1.6	@2.50

VIDEO NOIRE
Sept., 2001
TPB ... 9.95

VIOLENT CASES
Oct. 2003
TPB NGa,DMc ... 14.95

VIRUS
1993
1 MP(c),F:The Wan Xuan & the crew of the Electra	3.00
2 MP(c),V:Captian Powell	3.00
3 MP(c),V:Virus	3.00
4 MP(c),Last issue	3.00
TPB rep.#1–#4	16.95

VORTEX, THE
1 ... 2.00

WALTER: CAMPAIGN OF TERROR
1	2.50
2 and 3	@2.50

WARRIOR OF WAVERLY STREET, THE
Nov., 1996
1 (of 2) by M.Coto & J. Stokes	2.95
1-shot Broodstorm	2.95

WARWORLD!
(B&W) 1989
1 ... 2.00

WHAT'S MICHAEL?
(B&W) Manga
TPB by Makoto Kobayashi	5.95
TPB Living Together	5.95
TPB Off the Deep End	5.95
TPB A Hard Day's Life (2002)	8.95
TPB Show Time	8.95
TPB Fat Cat in the City	8.95

The Warrior of Waverly Street #1
© *Dark Horse Comics*

WHITE LIKE SHE
(B&W) 1994
1 by Bob Fingerman	2.95
2 thru 4	@2.95

WILL EISNER'S HAWKS OF THE SEAS
July 2003
TPB b&w ... 19.95

WILL TO POWER
Comics' Greatest World 1994
1 BS, A:X	2.25
2 BS, A:X,Monster	2.25
3 BS, A:X	2.25
4 BS, In Steel Harbor	2.25
5 V:Wolfgang	2.25
6 V:Motorhead	2.25
7 JOy(c),V:Amazing Grace	2.25
8 V:Catalyst	2.25
9 Titan, Grace	2.25
10 Vortex alien, Grace	2.25
11 Vortex alien, King Titan	2.25
12 Vortex alien	2.25

WITCHBLADE/ALIENS/ DARKNESS/PREDATOR: MINDHUNTER
Dec., 2000
1 (of 3)	3.00
2	3.00
2a variant TnD (c)	3.00
3 concl	3.00
TPB 96-pg.	12.95

WIZARD OF FOURTH STREET
(B&W) 1987
1	2.25
2 thru 4	@2.25

WOLF & RED
1995
1 Looney Tunes	2.50
2 Watchdog Wolf	2.50
3 Red Hot Riding Hood	2.50

DARK HORSE

The World Below #4
© Dark Horse Comics

WOLVERTON IN SPACE
(B&W) April, 1997
TPB by Basil Wolverton 16.95

WORLD BELOW, THE
March, 1999
1 PC 2.50
2 thru 4 PC . . . . @2.50

WORLD BELOW II, THE
Dec., 1999
1 (of 4) PC 2.95
2 . . . . 2.95
3 PC,Deeper and Stranger 2.95
4 PC,Deeper and Stranger 2.95

X
Comics' Greatest World 1994
1 B:StG(s),DoM,JP,I:X-Killer 3.00
2 DoM,JP,V:X-Killer 2.50
3 DoM,JP,A:Pit Bulls 2.50
4 DoM,JP 2.50
5 DoM,JP,V:Chaos Riders 2.50
6 Cyberassassins 2.50
7 Alamout 2.50
8 A:Ghost 2.50
9 War for Arcadia 2.50
10 War for Arcadia 2.50
11 I:Coffin, War 2.50
12 V:Coffin, A:Monster 2.50
13 D:X 2.50
14 conclusion to War 2.50
15 JS,SiG,war survivors 2.50
16 V:Headhunter 2.50
17 . . . . 2.50
18 V:Predator 2.50
19 V:Challenge 2.50
20 thru 25 . . . . @2.50
Spec. #1 One Shot to the Head . . . 2.50

XENA:
WARRIOR PRINCESS
Aug., 1999
1 . . . . 3.00
2 thru 9 . . . . @3.00
10 IEd,MD2,wayward viking 3.00
11 IEd,MD2,V:Lamia 3.00
12 IEd,MD2,Darkness Falls,concl. . 3.00
13 IEd,MD2,F:Legion 3.00

14 conclusion 3.00
1 to 14 newsstand photo(c) . . . . . @3.00
TPB Slave 10.00
TPB The Warrior Way of Death. . . 10.00
TPB Blood and Shadows 11.95

XXX
1 . . . . 3.95
2 V:Dr. Zemph 3.95
3 . . . . 3.95
4 V:Rhine Lords 3.95
5 I:Klaar 3.95
6 Klaar captured 4.95
7 Revolution Consequences 4.95

XENOXOIC TALES
Apr. 2003
TPB Vol. 1 rep 14.95
TPB Vol. 2 rep 14.95

YOUNG CYNICS CLUB
(B&W) 1993
1 by Glenn Wong 2.50

THE YOUNG INDIANA JONES CHRONICLES
1992
1 DBa,FS,TV Movie Adapt 3.25
2 DBa,TV Movie Adapt 2.75
3 DBa,GM 2.75
4 DBa,GM 2.75
5 DBa,GM 2.75
6 BBa,GM,WW1,French Army . . . 2.75
7 The Congo 2.75
8 Africa,A:A.Schweitzer 2.50
9 Vienna,Sophie-daughter of Arch-
 Duke Ferdinand 2.50
10 In Vienna continued 2.50
11 Far East 2.50
12 Fever Issue 2.50

YOU'RE UNDER ARREST!
(B&W) Manga 1995–96
1 by Kosuke Fujishima 2.95
2 thru 8 . . . . @2.95
TPB rep 12.95

You're Under Arrest! #8
© Dark Horse Comics

ZombieWorld: The Tree of Death #3
© Dark Horse Comics

ZOMBIEWORLD:
1-shot Eat Your Heart Out, KJo. . . . 3.00
1-shot Home for the Holidays 3.00

ZOMBIEWORLD:
DEAD END
Jan., 1998
1 (of 2) by Stephen Blue 3.00
2 . . . . @3.00

ZOMBIEWORLD:
CHAMPION
OF THE WORMS
Sept., 1997
1 (of 3) MMi 3.00
2 and 3 . . . . @3.00
Spec. Home for the Holidays 3.00
TPB 8.95

ZOMBIEWORLD:
THE TREE OF DEATH
May, 1999
1 (of 4) by P. Mills & J.Deadstock . 3.00
2 thru 4 . . . . @3.00

ZOMBIEWORLD:
WINTER'S DREGS
May, 1998
1 (of 4) by Fingerman & Edwards . 3.00
2 thru 4 . . . . @3.00

ZONE, THE
B&W 1990
1-shot 3.00

IMAGE

AARON STRIPS
(B&W) April, 1997
1 thru 4 rep. from Sunday comic
  strips, by Aaron Warner..... @2.95

ACTION PLANET
(B&W) Sept., 1997
Prev. Action Planet Comics
3 .... 3.95

ADRENALYNN
Aug., 1999
1 F:Sabina Nikoli.............. 2.50
2 TnD,V:Russian monster androids 2.50
3 TnD,V:last 2 Monster-cyborgs... 2.50
4 TnD,the real Sabina 2.50

ADVENTURES OF AARON
March, 1997
(B&W) by Aaron Warner
1 'Baby-sitter Gone Bad' 2.95
2 'Thunder Thighs of the
  Terrordome'................ 2.95
3 'Baby-sitter Gone Bad,' concl.... 2.95
100 Super Special 2.95
Christmas Spectacular #1........ 2.95

ADVENTURES OF BARRY WEEN, BOY GENIUS, THE
(B&W) March, 1999
1 (of 3) by Judd Winick 2.95
2 Growing Pains 2.95
3 School 2.95

ADVENTURE STRIP DIGEST
(B&W) April, 1998
1 by Randy Reynaldo 2.95
2 F:Rob Hanes, detective 2.95

AGENTS, THE
April 2003
1 (of 6) BDn, b&w............. 2.95
2 thru 6 .... @2.95

AGE OF BRONZE
(B&W) Nov., 1998
1 EiS,The Trojan War 3.00
2 EiS,Death of Paris 3.00
3 EiS,F:Herakles, Hektor........ 3.00
4 EiS,I:Helen................. 3.00
5 EiS,Achilles disguised......... 3.00
6 EiS,Helen gone 3.50
7 EiS,Odysseus mad?.......... 3.50
8 EiS,Achilles missing 3.50
9 EiS,Will war start?........... 3.50
10 EiS,Sacrifice,pt.1 .... 3.50
11 EiS,Sacrifice,pt.2 .... 3.50
12 EiS,You're not the Trojans? 3.50
13 thru 18 EiS,Sacrifice,pt.4–pt.9 @3.50
Spec.1-shot Behind the Scenes .. 3.50
Spec.#1 EiS, House of Horror..... 3.00
Spec.#2 .... 3.00
TPB Vol.1 A Thousand Ships 19.95

AGE OF HEROES, THE
Halloween, 1996
(B&W)
1 JHI & JRy................. 3.00
2 JHI & JRy................. 3.00
3 JHI & JRy,Luko,Trickster &
  Aerwyn try to steal treasure ... 3.00
4 JHI & JRy,Drake, the blind
  swordsman returns.......... 3.00
5 JHI & JRy,O:Conor One-Arm ... 3.00
Spec. #1 rep. #1 & #2.......... 4.95
Spec. #2 rep. #3 & #4.......... 6.95

AGE OF HEROES: WEX
(B&W) Aug., 1998
1 by JHI,Vurtex 2.95

AGENCY, THE
Top Cow, July, 2001
1 (of 6) PJe................. 4.00
1a variant(c) 4.00
1b variant MS(c) 4.00
2 PJe 2.50
3 PJe 2.50
4 PJe,A Virtual Secret 2.95
5 PJe,Virtual................. 2.95
6 PJe,concl. 48-pg........... 4.95

ALLEGRA
WildStorm, 1996
1 ScC,SSe.................. 2.50
2 thru 4 .... @2.50

ALLEY CAT
July, 1999
1 BNa,MHw,F:Alley Baggett...... 2.50
1a variant painted cover (1:4) ... 3.50
2 BNa,MHw,women murdered 2.50
3 photo(c).................. 2.50
3a variant JJu cover (1:4) 2.50
4 into darkness 2.50
5 The Martyr,pt.1 .... 3.00
6 The Martyr,pt.2 .... 3.00
7 The Martyr,pt.3............. 2.50
Wizard World Spec.#1 .... 2.50
Lingerie Edition............... 4.95

ALLIANCE, THE
Shadowline, 1995
1 JV,I:The Alliance, A Call
  to Arms 2.50
2 JV,Team comes together 'Like
  Pieces of a Puzzle'........... 2.50
3 I:Slash C 2.50
4 .... 2.50
1a thru 4a variant covers ...... @2.50

ALLIES, THE
Extreme, 1995
1 mini-series 2.50
2 thru 4 .... @2.50

ALONE IN THE DARK
July, 2002
GN 1-shot, 48-pg............. 4.95

ALTERED IMAGE
April, 1998
1 JV,The Day Reality Went Wild .. 2.50
2 JV,F:Everybody smooshed 2.50
3 JV,Middle Age Crisis, concl. 2.50
TPB F:everybody 9.95

AMANDA AND GUNN
(B&W) April, 1997
1 JeR, Montana 2036 .... 2.95
2 (of 4) JeR................. 2.95
3 (of 4) JeR................. 2.95
4 (of 4) JeR, conclusion........ 2.95

ANGELA
TMP, 1994–95
1 NGa(s),GCa,A:Spawn. 15.00
2 NGa(s),GCa,Angela's trial 14.00
3 NGa(s),GCa,In Hell. 12.00
Spec. Pirate Spawn(c) 32.00
Spec. Pirate Angela(c) (1995).... 30.00
TPB Rep.#1–#3 .... 9.95

ANGELA/GLORY: RAGE OF ANGELS
TMP/Extreme, 1996
1 x-over begins 5.00

APHRODITE IX
Top Cow, Aug., 2000
1 by David Finch............. 4.00
1a variant JBz(c)............. 4.00
1a signed 20.00
1b variant Michale Turner(c) 4.00
1c variant MS(c) 4.00
2 amnesia 3.50
3 conspiracy 3.50
0 with pin-up & poster 3.00
4 Who is she? 48-pg. 5.50
Spec.1 Convention spec., signed . 20.00
Preview ed., signed 5.00

Aphrodite IX #2 © Tpo Cow

ARCANUM
Top Cow, March, 1997
[Mini-series]
1 BPe, from Medieval
 Spawn/Witchblade 3.00
1a variant MS(s) (1:4)........ 2.50
2 BPe, Chi in Asylum......... 2.50
3 BPe, Ming Chang captive in
 Atlantis.................. 2.50
4 BPe,'The End?' 2.50
5 BPe,Royale's secret journal ... 2.50
6 BPe,Safe Haven?........... 2.50
7 BPe,Egypt 2.50

AREA 52
Jan., 2001
1 .... 2.95
2 The Gloves are off 2.95
3 Out of the Frying Pan and
 into the Fire 2.95
4 Beginning of the End 2.95

ARIA
Avalon Nov., 1998
1 by Brian Holguin & Jay Anacleto . 3.00
1a variant cover............... 4.00
2 A:Mad Gwynnion 3.00
3 English Countryside 3.00
4 V:Dark One 3.00
4a glow-in-the-dark(c)........ 15.00
5 London, 1966............... 2.50
6 Subterranean Homesick Blues .. 2.50
7 Mad Gods and Irish Men 2.50
Preview ed. F:Kildare 2.95
Spec.#1 Blanc & Noir, sketchbook . 2.95
Spec.#1 alternate cover 6.95
Spec.#2 Blanc & Noir.......... 2.50
Sketchbook by Jay Anacleto..... 5.95
TPB The Magic of Aria 13.95
Coll.Ed.#1, rep.#1−#2.......... 5.95

ARIA/ANGELA: HEAVENLY CREATURES
Feb., 2000
1 (of 2) x-over 5.00
1a variant JQ(c) (1:4).......... 3.00
1b variant J.G. Jones(c) (1:4) ... 4.00
1c variant Jay Anacleto(c) (1:4) ... 3.00
1 B&W 3.00
2 x-over concl................ 3.00
2a variant(c).................. 4.00
Museum edition 125.00

ARIA: THE SOUL MARKET
March, 2001
1 Legend continues............ 4.00
1a Museum edition.......... 125.00
2 F:Robin Goodfellow 3.00
3 A Dark Rider Approaches 3.00
4 Auction of imprisoned souls ... 3.00
5 What price a soul?........... 3.00
6 Mortality 3.00
GN A Midwinter's Dream,40-pg. ... 4.95

ARIA: A SUMMER SPELL
March, 2002
1 (of 2) London, summer 1967.... 3.00
2 Kildare is in love............. 3.00

ARIA: THE USES OF ENCHANTMENT
Feb. 2003
1 (of 4) 2.95
2 thru 4 .... @2.95

ARKAGA
Sept., 1997
1 by Arnie Tang Jorgensen 3.00
2 Desire for revenge 3.00

ART OF ERIK LARSEN
1 Sketchbook 4.95

ART OF HOMAGE STUDIOS
1 Various Pin-ups 4.95

ART OF JAY ANACLETO
Image
1-shot 48-pg. 5.95

ASCENSION
Top Cow, Sept., 1997
1 by David Finch,F:Angels....... 4.00
2 Andromeda fights alone 3.00
3 reunited with Lucien 3.00
4 .... 3.00
5 Gregorieff and Dayak Army..... 3.00
6 Voivodul returns, concl........ 3.00
7 Andy's problems worsen....... 2.50
8 revenge on Dayaks & Mineans .. 2.50
9 Andy exiled................. 2.50
10 A:D. Gavin Taylor........... 2.50
11 A:D. Gavin Taylor........... 2.50
12 A:turning point 2.50
13 A:Grigorieff, Petra 2.50
14 V:Marcus,A:Andromeda...... 2.50
15 Rowena's secrets 2.50
16 Petra joins Lucien 2.50
17 a schism 2.50
18 V:new entity............... 2.50
19 to Petra's Minean home...... 2.50
20 Resurrection,pt.1 .... 2.50
21 Resurrection,pt.2 .... 2.50
22 trapped 2.95
23 Andromeda's new outfit 2.95
Coll.Ed.#1, rep.#1−#2.......... 4.95
Coll.Ed.#2 .... 4.95

ASTOUNDING SPACE THRILLS
April, 2000
1 Ken Kelly(c),Cydonian Contant .. 2.95
2 The Criminal Code 2.95
3 Gordo:Earthling Prime,
 flip-book................... 2.95
4 The Craving of Consumorr,
 flip-book................... 2.95
5 Attack of the Macrobes........ 2.95

ASTRO CITY
See: KURT BUSIEK'S ASTRO CITY

ATHENA INC.
2002
1-shot Agents Roster,48-pg....... 6.00
The Beginning, 48-pg. 6.00
1 reoffered................... 3.00
2 Gwen has a stalker........... 3.00
2a variant(c).................. 3.00
3 Gwen hearing voices 3.00
3a variant(c).................. 3.00
4 Revelations 3.00
4a variant(c).................. 3.00
5 The Belly of the Beast 2.95
6 All Hell Breaks Loose 2.95
5a− a variant (c).............. @2.95

TPB Vol. 1 Manhunter Project.... 19.95

ATOMIC TOYBOX
April, 1999
Odyssey Line
1 AaL,F:Ken Logan 3.00
2 AaL,The Aliens are comming ... 3.00

AUTOMATION
Flypaper, 1998
1 Robots sent to Mars, and back .. 3.00
2 One goes mad 3.00
3 Sherzad vs. Konak 3.00
TPB rep. #1−#3 .... 12.95

AVIGON
(B&W) Oct., 2000
Spec. 56-pg. 5.95
GN 5.95

THE AWAKENING
(B&W) Oct., 1997
1 (of 4) by Stephen Blue 3.00
2 thru 4 .... @3.00
TPB rep. #1−#4 .... 9.95

BACKLASH
WildStorm, 1994−97
1 Taboo, 2 diff. covers 4.00
1a variant edition, 2 covers 3.00
2 Savage Dragon 2.50
3 V:Savage Dragon 2.50
4 SRf,A:Wetworks 2.50
5 SRf,A:Dane 2.50
6 BBh,SRf,A:Wetworks 2.50
7 BBh,SRf,V:Bounty Hunters 2.50
8 RMz,BBh,BWS(c),WildStorm
 Rising,pt.8,w/2 cards 2.50
8a Newsstand ed............... 2.25
9 F:Taboo,Dingo,V:Chasers...... 2.50
10 I:Crimson................... 2.50
11 R:Bloodmoon............... 2.50
12 R:Taboo,Crimson's Costume ... 3.00
13 Taboo to the Rescue 2.50
14 A:Deathblow 2.50
15 F:Cyberjack................. 2.50
16 F:Cole,Marc................. 2.50
17 F:Marc,Kink................. 2.50

Backlash #23
© *WildStorm*

IMAGE

Backlash–Battle

#	Price
18	2.50
19 Fire From Heaven,pt.2	2.50
20 SRf,BBh,Fire From Heaven,pt.10	2.50
21 SRf,BBh	2.50
22 SRf,BBh	2.50
23 SRf,BBh	2.50
24 SRf,BBh,return of Dingo	2.50
25 SRf,BBh,56-pg.. special	4.00
26 SRf,BBh,IR:Gramalkin	2.50
27 SRf,BBh	2.50
28 SRf,BBh,Backlash leads PSI team to Europe	2.50
29 SRf,BBh,Haroth raises the remnants of Atlantis	2.50
30 SRf,BBh,Backlash confronts Kherubim lords	2.50
31 SRf,BBh,team returns to PSI	2.50
32 SRf,BBh,earth-shattering final issue	2.50
TPB Backlash/Spider-Man, Webs & Whips, x-over	4.95
TPB The Drahn War, rep.#27–#32	15.00

BACKLASH/SPIDER-MAN
WildStorm/Marvel, 1996

#	Price
1 x-over,pt.1	2.50
1a variant cover	3.00
2 x-over,pt.2	2.50

BADGER
(B&W) May, 1997

#	Price
1 MBn,'Betelgeuse'	2.95
2 MBn,'Beefalo don't like fences'	2.95
3 MBn,'Loose Eel'	2.95
4 MBn,'Hot House'	2.95
5 MBn,Octopi in the hot tub	2.95
6 MBn,Prime Minister of Klactoveedesteen	2.95
7 MBn,Crime Comics	2.95
8 MBn,Root	2.95
9 MBn	2.95
10 MBn,Tuesday Ruby	2.95
11 MBn,Watch the Skies	2.95
12 MBn,The Lady Cobras	2.95
13 MBn,Horse Police	2.95
14 MBn,Badger Sells Out	2.95

BADROCK
Extreme, 1995

#	Price
1a RLd(p),TM(c),A:Dragon	2.25
1b SPa(ic),A:Savage Dragon	2.25
1c DF(ic)	2.25
2 RLd,ErS(s),V:Girth,A:Savage Dragon, flip-book-Grifter/Badrock #2	2.50
3 RLd,ErS,V:The Overlord	2.50
Ann.#1 I:Gunner, 48-pg.	2.95
Super-Spec. #1 A:Grifter & The Dragon	2.50

BADROCK AND COMPANY
Extreme, 1994–95

#	Price
1 KG(s)	2.50
1a San Diego Comic Con ed.	3.00
2 RLd(c),Fuji	2.50
3 Overtkill,'Overt Operations'	2.50
4 TBm,MBm,TNu,A:Velocity	2.50
5 A:Grifter	2.50
6 Finale,A:ShadowHawk	2.50

BALLISTIC
Top Cow, 1995

#	Price
1 F:Wetworks	3.00
2 F:Wetworks,Jesters	

Badrock and Company #1
© Extreme

#	Price
Transformation	3.00
3 F:Wetworks,final issue	3.00

BALLISTIC ACTION
Top Cow, 1996

#	Price
1 MSi(c), pin-ups	3.00

BALLISTIC IMAGERY
Top Cow, 1995

#	Price
1 F:Hellcop,Heavy Space, Cyberforce,anthology	3.00

BALLISTIC/WOLVERINE
Top Cow/Marvel, 1996

#	Price
1 Devil's Reign,pt.4,x-over	4.00

BANISHED KNIGHTS
Dec., 2001

#	Price
1 vampire civil war	3.00
1A variant(c)	3.00
1B holofoil(c)	5.00
2 F:Greyson & Belmiro	3.00
TPB Vol. 1 Samurai Noir	12.95

BASTARD SAMURAI
April, 2002

#	Price
1 (of 3)	3.00
2 F:Toshi	3.00
3 concl.	3.00

BATTLESTONE
Extreme, 1994

#	Price
1 RLd,ErS,MMy,AV	2.50
1a variant cover	3.00
2 RLd,ErS,MMy,AV,I&D:Roarke, finale	2.50

BATTLE CHASERS
Cliffhanger, April, 1998

#	Price
1 JMd, fantasy, team-up	9.00
1a Chromium ed. (5,000 made)	46.00
2 JMd,F:Gully	5.00
3 JMd,new ally	4.00
4 JMd,Red Monika	4.00
4a,b,c JMd variant covers	@3.00
5 JMd,V:Lord August,with 8-pg. Planetary #0	3.00

#	Price
6 JMd	3.00
6a variant AWa(c)	4.00

WildStorm/DC, Nov., 2000

#	Price
7 JMd(c)(1:2)	3.00
7a variant JSC(c) (1:4)	4.00
7b variant HuR(c) (1:4)	7.00
8 JMd,V:Harvester	3.00
TPB Coll.Ed.#1, rep.#1 & #2	5.95
TPB Coll.Ed #2	6.00
TPB A Gathering of Heroes	14.95
Prelude #1, JMd, 16-pg.	10.00

BATTLE OF THE PLANETS
Top Cow, July, 2002

#	Price
1 AxR	3.00
1a-c variant(c)s	@3.00
1d convention(c)	3.00
1e holofoil edition	6.00
2 AxR,attack on earth begins	3.00
3 AxR,The Firey Phoenix	3.00
4 Zoltar	3.00
5 Spectra connected to suicides	3.00
6 Under A Blood Red Sky,pt.1	3.00
7 Under A Blood Red Sky,pt.2	3.00
8 Under A Blood Red Sky,pt.3	3.00
9 Under A Blood Red Sky,pt.4	3.00
10 Aftermath	3.00
11 Second Encounters	3.00
12 concl., 48-pg.	5.00
1-shot flip-book Thundercats	5.00
1-shot Mark	3.00
1-shot Battle Book	5.00
1-shot Hell, 48-pg.	5.00
2 animation (c)	
1/2 reprint	3.00
TPB Destroy All Monsters	20.00
TPB Trial by Fire	8.00
TPB Blood Red Sky	16.95

BATTLE OF THE PLANETS: MANGA
Image/Top Cow Oct. 2003

#	Price
1	3.00
2	3.00

BATTLE OF THE PLANETS: WITCHBLADE
Image/Top Cow Jan. 2003

#	Price
1 48-pg.	7.00

Battle Chasers #3
© Image

All comics prices listed are for *Near Mint* condition.

Beetleborgs–Bloodwulf

IMAGE

BEETLEBORGS
Extreme, Nov., 1996
1 from TV show 2.50

BERZERKERS
Extreme, 1995
1 F:Greylore,Hatchet,Psi-Storm,
Cross,Wildmane,Youngblood#2 2.50
2 Into the Darkness 2.50
3 Slay Ride 2.50
4 final issue 2.50

BIG BANG COMICS
Big Bang Studios, 1996
(B&W) Prev.: Caliber
1 F:Mighty Man 2.25
2 Silver Age Shadowhawk 2.25
3 . . . . 2.25
4 . . . . 3.00
5 Top Secret Origins 3.00
6 Round Table of America and
Knights of Justice meet, orig.
mini-series #3 (color) 3.00
7 . . . . 3.00
8 F:Mister U.S. 3.00
9 I:Peter Chefren 3.00
10 F:Galahad 3.00
11 Faulty Towers is destroying
Midway City 3.00
12 F:The Savage Dragon 3.00
13 by Jeff Weigel, 40-pg.spec. 3.00
14 RB,A:The Savage Dragon 3.00
15 SBi(c),F:Dr. Weird 3.00
16 F:Thunder Girl 3.00
17 . . . . 3.00
18 Savage Dragon on Trial 3.00
19 O:Beacon,Hummingbird. 3.00
20 F:Knight Watchman,Blitz 3.00
21 F:Shadow Lady 3.00
22 The Bird-Man of Midway City . . . 3.00
23 Riddle of the Sphinx, sequel . . . 3.00
24 History of Big Bang,Vol.1 . . . . . . 4.00
25 Anniv. iss. 4.00
26 Murder by Microphone, concl. . . 3.00
27 History of Big Bang,Vol.2 . . . . . . 4.00
28 Knight of the Living Dead,pt.1 . . 4.00
29 Knight of the Living Dead,pt.2 . . 4.00
30 F:Knight Watchman 4.00
31 F:Knight-Sprite 4.00
32 F:Pink Flamingo 4.00
33 Peril of Parallel Planets 4.00
34 To Save the Gods 4.00
35 Big Bang vs. 1963 . . . . 4.00
Giant Sz. Ann.#1 Ultiman 5.00
TPB rep. 1994 mini-series. 11.00
Summer Spec.b&w, 48-pg. (2003) . 4.95

BIG BRUISERS
WildStorm, 1996
1 F:Maul,Impact,Badrock 3.50

BIG HAIR PRODUCTIONS
B&W Feb., 2000
1 by Andy Suriano,F:Astro-Bug . . 3.50
2 . . . . 3.50

BLACK AND WHITE
Hack Studios, 1996
1 ATi,New heroes,'Beginnings' . . . 2.25
2 ATi(p),apparent death 2.25
3 V:Chang 2.25
Ashcan 5.00

BLACK ANVIL
Top Cow, 1996
1 & 2 . . . . 2.50

BLACK FLAG
Extreme, 1994
1 B&W Preview 3.00

BLACK OPS
WildStorm, 1996
1 . . . . 2.50
2 thru 5 . . . . @2.50
TPB, rep.#1–#5 . . . . 14.95

BLACK TIDE
Nov., 2001
1 . . . . 3.00
1a variant(c) 3.00
1b variant(c) 3.00
2 Balance of Power 3.50
3 One Man's Enemy 3.50
4 Deception, Secrets and Lies . . . 3.50

BLAIR WITCH: DARK TESTAMENTS
Oct., 2000
Spec. IEd,CAd 2.95

BLINDSIDE
Extreme, Aug., 1996
1 MMy & AV, F:Nucgaek Jeno . . . 2.50
2 MMy & AV, Origin continues 2.50

BLISS ALLEY
(B&W) July, 1997
1 BML 3.00
2 BML,F:Wizard Walker 3.00
3 BML,Inky-Dinks 3.00

BLOKHEDZ
Nov. 2003
1 (of 4) 2.95

BLOODHUNTER
Extreme, Nov., 1996
1 RV, Cabbot Stone rises from the
slab 2.95

BLOOD LEGACY
Top Cow, April, 2000
1 MHw,The Story of Ryan 2.50
1a variant Keu Cha(c) 2.50
1b variant Mike Turner(c). 2.50
2 MHw,F:Dr. Susan Ryerson 2.50
3 MHw 2.50
4 MHw 2.50
1-shot The Young Ones (2003). . . . 4.00

BLOODPOOL
Exteme 1995
1 I:Seoul,Rubbe,Wylder,
'Discharged'. 2.50
1a variant cover. 2.50
2 The Hills Are Alive 2.50
3 Walk Like an Egyptian 2.50
4 final issue 2.50
TPB Rep. #1-#4 . . . . 12.95
[Regular Series] 1996
1 thru 3 JDy . . . . @2.50

Bloodstrike #2
© *Extreme*

BLOODSTRIKE
Extreme, 1993
1 A:Brigade,Rub the Blood(c)
Blood Brother prelude,x-over . . 3.50
2 I:Lethal,V:Brigade,BloodBrothers,
pt.2,B:BU:Knight 3.00
3 B:ErS(s),ATi(c),V:Coldsnap,Blood
Brothers,pt.4,'Turning Point' . . 3.00
4 ErS(s) 3.00
5 KG,I:Noble,A:Supreme 3.00
6 KG(s),CAx,C&J:Chapel,'Inside
Project:Born Again' 3.00
7 KG,RHe,A:Badrock,'Changing
of the Guard' 3.00
8 RHe,A:Spawn,Sleeping & Waking 3.00
9 RHe,Extreme Prejudice,pt.3,
I:Extreme Warrior,ATh,BU: Black
& White 3.00
10 Extreme Prejudice,pt.7,
V:Brigade, B:BU:Knight 3.00
25 I:Cabbot Bloodstrike 3.00
11 ErS(s),ATi(c),V:Coldsnap 3.00
12 ErS(s) 3.00
13 KG,A:Supreme,'BetterOffDead' . 3.00
14 KG(s),CAx,C&J:Chapel 3.00
15 KG,RHe,A:Badrock,War Games,
pt.1,Extreme Sacrifice begins . . 3.00
16 KG,RHe, War Games,pt.3,Extreme
Sacrifice ignites 3.00
17 KIA,V:The Horde 3.00
18 ExtremeSacrifice,pt.3,x-over . . 3.00
19 V:The Horde 3.00
20 R:Deadlock New Order 3.00
21 KA,V:Epiphany New Order. . . . 3.00
22 V:The Horde, last issue 3.00
25 see above, after #10
Ashcan 3.00

BLOODSTRIKE: ASSASSIN
Extreme, 1995
0 R:Battlestone 3.00
1 Debut new series 3.00
1a alternate cover 3.00
2 V:M.D.K. Assassins 3.00
3 V:Persuasion 3.00

BLOODWULF
Extreme, 1995
1 RLd,R:Bloodwulf 2.50
1b Run OJ Run 2.50

CVA Page 526   All comics prices listed are for *Near Mint* condition.

1c Alternate cover	2.50
1d Alternate cover	2.50
2 A:Hot Blood	2.50
3 Slippery When Wet.	2.50
4 Darkness Gnaws at my Soul, final issue.	2.50
Summer Spec.#1 V:Supreme Freeferall (1995).	2.50

BLUE
Aug., 1999

1 Android teenager	2.50
2 by Greg Aronowitz	2.50
3 rescue mission	2.50

BLUNTMAN AND CHRONIC
Aug., 2001

| GN MiA | 15.00 |

BODYCOUNT
March, 1996

1 KEa,SBs	2.50
2 thru 4 KEa,SBs	@2.50
TPB series rep..	17.95

BOHOS
Flypaper (B&W) 1998

1 by Maggie Whorf & B.Penaranda	2.95
2 F:teenage bohemians	2.95
3 concl.	2.95
TPB Bohos	12.95

BONE
(B&W) Dec., 1995
[Prev.: Cartoon Books]

21 thru 25	@3.00
26 The Turning	3.00
27 end of Dragonslayer storyline.	3.00
Bone Sourcebook	.25

reprints with new covers

| #1 thru #9 | @3.00 |
| 10 rep. 'Great Cow Race' | 3.00 |

Cartoon Books

11 Aftermath of the Great Cow Race	3.00
12	3.00
13 Thar she blows	3.00

Bone #22 © Cartoon Books

14	3.00
15 Double or nothing	3.00
16 hiding from the Rat Creatures	3.00
17 with 5 new pages.	3.00
18 Betrayed	3.00
19 'Three cheers for Dragon-slayer Phoney Bone'.	3.00
20 Phoney Bone vs. Lucius	3.00

BOOF
TMP, 1994

1	2.25
2 Meathook	2.25
3 Joyride.	2.25
4 Beach.	2.25
5 Down on the Farm	2.25
6 V:Gangster Chimps	2.25

BOOF AND THE BRUISE CREW
TMP, 1994

1	2.25
2 thru 5	@2.25
6 I:Mortar,O:Bruise Crew	2.25

BRASS
WildStorm, 1996

1 Rib,AWa,Folio Edition	3.50
2 Rib,AWa	2.50
3 Rib,AWa,concl.	2.50

BRIGADE
Extreme, 1993
[1st Series]

1 RLd(s),MMy,I:Brigade,Genocide	3.50
1a Gold ed.	4.00
2 RLd(s),V:Genocide,w/coupon#4	4.00
2a w/o coupon.	1.50
2b Gold ed.	4.00
3 I:Birds of Prey,V:Genocide	2.25
4 CyP,Youngblood#5 flip	2.25

[2nd Series]

0 RLd(s),ATi(c),JMs,NRd,I:Warcry, A:Emp,V:Youngblood	2.25
1 I:Boone,Hacker,V:Bloodstrike, Blood Brothers,pt.1.	2.75
1a Gold ed.	3.00
2 C:Coldsnap,Blood Brothers,pt.3	3.00
3 ErS(s),GP(c),MMy,NRd(i),I:Roman V:Bloodstrike,Blood Brothers, pt.5	2.25
4 Rip(s),MMy,RHe,Changes, BU:Lethal.	2.25
5 Rip(s),MMy,It's A VeryDeepSea.	2.25
6 Rip(s),MMy,I:Coral,Warlok, BU:Hackers Tale.	2.25
7 Rip(s),MMy,V:Warlok	2.25
8 ErS(s),MMy,Extreme Prejudice, pt.2,BU:Black & White,pt.5	2.25
9 ErS(s),MMy,Extreme Prejudice pt.6,ATh,BU:Black & White	2.25
25 ErS(s),MMy,D:Kayo,Coldsnap, Thermal.	2.25
26 Images of Tomorrow	2.25
10 Extreme Prejudice	2.00
11 WildC.A.T.S	2.50
12 Battlestone	2.50
13 Thermal.	2.00
14 Teamate deaths.	2.00
15 MWm,R:Roman Birds of Prey	2.00
16 ExtremeSacrifice,pt.4,x-over	2.50
17 MWn,I:New Team	2.50
18 I:The Shape New Order.	2.50
19 MWn,F:Troll,Glory	2.50
20 MWn,alien cult saga,concl.	2.50
21 F:ShadowHawk	2.50

Brigade #9 © Extreme

22 Supreme Apocalypse,pt.4	2.50
23	2.50
24	2.50
25 & 26 see above	
27 Extreme Babewatch.	2.50
Sourcebook	2.95

BRIT
July 2003

| 1-shot b&w, 48-pg. | 4.95 |

BUGBOY
(B&W) June, 1998

| 1-shot, by Mark Lewis, 48-pg. | 4.00 |

BULLETPROOF MONK
Flypaper, Nov., 1998

1 in San Francisco.	3.00
2 N.Y. Chinatown.	3.00
3 conclusion	3.00
TPB 80-pg.	9.95
1-shot Tales of the B P M	2.95

BUNKER, THE
April 2003

| GN 96-pg. | 9.95 |

BUTCHER KNIGHT
Top Cow, July, 2000

1 DT,F:Luther Washington	2.50
1a variant(c) MS (1:3)	2.50
1b variant(c) DT (1:3)	2.50
2 DT	2.50
3 DT,Blood & Gore	2.50
4 DT,concl.	2.95

CAPES
Sept. 2003

1 (of 3)	2.95
2	2.95
3	2.95

CARVERS
Flypaper, Oct., 1998

1 F:five snowboarders	3.00
2 J:Crazy Jack.	3.00
3 V:Evil Yeti.	3.00
TPB rep. #1–#3	9.95

IMAGE

CASEFILES: SAM AND TWITCH
May 2003
1 Have You Seen Me?,pt.1 ...... 2.95
2 thru 6 Have You Seen
  Me?, pt.2 thru pt.6 .... @2.95
7 .... 2.95

CASUAL HEROES
Motown, 1996
1 .... 2.50
2 thru 6 .... @2.50

CATHEDRAL CHILD
1998
GN by Lea Hernandez 9.95
GN 2nd printing 9.95

CELESTINE
Extreme, 1996
1 .... 2.50
2 .... 2.50

CHANNEL ZERO
(B&W) 1998
1 by Brian Wood 3.00
2 .... 3.00
3 gone global 3.00
4 Filter.................... 3.00
5 Brink of Millennium crash 3.00
6 Sound system 3.00
TPB Collection 11.95

CHAPEL
Extreme, 1995
1 BWn,F:Chapel 3.50
2 V:Colonel Black 3.00
2a variant cover............ 2.50
[Regular Series]
1 BWn,F:Chapel 2.50
1a variant cover............ 2.50
2 V:Giger.................. 2.50
3 V:Giger.................. 2.50
4 Extreme Babewatch......... 2.50
5 Hell on Earth,pt.1 .... 2.50
6 Hell on Earth,pt.2 .... 2.50
7 Shadowhunt x-over,pt.2 .... 2.50

CHASING DOGMA
June, 2001
TPB DFg,120-pg. 12.95

CHASSIS
Nov., 1999
1 F:Chassis McBain........... 3.00
2 .... 3.00
2a variant Matt Busch(c) 3.00
3 Gizmotech Industries 3.00
4 .... 3.00
4a Collector's variant(c)...... 3.95
5 Slic's One Shot, flip-cover..... 3.00

CHILDHOOD'S END
(B&W) Oct., 1997
1 (of 5) JCf,community playground 3.00

CHILLER
Dec., 1998
TPB JHl,F:Brian Marx 17.95

THE C.H.I.X. THAT TIME FORGOT
Studiosaurus, Aug., 1998
1 F:Good Girl 3.00

CITY OF SILENCE
May, 2000
1 (of 3) WEI,GEr,F:Silencers 2.50
1a variant GEr,3-D(c)(1:4) 2.50
2 WEI,GEr.................. 2.50
3 WEI,GEr.................. 2.50

CLERKS
Image, July, 2001
TPB 10.95

CLOCK MAKER, THE
Jan 2003
1 (of 12) 2.50
2 thru 7 .... @2.50

CLOCKWORK ANGELS
(B&W) March, 1999
GN seq. to Cathedral Child....... 9.95

CLOUDFALL
Nov. 2003
1-shot b&w 48-pg. 4.95

CODE BLUE
(B&W) April, 1998
1 by Jimmie Robinson......... 2.95
2 F.I.T.E. creates havoc 2.95

CODENAME: STYKE FORCE
Top Cow, 1994
1A MS(s),BPe,JRu(i) 3.50
1B Gold Embossed Cover 6.00
1C Blue Embossed Cover 9.00
2 MS(s),BPe,JRu(i) 2.50
3 MS(s),BPe,JRu(i) 2.50
4 MS(s),BPe,JRu(i) 2.50
5 MS(s),BPe,JRu(i) 2.50
6 MS(s),BPe,JRu(i) 2.25
7 MS(s),BPe,JRu(i) 2.25
8A Cyblade poster (Tucci) 4.00
8B Shi poster (Silvestri) 4.00
8C Tempest poster (Tan) 2.25
9 New Teamate 2.25
10 SvG, B:New Adventure 2.25
11 F:Bloodbow 2.25
12 F:Stryker................ 2.25
13 SvG(s),F:Strkyer 2.25
14 New Jobs 2.25
Spec.#0 O:Stryke Force 2.50
TPB rep. Death's Angel Saga 9.95

COMBAT
Jan., 1996
1 .... 2.50
2 .... 2.50

COMPLETE ALEX TOTH ZORRO
(B&W) April, 1999
TPB Complete Alex Toth Zorro ... 18.95

COSMIC RAY
June, 1999
1 by Stephen Blue............ 3.00
1a alternate cover (1:2) 3.00
2 F:Raymond Mann.......... 3.00
3 F:Star Marshalls............ 3.00

Cosmic Ray #2
© Cliffhanger

COW, THE
Top Cow, April, 2000
1 Spring edition.............. 2.95
2 Summer edition 2.95
3 Spring edition 2001......... 2.95

CREECH, THE
TMP, Oct., 1997
1 GCa,DaM,F:Chirs Rafferty 2.50
2 GCa,DaM,F:Dennis Dross 2.50
TPB Race Against Death 9.95

[GREG CAPULLO'S ORIGINAL] CREECH
TMP, Aug., 2001
1 A Vision of Death 2.50
2 Awakenings 2.50
3 The Resurrection 2.50

CREECH, THE: OUT FOR BLOOD
Image, July, 2001
1 GCa,Out for Blood, Book 1..... 4.95
2 GCa,48-pg................. 4.95
3 GCa,Killing Machine perfected .. 4.95

CREED: UTOPIATE
Jan., 2002
1 (of 4) TKn................. 3.50
2 TKn,disorder in dreamworld 3.00
3 TKn,fantasy vs. reality 3.00
4 TKn,Death of Creed 3.00

CREEPS
Oct., 2001
1 (of 4) TMd 3.50
2 TMd,I:Gurgle,Chitter.......... 3.00
3 TMd,Genesys Corporation 3.00
4 TMd,through their eyes....... 3.00

IMAGE

Crimson–Cyberforce

Crimson #4 © Image

CRIMSON
Cliffhanger, May, 1998
1 BAu,HuR,F:Alex Elder, vampire
  'Dawn to Dusk' 5.00
1a variant AWa(c) 7.00
1b Chromium Edition 12.00
2 BAu,HuR,V:Jelly-Bats,
  'Unlife Story'. 3.00
2a variant AAd(c). 6.00
3 BAu,HuR,V:Rose,Payment
  in Blood 4.00
4 BAu,HuR,F:Red Hood,Children
  of Judas,pt.1 . . . . 3.50
5 BAu,HuR,A:Red Hood,Children
  of Judas,pt.2 . . . . 3.50
6 BAu,HuR,A:Red Hood,Children
  of Judas,pt.3 . . . . 3.50
7 BAu,HuR,Christmas day 3.00
fi Dynamic Forces exclusive 4.00

WildStorm/DC, 1999
8 thru 23 BAu,HuR. . . . . @2.50
24 BAu,HuR, final issue 3.50
Spec.#1 Scarlet X: Blood on the
  Moon, BAu,HuR,one-shot. . . . 4.00
Spec. Crimson Sourcebook #1 . . 2.95
TPB Crimson, rep.#1–#6 . . . . . . 13.00
TPB Heaven & Earth,rep#7–#12 . . 14.95
TPB Loyalty & Loss 12.95
TPB Earth Angel,rep.#13-#18 . . . . 14.95
TPB Redemption,160-pg. 14.95

CRIMSON PLAGUE
June, 2000
1 GP,64-pg. 3.00
2 GP,Sole Survivor 2.50
3 GP,Blood trail 2.50
4 GP,Plague hits home 2.50

CROW, THE
TMP, Feb., 1999
1 JMu,F:Eric Draven 3.00
1a variant TP cover (1:4) 3.00
2 JMu,hunt for killers 3.00
3 JMu,justice for killers 3.00
4 JMu,Line Between Devil's Teeth . . 3.00
5 JMu,Skin of an Angel,pt.1 . . . . . 3.00
6 JMu,Skin of an Angel,pt.2. . . . . 3.00
7 JMu,Touch of Evil,pt.1. . . . . 3.00
8 JMu,Touch of Evil,pt.2. . . . . 3.00
9 JMu,Wings and Black Feathers. . 3.00

TPB Vol. 1 Vengeance 10.95
TPB Vol. 2 Evil Beyond Reach . . . 10.95
Crow Mag.#1, 56-pg. rep. 4.95
Crow Mag.#2 . . . . 4.95
Crow Mag.#3 . . . . 4.95

CRUSH, THE
Motown Jan., 1996
1 Mini-series 3.00
2 Let Me Light Your Fire 3.00
3 Million Dollar Smile. 3.00
4 . . . . 3.00
5 The Hip Hop Slide 3.00

CRYPT
Extreme, 1995
1 A:Prophet. 2.50
1a variant cover. 2.50
2 A:Prophet. 2.50

[JIM LEE'S]
C-23
WildStorm, April, 1998
1 BCi,JMi,F:Corben Helix. 2.50
2 JMi,TC(c),V:Angelans. 2.50
3 JMi,TC(c),with game card. 2.50
4 JMi,Corbin, banished 2.50
5 JMi,RCo(c),Queen Mother 2.50
5a variant JLe(c) (1:4) 2.50
6 JMi,RCo(c),V:Hyper Shock
  Troopers 2.50
7 JMi,RCo(c),Hail to the Queen . . . 2.50
8 JMi,RCo(c),Long Live the King . . 2.50

CURSED
Image/Top Cow Sept. 2003
1 (of 4) It is Coming. 3.00
2 The Walking Dead 3.00

CURSE OF THE SPAWN
TMP, Sept., 1996
1 DT,DaM,F:Daniel Lianso 6.00
1a B&W variant 20.00
2 DT,DaM,Dark Future,pt.2:
  Blood Lust 5.00
3 DT,DaM,Dark Future,pt.3:
  Corpse Candles 5.00
4 DT,DaM 4.00
5 DT,DaM,Sam & Twitch search
  for Gretchen Culver 3.00
6 DT,DaM,Sam & Twitch pursue
  Suture 3.00
7 DT,DaM,Suture is captured. . . . 3.00
8 DT,DaM,Suture escapes police
  custody 3.00
9 DT,DaM,Angela's secret origin . . 5.00
10 DT,DaM,Angela, Spawn Slayer . . 3.50
11 DT,DaM,Angela's story, concl. . . 3.50
12 DT,DaM,Jessica Priest, movie
  photo(c) 3.50
13 DT,DaM 'Heart of Darkness'. . . . 3.50
14 DT,DaM,Jessica, concl. 3.50
15 DT,DaM,Tempt an Angel,pt.1 . . 3.50
16 DT,DaM,Tempt an Angel,pt.2 . . 3.50
17 DT,DaM. 3.50
18 DT,DaM,F:Tony Twist. 3.50
19 DT,Curse & Tony Twist. 3.50
20 DT,DaM,Monsters & Mythology . 3.50
21 DT,DaM,Zeus Must Die 3.50
22 DT,F:Ryan Hatchett 3.50
23 DT,TM,R:Overtkill. 3.50
24 DT,TM,Pandemic 3.50
25 DT,TM,'Heart of Hell' 2.25
26 DT,TM,V:The Crocodile 2.25
27 DT,TM,F:Marc Simmons 2.25
28 DT,TM,V:Suture 2.25

29 DT,TM,A:Jonathan Edward
  Custer 2.25
TPB Vol. 1 Sacrifice the Soul 9.95
TPB Vol. 2 Blood & Sutures 9.95
TPB Vol. 3 Shades of Gray. 9.95
TPB Vol. 4 Lost Values 9.95
TPB Vol. 5 Penumbra 9.95

CYBERFORCE
Top Cow, 1992–93
[Limited Series]
0 WS,O:Cyber Force 2.50
1 MS,I:Cyberforce,w/coupon#3 . . . 5.00
1a w/o coupon. 3.00
2 MS,V:C.O.P.S. 3.50
3 MS. 2.50
4 MS,V:C.O.P.S,BU:Codename
  Styke Force. 2.50
TPB Rep. mini-series 12.95

[Regular Series] 1993
1 EcS(s),MS,SW 2.50
1B Gold Foil Logo 6.00
2 EcS(s),MS,SW,Killer Instinct
  #2,A:Warblade 2.25
2B Silver Embossed Cover 6.00
3 EcS(s),MS,SW,Killer Instinct #4,
  A:WildC.A.T.S. 2.25
3B Gold Embossed Cover 6.00
4 EcS(s),MS,Ballistic 2.50
5 EcS(s),MS 2.50
6 EcS(s),MS,Ballistic's Past. 2.50
7 S.H.O.C.s. 2.50
8 . . . . 2.50
9 A:Huntsman 2.50
10 A:Huntsman 2.50
10a Alternate Cover 4.00
10b Silver Seal Oz-Con 500c 9.00
11 . . . . 2.50
12 T.I.M.M.I.E. goes wild. 2.50
13 EcS,MS,O:Cyberdata. 2.50
14 EcS,MSI,V:T.I.M.M.I.E. 2.50
15 New Cyberdata Threat. 2.50
16 O:Ripclaw 2.50
17 Regrouping 2.50
18 thru 24 . . . . @2.50
25 . . . . 3.95
26 KWo 2.50
27 F:Ash 2.50
27a variant JQ&JP(c) (1:4) 4.00

Top Cow, 1996
28 A:Gabriel 2.50
29 . . . . 2.50

Cyberforce #28 © Top Cow

Cyberforce–Darker / IMAGE / Comics Values Annual

30 ScL,'Devil's Reign' tie-in 2.50
31 The team in conflict 2.50
32 Cyblade leads rejuvenated team 2.50
33 KWo, Cheleene in midst of
  civil war 2.50
34 KWo,Royal Blood,pt.3 . . . . 2.50
35 BTn,Royal Blood, concl. 2.50
Ashcan 1 (San Diego) 4.00
Ashcan 1 (signed) 6.00
Sourcebook 1 . . . . 2.50
Sourcebook 2 I:W.Zero 2.50
Ann.#1 O:Velocity 2.50
Ann.#2 . . . . 2.95
TPB new art 12.95
TPB EcS,MS,SW,Assault with a
  Deadly Woman 9.95

CYBERFORCE/ CODENAME STRYKEFORCE: OPPOSING FORCES
Sept., 1995
1 V:Dangerous Threat 2.50
2 Team vs. Team 2.50

CYBERFORCE ORIGINS
Top Cow, 1995
1 O:Cyblade 2.50
1B Gold Seal 1000c 6.00
2 O:Stryker 2.50
3 O:Impact 2.50
4 Misery 3.00

CYBERFORCE UNIVERSE SOURCEBOOK
Top Cow, 1994–95
1 . . . . 2.50
2 MS,BTn 2.50

CYBERNARY
WildStorm, 1995–96
1 (of 5) mini-series 2.50
2 thru 5 . . . . @2.50

CYBERPUNX
Extreme, 1996
1 and 2 . . . . @3.00
3 RLe & Ching Lau,F:Drake 3.00

Damned #2 © Homage

CYBLADE/SHI
1995
1 The Battle for Independents 2.95

CY-GOR
TMP, July, 1999
1 RV,I:Fatima,Frankie & Zevon . . . 2.50
2 RV,Fire in the Mind,pt.2 . . . . 2.50
3 RV,Needles and Pins 2.50
4 RV, Exquisite Corpse 2.50
5 RV 2.50
6 RV, the Terraplane 2.50
7 RV,Young Doctor Acula 2.50

DAMNED
Homage, June, 1997
1 (of 4) StG, MZ & DRo 2.50
2 StG, MZ & DRo,F:Mick Thorne . . 2.50
3 StG, MZ & DRo 2.50
4 StG, MZ & DRo 2.50

DANGER GIRL
WildStorm/Cliffhanger 1998
1 JSC,AGo,'Dangerously Yours,'
  40-pg. 8.00
1a chromium edition, 40-pg. 55.00
1b Tour Edition 25.00
2 I:Johnny Barracuda,'Dangerous
  Liaisons' 5.00
3 in Switzerland 4.00
3a variant AH(c) 5.00
3b variant TC(c) 5.00
4 I:Major Maxim 3.00
5 JSC,AGo 2.50
5a variant JMd(c) 9.00

WildStorm/DC, 1999
6 JSC,SW 2.50
6a variant JMd(c) 5.00
6b variant HuR(c) 4.00
7 JSC,SW,concl.,48-pg. 6.00
TPB Dangerous Coll.,Vol.1 . . . . . . 5.95
TPB Dangerous Coll.,Vol.2,rep.2&3 5.95
J. Scott Campbell Danger Girl
  Sketchbook, 56-pg. 6.95

DARING ESCAPES
TMP, 1998
1 ANi,F:Harry Houdini 3.00
2 ANi,search for Mystical Heart . . . 2.50
3 A:Kimiel 2.50
4 conclusion 2.50

DARK ANGEL: PHOENIX RESURRECTION
May, 2000
1 by Kia Asamiya, color manga . . . 3.00
2 thru 4 . . . . @3.00
1a thru 3a variant(c) . . . . @3.00

DARKCHYLDE
See: Maximum, 1996
1 Image reoffer 5.00
1C flip-book-Glory/Angel,Angels in
  Hell,pt.1, San Diego Con 4.00
1D remastered, RLd(c) 6.00
2 Image reoffer 5.00
2a variant cover 3.00
2b remastered, with poster 2.50
3 Image reoffer 3.50
3a remastered, with poster 2.50

Image, 1997
4 RQu,Ariel & Kauldron's past 5.00
5 RQu,No one here gets out alive . 4.00
TPB Rep. #1–#5 . . . . 12.95

Darkchyld: Swimsuit Illustrated © Image/Homage

Homage, 1998
0 RQu,Ariel's back, Ariel's past . . . 2.50

DARKCHYLDE/GLORY
Extreme
1-shot, four variant covers, by
  RLd, RQu, JDy & PtL 2.95

DARKCHYLDE: THE DIARY
May, 1997
1-shot, RQu et al,diary excerpts . . 5.00

DARKCHYLDE: THE LEGACY
WildStorm, 1998
1 RQu,F:Ariel 2.50
2 RQu 2.50

WildStorm/DC, 1999
3 RQu,A:Silencer 2.50
4 RQu,Carnival of Fools 2.50
4a RQu,AAd(c), variant 2.50
Summer Swimsuit Spectacular #1. . 4.00
Spec.Dreams of the Darkchylde #0. 2.50
TPB Darkchylde 20.00

DARKCHYLDE/ WITCHBLADE
Top Cow, July, 2000
1 RQu,Nightmare City 2.50

DARK CROSSINGS
Top Cow, May, 2000
Spec. #1 Dark Cloud Rising 5.95
Spec. #2 Dark Cloud Overhead . . . 5.95

DARKER IMAGE
1993
1 BML,BCi(s),RLd,SK,JLe,I:Blood
  Wulf,Deathblow,Maxx 4.00
1a Gold logo(c) 8.00
1b White(c) 6.00
Ashcan 1 . . . . 4.00

CVA Page 530 — All comics prices listed are for *Near Mint* condition.

DARKMINDS
1998
1 PtL,cyberpunk,detective 8.00
2 Neon Dragon 5.00
2a variant cover. 2.50
3 PtL,A:Neon Dragons. 2.50
4 PtL,Paradox killer 2.50
5 PtL,Unlikely friends, enemies . . 2.95
6 PtL,Aurora Industries 2.95
7 PtL,V:Mamuro Hayabusa 3.00
8 Conclusion,1st story arc 2.50
fi PtL,Cyborg dreams 2.50
TPB Collection #1 rep. #1–#3 . . . . 7.95
TPB Collection #2 rep. #4–#6 . . . . 7.95
TPB Collection #3 rep. #7 & #8. . . . 5.95
TPB Vol. I, rep.#1–#8 . . . . 18.95

VOL. II Feb., 2000
1 JMd(c) one year later 2.50
1a variant PtL(c) 2.50
1b variant Omar Dogan(c) 2.50
2 Changing Faces 2.50
2a variant PtL(c) 2.50
2b variant Michael Turner(c) 2.50
2c variant(c) 2.50
3 PtL(c),F:Reiko Tetsunori 2.50
3a variant Omar Dogan(c) 2.50
3b variant JQ(c). 2.50
4 PtL,cyborg attack 2.50
5 PtL,The Prize 2.50
6 PtL,9mm Answers. 2.50
7 PtL,The Hunger 2.50
8 PtL,Born Again 2.50
9 PtL,A Million and One 2.50
10 PtL,concl. 2.50
#0 The Bullet 2.50
#0a variant(c) 2.50
TPB Vol.1,Paradox, rep. 19.95
TPB Coming of Age 15.00

DARKNESS
Top Cow, Nov., 2002
1 PJe,DK. 3.00
1a holofoil(c) 5.95
2 DK 3.00
2 Megacon edition . . . .
3 DK 3.00
4 Under Cover of Darkness 3.00
5 You Lose Some 3.00
6 As the World Turns 3.00
1-shot Wanted Dead 3.00

DARKMINDS: MACROPOLIS
Jan., 2002
1 (of 8) PtL 2.95
1a variant(c) 2.95
2 F:Tiny 2.95
2a variant PtL(c) 2.95

DARKNESS, THE
Top Cow, 1996
0 Preview edition,B&W 15.00
fi 15.00
fi variant cover. 25.00
1/2 rep.+new story (2001),MS. . . . 2.95
1 GEn,MS,Coming of Age 9.00
1a Dark cover 9.00
1b Platinum cover 20.00
2 GEn,MS 8.00
3 GEn,MS,Jackie pursued by
 many foes 6.00
4 GEn,MS,Jackie explores
 Darkness power 6.00
5 GEn,MS,New York gangs on
 verge of all-out war 5.00
6 GEn,MS,F:JackieEstacado,concl. 4.00
7 MS 4.00

Darkness #27 © Top Cow

7a variant(c) 7.00
8 JBz,retribution 3.00
8a MS(c)(1:4) 5.00
9 Family Ties,pt.2,x-over 5.00
10 Family Ties,pt.3,x-over 6.00
11 GEn,MS,Hearts of Darkness . . 3.50
11a Chromium(c) 20.00
11b variant(c). 5.00
12 GEn,Hearts of Darkness 3.00
13 GEn,Hearts of Darkness 3.00
14 GEn,JBz,Hearts of Darkness . . 3.00
15 JBz,Spear of Destiny,pt.1 . . . . . 3.00
16 JBz,Spear of Destiny,pt.2 . . . . . 3.00
17 JBz,Spear of Destiny,pt.3 . . . . . 3.00
18 JBz,aftermath 3.00
19 JBz,No Mercy,pt.1 . . . . 2.50
20 JBz,No Mercy,pt.2 . . . . 2.50
21 JBz,Wynnwood 2.50
22 JBz,Where is Jenny? 2.50
23 JBz,SLo,new characters 2.50
24 JBz,SLo,road trip to Vegas. . . . 2.50
25 JBz,SLo,48-pg. 3.50
26 JBz,SLo,A:Joey Scarpaggio . . . 2.50
27 SLo,FBI continues assault 2.50
28 Darkness/Witchblade,pt.4,x-over 2.50
29 SLo,High Noon,pt.1 . . . . 2.50
30 SLo,High Noon,pt.2 . . . . 2.50
31 SLo,High Noon,pt.3 . . . . 2.50
32 SLo,Dark Days Ahead 2.50
33 SLo,Capris Castagliano,pt.1 . . . 2.50
34 SLo,Capris Castagliano,pt.2 . . . 2.50
35 SLo,tour of his life 2.50
36 SLo,Ripclaw,pt.3 . . . . 2.50
37 SLo,F:Robert Bearclaw 2.50
38 SLo,V:Conquistator 2.50
39 SLo,Jackie & Capris combine . . 2.50
40 DK,Darkness falls? 2.50
40a variant MS(c). 2.50
various foil (c) . . . . @9.00
Coll.Ed.#1,rep. #1–#2. . . . . 4.95
Coll.Ed.#2,rep. #3–#4, 56-pg. 4.95
Coll.Ed.#3,rep. #5–#6, 56-pg. 4.95
Coll.Ed.#3, with slipcase. 10.00
Coll.Ed.#4,rep. #7–#8 . . . . 4.95
Slipcase and all 3 GNs 25.00
Signed Slipcase and all 3 GNs . . 50.00
Coll.Ed.#1,deluxe,rep.#1–#6 . . . . 14.95
Coll.Ed.#5,rep.#11–#12 . . . . 5.95
Coll.Ed.#6,rep.#13–#14 . . . . 5.95
Spec. Infinity, SLo. 3.50
Darkness/Witchblade,pt.3 x-over . . 3.95
Spec.#1, Dark Ages 4.95
TPB Vol.1 Spear of Destiny 12.95
TPB Vol.2 Heart of Darkness . . . 14.95

DARKNESS, THE/BATMAN
Top Cow, April, 1999
Spec. SLo,MS, x-over. 6.00

DARK REALM
Oct., 2000
1 by Taeson Chang 3.00
2 S.F.P.D. in chaos 3.00
3 flip-book 3.00
4 Prophecy is fulfilled. 3.00

DART
1996
1 thru 3 Jozef Szekeres . . . . @3.00

DAVID AND GOLIATH
Sept. 2003
1 . . . . 2.95

DAWN
March, 2002
TPB Return of the Goddess 12.95
Spec. Convention Sketchbook 3.00
Spec. 2003 Convention Sketchbook 2.95

DAWN: THREE TIERS
June 2003
1 thru 3 JLi . . . . @2.95

DEADLANDS
July, 1999
GN 1-shot role-play tie-in 6.95

DEADLY DUO, THE
Highbrow, 1994–95
1 A:Kill-Cat 2.50
2 A:Pitt, O:Kid Avenger 2.50
3 A:Roman, O:Kill-Cat 2.50
[Second Series] 1995
1 A:Spawn. 2.50
2 A:Savage Dragon 2.50
3 A:Grunge, Gen13 . . . . 2.50
4 Movie Mayhem 2.50

DEATHBLOW
WildStorm, 1993–96
1 JLe,MN,I:Cybernary 3.00
2 JLe,BU:Cybernary 2.50
3 JLe(a&s),BU:Cybernary 3.00
4 JLe(s),TSe,BU:Cybernary 2.50
5 JLe(s),TSe,BU:Cybernary 2.50
5a different cover. 5.00
6 Black Angel 2.25
7 . . . . 2.25
8 Black Angel 2.25
9 The Four Horsemen 2.25
10 Michael Cray, Sister Mary 2.25
11 A:Four Horsemen. 2.25
12 Final Battle 2.50
13 New Story Arc 2.50
14 A:Johnny Savoy. 2.50
15 F:Michael Cray 2.50
16 TVs,BWS(c),WildStorm
 Rising,pt.6,w/2 cards 2.50
16a Newsstand ed. 2.25
17 V:Gammorran Hunter Killers . . 2.50
18 F:Cybernary. 2.50
19 F:Cybernary. 2.50
20 A:Gen 13. . . . . 2.50
21 Brothers in Arms,pt.2,A:Gen13. . 3.50
22 Brothers in Arms,pt.3. . . . . 2.50
23 Brothers in Arms,pt.4. . . . . 2.50
24 Brothers in Arms,pt.5 . . . . 3.00

All comics prices listed are for *Near Mint* condition.

Deathblow–Divine Right | IMAGE | Comics Values Annual

Deathblow #29
© WildStorm

25 Brothers in Arms,pt.6 . . . . 2.50
26 Fire From Heaven prelude 2.50
27 Fire From Heaven,pt.8 . . . . 3.00
28 Fire From Heaven,finale,pt.3 . . . 2.50
29 last issue 2.50
Ashcan 1 . . . . 4.00
TPB Dark Angel Saga,rep.,216-pg. 29.95
TPB Sinners and Saints, rep. 19.95

DEATHBLOW/WOLVERINE
WildStorm, Sept., 1996
1 RiB, AWs,x-over, set in San
   Francisco's Chinatown 2.50
2 RiB, AWs,concl. 2.50
TPB rep. series 8.95

DEATHMATE X-OVER
See: Acclaim/Valiant

DECEPTION, THE
(B&W) Flypaper, Jan., 1999
1 (of 3) F:Jordan Risk, magician . . 3.00
2 Framed for murder 3.00
3 V:South American Drug Cartel . . 3.00

DEFCON 4
WildStorm, 1996
1 mini-series 2.50
2 thru 4 . . . . @2.50

DEFIANCE
Feb., 2002
1 The Messenger,pt.1 . . . . 3.00
2 thru 4 The Messenger,pt.2–pt.4 @3.00
5 thru 8 The Scabbard,pt.1–pt.4 . @3.00

DEITY
May, 1999
Coll.Ed. Vol. 1. . . . . 9.95
Coll.Ed. Vol. 2. . . . . 9.95

DEITY: REVELATIONS
June, 1999
1 F:Jamie 3.00
2 F:Joe Tripoli 3.00
3 A legend reborn 3.00
3a variant cover (1:10). 3.00

DEMONSLAYER
Nov., 1999
1 MMy. 3.00
2 Jaclyn begins her quest 3.00
3 MMy, Michael & the Demon 3.00
Shadow Edition,pt.1 B&W. 4.95
VOL II
1 MMy,Into Hell,pt.1. . . . . 3.00
1a variant(c) (1:4) 3.00
2 MMy 3.00
3 MMy, enter Ebon 3.00

DERRING RISK
June, 1999
1 Fantasy Adventure 2.50
1a AWa variant(c) 2.50

DESPERADOS
Homage, Sept., 1997
1 by JMi & John Cassaday 7.00
2 V:Leander Peik. 3.00
2a 2nd printing 2.50
3 V:Leander Peik. 3.00
4 V:Leander Peik, concl. 3.00
5 V:Gideon Brood,pt.1. . . . . 3.00
TPB A Moment's Sunlight,rep.
   #1–#5. . . . . 16.95

DESPERATE TIMES
(B&W) June, 1998
1 by Chris Eliopoulos. 3.00
2 Strip joint 3.00
3 EL(c) 3.00
4 Christmas special 3.00
5 EL(c), sideways 3.00
6 . . . . 3.00
TPB 12.95

DETECTIVES INC.
March, 1999
TPB Vol. 1 . . . . 14.95
TPB Vol. 2 A Terror of Dying 19.95

DEVASTATOR
(B&W) April, 1998
1 JHI and Greg Horn 3.00
2 book 1,pt.2 . . . . 3.00
3 concl. to book 1 . . . . 3.00

DEVIL'S DUE STUDIOS
March 2003
1-shot 2003 Preview 1.00

DISCIPLES, THE
April, 2001
1 The new magic 3.00
2 Recruit Her or Kill Her 3.00
3 Viva Las Vegas 3.00
4 The Apples of Sodom 3.00

A DISTANT SOIL
(B&W) Highbrow, Aug., 1993
Prev: Aria Comics
15 CDo,Ascension,pt.3 . . . . 3.00
16 CDo,A:Bast, Avatar 3.00
17 CDo,D'mer & Bast conflict 3.00
18 CDo,'Ascension' finale 3.00
19 CDo,'Spires of Heaven,'pt.1 . . . 3.00
20 CDo,Lord Merai's suicide
   weakens Hierachy 3.00
21 CDo,'Exile for D'mer?' 3.00
22 CDo,Avatar's secrets,32-pg. . . 3.00
23 CDo,three stories. 3.00
24 CDo,malfunctioning spacesuit . . 3.00
25 CDo,NGa,Troll Bridge,48-pg. . . 4.00
26 CDo,B.U.:Red-Cloak by
   E.Kushner 3.00
27 CDo,B.U.:Liaden tale 3.00
28 CDo,B.U.:Liaden tale, concl. . . 3.00
29 CDo,B.U.:Delia Sherman story . . 3.00
30 . . . . 4.00
31 Sometimes the good guys lose . 4.00
32 F:Prince D'mer 4.00
33 Rebellion's final stand 4.00
34 CDo, 64-pg. 5.00
35 CDo, 32-pg. 4.00
36 CDo. 3.95
Images of A Distant Soil 3.00
Images of A Distant Soil, signed . . 34.95
GN The Gathering, rep.#1–#11 . . 18.95
GN The Gathering, 2nd printing . . 19.95
TPB The Ascendant, rep.#13–#24 18.95
TPB The Gathering. 19.95
TPB Vol.3, The Aria 16.95

DIVINE RIGHT:
THE ADVENTURES OF
MAX FARADAY
WildStorm, Sept., 1997
1 JLe,SW,Blaze of Glory 7.00
1a variant cover 7.50
1b variant, signed 29.95
1c Voyager pollybaged pack 6.00
1d Spanish edition 5.00
2 JLe,SW,Disco Inferno 5.00
2a variant(c) 5.00
3 JLe,SW,F:Christie Blaze,Enemies
   of the State 4.00
4 JLe,SW,F:Lynch,The Love
   Connection. 2.50
4a variant(c) 4.00
5 JLe,SW,V:Dominique Faust,Party
   Crashers 3.00
6 JLe,SW,Truth or Consequences,
   Susanna Chaste located. 3.00
7 JLe,SW,Into the Hollow Realm . . 3.00
8 JLe,SW,Tobru,V:Acheron 3.00
8a variant SW(c) 3.00
Preview edition, JLe(c) (1997) . . . 5.00
Coll.Ed.#1 . . . . 5.95
Coll.Ed.#2 . . . . 5.95
WildStorm/DC, 1999
9 JLe,SWi,Final Stand in
   Hollow Realm 3.00

*Divine Right: The Adventures of
Max Faraday #1 © WildStorm*

CVA Page 532 All comics prices listed are for *Near Mint* condition.

IMAGE

10 JLe,SWi	3.00
11 JLe,SWi,Divine Intervention	3.00
12 JLe,SWi,Divine Intervention	3.00
Coll.Ed.#3, rep.#5 & #6.	6.00
TPB Book 1 JLe (2002)	17.95
TPB Book 2 JLe (2002)	17.95

DOLLZ
April, 2001

1 RGr,TSg	3.00
1a-1c variant(c)s	3.00
2 RGr	3.00
3 RGr	3.00

DOMINION
Jan. 2003

1 KG	2.95
2 thru 5 KG	@2.95

DOOM'S IV
Extreme, 1994

1 RL(s),MPa, I:Doom's IV	2.50
1a variant(c),left side of art	2.50
1b variant(c),right side of art	2.50
2 Rld(s),MPa,MECH-MAX	2.50
2a variant (c)	2.50
3 Dr. Lychee, Brick	2.50
4 Dr. Lychee, Syber-idol	2.50
Sourcebook	2.50

DOUBLE IMAGE
Feb., 2001

1 The Bod, flip-book, Codeflesh	3.00
2 The Bod/Codeflesh	3.00
3 The Bod/Codeflesh	3.00
4 The Bod/Codeflesh	3.00
5 Trust in Me/Codeflesh	3.00

DRACULA VS. ZORRO
(B&W) Sept., 1998

1 DMG,RM	3.00
2 DMG,RM, conclusion	3.00

DRAGON, THE
March, 1995

1 rep. of Savage Dragon	2.25
2 thru 5 rep. of Savage Dragon	@2.25

THE DRAGON: BLOOD AND GUTS
Highbrow, 1995

1 I:Grip	2.50
2 JPn,KIS	2.50
3 JPn,KIS	2.50
TPB series rep.	7.95

DUNCAN'S KINGDOM
(B&W) Oct., 1999

1 by Gene Yang & Derek Kirk	3.00
2	3.00

DUSTY STAR
(B&W) April, 1997

0 sci-fi,western,adventure	3.00
1 thru 3	@3.00

DV8
WildStorm, 1996

1 WEl(s),HuR,'Lust for Life'	4.00
1a JLe(c)	5.00
1b Kevin Nowlan(c)	4.00

DV81 © WildStorm

2 WEl(s),HuR,Gen-active serial killers,'Some Weird Sin'	3.00
3 WEl(s), Neighborhood Threat	3.00
4 WEl(s),HuR,Miss Drugstore	3.00
5 Ivana sends DV8 to Japan	2.50
6 idle hands are the devil's tools	2.50
7 WEl(s),'Shades'	2.50
8 HuR,Sublime, Evo & Frostbite abandoned,'Three'	2.50
9 MHs,'Evolution'	2.50
10 MHs,'In Service to Nothing'	2.50
11 MHs,F:Copycat,'Facets'	2.50
12 MHs,F:Freestyle,V:Sen.Killory	2.50
13 MHs,'The Sad Tales of Senator Killory'	2.50
14 MHs,TR,New Horizon,TR(c),'Barely Legal'	5.00
14a TC(c)	2.50
14b Voyager bagged pack	3.50
15 MHs,F:Ivana Baiul,'Settling Accounts'	2.50
16 MHs,V:Dominique Faust 'Intersection'	2.50
17 MHs,Gen-Passive	2.50
18 MHs,Team 7,A:Grifter,'Same as It Ever Was'	2.50
19 MHs,First Mision,pt.1,'Larger Concerns'	2.50
20 MHs,First Mision,pt.2,'Lounging in the Ammo Dump'	2.50
21 MHs,First Mision,pt.3,V:Anthrax	2.50
22 MHs,V:Copycat,'Choices'	2.50
22a variant(c) JMd(1:4)	3.00
23 MHs,F:Threshold,'Gone to Ground'	2.50
24 MHs,F:Sublime,'Slip Stream,' prologue	2.50
25 MHs,Slipstream,pt.1	2.50
DV8 Rave,preview (1996)	3.00
Ann.#1 'Head Trips' (1998)	3.00

WildStorm/DC, 1999

26 MHs,TVs	2.50
27 MHs,TVs,V:Gen-Actives	2.50
28 MHs,TVs,F:Evo	2.50
29 MHs,TVs	2.50
30 MHs,TVs,Things Fall Apart,pt.1	2.50
31 MHs,TVs,Things Fall Apart,pt.2	2.50
32 MHs,TVs,Things Fall Apart,pt.3	2.50
Ann.'99 Slipstream	3.50
#0 40-pg.	3.00
TPB Neighborhood Threat (2002)	14.95

Divine Right–E.V.E.

DV8 VS. BLACK OPS
WildStorm, Oct., 1997

1 Techromis Design,pt.1	3.00
2 Techromis Design,pt.2	3.00
3 Techromis Design,pt.3	3.00

ECHO
March, 2000

1 A Broken World	2.50
1a variant(c)	2.50
2 Sacrifices	2.50
2a variant PtL(c)	2.50
3 Deadly new echo	2.50
3a variant PtL(c)	2.50
4 PtL,Desperate Times	2.50
5 PtL,Welcoming Party	2.50
6 Conspiracy Theory	2.50
6a variant PtL(c)	2.50
7 Anarchy,pt.1	2.50
8 A Life Worth Living	2.95
#0 Thick as Thieves	2.50
#0a variant(c)	2.50
#1 Holochrome edition	6.95

ELECTROPOLIS
May, 2001

1 DMt, Infernal Machine,pt.1	3.00
2 DMt, Infernal Machine,pt.2	3.00
3 DMt, Heavy Meddle	3.00
4 DMt, Infernal Machine,pt.4	3.00

ELEKTRA/CYBLADE
Top Cow/Marvel, 1997

1-shot 'Devil's Reign,'pt.7 (of 8) x-over	3.00

EMPIRE
May, 2000

1 MWa,BKi,F:Golgoth	5.00
2 MWa,BKi,F:Xanna	4.00
3 MWa,BKi,F:Lohkyn	4.00
4 MWa,BKi,Nature vs. nurture	4.00

ESPERS
April, 1997
(B&W) Vol. 3

1 JHl,A:Brian Marx,V:Architects	3.00
1a 2nd printing	3.00
2 JHl	3.00
3 JHl,Black Magic	3.00
4 JHl,Black Magic, concl.	3.00
5 JHl,two stories	3.00
6 JHl,F:Simon Ashley,Alan Black	3.00
7 JHl,Feel the Rapture.	3.00
8 JHl, trip to Hong Kong	3.00
9 JHl,V:Architects	3.00
TPB Undertow, rep.Halloween Comics series.	14.95
TPB Black Magic, rep.Vol.3,#1–4	14.95
TPB The Storm, rep.	15.95
TPB Interface, rep.2nd series	15.95

E.V.E. PROTOMECHA
Top Cow, Feb., 2000

1	3.00
1a variant JMd(c)	3.00
1b variant David Finch(c)	3.00
2 Gunner Unleashed	3.00
2a variant Michael Turner(c)	3.00
2b variant SPa(c)	3.00
3 thru 6	@3.00
TPB Vol.1 Sins of the Daughter	17.95

All comics prices listed are for *Near Mint* condition.

IMAGE

[ADVENTURES OF] EVIL AND MALICE
June, 1999
1 by Jimmie Robinson 3.50
2 F:Max 2000 . . . . 3.50
3 V:Cold Heart & Le'Chef 3.50
4 final showdown 3.50
TPB F:Evelyn & Malinda 12.95

EVO
Top Cow
1 MS,Endgame,pt.3 x-over 3.00

Exposure #2a © Image

EXPOSURE
July, 1999
1 F:Shawna & Lisa 2.50
2 Mirrors to the Soul 2.50
2a alternate photo(c) (1:2) 2.50
3 . . . . 2.50
3a alternate photo(c) (1:2) 2.50
4 Spark-Spangled See-Through Girl 2.50
4a alternate photo(c) (1:2) 2.50
Prelude 16-pg. 6.95
Prelude holo-foil 14.95

EXTREME ANTHOLOGY
1 . . . . 2.50

EXTREME CHRISTMAS SPECIAL
Various artists, new work 2.95

EXTREME DESTROYER
Extreme, 1996
1 prologue, x-over,bagged with card 2.50
2 epilogue, x-over 2.50

EXTREME HERO
1 . . . . 2.95

EXTREME PREJUDICE
Extreme, Nov., 1994
0 Prelude to X-over 3.00

EXTREME SACRIFICE
Extreme, Jan., 1995
Prelude,x-over,pt.1, A:Everyone with trading card 2.50
Epiloque, x-over,pt.8, conclusion with trading card 2.50
TPB Rep. whole x-over series 16.95

EXTREME 3000
Prelude 2.50

EXTREME TOUR BOOK
Tour Book 1992 . . . . 3.00
Tour Book 1994 . . . . 25.00

EXTREMELY YOUNGBLOOD
Extreme, Sept 1997
1 TBm&MBm(s) 3.50

EXTREME ZERO
0 RLd,CYp,ATi(i),I:Cybrid, Law & Order, Risk, Code 9, Lancers, Black Flag 3.00
0a Variant cover 3.00

FACTION PARADOX
Aug. 2003
1 War in Heaven 2.95
2 . . . . 2.95

FALLING MAN
(B&W) Dec., 1997
1 (of 3) BMC,PhH 3.00
2 Floyd vs. Duncan 3.00
3 . . . . 3.00

FATHOM
Top Cow, 1998
1 by Michael Turner,F:Aspen 7.00
2 war beneath the waves 3.50
3 Life changed forever 3.50
4 Connection to water 3.00
5 Aspen's connection to water . . . 3.00
6 Admiral's plans revealed 3.00
7 Finale,pt.1 . . . . 3.00
8 Finale,pt.2 . . . . 3.00
9 Finale, conclusion, end 3.00

Fathom #3 © Top Cow

10 Fathom returns 3.00
11 Fathom returns,pt.2 . . . . 3.00
12 Tomb Raider & Witchblade x-over,pt.1 . . . . 3.00
12a variant(c) 5.00
13 x-over,pt.2 . . . . 3.00
13a variant(c) 5.00
14 Aspen & Vana, concl. 3.00
14a variant(c) 5.00
15 Killian's Blue Sun 2.50
15a variant(c) 5.00
16 Admiral's subterfuge discovered . 2.50
#0 rep. new Mike Turner(c) 2.50
1/2 . . . . 3.00
Spec. Swimsuit ed. 2.95
Fathom 2000 swimsuit calendar . . . 2.95
Fathom 2000 smimsuit Spec. 2.95
TPB Coll.Ed.#1, rep.#1 . . . . 5.95
TPB Coll.Ed.#2, rep.#2–#3 . . . . . . 5.95
TPB Coll.Ed.#3, rep.#4–#5 . . . . . . 5.95
TPB Coll.Ed.#4, rep.#6–#7 . . . . . . 5.95
TPB Coll.Ed.#5, rep.#8–#9 . . . . . . 5.95
TPB Vol. 1, rep. #1–#9 . . . . 24.95

FATHOM: KILLIAN'S TIDE
Top Cow, March, 2001
1 (of 4) 5.00
1a variant(c) 4.00
2 thru 4 . . . . @3.00

FEAR EFFECT
Top Cow, March, 2000
1-shot MHw, video game tie-in . . . 5.00

FEAR EFFECT SPECIAL: RETRO HELIX
Top Cow, March, 2001
1 . . . . 3.00

FEATHER
Aug. 2003
1 (of 6) 2.95
2 . . . . 2.95

FELON
Top Cow, Oct., 2001
1 (of 4) 3.00
2 . . . . 3.00
3 concl. 3.00
4 I:Elizabeth Freeh 3.00

FUSED!
March, 2002
1 Canned Heat,pt.1 (of 4) 3.00
1a variant(c) 3.00
2 Canned Heat,pt.2 . . . . 3.00
3 Canned Heat,pt.3 . . . . 3.00
4 Canned Heat,pt.4 . . . . 3.00

F5
April, 2000
1 TnD,48-pg. 2.95
2 TnD,life or death 2.50
3 TnD 2.50
4 TnD, betrayed 2.50
Preview Book, TnD,24-pg. 2.50

FIRE
(B&W) Dec., 1998
TPB International intelligence 9.95
TPB The Definitive Collection 9.95

CVA Page 534 — All comics prices listed are for *Near Mint* condition.

IMAGE

FIREBREATHER
Jan 2003
1 (of 4) PhH(s) 2.95
2 thru 4 PhH(s) . . . . @2.95

FIRE FROM HEAVEN
WildStorm, 1996
1 x-over,Chapter 1 . . . . 3.50
2 x-over,Finale 2 . . . . 2.50

FIRSTMAN
April, 1997
1 ASm,LukeHenry becomesApollo . 2.50

FOOT SOLDIERS, THE
(B&W) Sept., 1997
Prev.: Dark Horse
1 by Jim Krueger, Graveyard of
   Forgotten Heroes 3.00
2 Tragedy o/t Travesty Tapestry . . . 3.00
3 Arch enemies,pt.3 . . . . 3.00
4 'It's a Wicked World Afterall' 3.00
5 Loose Ends 2.95

FOREVER AMBER
(B&W) July, 1999
1 by Don Hudson 2.95
1a variant cover (1:2) 2.95
2 Lady fights back 2.95
3 Amber sent to jail 2.25
4 Amber's revenge, concl. 2.95

40 OZ COLLECTED
Nov. 2003
TPB b&w 9.95

FRANKENSTEIN MOBSTER
Oct. 2003
0 . . . . 2.95
0a variant (c) 2.95

FREAK FORCE
Highbrow, 1993–95
1 EL(s),KG 3.00
2 EL(s),KG 3.00
3 EL(s),KG 3.00
4 EL(s),KG,A:Vanguard 3.00
5 EL(s),KG 3.00
6 EL(s),KG 3.00
7 EL(s),KG 3.00
8 EL(s),space ants 3.00
9 EL(s),Cyberforce 3.00
10 EL(s),Savage Dragon 3.00
11 EL(s),Invasion,pt.1 . . . . 3.00
12 EL(s),Invasion,pt.2 . . . . 3.00
13 EL(s),Invasion,pt.3 . . . . 3.00
14 EL(s),Team Defeated 3.00
15 EL(s),F:Barbaric 3.00
16 KG,EL(s),V:Chelsea Nirvana . . . 3.00
17 EL,KG,major plots converge . . . 3.00
18 Final Issue 3.00
TPB 448-pg 29.95

[Series Two] March, 1997
1 EL,Star joins team,V:The
   Frightening Force 3.00
2 EL,Dart quits team 3.00
3 EL,'Lo there shall come..an
   ending' 3.00

FRIENDS OF MAXX
I Before E, April, 1996
1 thru 3 WML&SK . . . . @3.00

FUSED!
March, 2002
1 Canned Heat,pt.1 (of 4) 3.00
1a variant(c) 3.00
2 thru 4 Canned Heat,pt.2–pt.4 . @3.00

GALAXY-SIZE ASTOUNDING SPACE THIRLLS
March, 2001
1 Galaxy Size Showdown, 48-pg.
   flip-book 4.95

GAMORRA SWIMSUIT SPECIAL
WildStorm, 1996
Spec.#1 . . . . 2.50

GAZILLION
Nov., 1998
1 HSm, Mars vs. Xof 2.50
1a variant cover (1:4) 2.50

GEAR STATION, THE
March, 2000
1 DaF,Dominion of Souls 6.00
1a variant AxR(c) 2.50
1b variant PtL(c) 2.50
1c variant Michael Turner(c) 2.50
2 DaF,23rd Gear 2.50
2a variant AAd(c) 2.50
3 DaF,Who is Fable 2.50
4 DaF,first showdown 2.50
5 DaF,Gear Station Prime 2.50
6 DaF 2.50

GEEKSVILLE
(B&W) March, 2000
#0 by R.Koslowski & G.Sassaman . 3.00
1 Breaking into the Biz,pt.1 . . . . . . 3.00
2 Breaking into the Biz,pt.2 . . . . . . 3.00
3 Back to the Con 3.00
4 Breaking into the Biz. 3.00
5 Dark Sky 3.00
6 End of 3 Geeks 3.00

GEMINAR
B&W June, 2000
1 . . . . 5.00
2 F:Captain Champion 5.00

GEN 13
WildStorm, 1994
0 Individual Hero Stories 4.00
1 JLe(s),BCi(s),I:Fairchild,Grunge,
   Freefall,Burnout 20.00
1a 2nd printing 4.00
2 JLe(s),BCi(s) 16.00
3 JLe(s),BCi(s),A:Pitt,'Payback' . . 10.00
4 JLe(s),BCi(s),'Free for All' 8.00
5 Final issue 5.00
5a WP variant cover 10.00
TPB Gen13 Coll.Ed. 12.95

[Regular Series] 1995
1a BCi(s),V:Mercenaries 5.00
1b Common Cover 2 . . . . 5.00
1c Heavy Metal Gen 8.00

Gen13 #30 © WildStorm

1d Pulp Fiction Parody 10.00
1e Gen 13 Bunch 8.00
1f Lin-Gen-re 10.00
1g Lil Gen 13 . . . . 8.00
1h Friendly Neighbor Grunge 8.00
1i Gen 13 Madison Ave 10.00
1j Gen-Et Jackson 8.00
1k Gen Dress Up cover 8.00
1l Verti-Gen 8.00
1m Do It Yourself Cover 8.00
2 BCi,BWS(c),WildStorm Rising,
   pt.4, w/2 cards 3.00
2a newsstand ed. 2.25
3 BCi,'Magical Mystery Tour' 3.00
4 BCi,'Tourist Trap' 3.00
5 BCi,I:New Member,Family Feud . 3.00
6 BCi,JLe,I:The Deviants,
   'Roman Holiday' 3.00
7 BCi,JLe,European Vacation,pt.2
   'Veni, Vidi, Vici' 3.00
8 BCi,'Bewitched,Bothered
   and Bewildered' 3.00
9 . . . . 3.00
10 Fire From Heaven,pt.3 . . . . 3.00
11 Fire From Heaven,pt.9 . . . . 3.00
12 F:Caitlin,her dad 3.00
13 A, B & C, each . . . . @3.00
14 'Higher Learning' 2.50
15 Fraternity and Sorority rush . . . 2.50
16 . . . . 2.50
17 BCi,JSC,AGo,battle royale in
   Tower of Luv,'Toy Soldiers' 2.50
18 BCi,JSC,AGo,V:Keepers,
   'Hello & Good-Byes' 2.50
19 BCi,JSC,AGo,Lynch & kids flee
   to Antarctica,'Bon Voyage' 2.50
20 BCi,JSC,AGo,'To Boldly Go' . . . 2.50
21 BCi,JSC,AGo,V:D'Rahn,'Lost
   in Space' 2.50
22 BCi,civil war,'Homecoming' . . . 2.50
23 BCi,21st century 2.50
24 BCi,V:D'Rahn,'Judgment Day' . . 2.50
25 BCi,Homecoming,JsC(c) 3.50
25a TC(c),'Where Angels Fear
   to Tread' 3.50
25b Voyager bagged pack 3.50
26 JAr,GFr,CaS,When Worlds
   Collide 2.50
27 JAr,GFr,CaS,'Search & Seizure' . 2.50
28 JAr,GFr,CaS, 'Remote Control' . . 2.50
29 JAr,GFr,CaS,I:Tindalos,
   'A Firm Grip on Reality' 2.50
30 JAr,GFr,CaS,'Stranger Than
   Fiction' 2.50

Gen 13–G.I. Joe

31 JAr,GFr,CaS,Roxy's Big Score,
'Paradigm Shift' 2.50
32 JAr,GFr,CaS,'Red Skies at
Morning' 2.50
33 JAr,GFr,CaS,aftermaths, 'Burning
the Candle at Both Ends',
with 8-page Planetary #0 . . . . . 4.00
34 JAr,GFr,CaS,AAd,A:Roxy
& Sarah,'Overture' 2.50
35 JAr,GFr,CaS,John Lynch resigns,
'But You Can't Hide' 2.50
36 JAr,GFr,CaS,F:John Lynch,
'That Was Then' 2.50
College Yearbook 1997, Superheroes
at Large 2.50
Ann. #1 WEI,SDi'London'sBrilliant' . 3.00
1-Shot Gen13:Unreal World (1996). 3.00
Gen13 3-D Special (1997) 5.00
3-D Spec. #1, (1997) 5.00
3-D Spec. #1, variant cover 5.00
3-D Spec. #1, (1998) 5.00
TPB rep.1–#5 of original mini-
series, 3rd printing 12.95
TPB Lost in Paradise, rep. #3–#5 . . 6.95
TPB EuropeanVacation,rep.#6–#7 . 6.95
TPB rep. #13 A, B & C 6.95
TPB Ordinary Heroes 12.95
TPB WildStorm Archives, rep. mini-
series, #0–#13, covers, etc. . . 13.00

WildStorm/DC, 1999

37 JAr,GFr,CaS,Reaper 2.50
38 JAr,GFr,CaS,BU:Grunge 2.50
38a variant cover 2.50
39 JAr,GFr,CaS,Genocide. 2.50
40 JAr,GFr,CaS,V:Reaper. 2.50
41 JAr,GFr,CaS 2.50
42 JoC(s),KM,pro wrestlers. 2.50
43 AWa(s&c),F:Fairchild 2.50
44 AWa(s&c),A:Mr.Magestic 2.50
45 SLo,EBe,JSb,fashion show 2.50
46 SLo,EBe,JSb,MightyJoeGrunge . 2.50
47 SLo,EBe,JSb. 2.50
48 SLo,EBe,JSb. 2.50
49 SLo,EBe,JSb. 2.50
50 SLo,EBe,JSb,48-pg. 4.00
50a variant JLe,SW(c) (1:4) 4.00
51 SLo,breather 2.50
52 SLo,F:Caitlin Fairchild 2.50
53 F:all Villains issue 2.50
54 SLo,EBe,SWi,F:Fairchild 2.50
55 EBe,Return to Reed 9,pt.2 . . . . 2.50
56 EBe,Fairchild,pt.3 . . . . 2.50
57 BRa,EBe,Tokyo in danger 2.50
58 BRa,EBe,mini-monster
massacre 2.50
59 BRa,EBe,V:Gaijin13. . . . . 2.50
60 AWa,Behind the Power 2.50
61 AWa,Goin' back to Cali 2.50
62 AWa,fast food 2.50
63 AWa,EBe,sailboat outing 2.50
64 AWa,Superhuman Like You,pt.1 . 2.50
65 AWa,Superhuman Like You,pt.2 . 2.50
66 AWa,8 guest artists 2.50
67 AWa,EBe,ColdAir on MyBehind . 2.50
68 AWa,Slave to Love,pt.1 . . . . . . 2.50
69 AWa,Slave to Love,pt.2 . . . . . . 2.50
70 AWa,F:Sara Rainmaker 2.50
71 AWa,Think Like A Gun,pt.1. . . . 2.50
72 AWa,Think Like A Gun,pt.2. . . . 2.50
73 AWa,Think Like A Gun,pt.3. . . . 2.50
74 AWa,Think Like A Gun,pt.4. . . . 2.50
75 AWa,How the Story Ends,pt.1 . 2.50
76 AWa,How the Story Ends,pt.2 . . 2.50
77 AWa,Story Ends,pt.3, 40-pg. . . 3.50
Annual'99 JAr(s). 3.50
Ann. 2000 #1, Devil's
Night x-over,pt.1 . . . . 3.50
Spec. Wired 2.50
Spec.#1 3-D AAd 4.95
Spec.#1a variant(c) 4.95
Spec. Carny Folk 3.50

Spec. 1-shot Going West 2.50
GN Grunge Saves the World 6.00
GN Bootleg: Grunge— The Movie. 10.00
GN Medicine Song, 48-pg. 5.95
GN Gen13/Fantastic Four. 5.95
GN Science Friction, 48-pg. 5.95
GN London,New York,Hell 6.95
GN A Christmas Caper (2002) . . . 5.95
TPB Gen13 . . . . 13.00
TPB Interactive Plus 12.00
TPB Starting Over 15.00
TPB I Love New York 9.95
TPB We'll Take Manhattan 14.95
TPB Super-Human Like You 12.95

Gen^{13} Bootleg #7 © WildStorm

GEN^{13} BOOTLEG
WildStorm, Nov., 1996

1 MFm&AD,lost in the 'Linquist
Fault,'pt.1 . . . . 3.00
1a signed 15.00
2 'Linquist Fault,'pt.2 . . . . 3.50
3 Gen13 Fairy Tale 3.50
4 WS&LSi,F:Valaria,'Little Girl
Lost'. 3.50
5 F:Fairchild,'Timesick,'pt.1 . . . . 3.50
6 F:Fairchild,'Timesick,'pt.2 . . . . 3.50
7 'Renaissance Ruckus' 3.50
8 AWa,'Grunge's Movie,'pt.1 . . . . 4.00
9 AWa,'Grunge's Movie,'pt.2 . . . . 4.00
10 AWa,'Grunge's Movie,'pt.3 . . . . 4.00
11 AaL,WS,Chupacabra,pt.1 . . . . . 2.50
12 AaL,WS,Chupacabra,pt.2. . . . . 2.50
13 F:Grunge,'The Trickster' 2.50
14 JMi,JoP,GL,bad neighbors 2.50
15 KNo,V:Trance,'Hanging,'pt.1 . . 2.50
16 KNo,V:Trance,'Hanging,'pt.2 . . 2.50
17 'Virgil Chu's Reality 2.50
18 MFm,'A Day at the Beach' 2.50
19 BKs,JhB,Satyr 2.50
20 CAd,F:John Lynch,'Numbskulls' . 2.50
Ann.#1 WEI,SDi, to NYC 2.95
TPB Grunge: The Movie,AWa. . . . 9.95
TPB Vol.1, rep.#1–#4 . . . . 11.95

GEN^{13}: INTERACTIVE
WildStorm, Oct., 1997

1 vote via Internet 4.00
2 MHs,vote via Internet 3.00
3 MHs,conclusion 3.00
TPB Gen13 Interactive Plus, rep. . 11.95

GEN^{13}/ GENERATION X
WildStorm, July, 1997

1 BCi&AAd,'Generation Gap' 3.00
1a variant JSC(c). 3.00
3-D edition, with glasses. 5.00
3-Da variant cover, with glasses . . 5.00

GEN^{13}: MAGICAL DRAMA QUEEN ROXY
WildStorm, Oct., 1998

1 (of 3) AWa,Mall of Doom. 4.00
2 AWa,V:Caitlin 4.00
3 AWa,dream sequence concl.. . . 4.00

GEN^{13}/THE MAXX
WildStorm, 1995

Spec.#1 BML,x-over. 4.00

GEN^{13}/MONKEY MAN & O'BRIEN
WildStorm, June, 1998

1 (of 2) AAd. 3.00
1a chromium edition 4.50
2 AAd,alternate universe, concl.. . . 3.00
2a variant AAd(c). 2.50

GEN^{13}: ORDINARY HEROES
WildStorm, 1996

1 & 2 . . . . @3.00

GEN^{12}
WildStorm, Feb., 1998

1 BCi,Team 7 tie-in,'The Legacy' . . 3.00
2 BCi,F:Morgan of I.O. 3.00
3 BCi,Dominique Faust 3.00
4 BCi,F:Miles Craven. 3.00
5 BCi,Team 7 re-unites 3.00

G.I. JOE
Sept., 2001

1 JSC(c) Reinstated,pt.1 . . . . . . 15.00
2 Reinstated,pt.2 . . . . 6.00
3 JSC(c),Reinstated,pt.3 . . . . 5.00
4 JSC(c),Reinstated,pt.4 . . . . 5.00
5 F:Duke. 3.50
6 Reckonings,pt.1 . . . . 3.00
7 Storm Shadow 3.00
8 Destro & Cobra Commander. . . . 3.00
9 Snake-eyes vs. Storm Shadow. . 3.00
10 Dreadnoks. 3.00
11 Mob rule in Chicago. 3.00
12 JBz(c),V:Android Trooper. 3.00
13 JBz(c),V:Firefly 2.95
14 Cobra Suburbs Return. 2.95
15 Reunion. 2.95
16 missing child 2.95
17 kidnap Flint & Baroness. 2.95
18 search for Flint & Baroness . . . 2.95
19 . . . . 2.95
20 Storm Shadow. 2.95
21 Snake-Eyes. 2.95
22 Return of Serpentor,pt.1. . . . . . 2.95
23 Return of Serpentor,pt.2. . . . . . 2.95
24 Return of Serpentor,pt.3. . . . . . 2.95
24a variant(c) 2.95
Spec. M.I.A., rep. #1 & #2. . . . . . 4.95
TPB Vol.1 Reinstated 14.95
TPB Vol. 2 Reckonings 12.95
TPB Vol. 3 Malfunction 12.95

IMAGE

G.I. JOE: BATTLE FILES
April, 2002
1 (of 3) G.I. Joe, 48-pg. 6.00
2 F:Cobra 6.00
3 F:Vehicles and Tech 6.00
TPB 14.95

G.I. JOE FRONTLINE
Oct., 2002
1 LHa(s),DJu,BL,DvD(c) 3.00
2 DJu,BL,DvD(c) V:Destro 3.00
3 DJu,BL,DvD(c) V:Destro 2.95
4 DJu,BL,Silent Castle 2.95
5 Icebound 2.95
6 Icebound,pt.2 . . . . 2.95
7 Icebound,pt.3 . . . . 2.95
8 Icebound,pt.4 . . . . 2.95
9 Kansas City 2.95
10 . . . . 2.95
11 Chuckles 2.95
12 Chuckles 2.95
13 Chuckles 2.95
14 Chuckles 2.95
15 F:Stalker 2.95
16 Night Creepers 2.95
17 PJe,F:Beachhead 2.95
16a–17a variant (c) . . . . @2.95
TPB Vol. 1 . . . . 12.95

G.I. JOE VS. TRANSFORMERS
June 2003
1 . . . . 2.95
2thru 6 . . . . @2.95
1a–6a variant (c) . . . . @2.95

GLORY
Extreme, 1995
0 JDy 2.50
1 JDy,F:Glory 4.00
1a variant cover 4.00
2 JDy,V:Demon Father 3.00
3 JDy,A:Rumble & Vandal 2.50
4 Vandal vs. Demon Horde 2.50
4a JDy variant cover 3.00
5 Supreme Apocalypse,pt.3,
 F:Vandal 2.50
6 Drug Problem 2.50
7 F:Superpatriot 2.50
8 Extreme Babewatch 2.50
9 Extreme Destroyer,pt.5,
 x-over, bagged with card 2.50
10 . . . . 2.50
11 . . . . 2.50
12 JDy, EBe & JSb 3.50
13 JDy, EBe & JSb 2.50
14 JDy, EBe & JSb 2.50
15 JDy, EBe & JSb, Out for
 vengeance 2.50
TPB rep.#1-#4 . . . . 9.95
continued: see Color Comics section

GLORY/ANGELA ANGELS IN HELL
Extreme, 1996
1 . . . . 4.00

GLORY/AVENGELYNE
Extreme, 1996
1 V:B'lial,I:Faith 4.00
1a no chrome(c) 3.00

GLORY/AVENGELYNE: THE GODYSSEY
Extreme
1 RLd & JDy 3.00
1a photo(c) 4.00

GLORY/CELESTINE: DARK ANGEL
Extreme, Sept., 1996
1 (of 3) JDy,PtL,sequel to Rage of
 Angels, A:Maximage 2.50
2 JDy,PtL,'Doomsday+1' 2.50
3 JDy,PtL, conclusion 2.50

GLORY & FRIENDS
Extreme, 1995
Bikini Fest #1 . . . . 2.50
Bikini Fest #2 . . . . 2.50
Lingerie Special #1 (1995) 3.00
Christmas Special #1 (1995) 2.50

GO GIRL!
Aug., 2000
1 TrR,F:Lindsay Goldman 3.50
2 TrR,wonderful life? 3.50
3 TrR,The Teacher from Hell 3.50
4 TrR,Vacation at dude ranch . . . 3.50
5 TrR,origin of powers 3.50

GOLDFISH
(B&W) 1998
TPB by Brian Michael Bendis . . . 16.95
TPB 272-pg. Definitive Colleciton . 19.95

GREASE MONKEY
March, 1998
1 TEl 2.95
2 TEl 2.95
3 TEl, The Calling; Rewards 2.95

GRIFTER
WildStorm, 1995–96
1 BWS(c), WildStorm
 Rising,pt.5,w/2 cards 2.50
1a Newsstand ed. 2.25
2 V:Diabolik,pt.1 . . . . 3.00
3 V:Diabolik,pt.2 . . . . 3.00
4 R:Forgotten Hero 3.00
5 Rampage of a Fallen Hero 3.00
6 V:Poerhouse 3.00
7 City of Angels,pt.1 . . . . 3.00
8 City of Angels,pt.2 . . . . 3.00
9 City of Angels,pt.3 . . . . 3.00
10 City of Angels,pt.4 . . . . 3.00

GRIFTER/BADROCK
Extreme, 1995
1 To Save Badrock's Mom 3.00
1a Variant cover 2.50
2 flip-book-Badrock #2 . . . . 3.00
3 double-size 3.50

GRIFTER-ONE SHOT
WildStorm, 1995
1 SS,DN 5.00

GRIFTER
WildStorm, 1996
1 StG 4.00
2 StG,V:Joe the Dead 3.00
3 StG,captured by MadJackPower . 3.00
4 StG,vs. Condition Red 3.00
5 StG,Grifter meets his dad,
 F:Molly Ingram 3.00
6 StG,A:Santini 3.00
7 StG,MtB,I:Charlatan 3.00
8 StG,MtB,Zealot
 disappears,V:Soldier 3.00
9 StG,Zealot captured?, secret
 history of Quiet Men 3.00
10 StG,Grifter & Soldier go to
 rescue Zealot 3.00
11 StG, renegade former agent . . 3.00
12 StG,'Who is Tanager?' 3.00
13 StG,F:Condition Red,'Family
 Feud' 3.00
14 StG,V:Joe the Dead 3.00

GRIFTER/SHI
WildStorm, 1996
1 BCi,JLe,TC 3.00
2 BCi,JLe,TC 3.00

GROO
1994–95
1 SA 3.50
2 A:Arba, Dakarba 3.50
3 The Generals Hat 3.50
4 A Drink of Water 3.50
5 SA,A Simple Invasion 3.50

Grifter #7 © WildStorm

Glory #15 © Extreme

Groo–Hong

6 SA,A Little Invention 3.50
7 The Plight of the Drazils 3.50
8 . . . . 3.50
9 I:Arfetto 3.50
10 The Sinkes 3.50
11 The Gamblers 3.50
12 . . . . 3.50

GRRL SCOUTS
Feb. 2003
1 (of 4) Work Sucks, b&w 2.95
2 thru 4 . . . . @2.95
TPB Vol. 1 . . . . 12.95

GUARDIAN ANGEL
May, 2002
1 (of 4) AWs,F:ChristianAngelos . . 3.00
2 AWs,no place like home 3.00
3 AWs,Our onlyhope 3.00
4 concl. 3.00

HAMMER OF THE GODS
Sept., 2002
TPB: Mortal Enemy, 176-pg. 18.95

HAMMER OF THE GODS: HAMMER HITS CHINA
Feb. 2003
1 thru 3 . . . . @2.95

HAWAIIAN DICK
Dec. 2002
1 thru 3 Hawaii in 1953 . . . . @2.95
TPB Vol. 1 Byrd of Paradise 14.95

HAWAIIAN DICK: THE LAST RESORT
Sept. 2003
1 (of 4) 2.95
2 . . . . 2.95
3 . . . . 2.95

HAWKSHAWS
March, 2000
1 by Dietrich Smith 2.95
1a variant movie poster(c) 2.95
2 and 3 . . . . @2.95

Hazard #4 © WildStorm

IMAGE

HAZARD
WildStorm, 1996
1 JMi,RMr 3.00
2 JMi,RMr 3.00
3 JMi,RMr 3.00
4 JMi,RMr 3.00
5 JMi,RMr,Hazard finds Dr. D'Oro . 3.00
6 JMi,RMr 3.00
7 JMi,RMr,Hazard meets Prism . . . 3.00

HEADHUNTERS
(B&W) April, 1997
1 ChM,V:Army of Wrath 3.00
2 ChM,V:undead militia 3.00
3 ChM,'Slaughterground' 3.00

HEARTBREAKERS
**July, 1998
Superdigest, 6'x9'**
1 B&W and color 104-pg.. . . . . . . 9.95

HEARTBREAKERS VERSUS BIOVOC
Image
TPB 'Bust Out' 9.95
TPB PGn 14.95

HEAVEN'S DEVILS
Sept. 2003
1 (of 4) 2.95
2 . . . . 2.95

HEAVEN'S WAR
Image
GN b&w, 120-pg. 12.95

HEDGE KNIGHT, THE
Aug. 2003
1 (of 6) MsM 2.95
1a variant (c) 2.95
2 . . . . 2.95
2a cardstock(c) 5.95
3 . . . . 2.95
3a holofoil (c) 5.95
4 MsM 2.95
4a variant holofoil (c) 5.95

HEIRS OF ETERNITY
April 2003
1 (of 5) 2.95
2 thru 5 . . . . @2.95

HELLCOP
Avalon, Oct., 1998
1 JoC,F:Virgil Hilts 2.50
2 JoC,It's a small underwold
  after all 2.50
3 JoC,new circles of Hell 2.50
4 JoC,secrets of Hell revealed 2.50
5 JoC,Hell & High Water 2.50
5a variant cover 2.95

HELLHOLE
Top Cow, May, 1999
1 SLo,AdP,F:Michael Cabrini 2.50
2 SLo,AdP,The Devil's Candy 2.50
3 SLo,AdP,power brokers 2.50

Comics Values Annual

HELLHOUNDS
Aug. 2003
1 Hadean Gates 2.95
2 thru 4 . . . . @2.95
1a and 2a variant (c) . . . . @2.95

HELLSHOCK
1994
1 I:Hellshock 3.50
2 Powers & Origin 3.50
3 New foe 3.50
4 . . . . 3.50

HELLSHOCK
Jan., 1997
1 JaL,Something wrong with
  Daniel, 48-pg. 3.00
2 JaL,Daniel learns to control
  powers. 2.50
3 JaL,Daniel free of madness 2.50
4 JaL,Daniel searches for his
  mother, Jonakand plans escape
  from Hell 2.50
5 JaL,Jonakand and fallen angels
  tear hell apart 2.50
6 JaL,'The Milk of Paradise' 2.50
7 JaL,'A Mother's Story',
  double size 3.95
8 JaL,House of Torture 2.50

HELLSPAWN
TMP, July, 2000
1 The Clown,pt.1 . . . . 3.00
2 The Clown,pt.2 . . . . 2.50
3 Hate Me 2.50
4 Hate You 2.50
5 Selling Fear 2.50
6 Angels 4.00
7 The Group 2.50
8 The Suicide Gate 2.50
9 Chains 2.50
10 Clash 2.50
11 Conflicts of Interest 2.50
12 Monsters and Miracles 2.50
13 Heaven & Hell 2.50
14 Light of Day 2.50
15 Blinded 2.50
16 Hellworld,pt.4 . . . . 2.50
17 The Killing Hand,pt.1 . . . . 2.50
18 The Killing Hand,pt.2 . . . . 2.50
19 The Killing Hand,pt.3 . . . . 2.50
20 The Collection 2.50
21 The Collection,pt.2 . . . . 2.50
22 Love Lost,pt.1 . . . . 2.95
23 Love Lost,pt.2 . . . . 2.50
24 In the Grip of Shadows 2.50
25 Remember Me? 2.50

HOLY TERROR, THE
Aug., 2002
1 (of 4) PhH 2.95
2 thru 3 PhH . . . . @2.95

HOMAGE STUDIOS
April, 1993
Swimsuit Spec.#1 JLe,WPo, MS . . . 2.25

HONG ON THE RANGE
Matinee Entertainment/ Flypaper, Dec., 1997
1 (of 3) by William Wu & Jeff
  Lafferty 2.50
2 in Washout 2.50
3 Duke Goslin 2.50
TPB Hong on the Range 12.95

All comics prices listed are for Near Mint condition.

IMAGE

Image–Kabuki

Image Introduces: Dog Soldiers
© Image

IMAGE INTRODUCES:
Oct. 2001

1 Primate	3.00
1b variant AGo(c)	3.00
(2) Legend of Isis	3.00
(3) The Believer	3.00
(4) Cryptopia	3.00
(5) Dog Soldiers	3.00

IMAGE TWO-IN-ONE
B&W, March, 2001

1 EL,48-pg. F:Herculian & Duncan. 3.00

IMAGE ZERO
1993

0 I:Troll,Deathtrap,Pin-ups,rep. Savage Dragon #4,O:Stryker, F:ShadowHawk 15.00

IMAGES OF SHADOWHAWK
1993–94

1 KG,V:Trencher	2.25
2 thru 3 V:Trencher	2.25

IMMORTAL TWO
May, 1997
(B&W) Half-Tone

1 MsM,F:Gaijin & Gabrielle	2.50
2 MsM	2.50
3 MsM	2.50
4 MsM,V:Okami Red	2.50
5 MsM,new drug epidemic	2.50
6 MsM,First Order, cont.	2.50
7 MsM,vs. impossible odds	2.50
7 MsM,flip photo cover	2.50

INFERNO: HELLBOUND
Top Cow, Nov., 2001

1 MS,DT,Hell loose on Earth	2.50
1a-1f variant(c)	@2.50
2 MS	2.50
3 MS	3.00
4 MS	2.50
#0 MS 16-pg., signed	19.95

INTRIGUE
Aug., 1999

1 F:Kirk Best	2.50
1a variant cover (1:4)	2.50
2 on the run from the law	2.50
3 V:NYPD SWAT team	2.50
3a variant HuR cover (1:4)	2.50
4	2.50
5	2.95
5a variant Mike Wieringo(c)	2.95

INVINCIBLE
Jan. 2003

1 O:Mark Grayson	2.95
2	2.95
3 quality time	2.95
4 human bombs	2.95
5 It Came From Outer Space	2.95
6	2.95
7 Guardians of the Globe	2.95
8 shperhero funeral	2.95
9	2.95
TPB Vol. 1 Family Matters	12.95

INVISIBLE 9
Flypaper, May, 1998

TPB 12.95

IRON WINGS
March, 2000

1 Legends of Iron Wings	2.50
1a variant Andy Park(c)	2.50
2 V:Amaxus	2.50
3 Nightmares	2.50

JACKIE CHAN'S SPARTAN X
(B&W) March, 1998

1 MGo,RM,Hell-Bent Hero for Hire.	2.95
2 MGo,to Russia	2.95
3 MGo,V:Kenshi	2.95
4 MGo,RM, in Istanbul	2.95
5 MGo,RM, Mind of God	2.95
5a MGo,RM, photo cover	2.95
6 MGo,RM, The Armor of Heaven	2.95
6a MGo,RM, photo cover	2.95

JACK STAFF
Feb. 2003

1 Britain's Greatest hero	2.95
2 thru 5	@2.95

JADE WARRIORS
Aug., 1999

1 MD2,Destruction of Japan	2.50
2 MD2,V:Ramthar	2.50
3 MD2,Blood of the Children	2.50
1a thru 3a photo(c)	@2.50
3b movie poster style(c)	2.50

JINX
Jan., 2000

1 F:Karen Lane	3.00
2 and 3	@3.00
1a thru 2a variant cover	@3.00

JINX
(B&W) June, 1997

1 by Brian Michael Bendis	3.00
1a 2nd printing	3.00
2 F:Jinx, female bounty hunter	3.00
3 thru 5	@4.00

Spec.#1 Buried Treasure	4.00
Spec.#1 True Crime Confessions	4.00
TPB rep. prev. #1–#4	9.95
TPB The Essential Collection	17.95
TPB 480-pg.	24.95

JINX: TORSO
(B&W) Aug., 1998

1 by Brian Michael Bendis, 48-pg.	4.00
2 search continues	4.00
3 Torso Killer	4.00
4 breaking the law	4.00
5 48-pg.	5.00
6 conclusion, 48-pg.	5.00
Spec. #@%!! short stories	3.95

JOURNEYMAN
Aug., 1999

1 by Brandon McKinney	3.00
2 enemies become allies	3.00
3 V:Dragon King	3.00

J.U.D.G.E.
March, 2000

1 by Greg Horn,F:Victoria Grace	2.95
1a variant cover	2.95
2 V:John Lawson	2.95
3 Secret Rage,pt.3	2.95

JUNKBOTZ ROTOGIN
Feb. 2003

1 . . . . 2.50

KABUKI
Sept., 1997

1 DMk,O:Kabuki	7.00
1a variant JSo(c)	7.00
2 DMk,O:Kabuki, pg.2	5.00
3 DMk,surprise visitor	5.00
4 DMk,Akemi, romance	7.00
5 DMk,action	4.00
6 DMk	3.00
7 DMk	3.00
7a DMK variant cover (1:2)	3.00
8 DMk	3.00
9 DMk, finale	3.00
TPB Circle of Blood,rep. orig. series plus 'Fear the Reaper', B&W	17.95
TPB Masks of the Noh	10.95
TPB Masks of the Noh, 2nd pr.	12.95
TPB Images, part rep. #1, 48-pg.	4.95
TPB Dreams	10.00
TPB Vol.2 Dreams	12.95
TPB Vol.4 Skin Deep	9.95
TPB Vol.4 Skin Deep, 2nd pr.	10.95
TPB Vol.4 Skin Deep, rep.	12.95
TPB Vol.5 Metamorphosis	24.95
TPB Vol. 6 Scarab	19.95
GN Reflections #1, 48-pg.	4.95
GN Reflections #1 signed	7.95
GN Reflections #2 art & stories	4.95
GN Reflections,Vol.3.	4.95
GN Reflections,Vol.4.	4.95
Spec. 1-shot The Ghost Play	2.95
Spec. #2 Images, rep. #2 & #3	5.95
Kabuki 1/2 Wizard Mail-in	2.95
Kabuki 1/2 signed	5.95

KABUKI AGENTS
(B&W) Aug., 1999

1 DMk,F:Scarab	3.00
1a JQ(c), DMk signed	7.00
2 DMk,F:Scarab, Tiger Lily	3.00
3 DMk,F:Scarab, Tiger Lily	3.00
4 DMk,F:Scarab, Tiger Lily	3.00

Kabuki–Kurt Busiek — IMAGE

5 thru 8 DMk . . . . @3.00
Artbook 4.95
Kabuki Agents: Scarab #1 signed . . 5.95

KABUKI CLASSICS
Feb., 1999
1 Fear the Reaper, rep. 10.00
2 Dance of Death 3.00
3 Circle of Blood, act 1, 48-pg. . . . 6.00
4 Circle of Blood, act 2 . . . . 4.00
5 Circle of Blood, act 3 . . . . 3.00
6 Circle of Blood, act 4 . . . . 3.00
7 Circle of Blood, act 5 . . . . 3.00
8 Circle of Blood, conclusion 3.00
9 Masks of the Noh, Act 1 . . . . . . 3.00
10 Masks of the Noh, Act 2. . . . . . 3.00
11 Masks of the Noh, Act 3 . . . . . . 3.00
12 Masks of the Noh, concl. 3.00
Kabuki Classics #1 signed 6.95

KARZA
Feb. 2003
1 Micronauts spin-off 2.95
2 thru 4 . . . . @2.95

KID SUPREME
Supreme 1996–97
1 & 2. . . . . 2.50
3 DaF,ErS. 2.50
4 DaF,ErS,Party time. 2.50
5 DaF,ErS,'Birds of a Feather' . . 2.50
6 DaF,ErS,I: The Sensational
   Spinner 2.50
7 DaF,ErS,Everything falls apart . . 2.50

KID TERRIFIC
(B&W) Nov., 1998
1 A:Snedak & Manny Stellar 3.00

KILLER INSTINCT TOUR BOOK
1 All Homage Artist,I:Crusade 5.00
1a signed 45.00

KILLRAZOR SPECIAL
Aug., 1995
1 O:Killrazor 2.50

KIN
Top Cow, Feb., 2000
1 GFr,Neanderthal. 3.00
2 GFr,F:McLoon 3.00
3 GFr,Alaska revenge 3.00
4 GFr 3.00
5 GFr,Born Free 3.00
6 GFr,40-pg.,The End? 4.00
6a variant AAd(c). 4.00
1st 6 as set, signed GFr. 24.95
TPB Descent of Man 17.95

KINDRED
WildStorm, 1994
1 JLe,BCi(s),BBh,I:Knidred 5.00
2 JLe,BCi(s),BBh,V:Knidred. 3.50
3 JLe,BCi(s),BBh,V:Knidred. 3.00
3a WPo(c),Alternate(c) 6.00
4 JLe,BCi(s),BBh,V:Knidred. 3.00
TPB rep. #1–#4. . . . . 9.95

'KINI
Flypaper, Feb., 1999
1 KK, BKs,F:Kim Walters 2.50

Kindred #2 © WildStorm

KISS: THE PSYCHO CIRCUS
TMP, July, 1997
1 SvG,AMe 8.00
2 AMe, unearthly origins 6.00
3 AMe, Judgment o/t Elementals . . . 5.00
4 AMe,Smoke and Mirrors,pt.1. . . . 4.00
5 AMe,Smoke and Mirrors,pt.2. . . . 4.00
6 AMe,Smoke and Mirrors, concl. . . 4.00
7 AMe,Creatures of the Night. 3.00
8 AMe,Forever. 3.00
9 AMe,Four Sides to Every Story . . 3.00
10 AMe,Destroyer,pt.1 . . . . 3.00
11 AMe,Destroyer,pt.2 . . . . 3.00
12 AMe,Destroyer,pt.3 (of 4) 3.00
13 AMe, Destroyer,pt.4 . . . . 3.00
14 AMe, in Feudal Japan 3.00
15 AMe, in Feudal Japan, choices . . 2.50
16 AMe, Ticket for Terror. 2.50
17 AMe, World Without Heroes,pt.2 2.50
18 AMe, Sunburst Finish. 2.50
19 Fate of the Psycho Circus 2.50
20 Mr. Makebelieve 2.50
21 Don't Talk to Strangers 2.50
22 Twin sisters 2.50
23 Tribunal of souls 2.50
24 Cat's Eye. 2.50
25 . . . . 2.50
26 Nightingale's Song,pt.1 . . . . . . 2.50
27 Nightingale's Song,pt.2 . . . . . . 2.50
28 Perdition Blues 2.50
29 Shadow of the Moon,pt.1. . . . . . 2.50
30 Shadow of the Moon,pt.2. . . . . . 2.50
31 Sins of Omission 2.50
32 Gallery of God's Mistakes 2.50
33 Gallery of God's Mistakes,pt.2 . . 2.50
34 Far Corners of Night 2.50
TPB Vol. I, rep. #1–#6 . . . . 12.95
TPB Vol. II rep. #10–#13. . . . . . . 9.95
TPB Vol.3 Whispered Scream. . . . 9.95
TPB Vol.4 Legends & Nightmares. . 9.95
Kiss Mag.#5 rep. 4.95

KNIGHTMARE
Extreme, 1995
0 O:Knightmare. 2.50
1 I:Knightmare MMy 2.50
2 I:Caine. 2.50
3 RLd,AV,The New Order,
   F:Detective Murtaugh. 2.50
4 RLd,AV,MMy,I:Thrillkill. 2.50
5 V:Thrillkill 2.50

6 Extreme Babewatch 2.50
7 . . . . 2.50
8 I:Acid 2.50

KNIGHTSTRIKE
Extreme, 1996
1 Extreme Destroyer,pt.6
   x-over, bagged with card 2.50

KNIGHT WATCHMAN
(B&W) May, 1998
1 by Gary Carlson & Chris Ecker . . 2.95
2 thru 4 Graveyard Shift,pt.2–pt.3@2.95

KORE
April 2003
1 . . . . 2.95
1a variant (c). 2.95
2 thru 5 . . . . @2.95

KOSMIC KAT
July, 1999
Activity Book. 2.95

KURT BUSIEK'S ASTRO CITY
Juke Box, 1995–96
1 I:Samaritan,'In Dreams' 12.00
1a 2nd printing 2.25
2 I:Silver Agent,V:Shirak
   the Devourer 10.00
3 F:Jack in the Box 10.00
4 I:Hanged Man,Safeguards 11.00
5 I:Crackerjack 12.00
6 O:Samaritan,F:Winged Victory . 14.00
TPB 19.95
[Vol. 2] Homage, 1996
fi F:Hanged Man (1996). 5.00
1 KBk(s),BA,Welcome to
   Astro City. 9.00
1a Trunk(c) 8.00
1b 2nd printing 2.50
2 KBk(s),BA,O:First Family,
   F:Astra, Everyday Life 7.00
2b 2nd printing 2.50
3 KBk(s),BA,Adventures in
   Other Worlds 7.00

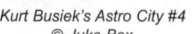

*Kurt Busiek's Astro City #4
© Juke Box*

CVA Page 540 — All comics prices listed are for *Near Mint* condition.

Comics Values Annual

IMAGE

Kurt Busiek–Lovebunny

Homage, Dec., 1996
4 KBk,BA,Teenager seeks to
  become teen sidekick,pt.1 (of 6) 6.00
5 Learning the Game. 5.00
6 V: creatures of Shadow Hill. 5.00
7 Aliens invade Astro City 4.00
8 The aliens are out there 4.00
9 Honor Guard vs. Aliens finale . . . 4.00
10 meet the junkman 4.00
11 Serpent's Teeth 4.00
12 F:Jack-In-The-Box 3.00
13 F:Looney Leo 3.00
14 F:Steeljack 3.00
15 F:supervillains 3.00
16 F:El Hombre 2.50
17 F:Steeljack, staying straight 2.50
TPB Confession, rep.#4–#9 . . . . . 19.95
3-D #1 . . . . 4.95
TPB Life in the Big City. 19.95
TPB Family Album 19.95

Homage/DC, 1999
VOLUME 2
16 KBk(s), El Hombre 3.00
17 KBk(s), Mock Turtle 3.00
18 KBk(s), F:Steeljack 3.00
19 KBk(s), F:Steeljack 3.00
20 KBk(s) 3.00
21 KBk(s),F:Crackerjack. 3.00
22 KBk(s),F:Samaritan 3.00
Spec.1/2 KBk(s) 3.00

LABMAN
1996
1 I:Labman 4.00
1a variant cover. 4.00
2 & 3 . . . . @4.00

LADY PENDRAGON
Nov., 1998
1 MHw,Destiny's Embrace 2.50
1a remastered, new cover 2.50
1b Dynamic Forces variant cover. . 6.95
1c JeL(c) glow-in-the-dark 19.95
1d Tour Edition 5.00
2 MHw,Destiny's Embrace,pt.2 . . . 3.00
3 MHw,Destiny's Embrace,pt.3 . . . 3.00
3a variant cover (1:4). 2.50
0 MHw, Secrets & Origins 2.50
0a Eurosketch cover 10.00
Preview (Wizard, Chicago Comicon) 4.95

Lady Pendragon Vol. 2 #3
© *Image*

TPB Special, 64-pg. (2002). 7.95

LADY PENDRAGON: DRAGON BLADE
April, 1999
1 MHw,Merlin trains Jennifer 2.50
1a variant cover (1:4). 2.50
1b Chrome Edition. 5.00
2 MHw,F:Morgana 2.50
2a variant cover (1:4). 2.50
3 MHw,B.U.I:Alley Cat 3.00
4 MHw,Morgana returns 2.50
5 MHw,Spear of Destiny 2.50
6 MHw,Jennifer Drake resigns . . . 2.50
7 MHw,Future Prophecy,pt.1 . . . . . 4.00
8 MHw,Future Prophecy,pt.2 . . . . . 2.50
9 MHw,Future Prophecy,pt.3 . . . . . 2.50
10 MHw,Messianic Lineage,pt.1 . . 2.50
11 MHw,Messianic Lineage,pt.2 . . 2.50
12 MHw,Messianic Lineage,pt.3 . . 2.50
1a Glow-in-the-dark JaL(c) . . . .
Gallery Ed.#1 . . . . 2.95
Gallery Ed.#1a photo(c) 2.95

LADY PENDRAGON: MORE THAN MORTAL
May, 1999
1 MHw,Pendragon vs. Protector. . . 2.50
1a variant cover (1:4). 6.95
1b Gold foil(c) 6.95

LADY SUPREME
Extreme, 1996
1 TMr 2.50
2 TMr,Die & Let Die,pt.2 . . . . 2.50
3 TMr,V:Manassa 2.50
4 TMr,'Lady Supreme goes
  undercover' 2.50

LAST SHOT
Image, Aug., 2001
1 Foodchain,pt.1 . . . . 3.00
2 Metal in his Heart 3.00
3 Six String Noose. 3.00
4 Angel of Death 3.00

LAST SHOT: FIRST DRAW
Image, May, 2001
1 First Draw Revolver 3.00

LAZARUS CHURCHYARD: THE FINAL CUT
2000
Gn WEl 14.95

LEAVE IT TO CHANCE
Homage, 1996–98
1 JeR,PS,I:Chance Falconer 5.00
2 JeR,PS,Dragons are a Girl's
  Best Friend 5.00
Homage
3 JeR,PS,Chance and St. George
  race against time 5.00
4 JeR,PS. 3.00
5 JeR,PS,'Trick or Threat' 3.00
6 JeR,PS,Return of Cap'n Hitch. . . 3.00
7 JeR,PS,'And Not a Drop to Drink 3.00
8 JeR,PS,Phantom of the Mall 3.00
9 JeR,PS,Midnite Monster
  Madness 3.00
10 JeR,PS,'Destroy All Monsters' . . 3.00

11 JeR,PS,Dead Men Can't Skate . 3.00
12 JeR,PS,visits her friend Dash. . . 3.00
13 JeR,PS,Reunion,48-pg. 5.00
TPB rep. #1–#4 . . . . 9.95
TPB Vol. II, rep. #5–#8 . . . . 12.95
TPB Trick or Threat 12.95

LEGACY
May 2003
1 . . . . 2.95
2 thru 4 . . . . @2.95
4a variant (c). 2.95

LEGEND OF ISIS
Feb., 2002
1 Origin of Isis 2.95

LEGEND OF SUPREME
Dec., 1994
1 KG(s),JJ,DPs,Revelations,pt.1 . . 2.50
2 Revelations,pt.2 . . . . 2.50
3 Conclusion 2.50

LETHAL
1996
1 . . . . 2.50
2 . . . . 2.50

LIBERTY MEADOWS
July, 2002
27 comic book convention 3.00
28 Ralph's Genetic Breakthrough . . 3.00
29 Brandy's Christmas Surprise . . 2.95
30 Long Cold Winter,pt.1 . . . . 2.95
31 Long Cold Winter,pt.2 . . . . 2.95
32 The Cow is Back 2.95
33 Mad Cow, pt.2 . . . . 2.95
34 . . . . 2.95
TPB Book #1 Eden, rep.#1–9 . . . 14.95

LITTLE-GREYMAN
(B&W)
TPB by C. Scott Morse 6.95

LITTLE RED HOT: BOUND
Image, July, 2001
1 (of 3) by Dawn Brown 3.00
2 . . . . 3.00
3 concl. 3.00

LITTLE RED HOT: CHANE OF FOOLS
(B&W) Feb., 1999
1 (of 3) by Dawn Brown, F:Chane . 3.00
2 stranded in desert. 3.00
3 Heaven vs. Hell 3.00
TPB The Foolish Collection, rep. . . 12.95

LOST ONES, THE
March, 2000
1 by Ken Penders 3.00
2 . . . . 3.00

LOVEBUNNY & MR. HELL
Feb. 2003
1-shot 2.95
1-shot Savage Love 2.95

All comics prices listed are for Near Mint condition.

LYNCH
WildStorm, June, 1997
1 TVs,'Terror in the Jungle' 2.50

MACE GRIFFIN: BOUNTY HUNTER
Image/Top Cow April 2003
1-shot 3.00

MAGDALENA
Top Cow, March, 2000
1 JBz,Darkness spin-off 4.00
1a variant MS(c) 4.00
1b variant Michael Turner(c) 4.00
2 JBz,secret revealed 2.50
3 JBz,Blood Divine,pt.3 .... 2.50
TPB JBz, 112-pg. 10.00

MAGDALENA
Image/Top Cow July 2003
1 (of 4) 3.00
2 thru 4 .... @3.00
1a and 2a variant (c) .... @3.00
Spec. Con. Preview ....

MAGDALENA/ANGELUS
Top Cow, Oct., 2001
1/2 The Light and the Glory 3.00

MAGDALENA/ BLOOD LEGACY
Top Cow, June, 2000
Preview 22-pg. 3.00

MAGDALENA/ VAMPIRELLA
Image/Top Cow June 2003
1-shot. 3.00
1-shotA variant (c) 1:4 .... 3.00

MAGE: THE HERO DEFINED
1997
1 MWg,F:Kevin Matchstick 5.00

Mage #13 © Image

IMAGE

2 MWg,Kirby Hero, V:harpies. 4.00
3 MWg,Isis, Gretch 3.00
4 MWg,Isis, drug 3.00
5 MWg,into Canada. 3.00
6 MWg,V:Dragonslayer 2.50
7 MWg 2.50
8 MWg,V:Red Caps. 2.50
9 MWg,Sibling Trio 2.50
10 MWg,enchanted by a succubus . 2.50
11 MWg,Joe Phat, missing 2.50
12 MWg,Pale Incanter's Lair. ... 2.50
13 MWg,What color is magic 2.50
14 MWg,Man Mountain of???? 2.50
15 MWg, 48-pg. concl. 6.00
Spec. 3-D #1 (1998) 4.95
TPB Vol. 1 rep. 9.95
TPB Vol. II, rep. #5–#8 .... 9.95
TPB Vol. 3, rep. #9–#12 .... 12.95
TPB Vol. 4, rep. #13—#15 ...... 14.95
Coll.Ed.Vol.1,rep.#1–#2 .... 5.95
Coll.Ed.Vol.2,rep.#3–#4 .... 5.95
Coll.Ed.Vol.3,rep.#5–#6 .... 5.95
Coll.Ed.Vol.4,rep.#7–#8 .... 4.95
Coll.Ed.Vol.5,rep.#9–#10 .... 4.95
Coll.Ed.Vol.6,rep.#11–#12 ...... 4.95
Coll.Ed.Vol.7,rep.#13–#14 ...... 5.50
Coll.Ed.Vol.8,rep.#15–#16 ...... 4.95

MAN AGAINST TIME
Motown 1996
1 'Every Hero' 2.50
2 .... 2.50
3 'Pro Patria Mori' 2.50

MARS ATTACKS
1996
1 KG,BSz(of 4) 2.50
2 & 3 .... @2.50
4 End of their world as they
  knew it 2.50

MASK OF ZORRO, THE
July, 1998
1 (of 4) DMG,RoW,RM,MGo(c), ... 3.00
2 DMG,RoW,RM,MGo(c). 3.00
3 DMG,RoW,MGo(c). 3.00
4 DMG,RoW,MGo concl. 3.00
4a photo cover 3.00

MASTERS OF THE UNIVERSE
2002
1 He-Man returns 3.00
1b variant JSC(c). 3.00
1b variant EN(c). 3.00
2 thru 4 .... @2.95
2a–4a variant (c) .... @2.95
Volume II
1 .... 2.95
2 thru 6 .... @2.95
1a–2a variant (c) .... @2.95
3a–4a holofoil (c). .... @5.95
1-shot Icons of Evil: Beast Man. 4.95

MAXIMAGE
Extreme, 1995–96
1 RLe(c) 2.50
2 Extreme Destroyer,pt.2,
  x-over, bagged with card 2.50
3 .... 2.50
4 A:Angela,Glory 2.50
5 thru 8 .... @2.50
9 BML, Sex Slaves of Bomba
  Island 2.50
10 BML, The King of Emotion is
  back. 2.50

MAXX, THE
1993
1/2 SK,from Wizard 10.00
1 SK,I:The Maxx 5.00
1a glow in the dark(c) 15.00
2 SK,V:Mr.Gone 4.00
3 SK,V:Mr.Gone 4.00
4 SK 4.00
5 SK 3.00
6 SK 3.00
7 SK,A:Pitt. 3.50
8 SK,V:Pitt. 3.50
9 SK 3.00
10 SK 3.00
11 SK 2.50
12 SK 2.50
13 Maxx Wanders in Dreams 2.50
14 R:Julie 4.00
15 Julia's Pregnant 4.00
16 SK,Is Maxx in Danger? 4.00
17 SK,Gardener Maxx 4.00
18 SK,'Beware The Hooley' 2.50
19 SK,V:Hooley,'Last Fairy Tale' 2.50
20 SK,Questions are answered.... 2.50
21 AM(s),SK. 2.50
22 SK,'Other Peoples' Crap' 2.50
23 SK,'Having to Believe' 2.50
24 SK. 2.50
25 SK,'Lost and Found' 2.50
26 SK. 2.50
27 V:Iago the Killer Slug 2.50
28 Sara and Norberg look for Julie 2.50
29 Sara and Gone defeat Iago the
  Slug 2.50
30 Lil' Sara faces her fears ... 2.50
31 F:The Library girl 2.50
32 F:The Library girl,pt.2. .... 2.50
33 Sara's back 2.50
34 Mark and Julia. 2.50
35 who knows? 2.50
36 bumfuzzled 2.50
37 Megan's story concl. 2.50
38 Mark,Julie,Larry,pt.1 (of 4) . 2.50
Spec. Friends of Maxx,F:Dude
  Japan. 3.00
The Maxx 3-D #1 .... 5.00
TPB Rep. #1–#5 .... 12.95
TPB Vol. 2 .... 12.95

MECHANIC, THE
Homage, Aug., 1998
GN JCh,JPe,time travel 6.00

MECH DESTROYER
Image, March, 2001
1 (of 4) Battle for Earth 3.00
2 Face of the Enemy 3.00
3 rescue the captives. 3.00
4 V:The Crimson Death 3.00

MEDIEVAL SPAWN/ WITCHBLADE
May, 1996
1 thru 3 .... @5.00
TPB series rep. 9.95

MEGADRAGON & TIGER
March, 1999
1 by Tony Wong, from Hong Kong . 3.00
2 F:Red Tiger 3.00
3 V:Single-Minded Arhat 3.00
4 V:Fiery Lord 3.00
5 F:Gigi 3.00

IMAGE

Megahurtz #2 © Image

MEGAHURTZ
(B&W) Aug., 1997
1 JPi,I:Megahurtz 3.00
2 JPi,visit to Wonderland 3.00
3 JPi,V:N-Filtraitors 3.00
4 JPi,Liberaiders 3.00

MEGATON MAN: BOMBSHELL
July, 1999
1 DSs,V:Unleash 3.00

MEGATON MAN: HARDCOPY
Fiasco (B&W) Feb., 1999
1 by Don Simpson 3.00
2 with 6 new pages 3.00

MESSENGER, THE
July, 2000
1-shot JOy, 48-pg. 6.00

MICRONAUTS
June, 2002
1 . . . . 3.00
2 . . . . 3.00
3 Revolution 3.00
4 Revolution 2.95
5 Revolution 2.95
6 Star Chamber,pt.1 . . . . 2.95
7 Star Chamber,pt.2 . . . . 2.95
8 Invasion Earth,pt.1 . . . . 2.95
9 Invasion Earth,pt.2 . . . . 2.95
10 Invasion Earth,pt.3 . . . . 2.95
11 Invasion Earth,pt.4 . . . . 2.95
TPB Vol. 1 Rebellion 10.95
Spec. 2002 Con Special . . . .

MIDNIGHT NATION
Top Cow, Sept., 2000
1 MSz 4.00
1a variant GrF(c) 4.00
2 MSz,GrF, on the run 3.00
3 MSz,GrF, To Hell and inbetween . 3.50
4 MSz,GrF, V:Walkers 3.50
5 MSz,GrF, Find your soul 3.00
6 MSz,GrF, Halfway 3.00
7 MSz,GrF, Change has begun . . . 3.00

8 MSz,GrF, Road gets worse 3.00
9 MSz,GrF, New York, New York . . 3.00
10 MSz,GrF, Soul's price 3.00
11 MSz,GrF, Still the Road to Hell . . 3.00
12 MSz,GrF, The End of the Road . 3.00
TPB series rep.288-pg 30.00

MIKE GRELL'S MAGGIE THE CAT
Jan., 1996
1 (of 4) Master Piece,pt.1 . . . . 2.50
2 Master Piece,pt.2 . . . . 2.50

MINISTRY OF SPACE
April, 2001
1 (of 3) WEI,CWn,World War II . . . 3.00
2 WEI,CWn 3.00
3 WEI,CWn,concl. 3.00

MISERY SPECIAL
Dec., 1995
1 Cyberforce Origins 2.95

MISPLACED
May 2003
1 . . . . 2.95
1a variant (c)s 2.95
2 . . . . 2.95
3 . . . . 2.95

MONSTER FIGHTERS, INC.
April, 1999
1 Who you gonna call 3.00
2 Wake the dead 3.00
1-shot The Black Book 3.50

MONSTER FIGHTERS INC.: THE GHOSTS OF CHRISTMAS
Dec., 1999
1 The Fright Before Christmas 4.00

MONSTERMAN
(B&W) Sept., 1997
1 MM,from Action Planet 3.00
2 MM,Inhuman monsters 3.00
3 MM,King of Monsters 3.00
4 MM, conclusion 3.00

MORE THAN MORTAL/ LADY PENDRAGON
June, 1999
1 MHw,x-over 2.50
Prev. Edition 16-pg., B&W 4.95

MORE THAN MORTAL: OTHERWORLDS
Liar Comics, July 1999
1 F:Derdre & Morand 3.00
1a variant cover (1:2) 5.00
2 in Otherworld 3.00
2a variant cover (1:2) 4.00
3 Lady in white 3.00
3a variant Derdre cover (1:2) 3.00
4 Woman in white, concl 3.00
5 Famine,pt.1 . . . . 3.00
6 Famine,pt.2 . . . . 3.00
7 Famine,pt.3 . . . . 3.00
Art Gallery #1 . . . . 3.50
TPB Vol. 1, rep. #1 & #2 . . . . 6.95

TPB Vol. 2 . . . . 6.95
TPB Vol. 3, Truths & Legends 5.95

MR. MONSTER VS. GORZILLA
(2 color) July, 1998
1-shot, MGi 3.00

MR. MONSTER'S GAL FRIDAY: KELLY
B&W Jan., 2000
1 MGi 3.50
2 MGi 3.50
3 MGi,AMo(s) 3.50

MR. RIGHT
Aug., 2001
1 TDF,RF,flip-book 2.95
2 TDF,RF,F:General Public 2.95

MOTH
July 2003
1-shot 48-pg 5.95

M-REX
Nov., 1999
1 by Joe Kelly & Duncan Rouleau . 3.00
2 thru 5 . . . . @3.00
4a and 5a variant cover . . . . @3.00
#1 Limited Tour Edition 5.00
Preview, B&W, 16-pg 5.00

MS. FORTUNE
(B&W) 1998
1 by Chris Marrinan 3.00
2 Carnage in the Caribbean 3.00
3 Doom at the Dawn of Time 3.00

MUTANT EARTH
May, 2002
1 (of 4) F:Trakk 3.00
2 F:Zeithian warlord, Gallowz 3.00
3 . . . . 3.00
4 concl. 3.00
1a thru 4a variant (c) . . . . @3.00
TPB Vol. 1 Trakk, sgn.& num. . . . 16.95

MYSTERY, INC.
Ashcan 1 . . . . 4.00

MYTHSTALKERS
March 2003
1 The Labyrinth,pt.1 . . . . 2.95
2 The Labyrinth,pt.2 . . . . 2.95
3 The Labyrinth,pt.3 . . . . 2.95
4 The Labyrinth,pt.4 . . . . 2.95
5 London Nights 2.95
6 London Nights,pt.2 . . . . 2.95
7 Gangs of London 2.95

NAMELESS, THE
(B&W) May, 1997
1 PhH,I:The Nameless, protector of Mexico City's lost children 2.95
2 thru 5 . . . . @2.95

NASH
July, 1999
1 MMy, by & starring Kevin Nash . . 2.50
1a variant cover (1:2) 3.00

Nash–Obergeist   IMAGE   Comics Values Annual

2 MMy, the end of Nash?....... 2.50
2a variant cover (1:2)........ 2.50
#1 Photo-Split edition 3.00
Preview edition MMy,F:Kevin Nash . 2.50
Preview ed.A variant cover (1:2)... 2.50

NEON CYBER
July, 1999
1 F:Neon Dragons............ 2.50
1a variant cover (1:2)......... 2.50
1b glow-in-the-dark edition...... 6.95
2 gang alliance 2.50
2a variant cover (1:2)......... 2.50
3 Neon a suspect 2.50
4 who framed Neon?.......... 2.50
5 .... 2.50
6 V:Mohawks............... 2.50
7 .... 2.50
8 conclusion of Vol. 1 .... 2.50

NEW ADVENTURES OF ABRAHAM LINCOLN
Homage, Feb., 1998
TPB SMI, 144-pg............ 19.95

NEWFORCE
Extreme, 1996
1 Extreme Destroyer,pt.8
 x-over, bagged with card 2.50
2 .... 2.50
3 .... 2.50
4 Team disbands............ 2.50

NEWMAN
Extreme, 1996
1 Extreme Destroyer,pt.3
 x-over, bagged with card 2.50
2 .... 2.50
3 .... 2.50
4 Shadowhunt x-over,pt.5 ...... 2.50

NEWMEN
Extreme, 1994
1 JMs 3.00
2 JMs,I:Girth 2.50
3 JMs,V:Girth,I:Ikonna 2.50
4 JMs,A:Ripclaw 2.50
5 JMs,Ripclaw,V:Ikonn......... 2.50
6 JMs 2.50
7 JMs 2.50
8 JMs,Team Youngblood 2.50
9 ErS(s),JMs,Kodiak Kidnapped . 2.50
10 ExtremeSacrifice,pt.5,x-over ... 2.50
11 F:Reign 2.50
12 R:Elemental.............. 2.50
13 ErS,I:Bootleg............. 2.50
14 ErS,Dominion's Secret....... 2.50
15 I:Time Guild.............. 2.50
16 .... 2.50
16a variant cover 3.00
17 R:Girth................. 2.50
18 F:Byrd 2.50
19 I:Bordda Khan,Shepherd 2.50
20 Extreme Babewatch......... 2.50
21 ErS,CSp,(1 of 5) 2.50
22 ErS,CSp, Who Needs the
 Newmen?................ 2.50
23 ErS,CSp,Who are the Newmen? 2.50

THE NEW ORDER HANDBOOK
Various artists............... 2.25

NEW SHADOWHAWK, THE
June, 1995
1 KBk,I:New ShadowHawk 3.00
2 KBk,V:Mutants 3.00
3 KBk,I:Trophy.............. 3.00
4 KBk,V:Blowfish 3.00
5 KBk,................... 3.00
6 KBk,................... 3.00
7 KBk,................... 3.00

NINE RINGS OF WU-TANG, THE
Nov., 1999
1 by Brian Haberlin 4.00
2 .... 3.00
3 Bringers of Sleep 3.00
4 F:Mza.................. 3.00
4a variant cover............. 3.00
5 .... 3.00
#1 limited tour edition 5.00
Preview, B&W, 16-pg 5.00
TPB Book of Days 19.95

NINE RINGS OF WU-TANG, THE: FATIMA'S REVENGE
May, 2000
1 by Brian Haberlin 2.95

1963 Book 4 © Image

1963
April, 1993
1 Mystery Incorporated, AnM(s),
 RV,DGb 2.50
1a Gold ed................ 4.00
1b Bronze ed............... 3.00
2 No One Escapes...The Fury,
 RV,SBi,DGb,JV,I:The Fury 2.25
3 Tales of the Uncanny,
 RV,SBi,I:U.S.A. 2.25
4 Tales From Beyond
 JV,SBi,I:N-Man, Johnny Beyond 2.25
5 Horus, Lord of Light,
 JV,SBi,I:Horus 2.25
6 Tomorrow Syndicate,
 JV,SBi,C:Shaft 2.25
Ashcan #1 .... 3.00
Ashcan #2 .... 2.50
Ashcan #4 .... 2.00

NINE VOLT
Top Cow, 1997
1 ACh................... 3.00
1a Variant(c) 4.00
2 ACh................... 3.00
3 ACh,V:crazed junkie terrorists .. 2.50
4 ACh,V:Rev. Cyril Gibson 2.50

NOBLE CAUSES
Sept., 2001
1-shot First Impressions 3.00
1 two stories 3.00
2 .... 3.00
2a variant RGr(c)............ 3.00
3 three's a crowd............ 3.00
3a variant Ccs(c)............ 3.00
4 In Sickness and in Health,pt.4. . . 3.00
4a variant(c) 3.00
TPB In Sickness and in Health ... 12.95
1-shot Extended Family, 80-pg.... 4.95

NOBLE CAUSES: DISTANT RELATIVES
July 2003
1 (of 4) 2.95
2 thru 4 .... @2.95

NOBLE CAUSES: FAMILY SECRETS
Oct., 2002
1 (of 4) F:Liz Donnelly-Noble..... 3.00
1a variant(c) 3.00
2 spin control............... 3.00
2a variant(c)............... 3.00
3 guest stars galore.......... 2.95
4 .... 2.95
3a– a variant(c) .... @2.95

NO HONOR
Top Cow, Feb., 2001
1 (of 4) F:Tanne Yojimbo 5.00
2 .... 5.00
3 .... 2.50
4 concl.................. 2.50
Prev. 16-pg. B&W........... 5.00
TPB 96-pg................ 13.00

NO HONOR: MAKYO
Top Cow, Nov., 2001
1 .... 3.95

NORMAL MAN/ MEGATON MAN SPECIAL
1 .... 2.50

NOWHERESVILLE
March, 2002
TPB MRc, 192-pg. b&w 14.95

OBERGEIST: RAGNAROK HIGHWAY
Top Cow/Minotaur 2001
1 TyH 3.00
2 TyH 3.00
3 TyH 3.00
4 TyH 3.00
5 TyH,Ambushed............ 3.00
6 TyH,His memory, Abyss's flame . 3.00
TPB Directors' Cut 19.95

CVA Page 544   All comics prices listed are for *Near Mint* condition.

IMAGE

OBERGEIST: THE EMPTY LOCKET
Top Cow/Minotaur, 2002
1 TyH 2.95

OBJECTIVE FIVE
July, 2000
1 biological weapons 3.00
2 F:Lark, Alexis & DJ 3.00
3 Airborne Virus 3.00
4 Reunion 3.00
5 Hidden Enemies 3.00
6 in China 3.00
7 Origins 3.00

OPERATION KNIGHTSTRIKE
May, 1995
1 RHe,A:Chapel,Bravo,Battlestone 2.50
2 In Afganistan 2.50
3 final issue 2.50

THE OTHERS
March, 1995
0 JV(s),From ShadowHawk 2.50
1 JV(s)V:Mongrel 2.50
2 JV,Mongrel takes weapons 2.50
3 War 2.50
4 O:Clone 2.50

OVERKILL
Top Cow, Oct., 2000
1 PJe,x-over,A:Aliens,Predator ... 6.00
2 PJe,x-over,A:Aliens,Predator ... 6.00

OXIDO
Sept. 2003
1 (of 6) LHa(s) 2.95
2 LHa(s) 2.95

PACT
1994
1 JV(s),WMc,I:Pact, C:Youngblood 2.25
2 JV(s),V:Youngblood 2.25
3 JV(s),V:Atrocity 2.25

PARADIGM
Sept., 2002
1 F:Chris Howells, 48-pg. b&w ... 3.50
2 40-pg. b&w 3.50
3 40-pg. b&w 3.50
4 40-pg 3.50
5 .... 2.95
6 All About the Community 2.95
7 40-pg 2.95
8 Swirly Things 2.95
9 Real Swirly Things 2.95
10 .... 2.95
11 40-pg 3.50
12 40-pg 3.50
TPB Vol. 1 Segue to an Interlude . 13.95

PARLIAMENT OF JUSTICE, THE
March 2003
1-shot b&w, 56-pg 5.95

PARTS UNKNOWN: KILLING ATTRACTION
(B&W) April, 2000
1 Sci-Fi/UFO adventure 3.00

PARTS UNKNOWN: HOSTILE TAKEOVER
(B&W) June, 2000
1 by Beau Smith & Brad Gorby ... 3.00
2 .... 3.00
3 & 4 .... @3.00

PHANTOM FORCE
Dec., 1993
1 RLd,JK,w/card 2.75
2 JK,V:Darkfire 1.95
See also Color Comics section

PHANTOM GUARD
WildStorm, Oct., 1997
1 by Sean Ruffner, Ryan Benjamin 3.00
1a variant cover 3.00
1b Voyager bagged pack 3.50
2 Martian wasteland 3.00
3 Lowell Zerium Mines 3.00
4 'Target Locked' 3.00
5 V:Vanox 3.00
6 Countdown to Armageddon ... 3.00

Pitt #2 © Top Cow

PITT
Top Cow, 1993–95
1 DK,I:Pitt,Timmy 4.00
2 DK,V:Quagg 3.00
3 DK,V:Zoyvod 4.00
4 DK,V:Zoyvod 3.00
5 DK 2.50
6 DK 2.50
7 DK 2.50
8 Ransom 2.50
9 DK,Artic Adventures 2.00
Ashcan 1 .... 3.00

POWER OF THE MARK
1 I:Ted Miller 2.50
2 V:The Fuse 2.50
3 TMB(s), The Mark 2.50
4 TMB,Mark's secrets revealed ... 2.50

POWER RANGERS ZEO
Extreme, Sept., 1997
1 thru 3 TBm&MBm(s),TNu,NRd @2.50

POWER RANGERS ZEO YOUNGBLOOD
Extreme, Oct., 1997
1 thru 2 RLd,TBm,MBm .... @2.95

POWERS
April, 2000
1 Who killed Retro Girl,pt.1 ..... 15.00
2 Who killed Retro Girl,pt.2 ..... 20.00
3 Who killed Retro Girl,pt.3 ..... 15.00
4 .... 8.00
5 A murder solved 8.00
6 .... 8.00
7 WEl, Ride Along 7.00
8 Role Play,pt.1 .... 7.00
9 Role Play,pt.2 .... 7.00
10 Role Play,pt.3 .... 7.00
11 .... 5.00
12 Groupies 5.00
13 Groupies,pt.2 .... 5.00
14 Groupies,pt.3 .... 5.00
15 Supergroup,pt.1 .... 5.00
16 Supergroup 5.00
17 incl. Bastard Samurai prequel . 5.00
18 superhero wanted for murder . 5.00
19 supergroup shocking concl ... 5.00
20 supergroup explosive concl ... 5.00
21 Anarchy,pt.1 .... 3.00
22 Anarchy,pt.2 .... 3.00
23 Anarchy,pt.3 .... 3.00
24 Anarchy,pt.4 .... 3.00
25 The Sellouts,pt.1 .... 3.00
26 The Sellouts,pt.2 .... 3.00
27 The Sellouts,pt.3 .... 2.95
28 The Sellouts,pt.4 .... 2.95
29 The Sellouts,pt.5 .... 2.95
30 The Sellouts,pt.6 .... 2.95
31 Forever,pt.1 .... 2.95
32 Forever,pt.2 .... 2.95
33 Forever,pt.3 .... 2.95
34 Forever,pt.4 .... 2.95
35 Forever,pt.5 .... 2.95
36 Forever,pt.6 .... 2.95
Spec.-1 Coloring & Activity Book .. 2.25
1/2 Wizard story + new 3.00
Scriptbook 344-pg 19.95
TPB Vol.1 Who Killed Retro Girl . 19.95
TPB Vol.1 Who Killed Retro Girl . 21.95
TPB Vol.1 readers addition 15.95
TPB Vol.2 Roleplay 13.95
TPB Vol.2 Roleplay, 2nd pr 13.95
TPB Vol.3 Little Deaths 24.95
TPB Vol.4 Supergroup 19.95
TPB Vol.5 Anarchy 14.95

PRIMAL INSTINCT
March, 2000
Preview 2.50

PRO, THE
July, 2002
GN 1-shot GEn,ACo,JP 56-pg 8.00
Con. Ed. signed, numbered 24.95

PROPHET
Extreme, 1993–95
0 San Diego Comic-Con ed 4.00
1 RLd(s)DPs,O:Prophet,I:Mary McCormick 3.00
1a Gold ed 4.00
2 RLd(s),DPs,C:Bloodstrike 2.50

IMAGE

Prophet–Rising — Comics Values Annual

Prophet #10 © Extreme

3 RLd(s),DPs, V:Bloodstrike,
  I:Judas 2.50
4 RLd(s),DPs,I:Omen,A:Judas 2.50
4a SPa(c),Limited ed. 3.00
5 SPa,Supreme Apocalypse,pt.2 .. 3.00
6 SPa 2.50
7 SPa War Games,pt.1 .... 2.25
8 SPa War Games,pt.2 .... 2.50
9 SPa,Extreme Sacrifice Prelude .. 2.50
10 ExtremeSacrifice,pt.7,x-over ... 2.50
Sourcebook 3.00
Ashcan #1 .... 3.00
Ashcan #2 .... 3.00

[Second Series] 1995
1 SPl, New Series 3.50
2 SPl, New Direction 2.50
2a variant cover. 2.50
3 True Nature 2.50
4 The Dying Factor 2.50
5 .... 2.50
6 .... 2.50
7 CDi,SPa 2.50
8 .... 2.50
9 .... 2.50
TPB 12.95
Ann.#1 Supreme Apocalypse 2.50
Spec.#1 Babewatch special (1995). 2.50

PROPHET/CHAPEL: SUPER SOLDIERS
May, 1996
1 .... 2.50
1A variant(c) b&w 2.50
2 .... 2.50

PUFFED
July 2003
1 (of 3) 2.95
2 .... 2.95
3 .... 2.95

PVP
March 2003
1 Player vs. Player 2.95
2 Lord of the Schwing 2.95
3 Lost and Found 2.95
4 V:Devilfish 2.95
5 Max Powers 2.95

Q-UNIT: REVENGE
Oct., 1999
1 KIA,BNa 2.95
1a variant cover (1:2). 2.95
2 KIA,BNa 2.95
2a variant cover (1:2). 2.95

RADISKULL AND DEVIL DOLL
Dec. 2002
1-shot b&w 2.50
1-shot Radiskull Hate Love ... 2.95

RADIX
Dec., 2001
1 mysterious new force 3.00
2 F:Val Fiores 3.00
3 .... 3.00
4 mysterious object 3.00

RAGMOP
(B&W)
Vol.2 #1 by Rob Walton 3.00
Vol.2 #2 .... 3.00

RAIL
June, 2001
GN DvD, 48-pg. 6.00

RANDY O'DONNEL IS THE MAN
Image, May, 2001
1 TDF,RLm,flip-book 3.00
2 TDF,RLm,The Chosen 3.00
3 TDF,RLm,Terror of the
  Warrior Toads. 3.00
4 TDF,Merciless are the Malok. 3.00

REALM OF THE CLAW
Oct. 2003
1 (of 6) 2.95
1a variant (c). 2.95

RED STAR, THE
June, 2000
1 by Christian Gossett 8.00
2 Project: Antares 6.00
3 Fall of the Red Fleet 4.00
4 Marcus' mystic revelation .. 4.00
5 A worker's Tale 4.00
6 War torn Nokgorka 3.00
7 Nokgorka,pt.2. .... 3.00
8 Nokgorka,pt.3. .... 3.00
9 Marcus Antares is alive. ... 3.00
9a variant(c) 3.00
Spec.#1 3-D Transformation ... 3.00
TPB Vol.1 Battle of Kar
  Dathra's Gate, 144-pg. 24.95

REGULATORS
June, 1995
1 F:Blackjack,'Touch of Scandal' . 2.50
2 F:Vortex 2.50
3 F:Arson 2.50
4 F:Scandal. 2.50

REPLACEMENT GOD AND OTHER STORIES, THE
(B&W) May, 1997
1 Knute vs. King Ursus 3.00
2 by Zander Cannon 3.00

Replacement God #5 © Image

3 thru 5 .... @3.00

RESIDENT EVIL
Wildstorm March, 1998
1 comic/game magazine 56-pg. . 6.00
2 thru 4 comic/game mag. 56-pg. @5.50
TPB Collection 1, series rep. . 14.95

REX MUNDI
Aug., 2002
0 .... 3.00
1 Unexpected visitor 2.95
2 Puzzle in the Painting 2.95
3 The Archbiship and the Pimp. 2.95
4 Shadows Beneath the City ... 2.95
5 Shadows Beneath the City ... 2.95
6 Secrets Revealed 2.95
7 Father of Wisdom 2.95
8 Suspicion grows 2.95

RIPCLAW
Top Cow, 1995
1/2 Prelude to Series (Wizard) . 3.00
1/2a Con versions 7.00
1 A:Killjoy, I:Shadowblade ... 3.00
2 Cyblade, Heatwave 2.50
3 EcS,BPe,AV,Alliance with
  S.H.O.C.s. 2.50
4 conclusion 2.50
Spec.#1 I:Ripclaw's Brother .. 3.00

[1st Regular Series]
1 thru 5 .... @2.50

RIPTIDE
1995
1 O:Riptide 2.50
2 O:Riptide 2.50

RISING STARS
Top Cow, March, 1999
1 A celestial event 10.00
1a, b, & c variant covers 9.00
2 life & death of Peter Dawson 9.00
3 new special 8.00
4 .... 8.00
5 To the netherworld 8.00
6 Things Fall Apart,pt.1 ..... 8.00
7 Things Fall Apart,pt.2 ..... 8.00
8 Things Fall Apart,pt.3 ..... 5.00
9 Act Two,pt.1 .... 5.00

CVA Page 546 — All comics prices listed are for *Near Mint* condition.

IMAGE

Rising–Savage

10 years later	3.50
11 Specials out of control	3.00
12 War for Chicago	3.00
12a Monstermart edition	9.95
12b Monstermart gold foil	16.95
12c Monstermart holofoil	24.95
13 Brothers	3.00
14 Patriot vs. Matthew Bright	3.00
15 The Secret	3.00
16 finale	3.00
17 campaign to change the world	3.00
18 will they change the world	3.00
19 MSz,government vs. Specials	3.00
20 MSz	3.00
21 MSz	3.00
1/2 rep	3.00
#0 rep. from Wizard	2.50
Preview MSz, 16-pg., B&W	5.00
Prelude	2.95
TPB Deluxe,rep.#1–#8	19.95
TPB Vol.2, rep.#9–#16	19.95
TPB Vol.3 Visitations	9.00

RISING STARS: BRIGHT
Image/Top Cow Feb. 2003

1 (of 3)	3.00
2 Authority	3.00
3 Civilian Casualties	3.00

RISING STARS: UNTOUCHABLE
Image/Top Cow Sept. 2003

1 Story of Laurel Darkhaven	3.00

ROTOGIN: JUNKBOTZ
April 2003

1 (of 8)	2.95
2 thru 4	@2.95
1a variant(c)	2.95

RUMBLE GIRLS
(B&W) April, 2000

1 (of 8) Silky Warrior Tansie	3.50
2	3.50
3 Sugar and Wax	3.50
4 Sapphire Bullets	3.50
5 It's Not Romantic	3.50
6 Boy, Girl, Boy Girl	3.50
7 The Life of My Time, concl.	3.95

SABRE
(B&W) 1998

TPB 20th Anniversary	12.95

SAFFIRE
April, 2000

1 MtB,SRf,F:Melanie,Lyssa,Priscilla	3.00
1a variant JMd(c)	3.00
1b Mat Broome blue foil(c)	11.50
1c Joe Mac blue foil(c)	12.95
2 MtB,SRf,V:The Kraken	3.00
2a randy green(c)	8.95
2b signed & number	10.95
3 MtB,SRf,Hades Gate	3.00

SAINT ANGEL
2000

Preview	3.00
1 KIA,BNa,40-pg.,flip-book	4.00
1a variant(c)	4.00
2 KIA,BNa,40-pg.,flip-book	4.00
3 KIA,BNa,40-pg.,flip-book	4.00
4 KIA,BNa,40-pg.,flip-book	4.00

SAM & TWITCH
TMP, Aug., 1999

1 AMe,Spawn tie-in	2.75
2 AMe,The Udaku,pt.2	2.50
3 AMe,The Udaku,pt.3	2.50
4 AMe,The Udaku,pt.4	2.50
5 AMe,The Udaku,pt.5	2.50
6 AMe,The Udaku,pt.6	2.50
7 AMe,The Udaku,pt.7	2.50
8 AMe,The Udaku,pt.8	2.50
9 One Really Bad Day	2.50
10 Witch Hunter,pt.1	2.50
11 Witch Hunter,pt.2	2.50
12 Witch Hunter,pt.3	2.50
13 Witch Hunter,pt.4	2.50
14 Dumb Laws and Egg	2.50
15 Bounty Hunter Wars,pt.1	2.50
16 Bounty Hunter Wars,pt.2	2.50
17 Bounty Hunter Wars,pt.3	2.50
18 Bounty Hunter Wars,pt.4	2.50
19 Bounty Hunter Wars,pt.5	2.50
20 Jon Doe Affair,pt.1	2.50
21 Jon Doe Affair,pt.2	2.50
22 Jon Doe Affair,pt.3	2.50
23 Jon Doe Affair,pt.4	2.50
24 Jon Doe Affair,pt.5	2.50
25 Jon Doe Affair,pt.6	2.50
26 Jon Doe Affair,pt.7	2.50
27 Death Row Confessions	2.50
TPB Vol.1 Udaku, rep.#1–#8	21.95

SAMMY: TOURIST TRAP
Feb. 2003

1 (of 4)	2.95
2	2.95
3 Fight! Fight! Fight!	2.95
4 concl.	2.95

SAM STORIES: LEGS
Dec., 1999

1-shot SK, 24-pg	2.50

SAVAGE DRAGON
Highbrow, July, 1992

1 EL,I:Savage Dragon	3.00
2 EL,I:Supertpatriot	3.50
3 EL,V:Bedrock,with coupon#6	3.00
3a EL,w/o coupon	3.00
Spec. Savage Dragon Versus Savage Megaton Man #1 EL,DSm	3.00
Gold ed.	12.00
TPB	9.95

[2nd Series] June, 1993

1 EL,I:Freaks	4.00
2 EL,V:Teen.Mutant Ninja Turtles, Flip book Vanguard #0	3.00
3 EL,A:Freaks	3.00
4 EL,A:Freaks	3.00
5 EL,Might Man flip book	3.00
6 EL,A:Freaks	3.00
7 EL,Overlord	3.00
8 EL,V:Cutthroat,Hellrazor	3.00
9 EL	3.00
10 EL	3.00
11 EL,A:Overlord	3.00
12 EL	3.00
13 EL,Mighty Man,Star,I:Widow (appeared after issue #20)	3.00
13a Larsen version of 13	3.00
14 Possessed,pt.1	3.00
15 Possessed,pt.2	3.00
16 Possessed,pt.3,V:Mace	3.00
17 V:Dragonslayer	3.50
18 R:The Fiend	3.00
19 V:The Fiend	3.00
20 Rematch with Overlord	3.00
21 V:Overlord	3.00
22 A:Teenage Mutant Turtles	3.00
23 Rapture vs. SheDragon	3.00
24 Gang War,pt.1	3.00
25 Gang War,pt.2 double size	4.00
26	3.00
27	3.00
28	3.00
29	3.00
30 EL,'Overlord Reborn'	3.00
31 'The Dragon is trapped in Hell'	3.00
32 Kill-Cat vs. Justice	3.00
33 fatherhood	3.00
34 F:Hellboy,pt.1	3.50
35 F:Hellboy,pt.2	3.00
36 Dragon & Star try to rescue Peter Klaptin	3.00
37 mutants struggle in ruins of Chicago	3.00
38 Dragon vs. Cyberface	3.00
39 Dragon vs. Dung	3.00
40 'G-Man'	3.00
41 Wedding issue	3.00
42 V:Darklord	3.00
43 Stranded on another world	3.00
44 in flying saucer	3.00
45	3.00
46 She-Dragon vs. Vicious Circle	3.00
47 A knight and a mummy	3.00
48 Unfinished Business,pt.1	3.00
49 Unfinished Business,pt.2	3.00
50 Unfinished Business,pt.3, some reps., 96-pg.	6.00
51 F:She-Dragon	3.00
52 F:She-Dragon,V:Hercules	3.00
53 EL,F:She Dragon	3.00
54 EL,V:imposter Dragon	3.00
55 EL,Dragon & She-Dragon	3.00
56 EL,Rita Medermade kidnapped	3.00
57 EL,V:Overlord	3.00
58 EL,Dragon's Resurrection	3.00
59 EL,return of Savage Dragon	3.00
60 EL,R:Devastator	3.00
61 EL,R:Rapture	3.00
62 EL,Savage Dragon married	3.00
63 EL,Dragon's honeymoon	3.00
64 EL,Overlord's secrets	3.00
65 EL,Possessed	3.00
66 EL,Dragon shrunk	3.00
67 EL,A:SuperPatriot	3.00
68 EL,V:PowerHouse	3.00
69 EL	3.00
70 EL, Hell on Earth	3.00
71 EL,End of the World,prequel	3.00
72 EL,End of the World,prequel	3.50

Savage Dragon #30 © Erik Larsen

All comics prices listed are for *Near Mint* condition.

Savage–Shadowhawk — IMAGE — Comics Values Annual

Savage Dragon #66 © Erik Larsen

73 EL,End of the World,pt.1 . . . . . . 3.50
74 EL,End of the World,pt.2 . . . . . . 3.50
75 EL,End of the World,pt.3 . . . . 5.00
76 EL,Hell on Earth begins 3.50
77 EL,Wildstar Returns 3.50
77a Variant JOy(c) 3.50
78 EL,Mind-slaves of the
  Brain-Child 3.50
79 EL,Girl Trouble 3.50
80 EL,Lurkers beneath Lake Fear . . 3.50
81 EL,The Land Down Under 3.50
82 EL,The Bug Riders 3.50
83 EL,F:Madman 3.50
84 EL,F:Madman 3.50
85 EL,Peril in Pittsburgh 3.50
86 EL,Mighty Man returns 3.50
87 EL,Havoc in the Hidden City . . . 3.50
88 EL,To Challenge the Gods 3.50
89 EL,Panic in Detroit 3.50
90 EL,Return to Chicago 3.50
91 EL,Rapture returns 3.50
92 EL,Reclaim the Earth,pt.1 . . . . . 3.50
93 EL,Reclaim the Earth,pt.2 . . . . . 3.50
94 EL,V:CyberFace 3.50
95 EL,V:Sebastian Khan,concl. 3.50
96 EL,V:The Creator 3.50
97 EL,F:She-Dragon 3.50
98 EL,return home 3.50
99 EL,Evil Twins 3.50
100 EL, Torn Between Two
  Worlds, 100-pg. 10.00
101 EL,F:son of Dragon 3.00
102 EL,V:Afterbirth 3.00
103 EL,Dragon & son 3.00
104 EL,secrets 3.00
105 EL,F:The Candyman 3.00
106 EL,Dragon as Santa 2.95
107 EL,flipcover Major Damage . . . 3.95
108 EL,Flying Shoes Incident 2.95
109 EL,Danger in Dimension X . . . 2.95
110 EL,Lost in Dimension X 2.95
111 EL,Mako the man-shark 2.95
112 EL,V:Octopus & OpenFace . . . 2.95
113 EL,Vicious Circle 2.95
TPB A Talk With God 17.95
  TPB A Talk with God, 2nd pr. . . 19.95
TPB The Fallen, rep.#7–#11 . . . . 12.95
TPB Possessed, rep.#12–#16. . . . 12.95
TPB Archives #2, B&W,1982 rep. . . 2.95
TPB Archives #3, B&W,1984 rep. . . 2.95
TPB Archives #4, B&W,1986 rep. . . 2.95
TPB Revenge 13.95
TPB Greatest Team-ups 19.95
TPB Book 1 Baptism of Fire 14.95

TPB Baptism of Fire (2002) . . 14.95
TPB Gang War 16.95
TPB This Savage World 15.95
TPB Vol.9, Worlds at War 16.95
Spec. 1-shot Savage Dragon
  Companion,64-pg. 2.95
Spec. 1-shot Savage Dragon/
  Hellboy, collected ed. 5.95

SAVAGE DRAGON DESTROYER DUCK
Nov., 1996
1 SvG,ChM,EL 4.00

SAVAGE DRAGON, THE: RED HORIZON
Comics Feb., 1997
1 MsM 3.00
2 MsM,Dragon in the ER,A:Freak
  Force 3.00
3 (of 3) MsM,Freak Force beaten . . 3.00

SAVAGE DRAGON: MARSHAL LAW
(B&W) July, 1997
1 (of 2) PMs,KON,F:Marshal Law . 3.00
2 PMs,KON, concl. 3.00

SAVAGE DRAGON: SEX & VIOLENCE
July, 1997
1 (of 2) TBm,MBm 3.00
2 TBm,MBm,AH, concl. 3.00

SAVAGE DRAGONBERT: FULL FRONTAL NERDITY
Oct., 2002
GN 80-pg. b&w 5.95

SAVANT GARDE
WildStorm, March, 1997
1 'A team without a rule book' . . . 2.50
2 Between killer & killer cat 2.50
3 V: strange Tapestry 2.50
4 'Any super-villain can take
  over the world' 2.50
5 'The Final Showdown' 2.50
6 BKs,Guilty until proven innocent . 2.50
7 BKs,death of John Colt 2.50
Fan Edition #1, with Fan #22 . . . . 3.00
Fan Edition #2, with Fan #23 . . . . 3.00
Fan Edition #3, with Fan #24 . . . . 3.00

SECTION ZERO
June, 2000
1 KK,TG,UFO's etc. 2.50
2 KK,TG,Sargasso sea 2.50
3 KK,TG,Curse of Sargasso 2.50
4 KK,TG,Ground Zero revealed . . . 2.50
5 KK,TG,Sargasso vs. Crust 2.95
6 KK,TG,Fire and Rain 2.95

SEI: DEATH & LEGEND
Nov. 2003
GN Manga 6.95

SEMANTIC LACE
June 2003
GN b&w, 112-pg. 9.95

Shadowhawk #3 © Image

SHADOWHAWK
Shadowline, Aug., 1992
1 JV,I:ShadowHawk,Black Foil(c),
  Pin-up, with coupon#1 . . . . . . 4.00
1a w/o coupon 2.25
2 JV,V:Arsenal,A:Spawn, I:Infiniti . . 3.00
3 JV,V:Arsenal,w/glow-in-the-
  dark(c) 3.50
4 V:Savage Dragon 2.50
TPB rep.#1-4 . . . . 19.95
Ashcan #1 . . . . 2.50
Ashcan #2 . . . . 2.50
Ashcan #3 . . . . 2.50
Ashcan #4 . . . . 2.50

[2nd Series] 1993
1 JV,Die Cut(c) 2.50
1a Gold ed. 3.00
2 JV,ShadowHawk I.D. 2.50
2a Gold ed. 2.50
3 Poster(c),JV,w/Ash Can 2.50
TPB 19.95

[3rd Series] 1993
0 Zero issue 2.25
1 JV,CWf,V:Vortex,Hardedge,
  Red Foil(c) 2.50
1a Gold ed. 3.00
1b signed 6.00
2 JV,CWf,MA,I:Deadline,
  BU&I:US Male 2.50
3 JV(a&s),ShadowHawk has AIDS,
  V:Hardedge,Blackjak 2.25
4 JV(a&s),V:Hardedge 2.25
Note: #5 to #11 not used; #12 below
  is the next issue, the 12th overall.
12 Monster Within,pt.1 . . . . 2.25
13 Monster Within,pt.2 . . . . 2.25
14 Monster Within,pt.3 . . . . 2.50
15 Monster Within,pt.4 . . . . 2.50
16 Monster Within,pt.5 . . . . 2.50
17 Monster Within,pt.6 . . . . 2.50
18 JV,D:ShadowHawk 2.50
Spec.#1 . . . . 3.50
Gallery#1 . . . . 2.00

SHADOWHAWK/ VAMPIRELLA
Feb., 1995
Book 2 V:Kaul 4.95
Book #1: see Vampi/ShadowHawk

IMAGE

SHADOWHUNT SPECIAL
Extreme, 1996
1 Shadowhunt x-over,pt.1 . . . . 2.50

SHADOWS
Feb. 2003
1 . . . . 2.95
2 . . . . 2.95
3 . . . . 2.95
4 b&w 2.95
5 b&w 2.95

SHAMAN'S TEARS
Creative Fire, 1993–96
0 MGr 2.50
1 MGr,I:Shaman,B:Origin 3.00
1a Siver Prism ed. 5.00
2 MGr,Poster(c) 2.50
3 MGr,V:Bar Sinister 2.50
4 MGr,V:Bar Sinister,E:Origin. 2.25
5 MGr,R:Jon Sable 2.25
6 MGr,V:Jon Sable 2.25
7 MGr,V:Rabids 2.25
8 MGr,A:Sable. 2.25
9 MGr,Becoming of Broadarrow. . . 2.25
10 Becoming of Broadarrow,pt.2 . . . 2.50
11 Becoming of Broadarrow,pt.3 . . . 2.50
12 Becoming of Broadarrow,pt.4 . . . 2.50
13 The Offspring,pt.1 . . . . 2.50

SHARKY
1998
1 by Dave Elliott & Alex Horley . . . 2.50
1a variant cover (5,000 made) . . . 3.00
2 coma over 2.50
2a variant cover. 2.95
3 R:Blazin' Glory 2.50
3a variant SBi(c) 2.50
4 tons of guest stars, concl 2.50
4a variant DAy(c) 2.50

SHATTERED IMAGE
WildStorm, 1996
1 KBk,TnD,crossover. 2.50
2 KBk 2.50
3 KBk 2.50
4 KBk,TnD,concl. 2.50

SHIDIMA
Jan. 2001
1 PtL, A Warlands saga 3.00
1a variant(c) 3.00
1b stormkote(c) 8.00
2 PtL 3.00
2a variant(c) 3.00
2b variant(c) 3.00
3 PtL 3.00
3a variant(c) 3.00
3b variant(c) 3.00
4 . . . . 3.00
5 . . . . 3.00
6 . . . . 3.00
0 24-pg. 2.25
0 variant(c) 2.25

SHIP OF FOOLS
(B&W) Sept., 1997
0 Bryan J.L. Glass, Michael
  Avon Oeming. 3.00
1 Death & Taxes,pt.1 . . . . 3.00
2 Death & Taxes,pt.2 . . . . 3.00
3 Death & Taxes,pt.3 . . . . 3.00
4 Death & Taxes,pt.4 . . . . 3.00
TPB rep. Caliber series. 14.95

SHOCKROCKETS
April, 2000
1 (of 6) KBk,SI. 2.50
2 KBk,SI,Command Decision. 2.50
3 KBk,SI,The Triangle Trade 2.50
4 KBk,SI,Rocket Science. 2.50
5 KBk,SI,sneak attack 2.50
6 KBk,SI,Final Battle,flip-book 2.50

SHUT UP & DIE
(B&W) 1998
1 JHI and Kevin Stokes 3.00
2 JHI,Angry White Man 3.00
3 JHI,Wife abducted 3.00
4 JHI 3.00
5 JHI,A:Earl Jackson 3.00

SIEGE
WildStorm, 1997
1 JPe,AV,Nothing you believe
  is real. 2.50
2 JPe,AV,Omega goes to Hawaii
  for funeral. 2.50
3 JPe,AV,Zontarian Crab Ships vs.
  Drop Ship. 2.50
4 JPe,AV,Rescue of Omega Squad 2.50

Sigma #3 © WildStorm

SIGMA
WildStorm, 1996
1 BCi,Fire From Heaven prelude . . 2.50
2 BCi,Fire From Heaven,pt.6 . . . . . 2.50
3 BCi,Fire From Heaven,pt.14 . . . . 2.50

SILENT SCREAMERS
Oct., 2000
1 Nosferatu, 40-pg. 4.95

SINKING
March, 1999
GN JHI 14.95

SIREN
(B&W) May, 1998
1 by J. Torres & Tim Levins 2.95
2 F:Zara Rush, private eye 2.95
3 cpmc;isopm 2.95
TPB rep. Shapes 9.95

SKINNERS
TMP, July, 2000
1 MtB,JMd. 3.00
1a variant PtL(c) 3.00
1b variant Andy Park(c). 3.00
1c variant MtB(c) 2-D. 3.00
1d limited ed. Broom(c) 8.95
1e limited ed., signed. 10.95
2 MtB,SRf 3.00
2a variant JBz(c) 3.00

SOLAR LORD
March, 1999
1 by Khoo Fuk Lung 2.50
2 Nickson is Solar Lord 2.50
3 V:5 enemies 2.50
4 V:5 enemies 2.50
5 V:The Emperor of Darkness 2.50
6 O:Nickson 2.50
7 concl., book one 2.50

SOMETHING WICKED
Oct. 2003
1 (of 4) b&w 2.95

SOUL OF A SAMURAI
April 2003
1 (of 4) b&w, 48-pg. 3.95
2 . . . . 3.95
3 48-pg 5.95

SOUL REAVER: LEGACY OF KAIN
Top Cow, June, 2000
1-shot MHw,video game tie-in. . . . 2.50

SOUL SAGA
Top Cow, 2000
1 SPa,F:Aries, Soulblade. 5.00
1a variant(c) JMd (1:4) 5.00
1b variant Michael Turner(c) (1:4) . 5.00
2 SPa,death in the family. 3.50
2a variant David Finch(c). 3.50
2b variant Pat Lee(c) 3.50
3 SPa, Khan Hordes 2.50
4 SPa, Dominion vs. Khan. 2.50
5 SPa, F:Ares 2.50
Coll.Ed.Vol.1 . . . . 5.95

SOULWIND
(B&W) March, 1997
1 quest for Soulwind begins. 3.00
2 Nick becomes 'Captain Crash' . . 3.00
3 Captain Crash & Poke pursue
  Soulwind info 3.00
4 concl. of story arc 3.00
5 The Day I Tried to Live,pt.1 . . . . . 3.00
6 The Day I Tried to Live,pt.2 . . . . . 3.00
7 The Day I Tried to Live,pt.3 . . . . . 3.00
8 The Day I Tried to Live,pt.4 . . . . . 3.00
TPB rep #1–#4 . . . . 9.95

SPARTAN: WARRIOR SPIRIT
July, 1995
1 thru 4 . . . . @3.00

SPARTAN X
(B&W) Sept., 1998
1 MGo,RM,'Plague Train'. 2.95
2 MGo,RM,'Plague Train',pt.2 . . . . 2.95
3 MGo,RM,'Plague Train',pt.3 . . . . 2.95

SPAWN
TMP, May, 1992
1 TM,I:Spawn,w/GP,DK pinups... 11.00
1a black & white.............. 23.00
2 TM,V:The Violator........... 10.00
3 TM,V:The Violator........... 10.00
4 TM,V:The Violator,+coupon #2 . 8.00
4a w/o coupon................ 3.00
5 TM,O:Billy Kincaid........... 8.00
6 TM,I:Overt-Kill.............. 5.00
7 TM,V:Overt-Kill.............. 5.00
8 TM,AMo(s),F:Billy Kincaid..... 5.00
9 NGa(s),TM,I:Angela.......... 6.00
10 DS(s),TM,A:Cerebus......... 4.00
11 FM(s),TM, Home Story....... 4.00
12 TM,Chapel killed Spawn..... 4.00
13 TM,A:Youngblood........... 4.00
14 TM,A:The Violator........... 5.00
15 TM, Myths II................ 4.00
16 GCa,I:Anti-Spawn........... 5.00
17 GCa,V:Anti-Spawn........... 7.00
18 GCa,ATi,D:Anti-Spawn....... 9.00
19 & 20 see after #25
21 TM,The Hunt,pt.1............ 9.00
22 TM,The Hunt,pt.2............ 3.00
23 TM,The Hunt,pt.3............ 3.00
24 TM,The Hunt,pt.4............ 3.00
25 Image X Book,MS,BTn....... 5.00
19 I:Houdini.................... 4.00
20 J:Houdini................... 6.00
26 TM........................ 4.00
27 I:The Curse................. 4.00
28 Faces Wanda............... 4.00
29 Returns From Angela........ 4.00
30 A:KKK..................... 4.00
31 R:Redeemer................ 3.00
32 TM,GCa,New Costume....... 4.00
33 R:Violator.................. 3.00
34 V:Violator.................. 3.00
35 F:Sam & Twitch............. 3.00
36 Talks to Wanda............. 3.00
37 I:The Freak................. 3.00
38.......................... 3.00
39.......................... 3.00
40 V:Curse................... 3.00
41 V:Curse................... 3.00
42 thru 49................... @3.00
50 48-pg..................... 4.00
51.......................... 3.00
52.......................... 3.00
53 A:Malebolgia............... 3.00
54 return to New York, alliance
   with Terry Fitzgerald......... 3.00
55 plans to defeat Jason Wynn... 3.00
56 efforts to defeat Jason Wynn.. 3.00
57.......................... 3.00
58 sequel to Spawn #29........ 3.00
59.......................... 3.00
60 battle between Spawn and
   Clown cont................. 3.00
61 battle with Clown concl...... 3.00
62 Spawn is Al Simmons for 1 day . 3.00
63 Operation: Wynn fall,pt.1.... 3.00
64 Wynn falls, bagged with toy
   catalog................... 2.50
65 recap issue................ 2.50
66 TM,GCa,lives of alley bums... 2.50
67 TM,GCa,Sam and Twitch..... 2.50
68 TM,GCa,R:Freak............ 2.50
69 TM,GCa,F:Freak............ 2.50
70 TM,GCa.................... 2.50
71 TM,GCa,Cold Blooded Truth . 2.50
72 TM,GCa,Haunting of the Heap. 2.50
73 TM,GCa,R:The Heap......... 2.50
74 TM,GCa,pathway to misery... 2.50
75 TM,GCa,Deadly Revelations.. 2.50
76 TM,GCa,Granny Blake....... 2.50
77 TM,GCa,confronts........... 2.50
78 TM,GCa,DaM,'Sins of Excess'.. 2.50
79 TM,GCa,DaM,Killer in N.Y..... 2.50
80 TM,GCa,DaM,F:Sam & Twitch.. 2.50

Spawn #84 © Todd McFarlane

81 TM,GCa,DaM,Sins are reborn . 2.50
82 TM,GCa,DaM,sea of self-doubt . 2.50
83 TM,GCa,V:Jason Wynn...... 2.50
84 TM,GCa,DaM,Helle's Belles... 2.50
85 TM,GCa,DaM,Legend of
   Hellspawn.................. 2.50
86 TM,GCa,DaM,V:Al Simmons... 2.50
87 TM,GCa,DaM,Al Simmons fate . 2.50
88 TM,GCa,DaM,Seasons of
   change.................... 2.50
89 TM,GCa,DaM,secrets revealed . 2.50
90 TM,GCa,DaM,three stories... 2.50
91 TM,GCa,DaM,Black Cat
   Bones,pt.1................. 2.50
92 TM,GCa,DaM,Black Cat
   Bones,pt.2................. 2.50
93 TM,GCa,DaM,Devil's Banquet.. 2.50
94 TM,GCa,DaM,Children's Hour . 2.50
95 TM,GCa,DaM,Cracks in the
   Foundation................. 2.50
96 TM,GCa,DaM,Rules of
   Engagement................ 2.50
97 TM,GCa,DaM,Heaven's Folly... 2.50
98 TM,GCa,DaM,The Trouble
   with Angels................. 2.50
99 TM,GCa,DaM,Edge of Darkness 2.50
100A TM,GCa,DaM,TM(c)She dies 10.00
100B TM,GCa,DaM,FM(c)....... 5.00
100C TM,GCa,DaM,GCa(c)...... 5.00
100D TM,GCa,DaM,AshleyWood(c) 5.00
100E TM,GCa,DaM,MMi(c)....... 5.00
100F TM,GCa,DaM,AxR(c)....... 5.00
101 TM,AMe,DaM,The Speed
   of Night................... 2.50
102 TM,AMe,DaM,Remains...... 2.50
103 TM,AMe,DaM,A Town Called
   Malice..................... 2.50
104 TM,Retribution Overdrive,pt.1 . 2.50
105 TM,Retribution Overdrive,pt.2 . 2.50
106 TM,The Kingdom,pt.1....... 2.50
107 TM,The Kingdom,pt.2....... 2.50
108 TM,The Kingdom,pt.3....... 2.50
109 TM,Hour of Cleansing
   Approaches................ 2.50
110 TM,The Kingdom,pt.4....... 2.50
111 TM,The Kingdom,pt.5....... 2.50
112 TM,The Kingdom,pt.6....... 2.50
113 TM,The Kingdom,pt.7....... 2.50
114 TM,The Bridge,pt.1......... 2.50
115 TM,The Bridge,pt.2......... 2.50
116 TM,Consequences......... 2.50
117 TM,A Season in Hell........ 2.50
118 TM,A Season in Hell,pt.2.... 2.50
119 TM,A Season in Hell,pt.3.... 2.50
120 TM,A Season in Hell,pt.4.... 2.50
121 TM,The Devil His Due....... 2.50
122 TM,Salvation Road......... 2.50
123 TM,Freedom in Nothingness . 2.50
124 TM,Through These Eyes.... 2.50
125 TM,Wake Up Dreaming,pt.1... 2.50
126 TM,Wake Up Dreaming,pt.2... 2.50
127 TM Loose Threads,pt.1..... 2.50
128 TM,Loose Threads,pt.2..... 2.50
129 TM,Loose Threads,pt.3..... 2.50
130 TM,Loose Threads,pt.4..... 2.95
131 TM,God is a Bullet,pt.1..... 2.95
132 TM,God is a Bullet,pt.2..... 2.50
133 TM,God is a Bullet,pt.3..... 2.50
134 TM,God is a Bullet,pt.4..... 2.50
135 TM,Mad Shadows,pt.1...... 2.50
136 TM,Mad Shadows,pt.2...... 2.50
137 TM,Mad Shadows,pt.3...... 2.50
138 TM,Mad Shadows,pt.4...... 2.50
139 TM,Asunder,pt.1........... 2.50
140 TM,Asunder,pt.2........... 2.50
Ann.#1 Blood & Shadows, 64-pg... 4.95
GN Spawn Movie adapt........ 5.00
TPB Capital Collection rep.#1-3
   limited to 1,200 copies..... 300.00
TPB TM,rep.#1–#5............ 9.95
TPB Spawn III rep. #12–#15... 9.95
TPB Spawn IV rep. #16–#20... 9.95
TPB Spawn V rep.#21–#25.... 9.95
TPB Spawn VI, rep.#26–#30... 9.95
TPB Vol. VII Deadman's Touch... 9.95
TPB Vol. VIII Betrayal of Blood.... 9.95
TPB Angela's Hunt............ 9.95
TPB Vol.9 Urban Jungle....... 9.95
TPB Vol.10 Vengeance of the Dead 9.95
TPB Vol.11 Crossroads........ 9.95
TPB Vol.12 Immortality........ 10.95
GN Spawn: Blood and Salvation... 4.95
Fan Edition #1, with Fan #16..... 3.00
Fan Edition #1a variant cover..... 4.00
Fan Edition #1b gold logo,retailer.. 5.00
Fan Edition #2, with Fan #17..... 3.00
Fan Edition #2a variant cover..... 4.00
Fan Edition #2b gold logo,retailer.. 5.00
Fan Edition #2c platinum Foil logo . 5.00
Fan Edition #2, with Fan #18..... 3.00
Fan Edition #2a variant cover..... 4.00
Fan Edition #3b gold logo,retailer.. 5.00

SPAWN/BATMAN
Image/DC 1994
1 FM(s),TM................... 5.00

SPAWN BLOOD FEUD
June, 1995
1 V:Vampires................. 4.00
2.......................... 4.00
3 Hunted as a Vampire........ 4.00
4 V:Heartless John............. 4.00

SPAWN BIBLE
TMP, Aug., 1996
1 TM,GCa.................... 2.25
2 Book of the Dead, 56-pg...... 4.95

SPAWN: THE DARK AGES
TMP, March, 1999
1 GF,LSh, from 12th century.... 2.50
1a variant TM(c) (1:4)......... 7.00
2 LSh,A:Black Knight........... 2.50
3 LSh,A:Black Knight........... 2.50
4 LSh,Lord Covenant.......... 2.50
5 LSh,Lord Covenant.......... 2.50
6 LSh,Sister Immaculata....... 2.50
7 LSh,Cogliostro.............. 2.50
8 LSh,Acts of Contrition........ 2.50
9 LSh....................... 2.50

IMAGE

Spawn–Stormwatch

10 LSh,F:Lord Covenant. 2.50
11 LSh,Ghost on the Hill 2.50
12 LSh,The Faithful 2.50
13 LSh,Blood and Glory 2.50
14 LSh,The Innocent 2.50
15 LSh,New Beginnings 2.50
16 CWf,Heart of the HellSpawn . . . 2.50
17 CWf,The Circle and the Worm . . 2.50
18 CWf,Crucified 2.50
19 CWf,Like Any Other Man 2.50
20 Voices in the Dark 2.50
21 Sins of the Hellspawn 2.50
22 The Seedling 2.50
23 The Beast 2.50
24 Bleed, Pagan, Bleed 2.50
25 The Plague of Man 2.50
26 Lesion 2.50
27 Bubonic Nights 2.50
28 Stonehaven,pt.1 . . . . 2.50
29 Stonehaven,pt.2 . . . . 2.50
30 The Beast of the Wood 2.50
31 Home to Roost 2.50

SPAWN THE IMPALER
TMP Oct., 1996
1 (of 3) MGr, fully painted 4.00
2 MGr 4.00
3 MGr 4.00

SPAWN: THE UNDEAD
TMP, May, 1999
1 PJe,DT,CWf,F:Spawn 2.25
2 PJe,DT,CWf,F:Travis Ward 2.25
3 PJe,DT,CWf,Heaven vs. Hell . . . 2.25
4 PJe,DT,CWf,suicide cult 2.25
5 PJe,DT,CWf,The Wind That
   Shakes the Barley 2.25
6 PJe,DT,CWf 2.25
7 PJe,DT,CWf,Up the Down Stairs 2.25
8 PJe,DT,CWf,One Lunch to Live. . 2.25
9 PJe,DT,CWf,Waiting 2.25
10 PJe,DT,CWf,How to Win Friends
    and Influence People 2.25
11 PJe,DT,CWf,Heaven and Hell
    and In Between 2.25

SPAWN/WILDC.A.T.S
Jan., 1996
1 AMo(s),Devilday, pt.1, x-over . . . 3.50
2 AMo(s),Devilday, pt.2 . . . . 3.50
3 AMo(s),Devilday, pt.3 . . . . 3.50
4 AMo(s),Devilday, pt.4 . . . . 3.50

SPIRIT OF THE TAO
Top Cow, May, 1998
1 BTn,F:Lance & Jasmine 2.50
2 BTn,mission to destroy base. . . . 2.50
3 BTn,V:Jaikap Clan 2.50
4 BTn,F:Jasmine & Lance 2.50
5 BTn, Antidote to virus 2.50
6 BTn, Tao grows stronger. 2.50
7 BTn, V:Menicus 2.50
8 BTn, A:Messiah 2.50
9 BTn, The Dragon is Loose 2.50
10 BTn, Jasmine out of control 2.50
11 BTn, Dragon ash race 2.50
12 BTn, F:Disciple 2.50
13 BTn, friend or foe 2.50
14 BTn, must one die? 2.50
15 BTn,conclusion, 48-pg. 3.95

SPLITTING IMAGE
March, 1993
1 DsM,A:Marginal Seven 2.25
2 DsM,A:Marginal Seven 2.25

STAR
June, 1995
1 F:Star from Savage Dragon 2.50
2 Buried Alive 2.50
3 A:Savage Dragon,Rapture 2.50
4 A:Savage Dragon,Rapture 2.50

STARCHILD: MYTHOPOLIS
(B&W) 1997
0 JOn, 'Prologue'. 2.95
1 JOn, 'Pinehead' 2.95
2 JOn, 'Pinehead,'pt.2 . . . . 2.95
3 JOn, 'Pinehead,'pt.3 . . . . 2.95
4 JOn, 'Fisher King,'pt.1 . . . . 2.95
5 JOn, 'Fisher King,'pt.2 . . . . 2.95

Stone Vol. 2, #3 © Avalon

STONE
Avalon Sept., 1998
2 WPo,V:Rook 2.50
3 WPo,A:Bann 2.50
4 WPo, conclusion 2.50

[VOL. II] Aug., 1999
1 WPo 2.50
1a Chromium Edition 6.95
2 WPo, search for murderer 2.50
2 Stonechrome edition 14.95
3 WPo,Blood from a Stone 2.50
4 WPo,A Rose by Any Other Name 2.50
5 Wpo, series resumes 2.95

STORMWATCH
WildStorm, 1993
0 JSc(c),O:StormWatch,
   V:Terrorists,w/card 2.50
1 JLe(c&s),ScC,TvS(i),
   I:StormWatch 2.25
1a Gold ed 4.00
2 JLe(c&s),ScC,TvS(i),I:Cannon,
   Winter,Fahrenheit,Regent 2.25
3 JLe(c&s),ScC,TvS(i),V:Regent,
   I:Backlash 3.00
4 V:Daemonites 2.50
5 SRf(s),BBh,V:Daemonites 2.25
6 BCi,ScC,TC,A:Mercs 2.25
7 BCi,ScC,TC,A:Mercs 2.50
8 BCi,ScC,TC,A:Mercs 2.50
9 BCi,I:Defile 2.50
10 V:Talos 2.00
10a variant(c) 5.00

11 RMz(s),the end? 2.00
12 RMz(s),V:Hellstrike,'Visions
    of Deathtrap' 2.00
13 V:M.A.D.-1 . . . . 2.00
14 Despot 2.00
15 Batallion, Flashpoint 2.00
16 V:Defile 2.00
17 D:Batallion 2.50
18 R:Argos 2.50
19 R:M.A.D.-1,L:Winter 2.50
20 F:Cannon,Winter,Bendix 2.50
21 V:Wildcats 2.50
22 RMz,BWS(c),WildStorm
    Rising,pt.9,w/2 cards 2.50
22a Newsstand ed 1.95
23 RMz(s),R:Despot,Warguard . . . 2.50
24 V:Despot 2.50
25 SSe,ScC,BCi,A:Spartan 2.75
25a 2nd printing 2.50
26 V:Despot 2.50
27 V:Despot,Rebuilding,'And in
    the End' 2.50
28 F:Blademaster,Swift,Flint,
    Comanche,New Adventures . . . 2.50
29 I:Prism,Reorganization 2.50
30 V:Heaven's Fist 2.50
31 V:Middle Eastern Terrorists 2.50
32 . . . . 2.50
33 inc. Winters Journey 2.50
34 . . . . 2.50
35 Fire From Heaven,pt.5 . . . . 2.50
36 Fire From Heaven,pt.12 . . . . . . 2.50
37 Double size,F:Weatherman One,
    I:Rose Tatoo 10.00
38 WEl(s) 5.00
39 WEl(s) 5.00
40 WEl(s),virus 5.00
41 WEl(s) 5.00
42 WEl(s),Weatherman discovers a
    conspiracy 5.00
43 WEl(s) 5.00
44 WEl(s),history of Jenny Sparks . 5.00
45 WEl(s),Battalion visits
    his family 5.00
46 WEl(s),secrets and more
    secrets, prologue 5.00
47 WEl(s), JLe, SW, dangerous
    experiment gone awry 5.00
48 WEl(s),'Change or Die'pt.1 . . . . . 5.00
49 WEl(s),'Change or Die'pt.2 . . . . . 5.00
50 WEl(s),'Change or Die' concl.
    large size 8.00
Sourcebok JLe(s),DT 2.75
Spec.#1 RMz(s),DT 4.25
Spec.#2 F:Fleshpoint 2.50
Ashcan 1 . . . . 3.00
TPB Change the World 9.95
TPB A Finer World 14.95
TPB Change or Die 14.95
TPB Force of Nature 14.95
TPB Lightning Strikes 14.95

STORMWATCH
WildStorm, Oct., 1997
1 WEl,bacterial horror,'Strange
   Weather,'pt.1,'Hard Rain' 5.00
1a Variant cover 5.00
1b Voyager bagged pack 5.00
2 WEl,Stormwatch Black team,
   'Strange Weather,'pt.2 . . . . 5.00
3 WEl,Black team,'Strange
   Weather,'pt.3,'A Storm Coming' 5.00
4 WEl,A Finer World,pt.1 . . . . 5.00
5 WEl,A Finer World,pt.2 . . . . 5.00
6 WEl,A Finer World,pt.3 . . . . 5.00
7 WEl,Bleed,pt.1 . . . . 5.00
8 WEl,Bleed,pt.2 . . . . 5.00
9 WEl,Bleed,pt.3 . . . . 5.00
10 WEl,'No Reason' 10.00
11 WEl,BHi,PNe,F:Jackson King,

Stormwatch–Team 1

'No Direction Home' 10.00
TPB Change or Die 15.00
TPB Force of Nature,(DC) 14.95
TPB Final Orbit, 96-pg. (DC). 9.95

STRANGERS
March 2003
1 (of 6) 2.95
2 In the Inwards of the Night . . . 2.95
3 Caresses such as Snakes Give . 2.95
4 The Livid Daylights 2.95
5 Icy till the Evening 2.95
6 Icy till the Evening 2.95
2a–6a variant (c) 2.95

STRANGERS IN PARADISE VOL. 3
Homage,1996
1 TMr 5.00
2 TMr 4.00
Homage,1996–97
3 TMr,David & Katchoo fight 3.50
4 TMr,Katchoo makes startling discovery 3.50
5 TMr,Francine's college days . . . 3.50
6 TMr,Katchoo searches for David . 3.50
7 TMr 3.50
8 TMr,demons of the past 3.50

STREET FIGHTER
Sept. 2003
1 Round One! Fight! 2.95
2 . . . . 2.95
3 . . . . 2.95
1a–3a variant (c) . . . . @2.95

STREETS
April, 1999
TPB Streets 16.95

STRIKEBACK!
WildStorm, 1996
1 rep & new art 2.50
2 thru 5 . . . . @2.50

STUPID COMICS
Sept., 2002
1-shot by Jim Mahfood,b&w 2.95
1-shot #2 . . . . 2.95

SUPER-PATRIOT
July, 1993
1 N:Super-Patriot. 2.25
2 KN(i),O:Super-Patriot 2.25
3 A:Youngblood 2.25
4 . . . . 2.00

SUPER-PATRIOT: LIBERTY AND JUSTICE
June, 1995
1 R:Covenant 2.50
2 Tokyo 2.50
3 Tokyo gets Trashed 2.50
4 Final issue 2.50
TPB Liberty and Justice, 112-pg. . 12.95

SUPERPATRIOT: AMERICA'S FIGHTING FORCE
July, 2002
1 (of 4) F:Johnny Armstrong 2.95

IMAGE

2 patriotic pandemonium 2.95
3 High Anxiety 2.95
4 The Final Battle, concl. 2.95

SUPERSTAR: AS SEEN ON TV
Jan., 2001
Spec. KBk,Sl,48-pg. 5.95

Supreme Vol. 2, #29
© Image

SUPREME
Supreme 1992
0 O:Supreme. 2.50
1 B:RLd(s&i),BrM, V:Youngblood . . 3.00
1a Gold ed. 5.00
2 BrM,I:Heavy Mettle,Grizlock . . . 2.50
3 BrM,I:Khrome 2.50
4 BrM 2.50
5 BrM(a&s),Clv(i),I:Thor,V:Chrome . 2.50
6 BrM,Clv(i),I:Starguard, A:Thor,V:Chrome 2.50
7 Rip,ErS(s),SwM,A:Starguard, A:Thor 2.50
8 Rip(s),SwM,V:Thor 2.50
9 Rip&KtH(s),BrM,Clv(i), V:Thor. . 2.50
10 KrH(s),BrM,JRu(i), BU:I:Black & White 2.50
11 Extreme Prejudice,pt.4, I:Newmen. 2.50
12 SPa(c),RLd(s),SwM 4.00
25 SPa(c),RLd(s),SwM,V:Simple Simon,Images of Tomorrow . . . 6.00
13 B:Supreme Madness 2.50
14 Supreme Madness,pt.2 . . . . . . 2.50
15 RLd(s)A:Spawn 2.50
16 V:StormWatch 2.50
17 Supreme Madness,pt.5 . . . . . . 2.50
18 E:Supreme Madness 2.50
19 V:The Underworld 2.50
20 V:The Underworld. 2.50
21 God Wars 2.50
22 RLd,CNn,God Wars, V:Thor. . . . 2.50
23 ExtremeSacrifice,pt.2,x-over . . . 2.50
24 Identity Questions 2.50
#25, see above, after #12
26 F:Kid Supreme 2.50
27 Rising Son,I:Cortex 2.50
28 Supreme Apocalypse:Prelude . . 2.50
29 Supreme Apocalypse,pt.1 . . . . . 2.50
30 Supreme Apocalypse,pt.5 . . . . . 2.50
31 V:Equinox 2.50
32 V:Cortex 2.50
33 Extreme Babewatch. 2.50

Comics Values Annual

34 She-Supreme 2.50
35 Extreme Destroyer,pt.7 x-over, bagged with card 2.50
36 . . . . 2.50
37 . . . . 2.50
38 . . . . 2.50
39 AMo. 2.50
40 AMo. 2.50
41 AMo. 5.00
42 AMo,'Secret Origins' 5.00
43 AMo,'Secrets of the Citadel Supreme'. 2.50
44 See Color Comics section
Ann.#1 TMB,CAd,KG,I:Vergessen. . 2.95
Ashcan #1 . . . . 3.00
Ashcan #2 . . . . 2.00

SUPREME: GLORY DAYS
Oct., 1994
1 Supreme in WWI 2.95
2 (of 2) BNa&KlA(s),DdW,GyM, A:Superpatriot 2.95

SWORD OF DAMOCLES
WildStorm, 1996
1 prelude to Fire From Heaven x-over. 2.50
2 Fire From Heaven,Finale,pt.2 . . . 2.50

SWORD OF DRACULA
Image Oct. 2003
1 . . . . 2.95

TALES OF THE DARKNESS
Top Cow, April, 1998
1 WPo,F:Jackie Estacado 3.00
2 WPo,concl. first story 3.00
3 Dungeon, Fire, and Sword,pt.1 . . 3.00
4 Dungeon, Fire & Sword 3.00
5 in Dark Ages. 3.00
6 futuristic story. 3.00
1/2 . . . . 3.00

TALES OF TELLOS: MAIDEN VOYAGE
Image, March, 2001
1 48-pg.. . . . . 3.95

TALES OF THE WITCHBLADE
Top Cow, 1996
1 TnD,F:Anne Bonney 9.00
1a TnD, variant cover (1:4) 12.00
1a signed, variant 20.00
2 TnD,F:Annabella. 6.00
3 WEl,BTn,future. 6.00
4 WEl,BTn,future,pt.2. . . . . 5.00
5 RiB,past 5.00
6 RGr, time of Celts. 3.00
7 in Ancient Egypt 3.00
7a variant cover (1:4). 10.00
8 ancient Egypt,pt.2. . . . . 3.00
9 ancient Egypt,pt.3. . . . . 3.00
Coll.Ed.#1, rep. #1–#2 . . . . 4.95
Coll.Ed.#2, rep.#3–#4 . . . . 5.95

TEAM 1: STORMWATCH
June, 1995
1 I:First StormWatch Team. 2.50
2 V:Helspont,D:Think Tank. 2.50

CVA Page 552 All comics prices listed are for *Near Mint* condition.

IMAGE

TEAM 1: WILDC.A.T.S
July, 1995
1 I:First Wildcats Team 2.50
2 B:Cabal 2.50

TEAM 7
WildStorm, 1994–95
1 New team. 4.00
2 New powers 2.50
3 Members go insane 2.50
4 final issue,V:A Nuke 2.50
Ashcan 2.00
TPB 9.95

TEAM 7 OBJECTIVE: HELL
May, 1995
1 CDi,CW,BWS(c),WildStorm Rising,Prologue,w/2 cards 2.50
1a Newsstand ed. 2.00
2 Cambodia. 2.50

TEAM 7: DEAD REACONING
Jan., 1996
1 CDi. 2.50
2 thru 4 CDi. . . . . @2.50

TEAM YOUNGBLOOD
Extreme, 1993
1 B:ErS(s),ATi(c),CYp,NRD(i), I:Masada,Dutch,V:Giger 2.50
2 ATi(c),CYp,NRd(i),V:Giger. 2.50
3 RLd(s),CYp,NRd(i),C:Spawn, V:Giger. 2.50
4 ErS(s). 2.50
5 ErS(s),CNn,I:Lynx. 2.50
6 ErS(s),N:Psi-Fire, BU:Black&White. 2.50
7 ErS(s),CYp,ATh,Extreme Prejudice,pt.1,I:Quantum, BU:Black & White. 2.50
8 ErS(s),CYp,ATh,Extreme Prejudice,pt.5, V:Quantum, BU:Black & White 2.50
9 RLd 2.50
10 ErS(s),CYp,ATh 2.50
11 RLd,ErS,Cyp 2.50

Team Youngblood #17
© Extreme

12 RLd,ErS,Cyp 2.50
13 ErS,Cyp. 2.50
14 RLd,ErS,Cya 2.50
15 New Blood. 2.50
16 RLd,ErS,TNu,I:New Sentinel, A:Bloodpool 2.50
17 ExtremeSacrifice,pt.6,x-over . . . 2.50
18 MS, membership drive. 2.50
19 R:Brahma 2.50
20 Contact,pt.1 1000 yr Badrock. . . 2.50
21 Contact,pt.2. . . . . 2.50
22 Shadowhunt x-over,pt.4 . . . . . 2.50

TECH JACKET
2002
1 Origin issue 2.95
2 thru 8 . . . . @2.95
TPB Vol.1 Lost and Found 12.95

TEENAGE MUTANT NINJA TURTLES
(B&W) Highbrow, June, 1996
1 . . . . 2.25
2 . . . . 2.25
3 . . . . 2.25
4 Donatello resurrected 2.25
5 FFo,Warlord Komodo uses Splinter as guinea pig. 2.50
6 FFo 2.50
7 FFo,Raphael joins Foot Clan? . . 2.50
8 FFo,Michelangelo tries to rescue Casey Jones' daughter 2.95
9 Enter: the Knight Watchman 2.95
10 'Enter: The Dragon' 2.95
11 V:DeathWatch,A:Vanguard. . . . 2.95
12 F:Raph, Foot Gang warfare . . . 2.95
13 Shredder is back!. 2.95
14 Shredder vs. Splinter 2.95
15 F:Donatello 2.95
16 reunited with Splinter 2.95
17 F:Leonardo 2.95
18 UFO Sightings 2.95
19 F:Leatherhead 2.95
20 F:Triceraton 2.95
21 A:Pimiko 2.95
22 F:Lady Shredder 2.95
23 F:Lady Shredder 2.95
TPB A New Beginning 9.95

TEKKEN FOREVER
Dec., 2001
1 (of 4) from Tekken 4 video game. 2.95
1a variant(c) 2.95
2 Iron Fist tournament 2.95

TELLOS
May, 1999
1 TDz, The Joining, part 1 . . . . . . 3.00
2 TDz, The Joining, part 2 . . . . . . 2.50
3 TDz, The Joining, part 3 . . . . . . 2.50
4 TDz,Hawke & Rikk 2.50
4a variant JaL cover (1:4) 2.50
4b variant AAd cover (1:4) 2.50
4c variant RGr cover (1:4) 2.50
5 TDz,all-out battle 2.50
6 TDz,Aftermath 2.50
7 TDz,Darkness & Light. 2.50
8 TDz,Tellos Joins Gorilla 2.50
8a variant Kia Asamiya(c) 2.50
8b variant HuR(c) 2.50
9 TDz,Jarek vs. Malesur 2.50
10 TDz, concl. 2.95
Coll.Ed.#1 The Joining 8.95
Prelude 16-pg. 6.95
Prelude holo-foil 14.95

Team 1–Tenth

Teenage Mutant Ninja Turtle #2
© Highbrow

GN Maiden Voyage 5.95
GN The Last Heist, 48-pg. 5.95
GN Sons & Moons, 48-pg. 5.95
TPB Vol.1 Reluctant Heroes 17.95
TPB Vol.2 Kindred Spirits 17.95

TENTH, THE
Jan.,, 1997
1 BSt, TnD,Last stand against Hell on Earth 6.00
2 BSt,TnD,invasion of Darklon Corp. begins. 5.00
3 BSt,TnD,Tenth & Espy team-up . 4.00
4 BSt,TmD.confrontation with possible Armageddon. 4.00
TPB rep.#1–#4 . . . . 10.95
[Regular Series] Aug., 1997
1 TnD,BSt,V:Blackspell 5.00
2 TnD,BSt,V:Blackspell 4.00
3 TnD,BSt,Gozza,Eve 4.00
4 TnD,BSt,teleported to Japan. . . . 4.00
5 TnD,BSt 3.50
6 TnD,BSt,CollateralDamage,pt.1 . 3.50
7 TnD,BSt,CollateralDamage,pt.2 . 4.00
8 TnD,BSt,Dark Wind At Your Back 3.00
9 TnD,BSt,F:Adrenalynn 3.00
10 TnD,pt.1 (of 3) 3.00
10a variant TnD(c) 3.00
11 TnD,Victor retains Tenth 3.00
11a variant cover 3.00
12 TnD,Black reign begins 3.00
13 TnD,V:Rhazes Darkk 3.00
14 TnD,V:Rhazes Darkk 3.00
Coll.Ed.Vol.1 rep. #1–#2 . . . . 4.95
Spec.Configuration#1, sourcebook . 2.50
TPB rep.#1–#4 . . . . 11.95

TENTH, THE: BLACK EMBRACE
Feb., 1999
1 TnD,SLo, V:Gozza 4.00
1a variant cover (1:2). 12.00
2 TnD,SLo, F:Esperanza 2.50
3 TnD,SLo, F:Adrenalynn 2.50
4 TnD, SLo, conclusion. 2.50

All comics prices listed are for *Near Mint* condition.

TENTH, THE: EVIL'S CHILD
Sept., 1999
1 TnD, F:Gozza........... 3.00
1a variant cover (1:3)......... 3.00
1b variant cover (1:3)......... 3.00
2 TnD, F:Twisted 3 .... 2.50
3 TnD 2.50
4 TnD, someone dies 2.50
Spec.Ed.#1, rep.#0 & #1/2 ...... 2.95

10TH MUSE, THE
Nov., 2000
1 MWn,KeL............. 3.50
1a variant(c) 3.50
2 MWn,KeL,flip-book......... 3.50
2a variant(c) 3.50
2b photo(c) 3.50
3 MWn, critically wounded...... 3.50
3a variant(c) 3.50
3b photo(c) 3.50
4 MWn,Who is Medusa?........ 3.50
5 MWn,The Savage World....... 3.50
6 MWn,RCz,A:Serra 3.50
6 photo(c) 3.50
7 MWn,RCz,Maxwell Gideon 3.50
7a photo(c) 3.50
8 MWn,Assault on Olympus...... 3.50
8a photo(c) 3.50
9 MWn,San Francisco battle 3.50
9a photo(c) 3.50
10 MWn,RCr,I:The Odyssey 3.50
10a variant(c) 3.50
10b variant CBa(c) 3.50
11 RCr,The Endgame 3.50

TIMESEEKERS
Aug. 2003
1 .... 2.95

TINCAN MAN
Jan., 2000
1 F:Alex Darkstar........... 3.00
1a variant GfD(c) (1:4)......... 3.00
2 no mercy 3.00
3 .... 3.00
Preview Book, 24-pg 3.00

TOMB RAIDER
Top Cow, Nov., 1999
1 DJu,JSb............... 4.00
2 DJu,JSb,quest for Medusa Mask 3.00
3 DJu,JSb,secret of Medusa Mask. 3.00
4 DJu,JSb,Medusa Mask found ... 3.00
5 DJu,JSb,Ancient Futures 3.00
6 DJu,JSb,Death Dance 3.00
7 DJu,JSb,Dead Center,pt.1(of4).. 3.00
8 DJu,JSb,Dead Center,pt.2 ..... 3.00
9 DJu,JSb,Death by Midnight..... 3.00
9a variant(c) 7.00
10 DJu, JSb,Eye of Creation 3.00
11 DJu,BTn 3.00
12 DJu,BTn 3.00
13 DJu,JSb,Honduras,pt.1 ...... 3.00
14 DJu,JSb,Honduras,pt.2 ...... 3.00
15 DJu,JSb,Without Limit 3.00
16 DJu,JSb,Pieces of Zero,pt.1... 3.00
17 DJu,JSb,Pieces of Zero,pt.2... 3.00
18 DJu,JSb,Pieces of Zero,pt.3... 3.00
19 DJu,Pieces of Eight,pt.1...... 3.00
20 DJu,Pieces of Zero,pt.4 ..... 3.00
21 Hunt for Black Mandala 3.00
22 The Trap,pt.2........... 3.00
23 Path of the Tiger,pt.3 ...... 3.00
24 Isle of Hydra 3.00
25 Endgame,pt.1 .... 3.00

26 Abyss,pt.1 .... 3.00
27 Abyss,pt.2 .... 3.00
28 Abyss,pt.3, Tempting Fate 3.00
29 V:Lord Vymes 3.00
30 Strange Flesh, 48-pg........ 5.00
31 Conquista 3.00
32 Angel of Darkness,pt.1....... 3.00
33 Angel of Darkness,pt.2....... 3.00
34 Angel of Darkness,pt.3....... 3.00
35 Black Legion,pt.1 .... 3.00
36 Black Legion,pt.2 .... 3.00
TPB Saga of the Medusa Mask .. 12.95
TPB Vol.2 Mystic Artifacts...... 19.95
TPB Tomb Raider/Witchblade.... 12.95
GN The Greatest Treasure of All.. 5.95
Spec. Gallery 2.95
Preview, B&W 16-pg.
0 Lara goes fishing 2.50
1/2 DJu, new(c)............ 2.95
TPB Vol.3 Chasing Shangri-La ... 12.95
Spec. Tomb Raider vs. Darkness . 3.00
1-shot The Greatest Pleasure of
  All, Prelude, DJu,JJu (2002)... 5.00
1-shot Takeover 3.00
1-shot Epiphany 5.00

TOMB RAIDER: JOURNEYS
Top Cow, Dec., 2001
1 (of 12) more Lara Croft........ 3.00
1A variant AH(c) 3.00
2 washed ashore in El Dorado... 3.00
3 Sodom and Gomorrah 3.00
4 Deja vu............... 3.00
5 Who's in your yearbook? 3.00
6 .... 3.00
7 Maori Dream-Spear 3.00
8 way to the Underworld 3.00
9 Akio 3.00
10 .... 3.00
11 .... 3.00
12 Settling Old Scores 3.00

TOMB RAIDER MAGAZINE
Top Cow, Feb., 2001
1 56-pg................ 4.95
2 56-pg................ 4.95

TOMB RAIDER/ WITCHBLADE
Top Cow, June, 2000
1/2 rep.................. 3.00

TOMB RAIDER/ WITCHBLADE REVISITED
Top Cow, Dec., 1998
1 Video game tie-in 3.00

TOM JUDGE: END OF DAYS
Image/Top Cow Dec. 2002
1 PJe,40-pg.............. 4.00

TOOTH & CLAW
Aug., 1999
1 Reborn to rage 3.00
2 MPa................. 3.00
3 MPa,Retribution,concl........ 3.00

TOP COW/BALLISTIC
Swimsuit Spec.#1 MS(c) (1995)... 4.00

TOP COW'S CALIFORNIA CHRISTMAS SPECTACULAR
Top Cow, 2001
Spec. Pin-ups.............. 3.00

TOP COW CLASSICS
Top Cow, 2000
Witchblade #1 B&W 3.00
The Darkness #1 B&W 3.00
Ascension #1 .... 3.00
Fathom #1 .... 3.00
Rising Stars #1 B&W 3.00
Cyberforce #1 B&W 3.00
Tomb Raider #1 B&W 3.00
Tomb Raider #1 B&W, signed.... 19.95
Aphrodite IX #1, B&W......... 3.00
Midnight Nation #1, B&W 3.00
Witchblade #25, B&W......... 3.00
Magdalena #1 JBz,b&w 3.00
Tomb Raider/Wtchblace #1...... 3.00
TPB Tomb Raider/Witchblade:
  Trouble Seekers.......... 7.95
  Trouble Seekers.......... 7.95
Battle of the Planets #1 .... 3.00
1-shot Book of Revelations (2003) . 4.00

TOP COW SECRETS
Jan., 1996
Winter Lingerie Spec........... 3.00

TOTAL SELL OUT
Dec. 2003
TPB BMB................ 14.95

A TOUCH OF SILVER
(B&W) Jan., 1997
1 JV,'Birthday'............. 3.00
2 JV,'Dance' 3.00
3 JV,'Bullies' 3.00
4 JV,'Separation'........... 3.00
5 JV,inc. Tomorrow Syndicate vs.
  Round Table of America, 12-pg.
  color section............ 3.00
6 JV 'Choices' Aug., 1963 ...... 3.00
TPB A Sociopath in Training 12.95

TRAKK: MONSTER HUNTER
Sept. 2003
- 1 (of 6) 2.95
- 1a variant (c) 2.95
- 2 .... 2.95
- 2a variant (c) 2.95
- 2b variant SBs(c) 2.95

TREKKER
May, 1999
- 1 RoR, in New Gelaph 3.00

TRENCHER
May, 1993
- 1 KG,I:Trencher 2.25
- 2 KG 2.25
- 3 KG,V:Supreme 2.25
- 4 KG,V:Elvis 2.25

TRIBE
March, 1993
- 1 TJn(s),LSn,I:The Tribe 2.50
- 1a Ivory(White) Editon 3.00
- 2 .... 2.25
- Ashcan 1 .... 3.00

TROLL
Extreme, Dec., 1993
- 1 RLd(s),JMs,I:Evangeliste, V:Katellan Command 2.50
- 2 .... 2.50
- Halloween Spec.#1 .... 2.50
- X-Mas Stocking Stuffer #1 ..... 2.95

Trool: Once A Hero #1 © Image

TROLL: ONCE A HERO
Aug., 1994
- 1 Troll in WWII 2.50

TROUBLEMAN
Motown June, 1996
- 1 Charles Drost 2.50
- 2 .... 2.50

TSUNAMI GIRL
Flypaper Jan., 1999
- 1 F:Michelle Vincent 3.00

IMAGE

- 2 Sorayama(c), A:Alan Poe 3.00
- 3 Sorayama(c), Surreal conspiracy 3.00

TUG & BUSTER
(B&W) June, 1998
- 1 MaH, humor, F:Stinkfinger 2.95

'21'
Top Cow, Feb., 1996
- 1 LWn,MDa 2.50
- 2 LWn,MDa 2.50
- 3 LWn,MDa 2.50
- 4 LWn,MDa,'Time Bomb',pt.1 ... 2.50
- 5 LWn,MDa,'Time Bomb',pt.2 ... 2.50
- 6 LWn,MDa,'Time Bomb',pt.3 'Detonation' 2.50

UNBOUND
(B&W) Jan., 1998
- 1 by Joe Pruett & Michael Peters ... 3.00
- 2 .... 3.00
- 3 F:Marta & Erik 3.00

UNION
WildStorm, Feb., 1995
- 0 O:Union 2.50
- 0a WPo(c) 5.00
- 1 MT,I:Union,A:StormWatch 2.75
- 2 MT 2.75
- 3 MT 2.75
- 4 MT, Good Intentions 2.75

Regular Series 1995
- 1 R:Union, Crusade 2.50
- 2 V:Crusade & Mnemo 2.50
- 3 A:Savage Dragon 2.50
- 4 JRo,BWS(c), WildStorm Rising,pt.3,w/2 cards 2.50
- 4a Newsstand ed 2.00
- 5 V:Necros 2.50
- 6 V:Necros 2.50
- 7 Jill's Surprise 2.50
- 8 Regal Vengeance,pt.1 .... 2.50
- 9 Regal Vengeance,pt.2 .... 2.50
- 10 Regal Vengeance,pt.3 ...... 2.50
- 1-shot Final Vengeance, MHs, V:Regent (1997) 2.50

UNION
WildStorm, 1996
- 1 MHs,RBn,'Knight of Faith' 2.50
- 2 MHs,RBn 2.50
- 3 MHs,RBn 2.00

UNIVERSE
Top Cow, Aug., 2001
- 1 PJe,The Triad of Powers 2.50
- 1 variant foil(c) 12.00
- 2 PJe,Pilgrimage into the Inferno .. 2.50
- 3 PJe,Judge finds Hell 2.50
- 4 PJe,plan for mankind's fate 2.50
- 5 PJe,express train to hell 2.50
- 6 PJe,family held hostage 2.50
- 7 PJe,successor to the devil 2.50
- 8 PJe, Stairway to Heaven,48-pg .. 5.00

VAGABOND
Aug., 2000
- 1 RBn,SRf,F:Sharon Armstrong ... 2.95
- 1a variant(c) 2.95
- 1b deluxe 8.95
- 1c signed 10.95
- 1d ruby red foil(c) 11.50
- 2 RBn,SRf 2.95

VAGRANT STORY
Top Cow, Sept., 2000
- 1 video game tie-in 2.95

VAMPIRE'S CHRISTMAS
- GN JLi 48-pg 5.95

VANGUARD
Highbrow, 1993–94
- 1 EL(s),BU:I:Vanguard 3.00
- 2 EL(s),Roxann 3.00
- 3 AMe 3.00
- 4 AMe 3.00
- 5 AMe,V:Aliens 3.00
- 6 V:Bank Robber 3.00
- Spec. B&W 48-pg 5.95

Vanguard: Strange Visitors #1 © Image

VANGUARD: STRANGE VISITORS
(B&W) 1996
- 1 (of 4) SEa,BAn,A:Amok,'Strange Visitors' 3.00
- 2 SEa,BAn 3.00
- 3 SEa,BAn 3.00
- 4 SEa,BAn,finale 3.00

VELOCITY
Top Cow, 1995–95
- 1 V:Morphing Opponent 3.00
- 2 V:Charnel 3.00
- 3 .... 3.00
- 4 .... 3.00

VENTURE
Jan. 2003
- 1 .... 2.95
- 2 thru 4 .... @2.95

VICTORY
May 2003
- 1 thru 3 .... @2.95
- 1a–3a variant (c) .... @2.95

VIOLATOR
TMP, 1994
- 1 AMo(s),BS,I:Admonisher 5.00

Violator–Wetworks

2 AMo(s),BS 4.00
3 AMo(s),BS,last issue. 4.00

VIOLATOR/BADROCK
Extreme, 1995

1 AMo(s),RLe(c),A:Celestine,'Rocks and Hard Places,'pt.1 . . . . 2.50
2 AMo(s),RLe(c),V:Celestine,'Mondo Inferno'. 2.50
3 RLe(c),F:Dr. McAllister,'Where Angels Fear to Tread'. 2.50
4 RLe(c),'Badrock's Bogus Journey,' final issue. 2.50
TPB Rep. 9.95

VIOLENT MESSIAHS
June, 2000

1 F:Rankor Island 4.00
1a variant AMe(c) (1:4) 6.00
2 . . . . 5.00
2a variant(c) 6.00
3 V:Citizen Pain. 4.00
4 V:Jeremiah Parker 3.00
5 flip-book 3.00
6 Tonight The Door Opens. 3.00
7 In the Final Stretch. 3.00
8 North End Mansion. 3.00
Spec. Genesis, 56-pg. 5.00
TPB Vol. 1 The Book of Job 24.95

VIOLENT MESSIAHS: LAMENTING PAIN
Sept., 2002

1 (of 4) F:Lt. Cheri Major 3.00
2 thru 4 . . . . @3.00
1a–4a variant (c) . . . . @3.00

VISITATIONS
(B&W) 1997

GN by C. Stott Morse 6.95

VOGUE
Extreme, 1995–96

1 F:Vogue,I:Redbloods 2.50
2 . . . . 2.50
3 conclusion 2.50

IMAGE

VOLTRON: DEFENDER OF THE UNIVERSE
May 2003

0 . . . . 2.50
1 Revelations,pt.1 . . . . 2.95
1a variant (c)s 2.95
2 thru 5 Revelations,pt.2–pt.5. . . @2.95

VOODOO
WildStorm, Nov., 1997

1 AMo(s),WildStorm universe. . . . 2.50
2 AMo(s),in old New Orleans . . . 2.50
3 AMo(s),Samedi 2.50
4 AMo(s), Christian Charles. 2.50
TPB Voodoo Dancing in the Dark . 10.00

WAHOO MORRIS
B&W March, 2000

1 Rock & Roll fantasy 3.00
2 . . . . 3.00

WALKING DEAD
Oct. 2003

1 . . . . 2.95
2 City of the Damned. 2.95

WARBLADE: ENDANGERED SPECIES
WildStorm, 1995

1 I:Pillar. 2.95
2 V:Ripclaw 2.50
3 I:Skinner. 2.50
4 final issue. 2.50

WARLANDS
Aug., 1999

1 by Pat Lee 2.50
1a, b & c variant covers. 2.50
1d Armore Chrome edition 12.95
2 help from the Elves? 2.50
2a variant cover (1:2). 2.50
3 the Dataran invasion. 2.50
3a variant cover (1:2). 2.50
4 . . . . 2.50
5 trapped between enemies. 2.50
6 enemies clash 2.95
7 the Dataran Horde 2.50
8 . . . . 2.50
9 final battle begins 2.50
10 flip-book 3.00
11 . . . . 2.50
12 concl. 2.50
Spec. Three stories 5.95
Chronicles Vol.1, rep.#1–#3 . . . . 7.95
Chronicles Vol.2, rep.#4–#6 . . . . 7.95
TPB Vol.1, 184-pg. 14.95

WARLANDS: AGE OF ICE
Image, July, 2001

1 Awakening 3.00
2 flip-book 3.00
3 thru 5 . . . . @3.00
1a and 2a variant covers . . . . . . @3.00
Spec. #0 (2002) 3.00
Spec. #1/2 (2002). 3.00

WEAPON ZERO
Top Cow, 1995

T-Minus-4 WS 8.00
T-Minus-3 Alien Invasion. 5.00
T-Minus-2 Formation of a Team . . 5.00
T-Minus-1 Alien Invasion. 5.00

Comics Values Annual

0 Whole Team Together. 4.00
1 . . . . 5.00
2 . . . . 3.50
3 . . . . 3.50
4 thru 9 WS,JBz . . . . @3.00
10 WS,ScL,'Devil's Reign' tie-in . . . 3.00
11 WS,JBz,Weapon Zero & Lilith return to T'srii moonbase . . . 3.00
12 WS,JBz, What's wrong with Jamie. 3.00
13 WS,JBz,problems with Jamie. . . 3.00
14 JBz,T'Srrii have returned 3.00
15 JBz,T'Srrii,concl.,48-pg. 3.50
Weapon Zero/Silver Surfer Spec. x-over (1997) 3.00

WEASEL GUY: ROADTRIP
(B&W) Aug., 1999

1 by Steve Buccellato 3.00
1a variant cover (1:4). 3.00
2 Peril in Pennsylvania 3.00
2a variant cover (1:4). 3.00
3 Don't Mess With Texas 3.00
3a variant cover (1:4). 3.00
4 48-pg, guest stars. 5.00
4a variant KIA(c) (1:4) 5.00

Wetworks #12 © WildStorm

WETWORKS
WildStorm, 1994

1 WPo,Rebirth. 4.00
2 WPo,BCi,Brakken,Blood Queen . 3.00
3 WPo,BCi,V:Vampire 3.00
4 WPo,BCi,Dozer 2.50
5 WPo,BCi,Pilgrim's Turn. 2.50
6 WPo,BCi,Civil War 2.50
7 WPo,BCi,F:Pilgrim 2.50
8 WPo,SW,BWS(c), WildStorm Rising,pt.7,w/2 cards 2.50
8a Newsstand ed. 2.25
9 F:Jester,Pilgrim Dozer 2.50
10 R:Dozer to Action. 2.50
11 Blood Queen Vs. Dane 2.50
12 V:Vampire Nation. 2.50
13 WPo(c) 2.50
14 . . . . 2.50
15 . . . . 2.50
16 Fire From Heaven,pt.4. . . . . . . 2.50
17 FTa,Fire From Heaven,pt.11. . . 2.50
18 FTa 2.50
19 FTa 2.50
20 FTa 2.50
21 FTa 2.50
22 FTa,Dave vs.Bloodqueen concl. . 2.50

Vogue #3 © Image

CVA Page 556 — All comics prices listed are for *Near Mint* condition.

IMAGE

Wetworks–WildC.A.T.S

23 FTa,Flattop & Crossbones,
V:Lady Feign 2.50
24 FTa 2.50
25 FTa,Can Pilgrim withstand the
beast that lurks within her,
double size. 4.50
26 team parts ways with Armand
Waering 2.50
27 V:Craven, no rest for the weary . 2.50
28 Vampire tracked in Pacific
Northwest,A:Johnny Savoy. . . . 2.50
29 V:Soulbender,'Power Surge'. . . . 2.50
30 'Secret of the Siynn'. 2.50
31 'Ashes to Ashes' 2.50
32 StG,PtL,V:Drakkar,'Sacrements
of Damnation,'pt.1 . . . . 2.50
32a Voyager pack, bagged with
Phantom Guard preview. 3.50
33 StG,PtL,Sacraments,pt.2 . . . . . . 2.50
34 StG,PtL,Sacraments,pt.3 . . . . . . 2.50
35 StG,PtL,Sacraments,pt.4 . . . . . . 2.50
36 StG,'Maximum Security'. 2.50
37 StG,V:St.Crispin,'Diversionary
Tactics,'pt.1 . . . . 2.50
38 StG,'DiversionaryTactics,'pt.2. . . 2.50
39 StG,'Symbiote Seizure' 2.50
40 StG,'Drawn Swords'. 2.50
41 StG,V:Stormwatch,'Drawn
Swords,' conclusion 2.50
42 StG,'Flash Back,'pt.1 . . . . 2.50
43 StG,'Flash Back,'conclusion 2.50
3-D Spec.#1 (1998) 5.00
Sourcebook #1 (1994) 2.50
Hero Ashcan. 3.00
Promo Ashcans #1,#2,#3 . . . . . . @3.00
TPB Rebirth,rep. #1–#3 & preview . 9.95

WETWORKS/VAMPIRELLA
WildStorm1997
1 JMi & GK, x-over 3.00

WHISKEY DICKEL, INTERNATIONAL COWGIRL
Aug. 2003
TPB b&w 120-pg. 12.95

WHIZ KIDS
April 2003
1-shot b&w, 48-pg. 4.95

WICKED, THE
Dec., 1999
1 RMr,FTa,supernatural thriller. . . . 3.00
1a variant Jay Anacleto(c)(1:4) . . . 3.00
2 thru 7 . . . . @3.00
3a & 4a variant covers . . . . @3.00
Special Medusa's Tale. 3.95
TPB Vol. 1 Omnibus 19.95

WILDC.A.T.S.
WildStorm, 1992
1 B:BCi(s),JLe, SW(i), I:Wild-
C.A.T.S. 5.00
1a Gold ed. 9.00
1b Gold and Signed. 10.00
2 JLe,SW(i),V:Master Gnome,
I:Wetworks, Prism foil(c),
with coupon #5. . . . . 4.00
2a w/o coupon. 2.00
3 RLd(c),JLe,SW(i), V:Youngblood. 3.50
4 E:BCi(s),JLe,LSn,SW(i),w/card,
A:Youngblood,BU:Tribe. 3.50
4a w/red card 5.00
5 BCi(s),JLe,SW,I:Misery. 3.00

WildC.A.T.S. #20
© Wildstorm

6 BCi(s),JLe,SW,Killer Instinct,
A:Misery,C:Ripclaw. 3.00
7 BCi(s),JLe,SW, A:Cyberforce . . . 3.00
8 BCi(s),JLe,SW 5.00
9 BCi(s),JLe,SW 3.00
10 CCi(s),JLe,SW,I:Huntsman 3.00
11 CCi(s),JLe,SW,V:Triad,
A:Huntsman 3.00
11a WPo(c) 5.00
12 JLe,CCi,A:Huntsman 3.00
13 JLe,CCi,A:Huntsman 3.00
14 X book. 3.00
15 F:Black Razors 3.00
16 Black Razors 3.00
17 A:StormWatch 3.00
18 R:Hightower. 3.00
19 V:Hightower. 3.00
20 TC,JeR,BWS(c),WildStorm
Rising,pt.2,w/2 cards 3.00
20a Newsstand ed. 2.50
21 Into Space Back Home 3.00
22 Space Adventures 3.00
23 F:Mr. Majestic's Team 3.00
24 O:Maul 3.00
25 double sized 5.00
26 AMo. 3.00
27 AMo. 3.00
28 AMo. 3.00
29 AMo,Fire From Heaven,pt.7 . . . 3.00
30 AMo,BKs,Fire From
Heaven,pt.13 . . . . 3.00
31 AMo,BKs,'Cats & Dogs' 3.00
32 AMo,BKs,'Catharsis' 3.00
33 AMo,BKs,'Belling the Cat' 3.00
34 AMo,MtB,New York seconds
away from nuclear disaster. . . . 3.00
35 AMo,MtB,BKs,V:Crusade 3.00
36 AMo,MtB,BKs,V:Crusade,
A:Union,pt.2 . . . . 3.00
37 BCi,JPe,MtB,WildC.A.T.s
team divided. 3.00
38 BCi,JPe,MtB,Puritans debut . . . 3.00
39 BCi,JPe,MtB,'C.A.T. Fight' 3.00
40 BCi,JPe,MtB,MtB(c),'Fight
of Flight'. 3.00
40a variant cover by TC 3.50
41 BCi,JPe,MtB,backwards in time . 3.00
42 BCi,JPe,MTb,in WWI 3.00
43 BCi,JPe,MTb,in ancient China . . 3.00
44 BCi,JPe,MTb,'Paradise Lost' . . . 3.00
45 BCi,JPe,MTb,'Circus Maximus' . 3.00
46 BCi,JPe,MTb,escape from
Rome. 3.00
47 BCi,JPe,MTb,time trip concl. . . . 3.00

47a variant JMd(c) 3.00
48 BCi,JPe,trapped in mothership. . 3.00
49 BCi,JPe,return to present. 3.00
50 BCi,JPe,AMo,new
costumes,40-pg.(June, 1998) . . 3.50
TPB A Gathering of Eagles. 9.95
Spec.#1 SrG(s),TC,SW,I:Destine,
Pin-ups 3.50
Spec.#2 . . . . 2.50
3-D #1 rep. #1 (1997) 4.95
3-Da variant cover 4.95
TPB rep. #1-4,w/0. . . . . 11.00
TPB Homecoming rep.#21–#27 . . 19.95
Ann.#1 JRo,LSn (1998) 2.95
TPB WildC.A.T.S/Cyberforce
Killer Instinct. 16.95
TPB Gathering of Eagles 9.95
TPB Gang War,rep.#28–34. . . . . . 16.95
TPB VOL. II Way of the Coda 12.95
Volume 2: See COLOR

WILDC.A.T.S ADVENTURES
WildStorm, 1994
1 From animated TV series 3.00
2 Helspont,Troika 2.50
3 Caught in war. 2.50
4 V:The President 2.50
5 I:Lonely 2.50
6 I:Majestics 2.50
7 . . . . 2.50
8 Betrayed. 2.50
9 V:Black Razors 2.50
10 F:Voodoo. 2.50
Sourcebook (JS(c) 2.95

WILDC.A.T.S/ALIENS
WildStorm, 1998
1-shot WEl,CSp,KN 9.00
1-shotA, variant GK&KN(c)(1:4) . . 11.00

WILDC.A.T.S. TRILOGY
June, 1993
1 BCi(s),JaL,V:Artemis. 2.50
2 BCi(s),JaL,V:Artemis. 2.25
3 BCi(s),JaL,V:Artemis. 2.25

WILDC.A.T.S/X-MEN
WildStorm, Feb., 1997
1 (of 4) SLo,TC, giant Marvel/
Image x-over 5.00
1a alternate cover by JLe 5.00
2 & 4 see Marvel
TPB WildC.A.T.S/X-Men, rep. 18.50

WILDC.A.T.S/X-MEN
WildStorm/Marvel, 1997
Golden Age #1,SLo,TC. 5.00
Golden Age #1a variant JLe(c) 5.00
3-D Golden Age #1, with glasses . . 5.00
3-D Golden Age #1, variant cover . . 5.00
Silver Age #1 SLo, JLe & SW,
x- over 4.50
Silver Age #1a NA&SW(c) 4.50
Silver Age #1b signed 19.95
Silver Age #1c signed, deluxe 29.95
3-D Silver Age #1, with glasses. . . . 6.50
3-D Silver Age #1, NA(c) variant . . . 6.50
Modern Age #1, JRo,AHu,MFm,
V:Hellfire Club 4.50
Modern Age #1a variant cover 4.50
3-D Modern Age #1, with glasses . . 4.95
3-D Modern Age #1, variant cover. . 4.95

All comics prices listed are for Near Mint condition.

CVA Page 557

IMAGE

Wildcore–Witchblade

Wildcore #1 © WildStorm

WILDCORE
WildStorm, 1997–98
1 BBh,SRf,BBh(c),V:Drahn 2.50
1a variant TC(c) 2.50
1b Voyager bagged pack 3.00
2 BBh,SRf,Brawl joins 2.50
3 BBh,SRf,V:D'rahn 2.50
4 BBh,SRf,A:Majestic 2.50
5 BBh,SRf,Tapestry 2.50
6 BBh,SRf,Zealot missing 2.50
7 BBh,SRf,caught in fantasy world. 2.50
8 RBn,SRf,V:Tapestry 2.50
9 RBn,SRf,Zealot's soul restored. . 2.50
10 RBn,SRf,Trans-dimensional
  trauma 2.50
GN Backlash & Taboo's African
  Vacation 6.00

WILDGUARD: CASTING CALL
Sept. 2003
1 (of 6) TNu 2.95
2 TNu 2.95
3 TNu 2.95
1a–3a variant (c)s . . . . @2.95

WILDSTAR: SKY ZERO
March, 1993
1 JOy,AG,I:WildStar 2.25
1a Gold ed. 3.00
2 JOy,AG 2.25
3 JOy,AG,V:Savage Dragon,
  D:WildStar 2.25
4 JOy,AG,Last Issue,Pin-ups 2.25
TPB WildStar Sky Zero (1994) . . 12.95
[Regular Series] Sept., 1995
1 R:WildStar 2.50
2 V:Mighty Man 2.50
3 . . . . 2.50
Ashcan 1.00

WILDSTORM!
WildStorm, Aug., 1995
1 F:Spartan,Black Razors 2.50
2 F:Deathblow 2.50
3 F:Taboo,Spartan 2.50
4 F:Nautika,Sunburst 2.50
Winter Wonderfest Spec.#1 . . . . 3.50
Spec.#1 Chamber of Horrors(1995) 3.50
Spec. Swimsuit Special '97 . . . . . 2.50

Spec. Ultimate Sports Official
  Program 2.50
Sketchbook 2.95
Spec. Halloween '97 . . . . 2.50
GN Thunderbook #1 . . . . 6.95
GN Summer Spec., 48-pg. (DC) . . 5.95

WILDSTORM ARCHIVES GENESIS
WildStorm, June, 1998
1 The #1 Collection, 238 pg. 7.00

WILDSTORM RISING
WildStorm, May, 1995
1 JeR,BWS(c&a) WildStorm Rising,
  pt.1:Tricked by Defile,w/2 cards 2.50
1a Newsstand ed. 2.25
2 RMz,BBo,BWS(c) WildStorm
  Rising,pt.10,w/2 cards 2.50
2a Newsstand ed. 2.25
WildStorm Sourcebook #1 . . . . . . 2.50
TPB Rep. Mini-series 16.95

WILDSTORM SPOTLIGHT
WildStorm, Feb., 1997
1 AMo,F:Majestic, at the end of
  time 2.50
2 StG,RMr,Loner returns 2.50
3 StG,RMr,Secret past of original
  Loner 2.50
4 F:Hellstrike,Stormwatch 2.50

WILDSTORM ULTIMATE SPORTS
WildStorm, 1997
Official Program #1 . . . . 2.50

WILDSTORM UNIVERSE '97
WildStorm, Nov., 1997
Sourcebook #1 thru #3 . . . . @2.50

WITCHBLADE
Top Cow, 1995–96
1 I:Witchblade 40.00
1A Special retailer edition 40.00
1B Wizard Ace edition,acetate(c) . 25.00
2 . . . . 25.00
2 encore edition 7.00
3 . . . . 20.00
4 . . . . 15.00
5 . . . . 12.00
6 thru 8 . . . . @10.00
Top Cow, 1996
9 . . . . 10.00
9A variant cover 12.00
10 I:Darkness (Jackie Estacado) . 12.00
10a variant Darkness cover (1:4) . 16.00
11 . . . . 6.00
12 Connection between Lisa,
  Microwave Murderer and
  Kenneth Irons 6.00
Witchblade 1/2 mail-in offer
  from Fan #8 . . . . 4.00
Top Cow, 1997
13 Dannette Boucher's secret past . 6.00
14 Sara searches for Microwave
  Murderer 5.00
15 'There is a war brewing...' 4.00
16 'Will Witchblade come between
  Sarah and Jake?' 4.00
17 New York City in shambles . . . 4.00
18 Family Ties,pt.1,x-over 4.00

Witchblade #16 © Top Cow

18a variant(c) 6.00
19 Family Ties,pt.4,x-over 4.00
20 Chief Siry, Ian Nottingham 3.00
21 another big surprise 3.00
22 F:Sara 3.00
23 F:Ian Nottingham 3.00
24 JPn,Sara learns truth 3.00
25 Save Jake's Life, 32 pg 3.50
26 'Grey' 3.00
27 A:Kenneth Irons 3.00
27a variant cover, all villains 9.00
28 A:Jackie Estacado 2.50
29 A:Kenneth Irons 2.50
30 Siry & Irons 2.50
31 How Sara's father died 2.50
32 answers and questions 2.50
33 F:Eric 2.50
34 F:Tommy Gallo 2.50
35 Sara gets who she wants 2.50
36 The Darkness,pt.1 x-over 2.50
37 V:wicked creatures 2.50
38 V:Demons of the Underworld . . 2.50
39 V:Demons of the Underworld . . 2.50
40 PJe,RV 2.50
41 PJe,RV,arsonist 2.50
42 PJe,pez dispensers 2.50
43 PJe,Impossible Murders 2.50
44 PJe,Impossible Murders 2.50
45 PJe 2.50
46 PJe 2.50
47 PJe 2.50
48 PJe 2.50
49 PJe,Firestarter is back 2.50
50 PJe,48-pg. 5.00
50a variant DK(c) 12.00
50b variant MS(c) 12.00
50c variant(c) 12.00
51 PJe,What is the Witchblade? . . 2.50
52 PJe,The Inferno is Coming 2.50
53 PJe 2.50
54 Ian Nottingham resurrected . . . 2.50
55 Tora No Shi 2.50
55a Battle of the Planets(c) 7.00
55b Battle(c) signed 7.00
56 Nottingham vs. Tora No Shi . . . 2.50
57 Sonatine,pt.4 . . . . 2.50
58 Sara & Joe Siry 2.50
59 Jackie Estacado is dead? 2.50
60 Endgame,pt.2 x-over 3.00
61 Julie returns 3.00
62 F:Magdalena 3.00
63 F:Magdalena 3.00
64 F:Magdalena 3.00
65 F:Magdalena,concl. 3.00

All comics prices listed are for Near Mint condition.

Witchblade–Zorro

66		3.00
67 Mother's Meat		3.00
68 Road Trip,pt.1		3.00
69 Road Trip,pt.2		3.00
70 return from trip		3.00
71 V:Shine		3.00
Spec. 1 Movie edition, photo(c)		9.95
Spec. 1a Movie, foil(c)		16.95
Spec. 1b Movie, holofoil(c)		24.95
Coll.Ed.Vol.#1		5.00
Coll.Ed.Vol.#2		5.00
Coll.Ed.Vol.#3		5.00
Coll.Ed.Vol.#4, rep. #7 & #8		5.00
Coll.Ed.Vol.#5, rep. #9 & #10		5.00
Coll.Ed.Vol.#6, rep. #11 & #12		5.00
Coll.Ed.Vol.#7, rep. #13 & #14		5.00
Coll.Ed.Vol.#8, rep. #15–#17		6.95
Delux Coll. Ed. rep.1–#8		24.95
Spec. Infinity SLo,AdP		3.50
Spec.#40 Preview book, B&W		5.00
Spec.#1 rep.movie photo cover		2.50
Spec.Witchblade/Darkness,pt.2 x-over, 48-pg.		3.95
Spec. Witchblade/Darkminds x-over		6.00
Gallery Edition #1		3.00
TPB Collects Witchblade/Darkness Family Ties x-over		10.00
TPB Vol.3 Prevailing, deluxe		14.95
TPB Vol.3 Prevailing, deluxe		14.95
TPB Revelations, deluxe		24.95
TPB Revelations, deluxe		24.95
TPB Distinctions		14.95
Spec.1 Lady Death x-over		4.95
Spec. Tomb Raider		3.95
TPB Obakemono		10.00
1/2 24-pg.		3.00
1-shot Nottingham, 48-pg.		5.00
1-shot Witchblade Animated		3.00
TPB Vlood Relations		13.00

WITCHBLADE: DESTINY'S CHILD
Top Cow, April, 2000
1 (of 3) O:Witchblade,pt.1		3.00
2 O:Witchblade,pt.2		3.00
3 O:Witchblade, concl.		3.00

WITCHFINDER, THE
Liar, Oct. 1999
1 by R. Lugibihl & S. Scott		3.00
1a variant cover (1:2)		3.00
2		3.00
3 Concl.		3.00

WIZARDS TALE, THE
Homage, 1997
TPB KBk,DWe		20.00
TPB 2nd printing		20.00

WOLVERINE/ WITCHBLADE
Top Cow, Jan., 1997
1-shot 'Devil's Reign'pt.5 (of 8)		4.00

WORLD CLASS COMICS
Aug., 2002
1-shot, 40-pg. b&w		4.95

WYNONNA EARP
WildStorm, 1996–97
1 BSt,'Violent Territory'		2.50
2 BSt,The Law comes to San Diablo		2.50

IMAGE

Wynonna Earp #2 © WildStorm

3 BSt,desperate to stop Hemo from going nationwide		2.50
4 BSt,goes to New York, V:ancient evil		2.50
5 BSt,battle with Raduk—Eater of the Dead concl.		2.50

YOUNGBLOOD
Extreme, April, 1992
0 RLd,O:Youngblood,w/coupon#7		3.00
0a without coupon		1.50
0b gold coupon		9.00
1 RLd,I:Youngblood (flipbook)		5.00
1a 2nd print.,gold border		2.50
1b RLD,Silent Edition		12.95
2 RLd,I:ShadowHawk		5.00
3 RLd,I:Supreme,Showdown		3.00
4 RLd,DK,A:Prophet,BU:Pitt		3.00
5 RLd,Flip book,w/Brigade #4		2.50
6 RLd(a&s),J:Troll,Knight Sabre, 2nd Die Hard, Proposal to Girl friend		3.50
7 Badrock, V:Overtkill		2.50
8 Chapel, V:Spawn		2.50
9		2.50
9a variant cover.		5.00
10 Bravo, Badrock, Troll		2.50
Yr.Bk.#1 CYp,I:Tyrax,Kaman.		2.75
Ashcan #1		8.00
Ashcan #2		4.00
TPB rep. #1-#5		16.95

[Volume 2] 1995
1 New Roster		2.50
2 The Program Continues		2.50
3 Extreme Babewatch		2.50
4 Extreme Destroyer,pt.4 x-over, bagged with card		2.50
5		2.50
6		2.50
7 Shadowhunt x-over,pt.3		2.50
8 ErS,RCz		2.50
9 ErS,RCz		2.50
10 ErS,RCz		2.50
TPB Baptism of Fire, F:Spawn See Color Pub. section		

YOUNGBLOOD BATTLEZONE
April, 1993
1 BrM		2.25
2		2.95

YOUNGBLOOD STRIKEFILE
Extreme, 1993
1 JaL,RLd,I:Allies,A:Al Simmons (Spawn)I:Giger,Glory		3.00
1a Gold ed.		4.00
2 JaL,RLd,V:Super Patriot, Giger		3.00
2a Gold ed.		3.50
3 RLd,JaL,DaM(i), A:Super Partiot		3.00
4 I:Overtkill		3.00
5		3.00
6 and 7 flip books		@3.00
8 Shaft		3.00
9 Knight Sabre		3.00
10 RLd,TNu,I:Bloodpool,Task, Psilence,Wylder,Rubble		3.50
11 ExtremeSacrifice,pt.0,x-over O:Link Crypt		2.50
TPB rep.#1-#3,sketchbook		12.95
Ashcan		3.00

YOUNGBLOOD/X-FORCE
Extreme/Marvel, 1996
1-shot Mojo visits Image x-over		5.00
1-shot RLd variant cover		5.00

YOUNGBLOOD: YEAR ONE
1 KBk(s),RLd, the early years		2.50
2 KBk(s),RLd,V:Giger,Cybernet		2.50

ZEALOT
WildStorm, 1995
1 O:Zealot		2.50
2 In Japan		2.50
3 V:Prometheus		2.50

ZERO GIRL
WildStorm/Homage, 2000
1 thru 4		@3.00

ZORRO
(B&W) 1998
TPB #1 rep. classic Alex Toth		15.95
TPB #2 rep. classic Alex Toth		15.95
TPB The Lady Wears Red		12.95

ZORRO
(B&W) Sept., 2001
TPB The Dailies, 248-pg.		18.95
TPB The Complete Alex Toth		18.95

ZORRO MANTANZAS
Sept., 1999
1 (of 4) DMG & Mike Mayhew		2.95
2 DMG,V:Machete		2.95

ZORRO'S LADY RAWHIDE: OTHER PEOPLE'S BLOOD
(B&W) Feb., 1999
1 DMG,EM,JuB(c),cont. from Topps		2.95
2 DMG,EM,V:Scarlet Fever		2.95
3 DMG,EM,V:Ansel Plague		2.95
4 DMG,EM,V:Scarlet Fever		2.95
5 DMG,EM,Whiplash		2.95

ZORRO'S RENEGADES
Image 1998
TPB Zorro's Renegades, B&W		14.95
TPB Vol. 2, Lady Rawhide		14.95

All comics prices listed are for *Near Mint* condition.

COLOR COMICS

ABBOTT AND COSTELLO
Charlton Comics, 1968ñ71
1 .... 110.00
2 thru 9 .... @55.00
10 thru 21 .... @40.00
22 .... 30.00

ACES HIGH
Gemstone, 1999
1 (of 5) EC Comics reprint 2.50
2 .... 2.50
3 .... 2.50
4 .... 2.50
5 .... 2.50
Annual rep. #1–#5 .... 13.50

ACME NOVELTY LIBRARY
Fantagraphics, 1994–98
1 thru 5 .... @4.50
6 thru 11 Jimmy Corrigan Meets
   His Dad, pt. 1 – pt. 6 (of 8) .. @4.50
12 Jimmy & Dad have lunch 4.95
13 Jimmy's Grandfather, 80-page . 10.95
14 F:Jimmy Corrigan 10.95
15 .... 9.95
1 thru 7, 2nd printings .... @3.95

A.D.A.M.
Toyman, 1998
1 .... 2.50
2 .... 2.50

ADAM-12
Gold Key, 1973–76
1 Photo(c), From TV show 100.00
2 thru 9 .... @40.00
10 .... 35.00

ADDAMS FAMILY
Gold Key, 1974–75
1 TV cartoon adapt. 125.00
2 .... 75.00
3 .... 50.00

ADLAI STEVENSON
Dell Publishing Co., Dec., 1966
1 Political Life Story 50.00

ADVENTURES OF BARON MUNCHAUSEN
Now Comics, 1989
1 thru 4 movie adapt. series .... @2.00

ADVENTURES OF FELIX THE CAT
Harvey, 1992
1 Short Stories 2.00

ADVENTURES OF KUNG FU PIG NINJA FLOUNDER AND 4-D MONKEY
1 thru 6 .... @1.80
7 thru 10 .... @2.00

ADVENTURES OF ROBIN HOOD
Gold Key, 1974–75
1 From Disney cartoon 25.00
2 thru 7 .... @15.00

Adventures of the Fly #1
© Archie Publications

ADVENTURES OF THE FLY
Archie Publications/ Radio Comics, 1959–65
1 JSm/JK,O:Fly,I:SpiderSpry
   A:Lancelot Strong/Shield ... 800.00
2 JSm/JK,DAy,AW 475.00
3 Jack Davis Art, O:Fly 350.00
4 V:Dazzler NA panel. 200.00
5 A:Spider Spry 125.00
6 V:Moon Men 125.00
7 A:Black Hood 150.00
8 A:Lancelot Strong/Shield 150.00
9 A:Lancelot Strong/Shield
   I:Cat Girl. 125.00
10 A:Spider Spry. 125.00
11 V:Rock Men 75.00
12 V:Brute Invaders 75.00
13 I:Kim Brand 80.00
14 I:Fly-Girl(Kim Brand) 100.00
15 A:Spider. 75.00
16 A:Fly-Girl 75.00
17 A:Fly-Girl 75.00
18 A:Fly-Girl 75.00
19 A:Fly-Girl 75.00
20 O:Fly-Girl. 80.00
21 A:Fly-Girl 50.00
22 A:Fly-Girl 50.00
23 A:Fly-Girl,Jaguar 50.00
24 A:Fly-Girl 50.00
25 A:Fly-Girl 50.00
26 A:Fly-Girl,Black Hood. 50.00
27 A:Fly-Girl,Black Hood. 50.00
28 A:Black Hood. 50.00
29 A:Fly-Girl,Black Hood. 50.00
30 A:Fly-Girl,R:Comet. 75.00
31 A:Black Hood, Shield, Comet .. 80.00
Becomes:

FLYMAN

ADVENTURES OF THE JAGUAR
Archie Publications/ Radio Comics, 1961–63
1 I:Ralph Hardy/Jaguar 275.00
2 10 cent cover 150.00
3 Last 10 cent cover 100.00
4 A:Cat-Girl 75.00
5 A:Cat-Girl 75.00
6 A:Cat-Girl 65.00
7 .... 55.00
8 .... 55.00
9 .... 55.00
10 .... 55.00
11 .... 55.00
12 A:Black Hood. 55.00
13 A:Cat-Girl,A:Black Hood. ... 55.00
14 A:Black Hood. 55.00
15 V:Human Octopus,last issue .. 55.00

ADVENTURES OF YOUNG DR. MASTERS
Archie Comics, 1964
1 .... 50.00
2 .... 25.00

ADVENTUROUS UNCLE SCROOGE McDUCK
Gladstone, Oct., 1997
1 .... 2.00
2 Don Rosa, A Little Something
   Special 2.00
3 The Black Widow 2.00

AFTERMATH
Chaos! Comics, 2000
1 sequel to Armageddon 2.95
1 premium. 10.00
Ashcan, Yellow 10.00
Ashcan, Blue 25.00

AGAINST BLACKSHARD
Sirius Comics, Aug., 1986
1 3-D. 2.25

AGENT: AMERICA
Awesome Entertainment, 1997
1 RLe 2.50
2 RLe,JSb,JLb,F:Supreme,
   V:Smash 2.50

AIRBOY
Eclipse, 1986–89
1 TT/TY,D:Golden Age Airboy
   O:New Airboy. 3.25
2 TT/TY,I:Marisa,R:SkyWolf 2.25
3 A:The Heap 2.50
4 A:Misery 2.50
5 DSt(c),R:Valkyrie 4.00
6 R:Iron Ace,I:Marlene 3.00
7 PG(c), ... 2.50
8 FH/TT(c). 2.50
9 R:Flying Fool, Riot, O'Hara
   Cocky, Judge & Turtle. 2.00
10 I:Manic,D:Cocky, Judge & Turtle . 2.00
11 O:Birdie 2.00
12 R:Flying Fool 2.00
13 I:New Bald Eagle 2.00

CVA Page 560   All comics prices listed are for *Near Mint* condition.

COLOR PUB. — Air–Alien

14 A:Sky Wolf, Iron Ace 2.00
15 A:Ku Klux Klan. 2.00
16 D:Manic,A:Ku Klux Klan. 2.00
17 A:HarryS.Truman,Misery 2.00
18 A:Gold.Age Black Angel 2.00
19 A:Gold.Age Rats 2.00
20 Rat storyline 2.00
21 I:Lester Mansfield (rel. of Gold.Age Rackman), Artic Deathzone #1. . . . . 2.00
22 DSp,Artic Deathzone #2 . . . . . 2.00
23 A:Gold.Age Black Angle, Artic Deathzone #3. . . . . 2.00
24 A: Heap 2.00
25 TY,I:Manure Man,A:Heap 2.00
26 R:Flying Dutchman 2.00
27 A:Iron Ace, Heap 2.00
28 A:Heap 2.00
29 . . . . 2.00
30 A:Iron Ace; Sky Wolf story 2.00
31 A:Valkyrie; Sky Wolf story 2.00
32 Hostage Virus, ... 2.00
33 DSp,SkyWolf sty,A:Sgt.Strike . . . 2.00
34 DSp,A:La Lupina 2.00
35 DSp,A:La Lupina, Sky Wolf 2.00
36 . . . . 2.00
37 DSp. 2.00
38 CI, Heap story 2.00
39 CI, Heap story 2.00
40 CI, Heap story 2.00
41 V:Steel Fox, Golden Age rep. O:Valkyrie. 2.00
42 A:Rackman 2.00
43 Sky Wolf sty, A:Flying Fool. 2.00
44 A:Rackman 2.00
45 . . . . 2.00
46 EC,Airboy Diary #1 . . . . 2.00
47 EC,Airboy Diary #2 . . . . 2.00
48 EC,Airboy Diary #3 . . . . 2.00
49 EC,Airboy Diary #4 . . . . 2.00
50 AKu/NKu,double-size 3.95
Spec. Meets the Prowler. 2.00
Spec. Mr. Monster 2.00
Spec. Vs Airmaidens 2.00

AIR FIGHTERS, SGT. STRIKE SPECIAL
Eclipse, 1988
1 A:Airboy,Valkyrie. 2.00

AIRMAIDENS SPECIAL
Eclipse Comics, 1987
1 A:Valkyrie 2.00

AIRMAN
Malibu 1993
1 I:Thresher. 2.25

AIR WAR STORIES
Dell Publishing Co., 1964
1 . . . . 65.00
2 . . . . 50.00
3 thru 8 . . . . @40.00

AKEMI
Brainstorm Comics, 1997
1 . . . . 2.95

ALADDIN
Walt Disney
Prestige. Movie Adapt. 4.95

Airman #1 © Malibu

ALAN MOORE'S AWESOME ADVENTURES
Awesome Entertainment, 1999
1 AMo 2.50
1a alternate AxR cover 6.95
2 F:Young Guns 3.00
Spec. Awesome Univ. Handbook . . 2.95
Spec.A alternate AxR cover 2.95

ALAN MOORE'S GLORY
Comic Cavalcade, 2001
0 Park (c) 3.50
0a MHy (c) 3.50
0b Martin (c) 3.50
0c MMy (c) 3.50
0d white leather (c) 25.00
0e Lush Lands edition 5.95
0f Finch Prism Foil (c) 12.95
Avatar Press, 2001
Preview B&W 16-page 2.00
Preview signed gold (c) 8.95
1 (of 4) JLi(c). 3.50
1a Finch (c). 3.50
1b Haley (c). 3.50
1c MMy(c). 3.50
1d Martin (c) 3.50
1e Wraparound (c) 3.50
1f Red velvet BPe (c). 25.00
1g Finch Prism Foil (c). 12.95
1h Andy Park (c) 5.95
1i SSh(c). 5.95
1j Royal Blue Edition 75.00
1k Defender (c) 5.95
2 AMo,MMy, Finch (c) 3.50
2a Park (c) 3.50
2b Haley (c). 3.50
2c Martin (c) 3.50
2d MMy (c) 3.50
2e Glory Freedom (c) 5.95
2f Hall painted (c) 5.95

ALARMING ADVENTURES
Harvey Publications, 1962–63
1 AW,RC,JSe. 125.00
2 AW,BP,RC,JSe 75.00
3 JSe 75.00

ALARMING TALES
Harvey Publications, 1957–58
1 JK,JK(c) 275.00

2 JK,JK(c) 200.00
3 JK 150.00
4 JK,BP. 150.00
5 JK,AW 160.00
6 JK 150.00

ALBEDO, VOL. 3
Antarctic Press, 1994–95
Vol. 1 and II, See B&W
1 thru 4 Various Artists . . . . @2.95

ALBINO SPIDER OF DAJETTE
Verotik, 1998
0 by Glenn Danzig & Wayne Robertson 2.95
0a alternate cover 5.00
1 fan club cover. 5.00

ALIAS
Now Comics, 1990
1 . . . . 2.00
2 thru 5 . . . . @1.75

ALIAS: AGENT BRSITOW
Arcade Comics 2003
0 RLd 3.00
0a photo (c). 3.00
0b Dlx. Foil photo (c) 10.00
0c Chromium (c) 15.00
0d sgn art (c). 50.00
1 . . . . 3.00
1a photo (c). 3.00
1b Dlx. Foil photo (c) 10.00

ALIAS: STORMFRONT
Now Comics
1 . . . . 2.00
2 . . . . 2.00

ALIEN ARENA
Atomeka, 2002
1 (of 2) 3.00
2 . . . . 3.00
1a thru 2a variant (c) . . . . @3.00

ALIEN ENCOUNTERS
Eclipse Comics, 1985–87
1 . . . . 4.00
2 . . . . 3.00
3 'I Shot the Last Martian' 3.00
4 JBo(c) 3.00
5 RCo,'Night of the Monkey' 3.00
6 'Now You See It,''Freefall' 3.00
7 . . . . 3.00
8 TY,'Take One Capsule Every Million Years,M.Monroe(c) 3.00
9 The Conquered 3.00
10 . . . . 3.00
11 TT,'Old Soldiers' 3.00
12 'What A Relief,''Eyes of the Sibyl' 3.00
13 GN,'The Light at the End' 3.00
14 JRy,GN,TL,RT,'Still born' 3.00

ALIEN TERROR
Eclipse, 1986
3-D #1 'Standard Procedure' 2.00

ALIEN WORLDS
Pacific, 1982
1 AW,VM,NR 4.00

All comics prices listed are for *Near Mint* condition.

Alien–American — COLOR PUB. — Comics Values Annual

2 DSt	3.50
3	3.00
4 DSt(i)	3.00
5	3.00
6	3.00
7	3.00
3-D #1 AAd,DSt	5.50

Eclipse, 1985
8 AW	2.50
9	2.50

[CAPTAIN JOHNER AND] ALIENS, THE
Gold Key, 1967
1 Rep. Magnus Robot Fighter	50.00

ALISTER THE SLAYER
Midnight Press, 1995
1 I:Alister The Slayer	2.50
2 V:Lady Hate	2.50
3 JQ&JP(c) V:Subterranean Vampire Bikers	2.50

ALL AMERICAN SPORTS
Charlton, 1967
1	40.00

ALL HALLOWS EVE
Innovation, 1991
1	4.95

ALLEY OOP
Dell Publishing Co., 1962–63
1	100.00
2	75.00

ALLEY OOP ADVENTURES
Antarctic Press, 1998
1	3.00
2	3.00
3 I:Granny Green	3.00
TPB	11.00

ALLIES
Awesome Entertainment, 1999
1 RLe,AMo	2.50
1a alternate RLe cover	6.95

ALL NEW EXILES
Malibu Ultraverse 1995–96
Infinity F:Juggernaut,Blaze	2.50
1 TKa,KeL,Beginning the Quest	2.25
1a Computer painted cover (1:6)	2.50
1b signed edition	4.00
2 I:Hellblade, Phoenix flip issue	2.25
3 TKa,KeL,Phoenix Resurrection	2.25
4 & 5	@2.25
6 I:Moloch	2.25
7	2.25
8 I:Maxis	2.25
9	2.25
10 'Aladdin Attacks'	2.25
11 V:Maxis,A:Ripfire	2.25

ALPHA KORPS
Diversity Comics, 1996
1 I:Alpha Korps	3.00
1 signed	4.95
2 'The Price of Freedom,' pt.2	2.50
2 signed	4.95
3 'The Price of Freedom,' pt.3	2.50
3 signed	4.95
4 'The Price of Freedom,' pt.4	2.50

ALPHA WAVE
Darkline, 1987
1	2.00

Alter Ego #2 © First

ALTER EGO
First, 1986
1 RTs, Ron Harris	2.00
2 thru 4	@2.00

ALVIN (& THE CHIPMUNKS)
Dell Publishing Co., 1962–73
1	125.00
2	80.00
3	75.00
4 thru 10	@60.00
11 thru 20	@50.00
21 thru 28	@45.00
1 Alvin for President & his pals in Merry Christmas with Clyde Crashcup & Leonardo	40.00

AMAZING CHAN & THE CHAN CLAN
Gold Key, 1973
1	35.00
2	25.00
3 and 4	@20.00

AMAZING HEROES SWIMSUIT ANNUALS
Fantagraphics, 1990–93
1990 Spec. A:Dawn	25.00
1990 2nd printing	15.00
1991 A: Dawn	20.00
1992 A: Dawn	20.00
1993 A: Dawn	20.00

AMAZON, THE
Comico, 1989
1	2.00
2	2.00
3 end mini-series	2.00

AMELIA RULES!
Renaissance Press, 2001
1 by Jimmy Gownley	2.95
2	2.95
3	2.95
4 thru 11	@2.95
TPB Vol. 1 In with the Out Crowd	14.95
TPB Orig. Art edition	60.00
TPB The Whole World's Crazy	17.95

AMELIA RULES!: SUPERHEROES
Renaissance Press 2003
1 (of 6)	2.95

AMERICAN FLAGG
First, 1983–88
1 HC,I:American Flagg, Hard Times, pt.1	5.00
2 HC,Hard Times,pt.2	3.50
3 HC,Hard Times,pt.3	3.50
4 HC,Southern Comfort,pt.1	3.50
5 HC,Southern Comfort,pt.2	3.50
6 HC,Southern Comfort,pt.3	3.50
7 HC,State of the Union,pt.1	3.50
8 HC,State of the Union,pt.2	3.50
9 HC,State of the Union,pt.3	3.50
10 HC,Solidarity-For Now,pt.1 I:Luthor Ironheart	3.50
11 HC,Solidarity-For Now,pt.2	3.50
12 HC,Solidarity-For Now,pt.3	3.50
13 HC	3.00
14 PB	3.00
15 HC,American Flagg A Complete story,pt.1	3.00
16 HC,Complete Story,pt.2	3.00
17 HC,Complete Story,pt.3	3.00
18 HC,Complete Story,pt.4	3.00
19 HC,Bullets & Ballots, pt.1	3.00
20 HC,LSn,Bullets & Ballots,pt.2	3.00
21 AMo,HC,LSn,Bull&Ballots,pt.3	3.00
22 AMo,HC,LSn,Bull&Ballots,pt.4	3.00
23 AMo,HC,LSn,England Swings, pt.1	3.00
24 AMo,HC,England Swings,pt.2	3.00
25 AMo,HC,England Swings,pt.3	3.00
26 AMO,HC,England Swings,pt.4	3.00
27 AMo with Raul the Cat	3.00
28 BWg	3.00
29 JSon	3.00
30 JSon	3.00
31 JSon,O:Bob Violence	3.00
32 JSon,A:Bob Violence	3.00
33 A:Bob Violence	3.00
34 A:Bob Violence	3.00
35 A:Bob Violence	3.00
36 A:Bob Violence	3.00
37 A:Bob Violence	3.00
38 New Direction	3.00
39 JSon,A:Bob Violence	3.00
40 A:Bob Violence	3.00
41	3.00
42 F:Luther Ironheart	3.00
43	3.00
44	3.00
45	3.00
46 PS	3.00
47 PS	3.00
48 PS	3.00
49	3.00
50 HC,last issue	3.00
Special #1 HC,I:Time2	4.00

See Also: Howard Chaykin's American Flagg

AMERICOMICS
AC Comics, 1983
1 GP(c),O:Shade............ 3.00
2 .... 2.00
3 Blue Beetle................ 2.00
4 O:Dragonfly 2.00
5 and 6 .... @2.00
Spec.#1 Capt.Atom,BlueBeetle.... 2.00

AMERICA'S BEST COMICS
WildStorm/DC, Nov., 2000
Spec.#1 64-page 6.95
America's Best Comics Sketchbook 5.95

AMERICAN WOMAN
Antarctic Press, 1998
1 by Richard Stockton & Brian
  Denham.................. 2.95
2 .... 2.95
2a deluxe 5.95

ANDROMEDA
Andromeda, 1995
1 I:Andromeda............... 2.50
2 Andromeda vs. Elite Force 2.50

ANGEL FIRE
Crusade Comics, 1997
1 BiT, from Shi #12, BiT(c)...... 2.95
1a with Roberto Flores cover..... 2.95
1b with photo cover 2.95
2 F:Shi 2.95
3 F:Shi, concl. 2.95

ANGEL OF DESTRUCTION
Malibu Oct., 1996
1 .... 2.50

ANIMAL MYSTIC: WATER WARS
Sirius, 1996
1 (of 6) DOe 4.00
2 thru 6 DOe .... @3.00
TPB rep................... 19.95
TPB Klor 9.95
GN Dark One's Animal
  Mystic Field Guide 9.95

ANNE McCAFFREY'S THE UNICORN GIRL
Big Entertainment, 1997
GN F:Acorna 22.00

ANNE RICE'S THE TALE OF THE BODY THIEF
Sicilian Dragon, 1999
1 (of 12) 2.95
2 F:Lestat 2.95
3 thru 6 .... @2.95
7 F:Gretchen 2.95
TPB 19.95
TPB Exclusive 19.95

ANYTHING GOES
Fantagraphics, 1986
1 GK,FlamingCarot,Savage...... 3.50
2 S:AnM,JK,JSt,SK 3.50
3 DS,NA(c),A:Cerebus......... 3.00
4 .... 2.50
5 A:TMNTurtles 5.00
6 .... 3.00

COLOR PUB.

APE NATION
Adventure Comics, 1991
1 Aliens land on Planet of
  the Apes 3.00
2 General Ollo............... 3.00
3 V:Gen.Ollo,Danada.......... 2.50
4 D:Danada................. 2.50

APOLLO SMILE
Eagle Wing, 1998
1 When the Levee Breaks 3.00
2 When the Levee Breaks, pt.2 .. 3.00
3 When the Levee Breaks, pt.3 .. 3.00

ARACHNAPHOBIA
Walt Disney, 1990
1 Movie Adapt 5.95
1a Newsstand 2.95

ARACHNID FOUNDATION
Quantum Comics, 1998
1 .... 2.95

ARAKNIS
Mushroom Comics, 1995–96
1 I:Araknis, Shades of Evil pt.1 .. 3.50
2 Shades of Evil pt.2 .... 3.50
3 with pin-ups 2.50
4 .... 2.50

ARAKNIS
Mushroom Comics, 1996
0 Michael & Mario Ortiz 3.00
0 signed 4.00
1 .... 2.50
1 special edition............. 10.00
Mystic Comics
2 thru 6 .... @2.50

ARAKNIS: RETRIBUTION
Morning Star Productions, 1997
1 (of 4) by Michael & Mario Ortiz .. 2.50
1 signed 10.00
2 thru 4 .... @2.50

ARAKNIS: SHADES OF EVIL
Morning Star Productions
1 thru 4 .... @2.50

ARCHANGELS: THE SAGA
Eternal Studios
1 I:Cameron 2.50
2 V:Demons 2.50
3 and 4 .... @2.75
5 and 6 .... @2.50
7 .... 3.50
8 .... 4.50

ARCHARD'S AGENTS
Crossgen Comics 2002
1 CDi(s) spin-off from Ruse 3.50

ARCHER & ARMSTRONG
Valiant 1992
0 JiS(s),BWS,BL,I&O:Archer,
  I:Armstrong,The Sec. 3.00
0 Gold Ed. 5 .... 4.00
1 FM(c),B:JiS(s),BWS,BL,Unity #3,
  A:Eternal Warrior 2.25
2 WS(c),E:JiS(s),BWS,BL,Unity

Archer & Armstrong #6 © Valiant

#11,2nd A:Turok,A:X-O........ 2.25
3 B:BWS(a&s), BWi, V:Sect in
  Rome 2.25
4 BWS,BWi,V:Sect in Rome 2.25
5 BWS,BWi,I:Andromeda......... 2.25
6 BWS,BWi, A:Andromeda,
  V:Medoc. 2.25
7 BWS,ANi,BWi,V:Sect in England 2.25
8 BWS,as Eternal Warrior #8,
  Three Musketeers,I:Ivan...... 2.25
9 BCh,BWi,in Britain 2.25
10 BWS,A:Ivar............... 2.25
11 BWS,A:Solar,Ivar........... 2.25
12 BWS,V:The Avenger......... 2.25
13 B:MBn(s),RgM,In Los Angeles .. 2.25
14 In Los Angeles............. 2.25
15 E:MBn(s),In LasVegas, I:Duerst . 2.25
16 V:Sect 2.25
17 B:MBn(s),In Florida 2.25
18 MV,in Heaven 2.25
19 MV,V:MircoboticCult,D:Duerst .. 2.25
20 MV,Christmas Issue.......... 2.25
21 MV,A:Shadowman,Master
   Darque................... 2.25
22 MV,A:Shadowman,Master
   Darque,w/Valiant Era card 2.25
23 MV 2.25
24 MV 2.25
25 MV,A:Eternal Warrior......... 2.25
26 Chaos Effect-Gamma #4, A:Ivar,
   Et. Warrior............... 2.25

ARCHIE
Archie Publications, 1981
1 thru 300 see Golden Age
301 thru 350 .... @6.50
351 thru 400 .... @6.50
401 thru 429 .... @5.00
430 thru 529 .... @2.00
530 thru 543 .... @2.20
Archie's Christmas Stocking #4.... 2.00
Archie's Christmas Stocking #5.... 2.00
Archie's Christmas Stocking #6.... 2.25
Archie's Christmas Stocking #7.... 2.29
Archie's Spring Break Spec.1 ..... 2.00
Archie's Spring Break Spec.2 ..... 2.00
Archie's Spring Break Spec.3 ..... 2.25
Archie's Spring Break Spec.4(1999) 2.25
Archie's Spring Break Spec.5(2000) 2.49
Archie's Vacation Spec.#4 .... 2.00
Archie's Vacation Spec.#5 .... 2.00
Archie's Vacation Spec.#6 .... 2.25
Archie's Vacation Spec.#7 .... 2.25
Archie's Vacation Spec.#8 .... 2.49

ARCHIE AND FRIENDS
Archie Publications, 1992—98
1 thru 10 . . . . @5.00
11 thru 20 . . . . @4.00
20 thru 26 . . . . @2.50
27 thru 37 . . . . @2.00
38 thru 44 . . . . @2.00
45 thru 48 . . . . @2.00
49 thru 56 Archie & Friends, Featuring Josie and the Pussy Cats . . . @2.00
57 thru 64 . . . . @2.00
65 thru 78 . . . . @2.20

ARCHIE AND ME
Archie Publications, 1964–87
1 . . . . 250.00
2 . . . . 125.00
3 . . . . 75.00
4 . . . . 60.00
5 . . . . 60.00
6 thru 10 . . . . @50.00
11 thru 20 . . . . @25.00
21 thru 100 . . . . @10.00
101 thru 162 . . . . @8.00

ARCHIE AS PUREHEART THE POWERFUL
Archie Publications, 1966–67
1 superhero parody 125.00
2 . . . . 75.00
3 thru 6 Captain Pureheart. . . . @50.00

Archie at Riverdale High #55
© Archie Publications

ARCHIE AT RIVERDALE HIGH
Archie Publications, 1972
1 . . . . 80.00
2 . . . . 45.00
3 . . . . 30.00
4 . . . . 20.00
5 . . . . 20.00
6 thru 10 . . . . @10.00
11 thru 30 . . . . @9.00
31 . . . . 11.00
32 thru 114 . . . . @6.00

ARCHIE COMICS DIGEST
Archie Comics Digest, 1973
1 . . . . 125.00
2 . . . . 75.00

COLOR PUB.

3 . . . . 30.00
4 . . . . 15.00
5 thru 10 . . . . @8.00
11 thru 88 . . . . @5.00

ARCHIE MEETS THE PUNISHER
Archie/Marvel, 1994
1-shot crossover, same contents as Punisher meets Archie 3.00

ARCHIE'S MADHOUSE
Archie Publications, 1959–69
1 . . . . 325.00
2 . . . . 165.00
3 thru 5 . . . . @125.00
6 thru 10 . . . . @75.00
11 thru 16 . . . . @60.00
17 thru 21 . . . . @30.00
22 . . . . 75.00
23 thru 30 . . . . @30.00
31 thru 40 . . . . @10.00
41 thru 66 . . . . @8.00

ARCHIE'S PAL JUGHEAD
SEE: JUGHEAD

ARCHIE'S SUPERHERO MAGAZINE
Archie Publications, 1979
1 JSm/SK,Rept.Double of Capt. Strong #1,Fly,Black Hood . . . 25.00
2 GM,NA/DG,AMc,I:'70's Black Hood, Superhero rept. 30.00

ARCHIE'S TV LAUGH-OUT
Archie Publications, 1969–86
1 . . . . 125.00
2 . . . . 75.00
3 . . . . 40.00
4 . . . . 40.00
5 . . . . 40.00
6 thru 10 . . . . @15.00
11 thru 106 . . . . @10.00

ARCHIE 3000
Archie Publications, 1989–1991
1 thru 16 . . . . 2.00

ARCHIE'S WEIRD MYSTERIES
Archie Comics, 1999
1 from animated series 2.00
2 Shriek. 2.00
3 thru 10 . . . . @2.00
11 thru 20 . . . . @2.00
21 thru 24 . . . . @2.00
25 . . . . 2.20
Becomes

ARCHIE'S MYSTERIES
26 thru 32 . . . . @2.20

ARENA, THE
Alchemy, 1990
1 . . . . 2.00
1a signed, numbered, limited 3.00
2 . . . . 2.00

ARIANE & BLUEBEARD
Eclipse, 1988
Spec. CR 3.95

ARISTOKITTENS, THE
Gold Key, 1971–75
1 Disney 35.00
2 thru 9 . . . . @20.00

ARKANIUM
Dreamwave, 2002
1 triple gatefold cover 2.95
2 thru 6 . . . . @2.95

ARMAGEDDON
Chaos! Comics, 1999
1 (of 4) F:Lady Death, Evil Ernie . . 2.95
1a Premium edition 10.00
2 O:Chaos. 2.95
3 . . . . 2.95
4 concl. 2.95
TPB 12.95

ARMAGEDDON FACTOR
AC Comics, 1987
1 Sentinels of Justice. 2.00
2 . . . . 2.00
3 (1990) 4.00

ARMOR
Continuity, 1985
1 TGr,NA,A:Silver Streak, silver logo. 5.00
1a 2nd printing,red logo 2.50
2 TGr,NA(c) 2.50
3 TGr,NA(c) 2.50
4 TGr,NA(c) 2.50
5 BS,NA(c) 2.50
6 TVE,NA(c) 2.50
7 NA(c) 2.50
8 FS,NA(c) 2.50
9 FS,NA&KN(c) 2.50
10 FS,NA&KN(c) 2.50
11 SDr(i),KN(c). 2.50
12 KN(c). 2.50
13 NA(c),direct sales 2.50
14 KN(c), newsstand 2.50
[2nd Series]
1 V:Hellbender,Trading Card 2.50
[3rd Series, Deathwatch 2000]
1 Deathwatch 2000 pt.3,w/card . . . 4.00
2 Deathwatch 2000 pt.9,w/card . . . 2.50
3 Deathwatch 2000 pt.15,w/card . . 2.50
4 . . . . 2.50
5 Rise of Magic 2.50
6 Rise of Magic 2.50

ARMORED TROOPER VOTOMS
CPM Comics, 1996
1 TEl 2.95
2 TEl 2.95
3 TEl 2.95
4 TEl 2.95
GN Supreme Survivor. 16.95

ARMORINES
Valiant 1994
0 (from X-O #25),Card Stock (c), Diamond Distributors 'Fall Fling' Retailer Meeting 2.50
0a Gold Ed. 3.00
1 JGz(s),JCf,B:White Death 2.25
2 JGz(s),JCf,E:White Death 2.25
3 JGz(s),JCf,V:Spider Aliens 2.25
4 JCf, V: Spider Aliens 2.25
5 JCf, Chaos Effect-Delta #2, A:H.A.R.D. Corp. 2.25

Armorines–Asylum

6 Spider Alien Mothership 2.25
7 Rescue. 2.25
8 Rescue in Iraq 2.25
9 . . . . 2.25
10 Protect Fidel Castro. 2.25
11 V: Spider Super Suit 2.25
12 F: Sirot 2.25
Yearbook I:Linoff. 3.00

VOLUME 2
1 48-pg.. . . . . 3.95
2 . . . . 3.95
3 and 4 . . . . @2.50

ARMY ATTACK
Charlton, 1964
1 SG 50.00
2 SG 30.00
3 SG. 25.00
4 thru 47 . . . . @15.00

ARMY WAR HEROES
Charlton, 1963–70
1 . . . . 60.00
2 . . . . 35.00
3 thru 21 . . . . @30.00
22 GS,O&I:Iron Corporal. 35.00
23 thru 38 . . . . @20.00

ARROW
Malibu 1992
1 V:Dr.Sheldon,A:Man O'War. 2.25

ARROWSMITH
Wildstorm/DC July 2003
1 (of 6) KBk(s),CPa 2.95
2 KBk(s),mystical aviator 2.95
3 KBk(s) thru 5. . . . . @2.95

ARTESIA
Sirius, 1999
1 (of 6) by Mark Smylie 2.95
1a limited edition 10.00
2 thru 6 . . . . @2.95
Ann.#1 . . . . 3.50
Ann.#2 . . . . 3.95
TPB Vol. 1 . . . . 19.95

ARTESIA AFIELD
Sirius, 2000
1 (of 6) by Mark Smylie 2.95
1a Limited Ed. 5.95
2 thru 4 . . . . @2.95
5 Becomes A Wolf. 2.95
6 Becomes A Queen 2.95

ARTESIA AFIRE
Archaia Studios Press 2003
1 (of 6) by Mark Smylie 3.95
2 thru 4 . . . . @3.95
TPB Vol. 1 . . . . 24.95
TPB Artesia Afield 24.95
Map Set Artesia: Know World 24.95

ASH
Event Comics, 1994
1 JQ,JP,Fire and Crossfire,pt.1 . . 12.00
1a David Finch/Batt(c). 3.00
1b omnichrome commemorative . 14.95
1c omnichrom signed & numbered 29.95
2 JQ,JP,Fire and Crossfire,pt.2 . . . 7.00
2a David Finch/Batt (c) 3.00
3 JQ,JP,Secret of Origin 4.50
4 I:Actor 3.00

COLOR PUB.

5 I:New Character 3.00
6 V:Gabriel 3.00
0 Red Laser ed., Current Ash (c) . 10.00
0 Red Laser ed., Future Ash (c) . . 10.00
TPB rep. #1–#5 . . . . 14.95
TPB Vol. 1, JQ,JP,sgn. lim. 34.95

ASH: CINDER AND SMOKE
Event Comics, 1997
1 MWa,BAu,HuR,JP 3.00
1a autographed virgin JQ cover . . 10.00
1b signed limited edition 12.00
2 HuR(c) 3.00
2 JQ(c) 3.00
3 (of 6) JQ&JP(c) 3.00
4 (of 6) JQ&JP(c) 3.00
5 (of 6) JQ&JP(c) 3.00
6 (of 6) JQ&JP(c) 3.00
3a thru 6a variant JP&HuR(c)s. . @3.00

ASH FILES, THE
Event Comics, 1997
1 JQ,JP. 2.95
1 signed, limited 19.95

ASH: FIRE AND CROSSFIRE
Event Comics, 1998
1 (of 5) JQ,JP 2.95
1a signed & numbered. 24.95
2 . . . . 2.95

ASH: THE FIRE WITHIN
Event Comics
2 JQ,JP. 2.95
3 JQ,JP, Ash Rooftop cover 2.95
3a JQ,JP, Ash Firefighter cover . . 2.95

ASH/22 BRIDES
Event Comics, 1996
1 FaN,HuR,JP. 2.95

ASSASSIN
Archangel Studios 2003
1 (of 4) 3.00
1a variant (c). 3.00
2 . . . . 3.00

ASSASSIN, INC.
Solson
1 thru 4 . . . . @2.00

ASSASSIN SCHOOL
APC 2003
1 . . . . 3.50
2 thru 5 . . . . @3.50

ASTER
Entity Comics, 1995
0 O:Aster the Celestial Knight 4.50
1 I:Celestial Knight 5.00
1b 2nd printing 3.00
2 . . . . 3.50
3 V:Tolmek 3.25
3a Variant cover 7.00
4 Final Issue 3.00
TPB Rep.#1–#4 + pin-up gallery . . 12.95

ASTER THE LAST CELESTIAL KNIGHT
Entity Comics, 1995
1 R:Aster Chromium Cover 2.50
1a Clear Chromium Edition 4.00
1b Holo Chrome Edition. 5.00
2 World Defender 2.50

Astro Boy #1
© Gold Key

ASTRO BOY
Gold Key, Aug., 1965
1 I:Astro Boy 700.00

ASTRO BOY
Now
Prev. Original Astro Boy
18 . . . . 2.00
19 . . . . 2.00
20 . . . . 2.00

ASTRO CITY: LOCAL HEROES
Homage/DC Feb. 2003
1 (of 5) KBk,BA 2.95
2 KBk,BA 2.95
3 KBk,BA 2.95
4 KBk,BA 2.95
5 KBk,BA,conclusion 2.95

ASYLUM
Pendragon, 1995
1 . . . . 2.95
2 . . . . 2.95
3 three stories 2.95

ASYLUM
Maximum Press, Dec., 1995
1 Warchild, Beanworld, Avengelyne,
 Battlestar Galactica 3.00
2 I:Deathkiss 3.00
3 . . . . 3.00
4 RLd,A:Cybrid 3.00
5 I:Black Seed 3.00
6 R:Steve Austin & Jaime
 Sommers 3.00
7 RLe,F:Bloodwulf 3.00
8 RLd 3.00
9 RLd 3.00
10 . . . . 3.00

Asylum–Avengelyne

11 . . . . 3.00
12 MMy,F:Blindside 3.00
13 . . . . 3.00

ATLAS
Avatar Press, 2002
1 Gossett (c) 3.50
1b thru 1e variant (c)s . . . . @3.50
2 Brooks (c). 3.50
2b variant (c). 3.50

ATOM ANT
Gold Key, Jan., 1966
1 . . . . 500.00

ATOM-AGE COMBAT
Fago Magazines, 1958–59
1 . . . . 275.00
2 . . . . 200.00
3 . . . . 175.00

ATOMIC RABBIT
Charlton Comics, 1955–58
1 . . . . 300.00
2 . . . . 150.00
3 thru 10 . . . . @75.00
11 . . . . 125.00
Becomes:

ATOMIC BUNNY
12 . . . . 150.00
13 thru 18. . . . . @75.00
19 Dec., 1959. . . . . 75.00

ATOMICS, THE
AAA Pop Comics, 1999
1 by Mike Allred. 2.95
2 Zapman 2.95
3 Mutant Street Beatniks 2.95
4 refugees from the Innerverse . . . 2.95
5 The Light 2.95
6 The Physical. 2.95
7 I:The Skunk 2.95
8 F:The Laser 2.95
9 taken hostage. 2.95
10 . . . . 2.95
11 Heroes divided. 2.95
12 with poster. 3.50
13 World of Savage Dragon 3.50
14 World of Savage Dragon,pt.4 . . 3.50
15 World of Savage Dragon,pt.5 . . 3.50
16 World of Savage Dragon,pt.6 . . 3.50
King Size Giant. 10.00
King-Size Spec. Lessons in Light
  Lava & Lasers 8.95
King-Size Spec. Jigsaw 10.00
King-Size Vol. 3 . . . . 8.95
King-Size Vol. 4, 80-page 8.95

ATOMIK ANGELS
Crusade Entertainment, 1996
1 BiT 2.95
1 variant cover (1:25). 5.00
2 BiT. 2.95
3 BiT. 2.95
4 BiT, conclusion 2.95

AUTHORITY, THE
WildStorm/DC, 1999
1 WEl(s),BHi,PNe 17.00
2 WEl(s),BHi,PNe,V:Kaizen
  Gamorra. 11.00
3 WEl(s),BHi,PNe,destruction . . 11.00
4 WEl(s),BHi,PNe,save L.A.. . . . 11.00
5 WEl(s),BHi,PNe,Swiftships,pt.1 . 11.00

COLOR PUB.

6 WEl(s),BHi,PNe 7.00
7 WEl(s),BHi,PNe 7.00
8 WEl(s),BHi,PNe 7.00
9 WEl(s),BHi,PNe,OuterDark,pt.1 . 7.00
10 WEl(s),BHi,PNe,OuterDark,pt.2 . 7.00
11 WEl(s),BHi,PNe,OuterDark,pt.3 . 7.00
12 WEl(s),BHi,PNe,OuterDark,pt.4 . 7.00
13 MMr(s),TvS,Nativity,pt.1. . . . . . 9.00
14 MMr(s),TvS,Nativity,pt.2. . . . . . 6.00
15 MMr(s),TvS,Nativity,pt.3. . . . . . 6.00
16 MMr(s),TvS,Nativity,pt.4. . . . . . 6.00
17 MMr(s),TvS,Earth Inferno,pt.1 . . 6.00
18 MMr(s),TvS,Earth Inferno,pt.2 . . 6.00
19 MMr(s),TvS,Earth Inferno,pt.3 . . 6.00
20 MMr(s),TvS,Earth Inferno,pt.4 . . 6.00
21 JMC,All Tomorrow's Parties 6.00
22 MMr(s),TvS,Brave New World,
  pt.1 (of 4) 6.00
23 TPe(s),Brave-World,pt.2. . . . . . 6.00
24 TPe(s),BU:Establishment,40-pg . 3.50
25 TPe(s),Re-Space. 3.50
26 TPe(s),F:Old Authority 3.50
27 MMr(s),New World Order,pt.2 . . 3.50

Authority #13
© *WildStorm*

28 MMr(s),AAd,F:Seth 3.50
29 New World Order,pt.4 . . . . 3.50
Ann. 2000 #1, Devil's
  Night x-over, pt.2 . . . . 5.00
GN The Authority: Kev (2002). 4.95
GN Scorched Earth 4.95
TPB The Authority: Relentless . . . 17.95
TPB Under New Management . . . 17.95
TPB Widescreen, 48-page 5.95
TPB Earth Inferno (2002) 14.95
TPB Transfer of Power (2002) . . . 17.95
Volume 2
1 DT,F:Jack Hawksmoor, etc.. . . . . 2.95
2 thru 7 DT . . . . @2.95
Spec. #0, 40-pg.. . . . . 2.95

AUTOMATIC KAFKA
WildStorm/DC, July, 2002
1 JoC, Eye of the Storm 2.95
2 JoC,NPS agents. 2.95
3 JoC,TV game show host. 2.95
4 JoC,. 2.95
5 JoC,. 2.95
6 JoC,. 2.95
7 JoC,who is Galaxia. 2.95
8 JoC 2.95
9 JoC 2.95

Comics Values Annual

AVENGEBLADE
Maximum Press, 1996
1 RLe 3.00
2 RLe 3.00

AVENGELYNE
Maximum Press, 1995
1 RLd,I:Avengelyne Dir ed. 12.00
1a Newstand Edition 5.00
1b Holochrome Edition 15.00
1 gold edition. 10.00
2 V:B'Lial. 4.00
3 I:Magoci 4.00
3 variant cover, pin-up 5.00
TPB rep. #1–#3 . . . . 10.00
Regular Series, April, 1996
0 RLd,O:Avengelyne 5.00
1 RLd,BNa,F:Devlin. 4.00
1 variant photo cover. 4.00
2 I:Darkchylde. 10.00
2a variant photo cover 12.00
3 . . . . 3.50
4 A:Cybrid 3.50
5 A:Cybrid, ... 3.50
6 RLd,F:Divinity. 3.50
7 RLd,F:Divinity. 3.50
8 RLd, ... 3.50
9 RLd, ... 3.50
10 BNa,`The Possession,' pt.1 . . . . 3.50
11 BNa,`The Possession,' pt.2 . . . . 3.50
12 BNa,`The Possession,' pt.3 . . . . 3.50
13 BNa,`The Possession,' pt.4 . . . . 3.50
14 A:Bloodwulf 3.50
15 A:Glory, Prophet 3.50
Swimsuit Edition 3.50
Swimsuit book, American
  Entertainment exclusive 7.50

AVENGELYNE
Awesome Entertainment, 1999
Prelude 2.50
1 RLe,RNa 2.50
1a, b & c variant covers. 2.50
2 RLe, ... 2.50
3 . . . . 2.50
Spec. Swimsuit, 1999 . . . . 3.00
Spec.#1-shot Demonslayer (2000) . 2.95
Spec.#1a Demonslayer variant (c) . 2.95
Spec.#1b Demonslayer variant (c) . 2.95
Spec.#1c Demonslayer variant (c) . 2.95

AVENGELYNE: ARMAGEDDON
Maximum Press, 1996–97
1 (of 3) RLd. 3.00
2 RLd, ... 3.00
3 BNa,ScC, finale 3.00

AVENGELYNE: BAD BLOOD
Avatar, 2000
1 Matt Haley (c). 3.50
1a Al Rio (c) 3.50
1b Tim Vigil (c) 3.50
1c prism foil (c) previews excl.. . . 12.95
1d Al Rio velvet (c) 19.95
1e leather (c). 25.00
1f platinum (c). 7.95
1g Ruby Red ed. 19.95
1h Royal Blue edition. 75.00
2 . . . . 3.50
2a Haley (c). 3.50
2b Moline (c). 3.50
Prelude Rick Lyon (c) 4.95
Prelude Al Rio (c) 4.95
Prelude Bikini (c) 5.95

Comics Values Annual

Prelude prism foil(c) 16-page 12.95
Prelude variant SSh(c) 5.95

AVENGELYNE BIBLE: REVELATIONS
Maximum Press
one-shot RLd, ... 3.50

AVENGELYNE: DARK DEPTHS
Avatar Press, 2001
1 (of 2) Rio(c) 3.50
1a MMy(c). 3.50
1b Martin (c) 3.50
1c blue velvet (c). 25.00
1d prism foil exclusive (c) 12.95
1e Heavenly Body edition 5.95
1f Royal Blue (c) 75.00
2 (of 2) Rio(c) 3.50
2a MMy(c) 3.50
2b Lyon (c) 3.50
2c Blue leather (c). 25.00
1/2 Rio (c) 16-page. 4.95
1/2 Lloyd painted (c)........... 4.95
1/2 Frillion (c). 4.95
1/2 Midnight Prayer (c)......... 5.95
1/2 Prism foil exclusive (c) 12.95

AVENGELYNE: DEADLY SINS
Maximum Press, 1996
1 RLd (c)..................... 3.00
1 photo (c). 3.00
2 RLd(c)..................... 3.00

AVENGELYNE: DRAGON REALM
Avatar Press, 2001
1/2 Rio (c) 4.95
1/2 Carrie Hall (c) 4.95
1/2 Lloyd (c) 4.95
1/2 Martin (c). 4.95
1/2 Dying Breath ed. 5.95
1/2 Prism foil ed. 12.95
1 (of 2) Rio(c) 3.50
1a Martin (c) 3.50
1b Vigil (c). 3.50
1c red leather (c). 25.00
1d bondage (c) 6.00
1e prism foil (c) 13.00
1f venomous edition 6.00
1g venomous emerald foil 14.00
1h Fearless edition 5.00
2 Rio(c). 3.50
2a Martin (c) 3.50
2b MMy (c) 3.50
2c Shaw (c). 3.50
2d Ron Adrian (c) 5.95

AVENGELYNE/GLORY
Maximum Press, 1995
1 V:B'Lial..................... 4.00
1a variant cover. 5.00
Swimsuit Spec. #1 .... 2.95

AVENGELYNE/GLORY: THE GODYSSEY
Maximum Press, 1996
1 RLd,BNa 3.00
2 thru 5 RLd. .... @3.00

COLOR PUB.

AVENGELYNE/PANDORA
Avatar, 2000
Spec. x-over. 3.50
Spec.Preview exclusive 3.50
Spec.Preview Bikini ed. 6.00
Spec.McDaniel (c). 6.00
Spec.Previews exlusive Prism ed.. 13.00
Spec.Red Velvet. 25.00
Spec.Ruby Red edition 20.00
Spec.Royal Blue............... 75.00

Avengelyne/Power #2
© *Maximum*

AVENGELYNE/POWER
Maximum Press, 1995–96
1 RLd,V:Hollywood 3.00
1 variant cover. 3.50
2 RLd(c) 3.00
3 .... 3.00
3a photo (c). 3.00

AVENGELYNE/PROPHET
Maximum Press, April, 1996
1 RLd,BNa,MD2 .... 3.00
Awesome Entertainment, 2000
Rage of Furies #1 RLe(c)........ 3.00
#1a IaC(c). 3.00
#1b Grant(c). 3.00
#1c Walker Bros.(c) 3.00
#1d Wizard world ed. 5.00
#1e Wizard world, signed 10.00

AVENGELYNE: REVELATION
Avatar, 2000
1 Rio (c) 3.50
1a Haley (c). 3.50
1b Wraparound (c) 3.50
1c leather (c). 25.00
1d Matt Martin (c) 5.95
1e royal blue (c) 75.00
Previews prism foil (c)......... 12.95
Prelude Lyon (c) 5.95
Prelude platinum signed 10.95

AVENGELYNE: SERAPHACIDE
Avatar Press, 2001
1/2 Lyon (c)................... 5.00
1/2 Martin (c). 5.00
1/2 Rio (c). 5.00

Avengelyne–Axis

1/2 Shaw (c) 5.00
1/2 Bound edition 6.00
1/2 Pax Romana (c) 5.95
1/2 Ron Adrian (c) 5.95
1 (of 2) Rio (c) 3.50
1a Hall (c) 3.50
1b Martin (c) 3.50
1c Lyon (c) 3.50
1d White Velvet (c) 25.00
1e Adam & Eve edition 5.95
1f Hard Woman (c) 5.95
1g Bikini (c). 5.95

AVENGELYNE/SHI
Avatar Press, 2001
1/2 RLd (c) 16-page 4.00
1/2a Rio (c) 4.00
1/2b MMy (c). 4.00
1/2c Martin (c). 4.00
1/2d Victory (c) 5.95
1/2e Sean Shaw, Cross cover 5.95
1 Finch (c) x-over 3.50
1a Martin (c) 3.50
1b Rio (c) 3.50
1c Shaw (c). 3.50
1d BTi wraparound (c). 3.50
1e Red Leather (c) 25.00
1f Prism foil (c) 12.95
1g Royal Blue edition. 75.00
1h Waller (c) 5.95
1i Face off cover 5.95
1j ruby red edition 24.95

AVENGELYNE/SUPREMA
Awesome Entertainment, 2000
Rage of Furies #1 (2000) 4.00
1a Wizard world ed. 5.00
1b signed 10.00

AVENGELYNE/ WARRIOR NUN AREALA
Maximum Press, 1997
Spec. 3.00
Awesome Entertainment, 1997
Spec. #2 The Nazarene Affair..... 3.00

AVENGERS, THE
Gold Key, Nov., 1968
1 .... 400.00

AWESOME
Awesome Entertainment, 1997
Holiday Spec. #1 .... 2.50
Holiday Spec.'99 .... 4.95
Spring '99 Tourbook 4.95

AXA
Eclipse, 1987
1 `Axa the Adopted'............ 2.00
2 .... 2.00

AXEL PRESSBUTTON
Eclipse, 1984
1 BB(c),Origin................. 2.00
2 .... 2.00
3 thru 4 .... @2.00
Becomes:
PRESSBUTTON

AXIS ALPHA
Axis Comics, 1994
1 LSn,I:BEASTIES,Dethgrip,
Shelter,W 2.75

All comics prices listed are for *Near Mint* condition.

CVA Page 567

AZTEC ACE
Eclipse, 1984
1 NR(i),I:AztecAce............ 3.50
2 NR(i) 3.50
3 NR(i) 3.00
4 NR(i) 3.00
5 NR(i) 3.00
6 NR(i) 3.00
7 NR(i) 3.00
8 NR(i) 3.00
9 NR(i) 3.00
10 NR(i) 2.00
11 .... 3.50
12 .... 2.50
13 .... 2.50
14 .... 2.50
15 F:Bridget 2.50

BABES OF BROADWAY
Broadway, 1996
1 .... 2.95

BABY HUEY, THE BABY GIANT
Harvey Publications, 1956–80
1 .... 600.00
2 .... 300.00
3 .... 175.00
4 .... 150.00
5 .... 150.00
6 thru 10 .... @75.00
11 thru 20 .... @50.00
21 thru 40 .... @40.00
41 thru 60 .... @25.00
61 thru 79 .... @20.00
80 .... 20.00
81 thru 95 .... @10.00
96 Giant size 12.00
97 Giant size 12.00
98 .... 8.00
99 .... 8.00

BABY HUEY AND PAPA
Harvey Publications, 1962–68
1 .... 250.00
2 .... 125.00
3 .... 75.00
4 .... 75.00
5 .... 75.00
6 .... 30.00
7 .... 30.00
8 .... 30.00
9 .... 30.00
10 .... 30.00
11 thru 20 .... @10.00
21 thru 33 .... @8.00

BABY HUEY DUCKLAND
Harvey Publications, 1962–66
1 .... 175.00
2 .... 75.00
3 .... 75.00
4 .... 75.00
5 .... 75.00
6 thru 14 .... @20.00
15 .... 20.00

BACHELOR FATHER
Dell Publishing Co., 1962
1 .... 125.00
2 .... 100.00

BACK TO THE FUTURE
Harvey, 1991
1 Chicago 1927 .... 2.00

COLOR PUB.

2 Cretaceous Period 2.00
3 World War I 2.00
4 Doc Retires 2.00

BAD BOY
Oni Press, 1997
GN Frank Miller & Simon Bisley . . . 4.95

BAD COMPANY
Quality, 1988
1 thru 19 .... @2.00

BAD EGGS
Acclaim 1996
1 thru 4 BL,DP,'That Dirty Yellow Mustard' .... @2.95

Badger #3
© Capital

BADGER
Capital, 1983
1 JBt,I:Badger,Ham,Daisy Yak,Yeti. 3.00
2 JBt,I:Riley,A:YakYeti 3.00
3 JBt,O:Badger,Ham 3.00
4 JBt,A'Ham 3.00

First, 1984–91
5 BR,DruidTree Pt1 .... 2.50
6 BR,DruidTree Pt2 .... 2.50
7 BR,I:Wonktendonk,Lord Weterlackus 2.50
8 BR,V:Demon 2.50
9 BR,I:Connie,WOatesCbra 2.50
10 BR,A:Wonktendonk, I:Hodag Meldrum. 2.50
11 BR,V:Hodag,L.W'lackus 2.50
12 BR,V:Hodag,L.W'lackus 2.50
13 BR,A:L.W'lakus,Clonezone, Judah. 2.50
14 BR,I:HerbNg 2.50
15 BR,I:Wombat,JMoranIbob ... 2.50
16 BR,A:Yak,Yeti 2.50
17 JBt,I:Lamont 3.00
18 BR,I:SpudsGroganA:Cbra ... 2.50
19 BR,I:Senator1,ClZone 2.50
20 BR,Billionaire'sPicnic 2.50
21 BR,I&O:Phantom 2.50
22 BR,I:Dr.Buick Riviera 2.50
23 I:BobDobb,A:Yeti 2.50
24 BR,A:Riley 2.50
25 BR,I:Killdozer. 2.50
26 BR,I:RoachWranger 2.50
27 BR,O:RoachWranger 2.50

28 BR,A:Yeti 2.50
29 A:Clonezone,C:GrimJack 2.50
30 BR,I:Dorgan. 2.00
31 BR,I:HopLingSung 2.00
32 BR,D:Dorgan,HopLingSng ... 2.00
33 RLm/AN,I:KidKang 3.00
34 RLm,I:Count Kohler 3.00
35 RLm,I:Count Kohler 3.00
36 RLm,V:Dire Wolf 3.00
37 AMe,A:Lamont 2.50
38 Animal Band 2.00
39 I:Buddy McBride 2.00
40 RLm,I:Sister Twyster 3.50
41 RLm,D:Sister Twyster 3.50
42 RLm,A:Paul Bunyan 3.50
43 RLm,V:Vampires 3.50
44 RLm,V:Vampires 3.50
45 RLm,V:Dr.Buick Riviera 3.50
46 RLm,V:Lort Weterlackus 3.50
47 RLm,Hmds.Sacr.BloodI 3.50
48 RLm,Hmds.Sacr.BloodII 3.50
49 RLm,TRoof off SuckerI 3.50
50 RLm,TRoof off SuckerII 5.00
51 RLm,V:Demon 3.00
52 TV,Tinku 4.00
53 TV,I:Shaza,Badass 4.00
54 TV,D:Shaza 4.00
55 I:Morris Myer 2.00
56 I:Dominance 2.00
57 A:KKang,V:L.W'lackus 2.00
58 A:Lamont,W'bat,V:SpudsJack . 2.00
59 Bad Art Issue 2.00
60 I:ChisumBros 2.25
61 V:ChismBros 2.00
62 I:Shanks 2.00
63 V:Shanks 2.00
64 A:Mavis Sykes 2.25
65 A:BruceLee 2.25
66 I:Joe Nappleseed. 2.25
67 Babysitting. 2.25
68 V:GiantFoot 2.25
69 O:Mavis 2.25
70 BR:Klaus(last monthly) 2.25
Graphic Nov.BR,I:Mazis Sykes,D:Hodag 10.00
Badger Bedlam............... 4.95

BADGER GOES BERSERK
First, 1989
1 I:Larry,Jessie 4.00
2 MZ,V:Larry,Jessie. 3.50
3 JBt/MZ,V:Larry,Jessie. 3.00
4 JBt/MZ,V:Larry,Jessie. 3.00

BAD GIRLS OF BLACKOUT
Blackout Comics, 1995
0 .... 3.50
1 I:Ms. Cyanide, Ice. 3.50
Ann.#1 Hari Kari, Lady Vampre. .. 3.50
Ann.#1 Commemorative ed. 9.95

BAD KITTY
Chaos! Comics, 2001
1 BnP 3.00
1a premium edition 10.00
2 .... 3.00
3 .... 3.00
Ashcan. 6.00
Script #1 .... 5.00
Script #1 premium 20.00

BAD KITTY: MISCHIEF NIGHT
Chaos! Comics, 2001
1 .... 3.00

COLOR PUB.

BARNEY AND BETTY RUBBLE
Charlton Comics, 1973–76
1 .... 75.00
2 .... 30.00
3 .... 30.00
4 .... 30.00
5 .... 30.00
6 thru 10 .... @20.00
11 thru 23 .... @15.00

BARRY M. GOLDWATER
Dell Publishing Co., March, 1965
1 .... 60.00

BAR SINISTER
Windjammer 1995
1 From Shaman's Tears........ 2.50
2 V:SWAT Team 2.50
3 F: Animus Prime............ 2.50
4 MGe,RHo,V:Jabbersnatch 2.50

BART-MAN
Bongo, 1993
1 Foil(c),I:Bart-Man 4.00
2 I:Penalizer 2.25
3 When Bongos Collide,pt.3,
  with card 2.25
4 Crime-Time,pt.1 .... 2.25
5 Bad Guys Strike Back........ 2.25

BART SIMPSON COMICS
Bongo Comics, 2000
1 .... 2.50
2 .... 2.50
3 Bart Simpson in space 2.50
4 Lisa on game show 2.50
5 Wild wild west.............. 2.50
6 Supercat of Springfield 2.50
7 Science contest 2.50
8 Dan DeCarlo Issue........... 2.50
9 Grows a beard 2.50
10 Krusty the Clown video 2.50
11 Mail order bride 2.50
12 thru 13 .... @2.50
14 .... 3.00
TPB The Big Book of Bart Simpson 11.95
TPB Big Bad Book of Bart Simpson.... 12.95

BART SIMPSONS TREEHOUSE OF HORROR
Bongo Comics, 1995
1 Bart People 2.95
2 thru 4 .... @2.95
5 48-pg....................... 3.50
6 and 7 64-page 0.50
8 .... @3.50
9 .... 5.00
1-shot Treehouse of Terror ... 2.50

BASEBALL
Kitchen Sink, 1991
1 WE (c) reprint of 1949 orig..... 3.95
2 Ray Gotto (c), w/4 BB cards.... 2.95

BAT, THE
Adventure
1 R:The Bat,inspiration for Batman says Bob Kane............. 2.50

Comics Values Annual

1a premium edition 13.00
1b super premium edition 20.00

BAD KITTY: RELOADED
Chaos! Comics, 2001
1 .... 3.00
1a premium ed................ 10.00
2 F:Chastity.................. 3.00
3 .... 3.00
4 .... 4.00
2a thru 4a variant (c) ...... @7.50

BADROCK/WOLVERINE
Awesome Entertainment, 1997
Spec. #1 JV,CYp,V:Sauron,48pg... 4.95

BAKER STREET
Caliber, 1989
1 .... 3.00
2 thru 10 .... @2.50
TPB Vol. 1 .... 14.95
TPB Vol. 2 .... 14.95

BALLAD OF HALO JONES
Quality, 1987
1 IG Alan Moore story 2.00
1a IG rep. 2.00
2 thru 12 .... @2.00

BAMM-BAMM & PEBBLES FLINTSTONE
Gold Key, Oct., 1964
1 .... 125.00

BANZAI GIRL
Sirius Entertainment, 2002
Preview book, lim. ed. 5.00
1 (of 4) by Jinky Coronado...... 2.95
1a panty pack ed. 19.95
2 thru 4 .... @2.95
2a thru 4a limited, signed, ph(c) @12.00
Sketchbook, limited 7.95

BARBARIANS, THE
Atlas, June, 1975
1 O: Andrax,F:Iron Jaw 25.00

BARBIE & KEN
Dell Publishing Co.
May-July, 1962
1 .... 600.00
2 .... 500.00
3 .... 500.00
4 .... 500.00
5 .... 550.00

BARBIE TWINS ADVENTURES, THE
Topps, 1995
1 I:Shane, Sia 2.50

BARBI TWINS ADVENTURES
Studio Chikara, 1998
Color Spec. The Roswell Incident.. 3.95

Bad–Battle

Baseball Comics #1
© Kitchen Sink

BATTLEBOOKS
Battlebooks Inc., 1999
all BTi(c)
Bubba-Busters Battlebook 5.00
Captain America Battlebook
  Blue print, signed edition 10.00
Colossus Battlebook............ 4.00
Daredevil Battlebook BTi(c) 4.00
Daredevil Battlebook JQ&JP(c)... 4.00
Darkchylde A Battlebook........ 4.00
Darkchylde B Battlebook........ 4.00
The Darkness Battlebook 4.00
Dr. Doom Battlebook 4.00
Elektra Battlebook 4.00
  Blue print, signed edition ... 12.95
Elektra Battlebook, revised ... 4.00
Gambit Battlebook 4.00
Green Goblin Battlebook........ 4.00
Iron Man Battlebook
  Blue print, signed edition ... 12.95
  Blue print, signed edition ... 12.95
The Incredible Hulk Battlebook 4.00
  Blue print, signed edition ... 12.95
Magneto Battlebook 4.00
President Clinton Battlebook... 5.00
Rogue Battlebook............... 4.00
  Blue print, signed edition ... 12.95
Sabretooth Battlebook 4.00
Shi: The Spirit of Benkei Battlebook 4.00
  Blue print, signed edition ... 10.00
Spider-Man Battlebook
  Blue print, signed edition ... 12.95
Storm Battlebook............... 4.00
The Thing Battlebook 4.00
Tomoe: Fan's of Fury Battlebook.. 4.00
Vampirella Hell on Earth Battlebook 4.00
White Queen Battlebook......... 4.00
Witchblade Battlebook 4.00
Wolverine Battlebook 4.00
Wolverine with Bone Claws Battlebook
  Blue print, signed edition ... 12.95

BATTLE FORCE
Blackthorne, 1987
1 and 2 .... @2.00
3 .... 2.00

BATTLE OF THE PLANETS
Gold Key, June, 1979
1 TV Cartoon................. 35.00

All comics prices listed are for *Near Mint* condition.

Battle–Beauty / COLOR PUB.

2	25.00
3	25.00
4	25.00
5	25.00

Whitman

6	15.00
7 thru 10	@15.00

BATTLESTAR GALACTICA
Maximum Press, 1995

1 Finds Earth	2.50
2 Council of Twelve	2.50
3 R:Adama	2.50
4 Pyramid Secrets	2.50
TPB series rep	12.95
Spec. Ed. Painted Book (1997)	3.00
Battlestar Galactica: The Compendium #1 rep. from Asylum	3.00

BATTLESTAR GALACTICA
Realm Press, 1997

1 by Chris Scalf	3.00
1a variant cover	3.00
2 Law of Volhad	3.00
3 Prison of Souls, pt.1	3.00
3a alternate cover	3.00
4 Prison of Souls, pt.2	3.00
5	3.00
6 A Path of Darkness, pt.1	3.00
7 A Path of Darkness, pt.2	3.00
7a photo (c)	3.00
7b signed and numbered	6.00
8 Centurion Prime	3.00
Spec.#1 20 Yahren Reunion	5.00
Spec.#1 No Memory of Earth	3.00
Spec.#1 CenturionPrime,Scott(c)	3.00
Spec.#1 CenturionPrime,Parsons(c)	3.00
Spec.#2 Centurion Prime	3.00
Spec. 1999 Tourbook	3.00
Spec. 1999 Tourbook con. ed.	7.00
Spec. 1999 Tourbook sign	30.00
Spec. Gallery #1	4.00
Tech Journal: The Galactica	4.00
Tech Journal: Ships of Fleet	4.00
Spec.No Man's Land	4.00
Spec.No Man's Land, deluxe	5.00
Cylon Dawn Spec. (2000)	4.00
Cylon Dawn Spec. deluxe	5.00
Darkest Night Spec. (2000)	4.00
Darkest Night Spec. variant (c)	5.00
Dire Prophecy Spec. (2000)	4.00
Dire Prophecy Spec. deluxe	5.00
Eve of Destruction Prelude(1999)	4.00
Spec.#1 Triad Triumph (2000)	4.00
Spec.#1a Triad Triumph,deluxe	5.00
TPB New Beginnings, rep. #1–#4	14.00

BATTLESTAR GALACTICA APOLLO'S JOURNEY
Maximum Press, April, 1996

1 story by Richard Hatch	2.95
2	2.50
3	2.50

BATTLESTAR GALACTICA THE ENEMY WITHIN
Maximum Press, Feb., 1996

1	3.00
2	2.50
3	2.50

BATTLESTAR GALACTICA JOURNEY'S END
Maximum Press, 1996

1 (of 4) RLd	3.00

Battlestar Galactica: Search for Sanctuary #1 © Maximum

2 RLd	3.00
3 RLd, the end of Galactica?	3.00
4 RLd, conclusion	3.00

BATTLESTAR GALACTICA SEARCH FOR SANCTUARY
Realm Press, 1998

1 (of 4)	3.00
2 Path of Darkness	3.00
3 tensions grow	3.00
4	3.00

BATTLESTAR GALACTICA SEASON THREE
Real Press, 1999

1	3.00
1a alternate JaL(c)	5.00
1b Cylon Attack (c)	5.00
1c Cylon Attack (c) signed	35.00
2	3.00
2a alternate cover	5.00
2b pencil sketch cover	5.00
2c convention edition	5.00
3 Fire in the Sky	3.00
3a alternate cover	5.00
3b convention edition	5.00
4 Scott (c)	3.00
4a Parsons (c)	3.00
5 Busch (c)	3.00
5a Parsons (c)	3.00
6	3.00
6a	3.00
7	3.00
7a deluxe	5.00
8	3.00
8a deluxe	5.00
Spec. 80-page Juggernaut	9.00
Tour Book Sketch ed.	25.00

BATTLESTAR GALACTICA STARBUCK
Maximum Press, 1997

1 (of 3) RLd	2.50
2 RLd	2.95
3 RLd, the end of Galactica?	2.95

BATTLETECH
Blackthorne, 1987

1	2.00
2 thru 6	@2.00

(Changed to Black & White)

1 3-D	2.50
2 3-D	2.50

BATTLETECH
Malibu Feb., 1995

0	2.95

BATTLETECH: FALLOUT
Malibu Dec., 1994–Mar. 1995

1 3 tales, Based on FASA game	3.00
1a gold foil limited edition	3.50
1b limited holographic editon	5.00
2 V:Clan Jade Falcon	3.00
3 R:Lea	3.00
4 Conclusion	3.00

BAY CITY JIVE
WildStorm/DC, May, 2001

1 (of 3) F:Sugah Rollins	2.95
1a variant (c) (1:4)	2.95
2 1976 streets of San Francisco	2.95
3 Hell on Earth, concl.	2.95

BEAGLE BOYS, THE
Gold Key, 1964–79

1	60.00
2 thru 5	@35.00
6 thru 10	@25.00
11 thru 20	@20.00
21 thru 46	@15.00
47	15.00

BEANIE THE MEANIE
Fargo Publications, 1958

1 thru 3	@40.00

B.E.A.S.T.I.E.S.
Axis Comics, 1994

1 JS(a&s),I:Beasties	2.25

THE BEATLES, LIFE STORY
Dell Publishing Co., 1964

1	700.00

BEAUTIFUL KILLER
Black Bull Entertainment, 2001

1 JP(s)	5.00
1a variant (c)	4.00
2 JP(s)	4.00
3 JP(s)	4.00
Preview Edition, limited	5.00

BEAUTY AND THE BEAST
Innovation, 1993

1 From TV series	2.50
1a Deluxe	3.95
2	2.50
3	2.50
4 Siege	2.50
5 Siege	2.50
6 Halloween	2.50
7	2.50

BEAUTY AND THE BEAST PORTRAIT OF LOVE
First, 1989–90
1 WP,TV tie in 12.00
2 .... 8.00
Book II:Night of Beauty......... 5.95

BEAUTY AND THE BEAST
Walt Disney, 1992
Movie adapt.(Prestige) 4.95
Movie adapt.(newsstand) 2.50
mini-series
1 Bewitched 2.00
2 Elsewhere 2.00
3 A:Catherine 2.50

BEDLAM!
Eclipse, 1985
1 SBi,RV,reprint horror 2.00
2 SBi,RV,reprint horror 2.00

BEETLE BAILEY
Harvey, 1992
1 F:Mort Walker's B.Bailey....... 2.00
2 Beetle builds a bridge......... 2.00
3 thru 12 .... 2.00

BEETLEJUICE
Harvey, 1991
1 EC,'This is your lice'.......... 2.00
Holiday Special #1 .... 2.00

BEN CASEY
Dell Publishing Co., June-July, 1962
1 Ph(c) 80.00
2 Ph(c) 60.00
3 Ph(c) 40.00
4 Drug, Ph(c)................ 45.00
5 Ph(c) 40.00
6 thru 10 Ph(c)............. @40.00

BERNI WRIGHTSON MASTER OF THE MACABRE
Pacific
1 BWr 5.25
2 BWr 3.75
3 BWr 3.50
4 BWr 3.50
Eclipse, 1984
5 BWr 3.50

BEST FROM BOY'S LIFE
Gilberton Company, Oct., 1957
1 .... 125.00
2 .... 75.00
3 .... 50.00
4 LbC 85.00
5 .... 50.00

BEST OF BUGS BUNNY
Gold Key, 1966–68
1 Both Giants 65.00
2 .... 50.00

COLOR PUB.

BEST OF DENNIS THE MENACE, THE
Hallden/Fawcett Publ., Summer, 1959–Spring, 1961
1 .... 100.00
2 thru 5 .... @50.00

BEST OF DONALD DUCK & UNCLE SCROOGE
Gold Key, 1964–67
1 .... 125.00
2 .... 100.00

BEST OF DONALD DUCK
Gold Key, Nov., 1965
1 .... 125.00

BETTA: TIME WARRIOR
Immortal Comics, 1997
1 (of 3)Beginnings's End,pt.1 .... 2.95
2 The Beginnings's End,pt.2 .... 2.95

BETTI COZMO
Antarctic Press, 1999
1 (of 3) 3.00
2 .... 3.00
3 Raygun For Hire............. 3.00

BETTY
Archie Publications, 1992
1 thru 39 .... @2.00
40 thru 60 .... @2.00
61 thru 80 .... @2.00
81 thru 100 .... @2.00
101 thru 119 .... @2.00
120 thru 133 .... @2.20

BETTY AND ME
Archie Publications, 1965–92
1 .... 125.00
2 .... 75.00
3 .... 40.00
4 .... 40.00
5 .... 40.00
6 thru 10 .... @25.00
11 thru 30 .... @15.00
31 thru 50 .... @10.00
51 thru 55 .... @8.00
56 thru 200 .... @5.00

BETTY AND VERONICA
Archie Publications, June, 1987
1 thru 100 .... @5.00
101 thru 104 .... @4.00
105 thru 119 .... @3.00
120 thru 141 .... @5.00
142 thru 160 .... @2.00
161 thru 181 .... @2.00
182 thru 195 .... @2.20
Summer Fun Special #5 .... 2.25
Summer Fun Special #6 .... 2.25
Summer Fun Special #7 .... 2.49
TPB Summer Fun Volume 1 ..... 10.95

BETTY & VERONICA SPECTACULAR
Archie Publications, 1992
1 thru 25 .... @2.00
26 thru 40 .... @2.00
41 thru 50 .... @2.00
51 thru 57 .... @2.00

Betty and Veronica #81
© Archie Publications

BETTY BOOP'S SUNDAY BEST
Kitchen Sink, 1998
TPB Complete Color Comics,
1934–36, new printing 19.95

BEVERLY HILLBILLYS
Dell Publishing Co., April-June, 1963
1 Ph(c) 250.00
2 Ph(c) 150.00
3 Ph(c) 100.00
4 .... 50.00
5 .... 100.00
6 .... 100.00
7 .... 100.00
8 Ph(c) 100.00
9 Ph(c) 100.00
10 Ph(c) 100.00
11 Ph(c) 100.00
12 Ph(c) 100.00
13 Ph(c) 100.00
14 Ph(c) 100.00
15 .... 75.00
16 .... 75.00
17 Ph(c) 75.00
18 Ph(c) 75.00
19 Ph(c) 75.00
20 Ph(c) 75.00
21 Ph(c) 75.00

BEWITCHED
Dell Publishing Co., April-June, 1965
1 .... 225.00
2 .... 150.00
3 Ph(c) 100.00
4 Ph(c) 100.00
5 Ph(c) 100.00
6 Ph(c) 100.00
7 Ph(c) 100.00
8 Ph(c) 100.00
9 Ph(c) 100.00
10 Ph(c) 100.00
11 Ph(c) 100.00
12 Ph(c) 100.00
13 Ph(c) 100.00
14 .... 60.00

BEYOND THE GRAVE
Charlton Comics, 1975–84
1 SD,TS(c),P(c)............ 40.00
2 thru 5.................. @25.00
6 thru 17................. @20.00

BIG BANG
Caliber Press, 1994
0 Whole Timeline inc........... 2.95
1.............................. 2.00
2.............................. 2.00
3.............................. 2.00
4 25 years after #3............ 2.00

BIG VALLEY, THE
Dell Publishing Co., June, 1966
1 Ph(c)....................... 75.00
2............................. 40.00
3............................. 40.00
4............................. 40.00
5............................. 40.00
6............................. 40.00

BILL BLACK'S FUN COMICS
AC Comics
1 Cpt.Paragon,B&W............. 2.50
2 and 3 B&W.................. @2.25
4 Color....................... 2.25

BILL THE GALACTIC HERO
Topps, 1994
1 thru 3 Harry Harrison adapt... @4.95

BILLY THE KID
Charlton Publ. Co., 1957–83
9............................ 100.00
10............................ 60.00
11 O:Ghost Train.............. 85.00
12............................ 60.00
13 AW,AT...................... 75.00
14............................ 60.00
15 AW,O:Billy the Kid......... 75.00
16 AW......................... 75.00
17............................ 60.00
18............................ 60.00
19............................ 60.00
20 JSe........................ 75.00
21 JSe........................ 75.00
22 JSe........................ 75.00
23 JSe........................ 75.00
24 JSe........................ 75.00
25 JSe........................ 75.00
26 JSe........................ 75.00
27............................ 25.00
28............................ 25.00
29............................ 25.00
30............................ 25.00
31 thru 40................... @20.00
41 thru 60................... @15.00
61 thru 80................... @12.00
81 thru 153.................. @10.00

BIONEERS
Mirage/Next, 1994
1 New Heroes.................. 2.75
2............................. 2.75
3 All-out War................. 2.75

BIONIC WOMAN, THE
Charlton, 1977
1 Oct, 1977, TV show adapt.... 25.00

2............................ 15.00
3............................ 15.00
4............................ 15.00
5............................ 15.00

BIONIX
Maximum Press, 1996
1 (of 3) RLd,F:Steve Austin &
   Jaime Sommers.............. 3.00
2 RLd,........................ 3.00

BIZARRE 3-D ZONE
Blackthorne, 1986
1............................. 2.50

BLACKBALL COMICS
Blackball Comics, 1994
1 KG,A:Trencher............... 3.25

[ORIGINAL] BLACK CAT
1 Reprints.................... 2.00
2 MA(c) rep................... 2.00
3 rep......................... 2.00

Black Diamond #1
© AC Comics

BLACK DIAMOND
AC Comics, 1983
1 Colt B..U. story............ 3.00
2 PG(c)....................... 2.00
3 PG(c)....................... 2.00
4 PG(c)....................... 2.00
5 PG(c)....................... 2.00

BLACK ENCHANTRESS
Heroic Publishing
1 and 2 Date Rape issues..... @2.00

BLACK FLAG
Maximum Press, 1995
1 Dan Fraga................... 3.00
2 I:New Character............. 2.50
3 V:Network, I:Glitz.......... 2.50
4 V:Glitz, Network............ 2.50
5 I:Jammers................... 2.50
6 I:Alphabots................. 2.50

BLACK FURY
Charlton Comics, May, 1955
1............................ 65.00
2............................ 30.00
3 thru 15................... @25.00
16 SD........................ 75.00
17 SD........................ 75.00
18 SD........................ 75.00
19 and 20................... @15.00
21 thru 30.................. @12.00
31 thru 56.................. @12.00
57 March-April, 1966......... 12.00

BLACK HOLE, THE
Whitman, 1980
1 & 2 movie adaptation...... @2.00
3 & 4 new stories........... @2.00

BLACK HOOD
Archie/Red Circle, 1983
1 ATh,GM,DW................... 2.00
2 ATh,DSp,A:Fox............... 2.00
3 ATh,GM...................... 2.00

BLACK JACK
Charlton Comics, 1957–59
20........................... 90.00
21........................... 50.00
22........................... 75.00
23 AW,AT..................... 75.00
24 SD....................... 100.00
25 SD....................... 100.00
26 SD....................... 100.00
27........................... 50.00
28 SD....................... 100.00
29........................... 50.00
30........................... 50.00

BLACKJACK: BLOOD & HONOR
Dark Angel, 1997
1 by Alex Simmons,JoB, 1930s
   Adventure, Hildebrandts(c).. 2.95
2 KeL,........................ 2.95
3 Tim Cheng disappears........ 2.95
4............................. 2.95

BLACK PHANTOM
AC Comics
1 F:Red Mask.................. 2.50
2 F:Red Mask.................. 2.50

BLACK RAVEN
Mad Monkey Press, 1996
1 Blueprints pt.1............. 2.95
2 Blueprints pt.2............. 2.95
3 V:Temple Assassins.......... 2.95
4 Blueprints pt.4............. 2.95
GN#1 Blueprints............... 6.95
GN#2 Blueprints............... 4.95

BLACK SEPTEMBER
Malibu Ultraverse, 1995
Infinity End of Black September... 3.00

BLACK SUN
WildStorm/DC, Sept., 2002
Eye of the Storm
1 (of 6) TvS,F:Maggie Sun..... 2.95
2 TvS......................... 2.95
3 TvS......................... 2.95
4 TvS......................... 2.95

BLACK TERROR
Eclipse, 1989–90
1 . . . . 3.95
2 . . . . 3.95
3 . . . . 4.95

BLACK TIDE
Avatar Press, 2002
1A Park (c) 3.50
2 Miller (c) 3.50
3 Miller (c) 3.50
1a thru 3a variant (c)s . . . . @3.50
Angel Gate Press
4 thru 8 . . . . @3.50
4a thru 8a variant (c) 3.50
TPB Vol. 1 Awakening the Key . . . 20.95
GN Vol. 1 Enter the Game 7.95

BLACK WEB
Inks Comics
1 thru 3 V:Seeker. . . . . @2.50

BLAST-OFF
Harvey Publications, Oct., 1965
1 JK,AW 75.00

BLAZING COMBAT
Warren Publishing Co., 1965–66
1 FF(c) 225.00
2 FF(c) 75.00
3 FF(c) 60.00
4 FF(c) 75.00

BLAZING SIX-GUNS
Skywald Comics, 1971
1 F: Red Mask, Sundance Kid . . . 25.00
2 Jesse James 20.00

BLONDIE
See: Golden Age Section

BLOOD & ROSES
Sky Comics, 1993
1 I:Blood,Rose. 2.75

BLOODBATH
Samson Comics
1 I:Alien,V:Starguile 2.50

BLOODCHILDE
Millennium, 1994
0 O:Bloodchilde. 2.95
1 Neil Gaiman, Vampires 2.95
1 signed (lim. to 500). 4.95
2 Neil Gaiman, Vampires 2.95
3 Neil Gaiman, Vampires 2.95
4 . . . . 2.95
5 Talk Show Host 2.95

BLOODFIRE
Lightning Comics, 1993
0 O:Bloodfire. 3.00
1 JZy(s),JJn, red foil 5.00
1a Platinum foil Ed. 5.00
1b B&W Promo Ed. Silver ink . . . 4.00
1c B&W Promo Ed. Gold ink 6.00
2 JZy(s),JJn,O:Bloodfire 4.00
3 JZy(s),JJn,I:Dreadwolf, Judgement Day,Overthrow 3.00
4 JZy(s),JJn,A:Dreadwolf, ... 3.00
5 JZy(s),JJn,I:Bloodstorm, w/card . 3.00
6 SZ(s),TLw,V:Storman 3.00
7 SZ(s),TLw,A:Pres.Clinton 3.00
8 SZ(s),TLw,O:Prodigal 3.00
9 SZ(s),TLw,I:Prodigal (in Costume). 3.00
10 SZ(s),TLw,B:Rampage,I:Thorpe. 3.00
11 . . . . 2.95
12 . . . . 2.95

BLOODFIRE/HELLINA
Lightning Comics, 1995
1 V:Slaughterhouse 3.00

BLOODLORE
Brave New Worlds
1 Dreamweavers 2.00
2 A Blow to the Crown 2.00

Bloodshot #17
© Valiant

BLOODSCENT
Comico, 1988
1 GC 2.00

BLOODSHOT
Valiant 1992
0 KVH(a&s),DG(i),Chromium (c), O:Bloodshot,A:Eternal Warrior . 3.00
0a Gold Ed.,w/Diamond 'Fall Fling' logo 4.00
1 BWS(c),B:KVH(s),DP,BWi, V:Mafia, I:Carboni,1st Chromium(c) 2.50
2 DP,I:Durkins,V:Ax 2.50
3 DP,V:The Mob 2.50
4 DP,A:Eternal Warrior. 2.25
5 DP,A:Eternal Warrior,Rai. 2.25
6 DP,I:Ninjak (Not in Costume) . . . 2.25
7 DP,JDx,A:Ninjak (1st appearance in costume) 2.25
8 DP,JDx,A:Geoff. 2.25
9 DP,JDx,V:Slavery Ring 2.25
10 DP,JDx,V:Tunnel Rat 2.25
11 DP,JDx,V:Iwatsu 2.25
12 DP,JDx,Day Off 2.25
13 DP,JDx,V:Webnet 2.25
14 DP,JDx,V:Carboni 2.25
15 DP,JDx,V:Cinder 2.25
16 DP,JDx,w/Valiant Era Card. . . . 2.25
17 DP,JDx,A:H.A.R.D.Corps 2.25
18 DP,KVH,After the Missile 2.25
19 DP,KVH,I:Uzzi the Clown 2.25
20 DP,KVH, Chaos Effect-Gamma #1, V:Immortal Enemy 2.25
21 DP,V: Immortal Enemy, Ax 2.25
22 Immortal Enemy 2.25
23 Cinder 2.25
24 Geomancer, Immortal Enemy. . . 2.25
25 V:Uzzi the Clown 2.25
26 V:Uzzi the Clown 2.25
27 Rampage,pt. 1 . . . . 2.25
28 Rampage,pt. 3 . . . . 2.25
29 Rampage Conc. A:Ninjak 2.25
30 V:Shape Shifter 2.25
31 Nanite Killer. 2.25
32 KVH,SCh,V: Vampires 2.25
33 KVH,SCh,V: Vampires 2.25
34 NBy,KVH,new villains spawned . 2.25
35 NBY,KVH,attempts to control . . . 2.25
36 V:Voodoo Drug Dealer 2.25
37 V:Voodoo Drug Dealer 2.25
38 V:Rampage 2.25
39 V:Rampage 2.25
40 USA wants Bloodshot 2.25
41 F:Jillian Alcott 2.25
42 Virtual Nightmare. 2.25
43 V:U.S. Troops 2.25
44 I:Deathangel, V:Speedshots. . . . 2.25
45 thru 51 . . . . @2.25
Yearbook #1 KVH,briefcase bomb . 4.25
Yearbook 1995 Villagers 2.95
Spec.GN Last Stand. 5.95

BLOODSHOT Series Two
Acclaim March, 1997
1 LKa(s),SaV 'Behold, a Pale Horseman' 2.50
1a variant cover. 3.00
2 LKa(s),SaV, 'Dead Man Walking' 2.50
3 LKa(s),SaV 'ChainsawMassacre' 2.50
4 LKa(s),SaV Search for Identity . . 2.50
5 LKa(s),SaV V:Simon Oreck 2.50
6 LKa(s),SaV 'Bloodwhispers' . . . 2.50
7 LKa(s),SaV 'To the Bitter End..', pt.1 . . . . 2.50
8 LKa(s),SaV 'To the Bitter End..', pt.2 . . . . 2.50
9 LKa(s),SaV 'Suicide'. 2.50
10 LKa(s),SaV 'Dreamland'. 2.50
11 LKa(s),SaV 2.50
12 LKa(s),SaV 'Cat Scratch Fever' . 2.50
13 LKa(s),SaV In Russia. 2.50
14 LKa(s),SaV to the Vatican 2.50
15 LKa(s),SaV DOA Headquarters . 2.50
16 LKa(s),SaV final issue 2.50

BLOOD SWORD
Jademan, 1988
1 . . . . 3.00
2 . . . . 2.50
3 thru 5 . . . . @2.00
6 thru 9 . . . . @2.50
10 thru 21 . . . . @2.50
22 thru 45 . . . . @2.00
46 V:Cannibal. 2.50
47 thru 53 . . . . @2.00

BLOOD SWORD DYNASTY
Jademan, 1989
1 . . . . 2.25
2 thru 6 . . . . @2.00
7 thru 18 MB . . . . @2.00
19 thru 40 . . . . @2.00

BLUE BEETLE
Charlton Comics, June, 1964
(1st Silver Age Series)
1 O:Dan Garrett/BlueBeetle 135.00
2 .... 75.00
3 V:Mr.Thunderbolt 80.00
4 V:Praying Mantis Man 75.00
5 V:Red Knight 75.00
(2nd S.A. Series), July, 1965
Previously: UNUSUAL TALES
50 V:Scorpion 65.00
51 V:Mentor 65.00
52 V:Magno 65.00
53 V:Praying Mantis Man 65.00
54 V:Eye of Horus 65.00
Becomes:

GHOSTLY TALES
(3rd S.A. Series), 1967
1 SD,I:Question 75.00
2 SD,O:TedKord,D:DanGarrett ... 35.00
3 SD,I:Madmen,A:Question 25.00
4 SD,A:Question 25.00
5 SD,VicSage(Question) app.
   in Blue Beetle Story 25.00

BLUE PHANTOM, THE
Dell Publishing Co.,
June-Aug., 1962
1 .... 65.00

BLUE RIBBON
Archie/Red Circle, 1983
1 JK,AV,O:Fly rep. 2.00
2 TVe,Mr.Justice 2.00
3 EB/TD,O:Steel Sterling 2.00
4 .... 2.00
5 S&K,Shield rep. 2.00
6 DAy/TD,Fox 2.00
7 TD,Fox 2.00
8 NA,GM,Blackhood 2.00
9 thru 11 .... @2.00
12 SD,ThunderAgents 2.00
13 Thunderbunny 2.00
14 Web & Jaguar 2.00

BOLD ADVENTURE
Pacific, 1987
1 .... 2.00
2 .... 2.00

Bombast #1
© Topps

COLOR PUB.

3 JSe 2.00

BOLT & STARFORCE SIX
AC Comics, 1984
1 .... 2.00
Bolt Special #1 .... 2.00

BOMBAST
Topps, 1993
1 V:Savage Dragon,Trading Card . 3.25

BONANZA
Dell Publishing Co.,
June-Aug., 1960
1 .... 275.00
2 .... 150.00
3 thru 10 .... @125.00
11 thru 20 .... @100.00
21 thru 37 .... @80.00

BORIS KARLOFF TALES OF MYSTERY
Gold Key, 1963–80
1 (Thriller) 125.00
2 (Thriller) 100.00
3 thru 8 .... @60.00
9 WW 75.00
10 .... 35.00
11 AW,JO 60.00
12 AT,AMc,JO 50.00
13 & 14. .... @35.00
15 RC,GE. 35.00
16 thru 20 .... @35.00
21 JJ,Screaming Skull 75.00
22 thru 50 .... @25.00
51 thru 74 .... @20.00
75 thru 97 .... @15.00

BOZO
Innovation
1 1950's reprint stories 6.95

BOZO THE CLOWN
Blackthorne
1 3-D. 2.50
2 3-D. 2.50

BRADY BUNCH, THE
Dell Publishing Co., Feb., 1970
1 .... 150.00
2 .... 125.00

BRAIN BOY
Dell Publishing Co.,
April-June, 1962
1 .... 175.00
2 .... 150.00
3 .... 125.00
4 .... 125.00
5 .... 125.00
6 .... 125.00

BRAM STOKER'S BURIAL OF THE RATS
Roger Corman's Comics, 1995
1 thru 3 film adaptation ..... @2.50

BRASS
WildStorm/DC, June, 2000
1 (of 6) JAr,RiB 2.50
2 JAr,RiB. 2.50

3 JAr,RiB. 2.50
4 JAr,RiB. 2.50
5 JAr,RiB,war is over 2.50
6 JAr,RiB,concl. 2.50

BRATH
Crossgen Comics 2003
Prequel CDi(s) 3.00
1 CDi(s). 3.50
2 thru 10 CDi(s) .... @3.00
TPB Brath Traveler. 9.95

BRAVURA
Malibu 1995
0 Preview book, mail-in 5.00

BREAK-THRU
Malibu Ultraverse, 1993–94
1 GJ(s),GP,AV(i),A:All Ultraverse
   Heroes 2.75
1a Foil Edition 7.50
2 GJ(s),GP,AV(i),A:All Ultraverse
   Heroes 2.75

'BREED
Malibu Bravura
[Limited Series] 1994
1 JSn(a&s),Black(c),I:Stoner ... 3.00
2 JSn(a&s),I:Rachel. 3.00
3 JSn(a&s),V:Rachel 3.00
4 JSn(a&s),I:Stoner's Mom 3.00
5 JSn(a&s),V:Rachel 3.00
6 JSn(a&s),final issue 3.00
TPB Book of Genesis, rep.#1-#6. . 12.95

'BREED II
Malibu Bravura
[Limited Series] 1994–95
1 JSn,The Book of Revelation ... 3.00
1a gold foil edition 4.00
2 JSn,A:Rachel 3.00
3 JSn,V:Actual Demon. 3.00
4 JSn,Language of Demons 3.00
5 JSn,R:Rachael 3.00
6 JSn,final issue 3.00

BREEDING GROUND
Samson Comics
1 I:Mazit, Zero. 2.50

BRENDA LEE STORY, THE
Dell Publishing Co., Sept., 1962
1 .... 125.00

BRENDA STARR REPORTER
Dell Publishing Co., Oct., 1963
1 .... 250.00

BRIAN BOLLAND'S BLACK BOOK
Eclipse, 1985
1 BB 2.50

BRIDES IN LOVE
Charlton Comics, 1956–65
1 .... 100.00
2 .... 60.00
3 thru 10 .... @40.00
11 thru 30 .... @35.00

COLOR PUB.

Brides–Captain

31 thru 44 . . . . @25.00
45 . . . . 20.00

BRIGADE
Awesome Entertainment
Vol II, 2000
1 A:Badrock 3.00

BRUCE LEE
Malibu 1994
1 MBn(s), Stories of B.Lee 5.00
2 MBn(s) 5.00
3 MBn(s) 5.00
4 thru 6 . . . . @5.00

BRUTE, THE
Atlas, Feb.–July, 1975
1 thru 3 . . . . @25.00

BUCK ROGERS
Gold Key, 1964
1 P(c) 135.00
2 AMc,FBe,P(c),movie adapt 25.00
3 AMc,FBe,P(c),movie adapt 25.00
4 FBe,P(c) 25.00
5 AMc,P(c) 20.00
6 AMc,P(c) 20.00
Whitman
7 thru 9 AMc,P(c) . . . . @30.00
10 and 11 AMc,P(c) . . . . @15.00
12 and 13 P(c) . . . . @10.00
14 thru 16 . . . . @8.00

BUCK ROGERS
TSR, 1990–91
1 thru 3 O:Buck Rogers . . . . @3.00
4 thru 6 Black Barney . . . . @3.00
7 thru 10 The Martian Wars . . . . @3.00

BUCKY O'HARE
Continuity, 1991
1 MGo 2.75
2 thru 5 . . . . @2.00

BUFFALO BILL JR.
Dell Publishing Co., 1956
1 . . . . 100.00
2 . . . . 75.00
3 . . . . 75.00
4 thru 6 . . . . 75.00
7 thru 13 . . . . @60.00

BUGGED-OUT ADVENTURES OF RALFY ROACH
Bugged Out Comics
1 I: Ralfy Roach 2.95

BULLWINKLE
Gold Key, 1962
1 Bullwinkle & Rocky 250.00
2 . . . . 150.00
3 thru 5 . . . . @80.00
6 and 7, rep. . . . . @75.00
8 thru 11 . . . . 80.00
12 rep. 50.00
13 and 14 . . . . @60.00
15 thru 19 . . . . @50.00
20 thru 24, rep. . . . . @25.00
25 . . . . 35.00

Bullwinkle and Rocky #2
© *Charlton Comics*

BULLWINKLE
Charlton Comics, July, 1970
1 . . . . 75.00
Becomes:

BULLWINKLE AND ROCKY
Charlton Comics, 1970–71
2 thru 7 . . . . @60.00

BULLWINKLE & ROCKY
Eclipse
3-D 25.00

BULLWINKLE FOR PRESIDENT
Blackthorne
1 3-D Special 2.50

BURKE'S LAW
Dell Publishing Co., 1964
1 from TV Show 75.00
2 . . . . 50.00
3 . . . . 50.00

BUTCH CASSIDY
Skywald Comics, 1971
1 . . . . 25.00
2 & 3 . . . . @20.00

CABBOT: BLOODHUNTER
Maximum Press, 1997
1 thru 4 RV . . . . @2.50

CADILLACS & DINOSAURS
Kitchen Sink
1 Rep. from Xenozoic Tales in 3-D. 6.00
Topps, 1994
BLOOD & BONES
1 thru 3 rep. Xenozoic Tales,
 all covers . . . . @2.50
MAN-EATER
1 thru 3, all covers 2.50
THE WILD ONES
1 thru 3, all covers 2.50

CAGES
Tundra
1 DMc 14.00
2 DMc 11.00
3 DMc 7.50
4 DMc 7.50
5 thru 7 DMc 5.00

CAIN
Harris, 1993
1 B:DQ(s),I:Cain,Frenzy 5.00
2 BSz(c),HBk,V:Mortatira 3.25

CAIN'S HUNDRED
Dell Publishing Co., May-July, 1962
1 . . . . 40.00
2 . . . . 25.00

CALIFORNIA RAISINS
Blackthorne, 1987
1 thru 4 3-D . . . . @2.50
5 3-D,O:Calif.Raisins 2.50
6 thru 8 3-D . . . . @2.50

CALVIN & THE COLONEL
Dell Publishing Co., April-June, 1962
1 . . . . 125.00
2 . . . . 100.00

CAP'N QUICK & FOOZLE
Eclipse, 1984–85
1 . . . . 2.00
2 and 3 . . . . @2.50

CAPT. ELECTRON
Brick Computers Inc.
1 . . . . 2.00
2 . . . . 2.25

CAPTAIN ATOM
See: STRANGE SUSPENSE STORIES

CAPTAIN CANUCK
Comely Comix, 1975–81
1 I:Blue Fox 25.00
2 I:Red Coat 20.00
3 I:Heather 20.00
4 thru 14 . . . . 15.00
Summer Spec. #1 . . . . 15.00

CAPTAIN GLORY
Topps, 1993
1 A:Bombast,Night Glider,
 Trading Card 3.25

CAPTAIN GRAVITY
Penny Farthing Press, 1998
1 by S.Vrattos & K. Martin 2.75
2 No one escapes Law of Gravity . 2.75
3 . . . . 2.75
4 . . . . 2.75
TPB 19.95
Spec. One True Hero 2.95

All comics prices listed are for *Near Mint* condition.

COLOR PUB.

CAPTAIN HARLOCK: FALL OF THE EMPIRE
Eternity, 1992
1 R:Captain Harlock 2.50
2 V:Tadashi 2.50
3 Bomb on the Arcadia 2.50
4 Final issue 2.50

CAPTAIN JOHNER & THE ALIENS
Valiant May, 1995
1 Rep. Magnus Robot Fighter #1–7
(Gold Key 1963–64) 2.95
2 Russ Manning rep. 2.95

CAPTAIN MARVEL
M. F. Enterprises, April, 1966
1 . . . . 50.00
2 . . . . 40.00
3 Fights The Bat 35.00
4 . . . . 35.00
5 Captain Marvel Presents the
Terrible Five 35.00

CAPTAIN NAUTICUS
Entity, 1994
1 V:Fathom 2.95
2 V:Fathom's Henchman 2.95
3 Surf's Up 2.00

CAPTAIN NICE
Gold Key, Nov., 1967
1 Ph(c) 100.00

CAPTAIN PARAGON
Americomics, 1983
1 thru 4 . . . . @2.00

CAPTAIN POWER
Continuity, 1988
1a NA,TVtie-in(direct sale) 2.00
1b NA,TVtie-in(newsstand) 2.00
2 NA 2.00

CAPTAIN STERN
Kitchen Sink Press
1 BWr,R:Captain Stern 5.25
2 BWr,Running Out of Time 4.35

CAPTAIN THUNDER AND BLUE BOLT
Hero Graphics
1 I:Capt.Thunder & Paul Fremont . 2.00
2 Paul becomes Blue Bolt 2.00
3 O:Capt.Thunder 2.00
4 V:Iguana Boys 2.00
5 V:Ian Shriver, in Scotland 2.00
6 V:Krakatoa 2.00
7 V:Krakatoa 2.00
8 A:Sparkplug (from League
of Champions) 2.00
9 A:Sparkplug 2.00
10 A:Sparkplug 2.00

CAPTAIN VENTURE & THE LAND BENEATH THE SEA
Gold Key, Oct., 1968
1 . . . . 75.00
2 . . . . 50.00

Captain Victory and the Galactic Rangers #3 © Pacific Comics

CAPTAIN VICTORY AND THE GALACTIC RANGERS
Pacific, 1982
1 JK 2.50
2 JK 2.00
3 JK,BU:NA,I:Ms.Mystic 2.00
4 JK 2.00
5 JK 2.00
6 JK,SD 2.00
7 thru 13 JK . . . . @2.00
Spec.#1 JK 2.00

CAR 54, WHERE ARE YOU?
Dell Publishing Co., March-May, 1962
1 Ph(c) 150.00
2 thru 7 Ph(c) . . . . @75.00

CARCA JOU RENAISSANCE
1 and 2 . . . . @2.00

CARNOSAUR CARNAGE
Atomeka, 1993
TPB 4.95

CAROLINE KENNEDY
Charlton Comics, 1961
1 . . . . 150.00

CASEY JONES & RAPHAEL
Mirage, 1994
1 Family War 2.75
2 Johnny Woo Woo 2.75
3 V:Johnny Woo Woo 2.75
4 9mm Raphael 2.75

CASPER & FRIENDS
Harvey, 1991
1 thru 4 . . . . @2.00
5 short stories, cont 2.00

CASPER & WENDY
Harvey, 1972–73
1 52-pg. giant 35.00
2 thru 5 . . . . @20.00
6 thru 8 . . . . @15.00

CASPER ENCHANTED TALES
Harvey, 1992
1 short stories 2.00

CASPER, THE FRIENDLY GHOST, 1988
Blackthorne
1 3-D 2.50

CASPER GHOSTLAND
Harvey
1 short stories 2.00

CASPER'S GHOSTLAND
Harvey Publications, Winter, 1958-59
1 . . . . 250.00
2 . . . . 150.00
3 thru 10 . . . . 100.00
11 thru 20 . . . . @75.00
21 thru 40 . . . . @40.00
41 thru 61 . . . . @30.00
62 thru 77 . . . . @25.00
78 thru 97 . . . . @20.00
98 Dec., 1979 . . . . 20.00

CASPER THE FRIENDLY GHOST
Harvey, 1990–91
Prev: The Friendly Ghost Casper
254 thru 260 . . . . @2.00
[Second Series], 1991–94
1 thru 14 . . . . @2.00
15 thru 28 . . . . @2.00

CATSEYE
Awesome/Hyperwerks, 1999
0 KIA,BNa,O:Catseye 2.95

CAT TALES
Eternity
1 3-D F:Felix 2.00

CAULDRON
Real Comics, 1995
1 Movie Style Comic 2.95
1a Variat cover 2.95

CAVE GIRL
AC Comics
1 . . . . 2.95

CAVE KIDS
Gold Key, 1963
1 . . . . 100.00
2 . . . . 50.00
3 . . . . 50.00
4 . . . . 50.00
5 . . . . 50.00
6 . . . . 35.00
7 A:Pebbles & Bamm Bamm . . . 45.00
8 thru 10 . . . . @30.00
11 thru 16 . . . . @30.00

COLOR PUB.

CAVEWOMAN
Avatar, 1999
Color Spec. 3.50
Color Spec. Fauna (c) 3.50
Color Spec. prism foil (c) 12.95
Color Spec. Royal Blue. 75.00

CENTURY
Awesome Entertainment, 2000
1 RLe 3.00
1a Millennium edition........... 4.95
2 .... 3.00
2a Millennium edition........... 4.95
2b signed 13.00
3 .... 3.00

CHAINS OF CHAOS
Harris, 1994
1 Vampirella, Rook 5.00
2 V:Chaoschild 3.25
3 Final issue 3.25

CHAMPIONS
Eclipse, 1986–87
1 I:Flare,League of Champions Foxbat, Dr.Arcane 12.00
2 I:Dark Malice 12.00
3 I:Lady Arcane 8.00
4 O:Dark Malice................ 12.00
5 O:Flare...................... 6.00
6 D:Giant Demonmaster 6.00

[New Series]
Hero Graphics, 1987–88
1 EL,I:Madame Synn,Galloping Galooper 5.00
2 I:Fat Man, Black Enchantress ... 2.25
3 I:Sparkplug&Icicle,O:Flare 2.25
4 I:Exo-Skeleton Man 2.25
5 A:Foxbat..................... 2.25
6 I:Mechanon, C:Foxbat 2.00
7 A:Mechanon,J:Sparkplug,Icicle . 2.00
8 O:Foxbat 2.00
9 Flare #0 (Flare preview) 2.00
10 Olympus Saga #1 .... 2.00
11 Olympus Saga #2 .... 2.00
12 Olympus Saga #3 .... 2.00
Ann.#1 O:Giant & DarkMalice..... 2.75
Ann.#2 .... 3.95

CHAMPIONS CLASSIC
Hero Graphics
1 GP(c),Rep.1st champions series . 2.00

CHAOS! BIBLE
Chaos! Comics, 1995
1 Character Profiles............ 3.50

CHAOS! CHRONICLES– THE HISTORY OF A COSMOS
Chaos! Comics, 1999
Spec. 3.50
Spec. signed premium 15.00

CHAOS EFFECT
Valiant 1994
Alpha DJ(c), BCh, JOy, A:All Valiant Characters 2.25
Alpha Red (c).................. 3.50
Omega DJ(c), BCh, JOy, A:All Valiant Characters 2.25
Omega Gold(c)................. 3.50

Epilogue,pt.1 .... 2.95
Epilogue,pt.2 .... 2.95

CHAOS! GALLERY
Chaos! Comics, 1997
1 .... 2.95

CHAOS! NIGHTMARE THEATER
Chaos! Comics, 1997
1 (of 4) BWr(c) 2.50
2 BWr(c) 2.50
3 BWr(c) 2.50
4 BWr(c) 2.50

CHAOS QUARTERLY
Harris Comics, 1995
1 F:Lady Death 4.95
1a Premium Edition 10.95
1b Signed,limited edition 20.00

CHAPEL
Awesome Entertainment, 1997
1 BNa, from Spawn,Youngblood .. 2.95

CHARLEMAGNE
Defiant, 1994
1 JiS(s),From Hero 2.00
2 JiS(s),I:Charles Smith........ 2.75
3 JiS(s),A:War Dancer.......... 2.75
4 DGC(s),V:Dark Powers........ 2.75
5 Schism prequel............... 2.75
6 V:Wardancer 2.75
7 R:To Vietnam 2.75

CHARLIE CHAN
Dell Publishing Co., Oct.-Dec., 1965
1 .... 75.00
2 .... 50.00

CHARLTON BULLSEYE
Charlton, 1981–82
1 Blue Beetle, I:Rocket Rabbit.... 3.50
2 Capt. Catnip; Nell the Horse ... 2.50
3 Grundar..................... 2.50
4 Vanguards 2.50

Charlton Bullseye Vol. 2, #8
© Charlton Comics

5 Warhund 2.50
6 Thunder-bunny 2.50
7 Captain Atom 2.50
8 weird stories................. 2.50
9 and 10 .... @2.50
Spec. #1...................... 2.00
Spec. #2 Atomic Mouse 2.00

CHARLTON SPORT LIBRARY
Charlton, 1970
1 Professional Football 40.00

CHASSIS
Millennium/Expand, 1995
1 I:Chassis McBain, Aero Run 2.95
1 2nd printing 2.95
1 chrome cover 9.95
2 .... 2.95
2a with racing card 4.95
2b Amanda Conner cover 2.95
2c Amanda Conner cover, signed . 9.95
2d foil cover, signed............ 7.95
[Vol. 2] Hurricane Comics, 1998
0 by Joshua Dysart & Wm.O'Neill . 2.95
0a variant cover................ 2.95
1 thru 3 .... @2.95

CHASTITY
Chaos! Comics, 2000
1/2 .... 2.95
1/2a premium ed., tattoo (c) 9.95
1/2b chromium edition 16.00
1/2 Ashcan 6.66
1 premium edition 9.95
Spec. #1 Reign of Terror (2000) ... 2.95
Spec. #1 Reign of Terror, premium . 9.95
Spec. #1 Love Bites (2001) 3.00
Spec. #1 Love Bites, premium ed. 10.00
Ashcan Love Bites (2001)....... 6.00

CHASTITY: CRAZYTOWN
Chaos! Comics, 2002
Ashcan b&w................... 6.00
1 (of 3) 3.00
1a premium edition 10.00
1b foil edition................. 20.00
2 .... 3.00
3 .... 3.00
2a and 3a variant (c) .... @7.50

CHASTITY: HEARTBREAKER
Chaos! Comics, 2002
1 .... 3.00
1a premium edition 10.00
1b super premium edition 20.00

CHASTITY LUST FOR LIFE
Chaos! Comics, 1999
1 (of 4) PNu 2.95
1a alternate cover 6.95
1b alternate cover, signed 20.00
1c premium edition 10.00
2 V:Hemlock 2.95
3 .... 2.95

CHASTITY: RE-IMAGINED
Chaos! Comics, 2002
1 Gothic tale 3.00
1a premium edition 10.00
1b super premium edition 20.00
Ashcan re-imagined b&w 6.00

All comics prices listed are for *Near Mint* condition.

CHASTITY ROCKED
Chaos! Comics, 1998
1 (of 4) PNu	2.95
1a & 1b variant covers	2.95
2 V:Jade	2.95
3 V:Jade	2.95
4 conclusion	2.95
Chastity/Cremator Preview Book, B&W	5.00

CHASTITY: SHATTERED
Chaos! Comics, 2001
1 BnP,LKa	3.00
1a premium edition	10.00
2	3.00
3	3.00
Ashcan	6.00

CHASTITY: THEATRE OF PAIN
Chaos! Comics, 1997
1 (of 3) BnP,	6.00
1a premium edition	15.00
2	3.00
3	3.00
3a premium edition	15.00
TPB rep.#1–#3, Sketchbook	9.95

CHEAP SHODDY ROBOT TOYS
Eclipse
1 A:Ronald Reagan	2.00

CHECKMATE
Gold Key, Oct., 1962
1 Ph(c)	75.00
2 Ph(c)	60.00

CHEMICAL MAN
1	2.00

CHERYL BLOSSOM
Archie Comics, April, 1996
1	2.00
2 thru 5	@2.00
6 thru 10	@2.00
11 thru 37	@2.00

CHERYL BLOSSOM GOES HOLLYWOOD
Archie Comics, 1996
1 (of 3) by Dan Parent & Bill Golliher	2.00
2 and 3	@2.00

CHEYENNE
Dell Publishing Co., Oct., 1956
1 Ph(c) all	250.00
2	150.00
3	100.00
4 thru 12	@75.00
13 thru 25	@65.00

CHEYENNE KID
(see WILD FRONTIER)

CHI-CHIAN
Sirius, 1997
1 (of 6) by Voltaire	2.95
2 thru 6	@2.95

COLOR PUB.

CHILD'S PLAY 2
Innovation
1 Movie Adapt Pt 1	2.50
2 Adapt Pt 2	2.50
3 Adapt Pt 3	2.50

CHILD'S PLAY 3
Innovation
1 Movie Adapt Pt 1	2.50
2 Movie Adapt Pt.2	2.50

CHILD'S PLAY: THE SERIES
Innovation
1 Chucky's Back	2.50
2 Straight Jacket Blues	2.50
3 M.A.R.K.E.D.	2.50
4 Chucky in Toys 4 You	2.50
5 Chucky in Hollywood	2.50

Chilling Adventures in Sorcery as Told by Sabrina #2 © Archie Comics

CHILDREN OF FIRE
Fantagor
1 thru 3 RCo	@2.00

CHILLING ADVENTURES IN SORCERY AS TOLD BY SABRINA
Archie, 1972–74
1	50.00
2	40.00
3 thru 5	@30.00

CHIMERA
Crossgen Comics 2003
1 RMz,BPe	3.00
2 thru 4	@3.00
TPB 160-pg.	15.95

CHIP 'N DALE
Dell Publishing, 1955–66
4	75.00
5 thru 10	@60.00
11 thru 30	@50.00

Gold Key, 1967
1 reprints	30.00
2 thru 10	@20.00
11 thru 20	@10.00

21 thru 83	@8.00

CHIP 'N DALE RESCUE RANGERS
Walt Disney, 1990
1 Rescue Rangers to the Rescue, pt.1	3.50
2 Rescue Rangers to the Rescue, pt.2	3.00
3 thru 7	@2.50
8 Coast to Coast Pt 1	2.00
9 Coast to Coast Pt 2	2.00
10 Coast to Coast Pt 3	2.00
11 Coast to Coast Pt 4	2.00
12 'Showdown at Hoedown'	2.00
13 Raining Cats & Dogs	2.00
14 'Cobra Kadabra'	2.00
15 I:Techno-Rats,WaspPatrol Fearless Frogs Pt.1	2.00
16 A:Techno-Rats,WaspPatrol, Fearless Frogs Pt.2	2.00
17 'For the Love of Cheese'	2.00
18 'Ghastly Goat of Quiver Moore, Pt.1	2.00

CHOO CHOO CHARLIE
Gold Key, Dec., 1969
1	150.00

CHOPPER: EARTH, WIND, AND FIRE
Fleetway
1 F:Chopper	2.95

CHOSEN, THE
Click Comics, 1995
1 I:The Chosen	2.50
2 I:Herman Cortez	2.50

CHRISTIAN
Maximum Press, 1996
1 and 2 (of 3) RLd	@2.95

CHRISTMAS PARADE
Gladstone
1 GiantEdition	4.00
2	3.50

CHRISTMAS SPIRIT, THE
Kitchen Sink
TPB Will Eisner art	15.00

CHROMA-TICK SPECIAL EDITION
New England Press, 1992
1 Rep.Tick#1,new stories	4.00
2 Rep.Tick#2,new stories	5.00
3 thru 8 Reps.& new stories	@3.50

CHROME
Hot Comics, 1986
1 Machine Man	3.50
2 thru 4	@2.00

CHROME WARRIORS IN A '59 CHEVY
Black Out Comics, 1998
0	2.95
1 Rob Roman & Tommy Castillo	2.95

CVA Page 578 — All comics prices listed are for *Near Mint* condition.

COLOR PUB.

CHROMIUM MAN, THE
Triumphant Comics, 1994
0 Blue Logo 6.00
0 Regular 2.50
1 I:Chromium Man,Mr.Death 3.50
2 I:Prince Vandal 3.00
3 I:Candi,Breaker,Coil 2.50
4 JnR(s),AdP,Unleashed 2.50
5 JnR(s),AdP,Unleashed 2.50
6 JnR(s),Courier,pt.1 .... 2.50
7 JnR(s),Courier,pt.2 .... 2.50
8 JnR(s),Chromium finds peace... 2.50
9 V:Tarsak 2.50
10 .... 2.50
11 Prince Vandal #8 .... 2.50
12 Prince Vandal #9 .... 2.50
13 V:Realm 2.50
14 A:Light 2.50
15 .... 2.50

CHROMIUM MAN: VIOLENT PAST
Triumphant Comics
1 thru 4 JnR(s) .... @2.50

Chronicles of Corum #3
© First

CHRONICLES OF CORUM
First, 1987–88
1 Michael Moorcock adapt. 2.25
2 thru 12 .... @2.00

CICERO'S CAT
Dell Publishing Co., July-Aug., 1959
1 .... 60.00
2 .... 50.00

CICI
Spilled Milk, 2002
1 (of 4) 3.00
2 thru 4 .... 2.50
Variant (c) .... @2.50

CIMMARON STRIP
Dell Publishing Co., Jan., 1968
1 .... 65.00

CITY KNIGHTS, THE
Windjammer 1995
1 I:Michael Walker 2.50
2 I:Herald 2.50
3 & 4 V:Herald .... @2.50

CITY PERILOUS
Broadway Comics
1 GI,Remember the Future,pt.1 .. 2.95
2 GI,Remember the Future,pt.2 .. 2.95
Becomes:
KNIGHTS ON BROADWAY
3 thru 5 GI .... @2.95

CLASSICS ILLUSTRATED
See Also: CLASSICS ILLUSTRATED SECTION

CLASSICS ILLUSTRATED
First, 1990
1 GW,The Raven 5.00
2 RG,Great Expectations 5.00
3 KB,Thru the Looking Glass ... 5.00
4 BSz,Moby Dick 5.00
5 SG,TM,KE, Hamlet 5.00
6 PCr,JT, Scarlet Letter 5.00
7 DSp,Count of Monte Cristo ... 5.00
8 Dr.Jekyll & Mr.Hyde 5.00
9 MP,Tom Sawyer 5.00
10 Call of the Wild 5.00
11 Rip Van Winkle 5.00
12 Dr. Moreau 5.00
13 Wuthering Heights 5.00
14 Fall of House of Usher 5.00
15 Gift of the Magi 5.00
16 A: Christmas Carol 5.00
17 Treasure Island 5.00
18 The Devils Dictionary 5.00
19 The Secret Agent 5.00
20 The Invisible Man 5.00
21 Cyrano de Bergerac 5.00
22 The Jungle Book 5.00
23 Swiss Family Robinson 5.00
24 Rime of Ancient Mariner ... 5.00
25 Ivanhoe 5.00
26 Aesop's Fables 5.00
27 The Jungle 5.00

CLASSICS ILLUSTRATED JUNIOR
Classics Illustrated Junior 2003
501 Show White & Seven Dwarfs .. 4.00
514 Steadfast Tin Soldier 4.00
519 Paul Bunyan 4.00
530 The Golden Bird 4.00
536 The Chimney Sweep 4.00
540 Tinder Box 4.00
546 The Elves and the Shoemaker. 4.00
563 The Wishing Well 4.00
564 Salt Mountain 4.00
570 Pearl Princess 4.00

CLASSWAR
Com.X, 2001
1 .... 3.00
2 thru 4 .... @3.00
TPB Vol. 1 .... 12.95
1 Metal edition 50.00

CLAUS
Draco, 1997
1 by Bowden & Guichardon 2.95
2 thru 4 .... @3.25

Chromium–Colour

CLIVE BARKER'S DREAD
Eclipse
Graphic Album 7.95

CLIVE BARKER'S TAPPING THE VEIN
Eclipse
1 .... 10.00
2 thru 5 .... @8.50

CLYDE CRASHCUP
Dell Publishing Co., Aug.-Oct., 1963
1 .... 200.00
2 .... 175.00
3 thru 5 .... @160.00

COBALT 60
Innovation
1 reprints 4.95

COBALT BLUE
Innovation, 1989
Spec.#1 .... 2.00
Spec.#2 .... 2.00
1 and 2 .... @2.00

CODENAME: DANGER
Lodestone, 1985
1 RB/BMc,I:Makor 2.50
2 KB,I:Capt.Energy 2.00
3 PS/RB 2.00
4 PG 2.00

CODE NAME: DOUBLE IMPACT
High Impact, 1997
1 RCI 3.00
1 variant cover 10.00
1 signed holofoil cover 14.95

CODENAME: STRIKEFORCE
Spectrum, 1984
1 .... 2.00

CODENAME: FIREARM
Malibu Ultraverse, 1995
0 I:New Firearm 3.00
1 F:Alec Swan 3.00
2 Dual Identity 3.00
3 F:Hitch and Lopez 3.00
4 F:Hitch and Lopez 3.00
5 Working Together 3.00

COLLECTOR'S DRACULA
Millennium
1 .... 4.25

COLOSSAL SHOW, THE
Gold Key, Oct., 1969
1 .... 65.00

COLOUR OF MAGIC
Innovation
1 Terry Pratchet novel adapt .. 3.00

All comics prices listed are for Near Mint condition.

Colour–Coven

2 'The Sending of Eight' 2.50
3 'Lure of the Worm 2.50
4 final issue 2.50

COLT .45
Dell Publishing Co., 1958
1 Ph(c) all 150.00
2 . . . . 135.00
3 . . . . 125.00
4 . . . . 125.00
5 . . . . 125.00
6 ATh 150.00
7 . . . . 125.00
8 . . . . 125.00
9 . . . . 125.00

COLT SPECIAL
AC Comics, 1985
1 . . . . 2.00
2 . . . . 2.00
3 . . . . 2.00

COMBAT
Dell Publishing Co., 1961
1 SG 75.00
2 SG 50.00
3 SG 50.00
4 JFK cover, Story 2-D 60.00
5 SG 50.00
6 SG 35.00
7 SG 35.00
8 SG 35.00
9 SG 35.00
10 SG 35.00
11 thru 27 SG . . . . @30.00
28 thru 40 SG . . . . @25.00

COMET, THE
Archie/Red Circle, 1983
1 AN,CI,O:Comet 2.00
2 AN,CI,D:Hangman 2.00

COMIC ALBUM
Dell Publishing Co., March–May, 1958
1 Donald Duck 150.00
2 Bugs Bunny 75.00
3 Donald Duck 100.00
4 Tom & Jerry 75.00
5 Woody Woodpecker 75.00
6 Bugs Bunny 75.00
7 Popeye 85.00
8 Tom & Jerry 75.00
9 Woody Woodpecker 75.00
10 Bugs Bunny 75.00
11 Popeye 85.00
12 Tom & Jerry 60.00
13 Woody Woodpecker 60.00
14 Bugs Bunny 60.00
15 Popeye 75.00
16 Flintstones 125.00
17 Space Mouse 75.00
18 3 Stooges,Ph(c) 125.00

COMICO X-MAS SPECIAL
Comico, 1988
1 SR/AW/DSt(c) 2.00

COMIX INTERNATIONAL
Warren Magazines, July, 1974
1 . . . . 125.00
2 WW,BW 75.00
3 . . . . 40.00

COLOR PUB.

4 RC 40.00
5 Spring, 1977 . . . . 35.00

CONCRETE JUNGLE: THE LEGEND OF THE BLACK LION
Acclaim 1998
1 (of 6) CPr,JFy,F:Terry Smalls . . . 2.50
2 CPr,JFy,Black Lion Order 2.50
3 CPr,JFy,The Man 2.50
4 CPr,JFy 2.50
5 CPr,JFy 2.50

CONSTRUCT
Mirage
1 I:Constructs 2.75
2 F:Sect.Eight, Armor 2.75
3 O:Constructs 2.75
4 Fist-O-God 2.75

CORBEN SPECIAL
Pacific
1 RCo 2.00

CORUM: THE BULL & THE SPEAR
First, 1989
1 thru 4 Michael Moorcock adapt.@2.00

COSMONEERS SPECIAL
1 . . . . 2.00

The Cougar #1
© Atlas Comics

COUGAR, THE
Atlas, April–July, 1975
1 . . . . 25.00
2 O:Cougar 25.00

COUNTDOWN
WildStorm/DC, 2000
1 (of 8) JMi,AaL 2.50
2 JMi,AaL 2.50
3 JMi,AaL 2.50
4 JMi,AaL 2.50
5 JMi,AaL 2.50
6 JMi,AaL 2.50

Comics Values Annual

7 JMi,AaL,RyE,supercriminals 2.50
8 JMi,AAl,RyE,concl. 2.95

COUNTER-OPS
Antarctic Press 2003
1 . . . . 3.95
2 thru 5 . . . . @3.95

COUNTER-STRIKE
Infinity Comics, 2000
1 (of 4) 2.50
1a premium chroma-foil (c) 12.00
2 thru 4 . . . . @2.50

COURTSHIP OF EDDIE'S FATHER
Dell Publishing Co., 1970
1 Ph(c) 65.00
2 Ph(c) 50.00

COVEN
Awesome Entertainment, 1997
1 IaC,JLb,JSb,V:The Pentad 8.00
1a variant covers 8.00
2 IaC,JLb,Who is Spellcaster? . . . 5.00
3 IaC,JLb,V:The Pentad 5.00
4 IaC,JLb,Pentad, concl. 4.00
5 IaC,JLb, ... 4.00
5 gold foil cover 8.00
6 IaC,JLb,Mardi Gras madness . . . 3.00
6 gold foil edition 8.00
7 IaC,JLb,V:Babylon 2.50
8 IaC,JLb,F:Thor, the God
  of Thunder 2.50
9 IaC,JLb, ... 2.50
Coll.Ed. #1, rep. #1–#2,
  new IaC(c) 4.95
Fan Appreciation #1, rep. #1,
  new cover 2.50
Coven/Menace S.D.Con
  preview book 5.00
TPB The Gathering 17.00

VOL 2
1 IaC,JLb 2.50
1a, b & c variant covers 2.50
1d chrome edition 10.00
1e gold foil cover 8.00
2 IaC,JLb,V:Supreme 2.50
2a Lionheart (c) 8.00
2b signed 20.00
3 IaC,JLb, Long Flight Home . . . 2.50
3 Ruby red edition 14.95
4 IaC,JLb 2.50
5 thru 7 . . . . @3.00
Coven Sourcebook #1 . . . . 3.00

COVEN 13
No Mercy Comics, 1997
1 by Rikki Rockett & Matt Busch . . 2.50
2 . . . . 2.50
3 . . . . 2.50
4 . . . . 2.50

COVEN/RE:GEX
Awesome Entertainment, 1999
1 (of 2) RLe,JLb,IaC 2.50
1a alternate IaC cover 6.95
2 JLb, conclusion 2.50

COVEN: DARK ORIGINS
Awesome Entertainment, 1999
1 . . . . 2.50
1a & b variant covers 2.50

COVEN: DARK SISTER
Avatar Press, 2001
1/2 Rio (c)	3.95
1/2 Shaw (c)	3.95
1/2 Martin (c)	3.95
1/2 Raptor attack (c)	4.95
1/2 Previews Raptor prism foil (c)	12.95
1/2 Bad Vibes (c)	5.95
1 Park (c)	3.50
1a Rio (c)	3.50
1b Martin (c)	3.50
1c wraparound (c)	3.95
1d Blue leather (c)	25.00
1e Royal Blue edition, in case	75.00
1f Haunting Vision edition	5.95
1g Prism foil edition	12.95
1h Embrace edition	5.95
1i Embrace edition, emerald (c)	13.95
2 Adrian (c) edition	5.95

COVEN: SPELLCASTER
Avatar Press, 2001
1/2 Bewitched edition	5.95
1/2 Bikini edition	5.95
1/2 Rio Royal Blue (c)	75.00
1 Finch (c)	3.50
1a Rio (c)	3.50
1b Martin (c)	3.50
1c Wraparound (c)	3.95
1d Leather	25.00
1e Finch Ruby Red(c)	24.95
1f Rio prism foil (c)	12.95
1g Royal Blue edition	75.00
2 Rio (c)	3.50
2a Shaw (c)	3.50
2b Martin (c)	3.50
2c Lyon (c)	3.50
Spec. #1 Free Spirit edition	5.96

COVEN: TOOTH & NAIL
Avatar Press, 2001
1 Adrian (c)	3.50
1a Rio (c)	3.50
1b Waller (c)	3.50
1c MMy(c)	3.50
1d Wraparound (c)	3.50
1e leather (c)	25.00
1f Royal Blue (c)	75.00
1g Bikini Edition (c)	5.95
1h Bad Ladies (c)	5.95
1i Prism exclusive (c)	12.95
1j Fantom (c)	5.95
1k Training Day (c)	5.95
1/2 Woman Scorned (c)	5.95
1/2a Prism Foil edition	12.95
1/2b Fantom edition	5.95
1/2c Adrian (c) 16-pg.	3.95
1/2d Waller (c)	3.95
1/2e MMy(c)	3.95
1/2f Martin (c)	3.95

COWBOY IN AFRICA
Gold Key, March, 1968
1 Chuck Conners,Ph(c)	65.00

CRACKED
Major Magazines, Feb.-Mar., 1958
1 AW	200.00
2	100.00
3 thru 6	@125.00
7 thru 10	@100.00
11 thru 20	@75.00
21 thru 30	@60.00
31 thru 60	@50.00
61 thru 99	@40.00
100	50.00
101 thru 145	@25.00
146 thru 148	@35.00
149 thru 162	@15.00
163	30.00
164 thru 174	@15.00
175 thru 200	@10.00
201 thru 252	@8.00
253 thru 300	@7.00
301 thru 348	@5.00

Crash Dummies #1
© Harvey

[THE INCREDIBLE] CRASH DUMMIES
Harvey, 1993
1 thru 3, from the toy series	@2.00

CRAZYMAN
Continuity, 1992
[1st Series]
1 Embossed(c),NA/RT(i), O:Crazyman	6.00
2 NA/BB(c)	2.50
3 DBa,V:Terrorists	2.50

[2nd Series], 1993
1 Die Cut(c)	2.50
2 thru 3	2.50
4 In Demon World	2.50

CREATURE
Antarctic Press, Oct., 1997
1 (of 2) by D.Walker&J.Maranto	2.95
2 concl.	2.95

CREED/TEENAGE MUTANT NINJA TURTLES
Lightning Comics, April, 1996
1	3.00
1 variant cover	3.00

CREED: CRANIAL DISORDER
Lightning Comics, 1996
1 (of 3)	3.00
1a variant cover, *Previews* exclusive	3.00
1b Platinum edition	9.00
1c Platinum edition, autographed	16.00
2	3.00
2a variant cover	3.00

CREMATOR: HELL'S GUARDIAN
Chaos! Comics, 1998
1 (of 5) LJi	2.95
2	2.95
3 V:Asteroth	2.95
4	2.95
5	2.95

CRIME MACHINE
Skywald Publications, Feb., 1971
1 JK	75.00
2 AT	50.00

CRIME PATROL
Gemstone, 2000
1 rep.	2.50
2 rep. Fall 1948	2.50
3 rep. Winter 1948	2.50
4 rep. Feb. 1949	2.50
5 rep.	2.50
6 rep.	2.50
7 rep.	2.50
8 rep. Oct. 1949	2.50
9 rep. Dec. 1949	2.50
10 rep. Feb. 1950 issue	2.50
'Annuals'
TPB Vol.#1 rep. #1–#5	13.50
TPB Vol.#2 rep. #6–#10	13.50

CRIME SUSPENSE STORIES
Russ Cochran, 1992
1 Rep. C.S.S. #1 (1950)	2.00
2 Rep. C.S.S.	2.00
3 Rep. C.S.S.	2.00
4 thru 6 Rep. C.S.S	@2.00
7 Rep. C.S.S.	2.00
8 thru 15 Rep.	@2.00

Gemstone, 1996
16 thru 27 EC comics reprint	@2.50
Ann.#1, rep. #1–#5	8.95
Ann.#2, rep. #6–#10	8.95
Ann.#3, rep. #11–#15	9.95
Ann.#4, rep. #16–#19	10.50
Ann.#5, rep. #20–#23	10.95
Ann.#6 rebinding #24–#27	10.95

CRIMSON NUN
Antarctic Press, 1997
1 (of 4)	2.95
2	2.95
3	2.95
4 concl	2.95

CRIMSON PLAGUE
Event Comics, 1997
1 GP,F:DiNA: Simmons	2.95
2 GP,	2.95

CROSSFIRE
Eclipse, 1984–86
1 DSp	3.00
2 DSp	2.50
3 DSp	2.00
4 DSp	2.00
5 DSp	2.00
6 DSp	2.00
7 DSp	2.50
8 DSp	2.50
9 DSp	2.00
10 DSp	2.00
11 DSp	2.00

All comics prices listed are for *Near Mint* condition.

Crossfire–Cybernary / COLOR PUB. / Comics Values Annual

Crossfire–Cybernary (cont.)
12 DSp,DSt(c),M.Monroe cover
 & story 2.50
13 DSp 2.00
14 DSp 2.00
15 DSp,O:Crossfire 2.00
16 DSp,'The Comedy Place' 2.00
17 DSp,'Comedy Place' Pt.2 ..... 2.00
See B&W

CROSSFIRE & RAINBOW
Eclipse, 1986
1 DSp,V:Marx Brothers 2.00
2 DSp,PG(c),V:Marx Brothers 2.00
3 DSp,HC(c),A:Witness 2.00
4 DSp,DSt(c),'This Isn't Elvis' 3.50

Crossgen Chronicles #2
© *Crossgen Comics*

CROSSGEN CHRONICLES
Crossgen Comics, 2000
1 48-pg. 4.50
2 RMz,GP 4.00
2a 2nd printing 11.00
3 BKs,GP, 48-page 5.00
4 MWa,GP, 48-page 4.00
5 RMz,GP 4.00
6 thru 8 .... @3.95

CROSSOVERS, THE
CG Entertainment 2003
1 (of 6) Cross Currents 3.00
2 thru 11 .... @3.00
TPB Vol. 1 Cross Currents 9.95

CROSSROADS
First, 1988
1 Sable,Whisper 4.00
2 Sable,Badger 4.00
3 JSon,JAl,Badger/Luther Ironheart 4.00
4 Grimjack/Judah Macabee 4.00
5 LM,Grimjack/Dreadstar/Nexus .. 4.00

CROUCHING TIGER, HIDDEN DRAGON
Comicson, 2002
GN #1 .... 13.95
GN #2 thru #4 .... @13.95

CROW, THE: CITY OF ANGELS
Kitchen Sink, 1996
1 thru 3 movie adaptation ..... @2.95
1 thru 3 movie adaptation,
 photo covers .... @2.95
TPB The Crow, The Movie, new
 printing 18.95

CRUX
Crossgen Comics, 2001
1 MWa,SEp 7.00
2 MWa,SEp 5.00
3 thru 8 MWa,SEp .... @3.00
9 thru 20 .... @3.00
21 thru 32 .... @2.95
TPB Vol. 1 .... 15.95
TPB Vol. 2 .... 15.95
TPB Vol. 3 Strangers in Atlantis . 15.95
TPB Vol. 4 Chaos Reborn 15.95

CRYBABY
Event Comics, 1999
1 GrL,SLo 2.95
1a limited, signed 10.00

CRYING FREEMAN III
Viz, 1991
1 A:Dark Eyes,Oshu 6.00
2 A:Dark Eyes,V:Oshu 5.25
3 Freeman vs. Oshu 5.25
4 Freeman Defeated 5.25
5 Freeman clones, A:Nitta 5.25
6 V:Nitta 5.25
7 thru 9 .... @4.95

CRYING FREEMAN IV
Viz, 1992
1 B:The Pomegranate 4.95
2 thru 7 .... @2.75
8 E:The Pomegranate 2.75
[2nd Series]
1 The Festival 2.50

CRYPT OF DAWN
Sirius, 1996
1 JLi 6.00
2 JLi 4.00
3 thru 6 .... @3.00

CRYPTIC WRITINGS OF MEGADETH
Chaos! Comics, 1997
1 BnP 2.95
1a Tour Edition, leather 20.00
1b Tour Edition, deluxe 30.00
2 BnP 2.95
3 BnP 2.95
4 BnP 2.95
TPB 12.95

CSI: CRIME SCENE INVESTIGATION
IDW Publishing 2003
1 (of 5) 5.00
1a photo(c) 8.00
2 thru 3 .... @5.00
4 thru 5 .... @4.00
GN Thicker Than Blood 7.00
GN Miami–Smoking Gun 7.00
TPB Vol. 1 Serial 20.00

CSI: CRIME SCENE INVESTIGATION: BAD RAP
IDW Publishing 2003
1 (of 5) 4.00
2 thru 5 .... @4.00

CURSE OF RUNE
Malibu Ultraverse, 1995
1A CU,Rune/Silver Surfer tie-in ... 2.50
1B CU, alternate cover 2.50
2 COntrol of the Soul Gem 2.50
3 F:Marvel's Adam Warlock 2.50
4 N:Adam Warlock 2.50

CVO: COVERT VAMPIRIC OPERATIONS–ARTIFACT
IDW Publishing 2003
1 .... 4.00
2 .... 4.00
GN 6.00

CYBER CITY: PART ONE
CPM Comics, 1995
1 I:Oedo City 2.95
2 Sengoku 2.95
Part Two
1 Based on Animated Movie 2.95

CYBERCRUSH: ROBOTS IN REVOLT
Fleetway/Quality
1 inc.Robo-Hunter,Ro-Busters ... 2.00
2 and 3 .... @2.00
4 and 5 V:Terraneks .... @2.00

CYBERFROG
Harris, 1995
0 O:Cyberfrog 2.95
0 AAd(c), signed 19.95
0 Alternate AAd(c) 9.95
1 .... 2.00
1a Signed,numbered 24.95
1b Ultra Violent Cover 49.95
2 .... 2.95
3 .... 2.95
4 .... 2.95
4a alternate cover, signed
 & numbered (#300) 29.95

CYBERFROG: RESERVOIR FROG
Harris, 1996
1 Preview Ashcan, signed
 & numbered 15.00
1 EL(c),V:the Swarm,
 Mr. Skorpeone 2.95
1 Signed & numbered (#250) 19.95
2 .... 2.95
1 & 2 Signed & numbered, in
 binder (#250) 39.95

CYBERHOOD
Entity Comics, 1995
1 R:Cyberhood 2.50
1a with PC Game 6.95

CYBERNARY 2.0
WildStorm/DC, July, 2001
1 (of 6) R:Yumiko Gamorra 2.95

COLOR PUB.

2 F:MechaMax 2.95
3 F:Toshiro 2.95
4 secret race of cyborgs 2.95
5 revolution or evolution. 2.95
6 Kaizen Gamorra, concl. 2.95

CYBERPUNK
Innovation
1 . . . . 2.00
2 . . . . 2.00
Book 2,#1. . . . . 2.25
Book 2,#2. . . . . 2.25

CYBERPUNK: THE SERAPHIM FILES
Innovation, 1990
1 . . . . 2.50
2 . . . . 2.50

CYBERPUNX
Maximum Press, 1997
1 MHw, ... 2.50

CYBERRAD
Continuity, 1991
1 NA layouts,I:Cyberran. 3.00
2 NA I/o 2.50
3 NA I/o. 2.50
4 NA I/o. 2.50
5 NA I/o Glow in the Dark cov . . . 5.00
6 NA I/o,Pullout poster. 2.50
7 NA I/o,See-thru(c). 2.50
[2nd Series], 1992
1 Hologram cover 2.00
2 NA(c),`The Disassembled Man' . 2.00
[3rd Series]
1 Holo.(c),just say no. 3.50
[4th Series], 1993 Deathwatch 2000]
1 Deathwatch 2000 pt.8,w/card . . 2.50
2 Deathwatch 2000 pt. w/card . . . 2.50

CYBRID
Maximum Press, 1995
1 F:Cybrid, I:The Clan 2.95

CYBRID
Maximum Press, 1997
0 RLd, 48pg 3.50
1 MsM,BNa. 3.00
2 MsM,BNa. 3.00

CYNDER
Immortelle Studios, 1996
1 thru 3: see B&W
Ann. #1 . . . . 2.95
Series II, 1997
1 A:Nira X 2.95

CYNDER/NIRA X
Immortelle Studios, 1996
1 x-over. 2.95
1 variant cover. 3.00
1 gold edition. 10.00

DAEMONSTORM
Caliber, 1997
1 TM(c),JMt. 3.95
1 signed 3.95
1 gold edition. 19.95

Daemonstorm 31
© Caliber

DAEMONSTORM: DEADWORLD
Caliber
one-shot 3.95

DAEMONSTORM: OZ
Caliber, 1997
1 . . . . 3.95

DAGAR THE INVINCIBLE
Gold Key, 1972–82
1 O:Daggar;I:Villians Olstellon
  & Scorpio 35.00
2 . . . . 20.00
3 I:Graylon 15.00
4 . . . . 15.00
5 . . . . 15.00
6 1st Dark Gods story 12.00
7 . . . . 12.00
8 . . . . 12.00
9 . . . . 12.00
10 . . . . 12.00
11 thru 19 . . . . @10.00

DAI KAMIKAZE
Now, 1987–88
1 Speed Racer 7.00
1a 2nd printing 2.00
2 . . . . 2.00
3 . . . . 2.00
4 . . . . 2.00
5 . . . . 2.00
6 thru 12 . . . . @2.00

DAKTARI
Dell Publishing Co., July, 1967
1 . . . . 50.00
2 . . . . 35.00
3 . . . . 35.00
4 . . . . 35.00

DALGODA
Fantagraphics, 1984–86
1 . . . . 3.50
2 KN,I:Grinwood'Daughter 3.00
3 KN 2.50
4 thru 8 . . . . @2.25

DALKIEL: THE PROPHECY
Verotik, 1998
1-shot, prequel to Satanika 3.95

DANGER
Charlton Comics, June, 1955
12 . . . . 100.00
13 . . . . 75.00
14 . . . . 75.00
Becomes:

JIM BOWIE
15 . . . . 40.00
16 . . . . 30.00
17 . . . . 30.00
18 . . . . 30.00
19 April, 1957 . . . . 30.00

DANGER GIRL: KAMIKAZE
WildStorm/DC, Dec., 2000
1 (of 2) 2.95
1a variant(c) 2.95
2 concl. 2.95
GN Viva Las Danger. 4.95
Spec. Danger Girl 3-D 4.95
Spec. Hawaiian Punch 4.95

DANGER RANGER
Checker Comics, 1998
1 I:Kirby Jackson, BSz(c). 2.00
2 . . . . 2.00

DANIEL BOONE
Gold Key, 1965–69
1 . . . . 125.00
2 thru 5 . . . . @75.00
6 thru 14 . . . . @50.00
15 . . . . 40.00

DANNY BLAZE
Charlton Comics, Aug., 1955
1 . . . . 125.00
2 . . . . 90.00
Becomes:

NATURE BOY
3 JB,O:Blue Beetle 175.00
4 . . . . 125.00
5 Feb., 1957 . . . . 100.00

DARE
Fantagraphics
1 F:Dan Dare 2.75
2 F:Dan Dare 2.75
3 F:Dan Dare 2.50
4 F:Dan Dare 2.50

DARE THE IMPOSSIBLE
Fleetway/Quality
1 DGb,rep.Dan Dare from 2000AD 2.00
2 DGb, Dare on Waterworld. 2.00
3 DGb. 2.00
4 DGb. 2.00
5 DGb,"The Garden of Eden". . . . 2.00
6 DGb. 2.00
7 DGb,V:Deadly Primitives. 2.00
8 DGb,The Doomsday Machine . . 2.00
9 thru 14 DGb . . . . @2.00

DARK, THE
Continuum, 1990
1 LSn(c),MBr,V:Futura 4.00
2 LSn,Shot by Futura. 3.00
3 MBr,Dark has amnesia 3.00

All comics prices listed are for Near Mint condition.

4 GT(c),MBr,O:The Dark 3.00
Convention Book 1992 MBr,GP,
  MFm,MMi,VS,LSn,TV...... 5.00
Convention Book 1993 MBr,PC,
  ECh,BS,BWi,GP(c),Foil(c),.... 4.00
[2nd Series], 1994
1 Dark Regains Memory 3.00
1a Signed, Foil Cover 2.75
1 BS(c),Red Foil(c),............ 3.00
1a BS(c),newstand ed. 3.00
1b BS(c),Blue foil................ 3.00
2 War on Crime................. 2.75
3 Geoffery Stockton............ 2.50
3 BS(c),Foil(c),................. 3.00
4 I:First Monster 2.50
4 GP(c),Foil(c),w/cards 3.00
5 thru 9 .... @2.50

DARK ADVENTURES
Darkline
1 thru 3 .... @2.00

DARK CHYLDE
Maximum Press, June, 1996
1 RQu....................... 16.00
1a American Entertainment edition 15.00
1b variant cover................ 15.00
2 RQu....................... 12.00
2 Variant cover 14.00
3 RQu....................... 10.00
3 Variant cover 12.00
4 RQu......................... 5.00
5 RQu,`No One Here Gets Out
  Alive' 12.00
Spec. Dark Chylde/Avengelyne RLd,
  RQu,I:Witch Tower 3.00
Spec. Dark Chylde/Glory RQu,.... 3.00
Darkchylde Entertainment, 2001
0 remastered, RQu (2001)....... 2.95
Last Issue special (2002) 3.95
Last issue exclusive variant(c) ... 3.95

DARKCHYLDE REDEMPTION
Darkchylde Entertainment, 2001
1 RQu 2.95
2 .... 2.95
3 .... 2.95

DARK DAYS
IDW Publishing 2003
1 (of 6) 4.50
2 thru 5 .... @4.25

DARK DOMINION
Defiant, 1993–94
1 SD,I:Michael Alexander........ 3.25
2 LWn(s),SLi(i),................ 2.75
3 LWn(s),SLi(i),................ 2.75
4 LWn(s),B:Hoxhunt 3.00
5 LWn(s),I:Puritan,Judah 2.75
6 LWn(s),I:Lurk 2.75
7 LWn(s),V:Glimmer 2.75
8 LWn(s),V:Glimmer 2.50
9 LWn(s)V:Puritan............... 2.50
10 LWn(s),Schism Prequel....... 2.50
11 LWn(s), X-Over 2.50
12 LWn(s), V:Chasm............. 2.50

DARKHAM VALE
APC 2003
1 (of 10) by Jack Lawrence 3.50

COLOR PUB.

2 thru 5 .... @3.50

DARKLON THE MYSTIC
Pacific, 1983
1 JSn 2.00

DARKMINDS: MACROPOLIS
Dreamwave 2002
1 .... 2.95
2 .... 2.95
3 .... 2.95
3a variant Pat Lee (c) 2.95
4 .... 2.95
TPB Vol. 1 .... 9.95

DARK ONE'S THIRD EYE
Sirius, April, 1996
one-shot Vol. 1 DOe............ 4.95
Vol. 2 DOe 4.95

DARK SHADOWS
Gold Key, March, 1969
1 W/Poster,Ph(c)............ 400.00
2 Ph(c) 150.00
3 W/Poster,Ph(c) 200.00
4 thru 7,Ph(c)............. @100.00
8 thru 10 .... @90.00
11 thru 20 .... @75.00
21 thru 35 .... @60.00

DARK SHADOWS
Innovation, 1992
1 Based on 1990's TV series..... 3.50
2 O:Victoria Winters............. 2.50
3 Barnabus Imprisoned 2.50
4 V: Redmond Swann 2.75
[2nd Series]
1 A:Nathan 2.75
2 thru 4 .... 2.75
Dark Shadows:Resurrected 15.95

DARK SIDE
Maximum Press, 1997
1 RLd,RQu 3.00

DARKSHRINE
Antarctic Press, 1999
1 by Shelby Robertson 3.00
1a deluxe 6.00
2 16-page 2.50

DARK TOWN
Mad Monkey Press
1 (of 13) 3.95
2 thru 7 .... @3.95

DARKWING DUCK
Walt Disney, 1991
1 I:Darkwing Duck.............. 2.00
2 V:Taurus Bulba............... 2.00
3 `Fowl Play'.................. 2.00
4 `End o/t beginning,'final issue ... 2.00

DARKWOOD
Aircel
1 thru 5 .... @2.00

Darkwing Duck #3
© Walt Disney

DARQUE PASSAGES
Acclaim 1997
1 (of 4) sequal to Master Darque .. 2.50
1 signed edition................ 4.00
2 .... 2.50
3 A:Pere Jean, Voodoo King 2.50
4 conclusion 2.50

DAUGHTERS OF TIME
3-D Zone
1 I:Kris,Cori,Lhana 3.95

FRONTIER FIGHTER
Charlton Comics, Aug., 1955
1 JK 100.00
2 JK 50.00
Becomes:

DAVY CROCKETT
3 thru 7 JK................. @75.00
8 Jan., 1957 JK............... 50.00
Becomes:

KID MONTANA
9 .... 65.00
10 .... 50.00
11 .... 35.00
12 .... 35.00
13 AW 40.00
14 thru 20 .... @35.00
21 thru 35 .... @30.00
36 thru 49 .... @20.00
50 March, 1965 .... 20.00

DAWN
Sirius, 1995–97
? Wizard mail-in............... 10.00
? variant 25.00
1 JLi,R:Dawn.................. 12.00
1a white trash edition........... 35.00
1b black light edition 25.00
1c look sharp edition 45.00
2 JLi, Trip to Hell 7.00
2 variant cover................ 30.00
3 JLi 6.00
3 limited edition 30.00
4 JLi, `The Gauntlet'............. 5.00
4a variant cover................ 20.00
5 JLi,`Everybody Dies'........... 4.00
5a variant cover................ 20.00
6 (of 6) JLi..................... 4.00
6a variant cover................ 15.00

Comics Values Annual / COLOR PUB. / Dawn–Deliverer

TPB Lucifer's Halo 20.00
TPB Tears of Dawn 18.00
10th Anniv. Spec. 2.95
10th Anniv. Spec, sgn,num. 5.00
Portable Dawn, art work 9.95

DAWN: PIN-UP GODDESS
Linsner.com, 2001
Spec. 2.95
Spec. Limited, signed 12.00

DAWN: THE RETURN OF THE GODDESS
Sirius, 1999
1 (of 4) JLi. 3.00
1a limited, signed 25.00
2 A:Marinen. 3.00
3 .... 3.00
4 .... 3.00
2a thru 4a deluxe .... @20.00

DAZEY'S DIARY
Dell Publishing Co., June-Aug., 1962
1 .... 50.00

DEAD BOYS: DEATH'S EMBRACE
London Night, 1996
1 EHr 3.00
1 platinum edition 6.00

DEAD CLOWN
Malibu Oct., 1996
1 I:Force America 2.50
2 I:Sadistic Six. 2.50
3 TMs(s),last issue 2.50

DEADFORCE
Antarctic Press, 1999
1 (of 3) by Roy Burdine 3.00
2 .... 3.00
3 .... 3.00

DEAD KING
Chaos! Comics, 1997
1 (of 4) Burnt, pt.1, F:Homicide ... 3.00
2 Burnt, pt.2 .... 2.95
3 Burnt, pt.3 .... 2.95
4 Burnt, pt.4, concl. 2.95
TPB Dead King Burnt 12.95

DEADSIDE
Acclaim 1998
1 (of 4) PJe. 2.50
2 thru 4 .... @2.50

DEAMON DREAMS
Pacific
1 .... 2.00
2 .... 2.00

DEAR NANCY PARKER
Gold Key, 1963
1 P(c) 35.00
2 P(c) 30.00

DEATHBLOW: BY BLOWS
WildStorm/DC October, 1999
1 (of 3) AMo,JBa 2.95

2 AMo,JBa. 2.95

DEATHDEALER
Verotika, 1995
1 FF(c), I:Deathdealer 15.00
2 thru 4 FF(c). .... @12.00

DEATHMASK
Future Comics 2003
1 DvM,DG,BL 3.00
2 thru 9 .... @3.00

DEATHMATE
Valiant/Image 1993
Preview (Advanced Comics). 2.25
Preview (Previews). 2.25
Preview (Comic Defense Fund) .. 4.00
Prologue BL,JLe,RLd,Solar meets
    Void 3.25
Prologue Gold 4.00
Blue SCh, HSn, F:Solar, Magnus,
    Battlestone, Livewire, Stronghold,
    Impact, Striker, Harbinger,
    Brigade, Supreme 3.00
Blue Gold Ed. 4.00
Yellow BCh,MLe,DP,F:Armstrong,
    H.A.R.D.C.A.T.S.,Ninjak,Zealot,
    Shadowman,Grifter,Ivar 3.00
Yellow Gold Ed. 4.00
Black JLe,MS,F:Warblade,Ripclaw,
    Turok,X-O Manowar 4.00
Black Gold Ed. 6.00
Red RLd,JMs 4.00
Red Gold Ed. 3.00
Epilogue 2.50
Epilogue Gold. 3.00

DEATH OF HARI KARI
Blackout Comics, 1997
0 .... 2.95
0 super Sexy Kari Cover 9.95
0 3-D super Sexy Kari Cover ... 14.95

DEATHRACE 2020
Cosmic Comics, 1995
1 Pat Mills, Tony Skinner 2.50
2 V:Spyda, Sawmill Jones 2.50
3 O:Frankenstein. 2.50
4 Deathrace cont. 2.50
5 F:Death Racers, D:Alchoholic ... 2.50
6 V:Indestructiman. 2.50
7 Smallville Mall 2.50

DEATH OF LADY VAMPRE
Blackout Comics, 1995
1 V:Baraclaw. 2.95
1 Commemorative Issue 9.95

DEATH RATTLE
Kitchen Sink, 1985–88
1 thru 7 .... @2.00
8 I:Xenozoic Tales 5.00
9 thru 18 .... @2.00

DECOY
Penny Farthing Press, 1999
1 (of 4) 2.75
2 .... 2.75
3 .... 2.75
4 .... 2.75
TPB 15.95

DECOY: STORM OF THE CENTURY
Pennyfarthing Press, 2002
1 thru 4 .... @2.95

DEFENDERS, THE
Dell Publishing Co., Sept.-Nov., 1962
1 .... 60.00
2 .... 40.00

DEFIANT: ORIGIN OF A UNIVERSE
Defiant, 1993
1 Giveaway 2.00

Deity Vol. 2, #3
© Hyperworks

DEITY
Hyperwerks, Sept., 1997
0 .... 3.00
1 KIA. 5.00
1a Director's Cut 3.00
2 thru 6 KIA .... @3.00
TPB rep. #1–#3 .... 7.95
TPB rep. #4–#6 .... 7.95

VOL II Awesome/Hyperworks, 1998
1 KIA,BNa, F:Jamie 2.95
1a Limited edition 7.95
1b Silver Foil edition 12.95
1c Gold Edition 19.95
2 KIA,BNa, A:Diamond Diaz. 2.95
3 KIA,BNa, The Soul Crusher ... 2.95
4 KIA,BNa, A:Ogden 2.95
5 KLa,BNa,V:Ma'Shiva 2.95
6 KIA,BNa. 2.95

DEITY II: CATSEYE
Hyperwerks, 1998
1 KIA,BNa,F:Digby. 2.95
2 KIA,BNa,A:II. 2.95
3 KIA,BNa,F:Catseye. 2.95
4 KIA,BNa,conclusion 2.95

DELIVERER
Zion Comics
1 thru 3 .... @2.00
4 F:Gabriel 2.00
5 V:Division 2.00

All comics prices listed are for *Near Mint* condition.

DEMON-HUNTER
Atlas, 1975
1 The Harvester of Eyes 15.00

DEMONIC TOYS
Eternity, 1992
1 Based on 1992 movie. 2.50
2 thru 4 . . . . @2.50

DEMONIQUE
London Night, 1996
0 Manga 3.00
1 EHr 3.00
2 (of 2) 3.00

DEMONSLAYER
Avatar Press, 2001
0 16-page, signed 5.95
TPB Vol. 1 . . . . 19.95

DEMONSLAYER: FUTURE SHOCK
Avatar Press, 2002
1/2 Eradicate Edition 5.95

DEMONSLAYER: PATH OF TIME
Avatar, 2002
1 MMy 3.50
1a Medieval (c) 3.50
1b Ninja (c) 3.50
1c Western (c). 3.50
1d Matt Martin (c) 3.50
1e Serenity (c). 5.95
1f bondage (c). 6.00
1g Prism foil (c) 12.95
1/2 . . . . 3.95
1/2 Pirate (c) 3.95
1/2 Cave Girl (c) 3.95
1/2 Bikini (c) 3.95
1/2 Martin (c) 3.95

DEMONSLAYER: PROPHECY
Avatar Press, 2001
1 MMy. 3.50
1a Celtic (c). 3.50
1b Hell on Wheels (c) 3.50
1c Leather (c) 20.00
1d lace edition 5.95
1e Bad Omens (c). 5.95
1f Mouth of Evil edition 5.95
1g Prism foil (c) 12.95
1h Royal blue edition. 75.00

DEMONSLAYER: RAVE
Avatar Press, 2001
Spec. 3.50
Spec. Bad Schoolgirl (c) 3.50
Spec. Silent Moment (c) 3.50
Rave in Style (c). 5.95
Rave Previews prism foil (c) 12.95

DEMONSLAYER: REBIRTH
Awesome Entertainment, 2000
1 . . . . 3.00

COLOR PUB.

DEMONSLAYER: VENGEANCE
Avatar Press, 2001
1 (of 2) MMy (c). 3.50
1a Park (c) 3.50
1b Wraparound (c) 3.95
1c Red Velvet (c). 20.00
1d prism foil (c) 12.95
1e fire (c). 5.95
1f ice (c) 5.95
1g Royal Blue edition. 75.00
2 MMy, concl. 3.50
2a Bikini (c). 3.50
2b Jungle Girl (c). 3.50
2c Ruins edition. 5.95

DEMONWARS: EYE FOR AN EYE
Crossgen Comics 2003
1 (of 5) 3.00
2 thru 5 . . . . @3.00

DEMONWARS: TRIAL BY FIRE
Crossgen Comics 2002
2 thru 5 . . . . @3.00
TPB Vol. 1 Trial by Fire. 12.95

DEN
Fantagor
1 thru 10 RCo . . . . @2.00

DEN SAGA
Tundra/Fantagor
1 RCo,O:Den begins 4.95

DENNIS THE MENACE
Fawcett, 1960-61
Fun Book #1. . . . . 75.00
And his Pal Joey #1 . . . . 50.00
And his Dog Ruff #1 . . . . 50.00
Television Special #1 . . . . 60.00
Triple Feature #1 . . . . 60.00
Television Special #2 . . . . 35.00

Dennis the Menace and His Friends #16 © Fawcett

DENNIS THE MENACE AND HIS FRIENDS
[VARIOUS SUBTITLES]
Fawcett, 1969-1980
1 thru 10 rep. . . . . @35.00
11 thru 20 rep.. . . . . @20.00
21 thru 46 rep. . . . . @15.00

DENNIS THE MENACE GIANTS
[VARIOUS SUBTITLES]
Fawcett, 1955-69
N# Vacation Special 150.00
N# Christmas 125.00
2 thru 10 . . . . @100.00
11 thru 20 . . . . @75.00
21 thru 30 . . . . @50.00
31 thru 40 . . . . @30.00
41 thru 75 . . . . @25.00
Becomes:

DENNIS THE MENACE BONUS MAGAZINE
[VARIOUS SUBTITLES]
Fawcett, 1970-79
76 thru 100 . . . . @8.00
101 thru 120 . . . . @5.00
121 thru 185 . . . . @3.00
186 thru 196 Big Bonus Series . . @3.00
Becomes:

DENNIS THE MENACE
Fawcett, 1979-80
#16 Fun Fest 5.00
#17 Fun Fest 5.00
#10 Big Bonus Series 5.00
#11 Big Bonus Series 5.00

DEPUTY DAWG
Gold Key, Aug., 1965
1 . . . . 200.00

DER VANDALE
Innervision, 1998
1 (of 3) 2.50
2 (of 3) 2.50
3 (of 3) 2.50
3 variant cover 2.50

DESERT STORM JOURNAL
Apple Comics, 1991
1 Hussein on (c) 2.75
1a Schwartzkopf on (c) 2.75
2 thru 8 . . . . @2.75

DESTROYER
Valiant 1994
0 MM 41st Century 2.95

DESTROYER DUCK
Eclipse, 1982-84
1 JK,AA,SA,I:Groo. 12.00
2 JK,AA,Starling 2.00
3 thru 5 JK. . . . . @2.00
6 thru 7 JK. . . . . @2.00

DESTRUCTOR, THE
Atlas, Feb.-Aug., 1975
1 thru 4 WW,SD. . . . . @25.00

DETECTIVES, INC.
Eclipse, 1985
1 MR,rep.GraphicNovel 3.00
2 MR 2.25
[2nd Series]
1 GC,'A Terror of Dying Dreams' . . 2.50
2 GC 2.25
3 GC,'Cut to the Bone' 2.00

DETONATOR
Chaos! Comics, 1994–95
1 I:Detonator 2.95
2 V:Messiah & Mindbender 2.75

DEVIL KIDS STARRING HOT STUFF
Harvey Publications, 1962–81
1 . . . . 175.00
2 . . . . 100.00
3 thru 10 . . . . @75.00
11 thru 20 . . . . @35.00
21 thru 30 . . . . @30.00
31 thru 40 . . . . @25.00
41 thru 50 68 pgs. . . . . @25.00
51 thru 55 62 pgs. . . . . @20.00
56 thru 70 . . . . @15.00
71 thru 100 . . . . @10.00
101 thru 106 . . . . @7.00
107 . . . . 7.00

DEVILMAN
Verotika, 1995
1 Go Nagi 2.95
1a San Diego Con Gatefold edition 4.95
2 F:Devilman 2.95
3 Through History 2.95
4 French Revolution 2.95
5 Custer's Last Stand 2.95

DEVLIN
Maximum Press, 1996
1 A:Avengelyne,3-part mini-series . . 2.50
2 (of 3) RLd,BNa,A:Avengelyne . . . 2.50

DICK TRACY
Blackthorne, 1986
1 3-D 2.50

DICK TRACY: BIG CITY BLUES
1 Mini Series 3.95
2 Mini Series 5.95
3 Mini Series 5.95

DINO ISLAND
Mirage, 1993
1 thru 2 . . . . 2.75

DINOSAUR REX
Upshot/Fantagraphics, 1987
1 thru 3 by Jan Strand &
   Henry Mayo . . . . @2.00

DINOSAURS
Walt Disney
1 Citizen Robbie(From TV) 2.95

DINOSAURS ATTACK
Eclipse, 1991
1 HT,Based on Topps cards 3.50

2 and 3 HT,Based on cards . . . . @3.50

DINOSAURS FOR HIRE
Malibu
1 3-D rep. B&W 3.00
[2nd Series] 1993–94
1 B:TMs(s),A:Reese,Archie,
   Lorenzo 3.00
2 BU:Dinosaurs 2099 . . . . 2.50
3 A:Ex-Mutants 2.50
4 V:Poacher,Revenue 2.50
5 . . . . 2.50
6 V:Samantha 2.50
7 V:Turret 2.50
8 Genesis #2, with Skycap 2.50
9 Genesis #5 . . . . 2.50
10 Flip(c) 2.50
11 V:Tiny Lorenzo 2.50
12 I:Manhatten Bob 2.50
13 I:Lil' Billy Frankenstein 2.50
14 final issue 2.50

DISNEY ADVENTURES
Walt Disney
1 . . . . 2.75
2 . . . . 2.50
3 thru 13 . . . . @2.25
14 thru 28 . . . . @2.00

DISNEY COLOSSAL COMICS COLLECTION
Walt Disney
1 inc.DuckTales, Chip'n'Dale 2.25
2 thru 9 . . . . @2.00

DISNEY COMICS IN 3-D
Walt Disney
1 . . . . 2.95

DISNEY COMICS SPEC: DONALD & SCROOGE
1 inc."Return to Xanadu" 8.95

DISNEYLAND BIRTHDAY PARTY
Gladstone, 1985
1 CB 10.00

DIVER DAN
Dell Publishing Co., Feb.-April, 1962
1 . . . . 75.00
2 . . . . 60.00

DIVINE INTERVENTION
WildStorm/DC, 1999
1 . . . . 2.50
Wildcats, pt.2, JLe,SLo,RiB 2.50
Gen13, pt.3, JLe,SLo,RiB 2.50

DIVINE MADNESS
Dark Moon
1 Human Flesh Artist 2.50
2 . . . . 2.50
3 Ancient Cult 2.50

DNAGENTS
Eclipse, 1983–85
1 O:DNAgents 4.00
2 . . . . 3.00

DNAgents 320
© Eclipse

3 . . . . 2.50
4 . . . . 2.50
5 . . . . 2.50
6 . . . . 2.50
7 . . . . 2.50
8 . . . . 2.50
9 DSp 2.50
10 . . . . 2.00
11 . . . . 2.50
12 . . . . 2.50
13 . . . . 2.00
14 . . . . 2.00
15 . . . . 2.50
16 . . . . 2.50
17 thru 25 . . . . @2.00
See also: NEW DNAGENTS

DON BLUTH'S DRAGON'S LAIR
Crossgen Comics 2003
1 (of 6) Singe's Revenge 2.95
2 thru 3 . . . . @2.95

DON BLUTH'S SPACE ACE
Crossgen Comics 2003
1 (of 6) Defender of the Universe . . 2.95
2 thru 3 . . . . @2.95

DO YOU BELIEVE IN NIGHTMARES?
St. John Publishing Co., 1957–58
1 SD 600.00
2 DAy 350.00

DOBER-MAN
1 . . . . 2.50

DOC SAVAGE
Gold Key, 1966
1 . . . . 45.00

DOC SAVAGE
Millennium
1 V:Russians 2.50

DOC SAVAGE, THE MAN OF BRONZE
Millennium
1 Monarch of Armageddon,pt.1 . . . 3.00
2 Monarch of Armageddon,pt.2 . . . 2.75
3 Monarch of Armageddon,pt.3 . . . 2.75
4 Monarch of Armageddon,pt.4 . . . 2.75

DOC SAVAGE: THE DEVIL'S THOUGHTS
Millennium
1 V:Hanoi Shan 2.50
2 V:Hanoi Shan 2.50
3 Final issue 2.50

DOC SAVAGE: DOOM DYNASTY
Millennium, 1991
1 . . . . 2.50
2 . . . . 2.50

DOC SAVAGE: MANUAL OF BRONZE
Millennium
1 Fact File 2.50

DOC SAVAGE: REPEL
Innovation
1 DvD(c) 2.50

DOCTOR BOOGIE
Media Arts
1 and 2 . . . . @2.00

DOCTOR CHAOS
Triumphant Comics, 1993
1 JnR(s),I:Doctor Chaos 2.50
2 JnR(s), ... 2.50
3 JnR(s),The Coming of the Cry,pt.1,I:Cry 2.50
4 JnR(s),The Coming of the Cry,pt.2,b:Ky'Li 2.50
5 JnR(s),E:Coming of the Cry,pt.3,V:Cry 2.50
6 Recovery 2.50
7 w/coupon 2.50
8 w/coupon 2.50
9 V:Mirth 2.50
10 Co. X #3 . . . . 2.50
11 Co. X #4 . . . . 2.50
12 A:Charlotte 2.50

DR. KILDARE
Dell Publishing Co., April-June, 1962
1 . . . . 125.00
2 . . . . 100.00
3 . . . . 100.00
4 . . . . 100.00
5 . . . . 100.00
6 . . . . 100.00
7 . . . . 100.00
8 . . . . 100.00
9 . . . . 100.00

DOCTOR SOLAR MAN OF THE ATOM
Gold Key, 1962
1 BF,I:Dr. Solar 325.00
2 BF,I:Prof.Harbinger 125.00
3 BF,The Hidden Hands 80.00
4 BF,The Deadly Sea 80.00
5 BF,I:Dr.Solar in costume 90.00
6 FBe,I:Nuro 60.00
7 FBe,Vanishing Oceans 60.00
8 FBe,Thought Controller 60.00
9 FBe,Transivac The Energy Consuming Computer 60.00
10 FBe,The Sun Giant 60.00
11 FBe,V:Nuro 40.00
12 FBe,The Mystery of the Vanishing Silver 40.00
13 FBe,Meteor from 100 Mill.BC . . 40.00
14 FBe,Solar's Midas Touch 40.00
15 FBe O:Dr.Solar 50.00
16 FBe,V:Nuro 40.00
17 FBe,The Fatal Foe 40.00
18 FBe,The Mind Master 40.00
19 FBe,SolarV:Solar 40.00
20 AMc,Atomic Nightmares 40.00
21 AMc,Challenge from Outer Space 35.00
22 AMc,Nuro,I:King Cybernoid . . . 35.00
23 AMc,A:King Cybernoid 35.00
24 EC,The Deadly Trio 35.00
25 EC,The Lost Dimension 35.00
26 EC,When Dimensions Collide . 35.00
27 (1969) The Ladder to Mars . . . 35.00
28 (1981),1-pg AMc,The Dome of Mystery 20.00
29 DSp,FBe,Magnus 20.00
30 DSp,FBe,Magnus 20.00

DR. TOMORROW
Acclaim May, 1997
1 (of 12) BL,Bart Simms finds Angel Computer 2.50
2 BL,V:Teutonic Knight 2.50
3 BL,V:Teutonic Knight concl. . . . 2.50
4 BL,V:Joe McCarthy 2.50
5 BL,V:J. Edgar Hoover 2.50
6 BL,DG,V:Mushroom Cloud 2.50
7 BL,DG,A:Mushroom Cloud 2.50
8 BL,GK,Vietnam 2.50
9 BL 2.50
10 BL,SMc,on *Oprah* 2.50
11 BL,the time capsule 2.50
12 BL,MBu(c),final issue 2.50

DOGHEAD
Tundra
1 Al Columbia,"Poster Child" 4.95

DOGS OF WAR
Defiant, 1994
1 F:Shooter,Ironhead 2.75
2 . . . . 2.50
3 Mouse Deserts 2.50
4 Schism Prequel 2.50
5 X-over 2.50
6 Aftermath 2.50

DOLLMAN
Eternity, 1991
1 Movie adapt. sequel 2.50
2 V:Sprug & Braindead Gang 2.50
3 Toni Costa Kidnapped 2.50
4 . . . . 2.50

DONALD DUCK
Dell/Gold Key, Dec., 1962
85 thru 97 . . . . 60.00
98 rep. #46 CB 60.00
99 . . . . 50.00
100 . . . . 35.00
101 . . . . 32.00
102 A:Super Goog 32.00
103 thru 110 . . . . @32.00
111 . . . . 32.00
112 I:Moby Duck 32.00
113 thru 133 . . . . @32.00
134 CB rep. 32.00
135 CB rep. 32.00
136 thru 156 . . . . @25.00
157 CB rep. 22.00
158 thru 163 . . . . @20.00
164 CB rep. 20.00
165 thru 216 . . . . @15.00

Whitman
217 . . . . 15.00
218 . . . . 15.00
219 CB rep. 15.00
220 and 221 . . . . @35.00
222 scarce 250.00
223 thru 228 . . . . @25.00
229 thru 240 . . . . @15.00
241 thru 245 . . . . @20.00

Gladstone
246 CB,Gilded Man 22.00
247 CB 15.00
248 CB,Forbidden Valley 15.00
249 CB 15.00
250 CB,Pirate Gold 20.00
251 CB,Donald's Best Xmas 15.00
252 CB,Trail o/t Unicorn 8.00
253 CB 8.00
254 CB, in old Calif. 9.00
255 CB 8.00
256 CB,Volcano Valley 8.00
257 CB,Forest Fire 8.00
258 thru 260 CB . . . . @8.00
261 thru 266 CB . . . . @8.00
267 thru 277 CB . . . . @8.00
278 CB 9.00
279 CB 9.00
280 thru 298 CB rep. . . . . @6.00
299 'Life Guard Daze' 4.00
300 'Donald's 300th Triumph' 48pg. 4.50
301 'The Gold Finder' 4.00
302 'Monkey Business' 4.00
303 'The Cantankerous Cat' 4.00
304 'Donald Duck Rants about Ants' 4.00
305 'Mockingbird Ridge' 4.00
306 'Worst Class Mail' 3.00
307 'Going to Sea' 3.00
308 'Worst Class Mail' 3.00

Dollman #3
© Eternity

DONALD DUCK ADVENTURES
Gladstone, Nov., 1987
1 CB,Jungle Hi-Jinks 8.00
2 CB,Dangerous Disquise 6.00
3 CB,Lost in the Andes 6.00
4 CB,Frozen Gold 6.00
5 CB,Rosa. 6.00
6 CB 3.00
7 CB 3.00
8 CB,Rosa. 6.00
9 CB 3.00
10 CB. 3.00
11 CB. 3.00
12 CB,Rosa,Giant-size 6.00
13 CB,Rosa(c) 3.50
14 CB. 3.00
15 CB. 3.00
16 CB. 3.00
17 CB. 3.00
18 CB,No Such Varmint 3.00
19 CB. 4.00
20 CB,Giant-size (1990) 4.00
21 CB,Rosa(c) (1993). 4.00
22 CB,The Pixilated Parrot 4.00
23 thru 30 . . . . @4.00
31 thru 40 . . . . @3.00
41 `Bruce McDuck' 3.00
42 `The Saga of Sourdough Sam'. . 3.00
43 `The Lost Charts of Columbus' . . 3.00
44 `The Kitchy-Kaw Diamond' 3.00
45 `The Red Duck' 3.00
46 . . . . 3.00
47 CB,`Trick or Treat' 3.00
48 `The Saphead Factor' 3.00

DONALD DUCK ADVENTURES
Walt Disney, June, 1990
1 Don Rosa, `The Money Pit' 6.00
2 CB 3.00
3 . . . . 3.00
4 CB 3.00
5 . . . . 3.00
6 . . . . 3.00
7 . . . . 3.00
8 . . . . 3.00
9 CB 3.00
10 `Run-Down Runner' 3.00
11 `Whats for Lunch-Supper' 3.00
12 `Head of Rama Putra' 3.00
13 `JustAHumble,BumblingDuck' . . 3.00
14 CB,`Day Gladstone's Luck
   Ran Out' 4.00
15 `A Tuft Luck Tale' 3.00
16 `Magica's Missin'Magic' 3.00
17 CB,`Secret of Atlantis' 4.00
18 `Crocodile Donald' 3.00
19 `Not So Silent Service' 3.00
20 `Ghost of Kamikaze Ridge' 3.00
21 CB,`The Golden Christmas Tree' 4.00
22 `The Master Landscapist' 5.00
23 `The Lost Peg Leg Mine' 3.00
24 `On Stolen Time' 4.00
25 Sense of Humor 3.00
26 CB,Race to the South Seas 4.00
27 CB,Nap in Nature 4.00
28 Olympic Tryout 3.00
29 CB,rep.March of Comics#20 . . . 4.00
30 A:The Vikings 3.00
31 The Sobbing Serpent of Loch
   McDuck 3.00
32 It Was No Occident 3.00
33 Crazy Christmas on Bear
   Mountain 3.00
34 Sup.Snooper Strikes Again 4.00
35 CB rep. 4.00
36 CB rep. 4.00
37 CB rep. 3.00

COLOR PUB.

38 CB rep. 4.00
Gemstone Publishing 2003
TPB Vol. 1 . . . . 7.95
TPB Vol. 2 thru Vol. 3 . . . . 7.95

DONALD DUCK ALBUM
Dell Publishing Co., May-July, 1959
1 CB(c) 75.00
2 . . . . 60.00

DONALD DUCK AND FRIENDS
Gemstone Publishing 2003
308 . . . . 2.95
309 . . . . 2.95
310 . . . . 2.95

DONATELLO
Mirage
1 . . . . 10.00

DONNA MIA
Dark Fantasy Prod., 1995
1 I:Donna Mia 4.00
1a Deluxe Edition 5.00
1b signed & num'd (100 copies). . 8.95
2 . . . . 3.00

Doomsday +1 Vol. 2, #4
© Charlton Comics

DOOMSDAY + 1
Charlton, 1975–79
1 JBy,JBy(c) 25.00
2 JBy(c),P(c) 20.00
3 JBy,JBy(c),P(c) 15.00
4 JBy,JBy(c),P(c),I:Lok 15.00
5 and 6 JBy,JBy(c),P(c) . . . . . . @15.00
7 thru 12 JBy,JBy(c),rep . . . . . . @7.00

DOOMSDAY SQUAD
Fantagraphics, 1986
1 rep. JBy 2.00
2 rep. JBy 2.00
3 rep. SS,A:Usagi Yojimbo 4.00
4 thru 7, rep. JBy . . . . @2.00

DOUBLE DARE ADVENTURES
Harvey Publications, 1966
1 I:B-man,Glowing Gladiator,
   Magicmaster. 100.00
2 AW/RC rep. A:B-Man,Glowing
   Gladiator, Magicmaster. 75.00

DOUBLE IMPACT
High Impact Studios, 1995–96
1 RCI,I:China & Jazz, chrome(c) . . 7.00
1 holographic rainbow (c) with
   certificate 15.00
1 rainbow (c), no certificate 10.00
1 chromium variant (c). 8.00
2 RCI,V:Castillo 3.00
2a signed, with certificate 4.00
3 China on cover 5.00
3a Jazzler on cover 3.00
3b Nikki on cover 3.00
3c `Blondage' 6.00
4 F:Mordred, The Rattler 2.95
4a `Phoenix' variant (c) 6.00
5 RCI 3.00
6 `Buttshots' 4.00
6a Jazz (c) 3.00
6a signed 6.00
7 I:Nikki Blade 3.00
8 . . . . 3.00
8a variant (c) 4.00
Gold edition, Lingerie special 3.00
Volume 2, 1996–97
0 RCI 3.00
1 RCI. 3.00
1a deluxe edition 4.00
1b prism foil (c) 5.00
1c gold foil (c) 5.00
2 RCI 3.00
3 . . . . 2.95
3a special edition RCI(c) 8.00

DOUBLE IMPACT: ALIVE
ABC Studios, 1999
1 RCI,F:China & Jazz 3.00
1a deluxe 8.00

DOUBLE IMPACT/ HELLINA
High Impact, 1996
1-shot RCI. 3.00

DOUBLE IMPACT/ LETHAL STRYKE: DOUBLE STRIKE
High Impact/London Night, 1996
1-shot RCI. 3.00

DOUBLE IMPACT SUICIDE RUN
High Impact, 1997
1 RCI. 3.00
1 gold edition 10.00
1 platinum edition 20.00
2 . . . . 3.00
2a Suicide Cover 10.00

DOUBLE IMPACT: 2069
ABC Studios, 1999
1 RCI,Independent Day 3.00
1a premium edition 5.00
1b Sexy China ed. 5.00

COLOR PUB.

DOUBLE LIFE OF PRIVATE STRONG
Archie Publications, 1959
1 JSm/JK,I:Lancelot Strong/
Shield, The Fly 750.00
2 JSm/JK,GT A:Fly 500.00

DRACULA
Dell Publishing Co., Nov., 1966
2 O:Dracula 50.00
3 . . . . 35.00
4 . . . . 35.00
6 . . . . 30.00
7 . . . . 25.00
8 . . . . 25.00

DRACULA
Topps, 1992
1 MMi,Movie adaptation (trading
 cards in each issue) 5.00
1a Red Foil Logo 10.00
1b 2nd Print. 2.95
2 MMi,Movie adapt.contd. 4.00
3 MMi,Movie adapt.contd. 4.00
4 MMi,Movie adapt.concludes . . . 4.00
TPB Collected Album 13.95

DRACULA CHRONICLES
Topps
1 True Story of Dracula 2.50
2 RTs,rep. Vlad #2 . . . . 2.50
3 RTs,rep. Vlad #3 . . . . 2.50

DRACULA VS. ZORRO
Topps, 1993
1 DMg(s),TY,Black(c), ... 3.25
2 DMg(s),TY,w/Zorro #0 . . . . 2.95
TPB 5.95

DRACULA: VLAD THE IMPALER
Topps, 1993
1 EM,I:Vlad Dracua, w/cards 3.25
1a Red Foil 10.00
2 EM, w/cards 3.25

Dragonflight #3
© *Eclipse*

DRAGONCHIANG
Eclipse
1 TT 2.95

DRAGONFLIGHT
Eclipse, 1991
1 Anne McCaffrey adapt. 4.95
2 novel adapt 4.95
3 novel adapt 4.95

DRAGONFLY
AC Comics, 1985
1 . . . . 3.50
2 and 3 . . . . @2.00
4 thru 8 . . . . @2.00

DRAGONRING
Aircel, 1987–88, Vol. 2
1 . . . . 3.50
2 O:Dragonring 2.50
3 thru 15 . . . . @2.00
See also: B&W

DRAKKON WARS, THE
Realm Press, 1997
0 by Richard Hatch & Chris Scalf . . 3.00
1 . . . . 3.00

DREADSTAR
First, 1986–91
27 JSn,from Epic,traitor 3.00
28 JSn 3.00
29 JSn,V:Lord Papal 3.00
30 JSn,D:Lord Papal 3.00
31 JSn,I:The Power 3.00
32 JSn 3.00
33 . . . . 3.00
34 LM/VM,A:Malchek 3.00
35 LM/VM. 3.00
36 LM/VM. 3.00
37 LM/VM,A:Last Laugh 3.00
38 LM/VM. 3.00
39 AMc,Crossroads tie-in 3.00
40 LM/VM. 3.00
41 AMe. 3.00
42 JSn,AMe,B.U.Pawns begins . . . 3.00
43 JSn,AMe,Pawns,pt.2 . . . . 3.00
44 JSn,AMe,Pawns,pt.3 . . . . 3.00
45 JSn,AMe,Pawns,pt.4 . . . . 3.00
46 JSn,AMe,Pawns,pt.5 . . . . 3.00
47 JSn,AMe,Pawns,pt.6 . . . . 3.00
48 JSn,AMe,Pawns,pt.7 . . . . 3.00
49 JSn,AMe,Pawns,pt.8 . . . . 3.00
50 JSn,AMe,Pawns,pt.9 prestige . . 4.25
51 PDd,Woj,Pawns,pt.10, Paladox
 epic begins. 4.00
52 AMe. 4.00
53 AMe,`Messing with Peoples
 Minds' 4.00
54 JSn,AMe,Pawns ends 4.00
55 AMe,I:Iron Angel 4.00
56 AMe,A:Iron Angel 4.00
57 A:Iron Angel. 4.00
58 A:Iron Angel. 4.00
59 A:Iron Angel. 4.00
60 AMe,Paladox epic ends 4.00
61 AME,A:Iron Angel 4.00
62 O:Dreadstar,I:Youngscuz 4.00
63 AMe,A:Youngscuz 4.00
64 AMe,A:Youngscuz 4.00

DREADSTAR
Malibu Bravura, 1994–95
1 JSn(c),PDd(s),EC,I:New Dreadstar
 (Kalla),w/stamp 2.75

2 JSn(c),PDd(s),EC,w/stamp 2.50
3 JSn(c),PDd(s),EC,w/stamp 2.75
4 PDd,EC,Kalla's origin,w/stamp . . 2.50
5 PDd,F:Vanth,w/stamp 2.50
6 PDd,w/stamp 2.50

DREAMS OF THE DARKCHYLDE
Darkchylde Entertainment, 2000
1 RQu,BPe 2.95
2 . . . . 2.95
3 . . . . 2.95
4 . . . . 2.95
4a Fear 2001 edition 5.95
4b Fear 2001 ruby red 29.95
5 . . . . 2.95
6 . . . . 2.95

DREDD RULES
Fleetway/Quality
1 SBs(c),JBy,Prev.unpubl. in USA . 5.00
2 inc.`Eldster Ninja Mud Wrestling
 Vigilantes'. 3.50
3 inc.`That Sweet Stuff' 3.50
4 Our Man in Hondo City. 3.50
5 . . . . 3.25
6 BKi,DBw. 3.25
7 "Banana City" 3.25
8 "Over the Top" 3.25
9 "Shooting Match" 3.25
10 SBs,inc.Mega-City primer 3.25
11 SBs,Legend/Johnny Biker 3.25
12 SBs,Rock on Tommy Who 3.25
13 BMy,The Ballad of Toad
 McFarlane 3.25
14 thru 15 . . . . @3.25
16 A:Russians 3.25
17 F:Young Giant 3.25
18 F:Jonny Cool. 2.95
19 V:Hunter's Club 2.95

DRIFT MARLO
Dell Publishing Co., May–July, 1962
1 . . . . 35.00
2 . . . . 25.00

DRUG WARS
Pioneer
1 . . . . 2.00
2 . . . . 2.00
3 . . . . 2.00

DRUNKEN FIST
Jademan, 1988
1 . . . . 3.25
2 . . . . 2.50
3 . . . . 2.00
4 . . . . 2.00
5 . . . . 2.00
6 thru 9 . . . . @2.00
10 thru 27. . . . . @2.00
28 D:Mack. 2.00
29 . . . . 2.00
30 . . . . 2.00
31 . . . . 2.00
32 Wong Mo-Gei vs.Swordsman. . . 2.00
33 Mo-Gei commits suicide. 2.00
34 . . . . 2.00
35 . . . . 2.00
36 D:Fire Oak. 2.00
37 Iron Law Kills Elephant-Man . . . 2.00
38 A:Wayne Chan. 2.00
39 D:Wayne Chan 2.00
40 D:Toro Yamamoto 2.00

COLOR PUB.

DUNGEONS & DRAGONS: THE LOST CITY
Twenty First Century, 1999
1 (of 6) game tie-in 4.95
2 thru 6 . . . . @4.95

DUNGEONS & DRAGONS: AMBER CASTLE
Twenty First Century, 2000
1 (of 6) game tie-in 4.95

DUNGEONS & DRAGONS: TEMPEST'S GATE
Kenzer & Company, 2001
1 (of 4) Born of Fire 3.00
2 Forged in Tears 3.00
3 Tempered in Fellowship 3.00
4 Sheathed in Justice 3.00
TPB 15.00

DUNGEONS AND DRAGONS: WHERE SHADOWS FALL
Kenzer & Company 2003
1 (of 5) 3.50
2 thru 4 . . . . @3.50

DWIGHT D. EISENHOWER
Dell Publishing Co., Dec., 1969
1 . . . . 60.00

DYNAMO
Tower Comics, Aug., 1966
1 WW,MSy,RC,SD,I:Andor 125.00
2 WW,DA,GT,MSy,Weed solo
  story A:Iron Maiden 75.00
3 WW,GT,Weed solo story,
  A:Iron Maiden. 75.00
4 WW,DA,A:Iron Maiden 75.00

DYNAMO JOE
First, 1986–87
1 . . . . 3.00
2 . . . . 2.00
3 thru 14 . . . . @2.00

Dynamo Joe #7
© First

Comics Values Annual

41 Lord Algol vs. Ghing Mob. 2.00
42 . . . . 2.00
43 D:Yamamoto,Swordsman in USA 2.00
44 `Cool Hand Wong'. 2.00
45 `Black Cult Rising' 2.00
46 . . . . 2.00
47 . . . . 2.00
48 Evil Child 2.00
49 I:Hurricane Child 2.00
50 Lord Algol vs.Diabol.Ent. 2.00
51 F:Flying Thunder 2.00
52 Madcap vs.Yama 2.00
53 Swordsman vs.Catman 2.00

DUCKMAN
Topps, 1994
1 USA Cartoon 2.50
2 XXX Files 2.50
3 I:King Chicken 2.50
4 V:Toys 2.50
5 F:Cornfed 2.50
6 Star Trek Parody 2.50
7 rep. 1990 B&W 1st app., now
  in color. 2.50

DUCKMAN: THE MOB FROG SAGA
Topps, 1994
1 I:Mob Frog 2.50
2 D:Mob Frog 2.50
3 In the Name of the Duck. 2.50

DUCK TALES
Gladstone, 1990
1 CB(r)I:LaunchpadMcQuck. 7.00
2 CB(r) 4.00
3 . . . . 4.00
4 CB(r) 4.00
5 thru 11 . . . . @4.00
12 . . . . 5.00
13 . . . . 5.00

DUCK TALES
Walt Disney
1 . . . . 4.00
2 . . . . 3.00
3 . . . . 2.50
4 . . . . 2.50
5 Scrooges'Quest 2.50
6 Scrooges'Quest 2.50
7 Return to Duckburg 2.50
8 . . . . 2.50
9 7 Sojourns of Scrooge 2.50
10 Moon of Gold. 2.50
11 Once & Future Warlock 2.50
12 Lost Beyond the MilkyWay. . . . 2.50
13 The Doomed of Sarras 2.50
14 Planet Blues 2.50
15 The Odyssey Ends 2.50
16 The Great Chase 2.50
17 Duck in Time Pt.1 . . . . 2.50
18 Duck in Time Pt.2 . . . . 2.50
19 Bail Out 2.50

DUDLEY DO-RIGHT
Charlton Comics, 1970–71
1 . . . . 125.00
2 thru 7 . . . . @100.00

DUNC & LOO
Dell Publishing Co., Oct.-Dec., 1961
1 . . . . 125.00
2 . . . . 100.00
3 thru 8 . . . . @75.00

Drunken–Edge

Spec.#1 . . . . 2.00

EARLY DAYS OF SOUTHERN KNIGHTS
Vol. 2 Graphic Novel. 5.00

EARTH 4
Continuity, 1993
[1st Series, Deathwatch 2000]
1 Deathwatch 2000 Pt.6,w/card . . . 2.50
2 Deathwatch 2000 Pt.11,w/card . . 2.50
3 V:Hellbenders, w/card. 2.50
[2nd Series]
1 WMc, ... 2.50
2 . . . . 2.50
3 . . . . 2.50

EAST MEETS WEST
Innovation
1 . . . . 2.50
2 . . . . 2.50
3 . . . . 2.50

EBONY WARRIOR
Africa Rising
1 I:Ebony Warrior 2.00

ECHO OF FUTUREPAST
Continuity, 1984–85
1 NA,MGo,I:Bucky O'Hare,
  Frankenstein 4.00
2 NA,MGo,A: Bucky O'Hare, Dracula,
  Werewolf. 3.50
3 NA,MGo,A:Bucky 3.50
4 NA,MGo,A:Bucky 3.50
5 NA,MGo,A:Drawla&Bucky. 3.50
6 Ath,B:Torpedo. 3.50
7 ATh 3.50
8 Ath, ... 3.25
9 Ath,Last issue. 3.25

ECLIPSE GRAPHIC NOVELS
Eclipse
1 Axa. 7.00
2 MR,I Am Coyote 7.00
3 DSt,Rocketeer 10.00
3a hard cover 40.00
4 Silver Heels 9.00
4a hard cover 40.00
5 Sisterhood of Steel 10.00
6 Zorro in Old Calif. 8.00

ECLIPSE MONTHLY
Eclipse, 1983–84
1 SD,DW,I:Static&Rio 2.00
2 GC,DW 2.00
3 thru 8 DW . . . . @2.00
9 DW. 2.00
10 DW. 2.00

EDGE
Malibu Bravura, 1994–95
1 GK,I:Edge 2.50
2 GK,STg,Gold Stamp. 2.50
3 GK,The Ultimates 2.50
4 GK,V:Mr. Ultimate. 2.50

EDGE
Crossgen Comics, 2002
TPB #1 224-page 9.95
TPB #2 256-page. 9.95

All comics prices listed are for Near Mint condition.

Edge–Elfquest / COLOR PUB. / Comics Values Annual

TPB #3 272-page 9.95
TPB #4 thru 8 . . . . @11.95
TPB #9 thru 13 192-page . . . . . . @7.95
becomes:

VECTOR
TPB #14 . . . . 7.95

EDGE OF CHAOS
Pacific, 1983
1 GM. 2.00
2 GM. 2.00
3 GM. 2.00

EIGHT LEGGED FREAKS
WildStorm/DC, July, 2002
Spec. movie adapt. 64-pg. 6.95

87th PRECINCT
Dell Publishing Co., April-June, 1962
1 BK 150.00
2 . . . . 125.00

EL CAZADOR
Crossgen Comics 2003
1 CDi,SEp 2.95
2 thru 3 CDi,SEp . . . . @2.95

ELEMENTALS
Comico, 1984–88
1 BWg,I:Destroyers 5.00
2 BWg 3.00
3 BWg 3.00
4 BWg 2.50
5 BWg 2.50
6 thru 12 BWg . . . . @2.00
13 thru 22 . . . . @2.00
23 thru 29 . . . . @2.00
Spec.#1 . . . . 2.00
Spec.#2 . . . . 2.00

[Second Series], 1989–94
1 . . . . 2.25
2 thru 4 . . . . @2.00
5 thru 28 . . . . @2.50
Spec.#1 Lingerie special. 2.95
GN The Natural Order, rep. 9.95
GN Death & Resurrection 12.95

[Third Series], 1995
1 R:Elementals, polybagged with
 Chrysalis promo card 2.50
2 R:Original Monolith, polybagged
 with Chrysalis promo card 2.50
3A Destroy the Shadowspear. . . . 2.50
3B variant cover 2.50
4 Memoirs,pt.1 . . . . 2.95
5 Memoirs,pt.2 . . . . 2.95
GN Ghost of a Chance 5.95
Spec. `Babes,' photo multimedia
 bikini special. 3.95
Spec. Hot Bikini Valentine. 3.95
Spec. All New Summer Special. . . 4.95
Spec.#1 Lingerie Metalite 3.95

ELEMENTALS: HOW THE WAR WAS ONE
Comico, 1996
1 thru 4 . . . . @2.95

ELEMENTALS: THE VAMPIRE'S REVENGE
Comico, 1996–97
1 thru 4 . . . . @2.95

ELEMENTALS VS. THE CHARNEL PRIESTS
Comico, 1996
Spec. 1 (of 2) 2.95
2 . . . . 2.95

ELEVEN OR ONE
Sirius, 1995
1 JLi 5.00

ELFLORD
Aircel, 1986–88
Volume 1: *See B&W*
Volume II
1 . . . . 3.50
2 . . . . 2.50
3 thru 20 . . . . @2.00
21 double size 4.95
22 thru 24 . . . . @2.00
Spec.#1 . . . . 2.00
25 thru 32, see B&W

ELFQUEST
Warp Graphics, 1998
TPB 20th Anniv. Special 8.95
TPB Scores, WPi, best of Elfquest
 stories 19.95

ELFQUEST: BLOOD OF TEN CHIEFS
Warp Graphics, 1993–95
1 WP 2.50
2 WP 2.50
3 WP,B:Swift Spear pt. 1 . . . . 2.50
4 WP,B:Swift Spear pt. 2 . . . . 2.50
5 V:Dinosaurs 2.50
6 Snowbeast 2.50
7 . . . . 2.50
8 Spirit Quest 2.50
9 Shadow Shifter. 2.50
10 Spheres pt. 1. . . . . 2.50
11 Spheres pt. 2. . . . . 2.50
12 . . . . 2.50
13 Forest 2.50
14 F:Mantricker 2.50
15 F:Bearclaw 2.50
16 Scar Vs. Bearclaw. 2.50
17 F:Eldolil,`Howl for Eldoril' 2.50
18 F:Finder. 2.50
19 F:Cutter & Skywise 2.50
20 final issue 2.50

ELFQUEST: HIDDEN YEARS
Warp Graphics
1 WP 3.00
2 WP, w/coupon promo. 2.75
3 WP, w/coupon promo.Cont.sty.
 previewed in Harbinger#11 . . . 3.25
4 WP,w/coupon 2.50
5 WP,O:Skywise 2.50
6 WP,F:Timmain 2.50
7 F:Timmain 2.50
8 Daughter's Day 2.50
9 WP(s),Enemy Face 2.50
9 1/2 WP,JBy,Holiday Spec. 3.50
10 thru 14 WP. . . . . @2.50
15 WP Wolfrider Tribe Splits 3.50
16 thru 18 WP 2.25
19 Mousehunt 2.25
20 F:Recognition 2.25
21 F:Teir, Messenger 2.50
22 F:Embu, Making a Point. 2.50
23 Not Wolf And Teir. 2.50
24 Magic Menace 2.50
25 B&W Wolfrider's Death 2.25
26 thru 29 B&W finale . . . . @2.25

ELFQUEST: JINK
Warp Graphics, 1994–96
1 Future 3.00
2 Future 2.50
3 Neverending Story 2.50
4 Neverending Story 2.50
5 V:True Sons, Hide and Seek. . . . 2.50
6 V:Truth Holder, Should Auld
 Acquaintance 2.50
7 F:Black Snakes 2.50
8 B&W V:Black Snakes 2.50
9 thru 12 . . . . 2.50

Elfquest: New Blook #17
© *Warp Graphics*

ELFQUEST: NEW BLOOD
Warp Graphics, 1992–96
1 JBy,artists try Elfquest 5.00
2 Barry Blair story 3.50
3 thru 5 . . . . @2.50
6 thru 24 . . . . @2.50
25 Forevergreen pt. 13. . . . . 2.50
26 V:Humans 2.50
27 V:Door. 2.50
28 I:Windkin, Triompe and Defeat. . 2.50
29 F:Windkin 2.50
30 V:Door. 2.50
31 F:The Wanderer 2.50
32 B&W Sorrow's End 2.50
33 thru 35 B&W 2.50
Summer Spec.1993 . . . . 4.25

ELFQUEST: THE REBELS
Warp Graphics, 1994–96
1 Aliens, set several hundred
 years in future 2.75
2 Escape. 2.50
3 He That Goes. 2.50
4 Reasons. 2.50
5 V:Skyward 2.50
6 F:Shimmer, The Edge. 2.50
7 . . . . 2.50
8 Squatters & Defenders 2.50
9 B&W Brother vs. Brother 2.50
10 thru 12 . . . . @2.50

ELFQUEST: SHARDS
Warp Graphics, 1994–96
1 Division 3.00
2 thru 5 . . . . @2.50
6 F:Two-Edge 2.50
7 F:Shuma 2.50
8 WP,Turnabout,pt.1 . . . . 2.50
9 WP,Turnabout,pt.2,V:Djun 2.50
10 Revelations,pt.1 . . . . 2.50
11 V:Humans 2.50
12 B&W F:High One Timmain 2.50
13 thru 16 B&W finale . . . . @2.50

ELFQUEST: WAVE DANCERS
Warp Graphics, 1993–96
1 Foil enhanced 3.25
2 thru 6 . . . . @2.50
Spec. #1 . . . . 3.00

ELIMINATOR COLOR SPECIAL
Eternity, 1991
1 DDo(c) set in the future 2.95

ELIMINATOR
Malibu Ultraverse, 1995
0 Man,DJa,MZ,Zothros tries to re-open passage to the Godwheel 2.95
1 MZ,Man,DRo, The Search for the Missing Infinity Gems,I:Siren . . 2.95
1a Black Cover ed. 3.95
2 MZ 2.50
3 MZ, Infinity Gem tie-in,finale . . . 2.50

ELRIC
Pacific, 1983–84
1 CR 4.00
2 CR 3.00
3 thru 6 CR . . . . @2.50

ELRIC
Topps, April, 1996
0 NGa,CPR, 'One Life,' based on Michael Moorcock character . . . 2.95

ELRIC, BANE OF THE BLACK SWORD
First, 1988–89
1 Michael Moorcock adapt. 2.00
2 . . . . 2.00
3 thru 5 . . . . @2.00

ELRIC, SAILOR ON THE SEAS OF FATE
First, 1985–86
1 Michael Moorcock adapt. 4.00
2 . . . . 3.00
3 thru 7 . . . . @2.00

ELRIC–VANISHING TOWER
First, 1987–88
1 Michael Moorcock adapt. 2.50
2 thru 6 . . . . @2.00

ELRIC, WEIRD OF THE WHITE WOLF
First, 1986–87
1 Michael Moorcock adapt. 3.00
2 thru 5 . . . . @2.00
Graphic Novel CR 7.00

ELVEN
Malibu Ultraverse, 1994
0 Rep.,A:Prime, double size 2.95
[Mini-Series] 1994–95
1 A:Prime, Primevil 2.50
2 AaL,R:Maxi-Man 2.50
3 AaL,V:Duey, Primevil 2.50
4 AaL,F:Primevil 2.50

E-Man #1
© Charlton Comics

E-MAN
Charlton Comics, 1973–75
1 JSon,O:E-Man 35.00
2 SD 20.00
3 . . . . 20.00
4 SD 20.00
5 SD,Miss Liberty Belle 20.00
6 JBy,Rog 2000 . . . . 20.00
7 JBy,Rog 2000 . . . . 20.00
8 J:Nova 25.00
9 JBy,Rog 2000 . . . . 20.00
10 JBy,Rog 2000 . . . . 20.00

E-MAN
First, 1983
1 JSon,O:E-Man & Nova, A:Rog 2000, 1 pg. JBy 2.50
2 JSon,I:F-Men (X-Men satire) 1-page Mike Mist 2.50
3 JSon, V:F-Men 2.50
4 JSon,Michael Mauser solo 2.50
5 JSon,I:Psychobabbler,A:Omaha, The Cat Dancer 2.50
6 JSon,O:E-Man,V:Feeder 2.50
7 JSon,V:Feeder 2.50
8 JSon,V:HotWax,A:CuteyBunny . . 2.50
9 JSon,I:Tyger Lili 2.50
10 JSon,O:Nova Kane pt.1 . . . . . . 2.50
11 JSon,O:Nova Kane pt.2 . . . . . . 2.50
12 JSon,A:Tyger Lili 2.50
13 JSon,V:Warp'sPrinceChaos . . . 2.50
14 JSon,V:Randarr 2.50
15 JSon,V:Samuel Boar 2.50
16 JSon,V:Samuel Boar 2.50
17 JSon,'Smeltquest' satire 2.50
18 JSon,'Rosemary..& Time' 2.50
19 JSon, 'Hoodoo Blues' 2.50
20 JSon,A:Donald Duke 2.50
21 JSon,A:B-Team,(satire) 2.50
22 JSon,A:Teddy Q. 2.50
23 JSon,A:TygerLili,B-Team 2.50
24 JSon,O:Michael Mauser 2.50
25 JSon,last issue 2.50
Spec. #1 . . . . 2.75

E-MAN
Comico, 1989–90
1 JSon 2.75
2 and 3 JSon . . . . @2.50

E-MAN
Alpha Productions, 1993
1 JSon 2.75

EMERGENCY
Charlton Comics, 1976
1 JSon(c),JBy 35.00
2 JSon 20.00
3 Thru 4 . . . . 20.00

ENCHANTED: THE AWAKENING
Sirius, 1998
1 by Robert Chang 2.95
2 . . . . 2.95
3 conclusion 2.95

ENGIN
Samson Comics
1 I:The Mesh 2.50

ENGINE
Shadow Planet, 2002
1 by Tim Tyler 3.50
1a signed sketch edition 9.95
2 thru 3 . . . . @2.95

ENSIGN O'TOOLE
Dell Publishing Co., Aug.-Oct., 1962
1 . . . . 35.00
2 . . . . 30.00

EPSILON WAVE
Independent
1 . . . . 3.00
2 . . . . 2.50
3 . . . . 2.25
4 . . . . 2.00
Elite Comics
5 thru 10 . . . . @2.00

ESC.(ESCAPE)
Comico, 1996
1 SPr 2.95
2 SPr 2.95
3 SPr 2.95
4 SPr 2.95
TPB SPr Rep. #1–#4 . . . . 14.95

ESC: NO EXIT
Comico, 1997
1 . . . . 2.95
1 medallion edition 9.95
2 . . . . 2.95

ESPERS
Eclipse, 1986
1 I:ESPers. 2.00
2 JBo(c),V:Terrorists 2.00
3 V:Terrorists 2.00
4 Beirut 2.00
5 'The Liquidators'. 2.00
6 V:Benito Giovanetti. 2.00

ESPIONAGE
Dell Publishing Co., May-July, 1964
1 . . . . 45.00
2 . . . . 35.00

ESTABLISHMENT, THE
WildStorm/DC, Sept., 2001
1 IEd,CAd,F:Charlie Arrows 2.50
2 IEd,CAd 2.50
3 IEd,CAd 2.50
4 IEd,CAd 2.50
5 IEd,CAd 2.50
6 IEd,CAd 2.50
7 IEd,CAd 2.50
8 IEd,CAd, in Russia 2.50
9 IEd,CAd, demon-god embryos . . 2.50
10 IEd,CAd, Charlie Arrows 2.50
11 IEd,CAd, DeadSpace. 2.50
12 IEd,CAd, Moonbase Straker. . . . 2.50
13 IEd,CAd, final issue 2.50

ETERNAL WARRIOR
Valiant 1992
1 FM(c),JDx,Unity #2,O:Eternal Warrior,Armstrong 3.00
1a Gold Ed. 4.00
1b Gold Foil Logo 5.00
2 WS(c),JDx,Unity #10,A:Solar, Harbinger,Eternal Warrior of 4001. . . . . 2.50
3 JDx,V:Armstrong,I:Astrea 2.50
4 JDx(i),I:Caldone, C:Bloodshot . . . 2.50
5 JDx,I:Bloodshot,V:Iwatsu's Men . 2.50
6 BWS,JDx,V:Master Darque. 2.50
7 BWS,V:Master Darque, D:Uncle Buck 2.50
8 BWS,as Archer & Armstrong #8 Three Musketeers,I:Ivar 2.50
9 MMo,JDx,B:Book of the Geomancer 2.50
10 JDx,E:Bk. o/t Geomancer. 2.50
11 B:KVH(s),JDx(i), V:Neo-Nazis . . 2.50
12 JDx(i),V:Caldone 2.50
13 MMo,JDx(i),V:Caldone, A:Bloodshot 2.50
14 E:KVH(s),MMo,V:Caldone, A:Geoff. 2.50
15 YG,A:Bloodshot,V:Tanaka 2.50
16 YG,A:Bloodshot. 2.50
17 A:Master Darque 2.50
18 C:Doctor Mirage 2.50
19 KVH(s),TeH,A:Doctor Mirage . . 2.50
20 KVH(s),Access Denied 2.50
21 KVH(s),TeH,V:Dr. Steiner. 2.50
22 V:Master Darque,w/Valiant Era Card. 2.50
23 KVH(s),TeH,Blind Fate. 2.50
24 KVH(s),TeH,V:Immortal Enemy . 2.50
25 MBn(s),A:Archer,Armstrong 2.50
26 Double(c), Chaos Effect-Gamma #4, A:Archer, Armstrong, Ivar . . 3.00
27 JOs(s). 2.25
28 War on Drugs 2.25
29 Immortal Enemy 2.25
30 Lt. Morgan. 2.25
31 JD,JOs 2.25
32 . . . . 2.25
33 Mortal Kin,pt.1 . . . . 2.25

Eternal Warrior #16
© Valiant

34 Mortal Kin,pt.2 . . . . 2.25
35 Mortal Kin Finale 2.50
36 Fenris League 2.50
37 Youthful Tale 2.50
38 V:Niala, The Dead Queen 2.50
39 JOs,JG,PG(c),V:body thieves. . . 2.50
40 JOs,JG,PG(c),finds organ farm . 2.50
41 War in Herznia. 2.50
42 I: Brisbane. 2.50
43 V:Neo Nazi 2.50
44 V:Neo Nazi 2.50
45 R:Fenris Society 2.50
46 V:Fenris Society 2.50
47 Jihad. 2.50
48 Immortal Life in Danger 2.50
49 JOs,JG,Hallucinations 2.50
50 . . . . 2.50
Yearbook #1 . . . . 4.25
Yearbook #2 . . . . 4.00
Wings of Justice WWI 2.50
Quarterly
Time and Treachery 3.95
Digital Alchemy. 3.95
Spec. Blackworks AHo 4.00

ETERNAL WARRIORS
Acclaim 1997 (Quarterly)
Archer & Armstrong AHo. 3.95
Mog AHo 3.95
The Immortal Enemy AHo. 3.95

ETERNITY SMITH
Hero
1 . . . . 2.00
2 . . . . 2.00
3 . . . . 2.00
4 Knightshade solo 2.00
5 Knightshade solo 2.00
6 . . . . 2.00
7 . . . . 2.00
8 I:Indigo. 2.00
9 A:Walter Koenig 2.00
10 . . . . 2.00
Heroic Publishing
1 Man Vs. Machine 2.00
2 Man Vs. Machine 2.00

EVA THE IMP
Red Top Comic/Decker, 1957
1 . . . . 35.00
2 . . . . 30.00

EVANGELINE
Comico, 1984
1 Guns of Mars 4.00
2 . . . . 3.00
Lodestone, 1986
1 . . . . 2.50
2 . . . . 2.50
First, 1988
1 . . . . 3.00
2 thru 9 . . . . @2.00
10 . . . . 2.00
11 . . . . 2.00
12 . . . . 2.00

EVERQUEST
WildStorm/DC, Dec., 2001
GN The Ruins of Kunark, JLe 5.95
GN Transformation 5.95

EVERYTHING'S ARCHIE
Archie Publications, May, 1969
1 . . . . 125.00
2 . . . . 75.00
3 thru 5 . . . . @50.00
6 thru 10 . . . . @35.00
11 thru 20 . . . . @25.00
21 thru 40 . . . . @15.00
41 thru 134 . . . . @10.00

EVIL ERNIE
See: B&W

EVIL ERNIE (THE SERIES)
Chaos! Comics, 1998
1 V:Purgatori 3.00
2 Search for Chastity, A:Savior . . . 3.00
3 V:Purgatori 3.00
4 return to New Jersey 3.00
5 two beings 3.00
6 heart of America 3.00
7 Unholy Nights. 3.00
8 Trauma,pt.1 . . . . 3.00
9 Trauma,pt.2 . . . . 3.00
10 Trauma,pt.3 . . . . 3.00

EVIL ERNIE: DEPRAVED
Chaos! Comics, 1999
1 (of 3) 4.00
1a premium edition 10.00
2 . . . . 3.00
3 . . . . 3.00

EVIL ERNIE: DESTROYER
Chaos! Comics, 1997
Prev.#1 . . . . 3.00
1 (of 9) BnP. 3.00
2 BnP 3.00
3 to Atlanta 3.00
4 siege of Atlanta. 3.00
5 . . . . 3.00
6 Nuclear launch codes 3.00
7 Nuclear attack 3.00
8 Nuclear attack continues. 3.00
9 New forms of living dead, concl. . 3.00

EVIL ERNIE: REVENGE
Chaos! Comics, 1994–95
1 SHu,BnP,A:LadyDeath,glow(c) . . 7.00
1a limited, glow-in-the-dark (c) . . 20.00
1a Commemorative edition 15.00
2 SHu,BnP,Loses Smiley 6.00
3 SHu,BnP,V:Dr. Price 5.00
4 SHu,BnP,Final Issue 5.00

COLOR PUB.

Evil–Famous

TPB Rep. #1-#4 . . . . 12.95
TPB Revenge #2, signed 20.00

EVIL ERNIE: STRAIGHT TO HELL
Chaos! Comics, 1995–96
1 Rampage in Hell, coffin(c). 4.00
1 limited, chromium edition 17.00
2 Cremator 4.00
3 . . . . 4.00
3a Chastity (c). 17.00
4 and 5 . . . . @4.00
Ashcan. 1.50
Spec. 17.00

EVIL ERNIE: THE RESURRECTION
Chaos! Comics, 1993–94
1 R:Evil Ernie 15.00
1a gold edition. 35.00
2 Enhanced Cover. 11.00
3 `Massive Mayhem' Lady Death poster. 11.00
4 final issue, extra pages 11.00
TPB Rep. #1-#4 . . . . 14.95
Ashcan Resurrection (2001) 20.00

EVIL ERNIE VS. THE MOVIE MONSTERS
Chaos! Comics
1 one-shot 3.00
1 omega edition 5.00
1 premium edition, signed 15.00

EVIL ERNIE VS. THE SUPER-HEROES
Chaos! Comics, 1995
1 one-shot 3.50
1a foil (c). 30.00
1b limited. 10.00
Spec. #2 by Hart Fisher & Steve Butler 3.00
Spec. #2, Premium edition 10.00

EVIL ERNIE: WAR OF THE DEAD
Chaos! Comics, 1999
1 (of 3) 3.00
1a premium 10.00
2 . . . . 3.00
3 concl. 3.00

EVIL ERNIE'S BADDEST BATTLES
Chaos! Comics, 1996
1-shot, imaginary battles 2.00

EXECUTIONER
Innovation, 1993
1 Don Pendleton(s),F:Mack Bolan . 3.95
1a Collector's Gold Ed. 2.95
1b Tyvek cover 3.95
2 War against Mafia. 2.75
3 War against Mafia,pt.2 . . . . 2.75

EXEMPLARS
1 and 2 . . . . @2.00

Exiles #2
© Malibu

EXILES
Malibu Ultraverse, 1993
1 TMs(s),PaP,I:Exiles. 4.00
1a w/out card 2.25
1b Gold hologram ed. 10.00
1c Ultra-limited 12.00
2 V:Kort. 3.00
3 BWS,Mastodon,BU:Rune 4.00
4 V:Kort. 3.00

EX-MUTANTS
Malibu Nov., 1992–Apr. 1994
1 I&O:Ex-Mutants 2.25
2 V:El Motho,Beafcake,Brickhouse 2.25
3 A:Sliggo,Zygote 2.25
4 . . . . 2.25
5 Piper Kidnapped. 2.25
6 A:Dr.Kildare 2.25
7 V:Dr.Kildare 2.25
8 O:Gelson 2.25
9 F:Dillion 2.25
10 F:Sluggtown 2.25
11 Man(s),Genesis#1,w/card. . . . 2.25
12 R0M(s),Genesis#4 . . . . 2.25
13 J:Gravestone,Arc. 2.25
14 C:Eye 2.25
15 A:Arrow 2.50
16 A:Arrow,I:KillCorp. 2.50
17 A:Arrow,V:KillCorp 2.50
18 A:Arrow,V:KillCorp 2.50

EXODUS, THE
Conquest Comics
1 V:Aliens 2.50

EXO-SQUAD
Topps, 1994
[Mini-Series]
0 . . . . 2.00
1 From Animated Series 2.50
2 F:Nara Burns 2.50
3 V:Neo-Sapiens 2.50

EXPLORERS
Explorer Press, 1995
1 I:Explorers 2.95
2 The Cellar 2.95

EXPOSURE SPECIAL
Avatar Press, 2000
1 . . . . 3.50
1a photo(c) 3.50

EXPOSURE: SECOND COMING
Avatar Press, 2000
1 (of 2) Angel (c) 40-page 5.00

EXTINCTIONERS
Vision Comics, 1998
1 by Shawntae Howard & Malcolm Earle 3.95
2 . . . . 3.95

EXTINCTION EVENT
Wildstorm/DC July 2003
1 (of 5) BBh,humans vs. dinos. . . . 2.50
2 thru 5 BBh . . . . @2.50

EXTREMES VIOLET
Blackout Comics, 1995
0 I:Violet 2.95
Becomes:

EXTREMES OF VIOLET
Blackout Comics, 1995
1 V:Drug Lords 2.95
2 A:Matt Chaney 2.95

EXTRA
Gemstone, 1999
1 (of 5) 2.50
2 . . . . 2.50
3 . . . . 2.50
4 . . . . 2.50
5 final issue. 2.50
`Annuals'
TPB Vol. 1 . . . . 13.50

EYE OF THE STORM
Rival Productions
1 I:Killian, Recon, Finesse, Stray . . 2.95
2 Conspiracy. 2.95
3 3-D Comic Background. 2.95
4 F:Recon 2.95
5 Sinclair & Rott 2.95
Ann. 48-pg. 4.95

FALCON, THE
Aircel
Spec. #1. 2.00

FAMILY AFFAIR
Gold Key, Feb., 1970
1 W/Poster,Ph(c) 85.00
2 . . . . 35.00
3 Ph(c) 40.00
4 Ph(c) 40.00

FAMILY MATTER
Kitchen Sink, 1998
GN by Will Eisner 16.00

FAMOUS INDIAN TRIBES
Dell Publishing Co., July-Sept., 1962
1 . . . . 30.00
2 . . . . 15.00

FANG
Sirius
1 V:Vampires, I:Fang 4.00
2 5 .... 3.25
3 V:The Master 2.95

FANTASTIC VOYAGES OF SINBAD, THE
Gold Key, Oct., 1965
1 Ph(c) 75.00
2 June, 1967 .... 65.00

FANTASY FEATURES
AC Comics, 1987
1 .... 2.00
2 .... 2.00

FARSCAPE: WAR TORN
WildStorm/DC, Oct., 2001
1 (of 2) MWm, F:John Crichton ... 4.95
2 MWm,48-page 4.95

FASHION IN ACTION
Eclipse
Summer Special #1 .... 2.00
Winter Special #1 .... 2.00

FAT ALBERT
Gold Key, 1974–79
1 .... 40.00
2 thru 10 .... @25.00
11 thru 29 .... @20.00

FATALE
Broadway, 1995
1 thru 6 JJo, `Inherit the Earth,' pt.5 .... @2.95
7 Fatale now Queen of the World . 2.95
8 `Crown of Thorns,' pt.1 .... 2.95
9 `Crown of Thorns,' pt.3 .... 2.95
TPB Inherit the Earth 14.95

FATE'S FIVE
Innervision, 1998
1 (of 4) 2.50
1 variant cover 2.50
2 (of 4) 2.50
3 (of 4) 2.50

FATHOM
Comico, 1987
1 thru 3 From Elementals ...... @2.50
[2nd Series], 1993
1 thru 3 .... @2.50

FATMAN, THE HUMAN FLYING SAUCER
Lightning Comics, April, 1967
1 CCB,O:Fatman & Tin Man 90.00
2 CCB 60.00
3 CCB,(Scarce) 65.00

FAUST: BOOK OF M
Avatar Press, 1999
1 (of 3) DQ,TV. 3.95
1a (of 3) prism foil (c) 12.95
1b signed, leather cover 20.00
1c Royal Blue edition 75.00
2 .... 3.95
3 .... 3.95

COLOR PUB.

FAZE ONE
AC Comics
1 .... 2.00

FAZE ONE FAZERS
AC Comics
1 .... 5.00
2 .... 3.00
3 thru 6 .... @2.00

FEARBOOK
Eclipse
1 SBi,RV,`A Dead Ringer' 2.00

FELIX THE CAT
Harvey
1 thru 4 .... @2.00
5 thru 7 .... @2.00

FELIX THE CAT: THE MOVIE
Felix Comics, 1998
1-shot, issued a mere 10 years after movie 3.95

Felix's Nephews Inky & Dinky #7
© Harvey Publications

FELIX'S NEPHEWS INKY & DINKY
Harvey Publications, Sept., 1957
1 .... 100.00
2 thru 7 .... @50.00

FEM 5
Entity, 1995
1 thru 4 five-part series ...... @2.95
1 signed & numbered 12.95

FEMFORCE
AC Comics
1 O:Femforce 8.00
2 A:Captain Paragon 4.00
3 `Skin Game' 3.50
4 `Skin Game' 3.50
5 Back in the Past 3.50
6 EL,Back in the Past 3.50
7 HB,O:Captain Paragon 3.50
8 V:Shade 3.50
9 V:Dr.Rivits 3.50
10 V:Dr.Rivits 3.50
11 D:Haunted Horsemen 3.00
12 V:Dr.Rivits 3.00
13 V:She-Cat 3.00
14 V:Alizarin Crimson 3.00
15 V:Alizarin Crimson 3.00
16 thru 56 See Black & White Pub.
57 V:Goat God 2.75
58 I:New Sentinels 2.75
59 I:Paragon. 2.75
60 V:Sentinels 2.75
61 F:Tara 2.75
62 V:Valkyra 2.75
63 I:Rayda 2.75
64 thru 67 .... @2.75
68 `Spellbound' 2.75
69 `She-Cat Possessed' 2.75
70 `Island Out of Time' 2.75
71 .... 2.75
72 w/Sentinels of Justice 4.00
72a no extras 3.00
73 w/Compact Comic 4.00
73a Regular edition 3.00
74 Daughter of Darkness 4.00
74a Regular edition 3.00
75 Gorby Poster 5.00
75a Regular edition 3.00
76 Daughters pt. 3, polybagged with Compact Comic 4.00
76a no bag or comic 3.00
77 V:Sea Monster 3.00
78 V:Gorgana, bagged with comic . 5.00
78a no bag or comic 3.00
79 V:Iron Jaw, polybagged with Index 5.00
79a no bag or index 3.00
80 polybagged with Index 6.00
80a F:Mr. Brimstone, Rad 3.00
81 polybagged with Index 6.00
81a Valentines Day Spec. 3.00
82 polybagged with Index 6.00
82a F:Ms. Victory 3.00
83 F:Paragon 3.00
84 The Death of Joan Wayne polybagged with index #4B ... 6.00
84a no bag or index 3.00
85 Synn vs. Narett, polybagged with card 5.00
85a no bag or card 3.00
86 polybagged with index #5 .... 5.00
86a unbagged, no suplements ... 3.00
87 Pandemonium in Paradise, polybagged with plate 10.00
87a unbagged, no plate 3.00
88 F:Garganta, polybagged with index #6 .... 6.00
88a unbagged, no index 3.00
89 polybagged with index 6.00
89a unbagged, no index 3.00
90 polybagged with index 6.00
90a unbagged, no index 3.00
91 polybagged with index 6.00
91a unbagged, no index 3.00
92 polybagged with index 6.00
92a unbagged, no index 3.00
93 on see Black & White Pub.
Spec.#1 .... 2.00
Untold Origin Spec #1 .... 4.95

FEMFORCE: UP CLOSE
AC Comics, 1992–95
1 F:Stardust 3.00
2 F:Stardust 3.00
3 .... 3.00
4 .... 3.00
5 with Sticker 4.00
5a Regular Edition 3.00
6 with Sticker 4.00
6a Regular Edition 3.00
7 with Sticker 4.00

Comics Values Annual — COLOR PUB. — Femforce–Flare

```
7a Regular Edition............. 3.00
8 with Sticker................. 4.00
8a Regular Edition............. 3.00
9 thru 11 ..................... @3.00
```

FENRY
Raven Publications
```
1 ............................. 6.95
1a Platinum Ed................. 15.00
```

FERRET
Malibu 1992
```
1 (From Protectors),DZ,V:Purple
   Dragon Tong,A:Iron Skull .... 2.25
```
[Regular Series] 1992–93
```
1 thru 3 ...................... 2.50
4 V:Toxin ..................... 2.50
4a Newstand ed. ............... 2.25
5 SEr,Genesis ................. 2.25
6 SEr,Genesis crossover ....... 2.25
7 V:Airman .................... 2.25
8 I:Posse ..................... 2.25
9 DZ,R:Iron Skull,I:Deathsong . 2.25
10 DZ ......................... 2.25
11 ............................ 2.25
```

FIGHT THE ENEMY
Tower Comics, Aug., 1966
```
1 BV,Lucky 7 .................. 50.00
2 AMc ......................... 40.00
3 WW,AMc ...................... 40.00
```

FIGHTING AMERICAN
Harvey, 1966
```
1 SK,Rep Fighting American
   from 1950's ................ 75.00
```

Fighting American #1
© Awesome Entertainment

FIGHTING AMERICAN
Awesome Entertainment
```
1 ............................. 5.00
1a variant (c) ................ 4.00
1b Platinum (c) ............... 15.00
2 ............................. 4.00
Coll.Ed.#1 rep.#1–#2 .......... 5.00
Spec.#1 Fighting American: Cold War
   RLe,JLb .................... 2.50
```

COLOR PUB.

FIGHTING AMERICAN: DOGS OF WAR
Awesome Entertainment, 1998
```
1 JSn,SPa,F:John Flagg ........ 2.50
1a Tour Edition, RLe cover .... 5.00
1b Tour Edition, signed ....... 12.00
2 JSn,SPa,other super-soldiers. 2.50
2a variant cover .............. 2.50
3 A:Crimson Dragon ............ 2.50
4 Who is No Name? ............. 2.50
Spec.'98 Con preview,b&w,16-page 5.00
```

FIGHTING AMERICAN: RULES OF THE GAME
Awesome Entertainment, 1997
```
1 JLb ......................... 3.00
2 JLb ......................... 2.50
3 JLb, Baby Buzz Bomber ....... 2.50
TPB ........................... 13.00
```

FIREARM
Malibu Ultraverse, 1993–95
```
0 w/video,I:Duet .............. 3.00
1 I:Firearm,Alec Swan ......... 2.50
1 silver foil, limited edition. 4.00
2 BWS,A:Hardcase,BU:Rune ...... 2.75
3 V:Sportsmen ................. 2.25
4 HC,Break-Thru x-over ........ 2.25
5 O:Prime,I:Ellen ............. 2.25
6 A:Prime ..................... 2.25
7 V:Killer .................... 2.25
8 DIB(c) ...................... 2.25
9 at the Rose Bowl ............ 2.25
10 The Lodge .................. 2.25
11 Ultraverse Premier #5,BU:Prime 3.50
12 Rafferty Saga,pt.1 ......... 2.25
13 Rafferty Saga,pt.2 ......... 2.25
14 Swan ....................... 2.25
15 Rafferty Saga,pt.3 ......... 2.25
16 Rafferty Saga,pt.4 ......... 2.25
17 Rafferty Saga,pt.5 ......... 2.25
18 JeR,HC(c),Rafferty Saga,finale 2.50
```

FIRST, THE
Crossgen Comics, Nov., 2000
```
1 BKs,BS ...................... 4.00
2 thru 13 BKs,BS .............. @3.50
14 thru 25 .................... @3.00
26 thru 36 .................... @3.00
37 Atwaal returns ............. 3.00
TPB Vol. 1 192-page ........... 20.00
TPB Vol. 2 rep. #8–#13 ........ 19.95
TPB Vol. 3 Sinister Motives ... 15.95
```

FIRST ADVENTURES
First
```
1 thru 5 ...................... @2.00
```

FIRST GRAPHIC NOVELS
First 1984
```
1 JBi,Beowolf ................. 8.00
1a 2nd Printing ............... 7.00
2 TT,Time Beavers ............. 10.00
3 HC,American Flag Hard Times . 12.00
4 Nexus,SR .................... 10.00
5 Elric,CR .................... 20.00
6 Enchanted Apples of Oz ...... 6.00
7 Secret Island of Oz ......... 10.00
8 HC,Time 2 ................... 28.00
9 TMNT ........................ 20.00
10 TMNT II .................... 18.00
11 Sailor on the Sea .......... 15.00
12 HC,American Flagg .......... 12.00
```

```
13 Ice Ring ................... 10.00
14 TMNT III ................... 14.00
15 Hex Breaker ................ 10.00
16 Forgotten Forest ........... 11.00
17 Mazinger ................... 11.00
18 TMNT IV .................... 13.00
19 O;Nexus .................... 10.00
20 American Flagg ............. 12.00
```

1st FOLIO
Pacific, 1984
```
1 Joe Kubert School ........... 2.00
```

FIRST WAVE: HEART OF A KILLER
Andromeda Entertainment, 2000
```
1 by Dan Parsons, TV tie-in ... 3.00
1a photo (c) .................. 3.00
2 ............................. 4.00
2a photo (c) .................. 4.00
2b signed ..................... 10.00
2c sketch edition ............. 20.00
TPB Vol. 1 Heart of a Killer .. 8.95
```

FIRST WAVE: IN THE BEGINNING
Andromeda Entertainment, 2001
```
1 ............................. 3.00
1a photo (c) .................. 3.00
```

FIRST WAVE: JORDAN RADCLIFFE
Andromeda Entertainment, 2001
```
1 painted (c) ................. 3.00
1a photo (c) .................. 3.00
1b limited foil (c) ........... 10.00
```

FISH POLICE
Comico, 1987
```
Vol 2 #6 thru #15 rep ......... @2.50
Vol 2 #16 rep ................. 3.00
Vol 2 #17 rep.,AuA ............ 3.00
1 Color Special (July 1987) ... 3.50
```

FIST OF THE NORTH STAR
Gutsoon! Entertainment 2003
```
TPB Vol.1 & 2 The Master Edition
   ........................... @14.75
TPB Vol.3 thru 7 Master Edition @17.95
```

FLAMEHEAD
JNCO Comics, 1998
```
1 I:Flamehead ................. 2.00
2 thru 5 ...................... @2.00
```

FLARE
Hero Graphics
```
1 I:Darkon&Prof.Pomegranite ... 4.00
2 Blonde Bombshell,A:Galooper . 3.00
3 I:Sky Marshall .............. 3.00
Ann.#1 ........................ 4.50
```
[2nd Series]
```
1 A:Galloping Galooper ........ 3.00
2 A:Lady Arcane ............... 3.00
3 I:Britannia ................. 3.00
4 A:Indigo .................... 2.50
5 R:Eternity Smith,O:Die Kriegerin 3.95
```

All comics prices listed are for Near Mint condition.

Flare–Force / COLOR PUB. / Comics Values Annual

6 I:Tigress 3.50
7 V:The Enemies 3.95
8 Morrigan Wars#4,A:Icicle Dragon 3.50
9 Morrigan Wars Pt.7 (B&W) 3.50

FLARE ADVENTURES
Hero Graphics, 1992
1 rep. 2.95
2 flipbook w/Champions Classics . . 2.95
3 flipbook w/Champions Classics . . 2.95
Becomes: B&W

FLASH GORDON
Gold Key, June, 1965
1 . . . . 75.00

FLASH GORDON
King, 1966–69
1 AW,DH,A:Mandrake 90.00
1a Comp. Army giveaway 60.00
2 FBe,A:Mandrake,R:Ming. 50.00
3 RE,"Lost in the Land of
  The Lizardmen" 55.00
4 AW,B:Secret Agent X-9 . . . . 60.00
5 AW 60.00
6 RC,On the Lost Continent
  of Mongo 55.00
7 MR, rep. `In the Human Forest'. 55.00
8 RC,JAp. 55.00
9 AR,rep 60.00
10 AR,rep. 60.00
11 RC 50.00
Charlton, 1969–70
12 RC. 40.00
13 JJ 40.00
14 . . . . 30.00
15 . . . . 30.00
16 . . . . 30.00
17 Brick Bradford story 30.00
18 MK,`Attack of the Locust Men'. 30.00
Gold Key, Oct.-Nov., 1975
19 Flash returns to Mongo 15.00
20 thru 30 . . . . @10.00
31 thru 37 AW movie adapt. . . . . @8.00

FLATLINE COMICS
Flatline Comics
1 Three stories River Prairie 2.50

Flesh & Bones 32
© *UpShot*

FLAXEN: ALTER EGO
Caliber
1 V:Dark Flaxen. 2.95

FLESH AND BONES
UpShot, 1986
1 Moore 2.50
2 thru 4 Moore . . . . @2.00

FLINTSTONES
Harvey
1 . . . . 2.00
2 Romeo and Juliet 2.00

FLINTSTONES
Archie, 1995
1 thru 10 . . . . @2.00
11 thru 14 . . . . @2.00
15 `Frankenstone's Monster'. 2.00
20 `An Heir-Raising Tale' 2.00
21 `King Fred The Last' 2.00
22 `Something Gruesome This
  Way Comes'. 2.00

FLINTSTONES, THE
**Dell Publishing Co.,
Nov.-Dec., 1961**
#1 *see Dell Giant*
2 . . . . 165.00
3 . . . . 100.00
4 . . . . 100.00
5 and 6 . . . . @75.00
Gold Key
7 . . . . 100.00
8 A:Mr.& Mrs J. Evil Scientists . . 75.00
9 A:Mr.& Mrs.J. Evil Scientists . . 75.00
10 A:Mr.& Mrs.J. Evil Scientists. . 75.00
11 I:Pebbles 125.00
12 `The Too-Old Cowhand' 65.00
13 thru 15 . . . . @65.00
16 I:Bamm-Bamm. 125.00
17 thru 20 . . . . @65.00
21 thru 23. . . . . @50.00
24 I:Gruesomes 55.00
25 thru 29 . . . . @50.00
30 `Dude Ranch Roundup' 50.00
31 Christmas(c) 50.00
32 . . . . 40.00
33 A:Dracula & Frankenstein 50.00
34 I:The Great Gazoo. 100.00
35 . . . . 40.00
36 `The Man Called Flintstone' . . 40.00
37 thru 40 . . . . @40.00
41 thru 60 . . . . @40.00

FLINTSTONES, THE
Charlton Comics, 1970
1 . . . . 125.00
2 . . . . 60.00
3 thru 7 . . . . @40.00
8 Summer Vacation 75.00
9 . . . . 40.00
10 . . . . 40.00
11 thru 20 . . . . @35.00
21 thru 50 . . . . @30.00

FLINTSTONES IN 3-D
Blackthorne
1 thru 5 . . . . @2.50

FLIPPER
Gold Key, April, 1966
1 Ph(c) from TV series. 100.00
2 and 3 Ph(c). . . . . @65.00

FLOOD RELIEF
Malibu Ultraverse, 1994
TPB Ultraverse Heroes 5.00

FLY IN MY EYE EXPOSED
Eclipse
1 JJo(c),"Our Visitor" 4.95

FLY, THE
Archie/Red Circle, 1983
1 JSn,A:Mr.Justice. 2.00
2 thru 9 RB,SD . . . . @2.00

FLYING SAUCERS
Dell, April, 1967
1 . . . . 75.00
2 thru 5 . . . . @40.00

FLYMAN
**Archie Publications
{Prev: Adventures of the Fly}**
31 I:Shield (Bill Higgins), A:Comet,
  Black Hood. 60.00
32 I:Mighty Crusaders. 50.00
33 A:Mighty Crusaders, R:Hangman
  Wizard 50.00
34 MSy,A:Black Hood,Shield,Comet
  Shield back-up story begins . . 45.00
35 O:Black Hood 45.00
36 O:Web,A:Hangman in Shield
  strip 45.00
37 A:Shield. 45.00
38 A:Web 40.00
39 A:Steel Sterling 40.00

FOES
Ram Comics
1 TheMaster's Game 2.00
2 TheMaster's Game #2 . . . . 2.00

FOODANG
Aug. House
1 I:Foodang 2.00
1a Signed, Foil cover 2.50
2 I:Maude 2.50
3 V:Undead Clown Man. 2.50
4 V:Executioner 2.50

FOOTSOLDIERS
Maximum Press, 1996
1 KJo,PhH, ... 2.75

FOOZLE
Eclipse, 1985
1 . . . . 2.50

FORBIDDEN PLANET
Innovation, 1992
1 Movie Adapt 2.50
2 Movie adapt.contd. 2.50
3 Movie adapt.contd. 2.50
4 Movie adapt.concl. 2.50
GN rep.#1–#4 (1997) 8.95

FORCE OF THE BUDDHA'S PALM
Jademan
1 . . . . 3.00
2 . . . . 2.25

All comics prices listed are for Near Mint condition.

COLOR PUB.

3 thru 10 . . . . @2.00
11 thru 24 . . . . @2.00
25 V:Maskman 2.00
26 V:Maskman 2.00
27 A:SmilingDemon 2.00
28 Maskman v 10 Demons 2.00
29 Giant Bat 2.00
30 . . . . 2.00
31 . . . . 2.00
32 'White Crane Villa' 2.00
33 Devilito defeats White Crane
 & Giant Bat 2.00
34 Samsun vs. Devilito 2.00
35 Samsun vs. Devilito 2.00
36 Samsun vs. Devilito 2.00
37 D:Galacial Moon 2.00
38 Persian Elders, Iron Boy 2.00
39 V:Mad Gen.,White Crane,
 Iron Boy 2.00
40 D:Heaven & Earth Elders 2.00
41 thru 43 . . . . @2.00
44 D:White Crane 2.95
45 V:Iron Boy 2.00
46 thru 48 . . . . @2.00
49 Iron Boy vs Sainted Jade 2.00
50 Iron Boy & The Holy Blaze 2.00
51 D:Aquarius 2.00
52 V:Son o/t Gemini Lord 2.00
53 Nine Continent's return to
 full powers 2.00

4-D MONKEY
Dr. Leung's, 1988–90
1 thru 11 . . . . @2.00

FOREVER WAR, THE
NBM
GN Vol. 1 Joe Haldeman adapt. . . . 8.95
GN Vol. 2 Joe Haldeman adapt. . . . 8.95
GN Vol. 3 Joe Haldeman adapt. . . . 8.95

FORGE
Crossgen Comics, 2002
TPB #1 224-page 9.95
TPB #2 256-page 9.95
TPB #3 272-page 9.95
TPB #4 thru #8 . . . . @11.95
TPB #9 thru #16 192-page . . . . . @7.95

FOXFIRE
Malibu Ultraverse, 1996
1 From Phoenix Resurrection 2.25
2 Fate of Mastodon revealed 2.25
3 & 4 . . . . @1.50

FRANK
Nemesis, 1994
1 thru 4 DGc(s),GgP . . . . @2.50
1a thru 4a variant(c) . . . . @2.50

FRANKENSTEIN
Malibu
1 thru 3 movie promo . . . . @2.50

FRANK FRAZETTA
FANTASY ILLUSTRATED
Frank Frazetta, 1998
1 . . . . 6.00
1a variant cover 8.00
3 . . . . 6.00
3 Neil Gaiman signed &
 numbered 24.95
3 Daniel signed & numbered 19.95
4 thru 9 . . . . @6.00

FRANK FRAZETTA
DEATH DEALER
Verotik, 1997
1 thru 4 by Glenn Danzig . . . . . @6.95

FRANK IN THE RIVER
Tundra
1 Avery/Jones style cartoons 2.95

FRANK MERRIWELL
AT YALE
Charlton Comics, 1955–56
1 . . . . 60.00
2 thru 4 . . . . @40.00

FRANK MILLER'S
ROBOCOP
Avatar Press/Pulsar Press 2003
1 . . . . 3.50
1b robosteel (c) 14.95
2 thru 5 . . . . @3.50
1a thru 5a wraparound (c) . . . . . @3.95

FRANKENSTEIN
Dell Publishing Co., 1964
1 . . . . 75.00
2 . . . . 40.00
3 and 4 . . . . @30.00

FRANKENSTEIN
Caliber
Novel Adaptation 2.95

FRANKENSTEIN
Topps, 1994
1 thru 4 . . . . @3.00

FRANKENSTEIN
DRACULA WAR
Topps
1 Frank Vs. Drac 2.50
2 F:Saint Germaine 2.50
3 Frank Vs. Drac 2.50

FREDDY
Dell Publishing Co., 1963
1 . . . . 35.00
2 and 3 . . . . @20.00

FREDDY'S DEAD:
THE FINAL NIGHTMARE
Innovation
1 Movie adaption, Pt.1 . . . . 2.50
2 Movie adaption, Pt.2 . . . . 2.50
GN Movie Adapt. 6.95
3-D Special 2.50

FREEMIND
Future Comics 2003
5 and 6 . . . . @3.50
7 thru 13 . . . . @3.00
TPB Origin of Freemind 16.95

FREEX
Malibu Ultraverse, 1993–95
1 I:Freex w/Ultraverse card 3.00
1a Ultra-Limited 4.00
1b Full Hologram(c) 5.00

Freex #4
© Malibu

2 L:Valerie,I:Rush 3.00
3 A:Rush 3.00
4 GJ(s),DdW,BWS,BU:Rune 2.75
5 GJ(s),V:Master of the Hunt 2.50
6 GJ(s),BH,Break Thru x-over,
 A:Night Man 2.25
7 BHr,MZ,O:Hardcase 2.25
8 BHr,V:Lost Angel 2.25
9 BHr,A:Old Man 2.25
10 BHr,V:Ms. Contrary 2.25
11 BHr,E:Origins 2.25
12 GJ,Ultraforce 2.00
13 New look 2.00
14 R:Boomboy 2.00
15 Death of Teamate 3.50
16 Prelude to Godwheel 2.00
17 A:Rune 2.50
18 GJ,A:Contray, Cayman, Juice . . 2.50
Giant Size#1 A:Prime 2.50

FRIDAY FOSTER
Dell Publishing Co., Oct., 1972
1 . . . . 40.00

FRIENDLY GHOST
CASPER, THE
Harvey Publications, 1958
1 . . . . 500.00
2 . . . . 200.00
3 thru 10 . . . . @125.00
11 thru 20 . . . . @100.00
21 thru 30 . . . . @75.00
31 thru 50 . . . . @60.00
51 thru 100 . . . . @40.00
101 thru 159 . . . . @30.00
160 thru 163 52 pgs. . . . . @20.00
164 thru 253 . . . . @10.00
Becomes:

CASPER
THE FRIENDLY GHOST

FRIGHT NIGHT
Now, 1988–90
1 thru 22 . . . . @2.00

FRIGHT NIGHT 3-D
Now, 1992
1 Dracula,w/3-D Glasses 2.95
2 . . . . 2.95

All comics prices listed are for *Near Mint* condition.

Fright–Gene

COLOR PUB.

FRIGHT NIGHT II
Now
Movie Adaptation 3.95

FRISKY ANIMALS ON PARADE
Ajax-Farrell Publ., Sept., 1957
1 LbC(c) 200.00
2 . . . . 125.00
3 LbC(c) 175.00

FROGMEN, THE
Dell Publishing Co., 1962
1 GE,Ph(c) 100.00
2 GE,FF 75.00
3 GE,FF 75.00
4 . . . . 50.00
5 ATh 60.00
6 thru 11 . . . . @45.00

FROM HERE TO INSANITY
Charlton Comics, Feb., 1955
8 . . . . 200.00
9 . . . . 150.00
10 SD(c) 250.00
11 JK 250.00
12 JK 250.00
3-1 . . . . 350.00

FRONTLINE COMBAT
EC Comics, 1995
1 thru 4 rep. . . . . @2.00
Gemstone, 1996
5 thru 13 rep . . . . @2.50
14 WW(c) 2.50
15 . . . . 2.50
`Annuals'
TPB Vol. 1 rebinding of #1–#5 . . . 10.95
TPB Vol. 2 rebinding of #6–#10 . . 12.95
TPB Vol. 3 rebinding of #11–#15. . 13.95

F-TROOP
Dell Publishing Co., 1966
1 Ph(c) 150.00
2 thru 7 Ph(c). . . . . @75.00

FUN-IN
Gold Key, 1970–74
1 . . . . 100.00
2 thru 6 . . . . @50.00
7 thru 10 . . . . @40.00
11 thru 15 . . . . @40.00

FUNKY PHANTOM
Gold Key, 1972–75
1 . . . . 75.00
2 thru 5 . . . . @40.00
6 thru 13 . . . . @30.00

FURRY NINJA HIGH SCHOOL STRIKES BACK
Shanda Fantasy Arts 2003
1 (of 2) 5.00
2 . . . . 5.00

FUTURAMA COMICS
Bongo Comics, 2000
1 thru 6 . . . . @2.50
7 thru 10 . . . . @2.50
11 thru 15 . . . . @2.50
TPB Vol. 1 . . . . 12.95

Spec. Futurama/Simpsons: Infinity Secret Crossover Crisis, pt.1 . . 2.50
Spec. Futurama/Simpsons Crossover Crisis, pt.2 . . . . 2.50

FUTURIANS
Lodestone, 1985
1 DC,I:Dr.Zeus 2.00
2 DC,I:MsMercury 2.00
3 DC 2.00
Eternity Graphic Novel, DC, Rep. +new material. 9.95

GALACTICA: THE NEW MILLENNIUM
Realm Press, 1999
1 Battlestar Galactica 3.00
1 convention edition. 5.00
1a signed 15.00
2 Busch (c) 3.00
2a Scalf (c) 3.00
2b convention edition. 5.00
3 . . . . 3.00
3a 3.00
4 . . . . 3.00
4a deluxe 5.00
Spec. Fangs of the Beast 4.00
Spec. Fangs of the Beast,deluxe . . 5.00
Tour Book, Conv. Ed., signed . . 15.00
Spec.Search for Sanctuary 4.00

GALL FORCE: ETERNAL STORY
CPM, 1995
1 F:Solnoids 2.95
2 V:Paranoid 2.95
3 . . . . 2.95
4 Implant Secrets 2.95

GALLANT MEN, THE
Gold Key, Oct., 1963
1 RsM 40.00

GALLEGHER BOY REPORTER
Gold Key, May, 1965
1 . . . . 30.00

GARRISON
Zion Comics
1 I:Wage, Garrison 2.50

GARRISON'S GORRILLAS
Dell Publishing Co., Jan., 1968
1 Ph(c) 75.00
2 thru 5 Ph(c). . . . . @40.00

GASP!
American Comics Group March, 1967
1 . . . . 50.00
2 thru 4, Aug. 1967 . . . . @30.00

GATE CRASHER
Black Bull Entertainment, 2000
1 (of 4) MWa,ACo,JP. 2.50
1a variant (c). 5.00
2 MWa,ACo,JP 2.50
3 MWa,ACo,JP 2.50
4 MWa,ACo,JP, concl. 2.50
3a and 4a variant (c)s . . . . @2.50

Gate Crasher #1
© Black Bull Entertainment

GATE CRASHER
Black Bull Entertainment, 2000
1 MWa,JP,ACo,F:Alex Wagner. . . . 2.50
1a variant Wizard World (c) 5.00
2 MWa,JP,ACo,Blue Tonya, Otmar. 2.50
2a variant (c). 2.50
3 MWa,JP,ACo,F:Hazard 2.50
3a variant ACo(c). 2.50
4 MWa,JP,ACo,ACo(c). 2.50
4a variant Greg Hildebrandt(c). . . 2.50
5 MWa,JP,ACo,AAd(c). 2.50
5a variant ACo(c). 2.50
6 MWa,JP,ACo 2.50
6a variant ACo(c). 2.50
TPB Ring of Fire, 104-page 12.95

GEN-ACTIVE
WildStorm/DC, March, 2000
1 V:DV8,48-pg.quarterly 3.95
2 several stories 3.95
2a variant JPn (c) 3.95
3 BSz,JLe(c) 3.95
3a variant Lee Bermejo (c) 3.95
4 R:Wildcore 3.95
4a variant (c) 3.95
5 F:Sublime 3.95
5a variant (c) (1:2) 3.95
6 Freakville 3.95

GENE FUSION
Beckett Entertainment 2003
1 Monsters on Parade,pt.1. . . . . . 2.95
2 Monsters on Parade,pt.2. . . . . . 2.95
3 Monsters on Parade,pt.3. . . . . . 2.95
4 Battle under the Big Tent 2.95

GENE RODDENBERRY'S LOST UNIVERSE
Teckno-Comics, 1994
0 I:Sensua. 2.50
1 Gene Roddenberry's. 2.50
2 Grange Discovered. 2.25
3 Secrets Revealed 2.00
4 F:Penultra 2.00
5 I:New Alien Race 2.00
6 Two Doctor Granges. 2.00
7 F:Alaa Chi Tskare 2.00

GENE RODDENBERRY'S XANDER IN LOST UNIVERSE
Teckno-Comics, 1995
1 V:Black Ghost. 2.25
2 V:Walker. 2.25
3 V:Lady Sensua 2.25
4 thru 7 . . . . @2.25
8 F:Lady Sensua 2.25

[Mini-Series], 1995
1 RoR,F:L.Nimoy's Primortals 2.25

GENESIS
Malibu Oct., 1993
0 GP,w/Pog,F:Widowmaker, A:Arrow 3.50
0a Gold ed. 5.00

GENSAGA: ANCIENT WARRIOR
Entity Comics, 1995
1 I:Gensaga 2.50
1a with Computer Games 2.50
2 V:Dinosaurs 2.50
3 V:Lord Abyss 2.50

GEN13
WildStorm/DC, Sept., 2002
1 CCI,Dylon & Ethan York 2.95
2 CCI,Herod strikes 2.95
3 CCI,Herod strikes 2.95
4 CCI,Hamza. 2.95
5 CCI,V:Preston Kills 2.95
6 CCI,V:Purple Haze 2.95
7 CCI,V:The Chrome 2.95
8 CCI,V:The Chrome 2.95
9 CCI,the alter or the morgue. 2.95
10 CCI,October Surprise,pt.4 . . . . . 2.95
11 CCI,Two Caitlins 2.95
12 CCI,G-Nome 2.95
13 CCI,G-Nome 2.95
14 CCI,F:Caitlin 2.95
15 CCI,V:The Clique 2.95
Spec. #0 CCI,JP, preview 0.13
TPB Meanwhile 17.95
TPB September Song. 19.95
See also Image Comics section

GEN13 MOVIE ADAPTATION
WildStorm/DC, Nov., 2001
1 JMi, animated movie adapt. 2.50

GENTLE BEN
Dell Publishing Co., Feb., 1968
1 Ph(c) 50.00
2 . . . . 35.00
3 thru 5 . . . . @30.00

GEOMANCER
Valiant 1994
1 RgM, I:Geomancer 3.00
2 RgM, Eternal Warrior 2.25
3 RgM, Darque Elementals 2.25
4 RgM 2.25
5 Riot Gear,pt. 1 . . . . 2.25
6 Riot Gear,pt. 2 . . . . 2.25
7 F:Zorn 2.25
8 v:Zorn. 2.25

GEORGE OF THE JUNGLE
Gold Key, Feb., 1969
1 From animated TV show 200.00
2 . . . . 150.00

GE ROUGE
Verotik, 1997
1 by Glenn Danzig & Calvin Irving . 2.95
1 fan club cover (2000) 5.00
2 and 3 . . . . @2.95
Biz:GE Rouge #? SBs 2.95

GET SMART
Dell Publishing Co., June, 1966
1 Ph(c) all 150.00
2 SD 100.00
3 SD 90.00
4 thru 8 . . . . @85.00

Ghostbusters #4
© First

[FILMATION'S] GHOSTBUSTERS
First, 1987
1 thru 4 . . . . @2.00

GHOST BUSTERS II
Now, 1989
1 thru 3 Mini-series . . . . @2.00

GHOST STORIES
Dell Publishing Co., Sept.-Nov., 1962
1 . . . . 75.00
2 . . . . 40.00
3 thru 10 . . . . @35.00
11 . . . . 30.00
12 thru 19 . . . . @25.00
20 . . . . 30.00
21 thru 33 . . . . @25.00
34 rep. 25.00
35 rep. 30.00
36 rep. 25.00
37 rep. 25.00

GHOSTLY TALES
Charlton, 1966
Previously: Blue Beetle
55 I&O Dr. Graves 60.00

56 thru 70 . . . . @30.00
71 thru 100 . . . . @20.00
101 thru 169 . . . . @15.00

GIANT COMICS
Charlton Comics Summer, 1957
1 A:Atomic Mouse,Hoppy 225.00
2 A:Atomic Mouse 200.00
3 . . . . 200.00

GIDGET
Dell Publishing Co., April, 1966
1 Ph(c),Sally Field 150.00
2 Ph(c),Sally Field 100.00

GIFT, THE
First, 1990
Holiday Special. 6.00

GIGANTOR
Antarctic Press, 2000
1 (of 12) BDn. 2.50
2 V:Red Reich 2.50
3 . . . . 2.50
4 Doppleganger,pt.1 . . . . 2.50
5 Doppleganger,pt.2 . . . . 2.50
6 Doppleganger,pt.3 . . . . 2.50
7 Rulers of the Sea 2.50
8 . . . . 2.50
9 Sting of the Spider 2.95
10 Sting of the Spider, pt.2 . . . . . . 2.95
11 Badge of Danger, pt.1 . . . . 2.95
12 Badge of Danger, pt.2, concl. . . 2.95

G.I. JOE 3-D
Blackthorne, 1987
1 . . . . 3.00
2 thru 5 . . . . @2.50
Ann. #1 . . . . 2.50

GIL THORPE
Dell Publishing Co., 1963
1 . . . . 50.00

GINGER FOX
Comico, 1988
1 thru 4 . . . . @2.00

GIN-RYU
Believe In Yourself, 1995
1 F:Japanese Sword 2.75
2 Identity Revealed 2.75
3 . . . . 2.75
4 Manhunt For Gin-Ryu 2.75

G.I. R.A.M.B.O.T.
Wonder Color, 1987
1 thru 3 . . . . @2.00

G.I. ROBOT
Eternity
1 . . . . 2.00

GIRL FROM U.N.C.L.E.
Gold Key, Jan., 1967
1 `The Fatal Accidents Affair' . . . 150.00
2 `The Kid Commandos Caper' . 100.00
3 `The Captain Kidd Affair' 100.00
4 `One-Way Tourist Affair' 100.00
5 `The Harem-Scarem Affair' . . . 100.00

GIRL GENIUS
Studio Foglio, 2001
0 Secret Blueprints Preview B&W . 1.50
1 by Phil & Kaja Foglio 2.95
2 and 3 . . . . @2.95
4 40-page 3.95
5 . . . . 2.95
6 40-page (cancelled?) 3.95
7 40-page 3.95

GLOBAL FORCE
Silverline
1 thru 4 . . . . @2.00

GLOBAL FREQUENCY
WildStorm/DC, Oct., 2002
1 (of 12) WEI 2.95
2 WEI,SDi 2.95
3 WEI,LSh 2.95
4 WEI,RMr 2.50
5 WEI,JMu 2.50
6 WEI, ... 2.50
7 WEI,Detonation 2.50
8 WEI,Miranda Zero disappears . . 2.50
9 WEI,Cathedral Lung 2.50
10 WEI,Superviolence 2.50
11 WEI,Aleph 2.50
12 WEI,concl 2.50

GLORY
Maximum Press, 1996
1–15 see Image
16 JDy 2.50
17 JDy 2.50
18 JDy 2.50
19 JDy,A:Demeter, Silverfall 2.50
20 JDy,A:Silverfall 2.50
21 JDy 2.50
22 JDy 2.50
23 A:Prophet 2.50
TPB Vol. 2, rep. 16.95
TPB Glory/Angela RLd,JDy 16.95

Awesome Entertainment, 1999
0 AMo 2.50
0a & b alternate covers 2.50
0c Timeless Beauty MMy(c) 5.95
1 AMo & ATi 3.50
2 AMo & ATi 3.00

GLORY/CELESTINE: DARK ANGEL
Maximum Press, 1996
1 & 2 See: Image
3 (of 3) JDy 2.50

GLORY/LIONHEART: RAGE OF FURIES
Awesome Entertainment, 2000
1 . . . . 3.00

G-MAN
Conquest Comics
1 I:Richard Glenn 2.50

GOAT, THE: H.A.E.D.U.S.
Acclaim 1998
Spec. CPr,KG,F:Vincent Van Goat . 3.95

GOBLIN LORD, THE
Goblin Studios, 1996
1 (of 6) sci-fi/fantasy 2.50
2 signed & numbered 9.95

3 . . . . 2.50
3a signed & numbered 9.95
4 thru 6 . . . . @2.50

Gods For Hire #2
© Hot Comics

GODS FOR HIRE
Hot Comics, 1986
1 thru 7 . . . . @2.00

GODWHEEL
Malibu Ultraverse, 1995
0 R:Argus to Godwheel 2.50
1 I:Primevil 2.50
2 Hardcase new costume 2.50
3 F:Lord Pumpkin 2.50
TPB Wheel of Thunder,rep.#0–#3 . . 9.95

GO-GO
Charlton Comics, June, 1966
1 Miss Bikini Luv 100.00
2 Beatles 125.00
3 Blooperman 50.00
4 . . . . 50.00
5 . . . . 50.00
6 JAp,Petula Clark, Ph(c) 75.00
7 Beach Boys 65.00
8 JAp,Monkees, Ph(c) 75.00
9 Ph(c),Oct., 1967 . . . . 50.00

GOLD DIGGER
Antarctic Press, 1999
VOL 2
1 by Fred Perry, F:Gina Diggers . . 2.50
2 . . . . 2.50
3 by Fred Perry 2.50
4 tinted glass is magical 2.50
5 . . . . 2.50
6 ancient cauldrons 2.50
7 Halls of the Extremely Dead . . . 2.50
8 Gone Fishing 2.50
9 Fauntleroy..a God? 2.50
10 Arms Master of Jade 2.50
11 Arms Master of Jade 2.50
12 Arms Master of Jade 2.95
13 Tournament of Arms 2.95
14 Tournament of Arms 2.95
15 . . . . 2.95
16 thru 26 . . . . @2.95
27 thru 37 . . . . @3.00
38 thru 42 . . . . @3.50
43 thru 47 . . . . @3.00

Ann. 2003 B&W 4.95
Swimsuit Spec. #1 . . . . 4.50
Swimsuit Spec. 2001 . . . . 4.50
Spec. Swimsuit 2003 . . . . 4.50
Spec. End of Summer Swimsuit . . 4.50
Spec. Perfect Memory Vol. 3 . . . . 5.95
Spec. Swimsuit 2002 . . . . 4.50
Spec. Swimsuit End of Summer . . 4.50
GN Perfect Memory Vol. 2 . . . . . 5.95
TPB Gold Brick collection 49.95
TPB Gold Brick collection, signed . 60.00
TPB Gold Brick Vol. 2 . . . . 49.95
TPB Color series, Vol.1 . . . . . . 15.95
TPB Color Series, Vol.2 . . . . . . 15.95
TPB Pocket Manga #1 . . . . 12.95
TPB Pocket Manga #10 . . . . . . 12.95
TPB Pocket Manga #11 . . . . . . 12.95

GOLD DIGGER BETA
Antarctic Press, 1998
Spec. 0 by Ben Dunn, Special
  Origin Issue, 24pg 2.00
1A bu Fred Perry, John Pound (c) . 2.95
1B Jeff Henderson (c) 2.95
2 and 3 . . . . @2.95

GOLDEN COMICS DIGEST
Gold Key, 1969–76
1 Tom & Jerry,Woody Woodpecker,
  Bugs Bunny 60.00
2 Hanna-Barbera,TV Fun
  Favorites 100.00
3 Tom & Jerry, Woody
  Woodpecker 50.00
4 Tarzan 50.00
5 Tom & Jerry, Woody Woodpecker,
  Bugs Bunny 30.00
6 Bugs Bunny 30.00
7 Hanna-Barbera,TV Fun
  Favorites 60.00
8 Tom & Jerry, Woody Woodpecker,
  Bugs Bunny 25.00
9 Tarzan 50.00
10 Bugs Bunny 25.00
11 Hanna-Barbera,TV Fun
  Favorites 60.00
12 Tom & Jerry,Bugs Bunny 25.00
13 Tom & Jerry 25.00
14 Bugs Bunny,Fun Packed
  Funnies 25.00
15 Tom & Jerry, Woody
  Woodpecker, Bugs Bunny 25.00
16 Woody Woodpecker 25.00
17 Bugs Bunny 25.00
18 Tom & Jerry, ... 25.00
19 Little Lulu 45.00
20 Woody Woodpecker 25.00
21 Bugs Bunny Showtime 25.00
22 Tom & Jerry Winter Wingding . . 25.00
23 Little Lulu & Tubby Fun Fling . . 50.00
24 Woody Woodpecker Fun
  Festival 20.00
25 Tom & Jerry 20.00
26 Bugs Bunny Halloween Hulla-
  Boo-Loo,Dr. Spektor article . . . 20.00
27 Little Lulu & Tubby in Hawaii . . 40.00
28 Tom & Jerry 20.00
29 Little Lulu & Tubby 40.00
30 Bugs Bunny Vacation Funnies . 20.00
31 Turk, Son of Stone 45.00
32 Woody Woodpecker
  SummerFun 20.00
33 Little Lulu & Tubby Halloween
  Fun 40.00
34 Bugs Bunny Winter Funnies . . . 20.00
35 Tom & Jerry Snowtime Funtime 20.00
36 Little Lulu & Her Friends 40.00
37 WoodyWoodpecker County Fair 20.00

38 The Pink Panther........... 20.00
39 Bugs Bunny Summer Fun 20.00
40 Little Lulu................. 40.00
41 Tom & Jerry Winter Carnival .. 20.00
42 Bugs Bunny................ 20.00
43 Little Lulu in Paris.......... 40.00
44 Woody Woodpecker Family Fun
   Festival.................. 20.00
45 The Pink Panther........... 20.00
46 Little Lulu & Tubby.......... 40.00
47 Bugs Bunny................ 20.00
48 The Lone Ranger........... 20.00

GOLDEN PICTURE STORY BOOK
Racine Press (Western), Dec., 1961
1 Huckleberry Hound......... 300.00
2 Yogi Bear................. 300.00
3 Babes In Toy Land......... 325.00
4 Walt Disney............... 300.00

GOMER PYLE
Gold Key, July, 1966
1 Ph(c) from TV show........ 150.00
2 and 3 .... @100.00

GOOD GUYS
Defiant, 1993
1 JiS(s),I:Good Guys........... 3.75
2 JiS(s),V:Mulchmorg 3.25
3 V:Chasm................... 2.75
4 Seduction of the Innocent..... 3.25
5 I:Truc..................... 2.75
6 A:Charlemagne.............. 2.75
7 JiS(s),V:Scourge 2.50
8 thru 11 .... @2.50

GOOFY ADVENTURES
Walt Disney, 1990
1 `Balboa de Goofy'............ 2.50
2 .... 2.00
3 thru 9 .... @2.00
10 Samurai................... 2.00
11 Goofis Khan................ 2.00
12 `Arizona Goof' Pt. 1 .... 2.00
13 `Arizona Goof' Pt. 2 .... 2.00
14 `Goofylution'............... 2.00
15 `Super Goof Vs.Cold Ray' 2.00
16 `Sheerluck Holmes' 2.00
17 GC,TP,`Tomb of Goofula'..... 2.00

GOOP, THE
JNCO Comics, 1998
1 .... 2.00
2 thru 4 .... @2.00

GORGO
Charlton Comics, 1961–65
1 SD...................... 325.00
2 SD,SD(c) 175.00
3 SD,SD(c) 150.00
4 SD(c) 100.00
5 thru 10 .... @100.00
11 .... 100.00
12 .... 75.00
13 thru 15 .... @75.00
16 SD...................... 75.00
17 thru 23................ @60.00

GORGO'S REVENGE
Charlton Comics, 1962
1 .... 75.00
Becomes:

COLOR PUB.

THE RETURN OF GORGO
2 .... 60.00
3 .... 60.00

G.O.T.H.
Verotik, 1995
1 thru 3 mini-series .... @2.95
TPB SBi, rep. of series......... 9.95

THE GOTHIC SCROLLS, DRAYVEN
Davdez Arts, 1997
1 16pg...................... 2.00
1a limited edition, new cover 2.95
2 and 3 .... 2.50
4 V:Lucifer................... 2.50
GN 12.95

Grateful Dead #2
© Kitchen Sink

GRATEFUL DEAD COMIX
Kitchen Sink 1993
1 TT,inc.DireWolf(large format) ... 5.50
2 TT,inc.Jack Straw............ 4.95
3 TT,inc. Sugaree 4.95
4 TT,inc. Sugaree 4.95
5 TT,Uncle John's Band........ 4.95
6 TT,Eagle Mall #1............. 4.95

GRAVESTONE
Malibu July, 1993–Feb., 1994
1 D:Gravestone,V:Wisecrack 2.25
1a Newstand ed............... 2.25
2 A:Eternal Man, V:Night Plague .. 2.25
2a Newstand ed............... 2.25
3 Genesis Tie in,w/skycap 2.25
4 Genesis 2.25
5 V:Scythe................... 2.25
6 V:Jug 2.25
7 R:Bogg.................... 2.25
8 & 9 .... @2.25

GREASE MONKEY
Kitchen Sink, 1997
1 by Tim Elred................ 3.50
2 by Tim Elred................ 3.50

GREAT AMERICAN WESTERN
AC Comics
1 .... 2.00
2 and 3 .... @2.95
4 .... 3.50

GREAT EXPLOITS
Decker Publ./Red Top, Oct., 1957
91 BK...................... 75.00

GREEN HORNET, THE
Gold Key, Feb., 1967
1 Bruce Lee,Ph(c).......... 350.00
2 Ph(c) 300.00
3 Ph(c) 250.00

GREEN HORNET
Now, 1989
1 O:40's Green Hornet 7.00
1a 2nd Printing 4.00
2 O:60's Green Hornet 5.00
3 thru 5 .... @4.00
6 .... 3.00
7 BSz(c),I:New Kato 3.00
8 thru 12 .... @3.50
13 V:Ecoterrorists............. 3.50
14 V:Ecoterrorists............. 3.50
Spec.#1 .... 2.50
Spec.#2 .... 2.25

[2nd Series], 1991
1 V:Johnny Dollar Pt.1.......... 2.25
2 V:Johnny Dollar Pt.2.......... 2.25
3 V:Johnny Dollar Pt.3.......... 2.25
4 V:Ex-Con/Politician 2.00
5 V:Ex-Con/Politician 2.00
6 Arkansas Vigilante 2.00
7 thru 9 The Beast .... @2.00
10 Green Hornet-prey.......... 2.00
11 F:Crimson Wasp 2.00
12 Crimson Wasp/Johnny Dollar
   Pt.1,polybagged w/Button... 2.50
13 TD(i),Wasp/Dollar Pt.2....... 2.50
14 TD(i),Wasp/Dollar Pt.3....... 2.50
15 TD(i),Secondsight 2.00
16 A:Commissioner Hamiliton.... 2.00
17 V:Gunslinger............... 2.00
18 V:Sister-Hood 2.00
19 V:Jewel Thief............... 2.00
20 F:Paul's Friend 2.00
21 V:Brick Arcade 2.00
22 V:Animal Testers, with
   Hologravure card 2.95
23 with Hologravure card 2.95
24 thru 25 Karate Wars ...... @2.00
26 B:City under Siege.......... 2.00
27 with Hologravure card 2.00
28 V:Gangs 2.00
29 V:Gangs 2.00
30 thru 37................. @2.00
38 R:Mei Li................... 2.50
39 Crimson Wasp.............. 2.50
40 .... 2.50
41 .... 2.50
42 Baby Killer................. 2.50
43 Wedding Disasters.......... 2.50
44 F:Amy Hamilton............. 2.50
45 Plane Hijacking 2.50
46 Airport Terrorists 2.50
Ann.#1 The Blue & the Green.... 2.50
1993 Ann 2.95

Bonus Books
TPB rep. Now comics #1–#12,
   296pg................... 10.00
TPB deluxe rep. Now comics
   #1–#12, 296pg........... 19.95

GREEN HORNET: DARK TOMORROW
Now, 1993
1 thru 3 Hornet Vs Kato . . . . @2.50

GREEN HORNET: SOLITARY SENTINAL
Now, 1992
1 Strike Force 2.50
2 thru 3 . . . . @2.50

GREENHAVEN
Aircel
1 . . . . 3.00
2 . . . . 2.50
3 . . . . 2.00

GREEN PLANET
Charlton, 1962
1 DG 100.00

GRENDEL
Comico, 1986–91
1 MW 9.00
1a 2nd printing 2.00
2 MW 6.00
3 thru 6 MW . . . . @5.00
7 MW 5.00
8 thru 12 MW . . . . @4.50
13 KSy(c) MW 4.00
14 KSy(c) MW 3.00
15 KSy(c) MW 3.00
16 MW,Mage 6.00
17 thru 19 MW,Mage . . . . @5.00
20 thru 32 MW . . . . @3.00
33 MW,giant-size 3.50
34 thru 36 MW . . . . @3.00
37 MW 5.00
38 MW 9.00
39 MW,D:Grendel 10.00
40 MW,D:Orion Assante 30.00

GREYLORE
Sirius, 1985–86
1 thru 5 . . . . @2.00

GREYSHIRT: INDIGO SUNSET
WildStorm/DC, Oct., 2001
America's Best Comics
1 (of 6) RV 3.50
2 RV 3.50
3 RV 3.50
4 RV, Star of Indigo 3.50
5 RV, Fanman 3.50
6 RV, Black Jack Hawkins 3.50
TPB Indigo Sunset 19.95

GRIMJACK
First, 1984–91
1 TT Teenage suicide story 3.00
2 TT A:Munden's Bar 2.50
3 TT A:Munden's Bar 2.00
4 TT A:Munden's Bar 2.00
5 TT,JSon,A:Munden's Bar 2.00
6 TT,SR,A:Munden's Bar 2.00
7 TT,A:Munden's Bar 2.00
8 TT,A:Munden's Bar 2.00
9 TT `My Sins Remembered' . . . 2.00
10 TT,JOy,A:Munden's Bar 2.00
11 TT,A:Munden'sBar 2.00
12 TT,A:Munden'sBar 2.00
13 TT,A:Munden'sBar 2.00
14 TT,A:Munden'sBar 2.00
15 TT,A:Munden'sBar 2.00
16 TT,A:Munden'sBar 2.00
17 TT,A:Munden'sBar 2.00
18 TT,A:Munden'sBar 2.00
19 TT,A:Munden'sBar 2.00
20 TT,A:Munden'sBar 2.00
21 TS,A:Munden's Bar 2.00
22 A:Munden's Bar 2.00
23 TS,A:Munden's Bar 2.00
24 PS,TT,rep.Starslayer10-11 . . . 2.00
25 TS,A:Munden's Bar 2.00
26 1st color TMNTurtles 10.00
27 TS,A:Munden's Bar 2.00
28 TS,A:Munden's Bar 2.00
29 A:Munden's Bar 2.00
30 A:Munden's Bar 2.00
31 A:Munden's Bar 2.00
32 A:Spook 2.00
33 JSon,Munden'sBar
  Christmas Tale 2.00
34 V:Spook 2.00
35 A:Munden's Bar 2.00
36 3rd Anniv.IssueD:Grimjack 2.50
37 A:Munden's Bar 2.00
38 A:Munden's Bar 2.00
39 R.Grimjack 2.00
40 . . . . 2.00
41 `Weeping Bride' 2.00
42 `Hardball' 2.00
43 `Beneath the Surface' 2.00
44 Shadow Wars 2.00
45 Shadow Wars 2.00
46 Shadow Wars 2.00
47 Shadow Wars,A:EddyCurrent . . 2.00
48 Shadow Wars 2.00
49 Shadow Wars 2.00
50 V:Dancer,ShadowWars ends . . 2.00
51 Crossroads tie-in,
  A:Judah Macabee 2.00
52 . . . . 2.00
53 Time Story 2.00
54 . . . . 2.50
55 FH 2.00
56 FH 2.00
57 FH 2.00
58 FH 2.00
59 FH 2.00
60 FH,Reunion Pt.1 . . . . 2.00
61 FH,Reunion Pt.2 . . . . 2.00
62 FH,Reunion Pt.3 . . . . 2.00
63 FH,A:Justice Drok 2.00
64 FH,O:Multiverse 2.00
65 FH 2.00
66 FH(c),Demon Wars Pt.1 . . . . . 2.00
67 FH(c),Demon Wars Pt.2 . . . . . 2.00
68 Demon Wars Pt.3 . . . . 2.00
69 Demon Wars Pt.4 . . . . 2.00
70 FH,I:Youngblood 2.00
71 FH,A:Youngblood 2.00
72 . . . . 2.00
73 FH(c) 2.00
74 FH(c) 2.00
75 FH,TS,V:The Major 2.00
76 FH,A:Youngblood 2.00
77 FH,A:Youngblood 2.25
78 . . . . 2.25
79 FH,Family Business #1 . . . . . 2.25
80 FH,Family Business #2 . . . . . 2.25
81 FH,Family Business #3 . . . . . 2.25

GRIMJACK CASEFILE
First, 1990
1 thru 5 rep. . . . . @2.00

GRIMM'S GHOST STORIES
Gold Key/Whitman, 1972–82
1 . . . . 35.00
2 . . . . 25.00
3 . . . . 25.00
4 . . . . 25.00
5 AW 30.00
6 . . . . 15.00
7 . . . . 15.00
8 AW 20.00
9 . . . . 15.00
10 . . . . 15.00
11 thru 16 . . . . @12.00
17 RC 15.00
18 thru 60 . . . . @10.00

GROO THE WANDERER
Pacific, 1982–84
1 SA,I:Sage,Taranto 25.00
2 SA,A:Sage 15.00
3 SA,C:Taranto 13.00
4 SA,C:Sage 13.00
5 SA,I:Ahax 13.00
6 SA,I:Gratic 15.00
7 SA,I:Chakala 15.00
8 SA,A:Chakala 15.00
Eclipse
Spec.#1 SA,O:Groo,rep Destroyer
  Duck #1 . . . . 23.00

GROUP LARUE
Innovation, 1989
1 . . . . 2.00
2 . . . . 2.00
3 . . . . 2.00

GUILLOTIN
ABC, 1997
1 JQ(c) 3.00
1a RCl(c) 6.00
1b gold cover, polybagged with
  trading card 10.00
2 . . . . 3.00
2a Serpent (c) 6.00
2b Cold Series (c) 6.00

GULLIVER'S TRAVELS
Dell Publishing Co.,
Sept.-Nov., 1965
1 . . . . 75.00
2 and 3 . . . . @50.00

Grimjack #66
© First

COLOR PUB.

GUMBY
Comico, 1987
1 AAd,Summer Fun Special......5.00
2 AAd,Winter Fun Special.......3.50

GUMBY IN 3-D
Blackthorne
Spec.#1 ....4.00
2 thru 7 ....@2.50

GUNSMOKE
Dell Publishing Co., Feb., 1956
1 J.Arness Ph(c) all..........250.00
2 ....150.00
3 ....150.00
4 ....150.00
5 ....150.00
6 ....100.00
7 ....100.00
8 ....125.00
9 ....125.00
10 AW,RC...................135.00
11 ....125.00
12 AW 135.00
13 thru 27 ....@100.00

GUY WITH A GUN:
A ZOMBIE NIGHTMARE
Alpha Productions
1 V:Gracel, Zombies...........2.75

HALL OF FAME
J.C. Productions
1 WW,GK,ThunderAgents.......2.00
2 WW,GK,ThunderAgents.......2.00
3 WW,Thunder Agents.........2.00

HALLOWEEN
Chaos! Comics, 2000
1 premium glow-in-the-dark (c)...12.95
1 chromium edition...........15.95

HALLOWEEN:
BEHIND THE MASK
Chaos! Comics, 2000
1 photo (c)...................2.95

HALLOWEEN II:
THE BLACKEST EYE
Chaos! Comics, 2001
Spec. 3.00
Spec. premium...............10.00

HALLOWEEN III:
THE DEVIL'S EYES
Chaos! Comics, 2001
Spec. 3.00
Spec. variant (c)..............3.00
Spec. Previews exclusive.......3.00

HALLOWEEN HORROR
Eclipse, 1987
1 ....2.00

HALO:
AN ANGEL'S STORY
Sirius, April, 1996
1 thru 3 by Chris Knowles.....@2.95
TPB rep. #1–#3 ....12.95

Hammer of God, Sword of Justice #1
© First Comics

HAMMER OF GOD
First
1 thru 4 ....@2.00
Deluxe #1`Sword of Justice Bk#1'...4.95
Deluxe #2`Sword of Justice Bk#2'...4.95

HAMSTER VICE
Blackthorne, 1985–87
1 thru 10 ....@2.00
3-D #1 ....2.50

HAND OF FATE
Eclipse, 1988
1 I:Artemus Fate..............1.75
2 F:Artemis & Alexis...........2.00
3 Mystery & Suspense..........2.00

HANDS OF THE DRAGON
Atlas, June, 1975
1 ....20.00

HANNA-BARBERA
ALL-STARS
Archie, 1995
1 thru 5 ....2.00

HANNA-BARBERA
BAND WAGON
Gold Key, 1962–63
1 ....200.00
2 ....150.00
3 ....100.00

HANNA-BARBERA
PARADE
Charlton Comics, 1971–72
1 ....125.00
2 thru 10 ....@75.00

HANNA-BARBERA
PRESENTS
Archie, 1995
1 thru 15 ....@2.00

HANNA-BARBERA
SUPER TV HEROES
Gold Key, April, 1968
1 B:Birdman,Herculiods,Moby Dick,
Young Samson & Goliath......250.00
2 ....175.00
3 thru 7 Oct. 1969 ....@150.00

HARBINGER
Valiant 1992
0 DL,O:Sting,V:Harada, from TPB
(Blue Bird Ed.) 2.25
0 from coupons...............4.00
1 DL,JDx,I:Sting,Torque,
Zeppelin,Flamingo,Kris.......3.00
1a w/o coupon...............1.00
2 DL,JDx,V:Harbinger Foundation,
I:Dr.Heyward................2.25
2a w/o coupon...............1.00
3 DL,JDx,I:Ax,Rexo, V:Spider
Aliens......................2.25
3a w/o coupon...............1.00
4 DL,JDx,V:Ax,I:Fort,
Spikeman,Dog,Bazooka........2.25
4a w/o coupon...............1.00
5 DL,JDx,I:Puff,Thumper,
A:Solar,V:Harada.............2.25
5a w/o coupon...............1.00
6 DL,D:Torque,A:Solar,
V:Harada,Eggbreakers........2.25
6a w/o coupon...............1.00
7 DL,Torque's Funeral........2.25
8 FM(c),DL,JDx,Unity#8,
A:Magnus,Eternal Warrior.....2.25
9 WS(c),DL,Unity #16,
A:Magnus,Armstrong,Rai,
Archer,Eternal Warrior 2.25
10 DL,I:H.A.R.D.Corps, Daryl,
Shetiqua....................2.25
11 DL,V:H.A.R.D.Corps........2.25
12 DL,F:Zeppelin,A:Elfquest....2.25
13 Flamingo Vs. Rock..........2.25
14 A:Magnus(Dream Sequence),
C:Stronghold................2.25
15 I:Livewire,Stronghold......2.25
16 A:Livewire,Stronghold......2.25
17 HSn,I:Simon...............2.25
18 HSn,I:Screen..............2.25
19 HSn,I:Caliph..............2.25
20 HSn,V:Caliph..............2.25
21 I:Pete's Father............2.25
22 HSn,A:Archer & Armstrong...2.25
23 HSn,B:Twilight of the
Eighth Day.................2.25
24 HSn,V:Eggbreakers.........2.25
25 HSn,V:Harada,E:Twlight of the
Eighth Day.................2.50
26 SCh,AdW,I:Jolt,Amazon,
Mircowave,Anvil,Sonix.......2.25
27 SCh,AdW,Christmas issue....2.25
28 SCh,AdW,O:Sonix,J:Tyger....2.25
29 SCh,AdW,A:Livewire,Stronghold,
w/Valiant Era card..........2.25
30 SCh,AdW,A:Livewire,Stronghold 2.25
31 SCh,AdW,V:H.A.R.D.Corps....2.25
32 SCh,AdW,A:Eternal Warrior...2.25
33 SCh, V:Dr. Eclipse.........2.25
34 SCh,Chaos Effect-Delta#1, A:X-
O, Dr. Eclipse..............2.25
35 Zephyr...................2.25
36 Zephyr, Magnus............2.25
37 Magnus, Harada...........2.25
38 A:Spikeman...............2.25
39 Zepplin vs. Harada........2.25
40 V:Harbinger...............2.25
41 V:Harbinger...............2.25
TPB w/#0,rep#1-4.............25.00
TPB 2nd Printing w/o #0.......9.95
TPB #2, Rep. 6-7,10-11........9.95

Harbinger–Harvey COLOR PUB. Comics Values Annual

HARBINGER FILES: HARADA
Valiant 1994
1 BL,DC,O:Harada 2.75
2 Harada's ultimate weapon 2.50

HARDCASE
Malibu Ultraverse, 1993–95
1 I:Hardcase,D:The Squad 3.00
1a Ultra-Limited, silver foil 4.00
1b Full Hologram(c). 6.00
1c Platinum edition 3.50
2 w/Ultraverse card 3.00
3 Hard decisions 2.75
4 A:Strangers 2.75
5 BWS,V:Hardwire,BU:Rune 2.75
6 V:Hardwire 2.50
7 ScB,Break-Thru x-over,
  I:Nanotech,A:Solution 2.25
8 GP,O:Solitare 2.25
9 B:O:Choice,I:Turf 2.25
10 O:Choice 2.25
11 ScB,V:Aladdin 2.25
12 AV,A:Choice. 2.25
13 A:Choice 2.25
14 A:Choice 2.25
15 Hardwires, NIM-E 2.25
16 NIM-E 3.50
17 Prime,NIM-E 2.25
18 V:Nim-E, Battle Royale 2.25
19 Prelude to Godwheel 2.25
20 R:Rex Mindi. 2.50
21 Mundiquest prelude 2.50
22 Mundiquest. 2.50
23 A:Loki 2.50
24 Mundiquest,pt.3. . . . . 2.50
25 Mundiquest,concl. 2.95
26 Time Gem Disaster 2.95

H.A.R.D. CORPS
Valiant 1992
1 JLe(c),DL,BL,V:Harbinger
  Foundation,I:Flatline,D:Maniac . 2.50
1a Gold Ed. 2.50
2 DL,BL,V:Harb.Foundation 2.50
3 DL,BL,J:Flatline 2.50
4 BL 2.50
5 BCh,BL(i),A:Bloodshot 2.50
5a Comic Defense System Ed. . . . 2.50
6 MLe,A:Spider Aliens 2.50
7 MLe,V:Spider Aliens, I:Hotshot . 2.50
8 MLe,V:Harada,J:Hotshot. 2.50
9 MLe,V:Harada,A:Turok 2.25
10 MLe,A:Turok,V:Dinosaurs 2.25
11 YG,I:Otherman. 2.25
12 MLe,V:Otherman 2.25
13 YG,D:Superstar 2.50
14 DvM(s),YG,V:Edie Simkus 2.25
15 DvM(s),YG,V:Edie Simkus 2.25
16 DvM(s),YG 2.25
17 DvM(s),RLe,V:Armorines. 2.25
18 DvM(s),RLe,V:Armorines,
  w/Valiant Era card 2.25
19 RLe,A:Harada 2.25
20 RLe,V:Harbingers 2.25
21 RLe,New Direction. 2.25
22 RLe,V:Midnight Earl 2.25
23 RLe,Chaos Effect-Delta #4,
  A:Armorines, X-O. 2.25
24 Ironhead 2.25
25 Midnight Earl 2.25
26 Heydrich, Omen. 2.25
27 Heydrich shows evil. 2.25
28 New H.A.R.D.corps 2.25
29 V:New Guard. 2.25
30 Final Issue. 2.25

HARDY BOYS, THE
Gold Key, April, 1970
1 . . . . 75.00
2 thru 4 . . . . @40.00

HARI KARI
Blackout Comics, 1995
0 I:Hari Kari. 2.95
1 . . . . 2.95
1a commemorative, variant(c) . . . 10.00
Specials & 1-shots
1 The Beginning, O:Kari (1996) . . . 2.95
1a The Beginning, commemorative,
  signed 9.95
1 Bloodshed (1996). 3.00
1a Bloodshed, deluxe, variant(c) . 10.00
1 Live & Untamed! (1996) 2.95
1 Rebirth (1996) 2.95
0 The Silence of Evil (1996). 2.95
0 The Silence of Evil, limited,
  foil stamped 12.95

Hari Kari The Beginning #1
© Blackout Comics

? The Diary of Kari Sun (1997) . . . 2.95
? The Diary of Kari Sun, deluxe. . . 9.95
0 Life or Death (1997) 2.95
0a Life or Death, super sexy
  parody edition. 12.95
1 Passion & Death (1997) 2.95
1 Passion & Death, photo(c) 9.95
1 Possessed by Evil (1997). 2.95
1 Resurrection (1997) 2.95

HARLEM GLOBETROTTERS
Gold Key, April, 1972
1 . . . . 40.00
2 thru 12, Jan. 1975. . . . . @30.00

HARRIERS
Entity, 1995
1 I:Macedon Arsenal, Cardinal. . . . 2.95
1a with Video Game 6.95
2 . . . . 2.50
3 V:Kr'llyn 2.50

HARSH REALM
Harris, 1994
1 thru 6 JHi(s), ... @2.95
TPB 14.95

HARVEY HITS
Harvey Publications, 1957–67
1 The Phantom 400.00
2 Rags Rabbit 60.00
3 Richie Rich 1,400.00
4 Little Dot's Uncles 225.00
5 Stevie Mazie's Boy Friend 50.00
6 JK(c),BP,The Phantom 250.00
7 Wendy the Witch 300.00
8 Sad Sack's Army Life 100.00
9 Richie Rich's Golden Deeds . 600.00
10 Little Lotta 125.00
11 Little Audrey Summer Fun . . . 100.00
12 The Phantom. 250.00
13 Little Dot's Uncles 100.00
14 Herman & Katnip 50.00
15 The Phantom. 250.00
16 Wendy the Witch 200.00
17 Sad Sack's Army Life. 75.00
18 Buzzy & the Crow 50.00
19 Little Audrey. 75.00
20 Casper & Spooky 100.00
21 Wendy the Witch 100.00
22 Sad Sack's Army Life. 75.00
23 Wendy the Witch 100.00
24 Little Dot's Uncles 150.00
25 Herman & Katnip 50.00
26 The Phantom. 200.00
27 Wendy the Good Little Witch . 100.00
28 Sad Sack's Army Life. 35.00
29 Harvey-Toon 50.00
30 Wendy the Witch 100.00
31 Herman & Katnip 30.00
32 Sad Sack's Army Life. 30.00
33 Wendy the Witch 40.00
34 Harvey-Toon 30.00
35 Funday Funnies 30.00
36 The Phantom. 175.00
37 Casper & Nightmare 50.00
38 Harvey-Toon 30.00
39 Sad Sack's Army Life. 30.00
40 Funday Funnies 25.00
41 Herman & Katnip 30.00
42 Harvey-Toon 30.00
43 Sad Sack's Army Life. 30.00
44 The Phantom. 175.00
45 Casper & Nightmare 50.00
46 Harvey-Toon 30.00
47 Sad Sack's Army Life. 30.00
48 The Phantom. 175.00
49 Stumbo the Giant. 125.00
50 Harvey-Toon 25.00
51 Sad Sack's Army Life. 25.00
52 Casper & Nightmare 30.00
53 Harvey-Toons 25.00
54 Stumbo the Giant. 60.00
55 Sad Sack's Army Life. 25.00
56 Casper & Nightmare 25.00
57 Stumbo the Giant. 50.00
58 Sad Sack's Army Life. 25.00
59 Casper & Nightmare 25.00
60 Stumbo the Giant 40.00
61 Sad Sack's Army Life. 25.00
62 Casper & Nightmare 25.00
63 Stumbo the Giant. 35.00
64 Sad Sack's Army Life. 25.00
65 Casper & Nightmare 25.00
66 Stumbo the Giant. 35.00
67 Sad Sack's Army Life. 25.00
68 Casper & Nightmare 25.00
69 Stumbo the Giant. 35.00
70 Sad Sack's Army Life 25.00
71 Casper & Nightmare 25.00
72 Stumbo the Giant. 35.00
73 Little Sad Sack 25.00
74 Sad Sack's Muttsy. 25.00
75 Casper & Nightmare 25.00
76 Little Sad Sack 25.00
77 Sad Sack's Muttsy 25.00
78 Stumbo the Giant. 35.00
79 Little Sad Sack 25.00

All comics prices listed are for *Near Mint* condition.

COLOR PUB.

Harvey–Heavy

80 Sad Sack's Muttsy	25.00
81 Little Sad Sack	25.00
82 Sad Sack's Muttsy	25.00
83 Little Sad Sack	25.00
84 Sad Sack's Muttsy	25.00
85 Gabby Gob	25.00
86 G.I. Juniors	25.00
87 Sad Sack's Muttsy	25.00
88 Stumbo the Giant	30.00
89 Sad Sack's Muttsy	20.00
90 Gabby Goo	20.00
91 G.I. Juniors	20.00
92 Sad Sack's Muttsy	20.00
93 Sadie Sack	20.00
94 Gabby Goo	20.00
95 G.I. Juniors	20.00
96 Sad Sack's Muttsy	20.00
97 Gabby Goo	20.00
98 G.I. Juniors	20.00
99 Sad Sack's Muttsy	20.00
100 Gabby Goo	20.00
101 G.I. Juniors	15.00
102 Sad Sack's Muttsy	15.00
103 Gabby Goo	15.00
104 G.I. Juniors	15.00
105 Sad Sack's Muttsy	15.00
106 Gabby Goo	15.00
107 G.I. Juniors	15.00
108 Sad Sack's Muttsy	15.00
109 Gabby Goo	15.00
110 G.I. Juniors	15.00
111 Sad Sack's Muttsy	15.00
112 G.I. Juniors	15.00
113 Sad Sack's Muttsy	15.00
114 G.I. Juniors	15.00
115 Sad Sack's Muttsy	15.00
116 G.I. Juniors	15.00
117 Sad Sack's Muttsy	15.00
118 G.I. Juniors	15.00
119 Sad Sack's Muttsy	15.00
120 G.I. Juniors	15.00
121 Sad Sack's Muttsy	15.00
122 G.I. Juniors	15.00

HATE
Fantagraphics, 1990
1 thru 15, see B&W

16 thru 29	@2.95
30 48pg.	3.95
Ann.#1 48-page (2000)	3.95
Ann.#2 (2001)	3.95
Ann.#3 (2002)	3.95
Ann.#4 (2003)	4.95
TPB Vol.1 Hey, Buddy!, rep. #1–#5	12.95
TPB Vol.1 Hey, Buddy! signed	12.95
TPB Vol.2 Buddy the Dreamer, rep. #6–#10	12.95
TPB Vol.2 Buddy the Dreamer, sgn	12.95
TPB Vol.3 Fun with Buddy & Lisa.	12.95
TPB Vol.4 Buddy Go Home	16.95
TPB Vol.4 Buddy Go Home! signed	16.95
TPB Vol.5 Buddy's Got Three Moms.	16.95
TPB Vol.6 Buddy Bites the Bullet	16.95

HAUNTED
Charlton, 1971–84

1	45.00
2	30.00
3 thru 5	@30.00
6 thru 10	@25.00
11 thru 20	@15.00
21 thru 50	@10.00
51 thru 75	@8.00

HAUNTED, THE
Chaos! Comics, 2001

1 (of 4) PDd	3.00
1a variant Nat Jones (c)	3.00
1b premium ed.	10.00
2 PDd	3.00
2a variant Molenaar (c)	7.50
3 PDd	3.00
3a variant (c)	7.50
4	3.00
4a variant (c)	7.50
Ashcan, b&w	6.00

HAUNTED, THE: GRAY MATTERS
Chaos! Comics, 2002

1	3.00
1a premium edition	10.00

HAUNTED LOVE
Charlton, 1973–75

1	60.00
2	30.00
3 thru 5	@25.00
6 thru 11	@20.00

HAUNT OF FEAR
Gladstone, 1991

1 EC Rep. H of F #17,WS#28	3.00
2 EC Rep. H of F #5,WS #29.	2.50

HAUNT OF FEAR
Russ Cochran, 1991

1 EC Rep. H of F #15	1.50
2 thru 5 EC Rep. H of F	@1.50

Second Series, 1992

1 EC Rep. H of F #14,WS#13	2.25
2 EC Rep. H of F #18,WF#14	2.00
3 EC Rep. H of F #19,WF#18	2.00
4 EC Rep. H of F #16,WF#15	2.00
5 EC Rep. H of F #5,WF#22	2.00
6 EC Rep. H of F.	2.00
7 EC Rep. H of F.	2.00
8 thru 15 Rep.	@2.00

Gemstone

16 thru 28 EC comics reprint	@2.50

'Annuals'

TPB Vol. 1 rebinding of #1–#5	8.95
TPB Vol. 2 rebinding of #6–#10	8.95
TPB Vol. 3 rebinding of #11–#15	8.95
TPB Vol. 4 rebinding of #16–#20	12.95
TPB Vol. 5 rebinding of #21–#25	13.50
TPB Vol. 6 rebinding of #26–#28	8.95

HAVE GUN, WILL TRAVEL
Dell Publishing Co., Aug., 1958

1 Richard Boone Ph(c) all	250.00
2	200.00
3	200.00
4 thru 14	@150.00

HAWKMOON, COUNT BRASS
First

1 Michael Moorcock adapt.	2.00
2 thru 4	@2.00

HAWKMOON JEWEL IN THE SKULL
First, 1986

1 Michael Moorcock adapt.	3.00
2	2.50
3	2.00
4	2.00

HAWKMOON, MAD GOD'S AMULET
First, 1987

1 Michael Moorcock adapt.	2.00
2	2.00
3	2.00
4	2.00

HAWKMOON, SWORD OF THE DAWN
First, 1987

1 Michael Moorcock adapt.	2.00
2 thru 4	@2.00

HAWKMOON, THE RUNESTAFF
First, 1988

1 Michael Moorcock adapt.	2.00
2	2.00
3	2.00
4	2.00

HEADMAN
Innovation

1	2.50
2	2.50

HEARTSTOPPER
Millennium

1 V:Demons	2.95
2 V:Demons	2.95
3 F:Hellfire.	2.95

HEAVEN SWORD & DRAGON SABRE
Comicsone.com 2002

TPB Vol. 4 thru Vol. 7	@13.95

HEAVY METAL MONSTERS
3-D-Zone, 1992

1 w/3-D glasses	3.95

Haunt of Fear #3
© Russ Cochran

All comics prices listed are for Near Mint condition.

HECTOR HEATHCOTE
Gold Key, March, 1964
1 . . . . 125.00

HEDG
Papyrus Media, 2002
1 by Patrick Sherman 2.95
1 signed 2.95
2 thru 4 . . . . @2.95
TPB Vol 1 . . . . 19.95

HELDEN
Caption Comics, 2001
1 (of 6) by Ralf Paul 2.95
2 thru 4 . . . . @2.95
5 . . . . 2.95
6 concl. 52-pg. 3.95

HELLINA
See Also B&W

HELLINA/ DOUBLE IMPACT
Lightning, 1996
1-shot JCy(c) 3.00
1-shot variant (c) 3.00

HELLINA: HEART OF THORNS
Lightning Comics, 1996
1 . . . . 3.00
1 autographed edition 10.00
2 . . . . 3.00
2 variant cover 3.00
2 platinum edition 5.95

HELLINA: HELLBORN
Lightning, 1997
1 . . . . 2.95
1 autographed edition 9.95

HELLINA/NIRA X: ANGEL OF DEATH
Lightning, 1996
1A cover A 3.00
1B cover B 3.00
1C Platinum cover 9.00
1D signed 9.00

HELLINA/NIRA X: CYBERANGEL
Lightning, 1996
1 autographed edition 9.95

HERBIE
American Comics Group April-May, 1964
1 . . . . 250.00
2 . . . . 125.00
3 . . . . 125.00
4 . . . . 125.00
5 A:Beatles,Dean Martin, Frank Sinatra 150.00
6 . . . . 100.00
7 . . . . 100.00
8 O:Fat Fury 130.00
9 . . . . 100.00
10 . . . . 100.00
11 . . . . 75.00

COLOR PUB.

12 . . . . 75.00
13 thru 22 . . . . @75.00
23 Feb., 1967 . . . . 75.00

Hercules #1
© Charlton Comics

HERCULES
Charlton Comics, Oct., 1967
1 . . . . 50.00
2 thru 7 . . . . @30.00
8 scarce 40.00
9 thru 13 Sept. 1969 . . . . @30.00

HERCULES: THE LEGENDARY JOURNEYS
Topps, 1996
1 & 2 . . . . @3.00
3 RTs,JBt,SeM,The Shaper,pt.1 . . . 5.00
3a Xena Ph(c) 15.00
4 RTs,JBt,SeM,The Shaper,pt.2 . . . 5.00
5 RTs,JBt,SeM,The Shaper,pt.3 . . . 5.00

HERE COMES THE BIG PEOPLE
Event Comics, 1997
1 ACo&JP(c) 2.95
1b JfD(c) 2.95
1c JQ&JP alternate (c) 9.95
1d JQ&JP alternate (c) signed . . . 29.95

HERO ALLIANCE
Wonder Color Comics, 1987
1 . . . . 2.00
Innovation, 1989-91
1 RLm,BS(c),R:HeroAlliance 6.00
2 RLm,BS(c),Victor vs.Rage 5.00
3 RLm,A:Stargrazers 4.00
4 . . . . 3.00
5 RLm(c) 2.50
6 BS(c),RLm pin-up 3.25
7 V:Magnetron 2.50
8 I:Vector 2.50
9 BS(c),V:Apostate 2.50
10 A:Sentry 2.25
11 . . . . 2.25
12 I:Bombshell 2.25
13 V:Bombshell 2.25
14 Kris Solo Story 2.25
15 JLA Parody Issue 2.25
16 V:Sepulchre 2.25
17 O:Victor,I&D:Misty 2.25

Annual #1 PS,BS,RLm 3.00
Spec.#1 Hero Alliance update 2.50
Spec.Hero Alliance & Justice Machine:
Identity Crises 2.50

HERO ALLIANCE: THE END OF THE GOLDEN AGE
Pied Piper, 1986
1 Bart Sears/Ron Lim 20.00
1a signed 25.00
1b 2nd printing 2.50
2 . . . . 12.00
3 . . . . 3.00
Graphic Novel 10.00
Innovation, 1989
1 RLm 5.00
1A 2nd printing 2.50
2 RLm 4.00
3 RLm 3.00

HERO ALLIANCE QUARTERLY
Innovation
1 Hero Alliance stories 2.75
2 inc.`Girl Happy' 2.75
3 inc.`Child Engagement' 2.75
4 . . . . 2.75

HIGH CHAPPARAL
Gold Key, Aug., 1968
1 . . . . 65.00

HIGH ROADS
WildStorm/DC, April, 2002
Cliffhanger Productions
1 (of 6),SLo(s),F:Nick Highroad . . . 2.95
2 SLo(s),Paris 2.95
3 SLo(s),Nic Highroad 2.95
4 SLo(s),Iron Cross Brotherhood . . 2.95
5 SLo(s),Sloan,Bombridge 2.95
6 SLo(s),concl. 2.95
TPB 14.95

HIGH SCHOOL CONFIDENTIAL DIARY
Charlton Comics, June, 1960
1 . . . . 55.00
2 thru 11 . . . . @35.00
Becomes:

CONFIDENTIAL DIARY
12 . . . . 40.00
13 thru 17 March, 1963 . . . . . @30.00

HIGH VOLTAGE
Blackout, 1996
0 . . . . 2.95

HILLBILLY COMICS
Charlton Comics, Aug., 1955
1 . . . . 90.00
2 thru 4 July 1956 . . . . @50.00

HI-SCHOOL ROMANCE DATE BOOK
Harvey Publications, Nov., 1962
1 BP 60.00
2 . . . . 35.00
3 March, 1963 . . . . 35.00

HIS NAME IS ROG... ROG 2000
A Plus Comics
1 . . . . 2.00

HOBBIT, THE
Eclipse
1 . . . . 8.00
1a 2ndPrinting 6.00
2 . . . . 7.00
2a 2ndPrinting 5.00
3 . . . . 6.00

HOGAN'S HEROES
Dell Publishing Co., June, 1966
1 Ph(c) 125.00
2 Ph(c) 75.00
3 JD,Ph(c) 75.00
4 thru 8 Ph(c) . . . . @50.00
8 and 9 . . . . @50.00

HONEY WEST
Gold Key, Sept., 1966
1 . . . . 150.00

HONEYMOONERS
Lodestone, 1986
1 . . . . 4.00
5 Mag. 2.50

[2nd Series] Triad, 1987
1 'They Know What They Like' . . . 3.00
2 'The Life You Save' 2.50
3 X-mas special,inc.Art Carney
  interview. 3.50
4 'In the Pink' 3.00
5 'Bang, Zoom, To the Moon'. 2.00
6 'Everyone Needs a Hero' inc.
  Will Eisner interview 2.00
7 . . . . 2.00
8 . . . . 2.00
9 Jack Davis(c) 4.50
10 thru 13. . . . . @2.00

HONG KONG
Blackout Comics, 1996
0 A:Hari Kari 2.95
0 limited commemorative edition . . 9.95

HORSEMEN
Griot Enterprises, 2002
1 (of 3) 2.95
2 thru 3 . . . . @2.95
3.5 . . . . 2.95

HOT COMICS PREMIERE
Hot Comics
1 F:Thunderkill, Jacknife 2.00

HOT ROD RACERS
Charlton Comics, Dec., 1964
1 . . . . 125.00
2 thru 5 . . . . @75.00
6 thru 15 July, 1967 . . . . @50.00

HOT STUFF, THE LITTLE DEVIL
Harvey Publications, Oct., 1957
1 . . . . 550.00
2 1st Stumbo the Giant 300.00
3 thru 5 . . . . @200.00
6 thru 10 . . . . @150.00

COLOR PUB.

Hot Stuff, The Little Devil #66
© Harvey

11 thru 20 . . . . @125.00
21 thru 40 . . . . @75.00
41 thru 60 . . . . @40.00
61 thru 100 . . . . @30.00
101 thru 105 . . . . @25.00
106 thru 112 52 pg Giants . . . . @30.00
113 thru 172 . . . . @5.00

HOT STUFF SIZZLERS
Harvey Publications, July, 1960
1 B:68 pgs. 200.00
2 thru 5 . . . . @100.00
6 thru 10 . . . . @60.00
11 thru 20 . . . . @50.00
21 thru 30 . . . . @35.00
31 thru 44 . . . . @25.00
45 E:68 pgs 15.00
46 thru 50 . . . . @15.00
51 thru 59 . . . . @10.00

HOTSHOTS
1 thru 4 . . . . @2.00

HOTSPUR
Eclipse
1 RT(i),I:Josef Quist 2.00
2 RT(i),Amulet of Kothique Stolen . 2.00
3 RT(i),Curse of the SexGoddess . 2.00

HOWARD CHAYKIN'S AMERICAN FLAGG!
First
1 thru 9 . . . . @2.00
10 thru 12. . . . . @2.00

H.P.LOVECRAFT'S CTHULHU
Millennium
1 I:Miskatonic Project,V:Mi-Go. . . . 2.50
2 Arkham, trading cards. 2.50

H.R. PUFNSTUF
Gold Key, 1970
1 . . . . 300.00
2 & 3 . . . . @150.00
4 thru 8 . . . . @125.00

His–I Spy

HUCK & YOGI JAMBOREE
Dell Publishing Co., March, 1961
1 . . . . 150.00

HUCKLEBERRY HOUND
Charlton, Nov., 1970
1 . . . . 75.00
2 thru 7 . . . . @40.00
3 Jan., 1972 . . . . 50.00

HUCKLEBERRY HOUND
Dell Publishing Co., May-July, 1959
1 . . . . 175.00
2 . . . . 125.00
3 thru 7 . . . . @100.00
8 thru 10 . . . . @75.00
11 thru 17 . . . . @60.00

Gold Key
18 Chuckleberry Tales 125.00
19 Chuckleberry Tales 100.00
20 Chuckleberry Tales 60.00
21 thru 30 . . . . @40.00
31 thru 43 . . . . @30.00

HUEY, DEWEY & LOUIE JUNIOR WOODCHUCKS
Gold Key, Aug., 1966
1 . . . . 85.00
2 thru 5 . . . . @50.00
6 thru 17 . . . . @40.00
18 . . . . 30.00
19 thru 25 . . . . @35.00
26 thru 30 . . . . @30.00
31 thru 57 . . . . @30.00
58 . . . . 25.00
59 . . . . 25.00
60 thru 80 . . . . @20.00
81 1984 . . . . 20.00

HYBRIDS
Continuity, 1993
0 Deathwatch 2000 prologue 5.00
1 Deathwatch 2000 pt.4,w/card . . . 2.50
2 Deathwatch 2000 pt.13,w/card . . 2.50
3 Deathwatch 2000 w/card 2.50
4 A:Valeria. 2.50
5 O:Valeria 2.50

[2nd Series], 1994
1 Rise of Magic 2.50

HYBRIDS: ORIGIN
Continuity, 1993
1 thru 5 . . . . @2.50

HYDE-25
Harris, 1995
1 New Drug 2.95

I DREAM OF JEANNIE
Dell Publishing Co., April, 1965
1 Ph(c),B.Eden 250.00
2 Ph(c),B.Eden 175.00

I SPY
Gold Key, Aug., 1966
1 Bill Cosby Ph(c) 350.00
2 Ph(c) 250.00
3 thru 4 AMc,Ph(c) . . . . @200.00
5 thru 6 Ph(c) Sept.1968 . . . . @200.00

I'M DICKENS – HE'S FENSTER
Dell Publishing Co., May-July, 1963
1 Ph(c) 75.00
2 Ph(c) 60.00

I-BOTS
Big Comics, 1996
1 F:Lady Justice 2.25
2 thru 4 . . . . @2.25
5 StG(s),PB. 2.25
6 StG(s),PB. 2.25
7 PB,`Rebirth,'pt.1, triptych (c) . . . 2.25
8 PB,`Rebirth,'pt.2, triptych (c) . . . 2.25
9 PB,`Rebirth,'pt.3, Original I-Bots return, triptych (c) 2.25

ICICLE
Hero Graphics
1 A:Flare,Lady Arcane, V:Eraserhead 4.95

IMP
Slave Labor, 1994
1 . . . . 2.25

IMPACT
Gemstone, 1999
1 EC Comic reprint 2.50
2 thru 5 . . . . @2.50
Annual #1 rep. #1–#5 . . . . 13.50

INCAL
Humanoids Publishing, 2001
1 . . . . 2.95
2 thru 6 . . . . @2.95
7 thru 13 . . . . 2.95
TPB Vol.1 Orphan of the City Shaft 17.95
TPB Vol.2 John Difool Detective . . 17.95
TPB Vol.3 The Epic Consipiracy . . 17.95

INMATES: PRISONERS OF SOCIETY
Delta Comics, 1997
1 (of 4) 2.95
2 thru 4 . . . . @2.95

INNER CIRCLE
Mushroom Comics, 1995
1.1 I:Point Blank 2.50
1.2 V:Deathcom 2.50
1.3 V:Deathcom 2.50
1.4 V:Deathcom 2.50

INNOCENTS
Radical Comics, 1995
1 I:Innocent 2.50

INNOVATORS
Dark Moon, 1995
1 I:Innovator, LeoShan 2.50
2 O:Mr. Void 2.50
3 I:Quill 2.50

INSANE CLOWN POSSE
Chaos Comics, 1999
1 . . . . 2.95
1 premium edition 10.00
1 Jeckel Brothers premium ed. . . . 10.00

3 Raze the Desertz of Glass 2.95
3a variant (c) 10.00
Spec. The Amazing Jeckel Brothers 2.95
TPB Vol. 1 . . . . 8.95

INSANE CLOWN POSSE: DARK CARNIVAL
Chaos! Comics, 2002
1 . . . . 3.00
1a premium edition 10.00

INSANE CLOWN POSSE: MR. JOHNSON'S HEAD
Chaos Comics, 2002
Ashcan 6.00
1 (of 2) 3.00
1a premium edition 10.00

INSANE CLOWN POSSE: THE PENDULUM
Chaos! Comics, 2000
1 polybagged with CD single 5.95
1a variant (c) 10.00
2 polybagged 5.95
3 polybagged 5.95
4 polybagged 5.95
5 Road Rage, polybagged 5.95
6 . . . . 5.95
7 Pendulum's Promise 6.00
8 Sport hunting, with CD-ROM. . . 6.00
9 Glimpse of Crystal Death 6.00
10 . . . . 6.00
11 with CD-ROM 6.00
12 . . . . 6.00
Spec. #1 Hallowicket 3.00
TPB Vol. 1 . . . . 8.95
TPB Vol. 2 . . . . 9.00

INTERVIEW WITH A VAMPIRE
Innovation, 1991
1 based on novel,preq.to Vampire Chronicles 3.50
2 . . . . 3.00
3 Death & Betrayal 3.00
4 . . . . 3.00
5 D:Lestat 2.50
6 Transylvania Revelation 2.50
7 Louis & Claudia in Paris 2.50
8 thru 10 . . . . @2.50
11 . . . . 2.50

INTERVIEW WITH A VAMPIRE
Innovation
1 based on novel, preq. to Vampire Chronicles 3.50
2 . . . . 3.00
3 Death & Betrayal 3.00
4 . . . . 3.00
5 D:Lestat 2.50
6 Transylvania Revelation 2.50
7 Louis & Claudia in Paris 2.50

INTIMATE
Charlton Comics, Dec., 1957
1 thru 3 . . . . @35.00
Becomes:

TEEN-AGE LOVE
4 . . . . 30.00
5 thru 9 . . . . @25.00
10 thru 35 . . . . @15.00
36 thru 96 . . . . @15.00

Invaders From Home, Book 1
© Piranha Press

INTRUDER
TSR, 1990–91
1 thru 4 . . . . @2.95
5 thru 8 The Next Dimension . . . @2.95

INVADERS FROM HOME
Piranha Press, 1990
1 thru 6 . . . . @2.50

INVADERS, THE
Gold Key, Oct., 1967
1 Ph(c),DSp 150.00
2 Ph(c),DSp 100.00
3 Ph(c),DSp 100.00
4 Ph(c),DSp 100.00

INVINCIBLE FOUR OF KUNG FU & NINJA
Dr. Leungs
1 . . . . 2.75
2 and 3 . . . . @2.50
4 . . . . 2.00
5 thru 11 . . . . @2.00

IO
Invictus Studios, 1994
1 I:IO 2.25
2 . . . . 2.25
3 V:Major Damage 2.25

IRON HORSE
Dell Publishing Co., March, 1967
1 . . . . 35.00
2 . . . . 35.00

IRONJAW
Atlas, Jan.–July, 1975
1 NA(c),MSy 20.00
2 NA(c) 15.00
3 . . . . 15.00
4 O:IronJaw 15.00

IRON MARSHAL
Jademan, 1990
1 . . . . 2.00

2 .... 2.00
3 .... 2.00
4 .... 2.00
5 .... 2.00
6 V:Bloody Duke 2.00
7 .... 2.00
8 .... 2.00
9 The Unicorn Sword 2.00
10 The Great Thor 2.00
11 A:Exterminator 2.00
12 Bloody Duke vs. Exterminator .. 2.00
13 Secret of Unicorn Supreme 2.00
14 A:The Great Thor 2.00
15 A:The Great Thor 2.00
16 V:Tienway Champ 2.00
17 thru 20 .... @2.00
21 Bloody Duke wounded 2.00
22 A:Great Thor 2.00
23 .... 2.00
24 .... 2.00
25 .... 2.00
26 Iron Marshal Betrayed 2.00
27 thru 32 .... @2.00

IRREGULARS, THE: BATTLETECH Miniseries
Blackthorne
1 .... 2.00
2 .... 2.00
3 B&W 2.00

IRUKASHI
1 .... 2.00

ISAAC ASIMOV'S I-BOTS
Tekno-Comix, 1995
1 I:I-Bots 2.00
2 O:I-Bots 2.00
3 V:Black OP 2.25

IT! TERROR FROM BEYOND SPACE
Millennium
1 .... 2.50
2 .... 2.50

IT'S ABOUT TIME
Gold Key, Jan., 1967
1 Ph(c) 65.00

ITCHY & SCRATCHY
Bongo Comics, 1993
1 DaC(s) 2.25
2 DaC(s) 2.25
3 .... 2.25

IVANHOE
Dell Publishing Co., July-Sept., 1963
1 .... 50.00

JACK
Med Systems Company
1 Anubis in the 90's 2.95
2 Modern Society 2.95

JACK HUNTER
Blackthorne, 1988
1 .... 2.00
2 .... 2.00
3 .... 2.00

JACKIE CHAN'S SPARTAN X
Topps, 1997
1 'The Armor of Heaven,' pt.1 .... 2.95
2 'The Armor of Heaven,' pt.2 .... 2.95
3 (of 6) 2.95

JADE
Chaos! Comics, 2001
1 .... 3.00
1a premium edition 10.00
2 .... 3.00
3 .... 3.00
4 .... 3.00
4a variant 7.50
Preview book 2.00
Preview book, premium 6.00
Ashcan Jade #1 .... 6.00

JADE: REDEMPTION
Chaos! Comics, 2001
1 (of 4) 3.00
1 premium edition 10.00
2 .... 3.00
3 .... 3.00
4 .... 3.00
2a thru 4a variant (c) .... @7.50
Ashcan 6.00

JADEMAN COLLECTION
1 .... 4.50
2 .... 3.00
3 .... 2.50
4 .... 2.50
5 .... 2.50

JADEMAN KUNG FU SPECIAL
1 I:Oriental Heroes, Blood Sword, Drunken Fist 5.00

JADE WARRIORS: SLAVE OF THE DRAGON
Avatar Press, 2000
1 (of 3) MD2, 40-page 3.50
1a photo (c) 3.50
1b wraparound (c) 3.50
2 MD2 .... 3.50
2a photo (c) 3.50

JAGUAR GOD
Verotika, 1995
1 Frazetta, I:Jaquar God 2.95
2 V:Yi-Cha 2.95
3 V:Yi-Cha 2.95
4 V:Yi-Cha 2.95
5 AOI 2.95
6 LSh,AOI 2.95
7 LSh,AOI 2.95
8 AOI 2.95
Spec.#1 Return to X'ibala,RCo 4.95
Spec. Jaguar God Illustrations ... 3.95
Spec. fan club edition 10.00

JAKE TRASH
Aircel
1 thru 3 .... @2.00

JAMES BOND 007
Eclipse, 1991
1 MGr,PerfectBound 5.50
2 MGr 5.00
3 MGr,end series 5.00
GN Licence to Kill, MGr I/o 8.00

JAMES BOND: GOLDENEYE
Topps, 1995
1 Movie adaptation 2.95
2 thru 3 Movie adaptation ..... @2.95

JAM SPECIAL
Comico
1 .... 2.50

JASON GOES TO HELL
Topps, 1993
1 Movie adapt.,w/3 cards 3.25
2 Movie adapt.,w/3 cards 3.25
3 Movie adapt.,w/3 cards 3.25

JASON VS. LEATHERFACE
Topps, 1995
1 Jason Meets Leatherface 2.95
2 SBi(c) Leatherface's family ... 2.95
3 SBi(c),conclusion 2.95

Javerts #1
© Firstlight

JAVERTS
Firstlight, 1994
1 New Series 2.95
2 thru 5 Pieces of an Icon .... @2.95

JENNY SPARKS: THE SECRET HISTORY OF THE AUTHORITY
WildStorm/DC, June, 2000
1 (of 5) MMr,JMC 2.50
1a variant (c) (1:4) 2.50
2 MMr,JMC 2.50
3 MMr,JMC,O:Jack Hawksmoor ... 2.50
4 MMr,JMC 2.50
5 MMr,JMC,conclusion 2.50
TPB 120-page, rep. 14.95

JET
WildStorm/DC, Sept., 2000
1 (of 4) DAn,ALa,F:Jodi Slayton ... 2.50

Jet–Jon Sable / COLOR PUB. / Comics Values Annual

2 DAn,ALa,Midnight to Midnight . . . 2.50
3 DAn,ALa,V:Timewaster 2.50
4 DAn,ALa,concl 2.50

JET DREAM
Gold Key, June, 1968
1 . . . . 50.00

JETSONS, THE
Gold Key, Jan., 1963
1 . . . . 350.00
2 . . . . 200.00
3 thru 10 . . . . @150.00
11 thru 20 . . . . @100.00
21 thru 36 Oct. 1970 . . . . @75.00

JETSONS, THE
Charlton Comics, Nov., 1970
1 from Hanna-Barbera TV show. 125.00
2 . . . . 60.00
3 thru 10 . . . . @45.00
11 thru 20 Dec. 1973 . . . . @35.00

JETSONS, THE
Harvey Comics, 1991–92
1 thru 5 . . . . @2.00

JETSONS, THE
Archie, 1995
1 thru 17 . . . . @2.00

JEZEBELLE
WildStorm/DC, Jan., 2001
1 (of 6) F:Harper Harrison 2.50
1a variant(c) (1:2) 2.50
2 BRa(s) 2.50
3 BRa(s) F:Harper Harrison 2.50
4 BRa(s),Seance&Sensibility,pt.1 . . 2.50
5 BRa(s),Seance&Sensibility,pt.2 . . 2.50
6 BRa(s),concl. 2.50

JEZEBEL JADE
Comico, 1988
1 AKu,A:Race Bannon 2.00
2 AKu 2.00
3 AKu 2.00

JIGSAW
Harvey Publications, Sept., 1966
1 . . . . 35.00
2 . . . . 25.00

JIMBO
Bongo Comics
1 R:Jimbo 2.95
2 thru 4 . . . . @2.95

JIMMY CORRIGAN
Fantagraphics
1 Chris Ware 3.95

J. N. WILLIAMSON'S MASQUES
Innovation
1 TV,From horror anthology 4.95
2 Olivia(c) inc.Better Than One . . . 4.95

COLOR PUB.

JOHN BOLTON, HALLS OF HORROR
Eclipse
1 JBo 2.00
2 JBo 2.00

JOHN CARTER OF MARS
Gold Key, 1964
1 . . . . 100.00
2 & 3 . . . . @60.00

JOHN F. KENNEDY LIFE STORY
(WITH 2 REPRINTS)
Dell Publishing Co., Aug.-Oct., 1964
1 . . . . 75.00
2 . . . . 50.00
3 . . . . 50.00

John Jakes Mullkon Empire #6
© Tekno Comix

JOHN JAKES MULLKON EMPIRE
Tekno Comix, 1995
1 I:Mulkons 2.25
2 O:Mulkons 2.00
3 D:Company Man 2.00
4 Disposal Problems 2.00
5 F:Granny 2.00
6 Where's Karma 2.25

JOHN LAW
Eclipse, 1983
1 WE 2.00

JOHNNY GAMBIT
Hot
1 . . . . 2.00

JOHNNY JASON TEEN REPORTER
Dell Publishing Co., 1962
1 . . . . 50.00
2 . . . . 40.00

JOHNNY NEMO
Eclipse, 1985–86
1 I:Johnny Nemo 2.00
2 . . . . 2.00
3 F:Sindy Shade 2.50

JOHN STEELE SECRET AGENT
Gold Key, Dec., 1964
1 . . . . 125.00

JONNY QUEST
Gold Key, Dec., 1964
1 TV show 500.00

JONNY QUEST
Comico, June, 1986
1 DW,SR,A:Dr.Zin 4.50
2 WP/JSon,O:RaceBannon 3.50
3 DSt(c) 3.00
4 TY/AW,DSt(i) 2.50
5 DSt(c)A:JezebelJade 2.50
6 AKu 2.00
7 . . . . 2.00
8 KSy 2.00
9 MA 2.00
10 King Richard III 2.00
11 JSon,BSz(c) 2.00
12 DSp 2.00
12 DSp 2.00
13 CI 2.00
14 . . . . 2.00
15 thru 31 . . . . @2.00
Spec.#1 . . . . 2.00
Spec.#2 . . . . 2.00

JONNY QUEST CLASSICS
Comico
1 DW 2.00
2 DW,O:Hadji 2.00
3 DW 2.00

JON SABLE
First, 1983
1 MGr,A:President 4.50
2 MGr,Alcohol Issue 3.50
3 MGr,O:Jon Sable 3.00
4 MGr,O:Jon Sable 3.00
5 MGr,O:Jon Sable 3.00
6 MGr,O:Jon Sable 3.00
7 MGr,The Target 2.50
8 MGr,Nuclear Energy 2.50
9 MGr,Nuclear Energy 2.50
10 MGr,Tripitych 2.50
11 MGr,I:Maggie 2.50
12 MGr,Vietnam 2.50
13 MGr,Vietnam 2.50
14 MGr,East Germany 2.50
15 MGr,Nicaragua 2.50
16 MGr,A:Maggie 2.50
17 MGr,1984 Olympics 2.50
18 MGr,1984 Olympics 2.50
19 MGr,The Widow 2.50
20 MGr,The Rookie 2.50
21 MGr,Africa 2.25
22 MGr,V:Sparrow 2.25
23 MGr,V:Sparrow 2.25
24 MGr,V:Sparrow 2.25
25 MGr,Shatter 3.00
26 MGr,Shatter 3.00
27 MGr,Shatter 3.00
28 MGr,Shatter 3.00
29 MGr,Shatter 3.00
30 MGr,Shatter 2.25

All comics prices listed are for *Near Mint* condition.

31 MGr,Nicaragua	2.00
32 MGr,Nicaragua	2.00
33 MGr,SA,Leprechauns	2.25
34 MGr,Indians	2.00
35 MGr,Indians	2.00
36 MGr,Africa	2.00
37 MGr,Africa	2.00
38 MGr,Africa	2.00
39 MGr,Africa	2.00
40 MGr,1st Case	2.00
41 MGr,1st Case	2.00
42 MGr,V:Sparrow	2.00
43 MGr,V:Sparrow	2.00
44 Hard Way	2.00
45 Hard Way II	2.00
46 MM,The Tower pt.1	2.00
47 MM,The Tower pt.2	2.00
48 MM,Prince Charles	2.00
49 MM,Prince Charles	2.00
50 A:Maggie the Cat	2.00
51 Jon Sable,babysitter pt.1	2.00
52 Jon Sable,babysitter pt.2	2.00
53 MGr	2.00
54 Jacklight pt.1	2.00
55 Jacklight pt.2	2.00
56 Jacklight pt.3	2.00

JOSIE
Archie Publications, Feb., 1963

1	250.00
2	150.00
3	75.00
4	60.00
5	75.00
6 thru 10	@55.00
11 thru 20	@40.00
21 thru 30	@35.00
31 thru 40	@30.00
41 thru 54	@30.00
55 thru 74	@20.00
75 thru 105	@20.00
106 Oct., 1962	20.00

JUDGE COLT
Gold Key, Oct., 1969

1	35.00
2	20.00
3	20.00
4 Sept., 1970	20.00

JUDGE DREDD
Eagle, 1983

1 BB,I:Judge Death(in USA)	10.00
2 BB(c&a),The Oxygen Board	8.00
3 BB(c),Judge Dredd Lives	7.00
4 BB(c),V:Perps	7.00
5 BB(c),V:Perps	5.00
6 BB(c),V:Perps	5.00
7 BB(c),V:Perps	5.00
8 BB(c),V:Perps	5.00
9 BB(c),V:Perps	5.00
10 BB(c),V:Perps	5.00
11 BB(c)	4.00
12 BB(c)	4.00
13 BB(c), The Day the Law Died, pt.5	4.00
14 BB(c),Dredd vs. Dredd	4.00
15 BB(c)	4.00
16 BB(c)	4.00
17 BB(c)	4.00
18 BB(c)	4.00
19 BB(c)	4.00
20 BB(c)	4.00
21 BB(c)	4.00
22 BB(c),V:Perps	3.00
23 BB(c),V:Perps	3.00
24 BB(c),V:Perps	3.00
25 BB(c),V:Perps	3.00
26 BB(c),V:Perps	3.00
27 BB(c),V:Perps	3.00
28 A:Judge Anderson,V:Megaman	4.00
29 A:Monty, the guinea pig	3.00
30 V:Perps	3.00
31 Destiny's Angel, Pt. 1	3.00
32 Destiny's Angel, Pt. 2	3.00
33 V:League of Fatties	3.00
34 V:Executioner	3.00

Judge Dredd #2
© Quality Press

JUDGE DREDD
Quality Press, 1986

1 Cry of the Werewolf Pt.1	6.00
2 Cry of the Werewolf Pt.2	5.00
3 Anti-smoking	4.00
4 Wreckers	4.00
5 Highwayman	4.00
6	3.00
7	3.00
8	3.00
9	3.00
10	3.00
11	3.00
12 Starborn Thing, Pt.1	3.00
13 Starborn Thing, Pt.2	3.00
14 BB, V:50 foot woman	3.00
15 City of the Damned Pt.1	3.00
16 City of the Damned Pt.2	3.00
17 City of the Damned conc.	3.00
18 V:Mean Machine Angel	3.00
19 Dredd Angel	3.00
20 V:Perps	3.00
21 V:Perps	3.00
22/23 Booby Trap	3.00
24 Junk food fiasco	3.00
25/26 V:Perps	3.00
27 V:Perps	3.00
28 Dredd Syndrome	3.00
29 V:Perps	3.00
30 V:Perps	3.00
31 Hunt Pudge Dempsey's killer	3.00
32 V:Mutated Sewer Alligator	3.00
33 V:Perps	3.00
34 V:Executioner	3.00
35 V:Shojan	3.00
36 V:Shojan	3.00
37 V:Perps	3.00
38 V:Perps	3.00
39 V:Perps	3.00
40 V:Perps	3.00
41 V:Perps	3.00
42 V:Perps	3.00
43 V:Perps	3.00
44 V:Perps	3.00
45 V:DNA Man	2.50
46 Genie lamp sty	2.50
47 V:Perps	2.50
48 Murder in Mega-City One	2.50
49 V:Perps	2.50
50 V:Perps	2.50
51 V:Perps	2.50
52 V:Perps	2.50
53 V:Perps	2.50
54 V:Perps	2.50
55 V:Perps	2.50
56 inc.JudgeDredd Postcards	2.50
57 V:Perps	2.50
58 V:370lb Maniac	2.50
59 V:Perps	2.50
60 Social Misfit	2.50
61 V:Perps	2.50

Becomes:

JUDGE DREDD CLASSICS

62	2.50
63 Mutants from the Radlands	2.50
64	2.50
65	2.50
66 Wit and wisdom of Dredd	2.50
67 V:Otto Sump	2.50
68 V:Otto Sump	2.50
69	2.50
70 Dinosaurs in Mega City 1	2.50
71	2.50
72 Pirates of the Black Atlantic	2.50
73	2.50
74	2.50
75	2.50
76 Diary of a Mad Citizen	3.00
TPB:Democracy Now	10.95
TPB:Rapture	12.95
Judge Dredd Special #1	2.50
GN Bad Science	7.95
GN Hall of Justice	7.95
GN Metal Fatigue	7.95

JUDGE DREDD
Titan, 2001

TPB The Emerald Isle	15.00
TPB Death Aid	15.00
TPB Goodnight Kiss (2002)	15.00
TPB Helter Skelter (2002)	15.00
TPB Justice One (2002)	15.00
GN Muzak Killer (2002)	14.95
GN Innocents Abroad (2002)	14.95
GN Necropolis Book One	14.95
GN Necropolis Book Two	19.95
GN Cursed Earth	19.95
GN The Complete America	16.95
GN Judge Dredd vs. Judge Dredd	12.95

JUDGE DREDD: AMERICA
Fleetway

1 I:America	3.50

JUDGE DREDD: JUDGE CHILD QUEST
Eagle

1 thru 3	@3.00
4 BB(c)	3.00
5	3.00

JUDGE DREDD'S CRIME FILE
Eagle, 1984

1 Ron Smith, 'The Perp Runners'	2.50
2 thru 6	@2.50

Quality (Prestige format)

1 A:Rogue Trooper	6.50

All comics prices listed are for Near Mint condition.

JUDGE DREDD'S EARLY CASES
Eagle
1 Robot Wars, Pt.1 . . . . 4.00
2 Robot Wars, Pt.2 . . . . 3.00
3 V:Perps 3.00
4 IG, Judge Giant 3.00
5 V:Perps 3.00
6 V:Judge killing car Elvis 3.00

2 IG,V:Fatties, Energy Vampires & Super Fleas 5.95
3 Battles foes from dead A:Judge Anderson 5.95

JUDGE DREDD'S HARDCASE PAPERS
Fleetway/Quality
1 V:The Tarantula 7.50
2 Junkies & Psychos 6.50
3 Crime Call Vid. Show 6.50
4 `Real Coffee',A:Johnny Alpha . . 6.50

JUDGE DREDD: THE MEGAZINE
Fleetway/Quality, 1991
1 Midnite's Children Pt.1 A:Chopper, Young Death 5.25
2 Midnite's Children Pt.2 . . . . 4.95
3 . . . . 4.95
23 thru 34 . . . . @3.95
35 thru 43 . . . . @5.25
44 thru 45 . . . . @6.95
Egmont Fleetway Limited
46 thru 75 . . . . @6.95

JUDGE PARKER
Argo, Feb., 1956
1 . . . . 50.00
2 . . . . 35.00

JUDGMENT DAY
Lightning Comics, 1993
1 B:JZy(s),KIK,V:Razorr,Rift, Nightmare, red prism(c) 5.00
1a Gold Prism(c) 5.00
1b Purple Prism(c) 7.00
1c Misprint,Red Prism(c), Bloodfire Credits inside 8.00
1d Misprint,Gold Prism(c), Bloodfire Credits inside 8.00
1e Misprint,Green Prism(c), Bloodfire Credits inside 8.00
1f B&W promo ed. Gold ink 5.00
1g B&W promo ed. platinum ed. . . 7.00
2 TLw,I:War Party,BU:Perg, w/Perg card 4.00
3 ErP,O:X-Treme 3.25
4 ErP,In Hell 3.25
5 TLw,In Hell 3.25
6 TLw,I:Red Front,O:Salurio 3.25
7 O:Safeguard 3.25
8 . . . . 2.95
9 . . . . 2.95
10 . . . . 2.95

JUDGMENT DAY
Maximum Press, 1997
Alpha AMo(s) 2.50
Alpha variant cover 2.50
Omega AMo(s) 2.50
Omega variant cover 2.50
Final Judgment AMo(s) 2.50
Final Judgment variant cover 2.50

JUDOMASTER
Charlton Comics, 1966
(Special War Series #4)
I:Judomaster 15.00
89 FMc,War stories begin 7.00
89 (90) FMc,A:Thunderbolt 6.00
91 FMc,DG,A:Sarge Steel 6.00
92 FMc,DG,A:Sarge Steel 6.00
93 FMc,DG,I:Tiger 6.00
94 FMc,DG,A:Sarge Steel 6.00
95 FMc,DG,A:Sarge Steel 5.00
96 FMc,DG,A:Sarge Steel 5.00
97 FMc,A:Sarge Steel 4.00
98 FMc,A:Sarge Steel 4.00

Jughead #199
© *Archie Publications*

JUGHEAD
Archie Publications Dec., 1965–June, 1987
127 thru 130 . . . . @35.00
131 thru 150 . . . . @30.00
151 thru 160 . . . . @15.00
161 thru 200 . . . . @12.00
201 thru 250 . . . . @10.00
251 thru 300 . . . . @8.00
301 thru 352 . . . . @5.00

JUGHEAD
Archie Publications [2nd Series], Aug., 1987
1 thru 45 . . . . @3.00
Becomes:

ARCHIE'S PAL JUGHEAD
June, 1993
46 thru 50 . . . . @2.00
51 thru 70 . . . . @2.00
71 thru 99 . . . . @2.00
100 A Storm Over Uniforms, x-over (Betty #57, Archie #467) 2.00
101 thru 122 . . . . @2.00
123 thru 125 . . . . @1.80
126 thru 133 . . . . @2.00
134 thru 147 . . . . @2.00
148 thru 155 . . . . @2.20

JUGHEAD AS CAPTAIN HERO
Archie Publications, Oct., 1966
1 . . . . 75.00
2 . . . . 50.00
3 thru 7 . . . . @35.00

JUGHEAD'S FANTASY
Archie Publications, Aug., 1960
1 . . . . 250.00
2 . . . . 175.00
3 . . . . 150.00

JUGHEAD'S JOKES
Archie Publications, Aug., 1967
1 . . . . 100.00
2 . . . . 75.00
3 thru 5 . . . . @40.00
6 thru 10 . . . . @35.00
11 thru 30 . . . . @25.00
31 thru 77 . . . . @10.00
78 Sept., 1982 . . . . 10.00

JUGHEAD WITH ARCHIE DIGEST
Archie Publications, March, 1974
1 . . . . 65.00
2 . . . . 50.00
3 thru 10 . . . . @25.00
11 thru 91 . . . . @10.00
92 thru 129 . . . . @8.00
130 thru 138 . . . . @7.00
139 thru 144 . . . . @7.00
145 thru 155 . . . . @5.00
156 thru 171 . . . . @3.00
172 thru 179 . . . . @3.00

JUNCTION 17
Antarctic Press 2003
1 . . . . 3.50
2 thru 4 . . . . @3.00

JUNGLE ADVENTURES
Skywald, March–June, 1971
1 F:Zangar,Jo-Jo,Blue Gorilla . . . 40.00
2 F:Sheena, Jo-Jo,Zangar 35.00
3 F:Zangar,Jo-Jo,White Princess . 35.00

JUNGLE BOOK, THE
NBM, 1997
TPB CR,Kipling adapt. 16.95

JUNGLE COMICS
Blackthorne, 1988
1 DSt(c) 2.00
2 . . . . 2.00
3 . . . . 2.00
See B&W

JUNGLE JIM
Charlton, 1969–70
22 . . . . 45.00
23 . . . . 25.00
24 . . . . 25.00
25 . . . . 25.00
26 . . . . 25.00
27 . . . . 35.00
28 . . . . 35.00

JUNGLE TALES OF TARZAN
Charlton Comics, Dec., 1964
1 . . . . 75.00
2 . . . . 50.00
3 . . . . 50.00
4 July, 1965 . . . . 50.00

JUNGLE WAR STORIES
Dell Publishing Co., July-Sept., 1962
1 P(c) all 45.00
2 .... 30.00
3 .... 30.00
4 .... 30.00
5 .... 30.00
6 .... 30.00
7 .... 30.00
8 .... 30.00
9 .... 30.00
10 .... 30.00
11 .... 30.00
Becomes:
GUERRILLA WAR
12 thru 14 .... @35.00

JUNIOR WOODCHUCKS
Walt Disney, 1991
1 CB,`Bubbleweight Champ' 2.00
2 CB,`Swamp of no Return'..... 2.00
3 `Rescue Run-Around'......... 2.00
4 `Cave Caper' 2.00

JURASSIC PARK
Topps, 1993
1 Movie Adapt.,w/card 5.00
1a Newsstand Ed................ 4.00
2 Movie Adapt.,w/card 3.25
3 Movie Adapt.,w/card 3.25
4 Movie Adapt.,w/card 3.25
2a thru 4a Newsstand Ed. ..... @2.75
Ann.#1 Death Lizards 3.95

JURASSIC PARK: ADVENTURES
Topps, 1994
1 thru 10 reprints titles .... @2.00

JURASSIC PARK: RAPTOR
Topps, 1993
1 SE w/Zorro #0 ashcan & cards .. 3.25
2 w/3 cards..................... 2.95

JURASSIC PARK: RAPTORS ATTACK
Topps, 1994
1 SEt(s), ... 2.75
2 SEt(s), ... 2.75
3 SEt(s), ... 2.75
4 SEt(s), ... 2.75

JURASSIC PARK: RAPTOR HIJACK
Topps
1 SEt(s), ... 2.50
2 SEt(s), ... 2.50
3 SEt(s), ... 2.50
4 SEt(s), ... 2.50

[JURASSIC PARK:] THE LOST WORLD
Topps, 1997
1 (of 4) movie adapt 2.95
2 thru 4 .... @2.95

JUST A PILGRIM
Black Bull Entertainment, 2001
1 GEn,MT(c)..................... 6.00
1a variant (c)................. 12.00
2 GEn,GF(c) 4.00
3 GEn,KN(c), Bloody Baskets 4.00
4 GEn,BSz(c) Firestarter 4.00
5 GEn,JMC(c)................... 4.00
Preview Ed..................... 7.00
TPB GEn,MT(c) 13.00

JUST A PILGRIM: GARDEN OF EDEN
Black Bull Entertainment, 2002
1 GEn,JJu(c).................... 7.00
1a variant GF (c)............... 4.00
2 GEn,CE 4.00
3 GEn,CE 4.00
4 GEn,CE 4.00
Preview ed. limited 7.00
TPB series rep................. 13.00

Justice Machine #1
© Noble Comics

JUSTICE MACHINE
Noble Comics, 1981–85
1 JBy(c) Mag size,B&W 30.00
2 MGu,Mag size,B&W 16.00
3 MGu,Mag size,B&W 10.00
4 MGu,Bluecobalt 8.00
5 MGu.......................... 7.00
Texas Comics
Ann.#1:BWG,I:Elementals,
  A: Thunder Agents 5.00

JUSTICE MACHINE
[Featuring the Elementals]
Comico, 1986
1 thru 4 .... @2.50

JUSTICE MACHINE
Comico, 1987–89
1 MGu.......................... 2.50
2 MGu.......................... 2.00
3 thru 14 MGu .... @2.00
15 thru 27 MGu .... @2.00
28 MGu 2.00
29 MGu,IW...................... 2.00
Ann.#1 .... 2.50
SummerSpectacular 1 .... 2.75
MINI SERIES, 1990
1 thru 4 F:Elementals......... @2.00

Innovation, 1990
1 .... 2.00
2 thru 4 The Ragnarok Portfolio . @2.00
5 thru 7 Demon trilogy .... @2.00

JUSTICE MACHINE: CHIMERA CONSPIRACY
Millennium
1 AH,R&N:Justice Machine,
  wraparound cover............ 2.50

JUST MARRIED
Charlton Comics, Jan., 1958
1 .... 100.00
2 .... 60.00
3 thru 10 .... @40.00
11 thru 30 .... @25.00
31 thru 113 .... @15.00
114 Dec., 1976................ 10.00

KABOOM
Awesome Entertainment, 1997
1 JLb,JMs,..................... 5.00
1a variant (c)s................ 6.00
2 JLb,JMs,..................... 3.00
3 JLb,JMs,..................... 4.00
4 JLb,JMs,Kaboom the
  Barbarian,pt.1 (of 3)........ 2.50
5 JLb,JMs,Barbarian,pt.2....... 2.50
6 JLb,JMs,Barbarian,pt.3....... 2.50
VOL II
1 (of 3) 2.50
2 JLe,JLb,F:Kyra 2.50
3 JLe,JLb, conclusion 2.50
Collected #1 & #2.............. 5.95

KABUKI
Caliber Press
1 Color Gallery,32 paintings... 7.00
1-shot Color Special, inc.
  pin-up gallery 3.00
1-shot Fear the Reaper (1994)... 7.00

KABUKI: SKIN DEEP
Caliber, 1996
1 DMk.......................... 4.00
2 DMk(c)....................... 3.50
2 AxR(c)....................... 6.00
3 Origin issue 3.50
4 .... 3.50

KAMIKAZE: 1946
Antarctic Press, 2000
1 Pickadon 2.95
2 Operation Olympic 2.95
3 Queens of the Seas 2.95
4 Operation Coronet 2.95
5 Kaitens...................... 2.95
6 Fortress Japan 2.95

KAMIKAZE
Wildstorm/DC Oct. 2003
1 (of 5) extreme sport 2.95
2 .... 2.95

KATO OF THE GREEN HORNET
Now, 1991
1 BA,1st Kato solo story 2.50
2 BA,Kato in China contd....... 2.50
3 Kato in China contd 2.50
4 Final Issue 2.50

Kato–Korak / COLOR PUB. / Comics Values Annual

KATO II
Now, 1992
1 VM,JSh,A:Karthage 2.50
2 VM,JSh,V:Karthage 2.50
3 VM,JSh,V:Karthage 2.50

KATY KEENE FASHION BOOK MAGAZINE
Archie Publications, 1955
1 Woggon(a&c) 600.00
2 .... 350.00
3 thru 10 not published
11 thru 18 .... @250.00
19 .... 200.00
20 .... 200.00
21 .... 200.00
22 .... 200.00
23 Winter 1958-59 .... 200.00

KATY KEENE PINUP PARADE
Archie Publications, 1955
1 .... 600.00
2 .... 300.00
3 .... 250.00
4 .... 250.00
5 .... 250.00
6 .... 225.00
7 .... 225.00
8 .... 225.00
9 .... 225.00
10 Woggon art 225.00
11 Story on comics 250.00
12 .... 225.00
13 .... 225.00
14 .... 225.00
15 Sept., 1961 .... 500.00

KELLY GREEN
Eclipse
1 SDr,O:Kelly Green 2.50
2 SDr,'One,Two,Three' 2.00
3 SDr,'Million Dollar Hit' .. 2.00
4 SDr,Rare 4.00

KELVIN MACE
Vortex
1 .... 6.50
1a 2nd printing 2.00
2 .... 4.00

KEN LASHLEY'S LEGENDS
DHJ Comics, 2002
1 (of 6) by Ken Lashley 2.95
1a variant (c) 2.95
1b previews exclusive 4.95
2 .... 2.95

KID DEATH & FLUFFY
Event Comics, 1997
Spec.#1 Halloween Spec. John
  Cebollero(c) 2.95
Spec.#1a Halloween Spec. JQ(c) .. 2.95

KILLER INSTINCT
Acclaim
1 thru 3 .... @2.50
Spec. Brothers by Art Holcomb 2.50

Killer Instict #3
© Acclaim

KILLER TALES
Eclipse, 1985
1 Tim Truman 3.00

KINDRED II
WildStorm/DC, Jan., 2002
1 (of 4) BBh 2.50
2 BBh 2.50
3 BBh,Backlash & Grifter 2.50
4 BBh,concl. 2.50

KING COMICS PRESENTS
King Comics
1 I:Rick Dees, Angel Lopez 2.00

KING LEONARDO AND HIS SHORT SUBJECTS
Dell Publishing Co., Nov.-Jan., 1961-62
1 .... 225.00
2 .... 150.00
3 .... 175.00
4 .... 150.00

KING LOUIE & MOWGLI
Gold Key, May, 1968
1 .... 40.00

KING OF DIAMONDS
Dell Publishing Co., July-Sept., 1962
1 Ph(c) 50.00

KIT KARTER
Dell Publishing Co., May-July, 1962
1 .... 40.00

KNIGHTHAWK
Windjammer 1995
1 NA(c&a),I:Knighthawk the
  Protector,V:Nemo 2.75
2 NA(c&a),Birth of Nemo 2.50
3 NA,V:Nemo 2.50
4 NA,V:Nemo 2.50
5 I:Cannon, Brick 2.50
6 V:Cannon, Brick 2.50

KNIGHTS OF THE ROUND TABLE
Dell Publishing Co., Nov.-Jan., 1963-64
1 P(c) 50.00

KNUCKLES
Archie Comics, 1997
1 .... 2.00
2 thru 31 .... @2.00
32 thru 33 .... @1.80

KOL MANIQUE RENAISSANCE
1 .... 2.00
2 .... 2.00

KOMAH
Anubis Press
1 Urban Decay Title 2.75

KOMBAT
Random Comics
1 (of 2) by Marcu Marshall
  & Pablo Villalobos 2.95
2 concl 2.95

KONA
Dell Publishing Co., Feb.-April, 1962
1 P(c) all,SG 125.00
2 SG 60.00
3 SG 60.00
4 SG,B:Anak 60.00
5 SG 60.00
6 SG 60.00
7 SG 60.00
8 SG 60.00
9 SG 60.00
10 SG 60.00
11 thru 21 SG .... @40.00

KONGA
Charlton Comics, 1960–65
1 SD,DG(c), movie adapt. ... 350.00
2 DG(c) 175.00
3 SD 150.00
4 SD 150.00
5 SD 150.00
6 thru 15 SD .... @100.00
16 thru 23 .... @75.00

KONGA'S REVENGE
Charlton Comics
2 Summer, 1962 .... 75.00
3 SD,Fall, 1964 .... 50.00
1 Dec., 1968 .... 35.00

KOOKIE
Dell Publishing Co., Feb.-April, 1962
1 .... 125.00
2 .... 100.00

KORAK, SON OF TARZAN
Gold Key, Jan., 1964
1 .... 100.00

COLOR PUB.

```
                                                    2 thru 11 . . . . . . . . . . . . . . . . . . @50.00
                                                    12 thru 21 . . . . . . . . . . . . . . . . . @35.00
                                                    22 thru 30 . . . . . . . . . . . . . . . . . @30.00
                                                    31 thru 40 . . . . . . . . . . . . . . . . . @25.00
                                                    41 thru 44 . . . . . . . . . . . . . . . . . @20.00
                                                    45 Jan., 1972 . . . . . . . . . . . . . . . . 20.00
                                                    Continued by DC
```

KRUSTY COMICS
Bongo Comics, 1995
1 Rise and Fall of Krustyland 2.25
2 Rise and Fall of Krustyland 2.25
3 Rise and Fall of Krustyland 2.25

KULL IN 3-D
Blackthorne
1 . . . . 2.50
2 . . . . 2.50
3 . . . . 2.50

LAD: A DOG
Dell Publishing Co., 1961
1 . . . . 60.00
2 . . . . 50.00

LADY ARCANE
Hero Graphics
1 A: Flare,BU:O:Giant 4.95
2 thru 3 . . . . @2.95

LADY DEATH
Chaos! Comics, Jan., 1994
1 BnP, A:Evil Ernie 15.00
1a signed gold foil 20.00
2 BnP 15.00
3 BnP 10.00
TPB Rep. #1–3 . . . . 6.95
TPB The Reckoning 12.95
TPB The Reckoning, revised,
    BnP,Shu 12.95
Specials & 1-shots
1 Swimsuit Edition 10.00
1a Velvet Edition 18.00
1 reprint with 8-page pin-up gallery 2.95
1 Lady Death in Lingerie,
    various artists 5.00
1 Lady Death & the Women of
    Chaos! Gallery, pin-ups (1996) . 2.25
1-shot Dragon Wars (1998) 2.95

Lady Death #3
© Chaos! Comics

1-shotA Dragon Wars, Premium Ed,
    Sketchbook cover 15.00
1-shot Retribution (1998) 2.95
1-shotA Retribution (1998) variant
    cover 2.95
1-shotB Retribution, premium ed. . 10.00

LADY DEATH
Chaos! Comics, 1998
? signed, limited 15.00
1 . . . . 3.00
1a signed, limited 10.00
2 R:Lady Demon 3.00
3 V:Levithia 3.00
4 V:Pagan 3.00
5 The Harrowing, pt.1 . . . . 3.00
6 V:Uriel 3.00
7 V:Moloch 3.00
8 time to sieze Hell 3.00
9 world scythe of the covenant . . 3.00
10 Goddess War,pt.2 x-over 3.00
11 V:Cremator 3.00
12 Unholy Nights 3.00
13 MD2,DQ,Inferno, pt.1 . . . . 3.00
13a signed 19.95
14 MD2,DQ,Inferno, pt.2 . . . . 2.95
15 MD2,DQ,Inferno, pt.3 . . . . 2.95
15a variant cover 6.00
16 MD2,DQ,Inferno, pt.4 . . . . 2.95
Swimsuit Spec.#1, signed 20.00

LADY DEATH
Chaos! Comics, 1999
1/2 Tribute Book 13.95
0 ashcan, yellow 10.00
0 ashcan, yellow, signed 20.00
0 ashcan, blue 25.00
1 (of 12) by Steve Hughes 2.95
1a signed 15.00
1b deluxe Steve Hughes (c) 15.95
Spec. Swimsuit 2001 #1 . . . . 3.00
Spec. Swimsuit 2001 #1 premium. 11.00
Vol. 1 Lady Death's Black Book . . 10.00
Vol. 1 Black Book,premium ed. . . . 15.00
Halloween Special Ashcan 6.00
Halloween Spec. Ashcan, premium 20.00
Halloween Spec. #1 . . . . 3.00
Halloween Spec. #1a premium ed. 10.00
Halloween Spec. #1b
    super-premium edition 20.00
Halloween Spec. 1c foil edition . . . 20.00

LADY DEATH
Crossgen Code 6 Comics 2003
1 thru 10 A Medieval Tale . . . . . . @2.95
GN Vol. 1 A Medieval Tale 9.95

LADY DEATH: ALIVE
Chaos! Comics, 2001
1 (of 4) 3.00
1a premium edition 12.00
2 . . . . 3.00
3 . . . . 3.00
4 concl. 3.00
4a variant Scott Lewis (c) 7.50
Ashcan 6.00

LADY DEATH/BAD KITTY
Chaos! Comics, 2001
1 . . . . 3.00
1a premium ed. 10.00
2 . . . . 3.00

LADY DEATH BEDLAM
Chaos! Comics, 2002
1 BAu 3.00

1a premium edition 10.00

LADY DEATH II: BETWEEN HEAVEN & HELL
Chaos! Comics, 1995
1 V:Purgatori 5.00
1a Limited Edition 5,000c. 25.00
1b premium velvet cover, signed . 30.00
2 Lives As Hope 4.00
3 V:Purgatori 4.00
4 final issue 4.00
TPB 12.95

LADY DEATH/CHASTITY
Chaos! Comics, 2001
1 x-over 3.00
1a premium edition 10.00

LADY DEATH/CHASTITY/ BAD KITTY: UNITED
Chaos! Comics, 2002
1 . . . . 3.00
1a premium edition 10.00

LADY DEATH/THE CROW
Chaos! Comics, 2002
1 . . . . 3.00
1a premium edition 10.00
1b super premium edition 20.00
Script #1 . . . . 5.00
Script #1 premium edition 20.00
Ashcan 6.00
Ashcan, premium edition 20.00
Preview book b&w 2.00
Preview book, premium edition . . 6.00

LADY DEATH: THE CRUCIBLE
Chaos! Comics, 1996
1 (of 6) BnP,SHu, ... 3.50
1 leather limited edition 15.00
2 BnP,SHu, ... 3.50
3 BnP,SHu, ... 3.50
4 BnP,SHu, ... 3.50
5 BnP,SHu, ... 3.50
6 BnP,SHu,V:Genocide,concl. . . . 2.95
GN Collected ed. Vol. 1 . . . . 5.95
GN Collected ed. Vol. 2 . . . . 5.95
GN Collected ed. Vol. 3 . . . . 6.00
TPB rep.#1–#6 . . . . 19.95
Spec. Script 5.00
Spec. Script, premium ed. 20.00

LADY DEATH: DARK ALLIANCE
Chaos! Comics, 2002
Ashcan b&w 6.00
Ashcan premium edition 15.00
1 (of 5) F:everybody 3.00
1a premium edition 10.00
2 thru 5 . . . . @3.00
2a thru 5a Alternate cover (c) . . . @7.50

LADY DEATH: DARK MILLENNIUM
Chaos! Comics, 2000
1 (of 3) 3.00
1a premium edition 7.00
1a signed, limited 10.00
2 . . . . 3.00
3 . . . . 3.00
Preview Book B&W 5.00

Lady Death–Lady Demon / COLOR PUB.

Lady Death The Crucible #4
© *Chaos! Comics*

LADY DEATH: DEATH BECOMES HER
Chaos! Comics, 1997
0 follows the *Crucible*, leads to
  Wicked Ways 3.00

LADY DEATH/EVIL ERNIE
Chaos! Comics, 2002
Ashcan 6.00
Ashcan premium edition 20.00
1 BnP, sequel to Dark Alliance . . . 3.50
1a premium edition 10.00
1b super premium edition 20.00
1c foil edition 20.00

LADY DEATH: THE GAUNTLET
Chaos! Comics, 2002
Ashcan b&w 6.00
1 (of 4) 3.00
1a premium edition 10.00
1b foil edition 20.00
2 . . . . 3.00
2a Variant JSC (c) 7.50

LADY DEATH: THE GODDESS RETURNS
Chaos! Chomics, 2002
1 (of 2) JOs 3.00
1a premium edition 10.00
2 . . . . 3.00
2a variant (c) 7.50

LADY DEATH: HEARTBREAKER
Chaos! Comics, 2002
1 . . . . 3.00
1a premium edition 10.00
1b super premium edition 20.00
1c foil (c) 20.00
1d MegaCon foil edition 25.00

LADY DEATH/JADE
Chaos! Comics, 2002
1 . . . . 3.00
1 premium edition 10.00

LADY DEATH: JUDGMENT WAR
Chaos! Comics, 1999
Prelude 3.00
1 (of 3) 3.00
1a premium 10.00
2 . . . . 3.00
3 Hell is vanquished, concl. 3.00
Preview Book B&W 5.00

LADY DEATH: LAST RITES
Chaos! Comics, 2001
1 (of 4) RCl(c) 3.00
1 premium ed. RCl(c) 15.00
2 . . . . 3.00
2 variant DkG(c) 7.50
3 . . . . 3.00
3a variant (c) 7.50
4 . . . . 3.00
4a variant (c) 7.50

LADY DEATH: LOVE BITES
Chaos! Comics, 2001
1 . . . . 3.00
1 premium edition 10.00
Ashcan 6.00

LADY DEATH/ MEDIEVAL WITCHBLADE
Chaos! Comics, 2001
1 BAu, x-over 3.50
1a variant MS (c) (1:4) 3.50
1b premium edition 10.00
1c super premium 20.00
Preview book 2.00
Preview book, premium ed. 5.00
Ashcan 12-page, B&W 6.00

LADY DEATH: MISCHIEF NIGHT
Chaos! Comics, 2001
1 . . . . 3.00
1a premium edition 13.00
1b super premium edition 20.00

LADY DEATH: THE MOURNING
Chaos! Comics, 2002
Ashcan 6.00
1 (of 2) 3.00
1a premium edition 10.00
2 . . . . 3.00
2a variant (c) 7.50

LADY DEATH: THE ODYSSEY
Chaos! Comics, 1996
Sneak Peek Preview 2.00
1 embossed cover 5.00
1 SHu(c) premium edition 15.00
2 . . . . 3.00
3 . . . . 3.00
4 . . . . 3.00
4a variant cover 15.00
Micro Premium Preview Book . . . 15.00
TPB 9.95

LADY DEATH: THE RAPTURE
Chaos! Comics, 1999
1 (of 4) BnP,V:Father Orbec 3.00
1a dynamic forces cover 7.00
1b dynamic forces, signed 15.00
1c premium edition 9.00
2 Heaven vs. Hell 3.00
3 V:Asteroth 3.00
4 BnP 3.00
Preview Book B&W 5.00
Collected ed. Vol. 1 . . . . 5.95
Collected ed. Vol. 2 . . . . 6.00

LADY DEATH: RE-IMAGINED
Chaos! Comics, 2002
1 Spanish Inquisition 3.00
1a premium edition 10.00
1b super premium edition 20.00
Ashcan Re-imagined (b&w) 6.00

LADY DEATH: RIVER OF FEAR
Chaos! Comics, Nov., 2001
1 . . . . 3.00
1a premium ed. 10.00

LADY DEATH: TRIBULATION
Chaos! Comics, Nov., 2000
1 . . . . 3.00
1a premium edition, tattoo (c) . . . 10.00
1b chromium (c) 16.00
1c chrome (c) signed 21.00
2 . . . . 3.00
3 . . . . 3.00
4 concl. 3.00
Ashcan B&W 6.66

LADY DEATH/ VAMPIRELLA: DARK HEARTS
Chaos!/Harris, 1999
Spec. x-over, 40-page 3.50
Spec. Premium Edition 10.00

LADY DEATH VS. PURGATORI
Chaos! Comics, 2000
1 gold foil 29.95
1 premium ed. 10.00

LADY DEATH VS. VAMPIRELLA II
Chaos!/Harris, 2000
1 x-over 3.50
1a premium ed. 10.00
1b Gold foil ed. 29.95
1c Blue foil ed.. . . . . 59.95

LADY DEMON
Chaos! Comics, 2000
1 (of 3) 2.95
1a premium ed. 10.00
2 . . . . 2.95
3 concl. 2.95
Preview book B&W 5.00

CVA Page 618   All comics prices listed are for *Near Mint* condition.

LADY PENDRAGON
Maximum Press, 1996
1 mini-series 2.50
2 . . . . 2.50
3 (of 3) MD2 . . . . 2.50

LADY RAWHIDE
Topps, 1995
1 All New Solo series. 5.00
2 It Can't Happen Here,pt.2 . . . . 3.50
3 . . . . 3.00
4 . . . . 3.00
5 conclusion 3.00
Spec.#1 Rep. Zorro #2-#3 . . . . . 6.50

LADY RAWHIDE
Topps, 1996
Mini-Series
1 DMG 4.00
1a DMG,signed, numbered 10.00
2 DMG 3.00
3 DMG 3.00
4 DMG, EM, `Intimate Wounds' . . . 3.00
5 DMG, EM 3.00
6 DMG 3.00
7 DMG 3.00
TPB 10.95

LADY RAWHIDE: OTHER PEOPLE'S BLOOD
Topps, 1996
Mini-Series
1 DMG,EM,`A Slice of Breast' 3.00

LADY VAMPRE
Blackout, 1995
0 B&W 3.50
1 . . . . 3.00

LANCELOT STRONG, THE SHIELD
Red Circle, 1983
1 A:Steel Sterling 3.50
2 A:Steel Sterling 2.00
3 AN/EB,D:Lancelot Strong 2.00

LANDSALE & TRUMAN'S DEAD FOLKS
Avatar Press 2003
1 . . . . 3.50
1a wraparound (c) 3.95
2 thru 3 . . . . @3.50
2a thru 3a wraparound (c) . . . . . @3.95

LARS OF MARS
Eclipse, 1987
1 3-D MA 3.00

LASER ERASER & PRESSBUTTON
Eclipse, 1985–87
1 GL,R:Laser Eraser 2.00
2 GL 2.00
3 GL,CK,`Tsultrine' 2.00
4 MC,`Death' 2.00
5 MC,JRy,`Gates of Hell' 2.00
6 `Corsairs of Illunium' 2.00
3-D#1 MC,GL(c),`Triple Cross' 2.00

LASH LARUE WESTERN
AC Comics
1 . . . . 3.50
Annual 2.95

LAST OF THE VIKING HEROES
Genesis West, 1987
1 JK 4.00
2 JK 3.50
3 . . . . 3.50
4 . . . . 3.50
5A sexy cover 4.00
5B mild cover 3.50
6 . . . . 3.50
7 AA(c) 3.50
8 . . . . 3.50
9 Great Battle of Nidhogger 3.50
10 `Death Among the Heroes' . . . 3.50
Summer Spec.#1 FF,JK 3.50
Summer Spec.#2 . . . . 3.00
Summer Spec.#3,A:TMNT 2.50

LAUGH
Archie, 1987–91
1 thru 29 . . . . @2.00

LAUREL AND HARDY
Dell Publishing Co., Oct., 1962
1 . . . . 90.00
2 . . . . 60.00
3 . . . . 60.00
4 . . . . 60.00

LAUREL & HARDY
Gold Key, Jan., 1967
1 . . . . 75.00
2 Oct., 1967 . . . . 50.00

LAWMAN
Dell Publishing Co., Feb., 1959
1 Ph(c) all 200.00
2 . . . . 100.00
3 ATh 110.00
4 . . . . 75.00
5 thru 7 . . . . @75.00
8 thru 11 . . . . @75.00

Law and Order #1
© *Maximum Press*

LAW AND ORDER
Maximum Press, 1995
1 MMy,D:Law,I:New Law, Order . . . 2.50
2 V:Max Spur 2.50
3 V:Law's Murderer 2.50

LAW OF DREDD
Quality
1 V:Perps 5.00
2 BB,Lunar Olympics 4.00
3 BB,V:Judge Death 3.00
4 V:Father Earth 3.00
5 Cursed Earth 3.00
6 V:Perps 3.00
7 V:Perps 3.00

Fleetway
8 Blockmania 3.00
9 BB,DGi,Framed for murders . . . 3.00
10 BB,Day the Law Died Pt.1 . . . . 2.50
11 BB,Day the Law Died Pt.2 . . . . 2.50
12 BB,V:Judge Cal 2.50
13 V:Judge Caligula 2.50
14 BB, V:Perps 2.50
15 Under investigation 2.50
16 V:Alien Mercenary 2.50
17 thru 24 . . . . @2.50
25 Ugly Clinic 2.50
26 Judge Dredd & Gavel? 2.50
27 Cycles,Lunatics & Graffiti
  Guerillas 2.50
28 Cadet Training Mission 2.50
29 `Guinea Pig that changed
  the world 2.50
30 Meka-City,V:Robot 2.50
31 Iso-Block 666 . . . . 2.50
32 Missing Game Show Hosts . . . 2.50
33 League of Fatties,final issue . . . 3.00

LAZARUS CHURCHYARD
Tundra
1 From UK Blast anthology 4.50
2 Goodnight Ladies 4.50

LAZARUS: THE MANY REINCARNATIONS
Lodestone Publishing, 2000
1 by Zak Hennessey 2.95
2 . . . . 2.95
4 thru 7 . . . . @2.75

LEAGUE OF CHAMPIONS
Hero Graphics, 1990
{Cont. from Champions #12}
1 Olympus Saga #4 . . . . 2.95
2 Olympus Saga #5,O:Malice 2.95
3 Olympus Saga ends 2.95

LEAGUE OF EXTRA-ORDINARY GENTLEMEN
WildStorm/DC, 1999
America's Best Comics
1 (of 6) AMo(s),KON 3.00
2 AMo(s),KON 3.00
3 AMo(s),KON 3.00
4 AMo(s),KON 3.00
5 AMo(s),KON 2.95
6 AMo(s),KON, concl. 2.95
GN Collected Edition 6.00
Vol. II (July, 2002)
1 AMo(s),KON 3.50
2 AMo(s),KON,Martian marauders . 3.50

League–Life

3 AMo(s),KON,traitor 3.50
4 AMo(s),KON, ... 3.50
5 AMo(s),KON, one dies 3.50
6 AMo(s),KON,finale 3.50
TPB Book One 14.95

LEATHERFACE
North Star
1 thru 3 . . . . @2.75

LEGACY
Majestic, 1993
0 platinum 10.00
1 I:Legacy 2.25
2 . . . . 2.25

LEGACY
Antarctic Press, 1999
1 by Fred Perry 3.00
2 thru 5 . . . . @3.00

LEGEND OF CUSTER, THE
Dell Publishing Co., Jan., 1968
1 Ph(c) 35.00

LEGEND OF SLEEPY HOLLOW
Tundra
One shot.BHa,W.Irving adapt. 6.95

LEGEND OF THE ELFLORD
Davdez Arts, 1998
1 by Barry Blair & Colin Chan 2.95
2 . . . . 2.50
3 . . . . 2.95
4 . . . . 2.95
GN Vol. 1 112-page 11.95

LEGEND OF THE SAGE
Chaos! Comics, 2001
1 (of 4) F:Victoria Noble. 3.00
1a premium edition 10.00
2 . . . . 3.00
2a variant (c). 7.50
3 . . . . 3.00
3a variant (c). 7.50
4 . . . . 3.00
4a variant (c). 7.50
Preview Book 2.00
Preview Book, premium edition. . . . 6.00

LEGENDS OF JESSE JAMES, THE
Gold Key, Feb., 1966
1 . . . . 40.00

LEGENDS OF LUXURA
Comic Cavalcade, 1998
Commemorative #1 by Kirk Lindo . . 5.95
Commemorative #1a deluxe 14.95

LEGENDS OF NASCAR
Vortex
1 HT,Bill Eliott ($1.50 cover Price) 15,000 copies. 10.00
1a ($2.00 cover price) 45,000 copies 5.00
1b 3rd pr., 80,000 copies 4.00
2 Richard Petty 4.00
3 Ken Schroder 3.50

COLOR PUB.

4 Bob Alison 3.00
5 Bill Elliott 3.00
6 Jr. Johnson. 3.00
7 Sterling Marlin 3.00
8 Benny Parsons 3.00
9 Rusty Wallace 3.00
10 thru 14 . . . . @3.00

LEGENDS OF THE STARGRAZERS
Innovation, 1989
1 thru 5 . . . . @2.00

LEJENTIA
Opus
1 . . . . 2.00
2 . . . . 2.25

LEMONADE KID
AC Comics
1 . . . . 2.50

Leonard Nimoy's Primortals #13
© Teckno-Comics

LEONARD NIMOY'S PRIMORTALS
Teckno-Comics, 1994
1 I:Primortals. 5.50
2 Zeerus Reveals Himself 4.00
3 Contact 2.50
4 Message Deciphered 2.25
5 Place & Time Announced 2.25
6 Zeerus Arrives on Earth 2.25
7 Zeerus Recieved 2.25
8 Hyperspace Escape 2.25
9 Pristar Lands on Earth 2.00
10 V:U.S. Army. 2.00
11 V:U.S. Army 2.00
12 V:Zeerus 2.25
13 thru 15. . . . . @2.25
Big Entertainment, April, 1996
0 SEa,MKb 2.25
1 . . . . 2.25
2 KWo,ANi 2.25
3 KWo,ANi 2.25
4 KWo,ANi 2.25
5 KWo,ANi 2.25
6 KWo,`Scorched Earth,' concl. . . . 2.25
7 PB,KWo&ANi(c),Zeerus & Narab together again 2.25

LEONARDO
Mirage, 1986
1 TMNT Character 5.00

LEOPARD
Millennium
1 I:Leopard 2.95
1a Gold Cover. 3.95
2 O:Leopard,V:Razor's Edge 2.95

LETHAL STRYKE
London Night Studios, 1995
1 F:Stryke 3.00
1a commemorative (1999). 5.95
2 O:Stryke. 3.00
Ann. #1 EHr 3.00
Ann. #1 platinum edition 10.00

LETHAL STRIKE/ DOUBLE IMPACT: LETHAL IMPACT
London Night, April, 1996
1 by Jude Millien 3.00
1 limited 5.00

LIBERTY PROJECT, THE
Eclipse, 1987–88
1 I:Liberty Project 2.50
2 . . . . 2.00
3 V:Silver City Wranglers. 2.00
4 . . . . 2.00
5 . . . . 2.00
6 F:Cimarron,`Misery and Gin' 2.00
7 I:Menace 2.00
8 V:Savage 2.00

LIDSVILLE
Gold Key, Oct., 1972
1 . . . . 60.00
2 . . . . 40.00
3 and 4 . . . . @40.00
5 Oct., 1973 . . . . 40.00

LIEUTENANT, THE
Dell Publishing Co., April-June, 1962
1 Ph(c) 50.00

LIFE & ADVENTURES OF SANTA CLAUS
Tundra
GN MP,L.Frank Baum adapt. 24.95

LIFE IN HELL
Blackthorne
1 3-D. 2.50

LIFE WITH ARCHIE
Archie Publications, Sept., 1958
1 . . . . 400.00
2 . . . . 200.00
3 . . . . 150.00
4 . . . . 150.00
5 . . . . 150.00
6 . . . . 100.00
7 . . . . 100.00
8 . . . . 100.00
9 . . . . 100.00
10 . . . . 100.00
11 thru 20 . . . . @75.00

All comics prices listed are for Near Mint condition.

COLOR PUB.

Comics Values Annual — Life–Little

21 thru 30 . . . . @50.00
31 thru 40 . . . . @40.00
41 . . . . 30.00
42 B:Pureheart 100.00
43 . . . . 60.00
44 . . . . 60.00
45 R.I.V.E.R.D.A.L.E. 75.00
46 O:Pureheart 60.00
47 thru 59 . . . . @40.00
60 thru 100 . . . . @35.00
101 thru 200 . . . . @15.00
201 thru 285 . . . . @10.00

LIGHT FANTASTIC, THE
Innovation, 1992
1 Terry Pratchett adapt. 2.50
2 Adaptation continues 2.50
3 Adaptation continues 2.50
4 Adapt.conclusion 2.50

LIGHTNING COMICS PRESENTS
Lightning Comics, 1994
1 B&W Promo Ed. 3.50
1a B&W Promo Ed. Platinum 3.50
1b B&W Promo Ed. Gold 3.50

LILLITH: DEMON PRINCESS
Antarctic Press, 1996
1 (of 3) from Warrior Nun Areala . . 2.95
1a Commemorative Edition (1999) . 5.95
2 and 3 . . . . @2.95

LIMBO CITY
Dreamwave, 2002
1 BAu,BBh 2.95
2 thru 3 . . . . @2.95

LINCOLN-16
Skarwood Productions, 1997
1 GI 2.95
2 GI 2.95
3 GI 2.95

LINDA LARK
Dell Publishing Co., Oct.-Dec., 1961
1 . . . . 35.00
2 . . . . 20.00
3 . . . . 20.00
4 . . . . 20.00
5 . . . . 20.00
6 . . . . 20.00
7 . . . . 20.00
8 . . . . 20.00

LINUS, THE LIONHEARTED
Gold Key, Sept., 1965
1 . . . . 150.00

LIONHEART
Awesome Entertainment, 1999
1 IaC,JLb, from *The Coven* 2.50
1 Wizard World exclusive 5.50
2 IaC,JLb 2.50
2a variant cover 2.50
2b variant IaC cover 6.95
3 concl 3.00

LIPPY THE LION AND HARDY HAR HAR
Gold Key, March, 1963
1 . . . . 160.00

LISA COMICS
Bongo Comics, 1995
1 F:Lisa Simpson 2.25

LITA FORD
Malibu/Rock-It Comix
1 JBa 3.95

LITTLE AMBROSE
Archie Publications, Sept., 1958
1 . . . . 150.00

Little Archie #137
© Archie Publications

LITTLE ARCHIE
Archie Publications, 1956
1 . . . . 1,000.00
2 . . . . 350.00
3 . . . . 200.00
4 . . . . 200.00
5 . . . . 200.00
6 thru 10 . . . . @150.00
11 thru 20 . . . . @100.00
21 thru 30 . . . . @75.00
31 thru 40 . . . . @65.00
41 thru 60 . . . . @60.00
61 thru 80 . . . . @40.00
81 thru 100 . . . . @15.00
101 thru 180 . . . . @10.00

LITTLE ARCHIE MYSTERY
Archie Publications, May, 1963
1 . . . . 150.00
2 Oct., 1963 . . . . 100.00

LITTLE AUDREY & MELVIN
Harvey Publications, May, 1962
1 . . . . 125.00
2 thru 5 . . . . @60.00
6 thru 10 . . . . @50.00
11 thru 20 . . . . @35.00

21 thru 40 . . . . @18.00
41 thru 50 . . . . @15.00
51 thru 53 52 pgs Giant size . . . @15.00
54 thru 60 . . . . @20.00
61 Dec., 1973 . . . . 15.00

LITTLE AUDREY TV FUNTIME
Harvey Publications, Sept., 1962
1 A:Richie Rich 125.00
2 same 75.00
3 same 60.00
4 . . . . 60.00
5 . . . . 60.00
6 thru 10 . . . . @35.00
11 thru 20 . . . . @25.00
21 thru 32 . . . . @20.00
33 Oct., 1971 . . . . 20.00

LITTLE DOT DOTLAND
Harvey Publications, July, 1962
1 . . . . 150.00
2 . . . . 75.00
3 . . . . 60.00
4 . . . . 45.00
5 . . . . 45.00
6 thru 10 . . . . @45.00
11 thru 20 . . . . @35.00
21 thru 50 . . . . @20.00
51 thru 60 . . . . @15.00
61 Dec., 1973 . . . . 15.00

LITTLE DOT'S UNCLES & AUNTS
Harvey Enterprises, Oct., 1961
1 . . . . 175.00
2 . . . . 100.00
3 . . . . 75.00
4 . . . . 65.00
5 . . . . 65.00
6 thru 10 . . . . @50.00
11 thru 20 . . . . @40.00
21 thru 40 . . . . @30.00
41 thru 51 . . . . @20.00
52 April, 1974 . . . . 20.00

LITTLE LOTTA
Harvey Publications, Nov., 1955
1 B:Richie Rich and Little Lotta . 450.00
2 . . . . 200.00
3 . . . . 150.00
4 . . . . 100.00
5 . . . . 100.00
6 . . . . 75.00
7 . . . . 75.00
8 . . . . 75.00
9 . . . . 75.00
10 . . . . 75.00
11 thru 20 . . . . @60.00
21 thru 40 . . . . @35.00
41 thru 60 . . . . @30.00
61 thru 80 . . . . @25.00
81 thru 99 . . . . @20.00
100 thru 103 52 pgs . . . . @15.00
104 thru 120 . . . . @15.00
121 May, 1976 . . . . 15.00

LITTLE LOTTA FOODLAND
Harvey Publications, Sept., 1963
1 68 pgs 175.00
2 . . . . 100.00
3 . . . . 75.00

Little–Ludwig / COLOR PUB. / Comics Values Annual

4 . . . . 50.00		
5 . . . . 50.00		
6 thru 10 . . . . @35.00		
11 thru 20 . . . . @25.00		
21 thru 26 . . . . @20.00		
27 . . . . 12.00		
28 . . . . 12.00		
29 Oct., 1972 . . . . 12.00		

LITTLE MERMAID
Walt Disney, 1992
1 based on movie 3.00
2 'Serpent Teen' 3.00
3 'Guppy Love' 3.00
4 . . . . 3.00

LITTLE MONSTERS, THE
Gold Key, Nov., 1964
1 . . . . 100.00
2 . . . . 50.00
3 thru 10 . . . . @35.00
11 thru 20 . . . . @25.00
21 thru 43 . . . . @25.00
44 Feb., 1978 . . . . 25.00

LITTLE MONSTERS
Now, 1990
1 thru 6 . . . . @2.00

LITTLE REDBIRDS
1 . . . . 2.50
2 . . . . 2.50
3 . . . . 2.50
4 . . . . 2.50

LITTLE SAD SACK
Harvey Publications, Oct., 1964
1 Richie Rich(c) 60.00
2 . . . . 40.00
3 . . . . 40.00
4 . . . . 40.00
5 . . . . 40.00
6 thru 19 Nov. 1967 . . . . @40.00

LITTLE STOOGES, THE
Gold Key, Sept., 1972
1 . . . . 45.00
2 . . . . 30.00
3 . . . . 25.00
4 . . . . 25.00
5 . . . . 25.00
6 and 7 March, 1974 . . . . @25.00

LLOYD LLEWELLYN
Fantagraphics, 1987
Spec. #1 . . . . 2.00

LOBO
Dell Publishing Co., Dec., 1965
1 . . . . 40.00
2 . . . . 30.00

LOCKE
Blackthorne
1 PO:Jones 2.00
2 TD 2.00
3 . . . . 2.00
4 . . . . 2.00
5 . . . . 2.00

LONE RANGER, THE
Gold Key, Sept., 1964
1 . . . . 85.00
2 . . . . 50.00
3 thru 5 . . . . @40.00
6 thru 10 . . . . @30.00
11 thru 18 . . . . @30.00
19 thru 27 . . . . @20.00
28 March, 1977 . . . . 20.00

Lone Ranger and Tonto #4
© Topps Comics

LONE RANGER AND TONTO, THE
Topps, 1994
1 JLd,TT,RM,The Last Battle 2.50
2 JLd,TT,RM 2.50
3 JLd,TT,RM, O:Lone Ranger . . . 2.50
4 JLd,TT,RM, It Crawls 2.50
TPB rep. #1–#4 . . . . 9.95

LOOKERS
Avatar
Combo Spec. 16pg. 3.00
Combo Spec. Platinum 9.95

LORD PUMPKIN
Malibu Oct., 1994
0 Sludge 2.50

LOST HEROES
Davdez Arts, 1998
0 by Rob Prior, lost SF heroes . . . 2.95
1 thru 5 . . . . @2.50
6 . . . . 2.95
GN 5/6 56-page 7.95

LOST IN SPACE
**Innovation, 1991
{based on TV series}**
1 O:Jupiter II Project 3.00
2 'Cavern of IdyllicSummersLost' . . 2.75
2a Special Edition 2.50
3 Do Not Go Gently into that Good
 Night',Bill Mumy script 2.50
4 'People are Strange' 2.50
5 The Perils of Penelope 2.50
6 Time Warp 2.50
7 thru 9 . . . . @2.50
10 inc.Afterthought 2.50

11 F:Judy Robinson 2.50
12 . . . . 2.95
Project Krell 2.50
Ann.#1 (1991) 2.95
Ann.#2 (1992) 2.95
1Spec.#1 & #2 rep. Seduction of
 the Innocent . . . . @2.50
GN Strangers among Strangers . . . 6.00
1-shot Project Robinson, follows
 story in issue #12 (1993) 2.50
Becomes:

LOST IN SPACE: VOYAGE TO THE BOTTOM OF THE SOUL
Innovation, 1993–94
13 . . . . 2.95
14 thru 18 . . . . @2.95

LOST PLANET
Eclipse, 1987–88
1 BHa,I:Tyler FLynn 2.50
2 BHa,R:Amelia Earhart 2.00
3 BHa 2.00
4 BHa,'Devil's Eye' 2.00
5 BHa,A:Amelia Earhart 2.00
6 . . . . 2.00

LOVECRAFT
Adventure Comics
1 'The Lurking Fear' adapt 2.95
2 Beyond the Wall of Sleep 2.95
3 The Tomb 2.95
4 The Alchemist 2.95

LOVE DIARY
Charlton Comics, July, 1958
1 . . . . 75.00
2 . . . . 50.00
3 . . . . 35.00
4 . . . . 35.00
5 . . . . 30.00
6 . . . . 35.00
7 thru 10 . . . . @30.00
11 thru 15 . . . . @30.00
16 thru 20 . . . . @30.00
21 thru 40 . . . . @15.00
41 thru 102 . . . . @10.00

LOVE SHOWDOWN COLLECTION
Archie Comics, 1997
TPB x-over rep. Archie #429 (pt.1),
 Betty #19 (pt.2), Betty & Veronica
 #82, (pt.3), Veronica #39 (pt.4)
 Return of Cheryl Blossom 4.95

LUCIFER'S HAMMER
Innovation, 1993–94
1 thru 6 Larry Niven & Jerry
 Pournelle novel adaptation . . @2.50

LUCY SHOW, THE
Gold Key, June, 1963
1 Ph(c) 225.00
2 Ph(c) 150.00
3 thru 5 . . . . @125.00

LUDWIG VON DRAKE
Dell Publishing Co., Nov.–Dec., 1961
1 . . . . 100.00
2 thru 4 . . . . @75.00

LUFTWAFFE 1946
Antarctic Press, 1998
1 color special, by Ted Namura . . . 2.95

LUGER
Eclipse, 1986–87
1 TY,I:Luger,mini-series 2.00
2 TY 2.00
3 TY,BHa,V:Sharks 2.00

LUNATIC FRINGE
Innovation, July, 1989
1 . . . . 2.00
2 . . . . 2.00

LUXURA
Comic Cavalcade, 1998
Commemorative #1 by Kirk Lindo . . 5.95
Commemorative #1a deluxe 14.95

LUXURA COLLECTION
Brainstorm
Commemorative edition, red foil cover, 48pg. 10.00

LYNCH MOB
Chaos! Comics, 1994
1 GCa(c), I:Mother Mayhem 3.00
2 Lynch Mob Loses 2.50
3 1994 Time Trip 2.50
3a Gold cover 3.00
4 Mother Mayhem at UN 2.50

LYNDON B. JOHNSON
Dell Publishing Co., March, 1965
1 Ph(c) 50.00

M
Eclipse, 1990–91
1 thru 4 JMu . . . . @4.95

MACROSS
Comico
1 . . . . 35.00
Becomes:

ROBOTECH, THE MACROSS SAGA

MAD FOLLIES
E.C. Comics, 1963
(N#) 350.00
2 1964 . . . . 250.00
3 1965 . . . . 200.00
4 1966 . . . . 225.00
5 1967 . . . . 150.00
6 1968 . . . . 125.00
7 1969 . . . . 125.00

MAD HOUSE
Red Circle, 1974–82
95 thru 97 Horror stories . . . . . @22.00
98 thru 130 Humor stories . . . . @15.00
Annual #8 thru #11 . . . . @18.00

MADMAN
Tundra, 1992
1 . . . . 15.00
2 . . . . 12.00
3 . . . . 7.00

COLOR PUB.

Oni Press 2003
King-Size Super Special 6.95

MADMAN ADVENTURES
Tundra, 1992
1 R & N:Madman 9.00
2 . . . . 7.00
3 . . . . 7.00

MADMAN PICTURE EXHIBITION
AAA Pop Comics, 2002
1 (of 4) 3.95
2 thru 4 . . . . 3.95

MADRAVEN HALLOWEEN SPECIAL
Hamilton Comics, 1995
1 Song of the Silkies 2.95

MAD SPECIAL
E.C. Publications, Inc., 1970
1 . . . . 125.00
2 . . . . 75.00
3 . . . . 70.00
4 thru 8 . . . . @70.00
9 thru 13 . . . . @50.00
14 . . . . 40.00
15 . . . . 40.00
16 . . . . 35.00
17 . . . . 35.00
18 . . . . 32.00
19 thru 21 . . . . @32.00
22 thru 31 . . . . @25.00
32 . . . . 25.00
33 thru 58 . . . . @10.00

MAGE
Comico, 1984–86
1 MWg,I:Kevin Matchstick 35.00
2 MWg,I:Edsel 18.00
3 MWg,V:Umbra Sprite 15.00
4 MWg,V:Umbra Sprite 15.00
5 MWg,I:Sean (Spook) 15.00
6 MWg,Grendel begins 35.00
7 MWg,Grendel 15.00
8 MWg,Grendel 12.00
9 MWg,Grendel 12.00

Mage #9
© Comico

Luftwaffe–Magic

10 MWg,Grendel,Styx 12.00
11 MWg,Grendel,Styx 12.00
12 MWg,D:Sean,Grendel 12.00
13 MWg,D:Edsel,Grendel 12.00
14 MWg,Grendel,O:Kevin 12.00
15 MWg,D:Umbra Sprite 15.00

MAGEBOOK
Comico
1 rep. Mage #1-4 . . . . 8.95
2 rep. Mage #5-8 . . . . 8.95

MAGE KNIGHT: STOLEN DESTINY
IDW Publishing, 2002
1 (of 5) by TDz & D.Cabrera 3.50
2 thru 5 . . . . @3.50

MAGIC FLUTE
Eclipse, 1989
1 CR 4.95

MAGIC THE GATHERING: ANTIQUITIES WAR
Armada 1995
1 Based on the Antiquities Set 2.75
2 F:Urza, Mishra 2.50
3 I:Tawnos, Ashod 2.50
4 The War Begins 2.50

MAGIC THE GATHERING: ARABIAN KNIGHTS
Armada 1995
1 Based on Rare Card set 2.75
2 V:Queen Nailah 2.50

MAGIC THE GATHERING: CONVOCATIONS
Armada 1995
1 Gallery of Art from Game 2.50

MAGIC THE GATHERING: FALLEN EMPIRES
[Mini-series] Armada
1 with pack of cards 2.75
2 F:Tymolin 2.50
TPB Rep. #1-#2 . . . . 4.95

MAGIC THE GATHERING: HOMELANDS
Armada 1995
1 I:Feroz, Serra 5.95

MAGIC THE GATHERING: ICE AGE
Armada 1995
1 Dominaia, from card game 3.00
2 Ice Age Adventures 2.50
3 CV(c) Planeswalker battles 2.50
4 final issue 2.50
TPB Rep. #1-#2 . . . . 4.95
TPB Rep. #3-#4 . . . . 4.95

MAGIC THE GATHERING: SHADOW MAGE
Armada 1995
1 I:Jared 3.00
2 F:Hurloon the Minotaur 2.75

Magic–Magnus

3 VMk(c&a),V:Juggernaut 2.50
4 Final issue 2.50
TPB Rep. #1-#2 .... 4.95
TPB Rep. #3-#4 .... 4.95

MAGIC THE GATHERING: THE URZA-MISHRA WAR
Armada
1 & 2 with Ice Age II card 5.95

MAGIC THE GATHERING: WAYFARER
Armada 1995
1 R:Jared 2.75
2 I:New Land................. 2.50
3 R:Liana, Ravidel............. 2.50
4 I:Golthonor 2.50
5 .... 2.50

MAGIC THE GATHERING: THE LEGENDS OF:
THE ELDER DRAGONS
1 & 2 .... @2.50
JEDIT OJANEN
1 & 2 .... @2.50
SHANDALAR
1 & 2 .... @2.50

[ON THE WORLD OF] MAGIC THE GATHERING
GN Serra Angel + card 5.95
GN Legend of the Fallen Angel + card 5.95
GN Dakkon Blackblade + card ... 5.95

MAGILLA GORILLA
Gold Key, May, 1964
1 .... 150.00
2 thru 10 Dec. 1968 .... @100.00

MAGILLA GORILLA
Charlton Comics, Nov., 1970
1 .... 75.00
2 thru 5 .... @40.00

MAGIQUE
WildStorm/DC, 2000
Ann. 2000 #1, Devil's Night x-over, pt.4 .... 3.50

MAGNUS: ROBOT FIGHTER
Gold Key, Feb., 1963
1 RM,I:Magnus,Teeja,A-1, I&B:Capt.Johner&aliens 350.00
2 RM,I:Sen.Zeremiah Clane.... 150.00
3 RM,I:Xyrkol................ 150.00
4 RM,I:Mekamn,Elzy 100.00
5 RM,The Immortal One 100.00
6 RM,I:Talpa 90.00
7 RM,I:Malev-6,ViXyrkol....... 125.00
8 RM,I:Outsiders(Chet, Horio, Toun, Malf)................ 90.00
9 RM, I:Madmot.............. 90.00
10 RM,Mysterious Octo-Rob..... 90.00
11 RM,I:Danae,Neo-Animals.... 75.00
12 RM,The Volcano Makers 75.00
13 RM,I:Dr Lazlo Noel 80.00
14 RM,The Monster Robs....... 75.00
15 RM,I:Mogul Radur 75.00
16 RM,I:Gophs 75.00

COLOR PUB.

17 RM,I:Zypex 75.00
18 RM,I:V'ril Trent.............. 75.00
19 RM,Fear Unlimited.......... 75.00
20 RM,I:Bunda the Great 75.00
21 RM, Space Spectre 75.00
22 Rep. #1 .... 50.00
23 DSp,Mission Disaster 50.00
24 Pied Piper of North Am 50.00
25 The Micro Giants 50.00
26 The Venomous Vaper 50.00
27 Panic in Pacifica 50.00
28 Threats from the Depths 50.00
29 Rep. #7 .... 20.00
30 Rep. #15 .... 20.00
31 Rep. #14 .... 20.00
32 Rep. #2 .... 20.00
33 Rep. #21 .... 20.00
34 Rep. #13 .... 20.00
35 Rep. #6 .... 20.00
36 Rep. #8 .... 20.00
37 Rep. #11 .... 20.00
38 Rep. #12 .... 20.00
39 Rep. #16 .... 20.00
40 Rep. #17 .... 20.00

Magnus Robot Fighter #20
© Gold Key

41 Rep. #18 .... 20.00
42 Rep. #19 .... 20.00
43 Rep. #20 .... 20.00
44 Rep. #23 .... 20.00
45 Rep. #24 .... 20.00
46 Rep. #25 .... 20.00

MAGNUS: ROBOT FIGHTER
Valiant 1991
0 PCu,BL,'Emancipator',w/ BWS card 6.00
0a PCu,BL,w/o card............ 3.00
1 ANi,BL,B:Steel Nation........ 4.00
1a w/o coupon................ 2.00
2 ANi,BL,Steel Nation #2 .... 3.00
2a w/o coupon................ 2.00
3 ANi,BL,Steel Nation #3 .... 3.00
3a w/o coupon................ 2.00
4 ANi,BL,E:Steel Nation........ 3.00
4a w/o coupon................ 2.00
5 DL,BL(i),I:Rai(#1),V:Slagger Flipbook format 3.00
5a w/o coupon................ 2.00
6 DL,A:Solar,V:Grandmother A:Rai(#2) 2.50
6a w/o coupon................ 2.00
7 DL,EC,V:Rai(#3)............. 2.50
7a w/o coupon................ 2.00

Comics Values Annual

8 DL,A:Rai(#4),Solar,X-O Armor.E:Flipbooks 2.50
8a w/o coupon................ 2.00
9 EC,V:Xyrkol,E-7 .... 2.50
10 V:Xyrkol................... 2.50
11 V:Xyrkol................... 2.50
12 I:Turok,V:Dr. Noel, I:Asylum,40-pg. 6.00
13 EC,Asylum,pt 1 .... 2.50
14 EC,Asylum,pt2............. 2.50
15 FM(c),EC,Unity#4,I:Eternal Warrior of 4001, O:Unity..... 2.50
16 WS(c),EC,Unity#12,A:Solar, Archer,Armstrong,Harbinger, X-O,Rai,Eternal Warrior 2.50
17 JaB,V:Talpa 2.50
18 SD,R:Mekman,V:E-7 .... 2.50
19 SD,V:Mekmen 2.50
20 EC,Tale of Magnus' past 2.50
21 JaB,R:Malevalents, Grand- mother 3.00
21a Gold Ed. 4.00
22 JaB,D:Felina,V:Malevalents, Grandmother 2.50
23 V:Malevolents 2.50
24 V:Malevolents 2.50
25 N:Magnus,R:1-A,silver-foil(c) .. 3.00
26 I:Young Wolves 2.50
27 V:Dr.Lazlo Noel 2.50
28 V:The Malevs 2.25
29 JCf,A:Eternal Warrior 2.25
30 JCf,V:The Malevs 2.25
31 JCf,V:The Malevs 2.25
32 JCf,Battle for South Am 2.25
33 B:JOs(s),JCf,A:Ivar 2.25
34 JCf,Captured 2.25
35 JCf,V:Mekman 2.25
36 JCf,w/Valiant Era Card...... 2.25
37 JCf,A:Starwatchers 2.25
38 JCf 2.25
39 JCf,F:Torque 2.25
40 JCf,F:Torque, A:Rai 2.25
41 JCf,Chaos Effect-Epsilon#4 A:Solar, Psi-Lords,Rai 2.50
42 JCf, F:Torque,A:Takashi..... 2.25
43 JCf,F:Torque,Immortal E 2.25
44 JCf,F:Torque,Stagger....... 2.25
45 V:Immortal Enemy 2.25
46 V:Immortal Enemy 2.25
47 Cold Blooded,pt.1 .... 2.25
48 Cold Blooded,pt.2 .... 2.25
49 F:Slagger.................. 2.25
50 V:Invisible Legion. 2.25
51 KoK,RyR,Return of the Robots,pt.1................ 2.25
52 KoK,RyR,Robots,pt.2........ 2.25
53 KoK,RyR,Robots,pt.3........ 2.25
54 KoK,RyR,Robots,pt.4........ 2.25
55 KG,A:Rai.................. 2.50
56 Magnus in Japan 2.50
57 .... 2.50
58 .... 2.50
59 V:Rai..................... 2.50
60 R:The Malevs 2.50
61 Secrets of the Malevs 2.50
62 V:Leeja 2.50
63 R:Destroyer 2.50
64 Ultimatum, F:Destroyer 2.50
Yearbook #1................. 3.95
TPB 1-4 .... 9.95

MAGNUS (ROBOT FIGHTER)
Acclaim Jan. 1997
1 Magnus back from the future ... 2.50
2 'Tomorrow Never Knows' 2.50
3 'Tomorrow Never Knows' 2.50
4 'Tomorrow Never Knows' 2.50
5 'Tomorrow Never Knows' 2.50
6 A:Janice Whitcraft........... 2.50

Comics Values Annual — COLOR PUB. — Magnus–Mantra

7 'When Titans Clash' 2.50
8 TPe,DdB,'When Titans Clash' ... 2.50
9 TPe,'See Tirana and Die' 2.50
10 TPe,'The Memory' 2.50
11 TPe,'Where Angels Fear' 2.50
12 TPe,'Showdown' 2.50
13 TPe 2.50
14 TPe,'Wild in the Streets' 2.50
15 TPe,Magnus stands alone 2.50
16 TPe,'Hart's Home' 2.50
17 TPe,'Invasive Procedures' 2.50
18 TPe,'Welcome to Salvation' 2.50

MAJOR DAMAGE
Invictus Studios, 1994
1 I:Major Damage 2.25
2 V:Godkin 2.25
3 First Contact Conclusion 2.25

MALICE
Heroic Publishing
1 I:Queen of the Dead 2.00

MAN CALLED A-X
Malibu Bravura, 1994–95
[Limited Series]
0 1st Puzzle piece 2.95
1 MWn,SwM 2.95
1a Gold foil Edition 4.00
2 MWn,SwM,VLElectobot 2.95
3 MWn,SwM,Mercy Island 2.95
4 MWn,SwM,One Who Came
 Before 2.95
5 MWn,SwM,Climax 2.95

MANDRAKE THE MAGICIAN
King Comics, 1966
1 .... 75.00
2 .... 50.00
3 .... 50.00
4 A:Girl Phantom 50.00
5 Cape Cod Caper 50.00
6 .... 50.00
7 O:Lothar 50.00
8 .... 60.00
9 A:Brick Bradford 50.00
10 A:Rip Kirby 60.00

MAN FROM PLANET X
Planet X Prod.
1 .... 3.00

MAN FROM U.N.C.L.E.
Gold Key, Feb., 1965
1 `The Explosive Affair' 250.00
2 `The Forthur Cookie Affair' ... 125.00
3 `The Deadly Devices Affair' 75.00
4 `The Rip Van Solo Affair' 75.00
5 `Ten Little Uncles Affair' 75.00
6 `The Three Blind Mice Affair' .. 75.00
7 `The Pixilated Puzzle Affair'
 I:Jet Dream (back-up begins) . 80.00
8 `The Floating People Affair' ... 75.00
9 `Spirit of St.Louis Affair' 75.00
10 `The Trojan Horse Affair' 75.00
11 `Three-Story Giant Affair' 60.00
12 `Dead Man's Diary Affair' 60.00
13 `The Flying Clowns Affair' ... 60.00
14 `Great Brain Drain Affair' 60.00
15 `The Animal Agents Affair' ... 60.00
16 `Instant Disaster Affair' 60.00
17 `The Deadly Visions Affair' .. 60.00
18 `The Alien Affair' 60.00

19 `Knight in Shining
 Armor Affair' 60.00
20 `Deep Freeze Affair' 60.00
21 rep. #10 .... 55.00
22 rep. #7 .... 55.00

MAN FROM U.N.C.L.E.
Entertainment, 1987
1 thru 11 .... @2.00

Man From U.N.C.L.E. 32
© Millennium

MAN FROM U.N.C.L.E.
Millennium, 1993
1 The Birds of Prey Affair,pt.1 .... 2.95
2 The Birds of Prey Affair,pt.2 .... 2.95

MANGA SHI, 2000
Crusade Entertainment, 1997
1 (of 3) BiT, `Final Jihad' flip-book
 Shi: Heaven and Earth 2.95
2 BiT, flip-book Tomoe:
 Unforgettable Fire preview 2.95
3 BiT, conclusion 2.95

MANGLE TANGLE TALES
Innovation
1 .... 2.95

MAN IN BLACK
Harvey Publications, Sept., 1957
1 BP 200.00
2 BP 150.00
3 BP 150.00
4 BP, March, 1958 .... 150.00

MANIK
Millennium/Expand (1995)
1 I:Macedon, Arsenal,Cardinal 2.95

MANKIND
Chaos! Comics, 1999
1-shot StG 2.95
1-shotA photo cover 2.95
1-shotB variant cover 6.95
1-shotC variant cover, signed ... 60.00

MAN OF THE ATOM
Valiant Heroes Special Project
Acclaim Jan 1997
Spec 3.95
TPB The Rebirth of Solar 8.00

MAN OF WAR
Eclipse, 1987–88
1 thru 3 .... @2.00

MAN OF WAR
Malibu 1993–94
1 thru 3 V:Lift 2.50
1a thru 5a Newsstand ed 2.00
4 w/poster 2.50
5 V:Killiner 2.50
6 KM,Genesis Crossover 2.50
7 DJu,Genesis Crossover 2.50
8 TMs(s),A:Rocket Ranger 2.25
9 thru 12 .... @2.25

MANTRA
Malibu Ultraverse, 1993–95
1 AV,I:Mantra,w/Ultraverse card ... 3.00
1a Full Hologram(c) 10.00
1b Silver foil(c) 5.00
2 AV,V:Warstrike 3.00
3 AV,V:Kismet Deadly 3.00
4 BWS,Mantra's marriage,
 BU:Rune story 2.50
5 MiB(s),AV(i),V:Wiley Wolf 2.25
6 MiB(s),AV(i),Break Thru x-over .. 2.25
7 DJu,TA,A:Prime, O:Prototype ... 2.25
8 B:MiB(s),A:Warstrike 2.25
9 V:Iron Knight,Puppeteer 2.25
10 NBy(c),DaR,B:Archmage Quest,
 Flip/UltraversePremiere #2 .... 4.00
11 MiB(s),V:Boneyard 2.25
12 MiB(s),A:Strangers 2.25
13 Topaz, Boneyard 2.25
14 Tradesmen, Boneyard 2.25
15 A:Prime,Doc Gross 2.25
16 A:Prime 2.25
17 A:Necromantra 2.50
18 Pregnancy 2.50
19 MiB,Pregnancy 2.50
20 Aftermath of Godwheel 2.50
21 TyD,MiB,Mantra goes bad ... 2.50
22 A:Marvel's Loki 2.50
23 I:Tremblor, A:Prime 2.50
24 V:Topaz 2.50
Giant Sized#1 GP(c),I:Topaz ... 2.25

MANTRA
Malibu Ultraverse, 1995–96
Infinity N:Mantra 2.50
1 Mantra in all Female Body 2.25
1a Computer Painted Cover 2.25
2 Phoenix flip issue 2.25
3 Phoenix Resurrection 2.25
4 .... 2.25
5 .... 2.25
6 TMs,I:Tattoo,A:Rush 2.25
7 .... 2.25

MANTRA: SPEAR OF DESTINY
Malibu Ultraverse, 1995
1 Search for Artifact 2.50
2 MiB,Eden vs. Aladdin 2.50

All comics prices listed are for Near Mint condition.

MANY WORLDS OF TESLA STRONG, THE
Wildstorm/DC May 2003
1 through the dimensions 5.95

MARK OF CHARON
Grossgen Comics 2003
1 (of 5) JoB 2.95
2 thru 5 .... @2.95

MARK RAND'S SKY TECHNOLOGIES INC.
Red Mercenary, 1995
1 I:Jae,Elliot,Firnn 2.95

MARKSMAN, THE
Hero Graphics, 1988
1 O:Marksman, Pt.#1 .... 2.00
2 O:Marksman, Pt.#2 .... 2.00
3 O:Marksman ends.I:Basilisk ... 2.00
4 A:Flare 2.00
5 I:Radar,Sonar 2.00
Ann. #1, A:Champions 2.00

MARRIED... WITH CHILDREN
Now, 1990
1 .... 4.00
1a 2nd printing 2.00
2 Ph(c) 3.00
3 .... 3.00
4 .... 2.50
5 Ph(c) 2.50
6 Ph(c) 2.00
7 .... 2.50

[2nd Series], 1991
1 Peg-Host of Radio Show 2.25
2 The Bundy Invention 2.00
3 Psychodad,(photo cover) 2.00
4 Mother-In-Law,(photo cover) . 2.00
5 Bundy the Crusader 2.00
6 Bundy J: The Order of the Mighty Warthog 2.00
7 Kelly the VJ 2.00
Spec. Ph(c) (1992) 2.00
Spec. Bud Bundy, Fanboy in Paradise 2.95
3-D Spec.(1993) 2.50

MARRIED WITH CHILDREN: DYSFUNCTIONAL FAMILY
Now
1 I:The Bundies 2.50
2 TV Appearance 2.50
3 Morally Pure Bundys 2.50

MARRIED WITH CHILDREN: FLASHBACK SPECIAL
Now, 1993
1 Peg and Al's first date 2.00
2 and 3 .... @2.00

MARRIED WITH CHILDREN: KELLY BUNDY SPECIAL
Now, 1992
1 with poster 2.00

2 and 3 with poster .... @2.00

MARRIED... WITH CHILDREN: QUANTUM QUARTET
Now, 1993
1 thru 4 Fantastic Four parody .. @2.00
Fall 1994 Spec., flip book 2.00

MARRIED WITH CHILDREN 2099
Mirage, 1993
1 thru 3 Cable Parody .... @2.50

MARS
First, 1984
1 thru 12 .... @2.00

Mars Attacks #3
© Topps Comics

MARS ATTACKS
Topps, 1994
1 KG(s) 5.00
2 .... 4.00
3 thru 6 KG(s) .... @4.00

[Series 2], 1995
1 Counterstrike 3.50
2 Counterstrike,pt.2 .... 2.95
3 Counterstrike,pt.3 .... 2.95
4 Counterstrike,pt.4 Convictions . 2.95
5 Counterstrike concl. 2.95
6 `Rescue of Janice Brown,'pt.1 . 2.95
7 `Rescue of Janice Brown,'pt.2 . 2.95
8 .... 2.95
Spec. Baseball 3.00

MARS ATTACKS HIGH SCHOOL
Topps, 1997
Spec. #1 (of 2) BSz(c) 2.95
Spec. #2 .... 2.95

MARS ATTACKS THE SAVAGE DRAGON
Topps, 1996
1 .... 3.00
2 thru 4 .... @3.00

MARVEL/ULTRAVERSE BATTLEZONES
Malibu Ultraverse, 1996
1 DPs(c),The Battle of the Heroes . 3.95

MARY WORTH
ARGO, March, 1956
1 .... 65.00

MASKED MAN
Eclipse, 1985–88
1 .... 3.00
2 thru 10 .... @2.00

MASTER DARQUE
Acclaim 1997
Spec. F:Brixton Sound, 48-pg. ... 4.00

MASTERS OF THE UNIVERSE
Crossgen Comics 2003
Spec. The Power of Fear 2.95
1 Rise of the Snake Men 2.95
TPB Traveler #1 Shard of Darkness 9.95

MASTERS OF THE UNIVERSE: ICONS OF EVIL
Crossgen Comics 2003
Spec. Tri-Klops 2.95
1 Mer-Man 4.95
1 Trapjaw 4.95

MASTERWORK SERIES
Seagate DC, 1983
1 FFrep.DC,Shining Knight 2.00
2 FFrep.DC,Shining Knight 2.00
3 BWr,Horror DC rep 2.00

MATT BUSCH'S DARIA JONTAK
Realm Press, 2000
1 sexy sci-fi 4.00
1a deluxe 5.00
2 .... 4.00
2a deluxe 5.00
Companion Book 3.00
Companion Book , deluxe 4.00

Andromeda Entertainment/ PlanetMatt, 2001
Spec. Where Angels Fear to Tread . 4.00
Spec. deluxe 5.00

MAVERICK
Dell Publishing Co., April, 1958
1 Ph(c) Garner photos 400.00
2 Ph(c) 150.00
3 Ph(c) 150.00
4 Ph(c) 150.00
5 Ph(c) 150.00
6 thru 14 Ph(c) last Garner ... @125.00
15 thru 19 Ph(c) R. Moore .... @100.00

MAVERICK MARSHALL
Charlton Comics, Nov., 1958
1 .... 50.00
2 thru 6 .... @35.00
7 May, 1960 .... 35.00

COLOR PUB.

MAVERICKS
Dagger, 1994
1 PuD,RkL, I:Mavericks 2.50
2 PuD,RkL 2.50
3 thru 5 . . . . @2.50

MAXIMORTAL
King Hell/Tundra, 1992
1 RV,A:True-Man 4.50
2 Crack in the New World 4.25
3 RV,Secret of the Manhattan
   Project revealed 4.25
4 . . . . 4.25
5 A:True Man 3.25
6 A:El Guano 3.25

MAXIMUM FORCE
Atomeka, 2002
Spec. #1 SBs, ... 3.00

MAYA
Gold Key, March, 1968
1 . . . . 35.00

MAZE AGENCY
Comico, 1988–91
1 O:Maze Agency 3.00
2 thru 6 . . . . @2.50
7 . . . . 2.75
8 thru 11 . . . . @2.00
12 . . . . 2.50
13 thru 15 . . . . @2.00
16 thru 23 . . . . @2.50
Spec. #1 . . . . 2.75

McHALE'S NAVY
Dell Publishing Co.
May-July, 1963
1 Ph(c) from TV show 100.00
2 Ph(c) 75.00
3 Ph(c) 75.00

McKEEVER & THE COLONEL
Dell Publishing Co.,
Feb.-April, 1963
1 Ph(c) 90.00
2 Ph(c) 60.00
3 Ph(c) 60.00

M.D.
Gemstone, 1999
1 (of 5) New Direction 2.50
2 . . . . 2.50
3 . . . . 2.50
4 . . . . 2.50
Annual #1 . . . . 13.50

M.D. GEIST
CPM, 1995
1 Cartoon Adaptation 2.95
2 J:Army 2.95
3 V:Final Terminator 2.95

M.D. GEIST: GROUND ZERO
CPM, 1996
1 thru 3 . . . . @2.95

MECHANICS
Fantagraphics
1 HB,rep.Love & Rockets 3.00
2 HB,rep.Love & Rockets 2.50
3 HB,rep.Love & Rockets 2.50

MEDIA STARR
Innovation, 1989
1 thru 3 . . . . @2.00

MEGADETH
Malibu Rock-it Comix
1 . . . . 4.25

Megalith #3
© Continuity

MEGALITH
Continuity, 1990
1 MT 6.00
2 MT 4.00
3 MT, Painted issue 2.50
4 NA,TVE 2.50
5 NA,TVE 2.50
6 MN 2.50
7 MN 2.50
8 . . . . 2.50
9 SDr(i) 2.50
10 . . . . 2.50
[2nd Series], 1993
Deathwatch 2000
0 Deathwatch 2000 prologue 5.00
1 Deathwatch 2000 Pt.5,w/card . . 2.50
2 Deathwatch 2000 Pt.10,w/card . 2.50
3 pt.16,Indestructible(c),w/card . . 2.50
4 & 5 Rise of Magic . . . . @2.50
6 & 7 . . . . @2.50

MEGAMAN
Dreamwave 2003
1 . . . . 2.95
1a holofoil (c) 5.95
2 thru 3 . . . . @2.50

MEGATON
Megaton, 1983
1 . . . . 4.00
Entity Comics, 1993
Holiday Spec. w/card 2.95

MEGATON EXPLOSION
1 RLd,AMe,I:Youngblood preview 25.00

MEGATON MAN
Kitchen Sink, 1984
1 Don Simpson art,I:MegatonMan . 6.00
1a rep. B&W 2.00
2 . . . . 4.00
3 and 4 . . . . @3.00
5 . . . . 2.50
6 Border Worlds 2.50
7 Border Worlds 2.50
8 Border Worlds 2.50
9 Border Worlds 2.50
10 final issue, 1986 . . . . 2.50

MEK
DC/Homage Nov. 2002
2 WEl 2.95
3 WEl, concl 2.95

MELTING POT
Kitchen Sink, 1993
1 . . . . 4.00
2 and 3 . . . . @2.95
4 . . . . 3.50
TPB KEa,SBs, rep 19.95

MELVIN MONSTER
Dell Publishing Co.,
April-June, 1965
1 . . . . 150.00
2 thru 10 . . . . @100.00

[Katshuiro Otomo's] MEMORIES
Epic, 1992
1 . . . . 2.50

MEN FROM EARTH
Future Fun
1 based on Matt Mason toy 6.50

MENACE
Awesome Entertainment, 1998
1 by Jada Pinkett & Don Fraga . . 2.50
1a signed 20.00
2 . . . . 2.50
3 . . . . 2.50

MERCENARY
NBM, 1998
TPB The Voyage 10.95
TPB The Black Globe 9.95
TPB The Fortress 9.95
TPB Giants, 48-pg 10.95
TPB Year 1000, 48-pg 11.95
TPB Lost Civilization 10.95

MERCHANTS OF DEATH
Eclipse, 1988
1 King's Castle, The Hero 3.50
2 King's Castle,Soldiers of Fortune 3.50
3 Ransom, Soldier of Fortune . . . 3.50
4 ATh(c),Ransom, Men o/t Legion . 3.50
5 Ransom,New York City Blues . . . 3.50

MERIDIAN
Crossgen Comics, 2000
1 BKs 4.50
2 BKs 4.50

Meridian–Mighty / COLOR PUB.

3 BKs	4.00
4 BKs	4.00
5 BKs	4.00
6 thru 11 BKs	@3.50
12 thru 18 BKs	@3.00
19 thru 30 BKs	@2.95
31 thru 42 BKs	@2.95
TPB rep #1–#7	19.95
TPB Vol. 2 192-pg.	19.95
TPB Vol. 3 160-pg.	15.95
TPB Vol. 4	15.95
TPB Vol. 5 Minister of Cadador	15.95
TPB Vol. 6 Changing Course	15.95
GN Meridian Traveler Vol.1	9.95
GN Meridian Traveler Vol.3	9.95
GN Meridian Traveler Vol.4	9.95

MERLIN REALM
Blackthorne, 1985

1 3-D	2.50

METABARONS
Humanoids Publishing, 2000

1	2.95
2 thru 9	@2.95
10 thru 17	@2.95
TPB Vol. 1 Path of the Warrior	14.95
TPB Vol. 2 Blood and Steel	14.95
TPB Vol. 3 Poet & Killer	11.95
TPB Vol. 4 Immaculate Conception	9.95
GN Alpha/Omega, 48-pg.	9.95

META 4
First 1990

1 IG	3.95
2 IG	2.25
3 IG/JSon,final monthly	2.25

METALLICA
Malibu Rock-it Comix

1	4.25

METALLIX
Future Comics 2003

0	3.50
4 thru 5	@3.50
6 thru 12	@3.00

METAL MILITIA
Entity Comics, 1995

1 I:Metal Militia	2.50
1a with Video Game	6.95
2 ICO	2.50
3 F:Detective Calahan	2.50
Ashcan	2.50

METAPHYSIQUE
Malibu Bravura, 1995

1 NBy,I:Metaphysique	2.95
1a Gold foil edition	4.00
2 NBy,Mandelbrot malfunctions	2.95
3 I:Harridas	2.95
4 D:Maj.Character,B:Superious	2.95
5 V:Astral Kid	2.95
6 Apocalyptic Armageddon, finale	2.95

MICHAELANGELO
Mirage

1 TMNT Character	15.00

MICKEY & DONALD
Gladstone, 1988

1 1449 Firestone	8.00

2	4.00
3 Man of Tomorrow	3.00
4 thru 15	@2.50
16 giant-size	2.50
17	3.00
18	4.00

Becomes:

DONALD AND MICKEY

19 thru 26	@2.00

MICKEY MANTLE COMICS
Magnum, 1991

1 JSt,Rise to Big Leagues	4.00

MICKEY MOUSE
Gladstone, 1986

219 FG,Seven Ghosts	20.00
220 FG,Seven Ghosts	10.00
221 FG,Seven Ghosts	10.00
222 FG,Editor in Grief	5.00
223 FG,Editor in Grief	4.00
224 FG,Crazy Crime Wave	4.00
225 FG,Crazy Crime Wave	4.00
226 FG,Captive Castaways	4.00
227 FG,Captive Castaways	4.00
228 FG,Captive Castaways	4.00
229 FG,Bat Bandit	4.00
230 FG,Bat Bandit	3.00
231 FG,Bobo the Elephant	3.00
232 FG,Bobo the Elephant	3.00
233 FG,Pirate Submarine	3.00
234 FG,Pirate Submarine	3.00
235 FG,Photo Racer	3.00
236 FG,Photo Racer	3.00
237 FG,Race for Riches	3.00
238 FG,Race for Riches	3.00
239 FG,Race for Riches	3.00
240 FG,March of Comics	3.00
241 FG	4.00
242 FG	3.00
243 FG	3.00
244 FG,60th Anniv	5.00
245 FG,Giant Ants	4.00
246 FG	3.00
247 FG	3.00
248 FG	3.00
249 FG	5.00
250 FG	3.00
251 FG	3.00
252 FG	3.00
253 FG	3.00
254 FG	3.00
255 FG	4.00
256 FG	4.00

MICKEY MOUSE
Walt Disney, 1990

1 'The Phantom Gondolier'	3.50
2	3.00
3 V:Phantom Blot	2.50
4	2.50
5	2.50
6	2.50
7 Phantom Blot	2.50
8 Phantom Blot	3.00
9 Fantasia 50th Anniversary	3.00
10 Sky Adventure	2.50
11 When Mouston Freezes Over	2.50
12 Hail & Farewell	2.50
13 'What's Shakin''	2.50
14 Mouseton,Eagle-Landing	2.50
15 'Lost Palace of Kashi'	2.50
16 'Scoundrels in Space'	2.50
17 'Sound of Blunder' Pt.1	2.50
18 'Sound of Blunder' Pt.2	2.50
19 50th Ann. Fantasia Celebration Sorcerer's Apprentice adapt	2.50

MICKEY MOUSE AND FRIENDS
Gemstone Publishing 2003

257	2.95
258	2.95
259	2.95

Mickey Spillane's Mike Danger 33
© Big Entertainment

MICKEY SPILLANE'S MIKE DANGER
Tekno Comix, 1995

1 I:Mike Danger	2.25
2 Underside of the City	2.00
3 Judicial System	2.00
4 Mike's First Job	2.00
5 Old New York	2.00
6 Sin Syndicate Leader	2.25
7 thru 11	@2.25

Big Entertainment, 1996

1	2.25
2	2.25
3 MCn,PGr,TBe,EB	2.25
4	2.25
5 'Time Heels'	2.25
6 TBe,'Paradox Rule'	2.25
7 TBe,'Red Menace,' pt.1	2.25
8 TBe,'Red Menace,' pt.2	2.25
9 TBe,'Red Menace,' pt.3	2.25
10 TBe,'Red Menace,' concl.	2.25

MICROBOTS, THE
Gold Key, Dec., 1971

1	30.00

MIDNIGHT EYE: GOKU PRIVATE INVESTIGATOR
Viz

1 A.D. 2014: Tokyo city	5.25
2 V:Hakuryu,A:Yoko	4.95
3 A:Ryoko,Search for Ryu	4.95
4 Goku vs. Ryu	4.95
5 Leilah Abducted	4.95
6 Lisa's I.D. discovered	4.95

MIGHTY COMICS
Archie, 1966
{Prev: Flyman}

40 A:Web	40.00
41 A:Shield, Black Hood	35.00

All comics prices listed are for Near Mint condition.

Mighty–Miss

42 A:Black Hood............. 35.00
43 A:Shield, Black Hood,Web.... 35.00
44 A:Black Hood, Steel Sterling
  Shield................. 35.00
45 Shield-Black Hood team-up
  O:Web................. 35.00
46 A:Steel Sterling, Black
  Hood, Web............ 35.00
47 A:Black Hood & Mr.Justice.... 35.00
48 A:Shield & Hangman........ 35.00
49 Steel Sterling-Black Hood
  team-up, A:Fox............ 35.00

[ALL NEW ADVENTURES OF] THE MIGHTY CRUSADERS
Archie/Red Circle, 1965
[1st Series]
1 O:Shield (Joe Higgins & Bill
  Higgins)................. 80.00
2 MSy,O:Comet.............. 50.00
3 O:Fly-Man................. 40.00
4 A:Fireball,Jaguar,Web,Fox,
  Blackjack Hangman & more
  Golden Age Archie Heroes... 45.00
5 I:Ultra-Men&TerrificThree..... 40.00
6 V:Maestro,A:Steel Sterling..... 40.00
7 O:Fly-Girl,A:Steel Sterling..... 40.00

[2nd Series], 1983
1 RB,R:Joe Higgins & Lancelot
  Strong as the SHIELD, Mighty
  Crusaders, A:Mr.Midnight..... 2.00
2 RB,V:Brain Emperor & Eterno... 2.00
3 RB,I:Darkling................ 2.00
4 DAy,TD................... 2.00
5 .... 2.00
6 DAy,TD,Shield.............. 2.00
7 .... 2.00
8 .... 2.00
9 Trial of the Shield............ 2.00
10 .... 2.00
11 DAy,D:Gold Age Black Hood, I:
  Riot Squad, series based on
  toy lines.................. 2.00
12 DAy,I:She-Fox.............. 2.00
13 Last issue................. 2.00
TPB Origin of Super Team (2003). 12.95

MIGHTY HERCULES, THE
Gold Key,, July, 1963
1 .... 225.00
2 .... 200.00

MIGHTY MAGNOR, THE
Malibu April, 1993
1 .... 2.00
2 thru 6 SA................. @2.00

MIGHTY MORPHIN POWER RANGERS
Hamilton, 1994–95
1 From TV Series.............. 2.75
2 Switcheroo................. 2.50
3 .... 2.25
4 F:White Ranger.............. 2.00
5 F:Pink Ranger............... 2.00
6 V:Garganturon.............. 2.00
TPB Re. #1-#6 photo (c)......... 9.95

[Series 2], 1995
1 Unstoppable Force............ 2.00
2 V:Mechanical Octopus......... 2.00
3 .... 2.00
4 Lost Ranger................. 2.00

[Series 3], 1995
1 O:Green Ranger.............. 2.00

COLOR PUB.

2 O:Green Ranger............. 2.00
3 I:New Megazords............ 2.00

MIGHTY MOUSE
Spotlight, 1987
1 FMc,PC(c)................. 2.00
2 FMc,CS(c)................. 2.00
1 Holiday Special.............. 2.00

MIGHTY MUTANIMALS
Archie Publications
[Mini-Series]
1 Cont.from TMNT Adventures#19,
  A:Raphael, Man Ray, Leather-
  head, Mondo Gecko,Deadman,
  Wingnut & Screwloose....... 2.00
2 V:Mr.Null,Malinga,Soul and Bean
  and the Malignoid Army..... 2.00
3 Alien Invasion help off, Raphael
  returns to Earth............ 2.00
4 `Days of Future Past'.......... 2.00
5 `Into the Sun'............... 2.00
6 V:Null & 4 Horsemen Pt#2..... 2.00
7 Jaws of Doom............... 2.00
Spec.#1 rep. all #1-3 +SBi pin-ups. 2.95

MIGHTY MUTANIMALS
Archie
1 Quest for Jagwar's Mother..... 2.00
2 V:Snake Eyes................ 2.00
3 .... 2.00
4 `Days of Future Past'.......... 2.00
5 `Into the Sun'............... 2.00
6 V:Null & 4 Horsemen Pt#2..... 2.00
7 Jaws of Doom............... 2.00

Mighty Samson #17
© Gold Key

MIGHTY SAMSON
Gold Key, 1964–82
1 O:Mighty Samson........... 125.00
2 thru 5.................... @75.00
6 thru 10................... @40.00
11 thru 20.................. @35.00
21 thru 32.................. @30.00

MIKE GRELL'S SABLE
First, 1990
1 thru 8 rep................. @2.00
9 .... 2.00
10 Triptych.................. 2.00

MIKE SHAYNE PRIVATE EYE
Dell Publishing Co.,
Nov.–Jan., 1961-62
1 .... 50.00
2 .... 30.00
3 .... 30.00

MILLENNIUM INDEX
Independent Comics, 1988
1 and 2.................... @2.00

MILTON THE MONSTER & FEARLESS FLY
Gold Key, May, 1966
1 .... 150.00

MIRACLEMAN
Eclipse, 1985–94
1 R:Miracleman............... 10.00
2 AD,Moore,V:Kid Miracleman.... 9.00
3 AD,Moore,V:Big Ben.......... 9.00
4 AD,Moore,R:Dr.Gargunza..... 9.00
5 AD,Moore,O:Miracleman..... 9.00
6 Moore,V:Miracledog, D:Evelyn
  Cream.................. 8.00
7 Moore,D:Dr.Gargunza........ 8.00
8 Moore..................... 8.00
9 RV,Moore,Birth of Miracebaby.. 8.00
10 JRy,RV,Moore.............. 8.00
11 JTo,Moore,Book III,
  I:Miraclewoman........... 8.00
12 thru 14 Moore............. @30.00
15 Moore................... 75.00
16 .... 30.00
17 .... 15.00
18 .... 12.00
19 thru 22.................. @7.00
23 .... 20.00
24 BWS(c),NGa(s),........... 5.00
25 .... 10.00
26 thru 28.................. @3.00
3-D Special #1............... 2.75
Graphic Albums
TPB Book 1 A Dream of Flying... 25.00
TPB Book 2 The Red Kings
  Syndrome................ 25.00
TPB Book 3 Olympus.......... 75.00
TPB Book 3................. 25.00

MIRACLEMAN APOCRYPHA
Eclipse, 1991–92
1 inc.`Rascal Prince'........... 7.00
2 Miracleman, Family Stories..... 7.00
3 .... 7.00

MIRACLEMAN FAMILY
Eclipse, 1988
1 British Rep.,A:Kid Miracleman... 2.00
2 Alan Moore (s)............... 2.00

MIRACLE SQUAD, THE
Upshot/Fantagraphics, 1986
1 Hollywood 30's.............. 2.00
2 thru 4.................... @2.00

MISS FURY
Adventure Comics, 1991
1 O:Cat Suit.................. 2.50
2 Miss Fury impersonator....... 2.50
3 A:Three Miss Fury's........... 2.50
4 conclusion................. 2.50

All comics prices listed are for Near Mint condition.

MISSION IMPOSSIBLE
Dell Publishing Co., May, 1967
1 Ph(c) 150.00
2 Ph(c) 125.00
3 Ph(c) 100.00
4 Ph(c) 100.00
5 Ph(c) 100.00

MISSIONS IN TIBET
Dimension Comics, 1995
1 I:New Series................. 2.50
2 F:Orlando,Ting,Alex 2.50
3 Two Worlds Collide.......... 2.50
4 V:Sada..................... 2.50

MISS PEACH
(& SPECIAL ISSUES)
Dell Publishing Co., 1963
1 .... 125.00

MR. AND MRS. J. EVIL SCIENTIST
Gold Key, Nov., 1963
1 .... 125.00
2 .... 75.00
3 .... 75.00
4 .... 75.00

MR. MAJESTIC
WildStorm/DC, 1999
1 JoC,A:Desmond 2.50
1a variant cover................ 3.00
2 JoC,time gone berserk 2.50
3 JoC,F:Maxine Manchester 2.50
4 JoC,F:Junior Majestic........ 2.50
5 JoC 2.50
6 JoC,F:Desmond 2.50
7 JoC,Universal Law,pt.1 ...... 2.50
8 JoC,Universal Law,pt.2 ...... 2.50
9 JoC,Universal Law,pt.3,
 final issue.................. 2.50
TPB 14.95

MR. MONSTER
Eclipse, 1985–87
1 I:Mr. Monster 7.00
2 DSt(c)....................... 5.00
3 V:Dr. NoZone 3.50
4 'Trapped in Dimension X'..... 3.00
5 V:Flesh-eating Amoebo........ 3.00
6 KG,SD,reprints 3.00
7 .... 3.00
8 V:Monster in the Atomic Telling
 Machine 3.00
9 V:Giant Clams 3.00
10 R:Dr.No Zone, 3-D 2.00

MR. MONSTER ATTACKS
Tundra, 1992
1 DGb,SK,short stories 4.25
2 SK,short stories cont......... 4.25
3 DGb,last issue 4.25

MR. MONSTER SUPERDUPER SPECIAL
Eclipse, 1986–87
1 .... 2.50
2 .... 2.00
3 .... 2.00
4 .... 2.00
5 .... 2.00

COLOR PUB.

6 .... 2.00
Hi-Voltage Super Science........ 2.00
3-D Spec. Hi-Octane Horror,JKu,
 'Touch of Death' reprint 2.00
Triple Treat................... 3.95

MR. MONSTER TRUE CRIME
Eclipse, 1986
1 .... 2.00
2 .... 2.00
3-D Spec. #1 .... 2.00

MR. MUSCLES
Charlton Comics, 1956
22 .... 65.00
23 .... 55.00

MR. MYSTIC
Eclipse
1 .... 2.00
2 .... 2.00
3 .... 2.00

MR. T AND THE T FORCE
Now, 1993
1 NA,R:Mr.T,V:Street Gangs 2.50
1a Gold Ed................... 10.00
2 NA,V:Demons................ 2.25
3 NBy,w/card.................. 2.25
4 NBy,In Urban America 2.25
5 thru 10, with card .... @2.25

MISTER X
Vortex, 1984
1 HB 7.00
2 HB 5.00
3 HB 3.50
4 HB 3.00
5 .... 3.00
6 thru 10 .... @2.50
11 thru 13 .... @2.00
14 .... 2.25

MOD SQUAD
Dell Publishing Co., 1969–71
1 .... 100.00
2 .... 50.00
3 .... 50.00
4 thru 8 .... @50.00

MOD WHEELS
Gold Key, 1971–76
1 .... 50.00
2 thru 18 .... @25.00
19 .... 20.00

MONARCHY
WildStorm/DC, Feb., 2001
1 JMC,V:Young Authoritans 2.50
2 JMC,F:Union 2.50
3 JMC,Vox Populi,pt.1 .... 2.50
4 JMC,Vox Populi,pt.2 .... 2.50
5 JMC,Boy Who Talked to Spiders. 2.50
6 JMC,Making the Metropolitan ... 2.50
7 JMC,Making the Metropolitan ... 2.50
8 JMC,Making the Metropolitan ... 2.50
9 JMC,Metropolitan epilog 2.50
10 JMC,V:Chimera 2.50
11 JMC,V:Higher Power 2.50
12 JMC,final issue 2.50
TPB Bullets over Babylon....... 12.95

Mod Squad #7
© Dell Publishing Co.

MONKEE'S, THE
Dell Publishing Co., 1967
1 Ph(c) 150.00
2 Ph(c) 125.00
3 Ph(c) 125.00
4 Ph(c) 125.00
5 .... 90.00
6 Ph(c) 100.00
7 Ph(c) 100.00
8 and 9 .... @90.00
10 Ph(c) 100.00
11 thru 17 .... @75.00

MONOLITH
Comico, 1991
1 From Elementals 2.50
2 'Seven Levels of Hell'........ 2.50
3 'Fugue and Variation' 2.50
4 'Fugue and Variation' 2.50

MONROE'S, THE
Dell Publishing Co., April, 1967
1 Ph(c) 35.00

MONSTER CLUB
Autumn Press 2003
1 .... 3.50
2 thru 4 .... @3.50
5 thru 11 .... @3.50
12 40-pg..................... 3.50
TPB Vol. 1 .... 19.95
TPB Vol. 2 .... 20.00

MONSTER MASSACRE
Atomeka
1 SBs, DBr,DGb 8.50
1a Black Edition............. 35.00

MONSTERS, INC.
Tokyopop Press, 2002
GN Vol.1 Disney manga adaptation 8.00

MONSTER WORLD
WildStorm/DC, May, 2001
1 (of 4) SLo,.................. 2.95
2 SLo, 5 young heroes 2.95
3 SLo, ... 2.95
4 SLo,concl. 2.95

MOONWALKER IN 3-D
Blackthorne
1 thru 3 . . . . @2.50

MORBID ANGEL
London Night, 1996
? Angel's Tear, signed 10.00
1 Commemorative (1999) 5.95

MORBID ANGEL: PENANCE
London Night, 1996
Revised Color Spec., double size . . 4.00

More Than Mortal #5
© Liar Comics

MORE THAN MORTAL
Liar Comics, 1997
1 . . . . 2.95
1a 2nd printing 2.95
1b convention, sign, num. 9.95
2 Derdre vs. the Host 2.95
2a variant painted cover 5.95
3 MS(c) 2.95
4 concl. 2.95
TPB rep. #1–#4 . . . . 14.95

MORE THAN MORTAL: SAGAS
Liar Comics, 1998
1 by Sharon Scott & Romano
  Molenaar 2.95
1a variant Tim Vigil(c) 2.95
1b variant JLi(c). 9.95
2 . . . . 2.95
3 conclusion 2.95

MORE THAN MORTAL: TRUTHS AND LEGENDS
Liar Comics, 1998
1 by Sharon Scott, Steve Firchow,
  Mark Prudeaux, O:Witchfinder . 3.00
1a signed 9.95
2 . . . . 3.00
3 . . . . 3.00
4 . . . . 3.00
5 . . . . 3.00
5a variant cover (1:4). 3.00
6 . . . . 3.00

COLOR PUB.

MORLOCK 2001
Atlas, Feb.–July, 1975
1 thru 2 O:Morlock . . . . @25.00
3 SD,BW,F:Midnight Men. 35.00

MORRIGAN
Sirius, 1997
1 by Lorenzo Bartoli & Saverio
  Tenuta 2.95
2 and 3 . . . . @2.95
GN rep. #1–#3 . . . . 9.95

MORTAL KOMBAT
Malibu 1994
0 Four stories 2.95
1 Based on the Video Game 2.95
1a Foil Ed 4.00
1b with new material 2.95
2 . . . . 2.95
3 . . . . 2.95
4 . . . . 2.95
5 I:Mortal Kombat II. 2.95
6 Climax 2.95
Spec. #1 Tournament edition 3.95
Spec. #2 Tournament edition II . . . 3.95
TPB rep. #1–#6 . . . . 14.95

MORTAL KOMBAT: BARAKA
Malibu 1995
1 V:Scorpion 2.95

MORTAL KOMBAT: BATTLEWAVE
Malibu 1995
1 New series 2.95
2 Action, Action, Action 2.95
3 The Gathering 2.95
4 F:Goro 2.95
5 F:Scorpion 2.95
6 final issue. 2.95

MORTAL KOMBAT: GORO, PRINCE OF PAIN
Malibu Sept., 1994
1 Goro. 2.95
1a Platinum Edition 6.25
2 Goro, V:Kombatant. 2.95
3 Goro, V:God of Pain 2.95

MORTAL KOMBAT: KITANA & MILEENA
Malibu 1995
1 Secrets of Outworld 2.95

MORTAL KOMBAT: KUNG LAO
Malibu 1995
1 one-shot Battlewave tie-in. 2.95

MORTAL KOMBAT: RAYDEN AND KANO
Malibu 1995
1 J:Rayden Kano. 2.95
1a Deluxe Edition 4.95
2 A:Reptile. 2.95
3 Kano, conclusion 2.95

MORTAL KOMBAT: U.S. SPECIAL FORCES
Malibu 1995
1 V:Black Dragon 3.50
2 V:Black Dragon 2.95

MOSTLY WANTED
WildStorm/DC, May, 2000
1 (of 4) SLo,F:Sister Crenn 2.50
2 SLo(s),F:Andi Mooncrest 2.50
3 SLo(s), ... 2.50
4 SLo(s),conclusion. 2.50

MOTORBIKE PUPPIES
Dark Zulu Lies, 1992
1 I:Motorbike Puppies 2.50

MOVIE COMICS
Gold Key/Whitman, Oct., 1962
Alice in Wonderland 50.00
Aristocats 125.00
Bambi 1 . . . . 50.00
Bambi 2 . . . . 40.00
Beneath the Planet of the Apes. . 150.00
Big Red 50.00
Blackbeard's Ghost. 50.00
Buck Rogers Giant Movie Edition . 35.00
Bullwhip Griffin 50.00
Captain Sinbad. 100.00
Chitty, Chitty Bang Bang. 100.00
Cinderella. 50.00
Darby O'Gill & the Little People. . . 75.00
Dumbo 50.00
Emil & the Detectives 45.00
Escapade in Florence 125.00
Fall of the Roman Empire. 50.00
Fantastic Voyage 70.00
55 Days at Peking 50.00
Fighting Prince of Donegal 40.00
First Men of the Moon. 50.00
Gay Purr-ee 75.00
Gnome Mobile 50.00
Goodbye, Mr. Chips 50.00
Happiest Millionaire 50.00
Hey There, It's Yogi Bear 100.00
Horse Without a Head 40.00
How the West Was Won 50.00
In Search of the Castaways 100.00
Jungle Book, The 100.00
Kidnapped 50.00
King Kong 50.00
King Kong N# 75.00
Lady and the Tramp 50.00
Lady and the Tramp 1. . . . . 75.00
Lady and the Tramp 2. . . . . 35.00
Legend of Lobo, The 35.00
Lt. Robin Crusoe 35.00
Lion, The 35.00
Lord Jim 40.00
Love Bug, The 40.00
Mary Poppins 55.00
Mary Poppins 1 . . . . 100.00
McLintock 175.00
Merlin Jones as the Monkey's
  Uncle 75.00
Miracle of the White Stallions . . . 40.00
Misadventures of Merlin Jones . . . 75.00
Moon-Spinners, The 100.00
Mutiny on the Bounty 50.00
Nikki, Wild Dog of the North 35.00
Old Yeller 35.00
One Hundred & One Dalmatians. . 40.00
Peter Pan 1 . . . . 50.00
Peter Pan 2 . . . . 35.00
P.T. 109 . . . . 75.00
Rio Conchos. 80.00
Robin Hood 50.00

All comics prices listed are for Near Mint condition.

Movie–Mysteries / COLOR PUB. / Comics Values Annual

Shaggy Dog & the Absent-Minded
  Professor 75.00
Sleeping Beauty 100.00
Snow White & the Seven Dwarfs . 50.00
Son of Flubber 50.00
Summer Magic 100.00
Swiss Family Robinson 40.00
Sword in the Stone 100.00
That Darn Cat 100.00
Those Magnificent Men in Their
  Flying Machines 50.00
Three Stooges in Orbit 150.00
Tiger Walks, A 60.00
Toby Tyler 40.00
Treasure Island 40.00
20,000 Leagues Under the Sea . . 40.00
Wonderful Adventures of
  Pinocchio 50.00
Wonderful World of Brothers
  Grimm 60.00
X, the Man with the X-Ray Eyes 125.00
Yellow Submarine w/poster 450.00

MS. MYSTIC
Pacific
1 NA,Origin 8.00
2 NA,Origin,I:Urth 4 . . . . 6.00

Continuity, 1988
1 NA,Origin rep. 2.00
2 NA,Origin,I:Urth 4 rep 2.00
3 NA,New material 2.00
4 TSh 2.00
5 DT 2.00
6 . . . . 2.00
7 . . . . 2.00
8 CH/Sdr,B:Love Story 2.00
9 DB 2.00
9a Newsstand(c) 2.00

[3rd Series], 1993
1 O:Ms.Mystic 2.50
2 A:Hybrid 2.50
3 . . . . 2.50
4 . . . . 2.50

[4th Series, Deathwatch 2000]
1 Deathwatch 2000 pt.8,w/card . . . 2.50
2 Deathwatch 2000 w/card 2.50
3 Indestructible cover, w/card 2.50

MS. TREE'S THRILLING DETECTIVE ADVENTURES
Eclipse, 1983
1 Miller pin up 4.00
2 . . . . 2.50
3 . . . . 2.00
Becomes:

MS. TREE
Eclipse, 1983
4 thru 6 . . . . @2.00
7 . . . . 2.50
8 . . . . 8.00
9 . . . . 2.00

Aardvark–Vanaheim, 1984
10 . . . . 2.00

Renegade
1 3-D. 2.00

MS. VICTORY GOLDEN ANNIVERSARY
AC Comics
1 Ms.Victory celebration 5.00

MS. VICTORY SPECIAL
AC Comics
1 . . . . 2.00

MUMMY ARCHIVES
Millennium, 1992
1.JM,Features,articles 2.50

The Mummy, Or Ramses the Damned #11 © Millennium

MUMMY, OR RAMSES THE DAMNED, THE
Millennium, 1992
1 Anne Rice Adapt. 5.00
2 JM,`Mummy in Mayfair'. 3.75
3 JM 3.25
4 JM, To Egypt 3.00
5 JM`The Mummy's Hand' 2.50
6 JM 20th Century Egypt 2.50
7 JM,More Ramses Past Revealed 2.50
8 JM,Hunt for Cleopatra 2.50
9 JM,Cleopatra's Wrath contd. . . . 2.50
10 JM,Subterranian World 2.50
11 JM. 2.50

MUMMY, THE: VALLEY OF THE GODS
Chaos! Comics, 2001
1 (of 3) MWn,MtB, movie tie-in . . . 3.00
1a variant (c) 3.00
1b premium 10.00
2 . . . . 3.00
2a Scorpion King photo (c) 3.00
3 . . . . 3.00
3a Imhotep phoco (c). 3.00
Ashcan 6.00

MUNDEN'S BAR ANNUAL
First, 1988
1 BB,JOy,JSn,SR 2.95

MUNSTERS, THE
Gold Key, 1965–68
1 . . . . 300.00
2 . . . . 150.00
3 thru 5 . . . . @125.00
6 thru 16 . . . . @100.00

MUPPET BABIES
Harvey, 1993
1 Return of Muppet Babies 2.00

MURCIELAGA/SHE-BAT
Studio G, 2001
1 by D.Gross & R.Lopez 2.95
2 thru 4 . . . . @2.95

MUTANT CHRONICLES—GOLGOTHA
Valiant
1 thru 4 + game trading card . . . @2.95
TPB, Vol. 1 rep.,pt.#1–#4 . . . . . . 10.95

MUTANTS & MISFITS
Silverline
1 thru 4 . . . . @2.00

MY FAVORITE MARTIAN
Gold Key, 1964–66
1 . . . . 200.00
2 . . . . 125.00
3 thru 9 . . . . @100.00

MY LITTLE MARGIE
Charlton Comics, 1954–65
1 Ph(c) 350.00
2 Ph(c) 175.00
3 . . . . 100.00
4 . . . . 100.00
5 . . . . 100.00
6 . . . . 100.00
7 . . . . 100.00
8 . . . . 100.00
9 . . . . 90.00
10 . . . . 75.00
11 . . . . 65.00
12 . . . . 65.00
13 . . . . 65.00
14 thru 19 . . . . @50.00
20 Giant Size 125.00
21 thru 35 . . . . @50.00
36 thru 53 . . . . @40.00
54 Beatles (c) 225.00

MYSTERIES OF UNEXPLORED WORLDS/ SON OF VULCAN
Charlton Comics, 1956
1 . . . . 400.00
2 . . . . 150.00
3 SD,SD(c) 300.00
4 SD,Forbidden Room 350.00
5 SD,SD(c) 300.00
6 SD 300.00
7 SD 300.00
8 SD 300.00
9 SD 300.00
10 SD,SD(c) 300.00
11 SD,SD(c) 300.00
12 SD,Charm Bracelet 250.00
13 thru 18 . . . . @75.00
19 SD(c) 165.00
20 . . . . 45.00
21 thru 24 SD . . . . @200.00
25 . . . . 35.00
26 SD 165.00
27 thru 30 . . . . @50.00
31 thru 45 . . . . @30.00
46 I:Son ofVulcan,Dr.Kong(1965) . 60.00
47 V:King Midas 30.00
48 V:Captain Tuska 30.00
Becomes:

SON OF VULCAN
49 DC redesigns costume 15.00
50 V:Dr.Kong 15.00

COLOR PUB.

MYSTERIOUS SUSPENSE
Charlton, 1968
1 SD,F:Question 100.00

MYSTERY COMICS DIGEST
Gold Key, March, 1972–75
1 WW,Riley's Believe It Or Not. . . 60.00
2 WW,Boris Karloff 55.00
3 RC,GEv,Twilight Zone. 50.00
4 Ripley's Believe It or Not. 45.00
5 Boris Karloff 45.00
6 Twilight Zone 45.00
7 Believe It Or Not. 45.00
8 RC,AW,Boris Karloff 45.00
9 Twilight Zone 45.00
10 thru 13 ....@45.00
14 1st Xorkon. 45.00
15 thru 20 ....@45.00
21 thru 26 ....@30.00

MYSTIC
Crosgen Comics, 2000
1 RMz,BPe 6.00
2 RMz,BPe 5.00
3 RMz,BPe 4.00
4 RMz,BPe 3.25
5 RMz,BPe 3.25
6 thru 10 ....@3.25
11 .... 4.00
12 thru 30 ....@3.00
31 thru 42 ....@3.00
TPB Vol. 1 .... 19.95
TPB Vol. 2 .... 19.95
TPB Vol. 3 Siege of Scales. 15.95
TPB Vol. 4 Out All Night 15.95
TPB Vol. 5 Master Class. 15.95

MYSTIC EDGE
Antarctic Press, 1998
1 by Ryan Kinnaird, F:Risa
& Symattra. 2.95

NANCY & SLUGGO
Dell Publishing Co., 1957
146 B:Peanuts 70.00
147 .... 65.00
148 .... 65.00
149 .... 65.00
150 thru 161 ....@65.00
162 thru 165 ....@100.00
166 thru 176 A:OONA . . . . . . @125.00
177 thru 180 ....@65.00
181 thru 187 ....@65.00

NATIONAL VELVET
Dell Publishing Co., May-July, 1961
1 Ph(c) 125.00
2 Ph(c) 60.00

NEAT STUFF
Fantagraphics, 1986
1 .... 4.50
2 .... 3.00
3 thru 5 ....@2.50
6 .... 2.25
7 .... 2.25

NECROMANTRA/ LORD PUMPKIN
Malibu Ultraverse, 1995
1 A:Loki (from Marvel) 2.95

2 MiB,V:Godwheel, flipbook. 2.95
3 O:Lord Pumpkin 2.95
4 Infinity Gem tie-in 2.95
4a variant cover. 3.50

NECROPOLIS
Fleetway
1 SBs(c),CE,A:Dark Judges/
Sisters Of Death. 2.95
2 .... 2.95
3 thru 9 ....@2.95

NECROSCOPE
Malibu Oct., 1992
1 Novel adapt., holo(c) 3.25
1a 2nd printing 2.95
2 thru 4 Adapt. cont. . . . . @2.95
Book II Oct., 1994
1 thru 5 .... 2.95

NECROWAR
Dreamwave 2003
1 .... 2.95
2 thru 4 ....@2.95

NEGATION
Crossgen Comics, 2001
1 MWa,PaP,F:Obregon Kaine 3.00
2 MWa,PaP,Kaine's master-plan . . 3.00
3 MWa,PaP,F:Captain Fluxor. 3.00
4 thru 12 PaP ....@3.00
13 thru 24 ....@2.95
Spec. #1 Negation: Lawbringer. . . . 3.00
Prequel MWa,PaP 3.00
TPB Vol. 1 Bohica 19.95
TPB Vol. 2 Baptism of Fire 15.95
TPB Vol. 3 Hounded 15.95

NEGATIVE EXPOSURE
Humanoids Publishing, 2001
1 by Enrico Mirini. 2.95
2 .... 2.95
3 thru 4 ....@2.95
TPB 18.95

NEIL GAIMAN'S LADY JUSTICE
Tekno Comix (1995)
1 I:Lady Justice 2.50
1a 6.00
2 V:Blood Pirate 2.00
3 V:Blood Pirate 2.00
4 New Story Arc 2.00
5 Street Gang War 2.00
6 Street Gang War 2.25
7 thru 11 ....@2.25
Big Entertainment, April, 1996
1 thru 4 ....@2.25
5 DIB(s). 2.25
6 DIB(s),'Woman About Town,' pt.1 2.25
7 DIB(s),'Woman About Town,' pt.2 2.25
8 DIB(s),'Woman About Town,' pt.3 2.25

NEIL GAIMAN'S MR. HERO THE NEWMATIC MAN
Tekno-Comics, 1994
1 I:Mr. Hero, Tecknophage. 2.50
2 A:Tecknophage. 2.25
3 I:Adam Kaine 2.00
4 I:New Body. 2.00
5 Earthquake. 2.00
6 I:New Character 2.00

Neil Gaiman's Mr. Hero the Newmatic Man #16 © Tekno Comics

7 I:Deadbolt, Bloodboil. 2.00
8 V:Avatar 2.00
9 in London. 2.00
10 V:Demon 2.00
11 V:Monster 2.00
12 The Great Goward. 2.25
13 thru 17 ....@2.25

NEIL GAIMAN'S PHAGE
Tekno-Comics, 1996
1 .... 2.25

NEIL GAIMAN'S PHAGE: SHADOW DEATH
Big Entertainment
1 thru 4 ....@2.25
5 O:Orlando Holmes,A:Lady
Messalina. 2.25
6 conclusion 2.25

NEIL GAIMAN'S TECKNOPHAGE
Teckno-Comics, 1995
1 I:Kalighoul, Tom Vietch 2.00
1a Steel Edition. 3.95
2 F:Mayor of New Yorick 2.00
3 Phange Building 2.00
4 Horde eevils 2.00
5 Middle Management 2.00
6 Escape from Phange 2.00
7 Mecca 2.25

NEIL GAIMAN'S WHEEL OF WORLDS
Teckno-Comics, 1995
0 Deluxe Edition w/Posters 2.95
0a I:Lady Justice 2.00
1 .... 3.25

NEMESIS THE WARLOCK
Eagle, 1984
1 .... 2.00
2 thru 8 ....@2.00

NEOTOPIA
Antarctic Press 2003
1 Princess for a Day 3.95
2 Philios to the Rescue 3.95
3 thru 5 . . . . @3.95
Vol. 2
1 (of 6) 3.00
2 . . . . 3.00
3 . . . . 3.95
4 thru 5 . . . . @3.00

NEW ADVENTURES OF FELIX THE CAT
Felix Comics, Inc., 1992
1 New stories 2.25
2 'The Magic Paint Brush' 2.25

NEW ADVENTURES OF PINOCCHIO
Dell Publishing Co., 1962
1 . . . . 125.00
2 and 3 . . . . @100.00

NEW ADVENTURES OF SPEED RACER
Now
0 Premiere, 3-D cover 2.00
1 thru 11 . . . . @2.00

NEW AMERICA
Eclipse, 1987–88
1 A:Scout 2.00
2 A:Scout 2.00
3 A:Roman Catholic Pope 2.00
4 A:Scout 2.00

NEW BREED
Pied Piper
1 . . . . 2.75
2 . . . . 2.25

NEW DNAGENTS, THE
Eclipse, 1985–87
1 R:DNAgents 2.00
2 F:Tank 2.00
3 Repopulating the World 2.00
4 Major Catastrophe for Earth . . . 2.00
5 'Last Place on Earth' 2.00
6 JOy(c),'Postscript' 2.00
7 V:Venimus 2.00
8 DSp,V:Venimus 2.00
9 V:Venimus,I:New Wave 2.00
10 I:New Airboy 2.00
11 Summer Fun Issue 2.00
12 V:Worm 2.00
13 EL,F:Tank 2.00
14 EL,Nudity,'Grounded' 2.00
15 thru 17 . . . . @2.00
3-D #1 . . . . 2.50

NEW JUSTICE MACHINE
Innovation, 1989
1 and 2 . . . . @2.00
2 . . . . 2.00

NEW KABOOM
Awesome Entertainment, 1999
1 RLe,JLb 2.50

COLOR PUB.

NEWMEN
Maximum Press, 1997
1–22 see Image
23 ErS,CSp,AG,'Anthem,' pt.3 . . . . 2.50
24 ErS,CSp,AG,'Anthem,' pt.4 . . . . 2.50
25 ErS,CSp,AG,'Anthem,' pt.5 . . . . 2.50

NEW ORLEANS SAINTS
1 Playoff season(football team) . . . 6.00

NEW STATESMEN
Fleetway
1 . . . . 4.50
2 thru 5 . . . . @3.95

NEWSTRALIA
Innovation, 1989
1 and 2 . . . . @2.00
3 . . . . 2.00

NEW TERRYTOONS
Dell Publishing Co., 1960–61
1 . . . . 85.00
2 thru 8 . . . . @50.00
Gold Key, 1962
1 F:Heckle & Jeckle 125.00
2 . . . . 100.00
3 thru 10 . . . . @50.00
11 thru 20 . . . . @40.00
21 thru 30 . . . . @25.00
31 thru 40 . . . . @20.00
41 thru 54 . . . . @15.00

NEW WAVE, THE
Eclipse, 1986–87
1 Error Pages 2.00
1a Correction 2.00
2 . . . . 2.00
3 'Space Station Called Hell' 2.00
4 Birth of Megabyte 2.00
5 PG(c),O:Avalon 2.00
6 O:Megabyte 2.00
7 Avalon disappears 2.00
8 V:Heap,V:Druids 2.00
9 . . . . 2.00
10 V:Heap Team 2.00
11 . . . . 2.00
12 . . . . 2.00
13 V:Volunteers 2.00

The Next Man #3
© Comico

14 1/3 issue 2.00

NEW WAVE vs. THE VOLUNTEERS
Eclipse, 1987
1 3-D,V:Volunteers 2.50
2 3-D,V:Volunteers 2.50

NEXT MAN
Comico, 1985
1 I&O:Next Man 2.50
2 . . . . 2.00
3 . . . . 2.00
4 . . . . 2.00
5 . . . . 2.00

NEXT NEXUS
First, 1989
1 SR 2.00
2 SR 2.00
3 SR 2.00
4 SR 2.00

NEXUS
Capital, 1983
1 SR,I:Judah Maccabee 5.00
2 SR,Origin,V:Bellows 4.00
3 SR,Sundra Captive 4.00
4 SR,V:Ziggurat 4.00
5 SR,'I'm Bored!' 4.00
6 SR,A:Badger,TrialogueTrilogy#1 . 4.00
First
7 SR,A:Badger,TrialogueTrilogy#2 . 4.00
8 SR,A:Badger,TrialogueTrilogy#3 . 3.00
9 SR,Teen Angel 2.50
10 SR,BWg,Talking Heads 2.00
11 SR,V:Clausius 2.00
12 SR,V:The Old General 2.00
13 SR,Sundra Peale solo 2.00
14 SR,A:Clonezone,Hilariator 2.00
15 SR,A:Clonezone 2.00
16 SR,A:Clonezone 2.00
17 Judah vs. Jacque,the Anvil 2.00
18 SR,A:Clonezone 2.00
19 SR,A:Clonezone 2.00
20 SR,A:Clonezone 2.00
21 SR,A:Clonezone 2.00
22 KG,A:Badger 2.00
23 SR,A:Clonezone 2.00
24 SR,A:Clonezone 2.00
25 SR,A:Clonezone 2.00
26 SR,A:Clonezone 2.00
27 SR,A:Clonezone 2.00
28 MMi 2.00
29 A:Kreed & Sinclair 2.00
30 JL,C:Badger 2.50
31 Judah solo story 2.00
32 JG,Judah solo story 2.00
33 SR,A:Kreed & Sinclair 2.00
34 SR,Judah solo story 2.00
35 SR,Judah solo story 2.00
36 SR 2.00
37 PS 2.00
38 . . . . 2.00
39 SR, The Boom Search 2.00
40 SR 2.00
41 SR 2.00
42 SR,Bowl-Shaped world 2.00
43 PS 2.00
44 PS 2.00
45 SR,A:Badger Pt.1 . . . . 2.00
46 SR,A:Badger Pt.2 . . . . 2.00
47 SR,A:Badger Pt.3 . . . . 2.00
48 SR,A:Badger Pt.4 . . . . 2.00
49 PS,A:Badger Pt.5 . . . . 2.00
50 SF,double size,A:Badger Pt.6
    Crossroads tie-in 3.50

COLOR PUB.

Nexus–Night

51 PS. 2.00	9 V:Werewolf. 2.50	6 . . . . 2.50
52 PS. 2.00	10 . . . . 2.50	
53 PS. 2.00	11. . . . . 2.50	### NIGHTMARES
54 PS. 2.00	12 . . . . 2.50	**Eclipse, 1985**
55 PS. 2.00	13 . . . . 2.50	1 . . . . 2.50
56 . . . . 2.00	14 V:Rafferty 2.50	2 . . . . 2.00
57 AH. 2.00	15 I:Rigoletto 2.50	
58 Sr,I:Stanislaus Korivitsky	16 I:Bloodfly 4.00	### NIGHT MUSIC
as Nexus 2.00	17 D:Playland. 2.50	**Eclipse, 1984–88**
59 SR. 2.00	18 DZ,SEt,V:Bloodfly 2.50	1 . . . . 2.50
60 SR. 2.00	19 DZ,SEt,V:Deathmask. 2.50	2 . . . . 2.50
61 . . . . 2.00	20 DZ,V:Bloody fly 2.50	3 CR, Jungle Bear. 3.00
62 . . . . 2.00	21 Identity Revealed. 2.50	4 Pelias & Melisande. 2.00
63 V:Elvonic Order. 2.00	22 Infinity Gem tie-in,A:Loki 2.50	5 Pelias. 2.00
64 V:Elvonic Order. 2.00	23 R:Rhianon 2.50	6 same as Salome #1
65 V:Elvonic Order. 2.00	Ann.#1 V:Pilgrim, 64-pg.. . . . . 3.95	7 same as Red Dog #1
66 V:Elvonic Order. 2.00		Graphic Novel 8.00
67 V:Elvonic Order. 2.00	### NIGHT MAN, THE	
68 LM. 2.00	**Malibu Ultraverse, 1995**	### NIGHTS INTO DREAMS
69 . . . . 2.00	Infinity Night Man vs. Night Man . . . 2.50	**Archie Comics, 1997**
70 . . . . 2.00	1 Discovers New powers. 2.25	1 based on Sega game 2.00
71 V:Bad Brains 2.00	1a Computer Painted Cover 2.25	2 thru 6 . . . . @2.00
72 V:Renegade heads 2.00	2 phoenix flip issue 2.25	
73 Horatio returns to Ylum 2.00	3 Phoenix Resurrection 2.25	### NIGHTSHADE
74 Horatio vs. Stan. 2.00	4 final issue. 2.25	**No Mercy Comics, 1997**
75 Horatio vs. Stan. 2.00		1 by Mark Williams 2.50
76 . . . . 2.25	### NIGHT MAN/GAMBIT	2 and 3 . . . . @2.50
77 . . . . 2.25	**Malibu 1996**	
78 O:Nexus,Nexus Files Pt#1 . . . . 2.25	1 thru 3 . . . . @2.50	### NIGHT TRIBES
79 Nexus Files Pt#2 . . . . 2.25		**WildStorm/DC, 1999**
80 Nexus.Files Pt#3,last iss. 2.25	### NIGHTMARE	1-shot Night Tribes unite. 5.00
	Innovation, 1989	
### NEXUS LEGENDS	1 AN 2.50	### NIGHTVEIL
First, 1989		**AC Comics, 1984**
1 thru 13 rep.Nexus . . . . @2.00	### NIGHTMARE AND	1 . . . . 3.50
14 rep.Nexus 2.00	### CASPER	2 . . . . 2.50
15 rep.Nexus 2.00	**Harvey Publications, 1963**	3 . . . . 2.25
16 rep.Nexus 2.00	1 . . . . 100.00	4 . . . . 2.25
17 rep.Nexus 2.00	2 . . . . 65.00	5 . . . . 2.25
18 rep.Nexus 2.00	3 . . . . 65.00	6 . . . . 2.00
19 rep.Nexus 2.00	4 . . . . 65.00	7 . . . . 2.00
20 SR,Sanctuary 2.00	5 . . . . 65.00	Spec.#1 . . . . 2.00
21 thru 23 SR . . . . @2.00	Becomes:	
	### CASPER AND	### NIGHT WALKER
### NICK HALIDAY	### NIGHTMARE	**Fleetway**
Argo, May, 1956	6 B:68 pgs. 25.00	1 thru 2 rep. . . . . @2.95
1 Strip reprints. 75.00	7 . . . . 15.00	
	8 . . . . 15.00	
### NICKI SHADOW	9 . . . . 15.00	
Relentless Comics, 1997	10 . . . . 15.00	
1 by Eric Burnham & Ted Naifeh . . 2.50	11 thru 20 . . . . @10.00	
2 Killing Zone, pt.2. . . . . 2.50	21 thru 30 . . . . @8.00	
3 Killing Zone, pt.3. . . . . 2.50	31 . . . . 8.00	
4 Killing Zone, concl. 2.50	32 E:68 pgs 8.00	
	33 thru 45. . . . . @5.00	
### NIGHT GLIDER	46 Aug., 1974. . . . . 5.00	
Topps, 1993		
1 V:Bombast,C:Captain Glory,	### NIGHTMARE ON	
Trading Card 3.25	### ELM STREET	
	Blackthorne, 1991	
### NIGHTHUNTER	1 3-D. 2.50	
Empire Comics, 2001	2 3-D. 2.50	
1 (of 12) 3.75	3 3-D. 2.50	
2 thru 4 . . . . @3.75		
	### NIGHTMARES ON	
### NIGHT MAN, THE	### ELM STREET	
Malibu Ultraverse, 1993–95	**Innovation**	
1 I:Night Man,Deathmask 2.75	1 Yours Truly, Freddy Krueger Pt.1 3.00	
1a Silver foil(c) 5.00	2 Yours Truly ,Freddy Krueger Pt.2 2.50	
2 GeH,V:Mangle 2.50	3 Loose Ends Pt.1,Return to	
3 SEt,GeH,A:Freex,Mangle 2.50	Springwood 2.50	
4 HC,I:Scrapyard,O:Firearm 2.50	4 Loose Ends Pt 2. . . . . 2.50	
5 SEt(s). 2.50	5 . . . . 2.50	
6 V:TNTNT 2.50		
7 V:Nick 2.50		*Nightveil #1*
8 V:Werewolf. 2.50		*© AC Comics*

Night–Nocturnals

NIGHTWOLF
Entropy
1 .... 2.00
2 .... 2.00

9 LIVES OF FELIX
Harvey
1 thru 4 .... @2.00

NINJA BOY
WildStorm/DC, Aug., 2001
1 Ancient Japan, 40-pg.......... 3.50
2 .... 2.95
3 .... 2.95
4 .... 2.95
5 .... 2.95
6 Bishamon, God of War 2.95
TPB Faded Dreams 14.95

NINJA HIGH SCHOOL
Eternity, 1992
1 Reps.orig.N.H.S.in color 2.00
2 thru 13 reprints .... @2.00

NINJA HIGH SCHOOL
Antarctic Press, 2000
1 thru 74 see B&W
75 .... 2.95
76 Quagmire gang 2.95
77 .... 2.95
78 World Domination Tour 2.95
79 Dog Supreme 2.95
80 Jeremy Feeple is back........ 2.95
81 F:Diamond Diane............. 2.95
82 F:Quagmire Koalas 2.95
83 Time passes 2.95
84 Past, Present, Future........ 2.95
85 Time has past 2.95
86 Queen of the Conglomerate... 2.95
87 Invaded by the Shallrams 2.95
88 Battle Chef battle 3.00
89 Sammie's secret 3.00
90 Earth's champion............ 3.00
91 The Toughest Contest 3.00
92 Round 2 .... 3.00
93 Round 3 .... 3.00
94 F:Red Ninja,V:Lendo Rivalsan .. 3.00
95 Ichi in a new place.......... 3.00
96 Dash the Impede............. 3.00
97 F:Asrial, Jeremy............. 3.00
98 Asrial found 3.00
99 F:Lendo Rivalson dies 3.00
100 F:Asrial, Jeremy, & Ichi
  BDn(c) 48-pg.............. 4.95
100a Fred Perry (c) 4.95
100b Robert Dejesus (c)......... 4.95
100c Rod Espinosa (c) 4.95
101 thru 111 .... @3.50
Yearbook 2001 .... 3.95
Yearbook 2002................... 3.95
Yearbook 2003 .... 3.95
TPB Textbook Vol. 2, 600-pg. .. 49.95
Spec. Swimsuit special 2002 ..... 4.50
TPB Vol. Pocket Manga 10.00

NINJA HIGH SCHOOL VERSION 2
Antarctic Press, 1999
1 by Ben Dunn 7.00
2 .... 5.00
3 .... 4.00
4 .... 3.00
5 thru 8 .... @2.50
9 Yumei strikes back 2.50
10 .... 2.50

11 Time & space distorted 2.50
12 When Worlds Colide, last issue . 2.50

NINJA HIGH SCHOOL FEATURING SPEED RACER
Eternity, 1993
1B 2.95
2B 2.95

Ninjack #3
© Valiant

NINJAK
Valiant 1994
0: O:Ninjak,pt. 1 .... 2.50
00: O:Ninjak,pt.2............... 2.50
1 B:MMo(s),JQ,JP,Chromium(c),
  I:Dr.Silk,Webnet............ 3.00
1a Gold Ed 4.00
2 JQ,JP,V:Dr.Silk,Webnet...... 2.50
3 JQ,JP,I:Seventh Dragon 2.25
4 MMo(a&s),V:Seventh Dragon,
  w/Valiant Era card 2.25
5 MMo(a&s),A:X-O Manowar..... 2.25
6 MMo(a&s),A:X-O Manowar,
  V:Dr.Silk,Webnet............ 2.25
7 MMo(a&s),I:Rhaman........ 2.25
8 MMo(a&s),Chaos Effect-Gamma
  #3, A:Madame Noir.......... 2.25
9 Dogs of War 2.25
10 Cantebury Tale #1 .... 2.25
11 Cantebury Tale #2 .... 2.25
12 .... 2.25
13 Mad Dogs and English....... 2.25
14 Cry Wolf,pt. 1 .... 2.25
15 Cry Wolf,pt. 2 .... 2.25
16 Plague,pt. 1.................. 2.25
17 Plague,pt. 2.................. 2.25
18 Computer Virus 2.25
19 DAn,ALa,MM,Breaking the
  Web,pt.1 .... 2.25
20 DAn,ALa,MM,Breaking the
  Web,pt.2 .... 2.25
21 DAn,ALa,MM,Breaking the
  Web,pt.3 .... 2.25
22 Bitter Wind................... 2.25
23 w/o arsenal 2.25
24 Unusual sidekick 2.25
25 .... 2.25
26 .... 2.25
27 Diamond Smugglers 2.25
28 F:Sister Gabriela 2.25
Yearbook #1, Dr. Silk 3.95

COLOR PUB.

NINJAK
Acclaim 1996
1 KBk(s), Denny Meechum
  becomes Ninjak 2.50
2 KBk(s) video game spin-off..... 2.50
3 KBk(s) video game spin-off..... 2.50
4 KBk(s) video game spin-off..... 2.50
5 KBk(s) video game spin-off..... 2.50
6 KBk(s) 'The World's Finest'.... 2.50
7 KBk(s) video game spin-off..... 2.50
8 KBk(s) video game spin-off..... 2.50
9 KBk(s) video game spin-off..... 2.50
10 KBk(s) F:Maria Barbella....... 2.50
11 KBk(s) Trial Continues 2.50
12 KBk(s) final issue............ 2.50

N.I.O.
Acclaim 1998
1 (of 4) by Shon Bury & JPi...... 2.50
2 .... 2.50
3 .... 2.50
4 conclusion 2.50

NIRA X: ANIME
Entity Comics, 1997
1 BMs........................... 2.95
1a deluxe, foil cover 3.50
2 BMs........................... 2.95
2a deluxe, foil cover 3.50
Swimsuit #0 .... 2.75
Swimsuit #0 Manga (c).......... 2.75

NIRA X: CYBERANGEL
Entity, 1994
1 From pages of Zen............ 2.95
1a 2nd printing 2.75
2 V:Parradox.................... 2.50
3 In Hydro-Dams................ 2.50
4 final issue..................... 2.50
4a with computer game 6.95
Ashcan.......................... 2.50
TPB Birth of an Angel 12.95

[Series 2], 1995
1 R:Nira X 3.75
1a Clear Chromium Edition 8.00
1b Holo-Chrome edition......... 10.00
2 Alien Invasion................. 2.50
3 Mecha New York 2.50
4 Final Issue 2.50

[Series 3], 1996
0 .... 2.75
0a signed & numbered 8.00
1 .... 2.50
1a gold edition, signed & numb... 5.00
2 .... 2.50
3 .... 3.00

NIRA X/CYNDER: ENDANGERED SPECIES
Entity Comics, 1996
1 .... 3.00
1a gold ink enhanced, bagged... 13.00

NOCTURNALS
Malibu Bravura, 1995
1 DIB,I:Nocturnals 2.95
1a Glow-in-the-Dark 4.00
2 DIB,I:Komodo, Mister Fane..... 2.95
3 DIB,F:Raccoon 2.95
4 DIB,I:The Old Wolf 2.95
5 Discovered by Police 2.95
6 DIB............................ 2.95

NOCTURNALS: THE DARK FOREVER
Oni Press, 2001
1 by Dan Brereton 2.95
2 . . . . 2.95
3 . . . . 2.95
TPB The Dark Forever (2002) 9.95
TPB Unhallowed Eve (2002) 9.95
TPB Black Planet (1998) 19.95

NOID IN 3-D
Blackthorne
1 thru 3 . . . . @2.50

NOMAN
Tower Comics, 1966
1 GK,OW,WW,AW 125.00
2 OW,WW,A:Dynamo 75.00

NOOGIE KOOTCH: SECRET AGENT MAN
Hobo Comics
1 I:Noogie Kootch 2.75
2 F:Celutron CIty 2.75

NO TIME FOR SERGEANTS
Dell Publishing Co.,, July, 1958
1 Ph(c) 150.00
2 Ph(c) 90.00
3 Ph(c) 75.00

NOVA HUNTER
Ryal Comics
1 thru 3 . . . . @2.50
4 Climax 2.50
5 Death and Betrayal 2.50

NUBIAN KNIGHT
Samson Comics
1 I:Shandai 2.50

NURSES, THE
Gold Key, April, 1963
1 . . . . 55.00
2 . . . . 35.00
3 . . . . 35.00

NYOKA, JUNGLE GIRL
Charlton Comics, 1955–57
14 . . . . 125.00
15 . . . . 100.00
16 . . . . 100.00
17 . . . . 100.00
18 . . . . 100.00
19 . . . . 100.00
20 . . . . 100.00
21 . . . . 100.00
22 . . . . 100.00

NYOKA, THE JUNGLE GIRL
AC Comics
1 and 2 . . . . @2.00

OBLIVION
Comico, 1995
1 R:The Elementals 2.50
2 I:Thunderboy, Lilith 2.50

COLOR PUB.

3 I:Fen, Ferril 2.50
4 War 2.95
5 The Unholy Trilogy 2.95

OCCULT FILES OF DR. SPEKTOR
Gold Key, April, 1973
1 I:Lakot 50.00
2 thru 5 . . . . @25.00
6 thru 10 . . . . @25.00
11 I:Spertor as Werewolf 25.00
12 and 13 . . . . @20.00
14 A:Dr. Solar 35.00
15 thru 24 . . . . @15.00
Whitman
25 rep 10.00

ODYSSEY, THE
Avatar/TidalWave Studios, 2002
1A RCz (c) 3.50
1B MMy (c) 3.50
1C Parajullo (c) 3.50
1D Murphy (c) 3.50

O.G. WHIZ
Gold Key, 1971–79
1 . . . . 75.00
2 . . . . 50.00
3 thru 6 . . . . @40.00
7 thru 11 . . . . @30.00

OINK: BLOOD AND CIRCUS
Kitchen Sink, 1997
1 (of 4) by John Mueller 4.95
2 . . . . 4.95
3 . . . . 4.95
4 conclusion 4.95

O'MALLEY AND THE ALLEY CATS
Gold Key, 1971–74
1 . . . . 35.00
2 thru 9 . . . . @30.00

OMEGA 7
Omega 7
1 V:Exterminator X 3.95
? by Alonzo L. Washington 3.95
0 . . . . 3.00

OMEGA SAGA, THE
Southpaw Publishing, 1998
0 by Mike Gerardo & Chris Navetta 3.00
1 Episode One, pt.1 . . . . 3.00
2 Episode One, pt.2 . . . . 3.00
Axess Comics
3 by Mike Gerardo, Heroes (c) . . . 3.00
3b Villains (c) 3.00

OMEN, THE
Chaos! Comics, 1998
Preview Book, BnP 2.00
1 by PNu & Justiniano 2.95
2 . . . . 2.95
3 . . . . 2.95
4 . . . . 2.95
5 concl 2.95
1-shot The Omen Vexed 2.95
TPB The Omen 12.95

ON A PALE HORSE
Innovation
1 Piers Anthony adapt 4.95
2 `Magician',I:Kronos 4.95
3 . . . . 4.95
4 VV, ... 4.95
5 . . . . 4.95
6 . . . . 4.95

ONE-ARM SWORDSMAN
Dr. Leung's
1 . . . . 2.95
2 . . . . 2.95
3 . . . . 2.75
4 thru 11 . . . . @2.00

Operation Stormbreaker 31
© *Acclaim*

OPERATION: STORMBREAKER
Acclaim Spec.Event, Apr., 1997
Spec. F:Teutonic Knight 3.95

ORBIT
Eclipse, 1990
1 DSt(c) 3.95
2 . . . . 3.95
3 . . . . 4.95

ORIENTAL HEROES
Jademan, 1988–92
1 by Tony Wong & MBn 2.50
2 . . . . 2.00
3 thru 13 . . . . @2.00
14 thru 27 . . . . @2.00
28 V:Skeleton Secretary 2.00
29 Barbarian vs.Lone Kwoon 2.00
30 Barbarian vs.Lone Kwoon 2.00
31 SkeletonSecretaryUprisng 2.00
32 Uprising Continues 2.00
33 Jupiter Kills His Brother 2.00
34 Skeleton Sec. Suicide 2.00
35 Red Sect Vs. Global Cult 2.00
36 A:Tiger 2.00
37 Old Supreme 2.00
38 Tiger vs. 4 Hitmen 2.00
39 D:Infinite White, V:Red Sect . . . 2.00
40 The Golden Buddhha Temple . . 2.00
41 thru 43 . . . . 2.00
44 SilverChime rescue 2.00
45 Global Cult Battle 2.00
46 thru 48 . . . . @2.00

All comics prices listed are for *Near Mint* condition.

Oriental–Painkiller

49 F:GoldDragon/SilverChime 2.00
50 Return to Global Cult 2.00
51 Gang Of Three Vs.White Beau
  & Lone Kwoon-Tin 2.00
52 Global Cult vs Red Sect. 2.00
53 Global Cult vs.Red Sect. 2.00

ORIGINAL ASTRO BOY
Now, 1987
1 KSy 3.00
2 thru 5 KSy .... @2.00
6 thru 17 KSy .... @2.00

ORIGINAL DICK TRACY
Gladestone, 1990
1 rep.V:Mrs.Pruneface 2.00
2 rep.V:Influence 2.00
3 rep.V:TheMole 2.00
4 rep.V:ItchyOliver 2.00
5 rep.V:Shoulders 2.00

ORIGINAL DR. SOLAR MAN OF THE ATOM
Valiant 1995
1 Reprint 2.95
2 Reprints 2.95
3 Reprints 2.95

ORIGINAL E-MAN
First, 1985
{rep. Charlton stories}
1 JSon,O:E-Man & Nova 2.00
2 JSon,V:Battery,SamuelBoar 2.00
3 JSon,`City in the Sand' 2.00
4 JSon,A:Brain from Sirius 2.00
5 JSon,V:T.V. Man 2.00
6 JSon,I:Teddy Q. 2.00
7 JSon,Vamfire 2.00

ORIGINAL MAGNUS ROBOT FIGHTER
Valiant 1995
1 Reprint 2.95
2 Russ Manning Art 2.95
3 Russ Manning 2.95

ORIGINAL SHIELD
ABC
1 DAy/TD,O:Shield 2.00
2 DAy,O:Dusty 2.00
3 DAy 2.00
4 DAy 2.00

ORIGINAL TUROK, SON OF STONE
Valiant 1995
1 Reprint 2.95
2 Alberto Gioletti art. 2.95
3 Alberto Gioletti 2.95
4 Reprints 2.95

ORIGIN OF THE DEFIANT UNIVERSE
Defiant, 1994
1 O:Defiant Characters 2.00

ORIGINS
Malibu Ultraverse
1 O:Ultraverse Heroes 2.25

COLOR PUB.

Out Breed 999 #2
© Blackout Comics

OUTBREED 999
Blackout Comics, 1994
1 thru 4 .... @2.95
5 Search For Daige 2.95

OUTCAST SPECIAL
Valiant 1995
1 R:The Outcast 2.50

OUTER LIMITS, THE
Dell Publishing Co., Jan.-March, 1964
1 P(c) 200.00
2 P(c) 125.00
3 P(c) 125.00
4 P(c) 125.00
5 P(c) 125.00
6 P(c) 75.00
7 P(c) 75.00
8 P(c) 75.00
9 P(c) 75.00
10 P(c) 75.00
11 thru 18 P(c) .... @60.00

OUTLAWS OF THE WEST
Charlton Comics, 1956–80
11 .... 75.00
12 .... 50.00
13 .... 50.00
14 Giant 85.00
15 .... 40.00
16 .... 40.00
17 .... 40.00
18 SD 100.00
19 .... 40.00
20 .... 40.00
21 thru 30 .... @35.00
31 thru 50 .... @30.00
51 thru 70 .... @25.00
71 thru 88 .... @20.00

OUT OF THIS WORLD
Charlton Comics, 1956–59
1 .... 300.00
2 .... 125.00
3 SD 350.00
4 SD 350.00
5 SD 350.00

6 SD 350.00
7 SD,SD(c) 375.00
8 SD 300.00
9 SD 250.00
10 SD,Perfect Forcaster 250.00
11 SD 300.00
12 SD 250.00
13 thru 15 .... @125.00
16 .... 325.00

OUTPOSTS
Blackthorne, 1997
1 thru 6 .... @2.00

OUT THERE
WildStorm/DC, May, 2001
1 HuR, Cliffhanger 2.50
2 HuR, ... 2.50
3 HuR 2.50
4 HuR 2.50
5 HuR 2.50
6 HuR 2.50
7 thru 9 HuR,Road to El
  Dorado,pt.1–pt.3 .... @2.50
10 thru 12 HuR,Road to El
  Dorado,pt.4–pt.6 .... @2.95
13 HuR,The War in Hell,pt.1 .... 2.95
14 HuR,The War in Hell,pt.2 .... 2.95
15 HuR,Draedalus's Domain 2.95
16 HuR,Dreadrealm 2.95
17 HuR,all-silent issue 2.95
18 HuR,V:Draedalus 2.95
TPB The Evil Within, rep.#1-#6 . 12.95

OWL, THE
Gold Key, April, 1967
1 .... 90.00
2 April, 1968 .... 65.00

OZZY OSBORNE
Malibu Rock-It Comix
1 w/guitar pick 3.95

PACIFIC PRESENTS
Pacific, 1992
1 DSt,Rocketeer,(3rd App.) 12.00
2 DSt,Rocketeer,(4th App.) 9.00
3 SD,I:Vanity 2.50
4 and 5 .... @2.00

P.A.C.
Artifacts Inc., 1993
1 I:P.A.C. 2.00

PAINKILLER JANE
Event Comics, 1997
1 JQ(c) 2.95
1 RL(c) 2.95
1 Red foil logo, signed 24.95
2 JQ&JP(c) 2.95
2 JP&RL(c) 2.95
3 JQ&JP(c) 2.95
3a JP&RL(c) 2.95
4 JQ&JP(c) A Too Bright Place
  For Dying 2.95
4a RL&JP(c) 2.95
5 JQ&JP(c) Purgatory
  Station—Next Stop Hell 2.95
5a RL&JP(c) 2.95
6 RL&JP(c) Blood Harvest 2.95
6a BSz&JP(c) 2.95
7 Jane in the Jungle,
  pt.1,BiT&JP(c) 2.95
7a RL&JP(c) 2.95
Spec.#0 O:Painkiller Jane,48-pg. . 3.95

COLOR PUB.

Painkiller–Perg

Spec.#0A signed. 30.00
Spec. Painkiller Jane/Hellboy
  Ancient Laughter (1998). 2.95
Spec. Painkiller Jane/Hellboy,
  signed 20.00
Spec. Painkiller Jane/The Darkness,
  signed, limited edition, JQ(c). . 29.95

PAINKILLER JANE/ DARKCHYLDE
Event Comics, 1998
1 BAu,RQu 2.95
1a signed & numbered. 30.00
1b Omnichrome edition 14.95
1c Omnichrome, signed. 30.00
1d Dynamic Forces cover 6.95

PAINKILLER JANE VS. THE DARKNESS: STRIPPER
Event Comics, 1997
1 GEn,JP,x-over, Amanda Connor
  cover. 2.95
1a Greg & Tim Hildebrandt 2.95
1b MS(c) 2.95
1c JQ(c) 2.95

PALADIN ALPHA
Firstlight
1 I:Paladin Alpha 2.95
2 V:Hellfire Triger. 2.95

PANDEMONIUM: DELIVERANCE
Chaos! Comics, 1998
1-shot by Jesse Leon McCann &
  Jack Jadson 2.95

PANIC
Gemstone, 1997
1 thru 12 EC Comics reprint. . . . @2.50
'Annuals'
TPB Vol. 1 rebinding #1–#4 . . . . 10.50
TPB Vol. 2 rebinding #5–#8 . . . . 10.95

PANTERA
Malibu Rock-it Comix, Aug., 1994
1 . . . . 3.95
1a Gold ed. 19.95

PANTHA
Harris Comics, 1997
1 (of 2) MT 3.50
1 Marilyn Monroe MT alt.cov. . . . 9.95
2 MT alternate (c) 9.95
2 photo (c). 9.95

PARADAX
Vortex, 1987
1 . . . . 2.25

PARADIGM
Gauntlet
1 A:Predator 2.95

PARADISE
Twenty First Century, 2000
1 thru 7 . . . . @2.95

Paragon Dark Apocalypse, Vol. 2 #1
© AC Comics

PARAGON DARK APOCALYPSE
AC, 1993
1 thru 4, Fem Force crossover . . @2.95

PARANOIA
Adventure Comics, 1991
1 (based on video game)'Clone1' . 3.25
2 King-R-Thr-2 . . . . 2.95
3 R:Happy Jack,V:N3F 2.95
4 V:The Computer 2.95
5 V:The Computer 2.95
6 V:Lance-R-Lot,last issue 2.95

PARTRIDGE FAMILY, THE
Charlton Comics, 1971–73
1 . . . . 90.00
2 thru 4 . . . . @40.00
5 Summer Special 100.00
6 thru 21 . . . . @35.00

PASSOVER
Maximum Press, 1996
1 (of 2) BNa 3.00
2 BNa,A:Avengelyne 3.00

PATH, THE
Crossgen Comics, 2002
1 . . . . 5.00
2 thru 4 . . . . @3.00
9 thru 21 . . . . @3.00
Prequel 48-pg. 2.95
TPB Vol. 1 Crisis of Faith 19.95
TPB Vol. 2 Blood on Snow 15.95
TPB Vol. 3 Death and Dishonor . . 15.95
TPB Traveler Vol. 2 Blood on Snow 9.95

PATHWAYS TO FANTASY
Pacific, 1984
1 BS,JJ art 3.00

PATRIOTS, THE
WildStorm/DC, Nov., 1999
1 BCi&JPe(s). 2.50
2 BCi&JPe(s). 2.50
3 BCi&JPe(s). 2.50
4 BCi&JPe(s). 2.50
5 BCi&JPe(s). 2.50
6 BCi&JPe(s). 2.50
7 BCi&JPe(s). 2.50
8 BCi&JPe(s),V:Stealthers 2.50
9 BCi&JPe(s). 2.50
10 JPe(s),final issue 2.50

PAT SAVAGE: WOMAN OF BRONZE
Millennium, 1992
1 F:Doc Savage's cousin 2.50

PEACEKEEPER
Future Comics 2003
1 . . . . 3.00
2 thru 5 . . . . @3.00

PEACEMAKER
Charlton, 1967
1 A:Fightin' 5 . . . . 5.00
2 A:Fightin' 5 . . . . 3.00
3 A:Fightin' 5 . . . . 3.00
4 O:Peacemaker,A:Fightin' 5 . . . . 4.00
5 A:Fightin' 5 . . . . 2.50

PEANUTS
Dell Publishing Co., 1958
1 . . . . 250.00
2 . . . . 200.00
3 . . . . 150.00
4 . . . . 125.00
5 thru 13 . . . . @100.00

PEANUTS
Gold Key, May, 1963
1 . . . . 200.00
2 thru 4 . . . . @150.00

PEARL HARBOR
Antarctic Press, 2001
1 by Ted Nomura, Movie tie-in . . . 3.95
2 movie tie-in, concl. 3.95
Spec. 60th Anniv. spec., 64-pg. . . 12.95
Spec. 60th Anniv., Japanese (c) . . 12.95

PEBBLES & BAMM-BAMM
Charlton Comics, 1972–76
1 . . . . 75.00
2 thru 10 . . . . @35.00
11 thru 36 . . . . @30.00

PEBBLES FLINTSTONE
Gold Key, Sept., 1963
1 'A Chip off the old block' 150.00

PERG
Lightning Comics, 1993
1 Glow in the dark(c),JS(c),
  B:JZy(s),KlK,I:Perg 3.75
1a Platinum Ed. 5.00
1b Gold Ed. 7.00
1 gold edition, glow-in-the-dark
  flip cover 30.00
2 KlK,O:Perg 3.25
2a Platinum Ed. 5.00
3 Flip Book (c), ... 3.25
3a Platinum Ed 5.00
4 TLw,I:Hellina 9.00
4a Platinum Ed 5.00
5 A:Hellina. 3.25

COLOR PUB.

Perg–Pitt

6 PIA,A:Hellina 3.25
7 .... 3.00
8 V:Police 3.00

PERRY MASON MYSTERY MAGAZINE
Dell Publishing Co., 1964
1 .... 75.00
2 Ray Burr Ph(c) 50.00

PETER PAN: RETURN TO NEVERNEVER LAND
Adventure
1 Peter in Mass. 2.50
2 V:Tiger Lily 2.50

PETER POTAMUS
Gold Key, Jan., 1965
1 .... 150.00

PETTICOAT JUNCTION
Dell Publishing Co., 1964
1 Ph(c) 100.00
2 Ph(c) 75.00
3 Ph(c) 75.00
4 .... 75.00
5 Ph(c) 75.00

PHANTOM, THE
Gold Key, 1962
1 RsM 250.00
2 B:King, Queen & Jack. ... 150.00
3 .... 125.00
4 .... 125.00
5 .... 125.00
6 .... 125.00
7 'The Super Apes' 125.00
8 .... 125.00
9 .... 125.00
10 'The Sleeping Giant' 125.00
11 E:King,Queen and Jack ... 100.00
12 B:Track Hunter. 100.00
13 .... 100.00
14 'The Historian' 100.00
15 .... 100.00
16 .... 100.00
17 'Samaris'. 100.00

King Comics, Sept., 1966
18 'The Treasure of the Skull Cave;'BU:Flash Gordon .. 100.00
19 'The Astronaut & the Pirates' .. 75.00
20 A:GirlPhantom,E:FlashGordon . 75.00
21 BU:Mandrake. 75.00
22 'Secret of Magic Mountain' . 75.00
23 .... 75.00
24 A:Girl Phantom 75.00
25 .... 60.00
26 .... 60.00
27 .... 60.00
28 .... 60.00
29 *never published*

Charlton Comics, 1969–77
30 .... 35.00
31 JAp,'Phantom of Shang-Ri-La'. 35.00
32 JAp,'The Pharaoh Phantom' . 35.00
33 The Jungle People 35.00
34 .... 32.00
35 .... 32.00
36 .... 32.00
37 .... 32.00
38 .... 32.00
39 .... 32.00
40 'The Ritual' 32.00
41 .... 25.00
42 .... 25.00

Phantom #47
© Charlton

43 .... 25.00
44 'To Right A Wrong'. 25.00
45 .... 25.00
46 I:Piranha 28.00
47 'The False Skull Cave'. ... 25.00
48 .... 25.00
49 .... 25.00
50 .... 25.00
51 'A Broken Vow' 25.00
52 .... 25.00
53 .... 25.00
54 .... 25.00
55 .... 25.00
56 .... 25.00
57 NightmareMedicine in Bengali . 25.00
58 .... 25.00
59 .... 25.00
60 .... 25.00
61 'A Dead Man's Promise' ... 25.00
62 .... 25.00
63 .... 25.00
64 'Duel With Death' 25.00
65 .... 25.00
66 'Goldbeard the Pirate' 25.00
67 'Triumph of Evil' 28.00
68 .... 25.00
69 .... 25.00
70 .... 25.00
71 .... 25.00
72 'Man in the Shadows' 25.00
73 .... 20.00
74 .... 28.00

PHANTOM
Wolf Publishing, 1992
1 Drug Runners. 2.25
2 Mystery Child of the Sea. ... 2.25
3 inc.feature pages on Phantom/Merchandise ... 2.25
4 TV Jungle Crime Buster ... 2.25
5 Castle Vacula-Transylvania. .. 2.25
6 The Old West 2.25
7 Sercet of Colussus 2.75
8 Temple of the Sun God ... 2.75

PHANTOM, THE
Moonstone, 2002
GN #1 The Ghost Killer, 48-pg. ... 5.95
GN #2 The Singh Web 5.95
GN #3 The Treasures of Bangalla. . 6.95
GN #4 The Hunt 6.95
TPB Vol. 1 Ghost Who Walks 16.95

PHANTOM BOLT, THE
Gold Key, 1964–66
1 .... 75.00
2 .... 60.00
3 .... 40.00
4 .... 40.00
5 .... 40.00
6 .... 40.00
7 .... 40.00

PHANTOM FORCE
Genesis West, 1994
Previously: Image
0 JK/JLe(c) 2.75
3 thru 10 .... @2.50

PHAZE
Eclipse, 1988
1 BSz(c),Takes place in future 2.25
2 PG(c),V:The Pentagon 2.00
3 Schwieger Vs. Mammoth ... 2.00

PHOENIX
Atlas, 1975
1 thru 4 .... @6.00

PHOENIX RESURRECTION
Malibu Ultraverse, 1995–96
0 Intro to Phoenix Resurrection ... 2.00
Genesis, A:X-Men.......... 3.95
Revelations, A:X-Men....... 3.95
Aftermath, A:X-Men 3.95

PINK PANTHER, THE
Gold Key, April, 1971
1 .... 75.00
2 thru 10 .... @35.00
11 thru 30 .... @25.00
31 thru 74 .... @15.00
75 thru 80 .... @25.00
81 thru 87 .... @20.00

PIRACY
Gemstone, 1998
1 EC comics reprint 2.50
2 thru 7 EC comics reprints ... @2.50
'Annuals'
TPB Vol. 1 rebinding #1–#4 ... 10.50
TPB Vol. 2 rebinding #5–#7 ... 7.95

PIRATE CORP.
Eternity
1 thru 5 .... @2.00

P.I.'S, THE
First, 1985
1 JSon,Ms.Tree,M Mauser. ... 2.00
2 JSon,Ms.Tree,M Mauser. ... 2.00
3 JSon,Ms.Tree,M Mauser. ... 2.00

PITT
Full Bleed Studios, 1996
1 thru 9, see Image
10 thru 14 DK .... @2.50
14a variant cover 7.00
15 DK. 2.50
16 DK, Ugly Americans,pt.1 ... 2.50
17 DK, Ugly Americans,pt.2 ... 2.50
18 DK, Ugly Americans,pt.3, concl. 2.50
19 by Brian Dawson 2.95

Comics Values Annual — COLOR PUB. — Pitt–Possessed

20 DK, Urgral Thul 2.50
TPB Vol. 1, rep. ? &#1–#4 . . . . . . 10.95
TPB Vol. 2, rep. #5–#9 . . . . 11.95
Spec. In the Blood 2.50

PITT CREW
Full Bleed Studios, 1998
1 Monster 2.50
2 F:Rai-Kee 2.50
3 Tyrants 2.50
4 The Slayer 2.50
5 . . . . 2.50

PITT: BIOGENESIS
Full Bleed Studios, 2000
1 (of 3) DK 2.50
2 DK 2.50

PLANESWALKER WAR
Acclaim Aug., 1996
GN #1 Magic: The Gathering tie-in . 5.95

PLANETARY
WildStorm/DC, 1999
1 WEI 2.50
2 WEI 2.50
3 WEI 2.50
4 thru 12 WEI . . . . @2.50
13 WEI,secret history of
 Elijah Snow 2.50
14 WEI,The Four vs. Planetary 2.50
15 WEI,in Australia 2.50
16 WEI 2.50
17 WEI Elijah Snow's past 2.95
TPB All over the World 14.95
TPB The Fourth Man, 144-pg. . . . 14.95
GN Planetary/The Authority 5.95
GN Planetery/JLA, Terra
 Occulta, JOy (2002) 5.95
GN WEI(s) Planetary/Batman
 Night on Earth x-over (2003) . . 5.95

PLAN 9 FROM OUTER SPACE
Malibu
GNv Movie Adapt. 4.95

PLANET COMICS
Blackthorne, 1988
1 DSt(c) 2.00
2 thru 4 . . . . @2.00

PLANET OF VAMPIRES
Atlas, Feb.–July, 1975
1 NA(c),1st PB 25.00
2 NA(c) 25.00
3 RH 25.00

POGZ N SLAMMER
Blackout Comics, 1995
1 I:Pogz N Slammer 2.00
2 Contact Other Schools 2.00

POINT BLANK
WildStorm/DC, Aug., 2002
Eye of the Storm
1 (of 5) CWi, super-hero noir 2.95
2 CWi, ... 2.95
3 CWi,F:Jack Hawksmoor 2.95
4 CWi, ... 2.95
5 CWi,concl. 2.95
TPB 14.95

Planet of Vampires #3
© Atlas Comics

POISON ELVES
Sirius Entertainment, 1998
Color Special #1 by Drew Hayes . . 2.95
Color Spec.#1 limited 9.95

POIZON
London Night Studios, 1995
0 . . . . 3.00
0 signed gothchik edition 9.00
? O:Poizon 3.00
?a Commemorative (1999) 5.95
1 . . . . 3.00
1a signed 7.00
2 EHr 3.00

POIZON: CADILLACS AND GREEN TOMATOES
London Night, 1997
2 . . . . 3.00
3 . . . . 3.00
6 deluxe 5.00

POIZON: DEMON HUNTER
London Night, 1998
1 . . . . 3.00
1 Green Death edition 14.95

POIZON: LOST CHILD
London Night Studios, 1996
0 . . . . 3.00
1 mini series 3.00
1 signed 9.00
1 Green Death edition 14.95
2 thru 3 . . . . @3.00

POKEMAN TALES:
Viz Communications, 1999
(Boardbooks)
1 Charmander Sees a Ghost 4.95
2 Pikachu's Day 4.95
3 Come Out, Squirtle! 4.95
4 Bulbasaur's Trouble 4.95
5 . . . . 4.95
6 . . . . 4.95
7 . . . . 4.95
8 . . . . 4.95
9 Meet Mew 4.95
10 Snorlax's Snack 4.95
11 Jigglypuff's Magic Lullaby 4.95
12 Lapras Makes a Friend 4.95
13 Eevee's Weather Report 4.95
14 Diglett's Birthday Party 4.95
15 First Prize for Starmie 4.95
16 Seel to the Rescue 4.95
Gift Set Vol. 1 . . . . 19.95
Gift Set Vol. 2 . . . . 19.95
Movie Spec 4.95

POKEMAN THE MOVIE 2000: REVELATION LUGIA
Viz Communications, 2000
1 . . . . 3.95
2 . . . . 3.95
3 . . . . 3.95
Spec. Pikachu's Rescue Adventure . 3.95
Art of Pokeman The Movie 2000 . . . 9.95

POKEMAN: THE FIRST MOVIE
Viz Communications, 1999
1 (of 4) Mewtwo Strikes Back 3.95
2 . . . . 3.95
3 . . . . 3.95
4 conclusion 3.95
Spec. Pikachu's Vacation 3.95
Art of Pokeman: First Movie 8.95
TPB 15.95

POKEMON TV ANIMATION
Viz Comics, 2000
TPB Vol. 1 . . . . 10.95

POPEYE
Gold Key, 1962
1-65 See Golden Age Section
66 . . . . 100.00
67 . . . . 75.00
68 thru 80 . . . . @50.00
King Comics, 1966
81 thru 92 . . . . @35.00
Charlton, 1969
94 thru 99 . . . . @35.00
100 . . . . 40.00
101 thru 138 . . . . @25.00
Gold Key, 1978
139 thru 143 . . . . @15.00
144 50th Aniv. Spec 18.00
155 . . . . @15.00
Whitman
156 thru 157 . . . . @15.00
158 thru 159 . . . . @25.00
162 thru 168 . . . . @15.00
169 thru 171 . . . . @20.00

POPEYE
Harvey Comics, 1993–94
1 thru 7 . . . . @2.00
Summer Spec.#1 . . . . 2.25

POPEYE SPECIAL
Ocean, 1987–88
1 . . . . 2.00
2 . . . . 2.00

POSSESSED, THE
Wildstorm/DC July 2003
1 (of 6) LSh,demons 2.95
2 thru 5 LSh,demon-infested . . . @2.95

All comics prices listed are for Near Mint condition.

POWER & GLORY
Malibu Bravura, 1994
1A HC(a&s),I:American
 Powerhouse 3.00
1B alternate cover 3.00
1c Blue Foil(c) 5.00
1d w/seirgraph. 5.00
1e Newsstand 3.00
2 HC(a&s), O:American
 Powerhouse 2.75
3 HC(a&s) 2.50
4 HC(a&s) 2.50
Winter Special 2.95
TPB Series reprint, w/stamp 12.95

POWER FACTOR
Wonder Color Comics, 1986
1 . . . . 4.00
2 . . . . 3.00
3 . . . . 3.00

POWER FACTOR
Innovation, 1990
1 thru 4 . . . . @2.25

POWERKNIGHTS
Amara, 1995
P I:Powerknights 2.00

POWER OF PRIME
Malibu Ultraverse, 1995
1 O:Prime Powers,Godwheel tie-in 2.50
2 V:Doc Gross, Godwheel tie-in . . . 2.50
3 F:Prime Phade 2.50
4 F:Elven,Turbocharge 2.50

POWER RANGERS ZEO/YOUNGBLOOD
Maximum Press, 1997
1 TNu,NRd 3.00

POWERS THAT BE
Broadway Comics
Preview Editions, Sept., 1995
1 thru 3 B&W . . . . @2.50
Regular Series, Nov., 1995
1 JiS,I:Fatale, Star Seed 3.00
2 thru 4 . . . . @2.95
5 It's the End of the World As We
 Know It,pt.1 . . . . 2.95
6 End/World As We Know It,pt.2 . . 2.95
Becomes:

STAR SEED
7 End/World As We Know It,pt.3 . . 2.95
8 End/World As We Know It,pt.4 . . 2.95
9 End/World As We Know It,pt.5 . . 2.95
10 End/World As We Know It,pt.6. . 2.95
11 End/World As We Know It,pt.7... 2.95

PRESSBUTTON
Eclipse
(see Axel Pressbutton)
5 and 6 . . . . @2.00

PRIEST
Maximum Press, 1996
1 RLd, F:Michael O'Bannon 3.00
2 RLd,BNa, ... 3.00
3 RLd 3.00

COLOR PUB.

PRIMAL RAGE
Sirius, 1996
1 TAr,from video game 2.95
1 foil cover, limited edition 2.95
2 TAr,DOe(c) 2.95

Prime #12 © Malibu

PRIME
Malibu Ultraverse, 1993–95
1 B:GJ(s),I:Prime. 4.00
1a Ultra-Limited 5.00
1b Full Hologram(c) 5.00
2 V:Organism 8, with Ultraverse
 card 3.00
3 NBy,I:Prototype 3.00
4 NBy,V:Prototype 3.00
5 NBy,BWS,I:Maxi-Man, BU:Rune . 3.00
6 NBy,A:Pres. Clinton 2.75
7 NBy,Break-Thru x-over 2.25
8 NBy,A:Mantra 2.25
9 NBy,Atomic Lies 2.25
10 NBy,A:Firearm,N:Prime 2.25
11 NBy 2.25
12 NBy,(Ultraverse Premiere#3)
 I:Planet Class. 3.50
13 NBy,V:Kutt,Planet Class. 2.95
14 DaR,I:Voodoo Master. 2.25
15 abused kids 2.25
16 I:Turbo. 2.25
17 Atalon 2.25
18 Prime's new partner. 2.25
19 Prime accused. 2.25
20 GJ,LeS,A:Rafferty 2.50
21 GJ,LeS,World without Prime . . . 2.50
22 GJ,LeS,F:Primevil 2.50
23 F:Prime's Mother 2.50
24 F:Prime's Mother. 2.50
25 A:Chelsea Clinton 2.50
26 True Powers 2.50
Ashcan (first) 7.00
Ashcan #1 BV(c),B&W 75
Ann.#1 R:Doc Gross. 3.95
TPB Rep. #1-#4 . . . . 9.95

PRIME
Malibu Ultraverse, 1995–96
Infinty I:Spider-Prime 3.00
1 Spider-Prime vs. Lizard 2.25
1a Computer painted cover 2.25
2 Phoenix flip issue 2.25
3 Phoenix Resurrection 2.25
4 & 5 . . . . @2.25
6 Prime on Drugs,pt.1,F:Solitaire . . 2.25

Comics Values Annual
7 F:Solitaire,pt.2 . . . . 2.25
8 F:Solitaire,pt.3 . . . . 2.25
9 and 10 . . . . @2.25
11 'Absolute Power Corrupts?
 Absolutely!'. 2.25
12 HuR,KG,pt.3 (of 3). 2.25
13 KG,Prime exposed, V:Colonel
 Rinaldo 2.25
14 KG, Return of Lord Pumpkin . . . 2.25
15 Return of Lord Pumpkin 2.25

PRIME/ CAPTAIN AMERICA
Malibu Ultraverse, 1996
1 GJ,NBy 3.95

PRIME VS. HULK
Malibu
0 . . . . 10.00
0a signed premium edition 20.00

PRIMER
Comico, 1982–84
1 . . . . 9.00
2 I:Grendel 100.00
3 . . . . 10.00
4 C:Maxx 10.00
5 I:Maxx 35.00
6 I:Evangelyne 15.00
[Volume 2], 1996
1 F:Lady Bathory 3.00

PRIMUS
Charlton Comics, 1972
1 . . . . 25.00
2 thru 5 . . . . @15.00
6 thru 7 . . . . @12.00

PRINCESS SALLY
Archie Comics, 1995
1 thru 3 Sonic tie-in . . . . @3.00

PRINCE VANDAL
Triumphant
1 JnR(s), ... 2.50
2 JnR(s) 2.50
3 JnR(s),ShG,I:Claire,V:Nicket,
 Vandal goes to Boviden 2.50
4 JnR(s),ShG,Game's End 2.50
5 JnR(s),ShG,The Sickness, the
 rat appears 2.50
6 JnR(s),ShG,B:Gothic 2.50

PRIORITY: WHITE HEAT
AC Comics, 1986
1 thru 2 miniseries . . . . @2.00

PRIVATEERS
Vanguard Graphics
1 and 2 . . . . @2.00

PROFESSIONAL: GOGOL 13
Viz
1 . . . . 4.95
2 and 3 . . . . @4.95

PROFESSOR OM
Innovation, 1990
1 I:Rock Warrior 2.50
2 Samurai Drama 2.50

COLOR PUB.

PROJECT A-KO
Malibu March, 1994
1 thru 4 Based on anime movie . @2.95
Antarctic Press, 1994
0 digest size 5.00

PROJECT A-KO 2
CPM, 1995
1 Space Saga 2.95
2 Space Saga 2.95
3 Queen Margarita 2.95

PROJECT A-KO: VERSUS THE UNIVERSE
CPM, 1995
1 Based on Animation 2.95
2 strange magician 3.00
3 . . . . 3.00
4 (of 5) TEl 2.95

PROMETHEA
WildStorm/DC, 1999
America's Best Comics
1 AMo(s),F:Sophie Bangs,40-pg. . . 3.50
2 AMo(s),Judgment of Solomon . . . 3.00
3 AMo(s),Misty Magic Land 3.00
4 AMo(s),CV,JWi 2.95
5 AMo(s),JWi,F:WW1 . . . . 2.95
6 AMo(s),JWi,F:Grace Brannagh . . 2.95
7 AMo(s),JWi,F:Sophie Bangs 2.95
8 AMo(s),JWi,V:Goetic demons . . . 2.95
9 AMo(s),JWi,The Temple 2.95
10 AMo(s),JWi,Sex, Stars
  and Serpents 2.95
11 AMo(s),JWi,giant monster 2.95
12 AMo(s),JWi,flip-book 2.95
13 AMo(s),JWi, ... 2.95
14 AMo(s),JWi, Lunar Realm 2.95
15 AMo(s),JWi, ... 2.95
16 AMo(s),JWi,Five Swell Guys . . . 2.95
17 AMo(s),JWi,Stacia vs. Hell 2.95
18 AMo(s),JWi,double demonic. . . . 2.95
19 AMo(s),JWi,Tree of Life 2.95
20 AMo(s),JWi,edge of existence . . 2.95
21 AMo(s),JWi,Binah 2.95
22 AMo(s),JWi,Jack Foust 2.95
23 AMo(s),JWi,40-pg. 3.50
24 AMo(s),JWi 2.95
25 AMo(s),JWi,A Higher Court 2.95
26 AMo(s),JWi,Later 2.95
27 AMo(s),JWi,Tom Strong 2.95
28 AMo(s),JWi,Jack Faust 2.95
TPB Promethea Book One 14.95
TPB Promethea Book Two 14.95
TPB Promethea Book Three 14.95

PROPHECY
Immortelle Studios, 1998
1 by Hawk, Lovalle, & Wong,
  F:Cynder & War Dragon 2.95
2 . . . . 2.95

PROPHECY OF THE SOUL SORCERER
Arcane Comics, 1999
1 (of 4) by Eric Dean Seaton 2.95
2 . . . . 2.95
3 . . . . 2.95
4 . . . . 2.95
5 . . . . 2.95
6 Nighthawk vs. Morbid 2.95
3a thru 6a variant (c) . . . . @2.95
7 . . . . 2.95
TPB Vol. 1 . . . . 10.95

PROPHET II
Awesome Entertainment, 1999
1 . . . . 2.99
1a holochrome wraparound (c) . . 15.00
TPB Timetrap 12.99

PROPHET: LEGACY
Awesome Entertainment, 1999
1 RLe 2.99
2 . . . . 2.99
2a variant (c) 2.99
3 . . . . 2.99

PROPHET/CABLE
Maximum, 1997
1 (of 2) RLd x-over 3.50
2 RLd x-over,A:Domino, Kirby,
  Blaquesmith 3.50

PROPHET OF DREAMS
Broken Tree Publications, 2002
1 (of 6) by Lawler & Vasquez 3.50
2 thru 6 . . . . @2.95

Protectors #12
© Malibu

PROTECTORS
Malibu 1992–94
1 I:Protectors, inc. JBi poster
  (direct) 3.00
1a thru 12a Newsstand . . . . . . @2.25
2 V:Mr.Monday,w/poster 2.50
3 V:Steel Army,w/poster 2.50
4 V:Steel Army 2.50
5 Die Cut(c),V:Mr.Monday 2.50
6 V:Mr.Monday 2.50
7 A:Thresher 2.50
8 V:Wisecrack 2.25
9 V:Wisecrack 2.50
10 I:Mantoka 2.50
11 A:Ms.Fury,V:Black Fury 2.50
12 A:Arrow 2.50
13 RAJ(s),Genesis#3 . . . . 2.25
14 RB(c),RAJ(s),Genesis#6 . . . . . 2.25
15 RAJ(s),J:Chalice 2.25
16 So Help Me God 2.25
17 L:Ferret 2.25
18 V:Regulators,BU:Mantako, R:Mr.
  Monday 2.25
19 A:Gravestone,Arc. 2.50
20 V:Nowhere Man 2.50
Protectors Handbook 2.50

PROTOTYPE
Malibu Ultraverse, 1993–95
1 V:Ultra-Tech,w/card 2.50
1a Ultra-lim. silver foil(c) 5.00
1b Hologram 6.00
2 I:Backstabber 2.50
3 LeS(s),DvA,JmP,BWS, V:Ultra-
  Tech,BU:Rune 2.50
4 TMs(s),V:Wrath 2.25
5 TMs(s),A:Strangers,Break-
  Thru x-over 2.25
6 TMs(s),Origins Month C:Arena . . 2.25
7 TMs(s),V:Arena 2.25
8 TMs(s),V:Arena 2.25
9 Prototype Unplugged 2.25
10 TMs(s),V:Prototype 2.25
11 TMs(s),R:Glare 2.25
12 V:Ultratech 2.25
13 Ultraverse Premiere #6 . . . . . . 3.50
14 Jimmy Ruiz, new boss 2.25
15 Techuza, Donovan 2.25
16 New CEO for Terrordy 2.25
17 Ranger Vs. Engine 2.25
18 Turf War 2.50
G-Size, Hostile Takeover 2.50
Spec.#0 LeS,JQ/JP(c) 2.50

PROTOTYPE: TURF WAR
Malibu Ultraverse
1 LeS,V:Techuza 2.50
2 LeS,F:Ranger,Arena 2.50
3 . . . . 2.50

PROWLER
Eclipse, 1987
1 I:Prowler 2.00
2 GN,A:Original Prowler 2.00
3 GN 2.00
4 GN 2.00
5 GN, adaption of `Vampire Bat' . . 2.00
6 w/flexi-disk record 2.00

PROWLER IN `WHITE ZOMBIE', THE
Eclipse, 1988
1 . . . . 2.00

PRUDENCE & CAUTION
Defiant, 1994
1 CCi(s), ... 3.25
2 CCi(s), ... 2.50
3 CCi(s), ... 2.50
4 CCi(s), ... 2.50
5 CCi(s), ... 2.50

PSI-LORDS: REIGN OF THE STARWATCHERS
Valiant 1994
1 MLe,DG,Chromium(c),Valiant
  Vision,V:Spider Aliens 3.00
2 MLe,DG,V:Spider Aliens 2.25
3 MLe,DG,Chaos Effect-Epsilon#2,
  A:Solar 2.25
becomes:

PSI-LORDS
4 V:Ravenrok 2.25
5 V:Ravenrok 2.25
6 . . . . 2.25
7 Micro-Invasion 2.25
8 A:Solar the Destroyer 2.25

All comics prices listed are for Near Mint condition.

Psi-Lords–Purgatori

9 Frozen Harbingers 2.25
10 F:Ravenrok 2.25

PSYCHO
Innovation
1 Hitchcock movie adapt 2.50
2 continued 2.50
3 continued 2.50

PSYCHOANALYSIS
Gemstone, 1999
1 (of 4) 2.50
2 . . . . 2.50
3 . . . . 2.50
TPB Ann. #1 . . . . 10.95

PSYCHOBLAST
First, 1987
1 thru 9 . . . . @2.00

PUBLIC DEFENDER IN ACTION
Charlton Comics, 1957
7 . . . . 100.00
8 and 9 . . . . @75.00
10 thru 12, ... @75.00

PUDGE PIG
Charlton Comics, Sept., 1958
1 . . . . 50.00
2 . . . . 35.00

PUNCTURE
Com.X, 2001
1 (of 12) by R. Uttley & B.Oliver . . . 3.00
2 thru 4 . . . . @3.00
3 thru 6 . . . . @4.00

PUNX
Windjammer 1995
1 KG,I:Punx 2.50
2 KG,A:Harbinger 2.50
3 KG,F:P.M.S 2.50
4 KG,final issue 2.50
Spec.#1 . . . . 2.50

PUNX REDUX
1 thru 4 . . . . @2.50

PUNX
Acclaim Jan., 1997
One Shot Spec. F:Big Max 2.50

PUPPET MASTER
Eternity
1 Movie Adapt.Andre Toulon 2.50
2 Puppets Protecting Diary 2.50
3 R:Andre Toulon 2.50
4 . . . . 2.50

PUPPET MASTER: CHILDREN OF THE PUPPET MASTER
Eternity
1 Killer Puppets on the loose 2.50
2 concl. 2.50

COLOR PUB.

PURGATORI
Chaos! Comics, 1998
1 DQ from slave to Goddess? 3.00
2 Goddess War,pt.1, x-over 3.00
3 Goddess War, epilog 3.00
4 Unholy Nights 3.00
5 V:Karmilla 3.00
6 . . . . 3.00
7 V:Dracula 3.00
1-shot prelude 3.00
1-shot signed, limited + print 15.00
Coll. Vol. 1 . . . . 5.95
Coll. Vol. 2 . . . . 5.95
Coll. Vol. 3 . . . . 5.95
Coll. Vol. 4 . . . . 5.95

PURGATORI
Chaos! Comics, 2000
1/2 . . . . 3.00
1/2 premium edition, tattoo(c) . . . 10.00
1/2 chromium (c) 15.00
1/2 chromium signed 21.00
1/2 Ashcan 6.66
0 . . . . 3.00
0 premium edition 10.00
0 Ashcan 6.66

PURGATORI: DARKEST HOUR
Chaos! Comics, 2001
1 . . . . 3.00
1a premium ed. RCI(c) 10.00
2 . . . . 3.00
2a variant (c) 7.50

PURGATORI: THE DRACULA GAMBIT
Chaos! Comics, 1997
1 DQ & Brian LeBlanc 3.00
1a signed 20.00
1b premium 9.95
Sketchbook, b&w 3.50

PURGATORI: EMPIRE
Chaos! Comics, 2000
1 (of 3) 3.00
1a premium 10.00
1b Comic Legal Defense
 Fund ed. 10.00
2 . . . . 3.00
3 concl. 3.00
Preview Book B&W 5.00

PURGATORI: GODDESS RISING
Chaos! Comics, 1999
1 (of 4) MD2 . . . . 3.00
1a premium edition 10.00
2 . . . . 3.00
3 . . . . 3.00
4 conclusion 3.00
Preview Book B&W 5.00

PURGATORI: GOD HUNTER
Chaos! Comics, 2002
Ashcan b&w 6.00
1 (of 2) 3.00
1a premium edition 10.00
2 . . . . 3.00
2a variant Rio & Broeker (c) 7.50

Comics Values Annual

PURGATORI: GOD KILLER
Chaos! Comics, 2002
1 (of 2) 3.00
1a premium edition 10.00
2 . . . . 3.00
2a variant (c) 7.50

PURGATORI: HEART-BREAKER
Chaos! Comics, 2002
1 . . . . 3.00
1a premium edition 10.00
1b super premium edition 20.00
1c MegaCon foil edition 25.00

PURGATORI: LOVE BITES
Chaos! Comics, 2001
1 . . . . 3.00
1 premium edition 10.00
Ashcan 6.00

PURGATORI: MISCHIEF NIGHT
Chaos! Comics, 2001
1 . . . . 3.00
1a premium edition 13.00
1b super premium edition 20.00

PURGATORI: THE HUNTED
Chaos! Comics, 2001
1 . . . . 3.00
1a premium edition 10.00
2 . . . . 3.00
2a variant (c) 7.50
Ashcan 6.00

PURGATORI: RAVENOUS
Chaos! Comics, 2002
Ashcan b&w 6.00
1 (of 2) 3.00
1a premium edition 10.00

PURGATORI: RE-IMAGINED
Chaos! Comics, 2002
1 Salem witch trials 3.00
1a premium edition 10.00
1b super premium edition 20.00
Ashcan Purgatori re-imagined 6.00

PURGATORI: SANCTIFIED
Chaos! Comics, 2002
1 BnP 3.00
1 premium edition 10.00

PURGATORI: TRICK OR TREAT
Chaos! Comics, 2002
1 . . . . 3.00
1a premium edition 10.00
1b super premium edition 20.00

PURGATORI: THE VAMPIRES MYTH
Chaos! Comics, 1996
1 (of 2) 4.00
1-shot limited chromium edition . . 19.75
2 BnP,JBa 3.00

All comics prices listed are for *Near Mint* condition.

COLOR PUB.

Purgatori–Rai

3 BnP,JBa, final issue 3.00
TPB with CD................. 25.00
TPB 12.95
Micro Premium Preview Book 15.00

PURGATORI VS. CHASTITY
Chaos! Comics, 2000
1 Alpha ending 3.00
1a Omega ending 3.00
1b deluxe 12.00

PURGATORI VS. LADY DEATH
Chaos! Comics, 2000
1 .... 3.00
1a premium edition 10.00
Ashcan B&W 6.66

PURGATORI VS. VAMPIRELLA
Chaos! Comics, 2000
1 .... 3.00
1 premium................... 10.00

Quantum & Woody #7
© Acclaim

QUANTUM & WOODY
Acclaim Feb., 1997
1 CPr(s),MBr Woodrow Van
  Chelton & Eric Henderson
  become unlikely superheros ... 4.00
1a Variant (c)................. 5.00
2 CPr(s),MBr,World's worst
  superhero team 3.00
3 CPr(s),MBr,Woody buys a goat. . 3.00
4 CPr(s),MBr.................. 3.00
5 CPr(s),MBr.................. 2.75
6 CPr(s),MBr.................. 2.75
7 CPr(s),MBr.................. 2.75
8 CPr(s),MBr,R:Warrant........ 2.75
9 CPr(s),DCw,Woody is dying 2.75
10 CPr(s),MBr,trapped in each
  other's bodies, Goat month. ... 2.75
11 CPr(s),MBr,switched body
  delimma................... 2.50
12 CPr(s),MBr,switched bodies ... 2.50
13 CPr(s),MBr,back in own bodies . 2.50
14 CPr(s),MBr,Magnum Force,pt.1 . 2.50
15 CPr(s),MBr,Magnum Force,pt.2 . 2.50
16 CPr(s),MBr,Magnum Force,pt.3 . 2.50

17 CPr(s),MBr,Magnum Force,pt.4 . 2.50
32 Dr. Eclipse,pt.3 .... 2.50
18 thru 27.................... @2.50
TPB Director's Cut, rep.#1–#4 .... 8.00
TPB Kiss Your Ass Goodbye...... 8.00
TPB Holy S-word We're Cancelled . 8.00
TPB Magnum Force 8.00

QUANTUM LEAP
Innovation, 1991
{based on TV series}
1 1968 Memphis 3.50
1a Special Edition 2.50
2 Ohio 1962,`Freedom of
  the Press'................. 3.00
3 1958 `The $50,000 Quest' 3.00
4 `Small Miracles' 2.50
5 .... 2.50
6 .... 2.50
7 Golf Pro,School Bus Driver..... 2.50
8 1958,Bank Robber 2.50
9 NY 1969,Gay Rights......... 2.50
10 1960s' Stand-up Comic 2.50
11 1959,Dr.(LSD experiments) 2.50
12 .... 2.50

QUANTUM LEAP
Acclaim Jan., 1997
1 BML(s),'Into the Void,'pt.1..... 2.50
2 BML(s),'Into the Void,'pt.2..... 2.50
3 BML(s),'Into the Void,'pt.3..... 2.50
Spec. 'The Leaper Before........ 3.95

QUEEN OF THE DAMNED
Innovation, 1991
1 Anne Rice Adapt.`On the Road
  to the Vampire Lestat'........ 3.50
2 Adapt. continued............. 2.50
3 The Devils Minion............ 2.50
4 Adapt.continued 2.50
5 Adapt.continued 2.50
6 Adapt.continued 2.50
7 Adapt.continued 2.50
8 Adapt.continued 2.50

QUICK-DRAW McGRAW
Charlton Comics, 1970–72
1 TV Animated Cartoon 75.00
2 .... 40.00
3 .... 40.00
4 thru 8 .... @40.00

Q-UNIT
Harris
1 I:Q-Unit,w/card 3.25

RACE AGAINST TIME
Dark Ange., 1997
1 .... 2.50
2 .... 2.50

RACE FOR THE MOON
Harvey Publications, 1958
1 BP 150.00
2 JK,AW,JK/AW(c).......... 250.00
3 JK,AW,JK/AW(c).......... 275.00

RACER-X
Premiere
Now, 1988
Spec.#1 .... 5.00

1 thru 3 .... @2.50

4 thru 11 .... @2.00
[2nd Series], 1989
1 thru 10 .... @2.00

RACER X
WildStorm/DC, May, 2000
1 (of 3) Rex Racer's secrets 2.50
1a variant (c) (1:4)............. 2.50
2 racing thrills 2.50
3 conclusion 2.95

RACK & PAIN: KILLERS
Chaos! Comics, 1996
1 (of 4) JaL(c)................. 2.95
2 BnP,LJi,JaL(c)............... 2.95
3 (of 4) BnP,LJi,............... 2.95
4 BnP,LJi, final issue 2.95

RADICAL DREAMER
Blackball, 1994
0 .... 2.00
1 thru 5 V:Jorge Futran .... @2.50

RADIOACTIVE MAN
Bongo, 1993
1 I:Radioactive Man............ 4.00
1 80pg offered again 3.25
88 V:Lava Man................ 2.00
212 V:Hypno Head 2.00
412 V:Dr. Crab, with trading card .. 2.25
679 with trading card 2.25
1000 Final issue............... 2.25

RADIOACTIVE MAN
Bongo Comics, 2000
100 .... 2.50
136 .... 2.50
222 .... 2.50
4 .... 2.50
575 new Radioactive Man born.... 2.50
106 new Radioactive Man insane .. 2.50
7 .... 2.50
Spec. Movie Adaptation 3.00

RAEL
Eclipse
Vol 1........................ 6.95

RAFFERTY
Malibu
1 Ashcan.................... 1.00

RAGAMUFFINS
Eclipse, 1985
1 .... 3.00

RAI
Valiant 1991
0 DL,O:Bloodshot,I:2nd Rai,D:X-O,
  Archer,Shadowman,F:all Valiant
  heroes,bridges Valiant Universe
  1992-4001 .... 3.00
1 V:Grandmother.............. 5.00
2 V:Icespike.................. 2.50
3 V:Humanists,Makiko 3.00
4 V:Makiko,rarest Valiant 4.00
5 Rai leaves earth, C:Eternal
  Warrior 2.50
6 FM(c),Unity#7,V:Pierce........ 2.50
7 WS(c),Unity#15,V:Pierce,
  D:Rai,A:Magnus............ 2.50
8 Epilogue of Unity in 4001 ..... 2.50
Becomes:

All comics prices listed are for *Near Mint* condition.

CVA Page 645

RAI AND THE FUTURE FORCE
Valiant 1993
9 F:Rai,E.Warrior of 4001,Tekla,
    X-O Commander,Spylocke 2.50
9a Gold Ed. 3.00
10 Rai vs. Malev Emperor 2.25
11 SCh,V:Malevolents........... 2.25
12 V:Cyber Raiders 2.25
13 Spylocke Revealed 2.25
14 SCh,D:M'Ree 2.25
15 SCh,V:X-O. 2.25
16 SCh,V:Malevs 2.25
17 .... 2.25
18 JOs(s),Spk,V:Malevs 2.25
19 JCf,V:Malves 2.25
20 JOs(s),DR,V:Malves,Spylocke
    realed to be Spider Alien 2.25
21 DR,I:Starwatchers,b:Torque,
    w/Valiant Era card 2.25
22 DR,D:2nd Rai, A:Starwatchers.. 2.25
23 DR,A:Starwatchers 2.25
24 DR,in Tibet 2.25
25 DR,F:Spylocke. 2.25
26 DR,Chaos Effect-Epsilon#3,
    A:Solar Magnus,Psi-Lords 2.25
Becomes:

RAI
Valiant 1994
27 'Rising Son' 2.25
28 V:Takashi. 2.25
29 A:Rentaro Nakadai........... 2.25
30 Splocke 2.25
31 Bad Penny,pt. 1............ 2.25
32 Bad Penny,pt. 2, F:Axscan.... 2.25
33 F:Spylocke, Rentaro 2.25
TPB #0-#4 .... 11.95
TPB Star System ed. 11.95

RALPH SNART ADVENTURES
Now
[Volumes 1 & 2]
see B&W
9 and 10, color 2.50
[Volume 3], 1988
1 .... 4.00
2 thru 10 .... @3.00
11 thru 21 .... @2.00
22 thru 26 .... @2.00
TPB 9.95
[Volume 4], 1992
1 thru 3, with 1 of 2 trading cards.. 2.50
[Volume 5], 1993
1 thru 5, with 1 of 2 trading cards.. 2.50
3-D Spec.#1 with 3-D glasses and
    12 trading cards 3.50
TPB Let's Get Naked (2003)..... 24.95

RAMPANT
Manifest Destiny Comics
1/2 Various Artists............. 2.50

RANDOM 5
Amara Inc., 1995
1 I:Random 5 .... 2.00

RANGO
Dell Publishing Co., Aug., 1967
1 Tim Conway Ph(c) 45.00

RANMA 1/2
Viz, 1992
1 I:Ranma 50.00
2 I:Upperclassmen Kuno 30.00
3 F:Upperclassmen Kuno 25.00
4 Confusion 5.00
5 A:Ryoga.................. 5.00
6 Ryoga plots revenge.......... 9.00
7 Conclusion 5.00
[Part 2], 1992
1 .... 8.00
2 .... 5.00
3 thru 7 .... @4.00
8 .... 5.00
9 .... 6.00
10 and 11 .... @3.00
continued, see B&W Pub.

RAPHAEL
Mirage, 1987
1 TMNTurtle characters 8.00

RARE BREED
Dark Moon Productions, 1995
1 V:Anarchy................. 2.50
2 V:Anarchy................. 2.50

RAT BASTARD
Crucial Comics, 1997
1 by The Huja Brothers 2.00
2 thru 6 .... @2.00

RAT PATROL, THE
Dell Publishing Co., March, 1967
1 Ph(c) 100.00
2 .... 65.00
3 thru 6 Ph(c)................ @50.00

RAVEN
Renaissance Comics, 1993
1 I:Raven 2.50
2 V:Macallister............... 2.50
3 thru 5 .... @2.50
6 V:Nightmare Creatures 2.75

RAVENING
Avatar, 1998
? Busch (c) F:Ravyn & Glyph..... 3.00
?a Meadows(c) 3.00
?d Sketched Edition........... 60.00
?e Blood Red Foil, signed 9.00

RAVENS AND RAINBOWS
Pacific, 1983
1 .... 2.00

RAVER
Malibu April, 1993
1 Prism cover 3.00
1a Newsstand 2.25
2 .... 2.25
3 Walter Koenig(s)............ 2.25
4 and 5 .... @2.25

RAY BRADBURY CHRONICLES
Byron Press
1 short stories 10.00
2 short stories 10.00

Ravens and Rainbows #1
© Pacific Comics

3 short stories 10.00

RAY BRADBURY COMICS
Topps, 1993–94
1 thru 5 with Trading Card .... @3.25
Spec.#1 The Illustrated Man 3.00
Spec. Trilogy of Terror 2.50
Spec. The Martian Chronicles..... 3.00

R.A.Z.E.
Firstlight
1 I:R.A.Z.E., Secret Weapon 2.95
2 V:Exterminators 2.95

RAZOR
London Night Studios, 1992
0 .... 9.00
0a 2nd printing (Fathom 1992).... 4.00
0b reprint (1995) 3.00
1 I:Stryke (Fathom 1992)........ 9.00
1a second printing............ 3.00
2 J.O'Barr (c)................ 10.00
2a limited ed., red & blue....... 19.00
2b platinum ed............... 20.00
3 Jim Balent (c).............. 7.00
3a with poster 15.00
4 .... 4.00
4a with poster 9.00
5 .... 7.00
5a platinum ed............... 15.00
6 .... 5.00
7 .... 4.00
8 thru 10 .... @3.00
11 & 12 B&W, Rituals,pt.1&2 ... @3.00
1/2 (1995).................. 5.00
Ann.#1 I:Shi (1993)............ 25.00
Ann.#2 O:Razor B&W (1994) 35.00
Becomes:

RAZOR UNCUT
See: B&W

RAZOR
Volume 2
London Knight, 1996
1 DQ, ... 3.00
1a holochrome edition 5.00
2 DQ...................... 3.00
2a holochrome edition 4.00
3 thru 7 .... @3.00
Razor Analog Burn 2.50

COLOR PUB.

RAZOR AND SHI SPECIAL
London Night Studios, 1994
1 Rep. Razor Ann.#1 + new art . . . 5.00
1a platinum version 9.00

RAZOR ARCHIVES
London Night, 1997
1 & 2 see B&W
3 rep. Razor #10–12 . . . . 7.00

RAZOR BURN
London Night Studios, 1994
1 V:Styke. 3.00
1a signed 5.00
2 Searching for Styke 3.00
2a Platinum. 7.00
3 Stryke's War. 3.00
4 D:Razor, bagged 3.00
5 Epilogue. 3.00

RAZOR: CRY NO MORE
London Night Studios, 1995
1-shot 3.00
1a variant 4.00
1b Commemorative (1999) 5.95

RAZOR: HEX & VIOLENCE
EH! Productions, 2000
0 EHr 3.00

RAZOR/MORBID ANGEL: SOUL SEARCH
London Night, 1996
1 (of 3) 3.00
1 platinum edition 5.00
1 Chromium edition 7.00
2 . . . . 3.00
3 . . . . 3.00

RAZOR/POISON/ AREALA WARRIOR NUN: LITTLE BAD ANGELS
London Night, 1999
Spec. x-over Raxor cover 3.95
Spec.A Poison cover 3.95
Spec.B Areala cover 3.95

Razor Torture #5
© London Night Studios

RAZOR THE RAVENING
Avatar
1 . . . . 3.50
1a Previews cover. 3.50
1b Bondage cover 6.00

RAZOR: THE SUFFERING
London Night Studios, 1994
1 . . . . 4.00
1a Director's cut 3.00
1b signed, limited 9.00
2 . . . . 3.00
2a Director's cut 2.50
3 final chapter 3.00

RAZOR SWIMSUIT SPECIAL
London Night Studios, 1995
1 pin-ups. 3.00
1a platinum version 7.00
1b commemorative edition. 4.00

RAZOR: TORTURE
London Night Studios, 1995
0 Razor back from dead 4.00
0a signed edition 7.00
1 . . . . 3.00
1a Commemorative (1999) 5.95
2 . . . . 3.00
3 EHr 3.00
4 . . . . 3.00
5 alt. cover, signed 4.00
6 alt. cover, signed 4.00
7 . . . . 3.00

RAZOR/WARRIOR NUN AREALA: DARK MENACE
London Night, 1999
Spec. x-over 3.95
Spec.A x-over, variant cover 3.95

RAZOR/WARRIOR NUN AREALA: FAITH
London Night, 1996
1 by Jude Millien 3.00
1a variant cover. 4.00

REAL GHOSTBUSTERS
Now, 1988
1 KSy(c) 4.50
2 thru 7 . . . . @2.50
8 thru 24 . . . . @2.00
[2nd Series], 1991
1 Halloween Special 2.00
Ann. 3-D w/glasses & pinups 2.95

REALITY CHECK
Sirius, 1996
1 by Tavicat. 2.95
2 thru 8 . . . . @2.50
9 thru 12 Nonesuch Nonsense . . @2.95
TPB Vol. 1 . . . . 17.95
TPB Vol. 2, rep.#7–#12 . . . . 17.95

REAL WAR STORIES
Eclipse, 1987–91
1 BB 3.00
1a 2nd printing 2.00
2 . . . . 4.95

RE-ANIMATOR
Adventure Comics, 1991
1 movie adaption 2.95
2 movie adaption 2.95

RE-ANIMATOR
Adventure
1 Prequel to Orig movie. 2.50

RE-ANIMATOR: DAWN OF THE RE-ANIMATOR
Adventure, 1992
1 Prequel to movie 2.50
2 . . . . 2.50
3 . . . . 2.50
4 V:Erich Metler. 2.50

RE-ANIMATOR: TALES OF HERBERT WEST
Adventure Comics
1 H.P.Lovecraft stories. 4.95

RED
DC Wildstorm July 2003
America's Best Comics
1 (of 3) WEI,CHm 2.95
2 WEI,CHm 2.95
3 WEI,CHm. 2.95

RED DOG
Eclipse, 1988
1 CR,Mowgli `Jungle Book' story . . 2.00

RED DRAGON
Comico, 1995
1 SBs,I:Red Dragon. 2.50
2 How Soon is Nau? 2.95

REDEEMER, THE
Black Library, 2002
1 . . . . 3.50
2 thru 4 . . . . @3.50

REDEEMERS
Antarctic Press, 1997
1 (of 5) by Herb Mallette & Patrick Blain 2.95
2 . . . . 2.95

RED SONJA in 3-D
Blackthorne
1 thru 3 . . . . @2.50

RED SONJA
Cross Plains Comics, 1999
1 Death in Scarlet,pt.1 . . . . 2.95
1a photo (c). 2.95
2 Death in Scarlet,pt.2 . . . . 2.95
3 Death in Scarlet,pt.3 . . . . 2.95

RED STAR, THE
Archangel Studios 2002
Vol. 2
2 . . . . 2.95
3 . . . . 3.00
4 . . . . 3.00
TPB Red Star Collected Edition . . 24.95
Annual #1 foil (c) signed 10.00

REESE'S PIECES
Eclipse, 1985
1 reprint from Web of Horror 2.00
2 reprint from Web of Horror 2.00

Re: Gex 30
© Awesome Entertainment

RE: GEX
Awesome Entertainment, 1998
0 RLe, ... 2.50
0a Red Foil variant 4.00
1 RLe,JLb 2.50
1a Platinum cover 7.00
1b Red Foil cover 12.00
1c Variant RL cover 4.00
1d prime 2.99
1e prime millennium ed.. .... 4.95
2 RLe,JLb 2.50
2a prime 2.99
2b Millennium edition 4.95
3 RLe,A:The Coven,V:Youngblood . 2.50
Con Spec. '98. .... 5.00
Orlando Megacon ashcan. 10.00
Orlando Megacon ashcan, signed. 20.00
Arcade Comics, 2002
Ashcan #1, Museum Edition 60.00
Ashcan #1, Museum Ed., signed. . 80.00

REGGIE
Archie Publications, 1963–65
15 .... 75.00
16 .... 75.00
17 .... 75.00
18 .... 75.00
Becomes:

REGGIE AND ME
Archie Publications, 1966–80
19 .... 50.00
20 thru 23 .... @30.00
24 thru 40 .... @25.00
41 thru 50 .... @15.00
51 thru 99 .... @10.00
100 .... 15.00
101 thru 126 .... @8.00

REGGIE'S WISE GUY JOKES
Archie Publications, April, 1968
1 .... 60.00
2 .... 30.00
3 .... 30.00
4 .... 30.00

COLOR PUB.

5 thru 15 Giants .... @30.00
16 thru 28 Giants .... @25.00
29 thru 40 .... @15.00
41 thru 60 .... @12.00
11 thru 59 .... @10.00
60 Jan., 1982 .... 10.00

REIVERS
Enigma
1 thru 3 Rock 'n' Roll .... @2.95

RELOAD
DC Homage Mar. 2003
1 (of 3) WEI,JP 2.95
2 WEI,JP 2.95
3 WEI,JP, concl. 2.95

REPTILICUS
Charlton Comics, Aug., 1961
1 .... 275.00
2 .... 150.00
Becomes:

REPTISAURUS
1962
3 .... 100.00
4 .... 75.00
5 .... 75.00
6 .... 75.00
7 .... 75.00
8 Summer, 1963 .... 75.00

RESIDENT EVIL: FIRE & ICE
WildStorm/DC, 2000
1 (of 4) from videogame 2.50
2 .... 2.50
3 .... 2.50
4 concl. 2.50
TPB Codename Veronica, Vol. 1. . 14.95
TPB Codename Veronica, Vol. 3. . 14.95
TPB Code Veronica, Vol. 4 ..... 14.95

RESISTANCE, THE
WildStorm/DC, Sept., 2002
1 JP(s),techno sci-fi. 2.95
2 JP(s) 2.95
3 JP(s) 2.95
4 JP(s) 2.95
5 JP(s),V:Sampizi 2.95
6 JP(s),V:Sampizi & GCC 2.95
7 JP(s),F:Version Mary 2.95
8 JP(s),F:Version Mary 2.95

RETURN OF KONGA, THE
Charlton Comics, 1962
N# 100.00

RETURN OF MEGATON MAN
Kitchen Sink, 1988
1 Don Simpson art (1988) 2.00
2 Don Simpson art. 2.00
3 Don Simpson art. 2.00

RETURN TO JURASSIC PARK
Topps, 1995
1 R:Jurassic Park 2.50
2 V:Blosyn Team, Army 2.50
3 The Hunted 2.50
4 Army 2.50
5 Heirs to the Thunder,pt.1 ..... 2.95

6 Heirs to the Thunder,pt.2 ..... 2.95
7 Inquiring Minds,pt.1 .... 2.95
8 Photo Finish, concl. 2.95
9 Jurassic Jam issue 2.95

REVENGE OF THE PROWLER
Eclipse, 1988
1 GN,R:Prowler 2.00
2 GN,A:Fighting Devil Dogs with
  Flexi-Disk 2.50
3 GN,A:Devil Dogs 2.00
4 GN,V:Pirahna 2.00

REVENGERS
Continuity, 1985
1 NA,O:Megalith,I:Crazyman 4.00
2 NA,Megalith meets Armor & Silver
Streak,Origin Revengers#1....... 2.50
3 NA/NR,Origin Revengers #2. ... 2.50
4 NA,Origin Revengers #3. ...... 2.50
5 NA,Origin Revengers #4. ...... 2.50
6 I:Hybrids. 3.00
Spec. #1 F:Hybrids. 4.95

RIBIT
Comico
1 FT,Mini-series. 2.00
2 FT,Mini-series. 2.00
3 FT,Mini-series. 2.00
4 FT,Mini-series. 2.00

RICHIE RICH
Harvey Publications, 1960–91
1 .... 2,000.00
2 .... 750.00
3 .... 500.00
4 .... 500.00
5 .... 500.00
6 .... 250.00
7 .... 250.00
8 .... 250.00
9 .... 250.00
10 .... 250.00
11 thru 20 .... @200.00
21 thru 40 .... @150.00
41 thru 60 .... @125.00
61 thru 80 .... @100.00
81 thru 99 .... @40.00
100 .... 45.00
101 thru 111 .... @25.00
112 thru 116 52 pg Giants ..... @30.00
117 thru 120 .... @25.00
121 thru 140 .... @20.00
141 thru 160 .... @15.00
161 thru 180 .... @10.00
181 thru 254 .... @5.00

RICHIE RICH
Harvey, 1991
1 thru 15 .... @3.00
16 thru 28 .... @2.00

RICHIE RICH BANK BOOKS
Harvey, 1972–82
1 .... 75.00
2 thru 5 .... @50.00
6 thru 10 .... @35.00
11 thru 20 .... @25.00
21 thru 30 .... @15.00
31 thru 40 .... @10.00
41 thru 59 .... @8.00

COLOR PUB.

RICHIE RICH BILLIONS
Harvey, 1974–82
1 . . . . 50.00
2 thru 5 . . . . @30.00
6 thru 10 . . . . @25.00
11 thru 20 . . . . @15.00
21 thru 30 . . . . @10.00
31 thru 48 . . . . @8.00

RICHIE RICH DIAMONDS
Harvey, 1972–82
1 . . . . 75.00
2 thru 5 . . . . @35.00
6 thru 10 . . . . @30.00
11 thru 20 . . . . @25.00
21 thru 30 . . . . @12.00
31 thru 59 . . . . @10.00

RICHIE RICH DOLLARS & CENTS
Harvey Publications, 1963–82
1 . . . . 225.00
2 . . . . 125.00
3 thru 5 . . . . @75.00
6 thru 10 . . . . @50.00
11 thru 20 . . . . @35.00
21 thru 30 . . . . @30.00
31 thru 43 . . . . @25.00
44 thru 60 . . . . @20.00
61 thru 70 . . . . @15.00
71 thru 109 . . . . @10.00

RICHIE RICH FORTUNES
Harvey, 1971–82
1 . . . . 75.00
2 thru 5 . . . . @50.00
6 thru 10 . . . . @40.00
11 thru 20 . . . . @20.00
21 thru 30 . . . . @10.00
31 thru 63 . . . . @8.00

RICHIE RICH GEMS
Harvey, 1974–82
1 . . . . 50.00
2 thru 5 . . . . @30.00
6 thru 10 . . . . @25.00
11 thru 20 . . . . @20.00
21 thru 30 . . . . @10.00
31 thru 43 . . . . @8.00

RICHIE RICH JACKPOTS
Harvey, 1974–82
1 . . . . 75.00
2 thru 5 . . . . @50.00
6 thru 10 . . . . @30.00
11 thru 20 . . . . @25.00
21 thru 30 . . . . @12.00
31 thru 58 . . . . @10.00

RICHIE RICH MILLIONS
Harvey Publications, 1961–82
1 . . . . 275.00
2 . . . . 175.00
3 thru 10 . . . . @150.00
11 thru 20 . . . . @100.00
21 thru 30 . . . . @75.00
31 thru 48 . . . . @35.00

49 thru 60 . . . . @30.00
61 thru 64 . . . . @25.00
65 thru 74 . . . . @20.00
75 thru 94 . . . . @18.00
95 thru 113 . . . . @12.00

RICHIE RICH MONEY WORLD
Harvey, 1972–82
1 . . . . 75.00
2 thru 5 . . . . @50.00
6 thru 10 . . . . @35.00
11 thru 20 . . . . @18.00
21 thru 30 . . . . @10.00
31 thru 59 . . . . @8.00

Richie Rich Profits #14
© Harvey

RICHIE RICH PROFITS
Harvey, 1974–82
1 . . . . 60.00
2 thru 5 . . . . @30.00
6 thru 10 . . . . @25.00
11 thru 20 . . . . @20.00
21 thru 30 . . . . @10.00
31 thru 47 . . . . @8.00

RICHIE RICH RICHES
Harvey, 1972–82
1 . . . . 75.00
2 thru 5 . . . . @50.00
6 thru 10 . . . . @30.00
11 thru 20 . . . . @20.00
21 thru 30 . . . . @15.00
31 thru 59 . . . . @10.00

RICHIE RICH SUCCESS STORIES
Harvey Publications, 1964–82
1 . . . . 275.00
2 thru 5 . . . . @150.00
6 thru 10 . . . . @100.00
11 thru 30 . . . . @75.00
31 thru 38 . . . . @50.00
39 thru 55 . . . . @35.00
56 thru 66 . . . . @20.00
67 thru 105 . . . . @15.00

RICHIE RICH VAULT OF MYSTERY
Harvey, 1974–82
1 . . . . 40.00
2 thru 5 . . . . @25.00
6 thru 10 . . . . @15.00
11 thru 20 . . . . @10.00
21 thru 30 . . . . @10.00
31 thru 47 . . . . @10.00

RICHIE RICH ZILLIONZ
Harvey, 1976–82
1 . . . . 35.00
2 thru 5 . . . . @20.00
6 thru 10 . . . . @15.00
11 thru 20 . . . . @10.00
21 thru 33 . . . . @8.00

RIFLEMAN, THE
Dell Publishing Co., 1959
1 Chuck Connors Ph(c) all 350.00
2 . . . . 200.00
3 ATh 175.00
4 . . . . 165.00
5 . . . . 165.00
6 ATh 175.00
7 . . . . 150.00
8 . . . . 150.00
9 . . . . 150.00
10 . . . . 150.00
11 . . . . 125.00
12 . . . . 125.00
13 . . . . 125.00
14 . . . . 125.00
15 . . . . 125.00
16 . . . . 125.00
17 . . . . 125.00
18 . . . . 125.00
19 . . . . 125.00
20 . . . . 125.00

RIOT GEAR
Triumphant, 1993
1 JnR(s),I:Riot Gear 2.50
2 JnR(s),I:Rabin 2.50
3 JnR(s),I:Surzar 2.50
4 JnR(s),D:Captain Tich 2.50
5 JnR(s),reactions 2.50
6 JnR(s),Tich avenged 2.50
7 JnR(s),Information Age 2.50
8 JnR(s), ... 2.50

RIOT GEAR: VIOLENT PAST
Triumphant, 1994
1 and 2 . . . . @2.50

R.I.P.
TSR, 1990–91
1 thru 4 . . . . @2.95
5 thru 8 Brasher, Avenger of the Dead . . . . @2.95

RIPLEY'S BELIEVE IT OR NOT!
Gold Key, 1967–80
4 Ph(c),AMc 60.00
5 GE,JJ 40.00
6 AMc 40.00
7 . . . . 35.00
8 . . . . 40.00
9 . . . . 35.00

Ripley's–Robotech

10 GE	40.00
11	30.00
12	30.00
13	30.00
14	30.00
15 GE	35.00
16	30.00
17	30.00
18	30.00
19	30.00
20	30.00
21 thru 30	@25.00
31 thru 38	@20.00
39 RC	20.00
40 thru 50	@18.00
51 thru 94	@15.00

RISE OF THE SNAKEMEN
Crossgen Comics 2003
1	2.95
2	2.95

RISK
Maximum Press, 1995
1 V:Furious	2.50

ROB
Awesome Entertainment, 1999
1 RLe	2.50

ROBERT E. HOWARD'S
Cross Plains Comics, 1999
GN Marchers of Valhalla	6.95
GN Wolfshead	6.95
GN Worms of the Earth	9.35

ROBIN HOOD
Eclipse, 1991
1 TT,Historically accurate series	2.75
2 and 3 TT	@2.75

ROBO DOJO
WildStorm/DC, Feb., 2002
1 (of 6) MWn, 40-pg.	3.50
2 MWn,	2.95
3 MWn,	2.95
4 MWn,Techno Council	2.95
5 MWn,Robojin revolt	2.95
6 MWn,traitor revealed, concl.	2.95

ROBO HUNTER
Eagle
1	2.00
2 thru 5	@2.00

ROBOTECH
Antarctic Press, 1997
1 by Fred Perry & BDn	2.95
2	2.95
3	2.95
4 Rolling Thunder, pt.1	2.95
5 Rolling Thunder, pt.2	2.95
6 Rolling Thunder, pt.3	2.95
7 Rolling Thunder, pt.4	2.95
8 Variants, pt.1	2.95
9 Variants, pt.2	2.95
10 Variants, pt.3	2.95
11 Variants, pt.4	2.95
TPB Megastorm by Fred Perry & Ben Dunn	7.95
Spec.1-shot Robotech: Final Fire	2.95
Spec.1-shot Robotech: Class Reunion	2.95

COLOR PUB.

ROBOTECH
Wildstorm/DC 2002
0 JLe	2.50
1 (of 6) JLe	2.95
2	2.95
3	2.95
4	2.95
5	2.95
6 SeP, concl.	2.95
Spec. Robotech Sourcebook	2.95
TPB From the Stars	9.95

Robotech Genesis, The Legend of Zor #1 © Eternity

ROBOTECH: GENESIS
The Legend of Zor
Eternity
1 O:Robotech w/cards	2.95
1a Limited Edition,extra pages with cards #1 & #2	5.95
2 thru 6, each with cards	@2.50

ROBOTECH IN 3-D
Comico, 1985
1	2.50

ROBOTECH: LOVE AND WAR
Wildstorm/DC July 2003
1 (of 6) Max and Miriya	2.95
2 flight school	2.95
3 Max and Miriya meet	2.95
4 Max and Miriya fight	2.95
5 Dixon dead	2.95
6 conclusion	2.95

ROBOTECH, THE MACROSS SAGA
Comico, 1985–89 (formerly Macross)
2	5.00
3	4.00
4	3.00
5	2.50
6 J:Rick Hunter	2.50
7 V:Zentraedi	2.00
8 A:Rick Hunter	2.00
9 V:Zentraedi	2.00
10 `Blind Game'	2.00
11 V:Zentraedi	2.00

Comics Values Annual

12 V:Zentraedi	2.00
13 V:Zentraedi	2.00
14 `Gloval's Reports'	2.00
15 V:Zentraedi	2.00
16 V:Zentraedi	2.00
17 V:Zentraedi	2.00
18 D:Roy Fokker	2.00
19 V:Khyron	2.00
20 V:Zentraedi	2.00
21 `A New Dawn'	2.00
22 V:Zentraedi	2.00
23 `Reckless'	2.00
24 HB,V:Zentraedi	2.00
25 `Wedding Bells'	2.00
26 `The Messenger'	2.00
27 `Force of Arms'	2.00
28 `Reconstruction Blues'	2.00
29 `Robotech Masters'	2.00
30 `Viva Miriya'	2.00
31 `Khyron's Revenge'	2.00
32 `Broken Heart'	2.00
33 `A Rainy Night'	2.00
34 `Private Time'	2.00
35 `Season's Greetings'	2.00
36 last issue	2.00
Graphic Novel #1	6.00

ROBOTECH: THE MACROSS SAGA
Wildstorm/DC Jan. 2003
TPB Vol. 1	14.95
TPB Vol. 2	14.95
TPB Vol. 3	14.95
TPB Vol. 4	14.95

ROBOTECH MASTERS
Comico, 1985–88
1	4.00
2	3.00
3 Space Station Liberty	3.00
4 V:Bioroids	2.50
5 V:Flagship	2.50
6 `Prelude to Battle'	2.50
7 `The Trap'	2.50
8 F:Dana Sterling	2.50
9 `Star Dust'	2.50
10 V:Zor	2.50
11 A:De Ja Vu	2.00
12 2OR	2.00
13	2.00
14 `Clone Chamber,'V:Zor	2.00
15 `Love Song'	2.00
16 V:General Emerson	2.00
17 `Mind Games'	2.00
18 `Dana in Wonderland'	2.00
19	2.00
20 A:Zor,Musica	2.00
21 `Final Nightmare'	2.00
22 `The Invid Connection'	2.00
23 `Catastrophe,' final issue	2.00

ROBOTECH: THE NEW GENERATION
Comico, 1985–88
1	4.00
2 `The Lost City'	3.00
3 V:Yellow Dancer	3.00
4 A:Yellow Dancer	3.00
5 SK(i),A:Yellow Dancer	2.50
6 F:Rook Bartley	2.50
7 `Paper Hero'	2.00
8	2.00
9 KSy,`The Genesis Pit'	2.00
10 V:The Invid	2.00
11 F:Scott Bernard	2.00
12 V:The Invid	2.00
13 V:The Invid	2.00

CVA Page 650 — All comics prices listed are for *Near Mint* condition.

Comics Values Annual — COLOR PUB. — Robotech–Room

14 `Annie's Wedding'	2.00
15 `Seperate Ways'	2.00
16 `Metamorphosis'	2.00
17 `Midnight Sun'	2.00
18	2.00
19	2.00
20 `Birthday Blues'	2.00
21 `Hired Gun'	2.00
22 `The Big Apple'	2.00
23 Robotech Wars	2.00
24 Robotech Wars	2.00
25 V:Invid, last issue	2.00

ROBOTECH SPECIAL DANA'S STORY
Eclipse

1 .... 5.00

ROBOTECH II: THE SENTINELS
Eternity

Swimsuit Spec.#1 .... 2.95

ROCK 'N' ROLL
Revolutionary, 1990
Prev: Black & White

15 Poison	6.00
16 Van Halen	5.00
17 Madonna	6.00
18 AliceCooper	5.00
19 Public Enemy, 2 Live Crew	5.00
20 Queensryche	5.00
21 Prince	5.00
22 AC/DC	5.00
23 Living Color	5.00
24 Anthrax	5.00
25 Z.Z.Top	5.00
26 Doors	5.00
27 Doors	5.00
28 Ozzy Osbourne	5.00
29 The Cure	5.00
30	5.00
31 Vanilla Ice	5.00
32 Frank Zappa	5.00
33 Guns n' Roses	5.00
34 The Black Crowes	5.00
35 R.E.M.	5.00
36 Michael Jackson	5.00
37 Ice T	5.00
38 Rod Stewart	5.00
39 New Kids on the Block	5.00
40 N.W.A./Ice Cube	5.00
41 Paula Abdul	5.00
42 Metallica II	5.00
43 Guns `N' Roses	5.00
44 Scorpions	5.00
45 Greatful Dead	5.00
46 Grateful Dead	5.00
47 Grateful Dead	5.00
48 (now b/w),Queen	5.00
49 Rush	5.00
50 Bob Dylan Pt.1	5.00
51 Bob Dylan Pt.2	5.00
52 Bob Dylan Pt.3	5.00
53 Bruce Springsteen	5.00
54 U2 Pt.1	5.00
55 U2 Pt.2	5.00
56 David Bowie	5.00
57 thru 65	@4.00

ROCK 'N' ROLL HIGH SCHOOL
Cosmic Comics, 1995

1 Sequel to the movie 2.50

Rocketeer Movie Adaptation
© Walt Disney

ROCKETEER
Walt Disney, 1991

1 DSt(c)RH,MovieAdaptation 7.00
Newsstand Version 3.25

ROCKETEER ADVENTURE MAGAZINE
Comico, 1988

1 DSt,MK,Rocketeer(6thApp.) ... 10.00
2 DSt,MK,Rocketeer(7thApp.) 8.00

ROCKETEER SPECIAL
Eclipse, 1984

1 DSt, Rocketeer(5th App.) 15.00

ROCKET MAN: KING OF THE ROCKET MEN
Innovation

1 thru 4 Adapts movie series ... @2.50

ROCKET RANGER
Adventure Comics, 1991

1 (of 12) from computer game ... 2.95

ROCKMEEZ
Jzink Comics, 1992

1 I:Rockmeez,V:Pyrites 2.50
2 V:Pyrites,Silv.Embos.(c) 2.50

ROCKY HORROR PICTURE SHOW
Calibre/Tome, 1990

1	6.00
2	3.50
3 `The Conclusion'	3.25
Rocky Horror Collection reps	4.95

ROG 2000
Pacific, 1982

1 One-Shot, JBy 2.00

ROGER RABBIT
Walt Disney, 1990

1 I:Rick Flint, `The Trouble with Toons' 5.50

2	3.50
3	3.00
4	3.00
5	3.00
6 thru 9	@3.00
10 `Tuned-in-toons'	3.00
11 `Who Framed Rick Flint'	3.00
12 `Somebunny to Love	3.00
13 `Honey,I Stink with Kids	3.00
14 `Who Fired Jessica Rabbit'	3.00
15 `The Great Toon Detective'	3.00
16 `See you later Aviator'	3.00
17 Flying Saucers over Toontown	3.00
18 `I Have Seen the Future'	3.00

ROGER RABBIT'S TOONTOWN
Walt Disney, 1991

1 Baby Herman,Jessica stories ... 2.50
2 `Pre-Hysterical Roger' 2.50
3 `Lumberjack of tomorrow' 2.50
4 `The Longest Daze' 2.50

ROGUE TROOPER
Fleetway/Quality, 1986

1 thru 5	@2.00
6	2.00
7 thru 21	@2.00
22/23	2.00
24	2.00
25/26	2.00
27 thru 35	@2.00
36	2.00
37	2.00
38 thru 40	@2.00
41 thru 43	@2.00

ROGUE TROOPER: THE FINAL WARRIOR
Fleetway

1 RS,Golden Rebellion,pt 1 ...... 2.95
2 thru 3 .... @2.95
4 `Saharan Ice-Belt War 2.95

ROLAND: DAYS OF WRATH
Terra Major, 1999

1 (of 4) 2.95
2 thru 4 .... @2.95
TPB 17.95

ROMAN HOLIDAYS, THE
Gold Key, 1973

1	65.00
2	40.00
3	40.00
4	40.00

ROOK, THE
Harris Comics, 1995

0 O:Rook 2.95
1 N:Rook 2.95
2 I:Coffin 2.95
3 The Spider Obsidian 2.95

ROOM 222
Dell Publishing Co., Jan., 1970

1	75.00
2	50.00
3 Drug	60.00
4 Ph(c)	50.00

All comics prices listed are for Near Mint condition.

CVA Page 651

COLOR PUB.

ROSE
Cartoon Books, 2000
1 (of 3) 48-pg. 5.95
2 JSi,CV,48-pg. 5.95
3 JSi,CV,48-pg., concl. 5.95
TPB 19.95

ROSWELL
Bongo Comics, 1996
1 by Bill Morrison,'The Story
  of the Century' 2.95
2 'The Untold Story' 2.95
3 'The Untold Story,' concl. 2.95
4 V:Mutato. 2.95
5 .... 2.95
6 time-traveling comic collector . . . 2.95
TPB Roswell Walks Among Us . . . 12.95

ROUTE 666
Crossgen Comics, 2002
1 .... 3.00
2 thru 5 .... @3.00
6 thru 18 .... @3.00
TPB Vol. 1 Highway of Horror. . . . 15.95
TPB Vol. 2 Three-Ring Circus. . . . 15.95

ROY ROGERS WESTERN CLASSICS
AC Comics
1 .... 2.95
2 .... 2.95
3 .... 2.95
4 .... 3.95

RUFF AND READY
Dell Publishing Co., Sept., 1958
1 .... 200.00
2 .... 150.00
3 .... 150.00
4 .... 100.00
5 .... 100.00
6 .... 100.00
7 .... 100.00
8 .... 100.00
9 .... 100.00
10 thru 12 .... @100.00

RUGRATS COMIC ADVENTURES
New England Comics, 1999
VOL. 1
1 thru 10 .... @2.95
VOL. 2
1 thru 10 .... @2.95
VOL. 3
1 .... 2.95
2 thru 9 .... @2.95

RUN, BUDDY, RUN
Gold Key, June, 1967
1 .... 35.00

RUNE
Malibu Ultraverse, 1994–95
0 BWS(a&s) 4.00
1 BWS(a&s),from Ultraverse 2.50
1a Foil cover 4.00
2 CU(s),BWS,V:Aladdin 2.25
3 DaR,BWS,(Ultraverse Premiere
  #1), Flip book 3.75
4 BWS,V:Twins 2.25
5 BWS 2.25

6 BWS 2.25
7 CU,JS 2.25
8 Rise of Gods,pt.2 .... 2.25
9 Prelude to Godwheel 2.25
G-Size #1 .... 2.50
TPB BWS(c&a),CU,The Awakening,
  rep.#1–#5. .... 12.95

RUNE
Malibu Ultraverse, 1995–96
Infinity V:Annihilus 2.50
1 A:Adam Warlock 2.25
1a Computer painted cover 2.25
2 Phoenix flip issue,A:Adam
  Warlock 2.25
3 Phoenix Resurrection 2.25
4 .... 2.25
5 .... 2.25
6 LKa,A:Warlock 2.25
Spec. #1 Rune vs. Venom x-over . . 2.25

RUNE: HEARTS OF DARKNESS
Malibu Ultraverse, 1996
1 DgM(s),KHt,TBd, flip book 2.25
2 DgM,KHt,TBd, flip book 2.25
3 DgM,KHt,TBd, flip book 2.25

RUNE/ SILVER SURFER
Malibu Ultraverse, 1995
1 BWS(c),A:Adam Warlock 5.95
1a Lim. edition (5,000 made) 8.00
1b Standard ed.newsprint 2.95

RUSE
Crossgen Comics, 2001
1 MWa 8.00
2 MWa 3.50
3 thru 14 .... @3.00
15 thru 26 .... @3.00
TPB Vol. 1 Enter the Detective . . . 15.95
TPB Vol. 3 Criminal Intent. 15.95

RUST
Now, 1987
1 .... 4.00
2 .... 3.00

Rune #2
© Malibu

3 thru 11 .... @2.00
12 I:Terminator 10.00
13 thru 15 .... @2.00
[Volume 2], 1989
1 thru 10 .... @2.00

RUST
Malibu
1 O:Rust 2.95
2 V:Marion Labs 2.95
3 I:Ashe Sapphire,5th Anniv. 2.95
4 I:Rustmobile 2.95

SABLE
First, 1988–90
1 AIDS story 2.00
2 Sable in Iran 2.00
3 Pentathelon 2.00
4 .... 2.00
5 DCw,V:Tong Gangs 2.00
6 In Atlantic City 2.00
7 V:EnvironmentalTerrorists 2.00
8 In Argentina 2.00
9 In Kenya Pt.1 .... 2.00
10 In Kenya Pt.2 .... 2.00
11 Jon Sable bodyguard 2.00
12 In Cambodia Pt.1 .... 2.00
13 In Cambodia Pt.2 .... 2.00
14 Christmas story 2.00
15 A:Ted Koppel 2.00
16 Sable as `B.B.Flemm' rev. 2.00
17 Turning point issue 2.00
18 Richard Rockwell(i) 2.00
19 A:Maggie the Cat 2.00
20 A:Gary Adler 2.00
21 Richard Rockwell(i) 2.00
22 A:Eden Kendall 2.00
23 TV cover 2.00
24 TV cover 2.00
25 TV cover 2.00
26 TV cover 2.00
27 .... 2.00
28 last issue 2.00

SABRE
Eclipse, 1982–85
1 PG 2.50
2 PG 3.00
3 thru 14 .... @2.00

SABRINA, THE TEENAGE WITCH
Archie Publications, 1971–83
1 .... 200.00
2 Archie 100.00
3 Archie 75.00
4 .... 60.00
5 .... 60.00
6 thru 10 .... @60.00
11 thru 30 .... @40.00
31 thru 40 .... @20.00
41 thru 76 .... @12.00
77 .... 20.00

SABRINA THE TEENAGE WITCH
Archie Comics, 1996
one-shot photo cover 7.00
1 photo cover 5.00
2 'Trouble in Time' 5.00
3 photo cover 5.00
4 photo cover 5.00
5 'Driver's License' 5.00
6 'Treasure Troubles'. 5.00
7 'The Sculpture Switch' 5.00

8 'The Cable Girl' photo (c) 5.00
9 'Farewell Feline' 5.00
10 'No Brain, No Pain' 5.00
11 'Mirror, Mirror' 3.00
12 '' 3.00
13 'Kin You Believe It' 3.00
14 'Too Much Magic' 3.00
15 'Wedding or Not' 3.00
16 How does your garden grow? . . 3.00
17 F:Josie & The Pussycats 3.00
18 photo (c) 3.00
19 photo (c) 3.00
20 thru 27 photo (c) . . . . @3.00
28 A:Sonic The Hedgehog 2.00
29 thru 33 photo (c) . . . . @2.00
[Volume 2], 2000
1 thru 3 from animated series . . . @1.80
4 thru 38 . . . . @2.00
39 thru 52 . . . . @2.20
Halloween Spooktacular #1 . . . . . 2.00
Halloween Spooktacular #2 . . . . . 2.00
Holiday Spectacular #3 . . . . 2.00

Sad Sack and the Sarge #140
© Harvey Publications

SAD SACK AND THE SARGE
Harvey Publications, 1957–82
1 . . . . 200.00
2 . . . . 100.00
3 thru 10 . . . . @75.00
11 thru 20 . . . . @60.00
21 thru 40 . . . . @35.00
41 thru 50 . . . . @25.00
51 thru 90 . . . . @20.00
91 thru 96 52 pg Giants . . . . . . @15.00
97 thru 155 . . . . @10.00

SAD SACK'S ARMY LIFE
Harvey Publications, 1963–76
1 . . . . 90.00
2 thru 10 . . . . @50.00
11 thru 20 . . . . @30.00
21 thru 30 . . . . @25.00
31 thru 50 . . . . @18.00
51 thru 61 . . . . @15.00

SAD SACK'S FUNNY FRIENDS
Harvey Publications, 1955–69
1 . . . . 125.00
2 thru 10 . . . . @75.00

11 thru 20 . . . . @35.00
21 thru 30 . . . . @20.00
31 thru 40 . . . . @15.00
41 thru 75 . . . . @10.00

SAD SACK in 3-D
Blackthorne
1 and 2 . . . . @2.50

SAFETY-BELT MAN ALL HELL
Sirius, 1996
1 . . . . 2.95
2 . . . . 2.95
3 . . . . 2.95
4 Linsner back (c) 4.00
5 . . . . 2.95

SAGA OF THE METABARONS
Humanoids Publishing, 1999
1 (of 16) Sci-fi 2.95
2 thru 9 . . . . @2.95

SALOME
Eclipse, 1987
1 CR 2.00

SAM AND MAX, FREE-LANCE POLICE SPECIAL
Comico, 1987–89
1 . . . . 2.75

SAM SLADE ROBOHUNTER
Quality, 1986–89
1 . . . . 2.00
2 . . . . 2.00
3 Filby Case 2.00
4 . . . . 2.00
5 . . . . 2.00
6 Bax the Burner, Moore 2.00
7 . . . . 2.00
8 thru 21 . . . . @2.00
22/23 . . . . 2.00
24 . . . . 2.00
25/26 . . . . 2.00
27 thru 33 . . . . @2.00

SAMSONS
Samsons Comics, 1995
1/2 Various Artists 2.50

SAMUREE
Windjammer 1995
1 I:Samuree 2.50
2 V:The Dragon 2.50
3 V:The Dragon 2.50

SAMURAI
Eclipse
1 . . . . 2.00
2 . . . . 2.00
3 thru 5 . . . . @2.00

SAMURAI GUARD
Colburn Comics, 2000
1 by Kirk C. Abrigo 2.50
2 . . . . 2.50
3 . . . . 3.00

4 . . . . 2.95
5 . . . . 2.95

SAMUREE
Continuity, 1987
1 NA,A:Revengers 2.00
2 A:Revengers 2.00
3 NA,A:Revengers 2.00
4 A:Revengers 2.00
5 BSz(c),A:Revengers 2.00
6 A:Revengers 2.00
7 . . . . 2.00
8 Drug story 2.00
9 Drug story 2.00
[2nd Series], 1993
1 thru 3 Rise of Magic . . . . @2.50

SANDSCAPE
Dreamwave 2003
1 . . . . 2.95
2 thru 4 . . . . @2.95

SANTANA
Malibu Rock-it Comix, May, 1994
1 TT(c&s),TY 3.95

SARGE STEEL/ SECRET AGENT
Charlton, 1964–66
1 DG,I:SargeSteel & IvanChung . 50.00
2 DG,I:Werner Von Hess 30.00
3 DG,V:Smiling Skull 30.00
4 DG,V:Lynx 30.00
5 FMc,V:Ivan Chung 30.00
6 FMc,A:Judomaster 35.00
7 DG 30.00
8 V:Talon 30.00
Becomes:
SECRET AGENT
9 DG,A:The Lynx 40.00
10 DG,JAp,A:Tiffany Sinn 30.00

SATANIKA
Verotik, 1995
0 . . . . 3.00
1 New ongoing series 4.00
2 Femininity 3.50
3 thru 5 . . . . @3.00
6 thru 10 . . . . @2.95
10a Wingbird variant cover 5.00
11 SBi,final issue 3.95
11a Jason Blood variant (c) 10.00
11b Superfest 99 limited 15.00
1-shot Satanika X (adult) 5.00
1-shot Satanika vs.Shilene 9.95

SATAN'S SIX
Topps, 1993
1 F:Satan's Six,w/3 cards 3.25
2 V:Kalazarr,w/3 cards 2.95
3 w/3 cards 2.95
4 w/3 cards 2.95

SATURDAY KNIGHTS
Hot
1 . . . . 2.00
2 thru 4 . . . . @2.00

SAURAUS FAMILY
Blackthorne
1 3-D 2.00

SAURIANS: UNNATURAL SELECTION
Crossgen Comics, 2002
1 (of 2) 3.00
2 . . . . 3.00

SAVAGE COMBAT TALES
Atlas, Feb.–July, 1975
1 F:Sgt Strykers Death Squad . . . 20.00
2 ATh,A:Warhawk 25.00
3 final issue 15.00

SAVAGE DRAGON/ TEENAGE MUTANT NINJA TURLTES CROSSOVER
Mirage, 1993
1 EL(s) 2.75

SAVED BY THE BELL
Harvey, 1992
1 based on TV series 2.00
2 thru 5 . . . . @2.00

SCARLET CRUSH
Awesome Entertainment, 1998
1 by John Stinsman 2.50
2 . . . . 2.50
3 Icaria's decision 2.50
4 Nirasawa arrives 2.50

SCARY TALES
Charlton, 1975
1 . . . . 35.00
2 . . . . 15.00
3 SD,P(c) 15.00
4 TS,SD,P(c) 20.00
5 SD 20.00
6 . . . . 15.00
7 SD 18.00
8 SD 18.00
9 TS 20.00
10 . . . . 15.00
11 . . . . 15.00
12 . . . . 15.00
13 . . . . 12.00
14 . . . . 15.00

Scary Tales #26
© Charlton Comics

COLOR PUB.

15 . . . . 15.00
16 . . . . 15.00
17 . . . . 12.00
18 . . . . 15.00
19 . . . . 15.00
20 . . . . 10.00
21 . . . . 15.00
22 . . . . 9.00
23 thru 28 . . . . @8.00
30 thru 37 . . . . @6.00
38 Mr. Jigsaw 9.00
39 SD 12.00
40 thru 46 . . . . @8.00

SCAVENGERS
Quality, 1988–89
1 thru 7 . . . . @2.00
8 thru 14 . . . . @2.00

SCAVENGERS
Triumphant Comics, 1993–94
0 Fso(c),JnR(s), ... 2.50
0a `Free Copy' 2.50
0b Red Logo 2.50
1 JnR(s),I:Scavengers,Ximos,
  C:Doctor Chaos 2.50
1a 2nd Printing 2.50
2 JnR(s), ... 2.50
3 JnR(s),I:Lurok 2.50
4 JnR(s), ... 2.50
5 Fso(c),JnR(s),D:Jack Hanal . . . 2.50
6 JnR(s), ... 2.50
7 JnR(s),I:Zion 2.50
8 JnR(s),Nativity 2.50
9 JnR(s),The Challenge 2.50
10 JnR(s),Snowblind 2.50

SCHISM
Defiant
1 thru 4 Defiant's x-over . . . . . . @3.25

SCIENCE COMIC BOOK
Nature Publishing House, 1997
TPB Earth Adventures 8.95
TPB Car Adventure 8.95
TPB Volcano Adventures 8.95
TPB World of Dinosaurs 8.95
TPB Beyond the Star 8.95
TPB Weather Genie 8.95
TPB Rain Forest Adventure 8.95
TPB Wildlife Adventure 8.95

SCION
Crossgen Comics, 2000
1 RMz 5.00
2 RMz 5.00
3 RMz 4.50
4 & 5 . . . . 3.00
6 . . . . 4.00
7 thru 18 . . . . @3.00
19 thru 30 RMz . . . . @3.00
31 thru 42 RMz . . . . @3.00
TPB Vol. 1 rep. #1–#7 . . . . 19.95
TPB Vol. 2 . . . . 19.95
TPB Vol. 3 Divided Loyalties 15.95
TPB Vol. 4 Sanctuary 15.95
TPB Vol. 5 The Far Kingdom . . . 15.95
TPB Scion Traveler, Vol. 1 . . . . . . 9.95

SCI-TECH
WildStorm/DC, 1999
1 (of 4) BCi,Ebe, ... 2.50
2 BCi,EBe, ... 2.50
3 BCi,EBe 2.50
4 BCi,EBe,concl. 2.50

SCOOBY DOO
Gold Key, 1970–75
1 . . . . 150.00
2 . . . . 100.00
3 . . . . 75.00
4 . . . . 75.00
5 . . . . 75.00
6 . . . . 60.00
7 . . . . 60.00
8 . . . . 60.00
9 . . . . 60.00
10 . . . . 60.00
11 thru 20 . . . . @50.00
21 thru 30 . . . . @40.00

SCOOBY DOO
Charlton Comics, 1975–76
1 . . . . 75.00
2 . . . . 40.00
3 . . . . 40.00
4 . . . . 40.00
5 . . . . 40.00
6 . . . . 35.00
7 . . . . 35.00
8 . . . . 35.00
9 . . . . 35.00
10 . . . . 35.00
11 . . . . 35.00

SCOOBY DOO
Archie, 1995
1 thru 10 . . . . @2.00
11 thru 13 . . . . @2.00
14 `The Balloon Busters' 2.00
15 `On the Boardwalk in
   Atlantic City' 2.00
16 `The Ghost of Central Park' . . . 2.00
19 `Electric Monster' 2.00
20 `The Legend of Spooky Doo' . . 2.00
21 `Monster Park After Dark' 2.00

SCORCHED EARTH
Tundra, 1991
1 Earth 2025,I:Dr.EliotGodwin . . . 3.50
2 Hunt for Eliot 2.95
3 Mystical Transformation 2.95

SCORPION, THE
Atlas, 1975
1 HC, bondage cover 25.00
2 HC,BWi,MK 20.00
3 . . . . 15.00

SCORPION CORP.
Dagger, 1993
1 PuD,JRI,CH, ... 2.75
2 PuD,JRI,CH,V:Victor Kyner 2.75
3 PuD,BIH,V:Victor Kyner 2.75

SCORPIO ROSE
Eclipse, 1983
1 MR/TP,I:Dr.Orient 2.00
2 MR/TP 2.00

SCOUT
Eclipse, 1985–87
1 TT,I:Scout,Fash.In Action 6.00
2 TT,V:Buffalo Monster 3.00
3 TT,V:President Grail 2.50
4 TT,V:President Grail 2.50
5 TT,`Killin' Floor' 2.50
6 TT,V:President Grail 2.50
7 TT,TY,Rosanna's Diary 2.50
8 TT,TY 2.50

Comics Values Annual — COLOR PUB. — Scout–Seraphim

- 9 TT,TY,A:Airboy 2.50
- 10 TT,TY,I:Proj.Mountain Fire 2.00
- 11 TT,FH,V:Rangers 2.00
- 12 TT,FH,`Me and the Devil' 2.00
- 13 TT,FH,Monday:Eliminator 2.00
- 14 TT,FH,Monday:Eliminator 2.00
- 15 TT,FH,Monday:Eliminator 2.00
- 16 TT,3-D issue,F:Santana 3.00
- 17 TT,A:Beanworld 2.00
- 18 TT,FH,V:Lex Lucifer 2.00
- 19 TT,w/Record,V:Lex Lucifer 3.00
- 20 TT,A:Monday:Eliminator 2.00
- 21 TT,A:Monday:Eliminator 2.00
- 22 TT,A:Swords of Texas 2.00
- 23 TT,A:Swords of Texas 2.00
- 24 TT,last Issue 2.00

SCOUT: WAR SHAMAN
Eclipse, 1988–89
- 1 TT,R:Scout (now a father) 2.25
- 2 TT,I:Redwire 2.00
- 3 TT,V:Atuma Yuma 2.00
- 4 TT,`Rollin' on the River' 2.00
- 5 TT,Hopi Katchina dieties 2.00
- 6 TT,Scout vs. Rosa Winter 2.00
- 7 TT,R:Redwire 2.00
- 8 TT,R:Beau LaDuke 2.00
- 9 TT,V:Doodyists 2.00
- 10 TT,TY,V:Redwire 2.00
- 11 TT,V:Redwire 2.00
- 12 TT,V:Snow Leopards 2.00
- 13 TT,F:Beau LaDuke 2.00
- 14 TT,V:Redwire 2.00
- 15 TT,V:Redwire 2.00
- 16 TT,`Wall of Death,'last issue ... 2.00

SEADRAGON
Elite, 1986–87
- 1 .... 3.00
- 1a 2nd printing 2.00
- 2 thru 8 .... @2.00

SEA HUNT
Dell Publishing Co., 1958
- 1 L.BridgesPh(c) all 200.00
- 2 .... 150.00
- 3 ATh 165.00
- 4 RsM 150.00
- 5 RsM 150.00
- 6 RsM 150.00
- 7 .... 125.00
- 8 RsM 150.00
- 9 RsM 150.00
- 10 RsM 150.00
- 11 RsM 150.00
- 12 .... 150.00
- 13 RsM 150.00

SEAQUEST
Nemesis, 1994
- 1 HC(c),DGC,KP,AA,Based on TV Show 2.50

SEBASTIAN
Walt Disney
- 1 From Little Mermaid 2.00
- 2 `While da Crab's Away' 2.00

THE SECOND LIFE OF DR. MIRAGE
Valiant 1993
- 1 B:BL(s),BCh,V:Mast.Darque ... 2.50
- 1a Gold Ed. 3.00
- 2 BCh,V:Master Darque 2.50
- 3 BCh 2.50

Second Life of Doctor Mirage 34
© Valiant

- 4 BCh,V:Bhrama 2.50
- 5 BCh,A:Shadowman,V:Master Darque 2.50
- 6 BCh,V:Dr.Eclipse 2.50
- 7 BCh,V:Dr.Eclipse,w/card 2.50
- 8 BCh 2.50
- 9 BCh,A:Otherman 2.50
- 10 BCh,V:Otherman 2.50
- 11 BCh,Chaos Effect-Beta#2 ... 2.50
- 12 BCh 2.25
- 13 BCh 2.25
- 14 .... 2.25
- 15 Chaos Effect 2.25
- 16 & 17 .... @2.25
- 18 F:Deathsmith 2.25
- 19 R:Walt Wiley 2.25

SECRET AGENT
Gold Key, Nov., 1966
- 1 .... 200.00
- 2 .... 150.00

SECRET CITY SAGA
Topps, 1993
- 0 JK 3.25
- 0 Gold Ed. 15.00
- 0 Red 10.00
- 1 w/3 cards 3.25
- 2 w/3 cards 3.25
- 3 w/3 cards 3.25
- 4 w/3 cards 3.25

SECRETS OF THE VALIANT UNIVERSE
Valiant 1994
- 1 from Wizard 2.50
- 2 BH,Chaos Effect-Beta#4,A:Master Darque,Dr.Mirage,Max St.James, Dr. Eclipse 2.25

SECRET SQUIRREL
Gold Key, Oct., 1966
- 1 .... 165.00

SECRET WEAPONS
Valiant 1993
- 1 JSP(a&s),BWi(i),I:Dr.Eclipse, A:Master Darque,A:Geoff, Livewire,Stronghold,Solar,X-O,

---

- Bloodshot,Shadowman 2.75
- 1a Gold Ed. 4.00
- 2 JSP(a&s),V:Master Darque, Dr.Eclipse 2.25
- 3 JSP(a&s),V:Speedshots 2.25
- 4 JSP(a&s),V:Scatterbrain 2.25
- 5 JSP(a&s),A:Ninjak 2.25
- 6 JPS(s),JPh(pl),TeH, V:Spider Aliens 2.25
- 7 JPS(s),V:Spider Aliens 2.25
- 8 JSP(a&pl),V:Harbingers 2.25
- 9 JSP(a&s),V:Webnet, w/Valiant Era card 2.25
- 10 JSP(a&s),V:Webnet 2.25
- 11 PGr,New Line-up 2.25
- 12 PGr,A:Bloodshot 2.25
- 13 PGr,Chaos Effect-Gamma#2 .. 2.25
- 14 PGr,F:Bloodshot 2.25
- 15 .... 2.25
- 16 .... 2.25
- 17 V:Dr. Silk 2.25
- 18 Gigo 2.25
- 19 A:Ninjak 2.25
- 20 Bloodshot Rampage,pt.2 .... 2.25
- 21 Bloodshot Rampage,pt.4 .... 2.25
- 22 I:Gestalt, Pyroclast 2.25
- 23 A:Bloodshot 2.25

SECRET WEAPONS: PLAYING WITH FIRE
Valiant
- 1 & 2 .... @2.50

SEDUCTION OF THE INNOCENT
Eclipse, 1985–86
- 1 ATh,`Hanged by the Neck' reps. . 3.00
- 2 .... 3.00
- 3 ATh,`The Crushed Gardenia' . 3.00
- 4 ATh,NC,`World's Apart' 3.00
- 5 ATh,`The Phantom Ship' 3.00
- 6 ATh,RA,`Hands of Don Jose' . 3.00
- 3-D #1 DSt(c) 5.00
- 3-D #2 ATh,MB,BWr,`Man Who Was Always on Time' 5.00

SEEKER
Sky Comics, 1995
- 1 JMt(s),I:Seeker 2.50

SENSEI
First, 1989
- 1 Mini-Series 2.75
- 2 .... 2.75
- 3 .... 2.75
- 4 .... 2.75

SENTINELS OF JUSTICE
AC Comics, 1990
- 1 Capt.Paragon 2.00
- 2 .... 2.00
- 3 Erik Larson art 2.00
- 4 Erik Larson art 2.00
- 5 .... 2.00
- 6 .... 2.00
- 7 .... 2.00

SENTRY: SPECIAL
Innovation, 1991
- 1 .... 2.75

SERAPHIM
Innovation, 1990
- 1 and 2 .... @2.50

All comics prices listed are for Near Mint condition.

SERINA
Antarctic, 1996
1 . . . . 2.95

SERPENTINA
Lightning, 1997
1 . . . . 3.00
1a variant cover 3.00

SEVEN SISTERS
Zephyr Comics, 1997
1 by Curley, Cruickshank & Garcia. 2.95
2 . . . . 2.95
3 . . . . 2.95
4 . . . . 2.95

77 SUNSET STRIP
Dell Publishing Co., Jan.-March, 1960
1 Ph(c) 150.00
2 Ph(c),RsM 165.00

SHADE SPECIAL
AC Comics, 1984
1 . . . . 2.00

SHADOW, THE
Archie Comics, 1964–65
1 . . . . 100.00
2 thru 5 . . . . @75.00
6 and 8 . . . . @50.00

SHADOW COMICS
1 Guardians of Justice &
 The O-Force. 2.00

SHADOWMAN
Valiant 1992
0 BH,TmR,Chromium (c),O:Maxim
 St.James,Shadowman 3.00
0a Newsstand ed. 2.50
0b Gold Ed. 4.00
1 DL,JRu,I&O:Shadowman 5.00
2 DL,V:Serial Killer 3.00
3 V:Emil Sosa 3.00
4 DL,FM(c),Unity#6,A:Solar 2.50
5 DL,WS(c),Unity#14, A:Archer &
 Armstrong 2.50
6 SD,L:Lilora. 2.50
7 DL,V:Creature 2.50
8 JDx(i),I:Master Darque 3.00
9 JDx(i),V:Darque's Minions. 3.00
10 BH,I:Sandria 2.50
11 BH,N:Shadowman. 2.50
12 BH,V:Master Darque 2.50
13 BH,V:Rev.Shadow Man 2.50
14 BH,JDx,V:Bikers 2.50
15 BH,JDx,V:JB, Fake Shadow
 Man,C:Turok 2.50
16 BH,JDx,I:Dr.Mirage, Carmen . . 3.00
17 BH,JDx,A:Archer & Armstrong . 2.25
18 BH,JDx,A:Archer & Armstrong . 2.25
19 BH,A:Aerosmith. 2.25
20 BH,A:Master Darque,
 V:Shadowman's Father. 2.25
21 BH,I:Maxim St.James (1895
 Shadowman) 2.25
22 V:Master Darque 2.25
23 BH(a&s),A:Doctor Mirage,
 V:Master Darque 2.25
24 BH(a&s),V:H.A.T.E. 2.25
25 RgM,w/Valiant Era card 2.25
26 w/Valiant Era card 2.50
27 BH,V:Drug Lord 2.25
28 BH,A:Master Darque 2.25
29 Chaos Effect-Beta#1,V:Master
 Darque. 2.25
30 R:Rotwak. 2.25
31 thru 33 . . . . @2.25
34 Voodoo in Caribbean 2.25
35 A:Ishmael 2.25
36 F:Ishmael 2.25
37 A:X-O, V:Blister 2.25
38 V:Ishmael, Blister. 2.25
39 BH,TmR,Explores Powers 2.25
40 BH,TmR,I,Vampire! 2.25
41 A:Steve Massarsky 2.25
42 . . . . 2.25
43 V:Smilin Jack. 2.25
TPB rep.#1-#3,#6 . . . . 9.95

SHADOWMAN
Acclaim Nov., 1996
1 GEn(s),'Deadside,'pt.1 . . . . 2.50
2 GEn(s),'Deadside,'pt.2 . . . . 2.50
3 GEn(s),'Deadside,'pt.3 . . . . 2.50
4 GEn(s),'Deadside,'pt.4 . . . . 2.50
5 JaD,CAd,'Nothing is True,'pt.1 . 2.50
6 JaD,CAd,'Nothing is True,'pt.2 . 2.50
7 JaD,CAd,'Nothing is True,'pt.3 . 2.50
8 JaD,CAd,'Nothing is True,'pt.4 . 2.50
9 JaD,CAd,'The Buzz,'pt.1. . . . . . 2.50
10 JaD,CAd,'The Buzz,'pt.2 . . . . . 2.50
11 JaD,CAd,'ClearBlueSkies,'pt.1 . 2.50
12 JaD,CAd,'ClearBlueSkies,'pt.2 . 2.50
13 JaD,CAd,'Hoodoo Bash,'pt.1 . . 2.50
14 JaD,CAd,'Hoodoo Bash,'pt.2 . . 2.50
15 JaD,CAd,'Hoodoo Bash,'pt.3 . . 2.50
16 Mask of Shadows ripped out . . 2.50
17 Mask of Shadows,pt.2 . . . . 2.50
18 Claudine kidnapped? 2.50
19 pursuit of Mah 2.50
20 Deadside vortes. 2.50
VOLUME 3, 1999
1 DAn,ALa,48-pg. 3.95
2 . . . . 2.50
3 Flip-book 2.50
4 Flip-book 2.50
5 thru 7 . . . . @2.50

SHADOW OF THE TORTURER, THE
Innovation, 1991
1 thru 6 Gene Wolfe adapt. . . . . @2.00

SHADOW RAVEN
Poc-It Comics, 1995
1 I:Shadow Raven. 2.95

SHADOW REAVERS
Black Bull Entertainment, 2001
1 Nel,KM(c). 4.00
1a variant TDr(c) 12.00
2 Nel,GF(c) 3.00
2a variant TDr(c) 5.00
3 Nel. 3.00
3a variant TDr(c) 5.00
4 Nel. 3.00
4a variant limited master edition . . 5.00
5 Nel. 3.00
5a variant limited master edition . . 5.00
Preview Edition. 3.00
Preview Edition, limited. 5.00

SHADOW STATE
Preview Editions
1 and 2 B&W . . . . @2.50
Broadway, 1995
1 thru 4 F:BloodS.C.R.E.A.M. . . @2.50
5 JiS, 'Image Isn't Everything,' . . . 2.50
6 'Anger of Lovers' pt.1 . . . . 2.50
7 'Anger of Lovers' pt.2 . . . . 2.95

SHAFT
Maximum Press, 1997
1 RLd 2.50

SHAIANA
Entity, 1995
1 R:Shaiana from Aster 3.75
1a clear chromium. 8.00
1b Holochrome 10.00
2 Guardians of Earth 2.50

SHANGHAI BREEZE
1 . . . . 2.00

SHAOLIN
Black Tiger Press
1 I:Tiger. 2.95
2 I:Crane. 2.95

SHATTER
First, 1985–88
1 . . . . 3.00
2 . . . . 2.50
3 . . . . 2.50
4 and 5 . . . . @2.00
6 thru 14 . . . . @2.00
Spec. #1 Computer Comic 5.00
#1a 2nd Printing. 2.00

SHE-DEVILS ON WHEELS
Aircel
1 V:Man-Eaters 2.95
2 V:Man-Eaters 2.95
3 V:Man-Eaters 2.95

SHEENA: QUEEN OF THE JUNGLE
London Night
0 by Gabriel Cain & Wilson 3.00
0a Zebra Edition 5.00
0b Leopard Edition 5.00
0c Alligator Edition 5.00

ShadowMan Vol. 2, #9
© Acclaim

SHEENA: QUEEN OF THE JUNGLE: BOUND
London Night, 1998
1 (of 4) by Everette Hartsoe
 & Art Wetherell 3.00
1 ministry ed. 5.00
1 Leather retro edition 12.00

SHERIFF OF TOMBSTONE
Charlton Comics, 1958–61
1 AW,JSe. 100.00
2 . . . . 50.00
3 thru 10 . . . . @40.00
11 thru 17 . . . . @35.00

Shi (The Way of the Warrior) #2
© Crusade Entertainment

SHI (THE WAY OF THE WARRIOR)
Crusade Comics, 1994–97
1 BiT,HMo,I:Shi 9.00
2 BiT 5.00
2a BiT, reissue, new cover 2.95
3 BiT 5.00
4 BiT 4.00
5 V:Arashi 3.00
5a variant cover 6.00
6 V:Tomoe 3.00
7 V:Nara Warriors 3.00
8 New costume 3.00
9 thru 11 . . . . @3.00
12 'Way of the Warrior' concl, flip-
 book Angel Fire 5.00
TPB Shi:Way of the Warrior 12.95
TPB Vol. 1 revised rep.JuB(c) . . . 14.95
TPB Vol. 2, rep. #5–#8 . . . . . . 14.95
TPB rep. Shi #9–#12 & Shi vs.
 Tomoe 17.95
Spec. #1 Shi/Cyblade,Battle of the
 Independents (1995) 4.00
Spec.#1a Shi/Cyblade,variant(c). . . 6.00
Ashcan #1, sign & num. (2000). . . 10.00
1 signed Antiquities edition. 100.00
TPB Way of the Warrior, signed . . 14.95

SHI: THE SERIES
Crusade Entertainment, 1997
1 sequel to *Shi: Heaven and Earth*,
 F:Tomoe. 3.50

2 Unforgettable Fire, concl. 3.00
3 A Rock and a Hard Place, pt.1 . . 3.00
4 A Rock and a Hard Place, pt.2 . . 3.00
5 A Rock and a Hard Place, pt.3 . . 3.00
6 . . . . 3.00
7 Photographer's lucky picture . . . 3.00
8 V:Gemini Dawn twins 3.00
9 Bad Blood, pt.1 . . . . 3.00
9a variant BTi(c) 3.00
9b variant Ahn (c) 3.00
9c variant Kevin Lau (c) 3.00
10 Bad Blood, pt.2 . . . . 3.00
10a variant BTi(c) 3.00
10b variant Ahn (c) 3.00
10c variant Kevin Lau (c) 3.00
11 Bad Blood, pt.3 . . . . 3.00
12 The Dark Crusade, pt.1 (of 8) . . 3.00
13 The Dark Crusade, pt.2 (of 8) . . 3.00
14 The Dark Crusade, pt.3 (of 8) . . 3.00
15 The Dark Crusade, pt.4 (of 8) . . 3.00
16 The Dark Crusade, pt.5 (of 8) . . 3.00
1-shot The Essential Dark Crusade. 3.00
1-shot Shi:Five Year Celebration. . . 5.00
1-shotA,B,C,&D variant covers 5.00
#0 & Wolverine/Shi flip book 2.99
Spec. Shi/Vampirella,x-over(1997) . 2.95
Spec. Shi: Nightstalkers, VMk,
 F:T.C.B. (1997). 3.50
Spec. Shi: Masquerade (1997) 3.50
Spec. Shi: Art of War Tour Book
 Wizard Chicago con (1998) . . 5.95
G.I. Preview Edition (2001) 5.00
Spec. Through the Ashes (2001). . . 3.00
TPB Cover Gallery (2003). 30.00

SHI: AKAI
Crusade Entertainment, 2001
1 BTi, I:RAF Victoria Cross 3.00
1 antiques edition 100.00
Ashcan, signed & numbered 10.00

SHI: BLACK WHITE & RED
Crusade Entertainment, 1998
1 Night of the Rat, pt.1 . . . . 3.00
2 Night of the Rat, pt.2 . . . . 3.00
Coll. Ed. rep. #1–#2 . . . . 6.95

SHI: EAST WIND RAIN
Crusade Entertainment, 1997
1 BiT,MSo, fully painted 3.50
2 BiT, concl 3.50

SHI: HEAVEN AND EARTH
Crusade Entertainment, 1997
1 (of 3) BiT 2.95
1 variant cover 2.95
2 BiT 2.95
3 BiT 2.95
4 BiT 2.95
TPB rep. #1–#4 . . . . 15.95

SHI: HOT TARGET
Crusade Entertainment 2003
1 . . . . 3.00

SHI: PANDORA'S BOX
Avatar Press 2003
Preview Edition 16-pg. B&W 5.95
Preview BiT(c) 2.00
Preview prism foil (c) 12.95
1/2 prism foil (c) 12.95
1/2 royal blue (c) 75.00
1 BiT(c). 3.50
1a variant (c)s . . . . @3.50
1b prism foil (c) 12.95
1 royal blue edition 75.00

SHI: POISONED PARADISE
Avatar, 2002
Preview 16-pg., b&w. 2.00
Preview, Ron Adrian (c) 5.95
Preview, prism foil edition 12.95
1 (of 2) BiT,Karl Waller,Martin(c) . . 3.50
1a BiT(c) 3.50
1b Waller (c) 3.50
1c Wraparound exclusive (c) 3.50
1d royal blue (c) 75.00
1e Angel of Death (c) 5.95
1f Angel of Death ruby foil (c) . . . 8.95
1g prism (c). 12.95
2 BiT(c) 3.50
2a Martin (c) 3.50
2b Waller (c) 3.50
2c Shaw (c) 3.50
1/2 Blossom (c) 5.95
1/2 BTi(c) 3.95
1/2 Martin (c) 3.95
1/2 Waller (c) 3.95

SHI: REKISHI
Crusade Entertainment, 1997
1 (of 2) BiT 2.95
2 BiT, conclusion 2.95
Coll.Ed. Shi:Reshiki, sourcebook,
 MS(c). 4.95

SHI VS. TOMOE
Crusade, April, 1996
Spec. #1 BiT, double size 3.95
GN Unforgettable Fire, rep. 6.99

SHI-SENRYAKU
Crusade, 1995
1 BiT,R:Shi 3.00
1a variant cover 5.00
1 (of 3) 2nd edition 2.50
2 BiT,Arts of Warfare 3.00
2 2nd edition 2.50
3 BiT 3.00
3 2nd edition 2.50
TPB Rep.#1-#2. . . . . 12.95
TPB 13.95

SHI: YEAR OF THE SERPENT
Crusade Entertainment, 2001
Spec. Tour Book, B&W 5.00

SHI – YEAR OF THE DRAGON
Crusade Entertainment, 2000
1 (of 3) BiT 3.00
1a variant (c). 3.00
1b signed & numbered. 10.00
1c true colors ed. BiT 5.95
1d true colors ed. ruby red 29.95
2 Ana Tears (c) BiT 3.00
2a Death Incarnate (c) BiT 3.00
3 BTi, concl. 3.00
Ashcan, signed & numbered 10.00
Coll. Ed. Black,White,Red 6.95
GN #1 & #2 Black,White,Red . . . 6.00
Poster Book 3.00
TPB Year of the Dragon (2002) . . . 9.95

SHOCK SUSPENSE STORIES
Russ Cochran Press, 1992
1 reps.horror stories 2.00

Shock–Simpsons

COLOR PUB.

2 inc.Kickback 2.00
3 thru 4 . . . . @2.00
5 thru 7 reps.horror stories . . . . . @2.00
8 reps.horror stories 2.00

Gemstone
18 EC comics reprint 2.50
TPB Vol. 1 rebinding of #1–#5 . . . . 8.95
TPB Vol. 2 rebinding of #5–#10 . . 9.95
TPB Vol. 3 rebinding of #11–#15. . 8.95
TPB Vol. 4 rebinding of #16–#20 . . 9.95

SHOCK THE MONKEY
Millennium/Expand, 1995
1 Shock therapy 2.95

SHOGUNAUT
Firstlight
1 I:Shogunaut 2.95
2 V:Teckno Terror 2.95

SHOOTING STARS
1 . . . . 2.50

SHOTGUN MARY
Antarctic Press, 1995
1 I:Shotgun Mary. 2.95
1a with CD Soundtrack 8.95
1b Red Foil cover 8.00
2 . . . . 2.95
Spec. Shooting Gallery. 2.95
Spec. Deviltown 2.95
Spec. Deviltown, commem. (1999) . . 5.95

SHOTGUN MARY
Antarctic Press, 1998
1 by Herb Mallette & Kelsey
   Shannon 2.95
2 Early Days, pt.2 . . . . 2.95
3 Early Days, pt.3 . . . . 2.95

SHOTGUN MARY: BLOOD LORE
Antarctic Press, 1997
1 (of 4) by Herb Mallette
   & Neil Googe 2.95
2 . . . . 2.95
3 . . . . 2.95
4 concl. 2.95

SHOTGUN MARY: SON OF THE BEAST, DAUGHTER OF LIGHT
Antarctic Press, 1997
1 by Miljenko Horvatic
   & Esad T. Ribic. 2.95

SIEGEL & SHUSTER
Eclipse, 1984–85
1 . . . . 2.00
2 . . . . 2.00

SIGIL
Crossgen Comics, 2000
1 BKs 5.00
2 BKs 3.25
3 thru 5 BKs. . . . . @3.50
6 thru 12 BKs. . . . . @3.25
13 thru 18 MWa,SEa. . . . . @3.00
19 thru 30 SEa . . . . @2.95
31 thru 42 CDi(s) . . . . @2.95
TPB Vol. 1 . . . . 19.95

Shotgun Mary Blood Lore #4
© *Antarctic Press*

TPB Vol. 2 . . . . 19.95
TPB Vol. 3 The Lizard God 15.95
TPB Vol. 4 Hostage Planet 15.95
TPB Vol. 5 Death Match 15.95

SILENT MOBIUS
Viz, 1991–92
1 Katsumi 5.75
2 Katsumi vs. Spirit 5.25
3 Katsumi trapped within entity . . . 4.95
4 Nami vs. Dragon. 4.95
5 Kiddy vs. Wire 4.95
6 Search for Wire 4.95
GN 14.95

SILENT MOBIUS II
Viz, 1991
1 AMP Officers vs. Entities cont . . . 4.95
2 Entities in Amp H.Q. 4.95
3 V:Entity 4.95
4 The Esper Weapon 4.95
5 Last issue 4.95

SILENT MOBIUS III
Viz, 1992
1 F:Lebia/computer network 2.75
2 Lebia/computer link cont. 2.75
3 Lebia in danger 2.75
4 Return to Consciousness 2.75
5 Conclusion 2.75

SILKEN GHOST
Crossgen Comics 2003
1 (of 5) CDi 2.95
2 thru 5 . . . . @2.95

SILVERBACK
Comico, 1989–90
1 thru 3 . . . . @2.50

SILVER CROSS
Antarctic Press, 1997
1 (of 3) by Ben Dunn 2.95
2 . . . . 2.95

SILVERHEELS
Pacific, 1983–84
1 thru 3 . . . . @2.00

SILVER STAR
Pacific, 1983–84
1 thru 6 JK . . . . @2.00

SILVER STAR
Topps, 1993
1 w/Cards 2.95

SILVER STORM
Silverline, 1998
1 . . . . 2.95
2 . . . . 2.00
3 . . . . 2.00
4 . . . . 2.00

SIMPSONS COMICS
Bongo Comics, 1993
1 Colossal Horner 7.00
2 A:Sideshow Bob 4.00
3 F:Bart 4.00
4 F:Bart. 4.00
5 A:Itchy & Scratchy 4.00
6 F:Lisa 4.00
7 Circus in Town 4.00
8 Mr. Burns Voyage 4.00
9 Autobiographies 4.00
10 Tales of the Kwik-E-Mart 4.00
11 Ned Flanders Public Enemy 4.00
12 In the Blodome 4.00
13 F:Bart & Millhouse 4.00
14 Homer owns beer company 4.00
15 Waltons parody 4.00
16 thru 18 . . . . @4.00
19 thru 23 . . . . @4.00
24 . . . . 4.00
25 . . . . 4.00
26 Bart: action hero! 4.00
27 . . . . 4.00
28 Krusty the Clown, tax protest . . . 4.00
29 Captain Slamtastic 4.00
30 Montgomery Burns clones
    Smithers 4.00
31 Radioactive Homer 4.00
32 F:Lisa and her sax 4.00
33 Reality on the blink 4.00
34 C. Montgomery Burns
    International Games 4.00
35 20 kids 4.00
36 Three geeks computer company 4.00
37 Grampa Abe Simpson 4.00
38 chemically-engineered donuts . . 4.00
39 People vs. Homer Simpson
    and the Comic Book Guy 4.00
40 F:Krusty the Clown 4.00
41 Krusty Fun Factory 4.00
42 . . . . 4.00
43 Urban legends 4.00
44 substitute teachers 4.00
45 Santa's Little Helper 4.00
46 Sideshow Bob 4.00
47 30 years in the future 4.00
48 dating game 4.00
49 Lisa double feature 4.00
50 80-pg 6.00
51 Thanksgiving 2.50
52 Worst Christmas Ever 2.50
53 The Beer Boys 2.50
54 Homer drives tank to work 2.50
55 Simpson's new pool 2.50
56 New king of Sweden 2.50
57 Bart turns tattletale 2.50
58 Mayor Quimby scandal 2.50
59 Boy band phenomenon 2.50
60 F:Waylon Smithers 2.50
61 Control of print media 2.50
62 Bible stories 2.50
63 Golf fever 2.50
64 Who dispenses justice 2.50

CVA Page 658   All comics prices listed are for *Near Mint* condition.

Comics Values Annual — COLOR PUB. — Simpsons–Sludge

65 revolution in Bosqieverde...... 2.50
66 Set sail with Homer............ 2.50
67 Lisa beautifies Springfield..... 2.50
68 Money to Burns................. 2.50
69 Merchants of Vengeance........ 2.50
70 The Iliad...................... 2.50
71 F:Sideshow Cecil................ 2.50
72 Early retirement plan........... 2.50
73 collection give-away............ 2.50
74 Dr. the Clown.................. 2.50
75 Untold tales................... 2.50
76 Shakespeare................... 2.50
77 Sideshow Bob.................. 2.50
78 thru 85................... @2.50
86............................... 3.00
87 thru 88................... @2.50
TPB Rep.#1-#4................. 10.00
TPB Wing Ding, 120pg.......... 11.95
TPB Simpsons Comics on Parade
 (1998)........................ 11.95
TPB Simpsons Comics Big
 Bonanza..................... 11.95
TPB Comics A Go-Go............ 11.95
TPB Comics Extravaganza...... 10.00
TPB Bartman Best of the Best... 10.00
TPB Simpsons Comics Strike Back 10.95
TPB Comics Wing Ding.......... 11.95
TPB Simpsons Unchained (2002).. 14.95
TPB Madness................... 14.95
Comic Spectacular,Vol.1 Rep...... 10.00
Comic Spectacular,Vol.2 Rep...... 10.00

SIMPSONS COMICS & STORIES
Welsh Publishing, 1993
1 with poster..................... 4.00
1a without poster................ 2.50

Bongo Comics, 1998
1 F:Bartman, Itchy & Scratchy.... 2.95

SINTHIA
Lightning, 1997
1A by Joseph Adam, Daughter
 of Lucifer.................... 3.00
1B............................... 3.00
1c Platinum Edition............... 9.95
1d Autographed Edition........... 9.95
2 Sisters of Darkness............ 2.95
2a variant cover................. 2.95
3 Wagner(c)..................... 2.95
3a variant Abrams cover.......... 2.95
3b deluxe variant cover.......... 9.95

4 Wagner(c)..................... 2.95
4a variant John Cleary cover..... 2.95

SIREN
Malibu Ultraverse, 1995
Infinity V:War Machine............ 2.50
1 V:War Machine.................. 2.25
1a Computer painted cover....... 2.25
2 Phoenix flip issue.............. 2.25
3 Phoenix Resurrection........... 2.25
Spec. #1 O:Siren................. 2.25

SISTERS OF MERCY
Maximum, 1995–96
1................................ 2.50
1a variant(c).................... 2.50
2................................ 2.50
3................................ 2.50

No Mercy Comics
4................................ 2.50
5................................ 2.50
TPB rep. #1–#5.................. 14.95

SISTERS OF MERCY: PARADISE LOST
London Night, 1997
1 by Ricki Rockett & Mark Williams 2.50
2................................ 2.50
3................................ 2.50
4................................ 2.50

SISTERS OF MERCY: WHEN RAZORS CRY CRIMSON TEARS
No Mercy Comics, 1996
1................................ 2.50

SIX MILLION DOLLAR MAN, THE
Charlton, June, 1976
1 JSon,Lee Majors Ph(c)........ 35.00
2 NA(c),JSon,Ph(c)............. 20.00
3 Ph(c) HC,NA................. 22.00
4 thru 9 Ph(c)............... @20.00

666: MARK OF THE BEAST
Fleetway/Quality, 1986
1 I:Fludd, BU:Wolfie Smith....... 2.00
2 thru 18.................... @2.00

SIX STRING SAMURAI
Awesome Entertainment, 1998
1 RLe............................ 2.95

SKATEMAN
Pacific, 1983
1 NA............................. 2.00

SKY WOLF
Eclipse, 1988
1 V:Baron Von Tundra............ 2.00
2 TL,V:Baron Von Tundra......... 2.00
3 TL,cont. in Airboy #41......... 2.00

SLAINE THE BERSERKER
Quality, 1987–89
1 thru 14.................... @2.00

15/16............................ 2.00
17............................... 2.00
18/19............................ 2.00
20............................... 2.00
Becomes:

SLAINE THE KING
Quality, 1989
21 thru 26................... @2.00

SLAINE
Fleetway
1 thru 4 SBs,From 2000 AD.... @4.95

SLAINE THE HORNED GOD
Egmont Fleetway, 1998
1 (of 3) Pat Millagan & SBs, 68pg.. 7.00
2 (of 3) Pat Millagan & SBs, 68pg.. 7.00
3 68-pg., conclusion............ 7.00

SLEEPER
Wildstorm/DC Jan. 2003
1 SeP,F:Holden Carver........... 2.95
2 SeP........................... 2.95
3 SeP,O:Miss Misery............. 2.95
4 SeP,behind the curtain......... 2.95
5 SeP,F:Holden Carver........... 2.95
6 SeP,Holden's past............. 2.95
7 SeP,things get worse.......... 2.95
8 SeP,Doppelganger............. 2.95
9 SeP,secret records............ 2.95
10 SeP.......................... 2.95
11 SeP.......................... 2.95

SLIDERS
Valiant 1996
1................................ 2.50
2................................ 2.50

SLIDERS: DARKEST HOUR
1 DGC,DG........................ 2.50
2 DGC,DG........................ 2.50
3 DGC,DG, Concl................ 2.50
Spec. RgM, Montezuma IV rules the
 world........................ 3.95
Spec. #2 'Secrets'............... 3.95
TPB from TV show................ 9.00

SLIDERS: ULTIMATUM
Valiant 1996
1 & 2........................ @2.50

SLIMER
Now, 1989
1................................ 2.50
2 thru 15.................... @2.00
Becomes:

SLIMER & REAL GHOSTBUSTERS
16 thru 18................... @2.00

SLUDGE
Malibu Ultraverse, 1993–94
1 BWS,I:Sludge,BU:I:Rune......... 2.75
1a Ultra-Limited................. 5.00
2 AaL,I:Bloodstorm............... 2.25
3 AaL,V:River Men................ 2.50
4 AaL,Origins Month, V:Alligator.. 2.25
5 AaL,V:Garret Whale............. 2.25
6 AaL,A:Dragon Fang,Lord
 Pumpkin...................... 2.25

Siren #3
© Malibu

All comics prices listed are for *Near Mint* condition.

Sludge–Solar / COLOR PUB.

7 V:Frank Hoag 2.25
8 AaL,V:Monsters 2.25
9 AaL,O:Sludge 2.25
10 AaL,O:Sludge 2.25
11 AaL,V:Bash Brothers 2.25
12 AaL,V:Prime, w/flip book
 w/Ultraverse Premiere #8 . . . . . 3.50
13 . . . . 2.25
Red X-Mas 2.50

SMAX
Wildstorm/DC Aug. 2003
1 (of 5) AMo,F:Jeff Smax 2.95
2 AMo,O:Smax 2.95
3 AMo,funeral 2.95

SMILEY
Chaos! Comics, 1998
1 the Psychotic Button 2.95
Spec. Smiley Anti-Holiday Spec. . . . 2.95
Spec. Smiley Psychotic Button's
 Spring Break Road Trip 2.95
Spec. Whacky Wrestling Spec. 2.95

SMOKE
What's Next Entertainment, 2000
1 (of 12) by Ty Rawls 3.00
2 . . . . 3.25
3 . . . . 3.25
4 . . . . 2.95
5 . . . . 3.25
TPB Vol. 1 . . . . 19.95

SNAGGLEPUSS
Gold Key, 1962–63
1 . . . . 125.00
2 . . . . 100.00
3 . . . . 100.00
4 . . . . 100.00

SNAKE PLISSKEN CHRONICLES
Crossgen Comics 2003
1 . . . . 3.00
2 . . . . 3.00
3 . . . . 3.00

SNAK POSSE
HCom, 1994
1 . . . . 2.00
2 . . . . 2.00

SNOOPER AND BLABBER DETECTIVES
Gold Key, 1962–63
1 . . . . 125.00
2 . . . . 100.00
3 . . . . 100.00

SNOW WHITE & SEVEN DWARFS GOLDEN ANNIVERSARY
Gladstone, 1987
1 w/poster & stickers 24.00

SOAP OPERA ROMANCES
Charlton, 1982–83
1 . . . . 40.00
2 thru 5 . . . . @30.00

SO DARK THE ROSE
CFD, 1995
1 Fully Painted 2.95

SOJOURN
Dreamer Comics, 1998
1 by Jim Somerville, Stranger
 & Stranger, pt.1 . . . . 2.95
2 Stranger & Stranger, pt.2 . . . . . . 2.95
3 Malice in Wonderland 2.95
4 A Game of Conscience, pt.1 . . . . 2.95
5 A Game of Conscience, pt.2 . . . . 2.10
6 A Game of Conscience, pt.3 . . . . 3.15
7 A Game of Conscience, pt.4 . . . . 3.15
8 The Hunt 3.15
9 The Hunt, pt.2 . . . . 3.15
10 The Hunt, Bloodied 3.15

SOJOURN
Crossgen Comics, 2001
1 RMz 7.00
2 thru 5 RMz . . . . @5.00
6 thru 17 RMz 3.00
18 thru 24 . . . . @3.00
25 IEd 1.00
26 thru 29 . . . . @2.95
Collected Ed. #1 . . . . 4.00
Prequel RMz 3.00
TPB Vol. 1 rep. #1–#6 . . . . 19.95
TPB Vol. 2 Dragon's Tale 15.95
TPB Traveler Vol. 2 Dragon's Tale . 9.95
TPB Vol. 3 The Warrior's Tale . . . 15.95
TPB Vol. 4 The Thief's Tale 15.95

SOLAR: HELL ON EARTH
Acclaim 1997
1 (of 4) CPr,DCw,Seleski twins
 have power of God 2.50
2 CPr,Goat Month prelude 2.50
3 CPr,RT,V:Jimmy Six 2.50
4 CPr 2.50

SOLAR: MAN OF THE ATOM
Valiant 1991
1 BWS,DP,BL,B:2nd Death B:Alpha
 & Omega 4.00
2 BWS,DP,BL,V:Dr Solar 3.00
3 BWS,DP,BL,V:Harada I:Harbinger
 Foundation 3.00
4 BWS,DP,BL,E:2nd Death V:Dr
 Solar 2.50
5 BWS,EC,V:Alien Armada 2.50
6 BWS,DP,SDr, V:Alien Armada X-
 O Armor 2.50
7 BWS,DP,SDr, V:Alien Armada X-
 O Armor 2.50
8 BWS,V:Dragon of Bangkok 2.50
9 BWS,DP,SDr, V:Erica's Baby . . . 2.50
10 BWS,DP,SDr,JDx,I:Eternal
 Warrior,E:Alpha&Omega 3.00
10a 2nd printing . . . .
11 SDr,A:Eternal Warrior, Prequel
 to Unity #0 . . . . 3.00
12 SDr,FM(c),Unity#9,O:Pierce,
 Albert 2.50
13 DP,SDr,WS(c),Unity #17,
 V:Pierce 2.50
14 DP,SDr,I:Bender (becomes
 Dr.Eclipse) 3.00
15 SD,V:Bender 3.00
16 Solar moves to California 2.50
17 SDr(i),V:X-O Manowar 2.50
18 SDr(i),A:X-Manowar 2.50
19 SDr(i),V:Videogame 2.50

Solar, Man of the Atom #19
© Valiant

20 SDr(i),Dawn of the Malevolence. 2.50
21 SDr(i),Master Darque 2.50
22 SDr(i),V:Master Darque,A:
 Bender(Dr.Eclipse) 2.50
23 SDr(i),JQ(c),V:Master
 Darque,I:Solar War God 2.50
24 SDr(i),A:Solar War God 2.50
25 V:Dr.Eclpise 2.25
26 Phil and Gayle on vaction 2.25
27 in Austrialia 2.25
28 A:Solar War God 2.25
29 KVH(s),JP(i),Valiant Vision,
 A:Solar War God 2.50
30 KVH(s),JP,V:Energy Parasite . . . 2.25
31 KVH(s),JP,Christmas Issue 2.25
32 KVH(s),JP,Parent's Night 2.25
33 KVH(s),PGr,JP,B:Solar the
 Destroyer,w/Valiant Era card. . . 2.25
34 KVH(s),PGr,V:Spider Alien 2.25
35 KVH(s),PGr,JP,E:Solar the
 Destroyer,Valiant Vision 2.25
36 KVH(s),PGr,JP,B:Revenge times
 two,V:Doctor Eclipse, Ravenus. 2.25
37 PGr,JP,E:Revenge times two,
 V:Doctor Eclipse,Ravenus 2.25
38 PGr,JP,Chaos Effect-Epsilon#1 . 2.25
39 . . . . 2.25
40 . . . . 2.25
41 . . . . 2.25
42 Elements of Evil,pt.1 . . . . 2.25
43 Elements of Evil,pt.2 . . . . 2.25
44 I:New Character 2.25
45 Explores Powers 2.25
46 I:The Sentry 2.25
47 DJu,DG,Brave New World,pt.2 . . 2.25
48 DJu,DG,Brave New World,pt.3 . . 2.25
49 DJu,DG,Brave New World,pt.4 . . 2.25
50 DJu,DG,Brave New World,pt.5 . . 2.25
51 I:Aliens on the Moon 2.25
52 Solar Saves Earth 2.25
53 I:Marauder 2.25
54 V:Marauder 2.25
55 I:Black Star 2.25
56 V:Black Star 2.25
57 A:Armorines 2.25
58 I:Atman, The Inquisitor 2.25
59 and 60 KG . . . . @2.25
TPB #0 JiS,BWS,BL,Alpha and
 Omega rep. from Solar #1–#10 9.95
TPB #1 JiS,BWS,GL,V:Doctor Solar
 rep. from Solar #1–#4 . . . . 9.95

SOLDIERS OF FREEDOM
Americomics, 1987
1	2.00
2	2.00

SOLITAIRE
Malibu Ultraverse, 1993–94
1 black bagged edition with playing card: Ace of Clubs, Diamonds, Hearts or Spades	2.75
1d Newsstand edition,no card	2.25
2 GJ(s),JJ,Break-Thru x-over, V:Moon Man	2.25
3 Origins Month, I:Monkey-Woman	2.25
4 O:Solitaire	2.25
5 JJ,V:Djinn	2.25
6 JJ,V:Lone	2.25
7 JJ,I:Double Edge	2.25
8 GJ,I:Degenerate	2.25
9 GJ,Degenerate Rafferty	2.25
10 Hostile Takeover #2	2.25
11 V:Djinn	2.25
12 V:Anton Lowe	2.25

SOLOMON KANE
Blackthorne
1 3-D Special	2.50
2 3-D Special	2.50
1 thru 4	@2.50

SOLUS
Crossgen Comics 2003
1 BKs,GP,RM,48-pg	2.95
2 thru 9	@2.95
TPB Vol. 1 Genesis	15.95

Solution #1
© Malibu

SOLUTION
Malibu Ultraverse, 1993–95
0 DaR,O:Solution	4.00
1 DaR,I:Solution	2.50
1a foil cover	4.00
2 DaR,BWS,V:Rex Mundi,Quatro, BU:Rune	2.50
3 DaR,A:Hardcase,Choice	2.50
4 DaR,Break-Thru x-over, A:Hardcase,Choice	2.50
5 F:Dropkick	2.25
6 B:O:Solution	2.25
7 KM,O:Solution	2.25
8 KM(c),E:O:Solution	2.25
9 F:Shadowmage	2.25
10 V:Vyr	2.25
11 V:Vorlexx	2.25
12 JHi	2.25
13 Hostile Takeover,pt.3	2.25
14 old foes	2.25
15 V:Casino	2.25
16 Flip/UltraverePremiere#10	3.50
17 F:Casino, Dragons Claws	2.50

SOMERSET HOLMES
Pacific, 1983–84
1 BA,AW,I:Cliff Hanger & Somerset Holmes	2.50
2 thru 4 BA,AW	@2.00

Eclipse, 1984
5 BA,AW	2.00
6 BA	2.00

SONIC THE HEDGEHOG
Archie Publications, 1993
1 A:Mobius,V:Robotnik	20.00
2	7.00
3 thru 6	@6.00
7 thru 10	@5.00
11 thru 30	@3.00
31 thru 39	@3.00
40 thru 54	@3.00
55 thru 78	@2.00
79 and 80	@1.80
81 thru 99	@2.00
100	2.00
101 thru 116	@2.00
117 thru 130	@2.20
GN Sonic Firsts, rep.#0, #1/4 ashcan,#3,#4,#13	4.95
Sonic Live Spec.#1	2.00

SONIC QUEST: THE DEATH EGG SAGA
Archie Comics, 1997
1 (of 3) by Mike Gallagher & MaG, cont. from Sonic the Hedgehog #41	2.00
2 and 3	@2.00

SONIC THE HEDGEHOG PRESENTS KNUCKLES CHASTIC
Archie Comics, 1995
1 I:New Heroes	2.00
Sonic Versus Knuckles Battle Royal Spec.#1	2.00

SONIC THE HEDGEHOG PRESENTS TAILS
Archie Comics, 1995
1 F:Tails	2.00
2 F:Tails	2.00

SONIC'S FRIENDLY NEMESIS: KNUCKLES
Archie Comics, 1996
1	2.00

SONIC SUPER SPECIAL
Archie Comics, 1997
1 Brave New World	2.00
3 Sonic Firsts	2.00
4 The Return of the King	2.25
5 Sonic Kids	2.25
6 Expanded Sonic #50, 48pg	2.25
7 F:Shadowhawk, The Maxx, Savage Dragon	2.25
8 four stories, 48-pg	2.25
9 R:Sonic Kids	2.25
10 Some Enchantra Evening	2.25
11	2.30
12 48-pg	2.50
13 thru 15	@2.50

SON OF MUTANT WORLD
Fantagor, 1990
1 BA	2.00
2	2.00

SOULMAN
Quantum Comics, 1998
1	2.95
2	2.95
3 16-pg.	2.95
4 16-pg.	2.95
5 24-pg.	2.95

SOULQUEST
Innovation, 1989
1 BA	3.95

SOUPY SALES COMIC BOOK
Archie Publications, 1965
1	135.00

SPACE ADVENTURES
Charlton, 1967–79, Volume 3
1 (#60) O&I:Paul Mann & The Saucers From the Future	75.00
2 thru 8 (1968–69)	@40.00
9 thru 13 (1978–79)	@15.00

SPACE: ABOVE AND BEYOND
Topps, 1995
1 thru 3 TV pilot adaptation	@2.95

SPACE: ABOVE AND BEYOND— THE GAUNTLET
Topps, 1996
1 and 2	@2.95

SPACE ARK
AC Comics, 1985–87
1	3.00
2	2.00

SPACE FAMILY ROBINSON
Gold Key, Dec., 1962–69
1 DSp	350.00
2	200.00
3	125.00
4	125.00
5	125.00
6 B:Captain Venture.	100.00
7	100.00
8	100.00
9	100.00
10	100.00
11 thru 20	@75.00
21 thru 36	@45.00

SPACE GHOST
Gold Key, March, 1967
1 . . . . 500.00

SPACE GHOST
Comico, 1987
1 SR,V:Robot Master. 6.00

SPACE GIANTS, THE
Pyramid Comics, 1997
0 . . . . 2.00
0a deluxe 2.25
1 . . . . 2.00
3 by Jeff Newman 2.00

SPACE MAN
Dell Publishing Co., 1962–72
1 . . . . 125.00
2 . . . . 60.00
3 . . . . 60.00
4 . . . . 45.00
5 . . . . 45.00
6 . . . . 45.00
7 . . . . 45.00
8 . . . . 45.00
9 . . . . 45.00
10 . . . . 45.00

SPACE: 1999
Charlton, 1975–76
1 . . . . 25.00
2 JSon,'Survival' 22.00
3 JBy,'Bring Them Back Alive' . . . 15.00
4 JBy. 15.00
5 JBy. 15.00
6 JBy. 15.00
7 . . . . 15.00
8 B&W. 15.00

SPACE: 1999
A Plus Comics
1 GM,JBy 2.50

SPACE USAGI
Mirage, 1993
1 thru 3 From TMNT . . . . @2.75

SPACE WAR
Charlton Comics, Oct., 1959
1 . . . . 200.00
2 . . . . 100.00
3 . . . . 90.00
4 SD,SD(c) 200.00
5 SD,SD(c) 200.00
6 SD 200.00
7 . . . . 75.00
8 SD,SD(c) 200.00
9 . . . . 75.00
10 SD,SD(c) 200.00
11 . . . . 75.00
12 . . . . 75.00
13 thru 15 . . . . @75.00
16 thru 27 . . . . @50.00
Becomes:

FIGHTIN' FIVE
28 SD,SD(c). 60.00
29 SD,SD(c). 60.00
30 SD,SD(c). 75.00
31 SD,SD(c). 75.00
32 . . . . 20.00
33 SD,SD(c). 75.00
34 Sd,SD(c) 75.00

SPECTER 7
Antarctic Press 2002
1 (of 3) by Craig Babiar 4.95
2 and 3 . . . . @4.95

SPECTRUM COMICS PRESENTS
Spectrum, 1983
1 I:Survivors 3.50

SPECWAR
Peter Four Productions, 2002
1 . . . . 3.25
2 thru 5 . . . . @3.25
6 thru 8 . . . . @3.25

SPEED RACER
Now, 1987–90
1 . . . . 3.50
1a 2nd printing 2.00
2 thru 33 . . . . @2.00
34 thru 38 . . . . @2.00
Spec. #1 . . . . 2.50
#1 2nd printing 2.00
Spec. #2. . . . . 3.50
Classics, Vol #2 . . . . 3.95
Classics, Vol #3 . . . . 3.95

[2nd Series]
1 R:Speed Racer. 2.00
2 . . . . 2.00
3 V:Giant Crab 2.00
4 . . . . 2.00
5 Racer-X 2.00
6 . . . . 2.00
7 . . . . 2.00

SPEED RACER
WildStorm/DC, 1999
1 Demon on Wheels 2.50
2 . . . . 2.50
3 concl. 2.50
TPB Born to Race 9.95
TPB Original Manga 9.95

SPELLBINDERS
Quality, 1986–88
1 Nemesis the Warlock 2.00
2 thru 11 Nemesis the Warlock. . @2.00

S.P.I.C.E.
Awesome Entertainment, 1998
1 RLe,JLb,F:Kaboom. 2.50

SPIDER
Eclipse, 1991
1 TT,'Blood Dance' 7.00
2 TT,'Blood Mark' 6.00
3 TT,The Spider Unmasked 5.50

SPIDER: REIGN OF THE VAMPIRE KING
Eclipse, 1992
1 TT,I:Legion of Vermin 5.25
2 thru 4 TT. . . . . @2.50

SPIDERFEMME
Personality
1 Rep. parody 2.50

SPIDER-MAN/BADROCK
Maximum Press, 1997
1 (of 2) DJu,MMy x-over 3.00
2 DJu,DaF x-over 3.00

SPIRAL PATH
Eclipse, 1986
1 V:Tairngir 2.00
2 V:King Artuk 2.00

SPIRIT
Harvey, 1966
1 WE,O:Spirit. 100.00
2 WE,O:The Octopus. 75.00

Spirit #4
© Kitchen Sink

SPIRIT, THE
Kitchen Sink, 1983–92
1 WE(c) (1983) 5.25
2 WE(c). 4.25
3 WE(c) (1984) 4.00
4 WE(c) 4.00
5 WE(c) 3.00
6 WE(c) 3.00
7 WE(c) 3.00
8 thru 11 WE(c) (1985). . . . . . . @3.00
See: B&W Pub. section

SPIRIT, THE: THE NEW ADVENTURES
Kitchen Sink, 1997
1 AMo,DGb 3.95
2 Eisner/Stout cover 3.50
2a Eisner/Schultz cover 3.50
3 AMo,Last Night I Dreamed of
   Dr. Cobra 3.50
4 Dr. Broca von Bitelbaum 3.50
5 Cursed Beauty 3.50
6 Swami Vashti Bubu. 3.50
7 Central City 3.50
8 by Joe Lansdale 3.50
9 . . . . 3.50
10 CAd,BRa 3.50

SPIRIT OF THE AMAZON
NW Studios 2002
1 . . . . 2.95
2 thru 7 . . . . @2.95

Comics Values Annual — COLOR PUB. — Spooky–Starslayer

SPOOKY HAUNTED HOUSE
Harvey Publications, 1972–75
1 .... 40.00
2 .... 30.00
3 thru 5 .... @30.00
6 thru 10 .... @25.00
11 thru 15 .... @20.00

SPOOKY SPOOKTOWN
Harvey Publications, 1966–76
1 B:Casper,Spooky,68 pgs..... 225.00
2 .... 125.00
3 .... 75.00
4 .... 75.00
5 .... 75.00
6 thru 10 .... @60.00
11 thru 20 .... @40.00
21 thru 30 .... @40.00
31 thru 39 E:68 pgs. ...... @35.00
40 thru 45 .... @25.00
46 thru 66 .... @15.00

SPYMAN
Harvey, 1966
1 GT,JSo,1st prof work,
  I:Spyman 100.00
2 DAy,JSo,V:Cyclops 75.00
3 .... 60.00

SQUAD, THE
Malibu
0-A Hardcase's old team 2.50
0-B 2.50
0-C L.A.Riots 2.50

SQUALOR
First, 1989
1 .... 2.75
2 .... 2.75
3 .... 2.75

STAINLESS STEEL RAT
Eagle, 1986
1 Harry Harrison adapt. 2.25
2 thru 6 .... @2.00

STAR BLAZERS
Comico, 1989
1 .... 3.00
2 .... 2.00
3 .... 2.00
4 .... 2.00

[2nd Series]
1 .... 2.00
2 .... 2.00
3 thru 5 .... @2.50

STARBLAZERS
Argo Press, 1995
0 Battleship Yamato 2.95
1 F:Dereck Wildstar 2.95
2 After the Comet War 2.95
3 .... 2.95
4 TEI 2.95
5 .... 2.95
6 .... 2.95
7 Icarus, pt.2 .... 2.95
8 .... 2.95
9 .... 2.95
10 .... 2.95
11 .... 2.95
12 Nova captured 2.95

STARFORCE SIX SPECIAL
AC Comics, 1984
1 .... 2.00

Stargate #3
© Entity Comics

STARGATE
Entity Comics, 1996
1 .... 2.95
2 .... 2.95
3 .... 2.95
4 (of 4) 2.95
4a deluxe limited edition 3.50

STARGATE: DOOMSDAY WORLD
Entity Comics, 1996
1 new crew explores 2nd StarGate 2.95
1 prism-foil edition 3.50
2 .... 2.95
3 .... 2.95
3 deluxe 3.50

STARGATE SG1
Avatar 2003
Convention Spec 3.00
Convention Spec. Photo (c) 3.95
Spec. First Prime Edition 5.95

STARGODS
Antarctic Press, 1998
1 by Zachary, Clark & Beaty ... 2.95
1a deluxe 5.95
2 The Golden Bow 2.95
2a deluxe, with poster 5.95
Spec. Stargods Visions 2.95

STARK RAVEN
Hardline Studios, 2000
1 The Screaming Rain,pt.1 ..... 2.95
2 The Screaming Rain,pt.2 ..... 2.95
3 .... 2.95

Endless Horizons, 2000
4 .... 2.95
5 .... 2.95
6 Ken Kelly (c) 2.95
7 .... 2.95
8 .... 2.95

STAR MASTERS
AC Comics, 1994
1 .... 2.00

STAR REACH CLASSICS
Eclipse, 1984
1 JSn,NA(r) 2.00
2 AN 2.00
3 HC 2.00
4 FB(r) 2.00
5 .... 2.00
6 .... 2.00

STAR SEED
See: POWERS THAT BE

STAR SLAMMERS
Malibu Bravura, 1994
1 WS(a&s) 2.75
2 WS(a&s),F:Meredith 2.75
3 WS(a&s) 2.50
4 WS(a&s) 2.50
5 WS,Rojas Choice 2.50

STARSLAYER
Pacific, 1982–83
1 MGr,O:Starslayer 4.00
2 MGr,DSt,I:Rocketeer 10.00
3 DSt,MGr,A:Rocketeer(2ndApp.) . 6.00
4 MGr,Baraka Kuhr 2.00
5 MGr,SA,A:Groo 7.00
6 MGr.conclusion story 2.00

First, 1983–85
7 MGr layouts 2.00
8 MGr layouts, MG 2.00
9 MGr layouts, MG 2.25
10 TT,MG,I:Grimjack 4.00
11 TT,MG,A:Grimjack 2.00
12 TT,MG,A:Grimjack 2.00
13 TT,MG,A:Grimjack 2.00
14 TT,A:Grimjack 2.00
15 TT,A:Grimjack 2.00
16 TT,A:Grimjack 2.00
17 TT,A:Grimjack 2.00
18 TT,Grimjack x-over 2.00
19 TT,TS,A:Black Flame 2.00
20 TT,TS,A:Black Flame 2.00
21 TT,TS,A:Black Flame 2.00
22 TT,TS,A:Black Flame 2.00
23 TT,TS,A:Black Flame 2.00
24 TT,TS,A:Black Flame 2.00
25 TS,A:Black Flame 2.00
26 TS,Black Flame full story .. 2.00
27 A:Black Flame 2.00
28 A:Black Flame 2.00
29 TS,A:Black Flame 2.00
30 TS,A:Black Flame 2.00
31 2nd Anniversary Issue 2.00
32 TS,A:Black Flame 2.00
33 TS,A:Black Flame 2.00
34 last issue 2.00
Graphic Novel 9.95

STARSLAYER DIRECTORS CUT
Windjammer 1995
1 R:Starslayer, Mike Grell 2.50
2 I:New Star Slayer 2.50
3 Jolly Rodger 2.50
4 V:Battle Droids 2.50
5 I:Baraka Kuhi 2.50
6 V:Valkyrie 2.50
7 MGr(c&a),Can Torin destroy? . 2.50
8 MGr(c&a),JAI, Can Torin live with
  his deeds?,final issue 2.50

All comics prices listed are for *Near Mint* condition.

STAR TREK
Gold Key, 1967–79
1 Planet of No Return 750.00
2 Devil's Isle of Space 500.00
3 Invasion of City Builders 250.00
4 Peril of Planet Quick Change . 250.00
5 Ghost Planet. 250.00
6 When Planets Collide 210.00
7 Voodoo Planet 225.00
8 Youth Trap 200.00
9 Legacy of Lazarus 200.00
10 Sceptre of the Sun. 175.00
11 Brain Shockers 175.00
12 Flight of the Buccaneer 150.00
13 Dark Traveler. 150.00
14 Enterprise Mutiny. 150.00
15 Museum a/t End of Time 150.00
16 Day of the Inquisitors. 150.00
17 Cosmic Cavemen 150.00
18 The Hijacked Planet. 150.00
19 The Haunted Asteroid 150.00
20 A World Gone Mad. 150.00
21 The Mummies of Heitus VII . . 100.00
22 Siege in Superspace 100.00
23 Child's Play 100.00
24 The Trial of Capt. Kirk 100.00
25 Dwarf Planet 100.00
26 The Perfect Dream 100.00
27 Ice Journey 100.00
28 The Mimicking Menace 100.00
29 rep. Star Trek #1 . . . . 100.00
30 Death of a Star 75.00
31 'The Final Truth'. 75.00
32 'The Animal People'. 75.00
33 'The Choice' 75.00
34 'The Psychocrystals' 75.00
35 rep. Star Trek #4 . . . . 75.00
36 'A Bomb in Time' 75.00
37 rep. Star Trek #5 . . . . 60.00
38 'One of our Captains
  is Missing' 60.00
39 'Prophet of Peace' 60.00
40 AMc,Furlough to Fury, A:
  Barbara McCoy 60.00
41 AMc,The Evictors. 60.00
42 'World Against Time' 60.00
43 'World Beneath the Waves' . . . 60.00
44 'Prince Traitor' 60.00
45 rep. Star Trek #7 . . . . 60.00
46 'Mr. Oracle' 60.00
47 AMc, 'This Tree Bears Bitter
  Fruit' 60.00
48 AMc,Murder on Enterprise 60.00
49 AMc, 'A Warp in Space' 60.00
50 AMc, 'The Planet of No Life' . . . 60.00
51 AMc,DestinationAnnihilation6 . . 50.00
52 AMc, 'And A Child Shall
  Lead Them' 50.00
53 AMc, 'What Fools..Mortals Be' . 50.00
54 AMc, 'Sport of Knaves' 50.00
55 AMc,A World Against Itself . . . 50.00
56 AMc,No Time Like The Past,
  A:Guardian of Forever 50.00
57 AMc, 'Spore of the Devil' 50.00
58 AMc, 'Brain Damaged Planet' . . 50.00
59 AMc, 'To Err is Vulcan' 50.00
60 AMc, 'The Empire Man' 50.00
61 AMc, 'Operation Con Game' . . . 50.00

STAR TREK
WildStorm/DC, April, 2001
TPB Other Realities, 192-pg. 14.95

STAR TREK: ALL OF ME
WildStorm/DC, Feb., 2000
1-shot AaL,RyE 5.95

COLOR PUB.

STAR TREK: DEEP SPACE NINE
Malibu Aug., 1993
1 Direct ed. 3.25
1a Photo(c). 3.00
1b Gold foil 5.00
2 w/skycap 3.50
3 Murder on DS9. . . . . 2.75
4 MiB(s),F:Bashir,Dax 2.75
5 MiB(s),V:Slaves 2.75
6 MiB(s),Three Stories. 2.75
7 F:Kira 2.75
8 B:Requiem 2.75
9 E:Requiem 2.75
10 Descendants 2.50
11 A Short Fuse 2.75
12 Baby on Board. 2.50
13 Problems with Odo 2.75
14 on Bejor. 2.75
15 mythologic dilemma 2.75
16 Shanghied 2.50
17 Voyager preview 2.50

Star Trek Deep Space Nine #16
© Malibu

18 V:Gwyn 2.50
19 Wormhole Mystery 2.50
20 Sisko Injured 2.50
21 Smugglers attack DS9 . . . . . 2.50
22 Commander Quark 2.50
23 Secret of the Lost Orb,pt.1 . . 2.50
24 Secret of the Lost Orb,pt.2 . . 2.50
25 Secret of the Lost Orb,pt.3 . . 2.50
26 Mudd's Pets,pt.1 . . . . 2.50
27 Mudd's Pets,pt.2 . . . . 2.50
28 F:Ensign Ro 2.50
29 F:Thomas Riker,Tuvok 2.50
30 F:Thomas Riker. 2.50
31 thru 32 . . . . @2.50
Ann.#1 Looking Glass. 3.95
Spec. #1Collision Course 3.50
Spec. #0 Terok Nor. 3.00

STAR TREK: DEEP SPACE NINE CELEBRITY SERIES: BLOOD AND HONOR
Malibu May, 1995
1 Mark Lenard(s) 2.95
2 Rules of Diplomacy. 2.95

Comics Values Annual

STAR TREK: DEEP SPACE NINE: LIGHTSTORM
Malibu Dec., 1994
1 Direct ed. 3.50
1a Silver foil 8.00

STAR TREK: DEEP SPACE NINE: HEARTS AND MINDS
Malibu [Limited Series] June, 1994
1 . . . . 3.00
2 . . . . 2.50
3 Into the Abyss,X-over preview. . . 2.50
4 final issue 2.50

STAR TREK: DEEP SPACE NINE: THE MAQUIS
Malibu [Limited Series] 1995
1 Federation Renegades 2.50
1a Newsstand, photo(c) 2.50
2 Garack. 2.50
3 F:Quark, Bashir 2.50

STAR TREK: DEEP SPACE NINE — N-VECTOR
WildStorm/DC, June, 2000
1 (of 4),F:Kira 2.50
2 sabotage 2.50
3 N-Vector viroid 2.50
4 F:Quark,concl. 2.50

STAR TREK: DEEP SPACE NINE/ THE NEXT GENERATION
Malibu Oct., 1994
1 Prophet & Losses,pt.2 . . . . 2.50
2 Prophet & Losses,pt.4 . . . . 2.50

STAR TREK: DIVIDED WE FALL
WildStorm/DC, May, 2001
1 (of 4) TNG & DS9 x-over 2.95
2 . . . . 2.95
3 . . . . 2.95
4 concl. 2.95

STAR TREK: ENTER THE WOLVES
WildStorm/DC, Feb., 2001
1-shot, 48-pg. 5.95

STAR TREK SPECIAL
WildStorm/DC, Dec., 2000
GN #1 64-pg. 6.95

STAR TREK: THE NEXT GENERATION
WildStorm/DC, 2000
GN Embrace the Wolf, 48-pg. 5.95
TPB Enemy Unseen, 224-pg. . . . 17.95
TPB The Gorn Crisis (2002) 17.95
TPB Forgiveness (2002) 17.95

STAR TREK: NEW FRONTIER — TIME MANAGEMENT
WildStorm/DC, 2001
GN PDd, novel adapt........... 5.95

STAR TREK: THE NEXT GENERATION — THE KILLING SHADOWS
WildStorm/DC, 2000
1 (of 4) V:Bodai Shin, assassin ... 2.25
2 V:Bodai Shin 2.25
3 V:Bodai Shin 2.25
4 concl...................... 2.50

STAR TREK: THE NEXT GENERATION — PERCHANCE TO DREAM
WildStorm/DC, 1999
1 (of 4) 2.50
2 thru 4 .... @2.50

STAR TREK: VOYAGER
Malibu
A V:Maquis.................... 2.75
Aa Newsstand, photo(c) 2.50
B conclusion.................. 2.75
Ba Newsstand, photo(c) 2.50

STAR TREK: VOYAGER
WildStorm/DC, May, 2000
Spec. Elite Force 5.95
Spec. Avalon Rising 5.95
TPB Encounters with the Unknown 19.95

STAR TREK: VOYAGER — PLANET KILLER
WildStorm/DC, Jan., 2001
1 (of 3) F:Kirk,Janeway 2.95
2 Doomsday Machine 2.95
3 concl...................... 2.95

STAR WARS IN 3-D
Blackthorne, 1987
1 thru 7 .... @2.50

STARWATCHERS
Valiant
1 MLe,DG,Chromium(c),Valiant Vision....................... 3.50

STARWOLVES: JUPITER RUN
1 .... 2.00

S.T.A.T.
Majestic, 1993
1 FdS(s),PhH,I:S.T.A.T.......... 2.50

STATIC-X
Chaos! Comics, 2002
1 by BnP, with CD-Rom......... 6.00
1a photo (c) with CD-Rom...... 6.00
1b collector's edition 20.00
Vol. 2
1 with CD-Rom 6.00
1a collector's edition 20.00

COLOR PUB.

STEALTH SQUAD
Petra Comics, 1993
1 I:Stealth Squad............. 2.50

STEAMPUNK
WildStorm/DC Cliffhanger, Feb., 2000
1 CBa........................ 2.50
1 chromium edition.............
2 CBa,V:Absinthe 2.50
3 CBa,F:Cole Blaquesmith........ 2.50
4 CBa,CBa(c) 2.50
4a variant JSC (c) (1:4) 2.50
4b variant JMd (c) (1:4) 2.50
4c variant HuR (c) (1:4) 2.50
5 CBa,V:Abbey Monsters........ 2.50
6 Mechanica Sundown,pt.1 ..... 2.50
7 Mechanica Sundown,pt.2 ..... 2.50
8 Mechanica Sundown,pt.3 ..... 2.50
9 Mambutu X, pt.1............ 2.50
10 Mambutu X, pt.2 .... 2.50
11 CBa, Stonehenge secret 2.50
12 CBa, 40-pg. final issue....... 3.50
TPB Drama Obscura 14.95
TPB Manimatron.............. 14.95

Steed And Mrs. Peel #1
© Eclipse

STEED & MRS. PEEL
Eclipse, 1990
1 IG,The Golden Game 4.95
2 IG,The Golden Game 4.95
3 IG,The Golden Game 4.95

STEEL CLAW
Quality, 1986
1 H:Ken Bulmer................ 2.00
2 .... 2.00
3 .... 2.00
4 .... 2.00

STEEL STERLING
Archie Publications, 1984 (formerly LANCELOT STRONG)
4 EB 2.00
5 EB 2.00
6 EB 2.00
7 EB 2.00

STEVE CANYON 3-D
Kitchen Sink, 1986
Milton Caniff & Peter Poplaski(c), w/glasses (1985) 2.00

STEVE ZODIAC & THE FIREBALL XL-5
Gold Key, Jan., 1964
1 .... 150.00

STING OF THE GREEN HORNET
Now, 1992
1 Polybagged w/trading card 2.75
2 inc.Full color poster 2.75
3 inc.Full color poster 2.75

STINGER
1 .... 2.00

STITCH
Samsons Comics
1 I:Stitch.................... 2.50

STONE COLD STEVE AUSTIN
Chaos! Comics, 1999
1 (of 4) Whoop Ass personified ... 2.95
1b Premium.................. 10.00
2 .... 2.95
3 .... 2.95
4 .... 2.95
1a thru 4a photo (c) .... @2.95
TPB Vol. 1 .... 12.95

STORMQUEST
Caliber, 1994
1 I:Stormquest................ 2.00
2 Time Stone................. 2.00
3 BU:Seeker 2.00
4 F:Shalimar 2.00
5 Reunion 2.00
6 V:Samuroids................ 2.00

STORM RIDERS
Comicsone.com, 2001
GN #1 by Wing Shing Ma, 178-pg.. 9.95
GN #2 127-pg................. 9.95
GN #3 thru #5, 120-pg........ @11.95
GN #6 thru #8, 120-pg........ @13.95
GN #9 thru #12............. @13.95

STORMWATCH: TEAM ACHILLES
WildStorm/DC,, July, 2002
Eye of the Storm
1 WPo,SW,new team............ 2.95
2 WPo,SW,extremists vs. U.N..... 2.95
3 WPo,SW,military action........ 2.95
4 WPo,SW,hunt for Ivana Baiul ... 2.95
5 WPo,F:The Authority.......... 2.95
6 WPo,F:The Authority.......... 2.95
7 MT,V:Ivana Baiul............. 2.95
8 F:Jukko Hamalainen........... 2.95
9 WPo,V:super-human........... 2.95
10 WPo 2.95
11 WPo 2.95
12 WPo,funeral............... 2.95
13 BSz,The Suiciders........... 2.95
14 WPo,Citizen Soldier.......... 2.95
15 The Suiciders 2.95

STRANGE DAYS
Eclipse, 1984–85
1	3.50
2	2.50
3	2.00

Strangers #9
© Malibu

STRANGERS, THE
Malibu Ultraverse 1993–95
1 I:Strangers	3.00
1a Ultra-Limited	4.00
1b Full Hologram(c)	5.00
2 A:J.D.Hunt,w/Ultraverse card	3.00
3 I:TNTNT	2.50
4 A:Hardcase	2.50
5 BWS,BU:Rune	2.50
6 J:Yrial,I:Deathwish	2.25
7 Break-Thru x-over	2.25
8 RHo,ANi,O:Solution	2.25
9 AV(i),I:Ulta Pirates	2.25
10 AV(i),V:Bastinado	2.25
11 in Alderson Disk	2.25
12 O:Yrial	2.25
13 (Ultraverse Premiere#4)	3.50
14	2.25
15 Zip-Zap, Yrail	2.25
16 Ultras, Teknight	2.25
17 Rafferty	2.25
18 Ultra Pirates	2.25
19 V:Pilgrim	2.25
20 Stranger Destroyed	2.25
21 A:Rex Mundi	2.50
22 SEt,V:Guy Hunt	2.50
23 SEt,RHo,V:Tabboo	2.50
24 RHo,SEt,V:Taboo	2.50
25 V:Godwheel Aliens	2.50
26 RHo,SEt,V:Aladdin	2.50
Ann.#1 Death	3.95
TPB rep. #1-#4	9.95
Ashcan 1 (signed)	8.00
Ashcan 1 (unsigned)	7.00

STRANGE SUSPENSE STORIES/ CAPTAIN ATOM
Charlton Comics, 1965
75 SD,O:CaptainAtom,1960Rep	175.00
76 SD, Capt.Atom,1960Rep	100.00
77 SD, Capt.Atom,1960Rep	100.00

Becomes:

CAPTAIN ATOM
Charlton Comics, 1965–67
78 SD, new stories begin	125.00
79 SD,I:Dr.Spectro	90.00
80 SD	90.00
81 SD,V:Dr.Spectro	90.00
82 SD,I:Nightshade,Ghost	90.00
83 SD,I:Ted Kord/Blue Beetle	75.00
84 SD,N:Captain Atom	75.00
85 SD,A:Blue Beetle,I:Punch & Jewelee	75.00
86 SD,A:Ghost, Blue Beetle	75.00
87 SD,JAp,A:Nightshade	75.00
88 SD/FMc,JAp,A:Nightshade	75.00
89 SD/FMc,JAp,A:Nightshade, Ghost, last issue Dec.,1967	75.00

STRAW MEN
Innovation
1 & 2	@2.00

STREET FIGHTER
Ocean, 1986–87
1 thru 3	@2.00

STREET FIGHTER
Malibu
1 thru 3 Based on Video Game	@3.00

STREET SHARKS
Archie Comics, 1995
1 & 2 Based on Cartoons	@2.00

STRIKE!
Eclipse, 1988
1 TL,RT,I&O:New Strike	2.00
2 TL,RT	2.00
3 TL,RT	2.00
4 TL,RT,V:Renegade CIA Agents	2.00
5 TL,RT,V:Alien Bugs	2.00
6 TL,RT,`Legacy of the Lost'	2.00
Spec. #1 Strike vs. Sgt. Strike TL,RT,`The Man'	2.00

STRIKEBACK
Malibu Bravura 1994–95
1	2.95
2	2.95
3 V:Doberman	2.95
4 V:Dragonryder Island	2.95
Spec.#1 KM,JRu,V:Dragon	3.50

STRIKER
Viz
1 thru 2	@2.75

STRIKEFORCE AMERICA
Comico, 1995
1 ScC,SK(c),I:StrikeforceAmerica	2.50
2 V:Superior-prisoner	2.95
3 Breakout, pt.2	2.95

[Volume 2], 1995
1 ScC,polybagged with Chrysalis promo card	2.95

STRONG MAN
AC Comics
1	2.95

STRONTIUM DOG
[Mini Series] Eagle, 1985
1 thru 4	@2.00

[Regular Series] Quality, 1988
Story line continued from 2000 A.D.
7 thru 14	@2.00
15/16	2.00
17	2.00
18/19	2.00
20 thru 29	@2.00
Spec.#1	2.00

[2nd Series], 1997
1 thru 6	@2.00

STRYKE
London Night Studios, 1995
0 I:Stryke	5.00
1	4.00

STUMBO THE GIANT
Blackthorne
1 3-D	2.50

STUMBO TINYTOWN
Harvey Publications, 1963–66
1	200.00
2	150.00
3	100.00
4	100.00
5	100.00
6 thru 13	@75.00

STUPID HEROES
Next, 1994
1 PeL(s),w/ 2 card-strip	2.75
2	2.75
3 F:Cinder	2.75

STURM THE TROOPER
1	2.00
2	2.00
3	2.00

SUBSPECIES
Eternity, 1991
1 Movie Adaptation	3.00
2 Movie Adaptation	2.50
3 Movie Adaptation	2.50
4 Movie Adaptation	2.50

SUN GLASSES AFTER DARK
Verotik, 1995
1	2.95
2 and 3	@2.95
4 thru 6	@3.95
6 fan club cover	5.00
? prequel, San Diego Con ed.	2.95

SUN-RUNNERS
Pacific, 1984
1	2.50
2	2.00
3	2.00

Eclipse, 1984–86
4	2.00
5	2.00
6 `Sins of the Father'	2.00
7 `Dark Side of Mark Dancer'	2.00
Summer Special #1	2.00

SUNSET CARSON
AC Comics
1 Based on Cowboy Star........ 5.00

SUPERBABES: FEMFORCE
AC Comics
1 Various Artists............... 5.00

SUPER CAR
Gold Key, 1962–63
1 .... 325.00
2 .... 200.00
3 .... 200.00
4 .... 225.00

SUPERCOPS
Now, 1990
1 thru 4 .... @2.00

SUPER COPS, THE
Red Circle, 1974
1 .... 3.00

SUPER GOOF
Gold Key, 1965–82
1 .... 60.00
2 thru 10 .... @30.00
11 thru 20 .... @25.00
21 thru 30 .... @20.00
31 thru 74 .... @15.00

SUPER HEROES VERSUS SUPERVILLIANS
Archie Publications, July, 1966
1 A:Flyman,Black Hood,The Web, The Shield 80.00

SUPERHUMAN SAMURAI SYBER SQUAD
Hamilton Comics, 1995
0 Based on TV Show........... 2.95

SUPER MARIO BROS.
Valiant 1991
1 thru 6 .... @2.00
Spec. #1................... 2.00

SUPERNAUT
Anarchy, 1997
1 (of 3) 3.00
1 gold logo 6.00
2 by Rob Hand, Hand of Doom ... 3.00
2a gold logo 6.00

SUPREME
Maximum Press, 1997
#1–#43 see Image
44 AMo, JoB, A:Glory 3.00
45 AMo, JoB, A:Glory 3.00
46 AMo,Suprema 3.00
47 AMo...................... 3.00
48 AMo...................... 2.50
49 AMo...................... 2.50
50 double size 3.95
51 .... 3.50
52A AMo, Book 1 .... 3.50
52B AMo, Book 2, continuation.... 3.50
53 AMo,CSp,AG,V:Omniman 3.00
54 AMo,CSp,AG,Ballad of Judy

Supreme #54 Awesome Entertainment © Awesome Entertainment

Jordan 3.00
55 AMo,CSp,AG,Silence At Gettysburg............... 3.00
56 AMo,CSp,AG,Reflections,pt.1 .. 3.00
57 AMo,CSp,AG,Reflections,pt.2 .. 3.00
58 AMo,CSp,AG,A World of His Own................. 3.00
59 AMo,CSp,AG,Professor Night of the Prism World 3.00
60 AMo,CSp,AG,F:Radar in Puppy Love..................... 3.00
61 AMo,CSp,AG,Meet Mr. Meteor.. 3.00
Coll.Ed.#1, rep.#1–#2........... 4.95
Coll.Ed.#2, rep.............. 4.95
Coll.Ed.#3 rep. #45–#46, AMo 4.95
Classic Col.Ed.#1,rep.#1&#2 ..... 5.95
Classic Col.Ed.#2,rep.#43&#44.... 5.95
TPB Secret Origins, rep......... 16.95
TPB Supreme Madness 14.95
TPB rep. #41–#46, AMo 14.95

SUPREME: THE RETURN
Awesome Entertainment, 1999
1 AMo,CSp,AG 3.00
1a variant AxR cover 6.95
2 AMo,JSn,................... 3.00
3 .... 3.00
4 .... 3.00
5 .... 2.99
6 New York City.............. 2.99
7 .... 2.99
8 .... 2.99

SURGE
Eclipse, 1984
1 A:DNAgents 3.00
2 A:DNAgents 2.00
3 A:DNAgents 3.00
4 A:DNAgents 3.00

SURVIVORS
Spectrum
1 Mag. size 5.00
2 .... 3.50
3 The Old One 2.50
4 .... 2.50

SURVIVORS
Fantagraphics
1 thru 3 .... @2.50

SUSPIRA: THE GREAT WORKING
Chaos! Comics, 1997
1 (of 4) PNa 2.95
2 PNa....................... 2.95
3 PNa....................... 2.95
4 PNa....................... 2.95

SWORD OF VALOR
A Plus Comics
1 .... 2.50
2 .... 2.50
3 .... 2.50
4 .... 2.50

SWORDS OF TEXAS
Eclipse, 1987
1 FH,New America 2.00
2 FH,V:Baja Badlands 2.00
3 FH,TY(c),V:Dogs of Danger 2.00
4 FH,V:Samurai Master......... 2.00

SYMBOLS OF JUSTICE
High Impact Studios, 1995
1 I:Granger,Justice,Rayven 2.95
2 V:Devil's Brigade 2.95

SYPHONS
Now, 1988
1 .... 2.00
2 thru 7 .... @2.00

SYPHONS: COUNTDOWN
Now, 1994
1 F:Brigade.................. 2.95
2 Led By Cross............... 2.95
3 Blown Cover................ 2.95
1995 Ann. Doomsday Device 2.95

SYPHONS: THE STARGATE STRATAGEM
Now, 1994
1 thru 3 .... @2.95

TALES CALCULATED TO DRIVE YOU BATS
Archie Publications, 1961–62
1 .... 200.00
2 .... 100.00
3 thru 6 .... @75.00

TALES FROM THE CRYPT
Gladstone, 1990–91
1 E.C.rep.AW/FF,GS 5.00
2 rep....................... 4.00
3 rep....................... 3.50
4 rep....................... 3.00
5 rep.TFTC #45............... 3.00
6 rep.TFTC #42............... 3.00

TALES FROM THE CRYPT
Russ Cochran Publ, 1992
1 rep. TFTC #31,CSS#12 .... 3.00
2 rep. TFTC #34,CSS#15 .... 3.00
3 rep. TFTC, CSS 3.00
4 rep. TFTC #43,CSS#18 .... 3.00
5 rep. TFTC,CSS#23........... 3.00

[2nd Series]
- 1 rep.horror stories 3.00
- 2 inc.The Maestro's Hand 3.00
- 3 thru 6 . . . . @3.00
- 7 thru 8 . . . . @3.00

Gemstone, 1996
- 16 thru 30 EC comics reprint . . . . @3.00

`Annuals`
- TPB Vol. 1 rebinding of #1–#5 . . . . 8.95
- TPB Vol. 2 rebinding of #5–#10 . . . 8.95
- TPB Vol. 3 rebinding of #11–#15 . . . 8.95
- TPB Vol. 4 rebinding of #16–#20 . . 12.95
- TPB Vol. 5 rebinding of #21–#24 . . 13.95

TALES OF EVIL
Atlas Comics, 1975
- 1 Werewolf 25.00
- 2 Bog Beast 20.00
- 3 Man-Monster 20.00

TALES OF TERROR
Eclipse, 1985–87
- 1 . . . . 3.00
- 2 `Claustrophobia' 2.00
- 3 GM,`Eyes in the Darkness' 2.00
- 4 TT,TY,JBo(c),`The Slasher' 2.00
- 5 `Back Forty,''Shoe Button Eyes' . 2.00
- 6 `Good Neighbors' 2.00
- 7 SBi,JBo,SK(i),`Video' 2.00
- 8 HB,`Revenant,''Food for Thought' 2.00
- 9 . . . . 2.00
- 10 . . . . 2.00
- 11 TT,JBo(c),`Black Cullen' 2.00
- 12 JBo,FH,`Last of the Vampires' . . 2.00
- 13 . . . . 2.00

TALES OF THE GREEN BERET
Dell Publishing Co., Jan., 1967
- 1 SG 50.00
- 2 thru 4 . . . . @40.00
- 5 . . . . 40.00

TALES OF THE GREEN HORNET
Now, 1990
- 1 NA(c),O:Green Hornet Pt.1 . . . . . 3.00
- 2 O:Green Hornet Pt.2. . . . . 2.50
- 3 Gun Metal Green 2.50
- 4 Targets 2.00

TALES OF THE MYSTERIOUS TRAVELER
Charlton Comics, Aug., 1956
- 1 DG 600.00
- 2 SD 450.00
- 3 SD,SD(c) 425.00
- 4 SD,SD(c) 500.00
- 5 SD,SD(c) 500.00
- 6 SD,SD(c) 500.00
- 7 SD 450.00
- 8 SD 450.00
- 9 SD 450.00
- 10 SD,SD(c) 475.00
- 11 SD,SD(c) 475.00
- 12 . . . . 200.00
- 13 . . . . 225.00
- 14 (1985) 15.00
- 15 (1985) 15.00

TALES OF THE REALM
Crossgen Comics 2003
- 1 (of 6) 2.95

COLOR PUB.

- 2 . . . . 2.95

TALES OF THE SUN RUNNERS
Sirius Comics, 1986
- 1 . . . . 2.00
- 2 and 3 . . . . @2.00

TALESPIN
Walt Disney, 1991
(Reg.-Series)
- 1 `Sky-Raker' Pt.1 . . . . 2.50
- 2 `Sky-Raker' Pt.2 . . . . 2.00
- 3 `Idiots Abroad' 2.00
- 4 `Contractual Desperation' 2.00
- 5 `The Oldman & the Sea Duck' . . 2.00
- 6 `F'reeze a Jolly Good Fellow' . . . 2.00

Talespin #4
© *Walt Disney*

TALESPIN
Walt Disney, 1991
[Mini-Series]
- 1 Take-off Pt.1 . . . . 3.00
- 2 Take-off Pt 2 . . . . 3.00
- 3 Take-off Pt 3,Khan Job 2.00
- 4 Take-off pt 4 . . . . 2.00

TALEWEAVER
WildStorm/DC, Sept., 2001
- 1 (of 6) 40-pg. 3.50
- 2 . . . . 2.95
- 2a variant (c) 2.95
- 3 . . . . 2.95
- 4 . . . . 2.95
- 5 . . . . 2.95
- 6 . . . . 2.95

TANK GIRL
Titan, 2002
- TPB Vol. 1 128-pg. 17.00
- TPB Vol. 2 . . . . 17.00
- TPB Vol. 3 . . . . 14.95

TAOLAND
Severe Reality Productions
- 4 1st full color issue 5.95
- 5 48pg. 5.95

TAOLAND ADVENTURES
Antarctic Press, 1999
- 1 by Jeff Amano 3.00
- 2 . . . . 3.00

TARGET AIRBOY
Eclipse, 1988
- 1 SK,A:Clint 2.00

TARGITT
Atlas, March–July, 1975
- 1 thru 3 . . . . @6.00

TAROT WITCH OF THE BLACK ROSE
Broadsword Comics, 2000
- 1 JBa(c) 2.95
- 2 . . . . 2.95
- 3 . . . . 2.95
- 4 . . . . 2.95
- 5 JBa 2.95
- 6 Goulish Intentions. 2.95
- 7 Return of the Dark Witch,pt.1 . . . 2.95
- 8 Return of the Dark Witch,pt.2 . . . 2.95
- 9 Return of the Dark Witch,pt.3 . . . 2.95
- 2a thru 16a signed . . . . @10.00
- 1b, 4b, 6b, 8b deluxe . . . . @19.95
- 7b double-deluxe edition 24.95
- 9b thru 23b deluxe . . . . @20.00
- 10 Quest for the Black Rose Sword 2.95
- 11 Black Rose Sword,pt.2. . . . . 2.95
- 12 . . . . 2.95
- 13 . . . . 2.95
- 13b previews exlusive (c) 15.00
- 14 . . . . 2.95
- 15 . . . . 2.95
- 16 . . . . 2.95
- 17 Cold Spell 2.95
- 18 Diary of a Witch. 2.95
- 19 Mists of Darkness, pt.1 . . . . 2.95
- 19a photo (c) 10.00
- 20 Mists of Darkness, pt.2 . . . . 2.95
- 21 Mists of Darkness, pt.3 . . . . 2.95
- 22 Mists of Darkness, pt.4 . . . . 2.95
- 23 Ghouls Gone Wild 2.95
- TPB Vol. 1 . . . . 25.00
- TPB Vol. 1 deluxe 34.95

TARZAN OF THE APES
Gold Key, 1962–72
prev. Dell (see Golden Age)
- 132 . . . . 65.00
- 133 . . . . 50.00
- 134 . . . . 50.00
- 135 . . . . 55.00
- 136 . . . . 50.00
- 137 . . . . 50.00
- 138 . . . . 50.00
- 139 I:Korak 55.00
- 140 . . . . 50.00
- 141 . . . . 50.00
- 142 . . . . 50.00
- 143 . . . . 50.00
- 144 . . . . 50.00
- 145 . . . . 50.00
- 146 . . . . 50.00
- 147 . . . . 50.00
- 148 . . . . 50.00
- 149 . . . . 50.00
- 150 . . . . 50.00
- 151 . . . . 50.00
- 152 . . . . 50.00
- 153 . . . . 50.00
- 154 . . . . 50.00
- 155 O:Tarzan 60.00
- 156 . . . . 40.00

All comics prices listed are for *Near Mint* condition.

Comics Values Annual — COLOR PUB. — Tarzan–Teenage

157 Banlu, Dog o/t Arande, Pt.1 .. 40.00
158 Banlu, Dog o/t Arande, Pt.2 .. 40.00
159 Banlu, Dog o/t Arande, Pt.3 .. 40.00
160 .... 40.00
161 .... 40.00
162 TV photo (c). 50.00
163 .... 40.00
164 .... 40.00
165 TV photo (c) 50.00
166 .... 40.00
167 .... 40.00
168 TV photo (c). 50.00
169 A:Leopard Girl 40.00
170 .... 40.00
171 TV photo (c). 60.00
172 .... 30.00
173 .... 30.00
174 .... 30.00
175 .... 30.00
176 .... 30.00
177 .... 30.00
178 O:Tarzan, rep. #155........ 30.00
179 A:Leopard Girl 30.00
180 .... 30.00
181 .... 30.00
182 .... 30.00
183 Down Trails of Terror 30.00
184 .... 30.00
185 .... 30.00
186 .... 30.00
187 .... 30.00
188 .... 30.00
189 .... 30.00
190 .... 30.00
191 .... 30.00
192 Tarzan and the Foreign Legion
 adaptation 30.00
193 'Escape From Sumatra' 30.00
194 thru 199 .... @30.00
200 .... 40.00
201 thru 205 .... @30.00
206 last issue 30.00
Continued by DC; see also Marvel

TARZAN IN COLOR
NBM, 1997
TPB Vol. 1, 1931–1933, by
 Hal Foster 24.95
TPB Vol. 2, 1933–1935, by
 Hal Foster 24.95
TPB Vol. 3, 1935–1937, by
 Hal Foster 24.95

TARZAN: THE BECKONING
Malibu Nov., 1992
1 TY,I:The Spider Man 2.75
2 TY,Going back to Africa 2.50
3 thru 6 .... 2.50

TARZAN: LOVE, LIES, AND THE LOST CITY
Malibu Aug., 1992
1 MWg&WS(s),Short Stories 3.95
2 The lost city of Opar 2.50
3 Final issue 2.50

TARZAN THE WARRIOR
Malibu March, 1992
1 SBs(c),O:Tarzan 3.50
2 .... 2.75
3 .... 2.75
4 Wom'cha's Ship 2.75
5 .... 2.75

TASK FORCE ALPHA
Alpha Productions
1 Forged in Fire.............. 3.50

TASMANIAN DEVIL & HIS TASTY FRIENDS
Gold Key, Nov., 1962
1 .... 200.00

TASTEE-FREEZ COMICS
Harvey Comics, 1957
1 Little Dot. 60.00
2 Rags Rabbit 30.00
3 Casper 40.00
4 Sad Sack 30.00
5 Mazie 30.00
6 Dick Tracy 50.00

TEAM ANARCHY
Anarchy, 1993
1 I:Team Anarchy............. 2.75
2 thru 3 .... 2.75
4 PuD,MaS,I:Primal........... 2.75

TEAM YANKEE
First, 1989
1 Harold Coyle novel adapt.. ..... 2.00
2 thru 6 .... @2.00
Trade Paperback 12.95

T.E.C.H. BOYZ HYPERACTIVE
Dynasty Comics
1 I:T.E.C.H. Boyz............. 2.95
2 Man vs. Nature............. 2.95

TEEN-AGE CONFIDENTIAL CONFESSIONS
Charlton Comics, 1960–64
1 .... 50.00
2 thru 5 .... @35.00
6 thru 10 .... @30.00
11 thru 22 .... @25.00

TEENAGE HOTRODDERS
Charlton Comics, April, 1963
1 .... 75.00
2 thru 5 .... @40.00
6 thru 10 .... @38.00
11 thru 23 .... @35.00
24 .... 35.00
Becomes:

TOP ELIMINATOR
25 thru 29 .... @30.00
Becomes:

DRAG 'N' WHEELS
30 .... 60.00
31 thru 39................. 40.00
40 thru 50 Scot Jackson 35.00
51 thru 59 May, 1973 .... 25.00

TEENAGE MUTANT NINJA TURTLES
First
1 .... 6.00
2 .... 4.50
Graphic Novel................ 17.00

TEENAGE MUTANT NINJA TURTLES
Archie, 1988 (From T.V. Series)
1 O:TMNT,April O'Neil,Shredder
 Krang 6.00
2 V:Shredder,O:Bebop &
 Rocksteady 4.00
3 V:Shredder & Krang 3.00

Teenage Mutant Ninja Turtles #7
© Mirage

TEENAGE MUTANT NINJA TURTLES
Mirage, 1993
1 A:Casey Jones 3.00
2 JmL(a&s) 3.00
3 thru 8 .... @2.75
9 V:Baxter Bot............... 2.75
10 Mr. Braunze............... 2.75
11 V:Raphael 2.75
12 V:Darpa.................. 2.75
13 J:Triceraton............... 2.75

TEENAGE MUTANT NINJA TURTLES ADVENTURES
Archie, 1988 [2nd Series]
1 Shredder,Bebop,Rocksteady
 return to earth 5.00
2 I:Baxter Stockman 3.00
3 'Three Fragments' #1 .... 3.00
4 'Three Fragments' #2......... 2.50
5 Original adventures begin,
 I:Man Ray 2.50
6 I:Leatherhead,Mary Bones 2.50
7 I:Cuddley the Cowlick; Inter-
 Galactic wrestling issue 2.50
8 I:Wingnut & Screwloose 2.00
9 I:Chameleon. 2.00
10 I:Scumbug, Wyrm 2.00
11 I:Rat King & Sons of Silence;
 Krang returns to earth 2.00
12 Final Conflict #1, A:Leatherhead
 Wingnut,Screwloose,Trap,
 I:Malinga 2.00
13 Final Conflict #2 .... 2.00
14 Turtles go to Brazil;I:Jagwar
 Dreadman 2.00
15 I:Mr. Null 2.00
16 I&D:Bubbla,the Glubbab 2.00
17 Cap'n Mossback 2.00
18 'Man Who Sold World' 2.00

All comics prices listed are for *Near Mint* condition.

Teenage–Terminator

19 I: Mighty Mutanimals 2.00
20 V:Supersoldier,War.Dragon 2.00
21 V:Vid Vicious 2.00
22 GC,Donatello captured 2.00
23 V:Krang,I:Slash,Belly Bomb 2.00
24 V:Krang 2.00
25 . . . . 2.00
26 I:T'Pau & Keeper 2.00
27 I:Nevermore,Nocturno&Hallocat. 2.00
28 Turtle go to Spain, I:Nindar & Chein Klan 2.00
29 Warrior Dragon captured 2.00
30 TMNT/Fox Mutant Ninjara team-up 2.00
31 TMNT/Ninjara team-up cont. . . . 2.00
32 A:Sumo Wrestler Tatoo 2.00
33 The Karma of Katmandu 2.00
34 Search For Charlie Llama 2.00
35 . . . . 2.00
36 V:Shredder 2.00
37 V:Shredder 2.00
38 V:Null & 4 Horsemen Pt.1 . . . . . 2.00
39 V:Null & 4 Horseman Pt.3 . . . . . 2.00
40 1492,A:The Other 2.00
41 And Deliver us from Evil. 2.00
42 Time Tripping Trilogy #1. . . . . . . 2.00
43 thru 51 . . . . @2.00
52 thru 54 . . . . @2.00
55 thru 57 Terracide . . . . @2.00
58 thru 70 . . . . @2.00
1990 Movie adapt(direct) 5.50
1990 Movie adapt(newsstand) 2.50
1991 TMNT meet Archie. 2.50
1991 Movie Adapt II 2.50
Spec.#2 Ghost of 13 Mile Island . . . 2.50
Spec.#3 Night of the Monsterex . . . 2.50
TMNT Mutant Universe Sourcebook 2.00

TEENAGE MUTANT NINJA TURTLES ANIMATED
Dreamwave 2003

1 . . . . 2.95
2 thru 6 . . . . @2.95
TPB Vol. 1 . . . . 9.95

TEENAGE MUTANT NINJA TURTLES/ FLAMING CARROT
Mirage/Dark Horse, 1993

1 JmL 3.00
2 thru 3 JmL 3.00
4 JmL 3.00

TMNT PRESENTS: APRIL O'NEIL
Archie, 1993

1 A:Chien Khan,Vid Vicious 2.00
2 V:White Ninja,A:V.Vicious 2.00
3 V:Vhien Khan,concl. 2.00

TMNT: THE MALTESE TURTLE
Mirage

Spec. F:Raphael Detective 2.95

TMNT PRESENTS: DONATELLO AND LEATHERHEAD
Archie, 1993

1 thru 2 . . . . @2.00

COLOR PUB.

TMNT PRESENTS: MERDUDE VS. RAY FILLET
Archie, 1993

1 thru 3 . . . . @2.00

TMNT: APRIL O'NEIL THE MAY EAST SAGA
Archie

1 A:TMNT 2.00

TMNT: YEAR OF THE TURTLE
Archie Comics, 1995

1 All New Era 2.00

[JACK KIRBY'S] TEENAGENTS
Topps
[Mini-Series]

1 WS,AH,w/3 cards 2.95
2 NV,w/3 cards 2.95
3 NV,w/3 cards 2.95
4 NV,w/3 leftover? cards 2.95

TEEN CONFESSIONS
Charlton Comics, 1959–76

1 . . . . 125.00
2 . . . . 60.00
3 . . . . 35.00
4 . . . . 35.00
5 . . . . 35.00
6 . . . . 35.00
7 . . . . 35.00
8 . . . . 35.00
9 . . . . 35.00
10 . . . . 35.00
11 thru 30 . . . . @30.00
31 Beatles cover. 125.00
32 thru 36 . . . . @25.00
37 Beatles cover,Fan Club story . 175.00
38 thru 97 . . . . @20.00

TEEN SECRET DIARY
Charlton Comics, 1959–61

1 . . . . 65.00
2 . . . . 40.00
3 . . . . 35.00
4 . . . . 35.00
5 . . . . 35.00
6 . . . . 35.00
7 . . . . 35.00
8 . . . . 35.00
9 . . . . 35.00
10 . . . . 35.00
11 . . . . 35.00

TEKKEN 2
Knightstone, 1997

1 (of 4) Tekken Saga, pt.3 . . . . . . 2.95
2 . . . . 2.95
2a photo cover 2.95
3 . . . . 2.95
3a photo cover 2.95

TEKKEN SAGA
Knightstone, 1997

1 (of 8) 3.95
2 . . . . 2.95
3 . . . . 2.95
4 Paul vs. Kazuya 2.95

Comics Values Annual

5 Paul a prisoner. 2.95
Nightstone Unlimited & Tekken ? . . 2.95

TENSE SUSPENSE
Fargo Publications, 1958–59

1 . . . . 100.00
2 . . . . 75.00

10TH MUSE
Avatar/Tidal Wave Studios, 2002

1A MWn,RCz, Andy Park (c) 3.50
1B CBa(c) 3.50
1C RCz(c) 3.50
1D Mark Brooks (c) 3.50
1E Valdez (c) 3.50
2 RCz(c) 3.50
2a Caldwell (c) 3.50
2b Rousseau (c) 3.50
2 RCz(c) 3.50
2a Green (c) 3.50
2b Grant (c) 3.50
TPB Vol. 1 . . . . 13.95
TPB Vol. 1 photo (c) 13.95

Angel Gate 2003

TPB Vol. 1 Maze of the Minotaur . . 7.95
TPB Vol. 2 Round Two 15.00

Terminator #17
© Now Comics

TERMINATOR, THE
Now, 1988–89

1 . . . . 10.00
2 . . . . 5.00
3 . . . . 4.00
4 thru 11 . . . . @3.50
12 I:JohnConnor($1.75,cov,dbl.sz) . 3.50
13 thru 17. . . . . @3.50
Spec. #1. 3.50

TERMINATOR: ALL MY FUTURES PAST
Now, 1990

1 Painted Art 3.00
2 Painted Art 3.00

TERMINATOR: THE BURNING EARTH
Now, 1990

1 . . . . 18.00
2 . . . . 12.00

TERMINATOR 2: CYBERNETIC DAWN
Malibu 1995–96
1 thru 4 .... @2.50
0 flip-book/T2 Nuclear Twilight 2.50

TERMINATOR 2: NUCLEAR TWILIGHT
Malibu 1995–96
1 thru 4 .... @2.50
0 flip-book, see above

TERMINATOR 3
Beckett Entertainment 2003
1 Before the Rise 5.95
2 Before the Rise 5.95
3 Eyes of the Rise 5.95
4 Eyes of the Rise 5.95
5 Fragmented 5.95

TERRAFORMERS
Wonder Comics, 1987
1 .... 2.00
2 .... 2.00
3 .... 2.00
4 .... 2.00

TERRANAUTS
Fantasy General, 1986
1 .... 2.00
2 .... 2.00

TERRA OBSCURA
Wildstorm/DC June 2003
America's Best Comics
1 (of 6) AMo(s) 2.95
2 AMo(s),F:Grant Halford 2.95
3 thru 5 AMo(s) .... @2.95

TESS
1 .... 2.00

TEXAS RANGERS IN ACTION
Charlton Comics, 1956–70
5 .... 80.00
6 .... 50.00
7 .... 50.00
8 SD 100.00
9 .... 50.00
10 .... 50.00
11 AW. 100.00
12 .... 35.00
13 AW 75.00
14 thru 20 .... @35.00
21 thru 30 .... @30.00
31 thru 59 .... @25.00
60 B:Riley's Rangers 28.00
61 thru 79 .... @15.00

THAT WILKIN BOY
Archie Publications, Jan., 1969
1 .... 50.00
2 .... 30.00
3 .... 30.00
4 .... 30.00
5 .... 30.00

6 .... 30.00
7 .... 30.00
8 .... 30.00
9 .... 30.00
10 .... 30.00
11 thru 20 .... @20.00
21 thru 26 E:Giant size .... @15.00
27 thru 52 .... @15.00

30 DAYS OF NIGHT
IDW Publishing, 2002
1 by S.Niles & B.Templesmith ... 60.00
1a 2nd printing 7.00
2 .... 25.00
3 .... 7.00
TPB 18.00

THESPIAN
Dark Moon, 1995
1 I:Thespian 2.50
2 V:Lemming 2.50
3 Lord of Manhattan 2.50

THING: COLD FEAR
1 R:Thing 3.00
2 .... 2.75

THIRD WORLD WAR
Fleetway, 1990–91
1 HamburgerLady 2.50
2 .... 2.50
3 The Killing Yields 2.50
4 .... 2.50
5 .... 2.50
6 .... 2.50

13: ASSASSIN
TSR, 1990–91
1 thru 4 from game .... @2.95
5 thru 8 The Search for Maggie Darr .... @2.95

THOSE ANNOYING POST BROTHERS
Vortex
1 .... 3.00
2 .... 2.00
3 .... 2.00
4 .... 2.00
5 .... 2.00
6 thru 18 .... @2.00
See also B&W listings

3-D ZONE PRESENTS
Renegade, 1987–89
1 L.B.Cole(c) 2.00
2 .... 2.00
3 .... 2.00
4 .... 2.00
5 .... 2.00
12 3-D Presidents 2.50
13 Flash Gordon 2.50
14 Tyranostar 2.50
15 Tyranostar 2.50
16 SpaceVixen 2.50

3 LITTLE KITTENS
Broadsword Comics, 2002
1 JBa, Purrr-fect weapons 2.95
2 Puss N Bullets 2.95
3 Purrr-Fect Weapons 2.95
1a thru 3a deluxe .... @20.00
1b thru 3b signed .... @10.00

Three Stooges #23 © Gold Key

THREE STOOGES
Dell Publishing Co., Oct.-Dec., 1959
6 Ph(c),B:Prof. Putter 150.00
7 Ph(c) 150.00
8 Ph(c) 150.00
9 Ph(c) 150.00

Gold Key, 1962
10 Ph(c) 150.00
11 Ph(c) 125.00
12 Ph(c) 125.00
13 Ph(c) 125.00
14 Ph(c) 125.00
15 Ph(c) Go Around the World .. 150.00
16 Ph(c),E:Prof. Putter 125.00
17 Ph(c),B:Little Monsters ... 125.00
18 Ph(c) 125.00
19 Ph(c) 125.00
20 Ph(c) 125.00
21 Ph(c) 125.00
22 Ph(c),Movie Scenes 125.00
23 Ph(c) 100.00
24 Ph(c) 100.00
25 Ph(c) 100.00
26 Ph(c) 100.00
27 Ph(c) 100.00
28 Ph(c) 100.00
29 Ph(c) 100.00
30 Ph(c) 100.00
31 thru 50 Ph(c) .... @75.00
51 .... 70.00
52 Ph(c) 75.00
53 Ph(c) 75.00
54 Ph(c) 75.00
55 Ph(c) 75.00

THREE STOOGES 3-D
Eclipse, 1991
1 thru 3 reprints from 1953 ... @2.50
4 reprints from 1953 .... 3.50

THRILLING SCIENCE TALES
AC Comics, 1989
1 .... 3.50

THRILLOGY
Pacific, 1984
1 .... 2.00

Thrill-Time / COLOR PUB.

THRILL-O-RAMA
Harvey Publications, 1965–66
1 A:Man in Black(Fate),DW,AW . . 75.00
2 AW,A:Pirana,I:Clawfang,
 The Barbarian 50.00
3 A:Pirana, Fate 40.00

THUNDER AGENTS
Tower, 1965–69
1 WW,RC,MSy,GT,I:Thunder
 Agents,IronMaiden,Warlord. . . 275.00
2 WW,MSy,D:Egghead 150.00
3 WW,DA,MSy,V:Warlords 100.00
4 WW,MSy,RC,I:Lightning 100.00
5 WW,RC,GK,MSy. 100.00
6 WW,SD,MSy,I:Warp Wizard . . . 90.00
7 WW,MSy,SD,D:Menthor 90.00
8 WW,MSy,GT,DA,I:Raven 90.00
9 OW,WW,MSy,A:Andor 90.00
10 WW,MSy,OW,A:Andor 90.00
11 WW,DA,MSy 75.00
12 SD,WW,MSy 75.00
13 WW,OW,A:Undersea Agent . . . 75.00
14 SD,WW,GK,N:Raven,A:Andor . 75.00
15 WW,OW,GT,A:Andor 65.00
16 SD,GK,A:Andor 65.00
17 WW,OW,GT 65.00
18 SD,OW,RC 50.00
19 GT,I:Ghost. 50.00
20 WW,RC,MSy,all reprints 50.00

T.H.U.N.D.E.R. AGENTS
J.C. Productions, 1983
1 MA,Centerfold 2.00
2 I:Vulcan 2.00

T.H.U.N.D.E.R. AGENTS
Maximum, 1995
1 and 2. . . . . @2.95

THUNDERBOLT
Charlton Comics, 1966–67
1 PAM,O:Thuderbolt 50.00
Prev: Son of Vulcan
51 PAM,V:Evila. 35.00
52 PAM,V:Gore the Monster 25.00
53 PAM,V:The Tong 25.00
54 PAM,I:Sentinels 25.00
55 PAM,V:Sentinels 25.00
56 PAM,A:Sentinels 25.00
57 A:Sentinels 25.00
58 PAM,A:Sentinels 25.00
59 PAM,A:Sentinels 25.00
60 PAM,JAp,I:Prankster 30.00

THUNDERCATS
WildStorm/DC, Aug., 2002
0 JSC, preview issue. 5.00
1a (of 5) King Lion-O. 5.00
1b variant AAd (c) 3.50
2a V:Mumm-ra. 3.00
2b variant JLe(c) 3.00
3 F:Lion-O. 3.00
3a variant JMd(c). 3.00
4 F:New Thundera. 3.00
5 concl. 3.00
GN Thundercats/Battle
 of the Planets. 4.95
TPB Reclaiming Thundera 12.95
Sourcebook 3.00

THUNDERCATS: DOGS OF WAR
WildStorm/DC June 2003
1 (of 5) 10 years in future 3.00

2 New Thundera 3.00
3 thru 5 BBh,AV . . . . @3.00

THUNDERCATS: HAMMERHAND'S REVENGE
Wildstorm/DC Oct. 2003
1 (of 5) 3.00
2 F:Lion-O. 3.00
Spec. Superman/Thundercats. 5.95

THUNDERCATS: THE RETURN
Wildstorm/DC Feb. 2003
1 (of 5) EBe,F:Lion-O 3.00
2 EBe,V:Mumm-Ra 3.00
3 EBe 3.00
4 EBe,Wilykat 3.00
5 EBe, concl. 3.00

TICK, THE
Spec. digest size 4.50

TICK, THE
New England Comics, 2001
1 all new, all color 3.95
1a variant (c). 3.95
2 thru 5 . . . . @3.95
6 return of Proto-Tick. 3.95
TPB The Naked City, 2nd pr. 15.95
TPB Circus Maximus Giant ed. . . . 14.95
Spec. Big Halloween 2000 . . . . . 3.50
Spec. Big Halloween 2001 . . . . . 3.95
Spec. Introducing the Tick (2002) . . 3.95
Spec. Circus Maximus Update 3.95

TICK & ARTIE
New England Comics, 2002
1 . . . . 3.50
2 BEd(c) 3.50

TICK, THE: BIG XMAS TRILOGY
New England Comics, 2002
1 . . . . 4.00
2 thru 3 . . . . @4.00

TICK'S INCREDIBLE INTERNET COMIC, THE
New England Comics, 2001
1 . . . . 3.95

TIGER GIRL
Gold Key, Sept., 1968
1 . . . . 50.00

TIGER-MAN
Atlas, April–Sept., 1975
1 thru 3 . . . . @15.00

TIGERS OF TERRA
Antarctic Press, 2000
Vol. 3
1 (of 4) War Against the Sun 2.95
2 Night of the Amazons 2.95
3 . . . . 2.95
4 Planet of War 2.95

Tiger-Man #2
© Atlas Comics

TIME TUNNEL, THE
Gold Key, Feb., 1967
1 from TV show 125.00
2 . . . . 75.00

TIME TWISTERS
Quality, 1987–89
1 Alan Moore ser. 2.00
2 Alan Moore ser. 2.00
3 Alan Moore ser. 2.00
4 Alan Moore ser. 2.00
5 . . . . 2.00
6 Alan Moore ser. 2.00
7 Alan Moore ser. 2.00
8 . . . . 2.00
9 . . . . 2.00
10 . . . . 2.00
11 . . . . 2.00
12 . . . . 2.00
13 thru 21 . . . . @2.00

TIME 2
1 Graphic Novel 8.00

TIMEWALKER
Valiant 1994
0 BH,DP,O:3 Immortals 2.95
1 DP, BH 2.50
2 DP,BH 2.50
3 DP BH 2.50
4 Ten Commandments. 2.50
5 DP,BH 2.50
6 Harbinger Wars,pt.1 . . . . 2.50
7 Harbinger Wars,pt.2 . . . . 2.50
8 Harbinger Wars,pt.3 . . . . 2.50
9 V:Jahk rt. 2.50
10 Last God of Dura-Europus,pt.1
 time: 260 A.D. 2.50
11 Last God of Dura-Europus,pt.2. . 2.50
12 3RW,DP,Ashes to Ashes,pt.1 . . 2.50
13 3RW,DP,Ashes to Ashes,pt.2 . . 2.50
14 Meets Mozart. 2.50
15 26th Century 2.50
Yearbook F:Harada. 2.95
TPB F:Archer & Armstrong 9.95

TIME WARRIOR
Blazing Comics, 1993
1 . . . . 2.50

TIPPY'S FRIENDS GO-GO & ANIMAL
Tower Comics, 1966–69
1	100.00
2	65.00
3	65.00
4	65.00
5	65.00
6	65.00
7	65.00
8 Beatles on cover & back	125.00
9 thru 15	@50.00

TIPPY TEEN
Tower Comics, Nov., 1965–70
1	100.00
2 thru 27	@60.00

TOHUBOHU
New Breed Comics, 1999
1	3.25
2 thru 5	@3.00
6 A Serpent in the Garden	3.25

TO DIE FOR
1 3-D	2.50

TOKYO STORM WARNING
Wildstorm/DC June 2003
1 (of 3) giant robots	2.95
2 WEI	2.95
3 WEI	2.95

TOM & JERRY
Harvey, 1991–94
1	2.50
2 thru 18	@2.00

TOM MIX WESTERN
AC Comics, 1988
1	2.95

TOM TERRIFIC!
Pines Comics
Summer, 1957
1	250.00
2	175.00
3	175.00
4	175.00
5	175.00
6 Fall, 1958	175.00

TOMMI-GUNN
London Night, 1997
0	3.00
?	3.00
1 signed	15.00
1a, chromium, elite edition	19.95
2	3.00
3	3.00

TOMMI-GUNN: KILLER'S LUST
London Night, 1997
1	3.00
1 Japanese Chromium edition	12.00
2	3.00

COLOR PUB.

Tomoe #3
© Crusade Entertainment

TOMOE
Crusade Entertainment, 1996
0 BiT,	3.00
1 BiT,Fan Appreciation Edition	3.00
2	3.00
TPB rep.	13.95

TOMOE/WITCHBLADE: FIRE SERMON
Crusade Entertainment, 1996
1	5.00
1a Gold foil	10.00

TOMOE: UNFORGETTABLE FIRE
Crusade Entertainment, 1997
1 (of 3)	2.95

TOMORROW STORIES
WildStorm/DC, 1999
America's Best Comics
1 AMo,AxR(c) anthology	3.50
1a AxR(c),variant cover	3.50
2 AMo(s),KN,RV,JBa	3.00
3 AMo(s),KN,RV,JBa	3.00
4 AMo(s),KN,RV,JBa	3.00
5 AMo(s),KN,RV,JBa	3.00
6 AMo(s),RV,JBa	3.00
7 AMo(s),RV,JBa	3.00
8 AMo(s),RV,JBa	2.95
9 AMo(s),RV,JBa	2.95
10 AMo(s),RV,JBa,Jack B. Quick	2.95
11 AMo(s),RV,JBa,AAd,F:Cobweb	2.95
12 AMo(s),RV,JBa, x-over	2.95

TOM STRONG
WildStorm/DC, 1999
America's Best Comics
1 AMo(s),CSp,40-pg.	3.50
2 AMo(s),CSp,Millennium City	3.00
3 AMo(s),CSp,Millennium City	3.00
4 AMo,CSp,AAd,Berlin in WW2	3.00
5 AMo,CSp,Memories of Pangea	3.00
6 AMo,CSp,DGb, Dead Man's Hand	2.95
7 AMo,CSp,GFr.	2.95
8 AMo,CSp,Lost Mesa	2.95
9 AMo,CSp,	2.95
10 AMo,CSp,F:Warren Strong	2.95
11 AMo,CSp,F:Tom Strange	2.95
12 AMo,CSp,F:Tom Strange,pt.2	2.95
13 AMo,CSp,Warren Strong	2.95
14 AMo,CSp,Space Family Strong	2.95
15 AMo,CSp,Val Var Garm	2.95
16 AMo(s),CSp,KIS,Modular Man	2.95
17 AMo(s),CSp,KIS,Weird Rider	2.95
18 AMo(s),CSp,KIS,Weird Rider	2.95
19 AMo(s),CSp,KIS.	2.95
20 AMo(s),CSp,KIS,JOy,pt.1	2.95
21 AMo(s),CSp,KIS,JOy,pt.2	2.95
22 AMo(s),CSp,KIS,JOy,pt.3	2.95
23 CSp,KIS,rescue mission.	2.95
TPB Book One, 208-pg.	14.95
TPB Book Two, 192-pg.	14.95

TOM STRONG'S TERRIFIC TALES
WildStorm/DC, Nov., 2001
America's Best Comics
1 AMo,AAd	3.50
2 AMo,AAd	2.95
3 AMo,AAd,JOy.	2.95
4 AMo(s),AAd,Jonni Future	2.95
5 AMo(s),SA,AAd(c)	2.95
6 AMo(s),JOy,AAd	2.95
7 AMo(s),AAd	2.95
8 AMo(s),AAd, young Tom	2.95

TOOL AND DIE
Samson Comics
1 Autographed	4.95
1a Blue Edition	9.95

TOP CAT
Charlton Comics, 1970–73
1	75.00
2 thru 10	@50.00
11 thru 20	@30.00

TOP TEN
WildStorm/DC, 1999
America's Best Comics
1 AMo(s),GeH,40-pg.	3.50
2 AMo(s),GeH	3.00
3 thru 9 AMo(s),GeH	@2.95
10 AMo(s),GeH,killer revealed	2.95
11 AMo(s),GeH,aftermath	2.95
12 AMo(s),GeH,season finale	2.95
TPB AMo(s),GeH	14.95
TPB Top 10 Book Two	14.95

TOR IN 3-D
Eclipse, 1986
1 JKu	3.00
1a B&W limited 100 sign	5.00
2 JKu	3.00

TORI-SHI-KITA
Relative Burn
1 Hunter Prey	2.50

TORMENTRESS: MISTRESS OF HELL
Blackout Comics, 1977
0	2.95

TOTAL ECLIPSE
Eclipse, 1988–89
1 BHa,BSz(c),A:Airboy,Skywolf	3.95

Total–Troublemakers / COLOR PUB. / Comics Values Annual

2 BHa,BSz(c),A:New Wave, Liberty
   Project 3.95
3 BHa,BSz(c),A:Scout,Ms.Tree . . . 3.95
4 BHa,BSz(c),A:Miracleman,
   Prowler 3.95
5 BHa,BSz(c),A:Miracleman, Aztec
   Ace 3.95

TOTAL ECLIPSE, THE SERAPHIM OBJECTIVE
Eclipse, 1988
1 tie-in Total Eclipse #2 . . . . 2.00

M.A.R.S. Patrol (Total War) #9
© Gold Key

TOTAL WAR
Gold Key,, July, 1965
1 WW 100.00
2 WW 100.00
Becomes:

M.A.R.S. PATROL
3 WW 100.00
4 . . . . 60.00
5 . . . . 60.00
6 . . . . 60.00
7 . . . . 60.00
8 . . . . 60.00
9 . . . . 60.00
10 . . . . 60.00

TOY BOY
Continuity, 1986–91
1 NA.I&O:Toy Boy,A:Megalith 2.00
2 TVE 2.00
3 TVE 2.00
4 TVE 2.00
5 TVE 2.00
6 TVE 2.00
7 MG 2.00

TRANCERS: THE ADVENTURES OF JACK DETH
Eternity
1 I:Jack Deth 2.50
2 A:Whistler, final issue 2.50

TRANSFORMERS
1 Robotics 2.00
2 . . . . 2.00
3 . . . . 2.50

TRANSFORMERS
Titan, 2001
GN Vol. 1 All Fall Down 20.00
GN Vol. 2 End of the Road 20.00
GN Vol. 3 Primal Scream 20.00
GN Vol. 4 Matrix Quest 20.00
GN Vol. 4 Matrix Quest spec. (c) . . 25.00
GN Vol. 5 Target 2006 . . . . 20.00
GN Vol. 6 Dark Design 19.95
GN Vol. 7 Fallen Angel 19.95
GN Beginnings 16.95
GN Showdown 19.95
GN City of Fear 19.95
GN Space Pirates 16.95
GN New Order 16.95
GN Cybertron Redux 16.95
GN Time Wars 19.95

TRANSFORMERS: ARMADA
Dreamwave, 2002
1 . . . . 3.50
2 thru 5 . . . . @3.00
6 thru 17 . . . . @2.95
TPB Vol. 1 . . . . 13.95
TPB Vol. 2 . . . . 15.95

TRANSFORMERS: GENERATION ONE
Dreamwave, 2002
1 . . . . 7.00
1a exclusive holofoil (c) 20.00
2 thru 6 . . . . @3.00
5a thru 6a variant (c) . . . . @3.00
Preview book, exclusive (c) 3.95
TPB rep. #1–#6 . . . . 17.95
TPB Profile Book One 12.95
TPB Profile Book Two 12.95
TPB Transformers Genesis
   Art Book 29.45
Vol. 2
1 (of 6) 2.95
1a chrome edition 5.95
2 thru 6 . . . . @2.95
GN More than meets the Eye, guide 5.25
GN More than meets the Eye #3 . . . 5.25

TRANSFORMERS/G.I. JOE
Dreamwave 2003
1 . . . . 2.95
1a holofoil (c) 5.95
2 thru 4 . . . . @2.95

TRANSFORMERS: MORE THAN MEETS THE EYE
Dreamwave 2003
1 (of 8) 5.25
2 thru 7 . . . . @5.25
8 final issue 5.95

TRANSFORMERS: THE WAR WITHIN
Dreamwave, 2002
1 . . . . 3.00
2 . . . . 3.00
3 thru 6 . . . . @3.00
TPB Vol. 1 . . . . 15.95
Vol. 2 The Dark Ages
1 . . . . 3.00
2 . . . . 3.00

TRANSFORMERS in 3-D
Blackthorne
1 thru 5 . . . . @2.50

TRAVEL OF JAMIE McPHEETERS, THE
Gold Key, Dec., 1963
1 Kurt Russell 50.00

TRAVELLER
Maximum Press, 1996
1 (of 3) RLd,MHw, ... 3.00

TRIAL BY FIRE
Crossgen Comics 2002
1 (of 5) 2.95

TRIBE
Axis Comics, 1993–94
1 see Image Comics section
2 TJn(s),LSn,V:Alex 2.25
3 TJn(s),LSn, ... 2.00
Good Comics, 1996
0 TJn,LSn 2.95
1 TJn,LSn,Choice and
   Responsibility 2.95
2 TJn,LSn,Choice and
   Responsibility 2.95

TRIBULATION FORCE
Tyndale House, 2002
GN Vol. #1 . . . . 6.00
GN Vol. #2 thru Vol. 5 . . . . @6.00

TRINITY ANGELS
Acclaim March, 1997
1 KM,DPs, Maria, Gianna &
   Theresa Barbella become Trinity
   Angels 2.50
2 KM,DPs, V:The 99 . . . . 2.50
3 KM,DPs, looking for a little head . . 2.50
4 KM,DPs, V:Flaming Queen 2.50
5 KM, New costumes 2.50
6 KM, in Las Vegas 2.50
7 KM, in Las Vegas 2.50
8 KM, 'A Woman Scorned' 2.50
9 KM, A:Rumblin' Guys 2.50
10 KM, Mad Cow 2.50
11 KM, ... 2.50
12 KM, Final issue 2.50

TROLL LORDS
Comico, 1989–90
Spec. #1 . . . . 2.00
1 . . . . 2.00
2 and 3 . . . . @2.00
4 . . . . 2.50

TROUBLEMAKERS
Acclaim Dec., 1996
1 FaN(s) 2.50
2 FaN(s) go back in time 2.50
3 FaN(s) Jane has a big problem . . 2.50
4 FaN(s) Can Blur prevent parents
   divorce? 2.50
5 FaN(s) A:Ninjak 2.50
6 FaN(s) in outer space 2.50
7 FaN(s) I:The Rabble Rousers . . . 2.50
8 FaN(s) Rabble Rousers,pt.2 . . . . 2.50
9 FaN(s) F:Christine 2.50
10 FaN(s) F:Zach 2.50
11 FaN(s) F:Calamity Jane 2.50

Comics Values Annual — COLOR PUB. — Troublemakers–TV

12 FaN(s) a Troublemaker dead ... 2.50
13 FaN(s) F:XL 2.50
14 FaN(s) 2.50
15 FaN(s) Is Parker alive? 2.50
16 FaN(s) Andrew Chase 2.50
17 FaN(s) V:Turnabout 2.50
18 FaN(s) Jacinda Monroe 2.50
19 FaN(s) V:Rabblerousers 2.50

TROUBLE WITH GIRLS
Comico, 1987–88
1 .... 3.00
2 .... 2.50
3 .... 2.50
4 .... 2.00

TRUE LOVE
Eclipse, 1986
1 ATh,NC,DSt(c),reprints 2.00
2 ATh,NC,BA(c),reprints 2.00

TRUE ROMANCE
Pyramid Comics, 1997
1 .... 2.00
1a deluxe 2.25
2 thru 4 .... @2.00

TUFF GHOSTS STARRING SPOOKY
Harvey Publications, 1962–72
1 .... 175.00
2 .... 90.00
3 .... 90.00
4 .... 90.00
5 .... 90.00
6 .... 75.00
7 .... 75.00
8 .... 75.00
9 .... 75.00
10 .... 75.00
11 thru 20 .... @35.00
21 thru 30 .... @30.00
31 thru 39 .... @25.00
40 thru 42 52 pg. Giants .... @32.00
43 .... 32.00

TUROK: CHILD OF BLOOD
Acclaim 1997
1-shot FaN, 48-pg. 4.00

TUROK: DINOSAUR HUNTER
Valiant 1993
1 BS,Chromium(c),O:Turok retold,V:Monark 3.00
1a Gold Ed. 4.00
2 BS,V:Monark 2.75
3 BCh,V:Monark 2.75
4 TT(s),RgM,O:Turok. 2.75
5 TT(s),RgM,V:Dinosaurs 2.75
6 TT(s),RgM,V:Longhunter. 2.75
7 TT(a&s),B:People o/t Spider ... 2.75
8 TT(a&s),V:T-Rex. 2.75
9 TT(a&s),E:People o/t Spider ... 2.75
10 MBn,RgM,A:Bile 2.75
11 MBn,RgM,V:Chun Yee,w/card . 2.75
12 MBn,RgM,V:Dinosaur 2.75
13 B:TT(c&s),RgM 2.75
14 V:Dino-Pirate. 2.50
15 RgM,V:Dino-Pirate. 2.25
16 Chaos Effect-Beta#3, V:Evil Shaman 2.75
17 V:C.I.A. 2.50

Turok: Dinosaur Hunter 38 © Valiant

18 V:Bionosaurs 2.50
19 A:Manowar 2.50
20 Chichak. 2.50
21 Ripsaw 2.50
22 .... 2.50
23 A:Longhunter. 2.50
24 R:To The Lost Land 2.50
25 I:Warrior of Mother God 2.50
26 V:Overlord. 2.50
27 TT,RgM,Lost Land,pt.4. ..... 2.50
28 MBn,DEA hunts rogue T-Rex . 2.50
29 SFu,Manhunt,pt.1 .... 2.50
30 SFu,Manhunt,pt.2 .... 2.50
31 F:Darwin Challenger 2.50
32 V:Special Effects 2.50
33 V:Aliens 2.50
34 V:Alien Ooze 2.50
35 Early Years 2.50
36 Confronts Past. 2.50
37 V:Nazi Women. 2.50
38 V:Bigfoot 2.50
39 TT,Shainer Silver 2.50
40 A:Longhunter. 2.50
41 Church of the Poison Mind. ... 2.50
42 Church of the Poison Mind. ... 2.50
43 thru 47 .... @2.50
Yearbook #1 MBn(s),DC, N&V:Mon Ark. 4.25
Yearbook 1995 MGr,The Hunted. . 2.95
Spec. Tales of the Lost Land. 4.00
TPB FaN 112pgs.rep. game 10.00

TUROK
Acclaim 1998
1 FaN 3-D cover 2.50
2 FaN,A:Armorines 2.50
3 FaN,Lazarus Concordance 2.50
4 FaN, real President? 2.50
TPB Dinosaur Hunter, FaN 9.95

TUROK: COMIC BOOK MAGAZINE
Acclaim 1998
Seeds of Evil 5.00
Adon's Curse 5.00
Turok/Shadowman 5.00

TUROK: EVOLUTION
Acclaim Comics 2002
Spec. based on video game 2.50

TUROK: THE HUNTED
Valiant
1 .... 2.50
2 .... 2.50

TUROK QUARTERLY— REDPATH
March, 1997, FaN(s),'Spring Break in the Lost Land'. 3.95
June, 1997, FaN(s), Killer loose in Oklahoma City 3.95

TUROK/SHADOWMAN
Acclaim 1999
1-shot 3.95

TUROK 3: SHADOW OF OBLIVION
Acclaim 2000
Spec. 48-pg. 4.95

TUROK/SHAMAN'S TEARS
Valiant 1995
1 MGr,Ghost Dance,pt. 1 .... 2.50
2 MGr,JAl,White Buffalo kidnapped,V:Bar Sinister 2.50
3 V:Supremeists/Circle Sea 2.50

TUROK/TIMEWALKER
Acclaim 1997
1 of 2 FaN(s),'Seventh Sabbath' .. 2.50
2 of 2 FaN(s),'Seventh Sabbath' .. 2.50

TUROK: SON OF STONE
Gold Key, 1962
1 thru 29 see Golden Age
30 .... 100.00
31 Drug 100.00
32 thru 40 .... @75.00
41 thru 50 .... @65.00
51 thru 60 .... @50.00
61 thru 75 .... @45.00
76 thru 91 .... @35.00
Whitman
92 thru 130 .... @15.00
Giant #1 .... 125.00

TURTLE SOUP
Millennium, 1991
1 Book 1, short stories. 2.50
2 thru 4 .... @2.50

TV CASPER & COMPANY
Harvey Publications, 1963–74
1 B:68 pg. Giants 165.00
2 .... 80.00
3 .... 80.00
4 .... 80.00
5 .... 80.00
6 .... 75.00
7 .... 75.00
8 .... 75.00
9 .... 75.00
10 .... 75.00
11 thru 20 .... @40.00
21 thru 31 E:68 pg. Giants .... @30.00
32 thru 46 .... @25.00

All comics prices listed are for Near Mint condition.

TWEETY AND SYLVESTER
Gold Key, 1963–84
1 . . . . 50.00
2 thru 10 . . . . @30.00
11 thru 30 . . . . @25.00
31 thru 121 . . . . @10.00

21 DOWN
WildStorm/DC, Sept., 2002
1 JP,JJu(c),F:Preston Kills 2.95
2 JP,JJu(c),Herod 2.95
3 JP,JJu(c),Bear Mountain 2.95
4 JP,JJu(c) 2.95
5 JP,JJu(c) 2.95
6 JP,JJu(c),The Conduit 2.95
7 JP,JJu(c),secret of Herod 2.95
8 JP,Roadside Attractions,pt.1 . . . 2.95
9 JP,Roadside Attractions,pt.2 . . . 2.95
10 JP,Roadside Attractions,pt.3 . . . 2.95
11 JP,Roadside Attractions,pt.4 . . . 2.95
12 JP,Roadside Attractions,concl. . . 2.95
TPB rep. #1 thru #7 . . . . 19.95

22 BRIDES
Event, 1996
1 . . . . 3.00
2 . . . . 3.00
2a variant (c) 4.00
3 . . . . 3.00
3a variant (c) 4.00
4 . . . . 3.00

TWILIGHT AVENGER
Elite, 1986
1 thru 4 . . . . @2.00

TWILIGHT MAN
First, 1989
1 Mini-Series 2.75
2 Mini-Series 2.75
3 Mini-Series 2.75
4 Mini-Series 2.75

TWILIGHT X-TRA
Antarctic Press, 1999
1 (of 3) by Joe Wright 2.50
2 . . . . 2.50
3 conclusion 2.50

TWILIGHT ZONE, THE
Gold Key, Nov., 1962
See also: Four Color #1173 & #1288
1 RC,FF,GE,P(c) all 200.00
2 . . . . 125.00
3 ATh,MSy 85.00
4 ATh 85.00
5 . . . . 75.00
6 . . . . 75.00
7 . . . . 75.00
8 . . . . 75.00
9 ATh 90.00
10 . . . . 75.00
11 . . . . 75.00
12 AW 75.00
13 AW,RC,FBe,AMc 75.00
14 RC,JO,RC,AT 75.00
15 RC,JO 75.00
16 . . . . 45.00
17 . . . . 45.00
18 . . . . 45.00
19 JO 45.00
20 . . . . 30.00
21 RC 35.00
22 JO 35.00
23 JO 35.00
24 . . . . 30.00
25 GE,RC,ATh 30.00
26 RC,GE 30.00
27 GE 30.00
28 . . . . 25.00
29 . . . . 25.00
30 . . . . 25.00
31 . . . . 25.00
32 GE 30.00
33 . . . . 25.00
34 . . . . 25.00
35 . . . . 25.00
36 . . . . 25.00
37 . . . . 25.00
38 . . . . 25.00
39 WMc 25.00
40 . . . . 22.00
41 . . . . 22.00
42 . . . . 22.00
43 RC 25.00
44 . . . . 22.00
45 . . . . 22.00
46 . . . . 22.00
47 . . . . 22.00
48 . . . . 22.00
49 . . . . 22.00
50 FBe,WS 22.00
51 AW 25.00
52 . . . . 22.00
53 . . . . 22.00
54 . . . . 22.00
55 . . . . 22.00
56 . . . . 22.00
57 FBe 22.00
58 . . . . 22.00
59 FBe,AMc 25.00
60 . . . . 20.00
61 . . . . 20.00
62 . . . . 20.00
63 . . . . 20.00
64 . . . . 20.00
65 . . . . 20.00
66 . . . . 20.00
67 . . . . 20.00
68 . . . . 20.00
69 . . . . 20.00
70 . . . . 20.00
71 rep 15.00
72 . . . . 20.00
73 rep 15.00
74 . . . . 20.00
75 . . . . 20.00
76 . . . . 20.00
77 FBe 25.00
78 FBe,AMc,The Missing Mirage . 25.00
79 rep 15.00
80 FBe,AMc 22.00
81 . . . . 20.00
82 AMc 25.00
83 FBe,WS 25.00
84 FBe,AMc 25.00
85 . . . . 20.00
86 rep 15.00
87 thru 91 . . . . @20.00

TWILIGHT ZONE
Now, 1990
1 NA,BSz(c) 8.00
1a 2nd printing Prestige +Harlan
  Ellison story 6.00

[Volume 2]
#1 'The Big Dry' (direct) 2.50
#1a Newsstand 2.00
2 'Blind Alley' 2.00
3 Extraterrestrial 2.00
4 The Mysterious Biker 2.00
5 Queen of the Void 2.00
6 Insecticide 2.00
7 The Outcasts,Ghost Horse 2.00

Twilight Zone Vol. 2 #11
© Nov

8 Colonists on Alcor 2.00
9 Dirty Lyle's House of Fun
  (3-D Holo) 2.95
10 Stairway to Heaven,Key
  to Paradise 2.00
11 TD(i),Partial Recall 2.00
3-D Spec 2.50
Ann. #1 . . . . 2.75

[Volume 3]
1 thru 2 . . . . @2.50

TWISTED TALES
Pacific, 1982–84
1 RCo. 'Infected' 3.50
2 . . . . 2.00
3 . . . . 2.00
4 . . . . 2.00
5 . . . . 2.00
6 . . . . 2.00
7 . . . . 2.00
8 . . . . 2.00

Eclipse
9 . . . . 2.00
10 GM,BWr 2.00

TWISTED TALES OF BRUCE JONES
Eclipse, 1982–84
1 . . . . 2.00
2 . . . . 2.00
3 . . . . 2.00
4 . . . . 2.00

TWISTER
Harris
1 inc.Special newspaper/poster,
  and trading cards 2.95

TWO FISTED TALES
Russ Cochran, 1992
1 JSe,HK,WW,JCr,reps 2.00
2 Reps inc.War Story 2.00
3 rep 2.00
4 thru 6 rep . . . . @2.00
7 thru 8 rep . . . . @2.00

Gemstone
17 thru 24 EC comics reprints . . . @2.50
'Annuals'
TPB Vol.#4 reprint #16–#20 . . . . 12.95

TPB Vol. 2 rebinding of #5–#10 . . . 9.95
TPB Vol. 3 rebinding of #11–#15. . 10.95
TPB Vol. 4 rebinding. 10.95
TPB Vol. 5 rebinding. 10.95

2000 A.D. MONTHLY
Eagle, 1985
1 A:JudgeDredd. 4.00
2 A:JudgeDredd. 3.00
3 A:JudgeDredd. 2.00
4 A:JudgeDredd. 2.00
5 . . . . 2.00
6 . . . . 2.00

[2nd Series]
1 . . . . 2.00
2 . . . . 2.00
3 . . . . 2.00
4 . . . . 2.00

Quality
5 . . . . 2.00
6 . . . . 2.00
7 thru 27 . . . . @2.00
28/29 . . . . 2.00
30 . . . . 2.00
31/32 . . . . 2.00
33 . . . . 2.00
34 . . . . 2.00
35 . . . . 2.00
36 . . . . 2.00
37 . . . . 2.00
Becomes:

2000 A.D. SHOWCASE
38 . . . . 2.00
39 . . . . 2.00
40 . . . . 2.00
41 . . . . 2.00
42 . . . . 2.00
43 . . . . 2.00
44 . . . . 2.00
45 . . . . 2.00
46 . . . . 2.00
47 . . . . 2.00
48 thru 54 . . . . @2.00
TPB:Killing Time 12.95

TWO-STEP
Wildstorm/DC Oct. 2003
1 (of 3) WEI(s),ACo,JP 2.95
2 WEI(s),ACo,JP 2.95

TZU THE REAPER
Murim Studios, 1997
1 by Gary Cohn & C.S. Chun. 2.95
2 . . . . 2.95
3 . . . . 2.95
4 . . . . 2.95
5 . . . . 2.95

TZU: SPIRITS OF DEATH
Murim Studios, 1997
1 . . . . 2.95

UFO FLYING SAUCERS
Gold Key, Oct., 1968
1 . . . . 50.00
2 . . . . 30.00
3 thru 13 . . . . @25.00
Becomes:

UFO & OUTER SPACE
Gold Key, June, 1978
14 thru 25 . . . . @15.00

COLOR PUB.

ULTRAFORCE
Malibu Ultraverse, 1994–95
1 GP,Prime, Prototype 2.50
2 GP,Collision Course 2.25
3 GP,Head to Head 2.25
4 GP,Ghosts 2.25
5 GP,Last Stand,V:Atalon. 2.25
6 GP,Final Blow,V:Atalon 2.50
7 CU,GP(c),F:Ghoul 2.50
8 MWn,CV,GP,F:Black Knight 2.50
9 A:Marvel's Black Knight 2.50
10 . . . . 2.50
Spec.#0 . . . . 2.50

ULTRAFORCE
Malibu Ultraverse, 1995–96
Infinity Fant. Ultraforce Four 2.50
1 GP(c),Shot Down,pt.1. . . . . 2.25
1a Computer painted cover 2.25
2 Phoenix flip issue,I:Lament 2.25
3 Shot Down,pt.3. . . . . 2.25
4 . . . . 2.25
5 Smoke and Bone,pt.1 . . . . 2.25
6 Smoke and Bone,pt.2. . . . . 2.25
7 thru 9 . . . . @2.25
10 A:Sersi,Eliminator 2.25
11 . . . . 2.25
12 MD2,LWn, cont. from All-New
 Exiles #12 . . . . 2.25
13 LWn,MD2,new UltraForce lineup 2.25
14 LWn,MD2,Hardcase returns. . . . 2.25
15 LWn,MD2,D:Ripfire 2.25

ULTRAFORCE/AVENGERS
Malibu Ultraverse, Aug., 1995
1 GP,Black September prelude . . . 3.95

ULTRAFORCE/ SPIDER-MAN
Malibu Ultraverse, 1996
1 . . . . 3.95

ULTRAMAN
Nemesis, 1994
1 EC,O:Ultraman 2.25
2 . . . . 2.50
3 . . . . 2.50
4 V:Blue Ultraman 2.50

ULTRAMAN
Harvey/Ultracomics, 1993
1 with 1 of 3 cards 2.50
2 with 1 of 3 cards & virgin cover . 2.50
3 with 1 of 3 cards & virgin cover . 2.50

ULTRAVERSE DOUBLE FEATURE
Malibu Ultraverse, Jan., 1995
1 F:Prime, Solitaire 3.95

ULTRAVERSE FUTURE SHOCK
Malibu Ultraverse, 1996
1 one-shot,MPc,alternate futures . . 2.50

ULTRAVERSE ORIGINS
Malibu Ultraverse, Jan., 1994
1 O:Ultraverse Heroes 2.25
1a Silver foil cover 12.50

Ultraman 32
© Harvey/Ultracomics

ULTRAVERSE UNLIMITED
Malibu Ultraverse, 1996
1 F:Warlock. 2.25
2 LWn,KWe, A:All-New Exiles,
 V:Maxis 2.25

ULTRAVERSE: YEAR ZERO: THE DEATH OF THE SQUAD
Malibu Ultraverse, 1995
0-A hardcase's old team 2.50
0-B 2.50
0-C L.A. Riots 2.50
1 JHl,A:Squad, Mantra. 2.95
2 JHl,DaR(c) prequel to Prime#1 . . 2.95
3 Cont. Year Zero Story 2.95
4 I:NM-E 2.95

ULTRAVERSE: YEAR ONE
Malibu Ultraverse, 1995
1 Handbook, double size 4.95
2 Prime 2.25

ULTRAVERSE: YEAR TWO
Malibu Ultraverse, 1996
1 Marvel/Ultraverse/Info. 4.95

UNCLE SCROOGE
Dell/Gold Key, Dec., 1962
40 CB,X-Mas 150.00
41 . . . . 125.00
42 . . . . 125.00
43 CB. 125.00
44 CB. 125.00
45 CB. 125.00
46 Lost Beneath the Sea 125.00
47 CB. 125.00
48 CB. 125.00
49 CB,Loony Lunar Gold Rush . . 125.00
50 CB,Rug Riders in the Sky . . . 125.00
51 CB,How Green Was my
 Lettuce 110.00
52 CB,Great Wig Mystery 110.00
53 CB,Interplanetary Postman. . . 110.00
54 CB,Billion-Dollar Safari! 110.00
55 CB,McDuck of Arabia 110.00
56 CB,Mystery of the Ghost

All comics prices listed are for *Near Mint* condition.

Uncle Scrooge

Town Railroad. 110.00
57 CB,Swamp of No Return 110.00
58 CB,Giant Robot Robbers 110.00
59 CB,North of the Yukon 110.00
60 CB,Phantom of Notre Duck . . 110.00
61 CB,So Far and No Safari 100.00
62 CB,Queen of the Wild
  Dog Pack. 100.00
63 CB,House of Haunts! 100.00
64 CB,Treasure of Marco Polo!. . 125.00
65 CB,Micro-Ducks from
  OuterSpace 100.00
66 CB,Heedless Horseman. 100.00
67 CB rep. 100.00
68 CB,Hall of the Mermaid
  Queen!. 100.00
69 CB,Cattle King! 100.00
70 CB,The Doom Diamond! 100.00
71 CB. 100.00
72 CB rep. 100.00
73 CB rep. 100.00
74 thru 110 . . . . @75.00
111 thru 148 . . . . @40.00
149. . . . . 30.00
150 thru 168 . . . . @25.00
169 thru 173 . . . . @15.00

Whitman, 1980
174 thru 176 . . . . @35.00
177 and 178 . . . . @40.00
179 Rare 600.00
180 thru 182 . . . . @50.00
183 thru 195 . . . . @25.00
196 and 197 . . . . @30.00
1981 thru 209 . . . . @35.00

Gladstone, 1986
210 CB. 20.00
211 CB,Prize of Pizzaro 18.00
212 CB,city-golden roofs. 18.00
213 CB,city-golden roofs. 18.00
214 CB. 18.00
215 CB, a cold bargain 18.00
216 CB. 18.00
217 CB,7 cities of Cibola 18.00
218 CB. 18.00
219 Don Rosa,Son of Sun 28.00
220 CB,Don Rosa. 10.00
221 CB,A:BeagleBoys 4.00
222 CB,Mysterious Island. 4.00
223 CB. 4.00
224 CB,Rosa,Cash Flow. 7.00
225 CB. 4.00
226 CB,Rosa 5.00
227 CB,Rosa 5.00
228 CB. 4.00
229 CB. 4.00
230 CB. 5.00
231 CB,Rosa(c) 4.00
232 CB. 4.00
233 CB. 4.00
234 CB. 4.00
235 Rosa 7.00
236 CB. 4.00
237 CB. 4.00
238 CB. 4.00
239 CB. 4.00
240 CB. 4.00
241 CB,giant 7.00
242 CB,giant 7.00

Walt Disney, 1990
243 CB,`Pie in the Sky'. 4.00
244 . . . . 3.50
245 . . . . 3.50
246 . . . . 3.50
247 . . . . 3.50
248 . . . . 3.50
249 . . . . 3.50
250 CB. 5.00
251 . . . . 3.00
252 `No Room For Human Error' . . 3.00
253 `Fab.Philosophers Stone 3.00

COLOR PUB.

254 The Filling Station 3.00
255 The Flying Dutchman. 3.00
256 CB,`Status Seeker' 3.00
257 `Coffee,Louie or Me' 3.00
258 CB,`Swamp of no return' 3.00
259 `The only way to Go' 3.00
260 The Waves Above, The
  Gold Below 3.00
261 Rosa,`Return to Zanadu' Pt.1 . . 6.00
262 Rosa,`Return to Zanadu' Pt.2. . 6.00
263 Rosa,`Treasure Under Glass'. . 6.00
264 Snobs Club 3.00
265 CB,Ten Cent Valentine. 3.00
266 The Money Ocean,Pt.1 . . . . . . 3.00
267 The Money Ocean,Pt 2 . . . . . . 3.00
268 CB,Rosa,Island in the Sky 3.00
269 The Flowers. 3.00
270 V:Magica DeSpell 3.00
271 The Secret o/t Stone 3.00
272 Canute The Brute's Battle Axe . 3.00
273 CB,Uncle Scrooge-Ghost. 3.25
274 CB,Hall of the Mermaid Queen 3.25
275 CB,Rosa,Christmas Cheers,inc.

Uncle Scrooge #252
© Walt Disney

  D.Rosa centerspread 3.25
276 Rosa, thru 277 . . . . @7.00
278 thru 280 . . . . @3.00

Gladstone, 1993
281 Rosa 7.00
282 thru 284 . . . . @3.00
285 Rosa, Life & Times. 11.00
286 thru 293 Rosa, Life & Times . @6.00
294 thru 299 . . . . @3.00
300 Rosa & Barks 5.00
301 `Statuesque Spendthrifts'. 3.00
302. . . . . 3.00
303 `Rocks to Riches'. 3.00
304 `My Private Eye' 3.00
305 `The Vigilante of Pizen Bluff' . . 3.00
306. . . . . 3.00
307 `Temper Temper' 3.00
308 `Revenge of the Witch'. 3.00
Prestige format, 64pg.
309 `Whadalottajargon'. 8.00
310 `The Sign of the Triple
  Distelfink' 8.00
311 `The Last Lord of Eldorado' . . . 8.00
312 `The Hands of Zeus'. 8.00
313 `The Fantastic River Race'. . . . 8.00
314 . . . . 8.00
315 `The Flying Scot,' pt.1 . . . . 8.00
316 `The Flying Scot,' pt.2 . . . . 8.00
317 `Pawns of the Lamp Garou' . . . 8.00
318 `Cowboy Captain of Cutty Sark' 8.00

Comics Values Annual

319 `The Horse Radish Story'. 8.00
320 `The Mysterious Stone Ray'. . . 8.00
321 `The Giant Robot Robbers' . . . 8.00
322 `Secret of the Lost
  Dutchman's Mine'. 8.00

UNCLE SCROOGE
Gemstone Publishing 2003
319 The Dutchman's Secret 6.95
320 Fools of the Trade 6.95
321 Attaaack 6.95
322 The Utter Limits 6.95
323 . . . . 6.95
324 . . . . 6.95

UNCLE SCROOGE ADVENTURES
Gladstone, 1987
1 CB,McDuck of Arabia 9.00
2 translated from Danish 5.00
3 translated from Danish 5.00
4 CB 5.00
5 Rosa 5.00
6 CB 3.50
7 CB 3.00
8 CB 3.00
9 Rosa 3.50
10 CB. 3.00
11 CB. 3.00
12 CB. 3.00
13 CB. 3.00
14 Rosa 3.50
15 CB. 3.00
16 CB. 3.00
17 CB. 3.00
18 CB. 3.00
19 CB,Rosa(c) 3.50
20 CB,giant 6.00
21 CB,giant 6.00
22 Rosa(c) 6.00
23 CB,giant 4.00
24 thru 26 . . . . @2.50
27 Rosa,O:Jr. Woodchuck 4.00
28 giant 4.00
29 . . . . 2.50
30 giant 5.00
31 thru 32 . . . . @3.00
33 Barks. 5.00
34 thru 40 . . . . @3.00
41 . . . . 2.50
42 `The Dragon's Amulet' 2.50
43 `Queen of the Wild Dog Pack' . . 2.50
44 . . . . 2.50
45 `The Secret of the Duckburg
  Triangle'. 2.50
46 `The Tides Turn' 2.50
47 `The Menehune Mystery' 2.50
48 `The Tenth Avatar' 2.50
49 `Dead-Eye Duck' 2.50
50 CB,`The Secret of Atlantis'. . . . 3.00
51 . . . . 2.50
52 The Black Diamond 2.50
53 Secret of the Incas 2.50
54 Secret of the Incas, pt.2 . . . . . . 2.50

UNCLE SCROOGE ADVENTURES
Gladstone, 1997–98
Don Rosa Specials
Spec.#1 (of 4). 11.00
Spec.#2 thru #4 . . . . @10.00
Van Horn Specials
Spec.#1 . . . . 10.00
Spec.#2 . . . . 10.00
Spec.#3 . . . . 10.00
Spec.#4 . . . . 10.00

All comics prices listed are for *Near Mint* condition.

UNCLE SCROOGE ADVENTURES IN COLOR
Gladstone, 1987–98
Carl Barks reprints
1 thru 32 . . . . @10.00
33 thru 35.. . . . . @11.00
36 32pg.. . . . . 9.00
37 thru 53 . . . . @10.00
54 Hall of the Mermaid Queen . . . 10.00
55 The Doom Diamond. 10.00
56 two adventures 10.00

UNCLE SCROOGE & DONALD DUCK
Gold Key, 1965
1 rep.. 125.00

UNCLE SCROOGE AND DONALD DUCK
Gladstone, Oct., 1997
1 . . . . 2.50
2 Christmas stories 2.50
3 Back to Long Ago. 2.50
TPB Vol. 1 . . . . 9.95
TPB Vol. 2 . . . . 9.95
TPB Vol. 3 . . . . 9.95
TPB Vol. 4 . . . . 9.95

UNCLE SCROOGE GOES TO DISNEYLAND
Gladstone, 1985
1 CB,etc. 100pp. 13.00

UNDEAD, THE
Chaos! Comics Black Label, 2001
Ashcan 6.00
Ashcan, premium edition 20.00
1 zombie wasteland. 5.00
1a previews exclusive (c). 5.00
1b signed edition 15.00
1c premium edition 10.00
1d super-premium edition 20.00
1e foil (c). 20.00

UNDERDOG
Charlton, July, 1970
1 Planet Zot. 125.00
2 Simon Sez/The Molemen 75.00
3 Whisler's Father 75.00
4 The Witch of Pycoon 75.00
5 The Snowmen 75.00
6 The Big Shrink 75.00
7 The Marbleheads 75.00
8 The Phoney Booths 75.00
9 Tin Man Alley 75.00
10 Be My Valentine (Jan., 1972). . 75.00

UNDERDOG
Gold Key, March, 1975
1 The Big Boom 90.00
2 The Sock Singer Caper 50.00
3 The Ice Cream Scream. 50.00
4 . . . . 50.00
5 . . . . 50.00
6 Head in a Cloud 50.00
7 The Cosmic Canine 50.00
8 . . . . 50.00
9 . . . . 50.00
10 Bouble Trouble Gum 50.00
11 The Private Life of
    Shoeshine Boy. 35.00
12 The Deadly Fist of Fingers. . . . 35.00

13 . . . . 35.00
14 Shrink Shrank Shrunk 35.00
15 Polluter Palooka 35.00
16 The Soda Jerk. 35.00
17 Flee For Your Life 35.00
18 Rain Rain Go Away...Okay . . . 35.00
19 Journey To the Center of
    the Earth 35.00
20 The Six Million Dollar Dog 35.00
21 Smell of Success. 35.00
22 Antlers Away 35.00
23 Wedding Bells In Outer Space
    (Feb.,1979) 35.00

Underdog #1
© Spotlight

UNDERDOG
Spotlight, 1987
1 FMc,PC(c),The Eredicator 3.00
2 FMc,CS(c), Prisoner of Love/
    The Return of Fearo 3.00

UNDERDOG IN 3-D
Blackthorne
1 Wanted Dead or Alive. 2.50

UNDERSEA AGENT
Tower, 1966–97
1 F:Davy Jones,UnderseaAgent. 125.00
2 thru 4 . . . . @75.00
5 O&I:Merman. 85.00
6 GK,WW(c) 85.00

UNDERTAKER
Chaos! Comics, 1999
Preview BSt, WWF character. 2.50
Preview, photo (c) 2.50
1 Prophecy of the Dead. 2.95
1a photo cover 2.95
1b premium edition 10.00
1c Death Chrome cover. 14.95
1d Death Chrome cover, signed.. 19.95
2 V:Embalmer & Paul Bearer. 2.95
3 O:Undertaker 2.95
4 Kane 2.95
5 Jezebel 2.95
6 thru 12 . . . . @2.95
2a thru 12a photo covers . . . . . @2.95
Halloween Spec. 2.95
Halloween Spec. photo(c). 2.95
TPB Prophecy of the Dead,
    rep.#1–#4. . . . . 12.95
TPB Vol.2 rep.#5–#8. . . . . 12.95

UNEARTHLY SPECTACULARS
Harvey, 1965
1 DW,AT,I:Tiger Boy 50.00
2 WW,AW,GK,I:Earthman,Miracles,
    Inc. A:Clawfang,TigerBoy 75.00
3 RC,AW,JO,A:Miracles,Inc. 50.00

U.N. FORCE
Gauntlet Comics, 1995
0 BDC(s). 2.95
1 B:BDC(s),I:U.N.Force 2.95
2 O:Indigo 2.95
3 . . . . 2.95
4 A:Predator 2.95
5 B:Critial Mass. 2.95

U.N. FORCE FILES
Gauntlet Comics
1 KP(c),F:Hunter Seeker, Lotus . . . 2.95

UNION OF JUSTICE
Quantum Comics, 1998
1 by David Watkins & Steve Kurth . 2.95
2 . . . . 2.95
3 A:Golden Age Union 2.95

UNITY
Valiant 1992
0 BWS,BL,Chapter#1,A:All Valiant
    Heroes,V:Erica Pierce 3.00
0a Red ed.,w/red logo 4.00
1 BWS,BL,Chapter#18,A:All Valiant
    Heroes,D:Erica Pierce 3.00
1a Gold logo 4.00
1b Platinum 4.00
TPB Previews Exclusive,Vol.I
    Chap.#1-9 . . . . 8.00
TPB Previews Exclusive,Vol.II
    Chap.#10-18 . . . . 3.00
TPB #1 rep Chapters #1-4 . . . . . 10.95
TPB #2 rep Chapters #5-9 . . . . . . 9.95
TPB #3 rep Chapters #10-14 . . . . 9.95

UNITY 2000
Acclaim 1999
1 (of 6) 2.50
2 thru 5 . . . . @2.50

UNIVERSAL SOLDIER
Now, 1992
1 Based on Movie,Holo.(c). 2.75
2 Luc & Ronnie on the run
    from UniSols 2.50
2a Photo cover 2.00
3 Photo(c) 2.00

UNKNOWN WORLDS OF FRANK BRUNNER
Eclipse, 1985
1 and 2 FB. . . . . @2.50

UNLEASHED!
Triumphant
0 JnR(s),I:Skyfire. 2.50
1 JnR(s),. 2.50

UNLV
1 Championship season (basketball
    based on college team) 3.00

UNTAMED LOVE
Fantagraphics, 1987
1 FF 2.00

UNTOLD TALES OF
Chaos! Comics, 2000
Purgatori #1 . . . . 2.95
Purgatori #1 premium ed. 12.95
Chastity #1 . . . . 2.95
Chastity premium #1 . . . . 12.95
Lady Death #1 . . . . 2.95
Lady Death #1 premium 12.95
Lady Death #1 chromium ed. 15.95

UNUSUAL TALES
Charlton Comics, 1955–65
1 . . . . 300.00
2 . . . . 150.00
3 thru 5 . . . . @100.00
6 SD,SD(c) 225.00
7 SD,SD(c) 275.00
8 SD,SD(c) 275.00
9 SD,SD(c) 300.00
10 SD,SD(c) 325.00
11 SD 300.00
12 SD 200.00
13 . . . . 90.00
14 SD 200.00
15 SD,SD(c) 225.00
16 thru 20 . . . . @90.00
21 . . . . 75.00
22 SD 150.00
23 . . . . 75.00
24 . . . . 75.00
25 SD 135.00
26 SD 135.00
27 SD 135.00
28 . . . . 75.00
29 SD 125.00
30 thru 49 . . . . @65.00

URI-ON
1 and 2 . . . . @2.00

URTH 4
Continuity, 1990
1 TVE,NA(c) 2.00
2 TVE,NA 2.00
3 TVE,NA 2.00
4 NA,Last issue 2.00

USAGI YOJIMBO
Mirage, 1993
1 A:TMNT 6.00
2 thru 16 . . . . @5.00
17 . . . . 8.00

VALERIA THE SHE BAT
Continuity, 1993
1 NA,I:Valeria 10.00
2 thru 4 . . . . [NOT RELEASED]
5 Rise of Magic 2.50

VALERIA, THE SHE-BAT
Windjammer 1995
1 (of 2) NA,Valeria & 'Rilla 2.50
2 (of 2) NA,BSz, final issue 2.50

VALHALLA
Antarctic Press, 1999
1 BDn set in 1939 . . . . 3.00

VALIANT ERA
Valiant
TPB rep.Magnus #12,Shadowman #8, Solar #10-11,Eternal Warrior#4-5 . . . . 13.95

VALIANT READER: GUIDE TO THE VALIANT UNIVERSE
1 O:Valiant Universe 2.25

VALIANT VISION STARTER KIT
Valiant
1 w/3-D Glasses 2.95
2 F:Starwatchers 2.95

VALKYRIE
Eclipse, 1988
1 PG,I:Steelfox,C:Airboy, Sky Wolf. 3.00
2 PG,O:New Black Angel 2.50
3 PG 2.50

[2nd Series]
1 BA,V:Eurasian Slavers 2.00
2 and 3 BA,V:Cowgirl . . . . @2.00

Valley of the Dinosaurs #7
© *Charlton Comics*

VALLEY OF THE DINOSAURS
Charlton, 1975
1 Hanna-Barbera TV adapt. 30.00
2 thru 11 . . . . @20.00

VALOR
Gemstone, 1998
1 EC comics reprint 2.50
2 . . . . 2.50
3 AW, The Cloak of Command 2.50
4 WW(c) 2.50
5 final issue 3.50
Annual
TPB Vol. 1 rebinding of series 13.50

VAMPEROTICA
Brainstorm, 1996
1–16 see B&W
17 . . . . 3.00

17a signed 5.00
17 Holochrome cover 40.00
18 Blood of the Damned (color) . . . 3.00
18a signed 5.00
19 'Hunter's Blood' 3.00
19a deluxe 3.00
20 'Vampire Quest' 3.00
21 hunting & feeding 3.00
22 . . . . 3.00
TPB Red Reign, rep. 12.95

VAMPEROTICA LINGERIE
Comic Cavalcade, 1998
Commemorative #1 by Kirk Lindo . . 5.95
Commemorative #1a deluxe 14.95

VAMPI
Harris Comics, 2000
1/2 24-pg. 10.00
1/2 variant edition 20.00
1 Switchblade Kiss,pt.1 . . . . 3.00
1c signed & numbered 20.00
1d gold foil 30.00
1e convention special, B&W 10.00
1g limited holochrome edition . . . 25.00
1g royal blue edition 60.00
1h Platinum edition 19.95
1i limited edition 9.95
2 Switchblade Kiss,pt.2 . . . . 8.00
1b thru 2b limited chrome (c) . . @15.00
2c limited holochrome edition . . . 25.00
3 Switchblade Kiss,pt.3 . . . . 5.00
4 Dark Angel Rising,pt.1 . . . . 3.00
5 Dark Angel Rising,pt.2 . . . . 3.00
6 Dark Angel Rising,pt.3 . . . . 3.50
7 Underworld, pt.1 (of 3) 3.00
8 Underworld, pt.2 . . . . 3.00
9 Underworld, pt.3 . . . . 3.00
1a thru 9a deluxe . . . . @10.00
Ashcan Vampi Dark Angel Rising
  platinum leather limited B&W . 14.95
Ashcan Vampi Underworld preview. 6.00
Ashcan Tainted Love 5.95
Vampi #1 preview 2.95
TPB Vol. 1, rep. #1–#3 . . . . 19.95

Anarchy Studios, 2001
10 . . . . 3.00
10b convention ed. 10.00
10c convention ed., signed 19.95
11 . . . . 3.00
12 . . . . 3.00
12b holo-fx chrome ed. 14.95
12c gold-fx chrome 24.95
13 . . . . 3.00
14 framed, I:Xenocyde 3.00
15 V:Xenocyde 3.00
16 saved by Xenocide 3.00
17 Ultimatrix, pt.2 . . . . 3.00
18 Ultimatrix, pt.3 . . . . 3.00
19 Serpent's Kiss, pt.1 . . . . 3.00
20 Serpent's Kiss, pt.2 . . . . 3.00
21 Serpent's Kiss, pt.3 . . . . 3.00
22 Serpent's Kiss, pt.4 . . . . 3.00
23 Fallout, pt.1 . . . . 3.00
24 Fallout, pt.2 . . . . 3.00
25 . . . . 3.00
10a thru 16a deluxe . . . . @10.00
14a thru 25a limited . . . . @9.95
Sketchbook platinum leather. . . . 14.95
Ashcan Vampi:End Game. 5.95
Ashcan Vampi #19–#21 . . . . 5.95
Ashcan Ultimatrix Leather Gold. . . 14.95
Ashcan Vampi: Anarchy in the USA
  giant-sized, limited (2001) 6.00
TPB Vol. 1 Switchblade Kiss/
  Dark Angel Rising 14.95
TPB Underworld Tainted Love 14.95

COLOR PUB.

Vampi–Vampirella

Vampi #10
© Anarchy Studios

VAMPI (DIGITAL)
Harris Comics, 2001
1 digital art	3.00
1a limited ed.	10.00
Preview edition, digital	3.00
Ashcan, Underworld gold leather	15.00

VAMPI VICIOUS
Anarchy Studios 2003
Prototype Convention edition	9.95
1	3.00
1a variant (c)	3.00
1 royal blue edition	39.95
1 gold foil edition	29.95
2 thru 3	@3.00
2a thru 3a variant (c)	3.00

VAMPIRE LESTAT
Innovation, 1990–91
1 Anne Rice Adapt.	17.00
1a 2nd printing	4.00
1b 3rd printing	2.50
2	7.00
2a 2nd printing	4.00
2b 3rd printing	2.50
3	5.00
3a 2nd printing	2.50
4	5.00
4a 2nd printing	2.50
5	5.00
6	5.00
7	5.00
8	5.00
9 scarce	8.00
9a 2nd Printing	3.00
10	5.00
11 'Those Who Must Be Kept'	4.00
12 conclusion	4.00
Vampire Companion #1	4.00
Vampire Companion #2 (preview 'Interview With The Vampire'	3.00
Vampire Companion #3	3.00
GN rep.#1-#12 (Innovation)	24.95
GN rep.#1-#12 (Ballantine)	25.00

VAMPIRELLA
Warren Publishing Co., 1969–83
1 NA,FF(c),I:Vampirella	600.00
2 B:Amazonia	200.00
3 Very scarce	500.00
4	125.00
5 FF(c)	125.00
6	125.00
7 FF(c)	150.00
8 B:horror	125.00
9 BWS,BV(c),WW	135.00
10 No Vampirella,WW	75.00
11 TS,FF(c)O&I Pendragon	100.00
12 WW	100.00
13	90.00
14	90.00
15	90.00
16	90.00
17 B:Tomb of the Gods	90.00
18	90.00
19 WW,1973 Annual	100.00
20 thru 25	@90.00
26	75.00
27 1974 Annual	90.00
28 thru 30	@75.00
31 FF(c)	90.00
32 thru 36	@50.00
37 1975 Annual	60.00
38	50.00
39	50.00
40	50.00
41 thru 45	@40.00
46 O:Vampirella	50.00
47 thru 99	@40.00
100 Double Size	100.00
101 thru 110	@60.00
111 Giant Edition	75.00
112	60.00

VAMPIRELLA
Harris, 1992
0 Dracula Wars	5.00
0a Blue version	22.00
1 V:Forces of Chaos, w/coupon for DSt poster	20.00
1a 2nd printing	5.00
2 AH(c)	18.00
3 A:Dracula	7.00
4 A:Dracula	6.00
5	6.00
Spec. #1 Vampirella/Shadowhawk: Creatures of the Night (1995)	5.50
TPB The Dracula War signed & numbered	39.95

Harris Comics, 1996
0 gold foil signed & numbered	22.00
1 Commemorative Edition	3.00
1a Commemorative Edition, sgn & num.	10.00
25th Anniv. Spec., FF(c)	5.95
25th Anniv. Spec., lim.	6.95
25th Anniv. Spec., lim., signed	49.95
Spec. Death of Vampirella, memorial, chromium cover	19.95
Spec. Death of Vampirella, memorial, chromium cover, signed	29.95
Spec. 1-shot Vampirella/Cain, flipbook, 72-pg. (1996)	6.95
Spec. Vampirella Pin-up (1995)	3.50

VAMPIRELLA
Harris Comics, 1997
1 Ascending Evil, pt.1	3.00
1a ultra-violent cover	3.00
1b JaL(c)	10.00
1c signed & numbered	20.00
2 Ascending Evil, pt.2	3.00
2a JaL(c)	10.00
3 Ascending Evil, pt.3	3.00
3a JaL(c)	10.00
4 Holy War, pt.1	3.00
4a Crimson ed., Joe Linsner (c)	3.00
5 Holy War, pt.2	3.00
6 Holy War, pt.3	3.00
7 Queen's Gambit, pt.1	3.00
7a variant cover, signed	30.00
7b chromium Edition	11.00
8 Queen's Gambit, pt.2	3.00
8a San Diego Con variant cover	10.00
9 Queen's Gambit, pt.3, concl.	3.00
10 Hell on Earth, pt.1 (of 3) V:Nyx	3.00
10a signed and numbered	20.00
10b variant JaL cover	10.00
10c Holoplaid Chromium Ed.	20.00
11 Hell on Earth, pt.2	3.00
12 Hell on Earth, pt.3, New costume	3.00
12a variant cover, new costume	3.00
12b chromium cover	11.00
13 World's End,pt.1	3.00
13a variant cover	3.00
13b Pantha cover	10.00
14 World's End,pt.2	3.00
14a variant cover	3.00
15 World's End,pt.3	3.00
15a variant cover	3.00
16 Pantha #1	3.00
16a Pantha photo cover	3.00
16b limited photo ed.	10.00
16c Julie Strain photo (c) ed.	10.00
17 Pantha #2	3.00
17a Phantha photo cover	3.00
17b Julie Strain photo (c) ed.	10.00
18 Rebirth, pt.1,JaL(c)	3.00
18a alternate cover, signed & num.	30.00
19 Rebirth, pt.2,	3.00
20 Rebirth, pt.3.	3.00
21 Dangerous Games,pt.1	3.00
21a Julie Strain photo (c)	10.00
21b Linsner chrome ed.	15.00
21c Millennium ed.	20.00
22 Dangerous Games,pt.2	3.00
22a Dorian (c)	10.00
22b Julie Strain signed	20.00
22c Julie Strain photo (c)	10.00
22d Linsner chrome (c)	15.00
23 Vampirella/Lady Death: The Revenge, pt.1	3.00
23a limited ed.	10.00
23b limited chrome ed.	15.00
23b Hell's Angels, Vampirella (c)	3.00
24a Pantha (c)	3.00
24b penciled ed. sign & num.	15.00
25 Hells Angels, vol.2	3.00
25a alternate (c)	3.00
25b Monte Moore (c)	15.00
26 The End #1	3.00
26a alternate (c)	10.00
26b platinum ed.	20.00
Ashcan, Ascending Evil, b&w, 16pg.	1.50
Ashcan, Ascending Evil, b&w, signed, limited	25.00
Ashcan, Queen's Gambit,B&W	6.00
Ashcan, Queen's Gambit,signed	25.00
Ashcan World's End, B&W,16pg.	6.00
Ashcan Rebirth preview,B&W,16-pg	6.00
Vampirella/Lady Death Limited Preview Ashcan, B&W	6.00
Vampirella, Queen's Gambit #1 special edition, alternate (c)	10.00
Chromium Edition	11.00
Spec.#0 A:Lady Death,B.U.:Pantha.	3.00
Spec.#0a Pantha(c)	3.00
Spec.#0b Vampirella(c)	10.00
Spec.#0c Vampirella(c), signed	30.00
Spec.#0d Pantha(c)	10.00
Spec. Vampirella/Dracula: The Centennial, A:Pantha,16pg.	2.00
Spec. Vampirella/Dracula: The Centennial, 48pg. (1997)	5.00
Spec.#1 Dangerous Games, holochrome (2001)	15.00
TPB Ascending Evil	7.50
Ann.Ed.#2 Rebirth	10.00

All comics prices listed are for Near Mint condition.

Vampirella–Vampirella

Ann.Ed.#3 Rebirth,Bruce Timm(c).. 10.00
Julie Strain Special................ 4.00
Julie Strain Special variant(c)..... 10.00
Julie Strain Spec. chrome (c).... 15.00
Julie Strain Spec. holochrome(c).. 25.00

VAMPIRELLA
Harris Comics, 2001
0 Gold edition 19.95
1 Nowheresville, Mayhew (c)..... 2.95
1a JSC (c)....................... 2.95
1b Anacleto (c) 2.95
1c JaL (c) 2.95
1d commemorative ed. B&W, FF(c) 4.95
1e Chicago convention edition 9.95
1f Chicago convention, limited ... 19.95
1g photo edition, limited........ 9.95
1h gold edition................. 29.95
1i holographic chrome (c) 14.95
1j royal blue edition 59.95
1k gold-fx chrome (c).......... 24.95
1l Ascending evil gold (c)...... 19.95
2 .... 3.00
2a limited 9.95
2b photo edition, limited....... 9.95
3 .... 3.00
3a limited 9.95
3b photo edition, limited....... 9.95
4 .... 3.00
4a limited 9.95
4b photo edition, limited....... 9.95
4c holo FX chrome (c)......... 14.95
4d gold-fx chrome 29.95
5 thru 22 .... @3.00
5a thru 22a limited .... @9.95
5b thru 22b photo (c) .... @9.95
7c thru 10c limited Pantha MT(c) @9.95
7d Pantha holo fx MC(c) 14.95
Ashcan #1 giant-size 5.95
Ashcan #4–#6 giant-size, 16-pg... 5.95
Preview #7–#9 16-pg............ 2.95
Ashcan #7–#9 giant-size,16-pg. .. 5.95
Ashcan #11–#13 .... 6.00
Ashcan #11–#13 leather 14.95
1-shot Vampirella Genesis 2.95
TPB Nowheresville 12.95
TPB Vol. 1 Crimson Chronicles.. 14.95
TPB Vol. 2 Fear of Mirrors 14.95
Spec. Model Search 9.95

VAMPIRELLA: BLOOD LUST
Harris, 1997
1 (of 2) JeR & JJu 5.00
2 JJu(c)........................ 5.00
Book 1, JJu(c) Virgin edition 11.00
Book 2, JJu(c) Virgin edition 11.00

VAMPIRELLA CLASSIC
Harris Comics, 1995
1 Dark Angel................... 3.50
2 V:Demogorgon................ 3.25
3 V:Were Beast................. 3.25
4 R:Papa Voodoo 3.25
5 .... 3.00

VAMPIRELLA: CROSSOVER GALLERY
Harris, 1997
1 art gallery.................... 3.00
1a signed and numbered........ 19.95
1b chromium edition 10.00
1c Painkiller Jane JQ(c),signed .. 29.95
1d Holochrome cover.......... 20.00

COLOR PUB.

Vampirella Death & Destruction #1
© Harris Comics

VAMPIRELLA: DEATH AND DESTRUCTION
Harris
1 limited preview ashcan 4.00
1a limited preview ashcan, signed
   & numbered 20.00
1b 'The Dying of the Light'...... 3.00
1c signed & numbered.......... 3.00
1d satin edition 25.00
1e satin edition, signed & numb.. 50.00
1f Lim. Ed., Mark Beachum (c)... 10.00
2 'The Nature of the Beast' 3.00
3 (of 3) TSg,ACo,JP,JJu(c),Mistress
   Nyx kills Vampi............. 3.00
TPB 14.95

VAMPIRELLA GENESIS
Harris Comics, 2001
Preview #1 variant 9.95
Preview #1 variant, signed 19.95

VAMPIRELLA/ LADY DEATH
Harris/Chaos!, 1999
1 x-over....................... 3.50
1a Valentine ed................. 9.95
1b signed and numbered........ 20.00
1c gold edition................ 29.95
1d penciled edition............ 10.00
Spec.#1 TheEnd,chrome(c)(2000) 14.95
Spec.#1a TheEnd,holochrome(c).. 24.95
Spec.#1b TheEnd,Royal blue(c).. 59.95
Spec.#1 Revenge, chrome(c)(2000)... 14.95
Spec.#1a Revenge,holochrome(c) 24.95
Spec.#1b Revenge,royal blue(c).. 59.95

VAMPIRELLA LIVES
Harris, 1996–97
1 Linen Edition 7.00
1a Censored Photo cover edition.. 8.00
2 Vengeance edition 3.00
2 Model photo edition 3.00
2 alternate edition, AH(c)...... 10.00
2 alternate edition, AH(c) signed . 10.00
3 WEl(s),ACo,JP,Graveyard edition,
   JSC......................... 3.00
3 WEl(s),ACo,JP,Model photo
   edition 3.00
TPB Vampirella Lives (2002) 12.95

Comics Values Annual

VAMPIRELLA OF DRAKULON
Harris Comics, 1996
1 V:assassin 3.00
1a alternate MiB(c)............. 9.95
2 Dracula returns............... 3.00
2a signed & numbered 8.00
3 thru 5 .... @3.00

VAMPIRELLA/ PAINKILLER JANE
Harris, 1998
1 foil JQ(c) 3.50
1a signed & numbered......... 39.95
1b alternate RL&JP(c).......... 9.95
1c alternate RL&JP(c) signed &
   numbered 29.95
1d Gold Edition 24.95
Ashcan Preview, signed &
   numbered 29.95

VAMPIRELLA: SAD WINGS OF DESTINY
Harris, 1996
1 DQ(s),JJu(c)................. 4.00
1 signed & numbered (#1,500)... 5.00
Gold Emblem Seal Edition 4.00
Gold Emblem Seal Edition, signed 25.00

VAMPIRELLA/SHI
Harris, 1997
Ashcan #1, limited, 16pg 3.00
1 .... 2.95
1a Chromium Edition 7.00
1b signed & numbered......... 19.95
1c penciled cover 9.95
1d penciled cover, signed 29.95

VAMPIRELLA STRIKES
Harris Comics, 1995
1 The Prize,pt.1................ 3.00
1a limited, signed & numbered... 10.00
1b full moon background 3.50
2 V:Dante Corp.,A:Passion 3.00
3 V:subway stalker 3.00
4 IEd,RN 'Soul Food'............ 3.00
5 DQ,RN,F:Eudaemon............ 3.00
5 signed & numbered, (200) 10.00
6 .... 3.00
6 signed, alternate cover 10.00
6 signed & numbered 12.00
7 silver special flip book....... 3.00
Ann. #1 new cover 10.00
Ann. #1 new cover, signed &
   numbered 25.00

VAMPIRELLA VS. EUDAEMON
Harris, 1996
1 .... 10.00
1 signed & numbered 25.00

VAMPIRELLA VS. HEMORRHAGE
Harris, 1997
1 IEd,MIB 3.50
1 signed & numbered 12.00
1 Linen edition, signed & numb.. 25.00
1 MIB alternate cover........... 9.95
2 IEd,MIB 3.50
3 (of 3) IEd, MIB 3.50

VAMPIRELLA VS. PANTHA
Harris, 1997
Showcase #1 preview 2.00
1 MMr,MT, MT(c) Vampirella vs.
  Pantha 3.50
1 MMr,MT, MT(c) Pantha vs.
  Vampirella 3.50
1 MT(c) Vampirella vs. Pantha,
  signed 20.00
1 MT(c) Pantha vs. Vampirella,
  signed 20.00
1a MMr,MT, MT(c) 10.00
1a MMr,MT, MT(c) signed &
  numbered 30.00

VAMPIRELLA/WETWORKS
Harris, 1997
1 StG,SSh,image x-over 2.95
1 signed & numbered 17.95
1b Sean Shaw & Kevin Nowlan (c) 9.95

VAMPIRELLA/WITCH-BLADE
Harris Comics 2003
1 . . . . 3.00
1a variant (c) 9.95

VAMPIRE THE MASQUERADE
Moonstone, 2001
1-shot Toreador 5.95
1-shot Nosferatu (2002) 6.95
1-shot Beckett 6.95
1-shot Ventrue 6.95
1-shot Calebros 5.95
1-shot Giovanni 5.50
1-shot Assamite 5.50
1-shot Lasombra 5.50
1-shot Isabel 4.95
1-shot Lucita 4.95
TPB Vol. 1 . . . . 16.95
TPB Vol. 2 . . . . 20.95
TPB Vol. 3 Five Undead 20.95

VAMPRESS LUXURA, THE
Brainstorm, 1996
1 . . . . 3.00
1a gold edition 10.00
2 . . . . 2.95
2a gold foil 10.00

VANDALA
Chaos! Comics, 2000
1 . . . . 2.95
1 premium 9.99

VANDALA II
Chaos! Comics, 2001
1 PDa,EBe 3.00
1a premium ed. Matt Hughes (c) . 10.00

VANGUARD ILLUSTRATED
Pacific, 1983
1 . . . . 3.00
2 DSt(c) 3.00
3 thru 5 SR . . . . @3.00
6 Gl 3.00
7 GE,I:Mr.Monster 6.00

VANITY
Pacific, 1984
1 and 2 . . . . @2.00

VARICK: CHRONICLES OF THE DARK PRINCE
Q Comics, 1999
1 by Nick Marcari & Major Fareed . 2.00
2 32-pg 2.00
3 thru 6 . . . . @2.00

VAULT OF HORROR
Gladstone, 1990–91
1 Rep.GS,WW 5.00
2 Rep.VoH #27 & HoF #18 . . . . . . 3.00
3 Rep.VoH #13 & HoF #22 . . . . . . 3.00
4 Rep.VoH #23 & HoF #13 . . . . . . 3.00
5 Rep.VoH #19 & HoF #5 . . . . 3.00
6 Rep.VoH #32 & WF #6 . . . . 3.00
7 Rep.VoH #26 & WS #7 . . . . 3.00

Vault of Horror #26
© Gemstone

VAULT OF HORROR
Russ Cochran Publ., 1991–92
1 Rep.VoH #28 & WS #18 . . . . 3.00
2 Rep.VoH #33 & WS #20 . . . . 2.50
3 Rep.VoH #26 & WS #7 . . . . 2.50
4 Rep.VoH #35 & WS #15 . . . . 2.50
4 Rep.VoH #18 & WS #11 . . . . 2.50
5 Rep.VoH #18 & WS #11 . . . . 2.50
2nd Series
1 thru 7 Rep.VoH . . . . @2.50
8 . . . . 2.50
Gemstone
17 thru 29 EC comics reprints . . . @2.50
`Annuals'
TPB Vol. 1 rebinding of #1–#5 . . . 8.95
TPB Vol. 2 rebinding of #6–#10 . . 8.95
TPB Vol. 3 rebinding of #11–#15 . 10.95
TPB Vol. 4 rebinding of #16–#20 . 12.95
TPB Vol. 5 rebinding of #21–#25 . 13.50
TPB Vol. 6 reginding of #26–#29 . 10.95

VECTOR
Now, 1986
1 . . . . 2.50
2 thru 5 . . . . @2.00

VEGAS KNIGHTS
Pioneer, 1989
1 . . . . 2.00
2 . . . . 2.00
3 . . . . 2.00

VENGEANCE OF VAMPIRELLA
Harris, 1994
1 Hemmorhage 6.00
1a Gold Edition 9.00
1 gold edition, signed, numbered . 15.00
2 Dervish 3.00
3 On the Hunt 3.00
4 Teenage Vampries 3.00
5 Teenage Vampries 3.00
6 . . . . 3.00
7 . . . . 3.00
8 bagged w/card 3.00
9 . . . . 3.00
10 Bad Jack Rising 3.00
11 Pits of Hell, w/card 3.00
12 V:Passion 3.00
13 V:Passion 3.00
14 Prelude to the Walk,pt.2 . . . . . . 3.00
15 The Mystery Walk,pt.1 . . . . 3.25
16 The Mystery Walk,pt.2 . . . . 3.25
17 The Mystery Walk,pt.3 . . . . 3.25
18 The Mystery Walk,pt.4 . . . . 3.00
19 The Mystery Walk,pt.5 . . . . 3.00
20 Mystery Walk epilog 3.00
14a thru 19a Buzz . . . . @5.00
21 thru 24 . . . . @3.00
25 `The End' 3.00
25 variant cover, signed &
  numbered 8.00
25 signed & numbered (2,500) . . . 8.00
25 gold edition, signed & numb. . 20.00
25 alternate cover, signed by Jae
  Lee & numbered (#1,500) 15.00
Mini-comic gold foil, signed 20.00
TPB 1-3 Bloodshed 6.95

VENTURE
AC Comics, 1986
1 . . . . 2.00
2 thru 4 . . . . @2.00

VERONICA
Archie Publications, April, 1989
1 thru 50 . . . . @2.00
51 thru 71 . . . . @2.00
72 thru 93 . . . . @2.00
94 thru 97 . . . . @1.80
98 thru 120 . . . . @2.00
121 thru 133 . . . . @2.00
134 thru 147 . . . . @2.20

VEROTIKA
Verotika, 1995
1 thru 3 Jae Lee, Frazetta . . . . . @2.95
4 thru 9 . . . . @2.95
1-shot Rogues Gallery of Villians
  (1998) 3.95

VEROTIK ILLUSTRATED
Verotik, 1997
1 48pg 6.95
2 . . . . 6.95
3 . . . . 6.95
3a alternate cover 6.95
3 variant cover 10.00

VESPER
Acetylene Comics, 2001
Preview B&W................ 3.00
1 Girls Night Out............. 2.50
1a JOb (c)................... 2.50
2 .... 2.50
2a variant Wizardworld 2001(c)... 5.00
3 The Word for the Day........ 2.50
3a variant HbK(c)............. 2.50
4 .... 2.50
5 Soul Harvest................ 2.50
6 .... 2.50
6a variant (c)................ 2.50
7 Return of Gruel.............. 2.95

VESPERS
Mars Media Group, 1995
1 Tony Caputo................ 2.50
2 I:Dark Side................. 2.50

VIC FLINT
Argo Publ., Feb., 1956
1 .... 90.00
2 .... 75.00

VICKI
Atlas, Feb.–Aug., 1975
1 Rep...................... 50.00
2 thru 4.................. @40.00

VICTORIAN
Penny Farthing Press, 1999
1 .... 2.95
2 thru 5.................. @2.95
6 thru 13................. @2.95
14 thru 17................ @2.95
18 thru 21................ @2.95
TPB Vol. 2 Self-Immolation..... 19.95
TPB Act 3: Self Estrangement... 19.95

VILLAINS & VIGILANTES
Eclipse, 1986–87
1 A:Crusaders,Shadowman...... 2.00
2 A:Condor.................. 2.00
3 V:Crushers................. 2.00
4 V:Crushers................. 2.00

VINTAGE MAGNUS ROBOT FIGHTER
Valiant
1 rep. Gold Key Magnus #22
(which is #1)................ 5.00
2 rep. Gold Key Magnus #3..... 4.50
3 rep. Gold Key Magnus #13.... 3.50
4 rep. Gold Key Magnus #15.... 3.50

VIOLENT CASES
Tundra
1 20's Chicago............... 11.00

VIP
TV Comics, 2000
1 (of 3).................... 2.95
2 .... 2.95
3 .... 2.95
1a thru 3a photo (c)......... @2.95
TPB Collected Edition......... 8.95
Preview Edition.............. 5.95

VIRGINIAN, THE
Gold Key, June, 1963
1 .... 75.00

VIRTEX
Oktomica Entertainment, 1998
0 16-pg..................... 2.00
1 V:Ripnun.................. 2.50
2 V:Ripnun.................. 2.50
3 alternate endings........... 2.50
4 Night of the Ninjella,pt.1..... 2.50
5 Night of the Ninjella,pt.2..... 2.95
6 All My Sins Remembered...... 2.95

VIRTUA FIGHTER
Malibu Aug., 1995
1 New Video Game Comic...... 2.50

Visitor #12
© Valiant

VISITOR
Valiant 1994
1 New Series................. 2.50
2 F:The Harbinger............ 2.50
3 The Bomb................. 2.50
4 V:F/X Specialists............ 2.50
5 R:Harbinger................ 2.50
6 KVH,BS(c),V:Men in Black.... 2.50
7 KVH,BS(c),V:Men in Black,pt.2.. 2.50
8 KVH,V:Harbinger identity..... 2.50
9 KVH,A:Harbinger,Flamingo.... 2.50
10 Weather Problems.......... 2.50
11 V:Cannibals............... 2.50
12 V:Harada, Men in Black..... 2.50
13 Visitor is the Future Harbinger.. 2.50

VISITOR VS. VALIANT
Valiant 1994
1 V:Solar.................... 2.95
2 .... 2.95

VOLTRON
Solson, 1985
1 TV tie-in.................. 3.50
2 .... 3.50
3 .... 3.50

VORTEX
Vortex, 1982–88
1 Peter Hsu art............... 9.00
2 Mister X on cover........... 6.00
3 .... 4.00
4 .... 4.00
5 .... 3.00
6 thru 8................... @3.00
9 thru 13.................. @2.00

VORTEX
Comico, 1991
1 SBt,from Elementals.......... 2.50
2 SBt,...................... 2.50

VORTEX: THE SECOND COMING
Entity, 1996
1 (of 6).................... 2.95
1a variant cover.............. 2.95
2 .... 2.95

VOYAGE TO THE DEEP
Dell Publishing Co., Sept.–Nov., 1962
1 P(c)..................... 75.00
2 P(c)..................... 50.00
3 P(c)..................... 50.00
4 P(c)..................... 50.00

WACKY ADVENTURES OF CRACKY
Gold Key, 1972–75
1 .... 25.00
2 thru 11................. @15.00
12 .... 12.00

WACKY WITCH
Gold Key, 1971–75
1 .... 40.00
2 .... 25.00
3 thru 20................. @20.00
21 .... 15.00

WAGON TRAIN
Gold Key, Jan.–Oct., 1964
1 .... 100.00
2 .... 75.00
3 .... 75.00
4 .... 75.00

WALLY
Gold Key, 1962–63
1 .... 50.00
2 .... 35.00
3 .... 35.00
4 .... 35.00

WALLY WOOD'S THUNDER AGENTS
Delux, 1984–86
1 GP,KG,DC,SD,I:New Menth.... 4.00
2 GP,KG,DC,SD,`The Raven'.... 3.50
3 KG,DC,SD................. 3.50
4 GP,KG,RB,DA.............. 3.50
5 JOy,KG,A:CodenamDangr..... 3.50

WALT DISNEY ANNUALS
Walt Disney's Autumn Adventure.. 4.00
Walt Disney's Holiday Parade #1.. 3.50
Walt Disney's Spring Fever....... 3.50
Walt Disney's Summer Fun....... 3.50
Walt Disney's Holiday Parade #2.. 3.50

Comics Values Annual — COLOR PUB. — Walt Disney

WALT DISNEY'S AUTUMN ADVENTURE
1 Rep. CB 4.00

WALT DISNEY'S CHRISTMAS PARADE
Gemstone Publishing 2003
1 . . . . 8.95

WALT DISNEY'S COMICS AND STORIES
Dell/Gold Key, 1962
- 264 CB, Von Drake & Gearloose . . 50.00
- 265 CB, Von Drake & Gearloose . . 50.00
- 266 CB, Von Drake & Gearloose . . 50.00
- 267 CB, Von Drake & Gearloose . . 50.00
- 268 CB, Von Drake & Gearloose . . 50.00
- 269 CB, Von Drake & Gearloose . . 50.00
- 270 CB, Von Drake & Gearloose . . 50.00
- 271 CB, Von Drake & Gearloose . . 50.00
- 272 CB, Von Drake & Gearloose . . 50.00
- 273 CB, Von Drake & Gearloose . . 50.00
- 274 CB, Von Drake & Gearloose . . 50.00
- 275 CB 45.00
- 276 CB 45.00
- 277 CB 45.00
- 278 CB 45.00
- 279 CB 45.00
- 280 CB 45.00
- 281 CB 45.00
- 282 CB 45.00
- 283 CB 45.00
- 284 . . . . 25.00
- 285 . . . . 25.00
- 286 CB 30.00
- 287 . . . . 25.00
- 288 CB 30.00
- 289 CB 30.00
- 290 . . . . 25.00
- 291 CB 30.00
- 292 CB 30.00
- 293 CB; Grandma Duck's Farm Friends 30.00
- 294 CB 30.00
- 295 . . . . 25.00
- 296 . . . . 25.00
- 297 CB; Gyro Gearloose 30.00
- 298 CB; Daisy Duck's Dairy 30.00
- 299 CB rep. 30.00
- 300 CB rep. 30.00
- 301 CB rep. 30.00
- 302 CB rep. 30.00
- 303 CB rep. 30.00
- 304 CB rep. 30.00
- 305 CB rep. Gyro Gearloose 30.00
- 306 CB rep. 30.00
- 307 CB rep. 30.00
- 308 CB 30.00
- 309 CB 30.00
- 310 CB 30.00
- 311 CB 30.00
- 312 CB 30.00
- 313 thru 327 . . . . @25.00
- 328 CB rep. 30.00
- 329 . . . . 20.00
- 330 . . . . 20.00
- 331 . . . . 20.00
- 332 . . . . 20.00
- 333 . . . . 20.00
- 334 . . . . 20.00
- 335 CB rep. 25.00
- 336 . . . . 20.00
- 337 . . . . 20.00
- 338 . . . . 20.00
- 339 . . . . 20.00
- 340 . . . . 20.00
- 341 . . . . 20.00
- 342 thru 350 CB rep. . . . . @25.00
- 351 thru 361 CB rep. with poster @30.00
- 351a thru 361a. without poster . @25.00
- 361 thru 400 CB rep. . . . . @25.00
- 401 thru 409 CB rep. . . . . @20.00
- 410 CB rep. Annette Funichello . . . 20.00
- 411 thru 429 CB rep. . . . . @20.00
- 430 . . . . 10.00
- 431 CB rep. 15.00
- 432 CB rep. 15.00
- 433 . . . . 10.00
- 434 CB rep. 15.00
- 435 CB rep. 15.00
- 436 CB rep. 15.00
- 437 . . . . 10.00
- 438 . . . . 10.00
- 439 CB rep. 11.00
- 440 CB rep. 11.00
- 441 . . . . 10.00
- 442 CB rep. 11.00
- 443 CB rep. 11.00
- 444 . . . . 10.00
- 445 . . . . 10.00
- 446 thru 465 CB rep. . . . . @11.00
- 466 . . . . 11.00
- 467 thru 473 CB rep. . . . . @11.00

Walt Disney's Comics and Stories #305 © Gold Key

Whitman, 1980
- 474 thru 478 CB rep. . . . . @20.00
- 479 CB 50.00
- 480 CB Rare 100.00
- 481 thru 484 . . . . @50.00
- 485 thru 505 . . . . @25.00
- 506 . . . . 20.00
- 507 CB rep. 22.00
- 508 CB rep. 22.00
- 509 CB rep. 22.00
- 510 CB rep. 22.00

Gladstone, 1986
- 511 translation of Dutch 25.00
- 512 translation of Dutch 25.00
- 513 translation of Dutch 25.00
- 514 translation of Dutch 11.00
- 515 translation of Dutch 11.00
- 516 translation of Dutch 11.00
- 517 translation of Dutch 6.00
- 518 translation of Dutch 6.00
- 519 CB, Donald Duck 6.00
- 520 translation of Dutch, Rosa . . 11.00
- 521 Walt Kelly 6.00
- 522 CB, WK, nephews 6.00
- 523 Rosa, Donald Duck 15.00
- 524 Rosa, Donald Duck 15.00
- 525 translation of Dutch 15.00
- 526 Rosa, Donald Duck 10.00
- 527 CB 6.00
- 528 Rosa, Donald Duck 15.00
- 529 CB 6.00
- 530 Rosa, Donald Duck 7.00
- 531 WK(c), Rosa, CB 7.00
- 532 CB 6.00
- 533 CB 6.00
- 534 CB 6.00
- 535 CB 6.00
- 536 CB 6.00
- 537 CB 6.00
- 538 CB 6.00
- 539 CB 6.00
- 540 CB new art 6.00
- 541 double-size, WK(c) 6.00
- 542 CB 7.00
- 543 CB, WK(c) 6.00
- 544 CB, WK(c) 6.00
- 545 CB 6.00
- 546 CB, WK, giant 7.00
- 547 CB, WK, Rosa, giant 15.00

Walt Disney, 1990
- 548 CB, WK, `Home is the Hero'. . . 12.00
- 549 CB, ... 5.00
- 550 CB, prev.unpub.story! 8.00
- 551 . . . . 5.00
- 552 . . . . 5.00
- 553 . . . . 5.00
- 554 . . . . 5.00
- 555 . . . . 5.00
- 556 . . . . 5.00
- 557 . . . . 5.00
- 558 `Donald's Fix-it Shop'. 5.00
- 559 `Bugs' 5.00
- 560 CB, April Fools Story 5.00
- 561 CB, Donald the `Flipist' 5.00
- 562 CB, `3DirtyLittleDucks' 5.00
- 563 CB, `Donald Camping' 5.00
- 564 CB, `Dirk the Dinosaur' 5.00
- 565 CB, DonaldDuck, TruantOfficer . 5.00
- 566 CB, `Will O' the Wisp' 5.00
- 567 CB, `Turkey Shoot' 5.00
- 568 CB, `AChristmas Eve Story' . . . 5.00
- 569 CB, New Years Resolutions . . . 5.00
- 570 CB, Donald the Mailman +Poster 5.00
- 571 CB, `Atom Bomb' 8.00
- 572 CB, April Fools 5.00
- 573 TV Quiz Show 5.00
- 574 Pinnocchio, 64pgs 6.00
- 575 Olympic Torch Bearer, Li'l Bad Wolf, 64 pgs. 6.00
- 576 giant 6.00
- 577 A: Truant Officers, 64 pgs. 6.00
- 578 CB, Old Quacky Manor 5.00
- 579 CB, Turkey Hunt 5.00
- 580 CB, The Wise Little Red Hen, 64 pg.-Sunday page format . . . 5.50
- 581 CB, Duck Lake 5.00
- 582 giant 5.50
- 583 giant 5.50
- 584 . . . . 5.00
- 585 CB, giant 5.50

Gladstone, 1993
- 586 . . . . 5.00
- 587 thru 599 . . . . @5.00
- 600 CB 6.00
- 601 thru 605 prestige format . . . . @7.00
- 606 `Winging It' 7.00
- 607 `Number 401' 7.00
- 608 `Sleepless in Duckburg' 7.00
- 609 . . . . 7.00
- 610 `Treasures Untold' 7.00
- 611 `Romance at a Glance' 7.00
- 612 `The Sod Couple' 7.00
- 613 `Another Fine Mess' 7.00
- 614 `Airheads' 7.00
- 615 `Backyard Battlers' 7.00
- 616 . . . . 7.00
- 617 `Tree's A Crowd' 7.00
- 618 `A Dolt from the Blue' 7.00

All comics prices listed are for Near Mint condition.

Walt Disney–War / COLOR PUB.

| 619 'Queen of the Ant Farm'..... 7.00
| 620 'Caught in the Cold Rush'.... 7.00
| 621 'Room and Bored'........... 7.00
| 622 .... 7.00
| 623 'All Quacked Up'............ 7.00
| 624 'Their Loaded Forebear'..... 7.00
| 625 'Mummery's the Word'....... 7.00
| 626 'A Real Gone Guy'........... 7.00
| 627 'To Bee or Not to Bee'....... 7.00
| 628 'Officer for a Day'........... 7.00
| 629 'The Ghost Train'............ 7.00
| 630 two Donald Duck stories..... 7.00
| 631 'Music Hath Charms'......... 7.00
| 632 'A Day in a Duck's Life'...... 7.00
| 633 All Donald issue............. 7.00
| 634 'The Runaway Train'......... 7.00
| 635 'Volcano Valley'............. 7.00
| 636 'Mission to Codfish Cove'.... 7.00
| 637 'Pizen Springs Dude Ranch'.. 7.00

WALT DISNEY'S COMICS AND STORIES
Gemstone Publishing 2003

| 634 .... 6.95
| 635 Hound of the Moaning Hills... 6.95
| 636 Perchance to Dream......... 6.95
| 637 So We Reap................. 6.95
| 638 .... 6.95
| 639 .... 6.95

WALT DISNEY COMICS DIGEST
Gold Key, 1968–76
[All done by Carl Barks]

| 1 Rep,Uncle Scrooge......... 125.00
| 2 .... 75.00
| 3 .... 75.00
| 4 .... 75.00
| 5 .... 125.00
| 6 .... 60.00
| 7 .... 60.00
| 8 .... 60.00
| 9 .... 60.00
| 10 .... 60.00
| 11 .... 60.00
| 12 .... 60.00
| 13 .... 60.00
| 14 .... 35.00
| 15 .... 35.00
| 16 rep.Donald Duck #26....... 60.00
| 17 .... 45.00
| 18 .... 45.00
| 19 .... 45.00
| 20 .... 45.00
| 21 .... 35.00
| 22 .... 35.00
| 23 .... 35.00
| 24 .... 35.00
| 25 .... 35.00
| 26 .... 35.00
| 27 .... 35.00
| 28 .... 35.00
| 29 .... 35.00
| 30 .... 35.00
| 31 .... 35.00
| 32 .... 30.00
| 33 .... 35.00
| 34 rep.Four Color #318........ 35.00
| 35 .... 35.00
| 36 .... 35.00
| 37 .... 35.00
| 38 rep.Disneyland#1........... 35.00
| 39 .... 35.00
| 40 .... 30.00
| 41 .... 25.00
| 42 .... 30.00
| 43 .... 30.00
| 44 Rep. Four Color #29 & others.. 75.00

| 45 .... 25.00
| 46 CB......................... 25.00
| 47 .... 25.00
| 48 .... 25.00
| 49 .... 25.00
| 50 CB......................... 25.00
| 51 rep.Four Color #71......... 35.00
| 52 CB......................... 25.00
| 53 .... 25.00
| 54 .... 25.00
| 55 .... 25.00
| 56 CB,rep. Uncle Scrooge #32... 30.00
| 57 CB......................... 25.00

WALT DISNEY SHOWCASE
Gold Key, 1970–80

| 1 Boatniks (photo cover)....... 40.00
| 2 Moby Duck.................. 30.00
| 3 Bongo & Lumpjaw........... 25.00
| 4 Pluto....................... 25.00
| 5 $1,000,000 Duck (photo cover). 30.00
| 6 Bedknobs & Broomsticks..... 25.00
| 7 Pluto....................... 25.00
| 8 Daisy & Donald.............. 25.00
| 9 101 Dalmatians rep.......... 28.00
| 10 Napoleon & Samantha....... 20.00
| 11 Moby Duck rep............. 15.00
| 12 Dumbo rep................. 20.00
| 13 Pluto rep................... 20.00
| 14 World's Greatest Athlete.... 25.00
| 15 3 Little Pigs rep............ 25.00
| 16 Aristocats rep.............. 25.00
| 17 Mary Poppins rep........... 25.00
| 18 Gyro Gearloose rep......... 35.00
| 19 That Darn Cat rep.......... 25.00
| 20 Pluto rep................... 20.00
| 21 Li'l Bad Wolf & 3 Little Pigs.. 15.00
| 22 Unbirthday Party rep........ 25.00
| 23 Pluto rep................... 20.00
| 24 Herbie Rides Again rep...... 20.00
| 25 Old Yeller rep.............. 20.00
| 26 Lt. Robin Crusoe USN rep... 20.00
| 27 Island at the Top of the World. 25.00
| 28 Brer Rabbit, Bucky Bug rep.. 20.00
| 29 Escape to Witch Mountain... 25.00
| 30 Magica De Spell rep......... 35.00
| 31 Bambi rep.................. 25.00
| 32 Spin & Marty rep............ 25.00
| 33 Pluto rep................... 20.00
| 34 Paul Revere's Ride rep...... 15.00
| 35 Goofy rep.................. 15.00
| 36 Peter Pan rep.............. 15.00
| 37 Tinker Bell & Jiminy Cricket rep. 15.00
| 38 Mickey & the Sleuth, Pt. 1... 20.00
| 39 Mickey & the Sleuth, Pt. 2... 20.00
| 40 The Rescuers.............. 20.00
| 41 Herbie Goes to Monte Carlo. 20.00
| 42 Mickey & the Sleuth......... 20.00
| 43 Pete's Dragon.............. 25.00
| 44 Return From Witch Mountain
| & In Search of the Castaways. 25.00
| 45 The Jungle Book rep........ 25.00
| 46 The Cat From Outer Space.. 20.00
| 47 Mickey Mouse Surprise Party. 20.00
| 48 The Wonderful Adventures of
| Pinocchio.................. 20.00
| 49 North Avenue Irregulars; Zorro. 20.00
| 50 Bedknobs & Broomsticks rep.. 20.00
| 51 101 Dalmatians............. 20.00
| 52 Unidentified Flying Oddball... 20.00
| 53 The Scarecrow............. 20.00
| 54 The Black Hole............. 20.00

WALT DISNEY COMICS IN COLOR
Gladstone, 1998

| TPB Vol. 1................... 9.95

Comics Values Annual

| TPB Vol. 2................... 9.95
| TPB Vol. 3................... 9.95
| TPB Vol. 4................... 9.95

WALT KELLY'S CHRISTMAS CLASSICS
Eclipse, 1987

| 1 .... 2.00

WALT KELLY'S SPRINGTIME TALES
Eclipse, 1988

| 1 .... 2.50

WAR AGAINST CRIME
Gemstone, 2000

| 1 rep......................... 2.50
| 2 rep. Summer 1942.......... 2.50
| 3 rep. Fall 1948.............. 2.50
| 4 rep. Winter 1948............ 2.50
| 5 rep. Feb. 1949.............. 2.50
| 6 rep. June 1949.............. 2.50
| 7 rep......................... 2.50
| 8 rep. Aug. 1949.............. 2.50
| 9 rep. Oct. 1949.............. 2.50
| 10 rep. Dec. 1949 issue....... 2.50
| 11 rep. Feb. 1950 issue....... 2.50
| 'Annuals'
| TPB Vol. 1 rep. #1–#5......... 13.50
| TPB Vol. 2 rep. #6–#11........ 15.95

WARCAT SPECIAL
Entity Press, 1995

| 1 I:Warcat.................... 2.95

WARCHILD
Maximum Press, 1995

| 1 I:Sword, Stone.............. 3.50
| 2 I:Morganna Lefay........... 3.00
| 3 V: The Black Knight......... 2.50
| 4 Rescue Merlyn.............. 2.50
| **[2nd Series]**
| 1 .... 2.50

WAR DANCER
Defiant, 1994

| 1 B:JiS(s),I:Ahrq Tsolmec...... 2.75

Warp #2
© First

CVA Page 686 — All comics prices listed are for *Near Mint* condition.

COLOR PUB.

War–Warstrike

2 I:Massakur 2.75
3 V:Massakur 2.75
4 JiS(s),A:Nudge 3.25

WARHAWKS
TSR, 1990–91
1 thru 6 from game . . . . @2.95
7 thru 10 The Battle of Britain. . . @2.95

WARHAWKS 2050
TSR
1 Pt.1 . . . . 2.95

WAR HEROES
Charlton Comics, 1963–67
1 . . . . 50.00
2 J.F.Kennedy 45.00
3 thru 10 . . . . @25.00
11 thru 26 . . . . @20.00
27 Devils Brigade 30.00

WARLASH
CFD, 1995
1 Project Hardfire 2.95

WARMASTER
1 and 2 . . . . @3.95

WARP
First, March, 1983
1 FB,JSon,I:Lord Cumulus & Prince
 Chaos, play adapt pt.1 . . . . . . 2.00
2 FB,SD,play adapt pt.2. . . . . 2.00
3 FB,SD,play adapt pt.3. . . . . 2.00
4 FB,SD,I:Xander,play pt.4 . . . . . 2.00
5 FB, play adapt pt.5 . . . . 2.00
6 FB/MG, play adapt pt.6. . . . . . . 2.00
7 FB/MG, play adapt pt.7. . . . . . . 2.00
8 FB/MG,BWg,play adapt pt.8 . . . 2.00
9 FB/MG,BWg,play adapt conc. . . 2.00
10 JBi/MG,BWg, Second Saga,
 I:Outrider 2.00
11 JBi/MG,A:Outrider 2.00
12 JBi/MG,A:Outrider 2.00
13 JBi/MG,A:Outrider 2.00
14 JBi/MG,A:Outrider 2.00
15 JBi/MG/BWg 2.00
16 BWg/MG,A:Outrider. 2.00
17 JBi/MG,A:Outrider. 2.00
18 JBi/MG,A:Outrider&Sargon . . . 2.00
19 MG,last issue. 2.00
Spec. #1 HC,O:Chaos 2.00
Spec. #2 MS/MG,V:Ylem 2.00
Spec. #3 . . . . 2.00

WARRIOR BUGS, THE
Artcoda Productions, 2002
1 . . . . 2.95
2 thru 5 . . . . @2.95

WARRIOR NUN AREALA
Antarctic Press, 1995
1 V:Lilith 4.00
1a limited edition 8.00
2 V:Lilith 3.00
3 V:Hellmaster 3.00
3 silver edition 12.00
TPB Rep.#1-#3. . . . . 9.95

BOOK II: RITUALS, 1996
1 Land of Rising Sun 3.00
1 Red edition. 9.00
1 signed 10.00
2 I:Cheetah 3.00
3 Iraq, 1989. . . . . 3.00

4 . . . . 3.00
5 Rituals,pt.5 . . . . 3.00
6 . . . . 3.00
Spec. Warrior Nun Portraits 4.00
Spec. Warrior Nun Portraits
 Commemorative Edition (1999) 6.00
TPB Rituals 16.00

Warrior Nun Book 3, #2
© *Antarctic Press*

BOOK III, 1997
1 The Hammer & the Holocaust. . . 3.00
2 Hammer & the Holocaust,pt.2 . . . 3.00
3 Hammer & the Holocaust,pt.3 . . . 3.00
4 Holy Man, Holy Terror,pt.1 . . . . . 3.00
5 Holy Man, Holy Terror,pt.2 . . . . . 3.00
6 by Barry Lyga & Ben Dunn 3.00
TPB Vol. 1 . . . . 9.95
TPB Vol. 1 reprint 9.95
Spec. Warrior Nun Areala/Glory
 by Ben Dunn 2.95
Spec. poster edition 5.95
Spec. Warrior Nun Areala vs. Razor,
 BDn,JWf x-over 3.95
Spec.Warrior Nun Areala vs. Razor
 commemorative (1999). 5.95
Spec.Warrior Nun Areala/Avengelyne
 comm. edition (1999) 5.95

VOL 3
1 F:Sister Shannon Masters 2.50
2 . . . . 2.50
3 . . . . 2.50
4 Antichrist arrives 2.50
5 . . . . 2.50
6 Crimson Nun 2.50
7 V:Ruprecht Marsh. 2.50
8 V:Mr.Zhu 2.50
9 in the Vatican 2.50
10 V:Nebelhexa 2.50
11 A:Demoness Lillith 2.50
12 F:Lillith. 3.50
13 V:Julius Salvius 2.95
14 Rebirth, pt.2. . . . . 2.95
15 Rebirth, pt.3. . . . . 2.95
16 Rebirth, pt.4. . . . . 2.95
17 Seven Deadly Sins, pt.1. . . . . . 2.95
18 Seven Deadly Sins, pt.2. . . . . . 2.95
19 Seven Deadly Sins, pt.3. . . . . . 2.95
Ann.2000 b&W 3.95

WARRIOR NUN AREALA:
SCORPIO ROSE
Antarctic Press, 1996
1 SEt & BDn 2.95

1a commemorative (1999). 5.95
2 thru 4 (of 4). . . . . @2.95

WARRIOR NUN DEI:
AFTERTIME
Antarctic Press, 1997
1 (of 3) by Patrick Thornton 2.95
1 Commemorative edition (1999) . . 5.95
2 . . . . 2.95
3 . . . . 3.00

WARRIOR NUN: FRENZY
Antarctic Press, 1998
1 (of 2) by Miki Horvatic
 & Esad T. Ribic. 2.95
2 . . . . 2.95

WARRIOR NUN:
NO JUSTICE
Antarctic Press, 2002
1 F:Areala,V:The Judge 3.95

WARRIOR NUN:
RESURRECTION
Antarctic Press, 1998
1 by Ben Dunn 2.95
1a deluxe 5.95
2 quest for lost God Armor 3.00
3 . . . . 3.00

WARRIORS OF PLASM
Defiant, 1993–95
1 JiS(s),DL,A:Lorca 3.25
2 JiS(s),DL,Sedition Agenda 3.25
3 JiS(s),DL,Sedition Agenda 3.25
4 JiS(s),DL,Sedition Agenda 3.25
5 JiS(s),B:The Demons of
 Darkedge 2.75
6 JiS(s),The Demons of
 Darkedge,pt.2. . . . . 2.75
7 JiS(s),DL, ... 2.75
8 JiS(s),DL,40-pg. 3.00
9 JiS(s),LWn(s),DL,40-pg. 3.00
10 DL, ... 2.50
GN Home for the Holidays 5.95

WARRIOR'S WAY
Bench Press Studios, 1998
1 . . . . 3.00
2 . . . . 3.00
3 . . . . 3.00
4 . . . . 3.00
5 . . . . 3.00
6 V:Technoborgs 3.00
7 . . . . 3.00

WARSTRIKE
Malibu Ultraverse, 1994–95
1 HNg,TA,in South America 2.25
2 HNg,TA,Gatefold(c) 2.25
3 in Brazil 2.25
4 HNg,TA,V:Blind Faith 2.25
5 . . . . 2.25
6 Rafferty 2.25
7 Origin 2.25

WARSTRIKE:
PRELUDE TO GODWHEEL
Malibu Ultraverse, 1994
1 Blind Faith/Lord Pumpkin 2.25

All comics prices listed are for Near Mint condition.

WART AND THE WIZARD
Gold Key, Feb., 1964
1 . . . . 60.00

WATERDOGS
Roaring Studio, 2002
1 (of 3) 2.95
2 thru 3 . . . . @2.95

WATERWORLD
Acclaim 1997
1 of 4 V:Leviathan 2.50
2 of 4 'Children of Leviathan' 2.50
3 of 4 KoK 2.50
4 of 4 KoK 'Children of Leviathan' . 2.50

WAVE WARRIORS
Astroboys
1 . . . . 2.00
2 . . . . 2.00

WAXWORK in 3-D
Blackthorne
1 . . . . 2.50

WAYFARERS
Eternity
1 . . . . 2.00
2 . . . . 2.00

WAY OF THE RAT
Crossgen Comics, 2002
1 CDi 4.00
2 thru 7 CDi . . . . @3.00
8 thru 19 CDi . . . . @3.00
GN Traveler Vol. 1 Walls of Zhumar 9.95
TPB Vol. 1 The Walls of Zhumar . . 15.95
TPB Vol. 2 The Dragon's Wake . . . 15.95

WEAPONS OF THE GODS
Comicsone.com, 2002
TPB Vol. 1 by Tony Wong 13.95
TPB Vol. 2 thru Vol. 7 . . . . @13.95

WEAPON ZERO
See: Image

WEASEL GUY WITCHBLADE
Hyperwerks, 1998
1-shot by Steve Succellato 3.00
1a variant Jeff Matsuda(c) 5.00
1b variant Karl Altstoeter(c) 8.00

WEB-MAN
Argosy
1 flip book with Time Warrior 2.50

WEB OF HORROR
Major Magazines, Dec., 1969
1 JJ(c),Ph(c),BWr 125.00
2 JJ(c),Ph(c),BWr 100.00
3 BWr,April, 1970 . . . . 100.00

WEDDING OF POPEYE AND OLIVE, THE
Ocean Comics, 1999
1 PDa, ... 2.75
1a signed, numbered 15.95
Spec. Sketch edition 40.00

WEIRD FANTASY
Russ Cochran, 1992
1 Reps 3.50
2 Reps.inc.The Black Arts 3.00
3 thru 4 rep . . . . @3.00
5 thru 7 rep 3.00
8 . . . . 3.00
Gemstone
9 thru 22 EC comics reprint . . . . @3.00
`Annuals'
TPB Vol. #1 rebinding of #1–#5 . . 10.00
TPB Vol. #2 rebinding of #6–#10 . 11.00
TPB Vol. #3 rebinding of #11–#14 . 10.00
TPB Vol. #4 rebinding of #15–#18 . 11.00
TPB Vol. #5 rebinding of #19–#22 . 12.00

Weird Science #15
© Gladstone

WEIRD SCIENCE
Gladstone, 1990–91
1 Rep. #22 + Fantasy #1 . . . . 4.00
2 Rep. #16 + Fantasy #17 . . . . 3.50
3 Rep. #9 + Fantasy #14 . . . . 3.50
4 Rep. #27 + Fantasy #11 . . . . 3.00
Russ Cochran/Gemstone, 1992
1 thru 21 EC comics reprint . . . . @3.00
`Annuals'
TPB Vol. #1 rebinding of #1–#5 . . 8.95
TPB Vol. #2 rebinding of #6–#10 . 9.95
TPB Vol. #3 rebinding of #11–#15 . 8.95
TPB Vol. #4 rebinding of #16–#18 . 9.95
TPB Vol. #5 rebinding of #19–#22 . 10.50

WEIRD SCIENCE–FANTASY
Russ Cochran/Gemstone, 1992
1 Rep. W.S.F. #23 (1954) 3.50
2 Rep. Flying Saucer Invasion 3.00
3 Rep 3.00
4 thru 6 Rep . . . . @3.00
7 rep #29 . . . . 3.00
8 . . . . 3.00
Gemstone
`Annuals'
TPB Vol. #1 rebinding of #1–#5 . . . 8.95
TPB Vol. #2 rebinding of #6–#10 . . 12.95

WEIRD SUSPENSE
Atlas, Feb.–July, 1975
1 thru 3 F:Tarantula . . . . @25.00

WEIRD TALES ILLUSTRATED
Millennium, 1992
1 KJo,JBo,PCr,short stories 4.95

WENDY
Blackthorne
1 3-D 2.50

WENDY, THE GOOD LITTLE WITCH
Harvey Publications, 1960–76
1 . . . . 250.00
2 . . . . 125.00
3 . . . . 100.00
4 . . . . 100.00
5 . . . . 100.00
6 . . . . 75.00
7 . . . . 75.00
8 . . . . 75.00
9 . . . . 75.00
10 . . . . 75.00
11 thru 20 . . . . @60.00
21 thru 30 . . . . @35.00
31 thru 50 . . . . @30.00
51 thru 69 . . . . @25.00
70 thru 74 52 pg Giants . . . . . . @20.00
75 thru 93 . . . . @20.00

WENDY WITCH WORLD
Harvey Publications, 1961–74
1 . . . . 200.00
2 . . . . 100.00
3 . . . . 100.00
4 . . . . 100.00
5 . . . . 100.00
6 . . . . 75.00
7 . . . . 75.00
8 . . . . 75.00
9 . . . . 75.00
10 . . . . 75.00
11 thru 20 . . . . @50.00
21 thru 30 . . . . @45.00
31 thru 39 . . . . @30.00
40 thru 50 . . . . @20.00
51 thru 53 . . . . @20.00

WEREWOLF
Blackthorne
1 3-D 3.50

WESTERN ACTION
Atlas, Feb., 1975
1 F:Kid Cody,Comanche Kid 25.00

WESTWYND
Westwynd, 1995
1 I:Sable,Shiva,Outcast,Tojo 2.50

WHAM
1 . . . . 2.00

COLOR PUB.

Whisper–Wild

WHISPER
Capital, 1983–84
1 MG(c)....................... 8.00
2 .... 6.00

First
1 .... 2.50
2 .... 2.00
3 .... 2.00
4 .... 2.00
5 .... 2.00
6 thru 12 .... @2.00
13 thru 19 .... @2.00
20 O:Whisper................. 2.00
21 thru 26 .... @2.00
27 Ghost Dance #2 .... 2.00
28 Ghost Dance #3 .... 2.00
29 thru 37 .... @2.00
Spec. #1..................... 4.00

WHITE FANG
Walt Disney, 1990
1 Movie Adapt. 5.95

WHITE TRASH
Tundra
1 I:Elvis & Dean.............. 3.95
2 Trip to Las Vegas contd..... 3.95
3 V:Purple Heart Brigade...... 3.95

WHODUNNIT
Eclipse, 1986–87
1 DSp,A:Jay Endicott.......... 2.00
2 DSp,'Who Slew Kangaroo?'.... 2.00
3 DSp,'Who Offed Henry Croft'. 2.00

WIDOW MADE IN BRITAIN
N Studio
1 I:Widow 2.60
2 F:Widow 2.60
3 Rampage 2.60
4 In Jail..................... 2.60

WIDOW METAL GYPSIES
London Night Studios, 1995
1 I:Emma Drew................. 3.00
2 Father Love 3.00
3 Final issue 3.00

WILD ANIMALS
Pacific, 1982
1 .... 2.00

WILD BILL PECOS
AC Comics, 1989
1 .... 3.50

WILDCATS
WildStorm/DC, 1999
Previously from Image
VOLUME 2
1 SLo,TC,..................... 2.50
1a variant cover.............. 2.50
1b variant cover.............. 2.50
1c variant cover.............. 2.50
1d variant cover.............. 2.50
1e variant cover.............. 2.50
2 SLo,TC,..................... 2.50
3 SLo,TC,F:Grifter............ 2.50
4 SLo,TC, ... 2.50
5 SLo,BHi,PNe,................ 2.50
6 SLo,........................ 2.50
7 SLo,R:Pike.................. 2.50

Wildcats #1
© *Wildstorm*

8 JoC(s),SeP,TC(c) 2.50
8a variant JLe&SW(c) (1:4).... 2.50
9 JoC(s),SeP,TC(c),Las Vegas.. 2.50
10 JoC(s),SeP,TC(c),Las Vegas. 2.50
11 JoC(s),SeP,TC(c),R:Ladytron 2.50
12 JoC(s),SeP,TC(c),go west .. 2.50
13 JoC(s),SeP,F:Void 2.50
14 JoC(s),SeP,Serial Boxes,pt.1 2.50
15 JoC(s),SeP,Serial Boxes,pt.2 2.50
16 JoC,SeP,Serial Boxes,pt.3 . 2.50
17 JoC,SeP,Serial Boxes,pt.4 . 2.50
18 JoC,SeP,Serial Boxes,pt.5 . 2.50
19 JoC,SeP,Serial Boxes,pt.6 . 2.50
20 JoC,SDi,F:Grifter, Maul ... 2.50
21 JoC,SDi,F:Grifter, Maul, pt.2 2.50
22 JoC,SeP,R:Grifter.......... 2.50
23 JoC,SeP,F:Grifter.......... 2.50
23a variant WPo(c) (1:4)...... 2.50
24 JoC,SeP,F:Voodoo........... 2.50
25 JoC,SeP, 40-pg............. 3.50
26 JoC,SeP, control of Halo .. 2.50
27 JoC,SeP,Grifter vs. Zealot. 2.50
28 JoC,SeP,Voodoo,final issue. 2.50
Spec. WildC.A.T.s: Mosaic 3.95
Ann. 2000 #1, Devil's
  Night x-over, pt.3 .... 3.50
GN Ladytron................... 5.95
TPB WildC.A.T.S.: Compendium. 10.00
TPB WildC.A.T.S.: Homecoming. 20.00
TPB Gang War................ 16.95
TPB Homecoming 19.95
TPB Vicious Circles 14.95
TPB Serial Boxes, 144-pg..... 14.95
TPB Street Smart............. 14.95
TPB Battery Park 17.95

WILDCATS VERSION 3.0
Wildcats/DC, Aug., 2002
Eye of the Storm
1 JoC,old and new team members. 2.95
2 JoC,Jack Marlowe,Halo corp . 2.95
3 JoC 2.95
4 JoC,........................ 2.95
5 JoC 2.95
6 JoC 2.95
7 JoC,I:Beef Boys 2.95
8 JoC,BU:The Authority,pt.3... 2.95
9 JoC,new Grifter 2.95
10 JoC,new Grifter 2.95
11 JoC,Lights Out in Garfield. 2.95
12 JoC,Jack Marlowe........... 2.95
13 JoC,Mister Wax............. 2.95
14 JoC,Halo Corp.............. 2.95

15 JoC,Car of tomorrow 2.95
16 JoC,new assassin 2.95
TPB Brand Building 14.95

WILDFIRE
Zion Comics
1 thru 3 V:Mr. Reeves ...... @2.00
4 Lord D'Rune................. 2.00

WILD FRONTIER
Charlton Comics, Oct., 1955
1 Davy Crockett.............. 100.00
2 same 75.00
3 same 75.00
4 same 75.00
5 same 75.00
6 same 75.00
7 O:Cheyenne Kid 75.00
Becomes:

CHEYENNE KID
8 .... 75.00
9 .... 40.00
10 AW,AT,SD(c) 100.00
11 Giant,Geronimo 100.00
12 AW,AT 100.00
13 AW,AT 75.00
14 AW 75.00
15 .... 40.00
16 .... 40.00
17 .... 40.00
18 .... 40.00
19 .... 40.00
20 JSe 50.00
21 JSe 50.00
22 JSe 50.00
23 .... 20.00
24 JSe 40.00
25 JSe 40.00
26 JSe 35.00
27 .... 30.00
28 .... 30.00
29 .... 30.00
30 JSe 35.00
31 thru 59 .... @20.00
60 thru 98................. @20.00
99 Nov., 1973................ 20.00

WILD TIMES
WildStorm/DC, 1999
Deathblow 2.50
DV8 .... 2.50
Gen13 .... 2.50
Grifter....................... 2.50
Wetworks...................... 2.50

WILD WEST C.O.W.- BOYS OF MOO MESA
Archie, 1992–93
1 Based on TV cartoon 2.00
2 Cody kidnapped.............. 2.00
3 Law of the Year Parade,
  last issue 2.00
(Regular series)
1 Valley o/t Thunder Lizard .. 2.00
2 Plains, Trains & Dirty Deals. 2.00

WILD WESTERN ACTION
Skywald, 1971
1 thru 3 .... @30.00

WILD WILD WEST
Gold Key, 1966–69
1 TV show tie-in............. 200.00
2 .... 150.00

Wild–Xena / COLOR PUB. / Comics Values Annual

3	125.00
4	125.00
5	125.00
6	125.00
7	125.00

WILD WILD WEST
Millennium, 1990–91
1	2.95
2 thru 4	@2.95

WILL EISNER'S 3-D CLASSICS
Kitchen Sink, 1985
WE art, w/glasses (1985) 2.00

WIN A PRIZE COMICS
Charlton Comics, Feb., 1955
1 S&K,Edgar Allen adapt.	900.00
2 S&K	600.00

Becomes:

TIMMY THE TIMID GHOST
3	75.00
4	40.00
5	40.00
6	30.00
7	30.00
8	30.00
9	30.00
10	30.00
11	75.00
12	75.00
13 thru 20	@30.00
21 thru 44	@25.00
45 1966	25.00

WINDRAGE
1 and 2 . . . . @2.00

WINTERWORLD
Eclipse, 1987–88
1 JZ,I:Scully, Wynn	2.00
2 JZ,V:Slave Farmers	2.00
3 JZ,V:Slave Farmers	2.00

WIREHEADS
Fleetway
1 . . . . 2.95

WISP
Oktomica Entertainment, 1999
1 All Along the Watchtower,pt.1	2.50
2 All Along the Watchtower,pt.2	2.50
3 All Along the Watchtower,pt.3	2.95
4 The Acheron Protocol	2.95

WITCHBLADE
SEE: IMAGE

WITCHING HOUR, THE
Millennium/Comico, 1992
1 Anne Rice adaptation	2.50
2 thru 5	@2.50

WOODY WOODPECKER
Harvey, 1991–93
1 thru 5 . . . . @2.00

COLOR PUB.

WORLD OF ARCHIE
Archie, 1994
1 thru 21 . . . . @2.00

World of Wood #2
© Eclipse

WORLD OF WOOD
Eclipse, 1986–87
1 WW	2.00
2 WW,DSt(i)	2.00
3 WW	2.00
4 WW	2.00

WORLD WAR II: 1946
Antarctic Press, 1999
1 by Ted Nomura	4.00
2 Born to Die	4.00
3 Battle for Moscow	4.00
4 Flying Tigers	4.00
5	4.00
6 The Hunley vs. the Potsdam	4.00
7 The Yamato	4.00
8 Tuskegee Airmen	4.00
9 Firestorm	4.00
10 Destination: Space	4.00
11 Night Witches	4.00
12 Korea	4.00
Ann. 2000 b&w	3.95

WRATH
Malibu Ultraverse, 1994–95
1 B:MiB(s),DvA,JmP,C:Mantra	2.25
1a Silver foil	3.00
2 DvA,JmP,V:Hellion	2.25
3 DvA,JmP,V:Radicals, I:Slayer	2.25
4 DvA,JmP,V:Freex	2.25
5 DvA,JmP,V:Freex	2.25
6 DvA,JmP	2.25
7 DvA,JmP,I:Pierce,Ogre, Doc Virtual	2.25
8	2.25
9 A:Prime	2.25
G-Size #1	2.50

WULF THE BARBARIAN
Atlas, Feb.–Sept. 1975
1 O:Wulf	15.00
2 NA,I:Berithe The Swordsman	12.00
3 & 4	@8.00

WWF BATTLEMANIA
Valiant
1 WWF Action	2.50
2 thru 5	@2.50

WYATT EARP
Dell Publishing Co., Nov., 1957
1 RsM	175.00
2 RsM	125.00
3 RsM	110.00
4	100.00
5 Ph(c)	100.00
6	100.00
7	100.00
8	100.00
9	100.00
10	100.00
11	75.00
12 RsM	75.00
13 AT	75.00

XANADU
Eclipse, 1988
1 . . . . 2.00

XENYA
Sanctuary Press, 1994
1 Hildebrandt Brothers	4.00
2	3.25
3	3.25
4 conclusion, Homecoming	2.95

XENA: WARRIOR PRINCESS
Topps, 1997
1 RTs,Revenge of the Gorgons, pt.1	5.00
1a photo (c)	8.00
2 (of 2) rescue of Gabrielle	4.00
TPB	9.95

[VOL 2]
0 AaL Temple of the Dragon God	3.00
1 (of 3) Joxer, Warrior Prince, pt.1	5.00
1a deluxe	8.00
2 Joxer, Warrior Prince, pt.2	4.00
2a photo (c)	4.00
TPB rep. #0–#2	9.95

XENA: WARRIOR PRINCESS: BLOOD LINES
Topps, 1997
1 (of 3) ALo	3.00
1a photo (c)	3.00
2 (of 3) ALo	3.00
2a photo (c)	3.00

XENA: WARRIOR PRINCESS: CALLISTO
Topps, 1997
1 (of 3) RTs	3.00
1a photo (c)	3.00
2 (of 3) RTs	3.00
2a photo (c)	3.00
3 (of 3) RTs	3.00
3a photo (c)	3.00

COLOR PUB.

XENA: WARRIOR PRINCESS: ORPHEUS
Topps, 1998
1 (of 3) 3.00
1a photo (c). 3.00
2 (of 3) 3.00
2a photo (c). 3.00
3 (of 3) 3.00
3a photo (c). 3.00

XENA: WARRIOR PRINCESS: THE ORIGINAL OLYMPICS
Topps, 1998
1 (of 3) 3.00
1a photo cover 3.00
2 F:Hercules 3.00
2a photo cover 3.00
3 . . . . 3.00
3a photo cover 3.00

XENA: WARRIOR PRINCESS: THE WEDDING OF XENA & HERCULES
Topps, 1998
1-shot 3.00
1-shot photo (c) 3.00

XENA, WARRIOR PRINCESS: THE WRATH OF HERA
Topps, 1998
1 (of 2) 3.00
1a photo cover edition 3.00
2 conclusion 3.00
2a photo cover edition 3.00

XENA: WARRIOR PRINCESS: XENA AND THE DRAGON'S TEETH
Topps, 1997
1 (of 3) RTs, ... 3.00
1a photo (c). 3.00
2 (of 3) RTs, ... 3.00
2a photo (c). 3.00
3 (of 3) RTs, ... 3.00
3a photo (c). 3.00

XENO MEN
Blackthorne
1 . . . . 2.00

XENOTECH
Mirage, 1993–94
1 I:Xenotech 2.75
2 . . . . 2.75
3 w/2 card strip 2.75

X-FILES
Topps, 1994–97
1 From Fox TV Series 40.00
1a Newstand 30.00
2 Aliens Killing Witnesses 25.00
3 The Return 22.00
4 Firebird,pt.1 . . . . 15.00

5 Firebird,pt.2 . . . . 10.00
6 Firebird,pt.3 . . . . 8.00
7 Trepanning Opera. 7.00
8 Silent Cities of the Mind,pt.1 . . . 6.00
9 Silent Cities of the Mind,pt.2 . . . 5.00
10 Feeling of Unreality,pt.1 . . . . . . 5.00
11 Feeling of Unreality,pt.2 . . . . . . 5.00
12 Feeling of Unreality,pt.3 . . . . . . 5.00
13 A Boy and His Saucer 5.00
14 . . . . 4.00
15 Home of the Brave. 4.00
16 Home of the Brave,pt.2 . . . . 3.50
17 DgM,CAd. 3.50
18 thru 21 . . . . @3.50
22 JRz,CAd,`The Kanishibari' 3.00
23 JRz,CAd,`Donor' 3.00
24 JRz,`Silver Lining' 3.00
25 JRz,CAd,`Remote Control,'pt.1 . 3.00
26 JRz,CAd,`Remote Control,'pt.2 . 3.00
27 JRz,CAd,`Remote Control,'pt.3 . 3.00
28 JRz,`Be Prepared,' pt.1,
  V:Windigo. 3.00
29 JRz,`Be Prepared,' pt.2 . . . . 3.00
30 JRz,`Surrounded,' pt.1 . . . . 3.00

X-Files #20
© Topps Comics

31 JRz,`Surrounded,' pt.2 (of 2) . . . 3.00
32 . . . . 3.00
33 widows on San Francisco 3.00
33 variant photo (c) 3.00
34 Project HAARP 3.00
35 Near Death Experience 3.00
36 Near Death Experience, pt.2 . . 3.00
37 JRz,The Face of Extinction 3.00
38 JRz, ... 3.00
39 JRz, Widow's Peak 3.00
40 Devil's Advocate 3.00
40a photo cover 3.00
41 Severed. 3.00
41a photo cover 3.00
Ann.#1 Hollow Eve 5.00
Ann.#2 E.L.F.S. 4.50
Spec.#1 Rep. #1-#3 . . . . 6.00
Spec.#2 Rep. #4-#6 Firebird 5.00
Spec.#3 Rep. #7-#9 . . . . 5.00
Spec.#4 Rep. 5.00
TPB Vol. 2 . . . . 19.95
GN Afterflight 5.95
GN Official Movie Adapt. (1998) . . . 5.95

X-FILES DIGEST
Topps, 1995
1 All New Series, 96pg. 4.00
2 and 3 . . . . 4.00

X-FILES, THE: GROUND ZERO
Topps, 1997
1 (of 4) based on novel 3.00
2 . . . . 3.00
3 . . . . 3.00
4 . . . . 3.00

X-FILES, THE: SEASON ONE
Topps, 1997
1 RTs,JVF(c) `Deep Throat' 5.00
Deep Throat, variant (c) 7.50
2 RTs,JVF(c) `Squeeze'. 4.00
Squeeze, RTs, JVF(c). 5.00
3 RTs,SSc,`Conduit' 4.00
Conduit, RTs. 5.00
4 RTs, `The Jersey Devil' 4.00
5 RTs, `Shadows' 4.00
Shadows JVF(c). 5.00
6 `Fire' 4.00
Fire 5.00
7 RTs,JVF, `Ice' 4.00
Ice 5.00
8 RTs, `Space' 4.00
Space JVF(c) 5.00
Spec. Pilot Episode RTs,JVF
  new JVF(c). 5.00
Beyond the Sea JVF(c). 5.00

XIMOS: VIOLENT PAST
Triumphant, 1994
1 JnR(s) 2.50
2 JnR(s) 2.50

XIN
Anarchy Studios, 2002
Alpha Preview edition 2.50
Alpha Preview, collector's ed. . . . 9.95
Ashcan limited edition. 5.95
Ashcan gold foil leather 14.95
1 Legend of the Monkey King 3.00
1a variant JMd(c). 3.00
1b Royal blue edition 29.95
1c gold foil edition 29.95
1d holo foil fx edition 9.95
2 thru 3 . . . . @3.00
2a thru 3a variant limited (c). . . . @9.95
TPB Legend of the Monkey King. . 12.95

XIN: JOURNEY OF THE MONKEY KING
Anarchy Studios 2003
1 . . . . 3.00
1a variant (c). 3.00
2 thru 3 . . . . @3.00
2a thru 3a variant (c) 3.00
1b thru 3b limited edition . . . . . . @9.95

X-O MANOWAR
Valiant 1992
0 JQ,O:Aric,1st Full Chromium(c) . 3.00
0a Gold Ed. 3.50
1 BL,BWS,I:Aric,Ken 4.00
2 BL(i),V:Lydia,Wolf-Class Armor . 3.00
3 I:X-Caliber,A:Solar 3.00
4 MM,A:Harbinger,C:Shadowman
  (Jack Boniface) 3.00
5 BWS(c),V:AX 3.00
5a w/Pink logo. 3.00
6 SD,V:Ax(X-O Armor). 3.00
7 FM(c),Unity#5,V:Pierce 2.75
8 WS(c),Unity#13,V:Pierce 2.75
9 Aric in Italy,408 A.D. 2.75

X-O Manowar–Zak / COLOR PUB.

10 N:X-O Armor	2.75
11 V:Spider Aliens	2.50
12 A:Solar	2.50
13 V:Solar	2.50
14 BS,A:Turok,I:Randy Cartier	3.00
15 BS,A:Turok	2.50
15a Red Ed.	3.00
16 V:The Mob.	2.50
17 BL	2.50
18 JCf,V:CIA,A:Randy,I:Paul	2.50
19 JCf,V:US Government	2.50
20 A:Toyo Harada	2.50
21 V:Ax	2.50
22 Aria in S.America	2.50
23 Aria in S.America	2.50
24 Aria comes back	2.50
25 JCf,JGz,PaK,I:Armories, BU:Armories#0	3.00
26 JGz(s),RLv,F:Ken	2.50
27 JGz,RLe,A:Turok,Geomancer, Stronghold,Livewire	2.50
28 JGz,RLe,D:X-O,V:Spider Aliens,w/Valiant Era card	2.75
29 JGz,RLe,A:Turok,V:SpiderAliens	2.50
30 JGz,RLe,A:Solar	2.50
31 JGz,RLe	2.50
32 JGz,RLe,at Orb,Inc.	2.25
33 JGz,RLe,Chaos Effect-Delta#3, A:Armorines,H.A.R.D. Corps.	2.25
34 thru 36	@2.25
37 Wolfbridge Affair,pt.1	2.25
38 Wolfbridge Affair,pt.2	2.25
39 Wolfbridge Affair,pt.3	2.25
40 Wolfbridge Affair,pt.4	2.25
41 Aftermath	2.25
42 A:Shadowman Surprise	2.25
43 Chasitty's Boys	2.25
44 Bart Sears New Direction	2.50
45 RMz,V:Crescendo	2.50
46 RMz,V:Crescendo	2.50
47 RMz,V:Crescendo	2.50
48 RMz,BS,A:Turok	2.50
49 RMz,loses control of armor	2.50
50-X R:Paul, I:Alloy	2.50
50-O V:Alloy	2.50
51 V:Lummox	2.50
52 V:A Blast From the Past	2.50
53 Returns To Space	2.50
54 I:New Aliens	2.50
55 V:Aliens	2.50
56 V:Aliens	2.50
57 I:Gamin	2.50
58 I:Volt	2.50
59 thru 67	@2.50

TPB rep.#1–4,w/X-O Manual 11.00

X-O MANOWAR
Series Two, Acclaim, Oct., 1997

1 Rand Banion v. R.A.G.E.	2.50
2 v. R.A.G.E.	2.50
3	2.50
4 R.A.G.E. is back	2.50
5 Donovan Wylie vs. Internaut	2.50
6 Internaut controls X-O suit	2.50
7 SEa, Donovan wears his armor	2.50
8 SEa, V:Basilisk	2.50
9 SEa, A: new Hard Corps.	2.50
10 SEa, R:Bravado	2.50
11 BAu,MWa,SEa,alien creators	2.50
12 BAu,MWa,SEa,O:armor	2.50
13 BAu,SEa,V:Alien creators	2.50
14 BAu,SEa,V:Aliens of Unity	2.50
15 BAu,SEa,out of armor	2.50
16 BAu,SEa	2.50
17 DMD,SEa,civil war	2.50
18 DMD,SEa,Rand Banion	2.50
19 DMD,SEa,V:Master Blaster	2.50
20 DMD,trapped in a sleep-state	2.50
TPB MWa,BAu rep. #1–#4	10.00

YAKKY DOODLE & CHOPPER
Gold Key, Dec., 1962

1 ..... 125.00

YEAH!
Homage/DC, 1999

1 GHe 3.00

YIN FEI
Leung's Publications, 1988–90

5	2.00
6 thru 11	@2.00

YOGI BEAR
Dell, Feb.-March, 1962
#1 thru #6, See Dell Four Color

7 thru 9 ..... 100.00

Gold Key

10	120.00
11 Jellystone Follies	100.00
12	60.00
13 Surprise Party	100.00
14 thru 19	@50.00
20 thru 29	@40.00
30 thru 42	@35.00

YOGI BEAR
Charlton Comics, 1970–76

1	60.00
2 thru 10	@35.00
11 thru 35	30.00

YOGI BEAR
Archie Comics, 1997

1 ..... 2.00

YOSEMITE SAM
Gold Key/Whitman, 1970–84

1	60.00
2 thru 10	@35.00
11 thru 40	@25.00
41 thru 81	@20.00

YOUNGBLOOD
Maximum Press/Extreme
Volume 2, 1996
Vol. 1 & Vol. 2 #1–#10, see Image

11 RLd,RCz,	2.50
12 Rle, V:Lord Dredd,A:New Man,double size	3.50
13 RLd,RCz,F:Die-Hard	2.50
14 RLd,RCz,	2.50
Super Spec.#1 ErS,CSp,AG	3.00
TPB Youngblood, rep. orig. Youngblood #1–#5	16.95
TPB Baptism of Fire rep. Youngblood #6–#8, #10 & Team Youngblood #9–#11	16.95

YOUNGBLOOD
Awesome Entertainment, 1998

1 AMo,SSr.	2.50
1a variant covers, 7 different	@2.50
1b foil logo	6.00
1c plus custom illustration	72.00
2 AMo,SSr,Baptism of Fire.	2.50
3 AMo,SSr,V:Professor Night	2.50
4 AMo,SSr,Young Guns	2.50
5 AMo,SSr,Young Guns	2.50
TPB rep.#1–#10 orig. series	14.95
1-shot, Youngblood/X-Force x-over,48pg. (1998)	4.95

YOUNGBLOOD: BLOODSPORT
Arcade Comics, 2002

1 MMr,RLd, RLd(c)	4.00
1a variant Quietly (c)	4.00
1b variant Park (c).	4.00
1c Foil ed.	10.00
1d Foil ed., signed	20.00
1e Museum ed.	100.00
1f Museum ed., signed	125.00
1g convention sketch ed.	50.00
1h San Diego con lim. ed.	10.00
1i San Diego con lim. signed	20.00
1j ltd (c)	20.00
1k sgn & re-sketched (c)	50.00
2 MMr,RLd, RLd(c)	3.00
2a variant Quietly (c)	3.00
2b variant Park (c).	3.00
2c Foil ed.	10.00
2d Foil ed., signed	20.00
2e Museum ed.	100.00
2f Museum ed., signed	125.00

YOUNGBLOOD CLASSICS
Image/Extreme, Sept., 1996

1 RLd,ErS,series rewritten & redrawn, new cover	2.25
2 RLd,ErS	2.25
3 RLd,ErS	2.25

YOUNGBLOOD GENESIS
Awesome Entertainment, 2000

1	3.00
1a signature edition	6.00

ZAANAN
Mainstream Comics

1 The Collectio,I:Zaanan 2.50

ZAK RAVEN, ESQ.
Avatar/Tidalwave Studios, 2002

1A Cha (c).	3.50
1B Arlem (c)	3.50
1C Miller (c).	3.50

X-O Manowar, Series 2, #5
© Acclaim

CVA Page 692 — All comics prices listed are for *Near Mint* condition.

Comics Values Annual

1D Murphy (c) 3.50

ZEN
Zen Comics 2003
0 . . . . 2.95
1 . . . . 2.95
2 thru 4 . . . . @2.95
TPB Vol. 1 Return of the Alien Hero. . . . 14.95

ZENDRA
Pennyfarthing Press, 2001
Volume 2
1 (of 6) Windmills of the World. . . . 2.95
2 All the Flesh Inherits 2.95
3 thru 5 . . . . @2.95
6 . . . . 2.95
TPB Vol. 1 . . . . 17.95
TPB Vol. 2 Heart of Fire 24.95

ZEN INTERGALACTIC NINJA
Archie, 1992
1 Rumble in the Rain Forest prequel,inc.poster 2.00
2 Rumble in Rain Forest #1 . . . . . . 2.00
3 Rumble in Rain Forest #2 . . . . . . 2.00

Entity Comics, 1994
0 Chromium (c),JaL(c) 4.00
1 Joe Orbeta 2.50
1a Platinum Edition 20.00
2 Deluxe Edition w/card 4.95
3 V:Rawhead 3.00
4 thru 7 . . . . @3.25
GN A Fire Upon The Earth 12.95

[2nd Series]
1 Joe Orbeta 4.95
2 . . . . 4.95
3 thru 5 . . . . @2.50

Zen Comics, 1998
Commemorative Ed. #1 . . . . 5.95

ZEN INTERGALACTIC NINJA
Studio Chikara, 1999
1 . . . . 3.95
1 variant (c) 9.95
2 . . . . 3.95
3 . . . . 3.95

ZEN/NIRA X: HELLSPACE
Zen Comics
1 . . . . 2.95

ZEN: NOVELLA
Eternity Comics
1 thru 8 . . . . @2.95

ZEN SPECIALS
Eternity
Spring#1 V:Lord Contaminous 2.50
April Fools#1 parody issue 2.50
Color Spec.#0 . . . . 3.50

ZEN: WARRIOR
Eternity Comics, 1994
1 vicious video game 3.00

COLOR PUB.

ZENDRA
Pennyfarthing Press, 2001
1 (of 6) 2.95
2 thru 6 . . . . @2.95

ZENITH PHASE I
Fleetway
1 thru 3 . . . . @2.00

ZENITH PHASE II
Fleetway
1 thru 2 . . . . @2.00

ZERO GIRL: FULL CIRCLE
DC/Homage Nov. 2002
2 SK 2.95
3 SK 2.95
4 SK 2.95
5 SK, concl. 2.95
TPB Full Circle 17.95

Zero Patrol 31
© Continuity

ZERO PATROL
Continuity, 1984–90
1 EM,NA,O&I:Megalith 2.50
2 EM,NA 2.00
3 EM,NA,I:Shaman 2.00
4 EM,NA 2.00
5 EM 2.00
6 thru 8 EM . . . . @2.00

ZERO TOLERANCE
First, 1990–91
1 TV 3.50
2 TV 3.00
3 TV 2.25
4 TV 2.25

ZOONIVERSE
Eclipse, 1986–87
1 I:Kren Patrol,wrap-around(c) 2.00
2 . . . . 2.00
3 . . . . 2.00
4 V:Wedge City 2.00

Zak–Zoot

5 Spak vs. Agent Ty-rote 2.00
6 last issue 2.00

ZORRO
Dell Publ. Co., 1959–61
1 thru 8, see Dell 4-Color
8 . . . . 125.00
9 . . . . 150.00
10 . . . . 110.00
11 . . . . 110.00
12 ATh 150.00
13 . . . . 100.00
14 . . . . 100.00
15 . . . . 100.00

ZORRO
Gold Key, 1966–68
1 ATh,Rep. 100.00
2 Rep. 75.00
3 Rep. 75.00
4 Rep. 75.00
5 Rep. 75.00
6 Rep. 75.00
7 Rep. 75.00
8 Rep. 75.00
9 ATh,Rep. 75.00

ZORRO
Topps, Nov., 1993
0 BSf(c),DMG(s), came bagged with Jurassic Park Raptor #1 and Teenagents #4 . . . . 4.00
1 DMG(s),V:Machete 3.00
2 DMG(s) 5.00
3 DMG(s) I:Lady Rawhide 15.00
4 MGr(s),DMG(s),V:Moonstalker . . 2.50
5 MGr,DMG(s),V:Moonstalker 2.50
6 A:Lady Rawhide 8.00
7 A:Lady Rawhide 7.00
8 MGr(c),DMG(s). 3.00
9 A:Lady Rawhide 4.00
10 A:Lady Rawhide 4.50
11 A:Lady Rawhide 8.00

ZOT!
Eclipse, 1984–85
1 by Scott McCloud 7.00
2 . . . . 3.00
3 Art and Soul 3.00
4 Assault on Castle Dekko 3.00
5 Sirius Business 3.00
6 It's always darkest 2.00
7 Common Ground 2.50
8 Through the Door 2.00
9 Gorilla Warfare 2.50
10 T.K.O. The Final Round 2.00
10a B&W 6.00
10b 2nd printing 2.50
Original Zot! Book 1 . . . . 9.95
Book One TPB 24.95
(Changed to B & W)

ZOT!
Kitchen Sink
Book One TPB 24.95

All comics prices listed are for Near Mint condition.

B&W COMICS

A1
Atomeka Press, 1989ñ92
1 BWs,A:Flaming Carrot,Mr.X. . . . 10.00
2 BWs 9.75
3 . . . . 9.75
4 . . . . 5.95
5 . . . . 6.95
6a 4.95

AARDWOLF
Aardwolf, 1994
1 DC,GM(c) 2.95
1a Certificate ed. signed 12.00
2 World Toughest Milkman 2.95
3 R.Block(s),O:Aardwolf 2.95

AARON STRIPS
Amazing Aaron Prod., 1999
1 thru 4, see Image
5 thru 9 . . . . @2.95
10 48-pg 3.95

A.B.C. WARRIORS
Fleetway/Quality, 1990
1 thru 8 . . . . @2.00
Titan, 2002
TPB Vol. 1 The Mek-nificent Seven 20.00
TPB Vol. 2 Black Holel 19.95

ABSOLUTE ZERO
Antarctic Press, 1995
1 . . . . 2.95
2 Rooftop,Athena 2.95
3 Stan Sakai 3.50
4 3-D Man and Kirby 2.95
5 & 6 Super Powers . . . . @3.95

AC ANNUAL
Aircel, 1990
1 . . . . 3.95
2 Based on 1940's heroes 5.00
3 F:GoldenAge Heroes 3.50
4 F:Sentinels of Justice 3.95

ACE COMICS PRESENTS
Ace, 1987
1 thru 7 . . . . @2.00

ACE McCOY
ACG Comics, 1999
1 FF 2.95
2 FF, SD 2.95
3 FF 2.95
4 FF 2.95
TPB Collected ed. FF,rep.5 issues 12.95

ACES
Eclipse, 1988
1 thru 5, mag. size . . . . @3.95

ACG'S AMAZING COMICS
ACG Comics, 2000
1 (of 4) F:Dragon Lady 2.95
2 thru 5 . . . . @2.95

ACHILLES STORM
Brainstorm, 1997
1 by Sandra Chang 2.95

ACHILLES STORM: DARK SECRET
Brainstorm, 1997
1 by Sandra Chang 2.95
2 . . . . 2.95
2a luxury edition 5.00

ACME
Fandom House, 1985–89
1 thru 9 . . . . @2.00

ACOLYTE CHRONICLES
Azure Press, 1995
1 I:Korath 2.95
2 V:Korath 2.95

A COP CALLED TRACY
ACG Comics, 1998
1 by Chester Gould 2.95
2 thru 8 . . . . @2.95
9 . . . . 2.95
9a deluxe 2.95
10 thru 18 . . . . @2.95
19 thru 24 giant-size,64-pg . . . . @5.95
Ann.#1 . . . . 2.95

ACTION GIRL COMICS
Slave Labor Graphics, 1994
1 thru 7 . . . . @3.00
1 thru 7, later printings . . . . @2.75
8 thru 12 . . . . @2.95
13 Halloween issue 2.95
14 F:Elizabeth Lavin 2.95
15 . . . . 2.95
16 GoGo Gang,pt.1 . . . . 2.75
17 GoGo Gang,pt.2 . . . . 2.75
18 Blue Monday 2.95
19 Halloween 2.95

ADAM AND EVE A.D.
Bam, 1985–87
1 . . . . 3.00
2 thru 10 . . . . @2.00

ADDAM OMEGA
Antarctic Press, 1997
1 (of 4) by Bill Hughes 2.95
2 thru 4 . . . . @2.95

ADOLESCENT RADIOACTIVE BLACK-BELT HAMSTERS
Eclipse, 1986
1 I:Bruce,Chuck,Jackie,Clint 2.50
1a 2nd printing 2.00
2 A parody of a parody 2.00
3 I:Bad Gerbil 2.00
4 A:Heap (3-D),Abusement Park . 2.00
5 Abusement Park #2 . . . . 2.00
6 SK,Abusement Park #3 . . . . . . 2.00
7 SK,V:Toe-Jam Monsters 2.00

Addam Omega #1
© Antarctic Press

8 SK 2.00
9 All-Jam last issue 2.00
[2nd Series]
Parody Press
1 . . . . 2.50
2 Hamsters Go Hollywood 2.50

ADVENTURERS
Aircel/Adventure, 1986
0 Origin Issue 2.50
1 with Skeleton 7.00
1a Revised cover 5.00
1b 2nd printing 2.50
2 Peter Hsu (c) 2.50
3 Peter Hsu (c) 2.50
4 Peter Hsu (c) 2.00
5 Peter Hsu (c) 2.00
6 Peter Hsu (c) 2.00
7 thru 9 . . . . @2.00

ADVENTURERS BOOK II
Adventure Publ., 1987
0 O:Man Gods 2.00
1 . . . . 2.00
2 thru 9 . . . . @2.00

ADVENTURERS BOOK III
Adventure Publ., 1989
1A Lim.(c)Ian McCaig 2.25
1B Reg.(c)Mitch Foust 2.25
2 thru 6 . . . . @2.25

ADVENTURES INTO THE UNKNOWN
A Plus Comics, 1990
1 AW,WW, rep. classic horror . . . 2.95
2 AW 2.95
3 AW 2.95
Halloween Spec. reps. Charlton & American Comics GroupHorror . 2.50
ACG Comics, 1997
1 FF,AW, Charlton comics reprint . 2.95

CVA Page 694   All comics prices listed are for *Near Mint* condition.

ADVENTURES OF BARRY WEEN BOY GENIUS
Oni Press, 2000
1 (of 6) by Judd Winick 2.95
2 Monkey Tales,pt.2. . . . . 2.95
3 Monkey Tales,pt.3. . . . . 2.95
4 Monkey Tales,pt.4. . . . . 2.95
5 Monkey Tales,pt.5. . . . . 2.95
6 Monkey Tales,pt.6. . . . . 2.95
TPB Vol. 1 thru Vol. 4 . . . . @8.95

ADVENTURES OF CHRISSY CLAWS, THE
Heroic, 1991
1 thru 2 . . . . @3.25

ADVENTURES OF CHUK THE BARBARIC
White Wolf, 1987
1 & 2 . . . . @1.25

ADVENTURES OF LIBERAL MAN, THE
Political Comics, 1996
1 by Marcus Pierce & Pete Garcia . 2.95
2 V:Right Wing talk show hosts . . . 2.95
3 Contract with America,'pt.2 . . . . . 2.95
4 Terminate with Extreme
  Prejudice,'pt.2 . . . . 2.95
5 Extreme Prejudice,pt.3 . . . . 2.95
6 . . . . 2.95
7 1996 Election issue 2.95
9 . . . . 2.95
10 The Last Boy Scouts,pt.2. . . . . . 2.95
Sharkbait Press, 1999
TPB Final Mission. 14.95

ADVENTURES OF LUTHER ARKWRIGHT
Valkyrie Press, 1987–89
1 thru 9 . . . . @2.25
See Also: Dark Horse section

ADVENTURES OF THE AEROBIC DUO
Lost Cause Productions
1 thru 3 . . . . @2.25
4 Gopher Quest. 2.25
5 V:Stupid Guy 2.25

ADVENTURES OF THEOWN
Pyramid, 1986
1 thru 3, Limited series . . . . @1.75

AESOP'S FABLES
Fantagraphics, 1991
1 Selection of Fables. 2.25
2 Selection of Fables. 2.25
3 inc. Boy who cried wolf 2.25

AETOS
Hall of Heroes, 1997
1 by Dan Parsons 2.50
1 variant cover. 4.00
2 . . . . 2.50

AETOS THE EAGLE
Ground Zero, 1997
1 (of 3) by Dan Parsons. 3.00
2 . . . . 3.00
3 concl. 3.00

AETOS 2: CHILDREN OF THE GRAVES
Orphan Underground, 1995
1 A:Nightmare 2.50

Agent Unknown #3
© *Renegade*

AGENT UNKNOWN
Renegade, 1987
1 thru 3 . . . . @2.00

AGE OF HEROES, THE
Halloween Comics, 1996
1 JHI 3.50
1A signed 7.00
2 JHI 3.50
2A signed 7.00

AGONY ACRES
AA2 Entertainment, 1995
1 thru 3 . . . . @2.50
4 and 5 . . . . @2.95

AIRFIGHTERS CLASSICS
Eclipse, 1987
1 O:Airboy,rep.Air Fighters#2 . . . . 4.00
2 rep.Old Airboy appearances 4.00
3 thru 6 . . . . @3.95

AIRWAVES
Caliber, 1990
1 Radio Security 2.50
2 A:Paisley,Ganja 2.50
3 Formation of Rebel Alliance 2.50
4 Big Annie,pt. 1 . . . . 2.50
5 Big Annie,pt 2 . . . . 2.50

AKIKO
Sirius, 1996
1 MCi, Akiko on the Planet Smoo. . 6.00
2 MCi 4.00
3 thru 17 MCi. . . . . @3.00
18 Alia Rellapor, concl. 3.00
19 new story,pt.1 . . . . 3.00
20 F:Mr. Beeba. 3.00
21 On the Road 3.00
22 . . . . 3.00
23 space station Fognon-6 . . . . . . 3.00
24 escape spaceship 3.00
25 Done in One, 32pg. 3.00
26 reunited on planet Smoo 3.00
27 MCi,Bornstone's Elixir,pt.2 . . . . 3.00
28 MCi,Bornstone's Elixir,pt.3 . . . . 3.00
29 MCi,Bornstone's Elixir,pt.4 . . . . 3.00
30 MCi,Bornstone's Elixir,pt.5 . . . . 3.00
31 MCi,Bornstone's Elixir, concl. . . 3.00
32 MCi,On Planet Earth,pt.1 . . . . . 3.00
33 MCi,On Planet Earth,pt.2 . . . . . 3.00
34 MCi,On Planet Earth,pt.3 . . . . . 3.00
35 Moonshopping,pt.1 . . . . 3.00
36 Moonshopping,pt.2 . . . . 3.00
37 Moonshopping,pt.3 . . . . 3.00
38 Moonshopping,pt.4 . . . . 3.00
39 Big Bag of This and That 3.00
40 Battle of Boach's Keep,pt.1 . . . 3.00
41 Battle of Boach's Keep,pt.2 . . . 3.00
42 Battle of Boach's Keep,pt.3 . . . 3.00
43 Battle of Boach's Keep,pt.4 . . . 3.00
44 Battle of Boach's Keep,pt.5 . . . 3.00
45 Battle of Boach's Keep,pt.6 . . . 3.00
46 Battle of Boach's Keep,pt.7 . . . 3.00
47 Battle of Boach's Keep,pt.8 . . . 3.00
48 Akiko on Planet Earth,pt.1 . . . . 3.00
49 Akiko on Planet Earth,pt.2 . . . . 3.00
50 40-pg. 3.50
51 . . . . 2.95
TPB Vol. 1 rep. #1–#6 . . . . 14.95
TPB Vol. 2 rep. #8–#13. . . . . 11.95
TPB Vol. 3 rep. #14–#18. . . . . . . 11.95
TPB Vol. 4 rep. #19–#24. . . . . . . 14.95
TPB Vol. 5 . . . . 12.95
TPB Vol. 6 . . . . 14.95
TPB Vol. 1 Flights of Fancy. 14.95
GN Akiko on the Planet Smoo. . . . 14.95
Spec. Akiko on the Planet Smoo. . . 3.50

ALAN MOORE'S THE COURTYARD
Avatar Press 2003
1 and 2 . . . . @3.50
1a thru 2a wraparound (c) . . . . . @3.95

ALAN MOORE'S YUGGOTH CULTURES
Avatar Press 2003
1 thru 3 . . . . @3.50
1 thru 3a wraparound (c) 3.95

ALBEDO
Thoughts & Images, 1985–89
0 white cover, yellow drawing table
  Blade Runner 35.00
0a white(c) 15.00
0b blue(c),1st ptg 12.00
0c blue(c),2nd ptg 10.00
0d blue(c),3rd ptg 5.00
0e Photo(c),4th ptg.,inc. extra
  pages. 3.00
1 SS,I:Nilson Groundthumper,
  dull red cover 10.00
1a bright red cover 6.00
2 SS,I:Usagi Yojimbo 15.00
3 SS,Erma, Usagi 5.00
4 SS,Usagi 6.00
5 Nelson Groundthumper. 5.00
6 Erma, High Orbit. 4.00
7 . . . . 2.00
8 Erna Feldna 2.00
9 High Orbit,Harvest Venture 2.00
10 thru 14 . . . . @2.00

ALBEDO VOL. II
Antarctic Press, 1991–93
1 New Erma Story	3.00
2 E.D.F. HQ.	3.00
3 Birth of Erma's Child	3.00
4 Non action issue	3.00
5 The Outworlds	3.00
6 War preparations	3.00
7 Ekosiak in Anarchy	3.00
8 EDF High Command	3.00
Spec. Color	3.00

VOL. III
1 .... 3.50

ALIEN FIRE
Kitchen Sink Press, 1987
1 Eric Vincent art	3.50
2 Eric Vincent art	2.50
3 Eric Vincent art	2.00

ALIEN NATION: A BREED APART
Adventure Comics, 1990
1 Friar Kaddish	3.00
2 Friar Kaddish	2.50
3 The 'Vampires' Busted	2.50
4 Final Issue	2.50

ALIEN NATION: THE FIRSTCOMERS
Adventure Comics, 1991
1 New Mini-series	2.50
2 Assassin	2.50
3 Search for Saucer	2.50
4 Final Issue	2.50

ALIEN NATION: THE PUBLIC ENEMY
Adventure Comics, 1991
1 'Before the Fall'	2.50
2 Earth & Wehlnistrata	2.50
3 Killer on the Loose	2.50

ALIEN NATION: THE SKIN TRADE
Adventure Comics, 1991
1 'Case of the Missing Milksop'	2.50
2 'To Live And Die in L.A'	2.50
3 A:Dr. Jekyll	2.50
4 D.Methoraphan Exposed	2.50

ALIEN NATION: THE SPARTANS
Adventure Comics, 1990
1 JT/DPo,Yellow wrap	4.00
1a JT/DPo,Green wrap	4.00
1b JT/DPo,Pink wrap	4.00
1c JT/DPo,blue wrap	4.00
1d LTD collectors edition	7.00
2 JT,A:Ruth Lawrence	2.50
3 JT/SM,Spartans	2.50
4 JT/SM,conclusion	2.50

ALISON DARE, LITTLE MISS ADVENTURES
Oni Press, 2001
1 (of 3)	3.00
TPB	8.95

Alien Nation, The Spartans #2
© Adventure Comics

Vol. 2
1 (of 2) Heart of the Maiden	2.95
2 Heart of the Maiden	2.95
1-shot 48-pg. (2000)	4.50

ALL-NEW TENCHI MUYO
Viz Communications, 2002
Part 1
1 (of 5) by Hitoshi Okuda	2.95
2 thru 5	@2.95

Part 2
1 (of 5)	2.95
2 thru 5	@2.95
TPB Vol. 1 Alien Nation	8.95
TPB Vol. 2 Doom Time	8.95
TPB Vol. 3 Dark Washu	8.95

ALL-PRO SPORTS
All Pro Sports
1 Unauthorized Bio-Bo Jackson	2.50
2 Unauthorized Bio-Joe Montana	2.50

ALLURA AND THE CYBERANGELS
Avatar Press, 1998
Spec.#1 by Bill Maus 3.95

ALLY
Ally Winsor Productions, 1995
1 I&O: Ally	2.95
2 and 3	@2.95

ALTERNATE HEROES
Prelude Graphics, 1986
1 and 2 .... @2.00

AMAZING COMICS PREMIERES
Amazing, 1987
1 thru 9 .... @2.00

AMAZON WOMAN
Fantaco, 1994
1	3.00
2	3.00

VOL. 2 (1996)
1 thru 4	@3.00
Christmas Spec.	4.95
Beach Party	5.95
Amazing Colossal Amazon Woman #1	7.95
Amazing Colossal Amazon Album	12.95
Jungle Annual #1	5.95
Jungle Album	9.95
TPB Amazon Woman: The Art of Tom Simonton	9.95
TPB Amazon Woman, deluxe	19.95
Spec. Invaders of Terror (1996)	5.95
TPB Book One by Tom Simonton	14.95
TPB Book Two The Curse of the Amazon	14.95
1-shot Attack of the Amazon Girls, cont. nudity	4.95

AMAZONS GONZANGAS: BAD GIRLS OF THE JUNGLE
Academy Comics, 1995
0 Rites of passage,JWt 3.50

AMERICAN SPLENDOR
Harvey Bekar, 1976–90
1 thru 15 .... @3.25

Tundra, 1991
16 .... 3.95

AMERICAN WOMAN
Antarctic Press, 1998
1 by B.Denham & R.Stockton 2.95

AMERICA'S GREATEST COMICS
AC Comics, 2002
1 F:Phantom Lady, golden-age rep.	6.95
2 F:Mysta on the Moon	6.95
3 F:Spy Smasher	6.95
4 F:Yarko, Master Magician	6.95
5 F: Captain Science	6.95
6	6.95
7 F:Bob Lubbers	6.95

AMERIMAGNA
Ironcat 2002
Vol. 1
TPB #1	8.00
TPB #2 thru #3	@8.00

I.C. Entertainment 2003
TPB #4 thru #12 .... @8.00

AMUSING STORIES
Blackthorne
1 thru 3 .... @2.00

ANATOMIC BOMBS
Brainstorm, 1998
1 Angelissa, by Mike James	2.95
1a Bad Tabitha, by Mike James	2.95
1b Bad Tabitha, photo cover edition	3.95

ANGEL GIRL
Angel Entertainment, 1997
0 by David Campiti & Al Rio	2.95
1 by David Campiti & Richard Fraga	2.95
1 deluxe	5.95
1-shot Against All Evil	2.95

Spec. #1 Angels Illustrated Swimsuit
 Special. 5.00
1-shot Before the Wings 2.95
1-shot Demonworld, by Ellis Bell &
 Mark Kuettner 2.95
1-shot Doomsday, by Ellis Bell &
 Mark Kuettner 3.00

ANGEL GIRL: HEAVEN SENT
Angel Entertainment, 1997
0 by David Campiti & Al Rio. 2.95
1 . . . . 3.00

ANGELIC LAYER
Tokyopop Press, 2002
GN Vol. 1 (of 7) 10.00
GN Vol. 2 thru 5 . . . . 10.00

ANGEL OF DEATH
Innovation
1 thru 4 . . . . @2.25

ANIMAL MYSTIC
Cry For Dawn/Sirus, 1993–95
1 DOe. 32.00
1a variant, signed 47.00
1b 2nd printing, new (c). 7.00
2 I:Klor 30.00
2a 2nd printing, new (c) 6.00
3 . . . . 12.00
3a 2nd printing 5.00
4 last issue 4.00
4a special 15.00
TPB DOe 14.95

ANIMAL MYSTIC: KLOR
Sirius, 1999
1 (of 3) DOe 2.95
2 DOe 2.95
3 DOe, conclusion 2.95

ANIMERICA
Viz Comics
1 F:Bubble Gum Crisis 2.95
2 F:Bubble Gum Crisis 2.95
3 F:Bubble Gum Crisis 2.95

ANIMERICA
Viz Communications, 2000
Vol. 8
11 & 12 . . . . @4.95
Vol. 9, 2001
1 thru 10 . . . . @4.95
11/12 . . . . 4.95
Vol. 10, 2001
1 thru 12 . . . . @4.95
Vol. 11 Jan. 2003
1 thru 12 . . . . @4.95
TPB Best of Animerica 2003 . . . . . 12.95

ANIMERICA EXTRA
Viz Communications, 1998
1 & 2 . . . . @4.95
VOL. 2, 1998
1 thru 11 . . . . @4.95
VOL. 3, 1999
1 thru 12 . . . . @4.95
VOL. 4, 2000
1 thru 12 . . . . @4.95

B & W PUB.

Vol. 5, 2001
1 thru 12 . . . . @4.95
Vol. 6
1 thru 12 . . . . @4.95

ANTARES CIRCLE
Antarctic Press
1 . . . . 1.75
2 . . . . 1.75

ANUBIS
Unicorn Books
1 I:Anubis 2.50
2 F:Anubis. 2.50
3 . . . . 2.50
Didactic Chocolate Press
3 by Scott Berwanger 2.75
4 thru 6 . . . . @2.75
Adventure Comics
7 'Sandy's Plight'. 2.75
8 . . . . 2.95

A-OK #3
© *Antarctic Press*

A-OK
Antarctic Press, 1993
1 Ninja H.S. spin-off series 2.50
2 F:Paul,Moniko,James 2.50
3 Confrontation 2.50
4 . . . . 2.50

APATHY KAT
Entity, 1995
1 . . . . 2.75
1 signed, numbered. 9.95
1 2nd printing 2.75
2 . . . . 2.75
2 2nd printing 2.75
3 & 4 . . . . 2.75
TPB Kollection #1 . . . . 7.95

APE CITY
Adventure Comics
1 Monkey Business 3.00
2 thru 4 . . . . @2.50

APPARITION, THE
Caliber, 1995
1 thru 4 . . . . @2.95

Angel–Areala

5 'Black Clouds' 2.95

APPLESEED
Eclipse, 1988
1 MSh,rep. Japanese comic 9.00
2 MSh,arrival in Olympus City 6.00
3 MSh,Olympus City politics 5.00
4 MSh,V:Director 5.00
5 MSh,Deunan vs. Chiffon. 5.00
Book Two, 1989
1 MSh,AAd(c),Olympus City 4.00
2 MSh,AAd(c),Hitomi vs.EswatUnit 4.00
3 MSh,AAd(c),Deunan vs.Gaia . . . 4.00
4 MSh,AAd(c),V:Robot Spiders . . . 4.00
5 MSh,AAd(c),Hitome vs.Gaia 4.00
Book Three, 1989
1 MSh,Brigreos vs.Biodroid 5.00
2 MSh,V:Cuban Navy 4.00
3 MSh,'Benandanti'. 4.00
4 MSh,V:Renegade biodroid 4.00
5 MSh 4.00
Book Four, 1990
1 MSh,V:Munma Terrorists. 3.50
2 MSh,V:Drug-crazed Munma 3.50
3 Msh,V:Munma Drug Addicts 3.50
4 MSh,Deunan vs. Pani. 3.50

AQUA KNIGHT
Viz Communications, 2000
1 (of 6) by Yukito Kishiro 3.50
2 thru 6 . . . . @3.50
PART 2
1 (of 5) 3.50
2 thru 5 . . . . @3.50
PART 3, 2001
1 thru 5 . . . . @3.50
TPB Vol. 1 . . . . 16.95
TPB Vol. 2 . . . . 16.95
TPB Vol. 3 . . . . 16.95

AQUARIUM
CPM Manga, 2000
1 by Tomoko Taniguchi 2.95
2 thru 6 . . . . @2.95

ARAMIS WEEKLY
Comics Interview
1 mini-series 2.00
2 . . . . 2.00
3 . . . . 2.00

AREA 88
Eclipse, 1987
1 I:Shin Kazama 3.00
1a 2nd printing 1.50
2 Dangerous Mission 2.00
2a 2nd printing 1.50
3 O:Shin,Paris '78 . . . . 2.00
4 thru 8 . . . . @2.00
9 thru 36 . . . . @1.50
Viz Communications, 1988
37 thru 39 . . . . @1.50
40 . . . . 1.75
41 . . . . 1.75
42 . . . . 2.00

AREALA, ANGEL OF WAR
Antarctic Press, 1998
1 F:Warrior Nun Areala, color. 3.00
2 color. 3.00
3 b&w 3.00
4 b&w, conclusion 3.00

Argonauts–Athena

ARGONAUTS
Eternity
1 thru 5 .... @2.00

ARIK KHAN
A Plus Comics
1 I:Arik Khan 2.50
2 .... 2.50
ACG Comics, 1998
1 by Frank Reyes, heroic fantasy . 2.95

Aristocratic X-traterrestrial Time-Traveling Thieves #2
© Fictioneer Books

ARISTOCRATIC X-TRA-TERRESTRIAL TIME-TRAVELING THIEVES
Fictioneer Books, 1987
1 V:IRS 2.00
2 V:Realty 1.75
3 V:MDM 1.75
4 thru 12 .... @1.75

ARIZONA: A SIMPLE HORROR
London Night/EH Prod., 1998
1 (of 3) by Joe Kennedy &
 Jerry Beck 3.00
2 double sized 3.00
3 .... 3.00
1-shot Wild at Heart, signed
 alternate cover 10.00

A.R.M.
Adventure Comics, 1990
1 Larry Niven adapt. Death by
 Ecstasy,pt.1 .... 2.50
2 Death by Ecstasy,pt.2 .... 2.50
3 Death by Ecstasy,pt.3 .... 2.50

ARMAGEDDON PATROL
Alchemy Texts, 1999
Spec. The Shot 2.95
1 (of 2) Cherries 2.95
2 Cherries 2.95
Spec. Maiden America (2002) ... 3.00
Spec. Fatal Mistakes 3.00

B & W PUB.

ARMED & DANGEROUS
Valiant (B&W) 1995
1 thru 4 .... @2.95
Spec.#1 .... 2.95

ARMED & DANGEROUS
Acclaim (B&W) 1996
1 BH,Hell's Slaughterhouse,pt.1 . . 2.95
2 BH,Hell's Slaughterhouse,pt.2 . . 2.95
3 BH,Hell's Slaughterhouse,pt.3 . . 2.95
4 BH,Hell's Slaughterhouse,pt.4 . . 2.95

ARMED & DANGEROUS No. 2
Acclaim (B&W) Dec., 1996
1 BH,When Irish Eyes are
 Dying,pt.1 .... 2.95
2 thru 4 BH,When Irish
 Eyes,pt.2 thru pt.4 .... @2.95

ARROW SPOTLIGHT
Arrow Comics, 1998–99
Adventures of Simone & Ajax 2.95
Allison Chains 2.95
Descendants of Toshin 2.95
Max Velocity, by Jack Snider ... 2.95
Red Vengeance, by Chris Kemple . 2.95
Talonback 2.95

ARSENIC LULLABY
A Silent Comics, 1999
Spec. May '99 .... 2.50
Spec. July '99 .... 2.50
Spec. Sept.'99 .... 2.50
Spec. Jan. 2000 .... 2.50
8 thru 15 .... @2.50
Sept. 2001 .... 2.50
Nov. 2001 .... 2.65
Christmas 2001 .... 2.65
Spec. Christmas Special 2.50
Spec. Halloween Special 2.75
TPB The Devil Your Neighbor ... 13.00
TPB Arsenic Lullaby, Year Two .. 13.00
Volume 2, 2002
1 by Douglas Paszkiewicz 2.50
2 .... 2.65
3 .... 2.65
4 .... 2.75
TPB Vol. 1 Damned Laughter 13.00
TPB The Devil's hat Trick 18.95
AAA Milwaukee Publishing 2002
Lost issue, signed 4.00

ASHEN VICTOR
Viz Communications, 1998
1 (of 4) by Yukito Kishiro 2.95
2 thru 4 concl. .... @2.95
TPB 14.95

ASHES
Caliber, 1990–91
1 thru 6 .... @2.50

ASHLEY DUST
Knight Press, 1995
1 thru 3 .... @2.50
4 V:Allister Crowley 2.50
5 Metaphysical Adventure 2.50

ASRIAL VS. CHEETAH
Antarctic Press, 1995–96
1 & 2 Ninja High School Gold

Comics Values Annual

Digger x-over .... @2.95

ASSASSINATE HITLER!
New England Comics, 2001
1 (of 3) by Ron Ledwell 3.75
2 thru 3 .... @3.75

ASSASSINETTE
Pocket Change Comics, 1994
1 thru 3 .... @2.50
4 Psychic Realm 2.50
5 V:Nemesis 2.50
6 The Second Coming,pt.2 ..... 2.50
7 The Second Coming,pt.3 ..... 2.50
8 V:Crazy Actor 2.50
9 .... 2.50
10 final issue 2.50
Spec. Assassinette Returns 2.50
Spec. Assassinette Violated ... 2.50
Deluxe Assassinette Violated .. 4.25

ASSASSINETTE: HARDCORE 1995
Pocket Change Comics
1 By Shadow Slasher Team 2.50
2 V:Bolero 2.50

ASTOUNDING SPACE THRILLS
Day One Comics, 1998
1 by Steve Conley, The Codex
 Reckoning,pt.1 .... 2.95
2 Bros. Hildebrandt (c) 2.95
3 Aspects of Iron 2.95
4 The Robot Murders 2.95
5 Gordo returns 2.95

ASTRA
CPM Manga, 2001
1 .... 2.95
1a variant JBa (c) 2.95
1b variant JBa(c) signed 29.95
2 thru 5 .... @2.95
6 thru 8 .... @2.95
TPB Jerry Robinson's Astra 15.95

ASTRONAUTS IN TROUBLE: LIVE FROM THE MOON
Gun Dog Comics, 1999
1 (of 5) 2.95
2 thru 5 .... @2.95
AIT Comics, 1999
Spec.#1 Cool Ed's 2.95
Spec.#1 CAd, One Shot, One Beer. 7.95

ASTRONAUTS IN TROUBLE: SPACE:, 1959
AIT/Planetlar, 2000
1 (of 3) by Larry Young, CAd .. 2.95
2 .... 2.95
3 .... 2.95
TPB 72-pg 7.95
TPB Astronauts in Trouble 16.95

ATHENA
A.M. Works
7 thru 14 by Dean Hsieh ..... @2.95
TPB Vol. 1 .... 14.95
TPB Vol. 2 .... 15.95

ATOMIC CITY TALES
Kitchen Sink, 1996
1 thru 4 by Jay Stephens ...... @3.50
TPB Vol. 1 Go Power 12.95
TPB Vol. 1 signed & numbered ... 20.95
Oni Press, 2002
TPB Vol. 1 Go Power 12.95
TPB Vol. 2 Doc Phantom 12.95

ATOMIC COMICS
1 .... 1.50
Becomes:
MARK I

Atomic Man #1
© Blackthorne

ATOMIC MAN
Blackthorne, 1986
1 .... 3.00
2 .... 2.00
3 .... 1.75

ATOMIC MOUSE
A Plus Comics, 1990
1 A:Atomic Bunny 2.50

ATOMIC OVERDRIVE
Caliber
1 by Dave Darrigo & PGr. 2.95
2 1950s Sci-Fi,Horror,Humor 2.95
3 .... 2.95

A TRAVELLER'S TALE
Antarctic Press
1 I:Goshin the Traveller 2.50
2 .... 2.50

ATTACK OF THE MUTANT MONSTERS
A Plus Comics
1 SD,rep.Gorgo(Kegor) 2.50

AUGUST
Arrow Comics, 1998
1 by Scott Rosema 2.95
2 thru 4 .... @2.95

B & W PUB.

AUTUMN
Caliber Press, 1995
1 I:James Turell 2.95
GN 7"x10" 12.95

AVALON
Harrier, 1987
1 thru 3 .... @1.50

AVANT GUARD
Day 1 Comics, 1994
1 thru 4 F:Feedback .... @2.50

AVATARS
Avatar Press, 1998
1 (of 2) by Gregory & Holaso 3.95
2 F:Pandora & Atlas 3.50

AV IN 3D
Aardvark–Vanaheim, 1984
1 Color,A:FlamingCarot 6.00

AVELON
Kenzer & Company, 1998
1 .... 2.95
2 thru 5 .... @2.95
6 thru 11 Legacy of Thrain ..... @2.95
11 & 12 Heir to Legend .... @2.95

AVENUE X
Innovation
1 Based on NY radio drama 2.50
Purple Spiral
3 signed & numbered 3.00

AWAKENING COMICS
Awakening Comics, 1997
1 by Steve Peters 3.50
2 .... 3.50
3 .... 2.95
4 .... 2.95
Awakening Comics, 1999
1 by Steve Peters 3.50
Spec. Millennium Bug Fever 2.95

AWESOME COMICS
1 thru 3 .... @2.00

AXED FILES, THE
Entity Comics, 1995
1 X-Files Parody 2.50
1 3rd printing, parody 2.75

B-MOVIE PRESENTS
B-Movie Comics, 1986
1 .... 1.70
2 .... 1.70
3 Tasma, Queen of the Jungle ... 1.70
4 .... 1.70

BABES OF AREA 51
Blatant Comics, 1997
1 .... 2.95

BABY ANGEL X
Brainstorm, 1996
1 .... 2.95
2 .... 2.95
3 gold edition 5.00

Atomic–Ballad

3a signed edition 10.00

BABY ANGEL X: SCORCHED EARTH
Brainstorm, 1997
1 by Scott Harrison 2.95
2 .... 2.95

BABYLON CRUSH
Boneyard Press, 1995
1 I:Babylon Crush 2.95
2 V:A Gang 2.95
3 V:Mafiaso Brothers 2.95
4 & 5 .... @2.95
CFD
6 & 7 .... @3.95
Boneyard, 1998
1-shot Buddha, F:Lesbian dominatrix vigilante 4.95
Spec. Babylon Bondage Christmas . 2.95
Spec. Girlfriends 2.95
Spec. The Last Shepherd 2.95

BAD APPLES
High Impact, 1997
1 .... 2.95
1 Bad Candies cover 9.95
2 .... 2.95
2 deluxe 15.00
3 by Billy Patton 2.95
ABC Studios, 1999
VOL 2
1 RCl 3.00
1a deluxe variant 8.00
2 .... 3.00
VOL 3
1 by Greg Narvasa 3.00
1a gold manga 10.00

BAD APPLES: HIGH EXPECTATIONS
ABC Studios, 1999
1 .... 3.00
1a Beach Fun (c) 8.00
2 .... 3.00
2a deluxe 8.00

BAKER STREET
(Prev. color)
Caliber, 1989
3 .... 3.25
4 .... 2.00
5 Children of the Night,pt.1 ..... 2.00
6 Children of the Night,pt.2 ..... 2.00
7 thru 10 Children of the Night pt.3–pt.6 .... @2.50

BAKER STREET: GRAPHITTI
Caliber
1 'Elemenary, My Dear' 2.50

BALANCE OF POWER
MU Press, 1990–91
1 thru 4 .... @2.50

BALLAD OF UTOPIA
Black Daze, 2000
1 by B.Buchanan & M.Hoffman ... 2.95
2 thru 5 .... @2.95

All comics prices listed are for *Near Mint* condition.

Ballad–Battletech

TPB Vol. 1 . . . . 8.95

Antimatter/Hoffman International 2003
7 thru 8 . . . . @2.95

BANDY MAN, THE
Caliber, 1996
1 SPr,CAd 2.95
2 SPr,CAd,JIT 2.95
3 SPr,CAd,JIT, conclusion 2.95

BANANA FISH
Viz Communications, 1998
TPB by Akimi Yoshida 15.95
TPB Vol. 2 . . . . 15.95
TPB Vol. 3 . . . . 15.95
TPB Vol. 4 . . . . 15.95
TPB Vol. 5 . . . . 15.95
TPB Vol. 6 . . . . 15.95
TPB Vol. 7 . . . . 15.95

Baoh #5
© Viz Communications

BAOH
Viz, 1990
1 thru 8 . . . . @2.95
GN V:Juda Laboratory 14.95

BARABBAS
Slave Labor, 1986
1 . . . . 4.50
2 thru 4 . . . . @1.50

BARBARIANS
ACG Comics
1 by Jeff Jones, Mike Kaluta, Wayne Howard 2.95
2 WW 2.95

BARBARIC TALES
Pyramid
1 . . . . 3.00
2 and 3 . . . . @1.70

BASEBALL SUPERSTARS
Revolutionary, 1991–93
1 Nolan Ryan 2.50
2 Bo Jackson 2.50
3 Ken Griffey Jr. 2.50
4 Pete Rose 2.50

B & W PUB.

5 Rickey Henderson 2.50
6 Jose Canseco 2.50
7 Cal Ripkin Jr. 2.50
8 Carlton Fisk 2.50
9 George Brett 2.50
10 Darryl Strawberry 2.50
11 Frank Thomas 2.50
12 Ryne Sandberg (color) 2.75
13 Kirby Puckett (color) 2.75
14 Roberto & Sandy Alomar (color) . 2.75
15 Roger Clemens (color) 2.75
16 Mark McGuire 2.95
17 Avery & Glavin 2.95
18 Dennis Eckersley 2.95
19 Dave Winfield 2.95
20 Jim Abbott 2.95

BASTARD!!
Viz Communications, 2001
1 thru 2 Wizard . . . . @3.95
3 thru 5 Ninja . . . . @3.95
6 thru 8 Fighter . . . . @3.95
9 thru 10 Vampire . . . . @3.95
11 thru 12 Empress . . . . @3.95
13 thru 15 Empress . . . . @3.95
TPB Vol. 1 thru Vol. 3 . . . . @14.95
TPB Vol. 4 thru Vol. 5 . . . . @12.95

BATTLE ANGEL ALITA
Viz, 1992
1 I:Daisuka,Alita 8.00
2 Alita becomes warrior 6.00
3 A:Daiuke,V:Cyborg 4.00
4 Alita/Cyborg,A:Makaku 4.00
5 The Bounty Hunters Bar 4.00
6 Confrontation 4.00
7 Underground Sewers,A:Fang . . . 3.00
8 & 9 . . . . @2.75

Part Two, 1993
1 V:Zapan 3.00
2 V:Zapan 3.00
3 F:Ido 2.75
4 thru 7 V:Zapan . . . . @2.75
TPB Killing Angel 15.95

Part Three, 1993
1 thru 5 . . . . @2.75
6 . . . . 5.00
7 thru 13 . . . . @2.75

Part Four, 1994
1 thru 7 . . . . @2.75

Part Five, 1995
1 thru 6 . . . . @2.75
7 . . . . 2.95

Part Six, 1995–96
1 thru 8 YuK . . . . @2.95
TPB Angel of Chaos 15.95

Part Seven, 1996
1 thru 8 YuK . . . . @2.95

Part Eight, 1997
1 thru 9 YuK . . . . @2.95
TPB Vol. 2 Tears of an Agnel . . 15.95
TPB Vol. 4 Angel of Victory 15.95
TPB Vol. 5 . . . . 15.95
TPB Vol. 6 Angel of Death 15.95
TPB Vol. 7 Angel of Chaos 15.95
TPB Vol. 8 Fallen Angel 15.95
TPB Vol. 9 Angel's Ascension . . 16.95

BATTLE ANGEL ALITA: LAST ORDER
Viz Communicatons, 2002
Part 1
1 by Yukito Kishiro 2.95
2 thru 6 . . . . @2.95
GN Vol. 1 . . . . 9.95

Comics Values Annual

GN Vol. 2 . . . . 9.95
TPB Vol. 3 Killing Angel 15.95
TPB Vol. 5 Angle of Redemption . . 15.95

BATTLE ARMOR
Eternity, 1988
1 thru 4 . . . . @2.00

BATTLE BEASTS
Blackthorne, 1988
1 thru 4 . . . . @1.50

BATTLE GIRLZ
Antarctic Press, 2002
1 by Rod Espinosa 3.00
2 thru 6 . . . . @3.00

BATTLEGROUND EARTH
Best Comics, 1996
1 . . . . 2.50
2 . . . . 2.50
3 'Destiny Quest: The Vengeance' concl. 2.50
4 V:Conjura 2.50
5 'The Pit of Black Death' 2.50

BATTLE POPE
Funk-O-Tron, 2000
1 . . . . 2.95
2 thru 4 . . . . @2.95
Spec.#1 Shorts 4.95
Spec.#2 Shorts 4.95
Spec.#3 Shorts 2.95
Spec.#1 Christmas Popetacular . . 4.95
TPB Vol. 1 . . . . 12.95
TPB Vol. 2 . . . . 12.95
TPB Saint Michael (2001) 12.95

BATTLE POPE MAYHEM
Funk-O-Tron, 2001
1 (of 2) 2.95
2 . . . . 2.95

BATTLE POPE PRESENTS: SAINT MICHAEL
Funk-O-Tron, 2001
1 (of 3) 2.95
2 . . . . 2.95
3 . . . . 2.95

BATTLE POPE: WRATH OF GOD
Funk-O-Tron, 2002
1 (of 3) by R.Kirkman & T.Moore . . 3.50
2 thru 3 . . . . @3.50

BATTLESTAR BLACK & WHITE
Realm Press, 2000
1-shot Battlestar Galactica 2.99

BATTLETECH
Blackthorne, 1987
(Prev. Color)
7 thru 12 . . . . @1.75
Ann.#1 . . . . 4.50

All comics prices listed are for *Near Mint* condition.

BATTRON
NEC
1 WWII story 2.75
2 WWII contd. 2.75

BEAST WARRIOR OF SHAOLIN
Pied Piper, 1987
1 thru 5 . . . . @2.00

THE BEATLES EXPERIENCE
Revolutionary, 1991
1 Beatles 1960's 3.00
2 Beatles 1964-1966 . . . . 2.50
3 . . . . 2.50
4 Abbey Road, Let it be 2.50
5 The Solo Years 2.50
6 Paul McCartney & Wings 2.50
7 The Murder of John Lennon . . . 2.50
8 To 1992, final issue 2.50

BECK AND CAUL
Gauntlet, 1994
1 I:Beck and Caul 2.95
2 thru 6 . . . . @2.95
Ann.#1 A Single Step 3.50

BENZINE
Antarctic Press, 2000
1 manga, by Ben Dunn 4.95
2 thru 7 . . . . @4.95

BERLIN
Drawn & Quarterly, 1999
1 by Jason Lutes 2.95
2 thru 8 . . . . @2.95
9 thru 10 . . . . @3.50
TPB Book One 15.95

BERZERKER
Gauntlet (Caliber), 1993
1 thru 6 . . . . @2.95

BEST OF THE WEST
AC Comics, 1998
1 F:Durango Kid 4.95
2 F:The Haunted Horseman 4.95
3 F:The Haunted Horseman 4.95
4 F:Roy Rogers, 44-pg. 5.95
5 F:Durango Kid 5.95
6 F:Durango Kid 5.95
7 F:Monte Hale 5.95
8 . . . . 5.95
9 F:Sunset Carson 5.95
10 F:Durango Kid 5.95
11 F:Black Diamond 5.95
12 F:Latigo Kid 5.95
13 F:The Durango Kid 5.95
14 F:Haunted Horseman 5.95
15 F:Roy Rogers 5.95
16 O:The Whip 5.95
17 F:Lone Ranger 5.95
18 F:Black Bull 5.95
19 F:Rocky Lane 5.95
20 F:Durango Kid 5.95
21 F:Masked Marvel 5.95
22 F:Ken Maynard 5.95
23 F:Freaks of Fear 5.95
24 F:Redmask, Black Phantom . . 5.95
25 FF(c),F:Haunted horsemen . . 5.95
26 F:Lazo Kid, Lemonade Kid . . . 5.95
27 F:Roy Rogers 5.95
28 F:Red Mask 5.95
29 F:Jim Bowie 5.95
30 F:The Durango Kid 5.95
31 F:Haunted Horseman 5.95
32 F:Haunted Horseman 5.95
33 F:Zorro 6.95
34 Roy Rogers 6.95
35 The Haunted Horseman 6.95
36 Gene Autry 6.95
37 Origins Issue 6.95
38 Durango Kid 6.95

BETHANY THE VAMPFIRE
Brainstorm, 1997
0 O:Bethany 2.95
1 by Holly Galightly 2.95
1a luxury edition 5.00
2 . . . . 2.95
3 . . . . 2.95

BETTIE PAGE THE '50s RAGE
Illustration Studio, 2001
1 revised edition, Steve Woron . . . 3.25
2 all pin-up layout 3.25
2 tame cover 3.25
Ann.#1 revised 3.25

BEYOND MARS
Blackthorne
1 thru 5 . . . . @2.00

BIGGER
Free Lunch Comics, 1998
Spec.#1 . . . . 3.50
1 (of 4) The Devil's Concubine . . . 2.95
2 thru 4 Devil's Concubine,pt.2–4 . 2.95

BIG NUMBERS
Mad Love
1 BSz,AMo(s) 6.00
2 BSz,AMo(s) 5.50

BIG O, THE
Viz Communications, 2002
Part 1
1 (of 5) by Hitoshi Ariga 3.50
2 thru 5 . . . . @3.50
Part 2
1 (of 4) by Hitoshi Ariga 3.50
2 thru 4 . . . . 3.50
Part 3
1 (of 4) by Hitoshi Ariga 3.50
2 thru 4 . . . . @3.50
TPB Vol. 1 . . . . 15.95
Part 4
1 (of 4) by Hitoshi Ariga 3.50
2 thru 4 . . . . @3.50
TPB Vol. 2 thru Vol. 4 . . . . @9.95

BILL THE BULL
Burnt Cain, 1992
1 I:Bill the Bull 2.95
2 & 3 For Hire . . . . @2.95

BILL THE BULL: ONE SHOT, ONE BOURBON, ONE BEER
Boneyard, 1994
1 . . . . 2.95
2 . . . . 2.95

BILLY DOGMA
Millennium, 1997
1 by Dean Haspiel 2.95
1a signed print edition 4.95
2 . . . . 2.95
3 . . . . 2.95
4 They Found A Sawed-Off in My Afro 2.95

BILLY NGUYEN PRIVATE EYE
Caliber, 1990
1 . . . . 2.00
1a 2nd printing 2.00
2 thru 6 . . . . @2.00

Bio-Booster Armor Guyver #3
© Viz Communications

BIO-BOOSTER ARMOR GUYVER
Viz Communications
Part One, 1993
1 by Yoshiki Takaya 4.00
2 thru 12 . . . . @3.00
TPB Vol. 1 rep.Part One,#1–#6. . 15.95
TPB Vol. 2 Revenge of Chronos . . 15.95
Part Two, 1994–95
1 F:Sho 2.75
2 thru 7 . . . . @2.75
TPB Vol. 3 Dark Masters 15.95
Part Three, 1995
1 Sho Unconscious 2.75
2 thru 7 . . . . @2.75
TPB Vol. 4 Escape From Chronos 15.95
Part Four, 1995–96
1 thru 7 . . . . @2.95
TPB Vol. 5 Guyver Reborn 15.95
Part Five, 1996
1 thru 7 . . . . @2.95
TPB Vol. 6 Heart of Chronos 15.95
Part Six, 1996–97
1 thru 6 by Yoshiki Takaya . . . . . @2.95
TPB Vol. 7 Armageddon 15.95

BIRTHDAY BOY, THE
Beetlebomb Books, 1997
1 by Jason Lethcoe 2.95
2 . . . . 2.95
3 . . . . 2.95
4 16-pg. 2.95

All comics prices listed are for Near Mint condition.

Birthday–Bloodshed — B & W PUB. — Comics Values Annual

VOL 2
1 16-pg........................ 2.95
TPB 56 pg..................... 7.95

BIZARRE HEROES
Kitchen Sink, 1990
1 DSs, parody 2.50
Fiasco Comics
1 DSs, reprint 2.95

[Original] BLACK CAT
Recollections, 1991
4 rep............................ 2.00
5 A:Ted Parrish 2.00
6 50th Anniv. Issue 2.00
7 rep............................ 2.00

BLACK AND WHITE
Viz Communications, 1999
1 (of 5) by Taiyo Matsumoto 3.25
2 thru 5 .... @3.25
TPB Vol. 1 216-pg............ 15.95
TPB Vol. 2 208-pg............ 15.95
TPB Vol. 3 208-pg............ 15.95

BLACKENED
Enigma
1 V:Killing Machine 2.95
2 V:Killing Machine 2.95
3 Flaming Altar 2.95

BLACK HOLE
Kitchen Sink, 1995
1 by Charles Burns 3.50
1 new printing 4.50
2 .... 3.50
3 .... 3.50
3 2nd printing 4.50
Fantagraphics Books, 2000
5 by Charles Burns 3.95
6 .... 4.50
7 .... 4.50
8 .... 4.50
9 .... 4.50

BLACK JACK
Viz Communications, 1996
GN by Osamu Tezuka......... 15.95
GN Vol 2 Two-Fisted Surgeon.... 15.95
Spec. Operation Down Under..... 3.50
Spec. Under the Knife 3.25

BLACK KISS
Vortex, 1988
1 HC,Adult..................... 7.00
1a 2nd printing 4.00
1b 3rd printing 1.25
2 HC 6.00
2a 2nd printing 3.00
3 HC 5.00
4 HC 4.00
5 & 6 HC .... @2.00
7 thru 12 HC .... @1.50

BLACKMASK
Eastern Comics, 1988
1 thru 6 .... @1.75

BLACK MIST
Caliber Core, 1998
1 by James Pruett & Mike Perkins,
  Blood of Kali,pt.1 .... 2.95

Black Mist #1
© Caliber

1a variant MV(c) 2.95
1b variant Jordan Raskin(c)... 2.95
1c variant GyD(c) 2.95
1d premium edition, signed 9.95
2 thru 5 Blood of Kali,pt.2–pt.5 .. @2.95
Spec. Dawn of Armageddon, Blood
  of Kali,pt.6 & pt.7, 48-pg. .. 3.95

BLACK SCORPION
Special Studio, 1991
1 Knight of Justice 2.75
2 A Game for Old Men 2.75
3 Blackmailer's Auction 2.75

BLACKTHORNE 3 in 1
Blackthorne, 1987
1 & 2 .... @2.00

BLACK ZEPPELIN
Renegade, 1985
1 GD 2.50
2 thru 6 GD .... @2.00

BLADE OF SHURIKEN
Eternity, 1987
1 thru 8 .... @2.00

BLAIR WITCH PROJECT
Oni Press, 1999
Spec. Movie adapt............. 2.95

BLAIR WITCH CHRONICLES
Oni Press, 2000
1 (of 4) by Jen Van Meter
  & Guy Davis............... 2.95
2 thru 4 .... @2.95
TPB Rep...................... 15.95

BLIND FEAR
Eternity
1 thru 4 .... @2.00

BLONDE AVENGER
Blonde Avenger Comics, 1998
25 flip-book, Full Metal Corset 3.95

27 Full Metal Corset,pt.2....... 3.95
Spec. Short Blonde Girl with
  the Two Big Boobs 3.95

BLONDE AVENGER: DANGEROUS CONCLUSIONS
Brainstorm, 1997
1 V:Victor Von Fuchs......... 2.95
1a photo deluxe cover 3.95
2 .... 2.95
2a photo deluxe cover 3.95

BLOOD & ROSES ADVENTURES
Knight Press, 1995
1 F:Time Agents 2.95
2 F:Time Agents 2.95
3 Search for Time Agents 2.95
4 Time Adventures............ 2.95
TPB Vol. 1 .... 12.95
TPB Art of Blood & Roses..... 14.95

BLOOD 'N' GUTS
Aircel, 1990
1 thru 3 .... @2.50

BLOODBROTHERS
Eternity
1 thru 4 .... @2.00

BLOOD IS THE HARVEST
Eclipse, 1992
1 I:Nikita,Milo................. 4.50
2 V:M'Raud D:Nikita? 2.50
3 Milo captured 2.50
4 F:Nikita/Milo 2.50

BLOOD JUNKIES
Eternity, 1991
1 Vampires on Capitol Hill 2.50
2 final issue................... 2.50

BLOODLETTING
Fantaco
1 A Shilling for a Redcoat 2.95
2 .... 2.95
3 Flee 2.95
4 thru 10 (of 11) by Chynna
  Clugston.................... @3.95

BLOOD OF DRACULA
Apple, 1987–90
1 thru 7 .... @3.00
8 thru 14 .... @3.00
15 with Record & Mask........ 4.00
16 .... 5.00
17 thru 20 .... @4.50

BLOOD OF THE INNOCENT
Warp Graphics, 1986
1 thru 4 .... @2.50

BLOODSHED
Damage, 1993
1 Little Brother................ 2.95
1a Commemorative issue 4.00
1b Encore edition, gold foil(c).. 3.50
2 Little Brother............... 2.95

B & W PUB.

Bloodshed–Books

3 O:Bloodshed 2.95
3 'The Wastelands,' cont. 3.50
4 The City 3.50
5 the end is near 3.50
6 .... 3.50
7 Lies, concl. 3.50
'M' 3.50
'M' deluxe 5.00
Spec. Lunatics Fringe 3.50
Spec. Lies Epilogue, final issue .. 3.50
Spec. Chris Mass #1 .... 3.50
Spec. Requiem 3.50

BLOODTHIRSTY PIRATE TALES
Black Swan Press, 1995
1 .... 2.50
2 .... 2.50
3 .... 2.50
4 'Blockade of Charleston Harbor'. 2.50
5 'The Queen Anne's Revenge'... 2.50
6 Blackhand's Party 2.50
7 Battle of Ocracoke Inlet 2.95
8 final issue 2.95

BLOODWING
Eternity, 1988
1 thru 5 .... @2.00

BLOODY SCHOOL
Curtis Comics, 2002
Vol. 1 Manga
1 by S.Yang & K. Yoo 2.95
2 thru 5 .... @2.95

BLUDGEON
Aardwolf, 1997
1 by JPi & David Chylsetk 2.95
2 'Alise in Wonderland' 2.95
3 'Seeing Red' 2.95

BLUE BULLETEER
AC Comics, 1989
1 .... 2.25

BLUE MONDAY: ABSOLUTE BEGINNERS
Oni Press, 2000
1 thru 4 .... @2.95
Spec. Nobody's Fool 2.95
Spec. Lovecats (2002) 2.95
Spec. Dead Man's Party (2002) .. 2.95

BLUE MONDAY: THE KIDS ARE ALRIGHT
Oni Press, 2000
1 by Chynna Clugston-Major 2.95
2 .... 2.95
3 concl. 2.95

BOGIE MAN: CHINATOON
Atomeka
1 I:Francis Claine 2.95
2 F:Bogie Man. 2.95
3 thru 4 F:Bogie Man........... 2.95

BOGIE MAN: MANHATTEN PROJECT
Apocalypse
1-shot D.Quale Assassination Plot . 3.95

BONAFIDE
Bonafide Productions
1 F:Doxie 'th Mutt 3.50
2 F:Doxie 'th Mutt 3.50
3 F:Doxie 'th Mutt 3.50

BONE
Cartoon Books, 1991
1 by Jeff Smith,I:Bone 80.00
1a 2nd printing 10.00
1b 3rd Printing. 8.00
2 JSi,I:Thorn 45.00
2a 2nd printing 7.00
3 JSi 35.00
3a 2nd printing 5.00
4 JSi 22.00
5 JSi 20.00
6 JSi 20.00

Bone #11
© Cartoon Books

7 JSi 15.00
8 JSi,The Great Cow Race,pt.1 ... 9.00
9 JSi,The Great Cow Race,pt.2 ... 8.00
1c thru 9a later printings. ...... @3.00
10 JSi,The Great Cow Race,pt.3. .. 8.00
11 JSi. 4.00
12 JSi. 4.00
13 JSi. 8.00
14 thru 17 JSi, ... @4.00
18 JSi,V:Bar owner. 4.00
19 JSi,F:Phoney Bone 4.00
20 JSi,Dragonslayer Phoney Bone . 4.00
21 thru 27, see Image
21 thru 27 reprints. .... @3.00
28 JSi,`Rockjaw: Master of the Eastern Border' 3.00
29 JSi. 3.00
30 JSi. 3.00
31 JSi. 3.00
32 JSi,Bartleby the Rat Creature Cub saga, concl. 3.00
33 JSi,Phoney's fate. 3.00
34 JSi,Kingdok Slayer. 3.00
35 JSi,Return of Gran'ma Ben ... 3.00
36 JSi,Return of Rockjaw 3.00
37 JSi,Extravaganza Issue 3.00
38 JSi,48-pg. 5.00
39 JSi,Ghost Circles. 3.00
40 JSi,wrap-around cover. 3.00
41 JSi,Deep in enemy territory ... 3.00
42 JSi, ... 3.00
43 JSi,sacred wall of the old capital. 3.00

44 JSi,rooftop eatery 3.00
45 JSi,Inner Circle of Power 3.00
46 JSi,Rat Creature Army 3.00
47 JSi,Making money 3.00
48 JSi,Surrender or Die 3.00
49 JSi,The usurper Tarsil 3.00
50 JSi,War, Rat Creatures 3.00
51 JSi,Casualties 3.00
52 thru 53 .... @3.00
54 This Mortal Coil 3.00
Spec.10th Anniv. Ed.with PVC fig.. 5.95
TPB rep.#1-#4 .... 14.00
TPB Vol. 1 Rep.#1-#6. .... 12.95
TPB Vol. 2 Rep.#7-#12. .... 12.95
TPB Vol. 3 Eyes of the Storm ... 16.95
TPB Vol.4 Dragonslayer 16.95
TPB Vol. 5 Rock Jaw: Master of the Eastern Border 14.95
TPB Vol. 6 Old Man's Cave 17.95
TPB Vol. 7 Ghost Circles 24.95
TPB Bone Reader 9.95
TPB Vol. 8 Treasure Hunters 15.95

BONESHAKER
Caliber Press
1 Suicidal Wrestler 3.50

BONEYARD
NBM Books, 2001
1 by Richard Moore 2.95
2 thru 4 .... @2.95
5 thru 8 .... @2.95
9 thru 12 .... @2.95
Spec. Swimsuit Issue 2.95
TPB Vol. 1 .... 12.95
TPB Vol. 2 .... 10.95

BOOK, THE
DreamSmith Studios, 1998
1 epic fantasy 72pg. 3.50
2 .... 3.50
3 .... 3.95
4 .... 3.95
5 thru 7 .... @4.00
Ashcan Preview, 24-pg. 5.00
Ashcan Preview, GP(c). 10.00
Handbook, 32-pg. 2.00

BOOK OF BALLADS AND SAGAS
Green Man Press, 1995
1 False Knight in the Road 2.95
2 thru 4 .... 3.00
5 .... 3.50

BOOK OF THE TAROT
Caliber Tome Press, 1998
1 History/Development o/t Tarot... 3.95
1a 64pg. 4.95
1b signed 4.95

BOOKS OF LORE
Peregrine
Spec.#1 fantasy anthology 2.95
Spec.#2 .... 2.95
Spec.#3 .... 2.95
1-shot Shattered Lives 2.95

BOOKS OF LORE: THE KAYNIN GAMBIT
Peregrine, 1998
0 by Kevin Tucker & David Napoliello 2.95
1 (of 2) 2.95

All comics prices listed are for *Near Mint* condition.

CVA Page 703

BOOKS OF LORE: THE SHAPE OF EVIL
Peregrine Entertainment, 1999
1a Xavier (c) 2.95
2 thru 4 . . . . @2.95

BOOKS OF LORE: THE SHAPE OF EVIL
Peregrine Entertainment, 1999
1 (of 2) 2.95
2 . . . . 2.95

BOOKS OF LORE: THE STORYTELLER
Peregrine Entertainment, 2000
1 (of 3) by Kevin Tucker
 & Philip Xavier 2.95
2 . . . . 2.95
3 concl. 2.95

BOONDOGGLE
Knight Press, 1995
1 Waffle War 2.95
2 Waffle War 2.95
3 Waffle War 2.95

BOONDOGGLE
Caliber Tapestry, 1997
Spec. 2.95
Spec., signed 2.95
1 thru 3 . . . . @2.95
4 At Wo's 2.95

BORDER WORLDS
Kitchen Sink, 1986
1 adult 3.00
2 thru 7 . . . . @3.00
Spec.#1 Border Worlds: Marooned . 3.00

BORIS' ADVENTURE MAGAZINE
Nicotat, 1988
1 & 2 . . . . @2.00
3 thru 6 . . . . @2.95

BORIS THE BEAR
Nikotat, 1987
1–12: See Dark Horse section
13 thru 29 . . . . @2.00
30 thru 34 . . . . @2.50

BORN TO KILL
Aircel, 1991
1 thru 3 . . . . @2.50

BOSTON BOMBERS
Caliber
1 . . . . 2.00
2 . . . . 2.50
Spec.#1 . . . . 3.95
Note: other issues are flip-books with: Oz #17; The Searchers #5; Raven Chronicles #12; & LegendLore #6

BOUNTY
Caliber, 1991
1 `Bounty,''Navarro,'pt.1 . . . . 2.50
2 `Bounty,''Navarro,'pt.2 . . . . 2.50
3 `Bounty,''Navarro,'pt.3 . . . . 2.50

BOX OFFICE POISON
Antarctic Press, 1996
1 by Alex Robinson 9.00

---

2 . . . . 6.00
3 thru 5 . . . . @4.00
6 thru 10 . . . . @3.00
11 thru 21 . . . . @3.00
TPB 160-pg. 14.95
TPB 608-pg. 29.95
Big Super Spec.#1 . . . . 4.95

BRADLEYS, THE
Fantagraphics, 1999
1 (of 6) by Peter Bagge 2.95
2 thru 6 . . . . @2.95

BRAT PACK
King Hell Publications, 1990
1 . . . . 6.00
1a 2nd printing 3.00
2 thru 5 . . . . @4.00
Brat Pack Collection 13.00

BRATPACK/MAXIMORTAL
King Hell, 1996
Super Spec.#1 RV 3.00
Super Spec.#2 RV 3.00

BREAKFAST AFTER NOON
Oni Press, 2000
1 (of 6) by Andi Watson 2.95
2 thru 6 . . . . @2.95
TPB 19.95

BREAKNECK BLVD.
Slave Labor Graphics, 1995–96
1 thru 3 Jhonen Vasques art . . . @2.95
4 by Timothy Markin 2.95
5 . . . . 2.95
6 . . . . 2.95

BRENDA STARR, ACE REPORTER
ACG Comics, 1998
1 by Dale Messick, Charlton rep. . . 3.00
2 . . . . 2.95
Spec.#1 Pin-ups,rep. from 40s
 and 50s (1998) 2.95

BRILLIANT BOY
Circus Comics, 1997
1 . . . . 2.95
2 Drake,pt.1 (of 5) 2.95
3 Drake,pt.2 . . . . 2.50
4 Drake,pt.3 . . . . 2.50
5 Drake,pt.4 . . . . 2.50
6 Drake,pt.5 . . . . 2.50
7 The Great Thunder,pt.1 (of 6) . . 2.50
8 The Great Thunder,pt.2 . . . . . . 2.50

BROID
Eternity, 1990
1 thru 4 . . . . @2.25

BROKEN HALO: IS THERE NOTHING SACRED
Broken Halos Comics, 1998
1 by Donald J. Vigil & Tim Vigil . . . 2.95
2 . . . . 2.95
3 . . . . 2.95
Ashcan, limited ed. 16-pg. 6.95
TPB Vol. 1 by Joe & Tim Vigil,
 limited ed. 9.95

Broid #2
© Eternity

BROKEN HEROES
Sirius, 1998
1 by Fillbach Bros. 2.50
2 The Neon Graveyard 2.50
3 Rocket Man 2.50
4 thru 12 final issue . . . . @2.50
TPB Captain Freebird rep. #1–#12 19.95

BRONX
Eternity, 1991
1 A.Saichann Short Stories 2.50
2 & 3 . . . . @2.50

Aircel
Reprint 2.95

BROTHER MAN
New City Comics
1 . . . . 5.00
1a 2.00
2 thru 7 . . . . @2.00

BRUCE JONES' OUTER EDGE
Innovation, 1993
1 All reprints 2.50

BRUCE JONES: RAZORS EDGE
Innovation
1 All reprints 2.50
2 D:Grimm, Gritty 2.50

BRU-HED
Schism Comics, 1994
1 Blockhead 2.95
1a 2nd printing 2.75
2 Blockhead 2.95
Vol. 1 Bru-Hed's Bunnies, Baddies
 & Buddies (1998) 2.50
Vol. 1 Bru-Hed's Guide to Gettin'
 Girls Now 2.50
Vol. 2 Bru-Hed's Guide 2.50

BUCE-N-GAR
RAK
1 . . . . 1.75
2 and 3 . . . . @1.75

BUCK GODOT
Palliard Press
1 I:Buck Godot 2.95

BUCK GODOT: ZAP GUN FOR HIRE
Studio Foglio, 1993
1 thru 6 . . . . @2.95
7 by Phil Foglio & Barb Kaalberg . . 2.95
8 finale 3.50
TPB Gallimaufry Vol. 1 . . . . 12.50
TPB Gallimaufry Vol. 2 . . . . 14.95

BUFFALO WINGS
Antarctic Press, 1993
1 & 2 . . . . @2.50

BUG
Planet X Productions, 1997
1 . . . . 1.50
2 . . . . 1.50

B.U.G.G.S
Acetylene Comics, 2001
1 . . . . 2.50
1a variant San Diego Con (c) 3.00
2 . . . . 2.50
3 . . . . 2.50
3a variant (c) 2.50
4 . . . . 2.50
5 . . . . 2.50

BULLET CROW
Eclipse, 1987
1 & 2 Fowl of Fortune . . . . @2.50

BULWARK
Millennium, 1995
1 I:Bulwark 2.95
2 O:Bulwark 2.95

BUREAU OF MANA INVESTIGATION
Radio Comix, 2002
1 by C.Hanson & E.Garcia 3.00
2 thru 5 . . . . @3.00

BURNING BLUE, THE
Crusade Entertainment, 2001
1 BTi 3.00
1a computer gen (c) 3.00

BUSHIDO
Eternity, 1988
1 thru 6 . . . . @2.00

BUZZ
Kitchen Sink
1 Mark Landman (c) (1990) 2.95
2 Mark Landman (c) 2.95
3 Mark Landman (c) (1991) 2.95

BUZZARD
Cat Head Comics, 1990–95
1 thru 9 . . . . @2.75
10 thru 20 . . . . @3.50

Buzzard #7
© Cathouse Comics

CABLE TV
Parody Press
1 Cable Satire 2.50

CADILLACS AND DINOSAURS
Kitchen Sink, 1992
3-D comic 3.95

CALIBER CORE
Caliber, 1998
0 48pg 2.95
1 Gestalt cover 2.95
1a Rain People cover 2.95
1b Spiral cover 2.95
2 F:Al-Haquat 2.95

CALIBER DOUBLE FEATURE
Caliber, 2000
1 48-pg 3.95
2 . . . . 3.95
3 . . . . 3.95

CALIBER FOCUS
Caliber, 2000
1 48-pg 3.95
2 thru 4 . . . . @3.95

CALIBER PRESENTS
Caliber, 1989
1 TV,I:Crow 60.00
2 Deadworld 10.00
3 Realm 4.00
4 Baker Street 4.00
5 TV,Heart of Darkness, Fugitive . 3.50
6 TV,Heart of Darkness, Fugitive . 3.50
7 TV,Heart of Darkness,
  Dragonfeast 3.50
8 TV,Cuda,Fugitive 3.50
9 Baker Street,Sting Inc. 3.50
10 Fugitive, The Edge 3.50
11 Ashes,Random Thoughts 3.50
12 Fugitive,Random Thoughts . . . 3.50
13 Random Thoughts,Synergist . . 3.50
14 Random Thoughts,Fugitive . . . 3.50
15 Fringe, F:The Crow 4.00
16 Fugitive, The Verdict 3.50
17 Deadworld, The Verdict 3.50
18 Orlak,The Verdict 3.50
19 Taken Under,Go-Man 3.50
20 The Verdict,Go-Man 3.50
21 The Verdict,Go-Man 3.50
22 The Verdict,Go-Man 3.50
23 Go-Man,Heat Seeker 3.50
24 Heat Seeker,MacktheKnife 3.50
Christmas Spec. A:Crow,Deadworld
  Realm,Baker Street 10.00
Summer Spec. inc. the Silencers,
  Swords of Shar-Pei (preludes) . 3.95
1-Shot 2.50
1-shot Hybrid 2.50

CALIBER SPOTLIGHT
Caliber, 1995
1 F:Kabuki,Oz 3.00

CALIBRATIONS
Caliber, 1996
1 WEI,MCy,`Atmospherics,'pt.1 . . . 3.00
2 WEI,MCy,`Atmospherics,'pt.2 . . . 3.00
3 WEI,MCy,`Atmospherics,'pt.3 . . . 3.00
4 WEI,MCy,`Atmospherics,'pt.4 . . . 3.00
5 WEI,MCy,`Atmospherics,' concl . . 3.00

CALIFORNIA GIRLS
Eclipse, 1987
1 thru 8 . . . . @2.00

CALIGARI 2050
Monster
1 Gothic Horror 2.25
2 &3 Gothic Horror . . . . @2.25

CALL ME PRINCESS
CPM Manga, 1999
1 by Tomoko Taniguchi 2.95
1a variant cover 2.95
2 . . . . 2.95
3 . . . . 2.95
4 . . . . 2.95
5 . . . . 2.95
6 final issue 2.95
TPB Vol. 1 . . . . 15.95

CAMELOT ETERNAL
Caliber, 1990
1 . . . . 3.00
2 . . . . 2.50
3 . . . . 2.50
4 Launcelot & Guinevere 2.50
5 Mordred Escapes 2.50
6 MorganLeFay returns from dead. 2.50
7 Revenge of Morgan 2.50
8 Launcelot flees Camelot 2.50

CANTON KID
Millennium, 1997
1 . . . . 2.50

CAPTAIN CANUCK REBORN
Semple Comics, 1995–96
1 thru 3 by Richard Comely . . . . @2.50

CAPT. CONFEDERACY
Steel Dragon, 1985–88
1 adult 6.00
2 . . . . 2.50
3 . . . . 2.00
4 . . . . 2.00
4a 2.00
5 thru 8 . . . . @2.00

Captain–Cavewoman

9 thru 11 .... @2.00
12 .... 2.00

CAPT. ELECTRON
Brick Computers Inc., 1986
1 .... 2.50
2 .... 2.25

CAPTAIN HARLOCK
Eternity
1 BDn 3.00
1a 2nd printing 2.50
2 .... 2.50
3 .... 2.50
4 thru 13 .... @2.00
Christmas special 2.50
Spec.#1 The Machine People .. 2.50

CAPTAIN HARLOCK DEATHSHADOW RISING
Eternity, 1991
1 .... 2.75
2 .... 2.50
3 .... 2.25
4 Harlock/Nevich Truce 2.25
5 Reunited with Arcadia Crew .. 2.25
6 .... 2.95

[ADVENTURES OF] CAPTAIN JACK
Fantagraphics, 1986
1 .... 4.00
2 & 3 .... @2.50
4 thru 12 .... @2.00

CAPTAIN KOALA
Koala Comics, 1997
1 .... 2.95
2 thru 7 .... @2.50

CAPTAIN STERNN: RUNNING OUT OF TIME
Kitchen Sink, 1993
1 BWr(c) (1993) 6.00
2 BWr(c) 6.00
3 BWr(c) (1994) 6.00
4 BWr(c) 6.00

CAPTAIN THUNDER AND BLUE BOLT
Hero Graphics, 1987
1 New stories 3.50
2 Hard Targets 3.50

CARDCAPTOR SAKURA
Mixx Entertainment, 1999
1 by Clamp 2.95
2 thru 6 .... @2.50
TPB Pocket Mixx, Vol. 1 thru 5 .. @9.95
Tokyopop.Com, 2000
7 thru 25 .... @2.95
26 thru 34 .... @3.00
TPB Anime Vol. 1 .... 13.00
TPB Anime Vol. 2 .... 13.00
TPB Anime Vol. 5 .... 15.00
TPB Anime Vol. 6 thru 10 .. @15.00
TPB Art of Cardcaptor Sakura 3 .. 20.00
TPB Pocket Mixx, Vol. 6 ..... 10.00
GN Vol. 1 Passages 10.00
GN Vol. 2 Master of the Clow .. 10.00
GN Vol. 3 thru Vol. 6 ..... @10.00

B & W PUB.

CARTOON HISTORY OF THE UNIVERSE
Rip Off Press
1 Gonick art. 2.50
2 Sticks & Stones 2.50
3 River Realms 2.50
4 Old Testament 2.50
5 Brains & Bronze 2.50
6 These Athenians 2.50
7 All about Athens 2.50

CASES OF SHERLOCK HOLMES
Renegade, 1986
1 thru 18 .... @2.00
19 .... 2.25

CASTLE IN THE SKY
Viz Communications 2003
GN Vol. 1 .... 9.95
GN Vol. 2 thru Vol. 4 ..... @9.95

Castle Waiting #4
© Linda Medley

CASTLE WAITING
Olio, 1997
1 by Linda Medley 10.00
1a 2nd printing 3.00
2 .... 5.00
2a 2nd printing 3.00
3 Labors of Love 3.00
4 birth of Lady Jain's baby . 3.00
5 .... 3.00
6 City Mouse, Country Mouse,pt.1 . 3.00
7 City Mouse, Country Mouse,pt.2 . 3.00
Spec. The Curse of Brambly
  Hedge (1996) 3.00
Spec. Curse of Brambly Hedge,
  revised 1998, 96-pg. 9.00
TPB Vol. 1 Lucky Road 16.95
VOL. 2, 2000
1 by Linda Medley 2.95
2 Solicitine,pt.1 .... 2.95
3 thru 7 .... @2.95
#13 (Vol. 2, #6) 2.95
#14 (Vol. 2, #7) 2.95
#15 thru #16 .... @2.95
TPB Vol. 1 Lucky Road 17.95
TPB Vol. 2 Solicitine 17.95
GN The Curse of Brambly Hedge .. 9.00

Comics Values Annual

CAT & MOUSE
Aircel, 1989–92
1 .... 4.00
2 .... 3.00
3 thru 8 .... @2.25
9 Cat Reveals Identity 2.25
10 Tooth & Nail 2.25
11 Tooth & Nail 2.25
12 Tooth & Nail, Demon 2.25
13 'Good Times, Bad Times' .. 2.25
14 Mouse Alone 2.25
15 Champion ID revealed 2.25
16 Jerry Critically Ill 2.25
17 Kunoichi vs. Tooth 2.25
18 Search for Organ Donor ... 2.25
Graphic Novel 9.95

CAT CLAW
Eternity, 1990
1 O:Cat Claw 2.75
1a 2nd printing 2.50
2 thru 9 .... @2.50

CATFIGHT
Lightning Comics, 1996
1 V:Prince Nightmare 4.00
1a Gold Edition 6.00
Spec.#1 Dream Warrior,
  V:The Slasher 2.75
Spec.#1 Dream intoAction,A:Creed. 3.00
Spec.#1a signed and numbered .. 8.00
Spec.#1 Escape From Limbo ... 2.75
Spec.#1a variant cover (1996) . 2.75
Spec.#1b platinum cover 5.95
Spec.#1d variant nude cover . 8.00
Spec.#1 Sweet Revenge (1997) .. 2.95
Spec.#1a variant cover 2.95

CAT-MAN RETRO COMIC
AC Comics
0 by Bill Black & Mark Heike .. 5.95
1 thru 3 .... @5.95
Ashcan #1 I:Catman & Kitten . 5.95

CAVEWOMAN
Basement/Caliber, 1994–95
1 .... 70.00
1a by Budd Root 2nd printing . 4.00
1b 3rd printing, new cover .. 3.00
2 .... 40.00
2a 2nd printing 3.00
2 3rd printing, new cover ... 3.00
3 .... 35.00
4 .... 35.00
5 Cavewoman vs. Klyde,
  Round Two 25.00
6 .... 25.00

CAVEWOMAN INTERVENTION
Basement Comics, 2000
1 by Devon Massey 2.95
1a variant Budd Root (c) 8.95
1b gold foil alternate (c) .. 12.50
2 .... 2.95
2a variant (c) 8.95
2b Purple foil (c) 12.50
Spec. Klyde & Meriem 1-shot . 2.95
Spec. Klyde & Meriem, KDM(c) . 8.95
Spec. Klyde & Meriem green foil . 10.00
Spec. Klyde & Meriem, Beauty,
  Blizzard & the Beast 8.95
Spec. Beauty, Blizzard, gold foil . 12.50
Spec. Prehistoric Pin-ups ... 4.50
Spec. Prehistoric Pin-ups gold foil . 12.50

CVA Page 706   All comics prices listed are for *Near Mint* condition.

B & W PUB.

Cavewoman–Cerebus

Spec. Prehistoric Pin-ups, Book 2	4.50
Spec. Prehistoric Pin-ups 2,lim.	8.95
Spec. Prehistoric Pin-ups 2, gold foil.	11.50
Spec. Prehistoric Pin-ups 3	4.50
Spec. Prehistoric Pin-Ups 3 Spec.	8.95
Cavewoman Cover Gallery, 48-pg.	4.50
Cavewoman Cover Gallery spec.	8.95
1-shot He Said, She Said	3.50
1-shot He Said, She Said special	8.95
1-shot Cavewoman The Movie	3.25

CAVEWOMAN: JUNGLE TALES
Basement Comics, 2000

1 by Budd Root	3.00
1a Frank Cho (c)	10.95
2	2.95
2a spec. edition	8.95

CAVEWOMAN: MERIEM'S GALLERY
Basement Comics, 2001

1	3.50
1a Spec. lim. ed.	8.95
1b Gold foil edition	11.50
2 pin-up book	3.50
2a Special edition	8.95
2b gold special edition	11.50
3	2.95
3	8.95

CAVEWOMAN: MISSING LINK
Basement Comics, 1997

1 (of 4)	2.95
2 thru 4	@2.95
TPB 96-pg.	19.95
TPB 2nd printing	9.95

CAVEWOMAN: ODYSSEY
Caliber, 1999

1 (of 5)	2.95
2	2.95
3	2.95
4	2.95
Basement Comics, 2000	
1a front row seat (c) by Budd Root	8.95
1b foil (c)	12.50
2a variant (c)	5.95
2b jungle green foil (c)	12.50
1-shot spec.	2.95
1-shot spec. variant (c)	5.95
1-shot spec. foil (c)	12.50

CAVEWOMAN: PANGAEAN SEA
Basement Comics, 1999

0 Origin issue	2.95
0 variant AAd (c)	8.95
0 special Root (c)	10.00
0 green foil (c)	11.50
0 alternate gold foil (c)	11.50
1 by Bud Root	4.95
1a variant Massey (c)	8.95
1b Root Sea Blue Foil (c)	12.50
1c Cho Sea Blue Foil (c)	12.50
2	2.95
2 Spec. ed. (c)	8.95
2 Blue Foil (c)	11.50
3	3.25
3 silver foil (c)	11.50
4	3.25
4a special edition	8.95

4b red foil edition	11.50
5	3.25
5 special edition	8.95
5 red foil edition	11.50
6	3.25
6a special edition (c)	8.95
6b red foil (c)	9.95
7	3.25
7a special edition (c)	8.95
Spec. #1 Prehistoric Pin-ups	4.50
Prologue	2.95

CAVEWOMAN: RAIN
Caliber, 1996

1 by Budd Root	7.00
1a 2nd printing	3.00
2	5.00
2a 2nd printing	3.00
3	4.00
3a 2nd edition, new cover	3.00
4	4.00
4a 2nd edition, new cover	3.00
5	3.50
5 2nd edition, new cover	3.00
6 thru 8	@3.00

CAVEWOMEN: RAPTOR
Basement Comics, 2002

1 (of 2)	3.25
1a special edition	8.95
1b red foil edition	11.50
2	3.25
2a special edition	8.95
2b Purple foil (c)	11.50

CECIL KUNKLE
Darkline Comics, 1987

1	2.00

CELESTIAL MECHANICS
Innovation, 1990

1 thru 3	@2.25

CELESTIAL ZONE
Asiapac Books, 2000

1 by Wee Tian Beng	8.95
2 thru 8	@8.95
9 152-pg.	8.95
11 Fantasy on Moonlit Lotus	8.95
12 THe Battle of Maling	8.95
13 Assault on Mt. Dream-Cloud	9.95
14 An Onerous Battle	9.95
15 Capturing Mt. Dream-Cloud	9.95
16 Chi Xue & Xuan Hua injured	9.95
TCZ Studio, 2002	
17 thru 25 152-pg.	@9.95
Vol. 2	
1	9.95
2 thru 4	@9.50

CEMENT SHOOZ
Horse Feathers, 1991

1 with color pin-up	2.50

CEREBUS
Aardvark–Vanaheim, 1977

0	3.00
0a Gold Ed.	10.00
1 B:DS(s&a),I:Cerebus	325.00
1a Counterfeit	50.00
2 DS,V:Succubus	90.00
3 DS,I:Red Sophia	125.00
4 DS,I:Elrod	75.00
5 DS,A:The Pigts	60.00

Cement Shooz #1
© Horse Feathers

6 DS,I:Jaka	60.00
7 DS,R:Elrod	45.00
8 DS,A:Conniptins	45.00
9 DS,I&V:K'cor	45.00
10 DS,R:Red Sophia	45.00
11 DS,I:The Cockroach	30.00
12 DS,R:Elrod	30.00
13 DS,I:Necross	25.00
14 DS,V:Shadow Crawler	25.00
15 DS,V: Shadow Crawler	25.00
16 DS, at the Masque	20.00
17 DS,`Champion'	20.00
18 DS,Fluroc	20.00
19 DS,I:Perce & Greet-a	20.00
20 DS,Mind Game	20.00
21 DS,A:CaptCockroach,rare	40.00
22 DS,D:Elrod	20.00
23 DS,DuFort's school	10.00
24 DS,IR:Prof.Clarmont	10.00
25 DS,A:Woman-thing	10.00
26 DS,High Society	10.00
27 DS,Kidnapping of an Avrdvark	10.00
28 DS,Mind Game!!	10.00
29 DS,Reprocussions	10.00
30 DS,Debts	15.00
31 DS,Chasing Cootie	15.00
32 DS	8.00
33 DS,Friction	5.00
34 DS,Three Days Before	6.00
35 thru 50 DS	@6.00
51 DS,(scarce)	12.00
52 DS	5.00
53 DS,C:Wolveroach	7.00
54 DS,I:Wolveroach	9.00
55 DS,A:Wolveroach	8.00
56 DS,A:Wolveroach	8.00
57 DS	5.00
58 DS	5.00
59 DS,Memories,pt.V	5.00
60 DS,more vignettes	5.00
61 DS,A:Flaming Carrot	6.00
62 DS,A:Flaming Carrot	6.00
63 DS,Mind Game VI	5.00
64 DS,Never Fear for Change	5.00
65 DS,Papal Speech	5.00
66 DS,Thrill of Agony	5.00
67 thru 70 DS	@5.00
71 thru 74 DS	@4.00
75 DS,Terrible Analogies	4.00
76 DS,D:Weisshaupt	4.00
77 DS,Surreal daydream	4.00
78 DS,Surreal daydream	4.00
79 DS,Spinning Straw	4.00
80 DS,V:Stone Tarim	4.00

All comics prices listed are for Near Mint condition.

Cerebus–Charm / B & W PUB.

81 DS,A:Sacred Wars Roach	4.00
82 DS,A:Tarim	3.50
83 DS,A:Michele	3.50
84 DS,Weisshaupt's Letter	3.50
85 DS,A:Mick Jagger	3.50
86 DS,A:Mick Jagger	3.50
87 DS,Tower Climb	3.50
88 DS,D:Stone Tarim	3.50
89 DS,A:Cute Elf	3.50
90 DS,Anti-Apartheid(c)	3.50
91 DS	3.50
92 DS,A:Bill & Seth	3.50
93 DS,Astoria in Prison	3.50
94 DS,Rape of Astoria	3.50
95 DS,Sophia-Astoria Dream	3.50
96 DS,Astoria in Prison	3.50
97 DS,Escape Planned	3.50
98 DS,Astoria's Trial	3.50
99 DS,Sorcery in Court	3.50
100 DS,A:Cirin	3.50
101 DS,The Gold Sphere	3.00
102 DS,The Final Ascension	3.00
103 DS,On the Tower	3.00
104 DS,A:Flaming Carrot	3.00
105 DS,V:Fred & Ethel	3.00
106 DS,D:Fred & Ethel	3.00
107 DS,Judge on the Moon	3.00
108 DS,All History	3.00
109 DS,O:Universe	3.00
110 DS,More Universe	3.00
111 DS,Cerebus' Fate	3.00
112 DS,Memories	3.00
113 DS,Memories	3.00
114 DS,I:Rick Nash	3.00
115 DS,I:Pud Withers	3.00
116 DS,Rick Meets Cerebus	3.00
117 DS,Young Jaka Injured	3.00
118 DS,Cerebus Apologizes	3.00
119 DS,Jaka Opens Door	3.00
120 DS,I:Oscar	3.00
121 DS,Women Explained	3.00
122 DS,Iest History	3.00
123 DS,Each One's Dream	3.00
124 DS	3.00
125 DS,C:Lord Julius	3.00
126 DS,R:Old Vet'ran	2.50
127 DS,Jaka Dances	2.50
128 DS,L:Cerebus as Fred	2.50
129 DS,Jaka's Story	2.50
130 DS,D:Pud Withers	2.50
131 DS,Jaka Imprisoned	4.00
132 DS,A:Nurse	4.00
133 DS,I:Mrs. Thatcher	4.00
134 DS,Dancing Debate	4.00
135 DS,Jaka Signs	4.00
136 DS,L:Rick	4.00
137 DS,Like-a-Looks	4.00
138 DS,Maids'Gossip	4.00
139 DS,A:Misogynist-roach.	4.00
140 I:Old Oscar	4.00
141 A:Cerebus	4.00
142 C:Mick Jagger	4.00
143 DS,Oscars Forboding	4.00
144 DS,I:Doris	4.00
145 thru 146 DS	@4.00
147 Neil Gaiman, DS	6.00
148 DS	3.00
149 DS	3.00
150 DS	3.00
151 DS,B:Mothers & Daughters, Book 1: Flight,pt.1	4.00
151a 2nd printing	2.50
152 DS,Flight,pt.2	4.00
152a 2nd printing	2.50
153 DS,Flight,pt.3	4.00
153a 2nd printing	2.50
154 DS,Flight,pt.4	4.00
155 DS,Flight,pt.5	4.00
156 DS,Flight,pt.6	3.00
157 DS,Flight,pt.7	3.00
158 DS,Flight,pt.8	3.00
159 DS,Flight,pt.9	3.00
160 DS,Flight,pt.10	3.00
161 DS,Flight,pt.11, Bone story.	15.00
162 DS,E:M&D,Bk.1:Flight pt.12	3.00
163 DS,B:Mothers & Daughters Book 2: Women,pt.1	2.75
164 DS,Women,pt.2,inc. Tour Momentos	3.00
165 thru 174 Women,pt.3–12	@3.00
175 DS,B:Mothers & Daughters, Book 3: Reads,pt.1	3.00
175 thru 186 Reads,pt.1–12	@3.00
187 DS,B:Mothers & Daughters, Book 4:Minds,pt.1	3.00
188 thru 199 Minds,pt.5–13	@3.00
200	3.50
201 thru 219 Guys,pt.1 to pt.19	@3.00
220 thru 231 Rick'sStory,pt.1–12	@3.00
232 thru 265 GoingHome,pt.1–34	@2.50
266 thru 272 Latter Days, pt.1–pt.7 (of 35)	@2.50
273 thru 296 LatterDays,pt.8– pt.31	@2.50
Spec.#1 Cerebus Companion	3.95

TPBs

Vol.1 Cerebus, rep.#1–#25	25.00
Vol.2 High Society, rep.#26–#50	25.00
Vol.3 Church&StateI,rep.#52–#85	30.00

Cerebus #47
© Aardvark-Vanaheim

Vol.4 Church&StateII,rep.#86–#111	30.00
Vol.5 Jaka'sStory,rep.#114–#136.	25.00
Vol.6 Melmoth, rep.#139–#150	17.00
Vol.7, Flight, rep.#151–#162	17.00
Vol.8 Women, rep.#163–#174	17.00
Vol.9 Reads, rep.#175–#186	17.00
Vol.9 Reads, 2nd printing	15.00
Vol.9 Reads, signed & numb.	28.00
Vol.10 Minds, rep.#187–#199	16.00
Vol.11 Guys rep.#201–#219	30.00
Vol.11, 2nd printing	20.00
Vol.12 Rick's Story	17.00
Vol.12 signed	25.00
Vol.13 Going Home, 420-pg.	25.00
Vol.13 deluxe	37.00
Vol.14 Form & Void	25.00
Vol.14a deluxe	37.00
Vol. 15 Latter Days	30.00
Vol. 15 signed	40.00

CEREBUS CHURCH & STATE
Aardvark–Vanaheim, 1991

1 DS rep #51	2.25
2 thru 30 DS rep #52-#80	@2.00

CEREBUS HIGH SOCIETY
Aardvark–Vanaheim, 1990

1 thru 14 DS (biweekly)	@2.00
15 thru 24 DS rep.	@2.00
25 DS rep. #50, final.	2.00

CEREBUS JAM
Aardvark–Vanaheim, 1985

1 MA,BHa,TA,WE,A:Spirit	15.00

CEREBUS REPRINTS
Aardvark–Vanaheim

1A thru 28A DS rep	@2.00

See also: Church & State
See also: Swords of Cerebus

CERES, CELESTIAL LEGEND
Viz Communications, 2001

1 thru 6	@2.95
TPB Vol. 1 Aya	15.95

Part 2

1 thru 6	@2.95

Part 3

1 (of 4)	3.50
2 thru 4	@3.50

Part 4

1 (of 4) by Yu Watase	3.50
2	3.50
3 thru 4	@3.50

Part 5

1	3.50
TPB Vol. 1 Ayuhi.	15.95
TPB Vol. 2 Yuhi	15.95
TPB Vol. 3 Suzumi	15.95
TPB Vol. 4 Chidori	9.95
TPB Vol. 5 Mikage	9.95

CHAINSAW VIGILANTE
New England Press

1 Tick Spinoff	3.25
2 & 3	@2.75

CHAMPION OF KITARA: DUM DUM & DRAGONS
MU Press, 1992

1 Dragons Secret	2.95
2 Dragons Secret	2.95
3 Dragons Secret	2.95

CHANGE COMMANDER GOKU II
Antarctic Press, 1996

1 (of 4) by Ippongi Bang	2.95
2	2.95
3	2.95
TPB Vol 1, Change Commander Goku, rep. #1–#5	12.95

CHARLIE CHAN
Eternity, 1989

1 thru 4	@2.00
5 and 6	@2.25

CHARM SCHOOL
Amaze Ink/Slave Labor Graphics, 2000

1 by Elizabeth Watasin	2.95
2	2.95
4 Vampire Dragster Dean	2.95

CVA Page 708 — All comics prices listed are for *Near Mint* condition.

5 Vampire Dragster Dean 2.95
6 fight to the death 2.95
7 thru 9 . . . . 2.95
TPB Vol. 1 Magical Witch
  Girl Bunny 11.95

CHASER PLATOON
Aircel, 1990–91
1 Interstellar War 2.25
2 Ambush 2.25
3 New Weapon 2.25
4 Saringer Battle Robot 2.25
5 Behind Enemy Lines 2.25
6 Operation Youthtest 2.25

CHESTY SANCHEZ
Antarctic Press, 1995
1 & 2 . . . . @2.95
Giant Size Spec. #1 (1999) 6.00

CHIBI-POP MANGA
Chibi-Pop (1998)
2 thru 6 64-pg . . . . @3.95
VOL 2
1 72-pg 3.95
2 thru 6 . . . . @3.95

CHINA & JAZZ
ABC Comics, 1999
1 RCl 3.00
VOL. 2
1 (of 3) RCl 3.00
2 RCl 3.00
Spec. Raising Hell 5.00

CHINA & JAZZ CODE NAME DOUBLE IMPACT
High Impact, 1996
1 . . . . 3.00
2 . . . . 2.95

CHINA & JAZZ: TRIGGER HAPPY
ABC Comics, 1998
1 (of 4) by Clayton Henry 3.00
1a Jazz Bikini cover 3.95
1b China Bikini cover 3.95
1c gold variant cover 5.95
2 . . . . 3.00
2a Playtoy edition 5.95
2b Mercenary edition 5.95
2c Gold edition 5.95
Spec. Trigger Happy Special 3.00
Spec. A manga cover 8.00
Spec. China & Jazz 3.00

CHINA & JAZZ: SUPERSTARS
ABC Studios, 1999
1 (of 3) 3.00
Spec. China Platinum 3.00

CHIRALITY
CPM Manga Comics, 1997
6 by Satoshi Urushihara, SS(c) . . . 2.95
7 final battle for Shiori's life 2.95
8 . . . . 2.95
9 Adam transformed into
  duplicate Carol 2.95
10 . . . . 2.95

11 . . . . 2.95
12 V:Adam 2.95
13 toward Alaska 2.95
14 reach Gaia 2.95
15 Carol and Shiori 2.95
16 . . . . 2.95
17 descend into Gaia 2.95
18 final issue 2.95
Spec. Gallery, pin-up book 3.95
GN Book One rep. #1–#4 . . . . . . 9.95
GN Book Two rep. #4–#8 . . . . . . 9.95
TPB Book Three rep. #8–#12 . . . 15.95
TPB Book Four, rep. #13–#18 . . . 15.95

CHIRALITY: TO THE PROMISED LAND
CPM Comics, 1997
1 by Satoshi Urushihara 2.95
2 thru 4 . . . . @2.95

CHIRON
Annurel Studio Graphics
1 . . . . 2.50
1a 2nd printing 2.50
2 Transported to Doran 2.50
3 Transported to Doran 2.50
3a Gold Edition 4.00

CHOBITS
Tokyopop Press, 2002
TPB Vol. 1 authentic manga 10.00
TPB Vol. 2 thru 8 . . . . @10.00

CHRONICLES OF THE CURSED SWORD
Tokyopop Press 2003
TPB Vol. 1 . . . . 10.00
TPB Vol. 2 thru 3 . . . . @10.00

CIRCLE WEAVE, THE
Indigo Bean Productions, 1995
1 Apprentice to a God 2.00
2 Apprentice to a God, pt.2 . . . . . 2.00
3 Apprentice to a God, pt.3 . . . . . 2.00
4 Apprentice to a God, pt.4 . . . . . 2.00
5 Apprentice to a God, pt.5 . . . . . 2.50

CLAN APIS
Active Synapse, 1998
1 (of 5) by Jay Hosler, F:Bees 2.95
2 F:Nyuki, Zambur 2.95
3 . . . . 2.95
4 . . . . 2.95
5 conclusion 2.95
TPB 160-pg. 15.00

CLAMP SCHOOL DETECTIVES
Tokyopop Press 2003
TPB Vol. 1 (of 3) 10.00
TPB Vol. 2 thru Vol. 3 . . . . . . @10.00

CLANDE, INC.
Domain Publishing
1 I:Sam Davidson, Jeremy Clande . 2.95
2 V:Dias 2.95

CLERKS: THE COMIC BOOK
Oni Press, 1998
1 KSm & Jim Mahfood 12.00

1a 2nd printing 4.00
Spec. The Lost Scene 5.00
Holiday Special 5.00
TPB 10.95

CLIFFHANGER COMICS
AC Comics
1 rep 2.50
2 rep 2.50

CLINT THE HAMSTER
Eclipse
1 . . . . 2.50
2 . . . . 1.50

CLOVER
Tokyopop Press, 2001
TPB Pocket Mixx, Vol. 1 . . . . . . 14.95
TPB Pocket Mixx, Vol. 2 . . . . . . 14.95
TPB Pocket Mixx, Vol. 3 . . . . . . 14.95
TPB Pocket Mixx, Vol. 4 . . . . . . 14.95

COBRA
Viz, 1990–91
1 thru 6 . . . . @2.95
7 . . . . 3.25
8 V:SnowHawks 3.25
9 Zados 3.25
10 thru 12 . . . . @3.25

COFFIN
Oni Press, 2000
1 . . . . 2.95
2 thru 4 . . . . @2.95
TPB 112-pg. 11.95

COLD BLOODED CHAMELEON COMMANDOS
Blackthorne, 1986
1 . . . . 2.00
2 . . . . 1.50
3 . . . . 1.50
4 . . . . 1.75
5 . . . . 1.75
6 . . . . 2.00
7 . . . . 2.00

Cold Blooded Chameleon Commandos #3 © Blackthorne

COLD EDEN
Legacy, 1995
1 Last City on Earth............ 2.35
2 V:Mutant Hunting Pack........ 2.35
3 D6 Tower................... 2.35

COLE BLACK
Hartberg
1 .... 15.00
2 .... 10.00
3 .... 10.00
4 .... 10.00
5 .... 12.00

Vol. 2
1 .... 3.50
2 .... 2.00
3 .... 2.00

COLONEL KILGORE
Special Studios
1 WWII stories................ 2.50
2 Command Performance 2.50

COLT
K-Z Comics
1 .... 4.00
2 pin-up by Laird............. 6.00
2 pin-up by Henbeck.......... 2.00
3 thru 5................... @1.00

COMIC BOOK HEAVEN
Amaze Ink/Slave Labor Graphics, 2001
Vol. 2
1 .... 1.95
2 thru 5................... @1.95
6 thru 9................... @2.25

COMICS EXPRESS
Eclipse, 1989
1 thru 4................... @2.95
5 thru 11.................. @3.95

COMING OF APHRODITE
Hero Graphics
1 Aphrodite/modern day........ 3.95

COMMAND REVIEW
Thoughts & Images, 1986
1 rep. Albedo #1-4............ 6.00
2 rep. Albedo #5-8............ 4.00
3 rep. Albedo #9-13........... 4.00

CONDOM-MAN
Aaaahh!! Comics
1 I:Condom Man............... 3.50
2 F:Condom Man............... 3.50
3 V:Alien Army................ 3.50
4 Brother bought back to life ... 3.50
5 O:Condom-Man (Chris Swafford) 3.50

CONQUEROR
Harrier, 1984–86
1 .... 3.50
2 thru 4................... @2.00
5 thru 9................... @2.00

CONSPIRACY COMICS
Revolutionary, 1991
1 Marilyn Monroe.............. 2.50
2 Who Killed JFK.............. 2.50
3 Who Killed RFK.............. 2.50

CONSTELLATION GRAPHICS
STG
1 thru 4................... @2.00

CONSTRUCT
Caliber ¡New Worldsî, 1996
1 (of 6) PJe,LDu, sci-fi,48pg ... 3.95
2 PJe,LDu..................... 2.95
3 PJe,LDu..................... 2.95
4 PJe,LDu..................... 2.95
5 PJe,LDu..................... 2.95
6 PJe,LDu, conclusion......... 2.95

CORRECTOR YUI
Tokyopop Press, 2001
1 48-pg....................... 2.95
2 .... 2.95
3 .... 2.95
4 .... 2.95
TPB Pocket Mixx, Vol. 1....... 9.95
TPB Pocket, Vol. 2 thru Vol. 5 . @10.00

CORTO MALTESE: BALLAD OF THE SALT SEA
NBM, 1997
1 by Hugo Pratt............... 2.95
1 a 2nd printing 2.95
2 by Hugo Pratt............... 2.95
3 Escondida 2.95
4 .... 2.95
5 .... 2.95
6 .... 2.95
7 final issue 2.95
TPB by Hugo Pratt, `In Siberia'. 10.95
TPB `Fable of Venice'......... 10.95
TPB `Banana Conga' 8.95
TPB `Voodoo for the President'. 8.95
TPB `Midwinter's Morning' 8.95
TPB `In Africa' 8.95

COSMIC HEROES
Eternity, 1988
1 Buck Rogers rep............. 2.50
2 thru 6 Buck Rogers rep..... @2.25

7 thru 9 Buck Rogers rep..... @2.25
10 .... 3.50
11 .... 3.95

COUNTER PARTS
Tundra, 1993
1 thru 3................... @2.95

COURTNEY CRUMRIN & THE COVEN OF MYSTICS
Oni Press 2003
1 (of 4) by Ted Naifeh........ 2.95
2 thru 4................... @2.95
TPB Vol. 1 .... 11.95
TPB The Night Things......... 11.95

COVENTRY
Fantagraphics, 1996
1 BWg, `The Frogs of God' 3.95
2 BWg, `Thirteen Dead Guys Named Bob' 3.95
3 BWg........................ 3.95
4 .... 3.95

COWBOY BEBOP
Tokyopop Press, 2002
1 (of 4) by Yukata Nanten 2.95
2 .... 2.95
3 .... 3.00
4 .... 3.00
Spec. Complete Anime Guide #1 . 12.95
Spec. Complete Anime Guide #2–#6............. @13.00
GN Vol. 1 (of 3) authentic manga . 10.00
GN Vol. 2 thru Vol. 3........ @10.00

CRAY BABY ADVENTURES, THE
Electric Milk, 1997
1 by Art Baltazar.............. 3.00

TV Comics, 1997
1 2nd printing 3.00
2 .... 3.00
4 Captain Camel............... 3.00
5 .... 3.00
Advent.Spec.San Diego Con lim. ed.................. 5.00
TPB Vol. 1 rep. #1–#5........ 14.95

CRAY BABY ADVENTURES: WRATH OF THE PEDDIDLERS
TV Comics, 1998
1 (of 3) by Art Baltazar........ 3.00
2 .... 3.00
3 concl....................... 3.00

CREED
Hall of Heroes, 1994
1 TKn,I:Mark Farley........... 25.00
1A Wizard Ace edition rep..... 20.00
2 TKn,Camping................. 35.00
TPB The Void, Collected ed.... 5.95
TPB Deluxe 9.95

CREED
Lightning Comics, 1995
1-shot TKn retelling of #1&#2 ... 2.75
See also: Color

Conqueror #6
© Harrier

All comics prices listed are for *Near Mint* condition.

B & W PUB.

CREED/TEENAGE MUTANT NINJA TURTLES
Lightning Comics, 1996
- 1 TKn(c) 3.00
- 2 TKn(c) 3.00
- 1 Gold Collector's Edition 5.95
- 1 Platinum Edition 9.95

CREED: CRANIAL DISORDER
Lightning Comics, 1996
- 1 . . . . 4.00
- 1A Previews variant cover 3.00
- 1B Platinum Edition 6.00
- 1C signed platinum edition. 8.00
- 2 . . . . 3.00
- 2b variant cover. 3.00
- 3 . . . . 3.00
- 3b variant cover. 3.00
- 3c limited edition 10.00

CREED: THE GOOD SHIP & THE NEW JOURNEY HOME
Lightning Comics, 1998
- 1 . . . . 3.00
- 1a variant cover. 3.00
- 1b limited edition 10.00

CREED: MECHANICAL EVOLUTION
Gearbox Press, 2000
- 1 (of 2) 3.00
- 1a variant (c). 3.00
- 1b signed 10.00
- 2 . . . . 3.00

CREED: USE YOUR DELUSION
Avatar Press, 1998
- 1 (of 2) by Trent Kaniuga 3.00
- 1 white leather. 30.00
- 2 . . . . 3.00
- 2 deluxe 4.95
- GN rep. #1–#2 . . . . 3.95

CRIME BUSTER
AC Comics
- 0 from FemForce. 2.95
- 1 Rep. From Boys Illustrated 3.95

CRIMEBUSTER
ACG Comics, 2000
- 1 (of 3) F:Dick Tracy 2.95
- 2 & 3 . . . . @2.95

CRIME CLASSICS
Eternity, 1988
- 1 thru 11 rep. Shadow comic strip . . . . @2.00
- 12 . . . . 2.25

CRIMSON DREAMS
Crimson
- 1 thru 11 . . . . @2.00

CRITTERS
Fantagraphics Books, 1986–90
- 1 SS,Usagi Yojimbo,Cutey 7.00
- 2 Captain Jack,Birthright 6.00
- 3 SS,Usagi Yojimbo,Gnuff 5.00
- 4 Gnuff,Birthright 5.00
- 5 Birthright. 5.00
- 6 SS,Usagi Yojimbo,Birthright . . . 5.00
- 7 SS,Usagi Yojimbo,Jack Bunny . 5.00
- 8 SK,Animal Graffiti,Lizards 5.00
- 9 Animal Graffiti. 5.00
- 10 SS,Usagi Yojimbo 5.00
- 11 SS,Usagi Yojimbo, ... 3.00
- 12 Birthright II. 2.50
- 13 Birthright II,Gnuff. 2.50
- 14 SS,Usagi Yojimbo,BirthrightII . . 3.00
- 15 Birthright II,CareBears 2.50
- 16 SS,Groundthumper,Gnuff. 2.50
- 17 Birthright II,Lionheart 2.50
- 18 Dragon's 2.50
- 19 Gnuff,Dragon's 2.50
- 20 Gnuff 2.50
- 21 Gnuff. 2.50
- 22 Watchdogs,Gnuff. 2.50
- 23 Flexi-Disc,X-Mas Issue 4.00
- 24 Angst,Lizards,Gnuff 2.50
- 25 Lionheart,SBi,Gnuff 2.50
- 26 Angst,Gnuff 2.50
- 27 SS,Ground Thumper 2.50
- 28 Blue Beagle,Lionheart 2.50
- 29 Lionheart,Gnuff 2.50
- 30 Radical Dog,Gnuff 2.50
- 31 SBi,Gnuffs,Lizards 2.50
- 32 Lizards,Big Sneeze 2.50
- 33 Gnuff,Angst,Big Sneeze. 2.50
- 34 Blue Beagle vs. Robohop 2.50
- 35 Lionheart,Fission Chicken 2.50
- 36 Blue Beagle,Fission Chicken . . 2.50
- 37 Fission Chicken 2.50
- 38 SS,double size,Usagi Yojimbo . 4.00
- 39 Fission Chicken 2.00
- 40 Gnuff 2.00
- 41 Duck'Bill Platypus 2.00
- 42 Glass Onion 2.00
- 43 Lionheart 2.00
- 44 Watchdogs 2.00
- 45 Ambrose the Frog 2.00
- 46 Lionheart. 2.00
- 47 Birthright 2.00
- 48 Birthright 2.00
- 49 Birthright 2.00
- 50 SS,Neil the Horse, UsagiYojimbo 5.00
- Spec.1 Albedo,rep+new 10pgStory . 2.00

CROSSFIRE
Eclipse, 1987
Prev. Color
- 18 thru 26 DSp . . . . @2.00

CROW, THE
Caliber, 1989
- 1 . . . . 40.00
- 1a 2nd Printing 5.00
- 1b 3rd Printing. 5.00
- 2 . . . . 25.00
- 2a 2nd Printing 4.00
- 2b 3rd Printing. 4.00
- 3 . . . . 20.00
- 3a 2nd Printing 4.00
- 4 . . . . 20.00

Tundra, 1992
- 1 reps. Crow #1, #2. . . . . 15.00
- 2 . . . . 8.00
- 3 . . . . 10.00
- TPB 20.00

CROW, THE
Kitchen Sink, 1996
- TPB Flesh & Blood Collection . . . 10.95
- TPB The Crow Collection,
- 7th printing 224pg. 15.95

CROW, THE: DEAD TIME
Kitchen Sink, 1996
- 1 . . . . 5.00
- 2 . . . . 4.00
- 3 . . . . 3.00
- TPB Collection rep. 10.95

CROW, THE: DEMON IN DISGUISE
Kitchen Sink, 1997
- 1 (of 4) by John J. Miller & Dean Ormston 3.00
- 2 . . . . 3.00
- 3 . . . . 3.00

CROW, THE: FLESH AND BLOOD
Kitchen Sink, 1996
- 1 thru 3 . . . . @3.00
- TPB rep. 96-pg. 10.95

CROW, THE: WAKING NIGHTMARES
Kitchen Sink, 1997
- 1 PhH 3.00
- 2 thru 4 PhH . . . . @2.95

The Crow: Wild Justice #1
© Kitchen Sink

CROW, THE: WILD JUSTICE, 1996
Kitchen Sink
- 1 thru 3 . . . . @3.00

CROW/RAZOR: KILL THE PAIN
London Night, 1998
- 1 (of 3) JOb,EHr, ... 3.00
- 1b EHr & Jerry Beck, Director's Cut, 40pg. 5.00
- 1c black leather, signed & numbered 29.95
- 1d Ministry of Night (c). 5.00
- 1e Ministry (c) signed 15.00
- 1f black leather, red foil logos . . 20.00
- 2 . . . . 3.00

Crow–Cyborg / B & W PUB.

2a Ministry of Night (c). 5.00
2b Leather edition 10.00
3 . . . . 3.00
3a Ministry of Night (c). 5.00
4 . . . . 3.00
4a Ministry of Night (c). 6.00
4b Leather edition 15.00
4c Leather edition, signed 15.00
Spec. Finale 3.00
Spec. Finale, Ministry (c). 5.00
0 . . . . 3.00
0a Ministry (c) 5.00
0b Red Velvet Elite 20.00
1-shotA Tour Book, cover A. 5.00
1-shotB Tour Book, cover B 5.00
1-shotC Tour Book, cover C 5.00
1-shotD Tour Book, ministry edition. 5.00
1-shotE Tour Book, limited black
  leather 15.00
1-shotF Tour Book, signed 18.00
Spec. Nocturnal Masque 48-pg. . . 5.95
TPB Kill The Pain, 150-pg. 15.95

EH! Productions, 1999
Spec. The Lost Chapter 4.95
Spec. The Lost Chapter,
  Elite Fan Ed. 6.00

CROW OF THE BEAR CLAN
Blackthorne, 1986
1 . . . . 2.25
2 thru 6 . . . . @1.75

CRUSADERS
Guild, 1982
1 Southern Knights, Mag. size . . . 10.00

CRUSHER JOE
Ironcat, 1999
1 by Haruka Takachiho 2.95
2 thru 6 . . . . @2.95
TPB 15.95

CRY FOR DAWN
Cry For Dawn, 1989–90
1 . . . . 90.00
1a 2nd Printing 35.00
1b 3rd Printing. 25.00
2 . . . . 40.00
2a 2nd Printing 10.00
3 . . . . 30.00
4 . . . . 20.00
5 . . . . 20.00
6 . . . . 20.00
7 Corporate Ladder,Rock A
  Bye Baby 15.00
8 Decay,This is the Enemy 15.00
9 . . . . 15.00
1-shot Subtle Violents,F:Ryder . . . 3.00

CRYING FREEMAN
Viz, 1989
1 . . . . 4.00
2 . . . . 3.50
3 thru 5 . . . . @3.50
6 thru 8 . . . . @3.00

CRYING FREEMAN II
Viz, 1990–91
1 . . . . 4.00
2 . . . . 3.50
3 . . . . 3.50
4 thru 6 . . . . @3.00
7 V:Bugnug 3.00
8 Emu & The Samurai Sword . . . 3.00

9 Final Issue 3.00

CRYING FREEMAN III
Viz, 1991
1 thru 10 . . . . @4.00

CRYING FREEMAN IV
Viz, 1992
1 thru 3 . . . . @4.00
4 thru 8 . . . . @2.75

CRY FREEMAN V
Viz, 1993
1 Return to Japan 4.00
2 A:Tateoka-assassin. 4.00
3 . . . . 4.00
4 A:Bagwana 4.00
5 V:Tsunaike 4.00
6 V:Aido Family 4.00
7 V:Tsunaike 4.00
GN:Taste of Revenge 14.95

CRYPT OF DAWN
Sirius, 1996
1 JLi(c) 6.00
1 variant cover. 10.00
2 JLi(c) 4.00
3 . . . . 3.00
4 JLi(c) 3.00
5 JLi(c) 3.00
6 Vanguard of Comics 3.00

CRYSTAL BREEZE
High Impact, 1996
1 thru 3 . . . . @2.95
Spec.#1 Crystal Breeze Unleashed. 3.00
Spec.#1 Crystal Breeze Revenge . . 2.95
Spec.#1a gold edition cover 10.00

CUDA
Rebel Studios
1 I:Cuda,Zora,V:Shanga Bai 2.00
CUDA B.C. (Rebel Studios) signed 12.95

Avatar Press, 1998
1 (of 4) by Tim & Joe Vigil 3.50
1b Leather cover 20.00
1c signed. 15.00
1d Royal Blue edition 60.00
2 . . . . 3.50
3 . . . . 3.50
4 . . . . 3.50
1 thru 4 gore (c). . . . . @6.00
0 80-pg. 7.95
0a Gore (c) 8.95
0c prism foil (c) 12.95
0d Royal blue 75.00
TPB Vol. 1, 160-pg. 19.95

CUTEY BUNNY
Army Surplus Comix, 1982
1 . . . . 8.00
2 thru 4 . . . . @4.00

Eclipse, 1985
5 X-Men, Batman parody 3.00

CUTIE HONEY
Ironcat, 1997
1 crime fighting android 2.95
2 . . . . 2.95
3 Wonderful Mask 2.95
4 thru 6 . . . . @2.95

VOL 2, 1998
CUTIE HONEY '90
1 Sorayama cover 2.95
2 thru 6 . . . . @2.95

Cyber 7 Book 2, #6
© Rockland

CYBER 7
Eclipse, 1989
1 . . . . 2.50
2 thru 5 . . . . @2.00

Book 2: Rockland, 1990
1 thru 7 . . . . @2.00
8 thru 10 . . . . @2.50

CYBERFROG
Hall of Heroes, 1994
1 I:Cyberfrog 5.00
1a 2nd printing 2.50
2 V:Ben Riley 4.00
2a 2nd printing 2.50

CYBERFROG
Harris, 1997
1 3rd Anniv. Special 3.00
1a Walt Simonson(c). 6.00
1b signed & numbered. 10.00
2 . . . . 3.50
2a variant cover. 4.00
3 . . . . 3.50
4 . . . . 3.50
4a signed 10.00
Ashcan Cyberfrog: Amphibionix . . . 6.00
Spec. Cyberfrog Amphibionix(2001) 3.00

CYBERFROG VS CREED
Harris, 1997
1 . . . . 3.50
1 Creed vs. Cyberfrog, alternate
  edition 9.95

CYBERZONE
Jet Black Grafiks, 1994
1 thru 8 Never-never Land . . . . @2.50

CYBORG 009
Tokyopop Press 2003
GN Vol. 1 . . . . 10.00
GN Vol. 2 . . . . 10.00

CYCLOPS
Comics Interview, 1988
1 Mini-series, BSz 2.50
2 . . . . 2.50
3 . . . . 2.50

CYCLOPS
Blackthorne
1 Mini-series 2.50
2 . . . . 2.50
3 . . . . 2.50

CYGNUS X-1
Twisted Pearl Press
1 V:Yag'Nost 2.50
2 F:Rex and Bounty Hunters 2.50

CYNDER
Immortelle Studios, 1995
1 I:Cynder 5.00
2 . . . . 3.00
3 conclusion 2.50
Second Series, 1996
1 thru 3 . . . . 3.00

CYNDER/HELLINA
Immortelle Studios, 1996
Spec. 1 x-over 3.00

DAEMONIFUGE: THE SCREAMING CAGE
Black Library, 2002
1 by Kev Walker 2.50
2 and 3 . . . . @2.50

DAIKAZU
Ground Zero
1 . . . . 5.00
1a 2nd Printing 1.50
2 . . . . 3.00
2a 2nd Printing 1.50
3 . . . . 3.00
3a 2nd Printing 1.50
4 thru 7 . . . . @1.50
8 . . . . 1.75

DA'KOTA
Millennium, 1997
1 by Pavlet & Petersen 2.95
1 signed 4.95
1 foil edition 9.95
2 . . . . 2.95
2 foil edition 4.95
3 foil deluxe edition 6.95
3 . . . . 2.95
3a variant cover 2.95
Spec.#1 Orig.Art Edition 9.95

DAMONSTREIK
Imperial Comics
1 I:Damonstreik 2.00
2 V:Sonix 2.00
3 V:Sonix 2.00
4 J:Ohm 2.00
5 V:Drakkus 2.00

DANCE TIL TOMORROW
Viz Communications, 1998
TPB Vol. 1 by Naoki Yamanoto . . . 15.95
TPB Vol. 2 thru Vol. 5 . . . . @15.95
TPB Vol. 6 thru Vol. 7 . . . . @12.95

DANGEROUS TIMES
Evolution
1 MK 2.50
2 MA(c) 2.00
2a 2nd printing 1.75
3 MR(c) 2.00
3a 2nd printing 2.00
4 GP(c) 2.00

DAN TURNER HOLLYWOOD DETECTIVE
Eternity, 1991
1 'Darkstar of Death' 2.50
Spec.#1 Dan Turner, Homicide Hunch, Dan Turner Framed . . . 2.50
Spec.#1 Dan Turner, The Star Chamber, Death of Folly Hempstead 2.50

DARK ANGEL
Boneyard, 1991
1 by Hart Fisher 2.25
2 . . . . 2.25

DARK ANGEL
Boneyard, 1997
1 by H.Fisher & J.Helkowski 2.00
2 . . . . 2.00
3 by Hart Fisher & John Cassaday 2.00
4 The Quiet Demon 2.00
Spec.#1 Dark Angel/Bill the Bull, 48-pg. (1998) 4.95
Spec. 1999 . . . . 4.95
GN Last Decade Dead Century . . . 15.95
GN deluxe 19.95

DARK ANGEL
CPM Manga, 1999
1 by Kia Asamiya 2.95
2 thru 9 . . . . @2.95
10 thru 31 . . . . @2.95
TPB Vol. 1 rep. #1–#5 . . . . 15.95
TPB Vol. 2 . . . . 15.95
TPB Vol. 3 . . . . 15.95

DARK ASSASSIN
Silverwolf, 1987
1 thru 3 . . . . @1.50
Vol. 2
1 thru 5 . . . . @2.00

DARK CITY ANGEL
Freak Pit Productions
1 I:Lt.Michelle Constello 3.50
2 . . . . 3.50
3 Sex Doll is Prime Suspect 3.50

DARK FANTASIES
Dark Fantasy, 1994–97
0 Donna Mia foil (c) 8.00
0 Destiny Angel foil (c) 7.50
1 Jli (c) 9.00
1a test print Jli (c) 12.00
1 2nd printing 3.95
1 signed & numbered 7.95
2 Kevin J. Taylor Girl (c) 4.00
2a foil stamped 3.00
3 JOb Crow (c) 4.00
3a foil stamped 3.50
4 . . . . 4.00
4a foil stamped 3.50
5 . . . . 4.00
5a foil stamped 3.50

Dark Fantasies #6
© Dark Fantasy

6 Angel Destiny 4.00
6a foil stamped 3.50
7 . . . . 4.00
7a foil stamped 3.50
8 . . . . 4.00
8 Blue cover 3.50
8 Red cover 3.50
8 deluxe foil-enhanced 3.95
9 Destiny Angel (c) 3.50
9a Destiny Angel, red foil (c) 3.95
9b Horror (c) 3.50
9c Horror, red foil (c) 3.95
10 . . . . 3.50
10a red foil (c) 3.95
Spec.#1 Summers Eve Pin-up . . . 2.95
Spec.#1 foil-stamped 3.50

DARK FRINGE
Brainstorm, 1996
1 . . . . 2.95

DARK FRINGE: SPIRITS OF THE DEAD
Brainstorm, 1997
1 by Eman Torre & John Kisse 2.95
2 concl 2.95

DARK ISLAND
Davdez Arts, 1998
1 by Barry Blair & Colin Chan . . . 2.50
2 thru 4 . . . . @2.50

DARKLIGHT: PRELUDE
Sirius, 2000
1 (of 3) by Teri Sue Wood 2.95
2 . . . . 2.95
3 concl 2.95

DARK LORD
RAK
1 thru 3 . . . . @2.00

DARK MANGA
London Night
1 Featuring Demonique 4.95

DARK MUSE
Dark Muse Productions
1 with mini-comic............. 3.50
1a with mini-comic............ 5.00
2 .... 3.95
3 F:Coffin Joe 3.95

DARK OZ
Arrow Comics, 1997
1 (of 5) by Griffith, Kerr & Bryan... 2.75
2 .... 2.75
3 .... 2.75
4 .... 2.75
5 .... 2.75
Spec. Bill Bryan's Oz Collection ... 2.95

DARK REGIONS
White Wolf, 1987
1 .... 2.50
2 .... 2.50
3 Scarce 3.00
4 and 5 .... @2.00

DARK STAR
Rebel
1 I:Ran 2.25
2 thru 3 .... @2.25

DARK VISIONS
Pyramid, 1987
1 I:Wasteland Man............. 2.00
2 thru 4 .... @2.00

DARK WOLF
Eternity, 1988
1 and 2 .... @2.00
Volume 2
1 thru 14 .... @2.00
Ann. #1 .... 2.25

DARQUE RAZOR
London Night, 1996
? by Dan Membeila & Albert Holaso,
  Dark Birth................... 2.25
? necro-embossed edition 10.00
1 .... 3.00
2 .... 3.00
3 .... 3.00

DAYS OF DARKNESS
Apple
1 From Pearl Harbor
  to Midway.................... 2.75
2 Pearl Harbor Attack,cont..... 2.75
3 Japanese Juggernaut.......... 2.75
4 Bataan Peninsula............. 2.75
GN 14.95

DEADBEATS
Claypool Comics, 1993
1 thru 13 .... @2.50
14 New Ways to Dream 2.50
15 thru 25 .... @2.50
26 by Richard Howell & Ricardo
  Villagran, The Southland
  Family Saga.................. 2.50
27 Christine transformed into
  Predator..................... 2.50
28 .... 2.50
29 forbidden antiquities....... 2.50
30 V:Dracula 2.50
31 Reconstructing Deadbeats.... 2.50
32 New generation of Deadbeats . 2.50
33 Quiet Night in Fear City ... 2.50
34 Dagger of Deliverance 2.50
35 Deadbeats of Danger Street . 2.50
36 By His Majesty's Request ... 2.50
37 Carnival of Goals........... 2.50
38 HorrorFest begins 2.50
39 HorrorFest.................. 2.50
40 HorrorFest.................. 2.50
41 Guys Night Out 2.50
42 Dark Dealings 2.50
43 Dodging the Bullet 2.50
44 Town for Sale 2.50
45 thru 50 .... @2.50
51 thru 62 .... @2.50
TPB Rep. #1–#6................ 12.95
TPB Vol. 2 Tangy Treats, 160-pg. . 12.95

DEADKILLER
Caliber
1 Rep Deadworld 19 thru 21 ..... 2.95

DEADTIME STORIES
New Comics, 1987
1 AAd,WS 1.75

DEADWORLD
Arrow, 1986
1 Arrow Pyb.................... 5.00
2 .... 4.00
3 V:King Zombie 3.50
4 V:King Zombie 3.50
5 Team Rests 3.50
6 V:King Zombie 3.50
7 F:KZ & Deake, Graphic(c)..... 3.50
7a Tame cover.................. 2.00
8 V:Living Corpse, Graphic(c) .. 2.50
8a Tame cover.................. 2.00
9 V:Sadistic Punks, Graphic(c).. 2.50
9a Tame cover.................. 2.00
10 V:King Zombie, Graphic(c)... 2.50
10a Tame cover 2.00
11 V:King Zombie, Graphic(c)... 3.00
11a Tame cover 2.50
12 I:Percy, Graphic(c)......... 3.00
12a Tame cover 2.50
13 V:King Zombie, Graphic(c)... 3.00
13a Tame cover 2.50
14 V:Voodoo Cult,Graphic(c).... 3.00
14a Tame cover 2.50
15 Zombie stories,Graphic(c) .. 3.00
15a Tame cover 2.50
16 V:`Civilized' Community 2.50
17 V:King Zombie 2.50
18 V:King Zombie 2.50
19 V:Grakken 2.50
20 V:King Zombie 2.50
21 Dead Killer 2.50
22 L:Dan & Joey................ 2.50
23 V:King Zombie 2.50
24 .... 2.50
25 (R:Vince Locke)............. 2.50
26 .... 2.50
Caliber
1 thru 11 .... @2.95
12 thru 14 Death Call .... @2.95
15 Death Call,pt.6............. 2.95
Spec. Deadworld Archives, rep. . 2.50
Spec. Bits & Pieces, rep.
  Caliber Presents #2&#8 ...... 2.00
Spec. To Kill A King,R:Deadkiller... 2.95

DEATH ANGEL
Lightning, 1997
1 by J. Cleary & Anderson...... 2.95
1 variant cover................ 2.95
1 limited edition A 9.95
1 limited edition B 9.95

DEATHDREAMS OF DRACULA
Apple
1 Selection of short stories .. 2.50
2 short stories 2.50
3 Inc. Rep. BWr,'Breathless' .. 2.50
4 short stories 2.50

DEATH HUNT
Eternity
1 .... 2.00
2 .... 2.00

DEATHMARK
Lightning Comics, 1994
1 O:War Party 2.75

DEATH OF ANGEL GIRL
Angel Entertainment, 1997
1 by E.Bell & C.Forrest,F:Michelle . 2.95

DEATH OF BLOODFIRE
Lightning
1 .... 3.00
1a variant cover............... 3.00

DEATH RATTLE
Kitchen Sink, 1995 (Prev. Color)
1 thru 3 .... @3.50
4 .... 3.00
5 .... 2.50
6 Steve Bissette(c)............ 2.00
7 Ed Gein 2.00
8 I:Xenozoic Tales 10.00
9 BW,rep....................... 2.00
10 AW,rep...................... 2.00
11 thru 15 .... @2.00
16 BW,Spacehawk 2.00
17 Rand Holmes(c).............. 2.00
18 FMc......................... 2.00

DEATH'S HEAD
Crystal
1 thru 3 .... @2.00

DEATHWORLD
Adventure Comics, 1990
1 Harry Harrison adapt. 2.50
2 thru 4 . . . . @2.50
BOOK II, 1991
1 Harry Harrison adapt. 2.50
2 thru 4 . . . . @2.50
BOOK III, 1991
1 H.Harrison adapt.,colonization . . 2.50
2 Attack on the Lowlands. 2.50
3 Attack on the Lowlands contd. . . 2.50
4 last issue 2.50

DEE VEE
Dee Vee, 1997
1 ECa, F:Alex 2.95
2 ECa 2.95
3 ECa 2.95
4 thru 14 . . . . @2.95
Spec. #1 Life is Cheap 2.95

DEFENSELESS DEAD
Adventure Comics, 1991
1 Larry Niven adapt. A:Gil 2.50
2 A:Organlegger 2.50
3 A:Organlegger 2.50

DELTA TENN
Entertainment, 1987
1 thru 11 . . . . @2.00

DEMON BABY
SQP/666 Comics, 1997
1 by Rich Larson, seq. to Hell
   on Heels 2.95
1a deluxe 9.95
2 . . . . 2.95
2a deluxe 9.95
3 . . . . 2.95
3a deluxe 9.95
GN Hell on Heels 9.95
GN Hell on Heels, deluxe 19.95

DEMON BITCH
Forbidden, 1997–98
1-shot 2.95
Spec.#1 Demon Bitch vs.
   Angel Girl 2.95

B & W PUB.
Spec.#1 Demon Bitch: Devilspawn, by
   Angela Benoit & Nirut Chaswan 3.00
Spec.#1 Demon Bitch: Hellslave,
   Free on Earth cover 3.00
Spec.#1 Demon Bitch: Tales of
   the Damned 2.95

DEMON DIARY
Tokyopop Press 2003
GN Vol. 1 . . . . 10.00
GN Vol. 2 thru 4 . . . . @10.00

DEMONGATE
Sirius, 1996–97
1 thru 12 by Bao Lin Hum &
   Colin Chan . . . . @2.50

DEMON GUN
Crusade Entertainment, 1996
1 thru 3 GCh,KtH . . . . @2.95

DEMON HUNTER
Aircel, 1989
1 thru 4 . . . . @2.00

DEMON HUNTER
Davdez Arts, 1998
1 by Barry Blair & Colin Chan 2.50
2 F:Hunter Gordon 2.50
3 . . . . 2.50

DEMONIQUE
London Night, 1997
? by SKy Owens, A:Anvil 3.00
1 by Membeila & Owens 3.00
2 F:Viper 3.00
3 Mayhem 3.00
4 Final issue 3.00

DEMONIQUE: ANGEL OF NIGHT
London Night, 1997
1 (of 3) by Skylar Owens 3.00
2 . . . . 3.00
3 final issue 3.00

DEMONSLAYER: LORDS OF NIGHT
Avatar Press 2003
1/2 Fire Edition 5.95
1/2 Ice Edition 5.95
1/2 Attitude Edition 5.95
Preview 2.00
Preview variant (c)s 5.95
1 . . . . 3.50
1a variant (c)s 3.50
1b wraparound (c) 3.95

DEMON'S TAILS
Adventure
1 . . . . 2.50
2 A:Champion 2.50
3 V:Champion 2.50
4 V:Champion 2.50

DEMON WARRIOR
Eastern, 1987
1 thru 12 . . . . @2.00
13 and 14 . . . . @2.00

DENIZENS OF DEEP CITY
Jabberwocky, 1988
1 thru 8 . . . . @2.00

DERRECK WAYNE'S STRAPPED
Gothic Images
1 Confrontational Factor 2.25
2 Confrontational Factor 2.25

DESCENDING ANGELS
Millennium, 1995
1 I:3 Angels 2.00
2 F:Jim Johnson 2.95
3 F:Jim Johnson 2.95

DESERT PEACH
Thoughts & Images, 1988
1 thru 4 . . . . @2.00

DESTINY ANGEL
Dark Fantasy, 1996
1 (of 3) 3.95
1 2nd printing 3.95
1a deluxe 4.50
2 `Sunless Garden' 3.50
2a foil cover 3.95
2b photo cover 3.95

DESTROY
Eclipse, 1986
1 Large Size 4.95
2 Small Size,3-D 4.95

DETECTIVE, THE
Caliber, 1998
1 by Gerard Goffaux 2.95
2 . . . . 2.95
3 Clutches of the Past 2.95

DEVIL JACK
Doom Theatre, 1995
1 I:Devil Jack 2.95
1a Directors Cut 2.95
2 V:Belegosi 2.95
3 . . . . 3.00

DEVIL'S WORKSHOP
Blue Comet Press, 1995
1 Iron Cupcakes 2.95

DIABOLIK
Scorpion Productions, 1999
VOL. 1
1 Terror Aboard The Karima 5.95
2 Fight Against Time 5.95
3 Crumbs for the Scum 5.95
4 Family with no morals 5.95
5 . . . . 5.95
6 . . . . 5.95
VOL. 2
1 Target: Diabolik 5.95
2 One Crazy Love 5.95
3 . . . . 5.95
4 Interrupted Game 5.95

Demongate #3
© Sirius

All comics prices listed are for *Near Mint* condition.

DICK DANGER
Olsen Comics, 1998
1 by W.W. Olsen 2.95
2 F:Red Olga. 2.95
3 The Angel Murder. 2.95
4 Is Hitler Still Alive? 2.95
5 Nikita, The Cat Girl. 2.95

DICKS
Caliber, 1997
1 (of 4),GEn,JMC, ... 2.95
2 GEn,JMC 2.95
3 GEn,JMC 2.95
4 concl. 2.95
TPB GEn,JMC 12.95

DICK TRACY
Tony Raiola 2003
GN Purple Cross Gang. 9.50
GN Large Feature reprint #3–#6 . @9.50
GN Scottie of Scotland Yard 9.50
GN Kidnapped Princes 9.50

DICK TRACY CRIMEBUSTER
ACG Comics, 1998
1 by M.A.Collins & D.Locher 2.95
2 thru 9 . . . . @2.95
TPB rep. (2001) 19.95

DICK TRACY DETECTIVE
ACG Comics, 1999
1 (of 4) by Chester Gould 2.95
2 thru 4 . . . . @2.95

DICK TRACY MAGAZINE
1 V:Little Face Finnyo 3.95

DICK TRACY
Blackthorne, 1984–89
1 thru 12 . . . . @6.50
13 thru 25 . . . . @7.50
Becomes:

DICK TRACY MONTHLY/WEEKLY
Blackthorne, 1988
1 thru 25 monthly. . . . . @3.00
26 thru 108 weekly. . . . . @4.00
Unprinted Stories #3. . . . . 2.95
1 3-D Special 3.00
Spec. #1 . . . . 2.95
Spec. #2. . . . . 2.95
Spec. #3. . . . . 2.95

DICK TRACY: THE EARLY YEARS
Blackthorne, 1987
1 thru 3, 78-pg. . . . . @7.50
4 thru 6 . . . . @3.50
7 and 8 . . . . @4.00

DICK TRACY UNPRINTED STORIES
Blackthorne, 1987
1 thru 4 . . . . @3.00

DIGIMON
Tokyopop Press 2003
GN Vol. 1 (of 12) 10.00
GN Vol. 2 thru Vol. 5 . . . . @10.00

DIGITAL DRAGON
Peregrine Entertainment, 1999
1 by Bryan Heyboer. 2.95
2 thru 4 . . . . @2.95

DIM-WITTED DARRYL
Slave Labor Graphics, 1998
1 by Michael Bresnahan 2.95
2 thru 5 . . . . @2.95

DINOSAURS FOR HIRE
Eternity, 1988
1 . . . . 3.00
1a Rep. 2.00
2 thru 9 . . . . @2.00
Fall Classic #1 . . . . 2.25
Malibu, 1993
#1 3-D special 3.50

DIRTY PAIR
Eclipse, 1988
1 . . . . 9.00
2 . . . . 7.00
3 . . . . 6.00
4 end mini-series. 6.00
Vol. 2, 1989
1 thru 5 . . . . @5.00
Vol. 3, 1990
1 thru 5 . . . . @5.00

DIRTY PAIR: SIM EARTH
Eclipse
1 thru 4 . . . . @4.00

DISCIPLES
Caliber Core, 1998
1 Climate of fear 2.95
2 . . . . 2.95

A DISTANT SOIL
Warp Graphics, 1983
1 A:Panda Khan 10.00
2 . . . . 5.00
3 . . . . 4.00
4 . . . . 3.00

Ditko's World: Static
© Renegade

5 . . . . 3.00
6 thru 9 . . . . @3.00
Aria Press, 1991
1 F:Seasons of Spring. 6.00
1a-2nd to 4th printing. 2.50
2 Seasons of Spring,pt.2 . . . . 5.00
3 . . . . 3.00
4 . . . . 3.00
5 thru 8 . . . . @3.00
9 thru 11 Knights of the Angel . . @3.00
12 thru 14 . . . . @3.00
GN Knights of the Angel, deluxe . . 15.95
GN Immigrant Song rep.#1–#3 . . . . 6.95
See Image Comics

DITKO'S WORLD: STATIC
Renegade
1 thru 3 SD . . . . @2.00

DOCTOR
Ironcat, 1997
1 (of 5) by Bang Ippongi 2.95
2 . . . . 2.95
4 . . . . 2.95
5 Pay Back in the City of
   Santa La Paz 2.95
6 final issue 2.95

DR. GORPON
Eternity, 1991
1 I:Dr.Gorpon,V:Demon 2.25
2 A:Doofus,V:ChocolateBunny 2.50
3 D:Dr.Gorpon 2.50

DR. RADIUM
Silverline
1 . . . . 3.00
2 . . . . 2.00
3 and 4 . . . . @2.00

DR. RADIUM: MAN OF SCIENCE
Slave Labor, 1992
1 And Baby makes 2, BU: Dr.
   Radiums' Grim Future 2.50

DOC WEIRD'S THRILL BOOK
1 AW. 2.00
2 . . . . 2.00
3 . . . . 2.00

DOCTOR WEIRD
Caliber Press, 1994
1 V:Charnogg 2.50
2 V:Charnogg 2.50

DR. WONDER
Old Town Publishing, 1996
1 thur 5 . . . . @3.00

DODEKAIN
Antarctic Press, 1994
1 and 2 by Masayuki Fujihara . . @2.95
3 Rampage Vs. Zogerians 2.95
4 V:Zogerians 2.95
5 F:Takuma 2.95
6 Dan vs. Takuma 2.75
7 V:Okizon 2.75
8 V:Okizon 2.95

DOGAROO
Blackthorne, 1988
1 .... 2.00

DOGS O'WAR, THE
Crusade Entertainment, 1996–97
1 thru 3 (of 3). .... @2.95

DOLLS
Sirius, 1998
1-shot science fiction 2.95

DOMINION
Eclipse Manga, 1990
1 .... 3.00
2 thru 6 .... @2.00

DOMINO CHANCE
Chance, 1982
1 1,000 printed 10.00
1a 2nd printing 3.50
2 thru 6 .... @3.00
7 I:Gizmo 7.00
8 A:Gizmo 11.00
9 .... 2.50
[2nd Series]
1 .... 3.00
2 and 3 .... @2.00

DONATELLO
Mirage, 1986
1-shot A:TMNTurtles 12.00

DONNA MIA
Avatar Press, 1997
0 by Tevlin Utz. 3.00
0b leather cover. 15.00
0c signed 8.00
1 .... 3.95
1a signed 8.00
1b Royal Blue edition. 50.00
2 .... 3.95
2a deluxe 4.50
3 (of 3) 3.00
3a deluxe 8.00
Giant Size #1 .... 3.00
Giant Size #1 leather cover. . 15.00
Giant Size #1 signed 8.00
Giant Size #2 .... 3.95
Giant Size #2 Deluxe 10.00
TPB rep. #0–#3 & Giant
  Size #1–#2. .... 15.95
Spec. Infinity. 3.00
Spec.#1 Pin-up (1997) 3.00

DON SIMPSON'S BIZARRE HEROES
Fiasco Comics, 1990
0 thru 7 .... 2.95
8 V:Darkcease. 2.95
9 R:Yan Man 2.95
10 F:Mainstreamers 2.95
11 Search for Megaton Man ... 2.95
12 .... 2.95
13 House of Megaton Man 2.95
14 Cec Vs. Dark Cease 2.95
TPB Apocalypse Affiliation .. 12.95

DOOMSDAY + 1
ACG Comics, 1998
1 by JBn rep. Charlton. 2.95

B & W PUB.

2 A Faceless Foe. 2.95
3 .... 2.95
4 The Hidden Enemy. 2.95
5 Rule of Fear. 2.95
6 .... 2.95
7 NA(c), final issue 2.95

Dork #7
© *Slave Labor Graphics*

DORK
Amaze Ink/Slave Labor Graphics, 1993–2001
1 EDo 3.00
2 EDo 3.00
3 EDo 3.00
1 thru 3 2nd printings .... @3.00
4 .... 3.00
5 thru 7 .... @3.00
8 .... 3.50
9 .... 3.00
TPB Vol. 1 Who's Laughing Now. . 11.95
TPB Vol. 2 Circling the Drain .. 13.95

DORK TOWER
Corsair Publishing, 1998
1 by John Kovalic 3.00
2 thru 8 .... @3.50
Dork Storm, 2000
9 Angry Young Fan 3.00
10 Road Rules 3.00
11 World of Dorkness 3.00
12 and 13 .... @3.00
14 Gilly, Warrior Princess 3.00
15 .... 3.00
16 Trader of the Last Orc 3.00
17 Halloween in Mud Bay 3.00
17 At the Big Con 3.00
18 Understanding Games. 3.00
19 Junk Food Issue 3.00
20 Featuring Gilly. 3.00
21 20th Century Boy. 3.00
22 Daily Carson 3.00
23 Dork Tower Frag 3.00
24 .... 3.00
25 .... 4.00
26 Dice Fidelity. 3.00
27 Clanbook Mopey 3.00
Spec. Lord of the Rings 3.00
Swimsuit Special #1 .... 2.95
Best of Dork Tower #1 .... 2.95
TPB Vol. 1 Dork Covenant 15.95
TPB Vol. 2 Dork Shadows. 15.95
TPB Vol. 3 Heart of Dorkness.. 16.00
TPB Dork Tower 15.95

TPB Vol. 5 Understanding Gamers 16.00
TPB Vol. 6 1d6 Degrees of
  Spearation 16.00
1-shot Wizkids Special 3.00

DOUBLE EDGE DOUBLE
Double Edge
1 thru 3 .... 3.50
4 Heroes Inc. Rep.#1-#2 .... 2.95

DOUBLE IMPACT
High Impact Studios, 1995–96
1 I: China & Jazz. 5.00
1a Chromium (c) variant, signed .. 6.00
1b Rainbow (c) w/certificate... 15.00
1c Rainbow (c) w/o certificate .. 10.00
2 Castilo's Crime 3.00
2b silver version 10.00
2c signed, w/certificate 5.00
3 .... 5.00
3a Bondage (c) 15.00
4 .... 5.00
4a Phoenix (c). 15.00
5 .... 5.00
6 China cover 3.00
6a Jazz cover 3.00
6b signed China or Jazz(c) ... 15.00
6c bondage(c). 10.00
7 & 8 .... @3.00
8a variant (c). 8.00
2nd Series, 1996–97
0 .... 3.00
1 .... 3.00
1a chromium (c) 4.00
1b Chromium variant edition .. 14.95
1c Christmas (c) 10.00
2 .... 3.00
2a Sweedish Erotica(c) 10.00
Spec.#1 Double Impact/Lethal Strike:
  Double Strike, x-over 3.00
Spec.#1 Double Impact/Nikki Blade:
  Hard Core x-over (1997) 2.95
  Platinum variant RCI(c). .. 10.00
  Gold Metal variant RCI(c) .. 20.00
Spec.#1 Raising Hell, RCI,RkB .. 2.95
ABC Comics, 1998
1 encore 3.00
1a encore, Chicago cover 6.00
1b encore, San Diego nude cover . 6.00
Spec. Double Impact/Luxura (1998) 3.00
Spec. Vampeurotica edition.... 5.95
Bikini Spec. 3.00
Christmas Spec.. .... 3.00
Christmas Spec., gold foil 10.00
Coll.#1 .... 3.00
Coll.#1a x-mas 8.00
Spring Spec.#1. .... 3.00
Spring Spec.#1a manga cover .. 8.00
Summer Bikini Spec. 1999 .... 3.00
Gallery Collection #1 .... 5.00
Lingerie Special 3.00

DOUBLE IMPACT ALIVE
ABC Comics, 1999
1 (of 3) Double Impact Alive 2000 . 3.00
1a Double Impact Alive 2000,
  gold foil ed. 8.00
1b Red Leather 15.00
2 RCI............................ 3.00
2a Manga cover 8.00
2c silver embossed foil 10.00

DOUBLE IMPACT: ASSASSINS FOR HIRE
High Impact, 1997
1 RCI,RkB 3.00

All comics prices listed are for *Near Mint* condition.

Double–Dragon / B & W PUB.

2 .... 3.00
ABC Comics, 1998
1 .... 3.00

DOUBLE IMPACT: FROM THE ASHES
ABC Comics, 1998
1 (of 2) RCl 3.00
2 RCl. 3.00
2A variant cover A 5.95
2B variant cover B 5.95

DOUBLE IMPACT: HOT SHOTS
ABC Studios, 1999
1 RCl. 3.00
2 .... 3.00

DOUBLE IMPACT MERCS
ABC Comics, 1999
1 (of 3) RCl 3.00
1a deluxe 8.00
2 RCl. 3.00
2a deluxe 10.00

DOUBLE IMPACT: ONE STEP BEYOND
ABC Comics, 1998
1 (of 2) RCl 3.00
1a Leather cover 20.00

DOUBLE IMPACT RAW
ABC Comics, 1997
1 (of 3) RCl, adult 3.00
1b Star photo (c) 10.00
1A Wraparound cover A 5.95
1B Wraparound cover B 5.95
2 .... 2.95
3 concl. 2.95
3A Variant cover A 5.95

VOL. 2
1 (of 3) adult material 3.00

DOUBLE IMPACT/RAZOR
ABC Studios, 1999
1 (of 3) 3.25
1b Previews exclusive 8.00
1c Manga alt.(c) 8.00
2 .... 3.25

DOUBLE IMPACT SUICIDE RUN
ABC Comics, 1998
1 (of 2) RCl 3.00
1b Leather cover 15.00
2 adult material 3.00
Collected edition 3.00
Collected, gold foil 10.00

DOUBLE IMPACT 2069
ABC Comics, 1999
1 Virgin Encore Edition 3.00
1a Deluxe Erotica edition 8.00
Christmas Spec. 3.00
Christmas Spec. Previews (c). . 8.00

DOUBLE IMPACT X
ABC Comics, 2000
1 .... 5.95
1a alternate (c) 5.95

---

2 .... 5.95
2 deluxe, vinyl (c) 20.00
Intro 20.00

DRACULA
Eternity
1 .... 3.75
1a 2nd printing 2.50
2 thru 4 .... @2.50

DRACULA IN HELL
Apple
1 O:Dracula 2.50
2 O:Dracula contd. 2.50

DRACULA: SUICIDE CLUB
Adventure, 1992
1 I:Suicide Club in UK 2.50
2 Dracula/Suicide Club cont. . . 2.50
3 Club raid,A:Insp.Harrison . . . 2.50
4 Vision of Miss Fortune 2.50

DRACULA: THE LADY IN THE TOMB
Eternity
1 .... 2.50

DRACULA'S COZY COFFIN
Draculina Publishing, 1995
1 thru 4 Halloween issue ..... @2.95

DRAGON ARMS
Antarctic Press 2002
1 48-pg. 4.95
2 thru 6 .... @3.50
Pocket Manga TPB Vol. 1 ..... 10.00

DRAGONBALL
Viz Communications, 1998
1 (of 12) by Akira Toriyama ... 8.00
2 thru 4 .... @5.00
5 thru 12 .... @3.00
TPB Vol. 1 .... 14.95
TPB Vol. 2 rep. #7–#12. ..... 14.95

PART TWO, 1999
1 (of 15) by Akira Toriyama ... 5.00
2 thru 4 .... @4.00
5 thru 15 .... @3.00
TPB Vol. 3 rep.Vol.2 #3–#8. . . . 14.95
TPB Vol. 4 rep.Vol.2 #7–#13. . . 14.95

PART THREE, 2000
1 (of 14) by Akira Toriyama ... 3.00
2 thru 5 .... @3.00
8 thru 14 .... @3.00

PART FOUR, 2001
1 thru 4 (of 10). .... @3.00
5 thru 10 .... @3.00

PART FIVE, 2002
1 (of 7) 3.00
2 thru 6 .... @3.00
7 .... 2.95

Part 6
1 .... 3.50
2 .... 3.50
TPB Vol. 11 thru Vol. 13 ..... @7.95
TPB Vol. 1 thru 7 2nd print ... @7.95

DRAGONBALL Z
Viz Communications, 1998
1 (of 9) by Akira Toriyama 13.00

Comics Values Annual

Dragonball Z, Part 2, #10
© Viz Communications

2 thru 9 .... @5.00
TPB Vol. 1 .... 14.95
TPB Vol. 2 .... 14.95

PART TWO (1998)
1 (of 14) by Akira Toriyama 4.00
2 thru 9 .... @3.50
10 thru 14 .... @3.50
TPB Vol. 3 .... 14.95
TPB Vol. 4 .... 14.95

PART THREE (1999)
1 (of 10) by Akira Toriyama ... 3.50
2 thru 10 .... @3.00
TPB Vol. 5, Part 3, #1–#6 . . . . 12.95
TPB Vol. 6, Part 3, #7–#11 . . . . 12.95

PART 4 (2000)
1 thru 13 (of 15). .... @3.00

PART 5 (2001)
1 (of 12) 3.00
2 thru 10 .... @3.00
TPB Vol. 7 thru Vol. 10 . . . . . . @12.95
TPB Vol. 11 thru Vol. 12 . . . . . @7.95
TPB Vol. 1 thru Vol. 7 2nd print . . @7.95

DRAGONFORCE
Aircel, 1988
1 DK 6.00
2 thru 7 DK .... @4.00
8 thru 12 .... @4.00
13 .... 2.00

DRAGONFORCE CHRONICLES
Aircel, 1988
Vol. 1 thru Vol. 5 rep. ...... @2.95

DRAGON HUNTER
Tokyopop Press 2003
GN Vol. 1 (of 9) 10.00
GN Vol. 2 thru Vol. 3 .... @10.00

DRAGON KNIGHTS
Tokyopop Press, 2001
1 by Mineko Ohkami 3.00
2 thru 6 .... @3.00
GN Vol. 1 (of 17) authentic manga 10.00
GN Vol. 2 thru 11 .... @10.00

CVA Page 718 — All comics prices listed are for *Near Mint* condition.

DRAGONMIST
Raised Brow Publications
1 I:Dragonmist.............. 2.75
2 F:Assassin................ 2.75

DRAGON OF THE VALKYR
Rak
1 .... 2.00
2 thru 4 .... @2.00

DRAGON QUEST
Silverwolf
1 TV 15.00
2 TV 7.50
3 TV 6.50

DRAGONRING
[1st Series]
1 B.Blair,rare 110.00
Aircel, 1986
1 .... 3.50
2 .... 2.00
3 thru 6 .... @2.00
See Also Color Comics

DRAGONTOK SAGA
Hanthercraft
1 thru 10 .... @2.50

DRAGON WARS
Ironcat, 1998
1 by Ryukihei 2.95
2 thru 11 .... @2.95
TPB Vol. 1 .... 17.95

DRAGON WEEKLY
1 Southern Knights 2.00
2 and 3 .... @2.00

DREAD OF NIGHT
Hamilton
1 Horror story collection... 3.95
2 Json, inc.'Genocide'..... 3.95

DREAM ANGEL AND ANGEL GIRL
Angel Entertainment, 1998
1 .... 2.95

DREAM ANGEL: THE QUANTUM DREAMER
Angel Entertainment, 1997
1 by Mort Castle & Adriana Melo .. 2.95
2 .... 2.95

DREAM ANGEL: WORLD WITHOUT END
Angel Entertainment, 1998
1 Dream world cover 3.00

DREAMERY
Eclipse, 1986
1 thru 13 .... @2.25

DREAMGIRL
Angel Entertainment, 1996
0 by David Campitti & Al Rio 2.95

B & W PUB.

1 .... 2.95
1 deluxe 5.95
1 Manga cover 5.00

DREAMLANDS
Caliber ìNew Worldsî, 1996
1 .... 2.95
2 flip book with Boston Bombers #3 2.95

DREAMTIME
Blind Rat, 1995
1 Young Deserter........... 2.95
2 Gypsy Trouble 2.50

Dreamwalker #1
© *Caliber*

DREAMWALKER
Caliber Tapestry, 1997
1 thru 4 .... @3.00
5 by Jenni Gregory, 2nd story arc.. 3.00
6 2nd story arc, concl..... 3.00

DREAMWALKER: CAROUSEL
Avatar, 1998
0 .... 3.00
1 by Jenni Gregory 3.00
2 conclusion 3.00

DREAMWALKER: SUMMER RAIN
Avatar, 1999
1 by Jenni Gregory 3.00

DREAMWALKER: AUTUMN LEAVES
Avatar, 1999
1 by Jenni Gregory 3.00
2 conclusion 3.00

DREAMWOLVES
Dramenon Studios, 1994
1 .... 3.00
2 .... 3.00
3 F:Desiree 3.00
4 V:Venefica 3.00
5 V:Venefica 3.00
6 R:Carnifax 3.00

Dragonmist–Eagle

7 .... 3.00
8 F:Wendy Bascum 3.00

DRIFTERS
Infinity Graphics, 1986
1 .... 2.00

DRYWALL AND OSWALD SHOW, THE
Fireman Press, 1998
1 by Mandy Carter,Trent Kaniuga . 2.95

DUNGEONEERS
Silverwolf, 1986
1 thru 8 .... @2.00

DUNGEONS & DRAGONS: BLACK & WHITE
Kenzer & Company, 2002
1 (of 8) by J.Limke & R.Pereira ... 3.00
2 thru 6 .... @3.00

DUNGEONS & DRAGONS IN SHADOW OF DRAGONS
Kenzer & Company, 2001
1 (of 8) The Last of My Father 2.95
2 thru 4 .... @2.95
5 thru 8 .... @3.00

DWELLING, THE
Chaos! Comics/Black Label Graphics, 2002
Ashcan 6.00
1 BnP 5.00
1a premium edition 10.00
1b super premium edition .. 20.00
1c signed edition 15.00
Spec. #1 script edition 5.00
Spec. #1 premium script edition .. 20.00

EAGLE
Crystal, 1986
1 .... 3.00
1a signed & limited 5.00
2 thru 5 .... @2.75
6 thru 11 .... @2.50
12 .... 2.50
13 thru 17 .... @2.50
Apple, 1988
18 thru 26 .... @2.00

EAGLE
Viz Communications, 2000
1 (of 14) The Candidate,112-pg. .. 6.95
2 Scandal 6.95
3 The Vice-President....... 6.95
4 New Hampshire 6.95
5 On the Battlefield 6.95
6 King of New York 6.95
7 Pandora's Box 6.95
8 The Debate 6.95
9 Passion 6.95
10 Gone to Texas........... 6.95
11 Super Tuesday 6.95
12 Suspicion............... 6.95
13 Illegitimate child...... 6.95
14 Confession 6.95
15 The Nomination 6.95
16 The General 6.95
17 Coming Home 6.95
18 Frame Up 6.95
19 Fires in the Plain 6.95

Eagle–Elford / B & W PUB.

20 Someone You Can Trust 6.95
21 End of the Trail 6.95
22 Father & Son 6.95
TPB Vol. 1 424-pg. 19.95
TPB Vol. 2 .... 19.95
TPB Vol. 3 416-pg. 19.95
TPB Vol. 4 512-pg. 22.95

EAGLE: DARK MIRROR
Comic Zone
1 A:Eagle, inc reps 2.75
2 In Japan, V:Lord Kagami 2.75
3 .... 2.95
4 .... 2.95

EAGLES DARE
Aager Comics, 1994
1 thru 4 .... 2.00
5 V:Dragon 2.00

EARTH LORE: LEGEND OF BEK LARSON
Eternity
1 .... 1.80

EARTH LORE: REIGN OF DRAGON LORD
1 .... 1.80
2 .... 1.75

EARTH WAR
Newcomers Publishing, 1995
1 and 2 from Newcomers Illus. ... 2.95

EARTH: YEAR ZERO
Eclipse
1 thru 4 .... @2.00

EAT-MAN
Viz Communications, 1997
1 (of 6) by Akihito Yoshitami 2.95
2 thru 6 .... @2.95
Vol.1 Full Course Meal,rep.Pt.1. . . 15.95
PART TWO, 1998
1 (of 5) by Akihito Yoshitami 2.95
2 (of 5) 3.50
3 thru 5 .... @3.25
TPB Vol. 2 Second Course 15.95

EB'NN THE RAVEN
Now
1 .... 5.00
2 .... 3.00
3 .... 2.50
4 .... 2.00
5 thru 9 .... @2.00

EBONIX-FILES, THE
Blatant Comics, 1998
1A TV parody, cover A 3.95
1B TV parody, cover B 3.95

EDDIE CAMPELL'S BACCHUS
Eddie Campell Comics, 1995
1 V:Telchines 7.00
1 2nd printing 3.00
2 thru 10 V:Telchines 4.00
11 thru 26 ECa .... @3.00
27 thru 37 ECa .... @3.00
38 thru 46 .... @3.00

47 thru 56 .... @3.00
57 thru 60 .... @3.00
GN Collected Bacchus, Vol. 1 .... 9.95
GN Collected Bacchus, Vol. 2 .... 9.95
GN Collected Bacchus, Vol. 3,
   Doing the Islands 17.95
GN Collected Bacchus, Vol. 4,
   One Man Show 8.50
GN Collected Bacchus, Vol. 5
   Earth, Air, Water & Fire 9.95
GN Collected Bacchus, Vol. 6
   1001 Nights of Bacchus 9.95
GN Collected Bacchus, Vol. 9,
   King Bacchus 12.95
TPB 1001 Nights of Bacchus 13.50
TPB King Bacchus 13.95

EDDY CURRENT
Mad Dog, 1987
1 thru 12 .... @2.00

EDGAR ALLAN POE
Eternity, 1988
1 Black Cat 2.50
2 Pit & Pendulum 2.00
3 Masque of the Red Death...... 2.00
4 Murder in the Rue Morgue 2.00
5 Tell Tale Heart 2.00

EDGE
1 .... 3.00
Vol 2 #1 thru #3 .... @3.00
Vol 2 #4 thru #6 .... @2.00

Eightball #7
© Fantagraphics

EIGHTBALL
Fantagraphics, 1989
1 .... 13.00
2 .... 8.00
3 .... 7.00
4 .... 6.00
1a thru 4a later printings ...... @3.00
5 thru 8 .... @6.00
9 thru 10 .... @4.00
11 A:Ghost World 4.00
12 F:Ghost World 4.00
13 thru 17 .... @4.00
18 .... 4.00
19 .... 4.00
20 .... 5.00
21 48-pg. 5.00
TPB Orgy Bound, rep. #7–#14 ... 14.95

TPB Lout Rampage 14.95
TPB Pussey 8.95
TPB Velvet glove cast in iron ... 16.95
TPB Caricature 16.95

ELECTRIC GIRL
Mighty Gremlin, 1998
1 .... 3.50
2 thru 9 .... @2.95
AIT/Planet Lar, 2002
10 by Mike Brennan 2.95
TPB Vol. 1 .... 9.95
TPB Vol. 2 152-pg. 13.95

ELFORD
Aircel, 1986
1 I:Hawk 5.00
1a 2nd printing 3.50
2 .... 3.00
2a 2nd printing 2.00
3 V:Doran 3.00
4 V:Doran 3.00
5 V:Doran 2.00
6 V:Nendo 2.00
Compilation Book 4.95
(Vol 2), #1 to #24, see Color
25 thru 31 .... @2.00
32 .... 2.50

ELFORD
[3rd Series]
Nightwynd
1 .... 2.50
2 thru 4 .... @2.50

ELFORD
Warp Graphics, 1997
1 (of 4) by Barry Blair & Colin Chan 2.95
2 thru 4 .... @2.95

ELFORD: ALL THE LONELY PLACES
Warp Graphics, 1997
1 (of 4)Barry Blair & Colin Chan. .. 2.95
Becomes:
HAWK AND WINDBLADE: ALL THE LONELY PLACES
2 (of 2) 2.95

ELFORD CHRONICLES
Aircel, 1990
1 (of 12) thru 8 rep B.Blair ..... @2.50

ELFORD CUTS LOOSE
Warp Graphics, 1997
1 by Barry Blair and Colin Chan. . . 2.95
2 F:Hawk Erik-san 2.95
3 .... 2.95
4 all out attack 2.95
5 north to safety 2.95
6 homeward 2.95
7 back to Greenhaven 2.95
8 Greenhaven Siege 2.95
9 Felines, Nothing More Than
   Felines 2.95

ELFORD: HAWK
China Winds, 1998
1-shot by Barry Blair and
   Colin Chan 3.50

B & W PUB.

ELFLORE: THE HIGH SEAS
Raw Comics
4 by Barry Blair (500 copies) 4.50

ELFQUEST
Warp Graphics, 1979–85
1 WP 30.00
1a WP,2nd printing 10.00
1b WP,3rd printing 5.00
1c WP,4th printing (1989) 4.00
2 WP 15.00
2a WP,2nd printing 4.00
3 WP 12.00
3a WP,2nd printing 4.00
4 WP 12.00
4a WP,2nd printing 4.00
5 WP 12.00
5a WP,2nd printing 4.00
6 WP 12.00
6a WP,2nd printing 4.00
7 WP 10.00
8 WP 10.00
9 WP 10.00
2a thru 9a WP,later printings . . . @3.00
10 thru 15 . . . . @5.00
16 WP,I:DistantSoil 8.00
17 thru 21 WP . . . . @5.00
TPB Gatherum 19.95

ELFQUEST
Warp Graphics, 1996
4 thru 14 ed. RPi . . . . @5.00
15 . . . . 5.50
16 What if Cutter never
   became chief 5.50
17 F:Fire-Eye 5.50
18 Dreamtime, concl. 5.50
19 Wolfrider begins 5.50
20 . . . . 5.50
21 20th anniv. 5.50
22 F:Wolfrider 5.00
23 F:WaveDancers 5.00
24 F:Wolfrider 5.00
25 F:Wolfrider 5.00
26 Wild Hunt 5.00
27 . . . . 5.00
28 F:Ember & Teir 5.00
29 three new stories 5.00
30 new stories 5.00
31 new stories 5.00
32 Wild Hunt,pt.1, 24-pg. 3.50
33 Wild Hunt,pt.2 . . . . 3.50
34 Wild Hunt,pt.3 . . . . 3.50
35 Wild Hunt,pt.4 . . . . 3.50
Spec.#1 Worldpool,pt.1 (1997) . . . 3.50
Spec.#2 Worldpool,pt.2 (1997) . . . 3.50
READERS COLLECTIONS
TPB Vol.1 Fire & Flight 11.95
TPB Vol.2 The Forbidden Grove . . 11.95
TPB Vol.3 Captives of
   Blue Mountain 11.95
TPB Vol.4 Quest's End 11.95
TPB Vol.5 Siege at Blue Mountain 11.95
TPB Vol.6 Secret of Two-Edge . . 11.95
TPB Vol.7 Cry From Beyond 11.95
TPB Vol.8 Kings of the
   Broken Wheel 11.95
TPB Vol.8A Dreamtime 11.95
TPB Vol.8B In All But Blood 16.95
TPB Vol.9 Rogue's Curse 13.95
TPB Vol.9A Wolfrider 11.95
TPB Vol.9B Blood of Ten Chiefs . . 12.95
TPB Vol.9C Kahvi 13.95
TPB Vol.11A Huntress 11.95
TPB Vol.11B Ascent 12.95
TPB Vol.11C Shadowstalker 12.95
TPB Vol.12 Ascent 12.95
TPB Vol.12A Reunion 12.95
TPB Vol.13A Rebels 11.95
TPB Vol.13B Junk 11.95
TPB Vol.14 JINK 11.95
TPB Vol.14A Skyward Shadow . . 11.95
TPB Vol.14B Mindcoil 11.95
TPB Vol.15 Forevergreen 12.95
TPB Vol.15A Dreams End 12.95
TPB Vol.15B Phoenix 13.95
TPB Vol.16 Wave Dancers 11.95
TPB Vol.`?' Worldpool 12.95
TPB The Rebels, 176-pg. 11.95
GN Shards 13.95
GN Legacy (Hidden Years
   #16–#22) 11.95
GN A Gift of Her Own 16.95
TPB Wolfrider's Guide, revised . . 16.95
Spec. Metamorphosis, WP,
   RPi (1996) 2.95
Spec. Elfquest: Wolfrider 2.95
Summer Spec. 2001 Recognition . . 2.95
Summer Spec. 2001 Wolfshadow . . 3.95

ELFQUEST: KAHVI
Warp Graphics, 1995
1 thru 6 I:Kahvi . . . . @2.25

ELFQUEST: KINGS OF THE BROKEN WHEEL
Warp Graphics, 1990–92
1 WP 2.25
2 thru 9 WP . . . . @2.25

Elfquest: Seige at Blue Mountain #1
© *Warp Graphics*

ELFQUEST: SEIGE AT BLUE MOUNTAIN
Warp Graphics/Apple Comics, 1987–88
1 WP,JSo 9.00
1a 2nd printing 3.00
2 WP 6.00
2a 2nd printing 3.00
3 WP 5.00
3a 2nd printing 2.00
4 thru 8 WP . . . . @5.00

ELFQUEST: TWO SPEAR
Warp Graphics, 1995
1 thru 3 (of 5) Two-Spears past . @2.25

ELFQUEST: WORLDPOOL
Warp Graphics, 1997
Spec.#1 (of 2) 2.95
Spec.#2 (of 2) 2.95

ELFTREK
Dimension, 1986
1 Elfquest's Star Trek parody 2.00
2 . . . . 2.00

ELF WARRIOR
Adventure, 1987
1 . . . . 3.00
2 . . . . 2.50
3 thru 5 . . . . @2.00

EL HAZARD: THE MAGNIFICENT WORLD
Viz Communications, 2000
1 by Hidetomo Tsubura 2.95
2 . . . . 2.95
3 thru 5 . . . . @2.95
Part 2, 2001
1 thru 5 . . . . @2.95
Part 3, 2001
1 thru 5 (of 6) . . . . @2.95
6 . . . . 2.95
TPB Vol. 1 . . . . 15.95
TPB Vol. 2 . . . . 15.95
TPB Vol. 3 . . . . 15.95

ELIMINATOR
Eternity
1 `Drugs in the Future' 2.50
2 . . . . 2.50

ELVIRA, MISTRESS OF THE DARK
Claypool Comics, 1993
1 . . . . 7.00
2 thru 35 . . . . @4.00
36 thru 74 photo covers . . . . . . @3.50
75 Mistress of the Jungle,pt.1 . . . 3.50
76 Mistress of the Jungle,pt.2 . . . 3.50
77 Rome on the Range 3.50
78 thru 90 photo covers . . . . . . @3.50
91 thru 103 . . . . @3.00
104 thru 127 . . . . @3.00
TPB Elvira, Mistress of the Dark . . 12.95
TPB Vol. 2 Double Delights 12.95

ELVIRA
Eclipse
1 Rosalind Wyck 2.50

EMBRACE
London Night, 1996
1 NC17 edition, EHr, signed 10.00

EMBRACE: HUNGER OF THE FLESH
London Night, 1997
1 DQ,last of the original
   vampire race 3.00
1a DQ,deluxe 6.00
1b signed by Kevin West 15.00
2 DQ 3.00
2a DQ,deluxe 6.00
3 by Dan Membiela & Kevin
   West, concl. 3.00

All comics prices listed are for *Near Mint* condition.

EMERALDAS
Eternity, 1990
1 thru 4 .... @2.25

EMMA DAVENPORT
Lohamn Hill Press, 1995
1 I:Emma Davenport 2.75
2 .... 2.75
3 O:Hammerin Jim 2.75
4 Cookie Woofer War 2.75

EMPIRE
Eternity, 1988
1 thru 4 .... @2.00

EMPTY ZONE
Sirius, 1998
1 by Jason Alexander 3.00
1a limited edition 5.00
2 .... 2.50
3 .... 2.50
4 .... 2.50
TPB 11.95
TPB Vol. 2 .... 16.95
VOL. 2 TRANSMISSIONS, 1999
1 by Jason Alexander 2.95
2 thru 7 .... @2.95
8 History Lessions,pt.1 .... 2.95

EMPTY ZONE: CONVERSATIONS WITH THE DEAD
Sirius Entertainment, 2002
1 (of 5) by Jason Alexander...... 2.95
2 thru 3 .... @2.95

ENCHANTED
Sirius, 1997
1 (of 3) by Robert Chang........ 2.95
2 .... 2.95
3 concl....................... 2.95

ENCHANTED VALLEY
Blackthorne
1 .... 2.00
2 .... 2.00

Enchanted Valley #1
© Blackthorne

ENCHANTER
Eclipse, 1987
1 thru 3 .... @2.50

ENCHANTER: APOCALYPSE WIND NOVELLA
Entity
1 Foil Enhanced Cover 2.95

ENFORCERS
Dark Visions Publishing, 1995
0 From Anthology Title.......... 2.50

ENNIS AND MCCREA'S BIGGER DICKS
Avatar Press, 2002
1 (of 4) GEn,JMC,F:Dougie & Ivor . 4.95
1a Guaranteed to Offend cover ... 4.95
2 thru 4 .... @4.95
2a thru 4a offensive (c) .... @4.95

ENNIS AND MCCREA'S DICKS 2
Avatar Press, 2002
1 (of 4) 3.50
2 thru 4 .... @3.50
1a thru 4a offensive (c) .... @3.95
X-Mas Spec. #1 .... 3.50
X-Man Spec. #1 offensive (c) 3.95

ENTITY
Avatar
? Nira X cover................. 5.95
? Snowman cover 10.95
? Nira X silver cover 10.95
? Snowman silver cover........ 15.95

ENTROPY TALES
Entropy
1 .... 2.00
2 Domino Chance 2.00
3 thru 5 .... @2.00

EPSILON WAVE
Elite
1 .... 3.00
2 .... 2.00
3 thru 5 .... @1.60

EQUINE THE UNCIVILIZED
GraphXpress
1 .... 4.00
2 .... 2.50
3 thru 6 .... @2.00

EQUINOX CHRONICLES
Innovation, 1991
1 I:Team Equinox, Black Avatar . . . 2.25
2 Black Avatar Plans US conquest. 2.25

ERADICATORS
Greater Mercury, 1990–91
1 RLm (1st Work) 5.00
1a 2nd printing 1.50
2 .... 2.50
3 Vigil 2.00
4 thru 8 .... @1.50

ERIC PRESTON IS THE FLAME
B-Movie Comics, 1987
1 Son of G.A.Flame............ 2.00

ESCAPE TO THE STARS
Visionary
1 thru 7 .... @2.00
[2nd Series]
1 and 2 .... @2.00

ESCAPE VELOCITY
Escape Velocity Press, 1986
1 and 2 .... @2.00

ESMERALDAS
Eternity
1 thru 4 .... 2.25

ESP
Curtis Comics, 2002
Vol. 1 Manga
1 by Jihoon Park & Takyoung Lee . 2.95
2 thru 5 .... @2.95
Vol. 2
1 .... 2.95

ESPERS
Halloween Comics, 1996
1 JHI, R:ESPers 3.00
1 JHI,signed 3.00
2 JHI,signed 3.00
3 JHI, ... 3.00
3 JHI,signed 3.00
4 thru 6 JHI, conclusion .... @3.00
Volume 2
1 `Undertow' 2.95
2 .... 2.95

ESP ULTRA
Komics, Inc., 1999
TPB Vol. 1 .... 8.95
TPB Vol. 2 thru Vol. 7 .... @8.95

ETERNITY TRIPLE ACTION
Malibu B&W
1 F:Gazonga 2.00
2 F:Gigantor 2.50

EVENT PRESENTS THE ASH UNIVERSE
Event Comics, 1998
1-shot JQ,JP, 48pg 2.95

EVERETTE HARTSOE'S RAZOR
EH! Productions, 2000
1 .... 3.50
1a Ruby Foil 5.00
2 .... 3.95

EVIL ERNIE
Eternity, 1991–92
1 SHu,BnP,I&O:Evil Ernie,
   Lady Death................ 50.00
1a Spec. 1992 reprint, 16 extra
   pages................... 30.00

Comics Values Annual — B & W PUB. — Evil–Fantastic

2 Death & Revival of Ernie,
A:Lady Death, 1st (c) 30.00
3 Psycho Plague, A:Lady Death. . 28.00
4 A:Lady Death 22.00
5 A:Lady Death 20.00
TPB rep #1-5 . . . . 10.95

EVIL ERNIE
Chaos! Comics
1 thru 5 reprints . . . . @3.00
Spec. Youth Gone Wild, die-cut
cover, Director's cut 5.00
TPB Youth Gone Wild. 9.95
Chaos! Comics, 1996
1 encore presentation 3.00
2 thru 5 encore presentation 3.00
TPB Revenge. 12.95
Preview Book Depraved 5.00
Pieces of Me Script 4.95

EVIL ERNIE: THE HORROR
Chaos! Comics, 2002
Ashcan b&w 6.00
1 BnP 4.50
1a premium edition 10.00
1b signed edition 15.00
1c super-premium edition 20.00
Spec. Script edition. 5.00
Spec. Script Edition, premium. . . 20.00

EVIL ERNIE: MANHATTAN DEATH TRIP
Chaos! Comics, 2002
1 BnP 3.50
1a premium edition 10.00
1b super-premium edition 20.00
Spec. #1 script 5.00
Spec. #1 script, premium edition. . 20.00

EVIL ERNIE RETURNS
Chaos! Comics, 2001
1 BnP 4.00
1a premium edition 13.00
1b super premium edition 20.00
1c signed ed.. . . . . 15.00
Ashcan 6.00
Script #1 . . . . 5.00
Script #1 premium edition 20.00

EVIL ERNIE: YOUTH GONE WILD
Chaos! Comics, 2001
Script 25.00
Script, signed 35.00

EVIL EYE
Fantagraphics, 1998
1 by Richard Sala 3.00
2 Glass Scorpion,pt.2 . . . . 3.00
3 thru 7 . . . . @3.00
8 thru 10 . . . . @3.50

EXCEL SAGA
Viz Communications 2003
GN Vol. 1 . . . . 9.95
GN Vol. 2 thru Vol. 3 . . . . @9.95

EXIT
Caliber, 1995
1 I:New series 2.95
2 thru 4 `The Traitors,'pt.2–pt.4 . . 2.95
Epilogue. 2.95

GN rep. 320-pg. 19.95
GN rep. 160-pg. 14.95

Ex-Mutants #6
© Amazing Comics

EX-MUTANTS
Amazing Comics, 1986
1 AC/RLm 5.00
1a 2nd printing 2.00
2 and 3 . . . . @3.00
EC
4 and 5 . . . . @2.00
6 PP 2.00
7 . . . . 2.00
8 . . . . 2.00
Ann. #1 . . . . 2.00
Pin-Up Spec. #1 . . . . 2.00

EX-MUTANTS: THE SHATTERED EARTH CHRONICLES
Eternity, 1988
1 thru 3 . . . . @2.00
4 RLd(c) 2.75
5 RLd(c) 2.75
6 thru 14 . . . . @2.00
Winter Special #1 . . . . 2.00

EXPLORERS
Caliber Tapestry, 1997
1 . . . . 2.95
2 . . . . 2.95
3 `Nahuatl'. 2.95
4 `The Sky is Falling'. 2.95

EXTINCTIONERS
Shanda Fantasy Arts VOL 2, 1999
1 . . . . 2.95
2 thru 7 . . . . @2.95
8 . . . . 3.00
9 . . . . 3.00
10 48-pg. 5.00

EXTREMELY SILLY
Antarctic Press
1 . . . . 4.00
Vol. II, 1996
1 . . . . 2.00
2 . . . . 2.00

EYE OF MONGOMBO
Fantagraphics Books, 1990–91
1 . . . . 3.00
2 thru 7 . . . . @2.00

FAITH
Lightning Comics, 1997
1 (of 2) 2.95
1a variant cover. 2.95
1b Limited, cover A 9.95
1c Limited, cover B 9.95
1d signed & numbered 9.95
1 encore edition. 2.95
1a encore, cover B 2.95
1b deluxe encore edition, cover A . 9.95
1c deluxe encore edition, cover B . 9.95

FAKE
Tokyopop Press 2003
GN Vol. 1 (of 7) 10.00
GN Vol. 2 thru Vol. 4 . . . . @10.00

FANG: TESTAMENT
Sirius, 1997
1 by Kevin J. Taylor 2.50
2 . . . . 2.50
3 . . . . 2.50
4 (of 4) 2.50
TPB 11.95

FANGS OF THE WIDOW
London Night Studios, 1995
1 O:The Widow 3.00
1a platinum edition 5.00
2 Body Count 3.00
3 Emma Revealed. 3.00
4 and 5 . . . . @3.00
Ground Zero, 1995
7 thru 9 `Metal Gypsies,'pt.#1–#3 @3.00
10 thru 13 rep. Widow: Bound by
Blood #1–#4 + additional material . . 3.50
14 `Search and Destroy'pt.1 . . . . . 3.00
15 `Search and Destroy'pt.2 . . . . . 3.00
Ann. #1 Search and Destroy. . . . 5.95

FANTASCI
Warp Graphics-Apple, 1986
1 . . . . 2.50
2 and 3 . . . . @2.00
4 . . . . 4.00
5 thru 8 . . . . @2.00
9 `Apple Turnover'. 2.00

FANTASTIC ADVENTURES
1 thru 5 . . . . @2.00

FANTASTIC FABLES
Silver Wolf, 1987
1 and 2 . . . . @2.00

FANTASTIC PANIC
Antarctic, 1993–94
1 thru 8 Ganbear . . . . @2.75
Vol. 2, 1995
1 thru 4 . . . . @2.75
4 thru 9 . . . . @2.95
10 concl. 3.50

FANTASTIC STORIES
Basement Comics, 2001
1 F:Grakoom, the Forgotten God. . 2.95

Fantastic–Femforce — B & W PUB.

Fantastic Panic #4
© Antarctic

1a special edition............. 8.95
2 Lost Women of the Moon...... 2.95
2a special edition............. 8.95
3 .... 2.95
3a special edition............. 8.95

FANTASTIC WORLDS
Flashback Comics, 1995
1 Space Opera................. 2.95
2 F:Attu, Captain Courage...... 2.95

FANTASY QUARTERLY
Independent, 1976
1 1978 1st Elfquest........... 65.00

FART WARS: SPECIAL EDITION
Entity Comics, 1997
1 Star Wars trilogy parody,A:Nira X 2.75
1a Empire Attacks Back cover... 2.75
1b Return of the One-Eye cover... 2.75

FAR WEST
Antarctic Press, 1998
1 (of 4) by Richard Moore...... 2.95
2 thru 4 ....@3.00
VOL. 2
1 (of 4) 2.99
2 .... 2.50

FASTLANE ILLUSTRATED
Fastlane Studios, 1994
1 Super Powers & Hot Rods..... 2.50
2 & 3 ....@2.50

FATALIS
Caliber Core, 1998
1 by Mark Chadbourn
  & Vince Danks 2.95
1a signed & numbered 6.95
2 .... 2.95

FAT NINJA
Silver Wolf Comics, 1985–86
1 .... 2.50
2 Vigil 2.50
3 thru 8 ....@1.50

FAUST
Northstar, 1985
1 Vigil 25.00
1a Vigil,2nd Printing......... 5.00
1b Vigil,3rd Printing......... 2.00
1c Tour Edition 25.00
2 Vigil 15.00
2a Vigil,2nd Printing......... 3.00
2b Vigil,3rd Printing......... 2.50
3 Vigil 10.00
3a Vigil,2nd Printing......... 2.50
4 Vigil 5.00
5 Vigil 5.00
6 Vigil 5.00
Rebel Studios
7 Vigil 5.00
8 TV 3.50
9 TV,Love of the Damned 3.50
10 E:DQ(s),TV,Love o/t Damned... 3.50
VOL. II
1 TV,Love of the Damned 2.50

FAUST/777: THE WRATH
Avatar Press, 1998
0 by David Quinn & Tim Vigil,
  Darkness in Collision x-over... 3.00
0a wrap....................... 3.95
0b leather cover.............. 20.00
0c Royal Blue edition......... 60.00
0d Platinum edition 15.95
1 (of 4) 3.50
2 Darkness in Collision,pt.3 . 3.50
3 .... 3.50
4 .... 3.50
Faust Hornbook 4.95
TPB 112-pg.................... 16.95

FAUST: SINGHA'S TALONS
Avatar, 2000
1/2 .... 3.50
1/2 wraparound (c) 3.95
1/2 Beachum (c)............... 5.95
1/2 prism foil................ 12.95
1/2 royal blue edition........ 75.00
1/2 Blood Curse 5.00
1 (of 4) 3.95
1a wraparound (c) 4.50
1c red foil leather........... 25.00
1d prism foil................. 12.95
1 commemorative 5.95
2 thru 4 ....@3.95
2a thru 4a previews exclusives..@4.50
Preview Book 5.95

FELIX THE CAT B&W
Felix Comics, 1997
1 inc. Felix's Cafe 2.00
2 Crusin' for a Brusin' 2.00
3 Ah Choo..................... 2.00
4 inc. Spaced Out 2.00
5 Holiday/Winter issue........ 2.00
6 The Felix Force 2.25
7 A Rash of Trash 2.25
8 Halloween 2.25
Cat-A-Strophic Wrestling Spec.#1. 2.25
Felix Summer Splash #1........ 2.50

FELIX THE CAT TRUE CRIME STORIES
Felix Comics, 2000
1 .... 2.50
Spec.#1 Blockbuster movie
  bonanza..................... 2.50
Spec. Felix Jurassic Jamboree . 2.50
Spec. Felix Magic Bag of Tricks ... 2.50
Spec. Felix Laff-A-Palooza 2.50

FELIX THE CAT'S TV EXTRAVAGANZA
Felix Comics, 2002
1 .... 2.50

FEM FANTASTIQUE
AC Comics, 1988
1 .... 2.00

FEM FORCE
AC Comics, 1987
1 thru 15 See Color
16 I:Thunder Fox 3.00
17 F:She-Cat,Ms.Victory, giant . 3.00
18 double size 3.00
19 .... 3.00
20 V:RipJaw, Black Commando .. 3.00
21 V:Dr.Pretorius 3.00
22 V:Dr.Pretorius 3.00
23 V:Rad 3.00
24 A:Teen Femforce 3.00
25 V:Madame Boa 3.00
26 V:Black Shroud 3.00
27 V:Black Shroud 3.00
28 A:Arsenio Hall 3.00
29 V:Black Shroud 3.00
30 V:Garganta 3.00
31 I:Kronon Captain Paragon .. 3.00
32 V:Garganta 3.00
33 Personal Lives of team 3.00
34 V:Black Shroud 3.00
35 V:Black Shroud 3.00
36 giant,V:Dragonfly,Shade... 3.00
37 A:Blue Bulleteer,She-Cat .. 3.00
38 V:Lady Luger............... 3.00
39 F:She-Cat 3.00
40 V:Sehkmet................. 3.00
41 V:Captain Paragon 3.00
42 V:Alizarin Crimson 3.00
43 V:Glamazons of Galaxy G ... 3.00
44 V:Lady Luger,F:Garganta.... 5.00
45 Nightveil Rescued 3.00
46 V:Lady Luger............... 3.00
47 V:Alizarin Crimson 3.00
48 .... 3.00
49 I:New Msw.Victory 3.00
50 Ms.Victory Vs.Rad,flexi-disc... 3.00
51 .... 3.00
52 V:Claw & Clawites 3.00
53 I:Bulldog Deni,V:(Dick
  Briefer's)Frightenstein 3.00
54 The Orb of Bliss........... 3.00
55 R:Nightveil................ 3.00
56 V:Alizarin Crimson 3.00
57 thru 92 See Color
93 `Shattered Memories,'pt.2 . 3.00
93a deluxe 6.00
94 `Shattered Memories,'pt.3 . 3.00
94a deluxe 6.00
95 .... 3.00
95a deluxe 6.00
96 .... 3.00
96a deluxe 6.00
97 .... 3.00
98 deluxe 6.00
98 .... 3.00
98 deluxe 6.00
99 .... 3.00
99 deluxe 6.00
100 Anniv. issue, with poster..... 8.00
100A signed, with poster..... 12.00
100B no poster, not signed ... 4.00

THE YESTERDAY SYNDROME
101 Pt.1...................... 5.00
102 Pt.2...................... 5.00

CVA Page 724 — All comics prices listed are for *Near Mint* condition.

B & W PUB.

RETURN FROM THE ASHES
103 Pt.3 . . . . 5.00
104 pt.1 Firebeam, 44pg. 5.00
105 pt.2 . . . . 5.00
106 pt.3 concl. 5.00

DARKGODS: RAMPAGE
107 Darkgods: Rampage,pt.1 . . . . 5.00
108 Darkgods: Rampage,pt.2 . . . . . 5.00
109 Darkgods: Rampage,pt.3 . . . . . 6.00
110 thru 117 . . . . @5.95
118 44-pg. 6.95
118a spec. edition, 60-pg. 9.95
119 The Missing Mask 6.95
120 Superbabes,pt.1 . . . . 6.95
121 Superbabes,pt.2 . . . . 6.95
121a Femme Noir (c) 9.95
122 Superbabes,pt.3 . . . . 6.95
122a spec. editions, variant(c). . . @9.95
Spec.#1 FemForce Timelines,
 O:Femforce (1995) 2.95
Spec.#1 FemForce:Frightbook,
 Horror tales by Briefer,
 Ayers, Powell 2.95
Spec.#2 (2001) 5.95
Spec.#1 Femforce:Uncut (2001) . . . 9.95
Untold Origin of FemForce 4.95
GN The Capricorn Chronicles . . . 12.50
GN FemForce: Timestorm 9.95
GN, FemForce: Timestorm, deluxe 14.95
TPB Origins 12.95
TPB Origins, signed 13.95
TPB Sisters in Sin, lim. ed. 21.95
Secret Files of Femforce, deluxe. . . 4.95
Pulp Fiction Portfolio #2 . . . . 18.00
Spec. #1 Femforce vs. The Claw . . 6.95
Spec. #1 Rampaging She-Cat 6.95

FEMFORCE SPECIAL
AC Comics, 1999
1 Femforce Special: Rayda–
 The Cyberian Connection 2.95
1a Variant cover 2.95
1b Variant cover, signed 9.95
2 . . . . 2.95
3 conclusion 3.95

FEVER, THE
Dark Vision Publishing
1 O:The Fever. 2.50
2 Fever's Father 2.50

FIFTIES TERROR
Eternity, 1988
1 thru 6 . . . . @2.00

FIGHTING YANK
AC Comics, 2001
1 by Hack Koilby 5.95
2 thru 5 . . . . @5.95

FINAL CYCLE
Sirius
Graphic Novel 4.00
1 thru 4 . . . . @2.00

FINDER
Lightspeed Comics, 1996
1 thru 5 by Carla Speed McNeil . @2.95
6 thru 19 . . . . @2.95
20 thru 24 . . . . @2.95
25 thru 33 . . . . @2.95
TPB Vol. 1 Sin Eater 15.95
TPB Vol. 2 Sin-Eater 19.95
TPB Vol. 3 King of the Cats 13.95
TPB Vol. 4 Talisman 13.95
TPB Vol. 5 Dream Sequence . . . 20.95

FINDER FOOTNOTES
Lightspeed Press
1 thru 4 . . . . @6.00

FIRE TEAM
Aircel, 1990
1 thru 3 by Don Lomax. . . . . @2.50
4 V:Vietnamese Gangs 2.50
5 Cam in Vietnam 2.50
6 . . . . 2.50

FIRST WAVE
Andromeda Entertainment, 2001
1 Patriot or Traitor 3.00
1a signed 10.00
GN Through Alien Eyes 7.95

FIRST WAVE: DOUBLE VISION
Andromeda Entertainment, 2001
1 (of 2) 3.00
1a photo (c). 3.00

FIRST WAVE: GENESIS OF A GENIUS
Andromeda Entertainment, 2001
Spec. painted (c) 3.00
Spec. photo (c). 3.00

FISH POLICE
Fishwrap Productions, 1985
1 1st printing 7.00
1a 2nd printing 3.00
Becomes:

INSPECTOR GILL OF THE FISH POLICE
2 . . . . 5.00
3 thru 11 . . . . @4.00
[Vol 2]
Comico Publ., 1987
5 thru 12 . . . . @3.50
13 thru 17 see Color issues

Inspector Gill of the Fish Police@2
© Fishwrap Productions

Apple Publ.
18 thru 24 . . . . @2.50

FISH SHTICKS
Apple, 1991
1 and 2 Fish Police . . . . @2.75
3 and 4 . . . . @2.50

FIST OF GOD
Eternity, 1988
1 thru 4 . . . . @2.00

FIST OF THE BLUE SKY
Gutsoon! Entertainment 2003
TPB Vol. 1 . . . . 9.95
TPB Vol. 2 thru Vol. 3 . . . . @9.95

FIST OF THE NORTH STAR
Viz Select, 1996
1 thru 3 . . . . @3.25
4 . . . . 2.00
5 . . . . 3.25
6 . . . . 2.95
7 . . . . 2.95
TPB Vol. 2 Night of the Jackal, rep.16.95
Part Three
1 thru 5 by Buronson
 & Tetsuo Hara . . . . @2.95
Part Four, 1996
1 thru 7 . . . . @2.95
TPB Volume 2: Southern Cross . . 16.95

FLAG FIGHTERS
Ironcat, 1997
1 by Masaomi Kanzaki 2.95
2 Student Flagger,pt.1 . . . . 2.95
3 Student Flagger,pt.2 . . . . 2.95
4 Student Flagger,pt.3 . . . . 2.95
5 . . . . 2.95
6 Death Window 2.95
7 F:Murasame 2.95

FLAMING CARROT
Aardvark–Vanaheim, 1984
1 1981 Killian Barracks 50.00
1a 1984 . . . . 25.00
2 . . . . 25.00
3 . . . . 20.00
4 thru 6 . . . . @15.00
Renegade
7 . . . . 12.00
8 . . . . 10.00
9 . . . . 8.00
10 . . . . 8.00
11 and 12 . . . . @6.00
13 thru 15 . . . . @5.00
15a variant without cover price 8.00
16 and 17 . . . . @5.00
See: Dark Horse

FLARE
Hero Graphics
1 thru 8 . . . . @3.95
9 F:Sparkplug 3.95
10 thru 12 . . . . 2.95

FLARE ADVENTURES
Hero Graphics, 1988
1 Rep 1st issue Flare 2.00

All comics prices listed are for Near Mint condition.

Flare–From

FLARE ADVENTURES/ CHAMPIONS CLASSICS
Becomes:
2 thru 15 . . . . @3.95

FLARE VS. TIGRESS
Hero Graphics
1 and 2 . . . . @3.50

FORBIDDEN KINGDOM
1 thru 11 . . . . @2.00

FORBIDDEN VAMPIRE TALES
Forbidden, 1997
0 . . . . 2.95
1 sexy vampire 2.95
2 thru 5 . . . . @2.95
6 . . . . 3.00
7 Bloodlust and Bust cover 3.00
Spec.#1 Vault of Innocents 3.95

FORBIDDEN WORLDS
ACG, 1996
1 SD,JAp,rep. 2.50

FORCE SEVEN
Lone Star Press, 1999
1 thru 7 . . . . @2.95

FORCE 10
Crow Comics
0 Ash Can Preview 75
1 I:Force 10. . . . . 2.50
2 Children of the Revolution,pt#2 . . 2.50
3 Against all Odds 2.50

FORETERNITY
Antarctic Press, 1997
1 by Rod Espinoza 2.95
2 and 3 . . . . @2.95

FOREVER WARRIORS
Aardwolf, 1996
1 (of 3) RTs,RB 2.95
2 RTs,RB. 2.95
3 RTs,RB, concl. 2.95

FOREVER WARRIORS
CFD, 1997
1 RB,RTs 2.95
2 RB,RTs,KN 2.95
3 RB,RTs, finale 2.95

FORTY WINKS
Oddjobs Limited, 1997
1 (of 4) by Sneed & Peters 2.95
2 Everything Right is Wrong Again. 2.95
3 Where Your Eyes Don't Go. 2.95
4 There Might be Giants 2.95
Peregrine Entertainment, 1998
Christmas Spec. 2.95
TV Party Spec. 2.95
Spec.#1 Buzzboy (2000). 2.95

FORTY WINKS: MR. HORRIBLE
Peregrine Entertainment, 2000
1 and 2 . . . . @2.95

B & W PUB.

FORTY WINKS: THE FABLED PIRATE QUEEN OF THE SOUTH CHINA SEA
Peregrine Entertainment, 1999
1 by Vincent Sneed & Martinez . . . 2.95
2 . . . . 2.95
3 . . . . 2.95

Four Kunoichi: Enter the Sinja #1B
© *Lightning Comics*

FOUR KUNOICHI: ENTER THE SINJA
Lightning Comics, 1997
1 . . . . 2.95

FOX COMICS
1 Spec. 2.95
25 . . . . 2.95
26 . . . . 3.50

FRANK
Fantagraphics
1 JWo 3.00
2 JWo 4.00
3 . . . . 4.00
4 . . . . 4.00
GN rep. from various sources 14.95
TPB Vol. 1, signed 14.95
Vol. 2 partial color. 16.95

FRANKENSTEIN
Eternity
1 thru 3 . . . . @2.00

FRANKIES FRIGHTMARES
1 Celebrates Frank 60th Anniv. . . . 2.00

FRANK THE UNICORN
Fish Warp
1 thru 7 . . . . @2.00

FREAK-OUT ON INFANT EARTHS
Blackthorne, 1987
1 Don Chin 2.00
2 Don Chin 2.00

Comics Values Annual

FREAKS
Monster Comics
1 Movie adapt 2.50
2 Movie adapt.cont. 2.50
3 thru 4 Movie adapt. . . . . @2.50

FRED THE POSSESSED FLOWER
Happy Predator, 1998
1 The Plant Behind the Scenes . . . 2.95
2 . . . . 2.95
3 Interview with a Demon 2.95
4 The People vs. Hell 2.95
5 . . . . 2.95
6 The Origin of Fred 2.95

FRENCH ICE
Renegade Press, 1987
1 thru 15 . . . . @2.00

FRIENDS
Renegade, 1987
1 thru 5 . . . . @2.00

FRIGHT
Eternity
1 thru 13 . . . . @2.00

FRINGE
Caliber
1 thru 7 . . . . @2.50

FROM BEYOND
Studio Insidio
1 Short stories-horror. 2.25
2 inc.Clara Mutilares 2.50
3 inc.The Experiment. 2.50
4 inc.Positive Feedback. 2.50

FROM HELL
Tundra, 1991
1 . . . . 20.00
1a 2nd printing 10.00
2 . . . . 12.00
Kitchen Sink Volume Three
1 AMo,ECa 10.00
2 AMo,ECa 7.00
2a 2nd printing 6.00
3 . . . . 7.00
3a 2nd printing 6.00
4 . . . . 7.00
4 new printing 5.00
5 . . . . 7.00
5 new printing 5.00
6 . . . . 7.00
7 . . . . 7.00
8 . . . . 7.00
8 AMo,ECa,new printing 5.00
9 AMo,ECa 7.00
9 new printing 5.00
10 AMo,ECa. 7.00
10 new printing. 5.00
Spec. Dance of the Gull Catchers . . 4.95

FROM THE DARKNESS
Adventure Comics, 1990
1 JBa 25.00
2 . . . . 30.00
3 and 4 . . . . @12.00

All comics prices listed are for *Near Mint* condition.

FROM THE DARKNESS II BLOOD VOWS
Cry For Dawn
1 R:Ray Thorn,Desnoires 12.00
2 V:Desnoires 8.00
3 . . . . 8.00

FROM THE VOID
1 1st B.Blair,1982 . . . . 75.00

FROST: THE DYING BREED
Caliber
1 thru 3 Vietnam Flashbacks . . . @2.95

F–III BANDIT
Antarctic Press, 1995
1 F:Akira, Yoohoo 2.95
2 F:Yukio 2.95
3 F:Were-Women 2.95
4 . . . . 2.95
5 Romeo & Juliet story 2.95
6 thru 8 . . . . @2.95

FUGITOID
Mirage
1 TMNT Tie-in 8.00

FULL METAL FICTION
London Night, 1997
1 EHr 4.00
1a Nun with a Gun edition 10.00
1b dark room edition cover 4.00
2 . . . . 4.00
2a signed 10.00
3 `Hellborne' concl. 4.00
4 . . . . 4.00
5 EHr 4.00
6 . . . . 4.00
7 . . . . 4.00
8 . . . . 4.00

FURIES
Carbon-Based, 1996
1 thru 6 . . . . @2.75

FURRLOUGH
Antarctic Press, 1991
1 Funny Animal Military stories . . . 3.00
2 thru 10 . . . . @2.50
11 thru 20 . . . . @2.75
21 thru 33 . . . . @2.75
34 . . . . 2.95
35 48pg 4.00
36 thru 40 . . . . @2.95
41 thru 51 . . . . @2.95
Best of Furlough, Vol.1 . . . . 4.95
Best of Furlough, Vol.2 . . . . 4.95
Radio Comix
52 thru 75 . . . . @2.95
76 thru 99 . . . . @2.95
100 80-pg. 5.95
101 . . . . 2.95
102 . . . . 2.95
103 thru 131 . . . . @3.00
Furrlough's Finest Vol. 1 . . . . 6.00

FURRY NINJA HIGH SCHOOL
Shanda Fantasy Arts, 2002
1 (of 2) x-over (self) parody 5.00
2 x-over, concl. 5.00

Furrlough #71
© Radio Comix

FURY
Aircel
1 thru 3 . . . . @1.70

FURY OF HELLINA, THE
Lightning Comics, 1995
1 V:Luciver 3.50
1a limited & signed 8.00
1b platinum 8.00

FUSHIGI YUGI
Viz Communications, 1999
TPB by Yu Watase 15.95
TPB Vol. 2 Oracle 15.95
TPB Vol. 3 Disciple 15.95
TPB Vol. 5 Rival 15.95
TPB Vol. 6 Summoner 15.95
TPB Vol. 7 Castaway 15.95
TPB Vol. 8 . . . . 9.95
TPB Vol. 9 The Mysterious Play . . 9.95
TPB The Art of Fushigi Yugi 22.95

FUSION
Eclipse, 1987
1 . . . . 2.50
2 thru 17 . . . . @2.00

FUTABA-KUN CHANGE
Ironcat, 1998
1 by Hiroshi Aro 2.95
2 thru 6 . . . . @2.95
GN Vol. 1 . . . . 15.95
VOL. 2
1 . . . . 2.95
2 thru 6 . . . . @2.95
VOL. 3, 1999
1 . . . . 2.95
2 thru 6 . . . . @2.95
TPB Vol. 3 . . . . 15.95
VOL. 4, 2000
1 . . . . 2.95
2 thru 6 . . . . @2.95
VOL. 5, 2000
1 by Hiroshi Aro 2.95
2 thru 6 . . . . @2.95
VOL. 6, 2001
1 . . . . 2.95
2 thru 6 . . . . @2.95

TPB Vol. 4 . . . . 15.95
TPB Vol. 5 rep. 15.95
VOL. 7, 2001
1 . . . . 2.95
2 thru 6 . . . . @2.95
VOL. 8
1 thru 6 . . . . @2.95
TPB Vol. 5 . . . . 15.95
TPB Vol. 7 . . . . 15.95
TPB Vol. 8 . . . . 15.95

FUTURAMA
Slave Labor, 1989
1 thru 4 . . . . @2.50

FUTURETECH
Mushroom Comics, 1995
1 Automotive Hi-Tech 3.50
2 Cyber Trucks 3.50

FUTURIANS
Aardwolf, 1995
0 DC R:Futurians, sequel to
 Lodestone color series 2.95
0 second printing, DC 2.95

G-GUNDAM
Tokyopop Press 2003
GN Vol. 1 . . . . 10.00
GN Vol. 2 thru 3 . . . . @10.00

GAIJIN
Caliber, 1990
1-shot, 64pg. 3.50
1 thru 3 . . . . @2.00

GALAXION
Helikon, 1997
1 by Tara Jenkins, science fiction. . 2.75
2 . . . . 2.75
3 . . . . 2.75
4 Choices 2.75
5 . . . . 2.75
6 Communication 2.75
7 Song of Hiawatha 2.75
8 Persuasion 2.75
9 Deal with the Devil 2.75
10 . . . . 2.75
11 . . . . 2.75
Spec. #1, 16pg. 1.00
GN Vol 1 . . . . 15.95
Spec. Flip Book Galaxion
 & Amy Unbound 2.75

GALAXY EXPRESS
Viz Communications, 1998
TPB Vol. 1 232-pg. 16.95
TPB Vol. 2 . . . . 16.95
TPB Vol. 3 . . . . 16.95
TPB Vol. 4 . . . . 16.95
TPB Vol. 5 . . . . 18.95

GATEKEEPER
GK Publishing, 1987
1 . . . . 2.50
2 and 3 . . . . @2.95

GATES OF THE NIGHT
Jademan
1 thru 4 . . . . @3.50

GEAR
Fireman Press, 1998
1 (of 6) by Douglas TenNaple 2.95
2 thru 6 .... @2.95
TPB 14.95

GEISHA
Oni Press, 1998
1 (of 4) by Andi Watson 2.95
2 .... 2.95
3 .... 2.95
4 .... 2.95
TPB by Andi Watson 9.95

GEMS OF THE SAMURAI
Newcomers Publishing
1 I:Master Samurai 2.95

GENERIC COMIC BOOK
Comics Conspiracy, 2001
1 thru 4 .... @1.95
5 .... 1.95
5a Hyper Fanboy variant edition .. 5.95
6 thru 13 .... @1.95
TPB 8.95

GENOCYBER
Viz, 1993
1 I:Genocyber 2.75
2 thru 5 .... @2.75

GEOBREEDERS
CPM Manga, 1999
1 by Akhiro Ito 2.95
2 thru 6 .... @2.95
7 thru 20 .... @2.95
21 thru 33 .... @2.95
34 thru 36 .... @2.95
TPB Vol. 1 .... 15.95
TPB Vol. 2 rep. #8–#14 .... 15.95
TPB Vol. 3 .... 15.95
TPB Vol. 4 Unfriendly Skies 15.95
TPB #5 Big Trouble at Tokyo Tower... 15.95

GERIATRIC GANGRENE JUJITSU GERBILS
Planet X Productions
1 .... 2.50
2 .... 2.00

GHOSTS OF DRACULA
Eternity
1 A:Dracula & Houdini 2.50
2 A:Sherlock Holmes 2.50
3 A:Houdini 2.50
4 Count Dracula's Castle 2.50
5 Houdini, Van Helsing, Dracula team-up 2.50

GI GOVERNMENT ISSUED
Paranoid Press, 1994
1 thru 7 F:Mac, Jack .... @2.00

GIANT SHANDA ANIMAL
Shanda Fantasy Arts, 1998
1 .... 4.95
2 .... 4.95
3 .... 4.95
4 .... 4.50
5 .... 4.95
6 48-pg. 5.00

7 .... 5.00
8 .... 5.00

GIDEON HAWK
Big Shot Comics, 1995
1 I:Gideon Hawk, Max 9471..... 2.00
2 The Jewel of Shamboli,pt.2..... 2.00
3 The Jewel of Shamboli,pt.3..... 2.00
2 The Jewel of Shamboli,pt.4..... 2.50
3 The Jewel of Shamboli,pt.5..... 2.50

GIGANTOR
Antarctic Press, 2000
1 (of 12) by Ben Dunn 2.95
2 thru 8 .... @2.95

GIRL GENIUS
Studio Foglio, 2001
1 thru 5 .... @2.95
Airship Entertainment, 2002
6 thru 10 .... @3.95
TPB Vol. 1 Phil Foglio, 96-pg.... 10.00

GIRLS OF NINJA HIGH SCHOOL, 1997
Antarctic Press
Spec. 3.95
Spec. 1998 cover A 2.95
Spec. 1998 cover B 2.95
Spec. 1999 .... 3.00

GIZMO
Chance, 1986
1 .... 7.50

GIZMO
Mirage, 1987
1 .... 5.50
2 .... 3.00
3 .... 2.50
4 thru 7 .... @2.50

GIZMO & THE FUGITOID
Mirage, 1989
1 and 2 .... @1.75

GLOOM COOKIE
Slave Labor Graphics, 1999
1 by Serena Valentino & Ted Naifeh 3.00
2 .... 3.00
3 .... 3.00
4 .... 3.00
5 .... 3.00
6 Sebastian's Search 3.00
7 thru 9 .... @3.00
10 thru 17 .... @3.00
TPB Vol. 1 200-pg............ 17.95
TPB Vol. 2 192-pg............ 16.95
Color Spec. A Monster's Christmas. 3.95

GNATRAT
Prelude
1 .... 5.00
2 Early Years 2.00

GNATRAT: THE MOVIE
Innovation
1 .... 2.25

GOBBLEDYGOOK
Mirage, 1986
1 1st series, Rare 200.00
2 1st series, Rare 150.00
1 TMNT series reprint 5.00

GOJIN
Antarctic Press, 1995
1 F:Terran Defense Force 2.95
2 F:Terran Defense Force 2.95
3 V:Alien Monster 2.95
4 Aliens Bone 2.95
5 thru 8 .... @2.95

Gold Digger #14
© Antarctic Press

GOLD DIGGER
Antarctic Press, 1992
[Limited Series]
1 Geena & Cheetah in Peru...... 8.00
2 Adventures contd........... 6.00
3 Adventures contd........... 6.00
4 Adventures contd........... 5.00
GN Rep. #1–#4 + new material.... 9.95

[Volume 2], 1993
1 by Fred Perry 10.00
2 Fred Perry 8.00
3 Fred Perry 8.00
4 Fred Perry 6.00
5 misnumbered as #0 .... 5.00
6 thru 8 by Fred Perry .... @4.00
9 and 10 by Fred Perry .... @3.50
11 thru 27 by Fred Perry ...... @3.00
28 and 29 by Fred Perry ...... @2.75
30 .... 3.00
31 .... 3.00
32 Time Warp Part One 3.00
33 .... 3.00
34 .... 3.00
35 Time Warp Part Seven....... 3.00
36 .... 3.00
37 .... 2.95
38 V:Dynasty of Evil 2.95
39 .... 2.95
40 Wedding day 2.95
41 Gold Digger Beta........... 2.95
42 .... 2.95
43 Beta Phase phenomenon..... 2.95
44 Beta tool 2.95
45 F:Priestess Tanya 2.95
46 Agent M. 2.95
47 Old Dirty Bastard.......... 3.00

48 . . . . 3.00	25 . . . . 7.00	
49 The Library of Time 3.00	26 Emerald. 7.00	
50 . . . . 3.00	27 The Fog Robbers. 7.00	
50a deluxe 6.00	Becomes:	
Ann. 1995, 48-pg. 3.95		

MEN OF MYSTERY
AC Comics, 2000

Ann. 1996. . . . . 3.95
Ann. 1997. . . . . 3.95
Ann. 1998. . . . . 3.95
Ann. 2000 b&w. 3.95
Ann. 2001 . . . . 3.95
Ann. 2002 B&W 3.95
Best of Gold Digger Ann. Vol. 1 . . . 3.00
Collected Gold Digger,Vol.1 . . . . . 9.95
Collected Gold Digger,Vol.2 . . . . . 9.95
Collected Gold Digger,Vol.3 . . . . . 9.95
Collected Gold Digger,Vol.4 . . . . . 9.95
Collected Gold Digger,Vol.5 . . . . . 9.95
Collected Gold Digger,Vol.6 . . . . 10.95
Collected Gold Digger,Vol.7 . . . . 10.95
Collected Gold Digger,Vol.8 . . . . 10.95
Collected Gold Digger,Vol.9 . . . . 12.95
Mangazine Spec. #1. . . . . 3.00

28 F:Black Terror,Miss Masque. . . . 7.00
29 The Lynx, Wildfire 7.00
30 War Years 7.00
31 Speed and Space 7.00
32 Phantom Lady. 7.00
33 Red white and blue 7.00
34 Halloween Issue 7.00
35 F:Spy Smasher 7.00
36 F:Captain Flash 7.00
37 F:Cat-Man and Kitten. 7.00
38 Spy Smasher vs. Iron Mask . . . 6.95
39 Spy Smasher, Airboy 6.95
40 The Black Terror 6.95
41 Bulletman 6.95
42 Blue Bolt 6.95
43 The Flame. 6.95
44 Cat-Man and Bulletman 6.95
Coll. Ed. #7 . . . . 19.95
Digest Spec. #1 . . . . 15.95
Spotlight Spec. #1 . . . . 14.95

GOLD DIGGER/ NINJA HIGH SCHOOL
Antarctic Press 1998

Spec. Asrial vs. Cheetah Compilation, x-over rep. 4.95
Spec. Science Fair Compilation, x-over rep. 4.95
TPB Time Warp 15.95

GOLD DIGGER: EDGE GUARD
Radio Comix, 2000

1 (of 4) by John Barrett 2.95
2 thru 6 . . . . @2.95
7 finale 3.00

GOLDEN AGE GREATS
AC Comics, 1995

Vol.#1 thru #6 40s and 50s . . . . @9.95
Vol. 7 Best of the West. 9.95
Vol. 8 F:Phantom Lady, Miss Victory 9.95
Vol. 9 Fabulous Femmes of Fiction House 9.95
Vol. 11 Roy Rogers & The Silver Screen Cowboys 11.95
Vol. 12 Thrilling Science Fiction . . . 9.95
Vol. 13 . . . . 9.95
Vol. 14 The Comic Book Jungle . . 11.95

GOLDEN-AGE MEN OF MYSTERY
AC Comics

5 . . . . 7.00
7 . . . . 6.00
8 . . . . 6.00
9 . . . . 6.00
10 Masked comic book heroes, 52 pg. 7.00
11 rep. Cat-Man comics 7.00
12 Espionage, WE 7.00
13 F:Daredevil vs. The Claw. 7.00
14 F:Commando Yank 7.00
15 F:Captain 3-D 7.00
16 F:Mr. Scarlet, Airboy 7.00
17 F:Stuntman 7.00
18 . . . . 7.00
19 Space edition. 7.00
19a spec. ed. 68-pg. 11.00
20 F:Phantom Lady 7.00
21 Fawcett superheroes 7.00
22 Manhunter. 7.00
23 Skyman. 7.00
24 Captain Flash 7.00

GOLDEN WARRIOR
Industrial Design, 1997

1 by Eric Bansen & RB 2.95
2 and 3 . . . . @2.95

GOLDEN WARRIOR ICZER ONE
Antarctic, 1994

1 thru 5 . . . . @2.95

GOLDWYN 3-D
Blackthorne

1 . . . . 2.00

GO-MAN
Caliber

1 thru 4 . . . . @2.00
Graphic Novel 'N'. 9.95

GOOD GIRL COMICS
AC

1 F:Tara Fremont. 3.95

GOOD GIRLS
Fantagraphics, 1987

1 adult. 2.00
2 thru 4 . . . . @2.00

GOON, THE
Avatar Press, 1999

1 by Eric Powell. 3.00
2 . . . . 3.00
3 . . . . 3.00

GORE SHRIEK
Fantaco

1 . . . . 2.50
2 and 3 . . . . @1.50
4 +Mars Attacks. 2.95
5 . . . . 2.95
6 . . . . 3.50
Vol 2 #1 . . . . 2.50

Good Girls #1
© *Fantagraphics*

GOTHESS: DARK ECSTASY
SCC Entertainment, 1997

1 (of 3) 2.95
2 . . . . 2.95
3 . . . . 2.95

GRACKLE, THE
Acclaim (B&W) Sept., 1996

1 MBn,PG,Double Cross,pt.1 . . . . 2.95
2 MBn,PG,Double Cross,pt.2 . . . . 2.95
3 MBn,PG,Double Cross,pt.3 . . . . 2.95
4 MBn,PG,Double Cross,pt.4 . . . . 2.95

GRAPHIC CLASSICS
Eureka Productions, 2001

TPB Vol. 1 Edgar Allan Poe 7.95
TPB Vol. 2 Arthur Conan Doyle. . . 9.95
TPB Vol. 3 H.G. Wells 9.95
TPB Vol. 4 H.P. Lovecraft 9.95
TPB Vol. 5 Jack London 9.95
TPB Vol. 6 Ambrose Bierce. 9.95
TPB Vol. 7 Bram Stoker 9.95

GRAPHIC STORY MONTHLY
Fantagraphics

1 thru 7 . . . . @2.95

GRAPHIQUE MUSIQUE
Slave Labor, 1989–90

1 . . . . 35.00
2 . . . . 30.00
3 . . . . 25.00

GRAVEDIGGERS
Acclaim (B&W) 1996

1 (of 4) 2.95
2 thru 4 . . . . @2.95

GRAVE TALES
Hamilton, 1991

1 JSon,GM, mag. size 8.00
2 JSon,GM,short stories 6.00
3 JSon,GM, inc.'Stake Out' 6.00

GRAVITATION
Tokyopop Press 2003
GN Vol. 1 .... 10.00
GN Vol. 2 thru Vol. 3 .... @10.00

GREAT DETECTIVE STARRING SHERLOCK HOLMES
ACG Comics, 1999
1 by Otto Lagoni 2.95
2 thru 5 .... @2.95

GREEN BERETS
ACG, 2000
1 JKu 2.95
2 thru 7 JKu, Robin Moore .... @2.95
TPB Limited Signed 24.95

GREENLEAF IN EXILE
Cat's Paw Comics, 1998
1 by Doug Anderson 2.95
2 thru 7 .... @2.95

GREMLIN TROUBLE
Anti-Ballistic Pixelation
1 & 2 Airstrike on Gremlin Home @2.95
1 new printing 2.95
3 thru 5 .... @2.95
6 'Fun with Electricity' 2.95
7 'Cypher in Fairyland' 2.95
8 .... 2.95
9 F:Candy Tsai 2.95
10 The Tuberians are coming .. 2.95
11 V:X-the-Unmentionable 2.95
12 preemptive strike on Site X 2.95
13 Gremlin-Goblin war 2.95
14 .... 2.95
15 Battle of 5 Armies 2.95
16 .... 2.95
17 kidnapped to Fairyland 2.95
18 .... 2.95
19 The Sky Stone 2.95
20 Ring Fortress 2.95
21 A-Girls 2.95
22 Gremlin Guild 2.95
23 escape from Mordovania 2.95
24 thru 30 .... @2.95
TPB Vol.1 rep.#1–#6 .... 14.95
TPB Vol.2 rep.#7–#12 .... 12.95
TPB Vol.3 rep.#13–#18 .... 12.95
TPB Vol.4 rep. #19–#25 .... 12.95
TPB Vol.5 rep. #26–#30 .... 14.95
Spec. #1 Super Special 2.95

GRENDEL
Comico, 1983
1 MW,O:Hunter Rose, rare 90.00
2 MW,O:Argent, rare 75.00
3 MW,rare 70.00

GREY
Viz Select, 1989
Book 1 .... 5.00
Book 2 scarce 5.50
Book 3 .... 3.00
Book 4 .... 3.00
Book 5 .... 3.00
Book 6 thru Book 9 .... @2.50

GREYMATTER
Alaffinity Studios, 1993
1 thru 14 by Marcus Harwell ... @2.95

Greymatter #5
© Alaffinity Studios

GRIFFIN, THE
Slave Labor, 1988
1 .... 1.75
1a 2nd printing 1.75
2 thru 4 .... @1.75
5 .... 2.00

Amaze Ink, 1997
1 by DVa & Phil Allora 2.95
2 by DVa & Paul Way 2.95

GRIPS
Silver Wolf, 1986
1 Vigil 15.00
2 Vigil 12.00
3 Vigil 9.00
4 Vigil 8.00
Vol 1 #1 rep 2.50

Volume 2
1 .... 2.50
2 .... 2.50
3 thru 6 .... @2.00
7 .... 2.25
8 .... 2.25
9 thru 12 .... @2.50

GROUND ZERO
Eternity
1 Science Fiction mini-series . 2.50
2 Alien Invasion Aftermath ... 2.50

GRRL SCOUTS
Oni Press, 1999
1 (of 4) by Jim Mahfood 3.00
2 thru 4 .... @3.00
TPB 11.95

Amazing Aaron, 1999
1 Aaron Warner 2.95
2 .... 2.95

GTO
Tokyopop Press, 2002
GN Vol. 1 (of 20) authentic manga 10.00
GN Vol. 2 thru 15 .... @10.00

GUERRILA GROUNDHOG
Eclipse, 1987
1 .... 1.50
2 .... 1.50

GUILLOTIN
High Impact, 1997
Preview JQ,RCI 5.00
ABC Studios, 1999
Spec. Ed. 3.00
Spec. Ed. Serpent Ed. 8.00

GUILLOTINE
Silver Wolf
1 and 2 .... @1.50

GUN CRISIS
Ironcat, 1998
1 (of 3) by Masoami Kanzaki .. 2.95
2 .... 2.95
3 .... 2.95

GUNDAM WING
Mixx Entertainment, 2000
1 .... 5.00
2 thru 4 .... @4.00
TPB Pocket Mixx, Vol.1 .... 9.95
TPB Pocket Mixx, Vol.2 .... 9.95
TPB Pocket Mixx, Vol.3 .... 9.95
Tokyopop.Com, 2000
5 thru 8 .... @3.00
9 thru 12 .... @3.00
TPB Vol. 1 Blue Destiny Mixx . 12.95
TPB Gundam Technical Manual #1 13.00
TPB Gundam Technical Manual
  #2 thru #6 .... @13.00

GUNDAM WING: BATTLEFIELD OF PACIFISTS
Tokyopop Press, 2001
1 48-pg 3.00
2 .... 3.00
3 thru 5 .... @2.95
TPB Vol. 1 .... 9.95

GUNDAM WING: ENDLESS WALTZ
Tokyopop Press, 2002
1 (of 5) 3.00
2 thru 4 .... @3.00
TPB 184-pg 10.00

GUNDAM WING: G-UNIT
Tokyopop Press, 2002
1 (of 12) 3.00
2 .... 3.00

GUNDAM WING: THE LAST OUTPOST
Tokyopop Press, 2002
1 (of 12) 3.00
2 thru 4 .... @3.00
TPB Vol. 1 (of 3) 10.00
TPB Vol. 2 thru Vol. 3 .... @10.00

GUNDAM: THE ORIGIN
Viz Communications, 2002
GN #1 by Yoshikazu Yasuhiko .. 7.95
GN #2 thru #8 .... @7.95

GUNFIGHTERS IN HELL
Broken Halos, 1999
GN by Tim & Joe Vigil 19.95
GN leather(c), signed & numbered 34.95

HALL OF HEROES PRESENTS
Hall of Heroes, 1996–97
0 by Doug Brammer & Matt Roach,
'Slingers' by Matt Martin 2.50
1 . . . . 2.50
1a signed & numbered 4.00
2 'The Last Days' 2.50
3 'The Power of the Golem' 2.50
4 F:Turaxx the Trobbit 2.50
5 . . . . 2.50

HALLOWIENERS
Mirage
1 . . . . 2.00
2 . . . . 2.00

HALO BROTHERS
Fantagraphics
Special #1 . . . . 2.25

HAMMER GIRL
Brainstorm, 1996
1 dinosaur, sci-fi adventure 2.95
2 . . . . 2.95
2a deluxe 5.00

HAMSTER VICE
Blackthorne, 1986
1 . . . . 3.50
2 . . . . 2.50
3 thru 11 . . . . @2.00

New Series
Eternity, 1989
1 and 2 . . . . @2.00

HANGED MAN
Caliber, 1998
1 (of 2) by AIG & Arthur Ranson . . . 2.95
2 (of 2) 2.95
TPB 5.95

HAPPY MANIA
Tokyopop Press 2003
1 (of 11) 10.00
2 thru 5 . . . . @10.00

HARD GORE
Komics, Inc., 2000
TPB Vol. 1 . . . . 9.85
TPB Vol. 2 thru Vol. 7 . . . . @9.85

HARD ROCK COMICS
Revolutionary, 1992
1 Metallica-The Early Years 6.00
2 Motley Crew 4.00
3 Jane's Addiction 3.50
4 Nirvana 4.00
5 Kiss 9.00
5a 2nd printing 5.00
6 Def Leppard II 3.00
7 Red Hot Chili Peppers 3.00
8 Pearl Jam 3.00
9 Queen II 3.00
10 Birth of Punk 3.00
11 Pantera 3.00
12 Hendrix 3.00
13 Dead Kennedys 3.00
14 Van Halen II 2.50
15 Megadeath 2.50
16 Joan Jett 2.50
17 Not printed

Comics Values Annual

TPB Original Sin 7.95
TPB Original Sin, variant (c) 9.95
TPB Original Sin, special ed 11.95
TPB Leather Hell 19.95
TPB Leather Hell, signed 29.95

GUNFIGHTERS IN HELL: ORIGINAL SIN
Broken Halos, 2001
1 . . . . 3.95
1a variant (c) 5.95
1 limited edition 16-pg. 6.66
2 24-pg. 3.95
2a cardstock (c) 4.50
2b limited edition 5.95

GUN FURY
Aircel, 1989
1 thru 10 . . . . @2.00

GUN FURY RETURNS
Aircel, 1990
1 . . . . 2.95
2 . . . . 2.95
3 V:The Yes Men 2.25
4 . . . . 2.25

GUNNER
Gun Dog Comics, 1999
1 by Eric Yonge 2.95
2 thru 7 . . . . @2.95

GUNS OF SHAR-PEI
Caliber
1 The Good,the Bad & the Deadly . 2.95
2 & 3 . . . . @2.95

GUTWALLOW
Numbskull Press, 1998
1 by Dan Berger 2.95
2 thru 7 The Gingerbread Man . . @2.95

GUTWALLOW
Digital Webbing 2002
1 (of 3) 2.95
2 Fury of the Furry 2.95
3 concl. 2.95
TPB Fury of the Furry 12.95

GYRE
Abaculus, 1997
1 by Martin Shipp & Marc Laming . 2.95
2 . . . . 2.95
3 Soul Keeper, pt. 2.95
4 . . . . 2.95
5 . . . . 2.95
6 . . . . 2.95
Spec. Edition 56-pg. 4.50

HADES
Domain Publishing, 1995
1 F:Civil War Officer 3.00

HALL OF HEROES
Hall of Heroes, 1993
1 I:Dead Bolt 12.00
2 and 3 . . . . @4.50
Ashcan, 8-pg. 5.95
Halloween Horror Special 2.50
Halloween Horror Special '98 . . . . 2.50

B & W PUB.

Gunfighters–Hate

18 Queensryche 2.50
19 Tesla 2.50
20 The Sweet 2.50

HARI KARI
Blackout, 1995
1 . . . . 3.00
1a platinum 8.00
1-shot Possessed by Evil(1997) . . . 2.95
1-shot Hari Kari Goes Hollywood
(1997) 2.95
Deluxe 14.95
Spec #1 Sexy Summer Rampage,
gallery issue (1997) 2.95
Deluxe, super sexy cover 9.95
1-shot Cry of Darkness (1998) . . . 2.95
Variant photo ultra sexy ed. . . . 9.95
1-shot The Last Stand (1998) 2.95
Ultra sexy edition 9.95
Deluxe 14.95

HARI KARI MANGA
Blackout Comics, 1998
Spec. 0 Sex, Thugs & Rock 'n' Roll 2.95
1-shot Manga Adventures (1997) . . 2.95
1-shot Deadly Exposure, by Rob
Roman & Nigel Tully 2.95
Deluxe 14.95
1-shot Deadtime Stories, by Rob
Roman & Nigel Tully 2.95
Deluxe edition 14.95
1-shot Manga To Die For 2.95
Deluxe 14.95
1-shot Running From Poison 2.95

HARLEM BEAT
Tokyopop Press, 2001
GN Vol. 2 . . . . 9.95
GN Vol. 3 . . . . 9.95
GN Vol. 4 . . . . 9.95
TPB Pocket Mixx, Vol. 5 . . . . 9.95
TPB Pocket Mixx, Vol. 6 . . . . 9.95
TPB Pocket Mixx, Vol. 7 . . . . 9.95
TPB Pocket Mixx, Vol. 8 . . . . 9.95
TPB Pocket Mixx, Vol. 9 . . . . 9.95

HARPY: PRIZE OF THE OVERLORD
Ground Zero, 1996
1 (of 6) 3.00
2 thru 6 . . . . @3.00
1-shot Harpy Preview, prequel 3.00

Peregrine, 1998
TPB rep. #1–#6 . . . . 14.95
Spec. Harpy Pin-up Book 2.95

HARTE OF HARKNESS
Eternity
1 I:Dennis Harte,Vampire
private-eye 2.50
2 V:Satan's Blitz St.Gang 2.50
3 Jack Grissom/Vampire 2.50
4 V:Jack Grissom, concl. 2.50

HARVY FLIP BOOK
Blackthorne
1 . . . . 2.00
2 . . . . 2.00
3 . . . . 2.00

HATE
Fantagraphics, 1990
1 . . . . 15.00
2 . . . . 12.00

Hate–Herobear / B & W PUB. / Comics Values Annual

3	9.00
4	8.00
5	8.00
6	8.00
7	7.00
8 thru 10	@6.00
11 and 12	@5.00
1a to 12a reprints	@2.50
13 thru 15	@4.00
Hate Jamboree, 64-pg.	4.00

See Color

HAVOC, INC.
Radio Comix, 1998
1 by Mark Barnard & Terrie Smith	2.95
2 thru 6	@2.95
9	3.00
TPB Vol. 1 128-pg.	12.95

HEAD, THE
1 Old Airboy (1966)	2.00

HEAVY METAL MONSTERS
Revolutionary, 1992
1 `Up in Flames'	2.25

HE IS JUST A RAT
Exclaim Bound Comics, 1995
1 & 2 V:Jimmy and Billy Bob	2.75

HELLGIRL
Knight Press, 1995
1 I:Jazzmine Grayce	2.95
1-shot Demonseed II, Bob Hickey & Bill Nichols (1997)	2.95
1-shot Demonsong, Bob Hickey & Bill Nichols (1997)	2.95
1-shot Purgatory (1997)	2.95

HELLINA
Lightning Comics, 1994
1-shot I&O:Hellina	5.00
Commemorative	10.00
1996 rep. gold	5.00
Spec. Hellina: Genesis with poster (1996)	3.00
Platinum edition	4.00
Spec. Hellina: In the Flesh (1997) two diff. mild covers	@3.00
Spec. Hellina: Naked Desire (1997)	2.95
Cover B	2.95
Signed	2.95
Spec. Hellina: Taking Back the Night (1995) V:Michael Naynar	3.00
Spec. Hellina: Wicket Ways (1995) A:Perg	2.75
Encore editions	3.00
Encore variant (c)	3.00
Spec. Hellina: X-Mas in Hell (1996) two different covers	@3.00
Platinum edition	5.00
Spec. Hellina: The Relic	3.00
Variant cover	3.00
Spec. 1997 Pin-up	3.50
1997 Pin-up, cover B	3.50
X-Over Hellina/Catfight (1995) V:Prince of Sommia	2.75
Gold	4.00
Encore edition, mild covers, 2 different	@2.95
X-Over Hellina/Cynder (1997) covA	2.95
Cover B	2.95
Spec Hellina #1 Skybolt Toyz lim. ed. (1997)	2.00

TPB rep. Hellina appearances	8.95
TPB rep. one-shots	12.95

HELLINA
Avatar Press 2003
0	3.50
0a variant (c)	3.50
0b wraparound (c)	3.95
0c Hard Ruler Edition	5.95
0d Prism foil edition	12.95

HELLINA: HEART OF THORNS
Lightning Comics, 1996
1 (of 2)	3.00
1b autographed	5.00
2	2.75
2a variant cover	2.75
2b platinum edition	5.95

HELLINA: HELL'S ANGEL
Lightning Comics, 1996
1	2.75
1a platinum edition	8.00
1a platinum edition, signed	10.00
1c nude platinum edition	15.00
2	2.75
2a platinum edition	8.00
1 encore edition, cover A	2.95
1a encore edition, cover B	2.95
1b deluxe encore edition, cover A	5.00
1c deluxe encore edition, cover B	5.00

HELLINA: KISS OF DEATH
Lightning Comics, 1995
1-shot A:Perg	4.00
1-shot gold edition	10.00
1-shot Encore editions	3.00

Lightning, 1997
1A	2.95
1B variant cover	2.95
1 encore, signed & numbered	5.00

HELLINA: SEDUCTION
Avatar Press 2003
1/2 Carnage Edition	5.95
1/2 Statuesque Edition	5.95
Preview	2.00
Preview variant (c)	5.95
Preview Bad Girl edition	5.95
1	3.50
1a wraparound (c)	3.95

HELLINA VS PANDORA
Avatar Press 2003
Preview	2.00
Preview variant (c)	5.95

HELSING
Caliber Core, 1998
1W by Gary Reed & Low, Wozniak(c)	2.95
1L Loudon (c)	2.95
1 variant cover	8.95
1 premium, signed	9.95
2	2.95
3	2.95
4 Secrets and Lies	2.95
Spec. Dawn of Armageddon, Secrets & Lies, concl. 48-pg.	3.95

HELTER SKELTER
Antarctic Press, 1997
0 by Mike Harris & Duc Tran	2.95
1 (of 4)	2.95
2 thru 6	@2.95

Hepcats #6
© Antarctic Press

HEPCATS
Double Diamond, 1989
1	15.00
2	12.00
3 Snow Blind	12.00
4 thru 9	@9.00
10 thru 13	@3.50
14 Chapter 12	3.00
15 Snowblind Chp. 13	2.75

Antarctic Press, 1996
1 by Martin Wagner	3.00
2 `Trial by Intimacy'	3.00
3 Snowblind,pt.1	3.00
4 Snowblind,pt.2	3.00
5 Snowblind,pt.3	3.00
6 Snowblind,pt.4	3.00
7 Snowblind,pt.5 Intrusion	2.95
8 Snowblind,pt.6 Super Heroes	2.95
9 Snowblind,pt.7 Kevin & Kathryn	2.95
10 Snowblind,pt.8 Exorcism, Prelude	2.95
11 Snowblind,pt.10 Exorcism(a)	2.95
12 Snowblind,pt.10 Exorcism(b)	2.95
13 Snowbling,pt.11 It's a Garden of Eden	3.50
TPB Collected Hepcats	14.95

HERCULES
A Plus Comics
1 Hercules Saga	2.50

HERCULES PROJECT
Monster Comics, 1991
1 Origin issue,V:Mutants	2.00

HEROBEAR AND THE KID
Astonish Comics, 2000
1	15.00
2	12.00
1a and 2a 2nd printings	@3.50
3	3.50
4	3.50
5 Belief	3.50
TPB Vol. 1 The Inheritance	17.95

HEROES
Blackbird, 1987
1 .... 5.00
2 .... 3.00
3 .... 2.25
4 comic size 2.00
5 thru 7 .... @2.00

HEROES ANONYMOUS
Bongo Comics 2003
1 (of 6) 3.00
2 thru 3 .... @3.00

HEROES FROM WORDSMITH
Special Studios
1 WWI,F:Hunter Hawke......... 2.50

HEROES INCORPORATED
Double Edge Publishing
1 I:Heroes, Inc. 2.95
2 Betrayal 2.95

HEROIC TALES
Lone Star Press, 1997
1 by Robb Phipps & Bill Williams.. 2.50
2 Steel of a Soldier's Heart,pt.2 ... 2.50
3 Steel of a Soldier's Heart,pt.3 ... 2.50
4 .... 2.50
5 .... 2.50
6 The Belles of Freedom, prequel . 2.50
7 The Children of Atlas,pt.1 ...... 2.50
8 by Bill Williams & Jeff Parker,
   I:Atlas..................... 2.50

HEROINES, INC.
Avatar
1 thru 5 .... @1.75

HERO SANDWICH
Slave Labor, 1987
1 thru 4 .... @2.00
5 thru 8 .... @2.00
9 .... 2.00
Graphic Novel 7.95

HEY MISTER
Insomnia Comics, 1997
1 and 2 .... @2.50
Top Shelf
3 by Pete Sickman-Garner....... 2.95
4 .... 2.95
Spec. Behind the Green Door.... 2.95
Spec. The Trouble With Jesus ... 2.95
Spec. Eyes on the Prize 2.95
Spec. Dial "M" for Mister...... 3.50
TPB After School Special 4.95
TPB Celebrity Roast 144-pg. ... 9.95

HIGH CALIBER
Caliber, 1997
1 64pg....................... 4.00
1 signed edition.............. 4.00
2 64pg....................... 4.00
3 48pg....................... 4.00
4 .... 4.00

HIGH SCHOOL AGENT
Sun Comics, 1992
1 I:Kohsuke Kanamori.......... 2.50
2 Treasure Hunt at North Pole.... 2.50

High School Agent #4
© Sun Comics

3 and 4 .... @2.50

HIGH SHINING BRASS
Apple
1 thru 4 .... @2.75

HIGH SOCIETY
Aardvark–Vanaheim
1 DS,Cerebus 25.00

HIGHWAY 13
Amaze Ink/Slave Labor Graphics, 2000
1 thru 4 by Les McClaine...... @2.95
5 thru 11 .... @2.95

HILLY ROSE'S SPACE ADVENTURES
Astro Comics, 1995
1 confronts Steeltrap 6.00
1 2nd & 3rd pr. by B.C. Boyer 3.00
2 .... 5.00
2 2nd & 3rd printing.......... 3.00
3 .... 3.50
3 2nd printing 3.00
4 thru 9 .... @3.00
TPB Vol.1 Rocket Reporter...... 12.95

HIT THE BEACH
Antarctic, 1993
1 .... 2.95
1a deluxe edition............. 5.00
2 & 3 .... @2.95
Spec. funny animal............ 2.95
Spec. 32 pg 2.95
Spec. deluxe 3.95
Spec. deluxe poster edition.... 4.95
Spec. 48-pg., 1999............ 3.95
Spec. (#7) 48-pg., 2000 ...... 3.95
Ann. 2001.................... 3.95
Ann. 2002.................... 4.00
1-shot Hit the Beach 2003 ..... 5.00

HITOMI AND HER GIRL COMMANDOS
Antarctic Press, 1992
1 Shadowhunter,from Ninja HS ... 2.50

2 Synaptic Transducer......... 2.50
3 Shadowhunter in S.America ... 2.50
4 V:Mr.Akuma,last issue 2.50
[Series II]
1 thru 10 .... @2.75

HOLLYWOOD'S GOLDEN ERA, 1930S
A-List Comics, 1999
1 (of 3) 2.95
2 .... 2.95
3 .... 2.95

HOLO BROTHERS, THE
Monster Comics, 1991
1 thru 10 .... @2.00
Fantagraphics
Spec.#1 .... 2.25
TPB The Curse of the Bloated Toad 4.95

HOLY KNIGHT
Pocket Change Comics
1 thru 3 .... @2.50
4 V:His Past 2.50
5 V:Souljoiner 2.50
6 V:Demon Priest 2.50
7 Silent Scream,pt.2 .... 2.50
8 `Dragon Quest',pt.1 .... 2.50
9 `Dragon Quest',pt.2 .... 2.50
10 `Dragon Quest',pt.3 .... 2.50
11 `Dragon Quest',pt.4 .... 2.50

HONK
Fantagraphics, 1986
1 Don Martin................. 2.75
2 and 3 .... @2.75

HONOR AMONG THIEVES
Gateway Graphics, 1987
1 and 2 .... @2.00

HOON
Eenieweenie Comics, 1995
1 I:Hoon 2.50
2 Calazone Disaster 2.50
3 Reality Check............... 2.50
4 thru 8 .... @2.50

HOON, THE
Caliber Tapestry, 1996
1 .... 2.95
2 .... 2.95
3 .... 2.95

HOPELESS SAVAGES
Oni Press, 2001
1 thru 4 .... @2.95
TPB Vol. 1 .... 13.95
TPB Vol. 2 Ground Zero 11.95

HOPELESS SAVAGES: GROUND ZERO
Oni Press, 2002
1 (of 4) 2.95
2 thru 4 .... @2.95

HOROBI
Viz, 1990
1 .... 4.00
2 thru 8 .... @3.75

Book 2, 1990–91
1 by Yoshihisa Tagami 3.50
2 D:Okado,Shoko Kidnapped. 4.25
3 Madoka Attacks Zen 4.25
4 D:Abbess Mitsuko. 4.25
5 Catharsis!. 4.25
6 Shuichi Vs. Zen 4.25
7 Shuichi vs. Zen, conc. 4.25

HORROR IN THE DARK
Fantagor
1 RCo,Inc.Blood Birth 2.00
2 RCo,Inc.Bath of Blood 2.00
3 RCo 2.00
4 RCo,Inc.Tales of the
 Black Diamond. 2.00

HORROR SHOW
Caliber
1 GD,1977-80 reprint horror 3.50

HOUSE OF FRIGHTENSTEIN
AC Comics
1 . . . . 2.95

HOUSE OF HORROR
AC Comics
1 . . . . 2.50

HOWL
Eternity
1 & 2 . . . . @2.25

HOW TO DRAW TEENAGE MUTANT NINJA TURTLES
Solson
1 Lighter cover 10.00
1a Dark cover 5.00

H.P. LOVECRAFT'S THE CALL OF CTHULHU AND OTHERS
Cross Plains Comics, 1999
1-shot RTs,EM 5.95

H.P. LOVECRAFT'S THE DREAM-QUEST OF UNKNOWN KADATH
Mock Man Press, 1997
1 (of 5) by Jason Thompson 2.95
1 2nd printing 2.95
2 thru 5 . . . . @2.95

H.P. LOVECRAFT'S THE RETURN OF CTHULHU
Cross Plains Comics, 2000
1-shot RTs & EM 5.95

HUGO
Fantagraphics, 1985
1 . . . . 4.00
2 thru 4 . . . . @2.00

HUMAN GARGOYLES
Eternity, 1988
Book one 2.00
Book two 2.00

H.P. Lovecraft's The Dream-Quest of Unknown Kadath #1 © Mock Man

Book three 2.00
Book four 2.00

HUNT AND THE HUNTED, THE
Newcomers Publishing
1 I:Aramis Thiron 2.95
2 V:Werewolves 2.95
3 Rio De Janero 2.95
4 F:Aramis Thiron 2.95

HURRICANE GIRLS
Antarctic Press, 1995
1 & 2 Tale of Dinon . . . . @3.50
3 thru 7 seven part series. . . . . . @2.95

HUZZAH
1 I:Albedo'sErmaFelna. 50.00

HY-BREED
Division Publishing
1 thru 3 F:Cen Intel . . . . @2.25
4 thru 9 . . . . @2.50

HYPER DOLLS
Ironcat Manga, 1998
1 by Shinpei Itoh, F:Miyu & Maika . 2.95
2 thru 6 . . . . @2.95
VOL 2
1 . . . . 2.95
2 thru 6 . . . . @2.95
VOL 3
1 . . . . 2.95
2 thru 6 . . . . @2.95
VOL 4, 2000
1 . . . . 2.95
2 thru 6 . . . . @2.95
VOL 5, 2000
1 . . . . 2.95
2 thru 6 . . . . @2.95
TPB Vol. 1 . . . . 15.95
TPB Vol. 3 thru Vol. 5 . . . . @15.95

I.F.S. ZONE
1 thru 6 . . . . @2.00

I AM LEGEND
Eclipse, 1991
1 Novel adapt. aka Omega Man . . 5.95
2 thru 3 68-pg. . . . . @5.95

ICARUS
Aircel, 1987
1 thru 9 . . . . @2.00

ICON DEVIL
Spider
1 by Neil Hanson 2.00
2 . . . . 2.00
2nd Series
1 thru 5 . . . . @2.00

I DREAM OF JEANNIE
Airwave Comics, 2002
1 JJu(c). 2.95
1 special edition 5.95
2 . . . . 2.95
2a variant photo (c) 2.95
3 . . . . 2.95
Preview Book #1 . . . . 6.95
Spec. Trick-or-Treats Annual #1 . . 3.50
Spec.#1 Wishbook (2001). 2.95
Spec.#1 Wishbook, photo (c) . . . 2.95
Spec. Spring Spectacular 3.50
Spec. Spring Spectacular, photo(c). 3.50

ILIAD
Amaze Ink, 1997
1 by Darren Brady & Alex Ogle . . . 2.95
2 thru 7 . . . . @2.95

ILIAD II
MicMac
1 . . . . 3.00
1a 2nd cover variation 3.00
2 . . . . 2.00
3 . . . . 2.00
4 . . . . 2.00

ILLUMINATUS
Rip Off, 1990
1 . . . . 2.00
2 . . . . 2.50
3 . . . . 2.50

INDUSTRIACIDE
Broken Tree Publications, 2002
1 (of 6) by Sean Dietrich 2.95
2 thru 6 . . . . @2.95

INFERNO
Caliber Press, 1995
1 I:City of Inferno. 2.95
2 Search for Identity 2.95
3 V:Malateste 2.95
4 by MCy and Michael Gaydos . . . 2.95
5 . . . . 2.95

INITIAL D
Tokyopop Press, 2002
GN Vol. 1 authentic manga. 10.00
GN Vol. 2 thru 9 . . . . @10.00

INTERZONE
Brainstorm Comics
1 w/4 cards 2.50
2 w/4 cards 2.50

All comics prices listed are for Near Mint condition.

INTO THE STORM
Curtis Comics, 2002
Vol. 1 Manga
1 by Jihoon Park & Takyoung Lee . 2.95
2 thru 4 . . . . @2.95
Vol. 2
1 . . . . 2.95

INU YASHA
Viz Communications, 1997
1 thru 5 (of 10) by Rumiko
  Takahashi . . . . @2.95
PART TWO:
A FEUDAL FAIRY TALE
Viz Communications, 1998
1 (of 9) by Rumiko Takahashi 2.95
2 thru 7 . . . . @2.95
8 thru 15 (of 15) . . . . @3.25
TPB 15.95
TPB Vol. 2 . . . . 15.95
PART THREE, 1999
1 (of 7) thru 7 . . . . @3.25
TPB Vol. 3 . . . . 15.95
PART FOUR, 1999
1 (of 7) by Rumiko Takahashi 3.25
2 thru 7 . . . . @3.25
TPB Vol. 4 . . . . 15.95
PART FIVE, 2000
1 (of 11) by Rumiko Takahashi 2.95
2 thru 11 . . . . @2.95
TPB Vol. 5 . . . . 15.95
TPB Vol. 6 . . . . 15.95
PART SIX, 2001
1 (of 15) 2.95
2 thru 7 . . . . @2.95
8 thru 15 . . . . @2.95
PART SEVEN, 2002
1 (of 8) by Rumiko Takahashi 3.25
2 thru 7 . . . . @2.95
TPB Vol.8 rep. Vol.4 #6–Vol5 #3 . . 15.95
TPB Vol.9 . . . . 15.95
TPB Vol.10 thru 12 . . . . @15.95
TPB Vol.13 thru Vol. 15 . . . . @8.95
TPB Art of Inu-Yasha, color 22.95

INVADERS FROM MARS
Eternity, 1990
1 . . . . 2.50
2 . . . . 2.50
3 . . . . 2.50
BOOK II, 1991
1 Sequel to '50's SF classic 2.50
2 Pact of Tsukus/Humans 2.50
3 Last issue 2.50

INVASION '55
Apple, 1990
1 . . . . 2.25
2 . . . . 2.25
3 . . . . 2.25

INVISIBLE PEOPLE
Kitchen Sink
1 WE,I:Peacus Pleatnik 2.95
2 WE,The Power 2.95
3 WE,Final issue 2.95

INVU
Tokyopop Press, 2002
GN Vol. 1 by Kang-Won Kim 10.00
GN Vol. 2 176-pg 10.00

ISLAND
Tokyopop Press, 2001
1 48-pg 2.95
2 . . . . 2.95
3 . . . . 2.95
4 . . . . 2.95
TPB Pocket Mixx, Vol. 1 . . . . 14.95
TPB Pocket Mixx, Vol. 2 . . . . 14.95
TPB Pocket Mixx, Vol. 3 . . . . 10.00
TPB Pocket Mixx, Vol. 4 . . . . 10.00
GN Vol. 5 thru Vol. 7 . . . . @10.00

ISMET
Canis
1 Cartoon Dog 8.00
2 . . . . 5.00
3 Rare 5.00
4 . . . . 5.00

IT'S SCIENCE WITH DR. RADIUM
Slave Labor, 1986
1 thru 7 . . . . @2.00
8 . . . . 2.00
9 . . . . 2.00
Spec #1 . . . . 2.95

Jackaroo #1
© Eternity

JACKAROO
Eternity, 1990
1 GCh 2.25
2 GCh 2.25
3 GCh 2.25

JACK HUNTER
Blackthorne, 1987
1 . . . . 3.50
2 . . . . 3.50
3 . . . . 3.50

JACK OF NINES
1 . . . . 2.00
2 thru 4 . . . . @2.00
5 . . . . 2.00

JACK STAFF
Dancing Elephant Press, 2000
1 by Paul Grist 2.95
2 thru 4 . . . . @2.95

5 . . . . 2.95
6 . . . . 2.95
7 . . . . 2.95
8 36-pg 4.50
9 thru 12 . . . . @2.95
TPB Vol. 1 Yesterday's heroes . . . 15.95

JACK THE RIPPER
Eternity
1 thru 4 . . . . @2.25

JAM, THE
Slave Labor, 1989
1 . . . . 3.00
2 . . . . 3.00
3 thru 5 . . . . @3.00
Dark Horse, 1993
6 thru 8 . . . . 3.00
Caliber, 1995
9 . . . . 3.00
9 signed edition 3.00
10 It's a Kafka Thing 3.00
11 thru 14 . . . . @3.00
15 `The Kinetic,'pt.3 . . . . 3.00

JAMES O'BARR ORIGINAL SINS
ACG Comics, 2000
1 . . . . 2.95
2 . . . . 2.95

JAMES O'BARR TASTY BITES
ACG Comics, 1999
1 . . . . 2.95
1a signed 9.95

JANE'S WORLD
Girl Twirl 2003
1 by Paige Braddock 2.95
2 thru 8 . . . . @2.95
TPB Vol. 1 . . . . 14.95

JASON AND THE ARGONAUTS
Caliber
1 thru 5 . . . . @2.50

JAY & SILENT BOB
Oni Press, 1998
1 (of 4) by Kevin Smith & Duncan
  Fregedo 8.00
2 thru 4 . . . . @3.00
TPB rep. #1–#4 . . . . 11.95

JAZZ
High Impact, 1996
1 . . . . 3.00
1 Gold variant edition RCl(c) 9.95
2 . . . . 3.00
2a deluxe edition 9.95
3 . . . . 3.00
3a variant (c) 9.95

JAZZ THE SERIES
ABC Comics, 1999
1 RCl(c) 3.00
1a DOe(c) 3.00
2 . . . . 3.00

JAZZ: SOLITAIRE
ABC Comics, 1998
1 (of 4) by Jose Varese	3.00
1a photo cover	5.95
2	3.00
2a Variant Exotika (c)	5.95
2b Variant Naughty (c)	5.95
3	3.00
Collected Ed.	4.95

JAZZ: SUPERSTAR
ABC Comics, 1998
1 (of 3) by Jose Varese	3.00
1a JQ cover	6.00

JAZZ AGE CHRONICLES
Caliber, 1990
1 thru 6	@2.00
7	2.50

JCP FEATURES
J.C. Productions, 1982
1 1st MT;S&K,NA/DG rep.
A:T.H.U.N.D.E.R.Agents,
TheFly, Black Hood Mag.Size . 11.00

JENNY FINN
Oni Press, 1999
1 (of 4) by MMi & Troy Nixey	2.95
2 MMi	2.95
3 MMi	2.95
4 MMi, concl.	3.95

JEREMIAH
Fantagraphics, 1982–83
GN #1	35.00
GN #2	32.00

JEREMIAH: BIRDS OF PREY
Adventure Comics, 1991
1 I: Jeremiah,A:Kurdy	4.00
2 conclusion	4.00

JEREMIAH: EYES LIKE BURNING COALS
Adventure Comics, 1991
1 fourth series	4.00
2 conclusion	4.00

JEREMIAH: FIST FULL OF SAND
Adventure Comics
1 A:Captain Kenney	4.00
2 conclusion	4.00

JEREMIAH: THE HEIRS
Adventure Comics, 1991
1 Nathanial Bancroft estate	4.00
2 conclusion	4.00

JERRY IGERS FAMOUS FEATURES
Blackthorne
1	3.00
2 thru 4	@2.00

Pacific
5 thru 8	@2.00

JETCAT CLUBHOUSE
Oni Press, 2001
1 by Jay Stephens	3.25
2 thru 4	@3.25
5	3.25
TPB by Jay Stephens (2002)	10.95

JIM
Fantagraphics, 1987–90
1	15.00
2	12.00
3 and 4	@8.00

Second Series, 1994
1	4.00
1a 2nd printing	3.00
2	3.50
2a 2nd printing	3.00
3 thru 5	@3.00

JINGLE BELLE
Oni Press, 1999
1 (of 2) by PDi	3.00
2 PDi	3.00
All-Star Holiday Hullabaloo	5.00
1-shot Jingle Belle Jubilee	3.00
1-shot The Mighty Elves	3.00
1-shot Winter Wingding	2.95
TPB Naughty & Nice (2000)	9.50

JING KING OF BANDITS
Tokyopop Press 2003
GN Vol. 1 (of 7)	10.00
GN Vol. 2 thru Vol. 4	@10.00

J. O'BARR's THE CROW
Kitchen Sink, 1998
0 F:Eric Draven, 48-pg.	3.50
1	3.50
2 Demon in Disguise	3.50

JOE PSYCHO & MOO FROG
Goblin Studios, 1996
1 Fanatics Edition	2.50
1 Fanatics signed and numbered Edition	9.95
2	2.50
2 signed & numbered	9.95
3	2.50
4	2.50
4B San Diego Con cover	4.95
5	2.50
Spec. Psychosis Abnormalis	2.50

JOE R. LANSDALE'S THE DRIVE-IN
Avatar Press 2003
1 thru 2 (of 4)	@3.50
1a thru 2a wraparound (c)	@3.95

JOE SINN
Caliber
1 I:Joe Sinn,Nikki	2.95
2	2.95

JOHNNY ATOMIC
Eternity
1 I:Johnny A.Tomick	2.50
2 Project X-contingency plan	2.50
3	2.50

JOHNNY COMET
ACG Comics, 1999
1	2.95
2	2.95
3 FF, rep.	2.95
4 FF, rep.	2.95
5 FF, rep.	2.95

JOHNNY DARK
Double Edge
1 V:Biker Gang	2.95

JOHNNY THE HOMICIDAL MANIAC
Slave Labor, 1996
1 by Jhonen Vasquez	15.00
1 3rd printing	4.00
1 signed, limited	9.00
2	8.00
2 3rd printing	3.00
3	7.00
3 3rd printing	3.00
4	5.00
4 2nd & 3rd printing	3.00
5	4.00
5 2nd printing	3.00
6	3.00
7	3.00
TPB	19.95
TPB Director's Cut	19.95

JOURNEY
Aardvark–Vanaheim, 1983
1	7.00
2	6.00
3	5.00
4	3.00
5 thru 7	@3.00
8 thru 14	@2.50

Fantagraphics, 1985
15	2.50
16 thru 28	@2.00

JR. JACKALOPE
1 orange cover,1981	8.00
1a Yellow cover,1981	12.00
2	8.00

JUDGE DREDD
Hamlyn, 2001
TPB Doomsday for Mega-City One	25.00
TPB Doomsday for Dredd	20.00
TPB Wilderlands, 216-pg.	30.00
GN Judge Dredd: Pit	16.00
GN Judge Dredd: Fetish	10.00

Titan, 2001
TPB Judge Dredd: The Emerald Isle	15.00
TPB Judge Dredd: Death Aid	15.00

JULIE'S JOURNEY/ GRAVITY
Paper Live Studios, 1998
1 by David Keye	2.50
2 thru 6	@2.50

JULINE
Tokyopop Press, 2000
TPB Pocket Mixx, Vol. 1	9.95
TPB Pocket Mixx, Vol. 2	12.95
TPB Pocket Mixx, Vol. 3	14.95
TPB Pocket Mixx, Vol. 4	13.00
TPB Pocket Mixx, Vol. 5	13.00

JUNGLE COMICS
Blackthorne, 1988
4 thru 6 .... @2.00

JUNGLE COMICS
A-List Comics, 1997
1 reprint of golden age......... 2.95
2 thru 6 .... @2.95
TPB Book of Jungle Comics
 Covers, 1940–54 .... 7.95

JUNGLE FANTASY
Avatar Press, 2002
Preview 2.00
Preview, Fauna (c) 2.00
Preview, Wild (c)............. 5.95
1 .... 3.50
1b wraparound (c)............. 3.95
2 .... 3.50
3 .... 3.50
3b Back to the Hunt Edition...... 5.95
4 .... 3.50
1a thru 4a variant (c)s .... @3.50
1/2 Winged Death Edition........ 5.95

JUNGLE GIRLS
AC Comics, 1989–93
1 incGold.Age reps............. 3.00
2 .... 3.00
3 Greed,A:Tara 3.00
4 CaveGirl................... 3.00
5 Camilla.................... 3.00
6 TigerGirl 3.00
7 CaveGirl................... 3.00
8 Sheena Queen o/t Jungle...... 3.00
9 Wild Girl,Tiger Girl,Sheena 3.00
10 F:Tara,Cave Girl,Nyoka....... 3.00
11 F:Sheena,Tiger Girl,Nyoka..... 3.00
12 F:Sheena,Camilla,Tig.Girl 3.00
13 F:Tara, Tiger Girl 3.00

JUNIOR
Fantagraphics, 2000
1 (of 5) by Peter Bogge 3.00
2 thru 5 .... @3.00

JUPITER
Sandberg Publishing, 1999
1 by Jason Sandberg........... 2.95
2 thru 10 .... @2.95

JURASSIC JANE
London Night, 1997
1 by Sky Owens, F:Tira, elf
 princess of Atlantis 3.00
2 Sky Owens.................. 3.00
3 Sky Owens.................. 3.00
4 EHr, Sky Owens.............. 3.00
5 by Preston Owens 3.00
6 by Sky Owens 3.00
7 by Sky Owens 3.00
Coll. Ed..................... 5.00

JUSTICE
Newcomers Publishing, 1995
1 I:Judiciary Urban Strike Team ... 2.95

JUSTY
Viz Communications, 1988
1 thru 9 .... @1.75

KABUKI: CIRCLE OF BLOOD
Caliber Press, 1995
1 R:Kabuki 6.00
2 Kabuki Goes Rogue 5.00
3 V:Noh Agents 5.00
4 V:Noh Agents 3.50
5 V:Kai 3.00
6 .... 3.00
TPB Rep.#1-#6................ 16.95
TPB deluxe, signed, etc......... 24.95
TPB Compilation 7.95

KABUKI: DANCE OF DEATH
London Night Studios, 1995
1 1st Full series 8.00

KABUKI: MASKS OF THE NOH
Caliber, 1996
1A JQ(c) 3.00
1B Mays/Mack(c)............... 3.00
1C Buzz(c) 3.00
2 .... 3.00
3 DMk....................... 3.00
4 epilog..................... 3.00

KAFKA
Renegade, 1987
1 thru 6 .... @2.00
The Execution Spec............ 2.25

KAMUI
Eclipse, 1987
1 Sanpei Shirato Art 4.00
1a 2nd printing 2.50
2 Mystery of Hanbie 3.00
2a 2nd printing 2.00
3 V:Ichijiro................... 2.00
3a 2nd printing 2.00
4 thru 15 .... @2.00
16 thru 19................... @2.00
20 thru 37................... @2.00

KANE
Dancing Elephant
14 thru 17 by Paul Grist .... @3.50
18 thru 22................... @3.50
23 thru 33................... @2.95
TPB Book 1: rep. #1–#4 .... 11.95
TPB Book 2: Rabbit Hunt 12.50
TPB Book 3: Histories.......... 12.50
TPB Book 4: Thrity Ninth 19.95
TPB #5 Untouchable Rico Costas. 12.95

KANSAS THUNDER
Red Menace, 1997
1 .... 2.95

KAOS MOON
Caliber, 1996
1 by DdB.................... 3.50
1a 2nd edition 3.00
2 .... 3.50
2a 2nd edition, new cover 3.00
3 .... 5.00
4 Anubian Nights, Chapter 2 .... 5.00
GN Full Circle, rep #1–#2 .... 5.95

Kansas Thunder #1
© Red Menace

KAPTAIN KEEN
Vortex, 1986
1 thru 3 .... @1.75
4 and 5 .... @1.50
6 and 7 .... @1.75

KARE KANO
Tokyopop Press, 2002
GN Vol. 1 .... 10.00
GN Vol. 2 thru Vol. 6 .... @10.00

KATMANDU
Antarctic Press, 1993
1 thru 3 .... @2.75
4 & 5 Woman of Honor 2.75
6 F:Laska 2.75
Med Systems
7 and 8 .... @2.00
Vision Comics, 1996
9 `When Warriors Die,'pt.3(of 3)... 2.00
10 `The Curse of the Blood,'pt.1 .. 2.50
11 `The Curse of the Blood,'pt.2 .. 2.50
12 `The Curse of the Blood,' concl . 2.95
13 `The Search For Magic,'pt.1 .. 2.95
Shanda Fantasy Arts
14 `The Search For Magic,'pt.2.... 2.95
15 `The Search For Magic,'pt.3.... 2.95
16 `Ceremonies,'pt.1 (of 3)....... 2.95
17 `Ceremonies,'pt.2 .... 2.95
18 `Ceremonies,'pt.3 .... 2.95
19 `Peace Keeper,'pt.1 .... 2.95
20 `Peace Keeper,'pt.2 .... 2.95
21 `Peace Keeper,'pt.3 .... 2.95
22 .... 2.95
23 and 24 .... @3.00
25 thru 30 48-pg............. @5.00
Ann. #1 48-pg................ 4.95
Ann. #2 .... 5.00
Ann. #3 .... 5.00
Ann. #4 .... 5.00

KAZAN
Comicsone.com, 2001
TPB Vol.1 188-pg. by Gaku Miyao . 9.95
TPB Vol.2 187-pg.............. 9.95
TPB Vol.3 188-pg.............. 9.95
TPB Vol.4 188-pg.............. 9.95
TPB Vol.5 188-pg.............. 9.95

Kazan–Knights

TPB Vol.6 202-pg. 9.95
TPB Vol.7 202-pg. 9.95

KEIF LLAMA
Fantagraphics
1 thru 6 . . . . @2.00

KELLEY BELLE, POLICE DETECTIVE
Newcomers Publishing
1 Debut issue 2.95
2 Case of the Jeweled Scarab 2.95
3 Case o/t Jeweled Scarab,pt.2 . . . 2.95
TPB #1 . . . . 8.95

KID CANNIBAL
Eternity, 1991
1 I:Kid Cannibal 2.50
2 Hunt for Kid Cannibal 2.50
3 A:Janice 2.50
4 final issue 2.50

KIKU SAN
Aircel, 1988
1 thru 6 . . . . @2.00

KILLBOX
Antarctic Press 2002
1 . . . . 5.00
2 thru 3 . . . . @5.00

KILLING STROKE
Eternity, 1991
1 British horror tales 2.50
2 inc.'Blood calls to Blood'. 2.50
3 and 4 . . . . @2.50

KILROY
Caliber Core, 1998
1C by Joe Pruett & Feliciano
  Zecchin, John Cassaday(c) . . . 3.00
1P JoP (c) 3.00
1a premium edition 10.00
2 . . . . 3.00
3 . . . . 3.00
4 O:Kilroy 3.00
Spec. Dawn of Armageddon,
  x-over, 48-pg. 3.95
Spec.#1 The Origin 4.95
Spec.#2 The Origin,pt.2 . . . . 4.95
TPB Kilroy is Here: Pride, Prejudice
  & Persecution. 6.95

KILROY IS HERE
Caliber Press, 1995
1 Kilroy Rescues Infant 3.00
2 Reflections,pt.2. . . . . 3.00
3 Reflections,pt.3. . . . . 3.00
4 Lincoln Memorial 3.00
5 thru 8 . . . . @3.00
9 and 10 . . . . @3.00
11 WEI,RPc,'Screen' 3.00
12 Khymer Rouge 3.00
Spec. Kilroy: Daemonstorm (1997) . 3.00

KIMBER, PRINCE OF FELONS
Antarctic Press, 1992
1 I:Kimber 2.50
2 V:Lord Tyrex 2.50

B & W PUB.

KINDAICHI CASE FILES, THE
Tokyopop Press 2003
GN Vol. 1 (of 6) 10.00
GN Vol. 2 thru Vol. 4 . . . . @10.00

KINGDOM OF THE WICKED
Caliber, 1996
1 IEd 2.95
2 IEd 2.95
3 IEd 2.95
4 IEd 2.95
TPB rep. #1–#4 . . . . 12.95

King Kong #1
© Monster Comics

KING KONG
Monster Comics, 1991
1 thru 6 . . . . @2.50

KING OF HELL
Tokyopop Press 2003
GN Vol. 1 (of 3) 10.00
GN Vol. 2 thru Vol. 3 . . . . 10.00

KINGS IN DISGUISE
Kitchen Sink, 1988
1 thru 5 . . . . @2.00
6 end Mini-series. 2.00

KING ZOMBIE
Caliber, 1998
1L by Tom Sniegoski & Jacen
  Burroughs, VcL(c) 2.95
1M Meadows (c) 2.95
2 . . . . 2.95
3 . . . . 2.95

KIRBY KING OF THE SERIALS
Blackthorne, 1989
1 . . . . 2.00
2 . . . . 2.00
3 . . . . 2.00
4 . . . . 2.00

Comics Values Annual

KISSING CHAOS
Oni Press, 2001
1 (of 8) by Arthur Dela Cruz 2.50
2 16-pg 2.50
3 16-pg 2.50
4 . . . . 3.00
5 16-pg 2.50
6 16-pg 2.50
7 16-pg 2.50
8 24-pg 2.50
TPB Vol. 1 . . . . 17.95

KISSING CHAOS: NONSTOP BEAUTY
Oni Press 2002
3 thru 4 . . . . @3.00
TPB Vol. 2 . . . . 11.95
1-shot 1000 Words 3.00

KITZ 'N' KATZ
Phantasy
1 . . . . 3.50
Eclipse
2 . . . . 2.00
3 . . . . 2.00
4 and 5 . . . . @2.00

KLOWN SHOCK
North Star
1 Horror Stories 2.75

KNEWTS OF THE ROUND TABLE
Pan Entertainment, 1998
1 . . . . 2.50
2 thru 6 . . . . @2.50

KNIGHTMARE
Antarctic Press, 1994
1 . . . . 2.75
2 . . . . 2.75
3 Wedding Knight,pt.1 . . . . 2.75
4 Wedding Knight,pt.2 . . . . 2.75
5 F:Dream Shadow 2.75
6 V:Razorblast 2.75

KNIGHT MASTERS
1 thru 7 . . . . @2.00

KNIGHTS OF THE DINNER TABLE
Alderac Group, 1994
1 . . . . 50.00
2 . . . . 30.00
3 . . . . 20.00
Kenzer & Company, 1997
4 Have Dice Will Travel 15.00
5 Master of the Game 15.00
6 on the high seas 10.00
7 Lord of Steam 10.00
8 A:magic cow 5.00
9 To Dice for Sister Sara 5.00
16 thru 18 . . . . @5.00
19 thru 49 . . . . @3.00
50 double-size 5.00
51 thru 69 . . . . @3.00
70 thru 85 . . . . @4.00
TPB Vol. 1 Bundle of Trouble 9.95
TPB Vol. 2 Bundle of Trouble 9.95
TPB Vol. 3 Bundle of Trouble 9.95
TPB Vol. 4 Bundle of Trouble 9.95
TPB Vol. 5 Bundle of Trouble 9.95

B & W PUB.

TPB Vol. 6 Bundle of Trouble 9.95
TPB Vol. 7 Bundle of Trouble 9.95
TPB Vol. 8 Bundle of Trouble 9.95
TPB Vol. 9 Bundle of Trouble 10.00
TPB Vol. 10 Bundle of Trouble . . . 12.00
TPB Tales From the Vault 9.95
TPB Tales From the Vault, Vol.2 . . . 9.95
TPB Tales From the Vault, Vol.3 . . 12.95
TPB #4 Tales from the Vault 10.00
Spec. Black Hands Gaming Society 3.00
Spec. Origins 2003 . . . . 3.00

KNIGHTS OF THE DINNER TABLE: EVERKNIGHTS
Kenzer & Company, 2002
1 . . . . 3.00
2 thru 9 . . . . @3.00

KNIGHTS OF THE DINNER TABLE/FAANS
Six-Handed Press, 1999
X-over Spec. 3.00

KNIGHTS OF THE DINNER TABLE: HACKMASTERS
Kenzer & Company, 2000
1 . . . . 3.00
2 thru 8 . . . . @3.00
9 and 11 . . . . @3.00
11 . . . . 3.00
becomes:

KNIGHTS OF THE DINNER TABLE: HACKMASTERS OF EVERKNIGHT
11 thru 15 . . . . @3.00
TPB Vol. 1 Ultimate Hackmasters . 14.00

KNIGHTS OF THE DINNER TABLE ILLUSTRATED
Kenzer & Company, 2000
1 . . . . 3.00
2 thru 8 . . . . @3.00
9 thru 28 . . . . @3.00
Travelers Special #1 . . . . 3.00
TPB Vol. 1 Overkill 14.00

KNIGHTS OF THE DINNER TABLE MINI-SERIES
Kenzer & Company 2003
Vol. 1
1 (of 3) 3.00
2 thru 3 . . . . @3.00
1a thru 3a variant (c) . . . . @3.00

KNIGHT WATCHMAN
Caliber Press, 1994
1 Graveyard Shift,pt. 1 . . . . 3.00
2 Graveyard Shift,pt. 2 . . . . 3.00

KODOCHA: SANA'S STAGE
Tokyopop Press, 2002
1 (of 5) by Miho Obana 2.95
2 . . . . 2.95
3 thru 5 . . . . @3.00
GN Vol. 1 . . . . 10.00
GN Vol. 2 thru 10 . . . . @10.00

KOMODO & THE DEFIANTS
Victory
1 thru 6 . . . . @2.00

KORVUS
Human Monster Press, 1997
1 by Mick Fernette 2.95
2 . . . . 2.95

Arrow Comics, 1998
3 . . . . 2.95
VOL 2
1 . . . . 2.95
2 . . . . 2.95

KUNG FU WARRIORS
(Prev. ROBOWARRIORS)
CFW
12 . . . . 2.00
13 thru 19 . . . . @2.25

KUNOICHI
Lightning Comics, 1996
1 2 diff. mild covers 3.00
1 platinum edition 5.95
1 autographed edition 9.95

KYRA
Elsewhere, 1989
1 thru 5 by Robin Ator . . . . @2.00
TPB rep #1–#5 + pin-ups 6.95

L33T: COMICS FOR GAMERS
Keenspot Entertainment, 2002
1 . . . . 4.95
2 thru 4 . . . . @4.95
5 24-pg. 2.95
6 thru 11 . . . . @4.95

LABOR FORCE
Blackthorne, 1986
1 thru 4 . . . . @2.00
5 thru 8 . . . . @2.00

LA COSA NOSTROID
Fireman Press, 1997
1 by Don Harmon & Rob Schrab . 3.00
2 by Don Harmon & Edvis 3.00
3 . . . . 3.00
4 . . . . 3.00
5 . . . . 3.00
6 x-over madness 3.00
7 . . . . 3.00
8 . . . . 3.00
9 . . . . 3.00
10 final issue of Volume 1 . . . . 3.00

LACUNAE
CFD Produciton, 1995
1 thru 4 F:Monkey Boys 2.50
5 thru 10 . . . . @2.50
11 HMo 2.50
12 HMo 2.50

LADIES OF LONDON NIGHT
London Night, 1997
Fall Special 5.00
Winter Special 5.00

Knights–Land

Winter Wonderland Edition 7.00
Spring 98 Special 5.00
Spotlight: Devon Michaels 3.95

LADY ARCANE
Heroic Publishing
1 thru 4 . . . . @3.50

Lady Vampre #0
© Blackout Comics

LADY VAMPRE
Blackout Comics, 1996
0 (1995) 2.75
1 flip-book 2.95
0 Immortal No More (1998) 2.95
Spec.#1 In the Flesh (1996) 2.95
Spec.#1a photo sexy cover 9.95

LADY VAMPRE RETURNS
Blackout Comics, 1998
1 by Rob Roman & Kirk Manley . . 2.95
1a Deluxe edition 14.95

LAFFIN GAS
Blackthorne, 1986
1 . . . . 2.50
2 thru 12 . . . . @2.00

LANCE STANTON WAYWARD WARRIOR
1 and 2 . . . . @2.00

LANDER
Mermaid Producions
1 Power of the Dollar,pt.1 . . . . 2.25
2 Power of the Dollar,pt.2 . . . . 2.25
3 Power of the Dollar,pt.3 . . . . 2.25
Vol. 2
1 'By Whose Authority,'pt.1 . . . . . 2.75
2 'By Whose Authority,'pt.2 . . . . . 2.75

LAND OF OZ
Arrow Comics, 1998
1 by Gary Bishop & Bill Bryan 3.00
2 thru 6 . . . . @3.00

LAST DITCH
Edge Press
1 CCa(s),THa, ... 2.50

LAST GENERATION
Black Tie Studios, 1987
1 . . . . 5.00
2 . . . . 4.00
3 . . . . 2.25
4 . . . . 2.25
5 . . . . 2.25
Book One Rep. 6.95

LATEX ALICE
Basement Comics 2003
0 . . . . 2.95
0a special edition. 8.95
1 Blonde Ambition 2.95
1a Blonde Ambition, special. 8.95
Spec. Papercuts 2.95
Spec. #1 Paper Cuts 8.95
Bikini Bash Gallery #1 spec. 8.95

LEAGUE OF CHAMPIONS
Hero Comics, 1990
(cont. from Innovation L.of C. #3)
1 GP,F:Sparkplug,Icestar. 3.50
2 GP(i),F:Marksman,Flare,Icicle. . 3.50
3 . . . . 3.50
4 F:Sparkplug,League 3.50
5 Morrigan Wars,pt.#1 . . . . 3.50
6 Morrigan Wars,pt.#3 . . . . 3.50
7 Morrigan Wars,pt.#6 . . . . 3.50
8 Morrigan Wars Conclusion 3.50
9 A:Gargoyle 3.50
10 A:Rose 3.50
11 thru 12. . . . . 3.95
13 V:Malice 3.95
14 V:Olympians 3.95
15 V:Olympians 2.95

LE FEMME VAMPRIQUE
Brainstorm, 1997
1 . . . . 3.50

LEGENDLORE
Caliber ìNew Worldsî
1 JMt signed 2.95
3 JMt. 2.95
4 JMt 2.95
5 JMt. 2.95
6 flip book w/Boston Bombers #4 . 2.95
7 JMt 2.95
8 JMt. 2.95
TPB Tainted Soul, rep. #1–#4 . . . 12.95
TPB In Misery's Shadow,
  Rep. #5–#7 . . . . 9.95

LEGENDLORE: REALM WARS
Caliber ìNew Worldsî
1 by Joe Martin & Philip Xavier,
  Fawn cover by Xavier. 2.95
1a Falla cover by Boller 2.95
1b signed 2.95
2 . . . . 2.95
3 . . . . 2.95
4 concl. 2.95

LEGENDLORE: WRATH OF THE DRAGON
Caliber Fantasy, 1998
1 by JMt & Philip Xavier. 2.95

1 variant Philip Xavier(c) 2.95
2 . . . . 2.95
3 . . . . 2.95
4 . . . . 2.95
5 Prisoner set free 2.95
Spec. Handbook. 3.95
1-shot Legendlore: Slave of Fate
  by JMT & Philip Xavier 2.95
1-shot The Wind Spirits, 48-pg. . . 3.95
Giant Size Spec. 48-pg. 3.95

LEGENDS OF CAMELOT
Caliber Fantasy, 1999
Excalibur 2.95
Quest For Honor. 2.95
Merlin. 2.95
The Enchanted Lady 2.95
Sir Balin & The Dolorous Stroke . . . 2.95

LEGEND OF LEMNEAR
CPM Manga, 1997
1 . . . . 2.95
2 thru 17 . . . . @2.95
18 final issue 2.95
TPB Vol 1, 160-pg. 15.95
TPB Vol. 2 . . . . 15.95
TPB Vol. 3 176-pg. 15.95

LEGEND OF THE EIGHT DRAGON GODS
Komics, Inc., 2000
GN Vol. 1 . . . . 9.85
GN Vol. 2 . . . . 9.85
GN Vol. 3 . . . . 9.85
GN Vol. 4 181-pg. 9.85
GN Vol. 5 164-pg. 9.85
GN Vol. 6 164-pg. 9.85

Legends of Luxura #3
© Brainstorm

LEGENDS OF LUXURA
Brainstorm, 1996
1 platinum edition 5.00
2 gold edition. 5.00
3 . . . . 2.95
TPB #1. . . . . 12.95

LEGION ANTHOLOGY
Limelight, 1997
1 four stories 2.95
2 . . . . 2.95

3 F:Binary Angel 2.95
4 . . . . 2.95
5 Binary Angel. 2.95

LEGION X-I
Greater Mercury
1 McKinney. 5.00
2 McKinney,rare 15.00
Volume 2, 1989
1 thru 4 . . . . @2.00

LEGION X-2
Vol 2 #1 . . . . 2.00
Vol 2 #2 . . . . 2.00
Vol 2 #3 . . . . 2.00
Vol 2 #4 . . . . 2.00

LENORE
Slave Labor, 1998
1 by Roman Dirge 3.00
2 thru 10 . . . . @3.00
TPB 11.95
TPB Vol. 2 Wedgies! 13.95

LENSMAN
Eternity, 1990
1 E.E.`Doc' Smith adapt. 2.25
2 . . . . 2.25
3 . . . . 2.25
4 . . . . 2.25
5 On Radelix 2.25
6 . . . . 2.25
Collectors Spec #1, 56 pgs. 3.95
TPB Birth of a Lensman, rep. . . . 5.95
TPB Secret of the Lens, rep. . . . 5.95

LENSMAN: GALACTIC PATROL
Eternity, 1990
1 thru 7 E.E. `Doc' Smith adapt. . @2.25

LENSMAN: WAR OF THE GALAXIES
Eternity, 1990
1 thru 7 . . . . @2.25

LEONARDO
Mirage, 1986
1-shot TMNTurtles 13.00

LETHAL LADIES OF BRAINSTORM
Brainstorm, 1997
1 F:Luxura, Vampfire, etc. 2.95
1 luxury edition 5.00

LETHAL STRIKE ARCHIVES
London Night, 1997
1 rep. Razor #7, #10 & Uncut
  #19–#21. . . . . 3.00
TPB Lethal Strike (1998) 12.95

LETHAL STRIKE: SHADOW VIPER
London Night, 1998
1 (of 2) from Razor: Torture #4 . . . 3.00
1 leather 15.00

LETHARGIC LAD ADVENTURES
Crusade Entertainment, 1997
1 by Greg Hyland 2.95
2 . . . . 2.95
Becomes:

LETHARGIC LAD
TV Comics, 1997
3 by Greg Hyland 2.95
4 . . . . 2.95
5 . . . . 2.95
TPB Big Book of Lethargic Lad . . . 15.95
Lethargic Comics
6 by Greg Hyland 2.95
7 thru 14 . . . . @2.95

LEVEL X
Caliber, 1997
1 . . . . 2.95
2 32pg. 2.95
3 48pg. 3.95

LEVEL X: THE NEXT REALITY
Caliber, 1997
1 (of 2) by Dan Harbison & Randy
  Buccini, 64pg. 3.95
2 48pg. 3.95

LIBBY ELLIS
Eternity, 1988
1 thru 4 . . . . @2.00

LIBERATOR
Eternity
1 thru 6 . . . . @2.00

LIBERTY MEADOWS
Insight Studios, 1999
1 by Frank Cho 26.00
2 . . . . 15.00
3 . . . . 10.00
4 thru 10 . . . . @8.00
11 thru 20 . . . . @4.00
21 thru 23 . . . . @3.00
24 Virtual Reality Adventure 3.00
25 Pool Party 3.00
26 Fossil Dinosaurs 3.00
Spec. Wedding Album 3.00

L.I.F.E. BRIGADE
Blue Comet
1 A:Dr. Death. 2.00
1a 2nd printing 2.00
2 . . . . 2.00

LIFE OF A FETUS
Slave Labor, 1999
1 by Andy Ristaino. 2.95
2 thru 7 . . . . @2.95

LIFEQUEST
Caliber, 1997
1 by Matt Vanderpol 2.95
2 . . . . 2.95
3 . . . . 2.95
4 . . . . 2.95
5 . . . . 2.95
6 . . . . 2.95

LITTLE GLOOMY
Amaze Ink/Slave Labor Graphics, 1999
1 by Landry Walker & Eric Jones . . 2.95
2 thru 4 . . . . @2.95
5 . . . . 2.95
6 Mystery of the Invisible
  Men,pt.1 . . . . 2.95
Halloween Spec. 3.50
TPB Vol. 1 . . . . 12.95

LITTLE ORPHAN ANNIE
Tony Raiola 2001
TPB Man of Mystery 9.50
TPB Pro and the Con 9.50
TPB Little Worker 9.50
TPB The Dreamer 9.50
TPB Rich Man, Poor Man 9.50

LITTLE WHITE MOUSE (THE SERIES)
Caliber, 1998
1 by Paul Sizer 2.95
2 Fever Dreams 2.95
3 Filthy Jake 2.95
4 . . . . 2.95

LITTLE WHITE MOUSE: ENTROPY DREAMING
Blue Line Pro Comics, 2001
1 by Paul Sizer 2.95
2 Nuts and Bolts 2.95
3 . . . . 2.95
4 concl. 2.95

LITTLE WHITE MOUSE: OPEN SPACE
Blue Line Pro Comics, 2002
1 (of 4) by Paul Sizer. 2.95
2 thru 4 . . . . @2.95
TPB Vol. 3 . . . . 14.95

LIVINGSTONE MOUNTAIN
Adventure Comics, 1991
1 I:Scat,Dragon Rax 2.50
2 Scat & Rax Create Monsters . . . 2.50
3 Rax rescue attempt 2.50
4 Final issue 2.50

LLOYD LLEWELLYN
Fantagraphics, 1986
1 Mag Size 4.00
2 Mag Size 2.25
3 Mag Size 2.25
4 Mag Size 2.25
5 Mag Size 2.25
6 Mag Size 2.25
7 Regular Size 2.25

LOCO VS. PULVERINE
Eclipse, 1992
1 Parody 2.50

LODOSS WAR: CHRONICLES OF THE HEROIC KNIGHT
CPM Manga, 2000
1 by Ryo Mizuno & M. Natsumoto . 2.95
2 thru 15 . . . . @2.95
16 thru 19 . . . . @2.95
TPB Vol. 1 . . . . 15.95

TPB Vol. 2 thru Vol. 6 . . . . @15.95

LODOSS WAR: DEELIT'S TALE
CPM Manga, 2001
1 by R. Mizuno & S. Yoneyama . . . 2.95
1a signed & numbered. 14.95
2 thru 4 . . . . @2.95
5 thru 8 . . . . @2.95
TPB Vol. 1 Choices. 15.95
TPB Vol. 2 Forest of No Return . . . 15.95

LODOSS WAR: THE GREY WITCH
CPM Manga, 1998
1 by Ryo Mizuno & Yoshihiko Ochi 2.95
2 by Ryo Mizuno & Akikiro Yamada 2.95
3 thru 10 . . . . @2.95
11 thru 22 . . . . @2.95
TPB Vol. 2 . . . . 15.95
TPB Vol. 3 . . . . 15.95

LODOSS WAR: THE LADY OF PHARIS
CPM Manga, 1999
1 by Ryo Mizuno & Akikiro Yamada 2.95
2 thru 7 . . . . @2.95
TPB Vol. 1 208-pg. 15.95

Logan's Run #2
© *Adventure Comics*

LOGAN'S RUN
Adventure Comics, 1990
1 thru 6 Novel adapt. . . . . @2.95

LOGAN'S WORLD
Adventure Comics, 1991
1 Seq. to Logan's Run 2.50
2 thru 6 . . . . @2.50

LONER
Fleetway
1 Pt.1 (of 7) 2.00
2 Pt.2 . . . . 2.00
3 Pt.3 . . . . 2.00
4 Pt.4 . . . . 2.00
5 Pt.5 . . . . 2.00
6 Pt.6 . . . . 2.00

LONE WOLF & CUB
First, 1987–91
1 FM(c)	7.00
1a 2nd printing	2.50
1b 3rd printing	1.50
2	4.00
2a 2nd printing	2.00
3	4.00
4 thru 10	@4.00
11 thru 17	@3.00
18 thru 25	@3.00
26 thru 36	@3.00
37 and 38	@4.00
39 120-pg.	5.95
40	3.25
41 MP(c), 60-pg.	4.00
42 MP(c)	3.25
43 MP(c)	3.25
44 MP(c)	3.25
45 MP(c)	3.25

LOOKERS
Avatar Press, 1997
1	3.00
1 deluxe	5.00
1 signed	12.00
2	3.00
2 Deluxe cover	8.00
Spec. #1	3.00
Spec. #1 signed	8.00
Spec. Allure of the Serpent (1999)	3.50
Spec. Slaves of Anubis (1998)	3.50

LORD OF THE DEAD
Conquest
1 R.E.Howard adapt.	2.95

LORELEI
Power Comics, 1996
2 'Building the Perfect Beast,'pt.7	2.50
3 'Building the Perfect Beast,'pt.8	2.50
Vol.2
0 2nd printing	2.50
1	2.50
1a deluxe	3.95
1b signed	7.95

LORI LOVECRAFT
Caliber, 1997
1 MV, 48pg	3.95
1a signed	3.95
1-shot The Dark Lady (1997)	2.95
1-shot Repression (1998)	2.95
Spec. The Big Comeback (1998)	2.95
AV Publications, 2000
TPB Vol. 1 160-pg.	11.95

LOST, THE
Caliber, 1996
1	3.00
1a special ed.	7.00
1b signed	3.00
2 thru 4	@3.00

LOST CONTINENT
Eclipse, 1990
1 thru 5, Manga	@3.50

LOST STORIES
Creative Frontiers, 1998
1	2.95
2	2.95
3	2.95

---

4 The Big Horn Bruhaha	2.95
5 Strike Force O'Shea,pt.1	2.95
6 Strike Force O'Shea,pt.2	2.95
7 Gnome for a Day	2.95
8 A Vampire Too Far	2.95
9 The Undertroll Saga,pt.1	2.95

LOST WORLD, THE
Millennium, 1996
1 & 2 Arthur Conan Doyle adapt.	@2.95

LOTHAR
Powerhouse Graphics
1 I:Lothar,Galactic Bounty Hunter	2.50
2 I:Nightcap	2.50

LOUIS RIEL
Drawn & Quarterly, 1999
1 (of 10) by Chester Brown	2.95
2 thru 5	@2.95
6 thru 10	@2.95

LOVE AND ROCKETS
Fantagraphics Books, 1982–96
1 HB,B&W cover, adult	30.00
1a HB,Color cover	20.00
1b 2nd printing	4.00
2 HB	10.00
3 HB	6.00
4 HB	6.00
5 HB	6.00
6 HB	5.00
7 HB	6.00
8 HB	6.00
9 HB	5.00
10 HB	5.00
11 HB	3.00
12 HB	3.00
13 HB	3.00
14 HB	3.00
15 HB	3.00
16 thru 21 HB	@3.00
22 thru 39 HB	@3.00
40 thru 50	@3.00
Bonanza rep.	3.00
TPB Vol 9 Flies on the Ceiling, 2nd printing	16.95
TPB Vol 10	11.95
TPB Vol 11	14.95
TPB Vol 12	16.95
TPB Vol 14 Luba Conquers the World	14.95
TPB Vol 15	14.95

Love and Rockets #5
© Fantagraphics

Vol. 2, 2001
1 GHe,JHr,	3.95
1a 2nd printing	3.95
2	3.95
3	3.95
4 thru 9	@3.95

LOVE FIGHTS
Oni Press 2003
1	3.00
2 thru 4	@3.00
5	5.95

LOVE HINA
Tokyopop Press, 2002
1 (of 4) by Ken Akamatsu	3.00
2 thru 4	@3.00
GN Vol. 1 (of 14) authentic manga	10.00
GN Vol. 2 thru Vol. 14	@10.00

LOVE IN TIGHTS
Amaze Ink, 1998
1	2.95
Spec. Valentine's Day Special	2.95
Spec. Spring Fling	2.95
Anniv. #1	2.95
6	2.95
7	2.95

LOVELY PRUDENCE
Millennium, 1997
1 by Maze	2.95
2	2.95
3 Nightmares of Breeding	2.95
#M 24-pg.	1.95
#M 24-pg., signed	2.95
Spec. Swimsuit Special	2.95
Christmas Misery Spec.#1	2.95

LUBA
Fantagraphics, 1998
1 by Gilbert Hernandez	3.00
2 thru 5	@2.95
6 thru 7	@3.50
TPB Luba in America (2001)	19.95

LUBA'S COMICS & STORIES
Fantagraphics, 2000
1 by Gilbert Hernandez	3.00
2 GHe	3.50
3 GHe, Ofelia	3.50
6 GHe	3.50

LUFTWAFFE 1946
[Mini-Series]
Antarctic Press, 1996
1	5.00
2 thru 4	@4.00
TPB Vol.1, rep.mini-series #1–#4	10.95

Antarctic Press, 1997
1 by Ted Namura & BDn	3.00
2 Luftsturm,pt.2	3.00
3 Luftsturm,pt.3	3.00
4 Luftsturm,pt.4	3.00
5 new weapons	3.00
6 Projekt Saucer,pt.1	3.00
7 Projekt Saucer,pt.2	3.00
8 Projekt Saucer,pt.3	3.00
9 Projekt Saucer,pt.4	3.00
10 Projekt Saucer,pt.5	3.00
11 Projekt Saucer, epilogue	3.00
12 Richthofen's Flying Circus,pt.1	3.00

Comics Values Annual — B & W PUB. — Luftwaffe–Magic

13 Richthofen's Flying Circus,pt.2 . . 3.00
14 Jagdeschwader,pt.2 . . . . 3.00
15 Jagdeschwader,pt.3 . . . . 3.00
16 Jagdeschwader,pt.4 . . . . 3.00
17 Jagdeschwader,pt.5 . . . . 3.00
18 Schweinfurt 3.00
Tech Manual Vol. 1 . . . . 3.95
Tech Manual Vol. 2 . . . . 4.00
Tech Manual Vol. 3 Rocket Fighters 3.99
Tech Manual Vol. 4 Amerika
   Bombers 3.99
Tech Manual Vol. 5 Wonder
   Weapons 3.99
Tech. Manual Vol. 6 . . . . 6.00
Spec.#1 Triebflugel 2.95
Spec.#1 World War II: 1946 . . . . . . 3.95
Ann. #1 prototype artwork 2.95
TPB Vol.2, rep. #1–#5. . . . . 10.95
TPB Vol. 3, rep. 10.95
TPB Vol. 4, rep. #13–#18 . . . . 14.95
TPB 600-pg. 49.95

New Volume (2002)
1 Tigers of the Luftwaffe 5.95
2 thru 14 . . . . @5.95
Pocket Manga Vol. 1 . . . . 10.00
TPB Technical Manual 21.95

LUM*URUSEI YATSURA
Viz Communications
1 Art by Rumiko Takahashi 2.95
2 . . . . 2.95
3 . . . . 2.95
4 . . . . 2.95
5 . . . . 3.25
6 thru 8 . . . . @2.95

LUNAR DONUT
Cosmic Lunchbox Comics, 1996
1 thru 4 by Parham & Tucker . . . @2.95
Lunar Donut
5 . . . . 2.95
6 Powdered Sugar. 2.95

LUXURA
Brainstorm, 1996
Convention Book 2 . . . . 2.95
Ann.#1 48pg (1998) 3.95
Pin-up mag. Luxura: The Good, The
   Bad and the Beautiful (1999) . . 3.95
Spec.1 Luxura & Vampfire, x-over
   by Fauve (1997) 2.95
Luxura Leather, Platinum edition . . 5.00
Luxura Leather, Signed edition 8.00

LUXURA/BABY ANGEL X
Brainstorm, 1996
Spec. x-over 2.95
Spec. deluxe 5.00
Luxury edition 8.00
Deluxe luxury edition 12.00

LUXURA/WIDOW: BLOOD LUST
Brainstorm
Omega x-over pt.2 concl. 2.95
Omega Fusion cover 5.00
Luxury edition 8.00
Deluxe luxury edition 12.00
See: Widow/Luxura for pt.1

LYNX: AN ELFLORD TALE
Peregrin, 1999
1 by Barry Blair 2.95

---

2 by Barry Blair & Colin Chan 2.95
3 . . . . 2.95
4 . . . . 2.95

M.A.C.H. 1
Fleetway
1 I:John Probe-Secret Agent 2.00
2 thru 9 . . . . @2.00

MACKENZIE QUEEN
Matrix, 1985
1 thru 5 . . . . @3.75

MACROSS II
Viz Comics, 1992
1 Macross Saga sequel 2.75
2 A:Ishtar 2.75
3 F:Reporter Hibiki,Ishtar 2.75
4 V:Feff,The Marduk 2.75
5 . . . . 2.75
6 . . . . 2.75
7 Sylvie Confesses 2.75
8 F:Ishtar 2.75
9 V:Marduk Fleet 2.75
10 . . . . 2.75

MACROSS II: THE MICRON CONSPIRACY
Viz, 1994
1 Manga 2.75

Mad Dogs #1
© Eclipse

MAD DOGS
Eclipse, 1992
1 I:Mad Dogs(Cops) 2.50
2 V:Chinatown Hood 2.50
3 . . . . 2.50

MADMAN
Oni Press, 2002
TPB Madman Adventures (2002) . 14.95
TPB The Odyity Odyssey,
   10th Anniv. (2002) 15.95

MAD RACCOONS
MU Press, 1991
1 thru 7 by Cathy Hill, Angst of
   an Artist . . . . @2.95

MAELSTROM
Aircel, 1987
1 thru 5 . . . . @2.00
6 thru 13 . . . . @2.00

MAGGOTS
Hamilton, 1991
1 JSon, mag size 3.95
2 JSon, mag size 3.95
3 GM/JSon,inc.`Some Kinda
   Beautiful' 3.95

MAGICAL MATES
Antarctic Press, 1995
1 & 2 Manga, by Mio Odagi . . . . @2.95
3 thru 8 (of 8) . . . . @2.95

MAGICAL POKEMON JOURNEY
Viz Communications, 2000
1 How Do You Do, Pikachu 5.00
2 Cooking with Jigglypuff 5.00
3 Pokemon Holiday 5.00
4 Fun at the Beach 5.00
TPB Vol. 1 Party with Pikachu . . . 13.95
PART 2, 2000
1 thru 4 . . . . @5.00
PART 3, 2000
1 thru 4 . . . . @5.00
TPB Vol.3 Wal Comes Crashing
   Down 13.95
PART 4, 2001
1 thru 4 Love Potion Pursuit . . . . @5.00
TPB Vol.4 Friends & Family 13.95
PART 5, 2001
1 thru 4 . . . . @5.00
TPB Vol.5 Going Coconuts 13.95
PART 6, 2001
1 (of 4) 5.00
2 thru 4 . . . . @5.00
TPB Vol.6 Gold & Silver 13.95
PART 7, 2002
1 . . . . 4.95
2 thru 4 . . . . @5.00
TPB Vol.7 From the Heart 13.95

MAGIC KNIGHT RAYEARTH
Mixx Entertainment, 1999
Manga Vol. 2 . . . . 11.95
Manga Vol. 3 . . . . 11.95
Tokyopop Press, 2000
Vol. 4 . . . . 11.95
TPB Mixx Manga Vol. 5 . . . . 11.95
TPB Mixx Manga Vol. 6 . . . . 12.95
TPB Art of Magic Knight Rayearth . 20.00
TPB Art of Vol. 2 . . . . 20.00

MAGIC PRIEST
Antarctic Press, 1998
1 (of 3) by B.Lyga & N.Googe 2.95
2 . . . . 2.95

MAGIC WHISTLE
Alternative Press
Vol 2
1 by Sam Henderson 2.95
2 thru 8 . . . . @2.95

All comics prices listed are for *Near Mint* condition.

Magus–Marquis — B & W PUB.

MAGUS
Caliber Core, 1998
1L by Gary Reed & Craig Brasfield,
  VcL(c) 2.95
1D GyD(c). 2.95
1 premium edition, signed 9.95
2 Magus secrets 2.95
3 Lilith & Beezlebub. 2.95
1-shot Magus: The Forever King. . . 2.95
Spec. Dawn of Armageddon,
  x-over, 48-pg. 2.95

MAI, THE PSYCHIC GIRL
Eclipse, 1987
1 I:Mai,Alliance of 13 Sages 3.75
1a 2nd printing 2.50
2 V:Wisdom Alliance 2.50
2a 2nd printing 2.50
3 V:Kaieda,I:Ojii-San 2.50
4 . . . . 2.50
5 thru 19 . . . . @2.50
20 thru 28 . . . . @2.50

MAISON IKKOKU
Viz Comics, 1993
1 thru 7 Manga 2.95
[Part Two]
1 thru 6 . . . . 2.95
[Part Three]
1 thru 6 . . . . 2.95
[Part Four]
1 thru 6 F:Kyoko 2.95
7 thru 10 . . . . @2.95
[Part Six], 1996
1 thru 11 by Rumiko Takahashi . @3.50
[Part Seven], 1997
1 thru 8 by Rumiko Takahashi . . @3.25
9 thru 13 . . . . @3.50
[Part Eight], 1998
1 (of 8) 3.25
2 . . . . 3.50
3 thru 8 . . . . @3.25
[Part Nine], 1999
1 (of 10) 3.25
2 thru 10 . . . . @3.25
TPB Vol. 4 Good Housekeeping . . 15.95
TPB Vol. 5 Empty Nest. 15.95
TPB Vol. 6 Bedside Manners . . . 15.95
TPB Vol. 7 Intensive Care. 15.95
TPB Vol. 8 Domestic Dispute . . . 16.95
TPB Vol. 10 Dogged Pursuit 17.95
TPB Vol. 11 Student Affairs. 16.95
TPB Vol. 12 The Hounds of War . . 16.95
TPB Vol. 14 Welcome Home. . . . 16.95

MANDRAKE
1 . . . . 3.95
2 . . . . 3.95
3 . . . . 3.95
Ultimate Mandrake 14.95

MANDRAKE MONTHLY
1 . . . . 3.95
2 . . . . 3.95
3 . . . . 4.95
4 . . . . 4.95
5 . . . . 4.95
6 . . . . 6.95
Special #1 . . . . 6.95

MAN-EATING COW
New England Comics, 1992
1 Spin-off from the Tick 3.25
2 O:Mr.Krinkles,A:Lt.Valentine 2.75

Man-Eating Cow #2
© New England Comics

3 Final issue 2.75
Bonanza #1, 128pg (1996) 4.95
Bonanza #2, 100pg. 4.95

MAN-ELF
3 A:Jerry Cornelius 2.25

MAN FROM U.N.C.L.E.
Entertainment Publ., 1987
1 'Number One with a Bullet Affair. 3.50
2 'Number One with a Bullet Affair. 3.00
3 'The E-I-E-I-O Affair'. 3.00
4 'The E-I-E-I-O Affair,' concl. 3.00
5 'The Wasp Affair' 3.00
6 'Lost City of THRUSH Affair'. . . . 3.00
7 'The Wildwater Affair' 3.00
8 'The Wilder West Affair' 3.00
9 'The Canhadian Lightning Affair' . 3.00
10 'The Turncoat Affair' 3.00
11 'Craters of the Moon Affair' 3.00

MANGA EX
Antarctic Press, 2001
1 thru 5 . . . . @6.95
6 . . . . 6.95

MANGAPHILE
Radio Comix, 1999
1 thru 5 . . . . @2.95
6 thru 11 . . . . @2.95
12 48-pg. 3.95
13 48-pg. 4.00
14 thru 21 48-pg. 4.00

MANGA VIZION
Viz Communications
Vol. 1, 1995
1 thru 10 Ogre Slayer. . . . . @4.95
Vol. 2, 1996
1 thru 12 . . . . @4.95
Vol. 3, 1997
1 thru 8 . . . . @4.95
Vol. 4
1 thru 8 . . . . @4.95

MANGAZINE
Antarctic Press, 1985
1 newsprint cover 15.00

1a reprint. 3.00
2 . . . . 9.00
3 . . . . 8.00
4 . . . . 8.00
5 . . . . 8.00
New Series
1 . . . . 3.00
2 . . . . 3.00
3 . . . . 2.00
4 . . . . 2.00
5 thru 7 . . . . @2.00
8 thru 13 . . . . @2.25
14 New Format. 2.95
15 thru 44 . . . . @2.95
VOL. 3, 1999
1 thru 15 . . . . @9.00
16 thru 27 140+-pg. . . . . @9.00
28 thru 39 . . . . @9.00
40 thru 49 . . . . @10.00

MANIMAL
Renegade, 1986
1 EC,rep. 2.00

MAN OF RUST
Blackthorne, 1986
1 Cover A 2.00
1 Cover B 2.00

MANSLAUGHTER
Brainstorm, 1996
1 . . . . 2.95
1a gold foil edition 5.00

MANTUS FILES
Eternity
1 Sidney Williams novel adapt. . . . 2.50
2 Vampiric Figures. 2.50
3 Secarus' Mansion. 2.50
4 A:Secarus. 2.50

MARCANE
Eclipse
1 Book 1,JMu 5.95

MARK I
(Prev.: Atomic Comics)
2 . . . . 2.00

MARMALADE BOY
Tokyopop Press, 2001
1 (of 5) by Wataru Yoshizumi 2.95
2 . . . . 2.95
3 . . . . 2.95
4 and 5 . . . . 3.00
GN Vol. 1 (of 8) authentic manga . 10.00
GN Vol. 2 thru 8 . . . . @10.00

MARQUIS, THE
Caliber, 1997
1 GyD 3.00
1 spec. double gatefold cover 6.00
2 Marquis cover by Vincent Locke . 3.00
2a Marquis view of world GyD(c). . 3.00
3 . . . . 3.00
Spec. The Marquis, Gallery of
  Hell, GyD 3.95
Spec. The Marquis: Les Preludes,
  GyD prelude edition (1996). . . . 2.95
Spec.A Les Preludes, signed 2.95

CVA Page 744   All comics prices listed are for *Near Mint* condition.

MARQUIS, THE: DANSE MACABRE
Oni Press, 2000
1 (of 5) by Guy Davis 3.00
2 .... 3.00
3 thru 5 .... @3.00
TPB 18.95

MARS
Tokyopop Press, 2002
GN Vol. 1 (of 15) authentic manga 10.00
GN Vol. 2 thru Vol. 15 .... @10.00

MARTIAN SUCCESSOR NADESICO
CPM Manga, 1999
1 by Kia Asamiya............. 2.95
2 .... 2.95
3 .... 2.95
4 thru 15 .... @2.95
16 thru 26 .... @2.95
TPB Vol. 1 .... 15.95
TPB Book 2 176-pg........... 15.95
TPB Book 3 176-pg........... 15.95
TPB Book 4 208-pg........... 15.95

MASKED WARRIOR X
Antarctic Press, 1996
1 (of 6) by Masayuki Fujihara..... 3.50
2 .... 2.95
3 The Girls of Olympus,' pt.2 ..... 2.95
4 'Protect the Silver Fortress' 2.95

MASQUERADE
Eclipse
1 .... 2.00
2 .... 2.00
3 .... 2.00

MATAAK
K-Blamm, 1995
1 I:Mataak.................. 2.50
2 Spirit of Peace 2.50

MATT CHAMPION
Metro
1 EC...................... 2.00
2 EC...................... 2.00

MAVIS
Exhibit A, 1998
1 BLs, F:Wolff & Byrd's secretary.. 2.95
2 .... 2.95

MAXION
CPM, 1999
1 by Takeshi Takebayashi 2.95
2 thru 11 .... @2.95
12 thru 24 .... @2.95
25 .... 2.95
26 .... 2.95
TPB Book 1 .... 15.95
TPB Book 2 .... 15.95
TPB Book 3 Waves of Misfortune. 15.95
TPB Book 4 Maniac Obsessions.. 15.95

MAX OF THE REGULATORS
Atlantic
1 .... 4.00
2 .... 3.50

3 .... 3.50
4 .... 3.50

MAXWELL MOUSE FOLLIES
Renegade, 1986
1 Large format (1981) 4.00
1a Comic Size(1986)........... 3.00
2 thru 6 .... @2.00

MAYHEM
1 Mask(c) 9.00
2 thru 6 .... @8.00

MAZE AGENCY
Caliber, 1997
1 'The Death of Justice Girl'
reprint series 2.95
1a signed 2.95
2 stranded in a monastery, Gene
Gonzales(c) 2.95
2a Adam Hughes (c) 2.95
3G The Two Wrong Rhoades,
Gonzales(c) 2.95
3H Adam Hughes(c) 2.95

MEASLES
Fantagraphics, 1998
1 by Gilbert Hernandez 2.95
2 thru 8 .... @2.95

MEAT CAKE
Fantagraphics, 1995
1 thru 4 .... @2.50
5 thru 8 .... @3.00
9 thru 12 .... @4.00

MECHANOIDS
Caliber, 1991
1 .... 2.50
2 thru 5 .... @3.50

MECHARIDER: THE REGULAR SERIES
Castle
1 thru 3 F:Winter 2.95
Spec.#1 Limited Edition 2.95

MEDABOTS
Viz Communications, 2002
Part 1
1 (of 4) by Rin Horuma 2.75
2 thru 4 .... @2.75
Part 2
1 (of 4) New Challenges 2.75
2 thru 4 .... @2.75
Part 3
1 (of 4) 2.75
2 thru 4 .... @2.75
Part 4
1 by Horumarin 2.75
2 thru 4 .... 2.75
TPB Vol. 1 A Boy and His 'Bot 9.95
TPB Vol. 2 Let's Get Ready
to Robattle 9.95
TPB Vol. 3 The Medaforce 9.95
TPB Vol. 4 Finale 9.95

MEGATON
Megaton, 1983
1 JG(c),EL(1stProWork),GD,MG,

A:Ultragirl,Vanguard 9.00
2 EL,JG(pin-up),A:Vanguard 8.00
3 MG,AMe,JG,EL,I:Savage
Dragon................... 13.00
4 AMe,EL,2nd A:Savage Dragon
(inc.EL profile) 9.00
5 AMe,RLd(inside front cover) 3.00
6 AMe,JG(inside back cover),
EL(Back cover) 3.00
7 AMe 3.00
8 RLd,I:Youngblood(Preview).... 18.00

MEGATON MAN MEETS THE UNCATEGORIZABLE X-THEMS
Jabberwocky, 1989
1 .... 2.00

MEGATON MAN VS. FORBIDDEN FRANKENSTEIN
Fiasco Comics, 1996
1 by Don Simpson & Anton Drek .. 2.95

MELISSA MOORE: BODYGUARD
Draculina Publishing, 1995
1 thru 3 V:Machine Gun Eddie .. @2.95

MEMORY MAN
Emergency Stop Press, 1995
1 thru 2 Some of the Space Man .. 2.95

Men in Black #1
© Aircel

MEN IN BLACK
Aircel, 1991
1 by Lowell Cunningham & Sandy
Carruthers, basis of Movie ... 35.00
2 .... 20.00
3 F:Jay, Arbiter Doran 20.00
[Book II], 1991
1 .... 15.00
2 thru 3 .... @8.00

MEN IN BLACK: THE ROBORG INCIDENT
Castle
1 thru 3 . . . . @3.00

MERCEDES
Angus Publishing, 1995
8 thru 15 by Mike Friedland
 & Grant Fuhst . . . . @2.95
TPB Vol. 2 . . . . 10.95
TPB Vol. 3, rep. The Wicked
 from #11–#15 . . . . 10.95
VOL. 4
1 thru 4 . . . . @2.95
VOL. 5, 1997
1 . . . . 2.95
2 and 3 . . . . @2.95
Spec. Senseless Acts of
 Beauty (1998) 2.95

MERCHANTS OF DEATH
Eclipse, 1988
1 thru 5 . . . . @2.00

MERCY
Avatar Press, 1997
0 O:Mercy 3.00
0b leather cover. 30.00
1 (of 2) by Bill Maus 3.00
1 leather cover 25.00
1 signed 10.00

MERLIN
Adventure Comics, 1990
1 BMC,Merlin's Visions 2.50
2 V:Warlord Carados 2.50
3 . . . . 2.50
4 Ninevah 2.50
5 D:Hagus. 2.50
6 Final Issue 2.50
[2nd Series]
1 Journey of Rhiannon & Tryon . . . 2.50
2 Conclusion 2.50

MERMAID'S GAZE
Viz Comics, 1995
1 thru 3 V:Shingo. 2.75
4 final issue. 2.75
TPB 15.95

METACOPS
Monster Comics, 1991
1 and 2 . . . . @2.00

METAL GUARDIAN FAUST
Viz Communications, 1997
1 thru 5 (of 8) by Tetsuo Ueyama @2.95
6 thru 8 . . . . @2.95
TPB Vol. 1 . . . . 16.95

METROPOLIS
Caliber, 1997
0 movie adaptation, series
 prequel,48pg 3.95
1 The Last Fredersen, pt.1 . . . . . 2.95
2 The Last Fredersen, pt.2 . . . . . 2.95
3 The Last Fredersen, pt.3 . . . . . 2.95

METAPHYSIQUE
Eclipse
1 NB,Short Stories. 2.50

2 NB,Short Stories. 2.50

MIAMI MICE
Rip Off Press, 1986
1 1st printing 3.00
1a 2nd printing 2.00
3 . . . . 2.00
4 Record,A:TMNT 3.00

MICHELANGELO
Mirage, 1986
1 TMNT. 17.00
1a 2nd Printing 4.50

Micra #2
© Fictioneer

MICRA
Fictioneer, 1986
1 . . . . 4.00
2 . . . . 3.00
3 . . . . 3.00
4 . . . . 2.00
5 thru 7 . . . . @1.75
8 . . . . 2.25

MIDNIGHT
Blackthorne
1 thru 4 . . . . @1.75

MIDNIGHT PANTHER
CPM Comics, 1997
1 Manga, translated. 2.95
2 . . . . 2.95
3 . . . . 2.95
4 . . . . 2.95
5 . . . . 2.95
6 Den of Scoundrels 2.95
7 The Sleeping Town. 2.95
8 to Reincarnation City 2.95
9 O:Midnight Panthers. 2.95
10 . . . . 2.95
11 . . . . 2.95
12 . . . . 2.95
TPB Sex, Death and Rock 'n' Roll.
 rep #1–#6. . . . . 15.95
TPB Book 2: Feline Fanatics,
 rep.#7–#12. . . . . 15.95
Spec. Breaking Up is Hard to Do . 2.95

MIDNIGHT PANTHER: FEUDAL FANTASY
CPM Manga, 1998
1 by Yu Asagiri 2.95
2 thru 5 . . . . @2.95
TPB Book 4: Feudal Fantasy 15.95

MIDNIGHT PANTHER: SCHOOL DAZE
CPM Comics, 1998
1 (of 5) by Yu Asagiri 2.95
2 thru 5 . . . . @2.95
TPB Book 3: School Daze 15.95

MIDNITE SKULKER
Target, 1986
1 thru 7 . . . . @2.00

MIGHTY GUY
C&T, 1987
1 thru 6 . . . . @2.00
Summer Fun Spec #1 . . . . 2.50

MIGHTY MITES
Eternity, 1986
1 I:X-Mites. 2.00
2 & 3 . . . . @2.00

MIGHTY MOUSE ADVENTURE MAGAZINE
Spotlight, 1987
1 . . . . 5.00

MIGHTY TINY
Antarctic
1 thru 4 . . . . @2.00
5 . . . . 2.50
Mouse Marines Collection rep. 7.50

MIKE HOFFMAN'S LOST WORLDS OF FANTASY AND SCI-FI
Antimater/Hoffman Int. 2003
1 . . . . 2.95
1 spec. edition. 8.95
2 thru 7 . . . . @2.95
3 thru 4 special edition. 8.95

MIKE HOFFMAN'S MONSTERS AND MAIDENS
Antimater/Hoffman International 2003
1 . . . . 3.50
2 . . . . 2.95

MIKE HOFFMAN'S TIGRESS
Black Daze, 2000
1 by Mike Hoffman 2.95
Antimater/Hoffman Int. 2003
TPB Vol. 1 Journey to Caldathrea . . 9.95
Spec. Cover Gallery Spec. 8.95

MILK & CHEESE
Slave Labor, 1991–97
1 EDo, Milk Products gone bad . . 55.00

| 1a 2nd thru 7th printing 3.50
| 2 .... 32.00
| 2a 2nd thru 4th printing 10.00
| 3 .... 22.00
| 3a 2nd thru 4th printing 10.00
| 4 .... 15.00
| 4a 2nd & 3rd printing........... 3.00
| 5 .... 15.00
| 5a 2nd & 3rd printing........... 3.00
| 6 .... 10.00
| 6a 2nd printing 2.75
| Other #1....................... 2.75
| Third #1 .... 2.75
| Fourth #1 .... 2.75
| First #2....................... 2.75
| Six Six Six #1................. 2.75
| Six Six Six 2nd printing, EDo .. 2.75
| Latest Thing 2.95
| TPB Fun with Milk & Cheese, rep.
| 1st 4 issues 11.95

MILLINIUM 2.5: THE BUCK ROGERS SAGA
ACG Comics, 2000
1 by Dick Calkin 2.95
2 thru 4 .... @2.95

MILTON CANIFF'S TERRY & THE PIRATES
ACG Comics, 1999
1 by Milton Caniff 2.95
2 .... 2.95
3 .... 2.95
4 .... 2.95
TPB Spec. (2001)............... 12.95

MINIMUM WAGE
Fantagraphics, 1995
Vol. 1, new printing 11.00
Vol. 2, 1995
1 thru 4 .... @3.00
5 by Bob Fingerman 3.00
6 .... 3.00
7 .... 3.00
8 .... 3.00
9 Artsy Fartsy 3.00
10 .... 3.00
TPB Vol. 2, rep. #1–#5 .... 12.95

MIRACLE GIRLS
Tokyopop Press, 2000
1 .... 2.95
2 .... 2.95
3 thru 14 .... @2.95
15 thru 17.................. @2.95
18 thru 23.................. @3.00
TPB Pocket Mixx, Vol. 1
  thru Vol.3 .... @9.95
TPB Pocket Mixx, Vol. 4 ...... 10.00
TPB Pocket Mixx, Vol. 5 ...... 10.00
GN Vol. 6 thru Vol. 9 ...... @10.00

MIRACLE SQUAD BLOOD & DUST
Apple, 1989
1 thru 3 .... @2.35

MISTER BLANK
Amaze Ink, 1997
0 by Chris Hicks 2.25
0a 2nd printing 2.00
1 F:Sam Smith 2.95
2 thru 14 .... @2.95
TPB rep. #1–#14, 360-pg........ 29.95

B & W PUB.

MISTER X
Vortex, Vol 2, 1989–90
1 thru 11 .... @2.00

MITES
Continuum
1 .... 2.50
1a 2.00
2B 2.00
3 and 4 .... @2.00

MOBILE POLICE PATLABOR
Viz Communications, 1997
1 (of 12) by Masami Yuki........ 2.95
PART TWO, 1998
1 by Masami Yuki 2.95
2 thru 6 .... @2.95
TPB Vol. 1 .... 15.95
TPB Vol. 2 Basic Training 15.95

MOBILE SUIT GUNDAM 0079
Viz Communications, 1999
1 (of 8) by Kazhisa Kondo ..... @2.95
2 thru 7 .... @2.95
PART TWO, 1999
1 (of 5) 2.95
2 thru 5 .... @2.95
TPB Vol. 1 .... 15.95
TPB Vol. 1 2nd edition 9.95
TPB Vol. 2 .... 15.95
TPB Vol. 2 2nd edition 9.95
TPB Vol. 3 thru 9 .... @9.95

MOBILE SUIT GUNDAM WING: BLIND TARGET
Viz Communications, 2001
1 thru 4 .... @2.95
TPB 12.95

MOBILE SUIT GUNDAM WING: EPISODE ZERO
Viz Communications, 2001
1 thru 8 .... @2.95
TPB Art of Mobile Suit
  Gundam Wing 19.95
TPB (2002)................... 16.95

MOBILE SUIT GUNDAM WING: GROUND ZERO
Viz Communications, 2000
1 (of 4) by Reku Fuyynagi 2.95
2 thru 4 .... @2.95
TPB 144-pg.................... 14.95

MODERN PULP
Special Studio
1 Rep.from January Midnight..... 2.75

MOEBIUS COMICS
Caliber, 1996
1 Moe 3.00
2 Moe 3.00
3 Moe 3.00
4 Moe,MP 3.00
5 Moe,SL 3.00
6 Moe 3.00

MOGOBI DESERT RATS
Midnight Comics, 1991
1 I&O:Desert Rats 'Waste of the
  World' 2.25

MONNGA
Daikaiyu Enterprises, 1995
1 & 2 Titanic Omega 3.95

MONOGRAPHS
Coppervale, 1997
1 by James Owen 2.95
2 Bob Phantom 2.95
3 Sidekick Wanted—Benefits
  Available 2.95
4 thru 6 .... 2.95

Monster Boy #1
© Monster Comics

MONSTER BOY
Monster Comics
1 A:Monster Boy 2.25

MONSTER POSSE
Malibu Adventure 1992
1 I:Monster Posse 2.50
2 I:P.O.N.E,Wack Mack Dwac's
  sister,D-Vicious............ 2.50
3 .... 2.50

MONSTERS ATTACK
Globe
1 GM,JSe 2.00
2 GC 2.00
3 ATh,GC 2.00

MONSTERS FROM OUTER SPACE
Adventure, 1992
1 thru 3 .... @2.50

MORBID ANGEL: DESPERATE ANGELS
London Night, 1998
0 EHr, & Jude Millien.......... 3.00
0A Powell(c)................... 5.00
0B Powell(c)................... 5.00

All comics prices listed are for Near Mint condition.

MORBID ANGEL: PENANCE
London Night Studios, 1995
1 I:Brandon Watts 4.00

MORBID ANGEL: TO HELL AND BACK
London Night, 1996
1 (of 3) EHr. 4.00
2 and 3 . . . . @3.00

MORNING GLORY
Radio Comix, 1998
1 by Loran Gayton & Michael Vega 2.95
2 thru 6 . . . . @2.95

MORTAL COIL
Mermaid
1 thru 3 . . . . @2.25
4 F:Red-Line,Gift. 2.25
5 Pin-Up Issue. 2.25

MORTAR MAN
Marshall Comics, 1993
1 I:Mortar Man. 2.00
2 thru 3 . . . . @2.00

MOSAIC
Oktober Black Press
1 F:Halo,Daeva 2.25
2 "Gun Metal Gray" 2.50
3 . . . . 2.50
4 Elf(c) 2.50
5 Wisps 2.50

MOSAIC
Sirius, 1999
1 by Kyle Hotz. 2.95
2 thru 5 conclusion. . . . . @2.95
TPB 14.95

MOUNTAIN WORLD
Newcomers Press, 1995
1 I:Jeremiah Rainshadow 2.95

MR. BEAT ADVENTURES
Moordam Comics, 1997
1 . . . . 2.95
1 deluxe 5.00
Spec. House of Burning Jazz Love. 2.95
Spec. deluxe 5.00
Two-Fisted Atomic Action
    Super Spec. 2.95
Two-Fisted Atomic Action
    Super Spec., deluxe 10.00
Two-Fisted Atomic Action
    Super Spec., mega deluxe . . . 20.00
Spec. Mr. Beat: Superstar. 5.00
Spec. Mr. Beat: Superstar, deluxe. 10.00
Ann.#1 Babes and Bongos 2.95

MR. FIXITT
Apple, 1989
1 and 2 . . . . @2.00

MR. MYSTIC
Eclipse
1 Will Eisner 2.50

MR. NIGHTMARE'S WONDERFUL WORLD
Moonstone, 1995
1 thru 3 Dreams So Real,
    pt.1–pt.3 . . . . @2.95

MS. CHRIST
Draculina Publishing, 1995
1 I:Ms. Christ. 2.95

Ms. Tree #21
© Renegade

MS. TREE
Aardvark–Vanaheim, 1984
1-10 see Other Pub. (color)
11 thru 18 . . . . @2.00
Renegade, 1985
19 thru 49. . . . . @2.00
50 . . . . 4.50
1 3-D Classic. 2.95

MUMMY, THE
Monster Comics
1 A:Dr.Clarke,Prof.Belmore 2.00
2 Mummy's Curse 2.00
3 A:Carloph 2.00
4 V:Carloph, conc. 2.00

MUMMY'S CURSE
Aircel, 1990
1 thru 4 B.Blair. . . . . @2.25

MUNSTERS, THE
TV Comics, 1998
1 photo (c). 3.00
1a variant (c). 8.00
2 Beverly Owen(c). 3.00
2 Pat Priest (c) 3.00
2 Pat Priest (c) signed 19.95
3 . . . . 3.00
3a Celebrity autograph edition . . 22.95
4 . . . . 3.00
4a variant photo (c) 3.00
4b variant (c) celebrity autograph
    edition 22.95
5 Herman photo (c) 3.00
5 Grandpa photo (c) 3.00
Spec. Comic Con 9.95
Celebrity Autograph Edition: Butch
    Patrick 22.95
TPB Vol 1, rep. #1–#4 . . . . 10.95
Spec.#1 Herman/Grandpa (c) 3.00
Spec.#1a Grandpa (c) 3.00
Halloween Spec. Munsters 1313. . . 3.00
Golden Age Adventure Spec.A(c) . . 3.00
Golden Age Adventure Spec.B(c) . . 3.00

MUNSTERS CLASSICS
TV Comics
0 The Fregosi Emerald 3.00
0 variant (c). 7.95

MURCIELAGA: SHE-BAT
Hero Graphics, 1993
1 Daerick Gross reps. 2.00
2 Reps. contd 2.95

MURDER
Renegade, 1986
1 SD 2.00
2 Cl(c). 2.00
3 SD 2.00
[2nd series]
1 . . . . 2.00

MURDER CAN BE FUN
Slave Labor, 1996
1 thru 6 . . . . @2.95
2 2nd printing 2.95
7 . . . . 2.95
8 . . . . 2.95
9 Seedy Side of Sex 2.95
10 We Love Sports. 2.95
11 . . . . 2.95
12 Amusement Park Terror 2.95

MURDER ME DEAD
El Capitan Books, 2000
1 (of 8) by David Lapham 3.00
2 . . . . 3.00
3 thru 8 . . . . @3.00
9 64-pg. 5.00
TPB 19.95

MUTANT ZONE
Aircel, 1991
1 Future story 2.50
2 F.B.I. Drone Exterminators 2.50
3 conclusion 2.50

MYSTERY MAN
Slave Labor, 1988
1 thru 5 . . . . @2.00

MYTH ADVENTURES
Warp Graphics, 1984
1 Mag size 2.00
2 thru 4 . . . . @2.00
5 Comic size 2.00
6 thru 11 . . . . @2.00
12 . . . . 2.00

MYTH CONCEPTIONS
Apple, 1987
1 . . . . 2.00
2 . . . . 2.00
3 thru 8 . . . . @2.00

MYTHOGRAPHY
Bardic Press, 1966
1 F:Poison Elves	5.00
2 fantasy stories	5.00
3 fantasy stories, inc. Elfquest	5.00
4	4.50
5 72-pg.	4.50
6 F:Anubis Squadron 72pg.	4.00
7 80-pg.	4.50
8 72-pg.	4.50

MYTHOS
Wonder Comix, 1987
1 and 2	@2.00

NATURE OF THE BEAST
Caliber
1 thru 3 'The Beast'	@2.50

NAUGHTY BITS
Fantagraphics, 1996
20	2.95
21 I:Bitchy Butch	2.95
22	2.95
23 O:Bitchy Butch.	2.95
24	2.95
25 by Roberta Gregory	2.95
26 thru 38	@2.95
TPB Vol. 4: Bitchy's School Daze	9.95
TPB Vol. 5: Bitchy Butch.	9.95
TPB Work & Play with Bitchy Bitch	9.95
TPB A Bitch is Born, sgn.	9.95
TPB Vol.6 Burn, Bitchy, Burn	9.95

NAUSICAA OF THE VALLEY OF WIND
Viz Select, 1988
Book One	4.50
Book Two	5.50
Book Three	4.00
Book Four	3.00
Book Five	2.50
Book Six	2.95
Book Seven	2.95

[Part 2]
#1 thru #4	@2.95

[Part 3]
#1 thru #3	@2.95
TPB Vol. 4	17.95

NAZRAT
Imperial, 1986
1	2.50
2 thru 6	@2.00

NECROSCOPE
Caliber, 1997
1 Brian Lumley adapt.	2.95
1 signed	2.95
2	2.95
3	2.95
4	2.95

NEGATIVE BURN
Caliber, 1993
1 I:Matrix 7, Flaming Carrot	5.00
2	3.50
3 Bone preview	12.00
4 thru 12 various stories	@3.25
13 Strangers in Paradise	10.00
14 thru 18 various stories	@3.50
19 Flaming Carrot.	5.00
20 In the Park.	4.00
21 Trollords	4.00
22 Father the Dryad	4.00
23 I:The Creep	4.00
24 The Factor.	4.00
25 The Factor.	4.00
26 Very Vicki	4.00
27 Nancy Kate	4.00
28 Favorite Song	4.00
29 thru 33.	4.00
34 Kaos Moon	6.00
35 thru 38	@4.00
39 'Iron Empires,' pt. 4	4.00
40 'Suzi Romaine'	4.00
41 'Iron Empires,' cont.	4.00
42	4.00
43 'Iron Empires,' concl.	4.00
44 'Skeleton Key'.	4.00
45 'Divine Winds'	4.00
46 'A Bullet For Me'	4.00

Negative Burn #22
© Caliber

47	4.00
48 special 80-pg. issue	5.00
49 special 80-pg. issue	5.00
50 96-pg., final issue	7.00
TPB Best of Year One	9.95
TPB Best of Year Two.	9.95

NEIL THE HORSE
Aardvark–Vanaheim, 1983
1 Art:Arn Sara	5.00
1a 2nd printing	2.00
2	3.00
3	4.00
4	3.00
5 Video Warriors	2.50
6 Video Warriors	2.50
7 Video Warriors	2.50
8 Outer Space.	2.50
9 Conan	2.50
10	2.50

Renegade, 1985
11 Fred Astair.	2.00
12	2.00
13	2.00
14 Special	3.00
15	2.00

NEMESIS THE WARLOCK
Fleetway, 1989
1 thru 16	@2.00

NEON GENESIS EVANGELION
Viz Communication, 1997
1 (of 6) by Gainax & Yoshiyuki Sadamoto	3.25
1 special collectors edition	2.95
2 thru 6	@2.95
2 thru 6 special collectors ed.	@2.95
TPB Vol. 1	16.50
TPB Vol. 1 special collectors ed.	16.50

BOOK TWO, 1998
1 (of 5) by Yoshiyuki Sadamoto	2.95
1 special collectors edition	2.95
2 thru 5	@2.95
2 thru 5 special collectors ed.	@2.95
TPB Book 2	15.95
TPB Book 2, collector ed.	15.95

BOOK THREE, 1998
1 thru 6 by Yoshiyuki Sadamoto	@2.95
1a thru 6a Collectors edition	@2.95
GN Vol. 3 Evangelion	15.95
GN Vol. 3 Evangelion, coll. ed.	15.95

BOOK FOUR, 1999
1 thru 7 by Yoshiyuki Sadamoto	@2.95
1a thru 7a special collectors ed.	@2.95

BOOK FIVE, 2000
1	2.95
1a collectors ed.	2.95
2 thru 7	@2.95
2a thru 7a deluxe	@2.95
TPB Book 5	15.95
TPB Collect. Ed	15.95

BOOK SIX, 2001
1 thru 4	@3.50
1a thru 4a coll. ed.	@3.50
TPB Vol. 6	15.95
TPB Vol. 6 collector ed.	15.95

BOOK SEVEN
1 (of 7)	3.50
2 thru 5	@2.95
6	@3.50
2a thru 5a collector's edition.	@2.95
6a collector's edition	@3.50
TPB Vol. 7	15.95
TPB Vol. 7 collector ed.	15.95

NEON– THE FUTURE WARRIOR
Komics, Inc., 2000
TPB Vol. 1	12.85
TPB Vol. 2	12.85
TPB Vol. 3	12.85
TPB Vol. 4 187-pg.	12.85
TPB Vol. 5 183-pg.	12.85
TPB Vol. 6 186-pg.	12.85
TPB Vol. 7 185-pg.	12.85
TPB Vol. 8 185-pg.	12.85
TPB Vol. 9 185-pg., final	12.85

NERVOUS REX
Blackthorne, 1985
1	3.00
1a 2nd printing	2.00
2	3.00
3	3.00
4	2.50
5 thru 10	@2.00
GraphicNovel	3.00

NEW ADVENTURES OF TERRY & THE PIRATES
ACG Comics, 1998
1 by Bros. Hildebrandt	2.95
2 thru 7	@2.95

NEWCOMERS ILLUSTRATED
Newcomers Publishing
1 thru 5 various artists . . . . @2.95
6 Science Fiction 2.95
7 thru 8 . . . . @2.95
9 Shocking Machines 2.95
10 . . . . 2.95
11 Hitman 2.95
12 final issue 2.95

NEW ERADICATORS
Vol 2 #1 NewBeginnings 2.00
Vol 2 #2 NewBeginnings 2.00
Vol 2 #3 NewFriends 2.00

NEW FRONTIERS
1 CS(c) 3.00
1a 2nd Printing 2.00

NEW FRONTIERS
Evolution
1 A:Action Master, Green Ghost . . . 2.00
2 . . . . 2.00

NEW HERO COMICS
Pierce
1 and 2 . . . . @2.00

NEW HORIZONS
Shanda Fantasy Arts, 1997
1 . . . . 4.95
2 thru 5 . . . . @4.50
6 thru 9 . . . . @4.95
10 thru 15 . . . . @5.00

NEW HUMANS
Pied Piper, 1987
1 and 2 . . . . @2.00

NEW HUMANS
Eternity, 1987
1 . . . . 2.00
2 thru 15 . . . . @2.00
Ann. #1 . . . . 2.95

NEW HUMANS
1 Shattered Earth Chronicles 2.00

NEW LOVE
Fantagraphics, 1996
1 GHe, Love & Rockets tie-in 2.95
2 thru 3 GHe . . . . @2.95
4 thru 6 GHe . . . . @2.95

NEW PULP ADVENTURES SPECIAL
Dunewadd Comics
1 I:Kawala 2.50

NEW REALITY
1 thru 6 . . . . @2.00

NEWSTRALIA
Innovation, 1989
(Prev. Color)
4 . . . . 2.25
5 . . . . 2.25

New Triumph #3
© Matrix Graphics

NEW TRIUMPH
Matrix Graphics, 1985
1 F:Northguard 3.00
1a 2nd printing 2.00
2 thru 4 . . . . @2.00

NEW VAMPIRE MIYU
Ironcat, 1997
1 by Narumi Kakinouchi 2.95
2 thru 6 . . . . @2.95
7 The Past Lies Beyond a Door, finale 2.95
GN rep. #1–#7 . . . . 17.95
VOL. 2, 1998
1 by Narumi Kakinouchi 2.95
2 thru 6 . . . . @2.95
VOL. 3, 1998
1 . . . . 2.95
2 thru 7 . . . . @2.95
VOL. 4, 1999
1 by Narumi Kakinouchi 2.95
2 thru 6 . . . . @2.95
VOL. 5
1 . . . . 2.95
2 thru 7 . . . . @2.95
GN Vol. 4, The Return of Miyu . . . 17.95
GN Vol. 5, Wrath of Miyu 17.95

NEW WORLD DISORDER
Millennium, 1995
1 I:King Skin Gang 2.95

NEW WORLD ORDER
Blazer Studios, 1993
1 thru 8 . . . . @2.50

NEW YORK CITY OUTLAWS
Outlaw
1 thru 5 . . . . @2.50

NEW YORK, YEAR ZERO
Eclipse, 1988
1 thru 4 . . . . @2.00

NEXUS
Capital, 1981
1 SR,I:Nexus,large size 12.00
2 SR,Mag size 8.00
3 SR,Mag size 5.00

NIGHT
Amaze Ink, 1995
0 V:The Prince 2.00

NIGHT ANGEL
Substance Comics, 1995
1 I:Night Angel 2.95

NIGHT CRY
CFD Productions, 1995
1 Evil Ernie & Razor story 8.00
1 signed 9.00
2 . . . . 6.00
3 . . . . 5.00
4 . . . . 4.00
4a platinum (c) 6.00
5 . . . . 4.00
6 . . . . 2.75
6a signed 8.00

NIGHT LIFE
Caliber
1 thru 7 . . . . @2.00

NIGHT MASTER
Silver Wolf, 1987
1 Vigil 5.50
2 Vigil 2.50
3 . . . . 2.00

NIGHT OF THE LIVING DEAD
Fantaco
0 prelude 1.75
1 based on cult classic movie 4.95
2 Movie adapt,continued 4.95
3 Movie adapt,conclusion 4.95
5 . . . . 5.95
TPB Official Complete story, rep. . 24.95
TPB London, Clive Barker's story . 14.95

NIGHT'S CHILDREN
Fantaco
1 . . . . 3.50
2 . . . . 3.50
3 . . . . 3.50
4 . . . . 3.50

NIGHT'S CHILDREN
Millennium, 1995
1 The Ripper, Klaus Wulfe 3.95
Spec. High Noon (1996) 2.95
Spec. The Churchyard (1997) 3.25

NIGHT'S CHILDREN: THE VAMPIRE
Millennium, 1995
1 F:Klaus Wulfe 2.95
2 F:Klaus Wulfe 2.95

NIGHT STREETS
Arrow, 1986
1 . . . . 2.50
2 thru 4 . . . . @2.00

NIGHTVISION
London Night, 1996
1 DQ,KHt, All About Eve 3.00
1 signed 12.95
1a erotica edition. 10.00

NIGHT WARRIORS: DARKSTALKERS' REVENGE
Viz Communications, 1998
1 (of 6) by Run Ishida 2.95
2 . . . . 3.25
3 thru 6 . . . . @2.95
TPB 15.95

NIGHT ZERO
Fleetway
1 thru 4 . . . . @2.00

NIKKI BLADE
High Impact, 1997
0 . . . . 2.95
0a deluxe adult cover 10.00
0b gold edition variant cover . . . 14.95
Spec.#0 Nikki Blade: Forever Nikki
  (1997) MIB(c). 2.95
Deluxe RCI(c). 10.00
ABC Comics, 1998
Spec. Nikki Blade: Blades of Death
  (1998) by RCI & Clayton Henry. 3.00
Puzzle variant A cover 5.95
Puzzle variant B cover 5.95
Puzzle variant C cover 5.95
Spec. Nikki Blade: Revenge 3.00

NIMROD, THE
Fantagraphics, 1998
1 by Lewis Trondheim 2.95
2 thru 4 . . . . @2.95
5 . . . . 3.95
6 . . . . 3.50
7 . . . . 3.95

NINJA
Eternity
1 . . . . 3.00
2 thru 6 . . . . @2.00
7 thru 13 . . . . @2.00

NINJA ELITE
Adventure, 1987
1 thru 5 . . . . @2.00
6 thru 8 . . . . @2.00

NINJA FUNNIES
Eternity
1 and 2 . . . . @2.00
3 thru 5 . . . . @2.00

NINJA HIGH SCHOOL
Antarctic, 1987
1 . . . . 15.00
2 thru 4 . . . . @11.00
Eternity, 1988
5 thru 22 . . . . @3.00
23 Zardon Assassin 2.50
24 . . . . 2.50
25 Return of the Zetramen 2.50
26 Stanley the Demon 2.50
27 Return of the Zetramen 2.50
28 Threat of the super computer. . 2.50
29 V:Super Computer. 2.50
30 I:Akaru. 2.50
31 Jeremy V:Akaru 2.50
32 thru 34 V:Giant Monsters Pt.1
  thru Pt. 3 . . . . @2.50
35 thru 43 . . . . @2.50
44 Combat Cheerleaders 2.75
45 Cheerleader Competition 2.75
46 Monsters From Space 2.75
47 . . . . 2.75
48 F:Jeremy Feeple 2.75
49 thru 51 . . . . @2.95
52 thru 57 Time Warp, pt.4–pt.8 . @2.95
58 Zardon ambassador, BU:BDn . 2.95
59 Akaru overwhelmed 2.95
60 to the Himalayas 2.95
61 ancient Himalayan temple . . . 2.95
62 Hillbilly girl. 2.95
63 F:Tetsuo Rivalsan 2.95
64 Jeremy Feeple: Saboteur?. . . . 2.95
65 Quagmire Trial of the Century . 2.95
66 . . . . 2.95
67 F:Eolata. 3.00
68 F:Akaru & Asrial. 3.00
69 Guri-Guri Island. 3.00
70 Mad Bomber in Space 2.50
71 traitor in secret police. 2.99
72 . . . . 2.50
73 . . . . 2.50
74 Girl Scouts. 2.50
Special #1 . . . . 2.95
Special #2 . . . . 2.95
Special #3 . . . . 2.95
Special #3 1/2 . . . . 2.25
Ann. 1989. . . . . 2.95
Ann.#3 . . . . 3.95
TPB Vol. 1 rep. #1–3 . . . . 12.00
TPB Vol. 1, new edition. 14.95
TPB Vol. 2 rep. #4–7 . . . . 12.00
TPB Vol. 3 rep. #8–11. . . . . 9.00
TPB Vol. 3, rep. #8–#11 . . . . . . 10.95
TPB Vol. 4 rep. #12–15 . . . . 8.00
TPB Vol. 4, rep. #12–#15 . . . . . 10.95
TPB Vol. 5 rep. #16–18 . . . . 7.95
TPB Vol. 6 rep. #19–21 . . . . 7.95
TPB Vol. 7 rep. #22–24 . . . . 7.95
TPB Vol. 7, rep. #22–#24 The Ides
  of May 10.95
TPB Vol. 8 rep. #25–27 . . . . 7.95
TPB Vol. 9 rep. #28–31. . . . . . . 10.95
TPB Vol. 9, rep. #28–#31 Long
  Distance Bottle. 10.95
TPB Vol. 10 rep. #32–35. . . . . . 10.95
TPB Vol. 11 rep. #36–39. . . . . . 10.95
TPB Vol. 11, rep. #36–#39 Shades
  of Grey. 10.95
TPB Vol. 12 . . . . 10.95
TPB Vol. 15 three stories 7.95
Yearbook 1994 . . . . 4.00
Yearbook 1995 . . . . 3.95
Yearbook 1996 . . . . 3.95
Yearbook 1997, cover A 3.95
Yearbook 1997, cover B 3.95
Yearbook 1998, cover A 2.95
Yearbook 1998, cover B 2.95
Spec. Girls of Ninja High School
  (1997) 3.95
Spec. Girls of Ninja High School
  1998 cover A 2.95
  1998 cover B 2.95
Spec. 1999 . . . . 3.00
Spotlight #4 Rod Espinosa 3.00
Summer Spec.#1 . . . . 3.00
Antarctic Press, 2000
Swimsuit Spec. 2000 . . . . 4.50
Swimsuit Spec. 2001 . . . . 4.50
TPB Vol. 1, signed 19.95
TPB Textbook Vol. 1 600-pg. . . . 49.95

NINJA HIGH SCHOOL GIRLS
Antarctic Press
0 . . . . 2.75
1 and 2 rep. . . . . @2.75
3 thru 5 rep. . . . . @3.95
Yearbook 3.95

NINJA HIGH SCHOOL PERFECT MEMORY
Antarctic Press, 1993
1 thru 2, 96pg . . . . @4.95

NINJA HIGH SCHOOL SMALL BODIES
Antarctic Press
1 "Monopolize" 2.50
2 Omegadon Cannon 2.75
3 Omegadon Cannon 2.75
3a deluxe 4.50
4 Omegadon Cannon 2.75
5 Wrong Order 2.75
6 Chicken Rage. 2.95
7 . . . . 2.95

NIRA X: CYBERANGEL
Entity Comics, 1996
1 . . . . 5.00
1a deluxe 8.00
2 BMs 4.00
3 and 4 BMs . . . . @3.00
4a with PC Game 8.00
Ann.#1 BMs flip-cover. 2.75
2nd Mini Series, 1995
1 . . . . 4.00
1a 2nd printing 2.50
2 thru 4 . . . . @2.50
3rd Mini Series, 1995–96
1 . . . . 2.50
1a Gold(c). 5.00
2 . . . . 2.50
3 . . . . 3.00
Regular Series
1 . . . . 2.75
1a with game. 7.00
2 thru 4 . . . . @2.75
4a with game. 7.00
Spec. Nira X:Headwave, encore

Nira X Exodus #1
© Entity

Nira–Official

special toy edition. 2.50
Encore special toy edition,
signed & numbered 12.95
Spec. Nira X:Memoirs (1997) BMs . 2.75
Deluxe 3.50

NIRA X/HELLINA: HEAVEN & HELL
Entity Comics
1 San Diego Con edition, BMs 5.00
1a foil. 3.00

NIRA X: EXODUS
Avatar, 1997
0 (of 2) BMs 3.00
0a Leather cover. 20.00
0b signed 10.00
1 (of 2) 3.00
1a leather cover. 18.00
1b signed 9.00
2 . . . . 3.00
Spec. Shoot First 3.00
Spec. Summer Splash 4.95

NIRA X: HISTORY
Avatar Press, 1999
1 (of 2) by Bill Maus 3.50
2 . . . . 3.50

NIRA X: SOUL SKURGE
Entity, 1996
1 (of 3) BMs, A:Vortex 2.75
2 BMs, ... 2.75
3 . . . . 2.75

NOBODY
Oni Press, 1998
1 (of 4) 2.95
2 thru 4 . . . . @2.95
TPB Sacrifices 11.95
AIT/Planetlar, 2000
TPB 12.95

NODWICK
Henchman Publishing, 2000
1 by Aaron Williams. 2.95
2 & 3 . . . . @2.95
Dork Storm, 2000
1 by Aaron Williams. 2.95
5 . . . . 2.95
6 thru 11 . . . . @2.95
12 thru 24 . . . . @3.00
TPB Vol. 1 . . . . 15.95
TPB Vol. 2 Of Gods & Henchmen . 16.00
TPB Vol. 3 . . . . 16.00

NO GUTS, NO GLORY
Fantaco
1-shot, K.Eastman's 1st solo
work since TMNT 2.95

NOMADS OF ANTIQUITY
1 thru 6 . . . . @2.00

NO NEED FOR TENCHI
Viz Comics
PART ONE
1 thru 7 (of 7). . . . . @2.95
PART TWO, 1996
1 thru 7 by Hitoshi Okuda. . . . . @2.95
TPB Sword Play 15.95

B & W PUB.

No Need for Tenchi, Vol. 9, #6
© Viz Comics

PART THREE, 1997
1 (of 6) by Hitoshi Okuda. 2.95
2 . . . . 2.95
3 thru 6 . . . . @2.95
TPB Magical Girl Pretty Sammy . . 15.95
PART FOUR, 1997
1 (of 6) by Hitoshi Okuda. 2.95
2 thru 6 . . . . @2.95
TPB Vol. 4 Samurai Space Opera. 15.95
PART FIVE, 1998
1 (of 6) 2.95
2 thru 6 . . . . @2.95
TPB Vol. 5 Unreal Genius 15.95
PART SIX, 1998
1 (of 6) 2.95
2 thru 6 . . . . @2.95
TPB Vol. 6 Dream a Little Scheme 15.95
PART SEVEN, 1999
1 (of 6) 2.95
2 thru 6 . . . . @2.95
TPB Vol. 7 Tenchi in Love. 15.95
PART EIGHT, 1999
1 (of 5) by Hitoshi Okuda. 3.25
2 thru 5 . . . . @2.95
TPB Vol. 8 Chef of Iron. 15.95
PART NINE
1 (of 6) by Hitoshi Okuda. 2.95
2 thru 6 . . . . @2.95
TPB Vol. 9 Quest for More Money. 15.95
PART TEN, 2000
1 (of 7) 2.95
2 thru 7 . . . . @2.95
TPB Vol. 10 Mother Planet 15.95
PART ELEVEN, 2001
1 thru 4 . . . . @3.50
TPB Vol. 11 Ayeka's Heart 15.95
PART TWELVE, 2001
1 thru 4 (of 6). . . . . @3.50
5 thru 6 . . . . @2.95
TPB Vol. 12 . . . . 15.95

NORMAL MAN
Aardvark–Vanaheim, 1984
1 . . . . 4.00
2 thru 9 . . . . @2.75
Renegade
10 thru 19. . . . . @2.00

Comics Values Annual

NOSFERATU: PLAGUE OF TERROR
Millennium
1 I:Orlock 2.50
2 19th Century India,A:Sir W.
Longsword. 2.50
3 WWI/WWII to Viet Nam 2.50
4 O:Orlock,V:Longsword,conc. . . . 2.50

NOVA GIRLS
MN Design, 1998
1 The Immortality Quest, pt.1. . . . 2.00
1a JJu (c) 2.95
1b photo (c) 3.95
1 variant Starship Discover #0(c). . 3.95
1 variant Phazer #0 cover 3.95
2 The Immortality Quest, pt.2. . . . 2.95
2a deluxe 2.95
3 The Immortality Quest, pt.3. . . . 2.00
3a deluxe 2.95
Space 34–24–34 Gold Seal 10th
Anniv. Edition 74.95

NOWHERESVILLE
Caliber, 1996
1 thru 3 by MRc. . . . . @2.95
Spec. The History of Cool. 2.95

NYOKA THE JUNGLE GIRL
AC Comics
3 . . . . 2.25
4 . . . . 2.25
5 . . . . 2.50

OCTOBRIANA
Revolution Comics
0 16pg. 1.25
1 'The Octobriana Files,'pt.1 . . . . 2.95
2 'The Octobriana Files,'pt.2 . . . . 2.95
3 'The Octobriana Files,'pt.3 . . . . 2.95
4 'The Octobriana Files,'pt.4 . . . . 2.95
5 'The Octobriana Files,'pt.5 . . . . 2.95
Alchemy Texts, 2001
Spec. 30th Anniv. Spec. 3.00

ODD JOB
Amaze Ink/Slave Labor Graphics, 2000
1 by Ian Smith & Tyson Smith 2.95
2 thru 8 . . . . @2.95
TPB Vol. 1 . . . . 19.95

OFFERINGS
Cry For Dawn
1 Sword & Sorcery stories 7.00
2 and 3 . . . . @6.00

OFFICIAL BUZ SAWYER
Pioneer, 1988
1 . . . . 2.00
2 . . . . 2.00
3 . . . . 2.00
4 . . . . 2.00
5 . . . . 2.00
6 . . . . 2.00

OFFICIAL HOW TO DRAW G.I. JOE
Blackthorne, 1987
1 thru 5 . . . . @2.00

CVA Page 752 — All comics prices listed are for *Near Mint* condition.

OFFICIAL HOW TO DRAW ROBOTECH
Blackthorne, 1987
1 thru 11 .... @2.00
12 .... 2.95
13 thru 16 .... @2.00

OFFICIAL HOW TO DRAW TRANSFORMERS
Blackthorne, 1987
1 thru 7 .... @2.00

OFFICIAL JOHNNY HAZARD
Pioneer, 1988
1 thru 3 .... @2.00
4 .... 2.00
5 .... 2.00

OFFICIAL JUNGLE JIM
Pioneer, 1988
1 thru 5 AR,rep. .... @2.00
6 AR,rep. 2.00
7 thru 10 AR,rep. .... @2.00
11 thru 20 AR,rep. .... @2.50
Ann.#1 .... 2.00
Giant Size 3.95

OFFICIAL MANDRAKE
Pioneer, 1988
1 thru 5 .... @2.00
6 .... 2.00
7 thru 10 .... @2.00
11 .... 2.50
12 .... 2.00
13 thru 17 .... @2.50
Ann. #1 .... 3.95
King Size #1 .... 3.95
Giant Size #1 .... 3.95

OFFICIAL MODESTY BLAISE
Pioneer, 1988
1 thru 4 .... @2.00
5 .... 2.00
6 thru 14 .... @2.00
Ann. #1 .... 3.95
King Size #1 .... 3.95

OFFICIAL PRINCE VALIANT
Pioneer, 1988
1 Hal Foster,rep. 2.00
2 Hal Foster,rep. 2.00
3 Hal Foster,rep. 2.00
4 Hal Foster,rep. 2.00
5 Hal Foster,rep. 2.00
6 Hal Foster,rep. 2.00
7 .... 2.00
8 thru 14 .... @2.00
15 thru 24 .... @2.50
Ann. #1 .... 3.95
King Size #1 .... 3.95

OFFICIAL RIP KIRBY
Pioneer, 1988
1 thru 3 AR .... @2.00
4 AR 2.00
5 and 6 AR .... @2.00

Official Secret Agent #4
© *Pioneer*

OFFICIAL SECRET AGENT
Pioneer, 1988
1 thru 5 AW rep .... @2.00
6 AW 2.00
7 thru 9 AW .... @2.00

OF MIND AND SOUL
Rage Comics, 1997
0 .... 2.95
1 .... 2.50
2 .... 2.50
3 .... 2.00
Spec. Standing on a Beach ... 2.50
Spec. Soul'd Out` 2.95
Spec. A Day in Hell 2.95
Spec. 1-shot 1.50

OHM'S LAW
Imperial Comics
1 thru 2 .... @2.00
3 V:Men in Black 2.00
4 A:Damonstriek 2.00
5 F:Tryst 2.00

OH MY GOTH!
Sirius/Dog Star, 1998
1 by Voltaire 2.95
2 .... 2.95
3 .... 2.95
4 Goths in Space 2.95
TPB 13.00

OH MY GOTH: HUMANS SUCK!
Sirius Entertainment, 2000
1 (of 3) 2.95
1 deluxe 5.00
2 and 3 .... @2.95

OKTOBERFEST
Now & Then
1 (1976) Dave Sim 20.00

OMEGA
North Star
1 1st pr by Rebel,rare 50.00
1a Vigil(Yellow Cov.) 15.00
2 .... 2.00

OMEGA ELITE
Blackthorne
1 .... 2.00
2 .... 2.00

OMEN
North Star, 1987
1 .... 8.00
1a 2nd printing 2.00
2 thru 4 .... @3.50

OMICRON
Pyramid, 1987
1 and 2 .... @2.25
3 .... 2.50

OMNI MEN
Blackthorne, 1989
1 .... 2.00
2 .... 2.00

ONE-POUND GOSPEL
Viz Communications, 1996
1 .... 3.50
2 .... 3.50
3 .... 2.95
4 .... 2.95
TPB rep. 16.95
ROUND TWO, 1997
1 thru 8 by Rumiko Takahashi .. @2.95
TPB Vol. 1 .... 16.96
TPB Vol. 2 Hungry For Victory .. 15.95
TPB Vol. 3 Knuckle Sandwich ... 15.95
PART 7
1 (of 13) by Rumiko Takahashi ... 2.95

ONE SHOT WESTERN
Calibur
1-shot F:Savage Sisters, Tornpath Outlaw 2.50

ONI DOUBLE FEATURE
Oni Press, 1997
1 F:Secret Broadcast 12.00
1a 2nd printing 3.00
2 F:Car Crash on the 405 .... 3.50
3 F:Troy Nixey 3.50
4 F:A River in Egypt 3.50
5 F:Fan Girl From Hell 5.00
6 inc. NGa Only the End of the World, pt.1 .... 3.00
7 inc. NGa Only the End of the World, pt.2 .... 3.00
8 inc. NGa Only the End of the World, pt.3 .... 3.00
9 thru 11 .... @3.00
12 Bluntman & Chronic 8.00
13 .... 3.00

ONIGAMI
Antarctic Press, 1998
1 (of 3) by Michael Lacombe, sequel to Winter Jade storyline from Warrior Nun: Black and White .. 3.00
2 .... 3.00
3 concl. 3.00

OPEN SEASON
Renegade, 1987
1 thru 7 .... @2.00

OPTIC NERVE
Adrian Tomine, 1990
1 thru 5, mini-comic 12.00
6 . . . . 7.00
7 . . . . 5.00
8 . . . . 2.95
9 . . . . 3.95

OPTIC NERVE
Drawn & Quarterly, 1995
1 Summer Job 10.00
1a 2nd printing 6.00
2 . . . . 5.00
3 and 4 . . . . @3.00
5 thru 8 . . . . @3.50
TPB 32 Stories 9.95

ORACLE PRESENTS
Oracle, 1986
1 thru 4 . . . . @2.00

ORBIT
Eclipse, 1990
1 and 2 . . . . @5.00
3 . . . . 5.00

ORIGINAL TOM CORBETT
Eternity, 1990
1 thru 10 rep. newspaper strips . @2.95

ORIGINS OF REID FLEMING, WORLD'S TOUGHEST MILKMAN
Deep Sea Comics, 1998
1 by David Boswell 3.00

ORLAK: FLESH & STEEL
Caliber
1 '1991 A.D.' 2.50

ORLAK REDUX
Caliber, 1991
1 rep. Caliber Presents, 64-pg. . . . 3.95

OUTLAW OVERDRIVE
Blue Comet Press
1 Red Edition I:Deathrow 2.95
1a Black Edition 2.95
1b Blue Edition 2.95

OZ
Imperial Comics, 1996
1 Land of Oz Gone Mad 9.00
2 Land of Oz Gone Mad 7.00
3 Land of Oz Gone Mad 6.00
4 Tin Woodsmen 6.00
5 F:Pumkinhead 6.00
6 Emerald City 6.00
7 V:Bane Wolves 4.00
8 V:Nome Hordes 4.00
9 Freedom Fighters Vs. Heroes . . 4.00
10 thru 15 . . . . @4.00
16 . . . . 3.50
Spec.#1 . . . . 6.00
Spec. Scarecrow #1 . . . . 3.00
Spec. Lion #1 . . . . 3.00
Spec. Tin Man #1 . . . . 3.00
Spec. Freedom Fighters #1 . . . . 3.00
TPB Rep. #1-#4 . . . . 14.95
Caliber `New Worlds'
17 by Ralph Griffith, Stuart Kerr & Tim Holtrop 3.50
18 . . . . 3.00
19 . . . . 3.00
20 . . . . 3.00
21 'Witches War' pt.1 (of 5) 3.00
22 . . . . 2.95
GN Heroes of Oz 14.95

Oz Romance in Rags #1
© Caliber

OZ: ROMANCE IN RAGS
Caliber, 1996
1 thru 3 Bill Bryan . . . . @2.95

OZ SQUAD
Patchwork Press, 1992
1 . . . . 4.00
2 thru 6 . . . . @3.00
7 Time Train Destroyed 3.00
8 Old West 3.00

OZ: STRAW AND SORCERY
Caliber `New Worlds', 1997
1 thru 3 . . . . @2.95

PAKKINS' LAND
Caliber Tapestry, 1996
1 . . . . 6.00
1a signed edition 3.00
1a second edition, new cover . . . 3.00
2 . . . . 4.00
2a second edition, new cover . . . 3.00
3 . . . . 4.00
3 2nd edition, new cover 3.00
4 thru 6 . . . . @3.00
GN Book One: Paul's Adventure . . . 9.95
Pakkins Presents, 2000
TPB Vol.1 Paul'sAdventure revised 15.95
TPB Vol.2 Quest For Kings 15.95
TPB Vol.3 Forgotten Dreams . . . 15.95
TPV Vol.4 Tavitah 16.95

PAKKINS' LAND: FORGOTTEN DREAMS
Caliber, 1998
1 by Gary & Rhoda Shipman 3.00
2 thru 5 . . . . @3.00

PAKKINS' LAND: QUEST FOR KINGS
Caliber, 1997
1G by Gary & Rhoda Shipman,
  Shipman(c) 3.00
1J by Gary & Rhoda Shipman,
  JSi(c) 3.00
2 . . . . 3.00
3 Rahsha's city 3.00
4 . . . . 3.00
5 . . . . 3.00

PALANTINE
Gryphon Rampant, 1995
1 thru 5 V:Master of Basilisk 2.50

PALOOKA-VILLE
Drawn & Quarterly
1 third printing 2.95
1 10th Anniv. Ed. 3.75
10 by Seth 3.75
11 Clyde Fans, pt.2 . . . . 3.75
12 Clyde Fans, pt.3 . . . . 3.75
13 Clyde Fans 3.75
14 . . . . 3.75
15 . . . . 3.75
16 . . . . 4.75
TPB Its a Good Life If You
  Don't Weaken 12.95

PANDA KHAN
1 thru 4 . . . . @2.00

PANDEMONIUM
Curtis Comics, 2002
Vol. 1 Manga
1 by Jaeongtae Lee 2.95
2 thru 5 . . . . @2.95
Vol. 2
1 . . . . 2.95

PANDORA
Brainstorm, 1996
1 (of 2) 3.00

PANDORA
Avatar Press, 1997
0 . . . . 3.00
1 signed 12.00
2 (of 2) 3.00
2 deluxe 9.00
X-over Pandora/Ranzor:Devil Inside
  (1998) signed 12.00
  Haley (c) 5.00
X-over Pandora/Razor (1999) . . . 3.50
  Leather cover, signed 15.00
  Expanded Edition 5.00
X-over Pandora/Shotgun Mary:
  Demon Nation (1998) 3.00
  Deluxe 4.95
  Leather 20.00
  Royal Blue edition 50.00
X-over Pandora/Widow (1997) . . 3.95
  Leather cover 15.00
Spec. Arachnophobia 3.50
Spec. Pandora Special (1997) . . . 3.00
  Leather cover 15.00
  Avatar convention (c) ed. . . . 15.00
Spec. Pandora Pin-up (1997) . . . 3.00
  Signed 15.00
Spec. Nudes (1997) 3.50
GN Love and War (2003) 5.95

PANDORA'S CHEST
Avatar Press, 1999
1 (of 3) 2.75

PANDORA: DEMONOGRAPHY
Avatar Press, 1997
1 thru 3 . . . . @3.00

PANDORA DEVILS ADVOCATE
Avatar Press, 1999
1 (of 3) 3.50
1a Previews exclusive foil (c). . . . 12.95
2 . . . . 3.50
3 . . . . 3.50

PANDORA: PANDEMONIUM
Avatar Press, 1997
1 Pandora goes to Hell 3.00
1 leather cover 25.00
1 signed 10.00
2 (of 3) 3.00

PANTHEON
Lone Star Press, 1998
1 (of 12) 2.95
2 Welcome to the Machine 2.95
3 V:Death Boy 2.95
4 F:Tangeroa. 2.95
5 Under Pressure 2.95
6 All-villain issue 2.95
7 thru 9 . . . . @2.95
10 thru 12 . . . . @2.95
Spec. Ancient History (1999). 3.50

PAPER CUTS
1 E Starzer-1982 . . . . 15.00
2 and 3 . . . . @2.50

PARADISE KISS
Tokyopop Press, 2002
GN Vol. 1 (of 3) authentic manga . 10.00
GN Vol. 2 thru Vol. 4 . . . . @10.00

PARASYTE
Mixx Entertainment, 1999
TPB Vol.1 192-pg. 11.95
TPB Vol.2 192-pg. 11.95
Tokyopop Press, 2001
TPB Vol. 4 . . . . 11.95
TPB Vol. 5 . . . . 11.95
TPB Mixx Vol. 6 . . . . 12.95
TPB Mixx Vol. 7 . . . . 12.95
TPB Mixx Vol. 8 . . . . 12.95
TPB Pocket Vol. 9 . . . . 14.95
TPB Pocket Mixx Vol. 10 . . . . . 13.95
GN Vol. 11 . . . . 10.00
TPB Pocket Mixx Vol. 12 . . . . . 13.00

PARTICLE DREAMS
Fantagraphics, 1986
1 . . . . 3.00
2 thru 6 . . . . @2.25

PARTNERS IN PANDEMONIUM
Caliber
1 'Hell on Earth' 2.50

2 Sheldon&Murphy become mortal 2.50
3 A:Abra Cadaver 2.50

PARTS OF A HOLE
Caliber, 1991
1 Short Stories 2.50

PARTS UNKNOWN
Eclipse, 1992
1 I:Spurr,V:Aliens. 2.50
2 Aliens on Earth cont. 2.50

Parts Unknown: Dark Intentions #3
© Knight Press

PARTS UNKNOWN: DARK INTENTIONS
Knight Press, 1995
0 . . . . 2.95
1 I:Prelude to limited Series. 2.95
2 V:Luggnar. 2.95
3 V:Luggnar. 2.95
4 . . . . 2.95
1-shot, Handbook, The Roswell
  Agenda 2.95
Super-Ann. #1 . . . . 3.95

PATRICK THE WOLF BOY
Blindwolf Studios, 2000
1 by Art Baltazar & Franco. 2.95
Halloween Special 2.95
Next Halloween Special 2.95
Valentine's Day Special 2.95
Christmas Spec. 2.95
Mother's Day Special 2.95
Summer Spec. 2.95
Superhero Spec.(2002). 2.95
Sci-Fi Special (2002) 2.95
Another Halloween Special (2002) . 2.95
Spec. This Year's Halloween Special. . . 2.95
Spec. Grimm Reaper Super Special 2.95
Spec. Wedding Special. 2.95
Spec. After School Special 2.95
TPB Vol. 1 . . . . 10.00
TPB Vol. 2 . . . . 10.00

PATTY CAKE
Caliber Tapestry, 1996
1 by Scott Roberts. 2.95
2 . . . . 2.95
3 . . . . 2.95

4 . . . . 2.95
Christmas special 3.95

PATTY-CAKE & FRIENDS
Slave Labor, 1997
1 by Scott Roberts 2.95
2 thru 15 . . . . @2.95
Halloween Spec. 3.95
VOL. 2, 2000
1 by Scott Roberts, 48-pg. 4.95
2 thru 4 48-pg. . . . . @4.95
5 thru 9 . . . . @4.95
TPB Sugar & Spice..Mostly Spice . 13.95
TPB Vol. 2 And Everything Nice . . 13.95
TPB Vol. 3 Love is All Around . . . 13.95

PAUL THE SAMURAI
New England Comics, 1991
1 thru 3 . . . . @2.75
Bonanza #2 100pg. 4.95
GN Collected 8.95

PEACH GIRL
Tokyopop Press, 2000
TPB Pocket Mixx, Vol. 1 . . . . 9.95
TPB Pocket Mixx, Vol. 2 . . . . 9.95
TPB Pocket Mixx, Vol. 3 . . . . 9.95
TPB Pocket Vol. 4 thru Vol. 8 . . @10.00

PENDULUM
Adventure, 1993
1 Big Hand,Little Hand. 2.50
2 The Immortality Formula. 2.50
3 . . . . 2.50

PENNY CENTURY
Fantagraphics, 1997
1 by Jaime Hernandez. 2.95
2 thru 7 . . . . @2.95

PENTACLE: THE SIGN OF THE FIVE
Eternity, 1991
1 . . . . 2.25
2 Det.Sandler,H.Smitts 2.25
3 Det.Sandler becomes New
  Warlock 2.25
4 5 warlocks Vs. Kaji 2.50

PETE THE P.O.'D POSTAL WORKER
Sharkbait Press, 1998
1 by Marcus Pierce & Pete
  Garcia, Route 666 . . . . 2.95
2 prison mail 2.95
3 To Aliens with Love. 2.95
4 Special Delivery to
  Conad the Alien 2.95
5 England Vacation 2.95
6 Benedict Postman 2.95
7 Postman on Elm Street. 2.95
8 Postman on Elm Street. 2.95
9 Pete Meets Jerry Ringer. 2.95
10 Y2K Express 2.95
11 Postal Wars 2.95
12 . . . . 2.95
X-mas Spec.#1 . . . . 3.50
Spec. War Journal 2.95
TPB Pete Unplugged 12.95

PHANTOM
1 thru 3 . . . . @5.95
4 and 5 . . . . @6.95

Phantom–Poe — B & W PUB.

PHANTOM, THE
Tony Raiola, 2000
TPB Diamond Hunters 9.50
TPB The Little Toma 9.50
TPB Sea Horse 9.50
TPB Game of Alvar. 9.50
TPB Diana Aviatrix 9.50
TPB Phantom's Treasure 9.50

PHANTOM OF FEAR CITY
Claypool, 1994–95
1 thru 12 . . . . 2.50

PHANTOM OF THE OPERA
Eternity
1 . . . . 2.00

PHASE ONE
Victory, 1986
1 . . . . 3.00
2 . . . . 2.00
3 thru 5 . . . . @2.00

PHIGMENTS
Amazing, 1987
1 . . . . 5.00
2 . . . . 2.00
3 . . . . 2.00

PHONEY PAGES
Renegade
1 and 2 . . . . @2.00

PINEAPPLE ARMY
Viz Communications, 1988
1 thru 10 . . . . @2.00

PINK FLOYD EXPERIENCE
Revolutionary, 1991
1 based on rock group 2.50
2 Dark Side of the Moon 2.50
3 Dark Side of the Moon, Wish you
were here. 2.50
4 The Wall. 2.50
5 A Momentary lapse of reason . . . 2.50

PIRATE CORPS!
Eternity, 1987
6 and 7 . . . . @2.00
Spec. #1 . . . . 2.00

PIRANHA! IS LOOSE
Special Studio
1 Drug Runners,F:Piranha 2.95
2 Expedition into Terror 2.95

PIXY JUNKET
Viz, 1993
1 thru 6 . . . . @2.75

P.J. WARLOCK
Eclipse, 1986
1 thru 3 . . . . @2.00

PLANET COMICS
Blackthorne, 1988
(Prev. Color)
4 and 5 . . . . @2.00

PLANET COMICS
A-List Comics, 1997
1 by L.Hampton & R.Leonardo. . . . 2.50
2 rep. from 1940 . . . . 2.95
3 . . . . 2.95
5 . . . . 2.95
6 . . . . 2.95
TPB Book of Planet Comics
Covers, 1949–54 . . . . 7.95

PLANET COMICS
ACG Comics, 2000
1 WW, rep. 6.95
2 64-pg.. . . . . 5.95

PLANET LADDER
Tokyopop Press, 2002
GN Vol. 1 authentic manga 10.00
GN Vol. 2 thru Vol. 5 . . . . @10.00

PLANET OF THE APES
Adventure Comics, 1990
1 WD,collect.ed. 6.00
1 2 covers 4.00

Planet of the Apes #1
© Adventure Comics

1a 2nd printing 2.50
1b 3rd printing 2.25
2 . . . . 3.00
3 . . . . 3.00
4 . . . . 3.00
5 D:Alexander? 3.00
6 Welcome to Ape City 3.00
7 . . . . 3.00
8 Christmas Story 2.75
9 Swamp Ape Village. 2.75
10 Swamp Apes in Forbidden City . 2.75
11 Ape War continues. 2.75
12 W:Alexander & Coure 2.75
13 Planet of Apes/Alien Nation/Ape
City x-over 2.75
14 Countdown to Zero Pt.1. . . . . . 2.75
15 Countdown to Zero Pt.2. . . . . . 2.75
16 Countdown to Zero Pt.3. . . . . . 2.75
17 Countdown to Zero Pt.4. . . . . . 2.75
18 Ape City (after Ape Nation mini-
series 2.75
19 1991 'Conquest..' tie-in 2.75
20 Return of the Ape Riders 2.75
21 The Terror Beneath,Pt.1. . . . . . 2.75
22 The Terror Beneath,Pt.2. . . . . . 2.75
23 The Terror Beneath,Pt.3. . . . . . 2.75

Ann #1,'Day on Planet o/t Apes' . . . 3.50
Lim.Ed. #1 . . . . 5.00

PLANET OF THE APES: BLOOD OF THE APES
Adventure Comics, 1991
1 A:Tonus the Butcher 3.00
2 Valia/Taylorite Connection. 2.75
3 Ape Army in Phis 2.75
4 . . . . 2.75

PLANET OF THE APES: FORBIDDEN ZONE
Adventure
1 Battle for the Planet of the Apes
& Planet of the Apes tie-in 2.75
2 A:Juilus 2.75

PLANET OF THE APES: SINS OF THE FATHER
Adventure Comics, 1992
1 Conquest Tie-in 2.75

PLANET OF THE APES URCHAKS' FOLLY
Adventure Comics, 1991
1 . . . . 3.00
2 . . . . 2.75
3 'The Taylorites' 2.75
4 Conclusion 2.75

PLANET 29
Caliber
1 A Future Snarl Tale 2.50
2 A:Biff,Squakman 2.50

PLANET-X
Eternity, 1991
1 three horror stories 2.50

PLAN 9 FROM OUTER SPACE
Eternity, 1991
1 . . . . 2.50
2 and 3 . . . . @2.25

PLASTIC LITTLE
CPM Comics, 1997
1 (of 5) Manga, by Satoshi
Urushihara R:Captain Tita 2.95
2 F:Joshua Balboa 2.95
3 . . . . 2.95
4 . . . . 2.95
5 concl. 2.95
TPB Captain's Log, rep. #1–#5 . . . 15.95

PLASTRON CAFE
Mirage, 1992
1 RV,inc.North by Downeast 2.25
2 thru 4 . . . . @2.25

POE
Cheese Comics, 1996
1 by Jason Asala, reoffer 3.00
2 . . . . 3.00
3 'The System of Doctor Tarr and
Professor Fether' 3.00
4 thru 6 . . . . @3.00

CVA Page 756 — All comics prices listed are for *Near Mint* condition.

B & W PUB.

Poe–Pokemon

Sirius/Dog Star
TPB Vol. 1 . . . . 14.95

VOL 2, 1997
1 by Jason Asala 3.00
2 House of Usher, pt.1 (of 4) 3.00
3 House of Usher, pt.2 . . . . 3.00
4 House of Usher, pt.3 . . . . 3.00
5 House of Usher, pt.4 . . . . 3.00
6 . . . . 3.00
7 . . . . 3.00
8 Small Town 3.00
9 Small Town, pt.2 . . . . 3.00
10 Small Town, pt.3 . . . . 3.00
11 Gold & Lead, pt.1 . . . . 3.00
12 Gold and Lead, pt.2 . . . . 3.00
13 F:Pluto the cat 3.00
14 A:Mad Meg Mayflower 3.00
15 Airship 3.00
16 path of next demon 3.00
17 22 one-page stories 3.00
18 Airship 3.00
19 thru 24 Balloon Hoax . . . . @3.00

POINT BLANK
Acme/Eclipse, 1989
1 thru 5 . . . . @2.95

POISON ELVES
Mulehide Graphics, 1993–95
Previously: I, Lusipher
8 DHa(c&a) 12.00
9 DHa 10.00
10 DHa 10.00
11 DHa, comic size 10.00
12 DHa 10.00
13 DHa 15.00
14 and 15 DHa . . . . @15.00
15a 2nd printing 6.00
16 and 17 DHa . . . . @7.00
17a 2nd printing 6.00
18 DHa 7.00
19 DHa 7.00
20 DHa 7.00

2nd Series, Sirius, 1995–97
1 F:Lusipher 6.00
2 V:Assassins Guild 4.00
3 Sanctuary, pt.3 . . . . 4.00
4 Sanctuary, pt.4 . . . . 4.00
5 Sanctuary, pt.5 . . . . 4.00
6 I:Lester Gran 4.00
7 thru 24 . . . . @4.00
25 DHa 3.00
26 DHa 3.00
27 DHa 3.00
28 DHa,F:Lusiphur 3.00
29 DHa 3.00
30 DHa,F:Vido 3.00
31 DHa 3.00
32 DHa, Cassandra is dead 3.00
33 DHa, temporary truce 3.00
34 DHa, Lusiphur's feminine side . . 3.00
35 DHa, Purple Marauder
    reappears 3.00
36 DHa, Lusiphur tracked down . . . 3.00
37 DHa, questionable help 3.00
38 DHa 3.00
39 DHa 3.00
40 DHa, Sanctuary, concl. 3.00
41 DHa, on to Amrahly'nn 3.00
42 DHa, Just in Town
    for the Night,pt.1 . . . . 3.00
43 DHa, Town for the Night, pt.2 . . 3.00
44 DHa, Town for the Night, pt.3 . . 3.00
45 DHa, Petunia 3.00
46 DHa, High Price of
    Unemployment 2.50
47 The Fairy and the Imp 2.50
48 South for the Winter,pt.1 . . . . 2.50

Poison Elves #11
© *Sirius*

49 South for the Winter,pt.2 . . . . . 2.50
50 South for the Winter,pt.3 . . . . . 3.00
51 South for the Winter,pt.4 . . . . . 3.00
52 South for the Winter,pt.5 . . . . . 3.00
53 South for the Winter,pt.6 . . . . . 3.00
54 South for the Winter,pt.7 . . . . . 3.00
55 thru 60 . . . . @3.00
61 by The Fillbach Brothers 3.00
62 thru 68 . . . . @3.00
69 thru 75 . . . . @2.95
TPB Vol. 1 Requiem for an Elf . . 14.95
TPB Vol. 2 Traumatic Dogs 14.95
TPB Vol. 3 Desert of the Third Sin 14.95
TPB Vol. 4 Patrons, 48pg 4.95
TPB Vol. 5 rep. 272-pg. 14.95
TPB Vol. 6 rep. 280-pg. 14.95
TPB Vol. 7 . . . . 19.95
TPB Vol. 8 . . . . 15.95
TPB Vol. 9 Baptism by Fire 19.95
TPB The Muleskinner Years . . . 34.95
TPB Lusipher & Lirilith (2001) . . . 11.95
TPB Parintachin 8.95
Spec. Poison Elves Companion . . . 3.50
Sketchbook 2.95
Sketchbook, limited 13.00

POISON ELVES: LUSIPHER & LIRILITH
Sirius Entertainment, 2001
1 (of 4) by Drew Hayes 3.00
1a limited ed 10.00
2 . . . . 3.00
2a delux 10.00
3 . . . . 3.00
3a limited 6.50
4 . . . . 3.00
4a limited 6.50

POISON ELVES: PARINTACHIN
Sirius Entertainment, 2001
1 (of 3) 3.00
2 . . . . 3.00
3 . . . . 3.00

POIZON: DEMON HUNTER
London Night, 1998
1 . . . . 3.00
2 . . . . 3.00
3 . . . . 3.00

4 double sized finale 3.00

POKEMON ADVENTURES
Viz Communications, 1999
1 (of 5) Mysterious Mew 6.00
2 Wanted: Pikachu 6.00
3 The Snorlax Stop 6.00
4 . . . . 6.00
5 The Ghastly Ghosts 6.00

PART TWO, 2000
1 (of 6) Team Rocket Returns 3.00
2 The Hunt for Eevee 3.00
3 The Nidoking Safari 3.00
4 Mission: Magmar 3.00
5 The Dangerous Dragonite 3.00
6 The Mythical Moltres 3.00

PART THREE, 2000
1 . . . . 3.00
2 thru 7 . . . . @3.00

PART FOUR, 2001
Spec. 5.00

PART FIVE, 2001
1 thru 5 . . . . @5.00

PART SIX
1 (of 4) 5.00
2 thru 4 . . . . @5.00

PART SEVEN
1 (of 5) 5.00
2 thru 5 . . . . @5.00
TPB Pokemon: The Movie 2000 . . 15.95
TPB Art of Pokemon Third Movie . 12.95
TPB Vol. 1 Wanted: Pikachu 14.95
TPB Vol. 2 Legendary Pokemon . . 14.95
TPB Vol. 3 Saffron City Siege . . . 13.95
TPB Vol. 4 Trainer in Yellow 13.95
TPB Vol. 5 Making Waves 13.95
TPB Vol. 6 The Cave Campaign . . 13.95
TPB Vol. 7 Pokemon Elite 13.95

POKEMON: ELECTRIC PIKACHU BOOGALOO
Viz Communications, 1999
1 (of 4) by Toshihiro Ono, 48-pg. . . 3.50
2 . . . . 3.00
3 . . . . 3.00
4 finale 3.00
TPB 12.95

POKEMON: THE ELECTRIC TALE OF PIKACHU
Viz Communications, 1998
1 (of 4) by Toshihiro Ono 12.00
1a 2nd printing 4.00
2 . . . . 7.00
2a 2nd printing 4.00
3 . . . . 4.00
4 . . . . 4.00
GN The Electric Tale of Pikachu . . 12.95

POKEMON: PIKACHU SHOCKS BACK
Viz Communications, 1999
1 (of 4) by Toshihiro Ono 3.25
2 thru 4 . . . . @3.25

POKEMON: SURF'S UP PIKACHU
Viz Communications, 1999
1 (of 4) thru 3 . . . . @3.00
4 . . . . 3.50
TPB Vol. 3 . . . . 12.95

All comics prices listed are for *Near Mint* condition.

POKEMON TALES
Viz Communications, 2001
Prev. Color
17 Mewtwos Watching You 5.00
18 Magnemites Mission 5.00
19 Don't Laugh Charizard. 5.00
20 Onix Underground 5.00
Gold and Silver Board Books
Vol. 1 Chikorita. 5.50
Vol. 2 Cyndaquil. 5.50
Vol. 3 Totodile. 5.50
Vol. 4 Muddy Pichi 5.50
Vol. 5 Wobuffet Watches Clouds. . . 5.50
Vol. 6 Swinub's Nose 5.50
Vol. 7 Wake Up Lugia. 5.50
Vol. 8 Look Out Hondour 5.50
Vol. 9 Corsola's Brave New World . 5.50

POKEWOMON: GOTTA SHAG 'EM ALL!
Blatant Comics, 1999
1 by Mike Rosenzweig. 3.00

POOT
Fantagraphics, 1997
1 by Walt Holcombe 2.95
2 Swollen Holler, pt.2. . . . . 2.95
3 sex issue 2.95
4 final issue, 40-pg.. . . . . 3.95

POPCORN
Discovery, 1993
1 . . . . 3.95

POP PARODY
Studio Chikara, 1999
Big Fat Sci-Fi Spec.:Stawars 2.95
Pokymon–World Domination. 2.95
Dixxi Chix vs. Spice Galz 2.95
The Blair Snitch Project 3.95

PORTIA PRINZ OF THE GLAMAZONS
Eclipse, 1986
1 thru 6 . . . . @2.00

POST BROTHERS
Rip Off Press
15 thru 18. . . . . @2.00
19 and 20 . . . . @2.50

POWER COMICS
Power Comics, 1977
1 Smart-Early Aardvark 15.00
1a 2nd printing 7.00
2 I:Cobalt Blue. 10.00
3 and 4 . . . . @8.00
5 . . . . 8.00

POWER COMICS
Eclipse, 1988
1 BB,DGb,Powerbolt 2.50
2 BB,DGb 2.50
3 BB,DGb 2.50

PPV
Antarctic Press, 2002
1 by Tom Root & Jerzy Drozd 2.95
2 thru 3 . . . . @2.95

PREMIERE
Diversity Comics, 1995
1 F:Kolmec The Savage 2.75

PRETEEN DIRTY GENE KUNG FU KANGAROOS
Blackthorne, 1986
1 and 2 . . . . @2.00

PREY
Monster Comics
1 I:Prey,A:Andrina 2.25
2 V:Andrina 2.25
3 conclusion 2.25

PRICE, THE
1 Dreadstar mag. size 20.00

PRIEST
Tokyopop Press, 2002
GN Vol. 1 by Min-Woo Hyung 10.00
GN Vol. 2 thru Vol. 9 . . . . @10.00

PRIMITIVES
Spartive Studios, 1995
1 thru 3 On the Moon. . . . . @2.50

PRIME CUTS
Fantagraphics
1 adult. 3.50
2 thru 6 . . . . @3.50
7 thru 12 . . . . @3.95

PRIMER
Comico, 1982
1 . . . . 10.00
2 MW,I:Grendel 100.00
3 . . . . 9.00
4 . . . . 8.00
5 SK(1st work),I:Maxx 30.00
6 IN,Evangeline. 14.00

PRIME SLIME TALES
Mirage, 1986
1 . . . . 5.00
2 . . . . 2.50

Prime Slime Tales #2
© Mirage

PRINCE VALIANT
1 thru 4 . . . . @4.95
Spec #1 . . . . 6.95

PRINCE VALIANT MONTHLY
Pioneer
1 thru 6 . . . . @3.95
6 . . . . 4.95
7 . . . . 4.95
8 . . . . 4.95
9 . . . . 6.95

PRINCESS PRINCE
CPM Manga, 2000
1 . . . . 2.95
1a Leah Hernandez (c) 2.95
2 thru 14 . . . . @2.95
15 . . . . 2.95
16 . . . . 2.95

PRIVATE BEACH
Amaze Ink/Slave Labor Graphics, 2001
1 by David Hahn 2.95
2 . . . . 2.95
3 . . . . 2.95
4 . . . . 2.95
5 thru 8 . . . . @2.95
TPB Vol. 1 Fun & Perils 12.95
TPB Vol. 2 Secret Messages . . . 13.95

PRIVATE EYES
Eternity, 1988
1 Saint rep. 2.00
2 . . . . 2.00
3 . . . . 2.00
4 . . . . 2.00
5 . . . . 2.00

PROTHEUS
Caliber, 1986
1 . . . . 2.50
2 . . . . 2.50

PSI–JUDGE ANDERSON
Fleetway, 1989
1 thru 15 . . . . @2.00

PULP
Viz Communications, 1997
1 Manga anthology magazine 5.95
2 thru 5 . . . . @5.95
VOL. TWO
1 thru 12 . . . . @5.95
VOL. THREE
1 thru 11 . . . . @5.95
VOL. FOUR
1 . . . . 5.95
2 thru 12 . . . . @5.95
VOL. FIVE, 2000
1 . . . . 5.95
2 thru 12 . . . . @5.95
VOL SIX
1 thru 8 . . . . @5.95

PULP FICTION
A-List Comics, 1997
1 thru 2 rep. of golden age. . . . . @2.50

3 . . . . 2.95	**QUEST PRESENTS**	**RAIKA**
4 . . . . 2.95	**Quest, 1983**	**Sun Comics**
5 . . . . 2.95	1 JD 2.00	1 thru 12 . . . . @2.50
6 . . . . 2.95	2 JD 2.00	
7 . . . . 2.95	3 JD 2.00	**RAISING HELL**
Spec. Art of Pulp Fiction 2.95		**ABC Comics, 1997**
	QUICKEN FORBIDDEN	1 . . . . 2.95
PUMA BLUES	**Cryptic Press, 1998**	1a gold series, 2 extra pages. 3.00
Aardvark–Vanaheim, 1986	1 . . . . 2.95	2 RCI,F:China & Jazz 2.95
1 10,000 printed 4.00	2 . . . . 2.95	3 conclusion, A:Wild Things. 2.95
1a 2nd printing 2.00	3 . . . . 2.95	3 Baby Cheeks edition. 10.00
2 . . . . 3.00	4 . . . . 2.95	3 Baby Cheeks Gold Edition 14.95
3 . . . . 2.50	5 . . . . 2.95	
4 thru 19 . . . . @2.50	6 Trial Separation,pt.1 . . . . 2.95	
20 Special 2.50	7 Trial Separation,pt.2 . . . . 2.95	
Mirage	8 Trial Separation, concl. 2.95	
21 thru 24. . . . . @2.00	9 Anxiety Disorder, pt.1 . . . . 2.95	
25 . . . . 2.50	10 Anxiety Disorder, pt.2. . . . . 2.95	
26 thru 28. . . . . @2.00	11 thru 12 . . . . @2.95	
	TPB 152-pg. 14.95	
PVP		
Dork Storm Press, 2001	**RABID MONKEY**	
1 by Scott Kurtz. 2.95	**D.B.I. Comics, 1997**	
2 . . . . 2.95	1 thru 4 by Joel Steudler . . . . . . @2.25	
3 . . . . 2.95	5 thru 7 . . . . @2.25	
4 . . . . 2.95	8 thru 13 . . . . @2.50	
5 thru 8 . . . . @3.00	#1–#5 Autographed pack 12.00	
Collected ed. #1 Hat Trick. 3.00	**Dreamriders Workshop, 1998**	
TPB Vol. 1 Striptease 16.00	**Vol. 2**	
	1 . . . . 2.95	
QUACK!		
Star Reach, 1976	**RADICAL DREAMER**	
1 Duckaneer 11.00	**Mark's Giant Economy**	
1a 2nd printing 4.00	**Sized Comics, 1995–96**	
2 Newton the Rabbit Wonder 8.00	1 thru 3 F:Max Wrighter . . . . @3.00	
3 Dave Sim,The Beavers. 8.00	4 is Max the Devil? 3.00	
4 Dave Sim 8.00	**VOL 2, 1998**	
5 Dave Sim 8.00	1 (of 6) by Mark Wheatley, sci-fi. . . 3.00	*Ralph Snart #1*
6 . . . . 8.00		*© Now*
	RAGMOP	
QUANTUM MECHANICS	**Planet Lucy Press, 1995**	**RALPH SNART**
Avatar, 1999	See Image also	**Now, 1986**
1 (of 2) by Barry Gregory &	1 by Rob Walton, 3rd. printing 3.00	1 . . . . 5.00
Jacen Burrows 3.50	2 thru 8 reoffer . . . . @2.75	2 . . . . 4.00
1a wraparound cover. 3.95	8 . . . . 2.75	3 . . . . 4.00
2 conclusion 3.50	9 . . . . 2.75	**[Volume 2] 1986**
2a wraparound cover. 3.95	10 . . . . 2.75	1 . . . . 3.00
	VOL 2, 1997	2 thru 8 . . . . @1.50
QUEEN & COUNTRY	3 by Rob Walton 2.95	Trade Paperback 2.95
Oni Press, 2001	4 O-ring saga, pt. 2 (of 3) 2.95	
1 by Greg Rucka & Steve Rolston 10.00		**RAMBO**
2 . . . . 11.00	**RAGNAROK**	**Blackthorne, 1988**
3 thru 5 . . . . @5.00	**Sun Comics**	1 thru 5 . . . . @2.00
6 thru 12 . . . . @3.00	1 I:Ragnarok Guy,Honey 2.50	
13 thru 15 . . . . @3.00	2 The Melder Foundation. 2.50	**RAMBO III**
16 thru 21 . . . . @3.00	3 Guy/Honey mission contd. 2.50	**Blackthorne**
TPB Vol. 1 . . . . 11.95	4 I:Big Gossage. 2.50	1 . . . . 2.00
TPB Vol. 2 Morning Star 9.95		
TPB Vol. 3 Crystal Ball 14.95	**RAGNAROK**	**RAMM**
TPB Vol. 4 Operation Blackwell . . . 8.95	**Tokyopop Press, 2002**	**Megaton Comics, 1987**
	1 (of 4) by Myung Jin Lee 2.95	1 and 2 . . . . @2.00
QUEEN & COUNTRY:	2 thru 4 . . . . @3.00	
DECLASSIFIED	GN Vol. 1 . . . . 10.00	**RANMA 1/2**
Oni Press 2002	GN Vol. 2 thru Vol. 7 . . . . @10.00	**Viz, 1993**
1 (of 3) 2.95		*Parts 1 & 2, see color*
2 . . . . 2.95	**RAIJIN COMICS**	**PART 3, 1993–94**
3 . . . . 2.95	**Gutsoon! Entertainment 2002**	1 thru 13 . . . . @3.00
TPB Vol. 1 . . . . 8.95	1 manga 4.95	**PART 4, 1995**
	2 thru 36 . . . . @4.95	1 thru 11 . . . . @3.00
QUEST FOR	37 thru 39 . . . . @5.95	**PART 5, 1996**
DREAMS LOST		1 thru 9 . . . . @3.00
Literacy Vol. of Chicago, 1987		10 thru 12 . . . . @3.00
1-shot inc. TMNTurtles. 2.00		

Ranma–Razor

PART 6, 1996
1 thru 8 (of 14) . . . . @3.00
9 thru 14 . . . . @3.00
TPB Vol. 6 . . . . 15.95
TPB Vol. 7 . . . . 15.95
TPB Vol. 8 . . . . 15.95
TPB Vol. 9 . . . . 15.95
TPB Vol. 10 rep. Part Six, 1st half. 15.95
TPB Vol. 11 rep. Part Six, 2nd half 15.95

PART 7, 1998
1 (of 14) 2.95
2 thru 14 . . . . @2.95
TPB Vol. 12 . . . . 15.95
TPB Vol. 13 . . . . 15.95

PART 8, 1999
1 (of 13) thru 5 . . . . @2.95
6 thru 13 . . . . @2.95
TPB Vol. 14 . . . . 15.95
TPB Vol. 15 . . . . 16.95
TPB Vol. 16 . . . . 15.95

PART 9, 2000
1 (of 11) 2.95
2 thru 11 . . . . @2.95
TPB Vol. 17 rep. Vol.9, #1–#6 . . . 15.95
TPB Vol. 18 rep. Vol.9, #6–#11 . . 15.95

PART 10, 2001
1 (of 11) 2.95
2 thru 8 . . . . @2.95
9 thru 11 . . . . @2.95

PART 11, 2002
1 (of 11) 2.95
2 thru 11 . . . . 2.95
TPB Vol. 19 . . . . 15.95
TPB Vol. 20 . . . . 15.95
TPB Art of Ranma 1/2. . . . . 24.95

Part 12 (March 2003)
1 . . . . 2.95
TPB Vol. 21 . . . . 15.95
TPB Vol. 22 thru Vol. 24 . . . . @9.95

Raphael #1
© Mirage

RAPHAEL
Mirage, 1985
1 TMNT 17.50
1a 2nd printing 7.50

RAPTUS
High Impact
1 . . . . 3.00
1 2nd printing, new cover 3.00
2 . . . . 3.00
3 . . . . 3.00

B & W PUB.

RAPTUS: DEAD OF NIGHT
High Impact
1 . . . . 2.95
2 . . . . 2.95
3 . . . . 3.00

RAT FINK
World of Fandom
1 . . . . 2.50
2 & 3 . . . . @2.50

RAVAGER
Kosmic Comic, 1997
0 Ashcan 2.00
1 The First Coming 3.55
2 . . . . 3.55
3 . . . . 3.55
4 by Kirk Patrick & Babak Homayoun 3.55
5 . . . . 3.55
6 by Kirk Patrick & Romel Cruz . . . 3.55

RAVE
Tokyopop Press, 2002
GN Vol. 1 by Hiro Mashima 10.00
GN Vol. 2 thru Vol. 5 . . . . @10.00

RAVEN
Ariel Press 2003
1 . . . . 1.95
2 thru 6 . . . . @1.95

RAVEN CHRONICLES
Caliber Press, 1995
1 . . . . 3.00
1a Special Edition 6.00
2 Landing Zone 3.00
3 The Rain People 3.00
4 The Healer 3.00
5 thru 9 . . . . @3.00
Caliber 'New Worlds'
10 by Scott Andrews, Laurence Campbell & Tim Perkins 3.00
11 'The Ghost of Alanzo Mann' . . . 3.00
12 'The Compensators' flip book with Boston Bombers #1 . . . . . 3.00
13 48pg, bagged with back issue . . 4.00
14 . . . . 3.00
15 . . . . 3.00
16 inc. Black Mist 3.00
Spec. Heart of the Dragon 3.00
GN 192pg rep 16.95

RAVENING, THE
Avatar Press, 1997
0 Trevlin Utz (c) 3.95
0 Matt Martin (c) 3.95
0 Matt Haley (c) 3.95
0 leather cover 25.00
0 signed 15.00
1 . . . . 3.00
1 leather cover 25.00
1 Avatar con cover edition 15.00
2 (of 2) 3.00
Spec. Secrets of the Ravening . . . 2.75

RAW CITY
Dramenon Studios
1 I:Dya,Gino 3.00
2 V:Crucifier 3.00
3 The Siren's Past 3.00

Comics Values Annual

RAW MEDIA MAGS.
Rebel
1 TV,SK,short stories 5.00

RAZOR
London Night, 1992
6 signed 20.00
10 signed 15.00
TPB The Suffering, rep. #1–#3 . . . 12.95
GN Let Us Prey, rep. of Razor/Wild Child, 80pg 5.00
X-over Razor/Embrace: The Spawning (1997) 3.00
Carmen Electra photo (c) 3.00
Carmen Electra photo embossed (c), signed 19.00
Spec. Razor: Switchblade Symphony, Tour Book, limited black leather 15.00

RAZOR ANALOG BURN
London Night Studios, 1999
1 by Lee Duhig 2.50
2 . . . . 2.50

RAZOR: ARCHIVES
London Night, 1997
1 EHr, rep #1–#4 . . . . 5.00
1a signed 12.00
2 EHr, rep #5–#8 . . . . 5.00
3 EHr, rep #9–#15 . . . . 5.00
4 EHr, rep #16–#17 . . . . 5.00

RAZOR: BLEEDING HEART
Avatar Press, 2001
1 Fillion (c) 3.50
1a Martin (c) 3.50
1b Wraparound (c) 4.95
1c Adult (c) 6.00
1d Worship (c) 5.95

RAZOR/DARK ANGEL: THE FINAL NAIL
Boneyard/London Night
1 X-over (Boneyard Press) 4.00
2 X-over concl.(London Night) 3.00

RAZOR: THE DARKEST NIGHT
London Night, 1998
1 . . . . 4.95
1a white velvet 20.00
2 velvet edition 10.00
EH! Productions, 1999
1 . . . . 4.95
1a Velvet Edition, signed 25.00
2 . . . . 4.95
3 . . . . 4.95
3a Fan ed 6.00

RAZOR: THE FURIES
Avatar, 2000
1 48-pg 4.95
1a Previews Exclusive 4.95

RAZOR: GOTHIC
London Night, 1998
1 (of 4) by EHr and Scott Wilson . . 3.00
1 leather 12.00
2 EHr 3.00

B & W PUB.

Razor–Redmoon

2a Graphic/violent cover 6.00
2b Gothic/leather cover 15.00

EH! Productions
3 . . . . 3.00
3a Elite Fan ed. 5.00
4 . . . . 3.00
4a Elite Fan ed. 5.00
Spec. Gotherotica. 5.00

RAZOR: TILL I BLEED DAYLIGHT
Avatar, 2000
1 (of 2) Tim Vigil (c). 3.50
1a wraparound (c) 3.95
1b Vampire Razor (c). 5.00
1c adult (c) 6.00
1d prism foil. 12.95
1e expanded edition 5.00
2 . . . . 3.50
2a wraparound (c) 3.95
2b adult (c) 6.00
2c expanded edition, 56-pg. 5.00

RAZOR: TORTURE
London Night, 1995
0 chromium signed 4.00
1 platinum signed 3.00

RAZOR UNCUT
London Night Studios, 1995
Prev. RAZOR (Ind. Color)
13 . . . . 3.00
14 V:Child Killer 3.00
15 Questions About Father 3.00
16 Nicole's Life,pt.1 . . . . 3.00
17 Nicole's Life,pt.2 . . . . 3.00
18 . . . . 3.00
19 thru 21 Kiss from a Rose . . . . @3.00
22 thru 24 . . . . @3.00
25 mild cover I:Knyfe 3.00
25b signed 12.95
26 . . . . 3.00
27 A:Sade, pt.1. . . . . 3.00
28 A:Sade, pt.2. . . . . 3.00
29 . . . . 3.00
30 . . . . 3.00
31 'Strength by Numbers'. 3.00
32 double sized 3.50
33 'Let Us Prey,' pt.2 . . . . 3.00
34 'Let Us Prey,' pt.4 (of 2) 3.00

Razor Uncut #23
© London Night Studios

35 Let the battle begin 3.00
36 all-out war for Queen City 3.00
37 'After the Fall' pt.1 . . . . 3.00
38 'After the Fall,' pt.2 . . . . 3.00
39 'Money For Hire' 3.00
40 'Father's Bane,' pt.1 . . . . 3.00
41 'Father's Bane,' pt.2 . . . . 3.00
42 'Father's Bane,' pt.3 . . . . 3.00
43 'Father's Bane,' pt.4 . . . . 3.00
44 Razor finds abandoned child . . . 3.00
45 An American Tragedy, pt.1 (of 5) 3.00
45a commemmorative edition, EHr . 5.00
46 An American Tragedy, pt.2 . . . 3.00
47 An American Tragedy, pt.3 . . . 3.00
48 An American Tragedy, pt.4 . . . 3.00
49 An American Tragedy, pt.5 . . . 3.00
50 back in Asylum, Tony Daniel (c) . 3.00
50a Michael Bair (c) 5.00
50b Stephen Sandoval (c) 5.00
50c Blood Red Velvet EHr (c) . . . 25.00
Spec. Deep Cuts (1997) 5th Anniv.
   rep. #6,#13–#15, 80 pg 5.00

EH! Productions, 1999
51 . . . . 3.00

RAZORGUTS
Monster Comics, 1992
1 thru 4 . . . . 2.25

RAZOR'S EDGE
London Night, 1999
0 Razor/Stryke (c) 4.95
0b Night Vixen (c) 4.95
1 . . . . 4.95
1a Arizona (c) 4.95
2 Razorblaze (c) 4.95
2a Battle Girl (c) 6.00
2b Nightvixen (c) 4.95
3 . . . . 4.95
3a Nightvixen (c) 4.95
4 . . . . 4.95
4a (c) 4.95
5 . . . . 4.95
5a Stryke (c) 4.95

EH! Productions, 1999
6 48-pg. 4.95
7 . . . . 4.95
8 . . . . 4.95
9 . . . . 4.95

REACTOMAN
B-Movie Comics
1 . . . . 2.00
1a signed,numbered 2.75
2 thru 4 . . . . @2.00
collection 4.95

REAGAN'S RAIDERS
Solson
1 thru 6 . . . . @2.50

REAL BOUT HIGH SCHOOL
Tokyopop Press, 2002
TPB Vol. 1 (of 6) authentic manga 10.00
TBP Vol. 2 thru Vol. 5 . . . . @10.00

REALM
Arrow, 1986
1 Fantasy 6.00
2 . . . . 4.00
3 . . . . 3.00
4 TV,Deadworld. 21.00
5 I:L.Kazan 2.00

6 thru 13 . . . . @1.50
Caliber Press, 1990
14 thru 18 . . . . @2.00
19 . . . . 2.50

REAL STUFF
Fantagraphic, 1990
1 thru 12 . . . . 2.50

REAPER
Newcomers Publishing
1 V:The Chinde 2.95
2 . . . . 2.95
3 conclusion 2.95

REBELLION
Daikaiyu Enterprises, 1995
1 I:Rebellion 2.50

REBIRTH
Tokyopop Press 2003
GN Vol. 1 thru 5 (of 11) . . . . . . @10.00

REBOUND
Tokyopop Press 2003
GN Vol. 1 . . . . 10.00
GN Vol. 2 thru 5 . . . . @10.00

RECORD OF THE LODOSS WAR
CPM Manga, 2000
TPB Book 1 The Grey Witch. . . . 15.95
TPB Book 2 The Grey Witch. . . . 15.95
TPB The Lady of Pharis 15.95
TPB Welcome to Lodoss Island . . 15.95
TPB Vol.2 Welcome Lodoss Island 15.95

RED DIARY
Caliber, 1998
1 (of 4) F:Marilyn, JFK, Hoover,
  CIA 3.95
1a deluxe 6.95
2 . . . . 3.95
3 (of 4) 3.95
1 signed). 3.95
4 . . . . 3.95

RED FOX
Harrier, 1986
1 scarce 6.00
1a 2nd printing 2.50
2 rare 5.00
3 . . . . 3.00
4 I:White Fox. 3.00
5 I:Red Snail 3.00
6 . . . . 2.00
7 Wbolton 2.00
8 . . . . 2.00
9 Demosblurth. 2.00

RED & STUMPY
Parody Press
1 Ren & Stimpy parody 2.95

REDMOON
Comicsone.com, 2001
GN #1 196-pg. by Mina Hwang . . . 11.95
GN #2 196-pg. 11.95
GN #3 196-pg. 11.95
GN #4 200-pg. 11.95
GN #5 206-pg. 11.95

RE:GEX: BLACK & WHITE
Awesome Entertainment, 1999
1 RLe,JLb 2.95

REID FLEMING, WORLD'S TOUGHEST MILKMAN
Blackbird-Eclipse, 1986
1 David Boswell,I:Reid Fleming ... 5.00
1a 2nd printing 3.00
1b 3rd–5th printing .... @2.50
Volume 2, 1986
#1 Rogues to Riches Pt.1 .... 5.00
#2 Rogues to Riches Pt.2 (1987) .. 3.00
#2a Later printings 2.50
#3 Rogues to Riches Pt.3 (1988) .. 3.00
#3a Later printings 2.50
#4 Rogues to Riches Pt.4 (1989) .. 3.00
#5 Rogues to Riches Pt.5 (1990) .. 2.50
Deep-Sea Comics, 1987
3 'Rogue to Riches,' pt.2,4th pr ... 3.00
4 'Rogue to Riches,' pt.3,3rd pr ... 3.00
5 'Rogue to Riches,' pt.4,2nd pr ... 3.00
6 'Rogue to Riches,' pt.5,2nd pr ... 3.00
7 'Another Dawn,'Pt.1 .... 3.00
8 'Another Dawn,'Pt.2 .... 3.00
9 'Another Dawn,'Pt.3 .... 3.00
TPB Rogue to Riches rep. 13.95
Spec#1 Origins (1998) 3.00

REIVERS
Enigma
1 thru 2 Ch'tocc in Space 2.95

RENEGADES OF JUSTICE
Blue Masque
1 I:Monarch,Bloodshadow 2.50
2 Madfire 2.50
3 Television Chronicles 2.50
4 R:Karen Styles 2.50

RENFIELD
Caliber, 1994
1 thru 3 .... @3.00
GN Conclusion of series 8.95

REPENTANCE
Advantage Graphics, 1995
1 I:Repentance 2.00

REPLACEMENT GOD
Amaze Ink, 1995
1 Child in The Land of Man 6.00
1a 2nd & 3rd printing 3.00
2 Eye of Knute 4.00
3 & 4 'Bravery' .... @3.50
5 thru 7 .... @3.00
8 Fairie, book one, concl. 2.95
TPB rep. #1–#8 .... 19.95

REPLACEMENT GOD & OTHER STORIES
Handicraft Guild, 1998
Previously published by Image
6 by Zander Cannon, 80pg 6.95

RETALIATOR
Eclipse
1 I&O:Retaliator 2.50
2 O:Retaliator cont. 2.50

B & W PUB.

GN #6 208-pg. 11.95
3 thru 5 .... @2.50

RETIEF
Adventure, 1987–88
1 thru 6 Keith Laumer adapt. ... @2.00
[Vol. 2], 1989–90
1 thru 6 .... @2.25
Spec.#1 Retief:Garbage Invasion .. 2.50
Spec.#1 Retief:The Giant Killer,
  V:Giant Dinosaur (1991) 2.50
Spec.#1 Grime & Punishment,
  Planet Slunch (1991) 2.50

RETIEF OF THE CDT
Adventure, 1990
1 Keith Laumer Novel Adapt. 2.00
2 thru 6 .... @2.00

RETIEF AND THE WARLORDS
Adventure Comics
1 Keith Laumer Novel Adapt. 2.50
2 Haterakans 2.50
3 Retief Arrested for Treason 2.50
4 Final Battle (last issue) 2.50

RETIEF: DIPLOMATIC IMMUNITY
Adventure Comics, 1991
1 Groaci Invasion 2.50
2 Groaci story cont. 2.50

RETRO-DEAD
Blazer Unlimited, 1995
1 Dimensional Rift 2.95
2 by Dan Reed 2.95

RETROGRADE
Eternity
1 thru 4 .... @2.00

RETURN OF HAPPY THE CLOWN
Caliber Press
1 & 2 V:Oni 2.95

RETURN OF LUM URUSEI* YATSURA, THE
Viz Comics, 1994
1 thru 6 .... @3.00
TPB #1 .... 15.95
PART TWO, 1995
1 thru 13 .... @3.00
TPB Trouble Times Ten, rep.,pt#2 . 15.95
PART THREE, 1996
1 thru 11 by Rumiko Takahashi . @2.95
TPB Creature Features 15.95
PART FOUR, 1997
1 thru 11 by Rumiko Takahashi . @2.95
TPB Vol. 5 Feudal Furor 15.95
TPB Vol. 6 Creature Features ... 15.95
TPB Vol. 7 For Better or Curse .. 15.95
TPB Vol. 8 Ran Attacks 15.95

RETURN OF THE SKYMAN
Ace Comics, 1987
1 SD 2.00

Return of the Skyman #1
© Ace Comics

REVOLVER
Renegade, 1985
1 SD 2.00
2 thru 12 .... @2.00
Ann. #1 .... 2.00

REVOLVING DOORS
Blackthorne, 1986
1 .... 2.00
2 .... 2.00
3 .... 2.00
Graphic Novel 3.95

RHEINTOCHTER
Antarctic Press, 1998
1 by Y.Paquette & M.Lacombe ... 2.95
2 (of 2) concl. 2.95

RHUDIPRRT PRINCE OF FUR
MU Press, 1990–91
1 thru 6 .... @2.00

RICK RAYGUN
1 .... 2.00
2 thru 8 .... @2.00

RIO KID
Eternity
1 I:Rio Kid 2.50
2 V:Blow Torch Killer 2.50
3 .... 2.50

RIOT
Viz, 1995
1 F:Riot,Axel 2.75
2 & 3 .... 2.75
4 final issue 2.75
TPB Rep 15.95

RIOT ACT TWO
Viz Comics, 1996
1 thru 7 .... @2.95
TPB rep 15.95

RIP IN TIME
Fantagor, 1986
1 RCo,Limited series 3.00
2 RCo 2.00
3 RCo 2.00
4 RCo 2.00
5 RCo,Last 2.00

ROACHMILL
Blackthorne, 1986
1 . . . . 5.00
2 . . . . 3.00
3 . . . . 3.00
4 . . . . 3.00
See: Dark Horse

ROBERT E. HOWARD'S
Cross Plains Comics, 1999
1-shot Horror, 64-pg. 5.95
TPB Kull 19.95
1-shot Black Stone 3.95

ROBIN HOOD
Eternity, 1989
1 thru 4 . . . . @2.25

ROBO DEFENSE TEAM MECHA RIDER
Castle Comics
1 I:RDT Mecha Rider 2.95
2 Identity of Outlaw 2.95

ROBOTECH
Eternity
1-shot Untold Stories 2.50
Academy Comics, 1995–96
0 Robotech Information 2.50
Spec. Robotech: Macross Tempest F:Roy Fokker, Tempest (1995) . 3.00
Spec. Robotech: Mech Angel, I:Mech Angel (1995) 3.00
Spec. Robotech: The Misfits, from Southern Cross transferred to Africa 3.00
Spec. #1 & #2 Robotech The Movie, Benny R. Powell & Chi . . . . @3.00
Spec. Robotech Romance 3.00
Spec. Robotech: Sentinels Star Runners Carpenter's Journey (1996) . . . 3.00
GN The Threadbard Heart 9.35
Antarctic Press, 1998
Ann. #1 . . . . 3.00
Spec.#1 Robotech: Escape (1998) . 3.00

ROBOTECH: ACADEMY BLUES
Academy Comics
0 Classroom Blues 3.50
1 F:Lisa 3.00
2 Bomb at the Academy 3.00
3 Roy's Drinking Buddy 3.00

ROBOTECH: AFTERMATH
Academy Comics
1 thru 10 R:Bruce Lewis . . . . . . @3.00
11 Zentradi Traitor 3.00
12 and 13 . . . . @3.00

ROBOTECH: CLONE
Academy Comics
1 Dialect of Duality 3.00

2 V:Monte Yarrow 3.00
3 Ressurection 3.00
4 Ressurection 3.00
5 F:Bibi Ava 3.00

ROBOTECH: COVERT OPS
Antarctic Press, 1998
1 (of 2) by Greg Lane 3.00
2 . . . . 3.00

ROBOTECH: INVID WAR
Eternity, 1993
1 No Man's Land 2.50
2 V:Defoliators 2.50
3 V:The Invid,Reflex Point 2.50
4 V:The Invid 2.50

Robotech Invid War #8
© Eternity

5 Moonbase Aluce II 2.50
6 Moonbase-Zentraedi plot 2.50
7 Zentraedi plot contd 2.50
8 A:Lancer 2.50
9 A:Johnathan Wolfe 2.50
10 . . . . 2.50
11 F:Rand 2.50
12 thru 15 . . . . 2.50

ROBOTECH: INVID WAR AFTERMATH
Eternity
1 thru 6 F:Rand 2.75

ROBOTECH: MORDECAI
Academy Comics
1 . . . . 3.00
2 Annie meets her clone 3.00

ROBOTECH: RETURN TO MACROSS
Eternity, 1993
1 thru 12 . . . . @2.50
Academy Comics
13 thru 17 Roy Fokker . . . . @2.75
18 F:The Faithful 2.75
19 F:Lisa 2.75
20 F:Lisa 2.75

21 V:Killer Robot 2.95
22 War of the Believers 2.95
23 War of the Believers,pt.2 . . . . . 2.95
24 War of the Believers,pt.3 . . . . . 2.95
25 War of the Believers,pt.4 . . . . . 2.95
26 thru 30 . . . . @2.95
31 What is the Federalist Plan? . . 2.95
32 thru 34 . . . . @2.95
35 Typhoon threatens Macross Island 2.95
36 . . . . 2.95
37 round up of Federalist Agents . . 2.95

ROBOTECH: SENTINELS: RUBICON
Antarctic Press, 1998
1 (of 7) 2.95
2 Shadows of the Past 2.95

ROBOTECH II THE SENTINELS
Eternity, 1988
1 . . . . 3.00
1a 2nd printing 2.00
2 . . . . 2.50
2a 2nd printing 2.00
3 . . . . 2.50
3a 2nd printing 2.00
4 thru 16 . . . . @2.50
Book 2, 1990
1 thru 12 . . . . @2.25
13 thru 20 . . . . @2.50
Wedding Special #1 (1989) 2.00
Wedding Special #2 . . . . 2.00
Robotech II Handbook 2.50
Book Three
1 thru 8 V:Invid . . . . @2.50
Book Four
Academy Comics, 1995
1 by Jason Waltrip 2.95
2 thru 4 F:Tesla . . . . @2.75
5 JWp,JWt,interior of Haydon IV . . 2.95
6 thru 8 . . . . @2.95
9 JWp,JWt,Breetai, Wolf & Vince return to Tirol 2.95
10 JWp,JWt,Ark Angel attacked by The Black Death Destroyers . . . 2.95
11 JWp,JWt,Tirol, Wolff, Vince & Breetai on trial for treason 2.95
12 JWp,JWt,Dr. Lang exposes General Edwards' evil designs . 2.95
13 F:Tesla 2.75
14 V:Invid 2.75
15 . . . . 2.75
16 . . . . 2.75
17 V:Invid Mechas 2.75
18 F:"HIN" 2.95
19 V:Invid 2.95
20 Final Aplp. Invid Regiss 2.95
21 Predator and Prey 2.95
22 A Clockwork Planet 2.95
Halloween Special JWp,JWt, . . . 2.95

ROBOTECH II: THE SENTINELS: CYBERPIRATES
Eternity, 1991
1 The Hard Wired Coffin 2.25
2 thru 4 . . . . @2.25

All comics prices listed are for Near Mint condition.

Robotech–Sailor

B & W PUB.

Comics Values Annual

ROBOTECH II: THE SENTINELS: THE MALCONTENT UPRISING
Eternity
1 thru 12 . . . . @2.00

ROBOTECH: VERMILION
Antarctic Press, 1997
1 (of 4) by Duc Tran 3.00
2 Why did Hiro die? 3.00
3 . . . . 3.00
4 . . . . 3.00

ROBOTECH: WARRIORS
Academy Comics, 1995
1 F:Breetai 3.00
2 F:Mirya 3.00
3 F:Mirya 3.00
GN The Terror Maker 9.35

ROBOTECH: WINGS OF GIBRALTAR
Antarctic Press, 1998
1 (of 2) by Lee Duhig 3.00
2 . . . . 3.00

ROBO WARRIORS
CFW
1 thru 11 . . . . @2.00
Becomes:
KUNG FU WARRIORS

ROCK 'N' ROLL COMICS
Revolutionary, 1989
1 Guns & Roses 10.00
1a 2nd printing 3.50
1b 3rd printing 3.00
1c 4th-7th printing 3.00
2 Metalica 11.00
2a 2nd printing 3.00
2b 3rd-5th printing 3.00
3 Bon Jovi 9.00
4 Motley Crue 5.00
5 Def Leppard 5.00
6 Rolling Stones 8.00
6a 2nd-4th printing 3.00
7 The Who 5.00
7a 2nd-3rd printing 3.00
9 Kiss 15.00
9a 2nd-3rd Printing 5.00
10 Warrant/Whitesnake 6.00
10a 2nd Printing 3.00
11 Aerosmith 5.00
12 New Kids on Block 5.00
12a 2nd Printing 2.00
13 LedZeppelin 6.00
14 Sex Pistols 5.00
See Independent Color

ROCKET RANGERS
Adventure, 1992
1 . . . . 2.95
2 . . . . 2.95
3 . . . . 2.95

ROCKIN' ROLLIN' MINER ANTS
Fate Comics, 1992
1 As seen in TMNT #40 . . . . . . 2.35
1a Gold Variant copy 7.50

2 Elephant Hunting, A:Scorn, Blister 2.25
3 V:Scorn, Inc.,K.Eastman Ant pin-up 2.25
4 Animal Experiments,V:Loboto . . . 2.25

ROLLING STONES: THE SIXTIES
Personality
1 Regular Version 2.95
1a Deluxe Version,w/cards 6.95

ROOTER
Custom Comics of America, 1996–97
1 Sweatin' Bullets 2.95
2 Big Bad Beaver 2.95
3 The Big Izzy 2.95
4 Da Voodoo Blues 2.95
5 . . . . 2.95
6 Blues Power 2.95
Ann. #1, 120pg. 14.95
VOL 2, 1998
1 by Kelly Campbell 2.95
2 . . . . 2.95
3 Hot Rocks Mojo 2.95

ROSE
Hero Graphics, 1993
1 From The Champions 3.50
2 A:Huntsman 3.50
3 thru 5 . . . . @2.95

ROSE AND GUNN
London Night, 1996
1 . . . . 3.00
1b signed 10.00
2 . . . . 3.00
3 . . . . 3.00

ROSE AND GUNN: RECKONING
London Night
1 (of 2) 3.00

Rose 'N' Gunn, Creators Choice #1
© Bishop Press

ROSE 'N' GUNN
Bishop Pres, 1995
1 Deadly Duo 5.00
2 V:Marilyn Monroe 3.00
3 Presidential Affairs 3.00
4 Without Each Other 3.00
5 V:Red 3.00
6 & 7 . . . . @3.00
Creator's Choice Rep. #1 . . . . . 2.95
Creator's Choice Rep. #2 . . . . . 2.95
Creator's Choice Rep. #3 . . . . . 2.95

ROVERS
Eternity
1 thru 7 . . . . @2.00

RUBES REVIVED
Fish Warp
1 . . . . 2.00
2 and 3 . . . . @2.00

RUK BUD WEBSTER
Fish Warp
1 thru 3 . . . . @2.00

SABER MARIONETTE J
Tokyopop Press 2003
GN Vol. 1 . . . . 10.00
GN Vol. 2 thru 3 . . . . @10.00

SADE
Bishop Press, 1995
0 B:Adventures of Sade 3.00
1 . . . . 3.00
1a variant 6.00
2 . . . . 3.00

SADE SPECIAL
Bishop Press
1 V:Razor 5.00
1a signed 7.00

SADE
London Night, 1996
1 . . . . 3.00
2 thru 5 . . . . @3.00

SADE/ROSE AND GUNN
London Night, 1996
1 Confederate Mist 3.00

SADE: TESTAMENTS OF PAIN
London Night, 1997
1 (of 2) 3.00

SAGA OF THE MAN-ELF
Trident, 1989
1 thru 5 . . . . @2.25

SAGE
Fantaco, 1995
1 O:Sage 4.95

SAILOR MOON
Mixx Entertainment, 1998
1 by Naoko Tekeuchi 20.00
2 thru 5 . . . . @12.00
6 thru 11 . . . . @5.00

CVA Page 764   All comics prices listed are for *Near Mint* condition.

Sailor Moon #8
© Mixx Entertainment

12 thru 20 . . . . @5.00
Pocket #1 (of 18) 192-pg. 10.00
Pocket #2 rep. 10.00
Pocket #3 rep. 10.00
Pocket #4 rep. 10.00
Pocket #5 rep. #11–#13 . . . . 10.00
Pocket #6 rep. #14–#17 . . . . 10.00
Scout Guide: Sailor Mars: Fire . . . 12.95
Scout Guide: Sailor Venus: Love. . 12.95
Scout Guide: Sailor Jupiter:
  Thunder 12.95
Novel A Scout is Born 5.00
Novel The Power of Love 5.00
Novel 3: Mercury Rising 5.00

Tokyopop.Com, 2000
21 thru 25 . . . . @3.00
26 thru 35 . . . . @3.00
Pocket Mixx Vol. 7 thru 11 . . . . . @9.95
Pocket Mixx Stars, Vol.1 thru 3 . . @9.95
TPB Scout Guide-Meet Sailor
  Moon: Crystal 12.95
TPB Scout Guide-Meet Sailor
  Mercury: Ice 12.95
TPB Scout Guide-Meet Sailor
  Jupiter: Thunder 12.95

SAILOR MOON SUPER S
Mixx Entertainment, 1999
1 (of 18) 192-pg. 9.95
2 Pocket Mixx 9.95
3 Pocket Mixx 9.95
4 Pocket Mixx 9.95

SAINT
Kick Ass Comics
1 & 2 V:Cerran 2.50

SAINT GERMAINE
Caliber `Core', 1997
0 O:St. Germaine 4.00
1 VcL, two immortals, St. Germain
  cover 3.00
1 Lilith cover 3.00
2 VcL 3.00
3 VcL 3.00
3a signed 3.00
4 VcL 3.00
5 The Kilroy Mandate, VcL(c) 3.00
5a Meyer (c) 3.00
6 Kilroy Mandate 3.00

8 Ghost Dance 3.00
8 The Man in the Iron Mask. 3.00
10 The Tragedy of Falstaff 3.00
11 by Gary Reed & James Lyle. . . . 3.00
GN Shadows Fall, rep. #1–#4 . . . 14.95
Spec. Casanova's Lament, 48-pg. . 3.95
Spec. Restoration, VcL 3.95

SAINT GERMAINE: PRIOR ECHOES
Caliber `Core', 1998
1 (of 4) by Gary Reed 3.00
2 . . . . 3.00
3 . . . . 3.00

SAINT TAIL
Tokyopop Press, 2000
1 . . . . 2.95
2 thru 13 . . . . @2.95
14 thru 16 . . . . @2.95
17 thru 20 . . . . @3.00
TPB Pocket Mixx, Vol. 1 . . . . 9.95
TPB Pocket Mixx, Vol. 2 . . . . 9.95
TPB Pocket Vol. 3 thru Vol. 7 . . @10.00

SAMURAI (1st series)
1 . . . . 50.00
2 . . . . 25.00
3 . . . . 25.00
4 . . . . 25.00
5 . . . . 25.00

SAMURAI
Aircel, 1985
1 rare 6.00
1a 2nd printing 3.00
1b 3rd printing 2.00
2 . . . . 5.00
2a 2nd printing 2.50
3 . . . . 3.00
4 . . . . 3.00
5 thru 12 . . . . @2.00
13 DK (1st art) 4.00
14 thru 16 DK . . . . @4.00
17 thru 23 . . . . @2.00

[3rd series], 1988
#1 thru 3 . . . . @2.00
#4 thru 7 . . . . @2.00
Compilation Book 4.95

SAMURAI
Warp Graphics, 1997
1 by Barry Blair & Colin Chan 2.95
2 . . . . 2.95
3 . . . . 2.95
4 . . . . 2.95

SAMURAI DEEPER KYO
Tokyopop Press 2003
GN Vol. 1 . . . . 10.00
GN Vol. 2 thru Vol. 4 . . . . @10.00

SAMURAI FUNNIES
Solson
1 thru 3 . . . . @2.00

SAMURAI PENGUIN
Solson, 1986
1 . . . . 3.00
2 I:Dr.Radium 2.00
3 . . . . 2.00
4 . . . . 2.00
5 FC 2.00

6 color. 2.25
7 . . . . 2.25
8 . . . . 2.00
9 . . . . 2.00

SAMURAI 7
Gauntlet Comics
1 I: Samurai 7 . . . . 2.50

SAMURAI, SON OF DEATH
Eclipse
1 . . . . 3.95
1a 2nd printing 3.95

SANCTUARY
Viz Communications, 1993
1 World of Yakuza 5.00
2 thru 4 . . . . @5.00
5 thru 9 . . . . @5.00
[Part Two], 1994
1 thru 9 . . . . @5.00
[Part Three], 1994–95
1 thru 8 . . . . @3.50
[Part Four], 1995–96
1 thru 7 . . . . @3.50
[Part Five], 1996
7 thru 13 by Sho Fumimura &
  Ryoichi Ikegami . . . . @3.50
GN rep. ? of part 4 & ? part 5 . . . 16.95
GN Vol. 5 . . . . 17.95
GN Vol. 6 . . . . 17.95
GN Vol. 9 . . . . 16.95

SANTA CLAWS
Eternity
1 `Deck the Mall with Blood
  and Corpses' 2.95

SAPPHIRE
Ariel Press, 1996
1 by Vince Danks 2.95
6 . . . . 2.95
7 . . . . 2.95
8 . . . . 2.95
9 . . . . 2.95

SARAI
Comicsone.com, 2001
Vol. 1
TPB #1 by Masahiro Shibata 9.95
TPB #2 thru #4 186-pg. 9.95
GN #6 200-pg. 9.95
GN #7 188-pg. 9.95
GN #8 200-pg. 9.95

SAVAGE HENRY
Vortex, 1987
1 thru 13 . . . . @2.00
Rip Off Press, 1991
14 thru 15 . . . . @2.00
16 thru 24 . . . . @2.50

SCARLET IN GASLIGHT
Eternity, 1988
1 A:SherlockHolmes 4.00
2 . . . . 3.00
3 & 4 . . . . @2.50

Scarlet–Sentinel / B & W PUB. / Comics Values Annual

SCARLET SCORPION/ DARKSIDE
AC Comics, 1995
1 & 2 Flipbooks 3.50

SCARLET THUNDER
Amaze Ink, 1995
1 thru 3 .... @2.50

SCARY GODMOTHER
Sirius Entertainment, 2001
1 by Jill Thompson 2.95
2 thru 6 concl. .... @2.95
TPB Wild About Harry 9.95
TPB Ghouls Out For Summer 14.95

SCARY GODMOTHER: BLOODY VALENTINE
Sirius Entertainment, 1998
1 .... 3.95
1a signed and numbered 10.00
Holiday Spooktactular 2.95

SCARY GODMOTHER: WILD ABOUT HARRY
Sirius Entertainment, 2000
1 (of 3) by Jill Thompson 2.95
2 .... 2.95
3 concl. 2.95

SCIMIDAR
Eternity
1 .... 4.00
1a 2nd Printing 2.50
2 and 3 .... @3.00
4 HotCover 3.50
4A MildCover 3.00

SCOOTER GIRL
Oni Press 2003
1 (of 6) 3.00
2 thru 5 .... @3.00

SCORN
SCC Entertainment, 1996
Lingerie Spec. 2.95
Lingerie Spec. deluxe 9.95
Super Spec.#1 rep. Deadly
 Rebellion, Headwave, Fabric
 of the Mind 4.95
X-over Scorn/Ardy: Alien Influence
 (1997) by Rob Potchak & Timothy
 Johnson 3.95
 Bill Maus (c) 3.95
 Deluxe gold 9.95
X-over Scorn/Dracula: The Vampire's
 Blood (1997) 3.95
 Dracula cover 3.95
 Scorn cover 3.95
Spec.#1A Scorn; Dead or Alive
 (1997) Mike Morales(c) 3.95
 Andrea Seri(c) 3.95
Spec.# Scorn:Deadly Rebellion ... 3.95
 Birthday Suit cover 9.95
 Celebrity photo cover 9.95
Spec.#1 Scorb: Fractured (1997)
 Fear cover 3.95
 Rage cover 3.95
Spec: Scorn: Heatwave (1997) by
 Chris Crosby & Mike Morales .. 3.95
Spec: Scorn: Hostage 3.95
Spec: Scorn: Naked Truth (1997) .. 3.95

SCRATCH
Outside, 1986
1 .... 3.00
2 .... 2.00
3 .... 2.00
4 .... 2.00

SCRIMIDAR
CFD Productions, 1995
1 I:Bloody Mary 2.75

SCRYED
Tokyopop Press 2003
GN Vol. 1 thru 5 .... @10.00

SCUD: DISPOSABLE ASSASSIN
Fireman Press, 1994
1 I:Scud 10.00
1a 3rd printing 3.50
2 .... 7.00
3 .... 5.00
4 thru 6 F:Scud .... @5.00

Scud: Disposable Assassin #5
© Fireman Press

7 Lupine Thoughts 4.00
8 Scud Looks for His Arm 4.00
9 Scud Looks for His Arm 4.00
10 thru 16 by Rob Schrab ..... @3.00
17 .... 3.00
18 .... 3.00
19 .... 3.00
20 Horse series, concl. 3.00
TPB Rep.#1-#4 .... 12.95
TPB Programmed for Damage,
 rep.#5–#9 .... 14.95
TPB Solid Gold Bomb 17.95
TPB Yellow Horseman (2001) ... 14.95

SCUD: TALES FROM THE VENDING MACHINE
Fireman Press, 1998
1 .... 2.50
2 thru 5 .... @2.50

SEARCHERS
Caliber `New Worlds', 1996
1A Red cover, signed 3.00
1B Blue cover, signed 3.00
3 .... 3.00
4 .... 3.00
5 flip book with Boston Bombers .. 3.00

SEARCHERS: APOSTLE OF MERCY
Caliber, 1997
1 (of 2) 4.00
2 .... 4.00

Vol 2?
1 .... 3.00
2 .... 3.00
3 (of 3) 48pg 4.00

SECRET FILES
Angel Entertainment, 1996
0 gold edition 7.00
0 commemorative edition 2.95
1 .... 2.95
1 spooky silver foil edition .. 5.95
2 .... 2.95
2 deluxe 5.95
Spec. Secret Files vs. Vampire Girls:
 The Vampire Effece (1997) ... 2.95
Pin-up Book Secret Files: Erotic
 Experiments (1997) 2.95
Spec.#1 Secret Files: F.B.I.
 Conspiracy (1997)F:Sabrina
 & Susanna Sorenson 2.95

SECRET FILES: THE STRANGE CASE
Angel Entertainment, 1996
0 by David Campitti & Al Rio 2.95
1 by David Campitti & Al Rio 2.95

SECRET MESSAGES
NBM Books, 2001
1 Abductions, pt.1 .... 2.95
2 Abductions, pt.2 .... 2.95
3 Abductions, pt.3 .... 2.95
4 Abductions, pt.4 .... 2.95
5 Abductions, pt.5 .... 2.95

SECTION 8
Noir Press, 1995
1 Anthology series 2.50
2 thru 6 .... @2.50
7 `Retribution,' pt.1 .... 2.50
8 `Retribution,' pt.2 .... 2.50
9 .... 2.50
10 `Chance' 2.50

SEEKER
Caliber `Core', 1998
1M by Gary Reed & Chris
 Massarotto, Meadows(c) 2.95
1W David Williams(c) 2.95
1a variant Greg Louden (c) 2.95
1 premium, signed 9.95
2 .... 2.95
3 .... 2.95
4 .... 2.95
5 Gestalt vs. LeAnn Heywood ... 2.95
Spec. Dawn of Armageddon,
 x-over, 48-pg 3.95

SENTINEL
Harrier, 1986
1 .... 2.00
2 thru 4 .... @2.00

SERAPHIN
Newcomers Press, 1995
1 I:Roy Torres 2.95

7 GUYS OF JUSTICE, THE
False Idol Studios, 2000
1 Jerque Imperitive,pt.1 . . . . 2.00
2 Jerque Imperitive,pt.2 . . . . 2.00
3 Jerque Imperitive,pt.3 . . . . 2.00
4 thru 11 . . . . @2.00
12 thru 16 . . . . @2.00

777: THE WRATH
Avatar Press, 1998
1 (of 3) by David Quinn & Tim Vigil 3.00
1a wraparound cover 3.50
1c leather cover 6.00
1d royal blue foil logo 75.00
1e signed 15.00
1f foil platinum edition 16.95
2 . . . . 3.00
3 concl. 3.00
TPB 777:The Wrath/
  Faust Fearbook 15.95

SEVENTH SYSTEM, THE
Sirius Entertainment, 1997
1 (of 6) by Roel 2.95
2 thru 6 . . . . @2.95

SFA SPOTLIGHT
Shanda Fantasy Arts, 1999
4 Tales of the Morphing Period . . . 4.50
5 Zebra, by Carl Gafford 4.50
6 Women in Fur 1999 . . . . 4.95
7 Tales From Supermegatopia 4.95
8 Women in Fur 2000 . . . . 5.00
9 Knight & Mouse 5.00
10 Atomic Mouse 5.00
11 Plush Beauties 5.00
12 Courageous Man Adventures . . . 5.00
13 Women in Fur 2001 . . . . 5.00
14 Fission Chicken 5.00
15 Women in Fur 2002 . . . . 5.00
16 Star Quack 5.00

SF SHORT STORIES
Webb Graphics, 1991
1 . . . . 2.50
2 . . . . 2.50

SHADES OF BLUE
AMP Comics, 2001
1 . . . . 2.50
2 thru 4 . . . . @2.50
5 Silence, pt.3 . . . . 2.50
6 F:Heidi, Marcus 2.50
7 Winter, pt.1 . . . . 2.95
8 Winter, pt.2 . . . . 2.95
9 Winter, pt.3 . . . . 2.95
10 . . . . 2.95

SHADES OF BLUE
Digital Webbing 2003
1 . . . . 2.95
2 thru 4 . . . . @2.95
TPB Vol. 1 . . . . 11.95

SHADES OF GRAY COMICS AND STORIES
Caliber Tapestry, 1996
1 . . . . 2.95

2 . . . . 2.95
3 . . . . 2.95
4 . . . . 2.95
Super Summer Spec. rep. 3.95

SHADOW CROSS
Darkside Comics, 1995
1 I:Shadow Cross 4.95
2 thru 7 . . . . @2.50

SHADOWGEAR
Antarctic Press, 1999
1 by Locke 3.00
2 . . . . 3.00
3 conclusion 3.00

SHADOWALKER
Aircel
1 thru 4 . . . . @2.00

SHADOW SLASHER
Pocket Change Comics, 1994
1 I:Shadow Slasher 2.50
2 V:Riplash 2.50
3 F:Matt Baker 2.50
4 Evolution 2.50
5 F:Riplash 2.50
6 Next Victim 2.50
7 What Can Kill Him 2.50
8 . . . . 2.50
9 final issue 2.50

SHANDA [THE PANDA]
Mu, 1992
1 . . . . 2.50

Antarctic Press, 1993
1 thru 11 . . . . @2.75
12 thru 14 . . . . @2.95

Med Systems
15 and 16 . . . . @2.00

Vision Comics, 1996
17 by Mike Curtis & Michelle Light . 2.00
18 `Rocky Horror Picture Show' . . . 2.00
19 `Shine on Me, Cajun Moon' 2.50
20 falling in love 2.50
22 Bright Eyes 2.95

Shanda Fantasy, 1999
23 Sweet Young Things 2.95
24 graduation night 2.95
25 48-pg. 4.95
26 thru 30 . . . . @2.95
31 thru 33 . . . . @3.00
34 48-pg. 5.00
35 thru 39 . . . . @5.00

SHANGHAIED
Eternity
1 & 2 . . . . @2.00
3 & 4 . . . . @2.00

SHARDS
Acension Comics, 1994
1 I:Silver, Raptor, RIpple 2.50
2 F:Anomoly 2.50

SHATTERED EARTH
Eternity, 1988–89
1 thru 9 . . . . @2.00

Shattered Earth #8
© Eternity

SHATTERPOINT
Eternity, 1990
1 thru 4 Broid miniseries . . . . . . @2.25

SHEBA
Sirius Dogstar, 1997
VOL 2
1 by Walter S. Crane IV 2.50
2 . . . . 2.50
3 . . . . 2.50
4 . . . . 2.50

Sick Mind Press
5 . . . . 2.95
6 . . . . 2.95
7 . . . . 2.95
TPB Vol. 2 (2000) 15.95

Shanda Fantasy Arts, 2001
Vol. 3
1 by Walter Crane IV 5.00
2 thru 3 . . . . @5.00

SHE-CAT
AC Comics, 1989
1 thru 4 . . . . @2.50

SHE-DEVILS ON WHEELS
Aircel, 1992
1 thru 3 by Bill Marimon 2.95

SHERLOCK HOLMES
Eternity, 1988
1 thru 22 . . . . @2.00

SHERLOCK HOLMES
Caliber/Tome Press, 1997
1-shot Dr. Jekyll and Mr. Holmes by
  Steve Jones & Seppo Makinen . 2.95
1-shot Return of the Devil 3.95
1-shot Return of the Devil, signed . . 3.95
GN Adventure of the Opera Ghost . 6.95
TPB Case of Blind Fear 12.95
TPB Scarlet in Gaslight 12.95
TPB Sussex Vampire 12.95

All comics prices listed are for *Near Mint* condition.

SHERLOCK HOLMES CASEBOOK
Eternity
1 and 2 .... @2.25

SHERLOCK HOLMES: CHRONICLES OF CRIME AND MYSTERY
Northstar
1 'The Speckled Band' 2.25

SHERLOCK HOLMES: HOUND OF THE BASKERVILLES
Caliber/Tome Press, 1997
1 (of 3) by Martin Powell & PO ... 2.95

SHERLOCK HOLMES: MARK OF THE BEAST
Caliber/Tome Press, 1997
1 (of 3) by Martin Powell
 & Seppo Makinen 2.95
2 .... 2.95
GN 12.95

SHERLOCK HOLMES MYSTERIES
Moonstone, 1997
1-shot by Joe Gentile & Richard
 Gulick 2.95
1-shot Sherlock Holmes and the
 Clown Prince of London (2001) 2.95

SHERLOCK HOLMES OF THE '30's
Eternity
1 thru 7 strip rep. .... @2.95

SHERLOCK HOLMES READER
Caliber 'Tome Press', 1998
1 Curse of the Beast 3.95
2 The Loch Ness Horror 3.95

3 The Loch Ness Horror 3.95
4 The Loch Ness Horror 3.95
5 .... 3.95

SHERLOCK HOLMES: RETURN OF THE DEVIL
Adventure, 1992
1 V:Moriarty 2.50
2 V:Moriarty 2.50

SHERLOCK JUNIOR
Eternity
1 Rep.NewspaperStrips 2.00
2 Rep.NewspaperStrips 2.00
3 Rep.NewspaperStrips 2.00

SHI
Crusade, 1999
0 rough cut edition 5.00
0 ashcan, signed 10.00
Spec.#1 Black,White & Red 2.95
Spec. San Diego (Con) Art of War
 Tour Book 1998 .... 9.95
Spec. Lim. Ed. Shi/Daredevil
 Banzai 14.00
Spec.#1 Kaidan, macabre 2.95
Spec.#1 Kaidan, signed & numb. . 19.95
Spec. Shi/First Wave, Voices
 of the Dead x-over (2001) 3.00
Spec. Shi/FirstWave,variant BiT(c) . 3.00
Spec. Shi/FirstWave,signed 9.95
Spec. First Wave/Shi, Voices of
 the Dead, pt.2 x-over (2001) ... 3.00
Spec. FirstWave/Shi,variant BiT(c) . 3.00
Coll. Ed. Heaven & Earth,
 Yin & Yang,96-pg 5.99
Year of the Dragon preview book . 3.00
Year of the Dragon tour book 5.00
Year of the Dragon tour Wizard ... 5.00
Year of the Dragon tour San Diego . 5.00
Umadoshi Tour Book, 2002 ...... 5.00
Umadoshi, Tour Book, sketch (c) .. 5.00
Umadoshi Tour Book, Pittsburg ... 5.00

SHI: THE ILLUSTRATED WARRIOR
Crusade Entertainment, 2002
1 (of 7) BiT 3.00
2 BiT thru 7 .... @3.00

SHI: SEMPO
Avatar 2003
1/2 Prism Foil Edition 12.95
1/2 Royal Blue Edition 75.00
1/2 Prism Foil (c) 12.95
Preview edition 2.00
Preview variant (c) 5.95
Preview wraparound (c) 5.95
Preview prism foil (c) 12.95
1 .... 3.50
1a variant (c) 3.50
2 .... 3.50
2a variant (c) 3.50
2b wraparound (c) 3.95

SHIELA TRENT VAMPIRE HUNTER
Draculina Publishing
1 O:Sheild Trent 2.50

SHIP OF FOOLS
Caliber, 1996
1 signed edition 3.00

2 'Dante's Compass' 3.00
3 The Great Escape begins 3.00
4 MiA 3.00
5 MiA 3.00
Spec. #1, Bon Voyage, Go to Hell,
 Mama Hades 3.95
TPB sci-fi action/adventure 11.95
continued: See Image Comics

SHOCK THE MONKEY
Millennium
1 & 2 Entering the Psychotic Mind . 3.95

SHONEN JUMP
Viz Communications 2002
1 thru 8 .... @4.95
Vol. 2
1 thru 12 .... @4.95

SHRED
CFW
1 thru 10 .... @2.25

SHRIEK
Fantaco
1 .... 4.95
2 .... 4.95
3 .... 7.95

SHURIKEN
Victory, 1986
1 Reggi Byers 5.00
1a 2nd printing 1.50
2 .... 3.00
3 .... 2.00
4 .... 2.00
5 thru 13 .... @2.00
Graphic Nov. Reggie Byers 8.00

SHURIKEN
Eternity, 1991
1 Shuriken vs. Slate 2.50
2 Neutralizer, Meguomo 2.50
3 R:Slate 2.50
4 Morgan's Bodyguard Serrate .. 2.50
5 Slate as Shuriken & Megumo .. 2.50
6 Hunt for Bionauts, final issue ... 2.50

SHURIKEN: COLD STEEL
Eternity, 1989
1 .... 2.00
2 .... 2.00
3 thru 6 .... @2.00

SHURIKEN TEAM-UP
ETernity, 1989
1 thru 3 .... @2.00

SIEGEL & SHUSTER
Eclipse, 1984
1 .... 2.00
2 .... 2.00

SILBUSTER
Antarctic Press, 1994
1 thru 10 .... @3.50
11 I:Kizuki Sister 3.50
12 thru 14 .... @3.50
15 .... 3.95
16 thru 19 .... @3.50
TPB Rep. #1-#4 .... 10.95
TPB Vol.2 .... 10.95

Sherlock Holmes: Return of the Devil #2 © Adventure

SILENT INVASION
Renegade, 1986
1 . . . . 4.00
2 thru 12, final issue . . . . @3.00
Combined Ed. #1 & #2 . . . . 16.95

SILENT INVASION
Caliber
4 Red Shadows, pt.1 . . . . 3.00
5 Red Shadows, pt.2 . . . . 3.00

SILENT INVASION: ABDUCTIONS
Caliber, 1998
1 by Larry Hancock & Michael
   Cherkos 2.95

SILENT MOBIUS
Viz Communications
Part 1 thru Part 4: See Color
TPB by Kia Asamiya 16.95
TPB Vol. 2 . . . . 16.95
TPB Vol. 3 . . . . 16.95
TPB Vol. 4 Into the Labyrinth 16.95
TPB Vol. 5 . . . . 16.95
TPB Vol. 6 Catastrophe 15.95
TPB Vol. 7 . . . . 16.95
TPB Vol. 8 Adventures 15.95
TPB Vol. 9 Turnabout 15.95
Part 5 INTO THE LABYRINTH, 1999
1 (of 6) by Kia Asamiya 2.95
2 thru 4 . . . . @2.95
5 & 6 . . . . @3.25
Part 6 KARMA, 1999
1 (of 7) by Kia Asamiya 3.25
2 thru 7 . . . . @3.25
Part 7 CATASTROPHE, 2000
1 (of 6) by Kia Asamiya 2.95
2 thru 6 . . . . @2.95
Part 8 LOVE & CHAOS, 2000
1 thru 7 . . . . @2.95
Part 9 ADVENTURERS, 2001
1 thru 6 (of 6) . . . . @2.95
Part 10 TURNABOUT, 2002
1 (of 6) by Kia Asamiya 2.95
2 thru 6 . . . . @2.95
Part 11 BLOOD, 2002
1 (of 5) by Kia Asamiya 2.95
2 thru 5 . . . . @2.95
TPB Vol. 10 Blood 12.95
Part 12 HELL, 2003
1 thru 3 . . . . @2.95
TPB Vol. 11 Hell 12.95

SILENT RAPTURE
Brainstorm, 1996
1 Jacob Grimm vs. Six Devils
   of Twilight 3.00
1a Vicious variant edition 5.00
Avatar Press, 1997
2 by Jude Millien 3.00
2a deluxe (c) 10.00

SILLY DADDY
Joe Chiappetta, 1995
1 . . . . 3.50
2 thru 5 . . . . 3.00
6 thru 10 . . . . @2.75
11 thru 18 . . . . @2.75
TPB The Long Goodbye 7.95
TPB A Death in the Family 8.95

Silver Storm #4
© Aircel

SILVER STORM
Aircel, 1990
1 thru 4 . . . . @2.25

SIMON/KIRBY READER
1 . . . . 2.00

SINBAD
Adventure, 1989
1 . . . . 2.25
2 . . . . 2.25
3 . . . . 2.25
4 . . . . 2.25

SINBAD: HOUSE OF GOD
Adventure Comics, 1991
1 Caliph's Wife Kidnapped 2.50
2 Magical Genie 2.50
3 Escape From Madhi 2.50
4 A:Genie 2.50

SINNAMON
Catfish Comics, 1995
1 remastered 2.75
1a remastered deluxe 3.75
6 thru 8 . . . . @2.75
Mythic Comics
9 'Ashes to Ashes—The Pyre-Anna
   Saga', pt.2 . . . . 2.75
10 'Twas Beauty Bashed
    The Beast' 2.75
11 . . . . 2.75
12 M.G.Delaney (c) 2.75
12 Poliwko (c) 2.75
Archives #1 . . . . 2.75

SISTER ARMAGEDDON
Dramenon Studios
1 & 2 Nun with a Gun . . . . @2.50
3 Mother Superior 2.50
4 V:Apoligon 2.95

SKELETON KEY
Amaze Ink, 1995
1 1 I:Skeleton Key 4.00
1 2nd printing 3.00
2 F:Tansin 3.00

3 V:Japanese Burglar 3.00
4 V:Closet Monster 3.00
5 thru 10 . . . . @3.00
11 . . . . 3.00
12 . . . . 3.00
14 by Andi Watson 3.00
15 'The Celestial Calendar' 3.00
16 thru 30 . . . . @3.00
Spec. 4.95
TPB Vol. 1, Threshold rep.#1–#6. . 11.95
TPB Vol.2 Celestial Calendar,
   rep.#7–#18 . . . . 19.95
TPB Vol. 3, rep. #19–#24 . . . . . . 12.95
TPB Vol. 4, Cats & Dogs, rep.
   #25–#30 . . . . 12.95
Spec.Skeleton Key/Sugar Kat 2.95
VOL 2
1 (of 4) 2.95
2 . . . . 2.95
3 . . . . 2.95
4 conclusion 2.95

SKIN 13
Entity/Parody, 1995
1/2a Grungie/Spider-Man 2.50
1/2b Heavy Metal 2.50
1/2c Gen-Et Jackson 2.50

SKULL MAN
Tokyopop Press, 2000
1 (of 5) 2.95
2 thru 4 . . . . @2.95
5 . . . . 3.00
GN Vol. 1 (of 7) authentic manga . 10.00
GN Vol. 2 thru 4 . . . . @10.00

SKUNK, THE
Entity Comics, 1997
#Uno 2.75
5 BMs 2.75
6 BMs 2.75
Collection #1 rep. #1–#3 . . . . 4.95
Collection #1a signed & numbered . 9.95
Collection #2 rep. #4–#6 . . . . 4.95

SKUNK/FOODANG
FOODANG/SKUNK
Entity Comics
Spec. 1 BMs, BMs(c) 2.75
Spec. 1a BMs, Mike Duggan(c) . . . 2.75

SKYNN & BONES: DEADLY ANGELS
Brainstorm, 1996
1 . . . . 2.95

SKYNN & BONES: FLESH FOR FANTASY
Brainstorm, 1997
1 erotic missions 2.95
2 erotic missions 2.95
Spec. #1 Dare to Bare 3.00

SLACK
Legacy Comics
1 Slacker Anthology 2.50
2 Loser 2.50

SLACKER COMICS
Slave Labor, 1994
1 thru 15 by Doug Slack . . . . . . @3.00
16 . . . . 2.95

SLAUGHTERHOUSE
Caliber
1 Bizarre medical Operations..... 2.95
2 House of Death 2.95
3 House of Death 2.95
4 Dead Killer vs. Mosaic 2.95

SLAUGHTERMAN
Comico, 1983
1 .... 2.00
2 .... 2.00

SLAYERS
CPM Manga, 1998
1 by Hajime Kanzaka & Rui
  Araizumi.................. 2.95
2 thru 6 .... @2.95
TPB Book 1: Medieval Mayham .. 15.95
Spec. #1 F:Lina Inverse 2.95
Spec. #2 thru #6 .... @2.95
TPB Vol. 1 Touch of Evil (2001) .. 15.95
TPB Vol. 2 Notorious 15.95
TPB Vol. 3 Lesser of Two Evils... 15.95
TPB Vol. 4 Spellbound 15.95

SLAYERS: SUPER–EXPLOSIVE DEMON STORY
CPM Manga, 2001
1 by H. Kanzaka & S. Yoshinaka .. 2.95
2 .... 2.95
3 thru 6 .... @2.95
TPB Book 1 Legend of Darkness . 15.95
TPB Book 2 Legacy of the
  Dragon God 15.95

SMILE
Tokyopop Press, 2000
Vol. 3
1 magazine 2.95
2 thru 12 magazine .... @5.00
Vol. 4
1 magazine 5.00

Smith Brown Jones #1
© Kiwi Studios

CVA Page 770

B & W PUB.
2 thru 4 .... @5.00
5 thru 6 .... @6.00
7 .... 5.00

SMITH BROWN JONES
Kiwi Studios, 1997
1 thru 5 .... @2.95
TPB Calm, Cook, and Collected .. 12.95

SMITH BROWN JONES: ALIEN ACCOUNTANT
Slave Labor, 1998
1 by Jon Hastings 2.95
2 .... 2.95
3 .... 2.95
4 .... 2.95
Spec.#1 Halloween Special 2.95
Spec. Convention Mayhem...... 5.95

SNOWMAN
Hall of Heroes, 1996
1 .... 15.00
1a variant (c)............... 20.00
1 3rd printing................ 2.75
1 San Diego Con. ed. 5.00
2 .... 8.00
2a 2nd printing 2.75
2b variant (c)................ 9.00
3 .... 6.00
3a variant (c)................ 7.00

SNOWMAN
Avatar Press, 1997
0 by Matt Martin, O:Snowman 3.00
0a Frozen Fear extra-bloody 4.95
0b Leather cover 25.00
0c signed.................... 10.00
Spec.#1 Snowman 1944......... 3.95
Spec.#1 Snowman 1944, deluxe.. 4.95
Spec.#1 Snowman 1944, signed.. 10.00
1-shot Flurries, Glynn (c) 4.95
1-shotA Flurries, Snowman (c) .. 4.95
TPB Snowman rep. 128-pg. 13.95

SNOWMAN: DEAD & DYING
Avatar Press, 1997
1 (of 3) by Matt Martin 3.00
1 deluxe 4.95
1 signed 10.00
2 .... 3.00
2 deluxe 4.95
3 by Matt Martin 3.00
3 Frozen Fear 4.95
3 White Velvet 25.00

SNOWMAN: HORROR SHOW
Avatar Press, 1998
1 by Matt Martin 3.00
1a Frozen Fear (c)............. 4.95
1b Leather cover 25.00
1 deluxe 4.95

SNOWMAN: 1994
Entity, 1996
1 flip cover #0, by Matt Martin,
  O:Snowman................ 3.00
1 signed, numbered........... 7.00
3 .... 2.75
3 deluxe, variant, foil cover 3.50
4 .... 2.75
4 deluxe, variant, foil cover 3.50

SNOWMAN2
Avatar Press, 1997
1 (of 2) Snowman vs. Snowman ... 3.00
1a Face-off cover 4.95
1b Leather cover 25.00
1c Royal Blue edition.......... 50.00
2 concl. 3.00
2a Sudden Death variant cover ... 4.95

SOB: SPECIAL OPERATIONS BRANCH
Promethean Studios, 1994
1 I:SOB..................... 2.50

SOCKETEER
Kardia
Rocketeer parody............. 2.25

SOLD OUT
Fantaco, 1986
1 & 2...................... @2.00

SOLO EX-MUTANTS
Eternity
1 thru 6 .... @2.00

SOMETHING DIFFERENT
Wooga Central, 1991
1 .... 2.50
2 .... 2.50

SONAMBULO: SLEEP OF THE JUST
Ninth Circle Studios, 1999
1 (of 3) by Rafael Navarro 2.95
2 .... 2.95
3 (of 3) 2.95
TPB Sleep of the Just.......... 15.00
Spec. Strange Tales (2000) 4.00
Spec. Ghost of a Chance (2002)... 5.00

SONG OF THE CID
Calibre/Tome
1 Story of El Cid 2.95
2 Story of El Cid concl. 2.95

SONG OF THE SIRENS
Millennium
Earth 2.95
Earth, signed print edition........ 6.95
Fire 2.95
Fire, signed print edition 9.95
Wind 2.95
Wind collectors edition 4.95
Wind with trading card 4.95
Secrets, Lies, & Videotape Pin-Up
  Special................... 2.95
Secrets, Lies, & Videotape Pin-Up
  Special, foil logo............ 5.95
Secrets, Lies, & Videotape Pin-Up
  Special, deluxe............. 9.95

SORCERER HUNTERS
Tokyopop.com, 1999
TPB Mixx Manga, Vol. 1 .... 11.95
TPB Mixx Manga, Vol. 2 .... 11.95
TPB Mixx Manga, Vol. 3 thru 5 . @12.95
TPB Mixx Manga, Vol. 6 .... 9.95
TPB Mixx Manga, Vol. 7 & 8 ... @14.95
TPB Mixx Manga, Vol. 9 thru 13 @13.00

SOUL
Samson Comics
1 thru 3 F:Sabbeth . . . . @2.50

SOULFIRE
Aircel
1 mini-series 2.00
2 . . . . 2.00
3 . . . . 2.00

SOULSEARCHERS AND CO.
Claypool, 1993–98
1 thru 10 Peter David(s) . . . . @5.00
11 thru 20 . . . . @3.00
21 thru 24 . . . . @3.00
25 ACo&SL(c) 2.50
26 O:Soulsearchers, pt.1 . . . . 2.50
27 O:Soulsearchers, pt.2 . . . . 2.50
28 O:Soulsearchers, pt.3 . . . . 2.50
29 O:Soulsearchers, pt.4 . . . . 2.50
30 thru 63 . . . . @2.50
TPB 12.95

SOUTHERN KNIGHTS
Guild, 1983
1 See Crusaders
2 . . . . 7.00
3 and 4 . . . . @5.00
5 thru 7 . . . . @4.00
Fictioneer, 1985
8 thru 11 . . . . @3.00
12 thru 33 . . . . @3.00
34 . . . . 3.00
35 The Morrigan Wars Pt.#2 . . . . . 3.50
36 Morrigan Wars Pt.#5 . . . . 3.50
37 Hell in a Handbasket 3.00
Ann. #1 . . . . 2.50
DreadHalloweenSpec #1 . . . . 2.25
Primer #1 . . . . 2.25

SOUTHERN SQUADRON
Aircel, 1990
1 thru 4 . . . . @2.25
Eternity
1 I:SQUAD 2.50
2 . . . . 2.25
3 . . . . 2.25
4 . . . . 2.25

SOUTHERN SQUADRON FREEDOM OF INFO. ACT.
Aircel, 1992
1 F.F.#1 Parody/Tribute cov. 2.50
2 A:Waitangi Rangers 2.50
3 . . . . 2.50

SPACE ARK
Apple, 1986
1 & 2 see color
3 . . . . 2.25
4 . . . . 2.25
5 . . . . 2.25

SPACE BEAVER
Ten-Buck Comics, 1986
1 . . . . 2.50
2 . . . . 2.00
3 O&I:Stinger 2.00
4 A:Stinger 2.00
5 . . . . 2.00
6 O:Rodent 2.00

7 thru 12 . . . . @2.00

SPACED
Anthony Smith Publ., 1988
1 I:Zip; 800 printed 40.00
2 . . . . 25.00
3 I:Dark Teddy 15.00
4 . . . . 15.00
5 and 6 . . . . @5.00
7 and 8 . . . . @2.00
Eclipse
9 . . . . 2.00
10 . . . . 2.00
11 thru 13 . . . . @2.00

Space Patrol #3
© Adventure

SPACE PATROL
Adventure, 1992
1 thru 3 . . . . 2.50

SPACE USAGI
Mirage Studios, 1992
1 Stan Sakai,Future Usagi 3.00
2 Stan Sakai,Future Usagi 3.00
3 Stan Sakai,Future Usagi 3.00

SPACE WOLF
Antarctic Press
1 From Albedo,by Dan Flahive 2.50

SPANDEX TIGHTS
Lost Cause Prod.
Vol. 1, 1994
1 thru 6 . . . . @2.50
Vol. 2, 1997
1 . . . . 2.50
2 prelude to Space Opera 2.95
6 . . . . 2.95
Spec. Vs. Mighty Awful Sour
  Rangers, signed 2.95

SPANDEX TIGHTS PRESENTS: SPACE OPERA
Lost Cause Productions, 1997
Part 1 by Bryan J.L. Glass & Bob
  Dix, parody 2.95
Part 1, signed, Star Wars parody . . 2.95
Part 2 'Star Bored,' pt.2 . . . . 2.95
Part 3 . . . . 2.95

SPANDEX TIGHTS PRESENTS: THE GIRLS OF '95
Lost Cause Productions
1 The Good, Bad and Deadly,
  signed (1997) 3.95

SPANDEX TIGHTS PRESENTS: WIN A DREAM DATE WITH SPANDEX-GIRL
Lost Cause Productions
1 (of 3) (1998) 2.95
2 and 3 . . . . @2.95

SPANDEX TIGHTS: THE LOST ISSUES
Lost Cause Productions
1 (of 4) 2.95
2 . . . . 2.95
3 . . . . 2.95
4 concl. 2.95

SPANK THE MONKEY
Arrow Comics, 1999
1 by Randy Zimmerman 2.95
2 thru 6 . . . . @2.95
Skip Month Spec.#1 . . . . 2.95

SPANK THE MONKEY ON THE COMIC MARKET
Arrow Comics, 2000
1 (of 3) by Randy Zimmerman 3.25
2 and 3 . . . . @3.25

SPARKPLUG
Hero Graphics
1 From League of Champions 2.95

SPARKPLUG SPECIAL
Heroic Publishing
1 V:Overman 2.50

SPARROW
Millennium, 1995
1 I:Sparrow 2.95
2 . . . . 2.95
3 Valley of Fire 2.50

SPEED RACER CLASSICS
Now, 1998
1 . . . . 3.00
1a 2nd Printing 2.00

SPENCER SPOOK
A.C.E. Comics
1 and 2 . . . . @2.00
3 thru 8 . . . . @2.00

SPICY TALES
Eternity, 1998
1 thru 13 . . . . @2.00
14 thru 20 . . . . @2.25
Special #2 . . . . 2.25

SPIDER KISS
1 Harlan Ellison 3.95

SPINELESS MAN
Parody Press, 1992
1 Spider-Man 2099 spoof 2.50

SPIRIT, THE
Kitchen Sink, 1986
Note: #1 to #11 are in color
12 thru 86 WE,rep (1986–92) . . . @3.00
GN The Spirit Casebook 16.95
TPB Vol.2 All About P'Gell 18.95
GN The Spirit Jam, 50 artists in
   48-pg. (1998) 5.95

SPIRIT, THE: THE ORIGIN YEARS
Kitchen Sink, 1997
1 F:The Origin of the Spirit 3.00
2 F:The Black Queen's Army 3.00
3 F:Palyachi,The Killer Clown 3.00
4 F:The Return of the Orang 3.00
5 WE 3.00
6 WE,Kiss of Death 3.00
7 F:The Kidnapping of Ebony 3.00
8 F:Christmas Spirit of 1940 . . . . . 3.00
9 WE 3.00
10 F:The Substitute Spirits 3.00

SPIRITED AWAY
Viz Communications, 2002
TPB Vol. 2 thru Vol. 5 . . . . @9.95
TPB Picture Book (color) 19.95
TPB Art of Spirited Away 34.95

SPIRITS
Mindwalker, 1995
1 thru 3 Silver City 2.95
4 Caleb Escapes Zeus 2.95

SPITTIN' IMAGE
Eclipse, 1992
1 Marvel & Image parody 2.50

Spittin' Image
© Eclipse

B & W PUB.

SPONGEBOB SQUAREPANTS
Tokyopop Press 2003
GN Vol. 1 Krusty Krap Adventures . . 8.00
GN Vol. 2 Friends Forever 8.00

SQUEE
Slave Labor, 1997
1 by Jhonen Vasquez 5.00
1a 2nd printing 3.00
2 . . . . 3.00
3 . . . . 3.00
4 . . . . 3.00
TPB 15.95

STAIN
Fathom Press, 1998
1 Byler (c) 3.00
1a Vigil (c) 3.00
1b limited edition 7.95
2 . . . . 3.00
2a Vigil (c) 3.00
3 . . . . 3.00
3a Vigil (c) 3.00
4 . . . . 3.00
4a Vigil (c) 3.00
5 King cover 3.00
5a Ang cover 3.00
6 . . . . 3.00
7 . . . . 3.00

STAINLESS STEEL ARMIDILLO
Antarctic Press, 1995
1 I:Saisni, Tania Badan 2.95
2 V:Mirage 2.95
3 V:Mirage 2.95
4 Spirit of Gaia 2.95
5 V:Giant 2.95
6 finale 2.95

STAR BLEECH THE GENERATION GAP
Parody Press
1 Parody 3.95

STARCHILD
Taliesin Press, 1992–97
0 . . . . 15.00
1 . . . . 20.00
1a 2nd printing 4.00
2 . . . . 18.00
2a 2nd printing 4.00
3 . . . . 8.00
4 . . . . 6.00
5 thru 13 . . . . @5.00
14 . . . . 3.00
Coppervale
TPB Coll. Ed. Awakenings, rep.
   #1–#12 . . . . 5.00
Essential Starchild, Book 3 . . . . . . 6.95
Essential Starchild, Book 4 . . . . . . 6.95
Essential Starchild, Book 5 . . . . . . 6.95

STARCHILD: CROSSROADS
Coppervale, 1995
1 thru 4, reoffer, by James Owen @3.00
TPB Coll. Ed.112-pg. 12.00
Conoisseurs Edition 100.00

Comics Values Annual

STARGATE: THE NEW ADVENTURES COLLECTION
Entity, 1997
1 rep. Underworld; One Nation
   Under Ra 6.00
1a photo cover 4.95

STARGATE: ONE NATION UNDER RA
Entity, 1997
1 . . . . 3.00
1a deluxe 3.50

STARGATE: REBELLION
Entity, 1997
1 (of 3) from novel, sequel to movi 13.00
1 deluxe 3.50
2 . . . . 3.00
2 deluxe 3.50
3 (of 3) 3.00
3 foil cover 3.50
GN rep. 80-pg. 7.95
GN photo (c) 7.95

STARGATE: UNDERWORLD
Entity, 1997
1 . . . . 3.00
1a deluxe 3.50

STAR HAWKS
ACG Comics, 2000
1 by Ron Goulart & Gil Kane 2.95
2 . . . . 2.95
3 . . . . 2.95

STARK: FUTURE
Aircel, 1986
1 . . . . 2.50
2 thru 7 . . . . @2.00
8 . . . . 2.00
9 thru 14 . . . . @2.00

STARLIGHT AGENCY
Antarctic Press, 1991
1 I:Starlight Agency 2.00
2 Anderson Kidnapped 2.00
3 . . . . 2.00

STAR RANGERS
Adventure, 1987
1 thru 3 . . . . @3.00
4 . . . . 2.00

BOOK II
1 . . . . 2.00
2 . . . . 2.00

STAR REACH
Taliesin Press, 1974
1 HC,I:CodyStarbuck 15.00
2 DG,JSn,NA(c) 6.00
3 FB 6.00
4 HC,HC(c) 6.00
5 JSon,HC(c) 6.00
6 GD,Elric 6.00
7 DS 6.00
8 CR,KSy 6.00
9 KSy 6.00
10 KSy 6.00
11 GD 6.00

B & W PUB.

12 MN,SL	10.00
13 SL,KSy	10.00
14	10.00
15	10.00
16	9.00
17	9.00
18	9.00

STAR WESTERN
ACG Comics, 2000
1	5.95
2 John Wayne	5.95
3 Clint Eastwood	5.95
4 Clayton Moore	5.95
5 F:Tonto	5.95
6 F:Fess Parker	5.95
7 F:Masked Riders of the Plains	5.95
8 James Arness-Matt Dillon(c)	5.95
9 Sam Elliott photo (c)	5.95
10 Chuck "Rifleman" Connors	5.95
11 John Hart	5.95
12 Davy Crockett, Daniel Boone	5.95
13 Gabby Hayes	5.95
TPB Compendium, #1–#4	19.95

STATIC
1 SD	2.00
2 SD	2.00
3 SD	2.00

STEALTH FORCE
Malibu, 1987
1 thru 7	@2.00

Eternity, 1988
8	2.00

STEALTH SQUAD
Petra Comics, 1993
0 O:Stealth Squad	2.50
1 I:Stealth Squad	2.50
2 I:New Member	2.50

Volume II
1 F:Solar Blade	2.50
2 American Ranger Vs.Jericho	2.50

STEAM DETECTIVES
Viz Communications, 1999
TPB by Kia Asamiya	15.95
TPB Vol. 2	15.95
TPB Vol. 3	15.95
TPB Vol. 4	15.95
TPB Vol. 5	15.95

STEELE DESTINES
Nightscapes
1 & 2 I:One Eyed Stranger	2.95
3 Kidnapped by Aliens	2.95

STEVE CANYON
Kitchen Sink
1 thru 14 by Doug Allen	@5.00
3-D Spec. #1 (1986)	6.00

STEVE DITKO'S STRANGE AVENGING TALES
Fantagraphics, 1997
1 SD	2.95
2 SD	2.95

Steve Canyon #12
© *Kitchen Sink*

STEVE GRANT'S MORTAL SOULS
Avatar Press, 2002
1	3.50
1a wraparound (c)	3.95
2	3.50
2a wraparound (c)	3.95
3	3.50
3a wraparound (c)	3.95

STEVEN
Kitchen Sink
1	4.00
1a 2ndPrinting	2.95
2	4.00
3	2.95
4 and 5	@3.50
TPB The Best of Steven by Doug Allen (1998)	12.95

STICKBOY
Revolutionary
1	2.00
2 thru 5	@2.50

STIG'S INFERNO
Vortex, 1985
1	5.00
2	3.50
3	3.00
4	3.00
5	2.25

Eclipse
6	2.25
7	2.25

STINZ
Fantagraphics, 1989
1	4.00
2	4.00
3	4.00
4	4.00

[2nd series]
Brave New Words, 1990
1 thru 3	2.50

STORMBRINGER
Taliesin Press
1 thru 3	@2.00

STORMWATCHER
Eclipse, 1989
1 thru 4	@2.00

STRAIN
Viz Communications, 1998
GN Vol. 1	16.95
TPB Vol. 2	15.95
TPB Vol. 3	15.95
TPB Vol. 4	16.95
TPB Vol. 5	16.95

STRANGE BEHAVIOR
Twilite Tone Press
1 LSn,MBr,Short Stories	2.95

STRANGE BREW
Aardvark–Vanaheim
1	5.00

STRANGEHAVEN
Abiogenesis Press, 1995
1 Surrealistic Comic	2.95
2 Secret Brotherhood	2.95
3 thru 10 by Gary S. Millidge	@2.95
11 thru 15	@2.95
TPB Arcadia, rep. #1–#6	14.95
TPB Brotherhood, rep.#7–#12	14.95

STRANGE SPORTS STORIES
Adventure, 1992
1 w/2 card strip	2.50
2 The Pick-Up Game,w/cards	2.50
3 Spinning Wheels,w/cards	2.50
4 thru 6 w/cards	@2.50

STRANGE WEATHER LATELY
Metaphrog, 1997
1	3.50
2 thru 4	@3.50
5 thru 10	@3.00
TPB Vol. 1 rep. #1–#5	9.95
TPB Vol. 2	9.95

STRANGERS IN PARADISE
Antarctic Press, 1993–94
1 by Terry Moore,I:Katchoo	65.00
1a 2nd printing	15.00
1b 3rd printing	5.00
2	45.00
3	35.00

Abstract Studio, 1994
1 TMr, Gold Logo edition	15.00
1a 2nd printing	6.00
2 and 3, Gold Logo edition	@10.00
4	6.00
5 R:Mrs. Parker	6.00
6	5.00
7 Darcey Uses Francine	5.00
8 thru 13 TMr	@4.00

VOL. 2
1 TMr, Gold Logo edition, I Dream of You	3.00
2 thru 13 gold logo	@3.00
TPB I Dream of You	16.95

VOL III, 1997
1 thru 8 See Image
9 TMr,Detective Walsh returns	4.00

All comics prices listed are for *Near Mint* condition.

Strangers–Sugar / B & W PUB.

10 .... 4.00
11 .... 3.00
12 .... 3.00
13 High School, pt.1 (of 3) 3.00
14 High School, pt.2........... 10.00
15 High School, pt.3........... 3.00
16A Francine/Katchoo Princess
   Warrior (c) 22.00
16B Tambi Princess Warrior (c)... 25.00
17 .... 3.00
18 Francine & Datchoo........... 3.00
19 Lifesize nude of Francine...... 3.00
20 Night at the Opera........... 3.00
21 All not well in paradise....... 3.00
22 The Big Rift 3.00
23 Katchoo moves out 3.00
24 steamy affairs 3.00
25 All Beach, All the Time....... 3.00
26 .... 3.00
27 at odds with the Big Six...... 3.00
28 thru 35 .... @3.00
36 Katchoo vs. Veronica......... 3.00
37 return to Tennessee.......... 3.00
38 from rags to ritches 3.00
39 Good news and bad news 3.00
40 Engaged to right brother?..... 3.00
41 Expelled from college 3.00
42 Slumber Party 3.00
43 Tropic Of Desire 3.00
44 Marooned 3.00
45 Francine and Katchoo 3.00
46 Molly & Poo, Borderline Lover .. 3.00
47 Francine pregnant 3.00
48 Casey's Story 3.00
49 Molly & Poo................. 3.00
50 Celebrate #50 .... 3.00
51 .... 3.00
52 Francine & Katchoo 3.00
53 My Maiden Voyage 3.00
54 Girl Trouble, pt.1 .... 3.00
55 Girl Trouble, pt.2 .... 3.00
56 Girl Trouble, pt.3 .... 3.00
57 Blue Bird of Happiness 3.00
58 thru 61 .... @3.00
TPB Vol.4 Love Me Tender 12.95
TPB Vol.5 Immortal Enemies, rep.
   #6–#12.................. 12.95
TPB Vol. 6 High School 8.95
TPB Vol. 8 My Other Life 14.95
TPB Vol. 9 Child of Rage 15.95
TPB Vol. 10 Tropic of Desire..... 12.95
TPB Vol. 11 Brave New World ... 8.95
TPB Vol. 12 Field of GOld....... 12.95
TPB Vol. 13 Flower to Flame ... 15.95
Spec. Sourcebook 2.95
Spec. #93268 Songs & Lyrics..... 2.75

STRANGELOVE
Entity Comics, 1995
1 I:Strangelove 2.50
2 V:Hyper Bullies............... 2.50
3 I:Bogie 2.50

STRANGE WORLDS
Eternity
1 .... 3.95
2 thru 4 .... @3.95

STRATA
Renegade, 1986
1 .... 3.00
2 .... 2.50
3 .... 2.00
4 .... 2.00
5 .... 2.00
6 .... 2.00

STRAW MEN
All American, 1989
1 thru 5 .... @2.00
6 thru 8 .... @2.25

STRAY BULLETS
El Capitan, 1995
1 .... 15.00
1a 2nd & 3rd printing........... 4.00
2 .... 8.00
2a 2nd printing 3.50
3 .... 7.00
4 .... 7.00
5 Dysfunctional Family.......... 4.00
6 F:Amy Racecar............... 4.00
7 Virginias Freedom 4.00
8 DL,`Lucky to Have Her' 3.00
9 DL,'26 Guys Named Nick' 3.00
10 DL,`Here Comes the Circus' .. 3.00
11 DL,`How to Cheer Up Your
   Best Friend' 3.00
12 DL, People Will be Hurt 3.00
13 DL `Selling Candy'........... 3.00
14 DL,The Killers arrive,48pg 3.50
15 Sex and Violence............. 3.00
16 .... 3.00
17 While Ricky Fish Was Sleeping . 3.00
18 Sex and Violence, pt.2........ 3.00
19 Young and sexy 3.00
20 Motel...................... 3.00
21 .... 3.00
22 40-pg..................... 3.50
23 thru 30................... @3.50
31 thru 34................... @3.00
35 thru 36................... @3.50
TPB Vol. 1 Innocence of Nihilism . 11.95
TPB Vol. 2 .... 11.95
TPB Vol. 3 .... 11.95
TPB Vol. 4 rep. #13–#16........ 11.95
TPB Vol. 5 rep. #17–#20........ 11.95
TPB Vol. 6 .... 14.95
TPB Vol. 7 .... 14.95
TPB Vol. 8 .... 14.95

STREET FIGHTER
Ocean Comics, 1986
1 thru 4 limited series .... @2.00

STREET HEROES 2005
Eternity, 1989
1 thru 3 .... @2.00

STREET MUSIC
Fantagraphics
1 .... 2.75
2 .... 2.75
3 .... 2.95
4 .... 2.95
5 .... 2.50
6 .... 3.95

STREET POET RAY
Fantagraphics, 1989
1 .... 2.50
2 .... 2.00
3 .... 2.95
4 .... 2.95

STREET WOLF
Blackthorne, 1986
1 limited series 2.00
2 and 3 .... @2.00
Graphic Novel 6.95

STRIKER: SECRET OF THE BERSERKER
Viz
1 & 2 V:The Berserker .... @2.75
3 F:Yu and Maia 2.75

Striker: The Armored Warrior #2
© Viz Communications

STRIKER: THE ARMORED WARRIOR
Viz 1992
1 Overture.................... 2.75
2 V:Child Esper................ 2.75
3 Professor taken hostage....... 2.75
GN Vol.1 The Armored Warrior .. 16.95
GN Vol.2 Forest of No Return.... 15.95

STUPID, STUPID RAT TAILS:THE ADVENTURES OF BIGJOHNSON BONE
Cartoon Books, 1999
1 I:Big Johnson Bone,FrontierHero 2.95
2 .... 2.95
TPB 9.95

STYGMATA
Entity, 1994
0 .... 3.00
1 V:The Rodent................ 2.95
2 thru 3 .... @2.95
Yearbook #1 (1995) 3.00
TPB Dragon Prophet 6.95

SUBTLE VIOLENTS
CFD Productions, 1991
1 Linsner (c&a)............... 25.00
1a San Diego Con............. 80.00

SUGAR BUZZ
Slave Labor, 1998
1 by I.Carney & W. Phoenix 2.95
2 .... 2.95
3 .... 2.95
4 .... 2.95
5 .... 2.95
6 F:Ultra Spacers 2.95
7 I:Precious & Percival 2.95
8 thru 10 .... @2.95

SUGAR RAY FINHEAD
Wolf Press, 1992
1 I&O Sugar Ray Finhead 2.50
2 I:Bessie & Big-Foot Benny the
Pit Bull Man 2.95
3 thru 7 Mardi Gras . . . . @2.50
9 & 10 . . . . @2.50

SULTRY TEENAGE SUPER-FOXES
Solson, 1987
1 thru 4 RB,Woj . . . . @2.00

SUPERMODELS IN THE RAINFOREST
Sirius, 1998
1 (of 3) 2.95
2 and 3 . . . . @2.95

SUPERSWINE
Caliber
1 Parody, I:Superswine 2.50

SURVIVALIST CHRONICLES
Survival Art
1 . . . . 6.50
2 . . . . 6.50
3 I:Bessie & Big Foot Benny 2.00

SURROGATE SAVIOR
Hot Brazer Comic Pub.
1 I:Ralph 2.50
2 Baggage. 2.50

SWAN
Little Idylls, 1995
1 thru 3 Ghost of Lord Kaaren . . @2.95
4 V:Slake. 2.95

SWEET CHILDE BATTLE BOOK
Advantage Graphics, 1995
1 I:Tasha Radcliffe. 2.50

SWEET CHILDE: LOST CONFESSIONS
Anarchy Bridgeworks, 1997
1 F:Tasha Radcliffe 2.95

SWEET LUCY
Brainstorm Comics
1 with 4 cards 2.50
2 . . . . 2.50

SWERVE
Amaze Ink, 1995
1 thru 3 by Kyle Hunter . . . . @2.00

SWIFTSURE
Harrier Comics, 1985
1 . . . . 2.00
2 . . . . 2.00
3 thru 8 . . . . @2.00
9 . . . . 9.00
9a 2nd printing 2.00
10 . . . . 2.00
11 . . . . 2.00

B & W PUB.

SWITCH B.L.A.Z.E. MANGA
London Night, 1999
0 . . . . 3.50
? Con special 4.95
? Con special, Japanese (c) 6.00
1 . . . . 3.50
1a Elite fan ed. 6.00
1b Anime cell ed. 19.95

SWORD OF VALOR
A Plus Comics
1 JAp,rep.Thane of Bagarth 2.50
2 JAp/MK rep 2.50
3 & 4 . . . . @2.50

SWORDS AND SCIENCE
Pyramid
1 thru 3 . . . . @2.00

SWORDS OF CEREBUS
Aardvark–Vanaheim
1 rep. Cerebus 1-4 . . . . 15.00
1a reprint editions 10.00
2 rep. Cerebus 5-8 . . . . 12.00
2a reprint editions 8.00
3 rep. Cerebus 9-12. . . . . 12.00
3a reprint editions 8.00
4 rep. Cerebus 13-16. . . . . 12.00
4a reprint editions 8.00
5 rep. Cerebus 17-20. . . . . 12.00
5a reprint editions 8.00
6 rep. Cerebus 21-25. . . . . 12.00
6a reprint editions 8.00

SWORDS OF SHAR-PAI
Caliber, 1991
1 Mutant Ninja Dog 2.50
2 Shar-Pei. 2.50
3 Final issue 2.50

SWORDS OF VALORS: ROBIN HOOD
A Plus Comics
1 rep. of Charlton comics. 2.50
2 thru 4 . . . . @2.50

SYSTEM SEVEN
Arrow, 1987
1 thru 4 . . . . @2.00

TAKEN UNDER COMPENDIUM
Caliber
1 rep. Cal Presents #19-#22 . . . . 2.95

TALES FROM THE ANIVERSE
Arrow
1 7,400 printed 9.00
2 . . . . 4.00
3 10,000 printed 2.50
4 . . . . 2.50
[2nd series]
Massive Comics Group
1 thru 3 . . . . @2.00

System Seven #2
© Arrow

TALES FROM THE BOG
Aberation Press, 1995
1 thru 4 by Marcus Lusk. . . . . . @3.00
1a thru 4a Director's cut. . . . . . @4.00
5 thru 7 . . . . @4.00
1a Director's Cut, 32pg. 2.95
2a Director's Cut, 32pg. 3.95
3a Director's Cut, 48pg. 3.95
4a Director's Cut, 40pg. 3.95
8 . . . . 3.00

TALES FROM THE EDGE
Vanguard, 1993
5 . . . . 2.95
5a signed 5.95
6 . . . . 2.95
7 . . . . 2.95
7a signed 5.95
8 . . . . 2.95
8a signed 5.95
9 . . . . 2.95
10 . . . . 2.95
10a signed 5.95
11 F:Sacred Monkeys 2.95
12 spec.F:Steranko 4.00
12a signed, limited 15.00
13 F:Steranko. 2.95
14 . . . . 2.95
15 Sienkiewicz special 4.00
Spec. Nightstand Chillers Benefit
Edition 4.95
Spec. Nightstand Chillers, signed . 10.00
Spec. Sienkiewicz Special 10.00

TALES FROM THE HEART
Entropy, 1988–94
1 thru 5 . . . . @2.00
6 . . . . 2.00
7 . . . . 2.00

TALES OF THE BEANWORLD
Eclipse, 1985
1 . . . . 10.00
2 . . . . 4.00
3 . . . . 2.50
4 I:Beanish 2.00
5 thru 20 . . . . @2.00
21 . . . . 3.00

TALES OF THE FEHNRIK
Antarctic Press, 1995
1 I:Lady Zeista. 2.95

TALES OF THE JACKALOPE
Blackthorne, 1986
1 . . . . 4.00
2 . . . . 3.00
3 and 4 . . . . @2.50
5 thru 9 . . . . @2.00

TALES OF THE NINJA WARRIORS
CFW
1 thru 14 . . . . @2.00
15 thru 19 . . . . @2.35

TALES OF THE PLAGUE
Eclipse
1 RCo 4.00

TALES OF THE SUNRUNNERS
Sirius, 1986
Vol. 2
1 thru 3 . . . . @2.50
Christmas Spec. 2.50

TALES OF THE TEENAGE MUTANT NINJA TURTLES
Mirage, 1987
1 . . . . 8.00
1B 2nd printing 3.00
2 . . . . 8.00
3 . . . . 5.00
4 . . . . 5.00
5 . . . . 5.00
6 thru 9 . . . . @4.00

TALES TOO TERRIBLE TO TELL
New England Comics, 1991
1 thru 6 Pre-code horror stories . @3.50

Tales Too Terrible to Tell #4
© New England Comics

B & W PUB.

TALL TAILS
Vision Comics, 1998
1 Earth Shaking. 2.95
1a Anime Blast cover. 2.95
1b Spell Warrior cover. 2.95
1c signed 4.95
2 Fire Quest, Pt.1 . . . . 2.95
3 Fire Quest, Pt.2 . . . . 2.95
4 Pain and Compromises,pt.1 . . . 2.95
5 . . . . 2.95
6 Trail Blazing, pt.1 . . . . 2.95
7 Trail Blazing, pt.2 . . . . 2.95
8 When It Almost Happened 2.95
GN Vol. 1 . . . . 8.95

TANTALIZING STORIES
Tundra, 1992
1 F:Frank & Montgomery Wart. . . . 2.25
2 Frank & Mont.stories cont. 2.25

TAOLAND
Sunitek
1 V:The Crocodile Warlord. 2.00
2 & 3 I:New Enemy . . . . @3.25

TASK FORCE ALPHA
Academy Comics
1 I:Task Force Alpha 3.50

TEAM NIPPON
Aircel
1 thru 7 by Barry Blair . . . . @2.00

TECHNOPHILIA
Brainstorm Comics
1 with 4 cards 2.50

TEENAGE MUTANT NINJA TURTLES
Mirage Studios, 1981
*Counterfeits Exist - Beware
1 I:Turtles 200.00
1a 2nd printing 25.00
1b 3rd printing 20.00
1c 4th printing 12.00
1d 5th printing 4.00
2 . . . . 50.00
2a 2nd printing 12.00
2b 3rd printing 4.00
3 . . . . 30.00
3a 2nd printing 3.50
3b Special printing,rare 50.00
4 . . . . 20.00
4a 2nd printing 3.50
5 A:Fugitoid 8.00
5a 2nd printing 3.50
6 A:Fugitoid 7.00
6a 2nd printing 2.50
7 A:Fugitoid. 8.00
7a 2nd printing 2.50
8 A:Cerebus 9.00
9 . . . . 7.00
10 V:Shredder 7.00
11 A:Casey Jones. 6.00
12 thru 18 . . . . @6.00
19 Return to NY 4.00
20 Return to NY 4.00
21 Return to NY,D:Shredder. 4.00
22 thru 32 . . . . @4.00
33 color, Corben. 3.50
34 Toytle Anxiety 3.50
35 Souls Withering 3.50
36 Souls Wake 3.50
37 Twilight of the Rings 3.50

Comics Values Annual

38 Spaced Out Pt.1, A:President Bush 3.50
39 Spaced Out Pt.2 . . . . 3.50
40 Spaced Out concl.,I:Rockin' Rollin' Miner Ants (B.U. story). . 2.00
41 Turtle Dreams issue. 2.00
42 Juliets Revenge. 2.00
43 Halls of Lost Legends 2.00
44 V:Ninjas. 2.00
45 A:Leatherhead. 2.00
46 V:Samurai Dinosaur. 2.00
47 Space Usagi. 2.00
48 Shades of Grey Part 1 . . . . 2.00
49 Shades of Grey Part 2 . . . . 2.00
50 Eastman/Laird,new direction, inc.TM,EL,WS pin-ups 2.00
51 City at War #2 . . . . 2.00
52 City at War #3 . . . . 2.25
53 City at War #4 . . . . 2.25
54 City at War #5 . . . . 2.25
55 thru 65 . . . . @2.25
1990 Movie adaptation 6.50
Spec. The Haunted Pizza 2.25

Volume 2
1 thru 8 . . . . @2.75
9 V:Baxter Bot. 2.75
10 Mr. Braunze. 2.75
11 F:Raphael 2.75
12 V:DARPA. 2.75
13 J:Triceraton 2.75

Vol. 4, 2001
1 PLa & Jim Lawson 2.95
2 thru 12 PLa . . . . @2.95

TMNT TRAINING MANUAL
1 . . . . 5.00
2 thru 5 . . . . @3.00

TEMPEST COMICS PRESENTS
Academy Comics
1 I:Steeple, Nemesis 2.50

10TH MUSE/ DEMONSLAYER
Avatar Press, 2002
Preview, 16-pg.. . . . . 2.00
1 MMy(c). 3.50
1a Matt Martin (c) 3.50
1b SSh(c) 3.50
1c Karl Waller (c). 3.50
1d wraparound (c) 3.50
1e Red Leather (c) 25.00
1f prism foil edition 12.95
1g Aftermath (c). 5.95
1h Art Nouveau (c) 5.95
1/2 MMy bikini (c) 5.95
1/2 Conflict edition. 5.95
1/2 Catfight (c). 5.95

TERROR ON THE PLANET OF THE APES
Adventure Comics, 1991
1 MP,collectors edition 2.50
2 MP, the Forbidden Zone 2.50
3 . . . . 2.50

TERRY AND THE PIRATES
ACG Comics, 1998
1 by Georges Wunder, Charlton reprint 3.00
2 . . . . 2.95
3 . . . . 2.95

TERRY & THE PIRATES
Tony Raiola, 2001
Feature Comics #6, 1938 reprint... 7.95
Feature Comics #2 1937 reprint... 7.95
Feature Comics #28 1938 reprint.. 7.95
Raven Evermore 1941 reprint..... 7.95

TERRY MOORE'S PARADISE, TOO
Abstract Studio, 2000
1 .... 2.75
2 .... 2.95
3 .... 2.95
4 .... 2.95
5 thru 14 .... @2.95
TPB Vol. 1 Drunk Ducks....... 15.95
TPB Vol. 2 Checking for Weirdos. 15.95

TEX BENSON
Metro Comics
1 thru 4 .... @2.00

39 SCREAMS
Thunder Baas
1 thru 6 .... @2.00

THEY WERE 11
Viz
1 Galactic University 2.75
2 The Accident 2.75
3 Virus 2.75
4 V:Virus 2.75

THIEVES AND KINGS
I Box, 1994–97
1 F:Ruebel The Intrepid........ 8.00
1a 2nd printing 2.50
2 .... 6.00
2a 2nd printing 2.50
3 .... 5.00
3a 2nd printing 2.50
4 .... 4.00
5 .... 4.00
6 V:Shadow Lady 4.00
7 V:Shadow Lady 3.00
8 thru 18 by Mark Oakley...... @3.00
19 thru 24 .... @2.50
25 thru 36................ @2.50
37 thru 39................ @2.50
40 .... 3.00
41 thru 43 .... @2.95
TPB Vol. 1: The Red Book,
  rep.#1–#6............... 12.00
TPB Vol. 1: 2nd printing 13.50
TPB Vol. 2: The Green Book..... 14.00
TPB Vol. 2: 2nd printing 16.50
TPB Vol. 3: The Blue Book 16.50
TPB Vol. 4: Shadow Book....... 16.50

THORR SUERD OR SWORD OF THOR
Vincent
1 .... 3.00
1a 2nd printing 2.00
2 .... 2.00
3 .... 2.00

THOSE ANNOYING POST BROS.
1 thru 18 see Color
Becomes:

POST BROTHERS
Rip Off, 1991–94
19 thru 38 .... @2.95
Becomes:

THOSE ANNOYING POST BROS.
Vortex, 1994
39 thru 45 .... @2.50
46 thru 56................ @2.95
57 Russ working on chaos wave... 2.95
58 Fearsome chaos wave....... 2.95
59 Recondite Silicates 2.95
60 .... 2.95
61 Assassinate JFK's ghost 2.95
62 Post Digestion 64pg......... 5.95
63 .... 5.95
GN Distrub the Neighbors....... 10.00
Ann. #3 Before the Flood, 56pg... 4.95
TPB Das Loot.............. 14.95

THREAT
Fantagraphics, 1985
1 .... 5.00
2 .... 3.00
3 and 4 .... @2.00
5 thru 10 .... @2.25

3 X 3 EYES
Innovation
1 Labyrinth of the Demons
  Eye,Pt.1 .... 2.25
2 Demons Eye, Pt.2 .... 2.25
3 Demons Eye, Pt.3 .... 2.25
4 Demons Eye, Pt.4 .... 2.25
5 Demons Eye, concl.......... 2.25

THREE GEEKS, THE
3 Finger Prints, 1997
1 by Rich Koslowski, Going
  to the Con, pt.1 .... 9.00
2 Going to the Con, pt.2 .... 6.00
3 Going to the Con, pt.3 (of 3)... 4.00
4 .... 4.00
5 five more geeks 2.50
6 F:Allen 2.50
7 .... 2.50
8 48-pg.................. 4.00
9 24-pg.................. 2.50
10 Happy Birthday Allen 2.50
10a variant cover 3.50
11 Happy Birthday Allen, pt.2 .... 2.50
TPB 8.95

THREE ROCKETEERS
Eclipse
1 JK,AW,rep................ 2.00
2 JK,AW,rep................ 2.00

THREE STRIKES
Oni Press 2003
1 (of 5) 3.00
2 thru 5 .... @3.00

THRESHOLD
Sleeping Giant, 1996
1 .... 2.50
2 .... 2.50

[2nd Series], 1997
1 .... 2.50
2 .... 2.50
3 .... 2.50

Avatar Press, 1998
1 Snowman cover 4.50
1a Tales of the Cyberangels cover. 4.50
1b Furies cover 4.50
1c Fuzzie Dice cover.......... 4.50
2 Snowman cover 4.95
3 Ravening (c)............. 4.95
4 Donna Mia (c)............ 4.95
5 Black Reign (c)............ 4.95
6 Luna cover 4.95
7 Darkness in Collision,
  Cavewoman(c)........... 4.95
8 Vigil/Cuda (c) 4.95
9 August (c)............... 4.95
2a thru 9a variant (c)s .... @4.95
10 Calico (c).............. 4.95
11 Scythe (c) 4.95
12 Snowman (c)............ 4.95
13 Snowman (c)............ 4.95

Threshold #1
© Avatar

14 Kaos Moon (c)............ 4.95
15 Luna (c)............... 4.95
16 Scythe (c) 4.95
17 Cimmerian (c) 4.95
18 Nightvision (c)........... 4.95
19 Pandora (c)............. 4.95
20 Kaos Moon (c)........... 4.95
21 Jungle Girl (c) 4.95
22 .... 4.95
23 Ravening (c) 4.95
24 Faust: Singha's Talons...... 4.95
25 Dark Blue (c)............ 4.95
26 Dark Blue (c)............ 4.95
27 Dark blue (c) 4.95
28 Dark blue (c) 4.95
29 Dark Blue (c)............ 4.95
30 Dark Blue (c)............ 4.95
10a thru 30a variant (c)s ..... @4.95
31 Luna (c)............... 4.95
32 Ravening (c) 4.95
33 Pandora (c)............. 4.95
34 Pandora (c)............. 4.95
35 Pandora (c)............. 4.95
36 Pandora (c)............. 4.95
37 Pandora (c)............. 4.95
38 Pandora (c)............. 4.95
39 Razor (c).............. 4.95
40 Lookers (c) 4.95
41 Razor (c).............. 4.95
42 Razor (c).............. 4.95
43 Razor (c).............. 4.95
43 Razor (c).............. 4.95
45 Demonslayer (c) 4.95
46 Demonslayer (c) 4.95
47 Pandora (c)............. 4.95
31a thru 47a variant (c)s ..... @4.95

Threshold–Tigers

B & W PUB.

48 Pandora (c) 4.95
49 Pandora (c) 4.95
48a thru 49a connecting (c) 5.95
50 64-pg. 8.95
50 connecting (c)s 8.95
50a variant (c)s . . . . @8.95
51 . . . . 4.95
51a variant (c) 4.95
51 Pandora Western edition 5.95
TPB Razor X, 48-pg. 6.95
TPB Razor X, Vol. 2 . . . . 6.95

THRESHOLD OF REALITY
Maintech, 1986
1 5,000 printed 2.50
2 thru 4 . . . . @2.00

THUNDERBIRD
Newcomers Publishing
1 & 2 2 Stories. . . . . @2.95
3 . . . . 2.95
4 I:Mercer 2.95
5 R:Raven 2.95
6 & 7 . . . . @2.95
8 final issue. 3.50
Ann.#1 The Great Escape 3.50

THUNDER BUNNY
Mirage, 1985
1 O:Thunder Bunny 2.50
2 VO:Dr.Fog 2.00
3 I:GoldenMan. 2.00
4 V:Keeper 2.00
5 I:Moon Mess. 2.00
6 V:Mr.Endall. 2.00
7 VI:Dr.Fog 2.00
8 . . . . 2.00
9 VS:Gen. Agents 2.00
10 thru 12 . . . . @2.00

THUNDER MACE
Rak, 1986
1 Proto type-blue & red very
 rare:1,000 printed 15.00
1a four color cover. 3.00
2 thru 5 . . . . @2.00
6 . . . . 2.00
7 . . . . 2.00
Graphic Novel, rep.1-4 . . . . 5.00

TICK
New England Comics, 1988
1 BEd 45.00
1a 2nd printing 10.00
1b 3rd printing 8.00
1c 4th printing 5.00
2 BEd 50.00
2a 2nd printing 10.00
2b 3rd printing 4.00
2c 4th printing 2.50
3 BEd 10.00
3a 2nd printing 3.00
4 BEd 8.00
4a 2nd printing 3.00
5 BEd 8.00
6 BEd 7.00
7 BEd,A:Chairface Chippendale. . . 7.00
8 BEd 6.00
8a Spec.No Logo edition 12.00
9 BEd,A:Chainsaw Vigilante,
 Red Eye 5.00
10 BEd. 5.00
11 thru 12 BEd . . . . @4.00
9 thru 12, new printings . . . . @2.95
Spec. Ed. #1, I:Tick 25.00
Spec. Ed. #2, 2nd App. Tick 20.00
Spec. #1 Reprise edition. 5.95

Tick #7 (2nd printing)
© *New England Comics*

TPB Omnibus #1 rep. #1–#6. . . . 17.95
TPB Omnibus #2 BEd,fifth printing 14.95
TPB Omnibus #3 BEd. 10.95
TPB Omnibus #4 BEd. 10.95
The Tick Big Yule Log Special 1998 3.50
The Tick Big Yule Log Special 1999 3.50
Tick's Big Yule Log Special 2001 . . 3.50
Big Giant Summer Special #1, The
 Sidekicks are Revolting 3.50
Big Summer Annual #1. . . . . 3.50
Tick's Big Red-N-Green X-mas . . . 3.95
TPB Tick Bonanza #3. . . . . 4.95
TPB Tick Bonanza #4. . . . . 4.95
Spec.#1 Back to School 3.50
Big Halloween Special #1. . . . . . . 3.50
Massive Summer Double Spectacle
 Photo-Cover set of 2 . . . . 7.95
13 Pseudo-Tick, not by Edlund . . . 3.50
Big Year 2000 Spectacle. 3.50
Big Romantic Adventure #1, 2nd ed. 3.50
Big Tax Time Terror #1 . . . . 3.50
Big Mother's Day Spec. #1 . . . . . . 3.50
Big Halloween Special 2000 . . . . . 3.50
Big Father's Day Special 3.50
Big Cruise Ship Vacation Spec.#1 . 3.50
Massive Summer Double Spec.#1 . 3.50
Massive Summer Double Spec.#2 . 3.50

TICK AND ARTHUR, THE
New England Comics, 1999
1 by Sean Wang & Mike Baker . . . 3.50
2 Return of the Thorn,pt.2 . . . . . . 3.50
3 Return of the Thorn,pt.3 . . . . . . 3.50
4 Tick & Arthur meet Flea & Doyle . 3.50
5 Flea & Doyle superheroes? 3.50
6 Chainsaw Vigilantes 3.50
TPB Bonanza #1 rep. #1–#3. . . . . 5.50
TPB Bonanza #2 rep. #4–#6. . . . . 5.50

TICK, THE: BIG BLUE DESTINY
New England Comics, 1997
1 by Eli Stone, Keen edition. 3.00
1 Wicked Keen edition. 5.00
2A cover A. 3.00
3B cover B 3.00
3 . . . . 3.50
4 . . . . 3.50
5 The Chrysalis Crisis 3.50

Comics Values Annual

TICK CIRCUS MAXIMUS
New England Comics, 2000
1 (of 4) by Sean Wang. 3.50
2 . . . . 3.50
3 . . . . 3.50
4 concl. 3.50
Spec.#1 Circus Maximus
 Redux (2001). 3.50

TICK: GIANT CIRCUS OF THE MIGHTY
New England Press, 1992
1 A-O 3.00
2 P-Z 3.00
3 . . . . 3.00

TICK, THE: GOLDEN AGE
New England Comics, 2002
1 Entertaining cover. 4.95
1a Classic cover 4.95
2 extremely creepy cover. 4.95
2a Ferociously heroic cover 4.95
3 Bleeding Heart (c) 4.95
3a Criminally Maniacal (c) 4.95
TPB Golden Age giant edition. . . . 12.95

TICK, THE: HEROES OF THE CITY
New England Comics, 1999
1 three stories 3.50
2 . . . . 3.50
3 . . . . 3.50
4 . . . . 3.50
5 . . . . 3.50
6 . . . . 3.50
TPB Bonanza #1 rep. #1–#3. . . . . 5.50
TPB Bonanza #2 rep. #4–#6. . . . . 5.50

TICK: KARMA TORNADO
New England Press, 1993
1 . . . . 4.00
1 2nd printing 3.00
2 . . . . 3.50
2 2nd printing 3.00
3 thru 9 . . . . @3.50
3 thru 9 2nd printings . . . . @3.00
TPB #1 second edition 13.95
TPB Bonanza Edition, Vol.2 . . . . . . 4.95
TPB Bonanza Edition, Vol.3 . . . . . . 4.95

TICK, THE: LUNY BIN
New England Comics, 1998
1 (of 3) by Eli Stone, Back to
 the Luny Bin. 3.50
2 To the Rescue 3.50
3 Six Eyes in Tears 3.50
Preview Special, 32pg 2.00
TPB Luny Bin Trilogy 120-pg. 4.95

TICK OMNIBUS
New England Press
1 1 to 6 Rep. 14.95

TICK'S BACK, THE
New England Comics, 1997
0 by Eli Stone, V:Toy DeForce 3.00

TIGERS OF THE LUFTWAFTE
Antarctic Press, 2001
1 48-pg. 5.95
2 48-pg. 5.95

All comics prices listed are for *Near Mint* condition.

Comics Values Annual — B & W PUB. — Tigers–Tom

3 48-pg.. . . . . 5.95
4 Wild Angels, 48-pg. 5.95
5 Black Devil, 48-pg. 5.95
6 Black Devil, pt.2 . . . . 5.95
7 April Fools phoney issue. 5.95
8 Fighter General 5.95
9 Adolf Galland 5.95
10 final issue 5.95

TIGERS OF TERRA
Mind-Visions, 1992
1 6,000 printed 4.50
1a Signed & Num. 14.00
2 . . . . 2.00
2a Signed & Num. 11.00
5 thru 7 . . . . @3.50
8 thru 10 . . . . @3.75
Antarctic, 1993
11 and 12 . . . . @3.95
[Vol. 2], 1993
0 thru 14 . . . . @2.75
15 Totenkopf Police,pt.2 . . . . 2.75
16 Battleship Arizona,pt.3 . . . . . . 2.75
17 thru 22 . . . . @2.95
23 'Trouble with Tigers' pt.3 . . . . 2.95
24 48pg 10th Anniv. 3.95
25 'Battle for Terra' pt.1 . . . . 2.95
TPB Book Two 9.95
TPB Book Three. 9.95
TPB Book Four. 9.95

TIGER-X
Eternity, 1988
Special #1 . . . . 2.50
Spec. #1a 2nd printing 2.25
1 thru 3 . . . . @2.00
Book II, 1989
1 thru 4 . . . . @2.00

TIGRESS
Hero Graphics, 1992
1 Tigress vs. Flare. 4.00
2 . . . . 3.00
3 A:Lady Arcane 3.00
4 inc. B.U. Mudpie. 4.00
5 . . . . 4.00
6 . . . . 4.00

TIGRESS
Basement Comics, 1998
1 by Budd Root and Mike Hoffman 3.00
2 concl. 3.00
1-shot Mike Hoffman special. . . . 8.95
1-shot green foil edition 12.50
1-shot gold foil edition. 12.50

TIGRESS TALES
Amryl Entertainment, 2001
1 by Mike Hoffman 3.00
2 Slave Planet. 3.00
Basement Comics, 2001
1a spec. edition. 8.95
2 Special Edition 8.95
2 Blue foil (c). 12.50
3a Special ed. 8.95
3b special edition, purple foil . . . 11.50
4 . . . . 2.95
4a Special ed. 8.95
4b special edition, gold foil 11.50
5 . . . . 2.95
5a Special ed. 8.95
Pin-Up book (2001) 3.50
Pin-Up Book, special edition. . . . 8.95

TIGRESS: THE HIDDEN LANDS
Basement Comics, 2002
1 by Mike Hoffman 3.50

TIME DRIFTERS
Innovation, 1990
1 . . . . 2.25
2 . . . . 2.25
3 . . . . 2.25

TIME GATES
Double Edge
1 SF series,The Egg #1. . . . . 2.00
2 The Egg #2 . . . . 2.00
3 Spirit of the Dragon #1 . . . . . . 2.00
4 Spirit of the Dragon #2 . . . . . . 2.00
4a Var.cover 2.00

TIME JUMP WAR
Apple
1 thru 3 . . . . @2.00

TIME MACHINE
Eternity, 1990
1 thru 3 H.G. Wells adapt. . . . . @2.50

TIME TRAVELER AI
CPM Manga, 1999
1 by Ai Ijima &
 Takeshi Takebayashi 2.95
2 thru 13 . . . . @2.95
14 thru 21. . . . . @2.95
TPB Book One, rep. 15.95
TPB Sexy Pirates 15.95
TPB Vol. 2 Sexy Pirates 15.95
TPB Vol. 3 Sexy Ninja Girl 15.95

TIME WARRIORS
Fantasy General, 1986
1 rep.Alpha Track #1 . . . . 2.00
1a Bi-Weekly. 2.00
2 . . . . 2.00
3 . . . . 2.00

TIM VIGIL'S WEBWITCH
Avatar Press, 2002
Preview, 16-pg. 2.00
Preview, Temptress (c) 5.95
Preview, Serenity (c). 5.95
Preview, prism foil exclusive(c) . . 12.95
Preview Cave of Evil edition 5.95
1 (of 3) Finch(c). 3.50
2 Vigil(c) 3.50
3 Adrian (c) 3.50
1a thru 3a variant(c). . . . . @3.50
1b thru 3b wraparound (c)s . . . @3.95
Webwitch Companion 4.95
Webwitch Companion Waller (c) . . 4.95
Webwitch Companion Martin (c) . . 4.95

TITANESS
Draculina Publishing, 1995
1 I:Titaness,Tomboy. 2.95

TO BE ANNOUNCED
Strawberry Jam, 1986
1 thru 6 . . . . @2.00

TOKYO MEW MEW
Tokyopop Press 2003
GN Vol. 1 (of 4) 10.00
GN Vol. 2 thru Vol. 4 . . . . @10.00

Tomb Tales #4
© Cryptic Entertainment

TOMB TALES
Cryptic Entertainment, 1997
1 . . . . 3.00
2 . . . . 3.00
3 . . . . 3.00
4 A Rare Gem 3.00
5 . . . . 3.00
6 The Flame Game 3.00
7 Invasion of the Shoddy Snatchers 3.00

TOM CORBETT SPACE CADET
Eternity, 1990
1 . . . . 2.00
2 . . . . 2.00
3 . . . . 2.25
4 . . . . 2.25

TOM CORBETT II
Eternity, 1990
1 . . . . 2.25
2 . . . . 2.25
3 . . . . 2.25
4 . . . . 2.25

TOMMI GUNN: KILLERS LUST
London Night, 1997
1 . . . . 3.00
1 photo cover 6.00
Ann. #1 . . . . 3.00

TOM MIX HOLIDAY ALBUM
Amazing Comics
1 . . . . 3.50

TOM MIX WESTERN
AC Comics, 1988
1 . . . . 2.50
2 . . . . 2.50

All comics prices listed are for *Near Mint* condition.

TOMMY & THE MONSTERS
New Comics
1 thru 3 . . . . @2.00

TOMORROW MAN
Antarctic, 1993
1 R:Tommorrow Man 2.95
Spec.#1 48-pg. 3.95

TOMORROW MAN
Antarctic Press, 2000
1 Requiem for Nepton,pt.1. . . . . . . 5.00
2 Requiem for Nepton,pt.2. . . . . . . 2.95
3 Requiem for Nepton,pt.3. . . . . . . 2.95

TONY DIGEROLAMO'S JERSEY DEVIL
South Jersey Rebellion
1 by Tony DiGerolamo 2.95
2 . . . . 2.95
3 . . . . 2.25
4 . . . . 2.95
5 Robin Hood of the Pines,pt.1 . . . 2.25
6 Robin Hood of the Pines,pt.2 . . . 2.95

TONY DIGEROLAMO'S THE TRAVELERS
Kenzer & Company, 2000
1 thru 3 . . . . @2.25
7 . . . . 2.95
8 Vlad Tepes in Romania 2.95
9 Arcimedes & Time Machine 2.95
10 Strange storm 2.95
11 Wrath of the Imprechaun 2.95
12 thru 20 . . . . @3.00
Wingnut Comics 2003
21 thru 24 . . . . @3.00
TPB Vol. 1 Keg O' Fun 11.95

TONY DIGEROLAMO'S THE FIX
South Jersey Rebellion, 2001
1 (of 4) 2.50
2 thru 4 . . . . @2.50

TOO MUCH COFFEE MAN
Adhesive Comics, 1994
1 F:Too Much Coffee Man 16.00
1a 2nd printing 4.00
2 Wheeler (s&a) 8.00
3 Wheeler (s&a) 6.00
4 In love 6.00
5 thru 7 . . . . @4.00
8 thru 10 . . . . @3.00
Mag. #11 64-pg. 4.95
Mag. #12 . . . . 4.95
Mag. #13 thru #18. . . . . @4.95

TOO MUCH HOPELESS SAVAGES
Oni Press 2003
1 (of 4) 3.00
2 thru 3 . . . . @3.00

TORG
Adventure
1 Based on Role Playing Game . . . 2.50
2 thru 3 Based on Game . . . . . . @2.50

TOR JOHNSON: HOLLYWOOD STAR
Monster Comics
1 Biographical story 2.50

TORRID AFFAIRS
Eternity, 1988
1 . . . . 2.25
2 . . . . 2.25
3 thru 5, 60-pg. . . . . @2.95

TOTALLY ALIEN
Trigon
1 . . . . 15.00
2 . . . . 10.00
3 . . . . 8.00

TOUGH GUYS AND WILD WOMEN
Eternity, 1989
1 . . . . 2.25
2 . . . . 2.25

TRACKER
Blackthorne, 1988
1 . . . . 2.00
2 . . . . 2.00
3 . . . . 2.00
4 . . . . 2.00

TRANSFORMERS ARMADA CINEMANGA
Tokyopop Press 2003
GN Vol. 1 (of 3) 8.00
GN Vol. 2 . . . . 8.00
GN Vol. 3 . . . . 8.00

TRANSIT
Vortex, 1987
1 . . . . 2.00
2 thru 6 . . . . @2.00

TRICKSTER KING MONKEY
Eastern
1 thru 5 . . . . @2.00

TRIDENT
Trident, 1989
1 thru 7 . . . . @3.50
8 . . . . 4.50

TRIUMVERATE
Mermaid Productions
1 I:Trimverate 2.25
2 & 3 Team captured . . . . @2.25
4 V:Ord,Ael 2.25

TROLLORDS
Tru Studios, 1986
1 1st printing 5.00
1a 2nd printing 2.00
2 . . . . 3.00
3 . . . . 2.00
4 thru 15 . . . . @2.00
#1 special 2.00

Trollords #1
© Tru Studios

TROLLORDS
Apple Comics, 1989–90
1 thru 6 . . . . @2.50

TROLLORDS
Caliber Tapestry, 1996
1 and 2 . . . . @2.95

TROLLORDS: DEATH & KISSES
Apple Comics, 1989
1 . . . . 2.00
2 thru 5 . . . . @2.25

TROUBLE SHOOTERS
Nightwolf, 1995
1 I:Trouble Shooters 2.50
2 V:Ifrit,Djin,Ghul 2.50
3 V:Morgath. 2.50

TROUBLE WITH GIRLS
Eternity, 1989–91
1 . . . . 3.00
2 . . . . 2.50
3 thru 14 . . . . @2.25
15 thru 21 . . . . @2.25
22 Lester's Origin 2.25
Ann. #1 . . . . 2.95
Graphic Novel 7.95
Graphic Novel #2 . . . . 7.95
Xmas special `World of Girls' 2.95
NEW SERIES
1 thru 4 see color
5 thru 11 . . . . @2.00

TROUBLE WITH TIGERS
Antarctic Press, 1992
1 Ninja High School/Tigers x-over . 2.00
2 . . . . 2.00

TRUE CRIME
Eclipse
1 thru 2 . . . . @2.95

TRUFAN ADVENTURES THEATRE
Paragraphics, 1986
1 .... 7.00
2 3-D issue 5.00

TURTLE SOUP
Mirage, 1985
1 A:TMNTurtles 6.00

TURTLES TEACH KARATE
Solson
1 .... 4.00
2 .... 3.50

TUXEDO GIN
Viz Communications 2003
TPB Vol. 1 .... 9.95
TPB Vol. 2 thru Vol. 3 ..... @9.95

TV WESTERN
AC Comics, 2001
1 F:Jock Mahoney, Range Reed .. 5.95
Becomes:

WESTERN MOVIE HERO
AC Comics, 2001
2 F:Monte Hale 5.95
3 F:John Wayne 5.95
4 F:Rex Allen 6.95

TWILIGHT AVENGER
Eternity, 1988
1 thru 18 .... @2.00
Miracle Studios
Spec. Twilight Avenger Super Summer Special 2.75

TWILIGHT-X: INTERLUDE
Antarctic Press, 1992
1 thru 3 by Joseph Wright ..... @2.50
Vol. 2, 1993
1 thru 5 .... @2.50

TWILIGHT-X QUARTERLY
Antarctic Press, 1994
1 thru 3 by Joseph Wright ..... @2.95
4 Celebration 2.95

TWILIGHT X: STORM
Antarctic Press 2003
1 .... 3.50
2 thru 5 .... @3.50

TWIST
Kitchen Sink, 1988
1 .... 2.00
2 and 3 .... @2.00

TWISTED TANTRUMS OF THE PURPLE SNIT
Blackthorne, 1986
1 .... 2.50
2 .... 2.00

2001 NIGHTS
Viz, 1990–91
1 by Yukinobu Hoshino 5.00
2 .... 4.00

Twisted Tantrums of the Purple Snit #2 © Blackthorne

3 thru 5 .... @3.75
6 thru 10 .... @4.25

TYRANNY REX
Fleetway
GN reps. from 2000A.D. ... 7.95

ULTIMATE STRIKE
London Night, 1996
1 .... 2.00
1 holochrome edition 15.00
2 .... 2.00
3 .... 2.00
4 .... 2.00
5 .... 2.00
6 sequel to Strike #0 .... 2.00
7 by Kevin Hill, 'Strike: Year One' concl. 2.00
8 Year One, ... 2.00
9 Year One, cont. 2.00
10 .... 2.00
11 .... 2.00
12 .... 2.00

ULTRA KLUTZ
Onward Comics
1 .... 2.50
2 thru 18 .... @2.25
19 thru 24 .... @2.25
25 thru 30 .... @2.25
31 .... 3.00

Bad Habit
TBP Book One, rep. #1–#23 ..... 29.95

UNCANNY MAN-FROG
Mad Dog
1 and 2 .... @2.00

UNCENSORED MOUSE
Eternity, 1989
1 Mickey Mouse 10.00
2 Mickey Mouse 11.00

UNDER THE GLASS MOON
Tokyopop Press 2003
GN Vol. 1 (of 3) 10.00

GN Vol. 2 .... 10.00

UNFORGIVEN, THE
Trinity Comics Ministries Mission of Tranquility
1 thru 6 V:Dormian Grath ..... @2.00
7 I:Faith. 2.00

UNICORN ISLE
Genesis West, 1986
1 .... 2.50
2 .... 2.00
3 .... 2.00
Apple, 1987
4 thru 6 .... @2.00

UNLEASHED
Caliber Press
1 F:Carson Davis 2.95
2 V:North Harbor Crime 2.95

UNSUPERVISED EXISTENCE
Fantagraphics
1 .... 2.00
2 and 3 .... @2.50

UNTOLD TALES OF EVIL ERNIE
Chaos! Comics, 2000
Pieces of Me #1 .... 3.50
Black Death premium #1 ... 12.95
Evil Ernie:chromium #1 ... 15.95
Relentless 1 BnP (2002) 5.00
Relentless 1a premium ed. ... 10.00
Relentless 1b Super premium ed. .. 20.00
Relentless 1c signed ed. ... 15.00
Relentless, Script 5.00
Relentless Script, premium ed. ... 20.00

UNTOUCHABLES
1 thru 20 .... @2.00

UNTOUCHABLES
Caliber, 1997
1K by Joe Pruett & John Kissee, MK(c) 3.00
1S Showman (c) 3.00
2 .... 3.00
3 MK (c) 3.00
4 MK (c) 3.00
Spec. High Society Killer (1998) ... 3.95

USAGI YOJIMBO
Fantagraphics, 1987
1 SS 11.00
1a 2nd printing 5.00
2 SS, Samurai 8.00
3 SS, Samurai, A:Croakers ... 6.00
4 SS 5.00
5 thru 7 SS .... @5.00
8 SS, A Mother's Love 5.00
8a 2nd printing 3.00
9 SS 5.00
10 SS, A:Turtles 5.00
10a 2nd printing 3.00
11 thru 18 SS .... @4.00
19 SS, Frost & Fire, A:Nelson Groundthumper 4.00
20 thru 21 SS .... @4.00
22 SS, A:Panda Khan 4.00
23 SS, V:Ninja Bats 4.00

Usagi–Vampfire / B & W PUB.

24 SS	4.00
25 SS,A:Lionheart	4.00
26 SS,Gambling	4.00
27 SS	4.00
28 thru 31 SS,Circles pt.1–4	@4.00
32	4.00
33 SS,Ritual Murder	4.00
34 thru 37	@4.00
Spec.#1 SS,SummerSpec, C:Groo	45.00
TPB Vol 4, rep.	16.95
TPB Vol 6, rep., new printing	12.95
TPB Vol 7, Gen's Story	16.95

Radio Comix
Vol. 1 The Art of Usagi Yojimbo.... 3.95

VAGABOND
Viz Communications, 2001
Part 1
1 (of 8) by Takehiko Inoue	4.95
2 thru 16	@4.95
TPB Vol. 1 thru Vol. 4	@12.95
TPB Vol. 5 thru Vol. 7	@9.95

VALENTINO
Renegade, 1985
1	2.00
2 and 3	@2.00

VAMPEROTICA
Brainstorm Comics, 1994
1 I:Luxura	8.00
1a 2nd & 3rd printing	3.00
2	6.00
2 2nd printing	3.00
3	4.00
4 I:Blood Hunter	4.00
5 Deadshot	4.00
6 Deadshot	4.00
7 Baptism	4.00
8 Pains,Peepers	4.00
9 thru 11	@4.00
12 thru 16	@3.00
17 thru 22 see: color	
20 signed	5.00
23	3.00
23 encore edition	2.95
24	3.00
25	3.00
26	3.00
27	3.00
28 A:China & Jazz	3.00
29 mild cover	3.00
30 Legends of Luxura x-over, concl.	3.00
31 V:Red Militia	3.00
32	3.00
33 by Kirk Lindo	3.00
34 V:Pontius Vanthor	3.00
34a luxury edition	5.00
35	3.00
36 I:Countess Vladimira	3.00
36a photo cover edition	3.95
37	3.00
37a statue cover	3.00
38	3.00
39 Death From Above, pt.1	3.00
40 Death From Above, pt.2	3.00
41	3.00
42 Hostile Seduction	3.00
43 Harvest	3.00
44 F:Luxura	3.00
45 The Kindred Kill	3.00
45b photo cover	4.00
46 Murder Most Foul	3.00
47 Camelot	3.00
48 Reflections Over Blood	3.00
49 Love's Story	3.00
50 final issue, 48-pg.	5.00
50b commemorative edition, Julie	
Strain photo (c)	7.00
50c commem. signed	10.00
Commemorative Edition	2.95
Lingerie Special #1	2.95
Spec. Lingerie, encore edition	2.95
Spec. Lingerie, deluxe	3.95
Spec. Swimsuit, encore edition	2.95
Gallery #1	4.95
Gallery #2	4.95
Bondage Spec. #1	2.95
Bondage Spec. #1, manga	3.95
Ann. #1 Encore	3.00
Spec. #2 Dare to Bare	2.95
Spec. #4 Encore Edition, new(c)	2.95
Spec. #5 Encore Edition	2.95
Spec.#1 Vamperotica Presents: Countess Vladimira (1998)	3.00
Vamperotica Collector Vol. 1	3.95
Pin-Up #1 (2000)	2.95
Spec. Blood of Japan	3.00
1-shot Blond Goddess (2003)	2.95
GN Blood of the Impaler	7.95
1-shot Dark Fantasy	2.95
GN Deadly Vixens	7.95
1-shot Bondage Gallery	2.95

VAMPEROTICA: DARK FICTION
Vamperotica Ent., 2001
1 F:Vampress Luxura	2.95
1a adult (c)	3.95
1b premium edition	4.95
2	2.95
3	2.95
4	2.95
TPB Vamperotica Maximum Excitement (2001)	7.95
TPB Vamperotica Slave to Love (2000)	7.95

VAMPEROTICA: DIVIDE & CONQUER
Brainstorm, 1999
1 V:The Juicious Edicts	3.00
1b Commemorative #1	5.00
1c Commemorative #1 deluxe	7.00
2 conclusion	3.00

VAMPEROTICA ILLUSTRATED
Brainstorm
1 F:Vampress Luxura	2.95
1b premium ed.	4.95
1c premium signed	5.95
2	2.95
3	2.95
4	2.95
5	2.95
6	2.95

VAMPEROTICA LUST FOR LUXURA
Vamperotica, 2002
1 by Kirk Lindo	2.95
1a premium edition	4.95
2	2.95
3	2.95
1c Sketch cover edition	3.95
3a photo(c)	4.95

VAMPEROTICA MANGA
Brainstorm, 1998
1	2.95
2	3.00

VAMPEROTICA TALES
Brainstorm, 1998
1	2.95
2	2.95
3	3.00
4 Veiled Threat	3.00
5 A Night of Wine and Roses	3.00

VAMPEROTICA: TALES FROM THE BLOODVAULT
Vamperotica Ent., 2000
Mag. #1	4.95
Mag. #1b premium ed.	6.95

VAMPEROTICA: WHEN DARKNESS FALLS
Vamperotica Ent., 2002
1	2.95
1b premium edition	4.95
2	2.95
3	2.95
TPB Dark Ages, series rep..	7.95

VAMPFIRE
Brainstorm, 1996
1	2.95
1b commemorative photo cover	10.00
2	2.95
2b signed	5.00
2d Remastered	2.95
2e signed	10.00
2f deluxe with litho	19.95
3 remastered	3.95
3a signed	10.00
3b deluxe	19.95
Pin-Up Spec.	2.95
Pin-Up Spec. deluxe	3.95
Tour Book #1	2.95

VAMPFIRE: EROTIC ECHO
Brainstorm, 1997
1 by Fauve	2.95
1b photo cover	3.00
2	2.95
2b photo cover	2.95

Vampirella #1
© Harris

VAMPFIRE: NECROMANTIQUE
Brainstorm, 1997
1 by Holly Golightly 2.95
1b luxury edition, virgin cover 5.00
1c luxury edition, signed 15.00
1d regular, signed 8.00
2 by Fauve 2.95

VAMPIRE BITES
Brainstorm, 1995
1 . . . . 3.00
2 . . . . 2.95

VAMPIRE CONFESSIONS
Brainstorm, 1998
1 . . . . 3.00

VAMPIRE DAHLIA, THE
Ironcat, 2001
1 (of 6) by Narumi Kakinouchi 2.95
2 thru 6 . . . . @2.95
TPB Vol. 1 Death is a Kiss 16.95

VAMPIRE GAME
Tokyopop Press 2003
GN Vol. 1 (of 3) 10.00
GN Vol. 2 thru Vol. 3 . . . . 10.00

VAMPIRE GIRLS: CALIFORNIA 1969
Angel Entertainment, 1996
1 blood red foil deluxe edition 5.95
2 . . . . 2.95
2 deluxe 5.95
TPB 5.00

VAMPIRE GIRLS: NEW YORK 1979
Angel Entertainment, 1996
0 . . . . 2.95
0 gold edition 8.00
1 . . . . 2.95

VAMPIRE GIRLS: BUBBLEGUM & BLOOD
Angel Entertainment, 1996
1 . . . . 2.95
1 deluxe edition 5.95
2 . . . . 2.95
2 deluxe edition 5.95

VAMPIRE GIRLS EROTIQUE
Angel Entertainment, 1996
1 . . . . 2.95
2 . . . . 2.95
3 . . . . 2.95
4 . . . . 2.95
5 . . . . 2.95
6 . . . . 2.95
7 Bloodsucker cover 3.00
Spec. Gravedigger (1996) by
  Alexandra Scott & Bill Wylie . . . 3.00
Spec. Paris 1968 (1997) by
  Alexandra Scott & Dean Burnett 2.95
Spec. Titanic 1912 (1998) by
  Alexandra Scott & Dean Burnett 2.95

VAMPIRE GIRLS EROTIQUE: GRAVEDIGGER
Angel Entertainment, 1996
1 by Alexandra Scott & Bill Wylie . . 3.00

VAMPIRE GIRLS VS. ANGEL GIRL
Angel Entertainment, 1997
1 . . . . 2.95

VAMPIRELLA
Harris
1 DC,SL,Summer Nights,48pg. 3.95
Pantha Ashcan, 16-pg. 6.00
Dangerous Games Preview Ashcan 6.00
Hell on Earth, Leather Ashcan . . . 14.95
Hell on Earth, Leather Ashcan,
  signed 29.95
30th Ann. Spec. Julie
  Strain photo (c) 9.95
Painkiller Jane preview Ashcan 6.00
Spec.#1 Vampirella vs. Hemorrhage,
  Limited Preview Ashcan 5.00
Vampirella/Lady Death Ashcan
  16-pg., Rematch. 6.00
Vampirella/Lady Death Ashcan
  16-pg., Finale. 6.00
Vampirella/Lady Death Ashcan
  16-pg., Revenge, platinum . . . 19.95
Vampirella 2999 A.D.
  Manga Ashcan 7.95
Vampirella 2999 A.D. Manga
  Ashcan, leather edition 14.95
Vampirella 3000 A.D.
  Manga Ashcan 7.95
Vampirella 3000 A.D.Manga
  Ashcan, leather edition 14.95

VAMPIRELLA
Harris Comics, 2002
#1 magazine reprint from 1969 . . 29.95
#1 royal blue foil (c). 59.95
#1 platinum foil (c). 19.95
TPB Vampirella and the Blood Red
  Queen of Hearts, rep. from Warren
  Vampirella, 96pg. 9.95

VAMPIRELLA
Silver Anniversary Collection
Harris, 1996
0 Vampirella of Darkulon, EM 3.00
1 good girl edition 2.50
1a bad girl edition 2.50
2 good girl edition 2.50
2a bad girl edition 2.50
3 good girl edition 2.50
3a bad girl edition 2.50
4 Silkie(c) 2.50
4a MBc(c) 2.50

VAMPIRELLA COMICS MAGAZINE
Harris Comics 2003
1 . . . . 3.95
1a photo (c). 9.95
2 . . . . 3.95
2a photo (c). 9.95

Vampirella: Morning in America #1
© Harris

VAMPIRELLA: MORNING IN AMERICA
Harris/Dark Horse, 1991–92
Book 1 thru 4 . . . . @7.00
Book 2 thru 4 . . . . @5.00
TPB 25.00

VAMPIRELLA RETRO
Harris, 1998
1 (of 3) rep. Warren stories 2.50
2 (of 3) rep. Warren stories 2.50
3 (of 3) rep. Warren stories 2.50

VAMPIRELLA: LEGENDARY TALES
Harris Comics, 2000
1 . . . . 2.95
1a deluxe 9.95
1b Julie Strain photo (c). 9.95
2 . . . . 2.95
2a variant (c). 9.95
2b Julie Strain photo (c). 9.95

VAMPIRE MIYU
Antarctica Press, 1996
1 I:Vampire Princess Miyu 2.95
2 thru 5 . . . . @3.95
6 48pg. 4.95

VAMPIRE PRINCESS MIYU
Ironcat, 2000
VOL 1
1 by Narumi Kakinouchi. 2.95
2 thru 4 . . . . @2.95
TPB Vol. 1 (2001) 17.95
TPB Vol. 2 thru Vol. 3 . . . . @17.95
TPB Vol. 4 . . . . 17.95
TPB Vol. 5 Intrusions 15.95
TPB Vol. 6 . . . . 15.95
TPB Vol. 7 Vortex 15.95
Artbook (color) 25.00

VAMPIRE PRINCESSS YUI
Ironcat, 2000
Vol. 1
1 . . . . @2.95
2 thru 6 . . . . @2.95

Vampire–Visions

Vol. 2
1 .... 2.95
2 thru 6 .... @2.95

VAMPIRE YUI
Ironcat, 2000
Vol. 3
1 .... 2.95
2 thru 4 .... @2.95
5 thru 6 .... @2.95

Vol. 4 (2002)
1 thru 7 .... @2.95

Vol. 5
1 .... 2.95
2 thru 7 .... @2.95
TPB Vol. 1 .... 17.95
TPB Vol. 2 .... 17.95
TPB Vol. 3 .... 17.95
TPB Vol. 4 .... 15.95
TPB Vol. 5 .... 15.95

VAMPIRE'S TATTOO
London Night, 1997
1 (of 2) by Art Wetherell 3.00
2 .... 3.00
3 .... 3.00

VAMPIRE VERSES, THE
CFD Productions, 1995
1 thru 3 .... @3.00

VAMPIRE ZONE, THE
Brainstorm, 1998
1 .... 2.95

VAMPORNRELLA
Forbidden, 1997
1 parody 2.95

VAMPYRES
Eternity, 1988
1 thru 4 .... @2.25

VAPOR LOCH
Sky Comics, 1994
1 .... 2.50

Vengeance of the Aztecs #2
© Caliber

B & W PUB.

VENGEANCE OF DREADWOLF
Lightning Comics
1 O:Dreadwolf 2.75

VENGEANCE OF THE AZTECS
Caliber, 1993
1 .... 2.50
2 .... 2.50

VERDICT
Eternity, 1988
1 thru 4 .... @2.00

VEROTIKA
Verotika, 1995–97
1 Magical Times 12.00
2 .... 7.00
3 .... 5.00
4 thru 6 .... @4.00
7 thru 15 .... @3.00

VERY VICKY
Meet Danny Ocean, 1993
1 .... 3.50
1a 2nd printing 3.00
2 thru 8 .... @2.50
Spec. Calling All Hillbillies ... 2.50

VIC & BLOOD
Renegade, 1987
1 and 2 RCo,Ellison .... @2.00

VICKY VALENTINE
Renegade, 1985
1 thru 4 .... @2.00

VICTIM
Silver Wolf, 1987
1 & 2 .... @2.00

VICTIMS
Eternity, 1988
1 thru 5 .... @2.00

VIDEO CLASSICS
Eternity
1 Mighty Mouse 3.50
2 Mighty Mouse 3.50

VIDEO GIRL AI
Viz Communications, 1999
TPB by Masakazu Katsura ... 15.95
TPB Vol. 2 Mix Down 15.95
TPB Vol. 3 Recall 15.95
TPB Vol. 4 Offline 15.95
TPB Vol. 5 .... 15.95
TPB Vol. 6 Cutting Room ... 12.95

VIETNAM JOURNAL
Apple Comics, 1987
1 .... 5.00
1a 2nd printing 3.00
2 .... 3.00
3 thru 5 .... @3.00
6 thru 13 .... @3.00
14 thru 16 .... @3.00

Comics Values Annual

VIGIL
Duality Press, 1997
Baby Steps 2.95
Dirt, by A.Laudermilk & M.Iverson .. 2.95
Slash and Burn, Bloodline story ... 2.95
The Vegas Shuffle, Bloodline story . 2.95
Desertion 2.95
Outreach 2.95
Penetration 2.95
Daddy's Little Girl, final issue ... 2.95
TPB Vol. 1, rep. #1–#5 .... 19.95

VIGIL: DESERT FOXES
Millennium, 1995
1 & 2 F:Grace Kimble ...... @3.95

VIGIL: ERUPTION
Millennium, 1996
1 (of 2) vampire hunters 3.95
2 (of 2) 3.95

VIGIL: FALL FROM GRACE
Innovation, 1992
1 'State of Grace' 2.75
2 The Graceland Hunt 2.50

VIGIL: SCATTER SHOTS
Duality Press, 1997
1 by A.Laudermilk & M.Iverson ... 3.95
2 .... 3.95

VINSON WATSON'S RAGE
Trinity Visuals
1 I:Rena Helen 3.00

VINSON WATSON'S SWEET CHILDE
Advantage Graphics
Vol. 2
1 F:Spyder 2.00

VIRGIN: SLUMBER
Entity, 1997
1 BMs 2.75
1 deluxe 3.50

VIRGIN: SURROUNDED
Entity, 1997
1 BMs 2.75
1 deluxe 3.50

VIRGIN: TILL DEATH DO US PART
Entity, 1997
1 BMs 2.75
1 deluxe 3.50

VISIONS
Vision Publication, 1979–83
1 I:Flaming Carrot 50.00
2 Flaming Carrot 30.00
3 Flaming Carrot 15.00
4 Flaming Carrot 25.00

VISUAL ASSAULT OMNIBUS
Visual Assault Comics, 1995
1 thru 4 O:Dimensioner 3.00

VIXEN
Meteor Comics
1 & 2 Battle of the Vixens . . . . . . @2.95

VORTEX
Hall of Heroes, 1993
1 . . . . 15.00
1a commemorative 5.00
2 . . . . 10.00
3 thru 5 . . . . @3.50
6 V:The Reverend 3.00

VORTEX SPECIAL: CYBERSIN
Avatar Press, 1997
1 by Matt Martin & Bil Maus 3.00
1b velvet cover 15.00
1c signed 10.00
1d Snowman spec. (c) 5.00

VORTEX: DR. KILBOURN
Entity, 1997
1 by Matt Martin 3.00
1a deluxe 3.50

VORTEX: INTO THE DARK
Entity, 1997
1 . . . . 3.00
1 deluxe 3.50

VOX
Apple, 1989
1 JBy(c) 2.00
2 and 3 . . . . @2.00
4 and 5 . . . . @2.15

WABBIT WAMPAGE
Amazing Comics, 1987
1 . . . . 2.00

WAFFEN SS
New England Comics, 2000
1 by Ron Ledwell 3.50
2 thru 7 . . . . @3.50

WAITING PLACE, THE
Slave Labor, 1997
5 . . . . 3.00
6 . . . . 3.00
VOL. 2, 2000
1 . . . . 3.00
2 . . . . 3.00
3 A Sporting Chance 3.00
4 I Care 3.00
5 The Road Home 3.00
6 . . . . 3.00
7 . . . . 3.00
8 Under a Frozen Sky 3.00
9 Intrusions, pt.1 . . . . 3.00
10 Intrusions, pt.2 . . . . 3.00
11 Intrusions, pt.3 . . . . 3.00
TPB Vol. 1 . . . . 15.95
TPB Vol. 2 thru Vol. 3 . . . . @15.95

WALKING DEAD
Aircel
1 thru 4 . . . . @2.25
Zombie Spec. 1 . . . . 2.25

WALK THROUGH OCTOBER
Caliber
1 I:Mr. Balloon 2.95
2 . . . . 2.95
3 All Hallow's Eve 2.95

WALT THE WILDCAT
Motion Comics, 1995
1 I:Walt the Wildcat 2.50

WANDERING STAR
Pen & Ink, 1993
1 I:Casandra Andrews 12.00
1a 2nd & 3rd printing 3.00
2 . . . . 8.00
3 . . . . 5.00
4 . . . . 4.00
5 . . . . 4.00
6 . . . . 3.00
7 . . . . 3.00
8 and 9 F:Casandra Andrews 3.00
10 R:Mekron 3.00
11 . . . . 3.00
Sirius, 1995–97
12 thru 20 TWo . . . . @2.50
21 TWo, final issue 2.50
TPB Vol. 1 rep. #1–#7 . . . . 14.95
TPB Vol. 2 . . . . 14.95
TPB Vol. 3 168-pg 14.95

WANDERLUST
Antarctic Press, 2000
1 (of 3) by Bryant Shiu 2.50
2 . . . . 2.50
3 conclusion 2.50

WARCAT
Alliance Comics
1 thru 7 A:Ebonia 2.50

WARD: A BULLET SERIES
Liar Comics
1 Foresight,pt.1 . . . . 2.50
2 Foresight,pt.2 . . . . 2.50
3 Foresight,pt.3 . . . . 2.50

WARLOCK 5
Aircel, 1986
1 . . . . 6.00
2 . . . . 5.00
3 . . . . 6.00
4 . . . . 5.00
5 . . . . 5.00
6 thru 11 . . . . @4.00
12 . . . . 3.50
13 . . . . 3.50
14 thru 16 . . . . @3.00
17 . . . . 3.00
18 . . . . 3.00
19 thru 22 . . . . @3.00
Book 2 #1 thru #7 . . . . @3.00

WARLOCK 5
Sirius, 1997
1 (of 4) by Barry Blair & Colin Chan 2.50
2 . . . . 2.50
3 . . . . 2.50
4 finale 2.50

WARLOCKS
Aircel, 1988
1 thru 3 . . . . @2.00
4 thru 12 . . . . @2.00
Spec #1 Rep 2.25

WAR OF THE WORLDS
Eternity
1 TV tie-in 2.50
2 thru 6 . . . . @2.50

WAR OF THE WORLDS, THE
Caliber `New Worlds', 1996
1 from H.G. Wells 3.00
1a signed 3.00
2 war for Kansas City 3.00
3 Haven & The Hellweed 3.00
4 . . . . 3.00

Vox #1
© Apple

War of the Worlds #1
© Caliber

All comics prices listed are for *Near Mint* condition.

War–Warriors — B & W PUB.

War of the Worlds #4
© Caliber

5 . . . . 3.00
TPB rep. #1–#5 . . . . 14.95

WAR OF THE WORLDS: THE MEMPHIS FRONT
Arrow Comics, 1998
1 (of 5) by Randy Zimmerman & Richard Gulick 2.95
2 thru 5 . . . . @2.95
Spec.#1 signed & numbered. 2.95

WARREN ELLIS' ATMOSPHERICS
Avatar Press, 2002
GN 5.95

WARREN ELLIS' BAD SIGNAL
Avatar Press 2002
GN 6.95
GN Vol. 2 . . . . 6.95

WARREN ELLIS' BAD WORLD
Avatar Press, 2001
1 (of 3) 3.50
2 . . . . 3.50
3 . . . . 3.50
1a thru 3a wraparound (c) . . . . . @3.95
TPB series rep. 10.95

WARREN ELLIS' DARK BLUE
Avatar Press, 2000
GN 72-pg. 8.95
TPB Scriptbook 6.95

WARREN ELLIS' SCARS
Avatar Press, 2002
Sampler 0.75
1 (of 6) 3.50
1 wraparound (c) 3.95
2 thru 6 . . . . @3.50
2a–6a wraparound (c) 3.95

WARREN ELLIS' STRANGE KILLINGS
Avavar Press, 2002
1 (of 3) WEI 3.50
1a wraparound (c) 3.95
2 . . . . 3.50
2a wraparound (c) 3.95
3 . . . . 3.50
3a wraparound (c) 3.50
TPB 9.95

WARREN ELLIS' STRANGE KILLINGS: THE BODY ORCHARD
Avavar Press, 2002
1 (of 6) WEI 3.50
1a wraparound (c) 3.95
2 thru 6 WEI . . . . @3.50
2a thru 6a wraparound (c) . . . . . @3.95
TPB Body Orchard 16.95

WARREN ELLIS' STRANGE KILLINGS: STRONG MEDICINE
Avatar Press 2003
1 . . . . 3.50
2 thru 3 . . . . @3.50
1a thru 3a wraparound (c) . . . . . @3.95

WARREN ELLIS' STRANGE KISS
Avatar Press, 1999
1 . . . . 3.00
1a 3.95
1b signed 29.95
2 . . . . 2.00
2a wraparound (c) 3.95
3 . . . . 3.00
3a wraparound (c) 3.95
TPB 8.95

WARREN ELLIS' STRANGER KISSES
Avatar Press, 2000
1 (of 3) 3.00
1a leather signed 24.95
2 . . . . 3.00
3 . . . . 3.00
1a thru 3a wraparound (c) . . . . . @3.95
TPB series rep. 9.95

WARRIOR NUN AREALA: BOOKS OF PERIL
Antarctic Press, 2001
1 (of 4) 3.00
2 The Book of Sharate. 3.00
3 Book of Xitan 3.00
4 Devil's Deal 3.00
5 Scepter of the Crescent Moon . . 3.00
6 Scepter of the Crescent Moon . . 3.00
7 Scepter of the Crescent Moon . . 3.00
8 The Good Son, pt.1 . . . . 3.00
9 The Good Son, pt.2 . . . . 3.00
10 The Good Son, pt.3 . . . . 3.00
11 Dissension, pt.1 . . . . 3.00
12 Dissension, pt.2 . . . . 3.00
13 Dissension, pt.3 . . . . 3.00
14 Curse of Looming Plague,pt.1 . 3.50
15 Curse of Looming Plague,pt.2 . 3.50
16 Curse of Looming Plague,pt.3 . 3.50
17 Soul Reaper 3.50
18 Soul Reaper, pt.2 . . . . 3.50
19 Soul Reaper, pt.3 . . . . 3.50
20 thru 22 . . . . @3.50
Spec. Swimsuit Special (2002) . . . 3.95

WARRIOR NUN AREALA: DANGEROUS GAME
Antarctic Press, 2001
1 (of 3) 3.00
2 . . . . 3.00
3 . . . . 3.00

WARRIOR NUN AREALA: GHOSTS OF THE PAST
Antarctic Press, 2001
1 (of 4) 3.00
2 thru 4 . . . . @3.00

WARRIOR NUN AREALA/RAZOR: DARK PROPHECY
London Night, 1999
1 16-pg. 2.50
2 16-pg. 2.50
Antarctic Press
3 . . . . 2.50
4 . . . . 2.50

WARRIOR NUN AREALA: THE MANGA
Antarctic Press, 2000
1-shot 3.00

WARRIOR NUN BRIGANTIA
Antarctic Press, 2000
1 V:Fata Morgana 3.00
2 Sister Anna. 3.00
3 . . . . 3.00

WARRIOR NUN: BLACK AND WHITE
Antarctic Press, 1997
1 . . . . 3.00
2 . . . . 3.00
3 . . . . 3.00
4 Winter Jade, pt.1 F:Ninja Nun . . . 3.00
5 Winter Jade, pt.2 . . . . 3.00
6 Winter Jade, pt.3 . . . . 3.00
7 . . . . 3.00
8 . . . . 3.00
9 Return of the Redeemers 3.00
10 Return of Lillith 3.00
11 The Redeemers, cont. 3.00
12 The Redeemers, cont. 3.00
13 I:Sister Trinity. 3.00
14 Redeemers saga again 3.00
15 F:Sister Trinity 3.00
16 F:Sister Trinity 3.00
17 Showdown. 3.00
18 Reaction 3.00
19 Carnivale. 3.00
20 Twilight Earth. 3.00
21 Lost Souls of Blue Moon Mountain 2.50
Spec. Warrior Nun Areala/Razor: Revenge 3.00
Spec.A Revenge, deluxe. 6.00

WARRIORS
1 . . . . 2.50
2 thru 7 . . . . @2.00

All comics prices listed are for Near Mint condition.

WARZONE
Entity, 1995
1 I:Bella & Supra 2.95
2 F:Bladeback, Alloy, Granite 2.95
3 F:Bladeback 2.95

WEATHER WOMAN
CPM Manga, 2000
1 signed & limited 19.95
4 thru 8 . . . . @2.95

WEBWITCH
Avatar Press, 1997
0 by Raff Ienco 3.00
1 (of 2) signed 10.00
1 (of 2) 3.00
2 (of 2) 3.00
Boxed Set, all rare editions 35.00

WEBWITCH: PRELUDE TO WAR
Avatar Press, 1998
1 by Raff Jenco 3.00
1b Leather cover 30.00

WEBWITCH: WAR
Avatar Press, 1998
1 (of 2) by Bill Maus 3.00
1b Leather cover 30.00
2 conclusion 3.00

WEDDING PEACH
Viz Communications 2003
TPB Vol. 1 . . . . 9.95
TPB Vol. 2 thru Vol. 3 . . . . @9.95

WEIRDFALL
Antarctic Press, 1995
1 I:Weirdfall 2.75
2 O:Weirdfall 2.75
3 . . . . 2.75

WEIRDSVILLE
Blindwolf Studios, 1997
1 . . . . 3.50
1 2nd printing 2.95
2 . . . . 3.50
2 2nd printing 2.95
3 . . . . 3.50
3 2nd printing 2.95
4 . . . . 3.50
5 . . . . 3.00
6 The Usual Weirdoes, concl. 3.00
7 . . . . 3.00
8 An American Werewolf in
  Weirdsville, pt.1 (of 2). 3.00
9 An American Werewolf in
  Weirdsville, pt.2 . . . . 3.00
10 . . . . 3.00

WEIRDSVILLE/CRYBABY: HEY YOU TWO
Blindwolf Studios, 1999
1 . . . . 3.00

WEREWOLF
Blackthorne, 1988–89
1 TV tie-in 2.00
2 thru 7 . . . . @2.00

WHAT IS THE FACE?
A.C.E. Comics, 1986
1 SD/FMc,I:New Face 2.00
2 SD/FMc 2.00
3 SD 2.00

WHISPERS & SHADOWS
Oasis
1 8 1/2 x 11 . . . . 2.00
1a Regular size 2.00
2 8 1/2 x 11 . . . . 2.00
3 8 1/2 x 11 . . . . 2.00
4 thru 9 . . . . @2.00

WHITE DEVIL
Eternity, 1991
1 thru 6 adult . . . . @2.50

WHITE ORCHID, THE
Atlantis
1 (of 6) 2.95
2 . . . . 2.95
3 . . . . 2.95
4 . . . . 3.50
5 `Death Trap,' pt.1 . . . . 2.95
6 The Price of Vengeance 3.50

Whiteout #3
© Oni Press

WHITEOUT
Oni Press, 1998
1 (of 4) by Greg Rucka &
  Steve Leiber 3.00
2 . . . . 3.00
3 . . . . 3.00
4 conclusion 3.00
TPB 128-pg. 10.95

WHITEOUT: MELT
Oni Press, 1999
1 (of 4) by Greg Rucka &
  Steve Lieber 3.00
2 . . . . 3.00
3 . . . . 3.00
4 concl. 3.00
TPB 11.95

WHITE RAVEN
Visionary Publications
1 Government Intrigue 2.95

2 . . . . 2.95
3 Mystery Man Gets Wheels 2.95
4 Facility 2.95
5 V:Douglas. 2.95
6 . . . . 2.95
7 . . . . 2.95

WHITLEY STRIEBER'S BEYOND COMMUNION
Caliber, 1997
1 UFO Odyssey. 2.95
1 signed 2.95
1 special edition, signed
  by Strieber 6.95
1a 2nd printing 2.95
2 . . . . 2.95
3 . . . . 2.95
4 . . . . 2.95

WICKED
Millennium, 1994
1 thru 4 . . . . @2.50

WICKED: THE RECKONING
Millennium
1 R:Wicked 2.95
2 F:Rachel Blackstone. 2.95

WIDOW
Ground Zero, 1996
Cinegraphic Spec.#1: Daughter
  of Darkness 4.00

WIDOW/LUXURA: BLOOD LUST
Ground Zero, 1996
Alpha x-over, pt.1 . . . . 3.50
see Luxura/Widow for pt. 2

WIDOW: BOUND BY BLOOD
Ground Zero, 1996
1 thru 5 by Mike Wolfer . . . . @3.50

WIDOW: PROGENY
Ground Zero, 1997
1 by Mike Wolfer & Karl Moline . . . 3.00
2 (of 3) 3.00
3 concl. 3.00

WIDOW: THE COMPLETE WORKS
Ground Zero, 1996
Vol.1 Flesh and Blood 10.95
Vol.1 deluxe 16.95
Vol.2 Kill Me Again 10.95
Vol.2 deluxe 16.95
Vol.3 Metal Gypsies 10.95
Vol.3 deluxe 16.95

WIDOW
Avatar Press, 1997
0 by Mike Wolfer 3.95
0b Black leather cover 25.00
0 signed 10.00

WILD 7
Comicsone.com, 2001
GN #1 by Mikiya Mochizuki, 200-pg. 9.95
GN #2 185-pg. 9.95
GN #3 257-pg. 9.95
GN #4 256-pg. 9.95
GN #5 200-pg. 9.95
GN #6 200-pg. 9.95
GN #7 185-pg. 9.95

WILD THINGZ
ABC Comics, 1998
0 RCI & Armando Huerta 3.00
0a painted cover 6.00
0b Fan edition 5.95
0c Summer edition 5.95
0d Leather cover, original art . . . 55.00
1 (of 2) RCI 3.00
1b Leather cover 30.00
1c virgin cover 3.00
1d gold cover 5.95
1e Platinum cover 5.95

Widow The Origin #1
© Avatar

WIDOW: THE ORIGIN
Avatar Press, 1997
1 (of 3) by Mike Wolfer 3.95
1a leather cover 25.00
2 (of 3) 3.00

WILLOW
Angel Entertainment, 1996
0 commemorative edition. 2.95
1 . . . . 2.95
1 black magic foil edition 5.95
2 . . . . 2.95
2 gold edition 8.00
2 nude platinum cover 15.00

WILD, THE
1 and 2 . . . . @2.00
3 thru 7 . . . . @2.00

WIND BLADE
1 Elford 1st Blair 40.00

WILD ACT
Tokyopop Press 2003
GN Vol. 1 (of 13) 10.00
GN Vol. 2 thru Vol. 3 . . . . @10.00

WINGS
A-List Comics, 1997
1 rep. of golden age 2.50
2 . . . . 2.95
3 . . . . 2.95
4 . . . . 2.95
5 . . . . 2.95

WILDFLOWER
Sirius/Dog Star, 1998
1 by Billy Martinez 2.50
2 thru 6 . . . . @2.50
Neko Press, 2002
TPB Vol.1 Beginnings, rep.from1997 . . . 15.00

WINDRAVEN
Hero Graphics/Blue Comet
1 The Healing,(see Rough Raiders) 2.95

WISH
Tokyopop Press, 2002
GN Vol. 1 by Clamp 10.00
GN Vol. 2 . . . . 10.00
GN Vol. 3 . . . . 10.00

WILDFLOWER: TRIBAL SCREAMS
Neko Press, 2002
1 Martinez (c) 3.00
1a Dark One (c) 5.00
2 thru 4 . . . . @3.00
Spec. Wildflower Y2K, 16-pg. 10.00

WITCH
Amaze Ink/Slave Labor Graphics, 2001
1 by Lorna Miller 2.95
2 . . . . 2.95
3 thru 4 . . . . @2.95
TPB Vol. 1 . . . . 11.95

WILD KNIGHTS
Eternity, 1988
1 thru 10 . . . . @2.00
Shattered Earth Chron. #1 . . . . . . 2.00

WIZARD OF TIME
David House, 1986
1 . . . . 2.00
1a 2nd printing(blue) 2.00
2 and 3 . . . . @2.00

WILDLIFE
Antarctic, 1993
1 thru 12 . . . . @2.75

WIZARDS OF THE LAST RESORT
Blackthorne, 1987
1 . . . . 2.50

WILDMAN
Miller
1 and 2 . . . . @2.00
3 thru 6 . . . . @2.00

WOLFF & BYRD, COUNSELORS OF THE MACABRE
Exhibit A, 1994
1 . . . . 6.00
2 thru 4 . . . . @3.50
5 thru 11 . . . . @2.50
12 thru 16 BLs . . . . @2.50
17 thru 23 . . . . @2.50
TPB Casefiles Vol. I rep. #1–#4,
 3rd printing 9.95
TPB Casefiles Vol. 2 rep.#5–#8 . . . 9.95
TPB Casefiles Vol.III rep.#9–#12. . 10.95
TPB Casefiles Vol.IV rep.#13–#16 10.95
TPB Supernatural Law 7.95
TPB Supernatural Law rep. 7.95
TPB Fright Court rep. 9.95
Spec.#1 Greatest Writs (1997) BLs. 2.95
Spec. #1 Secretary Mavis (1998) . . 2.95
Spec. #2 Secretary Mavis (1999) . . 2.95
Becomes:

SUPERNATURAL LAW
Exhibit A Press, 2000
24 . . . . 2.50
25 The end of 1999 . . . . 2.50
26 Black Market Souls 2.50
27 Creatures of the Night,
 with lawyers 2.50
28 While the City Doesn't Sleep . . 2.50
29 thru 31 . . . . @2.50
32 . . . . 2.95
33 thru 35 . . . . @2.50
36 thru 39 . . . . @2.95
TPB Sonofawitch, rep. 14.95

WORDSMITH
Renegade, 1985
1 . . . . 3.00
2 thru 6 . . . . @2.00
7 thru 12 . . . . @2.00
Series 2, Caliber, 1996
1 thru 6 . . . . @3.00

WORLD HARDBALL LEAGUE
Titus Press, 1994
1 F:Big Bat 2.95
2 F:Big Bat 2.95
3 Mount Evrest 2.95
4 Juan Hernandez 2.95

WORLD OF ROBOTECH
Academy Comics, 1995
GN Tales of Planets 12.95

WORLD OF WOOD
Eclipse, 1986
1 thru 4 see color
5 Flying Saucers 2.00

WORLDS OF FANTASY
Newcomers Publishing, 1995
1 The Jenn Chronicles 2.95

WORLDS OF H.P. LOVECRAFT
Caliber Tome Press, 1997
1-shot The Alchemist 2.95
1-shot The Tomb 2.95
1-shot The Lurking Fear 2.95
1-shot Beyond the Walls of Sleep . 2.95

WORLD WAR 2
New England Comics, 2001
- 3 Eastern Front, pt.2 .... 3.50
- 4 Falaise Pocket 3.50
- 5 D-Day 3.50
- 6 Tarawa 3.50
- 7 Afrika Korps 3.50
- 8 Midway 3.50

WORLD WAR 2: STALINGRAD
New England Comics, 2000
- 1 by Ron Ledwell 3.50
- 2 .... 3.50

WOUNDED MAN
Comicsone.com, 2001
- GN #1 400-pg. by R. Ikegami 14.95
- GN #2 400-pg. 14.95
- GN #3 448-pg. 14.95
- GN #4 thru #9 200-pg. .... @9.95

WRETCH, THE
Caliber, 1996
- 1 PhH 2.95
- 2 PhH 2.95

Amaze Ink, 1997
- 3 PhH 2.95
- 4 PhH 2.95
- 5 PhH & Jim Woodyard 2.95
- 6 PhH & Bruce McCorkindale ... 2.95
- 7 PhH 2.95

WU WEI
Animus, 1995
- 1 'Debaser' 2.50
- 2 Blind Whisper 2.50
- 3 .... 2.50
- 4 .... 2.50
- 5 'Testament' pt.5 .... 2.50
- 6 by Oscar Stern 2.50
- 7 Explicador 2.95
- 8 Dead Skin 2.95
- 9 Apotheosis or Bang You're Dead. 2.95

WW2
New England Comics 2003
- 1-shot Snipers 3.95
- 1-shot War in the Air 3.95
- 1-shot Mercenaries 3.95
- 1-shot U-Boats 3.95

WYRD: THE RELUCTANT WARRIOR
Amaze Ink, 1999
- 1 (of 6) JSn 2.95
- 2 .... 2.95
- 3 Telemarketing Horrors 2.95
- 4 Maxi-Man 2.95
- 5 .... 2.95
- 6 .... 2.95
- TPB JSn, 132-pg. 16.95

XANADU
Thoughts & Images, 1988
- 1 thru 5 .... @2.00

XENON
Eclipse, 1987
- 1 .... 3.00
- 2 thru 23 .... @2.25

XENO'S ARROW
Cup O' Tea Studios, 1999
- 1 by Greg Beettam 2.50
- 2 thru 10 .... @2.50

Radio Comix, 2001
Book 2
- 1 (of 6) 2.95
- 2 and 3 .... @2.95
- 4 and 5 .... @3.00

XENOZOIC TALES
Kitchen Sink, 1986
- 1 by Mark Schultz 10.00
- 1a Reprint 2.50
- 2 .... 5.00
- 2a Reprint 2.50
- 3 .... 7.00
- 4 .... 6.00
- 5 thru 7 .... @4.00
- 8 thru 13 .... @3.00
- 14 MSh 3.00

Xenozoic Tales #3
© Kitchen Sink

X-BABES VS. JUSTICE BABES
Personality
- 1 Spoof/parody 2.95

X-CONS
Parody Press
- 1 X-Men satire,flip cover 2.50

X-DAY
Tokyopop Press 2003
- GN Vol. 1 thru Vol. 2 .... @10.00

XENO'S ARROW
Cup O' Tea Studios, 1999
- 1 by Greg Beettam 2.50
- 2 thru 10 .... @2.50

Radio Comix, 2001
Book 2
- 6 .... 3.00

X-FARCE
Eclipse, 1992
- One-Shot X-Force parody 3.00

X-FLIES BUG HUNT
Twist and Shout, 1997
- 1 Vampires 2.95
- 2 Monsters 2.95
- 3 Aliens 2.95
- 4 The Truth 2.95
- Conspiracy 2.95
- Spec. #1 Flies in Black 2.95

XIOLA
Zion Comics
- 1 thru 3 F:Kantasia .... @2.00
- 4 Visitor 2.00

XMEN
- 1 Parody 2.00

X-1999
Viz
- 1 I:Kamir Shiro 2.75
- 2 thru 5 F:Princess Hitane ... @2.75
- 6 Battle for X-1999 .... 2.75
- TPB Vol. 3 Serenade 15.95
- TPB Vol. 4 Intermezzo 15.95
- TPB Vol. 6 Duet 15.95
- TPB Vol. 7 Rhapsody 15.95
- TPB Vol. 8 Crescendo (2002) .. 15.95
- TPB Vol. 9 Requiem 15.95
- TPB Vol. 10 Fugue 9.95
- TPB Vol. 11 Interlude 9.95
- TPB Vol. 12 Movement 9.95

X-THIEVES
- 1 .... 3.00
- 2 .... 2.00
- 3 .... 2.00

YAHOO
Fantagraphics, 1988
- 1 thru 4 .... @2.00

YAKUZA
Eternity, 1987
- 1 thru 5 .... @2.00

YAWN
Parody Press
- 1 Spawn parody 2.50
Enigma
- 1 Spawn parody rep.? 2.75

YELLOW CABALLERO
Viz Communications, 2001
- 1 thru 4 Pikachu's New Partner . @2.95

YOUNG DRACULA: PRAYER OF THE VAMPIRE
Boneyard Press, 1997
- 1 (of 5) sequel to Young Dracula:
  Diary of a Vampire 2.95
- 2 Empire of Madness, pt.2 .... 2.95
- 3 Children of Madness 2.95
- 4 Madness Prime 2.95
- 5 V:Cartiphilus 3.95

YOUNG MASTERS
New Comics, 1987
1 thru 10 ....@2.00

YU-GI-OH!
Viz Communications 2003
TPB Vol. 1 The Millennium Puzzle . 7.95
TPB Vol. 2 thru Vol. 3 ....@7.95

YUYU HAKUSHO
Viz Communications 2003
TPB Vol. 1 Goodbye Material World 7.95
TPB Vol. 2 Lonesome Ghosts.....7.95

Z
Keystone Graphics, 1994
1 ....2.75
2 House of Windsor-Yakonaral ...2.75
3 House of Windsor-Yakonaral II ...2.75

ZELL THE SWORDDANCER
Thoughts & Images, 1986
1 Steve Gallacci 5.50
2 and 3 ....@2.00

ZEN ILLUSTRATED NOVELLA
Entity
1 thru 4 R:Bruce Lewis........@2.95
5 Immortal Combat 2.95
6 Bubble Economy 2.95
7 Zen City....................2.95
8 V:Assassins 2.95

ZEN, INTER-GALACTIC NINJA
Zen, 1987
1 ....15.00
2 ....9.00
3 thru 9 ....@9.00
X-mas Spec #1,V:Black Hole Bob..3.00
[2nd Series]
1 'Down to Earth' 3.00
2 RA, A:Jeremy Baker.........3.00
2a polybagged, limited.........5.00
3 thru 5 ....@3.00
[3rd Series]
0 ....3.00
1 thru 3 A:Niro ....@3.00
Sourcebook #1................3.50

ZEN INTERGALACTIC NINJA: STARQUEST
Entity
1 thru 6 V:Nolan the Destroyer..@3.00
7 V:Dimensional 3.00
8 thru 9 I:New Team..........@3.00
10 In Deep Space.............3.00
11 Dimensional Terrorists 3.00
TPB Rep. #1-#4 ....@6.95

ZEN INTERGALACTIC NINJA VS. MICHEAL JACK-ZEN
Entity
1 Cameos Galore 2.95

ZENISMS WIT AND WISDOMS
Entity
1 R:Bruce Lewis 2.95

ZEN: MISTRESS OF CHAOS
1 ....2.95

ZENITH: PHASE II
Fleetway
1 GMo(s),SY,Rep.2000 AD 2.00

ZERO ZERO
Fantagraphics, 1995
1 thru 7 ....@5.00
8 ....6.00
9 thru 15 ....@5.00
16 ....6.00
17 thru 22 ....@5.00
23 F:'Tired'..................5.00
24 F:Smilin' Ed 4.00
25 ....4.00
26 final issue, 56-pg. 5.00
27 really final 64-pg.............5.00

ZETRAMAN
Antarctic, 1991
1 thru 3 ....@2.00
[Vol. 2], 1992
1 and 2 ....@2.75

ZETRAMAN: REVIVAL
Antarctic Press, 1993
1 thru 3 ....@2.75

ZILLION
Eternity, 1993
1 thru 4 ....@2.50

ZODIAC P.I.
Tokyopop Press 2003
GN Vol. 1 ....10.00
GN Vol. 2 thru Vol. 4 ....@10.00

ZOIDS
Viz Communications, 2002
1 by Michiro Ueyama..........6.00
2 thru 14 ....@6.00
TPB New Century..............9.95

ZOLASTRAYA AND THE BARD
Twilight Twins, 1987
1 thru 5 ....@2.00

Zoot #5
© Fantagraphics

ZOMBIE WAR: EARTH MUST BE DESTROYED
Fantaco, 1993
1 thru 3 Kevin Eastman ....@3.95

ZONE CONTINUUM
Caliber
1 Master of the Waves..........2.95
2 ....2.95

ZOOT!
Fantagraphics, 1993
1 thru 5 ....@2.50

ZOT!
Eclipse, 1987
(#1-#10 See: Color)
11 New Series 3.00
12 thru 15 ....@3.00
16 A:De-Evolutionaries 3.00
17 thru 36 ....@3.00
Kitchen Sink
Book Two TPB rep. #11–#15, #17–#18..............19.95
Book Two TPB signed and numbered................34.95
Book Three TPB rep. #16, #21–#27...............19.95
Book Four TPB The Earth Stories................19.95

ZU
Mu Press, 1995
1 thru 11 ....@2.95
12 'The Monkey Tales' 2.95
13 ....2.95
14 ....2.95
15 'Curse of the Re-Possessed'...2.95
16 thru 19..................@2.95
20 final issue 2.95

Classics Illustrated

[Issued As Classic Comics]
001-THE THREE MUSKETEERS
By Alexandre Dumas

10/41 (—) MKd(a&c),
 Original,10¢ (c) Price 6,500.00
05/43 (10) MKd(a&c),
 No(c)Price; rep 400.00
11/43 (15) MKd(a&c),Long
 Island Independent Ed; 250.00
6/44 (18/20) MKd(a&c),
 Sunrise Times Edition;rep ... 200.00
7/44 (21) MKd(a&c),Richmond
 Courrier Edition;rep 175.00
6/46 (28) MKd(a&c),rep 150.00
4/47 (36) MKd(a&c),
 New ClLogo;rep 75.00
6/49 (60) MKd(a&c),Cl Logo;rep .. 50.00
10/49 (64) MKd(a&c),Cl Logo;rep . 50.00
12/50 (78) MKd(a&c),15¢(c)
 Price; Cl Logo;rep 30.00
03/52 (93) MKd(a&c),
 Cl Logo;rep 30.00
11/53 (114) Cl Logo;rep 25.00
09/56 (134) MKd(a&c),New
 P(c),Cl Logo,64 pgs;rep 30.00
03/58 (143) MKd(a&c),P(c),
 Cl Logo,64 pgs;rep 25.00
05/59 (150) GE&RC New Art,
 P(c),ClLogo;rep 25.00
03/61 (149) GE&RC,P(c),
 Cl Logo;rep 18.00
62-63 (167) GE&RC,P(c),
 Cl Logo;rep 18.00
04/64 (167) GE&RC,P(c),
 Cl Logo;rep 18.00
01/65 (167) GE&RC,P(c),
 Cl Logo;rep 18.00
03/66 (167) GE&RC,P(c),
 Cl Logo;rep 18.00
11/67 (166) GE&RC,P(c),
 Cl Logo;rep 18.00
Sp/69 (166) GE&RC,P(c),25¢(c)
 Price,ClLogo, Rigid(c);rep. ... 18.00

CI #1, The Three Musketeers
© Gilberton Publications

Sp/71 (169) GE&RC,P(c),
 Cl Logo,Rigid(c);rep 18.00

002-IVANHOE
By Sir Walter Scott

1941 (—) EA,MKd(c),Original . 3,000.00
05/43 (1) EA,MKd(c),word "Presents"
 Removed From(c);rep. 350.00
11/43 (15) EA,MKd(c),Long Island
 Independent Edition;rep 250.00
06/44 (18/20) EA,MKd(c),Sunrise
 Times Edition;rep 200.00
07/44 (21) EA,MKd(c),Richmond
 Courrier Edition;rep 175.00
06/46 (28) EA,MKd(c),rep 150.00
07/47 (36) EA,MKd(c),New
 Cl Logo; rep 100.00
06/49 (60) EA,MKd(c),Cl Logo;rep 50.00
10/49 (64) EA,MKd(c),Cl Logo;rep 40.00
12/50 (78) EA,MKd(c),15¢(c)
 Price; Cl Logo;rep 30.00
11/51 (89) EA,MKd(c),Cl Logo;rep 25.00
04/53 (106) EA,MKd(c),Cl
 Logo;rep 20.00
07/54 (121) EA,MKd(c),Cl
 Logo;rep 30.00
01/57 (136) NN New Art,New
 P(c),Cl Logo;rep 30.00
01/58 (142) NN,P(c),Cl Logo;rep. 18.00
11/59 (153) NN,P(c),Cl Logo;rep. 18.00
03/61 (149) NN,P(c),Cl Logo;rep. 15.00
62-63 (167) NN,P(c),Cl Logo;rep. 15.00
05/64 (167) NN,P(c),Cl Logo;rep. 15.00
01/65 (167) NN,P(c),Cl Logo;rep. 15.00
03/66 (167) NN,P(c),Cl Logo;rep. 15.00
09/67 (166) NN,P(c),Cl Logo;rep. 15.00
1968 (166) NN,P(c),Cl Logo;rep . 15.00
Wr/69 (169) NN,P(c),Cl
 Logo Rigid(c);rep 15.00
Wr/71 (169) NN,P(c),Cl
 Logo,Rigid(c);rep 15.00

003-THE COUNT OF MONTE CRISTO
By Alexandre Dumas

03/42 (—) ASm(a&c),Orig. 2,000.00
05/43 (10) ASm(a&c);rep 300.00
11/43 (15) ASm(a&c),Long Island
 Independent Edition;rep 250.00
06/44 (18/20) ASm(a&c),
 Sunrise Times Edition;rep ... 225.00
06/44 (20) ASm(a&c),Sunrise
 Times Edition;rep 200.00
07/44 (21) ASm(a&c),Richmond
 Courrier Edition;rep 175.00
06/46 (28) ASm(a&c);rep 150.00
04/47 (36) ASm(a&c),New
 Cl Logo; rep 75.00
06/49 (60) ASm(a&c),Cl
 Logo;rep 60.00
08/49 (62) ASm(a&c),Cl
 Logo;rep 75.00
05/50 (71) ASm(a&c),Cl
 Logo;rep 50.00
09/51 (87) ASm(a&c),15¢(c)
 Price, Cl Logo;rep 30.00
11/53 (113) ASm(a&c),
 Cl Logo; rep 25.00
11/56 (—) LC New Art,New
 P(c), Cl Logo;rep 25.00
03/58 (135) LC,P(c),Cl Logo;rep. 18.00
11/59 (153) LC,P(c),Cl Logo;rep. 18.00

03/61 (161) LC,P(c),Cl Logo;rep . 18.00
62/63 (167) LC,P(c),Cl Logo;rep . 15.00
07/64 (167) LC,P(c),Cl Logo;rep . 15.00
07/65 (167) LC,P(c),Cl Logo;rep . 15.00
07/66 (167) LC,P(c),Cl Logo;rep . 15.00
1968 (166) LC,P(c),25¢(c)
 Price, Cl Logo;rep 15.00
Wn/69 (169) LC,P(c),Cl Logo,
 Rigid(c);rep 15.00

004-THE LAST OF THE MOHICANS
By James Fenimore Cooper

08/42 (—) RR(a&c),Original .. 1,500.00
06/43 (12) RR(a&c),Price
 Balloon Deleted;rep 300.00
11/43 (15) RR(a&c),Long Island
 Independent Edition;rep 250.00
06/44 (20) RR(a&c),Long Island
 Independent Edition;rep 225.00
07/44 (21) RR(a&c),Queens
 Home News Edition;rep 200.00
06/46 (28) RR(a&c);rep. 150.00
04/47 (36) RR(a&c),New
 Cl Logo; rep 75.00
06/49 (60) RR(a&c),Cl Logo;rep . 50.00
10/49 (64) RR(a&c),Cl Logo;rep . 35.00
12/50 (78) RR(a&c),15¢(c)
 Price,Cl Logo rep 35.00
11/51 (89) RR(a&c),Cl Logo;rep . 30.00
03/54 (117) RR(a&c),Cl Logo;rep . 28.00
11/56 (135) RR,New P(c),
 Cl Logo; rep 28.00
11/57 (141) RR,P(c),Cl Logo;rep . 30.00
05/59 (150) JSe&StA New Art;
 P(c), Cl Logo;rep 28.00
03/61 (161) JSe&StA,P(c),Cl
 Logo; rep 15.00
62/63 (167) JSe&StA,P(c),Cl
 Logo; rep 15.00
06/64 (167) JSe&StA,P(c),Cl
 Logo; rep 15.00
08/65 (167) JSe&StA,P(c),Cl
 Logo; rep 15.00
08/66 (167) JSe&StA,P(c),Cl
 Logo; rep 15.00

CC #4, The Last of the Mohicans
© Gilberton Publications

All comics prices listed are for *Near Mint* condition.

Classics Illustrated

1967 **(166)** JSe&StA,P(c),25¢(c)
  Price, CI Logo;rep 15.00
Sp/69 **(169)** JSe&StA,P(c),CI
  Logo, Rigid(c);rep.......... 15.00

005-MOBY DICK
By Herman Melville
09/42 **(—)** LZ(a&c),Original... 2,100.00
05/43 **(10)** LZ(a&c),Conray Products
  Edition, No(c)Price;rep 350.00
11/43 **(15)** LZ(a&c),Long Island
  Independent Edition;rep 275.00
06/44 **(18/20)** LZ(a&c),Sunrise
  Times Edition;rep 250.00
07/44 **(20)** LZ(a&c),Sunrise
  Times Edition;rep 225.00
07/44 **(21)** LZ(a&c),Sunrise
  Times Edition;rep 200.00
06/46 **(28)** LZ(a&c);rep 150.00
04/47 **(36)** LZ(a&c),New CI
  Logo;rep................. 75.00
06/49 **(60)** LZ(a&c),CI Logo;rep .. 50.00
08/49 **(62)** LZ(a&c),CI Logo;rep .. 55.00
05/50 **(71)** LZ(a&c),CI Logo;rep .. 40.00
09/51 **(87)** LZ(a&c),15¢(c)
  Price, CI Logo;rep 30.00
04/54 **(118)** LZ(a&c),CI Logo;rep.. 25.00
03/56 **(131)** NN New Art,New
  P(c), CI Logo;rep 25.00
05/57 **(138)** NN,P(c),CI Logo;rep.. 18.00
01/59 **(148)** NN,P(c),CI Logo;rep.. 18.00
09/60 **(158)** NN,P(c),CI Logo;rep.. 18.00
62/63 **(167)** NN,P(c),CI Logo;rep.. 18.00
06/64 **(167)** NN,P(c),CI Logo;rep.. 18.00
07/65 **(167)** NN,P(c),CI Logo;rep.. 18.00
03/66 **(167)** NN,P(c),CI Logo;rep.. 18.00
09/67 **(166)** NN,P(c),CI Logo;rep.. 18.00
Wn/69 **(166)** NN,P(c),25¢(c) Price,
  CI Logo, Rigid(c);rep 25.00
Wn/71 **(169)** NN,P(c),CI Logo;rep. 20.00

006-A TALE OF TWO CITIES
By Charles Dickens
11/42 **(—)** StM(a&c),Original.. 1,500.00
09/43 **(14)** StM(a&c),No(c)
  Price; rep............... 300.00
03/44 **(18)** StM(a&c),Long Island
  Independent Edition;rep 275.00
06/44 **(20)** StM(a&c),Sunrise
  Times Edition;rep 235.00
06/46 **(28)** StM(a&c);rep 150.00
09/48 **(51)** StM(a&c),New CI
  Logo; rep 75.00
10/49 **(64)** StM(a&c),CI
  Logo;rep................. 40.00
12/50 **(78)** StM(a&c),15¢(c)
  Price, CI Logo; rep 30.00
11/51 **(89)** StM(a&c),CI Logo;rep.. 30.00
03/54 **(117)** StM(a&c),CI
  Logo;rep................. 25.00
05/56 **(132)** JO New Art,New
  P(c), CI Logo;rep 30.00
09/57 **(140)** JO,P(c),CI Logo;rep.. 15.00
11/57 **(147)** JO,P(c),CI Logo;rep.. 15.00
09/59 **(152)** JO,P(c),CI Logo;rep. 250.00
11/59 **(153)** JO,P(c),CI Logo;rep.. 18.00
03/61 **(149)** JO,P(c),CI Logo;rep.. 18.00
62/63 **(167)** JO,P(c),CI Logo;rep.. 110.00
06/64 **(167)** JO,P(c),CI Logo;rep.. 15.00
08/65 **(167)** JO,P(c),CI Logo;rep.. 15.00
05/67 **(166)** JO,P(c),CI Logo;rep.. 15.00
Fl/68 **(166)** JO,NN New P(c),
  25¢(c)Price,CI Logo;rep 25.00
Sr/70 **(169)** JO,NN P(c),CI
  Logo, Rigid(c);rep 20.00

007-ROBIN HOOD
By Howard Pyle
12/42 **(—)** LZ(a&c),Original... 1,400.00
06/43 **(12)** LZ(a&c),P.D.C.
  on(c) Deleted;rep 300.00
03/44 **(18)** LZ(a&c),Long Island
  Independent Edition;rep 225.00
06/44 **(20)** LZ(a&c),Nassau
  Bulletin Edition;rep........ 250.00
10/44 **(22)** LZ(a&c),Queens
  City Times Edition;rep...... 225.00
06/46 **(28)** LZ(a&c),rep 150.00
09/48 **(51)** LZ(a&c),New CI
  Logo;rep................. 75.00
06/49 **(60)** LZ(a&c),CI Logo;rep .. 35.00
10/49 **(64)** LZ(a&c),CI Logo;rep .. 32.00
12/50 **(78)** LZ(a&c),CI Logo;rep .. 32.00
07/52 **(97)** LZ(a&c),CI Logo;rep .. 35.00
03/53 **(106)** LZ(a&c),CI Logo;rep.. 30.00
07/54 **(121)** LZ(a&c),CI Logo;rep.. 30.00
11/55 **(129)** LZ,New P(c),
  CI Logo;rep 30.00
01/57 **(136)** JkS New Art,P(c);rep. 30.00
03/58 **(143)** JkS,P(c),CI Logo;rep. 18.00
11/59 **(153)** JkS,P(c),CI Logo;rep. 15.00
10/61 **(164)** JkS,P(c),CI Logo;rep. 15.00
62/63 **(167)** JkS,P(c),CI Logo;rep. 15.00
06/64 **(167)** JkS,P(c),CI Logo;rep. 20.00
05/65 **(167)** JkS,P(c),CI Logo;rep. 15.00
07/66 **(167)** JkS,P(c),CI Logo;rep. 15.00
12/67 **(166)** JkS,P(c),CI Logo;rep. 20.00
Sr/69 **(169)** JkS,P(c),CI
  Logo, Rigid(c);rep.......... 15.00

008-ARABIAN KNIGHTS
By Antoine Galland
03/43 **(—)** LCh(a&c),Original.. 2,200.00
09/43 **(14)** LCh(a&c);rep 700.00
01/44 **(17)** LCh(a&c),Long Island
  Independent Edition;rep 750.00
06/44 **(20)** LCh(a&c),Nassau
  Bulletin Edition,64 pgs;rep .. 600.00
06/46 **(28)** LCh(a&c);rep 400.00
09/48 **(51)** LCh(a&c),New CI
  Logo; rep 400.00
10/49 **(64)** LCh(a&c),CI
  Logo;rep................ 300.00
12/50 **(78)** LCh(a&c),CI
  Logo;rep................ 250.00
10/61 **(164)** ChB New Art,P(c),
  CI Logo;rep 225.00

CI #7, Robin Hood
© Gilberton Publications

009-LES MISERABLES
By Victor Hugo
03/43 **(—)** RLv(a&c),Original.. 1,300.00
09/43 **(14)** RLv(a&c);rep 300.00
03/44 **(18)** RLv(a&c),Nassau
  Bulletin Edition;rep........ 260.00
06/44 **(20)** RLv(a&c),Richmond
  Courier Edition;rep 250.00
06/46 **(28)** RLv(a&c);rep 200.00
09/48 **(51)** RLv(a&c),New CI
  Logo; rep 85.00
05/50 **(71)** RLv(a&c),CI
  Logo;rep................. 75.00
09/51 **(87)** RLv(a&c),CI Logo,
  15¢(c)Price;rep............ 60.00
03/61 **(161)** NN New Art,GMc
  New P(c), CI Logo;rep 60.00
09/63 **(167)** NN,GMc P(c),CI
  Logo; rep 35.00
12/65 **(167)** NN,GMc P(c),CI
  Logo; rep 35.00
1968 **(166)** NN,GMc P(c),25¢(c)
  Price, CI Logo;rep 35.00

010-ROBINSON CRUSOE
By Daniel Defoe
04/43 **(—)** StM(a&c),Original.. 1,100.00
09/43 **(14)** StM(a&c);rep 350.00
03/44 **(18)** StM(a&c),Nassau Bulletin
  Ed.,'Bill of Rights'Pge.64;rep. 300.00
06/44 **(20)** StM(a&c);Sunrise
  Home News Edition;rep 250.00
??/45 **(23)** StM(a&c);rep 150.00
06/46 **(28)** StM(a&c);rep 150.00
09/48 **(51)** StM(a&c),New CI
  Logo; rep 75.00
10/49 **(64)** StM(a&c),CI Logo;rep . 50.00
12/50 **(78)** StM(a&c),15¢(c)
  Price, CI Logo;rep 35.00
07/52 **(97)** StM(a&c),CI Logo;rep . 32.00
12/53 **(114)** StM(a&c),CI
  Logo;rep................. 30.00
01/56 **(130)** StM,New P(c),CI
  Logo; rep 32.00
09/57 **(140)** SmC New Art,P(c),
  CI Logo;rep 32.00
11/59 **(153)** SmC,P(c),CI Logo;rep 15.00
10/61 **(164)** SmC,P(c),CI Logo;rep 15.00
62/63 **(167)** SmC,P(c),CI Logo;rep 18.00
07/64 **(167)** SmC,P(c),CI Logo;rep 20.00
05/65 **(167)** SmC,P(c),CI Logo;rep 15.00
06/66 **(167)** SmC,P(c),CI Logo;rep 18.00
Fl/68 **(166)** SmC,P(c),CI Logo,
  25¢(c)Price;rep............ 18.00
1968 **(166)** SmC,P(c),CI Logo,No
  Twin Circle Ad;rep 15.00
Sr/70 **(169)** SmC,P(c),CI Logo,
  Rigid(c);rep 15.00

011-DON QUIXOTE
By Miguel de Cervantes Saavedra
05/43 **(—)** LZ(a&c),Original... 1,200.00
03/44 **(18)** LZ(a&c),Nassau
  Bulletin Edition;rep........ 300.00
07/44 **(21)** LZ(a&c),Queens
  Home News Edition;rep 250.00
06/46 **(28)** LZ(a&c);rep 150.00
08/53 **(110)** LZ,TO New P(c),New
  CI Logo;rep 45.00
05/60 **(156)** LZ,TO P(c),Pages
  Reduced to 48,CI Logo;rep... 30.00
1962 **(165)** LZ,TO P(c),CI Logo;rep 20.00
01/64 **(167)** LZ,TO P(c),CI
  Logo;rep................. 20.00
11/65 **(167)** LZ,TO P(c),CI
  Logo;rep................. 20.00
1968 **(166)** LZ,TO P(c),CI Logo,
  25¢(c)Price;rep............ 40.00

Classics Illustrated 012–019

012-RIP VAN WINKLE & THE HEADLESS HORSEMAN
By Washington Irving
06/43 (——) RLv(a&c),Original. 1,200.00
11/43 (15) RLv(a&c),Long Island Independent Edition;rep 275.00
06/44 (20) RLv(a&c),Long Island Independent Edition;rep 250.00
10/44 (22) RLv(a&c),Queens City Times Edition;rep 225.00
06/46 (28) RLv(a&c);rep 150.00
06/49 (60) RLv(a&c),New Cl Logo;rep. 75.00
08/49 (62) RLv(a&c),Cl Logo;rep. 45.00
05/50 (71) RLv(a&c),Cl Logo;rep. 35.00
11/51 (89) RLv(a&c),15¢(c) Price, Cl Logo;rep 30.00
04/54 (118) RLv(a&c),Cl Logo;rep. 32.00
05/56 (132) RLv,New P(c), Cl Logo; rep 35.00
05/59 (150) NN New Art;P(c), Cl Logo; rep 35.00
09/60 (158) NN,P(c),Cl Logo;rep.. 20.00
62/63 (167) NN,P(c),Cl Logo;rep.. 20.00
12/63 (167) NN,P(c),Cl Logo;rep.. 20.00
04/65 (167) NN,P(c),Cl Logo;rep.. 22.00
04/66 (167) NN,P(c),Cl Logo;rep.. 20.00
1969 (166) NN,P(c),Cl Logo, 25¢(c)Price,Rigid(c);rep 26.00
Sr/70 (169) NN,P(c),Cl Logo, Rigid(c);rep 25.00

013-DR. JEKYLL AND MR.HYDE
By Robert Louis Stevenson
08/43 (——) AdH(a&c),Original. . 1,500.00
11/43 (15) AdH(a&c),Long Island Independent Edition;rep 400.00
06/44 (20) AdH(a&c),Long Island Independent Edition;rep 275.00
06/46 (28) AdH(a&c),No(c) Price; rep 225.00
06/49 (60) AdH,HcK New(c),New Cl Logo,Pgs.reduced to 48;rep .. 75.00
08/49 (62) AdH,HcK(c),Cl Logo;rep. 45.00
05/50 (71) AdH,HcK(c),Cl Logo;rep. 40.00
09/51 (87) AdH,HcK(c),Erroneous Return of Original Date, Cl Logo;rep 40.00
10/53 (112) LC New Art,New P(c), Cl Logo;rep 40.00
11/59 (153) LC,P(c),Cl Logo;rep.. 20.00
03/61 (161) LC,P(c),Cl Logo;rep.. 20.00
62/63 (167) LC,P(c),Cl Logo;rep.. 20.00
08/64 (167) LC,P(c),Cl Logo;rep.. 20.00
11/65 (167) LC,P(c),Cl Logo;rep.. 20.00
1968 (166) LC,P(c),Cl Logo, 25¢(c)Price;rep............ 22.00
Wr/69 (169) LC,P(c),Cl Logo, Rigid(c);rep 20.00

014-WESTWARD HO!
By Charles Kingsley
09/43 (——) ASm(a&c),Orig. ... 2,500.00
11/43 (15) ASm(a&c),Long Island Independent Edition;rep 750.00
07/44 (21) ASm(a&c);rep 650.00
06/46 (28) ASm(a&c),No(c) Price; rep 450.00
11/48 (53) ASm(a&c),Pages reduced to 48, New Cl Logo;rep..... 400.00

015-UNCLE TOM'S CABIN
By Harriet Beecher Stowe
11/43 (——) RLv(a&c),Original .. 1,000.00
11/43 (15) RLv(a&c),Blank Price Circle, Long Island Independent Ed.;rep 300.00
07/44 (21) RLv(a&c),Nassau Bulliten Edition;rep 250.00
06/46 (28) RLv(a&c),No(c) Price; rep 200.00
11/48 (53) RLv(a&c),Pages Reduced to 48, New Cl Logo;rep...... 75.00
05/50 (71) RLv(a&c),Cl Logo . 45.00
11/51 (89) RLv(a&c),15¢(c) Price, Cl Logo;rep 45.00
03/54 (117) RLv,New P(c),Cl Logo, Lettering Changes;rep.. 32.00
09/55 (128) RLv,P(c),"Picture Progress"Promotion,Cl Logo;rep. 22.00
03/57 (137) RLv,P(c),Cl Logo;rep. 15.00
09/58 (146) RLv,P(c),Cl Logo;rep. 15.00
01/60 (154) RLv,P(c),Cl Logo;rep. 15.00
03/61 (161) RLv,P(c),Cl Logo;rep. 17.00
62/63 (167) RLv,P(c),Cl Logo;rep. 15.00
06/64 (167) RLv,P(c),Cl Logo;rep. 15.00
05/65 (167) RLv,P(c),Cl Logo;rep. 15.00
05/67 (166) RLv,P(c),Cl Logo;rep. 15.00
Wr/69 (166) RLv,P(c),Cl Logo, Rigid(c);rep 26.00
Sr/70 (169) RLv,P(c),Cl Logo, Rigid(c);rep 25.00

016-GULLIVER'S TRAVELS
By Johnathan Swift
12/43 (——) LCh(a&c),Original. 1,000.00
06/44 (18/20) LCh(a&c),Queen's Home News Edition,No(c)Price; rep 275.00
10/44 (22) LCh(a&c),Queen's Home News Editon;rep..... 225.00
06/46 (28) LCh(a&c);rep 150.00
06/49 (60) LCh(a&c),Pgs. Reduced To 48, New Cl Logo;rep 75.00
08/49 (62) LCh(a&c),Cl Logo;rep . 45.00
10/49 (64) LCh(a&c),Cl Logo;rep . 45.00
12/50 (78) LCh(a&c),15¢(c) Price, Cl Logo;rep 35.00
11/51 (89) LCh(a&c),Cl Logo;rep . 30.00
03/60 (155) LCh,New P(c),Cl Logo; rep 35.00
1962 (165) LCh,P(c),Cl Logo;rep . 20.00
05/64 (167) LCh,P(c),Cl Logo;rep . 20.00
11/65 (167) LCh,P(c),Cl Logo;rep . 20.00
1968 (166) LCh,P(c),Cl Logo, 25¢(c)Price;rep............ 20.00
Wr/69 (169) LCh,P(c),Cl Logo, Rigid(c);rep 20.00

017-THE DEERSLAYER
By James Fenimore Cooper
01/44 (——) LZ(a&c),Original ... 900.00
03/44 (18) LZ(a&c),No(c)Price; rep....................... 275.00
10/44 (22) LZ(a&c),Queen's City Times Edition;rep 200.00
06/46 (28) LZ(a&c);rep 150.00
06/49 (60) LZ(a&c),Pgs. Reduced to 48,New Cl Logo;rep....... 75.00
10/49 (64) LZ(a&c),Cl Logo;rep .. 35.00
07/51 (85) LZ(a&c),15¢(c) Price, Cl Logo;rep 30.00
04/54 (118) LZ(a&c),Cl Logo;rep. 28.00
05/56 (132) LZ(a&c),Cl Logo;rep. 25.00
11/66 (167) LZ(a&c),Cl Logo;rep. 25.00
1968 (166) LZ,StA New P(c),Cl Logo, 25¢(c)Price;rep 35.00

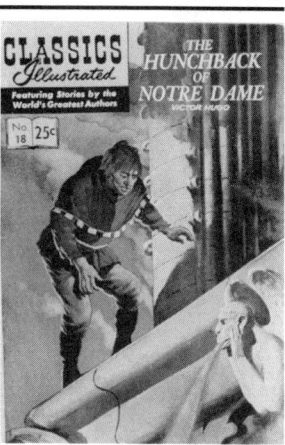

CC #18, The Hunchback of Notre Dame © Gilberton Publications

Sg/71 (169) LZ,StA P(c),Cl Logo, Rigid(c), Letters From Parents and Educators;rep 25.00

018-THE HUNCHBACK OF NOTRE DAME
By Victor Hugo
03/44 (——) ASm(a&c),Original Gilberton Edition 1,200.00
03/44 (——) ASm(a&c),Original Island Publications Edition . 1,000.00
06/44 (18/20) ASm(a&c),Queens Home News Edition;rep 300.00
10/44 (22) ASm(a&c),Queens City Times Edition;rep...... 250.00
06/46 (28) ASm(a&c);rep 225.00
06/49 (60) ASm,HcK New(c)8 Pgs. Deleted, New Cl Logo;ep ... 75.00
08/49 (62) ASm,HcK(c),Cl Logo;rep. 40.00
12/50 (78) ASm,HcK(c),15¢(c) Price, Cl Logo;rep 35.00
11/51 (89) ASm,HcK(c),Cl Logo;rep. 32.00
04/54 (118) ASm,HcK(c),Cl Logo;rep. 35.00
09/57 (140) ASm,New P(c),Cl Logo; rep 32.00
09/58 (146) ASm,P(c),Cl Logo;rep 32.00
09/60 (158) GE&RC New Art,GMc New P(c),Cl Logo;rep...... 20.00
1962 (165) GE&RC,GMc P(c),Cl Logo; rep 20.00
09/63 (167) GE&RC,GMc P(c),Cl Logo; rep 20.00
10/64 (167) GE&RC,GMc P(c),Cl Logo; rep 20.00
04/66 (167) GE&RC,GMc P(c),Cl Logo; rep 20.00
1968 (166) GE&RC,GMc P(c),Cl Logo, 25¢(c)Price;rep........ 20.00
Sr/70 (169) GE&RC,GMc P(c),Cl Logo, Rigid(c);rep........ 20.00

019-HUCKLEBERRY FINN
By Mark Twain
04/44 (——) LZ(a&c),Original Gilberton Edition.......... 750.00
04/44 (——) LZ(a&c),Original Island Publications Company Edition 800.00
03/44 (18) LZ(a&c),Nassau Bulliten Editon;rep 300.00

019–026 Classics Illustrated

10/44 **(22)** LZ(a&c),Queens City
  Times Edition;rep 250.00
06/46 **(28)** LZ(a&c);rep 200.00
06/49 **(60)** LZ(a&c),New CI Logo,
  Pgs.Reduced to 48;rep 75.00
08/49 **(62)** LZ(a&c),CI Logo;rep .. 40.00
12/50 **(78)** LZ(a&c),CI Logo;rep .. 35.00
11/51 **(89)** LZ(a&c),CI Logo;rep .. 30.00
03/54 **(117)** LZ(a&c),CI Logo;rep.. 30.00
03/56 **(131)** FrG New Art,New
  P(c), CI Logo; rep............ 30.00
09/57 **(140)** FrG,P(c),CI Logo;rep . 20.00
05/59 **(150)** FrG,P(c),CI Logo;rep . 20.00
09/60 **(158)** FrG,P(c),CI Logo;rep . 20.00
1962 **(165)** FrG,P(c),CI Logo;rep . 20.00
62/63 **(167)** FrG,P(c),CI Logo;rep . 20.00
06/64 **(167)** FrG,P(c),CI Logo;rep . 20.00
06/65 **(167)** FrG,P(c),CI Logo;rep . 20.00
10/65 **(167)** FrG,P(c),CI Logo;rep . 20.00
09/67 **(166)** FrG,P(c),CI Logo;rep . 20.00
Wr/69 **(166)** FrG,P(c),CI Logo,
  25¢(c)Price, Rigid(c);rep..... 20.00
Sr/70 **(169)** FrG,P(c),CI Logo,
  Rigid(c);rep 20.00

020-THE CORSICAN BROTHERS
By Alexandre Dumas
06/44 **(—)** ASm(a&c),Original
  Gilberton Edition........... 650.00
06/44 **(—)** ASm(a&c),Original
  Courier Edition 550.00
06/44 **(—)** ASm(a&c),Original Long
  Island Independent Edition .. 550.00
10/44 **(22)** ASm(a&c),Queens
  City Times Edition;rep....... 275.00
06/46 **(28)** ASm(a&c);rep 250.00
06/49 **(60)** ASm(a&c),No(c)Price,
  New CI Logo,Pgs. Reduced
  to 48;rep................... 225.00
08/49 **(62)** ASm(a&c),CI
  Logo;rep.................. 165.00
12/50 **(78)** ASm(a&c),15¢(c)
  Price, CI Logo;rep 150.00
07/52 **(97)** ASm(a&c),CI
  Logo;rep.................. 135.00

021-FAMOUS MYSTERIES
By Sir Arthur Conan Doyle
Guy de Maupassant
& Edgar Allan Poe
07/44 **(—)** AdH,LZ,ASm(a&c),
  Original Gilberton Edition.. 1,300.00
07/44 **(—)** AdH,LZ,ASm(a&c),
  Original Island Publications
  Edition; No Date or Indicia 1,350.00
07/44 **(—)** AdH,LZ,ASm(a&c),
  Original Richmond Courier
  Edition.................. 1,100.00
10/44 **(22)** AdH,LZ,ASm(a&c),
  Nassau Bulliten Edition;rep .. 450.00
09/46 **(30)** AdH,LZ,ASm(a&c);
  rep..................... 350.00
08/49 **(62)** AdH,LZ,ASm(a&c),
  New CI Logo;rep 300.00
04/50 **(70)** AdH,LZ,ASm(a&c),
  CI Logo;rep 275.00
07/51 **(85)** AdH,LZ,ASm(a&c),
  15¢(c) Price,CI Logo;rep.... 250.00
12/53 **(114)** ASm,AdH,LZ,New
  P(c), CI Logo;rep 250.00

022-THE PATHFINDER
By James Fenimore Cooper
10/44 **(—)** LZ(a&c),Original
  Gilberton Edition.......... 600.00
10/44 **(—)** LZ(a&c),Original
  Island Publications Edition;.. 450.00
10/44 **(—)** LZ(a&c),Original
  Queens County Times Edition 450.00
09/46 **(30)** LZ(a&c),No(c)
  Price;rep................. 150.00
06/49 **(60)** LZ(a&c),New CI Logo,
  Pgs.Reduced To 48;rep 50.00
08/49 **(62)** LZ(a&c),CI Logo;rep .. 45.00
04/50 **(70)** LZ(a&c),CI Logo;rep .. 35.00
07/51 **(85)** LZ(a&c),15¢(c)
  Price, CI Logo;rep 32.00
04/54 **(118)** LZ(a&c),CI Logo;rep.. 30.00
05/56 **(132)** LZ(a&c),CI Logo;rep.. 30.00
09/58 **(146)** LZ(a&c),CI Logo;rep.. 35.00
11/63 **(167)** LZ,NN New P(c),CI
  Logo; rep................. 30.00
12/65 **(167)** LZ,NN P(c),CI
  Logo;rep................. 30.00
08/67 **(166)** LZ,NN P(c),CI
  Logo;rep................. 30.00

023-OLIVER TWIST
By Charles Dickens
(First Classic produced by the Iger shop)
07/45 **(—)** AdH(a&c),Original ... 600.00
09/46 **(30)** AdH(a&c),Price
  Circle is Blank;rep 400.00
06/49 **(60)** AdH(a&c),Pgs. Reduced
  To 48, New CI Logo;rep 50.00
08/49 **(62)** AdH(a&c),CI
  Logo;rep.................. 45.00
05/50 **(71)** AdH(a&c),CI
  Logo;rep.................. 35.00
07/51 **(85)** AdH(a&c),15¢(c)
  Price CI Logo;rep.......... 32.00
04/52 **(94)** AdH(a&c),CI
  Logo;rep.................. 32.00
04/54 **(118)** AdH(a&c),CI
  Logo;rep.................. 30.00
01/57 **(136)** AdH,New P(c),CI
  Logo; rep................. 30.00
05/59 **(150)** AdH,P(c),CI Logo;rep . 25.00
1961 **(164)** AdH,P(c),CI Logo;rep . 25.00
10/61 **(164)** GE&RC New Art,P(c),
  CI Logo;rep............... 35.00
62/63 **(167)** GE&RC,P(c),CI
  Logo; rep................. 15.00
08/64 **(167)** GE&RC,P(c),CI
  Logo; rep................. 15.00
12/65 **(167)** GE&RC,P(c),
  CI Logo;rep............... 15.00

CI #24, A Connecticut Yankee in King Arthur's Court © Gilberton Publications

1968 **(166)** GE&RC,P(c),CI
  Logo, 25¢(c)Price;rep....... 15.00
Wr/69 **(169)** GE&RC,P(c),CI
  Logo, Rigid(c);rep.......... 15.00

024-A CONNECTICUT YANKEE IN KING ARTHUR'S COURT
By Mark Twain
09/45 **(—)** JH(a&c),Original 450.00
09/46 **(30)** JH(a&c),Price Circle
  Blank;rep................. 150.00
06/49 **(60)** JH(a&c),8 Pages
  Deleted,New CI Logo;rep 50.00
08/49 **(62)** JH(a&c),CI Logo;rep .. 45.00
05/50 **(71)** JH(a&c),CI Logo;rep .. 35.00
09/51 **(87)** JH(a&c),15¢(c) Price
  CI Logo;rep............... 30.00
07/54 **(121)** JH(a&c),CI Logo;rep . 30.00
09/57 **(140)** JkS New Art,New
  P(c),CI Logo; rep 35.00
11/59 **(153)** JkS,P(c),CI Logo;rep . 18.00
1961 **(164)** JkS,P(c),CI Logo;rep.. 15.00
62/63 **(167)** JkS,P(c),CI Logo;rep . 15.00
07/64 **(167)** JkS,P(c),CI Logo;rep . 15.00
06/66 **(167)** JkS,P(c),CI Logo;rep . 15.00
1968 **(166)** JkS,P(c),CI logo,
  25¢(c)Price;rep............ 15.00
Sg/71 **(169)** JkS,P(c),CI Logo,
  Rigid(c);rep 15.00

025-TWO YEARS BEFORE THE MAST
By Richard Henry Dana Jr.
10/45 **(—)** RWb,DvH,Original; .. 450.00
09/46 **(30)** RWb,DvH,Price Circle
  Blank................... 150.00
06/49 **(60)** RWb,DvH,8 Pages
  Deleted,New CI Logo;rep 50.00
08/49 **(62)** RWb,DvH,CI Logo;rep . 45.00
05/50 **(71)** RWb,DvH,CI Logo;rep . 35.00
07/51 **(85)** RWb,DvH,15¢(c) Price
  CI Logo;rep 30.00
12/53 **(114)** RWb,DvH,CI Logo;rep 28.00
05/60 **(156)** RWb,DvH,New P(c),
  CI Logo, 3 Pgs. Replaced
  By Fillers;rep............. 32.00
12/63 **(167)** RWb,DvH,P(c),CI
  Logo; rep................ 15.00
12/65 **(167)** RWb,DvH,P(c),CI
  Logo; rep................ 15.00
09/67 **(166)** RWb,DvH,P(c),CI
  Logo; rep................ 15.00
Wr/69 **(169)** RWb,DvH,P(c),25¢(c)
  Price, CI Logo,Rigid(c);rep ... 15.00

026-FRANKENSTEIN
By Mary Wollstonecraft Shelley
12/45 **(—)** RWb&ABr(a&c),
  Original................ 1,400.00
09/46 **(30)** RWb&ABr(a&c),
  Price Circle Blank;rep...... 350.00
06/49 **(60)** RWb&ABr(a&c),
  New CI Logo;rep 175.00
08/49 **(62)** RWb&ABr(a&c),
  CI Logo;rep 150.00
05/50 **(71)** RWb&ABr(a&c),
  CI Logo;rep 75.00
04/51 **(82)** RWb&ABr(a&c),
  15¢(c) Price,CI Logo;rep..... 65.00
03/54 **(117)** RWb&ABr(a&c),
  CI Logo;rep 30.00
09/58 **(146)** RWb&ABr,NS
  New P(c), CI Logo; rep...... 35.00
11/59 **(153)** RWb&ABr,NS
  P(c),CI Logo; rep 50.00

01/61 **(160)** RWb&ABr,NS
  P(c),CI Logo; rep 16.00
165 **(1962)** RWb&ABr,NS P(c),
  CI Logo; rep.............. 16.00
62/63 **(167)** RWb&ABr,NS P(c),
  CI Logo; rep.............. 15.00
06/64 **(167)** RWb&ABr,NS P(c),
  CI logo; rep 15.00
06/65 **(167)** RWb&ABr,NS P(c),
  CI Logo; rep.............. 15.00
10/65 **(167)** RWb&ABr,NS P(c),
  CI Logo; rep.............. 15.00
09/67 **(166)** RWb&ABr,NS P(c),
  CI Logo; rep.............. 15.00
Fl/69 **(169)** RWb&ABr,NS P(c),25¢(c)
  Price,CI Logo,Rigid(c);rep.... 15.00
Sg/71 **(169)** RWb&ABr,NS P(c),
  CI Logo, Rigid(c);rep 15.00

027-THE ADVENTURES MARCO POLO
By Marco Polo & Donn Byrne
04/46 **(—)** HFI(a&c);Original .. 500.00
09/46 **(30)** HFI(a&c);rep 150.00
04/50 **(70)** HFI(a&c),8 Pages Deleted,
  No(c) Price,New CI Logo;rep . 45.00
09/51 **(87)** HFI(a&c),15¢(c)
  Price,CI Logo;rep 30.00
03/54 **(117)** HFI(a&c),CILogo;rep . 25.00
01/60 **(154)** HFI,New P(c),CI
  Logo;rep.................. 25.00
1962 **(165)** HFI,P(c),CI Logo;rep.. 15.00
04/64 **(167)** HFI,P(c),CI Logo; rep . 15.00
06/66 **(167)** HFI,P(c),CI Logo; rep . 15.00
Sg/69 **(169)** HFI,P(c),CI Logo,
  25¢(c)Price,Rigid(c);rep 15.00

028-MICHAEL STROGOFF
By Jules Verne
06/46 **(—)** AdH(a&c),Original ... 500.00
09/48 **(51)** AdH(a&c),8 Pages
  Deleted,New CI Logo;rep ... 150.00
01/54 **(115)** AdH,New P(c),CI
  Logo; rep 45.00
03/60 **(155)** AdH,P(c),CI Logo;rep. 18.00
11/63 **(167)** AdH,P(c),CI Logo;rep. 18.00
07/66 **(167)** AdH,P(c),CI Logo; rep. 18.00
Sr/69 **(169)**AdH,NN,NewP(c),25¢(c)
  Price, CI Logo,Rigid(c);rep ... 28.00

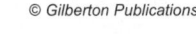
CI #31, The Black Arrow
© Gilberton Publications

029-THE PRINCE AND THE PAUPER
By Mark Twain
07/46 **(—)** AdH(a&c),Original ... 750.00
06/49 **(60)** AdH,New HcK(c),New CI
  Logo,8 Pages Deleted;rep ... 70.00
08/49 **(62)** AdH,HcK(c),CILogo;rep 50.00
05/50 **(71)** AdH,HcK(c),CILogo;rep 35.00
03/52 **(93)** AdH,HcK(c),CILogo;rep 32.00
12/53 **(114)** AdH,HcK(c),CI
  Logo;rep................... 30.00
09/55 **(128)** AdH,New P(c),CI
  Logo; rep 30.00
05/57 **(138)** AdH,P(c),CI Logo;rep . 18.00
05/59 **(150)** AdH,P(c),CI Logo;rep . 18.00
1961 **(164)** AdH,P(c),CI Logo;rep . 18.00
62/63 **(167)** AdH,P(c),CI Logo;rep . 18.00
07/64 **(167)** AdH,P(c),CI Logo;rep . 18.00
11/65 **(167)** AdH,P(c),CI Logo;rep . 18.00
1968 **(166)** AdH,P(c),CI Logo,
  25¢(c)Price;rep............ 18.00
Sr/70 **(169)** AdH,P(c),CI Logo,
  Rigid(c);rep 18.00

030-THE MOONSTONE
By William Wilkie Collins
09/46 **(—)** DRi(a&c),Original ... 500.00
06/49 **(60)** DRi(a&c),8 Pages
  Deleted,New CI Logo;rep ... 90.00
04/50 **(70)** DRi(a&c),CI Logo;rep.. 65.00
03/60 **(155)** DRi,LbC New P(c),
  CI Logo;rep................ 90.00
1962 **(165)** DRi,LbC P(c),CI Logo;
  rep....................... 35.00
01/64 **(167)** DRi,LbC P(c),CI Logo;
  rep....................... 28.00
09/65 **(167)** DRi,LbC P(c),CI Logo;
  rep....................... 20.00
1968 **(166)** DRi,LbC P(c),CI Logo,
  25¢(c)Price;rep............ 18.00

031-THE BLACK ARROW
By Robert Louis Stevenson
10/46 **(—)** AdH(a&c),Original ... 400.00
09/48 **(51)** AdH(a&c),8 Pages
  Deleted,New CI Logo;rep 50.00
10/49 **(64)** AdH(a&c),CI
  Logo;rep................... 35.00
09/51 **(87)** AdH(a&c),15¢(c)
  Price;CI Logo;rep 30.00
06/53 **(108)** AdH(a&c),CI
  Logo;rep................... 28.00
03/55 **(125)** AdH(a&c),CI
  Logo; rep 27.00
03/56 **(131)** AdH,New P(c),CI
  Logo; rep 22.00
09/57 **(140)** AdH,P(c),CI Logo;rep. 20.00
01/59 **(148)** AdH,P(c),CI Logo;rep. 20.00
03/61 **(161)** AdH,P(c),CI Logo;rep. 20.00
62/63 **(167)** AdH,P(c),CI Logo;rep. 20.00
07/64 **(167)** AdH,P(c),CI logo;rep . 20.00
11/65 **(167)** AdH,P(c),CI Logo;rep. 20.00
1968 **(166)** AdH,P(c),CI Logo,
  25¢(c)Price;rep............ 20.00

032-LORNA DOONE
By Richard Doddridge Blackmore
12/46 **(—)** MB(a&c),Original.... 450.00
10/49 **(53/64)** MB(a&c),8 Pages
  Deleted,New CI Logo;rep 90.00
07/51 **(85)** MB(a&c),15¢(c)
  Price, CI Logo;rep 65.00
04/54 **(118)** MB(a&c),CI Logo;rep . 35.00
05/57 **(138)** MB,New P(c); Old(c)
  Becomes New Splash Pge.,CI

  Logo;rep.................. 35.00
05/59 **(150)** MB,P(c),CI Logo;rep . 20.00
1962 **(165)** MB,P(c),CI Logo;rep .. 20.00
01/64 **(167)** MB,P(c),CI Logo;rep . 22.00
11/65 **(167)** MB,P(c),CI Logo;rep.. 22.00
1968 **(166)** MB,New P(c),
  CI Logo;rep................ 35.00

033-THE ADVENTURES OF SHERLOCK HOLMES
By Sir Arthur Conan Doyle
01/47 **(—)** LZ,HcK(c),Original . 1,500.00
11/48 **(53)** LZ,HcK(c),"A Study in Scarlet"
  Deleted,New CI Logo;rep ... 500.00
05/50 **(71)** LZ,HcK(c),CI Logo;rep 400.00
11/51 **(89)** LZ,HcK(c),15¢(c)
  Price,CI Logo;rep 350.00

034-MYSTERIOUS ISLAND
By Jules Verne
Last Classic Comic
02/47 **(—)** RWb&DvH,Original .. 500.00
06/49 **(60)** RWb&DvH,8 Pages
  Deleted,New CI Logo;rep 65.00
08/49 **(62)** RWb&DvH,CI Logo;rep 45.00
05/50 **(71)** RWb&DvH,CI Logo;rep 65.00
12/50 **(78)** RWb&DvH,15¢(c) Price,
  CI Logo;rep 35.00
02/52 **(92)** RWb&DvH,CI Logo;rep 35.00
03/54 **(117)** RWb&DvH,CI Logo;
  rep....................... 35.00
09/57 **(140)** RWb&DvH,New P(c),
  CI Logo;rep................ 35.00
05/60 **(156)** RWb&DvH,P(c),CI
  Logo;rep.................. 20.00
10/63 **(167)** RWb&DvH,P(c),CI
  Logo;rep.................. 20.00
05/64 **(167)** RWb&DvH,P(c),CI
  Logo;rep.................. 20.00
06/66 **(167)** RWb&DvH,P(c),CI
  logo;rep 20.00
1968 **(166)** RWb&DvH,P(c),CI Logo,
  25¢(c)Price;rep............ 20.00

035-LAST DAYS OF POMPEII
By Lord Edward Bulwer Lytton
First Classics Illustrated
03/47 **(—)** HcK(a&c),Original ... 500.00
03/61 **(161)** JK,New P(c),
  15¢(c)Price;rep............ 65.00
01/64 **(167)** JK,P(c);rep.......... 30.00
07/66 **(167)** JK,P(c);rep.......... 30.00
Sg/70 **(169)** JK,P(c),25¢(c)
  Price, Rigid(c);rep.......... 30.00

036-TYPEE
By Herman Melville
04/47 **(—)** EzW(a&c),Original... 275.00
10/49 **(64)** EzW(a&c),No(c)price,
  8 pages deleted;rep 90.00
03/60 **(155)** EzW,GMc New
  P(c);rep................... 35.00
09/63 **(167)** EzW,GMc P(c);rep... 25.00
07/65 **(167)** EzW,GMc P(c);rep... 25.00
Sr/69 **(169)** EzW,GMc P(c),25¢(c)
  Price, Rigid(c);rep.......... 25.00

037-THE PIONEERS
By James Fenimore Cooper
05/47 **(37)** RP(a&c),Original 250.00
08/49 **(62)** RP(a&c),8 Pages
  Deleted;rep 45.00
04/50 **(70)** RP(a&c);rep.......... 35.00

037–050 Classics Illustrated

02/52 **(92)** RP(a&c),15¢(c)price;
rep 35.00
04/54 **(118)** RP(a&c);rep 30.00
03/56 **(131)** RP(a&c);rep 30.00
05/56 **(132)** RP(a&c);rep 30.00
11/59 **(153)** RP(a&c);rep 25.00
05/64 **(167)** RP(a&c);rep 25.00
06/66 **(167)** RP(a&c);rep 25.00
1968 **(166)** RP,TO New P(c),
25¢(c)Price;rep 35.00

038-ADVENTURES OF CELLINI
By Benvenuto Cellini
06/47 **(—)** AgF(a&c),Original . . . 350.00
1961 **(164)** NN New Art,New P(c);
rep 35.00
12/63 **(167)** NN,P(c);rep 25.00
07/66 **(167)** NN,P(c);rep 25.00
Sg/70 **(169)** NN,P(c),25¢(c)
Price, Rigid(c);rep. 28.00

039-JANE EYRE
By Charlotte Bronte
07/47 **(—)** HyG(a&c),Original . . . 325.00
06/49 **(60)** HyG(a&c),No(c)Price,
8 pages deleted;rep 50.00
08/49 **(62)** HyG(a&c);rep. 45.00
05/50 **(71)** HyG(a&c);rep. 35.00
02/52 **(92)** HyG(a&c),15¢(c)
Price; rep 32.00
04/54 **(118)** HyG(a&c);rep. 32.00
01/58 **(142)** HyG,New P(c);rep . . 32.00
01/60 **(154)** HyG,P(c);rep 32.00
1962 **(165)** HjK New Art,P(c);rep. . 32.00
12/63 **(167)** HjK,P(c);rep 32.00
04/65 **(167)** HjK,P(c);rep 32.00
08/66 **(167)** HjK,P(c);rep 32.00
1968 **(166)** HjK,NN New P(c);rep . 75.00

040-MYSTERIES
(The Pit & the Pendulum, The Adventures of Hans Pfall, Fall of the House of Usher)
By Edgar Allan Poe
08/47 **(—)** AgF,HyG,HcK(a&c),
Original 800.00
08/49 **(62)** AgF,HyG,HcK(a&c),
8 Pages deleted;rep 350.00
09/50 **(75)** AgF,HyG,
HcK(a&c);rep 300.00
02/52 **(92)** AgF,HyG,HcK(a&c)
15¢(c) Price;rep 250.00

041-TWENTY YEARS AFTER
By Alexandre Dumas
09/47 **(—)** RBu(a&c),Original . . . 600.00
08/49 **(62)** RBu,HcK New(c),No(c)
Price, 8 Pages Deleted;rep . . . 65.00
12/50 **(78)** RBu,HcK(c),15¢(c)
Price; rep 45.00
05/60 **(156)** RBu,DgR New P(c);
rep 35.00
12/63 **(167)** RBu,DgR P(c);rep . . 50.00
11/66 **(167)** RBu,DgR P(c);rep . . 50.00
Sg/70 **(169)** RBu,DgR P(c),25¢(c)
Price, Rigid(c);rep. 50.00

042-SWISS FAMILY ROBINSON
By Johann Wyss
10/47 **(42)** HcK(a&c),Original . . . 275.00
08/49 **(62)** HcK(a&c),No(c)price,
8 Pages Deleted,Not Every Issue

Has 'Gift Box' Ad;rep 75.00
09/50 **(75)** HcK(a&c);rep 35.00
03/52 **(93)** HcK(a&c);rep 32.00
03/54 **(117)** HcK(a&c);rep. 30.00
03/56 **(131)** HcK,New P(c);rep . . 28.00
03/57 **(137)** HcK,P(c);rep 28.00
11/57 **(141)** HcK,P(c);rep 28.00
09/59 **(152)** NN New art,P(c);rep. . 28.00
09/60 **(158)** NN,P(c);rep 25.00
12/63 **(165)** NN,P(c);rep 30.00
12/63 **(167)** NN,P(c);rep 15.00
04/65 **(167)** NN,P(c);rep 15.00
05/66 **(167)** NN,P(c);rep 15.00
11/67 **(166)** NN,P(c);rep 15.00
Sg/69 **(169)** NN,P(c);rep 15.00

043-GREAT EXPECTATIONS
By Charles Dickens
11/47 **(—)** HcK(a&c),Original. . 1,400.00
08/49 **(62)** HcK(a&c),No(c)price;
8 pages deleted;rep 850.00

044-MYSTERIES OF PARIS
By Eugene Sue
12/47 **(44)** HcK(a&c),Original . . . 900.00
08/47 **(62)** HcK(a&c),No(c)Price,
8 Pages Deleted,Not Every Issue
Has'Gift Box'Ad;rep 350.00
12/50 **(78)** HcK(a&c),15¢(c)
Price; rep 300.00

045-TOM BROWN'S SCHOOL DAYS
By Thomas Hughes
01/48 **(44)** HFl(a&c),Original,
1st 48 Pge. Issue 200.00
10/49 **(64)** HFl(a&c),No(c)
Price;rep 60.00
03/61 **(161)** JTg New Art,GMc
New P(c);rep 30.00
02/64 **(167)** JTg,GMc P(c);rep. . . 20.00
08/66 **(167)** JTg,GMc P(c);rep. . . 20.00
1968 **(166)** JTg,GMc P(c),
25¢(c)Price;rep. 20.00

046-KIDNAPPED
By Robert Louis Stevenson
04/48 **(47)** RWb(a&c),Original . . . 165.00
08/49 **(62)** RWb(a&c),Red Circle
Either Blank or With 10¢;rep . . 90.00
12/50 **(78)** RWb(a&c),15¢(c)
Price; rep 35.00
09/51 **(87)** RWb(a&c),rep 32.00
04/54 **(118)** RWb(a&c);rep 30.00
03/56 **(131)** RWb,New P(c);rep . . 30.00
09/57 **(140)** RWb,P(c);rep 18.00
05/59 **(150)** RWb,P(c);rep 18.00
05/60 **(156)** RWb,P(c);rep 18.00
1961 **(164)** RWb,P(c),Reduced Pge.
Wdth;rep 18.00
62/63 **(167)** RWb,P(c);rep. 18.00
03/64 **(167)** RWb,P(c);rep. 18.00
06/65 **(167)** RWb,P(c);rep. 18.00
12/65 **(167)** RWb,P(c);rep. 18.00
09/67 **(167)** RWb,P(c);rep. 18.00
Wr/69 **(166)** RWb,P(c),25¢(c)
Price, Rigid(c);rep. 18.00
Sr/70 **(169)** RWb,P(c),Rigid(c);rep. 18.00

047-TWENTY THOUSAND LEAGUES UNDER THE SEA
By Jules Verne
05/58 **(47)** HcK(a&c),Original . . . 180.00
10/49 **(64)** HcK(a&c),No(c)
Price; rep 45.00
12/50 **(78)** HcK(a&c),15¢(c)
Price; rep 35.00
04/52 **(94)** HcK(a&c);rep. 35.00
04/54 **(118)** HcK(a&c);rep 30.00
09/55 **(128)** HcK,New P(c);rep . . 30.00
07/56 **(133)** HcK,P(c);rep 25.00
09/57 **(140)** HcK,P(c);rep 18.00
01/59 **(148)** HcK,P(c);rep 18.00
05/60 **(156)** HcK,P(c);rep 18.00
62/63 **(165)** HcK,P(c);rep. 18.00
05/48 **(167)** HcK,P(c);rep. 18.00
03/64 **(167)** HcK,P(c);rep. 18.00
08/65 **(167)** HcK,P(c);rep. 18.00
10/66 **(167)** HcK,P(c);rep. 18.00
1968 **(166)** HcK,NN New P(c),
25¢(c)Price;rep. 25.00
Sg/70 **(169)** HcK,NN P(c),
Rigid(c);rep 25.00

048-DAVID COPPERFIELD
By Charles Dickens
06/48 **(47)** HcK(a&c),Original . . . 165.00
10/49 **(64)** HcK(a&c),Price Circle
Replaced By Image of Boy
Reading;rep 45.00
09/51 **(87)** HcK(a&c),15¢(c)
Price; rep 35.00
07/54 **(121)** HcK,New P(c);rep . . 30.00
10/56 **(130)** HcK,P(c);rep 18.00
09/57 **(140)** HcK,P(c);rep 18.00
01/59 **(148)** HcK,P(c);rep 18.00
05/60 **(156)** HcK,P(c);rep 18.00
62/63 **(167)** HcK,P(c);rep. 18.00
04/64 **(167)** HcK,P(c);rep. 18.00
06/65 **(167)** HcK,P(c);rep. 18.00
05/67 **(166)** HcK,P(c);rep. 18.00
R/67 **(166)** HcK,P(c);rep. 25.00
Sg/69 **(166)** HcK,P(c),25¢(c)
Price, Rigid(c);rep. 18.00
Wr/69 **(169)** HcK,P(c),Rigid(c);rep. 18.00

049-ALICE IN WONDERLAND
By Lewis Carroll
07/48 **(47)** AB(a&c),Original 250.00
10/49 **(64)** AB(a&c),No(c)Price;
rep 60.00
07/51 **(85)** AB(a&c),15¢(c)Price;
rep 50.00
03/60 **(155)** AB,New P(c);rep . . . 50.00
1962 **(165)** AB,P(c);rep. 35.00
03/64 **(167)** AB,P(c);rep 30.00
06/66 **(167)** AB,P(c);rep 30.00
Fl/68 **(166)** AB,TO New P(c),25¢(c)
Price, New Soft(c);rep 50.00
Fl/68 **(166)** AB,P(c),Both Soft &
Rigid(c)s;rep. 100.00

050-ADVENTURES OF TOM SAWYER
By Mark Twain
08/48 **(51)** ARu(a&c),Original . . . 200.00
09/48 **(51)** ARu(a&c),Original . . . 225.00
10/49 **(64)** ARu(a&c),No(c)
Price; rep 35.00
12/50 **(78)** ARu(a&c),15¢(c)
Price; rep 30.00

Comics Values Annual — Classics Illustrated — 050–063

04/52 **(94)** ARu(a&c);rep 30.00
12/53 **(114)** ARu(a&c);rep 30.00
03/54 **(117)** ARu(a&c);rep 25.00
05/56 **(132)** ARu(a&c);rep 25.00
09/57 **(140)** ARu,New P(c);rep . . 22.00
05/59 **(150)** ARu,P(c);rep 25.00
10/61 **(164)** New Art,P(c);rep 15.00
62/63 **(167)** P(c);rep 15.00
01/65 **(167)** P(c);rep 15.00
05/66 **(167)** P(c);rep 15.00
12/67 **(166)** P(c);rep 15.00
Fl/69 **(169)** P(c),25¢(c) Price,
 Rigid(c);rep 15.00
Wr/71 **(169)** P(c);rep 15.00

051-THE SPY
By James Fenimore Cooper
09/48 **(51)** AdH(a&c),Original,
 Maroon(c). 165.00
09/48 **(51)** AdH(a&c),Original,
 Violet(c) 165.00
11/51 **(89)** AdH(a&c),15¢(c)
 Price; rep 35.00
07/54 **(121)** AdH(a&c);rep. 30.00
07/57 **(139)** AdH,New P(c);rep . . 30.00
05/60 **(156)** AdH,P(c);rep 18.00
11/63 **(167)** AdH,P(c);rep 18.00
07/66 **(167)** AdH,P(c);rep 18.00
Wr/69 **(166)** AdH,P(c),25¢(c)Price,
 Both Soft & Rigid(c)s;rep 35.00

052-THE HOUSE OF SEVEN GABLES
By Nathaniel Hawthorne
10/48 **(53)** HyG(a&c),Original . . . 165.00
11/51 **(89)** HyG(a&c),15¢(c)
 Price; rep 35.00
07/54 **(121)** HyG(a&c);rep 30.00
01/58 **(142)** GWb New Art,New
 P(c); rep 35.00
05/60 **(156)** GWb,P(c);rep. 18.00
1962 **(165)** GWb,P(c);rep 18.00
05/64 **(167)** GWb,P(c);rep. 18.00
03/66 **(167)** GWb,P(c);rep. 18.00
1968 **(166)** GWb,P(c),25¢(c)
 Price; rep 18.00
Sg/70 **(169)** GWb,P(c),Rigid(c);rep 18.00

053-A CHRISTMAS CAROL
By Charles Dickens
11/48 **(53)** HcK(a&c),Original . . . 250.00

054-MAN IN THE IRON MASK
By Alexandre Dumas
12/48 **(55)** AgF,HcK(c),Original . . . 165.00
03/52 **(93)** AgF,HcK(c),15¢(c)
 Price; rep 45.00
09/53 **(111)** AgF,HcK(c);rep 60.00
01/58 **(142)** KBa New Art,New
 P(c); rep 35.00
01/60 **(154)** KBa,P(c);rep 18.00
1962 **(165)** KBa,P(c);rep 18.00
05/64 **(167)** KBa,P(c);rep 18.00
04/66 **(167)** KBa,P(c);rep 18.00
Wr/69 **(166)** KBa,P(c),25¢(c)
 Price, Rigid(c);rep 18.00

055-SILAS MARINER
By George Eliot
01/49 **(55)** AdH,HcK(c),Original . . 165.00
09/50 **(75)** AdH,HcK(c),Price Circle
 Blank,'Coming next'Ad(not
 usually in reps.);rep 45.00

07/52 **(97)** AdH,HcK(c);rep 32.00
07/54 **(121)** AdH,New P(c);rep . . . 30.00
01/56 **(130)** AdH,P(c);rep 18.00
09/57 **(140)** AdH,P(c);rep 18.00
01/60 **(154)** AdH,P(c);rep 18.00
1962 **(165)** AdH,P(c);rep. 18.00
05/64 **(167)** AdH,P(c);rep 18.00
06/65 **(167)** AdH,P(c);rep 18.00
05/67 **(166)** AdH,P(c);rep 18.00
Wr/69 **(166)** AdH,P(c),25¢(c) Price,
 Rigid(c);rep,Soft & Stiff 35.00

056-THE TOILERS OF THE SEA
By Victor Hugo
02/49 **(55)** AgF(a&c),Original. . . . 275.00
01/62 **(165)** AT New Art,New
 P(c); rep. 60.00
03/64 **(167)** AT,P(c);rep. 35.00
10/66 **(167)** AT,P(c);rep. 35.00

057-THE SONG OF HIAWATHA
By Henry Wadsworth Longfellow
03/49 **(55)** AB(a&c),Original 165.00
09/50 **(75)** AB(a&c),No(c)price,'
 Coming Next'Ad(not usually
 found in reps.);rep 50.00
04/52 **(94)** AB(a&c),15¢(c)
 Price;rep 35.00
04/54 **(118)** AB(a&c);rep 32.00
09/56 **(134)** AB,New P(c);rep 30.00
07/57 **(139)** AB,P(c);rep 18.00
01/60 **(154)** AB,P(c);rep 18.00
62/63 **(167)** AB,P(c),Erroneosly
 Has Original Date;rep. 18.00
09/64 **(167)** AB,P(c);rep 18.00
10/65 **(167)** AB,P(c);rep 18.00
Fl/68 **(166)** AB,P(c),25¢(c)Price;
 rep. 18.00

058-THE PRAIRIE
By James Fenimore Cooper
04/49 **(60)** RP(a&c),Original 165.00
08/49 **(62)** RP(a&c);rep. 75.00
12/50 **(78)** RP(a&c),15¢(c) Price
 In Double Circle;rep 35.00
12/53 **(114)** RP(a&c);rep 30.00
03/56 **(131)** RP(a&c);rep. 30.00
05/56 **(132)** RP(a&c);rep. 30.00
09/58 **(146)** RP,New P(c);rep 30.00
03/60 **(155)** RP,P(c);rep 20.00
05/64 **(167)** RP,P(c);rep 18.00
04/66 **(167)** RP,P(c);rep 18.00
Sr/69 **(169)** RP,P(c),25¢(c)
 Price; Rigid(c);rep. 18.00

059-WUTHERING HEIGHTS
By Emily Bronte
05/49 **(60)** HcK(a&c),Original . . . 225.00
07/51 **(85)** HcK(a&c),15¢(c)
 Price; rep 50.00
05/60 **(156)** HcK,GB New P(c);rep 35.00
04/67 **(167)** HcK,GB P(c);rep 25.00
10/66 **(167)** HcK,GB P(c);rep 25.00
Sr/69 **(169)** HcK,GBP(c),25¢(c)
 Price, Rigid(c);rep. 22.00

060-BLACK BEAUTY
By Anna Sewell
06/49 **(62)** AgF(a&c),Original. . . . 165.00
08/49 **(62)** AgF(a&c);rep 225.00
07/51 **(85)** AgF(a&c),15¢(c) Price;
 rep 40.00

Cl #58 The Prairie
© Gilberton Publications

09/60 **(158)** LbC&NN&StA New
 Art, LbC New P(c);rep 35.00
02/64 **(167)** LbC&NN&StA,LbC
 P(c); rep 30.00
03/66 **(167)** LbC&NN&StA,LbC
 P(c); rep 30.00
03/66 **(167)** LbC&NN&StA,LbC
 P(c), 'Open Book'Blank;rep. . . 30.00
1968 **(166)** LbC&NN&StA,AIM New
 P(c) 25¢(c) Price;rep 75.00

061-THE WOMAN IN WHITE
By William Wilke Collins
07/49 **(62)** AB(a&c),Original,
 Maroon & Violet(c)s 175.00
05/60 **(156)** AB,DgR New P(c);rep 40.00
01/64 **(167)** AB,DgR P(c);rep 30.00
1968 **(166)** AB,DgR P(c),
 25¢(c)Price;rep. 30.00

062-WESTERN STORIES
(The Luck of Roaring Camp & The Outcasts of Poker Flat)
By Bret Harte
08/49 **(62)** HcK(a&c),Original . . . 165.00
11/51 **(89)** HcK(a&c),15¢(c)
 Price; rep 40.00
07/54 **(121)** HcK(a&c);rep 32.00
03/57 **(137)** HcK,New P(c);rep . . . 30.00
09/59 **(152)** HcK,P(c);rep 20.00
10/63 **(167)** HcK,P(c);rep. 20.00
06/64 **(167)** HcK,P(c);rep. 18.00
11/66 **(167)** HcK,P(c);rep. 18.00
1968 **(166)** HcK,TO New P(c),
 25¢ Price;rep 30.00

063-THE MAN WITHOUT A COUNTRY
By Edward Everett Hale
09/49 **(62)** HcK(a&c),Original . . . 165.00
12/50 **(78)** HcK(a&c),15¢(c)Price
 In Double Circles;rep 40.00
05/60 **(156)** HcK,GMc New P(c);
 rep 35.00
01/62 **(165)** AT New Art,GMc P(c),
 Added Text Pages;rep 32.00
03/64 **(167)** AT,GMc P(c);rep. 18.00
08/66 **(167)** AT,GMc P(c);rep. 18.00

All comics prices listed are for *Near Mint* condition.

063-078 Classics Illustrated

Sr/69 **(169)** AT,GMc P(c),25¢(c)
 Price, Rigid(c);rep 18.00

064-TREASURE ISLAND
By Robert Louis Stevenson
10/49 **(62)** AB(a&c),Original 165.00
04/51 **(82)** AB(a&c),15¢(c)
 Price;rep 40.00
03/54 **(117)** AB(a&c),rep 32.00
03/56 **(131)** AB,New P(c);rep 30.00
05/57 **(138)** AB,P(c);rep 18.00
09/58 **(146)** AB,P(c);rep 18.00
09/60 **(158)** AB,P(c);rep 18.00
1962 **(165)** AB,P(c);rep 18.00
62/63 **(167)** AB,P(c);rep 18.00
06/64 **(167)** AB,P(c);rep 18.00
12/65 **(167)** AB,P(c);rep 18.00
10/67 **(166)** AB,P(c);rep 22.00
10/67 **(166)** AB,P(c),GRIT Ad
 Stapled In Book;rep 100.00
Sg/69 **(169)** AB,P(c),25¢(c)
 Price, Rigid(c);rep 18.00

065-BENJAMIN FRANKLIN
By Benjamin Franklin
11/49 **(64)** AB,RtH,GS(Iger Shop),
 HcK(c),Original 165.00
03/56 **(131)** AB,RtH,GS(Iger Shop),
 New P(c) ;rep 35.00
01/60 **(154)** AB,RtH,GS(Iger Shop),
 P(c);rep 20.00
02/64 **(167)** AB,RtH,GS(Iger Shop),
 P(c);rep 18.00
04/66 **(167)** AB,RtH,GS(Iger Shop),
 P(c);rep 18.00
Fl/69 **(169)** AB,RtH,GS(Iger Shop),
 P(c), 25¢(c)Price,Rigid(c);rep . 20.00

066-THE CLOISTER AND THE HEARTH
By Charles Reade
12/49 **(67)** HcK(a&c),Original . . . 350.00

067-THE SCOTTISH CHIEFS
By Jane Porter
01/50 **(67)** AB(a&c),Original 165.00
07/51 **(85)** AB(a&c),15¢(c)
 Price;rep 40.00
04/54 **(118)** AB(a&c),rep 35.00
01/57 **(136)** AB,New P(c);rep 32.00
01/60 **(154)** AB,P(c);rep 20.00
11/63 **(167)** AB,P(c);rep 25.00
08/65 **(167)** AB,P(c);rep 20.00

068-JULIUS CEASAR
By William Shakespeare
02/50 **(70)** HcK(a&c),Original . . . 150.00
07/51 **(85)** HcK(a&c),15¢(c)
 Price; rep 40.00
06/53 **(108)** HcK(a&c);rep 32.00
05/60 **(156)** HcK,LbC New P(c);rep 35.00
1962 **(165)** GE&RC New Art,
 LbC P(c);rep 35.00
02/64 **(167)** GE&RC,LbC P(c);rep . 18.00
10/65 **(167)** GE&RC,LbC P(c),Tarzan
 Books Inside(c);rep 18.00
1967 **(166)** GE&RC,LbC P(c);rep . 18.00
Wr/69 **(169)** GE&RC,LbC P(c),
 Rigid(c);rep 18.00

069-AROUND THE WORLD IN 80 DAYS
By Jules Verne
03/50 **(70)** HcK(a&c),Original . . . 150.00
09/51 **(87)** HcK(a&c),15¢(c)
 Price; rep 45.00
03/55 **(125)** HcK(a&c);rep 32.00
01/57 **(136)** HcK,New P(c);rep . . . 32.00
09/58 **(146)** HcK,P(c),rep 20.00
09/59 **(152)** HcK,P(c);rep 20.00
1961 **(164)** HcK,P(c);rep 20.00
62/63 **(167)** HcK,P(c);rep 18.00
07/64 **(167)** HcK,P(c);rep 18.00
11/65 **(167)** HcK,P(c);rep 18.00
07/67 **(166)** HcK,P(c);rep 18.00
Sg/69 **(169)** HcK,P(c),25¢(c)
 Price, Rigid(c);rep 18.00

070-THE PILOT
By James Fenimore Cooper
04/50 **(71)** AB(a&c),Original 125.00
10/50 **(75)** AB(a&c),15¢(c)
 Price;rep 45.00
02/52 **(92)** AB(a&c);rep 32.00
03/55 **(125)** AB(a&c);rep 35.00
05/60 **(156)** AB,GMc New P(c);rep 30.00
02/64 **(167)** AB,GMc P(c);rep . . . 30.00
05/66 **(167)** AB,GMc P(c);rep . . . 28.00

071-THE MAN WHO LAUGHS
By Victor Hugo
05/50 **(71)** AB(a&c),Original 250.00
01/62 **(165)** NN,NN New P(c);rep 125.00
04/64 **(167)** NN,NN P(c);rep 100.00

072-THE OREGON TRAIL
By Francis Parkman
06/50 **(73)** HcK(a&c), Original . . . 150.00
11/51 **(89)** HcK(a&c),15¢(c)
 Price; rep 40.00
07/54 **(121)** HcK(a&c);rep 32.00
03/56 **(131)** HcK,New P(c);rep . . . 30.00
09/57 **(140)** HcK,P(c);rep 20.00
05/59 **(150)** HcK,P(c);rep 18.00
01/61 **(164)** HcK,P(c);rep 18.00
62/63 **(167)** HcK,P(c);rep 18.00
08/64 **(167)** HcK,P(c);rep 18.00
10/65 **(167)** HcK,P(c);rep 18.00
1968 **(166)** HcK,P(c),25¢(c)Price;
 rep 18.00

073-THE BLACK TULIP
By Alexandre Dumas
07/50 **(75)** AB(a&c),Original 400.00

074-MR. MIDSHIPMAN EASY
By Captain Frederick Marryat
08/50 **(75)** BbL,Original 400.00

075-THE LADY OF THE LAKE
By Sir Walter Scott
09/50 **(75)** HcK(a&c),Original . . . 125.00
07/51 **(85)** HcK(a&c),15¢(c)
 Price; rep 40.00
04/54 **(118)** HcK(a&c),rep 35.00
07/57 **(139)** HcK,New P(c);rep . . . 35.00
01/60 **(154)** HcK,P(c);rep 18.00
1962 **(165)** HcK,P(c);rep 18.00
04/64 **(167)** HcK,P(c);rep 18.00
05/66 **(167)** HcK,P(c);rep 18.00

Sg/69 **(169)** HcK,P(c),25¢(c)
 Price, Rigid(c);rep 18.00

076-THE PRISONER OF ZENDA
By Anthony Hope Hawkins
10/50 **(75)** HcK(a&c),Original . . . 125.00
07/51 **(85)** HcK(a&c),15¢(c) Price;
 rep 40.00
09/53 **(111)** HcK(a&c),rep 35.00
09/55 **(128)** HcK,New P(c);rep . . . 35.00
09/59 **(152)** HcK,P(c);rep 20.00
1962 **(165)** HcK,P(c);rep 18.00
04/64 **(167)** HcK,P(c);rep 18.00
09/66 **(167)** HcK,P(c);rep 18.00
Fl/69 **(169)** HcK,P(c),25¢(c) Price,
 Rigid(c);rep 18.00

CI #81, The Illiad
© Gilberton Publications

077-THE ILLIAD
By Homer
11/50 **(78)** AB(a&c),Original. 135.00
09/51 **(87)** AB(a&c),15¢(c)
 Price;rep 40.00
07/54 **(121)** AB(a&c);rep 35.00
07/57 **(139)** AB,New P(c);rep 35.00
05/59 **(150)** AB,P(c);rep 20.00
1962 **(165)** AB,P(c);rep 18.00
10/63 **(167)** AB,P(c);rep 18.00
07/64 **(167)** AB,P(c);rep 18.00
05/66 **(167)** AB,P(c);rep 18.00
1968 **(166)** AB,P(c),25¢(c)
 Price;rep 18.00

078-JOAN OF ARC
By Frederick Shiller
12/50 **(78)** HcK(a&c),Original . . . 125.00
09/51 **(87)** HcK(a&c),15¢(c)
 Price; rep 40.00
11/53 **(113)** HcK(a&c),rep 35.00
09/55 **(128)** HcK,New P(c);rep . . . 35.00
09/57 **(140)** HcK,P(c);rep 20.00
05/59 **(150)** HcK,P(c);rep 20.00
11/60 **(159)** HcK,P(c);rep 18.00
62/63 **(167)** HcK,P(c);rep 18.00
12/63 **(167)** HcK,P(c);rep 18.00
06/65 **(167)** HcK,P(c);rep 18.00
06/67 **(166)** HcK,P(c);rep 18.00
Wr/69 **(166)** HcK,TO New P(c),
 25¢(c)Price, Rigid(c);rep 35.00

079-CYRANO DE BERGERAC
By Edmond Rostand
01/51 **(78)** AB(a&c),Original,Movie
Promo Inside Front(c)...... 125.00
07/51 **(85)** AB(a&c),15¢(c)
Price;rep 40.00
04/54 **(118)** AB(a&c);rep 35.00
07/56 **(133)** AB,New P(c);rep 35.00
05/60 **(156)** AB,P(c);rep 30.00
08/64 **(167)** AB,P(c);rep 30.00

080-WHITE FANG
By Jack London
(Last Line Drawn (c)
02/51 **(79)** AB(a&c),Original 125.00
09/51 **(87)** AB(a&c);rep......... 40.00
03/55 **(125)** AB(a&c);rep 35.00
05/56 **(132)** AB,New P(c);rep ... 35.00
09/57 **(140)** AB,P(c);rep 20.00
11/59 **(153)** AB,P(c);rep 20.00
62/63 **(167)** AB,P(c);rep 18.00
09/64 **(167)** AB,P(c);rep 18.00
07/65 **(167)** AB,P(c);rep 18.00
06/67 **(166)** AB,P(c);rep 18.00
Fl/69 **(169)** AB,P(c),25¢(c)
Price, Rigid(c);rep........... 18.00

081-THE ODYSSEY
By Homer
(P(c)s From Now on)
03/51 **(82)** HyG,AB P(c),Original . 125.00
08/64 **(167)** HyG,AB P(c);rep 30.00
10/66 **(167)** HyG,AB P(c);rep 30.00
Sg/69 **(169)** HyG,TyT New P(c),
Rigid(c);rep 35.00

082-THE MASTER OF BALLANTRAE
By Robert Louis Stevenson
04/51 **(82)** LDr,AB P(c),Original.. 80.00
08/64 **(167)** LDr,AB P(c);rep 30.00
Fl/69 **(166)** LDr,Syk New P(c),
Rigid(c);rep 35.00

083-THE JUNGLE BOOK
By Rudyard Kipling
05/51 **(85)** WmB&AB,AB P(c),
Original 80.00
08/53 **(110)** WmB&AB,AB P(c);rep 20.00
03/55 **(125)** WmB&AB,AB P(c);rep 20.00
05/56 **(134)** WmB&AB,AB P(c);rep 20.00
01/58 **(142)** WmB&AB,AB P(c);rep 20.00
05/59 **(150)** WmB&AB,AB P(c);rep 18.00
11/60 **(159)** WmB&AB,AB P(c);rep 18.00
62/63 **(167)** WmB&AB,AB P(c);rep 18.00
03/65 **(167)** WmB&AB,AB P(c);rep 18.00
11/65 **(167)** WmB&AB,AB P(c);rep 18.00
05/66 **(167)** WmB&AB,AB P(c);rep 18.00
1968 **(166)** NN Art,NN New P(c),
Rigid(c);rep 35.00

084-THE GOLD BUG & OTHER STORIES
(The Gold Bug-The Telltale HeartThe Cask of Amontillado)
By Edgar Allan Poe
06/51 **(85)** AB,RP,JLv,AB P(c),
Original 165.00
07/64 **(127)** AB,RP,JLv,AB
P(c);rep 125.00

085-THE SEA WOLF
By Jack London
08/51 **(85)** AB,AB P(c),Original ... 75.00
07/54 **(121)** AB,AB P(c);rep...... 20.00
05/56 **(132)** AB,AB P(c);rep...... 20.00
11/57 **(141)** AB,AB P(c);rep...... 20.00
03/61 **(161)** AB,AB P(c);rep...... 18.00
02/64 **(167)** AB,AB P(c);rep...... 18.00
11/65 **(167)** AB,AB P(c);rep...... 18.00
Fl/69 **(169)** AB,AB P(c),25¢(c)
Price, Rigid(c);rep........... 18.00

086-UNDER TWO FLAGS
By Oiuda
08/51 **(87)** MDb,AB P(c),Original.. 60.00
03/54 **(117)** MDb,AB P(c);rep 25.00
07/57 **(139)** MDb,AB P(c);rep 20.00
09/60 **(158)** MDb,AB P(c);rep 20.00
02/64 **(167)** MDb,AB P(c);rep 18.00
08/66 **(167)** MDb,AB P(c);rep 18.00
Sr/69 **(169)** MDb,AB P(c),25¢(c)
Price, Rigid(c);rep........... 18.00

087-A MIDSUMMER NIGHTS DREAM
By William Shakespeare
09/51 **(87)** AB,AB P(c),Original ... 60.00
03/61 **(161)** AB,AB P(c);rep...... 20.00
04/64 **(167)** AB,AB P(c);rep...... 18.00
05/66 **(167)** AB,AB P(c);rep...... 18.00
Sr/69 **(169)** AB,AB P(c),25¢(c)
Price; rep 18.00

088-MEN OF IRON
By Howard Pyle
10/51 **(89)** HD,LDr,GS,Original ... 60.00
01/60 **(154)** HD,LDr,GS,P(c);rep .. 20.00
01/64 **(167)** HD,LDr,GS,P(c);rep .. 18.00
1968 **(166)** HD,LDr,GS,P(c),
25¢(c)Price;rep............ 18.00

089-CRIME AND PUNISHMENT
By Fedor Dostoevsky
11/51 **(89)** RP,AB P(c),Original ... 65.00
09/59 **(152)** RP,AB P(c);rep...... 25.00
04/64 **(167)** RP,AB P(c);rep...... 18.00
05/66 **(167)** RP,AB P(c);rep...... 18.00
Fl/69 **(169)** RP,AB P(c),25¢(c)
Price, Rigid(c);rep........... 18.00

090-GREEN MANSIONS
By William Henry Hudson
12/51 **(89)** AB,AB P(c),Original ... 65.00
01/59 **(148)** AB,New LbC P(c);rep. 30.00
1962 **(165)** AB,LbC P(c);rep 18.00
04/64 **(167)** AB,LbC P(c);rep..... 18.00
09/66 **(167)** AB,LbC P(c);rep..... 18.00
Sr/69 **(169)** AB,LbC P(c),25¢(c)
Price, Rigid(c);rep........... 18.00

091-THE CALL OF THE WILD
By Jack London
01/52 **(92)** MDb,P(c),Original 65.00
10/53 **(112)** MDb,P(c);rep....... 20.00
03/55(125)MDb,P(c),'PictureProgress'
Onn. Back(c);rep........... 20.00
09/56 **(134)** MDb,P(c);rep....... 20.00
03/58 **(143)** MDb,P(c);rep....... 18.00
1962 **(165)** MDb,P(c);rep........ 18.00
1962 **(167)** MDb,P(c);rep........ 18.00
04/65 **(167)** MDb,P(c);rep....... 18.00
03/66 **(167)** MDb,P(c);rep....... 18.00
03/66 **(167)** MDb,P(c),Record
Edition;rep 18.00
11/67 **(166)** MDb,P(c);rep 18.00
Sg/70 **(169)** MDb,P(c),25¢(c)
Price, Rigid(c);rep........... 18.00

092-THE COURTSHIP OF MILES STANDISH
By Henry Wadsworth Longfellow
02/52 **(92)** AB,AB P(c),Original ... 60.00
1962 **(165)** AB,AB P(c);rep 20.00
03/64 **(167)** AB,AB P(c);rep...... 20.00
05/67 **(166)** AB,AB P(c);rep...... 20.00
Wr/69 **(169)** AB,AB P(c),25¢(c)
Price, Rigid(c);rep........... 20.00

093-PUDD'NHEAD WILSON
By Mark Twain
03/52 **(94)** HcK,HcK P(c),Original . 65.00
1962 **(165)** HcK,GMc New P(c);rep 25.00
03/64 **(167)** HcK,GMc P(c);rep ... 20.00
1968 **(166)** HcK,GMc P(c),25¢(c)
Price, Soft(c);rep 20.00

094-DAVID BALFOUR
By Robert Louis Stevenson
04/52 **(94)** RP,P(c),Original 65.00
05/64 **(167)** RP,P(c);rep 25.00
1968 **(166)** RP,P(c),25¢(c)Price;rep 25.00

095-ALL QUIET ON THE WESTERN FRONT
By Erich Maria Remarque
05/52 **(96)** MDb,P(c),Original 165.00
05/52 **(99)** MDb,P(c),Original 85.00
10/64 **(167)** MDb,P(c);rep....... 35.00
11/66 **(167)** MDb,P(c);rep....... 35.00

096-DANIEL BOONE
By John Bakeless
06/52 **(97)** AB,P(c),Original 65.00
03/54 **(117)** AB,P(c);rep 20.00
09/55 **(128)** AB,P(c);rep 20.00
05/56 **(132)** AB,P(c);rep 20.00
—— **(134)** AB,P(c),'Story of
Jesus'on Back(c);rep 20.00
09/60 **(158)** AB,P(c);rep 20.00
01/64 **(167)** AB,P(c);rep 18.00
05/65 **(167)** AB,P(c);rep 18.00
11/66 **(167)** AB,P(c);rep 18.00
Wr/69 **(166)** AB,P(c),25¢(c)
Price, Rigid(c);rep........... 25.00

097-KING SOLOMON'S MINES
By H. Rider Haggard
07/52 **(96)** HcK,P(c),Original 60.00
04/54 **(118)** HcK,P(c);rep 20.00
03/56 **(131)** HcK,P(c);rep 20.00
09/51 **(141)** HcK,P(c);rep 20.00
09/60 **(158)** HcK,P(c);rep 18.00
02/64 **(167)** HcK,P(c);rep 18.00
09/65 **(167)** HcK,P(c);rep 18.00
Sr/69 **(169)** HcK,P(c),25¢(c)
Price; Rigid(c);rep........... 20.00

Classics Illustrated

CI #109, Pitcairn's Island
© Gilberton Publications

098-THE RED BADGE OF COURAGE
By Stephen Crane
08/52 **(98)** MDb,GS,P(c),Original . 65.00
04/54 **(118)** MDb,GS,P(c);rep 20.00
05/56 **(132)** MDb,GS,P(c);rep 20.00
01/58 **(142)** MDb,GS,P(c);rep 20.00
09/59 **(152)** MDb,GS,P(c);rep 20.00
03/61 **(161)** MDb,GS,P(c);rep 20.00
62/63 **(167)** MDb,GS,P(c),Erroneusly
 Has Original Date;rep....... 20.00
09/64 **(167)** MDb,GS,P(c);rep 20.00
10/65 **(167)** MDb,GS,P(c);rep 20.00
1968 **(166)** MDb,GS,P(c),25¢(c)
 Price, Rigid(c);rep.......... 30.00

099-HAMLET
By William Shakespeare
09/52 **(98)** AB,P(c),Original....... 65.00
07/54 **(121)** AB,P(c);rep 20.00
11/57 **(141)** AB,P(c);rep 20.00
09/60 **(158)** AB,P(c);rep 18.00
62/63 **(167)** AB,P(c),Erroneusly
 Has Original Date;rep....... 18.00
07/65 **(167)** AB,P(c);rep 18.00
04/67 **(166)** AB,P(c);rep 18.00
Sg/69 **(169)** AB,EdM New P(c),
 25¢(c)Price, Rigid(c);rep.... 30.00

100-MUTINY ON THE BOUNTY
By Charrles Nordhoff
10/52 **(100)** MsW,HcK P(c),Original 60.00
03/54 **(117)** MsW,HcK P(c);rep ... 20.00
05/56 **(132)** MsW,HcK P(c);rep ... 20.00
01/58 **(142)** MsW,HcK P(c);rep ... 20.00
03/60 **(155)** MsW,HcK P(c);rep ... 18.00
62/63 **(167)** MsW,HcK P(c),Erroneusly
 Has Original Date;rep....... 18.00
05/64 **(167)** MsW,HcK P(c);rep ... 18.00
03/66 **(167)** MsW,HcK P(c),N#
 or Price;rep 20.00
Sg/70 **(169)** MsW,HcK P(c),
 Rigid(c); rep 18.00

101-WILLIAM TELL
By Frederick Schiller
11/52 **(101)** MDb,HcK P(c),Original 60.00
04/54 **(118)** MDb,HcK P(c);rep ... 20.00
11/57 **(141)** MDb,HcK P(c);rep ... 20.00
09/60 **(158)** MDb,HcK P(c);rep ... 18.00
62/63 **(167)** MDb,HcK P(c),Erroneusly
 Has Original Date;rep....... 18.00
11/64 **(167)** MDb,HcK P(c);rep ... 18.00
04/67 **(166)** MDb,HcK P(c);rep ... 18.00
Wr/69 **(169)** MDb,HcK P(c)25¢(c)
 Price, Rigid(c);rep.......... 18.00

102-THE WHITE COMPANY
By Sir Arthur Conan Doyle
12/52 **(101)** AB,P(c),Original 125.00
1962 **(165)** AB,P(c);rep.......... 35.00
04/64 **(167)** AB,P(c);rep 35.00

103-MEN AGAINST THE SEA
By Charles Nordhoff
01/53 **(104)** RP,HcK P(c),Original . 65.00
12/53 **(114)** RP,HcK P(c);rep..... 30.00
03/56 **(131)** RP,New P(c);rep 35.00
03/59 **(149)** RP,HcK P(c);rep 30.00
09/60 **(158)** RP,P(c);rep 38.00
03/64 **(167)** RP,P(c);rep 25.00

104-BRING 'EM BACK ALIVE
By Frank Buck & Edward Anthony
02/53 **(105)** HcK,HcK P(c)Original. 65.00
04/54 **(118)** HcK,HcK P(c);rep.... 20.00
07/56 **(133)** HcK,HcK P(c);rep.... 20.00
05/59 **(150)** HcK,HcK P(c);rep.... 18.00
09/60 **(158)** HcK,HcK P(c);rep.... 18.00
10/63 **(167)** HcK,HcK P(c);rep.... 18.00
09/65 **(167)** HcK,HcK P(c);rep.... 18.00
Wr/69 **(169)** HcK,HcK P(c),25¢(c)
 Price, Rigid(c);rep.......... 18.00

105-FROM THE EARTH TO THE MOON
By Jules Verne
03/53 **(106)** AB,P(c),Original..... 65.00
04/54 **(118)** AB,P(c);rep 20.00
03/56 **(132)** AB,P(c);rep 20.00
11/57 **(141)** AB,P(c);rep 20.00
09/58 **(146)** AB,P(c);rep 20.00
05/60 **(156)** AB,P(c);rep 20.00
62/63 **(167)** AB,P(c),Erroneusly
 Has Original Date;rep....... 18.00
05/64 **(167)** AB,P(c);rep 18.00
05/65 **(167)** AB,P(c);rep 18.00
10/67 **(166)** AB,P(c);rep 18.00
Sr/69 **(169)** AB,P(c),25¢(c)
 Price, Rigid(c);rep.......... 18.00
Sg/71 **(169)** AB,P(c);rep 18.00

106-BUFFALO BILL
By William F. Cody
04/53 **(107)** MDb,P(c),Original ... 60.00
04/54 **(118)** MDb,P(c);rep 20.00
03/56 **(132)** MDb,P(c);rep 20.00
01/58 **(142)** MDb,P(c);rep 20.00
03/61 **(161)** MDb,P(c);rep 18.00
03/64 **(167)** MDb,P(c);rep 18.00
07/67 **(166)** MDb,P(c);rep 18.00
Fl/69 **(169)** MDb,P(c),Rigid(c);rep . 18.00

107-KING OF THE KHYBER RIFLES
By Talbot Mundy
05/53 **(108)** SMz,P(c),Original.... 60.00
04/54 **(118)** SMz,P(c);rep 20.00

09/58 **(146)** SMz,P(c);rep 20.00
09/60 **(158)** SMz,P(c);rep 18.00
62/63 **(167)** SMz,P(c),Erroneusly
 Has Original Date;rep....... 18.00
62/63 **(167)** SMz,P(c);rep 18.00
10/66 **(167)** SMz,P(c);rep 18.00

108-KNIGHTS OF THE ROUND TABLE
By Howard Pyle?
06/53 **(108)** AB,P(c),Original 65.00
06/53 **(109)** AB,P(c),Original 70.00
03/54 **(117)** AB,P(c);rep 20.00
11/59 **(153)** AB,P(c);rep 18.00
1962 **(165)** AB,P(c);rep.......... 18.00
04/64 **(167)** AB,P(c);rep 18.00
04/67 **(166)** AB,P(c);rep 18.00

109-PITCAIRN'S ISLAND
By Charles Nordhoff
07/53 **(110)** RP,P(c),Original 65.00
1962 **(165)** RP,P(c);rep 20.00
03/64 **(167)** RP,P(c);rep 20.00
06/67 **(166)** RP,P(c);rep 20.00

110-A STUDY IN SCARLET
By Sir Arthur Conan Doyle
08/53 **(111)** SMz,P(c),Original.... 150.00
1962 **(165)** SMz,P(c);rep........ 100.00

111-THE TALISMAN
By Sir Walter Scott
09/53 **(112)** HcK,HcK P(c),Original 75.00
1962 **(165)** HcK,HcK P(c);rep 20.00
05/64 **(167)** HcK,HcK P(c);rep.... 18.00
Fl/68 **(166)** HcK,HcK P(c),
 25¢(c)Price;rep............ 20.00

112-ADVENTURES OF KIT CARSON
By John S. C. Abbott
10/53 **(113)** RP,P(c),Original..... 65.00
11/55 **(129)** RP,P(c);rep 20.00
11/57 **(141)** RP,P(c);rep 20.00
09/59 **(152)** RP,P(c);rep 18.00
03/61 **(161)** RP,P(c);rep 18.00
62/63 **(167)** RP,P(c);rep 18.00
02/65 **(167)** RP,P(c);rep 18.00
05/66 **(167)** RP,P(c);rep 18.00
Wr/69 **(166)** RP,EdM New P(c),
 25¢(c)Price, Rigid(c);rep.... 25.00

113-THE FORTY-FIVE GUARDSMEN
By Alexandre Dumas
11/53 **(114)** MDb,P(c),Original... 100.00
07/66 **(166)** MDb,P(c);rep 50.00

114-THE RED ROVER
By James Fenimore Cooper
12/53 **(115)** PrC,JP P(c),Original . 100.00
07/67 **(166)** PrC,JP P(c);rep 50.00

115-HOW I FOUND LIVINGSTONE
By Sir Henry Stanley
01/54 **(116)** SF&ST,P(c),Original . 120.00
01/67 **(167)** SF&ST,P(c);rep 60.00

Classics Illustrated 116–137

116-THE BOTTLE IMP
By Robert Louis Stevenson
02/54 **(117)** LC,P(c),Original 120.00
01/67 **(167)** LC,P(c);rep 60.00

117-CAPTAINS COURAGEOUS
By Rudyard Kipling
03/54 **(118)** PrC,P(c),Original ... 125.00
02/67 **(167)** PrC,P(c);rep........ 32.00
Fl/69 **(169)** PrC,P(c),25¢(c)
Price, Rigid(c);rep.......... 30.00

118-ROB ROY
By Sir Walter Scott
04/54 **(119)** RP,WIP,P(c),Original. 120.00
02/67 **(167)** RP,WIP,P(c);rep..... 60.00

119-SOLDERS OF FORTUNE
By Richard Harding Davis
05/54 **(120)** KS,P(c),Original..... 90.00
03/67 **(166)** KS,P(c);rep 32.00
Sg/70 **(169)** KS,P(c),25¢(c)
Price, Rigid(c);rep.......... 30.00

120-THE HURRICANE
By Charles Nordhoff
1954 **(121)** LC,LC P(c),Original... 90.00
03/67 **(166)** LC,LC P(c);rep..... 45.00

121-WILD BILL HICKOCK
Author Unknown
07/54 **(122)** MI,ST,P(c),Original... 60.00
05/56 **(132)** MI,ST,P(c);rep 20.00
11/57 **(141)** MI,ST,P(c);rep 20.00
01/60 **(154)** MI,ST,P(c);rep 20.00
62/63 **(167)** MI,ST,P(c);rep 18.00
08/64 **(167)** MI,ST,P(c);rep 18.00
04/67 **(166)** MI,ST,P(c);rep 18.00
Wr/69 **(169)** MI,ST,P(c),Rigid
(c);rep 18.00

122-THE MUTINEERS
By Charles Boardman Hawes
09/54 **(123)** PrC,P(c),Original 65.00
01/57 **(136)** PrC,P(c);rep........ 20.00
09/58 **(146)** PrC,P(c);rep........ 20.00
09/60 **(158)** PrC,P(c);rep........ 18.00
11/63 **(167)** PrC,P(c);rep........ 18.00
03/65 **(167)** PrC,P(c);rep........ 18.00
08/67 **(166)** PrC,P(c);rep........ 18.00

123-FANG AND CLAW
By Frank Buck
11/54 **(124)** LnS,P(c),Original 65.00
07/56 **(133)** LnS,P(c);rep 20.00
03/58 **(143)** LnS,P(c);rep 20.00
01/60 **(154)** LnS,P(c);rep 18.00
62/63 **(167)** LnS,P(c),Erroneusly
Has Original Date;rep....... 18.00
09/65 **(167)** LnS,P(c);rep 18.00

124-THE WAR OF THE WORLDS
By H. G. Wells
01/55 **(125)** LC,LC P(c),Original .. 90.00
03/56 **(131)** LC,LC P(c);rep...... 20.00
11/57 **(141)** LC,LC P(c);rep...... 20.00
01/59 **(148)** LC,LC P(c);rep...... 20.00
05/60 **(156)** LC,LC P(c);rep...... 25.00
1962 **(165)** LC,LC P(c);rep...... 20.00
62/63 **(167)** LC,LC P(c);rep...... 20.00
11/64 **(167)** LC,LC P(c);rep...... 20.00
11/65 **(167)** LC,LC P(c);rep...... 20.00
1968 **(166)** LC,LC P(c),25¢(c)
Price; rep 20.00
Sr/70 **(169)** LC,LC P(c),Rigid
(c);rep 20.00

125-THE OX BOW INCIDENT
By Walter Van Tilberg Clark
03/55 **(—)** NN,P(c),Original 60.00
03/58 **(143)** NN,P(c);rep 20.00
09/59 **(152)** NN,P(c);rep 20.00
03/61 **(149)** NN,P(c);rep 20.00
62/63 **(167)** NN,P(c);rep 18.00
11/64 **(167)** NN,P(c);rep 18.00
04/67 **(166)** NN,P(c);rep 18.00
r/69 **(169)** NN,P(c),25¢(c)
Price, Rigid(c);rep.......... 18.00

126-THE DOWNFALL
By Emile Zola
05/55 **(—)** LC,LC P(c),Original,'
Picture Progress'Replaces
Reorder List 65.00
08/64 **(167)** LC,LC P(c);rep..... 25.00
1968 **(166)** LC,LC P(c),25¢(c)
Price;rep 25.00

127-THE KING OF THE MOUNTAINS
By Edmond About
07/55 **(128)** NN,P(c),Original..... 65.00
06/64 **(167)** NN,P(c);rep........ 22.00
Fl/68 **(166)** NN,P(c),25¢(c)
Price;rep 22.00

128-MACBETH
By William Shakespeare
09/55 **(128)** AB,P(c),Original 65.00
03/58 **(143)** AB,P(c);rep 20.00
09/60 **(158)** AB,P(c);rep 20.00
62/63 **(167)** AB,P(c);rep 18.00
06/64 **(167)** AB,P(c);rep 18.00
04/67 **(166)** AB,P(c);rep 18.00
1968 **(166)** AB,P(c),25¢(c)
Price;rep 18.00
Sg/70 **(169)** AB,P(c),Rigid(c);rep.. 18.00

129-DAVY CROCKETT
Author Unknown
11/55 **(129)** LC,P(c),Original 150.00
09/66 **(167)** LC,P(c);rep 100.00

130-CAESAR'S CONQUESTS
By Julius Caesar
01/56 **(130)** JO,P(c),Original 75.00
01/58 **(142)** JO,P(c);rep 20.00
09/59 **(152)** JO,P(c);rep 20.00
03/61 **(149)** JO,P(c);rep 20.00
62/63 **(167)** JO,P(c);rep 18.00
10/64 **(167)** JO,P(c);rep 18.00
04/66 **(167)** JO,P(c);rep 18.00

131-THE COVERED WAGON
By Emerson Hough
03/56 **(131)** NN,P(c),Original..... 60.00
03/58 **(143)** NN,P(c);rep 20.00

09/59 **(152)** NN,P(c);rep 20.00
09/60 **(158)** NN,P(c);rep 20.00
62/63 **(167)** NN,P(c);rep 18.00
11/64 **(167)** NN,P(c);rep 18.00
04/66 **(167)** NN,P(c);rep 18.00
Wr/69 **(169)** NN,P(c),25¢(c)
Price, Rigid(c);rep.......... 18.00

132-THE DARK FRIGATE
By Charles Boardman Hawes
05/56 **(132)** EW&RWb,P(c),Orig.. 65.00
05/59 **(150)** EW&RWb,P(c);rep ... 20.00
01/64 **(167)** EW&RWb,P(c);rep ... 20.00
05/67 **(166)** EW&RWb,P(c);rep ... 20.00

133-THE TIME MACHINE
By H. G. Wells
07/56 **(132)** LC,P(c),Original 80.00
01/58 **(142)** LC,P(c);rep 20.00
09/59 **(152)** LC,P(c);rep 20.00
09/60 **(158)** LC,P(c);rep 20.00
62/63 **(167)** LC,P(c);rep 20.00
06/64 **(167)** LC,P(c);rep 25.00
03/66 **(167)** LC,P(c);rep 20.00
03/66 **(167)** LC,P(c),N# Or Price;
rep 20.00
12/67 **(166)** LC,P(c);rep 20.00
Wr/71 **(169)** LC,P(c),25¢(c)
Price, Rigid(c);rep.......... 20.00

134-ROMEO AND JULIET
By William Shakespeare
09/56 **(134)** GE,P(c),Original 65.00
03/61 **(161)** GE,P(c);rep 20.00
09/63 **(167)** GE,P(c);rep 18.00
05/65 **(167)** GE,P(c);rep 18.00
06/67 **(166)** GE,P(c);rep 18.00
Wr/69 **(166)** GE,EdM New P(c),
25¢(c)Price, Rigid(c);rep..... 32.00

135-WATERLOO
By Emile Erckmann & Alexandre Chatrian
11/56 **(135)** Grl,AB P(c),Original .. 65.00
11/59 **(153)** Grl,AB P(c);rep 20.00
62/63 **(167)** Grl,AB P(c);rep 18.00
09/64 **(167)** Grl,AB P(c);rep 18.00
1968 **(166)** Grl,AB P(c),25¢(c)
Price; rep 18.00

136-LORD JIM
By Joseph Conrad
01/57 **(136)** GE,P(c),Original..... 65.00
62/63 **(165)** GE,P(c);rep 18.00
03/64 **(167)** GE,P(c);rep 18.00
09/66 **(167)** GE,P(c);rep 18.00
Sr/69 **(169)** GE,P(c),25¢(c)
Price, Rigid(c);rep.......... 18.00

137-THE LITTLE SAVAGE
By Captain Frederick Marryat
03/57 **(136)** GE,P(c),Original..... 65.00
01/59 **(148)** GE,P(c);rep 20.00
05/60 **(156)** GE,P(c);rep 20.00
62/63 **(167)** GE,P(c);rep 18.00
10/64 **(167)** GE,P(c);rep 18.00
08/67 **(166)** GE,P(c);rep 18.00
Sg/70 **(169)** GE,P(c),25¢(c)
Price, Rigid(c);rep.......... 18.00

All comics prices listed are for *Near Mint* condition.

138-A JOURNEY TO THE CENTER OF THE EARTH
By Jules Verne
05/57 **(136)** NN,P(c),Original..... 90.00
09/58 **(146)** NN,P(c);rep 20.00
05/60 **(156)** NN,P(c);rep 20.00
09/60 **(158)** NN,P(c);rep 20.00
62/63 **(167)** NN,P(c);rep 18.00
06/64 **(167)** NN,P(c);rep 20.00
04/66 **(167)** NN,P(c);rep 20.00
1968 **(166)** NN,P(c),25¢(c) Price;rep 18.00

139-IN THE REIGN OF TERROR
By George Alfred Henty
07/57 **(139)** GE,P(c),Original..... 60.00
01/60 **(154)** GE,P(c);rep 20.00
62/63 **(167)** GE,P(c),Erroneusly Has Original Date;rep....... 18.00
07/64 **(167)** GE,P(c);rep 20.00
1968 **(166)** GE,P(c),25¢(c) Price;rep 18.00

140-ON JUNGLE TRAILS
By Frank Buck
09/57 **(140)** NN,P(c),Original..... 60.00
05/59 **(150)** NN,P(c);rep 20.00
01/61 **(160)** NN,P(c);rep 20.00
09/63 **(167)** NN,P(c);rep 18.00
09/65 **(167)** NN,P(c);rep 18.00

141-CASTLE DANGEROUS
By Sir Walter Scott
11/57 **(141)** StC,P(c),Original 75.00
09/59 **(152)** STC,P(c);rep 20.00
62/63 **(167)** StC,P(c);rep........ 18.00
07/67 **(166)** StC,P(c);rep........ 18.00

142-ABRAHAM LINCOLN
By Benjamin Thomas
01/58 **(142)** NN,P(c),Original..... 70.00
01/60 **(154)** NN,P(c);rep 20.00
09/60 **(158)** NN,P(c);rep 20.00
10/63 **(167)** NN,P(c);rep 18.00
07/65 **(167)** NN,P(c);rep 18.00
11/67 **(166)** NN,P(c);rep 18.00
Fl/69 **(169)** NN,P(c),25¢(c) Price, Rigid(c);rep 18.00

143-KIM
By Rudyard Kipling
03/58 **(143)** JO,P(c)Original 65.00
62/63 **(165)** JO,P(c);rep 18.00
11/63 **(167)** JO,P(c);rep 18.00
08/65 **(167)** JO,P(c);rep 18.00
Wr/69 **(169)** JO,P(c),25¢(c) Price, Rigid(c);rep 18.00

144-THE FIRST MEN IN THE MOON
By H. G. Wells
05/58 **(143)** GWb,AW,AT,RKr, GMC P(c), Original....... 75.00
11/59 **(153)** GWb,AW,AT,RKr, GMC, P(c); rep............ 20.00
03/61 **(161)** GWb,AW,AT,RKr, GMC, P(c); rep............ 18.00
62/63 **(167)** GWb,AW,AT,RKr, GMC, P(c); rep............ 18.00
12/65 **(167)** GWb,AW,AT,RKr, GMC, P(c); rep............ 18.00

Cl #144, The First Men in the Moon © Gilberton Publications

Fl/68 **(166)** GWb,AW,AT,RKr,GMC P(c),25¢(c) Price,Rigid(c);rep . 18.00
Wr/69 **(169)** GWb,AW,AT,RKr,GMC P(c), Rigid(c);rep 28.00

145-THE CRISIS
by Winston Churchill
07/58 **(143)** GE,P(c),Original..... 65.00
05/60 **(156)** GE,P(c);rep 20.00
10/63 **(167)** GE,P(c);rep 18.00
03/65 **(167)** GE,P(c);rep 18.00
1968 **(166)** GE,P(c),25¢(c) Price;rep 18.00

146-WITH FIRE AND SWORD
By Henryk Sienkiewicz
09/58 **(143)** GWb,P(c),Original ... 70.00
05/60 **(156)** GWb,P(c);rep 25.00
11/63 **(167)** GWb,P(c);rep........ 20.00
03/65 **(167)** GWb,P(c);rep........ 20.00

147-BEN-HUR
By Lew Wallace
11/58 **(147)** JO,P(c),Original 60.00
11/59 **(153)** JO,P(c);rep 65.00
09/60 **(158)** JO,P(c);rep 20.00
62/63 **(167)** JO,P(c),Has the Original Date;rep 20.00
—— **(167)** JO,P(c);rep 18.00
02/65 **(167)** JO,P(c);rep 18.00
09/66 **(167)** JO,P(c);rep 18.00
Fl/68 **(166)** JO,P(c),25¢(c)Price, Both Rigid & Soft (c)s;rep.... 50.00

148-THE BUCKANEER
By Lyle Saxon
01/59 **(148)** GE&RJ,NS P(c),orig. . 60.00
—— **(568)** GE&RJ,NS P(c),Juniors List Only;rep.............. 20.00
62/63 **(167)** GE&RJ,NS P(c);rep . . 20.00
09/65 **(167)** GE&RJ,NS P(c);rep . . 20.00
Sr/69 **(169)** GE&RJ,NS P(c),25¢(c) Price, Rigid(c);rep 20.00

149-OFF ON A COMET
By Jules Verne
03/59 **(149)** GMc,P(c),Original ... 65.00
03/60 **(155)** GMc,P(c);rep 20.00
03/61 **(149)** GMc,P(c);rep 20.00
12/63 **(167)** GMc,P(c);rep 18.00
02/65 **(167)** GMc,P(c);rep 18.00
10/66 **(167)** GMc,P(c);rep 18.00
Fl/68 **(166)** GMc,EdM New P(c), 25¢(c)Price;rep............ 30.00

150-THE VIRGINIAN
By Owen Winster
05/59 **(150)** NN,DrG P(c),Original . 75.00
1961 **(164)** NN,DrG P(c);rep..... 30.00
62/63 **(167)** NN,DrG P(c);rep 35.00
12/65 **(167)** NN,DrG P(c);rep 30.00

151-WON BY THE SWORD
By George Alfred Henty
07/59 **(150)** JTg,P(c),Original 70.00
1961 **(164)** JTg,P(c);rep 25.00
10/63 **(167)** JTg,P(c);rep........ 25.00
1963 **(167)** JTg,P(c);rep 25.00
07/67 **(166)** JTg,P(c);rep........ 25.00

152-WILD ANIMALS I HAVE KNOWN
By Ernest Thompson Seton
09/59 **(152)** LbC,LbC P(c),Original 85.00
03/61 **(149)** LbC,LbC P(c);rep 20.00
09/63 **(167)** LbC,LbC P(c);rep.... 18.00
08/65 **(167)** LbC,LbC P(c);rep.... 18.00
fl/69 **(169)** LbC,LbC P(c),25¢(c) Price, Rigid(c);rep 18.00

153-THE INVISIBLE MAN
By H. G. Wells
11/59 **(153)** NN,GB P(c),Original . . 90.00
03/61 **(149)** NN,GB P(c);rep 20.00
62/63 **(167)** NN,GB P(c);rep 18.00
02/65 **(167)** NN,GB P(c);rep 18.00
09/66 **(167)** NN,GB P(c);rep 18.00
Wr/69 **(166)** NN,GB P(c),25¢(c) Price, Rigid(c);rep 18.00
Sg/71 **(169)** NN,GB P(c),Rigid(c), Words Spelling'Invisible Man' Are' Solid'Not'Invisible';rep ... 18.00

154-THE CONSPIRACY OF PONTIAC
By Francis Parkman
01/60 **(154)** GMc,GMc P(c), Original 75.00
11/63 **(167)** GMc,GMc P(c);rep ... 30.00
07/64 **(167)** GMc,GMc P(c);rep ... 30.00
12/67 **(166)** GMc,GMc P(c);rep ... 30.00

155-THE LION OF THE NORTH
By George Alfred Henty
03/60 **(154)** NN,GMc P(c),Original 70.00
01/64 **(167)** NN,GMc P(c);rep 25.00
1967 **(166)** NN,GMc P(c),25¢(c) Price; rep 20.00

156-THE CONQUEST OF MEXICO
By Bernal Diaz Del Castillo
05/60 **(156)** BPr,BPr P(c),Original . 70.00
01/64 **(167)** BPr,BPr P(c);rep 20.00
08/67 **(166)** BPr,BPr P(c);rep 20.00
Sg/70 **(169)** BPr,BPr P(c),25¢(c) Price; Rigid(c);rep 18.00

Classics Illustrated

157-LIVES OF THE HUNTED
By Ernest Thompson Seton
07/60 **(156)** NN,LbC P(c),Original . . 75.00
02/64 **(167)** NN,LbC P(c);rep 28.00
10/67 **(166)** NN,LbC P(c);rep 28.00

158-THE CONSPIRATORS
By Alexandre Dumas
09/60 **(156)** GMc,GMc P(c),
 Original 75.00
07/64 **(167)** GMc,GMc P(c);rep. . . . 28.00
10/67 **(166)** GMc,GMc P(c);rep. . . 28.00

159-THE OCTOPUS
By Frank Norris
11/60 **(159)** GM&GE,LbC P(c),
 Original 75.00
02/64 **(167)** GM&GE,LbC P(c);rep 28.00
166 **(1967)** GM&GE,LbC P(c),25¢(c)
 Price;rep 28.00

160-THE FOOD OF THE GODS
By H.G. Wells
01/61 **(159)** TyT,GMc P(c),Original 75.00
01/61 **(160)** TyT,GMc P(c),Original;
 Same Except For the HRN# . . 60.00
01/64 **(167)** TyT,GMc P(c);rep 28.00
06/67 **(166)** TyT,GMc P(c);rep 28.00

161-CLEOPATRA
By H. Rider Haggard
03/61 **(161)** NN,Pch P(c),Original . . 75.00
01/64 **(167)** NN,Pch P(c);rep. 30.00
08/67 **(166)** NN,Pch P(c);rep. 30.00

162-ROBUR THE CONQUEROR
By Jules Verne
05/61 **(162)** GM&DPn,CJ P(c),
 Original 75.00
07/64 **(167)** GM&DPn,CJ P(c);rep. 28.00
08/67 **(166)** GM&DPn,CJ P(c);rep. 28.00

163-MASTER OF THE WORLD
By Jules Verne
07/61 **(163)** GM,P(c),Original 75.00
01/65 **(167)** GM,P(c);rep 28.00
1968 **(166)** GM,P(c),25¢(c)
 Price;rep 28.00

164-THE COSSACK CHIEF
By Nicolai Gogol
1961 **(164)** SyM,P(c),Original 75.00
04/65 **(167)** SyM,P(c);rep 28.00
Fl/68 **(166)** SyM,P(c),25¢(c)
 Price;rep 28.00

165-THE QUEEN'S NECKLACE
by Alexandre Dumas
01/62 **(164)** GM,P(c),Original 75.00
04/65 **(167)** GM,P(c);rep 28.00
Fl/68 **(166)** GM,P(c),25¢(c)
 Price;rep 28.00

166-TIGERS AND TRAITORS
By Jules Verne
05/62 **(165)** NN,P(c),Original. . . . 125.00
02/64 **(167)** NN,P(c);rep 40.00
11/66 **(167)** NN,P(c);rep 40.00

167-FAUST
By Johann Wolfgang von Goethe
08/62 **(165)** NN,NN P(c),Original. 175.00
02/64 **(167)** NN,NN P(c);rep 75.00
06/67 **(166)** NN,NN P(c);rep 75.00

168-IN FREEDOM'S CAUSE
By George Alfred Henty
Wr/69 **(169)** GE&RC,P(c),
 Original, Rigid (c) 225.00

169-NEGRO AMERICANS THE EARLY YEARS
AUTHOR UNKNOWN
Sg/69 **(166)** NN,NN P(c),
 Original, Rigid(c). 175.00
Sg/69 **(169)** NN,NN P(c),
 Rigid; rep 85.00

CLASSICS ILLUSTRATED GIANTS
An Illustrated Library of Great
Adventure Stories -(reps. of
Issues 6,7,8,10). 2,000.00
An Illustrated Library of Exciting
Mystery Stories -(reps. of
Issues 30,21,40,13) 2,100.00
An Illustrated Library of Great
Indian Stories -(reps. of
Issues 4,17,22,37) 2,000.00

CLASSICS ILLUSTRATED JUNIOR
Oct., 1953–Spring., 1971
501-Snow White and the
 Seven Dwarves 125.00
502-The Ugly Duckling 75.00
503-Cinderella 50.00
504-The Pied Piper. 45.00
505-The Sleeping Beauty 45.00
506-The Three Little Pigs. 45.00
507-Jack and the Beanstalk 45.00
508-Goldilocks & the Three Bears. 45.00
509-Beauty and the Beast 45.00
510-Little Red Riding Hood. 45.00
511-Puss-N-Boots. 45.00
512-Rumpelstilskin 45.00
513-Pinnochio 55.00
514-The Steadfast Tin Soldier. . . 75.00
515-Johnny Appleseed 40.00
516-Alladin and His Lamp. 40.00
517-The Emperor's New Clothes . 40.00
518-The Golden Goose 40.00
519-Paul Bunyan 40.00
520-Thumbelina 45.00
521-King of the Golden River . . . 45.00
522-The Nightingale 35.00
523-The Gallant Tailor 35.00
524-The Wild Swans. 35.00
525-The Little Mermaid. 40.00
526-The Frog Prince. 40.00
527-The Golden-Haired Giant. . . 40.00
528-The Penny Prince 35.00
529-The Magic Servants. 35.00
530-The Golden Bird 35.00
531-Rapunzel. 40.00
532-The Dancing Princesses . . . 35.00
533-The Magic Fountain. 35.00
534-The Golden Touch 35.00
535-The Wizard of Oz. 75.00
536-The Chimney Sweep 40.00
537-The Three Faires. 35.00
538-Silly Hans 35.00
539-The Enchanted Fish. 50.00
540-The Tinder-Box 50.00
541-Snow White and Rose Red . . 35.00
542-The Donkey's Tail 35.00
543-The House in the Woods 32.00
544-The Golden Fleece 55.00
545-The Glass Mountain. 42.00
546-The Elves and the Shoemaker 35.00
547-The Wishing Table 35.00
548-The Magic Pitcher 30.00
549-Simple Kate. 30.00
550-The Singing Donkey 30.00
551-The Queen Bee. 30.00
552-The Three Little Dwarves. . . 40.00
553-King Thrushbeard 30.00
554-The Enchanted Deer 30.00
555-The Three Golden Apples . . 30.00
556-The Elf Mound 30.00
557-Silly Willy. 50.00
558-The Magic Dish,LbC(c) 50.00
559-The Japanese Lantern,LbC(c) 60.00
560-The Doll Princess,LbC(c) . . . 60.00
561-Hans Humdrum,LbC(c) 40.00
562-The Enchanted Pony,LbC(c) . 60.00
563-The Wishing Well,LbC(c) . . . 40.00
564-The Salt Mountain,LbC(c) . . . 40.00
565-The Silly Princess,LbC(c). . . 40.00
566-Clumsy Hans,LbC(c) 40.00
567-The Bearskin Soldier,LbC(c) . 40.00
568-The Happy Hedgehog,LbC(c). 40.00
569-The Three Giants. 40.00
570-The Pearl Princess 40.00
571-How Fire Came to the Indians 55.00
572-The Drummer Boy 55.00
573-The Crystal Ball 55.00
574-Brightboots 50.00
575-The Fearless Prince. 50.00
576-The Princess Who Saw
 Everything 65.00
577-The Runaway Dumpling. 75.00

CLASSICS ILLLUSTRATED SPECIAL ISSUE
Dec., 1955–July, 1962
N# United Nations 400.00
129-The Story of Jesus,Jesus on
 mountain(c) 100.00
129a-Three Camels(c) 125.00
129b-Mountain(c),HRN to 161 . . 75.00
129c-Mountain(c) (1968). 70.00
132A-The Story of America. 80.00
135A-The Ten Commandments. . 80.00
138A-Adventures in Science. . . . 75.00
138Aa-HRN to 149. . . . . 50.00
138Ab-rep.,12/61 . . . . 60.00
141A-GE,The Rough Rider. 75.00
144A-RC,GE,Blazing the Trails . . 75.00
147A-RC,GE,Crossing the Rockies 75.00
150A-Grl,Royal Canadian Police. . 75.00
153A-GE,Men, Guns, & Cattle . . 75.00
156A-GE,GM,The Atomic Age. . . . 75.00
159A-GE,GM,Rockets, Jets and
 Missles. 75.00
162A-RC,GE,War Between
 the States. 150.00
165A-RC/GE,JK,Grl,To the Stars . 80.00
166A-RC/GE,JK,Grl,World War II 125.00
167A-RC/GE,JK,Prehistoric
 World 125.00
167Aa-HRN to 167 . . . . 110.00

All comics prices listed are for *Near Mint* condition.

UNDERGROUND

AMAZING DOPE TALES
Greg Shaw
1 Untrimmed black and white pages, out of order;artist unknown . . 110.00
2 Trimmed and proper pages 95.00

AMERICAN SPLENDOR
Harvey Pekar May, 1976
1 B:Harvey Pekar Stories,
  HP,RCr,GDu,GBu 25.00
2 HP,RCr,GDu,GBu 10.00
3 HP,RCr,GDu,GBu 10.00
4 HP,RCr,GDu,GBu 8.00
5 HP,RCr,GDu,GBu 8.00
6 HP,RCr,GDu,GBu,GSh 7.00
7 HP,GSh,GDu,GBu 5.00
8 HP,GSh,GDu,GBu 3.00
9 and 10 HP,GSh,GDu,GBu . . . . @3.00
11 . . . . 3.00
12 . . . . 4.50
13 thru 19 . . . . @3.50
20 E:Harvey Pekar Stories 4.00

ANTHOLOGY OF SLOW DEATH
Wingnut Press/Last Gasp
1 140 pgs, RCr,RCo, GiS, DSh, Harlan Ellison VB,RTu 37.00

APEX TREASURY OF UNDERGROUND COMICS, THE
Links Books Inc. Oct.,1974
1 . . . . 40.00

APEX TREASURY OF UNDERGROUND COMICS –BEST OF BIJOU FUNNIES
Quick Fox 1981
1 Paperback,comix,various artists 21.00

ARCADE THE COMICS REVUE
Print Mint Inc. Spring, 1975
1 ASp,BG,RCr,SRo,SCW 25.00
2 ASp,BG,RCr,SRo 15.00
3 ASp,BG,RCr,RW,SCW 10.00
4 ASp,BG,RCr,WBu,RW,SCW . . . 10.00
5 thru 7 ASp,BG,SRo,RW,SCW . @7.50

BABYFAT
Comix World/Clay Geerdes 1978
1 B:8pg news parodies, one page comix by various artists 4.50
2 thru 9 same . . . . @3.00
10 thru 26 same . . . . @2.00

BATTLE OF THE TITANS
University of Illinois SF Society 1972
1 Sci-Fi;VB,JGa 50.00

BEST BUY COMICS
Last Gasp Eco-Funnies
1 Rep Whole Earth Review;RCr. . . 3.50

BEST OF BIJOU FUNNIES, THE
Links Books Inc. 1975
1 164 pgs,paperback 250.00

BEST OF RIP-OFF PRESS
Rip Off Press Inc. 1973
1 132 pgs paperback,SCW, RCr,SRo,RW 25.00
2 100 pgs,GS,FT 27.50
3 100 pgs,FS 10.75
4 132 pgs,GiS,DSh 13.00

BIG ASS
Rip Off Press 1969–71
1 28 pgs,RCr 80.00
2 RCr 50.00

BIJOU FUNNIES
Bijou Publishing Empire 1968
1 B:JLy,editor;RCr,GS SW 300.00
2 RCr,GS,SW 125.00
3 RCr,SWi,JsG 80.00
4 SWi,JsG 45.00
5 SWi,JsG 50.00
6 E:JLy,editor,SWi,RCr,JsG 40.00
7 and 8 . . . . @40.00

Bizarre Sex #9
© Kitchen Sink

BINKY BROWN MEETS THE HOLY VIRGIN MARY
Last Gasp Eco-Funnies March, 1972
N# Autobiography about Growing up w/a Catholic Neurosis,JsG . . . 25.00
2nd Printing:only text in bottom left panel 12.00

BIZARRE SEX
Kitchen Sink Komix May, 1972
1 B:DKi,editor,various artists 30.00
2 . . . . 25.00
3 . . . . 20.00
4 thru 6 . . . . @15.00
7 . . . . 6.00
8 . . . . 5.00
9 Omaha the Cat Dancer,RW . . . 25.00
10 inc.Omaha the Cat Dancer,RW 20.00

BLACK LAUGHTER
Black Laughter Pub. Co, Nov. 1972
1 James Dixon art 64.00

BLOOD FROM A STONE (GUIDE TO TAX REFORM)
New York Public Interest Research Group Inc. 1977
1 Tax reform proposals 8.50

BOBBY LONDON RETROSPECTIVE AND ART PORTFOLIO
Cartoonist Representatives
1 . . . . 19.50

BOBMAN AND TEDDY
Parrallax Comic Books Inc 1966
1 RFK & Ted Kennedy's struggle to control Democratic party 60.00

BODE'S CARTOON CONCERT
Dell Sept., 1973
1 132 pgs; VB 27.50

BOGEYMAN COMICS
San Fransisco Comic Book Co., 1969
1 Horror,RHa 65.00
2 Horror,RHa 50.00
The Company & Sons
3 . . . . 35.00

BUFFALO RAG/THE DEAD CONCERT COMIX
Kenny Laramey Dec. 1973
1 Alice in Wonderland parody . . . 60.00

CVA Page 804   All comics prices listed are for *Near Mint* condition.

UNDERGROUND

CAPTAIN GUTS
The Print Mint 1969
1 Super patriotV:Counter
culture 30.00
2 V:Black Panthers 20.00
3 V:Dope Smugglers 20.00

CAPTAIN STICKY
Captain Sticky 1974–75
1 Super lawyer V:SocialInjustice . 20.00

CARTOON HISTORY OF THE UNIVERSE
Rip Off Press Sept., 1978
1 Evolution of Everything;
B:Larry Gonick 8.00
2 Sticks and Stones 8.00
3 River Realms-Sumer & Egypt . . 8.00
4 Part of the Old Testament 5.00

Cherry Collection TPB #2
© Kitchen Sink

5 Brains and Bronze 5.00
6 Who are these Athenians 5.00

CASCADE COMIX MONTHLY
Everyman Studios March, 1978
1 Interviews,articles about
comix & comix artists 6.50
2 and 3 same. . . . . @6.50
4 thru 11 . . . . @3.00
12 thru 23 . . . . @2.25

CHECKERED DEMON
Last Gasp July, 1977
1 SCW 15.00
2 SCW 8.50
3 SCW 6.50

CHEECH WIZARD
Office of Student Publications, Syracuse U 1967
n/n VB 150.00

CHERRY
Kitchen Sink
1 by Larry Welz 10.00

2 . . . . 7.00
3 thru 5 . . . . @5.00
6 thru 10 . . . . @4.00
11 thru 15 . . . . @4.00
TPB Cherry Collection #1 . . . . . . 15.00
TPB Cherry Collection #2 . . . . . . 15.00
TPB Cherry Collection #3 . . . . . . 12.95
Cherry's Jubilee #1 thru #4 . . . . @3.00

CHICAGO MIRROR
Jay Lynch/Mirror Publishing Empire Autumn, 1967
1 B:Bijou Funnies 50.00
2 same 40.00
3 same 125.00

COLLECTED CHEECH WIZARD, THE
Company & Sons 1972
n/n VB. 60.00

COLLECTED TRASHMAN #1, THE
Fat City & The Red Mountain Tribe Productions
n/n SRo. 32.50

COMICS & COMIX
October, 1975
1 . . . . 15.00

COMIX BOOK
Magazine Management Co. Oct., 1974
1 Compilation for newsstand
distribution 20.00
2 and 3 . . . . @10.00
Kitchen Sink Enterprises
4 . . . . 20.00
5 . . . . 10.00

COMIX COLLECTOR, THE
Archival Press Inc. Dec., 1979
1 Fanzine 5.00
2 & 3 Fanzine . . . . @4.00

COMMIES FROM MARS
Kitchen Sink March, 1973
1 TB 40.00
Last Gasp
2 thru 5 TB. . . . . @15.00

COMPLETE FRITZ THE CAT
Belier Press 1978
n/n RCr,SRo,DSh 65.00

CONSPIRACY CAPERS
The Conspiracy 1969
1 Benefit Legal Defense of the
Chicago-8. . . . . 100.00

DAN O'NEIL'S COMICS & STORIES
Company & Sons, VOL.1
1 B:Dan O'Neill 50.00
2 & 3 . . . . @30.00

1971 VOL.2
1 . . . . 6.50
2 and E:Dan O'Neill . . . . @4.50

DAS KAMPF
Vaughn Bode May, 1963
N# 100 Loose pgs. 750.00
2nd Printing 52pgs.-produced by
W.Bachner & Bagginer,1977 . . 15.00

DEADBONE EROTICA
Bantam Books Inc. April, 1971
n/n 132 pgs VB 50.00

DEADCENTER CLEAVAGE
April, 1971
1 14 pgs 50.00

DEATH RATTLE
Kitchen Sink June, 1972
1 RCo,TB 25.00
2 TB 20.00
3 TB 16.00

DESPAIR
The Print Mint 1969
1 RCr 50.00

DIRTY DUCK BOOK, THE
Company & Sons March, 1972
1 Bobby London 30.00

DISNEY RAPES THE 1st AMENDMENT
Dan O'Neil 1974
1 Benefit Air Pirates V:Disney
Law suit; Dan O'Neill 15.00

DOPE COMIX
Kitchen Sink Feb., 1978
1 Drugs comix;various artists. . . . 10.00
2 same 7.00
3 & 4 LSD issue. . . . . @5.00
5 Omaha the Cat Dancer, RW . . . 10.00

DOPIN DAN
Last Gasp Eco-Funnies April, 1972
1 TR 15.00
2 and 3 TR. . . . . @10.00
4 Todays Army,TR 7.50

DR. ATOMIC
Last Gasp Eco-Funnies Sept., 1972
1 B:Larry S. Todd 15.00
2 and 3 . . . . @12.00
4 . . . . 10.00
5 E:Larry S. Todd 6.00

DR. ATOMIC'S MARIJUANA MULTIPLIER
Kistone Press 1974
1 How to grow great pot 10.00

UNDERGROUND

DRAWINGS BY S. CLAY WILSON
San Francisco Graphics
1 28 pgs 200.00

DYING DOLPHIN
The Print Mint 1970
n/n 20.00

EBON
San Francisco Comic Book Company
1 Comix version; RCr 30.00
1 Tabloid version 20.00

EL PERFECTO COMICS
The Print Mint 1973
N# Benefit Timothy Leary....... 30.00

The Fabulous Furry Freak Brothers #9
© Rip Off Press

2nd Printing-1975 .... 4.00

ETERNAL TRUTH
Sunday Funnies Comic Corp
1 Christian Comix 25.00

EVERMUCH WAVE
Atlantis Distributors
1 Nunzio the Narc; Adventures
   of God 60.00

FABULOUS FURRY FREAK BROTHERS, THE
COLLECTED ADVENTURES OF
Rip Off Press #1 Feb., 1971
1 GiS 90.00
FURTHER ADVENTURES OF
Rip Off Press #2
1 GiS,DSh 60.00
A YEAR PASSES LIKE NOTHING WITH
Rip Off Press #3
1 GiS....................... 25.00
BROTHER CAN YOU

SPARE $.75 FOR
Rip Off Press #4
1 GiS,DSh 20.00
FABULOUS FURRY FREAK BROTHERS, THE
Rip Off Press #5
1 GiS,DSh 15.00
SIX SNAPPY SOCKERS FROM THE ARCHIVES OF
Rip Off Press #6
1 GiS 10.00

FANTAGOR
1970
1 (Corben), fanzine 125.00
1a (Last Gasp) 22.00
2 & 3 .... @25.00
4 .... 35.00

THE ADVENTURES OF FAT FREDDY'S CAT,
Rip Off Press Feb., 1977
1 .... 20.00
2 .... 10.00
3 .... 12.00
4 .... 8.00
5 & 6 .... @8.00

FEDS 'N' HEADS
Gilbert Shelton/Print Mint 1968
N# I:Fabulous Furry Freak Bros.; Has no `Print Mint' Address
   24 pgs................. 400.00
2nd printing, 28 pgs......... 60.00
3rd printing, May, 1969 ..... 50.00
4th printing, Says `Forth Printing' 25.00
5th-12th printings.......... @8.00
13th printing 6.50
14th printing 4.75

FELCH
Keith Green
1 RW,SCW,RCr.............. 45.00

FEVER PITCH
Kitchen Sink Enterprises July, 1976
1 RCo 25.00
Jabberwocky Graphix
2 250 signed & numbered 20.00
3 400 signed & numbered 18.00
4 .... 10.00

50'S FUNNIES
Kitchen Sink Enterprises 1980
1 Larry Shell, editor,various
   artists 10.00

FLAMING CARROT
Kilian Barracks Free Press 1981
1 Bob Budden,various artists ... 15.00

FLASH THEATRE
Oogle Productions 1970
1 44 pgs 50.00

FLESHAPOIDS FROM EARTH
Popular Culture Dec., 1974
1 36 pgs 40.00

THE COMPLETE FOO!
Bijou Publishing Sept., 1980
1 RCr, Charles Crumb, r:Crumb
   brothers fanzines 50.00

FRITZ BUGS OUT
Ballentine Books 1972
n/n RCr 70.00

FRITZ THE CAT
Ballentine Books 1969
n/n RCr................... 125.00

FRITZ THE NO-GOOD
Ballentine Books 1972
n/n RCr 60.00

FRITZ: SECRET AGENT FOR THE CIA
Ballentine Books 1972
n/n RCr 60.00

FUNNY AMINALS
Apex Novelties/Don Donahue 1972
1 RCr 65.00

GAY COMIX
Kitchen Sink Sept., 1981
1 36 pgs 7.50
2 36 pgs 5.00

GEN OF HIROSHIMA
Educomics/Leonard Rifas Jan., 1980
1 Antiwar comix by Hiroshima
   survivor Keiji Nakawaza 9.50
2 same 6.50

GHOST MOTHER COMICS
John "Mad" Peck 1969
1 SCw,JsG 55.00

GIMMEABREAK COMIX
Rhuta Press Feb., 1971
2 48 pgs, #0 & #1 were advertised,but
may not have been printed 125.00

GIRLS & BOYS
Lynda J. Barry 1980
1 B:12 pgs with every other page
   blank, all Barry art 10.00
2 thru 10 same.............. @6.50
11 thru 20 same .... @4.50
20 thru 25 same .... @3.50

GOD NOSE
Jack Jackson/
Rip Off Press 1964
N# 42 pgs................. 125.00
2nd printing,Pinkish(c);44p..... 60.00
3rd printing,Blue Border(c)..... 30.00
4th printing,Red Border(c) 15.00

CVA Page 806 — All comics prices listed are for *Near Mint* condition.

UNDERGROUND

GOTHIC BLIMP WORKS LTD.
East Village Other/
Peter Leggieri 1969
1 VB,Editor,various artists 200.00
2 same 145.00
3 KDe,editor 135.00
4 KDe,editor 130.00
5 thru 7 KDe,editor........ @125.00
8 various artists 185.00

GREASER COMICS
Half-Ass Press Sept. 1971
1 28 pgs, George DiCaprio 25.00
Rip Off Press July 1972
2 George DiCaprio............ 15.00

GRIM WIT
Last Gasp 1972
1 RCo..................... 40.00
2 RCo..................... 30.00

HAROLD HEAD, THE COLLECTED ADVENTURES OF
Georgia Straight 1972
1 .... 50.00
2 .... 15.00

HARRY CHESS THAT MAN FROM A.U.N.T.I.E.
The Uncensored Adventures
Trojan Book Service 1966
N# 1st Comix By & For Gay Community 135.00

HEAR THE SOUND OF MY FEET WALKING....
Glide Urban Center 1969
1 Dan O'Neill, 128 pgs 70.00

HISTORY OF UNDERGROUND COMIX
Straight Arrow Books 1974
1 Book by Mark James Estren about Underground Comix 40.00

HOMEGROWN FUNNIES
Kitchen Sink 1971
1 RCr 55.00

HONKYTONK SUE, THE QUEEN OF COUNTRY SWING
Bob Boze Bell Feb., 1979
1 BBB 15.00
2 & 3 BBB .... @10.00

IKE LIVES
Warm Neck Funnies 1973
1 20 pgs,Mark Fisher......... 15.00

INSECT FEAR
Last Gasp 1970
1 SRo,GiS,RHa,JsG 75.00

Print Mint 1970–72
2 .... 30.00
3 .... 20.00

IT AIN'T ME BABE
Last Gasp Eco-Funnies July. 1970
n/n First all women comix
Womens Liberation theme ... 40.00

JAPANESE MONSTER
Carol Lay July, 1979
1 8pgs, Carol Lay 10.00

JESUS LOVES YOU
Zondervan Books/Craig Yoe 1972
1 Christian, RCr 35.00

THE NEW ADVENTURES OF JESUS
Rip Off Press Nov., 1971
1 44 pgs, FSt................ 50.00

JIZ
Apex Novelty 1969
1 36 pgs; RCr, SRo, VMo, SCW; hand trimmed and unevenly stapled 60.00

JUNKWAFFEL
The Print Mint 1971
1 VB 35.00
2 and 3 VB .... @30.00
4 VB,JJ 25.00

KANNED KORN KOMIX
Canned Heat Fan Club 1969
1 20pgs.................... 15.00

KAPTAIN AMERIKA KOMIX
Brief Candle Comix March 1970
1 anti U.S. involvement in Laos... 35.00

KING BEE
Apex/Don Donahue & Kerry Clark 1969
1 RCr,SCW 140.00

KURTZMAN COMIX
Kitchen Sink Sept., 1976
1 HK,RCr,GiS,DKi,WE........ 30.00

LAUGH IN THE DARK
Last Gasp
n/n KDe,RHa,SRo,SCW 20.00

LENNY OF LAVEDO
Sunbury Productions/Print Mint 1965
N# Green(c);1st Joel Beck-a ... 550.00
2nd printing, Orange(c) 400.00
3rd printing, White(c) 200.00

THE MACHINES
Office of Student Publications
Syracuse University 1967
1 VB 135.00

THE MAN
Office of Student Publications
Syracuse University 1966
1 VB 165.00

MAGGOTZINE
Charles Schneider May, 1981
1 Various Artists,conceptual maggot stuff 10.00

MANTICORE
Joe Kubert School of Cartooning & Graphic Arts Inc. Autumn, 1976
1 Fanzine,various artists 10.00

MEAN BITCH THRILLS
The Print Mint 1971
1 SRO..................... 15.00

MICKEY RAT
Los Angeles Comic Book Co. May, 1972
1 Robert Armstrong 35.00
2 same 35.00
3 same 15.00

MOM'S HOMEMADE COMICS
Kitchen Sink June 1969
1 DKi, RCr................. 130.00
The Print Mint
2 DKi..................... 40.00
Kitchen Sink Enterprises
3 DKi,RCr 30.00

MONDAY FUNNIES, THE
Monday Funnies 1977
1 8pgs,various artists 6.50
2 16pgs,various artists 9.00
3 16pgs,various artists 6.50
4 16pgs,various artists 5.50

MONDAY FUNNIES, THE
Passtime Publ. July–Aug., 1980
1 thru 8 Marc L.Reed......... @8.00

MOUSE LIBERATION FRONT
COMMUNIQUE #2 August, 1979
1 SRo, SCW, VMo,DKi; Disney's sues Dan O'Neil's Air Pirates 15.00

MOONCHILD COMICS
Nicola Cuti 1968
0 Nicola Cuti................ 35.00
2 Nicola Cuti................ 35.00
3 Nicola Cuti................ 35.00

MOONDOG
The Print Mint March, 1970
1 All George Metzer.......... 20.00

Moondog–Phantom UNDERGROUND Comics Values Annual

Mr. Natural #3
© R. Crumb

2 same 15.00
3 and 4 same. . . . . @10.00

MORE ADVENTURES OF FAT FREDDY'S CAT
Rip Off Press Jan., 1981
1 GiS. 14.00

MOTOR CITY COMICS
Rip Off Press April, 1969
1 RCr 180.00
2 RCr 130.00

MR. NATURAL
San Fransisco Comic Book Co. August, 1970
1 RCr 130.00
2 RCr 70.00
Kitchen Sink
3 RCr, (B&W) 35.00

NARD 'N' PAT, JAYZEY LYNCH'S
Cartoonists Cooperative Press March, 1974
1 Jay Lynch. 15.00
2 Jay Lynch. 10.00
Kitchen Sink Press 1972
3 . . . . 15.00

NEVERWHERE
Ariel Inc. Feb., 1978
1 RCo 25.00

NICKEL LIBRARY
Gary Arlington
1 1 pg heavy stock colored paper, Reed Crandall 5.00
2 Kim Deitch 2.25
3 Harrison Cady 2.25
4 Frank Frazetta 4.00
5 Will Eisner 4.00
6 Justin Green. 2.25
7 C.C. Beck 4.00
8 Wally Wood 4.00
9 Winsor McCay 2.25

Omaha, The Cat Dancer #3
© Reed Waller

10 Jim Osborne 2.25
11 Don Towlley 2.25
12 Frank Frazetta 4.00
13 Will Eisner 4.00
14 Bill Griffith 2.25
15 George Herriman 2.25
16 Cliff Sterrett 2.25
17 George Herriman. 2.25
18 Rory Hayes & Simon Deitch. . 2.25
19 Disney Studios 2.25
20 Alex Toth 2.25
21 Will Eisner 2.25
22 Jack Davis 3.00
23 Alex Toth 2.25
24 Michele Brand 2.25
25 Roger Brand 2.25
26 Arnold Roth 2.25
27 Murphy Anderson 2.25
28 Wally Wood 3.00
29 Jack Kirby 4.00
30 Harvey Kurtzman 3.00
31 Jay Kinney. 2.25
32 Bill Plimpton 2.25
33 . . . . 2.25
34 Charles Dallas 2.25
35 thru 39 . . . . @2.25
40 Bill Edwards 2.25
41 Larry S. Todd. 2.25
42 Charles Dallas 2.25
43 Jim Osborne 2.25
43 1/2 Larry S. Todd. 2.25
44 Jack Jackson. 2.25
45 Rick Griffin. 2.25
46 Justin Green 2.25
47 and 48 Larry S. Todd . . . . @2.25
49 Charles Dallas 2.25
50 Robert Crumb 3.00
51 Wally Wood 3.00
52 Charles Dallas 3.00
53 and 54 Larry S. Todd . . . . @2.25
55 Charles Dallas 2.25
56 Jim Chase 2.25
57 Charles Dallas 2.25
58 Larry S. Todd. 2.25
59 Dave Geiser 2.25
60 Charles Dallas 2.25

ODD WORLD OF RICHARD CORBEN
Warren Publishing 1977
1 84pgs paperback 20.00

Omaha, The Cat Dancer #11
© Reed Waller

O.K. COMICS
Kitchen Sink June, 1972
1 and 2 Bruce Walthers . . . . . . @10.00

O.K. COMICS
O.K. Comic Company 1972
1 Tabloid with comix, articles, reviews, nudie cuties photos. . 30.00
2 thru 18 . . . . @20.00

OMAHA THE CAT DANCER
Steel Dragon Press, 1984
1 RW,F:Omaha, Shelly, Chuck . . . 15.00
Kitchen Sink, 1986
1 RW. 10.00
2 RW 8.00
3 thru 5 . . . . 7.00
6 thru 10 . . . . 6.00
11 thru 20 . . . . 5.00
Spec.#0, 25th Anniv. Classic 15.00
Images of Omaha, RW benefit 8.00
Images No. 2 . . . . 7.00
TPB Collected Omaha #1, rep. . . . 15.00
TPB Collected Omaha #2, rep. . . . 13.00
TPB Collected Omaha #3, rep. . . . 13.00
TPB Collected Omaha #4, rep. . . . 13.00
TPB Collected Omaha #5, rep. . . . 13.00
Vol. 2, Fantagraphics, 1994
1 . . . . 5.00
2 . . . . 5.00

ORACLE COMIX
Thru Black Holes
Comix Productions Oct., 1980
1 and 2 Michael Roden . . . . . . @5.00

PENGUINS IN BONDAGE
Sorcerer Studio/ Wayne Gibson July, 1981
1 8pgs,Wayne Gibson 4.00

PHANTOM LADY
Randy Crawford June, 1978
1 Sex funnies 5.00

UNDERGROUND

PHUCKED UP FUNNIES
Suny Binghamton 1969
1 ASp;insert bound in yearbook . 400.00

PINK FLOYD, THE
October, 1974
1 sold at concerts 35.00

PLASTIC MAN
Randy Crawford May, 1977
1 Sex funnies,RandyCrawford . . . 10.00

PORK
Co-op Press May, 1974
1 SCW 15.00

PORTFOLIO OF UNDERGROUND ART
Schanes & Schanes 1980
1 SRo,SCW,VMo,RW and many others 13 loose sheets in folder, 32pg book, 1200 signed & numb. . . 75.00

POWERMAN AND POWER MOWER SAFETY
Frank Burgmeir, Co.
Outdoor Power Equipment
1 VB; educational comic about power mower safety 185.00

PROMETHIAN ENTERPRISES
Promethian Enterprises Memorial Day, 1969
1 B:Jim Vadeboncuor editor 75.00
2 same 60.00
3 thru 5 . . . . @25.00

PURE ART QUARTERLY
John A. Adams July, 1976
1 16pgs, All John A.Adams 10.00
2 thru 5 same. . . . .@10.00
6 thru 10 same. . . . . @8.00
11 thru 14 same . . . . @6.00

QUAGMIRE COMICS
Kitchen Sink Summer, 1970
1 DKi,Peter Poplaski 15.00

RAW
Raw Books 1980
1 36pgs,10pgs insert 310.00
2 36pgs,20pgs insert 185.00
3 52pgs,16pgs insert 155.00
4 44pgs,32pgs insert,Flexi disk record 125.00

R. CRUMB'S COMICS AND STORIES
Rip Off Press 1969
1 RCr. 125.00

RAWARARAWAR
Rip Off Press 1969
1 GSh. 60.00

RED SONJA & CONAN "HOT AND DRY"
Randy Crawford May, 1977
1 Sex funnies,Randy Crawford . . . 7.00

REID FLEMING WORLD'S TOUGHEST MILKMAN
David E. Boswell Dec., 1980
1 . . . . 6.00

RIP OFF COMIX
Rip Off Press April, 1977
1 GiS,FSt,JsG,DSh 20.00
2 thru 5 GiS,FSt. . . . . @12.00
6 thru 10 . . . . @6.00

ROWLF
Rip Off Press July, 1971
1 RCo 55.00

RUBBER DUCK TALES
The Print Mint March, 1971
1 Michael J Becker 20.00
2 Michael J Becker 15.00

S. CLAY WILSON TWENTY DRAWINGS
Abington Book Shop Inc. 1967
N# (a),Cowboy(c) 500.00
   (b),Pirate(c). 475.00
   (c),Motorcyclist(c) 475.00
   (d),Demon(c). 475.00
   (e),Deluxe with all 4 variations on same(c) with Gold Embossed Lettering . 675.00

SAN FRANCISCO COMIC BOOK
San Francisco Comic Book Co. Jan.-Feb., 1970
1 . . . . 120.00
2 . . . . 25.00
3 . . . . 20.00
4 thru 6 . . . . @15.00

SAVAGE HUMOR
The Print Mint 1973
1 . . . . 10.00

SAY WHAT?
Loring Park Shelter Community Cartooning Workshop April, 1979
1 B:Charles T. Smith,editor, various artists 10.00
2 thru 6 same . . . . @8.00

SCHIZOPHRENIA, CHEECH WIZARD
Last Gasp Eco-Funnies Jan., 1974
1 VB 30.00

SEX AND AFFECTION
C.P. Family Publishers 1974
1 Sex Education for Children 10.00

SHORT ORDER COMIX
Head Press/Family Fun 1973
1 50 cents,36pgs. 10.00
2 75 cents,44pgs. 5.00

SKULL COMICS
Last Gasp March, 1970
1 Horror,RHa 50.00
2 GiS,DSh,RCo 30.00
3 SRo,DSh,RCo 20.00
4 DSh,Lovecraft issue 20.00
5 SRo,RCo,Lovecraft issue 20.00
6 RCo,Herman Hesse 20.00

SLOW DEATH FUNNIES
Last Gasp April 1970
1 Ecological Awarness & Red Border on (c) 50.00
2nd-4th Printings White Border(c) 10.00
2 Silver(c);1st edition' 34 pgs . . . 100.00
2b Non Silver(c);Says 1st Edition, 34 pgs 20.00
2nd Amorphia Ad on pg 34 . . . . . 6.75
3rd Yellow Skull on (c) 7.00

San Francisco Comic Book #3
© R. Crumb

Skull #6
© Last Gasp Funnies

4th 'Mind Candy For the Masses'
  Ad on pg. 34 .... 7.00
5th $1.00(c) price 3.50
3 thru 5 .... @12.00
6 thru 10 .... @4.50

SMILE
Kitchen Sink Summer, 1970
1 Jim Mitchell 15.00
2 Jim Mitchell 12.00
3 Jim Mitchell 11.00

SNARF
Kitchen Sink Feb., 1972
1 DKi,editor,various artists 27.00
2 thru 5 same .... @15.00
6 thru 9 same .... @6.50

SNATCH COMICS
Apex Novelties 1968
1 RCr,SCW 320.00
2 RCr,SCW 160.00
3 RCr,SCW,RW 80.00

SNATCH SAMPLER
Keith Green 1979
n/n RCr,SCw,RW,RHa 35.00

SPACE INVADERS COMICS, DON CHIN'S
Comix World/Clay Geerdes April, 1972
1 8pgs 8.00

SPASM!
Last Gasp Eco-Funnies April, 1973
1 JJ 15.00

STONED PICTURE PARADE
San Francisco Comic Book Co., 1975
1 RCr,SRo,SCW,WE 22.00

SUBVERT COMICS
Rip Off Press Nov., 1970
1 SRo 25.00
2 SRo 20.00
3 SRo 12.00

TALES OF SEX & DEATH
Print Mint 1971
1 JsG,KDe.RHa,SRo 35.00
2 JsG,KDe.RHa,SRo 20.00

THRILLING MURDER COMICS
San Francisco Comic Book Co., 1971
1 SCW,KDe,RCr,SRo,Jim
  Arlington,editor 30.00

2 (TWO)
Keith Green Feb., 1975
1 SCW 10.00

VAMPIRELLA
Randy Crawford June, 1978
1 Sex Funnies 7.00

VAUGHN BODE THE PORTFOLIO
Northern Comfort Com. 1976
1 VB,16pgs 125.00

VAUGHN BODE PORTFOLIO #1
Vaughn Bode Productions 1978
1 VB,10 pgs 35.00

VAUGHN BODE'S CHEECH WIZARD, THE COLLECTED ADVENTURES OF THE CARTOON MESSIAH
Northern Comfort Com. 1976
1 VB,88pgs 55.00

VAUGHN BODE'S DEADBONE, THE FIRST TESTAMENT OF CHEECH WIZARD
Northern Comfort Com. 1975
1 VB 65.00

VIETNAM
N# 20pgs. Role of Blacks in
  the War,TG Lewis 125.00

WEIRDO
Last Gasp Eco-Funnies March, 1981
1 thru 3 RCr .... @12.00

WEIRDO, THE
Rodney Schroeter Oct., 1977
1 B:Rodney Schroezer,1pg 6.00
2 88pgs 6.00
3 44pgs 6.00

WIMMEN'S COMIX
Last Gasp Eco-Funnies Nov., 1972
1 All women artists&comix 15.00
2 thru 3 same .... @12.00
4 thru 7 same .... @8.00

WONDER WART-HOG AND THE NURDS OF NOVEMBER
Rip Off Press Sept., 1980
1 GiS 20.00

WONDER WART-HOG, CAPTAIN CRUD & OTHER SUPER STUFF
Fawcett Publications 1967
1 GiS,VB 25.00

Zap #3 © Apex Novelties

YELLOW DOG
The Print Mint May, 1968
1 4pgs,RCr 40.00
2 and 3 8pgs,RCr. .... @30.00
4 8pgs,RCr,SCW 30.00
5 8pgs,RCr,SCW,KDe 30.00
6 thru 12 .... @25.00
13/14 52pgs RCr,Jay Lynch 12.00
15 Don Scheneker,editor 59.00
16 .... 55.00
17 thru 24 .... @15.00

YOUNG AND LUSTLESS
San Francisco Comic Book Co., 1972
1 BG 20.00

YOUNG LUST
Company & Sons Oct., 1970
1 BG,ASp 30.00
2 BG 15.00
3 BG,JsG,RCr,ASp 15.00
4 KDe,BG,SRo 10.50
5 BG,SRo 7.50
6 SRo,KDe 5.50

YOW
Last Gasp April, 1978
1 BG 5.75
2 BG 4.75
Becomes:

ZIPPY
3 BG 6.50

ZAP COMIX
Apex Novelties Oct., 1967
0 RCr 360.00
1 RCr 350.00
2 RCr,SCW 135.00
3 RCr,SCW,VMo,SRo 60.00
4 VMo,RW,RCr,SCW.SRo,GiS ... 60.00
5 RW,GiS,RCr,SCW,SRo 50.00
6 RW,GiS,RCr,SCW,SRo 30.00
7 RW,GiS,RCr,SCW,SRo 20.00
8 RW,GiS,RCr,SCW,SRo 15.00
9 RW,GiS,RCr,SCW,SRo 20.00

Index 100–Am

Title	Page
100 Bullets	123
100 Greatest Marvels	290
100 Pages of Comics	439
100%	123
100% True?	124
101 Ways To End the Clone Saga	290
10th Muse	670
10th Muse, The	554
10th Muse/Demonslayer	776
13: Assassin	671
1963	544
2 (two)	811
2-Gun Kid	204
2000 A.D. Monthly	677
2000 A.D. Showcase	677
2001 Nights	781
2001: A Space Odyssey	332
2010	332
2020 Visions	173
2099 A.D.	332
2099 A.D. Unlimited	332
2099 Apocalypse	332
2099 Genesis	332
2099 Special: The World Of Doom	332
2099 Unlimited	332
2099: Manifest Destiny	331
2099: World of Tomorrow	332
"21"	555
21 Down	676
2112	520
22 Brides	676
3 Little Kittens	671
3 X 3 Eyes	520, 777
3-D Batman	171
3-D Zone Presents	671
3-D-Ell	469
30 Days of Night	672
300	520
39 Screams	777
4-D Monkey	599
40 Oz Collected	535
411	239
4most	400
50's Funnies	806
50's Terror	725
666: Mark of the Beast	659
7 Guys of Justice, The	767
77 Sunset Strip	656
777: The Wrath	767
80 Page Giants	72
87th Precinct	592
9 Lives of Felix	636
A Clueless Valentine	214
A Connecticut Yankee In King Arthur's Court	794
A Cop Called Tracy	694
A History of Violence	92
A Journey To the Center Of the Earth	802
A Man Called A^x	114
A Midsummer Nights Dream	799
A Moon, A Girl ...Romance	435
A Small Killing	491
A Study In Scarlet	800
A Tale of Two Cities	792
A Traveller's Tale	699
A. Bizarro	21
A.D.A.M.	560
A.R.M.	698
A-1	196
A-1 Comics	358
A-Next	196
A-OK	697
A-Team	197
A1	694
Aardwolf	694
Aaron Strips	523, 694
Abbie An'slats	358
Abbott and Costello	358, 560
ABC Warriors	694
Abe Sapien: Drums of the Dead	489
Abominations	187
Abraham Lincoln	802
Abraham Stone	187
Absolute Vertigo	21
Absolute Zero	694
Abyss, The	489
AC Annual	694
Accelerate	21
Accident Man	489
Ace Comics	358
Ace Comics Presents	694
Ace Mccoy	694
Aces	694
Aces High	359, 560
ACG's Amazing Comics	694
Achilles Storm	694
Achilles Storm: Dark Secret	694
Acme	694
Acme Novelty Library	560
Acolyte Chronicles	694
Action	21
Action Comics	25
Action Force	187
Action Girl Comics	694
Action Planet	523
Actual Confessions	264
Actual Romances	187
Adam and Eve A.D.	694
Adam Strange	26
Adam-12	560
Addam Omega	694
Addams Family	560
Adlai Stevenson	560
Adolescent Radioactive Black Belt Hamsters	694
Adrenalynn	523
Adrenalynn: Weapon of War	489
Advanced Dungeons & Dragons	26
Adventure Comics	26, 29
Adventure Into Fear	239
Adventure Into Mystery	187
Adventure Strip Digest	523
Adventurers	694
Adventurers Book II	694
Adventurers Book III	694
Adventures In the DC Universe	29
Adventures In the Rifle Brigade	29
Adventures In the Rifle Brigade: Operation Bollock	29
Adventures In Wonderland	359
Adventures Into Terror	258
Adventures Into Darkness	359
Adventures Into the Unknown	359, 694
Adventures Into Weird Worlds	187
Adventures Marco Polo, The	795
Adventures of Robin Hood	560
Adventures of Snake Plisskin	187
Adventures of the Mask	489
Adventures of the Thing	187
Adventures of Young Dr. Masters	560
Adventures of Aaron	523
Adventures of Alan Ladd	29
Adventures of Baron Munchausen	560
Adventures of Barry Ween Boy Genius 2.0	695
Adventures of Barry Ween, Boy Genius, The	523
Adventures of Bob Hope	29
Adventures of Captain America	187
Adventures of Cellini	796
Adventures of Chrissy Claws	695
Adventures of Chuk the Barbaric	695
Adventures of Cyclops & Phoenix	187
Adventures of Dean Martin And Jerry Lewis	29
Adventures of Felix the Cat	560
Adventures of Ford Fairlane	29
Adventures of Homer Ghost	187
Adventures of Jerry Lewis	29
Adventures of Kit Carson	800
Adventures of Kung Fu Pig Ninja Flounder and 4-D Monkey	560
Adventures of Liberal Man	695
Adventures of Luther Arkwright	489, 695
Adventures of Mighty Mouse	359
Adventures of Ozzie and Harriet	29
Adventures of Pinky Lee	187
Adventures of Rex, The Wonderdog	29
Adventures of Sherlock Holmes, The	795
Adventures of Spider-Man	187
Adventures of Superboy	152
Adventures of Superman	157
Adventures of the Aerobic Duo	695
Adventures of the Fly	560
Adventures of the Jaguar	560
Adventures of the Outsiders	29, 43
Adventures of the Planet of the Apes	187
Adventures of the Uncanny X-Men	187
Adventures of the X-Men	187
Adventures of Theown	695
Adventures of Tom Sawyer	796
Adventurous Uncle Scrooge Mcduck	560
Aesops Fables	695
Aetos	695
Aetos 2: Children of the Graves	695
Aetos the Eagle	695
Aftermath	560
Against Blackshard	560
Age of Bronze	523
Age of Heroes	523
Age of Heroes: Wex	523
Age of Innocence	188
Age of Reptiles	489
Age of Reptiles: The Hunt	489
Agency, The	523
Agent Liberty	30
Agent Unknown	695
Agent X	187
Agent: America	560
Agents of Law	489
Agents, The	523
Aggie Mack	359
Agony Acres	695
Air Ace	359
Air Fighters Comics	360
Air Fighters, Sgt. Strike Special	560
Air War Stories	560
Airboy	360, 560
Airfighters Classics	695
Airmaidens Special	561
Airman	561
Airtight Garage	188
Airwaves	695
Akemi	561
Akiko	695
Akira	188, 489
Al Capp's Dog Patch Comics	360
Al Capp's Li'l Abner: The Frazetta Sundays	489
Al Capp's Shmoo	360
Al Capp's Wolf Gal	360
Al Williamson: Hidden Lands	490
Aladdin	188, 561
Alan Moore's Awesome Adventures	561
Alan Moore's Glory	561
Alan Moore's the Courtyard	695
Alan Moore's Yuggoth Cultures	695
Alarming Adventures	561
Alarming Tales	561
Albedo	561, 695
Albedo Vol II	696
Albino Spider of Dajette	561
Alf	188
Alias	188, 561
Alias: Agent Brsitow	561
Alias: Stormfront	561
Alice In Wonderland	796
Alien 3	490
Alien Encounters	561
Alien Fire	696
Alien Legion	188
Alien Legion: Jugger Grimrod	189
Alien Legion: On the Edge	189
Alien Legion: One Planet At A Time	189
Alien Legion: Tenants of Hell	189
Alien Nation	30
Alien Nation: A Breed Apart	696
Alien Nation: The Firstcomers	696
Alien Nation: The Public Enemy	696
Alien Nation: The Skin Trade	696
Alien Nation: The Spartans	696
Alien Resurrection	489
Alien Terror	561
Alien Worlds	561
Aliens	489
Aliens II	489
Aliens Vs Predator	490
Aliens Vs. Predator Vs. the Terminator	490
Aliens Vs. Predator: Booty	490
Aliens Vs. Predator: Eternal	490
Aliens Vs. Predator: Duel	490
Aliens Vs. Predator: War	490
Aliens Vs. Predator: Xenogenesis	490
Aliens, The	562
Aliens: Colonial Marines	489
Aliens: Alchemy	489
Aliens: Apocalypse—The Destroying Angels	489
Aliens: Berserker	489
Aliens: Earth War	489
Aliens: Genocide	490
Aliens: Havoc	490
Aliens: Hive	490
Aliens: Kidnapped	490
Aliens: Labyrinth	490
Aliens: Rogue	490
Aliens: Stronghold	490
Aliens: Survival	490
Aliens: Xenogenesis	490
Aliens: Music of the Spears	490
Aliens: Newts Tale	490
Aliens: Tribes	490
Aliens/Predator: Deadliest of the Species	490
Alison Dare, Little Miss Adventures	696
Alister the Slayer	562
All American Sports	562
All Funny Comics	32
All Good Comics	360
All Great Comics	379
All Hallows Eve	562
All Hero Comics	361
All Humor Comics	361
All Love Romances	453
All Negro Comics	361
All New Exiles	562
All Quiet On the Western Front	799
All Star Comics	32
All Star Squadron	32
All Star Western	32, 33, 177
All Suprise	189
All Teen Comics	189
All Top Comics	361
All Western Winners	190
All Winners Comics	189, 190
All-American Comics	30, 31
All-American Men of War	30
All-American Western	30
All-Famous Crime	360
All-Famous Police Cases	360
All-Flash	31
All-New Comics	361
All-New Tenchi Muyo	696
All-Pro Sports	696
All-Select Comics	189
All-Star Comics	32
All-True Crime	289
All-Winners	190
Allegra	523
Alley Cat	523
Alley Oop	361, 562
Alley Oop Adventures	562
Alliance, The	523
Allies	562
Allies, The	523
Allura and the Cyberangels	696
Ally	696
Alone In the Dark	523
Alpha Centurion	33
Alpha Flight	190, 191
Alpha Flight Special	191
Alpha Korps	562
Alpha Wave	562
Alter Ego	562
Alternate Heroes	696
Alvin (& the Chipmunks)	562
Amanda & Gunn	523
Amazing Adult Fantasy	191
Amazing Adventure Funnies	361

CVA Page 811

Am–Ba Index — Comics Values Annual

Entry	Page
Amazing Adventures	191, 361
Amazing Chan & the Chan Clan	562
Amazing Comics	192, 696
Amazing Detective Cases	192
Amazing Dope Tales	804
Amazing Fantasy	191
Amazing Ghost Stories	480
Amazing Heroes Swimsuit Annuals	562
Amazing High Adventure	192
Amazing Mystery Funnies	361
Amazing Scarlet Spider	192
Amazing Screw-On Head, The	490
Amazing Spider-Man	192, 196
Amazing Spider-Man Collection	196
Amazing Willie Mays	361
Amazing X-Men, The	196
Amazing-Man Comics	361
Amazon	186
Amazon Woman	696
Amazon, The	562
Amber: The Guns of Avalon	33
Ambush Bug	33
Amelia Rules!	562
Amelia Rules!: Superheroes	562
America In Action	362
America Vs. Justice Society	33
America's Best Comics	361, 563
America's Biggest Comics Book	362
America's Greatest Comics	362
America's Greatest Comics	696
American Century	33
American Flagg	562
American Freak: A Tale of the Un-Men	33
American Library	361
American Splendor	491, 696, 804
American Splendor Windfall	491
American Splendor: Unsung Hero	491
American Tail II	196
American Woman	563, 696
American, The	490
American, The: Lost In America	490
Americomics	563
Amerimagna	696
Amethyst	33
Amusing Stories	696
Anarky	33
Anatomic Bombs	696
Ancient Joe	491
Andrew Vachss' Cross	496
Andrew Vachss' Underground	520
Andromeda	563
Andy Comics	453
Angel	362, 491
Angel & the Ape	33
Angel and the Ape	33
Angel Fire	563
Angel Girl	696
Angel Girl: Heaven Sent	697
Angel of Death	697
Angel of Destruction	563
Angela	523
Angela/Glory: Rage of Angels	523
Angelic Layer	697
Anima	33
Animal Antics	33, 362
Animal Comics	362
Animal Fables (ec)	362
Animal Fair	362
Animal Mystic	697
Animal Mystic: Klor	697
Animal Mystic: Water Wars	563
Animal-Man	33
Animaniacs	34
Animax	196
Animerica	697
Animerica Extra	697
Anne Mccaffrey's the Unicorn Girl	563
Anne Rice's the Tale of the Body Thief	563
Annex	196
Annie	196
Annie Oakley	196
Annie Oakley & Tagg	563
Another Chance To Get It Right	491
Ant-Man's Big Christmas	196
Antares Circle	697
Anthology of Slow Death	804
Anthro	34
Anubis	697
Anything Goes	563
Apache Skies	196
Apathy Kat	697
Ape City	697
Ape Nation	563
Apex Treasury of Underground Comics	804
Apex Treasury of Underground Comics -Best of Bijou Funnies:	804
Aphrodite Ix	523
Apocalypse Strikefiles	196
Apollo Smile	563
Apparition, The	697
Appleseed	491, 697
Appleseed Databook	491
Aqua Knight	697
Aquaman	34, 35
Aquaman: Time & Tide	35
Aquarium	697
Arabian Knights	792
Arachnaphobia	563
Arachnid Foundation	563
Arak	35
Araknis	563
Araknis: Retribution	563
Araknis: Shades of Evil	563
Aramis Weekly	697
Arcade the Comics Revue	804
Arcana: The Books of Magic	35
Arcanum	524
Archangel	196
Archangels: The Saga	563
Archer & Armstrong	563
Archie	563
Archie 3000	564
Archie and Friends	564
Archie and Me	564
Archie As Pureheart the Powerful	564
Archie At Riverdale High	564
Archie Comics	362
Archie Comics Digest	564
Archie's Giant Series Magazine	362
Archie's Girls Betty and Veronica	363
Archie's Joke Book Magazine	363
Archie's Madhouse	564
Archie's Mechanics	363
Archie's Pal, Jughead	363
Archie's Pals and Gals	363
Archie's Rival Reggie	363
Archie's Superhero Magazine	564
Archie's Tv Laugh-Out	564
Archie's Weird Mysteries	564
Area 52	524
Area 88	697
Areala, Angel of War	697
Arena, The	564
Argonauts	698
Argus	35
Aria	524
Aria: A Summer Spell	524
Aria: The Soul Market	524
Aria: The Uses of Enchantment	524
Aria/Angela: Heavenly Creatures	524
Ariane & Bluebeard	564
Arik Khan	698
Arion	36
Arion the Immortal	36
Arion, Lord of Atlantis	36
Aristocratic X-Traterrestrial Time-Traveling Thieves	698
Aristokittens, The	564
Arizona Kid	197
Arizona: A Simple Horror	698
Arkaga	524
Arkham Asylum: Living Hell	36
Armageddon	564
Armageddon 2001	36
Armageddon 2001 Armageddon: the Alien Agenda	36
Armageddon Factor	564
Armageddon Patrol	698
Armageddon: Inferno	36
Armed & Dangerous	698
Armed & Dangerous No. 2	698
Armor	564
Armored Trooper Votoms	564
Armorines	564
Army and Navy Comics	464
Army Attack	565
Around the World In 80 Days	798
Arrgh!	197
Arrow	565
Arrow Spotlight	698
Arrow, The	363
Arrowhead	197
Arsenal	36
Arsenic Lullaby	698
Art of Homage Studios	524
Art of Erik Larsen	524
Art of Jay Anacleto, The	524
Art of Joseph Michael Linsner	524
Artemis: Requiem	36
Artesia	565
Artesia Afield	565
Artesia Afire	565
Arzach	491
Ascension	524
Ash	565
Ash Files, The	565
Ash: Cinder and Smoke	565
Ash: Fire and Crossfire	565
Ash: The Fire Within	565
Ash/22 Brides	565
Ashen Victor	698
Ashes	698
Ashley Dust	698
Asrial Vs. Cheetah	698
Assassin	565
Assassin School	565
Assassin, Inc.	565
Assassinate Hitler!	698
Assassinette	698
Assassinette Violated	698
Assassinette Returns	698
Assassinette: Hardcore	698
Assassins	186
Aster	565
Aster the Last Celestial Knight	565
Astonishing	266
Astonishing Tales	197
Astonishing X-Men	197
Astonishing X-Men, The	197
Astounding Space Thrills	524, 698
Astra	698
Astro Boy	491, 565
Astro City: Local Heroes	565
Astronauts In Trouble: Live From the Moon	698
Astronauts In Trouble: Space: 1959	698
Asylum	565
Atari Force	36
Athena	698
Athena Inc.	524
Atlantis Chronicles	36
Atlas	491, 566
Atom & Hawkman	36
Atom Ant	566
Atom Special	36
Atom, The	36
Atom-Age Combat	566
Atoman	363
Atomic Age	197
Atomic Bunny	566
Atomic City Tales	699
Atomic Comics	363, 699
Atomic Man	699
Atomic Mouse	363, 699
Atomic Overdrive	699
Atomic Rabbit	566
Atomic Thunder Bolt, The	363
Atomic Toybox	524
Atomics, The	566
Atomik Angels	566
Attack of the Mutant Monsters	699
August	699
Authentic Police Cases	363
Authority, The	566
Autobiographix	491
Automatic Kafka	566
Automation	524
Autumn	699
Av In 3d	699
Avalon	699
Avant Guard	699
Avataars: Covenant of the Shield	197
Avatar	36
Avatars	699
Avelon	699
Avengeblade	566
Avengelyne	566
Avengelyne Bible: Revelations	567
Avengelyne: Armageddon	566
Avengelyne: Bad Blood	566
Avengelyne: Dark Depths	567
Avengelyne: Deadly Sins	567
Avengelyne: Dragon Realm	567
Avengelyne: Revelation	567
Avengelyne: Seraphacide	567
Avengelyne/Glory	567
Avengelyne/Glory: The Godyssey	567
Avengelyne/Pandora	567
Avengelyne/Power	567
Avengelyne/Prophet	567
Avengelyne/Shi	567
Avengelyne/Suprema: Rage of Furies	567
Avengelyne/Warrior Nun Areala	567
Avengers	197, 200
Avengers Forever	201
Avengers Icons: Tigra	201
Avengers Infinity	201
Avengers Log	201
Avengers Spotlight	201
Avengers Strikefile	201
Avengers Two: Wonder Man & the Beast	201
Avengers Universe	201
Avengers Unleashed	201
Avengers Unplugged	201
Avengers West Coast	201
Avengers, The	567
Avengers: Celestial Quest	201
Avengers: The Crossing	201
Avengers: The Terminatrix Objective	201
Avengers: Timeslide	201
Avengers: United They Stand	201
Avengers/JLA	36
Avengers/Ultraforce	201
Avenue X	699
Aviation and Model Building	473
Avigon	524
Avon One-Shots	364
Awakening Comics	699
Awakening, The	524
Awesome	567
Awesome Comics	699
Axa	567
Axed Files, The	699
Axel Pressbutton	567
Axis Alpha	567
Azrael Plus	37
Azrael/Ash	37
Azreal	36
Aztec Ace	568
Aztek: The Ultimate Man	37
B - Movie Presents	**699**
B.E.A.S.T.I.E.S.	570
B.U.G.G.S	705
B-Sides	206
Babe	364, 491
Babe 2	491
Babe Ruth Sports Comics	364
Babes of Area 51	699
Babes of Broadway	568
Baby Angel X	699
Baby Angel X: Scorched Earth	699
Baby Huey and Papa	568
Baby Huey Duckland	568
Baby Huey, The Baby Giant	568
Babyfat	804
Babylon 5	37
Babylon 5: In Valen's Name	37
Babylon Crush	699
Bacchus Color Special	491
Bachelor Father	568
Back To The Future	568
Backlash	524
Backlash/Spider-Man	525
Backpack Marvels:	202

CVA Page 812

Index Ba–Bi

Entry	Page
Bad Apples	699
Bad Apples: High Expectations	699
Bad Boy	568
Bad Company	568
Bad Eggs	568
Bad Girls	37
Bad Girls of Blackout	568
Bad Kitty	568
Bad Kitty: Mischief Night	568
Bad Kitty: Reloaded	569
Badger	525, 568
Badger Goes Berserk	568
Badger: Shattered Mirror	491
Badger: Zen Pop Funny Animal Version	491
Badlands	491
Badrock	525
Badrock and Company	525
Badrock/Wolverine	569
Baker Street	569, 699
Baker Street: Graphitti	699
Balance of Power	699
Balder the Brave	202
Ball and Chain	37
Ball XI-5	665
Ballad of Halo Jones	569
Ballad of Utopia	699
Ballistic	525
Ballistic Action	525
Ballistic Imagery	525
Ballistic/Wolverine	525
Bamm-Bamm & Pebbles Flintstone	569
Banana Fish	700
Bandy Man, The	700
Bang-Up Comics	364
Banished Knights	525
Banner	202
Banner Comics	364
Banzai Girl	569
Baoh	700
Bar Sinister	569
Barabbas	700
Barb Wire	492
Barb Wire: Ace of Spades	492
Barbarians	700
Barbarians, The	569
Barbaric Tales	700
Barbi Twins Adventures	569
Barbie	202
Barbie & Ken	569
Barbie Fashion	202
Barbie Twins Adventures, The	569
Barney and Betty Rubble	569
Barnyard Comics	364
Barry M. Goldwater	569
Barry Windsor-Smith: Storyteller	492
Bart Simpson Comics	569
Bart Simpsons Treehouse of Horror	569
Bart-Man	569
Baseball	569
Baseball Comics	364
Baseball Greats	492
Baseball Heros	364
Baseball Superstars	700
Baseball Thrills	364
Basil Wolverton In Space	492
Basil Wolverton's Fantastic Fables	492
Bast	135
Bastard Samurai	525
Bastard!!	700
Bat, The	569
Bat-Thing	186
Batgirl	37, 38
Batgirl Adventures	38
Batgirl: Year One	38
Batman	38
Batman & Superman Adventures	43
Batman & Superman: World's Finest	44
Batman Adventures	43
Batman Adventures: The Lost Years	43
Batman Adventures: The Lost Years	43
Batman and the Outsiders	43
Batman and Robin	
Adventures, The	43
Batman Beyond	44
Batman Black & White	44
Batman Chronicles	44
Batman Family	45
Batman Vs. Predator	48
Batman Vs. Predator II Bloodmatch	48
Batman Vs. the Incredible Hulk	43
Batman: Book of the Dead	44
Batman: Dark Knight of the Round Table	44
Batman: Gotham Adventures	45
Batman: Gotham Nights II	46
Batman: Bane of the Demon	44
Batman: City of Light	44
Batman: Dark Victory	45
Batman: Death and the Maidens	45
Batman: Family	45
Batman: Gcpd	45
Batman: Gordon of Gotham	45
Batman: Gordon's Law	45
Batman: Gotham Knights	46
Batman: Gotham Nights	46
Batman: Haunted Gotham	46
Batman: Huntress	43
Batman: It's Joker Time	46
Batman: Jazz	46
Batman: League of Batmen	46
Batman: Legends of the Dark Knight	46
Batman: Man-Bat	47
Batman: Nevermore	47
Batman: No Man's Land	47
Batman: Orpheus Rising	47
Batman: Outlaws	47
Batman: Run, Riddler Run	48
Batman: Shadow of the Bat	48
Batman: Sword of Azrael	48
Batman: Tenses	48
Batman: The Ankh	44
Batman: The Cult	44
Batman: The Dark Knight Returns	44
Batman: The Dark Knight Strikes Again	44
Batman: The Doom That Came To Gotham	45
Batman: The Long Halloween	47
Batman: Toyman	48
Batman: Turning Points	48
Batman/Aliens	492
Batman/Aliens II	43
Batman/Captain America	43
Batman/Deadman	43
Batman/Deathblow: After the Fire	45
Batman/Demon	43
Batman/Dracula	43
Batman/Green Arrow	43
Batman/Grendel: Devil's Masque & Devil's Riddle	46
Batman/Hellboy/Starman	46
Batman/Houdini	43
Batman/Huntress: Cry For Blood	46
Batman/Judge Dredd	43
Batman/Judge Dredd: Die Laughing	46
Batman/Lobo	43
Batman/Phantom Stranger	43
Batman/Predator III: Blood Ties	49
Batman/Predator III: Blood	49
Batman/Punisher	43
Batman/Spawn	43
Batman/Spider-Man	43
Batman/Superman/Wonder Woman: Trinity	48
Batman/Tarzan: Claws of the Catwoman	492
Batman/Wildcat	49
Battle	202
Battle Action	202
Battle Angel Alita	700
Battle Angel Alita: Last Order	700
Battle Armor	700
Battle Beasts	700
Battle Brady	279
Battle Chasers	525
Battle Classics	49
Battle Force	569
Battle Girlz	700
Battle Gods: Warriors of the	
Chaak	492
Battle of the Planets	569
Battle of the Planets	525
Battle of the Planets: Manga	525
Battle of the Planets: Witchblade	525
Battle of the Titans	804
Battle Pope	700
Battle Pope Mayhem	700
Battle Pope Presents: Saint Michael	700
Battle Pope: Wrath of God	700
Battleaxes	49
Battlebooks	202, 569
Battlefield	202
Battlefield Action	385
Battlefront	202
Battleground	203
Battleground Earth	700
Battlestar Black & White	700
Battlestar Galactica	203, 570
Battlestar Galactica Apollo's Journey	570
Battlestar Galactica Journey's End	570
Battlestar Galactica the Enemy Within	570
Battlestar Galactica: Search For Sanctuary	570
Battlestar Galactica: Season Three	570
Battlestar Glactica: Starbuck	570
Battlestone	525
Battletech	570, 700
Battletech: Fallout	570
Battletide	203
Battletide II	203
Battron	701
Bay City Jive	570
Beagle Boys, The	570
Beanie the Meanie	570
Beany & Cecil	364
Beast	203
Beast Boy	49
Beast Warrior of Shaolin	701
Beatles Experience, The	701
Beatles Life Story, The	570
Beautiful Killer	570
Beautiful Stories For Ugly Children	49
Beauty and the Beast	570, 571
Beauty and the Beast	203
Beauty and the Beast Portrait of Love	571
Beavis & Butt-Head	203
Beck and Caul	701
Bedlam	571
Beetle Bailey	571
Beetleborgs	526
Beetlejuice	571
Before the Fantastic 4: Grimm and Logan	203
Before the Fantastic 4: Reed Richards	203
Before the Fantastic 4: The Storms	203
Ben Bowie & His Mountain Men	364
Ben Casey	571
Ben-Hur	802
Benjamin Franklin	798
Benzine	701
Beowulf	49
Berlin	701
Berni Wrightson Master of the Macabre	571
Berserk	492
Berzerker	701
Berzerkers	526
Best Buy Comics	804
Best Comics	364
Best From Boy's Life	571
Best of Bijou Funnies	804
Best of Bijou Funnies	804
Best of Bugs Bunny	804
Best of Dennis the Menace, The	571
Best of Donald Duck	571
Best of Marvel '96	203
Best of Rip-Off Press	804
Best of the Brave & the Bold	49
Best of the West	701
Best Western	203
Bethany the Vampfire	701
Betta: Time Warrior	571
Betti Cozmo	571
Bettie Page	492
Bettie Page Comics: Spicy Adventure	492
Bettie Page the '50s Rage	701
Bettie Page: Queen of Hearts	492
Bettie Page: Queen of the Nile	492
Betty	571
Betty & Veronica Spectacular	571
Betty and Me	571
Betty and Veronica	571
Betty Boop's Sunday Best	571
Beverly Hillbillys	571
Beware	203, 373
Beware the Creeper	49
Bewitched	571
Beyond Communion	787
Beyond Mars	701
Beyond the Grave	572
Big	492
Big All-American Comic Book	49
Big Ass	804
Big Bang	572
Big Bang Comics	526
Big Blown Baby	492
Big Book of Conspiracies, The	49
Big Book of Death, The	49
Big Book of Fun Comics	49
Big Book of Hoaxes, The	49
Big Book of Little Criminals, The	49
Big Book of Losers, The	49
Big Book of Martyrs, The	49
Big Book of Scandal	49
Big Book of the Unexplained	49
Big Book of the Weird Wild West	49
Big Book of Thugs, The	49
Big Book of Urban Legends, The	49
Big Book of Weirdos, The	49
Big Bruisers	526
Big Chief Wahoo	365
Big Daddy Danger	49
Big Guy and Rusty the Robot Boy	492
Big Hair Productions	526
Big Hoax	492
Big Numbers	701
Big O, The	701
Big Shot Comics	365
Big Valley, The	572
Big-3	365
Bigg Time	49
Bigger	701
Bijou Funnies	804
Biker Mice From Mars	204
Bill & Ted's Bogus Journey	204
Bill & Ted's Excellent Comics	204
Bill Barnes, America's Air Ace	359
Bill Black's Fun Comics	572
Bill Boyd Western	365
Bill Stern's Sports Book	365
Bill the Bull	701
Bill the Bull: One Shot, One Bourbon, One Beer	701
Bill the Galactic Hero	572
Billi 99	492
Billy Buckskin Western	204
Billy Dogma	701
Billy Nguyen Private Eye	701
Billy the Kid	572
Billy the Kid Adventure Magazine	365
Bingo Comics	365
Binky Brown Meets the Holy Virgin Mary	804
Bioneers	572
Bionic Woman, The	572
Bionix	572
Bird: The Tattoo	492
Birds of Prey	49
Birds of Prey: Batgirl	50
Birds of Prey: Catwoman/Batgirl	50
Birds of Prey: Manhunt	49
Birthday Boy, The	701
Bishop	204
Bishop: The Last X-Man	204
Bishop: Xavier's Security Enforcer	204
Bizarre 3-D Zone	572

CVA Page 813

Bizarre Adventures 272
Bizarre Heroes 702
Bizarre Sex 804
Bizarro Comics 50
Black and White 526, 702
Black Anvil 526
Black Arrow, The 795
Black Axe 204
Black Beauty 797
Black Canary 50
Black Canary/Oracle: Birds of Prey 50
Black Cat 204, 572
Black Cat Comics 365
Black Cat Mystery 366
Black Cat Mystic 366
Black Cat Western 366
Black Condor 50
Black Cross: Dirty Work 492
Black Diamond 572
Black Diamond Western 381
Black Dragon 204
Black Dragon, The 492
Black Enchantress 572
Black Flag 526, 572
Black Fury 572
Black Goliath 204
Black Hole 702
Black Hole, The 572
Black Hood 51, 420, 572
Black Jack 572, 702
Black Kiss 702
Black Knight 204
Black Knight, The 204
Black Knight: Exodus 204
Black Lamb, The 51
Black Laughter 804
Black Lightning 51
Black Magic 492
Black Mask 52
Black Mist 702
Black Ops 526
Black Orchid 52
Black Panther 204
Black Pearl, The 492
Black Phantom 572
Black Raven 572
Black Rider 190
Black Rider Rides Again 205
Black Scorpion 702
Black September 572
Black Sun 572
Black Terror 367, 573
Black Tide 526, 573
Black Tulip, The 798
Black Web 573
Black Widow 205
Black Widow: Pale Little Spider 205
Black Zeppelin 702
Blackball Comics 572
Blackburne Covenant, The 492
Blackened 702
Blackhawk 50, 366
Blackjack: Blood & Honor 572
Blackmask 702
Blackstone, The Magician 205
Blackthorne 3 In 1 702
Blackwulf 205
Blade 205
Blade of Shuriken 702
Blade of the Immortal 492
Blade Runner 205
Blade, The Vampire Hunter 205
Blade: Vampire Hunter 205
Blair Which? 493
Blair Witch Chronicles 702
Blair Witch Project 702
Blair Witch: Dark Testaments 526
Blanche Goes To New York 493
Blast Corps 493
Blast-Off 573
Blasters Special 52
Blaze 205
Blaze Carson 206
Blaze of Glory 206
Blaze, The Wonder Collie 206
Blazing Combat 573
Blazing Comics 367
Blazing Six-Guns 573
Blind Fear 702
Blindside 526
Blink 206
Bliss Alley 526
Blokhedz 526
Blonde Avenger 702
Blonde Avenger: Dangerous Conclusions 702
Blonde Phantom 189
Blondie Comics 367
Blood 206
Blood 'n' Guts 702
Blood & Glory 206
Blood & Roses 573
Blood & Roses Adventures 702
Blood & Shadows 52
Blood and Water 52
Blood From A Stone 804
Blood Is the Harvest 702
Blood Junkies 702
Blood Legacy 526
Blood Legacy: The Young Ones 526
Blood of Dracula 702
Blood of the Innocent 702
Blood Sword 573
Blood Sword Dynasty 573
Blood Syndicate 52
Blood Ties 493
Blood World 493
Blood Wulf 526
Blood: A Tale 52
Bloodbath 52, 573
Bloodbrothers 702
Bloodfire 573
Bloodfire/Hellina 573
Bloodhunter 526
Bloodletting 702
Bloodlines 206
Bloodlore 573
Bloodpack 52
Bloodpool 526
Bloodscent 573
Bloodshed 702
Bloodshot 573
Bloodstone 206
Bloodstrike 526
Bloodstrike: Assassin 526
Bloodthirsty Pirate Tales 703
Bloodwing 703
Bloody Mary 52
Bloody Mary: Lady Liberty 52
Bloody School 703
Bludgeon 703
Blue 527
Blue Beetle 52, 468, 574
Blue Beetle, The 367
Blue Bolt 368
Blue Bulleteer 703
Blue Circle Comics 368
Blue Devil 53
Blue Lily 493
Blue Monday: Absolute Beginners 703
Blue Monday: The Kids Are Alright 703
Blue Phantom, The 574
Blue Ribbon 574
Blue Ribbon Comics 368
Bluntman and Chronic 527
Bo 368
Bob Burden's Original Mysterymen 508
Bob Colt 368
Bob the Galactic Bum 53
Bobby London Retrospective and Art Portfolio 804
Bobman and Teddy 804
Bode's Cartoon Concert 804
Body Bags 493
Body Count 527
Body Doubles 53
Bogeyman Comics 804
Bogie Man, The 53
Bogie Man: Chinatoon 703
Bogie Man: Manhatten Project .703
Bohos 527
Bold Adventure 574
Bold Stories 368
Bolt & Starforce Six 574
Bomba, The Jungle Boy 53
Bombast 574
Bomber Comics 368
Bonafide 703
Bonanza 574
Bone 527, 703
Boneshaker 703
Boneyard 703
Boof 527
Boof and the Bruise Crew 527
Boogeyman 512
Book of All Comics 369
Book of Ballads and Sagas 703
Book of Comics, The 369
Book of Fate, The 53
Book of Night 493
Book of the Damned 214
Book of the Dead 206
Book of the Tarot 703
Book, The 703
Books of Faerie 53
Books of Faerie, The 53
Books of Faerie, The: Auberon's Tale 53
Books of Lore 703
Books of Lore: The Kaynin Gambit 703
Books of Lore: The Shape of Evil 704
Books of Lore: The Storyteller .704
Books of Magic 53
Boondoggle 704
Booster Gold 53
Border Worlds 704
Boris Karloff Tales of Mystery 574
Boris the Bear 493, 704
Boris' Adventure Magazine 704
Born 206
Born To Kill 704
Boston Bombers 704
Bottle Imp, The 801
Bounty 704
Box Office Poison 704
Boy Comics 369
Boy Commandos 54
Boy Explorers 468
Bozo 574
Bozo the Clown 574
Bozz Chronicles, The 206
Bradleys, The 704
Brady Bunch, The 574
Brain Boy 574
Brainbanx 54
Bram Stoker's Burial of the Rats 574
Brass 527, 574
Brat Pack 704
Brath 574
Bratpack/Maximortal 704
Brats Bizarre 206
Brave 493
Brave and the Bold 54
Brave Old World 55
Bravura 574
Break the Chain 206
Break-Thru 574
Breakfast After Noon 704
Breakneck Blvd 704
Breathtaker 55
'Breed 574
'Breed II 574
Breeding Ground 574
Brenda Lee Story, The 574
Brenda Starr 369
Brenda Starr Reporter 574
Brenda Starr, Ace Reporter 704
Brian Bolland's Black Book 574
Brick Bradford 369
Brides In Love 574
Brigade 527, 575
Brilliant Boy 704
Bring 'em Back Alive 800
Brit 527
Broadway Romances 369
Broid 704
Broken Halo: Is There Nothing Sacred 704
Broken Heroes 704
Broncho Bill 369
Bronx 704
Brooklyn Dreams 55
Brother Man 704
Brother Power, The Geek 55
Brotherhood, The 206
Bru-Hed 704
Bruce Gentry 369
Bruce Jones: Razors Edge 704
Bruce Jones' Outer Edge 704
Bruce Lee 575
Bruce Wayne: Agent of S.H.I.E.L.D. 186
Brute Force 206
Brute, The 575
Bubble Gum Crisis: Grand Mal .493
Buccaneers 419
Buce-N-Gar 704
Buck Duck 206
Buck Godot 705
Buck Godot: Zap Gun For Hire .705
Buck Jones 369
Buck Rogers 369, 575
Buckaneer, The 802
Buckeroo Banzai 206
Bucky O'hare 575
Buffalo Bill 800
Buffalo Bill Jr. 575
Buffalo Rag/The Dead Concert Comix 804
Buffalo Wings 705
Buffy the Vampire Slayer: Angel 494
Buffy the Vampire Slayer: the Origin 494
Buffy the Vampire Slayer 493
Buffy the Vampire Slayer: Haunted 494
Buffy the Vampire Slayer: Oz 494
Buffy the Vampire Slayer: Willow and Tara — Wilderness 494
Bug 206, 705
Bug Movies 370
Bugboy 527
Bugged-Out Adventures of Ralfy Roach 575
Bugs Bunny 55, 370
Bullet Crow 705
Bulletman 370
Bulletproof Monk 527
Bullets & Bracelets 186
Bulls-Eye 453
Bullwinkle 575
Bullwinkle & Rocky 206, 575
Bullwinkle For President 575
Bulwark 705
Bunker, The 527
Burke's Law 575
Burning Blue, The 705
Bushido 705
Buster Crabbe 370
Butch Cassidy 575
Butcher Knight 527
Butcher, The 55
Buz Sawyer 370
Buzz 705
Buzzard 705
Buzzy 55
By Bizarre Hands 494
C.H.I.X. That Time Forgot, The 528
C-23 529
C-M-O Comics 374
Cabbot: Bloodhunter 575
Cable 206
Cable & Deadpool 207
Cable & X-Force 207
Cadillacs & Dinosaurs 575
Cadillacs & Dinosaurs 207
Cadillacs and Dinosaurs 705
Caesar's Conquests 801
Cage 207
Cages 575
Cain 494, 575
Cain's Hundred 575
Caliber Core 705
Caliber Double Feature 705
Caliber Focus 705
Caliber Presents 705
Caliber Spotlight 705
Calibrations 705
California Girls 705
California Raisins 575
Caligari 2050 705
Call Me Princess 705

Index

Ca–Co

Call of Duty: The Brother Hood .208
Call of the Wild, The 799
Call, The 208
Calling All Boys 370
Calling All Girls 370
Calling All Kids 370
Calvin & the Colonel 575
Camelot 3000 55
Camelot Eternal 705
Camera Comics 370
Camp Candy 208
Camp Comics 370
Cannon God Exaxxion 494
Canton Kid 705
Cap'n Quick & Foozle 575
Caper 56
Capes 527
Capt. Confederacy 705
Capt. Electron 575, 706
Capt. Savage & His Leather-
  neck Raiders 212
Captain Action 56
Captain Aero Comics 370
Captain America 208, 211
Captain America Comics 208
Captain America: Dead Man
  Running 211
Captain America: Sentinel of
  Liberty 211
Captain America: What
  Price Glory 211
Captain Atom 56, 575, 666
Captain Battle 371
Captain Battle, Jr. 371
Captain Britain Classics 211
Captain Canuck 575
Captain Carrot 56
Captain Confederacy 211
Captain Courageous Comics ..364
Captain Easy 371
Captain Fearless Comics 371
Captain Flash 371
Captain Fleet 371
Captain Flight Comics 371
Captain Gallant 371
Captain Glory 575
Captain Gravity 575
Captain Guts 805
Captain Harlock 706
Captain Harlock Death-
  shadow Rising 706
Captain Harlock: Fall of
  the Empire 576
Captain Jack 706
Captain Jet 371
Captain Johner & the Aliens ..576
Captain Justice 211
Captain Kidd 379
Captain Koala 706
Captain Marvel 211, 212, 576
Captain Marvel Adventures ...371
Captain Marvel Jr. 372
Captain Midnight 372
Captain Nauticus 576
Captain Nice 576
Captain Paragon 576
Captain Planet 212
Captain Power 576
Captain Pureheart 564
Captain Science 373
Captain Stern 576
Captain Sternn: Running Out
  of Time 706
Captain Steve Savage 373
Captain Sticky 805
Captain Storm 56
Captain Thunder and
  Blue Bolt 576, 706
Captain Venture & the Land
  Beneath the Sea 576
Captain Victory 576
Captain Video 373
Captain Wizard 373
Captains Courageous 801
Car 54, Where Are You? 576
Car Warriors 213
Caravan Kidd 494
Carca Jou Renaissance 576
Cardcaptor Sakura 706
Care Bears 212

Carnage 212
Carnival 453
Carnosaur Carnage 576
Caroline Kennedy 576
Carson of Venus 499
Cartoon Cartoons 56
Cartoon History of the
  Universe 706, 805
Cartoon Kids 212
Cartoon Network Starring ...56
Cartoon Network Presents ...56
Carvers 527
Cascade Comix Monthly 805
Casefiles: Sam and Twitch ..528
Cases of Sherlock Holmes ..706
Casey Jones & Raphael 576
Casey- Crime Photographer ..213
Casper 213
Casper & Friends 576
Casper & Wendy 576
Casper and Nightmare 635
Casper Enchanted Tales 576
Casper Ghostland 576
Casper the Friendly Ghost ..576
Casper, The Friendly Ghost ..373
Casper's Ghostland 576
Castle Dangerous 802
Castle In the Sky 706
Castle Waiting 706
Casual Heroes 528
Cat & Mouse 706
Cat Claw 706
Cat Tales 576
Cat, The 213
Cat-Man Comics 373
Cat-Man Retro Comic 706
Catalyst: Agents of Change ..494
Catfight 706
Catfight: Dream Into Action .706
Catfight: Sweet Revenge 706
Catfight: Dream Warrior ...706
Cathedral Child 528
Catseye 576
Catwoman 56, 57
Catwoman: Guardian of
  Gotham 57
Catwoman/Wildcat 57
Cauldron 576
Cave Girl 576
Cave Kids 576
Cavewoman 577, 706
Cavewoman Intervention ...706
Cavewoman: Jungle Tales ..707
Cavewoman: Meriem's Gallery .707
Cavewoman: Missing Link ..707
Cavewoman: Odyssey 707
Cavewoman: Pangaean Sea ..707
Cavewoman: Rain 707
Cavewoman: Raptor 707
Cecil Kunkle 707
Celestial Mechanics 707
Celestial Zone 707
Celestine 528
Cement Shooz 707
Centurions 57
Century 577
Century: Distant Sons 213
Cerebus 707
Cerebus Church & State 708
Cerebus High Society 708
Cerebus Jam 708
Cerebus Reprints 708
Ceres, Celestial Legend 708
Chain Gang War 57
Chains of Chaos 577
Chainsaw Vigilante 708
Challenger, The 374
Challengers of the Fantastic ..186
Challengers of the Unknown .57, 58
Chamber of Chills 213, 374
Chamber of Clues 374
Chamber of Darkness 213
Champ Comics 374
Champion Comics 374
Champion of Kitara: Dum
  Dum & Dragons 708
Champions 213, 577
Champions Classic 577
Change Commander Goku II ..708
Channel Zero 528

Chaos Bible 577
Chaos Effect 577
Chaos Quarterly 577
Chaos! Chronicles–the History
  of A Cosmos 577
Chaos! Gallery 577
Chaos! Nightmare Theater ..577
Chapel 528, 577
Charlemagne 577
Charlie Chan 577, 708
Charlie Mccarthy 374
Charlton Bullseye 577
Charlton Sport Library 577
Charm School 708
Chase 58
Chaser Platoon 709
Chasing Dogma 528
Chassis 528, 577
Chastity Lust For Life 577
Chastity Rocked 578
Chastity: Crazytown 577
Chastity: Heartbreaker 577
Chastity: Re-Imagined 577
Chastity: Shattered 578
Chastity: Theatre of Pain ...578
Cheap Shoddy 578
Checkered Demon 805
Checkmate 58
Cheech Wizard 805
Chemical Man 578
Cherry 805
Cheryl Blossom 578
Cheryl Blossom Goes
  Hollywood 578
Chesty Sanchez 709
Cheval Noir 494
Cheyenne 578
Cheyenne Kid 578, 689
Chi-Chian 578
Chiaroscuro: The Private Lives
  of Leonardo Davinci 58
Chibi-Pop Manga 709
Chicago Mirror 805
Chief, The 374
Child's Play 2 578
Child's Play 3 578
Child's Play: The Series ...578
Childhood's End 528
Children of Fire 578
Children of the Puppet Master .644
Children of the Voyage 213
Children's Crusade 58
Chili 213
Chiller 528
Chilling Adventures In Sorcery
  As Told By Sabrina 578
Chilling Tales 373
Chimera 578
China & Jazz 709
China & Jazz Code Name
  Double Impact 709
China & Jazz: Superstars ..578
China & Jazz: Trigger Happy .709
Chip 'n' Dale 578
Chirality 709
Chirality: To the Promised Land .709
Chiron 709
Chobits 709
Choice 374
Choo Choo Charlie 578
Chopper: Earth, Wind, and
  Fire 578
Chosen, The 578
Christian 578
Christmas Carol, A 797
Christmas Parade 578
Christmas Spirit, The 578
Christmas With the Super-
  Heroes 58
Chroma-Tick Special Edition ..709
Chrome 578
Chrome Warriors In A '59
  Chevy 578
Chromium Man 579
Chromium Man: Violent Past ..579
Chronicles of Conan, The ..494
Chronicles of Corum 579
Chronicles of the Cursed
  Sword 709
Chronos 58

Chronowar 494
Chuck Norris 213
Chuckle the Giggly Book of
  Comic Animals 374
Cicero's Cat 579
Cici 579
Cimmaron Strip 579
Cinder & Ashe 58
Cindy Comics 262
Cinema Comics Herald 374
Cinnamon: El Ciclo 59
Circle Weave, The 709
Circus the Comic Riot 374
Cisco Kid, The 374
Citizen V 213
Citizen V & the V Battalion:
  the Everlasting 213
City Knights, The 579
City of Silence 528
City Perilous 579
Claire Voyant 374
Clamp School Detectives ...709
Clan Apis 709
Clande, Inc. 709
Clandestine 214
Clash 59
Classic Conan 217
Classic Punisher 296
Classic Star Wars:
  Devilworlds 495
  Han Solo At Star's End ..495
  A Long Time Ago 495
  A New Hope 495
  Early Adventures 495
  Empire Strikes Back 495
  Return of the Jedi 495
  Vandelhelm Mission 495
Classic X-Men 354
Classics Illlustrated Special
  Issue 803
Classics Illustrated 579
Classics Illustrated Junior ...579
Classics Illustrated Giants ..803
Classics Illustrated Junior ...803
Classwar 579
Claus 579
Claw the Unconquered 59
Cleopatra 803
Clerks 528
Clerks: The Comic Book ...709
Cliffhanger Comics 709
Clint the Hamster 709
Clive Barker's Hellraiser ...214
Clive Barker's Book of the
  Damned 214
Clive Barker's Dread 579
Clive Barker's Tapping the Vein .579
Cloak & Dagger 214
Cloak and Dagger 374
Clock Maker, The 528
Clockwork Angels 528
Cloister and the Hearth, The ..798
Clonezone 495
Cloudfall 528
Clover 709
Clowns, The (pagliacci) ...495
Club 9 495
Clue Comics 374
Clyde Crashcup 579
Cobalt 60 579
Cobalt Blue 579
Cobra 709
Cocomalt Big Book of Comics .375
Code Blue 528
Code Name: Double Impact .579
Code Name: Spitfire 316
Code of Honor 214
Codename: Strikeforce ...579
Codename: Danger 579
Codename: Firearm 579
Codename: Genetix 214
Codename: Knockout 59
Codename: Styke Force ..528
Coffin 709
Cold Blooded Chameleon
  Commandos 709
Cold Eden 710
Cole Black 710
Collected Trashman #1, The ..805
Collected Cheech Wizard, The .805

CVA Page 815

Co–Da Index Comics Values Annual

Title	Page
Collector's Dracula	579
Colonel Kilgore	710
Colors In Black	495
Colossal Show, The	579
Colossus	214
Colossus Comics	375
Colossus: God's Country	214
Colour of Magic	579
Colt	710
Colt .45	580
Colt Special	580
Columbia Comics	375
Combat	214, 528, 580
Combat Casey	337
Combat Kelly	214
Comet Man	214
Comet, The	59, 580
Comic Album	580
Comic Book	495
Comic Book Heaven	710
Comic Cavalcade	59
Comic Pages	402
Comico X-Mas Special	580
Comics & Comix	805
Comics and Stories	495
Comics Express	710
Comics Greatest World	495
Comics Magazine	402
Comics On Parade	375
Comics, The	375
Coming of Aphrodite	710
Comix Book	215, 805
Comix Collector, The	805
Comix International	580
Comix Zone	215
Command Review	710
Commando Adventures	215
Commies From Mars	805
Complete Alex Toth Zorro	528
Complete Book of Comics and Funnies	375
Complete Book of True Crime Comics	375
Complete Comics	192
Complete Fritz the Cat	805
Complete Mystery	215
Completely Pip and Norton	496
Conan	215, 217
Conan Classics	217
Conan Death Covered In Gold	215
Conan Saga	217
Conan the Adventurer	215
Conan the Barbarian	215
Conan the King	217
Conan the Legend	496
Conan the Savage	218
Conan the Usurper	217
Conan: River of Blood	217
Conan: The Flame and the Fiend	217
Conan: The Scarlet Sword	217
Conan/Rune	217
Concrete	496
Concrete Jungle: The Legend of the Black Lion	580
Concrete: Strange Armor	496
Concrete: Eclectica	496
Concrete: Fragile Creature	496
Concrete: Killer Smile	496
Concrete: Think Like A Mountain	496
Condom-Man	710
Coneheads	218
Confessions of Romance	375
Confessions of Love	375
Confessions of Lovelorn	425
Confidential Diary	608
Congo Bill	59
Congorilla	59
Conjurors	59
Conqueror	710
Conqueror Comics	375
Conqueror of the Barren Earth	59
Conquest of Mexico, The	802
Conspiracy	218
Conspiracy Capers	805
Conspiracy Comics	710
Conspiracy of Pontiac, The	802
Constellation Graphics	710
Construct	580, 710
Contact Comics	375
Contest of Champions	218
Contest of Champions II	218
Coo Coo Comics	375
Cookie	375
Cool World	59
Cops	59
Cops: The Job	218
Corben Special	580
Cormac Mac Art	496
Corny's Fetish	496
Corrector Yui	710
Corsican Brothers, The	794
Corto Maltese: Ballad of the Salt Sea	710
Corum: The Bull & the Spear	580
Cosmic Boy	60
Cosmic Heroes	710
Cosmic Odyssey	60
Cosmic Powers	218
Cosmic Powers Unlimited	218
Cosmic Ray	528
Cosmo Cat	376
Cosmoneers Special	580
Cossack Chief, The	803
Cougar, The	580
Count Duckula	218
Count of Monte Cristo, The	791
Counter Parts	710
Counter-Ops	580
Counter-Strike	580
Courage Comics	376
Courtney Crumrin & the Coven of Mystics	710
Courtship of Eddie's Father	580
Courtship of Miles Standish	799
Coutoo	496
Coven	580
Coven 13	580
Coven: Dark Origins	580
Coven: Dark Sister	581
Coven: Spellcaster	581
Coven: Tooth & Nail	581
Coven/Re: Gex	580
Coventry	710
Covered Wagon, The	801
Cow Puncher	376
Cow, The	528
Cowboy Action	341
Cowboy Bebop	710
Cowboy Comics	460
Cowboy In Africa	581
Cowboy Romances	218
Cowboy Wally Show, The	60
Cowboy Western	486
Cowboy Western Comics	486
Cowboy Western Heroes	486
Cowboys 'n' Injuns	376
Cowgirl Romances	223, 376
Coyote	218
Crack Comics	376
Crack Western	376
Crackajack Funnies	376
Cracked	581
Crash Comics	377
Crash Dummies	581
Crash Ryan	218
Cray Baby Adventures, The	710
Cray Baby Adventures: Wrath of the Peddidlers	710
Crazy	218, 219
Crazyman	581
Creature	581
Creature Commandos	60
Creature From the Black Lagoon	496
Creatures On the Loose	330
Creech, The	528
Creech, The: Out For Blood	528
Creed	710
Creed: Cranial Disorder	711
Creed: Cranial Disorder	581
Creed: Mechanical Evolution	711
Creed: The Good Ship & the New Journey Home	711
Creed: Use Your Delusion	711
Creed: Utopiate	528
Creed/Teenage Mutant Ninja Turtles	581, 711
Creeper, The	60
Creeps	528
Creepy	496
Cremator: Hell's Guardian	581
Crew	219
Crime and Punishment	377, 799
Crime Buster	711
Crime Can't Win	262
Crime Classics	711
Crime Detective Comics	377
Crime Does Not Pay	455
Crime Fighters	219
Crime Illustrated	377
Crime Machine	581
Crime Must Stop	377
Crime Mysteries	377
Crime On the Waterfront	387
Crime Patrol	377, 581
Crime Reporter	378
Crime Smasher	378
Crime Smashers	378
Crime Suspense Stories	581
Crime Suspenstories	378
Crime-Fighting Detective	378
Crimebuster	711
Crimes By Women	378
Criminal Macabre	496
Criminals On the Run	378
Crimson	529
Crimson Avenger	60
Crimson Dreams	711
Crimson Dynamo	219
Crimson Nun	581
Crimson Plague	529, 581
Crimson Skies	529
Crisis On Infinite Earths	60
Crisis On Multiple Earths	60
Crisis, The	802
Critical Error	496
Critical Mass	219
Critters	711
Cross	496
Crossfire	581, 711
Crossfire & Rainbow	582
Crossgen Chronicles	582
Crossover Classics	219
Crossovers, The	582
Crossroads	582
Crouching Tiger, Hidden	582
Crow	711
Crow of Bearclan	712
Crow, The	529, 711
Crow, The: Demon In Disguise	711
Crow, The: Flesh and Blood	711
Crow, The: Waking Nightmares	711
Crow, The: Wild Justice	711
Crow, The: City of Angels	582
Crow, The: Dead Time	711
Crow/Razor: Kill the Pain	711
Crown Comics	378
Crucible	60
Cruel and Unusual	60
Crusader From Mars	378
Crusaders	60, 712
Crusades, The	60
Crush	496
Crush, The	529
Crusher Joe	712
Crux	582
Cry For Dawn	712
Crybaby	582
Cryin' Lion, The	379
Crying Freeman	712
Crying Freeman II	712
Crying Freeman III	582
Crying Freeman IV	582
Crypt	529
Crypt of Dawn	582
Crypt of Shadows	219
Crypt of Terror	377
Cryptic Writings of Megadeth	582
Crystal Breeze	712
CSI: Crime Scene Investigation	582
CSI: Crime Scene Investigation: Bad Rap	582
Cud Comics	496
Cupid	219
Curse of Dracula, The	496
Curse of Rune	582
Curse of the Spawn	529
Curse of the Weird	219
Cursed	529
Cutey Bunny	712
Cutie Honey	712
Cutting Edge	219
CVO: Covert Vampiric Operations–Artifact	582
Cy-Gor	530
Cyber 7	712
Cyber City: Part One	582
Cybercrush: Robots In Revolt	582
Cyberella	60
Cyberforce	529
Cyberforce Origins	530
Cyberforce Universe Sourcebook	530
Cyberforce/Codename Strykeforce: Opposing Forces	530
Cyberfrog	582, 712
Cyberfrog Vs Creed	712
Cyberfrog: Reservoir Frog	582
Cyberhood	582
Cybernary	530
Cybernary 2.0	582
Cyberpunk	583
Cyberpunx	530, 583
Cyberrad	583
Cyberspace 3000	219
Cyberzone	712
Cyblade	530
Cyborg 009	712
Cybrid	583
Cyclone Comics	379
Cyclops	219, 713
Cygnus X-1	713
Cynder	583, 713
Cynder/Hellina	713
Cynder/Nira X	583
Cyrano De Bergerac	799
D.P. 7	**230**
Da'kota	713
Daemonifuge: The Screaming Cage	713
Daemonstorm	583
Daemonstorm: Deadworld	583
Daemonstorm: Oz	583
Daffy	379
Daffy Duck	379
Dagar the Invincible	583
Dagger, Desert Hawk	379
Dagwood	379
Dai Kamikaze	583
Daikazu	713
Daily Bugle	219
Dakota North	219
Daktari	583
Dale Evans Comics	60
Dalgoda	583
Damage	61
Damage Control	219
Damned	530
Damonstreik	713
Dan O'Neil's Comics & Stories	805
Dan Turner Hollywood Detective	713
Dance Til Tomorrow	713
Dances With Demons	219
Danger	583
Danger and Adventure	469
Danger Girl	530
Danger Girl: Kamikaze	583
Danger Is Our Business	379
Danger Ranger	583
Danger Trail	61
Danger Unlimited	496
Dangerous Times	713
Daniel Boone	583, 799
Danny Blaze	583
Dare	583
Daredevil	219, 222
Daredevil Comics	379
Daredevil: Ninja	222
Daredevil: The Man Without Fear	222
Daredevil: The Target	222
Daredevil: Yellow	222
Daredevil/Shi	222
Daredevil/Spider-Man	222
Daring Comics	223
Daring Confessions	487
Daring Escapes	530

Index Da–Di

Entry	Page
Daring Mystery Comics	222
Daring New Adventures of Supergirl	153
Dark Adventures	584
Dark Angel	247, 713
Dark Angel: Phoenix Resurrection	530
Dark Assassin	713
Dark Chylde	584
Dark City Angel	713
Dark Claw Adventures, The	186
Dark Crossings	530
Dark Crystal	223
Dark Days	584
Dark Design	242
Dark Dominion	584
Dark Fantasies	713
Dark Frigate, The	801
Dark Fringe	713
Dark Fringe: Spirits of the Dead	713
Dark Guard	223
Dark Hawk	223
Dark Horse Classics:	
Aliens Versus Predator	496
Predator: Jungle Tales	496
Star Wars— Dark Empire	496
Godzilla	496
Terror of Godzilla	496
Dark Horse Comics	496
Dark Horse Downunder	497
Dark Horse Maverick	497
Dark Horse Monsters	497
Dark Horse Presents	497
Dark Horse Presents: Aliens	498
Dark Island	713
Dark Lord	713
Dark Man	223
Dark Manga	713
Dark Mansion of Forbidden Love, The	61
Dark Muse	714
Dark Mysteries	380
Dark One's Third Eye	584
Dark Oz	714
Dark Realm	531
Dark Regions	714
Dark Shadows	584
Dark Side	584
Dark Star	714
Dark Town	584
Dark Visions	714
Dark Wolf	714
Dark, The	583
Darkchylde	530
Darkchylde Redemption	584
Darkchylde: The Diary	530
Darkchylde: The Legacy	530
Darkchylde/Glory	530
Darkchylde/Witchblade	530
Darker Image	530
Darkham Vale	584
Darkhold	223
Darklight: Prelude	713
Darklon the Mystic	584
Darkman	223
Darkminds	531
Darkminds: Macropolis	531, 584
Darkness	531
Darkness Falls: The Tooth Fairy– the Tragic Life of Matilda	498
Darkness, The/Batman	531
Darkseid Vs. Galactus the Hunger	61
Darkshrine	584
Darkstars	61
Darkwing Duck	584
Darkwood	584
Darling Love	487
Darque Passages	584
Darque Razor	714
Dart	531
Das Kampf	805
Date With Mille	223
Date With Patsy	223
Daughters of Time	584
David and Goliath	531
David Balfour	799
David Copperfield	796
Davy Crockett	380, 584, 801
Dawn	531, 584
Dawn of the Re-Animator	647
Dawn: Pin-Up Goddess	585
Dawn: The Return of the Goddess	585
Dawn: Three Tiers	531
Day of Judgment	61
Daydreamers	223
Days of Darkness	714
Dazey's Diary	585
Dazzler	223
DC Challenge	61
DC Comics Presents	61
DC First	62
DC Graphic Novel	62
DC Millennium Editions	62
DC One Million	62
DC Replica Editions	62
DC Science Fiction Graphic Novel	62
DC Special	62
DC Special Series	62
DC Superstars	63
DC Two Thousand	63
DC Universe	63
DC Universe: Trinity	63
DC Versus Marvel	186
DC Vs. Marvel	63
DC/Marvel Crossover Classics	62
DC/Marvel: All Access	62
Dead Boys: Death's Embrace	585
Dead Clown	585
Dead Corps(e)	63
Dead End Crime Stories	380
Dead In the West	498
Dead King	585
Dead of Knight	224
Dead Or Alive— A Cyberpunk Western	498
Dead To Rights	498
Dead-Eye Western Comics	380
Deadbeats	714
Deadbone Erotica	805
Deadcenter Cleavage	805
Deadenders	63
Deadface: Doing Islands With Bacchus	498
Deadface: Earth, Water, Air & Fire	498
Deadforce	585
Deadkiller	714
Deadlands	531
Deadliest Heroes of Kung Fu	224
Deadline	224
Deadline Usa	498
Deadly Duo	531
Deadly Foes of Spider-Man	224
Deadly Hands of Kung Fu	224
Deadman	63
Deadman: Dead Again	63
Deadman: Exorcism	63
Deadman: Lost Souls	63
Deadman: Love After Death	63
Deadpool	224
Deadshot	63
Deadside	585
Deadtime Stories	714
Deadwood Gulch	380
Deadworld	714
Deamon Dreams	585
Dear Beatrice Fairfax	380
Dear Lonely Heart	380
Dear Lonely Hearts	380
Dear Nancy Parker	585
Dearly Beloved	380
Death Angel	714
Death Gallery	63
Death Hunt	714
Death Metal	225
Death Metal Vs Genetix	225
Death of Angel Girl	714
Death of Bloodfire	714
Death of Hari Kari, The	585
Death of Lady Vampre	585
Death of Superman	160
Death Rattle	585, 714, 805
Death: The High Cost of Living	64
Death: The Time of Your Life	64
Death's Head	225, 714
Death's Head II	225
Death's Head II/Killpower: Battletide	226
Death's Head II/Die Cut	226
Death-Wreck	226
Death3	225
Deathblow	531
Deathblow: By Blows	585
Deathblow/Wolverine	532
Deathdealer	585
Deathdreams of Dracula	714
Deathlok	225
Deathlok Special	225
Deathmark	714
Deathmask	585
Deathmate	585
Deathstroke	64
Deathstroke: The Hunted	64
Deathstroke: The Terminator	64
Deathwish	64
Deathworld	715
Deathworld Book II	715
Deathworld Book III	715
Debbie Dean, Career Girl	380
Decade of Dark Horse, A	498
Decapitator	498
Deception, The	532
Decoy	585
Decoy: Storm of the Century	585
Dee Vee	715
Deep, The	226
Deerslayer, The	793
Defcon 4	715
Defenders	226
Defenders of the Earth	227
Defenders of Dynatron City	227
Defenders, The	585
Defenseless Dead	715
Defiance	532
Defiant: Origin of A Universe	585
Deity	532, 585
Deity II: Catseye	585
Deity: Revelations	532
Delicate Creatures	532
Deliverer	585
Dell Giant Comics	380
Dell Giant Editions	380
Dell Junior Treasury	381, 478
Della Vision	227
Delta Tenn	715
Demolition Man	64
Demon	64
Demon Baby	715
Demon Bitch	715
Demon Diary	715
Demon Hunter	715
Demon Warrior	715
Demon, The: Driven Out	65
Demon's Tails	715
Demon-Hunter	586
Demonhunter	715
Demonic Toys	586
Demonique	586, 715
Demonique: Angel of Night	715
Demonslayer	532, 586
Demonslayer: Future Shock	586
Demonslayer: Lords of Night	586
Demonslayer: Path of Time	586
Demonslayer: Prophecy	586
Demonslayer: Rave	586
Demonslayer: Rebirth	586
Demonslayer: Vengeance	586
Demonwars: Eye For An Eye	586
Demonwars: Trial By Fire	586
Den	586
Den Saga	586
Denizens of Deep City	715
Dennis the Menace	227, 381, 586
Dennis the Menace and His Friends	586
Dennis the Menace Big Bonus Series	586
Dennis the Menace Giants	586
Deputy Dawg	586
Der Vandale	715
Derreck Wayne's Strapped	715
Derring Risk	532
Desert Peach	715
Desert Storm Journal	586
Despair	805
Desperado	381
Desperadoes: Epidemic	65
Desperadoes: Quiet of the Grave	65
Desperados	532
Desperate Times	532
Destiny Angel	715
Destiny: A Chronicle of Deaths Foretold	65
Destroy	715
Destroyer	586
Destroyer Duck	586
Destroyer, The	227
Destroyer, The: Terror	227
Destructor, The	586
Detective Picture Stories	381
Detective Comics	65
Detective Eye	381
Detective, The	715
Detectives Inc.	532
Detectives, Inc.	587
Detention Comics	69
Detonator	587
Devastator	532
Devil Chief	498
Devil Dinosaur	227
Devil Dinosaur Spring Fling	227
Devil Dogs	381
Devil Jack	715
Devil Kids Starring Hot Stuff	587
Devil's Due Studios	532
Devil's Footprints, The	498
Devil's Workshop	715
Devil-Dog Dugan	227
Devilman	587
Devlin	587
Dexter Comics	381
Dexter the Demon	278
Dexter's Laboratory	69
Dhampire: Stillborn	69
Diablo: Tales of Sanctuary	498
Diabolik	715
Diary Confessions	467
Diary Loves	381
Diary Secrets	466
Dick Cole	381
Dick Danger	716
Dick Tracy	587, 716
Dick Tracy Monthly/Weekly	716
Dick Tracy Comics Monthly	382
Dick Tracy Crimebuster	716
Dick Tracy Magazine	716
Dick Tracy Monthly	382
Dick Tracy Unprinted Stories	716
Dick Tracy: Big City Blues	587
Dick Tracy: The Early Years	716
Dickie Dare	381
Dicks	716
Die-Cut	227
Die-Cut Vs. G-Force	227
Digimon	498, 716
Digital Dragon	716
Digitek	227
Dim-Witted Darryl	716
Dime Comics	383
Ding Dong	383
Dinky Duck	383
Dino Island	587
Dino Riders	227
Dinosaur Rex	587
Dinosaurs	587
Dinosaurs Attack	587
Dinosaurs For Hire	587, 716
Dinosaurs: A Celebration	227
Dirty Duck Book, The	805
Dirty Pair	498, 716
Dirty Pair: Fatal But Not Serious	498
Dirty Pair: Run From the Future	498
Dirty Pair: Sim Earth	716
Dirty Pair: Sim Hell	498
Dirty Pair: Sim Hell: Remastered	498
Disavowed	69
Disciples	716
Disciples, The	532
Disney Adventures	587
Disney Afternoon	227
Disney Colossal Comics Collection	587
Disney Comic Hits	227
Disney Comics In 3-D	587
Disney Comics Spec	587

Disney Presents 227	Doomsday + 1 ....589, 717	Dragonforce Chronicles 718	Earth X 231
Disney Rapes the 1st	Doomsday Squad 589	Dragonlance 71	Earth: Year Zero 720
Amendment 805	Doorway To Nightmare 71	Dragonmist 719	Earthworm Jim 231
Disney's Atlantis the Lost	Dope Comix 805	Dragonring 590, 719	East Meets West 591
Empire 498	Dopey Duck 230	Dragonslayer 230	Eat Right To Work and Win ..385
Disney's Tarzan 498	Dopey Duck Comics 230	Dragontok Saga 719	Eat-Man 720
Disneyland Birthday Party ...587	Dopin Dan 805	Drakkon Wars, The 590	Eb'nn the Raven 720
Distant Soil, A 716	Dork 717	Drakuun 499	Ebon 806
Ditkos World: Static 716	Dork Tower 717	Drawing On Your Nightmares ..499	Ebonix-Files, The 720
Diver Dan 587	Dorothy Lamour 417	Drawings By S.Clay Wilson ..806	Ebony Warrior 591
Divine Intervention 587	Dotty Dripple 384	Dread of Night 719	Echo 533
Divine Madness 587	Double Action Comics 71	Dreadlands 230	Echo of Future Past 591
Divine Right: The Adventures	Double Comics 384	Dreadstar 230, 590	Eclipse Graphic Novels 591
of Max Faraday 532	Double Dare Adventures 589	Dreadstar & Company 230	Eclipse Monthly 591
Division 13 498	Double Dragon 230	Dream Angel and Angel Girl ..719	Eclipso 71
Dixie Dugan 383	Double Edge 230	Dream Angel: The Quantum	Eclipso: The Darkness 72
Dizzy Dames 383	Double Edge Double 717	Dreamer 719	Ectokid 231
Dizzy Don Comics 383	Double Image 533	Dream Angel: World Without	Edddie Stanky 385
Dizzy Duck 364	Double Impact 589, 717	End 719	Eddie Campell's Bacchus ...720
Dnagents 587	Double Impact 2069 718	Dream-Quest of Unknown	Eddy Current 720
Do You Believe In Nightmares? 587	Double Impact Alive 717	Kadath, The 734	Eden's Trail 231
Dober-Man 587	Double Impact Mercs 718	Dreamery 719	Edgar Allan Poe 720
Doc Carter V.D. Comics 383	Double Impact Raw 718	Dreamgirl 719	Edgar Rice Burroughs' Return
Doc Ock Vs. Spider-Man ...227	Double Impact Suicide	Dreaming, The 71	of Tarzan 499
Doc Samson 227	Run 589, 718	Dreamlands 719	Edgar Rice Burroughs' Tarzan .499
Doc Savage 69, 227, 228, 587, 588	Double Impact X 718	Dreams of the Darkchylde ...590	Edgar Rice Burroughs' Tarzan:
Doc Savage Comics 383	Double Impact: 2069 589	Dreamtime 719	the Lost Adventure 499
Doc Savage: Curse of the	Double Impact: Alive 589	Dreamwalker 719	Edgar Rice Burroughs' Tarzan—
Fire God 499	Double Impact: Assassins	Dreamwalker: Autumn Leaves .719	the Savage Heart 499
Doc Savage: Devil's Thoughts .588	For Hire 717	Dreamwalker: Carousel 719	Edgar Rice Burroughs' Tarzan:
Doc Savage: Doom Dynasty ..588	Double Impact: From the Ashes 718	Dreamwalker: Summer Rain ..719	The Rivers of Blood 499
Doc Savage: Manual of Bronze 588	Double Impact: Hot Shots 718	Dreamwolves 719	Edge 591, 720
Doc Savage: Repel 588	Double Impact: One Step	Dredd Rules 590	Edge of Chaos 592
Doc Weird's Thrill Book 716	Beyond 718	Drift Marlo 590	Eerie 385
Doctor 716	Double Impact/Lethal Strike ..717	Droids 230	Eerie Adventures 385
Doctor Boogie 588	Double Impact/Hellina 589	Dropsie Avenue: The	Egbert 386
Doctor Chaos 588	Double Impact/Luxura 717	Neighborhood 71	Egon 499
Doctor Fate 69	Double Impact/Nikki Blade ...717	Drug Wars 590	Egypt 72
Doctor Mid-Nite 70	Double Impact/Razor 718	Druid 230	Eh! 386
Doctor Octopus: Negative	Double Life of Private Strong ..590	Drunken Fist 590	Eight Legged Freaks 592
Exposuer 228	Double Up 384	Drywall and Oswald Show ...719	Eightball 720
Doctor Solar Man of the Atom .588	Down With Crime 385	Duck Tales 591	Eighth Wonder, The 500
Doctor Strange 229	Downfall, The 801	Duckman 591	El Bombo Comics 386
Doctor Strangefate 186	Dr. Anthony King Hollywood	Duckman: The Mob Frog Saga .591	El Cazador 592
Doctor Weird 716	Love Doctor 383	Dudley 385	El Diablo 72
Doctor Who 229	Dr. Atomic 805	Dudley Do-Right 591	El Hazard: The Magnificent
Dodekain 716	Dr. Atomic's Marijuana	Dumbo Weekly 385	World 721
Dogaroo 717	Multiplier 805	Dunc & Loo 806	El Perfecto Comics 806
Doghead 588	Dr. Fate 70	Duncan's Kingdom 533	Electric Girl 720
Dogs O'War, The 717	Dr. Giggles 499	Dune 230	Electric Undertow 231
Dogs of War 588	Dr. Gorpon 716	Dungeoneers 719	Electric Warrior 72
Doll Man 383	Dr. Jekyll and Mr.Hyde 793	Dungeons & Dragons:	Electropolis 533
Dollman 588	Dr. Kildare 588	Amber Castle 591	Elektra 231
Dolls 717	Dr. Radium 716	Dungeons & Dragons: Black	Elektra & Wolverine: The
Dolly Dill 229	Dr. Robot 499	& White 719	Redeemer 231
Dollz 533	Dr. Strange 228	Dungeons & Dragons:	Elektra Lives Again 231
Dome, The: Ground Zero ...70	Dr. Strange Classics 229	Tempest's Gate 591	Elektra: Assassin 231
Domination Factor 229	Dr. Tomorrow 588	Dungeons & Dragons: The	Elektra: Glimpse & Echo 231
Dominion 499, 533, 717	Dr. Wonder 716	Lost City 591	Elektra: Root of Evil 231
Dominion Special: Phantom	Dr.Radium: Man of Science ..716	Dungeons and Dragons:	Elektra: Saga 231
of the Audience 499	Dr.Strange: What Is It... 229	Where Shadows Fall 591	Elektra/Cyblade 533
Dominion: Conflict 1— No	Dr.Zero 229	Dungeons and Dragons In	Elektra/Witchblade 232
More Noise 499	Dracula 499, 590, 718	Shadow of Dragons 719	Elementals 592
Domino 229	Dracula Chronicles 590	Durango Kid 385	Elementals Vs. the Charnel
Domino Chance 717	Dracula In Hell 718	Dusty Star 533	Priests 592
Domu: A Child's Dreams 499	Dracula Lives 230	DV8 533	Elementals: How the War
Don Bluth's Dragon's Lair ...587	Dracula Vs. Zorro 533, 590	DV8 Vs. Black Ops 533	Was One 592
Don Bluth's Space Ace 587	Dracula: Lord of the Undead ..230	Dwelling, The 719	Elementals: The Vampire's
Don Fortune Magazine 384	Dracula: The Lady in the Tomb .718	Dwight D. Eisenhower 591	Revenge 592
Don Newcombe 384	Dracula: Vlad the Impaler ...590	Dying Dolphin 806	Eleven Or One 592
Don Quixote 792	Dracula's Cozy Coffin 718	Dylan Dog 499	Elf Warrior 721
Don Winslow of the Navy ...384	Draft, The 230	Dynamic Classics 71	Elford 592, 720
Donald and Mickey 628	Drag 'n' Wheels 669	Dynamic Comics 385	Elford Chronicles 720
Donald and Mickey Merry	Dragon Arms 718	Dynamite 385	Elford Cuts Loose 720
Christmas 384	Dragon Blood and Guts, The .533	Dynamo 591	Elford: All the Lonely Places ..720
Donald Duck 384, 588	Dragon Hunter 718	Dynamo Joe 591	Elford: Hawk 720
Donald Duck Adventures 589	Dragon Knights 718	Dynomutt 231	Elflore: The High Seas 721
Donald Duck Album 589	Dragon Lines 230	**E.V.E. Protomecha** **533**	Elfquest 232, 592, 721
Donald Duck and Friends ...589	Dragon of the Valkyr 719	E-Man 593	Elfquest: Wave Dancer 593
Donald Duck Giveaways 384	Dragon Quest 719	Eagle 385, 719	Elfquest: 25th Anniversary
Donatello 589, 717	Dragon Strike 230	Eagle, The 385	Edition 72
Donna Mia 589, 717	Dragon Wars 719	Eagle: Dark Mirror 720	Elfquest: Blood of Ten Chiefs .592
Doom 229	Dragon Weekly 719	Eagles Dare 720	Elfquest: Hidden Years 592
Doom 2099 229	Dragon, The 533	Early Days of Southern Knights 591	Elfquest: Jink 592
Doom 2099 A.D. 229	Dragon's Teeth/Dragon's Claws 230	Earth 4 591	Elfquest: Kahvi 721
Doom Force 70	Dragonball 718	Earth Lore: Legend of Bek	Elfquest: Kings of the Broken
Doom Patrol 70, 71, 118	Dragonball Z 718	Larson 720	Wheel 721
Doom: The Emperor Returns .230	Dragonchiang 590	Earth Lore: Reign of Dragon	Elfquest: New Blood 592
Doom's Iv 533	Dragonfly 590	Lord 720	Elfquest: Seige At Blue
Doomsday 71	Dragonforce 718	Earth War 720	Mountain 721

Comics Values Annual — Index — El–FI

Title	Page
Elfquest: Shards	593
Elfquest: The Rebels	592
Elfquest: Two Spear	721
Elfquest: Wolfrider	72
Elfquest: Worldpool	721
Elftrek	721
Eliminator	593
Eliminator Color Special	593
Ellery Queen	386
Elongated Man	72
Elric	593
Elric, Bane of the Black Sword	593
Elric, Sailor On the Seven Seas	593
Elric, Wierd of the White Wolf	593
Elric: One Life	593
Elric: Stormbringer	500
Elric-Vanishing Tower	593
Elsewhere Prince	232
Elseworld's Finest	72
Elsie the Cow	386
Elven	593
Elvira	72, 232, 721
Elvira, Mistress of the Dark	721
Embrace	721
Embrace: Hunger of the Flesh	721
Emeraldas	722
Emergency	593
Emma Davenport	722
Emma Frost	232
Empire	72, 533, 722
Empty Zone	722
Empty Zone: Conversations With the Dead	722
Enchanted	722
Enchanted Valley	722
Enchanted: The Awakening	593
Enchanter	722
Enchanter: Apocalypse Wind Novella	722
Enchanting Love	386
Enemy	500
Enemy Ace: War In Heaven	72
Enforcers	722
Engin	593
Engine	593
Enigma	72
Ennis and Mccrea's Bigger Dicks	722
Ennis and Mccrea's Dicks 2	722
Eno and Plum	500
Ensign O'Toole	593
Entity	722
Entropy Tales	232
Epic	232
Epic Graphic Novel	232
Epic Illustrated	232
Epic Lite	232
Epsilon Wave	593, 722
Equine the Uncivilized	722
Equinox Chronicles	722
Eradicator	72
Eradicators	722
Eric Preston Is the Flame	722
Ernie Comics	453
Esc. (Escape)	593
Esc: No Exit	593
Escape To the Stars	722
Escape Velocity	722
Esmeraldas	722
Esp	722
Esp Ultra	722
Espers	533, 594, 722
Espionage	594
Essential Vertigo: Swamp Thing	72
Essential Vertigo: The Sandman	594
Establishment, The	594
Eternal	232
Eternal Truth	806
Eternal Warrior	594
Eternal Warriors	594
Eternals	232
Eternals: Herod Factor	232
Eternity Smith	594
Eternity Triple Action	722
Etta Kett	386
Eudaemon	500
Eva the Imp	594
Evangeline	594
Event Presents the Ash Universe	722
Everette Hartsoe's Razor	722
Evermuch Wave	806
Everquest	594
Everyman	232
Everything's Archie	594
Evil and Malice	534
Evil Dead III: Army of Darkness	500
Evil Ernie	594, 722, 723
Evil Ernie Returns	723
Evil Ernie Vs. the Movie Monsters	595
Evil Ernie Vs. the Super-Heroes	595
Evil Ernie: Depraved	594
Evil Ernie: Destroyer	594
Evil Ernie: Manhattan Death Trip	723
Evil Ernie: Revenge	594
Evil Ernie: Straight To Hell	595
Evil Ernie: The Horror	723
Evil Ernie: The Resurrection	595
Evil Ernie: Youth Gone Wild	723
Evil Ernie's Baddest Battles	595
Evil Eye	723
Evo	534
Ewoks	232
Ex-Mutants	595, 723
Ex-Mutants: The Shattered Earth Chronicles	723
Excalibur	233
Excalibur: Sword of Power	233
Excel Saga	723
Exciting Comics	386
Exciting Romances	386
Exciting X-Patrol	186
Executioner	595
Exemplars	595
Exiles	233, 595
Exit	723
Exo-Squad	595
Exodus	595
Exotic Romances	475
Exotics, The	500
Explorer Joe	386
Explorers	595, 723
Exposed	386
Exposure	534
Exposure Special	595
Exposure: Second Coming	595
Extinctioners	595, 723
Extra	386, 595
Extra!	386
Extreme Christmas Special	534
Extreme 3000	534
Extreme Anthology	534
Extreme Destroyer	534
Extreme Hero	534
Extreme Justice	73
Extreme Prejudice	534
Extreme Sacrifice	534
Extreme Tour Book	534
Extreme Zero	534
Extremely Silly	723
Extremely Youngblood	534
Extremes Violet	595
Extremist	73
Eye of Mongombo	723
Eyeball Kid	500
F-Troop	600
F5	534
F5 Origin	500
Fables	73
Fabulous Furry Freak Brothers, The	806
Face, The	73, 387
Faction Paradox	534
Factor X	234
Fafhrd and the Gray Mouser	234
Fairy Tale Parade	387
Faith	73, 723
Faithful	234
Fake	723
Falcon	234
Falcon, The	595
Fallen Angel	73
Fallen Angels	234
Falling Man	534
Family Affair	595
Family Man	73
Family Matter	595
Famous Comics	387
Famous Crimes	387
Famous Fairy Tales	387
Famous Feature Stories	387
Famous Funnies	387
Famous Gang, Book of Comics	383
Famous Gangsters	387
Famous Indian Tribes	595
Famous Mysteries	794
Famous Stars	387
Famous Stories	388
Famous Western Badmen	450
Fanboy	73
Fang	596
Fang and Claw	801
Fang: Testament	723
Fangs of the Widow	723
Fantagor	806
Fantasci	723
Fantastic	373
Fantastic Adventures	723
Fantastic Comics	388
Fantastic Fables	723
Fantastic Firsts	234
Fantastic Five	234
Fantastic Force	234
Fantastic Four	234
Fantastic Four 2099	238
Fantastic Four Roast	238
Fantastic Four the World's Greatest Comic Magazine	238
Fantastic Four Unlimited	238
Fantastic Four Unplugged	238
Fantastic Four Vs. X-Men	238
Fantastic Four: 1 2 3 4	238
Fantastic Four: Atlantis Rising	238
Fantastic Four: Unstable Molecules	238
Fantastic Four's Big Town	238
Fantastic Panic	723
Fantastic Stories	723
Fantastic Voyages of Sinbad, The	596
Fantastic World of Hanna-Barbera	238
Fantastic Worlds	724
Fantasy Features	596
Fantasy Masterpieces	238
Fantasy Quarterly	724
Fantoman	361
Far West	724
Farewell Moonshadow	73
Farewell To Weapons	238
Fargo Kid	417
Farscape: War Torn	596
Fashion In Action	596
Fast Fiction	388
Fastlane Illustrated	724
Fat Albert	596
Fat Dog Mendoza	500
Fat Freddy's Cat,	806
Fat Ninja	724
Fatale	596
Fatalis	724
Fate	73
Fate's Five	596
Fathom	534, 596
Fathom: Killian's Tide	534
Fatman, The Human Flying Saucer	596
Fault Lines	73
Faust	724, 803
Faust: Book of M	596
Faust/777: The Wrath	724
Fawcett Funny Animals	388
Fawcett Movie Comics	388
Fax From Sarajevo	500
Faze One	596
Faze One Fazers	596
Fear	238
Fear Effect	534
Fear Effect Special: Retro Helix	534
Fearbook	596
Feather	534
Feature Books	388
Feature Comics	389
Feature Funnies	389
Federal Men Comics	389
Feds 'n' Heads Comics	806
Feeders	500
Felch	806
Felix the Cat	389, 596
Felix the Cat B&w	724
Felix the Cat True Crime Stories	724
Felix the Cat: The Movie	596
Felix the Cat's Greatest Hits	500
Felix the Cat's Tv Extravaganza	724
Felix's Nephews Inky & Dinky	596
Felon	534
Fem 5	596
Fem Fantastique	724
Fem Force	724
Femforce	596
Femforce Special	725
Femforce: The Yesterday Syndrome	725
Femforce: Up Close	596
Fenry	597
Ferdinand the Bull	390
Ferret	597
Feud	239
Fever Pitch	806
Fever, The	725
Fight Against the Guilty	390
Fight Against Crime	390
Fight Comics	390
Fight For Tomorrow	73
Fight Man	239
Fight the Enemy	597
Fightin' Five(b)	662
Fightin' Texan	468
Fighting American	73, 390, 597
Fighting American: Dogs of War	597
Fighting American: Rules of the Game	597
Fighting Davy Crockett	419
Fighting Indians of the Wild West	390
Fighting Leathernecks	597
Fighting Yank	391, 725
Film Star Romances	391
Filth, The	73
Final Cycle	725
Final Night, The	73
Finals	74
Finder	725
Finder Footnotes	725
Fire	534
Fire From Heaven	535
Fire Team	725
Firearm	597
Firebrand	74
Firebreather	535
Firehair Comics	391
Firestar	239
Firestorm	74
Firestorm, The Nuclear Man	74, 79
First Adventures	597
First Folio	597
First Graphic Novels	597
First Issue Special	74
First Men In the Moon, The	802
First Wave	725
First Wave: Double Vision	725
First Wave: Genesis of A Genius	725
First Wave: Heart of A Killer	597
First Wave: In the Beginning	597
First Wave: Jordan Radcliff	597
First, The	597
Firstman	535
Fish Police	239, 725
Fish Shticks	725
Fist of God	725
Fist of the Blue Sky	725
Fist of the North Star	597, 725
Flag Fighters	725
Flame, The	391
Flamehead	597
Flaming Carrot	500, 725
Flaming Carrot Comics	806
Flaming Love	391
Flare	597, 725
Flare Adventures	598, 725
Flare Vs. Tigress	726
Flash	75, 76
Flash & Green Lantern: The Brave & the Bold	77
Flash Comics	74

CVA Page 819

Flash Gordon . . .78, 239, 391, 598
Flash Theatre 806
Flashpoint 78
Flatline Comics 598
Flaxen 500
Flaxen: Alter Ego 598
Flesh and Bones 598
Fleshapoids From Earth 806
Flinch 78
Flintstone Kids 239
Flintstones 239, 598
Flintstones and the Jetsons 78
Flintstones In 3-D 598
Flintstones, The 598
Flip 391
Flipper 598
Floaters 500
Flood Relief 598
Flood! 500
Fly Boy 391
Fly In My Eye Exposed 598
Fly, The 78, 598
Flying A's Ranger Rider, The . .391
Flying Hero Barbie 239
Flying Saucers 598
Flyman 598
Foes .598
Food of the Gods, The 803
Foodang 598
Foodini 391
Foofur 239
Foolkiller 239
Foot Soldiers, The 500, 535
Football Thrills 391
Footsoldiers 598
Foozle 598
For Your Eyes Only 239
Forbidden Kingdom 726
Forbidden Love 391
Forbidden Planet 598
Forbidden Tales of Dark Mansion 78
Forbidden Vampire Tales 726
Forbidden Worlds 391, 726
Force 10 726
Force of the Buddha's Palm . . .598
Force Seven 726
Force Works 239
Foreign Intrigues 385
Foremost Boys 400
Foreternity 726
Forever Amber 535
Forever Maelstrom 78
Forever People 78
Forever War, The 599
Forever Warriors 726
Forge .599
Forgotten Realms 78
Formerly Known As the Justice League 78
Fort: Prophet of the Unexplained 500
Forty Winks 726
Forty Winks: Mr. Horrible 726
Forty Winks: The Fabled Pirate Queen of the South China Sea 726
Forty-Five Guardsmen, The . . .800
Four Color 392
Four Favorites 400
Four Horsemen 78
Four Star Battle Tales 78
Four Star Spetacular 78
Four Women 78
Fourth World Gallery 78
Fox and the Crow 78
Fox Comics 726
Foxfire 599
Fraggle Rock 239
Francis, Brother of the Universe 239
Frank 599, 726
Frank Frazetta Fantasy Illustrated 599
Frank In the River 599
Frank Merriwell At Yale 599
Frank Miller's Robocop 599
Frank the Unicorn 726
Frankenstein 281, 500, 599, 726, 794
Frankenstein Dracula War 599
Frankenstein Comics 400
Frankenstein Mobster 535
Frankies Frightmares 726
Freak Force 535
Freak-Out On Infant Earths . . .726
Freaks 726
Freakshow 500
Fred Hembeck 239
Fred the Possessed Flower . . .726
Freddy 599
Freddy's Dead: The Final Nightmare 599
Freedom Fighters 79
Freemind 599
Freex .599
French Ice 726
Friday Foster 599
Friendly Ghost 599
Friends 726
Friends of Maxx 535
Fright 239, 726
Fright Night 599
Fright Night 3-D 599
Fright Night II 600
Fringe 726
Frisky Animals 400
Frisky Animals On Parade 600
Frisky Fables 400
Fritz Bugs Out 806
Fritz the Cat 806
Fritz the No-Good 806
Fritz: Secret Agent For the CIA .806
Fritzi Ritz 400
Frogman Comics 401
Frogmen, The 600
From Beyond 726
From Beyond the Unknown 79
From Hell 726
From Here To Insanity 600
From the Darkness 726
From the Darkness II Blood Vows 727
From the Earth To the Moon . . .800
From the Void 727
Front Page Comic Book 401
Frontier Fighter 584
Frontier Romances 401
Frontier Western 239
Frontline Combat 401, 600
Frost: The Dying Breed 727
Fugitives From Justice 401
Fugitoid 727
Full Metal Fiction 727
Fun-In 600
Funky Phantom 600
Funnies, The 401
Funny Aminals 806
Funny Book 401
Funny Films 401
Funny Frolics 240
Funny Funnies 401
Funny Pages 402
Funny Picture Stories 402
Funny Stocking Stuffer 79
Funny Stuff 79
Funny Tunes 402
Funnyman 402
Furies 727
Furrlough 727
Furry Ninja High School 727
Furry Ninja High School Strikes Back 600
Further Adventures of Cyclops and Phoenix 240
Fury 240, 727
Fury of Firestorm 79
Fury of Hellina, The 727
Fury of S.H.I.E.L.D. 240
Fury/Agent 13 240
Fused! 535
Fushigi Yugi 727
Fusion 727
Futaba-Kun Change 727
Futurama 727
Futurama Comics 600
Future Comics 402
Future World 500
Future World Comics 402
Futuretech 727
Futurians 600, 727
F–III Bandit 727
G.I. Combat 81, 403
G.I. Jane 404
G.I. Joe 243, 404, 501, 536
G.I. Joe 3-D 601
G.I. Joe and the Transformers .244
G.I. Joe European Missions . . .244
G.I. Joe Frontline 537
G.I. Joe Special Missions 244
G.I. Joe Vs. Transformers 537
G.I. Joe: Battle Files 537
G.I. R.A.M.B.O.T. 601
G.I. Robot 601
G.I. Sweethearts 381
G.I. Tales 304
G.I. War Brides 404
G.I.Joe Universe 244
G.O.T.H. 603
G-Gundam 727
G-Man 602
Gabby Hayes Western 402
Gaijin .727
Galactic 500
Galactic Guardians 240
Galactica: The New Millennium .600
Galactus the Devourer 240
Galaxion 727
Galaxy Express 727
Galaxy-Size Astounding Space Thrills 535
Gall Force: Eternal Story 600
Gallant Men, The 600
Gallegher Boy Reporter 600
Gambit 240
Gambit & Bishop: Sons of the Atom 240
Gambit and the X-Ternals 240
Gamera 500
Gammarauders 80
Gamorra Swimsuit Special 535
Gang Busters 80
Gang World 402
Gangland 80
Gangsters and Gun Molls 402
Gangsters Can't Win 402
Gargoyle 240
Gargoyles 240
Garrison 600
Garrison's Gorrillas 600
Gary Gianni's Monstermen 500
Gasoline Alley 402
Gasp! .600
Gatecrasher 600
Gatekeeper 727
Gates of the Night 727
Gay Comix 806
Gazillion 535
Ge Rouge 601
Gear .728
Gear Station, The 535
Geeksville 535
Geisha 728
Gem Comics 402
Geminar 535
Gemini Blood 80
Gems of the Samurai 728
Gen 13 535
Gen 13 Bootleg 536
Gen 13: Interactive 536
Gen 13/Generation X 536
Gen of Hiroshima 806
Gen12 536
Gen13 601
Gen13 Movie Adaptation 601
Gen13: Ordinary Heroes 536
Gen13: Magical Dream Queen Roxy 536
Gen13/Maxx 536
Gen13/Monkey Man & O'Brien .536
Gene Autrey's Champion 403
Gene Autry Comics 402, 403
Gene Dogs 240
Gene Fusion 600
Gene Roddenberry's Lost Universe 600
Gene Roddenberry's Xander In Lost Universe 601
Generation Hex 186
Generation Next 240
Generation X 240
Generation X: Underground . . .241
Generation X/Gen 13 241
Generic Comic 241
Generic Comic Book 728
Genesis 80, 601
Genetix 241
Genocyber 728
Gensaga: Ancient Warrior 601
Gentle Ben 601
Geobreeders 728
Geomancer 601
George of the Jungle 601
George Pal's Puppetoon's 403
Georgie & Judy Comics 241
Georgie Comics 241
Gerald Mcboing-Boing and the Nearsighted Mr. Magoo . . .403
Geriatric Gangrene Jujitsu Gerbils 728
Geronimo 403
Get Lost 403
Get Smart 601
Getalong Gang 241
Ghost 403, 500
Ghost and the Shadow 501
Ghost Breakers 403
Ghost Busters II 601
Ghost In the Shell 501
Ghost In the Shell 2: Man-Machine Interface 501
Ghost Mother Comics 806
Ghost Rider 241
Ghost Rider 2099 243
Ghost Rider 2099 A.D. 243
Ghost Rider: Highway To Hell . .243
Ghost Rider: The Hammer Lane 243
Ghost Rider/Ballistic 242
Ghost Rider/Blaze Spirits of Vengeance 242
Ghost Rider/Captain America: Fear 242
Ghost Rider/Cyblade 243
Ghost Stories 601
Ghost/Batgirl 501
Ghost/Hellboy Collection 501
Ghostdancing 80
Ghostly Tales 574, 601
Ghostly Weird Stories 368
Ghosts 80
Ghosts of Dracula 728
Gi Government Issued 728
Giant Boy Book of Comics 403
Giant Comics 601
Giant Comics Edition 403
Giant Shanda Animal 728
Giant-Size Chillers 243
Giant-Size Dracula 243
Giant-Size Mini-Marvels: Starring Spidey 243
Giantkiller 81
Gideon Hawk 728
Gidget 601
Gift Comics 404
Gift, The 601
Gifts of the Night 82
Gigantor 601, 728
Giggle Comics 404
Gil Thorpe 601
Gilgamesh II 82
Gimmeabreak Comix 806
Gin-Ryu 601
Ginger 404
Ginger Fox 601
Girl Comics 244
Girl Confessions 244
Girl Crazy 501
Girl From U.N.C.L.E. 601
Girl Genius 602, 728
Girl Who Would Be Death, The .82
Girls & Boys 806
Girls In Love 381, 404
Girls Life 244
Girls of Ninja High School 1997 728
Give Me Liberty 501
Gizmo 728
Gizmo & the Fugitoid 728
Global Force 602
Global Frequency 602
Gloom Cookie 728
Glory 537, 602

Comics Values Annual — Index — Gl–Ha

Title	Page
Glory & Friends	537
Glory/Angela Angels In Hell	537
Glory/Avengelyne	537
Glory/Avengelyne: The Godyssey	537
Glory/Celestine: Dark Angel	537, 602
Gnatrat	728
Gnatrat: The Movie	728
Go Boy 7: Human Action Machine	501
Go Girl!	501, 537
Go-Go	602
Go-Man	729
Goat, The: H.A.E.D.U.S.	602
Gobbledy Gook	728
Goblin Lord, The	602
God Nose	806
Goddess	82
Gods For Hire	602
Godwheel	602
Godzilla	244, 501
Godzilla Color Special	501
Going Steady	467
Gojin	728
Gold Bug & Other Stories, The	799
Gold Digger	602, 728
Gold Digger Beta	602
Gold Digger: Edge Guard	729
Gold Digger/Ninja High School	729
Gold Medal Comics	404
Golden Age	82
Golden Age Greats	729
Golden Age of Marvel	245
Golden Arrow	404
Golden Comics Digest	602
Golden Lad	404
Golden Picture Story Book	603
Golden Warrior	729
Golden Warrior Iczer One	729
Golden West Love	404
Golden-Age Men of Mystery	729
Goldfish	537
Goldwyn 3-D	729
Gomer Pyle	603
Gon	82
Good Girl Comics	729
Good Girls	729
Good Guys	603
Goofy Adventures	603
Goofy Comics	404
Goon, The	501, 729
Goop, The	603
Gore Shriek	729
Gorgo	603
Gorgo's Revenge	603
Gotham Central	82
Gotham Girls	82
Gothess: Dark Ecstasy	729
Gothic Blimp Works Ltd.	807
Gothic Scrolls, Drayven, The	603
Grackle, The	729
Graphic Classics	729
Graphic Story Monthly	729
Graphique Musique	729
Grave Tales	729
Gravediggers	729
Gravestone	603
Gravitation	730
Grease Monkey	537, 603
Greaser Comics	807
Great Expectations	796
Great American Comics Presents- the Secret Voice	405
Great American Western	603
Great Comics	405
Great Detective Starring Sherlock Holmes	730
Great Exploits	603
Great Lover Romances	405
Greatest Spider-Man & Daredevil Team-Ups, The	245
Greatest Stories Ever Told	82
Greatful Dead Comix	603
Green Arrow	82
Green Arrow Longbow Hunters	83
Green Arrow: The Wonder Years	83
Green Berets	730
Green Candles	84
Green Giant Comics	405
Green Goblin	245
Green Hornet	603
Green Hornet Comics	405
Green Hornet: Dark Tomorrow	604
Green Hornet: Solitary Sentinal	604
Green Lama	405
Green Lantern	84, 85
Green Lantern Corps	85
Green Lantern Corps Quarterly	87
Green Lantern & Sentinel: Heart of Darkness	87
Green Lantern Vs. Aliens	501
Green Lantern: Circle of Fire	87
Green Lantern: Dragon Lord	87
Green Lantern: Emerald Dawn	87
Green Lantern: Evil's Might	87
Green Lantern: Mosaic	87
Green Lantern: The New Corps	87
Green Lantern/Green Arrow	87
Green Mansions	799
Green Mask, The	405
Green Planet	604
Greenhaven	604
Greenleaf In Exile	730
Greg Capullo's Original Creech	528
Gregory	87
Gremlin Trouble	730
Grendel	501, 604, 730
Grendel Classics	501
Grendel Tales: The Devil May Care	502
Grendel Tales: Devil's Apprentice	502
Grendel Tales: Devil's Choices	502
Grendel Tales: Devils and Deaths	502
Grendel Tales: Four Devils, One Hell	502
Grendel Tales: Homecoming	502
Grendel Tales: The Devil In Our Midst	502
Grendel Tales: The Devil's Hammer	502
Grendel: Black, White, and Red	501
Grendel: Devil By the Deed	502
Grendel: Devil Child	502
Grendel: Devil's Legacy	502
Grendel: God and the Devil	502
Grendel: Red, White, & Black	502
Grendel: The Devil Inside	502
Grendel: War Child	502
Grey	730
Greylore	604
Greymatter	730
Greyshirt: Indigo Sunset	604
Griffin	87
Griffin, The	730
Grifter	537
Grifter and the Mask	502
Grifter-One Shot	537
Grifter/Badrock	537
Grifter/Shi	537
Grim Wit	807
Grimjack	604
Grimjack Casefile	604
Grimm's Ghost Stories	604
Grip: The Strange World of Men	87
Grips	730
Groo	512, 537
Groo Chronicles	537
Groo The Wanderer	245, 604
Groo: Death and Taxes	502
Groo: Mightier Than the Sword	513
Groovy	245
Gross Point	87
Ground Zero	730
Group Larue	604
Grrl Scouts	537, 730
GTO	730
Guardian Angel	538
Guardians of Metropolis	88
Guardians of the Galaxy	245
Guerrila Groundhog	730
Guerrilla War	615
Guff	502
Guillotin	604, 730
Guillotine	87
Gulliver's Travels	604, 793
Gumby	605
Gumby In 3-D	605
Gumps, The	405
Gun Crisis	730
Gun Fury	731
Gun Fury Returns	731
Gun Theory	246
Gundam Wing	730
Gundam Wing: Battlefield of Pacifists	730
Gundam Wing: Endless Waltz	730
Gundam Wing: G-Unit	730
Gundam Wing: The Last Outpost	730
Gundam: The Origin	730
Gunfighters In Hell	730
Gunfighters In Hell: Original Sin	731
Gunfire	88
Gunhawk, The	206
Gunhawks	246
Gunner	731
Gunrunner	246
Guns Against Gangsters	405
Guns of Shar-Pei	731
Guns of the Dragon	88
Gunslinger	324
Gunslingers	246
Gunsmith Cats	502
Gunsmith Cats: Bad Trip	502
Gunsmith Cats: Bean Bandit	502
Gunsmith Cats: Bonnie & Clyde	502
Gunsmith Cats: Shades of Gray	503
Gunsmith Cats: The Return of Gray	503
Gunsmith Cats: Goldie Vs. Misty	503
Gunsmith Cats: Kidnapped	503
Gunsmith Cats: Mister V	503
Gunsmoke	405, 605
Gunsmoke Western	190
Gutwallow	731
Guy Gardner	88
Guy Gardner: Warrior	88
Guy Gardner: Reborn	88
Guy With A Gun: A Zombie Nightmare	605
Gyre	731
H.A.R.D. Corps	606
H.P. Lovecraft's the Call of Cthulhu and Others	734
H.P. Lovecraft's the Dream-Quest of Unknown Kadath	734
H.P. Lovecraft's the Return of Cthulhu	734
H.P.'S Rock City	504
H.R. Pufnstuf	609
H-E-R-O	91
Ha Ha Comics	405
Hacker Files	88
Hades	731
Hall of Fame	605
Hall of Heroes Presents	731
Halloween	605
Halloween Horror	605
Halloween II: The Blackest Eye	605
Halloween III: The Devil's Eyes	605
Halloween: Behind the Mask	605
Hallowieners	731
Halo Brothers	731
Halo: An Angel's Story	605
Hamlet	800
Hammer Girl	731
Hammer Locke	88
Hammer of God	605
Hammer of God: Butch	503
Hammer of God: Pentathlon	503
Hammer of the Gods	538
Hammer of the Gods: Hammer Hits China	538
Hammer, The: Uncle Alex	503
Hamster Vice	605, 731
Hand of Fate	406, 605
Hands of the Dragon, The	503
Hanged Man	731
Hangman Comics	420
Hanna-Barbera Band Wagon	605
Hanna-Barbera Parade	605
Hanna-Barbera All-Stars	605
Hanna-Barbera Presents	605
Hanna-Barbera Super TV Heroes	605
Hap Hazard Comics	406
Happy Birthday Martha Washington	503
Happy Comics	406
Happy Endings	503
Happy Houlihans	452
Happy Mania	731
Happy Rabbit	406
Harbinger	605
Harbinger Files: Harada	606
Hard Boiled	503
Hard Gore	731
Hard Looks	503
Hardcase	606
Hardcore Station	88
Hardware	88
Hardy Boys, The	606
Hari Kair: Possessed By Evil	731
Hari Kari	606
Hari Kari Goes Hollywood	731
Hari Kari Manga	731
Hari Kari Manga: Deadly Exposure	731
Hari Kari Manga: Deadtime Stories	731
Hari Kari Manga: Sex, Thugs, & Rock 'n' Roll	731
Hari Kari: Possessed By Evil	606
Hari Kari: Bloodshed	606
Hari Kari: Cry of Darkness	731
Hari Kari: Life Or Death	606
Hari Kari: Live & Untamed!	606
Hari Kari: Passion & Death	606
Hari Kari: Rebirth	606
Hari Kari: Resurrection	606
Hari Kari: Sexy Summer Rampage	731
Hari Kari: The Beginning	606
Hari Kari: The Diary of Kari Sun	606
Hari Kari: The Last Stand	731
Hari Kari: The Silence of Evil	606
Harlan Ellison's Dream Corridor Quarterly	503
Harlan Ellison's Dream Corridor	503
Harlem Beat	731
Harlem Globetrotters	606
Harley Quinn	89
Harold Head, The Collected Adventures Of	807
Harpy: Prize of the Overlord	731
Harriers	606
Harrowers	246
Harry Chess That Man From A.U.N.T.I.E.	807
Harsh Realm	606
Harte of Harkness	731
Harvey	246
Harvey Comic Hits	406
Harvey Hits	606
Harvey Presents: Casper	246
Harvy Flip Book	731
Hate	607, 731
Haunt of Fear	406, 607
Haunted	607
Haunted Love	607
Haunted Man, The	503
Haunted Thrills	406
Haunted, The	607
Haunted, The: Gray Matters	607
Have Gun, Will Travel	607
Haven: The Broken City	89
Havoc, Inc.	732
Havok & Wolverine	246
Hawallan Dick	538
Hawaiian Dick: The Last Resort	538
Hawk & Dove	89
Hawk and Windblade: All the Lonely Places	720
Hawk, The	406
Hawkeye	246
Hawkeye: Earth's Mightiest Marksman	246
Hawkman	89
Hawkmoon	607
Hawkmoon, Count Brass	607
Hawkmoon, Sword of the Dawn	607
Hawkmoon, The Hunestaff	607
Hawkshaws	538
Hawkworld	90
Haywire	90
Hazard	538

CVA Page 821

Index

Entry	Page
He Is Just A Rat	732
Head, The	732
Headhunters	538
Headline Comics	406
Headman	607
Headmasters	246
Hear the Sound of My Feet Walking	807
Heart of Empire: The Legacy of Luther Arkwright	503
Heart of the Beast	90
Heart Throbs	90, 407
Heartbreakers	503, 538
Heartbreakers Versus Biovoc	538
Heartland	90
Hearts of Darkness	242
Heartstopper	607
Heathcliff	246
Heathcliff's Funhouse	247
Heaven Sword & Dragon Sabre	607
Heaven's Devils	538
Heaven's War	538
Heavy Hitters	247
Heavy Liquid	90
Heavy Metal Monsters	732
Heavy Metal Monsters	607
Heckle and Jeckle	407
Heckler	90
Hector Heathcote	608
Hedg	608
Hedge Knight, The	538
Hedy Devine Comics	247
Hedy Wolfe	247
Heirs of Eternity	538
Helden	608
Hell	503
Hell's Angel	247
Hellblazer	90
Hellblazer Special: Bad Blood	91
Hellblazer Special: Lady Constantine	91
Hellbiazer/The Books of Magic	91
Hellboy	503
Hellboy Jr.	504
Hellboy: Almost Colossus	503
Hellboy: Box Full of Evil	503
Hellboy: Wake the Devil	504
Hellboy: Conqueror Worm	503
Hellboy: Seeds of Destruction	503
Hellboy: The Third Wish	504
Hellboy: Weird Tales	504
Hellcat	247
Hellcop	538
Hellgirl	732
Hellhole	538
Hellhound	247
Hellhounds	504, 538
Hellhounds: Panzer Corps	504
Hellina	732
Hellina Vs Pandora	732
Hellina: Heart of Thorns	608, 732
Hellina: Hell's Angel	732
Hellina: Hellborn	608
Hellina: Kiss of Death	732
Hellina: Seduction	732
Hellina/Double Impact	732
Hellina/Nira X: Angel of Death	608
Hellina/Nira X: Cyberangel	608
Hello Pal Comics	407
Hellraiser	214
Hellraiser III Hell On Earth	247
Hellshock	538
Hellsing	504
Hellspawn	538
Hellstorm, Prince of Lies	247
Helsing	732
Helter Skelter	732
Henry	407
Henry Aldrich Comics	407
Hepcats	732
Herbie	504, 608
Hercules	608, 732
Hercules and the Heart of Chaos	247
Hercules Prince of Power	247
Hercules Project	732
Hercules Unbound	91
Hercules: The Legendary Journeys	608
Heretic, The	504
Hermes Vs. the Eyeball Kid	504
Hero	247
Hero Alliance	608
Hero Alliance Quarterly	608
Hero Alliance: The End of the Golden Age	608
Hero For Hire	247
Hero Hotline	92
Hero Sandwich	733
Hero Zero	504
Herobear and the Kid	732
Heroes	91, 733
Heroes Against Hunger	92
Heroes Anonymous	733
Heroes For Hire	247
Heroes For Hope	248
Heroes From Wordsmith	733
Heroes Incorporated	733
Heroes Reborn: The Return	248
Heroic Comics	407
Heroic Tales	733
Heroines, Inc.	733
Hex	92
Hey Mister	733
Hi-Ho Comics	408
Hi-Jinx	408
Hi-Lite Comics	408
Hi-School Romance Date Book	608
Hickory	408
Hieroglyph	504
High Caliber	733
High Chapparal	608
High Roads	608
High School Confidential Diary	608
High School Agent	733
High Shining Brass	733
High Society	733
High Voltage	608
Highway 13	733
Hillbilly Comics	608
Hilly Rose's Space Adventures	733
His Name Is Rog... Rog 2000	609
History of DC Universe	92
History of Underground Comix	807
Hit Comics	408
Hit the Beach	733
Hitchhiker's Guide to the Galaxy	92
Hitman	92
Hitomi and Her Girl Commandos	733
Hobbit, The	609
Hogan's Heros	609
Hokum & Hex	248
Holiday Comics	248, 408
Hollywood Confessions	409
Hollywood Comics	409
Hollywood Diary	409
Hollywood Film Stories	409
Hollywood Secrets	409
Hollywood Superstars	248
Hollywood's Golden Era 1930s	733
Holo Brothers, The	733
Holy Knight	733
Holy Terror, The	538
Holyoke One-Shot	409
Homage Studios	538
Homegrown Funnies	807
Homer, The Happy Ghost	248
Honey West	609
Honeymoon Romance	409
Honeymooners	99, 609
Hong Kong	609
Hong On the Range	538
Honk	733
Honkytonk Sue, The Queen of Country Swing	807
Honor Among Thieves	733
Hood, The	248
Hooded Horseman	440
Hook	248
Hoon	733
Hopalong Cassidy	92, 409
Hopeless Savages	733
Hopeless Savages:	733
Hoppy the Marvel Bunny	409
Horace & Dotty Dripple	384
Horobi	733
Horrific	409
Horror From the Tomb	438
Horror In the Dark	734
Horrorist	93
Horrors, The	248, 409
Horse Feather Comics	409
Horsemen	609
Hot Comics Premiere	609
Hot Rod and Speedway Comics	410
Hot Rod Comics	410
Hot Rod King	410
Hot Rod Racers	609
Hot Shots	248
Hot Stuff Sizzlers	609
Hot Stuff, The Little Devil	609
Hot Wheels	93
Hotshots	609
Hotspur	609
Hourman	93
House II	248
House of Frightenstein	734
House of Horror	734
House of Mystery	93
House of Secrets	95, 96
House of Secrets: Facade	96
House of Seven Gables, The	797
House On the Borderlands, The	96
How I Found Livingstone	800
How Stalin Hopes We Will Destroy America	410
How To Draw Teenage Mutant Ninja Turtles	734
Howard Chaykin's American Flagg!	609
Howard the Duck	248
Howard the Duck Magazine	248
Howdy Doody	410
Howl	734
Huck & Yogi Jamboree	609
Huckleberry Finn	793
Huckleberry Hound	609
Huey, Dewey & Louie	609
Hugga Bunch	248
Hugo	734
Hulk 2099	249
Hulk 2099 A.D.	249
Hulk Smash	249
Hulk, The	249
Hulk: Grey	249
Hulk: Nightmerica	249
Hulk: The Movie Adaptation	249
Hulk/Wolverine: 6 Hours	249
Human Defense Corps	96
Human Fly	249
Human Gargoyles	734
Human Target	96
Human Target Special	96
Human Torch	249, 250
Human Torch Comics	250
Humbug	410
Humdinger	410
Humphrey Comics	410
Hunchback of Notre Dame	793
Hunt and the Hunted, The	734
Hunter's Heart	96
Huntress	97
Huntress, The	96
Hurricane Girls	734
Hurricane, The	801
Huzzah	734
Hy-Breed	734
Hybrids	609
Hybrids: Origin	609
Hyde-25	609
Hyper Dolls	734
Hyper Mystery Comics	410
Hyperkind	250
Hyperkind Unleashed	250
Hypersonic	504
I Am Legend	734
I Die At Midnight	97
I Dream of Jeannie	609, 734
I Love Lucy Comics	410
I Love You	411
I Loved	488
I Spy	609
I.F.S. Zone	734
I, Paparazzi	99
I'm Dickens – He's Fenster	610
I-Bots	610
Ibis, The Invincible	410
Icandy	97
Icarus	734
Iceman	250
Icicle	610
Icon	97
Icon Devil	734
Ideal	250
Ideal Comics	250
Ideal Romance	467
Idol	250
If the Devil Would Talk	410
Iguana, The	504
Ike Lives	807
Iliad	734
Iliad II	734
Illegal Alien	504
Illiad, The	798
Illuminator	250
Illuminatus	734
Illustrated Stories of the Opera	410
Image Comics	539
Image Introduces:	539
Image Two-In-One	539
Image Zero	539
Images of Shadowhawk	539
Immortal Dr. Fate	97
Immortal Two	539
Immortalis	250
Imp	610
Impact	410, 610
Impact Winter Special	97
Imperial Guard	250
Impossible Man Summer Vacation	250
Impulse	97
In Freedom's Cause	803
In Love	411
In the Reign of Terror	802
In the Shadow of Edgar Allan Poe	98
Incal	610
Incal, The	250
Incomplete Death's Head	250
Incredible Science Fiction	410
Incredible Hulk	248, 250
Incredible Hulk Megazine	253
Incredible Hulk Vs. Wolverine	253
Incredible Hulk: Future Imperfect	253
Incredible Hulk/Pitt	253
Incredible Science Fantasy	481
Independence Day	253
Indian Chief	410
Indian Fighter	410
Indian Warriors	440
Indiana Jones	253
Indiana Jones and the Last Crusade	253
Indiana Jones and the Sargasso Pirates	504
Indiana Jones and the Arms of Gold	504
Indiana Jones and the Fate of Atlantis	504
Indiana Jones and the Golden Fleece	504
Indiana Jones and the Iron Phoenix	504
Indiana Jones and the Shrine of the Sea Devil	504
Indiana Jones and the Spear of Destiny	504
Indiana Jones and the Temple of Doom	253
Indiana Jones: Thunder In the Orient	504
Indians	411
Indians On the Warpath	411
Industriacide	734
Industrial Gothic	98
Inferior Five	98
Inferno	98, 734
Inferno: Hellbound	539
Infinity Abyss	253
Infinity Crusade	253
Infinity Gauntlet	254
Infinity War	254
Infinity, Inc.	98
Informer, The	411
Ingrigue	539
Inhumanoids	254

Comics Values Annual — Index — In–Ju

Inhumans 254	Jack Staff 539, 735	Jingle Belle 736	Judge Dredd Vs. Aliens:
Initial D 734	Jack the Giant Killer 412	Jingle Jangle Comics 412	Incubus 505
Inmates: Prisoners of Society ..610	Jack the Ripper 735	Jinn 539	Judge Dredd: America 613
Inner Circle 610	Jackaroo 735	Jinx 539	Judge Dredd: Judge Child
Innocents 610	Jackie Chan's Spartan X ..539, 611	Jinx: Torso 539	Quest 613
Innovators 610	Jackie Gleason 412	Jiz 807	Judge Dredd: Legends of
Insane Clown Posse 610	Jackie Gleason and the 99	JLA 99	the Law 102
Insane Clown Posse: Dark	Jackie Robinson 412	JLA: Act of God 100	Judge Dredd: The Megazine ...614
Carnival 610	Jackpot Comics 412	JLA: Age of Wonder 100	Judge Dredd's Crime File 613
Insane Clown Posse: Mr.	Jade Warriors 539	JLA: Black Baptism 100	Judge Dredd's Early Cases ...614
Johnson's Head 610	Jade Warriors: Slave of	JLA: Created Equal 100	Judge Dredd's Hardcore
Insane Clown Posse: The	the Dragon 611	JLA: Destiny 100	Papers 614
Pendulum 610	Jade: Redemption 611	JLA: Gatekeeper 100	Judge Parker 614
Insect Fear 807	Jademan Collection 611	JLA: Incarnations 100	Judgement Day 614
Inspector Gill of the Fish Police 725	Jademan Kung Fu Special ...611	JLA: Paradise Lost 100	Judgment Day 614
Instant Piano 504	Jaguar 99	JLA: Scary Monsters 100	Judo Joe 414
Interface 254	Jaguar God 611	JLA: World Without Grown-Ups 101	Judomaster 614
International Crime Patrol ... 377	Jake Trash 611	JLA: Year One 101	Judy Canova 414
International Comics 377	Jam Special 611	JLA-Z 101	Juggernaut 259
Interview With A Vampire 610	Jam, The 735	JLA/Avengers 257	Juggernaut: The Eighth Day ...259
Interzone 734	Jamboree 412	JLA/Jsa 100	Jughead 614
Intimate 610	James Bond 007 611	JLA/The Spectre: Soul War ...101	Jughead As Captain Hero 614
Intimate Confessions 411	James Bond 007: A Silent	JLA/Titans 101	Jughead With Archie Digest ...614
Intimate Love 411	Armageddon 505	JLX 186	Jughead's Fantasy 614
Intimate Secrets of Romance ..411	James Bond 007: Quasimodo	JLX Unleashed 186	Jughead's Jokes 614
Into the Storm 735	Gambit 505	Jo-Jo Comics 413	Juke Box 414
Intron Depot 504	James Bond 007: Serpent's	Joan of Arc 798	Julie's Journey/Gravity 736
Intruder 610	Tooth 505	Joe College 412	Juline 736
Inu Yasha 735	James Bond 007: Shattered	Joe Louis 413	Julius Ceasar 798
Inu Yasha: A Feudal Fairy Tale .735	Helix 505	Joe Palooka 413	Jumbo Comics 414
Invaders 254	James Bond Jr. 257	Joe Psycho & Moo Frog 736	Junction 17 614
Invaders From Home 610	James Bond: Goldeneye 611	Joe R. Lansdale's the Drive-In .736	Jungle Action 259
Invaders From Mars 735	James O'Barr Original Sins ..735	Joe Sinn 736	Jungle Adventures 614
Invaders, The 610	James O'Barr Tasty Bites ... 735	Joe Yank 413	Jungle Book, The 614, 799
Invasion '55 735	Jane Arden 412	John Bolton, Halls of Horror ...612	Jungle Comics 415, 614, 737
Invasion! 98	Jane Eyre 796	John Bolton's Strange Wink .. 505	Jungle Fantasy 737
Invincible 539	Jane's World 735	John Byrne's Next Men 508	Jungle Girls 737
Invincible Ed: 504	Jann of the Jungle 259	John Carter of Mars 612	Jungle Jim 417
Invincible Four of Kung Fu	Japanese Monster 807	John Carter, Warlord of Mars .257	Jungle Jo 417
& Ninja 539	Jason and the Argonauts ... 735	John F. Kennedy Life Story ...612	Jungle Lil 417
Invisible Scarlet O'Neil 411	Jason Goes To Hell 611	John Hix Scrapbook 413	Jungle Tales 259
Invisible 9 539	Jason Vs. Leatherface 611	John Jakes Mullkon Empire ...612	Jungle Tales of Tarzan 614
Invisible Man, The 802	Javerts 611	John Law 612	Jungle Thrills 467
Invisible People 735	Jay & Silent Bob 735	John Steele Secret Agent ... 612	Jungle War Stories 615
Invisibles 98	Jazz 735	John Wayne Adventure Comics 413	Junie Prom 417
Invu 735	Jazz Age Chronicles 736	Johnny the Homicidal Maniac ..736	Junior 737
Io 610	Jazz the Series 735	Johnny Atomic 736	Junior Carrot Patrol 505
Iron Fist 254	Jazz: Solitaire 736	Johnny Comet 736	Junior Comics 417
Iron Fist/Wolverine 254	Jazz: Superstar 736	Johnny Danger 413	Junior Hoop Comics 417
Iron Hand of Almuric 505	Jcp Features 736	Johnny Dark 736	Junior Woodchucks 615
Iron Horse 610	Jeanie Comics 223	Johnny Dynamite 385, 505	Junk Culture 102
Iron Lantern 186	Jedit Ojanen 624	Johnny Gambit 612	Junkbotz Rotogin 539
Iron Man 254	Jeep Comics 412	Johnny Hazard 413	Junkwaffel 807
Iron Man & Submariner 257	Jeff Jordan, U.S. Agent 412	Johnny Jason Teen Reporter .612	Jupiter 737
Iron Man: Bad Blood 257	Jemm, Son of Saturn 99	Johnny Law, Sky Ranger ... 413	Jurassic Jane 737
Iron Man: The Iron Age 257	Jenny Finn 736	Johnny Nemo 612	Jurassic Park 615
Iron Marshal 610	Jenny Sparks: The Secret	Johnny Thunder 101	Jurassic Park: Adventures ...615
Iron Vic 411	History of the Authority ...611	Joker 101	Jurassic Park: Raptor 615
Iron Wings 539	Jeremiah: Birds of Prey 736	Joker Comics 258	Jurassic Park: Raptor Hijack ..615
Ironjaw 610	Jeremiah: Eyes Like Burning	Joker, The: Last Laugh 101	Jurassic Park: Raptors Attack ..615
Ironwolf 99	Coals 736	Joker/Mask 505	Jurassic Park: The Lost World .615
Ironwolf: Fires of the Revolution .99	Jeremiah: Fist Full of Sand ...736	Jolly Jingles 412	Just A Pilgrim 615
Irregulars, The: Battletech 611	Jeremiah: The Heirs 736	Jon Sable 612	Just A Pilgrim: Garden of Eden .615
Irukashi 611	Jerry Igers Famous Features ..736	Jonah Hex 101	Just Imagine... .... 102, 106
Isis 99	Jesse James 412	Jonah Hex and Other Western	Just Married 615
Island 735	Jest 412	Tales 259, 737	Justice 259, 737
Island of Dr. Moreau 257	Jesus Loves You 807	Jonah Hex: Shadows West ...102	Justice Comics 260
Ismet 735	Jet 611	Jonah Hex: Riders of the Worm 102	Justice League Adventures ..102
It Ain't Me Babe 807	Jet Aces 412	Jonah Hex: Two-Gun Mojo ...102	Justice League America 103
It Really Happened 411	Jet Dream 612	Jonni Thunder 102	Justice League Europe 103
It! Terror From Beyond Space ..611	Jet Fighters 412	Jonny Demon 505	Justice League
It's A Duck's Life 257	Jetcat Clubhouse 736	Jonny Double 102	International 103, 104
It's About Time 611	Jetsons, The 612	Jonny Quest 612	Justice League International
It's Gametime 99	Jetta of the 21st Century ... 412	Jonny Quest Classics 612	Quarterly 104
It's Science With Dr. Radium ..735	Jezebel Jade 612	Josie 613	Justice League of America ...104
Itchy & Scratchy 611	Jezebelle 612	Josie and the Pussy Cats ... 564	Justice League of America:
Ivanhoe 611, 791	Jiggs and Maggie 412	Joss Whedon's Fray 505	the Nail 104
J. O'Barr's the Crow 736	Jigsaw 612	Journey 736	Justice League Task Force ...106
J.N.Williamson's Masques ...612	Jihad 257	Journey Into Fear 414	Justice League: A
J.U.D.G.E. 539	Jim 736	Journey Into Mystery .258, 259, 327	Midsummer's Nightmare ..104
J-2 259	Jim Bowie 583	Journey Into Unknown Worlds .189	Justice Leagues 106
Jace Pearson of the Texas	Jim Hardy 412	Journeyman 539	Justice Machine 615
Rangers 411	Jim Lee's C-23 529	Jr. Jackalope 736	Justice Machine: Chimera
Jack 611	Jim Ray's Aviation Sketch Book 412	JSA 102	Conspiracy 615
Jack Armstrong 411	Jimbo 612	JSA: All-Stars 102	Justice Riders 106
Jack Hunter 611, 735	Jimmy Corrigan 612	JSA: The Liberty Files 102	Justice Society of America ...106
Jack In the Box 486	Jimmy Olsen: Adventures ... 99	JSA: The Unholy Three 102	Justice Traps of the Guilty ...417
Jack Kirby's Fourth World 99	Jimmy Wakely 99	Judge Colt 613	Justice, Inc. 102
Jack of Hearts 257	Jing King of Bandits 736	Judge Dredd 102, 613, 736	Justice: Four Balance 260
Jack of Nines 735	Jing Pals 412	Judge Dredd Classics 613	Justy 737

CVA Page 823

Ka'a'nga Comics . . . 417
Ka-Zar . . . 260
Kaboom . . . 615
Kabuki . . . 539
Kabuki Agents . . . 539
Kabuki Classics . . . 540
Kabuki Color Gallery . . . 615
Kabuki Color Special . . . 615
Kabuki Fear the Reaper . . . 615
Kabuki: Circle of Blood . . . 737
Kabuki: Dance of Death . . . 737
Kabuki: Masks of the Noh . . . 737
Kabuki: Skin Deep . . . 615
Kafka . . . 737
Kamandi, The Last Boy On Earth . . . 106
Kamandi: At Earth's End . . . 107
Kamikaze: 1946 . . . 615
Kamui . . . 737
Kane . . . 737
Kanned Korn Komix . . . 807
Kansas Thunder . . . 737
Kaos Moon . . . 737
Kaptain Amerika Komix . . . 807
Kaptain Keen . . . 737
Karate Kid . . . 107
Kare Kano . . . 737
Karza . . . 540
Kasco Comics . . . 418
Kathy . . . 260, 418
Katmandu . . . 737
Kato II . . . 616
Kato of the Green Hornet . . . 615
Katy Keene . . . 418
Katy Keene Pinup Parade . . . 616
Katy Keene Fashion Book Magazine . . . 616
Kayo . . . 453
Kazan . . . 737
Keen Detective Funnies . . . 418
Keen Komics . . . 418
Keen Teens . . . 418
Keif Llama . . . 738
Kelley Belle, Police Detective . . 738
Kelley Jones' the Hammer . . . 505
Kelley Jones' the Hammer: the Outsider . . . 505
Kelly Green . . . 616
Kellys, The . . . 261
Kelvin Mace . . . 616
Ken Lashley's Legends . . . 616
Ken Maynard Western . . . 418
Ken Shannon . . . 418
Kent Black of the Secret Service . . . 260
Kents, The . . . 107
Kerry Drake Detective Cases . . 418
Kewpies . . . 418
Key Comics . . . 418
Kickers Inc. . . . 260
Kid & Play . . . 260
Kid Cannibal . . . 738
Kid Colt Outlaw . . . 260
Kid Cowboy . . . 418
Kid Death & Fluffy . . . 616
Kid Eternity . . . 107, 418
Kid From Dodge City . . . 261
Kid From Texas . . . 261
Kid Komics . . . 261
Kid Montana . . . 584
Kid Movie Komics . . . 261
Kid Slade Gunfighter . . . 278
Kid Supreme . . . 540
Kid Terrific . . . 540
Kid Zoo Comics . . . 419
Kiddie Carnival . . . 418
Kidnapped . . . 796
Kiku San . . . 738
Kill Your Boyfriend . . . 107
Killbox . . . 738
Killer Instinct . . . 616
Killer Instinct Tour Book . . . 540
Killer Tales . . . 616
Killers. The . . . 419
Killfrenzy . . . 261
Killing Stroke . . . 738
Killpower: The Early Years . . . 261
Killraven . . . 261
Killrazor Special . . . 540
Kilroy . . . 738
Kilroy Is Here . . . 738
Kilroys, The . . . 419
Kim . . . 802
Kimber, Prince of Felons . . . 738
Kin . . . 540
Kindaichi Case Files, The . . . 738
Kindred . . . 540
Kindred II . . . 616
King Arthur & the Knights of Justice . . . 261
King Bee . . . 807
King Comics . . . 419
King Comics Presents . . . 616
King Conan . . . 217
King Kong . . . 738
King Louie & Mowgli . . . 616
King of Diamonds . . . 616
King of Hell . . . 738
King of the Khyber Rifles . . . 800
King of the Mountains, The . . . 801
King of the Royal Mounted . . . 419
King Solomon's Mines . . . 799
King Tiger/Motorhead . . . 505
King Zombie . . . 738
Kingdom Come . . . 107
Kingdom of the Wicked . . . 738
Kingdom, The . . . 107
Kingpin . . . 262
Kings In Disguise . . . 738
Kings of the Night . . . 505
'Kini . . . 540
Kirby King of the Serials . . . 738
Kiss . . . 505
Kiss: The Psycho Circus . . . 540
Kissing Chaos . . . 738
Kissing Chaos: Nonstop Beauty . . . 738
Kissyfur . . . 107
Kit Carson . . . 419
Kit Karter . . . 616
Kitty Pride & Wolverine . . . 262
Kitty Pryde: Agent of S.H.I.E.L.D. . . . 262
Kitz N Katz . . . 738
Kling Klang Klatch . . . 505
Knewts of the Round Table . . . 738
Knight Masters . . . 738
Knight Watchman . . . 540, 739
Knighthawk . . . 616
Knightmare . . . 540, 738
Knights of Pendragon . . . 262
Knights of the Dinner Table . . . 738
Knights of the Dinner Table Illustrated . . . 739
Knights of the Dinner Table Mini-Series . . . 739
Knights of the Dinner Table: Everknights . . . 739
Knights of the Dinner Table: Hackmasters . . . 739
Knights of the Dinner Table/ Faans . . . 739
Knights of the Round Table . . . 616, 800
Knights On Broadway . . . 579
Knightstrike . . . 540
Knuckles . . . 616
Ko Komics . . . 420
Kobalt . . . 107
Kobra . . . 107
Kodocha . . . 739
Koko and Kola . . . 419
Kol Manique Renaissance . . . 616
Komah . . . 616
Kombat . . . 616
Komik Pages . . . 453
Komodo & the Defiants . . . 739
Kona . . . 616
Kong the Untamed . . . 107
Konga . . . 616
Konga's Revenge . . . 616
Kookie . . . 616
Korak, Son of Tarzan . . . 107, 616
Kore . . . 540
Korvus . . . 739
Kosmic Kat . . . 540
Krazy Kat Comics . . . 420
Krazy Komics . . . 262
Krazy Krow . . . 262
Krazy Life . . . 442
Kree-Skrull War . . . 262
Krull . . . 262
Krusty Comics . . . 617
Krypton Chronicles . . . 107
Kull . . . 263
Kull and the Barbarians . . . 263
Kull In 3-D . . . 617
Kull the Conqueror . . . 262
Kung Fu Warriors . . . 739
Kunoichi . . . 739
Kurt Busiek's Astro City . . . 540
Kurtzman Comix . . . 807
Kyra . . . 739
L.A.W. . . . 108
L.E.G.I.O.N. '89-92 . . . 109
L.I.F.E. Brigade . . . 741
L33t: Comics For Gamers . . . 739
La Cosa Nostroid . . . 739
Lab Rats . . . 107
Labman . . . 541
Labor Force . . . 739
Labor Is A Partner . . . 420
Labrynth . . . 263
Lacunae . . . 739
Lad: A Dog . . . 617
Ladies of London Night . . . 739
Lady Arcane . . . 617, 739
Lady Death . . . 617
Lady Death & the Women of Chaos! Gallery . . . 617
Lady Death Bedlam . . . 617
Lady Death In Lingerie . . . 617
Lady Death Vs. Purgatori . . . 618
Lady Death Vs. Vampirella II . . 618
Lady Death: Alive . . . 617
Lady Death: Between Heaven & Hell . . . 617
Lady Death: Dark Alliance . . . 617
Lady Death: Dark Millennium . . 617
Lady Death: Death Becomes Her . . . 618
Lady Death: Dragon Wars . . . 617
Lady Death: Heartbreaker . . . 618
Lady Death: Judgment War . . . 618
Lady Death: Last Rites . . . 618
Lady Death: Love Bites . . . 618
Lady Death: Mischief Night . . . 618
Lady Death: Re-Imagined . . . 618
Lady Death: Retribution . . . 617
Lady Death: River of Fear . . . 618
Lady Death: The Crucible . . . 617
Lady Death: The Gauntlet . . . 618
Lady Death: The Goddess Returns . . . 618
Lady Death: The Mourning . . . 618
Lady Death: The Odyssey . . . 618
Lady Death: The Rapture . . . 618
Lady Death: Tribulation . . . 618
Lady Death/Medieval Witchblade . . . 618
Lady Death/Bad Kitty . . . 617
Lady Death/Chastity . . . 617
Lady Death/Chastity/Bad Kitty: United . . . 617
Lady Death/Evil Ernie . . . 618
Lady Death/Jade . . . 618
Lady Death/The Crow . . . 617
Lady Death/Vampirella: Dark Hearts . . . 618
Lady Demon . . . 618
Lady Justice . . . 633
Lady of the Lake, The . . . 798
Lady Pendragon . . . 541, 619
Lady Pendragon: Dragon Blade . . . 541
Lady Pendragon: More Than Mortal . . . 541
Lady Rawhide . . . 619
Lady Rawhide: Other People's Blood . . . 619
Lady Supreme . . . 541
Lady Vampre . . . 619, 739
Lady Vampre Returns . . . 739
Laff-A-Lympics . . . 263
Laffin Gas . . . 739
Laffy-Daffy Comics . . . 420
Lana . . . 263
Lance O'Casey . . . 420
Lance Stanton Wayward Warrior . . . 739
Lancelot Strong, The Shield . . 619
Land of Nod . . . 505
Land of Oz . . . 739
Land of the Lost . . . 420
Lander . . . 739
Landsale & Truman's Dead Folks . . . 619
Large Feature Comics . . . 420
Larry Doby, Baseball Hero . . . 420
Lars of Mars . . . 420, 619
Laser Eraser & Pressbutton . . 619
Lash Larue Western . . . 420, 619
Lassie . . . 420
Last American . . . 263
Last Avengers Story, The . . . 263
Last Day In Vietnam . . . 505
Last Days of Pompell . . . 795
Last Days of the Justice Society . . . 108
Last Ditch . . . 740
Last Generation . . . 740
Last of the Mohicans, The . . . 791
Last of the Viking Heroes . . . 619
Last One . . . 108
Last Shot . . . 541
Last Shot: First Draw . . . 541
Last Starfighter, The . . . 263
Last Temptation, The . . . 505
Latest Comics . . . 420
Latex Alice . . . 740
Laugh . . . 619
Laugh Comics . . . 421
Laugh Comix . . . 472
Laugh In the Dark . . . 807
Laurel & Hardy . . . 619
Laurel and Hardy . . . 421, 619
Law and Order . . . 619
Law of Dredd . . . 619
Law-Crime . . . 421
Lawbreakers . . . 421
Lawbreakers Always Lose . . . 421
Lawbreakers Always Lose! . . . 263
Lawbreakers Suspense Stories 421
Lawdog . . . 263
Lawdog & Grimrod: Terror At the Crossroads . . . 263
Lawman . . . 619
Lazarus Churchyard . . . 619
Lazarus Churchyard: The Final Cut . . . 541
Lazarus Five . . . 108
Lazarus: The Many Reincarnations . . . 619
Le Femme Vamprique . . . 740
Leading Comics . . . 108
League of Champions . . . 619, 740
League of Extraordinary Gentlemen . . . 619
League of Justice . . . 108
Leatherface . . . 620
Leave It To Binky . . . 108
Leave It To Chance . . . 541
Legacy . . . 541, 620
Legend of Sleepy Hollow . . . 620
Legend of Custer, The . . . 620
Legend of Isis . . . 541
Legend of Lemnear . . . 740
Legend of Supreme . . . 541
Legend of the Eight Dragon Gods . . . 740
Legend of the Elflord . . . 620
Legend of the Hawkman . . . 108
Legend of the Sage . . . 620
Legend of the Shield . . . 108
Legend of Wonder Woman . . . 108
Legendlore . . . 740
Legendlore: Realm Wars . . . 740
Legendlore: Wrath of the Dragon . . . 740
Legends . . . 108
Legends of Jesse James, The . 620
Legends of Camelot . . . 740
Legends of Daniel Boone, The . 108
Legends of Luxura . . . 620, 740
Legends of Nascar . . . 620
Legends of the Dark Claw . . . 186
Legends of the DC Universe . . . 108
Legends of the Legion . . . 109
Legends of the Stargrazers . . . 620
Legends of the World Finest . . . 109

Index Le–Ma

Title	Page
Legion Anthology	740
Legion Lost	109
Legion of Substitute Heroes	110
Legion of Monsters	263
Legion of Night	263
Legion of Super-Heroes	110
Legion X-2	740
Legion X-I	740
Legion, The	109
Legion: Science Police	112
Legionnaires	109
Legionnaires Three	110
Lejentia	620
Lemonade Kid	620
Lenny of Lavedo	807
Lenore	740
Lensman	740
Lensman: War of the Galaxies	740
Lensman: Galactic Patrol	740
Leonard Nimoy's Primortals	620
Leonardo	620, 740
Leopard	620
Leroy	421
Les Miserables	792
Let's Pretend	421
Lethal	541
Lethal Foes of Spiderman	263
Lethal Ladies of Brainstorm	740
Lethal Strike Archives	740
Lethal Strike: Shadow Viper	740
Lethal Strike/Double Impact: Lethal Impact	620
Lethal Stryke	620
Lethargic Lad	741
Lethargic Lad Adventures	741
Level X	741
Level X: The Next Reality	741
Li'l Abner	422
Li'l Genius	422
Li'l Kids	263
Li'l Pals	264
Li'l Pan	422
Libby Ellis	741
Liberator	741
Liberty Comics	421
Liberty Guards	421
Liberty Meadows	541, 741
Liberty Project, The	620
Liberty Scouts	421
Lidsville	620
Lieutenent, The	620
Life & Adventures of Santa Claus	620
Life In Hell	620
Life of A Fetus	741
Life of Captain Marvel	263
Life of Christ	263
Life of Pope John-Paul II	263
Life Story	421
Life With Snarky Parker	422
Life With Archie	620
Life With Millie	223
Life, The Universe and Everything	112
Lifequest	741
Light and Darkness War	263
Light Fantastic, The	621
Lightning Comics	422
Lightning Comics Presents	621
Lillith: Demon Princess	621
Limbo City	621
Limited Collectors Edition	112
Lincoln-16	621
Linda	443
Linda Carter, Student Nurse	263
Linda Lark	263
Linus, The Lionhearted	621
Lion King	263
Lion of the North, The	802
Lionheart	621
Lippy the Lion and Hardy Har Har	621
Lisa Comics	621
Lita Ford	621
Little Ambrose	621
Little Annie Fanny 1962–70	506
Little Archie	621
Little Archie Mystery	621
Little Asprin	264
Little Audrey	422

Title	Page
Little Audrey Tv Funtime	621
Little Audrey & Melvin	621
Little Bit	422
Little Dot	422
Little Dot Dotland	621
Little Dot's Uncles & Aunts	621
Little Endless	112
Little Eva	422
Little Giant Movie Funnies	422
Little Giant Comics	422
Little Giant Detective Funnies	422
Little Gloomy	741
Little Ike	423
Little Iodine	423
Little Jack Frost	423
Little Lana	263
Little Lenny	264
Little Lizzie	264
Little Lotta	621
Little Lotta Foodland	621
Little Lulu	430
Little Max Comics	423
Little Mermaid	622
Little Mermaid, The	423
Little Miss Muffet	423
Little Miss Sunbeam Comics	423
Little Monsters	622
Little Monsters, The	622
Little Orphan Annie	423, 741
Little Red Hot: Bound	541
Little Red Hot: Chane of Fools	541
Little Redbirds	622
Little Roquefort	423
Little Sad Sack	622
Little Savage, The	801
Little Scouts	423
Little Shop of Horrors	112
Little Stooges, The	622
Little White Mouse (the Series)	741
Little White Mouse: Entropy Dreaming	741
Little White Mouse: Open Space	741
Little-Greyman	541
Littlest Snowman	423
Lives of the Hunted	803
Living Bible, The	423
Livingstone Mountain	741
Lloyd Llewellyn	622, 741
Lobo	112, 622
Lobo the Duck	186
Lobo Unbound	113
Lobo: A Contract On Gawd	113
Lobo: Death & Taxes	113
Lobo: Unamerican Gladiators	113
Lobo: Infanticide	113
Lobo's Back	113
Lobo/Mask	113
Lobocop	113
Locke	622
Loco Vs Pulverine	741
Lodoss War: Chronicles Heroic Knight	741
Lodoss War: Deelit's Tale	741
Lodoss War: The Grey Witch	741
Lodoss War: The Lady of Pharis	741
Logan	264
Logan: Path of the Warrior	264
Logan: Shadow Society	264
Logan's Run	264, 741
Logan's World	741
Lois and Clark: The New Adventures of Superman	113
Lois Lane	113
Lone	506
Lone Eagle	423
Lone Gunmen, The	506
Lone Ranger	423
Lone Ranger, The	622
Lone Ranger's Companion Tonto, The	423
Lone Ranger's Famous Horse Hi-Yo Silver, The	423
Lone Rider	423
Lone Wolf & Cub	742
Lone Wolf 2100	506
Lone Wolf and Cub	506
Loner	741
Long Bow	424
Long Hot Summer, The	113

Title	Page
Longshot	264
Lookers	622, 742
Looney Tunes	113, 424
Looney Tunes and Merrie Melodies	424
Looney Tunes Mag.	113
Loose Cannon	113
Loose Cannons	264
Lord Jim	801
Lord of the Dead	742
Lord Pumpkin	622
Lords of Misrule	506
Lords of the Ultrarealm	113
Lorelei	742
Lori Lovecraft	742
Lorna Doone	795
Lorna, The Jungle Girl	264
Losers	113
Losers Special	113
Lost Continent	742
Lost Heroes	622
Lost In Space	506, 622
Lost Ones, The	541
Lost Planet	622
Lost Stories	742
Lost World	424, 506
Lost, The	742
Lothar	742
Louder Than Words	513
Louis Riel	742
Love Adventures	264
Love and Marriage	424
Love and Rockets	742
Love At First Sight	424
Love Confessions	424
Love Diary	424, 425, 622
Love Dramas	264
Love Fights	742
Love Hina	742
Love In Tights	742
Love Lessons	425
Love Letters	425
Love Memories	425
Love Mystery	425
Love Problems and Advice Illustrated	425
Love Romances	250
Love Scandals	425
Love Secrets	264, 425
Love Showdown Collection, The	622
Love Stories of Mary Worth	425
Lovebunny & Mr. Hell	541
Lovecraft	622
Lovelorn	425
Lovely Prudence	742
Lovers	189
Lovers Lane	425
Luba	742
Luba's Comics & Stories	742
Lucifer	113
Lucifer's Hammer	622
Lucky "7" Comics	426
Lucky Comics	426
Lucky Duck	426
Lucky Fights It Through	426
Lucky Star	426
Lucy Show, The	622
Lucy, The Real Gone Gal	426
Ludwig Von Drake	622
Luftwaffe 1946	623, 742
Luger	623
Lum*urusei Yatsura	743
Lunar Donut	743
Lunatic Fringe	623
Lunatik	264
Luxura	623, 743
Luxura Collection	623
Luxura/Baby Angel X	743
Luxura/Widow: Blood Lust	743
Lynch	542
Lynch Mob	623
Lyndon B. Johnson	623
Lynx: An Elflord Tale	743
M	**623**
M.A.R.S. Patrol	674
M.D.	627
M.D. Geist	627
M.D. Geist: Ground Zero	627
M-Rex	543
Mac Rayboy's Flash Gordon	506

Title	Page
Macbeth	801
Mace Griffin: Bounty Hunter	542
Mach 1	743
Machine Man	264
Machine Man 2020	264
Machine, The	506
Mackenzie Queen	743
Macross	623
Macross II the Micron Conspiracy	743
Mad	426
Mad About Millie	264
Mad Dog	264
Mad Dogs	743
Mad Follies	623
Mad Hatter, The	427
Mad Raccoons	743
Mad Special	623
Madame Xanadu	113
Madballs	264
Made Men	623
Madman	506, 623, 743
Madman Adventures	623
Madman Picture Exhibition	623
Madman/The Jam	506
Madwoman of the Sacred Heart, The	506
Maelstrom	743
Magdalena	542
Magdalena/Angelus	542
Magdalena/Blood Legacy	542
Magdalena/Vampirella	542
Mage	623
Mage Knight: Stolen Destiny	623
Mage: The Hero Defined	542
Magebook	623
Maggots	743
Maggotzine	807
Magic Comics	427
Magic Flute	623
Magic Knight Rayearth	743
Magic Priest	743
Magic the Gathering: Antiquities War	623
Arabian Knights	623
Convocations	623
Fallen Empires	623
Homelands	623
Ice Age	623
Shadow Mage	623
Legends Of: The Elder Dragons	624
Urza-Mishra War	624
Magic the Gathering: Wayfarer	624
Magic Whistle	743
Magic: The Gathering	506
Magical Mates	743
Magical Pokemon Journey	743
Magik	265
Magilla Gorilla	624
Magique	624
Magnetic Men Featuring Magneto	186
Magneto	265
Magneto & the Magnetic Men	186
Magneto Rex	265
Magneto: Dark Seduction	265
Magnus (robot Fighter)	624
Magnus: Robot Fighter	624
Magnus: Robotfighter	624
Magnus/Nexus	506
Magus	744
Mai the Psychic Girl	744
Maison Ikkoku	744
Major Bummer	113
Major Damage	625
Major Hoople Comics	427
Major Victory Comics	427
Malice	625
Man Against Time	542
Man Called A-X	625
Man Comics	265
Man Eating Cow	744
Man From Atlantis	265
Man From Planet X	625
Man From the Ciguiri	506
Man From U.N.C.L.E.	625, 744
Man Hunt!	427
Man In Black	625
Man In the Iron Mask	797

CVA Page 825

Man O'Mars 428	Marvel Double Feature ..270	Mask/Marshall Law 507	Men In Action 279
Man of Rust 744	Marvel Double-Shot 270	Masked Man 626	Men In Black 279, 745
Man of Steel 114	Marvel Family, The 430	Masked Marvel 431	Men In Black: Retribution ...279
Man of the Atom 625	Marvel Fanfare 270	Masked Ranger 431	Men In Black: The Roborg
Man of War 428, 625	Marvel Feature 270	Masked Warrior X 745	Incident 746
Man Who Laughs, The 798	Marvel Frontier Comics Special 270	Masquerade 745	Men of Iron 799
Man Without A Country, The ..797	Marvel Fumetti Book 270	Master Comics 431	Men of War 115
Man-Bat 114	Marvel Graphic Novel 270	Master Darque 626	Men's Adventures 331
Man-Bat Vs. Batman 114	Marvel Halloween: The	Master of Ballantrae, The ..799	Menace 278, 627
Man-Elf 744	Supernaturals Tour Book ..271	Master of Kung Fu, Special	Menz Insana 115
Man-Thing 265	Marvel Heroes 271	Marvel Ed. 277	Mephisto Vs. Four Heroes ...279
Mandrake 265, 744	Marvel Holiday Special ...271	Master of Kung Fu: Bleeding	Mercedes 746
Mandrake Monthly 744	Marvel Kids 271	Black 278	Mercenary 627
Manga Ex 744	Marvel Knights 271	Master of the World 803	Merchants of Death 627, 746
Manga Shi 2000 625	Marvel Knights Magazine ..271	Masters of Terror 278	Mercy 115, 746
Manga Vizion 744	Marvel Knights Tour Book ..271	Masters of the	Meridian 627
Mangaphile 744	Marvel Knights: Double-Shot .271	Universe ..114, 278, 542, 626	Merlin 746
Mangazine 744	Marvel Mangaverse 271	Masters of the Universe:	Merlin Realm 628
Mangle Tangle Tales 625	Marvel Masterpieces II	Icons of Evil 626	Mermaid's Gaze 746
Manhunter 114	Collection 271	Masterwork Series 626	Merry Mouse 433
Manik 625	Marvel Masterpieces Collection 271	Masterworks Series of Great	Merry-Go-Round Comics ...433
Manimal 744	Marvel Milestone Edition ..271	Comic Book Artists 115	Messenger, The 543
Mankind 625	Marvel Mini-Books 271	Mataak 745	Meta 4 628
Manslaughter 744	Marvel Movie Showcase	Matt Busch's Daria Jontak ..626	Metabarons 628
Manticore 807	Featuring Star Wars 272	Matt Champion 745	Metacops 746
Mantra 625	Marvel Movie Spotlight Featuring	Matt Slade Gunfighter 278	Metal Guardian Faust 746
Mantra: Spear of Destiny ...625	Raiders of the Lost Ark ..272	Maverick 278, 626	Metal Men 115
Mantus Files 744	Marvel Movie Premiere 272	Maverick Marshall 626	Metal Militia 628
Many Loves of Dobie Gillis ...114	Marvel Mystery Comics ...267	Mavericks 627	Metallica 628
Many Worlds of Tesla	Marvel Mystery Comics ...272	Mavis 745	Metallix 628
Strong, The 626	Marvel No-Prize Book 272	Max of the Regulators 745	Metamorpho 115
Marcane 744	Marvel Poster Book 272	Maximage 542	Metaphysique 628, 746
March of Comics 428	Marvel Premiere 272	Maximortal 627	Meteor Comics 433
Marge's Little Lulu 430	Marvel Presents 272	Maximum Force 627	Meteor Man 279
Marines At War 227	Marvel Preview 272	Maximum Overload 507	Metropol 279
Marines In Action 265	Marvel Remix 273	Maximum Security 278	Metropol A.D. 279
Marines In Battle 265	Marvel Saga 273	Maxion 745	Metropolis 507, 746
Mark Hazzard: Merc 266	Marvel Selects: Fantastic ..273	Maxwell Mouse Follies 745	Metropolis S.C.U. 115
Mark I 744	Marvel Selects: Spider-Man ..273	Maxx 542	Mezz Galactic Tour 507
Mark of Charon 626	Marvel Spotlight 273	Maya 627	Miami Mice 746
Mark Rand's Sky	Marvel Spotlight On Captain	Mayhem 507, 745	Michael Moorcock's Multiverse .115
Technologies Inc. 626	America 273	Maze Agency 627, 745	Michael Strogoff 795
Mark, The 506	Marvel Spotlight On Dr. Strange 273	Mazing Man 115	Michaelangelo 628, 746
Marksman, The 626	Marvel Spotlight On Silver	Mchale's Navy 627	Mickey & Donald 628
Marmaduke Mouse 430	Surfer 273	Mckeever & the Colonel ..627	Mickey Finn 433
Marmalade Boy 744	Marvel Sprectacular 273	MD 432	Mickey Mantle Comics 628
Marquis, The 744	Marvel Super Action 273	Measles 745	Mickey Mouse 433, 628
Marquis, The: Danse Macabre .745	Marvel Super Special 269	Meat Cake 745	Mickey Mouse and Friends ..628
Married With Children 2099 ..626	Marvel Superheroes ...273, 274	Mech Destroyer 542	Mickey Mouse Magazine ...433
Married With Children:	Marvel Superheroes Magazine .274	Mecha 507	Mickey Rat 807
Dysfunctional Family 626	Marvel Swimsuit 274	Mechanic, The 542	Mickey Spillane's Mike Danger .628
Married With Children:	Marvel Tails 274	Mechanics 627	Micra 746
Flashback Special 626	Marvel Tales 268, 274	Mechanoids 745	Microbots, The 628
Married... With Children ...626	Marvel Team-Up ...275, 276	Mecharider: The Regular Series 745	Micronauts 279, 543
Mars 626, 745	Marvel Treasury of Oz 276	Medabots 745	Midget Comics 433
Mars Attacks 626	Marvel Treasury Special ...276	Medal of Honor Comics ...432	Midnight 746
Mars Attacks High School ...626	Marvel Triple Action 276	Medal of Honor 507	Midnight Eye: Goku Private
Mars Attacks the Image	Marvel Two-In-One 276	Media Starr 627	Investigator 628
Universe 542	Marvel Universe 277	Medieval Spawn/Witchblade ..542	Midnight Men 279
Mars Attacks the Savage	Marvel Universe: Millennial	Meet Corliss Archer 432	Midnight Nation 543
Dragon 626	Visions 277	Meet Merton 432	Midnight Panther 746
Marshall Law 266, 506	Marvel Universe: The End ..277	Meet Miss Pepper 426	Midnight Panther: Feudal
Marshall Law: Cape Fear ...506	Marvel Valentine's Special ...277	Meet the New Post Gazette	Fantasy 746
Marshall Law: Secret Tribunal ..506	Marvel Versus DC 186	Sunday Funnies 432	Midnight Panther: School Daze 746
Martha Washington Goes	Marvel Visionaries 277	Megadeth 627	Midnight Sons Unlimited ...279
To War 507	Marvel X-Men Collection 277	Megadrane & Tiger 542	Midnight, Mass 115
Martha Washington Saves	Marvel: Heroes and	Megahurtz 543	Midnite Skulker 746
the World 507	Legends 1997 271	Megalith 627	Mighty Atom, The 444
Martha Washington Stranded	Marvel: Portraits of A Universe .272	Megaman 627	Mighty Comics 628
In Space 507	Marvel: Shadows & Light ..273	Megaton 627, 745	Mighty Crusaders 629
Martian Manhunter 114	Marvel: The Lost Generation ..273	Megaton Explosion 627	Mighty Guy 746
Martian Mystery 507	Marvel's Greatest Comics ...267	Megaton Man 627	Mighty Hercules, The 629
Martian Successor Nadesico .745	Marvel/Ultraverse Battlezones .626	Megaton Man Meets the	Mighty Heroes 280
Martin Kane 430	Marvelous Adventures of	Uncategorizable X-Thems .745	Mighty Magnor, The 629
Marvel 276	Gus Beezer 277	Megaton Man Vs. Forbidden	Mighty Marvel Western ...279
Marvel & DC Presents 266	Marvels 273	Frankenstein 745	Mighty Midget Comics 433
Marvel 1602 273	Marvels of Science 431	Megaton Man: Bombshell ...543	Mighty Mites 746
Marvel Action Hour: Fantastic	Marville 277	Megaton Man: Hardcopy ...543	Mighty Morphin Power
Four 266	Marvin Mouse 277	Mek 115, 627	Rangers 280, 629
Marvel Action Hour: Iron Man ..266	Mary Marvel Comics 431	Mekanix 278	Mighty Morphin Power
Marvel Action Universe 266	Mary Worth 626	Mel Allen Sports Comics ...433	Rangers: Ninja Rangers/
Marvel Adventures 266	Masakazu Katsura's Shadow	Melissa Moore: Bodyguard ..745	Vr Troopers 280
Marvel Boy 266	Lady I— Dangerous Love .507	Melting Pot 627	Mighty Mouse 280, 434, 629
Marvel Chillers 266	Mask 114	Melvin Monster 627	Mighty Mouse Adventure
Marvel Christmas Special ..267	Mask Comics 431	Melvin the Monster 278	Stories 434
Marvel Classics Comics ...267	Mask of Zorro, The 542	Memories 278, 627	Mighty Mouse Adventure
Marvel Collectors Item Classics 267	Mask Returns, The 507	Memory Man 746	Magazine 746
Marvel Comics 267	Mask, The 507	Men Against Crime 406	Mighty Mutanimals 629
Marvel Comics Super Special .269	Mask, The: Virtual Surreality ..507	Men Against the Sea 800	Mighty Samson 629
Marvel Comics Presents 268	Mask: Toys In the Attic 507	Men From Earth 627	Mighty Tiny 746

Index Mi–Ne

Mike Barnett, Man Against Crime .434	Monkeyshines Comics .435	Mr. and Mrs. J. Evil Scientist ..630
Mike Grell's Maggie the Cat ...543	Monnga .747	Mr. Anthony's Love Clinic 435
Mike Grell's Sable 629	Monographs .747	Mr. Beat Adventures .748
Mike Hoffman's Lost Worlds of Fantasy and Sci-Fi 746	Monolith .630	Mr. District Attorney .116
Mike Hoffman's Monsters and Maidens 746	Monroe's, The .630	Mr. Fixit .748
Mike Hoffman's Tigress 746	Monster .435	Mr. Majestic .630
Mike Mignola's B.P.R.D.: Hollow Earth 507	Monster Boy .747	Mr. Midshipman Easy 798
Mike Shayne Private Eye 629	Monster Club .630	Mr. Monster 508, 630
Military Comics 434	Monster Crime Comics 435	Mr. Monster Attacks 630
Milk & Cheese .746	Monster Fighters Inc.: The Ghosts of Christmas 543	Mr. Monster Superduper Special 630
Millennium .115	Monster Fighters, Inc. .543	Mr. Monster True Crime 630
Millennium Editions 62	Monster Massacre .630	Mr. Monster Vs. Gorzilla 543
Millennium Fever 116	Monster Menace .281	Mr. Monster's Gal Friday: Kelly .543
Millennium Index 629	Monster of Frankenstein .281	Mr. Muscles 468, 630
Millie the Model 280	Monster Posse .747	Mr. Mystic 630, 748
Millinium 2.5: The Buck Rogers Saga .747	Monster World .630	Mr. Natural .808
Milt Gross Funnies 434	Monsterman .543	Mr. Nightmare's Wonderful World 748
Milton Caniff's Terry & the Pirates 747	Monsters Attack .747	Mr. Right .543
Milton the Monster & Fearless Fly 629	Monsters From Outer Space ..747	Mr. T and the T Force 630
Minimum Wage .747	Monsters On the Prowl 213	Ms. Christ .748
Ministry of Space 543	Monsters Unleashed .281	Ms. Fortune .543
Minotaur's Tale, The 507	Monsters, Inc. 508, 630	Ms. Marvel .282
Minute Man 434	Monte Hale Western 431	Ms. Mystic .632
Minx, The .116	Monty Hall of the U.S. Marines .435	Ms. Tree 632, 748
Miracle Comics .435	Moon Girl and the Prince 435	Ms. Tree Thrilling Detective Adventures 632
Miracle Girls 747	Moon Knight 281, 282	Ms. Victory Golden Anniversary 632
Miracle Squad 629	Moon Knight: Divided We Fall ..282	Ms. Victory Special 632
Miracle Squad Blood & Dust ...747	Moonchild Comics .807	Ms.Tree Quarterly 117
Miracleman 629	Moondog .807	Mucha Lucha 117
Miracleman Family 629	Moonshadow 117, 282	Muggy-Doo, Boy Cat 436
Misery Special 543	Moonstone, The 795	Muktuk Wolfsbreath: Hard-Boiled Shaman 117
Misplaced .543	Moonwalker In 3-D 631	Mummy Archives 632
Miss America Comics 280	Moose Liberation Front 807	Mummy, The 748
Miss America Magazine 280	Mopsy .435	Mummy, The: Valley of the Gods 632
Miss Cairo Jones 435	Morbid Angel .631	Mummy: Ramses the Damned .632
Miss Fury .629	Morbid Angel: To Hell and Back 748	Mummy's Curse 748
Miss Fury Comics 280	Morbid Angel: Desperate Angels 747	Munden's Bar Annual 632
Miss Liberty 421	Morbius .282	Munsters Classics 748
Miss Peach 630	More Adventures of Fat Freddy's Cat 808	Munsters, The 632, 748
Mission Impossible 630	More Fun Comics 119	Muppet Babies 282, 632
Missions In Tibet 630	More Than Mortal 631	Muppets Take Manhattan 282
Mister Blank 747	More Than Mortal: Otherworlds 543	Murcielaga: She-Bat 748
Mister E 116	More Than Mortal: Sagas 631	Murcielaga/She-Bat 632
Mister Miracle 116	More Than Mortal: Truths and Legends 631	Murder .543
Mister Mystery 435	More Than Mortal/Lady Pendragon 543	Murder Can Be Fun 748
Mister Risk 405	Morlock 2001 631	Murder Me Dead 748
Mister Universe 435	Morlocks .282	Murder, Incorporated 436
Mister X 630, 747	Morning Glory 748	Murderous Gangsters 436
Misty .280	Morphos the Shape Changer ..508	Mutant Chronicles—Golgotha .632
Mites .747	Morrigan .631	Mutant Earth 543
Mitzi Comics 280	Mort the Dead Teenager 282	Mutant X 282, 283
Mitzi's Boyfriend 280	Mortal Coil 748	Mutant X: Future Shock 283
Mitzi's Romances 280	Mortal Kombat 631	Mutant Zone 748
Mobfire 117	Mortal Kombat: Baraka 631	Mutants & Misfits 632
Mobile Police Patlabor 747	Mortal Kombat: Battlewave ...631	Mutants: Generation Next 282
Mobile Suit Gundam 0079 747	Mortal Kombat: Goro, Prince of Pain 631	Mutants: The Amazing X-Men .282
Mobile Suit Gundam Wing: Blind Target 747	Mortal Kombat: Kitana & Mileena 631	Mutants: The Astonishing X-Men 282
Mobile Suit Gundam Wing: Episode Zero 747	Mortal Kombat: Kung Lao 631	Mutatis .283
Mobile Suit Gundam Wing: Ground Zero 747	Mortal Kombat: Rayden and Kano 631	Muties .283
Moby Dick 792	Mortal Kombat: U.S. Special Forces 631	Mutineers, The 801
Mod Squad 630	Mortar Man 748	Mutiny .437
Mod Wheels 630	Mortie .436	Mutiny On the Bounty 800
Modeling With Millie 223	Mosaic .748	Mutt and Jeff 117
Modern Comics 434	Mostly Wanted 631	My Confessions 482
Modern Love 435	Moth .543	My Date Comics 437
Modern Pulp 747	Mother Teresa 282	My Desire 437
Modesty Blaise 117	Mother, Come Home 508	My Diary 283
Modula Imperative 146, 147	Motion Picture Comics 436	My Favorite Martian 632
Moe & Shmoe Comics 435	Motion Pictures Funnies Weekly 436	My Great Love 437
Moebius 280	Motor City Comics 808	My Greatest Adventure 117
Moebius Comics 747	Motor Mouth & Killpower 282	My Intimate Affair 437
Moebius: Fusion 281	Motorbike Puppies 631	My Life 432
Molly Manton's Romances ...281	Motorhead 508	My Little Margie 632
Molly O'Day 435	Mountain World 748	My Love 437
Mom's Homemade Comics ..807	Movie Classics 436	My Love Affair 437
Moment of Silence 281	Movie Comics 117, 436, 631	My Love Life 488
Monarchy 630	Movie Love 436	My Love Memories 485
Monday Funnies, The 807	Movie Thrillers 436	My Love Story 437
Monkee's, The 630		My Name Is Chaos 118
Monkeyman & O'Brien 508		My Name Is Holocaust 118
		My Own Romance 283
		My Past Confessions 482
		My Private Life 437
		My Romance 283

My Secret .437	
My Secret Affair .437	
My Secret Life .437	
My Secret Love .443	
My Secret Marriage .437	
My Secret Romance .437	
My Secret Story .379	
My Story .487	
Mys-Tech Wars .283	
Myst: The Book of the Black Ships .508	
Mysteries .796	
Mysteries of Unexplored Worlds/Son of Vulcan ..632	
Mysteries of Paris .796	
Mysteries Weird and Strange ..437	
Mysterious Adventures .437	
Mysterious Island .795	
Mysterious Stories .438	
Mysterious Suspense .633	
Mysterious Traveler Comics ..438	
Mystery Comics .438	
Mystery Comics Digest .633	
Mystery In Space .118	
Mystery Man .748	
Mystery Men .508	
Mystery Men Comics .438	
Mystery Tales .283	
Mystery, Inc. .543	
Mysterymen .508	
Mystic .284, 633	
Mystic Comics .284	
Mystic Edge .633	
Mystical Tales .283	
Mystique .284	
Myth Adventures .748	
Myth Conceptions .748	
Mythography .749	
Mythos: The Final Tour .119	
Mythros .749	
Mythstalkers .543	
N.I.O. .636	
Nam Magazine .284	
Nam, The .284	
Name of the Game, The .119	
Nameless, The .543	
Names of Magic, The .119	
Namor .284	
Namor the Sub-Mariner .284	
Namora .284	
Nancy & Sluggo .633	
Nard N' Pat, Jayzey Lynch's ..808	
Nash .543	
Nathan Never .508	
Nathaniel Dusk .119	
Nathaniel Dusk II .119	
National Comics .119, 438	
National Velvet .633	
Nature Boy .583	
Nature of the Beast .749	
Naughty Bits .749	
Nausicaa of the Valley of Wind .749	
Navy Action .285	
Navy Combat .285	
Navy Tales .285	
Naz Rat .749	
Nazz, The .119	
Neat Stuff .633	
Nebbs, The .439	
Necromantra/Lord Pumpkin ..633	
Necropolis .633	
Necroscope .633, 749	
Necrowar .633	
Negation .633	
Negative Burn .749	
Negative Exposure .633	
Negro Americans the Early Years .803	
Negro Romances .439	
Neil Gaiman's Mr. Hero the Newmatic Man .633	
Neil Gaiman's Lady Justice ..633	
Neil Gaiman's Phage .633	
Neil Gaiman's Phage: Shadow Death .633	
Neil Gaiman's Tecknophage ..633	
Neil Gaiman's Wheel of Worlds 633	
Neil the Horse .749	
Nellie the Nurse .285	
Nemesis the Warlock .633, 749	

Index

Neon Cyber 544	Nick Fury, Versus S.H.I.E.L.D. .287	Relatives 544	OK Comics 439
Neon Genesis Evangelion 749	Nick Halliday 635	Noble Causes: Family Secrets .544	Oktane 509
Neon–the Future Warrior 749	Nickel Comics 439	Nobody 752	Oktoberfest 753
Neotopia 634	Nickel Library Series 808	Nocturnals 636	Oliver Twist 794
Nervous Rex 749	Nicki Shadow 635	Nocturnals: Witching Hour ...509	Olympians 289
Nevada 119	Night 750	Nocturnals: The Dark Forever .637	Omac 123
Nevermen, The 508	Night Angel 750	Nocturne 288	Omaha the Cat Dancer 808
Nevermen, The: Streets of	Night Before Christmask 509	Nodwick 752	Omega 753
Blood 508	Night Cry 750	Noid In 3-D 637	Omega 7 637
Neverwhere 808	Night Force 122	Nomad 288	Omega Elite 753
New Adventure Comics 119	Night Glider 635	Nomads of Antiquity 752	Omega Men 123
New Adventures of Speed	Night Life 750	Noman 637	Omega Saga, The 637
Racer 634	Night Man, The 635	Noogie Kootch: Secret	Omega the Unknown 289
New Adventures of Abraham	Night Man/Gambit 635	Agent Man 637	Omen 753
Lincoln 544	Night Master 750	Normal Man 752	Omen, The 637
New Adventures of Cholly	Night Music 635	Normal Man/Megaton Man	Omicron 753
& Flytrap 285	Night Nurse 288	Special 544	Omni Men 753
New Adventures of Felix	Night of the Living Dead 750	Northstar 288	On A Pale Horse 637
the Cat 634	Night Rider 288	Northwest Mounties 439	On Jungle Trails 802
New Adventures of Pinocchio .634	Night Streets 750	Nosferatu 509	On the Air 440
New Adventures of Superboy ..152	Night Thrasher 288	Nosferatu: Plague of Terror ..752	On the Spot 440
New Adventures of Terry &	Night Tribes 635	Not Brand Echh 288	One Bad Rat 509
the Pirates 749	Night Walker 635	Nothing Can Stop the	One Shot Western 753
New America 634	Night Warriors: Darkstalkers'	Juggernaut 289	One, The 290
New Book of Comics 119	Revenge 751	Nova 289	One-Arm Swordsman 637
New Breed 634	Night Zero 751	Nova Girls 752	One-Pound Gospel 753
New Comics 119	Night's Children 750	Nova Hunter 637	One-Trick Rip-Off 509
New Dnagents 634	Night's Children: The Vampire .750	Nowheresville 544, 752	Oni Double Feature 753
New Eradicators 750	Nightbreed 287	Nth Man 289	Onigami 753
New Eternals: Apocalypse Now 285	Nightcat 287	Nubian Knight 637	Onslaught 290
New Frontier 508	Nightcrawler 287	'Nuff Said 289	Onyx Overlord 290
New Frontiers 750	Nightfall: The Black Chronicles .122	Nursery Rhymes 439	Open Season 753
New Fun Comics 119	Nighthawk 287	Nurses, The 637	Open Space 290
New Funnies 401	Nighthunter 635	Nuts! 439	Operation Knightstrike 545
New Gods 120	Nightmare 288, 439, 480, 635	Nutsy Squirrel 123	Operation Peril 440
New Gods, The 120	Nightmare and Casper 635	Nutty Comics 439	Operation: Stormbreaker ...637
New Guardians 121	Nightmare Circus 288	Nutty Life 442	Optic Nerve 754
New Hero Comics 750	Nightmare On Elm Street .288, 635	Nyoka the Jungle Girl 752	Oracle Comix 808
New Horizons 750	Nightmares 635	Nyoka, Jungle Girl 637	Oracle Presents 754
New Humans 750	Nightmares On Elm Street ...635	Nyoka, The Jungle Girl ..439, 637	Orbit 637, 754
New Justice Machine 634	Nightmask 288	Nyx 289	Order, The 290
New Kaboom 634	Nights Into Dreams 635	O.G. Whiz 637	Oregon Trail, The 798
New Love 750	Nightshade 635	O.K. Comics 808	Oriental Heroes 637
New Man 544	Nightside 288	O'Malley and the Alley Cats ..637	Origin 290
New Mutants 286	Nightstalkers 288	Oaky Doaks 439	Origin of the Defiant Universe .638
New Mutants, The 285	Nightveil 635	Obergeist: Ragnarok Highway .544	Original Astro Boy 638
New Orleans Saints 634	Nightvision 751	Obergeist: The Empty Locket .545	Original Black Cat 572, 702
New Pulp Adventures Special .750	Nightwatch 288	Objective Five 545	Original Dick Tracy 638
New Reality 750	Nightwing 122	Oblivion 637	Original Dr. Solar Man of the
New Romances 439	Nightwing and Huntress 123	Obnoxio the Clown 289	Atom 638
New Shadowhawk, The 544	Nightwing: Alfred's Return ..123	Occult Files of Dr. Spektor ...637	Original E-Man 638
New Statesmen 634	Nightwolf 636	Octobriana 752	Original Ghost Rider 290
New T.H.U.N.D.E.R.	Nikki Blade 751	Octopus, The 803	Original Ghost Rider Rides
Agents, The 122	Nimrod, The 751	Odd Job 752	Again 290
New Teen Titans 121	Nina's New and Improved	Odd World of Richard Corben .808	Original Magnus Robot Fighter .638
New Terrytoons 634	All-Time Greatest 509	Odyssey, The 637, 799	Original Shield 638
New Titans 121	Nine Rings of Wu-Tang, The ..544	of Mind and Soul 753	Original Tom Corbett 754
New Triumph 750	Nine Rings of Wu-Tang, The:	Off On A Comet 802	Original Turok, Son of Stone ..638
New Two Fisted Tales: Vol II ..508	Fatima's Revenge 544	Offcastes 289	Origins 638
New Vampire Miyu 750	Nine Volt 544	Offerings 752	Origins of Marvel Comics ...290
New Warriors 286, 287	Ninja 751	Official Johnny Hazard 753	Origins of Reid Fleming,
New Wave Vs. the Volunteers .634	Ninja Boy 636	Official Buz Sawyer 752	World's Toughest Milkman 754
New Wave, The 634	Ninja Elite 751	Official Handbook of the	Orion 124, 509
New World Disorder 750	Ninja Funnies 636	Marvel Universe 277	Orlak Redux 754
New World Order 750	Ninja High School Girls 751	Official How To Draw G.I. Joe .752	Orlak: Flesh & Steel 754
New X-Men 353	Ninja High School 636, 751	Official How To Draw Robotech 753	Osborn Journals, The 290
New Year's Evil: 122	Ninja High School Featuring	Official How To Draw	Others, The 545
New York City Outlaws 750	Speed Racer 636	Transformers 753	Otis Goes Hollywood 510
New York Worlds Fair 122	Ninja High School Perfect	Official Jungle Jim 753	Otto Porfiri 510
New York, Year Zero 750	Memory 751	Official Mandrake 753	Our Army At War 124
Newcomers Illustrated 750	Ninja High School Small Bodies 751	Official Marvel Index To the	Our Fighting Forces 126
Newforce 544	Ninja High School Version 2 ..636	Avengers 289	Our Flag Comics 440
Newmen 544, 634	Ninjak 636	Official Marvel Index To the	Our Gang Comics 440
Newstralia 634, 750	Ninth Gland, The 509	Amazing Spider-Man 289	Our Love 290
Next Man 634	Nira X: Anime 636	Official Marvel Index To the	Our Love Story 290
Next Men 508	Nira X: Cyberangel 636, 752	Fantastic Four 289	Our Secret 437
Next Nexus 634	Nira X: Exodus 752	Official Marvel Index To the	Out For Blood 510
Nexus 634, 750	Nira X: History 752	X-Men 289	Out of the Night 440
Nexus Legends 635	Nira X: Soul Skurge 752	Official Marvel Timeline 289	Out of the Shadows 441
Nexus Meets Madman 508	Nira X/Cynder: Endangered	Official Modesty Blaise 753	Out of the Vortex 510
Nexus: Executioner's Song ..508	Species 636	Official Prince Valiant 753	Out of This World 638
Nexus: Nightmare In Blue 508	Nira X/Hellina: Heaven & Hell .752	Official Rip Kirby 753	Out There 638
Nexus: Alien Justice 508	No Escape 288	Official Secret Agent 753	Outbreed 999 638
Nexus: God Con 508	No Guts, No Glory 752	Official True Crime Cases ...289	Outcast Special 638
Nexus: Out of the Vortex 508	No Honor 544	Oh My Goddess! 509	Outcasts 127
Nexus: The Liberator 508	No Honor: Makyo 544	Oh My Goth: Humans Suck! ..753	Outer Limits, The 638
Nexus: The Origin 508	No Need For Tenchi 752	Oh My Goth! 753	Outlanders 510
Nexus: The Wages of Sin 509	No Time For Sergeants 637	Oh, Brother! 439	Outlanders: Epilogue 510
Nfl Superpro 287	Noble Causes 544	Ohm's Law 753	Outlaw 7 510
Nick Fury, Agent of S.H.I.E.L.D. 287	Noble Causes: Distant	Oink: Blood and Circus 637	Outlaw Fighters 290

Index Ou–Pr

Title	Page
Outlaw Kid	290
Outlaw Nation	127
Outlaw Overdrive	754
Outlaws	127, 440
Outlaws of the West	638
Outlaws, The	440
Outposts	638
Outsiders	127, 128
Over the Edge and Under A Buck	290
Overkill	545
Owl, The	638
Ox Bow Incident, The	801
Oxido	545
Oxydol-Dreft	441
Oz	510, 754
Oz Squad	754
Oz: Straw and Sorcery	754
Ozzie and Babs	441
Ozzy Osbourne	638
P.A.C.	**638**
P.I.'S, The	640
P.J. Warlock	756
Pacific Presents	638
Pact	545
Pageant of Comics	441
Painkiller Jane	638
Painkiller Jane Vs. the Darkness: Stripper	639
Painkiller Jane/Darkchylde	639
Painkiller Jane/Hellboy	639
Painkiller Jane/The Darkness	639
Pakkins' Land	754
Pakkins' Land: Forgotten Dreams	754
Pakkins' Land: Quest For Kings	754
Paladin Alpha	639
Palantine	754
Palooka-Ville	754
Panda Khan	754
Pandemonium	754
Pandemonium: Deliverance	639
Pandora	754
Pandora Devils Advocate	755
Pandora: Demonography	755
Pandora: Pandemonium	755
Pandora's Chest	755
Pandora/Racor: Devil Inside	755
Panhandle Pete and Jennifer	441
Panic	441, 639
Pantera	639
Pantha	639
Pantheon	755
Paper Cuts	755
Paradax	639
Paradigm	545, 639
Paradise	639
Paradise Kiss	755
Paradise X	291
Paradise X: The Heralds	290
Paradise X/Ragnarok	291
Paragon	291
Paragon Dark Apocalypse	639
Parallax: Emerald Night	128
Paramount Animated Comics	441
Paranoia	639
Parasyte	755
Parliament of Justice, The	545
Parole Breakers	441
Particle Dreams	755
Partners In Pandemonium	755
Partridge Family, The	639
Parts of A Hole	755
Parts Unknown	755
Parts Unknown: Dark Intentions	755
Parts Unknown: Hostile Takeover	545
Parts Unknown: Killing Attraction	545
Passover	639
Pat Savage: Woman of Bronze	639
Patches	441
Path, The	639
Pathfinder, The	794
Pathways To Fantasy	639
Patrick the Wolf Boy	755
Patsy & Hedy	291
Patsy & Her Pals	291
Patsy Walker	291
Patty Cake	755
Patty Powers	227
Patty-Cake & Friends	755
Paul the Samurai	755
Pawnee Bill	441
Pay-Off	441
Peacekeeper	639
Peacemaker	128, 639
Peach Girl	755
Peanuts	639
Pearl Harbor	639
Pebbles & Bamm-Bamm	639
Pebbles Flintstone	639
Pedro	441
Pelias & Melisande	635
Pendulum	755
Penguin Triumphant	128
Penguins In Bondage	808
Penny	441
Penny Century	755
Pentacle: The Sign of the Five	755
Pep Comics	441
Perfect Crime, The	442
Perfect Love	442
Perg	639
Perry Mason Mystery Magazine	640
Personal Love	442
Pete the P.O.'D Postal Worker	755
Pete Von Sholly's Morbid	510
Peter Cannon: Thunderbolt	128
Peter Cottontail	442
Peter Pan: Return To Nevernever Land	640
Peter Panda	128
Peter Parker, Spider-Man	312
Peter Parker, The Spectacular Spider-Man	291
Peter Parker: Spider-Man	292
Peter Paul's 4 In 1 Jumbo Comic Book	442
Peter Penny and His Magic Dollar	442
Peter Porkchops	128
Peter Porker	292
Peter Potamus	640
Peter Rabbit	442
Peter, The Little Pest	292
Petticoat Junction	640
Phantom	292, 640, 755
Phantom 2040	292
Phantom Bolt, The	640
Phantom Force	545, 640
Phantom Guard	545
Phantom Lady	443, 808
Phantom of Fear City	756
Phantom of the Opera	756
Phantom Stranger	128
Phantom Zone, The	128
Phantom, The	128, 640
Phase One	756
Phaze	640
Phigments	756
Phil Rizzuto	443
Phoenix	640
Phoenix (untold Story)	292
Phoenix Resurrection	640
Phoney Pages	756
Pi: The Book of Ants	510
Pictorial Confessions	443
Pictorial Love Stories	443
Pictorial Romances	443
Picture News	443
Picture Stories From Science	443
Picture Stories From the Bible	128
Picture Stories From World History	443
Piders	217
Pilgrim's Progress	292
Pilot, The	798
Pin-Up Pete	443
Pineapple Army	756
Pinhead	292
Pinhead and Foodini	443
Pinhead Vs. Marshall Law	292
Pink Floyd Experience	756
Pink Floyd, The	809
Pink Panther, The	640
Pinky and the Brain	128
Pinocchio & the Emperor of the Night	292
Pint-Sized X-Babies:	
Murderama	292
Pioneer Picture Stories	443
Pioneers, The	795
Piracy	443, 640
Piranha Is Loose	756
Pirate Comics	443
Pirate Corp.	640
Pirate Corps!	756
Pirates of Dark Waters	293
Pitcairn's Island	800
Pitt	545, 640
Pitt Crew	641
Pitt, The	293
Pitt: Biogenesis	641
Pixi Junket	756
Pixies, The	443
Plan 9 From Outer Space	641, 756
Planeswalker War	641
Planet 29	756
Planet Comics	444, 641, 756
Planet Ladder	756
Planet of the Apes	293, 510, 756
Planet of the Apes (movie)	510
Planet of the Apes Blood of the Apes	756
Planet of the Apes Urchaks' Folly	756
Planet of the Apes: Forbidden Zone	756
Planet of the Apes: Sins of the Father	756
Planet of the Apes: The Human War	510
Planet of Vampires	641
Planet Terry	293
Planet X	756
Planetary	641
Plasmer	293
Plastic Forks	293
Plastic Little	756
Plastic Man	128, 129, 444, 809
Plop!	129
Pocahontas	445
Pocket Comics	445
Poe	756
Pogo Possum	445
Pogz N Slammer	641
Point Blank	641, 757
Poison Elves	641, 757
Poison Elves: Lusipher & Lirilith	757
Poison Elves: Parintachin	757
Poizon	641
Poizon: Cadillacs and Green Tomatoes	641
Poizon: Demon Hunter	641, 757
Poizon: Lost Child	641
Pokeman Tales	641
Pokeman the Movie 2000: Revelation Lugia	641
Pokeman: The First Movie	641
Pokemon Adventures	757
Pokemon Tales	758
Pokemon Tv Animation	641
Pokemon: Electric Pikachu Boogaloo	757
Pokemon: Pikachu Shocks Back	757
Pokemon: Surf's Up Pikachu	757
Pokemon: The Electric Tale of Pikachu	757
Pokewomon: Gotta Shag 'em All!	758
Police Academy	293
Police Action	293
Police Badge	316
Police Comics	445
Police Line-Up	446
Police Trap	446
Polly Pigtails	446
Poot	758
Pop Gun War	510
Pop Parody	758
Popcorn	641
Popeye	446, 641
Popeye Special	641
Popeye the Sailor	641
Popples	293
Popular Comics	446
Popular Romances	446
Popular Teen-Agers	447
Pork	809
Portfolio of Underground Art	809
Portia Prinz of the Glamazons	758
Possessed, The	641
Post Brothers	758, 777
Powdered Toast-Man	293
Power & Glory	642
Power Comics	447, 758
Power Company, The	129
Power Factor	642
Power Girl	129
Power Line	293
Power Man	293
Power Man & Iron Fist	293
Power of Prime	642
Power of Shazam	129
Power of the Atom	129
Power of the Mark	545
Power Pachyderms	294
Power Pack	294
Power Pack: Peer Pressure	294
Power Rangers Zeo	545
Power Rangers Zeo/ Youngblood	545, 642
Powerhouse Pepper Comics	293
Powerknights	642
Powerman and Power Mower Safety	809
Powerpuff Girls	129
Powers	545
Powers That Be	642
PPV	758
Prairie, The	797
Preacher	129
Preacher Special: Saint of Killers	130
Predator	510
Predator 2	511
Predator Vs. Judge Dredd	511
Predator Vs. Magnus Robot Fighter	511
Predator: Hell & Hot Water	510
Predator: Home World	511
Predator: Bad Blood	510
Predator: Big Game	510
Predator: Bloody Sands of Time	510
Predator: Cold War	510
Predator: Dark River	510
Predator: Hell Come A Walkin'	511
Predator: Kindred	511
Predator: Nemesis	511
Predator: Primal	511
Predator: Xenogenesis	511
Predator: Race War	511
Premiere	758
Pressbutton	642
Preteen Dirty Gene Kung Fu Kangaroos	758
Prey	758
Prez	130
Price, The	758
Pride & Joy	130
Pride of the Yankees	447
Priest	642, 758
Primal	511
Primal Force	130
Primal Instinct	545
Primal Rage	642
Primate	539
Prime	642
Prime Cuts	758
Prime Slime Tales	758
Prime Vs. Hulk	642
Prime/Captain America	642
Primer	642, 758
Primitives	758
Primus	642
Prince	130
Prince and the Pauper, The	795
Prince Namor, The Sub-Mariner	294
Prince Valiant	294, 758
Prince Valiant Monthly	758
Prince Vandal	642
Princess Prince	758
Princess Sally	642
Priority: White Heat	642
Prison Break	447
Prisoner of Zenda, The	798
Prisoner, The	130
Private Beach	758

CVA Page 829

Index

Private Eye 294	Purgatori: Empire 644	Ranma 1/2 ....646, 759	Rebel Sword 511
Private Eyes 758	Purgatori: God Hunter 644	Raphael 646, 760	Rebellion 761
Privateers 642	Purgatori: God Killer 644	Raptus 760	Rebirth 761
Prize Comics 447	Purgatori: Goddess Rising 644	Raptus: Dead of Night 760	Rebound 761
Prize Comics Western 447	Purgatori: Heartbreaker 644	Rare Breed 646	Record Book of Famous
Pro, The 545	Purgatori: Love Bites 644	Rascals In Paradise 511	Police Cases 450
Professional: Gogol 13 642	Purgatori: Mischief Night 644	Rat Bastard 646	Record of the Lodoss War 761
Professor Om 642	Purgatori: Ravenous 644	Rat Fink 760	Red 647
Professor Xavier and the	Purgatori: Re-Imagined 644	Rat Patrol, The 646	Red Arrow 450
X-Men 294	Purgatori: Sanctified 644	Ravage 2099 298	Red Badge of Courage, The ...800
Project A-Ko 643	Purgatori: The Dracula Gambit .644	Ravage 2099 A.D. 298	Red Band Comics 450
Project A-Ko 2 643	Purgatori: The Hunted 644	Ravager 760	Red Circle Comics 450
Project A-Ko: Versus the	Purgatori: The Vampires Myth 644	Rave 760	Red Diary 761
Universe 643	Purgatori: Trick Or Treat 644	Raven 646, 760	Red Dog 647
Promethea 643	Purple Claw, The 448	Raven Chronicles 298	Red Dragon 647
Promethian Enterprises 809	Pussycat 297	Ravening 646	Red Dragon Comics 450
Propeller Man 511	Puzzle Fun Comics 448	Ravening, The 760	Red Fox 761
Prophecy 643	PVP 546, 759	Ravens and Rainbows 646	Red Mask 470
Prophecy of the Soul Sorcerer .643	**Q-Unit 645**	Raver 646	Red Rabbit 450
Prophet 545	Q-Unit: Revenge 546	Raw 809	Red Raven Comics 249
Prophet II 643	Quack 759	Raw City 760	Red Rocket 7 511
Prophet of Dreams 643	Quagmire Comics 809	Rawararawar 809	Red Rover, The 800
Prophet: Legacy 643	Quantum & Woody 645	Rawhide Kid 298, 299	Red Seal Comics 453
Prophet/Cable 643	Quantum Leap 645	Ray Bradbury Chronicles 646	Red Sonja 299, 647
Prophet/Chapel: Super	Quantum Mechanics 759	Ray Bradbury Comics 646	Red Sonja & Conan "Hot
Soldiers 546	Quasar 297	Ray, The 131	and Dry" 809
Proposition Player 130	Queen & Country 759	Razor 646, 760	Red Sonja In 3-D 647
Protectors 643	Queen & Country: Declassified .759	Razor Analog Burn 760	Red Star, The 546, 647
Protheus 758	Queen of the Damned 645	Razor and Shi Special 647	Red Tornado 131
Prototype 643	Queen of the West, Dale Evans 448	Razor Archives 647	Red Warrior 299
Prototype: Turf War 643	Queen's Necklace, The 803	Razor Burn 647	Red Wolf 299
Prowler 294, 643	Quest 298	Razor Swimsuit Special 647	Redblade 511
Prowler In "white Zombie" 643	Quest For Camelot 130	Razor the Ravening 647	Redeemer, The 647
Prudence & Caution 643	Quest For Dreams Lost 759	Razor Uncut 761	Redeemers 647
Psi Force 294	Quest Presents 759	Razor: Archives 760	Redmoon 761
Psi-Judge Anderson 758	Questprobe 298	Razor: Bleeding Heart 760	Redskin 450
Psi-Lords 643	Question Quarterly 130	Razor: Cry No More 647	Reese's Pieces 648
Psi-Lords: Reign of the	Question, The 130	Razor: Gothic 647	Reggie 648
Starwatchers 643	Quick-Draw Mcgraw 645	Razor: Hex & Violence 647	Reggie and Me 648
Psyba-Rats, The 130	Quick-Trigger Western 341	Razor: The Darkest Night 760	Reggie's Wise Guy Jokes 648
Psycho 130, 644	Quicken Forbidden 759	Razor: The Furies 646	Regulators 546
Psychoanalysis 447, 644	R. Crumb's Comics and	Razor: The Suffering 647	Reid Fleming World's
Psychoblast 644	Stories 809	Razor: Till I Bleed Daylight 761	Toughest Milkman 809
Psychonauts 295	R.A.Z.E. 646	Razor: Torture 647, 761	Reid Fleming, World's
Psylocke & Angel: Crimson	R.E.B.E.L.S '94 131	Razor's Edge 761	Toughest Milkman 762
Dawn 295	R.I.P. 649	Razor/Dark Angel: The Final	Reid Fleming/Flaming Carrot ..511
Public Defender In Action 644	R.I.P.D. 512	Nail 760	Reign of the Zodiac 131
Public Enemies 448	Rabid Monkey 759	Razor/Embrace: The Spawning 760	Reivers 648, 762
Pubo 511	Race Against Time 645	Razor/Morbid Angel: Soul	Relative Heroes 131
Pudd'nhead Wilson 799	Race For the Moon 645	Search 647	Reload 648
Pudge Pig 644	Race of Scorpions 511	Razor/Poison/Areala Warrior	Remarkable Worlds of Phineas
Puffed 546	Racer X 645	Nun: Little Bad Angels 647	B. Fuddle 131
Pulp 758	Racer-X 645	Razor/Warrior Nun Areala:	Remember Pearl Harbor 450
Pulp Fantastic 130	Rack & Pain 511	Dark Menace 647	Ren and Stimpy Show 299
Pulp Fiction 758	Rack & Pain: Killers 645	Razor/Warrior Nun Areala:	Renegades of Justice 762
Puma Blues 759	Racket Squad In Action 448	Faith 647	Renfield 762
Pumpkinhead 511	Radical Dreamer 645, 759	Razorguts 761	Repentance 762
Punch and Judy Comics 448	Radioactive Man 645	Razorline First Cut 299	Replacement God 762
Punch Comics 448	Radiskull and Devil Doll 546	Re: Gex 648	Replacement God & Other
Puncture 644	Radix 546	Re: Gex: Black & White 762	Stories 762
Punisher 295, 296	Rael 645	Re-Animator 647	Replacement God and Other
Punisher Meets Archie 296	Rafferty 645	Re-Animator: Dawn of the	Stories, The 546
Punisher 2099 296	Ragamuffins 645	Re-Animator 647	Reptilicus 648
Punisher 2099 A.D. 296	Raggety Ann and Andy 448	Re-Animator: Tales of Herbert	Reptisaurus 648
Punisher Armory 296	Ragman 130	West 647	Resident Evil 546
Punisher Kills the Marvel	Ragman: Cry of the Dead 131	Reactoman 761	Resident Evil: Fire & Ice 648
Universe 296	Ragmop 546, 759	Reagan's Raiders 761	Resistance, The 648
Punisher Magazine 296	Ragnarok 759	Real Adventures of Jonny	Restaurant At the End of
Punisher Movie Comic 296	Rai 645, 646	Quest, The 511	the Universe 131
Punisher P.O.V. 296	Rai and the Future Force 646	Real Bout High School 761	Resurrection Man 132
Punisher War Journal 296	Raiders of the Lost Ark 298	Real Clue Crime Stories 374	Retief 762
Punisher: No Escape 295	Raijin Comics 759	Real Experiences 324	Retief and the Warlords 762
Punisher: War Zone 297	Raika 759	Real Fact Comics 131	Retief of the Cdt 762
Punisher: Year One 297	Rail 546	Real Funnies 449	Retief: Diplomatic Immunity ..762
Punisher/Batman 295	Raising Hell 759	Real Ghostbusters 647	Retro-Dead 762
Punisher/Cap.America: Blood	Ralph Kiner Home Run King ...448	Real Heroes Comics 449	Retrograde 762
and Glory 296	Ralph Snart 759	Real Life Comics 449	Return of Gorgo, The 603
Punisher/Daredevil 295	Ralph Snart Adventures 646	Real Life Story of Fess Parker .449	Return of Happy the Clown 762
Punx 644	Ramar of the Jungle 448	Real Love 406	Return of Konga, The 648
Punx Redux 644	Rambo 759	Real Screen Comics 131	Return of Lum Urusei*
Puppet Comics 448	Rambo III 759	Real Stuff 761	Yatsura, The 762
Puppet Master 448	Ramm 759	Real War Stories 647	Return of Megaton Man 648
Puppet Master: Children of	Rampaging Hulk, The 298	Real West Romances 450	Return of the Jedi 299
the Puppet Master 644	Random 5 646	Real Western Hero 486	Return of the Outlaw 450
Pure Art Quarterly 809	Randy Bowen's Decapitator ..498	Realistic Romances 449	Return of the Skyman 762
Purgatori 644	Randy O'Donnel Is the Man ...546	Reality Check 647	Return To Jurassic Park 648
Purgatori Vs. Chastity 645	Range Romances 448	Realm 761	Reveal 512
Purgatori Vs. Lady Death 645	Rangers Comics 448	Realm of the Claw 546	Revealing Romances 450
Purgatori Vs. Vampirella 645	Rangers of Freedom 448	Realworlds 131	Revenge of the Prowler 648
Purgatori: Darkest Hour 644	Rango 646	Reaper 761	Revengers 648

CVA Page 830

Index

Re–Sc

Entry	Page
Revolver	762
Revolving Doors	762
Rex Allen Comics	450
Rex Dexter of Mars	450
Rex Hart	206
Rex Mundi	546
Rheintochter	762
Rhudiprrt Prince of Fur	762
Ribit	648
Ribtickler	450
Richard Dragon, Kung Fu Fighter	132
Richie Rich	299, 648
Richie Rich Dollars & Cents	649
Richie Rich Success Stories	649
Richie Rich Bank Books	648
Richie Rich Billions	649
Richie Rich Diamonds	649
Richie Rich Fortunes	649
Richie Rich Gems	649
Richie Rich Jackpots	649
Richie Rich Millions	649
Richie Rich Money World	649
Richie Rich Profits	649
Richie Rich Riches	649
Richie Rich Vault of Mystery	649
Rick Raygun	762
Rifleman, The	649
Rima, The Jungle Girl	132
Rin Tin Tin	450
Ring of Roses	512
Ring of the Niebelung	512
Ring, The	132, 512
Ringo Kid	299
Ringo Kid Western	299
Rio At Bay	512
Rio Kid	762
Riot	762
Riot Act Two	762
Riot Gear	649
Riot Gear: Violent Past	649
Rip Hunter, Time Master	132
Rip In Time	763
Rip Off Comix	809
Rip Van Winkle & the Headless Horseman	793
Ripclaw	546
Ripley's Believe It Or Not!	649
Ripley's Believe It Or Not	512
Riptide	546
Rise of the Snakemen	650
Rising Stars	546
Rising Stars: Bright	547
Rising Stars: Untouchable	547
Risk	650
Roachmill	512, 763
Road To Perdition	132
Rob	650
Rob Roy	801
Robert E. Howard's	650, 763
Robin	132
Robin 3000	133
Robin Hood	650, 763, 792
Robin Hood and His Merry Men	469
Robin Hood Tales	133
Robin Plus	133
Robin: Year One	133
Robinson Crusoe	792
Robo Defense Team Mecha Rider	763
Robo Dojo	650
Robo Hunter	650
Robo Warriors	764
Robocop	299
Robocop 3	512
Robocop II	300
Robocop Vs. Terminator	512
Robocop: Mortal Coils	512
Robocop: Prime Suspect	512
Robocop: Roulette	512
Robotech	650, 763
Robotech Defenders	133
Robotech II the Sentinels	763
Robotech II: The Sentinels: Cyberpirates	764
Robotech II: The Sentinels: the Malcontent Uprising	764
Robotech II: The Sentinels	651
Robotech In 3-D	650
Robotech Masters	650
Robotech Romance	763
Robotech Special Dana's Story	651
Robotech the Movie	763
Robotech Warriors: The Terror Maker	764
Robotech, The Macross Saga	650
Robotech: The Threadbare Heart	763
Robotech: Academy Blues	763
Robotech: Aftermath	763
Robotech: Clone	763
Robotech: Covert Ops	763
Robotech: Invid War	763
Robotech: Invid War Aftermath	763
Robotech: Love and War	650
Robotech: Return To Macross	763
Robotech: The Macross Saga	650
Robotech: The New Generation	650
Robotech: Untold Stories	763
Robotech: Vermilion	764
Robotech: Warriors	764
Robotech: Wings of Gibraltar	764
Robotech: Genesis	650
Robotech—the Sentinels: Rubicon	763
Robotix	300
Robur the Conqueror	803
Rock 'n' Roll	651
Rock 'n' Roll High School	651
Rock & Roll Comics	764
Rocket Comics	450
Rocket Kelly	450
Rocket Man: King of the Rocket Men	651
Rocket Raccoon	300
Rocket Ranger	651
Rocket Rangers	764
Rocket Ship X	450
Rocketeer	651
Rocketeer Adventure Magazine	512, 651
Rocketeer Special	651
Rocketman	450
Rockin Rollin Miner Ants	764
Rockmeez	651
Rocko's Modern Life	300
Rockstar Games' Oni	512
Rocky Horror Picture Show	651
Rocky Lane Western	451
Rod Cameron Western	451
Rog 2000	651
Rogan Gosh	133
Roger Rabbit	651
Roger Rabbit's: Toontown	651
Rogue	300
Rogue Trooper	651
Rogue Trooper: The Final Warrior	651
Roland: Days of Wrath	651
Rolling Stones: The Sixties	764
Roly Poly Comic-Book	451
Rom	300
Roman Holidays, The	651
Romance and Confession Stories	451
Romance Diary	300
Romance Tales	300
Romances of the West	300
Romantic Affairs	281
Romantic Love	451
Romantic Marriage	451
Romantic Picture Novelettes	451
Romantic Secrets	451
Romantic Story	451
Romantic Western	451
Romeo and Juliet	801
Romeo Tubbs	437
Ronin	133
Rook, The	651
Room 222	651
Rooter	764
Roots of the Swamp Thing	133
Rose	652, 764
Rose 'n' Gunn	764
Rose and Gunn	764
Rose and Gunn: Reckoning	764
Roswell	652
Rotogin: Junkbotz	547
Roundup	452
Route 666	652
Rovers	764
Rowlf	809
Roy Campanella, Baseball Hero	452
Roy Roger's Trigger	452
Roy Rogers	452
Roy Rogers and Trigger	452
Roy Rogers Western Classics	652
Royal Boy	300
Rubber Duck Tales	809
Rubes Revived	764
Rudolph the Red-Nosed Reindeer	133
Ruff and Ready	652
Rugged Action	300
Rugrats Comic Adventures	652
Ruins	300
Ruk Bud Webster	764
Rulah, Jungle Goddess	488
Rumble Girls	547
Run, Buddy, Run	652
Runaways	300
Rune	652
Rune: Hearts of Darkness	652
Rune/Silver Surfer	652
Ruse	652
Russian Roulette	133
Rust	652
Rusty Comics	261
S. Clay Wilson Twenty Drawings	809
S.C.I.-Spy	135
S.P.I.C.E.	662
S.T.A.R. Corps	142
S.T.A.T.	665
Saari, The Jungle Goddess	452
Saban's Mighty Morphin Power Rangers	280
Saban's Mighty Morphin Power Rangers: Ninja Rangers/ VR Troop	280
Saber Marionette J	764
Sable	652
Sabre	547, 652
Sabretooth	301
Sabretooth Classics	651
Sabretooth: Mary Shelley Overdrive	301
Sabrina the Teenage Witch	652
Sabu, Elephant Boy	452
Sachs & Violens	301
Sad Sack	452
Sad Sack and the Sarge	653
Sad Sack In 3-D	653
Sad Sack's Funny Friends	653
Sad Sack's Army Life	653
Saddle Justice	452
Saddle Romances	452
Sade	764
Sade Special	764
Sade: Testaments of Pain	764
Sade/Rose and Gunn	764
Safest Place, The	512
Safety-Belt Man All Hell	653
Saffire	547
Saga of Crystar	301
Saga of Original Human Torch	301
Saga of Ras Al Ghul	133
Saga of the Man-Elf	764
Saga of the Metabarons	653
Saga of the Swamp Thing	133
Sage	764
Sailor Moon	764
Sailor Moon Super S	765
Saint	765
Saint Angel	547
Saint Germaine	765
Saint Germaine: Prior Echoes	765
Saint Sinner	301
Saint Tail	765
Saint, The	452
Salome	653
Sam & Max Go To the Moon	301
Sam & Twitch	547
Sam and Max, Free Lance Police Special	653
Sam Hill Private Eye	452
Sam Slade Robohunter	653
Sam Stories: Legs	547
Sammy: Tourist Trap	765
Samson	452
Samsons	653
Samurai	653, 765
Samurai (1st Series)	765
Samurai 7	765
Samurai Cat	301
Samurai Deeper Kyo	765
Samurai Funnies	765
Samurai Guard	653
Samurai Jack	134
Samurai Penguin	765
Samurai, Son of Death	765
Samuree	653
San Fransisco Comic Book	809
Sanctuary	765
Sandman	134
Sandman Mystery Theatre	134
Sandman Presents:	135
Sandman Presents: Love Street	135
Sandman Presents: Lucifer	135
Sandman Presents: Dead Boy Detectives	135
Sandman Presents: Petrefax	135
Sandman Presents: The Corinthian	135
Sandman Presents: The Thessaliad	135
Sands of the South Pacific	452
Sandscape	653
Santa Claws	765
Santana	653
Sapphire	765
Sarai	765
Sarge Steel/Secret Agent	653
Satan's Six	653
Satana	301
Satanika	653
Saturday Knights	653
Saurus Family	653
Saurians: Unnatural Selection	654
Savage Combat Tales	654
Savage Dragon	547
Savage Dragon, The: Red Horizon	548
Savage Dragon: Marshal Law	548
Savage Dragon: Sex & Violence	548
Savage Dragon/Teenage Mutant Ninja Turtles Crossover	654
Savage Dragon/Destroyer Duck	548
Savage Henry	765
Savage Humor	809
Savage Sword of Conan	301
Savage Tales	303
Savant Garde	548
Saved By the Bell	654
Say What?	809
Scarab	135
Scare Tactics	135
Scarlet Crush	654
Scarlet In Gaslight	765
Scarlet Scorpion/Darkside	766
Scarlet Spider	303
Scarlet Spider Unlimited	303
Scarlet Thunder	766
Scarlet Witch	303
Scarlett	135
Scary Godmother	766
Scary Godmother: Bloody Valentine	766
Scary Godmother: Wild About Harry	766
Scary Tales	654
Scatterbrain	512
Scavengers	654
Scene of the Crime	135
Schism	654
Schizophrenia, Cheech Wizard	809
School Day Romances	447
Sci-Tech	654
Science Comic Book	654
Science Comics	452, 453
Scimidor	766
Scion	654
Scooby Doo	654
Scooby-Doo	135, 303
Scoop Comics	453
Scooter Girl	766
Scorched Earth	654
Scorn	766

CVA Page 831

Index

Sc–SI

Title	Page
Scorn/Ardy: Alien Influence	766
Scorn/Dracula: The Vampire's Blood	766
Scorpio Rose	654
Scorpion Corp.	654
Scorpion King, The	512
Scottish Chiefs, The	798
Scout	654
Scout: War Shaman	655
Scratch	766
Scream Comics	453
Scribbly	135
Scrimidar	766
Scryed	766
Scud: Disposable Assassin	766
Scud: Tales From the Vending Machine	766
Sea Devils	135
Sea Hound, The	453
Sea Hunt	655
Sea Wolf, The	799
Seadragon	655
Seaquest	655
Searchers	766
Searchers: Apostle of Mercy	766
Sebastian	655
Sebastian O	135
Secret Agent	653, 655
Secret City Saga	655
Secret Defenders	303
Secret Files	766
Secret Files & Origins	135
Secret Files: The Strange Case	766
Secret Hearts	136
Secret Loves	453
Secret Messages	766
Secret Mysteries	377
Secret of the Salamander	512
Secret Origins	136
Secret Society of Super-Heroes	136
Secret Society of Super-Villains	136
Secret Squirrel	655
Secret Wars	303
Secret Wars II	303
Secret Weapons	655
Secret Weapons: Playing With Fire	655
Secrets of Haunted House	136
Secrets of Sinister House	136
Secrets of the Legion of Super-Heroes	137
Secrets of the Valiant Universe	655
Sectaurs	303
Section 8	766
Section Zero	548
Seduction of the Innocent	655
Seeker	655, 766
Seeker 3000	303
Seekers	137
Seekers Into the Mystery	137
Sei: Death & Legend	548
Select Detective	453
Semantic Lace	548
Semper Fi	303
Sensation Comics	137
Sensation Mystery	137
Sensational Spider-Man	303
Sensei	655
Sentinel	304, 766
Sentinels of Justice	655
Sentry	304
Sentry: Special	655
Seraphic Feather	512
Seraphim	655
Seraphin	767
Sergeant Barney Barker	304
Sergeant Bilko	137
Sergeant Bilko's Pvt. Doberman	137
Sergeant Preston of the Yukon	453
Sergio Aragone's Groo	245
Sergio Aragones Actions Speak Louder Than Words	512
Sergio Aragones Massacres Marvel	305
Sergio Aragones' Boogeyman	512
Sergio Aragones' Day of the Dead	512
Sergio Aragones' Groo	512
Sergio Aragones' Groo & Rufferto	512
Sergio Aragones' Louder Than Words	513
Sergio Stomps Star Wars	513
Serina	656
Serpentina	656
Seven Block	305
Seven Seas Comics	453
Seven Sisters	656
Seventh System, The	767
Sex and Affection	809
Sex Warriors	513
Sf Short Stories	767
Sfa Spotlight	767
Sgt. Fury & His Howling Commandos	304
Sgt. Rock	126
Sgt. Rock Special	138
Sgt. Rocks Prize Battle Tales	138
Shade	138
Shade Special	656
Shade, The	138
Shade, The Changing Man	138
Shades of Blue	767
Shades of Gray Comics and Stories	767
Shado, Song of the Dragon	138
Shadow and the Mysterious 3, The	513
Shadow Cabinet	138
Shadow Comics	453, 656
Shadow Cross	767
Shadow Empire: Faith Conqures	513
Shadow of the Batman	139
Shadow of Batman	139
Shadow of the Torturer, The	656
Shadow Raven	656
Shadow Reavers	656
Shadow Slasher	767
Shadow Star	513
Shadow State	656
Shadow Strikes, The	139
Shadow War of Hawkman	139
Shadow, The	138, 513, 656
Shadow, The: Hell's Heat Wave	513
Shadow, The: In the Coils of Leviathan	513
Shadowalker	767
Shadowdragon Annual	139
Shadowgear	767
Shadowhawk	548
Shadowhawk/Vampirella	548
Shadowhawk Special	549
Shadowman	656
Shadowmasters	305
Shadowriders	305
Shadows	549
Shadows & Light	305
Shadows Fall	139
Shaft	656
Shaiana	656
Shaman's Tears	549
Shanda	767
Shandalar	624
Shang-Chi: Master of Kung Fu	305
Shanghai Breeze	656
Shanghied	767
Shanna, The She-Devil	305
Shaolin	656
Shards	767
Sharky	549
Sharp Comics	454
Shatter	656
Shattered Earth	767
Shattered Image	549
Shatterpoint	767
Shazam, The New Beginning	139
Shazam!	139
Shazam! Family	139
She Hulk: Ceremony	306
She-Cat	767
She-Devils On Wheels	656
She-Devils On Wheels	767
She-Hulk	305
Sheba	767
Sheena	305
Sheena, Queen of the Jungle	454
Sheena: Queen of the Jungle	656
Sheena: Queen of the Jungle: Bound	657
Sheriff of Tombstone	657
Sherlock Holmes	139, 767
Sherlock Holmes Casebook	768
Sherlock Holmes Mysteries	768
Sherlock Holmes of the '30's	768
Sherlock Holmes Reader	768
Sherlock Holmes: Hound of the Baskervilles	768
Sherlock Holmes: Mark of the Beast	768
Sherlock Holmes: Return of the Devil	768
Sherlock Junior	768
Sheva's War	139
Shi	657, 768
Shi Vs. Tomoe	657
Shi – Year of the Dragon	657
Shi: Akai	657
Shi: Black White & Red	657
Shi: East Wind Rain	657
Shi: Heaven and Earth	657
Shi: Hot Target	657
Shi: Pandora's Box	657
Shi: Poisoned Paradise	657
Shi: Rekishi	657
Shi: Sempo	768
Shi: The Illustrated Warrior	768
Shi: The Series	657
Shi: Year of the Serpent	657
Shi-Senryaku	657
Shidima	549
Shiela Trent Vampire Hunter	768
Shield	306
Shield Wizard Comics	454
Shinobi	513
Ship Ahoy	454
Ship of Fools	549, 768
Shock Detective Cases	378
Shock Suspense Stories	657
Shock Suspenstories	454
Shock the Monkey	658, 768
Shocking Mystery Cases	469
Shockrockets	549
Shogun Warriors	306
Shogunaut	658
Shonen Jump	768
Shooting Stars	658
Short Order Comix	809
Shotgun Mary	658
Shotgun Mary: Blood Lore	658
Shotgun Mary: Son of the Beast, Daughter of Light	658
Showcase	139
Showcase '94	140
Showcase '95	140
Showcase '96	140
Showcase '93	140
Shred	768
Shrek	513
Shriek	768
Shroud	306
Shuriken	768
Shuriken Team-Up	768
Shuriken: Cold Steel	768
Shut Up & Die	549
Siege	549
Siegel & Shuster	658, 768
Sigil	658
Sigma	549
Signal To Noise	513
Silas Mariner	797
Silbuster	768
Silent Invasion	769
Silent Invasion: Abductions	769
Silent Mobius	658, 769
Silent Mobius II	658
Silent Mobius III	658
Silent Rapture	769
Silent Screamers	549
Silke	513
Silken Ghost	658
Silly Daddy	769
Silver Age	140
Silver Age DC Classics	140
Silver Cross	658
Silver Sable	306
Silver Star	658
Silver Storm	658, 769
Silver Streak Comics	455
Silver Surfer	306, 307
Silver Surfer the Enslavers	307
Silver Surfer Vs. Dracula	307
Silver Surfer: Dangerous Artifacts	307
Silver Surfer: Innder Demons	307
Silver Surfer: Loftier Than Mortals	307
Silver Surfer/Superman	307
Silverback	658
Silverblade	140
Silverhawks	306
Silverheels	658
Simon/Kirby Reader	769
Simpsons Comics	658
Simpsons Comics & Stories	659
Sin City	513
Sin City: Big Fat Kill	513
Sin City: Hell and Back	513
Sin City: That Yellow Bastard	513
Sin City: A Dame To Kill For	513
Sin City: Just Another Saturday Night	513
Sinbad	769
Sinbad: House of God	769
Single Series	455
Sinister House of Secret Love	136
Sinking	549
Sinnamon	769
Sins of Youth	140
Sinthia	659
Siren	549, 659
Sister Armageddon	769
Sisterhood of Steel	307
Sisters of Mercy	659
Six From Sirius	308
Six From Sirius II	308
Six Million Dollar Man, The	659
Six String Samurai	659
Six-Gun Western	308
Skateman	659
Skeleton Hand	455
Skeleton Key	769
Skeleton Warriors	308
Skin 13	769
Skin Graft	141
Skinners	549
Skreemer	141
Skrull Kill Crew	308
Skull and Bones	141
Skull Comics	809
Skull Man	769
Skull, The Slayer	308
Skunk, The	769
Skunk/Foodang Foodang/Skunk	769
Sky Blazers	455
Sky Pilot	456
Sky Rocket	456
Sky Sheriff	456
Sky Wolf	659
Skyman	455
Skynn & Bones: Flesh For Fantasy	769
Skynn & Bones: Deadly Angels	769
Slack	769
Slacker Comics	769
Slaine	659
Slaine the Berserker	659
Slaine the Horned God	659
Slaine the King	659
Slam Bang Comics	456
Slapstick	308
Slapstick Comics	456
Slash Maraud	141
Slaughterhouse	770
Slaughterman	770
Slave Girl Comics	456
Slayers	770
Slayers: Super-Explosive Demon Story	770
Sledge Hammer	308
Sleeper	659
Sleepwalker	308
Sleeze Brothers	308
Slick Chick Comics	456
Sliders	659
Sliders: Darkest Hour	659
Sliders: Ultimatum	659
Slimer	659
Slimer & Real Ghostbusters	659
Slingers	308

Index

Sl–St

Slow Death Funnies 809
Sludge 659
Smallville 141
Smash Comics 141, 456
Smash Hits Sports Comics 456
Smax 141, 660
Smile 770, 810
Smiley 660
Smiley Burnette Western 456
Smilin' Jack 456
Smith Brown Jones 770
Smith Brown Jones: Alien
  Accountant 770
Smitty 457
Smoke 660
Smurfs 308
Snagglepuss 660
Snak Posse 660
Snake Plissken Chronicles 660
Snap 453
Snappy Comics 457
Snarf 810
Snatch Comics 810
Snatch Sampler 810
Sniffy the Pup 457
Snooper and Blabber
  Detectives 660
Snow White & Seven Dwarfs
  Golden Anniversary 660
Snowman 770
Snowman: 1994 770
Snowman: Dead & Dying 770
Snowman: Horror Show 770
Snowman2 770
So Dark the Rose 660
Soap Opera Romances 660
Sob: Special Operations
  Branch 770
Sock Monkey 514
Socketeer 770
Sojourn 660
Solar Lord 549
Solar: Hell On Earth 660
Solar: Man of the Atom 660
Solarman 308
Sold Out 770
Solders of Fortune 801
Soldier Comics 457
Soldier X 308
Soldiers of Fortune 457
Soldiers of Freedom 661
Solitaire 661
Solo 308, 514
Solo Avengers 308
Solo Ex-Mutants 770
Solomon Kane 309, 661
Solus 661
Solution 661
Somerset Holmes 661
Something Different 770
Son of Ambush Bug 141
Son of Mutant World 661
Son of Satan 309
Son of Sinbad 457
Son of Vulcan 632
Sonambulo: Sleep of the Just ..770
Song of Hiawatha, The 797
Song of the Cid 770
Song of the Sirens 770
Sonic Disruptors 141
Sonic Quest: The Death Egg
  Saga 661
Sonic Super Special 661
Sonic the Hedgehog 661
Sonic the Hedgehog Presents
  Knuckles Chaotic 661
Sonic the Hedgehog Presents
  Tails 661
Sonic's Friendly Nemesis:
  Knuckles 661
Sorcerer Hunters 770
Soul 771
Soul of A Samurai 549
Soul Reaver: Legacy of Kain ..549
Soul Saga 549
Soulfire 771
Soulman 661
Soulquest 661
Soulsearchers and Co. 771
Soulwind 549

Soupy Sales Comic Book 661
Southern Knights 771
Southern Squadron 771
Sovereign Seven 141
Soviet Super Soldiers 309
Space Action 457
Space Adventures 457, 661
Space Ark 661, 771
Space Beaver 771
Space Busters 457
Space Circus 514
Space Comics 402
Space Detective 457
Space Family Robinson 661
Space Ghost 662
Space Invaders Comics,
  Don Chin's 811
Space Jam 141
Space Man 662
Space Mouse 457
Space Patrol 457, 771
Space Squadron 309
Space Thrillers 457
Space Usagi 514, 662, 771
Space War 662
Space Western Comics 486
Space Wolf 771
Space Worlds 309
Space: 1999 662
Space: Above and Beyond ...661
Space: Above and Beyond—
  the Gauntlet 661
Spaced 771
Spacehawk 514
Spaceknights 309
Spaceman 309
Spandex Tights 771
Spandex Tights Presents:
  Space Opera 771
Spandex Tights Presents:
  the Girls of '95 771
Spandex Tights: The Lost
  Issues 771
Spank the Monkey 771
Spank the Monkey On the
  Comic Market 771
Spanner's Galaxy 141
Sparkler Comics 457
Sparkling Stars 458
Sparkman 458
Sparkplug 771
Sparkplug Special 771
Sparky Watts 458
Sparrow 771
Spartan X 549
Spartan: Warrior Spirit 549
Spasm! 811
Spawn 550
Spawn Bible 550
Spawn Blood Feud 550
Spawn the Impaler 551
Spawn: The Dark Ages 550
Spawn: The Undead 551
Spawn/Batman 550
Spawn/Wildc.A.T.S 551
Special Agent 458
Special Collector's Edition ..309
Special Comics 420
Special Edition Comics 458
Special Marvel Edition 309
Species 514
Species: Human Race 514
Spectacular Scarlet Spider ..309
Spectacular Spider-Man 310
Specter 7 662
Spectre, The 141, 142
Spectrum Comics Presents ..662
Specwar 662
Speed Comics 458
Speed Demon 186
Speed Force 142
Speed Racer 662
Speed Racer Classics 771
Speed Smith the Hot Rod King .458
Speedball 310
Spellbinders 662
Spellbound 310, 311
Spelljammer 142
Spencer Spook 771
Spicy Tales 771

Spider 662
Spider Kiss 772
Spider: Reign of the Vampire
  King 662
Spider-Boy 186
Spider-Boy Team-Up 186
Spider-Girl 311
Spider-Girl Presents: Darkdevil .311
Spider-Girl Presents: The Buzz .311
Spider-Man 311
Spider-Man Comics Magazine .313
Spider-Man & Wolverine ...312
Spider-Man & X-Factor:
  Shadow Games 315
Spider-Man 2099 314
Spider-Man 2099 A.D. 314
Spider-Man Adventures 312
Spider-Man Manga 313
Spider-Man Megazine 313
Spider-Man Super Size Special 314
Spider-Man Team-Up 314
Spider-Man Universe 314
Spider-Man Unlimited 314
Spider-Man Vs. Dracula 314
Spider-Man Unmasked 314
Spider-Man Vs. Dracula 314
Spider-Man, Chapter 1 312
Spider-Man: Mutant Agenda ..313
Spider-Man: The Arachnis
  Project 314
Spider-Man: The Clone
  Journals 314
Spider-Man: The Final
  Adventure 313
Spider-Man: Blue 312
Spider-Man: Dead Man's Hand .313
Spider-Man: Death & Destiny .313
Spider-Man: Friends and
  Enemies 313
Spider-Man: Get Kraven ...313
Spider-Man: Hobgoblin Lives ..313
Spider-Man: Legend of the
  Spider-Clan 313
Spider-Man: Lifeline 313
Spider-Man: Maximum Clonage 313
Spider-Man: Power of Terror ..313
Spider-Man: Quality of Life ...314
Spider-Man: Redemption ...314
Spider-Man: Revelations 312
Spider-Man: Revenge of the
  Green Goblin 314
Spider-Man: The Jackal Files .314
Spider-Man: The Lost Years ..314
Spider-Man: The Movie 313
Spider-Man: The Mysterio
  Manifesto 313
Spider-Man: The Parker Years .314
Spider-Man: The Venom Agenda 315
Spider-Man: Web of Doom ..315
Spider-Man/Badrock ...312, 662
Spider-Man/Batman 312
Spider-Man/Black Cat: The
  Evil That Men Do 312
Spider-Man/Gen13 313
Spider-Man/Punisher 314
Spider-Men: Funeral For An
  Octopus 313
Spider-Woman 315
Spiderfemme 662
Spiderman & Amazing Friends .312
Spiderman Saga 314
Spiderman Vs. Venom 315
Spiderman Vs. Wolverine ..315
Spiderman/Punisher/Sabertooth:
  Designer Genes 314
Spiderwoman 315
Spidey and the Mini Marvels ..315
Spidey Super Stories 315
Spineless Man 772
Spiral Path 662
Spirit 662
Spirit Casebook, The 772
Spirit Jam, The: 772
Spirit of the Amazon 662
Spirit of the Tao 551
Spirit of Wonder 514
Spirit, The 458, 459, 662, 772
Spirit, The: The New
  Adventures 662
Spirit, The: The Origin Years ..772
Spirited Away 772

Spiritman 459
Spirits 772
Spitfire and the Trouble-
  shooters 316
Spitfire Comics 459
Spitting Image 772
Splitting Image 551
Spongebob Squarepants ...772
Spoof 316
Spook Comics 459
Spook Detective Cases 378
Spook Suspense and Mystery .378
Spooky 459
Spooky Haunted House 663
Spooky Mysteries 459
Spooky Spooktown 663
Sport Comics 474
Sport Stars 316
Sports Action 316
Sports Thrills 381
Spotlight 316
Spotlight Comics 459
Spumco Comic Book 316
Spunky 459
Spy and Counter Spy 459
Spy Cases 261
Spy Fighters 316
Spy Hunters 459
Spy Smasher 460
Spy Thrillers 316
Spy, The 797
Spyboy 514
Spyboy 13: The M.A.N.G.A.
  Affair 514
Spyboy/Young Justice 514
Spyke 316
Spyman 663
Squad, The 663
Squadron Supreme 316
Squalor 663
Squee 772
Squeeks 460
St. George 301
Stain 772
Stainless Steel Armidillo ...772
Stainless Steel Rat 663
Stalker 142
Stalkers 316
Stamp Comics 460
Stan Shaw's Beauty & the
  Beast 514
Stanley & His Monster ..78, 142
Star 551
Star Blazers 663
Star Bleech the Generation
  Gap 772
Star Comics 460
Star Comics Magazine 316
Star Crossed 142
Star Hawks 772
Star Hunters 142
Star Master 316
Star Masters 663
Star Ranger 460
Star Ranger Funnies 460
Star Rangers 772
Star Reach 772
Star Reach Classics 663
Star Seed 642
Star Slammers 663
Star Spangled Comics 143
Star Spangled Comics 145
Star Spangled War Stories ..144
Star Studded 460
Star Trek 145, 317, 664
Star Trek the Next Generation
  Shadowheart 147
Star Trek Special 664
Star Trek the Next Generation
  Modala Imperative 147
Star Trek: 146
Star Trek: The Next Generation
  Deep Space Nine 146
Star Trek: The Next Generation
  Ill Wind 146
Star Trek: All of Me 664
Star Trek: Deep Space
  Nine 317, 664
Star Trek: Deep Space Nine
  Celebrity Series: Blood

and Honor 664
Star Trek: Deep Space Nine
 — N-Vector 664
Star Trek: Deep Space Nine:
 Hearts and Minds 664
Star Trek: Deep Space Nine:
 Lightstorm 664
Star Trek: Deep Space Nine/
 The Next Generation 664
Star Trek: Deep Spacenine:
 the Maquis 664
Star Trek: Divided We Fall ...664
Star Trek: Early Voyages 317
Star Trek: Enter the Wolves ...664
Star Trek: First Contact 317
Star Trek: Mirror, Mirror 317
Star Trek: New Frontier —
 Time Management 665
Star Trek: Next Generation 146
Star Trek: Operation
 Assimilation 317
Star Trek: Starfleet Academy ...317
Star Trek: Telepathy War 317
Star Trek: The Next Generation—
 riker Special 317
Star Trek: The Next Generation 664
Star Trek: The Next Generation —
 Perchance To Dream ...665
Star Trek: The Next Generation —
 the Killing Shadows 665
Star Trek: The Untold Voyages .317
Star Trek: Unlimited 317
Star Trek: Voyager 318, 665
Star Trek: Voyager — Planet
 Killer 665
Star Trek: Voyager:
 Splashdown 318
Star Trek/X-Men 318
Star Wars 318, 514
Star Wars Episode II—
 Attack of the Clones 516
Star Wars In 3-D 665
Star Wars Prelude To Rebellion 517
Star Wars Tales 517
Star Wars: A New Hope—
 Special Edition 515
Star Wars: Boba Fett—
 Enemy of the Empire ...515
Star Wars: Crimson Empire ...515
Star Wars: Empire's End 515
Star Wars: Heir To the Empire .516
Star Wars: Jedi Academy 516
Star Wars: Shadow Stalker 517
Star Wars: Vader's Quest 518
Star Wars: A New Hope—
 manga 515
Star Wars: A Valentine Story ...518
Star Wars: Battle of the
 Bounty Hunters 515
Star Wars: Boba Fett 515
Star Wars: Bounty Hunters 515
Star Wars: Chewbacca 515
Star Wars: Clone Wars 515
Star Wars: Dark Empire 515
Star Wars: Dark Force Rising ..515
Star Wars: Dark Forces 515
Star Wars: Darth Maul 515
Star Wars: Droids 515
Star Wars: Emissaries To
 Malastare 516
Star Wars: Empire 515
Star Wars: Episode I the
 Phantom Menace 516
Star Wars: Episode I the
 Phantom Menace—manga 516
Star Wars: Infinities — A New
 Hope 516
Star Wars: Infinities — Return
 of the Jedi 516
Star Wars: Infinities — the
 Empire Strikes Back 516
Star Wars: Jabba the Hutt 516
Star Wars: Jango Fett 516
Star Wars: Jango Fett—
 open Seasons 516
Star Wars: Jedi 516
Star Wars: Jedi Council —
 Acts of War 516
Star Wars: Jedi Quest 517
Star Wars: Jedi Vs. Sith 517

Star Wars: Mara Jade By the
 Emperor's Hand 517
Star Wars: Outlander 517
Star Wars: Qui-Gon & Obi-
 Wan—last Stand On
 Ord Mantell 517
Star Wars: Qui-Gon & Obi-
 Wan—the Auroient
 Express 517
Star Wars: Return of the Jedi
 —special Edition 517
Star Wars: River of Chaos 517
Star Wars: Shadows of the
 Empire — Evolution 517
Star Wars: Shadows of the
 Empire 517
Star Wars: Splinter of the
 Mind's Eye 517
Star Wars: Starfighter—
 crossbones 517
Star Wars: Tag & Bink
 Are Dead 517
Star Wars: Tales From
 Mos Eisley 517
Star Wars: Tales of the Jedi ...517
Star Wars: Tales of the Jedi:
 Dark Lords of the Sith ...517
Star Wars: Tales of the Jedi:
 the Freedon Nadd Uprising 517
Star Wars: Tales of the Jedi:
 the Redemption of Ulic
 Qel-Droma 518
Star Wars: Tales of the Jedi:
 the Sith War 517
Star Wars: Tales of the Jedi
 —the Fall of the Sith
 Empire 518
Star Wars: Tales of the Jedi—
 the Golden Age of the Sith 518
Star Wars: The Empire Strikes
 Back 516
Star Wars: The Hunt For
 Aurra Sing 516
Star Wars: The Last Command .517
Star Wars: The Protocol
 Offensive 517
Star Wars: The Return of
 the Jedi 517
Star Wars: The Stark
 Hyperspace War 518
Star Wars: Twilight 518
Star Wars: Underworld—
 the Yavin Vassilika 518
Star Wars: Union 518
Star Wars: X-Wing Rogue
 Squadron 518
Star Wars: Zam Wesell 518
Star Western 773
Star-Lord, Special Edition 316
Starblast 316
Starblazers 663
Starbrand 316
Starchild 772
Starchild: Crossroads 772
Starchild: Mythopolis 551
Stardust 142
Starfire 142
Starforce Six Special 663
Stargage Sg1 663
Stargate 663
Stargate: Doomsday World 663
Stargate: One Nation Under Ra 772
Stargate: Rebellion 772
Stargate: The New Adventures
 Collection 772
Stargate: Underworld 772
Stargods 663
Starjammers 316
Stark Raven 663
Stark: Future 772
Starlet O'Hara In Hollywood ...460
Starlight Agency 772
Starlord 316
Starlord Megazine 316
Starman 142
Starriors 316
Stars and S.T.R.I.P.E. 143
Stars and Stripes Comics 460
Starship Troopers 514
Starship Troopers: Dominant

Species 514
Starship Troopers: Brute
 Creations 514
Starship Troopers: Insect Touch 514
Starslayer 663
Starslayer Directors Cut 663
Starstruck 317, 514
Startling Comics 460
Startling Stories: The Thing—
 Night Falls On Yancy St. ..317
Startling Terror Tales 461
Starwatchers 665
Starwolves: Jupiter Run 665
Static 147, 773
Static Shock!: Rebirth of
 the Cool 147
Static-X 665
Stealth Force 773
Stealth Squad 665, 773
Steam Detectives 773
Steed & Mrs. Peel 665
Steel 147
Steel Claw 665
Steel Sterling Archie
 Publications 665
Steel, The Indestructible Man ..147
Steele Destines 773
Steelgrip Starkey 318
Steeltown Rockers 318
Steve Canyon 773
Steve Canyon 3-D 665
Steve Canyon Comics 461
Steve Ditko's Strange
 Avenging Tales 773
Steve Grant's Mortal Souls ...773
Steve Roper 461
Steve Saunders Special Agent .458
Steve Zodiac & the Fire 665
Steven 773
Stig's Inferno 773
Sting of the Green Hornet 665
Stinger 665
Stinz 773
Stitch 665
Stone 551
Stone Cold Steve Austin 665
Stoned Picture Parade 811
Stories By Famous Authors
 Illustrated 388
Storm 318
Storm Riders 665
Stormbringer 773
Stormquest 665
Stormwatch 551
Stormwatch: Team Achilles ...665
Stormwatcher 773
Story of Harry S. Truman, The .461
Straight Arrow 461
Strain 773
Strange Adventures 147, 149
Strange Behavior 773
Strange Brew 773
Strange Combat Tales 318
Strange Confessions 461
Strange Days 666
Strange Fantasy 461
Strange Sports Stories 773
Strange Sports Stories 149
Strange Stories From Another
 World 461
Strange Stories of Suspense ..300
Strange Suspense Stories ...462
Strange Suspense Stories/
 Captain Atom 666
Strange Suspense Stories 421, 461
Strange Tales 318, 319
Strange Tales of the Unusual ..319
Strange Tales: Dark Corners ..319
Strange Terrors 462
Strange Weather Lately 773
Strange World of Your Dreams .462
Strange Worlds 320, 462, 774
Strangehaven 773
Strangelove 774
Strangers 552
Strangers In Paradise 773
Strangers In Paradise Vol. 3 ..552
Strangers, The 666
Strata 774
Straw Men 666, 774

Strawberry Shortcake 320
Stray 149
Stray Bullets 774
Stray Toasters 320
Street Fighter 552, 666, 774
Street Heroes 2005 774
Street Music 774
Street Poet Ray 774
Street Sharks 666
Street Wolf 774
Streets 149, 552
Strictly Private 462
Strike! 666
Strikeback 666
Strikeback! 552
Strikeforce America 666
Strikeforce Morituri 320
Striker 666
Striker: Secret of the Berserker .774
Striker: The Armored Warrior ..774
Strong Guy Reborn 320
Strong Man 666
Strontium Dog 666
Stryfe's Strike File 320
Stryke 666
Stuck Rubber Baby 149
Stumbo the Giant 666
Stumbo Tinytown 666
Stuntman Comics 462
Stupid Comics 552
Stupid Heroes 666
Stupid, Stupid Rat Tails: The
 Adventures of Big Johnson
 Bone 774
Sturm the Trooper 666
Stygmata 774
Sub-Mariner 320
Sub-Mariner Comics 320
Subhuman 518
Subspecies 666
Subtle Violents 774
Suburban Jersey Ninja She-
 Devils 321
Subvert Comics 811
Sugar & Spike 149
Sugar Bowl Comics 462
Sugar Buzz 774
Sugar Ray Finhead 775
Suicide Squad 149, 150
Sultry Teenage Super-Foxes ..775
Sun Fun Komiks 462
Sun Glasses After Dark 666
Sun Runners 666
Sunny, America's Sweetheart .462
Sunset Carson 462, 667
Super Book of Comics 462
Super Car 667
Super Circus 463
Super Comics 463
Super Cops, The 667
Super DC Giant 153
Super Duck Comics 463
Super Friends 153
Super Funnies 463
Super Goof 667
Super Heroes Battle Super
 Gorilla 154
Super Heroes Versus
 Supervillians 667
Super Magician Comics 463
Super Manga Blast 518
Super Mario Bros. 667
Super Powers 166
Super Soldier: Man of War ...186
Super Soldiers 321
Super Spy 464
Super Western Comics 465
Super Western Funnies 463
Super World Comics 465
Super-Book of Comics 462
Super-Dooper Comics 463
Super-Mystery Comics 464
Super-Patriot 552
Super-Patriot: Liberty and
 Justice 552
Super-Soldier 186
Super-Team Family 166
Super-Villain Classics 321
Super-Villain Team-Up 321
Superbabes: Femforce 667

Index

Su–Th

Entry	Page
Superboy	150, 152
Superboy & the Legion of Super-Heroes	151
Superboy & the Ravers	152
Superboy Plus	153
Superboy's Legion	153
Superboy/Risk Double-Shot	153
Supercops	667
Supergirl	153
Superhuman Samurai Syber Squad	667
Superman	154, 158
Superman (miniature)	158
Superman & Batman: Generations — An Imaginary Tale	161
Superman & Batman: Generations III	161
Superman & Bugs Bunny	161
Superman Adventures	160
Superman and the Great Cleveland Fire	158
Superman Family, The	161
Superman For All Seasons	162
Superman Record Comic	158
Superman Red/Superman Blue	160
Superman Secret Files	160
Superman Spectacular	158
Superman Vs. Predator	165
Superman Vs. Spiderman	165
Superman Vs. the Terminator: Death To the Future	518
Superman Workbox	158
Superman, The Secret Years	165
Superman: Silver Banshee	164
Superman: The Doomsday Wars	161
Superman: The Man of Tomorrow	163
Superman: Birthright	161
Superman: Day of Doom	161
Superman: Last Son of Earth	162
Superman: Man of Steel	162
Superman: Metropolis	162
Superman: Red Son	163
Superman: Save the Planet	165
Superman: The Dark Side	161
Superman: The Death of Clark Kent	160
Superman: The Kansas Sighting	165
Superman: The Wedding Album	160
Superman's Buddy	158
Superman's Christmas Adventure	158
Superman's Girl Friend, Lois Lane	163
Superman's Nemesis, Lex Luthor	164
Superman's Pal, Jimmy Olsen	164
Superman-Tim Store Pamphlets	158
Superman/Aliens II	518
Superman/Batman	161
Superman/Doomsday: Hunter/Prey	161
Superman/Gen13	162
Superman/Madman Hullabaloo	518
Superman/Tarzan: Sons of the Jungle	518
Superman/Wonder Woman: Whom Gods Destroy	165
Supermen of America	165
Supermodels In the Rainforest	775
Supermouse	464
Supernatural Thrillers	321
Supernatural Law	788
Supernaturals	321
Supernaut	667
Supersnipe Comics	464
Superstar: As Seen On TV	552
Superswine	775
Supreme	552, 667
Supreme Power	321
Supreme: Glory Days	552
Supreme: The Return	667
Sure-Fire	422
Surge	667
Surrogate Savior	775
Survivalist Chronicles	775
Survivors	667
Suspense	321
Suspense Comics	465
Suspense Detective	465
Suspira: The Great Working	667
Suzie Comics	472
Swamp Thing	166, 167
Swan	775
Sweatshop	167
Sweeney	465
Sweet Childe Battle Book	775
Sweet Childe: Lost Confessions	775
Sweet Love	465
Sweet Lucy	775
Sweet Sixteen	465
Sweetheart Diary	465
Sweethearts	373
Swerve	775
Swift Arrow	465
Swiftsure	775
Swiss Family Robinson	796
Switch B.L.A.Z.E. Manga	775
Sword of Damocles	552
Sword of Dracula	552
Sword of Sorcery	167
Sword of the Atom	167
Sword of Valor	667, 775
Swords and Science	775
Swords of Cerebus	775
Swords of Shar-Pai	775
Swords of Texas	667
Swords of the Swashbucklers	321
Swords of Valors: Robin Hood	775
Symbols of Justice	667
Syn	519
Syphons	667
Syphons: Countdown	667
Syphons: The Stargate Stratagem	667
System Seven	775
System, The	167
T.E.C.H. Boyz Hyperactive	669
T.H.U.N.D.E.R. Agents	672
T-Man	471
Taffy	465
Tailgunner Jo	167
Tailspin	465, 668
Taken Under Compendium	775
Takion	167
Tale of One Bad Rat	519
Tale of the Marines	227
Tales Calculated To Drive You Bats	667
Tales From the Aniverse	775
Tales From the Bog	775
Tales From the Crypt	377, 667
Tales From the Edge	775
Tales From the Heart	775
Tales of Ordinary Madness	519
Tales of the Beanworld	775
Tales of the Jackalope	776
Tales of Asgard	322
Tales of Evil	668
Tales of G.I.Joe	322
Tales of Horror	465
Tales of Jace Pearson of the Texas Rangers	411
Tales of Justice	260
Tales of Sex & Death	811
Tales of Suspense	322
Tales of Tellos: Maiden Voyage	552
Tales of Terror	465, 668
Tales of Terror Annual	465
Tales of the Green Hornet	668
Tales of the Mysterious Traveler	668
Tales of the Age of Apocalypse	322
Tales of the Age of Apocalypse: Sinister Bloodline	322
Tales of the Darkness	552
Tales of the Fehnrik	776
Tales of the Green Beret	668
Tales of the Green Lantern Corps	167
Tales of the Legion of Super Heroes	167
Tales of the Marvels: Blockbuster	322
Tales of the Marvels: Inner Demons	322
Tales of the Marvels: Wonder Years	322
Tales of the New Teen Titans	167
Tales of the Ninja Warriors	776
Tales of the Plague	776
Tales of the Realm	668
Tales of the Sunrunners	668, 776
Tales of the Teen Titans	121, 167
Tales of the Teenage Mutant Ninja Turtles	776
Tales of the Unexpected	167
Tales of the Witchblade	552
Tales of the Zombie	322
Tales To Astonish	322, 323
Tales To Offend	519
Tales Too Terrible To Tell	776
Talisman, The	800
Tall Tails	776
Tally-Ho Comics	465
Talos of the Wilderness	169
Tangent '98	169
Tangent Comics	169
Tangled Web	323
Tank Girl	169, 519, 668
Tank Girl: Apocalypse	169
Tank Girl: The Odyssey	169
Tantalizing Stories	776
Taoland	776
Taoland Adventures	668
Target Airboy	668
Target Comics	466
Target Western Romances	466
Targitt	668
Tarot Witch of the Black Rose	668
Tarzan	169, 323, 466, 519
Tarzan Family	169
Tarzan In Color	669
Tarzan of the Apes	324, 668
Tarzan the Warrior	669
Tarzan Vs. Predator At the Earth's Core	519
Tarzan: Love, Lies, and the Lost City	669
Tarzan: The Beckoning	669
Tarzan: The Lost Adventure	499
Tarzan/John Carter: Warlords of Mars	519
Task Force Alpha	669, 776
Taskmaster	324
Tasmanian Devil & His Tasty Friends	669
Tastee-Freez Comics	669
Tattered Banners	169
Team 1: Stormwatch	552
Team 1: Wildcats	553
Team 7	553
Team 7 III: Dead Reacening	553
Team 7-Objective: Hell	553
Team America	324
Team Anarchy	669
Team Helix	324
Team Nippon	776
Team Titans	169
Team X 2000	324
Team X/Team 7	324
Team Yankee	669
Team Youngblood	553
Tean Beat	169
Tech Jacket	553
Technophilia	776
Teen Beam	169
Teen Comics	189
Teen Confessions	670
Teen Life	487
Teen Secret Diary	670
Teen Titans	170
Teen Titans Spotlight	170
Teen Titans Go!	170
Teen Titans, The	170
Teen Titans/Outsiders	170
Teen-Age Confidential	669
Teen-Age Diary Secrets	466
Teen-Age Love	610
Teen-Age Romances	467
Teen-Age Temptations	467
Teena	466
Teenage Hotrodders	669
Teenage Mutant Ninja Turtles	553, 669
Teenage Mutant Ninja Turtles Adventures	669
Teenage Mutant Ninja Turtles Animated	670
Teenage Mutant Ninja Turtles Training Manual	776
Teenage Mutant Ninja Turtles	776
Teenage Mutant Ninja Turtles/Flaming Carrot	670
Teenage Romance	283
Teenagents	670
Teenie Weenies, The	467
Tegra, Jungle Empress	488
Tekken 2	670
Tekken Forever	553
Tekken Saga	670
Television Comics	467
Television Puppet Show	467
Tell It To the Marines	467
Tellos	553
Tellos: Sons and Moons	553
Tempest	170
Tempest Comics Presents	776
Tempus Fugitive	170
Tender Romance	467
Tense Suspense	670
Tenth, The	553
Tenth, The: Black Embrace	553
Tenth, The: Evil's Child	554
Tenth, The: Nightwalker	519
Tenth, The: Resurrected	519
Terminal City	170
Terminal City: Aerial Graffiti	170
Terminal Point	519
Terminator	519, 670
Terminator 2: Cybernetic Dawn	671
Terminator 2: Nuclear Twilight	671
Terminator 3	671
Terminator II	324
Terminator: The Dark Years	519
Terminator: All My Futures Past	670
Terminator: End Game	519
Terminator: Enemy Within	519
Terminator: Hunters & Killers	519
Terminator: Secondary Objectives	519
Terminator: The Burning Earth	670
Terra Obscura	671
Terraformers	671
Terranauts	671
Terrarists	324
Terrific Comics	409, 467
Terrifying Tales	467
Territory, The	519
Terror Illustrated	467
Terror Inc.	324
Terror On the Planet of the Apes	776
Terrors of the Jungle	467
Terry & the Pirates	776
Terry and the Pirates	468, 776
Terry Moore's Paradise, Too	777
Terry-Bears Comics	468
Terrytoons Comics	468
Tess	671
Tessie the Typist	324
Tex Avery's Screwball Squirrel	519
Tex Avery's Droopy	519
Tex Benson	777
Tex Dawson, Gunslinger	324
Tex Farrell	468
Tex Granger	370
Tex Morgan	324
Tex Ritter Western	468
Tex Taylor	324
Texan, The	468
Texas Kid	324
Texas Rangers In Action	671
Thanos	324
Thanos Quest	324, 325
That Wilkin Boy	671
The Call of Duty: The Precinct	208
The Call of Duty: The Wagon	208
The Complete Foo!	806
The Flash Plus	77
The Horror of Collier County	504
The Legend of Mother Sarah	505
The Legend of Mother Sarah: City of the Angels	505
The Legend of Mother Sarah: City of the Children	506

CVA Page 835

Index

Th–Tw

Entry	Page
The Luck In the Head	506
The Machines	807
The Man	807
The New Adventures of Jesus	807
The New Order Handbook	544
The Phantom	756
The Second Life of Dr. Mirage	655
The Shadow and Doc Savage	513
The Witching Hour	178
Thespian	671
They Were 11	777
Thieves and Kings	777
Thing From Another World: Climate of Fear	519
Thing From Another World: Eternal Vows	520
Thing, The	325, 519
Thing, The: Freakshow	325
Thing!: Cold Fear	671
Thing!, The	468
Thing/She-Hulk	325
Third World War	671
Thirteen O'clock	520
This Is Suspense	421
This Is Suspense!	462
This Is War	468
This Magazine Is Haunted	468
Thor	325, 327
Thor Corps	328
Thor: Godstorm	328
Thor: Vikings	328
Thorion of the New Asgods	186
Thorr Suerd Or Sword of Thor	777
Those Annoying Post Bros.	777
Those Annoying Post Brothers	671
Threat	777
Three Geeks, The	777
Three Musketeers	328
Three Musketeers, The	791
Three Ring Comics	469
Three Rocketeers	777
Three Stooges	469, 671
Three Stooges 3-D	671
Three Strikes	777
Threshold	777
Threshold of Reality	778
Thrill-O-Rama	672
Thriller	171
Thrilling Adventures In Stamps	460
Thrilling Comics	171, 469
Thrilling Crime Cases	469
Thrilling Murder Comics	811
Thrilling Romances	469
Thrilling Science Tales	671
Thrilling True Story of the Baseball Giants	470
Thrillkiller	171
Thrillkillers '62	171
Thrillogy	671
Thrills of Tomorrow	471
Thunder Agents	672
Thunder Bunny	778
Thunder Mace	778
Thunderbird	778
Thunderbolt	672
Thunderbolts	328
Thundercats	328, 672
Thundercats: Dogs of War	292
Thundercats: Hammerhand's Revenge	672
Thundercats: The Return	672
Thunderstrike	328
Tick	778
Tick & Artie	672
Tick and Arthur, The	778
Tick Circus Maximus, The	778
Tick Omnibus	778
Tick Tock Tales	470
Tick, The	672
Tick, The: Big Blue Destiny	778
Tick, The: Big Xmas Trilogy	672
Tick, The: Golden Age	778
Tick, The: Heroes of the City	778
Tick, The: Luny Bin	778
Tick: Giant Circus of the Mighty	778
Tick: Karma Tornado	778
Tick's Back, The	778
Tick's Incredible Internet Comic, The	672
Tiger Girl	672
Tiger-Man	672
Tiger-X	779
Tigers and Traitors	803
Tigers of Terra	672, 779
Tigers of the Luftwaffe	778
Tigress	779
Tigress Tales	779
Tigress: The Hidden Lands	779
Tim Holt	470
Tim Tyler Cowboy	470
Tim Vigil's Webwitch	779
Timber Wolf	171
Time 2	672
Time Breakers	171
Time Cop	520
Time Drifters	779
Time Gates	779
Time Jump War	779
Time Machine	779
Time Machine, The	801
Time Masters	171
Time Tunnel, The	672
Time Twisters	672
Time Warp	171
Time Warrior	672
Time Warriors	779
Timely Presents: Human Torch Comics	329
Timeseekers	554
Timeslip Collection	329
Timeslip: The Coming of the Avengers	329
Timespirits	329
Timestryke	329
Timewalker	672
Timmy the Timid Ghost	690
Tincan Man	554
Tiny Tessie	324
Tiny Tots Comics	470
Tip Top Comics	470
Tippy Teen	673
Tippy's Friends Go-Go & Animal	673
Titan	520
Titan A.E.	520
Titaness	779
Titans	171
Titans, The/Legion of Super-Heroes: Universe Ablaze	171
Titans, The/Young Justice: Graduation Day	171
Tmnt Presents: Donatello and Leatherhead	670
Tmnt Presents: Merdude Vs. Ray Fillet	670
Tmnt Presents: April O'Neil	670
Tmnt: April O/Neil the May East Saga	670
Tmnt: The Maltese Turtle	670
Tmnt: Year of the Turtle	670
Tnt Comics	471
To Be Announced	779
To Die For	673
Today's Brides	471
Today's Romance	471
Tohubohu	673
Toilers of the Sea, The	797
Tokyo Mew Mew	779
Tokyo Storm Warning	673
Tom and Jerry	440, 471
Tom Brown's School Days	796
Tom Corbett Space Cadet	471
Tom Corbett II	779
Tom Corbett Space Cadet	779
Tom Judge: End of Days	554
Tom Mix	471
Tom Mix Commandos Comics	471
Tom Mix Holiday Album	779
Tom Mix Western	471, 673, 779
Tom Strong	673
Tom Strong's Terrific Tales	673
Tom Terrific!	673
Tom-Tom the Jungle Boy	472
Tomahawk	171
Tomb of Darkness	203
Tomb of Dracula	329, 330
Tomb of Dracula Magazine	330
Tomb of Terror	471
Tomb Raider	554
Tomb Raider Magazine	554
Tomb Raider: The Greatest Pleasure of All	554
Tomb Raider/Witchblade	554
Tomb Raider/Witchblade Revisited	554
Tomb Tales	779
Tommi Gunn: Killers Lust	779
Tommi-Gunn	673
Tommi-Gunn: Killer's Lust	673
Tommy & the Monsters	780
Tommy of the Big Top	472
Tomoe	673
Tomoe: Unforgettable Fire	673
Tomoe/Witchblade: Fire Sermon	673
Tomorrow Knights	330
Tomorrow Man	780
Tomorrow Stories	673
Tongue*lash	520
Tonto	423
Tony Daniel's F5	520
Tony Digerolamo's Jersey Devil	780
Tony Digerolamo's the Fix	780
Tony Digerolamo's Travelers	780
Tony Millionaire's Sock Monkey	520
Tony Trent	387
Too Much Coffee Man	520, 780
Too Much Hopeless Savages	780
Tool and Die	673
Toom Raider: Journeys	554
Tooth & Claw	554
Top Cat	673
Top Cow Classics	554
Top Cow Secrets	554
Top Cow: Book of Revelations	554
Top Cow's California Christmas Spectacular	554
Top Cow/Ballistic Studios	554
Top Dog	330
Top Eliminator	669
Top Flight Comics	472
Top Love Stories	472
Top Secret	472
Top Secrets	472
Top Spot Comics	473
Top Ten	673
Top-Notch Comics	472
Tops	472
Tops Comics	472
Tops In Adventure	473
Topsy-Turvy	473
Tor	172, 330, 473
Tor In 3-D	673
Tor Johnson: Hollywood Star	780
Torchy	473
Torg	780
Tori-Shi-Kita	673
Tormented, The	473
Tormentress: Mistress of Hell	673
Torrid Affairs	780
Total Eclipse	673
Total Eclipse, The Seraphim Objective	674
Total Justice	172
Total Recall	172
Total Sell Out	554
Total War	674
Totally Alien	780
Totems	172
Touch of Silver, A	554
Tough Guys and Wild Women	780
Tough Kid Squad Comics	330
Tower of Shadows	330
Toxic Avenger	330
Toxic Crusaders	330
Toxic Gumbo	172
Toy Boy	674
Toy Town Comics	473
Toyland Comics	473
Tracker	780
Trail Blazers	450
Trakk: Monster Hunter	555
Trancers: The Adventures of Jack Deth	673
Transformers	330, 674
Transformers Universe	331
Transformers Armada Cinemaster	780
Transformers Comics Magazine	331
Transformers In 3-D	674
Transformers, The Movie	331
Transformers: Armada	674
Transformers: Generation One	674
Transformers: More Than Meets the Eye	674
Transformers: The War Within	674
Transformers/G.I. Joe	674
Transit	780
Transmetropolitan	172
Transmutation of Ike Garuda	331
Travel of Jamie Mcpheeters	674
Traveller	674
Treasure Comics	473
Treasure Island	798
Treasury of Comics	473
Trekker	520, 555
Trenchcoat Brigade	173
Trencher	555
Trial By Fire	674
Tribe	555, 674
Tribulation Force	674
Trickster King Monkey	780
Trident	780
Trigun	520
Trinity Angels	674
Triple Threat	473
Triple°x	520
Triumph	173
Triumvirate	780
Troll	555
Troll Lords	674
Troll: Once A Hero	555
Trollords	780
Trollords: Death & Kisses	780
Trouble	331
Trouble Magnet	173
Trouble Shooters	780
Trouble With Girls	331, 675, 780
Troublemakers	674
Troubleman	555
True Adventures	331
True Aviation Picture Stories	473
True Comics	473
True Complete Mystery	215
True Confidences	474
True Crime	780
True Crime Comics	474
True Faith	173
True Life Romances	474
True Life Secrets	474
True Love	675
True Love Pictorial	474
True Movie and Television	474
True Romance	675
True Secrets	290
True Sport Picture Stories	474
True Sweetheart Secrets	474
True War Romances	475
True Western	331
True-To-Life Romances	475
Trufan Adventures Theatre	781
Truth: Red White Black	331
Try-Out Winner Book	331
Tsr Worlds	173
Tsunami Girl	555
Tuff Ghosts Starring Spooky	675
Tug & Buster	555
Turok	675
Turok 3: Shadow of Oblivion	675
Turok Quarterly—redpath	675
Turok, Son of Stone	475
Turok: Child of Blood	675
Turok: Comic Book Magazine	675
Turok: Dinosaur Hunter	675
Turok: Evolution	675
Turok: Son of Stone	675
Turok: The Hunted	675
Turok/Shadowman	675
Turok/Shaman's Tears	675
Turok/Timewalker	675
Turtle Soup	675, 781
Turtles Teach Karate	781
Tuxedo Gin	781
TV Casper & Company	675
TV Screen Cartoons	131
TV Stars	331
TV Western	475
Tweety and Sylvester	475, 676
Twenty Thousand Leagues Under the Sea	796
Twenty Years After	796

CVA Page 836

Index — Tw–Vi

Entry	Page
Twilight	173
Twilight Avenger	676, 781
Twilight Man	676
Twilight X: Storm	781
Twilight X-Tra	676
Twilight Zone	676
Twilight Zone, The	676
Twilight-X Quarterly	781
Twilight-X: Interlude	781
Twinkle Comics	475
Twist	781
Twisted Tales	676
Twisted Tales of Bruce Jones	676
Twisted Tantrums of the Purple Snit	781
Twister	676
Two Faces of Tomorrow, The	520
Two Fisted Tales	520, 676
Two Gun Western	213
Two Years Before the Mast	794
Two-Fisted Tales	475
Two-Gun Kid	331
Two-Gun Kid: Sunset Riders	332
Two-Gun Western	204
Typee	795
Typhoid	332
Tzu the Reaper	677
Tzu: Spirits of Death	677
U.N. Force	**679**
U.N. Force Files	679
U.S. 1	334
U.S. Agent	334
U.S. Jones	476
U.S. Marines In Action!	476
U.S. Tank Commandos	476
U.S. War Machine	334
U.S.A. Comics	334
UFO & Outer Space	677
UFO Flying Saucers	677
Ultimate Adventures	332
Ultimate Age of Apocalypse	332
Ultimate Daredevil & Elektra	332
Ultimate Marvel Magazine	332
Ultimate Marvel Team-Up	332
Ultimate Six	333
Ultimate Spider-Man	333
Ultimate Strike	781
Ultimate War	333
Ultimate X-Men	333
Ultimates, The	332
Ultra Girl	333
Ultra Klutz	781
Ultra X-Men Collection	333
Ultra X-Men III	333
Ultraforce	677
Ultraforce/Avengers	333, 677
Ultraforce/Spider-Man	677
Ultraman	677
Ultraman Tiga	520
Ultraverse Double Feature	677
Ultraverse Future Shock	677
Ultraverse Origins	677
Ultraverse Unlimited	677
Ultraverse: Year One	677
Ultraverse: Year Two	677
Ultraverse: Year Zero: The Death of the Squad	677
Ultron	333
Unauthorized Bio of Lex Luthor	173
Unbound	555
Uncanny Man-Frog	781
Uncanny Origins	333
Uncanny Tales	334
Uncanny Tales From the Grave	334
Uncanny X-Men	349
Uncensored Mouse	781
Uncle Charlie's Fables	475
Uncle Sam	173, 366
Uncle Scrooge	475, 677, 678
Uncle Scrooge Adventures	678
Uncle Scrooge Adventures In Color	679
Uncle Scrooge Adventures: Don Rosa 1997 Special	678
Uncle Scrooge and Donald Duck	679
Uncle Scrooge Goes To Disneyland	679
Uncle Tom's Cabin	793
Undead, The	679
Under the Glass Moon	781
Under Two Flags	799
Undercover Genie	173
Underdog	679
Underdog In 3-D	679
Underground	520
Undersea Agent	679
Undertaker	679
Underworld	173, 475
Underworld Unleashed	173
Underworld Crime	475
Unearthly Spectaculars	679
Unexpected, The	168
Unforgiven, The	781
Unicorn Isle	781
Union	555
Union Jack	334
Union of Justice	679
United Comics	475
United States Fighting Air Force	475
United States Marines	475
Unity	679
Unity 2000	679
Universal Monsters:	520
Universal Soldier	679
Universe	555
Universe X	334
Unkept Promise	476
Unknown Soldier	145, 173
Unknown World	461
Unknown Worlds of Frank Brunner	679
Unknown Worlds of Science Fiction	334
Unleashed	781
Unleashed!	679
UNLV	679
Unseen, The	476
Unsupervised Existence	781
Untamed	334
Untamed Love	476, 680
Untold Legend of Batman	173
Untold Legend of Captain Marvel, The	334
Untold Tales of Evil Ernie	781
Untold Tales of Spider-Man	335
Untouchables	781
Unusual Tales	680
Uri-On	680
Urth 4	680
Us War Machine 2.0	335
Usa Is Ready	476
Usagi Yojimbo	520, 521, 680, 781
Usagi Yojimbo Color Special: Green Persimmon	521
V	**173**
V For Vendetta	174
V...Comics	476
Vagabond	555, 782
Vagrant Story	555
Valentino	782
Valeria the She Bat	680
Valeria, The She-Bat	680
Valhalla	680
Valiant Era	680
Valiant Reader: Guide To the Valiant Universe	680
Valiant Vision Starter Kit	680
Valkyrie	335, 680
Valley of the Dinosaurs	680
Valor	173, 476, 680
Vamperotica	680, 782
Vamperotica Illustrated	782
Vamperotica Lingerie	680
Vamperotica Lust For Luxura	782
Vamperotica Manga	782
Vamperotica Tales	782
Vamperotica: Dark Fiction	782
Vamperotica: Divide & Conquer	782
Vamperotica: Tales From the Bloodvault	782
Vamperotica: When Darkness Falls	782
Vampfire	782
Vampfire: Erotic Echo	782
Vampfire: Necromantique	783
Vampi	680
Vampi (digital)	681
Vampi Vicious	681
Vampire Bites	783
Vampire Confessions	783
Vampire Dahlia, The	783
Vampire Game	783
Vampire Girls Erotique	783
Vampire Girls Erotique: Gravedigger	783
Vampire Girls: California 1969	783
Vampire Girls: New York 1979	783
Vampire Girls: Bubblegum & Blood	783
Vampire Lestat	681
Vampire Miyu	783
Vampire Princess Miyu	783
Vampire Princesss Yui	783
Vampire Tales	335
Vampire the Masquerade	683
Vampire Yui	784
Vampire Zone, The	784
Vampire's Christmas	555
Vampire's Tattoo	784
Vampirella	.521, 681, 682, 783, 811
Vampirella of Drakulon	682
Vampirella Classic	682
Vampirella Comics Magazine	783
Vampirella Genesis	682
Vampirella Lives	682
Vampirella Retro	783
Vampirella Strikes	682
Vampirella Vs. Eudaemon	682
Vampirella Vs. Hemorrhage	682
Vampirella Vs. Pantha	683
Vampirella: Morning In America	783
Vampirella: Sad Wings of Destiny	682
Vampirella: Blood Lust	682
Vampirella: Crossover Gallery	682
Vampirella: Death and Destruction	682
Vampirella: Legendary Tales	783
Vampirella/Lady Death	682
Vampirella/Painkiller Jane	682
Vampirella/Shi	682
Vampirella/Wetworks	683
Vampirella/Witchblade	683
Vampires	521
Vampornrella	784
Vampress Luxura, The	683
Vamps	174
Vamps: Hollywood & Vein	174
Vamps: Pumpkin Time	174
Vampyres	784
Vandala	683
Vandala II	683
Vanguard	555
Vanguard Illustrated	683
Vanguard: Strange Visitors	555
Vanity	683
Vapor Loch	784
Varick: Chronicles of the Dark Prince	683
Variety Comics	476
Vaughn Bode Productions Portfolio #1	811
Vaughn Bode the Portfolio	811
Vaughn Bode's Cheech Wizard the Collected Adventures of	811
Vaughn Bode's Deadbone the First Testament of Cheech Wizard	811
Vault of Evil	335
Vault of Horror	478, 683
Vector	683
Vegas Knights	683
Velocity	555
Vengeance of the A-Tech	784
Vengeance of Dreadwolf	784
Vengeance of Vampirella	683
Venom	335
Venom: Lethal Protector	335
Venom: Nights of Vengeance	336
Venom: Separation Anxiety	336
Venom: Sinner Takes All	336
Venom: The Enemy Within	335
Venom: Along Came A Spider	335
Venom: Carnage Unleashed	335
Venom: Finale	335
Venom: Funeral Pyre	335
Venom: License To Kill	336
Venom: On Trial	336
Venom: Seed of Darkness	336
Venom: Sign of the Boss	336
Venom: The Hunger	335
Venom: The Hunted	335
Venom: The Mace	336
Venom: The Madness	336
Venom: Tooth and Claw	336
Venture	555, 683
Venus	336
Venus Wars	521
Verdict	784
Veri Best Sure Shot Comics	476
Vermillion	174
Veronica	683
Verotik Illustrated	683
Verotika	683, 784
Version	521
Version II	521
Vertigo Gallery: Dreams and Nightmares	174
Vertigo Jam	174
Vertigo Pop!: London	174
Vertigo Pop!: Tokyo	174
Vertigo Preview	174
Vertigo Verite: Hell Eternal	174
Vertigo Verite: The System	174
Vertigo Verite: The Unseen Hand	174
Vertigo Visions: Dr. Occult	174
Vertigo Visions: Dr. Thirteen	174
Vertigo Visions: Phantom Stranger	174
Vertigo Visions: The Geek	174
Vertigo Visions: Tomahawk	174
Vertigo Voices: The Eaters	174
Vertigo: Winter's Edge	174
Very Best of Marvel Comics	336
Very Vicky	784
Vesper	684
Vespers	684
Vext	174
Vic & Blood	784
Vic Flint	476, 684
Vic Jordan	476
Vic Torry and His Flying Saucer	476
Vic Verity Magazine	476
Vicki	684
Vicky Valentine	784
Victim	784
Victims	784
Victorian	684
Victory	555
Victory Comics	476
Video Classics	784
Video Girl Ai	784
Video Jack	336
Video Noire	521
Viet Nam Journal	784
Vietnam	811
Vigil	784
Vigil: Desert Foxes	784
Vigil: Eruption	784
Vigil: Scatter Shots	784
Vigilante	174
Vigilante: City Lights, Prairie Justice	175
Villains & Vigilantes	684
Vinson Watson's Rage	784
Vinson Watson's Sweet Childe	784
Vintage Magnus Robot Fighter	684
Violator	555
Violator/Badrock	556
Violent Cases	521, 684
Violent Messiahs	556
Violent Messiahs: Lamenting Pain	556
Vip	684
Viper	175
Virgin: Slumber	784
Virgin: Surrounded	784
Virgin: Till Death Do Us Part	784
Virginian, The	684, 802
Virtex	684
Virtua Fighter	684
Virus	521
Vision	784
Vision & Scarlet Witch	336
Vision, The	336
Visionaries	336
Visitations	556

CVA Page 837

Index

Vi–Wi

Visitor 684
Visitor Vs. Valiant 684
Visual Assault Omnibus 785
Vixen 785
Vogue 556
Void Indigo 336
Voltron 684
Voltron: Defender of the
  Universe 556
Vooda 476
Voodoo 476, 556
Vortex 684, 785
Vortex Special: Cybersin 785
Vortex, The 521
Vortex: Dr. Kilborun 785
Vortex: Into the Dark 785
Vortex: The Second Coming .. 684
Vox 785
Voyage To the Deep 684
Wacky Adventures of Cracky .684
Wacky Duck 230, 384
Wacky Witch 684
Waffen Ss 785
Wagon Train 684
Wahoo Morris 556
Waiting Place, The 785
Walk Through October 785
Walking Dead 556, 785
Wally 684
Wally the Wizard 336
Wally Wood's Thunder Agents .684
Walt Disney Comics Digest .. 686
Walt Disney Annuals ... 477, 684
Walt Disney Comics In Color . 686
Walt Disney Dell Giant Editions 477
Walt Disney Presents 478
Walt Disney Showcase 686
Walt Disney's Comics & Stories 477
Walt Disney's Autumn
  Adventure 685
Walt Disney's Christmas
  Parade 685
Walt Disney's Comics and
  Stories 685, 686
Walt Kelly's Christmas Classics 686
Walt Kelly's Springtime Tales . 686
Walt the Wildcat 785
Walter: Campaign of Terror .. 521
Wambi the Jungle Boy 478
Wanderers 175
Wandering Star 785
Wanderlust 785
Wanted Comics 478
Wanted: The World's Most
  Dangerous Villians 175
War Action 336
War Adventures 336
War Against Crime 478, 686
War Battles 479
War Birds 479
War Combat 337
War Comics 337, 479
War Dancer 686
War Heroes 479, 687
War Is Hell 337
War Machine 338
War Man 338
War of the Gods 176
War of the Worlds 785
War of the Worlds, The . 785, 801
War of the Worlds: The
  Memphis Front 786
War Ships 479
War Stories 479
War Story 176
War Victory Adventures ... 479
War Victory Comics 479
War, The 336
Warblade: Endangered
  Species 556
Warcat 785
Warcat Special 686
Warchild 686
Ward: A Bullet Series 785
Warhawks 687
Warhawks 2050 687
Warheads 337
Warheads: Black Dawn ... 337
Warlands 556
Warlands: Age of Ice 556

Warlash 687
Warlock 337
Warlock 5 785
Warlock and the Infinity Watch .337
Warlock Chronicles 338
Warlocks 785
Warlord 175
Warmaster 687
Warp 687
Warpath 479
Warren Ellis' Atmospherics .. 786
Warren Ellis' Bad Signal ... 786
Warren Ellis' Bad World ... 786
Warren Ellis' Dark Blue ... 786
Warren Ellis' Scars 786
Warren Ellis' Strange Killings .786
Warren Ellis' Strange Killings:
  Strong Medicine 786
Warren Ellis' Strange Killings:
  The Body Orchard ... 786
Warren Ellis' Stranger Kiss .. 786
Warren Ellis' Stranger Kisses . 786
Warrior Bugs, The 687
Warrior Comics 479
Warrior Nun Areala 687
Warrior Nun Areala Vs. Razor . 687
Warrior Nun Areala: Books
  of Peril 786
Warrior Nun Areala:
  Dangerous Game 786
Warrior Nun Areala: Ghosts
  of the Past 786
Warrior Nun Areala: Scorpio
  Rose 687
Warrior Nun Areala: The Manga 786
Warrior Nun Areala/Glory ... 687
Warrior Nun Areala/Razor:
  Dark Prophecy 786
Warrior Nun Brigantia 786
Warrior Nun Dei: Aftertime ... 687
Warrior Nun: Black and White . 786
Warrior Nun: Frenzy 687
Warrior Nun: No Justice ... 687
Warrior Nun: Resurrection .. 687
Warrior of Waverly Street, The .521
Warrior of Waverly Street,
  The: Broodstorm 521
Warrior's Way 687
Warriors 786
Warriors of Plasm 687
Warstrike 687
Warstrike: Prelude To
  Godwheel 687
Wart and the Wizard 688
Wartime Romances 479
Warworld! 521
Warzone 787
Wasteland 176
Watchmen 176
Waterdogs 688
Waterloo 801
Waterworld 688
Wave Warriors 688
Waxwork In 3-D 688
Way of the Coda: The Collected
  Wildc.A.T.S 556
Way of the Rat 688
Wayfarers 688
Weapon X 338
Weapon Zero 556
Weapons of the Gods 688
Weasel Guy Witchblade ... 688
Weasel Guy: Roadtrip 556
Weather Woman 787
Weaveworld 338
Web 176
Web of Evil 479
Web of Horror 688
Web of Mystery 479
Web of Scarlet Spider 338
Web of Spider-Man 338
Web-Man 688
Webspinners: Tales of
  Spider-Man 339
Webwitch 787
Webwitch: Prelude To War .. 787
Webwitch: War 787
Wedding Bells 480
Wedding of Popeye and
  Olive, The 688

Wedding Peach 787
Weekender, The 480
Weird 176
Weird Adventures 480
Weird Chills 480
Weird Comics 480
Weird Fantasy 480, 688
Weird Horrors 480
Weird Mysteries 480
Weird Science 480, 688
Weird Science Fantasy . 481, 688
Weird Suspense 688
Weird Tales Illustrated ... 688
Weird Tales of the Future .. 481
Weird Terror 481
Weird Thrillers 481
Weird War Tales 176, 177
Weird Western Tales 177
Weird Wondertales 339
Weird Worlds 177
Weird, The 176
Weirdfall 787
Weirdo 811
Weirdo, The 811
Weirdsville 787
Weirdsville/Crybaby: Hey
  You Two 787
Wendy 688
Wendy Witch World 688
Wendy, The Good Little Witch .688
Werewolf 688, 787
Werewolf By Night 339
West Coast Avengers ... 340
Western Action 688
Western Action Thrillers ... 481
Western Adventures Comics . 481
Western Bandit Trails ... 481
Western Comics 177
Western Crime Cases ... 440
Western Crime-Busters ... 481
Western Fighters 481
Western Frontier 481
Western Gunfighters ... 340
Western Hearts 481
Western Hero 486
Western Kid 340
Western Love 482
Western Love Trails 481
Western Outlaws 340
Western Outlaws & Sheriffs . 203
Western Picture Stories ... 482
Western Stories 797
Western Tales 484
Western Tales of Black Rider . 190
Western Team-Up 341
Western Thrillers 341, 482
Western True Crime ... 482
Western Winners 190
Westerner, The 481
Westward Ho! 793
Westwynd 688
Wetworks 556
Wetworks/Vampirella ... 557
Whack 482
Wham 688
Wham Comics 482
What If? 341
What Is the Face? 787
What the -?! 342
What's Michael? 521
Where Creatures Roam .. 342
Where In the World Is
  Carmen Sandiego 177
Where Monsters Dwell ... 342
Whip Wilson 206
Whirlwind Comics 482
Whiskey Dickel, International
  Cowgirl 557
Whisper 689
Whispers & Shadows ... 787
White Company, The 800
White Devil 787
White Fang 689, 799
White Like She 521
White Orchid, The 787
White Princess of the Jungle . 482
White Raven 787
White Rider and Super Horse . 440
White Trash 689
Whiteout 787

Whiteout: Melt 787
Whitley Strieber's Beyond
  Communion 787
Whiz Comics 482
Whiz Kids 557
Who Is Next 483
Who's Who 178
Who's Who '88 178
Who's Who In Impact ... 178
Who's Who In Star Trek ... 178
Who's Who In the Legion ... 178
Who's Who Update '87 ... 178
Whodunit? 483
Whodunnit 689
Why I Hate Saturn 177
Wicked 787
Wicked, The 557
Wicked: The Reckoning ... 787
Widow 787, 788
Widow Made In Britain ... 689
Widow Metal Gypsies ... 689
Widow: Bound By Blood ... 788
Widow: Progeny 788
Widow: The Complete Works . 788
Widow: The Origin 788
Widow/Luxura: Blood Lust ... 788
Wilbur Comics 483
Wild 342
Wild 7 788
Wild Act 788
Wild Animals 689
Wild Animals I Have Known ... 802
Wild Bill Elliot 483
Wild Bill Hickock 801
Wild Bill Hickok 483
Wild Bill Hickok and Jingles .. 486
Wild Bill Pecos 689
Wild Boy of the Congo ... 483
Wild Cards 342
Wild Dog 178
Wild Frontier 689
Wild Knights 788
Wild Thing 342
Wild Thingz 788
Wild Times 689
Wild West 343
Wild West C.O.W.-Boys of
  Moo Mesa 689
Wild Western 343
Wild Wild West 178, 689, 690
Wild, The 788
Wildc.A.T.S Adventures ... 557
Wildc.A.T.S. Trilogy 557
Wildc.A.T.S/Aliens 557
Wildc.A.T.S/X-Men 557
Wildc.A.T.S/X-Men: The
  Dark Age 342
Wildcats 689
Wildcats Version 3.0 ... 689
Wildcore 558
Wildfire 689
Wildflower 788
Wildflower: Tribal Screams .. 788
Wildguard: Casting Call ... 558
Wildlife 788
Wildman 788
Wildstar 558
Wildstorm 558
Wildstorm Ultimate Sports .. 558
Wildstorm Archives Genesis .. 558
Wildstorm Rising 558
Wildstorm Spotlight 558
Wildstorm Universe '97 ... 558
Will Eisner Library 177
Will Eisner's 3-D Classics .. 690
Will Eisner's Hawks of
  the Seas 521
Will To Power 521
William Shatner's Tek World . 343
William Tell 800
Willie Comics 250
Willow 343, 788
Wimmen's Comix 811
Win A Prize Comics 690
Wind Blade 788
Windrage 690
Windraven 788
Windy & Willy 178
Wings 788

CVA Page 838

Index

Wi–Zu

Wings Comics	483
Winnie Winkle	484
Winterworld	690
Wireheads	690
Wise Son: The White Wolf	178
Wish	788
Wisp	690
Witch	788
Witchblade	558, 690
Witchblade: Destiny's Child	559
Witchblade/Aliens/Darkness/ Predator: Mindhunter	521
Witchcraft	178, 484
Witchcraft: La Terreur	178
Witches Tales	484
Witches Western Tales	484
Witchfinder, The	559
Witching Hour	690
With Fire and Sword	802
With the Marines On the Battlefronts of the World	484
Witness, The	343
Witty Comics	484
Wizard of Fourth Street	521
Wizard of Time	788
Wizards of the Last Resort	788
Wizards Tale, The	559
Wolf & Red	521
Wolff & Byrd, Counselors of the Macabre	788
Wolfpack	343
Wolverine	343, 344
Wolverine & Punisher: Damaging Evidence	344
Wolverine Encyclopedia	344
Wolverine Saga	345
Wolverine: Days of Future Past	344
Wolverine: Doombringer	344
Wolverine: Snikt!	345
Wolverine: The End	345
Wolverine: X-Isle	345
Wolverine/Doop	344
Wolverine/Gambit: Victims	345
Wolverine/Hulk	345
Wolverine/Netsuke	345
Wolverine/Punisher: Revelation	345
Wolverine/Witchblade	559
Wolverton In Space	522
Woman In White, The	797
Women In Love	484
Women Outlaws	484
Won By the Sword	802
Wonder Comics	485
Wonder Duck	345
Wonder Man	345
Wonder Wart-Hog and the Nurds of November	811
Wonder Wart-Hog, Captain Crud & Other Super Stuff	811
Wonder Woman	178, 180
Wonderboy	409
Wonderland Comics	485
Wonderman	345
Wonderworld Comics	485
Woody Woodpecker	690
Wordsmith	788
World Below II, The	522
World Below, The	522
World Championship Wrestling	345
World Class Comics	559
World Famous Heroes Magazine	485
World Hardball League	788
World of Archie	690
World of Fantasy	345
World of Krypton	181
World of Metropolis	181
World of Mystery	345
World of Robotech	788
World of Smallville	181
World of Suspense	345
World of Wood	690, 788
World War 2	789
World War 2: Stalingrad	789
World War II: 1946	690
World War III	485
World Without End	184
World's Best Comics	182
World's Finest	184
World's Finest Comics	182
World's Finest: Superboy/Robin	184
World's Greatest Stories	485
World's Greatest Super-Heroes	184
Worlds Collide	182
Worlds of Fantasy	788
Worlds of H.P. Lovecraft	788
Worlds Unknown	346
Wotalife	442
Wounded Man	789
Wow Comics	485
Wrath	690
Wrath of the Spectre	184
Wretch, The	789
Wu Wei	789
Wulf the Barbarian	690
Wuthering Heights	797
Ww2	789
Wwf Battlemania	690
Wyatt Earp	346, 690
Wynonna Earp	559
Wyrd: The Reluctant Warrior	789
X	**522**
X.S.E.	357
X: One Shot To the Head	522
X-1999	789
X-51	347
X-Babes Vs Justice Babes	789
X-Calibre	346
X-Cons	789
X-Day	789
X-Factor	346, 347
X-Files	691
X-Files Digest	691
X-Files, The: Ground Zero	691
X-Files, The: Season One	691
X-Flies Bug Hunt	789
X-Force	347
X-Force & Spider-Man: Sabotage	348
X-Force Megazine	348
X-Man	348
X-Men	349, 352
X-Men 2: The Movie	356
X-Men 2099	356
X-Men 2099 A.D.	356
X-Men Adventures	353
X-Men Archives: Captain	354
X-Men Archives: Captain Britain	354
X-Men At State Fair	354
X-Men Chronicles	354
X-Men Classics	354
X-Men Evolution	355
X-Men Firsts,	352
X-Men Forever	355
X-Men Icons: Chamber	355
X-Men Megazine	352
X-Men Omega	355
X-Men Prime	356
X-Men Rarities	352
X-Men Spotlight On Starjammers	356
X-Men Universe	356
X-Men Unlimited	356
X-Men Vs. Avengers	356
X-Men Vs. Dracula	352
X-Men Vs. the Brood	356
X-Men: Alpha	354
X-Men: Askani'son	354
X-Men: Black Sun	354
X-Men: Children of the Atom	354
X-Men: Days of Future Past	352
X-Men: Days of Future Present	352
X-Men: Early Years	355
X-Men: Hellfire Club	355
X-Men: Inferno	352
X-Men: Liberators	355
X-Men: Lost Tales	355
X-Men: Magik	355
X-Men: Mutant Massacre	352
X-Men: Phoenix	355
X-Men: Pryde & Wisdom	356
X-Men: Road To Onslaught	353
X-Men: Ronin	356
X-Men: The Hidden Years	355
X-Men: The Magneto War	356
X-Men: The Movie	355
X-Men: The Rise of Apocalypse	356
X-Men: The Search For Cyclops	356
X-Men: True Friends	356
X-Men: Wrath of Apocalypse	347
X-Men: X-Tinction Agenda	352
X-Men/Animation Special	354
X-Men/Alpha Flight	354
X-Men/Alpha Flight: The Gift	354
X-Men/Clandestine	354
X-Men/Micronauts	355
X-Nation 2099	357
X-O Manowar	691, 692
X-Patrol	186
X-Statix	357
X-Terminators	357
X-Thieves	789
X-Treme X-Men	357
X-Treme X-Men: Savage Land	357
X-Treme X-Men: X-Pose	357
X-Universe	357
Xanadu	690, 789
Xander In Lost Universe	601
Xavier Institute Alumni Yearbook	346
Xena: Warrior Princess	522, 690
Xena, Warrior Princess: Blood Lines	690
Callisto	690
Orpheus	691
The Original Olympics	691
The Wrath of Hera	691
The Wedding of Xena & Hercules	691
Xena and the Dragon's Teeth	691
Xeno Men	691
Xeno's Arrow	789
Xenobrood	184
Xenon	789
Xenotech	691
Xenoxoic Tales	522
Xenozoic Tales	789
Xenya	690
Xer	184
Ximos: Violent Past	691
Xin	691
Xin: Journey of the Monkey King	691
Xiola	789
Xmen	789
Xombi	184
XXX	522
Y: The Last Man	**184**
Yahoo	789
Yakuza	789
Yankee Comics	486
Yanky Doodle & Chopper	692
Yawn	789
Yeah!	184, 692
Yellow Caballero	789
Yellow Dog	811
Yellowjacket Comics	486
Yin Fei	692
Yogi Bear	357, 692
Yogi Berra	486
Yosemite Sam	692
You're Under Arrest!	522
Young All Stars	185
Young Allies Comics	357
Young and Lustless	811
Young Brides	486
Young Cynics Club	522
Young Dracula: Prayer of the Vampire	789
Young Eagle	487
Young Hearts	357
Young Heroes In Love	185
Young Indiana Jones	522
Young Justice	185
Young Justice: Sins of Youth	185
Young King Cole	487
Young Life	487
Young Love	185, 487
Young Lust	811
Young Masters	790
Young Men	218
Young Romance Comics	487
Youngblood	559, 692
Youngblood Strikefile	559
Youngblood Battlezone	559
Youngblood Classics	692
Youngblood Genesis	692
Youngblood Yearbook	559
Youngblood: Bloodsport	692
Youngblood: Year One	559
Youngblood/X-Force	559
Your United States	487
Youthful Heart	487
Youthful Romances	487
Yow	811
Yu-Gi-Oh!	790
Yuppies From Hell	357
Yuyu Hakusho	790
Z	**790**
Zaanan	692
Zachary Holmes	522
Zago, Jungle Prince	487
Zak Raven, Esq.	692
Zap Comix	811
Zatanna	185
Zealot	559
Zegra, Jungle Empress	488
Zell the Sworddancer	790
Zen	693
Zen Illustrated Novella	790
Zen Intergalactic	693
Zen Intergalactic Ninja	693
Zen Intergalactic Ninja Vs. Micheal Jack-Zen	790
Zen, Intergalactic Ninja: Starquest	790
Zen, Intergalactic Ninja	790
Zen: Mistress of Chaos	790
Zen: Novella	693
Zen: Warrior	693
Zen/Nira X: Hellspace	693
Zendra	693
Zenisms Wit and Wisdoms	790
Zenith Phase II	693
Zero Girl	185
Zero Girl: Full Circle	185, 693
Zero Hour: Crisis In Time	185
Zero Patrol	693
Zero Tolerance	693
Zero Zero	790
Zetraman	790
Zetraman: Revival	790
Zillion	790
Zip Comics	488
Zip-Jet	488
Zippy	811
Zodiac P.I.	790
Zoids	790
Zolastraya and the Bard	790
Zombie War	790
Zombieworld:	522
Zombieworld: Champion of the Worms	522
Zombieworld: Dead End	522
Zombieworld: Winter's Dregs	522
Zone Continuum	790
Zone, The	522
Zoom Comics	488
Zooniverse	693
Zoot Comics	488
Zorro	357, 559, 693
Zorro Mantanzas	559
Zorro's Lady Rawhide: Other People's Blood	559
Zorro's Renegades	559
Zot	693
Zot!	693, 790
Zu	790

OUR APOLOGIES

Last year's index was not updated when the page numbers were changed, just prior to printing, so that the listings began on page 29 instead of page 1. All of the index entries were off by 28 pages.

CVA GRADING GUIDE

Grading comics is an objective art. This grading guide outlines the many conditions you should look for when purchasing comics, from the highest grade and top condition to the lowest collectible grade and condition. Your own comics will fall into one of these categories. A more complete description and our comments on comics grades can be found inside. We would like to point out, however, that no reader or advertiser is required to follow this or any other standard. All prices in Comics Values Annual are for comics in Near Mint condition. Happy collecting!

Mint: Perfect, pristine, devoid of any trace of wear or printing or handling flaws. Covers must be fully lustrous with sharply pointed corners. No color fading. Must be well centered. Many "rack" comics are not "Mint" even when new.

Near Mint: Almost perfect with virtually no wear. No significant printing flaws. Covers must be essentially lustrous with sharp corners. Spine is a tight as new. In older comics, minimal color fading is acceptable, as is slight aging of the paper. Most price guides, including CVA, quote prices in this grade.

Very Fine: Well preserved, still pleasing in appearance. Small signs of wear, most particularly around the staples. Most luster is readily visible. Corners may no longer be sharp, but are not rounded. Typical of a comic read only a few times and then properly stored.

Fine: Clean, presentable, with noticeable signs of wear. Some white may show through enamel around staples, and moderate rounding of corners. No tape or writing damage. Book still lies flat.

Very Good: A well worn reading copy with some minor damage such as creasing, small tears or cover flaking. Some discoloration may be evident, with obvious wear around the staples. Little luster remains, and some rolling of the spine may be seen when comic is laid flat on the table.

Good: A fully intact comic with very heavy wear. Tears, cover creases and flaking, and rolled spine will all be evident. No tape repairs present. Only very scarce or valuable issues are collected in this state.

The adjoining price table shows the prices for the other collectible grades which correspond to any "near mint" price given in this book.

Mint	Near Mint	Very Fine	Fine	Very Good
$6,000	$5,000	$3,500	$2,000	$1,000
4,800	4,000	2,800	1,600	800
3,600	3,000	2,100	1,200	600
2,400	2,000	1,400	800	400
1,800	1,500	1,050	600	300
1,200	1,000	700	400	200
1,080	900	630	360	180
960	800	560	320	160
900	750	525	300	150
840	700	490	280	140
780	650	455	260	130
720	600	420	240	120
660	550	385	220	110
600	500	350	200	100
570	475	332	190	95
540	450	315	180	90
510	425	297	170	85
480	400	280	160	80
450	375	262	150	75
420	350	245	140	70
390	325	227	130	65
360	300	210	120	60
330	275	192	110	55
300	250	175	100	50
270	225	157	90	45
240	200	140	80	40
210	175	122	70	35
180	150	105	60	30
150	125	87	50	25
120	100	70	40	20
114	95	66	38	19
108	90	63	36	18
102	85	59	32	17
96	80	56	32	16
90	75	52	30	15
84	70	49	28	14
78	65	45	26	13
72	60	42	24	12
66	55	38	22	11
60	50	35	2	10
54	45	31	18	9
48	40	28	16	8
42	35	24	14	7
36	30	21	12	6
30	25	17	10	5
24	20	14	8	4
22	18	12	7	4
21	17	11	7	4
18	15	10	6	3
17	14	9	5	3
16	13	9	5	3
15	12	8	5	2
14	11	7	4	2
12	10	7	4	2
11	9	6	4	2
10	8	5	3	1
9	7	5	3	1
7	6	4	3	1
6	5	4	2	1
5	4	3	2	0
4	3	2	1	0
3	2	2	0	0
2	1	0	0	0